P9-EMQ-760

GRADUATE STUDY IN
PSYCHOLOGY

2017

American Psychological Association

South Huntington Public Library
145 Pidgeon Hill Road
Huntington Station, NY 11746

American Psychological Association
Washington, DC

Copyright © 2017 by the American Psychological Association. All rights reserved. Except as permitted under the United States Copyright Act of 1976, no part of this publication may be reproduced or distributed in any form or by any means, including, but not limited to, the process of scanning and digitization, or stored in a database or retrieval system, without the prior written permission of the publisher.

Published by
American Psychological Association
750 First Street, NE
Washington, DC 20002

www.apa.org

Typeset by Cadmus Communications, Baltimore, MD

Printer: United Book Press, Inc., Baltimore, MD
Cover Designer: Naylor Design, Washington, DC

ISBN-13: 978-1-4338-2642-9
ISBN-10: 1-4338-2642-9
ISSN: 2160-9527
50th edition

To order
APA Order Department
P.O. Box 92984
Washington, DC 20090-2984
Tel: (800) 374-2721, Direct: (202) 336-5510
Fax: (202) 336-5502, TDD/TTY: (202) 336-6123
Online: www.apa.org/pubs/books/
E-mail: order@apa.org

Printed in the United States of America

Contents

Contents

Foreword

This is the 50th edition of a book prepared to assist individuals interested in graduate study in psychology. The current edition provides information for more than 600 graduate departments, programs, and schools of psychology in the United States and Canada. The information was obtained from questionnaires sent to graduate departments and schools of psychology and was provided voluntarily. The American Psychological Association (APA) is not responsible for the accuracy of the information reported.

The purpose of this publication is to provide an information service, offering in one book information about the majority of graduate programs in psychology. Inclusion in this publication does not signify APA approval or endorsement of a graduate program, nor should it be assumed that a listing of a program in *Graduate Study in Psychology* means that its graduates are automatically qualified to sit for licensure as psychologists or are eligible for positions requiring a psychology degree.

However, programs listed in this publication have agreed to the following quality assurance provisions:

1. They have agreed to honor April 15 as the date allowed for graduate applicants to accept or reject an offer of admission and financial assistance for fall matriculation. This date adheres to national policy guidelines as stated by the Council of Graduate Schools and the Council of Graduate Departments of Psychology.

2. They have satisfied the following criteria: The program offers a graduate degree and is sponsored by a public or private higher education institution accredited by one of six regional accrediting bodies recognized by the U.S. Secretary of Education, or, in the case of Canadian programs, the institution is publicly recognized by the Association of Universities and Colleges of Canada as a member in good standing, or the program indicates that it meets *all* of the following criteria:

    A. The graduate program, wherever it may be administratively housed, is publicly labeled as a psychology program in pertinent institutional catalogs and brochures.

    B. The psychology program stands as a recognizable, coherent organizational entity within the institution.

    C. There is an identifiable core of full-time psychology faculty.

    D. Psychologists have clear authority and primary responsibility for the academic core and specialty preparation, whether or not the program involves multiple administrative lines.

    E. There is an identifiable body of graduate students who are enrolled in the program for the attainment of the graduate degree offered.

    F. The program is an organized, integrated sequence of study designed by the psychology faculty responsible for the program.

G. Programs leading to a doctoral degree require at least the equivalent of 3 full-time academic years of graduate study.

H. Doctoral programs ensure appropriate breadth and depth of education and training in psychology as follows:

    1) Methodology and history, including systematic preparation in scientific standards and responsibilities, research design and methodology, quantitative methods (e.g., statistics, psychometric methods), and historical foundations in psychology.

    2) Foundations in psychology, including

        a. biological bases of behavior (e.g., physiological psychology, comparative psychology, neuropsychology, psychopharmacology);

        b. cognitive–affective bases of behavior (e.g., learning, memory, perception, cognition, thinking, motivation, emotion);

        c. social bases of behavior (e.g., social psychology; cultural, ethnic, and group processes; sex roles; organizational behavior); and

        d. individual differences (e.g., personality theory, human development, individual differences, abnormal psychology, psychology of women, psychology of persons with disabilities, psychology of the minority experience).

    3) Additional preparation in the program's area of specialization, to include

        a. knowledge and application of ethical principles and guidelines and standards as may apply to scientific and professional practice activities;

        b. supervised practicum and/or laboratory experiences appropriate to the area of practice, teaching, or research in psychology; and

        c. advanced preparation appropriate to the area of specialization.

This publication may not answer all questions you have about graduate education in psychology. Some questions you may want to direct to particular graduate departments, programs, or schools of psychology. *For more information about general policies and for information related to graduate education, visit the APA Education website (http://www.apa.org/ed).*

Producing this annual publication involves the cooperation of many individuals each year. We wish to express appreciation to all graduate departments, programs, and schools that contributed information. We also wish to acknowledge the support and contributions by individuals in the Education Directorate, Internet Services, and Publications and Databases.

Caroline Cope, MA
Research Officer
Office of Graduate and Postgraduate Education and Training
Education Directorate
American Psychological Association

Considering Graduate Study

Psychology is a broad scientific discipline bridging the social and biological sciences. Psychology's applications include education and human development, health and human resilience, family and community relations, organizations and other work environments, engineering and technology, the arts and architecture, communications, and political and judiciary systems.

There are many types of graduate programs in psychology. Selecting a graduate program that is best for you requires thoughtful consideration. The American Psychological Association (APA) does not rank graduate programs in psychology. Rather, APA encourages selecting graduate programs based on the best match for you. Some programs focus on preparing students for an academic research career, while others focus on preparing students for applied research outside the university. Other programs prepare students to provide psychological services as licensed professional psychologists. Some programs offer professional development, in addition to a focus in psychology, to prepare students for a college teaching career. Psychology subfields of recent master's and doctoral graduates are illustrated in Figures 1 and 2.

Programs, Degrees, and Employment

Although employment in research, teaching, and human service positions is possible for those with a master's degree in psychology, the doctoral degree is considered the entry-level degree in psychology for the independent, licensed practice of psychology as a profession. The doctoral degree is the preferred degree for college and university faculty, and it has long been a requirement for faculty positions in research universities. For specific information about employment outcomes of a program's graduates, review the section entitled "Employment of Department Graduates" in each listing in this publication.

Figures 3 and 4 summarize the types of postdegree outcomes of graduates of master's and doctoral degree programs.

Figure 1. Master's Degrees Awarded by Psychology Subfield: 2014–2015

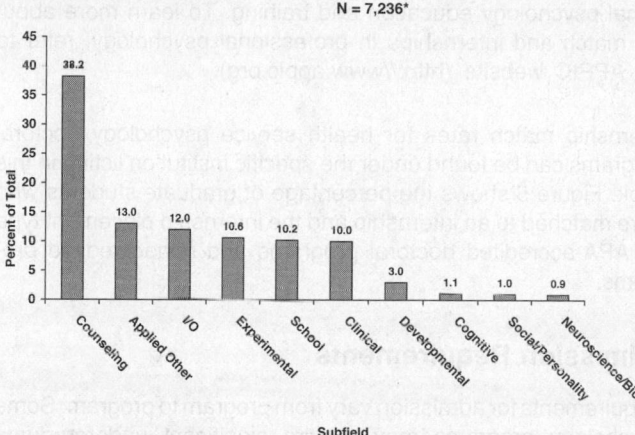

Source: *Graduate Study in Psychology, 2017 Edition* data. Prepared by the APA Office of Graduate and Postgraduate Education and Training. *Total includes MEd degrees in addition to MA/MS.

Figure 3. Employment and Outcomes of Master's Recipients: 2014–2015

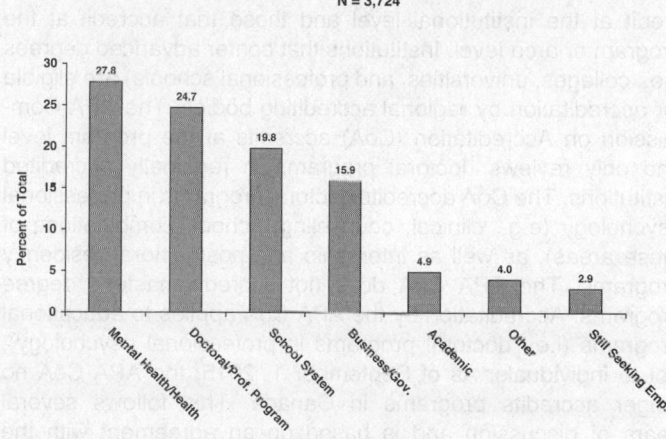

Source: *Graduate Study in Psychology, 2017 Edition* data. Prepared by the APA Office of Graduate and Postgraduate Education and Training.

Figure 2. Doctoral Degrees Awarded by Psychology Subfield: 2014–2015

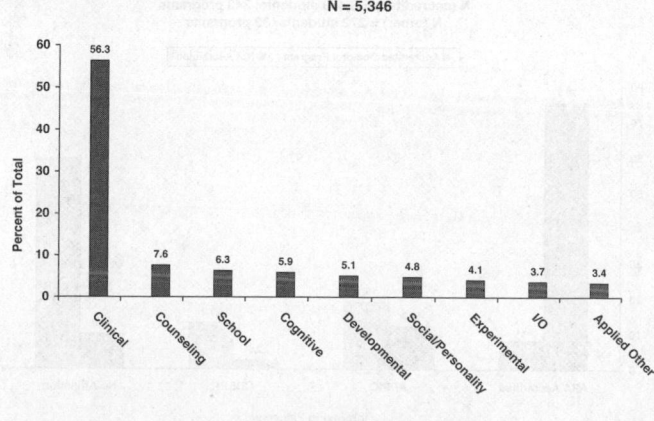

Source: *Graduate Study in Psychology, 2017 Edition* data. Prepared by the APA Office of Graduate and Postgraduate Education and Training.

Figure 4. Employment and Outcomes of Doctoral Recipients: 2014–2015

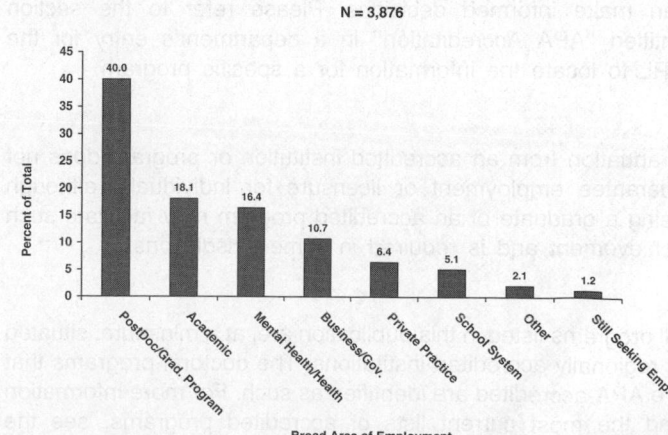

Source: *Graduate Study in Psychology, 2017 Edition* data. Prepared by the APA Office of Graduate and Postgraduate Education and Training.

Doctoral programs differ in the type of doctoral degree awarded. The two most common doctoral degrees are the PhD (Doctor of Philosophy) and the PsyD (Doctor of Psychology). Programs in colleges of education may offer the EdD (Doctor of Education) degree. The PhD is generally regarded as a research degree. Although many professional psychology programs award the PhD degree, especially those in university academic departments, these programs typically have an emphasis on research training integrated with applied or practice training. The PsyD is a professional degree in psychology (similar to the MD in medicine). Programs awarding the PsyD typically emphasize preparing their graduates for professional practice. About two thirds of all doctoral degrees in psychology are PhDs; of the degrees awarded in clinical psychology, about the same percentage receive PhDs as PsyDs.

Accreditation in Health Service Psychology

Accreditation is the mechanism by which students and the public are assured that the general quality of the education provided has met a set of educational and professional standards. Accreditation bodies include those that review and accredit at the institutional level and those that accredit at the program or area level. Institutions that confer advanced degrees (i.e., colleges, universities, and professional schools) are eligible for accreditation by regional accrediting bodies. The APA Commission on Accreditation (CoA) accredits at the program level and only reviews doctoral programs in regionally accredited institutions. The CoA accredits doctoral programs in professional psychology (e.g., clinical, counseling, school, combinations of these areas), as well as internship and postdoctoral residency programs. The APA CoA does not accredit master's degree programs. Accreditation by the APA CoA applies to educational programs (i.e., doctoral programs in professional psychology), not to individuals. As of September 1, 2015, the APA CoA no longer accredits programs in Canada. This follows several years of discussion and is based on an agreement with the Canadian Psychological Association (CPA). The CPA has their own accreditation system for programs in Canada. Doctoral programs accredited by the APA or the CPA are required to make publicly available information about the education and training outcomes of their students so that prospective students can make informed decisions. Please refer to the section entitled "APA Accreditation" in a department's entry for the URL to locate the information for a specific program.

Graduation from an accredited institution or program does not guarantee employment or licensure for individuals, although being a graduate of an accredited program may facilitate such achievement and is required in some jurisdictions.

All programs listed in this publication are, at a minimum, situated in regionally accredited institutions. The doctoral programs that are APA-accredited are identified as such. For more information and the most current lists of accredited programs, see the APA Office of Program Consultation and Accreditation website (http://www.apa.org/ed/accreditation).

Doctoral Internship Training in Professional Psychology

Doctoral programs that prepare their graduates for the professional practice of psychology, especially in health service provision, typically require a doctoral internship prior to the awarding of the doctorate. The health service psychology doctoral internship consists of 1 year (or the equivalent) of full-time supervised practice training. The internship is completed in a professional service agency training program that is typically not affiliated with the student's graduate program. Internship programs vary widely in terms of the settings and populations served as well as their models of training. Students sometimes relocate geographically to complete their internships. All accredited internship programs select students through a nationwide computerized matching process that has a standardized application and fixed deadlines administered by the Association of Psychology Postdoctoral and Internship Centers (APPIC). For many years the number of available internships has not grown at the rate the number of students has, resulting in an imbalance in which large numbers of students do not successfully match to an internship (e.g., 10% in 2015). While efforts are underway by the APA and the education and training community to address this, the imbalance is a significant issue facing professional psychology education and training. To learn more about the match and internships in professional psychology, refer to the APPIC website (http://www.appic.org).

Internship match rates for health service psychology doctoral programs can be found under the specific institution listing in this book. Figure 5 shows the percentage of graduate students who were matched to an internship and the internship placement type for APA-accredited doctoral programs and nonaccredited programs.

Admission Requirements

Requirements for admission vary from program to program. Some psychology programs may require significant undergraduate coursework in psychology, often the equivalent of a major or minor, while others do not.

Figure 5. Internship Placement by Program Type: 2014–2015

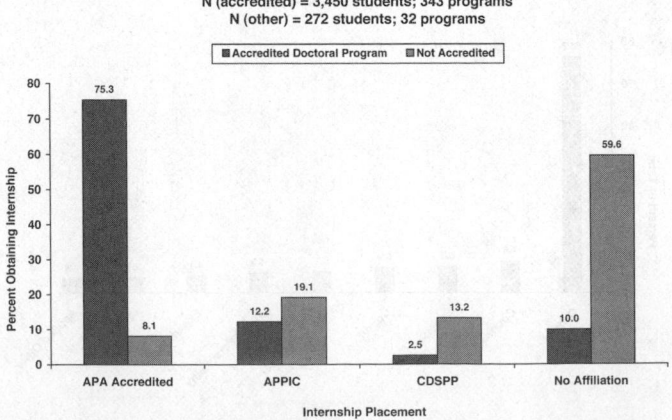

N (accredited) = 3,450 students; 343 programs
N (other) = 272 students; 32 programs

Source: *Graduate Study in Psychology, 2017 Edition* data. Prepared by the APA Office of Graduate and Postgraduate Education and Training.

Of the graduate departments listed in this publication that offer master's degrees, 77% require the Graduate Record Examination (GRE) Verbal (V) and Quantitative (Q) sections and 5% require the GRE-Subject (Psychology). Ninety-one percent of the doctoral programs listed require the GRE-V and Q sections, while 14% require the GRE-Subject (Psychology). If the programs in which you are interested require these standardized tests, you should take the GRE-V, GRE-Q, and GRE-Subject (Psychology) in time for the scores to be included with your application materials. The overall mean GRE scores reported for applicants admitted to master's degree programs listed in this publication are GRE-V: 154; GRE-Q: 150; and GRE-Subject: 582. The overall GRE scores reported for applicants admitted to doctoral degree programs listed in this publication are GRE-V: 158; GRE-Q: 155; and GRE-Subject: 485.

Other criteria considered as admission factors may include previous research activities, work experience, relevant public service, letters of recommendation, statement of goals and objectives, an interview, undergraduate psychology background, and undergraduate GPA. Figure 6 shows the ratings of importance of these other admissions criteria by master's and doctoral programs listed in this publication. A rating of 3 indicates that the individual admissions criterion is considered to be of high importance, while a rating of 0 indicates that the admissions criterion holds no importance in a program's admissions process. The three admissions criteria rated as of highest importance for both master's and doctoral programs are letters of recommendation, undergraduate GPA, and statement of goals and interests. The overall median undergraduate GPA reported for applicants admitted to master's degree programs listed in this publication is 3.43, while that for doctoral programs is 3.62.

The number of graduate school applicants typically exceeds the number of student openings. The number of applications received by a program and the number of students accepted provide a sense of the expected competition when applying to a particular department, program, or school. Figure 7 shows the percentage of students admitted in relationship to the number of applications for psychology programs in different areas. For more information, review the section entitled "Programs and Degrees Offered" for each of the programs of interest to you listed in this publication.

Application Information

An application to a department or program of study is a very important document. Always confirm (a) the deadline for filing the application, (b) what documents are required, and (c) who should receive the application. Include the required application fee. Information regarding required application materials is listed in the "Admissions Requirements" section for each department.

Most graduate programs in psychology accept students only for fall admission. However, if you are interested in winter, spring, or summer admission, check the application information listed in this publication for the program to which you are applying. Information about application deadlines in this publication is listed in the section entitled "Programs and Degrees Offered."

Time to Degree

Programs should be clear about the average number of years in full-time study (or part-time equivalent) required to complete the degree requirements. On average, graduate students take 6 years from entrance into a graduate program to complete the doctoral degree. Eighty percent of recent psychology PhD recipients also have master's degrees.

Tuition and Financial Assistance

Graduate education can be expensive. Figure 8 shows the average in-state and out-of-state public university and private university tuition rates for master's and doctoral level programs in psychology.

Figure 6.   Mean Rating of Importance of Various Admissions Criteria

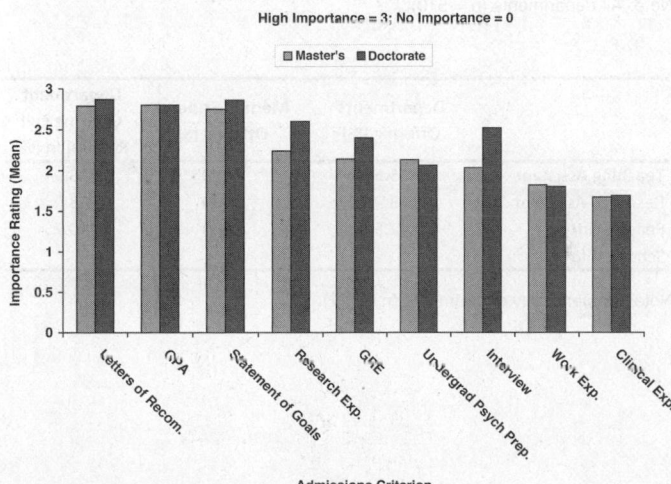

Source: *Graduate Study in Psychology, 2017 Edition* data. Prepared by the APA Office of Graduate and Postgraduate Education and Training.

Figure 7.   Percentage of Applicants Admitted to Graduate Programs by Selected Psychology Subfield: 2014–2015

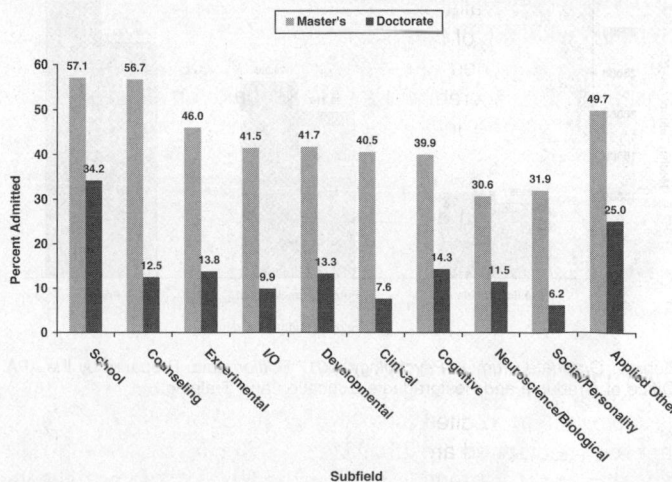

Source: *Graduate Study in Psychology, 2017 Edition* data. Prepared by the APA Office of Graduate and Postgraduate Education and Training.

The numbers in Figure 8 represent U.S. programs only. For universities in Canada, the median tuition for Canadian residents in a master's program is $5,593; for a PhD program, it is $7,271. For international students, the master's tuition is $14,635, and the tuition for doctoral programs is $15,267.

Financial assistance is available to graduate students to help cover the costs of graduate study. Many departments and programs offer teaching assistantships (TA) and research assistantships (RA) to their students. Students that are supported by a TA or RA receive a stipend in return for providing teaching services, or for providing research services. Some graduate students also receive fellowships or grants (FS), which provide funds to the student but do not require any particular service in return. Finally, some departments also offer tuition remission as part of the financial assistance, which means that a student's tuition costs are paid, and the amount of tuition covered may be partial or full. However, many students may still require loans to cover the costs of graduate study, especially if the combination of financial assistantships offered and tuition remission does not completely cover the costs of living and tuition.

Table 1 shows the percentage of departments that offered a TA, RA, or FS to students in the program. For departments that offered both doctoral and master's degrees, more than 80% offered TAs or RAs to students, and the median stipend was approximately $12,000. About 45% of departments reported that full tuition remission was available with these assistantships. For departments that offer only master's degrees, the percentage of departments that offered TAs or RAs was lower (45%), and the median salary was approximately $6,000. Full tuition remission was reported by less than 20% of master's-only departments for either TAs or RAs.

Figure 8. Median Tuition by Type of Institution/ Residency: 2014–2015

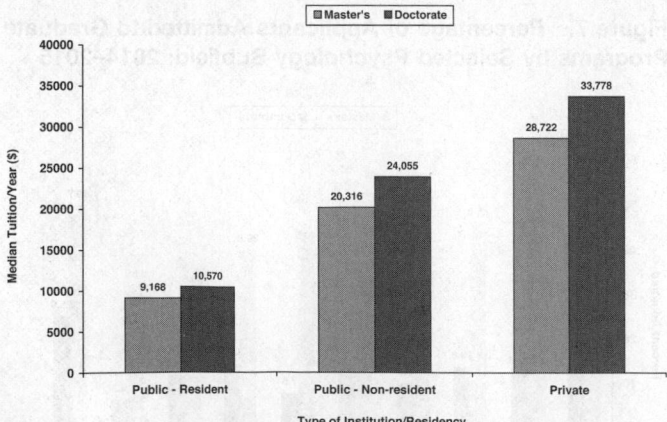

Source: *Graduate Study in Psychology, 2017 Edition* data. Prepared by the APA Office of Graduate and Postgraduate Education and Training.

Students should inquire, when receiving an offer of financial assistance, as to the amount to be given in terms of tuition remission (not requiring the student to pay tuition) versus a stipend (actual cash in hand).

For information about tuition costs and the types of assistance offered by departments and programs, review the section entitled "Financial Information/Assistance" for the programs of interest listed in this publication. You can review information listed on the APA Education website (http://www.apa.org/ed/graduate) for information about scholarships, fellowships, grants, and other funding opportunities.

The summary information presented in this introduction is based on the responses provided by the graduate programs listed in this publication. This information is not exhaustive in that a number of graduate programs in the United States and Canada are not listed in this publication and not all programs listed provide complete information to all questions. For this reason, you should look closely at the information provided by a specific program of interest to you and not rely exclusively on the group averages presented in this introduction.

Garth A. Fowler, PhD
Associate Executive Director
APA Education Directorate

Caroline Cope, MA
Research Officer
Office of Graduate and Postgraduate Education and Training
APA Education Directorate

Table 1. Financial Assistance Offered to Students, 2014–2015

	Departments Offering (%)	Median Stipend Offered ($)	Department Offering Full Remission (%)
Teaching Assistant	83.9	12000	45.5
Research Assistant	80.6	12149	45.1
Fellowship/ Scholarship	72.2	13030	35.7

Note: All departments (n = 510).

	Departments Offering (%)	Median Stipend Offered ($)	Department Offering Full Remission (%)
Teaching Assistant	65.6	6000	18.9
Research Assistant	63.9	5500	18.0
Fellowship/ Scholarship	47.5	2300	10.7

Note: Master's only departments (n = 122).

Rules for Acceptance of Offers for Admission and Financial Aid

The Council of Graduate Schools has adopted the following policy that provides guidance to students and graduate programs regarding offers of financial support. The policy was adopted by the Council of Graduate Schools in 1965 and reaffirmed in 1992. It was endorsed by the Council of Graduate Departments of Psychology in 1981 and reaffirmed in 2000. Graduate programs and schools currently listed in the book have agreed to honor the policy. The policy reads as follows:

> Acceptance of an offer of financial support (such as graduate scholarship, fellowship, traineeship, or assistantship) for the next academic year by a prospective or enrolled graduate student completes an agreement that both student and graduate school expect to honor. In that context, the conditions affecting such offers and their acceptance must be defined carefully and understood by all parties.

Students are under no obligation to respond to offers of financial support prior to April 15; earlier deadlines for acceptance of such offers violate the intent of this Resolution. In those instances in which the student accepts the offer before April 15 and subsequently desires to withdraw that acceptance, the student may submit in writing a resignation of the appointment at any time through April 15. However, an acceptance given or left in force after April 15 commits the student not to accept another offer without first obtaining a written release from the institution to which a commitment has been made. Similarly, an offer by an institution after April 15 is conditional on presentation by the student of the written release from any previously accepted offer. It is further agreed by the institutions and organizations subscribing to the above Resolution that a copy of this Resolution should accompany every scholarship, fellowship, traineeship, and assistantship offer.

Explanation of Program Listings

All information in *Graduate Study in Psychology, 2016* is self-reported by departments or schools. The following summarizes the information provide for each listing:

Contact Information

The name of the university or school, address, telephone number, name of the chairperson, e-mail, and website address are provided. There may be more than one department in an institution that offers degrees in psychology, and if so, each department is listed separately.

Orientation, Objectives, and Emphasis of Department

Each department or school writes a brief description of the orientation, objectives, and emphasis of its programs and any other helpful information about the training and education provided.

Programs and Degrees Offered

For each program or degree offered, this table lists the application deadline, the number of applications received during the previous application cycle, the number of applicants that subsequently enrolled, and the total number of students enrolled in the program. In addition, the number of degrees award for the most recent academic year is provided, along with the median number of years required for a degree and the number of students enrolled who were dismissed or voluntarily withdrew from the program before completing their degree requirements.

APA Accreditation

Whether a department or school has a program accredited in clinical psychology, counseling psychology, school psychology, or combined professional–scientific psychology is noted. Because changes in accreditation status may occur after publication, please contact the APA Office of Program Consultation and Accreditation, or review their website: (http://www.apa.org/ed/accreditation).

Internships/Practica

In this section, programs or departments provide information about internships or practica offered to students, and if internships or practica are required. Lastly, many departments provided additional information about the types of settings where students were located, the number of hours spent at the internship/practicum site, and other information. For those departments that have doctoral programs in health service psychology, information is included on the number of students who applied for an internship, the number who obtained an internship, and if the internship was paid or unpaid. In addition, the department was asked to indicate whether the student achieved an APA- or CPA-accredited internship, or if the internship was listed by the Association of Psychology Postdoctoral and Internship Centers or by the Council of Directors of School Psychology Programs (CDSPP).

Admissions

This table provides information reported on standardized test scores and GPA for each program, and if there are any required minimums for admission.

Admissions Requirements and Criteria

This section provides information regarding specific components required in an application, and a ranking of the importance of criteria used in making admission decisions.

Department Demographics

The table provides details about the number of full-time and part-time students, including information on the number of minority students in the department or school.

Financial Information/Assistance

Contact information for tuition and financial information is provided, as are tuition figures per year and per academic unit. Some schools and institutions have different fee structures for doctoral and master's students. The words *nonstate residents* are used by state universities that charge more for out-of-state residents than students who reside in the state. These fees should be used as rough guidelines and are subject to change.

Information on teaching assistantships, research assistantships, and fellowships/scholarships is reported. The data for each type of assistantship are listed for first-year and advanced students, and include the percentage of students that received each type of assistantship and whether the assistantship comes with any tuition remission.

The following definitions were used by departments when providing information:
  a) Teaching assistantship: Funds awarded to students in return for teaching services in the department or program.
  b) Research assistantship: Funds awarded to students in return for services related to research. These include funds from faculty research grants, general university funds, university training grants, and training grants given to students from funding agencies (i.e., National Institutes of Health Individual Training Grants).
  c) Fellowships/scholarships: Funds awarded to students that do not require any service in return.

Employment of Department Graduates

This section provides information about employment activities of graduates. Data presented by departments or schools include information about master's and doctoral degree graduates, such as enrollment in psychology doctoral programs and employment in academic positions, business, and government.

Additional Information

This section contains information that departments or schools provide regarding the availability of housing and day care services, information for students with disabilities, and application costs and a link to the online application (if available). In addition, departments and schools have the option of providing details regarding special facilities and resources available to students.

Also included in this section are statements related to personal behavior and religious beliefs that are considered a condition for admission to and retention in the program. In the interest of full disclosure to prospective students, therefore, departments, programs, or the institutions by which they are governed that have a statement to this effect are requested to cite the statement or provide a link at which it can be found.

2017

Graduate Study in Psychology

2017

Graduate
Study
in
Psychology

Alabama, University of
Department of Psychology
College of Arts and Sciences
Box 870348
Tuscaloosa, AL 35487-0348
Telephone: (205) 348-1919
Chairperson: Frances A. Conners

E-mail: mary.b.hubbard@ua.edu
Web: http://psychology.ua.edu/graduate-studies/

Orientation, Objectives, and Emphasis of Department
The University of Alabama doctoral program in psychology was founded in 1957 and trains students in clinical and experimental psychology. The clinical program has been continually accredited by the American Psychological Association since 1959. The department trains scientists and scientist–practitioners for a variety of roles: research, teaching, and applied practice. Both the clinical and the experimental programs strongly emphasize furthering psychology as a science. The clinical program has specialty areas in psychology-law, clinical-child, gerontology, and health and the experimental program has specialty areas in cognitive, social, and developmental. The social and developmental training areas involve exciting collaborations with other units on campus. The doctoral programs emphasize core knowledge in the social, cognitive, developmental, and biological aspects of behavior as well as methodological/statistical foundations. All students take additional courses designed to prepare them with the necessary knowledge and skills in their chosen specialty area. A further objective of the department is to promote independent scholarship and professional development. Coursework is supplemented by the active collaboration of faculty and students in ongoing research projects and clinical activities. The department maintains access to a wide range of settings in which students can refine their research and applied skills.

Programs and Degrees Offered

Program	Degree	Application Deadline	Applications Received	Accepted	New Admits Enrolled (PT)	Total Enrolled (PT)	Degrees Awarded in 2014–2015	Median Years to Complete Degree	Dismissed/Withdrew
Clinical Psychology	PhD	December 1 (Fall)	287	19	10	70	14	6	1
Cognitive Psychology	PhD	December 15 (Fall)	9	1	2 (0)	12 (0)	1	5	0
Social Psychology	PhD	December 15 (Fall)	22	8	5 (0)	21 (0)	3	5.5	2
Developmental Science	PhD	December 15 (Fall)	15	5	2 (0)	9 (0)	3	4.33	1

APA Accreditation
Clinical PhD: Student Outcome Data website: http://psychology.ua.edu/graduate-studies/clinical-psychology/.

Doctoral Degree (PhD Clinical Psychology): For those doctoral students for whom a professional internship was required in this program prior to graduation:
Total students who applied for an internship: 15
Total students who obtained an internship: 15
Total students who obtained a paid internship: 15
Total students who obtained an unpaid internship: 0
Total students who were placed in APA/CPA-accredited internships: 15
Total students placed in internships not APA/CPA-accredited, but listed with the Association of Psychology Postdoctoral and Internship Centers (APPIC): 0
Total students placed in internships conforming to guidelines of the Council of Directors of School Psychology Programs (CDSPP): 0
Total students placed in internships that were not APA/CPA-accredited, APPIC or CDSSP listed: 0

Internships/Practica
There are a number of practica available to graduate students. All doctoral students take PY695, a teaching internship, in which the student teaches an introductory psychology class under the supervision of a faculty member. Two semesters of basic psychotherapy

practicum are required of every doctoral student in clinical psychology. In this practicum, students conduct psychotherapy with four to six clients in the Department's Psychological Clinic. Students complete approximately 100 hours of direct client contact to fulfill this requirement. After basic psychotherapy practicum, doctoral clinical psychology students take either one or two (depending on specialty area) advanced practica in their area of specialization. Many of these practica are housed in community service agencies (e.g., state psychiatric hospital, community mental health center, University-operated treatment center for disturbed children). In addition to these formal practica, most doctoral students in the clinical program are financially supported at some time during their graduate school years through field placements in various community agencies. These students are supervised by either licensed psychologists employed by these agencies or by Department of Psychology clinical faculty. In addition to the intervention practica discussed above, all clinical doctoral students must take two of the three graduate psychological assessment courses offered.

Admissions

Entries appear in the following order: required test or GPA, minimum score (if required)/median score of students entering in 2015–2016.

Program	Degree	GRE-V	GRE-Q	GRE-Writing	GRE-Subject	Under-graduate GPA	Last 2 Years GPA	Psychol-ogy GPA	Master's GPA
Clinical Psychology	PhD	NA/161	NA/156	NA/5	Not specified	NA/3.8	Not specified	Not specified	Not specified
Cognitive Psychology	PhD	NA/151	NA/152	NA/3.75	Not specified	NA/3.3	Not specified	Not specified	Not specified
Social Psychology	PhD	NA/159	NA/158	NA/4	Not specified	NA/3.4	Not specified	Not specified	Not specified
Developmental Science	PhD	NA/151	NA/146	NA/4	Not specified	NA/3.9	Not specified	Not specified	Not specified

Admissions Requirements:

Degree	GRE	GRE-Subject	Letters of Recom-mendation	Research Statement	Writing Sample	CV	Interview
Doctoral	Required	Recom-mended	3	Required	Optional	Required	Required

Please note if these criteria vary for different programs: GRE Advanced Subject Test is preferred (but not required) for applicants to the Clinical Program.

Admissions Criteria:

GRE scores—high
Research experience—high
Work experience—low
Clinically related public service—low
GPA—medium

Letters of recommendation—high
Interview—medium
Statement of goals and objectives—high
Undergraduate psychology preparation—medium

For additional information on admission requirements, visit http://psychology.ua.edu/graduate-studies/graduate-admissions-process/.

Department Demographics

	Male (PT)	Female (PT)	Total	African-American/ Black (PT)	Hispanic/ Latino (PT)	Asian/ Pacific Islander (PT)	American Indian/ Alaska Native (PT)	Caucasian/ White (PT)	Unknown	Multiethnic (PT)	ADA (PT)	Int'l (PT)
Students	30 (0)	82 (0)	112	3 (0)	6 (0)	10 (0)	0 (0)	91 (0)	0 (0)	2 (0)	0 (0)	9 (0)

Financial Information/Assistance

Tuition: For information on tuition costs, visit https://studentaccounts.ua.edu/cost/. Tuition is subject to change. Additional fees are assessed to students beyond the costs of tuition for the following: course fee - $10.00 per hour; facility/technology fee - $9.50 per hour.

Doctoral:
State residents: $10,170 per academic year.
Nonstate residents: $25,950 per academic year.

Financial Assistance:

	Teaching Assistantship (% Receiving)	Teaching Assistantship Tuition Remission	Research Assistantship (% Receiving)	Research Assistantship Tuition Remission	Fellowship (% Receiving)	Fellowship Tuition Remission
First-Year Student	$14,562 (NA)	Full	$13,500 (NA)	Full	$15,000 (NA)	Full
Advanced Student	$14,562 (NA)	Full	$13,500 (NA)	Full	$15,000 (NA)	Full

For additional information on financial assistance, visit http://graduate.ua.edu/students/financial-support/.

Employment of Department Graduates

Doctoral:
Enrolled in a postdoctoral residency/fellowship: 5
Employed in independent practice: 2
Employed in an academic position at a university: 5
Employed in government agency: 8
Employed in a hospital/medical center: 1
Still seeking employment: 1
Total: 22

Additional Information

Housing and Day Care: No on-campus housing is available. On-campus day care facilities are available. See the following website for more information: http://www.hdfs.ches.ua.edu/childrens-program.html.

Information for Students With Physical Disabilities: See the following website: http://ods.ua.edu.

Special Facilities or Resources: The department is housed in a four-story building that it shares with the Department of Mathematics. It is directly connected to the University's Seebeck Computer Center. Facilities include faculty offices, student offices, classroom and seminar space, and research laboratories. Graduate students have access to microcomputers for research and word processing and videotaping capabilities for instruction and training. A major resource is the Psychology Clinic which recently moved to newly renovated space a short distance from the department offices. This clinic provides psychological assessment, referral, treatment planning, and direct intervention for a variety of clinical populations. The department's Child and Family Research Clinic serves as a specialized training and research laboratory and houses the departments Autism College Transition Program (UA-ACTS). Both clinics include observation facilities. Also affiliated with the department is the brand new Child Development Research Center, which has research, office, and training space, and runs a state-of-the-art preschool and where the department's Autism Clinic is located. Other affiliations on campus include the Alabama Research Institute on Aging, the Institute for Social Science Research, the Brewer-Porch Childrens Center, the Student Counseling Center, and the University Medical Center.

Application Information: Office of the Graduate School, University of Alabama, Box 870118, Tuscaloosa, AL 35487-0118. *Fee:* $50. *Online application:* http://graduate.ua.edu/application/.

Alabama, University of, at Birmingham
Department of Psychology
Arts and Sciences
415 Campbell Hall
Birmingham, AL 35294-1170
Telephone: (205) 934-3850
Chairperson: Karlene Ball, PhD

E-mail: kball@uab.edu
Web: http://www.uab.edu/cas/psychology/

Orientation, Objectives, and Emphasis of Department

The Department offers three doctoral programs: Clinical/Medical Psychology, Behavioral Neuroscience, and Developmental Psychology. The program promotes rigorous scientific training to produce scholars who are prepared to engage in independent research, clinical practice, and teaching. Medical/Clinical Psychology (co-sponsored and -administrated by the UAB School of Medicine) provides broad clinical training with an additional focus on behavioral and psychological factors in medical care and health as well as biological factors in mental illness. The Behavioral Neuroscience Program provides individualized, interdisciplinary training for research on the biological bases of behavior. The Developmental Program trains students to conduct research to discover and apply basic principles of developmental psychology across the lifespan in an interdisciplinary context. Students are exposed to the issues of development in its natural and social contexts, as well as in laboratories. Across the three programs, faculty research interests include: neuropsychology, psychophysiology, adult and developmental psychopathology, neuroimaging, sensation and perception, pain, spinal cord injury, control of movement, rehabilitation, aging, mental retardation/developmental disabilities, healthy aging, pediatric psychology, injury prevention, social ecology, cognitive development, caregiver and survivor issues, cancer, eating disorders, obesity, substance abuse, and psychopharmacology.

Programs and Degrees Offered

Program	Degree	Application Deadline	Applications Received	Accepted	New Admits Enrolled (PT)	Total Enrolled (PT)	Degrees Awarded in 2014–2015	Median Years to Complete Degree	Dismissed/ Withdrew
Behavioral Neuroscience	PhD	November 30 (Fall)	24	5	5	19 (0)	4	5.67	0
Lifespan Developmental Psychology	PhD	November 30 (Fall)	14	4	4 (0)	19 (0)	3	4.5	0
Medical/ Clinical Psychology	PhD	November 30 (Fall)	121	9	7 (0)	38 (0)	7	5	0

APA Accreditation

Clinical PhD: Student Outcome Data website: http://www.uab.edu/cas/psychology/graduate/medical-clinical-psychology.

Doctoral Degree (PhD Medical/Clinical Psychology): For those doctoral students for whom a professional internship was required in this program prior to graduation:
Total students who applied for an internship: 6
Total students who obtained an internship: 4
Total students who obtained a paid internship: 4
Total students who obtained an unpaid internship: 0
Total students who were placed in APA/CPA-accredited internships: 4
Total students placed in internships not APA/CPA-accredited, but listed with the Association of Psychology Postdoctoral and Internship Centers (APPIC): 0
Total students placed in internships conforming to guidelines of the Council of Directors of School Psychology Programs (CDSPP): 0
Total students placed in internships that were not APA/CPA-accredited, APPIC or CDSSP listed: 0

Internships/Practica

Students in the Medical/Clinical Psychology Program have opportunities for clinical practica with faculty distributed widely across the UAB campus. Participating faculty as well as clinical and research opportunities are located in the following departments and divisions, among others: Psychology, Psychiatry, Neurology, Pediatrics, Physical Medicine and Rehabilitation, Anesthesiology, Immunology and Rheumatology, and Gerontology, Geriatrics and Palliative Care. Interdisciplinary practicum opportunities are available in the Civitan-Sparks Clinics, the Center for Psychiatric Medicine, the Spain Rehabilitation Center, and throughout the UAB Medical Center as well as the adjacent Birmingham VA Medical Center and Children's of Alabama hospitals.

Admissions

Entries appear in the following order: required test or GPA, minimum score (if required)/median score of students entering in 2015–2016.

Program	Degree	GRE-V	GRE-Q	GRE-Writing	GRE-Subject	Undergraduate GPA	Last 2 Years GPA	Psychology GPA	Master's GPA
Behavioral Neuroscience	PhD	NA/160	NA/161	NA/4	Not specified	Not specified	Not specified	Not specified	Not specified

Admissions *cont'd*

Program	Degree	GRE-V	GRE-Q	GRE-Writing	GRE-Subject	Undergraduate GPA	Last 2 Years GPA	Psychology GPA	Master's GPA
Lifespan Developmental Psychology	PhD	NA/160	NA/156	NA/4.25	Not specified	NA/3.8	Not specified	Not specified	Not specified
Medical/Clinical Psychology	PhD	NA/162	NA/157	NA/5	NA/NA	NA/3.83	Not specified	Not specified	Not specified

Admissions Requirements:

Degree	GRE	GRE-Subject	Letters of Recommendation	Research Statement	Writing Sample	CV	Interview
Doctoral	Required	Recommended	3	Required	Optional	Required	Required

Please note if these criteria vary for different programs: GRE Psychology Subject Test is recommended for Medical/Clinical Psychology.

Admissions Criteria:

GRE scores—high
Research experience—high
Work experience—low
Clinically related public service—medium
GPA—high

Letters of recommendation—medium
Interview—medium
Statement of goals and objectives—high
Undergraduate psychology preparation—low

For additional information on admission requirements, visit https://www.uab.edu/cas/psychology/graduate-programs.

Department Demographics

	Male (PT)	Female (PT)	Total	African-American/ Black (PT)	Hispanic/ Latino (PT)	Asian/ Pacific Islander (PT)	American Indian/ Alaska Native (PT)	Caucasian/ White (PT)	Unknown	Multiethnic (PT)	ADA (PT)	Int'l (PT)
Students	18 (0)	58 (0)	76	4 (0)	2 (0)	3 (0)	0 (0)	66 (0)	0 (0)	1 (0)	2 (0)	2 (0)

Financial Information/Assistance

Tuition: For information on tuition costs, visit http://www.uab.edu/students/paying-for-uab/detailed-tuition-and-fees. Tuition is subject to change.

Doctoral:
State residents: $9,778 per academic year.
State residents: $383 per credit hour.
Nonstate residents: $899 per credit hour.

Financial Assistance:

	Teaching Assistantship (% Receiving)	Teaching Assistantship Tuition Remission	Research Assistantship (% Receiving)	Research Assistantship Tuition Remission	Fellowship (% Receiving)	Fellowship Tuition Remission
First-Year Student	NA (NA)	NA	NA (NA)	NA	$21,334 (100)	Full
Advanced Student	$21,335 (20)	Full	$21,768 (65)	Full	$22,293 (15)	Full

Employment of Department Graduates

Doctoral:
Enrolled in a postdoctoral residency/fellowship: 12
Employed in an academic position at a university: 1
Other employment position: 1
Total: 14

Additional Information

Housing and Day Care: On-campus housing is available. See the following website for more information: https://www.uab.edu/students/housing. On-campus day care facilities are available. See the following website for more information: http://www.uab.edu/humanresources/home/childdevelopmentcenter.

Information for Students With Physical Disabilities: See the following website: http://www.uab.edu/students/services/disability-support-services.

Special Facilities or Resources: The University of Alabama at Birmingham is a comprehensive, urban research university with an enrollment of approximately 18,000 students, including 6,000 graduate students. UAB receives approximately $500 million dollars in external funds annually for research support, and the UAB Psychology Department, in the College of Arts and Sciences, ranks among the top 100 psychology departments in the U.S. by NSF in federal/research funding. Facilities available to graduate students include academic and health sciences libraries with on- and off-campus electronic access, well-equipped laboratories in the Departments of Psychology, Neurology, Psychiatry and Behavioral Neurobiology, and Immunology and Rheumatology, as well as a 3-Tesla neuroimaging facility in the Civitan International Research Center. UAB's Center for Clinical and Translational Science provides support for genetic research as well as a variety of other research infrastructure needs. The UAB Medical Center and associated psychiatric, rehabilitation, pediatric, and veterans' hospitals provide ample access to patient populations and a culture that fosters interdisciplinary and collaborative research.

Application Information: Fee: $0. *Online application:* https://app.applyyourself.com/?id=uab-grad.

Alabama, University of, at Huntsville
Department of Psychology
College of Arts, Humanities, and Social Sciences
Morton Hall 335
Huntsville, AL 35899
Telephone: (256) 824-6191
Chairperson: Jeffrey Neuschatz

E-mail: carpens@email.uah.edu
Web: http://www.uah.edu/ahs/departments/psychology

Orientation, Objectives, and Emphasis of Department
The content of our program is directed toward the study of psychology as an intellectual and scientific pursuit, as contrasted with training directly applicable to counseling or psychology licensure and practice. Specialization areas include applied, social/personality, cognitive, developmental, and biological psychology. The program is designed for a small number of students who will work closely with individual faculty members and with each other. Although there are a few structured courses that are required of all students, a substantial portion of the students' program focuses on individual readings, research and a thesis.

Programs and Degrees Offered

Program	Degree	Application Deadline	Applications Received	Accepted	New Admits Enrolled (PT)	Total Enrolled (PT)	Degrees Awarded in 2014–2015	Median Years to Complete Degree	Dismissed/ Withdrew
General Experimental Psychology	MA/MS	June 1 (Fall), October 15 (Spring), March 15 (Summer)	15	8	8 (0)	1 (0)	4	2	0

Programs and Degrees Offered *cont'd*

Program	Degree	Application Deadline	Applica-tions Received	Accepted	New Admits Enrolled (PT)	Total Enrolled (PT)	Degrees Awarded in 2014–2015	Median Years to Complete Degree	Dismissed/Withdrew
I/O Psychology Specialization	MA/MS	June 1 (Fall), October 15 (Spring), March 15 (Summer)	6	2	4	4	2	2	0

Internships/Practica

Internships in academic student advising and in psychological test administration may be available for some students.

Admissions

Entries appear in the following order: required test or GPA, minimum score (if required)/median score of students entering in 2015–2016.

Program	Degree	GRE-V	GRE-Q	GRE-Writing	GRE-Subject	Under-graduate GPA	Last 2 Years GPA	Psychol-ogy GPA	Master's GPA
General Experimental Psychology	MA/MS	150/NA	150/NA	Not specified	Not specified	3.25/NA	Not specified	Not specified	Not specified
I/O Psychology Specialization	MA/MS	150/NA	150/NA	Not specified	Not specified	3.25/NA	NA/NA	Not specified	Not specified

Admissions Requirements:

Degree	GRE	GRE-Subject	Letters of Recom-mendation	Research Statement	Writing Sample	CV	Interview
Master's/Specialist	Required	None	3	Required	Required	Recom-mended	Required

Admissions Criteria:

GRE scores—high
Research experience—high
Work experience—low
Clinically related public service—low
GPA—high

Letters of recommendation—high
Statement of goals and objectives—high
Undergraduate psychology preparation—high
Empirical paper—high

For additional information on admission requirements, visit http://www.uah.edu/ahs/departments/psychology/programs/graduate.

Department Demographics

	Male (PT)	Female (PT)	Total	African-American/ Black (PT)	Hispanic/ Latino (PT)	Asian/ Pacific Islander (PT)	American Indian/ Alaska Native (PT)	Caucasian/ White (PT)	Unknown	Multiethnic (PT)	ADA (PT)	Int'l (PT)
Students	6 (1)	11 (3)	21	0 (0)	1 (0)	(0)	0 (0)	9 (4)	0 (0)	0 (0)	0 (0)	0 (0)

Financial Information/Assistance

Tuition: For information on tuition costs, visit http://www.uah.edu/bursar/tuition. Tuition is subject to change.

Master's:
State residents: $9,180 per academic year.
State residents: $655 per credit hour.
Nonstate residents: $22,320 per academic year.
Nonstate residents: $1,451 per credit hour.

Financial Assistance:

	Teaching Assistantship (% Receiving)	Teaching Assistantship Tuition Remission	Research Assistantship (% Receiving)	Research Assistantship Tuition Remission	Fellowship (% Receiving)	Fellowship Tuition Remission
First-Year Student	NA (NA)	NA	NA (NA)	Partial	NA (NA)	Partial
Advanced Student	$10,000 (NA)	Full	$10,000 (NA)	Partial	$4,000 (NA)	Full

For additional information on financial assistance, visit http://www.uah.edu/admissions/graduate/financial-aid.

Employment of Department Graduates

Master's:
Enrolled in a psychology doctoral program: 3
Enrolled in another graduate/professional program: 1
Other employment position: 2
Do not know: 1
Total: 7

Additional Information

Housing and Day Care: On-campus housing is available. See the following website for more information: http://www.uah.edu/housing/. On-campus day care facilities are available. See the following website for more information: http://www.uah.edu/ctc/child-care.

Information for Students With Physical Disabilities: See the following website: http://www.uah.edu/health-and-wellness/disability-support.

Special Facilities or Resources: Access to research facilities at NASA's Marshall Space Flight Center is available via an existing Space Act Agreement. Students also have access to archives at the National Children's Advocacy Center. Some students work collaboratively with the scientists in the Center for Simulation and Modeling on the UAH campus.

Application Information: Department Chair, Department of Psychology, Morton Hall 335, University of Alabama in Huntsville, Huntsville, AL 35899. *Fee:* $40. *Online application:* http://www.uah.edu/admissions/graduate/admission-process.

Auburn University
Department of Psychology
College of Liberal Arts
226 Thach Hall
Auburn University, AL 36849-5214
Telephone: (334) 844-4412
Department Head: Peter Chen

E-mail: bryangt@auburn.edu
Web: http://www.cla.auburn.edu/psychology/

Orientation, Objectives, and Emphasis of Department
Auburn's psychology programs offer training in basic research and in the application of knowledge and theory to societal problems. Faculty are committed to the premise that inquiry, breadth, and respect for the research process and the application of behavioral

science knowledge are valued elements in graduate education. Students work closely in laboratories with fellow students and faculty mentors. Students interested in applied work receive direct experience and supervision within community agencies and organizations where theory and technique can be practiced and refined. The Clinical Psychology training program applies a scientist–practitioner model that blends an empirical approach to knowledge within an experiential context. The Cognitive and Behavioral Sciences (CaBS) program provides training in Psychological Sciences. Top-notch animal and human laboratories are available in a number of settings. The Industrial/Organizational (I/O) program emphasizes a scientist–practitioner approach to improve both organizational effectiveness and the quality of work life of individual employees. The Applied Behavior Analysis (ABA) in Developmental Disabilities program (Master's) trains students to provide evidence-based behavioral services to individuals with developmental disabilities and prepares students to qualify for certification by the Behavior Analyst Certification Board. This 2-year program integrates foundational and specialized coursework with carefully designed practicum experiences.

Programs and Degrees Offered

Program	Degree	Application Deadline	Applications Received	Accepted	New Admits Enrolled (PT)	Total Enrolled (PT)	Degrees Awarded in 2014–2015	Median Years to Complete Degree	Dismissed/ Withdrew
Clinical Psychology	PhD	December 1 (Fall)	230	11	6 (0)	34 (0)	8	6	0
Cognitive and Behavioral Sciences	PhD	January 15 (Fall)	24	3	2 (0)	25 (0)	4	5.33	1
Industrial/ Organizational Psychology	PhD	January 15 (Fall)	64	6	4 (0)	19 (0)	4	6.33	0
ABA in Developmental Disabilities	MA/MS	February 1 (Fall)	64	12	12 (0)	12 (0)	10	1	0

APA Accreditation

Clinical PhD: Student Outcome Data website: http://www.cla.auburn.edu/psychology/clinical/student-admissions-outcomes-and-other-data1/.

Doctoral Degree (PhD Clinical Psychology): For those doctoral students for whom a professional internship was required in this program prior to graduation:
Total students who applied for an internship: 4
Total students who obtained an internship: 4
Total students who obtained a paid internship: 4
Total students who obtained an unpaid internship: 0
Total students who were placed in APA/CPA-accredited internships: 4
Total students placed in internships not APA/CPA-accredited, but listed with the Association of Psychology Postdoctoral and Internship Centers (APPIC): 0
Total students placed in internships conforming to guidelines of the Council of Directors of School Psychology Programs (CDSPP): 0
Total students placed in internships that were not APA/CPA-accredited, APPIC or CDSSP listed: 0

Master's Degree (MA/MS ABA in Developmental Disabilities): An internship experience, such as a final research project or "capstone" experience is required of graduates.

Internships/Practica

Current practicum sites that offer assistantships for clinical students are Auburn University Psychological Services Center, adolescent Correctional Facility, the Auburn University School System, Auburn University Student Counseling Services, Mt. Meigs Agency Program, the Central Alabama Veterans Health University macy, UAB/Montgomery Internal Medicine/Family Medicine Center Diabetes and Nutrition Center, and other Institute. West Central Georgia Regional Hospital, East Alabama training at a number of area organizations, including students may health settings. I/O psychology students receive paid placement, and the Fort Benning Field Station of the Disabilities at Montgomery's Center for Business and Economic internships before completing their doctoral including I/O students may participate in these and other students in the Master's Program in ABA Resources. participate in practica at the Army Research es various sites serving individuals with dev participate in an intensive practicum program arning Tree Tallassee Campus, and Lee local public schools, the Little Tree Presch

Admissions

Entries appear in the following order: required test or GPA, minimum score (if required)/median score of students entering in 2015–2016.

Program	Degree	GRE-V	GRE-Q	GRE-Writing	GRE-Subject	Undergraduate GPA	Last 2 Years GPA	Psychology GPA	Master's GPA
Clinical Psychology	PhD	NA/160	NA/155	NA/4.5	Not specified	NA/3.7	Not specified	Not specified	Not specified
Cognitive and Behavioral Sciences	PhD	NA/158	NA/152	NA/3.5	Not specified	NA/3.3	Not specified	Not specified	Not specified
Industrial/ Organizational Psychology	PhD	NA/159	NA/154	NA/3.75	Not specified	3/3.7	Not specified	Not specified	Not specified
ABA in Developmental Disabilities	MA/MS	NA/155	NA/157	NA/4	Not specified	NA/3.6	Not specified	Not specified	Not specified

Admissions Requirements:

Degree	GRE	GRE-Subject	Letters of Recommendation	Research Statement	Writing Sample	CV	Interview
Master's/Specialist	Required	None	3	Required	Optional	Required	Required
Doctoral	Required	None	3	Required	Optional	Required	Required

Please note if these criteria vary for different programs: For I/O and CaBS programs, clinically related public service has less significance. For I/O program, Undergraduate psychology preparation is of medium importance.

Admissions Criteria:

GRE scores—high
Research experience—high
Work experience—medium
Clinically related public service—medium
GPA—high

Letters of recommendation—high
Interview—high
Statement of goals and objectives—medium
Undergraduate psychology preparation—high

Department Demographics

	Male (PT)	Female (PT)	Total	African American/ Black (PT)	Hispanic/ Latin (PT)	Asian/ Pacific Islander (PT)	American Indian/ Alaska Native (PT)	Caucasian/ White (PT)	Unknown	Multiethnic (PT)	ADA (PT)	Int'l (PT)
Students	30 (0)	60 (0)	90	6 (0)	3 (0)	7	0 (0)	74 (0)	0 (0)	0 (0)	0 (0)	7 (0)

Financial Information/Assistance

Tuition

For information on tuition costs, visit http://www.auburn.edu/administration/business_office/sfs/. Tuition is subject to change. ... the following: $808 per semester Student Services Fee.

Fees are assessed to students beyond the costs of tuition ...

Doctoral
State re...
State re...
Nonstate 3,203 per academic year.
Nonstate ... per credit hour.
... .609 per academic year.
... 7 per credit hour.

Stu...
Stat...
No...dents: $13,203 per academic year.
Nong...s: $489 per credit hour.
...dents: $39,609 per academic year.
...s: $1,467 per credit hour.

Financial Assistance:

	Teaching Assistantship (% Receiving)	Teaching Assistantship Tuition Remission	Research Assistantship (% Receiving)	Research Assistantship Tuition Remission	Fellowship (% Receiving)	Fellowship Tuition Remission
First-Year Student	$13,680 (100)	Full	NA (NA)	NA	NA (NA)	NA
Advanced Student	$14,400 (40)	Full	$14,400 (40)	Full	NA (NA)	NA

Employment of Department Graduates

Master's:
Employed in academic position at a 2-year/4-year college: 1
Employed in other positions at a higher education institution: 1
Employed in a community mental health/counseling center: 8
Total: 10

Doctoral:
Enrolled in a postdoctoral residency/fellowship: 7
Employed in an academic position at a university: 1
Employed in academic position at a 2-year/4-year college: 3
Employed in business or industry: 3
Employed in government agency: 1
Still seeking employment: 1
Total: 16

Additional Information

Housing and Day Care: No on-campus housing is available. No on-campus day care facilities are available.

Information for Students With Physical Disabilities: See the following website: https://accessibility.auburn.edu/.

Special Facilities or Resources: The department administers a multipurpose psychological services center in a renovated and newly furnished building. Relationships with extra-university agencies and organizations facilitate training in applied research. A relationship with the Auburn University MRI Research Center allows us access to an open-bore 3T MRI scanner and a whole-body 7T MRI scanner for cutting-edge research in neuroimaging and cognitive neuroscience.

Application Information: Fee: $60. *Online application:* https://app.applyyourself.com/?id=auburn-g.

Auburn University
Special Education, Rehabilitation, Counseling
College of Education
2084 Haley Center
Auburn University, AL 36849-5222
Telephone: (334) 844-7676
E-mail: ask0002@auburn.edu
Department Head: Everett D. Martin   Web: http://www.education.auburn.edu/special-education-rehabilitation-and-counseling

Orientation, Objectives, and Emphasis of Department
The department values teaching, research, and outreach that contribute to the missions of the College and University. Further, the department seeks to foster a culture in which individual creativity and scholarship is reinforced and nurtured. Diversity is considered a core value in all that we do.

Programs and Degrees Offered

Program	Degree	Application Deadline	Applications Received	Accepted	New Admits Enrolled (PT)	Total Enrolled (PT)	Degrees Awarded in 2014–2015	Median Years to Complete Degree	Dismissed/ Withdrew
Counseling Psychology	PhD	December 11 (Fall)	72	11	7 (0)	45 (0)	5	5	1

APA Accreditation

Counseling PhD: Student Outcome Data website: http://www.education.auburn.edu/graduate-degree-cert/counseling-psychology-ph-d/.

Doctoral Degree (PhD Counseling Psychology): For those doctoral students for whom a professional internship was required in this program prior to graduation:

Total students who applied for an internship: 6
Total students who obtained an internship: 6
Total students who obtained a paid internship: 6
Total students who obtained an unpaid internship: 0
Total students who were placed in APA/CPA-accredited internships: 6
Total students placed in internships not APA/CPA-accredited, but listed with the Association of Psychology Postdoctoral and Internship Centers (APPIC): 0
Total students placed in internships conforming to guidelines of the Council of Directors of School Psychology Programs (CDSPP): 0
Total students placed in internships that were not APA/CPA-accredited, APPIC or CDSSP listed: 0

Internships/Practica

University counseling centers; community mental health centers; VAs; hospitals; community counseling agencies; jail/prison; military. Students participate in the APPIC match to apply to internship.

Admissions

Entries appear in the following order: required test or GPA, minimum score (if required)/median score of students entering in 2015–2016.

Program	Degree	GRE-V	GRE-Q	GRE-Writing	GRE-Subject	Under-graduate GPA	Last 2 Years GPA	Psychol-ogy GPA	Master's GPA
Counseling Psychology	PhD	NA/157	NA/155	NA/4.5	Not specified	NA/3.7	NA/NA	NA/NA	Not specified

Admissions Requirements:

Degree	GRE	GRE-Subject	Letters of Recommendation	Research Statement	Writing Sample	CV	Interview
Doctoral	Required	Optional	3	Required	Required	Required	Required

Please note if these criteria vary for different programs: The writing sample for the Counseling Psychology doctoral program is done at the time of the interview and provides information about how applicants think about information in a clinical way. We also look at how they communicate that information in written form. It is not a formal writing test. We do examine closely the scores on the Analytical Writing section of the GRE.

Admissions Criteria:

GRE scores—medium
Research experience—high
Work experience—medium
Clinically related public service—medium
GPA—high

Letters of recommendation—high
Interview—high
Statement of goals and objectives—high
Undergraduate psychology preparation—medium

For additional information on admission requirements, visit http://www.education.auburn.edu/sercapp-cop.

Department Demographics

	Male (PT)	Female (PT)	Total	African-American/ Black (PT)	Hispanic/ Latino (PT)	Asian/ Pacific Islander (PT)	American Indian/ Alaska Native (PT)	Caucasian/ White (PT)	Unknown	Multiethnic (PT)	ADA (PT)	Int'l (PT)
Students	10 (0)	35 (0)	45	9 (0)	1 (0)	3 (0)	0 (0)	31 (0)	0 (0)	1 (0)	1 (0)	2 (0)

Financial Information/Assistance

Tuition: For information on tuition costs, visit http://www.auburn.edu/administration/business_office/sfs/tuition-rates.html. Tuition is subject to change. Additional fees are assessed to students beyond the costs of tuition for the following: Approximately $2,400/year.

Doctoral:
State residents: $13,203 per academic year.
State residents: $489 per credit hour.
Nonstate residents: $39,609 per academic year.
Nonstate residents: $1,467 per credit hour.

Financial Assistance:

	Teaching Assistantship (% Receiving)	Teaching Assistantship Tuition Remission	Research Assistantship (% Receiving)	Research Assistantship Tuition Remission	Fellowship (% Receiving)	Fellowship Tuition Remission
First-Year Student	$6,100 (28)	Full	$6,100 (74)	Full	NA (NA)	Full
Advanced Student	$6,100 (8)	Full	$6,100 (50)	Full	NA (NA)	Full

For additional information on financial assistance, visit http://www.education.auburn.edu/serc-scholarship-information.

Employment of Department Graduates

Doctoral:
Enrolled in a postdoctoral residency/fellowship: 1
Employed in other positions at a higher education institution: 3
Employed in government agency: 1
Total: 5

Additional Information

Housing and Day Care: On-campus housing is available. See the following website for more information: http://auburn.edu/administration/housing/. No on-campus day care facilities are available.

Information for Students With Physical Disabilities: See the following website: http://accessibility.auburn.edu/.

Special Facilities or Resources: Interdisciplinary community. University partnership serving underserved, rural minority communities devoted to education, research and service. We also partner with University Student Affairs, Career Services, Housing, and the Athletic Department.

Application Information: Counseling Psychology, 2084 Haley Center, Auburn University, AL 36849-5222. *Fee:* $60. *Online application:* http://grad.auburn.edu/prospective.html.

Jacksonville State University
Department of Psychology
College of Graduate Studies
700 Pelham Road, North
Jacksonville, AL 36265-1602
Telephone: (256) 782-5402
Chairperson: Paige McKerchar, PhD, BCBA-D

E-mail: pmkerchar@jsu.edu
Web: http://www.jsu.edu/psychology/

Orientation, Objectives, and Emphasis of Department
JSU's master's program in psychology offers instruction and training in the analysis of behavior. Students complete courses in the experimental analysis of behavior and applied behavior analysis. Courses in the experimental analysis of behavior teach students about basic functional relations between environmental events and behavior, whereas courses in applied behavior analysis train

students in the application of those basic behavioral principles to human populations. Hands-on experience is available in our animal and human research facilities and local practicum sites. The program has a Behavior Analyst Certification Board (BACB)-approved course sequence and is accredited by the Association for Behavior Analysis International.

Programs and Degrees Offered

Program	Degree	Application Deadline	Applications Received	Accepted	New Admits Enrolled (PT)	Total Enrolled (PT)	Degrees Awarded in 2014–2015	Median Years to Complete Degree	Dismissed/ Withdrew
Applied Psychology	MA/MS	August 1 (Fall), Rolling	18	12	8 (0)	13 (2)	7	2	1

Internships/Practica

Applied Behavior Analysis practica are available in a variety of settings in which behavioral principles are used to improve human behavior. An Instructional Practicum is also available and allows outstanding students to gain teaching experience assisting a psychology professor.

Admissions

Entries appear in the following order: required test or GPA, minimum score (if required)/median score of students entering in 2015–2016.

Program	Degree	GRE-V	GRE-Q	GRE-Writing	GRE-Subject	Undergraduate GPA	Last 2 Years GPA	Psychology GPA	Master's GPA
Applied Psychology	MA/MS	NA/155	NA/145	NA/3	Not specified	NA/3.29	Not specified	Not specified	Not specified

Admissions Requirements:

Degree	GRE	GRE-Subject	Letters of Recommendation	Research Statement	Writing Sample	CV	Interview
Master's/Specialist	Required	None	3	Required	None	Required	None

Admissions Criteria:

GRE scores—high
Research experience—medium
Work experience—medium
Clinically related public service—medium

GPA—high
Letters of recommendation—high
Statement of goals and objectives—high
Undergraduate psychology preparation—high

For additional information on admission requirements, visit http://www.jsu.edu/psychology/gradfaq.html.

Department Demographics

	Male (PT)	Female (PT)	Total	African-American/ Black (PT)	Hispanic/ Latino (PT)	Asian/ Pacific Islander (PT)	American Indian/ Alaska Native (PT)	Caucasian/ White (PT)	Unknown	Multiethnic (PT)	ADA (PT)	Int'l (PT)
Students	1 (2)	12 (0)	15	1 (0)	0 (0)	0 (0)	0 (0)	11 (2)	1 (0)	0 (0)	0 (0)	0 (0)

Financial Information/Assistance

Tuition: For information on tuition costs, visit http://www.jsu.edu/bursar/fees/index.html. Tuition is subject to change. Additional fees are assessed to students beyond the costs of tuition for the following: $150 General University fee (per fall and spring only).

Master's:
State residents: $7,384 per academic year.
State residents: $371 per credit hour.
Nonstate residents: $14,062 per academic year.
Nonstate residents: $742 per credit hour.

Financial Assistance:

	Teaching Assistantship (% Receiving)	Teaching Assistantship Tuition Remission	Research Assistantship (% Receiving)	Research Assistantship Tuition Remission	Fellowship (% Receiving)	Fellowship Tuition Remission
First-Year Student	$7,000 (25)	NA	NA (NA)	NA	NA (16)	Partial
Advanced Student	$7,000 (25)	NA	$4,320 (16)	Partial	NA (NA)	NA

For additional information on financial assistance, visit http://www.jsu.edu/graduate/financial-aid.html.

Employment of Department Graduates

Master's:
Still seeking employment: 1
Other employment position: 6
Total: 7

Additional Information

Housing and Day Care: On-campus housing is available. See the following website for more information: http://www.jsu.edu/housing/Index.html. On-campus day care facilities are available. See the following website for more information: http://www.jsu.edu/edprof/fcs/cdc.html.

Information for Students With Physical Disabilities: See the following website: http://www.jsu.edu/dss/.

Special Facilities or Resources: Special facilities include a research suite with small-group classrooms and one-way mirrors, an animal room equipped with 15 pigeon chambers, and graduate student offices.

Application Information: Jacksonville State University, College of Graduate Studies, 700 Pelham Road North, Jacksonville, AL 36265-1602. *Fee:* $35. *Online application:* http://www.jsu.edu/graduate/admission/grad_app.html.

South Alabama, University of
Department of Psychology
Arts and Sciences
UCOM 1000, 307 University Boulevard North
Mobile, AL 36688
Telephone: (251) 460-6371
Chairperson: Elise Labbe, PhD

E-mail: elabbe@southalabama.edu
Web: http://www.southalabama.edu/psychology/

Orientation, Objectives, and Emphasis of Department
The University of South Alabama offers a combined Clinical/Counseling Psychology (CCP) doctoral program of studies integrating the missions and philosophies of clinical and counseling psychology. The CCP program will train students to provide the most effective types of psychological treatment and, upon completion of the program of studies, students will have a set of competencies enabling them to work successfully with a variety of professionals for the purpose of health promotion and treatment of mental illness. Students will be trained in the asset-strength model traditionally associated with counseling psychology and to conduct research and provide treatment for serious psychopathology traditionally associated with clinical psychology. The Department of Psychology currently accepts applicants to the Master of Science degree program with an interest in one or more areas of concentration in the Behavioral and Brain Sciences Psychology program. The available areas of concentration include: Behavioral Statistics/Computational Modeling, Cognitive and Perceptual Processing, Psychophysiology, Social/Developmental Psychology, and College Teaching Preparation.

Programs and Degrees Offered

Program	Degree	Application Deadline	Applica-tions Received	Accepted	New Admits Enrolled (PT)	Total Enrolled (PT)	Degrees Awarded in 2014–2015	Median Years to Complete Degree	Dismissed/ Withdrew
Brain and Behavior Sciences	MA/MS	February 15 (Fall)	7	4	2 (0)	5 (0)	0		0
Clinical/ Counseling Psychology	PhD	December 15 (Fall)	130	8	8 (0)	36 (0)	5	5	0

APA Accreditation

Combination PhD (Doctor of Philosophy).

Doctoral Degree (PhD Clinical/Counseling Psychology): For those doctoral students for whom a professional internship was required in this program prior to graduation:
Total students who applied for an internship: 4
Total students who obtained an internship: 4
Total students who obtained a paid internship: 4
Total students who obtained an unpaid internship: 0
Total students who were placed in APA/CPA-accredited internships: 1
Total students placed in internships not APA/CPA-accredited, but listed with the Association of Psychology Postdoctoral and Internship Centers (APPIC): 3
Total students placed in internships conforming to guidelines of the Council of Directors of School Psychology Programs (CDSPP):0
Total students placed in internships that were not APA/CPA-accredited, APPIC or CDSSP listed: 0

Master's Degree (MA/MS Brain and Behavior Sciences): An internship experience, such as a final research project or "capstone" experience is required of graduates.

Internships/Practica

Graduate students receive practical experience in the application of psychological assessment and treatment procedures in a variety of clinical settings. Emphasis is given to ethical and professional issues with intensive individual and group supervision. The Department of Psychology operates an outpatient teaching clinic where a variety of children and adults are seen for short-term assessment and treatment. External practicum placements are also available in a variety of community settings including a state mental hospital, an intellectual disabilities facility and community substance abuse programs.

Admissions

Entries appear in the following order: required test or GPA, minimum score (if required)/median score of students entering in 2015–2016.

Program	Degree	GRE-V	GRE-Q	GRE-Writing	GRE-Subject	Under-graduate GPA	Last 2 Years GPA	Psychol-ogy GPA	Master's GPA
Brain and Behavior Sciences	MA/MS	145/156	148/150	Not specified	Not specified	3.26/3.59	Not specified	3.46/3.78	Not specified
Clinical/ Counseling Psychology	PhD	154/157	145/154	3.5/4	Not specified	3.04/3.28	Not specified	NA/NA	3.4/3.79

Admissions Requirements:

Degree	GRE	GRE-Subject	Letters of Recom-mendation	Research Statement	Writing Sample	CV	Interview
Master's/Specialist	Required	None	3	Required	None	Required	Recom-mended

Admissions *cont'd*

Program	Degree	GRE-V	GRE-Q	GRE-Writing	GRE-Subject	Under-graduate GPA	Last 2 Years GPA	Psychology GPA	Master's GPA
Doctoral	Re-quired	None	3	Re-quired	None	Required	Re-quired		

Admissions Criteria:

GRE scores—high
Research experience—high
Work experience—low
Clinically related public service—low
GPA—high

Letters of recommendation—high
Interview—high
Statement of goals and objectives—high
Undergraduate psychology preparation—high

For additional information on admission requirements, visit http://www.southalabama.edu/colleges/artsandsci/psychology/app_procedures.html.

Department Demographics

	Male (PT)	Female (PT)	Total	African-American/ Black (PT)	Hispanic/ Latino (PT)	Asian/ Pacific Islander (PT)	American Indian/ Alaska Native (PT)	Caucasian/ White (PT)	Unknown	Multiethnic (PT)	ADA (PT)	Int'l (PT)
Students	15 (0)	23 (0)	38	3 (0)	1 (0)	1 (0)	1 (0)	31 (0)	0 (0)	1 (0)	0 (0)	0 (0)

Financial Information/Assistance

Tuition: For information on tuition costs, visit http://www.southalabama.edu/departments/financialaffairs/studentaccounting/tuition.html. Tuition is subject to change. Additional fees are assessed to students beyond the costs of tuition for the following: registration, student health, building, library, activity/athletic fee, transportation.

Doctoral:
State residents: $9,288 per academic year.
State residents: $387 per credit hour.
Nonstate residents: $18,576 per academic year.
Nonstate residents: $774 per credit hour.

Master's:
State residents: $9,288 per academic year.
State residents: $387 per credit hour.
Nonstate residents: $18,576 per academic year.
Nonstate residents: $774 per credit hour.

Financial Assistance:

	Teaching Assistantship (% Receiving)	Teaching Assistantship Tuition Remission	Research Assistantship (% Receiving)	Research Assistantship Tuition Remission	Fellowship (% Receiving)	Fellowship Tuition Remission
First-Year Student	NA (NA)	NA	$11,000 (50)	Full	$11,000 (50)	Full
Advanced Student	$11,000 (12)	Full	$10,044 (75)	Full	$11,000 (12)	Full

Employment of Department Graduates

Master's:
Enrolled in a psychology doctoral program: 1
Enrolled in another graduate/professional program: 1
Employed in a professional position in a school system: 1
Employed in business or industry: 1
Employed in a community mental health/counseling center: 1
Do not know: 1
Total: 6

Doctoral:
Employed in independent practice: 1
Employed in other positions at a higher education institution: 2
Employed in government agency: 1
Employed in a community mental health/counseling center: 1
Employed in a hospital/medical center: 1
Total: 6

Additional Information

Housing and Day Care: On-campus housing is available. See the following website for more information: http://www.southalabama.edu/housing/. No on-campus day care facilities are available.

Information for Students With Physical Disabilities: See the following website: http://www.southalabama.edu/dss/.

Special Facilities or Resources: In addition to the Psychological Clinic, the Psychology Department has laboratory facilities for neuropsychological and behavioral research and has access to both mainframe and personal computer facilities. An EEG/ERP laboratory is used for conducting research requiring the utilization of a dense array electrode cap. This laboratory is available for both faculty and graduate student research. A family interaction laboratory exists for studying parent-child interactions with the goal of enhancing parenting skills. A cognitive laboratory exists with the capability of studying linguistic enhancement. This laboratory also has an eye-tracking apparatus capable of being integrated into a variety of research projects. A social interaction laboratory exists to provide research into the dynamics of social interactions. A biofeedback laboratory exists for research into the treatment of issues such as headaches. A flight simulation laboratory exists for research into factors that influence flight safety.

Application Information: Director of Admission, 2500 Meisler Hall, University of South Alabama, Mobile, AL 36688-0002. *Fee:* $45. *Online application:* http://www.southalabama.edu/admissions/grad.shtml.

Alaska Pacific University

Department of Counseling Psychology
4101 University Drive
Anchorage, AK 99508
Telephone: (907) 564-8351
Chairperson: Dr. Kim Kjaersgaard

E-mail: admissions@alaskapacific.edu
Web: http://www.alaskapacific.edu/counseling-psychology/

Orientation, Objectives, and Emphasis of Department

The Master of Science in Counseling Psychology Program (MSCP) and the Psychology Doctorate programs are selective, rigorous programs for the creative adult who plans to become a licensed professional counselor or licensed psychologist. The MSCP program is eclectic in theoretical orientation and committed to celebrating diversity within the range of professional mental health approaches and techniques. The MSCP program encourages students to explore and develop their own special interests within the field. The program integrates theory and practice. The MSCP program meets the educational requirements for licensure as a Licensed Professional Counselor with the State of Alaska and other states throughout the U.S. The PsyD program was designed for professionals working in the field of mental health who desire further education or licensure as a psychologist. The program adheres to Alaska statutes and regulations for licensure and seeks to embrace recommendations for education promulgated by ASPPB and APA. The program is designed for students to be able to pursue individual areas of interest while completing required curriculum areas. The PsyD program is planning on submitting a self-study for APA accreditation in 2017.

Programs and Degrees Offered

Program	Degree	Application Deadline	Applica-tions Received	Accepted	New Admits Enrolled (PT)	Total Enrolled (PT)	Degrees Awarded In 2014–2015	Median Years to Complete Degree	Dismissed/ Withdrew
Counseling Psychology	MA/MS	February 15 (Fall)	28	17	15 (2)	23 (3)	12	2	1
Counseling Psychology	PsyD	October 15 (Summer)	15	9	4 (1)	16 (5)	7	3	4

Doctoral Degree (PsyD Counseling Psychology): For those doctoral students for whom a professional internship was required in this program prior to graduation:

Total students who applied for an internship: 9
Total students who obtained an internship: 9
Total students who obtained a paid internship: 7
Total students who obtained an unpaid internship: 2
Total students who were placed in APA/CPA-accredited internships: 0
Total students placed in internships not APA/CPA-accredited, but listed with the Association of Psychology Postdoctoral and Internship Centers (APPIC): 0
Total students placed in internships conforming to guidelines of the Council of Directors of School Psychology Programs (CDSPP): 0
Total students placed in internships that were not APA/CPA-accredited, APPIC or CDSSP listed: 9

Master's Degree (MA/MS Counseling Psychology): An internship experience, such as a final research project or "capstone" experience is required of graduates.

Internships/Practica

A significant part of a counselor's or psychologist's education occurs outside the classroom through practica and an internship experience. This is a unique opportunity for the student to begin applying theories and techniques of their classroom education as well as to focus their professional development in a specialized area of counseling. Internship opportunities are diverse in clientele and therapeutic context. In collaboration with the MSCP Director, PsyD Director, and faculty, students identify sites consistent with their needs. Past MSCP internship sites have included Southcentral Counseling Center, Anchorage School District, McLaughlin Youth Center, Southcentral Foundation, Catholic Social Services, Alaska Native Medical Center, Alaska Human Services, Salvation Army Clitheroe Center, Life Quest, Alaska Children's Services, Abused Women's Aid in Crisis, Providence Hospital Breakthrough Program, North Star Hospital, and Valley Women's Resource Center. Doctoral internships have been completed in integrated health settings, behavioral health departments in hospital settings, and private organizations.

Admissions

Entries appear in the following order: required test or GPA, minimum score (if required)/median score of students entering in 2015–2016.

Program	Degree	GRE-V	GRE-Q	GRE-Writing	GRE-Subject	Under-graduate GPA	Last 2 Years GPA	Psychol-ogy GPA	Master's GPA
Counseling Psychology	MA/MS	Not specified	Not specified	Not specified	Not specified	Not specified	Not specified	Not specified	Not specified
Counseling Psychology	PsyD	Not specified	Not specified	Not specified	Not specified	Not specified	Not specified	Not specified	3/NA

Admissions Requirements:

Degree	GRE	GRE-Subject	Letters of Recom-mendation	Research Statement	Writing Sample	CV	Interview
Master's/Specialist	None	None	3	Required	None	Required	Required
Doctoral	None	None	3	Required	Required	Required	Required

Please note if these criteria vary for different programs: MAT just used for the MSCP.

Admissions Criteria:

Research experience—low
Work experience—medium
Clinically related public service—medium
GPA—medium
Letters of recommendation—high

Interview—high
Statement of goals and objectives—high
Undergraduate psychology preparation—medium
MAT scores—medium

Department Demographics

	Male (PT)	Female (PT)	Total	African-American/ Black (PT)	Hispanic/ Latino (PT)	Asian/ Pacific Islander (PT)	American Indian/ Alaska Native (PT)	Caucasian/ White (PT)	Unknown	Multiethnic (PT)	ADA (PT)	Int'l (PT)
Students	17 (3)	22 (5)	47	0 (0)	0 (0)	0 (0)	0 (0)	0 (0)	39 (8)	0 (0)	0 (0)	1 (0)

Financial Information/Assistance

Tuition: For information on tuition costs, visit https://www.alaskapacific.edu/admissions/costs/. Tuition is subject to change. Tuition costs vary by program.

Doctoral:
State residents: $840 per credit hour.
Nonstate residents: $840 per credit hour.

Master's:
State residents: $630 per credit hour.
Nonstate residents: $630 per credit hour.

Financial Assistance:

	Teaching Assistantship (% Receiving)	Teaching Assistantship Tuition Remission	Research Assistantship (% Receiving)	Research Assistantship Tuition Remission	Fellowship (% Receiving)	Fellowship Tuition Remission
First-Year Student	NA (NA)	NA	NA (NA)	NA	NA (NA)	NA
Advanced Student	NA (20)	Partial	NA (NA)	NA	NA (NA)	NA

For additional information on financial assistance, visit http://www.alaskapacific.edu/student-financial-services/financial-aid/.

Employment of Department Graduates

Master's:
Enrolled in a psychology doctoral program: 3
Employed in a professional position in a school system: 2
Employed in business or industry: 1
Employed in government agency: 2
Employed in a community mental health/counseling center: 6
Employed in a hospital/medical center: 2
Total: 16

Doctoral:
Employed in independent practice: 4
Employed in a professional position in a school system: 1
Still seeking employment: 1
Not seeking employment: 1
Total: 7

Additional Information

Housing and Day Care: On-campus housing is available. See the following website for more information: https://www.alaskapacific.edu/campus-life/housing/. No on-campus day care facilities are available.

Special Facilities or Resources: We have counseling facilities with a one-way mirror and current recording technologies for providing feedback and learning. We also have a library of various current psychological tests and materials.

Application Information: Graduate Admissions: Alaska Pacific University, 4101 University Drive, Anchorage, AK 99508. *Fee:* $25. *Online application:* https://www.alaskapacific.edu/apply/.

Alaska, University of, Anchorage

MS in Clinical Psychology
College of Arts and Sciences
3211 Providence Drive
Anchorage, AK 99508
Telephone: (907) 786-1619
Director, Psychology Department: Dr. Claudia Lampman

E-mail: cblampman@uaa.alaska.edu
Web: http://www.uaa.alaska.edu/psych/

Orientation, Objectives, and Emphasis of Department

The mission of the MS program is to provide quality training to graduate students interested in mental health careers in diverse communities. The training seeks to produce graduates who are practitioner–scientists prepared to address local behavioral health needs in a context that is culturally sensitive and community focused.

Programs and Degrees Offered

Program	Degree	Application Deadline	Applications Received	Accepted	New Admits Enrolled (PT)	Total Enrolled (PT)	Degrees Awarded in 2014–2015	Median Years to Complete Degree	Dismissed/ Withdrew
Clinical Psychology	MA/MS	March 1 (Fall)	20	8	7 (0)	19 (1)	9	2.5	1

Internships/Practica

The psychology department maintains an in-house mental health clinic, the Psychological Services Center, where graduate students gain initial hands-on supervised psychotherapy experience. There are a variety of community internships available after completion of the first supervised practicum. The availability of community internships changes from year to year but we attempt to match student interests and internship experiences.

Admissions

Entries appear in the following order: required test or GPA, minimum score (if required)/median score of students entering in 2015–2016.

Program	Degree	GRE-V	GRE-Q	GRE-Writing	GRE-Subject	Under-graduate GPA	Last 2 Years GPA	Psychol-ogy GPA	Master's GPA
Clinical Psychology	MA/MS	Not specified	Not specified	Not specified	Not specified	3.2/3.7	Not specified	Not specified	Not specified

Admissions Requirements:

Degree	GRE	GRE-Subject	Letters of Recommendation	Research Statement	Writing Sample	CV	Interview
Master's/Specialist	None	None	3	Required	Required	Required	Optional

Admissions Criteria:

Research experience—low
Work experience—high
Clinically related public service—high
GPA—high

Letters of recommendation—high
Interview—medium
Statement of goals and objectives—high
Undergraduate psychology preparation—high

For additional information on admission requirements, visit http://www.uaa.alaska.edu/psych/Programs/admissions.cfm.

Department Demographics

	Male (PT)	Female (PT)	Total	African-American/ Black (PT)	Hispanic/ Latino (PT)	Asian/ Pacific Islander (PT)	American Indian/ Alaska Native (PT)	Caucasian/ White (PT)	Unknown	Multiethnic (PT)	ADA (PT)	Int'l (PT)
Students	2 (0)	17 (1)	20	0 (0)	1 (0)	1 (0)	0 (0)	14 (0)	0 (0)	3 (0)	0 (0)	0 (0)

Financial Information/Assistance

Tuition: For information on tuition costs, visit https://www.uaa.alaska.edu/records/registration/semester-expenses.cfm. Tuition is subject to change. Additional fees are assessed to students beyond the costs of tuition for the following: student life, student government, media, technology, network fee, concert fee.

Master's:
State residents: $423 per credit hour.
Nonstate residents: $864 per credit hour.

Financial Assistance:

	Teaching Assistantship (% Receiving)	Teaching Assistantship Tuition Remission	Research Assistantship (% Receiving)	Research Assistantship Tuition Remission	Fellowship (% Receiving)	Fellowship Tuition Remission
First-Year Student	$6,200 (NA)	Full	$6,200 (NA)	Full	NA (NA)	NA
Advanced Student	$6,200 (NA)	Full	$6,200 (NA)	Full	NA (NA)	NA

For additional information on financial assistance, visit http://www.uaa.alaska.edu/financialaid/.

Employment of Department Graduates

Master's:
Enrolled in a psychology doctoral program: 2
Employed in a community mental health/counseling center: 7
Total: 9

Additional Information

Housing and Day Care: On-campus housing is available. See the following website for more information: http://www.uaa.alaska.edu/housing/. No on-campus day care facilities are available.

Information for Students With Physical Disabilities: See the following website: http://www.uaa.alaska.edu/dss/.

Special Facilities or Resources: Center for Behavioral Health Research and Services (located in Institute for Social and Economic Research), Center for Human Development.

Application Information: University of Alaska Anchorage, MS Clinical Psychology Graduate Program, c/o Elly Gregory, SSB 352, 3211 Providence Drive, Anchorage, AK 99508. *Fee:* $80. *Online application:* http://www.uaa.alaska.edu/admissions/index.cfm.

Alaska, University of, Anchorage/Fairbanks
Joint PhD Program in Clinical-Community Psychology
UAA College of Arts & Sciences/UAF College of Liberal Arts
3211 Providence Drive
Anchorage, AK 99508
Telephone: (907) 786-1640
UAA Director of Clinical Training: Dr. James M. Fitterling

E-mail: aehauser@uaa.alaska.edu
Web: http://psyphd.alaska.edu

Orientation, Objectives, and Emphasis of Department
The UAF-UAA PhD Program in Clinical-Community Psychology is a scientist–practitioner program in clinical psychology that seeks to educate scholars and clinicians, who have strong commitments to research, evaluation, clinical practice, and community-based action, solidly grounded in the cultural contexts of all affected stakeholders. The program integrates clinical, community, and cultural psychology with a focus on rural, indigenous issues and an applied emphasis on the integration of research and practice. Through combining the spirit of clinical and community psychology, the program promotes contextually grounded and culturally appropriate research, evaluation, prevention, clinical service, community work, and social action, relevant to individuals, groups, families, and communities. The PhD Program in Clinical-Community Psychology with Rural, Indigenous Emphasis is a program jointly delivered and administered by the Departments of Psychology at the University of Alaska Fairbanks and the University of Alaska Anchorage. All program courses are co-taught across campuses via videoconference and all program components are delivered by faculty at both campuses. The program is designed such that the student experience is as similar as possible regardless of residence (Fairbanks or Anchorage).

Programs and Degrees Offered

Program	Degree	Application Deadline	Applica-tions Received	Accepted	New Admits Enrolled (PT)	Total Enrolled (PT)	Degrees Awarded in 2014–2015	Median Years to Complete Degree	Dismissed/Withdrew
Clinical-Community Psychology	PhD	January 15 (Fall)	43	10	10 (0)	52 (6)	2	5	0

APA Accreditation

Clinical PhD (Doctor of Philosophy).

Doctoral Degree (PhD Clinical-Community Psychology): For those doctoral students for whom a professional internship was required in this program prior to graduation:
Total students who applied for an internship: 8
Total students who obtained an internship: 8
Total students who obtained a paid internship: 8
Total students who obtained an unpaid internship: 0
Total students who were placed in APA/CPA-accredited internships: 8
Total students placed in internships not APA/CPA-accredited, but listed with the Association of Psychology Postdoctoral and Internship Centers (APPIC): 0
Total students placed in internships conforming to guidelines of the Council of Directors of School Psychology Programs (CDSPP): 0
Total students placed in internships that were not APA/CPA-accredited, APPIC or CDSSP listed: 0

Internships/Practica
Both campuses provide clinical practica through on-campus clinics and placements in local behavioral health centers. Community practica in a variety of community settings are also provided to all students. Internship placements in Alaska will also be available to students.

Admissions

Entries appear in the following order: required test or GPA, minimum score (if required)/median score of students entering in 2015–2016.

Program	Degree	GRE-V	GRE-Q	GRE-Writing	GRE-Subject	Under-graduate GPA	Last 2 Years GPA	Psychol-ogy GPA	Master's GPA
Clinical-Community Psychology	PhD	Not specified	Not specified	Not specified	Not specified	3/NA	Not specified	Not specified	Not specified

Admissions Requirements:

Degree	GRE	GRE-Subject	Letters of Recom-mendation	Research Statement	Writing Sample	CV	Interview
Doctoral	Optional	Optional	3	Required	Optional	Required	Required

Admissions Criteria:

GRE scores—low
Research experience—medium
Work experience—medium
Clinically related public service—medium
GPA—medium

Letters of recommendation—high
Interview—high
Statement of goals and objectives—high
Undergraduate psychology preparation—medium
Rural/indigenous interest—medium

For additional information on admission requirements, visit http://psyphd.alaska.edu/admissions.htm.

Department Demographics

	Male (PT)	Female (PT)	Total	African-American/ Black (PT)	Hispanic/ Latino (PT)	Asian/ Pacific Islander (PT)	American Indian/ Alaska Native (PT)	Caucasian/ White (PT)	Unknown	Multiethnic (PT)	ADA (PT)	Int'l (PT)
Students	15 (1)	37 (5)	58	1 (0)	3 (0)	4 (1)	7 (2)	35 (2)	0 (0)	2 (1)	1 (0)	1 (0)

Financial Information/Assistance

Tuition: For information on tuition costs, visit https://www.uaa.alaska.edu/records/registration/semester-expenses.cfm. Tuition is subject to change.

Doctoral:
State residents: $7,614 per academic year.
State residents: $423 per credit hour.
Nonstate residents: $7,938 per academic year.
Nonstate residents: $441 per credit hour.

Financial Assistance:

	Teaching Assistantship (% Receiving)	Teaching Assistantship Tuition Remission	Research Assistantship (% Receiving)	Research Assistantship Tuition Remission	Fellowship (% Receiving)	Fellowship Tuition Remission
First-Year Student	$26,322 (NA)	Partial	$26,322 (NA)	Partial	NA (NA)	NA
Advanced Student	$28,900 (NA)	Partial	$28,900 (NA)	Partial	NA (NA)	NA

For additional information on financial assistance, visit http://psyphd.alaska.edu/financial support.htm.

Employment of Department Graduates

Doctoral:
Employed in government agency: 1
Employed in a community mental health/counseling center: 1
Total: 2

Additional Information

Housing and Day Care: On-campus housing is available. See the following websites for more information: http://www.uaa.alaska. edu/housing/ and http://www.uaf.edu/reslife/graduate-family-housing/. On-campus day care facilities are available. See the following website for more information: http://www.ctc.uaf.edu/programs/BunnellHouse/.

Information for Students With Physical Disabilities: See the following website: http://www.uaa.alaska.edu/dss/ AND http://www. uaf.edu/disability/.

Special Facilities or Resources: At UAA, the academic facilities available to graduate students include two high definition video classrooms, individual study areas, clinical space in the Psychological Service Center, consisting of individual, family/group, child, and telehealth therapy rooms, and the Consortium Library, the major research library for southcentral Alaska. Research facilities available to graduate students include the Center for Behavioral Health Research and Services, a departmental laboratory and several university computer labs with PCs and Macs. At UAF, the academic facilities available to graduate students include two high definition video classrooms, individual study areas, and clinical space in the Psychology Department Clinic, consisting of individual, family/group, child, and telehealth therapy rooms. Other facilities available to graduate students include a departmental lab and several university labs with PCs and Macs. UAF is an international center for research in the Arctic and the North.

Application Information: Psychology PhD Program, University of Alaska Anchorage, 3211 Providence Drive, SSB 303, Anchorage, AK 99508. *Fee:* $75. *Online application:* https://uaonline.alaska.edu/.

Arizona School of Professional Psychology, Argosy University, Phoenix
Clinical Psychology
College of Clinical Psychology
Suite 150, 2233 West Dunlap Avenue
Phoenix, AZ 85021
Telephone: (602) 216-2600
Program Dean: Frederick S Wechsler, PhD, PsyD, ABPP (Clinical)
Web: http://clinical.argosy.edu/locations/phoenix/clinical-psychology-doctor-of-psychology

E-mail: fwechsler@argosy.edu

Orientation, Objectives, and Emphasis of Department
The mission of Argosy University/Phoenix is to educate and train students in clinical psychology and to prepare them for successful practitioner careers. The curriculum integrates theory, training, research, and practice and prepares students to work with a wide range of populations in need of psychological services. Faculty are both scholars and practitioners and guide students through coursework and field experiences so that they might understand how formal knowledge and practice operate to inform and enrich each other. The School follows a generalist practitioner-scholar orientation, exposing students to a broad array of clinical theories and interventions. Sensitivity to diverse populations, populations with specific needs, and multicultural awareness are important components of the school's training model.

Programs and Degrees Offered

Program	Degree	Application Deadline	Applications Received	Accepted	New Admits Enrolled (PT)	Total Enrolled (PT)	Degrees Awarded in 2014–2015	Median Years to Complete Degree	Dismissed/Withdrew
Clinical Psychology	PsyD	July 31 (Fall), December 1 (Spring)	86	40	40	183	33	5.57	0

APA Accreditation
Clinical PsyD: Student Outcome Data website: http://clinical.argosy.edu/locations/phoenix/clinical-psychology-doctor-of-psychology.

Doctoral Degree (PsyD Clinical Psychology): For those doctoral students for whom a professional internship was required in this program prior to graduation:
Total students who applied for an internship: 29
Total students who obtained an internship: 28
Total students who obtained a paid internship: 28
Total students who obtained an unpaid internship: 0
Total students who were placed in APA/CPA-accredited internships: 19
Total students placed in internships not APA/CPA-accredited, but listed with the Association of Psychology Postdoctoral and Internship Centers (APPIC): 8
Total students placed in internships conforming to guidelines of the Council of Directors of School Psychology Programs (CDSPP): 0
Total students placed in internships that were not APA/CPA-accredited, APPIC or CDSSP listed: 1

Internships/Practica
The School maintains an extensive clinical training network including public and private hospitals, community mental health agencies, private practices, substance abuse and rehabilitation agencies, correctional facilities, and the Indian Health Service.

Admissions
Entries appear in the following order: required test or GPA, minimum score (if required)/median score of students entering in 2015–2016.

Program	Degree	GRE-V	GRE-Q	GRE-Writing	GRE-Subject	Under-graduate GPA	Last 2 Years GPA	Psychology GPA	Master's GPA
Clinical Psychology	PsyD	Not specified	Not specified	Not specified	Not specified	3/3.4	Not specified	Not specified	3.25/3.5

Admissions Requirements:

Degree	GRE	GRE-Subject	Letters of Recommendation	Research Statement	Writing Sample	CV	Interview
Doctoral	Optional	Optional	3	Required	Optional	Required	Required

Admissions Criteria:

Research experience—low
Work experience—medium
Clinically related public service—medium
GPA—high

Letters of recommendation—high
Interview—high
Statement of goals and objectives—high
Undergraduate psychology preparation—medium

For additional information on admission requirements, visit http://clinical.argosy.edu/locations/phoenix/clinical-psychology-doctor-of-psychology/admissions.

Department Demographics

	Male (PT)	Female (PT)	Total	African-American/ Black (PT)	Hispanic/ Latino (PT)	Asian/ Pacific Islander (PT)	American Indian/ Alaska Native (PT)	Caucasian/ White (PT)	Unknown	Multiethnic (PT)	ADA (PT)	Int'l (PT)
Students	50 (0)	133 (0)	183	15 (0)	13 (0)	4 (0)	0 (0)	151 (0)	0 (0)	(0)	0 (0)	0 (0)

Financial Information/Assistance

Tuition: For information on tuition costs, visit https://www.argosy.edu/affordability/tuition-and-fees. Tuition is subject to change. Additional fees are assessed to students beyond the costs of tuition for the following: Total $745 - technology fee, student activity fee, graduation fee, add/drop fee, testing kit fee.

Doctoral:
State residents: $33,698 per academic year.
State residents: $1,162 per credit hour.
Nonstate residents: $33,698 per academic year.
Nonstate residents: $1,162 per credit hour.

Financial Assistance:

	Teaching Assistantship (% Receiving)	Teaching Assistantship Tuition Remission	Research Assistantship (% Receiving)	Research Assistantship Tuition Remission	Fellowship (% Receiving)	Fellowship Tuition Remission
First-Year Student	NA (8)	Partial	NA (NA)	NA	$5,400 (10)	Partial
Advanced Student	NA (8)	Partial	NA (NA)	NA	$5,400 (10)	NA

For additional information on financial assistance, visit https://www.argosy.edu/affordability.

Employment of Department Graduates

Doctoral:
Enrolled in a postdoctoral residency/fellowship: 1
Employed in independent practice: 5
Employed in an academic position at a university: 1
Employed in a professional position in a school system: 2
Employed in government agency: 3
Employed in a community mental health/counseling center: 8

Employed in a hospital/medical center: 9
Do not know: 4
Total: 33

Additional Information

Housing and Day Care: No on-campus housing is available. No on-campus day care facilities are available.

Application Information: MIchael Hohenstein, Arizona School of Professional Psychology, Argosy University/Phoenix, 2233 West Dunlap Avenue, Phoenix, AZ 85018. *Fee:* $50. *Online application:* https://www.argosy.edu/admissions/apply-online.

Arizona State University
Counseling & Counseling Psychology
College of Letters & Sciences
Payne Hall 446, MC-0811
Tempe, AZ 85287-0811
Telephone: (480) 965-8733
Faculty Head: Lisa Spanierman

E-mail: ccp@asu.edu
Web: https://cls.asu.edu/graduate/ccp

Orientation, Objectives, and Emphasis of Department
The faculty adheres to a scientist–practitioner model across all areas. Counseling Psychology doctoral program is APA-accredited and Master of Counseling is accredited by CACREP.

Programs and Degrees Offered

Program	Degree	Application Deadline	Applica-tions Received	Accepted	New Admits Enrolled (PT)	Total Enrolled (PT)	Degrees Awarded in 2014–2015	Median Years to Complete Degree	Dismissed/Withdrew
Counseling Psychology	PhD	December 1 (Fall)	142	8	7 (0)	44 (2)	2	5.5	0
Master Of Counseling	Other	January 4 (Fall)	115	96	51 (0)	92 (17)	37		1

APA Accreditation
Counseling PhD: Student Outcome Data website: https://cls.asu.edu/graduate/ccp/CP_Student-Resources.

Doctoral Degree (PhD Counseling Psychology): For those doctoral students for whom a professional internship was required in this program prior to graduation:
Total students who applied for an internship: 9
Total students who obtained an internship: 9
Total students who obtained a paid internship: 9
Total students who obtained an unpaid internship: 0
Total students who were placed in APA/CPA-accredited internships: 9
Total students placed in internships not APA/CPA-accredited, but listed with the Association of Psychology Postdoctoral and Internship Centers (APPIC): 0
Total students placed in internships conforming to guidelines of the Council of Directors of School Psychology Programs (CDSPP): 0
Total students placed in internships that were not APA/CPA-accredited, APPIC or CDSSP listed: 0

Master's Degree (Other Master of Counseling): An internship experience, such as a final research project or "capstone" experience is required of graduates.

Internships/Practica
Our doctoral internships include APA-approved sites throughout the nation. Sites include university counseling centers, community mental health clinics, and hospitals. Practica for doctoral and master's students typically are local (the greater Phoenix area) and include university counseling centers, community mental health clinics, and hospitals.

Admissions

Entries appear in the following order: required test or GPA, minimum score (if required)/median score of students entering in 2015–2016.

Program	Degree	GRE-V	GRE-Q	GRE-Writing	GRE-Subject	Under-graduate GPA	Last 2 Years GPA	Psychol-ogy GPA	Master's GPA
Counseling Psychology	PhD	148/155	150/153	Not specified	Not specified	Not specified	3.5/3.82	Not specified	Not specified
Master of Counseling	Other	145/154	145/149	Not specified	Not specified	Not specified	3/3.69	Not specified	Not specified

Admissions Requirements:

Degree	GRE	GRE-Subject	Letters of Recom-mendation	Research Statement	Writing Sample	CV	Interview
Master's/Specialist	Required	None	3	Required	None	Optional	None
Doctoral	Required	None	3	Required	Required	Required	Required

Please note if these criteria vary for different programs: Programs use the FRK index which combines GRE V+Q with undergraduate GPA. Minimum FRKs are set by faculty admissions committees.

Admissions Criteria:

GRE scores—medium
Research experience—high
Work experience—medium
Clinically related public service—high
GPA—high

Letters of recommendation—high
Interview—medium
Statement of goals and objectives—high
Undergraduate psychology preparation—low

Department Demographics

	Male (PT)	Female (PT)	Total	African-American/ Black (PT)	Hispanic/ Latino (PT)	Asian/ Pacific Islander (PT)	American Indian/ Alaska Native (PT)	Caucasian/ White (PT)	Unknown	Multiethnic (PT)	ADA (PT)	Int'l (PT)
Students	36 (3)	100 (16)	155	4 (1)	21 (1)	13 (0)	4 (0)	73 (14)	15 (3)	6 (0)	1 (0)	15 (3)

Financial Information/Assistance

Tuition: For information on tuition costs, visit https://students.asu.edu/tuitionandfees. Tuition is subject to change. Additional fees are assessed to students beyond the costs of tuition for the following: Master of Counseling program fee $300 per credit hour.

Doctoral:
State residents: $11,624 per academic year.
State residents: $645 per credit hour.
Nonstate residents: $21,016 per academic year.
Nonstate residents: $1,167 per credit hour.

Master's:
State residents: $11,624 per academic year.
State residents: $645 per credit hour.
Nonstate residents: $21,016 per academic year.
Nonstate residents: $1,167 per credit hour.

Financial Assistance:

	Teaching Assistantship (% Receiving)	Teaching Assistantship Tuition Remission	Research Assistantship (% Receiving)	Research Assistantship Tuition Remission	Fellowship (% Receiving)	Fellowship Tuition Remission
First-Year Student	$16,000 (NA)	Full	$14,900 (NA)	Full	$17,500 (NA)	Full
Advanced Student	$16,000 (NA)	Full	$14,900 (NA)	Full	NA (NA)	NA

For additional information on financial assistance, visit https://graduate.asu.edu/pay-for-college.

Employment of Department Graduates

Master's:
Enrolled in a psychology doctoral program: 1
Employed in academic position at a 2-year/4-year college: 2
Employed in a professional position in a school system: 3
Employed in business or industry: 2
Employed in government agency: 1
Employed in a community mental health/counseling center: 23
Still seeking employment: 3
Other employment position: 1
Total: 36

Doctoral:
Employed in other positions at a higher education institution: 1
Employed in government agency: 2
Employed in a hospital/medical center: 2
Total: 5

Additional Information

Housing and Day Care: No on-campus housing is available. On-campus day care facilities are available. See the following website for more information: https://eoss.asu.edu/students-families/oncampus.

Information for Students With Physical Disabilities: See the following website: https://eoss.asu.edu/drc.

Special Facilities or Resources: The Counseling Training Center is a state-of-the-art training facility for Master's and PhD-level counseling students. The center serves clients from both the university and the general public. In addition to training and clinical services, we conduct counseling process and outcome research at the Center.

Application Information: Fee: $70. Online application: http://asu.edu/gradapp.

Arizona State University
Department of Psychology
College of Liberal Arts and Sciences
Box 871104
Tempe, AZ 85287-1104
Telephone: (480) 965-7598
Chairperson: Keith Crnic

E-mail: laurie.chassin@asu.edu
Web: http://psychology.clas.asu.edu/

Orientation, Objectives, and Emphasis of Department
The department seeks to instill in students knowledge, skills, and an appreciation of psychology as a science and as a profession. To do so, it offers undergraduate and graduate programs emphasizing theory, research, and applied practice. The department encourages a multiplicity of theoretical viewpoints and research interests. The behavioral neuroscience area emphasizes the neural bases of motor disorders, drug abuse and recovery of function following brain damage. The clinical program includes areas of emphasis in health psychology, child-clinical psychology, and community-prevention. Also offered are classes in psychopathology, prevention, assessment and psychotherapy. The cognitive systems area includes cognitive psychology, adaptive systems, learning, sensation and perception, and cognitive development. The developmental area includes coursework and research experience in the core areas of cognitive and social development. The quantitative area focuses on design, measurement, and statistical analysis issues that arise in diverse areas of psychological research. The social area emphasizes theoretical and laboratory skills combined with program evaluation and applied social psychology. New interdisciplinary training opportunities are available in Arts, Media, and Engineering.

Programs and Degrees Offered

Program	Degree	Application Deadline	Applications Received	Accepted	New Admits Enrolled (PT)	Total Enrolled (PT)	Degrees Awarded in 2014–2015	Median Years to Complete Degree	Dismissed/ Withdrew
Clinical Psychology	PhD	December 1 (Fall)	268	5	5	51 (0)	7	6	1
Developmental Psychology	PhD	December 5 (Fall)	23	1	1 (0)	12 (0)	1	5	
Quantitative Psychology	PhD	December 5 (Fall)	37	0	0 (0)	13 (0)	1	8	1
Social Psychology	PhD	January 5 (Fall)	107	2	2 (0)	16 (0)	2	7	0
Behavioral Neuroscience	PhD	December 1 (Fall)	56	2	2	7	5	5	
Cognitive Science	PhD	January 5 (Fall)	22	1	1	16	4	5	0
Applied Behavioral Analysis	MA/MS	February 1 (Fall)	48	18	18	18	0		0

APA Accreditation

Clinical PhD: Student Outcome Data website: https://psychology.clas.asu.edu/content/psychology-clinical-phd.

Doctoral Degree (PhD Clinical Psychology): For those doctoral students for whom a professional internship was required in this program prior to graduation:
Total students who applied for an internship: 7
Total students who obtained an internship: 7
Total students who obtained a paid internship: 7
Total students who obtained an unpaid internship: 0
Total students who were placed in APA/CPA-accredited internships: 7
Total students placed in internships not APA/CPA-accredited, but listed with the Association of Psychology Postdoctoral and Internship Centers (APPIC): 0
Total students placed in internships conforming to guidelines of the Council of Directors of School Psychology Programs (CDSPP): 0
Total students placed in internships that were not APA/CPA-accredited, APPIC or CDSSP listed: 0

Master's Degree (MA/MS Applied Behavioral Analysis): An internship experience, such as a final research project or "capstone" experience is required of graduates.

Internships/Practica

Doctoral clinical students complete practica in community agencies and in our in-house training clinic

Admissions

Entries appear in the following order: required test or GPA, minimum score (if required)/median score of students entering in 2015–2016.

Program	Degree	GRE-V	GRE-Q	GRE-Writing	GRE-Subject	Undergraduate GPA	Last 2 Years GPA	Psychology GPA	Master's GPA
Clinical Psychology	PhD	NA/162	NA/158	NA/4.5	Not specified	3/3.78	Not specified	Not specified	Not specified
Developmental Psychology	PhD	Not specified	Not specified	Not specified	Not specified	Not specified	Not specified	Not specified	Not specified
Quantitative Psychology	PhD	Not specified	Not specified	Not specified	Not specified	Not specified	Not specified	Not specified	Not specified
Social Psychology	PhD	Not specified	Not specified	Not specified	Not specified	Not specified	Not specified	Not specified	Not specified

Admissions *cont'd*

Program	Degree	GRE-V	GRE-Q	GRE-Writing	GRE-Subject	Under-graduate GPA	Last 2 Years GPA	Psychology GPA	Master's GPA
Behavioral Neuroscience	PhD	Not specified	Not specified	Not specified	Not specified	3/NA	Not specified	Not specified	Not specified
Cognitive Science	PhD	Not specified	Not specified	Not specified	Not specified	Not specified	Not specified	Not specified	Not specified
Applied Behavioral Analysis	MA/MS	Not specified	Not specified	Not specified	Not specified	Not specified	Not specified	Not specified	Not specified

Admissions Requirements:

Degree	GRE	GRE-Subject	Letters of Recommendation	Research Statement	Writing Sample	CV	Interview
Master's/Specialist	Required	None	2	Required	None	Required	None
Doctoral	Required	Optional	3	Required	Optional	Required	Required

Admissions Criteria:

GRE scores—medium
Research experience—high
Work experience—low
Clinically related public service—medium
GPA—medium

Letters of recommendation—high
Interview—high
Statement of goals and objectives—high
Undergraduate psychology preparation—medium

For additional information on admission requirements, visit https://psychology.clas.asu.edu/admissions.

Department Demographics

	Male (PT)	Female (PT)	Total	African-American/ Black (PT)	Hispanic/ Latino (PT)	Asian/ Pacific Islander (PT)	American Indian/ Alaska Native (PT)	Caucasian/ White (PT)	Unknown	Multiethnic (PT)	ADA (PT)	Int'l (PT)
Students	36 (0)	79 (0)	115	2 (0)	11 (0)	17 (0)	4 (0)	80 (0)	1 (0)	0 (0)	0 (0)	8 (0)

Financial Information/Assistance

Tuition: For information on tuition costs, visit https://catalog.asu.edu/tuitionandfees/. Tuition is subject to change.

Doctoral:
State residents: $10,610 per academic year.
State residents: $758 per credit hour.
Nonstate residents: $27,086 per academic year.
Nonstate residents: $1,129 per credit hour.

Master's:
State residents: $758 per credit hour.
Nonstate residents: $1,129 per credit hour.

Financial Assistance:

	Teaching Assistantship (% Receiving)	Teaching Assistantship Tuition Remission	Research Assistantship (% Receiving)	Research Assistantship Tuition Remission	Fellowship (% Receiving)	Fellowship Tuition Remission
First-Year Student	$14,900 (NA)	Full	$14,900 (NA)	Full	NA (NA)	NA
Advanced Student	$15,900 (NA)	Full	$15,900 (NA)	Full	NA (NA)	NA

For additional information on financial assistance, visit https://graduate.asu.edu/pay-for-college.

Employment of Department Graduates

Doctoral:
Enrolled in a postdoctoral residency/fellowship: 11
Employed in an academic position at a university: 2
Employed in academic position at a 2-year/4-year college: 1
Employed in business or industry: 2
Employed in a community mental health/counseling center: 2
Still seeking employment: 1
Total: 19

Additional Information

Housing and Day Care: No on-campus housing is available. On-campus day care facilities are available. See the following website for more information: https://eoss.asu.edu/students-families/oncampus.

Information for Students With Physical Disabilities: See the following website: https://eoss.asu.edu/drc.

Special Facilities or Resources: The department has the Child Study Laboratory for training and research in developmental psychology, including both normal and clinical groups, particularly of preschool age; the Clinical Psychology Center, whose clients represent a wide range of psychological disorders and are not limited to the university community; and the experimental laboratories, with exceptional computer facilities for the study of speech perception, neural networks, categorization, memory, sensory processes and learning. The clinical and social programs maintain continuing liaisons with a wide range of off-campus agencies for research applications of psychological theory and research. Our NIMH-funded Preventive Intervention Research Center provides a site for training in the design, implementation, and evaluation of preventive interventions. Quantitatively-oriented students receive methodological experience in large-scale research programs and in our statistical laboratory.

Application Information: Graduate Coordinator, Department of Psychology, Arizona State University, PO Box 871104, Tempe, AZ 85287-1104. *Fee:* $70. *Online application:* http://asu.edu/gradapp.

Arizona State University
Human Systems Engineering, The Polytechnic School
Ira A. Fulton Schools of Engineering
Santa Catalina 150, 7271 East Sonoran Arroyo Mall
Mesa, AZ 85212
Telephone: (480) 727-4723
Program Chair: Nancy J. Cooke

E-mail: polygrad@asu.edu
Web: http://poly.engineering.asu.edu/hse/

Orientation, Objectives, and Emphasis of Department
The master's in Applied Psychology (Human Systems Engineering) in the Polytechnic School is a 2-year program that provides students with opportunities for practical experience in diverse laboratories as they master theory and methods associated with human factors and cognitive engineering. The program is hands-on and challenging, and the field is growing quickly, creating opportunities for further study and employment. The areas of application include: human-computer interaction, human-robot interaction, consumer psychology; team cognition, healthcare human factors, and sports psychology.

Programs and Degrees Offered

Program	Degree	Application Deadline	Applications Received	Accepted	New Admits Enrolled (PT)	Total Enrolled (PT)	Degrees Awarded in 2014–2015	Median Years to Complete Degree	Dismissed/ Withdrew
Applied Psychology	MA/MS	April 1 (Fall), September 15 (Spring)	18	7	7	20	4	2	0
Simulation, Modeling, and Applied Cognitive Sci	PhD	December 31 (Fall)	11	4	4	12	2	3.5	2

Internships/Practica

There are many opportunities for interaction with local industry.

Admissions

Entries appear in the following order: required test or GPA, minimum score (if required)/median score of students entering in 2015–2016.

Program	Degree	GRE-V	GRE-Q	GRE-Writing	GRE-Subject	Under-graduate GPA	Last 2 Years GPA	Psychology GPA	Master's GPA
Applied Psychology	MA/MS	Not specified	Not specified	Not specified	Not specified	Not specified	Not specified	Not specified	Not specified
Simulation, Modeling, and Applied Cognitive Sci	PhD	Not specified	Not specified	Not specified	Not specified	Not specified	Not specified	Not specified	Not specified

Admissions Requirements:

Degree	GRE	GRE-Subject	Letters of Recom-mendation	Research Statement	Writing Sample	CV	Interview
Master's/Specialist	Required	None	3	Required	None	Optional	None
Doctoral	Required	None	3	Required	None	Required	None

Admissions Criteria:

GRE scores—medium
Research experience—high
Work experience—medium
GPA—medium

Letters of recommendation—high
Statement of goals and objectives—high
Undergraduate psychology preparation—medium

Department Demographics

	Male (PT)	Female (PT)	Total	African-American/ Black (PT)	Hispanic/ Latino (PT)	Asian/ Pacific Islander (PT)	American Indian/ Alaska Native (PT)	Caucasian/ White (PT)	Unknown	Multiethnic (PT)	ADA (PT)	Int'l (PT)
Students	21 (0)	11 (0)	32	2 (0)	1 (0)	4 (0)	0 (0)	24 (0)	0 (0)	1 (0)	0 (0)	4 (0)

Financial Information/Assistance

Tuition: For information on tuition costs, visit https://students.asu.edu/tuition. Tuition is subject to change.

Doctoral:
State residents: $10,520 per academic year.
Nonstate residents: $23,119 per academic year.

Master's:
State residents: $10,520 per academic year.
Nonstate residents: $23,119 per academic year.

Financial Assistance:

	Teaching Assistantship (% Receiving)	Teaching Assistantship Tuition Remission	Research Assistantship (% Receiving)	Research Assistantship Tuition Remission	Fellowship (% Receiving)	Fellowship Tuition Remission
First-Year Student	NA (NA)	NA	$16,000 (25)	Full	NA (NA)	NA
Advanced Student	$16,000 (25)	Full	$16,000 (25)	Full	NA (NA)	NA

Employment of Department Graduates

Master's:
Enrolled in a psychology doctoral program: 1
Employed in business or industry: 5
Total: 6

Doctoral:
Employed in business or industry: 3
Total: 3

Additional Information

Housing and Day Care: On-campus housing is available. See the following website for more information: https://housing.asu.edu/. On-campus day care facilities are available. See the following website for more information: https://eoss.asu.edu/students-families/oncampus.

Information for Students With Physical Disabilities: See the following website: https://eoss.asu.edu/drc.

Special Facilities or Resources: Rich laboratory facilities that include flight simulators, team simulators, medical simulators, virtual reality equipment, and a driving simulator as well as computer labs. A human performance lab is available for user experience design and evaluation.

Application Information: Fee: $70. *Online application:* https://www.asu.edu/gradapp.

Arizona State University
Program in Family and Human Development
T. Denny Sanford School of Social and Family Dynamics
P.O. Box 873701
Tempe, AZ 85287-3701
Telephone: (480) 965-6978
Director: Richard Fabes

E-mail: graduatesanford@asu.edu
Web: https://thesanfordschool.asu.edu/degree-programs/graduate-programs

---

Orientation, Objectives, and Emphasis of Department
The doctoral degree program in Family and Human Development prepares researchers with a focus on social processes, family relationships, and infant, child, adolescent and emerging adult development. The doctoral program is designed for graduates to assume leadership roles as researchers and academicians in universities or other research-oriented settings, or as directors in public or privately funded mental health agencies, industry or government.

Programs and Degrees Offered

Program	Degree	Application Deadline	Applications Received	Accepted	New Admits Enrolled (PT)	Total Enrolled (PT)	Degrees Awarded in 2014–2015	Median Years to Complete Degree	Dismissed/Withdrew
Family and Human Development	PhD	December 1 (Fall)	39	19	5 (0)	49 (0)	8		0

Admissions
Entries appear in the following order: required test or GPA, minimum score (if required)/median score of students entering in 2015–2016.

Program	Degree	GRE-V	GRE-Q	GRE-Writing	GRE-Subject	Under-graduate GPA	Last 2 Years GPA	Psychology GPA	Master's GPA
Family and Human Development	PhD	NA/NA	NA/NA	NA/NA	Not specified	3/3.6	3/NA	Not specified	3/NA

Admissions Requirements:

Degree	GRE	GRE-Subject	Letters of Recommendation	Research Statement	Writing Sample	CV	Interview
Doctoral	Required	None	3	Required	Optional	Required	Required

Admissions Criteria:

GRE scores—high
Research experience—high
Work experience—medium
GPA—high
Letters of recommendation—high

Interview—high
Statement of goals and objectives—high
Undergraduate psychology preparation—low
Fit w/ available faculty—high

For additional information on admission requirements, visit https://thesanfordschool.asu.edu/family-and-human-development-phd.

Department Demographics

	Male (PT)	Female (PT)	Total	African-American/ Black (PT)	Hispanic/ Latino (PT)	Asian/ Pacific Islander (PT)	American Indian/ Alaska Native (PT)	Caucasian/ White (PT)	Unknown (PT)	Multiethnic (PT)	ADA (PT)	Int'l (PT)
Students	6 (0)	40 (0)	46	0 (0)	5 (0)	5 (0)	0 (0)	25 (0)	0 (0)	0 (0)	0 (0)	3 (0)

Financial Information/Assistance

Tuition: For information on tuition costs, visit https://students.asu.edu/tuitionandfees. Tuition is subject to change. Additional fees are assessed to students beyond the costs of tuition for the following: technology, health and wellness, program fees.

Doctoral:
State residents: $758 per credit hour.
Nonstate residents: $1,129 per credit hour.

Financial Assistance:

	Teaching Assistantship (% Receiving)	Teaching Assistantship Tuition Remission	Research Assistantship (% Receiving)	Research Assistantship Tuition Remission	Fellowship (% Receiving)	Fellowship Tuition Remission
First-Year Student	$15,500 (NA)	Full	$15,500 (NA)	Full	$15,500 (NA)	Full
Advanced Student	$20,100 (NA)	Full	$20,100 (NA)	Full	$20,100 (NA)	Full

Employment of Department Graduates

Doctoral:
Enrolled in a postdoctoral residency/fellowship: 4
Employed in other positions at a higher education institution: 2
Employed in business or industry: 1
Employed in government agency: 1
Total: 8

Additional Information

Housing and Day Care: No on-campus housing is available. On-campus day care facilities are available. See the following website for more information: https://eoss.asu.edu/students-families/oncampus.

Information for Students With Physical Disabilities: See the following website: https://eoss.asu.edu/drc.

Application Information: Fee: $70. Online application: http://asu.edu/gradapp.

Arizona, University of
Department of Psychology
College of Sciences
P.O. Box 210068
Tucson, AZ 85721
Telephone: (520) 621-7448
Head: Lee Ryan

E-mail: ryant@u.arizona.edu
Web: http://psychology.arizona.edu/

Orientation, Objectives, and Emphasis of Department
The Psychology Department is located in the School of Mind, Brain, and Behavior. Our objectives as a department are to contribute to the growth of knowledge about the mind and its workings, and the training of students to participate in this pursuit, as well as using this knowledge to benefit society. The department emphasizes research and training students headed toward both academic and research-related careers. Required courses provide breadth of coverage, but emphasis is on research within the area of specialization through independent work with individual faculty members. The interdisciplinary nature of the department within the School of Mind, Brain and Behavior fosters specialization in areas that cut across program boundaries and permits work with faculty members in other programs. The cognition and neural systems area emphasizes language, perception, attention, memory, aging, ensemble recording of neural activity, and human neuroimaging; the clinical area emphasizes clinical neuropsychology, psychotherapy research, sleep disorders, psychophysiology, and assessment; the social area emphasizes prejudice and stereotyping, cognitive dissonance, self-esteem, and motivational factors in thought and behavior; and the ethology and evolutionary area emphasizes quantitative ethology, invertebrate behavior and human behavioral ecology.

Programs and Degrees Offered

Program	Degree	Application Deadline	Applications Received	Accepted	New Admits Enrolled (PT)	Total Enrolled (PT)	Degrees Awarded in 2014–2015	Median Years to Complete Degree	Dismissed/ Withdrew
Clinical Psychology	PhD	December 15 (Fall)	183	6	6 (0)	42 (0)	4	7	0
Cognition and Neural Systems	PhD	December 15 (Fall)	47	5	5	26 (1)	5	5	1
Ethology and Evolutionary Psychology	PhD	December 15 (Fall)	8	0	0	6 (0)	1	13	0
Social Psychology	PhD	December 15 (Fall)	53	2	2	8 (1)	1	5	0

APA Accreditation
Clinical PhD: Student Outcome Data website. http://poyohology.arizona.edu/Clinical.

Doctoral Degree (PhD Clinical Psychology): For those doctoral students for whom a professional internship was required in this program prior to graduation:
Total students who applied for an internship: 6
Total students who obtained an internship: 6
Total students who obtained a paid internship: 6
Total students who obtained an unpaid internship: 0
Total students who were placed in APA/CPA-accredited internships: 6
Total students placed in internships not APA/CPA-accredited, but listed with the Association of Psychology Postdoctoral and Internship Centers (APPIC): 0
Total students placed in internships conforming to guidelines of the Council of Directors of School Psychology Programs (CDSPP): 0
Total students placed in internships that were not APA/CPA-accredited, APPIC or CDSSP listed: 0

Internships/Practica
Graduate students within the clinical program are required to do a one-year internship. The University Medical Center medical school offers internship positions, although most of our students leave campus for the internship. All of the clinical students are placed in APA-accredited internships. Students also participate in various clinical externships and practica available within the department as well as throughout the community as part of their graduate training.

Admissions

Entries appear in the following order: required test or GPA, minimum score (if required)/median score of students entering in 2015–2016.

Program	Degree	GRE-V	GRE-Q	GRE-Writing	GRE-Subject	Under-graduate GPA	Last 2 Years GPA	Psychol-ogy GPA	Master's GPA
Clinical Psychology	PhD	NA/160	NA/155	NA/4.7	NA/685	3/3.8	Not specified	Not specified	Not specified
Cognition and Neural Systems	PhD	NA/158	NA/161	NA/4.1	Not specified	Not specified	Not specified	Not specified	Not specified
Ethology and Evolutionary Psychology	PhD	NA/NA	NA/NA	Not specified	Not specified	Not specified	Not specified	Not specified	Not specified
Social Psychology	PhD	NA/153	NA/146	NA/3.5	Not specified	3/3.9	Not specified	Not specified	Not specified

Admissions Requirements:

Degree	GRE	GRE-Subject	Letters of Recom-mendation	Research Statement	Writing Sample	CV	Interview
Doctoral	Required	Recom-mended	3	Required	Recom-mended	Recom-mended	Required

Admissions Criteria:

GRE scores—medium
Research experience—high
Work experience—low
Clinically related public service—low
GPA—medium

Letters of recommendation—high
Interview—medium
Statement of goals and objectives—high
Undergraduate psychology preparation—medium

For additional information on admission requirements, visit http://psychology.arizona.edu/InfoforPhDApplicants.

Department Demographics

	Male (PT)	Female (PT)	Total	African-American/ Black (PT)	Hispanic/ Latino (PT)	Asian/ Pacific Islander (PT)	American Indian/ Alaska Native (PT)	Caucasian/ White (PT)	Unknown	Multiethnic (PT)	ADA (PT)	Int'l (PT)
Students	28 (0)	55 (2)	85	0 (0)	17 (0)	12 (0)	0 (0)	54 (2)	0 (0)	0 (0)	0 (0)	7 (0)

Financial Information/Assistance

Tuition: For information on tuition costs, visit http://bursar.arizona.edu/students/fees/index.asp. Tuition is subject to change. Additional fees are assessed to students beyond the costs of tuition for the following: Misc fees for all students range from $409.94 - $510.94.

Doctoral:
State residents: $11,040 per academic year.
State residents: $789 per credit hour.
Nonstate residents: $29,362 per academic year.
Nonstate residents: $1,631 per credit hour.

Financial Assistance:

	Teaching Assistantship (% Receiving)	Teaching Assistantship Tuition Remission	Research Assistantship (% Receiving)	Research Assistantship Tuition Remission	Fellowship (% Receiving)	Fellowship Tuition Remission
First-Year Student	$16,000 (NA)	Full	$16,000 (NA)	Full	$10,000 (NA)	Partial
Advanced Student	$16,000 (NA)	Full	$16,000 (NA)	Full	$10,000 (NA)	Partial

For additional information on financial assistance, visit http://financialaid.arizona.edu/graduate-students.

Employment of Department Graduates

Doctoral:
Enrolled in a postdoctoral residency/fellowship: 7
Employed in an academic position at a university: 1
Employed in academic position at a 2-year/4-year college: 1
Employed in government agency: 1
Do not know: 1
Total: 11

Additional Information

Housing and Day Care: On-campus housing is available. See the following website for more information: http://www.life.arizona.edu/home/graduate-housing/graduate-houslng-options. No on-campus day care facilities are available.

Information for Students With Physical Disabilities: See the following website: http://drc.arizona.edu/.

Special Facilities or Resources: The department has modern laboratories devoted to research in various areas of cognitive, clinical, neuroscientific, social, and comparative research. The department provides computing resources and technical assistance for teaching and research. There are a number of clinics within the department, bringing in patients associated with research projects on aging, sleep disorders, memory disorders, depression, and others. The department has ties with a number of other programs on campus, including the departments of Anatomy, Family and Community Medicine, Neurology, Ophthalmology, Pediatrics, Pharmacology, Physiology and Psychiatry in the College of Medicine, the departments of Ecology and Evolutionary Biology, Family Studies, Linguistics, Management and Policy, Mathematics, Philosophy, Renewable and Natural Resources, Speech and Hearing Sciences, and Physics on the main campus, and interdisciplinary programs including Cognitive Science, Statistics, and Neuroscience. Most of the department's faculty members are holders of research grants, permitting a significant proportion of the graduate students to serve as research assistants at various times during their training.

Application Information: *Fee:* $85. *Online application:* https://apply.grad.arizona.edu/.

Midwestern University
Clinical Psychology Program
College of Health Sciences
19555 North 59th Avenue
Glendale, AZ 85208
Telephone: (623) 572-3860
Program Director: Jared Chamberlain, PhD

E-mail: admissaz@midwestern.edu

Web: https://www.midwestern.edu/programs-and-admission/az-clinical-psychology.html

---

Orientation, Objectives, and Emphasis of Department
The Doctor of Psychology in Clinical Psychology Program follows the practitioner-scholar model of preparation that was accepted by the American Psychological Association at the Vail Conference. This model recognizes the ongoing need in society for expertly trained practitioners in the field of clinical psychology. The practitioner-scholar philosophy dictates that competent practitioners are required to have an extensive understanding of the theoretical principles in the clinical practice of psychology and the ability to utilize the knowledge in specific clinical situations. This program has the philosophy of educating and training individuals to enter

careers emphasizing the delivery of direct psychological services and consultation. Relevant theory, research, and field experiences are integrated toward the development of competent and ethical practitioners who are respectful of individual and cultural differences in the provision of psychological services. The Doctor of Psychology degree is designed to be a professional degree similar to the doctoral degrees provided in medicine, law, pharmacy, physical therapy, and dentistry. The PsyD has become the degree of choice for persons interested in becoming a high-level practitioner when pursuing a career in clinical psychology.

Programs and Degrees Offered

Program	Degree	Application Deadline	Applica-tions Received	Accepted	New Admits Enrolled (PT)	Total Enrolled (PT)	Degrees Awarded in 2014–2015	Median Years to Complete Degree	Dismissed/ Withdrew
Clinical Psychology	PsyD	July 15 (Fall), Rolling	71	27	27 (0)	61 (2)	8	4	5

APA Accreditation

Clinical PsyD: Student Outcome Data website: https://www.midwestern.edu/programs-and-admission/az-clinical-psychology.html.

Doctoral Degree (PsyD Clinical Psychology): For those doctoral students for whom a professional internship was required in this program prior to graduation:
Total students who applied for an internship: 11
Total students who obtained an internship: 11
Total students who obtained a paid internship: 11
Total students who obtained an unpaid internship: 0
Total students who were placed in APA/CPA-accredited internships: 1
Total students placed in internships not APA/CPA-accredited, but listed with the Association of Psychology Postdoctoral and Internship Centers (APPIC): 10
Total students placed in internships conforming to guidelines of the Council of Directors of School Psychology Programs (CDSPP): 0
Total students placed in internships that were not APA/CPA-accredited, APPIC or CDSSP listed: 0

Internships/Practica

All internships are placed through the APPIC match. Practicum placements occur at the Midwestern University Multispecialty Clinic as well as throughout the greater Phoenix area and may vary with regard to population served.

Admissions

Entries appear in the following order: required test or GPA, minimum score (if required)/median score of students entering in 2015–2016.

Program	Degree	GRE-V	GRE-Q	GRE-Writing	GRE-Subject	Under-graduate GPA	Last 2 Years GPA	Psychol-ogy GPA	Master's GPA
Clinical Psychology	PsyD	Not specified	Not specified	Not specified	Not specified	Not specified	Not specified	Not specified	Not specified

Admissions Requirements:

Degree	GRE	GRE-Subject	Letters of Recom-mendation	Research Statement	Writing Sample	CV	Interview
Doctoral	Required	Optional	3	Required	Optional	Required	Required

Admissions Criteria:

GRE scores—medium
Research experience—low
Work experience—high
Clinically related public service—high
GPA—high

Letters of recommendation—high
Interview—high
Statement of goals and objectives—high
Undergraduate psychology preparation—high

Department Demographics

	Male (PT)	Female (PT)	Total	African-American/ Black (PT)	Hispanic/ Latino (PT)	Asian/ Pacific Islander (PT)	American Indian/ Alaska Native (PT)	Caucasian/ White (PT)	Unknown	Multiethnic (PT)	ADA (PT)	Int'l (PT)
Students	12 (0)	49 (2)	63	4 (0)	2 (0)	4 (0)	1 (0)	50 (2)	0 (0)	0 (0)	0 (0)	3 (0)

Financial Information/Assistance

Doctoral:
State residents: $30,297 per academic year.
Nonstate residents: $30,297 per academic year.

Financial Assistance:

	Teaching Assistantship (% Receiving)	Teaching Assistantship Tuition Remission	Research Assistantship (% Receiving)	Research Assistantship Tuition Remission	Fellowship (% Receiving)	Fellowship Tuition Remission
First-Year Student	NA (NA)	NA	NA (NA)	NA	NA (NA)	NA
Advanced Student	NA (NA)	NA	NA (NA)	NA	NA (NA)	NA

Employment of Department Graduates

Doctoral:
Employed in independent practice: 4
Employed in a hospital/medical center: 1
Other employment position: 1
Do not know: 2
Total: 8

Additional Information

Housing and Day Care: On-campus housing is available. See the following website for more information: https://www.midwestern.edu/glendale-campus/housing.html. No on-campus day care facilities are available.

Special Facilities or Resources: Midwestern University's Multispecialty Clinic offers students a chance to train in a multidisciplinary setting at both the practicum and intern level.

Application Information: Midwestern University, Office of Admissions, 19555 North 59th Avenue, Glendale, AZ 85308. *Fee:* $0.
Online application: https://online.midwestern.edu/public/initapp.cgi?prog=AGCP&sess=FA&yr=2011.

Northcentral University
Department of Psychology
10000 East University Drive
Prescott Valley, AZ 86314
Telephone: (888) 327-2877
Chairperson: Bettina Shapira, PhD

E-mail: bshapira@ncu.edu
Web: http://www.ncu.edu/school-of-psychology

Orientation, Objectives, and Emphasis of Department
The department emphasizes applications of psychology. All instruction is carried out via distance learning in which students and faculty mentors work together in one-on-one relationships. Students need to be highly motivated, independent, and conscientious.

Programs and Degrees Offered

Program	Degree	Application Deadline	Applications Received	Accepted	New Admits Enrolled (PT)	Total Enrolled (PT)	Degrees Awarded in 2014–2015	Median Years to Complete Degree	Dismissed/ Withdrew
Psychology	MA/MS	Rolling	730	668	423 (0)	357 (0)	154	2.75	122
Psychology	PhD	Rolling	627	564	452 (0)	731 (0)	62	6.25	162

Admissions

Entries appear in the following order: required test or GPA, minimum score (if required)/median score of students entering in 2015–2016.

Program	Degree	GRE-V	GRE-Q	GRE-Writing	GRE-Subject	Under-graduate GPA	Last 2 Years GPA	Psychology GPA	Master's GPA
Psychology	MA/MS	Not specified	Not specified	Not specified	Not specified	Not specified	Not specified	Not specified	Not specified
Psychology	PhD	Not specified	Not specified	Not specified	Not specified	Not specified	Not specified	Not specified	Not specified

Admissions Requirements:

Degree	GRE	GRE-Subject	Letters of Recom-mendation	Research Statement	Writing Sample	CV	Interview
Master's/Specialist	None	None	N/A	None	None	None	None
Doctoral	None	None	N/A	None	None	Required	None

Admissions Criteria:

Research experience—low
Work experience—medium
Clinically related public service—medium
GPA—low

Letters of recommendation—low
Interview—low
Statement of goals and objectives—medium
Undergraduate psychology preparation—low

Department Demographics

	Male (PT)	Female (PT)	Total	African-American/ Black (PT)	Hispanic/ Latino (PT)	Asian/ Pacific Islander (PT)	American Indian/ Alaska Native (PT)	Caucasian/ White (PT)	Unknown	Multiethnic (PT)	ADA (PT)	Int'l (PT)
Students	218 (0)	870 (0)	1088	63 (0)	20 (0)	12 (0)	5 (0)	158 (0)	830 (0)	0 (0)	125 (0)	0 (0)

Financial Information/Assistance

Tuition: For information on tuition costs, visit http://www.ncu.edu/tuition-and-admissions/tuition. Tuition is subject to change. Tuition costs vary by program.

Doctoral:
State residents: $1,035 per credit hour.
Nonstate residents: $1,035 per credit hour.

Master's:
State residents: $752 per credit hour.
Nonstate residents: $752 per credit hour.

Financial Assistance:

	Teaching Assistantship (% Receiving)	Teaching Assistantship Tuition Remission	Research Assistantship (% Receiving)	Research Assistantship Tuition Remission	Fellowship (% Receiving)	Fellowship Tuition Remission
First-Year Student	NA (NA)	NA	NA (NA)	NA	NA (NA)	NA
Advanced Student	NA (NA)	NA	NA (NA)	NA	NA (NA)	NA

For additional information on financial assistance, visit http://www.ncu.edu/tuition-and-admissions/financing.

Employment of Department Graduates

Master's:
Enrolled in a psychology doctoral program: 15
Employed in an academic position at a university: 4
Employed in academic position at a 2-year/4-year college: 3
Employed in a professional position in a school system: 1
Employed in business or industry: 1
Employed in government agency: 7
Employed in a community mental health/counseling center: 3
Employed in a hospital/medical center: 1
Still seeking employment: 3
Not seeking employment: 2
Other employment position: 3
Do not know: 21
Total: 64

Doctoral:
Employed in an academic position at a university: 3
Employed in academic position at a 2-year/4-year college: 7
Employed in other positions at a higher education institution: 5
Employed in business or industry: 2
Employed in government agency: 3
Employed in a community mental health/counseling center: 2
Employed in a hospital/medical center: 3
Do not know: 25
Total: 50

Additional Information

Housing and Day Care: No on-campus housing is available. No on-campus day care facilities are available.

Application Information: Northcentral University, Attn: Enrollment, 8667 Hartford Drive, Scottsdale, AZ 85255. *Fee:* $0. *Online application:* https://apply.ncu.edu/.

Northern Arizona University
Department of Psychology
Social and Behavioral Sciences
NAU Box 15106
Flagstaff, AZ 86011
Telephone: (928) 523-3063
Chairperson: Rob Till

E-mail: ann.huffman@nau.edu
Web: http://nau.edu/sbs/psych/

Orientation, Objectives, and Emphasis of Department
The Psychological Sciences Department is committed to excellence in education at the graduate level, emphasizing teaching, scholarship, and service to the university and to the larger community. The department emphasizes theoretical foundations, empirical research, innovative curriculum, and practical hands-on applications of psychological knowledge.

Programs and Degrees Offered

Program	Degree	Application Deadline	Applications Received	Accepted	New Admits Enrolled (PT)	Total Enrolled (PT)	Degrees Awarded in 2014–2015	Median Years to Complete Degree	Dismissed/Withdrew
Psychological Sciences	MA/MS	February 1 (Fall)	40	15	15	30 (1)	12	2	1

Internships/Practica

Students may enroll in fieldwork placement that can range from applied health settings to teaching venues.

Admissions

Entries appear in the following order: required test or GPA, minimum score (if required)/median score of students entering in 2015–2016.

Program	Degree	GRE-V	GRE-Q	GRE-Writing	GRE-Subject	Under-graduate GPA	Last 2 Years GPA	Psychol-ogy GPA	Master's GPA
Psychological Sciences	MA/MS	Not specified	Not specified	Not specified	Not specified	Not specified	Not specified	Not specified	Not specified

Admissions Requirements:

Degree	GRE	GRE-Subject	Letters of Recom-mendation	Research Statement	Writing Sample	CV	Interview
Master's/Specialist	Required	None	3	Required	None	Required	None

Admissions Criteria:

GRE scores—high
Research experience—high
GPA—high

Letters of recommendation—high
Statement of goals and objectives—medium
Undergraduate psychology preparation—low

For additional information on admission requirements, visit http://nau.edu/SBS/Psych/Degrees-Programs/Graduate-Program/Admissions/.

Department Demographics

	Male (PT)	Female (PT)	Total	African-American/ Black (PT)	Hispanic/ Latino (PT)	Asian/ Pacific Islander (PT)	American Indian/ Alaska Native (PT)	Caucasian/ White (PT)	Unknown	Multiethnic (PT)	ADA (PT)	Int'l (PT)
Students	9 (0)	18 (0)	27	0 (0)	2 (0)	0 (0)	0 (1)	24 (0)	0 (0)	0 (0)	0 (0)	1 (0)

Financial Information/Assistance

Tuition: For information on tuition costs, visit http://nau.edu/SDAS/Tuition-Fees/. Tuition is subject to change.

Master's:
State residents: $9,552 per academic year.
State residents: $431 per credit hour.
Nonstate residents: $21,190 per academic year.
Nonstate residents: $1,130 per credit hour.

Financial Assistance:

	Teaching Assistantship (% Receiving)	Teaching Assistantship Tuition Remission	Research Assistantship (% Receiving)	Research Assistantship Tuition Remission	Fellowship (% Receiving)	Fellowship Tuition Remission
First-Year Student	NA (85)	Partial	NA (NA)	Partial	NA (15)	NA
Advanced Student	NA (85)	Partial	NA (NA)	Partial	NA (15)	NA

For additional information on financial assistance, visit http://nau.edu/finaid/.

Employment of Department Graduates

Master's:
Enrolled in a psychology doctoral program: 4
Enrolled in another graduate/professional program: 2
Employed in an academic position at a university: 1
Employed in a hospital/medical center: 2
Other employment position: 4
Do not know: 2
Total: 15

Additional Information

Housing and Day Care: On-campus housing is available. See the following website for more information: http://nau.edu/Residence-Life/. No on-campus day care facilities are available.

Information for Students With Physical Disabilities: See the following website: http://nau.edu/Disability-Resources/.

Special Facilities or Resources: Faculty research space accommodates graduate and undergraduate research students. All teaching rooms (located in a variety of NAU venues) are equipped with up-to-date technology.

Application Information: Department of Psychological Sciences, Graduate Program, Northern Arizona University, Box 15106, Flagstaff, AZ 86011. *Fee:* $50. *Online application:* https://www.applyweb.com/apply/northazg/.

Northern Arizona University
Educational Psychology
College of Education
P.O. Box 5774
Flagstaff, AZ 86011
Telephone: (928) 523-7103
Chairperson: Robert A. Horn

E-mail: Robert.Horn@nau.edu
Web: http://nau.edu/coe/ed-psych/

Orientation, Objectives, and Emphasis of Department
Because of the barriers to learning and living in our society, there is an increasing need for professionally trained counseling and school psychology personnel. Our graduate programs are based on a developmental, experiential training model that includes understanding theory, learning assessment and intervention skills, practicing skills in a supervised clinical setting, and performing skills in like settings. Integrated throughout our programs is a scientist–practitioner orientation that prepares students to ascertain the efficacy of assessment and intervention techniques.

Programs and Degrees Offered

Program	Degree	Application Deadline	Applications Received	Accepted	New Admits Enrolled (PT)	Total Enrolled (PT)	Degrees Awarded in 2014–2015	Median Years to Complete Degree	Dismissed/ Withdrew
Clinical Mental Health Counseling	MA/MS	February 15 (Fall), October 15 (Spring)	48	18	18 (1)	69 (26)	17	2.5	0
School Counseling	Med	February 15 (Fall)	10	4	7 (0)	27 (7)	28	2	0
Student Affairs	Med	February 15 (Fall)	49	22	20 (0)	32 (2)	11	2	0
Counseling Psychology	PhD	January 15 (Fall)	12	4	4 (0)	16 (10)	6	5	0
School Psychology	PhD	January 15 (Fall)	7	3	3 (0)	6 (4)	5	4	0

Programs and Degrees Offered *cont'd*

Program	Degree	Application Deadline	Applica-tions Received	Accepted	New Admits Enrolled (PT)	Total Enrolled (PT)	Degrees Awarded in 2014–2015	Median Years to Complete Degree	Dismissed/ Withdrew
Human Relations	Med	Rolling	150	145	30 (70)	76 (159)	84	2	0
School Psychology	EdS	January 15 (Fall)	20	6	6 (0)	27 (18)	6	2	0

Doctoral Degree (PhD Counseling Psychology): For those doctoral students for whom a professional internship was required in this program prior to graduation:
Total students who applied for an internship: 7
Total students who obtained an internship: 7
Total students who obtained a paid internship: 7
Total students who obtained an unpaid internship: 0
Total students who were placed in APA/CPA-accredited internships: 0
Total students placed in internships not APA/CPA-accredited, but listed with the Association of Psychology Postdoctoral and Internship Centers (APPIC): 4
Total students placed in internships conforming to guidelines of the Council of Directors of School Psychology Programs (CDSPP): 0
Total students placed in internships that were not APA/CPA-accredited, APPIC or CDSSP listed: 3

Doctoral Degree (PhD School Psychology): For those doctoral students for whom a professional internship was required in this program prior to graduation:
Total students who applied for an internship: 5
Total students who obtained an internship: 5
Total students who obtained a paid internship: 5
Total students who obtained an unpaid internship: 0
Total students who were placed in APA/CPA-accredited internships: 2
Total students placed in internships not APA/CPA-accredited, but listed with the Association of Psychology Postdoctoral and Internship Centers (APPIC): 1
Total students placed in internships conforming to guidelines of the Council of Directors of School Psychology Programs (CDSPP): 0
Total students placed in internships that were not APA/CPA-accredited, APPIC or CDSSP listed: 2

Master's Degree (MA/MS Clinical Mental Health Counseling): An internship experience, such as a final research project or "capstone" experience is required of graduates. Master's Degree (Med Student Affairs): An internship experience, such as a final research project or "capstone" experience is required of graduates.

Internships/Practica

Our programs are built on competency-based models and include closely supervised experiential practicum and internship components. Some of these experiences are offered in NAU's Counseling Center and the Institute for Human Development; student service facilities; public-school settings; reservation schools and communities; rural settings; and community agencies. In addition, the College of Education houses a Skills Lab that includes comprehensive testing and curriculum libraries and a practicum facility that uses both recorded and direct live feedback in the supervision of students working with clients.

Admissions

Entries appear in the following order: required test or GPA, minimum score (if required)/median score of students entering in 2015–2016.

Program	Degree	GRE-V	GRE-Q	GRE-Writing	GRE-Subject	Under-graduate GPA	Last 2 Years GPA	Psychol-ogy GPA	Master's GPA
Clinical Mental Health Counseling	MA/MS	NA/152	NA/147	Not specified	Not specified	NA/3.41	Not specified	Not specified	Not specified
School Counseling	Med	NA/151	NA/147	Not specified	Not specified	NA/3.5	Not specified	Not specified	Not specified
Student Affairs	Med	NA/150	NA/149	Not specified	Not specified	NA/3.39	Not specified	Not specified	Not specified

Admissions *cont'd*

Program	Degree	GRE-V	GRE-Q	GRE-Writing	GRE-Subject	Under-graduate GPA	Last 2 Years GPA	Psychol-ogy GPA	Master's GPA
Counseling Psychology	PhD	NA/152	NA/146	Not specified	Not specified	NA/3.86	Not specified	Not specified	Not specified
School Psychology	PhD	NA/152	NA/148	Not specified	Not specified	NA/3.65	Not specified	Not specified	Not specified
Human Relations	Med	Not specified	Not specified	Not specified	Not specified	3/NA	3/NA	Not specified	Not specified
School Psychology	EdS	NA/154	NA/151	Not specified	Not specified	NA/3.59	Not specified	Not specified	Not specified

Admissions Requirements:

Degree	GRE	GRE-Subject	Letters of Recom-mendation	Research Statement	Writing Sample	CV	Interview
Master's/Specialist	Required	None	3	Required	Required	Optional	Optional
Doctoral	Required	None	3	Required	Required	Optional	Optional

Admissions Criteria:

GRE scores—medium
Research experience—low
Work experience—medium
Clinically related public service—low
GPA—medium

Letters of recommendation—medium
Interview—medium
Statement of goals and objectives—high
Undergraduate psychology preparation—low

For additional information on admission requirements, visit http://nau.edu/COE/Ed-Psych/Degrees-Programs/.

Department Demographics

	Male (PT)	Female (PT)	Total	African-American/ Black (PT)	Hispanic/ Latino (PT)	Asian/ Pacific Islander (PT)	American Indian/ Alaska Native (PT)	Caucasian/ White (PT)	Unknown	Multiethnic (PT)	ADA (PT)	Int'l (PT)
Students	71 (54)	182 (172)	479	8 (13)	46 (48)	4 (6)	5 (6)	167 (145)	1 (3)	13 (5)	7 (6)	9 (0)

Financial Information/Assistance

Tuition: For information on tuition costs, visit http://nau.edu/SDAS/Tuition-Fees/. Tuition is subject to change. Additional fees are assessed to students beyond the costs of tuition for the following: FA Trust, Health/Rec, Activity, Info Tech, Green, ASNAU, and possible course fees.

Doctoral:
State residents: $7,758 per academic year.
State residents: $431 per credit hour.
Nonstate residents: $20,340 per academic year.
Nonstate residents: $1,130 per credit hour.

Master's:
State residents: $7,758 per academic year.
State residents: $431 per credit hour.
Nonstate residents: $20,340 per academic year.
Nonstate residents: $1,130 per credit hour.

Financial Assistance:

	Teaching Assistantship (% Receiving)	Teaching Assistantship Tuition Remission	Research Assistantship (% Receiving)	Research Assistantship Tuition Remission	Fellowship (% Receiving)	Fellowship Tuition Remission
First-Year Student	$10,012 (NA)	Full	$10,012 (NA)	Full	$500 (NA)	NA
Advanced Student	$10,012 (NA)	Full	$10,012 (NA)	Full	$500 (NA)	NA

For additional information on financial assistance, visit http://nau.edu/GradCol/Financing/.

Employment of Department Graduates

No information provided.

Additional Information

Housing and Day Care: On-campus housing is available. See the following website for more information: http://nau.edu/residence-life/. No on-campus day care facilities are available.

Information for Students With Physical Disabilities: See the following website: http://nau.edu/Disability-Resources/.

Special Facilities or Resources: Students in School Psychology programs (EdS and PhD) complete portions of their practicum at sites located on the Indian reservations and work with children and schools affiliated with the Navajo, Hopi, and Supai tribes. The EdS in School Psychology is also available at our Phoenix location. The MA Counseling and the MEd School Counseling programs are also available at other select sites in Arizona (i.e., Phoenix and Tucson). The MEd Human Relations program is an online 30 hr. program that does not lead to certification or licensure, but develops knowledge and skills in interpersonal, communication, critical thinking, research, and diversity awareness to assist individuals in careers in education, law enforcement, military, business, and other professions.

Application Information: Fee: $65. *Online application:* http://www.applyweb.com/apply/northazg/.

Affiliate Membership Application

Students | High School Teachers | Community College Teachers | International

Please complete the required information below. Return your completed application with payment to:
American Psychological Association, Service Center/Membership, 750 First Street, NE, Washington, DC 20002-4242

Applicant Information

Please print clearly or type.

Name (First/Middle/Last)_____

Contact Address_____

_____

City_____

State/Province/Country_____ Zip/Postal/Country Code_____

Phone (_____)_____ Fax (_____)_____

▶ E-mail_____

Add phone (include area/ country code), e-mail and school or institution.

▶ Name of School or Institution _____

▶ ☐ Your contact information will be listed in the APA Membership Directory. If you wish to publish <u>only your name</u> in the directory, please check here.

Membership Category

Please check the affiliate type that best describes you. See reverse side for requirements.

Student: ☐ Graduate $67.00*   Undergraduate ☐ $35.00 or ☐ $67.00*   ☐ High School $35.00

☐ Please check here if you attend a community college

*Includes membership in the American Psychological Association of Graduate Students (APAGS) and a subscription to *gradPSYCH*

Teacher: ☐ High School $50.00   ☐ Community College $50.00

International: ☐ Psychologists residing outside the U.S. or Canada $50.00

Name of the psychological association of the country of which you are a member; or give highest degree in psychology, date, institution, and major field of study **(required):**_____

_____

For Students Only

All <u>U.S.</u> graduate and undergraduate student applicants <u>must</u> complete sections A, B, and C.

Ⓐ Licensure/Ethics

If the graduate degree for which you are currently enrolled is a health service provider subfield (i.e., clinical, child clinical, counseling, school, geropsychology, or health), do you intend to seek licensure/certification by a state or provincial board of psychologist examiners for the independent practice of psychology?

☐ Yes, within the next year   ☐ Yes, eventually   ☐ No

☐ N/A, already licensed for the independent practice of psychology

Ⓑ Have you at any time been convicted of a felony, sanctioned by any professional ethics body, licensing board, or other regulatory body or by any professional or scientific organization? ☐ Yes *If yes, please provide an explanation on a separate sheet of paper.* ☐ No

In submitting this application, I subscribe to and will support the objectives of the American Psychological Association as set forth in Article 1 of the Bylaws, and the Ethical Principles of Psychologists and Code of Conduct, as adopted by the Association, and I affirm that the statements made in this application correctly represent my qualifications for election, and understand that if they do not, my affiliation may be voided.

The Ethical Principles of Psychologists and Code of Conduct is available on APA's website at http://www.apa.org/ethics/. The Bylaws are available at http://www.apa.org/about/governance/. Copies of these documents are also available to me upon request.

All students must sign the ethics statement (section C).

Ⓒ Signature _____ **Date** _____

Additional Information

The following items are <u>voluntary</u> and are used for research purposes only.

☐ Male   ☐ Female   ☐ Transgender   Date of birth (MM/DD/YY) _____

What is your race/ethnicity? *(U.S. residents, mark all that apply)*

☐ White
☐ Black, African American
☐ Hispanic/Latino(a)
☐ American Indian or Alaska Native

☐ Asian Indian
☐ Asian or Pacific Islander
☐ Chinese
☐ Filipino
☐ Japanese

☐ Korean
☐ Vietnamese
☐ Other Asian
☐ Native Hawaiian
☐ Guamanian or Chamorro

☐ Samoan
☐ Other Pacific Islander
☐ Other (specify)
_____

Payment Method

Applications will not be processed without payment. All payments must be drawn on a U.S. bank in U.S. dollars.

APA membership is based on the calendar year (January–December).

I am paying my total of $_____ by:

☐ Check or money order Check #_____ payable to the American Psychological Association

☐ American Express   ☐ MasterCard   ☐ Visa

Account Number_____ Expiration Date_____

Cardholder Name_____

Credit Card Billing Address_____

City/State/ZIP Code/Country_____

Daytime Telephone Number (include area code)_____

GS16

X Signature of Credit Card Holder (Required)_____

AMERICAN
PSYCHOLOGICAL
ASSOCIATION

Affiliate Membership Requirements Summary

Student requirements: High school, undergraduate, and graduate students taking psychology courses can become APA student affiliates. Graduate student affiliates are automatically enrolled in the American Psychological Association of Graduate Students (APAGS). Undergraduate affiliates may choose to join APAGS by paying the same rate as graduate students. Students must have a doctoral degree in psychology or a related field from a regionally accredited graduate or professional school (or a school that achieved such accreditation within 5 years of awarding of your doctoral degree, or a school of similar standing outside of the United States) to become a full **Member** of APA.

Teacher requirements: Teachers of psychology in high schools, junior colleges, and community colleges qualify as APA teacher affiliates. High school teacher affiliates are automatically members of Teachers of Psychology in Secondary Schools (TOPSS), an APA organization. Community college teacher affiliates receive membership in Psychology Teachers at Community Colleges (PT@CC), an APA organization.

Psychologists residing in countries other than the United States or Canada: May become APA international affiliates by providing required documentation indicating membership in your country's national psychology organization or evidence of appropriate qualifications.

Complete membership requirements: Requirements are available from APA's Service Center/Membership (see below for contact information).

Dues: Payment must accompany application. Applications without payment can not be processed. Payment must be made in U.S. dollars, drawn on a U.S. bank. APA affiliate dues (stated on the front of this application) are substantially discounted, over 75% off full member rates.

Membership term: APA membership is based on the calendar year (January–December). If your application is approved in September through December of the current year, your membership (including your subscriptions to the *Monitor on Psychology* and the *American Psychologist*) will automatically be extended to the end of the following year.

Standard inclusions: All APA affiliates receive a subscription to the *Monitor on Psychology* (11 issues*). Undergraduate and graduate students receive a subscription to *American Psychologist* (9 issues*). APAGS members receive a subscription to *gradPSYCH* (4 issues*).

Membership also includes substantial discounts (up to 60%) on various APA publications and electronic products. A detailed list of publications will be sent to you upon acceptance of your application.

Delivery of products and services: Allow 3–4 weeks for the processing of your application and 6–8 weeks for the initial delivery of your APA publications. International orders are sent via surface mail and may take longer.

APA Member and Affiliate Directory: Upon acceptance, your contact information will automatically be included in the official directory, which is a main source of member-to-member communication. To publish only your name in the directory, please check the appropriate box on the front of this application.

For questions or additional information:

Service Center/Membership: (202) 336-5580 or (800) 374-2721 or TDD/TTY: (202) 336-6123; Fax: (202) 336-5568; E-mail: membership@apa.org; Web: http://www.apa.org

Return your completed application to: American Psychological Association, Service Center/Membership, 750 First Street, NE, Washington, DC 20002-4242

*$6.00 of APA dues is allocated towards the *Monitor on Psychology* subscription and $12.00 of APA dues is allocated towards the *American Psychologist* subscription. If you receive *gradPSYCH*, $3.00 of APA dues is allocated towards the subscription.

Arkansas, University of
Department of Psychology
J. William Fulbright College of Arts and Science
216 Memorial Hall
Fayetteville, AR 72701
Telephone: (479) 575-4256
Chairperson: Douglas Behrend

E-mail: psycapp@uark.edu
Web: http://psyc.uark.edu/

Orientation, Objectives, and Emphasis of Department
The PhD program in clinical psychology is fully accredited by the American Psychological Association and follows the scientist/practitioner model of training. The program is based on the premise that clinical psychologists should be skilled practitioners and mental health service providers as well as competent researchers. To facilitate these goals, we strive to maximize the match between the clinical and research interests of the faculty with those of the graduate students. Courses and clinical experiences are designed to promote development in both areas. Our training is such that our graduates are competitive for academic, research, and direct service provision positions, as well positions that involve a combination of these responsibilities. The PhD program in Experimental Psychology serves as an umbrella under which four training tracks are offered in cognitive, developmental, neuroscience, and social content areas. Broad exposure to the field is provided via a core curriculum, with more specialized training offered in seminars and individualized programs of study. The courses, research experiences, and teaching opportunities we offer are designed to provide students with training in the scientific method and research skills needed to develop independent programs of research and to develop the skills relevant to the student's long-term goals and aspirations.

Programs and Degrees Offered

Program	Degree	Application Deadline	Applications Received	Accepted	New Admits Enrolled (PT)	Total Enrolled (PT)	Degrees Awarded in 2014–2015	Median Years to Complete Degree	Dismissed/Withdrew
Clinical Psychology	PhD	November 20 (Fall)	164	8	4	26 (0)	4	6	1
Experimental Psychology	PhD	December 1 (Fall)	25	7	5 (0)	21 (0)	2	5	0

APA Accreditation
Clinical PhD: Student Outcome Data website: http://fulbright.uark.edu/departments/psychological-science/graduate-programs/clinical-psychology/index.php.

Doctoral Degree (PhD Clinical Psychology): For those doctoral students for whom a professional internship was required in this program prior to graduation:
Total students who applied for an internship: 4
Total students who obtained an internship: 4
Total students who obtained a paid internship: 4
Total students who obtained an unpaid internship: 0
Total students who were placed in APA/CPA-accredited internships: 4
Total students placed in internships not APA/CPA-accredited, but listed with the Association of Psychology Postdoctoral and Internship Centers (APPIC): 0
Total students placed in internships conforming to guidelines of the Council of Directors of School Psychology Programs (CDSPP): 0
Total students placed in internships that were not APA/CPA-accredited, APPIC or CDSSP listed: 0

Internships/Practica
Doctoral students in the Clinical Training Program have always been able to obtain high-quality, APA-accredited predoctoral internships. Additionally, our students have numerous funded and volunteer placement opportunities throughout their tenure with us. These placements include a federally qualified health center, VA inpatient and outpatient units, a domestic violence shelter, University Counseling Center, medical neuropsychology setting, juvenile detention center, correctional center, and other clinical specialties.

Admissions

Entries appear in the following order: required test or GPA, minimum score (if required)/median score of students entering in 2015–2016.

Program	Degree	GRE-V	GRE-Q	GRE-Writing	GRE-Subject	Undergraduate GPA	Last 2 Years GPA	Psychology GPA	Master's GPA
Clinical Psychology	PhD	NA/156	NA/156	Not specified	Not specified	NA/3.88	Not specified	Not specified	Not specified
Experimental Psychology	PhD	NA/NA	NA/NA	NA/NA	Not specified	NA/3.67	Not specified	Not specified	Not specified

Admissions Requirements:

Degree	GRE	GRE-Subject	Letters of Recommendation	Research Statement	Writing Sample	CV	Interview
Doctoral	Required	Required	3	Required	Optional	Recommended	Recommended

Admissions Criteria:

GRE scores—high
Research experience—high
Work experience—low
Clinically related public service—low
GPA—high

Letters of recommendation—high
Interview—high
Statement of goals and objectives—high
Undergraduate psychology preparation—medium
Fit with faculty research—high

For additional information on admission requirements, visit http://fulbright.uark.edu/departments/psychological-science/graduate-programs/index.php.

Department Demographics

	Male (PT)	Female (PT)	Total	African-American/ Black (PT)	Hispanic/ Latino (PT)	Asian/ Pacific Islander (PT)	American Indian/ Alaska Native (PT)	Caucasian/ White (PT)	Unknown	Multiethnic (PT)	ADA (PT)	Int'l (PT)
Students	17 (0)	29 (0)	46	0 (0)	5 (0)	0 (0)	1 (0)	37 (0)	2 (0)	1 (0)	0 (0)	0 (0)

Financial Information/Assistance

Tuition: For information on tuition costs, visit http://finaid.uark.edu/office_information/cost-of-attendance.php. Tuition is subject to change. Additional fees are assessed to students beyond the costs of tuition for the following: student activity fees, technology fees.

Doctoral:
State residents: $9,598 per academic year.
State residents: $450 per credit hour.
Nonstate residents: $23,700 per academic year.
Nonstate residents: $1,037 per credit hour.

Financial Assistance:

	Teaching Assistantship (% Receiving)	Teaching Assistantship Tuition Remission	Research Assistantship (% Receiving)	Research Assistantship Tuition Remission	Fellowship (% Receiving)	Fellowship Tuition Remission
First-Year Student	$12,000 (NA)	Full	$12,000 (NA)	Full	$20,000 (NA)	Full
Advanced Student	$12,000 (NA)	Full	$12,000 (NA)	Full	$20,000 (NA)	Full

For additional information on financial assistance, visit http://fulbright.uark.edu/departments/psychological-science/graduate-programs/financial-aid.php.

Employment of Department Graduates

Doctoral:
Enrolled in a postdoctoral residency/fellowship: 3
Employed in academic position at a 2-year/4-year college: 2
Total: 5

Additional Information

Housing and Day Care: On-campus housing is available. See the following website for more information: http://housing.uark.edu/. On-campus day care facilities are available. See the following website for more information: http://jean-tyson-child-development-study-center.uark.edu.

Information for Students With Physical Disabilities: See the following website: http://cea.uark.edu/.

Special Facilities or Resources: The Department of Psychology is housed in Memorial Hall, a multilevel building with 58,000 square feet of office and research space for faculty and students. The building contains modern facilities for both human and small animal research, including specialized space for use with individuals and small groups of children and adults. The on-site Psychological Clinic is a state-of-the-art training and research facility dedicated to providing practicum and applied research experiences for clinical students. The clinic's treatment, testing, and research rooms are equipped with a closed-circuit videotaping system. Memorial Hall has comprehensive data analysis facilities, including numerous networked computers. Finally, the department is the beneficiary of a generous bequest that established the Marie Wilson Howells Fund, which provides funding for thesis and dissertation research, numerous research assistantships, student travel, and departmental colloquia. The department also nominates qualified students for supplemental Doctoral Fellowships available through the Graduate School.

Application Information: Graduate Studies Coordinator, Department of Psychology, 216 Memorial Hall, University of Arkansas, Fayetteville, AR 72701. *Fee:* $40. *Online application:* https://application.uark.edu/.

Central Arkansas, University of
Department of Psychology and Counseling
Health and Behavioral Sciences
201 Donaghey Avenue
Conway, AR 72035-0001
Telephone: (501) 450-3193
Chairperson: J. Arthur Gillaspy, Jr.

E-mail: ArtG@uca.edu
Web: http://uca.edu/psychology

Orientation, Objectives, and Emphasis of Department
The MS programs in Mental Health Counseling and School Psychology are designed to serve as terminal degrees with professional employment opportunities or as a firm foundation for prospective doctoral candidates. Broad training is offered in the understanding of psychological theories, assessment, and mental health interventions to enable graduates to function successfully in a variety of mental health and educational settings. The PhD in School Psychology is grounded in the scientist–practitioner model of training. Strong emphasis is placed on child mental health promotion, primary prevention, and intervention with a broad range of community related problems involving children, families, and schools. The program is responsive to ongoing societal concerns and issues pertaining to children, families, and schools. It prepares its graduates to function in schools, clinics, community agencies, and hospitals. The Counseling Psychology PhD program is based on the scientist–practitioner model of training and emphasizes community mental health intervention and prevention services for clients with a wide variety of mental health problems. Graduates will be prepared to provide evidence-based assessment and treatment services and to conduct research in clinical and university settings.

Programs and Degrees Offered

Program	Degree	Application Deadline	Applications Received	Accepted	New Admits Enrolled (PT)	Total Enrolled (PT)	Degrees Awarded in 2014–2015	Median Years to Complete Degree	Dismissed/ Withdrew
School Psychology	PhD	January 15 (Fall)	12	4	0 (0)	10 (0)	1	5	0
School Psychology	MA/MS	March 15 (Fall)	10	6	5 (0)	18 (0)	3	3	2
Counseling Psychology	PhD	January 15 (Fall), January 15 (Summer)	12	5	3 (0)	26 (0)	3	5	0
Mental Health Counseling	MA/MS	January 15 (Fall), January 15 (Summer)	29	23	13 (0)	57 (0)	17	2.5	3

APA Accreditation

School PhD: Student Outcome Data website: http://uca.edu/psychology/doc-school-psyc/.

Doctoral Degree (PhD School Psychology): For those doctoral students for whom a professional internship was required in this program prior to graduation:
Total students who applied for an internship: 2
Total students who obtained an internship: 2
Total students who obtained a paid internship: 2
Total students who obtained an unpaid internship: 0
Total students who were placed in APA/CPA-accredited internships: 2
Total students placed in internships not APA/CPA-accredited, but listed with the Association of Psychology Postdoctoral and Internship Centers (APPIC): 0
Total students placed in internships conforming to guidelines of the Council of Directors of School Psychology Programs (CDSPP): 0
Total students placed in internships that were not APA/CPA-accredited, APPIC or CDSSP listed: 0

Doctoral Degree (PhD Counseling Psychology): For those doctoral students for whom a professional internship was required in this program prior to graduation:
Total students who applied for an internship: 3
Total students who obtained an internship: 2
Total students who obtained a paid internship: 2
Total students who obtained an unpaid internship: 0
Total students who were placed in APA/CPA-accredited internships: 0
Total students placed in internships not APA/CPA-accredited, but listed with the Association of Psychology Postdoctoral and Internship Centers (APPIC): 2
Total students placed in internships conforming to guidelines of the Council of Directors of School Psychology Programs (CDSPP): 0
Total students placed in internships that were not APA/CPA-accredited, APPIC or CDSSP listed: 0

Master's Degree (MA/MS School Psychology): An internship experience, such as a final research project or "capstone" experience is required of graduates. Master's Degree (MA/MS Mental Health Counseling): An internship experience, such as a final research project or "capstone" experience is required of graduates.

Internships/Practica

Students are placed in a wide-range of practica and internships depending on their program of study, career aspirations, and match between the practicum/internship site and our program objectives. Examples of placements include schools, community agencies, hospitals, residential homes, university counseling centers, and clinics.

Admissions

Entries appear in the following order: required test or GPA, minimum score (if required)/median score of students entering in 2015–2016.

Program	Degree	GRE-V	GRE-Q	GRE-Writing	GRE-Subject	Under-graduate GPA	Last 2 Years GPA	Psychology GPA	Master's GPA
School Psychology	PhD	NA/150	NA/150	NA/4	Not specified	NA/3.7	Not specified	Not specified	Not specified
School Psychology	MA/MS	NA/148	NA/148	NA/4	Not specified	NA/3.5	Not specified	Not specified	Not specified
Counseling Psychology	PhD	NA/157	NA/149	NA/NA	Not specified	NA/3.76	Not specified	Not specified	Not specified
Mental Health Counseling	MA/MS	NA/151	NA/147	NA/3.5	Not specified	NA/3.57	Not specified	Not specified	Not specified

Admissions Requirements:

Degree	GRE	GRE-Subject	Letters of Recommendation	Research Statement	Writing Sample	CV	Interview
Master's/Specialist	Required	None	3	Required	Optional	Required	Required
Doctoral	Required	Optional	3	Required	Optional	Required	Required

Please note if these criteria vary for different programs: Doctoral programs place greater emphasis on previous research experience.

Admissions Criteria:

GRE scores—medium
Research experience—medium
Work experience—low
Clinically related public service—medium
GPA—high

Letters of recommendation—medium
Interview—high
Statement of goals and objectives—high
Undergraduate psychology preparation—medium

For additional information on admission requirements, visit http://uca.edu/psychology/graduate-programs/.

Department Demographics

	Male (PT)	Female (PT)	Total	African-American/ Black (PT)	Hispanic/ Latino (PT)	Asian/ Pacific Islander (PT)	American Indian/ Alaska Native (PT)	Caucasian/ White (PT)	Unknown	Multiethnic (PT)	ADA (PT)	Int'l (PT)
Students	28 (0)	61 (0)	89	13 (0)	1 (0)	2 (0)	0 (0)	69 (0)	0 (0)	4 (0)	0 (0)	3 (0)

Financial Information/Assistance

Tuition: For information on tuition costs, visit http://uca.edu/studentaccounts/tuition-and-fee-rates/. Tuition is subject to change.

Doctoral:
State residents: $418 per credit hour.
Nonstate residents: $661 per credit hour.

Master's:
State residents: $418 per credit hour.
Nonstate residents: $661 per credit hour.

Financial Assistance:

	Teaching Assistantship (% Receiving)	Teaching Assistantship Tuition Remission	Research Assistantship (% Receiving)	Research Assistantship Tuition Remission	Fellowship (% Receiving)	Fellowship Tuition Remission
First-Year Student	$8,000 (NA)	NA	$8,000 (NA)	NA	NA (NA)	NA
Advanced Student	$10,400 (NA)	NA	$8,000 (NA)	NA	NA (NA)	NA

For additional information on financial assistance, visit http://uca.edu/graduateschool/assistantships-and-other-aid/.

Employment of Department Graduates

Master's:
Enrolled in a psychology doctoral program: 1
Enrolled in another graduate/professional program: 7
Employed in a professional position in a school system: 3
Employed in a community mental health/counseling center: 28
Total: 39

Doctoral:
Employed in independent practice: 2
Employed in other positions at a higher education institution: 1
Employed in a professional position in a school system: 2
Employed in a community mental health/counseling center: 2
Total: 7

Additional Information

Housing and Day Care: On-campus housing is available. See the following website for more information: http://uca.edu/housing/. On-campus day care facilities are available. See the following website for more information: http://uca.edu/childstudy/.

Information for Students With Physical Disabilities: See the following website: http://uca.edu/disability/.

Special Facilities or Resources: The department has (a) a fully operational computer instruction/research room which can be used for onsite research purposes; (b) human and animal research labs; and (c) a multi-media computer system for research-related editing (e.g., self-modeling, therapy tapes). The department also operates the Psychology and Counseling Training Clinic that provides assessment services for the community.

Application Information: Director of Training, Department of Psychology & Counseling, Box 4915, University of Central Arkansas, Conway, AR 72035. *Fee:* $25. *Online application:* https://uca.edu/graduateschool/admission-process/.

Alliant International University: Fresno
Programs in Clinical Psychology & Clinical Counseling
California School of Professional Psychology
5130 East Clinton Way
Fresno, CA 93727
Telephone: (866) 825-5426
Executive Dean, California School of Professional Psychology: Teresa Chapa, PhD

E-mail: aerdman1@alliant.edu
Web: http://www.alliant.edu/cspp/

Orientation, Objectives, and Emphasis of Department
The clinical psychology PsyD program emphasizes training in clinical skills and clinical application of research knowledge and is designed for students who are interested in careers as practitioners, but also includes a research component. The program is multisystemically or ecosystemically oriented and trains students to consider the role of diverse systems in creating and/or remedying individual and social problems. An empirical PsyD dissertation is required and may focus on program development and/or evaluation, test development, survey research, or therapeutic outcomes. The clinical psychology PhD program puts equal weight on training in clinical, research, and teaching skills. The program is for students whose goal is an academic career in psychology. Emphasis areas offered are ecosystemic clinical child emphasis—trains students to work with infants, children, and adolescents, as well as with the adults in these clients' lives; health psychology emphasis—provides students with exposure to the expanding field of health psychology and behavioral medicine; forensic clinical psychology emphasis—prepares students to practice clinical psychology in a forensic environment. The master's program in clinical counseling trains students to provide competent professional therapeutic services in a variety of settings.

Programs and Degrees Offered

Program	Degree	Application Deadline	Applications Received	Accepted	New Admits Enrolled (PT)	Total Enrolled (PT)	Degrees Awarded in 2014–2015	Median Years to Complete Degree	Dismissed/ Withdrew
Clinical Psychology	PsyD	December 15 (Fall), Rolling	56	26	20 (0)	56 (6)	10	4.9	0
Clinical Psychology	PhD	December 15 (Fall), Rolling	29	16	5 (0)	39 (4)	8	5.22	0
Clinical Psychology	Respecialization Diploma	December 15 (Fall), Rolling	0	0	0 (0)	0 (0)	0		0
Clinical Counseling	MA/MS	April 1 (Fall), November 1 (Spring), Rolling	24	19	11 (0)	17 (0)	0		0

APA Accreditation
Clinical PsyD: Student Outcome Data website: http://www.alliant.edu/cspp/programs-degrees/clinical-psychology/clinical_psyd_fresno/index.php.
Clinical PhD: Student Outcome Data website: http://www.alliant.edu/cspp/programs-degrees/clinical-psychology/clinical_phd_fresno/index.php.

Doctoral Degree (PsyD Clinical Psychology): For those doctoral students for whom a professional internship was required in this program prior to graduation:
Total students who applied for an internship: 12
Total students who obtained an internship: 10
Total students who obtained a paid internship: 7
Total students who obtained an unpaid internship: 3

Total students who were placed in APA/CPA-accredited internships: 2
Total students placed in internships not APA/CPA-accredited, but listed with the Association of Psychology Postdoctoral and Internship Centers (APPIC): 3
Total students placed in internships conforming to guidelines of the Council of Directors of School Psychology Programs (CDSPP): 0
Total students placed in internships that were not APA/CPA-accredited, APPIC or CDSSP listed: 5

Doctoral Degree (PhD Clinical Psychology): For those doctoral students for whom a professional internship was required in this program prior to graduation:
Total students who applied for an internship: 9
Total students who obtained an internship: 7
Total students who obtained a paid internship: 6
Total students who obtained an unpaid internship: 1
Total students who were placed in APA/CPA-accredited internships: 3
Total students placed in internships not APA/CPA-accredited, but listed with the Association of Psychology Postdoctoral and Internship Centers (APPIC): 3
Total students placed in internships conforming to guidelines of the Council of Directors of School Psychology Programs (CDSPP): 0
Total students placed in internships that were not APA/CPA-accredited, APPIC or CDSSP listed: 1

Master's Degree (MA/MS Clinical Counseling): An internship experience, such as a final research project or "capstone" experience is required of graduates.

Internships/Practica

The clinical psychology programs emphasize the integration of academic coursework and research with clinical practice. In order to integrate appropriate skills with material learned in the classroom, students participate in a professional training placement experience beginning in the first year. The settings where students complete the professional training requirements include community mental health centers, clinics, inpatient mental health facilities, medical settings, specialized service centers, rehabilitation programs, residential/day care programs, forensic/correctional facilities, and educational programs. Third-year students will spend fifteen hours per week in a practicum either at CSPP's Psychological Service Center or at some other CSPP-approved agency. During their final year, clinical students complete a full year internship at an appropriate APA or APPIC internship. PhD students must also complete teaching practica. Clinical Counseling students conduct a minimum of 700 hours of direct and indirect supervised clinical experience counseling individuals, families or groups.

Admissions

Entries appear in the following order: required test or GPA, minimum score (if required)/median score of students entering in 2015–2016.

Program	Degree	GRE-V	GRE-Q	GRE-Writing	GRE-Subject	Under-graduate GPA	Last 2 Years GPA	Psychology GPA	Master's GPA
Clinical Psychology	PsyD	Not specified	Not specified	Not specified	Not specified	3/3.23	Not specified	3/NA	Not specified
Clinical Psychology	PhD	Not specified	Not specified	Not specified	Not specified	3/3.33	Not specified	3/NA	Not specified
Clinical Psychology	Respecial-ization Diploma	Not specified	Not specified	Not specified	Not specified	Not specified	Not specified	Not specified	Not specified
Clinical Counseling	MA/MS	Not specified	Not specified	Not specified	Not specified	Not specified	Not specified	Not specified	Not specified

Admissions Requirements:

Degree	GRE	GRE-Subject	Letters of Recom-mendation	Research Statement	Writing Sample	CV	Interview
Master's/Specialist	None	None	2	Required	None	Required	Required
Doctoral	Optional	Optional	2	Required	None	Required	Required

Please note if these criteria vary for different programs: Criteria differ by program and level.

Admissions Criteria:

GRE scores—low
Research experience—medium
Work experience—medium
Clinically related public service—medium
GPA—high

Letters of recommendation—high
Interview—high
Statement of goals and objectives—high
Undergraduate psychology preparation—medium

For additional information on admission requirements, visit http://www.alliant.edu/cspp/admissions/apply/index.php.

Department Demographics

	Male (PT)	Female (PT)	Total	African-American/ Black (PT)	Hispanic/ Latino (PT)	Asian/ Pacific Islander (PT)	American Indian/ Alaska Native (PT)	Caucasian/ White (PT)	Unknown	Multiethnic (PT)	ADA (PT)	Int'l (PT)
Students	36 (1)	76 (9)	122	6 (0)	31 (6)	7 (0)	0 (0)	52 (3)	6 (1)	10 (0)	2 (0)	4 (0)

Financial Information/Assistance

Tuition: For information on tuition costs, visit http://www.alliant.edu/admissions/tuition.php. Tuition is subject to change. Tuition costs vary by program.

Doctoral:
State residents: $1,160 per credit hour.
Nonstate residents: $1,160 per credit hour.

Master's:
State residents: $690 per credit hour.
Nonstate residents: $690 per credit hour.

Financial Assistance:

	Teaching Assistantship (% Receiving)	Teaching Assistantship Tuition Remission	Research Assistantship (% Receiving)	Research Assistantship Tuition Remission	Fellowship (% Receiving)	Fellowship Tuition Remission
First-Year Student	NA (NA)	NA	$1,000 (NA)	NA	$5,000 (NA)	NA
Advanced Student	$3,000 (NA)	NA	$1,000 (NA)	NA	$5,000 (NA)	NA

For additional information on financial assistance, visit http://www.alliant.edu/cspp/admissions/scholarships_financial_aid/index.php.

Employment of Department Graduates

No information provided.

Additional Information

Housing and Day Care: No on-campus housing is available. No on-campus day care facilities are available.

Information for Students With Physical Disabilities: See the following website: http://www.alliant.edu/consumer/disability-services/index.php.

Special Facilities or Resources: The Psychological Service Center serves the dual purpose of offering high quality psychological services to the community, particularly underserved segments, and continuing the tradition of education, training and service. The facility consists of eight therapy and two play therapy rooms, a large conference room, student work room, TV/monitor, and staff offices. The campus is also home to the Association for Play Therapy.

Application Information: Alliant International University, Admissions Processing Center, 10455 Pomerado Road, San Diego, CA 92131-1799. *Fee:* $65. *Online application:* https://www.applyweb.com/alliant/.

Alliant International University: Fresno
Programs in Organizational Psychology
California School of Professional Psychology
5130 East Clinton Way
Fresno, CA 93727-2014
Telephone: (866) 825-5426
Executive Dean, California School of Professional Psychology: Teresa Chapa, PhD
Web: http://www.alliant.edu/cspp/programs-degrees/organizational-psychology/

E-mail: aerdman1@alliant.edu

Orientation, Objectives, and Emphasis of Department
The doctoral program prepares students for careers as consultants, leaders/managers, or faculty in community colleges or other academic institutions. The program is 3 years post-master's and accessible to working adults. Students focus on the individual, on themes and cultures of organizations, and on practice in the global community. During the program they learn about managing change in complex organizations, examine and assess organizational procedures and processes, design interventions at the system/group/individual levels, and learn skills for OD consulting and conducting applied research. A PsyD project is a required part of the program. The PsyD program is accredited by the Organization Development Institute. The master's program is a 2-year program for working professionals and may be taken jointly with another doctoral program at Alliant in Fresno. The program has a practical curriculum related to management issues involving people and organizational processes.

Programs and Degrees Offered

Program	Degree	Application Deadline	Applica-tions Received	Accepted	New Admits Enrolled (PT)	Total Enrolled (PT)	Degrees Awarded in 2014–2015	Median Years to Complete Degree	Dismissed/Withdrew
Organization Development	PsyD	March 1 (Fall), October 1 (Spring), Rolling	13	12	3 (6)	12 (34)	6	4.4	0
Organizational Behavior	MA/MS	March 1 (Fall), October 1 (Spring), Rolling	9	7	0 (6)	1 (9)	6	1.74	0

Internships/Practica
The second and third years of the doctoral program involve a professional placement in organizational studies.

Admissions
Entries appear in the following order: required test or GPA, minimum score (if required)/median score of students entering in 2015–2016.

Program	Degree	GRE-V	GRE-Q	GRE-Writing	GRE-Subject	Under-graduate GPA	Last 2 Years GPA	Psychol-ogy GPA	Master's GPA
Organization Development	PsyD	Not specified	Not specified	Not specified	Not specified	3/3	Not specified	3/NA	Not specified
Organizational Behavior	MA/MS	Not specified	Not specified	Not specified	Not specified	3/3.22	Not specified	3/NA	Not specified

Admissions Requirements:

Degree	GRE	GRE-Subject	Letters of Recommendation	Research Statement	Writing Sample	CV	Interview
Master's/Specialist	Optional	None	2	Required	None	Required	Required
Doctoral	Optional	None	2	Required	None	Required	Required

Please note if these criteria vary for different programs: Criteria differ by program and level.

Admissions Criteria:

Research experience—low
Work experience—high
GPA—high
Letters of recommendation—high

Interview—high
Statement of goals and objectives—high
Undergraduate psychology preparation—medium

For additional information on admission requirements, visit http://www.alliant.edu/cspp/admissions/apply/op-app-req.php.

Department Demographics

	Male (PT)	Female (PT)	Total	African-American/ Black (PT)	Hispanic/ Latino (PT)	Asian/ Pacific Islander (PT)	American Indian/ Alaska Native (PT)	Caucasian/ White (PT)	Unknown	Multiethnic (PT)	ADA (PT)	Int'l (PT)
Students	7 (19)	6 (24)	56	3 (6)	3 (8)	0 (4)	0 (0)	5 (18)	2 (2)	0 (5)	0 (2)	2 (1)

Financial Information/Assistance

Tuition: For information on tuition costs, visit http://www.alliant.edu/admissions/tuition.php. Tuition is subject to change. Tuition costs vary by program.

Doctoral:
State residents: $1,160 per credit hour.
Nonstate residents: $1,160 per credit hour.

Master's:
State residents: $854 per credit hour.
Nonstate residents: $854 per credit hour.

Financial Assistance:

	Teaching Assistantship (% Receiving)	Teaching Assistantship Tuition Remission	Research Assistantship (% Receiving)	Research Assistantship Tuition Remission	Fellowship (% Receiving)	Fellowship Tuition Remission
First-Year Student	NA (NA)	NA	$1,000 (NA)	NA	$5,000 (NA)	NA
Advanced Student	$3,000 (NA)	NA	$1,000 (NA)	NA	$5,000 (NA)	NA

For additional information on financial assistance, visit http://www.alliant.edu/cspp/admissions/scholarships_financial_aid/index.php.

Employment of Department Graduates

No information provided.

Additional Information

Housing and Day Care: No on-campus housing is available. No on-campus day care facilities are available.

Information for Students With Physical Disabilities: See the following website: http://www.alliant.edu/consumer/disability-services/index.php.

Application Information: Alliant International University, Admissions Processing Center, 10455 Pomerado Road, San Diego, CA 92131-1799. *Fee:* $65. *Online application:* https://www.applyweb.com/alliant/.

Alliant International University: Irvine
Couple and Family Therapy Program
California School of Professional Psychology
Jamboree Building Center
2855 Michelle Drive, Suite 300
Irvine, CA 92606
Telephone: (866) 825-5426
Executive Dean, California School of Professional Psychology: Teresa Chapa, PhD
Web: http://www.alliant.edu/cspp/programs-degrees/couple-family-therapy/

E-mail: mgiovanini@alliant.edu

Orientation, Objectives, and Emphasis of Department
The mission of the Couple and Family Therapy Program is to prepare graduate students who are skilled in the theory, research, and clinical practice of the field of Marriage and Family Therapy and can integrate individual and systemic therapeutic models in an international, multicultural environment. The Couple and Family Therapy (CFT) programs provide students with the essential training needed to pursue a career as a professional Marriage and Family Therapist (MFT). The Master of Arts in MFT allows students to be licensed as an MFT and the Doctor of Psychology (PsyD) in MFT prepares students with academic and research experience. Students who complete the MFT master's at Alliant can apply all of their master's degree coursework and practicum hours toward the doctoral program. The programs are accredited by COAMFTE.

Programs and Degrees Offered

Program	Degree	Application Deadline	Applica-tions Received	Accepted	New Admits Enrolled (PT)	Total Enrolled (PT)	Degrees Awarded in 2014–2015	Median Years to Complete Degree	Dismissed/ Withdrew
Marital and Family Therapy	MA/MS	January 15 (Fall), October 1 (Spring), Rolling	49	33	23 (1)	39 (10)	21	2.07	1
Marital and Family Therapy	PsyD	January 15 (Fall), October 1 (Spring), Rolling	24	10	2 (1)	5 (46)	14	8.23	0

Internships/Practica
As part of the practicum experience, students complete 500 client contact hours, 250 of which must be with couples and families. Students receive at least 100 hours of individual and group supervision, 50 hours of which are based on direct observation, videotape, or audiotape. At least 25 of those hours must be videotape or direct observation. When students are ready to begin practicum, experienced faculty and staff assist students through each step in obtaining a field placement site approved by Alliant. While students are doing practicum training, they are required to perform marriage and family therapy under a California state licensed, AAMFT-approved supervisor or the equivalent.

Admissions
Entries appear in the following order: required test or GPA, minimum score (if required)/median score of students entering in 2015–2016.

Program	Degree	GRE-V	GRE-Q	GRE-Writing	GRE-Subject	Under-graduate GPA	Last 2 Years GPA	Psychol-ogy GPA	Master's GPA
Marital and Family Therapy	MA/MS	Not specified	Not specified	Not specified	Not specified	3/3.04	Not specified	3/NA	Not specified
Marital and Family Therapy	PsyD	Not specified	Not specified	Not specified	Not specified	3/3	Not specified	3/NA	Not specified

Admissions Requirements:

Degree	GRE	GRE-Subject	Letters of Recommendation	Research Statement	Writing Sample	CV	Interview
Master's/Specialist	Optional	None	2	Required	None	Required	Required
Doctoral	Optional	None	2	Required	None	Required	Required

Please note if these criteria vary for different programs: Criteria differ by program and level.

Admissions Criteria:

Research experience—medium
Work experience—medium
Clinically related public service—medium
GPA—high

Letters of recommendation—high
Interview—high
Statement of goals and objectives—high
Undergraduate psychology preparation—medium

For additional information on admission requirements, visit http://www.alliant.edu/cspp/admissions/apply/cft-app-req.php.

Department Demographics

	Male (PT)	Female (PT)	Total	African-American/ Black (PT)	Hispanic/ Latino (PT)	Asian/ Pacific Islander (PT)	American Indian/ Alaska Native (PT)	Caucasian/ White (PT)	Unknown (PT)	Multiethnic (PT)	ADA (PT)	Int'l (PT)
Students	13 (9)	31 (47)	100	1 (5)	8 (13)	6 (6)	0 (0)	20 (27)	6 (3)	3 (2)	0 (1)	3 (2)

Financial Information/Assistance

Tuition: For information on tuition costs, visit http://www.alliant.edu/admissions/tuition.php. Tuition is subject to change.

Doctoral:
State residents: $1,160 per credit hour.
Nonstate residents: $1,160 per credit hour.

Master's:
State residents: $1,160 per credit hour.
Nonstate residents: $1,160 per credit hour.

Financial Assistance:

	Teaching Assistantship (% Receiving)	Teaching Assistantship Tuition Remission	Research Assistantship (% Receiving)	Research Assistantship Tuition Remission	Fellowship (% Receiving)	Fellowship Tuition Remission
First-Year Student	NA (NA)	NA	$1,000 (NA)	NA	$2,500 (NA)	NA
Advanced Student	$3,000 (NA)	NA	$1,000 (NA)	NA	$2,500 (NA)	NA

For additional information on financial assistance, visit http://www.alliant.edu/cspp/admissions/scholarships_financial_aid/index.php.

Employment of Department Graduates

No information provided.

Additional Information

Housing and Day Care: No on-campus housing is available. No on-campus day care facilities are available.

Information for Students With Physical Disabilities: See the following website: http://www.alliant.edu/consumer/disability-services/index.php.

Application Information: Alliant International University, Admissions Processing Center, 10455 Pomerado Road, San Diego, CA 92131-1799. *Fee:* $65. *Online application:* https://www.applyweb.com/alliant/.

Alliant International University: Irvine

Programs in Educational and School Psychology and School Counseling
Hufstedler School of Education
Jamboree Building Center
2855 Michelle Drive, Suite 300
Irvine, CA 92606
Telephone: (866) 825-5426
Program Director: Donald Wofford, PsyD

E-mail: mgiovanini@alliant.edu
Web: http://www.alliant.edu/hsoe/

Orientation, Objectives, and Emphasis of Department

Programs train students with the skills necessary to work with students, teachers, parents, and other professionals in today's school environments. Curriculum includes professional skills, professional roles courses, applied research, and professional concepts. The master's degree program prepares students to gain the PPS (Pupil Personnel Services) credential that allows them to practice in California's schools. Students take evening classes and engage in fieldwork. At the doctoral level, students complete special focus area courses, examples of which include adolescent stress and coping, school culture and administration, pediatric psychology, infant and preschool mental health, child neuropsychology, and provision of services for children in alternative placement. Doctoral students also complete a PsyD project.

Programs and Degrees Offered

Program	Degree	Application Deadline	Applications Received	Accepted	New Admits Enrolled (PT)	Total Enrolled (PT)	Degrees Awarded in 2014–2015	Median Years to Complete Degree	Dismissed/Withdrew
Educational Psychology	PsyD	April 1 (Fall), Rolling	6	4	3 (1)	3 (7)	4	2.74	0
School Psychology	MA/MS	April 1 (Fall), Rolling	18	14	10 (2)	18 (5)	8	1.74	0
School Counseling	MA/MS	April 1 (Fall), Rolling	1	0	0 (0)	0 (0)	0		0

Internships/Practica

Students in the master's program have practica tied to their coursework beginning in the first semester of their programs. Internships are required of students seeking a Pupil Personnel Services (PPS) credential post-masters or as part of the doctoral program in educational psychology. The 1200 required internship hours for School Psychology and the 600 required internship hours for School Counseling are both completed at a public school district. Doctoral students interested in seeking clinical licensure must complete a separate psychology internship.

Admissions

Entries appear in the following order: required test or GPA, minimum score (if required)/median score of students entering in 2015–2016.

Program	Degree	GRE-V	GRE-Q	GRE-Writing	GRE-Subject	Under-graduate GPA	Last 2 Years GPA	Psychol-ogy GPA	Master's GPA
Educational Psychology	PsyD	Not specified	Not specified	Not specified	Not specified	3/3.07	Not specified	3/NA	Not specified
School Psychology	MA/MS	Not specified	Not specified	Not specified	Not specified	3/3.28	Not specified	3/NA	Not specified
School Counseling	MA/MS	Not specified	Not specified	Not specified	Not specified	Not specified	Not specified	Not specified	Not specified

Admissions Requirements:

Degree	GRE	GRE-Subject	Letters of Recommendation	Research Statement	Writing Sample	CV	Interview
Master's/Specialist	None	None	2	Required	None	Required	Required
Doctoral	None	None	2	Required	None	Required	Required

Please note if these criteria vary for different programs: Criteria differ by program and level.

Admissions Criteria:

Research experience—medium
Work experience—medium
Clinically related public service—medium
GPA—high

Letters of recommendation—high
Interview—high
Statement of goals and objectives—high
Undergraduate psychology preparation—medium

For additional information on admission requirements, visit http://www.alliant.edu/hsoe/hsoe-admissions/index.php.

Department Demographics

	Male (PT)	Female (PT)	Total	African-American/Black (PT)	Hispanic/Latino (PT)	Asian/Pacific Islander (PT)	American Indian/Alaska Native (PT)	Caucasian/White (PT)	Unknown (PT)	Multiethnic (PT)	ADA (PT)	Int'l (PT)
Students	4 (2)	17 (10)	33	1 (1)	8 (3)	2 (1)	0 (0)	8 (5)	1 (2)	1 (0)	0 (0)	0 (0)

Financial Information/Assistance

Tuition: For information on tuition costs, visit http://www.alliant.edu/admissions/tuition.php. Tuition is subject to change. Tuition costs vary by program.

Doctoral:
State residents: $1,055 per credit hour.
Nonstate residents: $1,055 per credit hour.

Master's:
State residents: $648 per credit hour.
Nonstate residents: $648 per credit hour.

Financial Assistance:

	Teaching Assistantship (% Receiving)	Teaching Assistantship Tuition Remission	Research Assistantship (% Receiving)	Research Assistantship Tuition Remission	Fellowship (% Receiving)	Fellowship Tuition Remission
First-Year Student	NA (NA)	NA	NA (NA)	NA	$1,000 (NA)	NA
Advanced Student	NA (NA)	NA	NA (NA)	NA	$2,500 (NA)	NA

For additional information on financial assistance, visit http://www.alliant.edu/hsoe/hsoe-admissions/hsoe-scholarships.php.

Employment of Department Graduates

No information provided.

Additional Information

Housing and Day Care: No on-campus housing is available. No on-campus day care facilities are available.

Information for Students With Physical Disabilities: See the following website: http://www.alliant.edu/consumer/disability-services/index.php.

Application Information: Alliant International University, Admissions Processing Center, 10455 Pomerado Road, San Diego, CA 92131-1799. *Fee:* $65. *Online application:* https://www.applyweb.com/alliant/.

Alliant International University: Los Angeles
Programs in Clinical Psychology and Couple and Family Therapy
California School of Professional Psychology
1000 South Fremont Avenue, Unit 5
Alhambra, CA 91803-1360
Telephone: (866) 825-5426
Executive Dean, California School of Professional Psychology: Teresa Chapa, PhD

E-mail: mgiovanini@alliant.edu
Web: http://www.alliant.edu/cspp/

Orientation, Objectives, and Emphasis of Department
The clinical psychology PsyD and PhD programs at the California School of Professional Psychology prepare students to function as multifaceted clinical psychologists through a curriculum based on an integration of psychological theory, research, and practice. Students develop competencies in eight areas: clinical health psychology; interpersonal/relationship; assessment; multifaceted multimodal intervention; research and evaluation; consultation/ teaching; management/supervision/training; and quality assurance. The PsyD program is a practitioner program where candidates gain relatively greater mastery in assessment, intervention, and management/supervision. The PhD program is a based on a scholar-practitioner model where practice and scholarship receive equal emphasis and includes the following guiding principles: the generation and application of knowledge must occur with an awareness of the sociocultural and sociopolitical contexts of mental health and mental illness; scholarship and practice must not only build upon existing literature but also maintain relevance to the diverse elements in our society and assume the challenges of attending to the complex social issues associated with psychological functioning; and methods of research and intervention must be appropriate to the culture in which they are conducted. Practicum and internship experiences are integrated throughout the programs.

Programs and Degrees Offered

Program	Degree	Application Deadline	Applications Received	Accepted	New Admits Enrolled (PT)	Total Enrolled (PT)	Degrees Awarded in 2014–2015	Median Years to Complete Degree	Dismissed/ Withdrew
Clinical Psychology	PsyD	December 15 (Fall), Rolling	240	75	40 (0)	152 (59)	43	4.44	2
Clinical Psychology	PhD	December 15 (Fall), Rolling	79	28	14 (0)	93 (21)	26	5.3	1
Marital and Family Therapy	MA/MS	January 15 (Fall), October 1 (Spring), Rolling	56	30	12 (4)	28 (8)	15	1.97	0
Marital and Family Therapy	PsyD	January 15 (Fall), October 1 (Spring), Rolling	36	23	7 (3)	17 (16)	0		0

APA Accreditation
Clinical PsyD: Student Outcome Data website: http://www.alliant.edu/cspp/programs-degrees/clinical-psychology/clinical_psyd_los-angeles/index.php.
Clinical PhD: Student Outcome Data website: http://www.alliant.edu/cspp/programs-degrees/clinical-psychology/clinical_phd_los_angeles/index.php.

Doctoral Degree (PsyD Clinical Psychology): For those doctoral students for whom a professional internship was required in this program prior to graduation:
Total students who applied for an internship: 53

Total students who obtained an internship: 41
Total students who obtained a paid internship: 30
Total students who obtained an unpaid internship: 11
Total students who were placed in APA/CPA-accredited internships: 15
Total students placed in internships not APA/CPA-accredited, but listed with the Association of Psychology Postdoctoral and Internship Centers (APPIC): 6
Total students placed in internships conforming to guidelines of the Council of Directors of School Psychology Programs (CDSPP): 0
Total students placed in internships that were not APA/CPA-accredited, APPIC or CDSSP listed: 20

Doctoral Degree (PhD Clinical Psychology): For those doctoral students for whom a professional internship was required in this program prior to graduation:
Total students who applied for an internship: 25
Total students who obtained an internship: 20
Total students who obtained a paid internship: 14
Total students who obtained an unpaid internship: 6
Total students who were placed in APA/CPA-accredited internships: 8
Total students placed in internships not APA/CPA-accredited, but listed with the Association of Psychology Postdoctoral and Internship Centers (APPIC): 2
Total students placed in internships conforming to guidelines of the Council of Directors of School Psychology Programs (CDSPP): 0
Total students placed in internships that were not APA/CPA-accredited, APPIC or CDSSP listed: 10

Internships/Practica

All students engage in practica and internships. Clinical psychology students complete 2000 predoctoral internship hours as part of their programs. The majority of the professional training sites are within 40 miles of the campus. These agencies serve a diverse range of individuals across ethnicity, culture, religion, and sexual orientation. These sites provide excellent training, offering a variety of theoretical orientations related to children, adolescents, adults, families and the elderly. Students who wish to pursue full-time internships are encouraged to make applications throughout the country. Couple and Family Therapy students complete 500 client contact hours, 250 of which must be with couples and families. Students receive at least 100 hours of individual and group supervision, 50 hours of which are based on direct observation, videotape, or audiotape. At least 25 of those hours must be videotape or direct observation. When students are ready to begin practicum, experienced faculty and staff assist students through each step in obtaining a field placement site approved by Alliant. While students are doing practicum training, they are required to perform marriage and family therapy under a California state licensed, AAMFT-approved supervisor or the equivalent.

Admissions

Entries appear in the following order: required test or GPA, minimum score (if required)/median score of students entering in 2015–2016.

Program	Degree	GRE-V	GRE-Q	GRE-Writing	GRE-Subject	Under-graduate GPA	Last 2 Years GPA	Psychol-ogy GPA	Master's GPA
Clinical Psychology	PsyD	Not specified	Not specified	Not specified	Not specified	3/3.42	Not specified	3/NA	Not specified
Clinical Psychology	PhD	Not specified	Not specified	Not specified	Not specified	3/3.18	Not specified	3/NA	Not specified
Marital and Family Therapy	MA/MS	Not specified	Not specified	Not specified	Not specified	3/3.1	Not specified	3/NA	Not specified
Marital and Family Therapy	PsyD	Not specified	Not specified	Not specified	Not specified	Not specified	Not specified	Not specified	Not specified

Admissions Requirements:

Degree	GRE	GRE-Subject	Letters of Recom-mendation	Research Statement	Writing Sample	CV	Interview
Master's/Specialist	Optional	None	2	Required	None	Required	Required
Doctoral	Optional	Optional	2	Required	None	Required	Required

Please note if these criteria vary for different programs: Criteria differ by program and level.

Admissions Criteria:

Research experience—medium
Work experience—medium
Clinically related public service—medium
GPA—high

Letters of recommendation—high
Interview—high
Statement of goals and objectives—high
Undergraduate psychology preparation—medium

For additional information on admission requirements, visit http://www.alliant.edu/cspp/admissions/apply/index.php.

Department Demographics

	Male (PT)	Female (PT)	Total	African-American/ Black (PT)	Hispanic/ Latino (PT)	Asian/ Pacific Islander (PT)	American Indian/ Alaska Native (PT)	Caucasian/ White (PT)	Unknown (PT)	Multiethnic (PT)	ADA (PT)	Int'l (PT)
Students	64 (20)	226 (84)	394	28 (4)	60 (27)	27 (8)	0 (0)	130 (54)	23 (4)	22 (7)	0 (0)	11 (1)

Financial Information/Assistance

Tuition: For information on tuition costs, visit http://www.alliant.edu/admissions/tuition.php. Tuition is subject to change.

Doctoral:
State residents: $1,160 per credit hour.
Nonstate residents: $1,160 per credit hour.

Master's:
State residents: $1,160 per credit hour.
Nonstate residents: $1,160 per credit hour.

Financial Assistance:

	Teaching Assistantship (% Receiving)	Teaching Assistantship Tuition Remission	Research Assistantship (% Receiving)	Research Assistantship Tuition Remission	Fellowship (% Receiving)	Fellowship Tuition Remission
First-Year Student	NA (NA)	NA	$1,000 (NA)	NA	$5,000 (NA)	NA
Advanced Student	$3,000 (NA)	NA	$1,000 (NA)	NA	$5,000 (NA)	NA

For additional information on financial assistance, visit http://www.alliant.edu/cspp/admissions/scholarships_financial_aid/index.php.

Employment of Department Graduates

No information provided.

Additional Information

Housing and Day Care: No on-campus housing is available. No on-campus day care facilities are available.

Information for Students With Physical Disabilities: See the following website: http://www.alliant.edu/consumer/disability-services/index.php.

Special Facilities or Resources: The Psychological Services Center (PSC) is charged with the mission of developing professional training, research, and consultation opportunities for CSPP faculty and students, while providing services to a variety of public/private agencies. It is committed to developing effective and innovative service strategies and resources that address the needs of a wide range of clients, with a particular focus on ethnically diverse, underserved populations. As a center "without walls," the PSC is the administrative umbrella for two major community-based programs: the Children, Youth, and Family Consortium and the School Court Accountability Project. These projects are designed to provide hands-on research, consulting, and clinical experience for students and to enhance the critically needed services to school-aged youth within the court system and school-aged populations. These programs enable participating CSPP faculty, staff, students, alumni/ae, and external consultant associates to provide services few other institutions can offer. Students also receive unique training and supervision that prepares them for critically needed roles as community advocates and leaders.

Application Information: Alliant International University, Admissions Processing Center, 10455 Pomerado Road, San Diego, CA 92131-1799. *Fee:* $65. *Online application:* https://www.applyweb.com/alliant/.

Alliant International University: Los Angeles
Programs in Educational and School Psychology and School Counseling
Hufstedler School of Education
1000 South Fremont Avenue, Unit 5
Alhambra, CA 91803-1360
Telephone: (866) 825-5426
Program Director: Carlton W. Parks, Jr. PhD

E-mail: mgiovanini@alliant.edu
Web: http://www.alliant.edu/hsoe/

Orientation, Objectives, and Emphasis of Department
Programs train students with the skills necessary to work with students, teachers, parents, and other professionals in today's school environments. The curriculum includes professional skills, professional roles courses, applied research, and professional concepts. The master's degree program prepares students to gain the PPS (Pupil Personnel Services) credential that allow them to practice in California's schools. Students take evening classes and engage in fieldwork. At the doctoral level, students complete special focus area courses, examples of which include adolescent stress and coping, school culture and administration, pediatric psychology, infant and preschool mental health, child neuropsychology, and provision of services for children in alternative placement. Doctoral students also complete a PsyD project.

Programs and Degrees Offered

Program	Degree	Application Deadline	Applications Received	Accepted	New Admits Enrolled (PT)	Total Enrolled (PT)	Degrees Awarded in 2014–2015	Median Years to Complete Degree	Dismissed/ Withdrew
School Psychology	MA/MS	April 1 (Fall), Rolling	12	12	3 (2)	5 (8)	4	1.74	0
Educational Psychology	PsyD	April 1 (Fall), Rolling	5	4	0 (3)	3 (8)	5	3.64	0
School Counseling	MA/MS	April 1 (Fall), Rolling	4	4	2 (0)	2 (0)	0		0

Internships/Practica
Students in the master's program have practica tied to their coursework beginning in the first semester of their programs. Internships are required of any students seeking the Pupil Personnel Services (PPS) credential post-masters or as part of the doctoral program in educational psychology. The 1200 internship hours for the School Psychology program and the 600 internship hours for the School Counseling program are completed at a public school district. Those in the doctoral program who are interested in clinical licensure must complete a separate psychology internship.

Admissions
Entries appear in the following order: required test or GPA, minimum score (if required)/median score of students entering in 2015–2016.

Program	Degree	GRE-V	GRE-Q	GRE-Writing	GRE-Subject	Under-graduate GPA	Last 2 Years GPA	Psychol-ogy GPA	Master's GPA
School Psychology	MA/MS	Not specified	Not specified	Not specified	Not specified	3/3	Not specified	3/NA	Not specified
Educational Psychology	PsyD	Not specified	Not specified	Not specified	Not specified	3/3	Not specified	3/NA	Not specified
School Counseling	MA/MS	Not specified	Not specified	Not specified	Not specified	Not specified	Not specified	Not specified	Not specified

Admissions Requirements:

Degree	GRE	GRE-Subject	Letters of Recommendation	Research Statement	Writing Sample	CV	Interview
Master's/Specialist	None	None	2	Required	None	Required	Required
Doctoral	None	None	2	Required	None	Required	Required

Please note if these criteria vary for different programs: Criteria differ by program and level.

Admissions Criteria:

Research experience—medium
Work experience—high
Clinically related public service—medium
GPA—high

Letters of recommendation—high
Interview—high
Statement of goals and objectives—high
Undergraduate psychology preparation—medium

For additional information on admission requirements, visit http://www.alliant.edu/hsoe/hsoe-admissions/index.php.

Department Demographics

	Male (PT)	Female (PT)	Total	African-American/ Black (PT)	Hispanic/ Latino (PT)	Asian/ Pacific Islander (PT)	American Indian/ Alaska Native (PT)	Caucasian/ White (PT)	Unknown	Multiethnic (PT)	ADA (PT)	Int'l (PT)
Students	3 (5)	7 (11)	26	4 (2)	6 (6)	0 (2)	0 (0)	0 (5)	0 (0)	0 (1)	0 (0)	0 (0)

Financial Information/Assistance

Tuition: For information on tuition costs, visit http://www.alliant.edu/admissions/tuition.php. Tuition is subject to change. Tuition costs vary by program.

Doctoral:
State residents: $1,055 per credit hour.
Nonstate residents: $1,055 per credit hour.

Master's:
State residents: $648 per credit hour.
Nonstate residents: $648 per credit hour.

Financial Assistance:

	Teaching Assistantship (% Receiving)	Teaching Assistantship Tuition Remission	Research Assistantship (% Receiving)	Research Assistantship Tuition Remission	Fellowship (% Receiving)	Fellowship Tuition Remission
First-Year Student	NA (NA)	NA	NA (NA)	NA	$1,000 (NA)	NA
Advanced Student	NA (NA)	NA	NA (NA)	NA	$2,500 (NA)	NA

For additional information on financial assistance, visit http://www.alliant.edu/hsoe/hsoe-admissions/hsoe-scholarships.php.

Employment of Department Graduates

No information provided.

Additional Information

Housing and Day Care: No on-campus housing is available. No on-campus day care facilities are available.

Information for Students With Physical Disabilities: See the following website: http://www.alliant.edu/consumer/disability-services/index.php.

Application Information: Alliant International University, Admissions Processing Center, 10455 Pomerado Road, San Diego, CA 93121-1799. *Fee:* $65. *Online application:* https://www.applyweb.com/alliant/.

Alliant International University: Los Angeles
Programs in Organizational Psychology
California School of Professional Psychology
1000 South Fremont Avenue, Unit 5
Alhambra, CA 91803-1360
Telephone: (866) 825-5426
Executive Dean, California School of Professional Psychology: Teresa Chapa, PhD
Web: http://www.alliant.edu/cspp/programs-degrees/organizational-psychology/

E-mail: mgiovanini@alliant.edu

Orientation, Objectives, and Emphasis of Department
The Master's program in Organizational Psychology provides in-depth education and training in the applied theory, research, and practice of organizational psychology and organizational development consulting. Graduates from this program have obtained careers as internally based organizational development consultants, training and development consultants, and human resources professionals. The Doctoral program in Organizational Psychology combines coursework in psychology and organizational theory with specialized courses in organizational change and development, industrial psychology, consulting to organizations, and human resources management. Doctoral students select either the Strategic Human Resource Management or the Executive Coaching concentration. Both of these programs are geared towards the working adult.

Programs and Degrees Offered

Program	Degree	Application Deadline	Applications Received	Accepted	New Admits Enrolled (PT)	Total Enrolled (PT)	Degrees Awarded in 2014–2015	Median Years to Complete Degree	Dismissed/ Withdrew
Organizational Psychology	PhD	March 1 (Fall), October 1 (Spring), Rolling	15	11	6 (1)	20 (19)	7	4.7	0
Organizational Psychology	MA/MS	March 1 (Fall), October 1 (Spring), Rolling	16	7	3 (1)	11 (2)	6	1.74	0

Internships/Practica
Doctoral students may begin their practical training though the Center for Innovation and Change, working with faculty on pro bono consulting projects. A doctoral-level field placement/internship is completed typically in the fourth year. Students spend 8-40 hours per week in a corporate, business, governmental, or non-profit setting. The majority of these are local to the student's campus; a few are outside the area, and are usually identified as part of a student's own career development interests. Students in the organizational psychology master's program have a one-semester practicum in organizational studies.

Admissions
Entries appear in the following order: required test or GPA, minimum score (if required)/median score of students entering in 2015–2016.

Program	Degree	GRE-V	GRE-Q	GRE-Writing	GRE-Subject	Under-graduate GPA	Last 2 Years GPA	Psychol-ogy GPA	Master's GPA
Organizational Psychology	PhD	Not specified	Not specified	Not specified	Not specified	3/3.34	Not specified	3/NA	Not specified
Organizational Psychology	MA/MS	Not specified	Not specified	Not specified	Not specified	3/3.31	Not specified	3/NA	Not specified

Admissions Requirements:

Degree	GRE	GRE-Subject	Letters of Recommendation	Research Statement	Writing Sample	CV	Interview
Master's/Specialist	Optional	Optional	2	Required	None	Required	Required
Doctoral	Optional	Optional	2	Required	None	Required	Required

Please note if these criteria vary for different programs: Criteria differ by program and level.

Admissions Criteria:

Research experience—high
Work experience—high
Clinically related public service—low
GPA—high

Letters of recommendation—high
Interview—high
Statement of goals and objectives—high
Undergraduate psychology preparation—medium

For additional information on admission requirements, visit http://www.alliant.edu/cspp/admissions/apply/op-app-req.php.

Department Demographics

	Male (PT)	Female (PT)	Total	African-American/ Black (PT)	Hispanic/ Latino (PT)	Asian/ Pacific Islander (PT)	American Indian/ Alaska Native (PT)	Caucasian/ White (PT)	Unknown	Multiethnic (PT)	ADA (PT)	Int'l (PT)
Students	6 (7)	25 (14)	52	0 (2)	6 (4)	3 (3)	0 (0)	15 (9)	3 (1)	4 (2)	0 (0)	1 (0)

Financial Information/Assistance

Tuition: For information on tuition costs, visit http://www.alliant.edu/admissions/tuition.php. Tuition is subject to change.

Doctoral:
State residents: $1,160 per credit hour.
Nonstate residents: $1,160 per credit hour.

Master's:
State residents: $1,160 per credit hour.
Nonstate residents: $1,160 per credit hour.

Financial Assistance:

	Teaching Assistantship (% Receiving)	Teaching Assistantship Tuition Remission	Research Assistantship (% Receiving)	Research Assistantship Tuition Remission	Fellowship (% Receiving)	Fellowship Tuition Remission
First-Year Student	NA (NA)	NA	$1,000 (NA)	NA	$5,000 (NA)	NA
Advanced Student	$3,000 (NA)	NA	$1,000 (NA)	NA	$5,000 (NA)	NA

For additional information on financial assistance, visit http://www.alliant.edu/cspp/admissions/scholarships_financial_aid/index.php.

Employment of Department Graduates

No information provided.

Additional Information

Housing and Day Care: No on-campus housing is available. No on-campus day care facilities are available.

Information for Students With Physical Disabilities: See the following website: http://www.alliant.edu/consumer/disability-services/index.php.

Special Facilities or Resources: At the Center for Innovation and Change in Los Angeles, graduate students apply what they are learning in the classroom by providing consulting services to non-profit organizations. Through the Center, first and second year students form consulting teams that provide pro bono service to clients in the Los Angeles area. Each consulting team works with a faculty supervisor. Thus students get practical training beginning early on in their programs.

Application Information: Alliant International University, Admissions Processing Center, 10455 Pomerado Road, San Diego, CA 92131-1799. *Fee:* $65. *Online application:* https://www.applyweb.com/alliant/.

Alliant International University: Sacramento

Programs in Clinical Psychology and Couple and Family Therapy
California School of Professional Psychology
2030 West El Camino Avenue, Suite 200
Sacramento, CA 95833
Telephone: (866) 825-5426
Executive Dean, California School of Professional Psychology: Teresa Chapa, PhD

E-mail: darrell.suha@alliant.edu
Web: http://www.alliant.edu/cspp/index.php

Orientation, Objectives, and Emphasis of Department

The clinical psychology PsyD program emphasizes training in clinical skills and clinical application of research knowledge and is designed for students who are interested in careers as practitioners, but it also includes a research component. An empirical PsyD dissertation is required and may focus on program development and/or evaluation, test development, survey research or therapeutic outcomes. The program offers a concentration in correctional psychology. The mission of the Couple and Family Therapy program is to prepare graduate students who are skilled in the theory, research, and clinical practice of the field of Marriage and Family Therapy and can integrate individual and systemic therapeutic models in an international, multicultural environment. The Couple and Family Therapy (CFT) programs provide students with the essential training needed to pursue a career as a professional Marriage and Family Therapist (MFT). The Master of Arts in MFT allows students to be licensed as an MFT and the Doctor of Psychology (PsyD) in MFT prepares students with academic and research experience. Students who complete the MFT master's at Alliant can apply all of their master's degree coursework and practicum hours toward the doctoral program. The programs are accredited by COAMFTE.

Programs and Degrees Offered

Program	Degree	Application Deadline	Applications Received	Accepted	New Admits Enrolled (PT)	Total Enrolled (PT)	Degrees Awarded in 2014–2015	Median Years to Complete Degree	Dismissed/ Withdrew
Marital and Family Therapy	MA/MS	January 15 (Fall), October 1 (Spring), Rolling	31	20	11 (0)	26 (8)	14	2.01	0
Marital and Family Therapy	PsyD	January 15 (Fall), October 1 (Spring), Rolling	9	7	5 (0)	9 (22)	0		0
Clinical Psychology	PsyD	December 15 (Fall), Rolling	71	22	13 (0)	46 (5)	13	5.78	0

APA Accreditation

Clinical PsyD: Student Outcome Data website: http://www.alliant.edu/cspp/programs-degrees/clinical-psychology/clinical_psyd_sacramento/index.php.

Doctoral Degree (PsyD Clinical Psychology): For those doctoral students for whom a professional internship was required in this program prior to graduation:
Total students who applied for an internship: 14
Total students who obtained an internship: 13
Total students who obtained a paid internship: 12

Total students who obtained an unpaid internship: 1
Total students who were placed in APA/CPA-accredited internships: 7
Total students placed in internships not APA/CPA-accredited, but listed with the Association of Psychology Postdoctoral and Internship Centers (APPIC): 1
Total students placed in internships conforming to guidelines of the Council of Directors of School Psychology Programs (CDSPP): 0
Total students placed in internships that were not APA/CPA-accredited, APPIC or CDSSP listed: 5

Internships/Practica

The clinical psychology program emphasizes the integration of academic coursework and research with clinical practice. In order to integrate appropriate skills with material learned in the classroom, students participate in a professional training placement experience beginning in the first year. The settings where students complete these requirements include community mental health centers, clinics, inpatient mental health facilities, medical settings, specialized service centers, rehabilitation programs, residential/day care programs, forensic/correctional facilities, and educational programs. During their final year, clinical students complete a full-year internship at an appropriate APA, APPIC, or CAPIC-approved site. As part of the practicum for the CFT program, students complete 500 client contact hours, 250 of which must be with couples and families. Students receive at least 100 hours of individual and group supervision, 50 hours of which are based on direct observation, videotape, or audiotape, and at least 25 of which must be videotape or direct observation. When students are ready to begin the practicum, experienced faculty and staff assist students through each step in obtaining a field placement site approved by Alliant. While student are doing practicum training they are required to perform marriage and family therapy under a California state-licensed, AAMFT-approved supervisor or the equivalent.

Admissions

Entries appear in the following order: required test or GPA, minimum score (if required)/median score of students entering in 2015–2016.

Program	Degree	GRE-V	GRE-Q	GRE-Writing	GRE-Subject	Under-graduate GPA	Last 2 Years GPA	Psychol-ogy GPA	Master's GPA
Marital and Family Therapy	MA/MS	Not specified	Not specified	Not specified	Not specified	3/3	Not specified	3/NA	Not specified
Marital and Family Therapy	PsyD	Not specified	Not specified	Not specified	Not specified	3/3	Not specified	3/NA	Not specified
Clinical Psychology	PsyD	Not specified	Not specified	Not specified	Not specified	3/3.45	Not specified	3/NA	Not specified

Admissions Requirements:

Degree	GRE	GRE-Subject	Letters of Recom-mendation	Research Statement	Writing Sample	CV	Interview
Master's/Specialist	Optional	None	2	Required	None	Required	Required
Doctoral	Optional	Optional	2	Required	None	Required	Required

Please note if these criteria vary for different programs: Criteria differ by program and level.

Admissions Criteria:

Research experience—medium
Work experience—medium
Clinically related public service—medium
GPA—high

Letters of recommendation—medium
Interview—high
Statement of goals and objectives—high
Undergraduate psychology preparation—medium

For additional information on admission requirements, visit http://www.alliant.edu/cspp/admissions/apply/index.php.

Department Demographics

	Male (PT)	Female (PT)	Total	African-American/ Black (PT)	Hispanic/ Latino (PT)	Asian/ Pacific Islander (PT)	American Indian/ Alaska Native (PT)	Caucasian/ White (PT)	Unknown	Multiethnic (PT)	ADA (PT)	Int'l (PT)
Students	14 (10)	67 (25)	116	6 (3)	16 (7)	11 (1)	0 (0)	32 (19)	6 (1)	10 (4)	0 (1)	4 (0)

Financial Information/Assistance

Tuition: For information on tuition costs, visit http://www.alliant.edu/admissions/tuition.php. Tuition is subject to change.

Doctoral:
State residents: $1,160 per credit hour.
Nonstate residents: $1,160 per credit hour.

Master's:
State residents: $1,160 per credit hour.
Nonstate residents: $1,160 per credit hour.

Financial Assistance:

	Teaching Assistantship (% Receiving)	Teaching Assistantship Tuition Remission	Research Assistantship (% Receiving)	Research Assistantship Tuition Remission	Fellowship (% Receiving)	Fellowship Tuition Remission
First-Year Student	NA (NA)	NA	NA (NA)	NA	$5,000 (NA)	NA
Advanced Student	$3,000 (NA)	NA	$1,000 (NA)	NA	$5,000 (NA)	NA

For additional information on financial assistance, visit http://www.alliant.edu/cspp/admissions/scholarships_financial aid/index.php.

Employment of Department Graduates

No information provided.

Additional Information

Housing and Day Care: No on-campus housing is available. No on-campus day care facilities are available.

Information for Students With Physical Disabilities: See the following website: http://www.alliant.edu/consumer/disability-services/index.php.

Application Information: Alliant International University Admissions Processing Center, 10455 Pomerado Road, San Diego, CA 92131-1799. *Fee:* $65. *Online application:* https://www.applyweb.com/alliant/.

Alliant International University: San Diego
Programs in Clinical Psychology and Couple and Family Therapy
California School of Professional Psychology
10455 Pomerado Road
San Diego, CA 92131-1799
Telephone: (866) 825-5426
Executive Dean, California School of Professional Psychology: Teresa Chapa, PhD

E-mail: acarter@alliant.edu
Web: http://www.alliant.edu/cspp/

Orientation, Objectives, and Emphasis of Department
The California School of Professional Psychology (CSPP) at Alliant International University offers comprehensive PhD and PsyD programs of instruction in professional psychology with an emphasis on doctoral training in clinical psychology in which academic requirements are integrated with supervised field experience. Students are evaluated by instructors and field supervisors on the

basis of their performance and participation throughout the year. Theory, personal growth, professional skill, humanities, investigatory skills courses, and field experience are designed to stimulate the graduate toward a scholarly as well as a professional contribution to society. Elective areas of emphasis in health psychology (PhD only), family and child psychology, clinical forensic psychology, psychodynamic, multicultural and international, and integrative psychology (PsyD only) are available within the clinical programs. Students in CSPP's Couple and Family Therapy MA and PsyD programs are trained to treat individuals, couples, and families with relational mental health issues from a systemic perspective. Skills are developed in mental health assessment, diagnosis, and treatment of individuals and relationship systems. The PsyD is based on the scholar-practitioner model; both degrees are offered in a format for working professionals. The CFT programs are accredited by COAMFTE.

Programs and Degrees Offered

Program	Degree	Application Deadline	Applications Received	Accepted	New Admits Enrolled (PT)	Total Enrolled (PT)	Degrees Awarded in 2014–2015	Median Years to Complete Degree	Dismissed/ Withdrew
Clinical Psychology	PsyD	December 15 (Fall), Rolling	190	61	32 (3)	126 (90)	39	5.68	1
Clinical Psychology	PhD	December 15 (Fall), Rolling	94	38	17 (1)	92 (66)	23	6.65	2
Clinical Psychology	Respecial- ization Diploma	December 15 (Fall), Rolling	2	2	0 (2)	2 (3)	1	5.31	0
Marital and Family Therapy	MA/MS	January 15 (Fall), October 1 (Spring), Rolling	93	61	25 (7)	59 (19)	35	1.97	0
Marital and Family Therapy	PsyD	January 15 (Fall), October 1 (Spring), Rolling	18	5	1 (2)	14 (29)	14	6.18	0

APA Accreditation

Clinical PsyD: Student Outcome Data website: http://www.alliant.edu/cspp/programs-degrees/clinical-psychology/psyd-sandiego. php.

Clinical PhD: Student Outcome Data website: http://www.alliant.edu/cspp/programs-degrees/clinical-psychology/clinical_phd_san-diego/index.php.

Doctoral Degree (PsyD Clinical Psychology): For those doctoral students for whom a professional internship was required in this program prior to graduation:

Total students who applied for an internship: 53

Total students who obtained an internship: 53

Total students who obtained a paid internship: 40

Total students who obtained an unpaid internship: 13

Total students who were placed in APA/CPA-accredited internships: 9

Total students placed in internships not APA/CPA-accredited, but listed with the Association of Psychology Postdoctoral and Internship Centers (APPIC): 2

Total students placed in internships conforming to guidelines of the Council of Directors of School Psychology Programs (CDSPP): 0

Total students placed in internships that were not APA/CPA-accredited, APPIC or CDSSP listed: 42

Doctoral Degree (PhD Clinical Psychology): For those doctoral students for whom a professional internship was required in this program prior to graduation:

Total students who applied for an internship: 26

Total students who obtained an internship: 21

Total students who obtained a paid internship: 19

Total students who obtained an unpaid internship: 2

Total students who were placed in APA/CPA-accredited internships: 12

Total students placed in internships not APA/CPA-accredited, but listed with the Association of Psychology Postdoctoral and Internship Centers (APPIC): 1

Total students placed in internships conforming to guidelines of the Council of Directors of School Psychology Programs (CDSPP): 0

Total students placed in internships that were not APA/CPA-accredited, APPIC or CDSSP listed: 8

Internships/Practica

Clinical psychology doctoral students receive practicum and internship experience at more than 80 agencies which meet the requirements for licensure set by the California Board of Psychology. Assignments to these agencies result from an application process conducted by year level, with third, fourth, and fifth year students receiving priority for licensable placements. The option of doing an APA-accredited full-time internship in the fourth or fifth years (depending on the program and year level requirements) is available and encouraged. Couple and family therapy students complete a required practicum including 500 client contact hours, 250 of which must be with couples and families. Students receive at least 100 hours of individual and group supervision, 50 hours of which are based on direct observation, videotape, or audiotape. At least 25 of those hours must be videotape or direct observation. While students are doing practicum training, they are required to perform marriage and family therapy under a California state-licensed, AAMFT-approved supervisor or the equivalent. CFT doctoral students complete a predoctoral internship.

Admissions

Entries appear in the following order: required test or GPA, minimum score (if required)/median score of students entering in 2015–2016.

Program	Degree	GRE-V	GRE-Q	GRE-Writing	GRE-Subject	Under-graduate GPA	Last 2 Years GPA	Psychol-ogy GPA	Master's GPA
Clinical Psychology	PsyD	Not specified	Not specified	Not specified	Not specified	3/3.29	Not specified	3/NA	3/3.78
Clinical Psychology	PhD	Not specified	Not specified	Not specified	Not specified	3/3.26	Not specified	3/NA	Not specified
Clinical Psychology	Respecial-ization Diploma	Not specified	Not specified	Not specified	Not specified	3/3.06	Not specified	3/NA	Not specified
Marital and Family Therapy	MA/MS	Not specified	Not specified	Not specified	Not specified	3/3.21	Not specified	3/NA	Not specified
Marital and Family Therapy	PsyD	Not specified	Not specified	Not specified	Not specified	3/3	Not specified	3/NA	Not specified

Admissions Requirements:

Degree	GRE	GRE-Subject	Letters of Recom-mendation	Research Statement	Writing Sample	CV	Interview
Master's/Specialist	Optional	None	2	Required	None	Required	Required
Doctoral	Optional	Optional	2	Required	None	Required	Required

Please note if these criteria vary for different programs: Criteria differ by program and level.

Admissions Criteria:

Research experience—medium
Work experience—medium
Clinically related public service—medium
GPA—high

Letters of recommendation—medium
Interview—high
Statement of goals and objectives—high
Undergraduate psychology preparation—medium

For additional information on admission requirements, visit http://www.alliant.edu/cssp/admissions/apply/index.php.

Department Demographics

	Male (PT)	Female (PT)	Total	African-American/ Black (PT)	Hispanic/ Latino (PT)	Asian/ Pacific Islander (PT)	American Indian/ Alaska Native (PT)	Caucasian/ White (PT)	Unknown	Multiethnic (PT)	ADA (PT)	Int'l (PT)
Students	52 (44)	241 (163)	500	15 (8)	51 (35)	20 (20)	1 (0)	168 (117)	25 (16)	13 (11)	3 (3)	9 (8)

Financial Information/Assistance

Tuition: For information on tuition costs, visit http://www.alliant.edu/admissions/tuition.php. Tuition is subject to change.

Doctoral:
State residents: $1,160 per credit hour.
Nonstate residents: $1,160 per credit hour.

Master's:
State residents: $1,160 per credit hour.
Nonstate residents: $1,160 per credit hour.

Financial Assistance:

	Teaching Assistantship (% Receiving)	Teaching Assistantship Tuition Remission	Research Assistantship (% Receiving)	Research Assistantship Tuition Remission	Fellowship (% Receiving)	Fellowship Tuition Remission
First-Year Student	NA (NA)	NA	$1,000 (NA)	NA	$5,000 (NA)	NA
Advanced Student	$3,000 (NA)	NA	$1,000 (NA)	NA	$5,000 (NA)	NA

For additional information on financial assistance, visit http://www.alliant.edu/cspp/admissions/scholarships_financial_aid/index.php.

Employment of Department Graduates

No information provided.

Additional Information

Housing and Day Care: On-campus housing is available. See the following website for more information: http://www.alliant.edu/locations/san-diego-campus/housing-dining.php. No on-campus day care facilities are available.

Information for Students With Physical Disabilities: See the following website: http://www.alliant.edu/consumer/disability-services/index.php.

Special Facilities or Resources: The Center for Applied Behavioral Services (CABS) is a multi-service and training center. The Center incorporates the expertise of CSPP faculty in the delivery of direct services and in modeling specific techniques of treatment and service for practicum students and interns. This is currently accomplished through an array of clinical and community services which are directed by faculty members.

Application Information: Alliant International University, Admissions Processing Center, 10455 Pomerado Road, San Diego, CA 92131-1799. *Fee:* $65. *Online application:* https://www.applyweb.com/alliant/.

Alliant International University: San Diego
Programs in Educational and School Psychology and School Counseling
Hufstedler School of Education
10455 Pomerado Road
San Diego, CA 92131-1799
Telephone: (866) 825-5426
Program Director: Steven Fisher, PsyD

E-mail: acarter@alliant.edu
Web: http://www.alliant.edu/hsoe/

Orientation, Objectives, and Emphasis of Department

Programs train students with the skills necessary to work with students, teachers, parents, and other professionals in today's school environments. Curriculum includes professional skills, professional roles courses, applied research, and professional concepts. The master's degree program prepares students to gain the PPS (Pupil Personnel Services) credential that allows them to practice in California's schools. Students take afternoon, evening, and weekend classes and engage in fieldwork. At the doctoral level, students complete special focus area courses, examples of which include adolescent stress and coping, school culture and administration, pediatric psychology, infant and preschool mental health, child neuropsychology, and provision of services for children in alternative placement. Doctoral students also complete a PsyD project.

Programs and Degrees Offered

Program	Degree	Application Deadline	Applica-tions Received	Accepted	New Admits Enrolled (PT)	Total Enrolled (PT)	Degrees Awarded in 2014–2015	Median Years to Complete Degree	Dismissed/ Withdrew
Educational Psychology	PsyD	April 1 (Fall), Rolling	3	1	0 (0)	1 (3)	0		0
School Psychology	MA/MS	April 1 (Fall), Rolling	29	22	10 (2)	17 (16)	12	1.74	0
School Counseling	MA/MS	April 1 (Fall), Rolling	9	8	5 (1)	7 (1)	0		1

Internships/Practica

Students in the master's program have practica tied to their coursework beginning in the first semester of their programs. Internships are required of students seeking a Pupil Personnel Services (PPS) credential post-masters or as part of the doctoral program in educational psychology. The 1200 required internship hours for the School Psychology program and the 600 required internship hours for the School Counseling program are completed at a public school district. Doctoral students interested in seeking clinical licensure must complete a separate psychology internship.

Admissions

Entries appear in the following order: required test or GPA, minimum score (if required)/median score of students entering in 2015–2016.

Program	Degree	GRE-V	GRE-Q	GRE-Writing	GRE-Subject	Under-graduate GPA	Last 2 Years GPA	Psychol-ogy GPA	Master's GPA
Educational Psychology	PsyD	Not specified	Not specified	Not specified	Not specified	3/NA	Not specified	3/NA	Not specified
School Psychology	MA/MS	Not specified	Not specified	Not specified	Not specified	3/3.27	Not specified	3/NA	Not specified
School Counseling	MA/MS	Not specified	Not specified	Not specified	Not specified	Not specified	Not specified	Not specified	Not specified

Admissions Requirements:

Degree	GRE	GRE-Subject	Letters of Recommendation	Research Statement	Writing Sample	CV	Interview
Master's/Specialist	None	None	2	Required	None	Required	Required
Doctoral	None	None	2	Required	None	Required	Required

Please note if these criteria vary for different programs: Criteria differ by program and level.

Admissions Criteria:

Research experience—medium
Work experience—medium
Clinically related public service—medium
GPA—high

Letters of recommendation—high
Interview—high
Statement of goals and objectives—high
Undergraduate psychology preparation—medium

For additional information on admission requirements, visit http://www.alliant.edu/hsoe/hsoe-admissions/index.php.

Department Demographics

	Male (PT)	Female (PT)	Total	African-American/ Black (PT)	Hispanic/ Latino (PT)	Asian/ Pacific Islander (PT)	American Indian/ Alaska Native (PT)	Caucasian/ White (PT)	Unknown	Multiethnic (PT)	ADA (PT)	Int'l (PT)
Students	4 (2)	21 (18)	45	0 (0)	9 (7)	0 (3)	0 (0)	11 (7)	2 (1)	3 (2)	0 (0)	1 (1)

Financial Information/Assistance

Tuition: For information on tuition costs, visit http://www.alliant.edu/admissions/tuition.php. Tuition is subject to change. Tuition costs vary by program.

Doctoral:
State residents: $1,055 per credit hour.
Nonstate residents: $1,055 per credit hour.

Master's:
State residents: $648 per credit hour.
Nonstate residents: $648 per credit hour.

Financial Assistance:

	Teaching Assistantship (% Receiving)	Teaching Assistantship Tuition Remission	Research Assistantship (% Receiving)	Research Assistantship Tuition Remission	Fellowship (% Receiving)	Fellowship Tuition Remission
First-Year Student	NA (NA)	NA	NA (NA)	NA	$1,000 (NA)	NA
Advanced Student	NA (NA)	NA	NA (NA)	NA	NA (NA)	NA

For additional information on financial assistance, visit http://www.alliant.edu/hsoe/hsoe-admissions/hsoe-scholarships.php.

Employment of Department Graduates

No information provided.

Additional Information

Housing and Day Care: On-campus housing is available. See the following website for more information: http://www.alliant.edu/locations/san-diego-campus/housing-dining.php. No on-campus day care facilities are available.

Information for Students With Physical Disabilities: See the following website: http://www.alliant.edu/consumer/disability-services/index.php.

Special Facilities or Resources: The Graduate School of Education at the San Diego campus houses the World Council of Curriculum and Instruction.

Application Information: Alliant International University, Admissions Processing Center, 10455 Pomerado Road, San Diego, CA 92131-1799. *Fee:* $65. *Online application:* https://www.applyweb.com/alliant/.

Alliant International University: San Diego
Programs in Organizational Psychology
California School of Professional Psychology
10455 Pomerado Road
San Diego, CA 92121-1799
Telephone: (866) 825-5426
Executive Dean, California School of Professional Psychology: Teresa Chapa, PhD
Web: http://www.alliant.edu/cspp/programs-degrees/organizational-psychology/

E-mail: acarter@alliant.edu

Orientation, Objectives, and Emphasis of Department

The Master's in Organizational Psychology program provides in-depth education and training in the applied theory, research, and practice of organizational psychology and organizational development consulting. Graduates from this program have obtained careers as internally-based organizational development consultants, training and development consultants, and human resources professionals. The doctoral program in Organizational Psychology combines coursework in psychology and organizational theory with specialized courses in organizational change and development, industrial psychology, consulting to organizations, and human resources management. Doctoral students select either the Strategic Human Resource Management or the Executive Coaching concentration. Students may also pursue the Consulting Psychology specialization, which builds on the Executive Coaching concentration. Both of these programs are geared towards the working adult.

Programs and Degrees Offered

Program	Degree	Application Deadline	Applications Received	Accepted	New Admits Enrolled (PT)	Total Enrolled (PT)	Degrees Awarded in 2014–2015	Median Years to Complete Degree	Dismissed/ Withdrew
Organizational Psychology	PhD	March 1 (Fall), October 1 (Spring), Rolling	14	10	7 (1)	15 (24)	0		0
Organizational Psychology	MA/MS	March 1 (Fall), October 1 (Spring), Rolling	8	5	2 (1)	12 (4)	4	2.51	0

Internships/Practica

Doctoral students participate in two half-time internships in the third and fourth years of the program; this allows for the integration of professional training with courses, seminars and research. Master's students have a one-semester practicum in the last term of their program.

Admissions

Entries appear in the following order: required test or GPA, minimum score (if required)/median score of students entering in 2015–2016.

Program	Degree	GRE-V	GRE-Q	GRE-Writing	GRE-Subject	Undergraduate GPA	Last 2 Years GPA	Psychology GPA	Master's GPA
Organizational Psychology	PhD	Not specified	Not specified	Not specified	Not specified	3/3.4	Not specified	3/NA	Not specified
Organizational Psychology	MA/MS	Not specified	Not specified	Not specified	Not specified	3/3.32	Not specified	3/NA	Not specified

Admissions Requirements:

Degree	GRE	GRE-Subject	Letters of Recommendation	Research Statement	Writing Sample	CV	Interview
Master's/Specialist	Optional	Optional	2	Required	None	Required	Required
Doctoral	Optional	Optional	2	Required	None	Required	Required

Please note if these criteria vary for different programs: Criteria vary by program. Research experience is more important for doctoral applicants; work experience is more important for master's programs.

Admissions Criteria:

Research experience—high
Work experience—medium
Clinically related public service—low
GPA—high

Letters of recommendation—high
Interview—high
Statement of goals and objectives—high
Undergraduate psychology preparation—medium

For additional information on admission requirements, visit http://www.alliant.edu/cspp/admissions/apply/op-app-req.php.

Department Demographics

	Male (PT)	Female (PT)	Total	African-American/ Black (PT)	Hispanic/ Latino (PT)	Asian/ Pacific Islander (PT)	American Indian/ Alaska Native (PT)	Caucasian/ White (PT)	Unknown	Multiethnic (PT)	ADA (PT)	Int'l (PT)
Students	7 (12)	20 (16)	55	2 (2)	2 (6)	3 (3)	0 (0)	9 (11)	8 (4)	3 (2)	0 (0)	2 (2)

Financial Information/Assistance

Tuition: For information on tuition costs, visit http://www.alliant.edu/admissions/tuition.php. Tuition is subject to change.

Doctoral:
State residents: $1,160 per credit hour.
Nonstate residents: $1,160 per credit hour.

Master's:
State residents: $1,160 per credit hour.
Nonstate residents: $1,160 per credit hour.

Financial Assistance:

	Teaching Assistantship (% Receiving)	Teaching Assistantship Tuition Remission	Research Assistantship (% Receiving)	Research Assistantship Tuition Remission	Fellowship (% Receiving)	Fellowship Tuition Remission
First-Year Student	NA (NA)	NA	$1,000 (NA)	NA	$5,000 (NA)	NA
Advanced Student	$3,000 (NA)	NA	$1,000 (NA)	NA	$5,000 (NA)	NA

For additional information on financial assistance, visit http://www.alliant.edu/cspp/admissions/scholarships_financial_aid/index.php.

Employment of Department Graduates

No information provided.

Additional Information

Housing and Day Care: On-campus housing is available. See the following website for more information: http://www.alliant.edu/locations/san-diego-campus/housing-dining.php. No on-campus day care facilities are available.

Information for Students With Physical Disabilities: See the following website: http://www.alliant.edu/consumer/disability-services/index.php.

Special Facilities or Resources: The Organizational Consulting Center (OCC) provides students with opportunities to participate with faculty and OCC associates on consulting projects during their programs.

Application Information: Alliant International University, Admissions Processing Center, 10455 Pomerado Road, San Diego, CA 92121-1799. *Fee:* $65. *Online application:* https://www.applyweb.com/alliant/.

Alliant International University: San Francisco
Programs in Clinical Psychology, Clinical Counseling, Couple & Family Therapy and Clinical Psychopharmacology
California School of Professional Psychology
One Beach Street, Suite 100
San Francisco, CA 94133-1221
Telephone: (866) 825-5426
Executive Dean, California School of Professional Psychology: Teresa Chapa, PhD

E-mail: aerdman1@alliant.edu
Web: http://www.alliant.edu/cspp/

Orientation, Objectives, and Emphasis of Department
CSPP's clinical psychology programs combine supervised field experiences with the study of psychological theory, clinical techniques, and applied research. The PsyD is a practitioner-oriented program. The PhD provides a balance of clinical and research training and is intended for students who expect independent research, teaching, and scholarship to be a significant part of their professional careers in addition to clinical work. In addition to the usual offerings, special training opportunities are available in five areas: family-child-adolescent psychology, health psychology, multicultural-community psychology, psychodynamic psychology, and gender studies (including psychology of women and men, and lesbian, gay, bisexual and transgender issues). The PsyD program also offers an intensive child and family track (focusing on child assessment, child therapy, and family therapy), a forensic family/child track (focusing on child abuse, child custody, delinquency, and family court services), and a social justice track (focusing on mental health services to historically underserved and culturally diverse populations). Students in the PsyD tracks are required to complete a specific sequence of courses, a dissertation, and an internship related to their track's focus. Other students in the PhD and PsyD programs can take many of these same training experiences on an elective basis.

Programs and Degrees Offered

Program	Degree	Application Deadline	Applications Received	Accepted	New Admits Enrolled (PT)	Total Enrolled (PT)	Degrees Awarded in 2014–2015	Median Years to Complete Degree	Dismissed/ Withdrew
Clinical Psychology	PsyD	December 15 (Fall), Rolling	145	73	40 (0)	165 (66)	56	4.99	1
Clinical Psychology	PhD	December 15 (Fall), Rolling	59	29	8 (0)	80 (18)	26	5.92	1
Clinical Psychology	Respecialization Diploma	December 15 (Fall), Rolling	3	1	0 (1)	0 (2)	0		0
Clinical Counseling	MA/MS	April 1 (Fall), November 1 (Spring), Rolling	41	23	9 (0)	16 (1)	7	1.97	1
Marital and Family Therapy	MA/MS	January 15 (Fall), October 1 (Spring), Rolling	32	15	4 (2)	10 (7)	0		1
Clinical Psychopharmacology	MA/MS	Rolling	41	40	0 (31)	2 (72)	26	2.41	0

APA Accreditation

Clinical PsyD: Student Outcome Data website: http://www.alliant.edu/cspp/programs-degrees/clinical-psychology/clinical_psyd_san_francisco/index.php.

Clinical PhD: Student Outcome Data website: http://www.alliant.edu/cspp/programs-degrees/clinical-psychology/clinical_phd_san-francisco/index.php.

Doctoral Degree (PsyD Clinical Psychology): For those doctoral students for whom a professional internship was required in this program prior to graduation:

Total students who applied for an internship: 70

Total students who obtained an internship: 67

Total students who obtained a paid internship: 50

Total students who obtained an unpaid internship: 17

Total students who were placed in APA/CPA-accredited internships: 17

Total students placed in internships not APA/CPA-accredited, but listed with the Association of Psychology Postdoctoral and Internship Centers (APPIC): 16

Total students placed in internships conforming to guidelines of the Council of Directors of School Psychology Programs (CDSPP): 0

Total students placed in internships that were not APA/CPA-accredited, APPIC or CDSSP listed: 34

Doctoral Degree (PhD Clinical Psychology): For those doctoral students for whom a professional internship was required in this program prior to graduation:

Total students who applied for an internship: 26

Total students who obtained an internship: 25

Total students who obtained a paid internship: 20

Total students who obtained an unpaid internship: 5

Total students who were placed in APA/CPA-accredited internships: 12

Total students placed in internships not APA/CPA-accredited, but listed with the Association of Psychology Postdoctoral and Internship Centers (APPIC): 7

Total students placed in internships conforming to guidelines of the Council of Directors of School Psychology Programs (CDSPP): 0

Total students placed in internships that were not APA/CPA-accredited, APPIC or CDSSP listed: 6

Master's Degree (MA/MS Clinical Counseling): An internship experience, such as a final research project or "capstone" experience is required of graduates.

Internships/Practica

During the first three years of the PsyD program and during the second and third years of the PhD program, students are engaged in field practica for 8-16 hours per week. All students get experience working with adults, children/adolescents, and persons with severe mental illness as well as more moderate forms of dysfunction. The tremendous ethnic/racial diversity of the San Francisco Bay Area insures that all students get exposure to working with clients from a variety of cultural groups. Practica are selected and approved by CSPP based on the quality of training and supervision provided for the students. They include community mental health centers, neuropsychology clinics, hospitals, child guidance clinics, college counseling centers, forensic settings, couple and family therapy agencies, residential treatment centers, infant/toddler mental health programs, corporate settings, and school programs for children and adolescents. Students begin the required internship in the fourth year (PsyD program) or the fifth year (PhD program). Full-time internship options include APA-accredited or APPIC-member training programs pursued through the national selection process, or local internship programs approved by the California Psychology Internship Council (CAPIC). Students have the option of completing the internship requirement in two years of half-time experience.

Admissions

Entries appear in the following order: required test or GPA, minimum score (if required)/median score of students entering in 2015–2016.

Program	Degree	GRE-V	GRE-Q	GRE-Writing	GRE-Subject	Under-graduate GPA	Last 2 Years GPA	Psychol-ogy GPA	Master's GPA
Clinical Psychology	PsyD	Not specified	Not specified	Not specified	Not specified	3/3.22	Not specified	3/NA	Not specified
Clinical Psychology	PhD	Not specified	Not specified	Not specified	Not specified	3/3.34	Not specified	3/NA	Not specified
Clinical Psychology	Respecial-ization Diploma	Not specified	Not specified	Not specified	Not specified	3/3.15	Not specified	NA/NA	Not specified

Admissions *(con't.)*

Program	Degree	GRE-V	GRE-Q	GRE-Writing	GRE-Subject	Under-graduate GPA	Last 2 Years GPA	Psychol-ogy GPA	Master's GPA
Clinical Counseling	MA/MS	Not specified	Not specified	Not specified	Not specified	Not specified	Not specified	Not specified	Not specified
Marital and Family Therapy	MA/MS	Not specified	Not specified	Not specified	Not specified	3/3	Not specified	3/NA	Not specified
Clinical Psycho-pharmacology	MA/MS	Not specified	Not specified	Not specified	Not specified	Not specified	Not specified	Not specified	Not specified

Admissions Requirements:

Degree	GRE	GRE-Subject	Letters of Recom-mendation	Research Statement	Writing Sample	CV	Interview
Master's/Specialist	Optional	None	2	Required	None	Required	Required
Doctoral	Optional	Optional	2	Required	None	Required	Required

Please note if these criteria vary for different programs: Criteria differ by program and level.

Admissions Criteria:

Research experience—high
Work experience—high
Clinically related public service—high
GPA—high

Letters of recommendation—high
Interview—high
Statement of goals and objectives—high
Undergraduate psychology preparation—medium

For additional information on admission requirements, visit http://www.alliant.edu/cspp/admissions/apply/index.php.

Department Demographics

	Male (PT)	Female (PT)	Total	African-American/ Black (PT)	Hispanic/ Latino (PT)	Asian/ Pacific Islander (PT)	American Indian/ Alaska Native (PT)	Caucasian/ White (PT)	Unknown (PT)	Multiethnic (PT)	ADA (PT)	Int'l (PT)
Students	70 (53)	203 (113)	439	15 (13)	31 (15)	44 (19)	0 (3)	140 (91)	25 (15)	18 (10)	6 (1)	13 (8)

Financial Information/Assistance

Tuition: For information on tuition costs, visit http://www.alliant.edu/admissions/tuition.php. Tuition is subject to change.

Doctoral:
State residents: $1,160 per credit hour.
Nonstate residents: $1,160 per credit hour.

Master's:
State residents: $1,160 per credit hour.
Nonstate residents: $1,160 per credit hour.

Financial Assistance:

	Teaching Assistantship (% Receiving)	Teaching Assistantship Tuition Remission	Research Assistantship (% Receiving)	Research Assistantship Tuition Remission	Fellowship (% Receiving)	Fellowship Tuition Remission
First-Year Student	NA (NA)	NA	$1,500 (NA)	NA	$5,000 (NA)	NA
Advanced Student	$3,000 (NA)	NA	$1,000 (NA)	NA	$5,000 (NA)	NA

For additional information on financial assistance, visit http://www.alliant.edu/cspp/admissions/scholarships_financial_aid/index.php.

Employment of Department Graduates

No information provided.

Additional Information

Housing and Day Care: No on-campus housing is available. No on-campus day care facilities are available.

Information for Students With Physical Disabilities: See the following website: http://www.alliant.edu/consumer/disability-services/index.php.

Special Facilities or Resources: Students can elect to receive supervised clinical experience through CSPP's Psychological Services Center (PSC)—a community mental health clinic that serves children, adults, couples, and families. The PSC enables faculty to model professional service delivery and to directly supervise and evaluate students' clinical work. Clinical services provided at the PSC include psychodiagnostic assessment and individual, couple, family, and group psychotherapy. The PSC has both Adult-Clinical and Child/Family-Clinical training programs. Students can also elect to gain additional assessment experience through the CSPP Psychological Assessment Clinic, which provides psychological testing and assessment services to infants and preschoolers, school-age children, adolescents, and adults from diverse cultural backgrounds in the San Francisco Bay Area. The Rockway Institute works to counter antigay prejudice and inform public policies affecting lesbian, gay, bisexual, and transgender (LGBT) people. The primary goals of the Institute are to convey accurate scientific and professional information about LGBT issues to the media, legislatures and the courts, and conduct research relevant to LGBT public policy questions in the areas of family relations, education, healthcare, social services, and the workplace. Computer labs are available to students and are fully equipped with SPSS and other statistical programs for research purposes.

Application Information: Alliant International University, Admissions Processing Center, 10455 Pomerado Road, San Diego, CA 92131. *Fee:* $65. *Online application:* https://www.applyweb.com/alliant/.

Alliant International University: San Francisco
Programs in Educational and School Psychology and School Counseling
Hufstedler School of Education
One Beach Street, Suite 100
San Francisco, CA 94133-1221
Telephone: (866) 825-5426
Program Director: James Adams, PsyD

E-mail: aerdman1@alliant.edu
Web: http://www.alliant.edu/hsoe/

Orientation, Objectives, and Emphasis of Department
Programs train students with the skills necessary to work with students, teachers, parents, and other professionals in today's school environments. The curriculum includes professional skills, professional roles courses, applied research, and professional concepts. The master's degree program prepares students to gain the PPS (Pupil Personnel Services) credential that allows them to practice in California's schools. Students take afternoon, evening and weekend classes and engage in fieldwork. At the doctoral level, students complete special focus area courses, examples of which include adolescent stress and coping, school culture and administration, pediatric psychology, infant and preschool mental health, child neuropsychology, and provision of services for children in alternative placement. Doctoral students also complete a PsyD project.

Programs and Degrees Offered

Program	Degree	Application Deadline	Applications Received	Accepted	New Admits Enrolled (PT)	Total Enrolled (PT)	Degrees Awarded in 2014–2015	Median Years to Complete Degree	Dismissed/ Withdrew
School Psychology	MA/MS	April 1 (Fall), Rolling	7	5	4 (0)	9 (8)	9	1.74	1
Educational Psychology	PsyD	April 1 (Fall), Rolling	7	6	0 (4)	0 (8)	4	2.68	0
School Counseling	MA/MS	April 1 (Fall), Rolling	4	3	2 (0)	2 (0)	0		1

Internships/Practica

Students in the master's program have practica tied to their coursework beginning in the first semester of their programs. Internships are required of any student seeking a Pupil Personnel Services (PPS) credential post-masters or as part of the doctoral program in educational psychology. The 1200 required internships hours for the School Psychology program and the 600 required internship hours for the School Counseling program are completed at public school districts. Those in the doctoral program who are interested in clinical licensure must complete a separate psychology internship.

Admissions

Entries appear in the following order: required test or GPA, minimum score (if required)/median score of students entering in 2015–2016.

Program	Degree	GRE-V	GRE-Q	GRE-Writing	GRE-Subject	Under-graduate GPA	Last 2 Years GPA	Psychol-ogy GPA	Master's GPA
School Psychology	MA/MS	Not specified	Not specified	Not specified	Not specified	3/3.18	Not specified	3/NA	Not specified
Educational Psychology	PsyD	Not specified	Not specified	Not specified	Not specified	3/3.2	Not specified	3/NA	Not specified
School Counseling	MA/MS	Not specified	Not specified	Not specified	Not specified	Not specified	Not specified	Not specified	Not specified

Admissions Requirements:

Degree	GRE	GRE-Subject	Letters of Recom-mendation	Research Statement	Writing Sample	CV	Interview
Master's/Specialist	None	None	2	Required	None	Required	Required
Doctoral	None	None	2	Required	None	Required	Required

Please note if these criteria vary for different programs: Criteria differ by program and level.

Admissions Criteria:

Research experience—medium
Work experience—high
Clinically related public service—medium
GPA—high

Letters of recommendation—high
Interview—high
Statement of goals and objectives—high
Undergraduate psychology preparation—medium

For additional information on admission requirements, visit http://www.alliant.edu/hsoe/hsoe-admissions/index.php.

Department Demographics

	Male (PT)	Female (PT)	Total	African-American/ Black (PT)	Hispanic/ Latino (PT)	Asian/ Pacific Islander (PT)	American Indian/ Alaska Native (PT)	Caucasian/ White (PT)	Unknown	Multiethnic (PT)	ADA (PT)	Int'l (PT)
Students	1 (7)	10 (9)	27	3 (1)	3 (2)	1 (2)	0 (0)	1 (7)	3 (0)	0 (4)	0 (0)	0 (0)

Financial Information/Assistance

Tuition: For information on tuition costs, visit http://www.alliant.edu/admissions/tuition.php. Tuition is subject to change.

Doctoral:
State residents: $1,055 per credit hour.
Nonstate residents: $1,055 per credit hour.

Master's:
State residents: $648 per credit hour.
Nonstate residents: $648 per credit hour.

Financial Assistance:

	Teaching Assistantship (% Receiving)	Teaching Assistantship Tuition Remission	Research Assistantship (% Receiving)	Research Assistantship Tuition Remission	Fellowship (% Receiving)	Fellowship Tuition Remission
First-Year Student	NA (NA)	NA	NA (NA)	NA	$1,000 (NA)	NA
Advanced Student	NA (NA)	NA	NA (NA)	NA	$2,500 (NA)	NA

For additional information on financial assistance, visit http://www.alliant.edu/hsoe/hsoe-admissions/hsoe-scholarships.php.

Employment of Department Graduates

No information provided.

Additional Information

Housing and Day Care: No on-campus housing is available. No on-campus day care facilities are available.

Information for Students With Physical Disabilities: See the following website: http://www.alliant.edu/consumer/disability-services/index.php.

Application Information: Alliant International University, Admissions Processing Center, 10455 Pomerado Road, San Diego, CA 92131-1799. *Fee:* $65. *Online application:* https://www.applyweb.com/alliant/.

American School of Professional Psychology at Argosy University/San Francisco Bay Area
Clinical Psychology
College of Clinical Psychology
1005 Atlantic Avenue
Alameda, CA 94501
Telephone: (510) 217-4871
Program Dean: Robert Perl, PsyD

E-mail: rperl@argosy.edu
Web: http://www.ASPPSanFrancisco.com

Orientation, Objectives, and Emphasis of Department

The PsyD in Clinical Psychology program is designed to educate and train students so they will be able to function effectively as clinical psychologists. To ensure that students are adequately prepared, the curriculum is designed to provide for the meaningful integration of psychological science, theory, and clinical practice. The program is designed to emphasize the development of knowledge, skills and attitudes essential in the training of professional psychologists who are committed to the ethical provision of quality, evidence-based services. The program follows a practitioner-scholar model and is based on the competencies developed by the National Council of Schools and Programs of Professional Psychology (NCSPP). The curriculum is designed to provide students with a broad array of theoretical perspectives in preparation for the general practice of clinical psychology. Required courses expose students to assessment and intervention strategies that are based on psychodynamic, cognitive-behavioral, systems, and experiential approaches. As a group, the program faculty is also representative of this diversity. Rather than being immersed in a single theoretical perspective, students are encouraged to consider these alternative perspectives, to critically evaluate the full range of theories and practices, and to apply them. The program is small in size and emphasizes a mentorship model.

Programs and Degrees Offered

Program	Degree	Application Deadline	Applications Received	Accepted	New Admits Enrolled (PT)	Total Enrolled (PT)	Degrees Awarded in 2014–2015	Median Years to Complete Degree	Dismissed/ Withdrew
Clinical Psychology	MA/MS	(Fall), (Spring), Rolling	1	1	0 (0)	0 (0)	0		1
Clinical Psychology	PsyD	(Fall), (Spring), Rolling	64	45	14	87	28	5.55	1

APA Accreditation

Clinical PsyD: Student Outcome Data website: http://clinical.argosy.edu/locations/san-francisco/clinical-psychology-doctor-of-psychology.

Doctoral Degree (PsyD Clinical Psychology): For those doctoral students for whom a professional internship was required in this program prior to graduation:
Total students who applied for an internship: 15
Total students who obtained an internship: 15
Total students who obtained a paid internship: 12
Total students who obtained an unpaid internship: 3
Total students who were placed in APA/CPA-accredited internships: 8
Total students placed in internships not APA/CPA-accredited, but listed with the Association of Psychology Postdoctoral and Internship Centers (APPIC): 4
Total students placed in internships conforming to guidelines of the Council of Directors of School Psychology Programs (CDSPP): 0
Total students placed in internships that were not APA/CPA-accredited, APPIC or CDSSP listed: 3

Master's Degree (MA/MS Clinical Psychology): An internship experience, such as a final research project or "capstone" experience is required of graduates.

Internships/Practica

Students in our PsyD program are expected to apply to APA internships, though APPIC and CAPIC (California Psychology Internship Council) internship opportunities are available for those who require them. PsyD students are encouraged to choose the internship experience that best meets their long term training goals, with APA as a priority. Students to have the option of applying to either a one-year full-time or a two-year half-time internship, but full-time is expected of most students. Practicum opportunities are organized through BAPIC or through our own in-house practicum program. Students are required to complete 3 years of practicum training prior to internship in the PsyD program and one year In the MA program. Our database of approved San Francisco Bay Area practicum sites includes community mental health centers, psychiatric hospitals, medical centers, VAs, university counseling centers, schools, correctional facilities, residential treatment programs, and other settings. Some sites serve the general population while others service specific populations or clinical problems (e.g., chemical dependency, eating disorders, medical and psychiatric rehabilitation, etc). Students are expected to seek varied practicum placements on a trajectory toward an accredited internship.

Admissions

Entries appear in the following order: required test or GPA, minimum score (if required)/median score of students entering in 2015–2016.

Program	Degree	GRE-V	GRE-Q	GRE-Writing	GRE-Subject	Under-graduate GPA	Last 2 Years GPA	Psychol-ogy GPA	Master's GPA
Clinical Psychology	MA/MS	Not specified	Not specified	Not specified	Not specified	3/NA	Not specified	Not specified	Not specified
Clinical Psychology	PsyD	NA/NA	NA/NA	NA/NA	Not specified	3/NA	Not specified	Not specified	Not specified

Admissions Requirements:

Degree	GRE	GRE-Subject	Letters of Recommendation	Research Statement	Writing Sample	CV	Interview
Master's/Specialist	Optional	Optional	3	Required	Required	Required	Required
Doctoral	Optional	Optional	3	Required	Required	Required	Required

Please note if these criteria vary for different programs: Based on qualifications, some PsyD applicants may be encouraged to consider the MA program. GRE scores are optional, but may strengthen applicant qualifications.

Admissions Criteria:

GRE scores—medium
Research experience—high
Work experience—medium
Clinically related public service—high
GPA—high

Letters of recommendation—high
Interview—high
Statement of goals and objectives—high
Undergraduate psychology preparation—high

Department Demographics

	Male (PT)	Female (PT)	Total	African-American/ Black (PT)	Hispanic/ Latino (PT)	Asian/ Pacific Islander (PT)	American Indian/ Alaska Native (PT)	Caucasian/ White (PT)	Unknown (PT)	Multiethnic (PT)	ADA (PT)	Int'l (PT)
Students	15 (0)	72 (0)	87	10 (0)	11 (0)	17 (0)	0 (0)	39 (0)	0 (0)	10 (0)	5 (0)	2 (0)

Financial Information/Assistance

Tuition: For information on tuition costs, visit https://www.argosy.edu/affordability/tuition-and-fees. Tuition is subject to change. Additional fees are assessed to students beyond the costs of tuition for the following: professional liability insurance, student activity fee, technology fee.

Doctoral:
State residents: $1,162 per credit hour.
Nonstate residents: $1,162 per credit hour.

Master's:
State residents: $1,162 per credit hour.
Nonstate residents: $1,162 per credit hour.

Financial Assistance:

	Teaching Assistantship (% Receiving)	Teaching Assistantship Tuition Remission	Research Assistantship (% Receiving)	Research Assistantship Tuition Remission	Fellowship (% Receiving)	Fellowship Tuition Remission
First-Year Student	NA (NA)	NA	NA (NA)	NA	$55,000 (NA)	Partial
Advanced Student	$5,000 (NA)	NA	NA (NA)	NA	$75,000 (NA)	Partial

For additional information on financial assistance, visit http://www.argosy.edu/affordability.

Employment of Department Graduates

No information provided.

Additional Information

Housing and Day Care: No on-campus housing is available. No on-campus day care facilities are available.

Special Facilities or Resources: Our program emphasizes a specialized hands-on clinical experience through our Intensive Clinical Training facility, offering clinical training beginning in the first year of the program. Through the Intensive Clinical Training program, students work directly with clients referred from the community while being observed by a team through a one-way mirror. The team consists of the instructor and fellow students who participate in pre- and post-therapy sessions in which they provide input and feedback about the therapeutic process. Each client session is guided by the instructor/assistant who, through the use of a microphone, provides clinical guidance and interventions directly to the student therapist through an earpiece worn by the student. As the session progresses, the instructor/assistant educates the team about the dynamics of the therapist/client interaction and the treatment approach. Students may participate on three levels: 1) as a clinical observer and a member of the team; 2) as a student therapist working directly with clients, and 3) as a clinical assistant in concert with our Supervision/Consultation course. Our program also houses an on-campus community clinic that serves as a practicum site for students or as an opportunity for supplemental assessment experience. The clinic provides assessment and therapy services.

Application Information: Patrick Bennett, Admissions Director, American School of Professional Psychology at Argosy University, 1005 Atlantic Avenue, Alameda, CA 94501. *Fee:* $50. *Online application:* https://apply.argosy.edu/.

American School of Professional Psychology at Argosy University/Southern California
Clinical Psychology
College of Clinical Psychology
601 South Lewis
Orange, CA 92868
Telephone: (714) 620-3701
Program Dean, Clinical Psychology: Gary Bruss, PhD

E-mail: gbruss@argosy.edu
Web: http://clinical.argosy.edu/locations/los-angeles-orange-county/

Orientation, Objectives, and Emphasis of Department
The graduate programs in psychology are designed to educate and train practitioners, with an additional emphasis on scholarly training in the doctoral programs. Courses and fieldwork experiences embrace multiple theoretical and intervention approaches, and a range of psychodiagnostic techniques (in the clinical programs), all of which are designed to serve a wide and diverse range of populations. PsyD concentrations are available in Forensic Psychology and Child/Adolescent Psychology. Students are taught by faculty with strong teaching and practitioner skills, with a strong focus on developing students with the fundamental clinical, counseling and relevant scholarly competencies required to pursue careers in psychology. Courses in applied and academic areas are considered to be critical in the development of practitioners with the skills to develop, innovate, implement, and assess delivery of services to clientele in clinical, counseling, and educational types of settings.

Programs and Degrees Offered

Program	Degree	Application Deadline	Applications Received	Accepted	New Admits Enrolled (PT)	Total Enrolled (PT)	Degrees Awarded in 2014–2015	Median Years to Complete Degree	Dismissed/ Withdrew
Clinical Psychology	PsyD	Rolling	121	48	38 (0)	145 (0)	27	5	5
Clinical Psychology	MA/MS	Rolling	9	4	(0)	6 (0)	4	2	0

APA Accreditation
Clinical PsyD: Student Outcome Data website: http://clinical.argosy.edu/locations/los-angeles-orange-county/clinical-psychology-doctor-of-psychology.

Doctoral Degree (PsyD Clinical Psychology): For those doctoral students for whom a professional internship was required in this program prior to graduation:
Total students who applied for an internship: 28
Total students who obtained an internship: 28
Total students who obtained a paid internship: 26
Total students who obtained an unpaid internship: 2
Total students who were placed in APA/CPA-accredited internships: 16
Total students placed in internships not APA/CPA-accredited, but listed with the Association of Psychology Postdoctoral and Internship Centers (APPIC): 6
Total students placed in internships conforming to guidelines of the Council of Directors of School Psychology Programs (CDSPP): 0
Total students placed in internships that were not APA/CPA-accredited, APPIC or CDSSP listed: 6

Master's Degree (MA/MS Clinical Psychology): An internship experience, such as a final research project or "capstone" experience is required of graduates.

Internships/Practica

The specific clinical focus of the practicum varies according to the student's program, training needs, professional interests and goals, and the availability of practicum sites. MA Clinical practica focus on training students counseling and therapy skills. The PsyD Clinical Psychology practica provide one year of psychodiagnostic assessment training and one year of therapy training. Students are also required to complete a third year of practicum training in either therapy or psychodiagnostic assessment, or a combination thereof. The program is committed to finding a wide range of practicum sites to provide many options for student professional exposure and development.

Admissions

Entries appear in the following order: required test or GPA, minimum score (if required)/median score of students entering in 2015–2016.

Program	Degree	GRE-V	GRE-Q	GRE-Writing	GRE-Subject	Under-graduate GPA	Last 2 Years GPA	Psychol-ogy GPA	Master's GPA
Clinical Psychology	PsyD	NA/NA	NA/NA	Not specified	Not specified	3/3.5	Not specified	Not specified	3.25/3.8
Clinical Psychology	MA/MS	Not specified	Not specified	Not specified	Not specified	3/NA	3/NA	Not specified	Not specified

Admissions Requirements:

Degree	GRE	GRE-Subject	Letters of Recom-mendation	Research Statement	Writing Sample	CV	Interview
Master's/Specialist	Optional	Optional	3	Required	Optional	Required	Required
Doctoral	Optional	Optional	3	Required	Optional	Required	Required

Please note if these criteria vary for different programs: High emphasis on work experience for doctoral programs, although outstanding presentation in areas related to GPA, recommendation letters, interview, and personal statement can offset a deficit in work experience. Letters of recommendation from work, prior training, and/or academic references are expected for all programs. Emphasis on both clinical and academic references for doctoral applicants.

Admissions Criteria:

GRE scores—medium
Research experience—medium
Work experience—medium
Clinically related public service—medium
GPA—high

Letters of recommendation—high
Interview—high
Statement of goals and objectives—high
Undergraduate psychology preparation—medium

Department Demographics

	Male (PT)	Female (PT)	Total	African-American/ Black (PT)	Hispanic/ Latino (PT)	Asian/ Pacific Islander (PT)	American Indian/ Alaska Native (PT)	Caucasian/ White (PT)	Unknown	Multiethnic (PT)	ADA (PT)	Int'l (PT)
Students	49 (0)	94 (0)	143					0 (0)	0 (0)		15 (0)	3 (0)

Financial Information/Assistance

Tuition: For information on tuition costs, visit https://www.argosy.edu/affordability/tuition-and-fees. Tuition is subject to change. Tuition costs vary by program.

Doctoral:
State residents: $37,184 per academic year.

Master's:
State residents: $1,162 per credit hour.

State residents: $1,162 per credit hour.
Nonstate residents: $37,184 per academic year.
Nonstate residents: $1,162 per credit hour.

Nonstate residents: $1,162 per credit hour.

Financial Assistance:

	Teaching Assistantship (% Receiving)	Teaching Assistantship Tuition Remission	Research Assistantship (% Receiving)	Research Assistantship Tuition Remission	Fellowship (% Receiving)	Fellowship Tuition Remission
First-Year Student	$1,000 (NA)	NA	NA (NA)	NA	$10,000 (NA)	Partial
Advanced Student	$1,000 (NA)	Partial	NA (NA)	NA	$10,000 (NA)	Partial

For additional information on financial assistance, visit https://www.argosy.edu/affordability.

Employment of Department Graduates

No information provided.

Additional Information

Housing and Day Care: No on-campus housing is available. No on-campus day care facilities are available.

Special Facilities or Resources: The campus has its own psychology clinic that is utilized for both clinical and research purposes.

Application Information: Director of Clinical Admissions, c/o American School of Professional Psychology at Argosy University/ Southern California, 601 South Lewis Street, Orange, CA 92868. *Fee:* $50. *Online application:* https://apply.argosy.edu/apply.

Antioch University Santa Barbara

Doctoral Program in Clinical Psychology
602 Anacapa Street
Santa Barbara, CA 93101
Telephone: (805) 962-8179
Chairperson: Ronald Pilato, PsyD

E-mail: rpilato@antioch.edu
Web: http://www.antiochsb.edu/

Orientation, Objectives, and Emphasis of Department

The Doctoral Program in Clinical Psychology at Antioch University Santa Barbara is a practitioner-scholar Doctor of Psychology (PsyD) Program. In addition to rigorous training in the broad and general scientific bases of psychology as well as the academic discipline and profession of clinical psychology, the curriculum integrates systemic, social justice, and multicultural perspectives with an emphasis in family psychology. Family forensic psychology coursework is offered for advanced students with training in assessing children and families, child custody evaluation, mediation and conflict resolution, family violence, forensic psychology, and expert witness testimony. Our practitioner-scholar program prepares students in a sequential fashion over the course of four years culminating in the full time internship in the fifth year. Students contribute to the base of research in professional psychology through their applied dissertations. Applicants may seek enrollment post bachelor's degree or post master's degree. Students entering with an earned master's degree in psychology, with equivalent courses, are given advanced standing and begin the program as second year students.

Programs and Degrees Offered

Program	Degree	Application Deadline	Applications Received	Accepted	New Admits Enrolled (PT)	Total Enrolled (PT)	Degrees Awarded in 2014–2015	Median Years to Complete Degree	Dismissed/ Withdrew
Clinical Psychology	PsyD	August 15 (Fall), Rolling	29	18	11 (0)	70 (0)	15	5.5	0

Doctoral Degree (PsyD Clinical Psychology): For those doctoral students for whom a professional internship was required in this program prior to graduation:

Total students who applied for an internship: 13
Total students who obtained an internship: 13
Total students who obtained a paid internship: 6
Total students who obtained an unpaid internship: 7
Total students who were placed in APA/CPA-accredited internships: 2
Total students placed in internships not APA/CPA-accredited, but listed with the Association of Psychology Postdoctoral and Internship Centers (APPIC): 2
Total students placed in internships conforming to guidelines of the Council of Directors of School Psychology Programs (CDSPP): 0
Total students placed in internships that were not APA/CPA-accredited, APPIC or CDSSP listed: 9

Internships/Practica

Practica are available in a variety of settings such as community agencies, schools, hospitals, and mental health clinics, in Santa Barbara, San Luis Obispo, Los Angeles and Ventura Counties. Doctoral candidates apply for full time internships through the national APPIC Match and through the CAPIC (California Psychology Internship Council) Match. Our applicants for internship have obtained APPIC member internships, APA accredited internships, and CAPIC member internships.

Admissions

Entries appear in the following order: required test or GPA, minimum score (if required)/median score of students entering in 2015–2016.

Program	Degree	GRE-V	GRE-Q	GRE-Writing	GRE-Subject	Undergraduate GPA	Last 2 Years GPA	Psychology GPA	Master's GPA
Clinical Psychology	PsyD	Not specified	Not specified	Not specified	Not specified	NA/NA	NA/NA	NA/NA	NA/NA

Admissions Requirements:

Degree	GRE	GRE-Subject	Letters of Recommendation	Research Statement	Writing Sample	CV	Interview
Doctoral	Optional	Optional	2	Optional	Required	Required	Required

Please note if these criteria vary for different programs: The doctoral program requires two essays that are used to assess analytic and critical thinking. An autobiographical essay is also required in order to assess for self-reflective capacity.

Admissions Criteria:

GRE scores—low
Research experience—low
Work experience—medium
Clinically related public service—high
GPA—medium

Letters of recommendation—high
Interview—high
Statement of goals and objectives—high
Undergraduate psychology preparation—medium
Writing sample—high

For additional information on admission requirements, visit http://www.antiochsb.edu/academic-programs/psyd-in-clinical-psychology/deadlines-criteria/.

Department Demographics

	Male (PT)	Female (PT)	Total	African-American/ Black (PT)	Hispanic/ Latino (PT)	Asian/ Pacific Islander (PT)	American Indian/ Alaska Native (PT)	Caucasian/ White (PT)	Unknown	Multiethnic (PT)	ADA (PT)	Int'l (PT)
Students	31 (0)	39 (0)	70	6 (0)	16 (0)	1 (0)	0 (0)	42 (0)	4 (0)	1 (0)	4 (0)	2 (0)

Financial Information/Assistance

Tuition: For information on tuition costs, visit http://www.antiochsb.edu/financial-aid/tuition/. Tuition is subject to change. Additional fees are assessed to students beyond the costs of tuition for the following: Testing supplies, practicum and materials fee, professional liability insurance, lab fee.

Doctoral:
State residents: $23,484 per academic year.
State residents: $785 per credit hour.
Nonstate residents: $23,484 per academic year.
Nonstate residents: $785 per credit hour.

Financial Assistance:

	Teaching Assistantship (% Receiving)	Teaching Assistantship Tuition Remission	Research Assistantship (% Receiving)	Research Assistantship Tuition Remission	Fellowship (% Receiving)	Fellowship Tuition Remission
First-Year Student	NA (NA)	NA	NA (NA)	NA	$3,500 (3)	Partial
Advanced Student	NA (NA)	NA	NA (NA)	NA	$1,750 (4)	Partial

For additional information on financial assistance, visit http://www.antiochsb.edu/financial-aid/.

Employment of Department Graduates

Doctoral:
Enrolled in a postdoctoral residency/fellowship: 7
Employed in independent practice: 2
Do not know: 6
Total: 15

Additional Information

Housing and Day Care: No on-campus housing is available. No on-campus day care facilities are available.

Special Facilities or Resources: Faculty are practicing professionals in their respective areas of expertise. Core faculty are engaged in a variety of research projects (according to their professional interests) which provide an opportunity for research assistantships for financial aid-eligible students.

Application Information: Admissions Office, Antioch University Santa Barbara, 602 Anacapa Street, Santa Barbara, CA 93101. *Fee:* $60. *Online application:* http://www.antiochsb.edu/admissions/apply-online/.

Azusa Pacific University (2015 data)

Department of Graduate Psychology
School of Behavioral and Applied Sciences
901 East Alosta, P.O. Box 7000
Azusa, CA 91702-7000
Telephone: (626) 815-5008
Chairperson: Marjorie Graham-Howard, PhD

E-mail: mlhoward@apu.edu
Web: http://www.apu.edu/bas/graduatepsychology/

Orientation, Objectives, and Emphasis of Department

The PsyD in Clinical Psychology with an emphasis in Family Psychology (APA-accredited) prepares students for the practice of professional psychology. The program adheres to a practitioner-scholar model of training and emphasizes development of the core competencies in clinical psychology adopted by the National Council of Schools and Programs of Professional Psychology. The program requires completion of a rigorous sequence of courses in the science and practice of psychology. Requirements include three years of clinical training, successful demonstration of clinical competency through examination, completion of a clinical dissertation, and a predoctoral internship. Pre-specialty education in family psychology and an emphasis in interdisciplinary studies, relating psychology to ethics, theology, and philosophy, are included. The program was designed to be consistent with the requirements of the Guidelines and Principles for Accreditation of Programs in Professional Psychology (APA, 1996). The MA in Clinical Psychology with an emphasis in Marriage and Family Therapy meets requirements for California MFT licensure. Concepts of individual psychology are integrated with interpersonal and ecological concepts of systems theory. Goals include cultivating the examined life, fostering theoretical mastery, developing practical clinical skills, encouraging clinically integrative strategies, and preparing psychotherapists to work in a culturally diverse world.

Programs and Degrees Offered

Program	Degree	Application Deadline	Applications Received	Accepted	New Admits Enrolled (PT)	Total Enrolled (PT)	Degrees Awarded in 2014–2015	Median Years to Complete Degree	Dismissed/ Withdrew
Clinical Psychology	MA/MS	March 1 (Fall), October 1 (Spring)	253	159	102 (13)	278 (48)	75	2.57	12
Clinical Psychology	PsyD	January 15 (Fall)	150	53	27 (0)	136 (13)	19	5	6

APA Accreditation

Clinical PsyD: Student Outcome Data website: http://www.apu.edu/bas/graduatepsychology/psyd/.

Doctoral Degree (PsyD Clinical Psychology): For those doctoral students for whom a professional internship was required in this program prior to graduation:
Total students who applied for an internship: 33
Total students who obtained an internship: 29
Total students who obtained a paid internship: 26
Total students who obtained an unpaid internship: 3
Total students who were placed in APA/CPA-accredited internships: 16
Total students placed in internships not APA/CPA-accredited, but listed with the Association of Psychology Postdoctoral and Internship Centers (APPIC): 10
Total students placed in internships conforming to guidelines of the Council of Directors of School Psychology Programs (CDSPP): 0
Total students placed in internships that were not APA/CPA-accredited, APPIC or CDSSP listed: 3

Internships/Practica

PsyD students are required to complete at least 3 years of practicum experience. These experiences are gained in placements throughout the Greater Los Angeles area which provides for a diverse clinical and multicultural experience. A sequence of clinical practicum courses is offered alongside practicum placements. All doctoral students are required to complete one full year predoctoral internship. APU interns match at a variety of sites (APA approved or those meeting APPIC standards) across the country. Students enrolled in the MA Program in Clinical Psychology complete a clinical training sequence that meets all requirements for future licensure as a Marriage and Family Therapist (MFT) in the state of California. Students complete 225 hours of direct client contact (75 of which may be client-centered advocacy) in diverse settings, such as community counseling centers, domestic violence clinics, and schools. Students receive training in individual, marital, and group therapy and exposure to treatments that have been demonstrated to be effective with specific problems. A sequence of clinical placement courses is offered simultaneously with the field placement experience. The APU Community Counseling Center provide a clinical training opportunity for both MA and PsyD students and serves as an outreach to the diverse area surrounding APU.

Admissions

Entries appear in the following order: required test or GPA, minimum score (if required)/median score of students entering in 2015–2016.

Program	Degree	GRE-V	GRE-Q	GRE-Writing	GRE-Subject	Under-graduate GPA	Last 2 Years GPA	Psychol-ogy GPA	Master's GPA
Clinical Psychology	MA/MS	Not specified	Not specified	Not specified	Not specified	2.7/3.3	Not specified	Not specified	Not specified
Clinical Psychology	PsyD	NA/NA	NA/NA	NA/NA	Not specified	3/3.52	Not specified	Not specified	3.5/3.6

Admissions Requirements:

Degree	GRE	GRE-Subject	Letters of Recommendation	Research Statement	Writing Sample	CV	Interview
Master's/Specialist	Optional	Optional	3	Required	Optional	Optional	Required
Doctoral	Required	Optional	3	Required	Optional	Required	Required

Please note if these criteria vary for different programs: No GRE scores required for MA; Work experience of medium importance for MA; Research experience of medium importance for MA; Clinically Related Public Service low for MA.

Admissions Criteria:

GRE scores—medium
Research experience—medium
Work experience—medium
Clinically related public service—medium

GPA—high
Letters of recommendation—high
Interview—high
Statement of goals and objectives—high

For additional information on admission requirements, visit http://www.apu.edu/bas/graduatepsychology/programs/.

Department Demographics

	Male (PT)	Female (PT)	Total	African-American/ Black (PT)	Hispanic/ Latino (PT)	Asian/ Pacific Islander (PT)	American Indian/ Alaska Native (PT)	Caucasian/ White (PT)	Unknown	Multiethnic (PT)	ADA (PT)	Int'l (PT)
Students	80 (21)	334 (40)	475	23 (5)	101 (14)	32 (4)	1 (0)	179 (29)	78 (9)	0 (0)	11 (0)	11 (0)

Financial Information/Assistance

Tuition: For information on tuition costs, visit http://www.apu.edu/graduateprofessionalcenter/sfs/costs/. Tuition is subject to change. Tuition costs vary by program.

Doctoral:
State residents: $937 per credit hour.
Nonstate residents: $937 per credit hour.

Master's:
State residents: $669 per credit hour.
Nonstate residents: $669 per credit hour.

Financial Assistance:

	Teaching Assistantship (% Receiving)	Teaching Assistantship Tuition Remission	Research Assistantship (% Receiving)	Research Assistantship Tuition Remission	Fellowship (% Receiving)	Fellowship Tuition Remission
First-Year Student	$6,250 (NA)	Partial	$6,250 (NA)	Partial	NA (NA)	NA
Advanced Student	$6,250 (NA)	Partial	$6,250 (NA)	Partial	NA (NA)	NA

For additional information on financial assistance, visit http://www.apu.edu/graduatecenter/sfs/financialaid/.

Employment of Department Graduates

Master's:
Employed in a professional position in a school system: 1
Employed in business or industry: 1
Employed in a community mental health/counseling center: 15
Employed in a hospital/medical center: 1
Still seeking employment: 1

Doctoral:
Enrolled in a postdoctoral residency/fellowship: 9
Employed in independent practice: 1
Employed in an academic position at a university: 1
Employed in government agency: 1
Employed in a community mental health/counseling center: 2

Not seeking employment: 1
Other employment position: 3
Do not know: 52
Total: 75

Employed in a hospital/medical center: 2
Do not know: 3
Total: 19

Additional Information

Housing and Day Care: No on-campus housing is available. No on-campus day care facilities are available.

Information for Students With Physical Disabilities: See the following website: http://www.apu.edu/lec/disabilities/.

Special Facilities or Resources: All students have access to the APA PsycINFO database and all APA journals full-text online as part of their student library privileges. The Darling Library provides an attractive and functional set of resources for the APU PsyD and MA. The library is technology-friendly and includes the Ahmanson Information Technology Center, an area with 75 computer desks. Each computer is wired into the university system for Internet and library catalog system searches. PsycINFO, as well as over 100 additional licensed databases, are available for student literature and subject searches. Eight "scholar rooms" were designed as a part of the Darling Graduate Library to be used for conducting research and writing. Doctoral students in the dissertation phase of their program are given priority in the reservation of these rooms. There are also several conference rooms in the Darling Library that may be reserved for student study groups or research teams. The Department of Graduate Psychology runs the Community Counseling Center (CCC) which offers a range of psychological services to residents of the local and surrounding communities. The CCC is also a viable mental health resource for both undergraduate and graduate students enrolled at Azusa Pacific University.

Application Information: Azusa Pacific University, Graduate Admissions, 901 E. Alosta, P.O. Box 7000, Azusa, CA 91702-7000. *Fee:* $45. *Online application:* http://www.apu.edu/apply/grad/.

Biola University
Rosemead School of Psychology
13800 Biola Avenue
La Mirada, CA 90639
Telephone: (562) 903-4867
Associate Dean and Director of Doctoral Programs: Tamara L. Anderson, PhD

E-mail: tamara.anderson@biola.edu
Web: http://www.rosemead.edu/

Orientation, Objectives, and Emphasis of Department
The historical theoretical orientation at Rosemead has been psychodynamic, and that model continues to be a cornerstone of training students to become excellent psychologists who provide high-quality psychotherapy services. The programs are based on the scholar-practitioner (PhD) and practitioner-scholar (PsyD) model of training in professional psychology. The substantive area is clinical psychology, and graduates are prepared to pursue postdoctoral training and become licensed to practice as clinical psychologists. The model of training leads to the formation of educational goals, which in turn lead to objectives and competencies. The goals, objectives, and competencies form a hierarchical educational structure that is stated in terms of student outcomes with increasing specificity for the competencies. The curriculum, including clinical training and required experiences, is designed to facilitate this educational structure. Achievement of program competencies is expected of all graduates.

Programs and Degrees Offered

Program	Degree	Application Deadline	Applications Received	Accepted	New Admits Enrolled (PT)	Total Enrolled (PT)	Degrees Awarded in 2014–2015	Median Years to Complete Degree	Dismissed/Withdrew
Clinical Psychology	PsyD	January 15 (Fall)	84	25	16 (0)	86 (0)	10	6	0
Clinical Psychology	PhD	December 1 (Fall)	85	17	12 (0)	51 (0)	7	6	1

APA Accreditation

Clinical PsyD (Doctor of Psychology).
Clinical PhD: Student Outcome Data website: http://www.rosemead.edu/programs/phd/.

Doctoral Degree (PsyD Clinical Psychology): For those doctoral students for whom a professional internship was required in this program prior to graduation:
Total students who applied for an internship: 13
Total students who obtained an internship: 11
Total students who obtained a paid internship: 11
Total students who obtained an unpaid internship: 0
Total students who were placed in APA/CPA-accredited internships: 6
Total students placed in internships not APA/CPA-accredited, but listed with the Association of Psychology Postdoctoral and Internship Centers (APPIC): 5
Total students placed in internships conforming to guidelines of the Council of Directors of School Psychology Programs (CDSPP): 0
Total students placed in internships that were not APA/CPA-accredited, APPIC or CDSSP listed: 0

Doctoral Degree (PhD Clinical Psychology): For those doctoral students for whom a professional internship was required in this program prior to graduation:
Total students who applied for an internship: 7
Total students who obtained an internship: 6
Total students who obtained a paid internship: 6
Total students who obtained an unpaid internship: 0
Total students who were placed in APA/CPA-accredited internships: 4
Total students placed in internships not APA/CPA-accredited, but listed with the Association of Psychology Postdoctoral and Internship Centers (APPIC): 2
Total students placed in internships conforming to guidelines of the Council of Directors of School Psychology Programs (CDSPP): 0
Total students placed in internships that were not APA/CPA-accredited, APPIC or CDSSP listed: 0

Internships/Practica

The location of Biola University in La Mirada, California allows students access to multiple and diverse practicum and internship training sites throughout the five very large and culturally diverse counties. Given this prime location, Rosemead enjoys over sixty practicum training sites that include community mental health clinics, several university counseling centers, VA, and other medical centers. Overall, students will complete more than 2,000 hours of practicum and internship before they graduate; ensuring students are well equipped to enter the mental health community.

Admissions

Entries appear in the following order: required test or GPA, minimum score (if required)/median score of students entering in 2015–2016.

Program	Degree	GRE-V	GRE-Q	GRE-Writing	GRE-Subject	Under-graduate GPA	Last 2 Years GPA	Psychology GPA	Master's GPA
Clinical Psychology	PsyD	NA/NA	NA/NA	Not specified	Not specified	3/3.59	NA/NA	NA/NA	3/3.65
Clinical Psychology	PhD	NA/NA	NA/NA	Not specified	Not specified	3/3.56	NA/NA	NA/NA	3/3.89

Admissions Requirements:

Degree	GRE	GRE-Subject	Letters of Recommendation	Research Statement	Writing Sample	CV	Interview
Doctoral	Required	Optional	4	Required	Optional	Optional	Required

Admissions Criteria:

GRE scores—high
Research experience—medium
Work experience—low
Clinically related public service—medium
GPA—high

Letters of recommendation—high
Interview—high
Statement of goals and objectives—medium
Undergraduate psychology preparation—medium
Essays—high

For additional information on admission requirements, visit http://www.rosemead.edu/admissions/steps-apply/.

Department Demographics

	Male (PT)	Female (PT)	Total	African-American/ Black (PT)	Hispanic/ Latino (PT)	Asian/ Pacific Islander (PT)	American Indian/ Alaska Native (PT)	Caucasian/ White (PT)	Unknown	Multiethnic (PT)	ADA (PT)	Int'l (PT)
Students	41 (0)	95 (0)	136	5 (0)	13 (0)	33 (0)	0 (0)	76 (0)	0 (0)	9 (0)	0 (0)	5 (0)

Financial Information/Assistance

Tuition: For information on tuition costs, visit http://www.rosemead.edu/tuition-financial-aid/tuition-and-fees/. Tuition is subject to change. Additional fees are assessed to students beyond the costs of tuition for the following: Professional Growth Fees.

Doctoral:
State residents: $24,090 per academic year.
State residents: $1,004 per credit hour.
Nonstate residents: $24,090 per academic year.
Nonstate residents: $1,004 per credit hour.

Financial Assistance:

	Teaching Assistantship (% Receiving)	Teaching Assistantship Tuition Remission	Research Assistantship (% Receiving)	Research Assistantship Tuition Remission	Fellowship (% Receiving)	Fellowship Tuition Remission
First-Year Student	$1,688 (NA)	NA	NA (NA)	NA	$2,500 (NA)	NA
Advanced Student	$2,310 (NA)	NA	NA (NA)	NA	$3,576 (NA)	NA

For additional information on financial assistance, visit http://rosemead.edu/tuition-financial-aid/financial-aid/.

Employment of Department Graduates

Doctoral:
Enrolled in a postdoctoral residency/fellowship: 7
Employed in independent practice: 4
Employed in other positions at a higher education institution: 1
Employed in government agency: 1
Employed in a community mental health/counseling center: 4
Employed in a hospital/medical center: 1
Not seeking employment: 1
Total: 19

Additional Information

Housing and Day Care: On-campus housing is available. See the following website for more information: http://rosemead.edu/about/student-life/housing/. No on-campus day care facilities are available.

Special Facilities or Resources: Rosemead is housed on the Biola University campus. This campus is a 100-acre undergraduate and graduate campus, which for 20 years has been ranked by U.S. News & World Report as a National University. The Carnegie Foundation also lists Biola University as a Doctoral Research University. Rose Hall houses all psychology faculty and includes 25 offices, four therapy/research rooms equipped with one-way mirrors, videotape equipment, seminar, conference, and classrooms, the testing room and administrative staff space, the Rosemead Student Lounge, as well as a room specifically equipped for family/child therapy and outfitted with toys. Also available in Rose Hall are two research labs. One is devoted to Neuro-feedback research, and the other houses twelve computers, a discussion area, and media equipment for presentations. Biola Counseling Center is located just off the edge of campus and is housed in a professional building. BCC services the university undergraduates, graduate students, faculty and staff, as well as the community at large. BCC serves as a training clinic for our doctoral students and includes 20 consulting rooms (two of which are fully stocked play therapy rooms), videotape equipment, one-way mirrors, computers for test scoring, and a large seminar room for student trainings and meetings.

Application Information: Office of Graduate Admissions, Biola University, Rosemead School of Psychology, 13800 Biola Avenue, La Mirada, CA 90639. *Fee:* $65. *Online application:* http://www.rosemead.edu/admissions/apply-now/.

California Lutheran University

PsyD Program in Clinical Psychology
Graduate School of Psychology
2201 Outlet Center Drive, Suite 600
Oxnard, CA 93036
Telephone: (805) 493-3675
Director, PsyD Program: Mindy Puopolo, PsyD

E-mail: mpuopolo@callutheran.edu
Web: http://www.callutheran.edu/academics/graduate/psyd-clinical-psychology/

Orientation, Objectives, and Emphasis of Department

California Lutheran University's Doctorate in Clinical Psychology (PsyD) is a five-year program that integrates science and practice in preparing students for careers as licensed clinical psychologists. The PsyD program upholds a strong commitment to diversity and inclusion, welcoming all students, faculty, and staff to our Southern California setting. Our program is housed within a top tier, private, not-for-profit university that has served Southern California for over 50 years. The latest technology, new facilities, small class sizes, and a stimulating curriculum are some of what makes our program outstanding.

Programs and Degrees Offered

Program	Degree	Application Deadline	Applica-tions Received	Accepted	New Admits Enrolled (PT)	Total Enrolled (PT)	Degrees Awarded in 2014–2015	Median Years to Complete Degree	Dismissed/ Withdrew
Clinical Psychology	PsyD	January 15 (Fall)	26	16	12 (0)	67 (0)	7	5	1

APA Accreditation

Clinical PsyD: Student Outcome Data website: http://www.callutheran.edu/academics/graduate/psyd-clinical-psychology/student-data.html.

Doctoral Degree (PsyD Clinical Psychology): For those doctoral students for whom a professional internship was required in this program prior to graduation:
Total students who applied for an internship: 8
Total students who obtained an internship: 7
Total students who obtained a paid internship: 6
Total students who obtained an unpaid internship: 1
Total students who were placed in APA/CPA-accredited internships: 1
Total students placed in internships not APA/CPA-accredited, but listed with the Association of Psychology Postdoctoral and Internship Centers (APPIC): 1
Total students placed in internships conforming to guidelines of the Council of Directors of School Psychology Programs (CDSPP): 0
Total students placed in internships that were not APA/CPA-accredited, APPIC or CDSSP listed: 5

Internships/Practica

The Graduate Psychology Programs at CLU are fortunate to have two fully operational training clinics that provide services to our community. Students have the choice of working with our traditional community or pursuing specialized training in dialectical behavior therapy (DBT) or intimate partner violence (IPV). The clinic facilities are fully equipped with individual and group rooms, play therapy rooms, state-of-the-art video recording equipment, record-keeping software, and computerized client outcome assessments, all of which contribute to a high-quality initial training experience. A collaborative and supportive atmosphere designed to facilitate both personal and professional growth is strongly valued. Students advance from the internal practicum experience to providing psychological services in the broader community with some of our many community partners. In this phase, students work alongside professionals in the field engaging in clinical and professional activities. We have formed partnerships with many agencies to provide these opportunities including community mental health centers, county clinics, hospitals or medical centers, residential treatment centers, substance abuse clinics, correctional facilities, and college counseling centers. Finally, students complete a formal internship prior to graduation where they consolidate their identity as doctoral-level clinicians.

Admissions

Entries appear in the following order: required test or GPA, minimum score (if required)/median score of students entering in 2015–2016.

Program	Degree	GRE-V	GRE-Q	GRE-Writing	GRE-Subject	Under-graduate GPA	Last 2 Years GPA	Psychology GPA	Master's GPA
Clinical Psychology	PsyD	NA/151	NA/143	NA/4	NA/NA	NA/3.39	Not specified	Not specified	Not specified

Admissions Requirements:

Degree	GRE	GRE-Subject	Letters of Recommendation	Research Statement	Writing Sample	CV	Interview
Doctoral	Required	Optional	2	Required	Required	Required	Required

Admissions Criteria:

GRE scores—medium
Research experience—medium
Work experience—medium
Clinically related public service—medium
GPA—high

Letters of recommendation—medium
Interview—high
Statement of goals and objectives—high
Undergraduate psychology preparation—high

For additional information on admission requirements, visit http://www.callutheran.edu/academics/graduate/psyd-clinical-psychology/admission-process.html.

Department Demographics

	Male (PT)	Female (PT)	Total	African-American/ Black (PT)	Hispanic/ Latino (PT)	Asian/ Pacific Islander (PT)	American Indian/ Alaska Native (PT)	Caucasian/ White (PT)	Unknown	Multiethnic (PT)	ADA (PT)	Int'l (PT)
Students	10 (0)	57 (0)	67	4 (0)	14 (0)	2 (0)	1 (0)	25 (0)	15 (0)	6 (0)	3 (0)	5 (0)

Financial Information/Assistance

Tuition: For information on tuition costs, visit http://www.callutheran.edu/academics/graduate/psyd-clinical-psychology/tuition-fees.html. Tuition is subject to change. Additional fees are assessed to students beyond the costs of tuition for the following: practicum fee; assessment lab fee; technology fee.

Doctoral:
State residents: $940 per credit hour.
Nonstate residents: $940 per credit hour.

Financial Assistance:

	Teaching Assistantship (% Receiving)	Teaching Assistantship Tuition Remission	Research Assistantship (% Receiving)	Research Assistantship Tuition Remission	Fellowship (% Receiving)	Fellowship Tuition Remission
First-Year Student	NA (NA)	NA	$1,200 (NA)	Partial	$2,500 (NA)	Partial
Advanced Student	NA (NA)	NA	$1,200 (NA)	Partial	$2,500 (NA)	Partial

For additional information on financial assistance, visit http://www.callutheran.edu/financial-aid/.

Employment of Department Graduates

Doctoral:
Enrolled in a postdoctoral residency/fellowship: 3
Employed in an academic position at a university: 2
Employed in business or industry: 1
Employed in a community mental health/counseling center: 1
Do not know: 1
Total: 8

Additional Information

Housing and Day Care: On-campus housing is available. See the following website for more information: http://www.callutheran.edu/admission/graduate/housing.html. On-campus day care facilities are available. See the following website for more information: https://earth.callutheran.edu/ecc/index.php.

Information for Students With Physical Disabilities: See the following website: http://www.callutheran.edu/students/disability-services/.

Special Facilities or Resources: In addition to the two Community Counseling and Parent Child Study Centers, CLU has a new Social and Behavioral Science Building complete with lab space and research facilities. The PsyD Program also benefits from close relationships with local mental health agencies, both private and public.

Application Information: Graduate Admissions, 60 W. Olsen Road, Thousand Oaks, CA 91360. *Fee:* $75. *Online application:* http://psych.callutheran.edu/apply.

California Polytechnic State University
Psychology and Child Development
Liberal Arts
1 Grand Avenue Building 47-24
San Luis Obispo, CA 93407
Telephone: (805) 756-2456
Chairperson: Jasna Jovanovic

E-mail: pgasser@calpoly.edu
Web: http://psycd.calpoly.edu/

Orientation, Objectives, and Emphasis of Department

The program is designed for persons who desire to practice in the field of clinical/counseling psychology. The program's mission is to provide the state of California with highly competent master's-level practitioners who are academically and clinically prepared to counsel individuals, couples, families, and groups in a multicultural society. The program fulfills the educational requirements for the state of California's Marriage and Family Therapist (MFT) License. Its mission is also to provide students who want to proceed on to doctoral programs in clinical or counseling psychology with sound research skills, thesis experience, and clinical intervention training. Graduates find career opportunities in the public sector such as in county Mental Health agencies and Departments of Social Services as well as in private non-profit and private practice agencies. Ten to twenty percent of graduates go on to doctoral programs in clinical or counseling psychology.

Programs and Degrees Offered

Program	Degree	Application Deadline	Applications Received	Accepted	New Admits Enrolled (PT)	Total Enrolled (PT)	Degrees Awarded in 2014–2015	Median Years to Complete Degree	Dismissed/ Withdrew
Counseling Marriage and Family	MA/MS	December 1 (Fall)	60	19	14 (0)	26 (13)	11	3	0

Internships/Practica

The program offers numerous well-supervised clinical practica and traineeship opportunities in a variety of public and private non-profit agencies. Training sites are selected based on their ability to provide: (a) quality supervision by a state-qualified licensed clinician; (b) assessment, diagnostic, and treatment experience with a wide variety of psychiatric disorders; (c) training in various treatment modalities (i.e., individual, couple, family, and group); and (d) exposure to a range of clients that represent the diversity of the community.

Admissions

Entries appear in the following order: required test or GPA, minimum score (if required)/median score of students entering in 2015–2016.

Program	Degree	GRE-V	GRE-Q	GRE-Writing	GRE-Subject	Under-graduate GPA	Last 2 Years GPA	Psychol-ogy GPA	Master's GPA
Counseling Marriage and Family	MA/MS	NA/150	NA/153	NA/4.2	Not specified	Not specified	NA/3.45	Not specified	Not specified

Admissions Requirements:

Degree	GRE	GRE-Subject	Letters of Recom-mendation	Research Statement	Writing Sample	CV	Interview
Master's/Specialist	Required	Optional	3	Required	Optional	Optional	Required

Admissions Criteria:

GRE scores—medium
Research experience—low
Work experience—high
Clinically related public service—high
GPA—medium

Letters of recommendation—high
Interview—high
Statement of goals and objectives—high
Undergraduate psychology preparation—low

For additional information on admission requirements, visit http://psycd.calpoly.edu/graduate/application-information.

Department Demographics

	Male (PT)	Female (PT)	Total	African-American/ Black (PT)	Hispanic/ Latino (PT)	Asian/ Pacific Islander (PT)	American Indian/ Alaska Native (PT)	Caucasian/ White (PT)	Unknown	Multiethnic (PT)	ADA (PT)	Int'l (PT)
Students	4 (1)	22 (12)	39	0 (0)	5 (3)	2 (0)	0 (0)	15 (8)	4 (0)	0 (2)	0 (0)	0 (0)

Financial Information/Assistance

Tuition: For information on tuition costs, visit http://www.afd.calpoly.edu/fees/index.asp. Tuition is subject to change.

Master's:
State residents: $9,924 per academic year.
Nonstate residents: $21,078 per academic year.

Financial Assistance:

	Teaching Assistantship (% Receiving)	Teaching Assistantship Tuition Remission	Research Assistantship (% Receiving)	Research Assistantship Tuition Remission	Fellowship (% Receiving)	Fellowship Tuition Remission
First-Year Student	NA (NA)	NA	NA (NA)	NA	NA (NA)	NA
Advanced Student	NA (NA)	NA	NA (NA)	NA	NA (NA)	NA

For additional information on financial assistance, visit http://financialaid.calpoly.edu/.

Employment of Department Graduates

No information provided.

Additional Information

Housing and Day Care: On-campus housing is available. See the following website for more information: http://www.housing. calpoly.edu/. On-campus day care facilities are available. See the following website for more information: http://www.asi.calpoly. edu/childrens_center.

Information for Students With Physical Disabilities: See the following website: http://drc.calpoly.edu/.

Special Facilities or Resources: Closely supervised, on-campus practicum experiences leading to challenging traineeships in diverse community agencies are the cornerstone of Cal Poly's preparation for the future clinician. The program hosts and operates a community counseling services clinic with three counseling offices and an observation room that provides direct viewing through one-way mirrors and remotely controlled video equipment. Our program is clinically intensive, where on-campus practicum experience prepares students for community traineeship, and both training requirements position students nicely for community internships once they've graduated.

Application Information: Cal Poly Admissions Office, 1 Grand Avenue, San Luis Obispo, CA 93407. *Fee:* $55. *Online application:* http://www.csumentor.edu/.

California State Polytechnic University-Pomona

Psychology & Sociology Department
College of Letters, Arts, and Social Sciences
3801 West Temple Avenue
Pomona, CA 91768
Telephone: (909) 869-3888
Director of MS in Psychology Program: Jeffery Scott Mio
Web: http://www.cpp.edu/~class/psychology-sociology/psychology/masters-program.shtml

E-mail: jsmio@cpp.edu

Orientation, Objectives, and Emphasis of Department

General marital and family orientation; eclectic.

Programs and Degrees Offered

Program	Degree	Application Deadline	Applications Received	Accepted	New Admits Enrolled (PT)	Total Enrolled (PT)	Degrees Awarded in 2014–2015	Median Years to Complete Degree	Dismissed/ Withdrew
Psychology	MA/MS	April 1 (Fall)	100	15	15	29	14	2	0

Internships/Practica

This is an MFT program, so we require students to complete traineeships as per BBS requirements.

Admissions

Entries appear in the following order: required test or GPA, minimum score (if required)/median score of students entering in 2015–2016.

Program	Degree	GRE-V	GRE-Q	GRE-Writing	GRE-Subject	Undergraduate GPA	Last 2 Years GPA	Psychology GPA	Master's GPA
Psychology	MA/MS	Not specified	Not specified	Not specified	Not specified	Not specified	Not specified	Not specified	Not specified

Admissions Requirements:

Degree	GRE	GRE-Subject	Letters of Recommendation	Research Statement	Writing Sample	CV	Interview
Master's/Specialist	None	None	3	Required	None	Optional	Required

Admissions Criteria:

GPA—high
Letters of recommendation—high
Interview—medium

Statement of goals and objectives—high
Undergraduate psychology preparation—high

Department Demographics

	Male (PT)	Female (PT)	Total	African-American/ Black (PT)	Hispanic/ Latino (PT)	Asian/ Pacific Islander (PT)	American Indian/ Alaska Native (PT)	Caucasian/ White (PT)	Unknown	Multiethnic (PT)	ADA (PT)	Int'l (PT)
Students	5 (0)	24 (0)	29	2 (0)	13 (0)	2 (0)	0 (0)	6 (0)	3 (0)	3 (0)	0 (0)	0 (0)

Financial Information/Assistance

Tuition: For information on tuition costs, visit http://www.cpp.edu/~student-accounting/tuition-fees/. Tuition is subject to change.

Master's:
State residents: $8,120 per academic year.
Nonstate residents: $19,280 per academic year.

Financial Assistance:

	Teaching Assistantship (% Receiving)	Teaching Assistantship Tuition Remission	Research Assistantship (% Receiving)	Research Assistantship Tuition Remission	Fellowship (% Receiving)	Fellowship Tuition Remission
First-Year Student	NA (NA)	NA	NA (NA)	NA	NA (NA)	NA
Advanced Student	NA (NA)	NA	NA (NA)	NA	$1,000 (NA)	NA

For additional information on financial assistance, visit http://www.cpp.edu/~financial-aid/index.shtml.

Employment of Department Graduates

Master's:
Employed in a community mental health/counseling center: 10
Do not know: 4
Total: 14

Additional Information

Housing and Day Care: On-campus housing is available. See the following website for more information: http://www.cpp.edu/~housing/. On-campus day care facilities are available. See the following website for more information: http://asi.cpp.edu/services/childrens-center/.

Information for Students With Physical Disabilities: See the following website: http://www.cpp.edu/~drc/index.shtml.

Application Information: Graduate Admissions, Psychology & Sociology Department, 3801 West Temple Avenue, Pomona, CA 91768. *Fee:* $55. *Online application:* http://www.cpp.edu/~admissions/apply-now.shtml.

California State University, Dominguez Hills

Department of Psychology
Natural and Behavioral Sciences
1000 East Victoria Street
Carson, CA 90747
Telephone: (310) 243-3427
Coordinator, MA in Psychology Program: Karen I. Wilson, PhD

E-mail: kmason@csudh.edu
Web: http://www4.csudh.edu/psychology/

Orientation, Objectives, and Emphasis of Department

The Clinical Psychology Master of Arts program provides you with a solid academic background in clinical psychology as it is applied within a community mental health framework. This program prepares you for a career in counseling, teaching and research in community settings, which includes public or private agencies. Eighteen units of additional coursework prepare you for practice as a marriage and family therapist. Our graduates are successful in gaining admission to and graduating from the doctoral programs of their choice.

Programs and Degrees Offered

Program	Degree	Application Deadline	Applica-tions Received	Accepted	New Admits Enrolled (PT)	Total Enrolled (PT)	Degrees Awarded in 2014–2015	Median Years to Complete Degree	Dismissed/ Withdrew
Clinical Psychology	MA/MS	March 1 (Fall)	80	30	17 (0)	71 (13)	15	2.5	1
Health Psychology	MA/MS	March 1 (Fall)	3	1	1	3	0		0

Internships/Practica

The Master of Arts in Psychology offers 550 supervised hours of practicum experience in a variety of settings.

Admissions

Entries appear in the following order: required test or GPA, minimum score (if required)/median score of students entering in 2015–2016.

Program	Degree	GRE-V	GRE-Q	GRE-Writing	GRE-Subject	Under-graduate GPA	Last 2 Years GPA	Psychol-ogy GPA	Master's GPA
Clinical Psychology	MA/MS	NA/NA	NA/NA	NA/NA	Not specified	NA/NA	3/NA	NA/NA	Not specified
Health Psychology	MA/MS	NA/NA	NA/NA	NA/NA	Not specified	NA/NA	3/NA	NA/NA	Not specified

Admissions Requirements:

Degree	GRE	GRE-Subject	Letters of Recom-mendation	Research Statement	Writing Sample	CV	Interview
Master's/Specialist	Required	Optional	3	Required	Optional	Optional	None

Admissions Criteria:

GRE scores—medium
Research experience—medium
Work experience—low
Clinically related public service—medium

GPA—high
Letters of recommendation—high
Interview—low
Statement of goals and objectives—high

For additional information on admission requirements, visit http://www4.csudh.edu/psychology/master/prospective/index.

Department Demographics

	Male (PT)	Female (PT)	Total	African-American/ Black (PT)	Hispanic/ Latino (PT)	Asian/ Pacific Islander (PT)	American Indian/ Alaska Native (PT)	Caucasian/ White (PT)	Unknown	Multiethnic (PT)	ADA (PT)	Int'l (PT)
Students	19 (4)	55 (9)	87	5 (2)	28 (3)	4 (0)	0 (0)	32 (8)	5 (0)	0 (0)	1 (0)	0 (0)

Financial Information/Assistance

Tuition: For information on tuition costs, visit http://www4.csudh.edu/accounting-services/student-financial-services/term-fees-information. Tuition is subject to change.

Master's:
State residents: $7,540 per academic year.
Nonstate residents: $372 per credit hour.

Financial Assistance:

	Teaching Assistantship (% Receiving)	Teaching Assistantship Tuition Remission	Research Assistantship (% Receiving)	Research Assistantship Tuition Remission	Fellowship (% Receiving)	Fellowship Tuition Remission
First-Year Student	NA (NA)	NA	NA (NA)	NA	$2,000 (NA)	NA
Advanced Student	NA (NA)	NA	NA (NA)	NA	$2,000 (NA)	NA

For additional information on financial assistance, visit http://www4.csudh.edu/financial-aid/.

Employment of Department Graduates

Master's:
Enrolled in a psychology doctoral program: 4
Enrolled in another graduate/professional program: 2
Do not know: 11
Total: 17

Additional Information

Housing and Day Care: On-campus housing is available. See the following website for more information: http://www4.csudh.edu/housing/. On-campus day care facilities are available. See the following website for more information: http://asicsudh.com/child-development-center/overview/.

Information for Students With Physical Disabilities: See the following website: http://www4.csudh.edu/dss/.

Application Information: Department of Psychology, California State University, Dominguez Hills, 1000 East Victoria Street, Carson, CA 90747. *Fee:* $55. *Online application:* http://www4.csudh.edu/admissions/.

California State University, Fresno

Psychology
College of Science and Mathematics
2576 East San Ramon Avenue ST11
Fresno, CA 93740
Telephone: (559) 278-2691
Chairperson: Constance Jones

E-mail: llachs@csufresno.edu
Web: http://www.fresnostate.edu/csm/psych/

Orientation, Objectives, and Emphasis of Department

Our graduate programs are built on a curriculum and a philosophy that strongly emphasize research and the empirical foundations of psychology. Students work closely with a faculty member whose research interests align with the student's own, allowing for training that is deep, rigorous and personalized to a graduate student's specific research goals.

Programs and Degrees Offered

Program	Degree	Application Deadline	Applica-tions Received	Accepted	New Admits Enrolled (PT)	Total Enrolled (PT)	Degrees Awarded in 2014–2015	Median Years to Complete Degree	Dismissed/ Withdrew
General Experimental Psychology	MA/MS	February 1 (Fall)	24	10	10	20	8	2	0
Applied Behavior Analysis	MA/MS	February 1 (Fall)	29	10	9	29	3	3	0
School Psychology	EdS	February 1 (Fall)	23	10	10	30	9	3	0

Internships/Practica

EdS program students are required to complete 500 hours of practicum and 1200 hours of internship.

Admissions

Entries appear in the following order: required test or GPA, minimum score (if required)/median score of students entering in 2015–2016.

Program	Degree	GRE-V	GRE-Q	GRE-Writing	GRE-Subject	Under-graduate GPA	Last 2 Years GPA	Psychol-ogy GPA	Master's GPA
General Experimental Psychology	MA/MS	NA/NA	NA/NA	NA/NA	Not specified	3/NA	NA/NA	3/NA	Not specified
Applied Behavior Analysis	MA/MS	NA/NA	NA/NA	NA/NA	Not specified	3/NA	NA/NA	3/NA	Not specified
School Psychology	EdS	NA/NA	NA/NA	NA/NA	Not specified	3/NA	NA/NA	3/NA	Not specified

Admissions Requirements:

Degree	GRE	GRE-Subject	Letters of Recom-mendation	Research Statement	Writing Sample	CV	Interview
Master's/Specialist	Required	None	3	Required	Optional	Required	Required

Admissions Criteria:

GRE scores—medium
Research experience—high
Work experience—low
Clinically related public service—low
GPA—high

Letters of recommendation—high
Interview—medium
Statement of goals and objectives—high
Undergraduate psychology preparation—medium

For additional information on admission requirements, visit http://www.fresnostate.edu/csm/psych/degrees-programs/graduate/requirements.html.

Department Demographics

	Male (PT)	Female (PT)	Total	African-American/ Black (PT)	Hispanic/ Latino (PT)	Asian/ Pacific Islander (PT)	American Indian/ Alaska Native (PT)	Caucasian/ White (PT)	Unknown	Multiethnic (PT)	ADA (PT)	Int'l (PT)
Students	25 (0)	29 (0)	54	0 (0)	23 (0)	5 (0)	0 (0)	23 (0)	0 (0)	2 (0)	0 (0)	0 (0)

Financial Information/Assistance

Tuition: For information on tuition costs, visit http://www.fresnostate.edu/adminserv/accountingservices/money/regfee.html. Tuition is subject to change.

Master's:
State residents: $7,582 per academic year.
Nonstate residents: $16,840 per academic year.

Financial Assistance:

	Teaching Assistantship (% Receiving)	Teaching Assistantship Tuition Remission	Research Assistantship (% Receiving)	Research Assistantship Tuition Remission	Fellowship (% Receiving)	Fellowship Tuition Remission
First-Year Student	$8,000 (NA)	NA	NA (NA)	NA	NA (NA)	NA
Advanced Student	$8,000 (NA)	NA	NA (NA)	NA	NA (NA)	NA

For additional information on financial assistance, visit http://www.fresnostate.edu/studentaffairs/financialaid/.

Employment of Department Graduates

No information provided.

Additional Information

Housing and Day Care: On-campus housing is available. See the following website for more information: http://www. universitycourtyard.org/. On-campus day care facilities are available. See the following website for more information: http://www. fresnostate.edu/academics/pfc/.

Information for Students With Physical Disabilities: See the following website: http://www.fresnostate.edu/studentaffairs/ssd/.

Special Facilities or Resources: Extensive computer facilities and test library available.

Application Information: Fee: $55. *Online application:* http://www.fresnostate.edu/academics/gradstudies/admission/applying.html.

California State University, Fullerton
Department of Psychology
Humanities and Social Sciences
P.O. Box 6846 (H-830M)
Fullerton, CA 92834-6846
Telephone: (657) 278-3589
Chairperson: Eriko Self

E-mail: ahayes@fullerton.edu
Web: http://psychology.fullerton.edu/

Orientation, Objectives, and Emphasis of Department

The MA program in psychological research provides advanced coursework and research training in core areas of psychology. Completion of the MA can facilitate application to PhD programs in psychology and provides skills important to careers in education, the health professions, and industry. The MS program in clinical psychology is intended to prepare students for work in a variety of mental health settings, and the program contains coursework relevant for the MFT and LPCC licenses in California. The program is also designed to prepare students for PhD work in both academic and professional schools of clinical psychology.

Programs and Degrees Offered

Program	Degree	Application Deadline	Applications Received	Accepted	New Admits Enrolled (PT)	Total Enrolled (PT)	Degrees Awarded in 2014–2015	Median Years to Complete Degree	Dismissed/ Withdrew
Clinical Psychology	MA/MS	March 1 (Fall)	54	18	18 (0)	50 (15)	11	3	2
Psychological Research	MA/MS	March 1 (Fall)	70	16	16	37 (13)	7	2	

Internships/Practica

A majority of the internships are done in agencies which do family therapy and substance abuse prevention and treatment. Many are community mental health centers. Most internships have live and videotape supervision. Students have done internships in schools, policy psychology, county clinics, and inpatient settings as well. Most agencies combine clinical and community work and serve low income and minority populations. Internship sites must meet California Board of Behavioral Sciences licensure requirements for supervision. Students enroll in Fieldwork classes on campus, in addition to their on-site supervision. Fieldwork classes entail additional consultation about cases and review of videos of students' therapy sessions.

Admissions

Entries appear in the following order: required test or GPA, minimum score (if required)/median score of students entering in 2015–2016.

Program	Degree	GRE-V	GRE-Q	GRE-Writing	GRE-Subject	Under-graduate GPA	Last 2 Years GPA	Psychol-ogy GPA	Master's GPA
Clinical Psychology	MA/MS	NA/152	NA/149	Not specified	NA/599	2.5/3.4	NA/3.6	3/3.5	Not specified
Psychological Research	MA/MS	NA/151	NA/151	Not specified	NA/NA	2.5/3.5	NA/NA	3/3.6	Not specified

Admissions Requirements:

Degree	GRE	GRE-Subject	Letters of Recommendation	Research Statement	Writing Sample	CV	Interview
Master's/Specialist	Required	Required	3	Required	Optional	Optional	Required

Please note if these criteria vary for different programs: The Clinical Psychology program requires an interview. There is no interview required for the General Psychology program.

Admissions Criteria:

GRE scores—high
Research experience—high
Clinically related public service—high
GPA—high

Letters of recommendation—high
Interview—high
Statement of goals and objectives—high
Undergraduate psychology preparation—high

For additional information on admission requirements, visit http://psychology.fullerton.edu/academics/graduate.aspx.

Department Demographics

	Male (PT)	Female (PT)	Total	African-American/ Black (PT)	Hispanic/ Latino (PT)	Asian/ Pacific Islander (PT)	American Indian/ Alaska Native (PT)	Caucasian/ White (PT)	Unknown (PT)	Multiethnic (PT)	ADA (PT)	Int'l (PT)
Students			0				0 (0)	0 (0)	0 (0)	(0)	0 (0)	

Financial Information/Assistance

Tuition: For information on tuition costs, visit http://sfs.fullerton.edu/feeinformation/.

Master's:
State residents: $7,830 per academic year.

Financial Assistance:

	Teaching Assistantship (% Receiving)	Teaching Assistantship Tuition Remission	Research Assistantship (% Receiving)	Research Assistantship Tuition Remission	Fellowship (% Receiving)	Fellowship Tuition Remission
First-Year Student	NA (NA)	NA	NA (NA)	NA	NA (NA)	NA
Advanced Student	NA (NA)	NA	NA (NA)	NA	NA (NA)	NA

For additional information on financial assistance, visit http://www.fullerton.edu/graduate/funding/.

Employment of Department Graduates

No information provided.

Additional Information

Housing and Day Care: On-campus housing is available. See the following website for more information: http://www.fullerton.edu/housing/. On-campus day care facilities are available. See the following website for more information: http://www.asi.fullerton.edu/cc/index.asp.

Information for Students With Physical Disabilities: See the following website: http://www.fullerton.edu/dss/.

Special Facilities or Resources: The department has laboratories for research in cognitive psychology, conditioning, perception, biopsychology, social psychology, psychological testing, and developmental psychology. The department also has extensive computer facilities, including a lab dedicated to grad student use.

Application Information: Graduate Office, Department of Psychology, California State Fullerton, P.O. Box 6846 (H-830M), Fullerton, CA 92834-6846. *Fee:* $55. *Online application:* http://www.fullerton.edu/graduate/prospectivestudents/application.asp.

California State University, Long Beach

Department of Psychology
College of Liberal Arts
1250 Bellflower Boulevard
Long Beach, CA 90840-0901
Telephone: (562) 985-5000
Chairperson: David J. Whitney

E-mail: psygrad@csulb.edu
Web: http://www.cla.csulb.edu/departments/psychology/

Orientation, Objectives, and Emphasis of Department

California State University Long Beach has three master's programs in psychology. The Master of Science in Psychology, Option in Human Factors (MSHF) prepares students to apply knowledge of psychology to the design of jobs, information systems, consumer products, workplaces and equipment in order to improve user performance, safety and comfort. Students acquire a background in the core areas of experimental psychology, research design and methodology, human factors, computer applications and applied research methods. The Master of Arts in Psychology, Option in Psychological Research (MAPR) prepares students for doctoral work in any psychology field or for master's-level research or teaching positions. Core seminars include cognition, learning, physiological and sensory psychology, social, personality, and developmental psychology, and quantitative methods. MAPR graduates who apply to doctoral programs have high acceptance rates with financial support. The Master of Science in Psychology, Option in Industrial and Organizational Psychology (MSIO) offers preparation for careers for which a background in industrial/organizational psychology is essential. These fields include personnel, organizational development, industrial relations, employee training, and marketing research.

Programs and Degrees Offered

Program	Degree	Application Deadline	Applications Received	Accepted	New Admits Enrolled (PT)	Total Enrolled (PT)	Degrees Awarded in 2014–2015	Median Years to Complete Degree	Dismissed/ Withdrew
Psychological Research	MA/MS	January 15 (Fall)	70	23	11 (0)	20 (1)	10	2	1
Industrial/ Organizational Psychology	MA/MS	December 1 (Fall)	84	22	11 (0)	22 (1)	17	2	0
Human Factors	MA/MS	January 15 (Fall)	34	20	9 (0)	18 (3)	6	2	0

Internships/Practica

Various internships in outside industrial and organizational settings are options for second-year MSIO students. Internships are available through Boeing, NASA and CUDA for MSHF students.

Admissions

Entries appear in the following order: required test or GPA, minimum score (if required)/median score of students entering in 2015–2016.

Program	Degree	GRE-V	GRE-Q	GRE-Writing	GRE-Subject	Under-graduate GPA	Last 2 Years GPA	Psychol-ogy GPA	Master's GPA
Psychological Research	MA/MS	NA/155	NA/153	NA/4.21	Not specified	Not specified	NA/3.63	NA/3.66	Not specified
Industrial/ Organizational Psychology	MA/MS	NA/155	NA/153	NA/4.3	Not specified	Not specified	NA/3.77	NA/3.81	Not specified
Human Factors	MA/MS	NA/155	NA/152	NA/3.94	Not specified	Not specified	NA/3.79	NA/3.83	Not specified

Admissions Requirements:

Degree	GRE	GRE-Subject	Letters of Recom-mendation	Research Statement	Writing Sample	CV	Interview
Master's/Specialist	Required	None	3	Required	None	None	None

Admissions Criteria:

GRE scores—high
Research experience—high
Work experience—low
GPA—high

Letters of recommendation—high
Statement of goals and objectives—high
Undergraduate psychology preparation—high

For additional information on admission requirements, visit http://www.cla.csulb.edu/departments/psychology/graduate-application/.

Department Demographics

	Male (PT)	Female (PT)	Total	African-American/ Black (PT)	Hispanic/ Latino (PT)	Asian/ Pacific Islander (PT)	American Indian/ Alaska Native (PT)	Caucasian/ White (PT)	Unknown	Multiethnic (PT)	ADA (PT)	Int'l (PT)
Students	24 (2)	36 (3)	65	1 (0)	15 (1)	15 (1)	2 (0)	27 (3)	0 (0)	0 (0)	0 (0)	2 (0)

Financial Information/Assistance

Tuition: For information on tuition costs, visit http://web.csulb.edu/depts/enrollment/registration/fees_basics.html. Tuition is subject to change.

Master's:
State residents: $7,718 per academic year.
Nonstate residents: $14,414 per academic year.

Financial Assistance:

	Teaching Assistantship (% Receiving)	Teaching Assistantship Tuition Remission	Research Assistantship (% Receiving)	Research Assistantship Tuition Remission	Fellowship (% Receiving)	Fellowship Tuition Remission
First-Year Student	NA (NA)	NA	$5,500 (NA)	NA	$2,500 (NA)	NA
Advanced Student	NA (NA)	NA	$5,500 (NA)	NA	$2,500 (NA)	NA

For additional information on financial assistance, visit http://www.cla.csulb.edu/departments/psychology/financial-sources/.

Employment of Department Graduates

No information provided.

Additional Information

Housing and Day Care: On-campus housing is available. See the following website for more information: http://web.csulb.edu/divisions/students/housing/. On-campus day care facilities are available. See the following website for more information: http://www.asicsulb.org/pages/child-development-center.

Information for Students With Physical Disabilities: See the following website: http://web.csulb.edu/divisions/students/dss.

Special Facilities or Resources: The Psychology Department is housed in a building that has wide and varied research facilities, including computer rooms and laboratories in clinical, developmental, human factors, industrial-organizational, behavioral neuroscience, social, and other areas of psychology. Computer facilities include many current software packages. The behavioral neuroscience area has access to a staffed university animal facility. For research in applied (e.g., community, health, industrial-organizational) and experimental (e.g., behavioral neuroscience, social) studies in psychology, there are many research suites and a test materials center. These facilities, located in the psychology building, are for research and training in interviewing, assessment, program and treatment evaluation, behavioral observation, collection and analysis of biological samples, and intervention strategies for hard-to-reach populations. Computer facilities are central to research in decision analysis, human-computer interface, statistical theory, assessment, and computer-aided instruction. Human factors labs include state-of-the-art air traffic control simulators (CHAAT - Center for Human Factors and Advanced Aeronautics Technologies), computerized tools for usability analyses (CUDA ' Center for Usability Design and Accessibility), eye and motion tracking systems, and other computerized systems for research and analysis. Our diversified facilities also accommodate research in managing diversity in the workplace and other topics in industrial/organizational psychology.

Application Information: Psychology Graduate Office, 1250 Bellflower Boulevard, Long Beach, CA 90840-0901. *Fee:* $55. *Online application:* http://www.csumentor.edu/.

California State University, Northridge

Department of Psychology
Social and Behavioral Sciences
18111 Nordhoff Street
Northridge, CA 91330-8255
Telephone: (818) 677-2827
Chairperson: Jill Razani

E-mail: jill.razani@csun.edu
Web: http://www.csun.edu/psychology

Orientation, Objectives, and Emphasis of Department

The Department of Psychology has, as a primary goal, the assurance that students receive a strong theoretical foundation as well as rigorous methodological and statistical coursework. In addition, all students must complete a project or a thesis in order to display their knowledge of their content area and their methodological sophistication. The General Experimental and Clinical programs emphasize the basic research and content knowledge required to enhance students' opportunities for entry into doctoral programs. The Applied Behavior Analysis (ABA) is a 2-year program during which students can obtain their MA degree and complete the Behavior Analyst Certification Board (BACB) coursework requirements to be able to practice as behavior analysts and/or pursue PhD programs in behavior analysis.

Programs and Degrees Offered

Program	Degree	Application Deadline	Applications Received	Accepted	New Admits Enrolled (PT)	Total Enrolled (PT)	Degrees Awarded in 2014–2015	Median Years to Complete Degree	Dismissed/Withdrew
Clinical Psychology	MA/MS	February 1 (Fall)	62	12	12 (0)	40 (0)	8	2	0
General Experimental Psychology	MA/MS	February 16 (Fall)	60	17	17 (0)	36 (0)	11	2	0
Applied Behavioral Analysis	MA/MS	January 18 (Fall)	100	35	33	60	31	2	2

Internships/Practica

Graduate students in applied fields have available an array of practicum experiences in the area. Direct clinical practicum experience is required of the Clinical students, who receive supervised training in three campus clinics specializing in Parent Child Interaction Training, Child and Adolescent Diagnostic Assessment, and Cognitive-Behavioral Psychotherapy. In addition, clinical internships are available in many community sites including the University Counseling Services and local mental health care facilities. General Experimental students work with departmental faculty as well as with those at neighboring universities. The Applied Behavior Analysis (ABA) graduate program offers practica and internships in community, school, clinics, and in-home settings. The purpose of the CSUN practicum program is to offer ABA students access to high quality supervised experiences during which students apply the skills acquired in their educational coursework.

Admissions

Entries appear in the following order: required test or GPA, minimum score (if required)/median score of students entering in 2015–2016.

Program	Degree	GRE-V	GRE-Q	GRE-Writing	GRE-Subject	Under-graduate GPA	Last 2 Years GPA	Psychology GPA	Master's GPA
Clinical Psychology	MA/MS	NA/NA	NA/NA	NA/NA	NA/NA	Not specified	Not specified	Not specified	Not specified
General Experimental Psychology	MA/MS	NA/NA	NA/NA	NA/NA	Not specified	Not specified	Not specified	Not specified	Not specified
Applied Behavioral Analysis	MA/MS	NA/NA	NA/NA	NA/NA	Not specified	3/3.5	3/3.5	3/3.5	Not specified

Admissions Requirements:

Degree	GRE	GRE-Subject	Letters of Recom-mendation	Research Statement	Writing Sample	CV	Interview
Master's/Specialist	Required	Required	3	Required	Optional	Required	Required

Please note if these criteria vary for different programs: Clinically Related Public Services is rated HIGH by the Clinical option; low relevance for the General Experimental option. Interviews are required by all three master's programs, either in-person (preferred) or via telephone (if necessary due to geographical restrictions). The GRE-Subject test is only required for applicants to the Clinical program.

Admissions Criteria:

GRE scores—medium
Research experience—high
Work experience—medium
Clinically related public service—medium
GPA—medium

Letters of recommendation—high
Interview—high
Statement of goals and objectives—high
Undergraduate psychology preparation—high

For additional information on admission requirements, visit http://www.csun.edu/social-behavioral-sciences/psychology/application-checklist.

Department Demographics

	Male (PT)	Female (PT)	Total	African-American/ Black (PT)	Hispanic/ Latino (PT)	Asian/ Pacific Islander (PT)	American Indian/ Alaska Native (PT)	Caucasian/ White (PT)	Unknown	Multiethnic (PT)	ADA (PT)	Int'l (PT)
Students	30 (0)	46 (0)	76	4 (0)	9 (0)	11 (0)	0 (0)	8 (0)	23 (0)	21 (0)	2 (0)	4 (0)

Financial Information/Assistance

Tuition: For information on tuition costs, visit http://www.csun.edu/financialaid/cost-attendance. Higher tuition cost for this program: Applied Behavior Analysis: $26,270 flat rate for entire program. Tuition is subject to change. Additional fees are assessed to students beyond the costs of tuition for the following: Non-residents are charged an additional $372.00 per credit. Tuition costs vary by program.

Master's:
State residents: $7,786 per academic year.

Financial Assistance:

	Teaching Assistantship (% Receiving)	Teaching Assistantship Tuition Remission	Research Assistantship (% Receiving)	Research Assistantship Tuition Remission	Fellowship (% Receiving)	Fellowship Tuition Remission
First-Year Student	NA (NA)	NA	NA (NA)	NA	NA (NA)	NA
Advanced Student	NA (NA)	NA	NA (NA)	NA	NA (NA)	NA

For additional information on financial assistance, visit http://www.csun.edu/research-graduate-studies/funding-sources.

Employment of Department Graduates

Master's:
Enrolled in a psychology doctoral program: 14
Enrolled in another graduate/professional program: 3
Do not know: 2
Total: 19

Additional Information

Housing and Day Care: On-campus housing is available. See the following website for more information: http://www.csun.edu/housing. On-campus day care facilities are available. See the following website for more information: http://www.csun.edu/as/childrens-center.

Information for Students With Physical Disabilities: See the following website: http://www.csun.edu/cod/.

Special Facilities or Resources: Some professors have federal or private grants that employ graduate students as research assistants. In addition, we have laboratories in Physiological Psychology (NeuroScan, BioPac), computer applications for Cognitive Psychology, multiple childcare sites for observation of children, and extensive research space. We also have a state-of-the-art Statistics Laboratory that can be used for data analysis for theses or projects.

Application Information: Psychology Graduate Office, California State University Northridge, 18111 Nordhoff Street, Northridge, CA 91330-8255. *Fee:* $55. *Online application:* http://www.csumentor.edu/admissionapp/grad_apply.asp.

California State University, Sacramento
Psychology
Social Sciences and Interdisciplinary Studies
6000 J Street
Sacramento, CA 95819-6007
Telephone: (916) 278-6254
Chairperson: Marya C. Endriga, PhD

E-mail: mendriga@csus.edu
Web: http://www.csus.edu/psyc/

Orientation, Objectives, and Emphasis of Department
Our mission is to educate, research, and practice in the field of Psychology with dedication and enthusiasm. We facilitate students' intellectual and personal growth. We prepare students for graduate studies, the workforce, managing citizenship responsibilities and life demands. We advance the many areas of our discipline through active and creative scholarship. We serve diverse communities through meaningful collaborations with people and organizations. Through teaching, scholarship, and service we promote human equity, health and well-being, effective functioning, and respect for diversity.

Programs and Degrees Offered

Program	Degree	Application Deadline	Applications Received	Accepted	New Admits Enrolled (PT)	Total Enrolled (PT)	Degrees Awarded in 2014–2015	Median Years to Complete Degree	Dismissed/ Withdrew
Psychology	MA/MS	January 15 (Fall)	101	17	15 (0)	34 (17)	13	4	2

Internships/Practica
Internships and practica are available for ABA and I/O students through local community agencies and state and county government departments.

Admissions
Entries appear in the following order: required test or GPA, minimum score (if required)/median score of students entering in 2015–2016.

Program	Degree	GRE-V	GRE-Q	GRE-Writing	GRE-Subject	Undergraduate GPA	Last 2 Years GPA	Psychology GPA	Master's GPA
Psychology	MA/MS	NA/152	NA/148	NA/3.8	NA/591	2.5/NA	Not specified	Not specified	Not specified

Admissions Requirements:

Degree	GRE	GRE-Subject	Letters of Recommendation	Research Statement	Writing Sample	CV	Interview
Master's/Specialist	Required	Required	3	Required	Optional	Required	Required

Please note if these criteria vary for different programs: Interview is required for the Applied Behavior Analysis track. GRE-Subject is required for the General Psychology track.

Admissions Criteria:

GRE scores—high
Research experience—high
Work experience—low
GPA—high

Letters of recommendation—high
Interview—low
Statement of goals and objectives—medium
Undergraduate psychology preparation—high

For additional information on admission requirements, visit http://www.csus.edu/psyc/Prospective Students.html.

Department Demographics

	Male (PT)	Female (PT)	Total	African-American/ Black (PT)	Hispanic/ Latino (PT)	Asian/ Pacific Islander (PT)	American Indian/ Alaska Native (PT)	Caucasian/ White (PT)	Unknown	Multiethnic (PT)	ADA (PT)	Int'l (PT)
Students	11 (10)	23 (7)	51					0 (0)	0 (0)			

Financial Information/Assistance

Tuition: Tuition is subject to change. Additional fees are assessed to students beyond the costs of tuition for the following: various, including athletics, student union, health facilities, $700 in mandatory fees.

Master's:
State residents: $8,138 per academic year.
Nonstate residents: $17,066 per academic year.

Financial Assistance:

	Teaching Assistantship (% Receiving)	Teaching Assistantship Tuition Remission	Research Assistantship (% Receiving)	Research Assistantship Tuition Remission	Fellowship (% Receiving)	Fellowship Tuition Remission
First-Year Student	NA (NA)	NA	NA (NA)	NA	NA (NA)	NA
Advanced Student	NA (NA)	NA	NA (NA)	NA	NA (NA)	NA

For additional information on financial assistance, visit http://www.csus.edu/faid/.

Employment of Department Graduates

No information provided.

Additional Information

Housing and Day Care: On-campus housing is available. See the following website for more information: http://www.csus.edu/housing/. On-campus day care facilities are available. See the following website for more information: http://www.asi.csus.edu/programs/childrens-center/.

Information for Students With Physical Disabilities: See the following website: http://www.csus.edu/sswd/.

Special Facilities or Resources: Department has a vivarium (rats), neuroscience labs, clinic facilities (for ABA, faculty research), after-school program for children with autism, trainee placements with community ABA programs, and research opportunities with state government departments.

Application Information: Graduate Coordinator, Department of Psychology, CSU Sacramento. *Fee:* $55. *Online application:* https://secure.csumentor.edu/admissionapp/grad_apply.asp.

California State University, San Marcos
Master of Arts in General Experimental Psychology
College of Humanities, Arts, Behavioral, & Social Sciences
333 South Twin Oaks Valley Road
San Marcos, CA 92096
Telephone: (760) 750-4102
Chairperson: Miriam Schustack

E-mail: stubiolo@csusm.edu
Web: http://www.csusm.edu/psychology/

Orientation, Objectives, and Emphasis of Department
Our Master of Arts degree is designed to accommodate students with a range of goals. The active research programs of our faculty, and our recognition of psychology as a scientific enterprise, provide graduate students with the intensive research training and coursework in primary content areas that are central to preparation for more advanced graduate work. Likewise, students who have aspirations for careers in community college teaching, community service, or business and industry, benefit from our program's emphasis on critical thinking, research methods, and advanced coursework.

Programs and Degrees Offered

Program	Degree	Application Deadline	Applications Received	Accepted	New Admits Enrolled (PT)	Total Enrolled (PT)	Degrees Awarded in 2014–2015	Median Years to Complete Degree	Dismissed/ Withdrew
General Experimental Psychology	MA/MS	February 1 (Fall)	55	18	14 (0)	25 (5)	9	2.75	0

Internships/Practica
All students take a course in the Teaching of Psychology and are individually responsible for breakout groups from the Introduction to Psychology class.

Admissions
Entries appear in the following order: required test or GPA, minimum score (if required)/median score of students entering in 2015–2016.

Program	Degree	GRE-V	GRE-Q	GRE-Writing	GRE-Subject	Under-graduate GPA	Last 2 Years GPA	Psychology GPA	Master's GPA
General Experimental Psychology	MA/MS	NA/NA	NA/NA	NA/NA	Not specified	2.5/NA	NA/NA	NA/NA	Not specified

Admissions Requirements:

Degree	GRE	GRE-Subject	Letters of Recommendation	Research Statement	Writing Sample	CV	Interview
Master's/Specialist	Required	Optional	3	Required	None	Optional	None

Please note if these criteria vary for different programs: While we do not have a cutoff, we strongly prefer candidates with GRE scores at or above the 50th percentile.

Admissions Criteria:

GRE scores—medium
Research experience—high
Work experience—low
GPA—high

Letters of recommendation—high
Statement of goals and objectives—high
Undergraduate psychology preparation—high

For additional information on admission requirements, visit http://www.csusm.edu/psychology/maprogram/index.html.

Department Demographics

	Male (PT)	Female (PT)	Total	African-American/ Black (PT)	Hispanic/ Latino (PT)	Asian/ Pacific Islander (PT)	American Indian/ Alaska Native (PT)	Caucasian/ White (PT)	Unknown	Multiethnic (PT)	ADA (PT)	Int'l (PT)
Students	9 (2)	16 (3)	30	0 (0)	11 (2)	0 (0)	0 (0)	14 (3)	0 (0)	0 (0)	0 (0)	0 (0)

Financial Information/Assistance

Tuition: For information on tuition costs, visit http://www.csusm.edu/schedule/spring_2016/fees_and_charges.html. Tuition is subject to change.

Master's:
State residents: $8,530 per academic year.
Nonstate residents: $15,226 per academic year.

Financial Assistance:

	Teaching Assistantship (% Receiving)	Teaching Assistantship Tuition Remission	Research Assistantship (% Receiving)	Research Assistantship Tuition Remission	Fellowship (% Receiving)	Fellowship Tuition Remission
First-Year Student	$4,000 (84)	NA	NA (16)	NA	NA (NA)	Partial
Advanced Student	$4,000 (80)	NA	NA (NA)	NA	NA (20)	Full

For additional information on financial assistance, visit http://www.csusm.edu/finaid/.

Employment of Department Graduates

Master's:
Enrolled in a psychology doctoral program: 3
Employed in business or industry: 2
Still seeking employment: 1
Other employment position: 1
Do not know: 2
Total: 9

Additional Information

Housing and Day Care: On-campus housing is available. See the following website for more information: http://www.csusm.edu/housing/. On-campus day care facilities are available. See the following website for more information: http://www.csusm.edu/ccf/.

Information for Students With Physical Disabilities: See the following website: http://www.csusm.edu/dss/.

Special Facilities or Resources: In addition to well-equipped classrooms and research space campus-wide, the Psychology Department offers high quality research facilities in the Social and Behavioral Sciences building, which opened in Fall 2011. This building includes a vivarium and observational and experimental research rooms designed with the research programs of our faculty and their students in mind.

Application Information: Fee: $55. *Online application:* http://www.csusm.edu/gsr/graduatestudies/future_applynow.html.

California, University of, Berkeley

Psychology Department
Letters & Sciences
3210 Tolman Hall
Berkeley, CA 94720-1650
Telephone: (510) 642-1382
Chairperson: Ann Kring

E-mail: psychgradinfo@berkeley.edu
Web: http://psychology.berkeley.edu/

Orientation, Objectives, and Emphasis of Department

The goal of the graduate program in Psychology at Berkeley is to produce scholar-researchers with sufficient breadth to retain perspective on the field of psychology and sufficient depth to permit successful independent and significant research. The members of the Department have organized themselves into six graduate training areas. These areas reflect a sense of intellectual community among the faculty and correspond, in general, with traditional designations in the field. However, each graduate training area has a distinctive stamp placed upon it by the faculty and students that make up the program. The majority of our students enter graduate training and fulfill the requirements established by the six existent training areas. These requirements vary from area to area but always involve a combination of courses, seminars, and supervised independent research. Students are also encouraged to take courses outside the Psychology Department, using the unique faculty strengths found on the Berkeley campus to enrich their graduate training.

Programs and Degrees Offered

Program	Degree	Application Deadline	Applications Received	Accepted	New Admits Enrolled (PT)	Total Enrolled (PT)	Degrees Awarded in 2014–2015	Median Years to Complete Degree	Dismissed/Withdrew
Cognition	PhD	November 21 (Fall)	20	2	1 (0)	12 (0)	0		0
Social-Personality	PhD	November 21 (Fall)	156	8	6 (0)	21 (0)	5	6	0
Developmental	PhD	November 21 (Fall)	33	4	2	9	3	5	0
Clinical Science	PhD	November 21 (Fall)	319	9	7 (0)	32 (0)	4	6	0
Behavioral and Systems Neuroscience	PhD	November 21 (Fall)	14	2	1	5 (0)	0		0
Cognitive Neuroscience	PhD	November 21 (Fall)	60	6	6	20	4	5	0

APA Accreditation

Clinical PhD: Student Outcome Data website: http://psychology.berkeley.edu/students/graduate-program/clinical-science.

Doctoral Degree (PhD Clinical Science): For those doctoral students for whom a professional internship was required in this program prior to graduation:
Total students who applied for an internship: 6
Total students who obtained an internship: 6
Total students who obtained a paid internship: 6
Total students who obtained an unpaid internship: 0
Total students who were placed in APA/CPA-accredited internships: 6
Total students placed in internships not APA/CPA-accredited, but listed with the Association of Psychology Postdoctoral and Internship Centers (APPIC): 0
Total students placed in internships conforming to guidelines of the Council of Directors of School Psychology Programs (CDSPP): 0
Total students placed in internships that were not APA/CPA-accredited, APPIC or CDSSP listed: 0

Internships/Practica

The sole practicum experience on-site is the Psychology Clinic, a pre-internship site for 2nd and 3rd year students in the Clinical Science program. A community clinic, operating on a sliding scale basis, for individuals and families in the Bay Area, the Clinic offers assessment, individual therapy, couples therapy, child/family therapy, and consultations.

Admissions

Entries appear in the following order: required test or GPA, minimum score (if required)/median score of students entering in 2015–2016.

Program	Degree	GRE-V	GRE-Q	GRE-Writing	GRE-Subject	Under-graduate GPA	Last 2 Years GPA	Psychol-ogy GPA	Master's GPA
Cognition	PhD	NA/161	NA/163	NA/4.5	Not specified	3/3.86	3/3.95	Not specified	Not specified
Social-Personality	PhD	NA/160	NA/158	NA/4.25	Not specified	3/3.83	3/4	Not specified	Not specified
Developmental	PhD	NA/168	NA/162	NA/5.5	Not specified	3/3.84	3/3.81	Not specified	Not specified
Clinical Science	PhD	NA/163	NA/159	NA/5	Not specified	3/3.77	3/3.84	Not specified	Not specified
Behavioral and Systems Neuroscience	PhD	NA/148	NA/167	NA/4	Not specified	3/3.4	3/3.45	Not specified	Not specified
Cognitive Neuroscience	PhD	Not specified	Not specified	Not specified	Not specified	Not specified	Not specified	Not specified	Not specified

Admissions Requirements:

Degree	GRE	GRE-Subject	Letters of Recom-mendation	Research Statement	Writing Sample	CV	Interview
Doctoral	Required	None	3	Required	Optional	Required	Required

Please note if these criteria vary for different programs: Clinical Science places heavier emphasis on clinical experience.

Admissions Criteria:

GRE scores—medium
Research experience—high
Work experience—medium
Clinically related public service—high
GPA—medium

Letters of recommendation—high
Interview—high
Statement of goals and objectives—high
Undergraduate psychology preparation—medium

For additional information on admission requirements, visit http://psychology.berkeley.edu/students/graduate-program/admissions.

Department Demographics

	Male (PT)	Female (PT)	Total	African-American/ Black (PT)	Hispanic/ Latino (PT)	Asian/ Pacific Islander (PT)	American Indian/ Alaska Native (PT)	Caucasian/ White (PT)	Unknown (PT)	Multiethnic (PT)	ADA (PT)	Int'l (PT)
Students	33 (0)	66 (0)	99	9 (0)	7 (0)	14 (0)	1 (0)	60 (0)	8 (0)	(0)	1 (0)	6 (0)

Financial Information/Assistance

Tuition: For information on tuition costs, visit http://registrar.berkeley.edu/current_students/registration_enrollment/feesched.html. Tuition is subject to change. Additional fees are assessed to students beyond the costs of tuition for the following: Health Insurance, Student Services, Campus, Transportation.

Doctoral:
State residents: $11,220 per academic year.
Nonstate residents: $26,322 per academic year.

Financial Assistance:

	Teaching Assistantship (% Receiving)	Teaching Assistantship Tuition Remission	Research Assistantship (% Receiving)	Research Assistantship Tuition Remission	Fellowship (% Receiving)	Fellowship Tuition Remission
First-Year Student	$21,300 (NA)	Partial	$24,000 (NA)	Full	$28,000 (NA)	Full
Advanced Student	$21,300 (NA)	Partial	$24,000 (NA)	Full	$26,000 (NA)	Full

For additional information on financial assistance, visit http://grad.berkeley.edu/financial/.

Employment of Department Graduates

No information provided.

Additional Information

Housing and Day Care: On-campus housing is available. See the following website for more information: http://housing2.berkeley.edu/graduate. On-campus day care facilities are available. See the following website for more information: http://ece.berkeley.edu/students.

Information for Students With Physical Disabilities: See the following website. http://dsp.berkeley.edu/.

Special Facilities or Resources: The Department of Psychology is housed in Tolman Hall, a building shared with the Graduate School of Education. A library devoted to books and journals in psychology and education is maintained on the second floor of this building. The main office of the Psychology Department, as well as faculty and teaching assistant offices, is on the third floor of Tolman Hall. Research rooms for carrying out a variety of studies with human subjects are on the basement, ground, fourth, and fifth floors. The basement also houses a human audition laboratory and an electronics shop. The Institute of Human Development is housed on the first floor of Tolman Hall, the Psychology Clinic on the second floor, and the Institute of Personality and Social Research on the fourth floor. The remaining research units—the Institute for Cognitive and Brain Sciences, the Field Station for the Study of Behavior, Ecology and Reproduction, the Helen Wills Neuroscience Institute, the Henry H. Wheeler Center for Brain Imaging, and the Northwest Animal Facility—are located elsewhere on campus and in the adjacent areas. The department will be moving in 2018 to a new building now under construction.

Application Information: Fee: $90. *Online application:* http://grad.berkeley.edu/admissions/apply/.

California, University of, Berkeley

School Psychology Program
Graduate School of Education
4511 Tolman Hall
Berkeley, CA 94720-1670
Telephone: (510) 642-7581
Program Director: Frank C. Worrell

E-mail: frankc@berkeley.edu
Web: http://gse.berkeley.edu/cognition-development/school-psychology

---

Orientation, Objectives, and Emphasis of Department

The school psychology program is a doctoral program within the cognition and development area. The program emphasizes the scientist-professional model of school psychological services, linking strong preparation in theory and research to applications in the professional context of schools and school systems. Through the thoughtful application of knowledge and skills, school psychologists work together with teachers and other school professionals to clarify and resolve problems regarding the educational and mental health needs of children in classrooms. Working as consultants and collaborators, school psychologists help others to accommodate the social systems of schools to the individual differences of students with the ultimate goal of promoting academic and social development. Graduate work within the program is supervised by professors from the Departments of Education and Psychology. Students fulfill all requirements for the academic PhD in human development, with additional coursework representing professional preparation for the specialty practice of school psychology. The program is accredited by APA.

Programs and Degrees Offered

Program	Degree	Application Deadline	Applications Received	Accepted	New Admits Enrolled (PT)	Total Enrolled (PT)	Degrees Awarded in 2014–2015	Median Years to Complete Degree	Dismissed/ Withdrew
School Psychology	PhD	December 1 (Fall)	48	12	5	32	4	6	2

APA Accreditation

School PhD: Student Outcome Data website: http://gse.berkeley.edu/student-admissions-outcomes-and-other-data-details.

Doctoral Degree (PhD School Psychology): For those doctoral students for whom a professional internship was required in this program prior to graduation:

Total students who applied for an internship: 9
Total students who obtained an internship: 9
Total students who obtained a paid internship: 5
Total students who obtained an unpaid internship: 4
Total students who were placed in APA/CPA-accredited internships: 0
Total students placed in internships not APA/CPA-accredited, but listed with the Association of Psychology Postdoctoral and Internship Centers (APPIC): 0
Total students placed in internships conforming to guidelines of the Council of Directors of School Psychology Programs (CDSPP): 9
Total students placed in internships that were not APA/CPA-accredited, APPIC or CDSSP listed: 0

Admissions

Entries appear in the following order: required test or GPA, minimum score (if required)/median score of students entering in 2015–2016.

Program	Degree	GRE-V	GRE-Q	GRE-Writing	GRE-Subject	Undergraduate GPA	Last 2 Years GPA	Psychology GPA	Master's GPA
School Psychology	PhD	NA/NA	NA/NA	Not specified	Not specified	NA/NA	Not specified	Not specified	Not specified

Admissions Requirements:

Degree	GRE	GRE-Subject	Letters of Recommendation	Research Statement	Writing Sample	CV	Interview
Doctoral	Required	Optional	3	Required	Optional	Optional	Required

Admissions Criteria:

GRE scores—high
Research experience—high
Work experience—medium
Clinically related public service—medium
GPA—high

Letters of recommendation—high
Interview—high
Statement of goals and objectives—high
Undergraduate psychology preparation—medium

For additional information on admission requirements, visit https://gse.berkeley.edu/admissions-application-instructions.

Department Demographics

	Male (PT)	Female (PT)	Total	African-American/ Black (PT)	Hispanic/ Latino (PT)	Asian/ Pacific Islander (PT)	American Indian/ Alaska Native (PT)	Caucasian/ White (PT)	Unknown (PT)	Multiethnic (PT)	ADA (PT)	Int'l (PT)
Students	7 (0)	25 (0)	32	4 (0)	3 (0)	6 (0)	0 (0)	17 (0)	0 (0)	2 (0)	0 (0)	2 (0)

Financial Information/Assistance

Tuition: For information on tuition costs, visit http://registrar.berkeley.edu/tuition-fees-residency/tuition-fees/fee-schedule. Tuition is subject to change.

Doctoral:
State residents: $17,357 per academic year.
Nonstate residents: $32,459 per academic year.

Financial Assistance:

	Teaching Assistantship (% Receiving)	Teaching Assistantship Tuition Remission	Research Assistantship (% Receiving)	Research Assistantship Tuition Remission	Fellowship (% Receiving)	Fellowship Tuition Remission
First-Year Student	$18,538 (NA)	Partial	$18,175 (NA)	Full	$17,600 (NA)	NA
Advanced Student	$20,512 (NA)	Partial	$20,935 (NA)	Full	$14,313 (NA)	NA

For additional information on financial assistance, visit http://gse.berkeley.edu/admissions-fees-and-financial-support.

Employment of Department Graduates

Doctoral:
Enrolled in a postdoctoral residency/fellowship: 1
Employed in a professional position in a school system: 3
Total: 4

Additional Information

Housing and Day Care: On-campus housing is available. See the following website for more information: http://housing2.berkeley.edu/graduate. On-campus day care facilities are available. See the following website for more information: http://ece.berkeley.edu/.

Information for Students With Physical Disabilities: See the following website: http://dsp.berkeley.edu.

Special Facilities or Resources: The school psychology program is based at the University of California, Berkeley, which is a major research university in a large metropolitan area of the country. Students have access to faculty research and university resources in countless topics and areas of specialization. The university and department sponsor numerous colloquia, speakers, and visiting lecturers from around the world throughout the year. Both intellectual and cultural resources abound. Ongoing research programs of faculty offer students opportunities to engage in applications of psychology to educational problems during their first three years of the program and in their dissertation research.

Application Information: Admission Office, Graduate School of Education. *Fee:* $90. *Online application:* http://grad.berkeley.edu/admissions/apply/.

California, University of, Davis (2015 data)
Department of Psychology
College of Letters and Science
1 Shields Avenue
Davis, CA 95616-8686
Telephone: (530) 752-9362
Chairperson: Paul Hastings

E-mail: klbales@ucdavis.edu
Web: http://psychology.ucdavis.edu

Orientation, Objectives, and Emphasis of Department
The department places strong emphasis on empirical research in five broad areas: (1) biological psychology (e.g., animal behavior, primatology, hormones and behavior, brain bases of social attachments, behavioral neuroscience); (2) perception, cognition, and cognitive neuroscience (e.g., memory, attention, language, consciousness); (3) personality, social psychology, and social neurosci-

ence (e.g., emotions, attitudes, prejudice, close relationships, cultural psychology, psychology of religion, brain bases of personality traits); (4) developmental psychology (cognitive, affective, and social development, personality development, effects of child abuse, brain bases of developmental disorders); and (5) quantitative psychology (e.g., psychometrics, multivariate statistics, hierarchical linear models, statistical models used in areas as diverse as neuroscience and longitudinal developmental research). Weekly colloquia in these five areas provide students with opportunities to hear about new research and present their own ideas and findings. Each student selects a three-person faculty advisory committee, which guides and evaluates the student's progress through the program. Major exams are tailored to each student by his or her advisory committee. Every faculty member has an active lab, permitting students to learn about anything from cellular recording and brain imaging to behavioral studies of development, perception, cognition, language, emotion, and both individual and social behavior, in both humans and nonhuman animals.

Programs and Degrees Offered

Program	Degree	Application Deadline	Applica-tions Received	Accepted	New Admits Enrolled (PT)	Total Enrolled (PT)	Degrees Awarded in 2014–2015	Median Years to Complete Degree	Dismissed/ Withdrew
Developmental Psychology	PhD	December 1 (Fall)	55	5	2 (0)	21 (0)	1	6.5	0
Social/ Personality Psychology	PhD	December 1 (Fall)	123	7	4 (0)	16 (0)	8	6.5	0
Quantitative Psychology	PhD	December 1 (Fall)	12	3	2	8	2	5.5	0
Biological Psychology	PhD	December 1 (Fall)	29	6	2	8	0		0
Perception, Cognition and Cognitive Neuroscience	PhD	December 1 (Fall)	109	6	1	25	2	5.5	0

Admissions

Entries appear in the following order: required test or GPA, minimum score (if required)/median score of students entering in 2015–2016.

Program	Degree	GRE-V	GRE-Q	GRE-Writing	GRE-Subject	Under-graduate GPA	Last 2 Years GPA	Psychol-ogy GPA	Master's GPA
Developmental Psychology	PhD	NA/NA	NA/NA	NA/NA	Not specified	3/NA	Not specified	Not specified	Not specified
Social/ Personality Psychology	PhD	NA/NA	NA/NA	NA/NA	Not specified	3/NA	Not specified	Not specified	Not specified
Quantitative Psychology	PhD	NA/NA	NA/NA	NA/NA	Not specified	3/NA	Not specified	Not specified	Not specified
Biological Psychology	PhD	NA/NA	NA/NA	NA/NA	Not specified	3/NA	Not specified	Not specified	Not specified
Perception, Cognition and Cognitive Neuroscience	PhD	NA/NA	NA/NA	NA/NA	Not specified	3/NA	Not specified	Not specified	Not specified

Admissions Requirements:

Degree	GRE	GRE-Subject	Letters of Recom-mendation	Research Statement	Writing Sample	CV	Interview
Doctoral	Required	Optional	3	Required	None	None	Required

Admissions Criteria:
GRE scores—high
Research experience—high
Work experience—low
GPA—high

Letters of recommendation—high
Interview—high
Statement of goals and objectives—high

For additional information on admission requirements, visit http://psychology.ucdavis.edu/graduate/?link=10.

Department Demographics

	Male (PT)	Female (PT)	Total	African-American/ Black (PT)	Hispanic/ Latino (PT)	Asian/ Pacific Islander (PT)	American Indian/ Alaska Native (PT)	Caucasian/ White (PT)	Unknown	Multiethnic (PT)	ADA (PT)	Int'l (PT)
Students	36 (0)	42 (0)	78	0 (0)	4 (0)	11 (0)	2 (0)	58 (0)	3 (0)	0 (0)	2 (0)	4 (0)

Financial Information/Assistance

Tuition: For information on tuition costs, visit http://budget.ucdavis.edu/studentfees. Tuition is subject to change.

Doctoral:
State residents: $16,540 per academic year.
Nonstate residents: $31,642 per academic year.

Financial Assistance:

	Teaching Assistantship (% Receiving)	Teaching Assistantship Tuition Remission	Research Assistantship (% Receiving)	Research Assistantship Tuition Remission	Fellowship (% Receiving)	Fellowship Tuition Remission
First-Year Student	$18,538 (NA)	Partial	$16,986 (NA)	Full	$25,000 (NA)	Full
Advanced Student	$18,538 (NA)	Partial	$18,349 (NA)	Full	$25,000 (NA)	Full

Employment of Department Graduates

Doctoral:
Enrolled in a postdoctoral residency/fellowship: 6
Employed in an academic position at a university: 4
Employed in other positions at a higher education institution: 1
Employed in government agency: 1
Still seeking employment: 1
Total: 13

Additional Information

Housing and Day Care: On-campus housing is available. See the following website for more information: http://housing.ucdavis.edu/prospective/graduate-professional-housing.asp. On-campus day care facilities are available. See the following website for more information: http://worklife-wellness.ucdavis.edu/family_care/children/childcareoptions.html.

Information for Students With Physical Disabilities: See the following website: http://sdc.ucdavis.edu/.

Special Facilities or Resources: The Psychology Department, which contains numerous state-of-the art laboratories, computer facilities, and a survey research facility, overlaps with several other major research centers on campus: California National Primate Research Center, a Center for Neuroscience, a Center for Mind and Brain, and the M.I.N.D. Institute for research on developmental disorders. Departmental faculty members participate in campus-wide graduate groups in psychology, human development, animal behavior, neuroscience, and other fields, and in a cross-university Bay Area Affective Sciences Training Program. The university includes a medical school, a veterinary school, a business school, and a law school, as well as exceptionally strong programs in all of the biological and social sciences. The Department of Psychology offers graduate students an education that is intellectually exciting, personally challenging, and very forward-looking, one that prepares new teacher-scientist-scholars to advance the study of mind, brain, and behavior.

Application Information: Graduate Program Coordinator, Psychology Department, University of California, One Shields Avenue, Davis, CA 95616-8686. *Fee:* $80. *Online application:* https://gs.ucdavis.edu/apply.

California, University of, Irvine
Psychology and Social Behavior
School of Social Ecology
4201 Social & Behavioral Sciences Gateway
Irvine, CA 92697-7085
Telephone: (949) 824-5574
Chairperson: Karen Rook

E-mail: rsilver@uci.edu
Web: http://psb.soceco.uci.edu/

Orientation, Objectives, and Emphasis of Department
The Department of Psychology and Social Behavior is united by an overarching interest in understanding the origins of human behavior as it develops across the life course and in diverse sociocultural contexts. The department has emphases in four areas (Health Psychology, Developmental Psychology, Social and Personality Psychology, and Affective Science). Our graduate program provides students with a foundation of the theories, methods, and knowledge base of these four core areas in order to understand the antecedents and developmental course of adaptive or maladaptive behavior in diverse sociocultural contexts. The multidisciplinary faculty, whose specialties include developmental, social, personality, health, psychology and law, biological, clinical, cultural, community, environmental, and ecological psychology, examines human health, well-being, and the ways in which individuals respond and adjust to changing circumstances over the lifespan. The faculty also share a strong commitment to interdisciplinary scholarship and to research that has the potential for application to important societal problems. Faculty interests include stress and coping, cognitive and biobehavioral processes in health behavior, subjective well-being, cognition and emotion, social development and developmental transitions across the lifespan, cultural influences on cognition and behavior, psychology and law, aging and health, and societal problems such as violence and disasters.

Programs and Degrees Offered

Program	Degree	Application Deadline	Applica-tions Received	Accepted	New Admits Enrolled (PT)	Total Enrolled (PT)	Degrees Awarded in 2014–2015	Median Years to Complete Degree	Dismissed/Withdrew
Psychology & Social Behavior	PhD	December 1 (Fall)	244	15	12 (0)	63 (0)	12	6	1

Internships/Practica
The school places a strong emphasis on training in conducting research that has both theoretical and practical applications. The school maintains a list of community agencies where students may seek various forms of research involvement.

Admissions
Entries appear in the following order: required test or GPA, minimum score (if required)/median score of students entering in 2015–2016.

Program	Degree	GRE-V	GRE-Q	GRE-Writing	GRE-Subject	Under-graduate GPA	Last 2 Years GPA	Psychol-ogy GPA	Master's GPA
Psychology & Social Behavior	PhD	154/163	148/161	Not specified	Not specified	3.19/3.7	Not specified	Not specified	Not specified

Admissions Requirements:

Degree	GRE	GRE-Subject	Letters of Recom-mendation	Research Statement	Writing Sample	CV	Interview
Doctoral	Required	None	3	Required	Optional	Optional	Required

Admissions Criteria:

GRE scores—high
Research experience—high
Work experience—low
GPA—high
Letters of recommendation—high

Interview—high
Statement of goals and objectives—high
Undergraduate psychology preparation—medium
Contribution to diversity—medium

For additional information on admission requirements, visit http://psb.soceco.uci.edu/pages/frequently-asked-questions.

Department Demographics

	Male (PT)	Female (PT)	Total	African-American/ Black (PT)	Hispanic/ Latino (PT)	Asian/ Pacific Islander (PT)	American Indian/ Alaska Native (PT)	Caucasian/ White (PT)	Unknown	Multiethnic (PT)	ADA (PT)	Int'l (PT)
Students	19 (0)	44 (0)	63	6 (0)	9 (0)	10 (0)	0 (0)	38 (0)	0 (0)	(0)	0 (0)	2 (0)

Financial Information/Assistance

Tuition: For information on tuition costs, visit http://www.reg.uci.edu/fees/. Tuition is subject to change.

Doctoral:
State residents: $16,495 per academic year.
Nonstate residents: $31,597 per academic year.

Financial Assistance:

	Teaching Assistantship (% Receiving)	Teaching Assistantship Tuition Remission	Research Assistantship (% Receiving)	Research Assistantship Tuition Remission	Fellowship (% Receiving)	Fellowship Tuition Remission
First-Year Student	$19,279 (94)	Full	$19,279 (NA)	Full	$25,000 (6)	Full
Advanced Student	$19,279 (60)	Full	$19,279 (16)	Full	$25,000 (24)	Full

For additional information on financial assistance, visit http://www.grad.uci.edu/funding/index.html.

Employment of Department Graduates

Doctoral:
Employed in an academic position at a university: 7
Employed in academic position at a 2-year/4-year college: 2
Employed in business or industry: 2
Employed in a hospital/medical center: 1
Total: 12

Additional Information

Housing and Day Care: On-campus housing is available. See the following website for more information: http://www.housing.uci.edu/. On-campus day care facilities are available. See the following website for more information: http://www.childcare.uci.edu/.

Information for Students With Physical Disabilities: See the following website: http://www.disability.uci.edu/.

Special Facilities or Resources: The Department maintains research facilities and equipment to support students and faculty in all aspects of their research. The Department has several laboratories equipped with observation stations, one-way mirrors, and audio-visual equipment. The rooms in these laboratories are configured to allow for observations of children, couples, families, or larger groups. Several faculty members also maintain laboratories with state-of-the-art equipment for both behavioral observation and psychophysiological assessments. The School also maintains two microcomputer laboratories, which are equipped with updated computers, laserjet and color printers, scanners, and a wide variety of software programs including SPSS (Statistical Package for the Social Sciences), SAS (Statistical Analysis System), SYSTAT, EQS, LISREL, and AMOS (structural equation modeling programs), and standard word processing, graphics, and speadsheet programs such as Microsoft Word, PowerPoint, Excel, and Corel WordPerfect. The computers are networked to the campus ethernet system to provide high-speed access to e-mail and the Internet. Graduate students and faculty are given unlimited free access to these computers, and orientation sessions offered in the fall quarter each year provide introductions to much of the statistical software available.

Application Information: Graduate Admissions, Psychology & Social Behavior, 4201 Social & Behavioral Sciences Gateway, Irvine, CA 92697-7085. *Fee:* $90. *Online application:* https://apps.grad.uci.edu/ogsa/.

California, University of, Los Angeles

Department of Psychology
Letters and Science
405 Hilgard Avenue
Los Angeles, CA 90095-1563
Telephone: (310) 825-2617
Chairperson: Gregory A. Miller

E-mail: gradadm@psych.ucla.edu
Web: http://www.psych.ucla.edu

Orientation, Objectives, and Emphasis of Department

Rigorous scientific training is the foundation of the PhD program. The graduate curriculum focuses on the usage of systematic methods of investigation to understand and quantify general principles of human behavior, pathology, cognition and emotion. More specifically, the department includes such research clusters as psychobiology and the brain; child-clinical and developmental psychology; adult psychopathology and family dynamics; cognition and memory; health, community, and political psychology; minority mental health; social cognition and intergroup relations; quantitative; and learning and behavior. In all these areas, the department's central aim is to train researchers dedicated to expanding the scientific knowledge upon which the discipline of psychology rests. This orientation also applies to the clinical program; while it offers excellent clinical training, its emphasis is on training researchers rather than private practitioners. In sum, the graduate training is designed to prepare research psychologists for careers in academic and applied settings—as college and university instructors; for leadership roles in community, government, and business organizations; and as professional research psychologists.

Programs and Degrees Offered

Program	Degree	Application Deadline	Applications Received	Accepted	New Admits Enrolled (PT)	Total Enrolled (PT)	Degrees Awarded in 2014–2015	Median Years to Complete Degree	Dismissed/ Withdrew
Behavioral Neuroscience	PhD	December 1 (Fall)	56	5	5 (0)	17 (0)	2	5	0
Clinical Psychology	PhD	December 1 (Fall)	298	13	13 (0)	69 (0)	22	6	0
Cognitive Psychology	PhD	December 1 (Fall)	100	4	4	32 (0)	4	5	0
Developmental Psychology	PhD	December 1 (Fall)	72	6	6	21 (0)	5	5	0
Learning and Behavior	PhD	December 1 (Fall)	9	2	2	7 (0)	1	5	0
Quantitative Psychology	PhD	December 1 (Fall)	22	2	1	7 (0)	1	5	0
Social Psychology	PhD	December 1 (Fall)	152	7	7	30 (0)	4	5	0
Health Psychology	PhD	December 1 (Fall)	44	3	3 (0)	16 (0)	2	5	0

APA Accreditation

Clinical PhD: Student Outcome Data website: http://www.psych.ucla.edu/graduate/prospective-students/clinical-student-data.

Doctoral Degree (PhD Clinical Psychology): For those doctoral students for whom a professional internship was required in this program prior to graduation:

Total students who applied for an internship: 8
Total students who obtained an internship: 8
Total students who obtained a paid internship: 8
Total students who obtained an unpaid internship: 0
Total students who were placed in APA/CPA-accredited internships: 8
Total students placed in internships not APA/CPA-accredited, but listed with the Association of Psychology Postdoctoral and Internship Centers (APPIC): 0
Total students placed in internships conforming to guidelines of the Council of Directors of School Psychology Programs (CDSPP): 0
Total students placed in internships that were not APA/CPA-accredited, APPIC or CDSSP listed: 0

Internships/Practica

VA Hospitals; San Fernando Valley Child Guidance Center; St. John's Child Development Center; Neuropsychiatric Institute/UCLA; UCLA Student Psych Services.

Admissions

Entries appear in the following order: required test or GPA, minimum score (if required)/median score of students entering in 2015–2016.

Program	Degree	GRE-V	GRE-Q	GRE-Writing	GRE-Subject	Under-graduate GPA	Last 2 Years GPA	Psychol-ogy GPA	Master's GPA
Behavioral Neuroscience	PhD	NA/NA	NA/NA	NA/NA	Not specified	NA/NA	Not specified	Not specified	Not specified
Clinical Psychology	PhD	NA/NA	NA/NA	NA/NA	NA/NA	NA/3.78	Not specified	Not specified	Not specified
Cognitive Psychology	PhD	NA/NA	NA/NA	NA/NA	Not specified	NA/NA	Not specified	Not specified	Not specified
Developmental Psychology	PhD	NA/NA	NA/NA	NA/NA	Not specified	NA/NA	Not specified	Not specified	Not specified
Learning and Behavior	PhD	NA/NA	NA/NA	NA/NA	Not specified	NA/NA	Not specified	Not specified	Not specified
Quantitative Psychology	PhD	NA/NA	NA/NA	NA/NA	Not specified	NA/NA	Not specified	Not specified	Not specified
Social Psychology	PhD	NA/NA	NA/NA	NA/NA	Not specified	NA/NA	Not specified	Not specified	Not specified
Health Psychology	PhD	NA/NA	NA/NA	NA/NA	Not specified	NA/NA	Not specified	Not specified	Not specified

Admissions Requirements:

Degree	GRE	GRE-Subject	Letters of Recom-mendation	Research Statement	Writing Sample	CV	Interview
Doctoral	Required	Required	3	Required	Recom-mended	Recom-mended	Required

Please note if these criteria vary for different programs: After an initial screening of applications, the areas invites selected candidates to an on-campus interview. The GRE-General test is required for all applicants. The GRE-Subject test is only required for Clinical applicants.

Admissions Criteria:

GRE scores—high
Research experience—high
Work experience—medium
Clinically related public service—medium

GPA—high
Letters of recommendation—high
Interview—high
Statement of goals and objectives—high

For additional information on admission requirements, visit https://www.psych.ucla.edu/graduate/prospective-students/application-instructions.

Department Demographics

	Male (PT)	Female (PT)	Total	African-American/ Black (PT)	Hispanic/ Latino (PT)	Asian/ Pacific Islander (PT)	American Indian/ Alaska Native (PT)	Caucasian/ White (PT)	Unknown	Multiethnic (PT)	ADA (PT)	Int'l (PT)
Students	62 (0)	137 (0)	199	5 (0)	13 (0)	30 (0)	1 (0)	135 (0)	4 (0)	11 (0)	0 (0)	4 (0)

Financial Information/Assistance

Tuition: For information on tuition costs, visit http://www.registrar.ucla.edu/fees/. Tuition is subject to change.

Doctoral:
State residents: $15,829 per academic year.
Nonstate residents: $30,931 per academic year.

Financial Assistance:

	Teaching Assistantship (% Receiving)	Teaching Assistantship Tuition Remission	Research Assistantship (% Receiving)	Research Assistantship Tuition Remission	Fellowship (% Receiving)	Fellowship Tuition Remission
First-Year Student	$19,279 (NA)	Partial	$14,179 (NA)	Partial	$21,000 (NA)	NA
Advanced Student	$21,519 (NA)	Partial	$18,117 (NA)	Partial	$20,000 (NA)	NA

For additional information on financial assistance, visit http://www.psych.ucla.edu/graduate/prospective-students/fellowships-other-support.

Employment of Department Graduates

Doctoral:
Enrolled in a postdoctoral residency/fellowship: 16
Employed in an academic position at a university: 4
Employed in business or industry: 2
Employed in government agency: 1
Do not know: 2
Total: 25

Additional Information

Housing and Day Care: On-campus housing is available. See the following website for more information: http://housing.ucla.edu. On-campus day care facilities are available. See the following website for more information: https://www.ece.ucla.edu/.

Information for Students With Physical Disabilities: See the following website: http://www.osd.ucla.edu/.

Special Facilities or Resources: The department is one of the largest on campus. Our three connected buildings (known collectively as Franz Hall) provide ample space (over 120,000 square feet) for psychological research. Laboratory facilities are of the highest quality. Precision equipment is available for electro-physiological stimulation and recording, magnetic resonance imaging (MRI), and for all major areas of sensory study. Specially designed laboratories exist for studies of group behavior and naturalistic observation. An extensive vivarium contains facilities for physiological animal studies. Computing facilities are leading-edge at all levels, from microcomputers to supercomputer clusters. The department also houses the Psychology Clinic, a training and research center for psychotherapy and diagnostics. Other resources include the Fernald Child Study Center (a research facility committed to investigating childhood behavioral disorders); the National Research Center for Asian American Mental Health; the California Self-Help Center; and the Center for Computer-Based Behavioral Studies. Departmental affiliations with the Brain Research Institute, the University Elementary School, the Neuropsychiatric Institute, and the local VA medical center also provide year-round research opportunities.

Application Information: Graduate Admissions Coordinator, Psychology Department, 405 Hilgard Avenue, 1285 Franz Hall, Los Angeles, CA 90095-1563. *Fee:* $90. *Online application:* https://app.applyyourself.com/?id=ucla-grad.

California, University of, Merced

Psychological Sciences
Social Sciences, Humanities, and Arts
5200 North Lake Road
Merced, CA 95343
Telephone: (209) 228-2252
Chairperson: Linda Cameron

E-mail: asong5@ucmerced.edu
Web: http://psychology.ucmerced.edu

Orientation, Objectives, and Emphasis of Department

UC Merced is the first research university built in the U.S. this century, and is one of the 10 campuses making up the premiere research university system of University of California. Our graduate training started in 2006, and is growing rapidly in developmental, health, and quantitative psychology. New psychology faculty are added every year. We are highly research-oriented, and do not offer any clinical training. We place priority on graduate students who desire a research career, but welcome applications from students with other aspirations as well. We employ a mentor model where a graduate student works closely with one faculty member (sometimes two) in his/her research program over the course of completing the program.

Programs and Degrees Offered

Program	Degree	Application Deadline	Applications Received	Accepted	New Admits Enrolled (PT)	Total Enrolled (PT)	Degrees Awarded in 2014–2015	Median Years to Complete Degree	Dismissed/ Withdrew
Developmental Psychology	PhD	December 15 (Fall)	19	3	2 (0)	9 (0)	2		0
Health Psychology	PhD	December 15 (Fall)	21	5	2 (0)	19 (0)	2	5	0
Quantitative Psychology	PhD	December 15 (Fall)	11	3	1 (0)	10 (0)	0		0

Admissions

Entries appear in the following order: required test or GPA, minimum score (if required)/median score of students entering in 2015–2016.

Program	Degree	GRE-V	GRE-Q	GRE-Writing	GRE-Subject	Under-graduate GPA	Last 2 Years GPA	Psychol-ogy GPA	Master's GPA
Developmental Psychology	PhD	NA/153	NA/150	NA/4	Not specified	3/3.5	Not specified	Not specified	Not specified
Health Psychology	PhD	NA/159	NA/152	NA/4.5	Not specified	3/3.7	Not specified	Not specified	Not specified
Quantitative Psychology	PhD	NA/161	NA/155	NA/4	Not specified	3/3.57	Not specified	Not specified	Not specified

Admissions Requirements:

Degree	GRE	GRE-Subject	Letters of Recom-mendation	Research Statement	Writing Sample	CV	Interview
Doctoral	Required	None	3	Required	Optional	Optional	Required

Please note if these criteria vary for different programs: Admission decisions are based on a combination of factors, including academic degrees and records, the statement of purpose, letters of recommendation, test scores, and relevant experience. We also consider the appropriateness of applicant's goals to the degree program in which you are interested and to the research interests of the program's faculty. In addition, consideration may be given to how your background and life experience would contribute significantly to an educationally beneficial blend of students.

Admissions Criteria:

GRE scores—medium

Research experience—high

Work experience—low

Clinically related public service—low

GPA—high

Letters of recommendation—medium

Interview—medium

Statement of goals and objectives—high

Undergraduate psychology preparation—low

For additional information on admission requirements, visit http://graduatedivision.ucmerced.edu/prospective-students/how-apply.

Department Demographics

	Male (PT)	Female (PT)	Total	African-American/ Black (PT)	Hispanic/ Latino (PT)	Asian/ Pacific Islander (PT)	American Indian/ Alaska Native (PT)	Caucasian/ White (PT)	Unknown	Multiethnic (PT)	ADA (PT)	Int'l (PT)
Students	14 (0)	24 (0)	38	3 (0)	4 (0)	2 (0)	1 (0)	27 (0)	0 (0)	0 (0)	0 (0)	1 (0)

Financial Information/Assistance

Tuition: Tuition is subject to change.

Doctoral:

State residents: $12,828 per academic year.

Nonstate residents: $27,930 per academic year.

Financial Assistance:

	Teaching Assistantship (% Receiving)	Teaching Assistantship Tuition Remission	Research Assistantship (% Receiving)	Research Assistantship Tuition Remission	Fellowship (% Receiving)	Fellowship Tuition Remission
First-Year Student	$18,000 (NA)	Full	$18,000 (NA)	Full	$18,000 (NA)	Full
Advanced Student	$20,000 (NA)	Full	$20,000 (NA)	Full	$20,000 (NA)	Full

For additional information on financial assistance, visit http://graduatedivision.ucmerced.edu/financial-support.

Employment of Department Graduates

Doctoral:

Enrolled in a postdoctoral residency/fellowship: 2

Employed in an academic position at a university: 1

Employed in business or industry: 2

Total: 5

Additional Information

Housing and Day Care: No on-campus housing is available. On-campus day care facilities are available. See the following website for more information: http://ecec.ucmerced.edu.

Information for Students With Physical Disabilities: See the following website: http://disabilityservices.ucmerced.edu/.

Special Facilities or Resources: We are located in a new Social Sciences and Management building, which has purpose-built psychology labs and views towards the Sierra Nevada mountains. Most students are assigned work space in this building. Relevant to those with health psychology interests is the Health Sciences Research Institute led by faculty in Public Health and Psychological Sciences.

Application Information: University of California, Merced, Attn: Graduate Division Application, 5200 N. Lake Road, Ste. KL 227, Merced, CA 95343. *Fee:* $80. *Online application:* http://graduatedivision.ucmerced.edu/node/89.

California, University of, Riverside

Department of Psychology
College of Humanties, Arts & Social Sciences
Psychology Building
Riverside, CA 92521-0426
Telephone: (951) 827-6306
Chairperson: Glenn Stanley

E-mail: ryan.lipinski@ucr.edu
Web: http://www.psych.ucr.edu

Orientation, Objectives, and Emphasis of Department

The orientation is toward theoretical and research training. Objectives are to provide the appropriate theoretical, quantitative, and methodological background to enable graduates of the program to engage in high-quality research. Additionally, training and experience in university-level teaching are provided. We also offer a minor in quantitative psychology which may be completed by any student in the PhD program in Psychology regardless of main area of interest. A concentration in health psychology is also offered in the social and developmental areas. The cognitive area has a strong concentration in cognitive modeling.

Programs and Degrees Offered

Program	Degree	Application Deadline	Applica-tions Received	Accepted	New Admits Enrolled (PT)	Total Enrolled (PT)	Degrees Awarded in 2014–2015	Median Years to Complete Degree	Dismissed/ Withdrew
Cognitive Psychology	PhD	December 1 (Fall)	23	4	4	20 (0)	0		0
Developmental Psychology	PhD	December 1 (Fall)	42	4	3	28 (0)	6	5	0
Social/ Personality Psychology	PhD	December 1 (Fall)	61	15	10	31 (0)	5	5	0
Systems Neuroscience	PhD	December 1 (Fall)	5	0	0	5 (0)	2	5	0

Admissions

Entries appear in the following order: required test or GPA, minimum score (if required)/median score of students entering in 2015–2016.

Program	Degree	GRE-V	GRE-Q	GRE-Writing	GRE-Subject	Under-graduate GPA	Last 2 Years GPA	Psychol-ogy GPA	Master's GPA
Cognitive Psychology	PhD	NA/NA	NA/NA	Not specified	Not specified	Not specified	NA/NA	Not specified	Not specified
Developmental Psychology	PhD	NA/NA	NA/NA	Not specified	Not specified	Not specified	NA/NA	Not specified	Not specified
Social/ Personality Psychology	PhD	NA/NA	NA/NA	Not specified	Not specified	Not specified	NA/NA	Not specified	Not specified
Systems Neuroscience	PhD	NA/NA	NA/NA	Not specified	Not specified	Not specified	NA/NA	Not specified	Not specified

Admissions Requirements:

Degree	GRE	GRE-Subject	Letters of Recom-mendation	Research Statement	Writing Sample	CV	Interview
Doctoral	Required	None	3	Required	Optional	Required	Required

Admissions Criteria:

GRE scores—medium
Research experience—high
Work experience—low
GPA—medium

Letters of recommendation—high
Interview—medium
Statement of goals and objectives—high
Undergraduate psychology preparation—medium

For additional information on admission requirements, visit http://www.psych.ucr.edu/grad/admissions.html.

Department Demographics

	Male (PT)	Female (PT)	Total	African-American/ Black (PT)	Hispanic/ Latino (PT)	Asian/ Pacific Islander (PT)	American Indian/ Alaska Native (PT)	Caucasian/ White (PT)	Unknown (PT)	Multiethnic (PT)	ADA (PT)	Int'l (PT)
Students	30 (0)	54 (0)	84	6 (0)	9 (0)	11 (0)	1 (0)	57 (0)	0 (0)	0 (0)	0 (0)	0 (0)

Financial Information/Assistance

Tuition: For information on tuition costs, visit http://registrar.ucr.edu/registrar/tuition-and-fees/index.html. Tuition is subject to change.

Doctoral:
State residents: $15,180 per academic year.
Nonstate residents: $39,888 per academic year.

Financial Assistance:

	Teaching Assistantship (% Receiving)	Teaching Assistantship Tuition Remission	Research Assistantship (% Receiving)	Research Assistantship Tuition Remission	Fellowship (% Receiving)	Fellowship Tuition Remission
First-Year Student	$17,427 (NA)	Full	$17,427 (NA)	Full	$17,000 (NA)	Full
Advanced Student	$17,427 (NA)	Full	$17,427 (NA)	Full	NA (NA)	NA

For additional information on financial assistance, visit http://www.psych.ucr.edu/grad/admissions.html.

Employment of Department Graduates

Doctoral:
Enrolled in a postdoctoral residency/fellowship: 2
Employed in an academic position at a university: 2
Employed in academic position at a 2-year/4-year college: 3
Employed in government agency: 1
Do not know: 1
Total: 9

Additional Information

Housing and Day Care: On-campus housing is available. See the following website for more information: http://housing.ucr.edu/. On-campus day care facilities are available. See the following website for more information: http://cdc.ucr.edu.

Information for Students With Physical Disabilities: See the following website: http://specialservices.ucr.edu/.

Special Facilities or Resources: The Psychology Department has recently moved into a new building built specifically for the department. The department has equipment and support systems to help students conduct research in all aspects of behavior. The neuroscience laboratories are equipped with the latest instrumentation for hormonal assays, extracellular and intracellular electrophysiology, and microscopic analysis of neuronal morphology. Research in the cognitive area incorporates computer-assisted experimental control for most any kind of reaction time experiment and has facilities for video and speech digitization and infrared eye-tracking. The developmental faculty have laboratory facilities to study parents and children, have access to the campus daycare center for studies that involve toddlers and preschool children, and have been very successful in conducting research in a culturally diverse local school system. The developmental faculty all participate in the Center for Family Studies, an interdisciplinary center. The social/personality psychology labs support research in social perception, nonverbal communication, health psychology, emotional expression, and attribution processes using audiovisual laboratories and observation rooms. Direct, free access is available to PsycINFO, PubMed, and many other online journals and databases.

Application Information: Graduate Admissions, Psychology Department, University of California, Riverside, Riverside, CA 92521. *Fee:* $80. *Online application:* http://graduate.ucr.edu/grad_admissions.html.

California, University of, San Diego

Department of Psychology
9500 Gilman Drive #0109
La Jolla, CA 92093-0109
Telephone: (858) 534-4416
Chairperson: Victor S. Ferreira

E-mail: psycphdinfo@ucsd.edu
Web: http://psychology.ucsd.edu/

Orientation, Objectives, and Emphasis of Department

The Department of Psychology at the University of California, San Diego provides advanced training in research in most aspects of experimental psychology. Modern laboratories and an attractive physical setting combine with a distinguished faculty, both within the Department of Psychology and in supporting disciplines, to provide research opportunities and training at the frontiers of psychological science. The graduate training program emphasizes and supports individual research, starting with the first year of study.

Programs and Degrees Offered

Program	Degree	Application Deadline	Applications Received	Accepted	New Admits Enrolled (PT)	Total Enrolled (PT)	Degrees Awarded In 2014–2015	Median Years to Complete Degree	Dismissed/Withdrew
Experimental Psychology	PhD	December 3 (Fall)	268	17	9 (0)	50 (0)	13	5.33	5

Admissions

Entries appear in the following order: required test or GPA, minimum score (if required)/median score of students entering in 2015–2016.

Program	Degree	GRE-V	GRE-Q	GRE-Writing	GRE-Subject	Undergraduate GPA	Last 2 Years GPA	Psychology GPA	Master's GPA
Experimental Psychology	PhD	NA/NA	NA/NA	Not specified	Not specified	NA/3.6	Not specified	Not specified	Not specified

Admissions Requirements:

Degree	GRE	GRE-Subject	Letters of Recommendation	Research Statement	Writing Sample	CV	Interview
Doctoral	Required	None	3	Required	Optional	Required	Required

Admissions Criteria:

GRE scores—high
Research experience—high
Work experience—medium
Clinically related public service—low
GPA—high

Letters of recommendation—high
Interview—high
Statement of goals and objectives—high
Undergraduate psychology preparation—medium

For additional information on admission requirements, visit http://psychology.ucsd.edu/graduate-program/prospective-students/admissions.html.

Department Demographics

	Male (PT)	Female (PT)	Total	African-American/ Black (PT)	Hispanic/ Latino (PT)	Asian/ Pacific Islander (PT)	American Indian/ Alaska Native (PT)	Caucasian/ White (PT)	Unknown	Multiethnic (PT)	ADA (PT)	Int'l (PT)
Students	31 (0)	19 (0)	50	0 (0)	1 (0)	11 (0)	1 (0)	34 (0)	3 (0)	0 (0)	2 (0)	5 (0)

Financial Information/Assistance

Tuition: For information on tuition costs, visit http://grad.ucsd.edu/financial/graduate-tuition-fees.html. Tuition is subject to change.

Doctoral:
State residents: $16,434 per academic year.
Nonstate residents: $31,536 per academic year.

Financial Assistance:

	Teaching Assistantship (% Receiving)	Teaching Assistantship Tuition Remission	Research Assistantship (% Receiving)	Research Assistantship Tuition Remission	Fellowship (% Receiving)	Fellowship Tuition Remission
First-Year Student	$14,506 (100)	Full	NA (NA)	NA	$8,993 (100)	NA
Advanced Student	$19,586 (100)	Full	NA (NA)	NA	$3,913 (100)	NA

For additional information on financial assistance, visit http://psychology.ucsd.edu/graduate-program/prospective-students/financial-support.html.

Employment of Department Graduates

Doctoral:
Enrolled in a postdoctoral residency/fellowship: 2
Employed in business or industry: 5
Not seeking employment: 1
Total: 8

Additional Information

Housing and Day Care: On-campus housing is available. See the following website for more information: http://hdh.ucsd.edu/arch/. On-campus day care facilities are available. See the following website for more information: http://child.ucsd.edu/programs/ecec/index.html.

Information for Students With Physical Disabilities: See the following website: http://disabilities.ucsd.edu.

Special Facilities or Resources: The Department shares research space and facilities with the Center for Brain and Cognition. Within the joint facilities, there are two computing facilities, a computational laboratory, visual and auditory laboratories, social psychology laboratories, cognitive laboratories, developmental laboratories, a clinic for autistic children, animal facilities, and extensive contacts with hospitals, industry, and the legal system. In addition to the numerous impressive libraries on campus, the Department also keeps a large selection of literature within our Mandler Library. Collaborative research is carried out with members of the Departments of Linguistics, Cognitive Science, Computer Science and Engineering, Sociology, Music, Ophthalmology, Neurosciences, members of the UCSD School of Medicine, Scripps Clinic and Research Foundation, and with the Salk Institute for Biological Studies and the Neurosciences Institute. The Scripps Institution of Oceanography, located on campus, provides facilities in neuroscience, as does the School of Medicine.

Application Information: Graduate Admission, Dept. of Psychology-0109, University of California-San Diego, La Jolla, CA 92093. *Fee:* $90. *Online application:* https://apply.grad.ucsd.edu/home.

California, University of, Santa Barbara

Counseling, Clinical, and School Psychology
Gevirtz Graduate School of Education
Santa Barbara, CA 93106-9490
Telephone: (805) 893-3375
Chairperson: Shane Jimerson

E-mail: ccspapp@education.ucsb.edu
Web: http://education.ucsb.edu/ccsp

Orientation, Objectives, and Emphasis of Department

The mission of the Department of Counseling, Clinical, and School Psychology is to generate and disseminate knowledge, provide expertise, and prepare the next generation of diverse scholars in applied psychology. The department strives to be recognized for excellence and innovation in research that fosters the psychological well-being and social equity of all people, especially vulnerable populations.

Programs and Degrees Offered

Program	Degree	Application Deadline	Applica-tions Received	Accepted	New Admits Enrolled (PT)	Total Enrolled (PT)	Degrees Awarded in 2014–2015	Median Years to Complete Degree	Dismissed/ Withdrew
Counseling/ Clinical/School	PhD	November 15 (Fall)	259	14	12 (0)	80 (0)	6	5	0

APA Accreditation

Combination PhD: Student Outcome Data website: http://education.ucsb.edu/ccsp/prospective-students.

Doctoral Degree (PhD Counseling/Clinical/School): For those doctoral students for whom a professional internship was required in this program prior to graduation:
Total students who applied for an internship: 18
Total students who obtained an internship: 15
Total students who obtained a paid internship: 15
Total students who obtained an unpaid internship: 0
Total students who were placed in APA/CPA-accredited internships: 15
Total students placed in internships not APA/CPA-accredited, but listed with the Association of Psychology Postdoctoral and Internship Centers (APPIC): 0
Total students placed in internships conforming to guidelines of the Council of Directors of School Psychology Programs (CDSPP): 0
Total students placed in internships that were not APA/CPA-accredited, APPIC or CDSSP listed: 0

Internships/Practica

During their first years in the program, students receive practicum experience in the Hosford Counseling and Psychological Services Clinic on campus, a sliding scale agency which serves adults, children, and families from the community. Advanced students receive experience as supervisors in the clinic. Students in the clinical emphasis have external practica in community-based settings, including an agency that serves families and children exposed to violence, a local hospital, and programs associated with county alcohol, drug and mental health services. Students in the counseling emphasis have external practica at UCSB's Counseling and Career Services centers. Students in the school emphasis have external practica in the schools. All doctoral students apply for predoctoral internships at APA-accredited sites across the country and participate in the APPIC match.

Admissions

Entries appear in the following order: required test or GPA, minimum score (if required)/median score of students entering in 2015–2016.

Program	Degree	GRE-V	GRE-Q	GRE-Writing	GRE-Subject	Under-graduate GPA	Last 2 Years GPA	Psychol-ogy GPA	Master's GPA
Counseling/ Clinical/School	PhD	NA/NA	NA/NA	NA/NA	Not specified	3/NA	Not specified	Not specified	Not specified

Admissions Requirements:

Degree	GRE	GRE-Subject	Letters of Recommendation	Research Statement	Writing Sample	CV	Interview
Doctoral	Required	Optional	3	Required	Required	Required	Required

Admissions Criteria:

GRE scores—medium
Research experience—high
Work experience—medium
Clinically related public service—medium
GPA—medium

Letters of recommendation—medium
Interview—high
Statement of goals and objectives—high
Undergraduate psychology preparation—low

For additional information on admission requirements, visit http://education.ucsb.edu/ccsp/prospective-students/how-apply.

Department Demographics

	Male (PT)	Female (PT)	Total	African-American/ Black (PT)	Hispanic/ Latino (PT)	Asian/ Pacific Islander (PT)	American Indian/ Alaska Native (PT)	Caucasian/ White (PT)	Unknown	Multiethnic (PT)	ADA (PT)	Int'l (PT)
Students	13 (0)	67 (0)	80	1 (0)	14 (0)	7 (0)	0 (0)	46 (0)	8 (0)	4 (0)	1 (0)	2 (0)

Financial Information/Assistance

Tuition: For information on tuition costs, visit http://registrar.sa.ucsb.edu/feechart.aspx. Tuition is subject to change.

Doctoral:
State residents: $13,193 per academic year.
Nonstate residents: $28,295 per academic year.

Financial Assistance:

	Teaching Assistantship (% Receiving)	Teaching Assistantship Tuition Remission	Research Assistantship (% Receiving)	Research Assistantship Tuition Remission	Fellowship (% Receiving)	Fellowship Tuition Remission
First-Year Student	$13,000 (NA)	Partial	$9,000 (NA)	Full	NA (NA)	Full
Advanced Student	$13,000 (NA)	Full	$9,000 (NA)	Full	$5,500 (NA)	Full

For additional information on financial assistance, visit http://education.ucsb.edu/ccsp/prospective-students/financial-assistance.

Employment of Department Graduates

Doctoral:
Enrolled in a postdoctoral residency/fellowship: 2
Employed in independent practice: 2
Employed in an academic position at a university: 1
Employed in other positions at a higher education institution: 1
Employed in a professional position in a school system: 1
Employed in a hospital/medical center: 1
Do not know: 5
Total: 13

Additional Information

Housing and Day Care: On-campus housing is available. See the following website for more information: http://www.housing.ucsb. edu/. On-campus day care facilities are available. See the following website for more information: http://childrenscenter.sa.ucsb.edu/.

Information for Students With Physical Disabilities: See the following website: http://dsp.sa.ucsb.edu/.

Special Facilities or Resources: The UCSB Combined Psychology program houses several training clinics: the Hosford Clinic serves community clients and is equipped with state-of-the-art equipment for recording, reviewing, editing, and live monitoring of assessment and counseling sessions; the Psychology Assessment Center provides psychological assessment services for the measurement of disorders that affect psychological, emotional, academic, and occupational functioning; and the Koegel Autism Center provides training in evidence-based practices for children with an autism spectrum disorder. Faculty have research labs in their areas of interest.

Application Information: Fee: $90. Online application: https://www.graddiv.ucsb.edu/eapp/.

California, University of, Santa Cruz

Psychology Department
273 Social Sciences 2
Santa Cruz, CA 95064
Telephone: (831) 459-4932
Chairperson: Campbell Leaper

E-mail: jhoward2@ucsc.edu
Web: http://psychology.ucsc.edu/

Orientation, Objectives, and Emphasis of Department

The Psychology Department at UC Santa Cruz offers a PhD degree with areas of specialization in cognitive, developmental, and social psychology. The program does not offer courses, training, or supervision in counseling or clinical psychology. Students are prepared for research, teaching, and administrative positions in colleges and universities, as well as positions in schools, government, and other public and private organizations. The PhD is a research degree. Students are required to demonstrate the ability to carry through to completion rigorous empirical research and to be active in research throughout their graduate career. Course requirements establish a foundation for critical evaluation of research literature and the design of conceptually important empirical research. To support students in achieving these goals, each student must be associated with one of the faculty, who serves as academic advisor and research sponsor.

Programs and Degrees Offered

Program	Degree	Application Deadline	Applications Received	Accepted	New Admits Enrolled (PT)	Total Enrolled (PT)	Degrees Awarded in 2014–2015	Median Years to Complete Degree	Dismissed/ Withdrew
Developmental Psychology	PhD	December 15 (Fall)	38	7	2	17	3	6.5	0
Social Psychology	PhD	December 15 (Fall)	106	6	4	21	?	6.6	0
Cognitive Psychology	PhD	December 15 (Fall)	51	8	5	21	4	5.5	2

Admissions

Entries appear in the following order: required test or GPA, minimum score (if required)/median score of students entering in 2015–2016.

Program	Degree	GRE-V	GRE-Q	GRE-Writing	GRE-Subject	Undergraduate GPA	Last 2 Years GPA	Psychology GPA	Master's GPA
Developmental Psychology	PhD	NA/158	NA/154	NA/4.4	Not specified	NA/3.65	Not specified	Not specified	Not specified
Social Psychology	PhD	NA/162	NA/158	NA/4.7	Not specified	NA/3.51	Not specified	Not specified	Not specified
Cognitive Psychology	PhD	NA/161	NA/159	NA/4	Not specified	NA/3.11	Not specified	Not specified	Not specified

Admissions Requirements:

Degree	GRE	GRE-Subject	Letters of Recommendation	Research Statement	Writing Sample	CV	Interview
Doctoral	Required	None	3	Required	None	Required	None

Admissions Criteria:

GRE scores—high
Research experience—high
Work experience—medium
GPA—high

Letters of recommendation—high
Statement of goals and objectives—high
Undergraduate psychology preparation—medium

For additional information on admission requirements, visit http://psychology.ucsc.edu/graduate/admission/index.html.

Department Demographics

	Male (PT)	Female (PT)	Total	African-American/ Black (PT)	Hispanic/ Latino (PT)	Asian/ Pacific Islander (PT)	American Indian/ Alaska Native (PT)	Caucasian/ White (PT)	Unknown	Multiethnic (PT)	ADA (PT)	Int'l (PT)
Students	19 (0)	46 (0)	65	7 (0)	9 (0)	7 (0)	2 (0)	27 (0)	5 (0)	8 (0)	0 (0)	0 (0)

Financial Information/Assistance

Tuition: For information on tuition costs, visit http://registrar.ucsc.edu/fees/registration/. Tuition is subject to change.

Doctoral:
State residents: $17,250 per academic year.
Nonstate residents: $32,352 per academic year.

Financial Assistance:

	Teaching Assistantship (% Receiving)	Teaching Assistantship Tuition Remission	Research Assistantship (% Receiving)	Research Assistantship Tuition Remission	Fellowship (% Receiving)	Fellowship Tuition Remission
First-Year Student	NA (NA)	Partial	NA (NA)	Full	NA (NA)	Full
Advanced Student	NA (NA)	Partial	NA (NA)	Full	NA (NA)	NA

For additional information on financial assistance, visit http://graddiv.ucsc.edu/financial-aid/.

Employment of Department Graduates

Doctoral:
Employed in an academic position at a university: 4
Total: 4

Additional Information

Housing and Day Care: On-campus housing is available. See the following website for more information: http://housing.ucsc.edu/gradhousing/index.html. On-campus day care facilities are available. See the following website for more information: http://childcare.ucsc.edu/index.html.

Information for Students With Physical Disabilities: See the following website: http://drc.ucsc.edu/.

Special Facilities or Resources: The department provides training to prepare the student for careers in academic and applied settings. Graduate students have the use of a variety of research facilities, including a number of computer-controlled experimental laboratories. Electronic equipment is available to allow the generation of sophisticated written and pictorial vision displays, musical sequences, and synthesized and visual speech patterns. There are observational facilities for developmental psychological research and a discourse analysis lab. A bilingual survey unit is under development which will utilize public opinion survey technology to study significant public policy, legal, and political issues that are critical to California's emerging majority population. Research opportunities exist with diverse sample groups in both laboratory and natural settings. The department has collaborative relationships with the National Center for Research on Cultural Diversity, Second Language Learning, and the Bilingual Research Center.

Application Information: UC Santa Cruz, Graduate Application Processing, 1156 High Street, Santa Cruz, CA 95064. *Fee:* $90. *Online application:* https://gradapp.ucsc.edu/.

Claremont Graduate University
Graduate Department of Psychology
Division of Behavioral and Organizational Sciences
123 East Eighth Street
Claremont, CA 91711-3955
Telephone: (909) 621-8084
Dean: Stewart I. Donaldson

E-mail: Stewart.Donaldson@cgu.edu
Web: http://www.cgu.edu/pages/154.asp

Orientation, Objectives, and Emphasis of Department
The program emphasizes contemporary human problems and social issues, and the organizations and systems involved in such issues, as well as on basic substantive research in social, organizational, developmental, and cognitive psychology and health behavior. Unusual specialty opportunities are available in positive psychology, organizational behavior, applied cognitive psychology, applied social psychology, health psychology, and program evaluation. The program offers preparation for careers in public service and business and industry as well as teaching and research. Research, theory, and practice are stressed in such policy and program areas as organizations and work; human social and physical environments; social service systems; psychological effects of educational computer technology; health and mental health systems; crime, delinquency, and law; and aging and life span education. Many opportunities are available for research, consulting, and field experiences in these and related areas. Strong emphasis is given to training in a broad range of research methodologies, from naturalistic observation to experimental design, with special attention to field research methods. Seminars, tutorials, independent research, individualized student program plans, practical field experience, and close advisory and collaborative relations with the faculty are designed to foster clarifications of individual goals, intellectual and professional growth, self-pacing, and attractive career opportunities.

Programs and Degrees Offered

Program	Degree	Application Deadline	Applications Received	Accepted	New Admits Enrolled (PT)	Total Enrolled (PT)	Degrees Awarded in 2014–2015	Median Years to Complete Degree	Dismissed/ Withdrew
Applied Social Psych/ Evaluation Co-Concentration	MA/MS	February 1 (Fall)	11	5	1	3 (7)	8	2	0
Cognitive Psychology/ Evaluation Co-Concentration	MA/MS	February 1 (Fall)	6	1	1	3 (1)	2	2	0
Organizational/ Evaluation Co-Concentration	MA/MS	February 1 (Fall)	34	26	9 (0)	12 (7)	7	2	0
Human Resources Design	MA/MS	February 1 (Fall)	10		5 (3)	10 (11)	21	2	0
Applied Cognitive Psychology	PhD	February 1 (Fall)	20	10	5	22 (6)	1	7	0

Programs and Degrees Offered (con't.)

Program	Degree	Application Deadline	Applica-tions Received	Accepted	New Admits Enrolled (PT)	Total Enrolled (PT)	Degrees Awarded in 2014–2015	Median Years to Complete Degree	Dismissed/ Withdrew
Applied Social Psychology	PhD	February 1 (Fall)	40	18	10 (1)	55 (18)	4	7	0
Evaluation and Applied Research Methods	PhD	February 1 (Fall)	14	7	2 (1)	15 (7)	2	7	0
Organizational Behavior	PhD	February 1 (Fall)	29	3	1 (1)	16 (8)	4	7	0
Health Behavior Research/ Evaluation	MA/MS	February 1 (Fall)	12	5	0 (0)	1 (0)	4	2	0
Positive Developmental Psychology	PhD	February 1 (Fall)	37	8	5	27 (15)	1		
Positive Organizational Psychology	PhD	February 1 (Fall)	39	9	5 (0)	12 (10)	0		
Positive Developmental Psych/ Evaluation Co-Concentration	MA/MS	February 1 (Fall)	21	15	4 (0)	7 (2)	11	2	
Positive Organizational Psych/ Evaluation Co-Concentration	MA/MS	February 1 (Fall)	35	25	8 (0)	13 (10)	9	2	
Health Evaluation	MA/MS	February 1 (Fall)							
Positive Health Psychology	MA/MS	February 1 (Fall)							
Educational Evaluation	MA/MS	February 1 (Fall)	4	1	1	0	0		

Internships/Practica

Research and consulting internships are available and encouraged for all students. Appropriate settings and roles are arranged according to the interests of individual students within the wide range of opportunities available in a large urban area. Typical settings include social service agencies; business and industrial organizations; hospitals, clinics, and mental health agencies; schools; governmental and regulatory agencies; and nonacademic research institutions, as well as numerous onsite research institutes.

Admissions

Entries appear in the following order: required test or GPA, minimum score (if required)/median score of students entering in 2015–2016.

Program	Degree	GRE-V	GRE-Q	GRE-Writing	GRE-Subject	Under-graduate GPA	Last 2 Years GPA	Psychol-ogy GPA	Master's GPA
Applied Social Psych/ Evaluation Co-Concentration	MA/MS	NA/NA	NA/NA	NA/NA	Not specified	NA/NA	Not specified	Not specified	Not specified

Admissions *(con't.)*

Program	Degree	GRE-V	GRE-Q	GRE-Writing	GRE-Subject	Under-graduate GPA	Last 2 Years GPA	Psychol-ogy GPA	Master's GPA
Cognitive Psychology/ Evaluation Co-Concentration	MA/MS	NA/NA	NA/NA	NA/NA	Not specified	NA/NA	Not specified	Not specified	Not specified
Organizational/ Evaluation Co-Concentration	MA/MS	NA/NA	NA/NA	NA/NA	Not specified	NA/NA	Not specified	Not specified	Not specified
Human Resources Design	MA/MS	NA/NA	NA/NA	Not specified	Not specified	Not specified	Not specified	Not specified	Not specified
Applied Cognitive Psychology	PhD	NA/NA	NA/NA	NA/NA	Not specified	NA/NA	Not specified	Not specified	Not specified
Applied Social Psychology	PhD	NA/NA	NA/NA	NA/NA	Not specified	NA/NA	Not specified	Not specified	Not specified
Evaluation and Applied Research Methods	PhD	NA/NA	NA/NA	NA/NA	Not specified	NA/NA	Not specified	Not specified	Not specified
Organizational Behavior	PhD	NA/NA	NA/NA	NA/NA	Not specified	NA/NA	Not specified	Not specified	Not specified
Health Behavior Research/ Evaluation	MA/MS	NA/NA	NA/NA	NA/NA	Not specified	NA/NA	Not specified	Not specified	Not specified
Positive Developmental Psychology	PhD	NA/NA	NA/NA	NA/NA	Not specified	NA/NA	Not specified	Not specified	Not specified
Positive Organizational Psychology	PhD	NA/NA	NA/NA	NA/NA	Not specified	NA/NA	Not specified	Not specified	Not specified
Positive Developmental Psych/ Evaluation Co-Concentration	MA/MS	NA/NA	NA/NA	NA/NA	Not specified	NA/NA	Not specified	Not specified	Not specified
Positive Organizational Psych/ Evaluation Co-Concentration	MA/MS	NA/NA	NA/NA	NA/NA	Not specified	NA/NA	Not specified	Not specified	Not specified
Health Evaluation	MA/MS	Not specified	Not specified	Not specified	Not specified	Not specified	Not specified	Not specified	Not specified
Positive Health Psychology	MA/MS	Not specified	Not specified	Not specified	Not specified	Not specified	Not specified	Not specified	Not specified
Educational Evaluation	MA/MS	Not specified	Not specified	Not specified	Not specified	Not specified	Not specified	Not specified	Not specified

Admissions Requirements:

Degree	GRE	GRE-Subject	Letters of Recommendation	Research Statement	Writing Sample	CV	Interview
Master's/Specialist	Required	None	3	Required	Optional	Required	None
Doctoral	Required	None	3	Required	Optional	Required	None

Please note if these criteria vary for different programs: HRD program does not require research experience but emphasizes work experience more strongly.

Admissions Criteria:

GRE scores—high
Research experience—medium
Work experience—medium
GPA—high

Letters of recommendation—high
Statement of goals and objectives—high
Undergraduate psychology preparation—medium

Department Demographics

	Male (PT)	Female (PT)	Total	African-American/ Black (PT)	Hispanic/ Latino (PT)	Asian/ Pacific Islander (PT)	American Indian/ Alaska Native (PT)	Caucasian/ White (PT)	Unknown	Multiethnic (PT)	ADA (PT)	Int'l (PT)
Students	83 (36)	136 (78)	333	13 (4)	17 (13)	21 (6)	2 (1)	105 (59)	25 (10)	7 (10)	3 (0)	25 (10)

Financial Information/Assistance

Tuition: For information on tuition costs, visit http://www.cgu.edu/pages/312.asp. Tuition is subject to change.

Doctoral:
State residents: $48,022 per academic year.
State residents: $1,847 per credit hour.
Nonstate residents: $48,022 per academic year.
Nonstate residents: $1,847 per credit hour.

Master's:
State residents: $48,022 per academic year.
State residents: $1,847 per credit hour.
Nonstate residents: $48,022 per academic year.
Nonstate residents: $1,847 per credit hour.

Financial Assistance:

	Teaching Assistantship (% Receiving)	Teaching Assistantship Tuition Remission	Research Assistantship (% Receiving)	Research Assistantship Tuition Remission	Fellowship (% Receiving)	Fellowship Tuition Remission
First-Year Student	$5,600 (NA)	NA	NA (NA)	NA	$8,761 (NA)	Partial
Advanced Student	$5,600 (NA)	NA	$5,200 (NA)	NA	$8,761 (NA)	Partial

For additional information on financial assistance, visit http://www.cgu.edu/pages/1003.asp.

Employment of Department Graduates

Master's:
Enrolled in another graduate/professional program: 1
Employed in an academic position at a university: 1
Employed in academic position at a 2-year/4-year college: 1
Employed in other positions at a higher education institution: 1
Employed in a professional position in a school system: 2
Employed in business or industry: 3

Doctoral:
Enrolled in a postdoctoral residency/fellowship: 4
Employed in an academic position at a university: 2
Employed in academic position at a 2-year/4-year college: 5
Employed in other positions at a higher education institution: 2
Employed in a professional position in a school system: 1
Employed in business or industry: 4

Employed in a community mental health/counseling center: 2
Employed in a hospital/medical center: 1
Other employment position: 1
Total: 13

Employed in a community mental health/counseling center: 2
Employed in a hospital/medical center: 2
Other employment position: 3
Total: 25

Additional Information

Housing and Day Care: On-campus housing is available. See the following website for more information: http://www.cgu.edu/pages/1156.asp. No on-campus day care facilities are available.

Information for Students With Physical Disabilities: See the following website: http://cgu.edu/pages/1154.asp.

Special Facilities or Resources: The school is equipped with labs for social, developmental, identity, health, positive psychology, and cognitive research, supplies and equipment for field research, a student lounge, and department library. The computer facilities are excellent, conveniently located, and include a wide variety of application programs. The department cooperates in overseeing research institutes for student-faculty grant or contract research, focusing on major problems of organizational and program evaluation research as well as research on social issues. Claremont Graduate University is a free-standing graduate institution within the context of the Claremont University Consortium of five colleges, the Graduate University, and the Keck Graduate Institute. This context allows the department to concentrate exclusively on graduate education in a relaxed, intimate context while enjoying the resources of a major university. In addition to the full-time graduate psychology faculty, there are more than 40 full-time faculty members from the undergraduate Claremont Colleges who participate in the graduate program and who are available to students for research, advising, and instruction. Resources from other programs within the Graduate University are also available to psychology students, in such areas as public policy, education, information sciences, business administration, executive management, economics, and government.

Application Information: Admissions Office, McManus Hall 131, Claremont Graduate University, Claremont, CA 91711. *Fee:* $70. *Online application:* http://app.applyyourself.com/?id=cgu.

Fielding Graduate University
School of Psychology
2020 de La Vina Street
Santa Barbara, CA 93105
Telephone: (800) 340-1099
Provost and Senior Vice President: Gerald Porter, PhD

E-mail: psyadmissions@fielding.edu
Web: http://www.fielding.edu/programs/psychology

Orientation, Objectives, and Emphasis of Department
Fielding Graduate University's School of Psychology enables adults to earn the PhD in clinical or media psychology as well as a postdoctoral certificate in neuropsychology or respecialization in clinical psychology. Our students bring a sense of autonomy, extensive personal and professional experience to their studies. The programs' scholar–practitioner model accommodates the special characteristics of adult students. Through coursework, seminars, face-to-face instruction and guided study, the adult learner pursues study while remaining in their community. Students in the PhD in clinical psychology and respecialization programs may choose among five concentrations: neuropsychology, forensic psychology, health psychology, violence prevention and control, and parent-infant mental health.

Programs and Degrees Offered

Program	Degree	Application Deadline	Applications Received	Accepted	New Admits Enrolled (PT)	Total Enrolled (PT)	Degrees Awarded in 2014–2015	Median Years to Complete Degree	Dismissed/Withdrew
Clinical Psychology	Respecialization Diploma	January 24 (Fall)	5	2	2 (0)	13 (0)	1	4.94	0
Clinical Psychology	PhD	January 15 (Fall)	253	95	71 (0)	415 (0)	40	8.62	23

Programs and Degrees Offered *(con't.)*

Program	Degree	Application Deadline	Applications Received	Accepted	New Admits Enrolled (PT)	Total Enrolled (PT)	Degrees Awarded in 2014–2015	Median Years to Complete Degree	Dismissed/Withdrew
Media Psychology	PhD	August 1 (Fall), November 1 (Spring), March 1 (Summer)	24	24	18 (0)	92 (0)	13	6.66	7
Postdoctoral Certificate in Neuro-psychology	Other	August 1 (Fall)	29	28	0 (19)	0 (58)	8	1.94	1
Media Psychology	MA/MS	August 15 (Fall), December 1 (Spring), April 1 (Summer)	39	37	24 (6)	41 (24)	12	1.68	9
Certificate in Clinical Psychology	Other	August 1 (Fall), December 1 (Spring), April 1 (Summer)	75	75	60 (1)	74 (1)	22	0.62	22
Certificate in Media Psychology	Other	August 1 (Fall), December 1 (Spring), April 1 (Summer)	31	31	28 (0)	28 (0)	0		5

APA Accreditation

Clinical PhD: Student Outcome Data website: http://www.fielding.edu/programs/psychology/psy/default.aspx.

Doctoral Degree (PhD Clinical Psychology): For those doctoral students for whom a professional internship was required in this program prior to graduation:
Total students who applied for an internship: 31
Total students who obtained an internship: 30
Total students who obtained a paid internship: 27
Total students who obtained an unpaid internship: 3
Total students who were placed in APA/CPA-accredited internships: 14
Total students placed in internships not APA/CPA-accredited, but listed with the Association of Psychology Postdoctoral and Internship Centers (APPIC): 7
Total students placed in internships conforming to guidelines of the Council of Directors of School Psychology Programs (CDSPP): 0
Total students placed in internships that were not APA/CPA-accredited, APPIC or CDSSP listed: 9

Master's Degree (MA/MS Media Psychology): An internship experience, such as a final research project or "capstone" experience is required of graduates.

Internships/Practica

Students in the doctoral and postdoctoral programs in clinical psychology apply through the APPIC Match to APA-accredited or APPIC-approved or comparable internship sites that offer organized training programs lasting one year full-time or two consecutive years half-time. Such internships provide a planned, integrated sequence of clinical and didactic experiences with the goal of providing sufficient training and supervision so that upon completion our graduates can function responsibly as postdoctoral psychologists.

Admissions

Entries appear in the following order: required test or GPA, minimum score (if required)/median score of students entering in 2015–2016.

Program	Degree	GRE-V	GRE-Q	GRE-Writing	GRE-Subject	Undergraduate GPA	Last 2 Years GPA	Psychology GPA	Master's GPA
Clinical Psychology	Respecialization Diploma	Not specified	Not specified	Not specified	Not specified	Not specified	Not specified	Not specified	Not specified
Clinical Psychology	PhD	Not specified	Not specified	Not specified	Not specified	2.02/3.36	Not specified	Not specified	3.07/3.82
Media Psychology	PhD	Not specified	Not specified	Not specified	Not specified	2.22/3.36	Not specified	Not specified	Not specified
Postdoctoral Certificate in Neuropsychology	Other	Not specified	Not specified	Not specified	Not specified	Not specified	Not specified	Not specified	Not specified
Media Psychology	MA/MS	Not specified	Not specified	Not specified	Not specified	2.26/3.51	Not specified	Not specified	Not specified
Certificate in Clinical Psychology	Other	Not specified	Not specified	Not specified	Not specified	Not specified	Not specified	Not specified	Not specified
Certificate in Media Psychology	Other	Not specified	Not specified	Not specified	Not specified	Not specified	Not specified	Not specified	Not specified

Admissions Requirements:

Degree	GRE	GRE-Subject	Letters of Recommendation	Research Statement	Writing Sample	CV	Interview
Master's/Specialist	None	None	3	Required	None	Required	None
Doctoral	None	None	3	Required	Required	Required	Required

Admissions Criteria:

Research experience—high
Work experience—high
Clinically related public service—high
GPA—medium
Letters of recommendation—high

Interview—high
Statement of goals and objectives—high
Undergraduate psychology preparation—medium
Writing Sample—medium

For additional information on admission requirements, visit http://www.fielding.edu/programs/psychology.

Department Demographics

	Male (PT)	Female (PT)	Total	African-American/ Black (PT)	Hispanic/ Latino (PT)	Asian/ Pacific Islander (PT)	American Indian/ Alaska Native (PT)	Caucasian/ White (PT)	Unknown	Multiethnic (PT)	ADA (PT)	Int'l (PT)
Students	175 (30)	482 (54)	741	98 (8)	23 (4)	27 (6)	6 (0)	335 (78)	63 (5)	76 (12)	31 (1)	3 (0)

Financial Information/Assistance

Tuition: For information on tuition costs, visit http://www.fielding.edu/financialAid/tuition.aspx. Tuition is subject to change. Additional fees are assessed to students beyond the costs of tuition for the following: Attendance of face-to-face sessions for doctoral programs. Tuition costs vary by program.

Doctoral:
State residents: $26,640 per academic year.
Nonstate residents: $26,640 per academic year.

Master's:
State residents: $560 per credit hour.
Nonstate residents: $560 per credit hour.

Financial Assistance:

	Teaching Assistantship (% Receiving)	Teaching Assistantship Tuition Remission	Research Assistantship (% Receiving)	Research Assistantship Tuition Remission	Fellowship (% Receiving)	Fellowship Tuition Remission
First-Year Student	NA (NA)	NA	NA (NA)	NA	$1,800 (3)	NA
Advanced Student	$1,600 (1)	NA	NA (NA)	NA	$1,950 (13)	NA

For additional information on financial assistance, visit http://www.fielding.edu/financialAid.

Employment of Department Graduates

No information provided.

Additional Information

Housing and Day Care: No on-campus housing is available. No on-campus day care facilities are available.

Special Facilities or Resources: In the clinical PhD program, students become members of a "cluster" in their geographical area consisting of a faculty member and other students. Meetings are held regularly and consist of a variety of learning activities including seminars, clinical and research training, dissertation support, faculty consultation, as well as peer contact and support. Three intensive week-long residential sessions are offered each year that bring together students, faculty, and other scholars who offer seminars and other educational and training events. Session activities include research training, dissertation seminars, instruction in the use of research libraries and electronic databases, face to face instruction in clinical and assessment courses, and lectures by invited research scholars. Additional assessment training in specialized assessment instruments or techniques is offered as well, often on a cluster level, or during a specialty training event, such as NeuroWeek.

Application Information: Psychology Admission Counselor, Fielding Graduate University, 2020 De La Vina Street, Santa Barbara, CA 93105. *Fee:* $75. *Online application:* http://www.fielding.edu/admission.

Fuller Theological Seminary
Department of Clinical Psychology
School of Psychology
180 North Oakland Avenue
Pasadena, CA 91101
Telephone: (626) 584-5500
Chairperson: Mari L. Clements, PhD

E-mail: clements@fuller.edu
Web: http://www.fuller.edu/sop/

Orientation, Objectives, and Emphasis of Department
The purpose of the Graduate School of Psychology is to prepare a distinctive kind of clinical psychologist: men and women whose understanding and action are deeply informed by both psychology and the Christian faith. It is based on the conviction that the coupling of Christian understanding with refined clinical and research skills will produce a psychologist with a special ability to help persons of faith on their journeys to wholeness. The school has adopted the scientist–practitioner model for its PhD program and the clinical-scientist model for its PsyD program.

Programs and Degrees Offered

Program	Degree	Application Deadline	Applications Received	Accepted	New Admits Enrolled (PT)	Total Enrolled (PT)	Degrees Awarded in 2014–2015	Median Years to Complete Degree	Dismissed/ Withdrew
Clinical Psychology	PhD	December 10 (Fall)	47	35	19 (0)	156 (0)	23	6	5
Clinical Psychology	PsyD	December 10 (Fall)	28	16	10 (0)	83 (0)	15	7	1
Psychology	PhD	December 10 (Fall)	4	1	0 (0)	2 (0)	0		0

APA Accreditation

Clinical PhD: Student Outcome Data website: http://fuller.edu/academics/school-of-psychology/clinical-psychology/doctor-of-philosophy/.

Clinical PsyD: Student Outcome Data website: http://fuller.edu/Academics/School-of-Psychology/Clinical-Psychology/Doctor-of-Psychology/.

Doctoral Degree (PhD Clinical Psychology): For those doctoral students for whom a professional internship was required in this program prior to graduation:

Total students who applied for an internship: 28
Total students who obtained an internship: 26
Total students who obtained a paid internship: 26
Total students who obtained an unpaid internship: 0
Total students who were placed in APA/CPA-accredited internships: 18
Total students placed in internships not APA/CPA-accredited, but listed with the Association of Psychology Postdoctoral and Internship Centers (APPIC): 8
Total students placed in internships conforming to guidelines of the Council of Directors of School Psychology Programs (CDSPP): 0
Total students placed in internships that were not APA/CPA-accredited, APPIC or CDSSP listed: 0

Doctoral Degree (PsyD Clinical Psychology): For those doctoral students for whom a professional internship was required in this program prior to graduation:

Total students who applied for an internship: 11
Total students who obtained an internship: 8
Total students who obtained a paid internship: 8
Total students who obtained an unpaid internship: 0
Total students who were placed in APA/CPA-accredited internships: 6
Total students placed in internships not APA/CPA-accredited, but listed with the Association of Psychology Postdoctoral and Internship Centers (APPIC): 1
Total students placed in internships conforming to guidelines of the Council of Directors of School Psychology Programs (CDSPP): 0
Total students placed in internships that were not APA/CPA-accredited, APPIC or CDSSP listed: 1

Internships/Practica

Students in the Clinical PhD and PsyD programs are placed in field training sites throughout their program including 2 years of practicum, 1 year of assessment clerkship, 1 year of pre-internship (PhD only), and a 1-year full-time clinical internship. Students are placed at Fuller Psychological and Family Services clinic as well as in over 60 sites throughout the L.A. metropolitan area. Because of our location, students are exposed to multiple methods of service delivery as well as to diverse ethnic, clinical, and age populations. Students obtain internships throughout the U.S. and Canada.

Admissions

Entries appear in the following order: required test or GPA, minimum score (if required)/median score of students entering in 2015–2016.

Program	Degree	GRE-V	GRE-Q	GRE-Writing	GRE-Subject	Under-graduate GPA	Last 2 Years GPA	Psychol-ogy GPA	Master's GPA
Clinical Psychology	PhD	NA/157	NA/159	NA/4.25	Not specified	Not specified	Not specified	NA/3.7	Not specified

Admissions *(con't.)*

Program	Degree	GRE-V	GRE-Q	GRE-Writing	GRE-Subject	Under-graduate GPA	Last 2 Years GPA	Psychology GPA	Master's GPA
Clinical Psychology	PsyD	NA/159	NA/156	NA/5	Not specified	Not specified	Not specified	NA/3.74	Not specified
Psychology	PhD	Not specified	Not specified	Not specified	Not specified	Not specified	Not specified	Not specified	Not specified

Admissions Requirements:

Degree	GRE	GRE-Subject	Letters of Recom-mendation	Research Statement	Writing Sample	CV	Interview
Doctoral	Required	Required	4	Required	Required	Required	Required

Please note if these criteria vary for different programs: Research experience is less important for PsyD candidates than for PhD candidates.

Admissions Criteria:

GRE scores—high
Research experience—high
Work experience—medium
Clinically related public service—medium
GPA—high

Letters of recommendation—high
Interview—high
Statement of goals and objectives—high
Undergraduate psychology preparation—medium
Integration experience—high

For additional information on admission requirements, visit http://fuller.edu/Admissions/.

Department Demographics

	Male (PT)	Female (PT)	Total	African-American/ Black (PT)	Hispanic/ Latino (PT)	Asian/ Pacific Islander (PT)	American Indian/ Alaska Native (PT)	Caucasian/ White (PT)	Unknown (PT)	Multiethnic (PT)	ADA (PT)	Int'l (PT)
Students	80 (0)	161 (0)	241	26 (0)	12 (0)	36 (0)	0 (0)	151 (0)	3 (0)	13 (0)	8 (0)	14 (0)

Financial Information/Assistance

Tuition: For information on tuition costs, visit http://fuller.edu/admissions/tuition-and-fees/. Tuition is subject to change. Additional fees are assessed to students beyond the costs of tuition for the following: $25 per quarter Student Life fee, $50 new student fee.

Doctoral:
State residents: $660 per credit hour.
Nonstate residents: $660 per credit hour.

Financial Assistance:

	Teaching Assistantship (% Receiving)	Teaching Assistantship Tuition Remission	Research Assistantship (% Receiving)	Research Assistantship Tuition Remission	Fellowship (% Receiving)	Fellowship Tuition Remission
First-Year Student	NA (NA)	NA	$15,000 (NA)	NA	$5,520 (NA)	NA
Advanced Student	$1,188 (NA)	NA	$15,000 (NA)	NA	$3,000 (25)	NA

For additional information on financial assistance, visit http://fuller.edu/sfs/.

Employment of Department Graduates

Doctoral:
Enrolled in a postdoctoral residency/fellowship: 21
Employed in independent practice: 4
Employed in an academic position at a university: 1
Employed in other positions at a higher education institution: 2
Employed in a professional position in a school system: 1
Employed in government agency: 1
Employed in a community mental health/counseling center: 3
Employed in a hospital/medical center: 3
Do not know: 2
Total: 38

Additional Information

Housing and Day Care: On-campus housing is available. See the following website for more information: http://fuller.edu/housing/.
No on-campus day care facilities are available.

Personal Behavior Statement: We are an evangelical Christian community and although we do not require a signed statement
of faith we do expect students to live within the standards of the community as described in our catalog.

Special Facilities or Resources: The Lee Edward Travis Research Institute (TRI) in the School of Psychology at Fuller Theological
Seminary is committed to fostering interdisciplinary research into the relationships between social systems, environmental situations,
personality, mental and affective states, biological processes, and spiritual and religious states and practices. Fuller Psychological &
Family Services clinic provides assistance to individuals, couples, and families, including services to children and adolescents.
Psychological interventions are offered for adjustment disorders, anxiety, depression, stress management, abuse and domestic
violence, and physical conditions affected by psychological factors. Student trainees may be placed in the clinic for practicum,
clerkship or pre-internship.

Application Information: Office of Admissions, Fuller Theological Seminary, 135 North Oakland Avenue, Pasadena, CA 91182.
Fee: $75. *Online application:* http://fuller.edu/admissions/online-application-for-admission/.

Golden Gate University
Psychology
536 Mission Street
San Francisco, CA 94005
Telephone: (800) 448-4968
Chairperson: Tom Wooldridge

E-mail: info@ggu.edu
Web: https://www.ggu.edu/programs/psychology/

Orientation, Objectives, and Emphasis of Department
Golden Gate University offers applied psychology degrees for students wishing to begin or enhance a career where they can make
a difference in society. Degree programs prepare students for a range of careers from licensed clinical therapists to organizational
consultants. Certificates in conflict resolution may be combined with degrees.

Programs and Degrees Offered

Program	Degree	Application Deadline	Applications Received	Accepted	New Admits Enrolled (PT)	Total Enrolled (PT)	Degrees Awarded in 2014–2015	Median Years to Complete Degree	Dismissed/ Withdrew
Counseling Psychology	MA/MS	Rolling	40	31	12 (7)	39 (55)	30		
Industrial-Organizational Psychology	MA/MS	Rolling	18	14	9 (2)	24 (20)	15		

Internships/Practica

Golden Gate University has relationships with over 80 San Francisco Bay Area clinics and agencies that provide clinical traineeships for our students and alumni. Located in a vigorous business community, Golden Gate University also assists Industrial/Organizational students with internship opportunities in businesses ranging from consulting to technology, as well as in government organizations.

Admissions

Entries appear in the following order: required test or GPA, minimum score (if required)/median score of students entering in 2015–2016.

Program	Degree	GRE-V	GRE-Q	GRE-Writing	GRE-Subject	Undergraduate GPA	Last 2 Years GPA	Psychology GPA	Master's GPA
Counseling Psychology	MA/MS	Not specified	Not specified	Not specified	Not specified	Not specified	Not specified	Not specified	Not specified
Industrial-Organizational Psychology	MA/MS	Not specified	Not specified	Not specified	Not specified	Not specified	Not specified	Not specified	Not specified

Admissions Requirements:

Degree	GRE	GRE-Subject	Letters of Recommendation	Research Statement	Writing Sample	CV	Interview
Master's/Specialist	Optional	None	Not Specified	Required	Optional	Optional	Optional

Admissions Criteria:

Work experience—medium
Clinically related public service—low
GPA—high
Letters of recommendation—low

Interview—low
Statement of goals and objectives—high
Undergraduate psychology preparation—low

For additional information on admission requirements, visit http://www.ggu.edu/graduate/enrollment/admission-requirements.

Department Demographics

	Male (PT)	Female (PT)	Total	African-American/ Black (PT)	Hispanic/ Latino (PT)	Asian/ Pacific Islander (PT)	American Indian/ Alaska Native (PT)	Caucasian/ White (PT)	Unknown	Multiethnic (PT)	ADA (PT)	Int'l (PT)
Students	5 (10)	20 (60)	95	3 (5)	0 (5)	12 (2)	0 (0)	8 (49)	1 (4)	1 (5)	1 (0)	12 (0)

Financial Information/Assistance

Tuition: For information on tuition costs, visit http://www.ggu.edu/enrollment/tuition-and-fees/tuition. Tuition is subject to change.

Master's:
State residents: $810 per credit hour.
Nonstate residents: $810 per credit hour.

Financial Assistance:

	Teaching Assistantship (% Receiving)	Teaching Assistantship Tuition Remission	Research Assistantship (% Receiving)	Research Assistantship Tuition Remission	Fellowship (% Receiving)	Fellowship Tuition Remission
First-Year Student	NA (NA)	NA	NA (NA)	NA	NA (NA)	NA
Advanced Student	NA (NA)	NA	NA (NA)	NA	NA (NA)	NA

For additional information on financial assistance, visit http://www.ggu.edu/enrollment/financial-aid.

Employment of Department Graduates

Master's:
Enrolled in a psychology doctoral program: 4
Employed in a professional position in a school system: 4
Employed in business or industry: 14
Employed in government agency: 1
Employed in a community mental health/counseling center: 35
Employed in a hospital/medical center: 1
Total: 59

Additional Information

Housing and Day Care: No on-campus housing is available. No on-campus day care facilities are available.

Application Information: Admissions, Golden Gate University, 536 Mission Street, San Francisco, CA 94005. *Fee:* $70. *Online application:* http://www.ggu.edu/admission/applydegree.do?type=G.

Humboldt State University (2015 data)
Department of Psychology
College of Professional Studies
1 Harpst Street
Arcata, CA 95521
Telephone: (707) 826-5264
Chairperson: William Reynolds, PhD

E-mail: kees@humboldt.edu
Web: http://www.humboldt.edu/psychology

Orientation, Objectives, and Emphasis of Department

The objectives of our department are to provide students with an understanding of principles and theories concerning human behavior and to the processes by which such information is obtained; to provide quality professional graduate education for students working toward California School Psychologist credentials, Marriage and Family Therapist licenses and other specialized occupational fields; and to provide a flexibility in our offerings that responds to changing societal agenda and student needs. Our Academic Research Master's program provides specializations in the following areas: Developmental Psychopathology, Biological Psychology, and Social and Environmental Psychology. Students should select one of these areas when they apply to the program.

Programs and Degrees Offered

Program	Degree	Application Deadline	Applica-tions Received	Accepted	New Admits Enrolled (PT)	Total Enrolled (PT)	Degrees Awarded in 2014–2015	Median Years to Complete Degree	Dismissed/ Withdrew
Academic Research	MA/MS	February 1 (Fall)	17	11	10 (0)	31 (0)	1	2	0
Counseling	MA/MS	February 1 (Fall)	27	11	8 (0)	25 (4)	7	2.6	
School Psychology	MA/MS	February 1 (Fall)	0	0	0 (0)	19 (0)	7	3	0

Internships/Practica

School Psychology internships (paid) are required of all students seeking the School Psychology credential. Counseling MA students are provided the opportunity to do fieldwork/practica in the department's community counseling clinic, as well as in several local mental health agencies.

Admissions

Entries appear in the following order: required test or GPA, minimum score (if required)/median score of students entering in 2015–2016.

Program	Degree	GRE-V	GRE-Q	GRE-Writing	GRE-Subject	Under-graduate GPA	Last 2 Years GPA	Psychol-ogy GPA	Master's GPA
Academic Research	MA/MS	Not specified	Not specified	Not specified	Not specified	3.25/NA	Not specified	3.25/NA	Not specified
Counseling	MA/MS	NA/NA	NA/NA	NA/NA	Not specified	3/NA	Not specified	Not specified	Not specified
School Psychology	MA/MS	Not specified	Not specified	Not specified	Not specified	3/NA	Not specified	Not specified	Not specified

Admissions Requirements:

Degree	GRE	GRE-Subject	Letters of Recom-mendation	Research Statement	Writing Sample	CV	Interview
Master's/Specialist	Required	None	3	Required	Optional	Optional	Required

Please note if these criteria vary for different programs: An interview is required for Counseling and School Psychology; research experience is important for Academic Research; clinically related public service or work experience is highly important for Counseling and School Psychology; school/child related work experience highly important for School Psychology.

Admissions Criteria:

GRE scores—low
Research experience—medium
Work experience—medium
Clinically related public service—medium
GPA—high

Letters of recommendation—high
Interview—medium
Statement of goals and objectives—high
Undergraduate psychology preparation—medium

For additional information on admission requirements, visit http://www2.humboldt.edu/psychology/programs/application-information.

Department Demographics

	Male (PT)	Female (PT)	Total	African-American/ Black (PT)	Hispanic/ Latino (PT)	Asian/ Pacific Islander (PT)	American Indian/ Alaska Native (PT)	Caucasian/ White (PT)	Unknown	Multiethnic (PT)	ADA (PT)	Int'l (PT)
Students	18 (1)	57 (3)	79	1 (0)	12 (2)	6 (0)	0 (0)	42 (2)	2 (0)	12 (0)	0 (0)	0 (0)

Financial Information/Assistance

Tuition: For information on tuition costs, visit http://www.humboldt.edu/studentfinancial/tuition_fees.html. Tuition is subject to change.

Master's:
State residents: $8,432 per academic year.
Nonstate residents: $8,432 per academic year.
Nonstate residents: $372 per credit hour.

Financial Assistance:

	Teaching Assistantship (% Receiving)	Teaching Assistantship Tuition Remission	Research Assistantship (% Receiving)	Research Assistantship Tuition Remission	Fellowship (% Receiving)	Fellowship Tuition Remission
First-Year Student	NA (NA)	NA	NA (NA)	NA	NA (NA)	NA
Advanced Student	NA (NA)	NA	NA (NA)	NA	NA (NA)	NA

For additional information on financial assistance, visit http://www.humboldt.edu/finaid/.

Employment of Department Graduates

Master's:
Enrolled in a psychology doctoral program: 2
Employed in a professional position in a school system: 7
Employed in a community mental health/counseling center: 6
Total: 15

Additional Information

Housing and Day Care: On-campus housing is available. See the following website for more information: http://www.humboldt.edu/housing/. On-campus day care facilities are available. See the following website for more information: http://www.humboldt.edu/childrencenter/.

Information for Students With Physical Disabilities: See the following website: http://www.humboldt.edu/disability/.

Special Facilities or Resources: The department has an on-campus clinic staffed by MA counseling students, an electronic equipment shop, a lab with biofeedback and EEG equipment, a lab equipped for research on motion sickness, observation and research access to an on-campus demonstration nursery school, a test library, and a computer laboratory. Our new Behavioral and Social Sciences Building provides exceptional research, instruction, faculty and student space for the Department of Psychology.

Application Information: Office of Admissions, Humboldt State University, Arcata, CA 95521. *Fee:* $55. *Online application:* http://www.humboldt.edu/gradprograms/future-students.

John F. Kennedy University
Graduate Psychology Programs
College of Graduate and Professional Studies
100 Ellinwood Way
Pleasant Hill, CA 94523
Telephone: (925) 969-3400
Dean: Gerardo Rodriguez-Menendez
E-mail: grodriguezmenendez@jfku.edu
Web: http://www.jfku.edu/Programs-and-Courses/College-of-Graduate-Professional-Studies.html

---

Orientation, Objectives, and Emphasis of Department
Our Graduate Psychology programs provide an academic environment that is rigorous, supportive, transformative. Students are offered an array of opportunities to develop the knowledge, skills, and understanding needed to reach their potential. We are committed to active learning and community service, and are guided by a commitment to traditionally underserved populations. Our graduate-level degree and certificate programs provide a solid foundation in the theoretical bases of the field of study, opportunities for specialized study, and an abundance of supervised internships and other types of field studies. The Doctor of Psychology (PsyD) program follows the practitioner-scholar model providing an educational and training program in clinical psychology at the doctoral level. The Sport Psychology program is an innovative program that integrates the core elements of performance enhancement, counseling skills, and sport science. Students may also enroll in the Dual MA/PsyD degree program and receive both the MA in Sports Psychology and the PsyD in Clinical Psychology. The Counseling Psychology program offers specializations in Marriage and Family Therapy and Professional Clinical Counseling. Our Holistic Counseling Psychology program adds a perspective that integrates body, mind, spirit and culture into its curriculum with five areas of study: Transpersonal, Somatic, Expressive Arts, Depth Psychology, Holistic Skills.

Programs and Degrees Offered

Program	Degree	Application Deadline	Applications Received	Accepted	New Admits Enrolled (PT)	Total Enrolled (PT)	Degrees Awarded in 2014–2015	Median Years to Complete Degree	Dismissed/Withdrew
Counseling Psychology	MA/MS	April 6 (Fall), October 6 (Spring)	152	74	38 (10)	123 (100)	86	2.67	8
Clinical Psychology	PsyD	January 16 (Fall)	111	49	25 (0)	67 (66)	18	5.67	5
Sport Psychology	MA/MS	April 6 (Fall), October 6 (Spring)	112	73	23 (15)	39 (70)	13	2.67	5
Counseling Psychology (Holistic)	MA/MS	April 6 (Fall), October 6 (Spring)	124	68	16 (23)	74 (156)	62	3.04	6

APA Accreditation

Clinical PsyD (Doctor of Psychology).

Doctoral Degree (PsyD Clinical Psychology): For those doctoral students for whom a professional internship was required in this program prior to graduation:
Total students who applied for an internship: 31
Total students who obtained an internship: 30
Total students who obtained a paid internship: 20
Total students who obtained an unpaid internship: 10
Total students who were placed in APA/CPA-accredited internships: 7
Total students placed in internships not APA/CPA-accredited, but listed with the Association of Psychology Postdoctoral and Internship Centers (APPIC): 8
Total students placed in internships conforming to guidelines of the Council of Directors of School Psychology Programs (CDSPP): 0
Total students placed in internships that were not APA/CPA-accredited, APPIC or CDSSP listed: 15

Master's Degree (MA/MS Counseling Psychology): An internship experience, such as a final research project or "capstone" experience is required of graduates. Master's Degree (MA/MS Sport Psychology): An internship experience, such as a final research project or "capstone" experience is required of graduates. Master's Degree (MA/MS Counseling Psychology (Holistic)): An internship experience, such as a final research project or "capstone" experience is required of graduates.

Internships/Practica

John F. Kennedy University has three community counseling centers, each located near one of our three campuses, which provide state-of-the-art supervision for students and provide thousands of hours of low-fee counseling each year. Additionally, approximately 150 external fieldwork sites, monitored by our faculty, are available in the surrounding counties. Students in the MA Counseling Psychology programs and the PsyD program accumulate hours toward their respective licenses at both the community counseling centers and the external sites. The MA in Sport Psychology program offers summer camps for incarcerated youth and youth sport teams which also serve as additional field placement sites for graduate students. In addition, the Sport Psychology program offers internship experiences for all onsite and online students. The MA Counseling Psychology program offers an Expressive Arts Camp for children ages 6-12 at two locations. This internship offers graduate students with an interest in the area of children and the creative process a practical hands-on experience. In 2014 JFKU was awarded an HHS grant that provides students in the MA Counseling Psychology programs with annual stipends of $10,000 for completing practicum hours at the University's three Community Counseling Centers in Concord, Oakland, and Sunnyvale.

Admissions

Entries appear in the following order: required test or GPA, minimum score (if required)/median score of students entering in 2015–2016.

Program	Degree	GRE-V	GRE-Q	GRE-Writing	GRE-Subject	Under-graduate GPA	Last 2 Years GPA	Psychol-ogy GPA	Master's GPA
Counseling Psychology	MA/MS	Not specified	Not specified	Not specified	Not specified	3/NA	Not specified	Not specified	Not specified
Clinical Psychology	PsyD	Not specified	Not specified	Not specified	Not specified	3/NA	Not specified	Not specified	Not specified
Sport Psychology	MA/MS	Not specified	Not specified	Not specified	Not specified	3/NA	Not specified	Not specified	Not specified
Counseling Psychology (Holistic)	MA/MS	Not specified	Not specified	Not specified	Not specified	3/NA	Not specified	Not specified	Not specified

Admissions Requirements:

Degree	GRE	GRE-Subject	Letters of Recom-mendation	Research Statement	Writing Sample	CV	Interview
Master's/Specialist	None	None	3	Required	Optional	Required	Required
Doctoral	Optional	Optional	3	Required	Required	Required	Required

Please note if these criteria vary for different programs: The quality of writing and GPA criteria are highly important to the PsyD program when evaluating applicants. The MA programs put a strong emphasis on the personal statement of goals and objectives and experience in public/social service. The Sport Psychology program looks for a strong personal statement and solid GPA for admission criteria.

Admissions Criteria:

Research experience—medium
Work experience—medium
Clinically related public service—high
GPA—medium

Letters of recommendation—high
Interview—high
Statement of goals and objectives—high
Undergraduate psychology preparation—medium

Department Demographics

	Male (PT)	Female (PT)	Total	African-American/ Black (PT)	Hispanic/ Latino (PT)	Asian/ Pacific Islander (PT)	American Indian/ Alaska Native (PT)	Caucasian/ White (PT)	Unknown (PT)	Multiethnic (PT)	ADA (PT)	Int'l (PT)
Students	88 (86)	257 (321)	752	29 (42)	38 (40)	42 (37)	3 (9)	168 (227)	35 (35)	30 (17)	10 (29)	13 (4)

Financial Information/Assistance

Tuition: For information on tuition costs, visit http://www.jfku.edu/Admissions/Tuition-and-Fees.html. Tuition is subject to change. Additional fees are assessed to students beyond the costs of tuition for the following: internship, comprehensive exams, student services, technology.

Doctoral:
State residents: $785 per credit hour.
Nonstate residents: $785 per credit hour.

Master's:
State residents: $655 per credit hour.
Nonstate residents: $655 per credit hour.

Financial Assistance:

	Teaching Assistantship (% Receiving)	Teaching Assistantship Tuition Remission	Research Assistantship (% Receiving)	Research Assistantship Tuition Remission	Fellowship (% Receiving)	Fellowship Tuition Remission
First-Year Student	NA (NA)	NA	NA (NA)	NA	$1,045 (9)	NA
Advanced Student	NA (NA)	NA	NA (NA)	NA	$1,045 (6)	NA

For additional information on financial assistance, visit http://www.jfku.edu/Admissions/Financial-Aid.html.

Employment of Department Graduates

No information provided.

Additional Information

Housing and Day Care: No on-campus housing is available. No on-campus day care facilities are available.

Special Facilities or Resources: As noted, the John F. Kennedy University community counseling centers serve a broad-based clientele throughout the surrounding communities. The programs in the school are actively engaged in community service. For example, the Sport Psychology program is an active participant in the Life Enhancement Through Athletic and Academic Participation (LEAP) in numerous Bay Area schools. Both MA Counseling Psychology programs provide opportunities for students to participate in school-based counseling services on elementary, middle and high school cmpuses.

Application Information: Admissions Office, John F. Kennedy University, 100 Ellinwood Way, Pleasant Hill, CA 94523-4817. *Fee:* $65. *Online application:* https://secure.jfku.edu/application/.

La Verne, University of

Psychology Department
College of Arts and Sciences
1950 Third Street
La Verne, CA 91750
Telephone: (909) 448-4179
PsyD Program Chair: Jerry L. Kernes, PhD

E-mail: nbrown2@laverne.edu
Web: http://sites.laverne.edu/psychology/psyd-program/

Orientation, Objectives, and Emphasis of Department

The clinical faculty consists of psychologists whose theoretical orientations include psychodynamic, humanistic, cognitive-behavioral, and multicultural, and who are clinically active in a range of clinical settings and populations. Faculty research interests include topics such as multiculturalism, psychotherapy outcome research, racial identity and acculturation, positive psychology, moral development and decision making, and violence and victimization. The curriculum of the PsyD program is anchored in a multi-cultural perspective and involves a multi-disciplinary faculty who are actively involved in clinical and research activities. The PsyD program meets all predoctoral requirements for California psychology licensure. Students proceed through the program in a cohort model, taking all but elective courses together with their entering group. This fosters a high level of cooperation among students. Student-faculty ratios are relatively small, resulting in multiple opportunities for mentoring by faculty and for student-faculty collaboration.

Programs and Degrees Offered

Program	Degree	Application Deadline	Applica-tions Received	Accepted	New Admits Enrolled (PT)	Total Enrolled (PT)	Degrees Awarded in 2014–2015	Median Years to Complete Degree	Dismissed/ Withdrew
Clinical Psychology	PsyD	December 31 (Fall)	77	35	14 (0)	41 (39)	25	6.32	3

APA Accreditation

Clinical PsyD (Doctor of Psychology).

Doctoral Degree (PsyD Clinical Psychology): For those doctoral students for whom a professional internship was required in this program prior to graduation:
Total students who applied for an internship: 21
Total students who obtained an internship: 20
Total students who obtained a paid internship: 18
Total students who obtained an unpaid internship: 2
Total students who were placed in APA/CPA-accredited internships: 12
Total students placed in internships not APA/CPA-accredited, but listed with the Association of Psychology Postdoctoral and Internship Centers (APPIC): 4
Total students placed in internships conforming to guidelines of the Council of Directors of School Psychology Programs (CDSPP): 0
Total students placed in internships that were not APA/CPA-accredited, APPIC or CDSSP listed: 4

Internships/Practica

The PsyD program includes required supervised practica in the second and third years of the program, with an optional fourth year practicum available. A minimum of 1500 hours of clinical practicum activities are required for the PsyD The culminating predoctoral internship in the fifth and final year of the program consists of an additional 1500 clinical hours. The Psychology department has an extensive network of practicum, fieldwork, and internship sites within mental health and educational settings throughout the Southern California area.

Admissions

Entries appear in the following order: required test or GPA, minimum score (if required)/median score of students entering in 2015–2016.

Program	Degree	GRE-V	GRE-Q	GRE-Writing	GRE-Subject	Under-graduate GPA	Last 2 Years GPA	Psychology GPA	Master's GPA
Clinical Psychology	PsyD	NA/153	NA/149	3.5/4	Not specified	3.1/3.63	Not specified	Not specified	Not specified

Admissions Requirements:

Degree	GRE	GRE-Subject	Letters of Recom-mendation	Research Statement	Writing Sample	CV	Interview
Doctoral	Required	None	3	Required	None	Required	Required

Please note if these criteria vary for different programs: On campus interviews are required for those being considered for admission. Students should have a minimum GRE score of 295 (Verbal and Quantitative combined).

Admissions Criteria:

GRE scores—high
Research experience—medium
Work experience—low
Clinically related public service—medium
GPA—high

Letters of recommendation—medium
Interview—high
Statement of goals and objectives—medium
Undergraduate psychology preparation—medium

For additional information on admission requirements, visit http://sites.laverne.edu/psychology/psyd-program/admissions/.

Department Demographics

	Male (PT)	Female (PT)	Total	African-American/ Black (PT)	Hispanic/ Latino (PT)	Asian/ Pacific Islander (PT)	American Indian/ Alaska Native (PT)	Caucasian/ White (PT)	Unknown	Multiethnic (PT)	ADA (PT)	Int'l (PT)
Students	6 (7)	35 (32)	80	4 (5)	7 (14)	5 (5)	0 (0)	22 (11)	2 (0)	1 (4)	0 (0)	0 (0)

Financial Information/Assistance

Tuition: For information on tuition costs, visit http://laverne.edu/tuition2/graduate/. Tuition is subject to change.

Doctoral:
State residents: $32,224 per academic year.
State residents: $1,007 per credit hour.
Nonstate residents: $32,224 per academic year.
Nonstate residents: $1,007 per credit hour.

Financial Assistance:

	Teaching Assistantship (% Receiving)	Teaching Assistantship Tuition Remission	Research Assistantship (% Receiving)	Research Assistantship Tuition Remission	Fellowship (% Receiving)	Fellowship Tuition Remission
First-Year Student	NA (NA)	NA	NA (NA)	NA	$10,000 (100)	Partial
Advanced Student	$4,000 (NA)	Partial	NA (NA)	NA	$2,000 (NA)	Partial

For additional information on financial assistance, visit http://sites.laverne.edu/psychology/psyd-program/financial-information/.

Employment of Department Graduates

Doctoral:
Enrolled in a postdoctoral residency/fellowship: 25
Total: 25

Additional Information

Housing and Day Care: On-campus housing is available. See the following website for more information: http://sites.laverne.edu/housing/. No on-campus day care facilities are available.

Information for Students With Physical Disabilities: See the following website: http://sites.laverne.edu/disabled-student-services/.

Special Facilities or Resources: Students have access to a wide network of local and regional clinical, research and library facilities in the metropolitan Los Angeles and Southern California area.

Application Information: Graduate Admissions, University of La Verne, 1950 Third Street, La Verne, CA 91750. *Fee:* $75. *Online application:* http://laverne.edu/admission/applyapply2/.

Loma Linda University

Department of Psychology
School of Behavioral Health
11130 Anderson Street
Loma Linda, CA 92350
Telephone: (909) 558-8577
Interim Chair: David A. Vermeersch, PhD

E-mail: psyc@llu.edu
Web: http://behavioralhealth.llu.edu/programs/psychology

Orientation, Objectives, and Emphasis of Department

Doctoral training at Loma Linda University takes place within the context of a holistic approach to human health and welfare. The University motto 'To make man whole' takes in every aspect of being human—the physical, psychological, spiritual, and social. Building on a University tradition of health sciences research, training, and service, the doctoral programs in the Department offer a combination of traditional and innovative training opportunities. The PhD in clinical psychology follows the traditional scientist–practitioner model and emphasizes research and clinical training. The PsyD is oriented toward clinical practice with emphasis on the understanding and application of the principles and research of psychological science.

Programs and Degrees Offered

Program	Degree	Application Deadline	Applica-tions Received	Accepted	New Admits Enrolled (PT)	Total Enrolled (PT)	Degrees Awarded in 2014–2015	Median Years to Complete Degree	Dismissed/ Withdrew
Clinical Psychology	PhD	December 31 (Fall)	49	13	12 (0)	72 (0)	9	7	3
Clinical Psychology	PsyD	December 31 (Fall)	70	14	14 (0)	61 (0)	11	6	0

APA Accreditation

Clinical PhD: Student Outcome Data website: http://behavioralhealth.llu.edu/programs/psychology/phd-clinical-psychology.
Clinical PsyD: Student Outcome Data website: http://behavioralhealth.llu.edu/programs/psychology/psyd-clinical-psychology.

Doctoral Degree (PhD Clinical Psychology): For those doctoral students for whom a professional internship was required in this program prior to graduation:
Total students who applied for an internship: 15
Total students who obtained an internship: 14
Total students who obtained a paid internship: 14
Total students who obtained an unpaid internship: 0
Total students who were placed in APA/CPA-accredited internships: 12
Total students placed in internships not APA/CPA-accredited, but listed with the Association of Psychology Postdoctoral and Internship Centers (APPIC): 2
Total students placed in internships conforming to guidelines of the Council of Directors of School Psychology Programs (CDSPP): 0
Total students placed in internships that were not APA/CPA-accredited, APPIC or CDSSP listed: 0

Doctoral Degree (PsyD Clinical Psychology): For those doctoral students for whom a professional internship was required in this program prior to graduation:
Total students who applied for an internship: 17
Total students who obtained an internship: 11
Total students who obtained a paid internship: 10
Total students who obtained an unpaid internship: 1
Total students who were placed in APA/CPA-accredited internships: 8
Total students placed in internships not APA/CPA-accredited, but listed with the Association of Psychology Postdoctoral and Internship Centers (APPIC): 3
Total students placed in internships conforming to guidelines of the Council of Directors of School Psychology Programs (CDSPP): 0
Total students placed in internships that were not APA/CPA-accredited, APPIC or CDSSP listed: 0

Internships/Practica

Internal practicum experiences are obtained at the Loma Linda Behavioral Health Institute, which houses our Department Training Clinic and serves extremely diverse patients from San Bernardino and Riverside Counties. Other department training experiences include the LLU Pediatrics Department population. Practicum students may also receive some supervised clinical training in area public and private school settings. The external practicum (20 hours per week, normally in the third year of the program) is entirely off the departmental campus. Students are expected to accumulate 950 to 1000 hours of supervised experience while on external practicum, with an absolute minimum of 250 hours being spent in direct service experiences with patients. External practicum students are presently placed in over 15 settings, including (1) The Rehabilitation Unit of the Loma Linda University Medical Center; (2) The San Bernardino County Department of Mental Health; (3) the Casa Colina Hospital for Rehabilitative Medicine; (4) LLU Department of Family Medicine-Primary Care; and (5) Local Indian Reservation. A full year (40 hours per week) of internship is required with sites available across the country. Students must complete an internship in either an APA-accredited or APPIC-member site.

Admissions

Entries appear in the following order: required test or GPA, minimum score (if required)/median score of students entering in 2015–2016.

Program	Degree	GRE-V	GRE-Q	GRE-Writing	GRE-Subject	Under-graduate GPA	Last 2 Years GPA	Psychol-ogy GPA	Master's GPA
Clinical Psychology	PhD	153/157	145/152	4/4.1	Not specified	3/3.5	Not specified	Not specified	Not specified
Clinical Psychology	PsyD	143/154	145/152	4/4.29	Not specified	3/3.37	NA/NA	Not specified	Not specified

Admissions Requirements:

Degree	GRE	GRE-Subject	Letters of Recommendation	Research Statement	Writing Sample	CV	Interview
Doctoral	Required	None	3	Required	None	Optional	Required

Please note if these criteria vary for different programs: For PhD applicants, research experience is highly desirable. For PsyD applicants, clinically-related experience is highly desirable.

Admissions Criteria:

GRE scores—high
Research experience—high
Work experience—medium
Clinically related public service—high
GPA—high

Letters of recommendation—high
Interview—high
Statement of goals and objectives—high
Undergraduate psychology preparation—high

For additional information on admission requirements, visit http://behavioralhealth.llu.edu/programs/psychology/admissions-and-application-psychology.

Department Demographics

	Male (PT)	Female (PT)	Total	African-American/ Black (PT)	Hispanic/ Latino (PT)	Asian/ Pacific Islander (PT)	American Indian/ Alaska Native (PT)	Caucasian/ White (PT)	Unknown	Multiethnic (PT)	ADA (PT)	Int'l (PT)
Students	38 (0)	95 (0)	133	11 (0)	17 (0)	30 (0)	1 (0)	74 (0)	0 (0)	0 (0)	1 (0)	0 (0)

Financial Information/Assistance

Tuition: For information on tuition costs, visit http://behavioralhealth.llu.edu/students/tuition-and-fees. Tuition is subject to change. Additional fees are assessed to students beyond the costs of tuition for the following: $3,472.00 (enrollment fee, lab fees and school fee).

Doctoral:
State residents: $36,639 per academic year.
Nonstate residents: $36,639 per academic year.

Financial Assistance:

	Teaching Assistantship (% Receiving)	Teaching Assistantship Tuition Remission	Research Assistantship (% Receiving)	Research Assistantship Tuition Remission	Fellowship (% Receiving)	Fellowship Tuition Remission
First-Year Student	NA (NA)	NA	$3,600 (5)	NA	NA (NA)	NA
Advanced Student	$1,000 (20)	NA	$5,000 (10)	NA	NA (NA)	NA

For additional information on financial assistance, visit http://home.llu.edu/campus-and-spiritual-life/student-services/financial-aid.

Employment of Department Graduates

Doctoral:
Enrolled in a postdoctoral residency/fellowship: 18
Employed in government agency: 2
Total: 20

Additional Information

Housing and Day Care: On-campus housing is available. See the following website for more information: http://home.llu.edu/campus-and-spiritual-life/housing-dining. No on-campus day care facilities are available.

Special Facilities or Resources: As a Health Sciences University, Loma Linda provides an ideal environment with resources for research and clinical training in such areas as health psychology/behavioral medicine and the delivery of health services. LLU Medical Center has nearly 900 beds, is staffed by more than 5000 people, and is the "flagship" of a system including hundreds of health care institutions around the world. In addition, a number of institutions in the area, such as the LLU Behavioral Medicine Center, Jerry L. Pettis VA Hospital, Patton State Hospital, and the San Bernardino County Mental Health Department represent numerous opportunities for research and clinical training in psychology.

Application Information: Loma Linda University, School of Behavioral Health, Office of Admissions, 11065 Campus Street Suite 217 (Griggs Hall), Loma Linda, CA 92350. *Fee:* $35. *Online application:* https://ssweb.llu.edu/apply.

Pacific, University of the
Department of Psychology
3601 Pacific Avenue
Stockton, CA 95211
Telephone: (209) 946-2133
Director of Graduate Studies: Carolynn Kohn, PhD, BCBA-D
E-mail: ckohn@pacific.edu
Web: http://www.pacific.edu/Academics/Schools-and-Colleges/College-of-the-Pacific/Academics/Departments-and-Programs/Psychology.html

---

Orientation, Objectives, and Emphasis of Department
The Psychology Department offers a program of graduate study leading to the MA degree in Psychology. Students accepted into our program plan to complete their MA degree and sit for the BCBA exam and/or plan to apply to doctoral programs in behavior analysis or clinical/counseling psychology with a behavioral focus. We do not offer an MFT or a Counseling MA. The overall program focus includes: a wide variety of applied experience in a number of different settings; intensive involvement in designing, conducting, and evaluating research; coursework in theoretical and research foundations of applied behavior analysis and behavior theory; and commitment to the development of student potential by active, supportive, and involved faculty.

Programs and Degrees Offered

Program	Degree	Application Deadline	Applications Received	Accepted	New Admits Enrolled (PT)	Total Enrolled (PT)	Degrees Awarded in 2014–2015	Median Years to Complete Degree	Dismissed/ Withdrew
Applied Behavior Analysis/ BCBA and Doctoral Prep	MA/MS	February 15 (Fall)	31	12	7 (1)	13	5	2.5	1

Internships/Practica
The department directs the Community Re-entry Program (contracted directly with the county), which provides a wide range of behaviorally based programs to assist the mentally disabled in becoming independent. This program provides half-time employment for eight graduate students per year. Students interested in developmental disabilities can work part-time with the Behavioral Instructional Service (in cooperation with Valley Mountain Regional Center, which serves these clients). We also have contracts with several outside agencies at which students can obtain practicum experience, including the Stockton Unified School District (ABA assessment and interventions for school problem behaviors) and BEST (early ABA interventions with children diagnosed with autism).

Admissions

Entries appear in the following order: required test or GPA, minimum score (if required)/median score of students entering in 2015–2016.

Program	Degree	GRE-V	GRE-Q	GRE-Writing	GRE-Subject	Under-graduate GPA	Last 2 Years GPA	Psychology GPA	Master's GPA
Applied Behavior Analysis/BCBA and Doctoral Prep	MA/MS	NA/155	NA/150	Not specified	Not specified	3/3.6	3/NA	3/NA	Not specified

Admissions Requirements:

Degree	GRE	GRE-Subject	Letters of Recommendation	Research Statement	Writing Sample	CV	Interview
Master's/Specialist	Required	None	3	Required	Optional	Required	Optional

Please note if these criteria vary for different programs: Applicants planning to take the BACB exam should have some relevant coursework and research in behavior analysis.

Admissions Criteria:

GRE scores—medium
Research experience—high
Work experience—medium
Clinically related public service—low
GPA—high

Letters of recommendation—high
Interview—low
Statement of goals and objectives—high
Undergraduate psychology preparation—high
Applied experience—medium

Department Demographics

	Male (PT)	Female (PT)	Total	African-American/Black (PT)	Hispanic/Latino (PT)	Asian/Pacific Islander (PT)	American Indian/Alaska Native (PT)	Caucasian/White (PT)	Unknown	Multiethnic (PT)	ADA (PT)	Int'l (PT)
Students	2 (0)	11 (0)	13	1 (0)	2 (0)	4 (0)	0 (0)	4 (0)	0 (0)	2 (0)	0 (0)	1 (0)

Financial Information/Assistance

Tuition: For information on tuition costs, visit http://www.pacific.edu/Campus-Life/Student-Services/Student-Accounts/Tuition-and-Fees.html. Tuition is subject to change.

Master's:
State residents: $19,648 per academic year.
State residents: $1,228 per credit hour.
Nonstate residents: $19,648 per academic year.
Nonstate residents: $1,228 per credit hour.

Financial Assistance:

	Teaching Assistantship (% Receiving)	Teaching Assistantship Tuition Remission	Research Assistantship (% Receiving)	Research Assistantship Tuition Remission	Fellowship (% Receiving)	Fellowship Tuition Remission
First-Year Student	$11,400 (100)	Partial	NA (NA)	NA	NA (NA)	NA
Advanced Student	$11,400 (100)	Partial	NA (NA)	NA	NA (NA)	NA

For additional information on financial assistance, visit http://www.pacific.edu/Admission/Graduate-Professional/Financial-Aid.html.

Employment of Department Graduates

Master's:
Enrolled in a psychology doctoral program: 4
Employed in a professional position in a school system: 2
Employed in a community mental health/counseling center: 1
Total: 7

Additional Information

Housing and Day Care: On-campus housing is available. See the following website for more information: http://www.pacific.edu/Campus-Life/Housing-and-Facilities.html. No on-campus day care facilities are available.

Special Facilities or Resources: The department provides office space for faculty and graduate students, computing equipment, and video equipment for research projects. Applied research projects are also conducted in community settings (e.g. schools, medical settings). The Community Re-entry Program and Valley Mountain Regional Center also provide rich opportunities for research in community settings.

Application Information: Dean of the Graduate School, University of the Pacific, 3601 Pacific Avenue, Stockton, CA 95211. *Fee:* $75. *Online application:* http://go.pacific.edu/apply/graduate.

Palo Alto University

Master's Programs
1791 Arastradero Road
Palo Alto, CA 94304
Telephone: (650) 417-2034
Director: Dr. William Snow

E-mail: MastersAdmissions@paloaltou.edu
Web: http://www.paloaltou.edu/graduate-programs/masters-degree-programs

---

Orientation, Objectives, and Emphasis of Department

The master's programs department exists to train master's-level researchers and clinicians in preparation for clinical and counseling work, further academic study, and other related careers.

Programs and Degrees Offered

Program	Degree	Application Deadline	Applications Received	Accepted	New Admits Enrolled (PT)	Total Enrolled (PT)	Degrees Awarded in 2014–2015	Median Years to Complete Degree	Dismissed/ Withdrew
Counseling	MA/MS	Rolling	164	151	37 (77)	154 (229)	34	2.22	19
Psychology	MA/MS	July 31 (Fall)	35	34	1 (24)	1 (50)	13	1.75	3

Internships/Practica

The counseling program requires a practicum during the second year of the program. The department offers students support with networking and applying for practicum placements.

Admissions

Entries appear in the following order: required test or GPA, minimum score (if required)/median score of students entering in 2015–2016.

Program	Degree	GRE-V	GRE-Q	GRE-Writing	GRE-Subject	Undergraduate GPA	Last 2 Years GPA	Psychology GPA	Master's GPA
Counseling	MA/MS	Not specified	Not specified	Not specified	Not specified	3/NA	Not specified	Not specified	Not specified
Psychology	MA/MS	Not specified	Not specified	Not specified	Not specified	3.3/NA	Not specified	Not specified	Not specified

Admissions Requirements:

Degree	GRE	GRE-Subject	Letters of Recommendation	Research Statement	Writing Sample	CV	Interview
Master's/Specialist	Optional	Optional	3	Required	None	Required	Required

Please note if these criteria vary for different programs: The counseling program focuses more strongly on counseling/clinical potential, while the psychology program focuses more strongly on academic performance and research experience, particularly for students who wish to go on to a doctoral program.

Admissions Criteria:

Research experience—low
Work experience—high
Clinically related public service—high
GPA—high

Letters of recommendation—high
Interview—high
Statement of goals and objectives—high
Undergraduate psychology preparation—medium

For additional information on admission requirements, visit http://www.paloaltou.edu/admissions/graduate-admissions.

Department Demographics

	Male (PT)	Female (PT)	Total	African-American/ Black (PT)	Hispanic/ Latino (PT)	Asian/ Pacific Islander (PT)	American Indian/ Alaska Native (PT)	Caucasian/ White (PT)	Unknown	Multiethnic (PT)	ADA (PT)	Int'l (PT)
Students	27 (59)	128 (220)	434	13 (13)	33 (40)	26 (48)	0 (1)	64 (113)	11 (57)	8 (7)	0 (0)	0 (0)

Financial Information/Assistance

Tuition: For information on tuition costs, visit http://www.paloaltou.edu/graduate-programs/choosing-graduate-program. Tuition is subject to change. Tuition costs vary by program.

Master's:
State residents: $20,150 per academic year.
State residents: $499 per credit hour.
Nonstate residents: $20,150 per academic year.
Nonstate residents: $499 per credit hour.

Financial Assistance:

	Teaching Assistantship (% Receiving)	Teaching Assistantship Tuition Remission	Research Assistantship (% Receiving)	Research Assistantship Tuition Remission	Fellowship (% Receiving)	Fellowship Tuition Remission
First-Year Student	NA (NA)	NA	NA (NA)	NA	NA (NA)	NA
Advanced Student	NA (NA)	NA	NA (NA)	NA	NA (NA)	NA

For additional information on financial assistance, visit http://www.paloaltou.edu/admissions/admissions-resources/financial-aid-and-scholarships.

Employment of Department Graduates

Master's:
Enrolled in a psychology doctoral program: 7
Enrolled in another graduate/professional program: 1
Employed in government agency: 1
Employed in a community mental health/counseling center: 26
Still seeking employment: 2
Not seeking employment: 3
Other employment position: 1
Do not know: 6
Total: 47

Additional Information

Housing and Day Care: No on-campus housing is available. No on-campus day care facilities are available.

Information for Students With Physical Disabilities: See the following website: http://www.paloaltou.edu/about/departments-and-offices/student-services.

Special Facilities or Resources: PAU offers an annual research forum and a network of many community mental health agencies throughout the greater Bay Area and Monterey Bay area.

Application Information: Palo Alto University, Office of Admissions, 1791 Arastradero Road, Palo Alto, CA 94304. *Fee:* $40. *Online application:* http://www.paloaltou.edu/apply.

Palo Alto University

PGSP - Stanford PsyD Consortium
1791 Arastradero Road
Palo Alto, CA 94304
Telephone: (800) 818-6136
Co-Directors of Clinical Training: Kimberly Hill, PhD and Steven Smith, PhD
Web: http://www.paloaltou.edu/graduate-programs/pgsp-psyd-stanford-consortium

E-mail: admissions@paloaltou.edu

Orientation, Objectives, and Emphasis of Department

The PGSP-Stanford PsyD Consortium is a practitioner-scholar program intended for individuals seeking careers devoted primarily to the direct delivery of clinical psychological services. The program provides a generalist education in clinical psychology, relegating the pursuit of more specialized training to students' later postdoctoral education. The Consortium training model emphasizes evidenced-based practice, and the priority we assign to evidenced-based practice is matched by our commitment to promote students' broad and general understanding of science and to foster students' ability to critically evaluate scientific theories, methods, and conclusions. As might be expected of an interdisciplinary faculty drawn from a medical school and an academic psychology department, the program takes a bio-psycho-social approach to psychology, striving for a balanced, integrated, contemporary understanding of the biological, social and psychological factors affecting human behavior. Thus, students' competent understanding of science and scientific methods represents a critical priority of the Consortium educational program.

Programs and Degrees Offered

Program	Degree	Application Deadline	Applications Received	Accepted	New Admits Enrolled (PT)	Total Enrolled (PT)	Degrees Awarded in 2014–2015	Median Years to Complete Degree	Dismissed/ Withdrew
Clinical Psychology	PsyD	January 2 (Fall)	328	49	32 (0)	167 (24)	26	4.96	0

APA Accreditation

Clinical PsyD: Student Outcome Data website: http://www.paloaltou.edu/graduate-programs/pgsp-psyd-stanford-consortium/student-admissions-outcomes-and-other-data.

Doctoral Degree (PsyD Clinical Psychology): For those doctoral students for whom a professional internship was required in this program prior to graduation:

Total students who applied for an internship: 30
Total students who obtained an internship: 29
Total students who obtained a paid internship: 29
Total students who obtained an unpaid internship: 0
Total students who were placed in APA/CPA-accredited internships: 29
Total students placed in internships not APA/CPA-accredited, but listed with the Association of Psychology Postdoctoral and Internship Centers (APPIC): 0
Total students placed in internships conforming to guidelines of the Council of Directors of School Psychology Programs (CDSPP): 0
Total students placed in internships that were not APA/CPA-accredited, APPIC or CDSSP listed: 0

Internships/Practica

The PGSP-Stanford Consortium provides students with experiences that are sequenced with increasing amounts of time spent in clinical work during each year of graduate training, with a total of approximately 2,000 clinical hours obtained prior to internship. In Year 1, students begin Supplemental Clinical Practica in the Stanford Psychiatry Department. In Year 2, students complete formal practica in captive training sites such as the PAU Gronowski Center, the Palo Alto VA, Stanford Inpatient Hospital, Stanford Faculty and Staff Help Center. In Years 3 and 4, students have many varied practica options spanning theoretical orientations, settings, populations, and locations across the Bay Area. At present there are approximately 40 approved practica sites to which third and fourth year students may apply including UCSF neuropsych, Santa Clara University College Counseling, Kaiser Permanente (child and adult), Children's Hospital Oakland, San Francisco VA, and the Palo Alto VA. In the fifth year, students are required to complete a 2,000-hour external APA-Accredited predoctoral internship.

Admissions

Entries appear in the following order: required test or GPA, minimum score (if required)/median score of students entering in 2015–2016.

Program	Degree	GRE-V	GRE-Q	GRE-Writing	GRE-Subject	Under-graduate GPA	Last 2 Years GPA	Psychol-ogy GPA	Master's GPA
Clinical Psychology	PsyD	NA/161	NA/156	NA/4.5	Not specified	NA/3.68	Not specified	Not specified	Not specified

Admissions Requirements:

Degree	GRE	GRE-Subject	Letters of Recommendation	Research Statement	Writing Sample	CV	Interview
Doctoral	Required	Recommended	3	Required	None	Required	Required

Admissions Criteria:

GRE scores—medium
Research experience—medium
Work experience—high
Clinically related public service—high
GPA—high

Letters of recommendation—high
Interview—high
Statement of goals and objectives—high
Undergraduate psychology preparation—high

For additional information on admission requirements, visit http://www.paloaltou.edu/graduate-programs/psyd-pgsp-stanford-consortium/admissions-requirements.

Department Demographics

	Male (PT)	Female (PT)	Total	African-American/ Black (PT)	Hispanic/ Latino (PT)	Asian/ Pacific Islander (PT)	American Indian/ Alaska Native (PT)	Caucasian/ White (PT)	Unknown	Multiethnic (PT)	ADA (PT)	Int'l (PT)
Students	21 (6)	146 (18)	191	7 (0)	14 (1)	24 (3)	0 (0)	94 (16)	23 (3)	5 (1)	8 (0)	3 (0)

Financial Information/Assistance

Tuition: For information on tuition costs, visit http://www.paloaltou.edu/admissions/admissions-resources/tuition-and-costs. Tuition is subject to change.

Doctoral:
State residents: $50,853 per academic year.
Nonstate residents: $50,853 per academic year.

Financial Assistance:

	Teaching Assistantship (% Receiving)	Teaching Assistantship Tuition Remission	Research Assistantship (% Receiving)	Research Assistantship Tuition Remission	Fellowship (% Receiving)	Fellowship Tuition Remission
First-Year Student	$3,000 (NA)	NA	$1,000 (NA)	NA	$5,000 (NA)	Partial
Advanced Student	$3,000 (NA)	NA	$1,000 (NA)	NA	$4,000 (NA)	Partial

For additional information on financial assistance, visit http://www.paloaltou.edu/admissions/admissions-resources/financial-aid.

Employment of Department Graduates

Doctoral:
Enrolled in a postdoctoral residency/fellowship: 21
Employed in a hospital/medical center: 4
Still seeking employment: 1
Total: 26

Additional Information

Housing and Day Care: No on-campus housing is available. No on-campus day care facilities are available.

Special Facilities or Resources: The PGSP-Stanford PsyD Consortium at Palo Alto University draws upon nationally renowned faculty and resources from the Pacific Graduate School of Psychology and the Stanford University School of Medicine's Department of Psychiatry and Behavioral Sciences. Among the unique features of the PGSP-Stanford Consortium is the context in which students are trained. In addition to its research and teaching facilities, the Stanford University Department of Psychiatry and Behavioral Sciences is the home of the largest clinic at the Stanford University Medical Center. Over 40,000 patient visits per year are completed at the Department of Psychiatry. The mission of the Stanford clinics involves the care of a wide variety of patients with diagnoses that span the spectrum from mood and anxiety disorders, to personality disorders, as well as bipolar disorder and schizophrenia. The majority of faculty who teach clinical courses also provide direct clinical care. Thus, instructors bring a fresh and vital perspective to their teaching. Almost all students elect to complete supplemental practica in the context of applied clinical research projects at the Stanford Psychiatry Department.

Application Information: Office of Admissions, Palo Alto University, 1791 Arastradero Road, Palo Alto, CA. 94304. *Fee:* $50. *Online application:* http://www.paloaltou.edu/apply.

Palo Alto University

PhD Clinical Psychology Program
1791 Arastradero Road
Palo Alto, CA 94304
Telephone: (800) 818-6136
Director of Clinical Training: Dr. Rowena Gomez
Web: http://www.paloaltou.edu/graduate-programs/phd-programs/phd-clinical-psychology

E-mail: admissions@paloaltou.edu

Orientation, Objectives, and Emphasis of Department

The PhD Clinical Psychology Program at Palo Alto University (PAU), Pacific Graduate School of Psychology (PGSP) is deeply committed to educating well-rounded clinical psychologists who are capable and competent as both researchers and clinicians. Students are taught to be science minded while appreciating the larger role of psychology in alleviating suffering in the world. This balance includes learning to value evidence-based clinical models while maintaining the responsibilities psychologists have to their community, society, and profession. An outstanding faculty of clinicians and researchers provides rigorous classroom instruction, clinical supervision, and research mentoring to help students find the right balance for them. Working within a training model best described as practitioner–scientist, students systematically move through 5 years of coursework and practica to acquire PhD-level competence and capability in areas of psychological theory, research, and practice.

Programs and Degrees Offered

Program	Degree	Application Deadline	Applica-tions Received	Accepted	New Admits Enrolled (PT)	Total Enrolled (PT)	Degrees Awarded in 2014–2015	Median Years to Complete Degree	Dismissed/ Withdrew
Clinical Psychology	PhD	January 2 (Fall)	340	210	87 (1)	431 (84)	55	4.97	3

APA Accreditation

Clinical PhD: Student Outcome Data website: http://www.paloaltou.edu/graduate-programs/phd-programs/phd-clinical-psychology/student-admissions-outcomes-and-other-data.

Doctoral Degree (PhD Clinical Psychology): For those doctoral students for whom a professional internship was required in this program prior to graduation:
Total students who applied for an internship: 74
Total students who obtained an internship: 70
Total students who obtained a paid internship: 69
Total students who obtained an unpaid internship: 1
Total students who were placed in APA/CPA-accredited internships: 61
Total students placed in internships not APA/CPA-accredited, but listed with the Association of Psychology Postdoctoral and Internship Centers (APPIC): 4
Total students placed in internships conforming to guidelines of the Council of Directors of School Psychology Programs (CDSPP): 0
Total students placed in internships that were not APA/CPA-accredited, APPIC or CDSSP listed: 5

Internships/Practica

All students take their second year of practicum at our Kurt and Barbara Gronowski Clinic, and their third and fourth year practicum training at community agencies. All PAU students are required to complete an APA-accredited internship in their fifth year of the program. Students who submit a waiver may opt to complete an APPIC or CAPIC-approved internship instead.

Admissions

Entries appear in the following order: required test or GPA, minimum score (if required)/median score of students entering in 2015–2016.

Program	Degree	GRE-V	GRE-Q	GRE-Writing	GRE-Subject	Under-graduate GPA	Last 2 Years GPA	Psychol-ogy GPA	Master's GPA
Clinical Psychology	PhD	NA/155	NA/152	NA/4	Not specified	NA/3.55	NA/NA	NA/NA	NA/3.7

Admissions Requirements:

Degree	GRE	GRE-Subject	Letters of Recommendation	Research Statement	Writing Sample	CV	Interview
Doctoral	Required	Optional	3	Required	None	Optional	Required

Admissions Criteria:

GRE scores—high

Research experience—medium

Work experience—medium

Clinically related public service—medium

GPA—high

Letters of recommendation—high

Interview—medium

Statement of goals and objectives—medium

For additional information on admission requirements, visit http://www.paloaltou.edu/graduate-programs/phd-programs/phd-clinical-psychology/admissions.

Department Demographics

	Male (PT)	Female (PT)	Total	African-American/ Black (PT)	Hispanic/ Latino (PT)	Asian/ Pacific Islander (PT)	American Indian/ Alaska Native (PT)	Caucasian/ White (PT)	Unknown	Multiethnic (PT)	ADA (PT)	Int'l (PT)
Students	100 (15)	331 (69)	515	20 (3)	43 (4)	61 (8)	2 (0)	220 (53)	79 (12)	6 (4)	36 (0)	25 (0)

Financial Information/Assistance

Tuition: For information on tuition costs, visit http://www.paloaltou.edu/admissions/admissions-resources/tuition-and-costs. Tuition is subject to change.

Doctoral:

State residents: $47,841 per academic year.

Nonstate residents: $47,841 per academic year.

Financial Assistance:

	Teaching Assistantship (% Receiving)	Teaching Assistantship Tuition Remission	Research Assistantship (% Receiving)	Research Assistantship Tuition Remission	Fellowship (% Receiving)	Fellowship Tuition Remission
First-Year Student	NA (NA)	NA	NA (NA)	NA	$10,000 (NA)	NA
Advanced Student	$3,000 (NA)	NA	$4,000 (NA)	NA	$5,000 (NA)	NA

For additional information on financial assistance, visit http://www.paloaltou.edu/admissions/admissions-resources/financial-aid-and-scholarships/graduate-students.

Employment of Department Graduates

Doctoral:

Enrolled in a postdoctoral residency/fellowship: 14

Employed in independent practice: 1

Employed in other positions at a higher education institution: 2

Employed in government agency: 2

Employed in a community mental health/counseling center: 8

Employed in a hospital/medical center: 12

Still seeking employment: 2

Do not know: 24

Total: 65

Additional Information

Housing and Day Care: No on-campus housing is available. No on-campus day care facilities are available.

Special Facilities or Resources: PAU's setting as a free-standing graduate school of psychology is much enhanced by our San Francisco Bay Area location. We provide students with access to local university libraries (e.g., Stanford, UC Berkeley). The range of clinical experience available to students is inexhaustible. Our faculty have active research programs in which students participate. Furthermore, PAU has a close relationship with local VAMCs, and the Gronowski clinic (a community-based psychology training clinic and treatment center dedicated to providing high quality, evidence-based, clinical services to adults, older adults, adolescents, children, and families in the community).

Application Information: Office of Admissions, Palo Alto University, 1791 Arastradero Road, Palo Alto, CA 94304. *Fee:* $50. *Online application:* http://www.paloaltou.edu/apply.

Pepperdine University

Psychology Division
Graduate School of Education and Psychology
6100 Center Drive, 5th Floor
Los Angeles, CA 90045
Telephone: (310) 568-5600
Associate Dean of Psychology: Dr. Robert A. deMayo

E-mail: mapsych@pepperdine.edu
Web: http://gsep.pepperdine.edu/

Orientation, Objectives, and Emphasis of Department

The psychology degree programs are designed to provide the student with a theoretical and practical understanding of the principles of psychology within the framework of a strong clinical emphasis. Courses present various aspects of the art and science of psychology as it is applied to the understanding of human behavior and to the prevention, diagnosis, and treatment of mental and emotional problems. The MA in psychology serves as the prerequisite for the PsyD degree, or for students seeking human services positions in community agencies and organizations. The MA in Clinical Psychology provides academic preparation for the Marriage and Family Therapy license. The PsyD program subscribes to a practitioner–scholar model of training.

Programs and Degrees Offered

Program	Degree	Application Deadline	Applications Received	Accepted	New Admits Enrolled (PT)	Total Enrolled (PT)	Degrees Awarded in 2014–2015	Median Years to Complete Degree	Dismissed/ Withdrew
Psychology	MA/MS	June 1 (Fall), October 1 (Spring), March 1 (Summer), Rolling	107	71	35 (0)	126 (23)	90	2	0
Clinical Psychology	PsyD	January 8 (Fall)	125	42	30 (0)	153 (4)	24	4	0
Clinical Psychology Mft Emphasis - Evening Format	MA/MS	June 1 (Fall), October 1 (Spring), March 1 (Summer), Rolling	239	176	85 (0)	395 (34)	135	3	0
Clinical Psychology Mft Emphasis - Day Format	MA/MS	February 1 (Fall)	158	81	46 (0)	85 (0)	40	2	0

Programs and Degrees Offered *(con't.)*

Program	Degree	Application Deadline	Applica-tions Received	Accepted	New Admits Enrolled (PT)	Total Enrolled (PT)	Degrees Awarded in 2014–2015	Median Years to Complete Degree	Dismissed/Withdrew
Clinical Psychology Mft Emphasis With Latinas/Os	MA/MS	June 1 (Fall), Rolling	17	14	12 (0)	44 (0)	0		0
Behavorial Psychology	MA/MS	June 1 (Fall), October 1 (Spring), March 1 (Summer)	0	0	0 (0)	0 (0)	0		0

APA Accreditation

Clinical PsyD: Student Outcome Data website: http://gsep.pepperdine.edu/doctorate-clinical-psychology/statistics/.

Doctoral Degree (PsyD Clinical Psychology): For those doctoral students for whom a professional internship was required in this program prior to graduation:
Total students who applied for an internship: 35
Total students who obtained an internship: 32
Total students who obtained a paid internship: 32
Total students who obtained an unpaid internship: 0
Total students who were placed in APA/CPA-accredited internships: 29
Total students placed in internships not APA/CPA-accredited, but listed with the Association of Psychology Postdoctoral and Internship Centers (APPIC): 1
Total students placed in internships conforming to guidelines of the Council of Directors of School Psychology Programs (CDSPP): 0
Total students placed in internships that were not APA/CPA-accredited, APPIC or CDSSP listed: 2

Master's Degree (MA/MS Clinical Psychology MFT Emphasis - Evening Format): An internship experience, such as a final research project or "capstone" experience is required of graduates. Master's Degree (MA/MS Clinical Psychology MFT Emphasis - Day Format): An internship experience, such as a final research project or "capstone" experience is required of graduates. Master's Degree (MA/MS Clinical Psychology MFT Emphasis with Latinas/os): An internship experience, such as a final research project or "capstone" experience is required of graduates.

Internships/Practica

Students in the PsyD and MA in Clinical Psychology programs complete practicum requirements at Pepperdine clinics or affiliated agencies in the community. PsyD students complete predoctoral internships in approved agencies. Pepperdine clinical training staff assist students in locating training positions.

Admissions

Entries appear in the following order: required test or GPA, minimum score (if required)/median score of students entering in 2015–2016.

Program	Degree	GRE-V	GRE-Q	GRE-Writing	GRE-Subject	Under-graduate GPA	Last 2 Years GPA	Psychol-ogy GPA	Master's GPA
Psychology	MA/MS	NA/151	NA/150	NA/3.8	Not specified	NA/3.29	Not specified	Not specified	Not specified
Clinical Psychology	PsyD	NA/152	NA/148	NA/3.9	Not specified	NA/3.2	Not specified	Not specified	NA/3.95
Clinical Psychology MFT Emphasis - Evening Format	MA/MS	NA/149	NA/147	NA/3.7	Not specified	NA/3.25	Not specified	Not specified	Not specified

Admissions *(con't.)*

Program	Degree	GRE-V	GRE-Q	GRE-Writing	GRE-Subject	Under-graduate GPA	Last 2 Years GPA	Psychol-ogy GPA	Master's GPA
Clinical Psychology MFT Emphasis - Day Format	MA/MS	NA/153	NA/150	NA/4.2	Not specified	NA/3.36	Not specified	Not specified	Not specified
Clinical Psychology MFT Emphasis with Latinas/os	MA/MS	NA/144	NA/141	NA/3.2	Not specified	NA/3.05	Not specified	Not specified	Not specified
Behavorial Psychology	MA/MS	Not specified	Not specified	Not specified	Not specified	Not specified	Not specified	Not specified	Not specified

Admissions Requirements:

Degree	GRE	GRE-Subject	Letters of Recom-mendation	Research Statement	Writing Sample	CV	Interview
Master's/Specialist	Optional	Optional	2	Required	None	None	None
Doctoral	Required	Required	2	Required	None	Required	Required

Please note if these criteria vary for different programs: Criteria vary by program. The admission criteria apply to our two evening format masters programs: the Master of Arts in Psychology and the Master of Arts in Clinical Psychology program with an Emphasis in Marriage and Family Therapy. Entrance to the daytime format Master of Arts in Clinical Psychology program requires an undergraduate major in psychology or related academic field and the GRE. Admission to our Doctor of Psychology program requires a master's degree in psychology or a closely related field. Clinical and research experience are regarded as highly important for admission to the doctoral program.

Admissions Criteria:

GRE scores—medium
Research experience—medium
Work experience—medium
Clinically related public service—medium
GPA—high

Letters of recommendation—high
Interview—low
Statement of goals and objectives—high
Undergraduate psychology preparation—medium

For additional information on admission requirements, visit http://gsep.pepperdine.edu/admission/.

Department Demographics

	Male (PT)	Female (PT)	Total	African-American/ Black (PT)	Hispanic/ Latino (PT)	Asian/ Pacific Islander (PT)	American Indian/ Alaska Native (PT)	Caucasian/ White (PT)	Unknown (PT)	Multiethnic (PT)	ADA (PT)	Int'l (PT)
Students	138 (11)	661 (50)	860	77 (3)	137 (13)	83 (7)	4 (0)	360 (20)	138 (18)	0 (0)	0 (0)	63 (0)

Financial Information/Assistance

Tuition: For information on tuition costs, visit http://gsep.pepperdine.edu/financial-aid/cost/. Higher tuition cost for this program: MA in Clinical Psychology, MFT Day Format, full-time program, $1440 per credit hour. Additional fees are assessed to students beyond the costs of tuition for the following: PsyD graduate association fee $40.

Doctoral:
State residents: $1,440 per credit hour.
Nonstate residents: $1,440 per credit hour.

Master's:
State residents: $1,145 per credit hour.
Nonstate residents: $1,145 per credit hour.

Financial Assistance:

	Teaching Assistantship (% Receiving)	Teaching Assistantship Tuition Remission	Research Assistantship (% Receiving)	Research Assistantship Tuition Remission	Fellowship (% Receiving)	Fellowship Tuition Remission
First-Year Student	$1,635 (16)	NA	$1,905 (5)	NA	$8,350 (NA)	NA
Advanced Student	$2,556 (34)	NA	$3,752 (14)	NA	$6,140 (NA)	NA

For additional information on financial assistance, visit http://gsep.pepperdine.edu/admission/financial-aid/.

Employment of Department Graduates

Master's:
Enrolled in a psychology doctoral program: 3
Enrolled in another graduate/professional program: 7
Employed in academic position at a 2-year/4-year college: 1
Employed in other positions at a higher education institution: 4
Employed in a professional position in a school system: 1
Employed in government agency: 3
Employed in a community mental health/counseling center: 14
Employed in a hospital/medical center: 4
Still seeking employment: 24
Not seeking employment: 11
Other employment position: 4
Do not know: 213
Total: 289

Doctoral:
Enrolled in a postdoctoral residency/fellowship: 2
Enrolled in another graduate/professional program: 1
Employed in independent practice: 2
Employed in other positions at a higher education institution: 2
Employed in a hospital/medical center: 3
Still seeking employment: 1
Not seeking employment: 7
Total: 18

Additional Information

Housing and Day Care: On-campus housing is available. See the following website for more information: http://community.pepperdine.edu/housing/grad-students/. No on-campus day care facilities are available.

Information for Students With Physical Disabilities: See the following website: http://www.pepperdine.edu/disabilityservices/.

Special Facilities or Resources: The Master of Arts in Psychology and Clinical Psychology programs at Pepperdine University are offered at four campuses throughout Southern California. Computer laboratories and libraries are available at all four campuses. Psychology clinics are located at the West Los Angeles Graduate Campus, the Irvine Graduate Campus and the Encino Graduate Campus, as well as a student counseling center on the Malibu Campus.

Application Information: Samantha Tarin, Admissions Specialist, 6100 Center Drive, 5th Floor, Los Angeles, CA 90045. *Fee:* $55. *Online application:* http://gsep.pepperdine.edu/admission/application/.

San Diego State University
Department of Psychology
College of Sciences
5500 Campanile Drive
San Diego, CA 92182-4611
Telephone: (619) 594-5359
Chairperson: Georg Matt

E-mail: jackie.jones@mail.sdsu.edu
Web: http://www.psychology.sdsu.edu/

Orientation, Objectives, and Emphasis of Department
The MA program in Psychology provides graduate level studies and preparation for PhD programs in several areas. It is particularly appropriate for students who need advanced work to strengthen their profiles for application to PhD programs, or for those wishing to explore graduate-level work before committing to PhD training. Areas of emphasis within the MA are: Behavioral Psychology, Social Psychology, Physical and/or Mental Health Research, Developmental Psychology, and Learning and Cognition. Students

take core classes in the major areas of psychology and electives in their areas of specialization. The MS Degree program in Applied Psychology has emphases in Program Evaluation and Industrial/Organizational Psychology. Our research-oriented program does not offer instruction in technical skills (e.g., intelligence testing) and does not have a counseling practicum or provide opportunities for development of clinical skills. Students gain valuable research experience, which may involve working with humans in non-clinical areas. Upon admission to the program students are assigned a faculty research mentor who guides them through the research process leading to the thesis. Students are prepared for professional careers in the public and private sectors or for doctoral-level training in Applied Psychology.

Programs and Degrees Offered

Program	Degree	Application Deadline	Applica-tions Received	Accepted	New Admits Enrolled (PT)	Total Enrolled (PT)	Degrees Awarded in 2014–2015	Median Years to Complete Degree	Dismissed/ Withdrew
Psychology	MA/MS	December 15 (Fall)	104	61	21 (0)	27 (0)	36	2.5	1
Applied Psychology	MA/MS	December 15 (Fall)	83	5	5 (0)	16	10	2.5	0

Internships/Practica

An essential component of graduate training in Applied Psychology is an internship experience that provides students with an opportunity to apply their classroom training and acquire new skills in a field setting. Interns are placed in a variety of settings, such as community-based organizations, consulting firms, city and county organizations, education, hospitality, high tech and private industry. Through the internship experience students also develop close contacts with other psychologists and practitioners working in their field. Internships are normally undertaken during the summer following the first year in the program and during the fall semester of the second year.

Admissions

Entries appear in the following order: required test or GPA, minimum score (if required)/median score of students entering in 2015–2016.

Program	Degree	GRE-V	GRE-Q	GRE-Writing	GRE-Subject	Under-graduate GPA	Last 2 Years GPA	Psychol-ogy GPA	Master's GPA
Psychology	MA/MS	Not specified	Not specified	Not specified	Not specified	Not specified	Not specified	Not specified	Not specified
Applied Psychology	MA/MS	Not specified	Not specified	Not specified	Not specified	Not specified	Not specified	Not specified	Not specified

Admissions Requirements:

Degree	GRE	GRE-Subject	Letters of Recom-mendation	Research Statement	Writing Sample	CV	Interview
Master's/Specialist	Required	None	3	Required	Optional	Required	Required

Please note if these criteria vary for different programs: Work experience is viewed more closely by the Applied Psychology (MS) faculty than by the MA faculty. Research experience is particularly important in the MA program as this is a predoctoral program.

Admissions Criteria:

GRE scores—high
Research experience—high
Work experience—medium
Clinically related public service—low
GPA—high

Letters of recommendation—high
Interview—high
Statement of goals and objectives—high
Undergraduate psychology preparation—medium

For additional information on admission requirements, visit http://www.psychology.sdsu.edu/graduate/masters-programs/prospective-students/application-procedures.

Department Demographics

	Male (PT)	Female (PT)	Total	African-American/ Black (PT)	Hispanic/ Latino (PT)	Asian/ Pacific Islander (PT)	American Indian/ Alaska Native (PT)	Caucasian/ White (PT)	Unknown	Multiethnic (PT)	ADA (PT)	Int'l (PT)
Students	21 (0)	37 (0)	58	0 (0)	4 (0)	8 (0)	0 (0)	41 (0)	3 (0)	2 (0)	0 (0)	2 (0)

Financial Information/Assistance

Tuition: For information on tuition costs, visit http://bfa.sdsu.edu/fm/co/sfs/registration.html. Tuition is subject to change.

Master's:
State residents: $8,242 per academic year.

Financial Assistance:

	Teaching Assistantship (% Receiving)	Teaching Assistantship Tuition Remission	Research Assistantship (% Receiving)	Research Assistantship Tuition Remission	Fellowship (% Receiving)	Fellowship Tuition Remission
First-Year Student	$12,360 (NA)	NA	$12,360 (NA)	NA	NA (NA)	NA
Advanced Student	$12,360 (NA)	NA	$12,360 (NA)	NA	NA (NA)	NA

For additional information on financial assistance, visit http://go.sdsu.edu/student_affairs/financialaid/Default.aspx.

Employment of Department Graduates

Master's:
Enrolled in a psychology doctoral program: 17
Enrolled in another graduate/professional program: 3
Employed in academic position at a 2-year/4-year college: 1
Employed in other positions at a higher education institution: 3
Employed in business or industry: 9
Employed in a community mental health/counseling center: 4
Employed in a hospital/medical center: 2
Still seeking employment: 1
Not seeking employment: 2
Other employment position: 1
Do not know: 3
Total: 46

Additional Information

Housing and Day Care: On-campus housing is available. See the following website for more information: http://housing.sdsu.edu/housing/. On-campus day care facilities are available. See the following website for more information: http://childcare.sdsu.edu/.

Information for Students With Physical Disabilities: See the following website: http://go.sdsu.edu/student_affairs/sds/.

Special Facilities or Resources: The following research labs welcome master's students: Anxiety and Depression in Children/Adolescents; Stereotype Threat, Aging/Dementia, Active Living/Healthy Eating; Alcohol Research; Behavioral Teratology; Brain Development Imaging; Categorical Distortions; Child Language/Emotion; Child and Adolescent Mental Health; Cognitive Development; Culture, Work Values/Organizational Behavior; Generational Differences; Child Abuse/Neglect; Health Outcomes; Intergroup Relations; Life-Span Human Senses; Measurement and Evaluation; Minority Community Health Intervention; Organizational Leadership/Citizenship; Organizational Research; Personality Assessment/Psychometrics; Personality Measurement Binge Drinking/intervention; Family Library Use/Lifelong Learning; Social Support and Education on Health/Well Being of People with Chronic Diseases; Psychosocial Factors in Coronary Heart Disease; Language/Cognitive Studies; Psychosocial, Chronic Illness adjustment; Smoking; Social Development; Social Influence and Group Dynamics; Social Rejection; Stress/Coping; and Activity for Adolescent Girls.

Students may conduct research at Children's Hospital, where several faculty members have their offices. Other resources include a community psychology clinic, the Center for Behavioral and Community Health Studies, Center for Behavioral Teratology, and the Center for Research in Mathematics and Science Education. Also available is an exchange program with the University of Mannheim, Germany. Students can choose to spend a semester or a year attending classes in Mannheim, and graduate students from Mannheim can spend a semester or a year taking classes here.

Application Information: Master's Programs Admissions Coordinator, Department of Psychology, San Diego State University, 5500 Campanile Drive, San Diego, CA 92182-4611. *Fee:* $55. *Online application:* http://arweb.sdsu.edu/es/admissions/grad/index.html.

San Diego State University/University of California, San Diego Joint Doctoral Program in Clinical Psychology

SDSU Department of Psychology/UCSD Department of Psychiatry
SDSU: College of Sciences UCSD: School of Medicine
6363 Alvarado Court, Suite #103
San Diego, CA 92120-4913
Telephone: (619) 594-2246
Co-Directors: Elizabeth Klonoff, PhD, Robert Heaton, PhD

E-mail: PsycJDP@mail.sdsu.edu
Web: http://clinpsyc.sdsu.edu/

Orientation, Objectives, and Emphasis of Department

Our PhD program is a cooperative venture of an academic Department of Psychology (SDSU) and a medical school Department of Psychiatry (UCSD). This partnership between two different departments in two universities provides unusual opportunities for interdisciplinary research. We currently offer concentrations in behavioral medicine, neuropsychology, and experimental psychopathology. The scientist–practitioner model on which the program is based involves a strong commitment to research as well as clinical training. The program aims to prepare students for leadership roles in academic and research settings. Our program is designed as a 5-year curriculum with a core of classroom instruction followed by apprenticeship training in specialty areas with appropriate seminars and tutorials. Clinical experiences are integrated with formal instruction throughout.

Programs and Degrees Offered

Program	Degree	Application Deadline	Applica-tions Received	Accepted	New Admits Enrolled (PT)	Total Enrolled (PT)	Degrees Awarded in 2014–2015	Median Years to Complete Degree	Dismissed/ Withdrew
Clinical Psychology	PhD	December 1 (Fall)	391	16	8 (0)	62 (0)	12	6	1

APA Accreditation

Clinical PhD: Student Outcome Data website: http://clinpsyc.sdsu.edu/admissions-2/student-admissions-outcome-and-other-data/.

Doctoral Degree (PhD Clinical Psychology): For those doctoral students for whom a professional internship was required in this program prior to graduation:
Total students who applied for an internship: 12
Total students who obtained an internship: 12
Total students who obtained a paid internship: 12
Total students who obtained an unpaid internship: 0
Total students who were placed in APA/CPA-accredited internships: 12
Total students placed in internships not APA/CPA-accredited, but listed with the Association of Psychology Postdoctoral and Internship Centers (APPIC): 0
Total students placed in internships conforming to guidelines of the Council of Directors of School Psychology Programs (CDSPP): 0
Total students placed in internships that were not APA/CPA-accredited, APPIC or CDSSP listed: 0

Internships/Practica

SDSU: Primary placement for all students in their second year is the Psychology Clinic. Students are taught general clinical skills. Therapy sessions are routinely videotaped for review in intensive weekly supervision session. UCSD: VA Outpatient Clinic: psychiatric outpatients—assessment and individual and group therapy. VA Medical Center: psychiatric inpatients—assessment, individual and group therapy. UCSD Outpatient Psychiatric Clinic: psychiatric outpatients—neuropsychological assessment and individual and group therapy. UCSD Medical Center: assessment and therapy of all types. All practicum placements are assigned for one full year beginning in the student's second year.

Admissions

Entries appear in the following order: required test or GPA, minimum score (if required)/median score of students entering in 2015–2016.

Program	Degree	GRE-V	GRE-Q	GRE-Writing	GRE-Subject	Under-graduate GPA	Last 2 Years GPA	Psychol-ogy GPA	Master's GPA
Clinical Psychology	PhD	153/162	153/159	Not specified	NA/745	3/3.72	Not specified	Not specified	Not specified

Admissions Requirements:

Degree	GRE	GRE-Subject	Letters of Recom-mendation	Research Statement	Writing Sample	CV	Interview
Doctoral	Required	Required	3	Required	None	Required	Required

Admissions Criteria:

GRE scores—medium
Research experience—high
Work experience—low
Clinically related public service—medium
GPA—high

Letters of recommendation—high
Interview—high
Statement of goals and objectives—high
Undergraduate psychology preparation—high

For additional information on admission requirements, visit http://clinpsyc.sdsu.edu/admissions-2/application-procedures/.

Department Demographics

	Male (PT)	Female (PT)	Total	African-American/ Black (PT)	Hispanic/ Latino (PT)	Asian/ Pacific Islander (PT)	American Indian/ Alaska Native (PT)	Caucasian/ White (PT)	Unknown	Multiethnic (PT)	ADA (PT)	Int'l (PT)
Students	4 (0)	58 (0)	62	2 (0)	6 (0)	6 (0)	0 (0)	38 (0)	5 (0)	5 (0)	2 (0)	1 (0)

Financial Information/Assistance

Tuition: For information on tuition costs, visit http://arweb.sdsu.edu/es/admissions/costs.html. Tuition is subject to change.

Doctoral:
State residents: $8,350 per academic year.
Nonstate residents: $15,046 per academic year.

Financial Assistance:

	Teaching Assistantship (% Receiving)	Teaching Assistantship Tuition Remission	Research Assistantship (% Receiving)	Research Assistantship Tuition Remission	Fellowship (% Receiving)	Fellowship Tuition Remission
First-Year Student	NA (NA)	NA	$18,000 (NA)	Full	$18,000 (NA)	Full
Advanced Student	$18,000 (NA)	Full	$18,000 (NA)	Full	$18,000 (NA)	Full

For additional information on financial assistance, visit http://clinpsyc.sdsu.edu/student-handbook/financial-information/student-fundingstipends/.

Employment of Department Graduates

Doctoral:
Enrolled in a postdoctoral residency/fellowship: 12
Total: 12

Additional Information

Housing and Day Care: On-campus housing is available. See the following website for more information: http://housing.sdsu.edu/housing/; http://hdh.ucsd.edu/arch/. On-campus day care facilities are available. See the following website for more information: https://childcare.sdsu.edu/; http://child.ucsd.edu/programs/ecec/index.html.

Information for Students With Physical Disabilities: See the following website: http://go.sdsu.edu/student_affairs/sds/; http://disabilities.ucsd.edu.

Special Facilities or Resources: The UCSD Department of Psychiatry, through the medical school, UCSD hospitals, and the VA Medical Center, has available all of the modern research and clinical facilities consistent with the School of Medicine's ranking among the top ten in the country in biomedical research. These include specialty laboratories (e.g., sleep labs), access to clinical trials, supercomputing facilities, and state-of-the-art neurochemical and biochemical laboratory facilities. Qualified students interested in MRI studies have access to a number of fully supported imagers. At SDSU, the Department of Psychology has a state-of-the-art video-equipped therapy training complex, as well as experiment rooms, equipment (e.g., computerized test administration capabilities), and supplies available for research, including computerized physiological assessment and biofeedback laboratories. Animal research can be conducted on campus, where small animals are housed in a modern vivarium staffed with a veterinarian. SDSU faculty also supervise research on more exotic species at Sea World and the San Diego Zoo. The College of Sciences maintains a completely equipped electronics shop, a wood shop, a metal shop, and computer support facilities with several high end UNIX servers, all staffed with full-time technicians. Collaborative relationships with faculty in the Graduate School of Public Health allow access to resources there as well.

Application Information: *Fee:* $55. *Online application:* https://app.applyyourself.com/?id=sdsu-grad.

San Francisco State University

Psychology
Science & Engineering
1600 Holloway Avenue
San Francisco, CA 94132
Telephone: (415) 338-2167
Chairperson: Jeffrey Cookston

E-mail: psych@sfsu.edu
Web: http://psychology.sfsu.edu

Orientation, Objectives, and Emphasis of Department

The theoretical orientation of the Clinical program is based on psychodynamic, developmental theory within a family and community systems framework. The Clinical program emphasizes training in psychotherapy and applied clinical experience. The Developmental program takes a life span approach. Research and courses emphasize family systems, attachment, social, cognitive and emotional development, and the development of diverse populations. Training is provided on developmental research methods. The Industrial/Organizational (I/O) MS program has a science-practice approach to work place issues. The program prepares graduates for professional work in business, industry, and government and for continuing education in I/O psychology. The Mind, Brain and Behavior program takes a basic scientific research approach, including the study of physiological issues. Prepares students for MA level careers and doctoral study. The School Psychology program emphasizes, within a cultural context, developmental and psychodynamic theories with an applied interpersonal relations and family systems approach. The Social psychology program, oriented toward research and applications in the public interest, prepares students for MA-level careers and doctoral study with training in both qualitative and quantitative methods.

Programs and Degrees Offered

Program	Degree	Application Deadline	Applica-tions Received	Accepted	New Admits Enrolled (PT)	Total Enrolled (PT)	Degrees Awarded in 2014–2015	Median Years to Complete Degree	Dismissed/Withdrew
Clinical Psychology	MA/MS	February 1 (Fall)	158	8	8	16	10	2	0

Programs and Degrees Offered *(con't.)*

Program	Degree	Application Deadline	Applica- tions Received	Accepted	New Admits Enrolled (PT)	Total Enrolled (PT)	Degrees Awarded in 2014– 2015	Median Years to Complete Degree	Dismissed/ Withdrew
Developmental Psychology	MA/MS	February 1 (Fall)	31	9	6	14	11	2	0
Industrial/ Organizational Psychology	MA/MS	February 1 (Fall)	79	10	6	15	10	2	0
Mind, Brain, and Behavior	MA/MS	February 1 (Fall)	62	19	10				0
School Psychology	MA/MS	February 1 (Fall)	36	11	8	8	10	3	0
Social Psychology	MA/MS	February 1 (Fall)	36	11	10	21	9	2	0

Internships/Practica

For clinical students, practicum in the first year is provided in the Psychology Clinic and at sites in San Francisco dealing with children and adolescents. Second year internships are located in mental health settings throughout the San Francisco Bay area. For I/O students, an internship is required during the second year of study. Students are placed in various work organizations throughout the San Francisco Bay Area. Students enrolled in the School Psychology program are placed in a first year school-based practicum by the program. Students apply for and are placed in schools throughout the San Francisco Bay Area in their second year. Students are required to complete a third year paid internship.

Admissions

Entries appear in the following order: required test or GPA, minimum score (if required)/median score of students entering in 2015–2016.

Program	Degree	GRE-V	GRE-Q	GRE-Writing	GRE-Subject	Under-graduate GPA	Last 2 Years GPA	Psychol-ogy GPA	Master's GPA
Clinical Psychology	MA/MS	NA/NA	NA/NA	NA/NA	Not specified	3/NA	3/NA	3/NA	Not specified
Developmental Psychology	MA/MS	NA/NA	NA/NA	NA/NA	Not specified	3/NA	3/NA	3/NA	Not specified
Industrial/ Organizational Psychology	MA/MS	NA/NA	NA/NA	NA/NA	Not specified	3/NA	3/NA	3/NA	Not specified
Mind, Brain, and Behavior	MA/MS	NA/NA	NA/NA	NA/NA	Not specified	3/NA	3/NA	3/NA	Not specified
School Psychology	MA/MS	NA/NA	NA/NA	NA/NA	Not specified	3/NA	3/NA	3/NA	Not specified
Social Psychology	MA/MS	NA/NA	NA/NA	NA/NA	Not specified	3/NA	3/NA	3/NA	Not specified

Admissions Requirements:

Degree	GRE	GRE-Subject	Letters of Recom-mendation	Research Statement	Writing Sample	CV	Interview
Master's/Specialist	Required	None	3	Required	Optional	Required	Required

Please note if these criteria vary for different programs: Applicants to the Clinical and School programs are required to submit a CV; it is optional for the other concentrations.

Admissions Criteria:

GRE scores—medium
Research experience—high
Work experience—medium
Clinically related public service—high
GPA—high

Letters of recommendation—high
Interview—high
Statement of goals and objectives—high
Undergraduate psychology preparation—medium

For additional information on admission requirements, visit http://psychology.sfsu.edu/graduate/application.html.

Department Demographics

	Male (PT)	Female (PT)	Total	African-American/ Black (PT)	Hispanic/ Latino (PT)	Asian/ Pacific Islander (PT)	American Indian/ Alaska Native (PT)	Caucasian/ White (PT)	Unknown	Multiethnic (PT)	ADA (PT)	Int'l (PT)
Students	29 (0)	45 (0)	74	3 (0)	5 (0)	6 (0)	0 (0)	50 (0)	0 (0)	10 (0)	0 (0)	5 (0)

Financial Information/Assistance

Tuition: For information on tuition costs, visit http://www.sfsu.edu/prospect/costs/fees.html. Tuition is subject to change.

Master's:
State residents: $7,542 per academic year.
Nonstate residents: $14,982 per academic year.

Financial Assistance:

	Teaching Assistantship (% Receiving)	Teaching Assistantship Tuition Remission	Research Assistantship (% Receiving)	Research Assistantship Tuition Remission	Fellowship (% Receiving)	Fellowship Tuition Remission
First-Year Student	NA (NA)	NA	NA (NA)	NA	NA (NA)	NA
Advanced Student	NA (NA)	NA	NA (NA)	NA	NA (NA)	NA

For additional information on financial assistance, visit http://www.sfsu.edu/~finaid/scholarships/.

Employment of Department Graduates

Master's:
Enrolled in a psychology doctoral program: 23
Enrolled in another graduate/professional program: 7
Employed in an academic position at a university: 3
Employed in academic position at a 2-year/4-year college: 1
Employed in other positions at a higher education institution: 1
Employed in a professional position in a school system: 3
Employed in business or industry: 7
Employed in government agency: 2
Employed in a community mental health/counseling center: 7
Employed in a hospital/medical center: 4
Still seeking employment: 2
Not seeking employment: 5
Other employment position: 1
Do not know: 8
Total: 74

Additional Information

Housing and Day Care: On-campus housing is available. See the following website for more information: http://housing.sfsu.edu/. On-campus day care facilities are available. See the following website for more information: http://childrenscampus.sfsu.edu/.

Information for Students With Physical Disabilities: See the following website: http://access.sfsu.edu/.

Special Facilities or Resources: Each full-time faculty member in the department has an active research lab in which students are active and essential members. There is a Psychology Clinic within the department which is a training facility for Clinical graduate students. The Clinic attracts clients from San Francisco State University and from the larger San Francisco Bay Area.

Application Information: Graduate Program Secretary, Department of Psychology, San Francisco State University, 1600 Holloway Avenue, EP 301, San Francisco, CA 94132. *Fee:* $55. *Online application:* http://www.csumentor.edu/AdmissionApp/grad_apply.asp.

Santa Clara University
Department of Counseling Psychology
School of Education and Counseling Psychology
500 El Camino Real - Loyola Hall 101
Santa Clara, CA 95053-0201
Telephone: (408) 551-1603
Chairperson: Lucila Ramos-Sánchez, PhD

E-mail: sbabbel@scu.edu
Web: http://www.scu.edu/ecp

Orientation, Objectives, and Emphasis of Department
Santa Clara University's graduate programs in counseling and counseling psychology are offered through the School of Education and Counseling Psychology. Programs lead to the Master of Arts in Counseling or the Master of Arts in Counseling Psychology, with the option of an emphasis in Health Psychology, Latino Counseling and Correctional Psychology. All of the Counseling Psychology (90-unit) programs prepare students for MFT licensure and/or the LPCC licensure through the California Board of Behavioral Sciences (BBS). The LPCC is more portable across the United States. Santa Clara is accredited by the Western Association of Schools and Colleges and is approved by the Board of Behavioral Science, Department of Consumer Affairs (California) to prepare students for MFT and LPCC licensure. The faculty represent a diverse set of clinical theories and perspectives, and students gain a broad exposure to a range of theories and practical applications in counseling.

Programs and Degrees Offered

Program	Degree	Application Deadline	Applica-tions Received	Accepted	New Admits Enrolled (PT)	Total Enrolled (PT)	Degrees Awarded in 2014–2015	Median Years to Complete Degree	Dismissed/ Withdrew
Counseling Psychology	MA/MS	Rolling	204	142	12 (8)	54 (78)	80	3.25	7
Counseling	MA/MS	Rolling	19	14	1 (1)	5 (10)	9	2.5	1

Internships/Practica
Supervised counseling experience designed specifically to meet California MFT and LPCC licensing requirements are required. Students will participate in weekly seminars for consultation and discussion with a licensed supervisor on such topics as case management and evaluation, referral procedures, ethical practices, professional and client interaction, confidential communication, and interprofessional ethical considerations.

Admissions
Entries appear in the following order: required test or GPA, minimum score (if required)/median score of students entering in 2015–2016.

Program	Degree	GRE-V	GRE-Q	GRE-Writing	GRE-Subject	Under-graduate GPA	Last 2 Years GPA	Psychology GPA	Master's GPA
Counseling Psychology	MA/MS	Not specified	Not specified	Not specified	Not specified	Not specified	Not specified	Not specified	Not specified
Counseling	MA/MS	Not specified	Not specified	Not specified	Not specified	Not specified	Not specified	Not specified	Not specified

Admissions Requirements:

Degree	GRE	GRE-Subject	Letters of Recommendation	Research Statement	Writing Sample	CV	Interview
Master's/Specialist	Optional	None	2	Required	Optional	Required	None

Admissions Criteria:

Research experience—low

Work experience—medium

Clinically related public service—high

GPA—medium

Letters of recommendation—medium

Statement of goals and objectives—high

For additional information on admission requirements, visit https://www.scu.edu/ecp/admissions/admissionrequirements/.

Department Demographics

	Male (PT)	Female (PT)	Total	African-American/ Black (PT)	Hispanic/ Latino (PT)	Asian/ Pacific Islander (PT)	American Indian/ Alaska Native (PT)	Caucasian/ White (PT)	Unknown	Multiethnic (PT)	ADA (PT)	Int'l (PT)
Students	14 (21)	45 (67)	147	5 (3)	10 (18)	7 (12)	0 (0)	20 (32)	15 (21)	2 (2)	2 (3)	7 (4)

Financial Information/Assistance

Tuition: For information on tuition costs, visit https://www.scu.edu/bursar/tuition/. Tuition is subject to change. Additional fees are assessed to students beyond the costs of tuition for the following: lab fees.

Master's:

State residents: $556 per credit hour.

Nonstate residents: $556 per credit hour.

Financial Assistance:

	Teaching Assistantship (% Receiving)	Teaching Assistantship Tuition Remission	Research Assistantship (% Receiving)	Research Assistantship Tuition Remission	Fellowship (% Receiving)	Fellowship Tuition Remission
First-Year Student	NA (NA)	NA	$600 (NA)	NA	$1,400 (NA)	NA
Advanced Student	NA (NA)	NA	$600 (NA)	NA	$1,400 (NA)	NA

For additional information on financial assistance, visit https://www.scu.edu/ecp/tuitionandaid/financialaid/.

Employment of Department Graduates

Master's:

Enrolled in a psychology doctoral program: 5

Enrolled in another graduate/professional program: 1

Employed in academic position at a 2-year/4-year college: 2

Employed in other positions at a higher education institution: 5

Employed in a professional position in a school system: 7

Employed in business or industry: 4

Employed in government agency: 2

Employed in a community mental health/counseling center: 8

Employed in a hospital/medical center: 1

Other employment position: 6

Do not know: 47

Total: 88

Additional Information

Housing and Day Care: On-campus housing is available. See the following website for more information: http://www.scu.edu/living/. On-campus day care facilities are available. See the following website for more information: https://www.scu.edu/kids-on-campus/.

Information for Students With Physical Disabilities: See the following website: https://www.scu.edu/disabilities/.

Special Facilities or Resources: Santa Clara University is located in the heart of Silicon Valley, with close connection to major business and academic resources in this area. The University has a complete complement of facilities including an excellent library, theater, museum and state of the art physical fitness center. The University has a dedication to educating the whole person and includes Centers of Distinction which explore diversity, ethics and the interface of technology and society.

Application Information: Graduate Admissions, School of ECP, Loyola Hall, Santa Clara University, 500 El Camino Real, Santa Clara, CA 95053-0201. *Fee:* $50. *Online application:* https://www.scu.edu/apply/edcp/handler.cfm?event=home.

Southern California, University of
Department of Psychology
College of Letters, Arts and Sciences
University Park - SGM 501
Los Angeles, CA 90089-1061
Telephone: (213) 740-2203
Chairperson: JoAnn Farver

E-mail: itakarag@usc.edu
Web: http://dornsife.usc.edu/psyc/

Orientation, Objectives, and Emphasis of Department
Graduate training in psychology prepares students for careers in research and teaching, as well as in empirically-oriented applied settings including health service, business, or other sectors. In addition to completing the required coursework, students in all specialty areas engage in empirical research throughout graduate study. Areas of specialization include: brain & cognitive science, clinical science, developmental psychology, quantitative methods, and social psychology. The clinical program, which is accredited by both APA and the Psychological Clinical Science Accreditation System (PCSAS), offers formal tracks in clinical-aging and child and family and a PhD/MPH dual degree.

Programs and Degrees Offered

Program	Degree	Application Deadline	Applications Received	Accepted	New Admits Enrolled (PT)	Total Enrolled (PT)	Degrees Awarded in 2014–2015	Median Years to Complete Degree	Dismissed/ Withdrew
Brain and Cognitive Sciences	PhD	December 1 (Fall)	73	2	1	12 (0)	5	5.31	0
Clinical Science	PhD	December 1 (Fall)	410	9	6	36	9	6.95	0
Developmental Psychology	PhD	December 1 (Fall)	33	2	0	3 (0)	1		0
Quantitative Methods	PhD	December 1 (Fall)	18	5	3	13	0		1
Social Psychology	PhD	December 1 (Fall)	123	5	4	16 (0)	1		0

APA Accreditation
Clinical PhD: Student Outcome Data website: http://dornsife.usc.edu/psyc/student-admissions-outcomes/.

Doctoral Degree (PhD Clinical Science): For those doctoral students for whom a professional internship was required in this program prior to graduation:
Total students who applied for an internship: 5

Total students who obtained an internship: 5
Total students who obtained a paid internship: 5
Total students who obtained an unpaid internship: 0
Total students who were placed in APA/CPA-accredited internships: 5
Total students placed in internships not APA/CPA-accredited, but listed with the Association of Psychology Postdoctoral and Internship Centers (APPIC): 0
Total students placed in internships conforming to guidelines of the Council of Directors of School Psychology Programs (CDSPP): 0
Total students placed in internships that were not APA/CPA-accredited, APPIC or CDSSP listed: 0

Internships/Practica

Students in the clinical psychology area take at least six semesters of clinical didactic practica, each of which involves instruction and supervised clinical service provision. Students receive both group and individual supervision of their cases. The first year practicum focuses on clinical interviewing and formal assessment. In the second and third year, students take practica based on their interests and specialty track. Practica are offered in general adult psychotherapy, psychotherapy with older adults, and child/family psychotherapy. After admission to doctoral candidacy, all students must complete a one-year, APA-approved clinical internship for which students separately apply at the time.

Admissions

Entries appear in the following order: required test or GPA, minimum score (if required)/median score of students entering in 2015–2016.

Program	Degree	GRE-V	GRE-Q	GRE-Writing	GRE-Subject	Under-graduate GPA	Last 2 Years GPA	Psychol-ogy GPA	Master's GPA
Brain and Cognitive Sciences	PhD	NA/163	146/164	NA/4.5	Not specified	Not specified	Not specified	Not specified	Not specified
Clinical Science	PhD	NA/164	146/159	NA/5	Not specified	Not specified	Not specified	Not specified	Not specified
Developmental Psychology	PhD	NA/161	146/152	NA/4	Not specified	Not specified	Not specified	Not specified	Not specified
Quantitative Methods	PhD	NA/157	146/164	NA/4	Not specified	Not specified	Not specified	Not specified	Not specified
Social Psychology	PhD	NA/168	146/162	NA/5	Not specified	Not specified	Not specified	Not specified	Not specified

Admissions Requirements:

Degree	GRE	GRE-Subject	Letters of Recom-mendation	Research Statement	Writing Sample	CV	Interview
Doctoral	Required	None	3	Required	None	Required	Required

Please note if these criteria vary for different programs: Interview and clinically related public service are very important for the Clinical Science program but less so for other areas.

Admissions Criteria:

GRE scores—high
Research experience—high
Work experience—medium
Clinically related public service—medium

GPA—high
Letters of recommendation—high
Statement of goals and objectives—high

For additional information on admission requirements, visit http://dornsife.usc.edu/psyc/admissions/.

Department Demographics

	Male (PT)	Female (PT)	Total	African-American/ Black (PT)	Hispanic/ Latino (PT)	Asian/ Pacific Islander (PT)	American Indian/ Alaska Native (PT)	Caucasian/ White (PT)	Unknown	Multiethnic (PT)	ADA (PT)	Int'l (PT)
Students	27 (0)	53 (0)	80	2 (0)	7 (0)	11 (0)	0 (0)	44 (0)	0 (0)	0 (0)	0 (0)	16 (0)

Financial Information/Assistance

Tuition: Tuition is subject to change. Additional fees are assessed to students beyond the costs of tuition for the following: One-time orientation fee of $55 + other mandatory fees (about $60) per semester.

Doctoral:
State residents: $39,984 per academic year.
State residents: $1,666 per credit hour.
Nonstate residents: $39,984 per academic year.
Nonstate residents: $1,666 per credit hour.

Financial Assistance:

	Teaching Assistantship (% Receiving)	Teaching Assistantship Tuition Remission	Research Assistantship (% Receiving)	Research Assistantship Tuition Remission	Fellowship (% Receiving)	Fellowship Tuition Remission
First-Year Student	$29,500 (14)	Full	$29,500 (0)	Full	$29,500 (85)	Full
Advanced Student	$24,800 (27)	Full	$25,600 (24)	Full	$29,100 (35)	Full

For additional information on financial assistance, visit http://dornsife.usc.edu/psyc/financial-aid/.

Employment of Department Graduates

Doctoral:
Enrolled in a postdoctoral residency/fellowship: 10
Employed in other positions at a higher education institution: 1
Employed in business or industry: 1
Employed in a community mental health/counseling center: 1
Employed in a hospital/medical center: 3
Total: 16

Additional Information

Housing and Day Care: On-campus housing is available. See the following website for more information: http://housing.usc.edu/. On-campus day care facilities are available. See the following website for more information: http://www.cclc.com/our-centers/los-angeles/ca/081041/.

Information for Students With Physical Disabilities: See the following website: http://dsp.usc.edu/.

Special Facilities or Resources: We are housed in the upper six floors of a 10-story building, which provides the department ample laboratory and office space. Most graduate students and faculty have offices and labs in the building. The department has state-of-the-art research facilities, including the Dana & David Dornsife Cognitive Neuroscience Imaging Center located in an adjacent building. A shared, communal social behavior laboratory of testing rooms and equipment is available for use by all faculty and students who are doing behavioral research. The clinical science program offers clinical services to the community through the on-campus Psychology Services Center.

Application Information: Irene Takaragawa, Graduate Advisor, Department of Psychology/SGM 508, University of Southern California, Los Angeles, CA 90089-1061. *Fee:* $85. *Online application:* http://www.usc.edu/admission/graduate/apply/.

Southern California, University of, Keck School of Medicine

Department of Preventive Medicine, Division of Health Behavior Research
USC Health Science Building, 2001 North Soto Street, 3rd Floor
Los Angeles, CA 90032
Telephone: (323) 442-8299
Director: Mary Ann Pentz

E-mail: barovich@usc.edu
Web: http://phdhbr.usc.edu/

Orientation, Objectives, and Emphasis of Department

The University of Southern California (USC) School of Medicine, Department of Preventive Medicine, Division of Health Behavior Research, offers a doctorate in health behavior research (HBR), providing academic and research training for students interested in pursuing career opportunities in the field of health promotion and disease prevention research. The specific objective of the program is to train exceptional researchers and scholars in the multidisciplinary field of health behavior research who will apply this knowledge creatively to the goal of primary and secondary prevention of disease. Students receive well-rounded training that encompasses theory and methods from many allied fields, including communication, psychology, preventive medicine, statistics, social network analysis, public/global health, and epidemiology. Students receive research experience participating in projects conducted through the USC Institute for Health Promotion and Disease Prevention Research (IPR). Required core courses include foundations of health behavior, data analysis, multivariate statistics in health behavior, biological basis of disease, basic theory and strategies in prevention, intervention research grant proposal development, health behavior research methods, and research seminar in health behavior. In addition to core course requirements, the curriculum includes content courses from the Department of Preventive Medicine's Divisions of Biostatistics and Epidemiology.

Programs and Degrees Offered

Program	Degree	Application Deadline	Applications Received	Accepted	New Admits Enrolled (PT)	Total Enrolled (PT)	Degrees Awarded in 2014–2015	Median Years to Complete Degree	Dismissed/Withdrew
Health Behavior Research	PhD	December 1 (Fall)	42	7	4 (0)	32 (1)	1	4	0

Admissions

Entries appear in the following order: required test or GPA, minimum score (if required)/median score of students entering in 2015–2016.

Program	Degree	GRE-V	GRE-Q	GRE-Writing	GRE-Subject	Under-graduate GPA	Last 2 Years GPA	Psychology GPA	Master's GPA
Health Behavior Research	PhD	158/158	147/152	Not specified	Not specified	3.2/3.62	Not specified	Not specified	3.4/3.87

Admissions Requirements:

Degree	GRE	GRE-Subject	Letters of Recommendation	Research Statement	Writing Sample	CV	Interview
Doctoral	Required	Required	3	Required	Optional	Required	Recommended

Please note if these criteria vary for different programs: Students are invited to interview, in-person or on the phone, but interviews are not required. (They are helpful, however.).

Admissions Criteria:

GRE scores—high
Research experience—medium
Work experience—medium
GPA—high

Letters of recommendation—high
Interview—medium
Statement of goals and objectives—high
Undergraduate psychology preparation—low

For additional information on admission requirements, visit https://phdhbr.usc.edu/admission.php.

Department Demographics

	Male (PT)	Female (PT)	Total	African-American/ Black (PT)	Hispanic/ Latino (PT)	Asian/ Pacific Islander (PT)	American Indian/ Alaska Native (PT)	Caucasian/ White (PT)	Unknown	Multiethnic (PT)	ADA (PT)	Int'l (PT)
Students	12 (1)	20 (0)	33	2 (0)	4 (0)	11 (1)	0 (0)	14 (0)	0 (0)	1 (0)	0 (0)	2 (0)

Financial Information/Assistance

Tuition: Additional fees are assessed to students beyond the costs of tuition for the following: programming, student services, and Norman Topping fee: currently $60 per semester.

Doctoral:
State residents: $23,324 per academic year.
State residents: $1,666 per credit hour.
Nonstate residents: $23,324 per academic year.
Nonstate residents: $1,666 per credit hour.

Financial Assistance:

	Teaching Assistantship (% Receiving)	Teaching Assistantship Tuition Remission	Research Assistantship (% Receiving)	Research Assistantship Tuition Remission	Fellowship (% Receiving)	Fellowship Tuition Remission
First-Year Student	$32,000 (0)	Full	$32,000 (0)	Full	$32,000 (100)	Full
Advanced Student	$32,000 (21)	Full	$32,000 (28)	Full	$32,000 (38)	Full

For additional information on financial assistance, visit https://phdhbr.usc.edu/financial_aid.php.

Employment of Department Graduates

Doctoral:
Enrolled in a postdoctoral residency/fellowship: 1
Total: 1

Additional Information

Housing and Day Care: On-campus housing is available. See the following website for more information: http://housing.usc.edu/. On-campus day care facilities are available. See the following website for more information: http://www.usc.edu/dept/hr/childcare/.

Information for Students With Physical Disabilities: See the following website: http://dsp.usc.edu/.

Special Facilities or Resources: Faculty and other researchers at IPR are recognized leaders in community-based approaches to health promotion and disease prevention. The research at IPR integrates the scientific perspectives of epidemiology, the behavioral sciences, biology, communication, and policy research in disease etiology and prevention. IPR enjoys research collaborations in 10 schools and 35 departments within USC and with noted researchers and public health leaders in leading universities across the U.S., Europe, Latin America, and Asia. IPR's faculty and researchers are world leaders in school- and community-based prevention, tobacco control, and cancer control and epidemiology; prevention of drug abuse, childhood obesity; promotion of improvements in nutrition and physical activity; research examining health disparities; and health communication campaigns for chronic disease prevention. In late 2013, USC, through the Department of Preventive Medicine and with primary involvement of IPR researchers, was one of 14 academic institutions designated to receive significant funding to contribute to a new regulatory science tobacco program intended to support tobacco product regulations. Other new research directions include developing mindfulness training in order to modify psychological stress and other mental/physical health symptoms and states and using mobile devices to investigate and influence activity and healthy eating.

Application Information: Fee: $85. *Online application:* http://www.usc.edu/admission/graduate/apply/.

Stanford University

Department of Psychology
Humanities & Sciences
450 Serra Mall, Jordan Hall, Building 420
Stanford, CA 94305-2130
Telephone: (650) 725-2400
Chairperson: Ian H. Gotlib

E-mail: psych-info@lists.stanford.edu
Web: https://psychology.stanford.edu/

Orientation, Objectives, and Emphasis of Department

The department focuses on a high-quality undergraduate program and a graduate program that emphasizes research training. There are five substantive content areas in the department: affective science, cognitive psychology, developmental psychology, social psychology, and neuroscience. Increasingly, faculty in all of these areas are involved in the use of neuroimaging as a research method. The department maintains its commitment to intellectual ties to other parts of the university. These relationships are especially close with psychiatry, biology, medicine, law, education, the graduate school of business, and the neuroscience institute.

Programs and Degrees Offered

Program	Degree	Application Deadline	Applica-tions Received	Accepted	New Admits Enrolled (PT)	Total Enrolled (PT)	Degrees Awarded in 2014–2015	Median Years to Complete Degree	Dismissed/ Withdrew
Cognitive Psychology	PhD	November 24 (Fall)	86	2	2 (0)	10 (0)	1	6	0
Social Psychology	PhD	November 24 (Fall)	216	4	4 (0)	18 (0)	4	6	0
Neuroscience	PhD	November 24 (Fall)	89	4	3 (0)	15 (0)	2	6	0
Developmental Psychology	PhD	November 24 (Fall)	59	3	0 (0)	10 (0)	1	6	0
Affective Science	PhD	November 24 (Fall)	127		4	17	3	6	

Admissions

Entries appear in the following order: required test or GPA, minimum score (if required)/median score of students entering in 2015–2016.

Program	Degree	GRE-V	GRE-Q	GRE-Writing	GRE-Subject	Under-graduate GPA	Last 2 Years GPA	Psychol-ogy GPA	Master's GPA
Cognitive Psychology	PhD	NA/NA	NA/NA	NA/NA	Not specified	NA/NA	Not specified	Not specified	NA/NA
Social Psychology	PhD	NA/NA	NA/NA	NA/NA	Not specified	NA/NA	Not specified	Not specified	NA/NA
Neuroscience	PhD	NA/NA	NA/NA	NA/NA	Not specified	NA/NA	Not specified	Not specified	NA/NA
Developmental Psychology	PhD	NA/NA	NA/NA	NA/NA	Not specified	NA/NA	Not specified	Not specified	NA/NA
Affective Science	PhD	NA/NA	NA/NA	NA/NA	Not specified	NA/NA	Not specified	Not specified	NA/NA

Admissions Requirements:

Degree	GRE	GRE-Subject	Letters of Recommendation	Research Statement	Writing Sample	CV	Interview
Doctoral	Required	Recommended	3	Required	Optional	Optional	Required

Admissions Criteria:

GRE scores—high
Research experience—high
Work experience—medium
Clinically related public service—medium
GPA—high

Letters of recommendation—high
Interview—high
Statement of goals and objectives—high
Undergraduate psychology preparation—medium

For additional information on admission requirements, visit https://psychology.stanford.edu/graduate_admissions.html.

Department Demographics

	Male (PT)	Female (PT)	Total	African-American/Black (PT)	Hispanic/Latino (PT)	Asian/Pacific Islander (PT)	American Indian/Alaska Native (PT)	Caucasian/White (PT)	Unknown	Multiethnic (PT)	ADA (PT)	Int'l (PT)
Students	33 (0)	37 (0)	70	2 (0)	3 (0)	18 (0)	0 (0)	36 (0)	11 (0)	0 (0)	0 (0)	15 (0)

Financial Information/Assistance

Tuition: For information on tuition costs, visit https://registrar.stanford.edu/students/tuition-and-fees.

Doctoral:
State residents: $39,640 per academic year.
Nonstate residents: $39,640 per academic year.

Financial Assistance:

	Teaching Assistantship (% Receiving)	Teaching Assistantship Tuition Remission	Research Assistantship (% Receiving)	Research Assistantship Tuition Remission	Fellowship (% Receiving)	Fellowship Tuition Remission
First-Year Student	NA (NA)	NA	$34,564 (100)	Full	$34,564 (100)	Full
Advanced Student	$34,564 (100)	Full	$34,564 (100)	Full	$34,564 (100)	Full

For additional information on financial assistance, visit http://financialaid.stanford.edu/grad/.

Employment of Department Graduates

Doctoral:
Enrolled in a postdoctoral residency/fellowship: 5
Employed in business or industry: 4
Do not know: 2
Total: 11

Additional Information

Housing and Day Care: On-campus housing is available. See the following website for more information: http://studenthousing.stanford.edu/. On-campus day care facilities are available. See the following website for more information: https://cardinalatwork.stanford.edu/benefits-rewards/worklife/children-family/on-site-child-care.

Information for Students With Physical Disabilities: See the following website: https://oae.stanford.edu/.

Special Facilities or Resources: The department has research and teaching facilities and personnel housed in Jordan Hall, where it maintains extensive laboratory and shop facilities, supervised by specialized technical assistants. These facilities include laboratories for behavioral and neural (fMRI, EEG, and TMS) research; The Center for Cognitive and Neurobiological Imaging, with a 3T scanner, is housed in the basement of Jordan Hall. Most of the laboratories are equipped with computer terminals linked directly to the university's computer center. The department also maintains a nursery school on campus that provides a laboratory for child observation, for training in nursery school practice, and for research.

Application Information: Admissions Committee, Department of Psychology, Stanford University, Jordan Hall, Building 420, 450 Serra Mall, Stanford, CA 94305-2130. *Fee:* $125. *Online application:* https://gradadmissions.stanford.edu/.

The Chicago School of Professional Psychology

Professional School
617 West 7th Street
Los Angeles, CA 90017
Telephone: (800) 721-8072
President: Michele Nealon-Woods

E-mail: admissions@thechicagoschool.edu
Web: http://www.thechicagoschool.edu

Orientation, Objectives, and Emphasis of Department

The Chicago School educates students to be competent practitioners by providing curricula that emphasize both a broad knowledge of the scientific and theoretical bases of psychology and the ability to apply that knowledge to specific employment situations. A student-centered environment, with personal advising and supervision provide opportunities for deepening awareness, knowledge, and skills. The programs are designed to integrate the study of cultural and individual differences and their impact in clinical and work settings. The professional and ethical development of the student is of foremost concern throughout the educational program.

Programs and Degrees Offered

Program	Degree	Application Deadline	Applications Received	Accepted	New Admits Enrolled (PT)	Total Enrolled (PT)	Degrees Awarded in 2014–2015	Median Years to Complete Degree	Dismissed/ Withdrew
Clinical Psychology	PsyD	March 15 (Fall), Rolling	388	168	79 (1)	425 (125)	100	5	13
Industrial/ Organizational Psychology	MA/MS	Rolling	218	205	111 (62)	258 (126)	128	1.8	44
Forensic Psychology	MA/MS	March 15 (Fall), Rolling	210	190	101 (55)	269 (132)	189	1.9	62
Business Psychology	PhD	March 15 (Fall), Rolling	85	73	29 (45)	128 (119)	18	4	28
School Psychology	EdS	March 15 (Fall)	89	81	40 (3)	115 (10)	82	2.9	8
BCBA- Board Certified Behavior Analyst	Respecial-ization Diploma	Rolling	31	29	19 (49)	32 (84)	67	1.1	22
Applied Behavior Analysis	PhD	March 15 (Fall)	69	57	26 (44)	46 (91)	5	5.2	12
Industrial/ Organizational Generalist Certificate	Other	Rolling	10	10	1 (17)	4 (28)	31	0.5	13

Programs and Degrees Offered (con't.)

Program	Degree	Application Deadline	Applications Received	Accepted	New Admits Enrolled (PT)	Total Enrolled (PT)	Degrees Awarded in 2014–2015	Median Years to Complete Degree	Dismissed/Withdrew
General Psychology	MA/MS	Rolling	38	37	26 (65)	157 (131)	137	2	42
Organizational Leadership	PhD	March 15 (Fall), Rolling	90	81	41 (35)	154 (164)	15	3.8	29
International Psychology	PhD	Rolling	87	75	21 (40)	93 (151)	19	4.1	32
Clinical Psychology, Marital and Family Therapy	MA/MS	March 15 (Fall)	114	110	57 (19)	149 (50)	4	3.1	20
Marital and Family Therapy	PsyD	March 15 (Fall)	41	39	13 (7)	79 (45)	3	4.9	12
Clinical Forensic Psychology	PsyD	March 15 (Fall), Rolling	130	74	40 (5)	190 (12)	39	3.9	28
Child and Adolescent Psychology Certificate	Other	Rolling	14	14	2 (31)	4 (45)	13	0.5	10
School Psychology	EdD	March 15 (Fall)	1	0	0 (0)	0 (10)	0		0
Counselor Ed & Supervision	PhD	March 15 (Fall), Rolling	17	11	3 (1)	13 (5)	0		0
Applied Clinical Psychology	PsyD	March 15 (Fall)	91	88	71 (10)	275 (34)	34	3.7	17
Applied Behavior Analysis	MA/MS	March 15 (Fall), Rolling	214	200	142 (72)	344 (139)	70	2	32
Organizational Leadership	MA/MS	Rolling	3	3	0 (7)	10 (7)	0		2
International Psychology	MA/MS	Rolling	11	10	0 (14)	7 (16)	0		2
Counseling Psychology	MA/MS	March 15 (Fall), Rolling	275	239	109 (38)	323 (97)	127	2.1	25
Clinical Mental Health Counseling	MA/MS	March 15 (Fall), Rolling	108	81	31 (70)	91 (85)	0		21
Educational Psychology & Technology	EdD	Rolling	8	7	0 (13)	6 (14)	0		1

APA Accreditation

Clinical PsyD: Student Outcome Data website: http://www.thechicagoschool.edu/chicago/programs/clinical-psychology/.

Doctoral Degree (PsyD Clinical Psychology): For those doctoral students for whom a professional internship was required in this program prior to graduation:

Total students who applied for an internship: 92
Total students who obtained an internship: 91
Total students who obtained a paid internship: 91
Total students who obtained an unpaid internship: 0
Total students who were placed in APA/CPA-accredited internships: 60
Total students placed in internships not APA/CPA-accredited, but listed with the Association of Psychology Postdoctoral and Internship Centers (APPIC): 31
Total students placed in internships conforming to guidelines of the Council of Directors of School Psychology Programs (CDSPP): 0
Total students placed in internships that were not APA/CPA-accredited, APPIC or CDSSP listed: 0

Master's Degree (MA/MS Industrial/Organizational Psychology): An internship experience, such as a final research project or "capstone" experience is required of graduates. Master's Degree (MA/MS Forensic Psychology): An internship experience, such as a final research project or "capstone" experience is required of graduates.

Internships/Practica

TCSPP engages with over 600 assessment and therapy sites across the country at which our students train.

Admissions

Entries appear in the following order: required test or GPA, minimum score (if required)/median score of students entering in 2015–2016.

Program	Degree	GRE-V	GRE-Q	GRE-Writing	GRE-Subject	Under-graduate GPA	Last 2 Years GPA	Psychol-ogy GPA	Master's GPA
Clinical Psychology	PsyD	NA/NA	NA/NA	Not specified	Not specified	Not specified	Not specified	Not specified	Not specified
Industrial/ Organizational Psychology	MA/MS	Not specified	Not specified	Not specified	Not specified	Not specified	Not specified	Not specified	Not specified
Forensic Psychology	MA/MS	Not specified	Not specified	Not specified	Not specified	Not specified	Not specified	Not specified	Not specified
Business Psychology	PhD	NA/NA	NA/NA	Not specified	Not specified	Not specified	Not specified	Not specified	Not specified
School Psychology	EdS	Not specified	Not specified	Not specified	Not specified	Not specified	Not specified	Not specified	Not specified
BCBA- Board Certified Behavior Analyst	Respecial-ization Diploma	Not specified	Not specified	Not specified	Not specified	Not specified	Not specified	Not specified	Not specified
Applied Behavior Analysis	PhD	NA/NA	NA/NA	Not specified	Not specified	Not specified	Not specified	Not specified	Not specified
Industrial/ Organizational Generalist Certificate	Other	Not specified	Not specified	Not specified	Not specified	Not specified	Not specified	Not specified	Not specified
General Psychology	MA/MS	Not specified	Not specified	Not specified	Not specified	Not specified	Not specified	Not specified	Not specified
Organizational Leadership	PhD	Not specified	Not specified	Not specified	Not specified	Not specified	Not specified	Not specified	Not specified
International Psychology	PhD	Not specified	Not specified	Not specified	Not specified	Not specified	Not specified	Not specified	Not specified

Admissions (con't.)

Program	Degree	GRE-V	GRE-Q	GRE-Writing	GRE-Subject	Under-graduate GPA	Last 2 Years GPA	Psychol-ogy GPA	Master's GPA
Clinical Psychology, Marital and Family Therapy	MA/MS	Not specified	Not specified	Not specified	Not specified	Not specified	Not specified	Not specified	Not specified
Marital and Family Therapy	PsyD	Not specified	Not specified	Not specified	Not specified	Not specified	Not specified	Not specified	Not specified
Clinical Forensic Psychology	PsyD	NA/NA	NA/NA	Not specified	Not specified	Not specified	Not specified	Not specified	Not specified
Child and Adolescent Psychology Certificate	Other	Not specified	Not specified	Not specified	Not specified	Not specified	Not specified	Not specified	Not specified
School Psychology	EdD	Not specified	Not specified	Not specified	Not specified	Not specified	Not specified	Not specified	Not specified
Counselor Ed & Supervision	PhD	Not specified	Not specified	Not specified	Not specified	Not specified	Not specified	Not specified	Not specified
Applied Clinical Psychology	PsyD	Not specified	Not specified	Not specified	Not specified	Not specified	Not specified	Not specified	Not specified
Applied Behavior Analysis	MA/MS	Not specified	Not specified	Not specified	Not specified	Not specified	Not specified	Not specified	Not specified
Organizational Leadership	MA/MS	Not specified	Not specified	Not specified	Not specified	Not specified	Not specified	Not specified	Not specified
International Psychology	MA/MS	Not specified	Not specified	Not specified	Not specified	Not specified	Not specified	Not specified	Not specified
Counseling Psychology	MA/MS	Not specified	Not specified	Not specified	Not specified	Not specified	Not specified	Not specified	Not specified
Clinical Mental Health Counseling	MA/MS	Not specified	Not specified	Not specified	Not specified	Not specified	Not specified	Not specified	Not specified
Educational Psychology & Technology	EdD	Not specified	Not specified	Not specified	Not specified	Not specified	Not specified	Not specified	Not specified

Admissions Requirements:

Degree	GRE	GRE-Subject	Letters of Recom-mendation	Research Statement	Writing Sample	CV	Interview
Master's/Specialist	Recom-mended	None	3	Required	None	Required	None
Doctoral	Required	Optional	3	Required	Optional	Required	Required

Please note if these criteria vary for different programs: The criteria listed below are summary of all programs. Please note the weighing may vary by program. Interviews are required and by invitation for select programs. The PsyD in Clinical Psychology program considers the GRE score as a high value criterion. The GRE is required for the following programs: PsyD in Clinical Psychology, PsyD in Clinical Forensic Psychology, PhD in Applied Behavior Analysis, and PsyD in Business Psychology.

Admissions Criteria:

GRE scores—medium	Letters of recommendation—medium
Research experience—medium	Interview—medium
Work experience—medium	Statement of goals and objectives—medium
Clinically related public service—medium	Undergraduate psychology preparation—low
GPA—medium	

For additional information on admission requirements, visit http://www.thechicagoschool.edu/admissions/.

Department Demographics

	Male (PT)	Female (PT)	Total	African-American/ Black (PT)	Hispanic/ Latino (PT)	Asian/ Pacific Islander (PT)	American Indian/ Alaska Native (PT)	Caucasian/ White (PT)	Unknown	Multiethnic (PT)	ADA (PT)	Int'l (PT)
Students	588 (397)	2611 (1376)	4972	654 (466)	524 (237)	186 (92)	15 (9)	1520 (773)	261 (153)	75 (66)	170 (16)	77 (10)

Financial Information/Assistance

Tuition: For information on tuition costs, visit http://www.thechicagoschool.edu/admissions/financial-aid/tuition-and-fees/. Tuition is subject to change. Additional fees are assessed to students beyond the costs of tuition for the following: Academic success lab, insitutional services, registration, eCollege. Tuition costs vary by program.

Doctoral:
State residents: $1,310 per credit hour.
Nonstate residents: $1,310 per credit hour.

Master's:
State residents: $1,051 per credit hour.
Nonstate residents: $1,051 per credit hour.

Financial Assistance:

	Teaching Assistantship (% Receiving)	Teaching Assistantship Tuition Remission	Research Assistantship (% Receiving)	Research Assistantship Tuition Remission	Fellowship (% Receiving)	Fellowship Tuition Remission
First-Year Student	NA (NA)	NA	NA (NA)	NA	$2,133 (NA)	NA
Advanced Student	NA (NA)	NA	NA (NA)	NA	$4,482 (NA)	NA

For additional information on financial assistance, visit http://www.thechicagoschool.edu/admissions/financial-aid/.

Employment of Department Graduates

No information provided.

Additional Information

Housing and Day Care: No on-campus housing is available. No on-campus day care facilities are available.

Special Facilities or Resources: TCSPP offers experiential learning opportunities through a variety of centers and institutes including the Center for Multicultural and Diversity Studies, the ConCISE student consulting center, the Forensic Training Institute, the Counseling Centers, the Center for Latino/a Mental Health, the Center for Military and Veteran Psychology, and the Naomi Ruth Cohen Institute. The mission of the Cohen Institute is to overcome the stigma associated with mental illness through culturally competent community outreach and educational programming. It offers one predoctoral fellowship to a TCSPP student annually.

Application Information: Admission Operations, c/o The Chicago School of Professional Psychology, 350 North Orleans Street, Suite 1050, Chicago, IL 60654-1822. *Fee:* $50. *Online application:* https://apply.thechicagoschool.edu/.

Wright Institute
Graduate School of Psychology
2728 Durant Avenue
Berkeley, CA 94704
Telephone: (510) 841-9230
Dean: Gilbert Newman, PhD

E-mail: info@wi.edu
Web: http://www.wi.edu/psyd-program

Orientation, Objectives, and Emphasis of Department

The goals of the Wright Institute are threefold: (1) to teach the scientific knowledge base of clinical psychology; (2) to teach and train students about the knowledge, skills, and attitudes necessary to become an exemplar practitioner of health service psychology, and in doing so; (3) to prepare students to recognize the multicultural dimensions of involved in being a clinical psychologist. Students apply critical thinking skills to three fundamental areas: the integration of clinical theory, practice and research; understanding of the self in social and cultural contexts, and appreciation of the interaction between clinician and client. Students are exposed to a number of clinical orientations learning to formulate and address clinical problems through assessment, careful treatment planning and evaluation. Coursework is integrated yearly with rigorous practicum experiences, providing for the systematic, progressive acquisition of skills and knowledge. Students actively participate in weekly, small-group professional seminars throughout 3 years of residency. These seminars provide mentoring and a rich forum for developing and integrating theory, technique, reflective judgment and ethical practice. Practicum and internship experiences consolidate the applied aspects of scientific knowledge and promote graduates toward the clinical leadership roles of the psychologist, clinician, supervisor, consultant, advocate, program design and implementation, and more.

Programs and Degrees Offered

Program	Degree	Application Deadline	Applica-tions Received	Accepted	New Admits Enrolled (PT)	Total Enrolled (PT)	Degrees Awarded in 2014– 2015	Median Years to Complete Degree	Dismissed/ Withdrew
Clinical Psychology	PsyD	January 15 (Fall)	276	129	61 (0)	383 (0)	46	4.92	4

APA Accreditation

Clinical PsyD: Student Outcome Data website: http://www.wi.edu/psyd-outcomes.

Doctoral Degree (PsyD Clinical Psychology): For those doctoral students for whom a professional internship was required in this program prior to graduation:
Total students who applied for an internship: 58
Total students who obtained an internship: 56
Total students who obtained a paid internship: 52
Total students who obtained an unpaid internship: 4
Total students who were placed in APA/CPA-accredited internships: 34
Total students placed in internships not APA/CPA-accredited, but listed with the Association of Psychology Postdoctoral and Internship Centers (APPIC): 11
Total students placed in internships conforming to guidelines of the Council of Directors of School Psychology Programs (CDSPP): 0
Total students placed in internships that were not APA/CPA-accredited, APPIC or CDSSP listed: 11

Internships/Practica

Through a minimum of 3 practicum years plus the internship, the Institute's training prepares students to integrate the knowledge base of psychology with clinical experience while working in a variety of roles. Beginning with the first year, students are required to perform 3 years of practicum training and many students elect to add non-required, supplemental practicum experiences. By the time students are ready to go to internship they have accrued nearly 2000 hours of supervised experience. Students work with a range of clinical populations, evidence-based treatment modalities, and train in a variety of clinical settings serving the ethno-culturally diverse populations of the San Francisco Bay Area. The Field Placement Office (FPO) operates an impressive clinical services program with outpatient and assessment clinics, jail-based, school-based, a recovery clinic, primary care health psychology services, and more. This eases the placement process significantly and furnishes extensive support to students in the practicum and internship application process. Since 2015, our program requires entering students to pursue an APA-accredited internship. Our internship match rate is rapidly increasing for students applying nationally for APA internships. Our students are valued by the most well-regarded internship sites in the Bay Area and throughout the nation.

Admissions

Entries appear in the following order: required test or GPA, minimum score (if required)/median score of students entering in 2015–2016.

Program	Degree	GRE-V	GRE-Q	GRE-Writing	GRE-Subject	Under-graduate GPA	Last 2 Years GPA	Psychol-ogy GPA	Master's GPA
Clinical Psychology	PsyD	NA/157	NA/150	NA/4.3	Not specified	3/3.5	Not specified	Not specified	Not specified

Admissions Requirements:

Degree	GRE	GRE-Subject	Letters of Recom-mendation	Research Statement	Writing Sample	CV	Interview
Doctoral	Required	None	3	Required	None	Required	Required

Admissions Criteria:

GRE scores—medium
Research experience—medium
Work experience—medium
Clinically related public service—high
GPA—high

Letters of recommendation—high
Interview—high
Statement of goals and objectives—high
Undergraduate psychology preparation—medium

For additional information on admission requirements, visit http://www.wi.edu/admission-psyd-info.

Department Demographics

	Male (PT)	Female (PT)	Total	African-American/ Black (PT)	Hispanic/ Latino (PT)	Asian/ Pacific Islander (PT)	American Indian/ Alaska Native (PT)	Caucasian/ White (PT)	Unknown	Multiethnic (PT)	ADA (PT)	Int'l (PT)
Students	96 (0)	287 (0)	383	18 (0)	28 (0)	48 (0)	4 (0)	250 (0)	4 (0)	31 (0)	26 (0)	13 (0)

Financial Information/Assistance

Tuition: For information on tuition costs, visit http://www.wi.edu/psyd-tuition-financial-aid. Tuition is subject to change.

Doctoral:
State residents: $32,500 per academic year.
Nonstate residents: $32,500 per academic year.

Financial Assistance:

	Teaching Assistantship (% Receiving)	Teaching Assistantship Tuition Remission	Research Assistantship (% Receiving)	Research Assistantship Tuition Remission	Fellowship (% Receiving)	Fellowship Tuition Remission
First-Year Student	NA (NA)	NA	$1,900 (2)	NA	NA (NA)	NA
Advanced Student	$2,100 (6)	NA	$1,900 (3)	NA	$1,800 (40)	NA

For additional information on financial assistance, visit http://www.wi.edu/psyd-tuition-financial-aid.

Employment of Department Graduates

Doctoral:
Enrolled in a postdoctoral residency/fellowship: 24
Employed in independent practice: 3
Employed in an academic position at a university: 2
Employed in a community mental health/counseling center: 4
Employed in a hospital/medical center: 4
Still seeking employment: 1
Other employment position: 2
Do not know: 6
Total: 46

Additional Information

Housing and Day Care: No on-campus housing is available. No on-campus day care facilities are available.

Special Facilities or Resources: The Wright Institute operates extensive evidence-based clinical services including traditional low-fee psychotherapy and assessment clinics as well as innovative programs in schools, primary care facilities, an addiction recovery program and other settings. Wright's psychodynamically-oriented clinical service has been in operation for over 40 years. Wright also operates a CBT/Mindfulness-based clinical service. The Wright Institute's clinical services enable students to work in communities challenged by violence, discrimination, poverty and a lack of health care access. We prepare our graduates to serve the most deserving, complex and multi-problem populations. One unique example is the Wright Institute's Integrated Health Psychology Training Program, where interns and practicum students learn primary care health psychology and perform as part of a multidisciplinary team, addressing the lifestyle and behavioral components contributing to poor health, and treating the co-occurring psychological disorders many patients experience. Through these clinics and programs, the Institute educates students to apply psychological knowledge and skills, not just to work with the problems and dysfunctions of underserved populations, but also to appreciate and cultivate those populations' strengths and aspirations. In so doing our students build a deeper multicultural perspective grounded in their own developing experience.

Application Information: The Wright Institute, Attn: Admissions, 2728 Durant Avenue, Berkeley, CA 94704. *Fee:* $50. *Online application:* http://www.wi.edu/admission-apply-online.

Colorado State University

Department of Psychology
Natural Sciences
200 West Lake Street, 1876 Campus Delivery
Fort Collins, CO 80523-1876
Telephone: (970) 491-6363
Chairperson: Don Rojas

E-mail: don.rojas@colostate.edu
Web: http://www.colostate.edu/Depts/Psychology/

Orientation, Objectives, and Emphasis of Department

Colorado State University offers graduate training leading to the MS and PhD degrees in applied social and health, cognitive, cognitive neuroscience, counseling, and industrial/organizational psychology. A core program of study is required of all students in the first years of graduate work to insure a broad and thorough grounding in psychology. Graduate students in applied social, cognitive and cognitive neuroscience areas take positions in academic, research, or government agencies. Industrial/Organizational has opportunities for students to have experiences in selection techniques, occupational health psychology, assessment centers, organizational climate and structure, and consultation. Counseling students are trained in academic and applied skills with opportunities in behavior therapy, group techniques, assessment, outreach, consultation, and supervision. Emphasis is on diversity and breadth.

Programs and Degrees Offered

Program	Degree	Application Deadline	Applications Received	Accepted	New Admits Enrolled (PT)	Total Enrolled (PT)	Degrees Awarded in 2014–2015	Median Years to Complete Degree	Dismissed/ Withdrew
Counseling Psychology	PhD	December 1 (Fall)	245	7	7 (0)	31 (0)	7	5	2
Industrial/ Organizational Psychology	PhD	December 1 (Fall)	112	3	3 (0)	24 (0)	5	6	0
Cognitive Psychology	PhD	January 15 (Fall)	65	2	2 (0)	10 (0)	1	6	1
Applied Social and Health Psychology	PhD	January 15 (Fall)	71	3	3 (0)	16 (0)	2	5.5	0
Cognitive Neuroscience	PhD	January 15 (Fall)	39	2	2 (0)	6 (0)	1	6	2
Applied Industrial/ Organizational Psychology	MA/MS	April 1 (Fall)	36	15	12	31	10	2	0

APA Accreditation

Counseling PhD: Student Outcome Data website: http://www.colostate.edu/Depts/Psychology/counseling/SAO.shtml.

Doctoral Degree (PhD Counseling Psychology): For those doctoral students for whom a professional internship was required in this program prior to graduation:
Total students who applied for an internship: 2
Total students who obtained an internship: 2
Total students who obtained a paid internship: 2
Total students who obtained an unpaid internship: 0
Total students who were placed in APA/CPA-accredited internships: 2
Total students placed in internships not APA/CPA-accredited, but listed with the Association of Psychology Postdoctoral and Internship Centers (APPIC): 0
Total students placed in internships conforming to guidelines of the Council of Directors of School Psychology Programs (CDSPP): 0
Total students placed in internships that were not APA/CPA-accredited, APPIC or CDSSP listed: 0

Master's Degree (MA/MS Applied Industrial/Organizational Psychology): An internship experience, such as a final research project or "capstone" experience is required of graduates.

Internships/Practica

There are a number of related practica for counseling students throughout Northern Colorado. The following are examples: neuropsychology, local community college, primary health care, and school districts. Industrial/Organizational students consult with a variety of businesses throughout the state including: United Airlines, HP, Sun Systems, IBM, microbreweries and hospitals. The Tri Ethnic Center for Prevention Research (TEC) is a part of the department.

Admissions

Entries appear in the following order: required test or GPA, minimum score (if required)/median score of students entering in 2015–2016.

Program	Degree	GRE-V	GRE-Q	GRE-Writing	GRE-Subject	Under-graduate GPA	Last 2 Years GPA	Psychology GPA	Master's GPA
Counseling Psychology	PhD	155/164	153/159	Not specified	Not specified	3.52/3.86	Not specified	Not specified	Not specified
Industrial/Organizational Psychology	PhD	155/155	150/153	Not specified	Not specified	3.82/3.82	Not specified	Not specified	Not specified
Cognitive Psychology	PhD	157/159	149/157	Not specified	Not specified	3.56/3.7	Not specified	Not specified	Not specified
Applied Social and Health Psychology	PhD	151/159	151/153	Not specified	Not specified	3.85/3.93	Not specified	Not specified	Not specified
Cognitive Neuroscience	PhD	153/158	154/155	Not specified	Not specified	3.2/3.22	Not specified	Not specified	Not specified
Applied Industrial/Organizational Psychology	MA/MS	Not specified	Not specified	Not specified	Not specified	Not specified	Not specified	Not specified	Not specified

Admissions Requirements:

Degree	GRE	GRE-Subject	Letters of Recommendation	Research Statement	Writing Sample	CV	Interview
Master's/Specialist	Required	Optional	3	Required	Required	Required	None
Doctoral	Required	Optional	3	Required	Required	Required	Required

Please note if these criteria vary for different programs: Scientific writing sample required by Applied Social and Industrial/Organizational Programs; optional for Cognitive and Cognitive Neuroscience. The subject test score is required by the Industrial/Organizational Psychology program and the MAIOP program only for applicants who did not major in psychology as an undergraduate.

Admissions Criteria:
GRE scores—high
Research experience—high
Work experience—medium
Clinically related public service—medium
GPA—high

Letters of recommendation—high
Interview—medium
Statement of goals and objectives—high
Undergraduate psychology preparation—medium

For additional information on admission requirements, visit http://www.colostate.edu/Depts/Psychology/apply.shtml.

Department Demographics

	Male (PT)	Female (PT)	Total	African-American/ Black (PT)	Hispanic/ Latino (PT)	Asian/ Pacific Islander (PT)	American Indian/ Alaska Native (PT)	Caucasian/ White (PT)	Unknown	Multiethnic (PT)	ADA (PT)	Int'l (PT)
Students	41 (0)	77 (0)	118	1 (0)	14 (0)	2 (0)	1 (0)	93 (0)	2 (0)	5 (0)	0 (0)	2 (0)

Financial Information/Assistance

Tuition: For information on tuition costs, visit http://registrar.colostate.edu/tuition-fees. Tuition is subject to change. Additional fees are assessed to students beyond the costs of tuition for the following: General Fees-$792.49, University Technology Fee-$25, University Facility Fee-$20.75/credit hour. Tuition costs vary by program.

Doctoral:
State residents: $9,347 per academic year.
Nonstate residents: $22,915 per academic year.

Financial Assistance:

	Teaching Assistantship (% Receiving)	Teaching Assistantship Tuition Remission	Research Assistantship (% Receiving)	Research Assistantship Tuition Remission	Fellowship (% Receiving)	Fellowship Tuition Remission
First-Year Student	$13,680 (NA)	Full	$13,680 (NA)	Full	$14,400 (NA)	NA
Advanced Student	$14,200 (NA)	Full	$14,200 (NA)	Full	NA (NA)	NA

For additional information on financial assistance, visit http://graduateschool.colostate.edu/financial-resources/.

Employment of Department Graduates

Doctoral:
Employed in independent practice: 1
Employed in an academic position at a university: 4
Employed in business or industry: 2
Employed in government agency: 1
Employed in a community mental health/counseling center: 3
Employed in a hospital/medical center: 4
Do not know: 1
Total: 16

Additional Information

Housing and Day Care: On-campus housing is available. See the following website for more information: http://www.housing.colostate.edu/. On-campus day care facilities are available. See the following website for more information: http://ecc.colostate.edu/.

Information for Students With Physical Disabilities: See the following website: http://www.rds.colostate.edu/.

Special Facilities or Resources: The Tri Ethnic Center for Prevention Research, a NIDA, CDC and Justice Department funded research center, focuses on adolescent issues such as substance use, violence, rural issues, and culturally appropriate prevention strategies. The Institute for Applied Prevention Research (IAPR), which is a Diversity Program of Research and Scholarly Excellence, is the umbrella group for a number of centers including Tri-Ethnic, CICRC, CFERT and CoAMP.

Application Information: Graduate Admissions Committee, Department of Psychology, Colorado State University, 1876 Campus Delivery, Fort Collins, CO 80526-1876. *Fee:* $50. *Online application:* https://psy.psych.colostate.edu/GradApp/.

Colorado, University of, Boulder

Department of Psychology and Neuroscience
Arts and Sciences
UCB 345, Muenzinger D244
Boulder, CO 80309-0345
Telephone: (303) 492-8662
Chairperson: Theresa D. Hernández

E-mail: info@psych.colorado.edu
Web: http://www.colorado.edu/psych-neuro/

Orientation, Objectives, and Emphasis of Department

Our emphasis is on training graduate students who have the capability to advance knowledge in the field, and who are committed to applying their knowledge. We emphasize rigorous training in both the theory and methods of psychological research.

Programs and Degrees Offered

Program	Degree	Application Deadline	Applications Received	Accepted	New Admits Enrolled (PT)	Total Enrolled (PT)	Degrees Awarded in 2014–2015	Median Years to Complete Degree	Dismissed/ Withdrew
Behavioral Genetics	PhD	December 1 (Fall)	10	0	0 (0)	11 (0)	2	6	0
Behavioral Neuroscience	PhD	December 1 (Fall)	108	3	3	12 (0)	5	6	0
Clinical Psychology	PhD	December 1 (Fall)	341	4	3 (0)	26 (0)	4	6	1
Cognitive Psychology	PhD	December 1 (Fall)	169	7	5	25	2	6	1
Social Psychology	PhD	December 1 (Fall)	137	5	2	15 (0)	2	6	0

APA Accreditation

Clinical PhD: Student Outcome Data website: http://www.colorado.edu/clinicalpsychology/student-admissions-outcomes-and-other-data.

Doctoral Degree (PhD Clinical Psychology): For those doctoral students for whom a professional internship was required in this program prior to graduation:
Total students who applied for an internship: 2
Total students who obtained an internship: 2
Total students who obtained a paid internship: 2
Total students who obtained an unpaid internship: 0
Total students who were placed in APA/CPA-accredited internships: 2
Total students placed in internships not APA/CPA-accredited, but listed with the Association of Psychology Postdoctoral and Internship Centers (APPIC): 0
Total students placed in internships conforming to guidelines of the Council of Directors of School Psychology Programs (CDSPP): 0
Total students placed in internships that were not APA/CPA-accredited, APPIC or CDSSP listed: 0

Internships/Practica

The Clinical Psychology PhD program requires a one year clinical internship in the final year of the program.

Admissions

Entries appear in the following order: required test or GPA, minimum score (if required)/median score of students entering in 2015–2016.

Program	Degree	GRE-V	GRE-Q	GRE-Writing	GRE-Subject	Undergraduate GPA	Last 2 Years GPA	Psychology GPA	Master's GPA
Behavioral Genetics	PhD	Not specified	Not specified	Not specified	Not specified	Not specified	Not specified	Not specified	Not specified

Admissions *(con't.)*

Program	Degree	GRE-V	GRE-Q	GRE-Writing	GRE-Subject	Under-graduate GPA	Last 2 Years GPA	Psychology GPA	Master's GPA
Behavioral Neuroscience	PhD	Not specified	Not specified	Not specified	Not specified	Not specified	Not specified	Not specified	Not specified
Clinical Psychology	PhD	NA/162	NA/163	Not specified	Not specified	Not specified	Not specified	Not specified	Not specified
Cognitive Psychology	PhD	Not specified	Not specified	Not specified	Not specified	Not specified	Not specified	Not specified	Not specified
Social Psychology	PhD	Not specified	Not specified	Not specified	Not specified	Not specified	Not specified	Not specified	Not specified

Admissions Requirements:

Degree	GRE	GRE-Subject	Letters of Recom-mendation	Research Statement	Writing Sample	CV	Interview
Doctoral	Required	Optional	3	Required	Optional	Required	Required

Please note if these criteria vary for different programs: Clinical work experience is only relevant in clinical program. Research experience is critical to admissions to all programs.

Admissions Criteria:

GRE scores—high
Research experience—high
Work experience—medium
Clinically related public service—medium
GPA—high

Letters of recommendation—high
Interview—high
Statement of goals and objectives—high
Undergraduate psychology preparation—medium

For additional information on admission requirements, visit http://www.colorado.edu/psych-neuro/graduates/application-information.

Department Demographics

	Male (PT)	Female (PT)	Total	African-American/ Black (PT)	Hispanic/ Latino (PT)	Asian/ Pacific Islander (PT)	American Indian/ Alaska Native (PT)	Caucasian/ White (PT)	Unknown (PT)	Multiethnic (PT)	ADA (PT)	Int'l (PT)
Students	37 (0)	52 (0)	89	0 (0)	4 (0)	7 (0)	0 (0)	78 (0)	0 (0)	0 (0)	0 (0)	3 (0)

Financial Information/Assistance

Tuition: For information on tuition costs, visit http://bursar.colorado.edu/tuition-fees/tuition-and-fees-rate-sheets/. Tuition is subject to change.

Doctoral:
State residents: $10,530 per academic year.
Nonstate residents: $27,828 per academic year.

Financial Assistance:

	Teaching Assistantship (% Receiving)	Teaching Assistantship Tuition Remission	Research Assistantship (% Receiving)	Research Assistantship Tuition Remission	Fellowship (% Receiving)	Fellowship Tuition Remission
First-Year Student	$17,909 (NA)	Full	$17,909 (NA)	Full	NA (NA)	NA
Advanced Student	$17,909 (NA)	Full	$19,263 (NA)	Full	NA (NA)	NA

For additional information on financial assistance, visit http://www.colorado.edu/financialaid/types-aid.

Employment of Department Graduates

Doctoral:
Enrolled in a postdoctoral residency/fellowship: 12
Employed in business or industry: 2
Employed in a hospital/medical center: 1
Total: 15

Additional Information

Housing and Day Care: On-campus housing is available. See the following website for more information: http://housing.colorado.edu/residences/graduate-family. On-campus day care facilities are available. See the following website for more information: https://childcare.colorado.edu/.

Information for Students With Physical Disabilities: See the following website: http://disabilityservices.colorado.edu/.

Special Facilities or Resources: The Department of Psychology & Neuroscience is housed in a large six-story building that contains space for offices, a clinic and research laboratories. There are extensive research facilities available to students, both in individual laboratories and from the department generally. The department has excellent laboratory facilities for human and animal research. The animal care facilities include those for mice, rats, and bullfrogs. The various labs in the department have access to state-of-the-art hardware, including fluorescent and confocal microscopy capability, CCD video camera for image analysis, and real time PCR optogenetics capabilities as well as various behavioral research setups. We have a new human imaging facility based on a Siemens 3T MRI imager that enables state-of-the-art cognitive neuroscience experiments. In terms of computing facilities, the department provides centralized facilities for departmental mailing lists, data analysis, model development and simulation, and many common computing tasks. The computing facility also has extensive support for development of and running real-time computer-controlled experiments. The facilities of the Institute of Behavioral Genetics, the Institute of Behavioral Science, the Institute of Cognitive Science and the Center for Neuroscience are available to students. Each of these institutes has its own laboratory space and specialized computer facilities.

Application Information: Fee: $50. Online application: http://www.colorado.edu/admissions/graduate/apply.

Colorado, University of, Colorado Springs
Department of Psychology
Letters, Arts, and Sciences
1420 Austin Bluffs Parkway
Colorado Springs, CO 80918
Telephone: (719) 255-4500
Chairperson: Dr. Michael Kisley

E-mail: ddubois@uccs.edu
Web: http://www.uccs.edu/psych

Orientation, Objectives, and Emphasis of Department
The MA program places special emphasis in general areas of applied clinical practice and general experimental psychology. The MA training will enable a student to prepare for a doctoral program, teach in community colleges, work under a licensed psychologist in private and public agencies, work in university counseling centers, or work as a researcher in a variety of organizations. A research thesis is required of all students. There is a broad range of faculty research interests including aging (e.g., psychopathology and psychological treatment of older adults, family dynamics, self-concept development, memory, cognition, and personality), social

psychology, psychology and the law, personality, program evaluation, prevention of child abuse, adolescent psychology and psychological trauma. There are optional tracks for Psychology and Law, Trauma Psychology, Cognitive Psychology, or Developmental Psychology for Masters Students. The accredited clinical PhD program offers two emphases, in geropsychology and trauma psychology.

Programs and Degrees Offered

Program	Degree	Application Deadline	Applications Received	Accepted	New Admits Enrolled (PT)	Total Enrolled (PT)	Degrees Awarded in 2014–2015	Median Years to Complete Degree	Dismissed/ Withdrew
Clinical Psychology	MA/MS	January 1 (Fall)	63	16	8 (0)	23 (0)	10	2	2
Clinical Psychology	PhD	December 1 (Fall)	171	8	5 (0)	19 (0)	4	5	1
Psychological Science	MA/MS	January 1 (Fall)	32	13	5 (0)	22 (0)	2	2	0

APA Accreditation

Clinical PhD: Student Outcome Data website: http://www.uccs.edu/psych/graduate/phd-program.html.

Doctoral Degree (PhD Clinical Psychology): For those doctoral students for whom a professional internship was required in this program prior to graduation:
Total students who applied for an internship: 2
Total students who obtained an internship: 2
Total students who obtained a paid internship: 2
Total students who obtained an unpaid internship: 0
Total students who were placed in APA/CPA-accredited internships: 2
Total students placed in internships not APA/CPA-accredited, but listed with the Association of Psychology Postdoctoral and Internship Centers (APPIC): 0
Total students placed in internships conforming to guidelines of the Council of Directors of School Psychology Programs (CDSPP): 0
Total students placed in internships that were not APA/CPA-accredited, APPIC or CDSSP listed: 0

Master's Degree (MA/MS Clinical Psychology): An internship experience, such as a final research project or "capstone" experience is required of graduates. Master's Degree (MA/MS Psychological Science): An internship experience, such as a final research project or "capstone" experience is required of graduates.

Internships/Practica

Required practicum experiences for MA Clinical and PhD Clinical are completed at the departmental CU Aging Center, the CU Counseling Center, or in community placements under licensed supervision (e.g., school settings, community health centers, state mental health facility, domestic violence center, impatient psychiatric hospital). The goal of these experiences is to expose students to clinical settings, to roles of clinical psychologists, and to begin the development of clinical skills.

Admissions

Entries appear in the following order: required test or GPA, minimum score (if required)/median score of students entering in 2015–2016.

Program	Degree	GRE-V	GRE-Q	GRE-Writing	GRE-Subject	Under-graduate GPA	Last 2 Years GPA	Psychol-ogy GPA	Master's GPA
Clinical Psychology	MA/MS	NA/158	NA/154	NA/4	Not specified	NA/3.7	Not specified	NA/NA	Not specified
Clinical Psychology	PhD	NA/161	NA/156	NA/4.5	Not specified	NA/3.35	Not specified	Not specified	Not specified
Psychological Science	MA/MS	NA/156	NA/151	NA/4	Not specified	NA/3.67	Not specified	NA/NA	Not specified

Admissions Requirements:

Degree	GRE	GRE-Subject	Letters of Recommendation	Research Statement	Writing Sample	CV	Interview
Master's/Specialist	Required	Recommended	4	Required	Optional	Required	None
Doctoral	Required	Recommended	4	Required	Optional	Required	Required

Please note if these criteria vary for different programs: For the Psychological Science MA program, clinically related public service is not required. Interviews are only for applicants to the doctoral program. MA applicants do not need to complete an interview as part of the application process.

Admissions Criteria:

GRE scores—high
Research experience—medium
Work experience—low
Clinically related public service—medium
GPA—medium

Letters of recommendation—medium
Interview—medium
Statement of goals and objectives—medium
Undergraduate psychology preparation—medium

Department Demographics

	Male (PT)	Female (PT)	Total	African-American/ Black (PT)	Hispanic/ Latino (PT)	Asian/ Pacific Islander (PT)	American Indian/ Alaska Native (PT)	Caucasian/ White (PT)	Unknown	Multiethnic (PT)	ADA (PT)	Int'l (PT)
Students	13 (0)	51 (0)	64	1 (0)	1 (0)	3 (0)	0 (0)	59 (0)	0 (0)	0 (0)	0 (0)	3 (0)

Financial Information/Assistance

Tuition: For information on tuition costs, visit http://www.uccs.edu/bursar/tuition-and-fees.html. Tuition is subject to change. Additional fees are assessed to students beyond the costs of tuition for the following: University set fees; psychology program fee. Tuition costs vary by program.

Doctoral:
State residents: $983 per credit hour.
Nonstate residents: $1,478 per credit hour.

Master's:
State residents: $882 per credit hour.
Nonstate residents: $1,405 per credit hour.

Financial Assistance:

	Teaching Assistantship (% Receiving)	Teaching Assistantship Tuition Remission	Research Assistantship (% Receiving)	Research Assistantship Tuition Remission	Fellowship (% Receiving)	Fellowship Tuition Remission
First-Year Student	$3,600 (NA)	NA	$5,000 (NA)	NA	$3,000 (NA)	NA
Advanced Student	$3,600 (NA)	NA	$5,000 (NA)	NA	$3,000 (NA)	NA

For additional information on financial assistance, visit http://www.uccs.edu/~finaid/.

Employment of Department Graduates

No information provided.

Additional Information

Housing and Day Care: On-campus housing is available. See the following website for more information: http://www.uccs.edu/~residence/. On-campus day care facilities are available. See the following website for more information: http://www.uccs.edu/~fdc/.

Information for Students With Physical Disabilities: See the following website: http://www.uccs.edu/~disability/.

Special Facilities or Resources: Research facilities include clinical training laboratories with observational capabilities, laboratories for individual and small group research, and a psychophysiological laboratory. Columbine Hall houses a 50-station computer lab that is available for general use. The CU Aging Center, administered through the Psychology Department, is a community-based nonprofit mental health clinic designed to serve the mental health needs of older adults and their families. The mission of the Center is to provide state-of-the-art psychological assessment and treatment services to older persons and their families, to study psychological aging processes, and to train students in clinical psychology and related disciplines.

Application Information: David DuBois, Program Assistant. *Fee:* $60. *Online application:* http://www.uccs.edu/graduateschool/prospective-students/admissions.html.

Colorado, University of, Denver

Department of Psychology
College of Liberal Arts and Sciences
Campus Box 173, P.O. Box 173364
Denver, CO 80217-3364
Telephone: (303) 556-8565
Chairperson: Peter Kaplan, PhD

E-mail: anne.beard@ucdenver.edu
Web: http://www.ucdenver.edu/academics/colleges/CLAS/Departments/psychology/

Orientation, Objectives, and Emphasis of Department

The Clinical Health Psychology program adheres to the scientist–practitioner model, and training emphasizes the contribution of research to the understanding, treatment, and prevention of human problems, and the application of knowledge that is grounded in scientific evidence. Students are trained to work within the community to use psychological tools and techniques to promote health, prevent and treat illness, and improve the health care system. In addition to coursework, students acquire expertise in research by completing a master's thesis and doctoral dissertation, and demonstrate competence in clinical assessment and intervention through a clinical competency examination along with several applied practicum experiences and a predoctoral internship.

Programs and Degrees Offered

Program	Degree	Application Deadline	Applica-tions Received	Accepted	New Admits Enrolled (PT)	Total Enrolled (PT)	Degrees Awarded in 2014–2015	Median Years to Complete Degree	Dismissed/Withdrew
Clinical Health Psychology	PhD	December 1 (Fall)	130	6	6	28	1	6	1

APA Accreditation

Clinical PhD: Student Outcome Data website: http://www.ucdenver.edu/academics/colleges/CLAS/Departments/psychology/Programs/PhD/Pages/Overview.aspx.

Doctoral Degree (PhD Clinical Health Psychology): For those doctoral students for whom a professional internship was required in this program prior to graduation:
Total students who applied for an internship: 4
Total students who obtained an internship: 4
Total students who obtained a paid internship: 4
Total students who obtained an unpaid internship: 0
Total students who were placed in APA/CPA-accredited internships: 4
Total students placed in internships not APA/CPA-accredited, but listed with the Association of Psychology Postdoctoral and Internship Centers (APPIC): 0
Total students placed in internships conforming to guidelines of the Council of Directors of School Psychology Programs (CDSPP): 0
Total students placed in internships that were not APA/CPA-accredited, APPIC or CDSSP listed: 0

Internships/Practica

Clinical practica are widely available at several community agencies. Past students have completed practica at local hospitals, mental health centers, residential treatment centers, and the division of corrections. All field placements must be approved by the program director in advance.

Admissions

Entries appear in the following order: required test or GPA, minimum score (if required)/median score of students entering in 2015–2016.

Program	Degree	GRE-V	GRE-Q	GRE-Writing	GRE-Subject	Undergraduate GPA	Last 2 Years GPA	Psychology GPA	Master's GPA
Clinical Health Psychology	PhD	NA/159	NA/152	Not specified	Not specified	NA/3.8	NA/3.9	Not specified	Not specified

Admissions Requirements:

Degree	GRE	GRE-Subject	Letters of Recommendation	Research Statement	Writing Sample	CV	Interview
Doctoral	Required	Optional	3	Required	Optional	Required	Required

Admissions Criteria:

GRE scores—high
Research experience—high
Work experience—medium
Clinically related public service—low
GPA—high

Letters of recommendation—high
Interview—high
Statement of goals and objectives—high
Undergraduate psychology preparation—medium

Department Demographics

	Male (PT)	Female (PT)	Total	African-American/ Black (PT)	Hispanic/ Latino (PT)	Asian/ Pacific Islander (PT)	American Indian/ Alaska Native (PT)	Caucasian/ White (PT)	Unknown	Multiethnic (PT)	ADA (PT)	Int'l (PT)
Students	3 (0)	25 (0)	28	0 (0)	1 (0)	2 (0)	0 (0)	25 (0)	0 (0)	0 (0)	0 (0)	0 (0)

Financial Information/Assistance

Tuition: For information on tuition costs, visit http://www.ucdenver.edu/student-services/resources/CostsAndFinancing. Tuition is subject to change. Additional fees are assessed to students beyond the costs of tuition for the following: transportation, technology, student services, etc.

Doctoral:
State residents: $8,936 per academic year.
State residents: $355 per credit hour.
Nonstate residents: $26,800 per academic year.
Nonstate residents: $1,055 per credit hour.

Financial Assistance:

	Teaching Assistantship (% Receiving)	Teaching Assistantship Tuition Remission	Research Assistantship (% Receiving)	Research Assistantship Tuition Remission	Fellowship (% Receiving)	Fellowship Tuition Remission
First-Year Student	$15,000 (NA)	Full	$15,000 (NA)	Full	$15,000 (NA)	Full
Advanced Student	$15,000 (NA)	Full	$15,000 (NA)	Full	$15,000 (NA)	Full

For additional information on financial assistance, visit http://www.ucdenver.edu/academics/colleges/CLAS/Departments/psychology/Programs/PhD/Pages/Costs-Student-Funding.aspx.

Employment of Department Graduates

Doctoral:
Enrolled in a postdoctoral residency/fellowship: 4
Employed in a community mental health/counseling center: 2
Total: 6

Additional Information

Housing and Day Care: No on-campus housing is available. On-campus day care facilities are available. See the following website for more information: http://www.ahec.edu/for-campus-faculty-staff/early-learning-center.

Information for Students With Physical Disabilities: See the following website: http://www.ucdenver.edu/disabilityresources.

Special Facilities or Resources: There are numerous possibilities for research collaborations with faculty at the Health Sciences Center (renamed Anschutz Medical Campus) in addition to the faculty members in our own department. There are also several affiliated institutions (e.g., AMC Cancer Research Center, The Children's Hospital and Kempe Center, Denver Health Medical Center, National Jewish Health, and the VA) in the area that provide additional opportunities for research collaborations and applied clinical work.

Application Information: Graduate School; University of Colorado Denver; Campus Box 163; 1380 Lawrence Street, Suite 1250; PO Box 173364; Denver, CO 80217-3364. *Fee:* $50. *Online application:* http://www.ucdenver.edu/admissions/doctoral/Pages/index.aspx.

Denver, University of
Child, Family, and School Psychology Program
Morgridge College of Education
1999 East Evans Avenue
Denver, CO 80208
Telephone: (303) 871-2473
Program Coordinator: Cynthia Hazel, PhD

E-mail: nora.mcpherson@du.edu
Web: http://morgridge.du.edu/programs/child-family-and-school-psychology/

Orientation, Objectives, and Emphasis of Department
The Child, Family, & School Psychology (CFSP) program, which stresses serving children in the context of their families and communities, teaches students about psychological factors that influence human development and learning. Students can be prepared for licensure as school psychologists through the National Association of School Psychologists (NASP) approved EdS degree program or the NASP-approved doctoral program; or for professional careers in a broad range of educational, medical, research, or treatment-oriented service systems serving children from birth through age 21. The program offers a distinctive opportunity to interested students to develop a specialization in early childhood development. The curriculum emphasizes strategies for supporting and intervening with children and families with diverse needs, as well as policy development, research, and program development and evaluation. The CFSP Program provides students expanded career options in schools and the community. As a student in this program, you will have the opportunity to work in a range of educational, medical, research, or treatment-oriented service systems at the local, state and national levels. You will also acquire a broad base of information about typical and atypical development, learning, and biological and environmental contexts that affect these areas.

Programs and Degrees Offered

Program	Degree	Application Deadline	Applica-tions Received	Accepted	New Admits Enrolled (PT)	Total Enrolled (PT)	Degrees Awarded in 2014–2015	Median Years to Complete Degree	Dismissed/Withdrew
Child, Family and School Psychology	MA/MS	January 1 (Fall)	12	5	0 (0)	3 (0)	2	2	0

Programs and Degrees Offered (con't.)

Program	Degree	Application Deadline	Applications Received	Accepted	New Admits Enrolled (PT)	Total Enrolled (PT)	Degrees Awarded in 2014–2015	Median Years to Complete Degree	Dismissed/ Withdrew
Child, Family and School Psychology	EdS	January 1 (Fall)	59	44	22 (0)	59 (0)	10	4	0
Child, Family and School Psychology	PhD	January 1 (Fall)	16	6	4 (0)	23 (0)	3	5.5	0

Doctoral Degree (PhD Child, Family and School Psychology): For those doctoral students for whom a professional internship was required in this program prior to graduation:
Total students who applied for an internship: 1
Total students who obtained an internship: 1
Total students who obtained a paid internship: 1
Total students who obtained an unpaid internship: 0
Total students who were placed in APA/CPA-accredited internships: 0
Total students placed in internships not APA/CPA-accredited, but listed with the Association of Psychology Postdoctoral and Internship Centers (APPIC): 0
Total students placed in internships conforming to guidelines of the Council of Directors of School Psychology Programs (CDSPP): 1
Total students placed in internships that were not APA/CPA-accredited, APPIC or CDSSP listed: 0

Master's Degree (MA/MS Child, Family and School Psychology): An internship experience, such as a final research project or "capstone" experience is required of graduates.

Internships/Practica
Integrated and well supervised field experiences taken during coursework and as independent placement courses are an integral part of the training of future school psychologists and child and family professionals. Such experiences in total provide opportunities for students to build and reflect upon professional roles and competencies and to master critical professional skills. Field coursework experiences are designed as a developmental Chain of Relevant Experiences (CoRE) where students progress from being Critical Observers, to Directed Participants, to Active Contributors, and ultimately to become Independent Practitioners. Although the structure and content of our field courses differ across degree programs, all students complete practica. EdS and PhD School Psychology Licensure students also complete a 1,200-hour (EdS) or 1,500-hour (PhD) Internship, which can occur over one full year or two consecutive years. Our programmatic field-based coursework includes training and practice in the following: comprehensive assessment of developmental strengths and weaknesses; direct and preventative interventions within home, school, and community settings; communication and collaboration with families and children with diverse life experiences; individual, group, and family crisis counseling; interdisciplinary and transdisciplinary team collaboration in school and community settings; delivery of in-service trainings and presentations; and system-wide program evaluation, research, and intervention.

Admissions
Entries appear in the following order: required test or GPA, minimum score (if required)/median score of students entering in 2015–2016.

Program	Degree	GRE-V	GRE-Q	GRE-Writing	GRE-Subject	Under-graduate GPA	Last 2 Years GPA	Psychology GPA	Master's GPA
Child, Family and School Psychology	MA/MS	Not specified	Not specified	Not specified	Not specified	Not specified	Not specified	Not specified	Not specified
Child, Family and School Psychology	EdS	Not specified	Not specified	Not specified	Not specified	Not specified	Not specified	Not specified	Not specified
Child, Family and School Psychology	PhD	Not specified	Not specified	Not specified	Not specified	Not specified	Not specified	Not specified	Not specified

Admissions Requirements:

Degree	GRE	GRE-Subject	Letters of Recommendation	Research Statement	Writing Sample	CV	Interview
Master's/Specialist	Required	Optional	2	Required	Optional	Required	Required
Doctoral	Required	Optional	3	Required	Optional	Required	Required

Admissions Criteria:

GRE scores—medium
Research experience—medium
Work experience—medium
Clinically related public service—medium
GPA—medium

Letters of recommendation—high
Interview—high
Statement of goals and objectives—high
Undergraduate psychology preparation—low

For additional information on admission requirements, visit http://morgridge.du.edu/apply/.

Department Demographics

	Male (PT)	Female (PT)	Total	African-American/ Black (PT)	Hispanic/ Latino (PT)	Asian/ Pacific Islander (PT)	American Indian/ Alaska Native (PT)	Caucasian/ White (PT)	Unknown (PT)	Multiethnic (PT)	ADA (PT)	Int'l (PT)
Students	7 (0)	76 (0)	83	0 (0)	1 (0)	0 (0)	1 (0)	81 (0)	0 (0)	0 (0)	0 (0)	0 (0)

Financial Information/Assistance

Tuition: For information on tuition costs, visit http://www.du.edu/registrar/registration/tuition.html. Tuition is subject to change. Additional fees are assessed to students beyond the costs of tuition for the following: Technology Fee of $4 per credit hour. Lab fees for certain classes.

Doctoral:
State residents: $1,142 per credit hour.
Nonstate residents: $1,142 per credit hour.

Master's:
State residents: $1,142 per credit hour.
Nonstate residents: $1,142 per credit hour.

Financial Assistance:

	Teaching Assistantship (% Receiving)	Teaching Assistantship Tuition Remission	Research Assistantship (% Receiving)	Research Assistantship Tuition Remission	Fellowship (% Receiving)	Fellowship Tuition Remission
First-Year Student	NA (NA)	NA	NA (NA)	Partial	NA (NA)	Partial
Advanced Student	NA (NA)	Partial	NA (NA)	Partial	NA (NA)	Partial

For additional information on financial assistance, visit http://morgridge.du.edu/financial-aid/.

Employment of Department Graduates

Master's:
Enrolled in a psychology doctoral program: 1
Enrolled in another graduate/professional program: 1
Total: 2

Doctoral:
Employed in a professional position in a school system: 3
Total: 3

Additional Information

Housing and Day Care: On-campus housing is available. See the following website for more information: http://www.du.edu/housing/. On-campus day care facilities are available. See the following website for more information: http://www.du.edu/fisher/.

Information for Students With Physical Disabilities: See the following website: http://www.du.edu/studentlife/disability-services/index.html.

Special Facilities or Resources: The Child, Family, and School Psychology Program resides in a recently constructed technology-rich building, Katherine A. Ruffatto Hall. Our new building provides teleconferencing capabilities, smart classrooms, interactive whiteboards, and a state-of-the-art space dedicated to the Counseling and Educational Services Clinic where students work with community clients. In addition, the Fisher Early Learning Center provides a wide range of supervised opportunities for our students including research, training, and practice with young children and their families.

Application Information: Morgridge College of Education, Office of Admissions, 1999 East Evans Avenue, Denver, CO 80208. *Fee:* $60. *Online application:* http://morgridge.du.edu/apply/.

Denver, University of
Counseling Psychology
Morgridge College of Education
1999 East Evans Avenue
Denver, CO 80208
Telephone: (303) 871-2484
Training Director: Maria Riva

E-mail: Maria.Riva@du.edu
Web: http://morgridge.du.edu/programs/counseling-psychology/

Orientation, Objectives, and Emphasis of Department
As a graduate student in the Counseling Psychology program, you'll develop the skills necessary to become an effective practitioner, researcher, and/or leader in your field. Our goal is to develop professionals who are insightful and self-reflective, who are innovative risk takers and superior critical thinkers. Our strong emphasis on multicultural and diversity competence is infused across the curriculum. Our highly selective doctoral program is accredited by the American Psychological Association and is well known for providing access to high quality practicum placements and having a high match rate with APA-accredited predoctoral internships across the country. Similarly, our master's program draws students from all over the U.S. and from several different countries. We not only want our students to demonstrate accurate and current knowledge, but to have expertise related to the many issues confronting society and to have the skills to create effective strategies and approaches to address these challenges. To work professionally in counseling psychology at the master's or doctoral level, you will need a strong background in the practice of counseling and psychotherapy, as well as knowledge of the scientific foundations of psychology in order to evaluate and think critically about your practice.

Programs and Degrees Offered

Program	Degree	Application Deadline	Applications Received	Accepted	New Admits Enrolled (PT)	Total Enrolled (PT)	Degrees Awarded in 2014–2015	Median Years to Complete Degree	Dismissed/Withdrew
Counseling	MA/MS	January 16 (Fall)	185	100	46 (2)	90 (4)	50	2	4
Counseling Psychology	PhD	December 1 (Fall)	180	16	8 (0)	35 (0)	6	4	1

APA Accreditation
Counseling PhD: Student Outcome Data website: http://morgridge.du.edu/programs/counseling-psychology/counseling-psychology-phd-student-admissions-outcomes-data/.

Doctoral Degree (PhD Counseling Psychology): For those doctoral students for whom a professional internship was required in this program prior to graduation:
Total students who applied for an internship: 6
Total students who obtained an internship: 6
Total students who obtained a paid internship: 6
Total students who obtained an unpaid internship: 0
Total students who were placed in APA/CPA-accredited internships: 6
Total students placed in internships not APA/CPA-accredited, but listed with the Association of Psychology Postdoctoral and Internship Centers (APPIC): 0
Total students placed in internships conforming to guidelines of the Council of Directors of School Psychology Programs (CDSPP): 0
Total students placed in internships that were not APA/CPA-accredited, APPIC or CDSSP listed: 0

Master's Degree (MA/MS Counseling): An internship experience, such as a final research project or "capstone" experience is required of graduates.

Internships/Practica

Both doctoral and master's students complete practica and internships in the community as well as in a campus clinic. Doctoral students must complete APA-approved internships (exceptions made in rare circumstances). Doctoral students have opportunities to complete advanced practica in a variety of settings including college counseling centers, hospitals, VA, and mental health agencies. MA students complete practica and internships in the Denver and surrounding communities. Sites include adolescent treatment facilities, mental health centers, women's crisis centers, schools, hospitals, etc.

Admissions

Entries appear in the following order: required test or GPA, minimum score (if required)/median score of students entering in 2015–2016.

Program	Degree	GRE-V	GRE-Q	GRE-Writing	GRE-Subject	Under-graduate GPA	Last 2 Years GPA	Psychology GPA	Master's GPA
Counseling	MA/MS	NA/NA	NA/NA	NA/NA	Not specified	NA/NA	Not specified	Not specified	Not specified
Counseling Psychology	PhD	NA/NA	NA/NA	NA/NA	Not specified	NA/NA	Not specified	Not specified	Not specified

Admissions Requirements:

Degree	GRE	GRE-Subject	Letters of Recom-mendation	Research Statement	Writing Sample	CV	Interview
Master's/Specialist	Required	Optional	2	Required	Optional	Required	Required
Doctoral	Required	Optional	3	Required	Optional	Required	Required

Admissions Criteria:

GRE scores—medium
Research experience—high
Work experience—high
Clinically related public service—medium
GPA—high

Letters of recommendation—high
Interview—high
Statement of goals and objectives—high
Undergraduate psychology preparation—medium

Department Demographics

	Male (PT)	Female (PT)	Total	African-American/ Black (PT)	Hispanic/ Latino (PT)	Asian/ Pacific Islander (PT)	American Indian/ Alaska Native (PT)	Caucasian/ White (PT)	Unknown	Multiethnic (PT)	ADA (PT)	Int'l (PT)
Students	25 (1)	100 (3)	129	4 (1)	8 (0)	10 (0)	4 (0)	94 (2)	0 (0)	5 (1)	1 (0)	8 (0)

Financial Information/Assistance

Tuition: For information on tuition costs, visit http://www.du.edu/registrar/registration/tuition.html. Tuition is subject to change. Additional fees are assessed to students beyond the costs of tuition for the following: $4/credit technology fee.

Doctoral:
State residents: $35,970 per academic year.
State residents: $1,199 per credit hour.
Nonstate residents: $35,970 per academic year.
Nonstate residents: $1,199 per credit hour.

Master's:
State residents: $1,199 per credit hour.
Nonstate residents: $1,199 per credit hour.

Financial Assistance:

	Teaching Assistantship (% Receiving)	Teaching Assistantship Tuition Remission	Research Assistantship (% Receiving)	Research Assistantship Tuition Remission	Fellowship (% Receiving)	Fellowship Tuition Remission
First-Year Student	$8,000 (NA)	Partial	$8,000 (NA)	Partial	$4,500 (NA)	Partial
Advanced Student	$8,000 (NA)	Partial	$8,000 (NA)	Partial	$8,000 (NA)	Partial

For additional information on financial assistance, visit http://morgridge.du.edu/financial-aid/.

Employment of Department Graduates

Master's:
Enrolled in a psychology doctoral program: 8
Enrolled in another graduate/professional program: 2
Employed in other positions at a higher education institution: 1
Employed in a professional position in a school system: 6
Employed in government agency: 1
Employed in a community mental health/counseling center: 12
Employed in a hospital/medical center: 3
Do not know: 16
Total: 49

Doctoral:
Enrolled in a postdoctoral residency/fellowship: 6
Total: 6

Additional Information

Housing and Day Care: On-campus housing is available. See the following website for more information: http://www.du.edu/housing/. On-campus day care facilities are available. See the following website for more information: http://www.du.edu/fisher/index.html.

Information for Students With Physical Disabilities: See the following website: http://www.du.edu/studentlife/disability-services/index.html.

Special Facilities or Resources: The Counseling Psychology Department is housed in a new beautiful building that is located in a residential area. We value community engagement and have practicum placements and internships in over 60+ agencies and schools. Our building, Katherine A. Ruffatto Hall, houses a computer lab and an in-house clinic along with comfortable study and meeting spaces for students and kitchens on every floor. There are available courses that lead to a concentration in addictions. Faculty welcome students to join their research groups. A multicultural and diversity focus is not only a strong value but it is also infused across the curriculum, in faculty research, and in our practicum/internship sites.

Application Information: Graduate Studies, Office of Admission, 2199 South University Boulevard, Denver, CO 80208-0302. *Fee:* $65. *Online application:* https://gradadmissions.du.edu/apply/.

Denver, University of
Department of Psychology
Arts, Humanities & Social Sciences
Frontier Hall, 2155 South Race Street
Denver, CO 80208
Telephone: (303) 871-2939
Chairperson: Anne P. DePrince

E-mail: anne.deprince@du.edu
Web: http://www.du.edu/psychology

Orientation, Objectives, and Emphasis of Department
Programs are oriented toward training students to pursue careers in research, teaching, and professional practice. They include Affective Science, Clinical Child, Cognitive, Developmental, and Social, as well as Developmental Cognitive Neuroscience, a program open to students in any of the other programs, that fosters an interdisciplinary approach to cognitive, affective, and social neuroscience. The department has one of the few APA-accredited clinical child programs, and has been ranked very highly in past rankings by

the American Psychological Society for publication impact. We value inclusive excellence and recognize that the success of our department and university depends on including a rich diversity of constituents. The department offers close collaborative relationships between faculty and students, with an emphasis on individualized tutorial relationships. The department's atmosphere encourages collaboration and offers students the freedom to seek out and work with multiple faculty members as fits the student's evolving interests. Our students are successful in publishing in prestigious journals, in winning predoctoral grants, and obtaining their first choice for clinical internships.

Programs and Degrees Offered

Program	Degree	Application Deadline	Applica- tions Received	Accepted	New Admits Enrolled (PT)	Total Enrolled (PT)	Degrees Awarded in 2014– 2015	Median Years to Complete Degree	Dismissed/ Withdrew
Clinical Child Psychology	PhD	December 1 (Fall)	243	8	5 (0)	29 (0)	2	6	0
Developmental Psychology	PhD	December 1 (Fall)	37	3	3	8 (0)	1	6	0
Social Psychology	PhD	December 1 (Fall)	40	2	0	8	0		1
Cognitive Psychology	PhD	December 1 (Fall)	19	1	0	4	0		0
Developmental Cognitive Neuroscience	PhD	December 1 (Fall)	70	10	7	26	2	6	0
Affective Science	PhD	December 1 (Fall)	40	2	0	8	0		1

APA Accreditation

Clinical PhD: Student Outcome Data website: http://www.du.edu/ahss/psychology/graduate/programs/clinicalchild/.

Doctoral Degree (PhD Clinical Child Psychology): For those doctoral students for whom a professional internship was required in this program prior to graduation:
Total students who applied for an internship: 4
Total students who obtained an internship: 4
Total students who obtained a paid internship: 4
Total students who obtained an unpaid internship: 0
Total students who were placed in APA/CPA-accredited internships: 4
Total students placed in internships not APA/CPA-accredited, but listed with the Association of Psychology Postdoctoral and Internship Centers (APPIC): 0
Total students placed in internships conforming to guidelines of the Council of Directors of School Psychology Programs (CDSPP): 0
Total students placed in internships that were not APA/CPA-accredited, APPIC or CDSSP listed: 0

Internships/Practica

The department offers two clinical training facilities: the Child and Family Clinic and the Developmental Neuropsychology Clinic. The Child and Family Clinic provides training in assessment and psychotherapy with children, families, and adults. The Neuropsychology Clinic provides specialized training in assessment of learning disorders, mainly in school-age children. Thus, a considerable amount of clinical training is provided within our Department by faculty supervisors, ensuring that each clinical student is solidly grounded in both assessment and treatment. Clinical students also typically do externships in the community, at sites such as local hospitals, day treatment programs, and other community agencies. Graduate students who are not in clinical can also get experience with patient populations either by internships in the neuropsychology clinic or through research in labs that study developmental disorders.

Admissions

Entries appear in the following order: required test or GPA, minimum score (if required)/median score of students entering in 2015–2016.

Program	Degree	GRE-V	GRE-Q	GRE-Writing	GRE-Subject	Under-graduate GPA	Last 2 Years GPA	Psychol-ogy GPA	Master's GPA
Clinical Child Psychology	PhD	NA/159	NA/155	NA/5	Not specified	Not specified	Not specified	Not specified	Not specified
Developmental Psychology	PhD	NA/165	NA/159	NA/4.5	Not specified	NA/3.66	Not specified	Not specified	Not specified
Social Psychology	PhD	NA/168	NA/160	NA/4.75	Not specified	Not specified	Not specified	Not specified	Not specified
Cognitive Psychology	PhD	NA/157	NA/155	NA/5	Not specified	Not specified	Not specified	Not specified	Not specified
Developmental Cognitive Neuroscience	PhD	NA/165	NA/159	NA/4.5	Not specified	Not specified	Not specified	Not specified	Not specified
Affective Science	PhD	NA/168	NA/160	NA/4.75	Not specified	NA/3.88	Not specified	Not specified	Not specified

Admissions Requirements:

Degree	GRE	GRE-Subject	Letters of Recom-mendation	Research Statement	Writing Sample	CV	Interview
Doctoral	Required	Required	3	Required	Required	Required	Required

Admissions Criteria:

GRE scores—high
Research experience—high
Work experience—medium
Clinically related public service—high

GPA—high
Letters of recommendation—high
Interview—high
Statement of goals and objectives—high

For additional information on admission requirements, visit http://www.du.edu/ahss/psychology/graduate/prospectivestudents/admission.html.

Department Demographics

	Male (PT)	Female (PT)	Total	African-American/ Black (PT)	Hispanic/ Latino (PT)	Asian/ Pacific Islander (PT)	American Indian/ Alaska Native (PT)	Caucasian/ White (PT)	Unknown	Multiethnic (PT)	ADA (PT)	Int'l (PT)
Students	6 (0)	41 (0)	47	2 (0)	2 (0)	6 (0)	0 (0)	35 (0)	0 (0)	2 (0)	0 (0)	3 (0)

Financial Information/Assistance

Tuition: For information on tuition costs, visit http://www.du.edu/registrar/registration/tuition.html.

Doctoral:
State residents: $35,970 per academic year.
State residents: $1,199 per credit hour.
Nonstate residents: $35,970 per academic year.
Nonstate residents: $1,199 per credit hour.

Financial Assistance:

	Teaching Assistantship (% Receiving)	Teaching Assistantship Tuition Remission	Research Assistantship (% Receiving)	Research Assistantship Tuition Remission	Fellowship (% Receiving)	Fellowship Tuition Remission
First-Year Student	$20,000 (NA)	Full	$20,000 (NA)	Full	NA (NA)	NA
Advanced Student	$20,000 (NA)	Full	$20,000 (NA)	Full	NA (NA)	NA

For additional information on financial assistance, visit http://www.du.edu/ahss/psychology/graduate/prospectivestudents/financial.html.

Employment of Department Graduates

Doctoral:
Enrolled in a postdoctoral residency/fellowship: 2
Employed in business or industry: 1
Total: 3

Additional Information

Housing and Day Care: On-campus housing is available. See the following website for more information: http://www.du.edu/housing/apartments/. On-campus day care facilities are available. See the following website for more information: http://www.du.edu/fisher/.

Information for Students With Physical Disabilities: See the following website: http://www.du.edu/studentlife/disability-services/index.html.

Special Facilities or Resources: Our labs include the AACT laboratory for study of automaticity, affect, control and thought, Affect and Decision Making Lab, Center for Marital and Family Studies, Child Health and Development Lab, Developmental Neuropsychology Lab, Emotion and Coping Lab, Family and Child Neuroscience Lab, L.E.a.R.N. Lab (Learning Exceptionalities and Related Neuropsychology), Neurodevelopmental Research Lab, PROTECT Lab (Promoting Resilience in Offspring and Targeting Early Childhood Trajectories), Relationship Center, Services for At-Risk Youth & Families Lab, Social Perception and Attitudes Lab, Traumatic Stress Studies Lab, Trust Lab, Visual Perception, Emotion & Cognition Lab. Labs are equipped with computers for controlling presentation of stimuli and collection of data, and some include equipment to measure EDA, ECG, EMG, and eye movements. FMRI studies are conducted nearby at U. of Colorado, Boulder. The Child Health Development Lab is equipped with a modified wet lab for processing saliva samples including a -80 freezer for storage. The Neurodevelopmental Research program collects and processes biological samples including blood and saliva from pregnant women, infants and children. In addition, we have a host of conventional laboratory rooms with one-way observation windows and up-to-date audio and video recording capabilities.

Application Information: Graduate Studies Office, University of Denver, 2199 South University Boulevard, MRB, Room 5, Denver, CO 80208. *Fee:* $65. *Online application:* http://www.du.edu/apply/graduates/applicationrequirements.html.

Denver, University of
Graduate School of Professional Psychology
2450 South Vine Street
Denver, CO 80210
Telephone: (303) 871-3736
Dean: Dr. Shelly Smith-Acuña

E-mail: gsppinfo@du.edu
Web: http://www.du.edu/gspp/

Orientation, Objectives, and Emphasis of Department
The Graduate School of Professional Psychology focuses on scientifically based training for applied professional work rather than on the more traditional academic-scientific approach to clinical training. In addition to the basic clinical curriculum, special emphases are available in several areas. Our students should have a probing, questioning stance toward human problems and, therefore, should be (1) knowledgeable about intra- and interpersonal theories, including assessment and intervention; (2) conversant with relevant issues and techniques in research; (3) sensitive to self and to interpersonal interactions as primary clinical tools; (4) skilled

in assessing and effectively intervening in human problems; (5) able to assess effectiveness of outcomes; and (6) aware of current professional and ethical issues. To these ends the programs focus on major social and psychological theories; research training directed toward the consumer rather than the producer of research; technical knowledge of assessment; and intervention in problems involving individuals, families, groups, and institutional systems. Strong emphasis is placed on practicum training.

Programs and Degrees Offered

Program	Degree	Application Deadline	Applications Received	Accepted	New Admits Enrolled (PT)	Total Enrolled (PT)	Degrees Awarded in 2014–2015	Median Years to Complete Degree	Dismissed/Withdrew
Forensic Psychology	MA/MS	January 5 (Fall)	87	44	26	52 (0)	25	2	0
Clinical Psychology	PsyD	December 5 (Fall)	450	75	36	111 (0)	23	4	3
International Disaster Psychology	MA/MS	(Fall), Rolling	46	25	15	34	17	2	0
Sport and Performance Psychology	MA/MS	January 5 (Fall)	102	56	26	52	25	2	0

APA Accreditation

Clinical PsyD: Student Outcome Data website: http://www.du.edu/gspp/programs/psyd-clinical/index.html.

Doctoral Degree (PsyD Clinical Psychology): For those doctoral students for whom a professional internship was required in this program prior to graduation:
Total students who applied for an internship: 40
Total students who obtained an internship: 37
Total students who obtained a paid internship: 37
Total students who obtained an unpaid internship: 0
Total students who were placed in APA/CPA-accredited internships: 37
Total students placed in internships not APA/CPA-accredited, but listed with the Association of Psychology Postdoctoral and Internship Centers (APPIC): 0
Total students placed in internships conforming to guidelines of the Council of Directors of School Psychology Programs (CDSPP): 0
Total students placed in internships that were not APA/CPA-accredited, APPIC or CDSSP listed: 0

Master's Degree (MA/MS Forensic Psychology): An internship experience, such as a final research project or "capstone" experience is required of graduates. Master's Degree (MA/MS International Disaster Psychology): An internship experience, such as a final research project or "capstone" experience is required of graduates. Master's Degree (MA/MS Sport and Performance Psychology): An internship experience, such as a final research project or "capstone" experience is required of graduates.

Internships/Practica

All GSPP academic programs require practica; there are over 150 possible training sites in the Denver area. Students in the GSPP PsyD program enjoy a very high match rate, especially with APA accredited programs - and those who choose to stay in Denver may apply to our APA-accredited affiliated internship program.

Admissions

Entries appear in the following order: required test or GPA, minimum score (if required)/median score of students entering in 2015–2016.

Program	Degree	GRE-V	GRE-Q	GRE-Writing	GRE-Subject	Under-graduate GPA	Last 2 Years GPA	Psychol-ogy GPA	Master's GPA
Forensic Psychology	MA/MS	NA/NA	NA/NA	NA/NA	Not specified	Not specified	Not specified	Not specified	Not specified
Clinical Psychology	PsyD	NA/158	NA/153	NA/4.3	Not specified	NA/NA	Not specified	Not specified	Not specified

Admissions *(con't.)*

Program	Degree	GRE-V	GRE-Q	GRE-Writing	GRE-Subject	Under-graduate GPA	Last 2 Years GPA	Psychol-ogy GPA	Master's GPA
International Disaster Psychology	MA/MS	NA/NA	NA/NA	NA/NA	Not specified	Not specified	Not specified	Not specified	Not specified
Sport and Performance Psychology	MA/MS	NA/NA	NA/NA	NA/NA	Not specified	Not specified	Not specified	Not specified	Not specified

Admissions Requirements:

Degree	GRE	GRE-Subject	Letters of Recom-mendation	Research Statement	Writing Sample	CV	Interview
Master's/Specialist	Required	Optional	2	Required	Optional	Required	Required
Doctoral	Required	Optional	2	Required	Optional	Required	Required

Admissions Criteria:

GRE scores—high
Research experience—medium
Work experience—high
Clinically related public service—high
GPA—high

Letters of recommendation—high
Interview—high
Statement of goals and objectives—high
Undergraduate psychology preparation—medium
Required essay responses—high

For additional information on admission requirements, visit http://www.du.edu/gspp/admissions/faq.html.

Department Demographics

	Male (PT)	Female (PT)	Total	African-American/ Black (PT)	Hispanic/ Latino (PT)	Asian/ Pacific Islander (PT)	American Indian/ Alaska Native (PT)	Caucasian/ White (PT)	Unknown	Multiethnic (PT)	ADA (PT)	Int'l (PT)
Students	54 (0)	195 (0)	249	9 (0)	10 (0)	21 (0)	3 (0)	181 (0)	18 (0)	6 (0)	1 (0)	14 (0)

Financial Information/Assistance

Tuition: For information on tuition costs, visit http://www.du.edu/registrar/registration/tuition.html. Tuition is subject to change. Tuition costs vary by program.

Doctoral:
State residents: $57,552 per academic year.
State residents: $1,199 per credit hour.
Nonstate residents: $57,552 per academic year.
Nonstate residents: $1,199 per credit hour.

Master's:
State residents: $43,164 per academic year.
State residents: $1,199 per credit hour.
Nonstate residents: $43,164 per academic year.
Nonstate residents: $1,199 per credit hour.

Financial Assistance:

	Teaching Assistantship (% Receiving)	Teaching Assistantship Tuition Remission	Research Assistantship (% Receiving)	Research Assistantship Tuition Remission	Fellowship (% Receiving)	Fellowship Tuition Remission
First-Year Student	NA (NA)	NA	$2,714 (7)	NA	$14,507 (35)	Partial
Advanced Student	$8,208 (33)	Partial	$2,714 (5)	NA	$25,905 (14)	Partial

For additional information on financial assistance, visit http://www.du.edu/financialaid/graduate/index.html.

Employment of Department Graduates

Doctoral:
Enrolled in a postdoctoral residency/fellowship: 14
Employed in independent practice: 13
Employed in an academic position at a university: 3
Employed in other positions at a higher education institution: 8
Employed in a professional position in a school system: 1
Employed in a community mental health/counseling center: 7
Employed in a hospital/medical center: 8
Other employment position: 10
Total: 64

Additional Information

Housing and Day Care: On-campus housing is available. See the following website for more information: http://www.du.edu/live/housing.html. On-campus day care facilities are available. See the following website for more information: http://www.du.edu/fisher/.

Information for Students With Physical Disabilities: See the following website: http://www.du.edu/studentlife/disability/.

Special Facilities or Resources: The program offers its own in-house training clinic, and varied opportunities are available in many community facilities for the required practicum experiences.

Application Information: Fee: $65. *Online application:* https://gradadmissions.du.edu/apply/.

Northern Colorado, University of
Department of Applied Psychology and Counselor Education
College of Education and Behavioral Sciences
501 20th Street, Box 131
Greeley, CO 80639
Telephone: (970) 351-2731
Coordinator and Director of Training: Stephen Wright

E-mail: diane.greenshields@unco.edu
Web: http://www.unco.edu/cebs/counspsych/

Orientation, Objectives, and Emphasis of Department
The Counseling Psychology PhD program's educational philosophy is based on the scientist–practitioner, or Boulder, model. Our program places emphasis on both training clinicians to work with diverse populations and becoming producers and consumers of research. The faculty view doctoral training as a developmental process in which, through course sequencing and mentoring relationships, students move from a learner role to one of increasing independence and responsibility.

Programs and Degrees Offered

Program	Degree	Application Deadline	Applications Received	Accepted	New Admits Enrolled (PT)	Total Enrolled (PT)	Degrees Awarded in 2014 2015	Median Years to Complete Degree	Dismissed/Withdrew
Counseling Psychology	PhD	December 1 (Fall)	97	7	7	35	10	5.5	0

APA Accreditation
Counseling PhD: Student Outcome Data website: http://www.unco.edu/cebs/counspsych/studentData.html.

Doctoral Degree (PhD Counseling Psychology): For those doctoral students for whom a professional internship was required in this program prior to graduation:
Total students who applied for an internship: 8
Total students who obtained an internship: 8
Total students who obtained a paid internship: 8
Total students who obtained an unpaid internship: 0
Total students who were placed in APA/CPA-accredited internships: 8
Total students placed in internships not APA/CPA-accredited, but listed with the Association of Psychology Postdoctoral and Internship Centers (APPIC): 0
Total students placed in internships conforming to guidelines of the Council of Directors of School Psychology Programs (CDSPP): 0
Total students placed in internships that were not APA/CPA-accredited, APPIC or CDSSP listed: 0

Internships/Practica

Practica in individual, couples and family, and group take place within our in-house clinic. After their second year, students may complete external practica in counseling centers, VAs, community agencies and other agencies. Students are required to do an APA-accredited internship.

Admissions

Entries appear in the following order: required test or GPA, minimum score (if required)/median score of students entering in 2015–2016.

Program	Degree	GRE-V	GRE-Q	GRE-Writing	GRE-Subject	Under-graduate GPA	Last 2 Years GPA	Psychol-ogy GPA	Master's GPA
Counseling Psychology	PhD	146/156	140/150	3.5/4	Not specified	3/3.76	3/3.76	Not specified	3/3.83

Admissions Requirements:

Degree	GRE	GRE-Subject	Letters of Recom-mendation	Research Statement	Writing Sample	CV	Interview
Doctoral	Required	None	3	Required	None	Required	Required

Admissions Criteria:

GRE scores—high
Research experience—medium
Work experience—medium
Clinically related public service—medium
GPA—medium

Letters of recommendation—high
Interview—high
Statement of goals and objectives—high
Undergraduate psychology preparation—medium

For additional information on admission requirements, visit http://www.unco.edu/cebs/counspsych/prospective.html.

Department Demographics

	Male (PT)	Female (PT)	Total	African-American/ Black (PT)	Hispanic/ Latino (PT)	Asian/ Pacific Islander (PT)	American Indian/ Alaska Native (PT)	Caucasian/ White (PT)	Unknown	Multiethnic (PT)	ADA (PT)	Int'l (PT)
Students	9 (0)	26 (0)	35	3 (0)	3 (0)	1 (0)	1 (0)	26 (0)	0 (0)	1 (0)	3 (0)	1 (0)

Financial Information/Assistance

Tuition: For information on tuition costs, visit http://www.unco.edu/costs/. Tuition is subject to change. Additional fees are assessed to students beyond the costs of tuition for the following: Total student fees are $79.44/credit hour. Other fees for practica and assessment classes may apply.

Doctoral:
State residents: $17,760 per academic year.
State residents: $592 per credit hour.
Nonstate residents: $36,240 per academic year.
Nonstate residents: $1,208 per credit hour.

Financial Assistance:

	Teaching Assistantship (% Receiving)	Teaching Assistantship Tuition Remission	Research Assistantship (% Receiving)	Research Assistantship Tuition Remission	Fellowship (% Receiving)	Fellowship Tuition Remission
First-Year Student	NA (NA)	NA	$7,705 (NA)	Partial	$1,000 (NA)	Partial
Advanced Student	$7,705 (NA)	Partial	$7,705 (NA)	Partial	$1,000 (NA)	Partial

For additional information on financial assistance, visit http://www.unco.edu/cebs/counspsych/cost.html.

Employment of Department Graduates

Doctoral:
Enrolled in a postdoctoral residency/fellowship: 2
Employed in independent practice: 2
Employed in a community mental health/counseling center: 4
Other employment position: 2
Total: 10

Additional Information

Housing and Day Care: On-campus housing is available. See the following website for more information: http://www.unco.edu/housing/. No on-campus day care facilities are available.

Information for Students With Physical Disabilities: See the following website: http://www.unco.edu/dss/.

Special Facilities or Resources: The Department has an in-house clinic with one-way mirror observation capabilities and all sessions can be video recorded and comments from licensed supervisors can be dubbed onto the video. We also use electronic medical records for all clinical records. This facility is built around a central observation area, from which eight counseling rooms, one testing room, two family therapy rooms, one group therapy room, and three play therapy rooms radiate. Our Diagnostic Materials Library has an excellent collection of current assessment instruments. The main university library has provided excellent support for the counseling psychology program. Many journals can be retrieved online and from the student's home. Additionally, funding is available for purchasing tests listed in the Mental Measurements Yearbook.

Application Information: The Graduate School, University of Northern Colorado, 501 20th Street, Campus Box 135, Greeley, CO 80639. *Fee:* $50. *Online application:* http://www.unco.edu/grad/admissions/apply.html.

Northern Colorado, University of
School Psychology
Education and Behavioral Sciences
501 20th Street, McKee 248
Greeley, CO 80639
Telephone: (970) 351-2731
Chairperson: Michelle Athanasiou

E-mail: michelle.athanasiou@unco.edu
Web: http://www.unco.edu/cebs/SchoolPsych/

Orientation, Objectives, and Emphasis of Department
The program's training philosophy is based on the scientist–practitioner model. Our goal is to develop professionals who are able to apply psychological and educational principles to improve the psychosocial environments of children (ages birth-21) and their families. Attention is directed toward the development of skills in the assessment of the intellectual, emotional, and social development of children; planning and implementing direct academic and social/emotional interventions with a focus on evidence-based and culturally sensitive practice; and providing individual and systems consultation within schools and the larger community. Foundational aspects of psychological practice, including human learning, development, relevant law, ethical principles and professional practice provide a basis upon which skills in assessment and intervention are built. The faculty believe strongly in the importance of science informing practice and vice versa. As such, we stress the importance of an evidence base for psychological practices, as well as measurement of outcomes in all aspects of practice.

Programs and Degrees Offered

Program	Degree	Application Deadline	Applications Received	Accepted	New Admits Enrolled (PT)	Total Enrolled (PT)	Degrees Awarded in 2014–2015	Median Years to Complete Degree	Dismissed/ Withdrew
School Psychology	PhD	December 15 (Fall)	28	15	7 (0)	33 (5)	10	5.4	0
School Psychology	EdS	December 15 (Fall)	45	38	18 (0)	39 (0)	16	3	0

APA Accreditation

School PhD: Student Outcome Data website: http://www.unco.edu/cebs/SchoolPsych/phd_psychology/phd_desc.html.

Doctoral Degree (PhD School Psychology): For those doctoral students for whom a professional internship was required in this program prior to graduation:

Total students who applied for an internship: 6

Total students who obtained an internship: 6

Total students who obtained a paid internship: 6

Total students who obtained an unpaid internship: 0

Total students who were placed in APA/CPA-accredited internships: 2

Total students placed in internships not APA/CPA-accredited, but listed with the Association of Psychology Postdoctoral and Internship Centers (APPIC): 0

Total students placed in internships conforming to guidelines of the Council of Directors of School Psychology Programs (CDSPP): 0

Total students placed in internships that were not APA/CPA-accredited, APPIC or CDSSP listed: 4

Internships/Practica

All students are required to complete numerous practicum courses prior to graduation. Each course is designed to provide hands-on experience related to skills-based competencies. Students will accrue an estimated 635-710 hours of practicum training prior to internship. Elective practica may be taken in the areas of couples and family counseling, neuropsychology, consultation, and play therapy. Requirements for the School Psychology Internship include at least 1,500 hours of supervised experience at the PhD level with supervision from a licensed psychologist/licensed school psychologist. The internship in School Psychology is intended to be an opportunity for students to progressively assume the professional role of a School Psychologist with supervision. The School Psychology internship will include experiences with a variety of populations from early childhood through high school in the areas of: direct and indirect interventions, child advocacy, program development and evaluation, and assessment and diagnosis from Child Find to staffing. It is highly recommended that students apply for an APA-accredited internship through APPIC.

Admissions

Entries appear in the following order: required test or GPA, minimum score (if required)/median score of students entering in 2015–2016.

Program	Degree	GRE-V	GRE-Q	GRE-Writing	GRE-Subject	Under-graduate GPA	Last 2 Years GPA	Psychol-ogy GPA	Master's GPA
School Psychology	PhD	148/156	146/147	4/4.5	Not specified	Not specified	3.13/ 3.82	Not specified	Not specified
School Psychology	EdS	141/155	135/148	Not specified	Not specified	3/3.6	Not specified	Not specified	Not specified

Admissions Requirements:

Degree	GRE	GRE-Subject	Letters of Recom-mendation	Research Statement	Writing Sample	CV	Interview
Master's/Specialist	Required	None	3	Required	Optional	Required	Required
Doctoral	Required	None	3	Required	Optional	Required	Required

Please note if these criteria vary for different programs: These criteria vary between the PhD and EdS For the PhD, there is a greater emphasis on GREs and research experience.

Admissions Criteria:

GRE scores—medium
Research experience—medium
Work experience—low
Clinically related public service—low

GPA—medium
Letters of recommendation—medium
Interview—high
Statement of goals and objectives—high

For additional information on admission requirements, visit http://www.unco.edu/cebs/SchoolPsych/admissions.html.

Department Demographics

	Male (PT)	Female (PT)	Total	African-American/ Black (PT)	Hispanic/ Latino (PT)	Asian/ Pacific Islander (PT)	American Indian/ Alaska Native (PT)	Caucasian/ White (PT)	Unknown	Multiethnic (PT)	ADA (PT)	Int'l (PT)
Students	13 (1)	59 (4)	77	3 (0)	5 (0)	3 (0)	0 (0)	61 (5)	0 (0)	0 (0)	1 (0)	1 (0)

Financial Information/Assistance

Tuition: For information on tuition costs, visit http://www.unco.edu/grad/funding/index.html. Tuition is subject to change. Additional fees are assessed to students beyond the costs of tuition for the following: Estimated fees per semester: $832.50.

Doctoral:
State residents: $10,656 per academic year.
State residents: $592 per credit hour.
Nonstate residents: $21,744 per academic year.
Nonstate residents: $1,208 per credit hour.

Master's:
State residents: $9,414 per academic year.
State residents: $523 per credit hour.
Nonstate residents: $19,044 per academic year.
Nonstate residents: $1,058 per credit hour.

Financial Assistance:

	Teaching Assistantship (% Receiving)	Teaching Assistantship Tuition Remission	Research Assistantship (% Receiving)	Research Assistantship Tuition Remission	Fellowship (% Receiving)	Fellowship Tuition Remission
First-Year Student	NA (NA)	NA	$7,705 (NA)	Partial	$1,000 (NA)	NA
Advanced Student	NA (NA)	NA	$7,705 (NA)	Partial	$1,000 (NA)	NA

For additional information on financial assistance, visit http://www.unco.edu/grad/funding/assistantships.html.

Employment of Department Graduates

No information provided.

Additional Information

Housing and Day Care: On-campus housing is available. See the following website for more information: http://www.unco.edu/housing/Grad_Students/index.html. No on-campus day care facilities are available.

Information for Students With Physical Disabilities: See the following website: http://www.unco.edu/dss/.

Special Facilities or Resources: The Diagnostic Materials Library (DML) is a library for the exclusive use of school psychology and counseling students and faculty. It contains tests, protocols, textbooks, and other materials that are needed for selected courses. Currently the DML has well over 100 different tests, and there are multiple copies of major academic, cognitive, neuropsychological, behavioral, and personality instruments.

Application Information: Graduate School and International Admissions, University of Northern Colorado, 501 20th Street, Campus Box 135, Greeley, CO 80639. *Fee:* $50. *Online application:* http://www.unco.edu/grad/admissions/apply.html.

Central Connecticut State University
Department of Psychological Science
1615 Stanley Street
New Britain, CT 06050-4010
Telephone: (860) 832-3100
Chairperson: Dr. Carolyn Fallahi

E-mail: fallahic@ccsu.edu
Web: http://www.ccsu.edu/psychology/

Orientation, Objectives, and Emphasis of Department
The Department of Psychological Science includes 20 faculty members whose interests cover a wide range of psychological areas. Collectively, the orientation of the department is toward applied areas (clinical, community, health, applied, developmental), with generally little emphasis on animal learning/behavior. The specialization in community psychology focuses heavily on primary prevention. The general specialization is intended to expose students to a broad range of applied areas in psychology, while the one in health psychology prepares students for careers in the field of health psychology. The three specializations have a strong research emphasis.

Programs and Degrees Offered

Program	Degree	Application Deadline	Applications Received	Accepted	New Admits Enrolled (PT)	Total Enrolled (PT)	Degrees Awarded in 2014–2015	Median Years to Complete Degree	Dismissed/ Withdrew
Community Psychology	MA/MS	April 1 (Fall), November 1 (Spring)	10	8	1 (3)	3 (5)	0		0
General Psychology	MA/MS	April 1 (Fall), November 1 (Spring)	25	15	2 (2)	8 (11)	1	4	0
Health Psychology	MA/MS	April 1 (Fall), November 1 (Spring)	17	13	7 (4)	14 (7)	4	5	0

Internships/Practica
We offer a variety of internships. For students in the community specialization, there are internships in prevention-oriented community programs dealing with substance abuse, teen pregnancy, etc. We also offer internships in developmental and counseling areas.

Admissions
Entries appear in the following order: required test or GPA, minimum score (if required)/median score of students entering in 2015–2016.

Program	Degree	GRE-V	GRE-Q	GRE-Writing	GRE-Subject	Undergraduate GPA	Last 2 Years GPA	Psychology GPA	Master's GPA
Community Psychology	MA/MS	Not specified	Not specified	Not specified	Not specified	2.75/NA	Not specified	3/NA	Not specified
General Psychology	MA/MS	Not specified	Not specified	Not specified	Not specified	2.75/NA	Not specified	3/NA	Not specified
Health Psychology	MA/MS	Not specified	Not specified	Not specified	Not specified	2.75/NA	Not specified	3/NA	Not specified

Admissions Requirements:

Degree	GRE	GRE-Subject	Letters of Recommendation	Research Statement	Writing Sample	CV	Interview
Master's/Specialist	None	None	3	Required	None	None	None

Admissions Criteria:

Research experience—medium
Work experience—medium
Clinically related public service—medium
GPA—high

Letters of recommendation—high
Statement of goals and objectives—high
Undergraduate psychology preparation—medium

For additional information on admission requirements, visit http://www.ccsu.edu/psychology/graduate/applyMA.html.

Department Demographics

	Male (PT)	Female (PT)	Total	African-American/ Black (PT)	Hispanic/ Latino (PT)	Asian/ Pacific Islander (PT)	American Indian/ Alaska Native (PT)	Caucasian/ White (PT)	Unknown (PT)	Multiethnic (PT)	ADA (PT)	Int'l (PT)
Students	13 (4)	12 (19)	48	2 (3)	4 (1)	0 (1)	0 (0)	15 (16)	2 (2)	2 (0)		0 (2)

Financial Information/Assistance

Tuition: For information on tuition costs, visit http://www.ccsu.edu/bursar/. Tuition is subject to change. Additional fees are assessed to students beyond the costs of tuition for the following: $65.00 per term registration fee for part-time students.

Master's:
State residents: $10,454 per academic year.
State residents: $577 per credit hour.
Nonstate residents: $22,666 per academic year.
Nonstate residents: $592 per credit hour.

Financial Assistance:

	Teaching Assistantship (% Receiving)	Teaching Assistantship Tuition Remission	Research Assistantship (% Receiving)	Research Assistantship Tuition Remission	Fellowship (% Receiving)	Fellowship Tuition Remission
First-Year Student	$3,000 (NA)	Partial	NA (NA)	NA	NA (NA)	NA
Advanced Student	$3,000 (NA)	Partial	NA (NA)	NA	NA (NA)	NA

For additional information on financial assistance, visit http://www.ccsu.edu/grad/assistantships.html.

Employment of Department Graduates

No information provided.

Additional Information

Housing and Day Care: On-campus housing is available. See the following website for more information: http://www.ccsu.edu/grad/housing.html. On-campus day care facilities are available. See the following website for more information: http://www.ccsu.edu/earlylearningprogram/.

Information for Students With Physical Disabilities: See the following website: http://www.ccsu.edu/sds/.

Special Facilities or Resources: The Department of Psychological Science has limited space available for human experimental research. The department has a computer laboratory, and the university has very good computer facilities available for student use. Students may also work on applied research projects with faculty through the Institute for Municipal and Regional Policy at the University.

Application Information: Office of Graduate Admissions, Central CT State University, 1615 Stanley Street, New Britain, CT 06050-4010. *Fee:* $50. *Online application:* https://www.applyweb.com/apply/ccsu/menu.html.

Connecticut, University of
Department of Psychological Sciences
College of Liberal Arts and Sciences
406 Babbidge Road, Unit 1020
Storrs, CT 06269-1020
Telephone: (860) 486-3515
Head: James A. Green

E-mail: Jackie.Soroka@uconn.edu
Web: http://psych.uconn.edu/

Orientation, Objectives, and Emphasis of Department
The department is focused on a dual mission of pursuing excellence in both research and teaching, while not losing sight of its broader mission to engage in meaningful outreach. The department is comprised of six divisions, each of which offers doctoral training in one or more areas of concentration as follows: (1) Behavioral Neuroscience (biopsychology, neuroscience); (2) Clinical Psychology; (3) Developmental Psychology; (4) Perception, Action, Cognition (ecological psychology, language, and cognition); (5) Industrial/Organizational Psychology; and (6) Social Psychology. Interdivisional areas of strength, and targets for future growth, include (a) quantitative research methods, (b) health psychology, (c) cognitive science, (d) neuropsychology, and (e) developmental psychopathology. The pursuit of new knowledge (i.e., discovery through research) is the dominant emphasis of the department. This emphasis relies heavily on the interactive contributions from faculty, graduate students, and undergraduate students. In addition, the department's Graduate Student Teacher Training Program provides multiple, mentored teaching experiences for graduate students interested in pursuing a career that combines research with teaching. Despite these varied emphases and endeavors, the department continues to maintain a collegial and supportive atmosphere where individual contributions are both recognized and rewarded.

Programs and Degrees Offered

Program	Degree	Application Deadline	Applications Received	Accepted	New Admits Enrolled (PT)	Total Enrolled (PT)	Degrees Awarded in 2014–2015	Median Years to Complete Degree	Dismissed/Withdrew
Behavioral Neuroscience	PhD	December 1 (Fall)	34	4	1 (0)	14 (0)	3	5	1
Developmental Psychology	PhD	December 1 (Fall)	9	2	0 (0)	18 (0)	0		1
Clinical Psychology	PhD	December 1 (Fall)	237	12	8 (0)	52 (0)	9	6.45	0
Perception, Action, Cognition	PhD	December 1 (Fall)	37	11	8 (0)	36 (0)	4	7	5
Industrial/ Organizational Psychology	PhD	December 1 (Fall)	62	8	2 (0)	18 (0)	7	5.75	2
Social Psychology	PhD	December 1 (Fall)	57	4	3 (0)	24 (0)	1	5	1

APA Accreditation
Clinical PhD: Student Outcome Data website: http://psych.uconn.edu/graduate/phd_clinical.php.

Doctoral Degree (PhD Clinical Psychology): For those doctoral students for whom a professional internship was required in this program prior to graduation:
Total students who applied for an internship: 9

Total students who obtained an internship: 9
Total students who obtained a paid internship: 9
Total students who obtained an unpaid internship: 0
Total students who were placed in APA/CPA-accredited internships: 9
Total students placed in internships not APA/CPA-accredited, but listed with the Association of Psychology Postdoctoral and Internship Centers (APPIC): 0
Total students placed in internships conforming to guidelines of the Council of Directors of School Psychology Programs (CDSPP): 0
Total students placed in internships that were not APA/CPA-accredited, APPIC or CDSSP listed: 0

Admissions

Entries appear in the following order: required test or GPA, minimum score (if required)/median score of students entering in 2015–2016.

Program	Degree	GRE-V	GRE-Q	GRE-Writing	GRE-Subject	Under-graduate GPA	Last 2 Years GPA	Psychol-ogy GPA	Master's GPA
Behavioral Neuroscience	PhD	NA/149	NA/167	NA/3	Not specified	Not specified	Not specified	Not specified	Not specified
Developmental Psychology	PhD	NA/NA	NA/NA	NA/NA	Not specified	Not specified	Not specified	Not specified	Not specified
Clinical Psychology	PhD	NA/164	NA/159	NA/4.8	Not specified	Not specified	Not specified	Not specified	Not specified
Perception, Action, Cognition	PhD	NA/159	NA/158	NA/4.4	Not specified	Not specified	Not specified	Not specified	Not specified
Industrial/ Organizational Psychology	PhD	NA/161	NA/158	NA/4.5	Not specified	Not specified	Not specified	Not specified	Not specified
Social Psychology	PhD	NA/156	NA/152	NA/4	Not specified	Not specified	Not specified	Not specified	Not specified

Admissions Requirements:

Degree	GRE	GRE-Subject	Letters of Recom-mendation	Research Statement	Writing Sample	CV	Interview
Doctoral	Required	Recom-mended	3	Required	Optional	Optional	None

Please note if these criteria vary for different programs: The Clinical Division interviews applicants by invitation only. The clinical interviews are considered to be high in importance of criteria used for offering admission. The Behavioral Neuroscience Division may interview by invitation or by applicant request, however interviews are not required. Developmental does not interview applicants in person as part of the admissions process. Perception, Action, and Cognition does not require interviews with applicants as part of the admissions process. Industrial/Organizational and Social divisions do not interview applicants as part of the admissions process.

Admissions Criteria:

GRE scores—medium
Research experience—high
Work experience—low
Clinically related public service—low

GPA—medium
Letters of recommendation—high
Interview—medium
Statement of goals and objectives—high

For additional information on admission requirements, visit http://grad.psych.uconn.edu/prospective/phd/application-requirements/.

Department Demographics

	Male (PT)	Female (PT)	Total	African-American/ Black (PT)	Hispanic/ Latino (PT)	Asian/ Pacific Islander (PT)	American Indian/ Alaska Native (PT)	Caucasian/ White (PT)	Unknown	Multiethnic (PT)	ADA (PT)	Int'l (PT)
Students	51 (0)	111 (0)	162	9 (0)	14 (0)	34 (0)	0 (0)	98 (0)	7 (0)	0 (0)	2 (0)	26 (0)

Financial Information/Assistance

Tuition: For information on tuition costs, visit http://bursar.uconn.edu/. Tuition is subject to change. Additional fees are assessed to students beyond the costs of tuition for the following: General University; Infrastructure/Maintenance; Student Activities; Matriculation; Transit; Technology.

Doctoral:
State residents: $13,026 per academic year.
State residents: $724 per credit hour.
Nonstate residents: $33,812 per academic year.
Nonstate residents: $1,878 per credit hour.

Financial Assistance:

	Teaching Assistantship (% Receiving)	Teaching Assistantship Tuition Remission	Research Assistantship (% Receiving)	Research Assistantship Tuition Remission	Fellowship (% Receiving)	Fellowship Tuition Remission
First-Year Student	$16,196 (NA)	Full	$16,196 (NA)	Full	$2,800 (NA)	NA
Advanced Student	$18,946 (NA)	Full	$18,946 (NA)	Full	$2,800 (NA)	NA

For additional information on financial assistance, visit http://grad.uconn.edu/financial-resources/internal-funding-opportunities/.

Employment of Department Graduates

Doctoral:
Enrolled in a postdoctoral residency/fellowship: 16
Enrolled in another graduate/professional program: 1
Employed in an academic position at a university: 1
Employed in other positions at a higher education institution: 1
Employed in business or industry: 4
Employed in government agency: 1
Total: 24

Additional Information

Housing and Day Care: No on-campus housing is available. On-campus day care facilities are available. See the following website for more information: http://childlabs.uconn.edu.

Information for Students With Physical Disabilities: See the following website: http://csd.uconn.edu/.

Special Facilities or Resources: Multiple facilities, resources, and opportunities for research and training endeavors are not only available, but also are encouraged, fostered, and strongly supported by the department. These opportunities include existing and strong research collaborations with the University of Connecticut Health Center, with Haskins Laboratories in New Haven, with the Olin Neuropsychiatry Research Center at the Institute of Living in Hartford, the Jackson Laboratory and with a wide variety of research and internship opportunities available at multiple industries, hospitals, mental institutions, and school systems located in Connecticut. In addition, the department makes available and encourages research and training opportunities with units located within the department and/or within the University, including the Center for Health Intervention and Prevention, the Psychological Services Clinic (PSC), the Industrial Psychology Applications Center (IPAC), the Center for the Ecological Study of Perception and Action (CESPA), The Jackson Laboratory, the Murine Behavioral Neurogenetics Facility, the CT Institute for the Brain and Cognitive

Sciences (IBACS) and a new on-campus fMRI facility. Collectively, these collaborative relationships provide graduate students with myriad opportunities to pursue their research and training experience objectives.

Application Information: Fee: $75. *Online application:* https://app.applyyourself.com/?id=uconngrad.

Connecticut, University of
School Psychology Program
NEAG School of Education
249 Glenbrook Road, Unit 3064
Storrs, CT 06269-3064
Telephone: (860) 486-4031
Director, School Psychology Program: Melissa Bray

E-mail: melissa.bray@uconn.edu
Web: http://schoolpsych.education.uconn.edu/

Orientation, Objectives, and Emphasis of Department
The Department of Educational Psychology sponsors master of arts/sixth-year and doctor of philosophy programs in school psychology. The programs are an integrated and organized preparation of psychologists whose primary professional interests involve children, families, and the educational process. The programs adhere to the scientist–practitioner model of training that assumes the effective practice of school psychology is based on knowledge gained from established methods of scientific inquiry. The faculty are committed to a learning environment that stresses an organized and explicit curriculum with clear expectations. In addition, the programs are designed to acquaint students with the diversity of theories and practices of school psychology, allowing students sufficient intellectual freedom to experiment with different delivery systems and various theoretical bases. The atmosphere is intended to foster informal student-faculty interactions, critical debate, and respect for theoretical diversity of practice, thus creating a more intense and exciting learning experience. It is believed that such a philosophy encourages and reinforces students' creativity and intellectual risk taking, which are fundamental in the further development of the professional practice of school psychology.

Programs and Degrees Offered

Program	Degree	Application Deadline	Applications Received	Accepted	New Admits Enrolled (PT)	Total Enrolled (PT)	Degrees Awarded in 2014–2015	Median Years to Complete Degree	Dismissed/ Withdrew
School Psychology	PhD	December 1 (Fall)	40	14	5 (0)	26 (0)	8	4.3	0
School Psychology	MA/MS	December 1 (Fall)	37	9	9 (0)	17 (0)	7	3	0

APA Accreditation
School PhD: Student Outcome Data website: http://schoolpsych.education.uconn.edu/student-admissions-outcomes-and-other-data/.

Doctoral Degree (PhD School Psychology): For those doctoral students for whom a professional internship was required in this program prior to graduation:
Total students who applied for an internship: 6
Total students who obtained an internship: 6
Total students who obtained a paid internship: 6
Total students who obtained an unpaid internship: 0
Total students who were placed in APA/CPA-accredited internships: 0
Total students placed in internships not APA/CPA-accredited, but listed with the Association of Psychology Postdoctoral and Internship Centers (APPIC): 0
Total students placed in internships conforming to guidelines of the Council of Directors of School Psychology Programs (CDSPP): 6
Total students placed in internships that were not APA/CPA-accredited, APPIC or CDSSP listed: 0

Master's Degree (MA/MS School Psychology): An internship experience, such as a final research project or "capstone" experience is required of graduates.

Internships/Practica
There are a number of practicum and internship placement opportunities for school psychology students at the University of Connecticut, as well as at affiliated sites and school districts. The overwhelming majority of internship placements are paid.

Admissions

Entries appear in the following order: required test or GPA, minimum score (if required)/median score of students entering in 2015–2016.

Program	Degree	GRE-V	GRE-Q	GRE-Writing	GRE-Subject	Under-graduate GPA	Last 2 Years GPA	Psychology GPA	Master's GPA
School Psychology	PhD	150/160	150/151	Not specified	Not specified	3/3.4	Not specified	Not specified	Not specified
School Psychology	MA/MS	150/152	150/156	Not specified	Not specified	3/3.4	Not specified	Not specified	Not specified

Admissions Requirements:

Degree	GRE	GRE-Subject	Letters of Recommendation	Research Statement	Writing Sample	CV	Interview
Master's/Specialist	Required	None	3	Required	Optional	Required	Required
Doctoral	Required	Optional	3	Required	Optional	Required	Required

Admissions Criteria:

GRE scores—high
Research experience—medium
Work experience—medium
Clinically related public service—low
GPA—medium

Letters of recommendation—high
Interview—high
Statement of goals and objectives—high
Undergraduate psychology preparation—low

For additional information on admission requirements, visit http://schoolpsych.education.uconn.edu/how-to-apply/.

Department Demographics

	Male (PT)	Female (PT)	Total	African-American/ Black (PT)	Hispanic/ Latino (PT)	Asian/ Pacific Islander (PT)	American Indian/ Alaska Native (PT)	Caucasian/ White (PT)	Unknown	Multiethnic (PT)	ADA (PT)	Int'l (PT)
Students	9 (0)	34 (0)	43	2 (0)	4 (0)	3 (0)	1 (0)	25 (0)	8 (0)	0 (0)	0 (0)	0 (0)

Financial Information/Assistance

Tuition: For information on tuition costs, visit http://bursar.uconn.edu/2015-2016-graduate-tuition-and-fees/. Additional fees are assessed to students beyond the costs of tuition for the following: General University, Infrastructure/Maintenance, Graduate Matriculation, Activity, Transit, Tech.

Doctoral:
State residents: $15,296 per academic year.
State residents: $425 per credit hour.
Nonstate residents: $36,084 per academic year.
Nonstate residents: $1,003 per credit hour.

Master's:
State residents: $15,296 per academic year.
State residents: $425 per credit hour.
Nonstate residents: $36,084 per academic year.
Nonstate residents: $1,003 per credit hour.

Financial Assistance:

	Teaching Assistantship (% Receiving)	Teaching Assistantship Tuition Remission	Research Assistantship (% Receiving)	Research Assistantship Tuition Remission	Fellowship (% Receiving)	Fellowship Tuition Remission
First-Year Student	NA (NA)	NA	$10,797 (92)	Full	NA (NA)	NA
Advanced Student	NA (NA)	NA	$11,996 (66)	Full	NA (NA)	NA

For additional information on financial assistance, visit http://grad.uconn.edu/financial-resources/internal-funding-opportunities/.

Employment of Department Graduates

Master's:
Enrolled in a psychology doctoral program: 1
Employed in a professional position in a school system: 6
Employed in government agency: 2
Employed in a community mental health/counseling center: 1
Total: 10

Doctoral:
Employed in an academic position at a university: 2
Employed in a professional position in a school system: 3
Total: 5

Additional Information

Housing and Day Care: On-campus housing is available. See the following website for more information: http://reslife.uconn.edu/graduate-housing/. On-campus day care facilities are available. See the following website for more information: http://childlabs.uconn.edu/.

Information for Students With Physical Disabilities: See the following website: http://csd.uconn.edu/.

Special Facilities or Resources: Research space, equipment and/or opportunities exist in the following center/labs: Center for Behavioral and Educational Research; the National Research Center on the Gifted and Talented; the Pappanikou Center for Excellence in Developmental Disabilities, Education, Research, and Service; the University's Program for Students with Learning Disabilities; and the University of Connecticut Educational Microcomputing Laboratory.

Application Information: Graduate Admissions, Room 108, Whetten Center Box U-6A, 438 Whitney Road Extension, Storrs, CT 06269-1006. *Fee:* $75. *Online application:* https://app.applyyourself.com/?id=uconngrad.

Hartford, University of
Department of Psychology
Arts & Sciences
200 Bloomfield Avenue, East Hall
West Hartford, CT 6117
Telephone: (860) 768-4544
Chairperson: Jack Powell, PhD

E-mail: jpowell@hartford.edu
Web: http://www.hartford.edu/A_and_S/departments/psychology/

Orientation, Objectives, and Emphasis of Department

The Department of Psychology at the University of Hartford is strongly student-centered and committed to engaging students in the understanding of behavior, cognition, emotion, and social interaction. Major emphasis is placed on the development of critical thinking and analytical skills so students become adept at formulating meaningful questions, implementing strategies to enhance growth and development, and solving problems of individual and group behavior. Students are encouraged to understand, appreciate, and embrace diversity and the need for community involvement. The Department promotes self-awareness and life-long learning aimed at developing well-rounded, resourceful, ethical, competent, and compassionate graduates at all levels of education.

Programs and Degrees Offered

Program	Degree	Application Deadline	Applications Received	Accepted	New Admits Enrolled (PT)	Total Enrolled (PT)	Degrees Awarded in 2014–2015	Median Years to Complete Degree	Dismissed/Withdrew
Clinical Practices in Psychology	MA/MS	February 15 (Fall)	65	34	14 (0)	24 (0)	6	2	0
School Psychology	MA/MS	February 15 (Fall)	29	14	11 (0)	31 (0)	19	3	0
Organizational Psychology	MA/MS	February 15 (Fall)	62	28	6 (11)	10 (26)	12	2	1
Organizational Psychology (Online)	MA/MS	Rolling	38	25	6 (18)	10 (29)	0		0

Internships/Practica

All Clinical Practices in Psychology students are assigned a half-time practicum in the second year of their academic program. The assignments for practica include mental health clinics, in- and out-patient services in hospitals, community centers, schools, and correctional institutions. Students are supervised both on-site by professional psychologists and at the University by the faculty. All School Psychology students are assigned a half-time practicum in their second year in a school setting and a full-time internship in their third year. Students are supervised by school psychologists on site and at the University by the faculty. Organizational Psychology students have an option of a one-semester practicum or capstone project.

Admissions

Entries appear in the following order: required test or GPA, minimum score (if required)/median score of students entering in 2015–2016.

Program	Degree	GRE-V	GRE-Q	GRE-Writing	GRE-Subject	Under-graduate GPA	Last 2 Years GPA	Psychology GPA	Master's GPA
Clinical Practices in Psychology	MA/MS	NA/155	NA/152	NA/4	NA/640	NA/NA	Not specified	Not specified	Not specified
School Psychology	MA/MS	NA/152	NA/145	NA/4	NA/540	NA/3.58	Not specified	Not specified	Not specified
Organizational Psychology	MA/MS	Not specified	Not specified	Not specified	Not specified	Not specified	Not specified	Not specified	Not specified
Organizational Psychology (Online)	MA/MS	Not specified	Not specified	Not specified	Not specified	Not specified	Not specified	Not specified	Not specified

Admissions Requirements:

Degree	GRE	GRE-Subject	Letters of Recommendation	Research Statement	Writing Sample	CV	Interview
Master's/Specialist	Required	Required	3	Required	Optional	Optional	Required

Please note if these criteria vary for different programs: Only the school psychology program requires an interview. Only Clinical Practices in Psychology program requires GRE Subject test; Organizational Psychology programs do not require GRE test.

Admissions Criteria:

GRE scores—medium
Research experience—medium
Work experience—medium
GPA—high

Letters of recommendation—high
Interview—high
Statement of goals and objectives—medium

Department Demographics

	Male (PT)	Female (PT)	Total	African-American/ Black (PT)	Hispanic/ Latino (PT)	Asian/ Pacific Islander (PT)	American Indian/ Alaska Native (PT)	Caucasian/ White (PT)	Unknown (PT)	Multiethnic (PT)	ADA (PT)	Int'l (PT)
Students	10 (6)	65 (49)	130	5 (11)	4 (7)	2 (2)	0 (0)	60 (31)	2 (2)	2 (2)	0 (0)	4 (0)

Financial Information/Assistance

Tuition: For information on tuition costs, visit http://www.hartford.edu/aboutuofh/finance_administration/financial_affairs/bursar/tuition/. Tuition is subject to change. Additional fees are assessed to students beyond the costs of tuition for the following: registration fee, technology fee.

Master's:
State residents: $556 per credit hour.
Nonstate residents: $556 per credit hour.

Financial Assistance:

	Teaching Assistantship (% Receiving)	Teaching Assistantship Tuition Remission	Research Assistantship (% Receiving)	Research Assistantship Tuition Remission	Fellowship (% Receiving)	Fellowship Tuition Remission
First-Year Student	$3,100 (NA)	NA	$3,100 (NA)	NA	NA (NA)	NA
Advanced Student	$3,100 (NA)	NA	$3,100 (NA)	NA	NA (NA)	NA

For additional information on financial assistance, visit http://admission.hartford.edu/finaid/.

Employment of Department Graduates

No information provided.

Additional Information

Housing and Day Care: On-campus housing is available. See the following website for more information: http://www.hartford.edu/res_life/. No on-campus day care facilities are available.

Information for Students With Physical Disabilities: See the following website: http://www.hartford.edu/academics/disability_services.aspx

Special Facilities or Resources: In addition to mock therapy observational studios, located within the Department of Psychology, there are research labs dedicated to the study of stress management, pain management, and attachment. Numerous community organizations are available for student internships and practica.

Application Information: University of Hartford, Graduate Admission, Computer Center and Administration Building, Second Floor, Suite 231, 200 Bloomfield Avenue, West Hartford, CT 06117. *Fee:* $50. *Online application:* http://www.hartford.edu/graduate/default.aspx.

Hartford, University of

Department of Psychology: Graduate Institute of Professional Psychology
Arts and Sciences
200 Bloomfield Avenue
West Hartford, CT 06117-1599
Telephone: (860) 768-4778
Program Director: John G. Mehm, PhD

E-mail: viereck@hartford.edu
Web: http://uhaweb.hartford.edu/gipppsyd/

Orientation, Objectives, and Emphasis of Department

The primary mission of the program is to prepare students for effective functioning in the multiple roles they will need to fill as practicing psychologists in these rapidly changing times. The program also espouses the principle of affirmative diversity, defined as upholding the fundamental values of human differences and the belief that respect for individual and cultural differences enhances and increases the quality of educational and interpersonal experiences.

Programs and Degrees Offered

Program	Degree	Application Deadline	Applications Received	Accepted	New Admits Enrolled (PT)	Total Enrolled (PT)	Degrees Awarded in 2014–2015	Median Years to Complete Degree	Dismissed/ Withdrew
Clinical Psychology	PsyD	December 1 (Fall)	169	61	23 (0)	146 (0)	24	5	2

APA Accreditation

Clinical PsyD (Doctor of Psychology).

Doctoral Degree (PsyD Clinical Psychology): For those doctoral students for whom a professional internship was required in this program prior to graduation:
Total students who applied for an internship: 25
Total students who obtained an internship: 21
Total students who obtained a paid internship: 21
Total students who obtained an unpaid internship: 0
Total students who were placed in APA/CPA-accredited internships: 19
Total students placed in internships not APA/CPA-accredited, but listed with the Association of Psychology Postdoctoral and Internship Centers (APPIC): 2
Total students placed in internships conforming to guidelines of the Council of Directors of School Psychology Programs (CDSPP): 0
Total students placed in internships that were not APA/CPA-accredited, APPIC or CDSSP listed: 0

Internships/Practica

Our practicum network is extensive (approximately 125 sites in four states) and includes child, adolescent, and adult placements. Students generally get their first or second choice of sites. Practicum placement is coordinated with the Professional Practice Seminars (second year) and Case Conference Seminars (third year) to insure students' clinical training needs are being met. Emphasis is placed upon the concept of "self-in-role" learning.

Admissions

Entries appear in the following order: required test or GPA, minimum score (if required)/median score of students entering in 2015–2016.

Program	Degree	GRE-V	GRE-Q	GRE-Writing	GRE-Subject	Under-graduate GPA	Last 2 Years GPA	Psychol-ogy GPA	Master's GPA
Clinical Psychology	PsyD	NA/154	NA/148	NA/4	NA/620	NA/3.5	Not specified	Not specified	Not specified

Admissions Requirements:

Degree	GRE	GRE-Subject	Letters of Recom-mendation	Research Statement	Writing Sample	CV	Interview
Doctoral	Required	Required	3	Required	Optional	Required	Required

Admissions Criteria:

GRE scores—medium
Research experience—medium
Work experience—medium
Clinically related public service—medium
GPA—high

Letters of recommendation—high
Interview—high
Statement of goals and objectives—high
Undergraduate psychology preparation—medium

For additional information on admission requirements, visit http://www.hartford.edu/A_and_S/departments/psychology/program_psyd/program_overview/faqs.aspx.

Department Demographics

	Male (PT)	Female (PT)	Total	African-American/ Black (PT)	Hispanic/ Latino (PT)	Asian/ Pacific Islander (PT)	American Indian/ Alaska Native (PT)	Caucasian/ White (PT)	Unknown	Multiethnic (PT)	ADA (PT)	Int'l (PT)
Students	29 (0)	117 (0)	146	8 (0)	14 (0)	15 (0)	0 (0)	109 (0)	0 (0)	0 (0)	2 (0)	3 (0)

Financial Information/Assistance

Tuition: For information on tuition costs, visit http://www.hartford.edu/aboutuofh/finance_administration/financial_affairs/bursar/tuition/. Tuition is subject to change. Additional fees are assessed to students beyond the costs of tuition for the following: registration fee, technology fee.

Doctoral:
State residents: $25,015 per academic year.
State residents: $1,005 per credit hour.
Nonstate residents: $25,015 per academic year.
Nonstate residents: $1,005 per credit hour.

Financial Assistance:

	Teaching Assistantship (% Receiving)	Teaching Assistantship Tuition Remission	Research Assistantship (% Receiving)	Research Assistantship Tuition Remission	Fellowship (% Receiving)	Fellowship Tuition Remission
First-Year Student	NA (NA)	NA	$3,100 (39)	NA	$4,400 (39)	NA
Advanced Student	$6,200 (35)	NA	$3,100 (6)	NA	$4,400 (31)	NA

For additional information on financial assistance, visit http://admission.hartford.edu/finaid/.

Employment of Department Graduates

Doctoral:
Enrolled in a postdoctoral residency/fellowship: 14
Employed in independent practice: 1
Employed in other positions at a higher education institution: 1
Employed in a community mental health/counseling center: 1
Other employment position: 4
Do not know: 3
Total: 24

Additional Information

Housing and Day Care: On-campus housing is available. See the following website for more information: http://www.hartford.edu/res_life/. No on-campus day care facilities are available.

Information for Students With Physical Disabilities: See the following website: http://www.hartford.edu/academics/disability_services.aspx.

Special Facilities or Resources: The Graduate Institute offers a Child and Adolescent Proficiency track. The goal of the track is to allow students to develop not only broad clinical skills, but also strong therapeutic, assessment, and program development skills in working specifically with children, adolescents, and families.

Application Information: University of Hartford, Graduate Admission, Computer Center and Administration Building, Second Floor, Suite 231, 200 Bloomfield Avenue, West Hartford, CT 06117. *Fee:* $50. *Online application:* http://www.hartford.edu/graduate/default.aspx.

New Haven, University of
Graduate Psychology
College of Arts and Sciences
300 Boston Post Road
West Haven, CT 6516
Telephone: (203) 932-7339
Chairperson: Alexandria E. Guzmán PhD

E-mail: aguzman@newhaven.edu
Web: http://www.newhaven.edu/4486/academic-departments/psychology/

Orientation, Objectives, and Emphasis of Department

The primary goal of the Master of Arts in Industrial and Organizational Psychology program is to provide students with the knowledge and experience necessary to improve the satisfaction and productivity of people at work. Graduates obtain challenging and rewarding positions in public and private corporations, consulting firms, and government agencies. Even though our program has a strong applied/career orientation we have been quite successful in providing those students who wish to pursue doctoral study with a strong research foundation.

Programs and Degrees Offered

Program	Degree	Application Deadline	Applica-tions Received	Accepted	New Admits Enrolled (PT)	Total Enrolled (PT)	Degrees Awarded in 2014–2015	Median Years to Complete Degree	Dismissed/ Withdrew
Industrial/ Organizational Psychology	MA/MS	(Fall), (Spring), Rolling	103	85	43 (15)	(11)	45	2	0
Community Psychology	MA/MS	(Fall), (Spring), Rolling	35	28	22 (0)	22 (0)	20	2	2

Internships/Practica

Most of the full time students complete an internship which allows the student to acquire special skills through coordinating formal coursework with an internship or practicum in an organizational setting. The internship gives the student with limited work experience the opportunity to work in cooperating organizations or consulting firms. We have longstanding relationships with a wide variety of business and community organizations that seek our students as interns.

Admissions

Entries appear in the following order: required test or GPA, minimum score (if required)/median score of students entering in 2015–2016.

Program	Degree	GRE-V	GRE-Q	GRE-Writing	GRE-Subject	Under-graduate GPA	Last 2 Years GPA	Psychol-ogy GPA	Master's GPA
Industrial/ Organizational Psychology	MA/MS	Not specified	Not specified	Not specified	Not specified	2.8/3.4	3/3.5	Not specified	Not specified
Community Psychology	MA/MS	Not specified	Not specified	Not specified	Not specified	2.8/3.5	3/3.5	Not specified	Not specified

Admissions Requirements:

Degree	GRE	GRE-Subject	Letters of Recom-mendation	Research Statement	Writing Sample	CV	Interview
Master's/Specialist	Optional	Optional	2	Required	Optional	Recom-mended	None

Admissions Criteria:

Research experience—medium
Work experience—medium
Clinically related public service—low
GPA—high

Letters of recommendation—high
Statement of goals and objectives—high
Undergraduate psychology preparation—medium

Department Demographics

	Male (PT)	Female (PT)	Total	African-American/ Black (PT)	Hispanic/ Latino (PT)	Asian/ Pacific Islander (PT)	American Indian/ Alaska Native (PT)	Caucasian/ White (PT)	Unknown (PT)	Multiethnic (PT)	ADA (PT)	Int'l (PT)
Students	28 (11)	81 (30)	150	11 (5)	5 (2)	8 (1)	0 (0)	59 (25)	26 (0)	2 (7)	0 (0)	11 (0)

Financial Information/Assistance

Tuition: For information on tuition costs, visit http://www.newhaven.edu/academics/resources/bursars/tuition/. Tuition is subject to change. Tuition costs vary by program.

Master's:
State residents: $22,000 per academic year.
State residents: $850 per credit hour.
Nonstate residents: $22,000 per academic year.
Nonstate residents: $850 per credit hour.

Financial Assistance:

	Teaching Assistantship (% Receiving)	Teaching Assistantship Tuition Remission	Research Assistantship (% Receiving)	Research Assistantship Tuition Remission	Fellowship (% Receiving)	Fellowship Tuition Remission
First-Year Student	NA (45)	Partial	NA (15)	Partial	NA (NA)	NA
Advanced Student	NA (NA)	Partial	NA (NA)	Partial	NA (NA)	NA

For additional information on financial assistance, visit http://www.newhaven.edu/admissions/gradadmissions/financial-aid/.

Employment of Department Graduates

Master's:
Enrolled in another graduate/professional program: 2
Employed in academic position at a 2-year/4-year college: 1
Employed in business or industry: 45
Employed in government agency: 5
Employed in a community mental health/counseling center: 11
Do not know: 10
Total: 74

Additional Information

Housing and Day Care: No on-campus housing is available. No on-campus day care facilities are available.

Information for Students With Physical Disabilities: See the following website: http://www.newhaven.edu/10569/.

Application Information: Graduate Admissions, 300 Boston Post Road, University of New Haven, West Haven, CT 06516. *Fee:* $50. *Online application:* http://www.newhaven.edu/admissions/gradadmissions/apply/.

Southern Connecticut State University

Department of Psychology
Arts and Sciences
501 Crescent Street
New Haven, CT 6515
Telephone: (203) 392-6868
Graduate Coordinator: W.J. Hauselt
E-mail: hauseltw1@southernct.edu
Web: http://www.southernct.edu/academics/schools/arts/departments/psychology/

Orientation, Objectives, and Emphasis of Department

This research-based academic program is designed to develop creative problem-solving skills that graduates can apply to a variety of clinical, industrial, and educational settings. Leading to a Master of Arts degree, this program is flexible enough to be completed on either a full- or part-time basis, meeting the needs of a wide range of candidates. For potential doctoral candidates who can enter neither a PhD nor a PsyD program at the present time, this program may provide the basis for later acceptance into a doctoral program. For those who are already working in clinical, educational, or industrial settings, it offers updated credentials. In addition, this program provides ideal training for people who want to explore their personal interest in obtaining employment in settings related to psychology. High school teachers may use the program to prepare themselves to teach psychology in addition to their current certification. The program emphasizes faculty advisement to help tailor the program to the needs of each individual student. With advisement, it may be completed in 1 year.

Programs and Degrees Offered

Program	Degree	Application Deadline	Applications Received	Accepted	New Admits Enrolled (PT)	Total Enrolled (PT)	Degrees Awarded in 2014–2015	Median Years to Complete Degree	Dismissed/ Withdrew
General Psychology	MA/MS	Rolling	27	10	6 (1)	17 (3)	13	2	0

Internships/Practica

With departmental permission, advanced MA students may arrange a one- or two-semester clinical or research internship (3 credits for one semester; 6 credits for two semesters). These are not available to students in their first semester. The internship is not required.

Admissions

Entries appear in the following order: required test or GPA, minimum score (if required)/median score of students entering in 2015–2016.

Program	Degree	GRE-V	GRE-Q	GRE-Writing	GRE-Subject	Under-graduate GPA	Last 2 Years GPA	Psychol-ogy GPA	Master's GPA
General Psychology	MA/MS	NA/NA	NA/NA	NA/NA	Not specified	3/NA	Not specified	3/NA	Not specified

Admissions Requirements:

Degree	GRE	GRE-Subject	Letters of Recom-mendation	Research Statement	Writing Sample	CV	Interview
Master's/Specialist	None	None	2	Required	None	None	None

Admissions Criteria:

Research experience—low
Work experience—low
GPA—high

Letters of recommendation—high
Statement of goals and objectives—high
Undergraduate psychology preparation—medium

For additional information on admission requirements, visit http://www.southernct.edu/academics/schools/arts/departments/psychology/graduate/AdmissionAppl.html.

Department Demographics

	Male (PT)	Female (PT)	Total	African-American/ Black (PT)	Hispanic/ Latino (PT)	Asian/ Pacific Islander (PT)	American Indian/ Alaska Native (PT)	Caucasian/ White (PT)	Unknown	Multiethnic (PT)	ADA (PT)	Int'l (PT)
Students	5 (1)	12 (2)	20	0 (0)	0 (0)	0 (0)	0 (0)	0 (0)	17 (3)	0 (0)	0 (0)	0 (0)

Financial Information/Assistance

Tuition: For information on tuition costs, visit http://www.southernct.edu/studentaccounts/tuitionfees.html. Tuition is subject to change.

Master's:
State residents: $10,704 per academic year.
State residents: $680 per credit hour.
Nonstate residents: $22,916 per academic year.
Nonstate residents: $703 per credit hour.

Financial Assistance:

	Teaching Assistantship (% Receiving)	Teaching Assistantship Tuition Remission	Research Assistantship (% Receiving)	Research Assistantship Tuition Remission	Fellowship (% Receiving)	Fellowship Tuition Remission
First-Year Student	$9,600 (NA)	Partial	NA (NA)	NA	NA (NA)	NA
Advanced Student	$9,600 (NA)	Partial	NA (NA)	NA	NA (NA)	NA

For additional information on financial assistance, visit http://www.southernct.edu/academics/graduate/graduate-admissions/financinged.html.

Employment of Department Graduates

Master's:
Enrolled in a psychology doctoral program: 3
Enrolled in another graduate/professional program: 4
Employed in a professional position in a school system: 1
Employed in business or industry: 2
Employed in a community mental health/counseling center: 1
Employed in a hospital/medical center: 1
Do not know: 1
Total: 13

Additional Information

Housing and Day Care: On-campus housing is available. See the following website for more information: http://www.southernct.edu/student-life/campus-life/residencelife/index.html. No on-campus day care facilities are available.

Information for Students With Physical Disabilities: See the following website: http://www.southernct.edu/student-life/support/drc/.

Application Information: Southern Connecticut State University, School of Graduate Studies, Application Processing Center, P.O. Box 8057, Portsmouth, NH 03802. *Fee:* $50. *Online application:* http://www.southernct.edu/academics/graduate/graduate-admissions/graduate-application/.

Yale University
Department of Psychology
P.O. Box 208205
New Haven, CT 06520-8205
Telephone: (203) 432-4518
Chairperson: Frank Keil

E-mail: lauretta.olivi@yale.edu
Web: http://psychology.yale.edu/

Orientation, Objectives, and Emphasis of Department
The chief goal of graduate education in psychology at Yale University is the training of research workers in academic and other settings who will broaden the basic scientific knowledge on which the discipline of psychology rests. Major emphasis is given to preparation for research; a definite effort is made to give students a background for teaching. The concentration of doctoral training

on research and teaching is consistent with a variety of career objectives in addition to traditional academics. The department believes that rigorous and balanced exposure to basic psychology is the best preparation for research careers. The first important aspect of graduate training is advanced study of general psychology, including method and psychological theory. The second is specialized training within a subfield. Third, the student is encouraged to take advantage of opportunities for wider training emphasizing research rather than practice. For the clinical area, research and practica are strongly integrated. Training is geared to the expectation that the majority of students will have research careers.

Programs and Degrees Offered

Program	Degree	Application Deadline	Applica-tions Received	Accepted	New Admits Enrolled (PT)	Total Enrolled (PT)	Degrees Awarded in 2014–2015	Median Years to Complete Degree	Dismissed/ Withdrew
Neuroscience	PhD	December 1 (Fall)	39	3	2 (0)	6 (0)	2	6	0
Clinical Psychology	PhD	December 1 (Fall)	288	7	5 (0)	23 (0)	3	7.5	0
Cognitive Psychology	PhD	December 1 (Fall)	79	5	3 (0)	14 (0)	2	5.5	0
Developmental Psychology	PhD	December 1 (Fall)	52	6	4 (0)	17 (0)	2	5.5	0
Social/ Personality Psychology	PhD	December 1 (Fall)	110	6	4 (0)	23 (0)	2	6	0

APA Accreditation
Clinical PhD: Student Outcome Data website: http://psychology.yale.edu/research/clinical-psychology.

Doctoral Degree (PhD Clinical Psychology): For those doctoral students for whom a professional internship was required in this program prior to graduation:
Total students who applied for an internship: 2
Total students who obtained an internship: 2
Total students who obtained a paid internship: 2
Total students who obtained an unpaid internship: 0
Total students who were placed in APA/CPA-accredited internships: 2
Total students placed in internships not APA/CPA-accredited, but listed with the Association of Psychology Postdoctoral and Internship Centers (APPIC): 0
Total students placed in internships conforming to guidelines of the Council of Directors of School Psychology Programs (CDSPP): 0
Total students placed in internships that were not APA/CPA-accredited, APPIC or CDSSP listed: 0

Internships/Practica
Local facilities for predoctoral internships are the Veterans Administration Center in West Haven, Yale Psychology Department Clinic, the Yale Child Study Center, and Yale Department of Psychiatry, with placement in the Connecticut Mental Health Center, Yale-New Haven Hospital, or the Yale Psychiatric Institute. Also, internships are arranged in accredited facilities throughout the United States.

Admissions
Entries appear in the following order: required test or GPA, minimum score (if required)/median score of students entering in 2015–2016.

Program	Degree	GRE-V	GRE-Q	GRE-Writing	GRE-Subject	Under-graduate GPA	Last 2 Years GPA	Psychol-ogy GPA	Master's GPA
Neuroscience	PhD	NA/NA	NA/NA	NA/NA	Not specified	NA/NA	NA/NA	NA/NA	NA/NA
Clinical Psychology	PhD	NA/164	NA/162	NA/5	Not specified	NA/NA	NA/NA	NA/NA	NA/NA
Cognitive Psychology	PhD	NA/NA	NA/NA	NA/NA	Not specified	NA/NA	NA/NA	NA/NA	NA/NA

Admissions *(con't.)*

Program	Degree	GRE-V	GRE-Q	GRE-Writing	GRE-Subject	Under-graduate GPA	Last 2 Years GPA	Psychol-ogy GPA	Master's GPA
Developmental Psychology	PhD	NA/NA	NA/NA	NA/NA	Not specified	NA/NA	NA/NA	NA/NA	NA/NA
Social/ Personality Psychology	PhD	NA/NA	NA/NA	NA/NA	Not specified	NA/NA	NA/NA	NA/NA	NA/NA

Admissions Requirements:

Degree	GRE	GRE-Subject	Letters of Recom-mendation	Research Statement	Writing Sample	CV	Interview
Doctoral	Required	None	3	Required	Recom-mended	Recom-mended	Required

Admissions Criteria:
GRE scores—high
Research experience—high
Work experience—low
Clinically related public service—low
GPA—high

Letters of recommendation—high
Interview—high
Statement of goals and objectives—high
Undergraduate psychology preparation—medium

For additional information on admission requirements, visit http://psychology.yale.edu/graduate/admissions/applying-admission.

Department Demographics

	Male (PT)	Female (PT)	Total	African-American/ Black (PT)	Hispanic/ Latino (PT)	Asian/ Pacific Islander (PT)	American Indian/ Alaska Native (PT)	Caucasian/ White (PT)	Unknown (PT)	Multiethnic (PT)	ADA (PT)	Int'l (PT)
Students	32 (0)	51 (0)	83	0 (0)	3 (0)	7 (0)	0 (0)	64 (0)	0 (0)	1 (0)	1 (0)	6 (0)

Financial Information/Assistance

Tuition: For information on tuition costs, visit http://gsas.yale.edu/funding-aid/tuition-living-costs. Tuition is subject to change.

Doctoral:
State residents: $38,700 per academic year.
Nonstate residents: $38,700 per academic year.

Financial Assistance:

	Teaching Assistantship (% Receiving)	Teaching Assistantship Tuition Remission	Research Assistantship (% Receiving)	Research Assistantship Tuition Remission	Fellowship (% Receiving)	Fellowship Tuition Remission
First-Year Student	NA (NA)	Full	NA (NA)	Full	NA (NA)	Full
Advanced Student	NA (NA)	Full	NA (NA)	Full	NA (NA)	Full

For additional information on financial assistance, visit http://gsas.yale.edu/funding-aid/office-financial-aid.

Employment of Department Graduates

Doctoral:
Enrolled in a postdoctoral residency/fellowship: 7
Employed in business or industry: 1
Employed in a community mental health/counseling center: 2
Still seeking employment: 1
Total: 11

Additional Information

Housing and Day Care: On-campus housing is available. See the following website for more information: http://housing.yale.edu/graduate-housing. On-campus day care facilities are available. See the following website for more information: http://www.yale.edu/hronline/worklife/ccd.html.

Information for Students With Physical Disabilities: See the following website: https://rod.ys.yale.edu/.

Special Facilities or Resources: Facilities available as adjuncts to research and teaching include The Yale Canine Cognition Lab, The Yale Parenting Center, The Yale Psychology Department Clinic, and The Yale Center for Emotional Intelligence. Other facilities include special rooms equipped for observation, intercommunication, and recording as required for clinical supervision or testing or for interview training and research. Also available to our students is an fMRI facility in the Yale University School of Medicine.

Application Information: Graduate School, Yale University, Office of Admissions, P.O. Box 208323, New Haven, CT 06520-8323. *Fee:* $100. *Online application:* https://www.yale.edu/graduateschool/admissions/apply_online.html.

Delaware, University of
Department of Psychological and Brain Sciences
College of Arts and Science
108 Wolf Hall
Newark, DE 19716
Telephone: (302) 831-2272
Chairperson: Robert F. Simons

E-mail: arielle@psych.udel.edu
Web: https://www.psych.udel.edu/

Orientation, Objectives, and Emphasis of Department
The department fosters a scientific approach to all areas of psychology. The training is organized around Behavioral Neuroscience, Clinical Science, Cognitive, and Social Areas, as well as an integrative developmental neuroscience focus that cuts across areas. The goal of this training is to prepare students to function as scientists and teachers in academic, applied, and clinical settings. Students in the Clinical Science program are additionally trained for full competence in independent practice, although that career path is not the goal of the program. Major current research interests are in these areas: (1) Behavioral Neuroscience: neuroanatomy; developmental psychobiology; psychopharmacology; and neurobiology of learning; (2) Clinical Science: development, evaluation, and dissemination of intervention/prevention programs for adults, adolescents, and children; basic research on effects of poverty; peer relations; intimate relationships; and brain mechanisms and psychophysiology of psychopathology; (3) Cognitive: attention; pattern recognition; psycholinguistics; visual information processing; memory; and cognitive development; (4) Social: intergroup relations; effects of being the victim of prejudice; social neuroscience; behavior in situations of social interdependence; and cultural and cross-cultural psychology. The PhD programs are flexible and encourage students to develop unique interests.

Programs and Degrees Offered

Program	Degree	Application Deadline	Applications Received	Accepted	New Admits Enrolled (PT)	Total Enrolled (PT)	Degrees Awarded in 2014–2015	Median Years to Complete Degree	Dismissed/ Withdrew
Clinical Science	PhD	December 15 (Fall)	158	8	4 (0)	26 (0)	4	6.5	0
Behavioral Neuroscience	PhD	December 15 (Fall)	38	7	3 (0)	15 (0)	1	5	0
Social Psychology	PhD	December 15 (Fall)	35	2	2 (0)	8 (0)	4	5.5	0
Cognitive Psychology	PhD	December 15 (Fall)	36	7	3 (0)	8 (0)	0		1

APA Accreditation
Clinical PhD: Student Outcome Data website: https://www.psych.udel.edu/graduate/areas-of-study/clinical-science/student-admissions-outcomes-and-other-data.

Doctoral Degree (PhD Clinical Science): For those doctoral students for whom a professional internship was required in this program prior to graduation:
Total students who applied for an internship: 8
Total students who obtained an internship: 8
Total students who obtained a paid internship: 8
Total students who obtained an unpaid internship: 0
Total students who were placed in APA/CPA-accredited internships: 8
Total students placed in internships not APA/CPA-accredited, but listed with the Association of Psychology Postdoctoral and Internship Centers (APPIC): 0
Total students placed in internships conforming to guidelines of the Council of Directors of School Psychology Programs (CDSPP): 0
Total students placed in internships that were not APA/CPA-accredited, APPIC or CDSSP listed: 0

Internships/Practica
A wide range of external practicum experiences are available for Clinical Science graduate students in their third year and beyond. In their first two years, students in the Clinical Science program are supervised by our faculty in our Psychological Services Training Center.

Admissions

Entries appear in the following order: required test or GPA, minimum score (if required)/median score of students entering in 2015–2016.

Program	Degree	GRE-V	GRE-Q	GRE-Writing	GRE-Subject	Under-graduate GPA	Last 2 Years GPA	Psychol-ogy GPA	Master's GPA
Clinical Science	PhD	NA/163	NA/157	NA/4.85	Not specified	NA/3.76	Not specified	Not specified	Not specified
Behavioral Neuroscience	PhD	NA/158	NA/159	NA/4.58	Not specified	Not specified	Not specified	Not specified	Not specified
Social Psychology	PhD	NA/157	NA/156	NA/3.83	Not specified	Not specified	Not specified	Not specified	Not specified
Cognitive Psychology	PhD	NA/159	NA/157	NA/3.92	Not specified	Not specified	Not specified	Not specified	Not specified

Admissions Requirements:

Degree	GRE	GRE-Subject	Letters of Recom-mendation	Research Statement	Writing Sample	CV	Interview
Doctoral	Required	None	3	Required	Optional	Optional	Required

Please note if these criteria vary for different programs: In the behavioral neuroscience, cognitive and social areas, GRE scores are emphasized less and research experience is emphasized more relative to the clinical area.

Admissions Criteria:

GRE scores—high
Research experience—high
Work experience—low
Clinically related public service—low
GPA—high

Letters of recommendation—high
Interview—high
Statement of goals and objectives—high
Undergraduate psychology preparation—medium

For additional information on admission requirements, visit https://www.psych.udel.edu/graduate/for-prospective-students.

Department Demographics

	Male (PT)	Female (PT)	Total	African-American/ Black (PT)	Hispanic/ Latino (PT)	Asian/ Pacific Islander (PT)	American Indian/ Alaska Native (PT)	Caucasian/ White (PT)	Unknown	Multiethnic (PT)	ADA (PT)	Int'l (PT)
Students	18 (0)	42 (0)	60	3 (0)	3 (0)	6 (0)	0 (0)	47 (0)	1 (0)	0 (0)	0 (0)	6 (0)

Financial Information/Assistance

Tuition: For information on tuition costs, visit http://grad.udel.edu/policies/tuition-rates/. Tuition is subject to change. Additional fees are assessed to students beyond the costs of tuition for the following: Student health and student service center fees.

Doctoral:
State residents: $30,132 per academic year.
State residents: $1,674 per credit hour.
Nonstate residents: $30,132 per academic year.
Nonstate residents: $1,674 per credit hour.

Financial Assistance:

	Teaching Assistantship (% Receiving)	Teaching Assistantship Tuition Remission	Research Assistantship (% Receiving)	Research Assistantship Tuition Remission	Fellowship (% Receiving)	Fellowship Tuition Remission
First-Year Student	$18,000 (NA)	Full	$18,000 (NA)	Full	$18,000 (NA)	Full
Advanced Student	$18,000 (NA)	Full	$18,000 (NA)	Full	$18,000 (NA)	Full

For additional information on financial assistance, visit http://grad.udel.edu/fees-and-funding/funding-opportunities/.

Employment of Department Graduates

Doctoral:
Enrolled in a postdoctoral residency/fellowship: 5
Employed in an academic position at a university: 2
Employed in business or industry: 1
Employed in government agency: 1
Total: 9

Additional Information

Housing and Day Care: On-campus housing is available. See the following website for more information: http://www.udel.edu/reslife/resources/students/grad.html. On-campus day care facilities are available. See the following website for more information: http://www.udel.edu/hr/childcare.html.

Information for Students With Physical Disabilities: See the following website: http://www.udel.edu/DSS/.

Special Facilities or Resources: The Department of Psychological and Brain Sciences is well equipped to handle departmental computing needs with a large assortment of Windows, Linux, and Macintosh computers and servers. A large capacity Community Cluster is also available. Graduate students will find strong laboratory resources appropriate to their research needs. Department laboratories are well equipped for the online control of experiments for human and animal subjects as well as for data analysis and modeling. Laboratories are equipped with video, acoustic, behavioral and physiological recording systems as appropriate. The Department also operates the Psychological Services Training Center for practicum training and research in clinical psychology; this is augmented by the Department's Center for Training, Evaluation and Community Collaboration (C-TECC).

Application Information: The Office of Graduate Studies, 234 Hullihen Hall, University of Delaware, Newark, DE 19716. *Fee:* $75. *Online application:* http://grad.udel.edu/apply/.

American University
Department of Psychology
College of Arts and Sciences
321 Asbury, 4400 Massachusetts Avenue, NW
Washington, DC 20016-8062
Telephone: (202) 885-1710
Chairperson: David A. F. Haaga

E-mail: psychology@american.edu
Web: http://www.american.edu/cas/psychology

Orientation, Objectives, and Emphasis of Department
The psychology department of American University offers three graduate programs. These are two separate PhD programs in clinical psychology and in behavior, cognition and neuroscience. The MA program has tracks in general, personality/social, and biological/experimental psychology. The doctoral program in clinical psychology trains psychologists to do therapy, assessment, research, university teaching, and consultation. The theoretical orientation is eclectic and follows the Boulder scientist–practitioner model. The doctoral program in behavioral neuroscience/experimental psychology involves intensive training in both pure and applied research settings. Students can work in laboratories exploring conditioning and learning, the experimental analysis of behavior, cognition and memory, physiological psychology, neuropsychology, and neuropharmacology. Study at the master's level provides the basis for further doctoral-level work and prepares students for immediate employment in a variety of careers including clinical-medical research, teaching, counseling and policy formulation, law enforcement, and government work. Our graduate students are expected to be professional, ethical, committed, full-time members of our psychology community.

Programs and Degrees Offered

Program	Degree	Application Deadline	Applica-tions Received	Accepted	New Admits Enrolled (PT)	Total Enrolled (PT)	Degrees Awarded in 2014–2015	Median Years to Complete Degree	Dismissed/ Withdrew
Behavior, Cognition and Neuroscience (Bcan)	PhD	December 1 (Fall)	27	8	5 (0)	24 (4)	8	4.38	1
Clinical Psychology	PhD	December 1 (Fall)	266	7	6 (0)	24 (7)	10	5.9	0
General Psychology	MA/MS	March 1 (Fall)	120	54	21 (0)	19 (19)	22	2	0

APA Accreditation
Clinical PhD: Student Outcome Data website: http://www.american.edu/cas/psychology/clinical/index.cfm.

Doctoral Degree (PhD Clinical Psychology): For those doctoral students for whom a professional internship was required in this program prior to graduation:
Total students who applied for an internship: 8
Total students who obtained an internship: 8
Total students who obtained a paid internship: 8
Total students who obtained an unpaid internship: 0
Total students who were placed in APA/CPA-accredited internships: 8
Total students placed in internships not APA/CPA-accredited, but listed with the Association of Psychology Postdoctoral and Internship Centers (APPIC): 0
Total students placed in internships conforming to guidelines of the Council of Directors of School Psychology Programs (CDSPP): 0
Total students placed in internships that were not APA/CPA-accredited, APPIC or CDSSP listed: 0

Internships/Practica
The greater Washington, DC metropolitan area provides a wealth of applied and research resources to complement our students' work in the classroom and faculty laboratories. These include the university's Counseling Center, local hospitals (Children's, St. Elizabeth's, Walter Reed, Georgetown University, National Rehabilitation), the Kennedy Institute, Gallaudet University, the NIH

(NIMH, NINDS, NIA, NCI), the National Zoo, and the national offices of many agencies (e.g., APA, APS, NAMI). Field work and short-term externships are available in many city, county, and private organizations, such as the Alexandria, VA Community Mental Health Center, the Montgomery County, MD Department of Addiction, Victim, and Mental Health Services, and the DC Rape Crisis Center. MA and PhD students can also earn degree credit while obtaining practical experience working in the private sector with autistic children, teaching self-management skills, or volunteering at shelters for battered women or the homeless. Many of these positions sometimes can provide funding. Clinical students participate in Rogerian, cognitive-behavioral, and psychodynamic therapy practica.

Admissions

Entries appear in the following order: required test or GPA, minimum score (if required)/median score of students entering in 2015–2016.

Program	Degree	GRE-V	GRE-Q	GRE-Writing	GRE-Subject	Under-graduate GPA	Last 2 Years GPA	Psychol-ogy GPA	Master's GPA
Behavior, Cognition and Neuroscience (BCAN)	PhD	158/158	152/155	5/5	NA/NA	3.64/3.7	Not specified	Not specified	Not specified
Clinical Psychology	PhD	162/162	158/157	4.83/5	Not specified	3.75/3.78	Not specified	Not specified	Not specified
General Psychology	MA/MS	158/158	155/155	4.1/4	Not specified	3.35/3.36	Not specified	Not specified	Not specified

Admissions Requirements:

Degree	GRE	GRE-Subject	Letters of Recom-mendation	Research Statement	Writing Sample	CV	Interview
Master's/Specialist	Required	Recom-mended	3	Required	Optional	Required	None
Doctoral	Required	Recom-mended	3	Required	Optional	Required	Required

Please note if these criteria vary for different programs: Clinically related public service not required for Behavior, Cognition, and Neuroscience program.

Admissions Criteria:

GRE scores—high
Research experience—high
Work experience—medium
Clinically related public service—low
GPA—high

Letters of recommendation—high
Interview—high
Statement of goals and objectives—high
Undergraduate psychology preparation—medium

Department Demographics

	Male (PT)	Female (PT)	Total	African-American/ Black (PT)	Hispanic/ Latino (PT)	Asian/ Pacific Islander (PT)	American Indian/ Alaska Native (PT)	Caucasian/ White (PT)	Unknown (PT)	Multiethnic (PT)	ADA (PT)	Int'l (PT)
Students	13 (9)	54 (21)	97	4 (0)	2 (0)	9 (1)	0 (0)	48 (29)	0 (0)	4 (0)	0 (0)	5 (0)

Financial Information/Assistance

Tuition: For information on tuition costs, visit http://www.american.edu/finance/studentaccounts/index.cfm. Tuition is subject to change.

Doctoral:
State residents: $1,579 per credit hour.
Nonstate residents: $1,579 per credit hour.

Master's:
State residents: $1,579 per credit hour.
Nonstate residents: $1,579 per credit hour.

Financial Assistance:

	Teaching Assistantship (% Receiving)	Teaching Assistantship Tuition Remission	Research Assistantship (% Receiving)	Research Assistantship Tuition Remission	Fellowship (% Receiving)	Fellowship Tuition Remission
First-Year Student	$19,200 (NA)	Full	NA (NA)	NA	NA (NA)	NA
Advanced Student	$19,200 (NA)	Full	NA (NA)	NA	NA (NA)	NA

For additional information on financial assistance, visit http://www.american.edu/cas/admissions/finance.cfm.

Employment of Department Graduates

Master's:
Enrolled in a psychology doctoral program: 7
Enrolled in another graduate/professional program: 2
Employed in an academic position at a university: 1
Employed in other positions at a higher education institution: 1
Employed in business or industry: 1
Employed in a community mental health/counseling center: 1
Employed in a hospital/medical center: 3
Still seeking employment: 1
Other employment position: 1
Do not know: 4
Total: 22

Doctoral:
Enrolled in a postdoctoral residency/fellowship: 7
Employed in independent practice: 2
Employed in an academic position at a university: 2
Employed in government agency: 1
Employed in a community mental health/counseling center: 1
Employed in a hospital/medical center: 1
Still seeking employment: 1
Other employment position: 1
Do not know: 1
Total: 17

Additional Information

Housing and Day Care: No on-campus housing is available. On-campus day care facilities are available. See the following website for more information: http://www.american.edu/hr/cdc.cfm.

Information for Students With Physical Disabilities: See the following website: http://www.american.edu/ocl/asac/index.cfm.

Special Facilities or Resources: Fifteen well-equipped laboratories investigate conditioning and learning, clinical and experimental neuropsychology, human cognition and memory, neuropharmacology, physiological psychology, social behavior, psychopathology, depression, anxiety disorders, emotion, eating disorders, parent-child interaction, addictive behavior, child development, and various other issues in applied experimental psychology and behavioral neuroscience. In addition, students train in the Department's cognitive behavioral training clinic. Close working relationships with laboratories at the National Institutes of Health, the Walter Reed Army Institutes of Research, and Georgetown University's Hospital and School of Medicine allow additional training opportunities. The Washington Research Library Consortium (WRLC) provides access to six local college and university libraries in addition to AU's Bender Library, the National Library of Medicine, and the Library of Congress.

Application Information: College of Arts and Sciences, American University, Mary Graydon Center, Room 301, 4400 Massachusetts Avenue, NW, Washington, DC 20016-8107. *Fee:* $55. *Online application:* http://www.american.edu/cas/admissions/apply.cfm.

Gallaudet University
Department of Psychology
College of Arts and Sciences
800 Florida Avenue, NE
Washington, DC 20002
Telephone: (202) 651-5540
Chairperson: Dennis B. Galvan, PhD

E-mail: dennis.galvan@gallaudet.edu
Web: http://www.gallaudet.edu/psychology.html

Orientation, Objectives, and Emphasis of Department

The Psychology Department at Gallaudet University offers graduate programs in school psychology and clinical psychology. The school psychology program awards a non-terminal Master of Arts degree in developmental psychology followed by a Specialist in School Psychology degree with specialization in deafness. The clinical psychology program is a scholar–practitioner model PhD program and trains generalist clinical psychologists to work with deaf, hard-of-hearing, and hearing populations. The school psychology program is both NCATE/NASP and NASDTEC-approved, and leads to certification as a school psychologist in the District of Columbia and approximately 24 states with reciprocity of certification. The full-time, 3-year program requires completion of at least 72 graduate semester hours, including a 1-year internship. The APA-accredited clinical psychology doctoral program is a 5-year program providing balanced training in research and clinical skills with a variety of age groups, including deaf and hard-of-hearing children, adults, and older adults. The fifth year is designed as a full-time clinical psychology internship. A research-based dissertation is required.

Programs and Degrees Offered

Program	Degree	Application Deadline	Applica-tions Received	Accepted	New Admits Enrolled (PT)	Total Enrolled (PT)	Degrees Awarded in 2014–2015	Median Years to Complete Degree	Dismissed/ Withdrew
Clinical Psychology	PhD	February 1 (Fall)	29	5	5 (0)	36 (5)	6	6	1
Specialist in School Psychology	Other	February 1 (Fall)	10	8	5 (0)	16 (0)	12	3	0

APA Accreditation

Clinical PhD: Student Outcome Data website: http://www.gallaudet.edu/psychology/graduate_programs/phd_clinical_psychology/student_admissions_outcomes_and_other_data.html.

Doctoral Degree (PhD Clinical Psychology): For those doctoral students for whom a professional internship was required in this program prior to graduation:

Total students who applied for an internship: 5

Total students who obtained an internship: 3

Total students who obtained a paid internship: 3

Total students who obtained an unpaid internship: 0

Total students who were placed in APA/CPA-accredited internships: 3

Total students placed in internships not APA/CPA-accredited, but listed with the Association of Psychology Postdoctoral and Internship Centers (APPIC): 0

Total students placed in internships conforming to guidelines of the Council of Directors of School Psychology Programs (CDSPP): 0

Total students placed in internships that were not APA/CPA-accredited, APPIC or CDSSP listed: 0

Internships/Practica

Students in the School Psychology program begin with a practicum experience in their first semester, visiting and observing school programs. During their second semester they are involved in doing cognitive assessments of deaf and hearing children (if appropriate) at laboratory schools on campus and a DC neighborhood school. The second year practicum requires 2 full days per week for a minimum of 14 weeks working with a school psychologist in the Washington Metropolitan area doing comprehensive assessments, some counseling if opportunities are available, and observation on a limited basis. The third year is spent in a full-time internship. These internships are typically located in both residential schools for the deaf as well as public school systems serving mainstreamed deaf youngsters all over the country. Students in the Clinical Psychology doctoral program begin practicum in their second year, conducted at the Gallaudet University Mental Health Center, which provides both student counseling and services to the community. Externship experiences in the third year and beyond are most often at off-campus agencies or hospitals; there are more than 50 such externship sites in the area. A 1-year, full-time internship is required (usually in the fifth or sixth year). APA-accredited programs are strongly preferred.

Admissions

Entries appear in the following order: required test or GPA, minimum score (if required)/median score of students entering in 2015–2016.

Program	Degree	GRE-V	GRE-Q	GRE-Writing	GRE-Subject	Under-graduate GPA	Last 2 Years GPA	Psychology GPA	Master's GPA
Clinical Psychology	PhD	NA/154	NA/150	NA/4	Not specified	3.6/3.59	Not specified	Not specified	Not specified
Specialist in School Psychology	Other	NA/NA	NA/NA	NA/NA	Not specified	3/3.98	Not specified	Not specified	Not specified

Admissions Requirements:

Degree	GRE	GRE-Subject	Letters of Recom-mendation	Research Statement	Writing Sample	CV	Interview
Master's/Specialist	Required	None	3	Required	Optional	Optional	None
Doctoral	Required	None	3	Required	Required	Required	Required

Please note if these criteria vary for different programs: Students with little experience with deaf people or sign language may be required to take sign language (ASL) courses prior to enrolling. Prior research experience and clinically related public service are rated high for clinical psychology doctoral program admissions and medium for school psychology admissions. GPA is rated high for the School Psychology program and medium for the doctoral program. Interview is low for School Psychology and high for the doctoral program.

Admissions Criteria:

GRE scores—medium
Research experience—medium
Work experience—medium
Clinically related public service—medium
GPA—high

Letters of recommendation—high
Interview—high
Statement of goals and objectives—high
Undergraduate psychology preparation—high

For additional information on admission requirements, visit http://www.gallaudet.edu/rgs/graduate_school/graduate_admissions/application_information.html.

Department Demographics

	Male (PT)	Female (PT)	Total	African-American/ Black (PT)	Hispanic/ Latino (PT)	Asian/ Pacific Islander (PT)	American Indian/ Alaska Native (PT)	Caucasian/ White (PT)	Unknown	Multiethnic (PT)	ADA (PT)	Int'l (PT)
Students	12 (1)	41 (3)	57	5 (2)	8 (0)	3 (0)	1 (0)	36 (2)	0 (0)	0 (0)	19 (2)	2 (0)

Financial Information/Assistance

Tuition: For information on tuition costs, visit http://www.gallaudet.edu/finance-office.html. Higher tuition cost for this program: International students pay higher tuition; higher for nondeveloping than developing countries. Tuition is subject to change. Additional fees are assessed to students beyond the costs of tuition for the following: health insurance and services.

Doctoral:
State residents: $16,596 per academic year.
Nonstate residents: $33,192 per academic year.

Master's:
State residents: $16,596 per academic year.
Nonstate residents: $33,192 per academic year.

Financial Assistance:

	Teaching Assistantship (% Receiving)	Teaching Assistantship Tuition Remission	Research Assistantship (% Receiving)	Research Assistantship Tuition Remission	Fellowship (% Receiving)	Fellowship Tuition Remission
First-Year Student	$4,500 (NA)	NA	$4,500 (NA)	NA	$12,000 (NA)	Partial
Advanced Student	$4,500 (NA)	NA	$4,500 (NA)	NA	$12,000 (NA)	Partial

For additional information on financial assistance, visit http://www.gallaudet.edu/financial_aid.html.

Employment of Department Graduates

Master's:
Employed in a professional position in a school system: 6
Total: 6

Doctoral:
Enrolled in a postdoctoral residency/fellowship: 4
Employed in other positions at a higher education institution: 1
Employed in a community mental health/counseling center: 1
Employed in a hospital/medical center: 1
Total: 7

Additional Information

Housing and Day Care: On-campus housing is available. See the following website for more information: http://www.gallaudet.edu/reslife.html. No on-campus day care facilities are available.

Information for Students With Physical Disabilities: See the following website: http://www.gallaudet.edu/office_for_students_with_disabilities.html.

Special Facilities or Resources: Gallaudet University is an internationally recognized center for research and training in areas related to deafness. With a diverse student body of approximately 1,800, the university trains deaf, hard-of-hearing, and hearing students in a variety of fields at the bachelor's, master's, and doctoral levels. Gallaudet programs are located on historic Kendall Green, in northeast Washington, DC near the U.S. Capitol, the Library of Congress, and the Smithsonian Institute. Also located on the campus are the Gallaudet University Mental Health Center, the Kendall Demonstration Elementary School, the Model Secondary School for the Deaf, the Gallaudet Research Institute, the Kellogg Conference Center, and the Gallaudet Library, which contains the largest collection of references on deafness in the world. Gallaudet faculty, including both deaf and hearing individuals, possess a unique combination of scholarly activity in their respective disciplines and experience with deaf clients and research on deafness. The University is committed to a working model of a bilingual (American Sign Language and English), multicultural community, where deaf, hard-of-hearing, and hearing people can work together without communication barriers.

Application Information: Office of Graduate Admissions, Gallaudet University, 800 Florida Avenue NE, Washington, DC 20002. *Fee:* $50. *Online application:* http://gradschool.gallaudet.edu/apply.

George Washington University
Department of Organizational Sciences and Communication/ I/O Psychology Program
Columbian College of Arts and Sciences
600 21st Street NW #201
Washington, DC 20052
Telephone: (202) 994-1875
Chairperson: Clay Warren
E-mail: orgsci@gwu.edu
Web: https://orgsciandcomm.columbian.gwu.edu/doctoral-program-industrialorganizational-psychology

---

Orientation, Objectives, and Emphasis of Department
The Department of Organizational Sciences and Communication is an interdisciplinary unit that builds on a broad range of disciplines including organizational management, psychology, communications, economics, and statistics. The Industrial/Organizational (I/O) Psychology doctoral program offers graduate training in areas such as personnel selection, training and development, work motivation, leadership, work teams, and organizational development. The program of study is designed in accordance with guidelines established by the Society for Industrial and Organizational Psychology (SIOP; Division 14, APA).

Programs and Degrees Offered

Program	Degree	Application Deadline	Applications Received	Accepted	New Admits Enrolled (PT)	Total Enrolled (PT)	Degrees Awarded in 2014–2015	Median Years to Complete Degree	Dismissed/ Withdrew
Industrial/ Organizational Psychology	PhD	December 15 (Fall)	100	3	3 (0)	16 (0)	2	5.5	0

Internships/Practica

Internships and applied work experiences are available at a wide variety of organizations including in the government, private practice, and the military, and in corporate, educational and non-profit sectors.

Admissions

Entries appear in the following order: required test or GPA, minimum score (if required)/median score of students entering in 2015–2016.

Program	Degree	GRE-V	GRE-Q	GRE-Writing	GRE-Subject	Under-graduate GPA	Last 2 Years GPA	Psychology GPA	Master's GPA
Industrial/ Organizational Psychology	PhD	NA/NA	NA/NA	NA/NA	Not specified	3/3.6	Not specified	Not specified	Not specified

Admissions Requirements:

Degree	GRE	GRE-Subject	Letters of Recom-mendation	Research Statement	Writing Sample	CV	Interview
Doctoral	Required	None	3	Required	Optional	Required	Required

Admissions Criteria:

GRE scores—high
Research experience—high
Work experience—low
GPA—high

Letters of recommendation—high
Interview—high
Statement of goals and objectives—high
Undergraduate psychology preparation—medium

For additional information on admission requirements, visit https://orgsciandcomm.columbian.gwu.edu/io-psychology-admissions.

Department Demographics

	Male (PT)	Female (PT)	Total	African-American/ Black (PT)	Hispanic/ Latino (PT)	Asian/ Pacific Islander (PT)	American Indian/ Alaska Native (PT)	Caucasian/ White (PT)	Unknown (PT)	Multiethnic (PT)	ADA (PT)	Int'l (PT)
Students	6 (0)	10 (0)	16	0 (0)	1 (0)	0 (0)	0 (0)	12 (0)	0 (0)	0 (0)	0 (0)	0 (0)

Financial Information/Assistance

Tuition: For information on tuition costs, visit http://studentaccounts.gwu.edu/graduate-tuition. Tuition is subject to change.

Doctoral:
State residents: $1,450 per credit hour.
Nonstate residents: $1,450 per credit hour.

Financial Assistance:

	Teaching Assistantship (% Receiving)	Teaching Assistantship Tuition Remission	Research Assistantship (% Receiving)	Research Assistantship Tuition Remission	Fellowship (% Receiving)	Fellowship Tuition Remission
First-Year Student	$6,000 (100)	Full	$6,000 (100)	Full	$10,000 (100)	Full
Advanced Student	$6,000 (75)	Full	$6,000 (75)	Full	$10,000 (75)	Full

For additional information on financial assistance, visit http://graduate.admissions.gwu.edu/financial-assistance.

Employment of Department Graduates

Doctoral:
Employed in an academic position at a university: 1
Employed in government agency: 1
Total: 2

Additional Information

Housing and Day Care: On-campus housing is available. See the following website for more information: http://living.gwu.edu/graduate-students. On-campus day care facilities are available.

Information for Students With Physical Disabilities: See the following website: http://www.gwu.edu/disability-support-services.

Application Information: Fee: $100. *Online application:* http://graduate.admissions.gwu.edu/.

George Washington University
Department of Psychology
Columbian College of Arts and Sciences
2125 G Street, NW
Washington, DC 20052
Telephone: (202) 994-6320
Chairperson: Carol Sigelman

E-mail: carol@gwu.edu
Web: http://psychology.columbian.gwu.edu

Orientation, Objectives, and Emphasis of Department
The department provides training in the basic science of psychology for each of its doctoral program areas: applied social psychology, clinical psychology, and cognitive neuroscience. The department's research centers on health promotion in diverse communities. The applied social program focuses on theories and methods of preventing high-risk social behaviors and addressing current health problems such as substance use, cancer, HIV, and obesity. The clinical program is an APA-approved program emphasizing both the basic science and applied aspects of clinical and community psychology. The focus of the program is health promotion and disease prevention in diverse urban communities. The cognitive neuroscience program focuses on perception, cognition, learning, and memory, with emphasis on the psychobiological underpinnings of these functions as revealed through neural imaging and other methodologies. Training in each program area addresses both scientific and professional objectives. Students are actively involved in research and are trained for careers in academic institutions, applied research, and professional practice.

Programs and Degrees Offered

Program	Degree	Application Deadline	Applica- tions Received	Accepted	New Admits Enrolled (PT)	Total Enrolled (PT)	Degrees Awarded in 2014– 2015	Median Years to Complete Degree	Dismissed/ Withdrew
Applied Social Psychology	PhD	December 1 (Fall)	36	1	1 (0)	10 (0)	1		0
Clinical Psychology	PhD	December 1 (Fall)	305	8	5 (0)	36 (0)	2	9.5	0

Programs and Degrees Offered (con't.)

Program	Degree	Application Deadline	Applica-tions Received	Accepted	New Admits Enrolled (PT)	Total Enrolled (PT)	Degrees Awarded in 2014–2015	Median Years to Complete Degree	Dismissed/Withdrew
Cognitive Neuroscience	PhD	December 1 (Fall)	34	0	0 (0)	11 (0)	1	5	0

APA Accreditation

Clinical PhD: Student Outcome Data website: http://psychology.columbian.gwu.edu/clinical.

Doctoral Degree (PhD Clinical Psychology): For those doctoral students for whom a professional internship was required in this program prior to graduation:

Total students who applied for an internship: 8

Total students who obtained an internship: 8

Total students who obtained a paid internship: 8

Total students who obtained an unpaid internship: 0

Total students who were placed in APA/CPA-accredited internships: 8

Total students placed in internships not APA/CPA-accredited, but listed with the Association of Psychology Postdoctoral and Internship Centers (APPIC): 0

Total students placed in internships conforming to guidelines of the Council of Directors of School Psychology Programs (CDSPP): 0

Total students placed in internships that were not APA/CPA-accredited, APPIC or CDSSP listed: 0

Internships/Practica

Many internships, training placements, and job opportunities are available in the Washington DC Metro area. Practicum placements are a required part of training in the clinical program and include the Department's own clinic, the Meltzer Center, as well as a host of community facilities. Some of our students also become involved with laboratories of the National Institutes of Health or work with hospitals, clinics, and research organizations in the area.

Admissions

Entries appear in the following order: required test or GPA, minimum score (if required)/median score of students entering in 2015–2016.

Program	Degree	GRE-V	GRE-Q	GRE-Writing	GRE-Subject	Under-graduate GPA	Last 2 Years GPA	Psychol-ogy GPA	Master's GPA
Applied Social Psychology	PhD	NA/NA	NA/NA	NA/NA	Not specified	NA/3.75	Not specified	Not specified	Not specified
Clinical Psychology	PhD	NA/161	NA/158	NA/4.4	Not specified	NA/3.54	Not specified	Not specified	Not specified
Cognitive Neuroscience	PhD	NA/NA	NA/NA	NA/NA	Not specified	NA/3.75	Not specified	Not specified	Not specified

Admissions Requirements:

Degree	GRE	GRE-Subject	Letters of Recom-mendation	Research Statement	Writing Sample	CV	Interview
Doctoral	Required	Optional	3	Required	Required	Required	Required

Admissions Criteria:

GRE scores—medium

Research experience—high

Work experience—medium

Clinically related public service—medium

GPA—high

Letters of recommendation—medium

Interview—high

Statement of goals and objectives—high

Undergraduate psychology preparation—medium

For additional information on admission requirements, visit http://psychology.columbian.gwu.edu/how-apply.

Department Demographics

	Male (PT)	Female (PT)	Total	African-American/ Black (PT)	Hispanic/ Latino (PT)	Asian/ Pacific Islander (PT)	American Indian/ Alaska Native (PT)	Caucasian/ White (PT)	Unknown	Multiethnic (PT)	ADA (PT)	Int'l (PT)
Students	14 (0)	43 (0)	57	8 (0)	6 (0)	10 (0)	0 (0)	33 (0)	0 (0)	0 (0)	0 (0)	2 (0)

Financial Information/Assistance

Tuition: For information on tuition costs, visit https://studentaccounts.gwu.edu/graduate-tuition. Tuition is subject to change. Additional fees are assessed to students beyond the costs of tuition for the following: Student activity fee of $2.00 per credit hour.

Doctoral:
State residents: $27,810 per academic year.
State residents: $1,545 per credit hour.
Nonstate residents: $27,810 per academic year.
Nonstate residents: $1,545 per credit hour.

Financial Assistance:

	Teaching Assistantship (% Receiving)	Teaching Assistantship Tuition Remission	Research Assistantship (% Receiving)	Research Assistantship Tuition Remission	Fellowship (% Receiving)	Fellowship Tuition Remission
First-Year Student	$22,500 (67)	Full	$22,500 (17)	Full	$25,000 (17)	Full
Advanced Student	$22,500 (70)	Full	$22,500 (8)	Full	$25,000 (20)	Full

For additional information on financial assistance, visit http://columbian.gwu.edu/graduate-funding-opportunities.

Employment of Department Graduates

Doctoral:
Enrolled in a postdoctoral residency/fellowship: 4
Employed in a hospital/medical center: 1
Total: 5

Additional Information

Housing and Day Care: On-campus housing is available. See the following website for more information: http://living.gwu.edu/graduate-students. On-campus day care facilities are available. See the following website for more information: https://hr.gwu.edu/childcare.

Information for Students With Physical Disabilities: See the following website: http://www.gwu.edu/disability-support-services.

Special Facilities or Resources: We have excellent on-campus computer facilities and laboratories in the department for social research, cognitive testing, and small animal research. There is convenient access to staff, libraries, and other facilities on campus.

Application Information: Graduate School, CCAS, George Washington University, Washington, DC 20052. *Fee:* $75. *Online application:* http://graduate.admissions.gwu.edu/.

George Washington University
Professional Psychology Program
Columbian College of Arts & Sciences
1922 F Street NW, Suite 130
Washington, DC 20052
Telephone: (202) 994-4929
Program Director: Loring J. Ingraham, PhD

E-mail: psyd@gwu.edu
Web: https://psyd.columbian.gwu.edu/

Orientation, Objectives, and Emphasis of Department

The mission of the PsyD program is to graduate practitioner-scholar professional psychologists who are exceptionally skilled as local clinical scientists in using a psychodynamic framework for the assessment and treatment of psychopathology. Our graduates know the clinical research methods necessary for new discoveries and base their professional practice in ongoing critical consumption of relevant research. We value openness, curiosity, diversity, tolerance, beneficence, humility, methodological ability and professional ethics in the discovery and equitable provision of effective clinical services. The program also offers an MA in Forensic Psychology. The MA addresses the nation's critical need for criminal profilers, competency experts, psychological evaluators, counselors, and related positions, to help solve crimes and prevent future criminal behavior. Potential employers include agencies involved in homeland security, federal and state law enforcement, correctional systems, and organizations that provide services to criminal offenders and their victims.

Programs and Degrees Offered

Program	Degree	Application Deadline	Applica-tions Received	Accepted	New Admits Enrolled (PT)	Total Enrolled (PT)	Degrees Awarded in 2014–2015	Median Years to Complete Degree	Dismissed/ Withdrew
Clinical Psychology	PsyD	December 1 (Fall)	143	38	18 (0)	110 (0)	32	4	0
Forensic Psychology	MA/MS	June 1 (Fall), November 1 (Spring)		81	43 (30)	69 (46)	11	1.5	1

APA Accreditation

On Probation PsyD: Student Outcome Data website: https://psyd.columbian.gwu.edu/student-admissions-outcomes-and-other-data.

Doctoral Degree (PsyD Clinical Psychology): For those doctoral students for whom a professional internship was required in this program prior to graduation:
Total students who applied for an internship: 28
Total students who obtained an internship: 27
Total students who obtained a paid internship: 27
Total students who obtained an unpaid internship: 0
Total students who were placed in APA/CPA-accredited internships: 11
Total students placed in internships not APA/CPA-accredited, but listed with the Association of Psychology Postdoctoral and Internship Centers (APPIC): 13
Total students placed in internships conforming to guidelines of the Council of Directors of School Psychology Programs (CDSPP): 0
Total students placed in internships that were not APA/CPA-accredited, APPIC or CDSSP listed: 3

Master's Degree (MA/MS Forensic Psychology): An internship experience, such as a final research project or "capstone" experience is required of graduates.

Internships/Practica

Professional Psychology program students participate in practica during every term of enrollment. The practicum component, the core experiential learning element of the PsyD program, provides doctoral candidates with the opportunity to integrate theory and practice. During their first year, students are immersed in the basics of psychological assessment and introduced to the psychodynamic approaches to psychotherapy. First-year doctoral students receive hands-on experience administering, scoring, interpreting, and writing reports involving both cognitive and personality assessments. Towards the end of the first year and after the first course in psychodynamic psychotherapy, students begin their supervised experience in conducting psychotherapy in our Center Clinic. In the second year of training, students serve as student clinical externs at the Center Clinic. Rising third-year students have the option of either continuing their training in the Clinic or pursuing an extramural externship outside the Clinic. Additionally, students begin a 1-year internship (or a 2-year internship, each year at least half time) early in the third year of full time study, after comprehensive exams. The Forensic Psychology program offers externship training, tailored to a student's professional interest, at a law enforcement agency, treatment site, correctional institution, public defender's office, prosecutor's office, or other similar setting.

Admissions

Entries appear in the following order: required test or GPA, minimum score (if required)/median score of students entering in 2015–2016.

Program	Degree	GRE-V	GRE-Q	GRE-Writing	GRE-Subject	Under-graduate GPA	Last 2 Years GPA	Psychol-ogy GPA	Master's GPA
Clinical Psychology	PsyD	NA/159	NA/153	NA/4	Not specified	NA/3.62	Not specified	Not specified	Not specified
Forensic Psychology	MA/MS	NA/157	NA/151	NA/4.25	Not specified	NA/3.5	Not specified	Not specified	Not specified

Admissions Requirements:

Degree	GRE	GRE-Subject	Letters of Recom-mendation	Research Statement	Writing Sample	CV	Interview
Master's/Specialist	Required	None	2	Required	Optional	Required	Required
Doctoral	Required	Required	3	Required	Optional	Required	Required

Please note if these criteria vary for different programs: The Forensic Psychology program's admissions criteria are different for the following: Undergraduate Psychology preparation—Low.

Admissions Criteria:

GRE scores—medium
Research experience—medium
Work experience—medium
Clinically related public service—medium
GPA—high

Letters of recommendation—high
Interview—high
Statement of goals and objectives—high
Undergraduate psychology preparation—high
Integrity and motivation—high

For additional information on admission requirements, visit https://psyd.columbian.gwu.edu/apply.

Department Demographics

	Male (PT)	Female (PT)	Total	African-American/ Black (PT)	Hispanic/ Latino (PT)	Asian/ Pacific Islander (PT)	American Indian/ Alaska Native (PT)	Caucasian/ White (PT)	Unknown	Multiethnic (PT)	ADA (PT)	Int'l (PT)
Students	64 (12)	115 (34)	225	11 (1)	5 (4)	5 (1)	0 (0)	154 (39)	0 (1)	4 (0)	3 (1)	6 (0)

Financial Information/Assistance

Tuition: For information on tuition costs, visit https://studentaccounts.gwu.edu/graduate-tuition. Tuition is subject to change. Additional fees are assessed to students beyond the costs of tuition for the following: $100 assessment materials for first year students.

Doctoral:
State residents: $41,160 per academic year.
State residents: $1,470 per credit hour.
Nonstate residents: $41,160 per academic year.
Nonstate residents: $1,470 per credit hour.

Master's:
State residents: $1,100 per credit hour.
Nonstate residents: $1,100 per credit hour.

Financial Assistance:

	Teaching Assistantship (% Receiving)	Teaching Assistantship Tuition Remission	Research Assistantship (% Receiving)	Research Assistantship Tuition Remission	Fellowship (% Receiving)	Fellowship Tuition Remission
First-Year Student	NA (NA)	NA	NA (NA)	NA	$7,000 (25)	Partial
Advanced Student	NA (NA)	NA	$3,600 (5)	NA	$5,000 (20)	Partial

For additional information on financial assistance, visit http://graduate.admissions.gwu.edu/financial-assistance.

Employment of Department Graduates

Doctoral:
Enrolled in a postdoctoral residency/fellowship: 8
Employed in independent practice: 2
Employed in other positions at a higher education institution: 5
Employed in a professional position in a school system: 1
Employed in a community mental health/counseling center: 4
Employed in a hospital/medical center: 2
Other employment position: 1
Total: 23

Additional Information

Housing and Day Care: On-campus housing is available. See the following website for more information: http://living.gwu.edu/graduate-students. No on-campus day care facilities are available.

Information for Students With Physical Disabilities: See the following website: http://www.gwu.edu/disability-support-services.

Special Facilities or Resources: The Professional Psychology program houses a Center Clinic, which provides mental health services to adults, adolescents, and children in the Washington, DC area who may otherwise not have access to needed care. These services include individual, couples, family, and group psychotherapy, as well as psychological assessment. Patients may also be referred for a psychiatric consultation through a partnership with the University's Department of Psychiatry and Behavioral Science. The Clinic also contributes to local community service agencies (such as public and charter schools, homeless shelters and addiction recovery programs) by providing needed consultation, assessment and therapeutic services free of charge. The Clinic is staffed by PsyD candidates who are supervised by licensed, highly experienced professionals. All PsyD candidates are required to complete a Clinic externship during their second year of training.

Application Information: Columbian College of Arts and Sciences, Graduate Admissions Office, The George Washington University, 801 22nd Street NW, Phillips Hall Room 107, Washington, DC 20052. *Fee:* $75. *Online application:* https://app.applyyourself.com/?id=GWUGRAD.

Georgetown University
Department of Psychology
Georgetown College
Box 571001, White Gravenor Hall 306
Washington, DC 20057
Telephone: (202) 687-4042
Chairperson: Chandan Vaidya

E-mail: psychology@georgetown.edu
Web: http://psychology.georgetown.edu/

Orientation, Objectives, and Emphasis of Department
We are an intellectually diverse community of scholars engaged in research addressing both basic psychological processes and social issues. We strive for excellence in our scholarship and teaching, and we seek to cultivate in our students a dedication to the highest standards in their endeavors. We are committed to collaboration within and across disciplinary lines and to sustaining professional links with relevant local, national, and global organizations.

Programs and Degrees Offered

Program	Degree	Application Deadline	Applica-tions Received	Accepted	New Admits Enrolled (PT)	Total Enrolled (PT)	Degrees Awarded in 2014–2015	Median Years to Complete Degree	Dismissed/ Withdrew
Human Development and Public Policy	PhD	December 1 (Fall)	75	1	1 (0)	9 (0)	2	5	0
Lifespan Cognitive Neuroscience	PhD	December 1 (Fall)	39	2	2 (0)	7 (0)	1	5	0

Admissions

Entries appear in the following order: required test or GPA, minimum score (if required)/median score of students entering in 2015–2016.

Program	Degree	GRE-V	GRE-Q	GRE-Writing	GRE-Subject	Under-graduate GPA	Last 2 Years GPA	Psychol-ogy GPA	Master's GPA
Human Development and Public Policy	PhD	NA/NA	NA/NA	Not specified	Not specified	NA/NA	Not specified	Not specified	Not specified
Lifespan Cognitive Neuroscience	PhD	NA/NA	NA/NA	Not specified	Not specified	NA/NA	Not specified	Not specified	Not specified

Admissions Requirements:

Degree	GRE	GRE-Subject	Letters of Recom-mendation	Research Statement	Writing Sample	CV	Interview
Doctoral	Required	None	3	Required	Required	Required	Required

Admissions Criteria:

GRE scores—high
Research experience—high
Work experience—low
Clinically related public service—low
GPA—high

Letters of recommendation—high
Interview—high
Statement of goals and objectives—high
Undergraduate psychology preparation—medium

For additional information on admission requirements, visit http://psychology.georgetown.edu/graduate/admissions/.

Department Demographics

	Male (PT)	Female (PT)	Total	African-American/ Black (PT)	Hispanic/ Latino (PT)	Asian/ Pacific Islander (PT)	American Indian/ Alaska Native (PT)	Caucasian/ White (PT)	Unknown	Multiethnic (PT)	ADA (PT)	Int'l (PT)
Students	4 (0)	12 (0)	16	0 (0)	2 (0)	0 (0)	0 (0)	14 (0)	0 (0)	0 (0)	0 (0)	0 (0)

Financial Information/Assistance

Tuition: For information on tuition costs, visit http://finaid.georgetown.edu/cost-of-attendance/graduate/. Tuition is subject to change. Additional fees are assessed to students beyond the costs of tuition for the following: health insurance, athletic access fee.

Doctoral:
State residents: $49,332 per academic year.
Nonstate residents: $49,332 per academic year.

Financial Assistance:

	Teaching Assistantship (% Receiving)	Teaching Assistantship Tuition Remission	Research Assistantship (% Receiving)	Research Assistantship Tuition Remission	Fellowship (% Receiving)	Fellowship Tuition Remission
First-Year Student	$26,000 (NA)	Full	NA (NA)	NA	NA (NA)	NA
Advanced Student	$26,000 (NA)	Full	NA (NA)	NA	NA (NA)	NA

For additional information on financial assistance, visit http://psychology.georgetown.edu/graduate/admissions/financial-support/.

Employment of Department Graduates

Doctoral:
Enrolled in a postdoctoral residency/fellowship: 2
Employed in business or industry: 1
Total: 3

Additional Information

Housing and Day Care: No on-campus housing is available. On-campus day care facilities are available. See the following website for more information: http://hoyakids.georgetown.edu.

Information for Students With Physical Disabilities: See the following website: http://academicsupport.georgetown.edu/disability/.

Special Facilities or Resources: Graduate students have office space in a graduate student suite or faculty laboratory space. They enter a rich interdisciplinary community in which psychology graduate students take courses with graduate students from public policy, neuroscience, linguistics, and other related disciplines. The Psychology Department has an observational laboratory facility as well as faculty laboratories investigating cognitive and developmental issues. The department also maintains the Georgetown Research Volunteer Project, a university-funded, Web-based facility for recruiting research participants across the lifespan. The Medical Center, which is immediately adjacent to the Main Campus, contains the Center for Functional and Molecular Imaging, affording the opportunity to conduct research using fMRI and other state-of-the-art neuroimaging technology.

Application Information: Georgetown Graduate School of Arts and Sciences. *Fee:* $80. *Online application:* https://app.applyyourself.com/?id=gtu-g.

The Catholic University of America
Psychology
Arts and Sciences
620 Michigan Avenue, NE
Washington, DC 20064
Telephone: (202) 319-5750
Chairperson: Marc Sebrechts, PhD

E-mail: barrueco@cua.edu
Web: http://psychology.cua.edu/

Orientation, Objectives, and Emphasis of Department
Our department is oriented to providing both graduate and undergraduate training in a variety of areas of psychology, with specialization at the doctoral level in Clinical, Applied Experimental, and Human Development. The applied-experimental psychology program at CUA offers advanced training in applied-experimental psychology and applied cognitive science to prepare individuals for career opportunities in industry, government, and universities. The PhD program in clinical psychology trains students toward four main goals: acquiring a broad base of knowledge in the science of psychology, acquiring competence in all aspects of conducting clinical research, acquiring competence in the practice of clinical psychology, and acquiring the professional attitudes and behaviors necessary for successful functioning as a psychologist. The Human Development PhD program provides students with a broad

base of knowledge in the science of psychology, and human development in particular. Students learn to conduct cutting-edge developmental research, understand and analyze developmental change within complex systems, work with diverse populations, and appreciate both basic and applied research. The program prepares students for careers as researchers, teachers, advocates, and more.

Programs and Degrees Offered

Program	Degree	Application Deadline	Applications Received	Accepted	New Admits Enrolled (PT)	Total Enrolled (PT)	Degrees Awarded in 2014–2015	Median Years to Complete Degree	Dismissed/ Withdrew
Clinical Psychology	PhD	December 1 (Fall)	191	12	6 (0)	40 (0)	7	6	0
Human Development	PhD	Rolling	10	0	0 (0)	3 (0)	0		0
Applied-Experimental Psychology	PhD	February 1 (Fall), Rolling	10	2	0 (0)	10 (0)	7	6	0
General Psychology	MA/MS	Rolling	35	31	12 (0)	22 (3)	13	2	0
Human Factors	MA/MS	February 1 (Fall), Rolling	5	1	1 (0)	4 (0)	0		0
Psychology and Law	MA/MS	Rolling	0	0	0 (0)	0 (0)	0		0

APA Accreditation
Clinical PhD: Student Outcome Data website: http://psychology.cua.edu/graduate/phdclprog.cfm.

Doctoral Degree (PhD Clinical Psychology): For those doctoral students for whom a professional internship was required in this program prior to graduation:
Total students who applied for an internship: 8
Total students who obtained an internship: 8
Total students who obtained a paid internship: 8
Total students who obtained an unpaid internship: 0
Total students who were placed in APA/CPA-accredited internships: 8
Total students placed in internships not APA/CPA-accredited, but listed with the Association of Psychology Postdoctoral and Internship Centers (APPIC): 0
Total students placed in internships conforming to guidelines of the Council of Directors of School Psychology Programs (CDSPP): 0
Total students placed in internships that were not APA/CPA-accredited, APPIC or CDSSP listed: 0

Master's Degree (MA/MS General Psychology): An internship experience, such as a final research project or "capstone" experience is required of graduates. Master's Degree (MA/MS Human Factors): An internship experience, such as a final research project or "capstone" experience is required of graduates. Master's Degree (MA/MS Psychology and Law): An internship experience, such as a final research project or "capstone" experience is required of graduates.

Internships/Practica
There are over 70 externships and practicum placement sites available for graduate students in the clinical psychology program. These are located in hospitals, universities, schools, and community clinics.

Admissions
Entries appear in the following order: required test or GPA, minimum score (if required)/median score of students entering in 2015–2016.

Program	Degree	GRE-V	GRE-Q	GRE-Writing	GRE-Subject	Undergraduate GPA	Last 2 Years GPA	Psychology GPA	Master's GPA
Clinical Psychology	PhD	Not specified	Not specified	Not specified	Not specified	Not specified	Not specified	Not specified	Not specified

Admissions (con't.)

Program	Degree	GRE-V	GRE-Q	GRE-Writing	GRE-Subject	Under-graduate GPA	Last 2 Years GPA	Psychol-ogy GPA	Master's GPA
Human Development	PhD	Not specified	Not specified	Not specified	Not specified	Not specified	Not specified	Not specified	Not specified
Applied-Experimental Psychology	PhD	Not specified	Not specified	Not specified	Not specified	Not specified	Not specified	Not specified	Not specified
General Psychology	MA/MS	Not specified	Not specified	Not specified	Not specified	Not specified	Not specified	Not specified	Not specified
Human Factors	MA/MS	Not specified	Not specified	Not specified	Not specified	Not specified	Not specified	Not specified	Not specified
Psychology and Law	MA/MS	Not specified	Not specified	Not specified	Not specified	Not specified	Not specified	Not specified	Not specified

Admissions Requirements:

Degree	GRE	GRE-Subject	Letters of Recom-mendation	Research Statement	Writing Sample	CV	Interview
Master's/Specialist	Required	Recom-mended	3	Required	Optional	Required	Optional
Doctoral	Required	Required	3	Required	Optional	Required	Required

Please note if these criteria vary for different programs: These criteria differ by the program area.

Admissions Criteria:
GRE scores—high
Research experience—high
Work experience—high
Clinically related public service—high
GPA—high

Letters of recommendation—high
Interview—high
Statement of goals and objectives—high
Undergraduate psychology preparation—high

For additional information on admission requirements, visit http://psychology.cua.edu/admissions/index.cfm.

Department Demographics

	Male (PT)	Female (PT)	Total	African-American/ Black (PT)	Hispanic/ Latino (PT)	Asian/ Pacific Islander (PT)	American Indian/ Alaska Native (PT)	Caucasian/ White (PT)	Unknown	Multiethnic (PT)	ADA (PT)	Int'l (PT)
Students	18 (0)	62 (0)	80	1 (0)	9 (0)	11 (0)	0 (0)	56 (0)	1 (0)	2 (0)	1 (0)	5 (0)

Financial Information/Assistance

Tuition: For information on tuition costs, visit http://enrollmentservices.cua.edu/Student-Financial-Information/Costs.cfm. Tuition is subject to change. Additional fees are assessed to students beyond the costs of tuition for the following: Activities fees, new student fees, and others. Tuition costs vary by program.

Doctoral:
State residents: $41,400 per academic year.
State residents: $1,650 per credit hour.
Nonstate residents: $41,400 per academic year.
Nonstate residents: $1,650 per credit hour.

Master's:
State residents: $41,400 per academic year.
State residents: $1,650 per credit hour.
Nonstate residents: $41,400 per academic year.
Nonstate residents: $1,650 per credit hour.

Financial Assistance:

	Teaching Assistantship (% Receiving)	Teaching Assistantship Tuition Remission	Research Assistantship (% Receiving)	Research Assistantship Tuition Remission	Fellowship (% Receiving)	Fellowship Tuition Remission
First-Year Student	$2,000 (5)	Full	$18,000 (9)	Full	NA (32)	Full
Advanced Student	$9,376 (38)	Full	$18,000 (7)	Full	NA (29)	Full

Employment of Department Graduates

Master's:
Enrolled in a psychology doctoral program: 3
Employed in other positions at a higher education institution: 1
Do not know: 13
Total: 17

Doctoral:
Enrolled in a postdoctoral residency/fellowship: 2
Employed in independent practice: 2
Employed in an academic position at a university: 1
Employed in government agency: 3
Employed in a community mental health/counseling center: 1
Employed in a hospital/medical center: 2
Do not know: 2
Total: 13

Additional Information

Housing and Day Care: On-campus housing is available. See the following website for more information: http://housing.cua.edu/livingatcua/gradlaw.cfm. No on-campus day care facilities are available.

Information for Students With Physical Disabilities: See the following website: http://dss.cua.edu.

Application Information: Fee: $60. *Online application:* https://app.applyyourself.com/?id=cuagrad.

Albizu University

PhD in Clinical Psychology
2173 Northwest 99th Avenue
Miami, FL 33172
Telephone: (305) 593-1223
Program Director: Carlos Perez Benitez
Web: http://www.albizu.edu/Academics/Degrees-in-Psychology/Clinical-Psychology-Ph-D/Clinical-Psychology-PhD-Program-Miami-Campus

E-mail: cperezbenitez@albizu.edu

Orientation, Objectives, and Emphasis of Department

The goal of the PhD program is to train students as clinical researchers and practitioners who are able to understand and approach psychological problems from a scientific perspective and to create knowledge through theoretical and empirical research. Students will develop strong research and clinical skills and a sense of social responsibility that will enable them to meaningfully contribute to the advancement of the science and practice of clinical psychology. Students will be able to pursue academic, research, or clinical careers. Through our program, students will be able to: demonstrate a scientific understanding of normal and abnormal behaviors of humans, taking into consideration the cultural and historical contexts in which they live; demonstrate comprehensive skills in and knowledge of psychological assessments and interventions, while acknowledging the role biological, psychological, and socio-cultural factors play in human functioning; demonstrate the ability to conduct clinical research and integrate scientific findings into clinical practice; demonstrate a thorough knowledge of and ability to apply ethical principles to clinical research and practice; and identify and understand issues related to cultural diversity and individual differences as they affect clinical and research competencies.

Programs and Degrees Offered

Program	Degree	Application Deadline	Applica-tions Received	Accepted	New Admits Enrolled (PT)	Total Enrolled (PT)	Degrees Awarded in 2014–2015	Median Years to Complete Degree	Dismissed/ Withdrew
Clinical Psychology	PhD	December 1 (Fall)	0	0	0 (0)	0 (0)	0		0

Doctoral Degree (PhD Clinical Psychology): For those doctoral students for whom a professional internship was required in this program prior to graduation:
Total students who applied for an internship: 0
Total students who obtained an internship: 0
Total students who obtained a paid internship: 0
Total students who obtained an unpaid internship: 0
Total students who were placed in APA/CPA-accredited internships: 0
Total students placed in internships not APA/CPA-accredited, but listed with the Association of Psychology Postdoctoral and Internship Centers (APPIC): 0
Total students placed in internships conforming to guidelines of the Council of Directors of School Psychology Programs (CDSPP): 0
Total students placed in internships that were not APA/CPA-accredited, APPIC or CDSSP listed: 0

Internships/Practica

In the second semester of the first year, PhD students begin their clinical practicum experience at the Goodman Psychological Services Center, AU's on-campus training clinic. Under the supervision of a licensed clinical psychologist, students conduct comprehensive psychological assessments and provide group and individual interventions to low-income clients following the scientist–practitioner model of training, which integrates science and practice. Further on in the program, students provide clinical services to the culturally diverse population of South Florida at over 35 program-approved external practicum training sites, including major and community hospitals, community mental health centers, community agencies, correctional facilities, and private practice offices. At all sites, students are directly supervised by licensed clinical psychologists. PhD students are also required to complete a predoctoral clinical internship during the fifth year of training. Students can apply for competitive internships nationwide at medical schools, community mental health centers, VA hospitals, university counseling centers, private hospitals, federal or state prisons, state psychiatric hospitals, and other training sites.

Admissions

Entries appear in the following order: required test or GPA, minimum score (if required)/median score of students entering in 2015–2016.

Program	Degree	GRE-V	GRE-Q	GRE-Writing	GRE-Subject	Under-graduate GPA	Last 2 Years GPA	Psychol-ogy GPA	Master's GPA
Clinical Psychology	PhD	Not specified	Not specified	Not specified	Not specified	Not specified	Not specified	Not specified	Not specified

Admissions Requirements:

Degree	GRE	GRE-Subject	Letters of Recom-mendation	Research Statement	Writing Sample	CV	Interview
Doctoral	Required	Required	2	Required	Optional	Required	Required

Admissions Criteria:

GRE scores—medium
Research experience—high
Work experience—medium
Clinically related public service—low
GPA—high

Letters of recommendation—high
Interview—high
Statement of goals and objectives—high
Undergraduate psychology preparation—high

Department Demographics

	Male (PT)	Female (PT)	Total	African-American/ Black (PT)	Hispanic/ Latino (PT)	Asian/ Pacific Islander (PT)	American Indian/ Alaska Native (PT)	Caucasian/ White (PT)	Unknown	Multiethnic (PT)	ADA (PT)	Int'l (PT)
Students	0 (0)	0 (0)	0	0 (0)	0 (0)	0 (0)	0 (0)	0 (0)	0 (0)	0 (0)	0 (0)	0 (0)

Financial Information/Assistance

Tuition: For information on tuition costs, visit http://www.albizu.edu/Finance/Tuition-and-Fees.

Doctoral:
State residents: $15,000 per academic year.
State residents: $750 per credit hour.
Nonstate residents: $15,000 per academic year.
Nonstate residents: $750 per credit hour.

Financial Assistance:

	Teaching Assistantship (% Receiving)	Teaching Assistantship Tuition Remission	Research Assistantship (% Receiving)	Research Assistantship Tuition Remission	Fellowship (% Receiving)	Fellowship Tuition Remission
First-Year Student	NA (NA)	NA	NA (NA)	NA	NA (NA)	NA
Advanced Student	$6,000 (NA)	NA	NA (NA)	NA	NA (NA)	NA

For additional information on financial assistance, visit http://www.albizu.edu/Admissions-and-Aid/Financial-Aid.

Employment of Department Graduates

No information provided.

Additional Information

Housing and Day Care: No on-campus housing is available. No on-campus day care facilities are available.

Special Facilities or Resources: The University has contracts with teaching hospitals in the area as well as community centers. The university is currently allocating more funds to conduct behavioral research.

Application Information: Albizu University (Miami Campus), Admissions Office, 2173 NW 99th Avenue, Suite 150, Miami, FL 33172. *Fee:* $50. *Online application:* https://apply.albizu.edu.

Barry University

Department of Psychology
College of Arts and Sciences
11300 Northeast 2nd Avenue
Miami Shores, FL 33161
Telephone: (305) 899-3270
Chairperson: Frank Muscarella, PhD

E-mail: fmuscarella@barry.edu
Web: https://www.barry.edu/psychology/clinical-psychology/

Orientation, Objectives, and Emphasis of Department

In the MS Clinical Psychology Program, students are expected to achieve competence in theory, assessment, therapy, and research. All clinical psychology students complete a thesis and a clinical practicum. Students who complete the 3-year, 60-credit program meet educational requirements for licensure as a Mental Health Counselor in Florida. In the third year these students complete a internship of 20 hours per week. The 36-credit option, a 2-year program, is the core of the 60-credit program. Students may opt to graduate with 36 credits if they are accepted into doctoral programs or make other career plan changes.

Programs and Degrees Offered

Program	Degree	Application Deadline	Applications Received	Accepted	New Admits Enrolled (PT)	Total Enrolled (PT)	Degrees Awarded in 2014–2015	Median Years to Complete Degree	Dismissed/ Withdrew
Clinical Psychology	MA/MS	February 15 (Fall)	60	20	10 (0)	30 (5)	10	3	0

Internships/Practica

All students enrolled in the MS Clinical Psychology program must complete a one-semester clinical practicum of 10 hours per week. Students in the 60-credit program must also complete a 50-week clinical internship of 20 hours per week. Because Barry University is located in a large, multi-cultural metropolitan area, the program is able to offer a significant number and variety of settings for the practicum and internship experiences. Sites include but are not limited to community mental health centers, assessment centers (primarily for the assessment of children), psychiatric hospitals, addiction treatment programs, geriatric in-home settings, forensic settings, and private practice settings. Supervision is provided both at the site and by a clinical supervisor on campus.

Admissions

Entries appear in the following order: required test or GPA, minimum score (if required)/median score of students entering in 2015–2016.

Program	Degree	GRE-V	GRE-Q	GRE-Writing	GRE-Subject	Under-graduate GPA	Last 2 Years GPA	Psychology GPA	Master's GPA
Clinical Psychology	MA/MS	NA/NA	NA/NA	NA/NA	Not specified	3/NA	Not specified	Not specified	Not specified

Admissions Requirements:

Degree	GRE	GRE-Subject	Letters of Recom-mendation	Research Statement	Writing Sample	CV	Interview
Master's/Specialist	Required	None	2	Required	Optional	Optional	None

Please note if these criteria vary for different programs: We look for verbal, quantitative, and analytical writing GRE scores at or above the 50th percentile.

Admissions Criteria:

GRE scores—medium
Research experience—low
Work experience—low
Clinically related public service—low

GPA—high
Letters of recommendation—high
Statement of goals and objectives—high
Undergraduate psychology preparation—medium

For additional information on admission requirements, visit http://www.barry.edu/psychology/clinical-psychology/admissions/admission-requirements.html.

Department Demographics

	Male (PT)	Female (PT)	Total	African-American/ Black (PT)	Hispanic/ Latino (PT)	Asian/ Pacific Islander (PT)	American Indian/ Alaska Native (PT)	Caucasian/ White (PT)	Unknown	Multiethnic (PT)	ADA (PT)	Int'l (PT)
Students	2 (1)	28 (4)	35	7 (0)	10 (1)	0 (0)	0 (0)	13 (4)	0 (0)	0 (0)	0 (0)	2 (0)

Financial Information/Assistance

Tuition: For information on tuition costs, visit http://www.barry.edu/psychology/clinical-psychology/admissions/tuition-fees.html. Tuition is subject to change.

Master's:
State residents: $990 per credit hour.
Nonstate residents: $990 per credit hour.

Financial Assistance:

	Teaching Assistantship (% Receiving)	Teaching Assistantship Tuition Remission	Research Assistantship (% Receiving)	Research Assistantship Tuition Remission	Fellowship (% Receiving)	Fellowship Tuition Remission
First-Year Student	$3,000 (20)	Partial	NA (NA)	NA	NA (NA)	NA
Advanced Student	$3,000 (20)	Partial	NA (NA)	NA	NA (NA)	NA

For additional information on financial assistance, visit http://www.barry.edu/psychology/clinical-psychology/financial-aid/.

Employment of Department Graduates

Master's:
Enrolled in a psychology doctoral program: 2
Employed in a community mental health/counseling center: 3
Employed in a hospital/medical center: 1
Other employment position: 4
Total: 10

Additional Information

Housing and Day Care: No on-campus housing is available. No on-campus day care facilities are available.

Information for Students With Physical Disabilities: See the following website: http://www.barry.edu/disability-services/.

Special Facilities or Resources: The Psychology Department has 8 full-time faculty members. The classes are small and offered in the evening to accommodate students' work schedules. There is a graduate student lab with computers and a printer and three observation rooms for clinical practice and training. A large-format printer is also available. The Department holds the Annual

Psychology Student Research Forum to showcase graduate student master's thesis research, encourages research presentations in professional venues, and provides some financial support for students who present their research at professional conferences.

Application Information: Office of Graduate Admissions, Barry University, 11300 NE 2nd Avenue, Miami Shores, FL 33161. *Fee:* $30. *Online application:* http://www.barry.edu/future-students/graduate/admissions/.

Central Florida, University of
Department of Psychology
College of Sciences
P.O. Box 161390
Orlando, FL 32816-1390
Telephone: (407) 823-4601
Chairperson: Jeffrey E. Cassisi, PhD

E-mail: psyinfo@ucf.edu
Web: http://psychology.cos.ucf.edu/

Orientation, Objectives, and Emphasis of Department
The PhD program in clinical psychology is an APA-accredited program, designed for individuals seeking a research-oriented career in the field of clinical psychology. The program also emphasizes training in consultation, teaching, supervision, and the design/evaluation of mental health programs. The MA program in clinical psychology has major emphases in assessment and evaluation skills; intervention, counseling, and psychotherapy skills; and an academic foundation in research methods. The program is designed to provide training and preparation for persons desiring to deliver clinical services at the master's level through community agencies. Graduates of this program meet the educational requirements for the mental health counselor state license. The MS program in Industrial/Organizational (I/O) psychology has major emphases in selection and training of employees, applied theories of organizational behavior, job satisfaction, test theory and construction; assessment center technology, statistics and experimental design. I/O students receive training in the 21 competence areas detailed by APA Division 14. The PhD program in applied experiment/human factors is patterned on the APA scientist–practitioner. It adheres to the guidelines for education and training established by the committee for Education and Training of APA's Division 21 (Applied Experimental and Engineering Psychology).

Programs and Degrees Offered

Program	Degree	Application Deadline	Applications Received	Accepted	New Admits Enrolled (PT)	Total Enrolled (PT)	Degrees Awarded in 2014–2015	Median Years to Complete Degree	Dismissed/Withdrew
Clinical Psychology	MA/MS	January 1 (Fall)	150	25	14	29	15	2	1
Industrial/ Organizational Psychology	MA/MS	January 15 (Fall)	135	32	13	28	18	2	0
Applied Experimental and Human Factors	PhD	December 15 (Fall)	51	7	7 (0)	47 (0)	7	7	3
Clinical Psychology	PhD	December 1 (Fall)	126	7	6 (0)	37 (0)	6	7	2
Industrial/ Organizational Psychology	PhD	December 15 (Fall)	108	10	5 (0)	28 (0)	6	5	2

APA Accreditation
Clinical PhD: Student Outcome Data website: http://psychology.cos.ucf.edu/graduate/ph-d-clinical/.

Doctoral Degree (PhD Clinical Psychology): For those doctoral students for whom a professional internship was required in this program prior to graduation:
Total students who applied for an internship: 7
Total students who obtained an internship: 7
Total students who obtained a paid internship: 7
Total students who obtained an unpaid internship: 0

Total students who were placed in APA/CPA-accredited internships: 6
Total students placed in internships not APA/CPA-accredited, but listed with the Association of Psychology Postdoctoral and Internship Centers (APPIC): 1
Total students placed in internships conforming to guidelines of the Council of Directors of School Psychology Programs (CDSPP): 0
Total students placed in internships that were not APA/CPA-accredited, APPIC or CDSSP listed: 0

Master's Degree (MA/MS Clinical Psychology): An internship experience, such as a final research project or "capstone" experience is required of graduates. Master's Degree (MA/MS Industrial/Organizational Psychology): An internship experience, such as a final research project or "capstone" experience is required of graduates.

Internships/Practica

Internships for clinical Master's students exist in community mental health centers and other agencies throughout Central Florida. Doctoral students complete their practica in our on-campus clinic as well as in a variety of community based clinical agencies. Human Factors students complete internships in a variety of government, business, and industry settings. I/O Master's students complete practicum placements in a variety of government, business and industry settings. Doctoral students complete an internship in a variety of business, industry and government settings.

Admissions

Entries appear in the following order: required test or GPA, minimum score (if required)/median score of students entering in 2015–2016.

Program	Degree	GRE-V	GRE-Q	GRE-Writing	GRE-Subject	Under-graduate GPA	Last 2 Years GPA	Psychology GPA	Master's GPA
Clinical Psychology	MA/MS	Not specified	Not specified	Not specified	Not specified	Not specified	Not specified	Not specified	Not specified
Industrial/ Organizational Psychology	MA/MS	150/155	152/154	Not specified	Not specified	3/3.5	Not specified	Not specified	Not specified
Applied Experimental and Human Factors	PhD	155/160	151/156	Not specified	Not specified	2.8/3.7	2.9/3.7	NA/NA	NA/NA
Clinical Psychology	PhD	155/159	146/154	Not specified	Not specified	3.5/3.75	Not specified	Not specified	Not specified
Industrial/ Organizational Psychology	PhD	157/161	154/157	Not specified	Not specified	3/3.4	NA/NA	NA/NA	Not specified

Admissions Requirements:

Degree	GRE	GRE-Subject	Letters of Recom-mendation	Research Statement	Writing Sample	CV	Interview
Master's/Specialist	Required	None	3	Required	Optional	Required	Required
Doctoral	Required	Required	3	Required	Optional	Required	Required

Please note if these criteria vary for different programs: Criteria vary by program. Only the Clinical PhD requires the GRE-Subject test. Clinical MA program requires an interview; I/O Master's does not.

Admissions Criteria:

GRE scores—high
Research experience—high
Work experience—low
Clinically related public service—medium
GPA—high

Letters of recommendation—high
Interview—high
Statement of goals and objectives—high
Undergraduate psychology preparation—medium

For additional information on admission requirements, visit https://psychology.cos.ucf.edu/graduate/.

Department Demographics

	Male (PT)	Female (PT)	Total	African-American/ Black (PT)	Hispanic/ Latino (PT)	Asian/ Pacific Islander (PT)	American Indian/ Alaska Native (PT)	Caucasian/ White (PT)	Unknown (PT)	Multiethnic (PT)	ADA (PT)	Int'l (PT)
Students	58 (0)	111 (0)	169	12 (0)	14 (0)	15 (0)	2 (0)	119 (0)	4 (0)	3 (0)	1 (0)	5 (0)

Financial Information/Assistance

Tuition: For information on tuition costs, visit http://tuitionfees.ikm.ucf.edu/. Tuition is subject to change. Additional fees are assessed to students beyond the costs of tuition for the following: additional fees are up to $100 depending on course.

Doctoral:
State residents: $8,068 per academic year.
State residents: $288 per credit hour.
Nonstate residents: $30,052 per academic year.
Nonstate residents: $1,073 per credit hour.

Master's:
State residents: $288 per credit hour.
Nonstate residents: $1,073 per credit hour.

Financial Assistance:

	Teaching Assistantship (% Receiving)	Teaching Assistantship Tuition Remission	Research Assistantship (% Receiving)	Research Assistantship Tuition Remission	Fellowship (% Receiving)	Fellowship Tuition Remission
First-Year Student	$12,000 (NA)	Full	$15,000 (NA)	Full	$13,500 (NA)	Full
Advanced Student	$12,000 (NA)	Full	$15,000 (NA)	Full	$13,500 (NA)	Full

For additional information on financial assistance, visit https://funding.graduate.ucf.edu/.

Employment of Department Graduates

Master's:
Enrolled in a psychology doctoral program: 4
Enrolled in another graduate/professional program: 1
Employed in other positions at a higher education institution: 1
Employed in business or industry: 13
Employed in government agency: 3
Employed in a community mental health/counseling center: 5
Employed in a hospital/medical center: 2
Other employment position: 2
Do not know: 2
Total: 33

Doctoral:
Enrolled in a postdoctoral residency/fellowship: 2
Employed in independent practice: 1
Employed in an academic position at a university: 4
Employed in other positions at a higher education institution: 2
Employed in business or industry: 3
Employed in government agency: 4
Employed in a hospital/medical center: 1
Still seeking employment: 1
Total: 18

Additional Information

Housing and Day Care: On-campus housing is available. See the following website for more information: http://www.housing.ucf.edu/. On-campus day care facilities are available. See the following website for more information: http://csc.sdes.ucf.edu/.

Information for Students With Physical Disabilities: See the following website: http://sds.sdes.ucf.edu/.

Special Facilities or Resources: The department's facilities and resources include extensive videotape capability, an intelligence and personality testing library, a statistics library, computer facilities within the department and in the computer center, a counseling and testing center, a creative school for children, and a communicative disorders clinic. Doctoral students have use of specialized equipment in the department-based Human Visual Performance Laboratory and Team Performance Laboratory. The clinical program has extensive ties to a number of community agencies for practica and assistantships as well as an on-site clinic.

Application Information: University of Central Florida, Department of Psychology-Attn: Graduate Admissions, P.O. Box 161390, Orlando, FL 32816-1390. *Fee:* $31. *Online application:* https://application.graduate.ucf.edu/.

Florida Atlantic University

Psychology
Charles E. Schmidt College of Science
777 Glades Road, P.O. Box 3091
Boca Raton, FL 33431-0991
Telephone: (561) 297-3360
Chairperson: David L. Wolgin

E-mail: laursen@fau.edu
Web: http://www.psy.fau.edu

Orientation, Objectives, and Emphasis of Department

The PhD program emphasizes research in several areas of experimental psychology. Students may select courses and conduct research in five areas: cognitive psychology, developmental psychology, evolutionary psychology, psychobiology/neuroscience, and social/personality psychology. Current research by faculty includes psycholinguistics, sentence processing, visual perception, and speech production and perception; the role of parent and peer relationships in individual adaptation; the relation between tool use and style of play in preschool children; mental synchronization in social interaction; neural mechanisms in recovery of function from brain damage, psychopharmacology, and nonlinear dynamics of brain and behavior; the use of traits to predict behavior, sex differences in mating, domestic violence, and the dynamics of social influence. The MA program is designed to prepare students for entry into doctoral-level programs in all areas of psychology. Research in developmental psychology uses a campus laboratory school for children in kindergarten through the eighth grade. Research in social/personality psychology uses laboratories with video and online computer facilities. The cognitive psychology laboratories include testing rooms with a network of PCs for online control of experiments in perception, learning, language, and cognition. The EEG laboratory includes an acoustic isolation chamber and a variety of amplifying and recording systems.

Programs and Degrees Offered

Program	Degree	Application Deadline	Applications Received	Accepted	New Admits Enrolled (PT)	Total Enrolled (PT)	Degrees Awarded in 2014–2015	Median Years to Complete Degree	Dismissed/ Withdrew
General-Experimental Psychology	MA/MS	May 1 (Fall)	70	20	10 (0)	23 (0)	10	2	6
Experimental Psychology	PhD	January 10 (Fall)	42	13	8 (0)	34 (7)	6	5.5	0

Admissions

Entries appear in the following order: required test or GPA, minimum score (if required)/median score of students entering in 2015–2016.

Program	Degree	GRE-V	GRE-Q	GRE-Writing	GRE-Subject	Undergraduate GPA	Last 2 Years GPA	Psychology GPA	Master's GPA
General-Experimental Psychology	MA/MS	150/NA	150/NA	Not specified	Not specified	Not specified	3/NA	Not specified	Not specified
Experimental Psychology	PhD	153/157	152/156	Not specified	Not specified	Not specified	3/NA	Not specified	Not specified

Admissions Requirements:

Degree	GRE	GRE-Subject	Letters of Recommendation	Research Statement	Writing Sample	CV	Interview
Master's/Specialist	Required	None	3	Required	None	None	None
Doctoral	Required	None	3	Required	None	None	None

Admissions Criteria:

GRE scores—high   Letters of recommendation—medium

Research experience—high

Statement of goals and objectives—high

Clinically related public service—low

Undergraduate psychology preparation—medium

GPA—high

For additional information on admission requirements, visit http://www.psy.fau.edu/graduate/ApplicationInfo.html.

Department Demographics

	Male (PT)	Female (PT)	Total	African-American/ Black (PT)	Hispanic/ Latino (PT)	Asian/ Pacific Islander (PT)	American Indian/ Alaska Native (PT)	Caucasian/ White (PT)	Unknown (PT)	Multiethnic (PT)	ADA (PT)	Int'l (PT)
Students	27 (0)	30 (0)	57	2 (0)	12 (0)	5 (0)	0 (0)	38 (0)	0 (0)	0 (0)	0 (0)	2 (0)

Financial Information/Assistance

Tuition: For information on tuition costs, visit http://www.fau.edu/controller/student_information/tuition_breakdown.php. Tuition is subject to change.

Doctoral:
State residents: $370 per credit hour.
Nonstate residents: $1,025 per credit hour.

Master's:
State residents: $370 per credit hour.
Nonstate residents: $1,025 per credit hour.

Financial Assistance:

	Teaching Assistantship (% Receiving)	Teaching Assistantship Tuition Remission	Research Assistantship (% Receiving)	Research Assistantship Tuition Remission	Fellowship (% Receiving)	Fellowship Tuition Remission
First-Year Student	$20,050 (90)	Partial	$20,050 (10)	Partial	$5,000 (30)	Partial
Advanced Student	$20,050 (90)	Partial	$20,050 (10)	Partial	$25,000 (10)	Partial

For additional information on financial assistance, visit www.fau.edu/finaid/getting-started/graduate-student.php.

Employment of Department Graduates

Master's:
Enrolled in a psychology doctoral program: 6
Enrolled in another graduate/professional program: 4
Employed in business or industry: 2
Employed in government agency: 1
Employed in a community mental health/counseling center: 2
Do not know: 2
Total: 17

Doctoral:
Enrolled in a postdoctoral residency/fellowship: 2
Employed in academic position at a 2-year/4-year college: 3
Employed in other positions at a higher education institution: 1
Total: 6

Additional Information

Housing and Day Care: On-campus housing is available. See the following website for more information: http://www.fau.edu/housing/. On-campus day care facilities are available. See the following website for more information: http://www.coe.fau.edu/SchoolAndK12Programs/ERCCD/.

Information for Students With Physical Disabilities: See the following website: http://www.fau.edu/sas/.

Special Facilities or Resources: Faculty in the Department of Psychology collaborate with scholars at the FAU Center for Complex Systems and Brain Sciences, the Max Planck Florida Institute, and the Torrey Pines Institute for Molecular Studies.

Application Information: Fee: $30. *Online application:* http://www.fau.edu/graduate/applyonline/index.php.

Florida Institute of Technology
School of Behavior Analysis
College of Psychology and Liberal Arts
150 West University Boulevard
Melbourne, FL 32901
Telephone: (321) 674-8372
Dean: Mary Beth Kenkel

E-mail: mwilbrandt@fit.edu
Web: http://cpla.fit.edu/aba/

Orientation, Objectives, and Emphasis of Department
The School of Behavior Analysis within the College of Psychology and Liberal Arts at Florida Institute of Technology offers MS and PhD in Behavior Analysis, MS in Organizational Behavior Management (OBM). The master's program in Applied Behavior Analysis (ABA) prepares graduates for employment in a variety of clinical settings. Upon graduation, students from the ABA program meet all the educational and supervised practicum requirements to seek certification as a BCBA. The Organizational Behavior Management MS program prepares behavior analysts for work as consultants in business/industry. The Behavior Analysis PhD program prepares students for teaching and research careers as well as senior supervising roles in treatment settings.

Programs and Degrees Offered

Program	Degree	Application Deadline	Applica-tions Received	Accepted	New Admits Enrolled (PT)	Total Enrolled (PT)	Degrees Awarded in 2014–2015	Median Years to Complete Degree	Dismissed/ Withdrew
Applied Behavior Analysis	MA/MS	February 15 (Fall)	81	51	26 (0)	63 (0)	15	2	1
Organizational Behavior Management	MA/MS	February 15 (Fall)	7	2	2 (0)	2 (0)	2	2.25	0
ABA + OBM	MA/MS	February 15 (Fall)	25	14	7 (0)	15 (0)	6	2.25	0
Behavior Analysis	PhD	January 15 (Fall)	30	4	4 (0)	13 (0)	3	3.25	0
Professional Behavior Analysis	MA/MS	June 15 (Fall), October 1 (Spring), March 1 (Summer), Rolling	145	134	134 (0)	124 (0)	14	2.5	10

Internships/Practica
The Applied Behavior Analysis program has practicum opportunities at Florida Tech's Scott Center for Autism Treatment, as well as other agencies working with children with developmental disabilities, serious emotional and behavioral disorders and autism. Students receive on-site supervision as well as ancillary supervision by program faculty. The (OBM) program has internships with local businesses and social service agencies.

Admissions
Entries appear in the following order: required test or GPA, minimum score (if required)/median score of students entering in 2015–2016.

Program	Degree	GRE-V	GRE-Q	GRE-Writing	GRE-Subject	Under-graduate GPA	Last 2 Years GPA	Psychol-ogy GPA	Master's GPA
Applied Behavior Analysis	MA/MS	Not specified	Not specified	Not specified	Not specified	Not specified	Not specified	Not specified	Not specified
Organizational Behavior Management	MA/MS	Not specified	Not specified	Not specified	Not specified	Not specified	Not specified	Not specified	Not specified

Admissions *(con't.)*

Program	Degree	GRE-V	GRE-Q	GRE-Writing	GRE-Subject	Under-graduate GPA	Last 2 Years GPA	Psychology GPA	Master's GPA
ABA + OBM	MA/MS	Not specified	Not specified	Not specified	Not specified	Not specified	Not specified	Not specified	Not specified
Behavior Analysis	PhD	Not specified	Not specified	Not specified	Not specified	Not specified	Not specified	Not specified	Not specified
Professional Behavior Analysis	MA/MS	Not specified	Not specified	Not specified	Not specified	Not specified	Not specified	Not specified	Not specified

Admissions Requirements:

Degree	GRE	GRE-Subject	Letters of Recommendation	Research Statement	Writing Sample	CV	Interview
Master's/Specialist	Required	None	3	Required	Required	Required	None
Doctoral	Required	None	3	Required	Required	Required	None

Please note if these criteria vary for different programs: Master of Arts degree program only requires three letters of recommendation, CV/resume, personal statement.

Admissions Criteria:

GRE scores—high
Research experience—low
Work experience—low
GPA—high

Letters of recommendation—high
Statement of goals and objectives—medium
Undergraduate psychology preparation—medium

Department Demographics

	Male (PT)	Female (PT)	Total	African-American/ Black (PT)	Hispanic/ Latino (PT)	Asian/ Pacific Islander (PT)	American Indian/ Alaska Native (PT)	Caucasian/ White (PT)	Unknown	Multiethnic (PT)	ADA (PT)	Int'l (PT)
Students	38 (0)	179 (0)	217	4 (0)	34 (0)	15 (0)	1 (0)	147 (0)	4 (0)	12 (0)	2 (0)	7 (0)

Financial Information/Assistance

Tuition: For information on tuition costs, visit http://www.fit.edu/registrar/registration/tuitionchrgs.php. Higher tuition cost for this program: Melbourne campus MS in Applied Behavior Analysis. Tuition costs vary by program.

Doctoral:
State residents: $21,690 per academic year.
State residents: $1,205 per credit hour.
Nonstate residents: $21,690 per academic year.
Nonstate residents: $1,205 per credit hour.

Master's:
State residents: $19,425 per academic year.
State residents: $925 per credit hour.
Nonstate residents: $19,425 per academic year.
Nonstate residents: $925 per credit hour.

Financial Assistance:

	Teaching Assistantship (% Receiving)	Teaching Assistantship Tuition Remission	Research Assistantship (% Receiving)	Research Assistantship Tuition Remission	Fellowship (% Receiving)	Fellowship Tuition Remission
First-Year Student	$4,000 (NA)	Partial	$4,000 (NA)	Partial	$10,500 (6)	Partial
Advanced Student	$4,000 (0)	Partial	$4,000 (13)	Partial	$8,000 (0)	Partial

For additional information on financial assistance, visit http://www.fit.edu/financialaid/.

Employment of Department Graduates

Master's:
Enrolled in a psychology doctoral program: 1
Enrolled in another graduate/professional program: 5
Employed in other positions at a higher education institution: 3
Employed in a professional position in a school system: 2
Employed in business or industry: 18
Employed in a community mental health/counseling center: 14
Other employment position: 12
Do not know: 4
Total: 59

Doctoral:
Enrolled in a postdoctoral residency/fellowship: 2
Employed in independent practice: 2
Employed in an academic position at a university: 2
Total: 6

Additional Information

Housing and Day Care: On-campus housing is available. See the following website for more information: http://www.fit.edu/housing/. No on-campus day care facilities are available.

Information for Students With Physical Disabilities: See the following website: http://www.fit.edu/disability/.

Special Facilities or Resources: The facilities of the School of Behavior Analysis include offices, classrooms, student meeting and work areas, research labs and computer labs in the new (2012) Florida Tech Commons facility. Additionally the Scott Center houses all the clinical services operations of the School. It includes facilities for autism treatment as well as general psychological services, including early intervention rooms, observation rooms, rooms for treatment of severe behavior problems and feeding problems, group training room, and group and individual treatment rooms. The University's Academic Computing Services-Microcenter provides computers and software, media conversion, digital graphic assistance, and professional editing of theses and papers for publication.

Application Information: Office of Graduate Admissions. *Fee:* $50. *Online application:* http://info.fit.edu/grad-apply-online.

Florida Institute of Technology
School of Psychology
College of Psychology and Liberal Arts
150 West University Boulevard
Melbourne, FL 32901-6988
Telephone: (321) 674-8104
Dean, College of Psychology and Liberal Arts: Mary Beth Kenkel

E-mail: mkenkel@fit.edu
Web: http://cpla.fit.edu/psych/

Orientation, Objectives, and Emphasis of Department
The School of Psychology at Florida Institute of Technology offers MS and PhD in Industrial/Organizational (I/O) Psychology, and PsyD in Clinical Psychology. The clinical PsyD program trains students based on a practitioner/scientist model focused on development of clinical skills. The program incorporates multiple theoretical orientations and has emphases in neuropsychology, integrated behavioral health psychology, child and family therapy, and forensic psychology. In the I/O Psychology program, students are trained in the scientist/practitioner framework in the core I/O content areas of personnel testing and selection, performance appraisal, motivation and emotion at work, and group and team processes. The program also has an elective concentration in international I/O psychology. Students also gain skills in advanced statistics and research methods in order to conduct organizational research. The program prepares graduates for a wide variety of careers in consulting and academics.

Programs and Degrees Offered

Program	Degree	Application Deadline	Applications Received	Accepted	New Admits Enrolled (PT)	Total Enrolled (PT)	Degrees Awarded in 2014–2015	Median Years to Complete Degree	Dismissed/ Withdrew
Clinical Psychology	PsyD	January 15 (Fall)	173	46	21 (0)	95 (1)	12	5	1
Industrial/ Organizational Psychology	MA/MS	January 15 (Fall)	96	17	8 (0)	14 (0)	11	2	0

Programs and Degrees Offered *(con't.)*

Program	Degree	Application Deadline	Applications Received	Accepted	New Admits Enrolled (PT)	Total Enrolled (PT)	Degrees Awarded in 2014–2015	Median Years to Complete Degree	Dismissed/ Withdrew
Industrial/ Organizational Psychology	PhD	January 15 (Fall)	78	23	7 (0)	29 (2)	3	5	0

APA Accreditation

Clinical PsyD: Student Outcome Data website: http://cpla.fit.edu/clinical/outcomes.php.

Doctoral Degree (PsyD Clinical Psychology): For those doctoral students for whom a professional internship was required in this program prior to graduation:
Total students who applied for an internship: 16
Total students who obtained an internship: 15
Total students who obtained a paid internship: 15
Total students who obtained an unpaid internship: 0
Total students who were placed in APA/CPA-accredited internships: 14
Total students placed in internships not APA/CPA-accredited, but listed with the Association of Psychology Postdoctoral and Internship Centers (APPIC): 1
Total students placed in internships conforming to guidelines of the Council of Directors of School Psychology Programs (CDSPP): 0
Total students placed in internships that were not APA/CPA-accredited, APPIC or CDSSP listed: 0

Internships/Practica

Students in the PsyD program complete a sequence of three or more separate practicum placements prior to internship. These include Florida Tech's Community Psychological Services Center and options at other outpatient and inpatient facilities. Inpatient sites include adult psychiatric hospitals, rehabilitation hospitals, children and adolescent inpatient units, behavioral medicine units within a medical hospital and prison setting. Outpatient sites include mental health centers, private practice settings, VA outpatient clinics, primary care clinics, and neuropsychological practices. Students gain experience in assessment and treatment of individuals, groups, couples, and families, in consultation and psychoeducational presentations. Treatment specialties include neuropsychology, aging, sexual abuse, domestic violence, PTSD, and behavioral health. The I/O program has ties to local business. Students are placed in a wide range of practicum sites including county and federal departments, aerospace and electronics industries, financial institutions, health care organizations, and management consulting firms.

Admissions

Entries appear in the following order: required test or GPA, minimum score (if required)/median score of students entering in 2015–2016.

Program	Degree	GRE-V	GRE-Q	GRE-Writing	GRE-Subject	Under-graduate GPA	Last 2 Years GPA	Psychology GPA	Master's GPA
Clinical Psychology	PsyD	NA/155	NA/150	NA/4	Not specified	3/3.62	NA/3.71	NA/3.62	3.2/3.94
Industrial/ Organizational Psychology	MA/MS	NA/155	NA/154	NA/4	Not specified	3/3.55	NA/3.77	NA/3.76	Not specified
Industrial/ Organizational Psychology	PhD	NA/154	NA/153	NA/4	Not specified	3/3.59	NA/3.56	NA/3.62	3.2/4

Admissions Requirements:

Degree	GRE	GRE-Subject	Letters of Recom-mendation	Research Statement	Writing Sample	CV	Interview
Master's/Specialist	Required	None	3	Required	Required	Required	None
Doctoral	Required	Recom-mended	3	Required	Required	Required	Recom-mended

Please note if these criteria vary for different programs: Only the Clinical PsyD program has an interview that is recommended. Only Clinical PsyD program recommends subject GRE scores.

Admissions Criteria:

GRE scores—medium
Research experience—medium
Work experience—high
Clinically related public service—high
GPA—high

Letters of recommendation—high
Interview—medium
Statement of goals and objectives—medium
Undergraduate psychology preparation—medium

Department Demographics

	Male (PT)	Female (PT)	Total	African-American/ Black (PT)	Hispanic/ Latino (PT)	Asian/ Pacific Islander (PT)	American Indian/ Alaska Native (PT)	Caucasian/ White (PT)	Unknown	Multiethnic (PT)	ADA (PT)	Int'l (PT)
Students	31 (1)	107 (2)	141	7 (0)	7 (0)	11 (0)	1 (0)	105 (3)	1 (0)	6 (0)	5 (0)	10 (0)

Financial Information/Assistance

Tuition: For information on tuition costs, visit http://www.fit.edu/registrar/registration/tuitionchrgs.php. Higher tuition cost for this program: PsyD program charges a flat $29,430 yearly tuition. Tuition is subject to change. Tuition costs vary by program.

Doctoral:
State residents: $33,507 per academic year.
State residents: $1,241 per credit hour.
Nonstate residents: $33,507 per academic year.
Nonstate residents: $1,241 per credit hour.

Master's:
State residents: $1,241 per credit hour.
Nonstate residents: $1,241 per credit hour.

Financial Assistance:

	Teaching Assistantship (% Receiving)	Teaching Assistantship Tuition Remission	Research Assistantship (% Receiving)	Research Assistantship Tuition Remission	Fellowship (% Receiving)	Fellowship Tuition Remission
First-Year Student	NA (NA)	NA	NA (NA)	NA	$7,000 (NA)	Partial
Advanced Student	$8,000 (NA)	NA	$4,000 (NA)	NA	$4,000 (NA)	Partial

For additional information on financial assistance, visit http://admission.fit.edu/graduate/university-aid.php.

Employment of Department Graduates

Master's:
Enrolled in a psychology doctoral program: 9
Employed in business or industry: 2
Total: 11

Doctoral:
Enrolled in a postdoctoral residency/fellowship: 8
Employed in independent practice: 1
Employed in business or industry: 1
Employed in government agency: 3
Other employment position: 1
Do not know: 1
Total: 15

Additional Information

Housing and Day Care: On-campus housing is available. See the following website for more information: http://www.fit.edu/housing/. No on-campus day care facilities are available.

Information for Students With Physical Disabilities: See the following website: http://www.fit.edu/disability/.

Special Facilities or Resources: The facilities of the School of Psychology include offices, classrooms, student work and meeting areas, research labs and computer labs in the new (2012) Florida Tech Commons facility. Additionally, the Scott Center houses all the clinical service operations of the School. It includes facilities for autism treatment as well as general psychological services, including early intervention rooms, observation rooms, play therapy rooms, and group and individual treatment rooms. A separate Neuropsychology Lab is also available. The University's Academic Computing Services-Microcenter provides computers and software, media conversion, digital graphic assistance, and professional editing of theses and papers for publication. Additionally, students receive training and conduct research in several community service programs operated by the School of Psychology. These include the Center for Organizational Effectiveness, a campus-based I/O consulting and research organization; East Central Florida Memory Clinic, through a contract with Holmes Regional Medical Center serves individuals with memory disorders by providing memory screenings, case management, education, wellness and support groups; and the Family Learning Program, which offers psychological assessment and treatment to child victims of sexual abuse and their family members.

Application Information: Florida Institute of Technology, Office of Graduate Admissions, 150 West University Boulevard, Melbourne, FL 32901. *Fee:* $60. *Online application:* http://info.fit.edu/grad-apply-online.

Florida International University
Psychology
Arts and Sciences
11200 SW 8th Street
Miami, FL 33199
Telephone: (305) 348-2880
Chairperson: William Pelham

E-mail: wpelham@fiu.edu
Web: http://psychology.fiu.edu/

Orientation, Objectives, and Emphasis of Department
The mission of the Department of Psychology at Florida International University is to create new knowledge about human behavior, apply what is known to improve the human condition, and educate and train students. Our graduate programs are designed to foster a commitment both to basic research and application as an integral part of the student's specialty area.

Programs and Degrees Offered

Program	Degree	Application Deadline	Applications Received	Accepted	New Admits Enrolled (PT)	Total Enrolled (PT)	Degrees Awarded in 2014–2015	Median Years to Complete Degree	Dismissed/ Withdrew
Developmental Science	PhD	December 15 (Fall)	15	8	5	18	9	5	0
Industrial/ Organizational Psychology	PhD	December 15 (Fall)	0	0	0	14	7	6	0
Legal Psychology	PhD	December 15 (Fall)	33	5	2	12	4	5	2
Counseling Psychology	MA/MS	February 15 (Fall)	119	35	29	58	20	2	0
Clinical Science	PhD	December 15 (Fall)	64	11	10	38	1	4	1
Cognitive Neuroscience	PhD	December 15 (Fall)	23	14	12	12	0		

Doctoral Degree (PhD Clinical Science): For those doctoral students for whom a professional internship was required in this program prior to graduation:
Total students who applied for an internship: 7
Total students who obtained an internship: 6
Total students who obtained a paid internship: 6
Total students who obtained an unpaid internship: 0
Total students who were placed in APA/CPA-accredited internships: 6
Total students placed in internships not APA/CPA-accredited, but listed with the Association of Psychology Postdoctoral and Internship Centers (APPIC): 0

Total students placed in internships conforming to guidelines of the Council of Directors of School Psychology Programs (CDSPP): 0
Total students placed in internships that were not APA/CPA-accredited, APPIC or CDSSP listed: 0

Master's Degree (MA/MS Counseling Psychology): An internship experience, such as a final research project or "capstone" experience is required of graduates.

Admissions

Entries appear in the following order: required test or GPA, minimum score (if required)/median score of students entering in 2015–2016.

Program	Degree	GRE-V	GRE-Q	GRE-Writing	GRE-Subject	Under-graduate GPA	Last 2 Years GPA	Psychol-ogy GPA	Master's GPA
Developmental Science	PhD	NA/NA	NA/NA	Not specified	Not specified	Not specified	3/3.75	Not specified	Not specified
Industrial/ Organizational Psychology	PhD	NA/NA	NA/NA	Not specified	Not specified	Not specified	3/3.65	Not specified	Not specified
Legal Psychology	PhD	NA/NA	NA/NA	Not specified	Not specified	Not specified	3/3.84	Not specified	Not specified
Counseling Psychology	MA/MS	NA/NA	NA/NA	Not specified	Not specified	Not specified	3/3.5	Not specified	Not specified
Clinical Science	PhD	NA/NA	NA/NA	Not specified	Not specified	Not specified	3/3.44	Not specified	Not specified
Cognitive Neuroscience	PhD	NA/NA	NA/NA	Not specified	Not specified	Not specified	3/3.23	Not specified	Not specified

Admissions Requirements:

Degree	GRE	GRE-Subject	Letters of Recom-mendation	Research Statement	Writing Sample	CV	Interview
Master's/Specialist	Required	None	3	Required	Required	Required	Required
Doctoral	Required	None	3	Required	Required	Required	Required

Admissions Criteria:

GRE scores—high
Research experience—high
Work experience—medium
Clinically related public service—low

GPA—high
Letters of recommendation—high
Statement of goals and objectives—high
Undergraduate psychology preparation—medium

For additional information on admission requirements, visit http://psychology.fiu.edu/graduate-programs/prospective-grad-students/.

Department Demographics

	Male (PT)	Female (PT)	Total	African-American/ Black (PT)	Hispanic/ Latino (PT)	Asian/ Pacific Islander (PT)	American Indian/ Alaska Native (PT)	Caucasian/ White (PT)	Unknown	Multiethnic (PT)	ADA (PT)	Int'l (PT)
Students	40 (0)	112 (0)	152	3 (0)	60 (0)	2 (0)	0 (0)	81 (0)	6 (0)	(0)	0 (0)	4 (0)

Financial Information/Assistance

Tuition: For information on tuition costs, visit http://onestop.fiu.edu/financial-aid/tuition-and-fees/. Tuition is subject to change.

Doctoral:
State residents: $10,920 per academic year.
State residents: $455 per credit hour.
Nonstate residents: $24,048 per academic year.
Nonstate residents: $1,002 per credit hour.

Master's:
State residents: $10,920 per academic year.
State residents: $455 per credit hour.
Nonstate residents: $24,048 per academic year.
Nonstate residents: $1,002 per credit hour.

Financial Assistance:

	Teaching Assistantship (% Receiving)	Teaching Assistantship Tuition Remission	Research Assistantship (% Receiving)	Research Assistantship Tuition Remission	Fellowship (% Receiving)	Fellowship Tuition Remission
First-Year Student	$19,194 (NA)	Partial	$19,194 (NA)	Partial	$30,000 (NA)	Partial
Advanced Student	$19,194 (NA)	Partial	$19,194 (NA)	Partial	$30,000 (NA)	Partial

For additional information on financial assistance, visit http://psychology.fiu.edu/graduate-programs/graduate-funding/.

Employment of Department Graduates

No information provided.

Additional Information

Housing and Day Care: On-campus housing is available. See the following website for more information: http://www.housing.fiu.edu/. On-campus day care facilities are available. See the following website for more information: http://children.fiu.edu/overview.html.

Information for Students With Physical Disabilities: See the following website: http://drc.fiu.edu/.

Application Information: FIU Graduate Admissions, Modesto A. Maidique Campus, PC 230, 11200 SW 8th Street, Miami, FL 33199. *Fee:* $30. *Online application:* http://gradschool.fiu.edu/admissions.shtml.

Florida School of Professional Psychology at Argosy University

1403 North Howard Avenue
Tampa, FL 33607
Telephone: (813) 463-7183
Program Dean: Crystal S. Collier, PsyD

E-mail: snobles@argosy.edu
Web: http://FSPPTampa.com

Orientation, Objectives, and Emphasis of Department

The Florida School of Professional Psychology (FSPP) at Argosy University, Tampa offers Clinical Psychology programs that are grounded in theory and research while also incorporating experiential elements that allow the student to learn through classroom exercises, personal reflection and supervised field experiences. Our programs follow the practitioner-scholar model, which prepares aspiring psychologists to develop the essential knowledge, skills and attitudes required for successful clinical practice. Whether our students' professional emphases are assessment, intervention or other professional activities, one of the keys to their development lies in the expert support and guidance of Argosy University's accomplished faculty. Through these relationships, students learn to apply their theoretical knowledge, implement clinical techniques and integrate research findings to enhance their abilities as clinicians. These close mentoring relationships extend beyond the classroom to collaborations on professional presentations and publications.

Programs and Degrees Offered

Program	Degree	Application Deadline	Applications Received	Accepted	New Admits Enrolled (PT)	Total Enrolled (PT)	Degrees Awarded in 2014–2015	Median Years to Complete Degree	Dismissed/ Withdrew
Clinical Psychology	PsyD	(Fall), Rolling	81	30	18	122	15	5.73	1

Programs and Degrees Offered *(con't.)*

Program	Degree	Application Deadline	Applica-tions Received	Accepted	New Admits Enrolled (PT)	Total Enrolled (PT)	Degrees Awarded in 2014–2015	Median Years to Complete Degree	Dismissed/ Withdrew
Clinical Psychology	MA/MS	(Fall), Rolling	18	16	7	13	1	2	2

APA Accreditation

Clinical PsyD: Student Outcome Data website: http://clinical.argosy.edu/locations/tampa/clinical-psychology-doctor-of-psychology.

Doctoral Degree (PsyD Clinical Psychology): For those doctoral students for whom a professional internship was required in this program prior to graduation:

Total students who applied for an internship: 17
Total students who obtained an internship: 17
Total students who obtained a paid internship: 17
Total students who obtained an unpaid internship: 0
Total students who were placed in APA/CPA-accredited internships: 12
Total students placed in internships not APA/CPA-accredited, but listed with the Association of Psychology Postdoctoral and Internship Centers (APPIC): 5
Total students placed in internships conforming to guidelines of the Council of Directors of School Psychology Programs (CDSPP): 0
Total students placed in internships that were not APA/CPA-accredited, APPIC or CDSSP listed: 0

Internships/Practica

The Florida School of Professional Psychology at Argosy University places students in a variety of clinical field sites, according to the interests and needs of our students. Approved practicum sites may include agencies such as: community mental health centers; psychiatric hospitals; schools & college campus counseling centers; outpatient clinics; private practices; residential treatment centers; court-ordered programs; and rehabilitation centers.

Admissions

Entries appear in the following order: required test or GPA, minimum score (if required)/median score of students entering in 2015–2016.

Program	Degree	GRE-V	GRE-Q	GRE-Writing	GRE-Subject	Under-graduate GPA	Last 2 Years GPA	Psychol-ogy GPA	Master's GPA
Clinical Psychology	PsyD	Not specified	Not specified	Not specified	Not specified	3/NA	Not specified	Not specified	3.25/NA
Clinical Psychology	MA/MS	Not specified	Not specified	Not specified	Not specified	3/NA	Not specified	Not specified	Not specified

Admissions Requirements:

Degree	GRE	GRE-Subject	Letters of Recom-mendation	Research Statement	Writing Sample	CV	Interview
Master's/Specialist	Optional	Optional	3	Required	Optional	Required	Required
Doctoral	Optional	Optional	3	Required	Optional	Required	Required

Admissions Criteria:

Research experience—medium
Work experience—medium
Clinically related public service—medium
GPA—high

Letters of recommendation—high
Interview—high
Statement of goals and objectives—high
Undergraduate psychology preparation—medium

For additional information on admission requirements, visit http://clinical.argosy.edu/locations/tampa/clinical-psychology-doctor-of-psychology/admissions.

Department Demographics

	Male (PT)	Female (PT)	Total	African-American/ Black (PT)	Hispanic/ Latino (PT)	Asian/ Pacific Islander (PT)	American Indian/ Alaska Native (PT)	Caucasian/ White (PT)	Unknown	Multiethnic (PT)	ADA (PT)	Int'l (PT)
Students	21 (0)	114 (0)	135	21 (0)	20 (0)	4 (0)	0 (0)	82 (0)	5 (0)	3 (0)	5 (0)	3 (0)

Financial Information/Assistance

Tuition: For information on tuition costs, visit https://www.argosy.edu/affordability/tuition-and-fees. Tuition is subject to change.

Doctoral:
State residents: $33,698 per academic year.
State residents: $1,162 per credit hour.
Nonstate residents: $33,698 per academic year.
Nonstate residents: $1,162 per credit hour.

Master's:
State residents: $30,212 per academic year.
State residents: $1,162 per credit hour.
Nonstate residents: $30,212 per academic year.
Nonstate residents: $1,162 per credit hour.

Financial Assistance:

	Teaching Assistantship (% Receiving)	Teaching Assistantship Tuition Remission	Research Assistantship (% Receiving)	Research Assistantship Tuition Remission	Fellowship (% Receiving)	Fellowship Tuition Remission
First-Year Student	NA (NA)	NA	NA (NA)	NA	NA (NA)	NA
Advanced Student	NA (NA)	NA	NA (NA)	NA	NA (NA)	NA

For additional information on financial assistance, visit https://www.argosy.edu/affordability/.

Employment of Department Graduates

Master's:
Employed in business or industry: 1
Total: 1

Doctoral:
Enrolled in a postdoctoral residency/fellowship: 11
Employed in independent practice: 1
Employed in government agency: 1
Employed in a community mental health/counseling center: 2
Total: 15

Additional Information

Housing and Day Care: No on-campus housing is available. No on-campus day care facilities are available.

Application Information: Sara Nobles, Clinical Assistant Director of Admissions, 1403 North Howard Avenue, Tampa, FL 33607. *Fee:* $50. *Online application:* https://apply.argosy.edu/apply.

Florida State University
Department of Psychology
Arts & Sciences
1107 West Call Street, P.O. Box 3064301
Tallahassee, FL 32306-4301
Telephone: (850) 644-2499
Chairperson: Jeanette Taylor

E-mail: grad-info@psy.fsu.edu
Web: http://www.psy.fsu.edu

Orientation, Objectives, and Emphasis of Department
This is a scientifically oriented department with considerable annual grant funding for basic and applied research. The Clinical Psychology program promotes a scientifically based approach to understanding; assessing; and ameliorating cognitive, emotional, behavioral, and health problems. Integrative training in clinical science and clinical service delivery is provided. Cognitive Psychology students develop research and analytical skills while learning to coordinate basic research with theory development and application. Current research includes expert performance, skill acquisition, reading, memory, attention, language processing, and cognitive aging. Students in Developmental Psychology conduct basic and applied research. A developmental perspective is interdisciplinary; consequently, developmental faculty members routinely hold appointments in one of our other doctoral programs. The Social Psychology program provides students with in-depth training in personality and social psychology, focusing on basic and applied research. Current research areas include the self, prejudice and stereotyping, romantic relationships, health psychology, and evolutionary perspectives. The interdisciplinary Neuroscience program offers students broad training in brain and behavior research. Areas of emphasis include sensory processes, neural development and plasticity, regulation of energy balance and social behaviors, behavioral pharmacology, and hormonal control of behavior. The terminal master's program in Applied Behavior Analysis focuses on analyzing and modifying behavior using well-established principles.

Programs and Degrees Offered

Program	Degree	Application Deadline	Applica-tions Received	Accepted	New Admits Enrolled (PT)	Total Enrolled (PT)	Degrees Awarded in 2014–2015	Median Years to Complete Degree	Dismissed/ Withdrew
Cognitive Psychology	PhD	December 15 (Fall)	44	4	3	25 (1)	1	7	1
Clinical Psychology	PhD	December 1 (Fall)	283	12	12 (0)	56 (3)	8	6.5	0
Neuroscience	PhD	December 1 (Fall)	37	7	3	19 (3)	3	5	2
Applied Behavior Analysis	MA/MS	January 16 (Fall)	72	33	16	32 (0)	17	2	0
Social Psychology	PhD	December 15 (Fall)	72	2	2	15 (1)	3	5	0
Developmental Psychology	PhD	December 15 (Fall)	20	2	0	6 (1)	2	5	0

APA Accreditation
Clinical PhD: Student Outcome Data website: https://psy.fsu.edu/clinical/index.htm.

Doctoral Degree (PhD Clinical Psychology): For those doctoral students for whom a professional internship was required in this program prior to graduation:
Total students who applied for an internship: 11
Total students who obtained an internship: 11
Total students who obtained a paid internship: 11
Total students who obtained an unpaid internship: 0
Total students who were placed in APA/CPA-accredited internships: 11
Total students placed in internships not APA/CPA-accredited, but listed with the Association of Psychology Postdoctoral and Internship Centers (APPIC): 0
Total students placed in internships conforming to guidelines of the Council of Directors of School Psychology Programs (CDSPP): 0
Total students placed in internships that were not APA/CPA-accredited, APPIC or CDSSP listed: 0

Master's Degree (MA/MS Applied Behavior Analysis): An internship experience, such as a final research project or "capstone" experience is required of graduates.

Internships/Practica
Community facilities provide a multitude of settings for practicum placements for clinical doctoral students and for master's students in applied behavior analysis. Clinical students receive a stipend and tuition waivers for their practicum work in the community as well as excellent supervised experience and opportunities for research. Practicum settings for clinical students include an inpatient psychiatric hospital, a comprehensive evaluation center for children, a juvenile treatment program, forensic facilities, and other agencies in the community. Clinical psychology students complete a required unpaid practicum at our nationally recognized on-campus Psychology Clinic during the second and, typically, third year of study. The clinic provides empirically based assessment

and therapy services to adults, children, and families in the north Florida region. Psychology faculty provide supervision. The clinical program culminates in a required one-year internship in an APA-approved facility. Clinical students from the FSU program have, over the years, been highly successful in obtaining excellent internships throughout the country. Applied Behavior Analysis master's students have diverse practicum sites from which to choose, including public schools, family homes, residential treatment facilities, businesses, consulting firms, and state agencies. Stipends and tuition waivers are available for many of the applied behavior analysis practicum settings.

Admissions

Entries appear in the following order: required test or GPA, minimum score (if required)/median score of students entering in 2015–2016.

Program	Degree	GRE-V	GRE-Q	GRE-Writing	GRE-Subject	Under-graduate GPA	Last 2 Years GPA	Psychology GPA	Master's GPA
Cognitive Psychology	PhD	150/160	146/158	Not specified	Not specified	Not specified	Not specified	Not specified	Not specified
Clinical Psychology	PhD	152/159	151/160	Not specified	Not specified	Not specified	Not specified	Not specified	Not specified
Neuroscience	PhD	152/157	151/157	Not specified	Not specified	Not specified	3/3.2	Not specified	Not specified
Applied Behavior Analysis	MA/MS	150/150	147/149	Not specified	Not specified	Not specified	Not specified	Not specified	Not specified
Social Psychology	PhD	153/157	148/155	Not specified	Not specified	Not specified	3/3.9	Not specified	Not specified
Developmental Psychology	PhD	150/150	146/145	Not specified	Not specified	Not specified	3/3.53	Not specified	Not specified

Admissions Requirements:

Degree	GRE	GRE-Subject	Letters of Recom-mendation	Research Statement	Writing Sample	CV	Interview
Master's/Specialist	Required	None	3	Required	Optional	Required	Optional
Doctoral	Required	Recom-mended	3	Required	Optional	Required	Required

Please note if these criteria vary for different programs: Research experience is not an important factor for admission to the Applied Behavior Analysis master's program; work or volunteer experience in behavior analysis is of high importance for this program.

Admissions Criteria:

GRE scores—high
Research experience—high
Work experience—low
Clinically related public service—low
GPA—high

Letters of recommendation—high
Interview—medium
Statement of goals and objectives—high
Undergraduate psychology preparation—medium
Match w/ faculty interest—high

For additional information on admission requirements, visit https://psy.fsu.edu/grad.prog/gradapp.html.

Department Demographics

	Male (PT)	Female (PT)	Total	African-American/ Black (PT)	Hispanic/ Latino (PT)	Asian/ Pacific Islander (PT)	American Indian/ Alaska Native (PT)	Caucasian/ White (PT)	Unknown	Multiethnic (PT)	ADA (PT)	Int'l (PT)
Students	48 (4)	105 (5)	162	6 (0)	15 (0)	7 (0)	0 (0)	117 (9)	3 (0)	5 (0)	3 (0)	2 (0)

Financial Information/Assistance

Tuition: For information on tuition costs, visit http://controller.vpfa.fsu.edu/student-business/tuition. Tuition is subject to change.

Doctoral:
State residents: $8,622 per academic year.
State residents: $479 per credit hour.
Nonstate residents: $19,980 per academic year.
Nonstate residents: $1,110 per credit hour.

Master's:
State residents: $8,622 per academic year.
State residents: $479 per credit hour.
Nonstate residents: $19,980 per academic year.
Nonstate residents: $1,110 per credit hour.

Financial Assistance:

	Teaching Assistantship (% Receiving)	Teaching Assistantship Tuition Remission	Research Assistantship (% Receiving)	Research Assistantship Tuition Remission	Fellowship (% Receiving)	Fellowship Tuition Remission
First-Year Student	$18,315 (NA)	Full	$22,000 (NA)	Full	$22,000 (NA)	Full
Advanced Student	$18,315 (NA)	Full	$22,000 (NA)	Full	$22,000 (NA)	Full

For additional information on financial assistance, visit https://psy.fsu.edu/grad.prog/financial.html.

Employment of Department Graduates

Master's:
Employed in a community mental health/counseling center: 17
Total: 17

Doctoral:
Enrolled in a postdoctoral residency/fellowship: 11
Employed in an academic position at a university: 5
Employed in other positions at a higher education institution: 1
Employed in a hospital/medical center: 2
Still seeking employment: 1
Do not know: 1
Total: 21

Additional Information

Housing and Day Care: On-campus housing is available. See the following website for more information: http://housing.fsu.edu/. On-campus day care facilities are available. See the following website for more information: http://www.childcare.fsu.edu/.

Information for Students With Physical Disabilities: See the following website: http://dos.fsu.edu/sdrc/.

Special Facilities or Resources: The department's technical staff and support facilities are some of the best in the country. Fully staffed and equipped electronic and machine shops support faculty and graduate student research. Highly trained staff provides assistance in graphic arts, photography, instrument and computer software design, and electronic communication services. A neurosurgical operating room and histological core laboratories are available. Faculty and students have available to them workstations offering human eye-tracking and brain wave and psychophysiological recording, among others. A molecular neuroscience laboratory provides equipment and training for studies of gene cloning and gene expression, as well as techniques to measure levels of hormones and neurotransmitters. The Clinical program administers an in-department outpatient clinic that offers empirically-based assessment and therapy services to members of the Tallahassee and surrounding communities. The department has been recognized by the APA for innovative practices in graduate education in psychology. This recognition was for the in-department clinic, which is a full-fledged clinical research laboratory. Based on research and case studies conducted at the clinic, faculty and students have published many books and peer-reviewed articles. The department and clinic are housed in a new, state-of-the-art building.

Application Information: Office of Admissions, Florida State University, 282 Champions Way, P.O. Box 3062400, Tallahassee, FL 32306-2400. *Fee:* $30. *Online application:* https://admissions.fsu.edu/gradapp/.

Florida State University
Psychological and Counseling Services (PCS)
Education
306 Stone Building
Tallahassee, FL 32306-4453
Telephone: (850) 644-4592
Director of Clinical Training: Steven Pfeiffer

E-mail: spfeiffer@fsu.edu
Web: http://coe.fsu.edu/

Orientation, Objectives, and Emphasis of Department

The Combined Doctoral Program in Counseling Psychology and School Psychology is fully accredited by the American Psychological Association. This unique program allows students to acquire knowledge and skills necessary for leadership positions in the practice of counseling psychology and school psychology in a variety of academic and applied settings. Students acquire basic competency in counseling psychology and school psychology, and advanced expertise in either counseling psychology or school psychology. The program prepares graduates for national certification and state licensure. Within the combined program, all students share a common core of experience in research and practice in counseling psychology and school psychology (70% shared coursework/ practica); students also are afforded the opportunity to concentrate in counseling psychology or school psychology (a few students decide to concentrate in both). The Combined Program embraces a scientist–practitioner model consistent with the mission of Florida State, a Research I University. The program faculty enjoy diverse research and clinical interests, providing students with a range of opportunities for professional development in the areas of mental health counseling, school psychology, career counseling, rehabilitation counseling, addictions counseling, prevention and early intervention, wellness, and psychology of the gifted.

Programs and Degrees Offered

Program	Degree	Application Deadline	Applica-tions Received	Accepted	New Admits Enrolled (PT)	Total Enrolled (PT)	Degrees Awarded in 2014–2015	Median Years to Complete Degree	Dismissed/ Withdrew
Combined Counseling and School Psychology	PhD	January 15 (Fall)	52	8	8 (0)	45 (0)	13	5	0
School Psychology	EdS	January 15 (Fall)	65	16	16	38	7	3	3

APA Accreditation

Combination PhD: Student Outcome Data website: http://education.fsu.edu/degrees-and-programs/counseling-psychology-and-school-psychology.

Doctoral Degree (PhD Combined Counseling and School Psychology): For those doctoral students for whom a professional internship was required in this program prior to graduation:
Total students who applied for an internship: 4
Total students who obtained an internship: 4
Total students who obtained a paid internship: 4
Total students who obtained an unpaid internship: 0
Total students who were placed in APA/CPA-accredited internships: 4
Total students placed in internships not APA/CPA-accredited, but listed with the Association of Psychology Postdoctoral and Internship Centers (APPIC): 0
Total students placed in internships conforming to guidelines of the Council of Directors of School Psychology Programs (CDSPP): 0
Total students placed in internships that were not APA/CPA-accredited, APPIC or CDSSP listed: 0

Internships/Practica

The program offers both on-campus and off-campus practicum experiences; on-campus clinical practica include a mental health clinic serving clients from the community; adult learning disability clinic serving college students and the community; student career counseling center; multidisciplinary center serving K–12 students from a number of school districts; university student counseling center; student disability resource center. Off-campus practica include a wide range of mental health, psychiatric, educational, and behavioral healthcare agencies and private practice settings.

Admissions

Entries appear in the following order: required test or GPA, minimum score (if required)/median score of students entering in 2015–2016.

Program	Degree	GRE-V	GRE-Q	GRE-Writing	GRE-Subject	Under-graduate GPA	Last 2 Years GPA	Psychol-ogy GPA	Master's GPA
Combined Counseling and School Psychology	PhD	NA/NA	NA/NA	Not specified	Not specified	3/3.64	NA/NA	Not specified	Not specified

Admissions *(con't.)*

Program	Degree	GRE-V	GRE-Q	GRE-Writing	GRE-Subject	Under-graduate GPA	Last 2 Years GPA	Psychology GPA	Master's GPA
School Psychology	EdS	142/NA	139/NA	Not specified	Not specified	3/NA	3.2/NA	Not specified	Not specified

Admissions Requirements:

Degree	GRE	GRE-Subject	Letters of Recommendation	Research Statement	Writing Sample	CV	Interview
Master's/Specialist	Required	Optional	3	Required	Optional	Required	Required
Doctoral	Required	Optional	3	Required	Optional	Required	Required

Please note if these criteria vary for different programs: Research experience and high interest are highly valued among successful applicants to the APA-accredited doctoral program in combined psychology.

Admissions Criteria:

GRE scores—high
Research experience—medium
Work experience—medium
Clinically related public service—medium
GPA—high

Letters of recommendation—high
Interview—high
Statement of goals and objectives—high
Undergraduate psychology preparation—low

For additional information on admission requirements, visit http://education.fsu.edu/admissions/graduate-admissions.

Department Demographics

	Male (PT)	Female (PT)	Total	African-American/ Black (PT)	Hispanic/ Latino (PT)	Asian/ Pacific Islander (PT)	American Indian/ Alaska Native (PT)	Caucasian/ White (PT)	Unknown	Multiethnic (PT)	ADA (PT)	Int'l (PT)
Students	13 (0)	70 (0)	83	4 (0)	7 (0)	4 (0)	0 (0)	67 (0)	0 (0)	1 (0)	1 (0)	3 (0)

Financial Information/Assistance

Tuition: For information on tuition costs, visit http://controller.vpfa.fsu.edu/student-business/tuition. Tuition is subject to change.

Doctoral:
State residents: $11,544 per academic year.
Nonstate residents: $26,698 per academic year.

Master's:
State residents: $11,544 per academic year.
Nonstate residents: $26,698 per academic year.

Financial Assistance:

	Teaching Assistantship (% Receiving)	Teaching Assistantship Tuition Remission	Research Assistantship (% Receiving)	Research Assistantship Tuition Remission	Fellowship (% Receiving)	Fellowship Tuition Remission
First-Year Student	$3,800 (NA)	Partial	$3,500 (NA)	Partial	$6,300 (NA)	Partial
Advanced Student	$3,800 (NA)	Partial	$3,500 (NA)	Partial	$6,300 (NA)	Partial

For additional information on financial assistance, visit http://gradschool.fsu.edu/Funding-Awards.

Employment of Department Graduates

Master's:
Employed in a professional position in a school system: 7
Total: 7

Doctoral:
Enrolled in a postdoctoral residency/fellowship: 4
Employed in independent practice: 1
Employed in business or industry: 1
Employed in government agency: 2
Employed in a community mental health/counseling center: 1
Total: 9

Additional Information

Housing and Day Care: On-campus housing is available. See the following website for more information: https://housing.fsu.edu/future-residents/graduate-and-non-traditional-student-housing. On-campus day care facilities are available. See the following website for more information: http://www.childcare.fsu.edu/.

Information for Students With Physical Disabilities: See the following website: http://dos.fsu.edu/sdrc/.

Special Facilities or Resources: The program uses the following clinic facilities for the development of assessment, counseling, and consultation skills: (1) The Human Services Center is a mental health training clinic that provides counseling services at no cost to residents of Tallahassee and surrounding communities. This center offers counseling for a wide range of mental health and psychiatric problems, social skill training, anger management, relationship counseling, family counseling, and personal growth and development. The center works with the juvenile justice system in providing services to court-referred cases. (2) The Adult Learning and Evaluation Center is a referral source for FSU, our other two local colleges, FAMU and TCC, and the community. It serves to assist adults in identifying ADHD, learning disabilities and related problems that may compromise the attainment of educational and career progress. It offers students practica and assistantships in psychological assessment and consultation. (3) The Career Center is located in the Dunlap Success Center and is one of the most technologically advanced career facilities in the nation. The Career Center provides opportunities for practica and internships as well as for student employment opportunities as career advisors. This Center serves as many as 6000 students per year with a variety of career concerns.

Application Information: Admissions Committee, Psychological and Counseling Services, Florida State University, Stone Building, Tallahassee, FL 32306-4453. *Fee:* $30. *Online application:* https://admissions.fsu.edu/gradapp/.

Florida, University of
Department of Clinical and Health Psychology
Public Health and Health Professions
Box 100165 HSC
Gainesville, FL 32610-0165
Telephone: (352) 273-6455
Chairperson: William W. Latimer

E-mail: progasstchp@phhp.ufl.edu
Web: http://chp.phhp.ufl.edu/

Orientation, Objectives, and Emphasis of Department
The program is designed to train doctoral-level professional psychologists in the scientist–practitioner model through the development of broad clinical skills and competencies, through mastery of broad areas of knowledge in psychology and clinical psychology, and through demonstrated competencies in contributing to that knowledge by research. Within these program objectives particular emphases can be identified: clinical health psychology, clinical neuropsychology, and clinical child/pediatric psychology. Courses, practica, conferences, committees, supervision, and settings are designed to augment each emphasis.

Programs and Degrees Offered

Program	Degree	Application Deadline	Applications Received	Accepted	New Admits Enrolled (PT)	Total Enrolled (PT)	Degrees Awarded in 2014–2015	Median Years to Complete Degree	Dismissed/ Withdrew
Clinical Psychology	PhD	December 15 (Fall)	291	15	13 (0)	83 (0)	13	5.9	0

APA Accreditation
Clinical PhD: Student Outcome Data website: http://chp.phhp.ufl.edu/academics/doctoral-in-clinical-psychology/student-admissions-outcomes-and-other-data/.

Doctoral Degree (PhD Clinical Psychology): For those doctoral students for whom a professional internship was required in this program prior to graduation:

Total students who applied for an internship: 15
Total students who obtained an internship: 15
Total students who obtained a paid internship: 15
Total students who obtained an unpaid internship: 0
Total students who were placed in APA/CPA-accredited internships: 15
Total students placed in internships not APA/CPA-accredited, but listed with the Association of Psychology Postdoctoral and Internship Centers (APPIC): 0
Total students placed in internships conforming to guidelines of the Council of Directors of School Psychology Programs (CDSPP): 0
Total students placed in internships that were not APA/CPA-accredited, APPIC or CDSSP listed: 0

Internships/Practica

The Department of Clinical and Health Psychology operates a Psychology Clinic which is part of Shands Hospital within the University of Florida Health Science Center. This clinic provides consultation, assessment, and intervention services to medical-surgical inpatients and outpatients, as well as community patients with emotional and behavioral problems. Major services include clinical health psychology, child/pediatric psychology and clinical neuropsychology.

Admissions

Entries appear in the following order: required test or GPA, minimum score (if required)/median score of students entering in 2015–2016.

Program	Degree	GRE-V	GRE-Q	GRE-Writing	GRE-Subject	Under-graduate GPA	Last 2 Years GPA	Psychol-ogy GPA	Master's GPA
Clinical Psychology	PhD	NA/160	NA/155	NA/4.6	Not specified	NA/3.75	Not specified	Not specified	Not specified

Admissions Requirements:

Degree	GRE	GRE-Subject	Letters of Recom-mendation	Research Statement	Writing Sample	CV	Interview
Doctoral	Required	None	3	Required	Optional	Required	Required

Admissions Criteria:

GRE scores—medium
Research experience—high
Work experience—medium
Clinically related public service—high

GPA—medium
Letters of recommendation—high
Interview—high
Statement of goals and objectives—high

For additional information on admission requirements, visit http://chp.phhp.ufl.edu/academics/doctoral-in-clinical-psychology/apply-to-the-program/.

Department Demographics

	Male (PT)	Female (PT)	Total	African-American/ Black (PT)	Hispanic/ Latino (PT)	Asian/ Pacific Islander (PT)	American Indian/ Alaska Native (PT)	Caucasian/ White (PT)	Unknown	Multiethnic (PT)	ADA (PT)	Int'l (PT)
Students	24 (0)	59 (0)	83	7 (0)	10 (0)	4 (0)	1 (0)	61 (0)	0 (0)	0 (0)	2 (0)	2 (0)

Financial Information/Assistance

Tuition: For information on tuition costs, visit http://www.fa.ufl.edu/bursar/current-students/. Tuition is subject to change.

Doctoral:
State residents: $12,642 per academic year.
State residents: $527 per credit hour.
Nonstate residents: $30,035 per academic year.
Nonstate residents: $1,251 per credit hour.

Financial Assistance:

	Teaching Assistantship (% Receiving)	Teaching Assistantship Tuition Remission	Research Assistantship (% Receiving)	Research Assistantship Tuition Remission	Fellowship (% Receiving)	Fellowship Tuition Remission
First-Year Student	NA (NA)	NA	$18,000 (67)	Full	$20,000 (33)	Full
Advanced Student	$18,000 (3)	Full	$18,000 (64)	Full	$20,000 (33)	Full

For additional information on financial assistance, visit http://chp.phhp.ufl.edu/academics/doctoral-in-clinical-psychology/financial-aid/.

Employment of Department Graduates

Doctoral:
Enrolled in a postdoctoral residency/fellowship: 11
Employed in government agency: 1
Employed in a hospital/medical center: 1
Total: 13

Additional Information

Housing and Day Care: On-campus housing is available. See the following website for more information: http://www.housing.ufl.edu/gfh/. On-campus day care facilities are available. See the following website for more information: http://babygator.ufl.edu/.

Information for Students With Physical Disabilities: See the following website: http://www.dso.ufl.edu/drc/.

Special Facilities or Resources: The Department and its parent College, the College of Public Health and Health Professions, is housed in a modern building that contains faculty offices, student work spaces, and state-of-the-art classroom facilities. In addition, department faculty currently occupy several thousand square feet of laboratory space for clinical and basic research. The Department is particularly strong in instrumentation and methodology for clinical research in pediatric and clinical child psychology, health psychology, and neuropsychology. Psychophysiological and neuroimaging capabilities are present and utilized by many faculty. The clinical psychology program uses the extensive resources of the campus and community. Sites utilized for clinical training include the department's Psychology Clinic, university student health services, the university counseling center; and the VA Medical Center in Gainesville. Agencies and centers throughout the state and nation are also available, principally for internship training for students. The use of these varied resources is consonant with the program objectives. The trainee is directly involved with a broad range of clinical and health problems, professionals, agencies, and settings.

Application Information: Graduate Admissions, Department of Clinical and Health Psychology, Box 100165 HSC, University of Florida, Gainesville, FL 32610-0165. *Fee:* $30. *Online application:* http://www.admissions.ufl.edu/start.html.

Florida, University of
Department of Psychology
Liberal Arts and Sciences
P.O. Box 112250
Gainesville, FL 32611-2250
Telephone: (352) 392-0601
Chairperson: Lise Abrams

E-mail: psych-info@ufl.edu
Web: http://www.psych.ufl.edu

Orientation, Objectives, and Emphasis of Department
The graduate program in psychology at the University of Florida is designed for those planning careers as researchers, teacher-scholars, and scientist–practitioners in psychology. In addition to specialized training in one or more areas, a core program of theories, methods, and research in general psychology insures that each student will be well prepared in the basic areas of psychology. The primary goal of the department is educating scientists who will help advance psychology as a science through teaching, research, and professional practice. Because the University of Florida is a broad spectrum university, including almost all the major academic departments as well as professional schools on a single campus, a unique atmosphere exists for the evolution

of the general program and the development of personal programs of study. Each student also receives training in at least one of the areas of specialization including counseling psychology, developmental, behavior analysis, behavioral and cognitive neuroscience, and social. One of the fundamental goals of the doctoral program is to engage the student as early as possible in the area of interest while ensuring a sound background of knowledge of theory, methodology, and major content areas so that maximum integration may be achieved.

Programs and Degrees Offered

Program	Degree	Application Deadline	Applications Received	Accepted	New Admits Enrolled (PT)	Total Enrolled (PT)	Degrees Awarded in 2014–2015	Median Years to Complete Degree	Dismissed/ Withdrew
Behavioral and Cognitive Neuroscience	PhD	December 1 (Fall)	45	9	8 (0)	23 (0)	4	5.5	0
Behavior Analysis	PhD	December 1 (Fall)	37	9	9 (0)	24 (0)	10	5	0
Counseling Psychology	PhD	December 1 (Fall)	150	9	4 (0)	30 (0)	5	5	0
Developmental Psychology	PhD	December 1 (Fall)	36	8	6 (0)	18 (0)	1	6	0
Social Psychology	PhD	December 1 (Fall)	38	0	0 (0)	6 (0)	1	4.5	0

APA Accreditation
Counseling PhD: Student Outcome Data website: http://www.psych.ufl.edu/coun/.

Doctoral Degree (PhD Counseling Psychology): For those doctoral students for whom a professional internship was required in this program prior to graduation:
Total students who applied for an internship: 7
Total students who obtained an internship: 7
Total students who obtained a paid internship: 7
Total students who obtained an unpaid internship: 0
Total students who were placed in APA/CPA-accredited internships: 7
Total students placed in internships not APA/CPA-accredited, but listed with the Association of Psychology Postdoctoral and Internship Centers (APPIC): 0
Total students placed in internships conforming to guidelines of the Council of Directors of School Psychology Programs (CDSPP): 0
Total students placed in internships that were not APA/CPA-accredited, APPIC or CDSSP listed: 0

Internships/Practica
University Counseling and Wellness Center, Family Practice Medical Group, Meridian Behavioral Healthcare, Alachua County Crisis Center, VA Medical Center, North Florida Treatment and Evaluation Center, and Northeast Florida State Hospital.

Admissions
Entries appear in the following order: required test or GPA, minimum score (if required)/median score of students entering in 2015–2016.

Program	Degree	GRE-V	GRE-Q	GRE-Writing	GRE-Subject	Undergraduate GPA	Last 2 Years GPA	Psychology GPA	Master's GPA
Behavioral and Cognitive Neuroscience	PhD	NA/158	NA/154	Not specified	Not specified	NA/3.5	Not specified	Not specified	Not specified
Behavior Analysis	PhD	NA/158	NA/156	Not specified	Not specified	NA/3.7	Not specified	Not specified	Not specified
Counseling Psychology	PhD	NA/158	NA/154	Not specified	Not specified	NA/3.6	Not specified	Not specified	Not specified

Admissions *(con't.)*

Program	Degree	GRE-V	GRE-Q	GRE-Writing	GRE-Subject	Under-graduate GPA	Last 2 Years GPA	Psychol-ogy GPA	Master's GPA
Developmental Psychology	PhD	NA/161	NA/155	Not specified	Not specified	NA/3.8	Not specified	Not specified	Not specified
Social Psychology	PhD	NA/163	NA/154	Not specified	Not specified	NA/3.85	NA/NA	Not specified	Not specified

Admissions Requirements:

Degree	GRE	GRE-Subject	Letters of Recommendation	Research Statement	Writing Sample	CV	Interview
Doctoral	Required	None	3	Required	Optional	Required	Recommended

Please note if these criteria vary for different programs: Only the Counseling Psychology program requires clinically related experience. Weight given to these criteria varies from area to area. Some programs do not conduct interviews every year.

Admissions Criteria:

GRE scores—medium
Research experience—high
Work experience—low
Clinically related public service—medium
GPA—medium

Letters of recommendation—medium
Interview—high
Statement of goals and objectives—high
Undergraduate psychology preparation—medium
Match w/ faculty research—high

For additional information on admission requirements, visit http://www.psych.ufl.edu/grad/admissions/.

Department Demographics

	Male (PT)	Female (PT)	Total	African-American/ Black (PT)	Hispanic/ Latino (PT)	Asian/ Pacific Islander (PT)	American Indian/ Alaska Native (PT)	Caucasian/ White (PT)	Unknown	Multiethnic (PT)	ADA (PT)	Int'l (PT)
Students	26 (0)	75 (0)	101	4 (0)	12 (0)	5 (0)	1 (0)	61 (0)	6 (0)	0 (0)	0 (0)	12 (0)

Financial Information/Assistance

Tuition: For information on tuition costs, visit http://www.fa.ufl.edu/bursar/current-students/. Tuition is subject to change. Additional fees are assessed to students beyond the costs of tuition for the following: Fees are $82 per credit hour.

Doctoral:
State residents: $8,082 per academic year.
State residents: $449 per credit hour.
Nonstate residents: $21,127 per academic year.
Nonstate residents: $1,174 per credit hour.

Financial Assistance:

	Teaching Assistantship (% Receiving)	Teaching Assistantship Tuition Remission	Research Assistantship (% Receiving)	Research Assistantship Tuition Remission	Fellowship (% Receiving)	Fellowship Tuition Remission
First-Year Student	$15,500 (37)	Full	$15,500 (7)	Full	$20,000 (55)	Full
Advanced Student	$16,000 (50)	Full	$16,000 (10)	Full	$20,000 (40)	Full

For additional information on financial assistance, visit http://www.psych.ufl.edu/grad/finances/.

Employment of Department Graduates

Doctoral:
Enrolled in a postdoctoral residency/fellowship: 8
Employed in independent practice: 3
Employed in an academic position at a university: 6
Employed in academic position at a 2-year/4-year college: 1
Employed in business or industry: 1
Employed in government agency: 2
Total: 21

Additional Information

Housing and Day Care: On-campus housing is available. See the following website for more information: http://www.housing.ufl.edu/gfh/choices/. On-campus day care facilities are available. See the following website for more information: http://babygator.ufl.edu/.

Information for Students With Physical Disabilities: See the following website: http://www.dso.ufl.edu/drc/.

Special Facilities or Resources: Special facilities in the department include laboratories in developmental (child, adolescent, aging), experimental analysis of behavior, cognitive and information processing, perception, behavioral neuroscience, and social; a vivarium; a statistical computation laboratory; a laboratory in neuropsychology and developmental learning disabilities; and the Computing Center.

Application Information: Fee: $30. *Online application:* http://www.admissions.ufl.edu/start.html.

Miami, University of
Department of Educational & Psychological Studies/Area of Counseling Psychology
Education
P.O. Box 248065
Coral Gables, FL 33124-2040
Telephone: (305) 284-3001
E-mail: l.buki@miami.edu
Chairperson: Laura Kohn-Wood, PhD   Web: http://www.education.miami.edu/department/departments.asp?Department_ID=2

Orientation, Objectives, and Emphasis of Department
Intellectual stimulation and cooperation characterize the academic culture within the Department of Educational and Psychological Studies. Due to our School's unique location, students can look forward to practical experiences working with diverse populations. Faculty and students create a community of scholars in which respect and professionalism are common goals. From this solid base of mutual support, students are encouraged to take risks to maximize learning. The Mental Health Counseling Program develops students' skills in assessment, prevention, and treatment of behavioral and emotional difficulties, as well as career and lifestyle issues. The program allows students to meet the academic requirements for licensure as a Mental Health Counselor in the State of Florida. The doctoral program follows the scientist–practitioner model. It seeks to prepare individuals who will contribute to knowledge in psychology through culturally informed research and scholarship, and who will be highly skilled, multiculturally competent clinicians.

Programs and Degrees Offered

Program	Degree	Application Deadline	Applications Received	Accepted	New Admits Enrolled (PT)	Total Enrolled (PT)	Degrees Awarded in 2014–2015	Median Years to Complete Degree	Dismissed/ Withdrew
Counseling Psychology	PhD	December 1 (Fall)	96	5	5 (0)	33 (0)	5	6	0
Marriage and Family Therapy	MA/MS	December 1 (Fall)	18	11	10 (1)	10 (4)	4	2	0
Mental Health Counseling	MA/MS	December 1 (Fall)	58	24	8 (0)	14 (8)	12	2.5	0

APA Accreditation

Counseling PhD: Student Outcome Data website: http://www.education.miami.edu/program/programs.asp?Program_ID=47.

Doctoral Degree (PhD Counseling Psychology): For those doctoral students for whom a professional internship was required in this program prior to graduation:

Total students who applied for an internship: 2
Total students who obtained an internship: 2
Total students who obtained a paid internship: 2
Total students who obtained an unpaid internship: 0
Total students who were placed in APA/CPA-accredited internships: 1
Total students placed in internships not APA/CPA-accredited, but listed with the Association of Psychology Postdoctoral and Internship Centers (APPIC): 1
Total students placed in internships conforming to guidelines of the Council of Directors of School Psychology Programs (CDSPP): 0
Total students placed in internships that were not APA/CPA-accredited, APPIC or CDSSP listed: 0

Master's Degree (MA/MS Marriage and Family Therapy): An internship experience, such as a final research project or "capstone" experience is required of graduates. Master's Degree (MA/MS Mental Health Counseling): An internship experience, such as a final research project or "capstone" experience is required of graduates.

Internships/Practica

Doctoral students complete two academic years of practicum: the first year in our on-campus, state of the art training clinic, and the second year in an agency or hospital setting located in the community. Practicum supervision is provided through weekly one-to-one meetings and group supervision meetings. Therapeutic modalities include individual, couple, and group therapies. The off-campus placement is tailored to the student's career goals. Many students also complete an optional advanced practicum with placements tailored to their career goals. Placements include university counseling centers, psychiatric facilities, VA hospitals, behavioral medicine settings, correctional facilities, and schools, among others.

Admissions

Entries appear in the following order: required test or GPA, minimum score (if required)/median score of students entering in 2015–2016.

Program	Degree	GRE-V	GRE-Q	GRE-Writing	GRE-Subject	Under-graduate GPA	Last 2 Years GPA	Psychology GPA	Master's GPA
Counseling Psychology	PhD	157/163	153/156	4/4.5	Not specified	3.55/3.72	NA/NA	NA/NA	3.5/3.85
Marriage and Family Therapy	MA/MS	153/150	148/146	4/4	Not specified	3/3.5	Not specified	Not specified	Not specified
Mental Health Counseling	MA/MS	153/150	148/146	4/4	Not specified	3/3.4	Not specified	Not specified	Not specified

Admissions Requirements:

Degree	GRE	GRE-Subject	Letters of Recom-mendation	Research Statement	Writing Sample	CV	Interview
Master's/Specialist	Required	None	3	Required	Optional	Required	Required
Doctoral	Required	None	3	Required	None	Required	Required

Admissions Criteria:

GRE scores—medium
Research experience—high
Work experience—medium
Clinically related public service—medium
GPA—high

Letters of recommendation—high
Interview—high
Statement of goals and objectives—high
Undergraduate psychology preparation—low

Department Demographics

	Male (PT)	Female (PT)	Total	African-American/ Black (PT)	Hispanic/ Latino (PT)	Asian/ Pacific Islander (PT)	American Indian/ Alaska Native (PT)	Caucasian/ White (PT)	Unknown	Multiethnic (PT)	ADA (PT)	Int'l (PT)
Students	12 (0)	45 (12)	69	5 (3)	17 (2)	4 (1)	0 (0)	26 (6)	0 (0)	5 (0)	4 (0)	3 (1)

Financial Information/Assistance

Tuition: For information on tuition costs, visit http://www.miami.edu/finance/index.php/student_account_services/tuition_and_fees/. Tuition is subject to change. Additional fees are assessed to students beyond the costs of tuition for the following: health insurance, wellness center.

Doctoral:
State residents: $1,850 per credit hour.
Nonstate residents: $1,850 per credit hour.

Master's:
State residents: $1,850 per credit hour.
Nonstate residents: $1,850 per credit hour.

Financial Assistance:

	Teaching Assistantship (% Receiving)	Teaching Assistantship Tuition Remission	Research Assistantship (% Receiving)	Research Assistantship Tuition Remission	Fellowship (% Receiving)	Fellowship Tuition Remission
First-Year Student	$20,250 (NA)	Full	$20,250 (100)	Full	$25,000 (NA)	Full
Advanced Student	$20,250 (10)	Full	$20,250 (70)	Full	$25,000 (20)	Full

For additional information on financial assistance, visit http://www.miami.edu/admission/index.php/ofas/graduate.

Employment of Department Graduates

Master's:
Enrolled in a psychology doctoral program: 3
Do not know: 13
Total: 16

Doctoral:
Enrolled in a postdoctoral residency/fellowship: 3
Employed in an academic position at a university: 2
Total: 5

Additional Information

Housing and Day Care: No on-campus housing is available. On-campus day care facilities are available. See the following website for more information: http://www.umcanterbury.com.

Information for Students With Physical Disabilities: See the following website: http://www.umarc.miami.edu/arc/ODS.html.

Special Facilities or Resources: The Institute for Individual and Family Counseling, a recently remodeled, state of the art on-campus clinic, is used as the primary practicum site. It is equipped with state-of-the-art facilities for audio, video, and live supervision. The multicultural clientele of the Institute and the other agencies and schools in the Miami area make it an ideal setting to develop clinical competence. Computer laboratories are available to students in the department. In addition, an assessment laboratory is an integral part of assessment training in the program.

Application Information: Lois Heffernan, Graduate Admissions Services, University of Miami, School of Education and Human Development, Max Orovitz Building, 1507 Levante Avenue, 3rd floor, Coral Gables, FL 33124. *Fee:* $65. *Online application:* https://www.applyweb.com/apply/miamigrd/index.html.

Miami, University of

Department of Psychology
College of Arts & Sciences
5665 Ponce de Leon Boulevard
Coral Gables, FL 33146
Telephone: (305) 284-2814
Chairperson: Philip M. McCabe

E-mail: pmccabe@miami.edu
Web: http://www.psy.miami.edu

Orientation, Objectives, and Emphasis of Department

The Department of Psychology's mission is to acquire, advance, and disseminate knowledge within the psychological and biobehavioral sciences. The Department seeks a balance among several academic endeavors including basic scientific research, applied research, undergraduate teaching, graduate teaching, professional training, and community service. The department offers courses leading to the degree of Doctor of Philosophy. The Clinical Psychology program, with tracks in adult, child, pediatric health, and health, uses a scientist–practitioner model of training with somewhat greater emphasis on the clinical science component. A mentor-model method of research training is employed. Prospective students in psychology are admitted to graduate study within the Adult, Child, or Health Divisions. The Adult Division houses the adult clinical track that includes a focus on personality–social psychology in addition to adult psychopathology and treatment. The Child Division houses the clinical child and pediatric health tracks of the clinical program and also the developmental program. The Health Division houses the health clinical track and the behavioral neuroscience and evolutionary psychology program. All students teach at least one undergraduate course as part of their graduate training. Students are supported via training grants, fellowships, teaching assistantships and research assistantships.

Programs and Degrees Offered

Program	Degree	Application Deadline	Applications Received	Accepted	New Admits Enrolled (PT)	Total Enrolled (PT)	Degrees Awarded in 2014–2015	Median Years to Complete Degree	Dismissed/ Withdrew
Developmental Psychology	PhD	December 1 (Fall)	29	2	1 (0)	10 (0)	4	6	0
Behavioral Neuroscience	PhD	December 1 (Fall)	24	5	3 (0)	8 (0)	2	5	0
Clinical Psychology	PhD	December 1 (Fall)	360	13	8 (0)	68 (0)	9	6	1

APA Accreditation

Clinical PhD: Student Outcome Data website: http://www.psy.miami.edu/graduate/clinical_training/.

Doctoral Degree (PhD Clinical Psychology): For those doctoral students for whom a professional internship was required in this program prior to graduation:
Total students who applied for an internship: 12
Total students who obtained an internship: 12
Total students who obtained a paid internship: 12
Total students who obtained an unpaid internship: 0
Total students who were placed in APA/CPA-accredited internships: 12
Total students placed in internships not APA/CPA-accredited, but listed with the Association of Psychology Postdoctoral and Internship Centers (APPIC): 0
Total students placed in internships conforming to guidelines of the Council of Directors of School Psychology Programs (CDSPP): 0
Total students placed in internships that were not APA/CPA-accredited, APPIC or CDSSP listed: 0

Internships/Practica

Practicum sites are available for students enrolled in our APA-accredited clinical program on the Coral Gables campus, Medical School campus and throughout Miami-Dade County. The department's Psychological Services Center represents a primary site for students developing skills in psychological assessment and empirically based interventions. Additional specialty practica are located in the Department of Pediatrics at the Medical School, the Veterans Administration Medical Center and various clinics throughout Miami-Dade County.

Admissions

Entries appear in the following order: required test or GPA, minimum score (if required)/median score of students entering in 2015–2016.

Program	Degree	GRE-V	GRE-Q	GRE-Writing	GRE-Subject	Under-graduate GPA	Last 2 Years GPA	Psychol-ogy GPA	Master's GPA
Developmental Psychology	PhD	NA/NA	NA/NA	NA/NA	Not specified	NA/NA	Not specified	Not specified	Not specified
Behavioral Neuroscience	PhD	NA/NA	NA/NA	NA/NA	Not specified	NA/NA	Not specified	Not specified	Not specified
Clinical Psychology	PhD	NA/161	NA/158	NA/NA	Not specified	NA/3.6	Not specified	Not specified	Not specified

Admissions Requirements:

Degree	GRE	GRE-Subject	Letters of Recom-mendation	Research Statement	Writing Sample	CV	Interview
Doctoral	Required	Recom-mended	3	Required	Optional	Recom-mended	Required

Please note if these criteria vary for different programs: Clinically related public service not weighted for non-clinical programs.

Admissions Criteria:

GRE scores—high
Research experience—high
Work experience—medium
Clinically related public service—medium
GPA—high

Letters of recommendation—high
Interview—high
Statement of goals and objectives—high
Undergraduate psychology preparation—medium

For additional information on admission requirements, visit http://www.psy.miami.edu/graduate/admissions/.

Department Demographics

	Male (PT)	Female (PT)	Total	African-American/ Black (PT)	Hispanic/ Latino (PT)	Asian/ Pacific Islander (PT)	American Indian/ Alaska Native (PT)	Caucasian/ White (PT)	Unknown (PT)	Multiethnic (PT)	ADA (PT)	Int'l (PT)
Students	17 (0)	69 (0)	86	6 (0)	13 (0)	7 (0)	0 (0)	55 (0)	1 (0)	4 (0)	1 (0)	2 (0)

Financial Information/Assistance

Tuition: For information on tuition costs, visit http://www.miami.edu/finance/index.php/student_account_services/tuition_and_fees/. Additional fees are assessed to students beyond the costs of tuition for the following: student activity fee.

Doctoral:
State residents: $40,700 per academic year.
State residents: $1,850 per credit hour.
Nonstate residents: $40,700 per academic year.
Nonstate residents: $1,850 per credit hour.

Financial Assistance:

	Teaching Assistantship (% Receiving)	Teaching Assistantship Tuition Remission	Research Assistantship (% Receiving)	Research Assistantship Tuition Remission	Fellowship (% Receiving)	Fellowship Tuition Remission
First-Year Student	$21,428 (NA)	Full	$23,376 (NA)	Full	$25,000 (NA)	Full
Advanced Student	$21,428 (NA)	Full	$23,376 (NA)	Full	$25,000 (NA)	Full

For additional information on financial assistance, visit http://www.psy.miami.edu/graduate/financing/.

Employment of Department Graduates

Doctoral:
Enrolled in a postdoctoral residency/fellowship: 8
Employed in independent practice: 2
Employed in an academic position at a university: 2
Do not know: 3
Total: 15

Additional Information

Housing and Day Care: No on-campus housing is available. On-campus day care facilities are available. See the following website for more information: http://www.umcanterbury.com/.

Information for Students With Physical Disabilities: See the following website: http://umarc.miami.edu/arc/ODS.html.

Special Facilities or Resources: The Psychological Services Center serves as a community-based mental health training clinic for clinical students. The Behavioral Medicine Research Building provides excellent research facilities for students in behavioral neuroscience and health psychology. The Behavioral Medicine Research Center located at the UM Miller School of Medicine Clinical Research Building provides state-of-the-art facilities for research in health psychology. The Linda Ray Intervention Center and the Center for Autism and Related Disabilities provide excellent research opportunities for students in our child programs. Faculty research is supported by more than $15 million yearly in federal and state funding. The department resides in a state-of-the-art research and teaching facility constructed for its use in 2003. A new research fMRI facility opened in 2013.

Application Information: Graduate Admissions, Department of Psychology, 5665 Ponce de Leon Boulevard, 5th Floor, Coral Gables, FL 33146. *Fee:* $65. *Online application:* https://www.applyweb.com/miamigrd/index.html.

North Florida, University of
Psychology/Master of Arts in General Psychology
College of Arts and Sciences
1 UNF Drive
Jacksonville, FL 32224
Telephone: (904) 620-2807
Chairperson: Lori Lange

E-mail: t.alloway@unf.edu

Web: https://www.unf.edu/coas/psychology/Master_of_Science_in_General_Psychology.aspx

---

Orientation, Objectives, and Emphasis of Department
The Master of Science in Psychological Science (MSPS) is broad-based and research-oriented. The program consists of rigorous coursework designed around a core curriculum of statistics, research design, and substantive areas of psychology, including social, personality, developmental, biological, and cognitive psychology. Students demonstrate knowledge, critical thinking, and scientific competency skills by completing a research-based thesis that constitutes a justifiable contribution to the discipline of psychology. Professional development is encouraged and fostered through such activities as scholarship, research conference presentations, teaching, departmental colloquia participation, and community engagement. Students completing the program are qualified to go on to further graduate work at universities offering a doctorate in psychology and/or find employment in jobs requiring master's-level expertise in psychology.

Programs and Degrees Offered

Program	Degree	Application Deadline	Applica-tions Received	Accepted	New Admits Enrolled (PT)	Total Enrolled (PT)	Degrees Awarded in 2014–2015	Median Years to Complete Degree	Dismissed/ Withdrew
Psychological Science	MA/MS	June 1 (Fall)	68	27	19 (0)	38 (0)	8	2.5	0

Admissions

Entries appear in the following order: required test or GPA, minimum score (if required)/median score of students entering in 2015–2016.

Program	Degree	GRE-V	GRE-Q	GRE-Writing	GRE-Subject	Under-graduate GPA	Last 2 Years GPA	Psychol-ogy GPA	Master's GPA
Psychological Science	MA/MS	150/NA	146/NA	NA/NA	Not specified	3/NA	Not specified	Not specified	Not specified

Admissions Requirements:

Degree	GRE	GRE-Subject	Letters of Recom-mendation	Research Statement	Writing Sample	CV	Interview
Master's/Specialist	Required	Optional	2	Required	Optional	Required	None

Admissions Criteria:

GRE scores—medium
Research experience—high
Work experience—low
GPA—high

Letters of recommendation—high
Statement of goals and objectives—high
Undergraduate psychology preparation—high

For additional information on admission requirements, visit http://www.unf.edu/graduateschool/academics/programs/General_Psychology.aspx.

Department Demographics

	Male (PT)	Female (PT)	Total	African-American/ Black (PT)	Hispanic/ Latino (PT)	Asian/ Pacific Islander (PT)	American Indian/ Alaska Native (PT)	Caucasian/ White (PT)	Unknown	Multiethnic (PT)	ADA (PT)	Int'l (PT)
Students	15 (0)	23 (0)	38	0 (0)	5 (0)	0 (0)	0 (0)	31 (0)	1 (0)	1 (0)	0 (0)	1 (0)

Financial Information/Assistance

Tuition: For information on tuition costs, visit http://www.unf.edu/tuition/. Tuition is subject to change.

Master's:
State residents: $9,867 per academic year.
State residents: $493 per credit hour.
Nonstate residents: $20,882 per academic year.
Nonstate residents: $1,044 per credit hour.

Financial Assistance:

	Teaching Assistantship (% Receiving)	Teaching Assistantship Tuition Remission	Research Assistantship (% Receiving)	Research Assistantship Tuition Remission	Fellowship (% Receiving)	Fellowship Tuition Remission
First-Year Student	$5,000 (11)	NA	NA (NA)	NA	NA (75)	Partial
Advanced Student	$10,000 (29)	NA	NA (NA)	NA	$500 (50)	NA

For additional information on financial assistance, visit http://www.unf.edu/graduateschool/prospective/funding/Scholarships.aspx.

Employment of Department Graduates

Master's:
Enrolled in a psychology doctoral program: 4
Employed in academic position at a 2-year/4-year college: 2
Employed in a professional position in a school system: 1
Employed in business or industry: 2
Employed in a community mental health/counseling center: 1
Employed in a hospital/medical center: 1
Do not know: 1
Total: 12

Additional Information

Housing and Day Care: On-campus housing is available. See the following website for more information: http://www.unf.edu/housing/. On-campus day care facilities are available. See the following website for more information: http://www.unf.edu/cdrc/.

Information for Students With Physical Disabilities: See the following website: http://www.unf.edu/drc/.

Special Facilities or Resources: Graduate library, research laboratories for all full-time faculty members and their lab members, shared lab space for larger research projects, community connections office.

Application Information: UNF Graduate School. *Fee:* $30. *Online application:* https://www.unf.edu/graduateschool/prospective/admissions/Apply_Today.aspx.

Nova Southeastern University
College of Psychology
3301 College Avenue, Maltz Building
Fort Lauderdale, FL 33314-7796
Telephone: (954) 262-5903
Dean: Karen S. Grosby, EdD

E-mail: ggayle1@nova.edu
Web: http://psychology.nova.edu

Orientation, Objectives, and Emphasis of Department
The Center for Psychological Studies (CPS) is committed to providing the highest quality educational experience to future psychologists and counseling professionals. These training experiences provide individuals with a sophisticated understanding of psychological research and the delivery of the highest-quality mental health care. Through the intimate interplay between CPS academic programs and the Nova Southeastern University (NSU) Psychology Services Center, learning becomes rooted in real problems, and research activities attempt to find answers to extant concerns. The center offers master's programs in counseling, mental health counseling, school counseling, general psychology, forensic psychology, specialist (PsyS) and doctoral (PsyD) programs in school psychology, and two APA-accredited doctoral programs in clinical psychology. The doctor of psychology (PsyD) program provides emphasis on training professionals to do service while the doctor of philosophy (PhD) program provides greater emphasis on applied research. In response to changes in health care delivery and the profession of psychology, the center developed concentrations at the doctoral level. Concentrations/tracks based on the existing PsyD and PhD curriculum are available in the areas of Clinical Neuropsychology, Clinical Health Psychology, Forensic Psychology, Psychodynamic Psychology, Psychology of Long-Term Mental Illness, Multicultural/diversity, and Child, Adolescent and Family.

Programs and Degrees Offered

Program	Degree	Application Deadline	Applications Received	Accepted	New Admits Enrolled (PT)	Total Enrolled (PT)	Degrees Awarded in 2014–2015	Median Years to Complete Degree	Dismissed/ Withdrew
Mental Health Counseling	MA/MS	Rolling	455	345	165	407 (46)	153	3	15
Clinical Psychology	PhD	January 8 (Fall)	221	18	15 (0)	73 (0)	14	6	0
Clinical Psychology	PsyD	January 8 (Fall)	346	160	86 (0)	424 (0)	60	5	12
School Counseling	MA/MS	Rolling	78	51	48 (0)	68 (10)	21	2	9
Specialist in School Psychology	Other	June 15 (Fall), November 15 (Winter)	27	14	14 (0)	49 (0)	15	4	3
School Psychology	PsyD	January 8 (Fall)	29	12	6 (0)	28 (0)	0		0
Counseling	MA/MS	June 15 (Fall), December 1 (Winter), March 29 (Summer)	400	257	240 (0)	420 (113)	150	2.5	40

APA Accreditation

Clinical PhD: Student Outcome Data website: http://psychology.nova.edu/graduate/clinical-psychology/phd/performance-outcomes.html.

Clinical PsyD: Student Outcome Data website: http://psychology.nova.edu/graduate/clinical-psychology/psyd/performance-outcomes.html.

Doctoral Degree (PhD Clinical Psychology): For those doctoral students for whom a professional internship was required in this program prior to graduation:

Total students who applied for an internship: 14
Total students who obtained an internship: 13
Total students who obtained a paid internship: 13
Total students who obtained an unpaid internship: 0
Total students who were placed in APA/CPA-accredited internships: 8
Total students placed in internships not APA/CPA-accredited, but listed with the Association of Psychology Postdoctoral and Internship Centers (APPIC): 5
Total students placed in internships conforming to guidelines of the Council of Directors of School Psychology Programs (CDSPP): 0
Total students placed in internships that were not APA/CPA-accredited, APPIC or CDSSP listed: 0

Doctoral Degree (PsyD Clinical Psychology): For those doctoral students for whom a professional internship was required in this program prior to graduation:

Total students who applied for an internship: 84
Total students who obtained an internship: 74
Total students who obtained a paid internship: 74
Total students who obtained an unpaid internship: 0
Total students who were placed in APA/CPA-accredited internships: 43
Total students placed in internships not APA/CPA-accredited, but listed with the Association of Psychology Postdoctoral and Internship Centers (APPIC): 31
Total students placed in internships conforming to guidelines of the Council of Directors of School Psychology Programs (CDSPP): 0
Total students placed in internships that were not APA/CPA-accredited, APPIC or CDSSP listed: 0

Master's Degree (MA/MS Mental Health Counseling): An internship experience, such as a final research project or "capstone" experience is required of graduates. Master's Degree (MA/MS School Counseling): An internship experience, such as a final research project or "capstone" experience is required of graduates. Master's Degree (MA/MS Counseling): An internship experience, such as a final research project or "capstone" experience is required of graduates.

Internships/Practica

Accredited by the American Psychological Association, the Psychology Services Center Internship Program offers doctoral candidates in psychology the opportunity to develop professionally, to enhance their ability to use scholarly research for informed practice, to develop proficiency in psychological assessment and psychotherapeutic intervention, and to acquire basic competence in the provision of supervision and consultation. In addition, the Center for Psychological Studies sponsors the Consortium Internship Program (APPIC member) that provides internship experiences in hospital and other settings within the South Florida Community. In addition to the extensive practicum placements available in the community, practicum opportunities for more than 100 students are provided through various CPS faculty supervised applied-research clinical programs located within the NSU Psychology Services Center. Areas of research include ADHD, alcohol and substance abuse, anxiety treatment, child and adolescent traumatic stress, clinical biofeedback, interpersonal violence, neuropsychological assessment, older adults, school psychology assessment and testing, the seriously emotionally disturbed, and trauma resolution integration.

Admissions

Entries appear in the following order: required test or GPA, minimum score (if required)/median score of students entering in 2015–2016.

Program	Degree	GRE-V	GRE-Q	GRE-Writing	GRE-Subject	Under-graduate GPA	Last 2 Years GPA	Psychol-ogy GPA	Master's GPA
Mental Health Counseling	MA/MS	Not specified	Not specified	Not specified	Not specified	Not specified	Not specified	Not specified	Not specified
Clinical Psychology	PhD	NA/159	NA/155	NA/4.4	Not specified	NA/3.6	Not specified	Not specified	Not specified
Clinical Psychology	PsyD	NA/153	NA/148	NA/4	Not specified	NA/3.48	Not specified	Not specified	Not specified
School Counseling	MA/MS	Not specified	Not specified	Not specified	Not specified	Not specified	Not specified	Not specified	Not specified
Specialist in School Psychology	Other	153/NA	144/NA	4/NA	Not specified	3/NA	Not specified	Not specified	Not specified
School Psychology	PsyD	153/NA	144/NA	4/NA	Not specified	3/NA	Not specified	Not specified	Not specified
Counseling	MA/MS	Not specified	Not specified	Not specified	Not specified	Not specified	Not specified	Not specified	Not specified

Admissions Requirements:

Degree	GRE	GRE-Subject	Letters of Recom-mendation	Research Statement	Writing Sample	CV	Interview
Master's/Specialist	Required	None	2	Required	Optional	Optional	Required
Doctoral	Required	Recom-mended	3	Required	Optional	Required	Required

Please note if these criteria vary for different programs: The importance of research is high for the PhD program; Undergraduate major in psychology is highly recommended for the PhD and PsyD programs. School PsyD recommends applicants take the GRE-Subject test.

Admissions Criteria:

GRE scores—high
Work experience—medium
Clinically related public service—medium
GPA—high

Letters of recommendation—high
Interview—high
Statement of goals and objectives—high
Undergraduate psychology preparation—medium

Department Demographics

	Male (PT)	Female (PT)	Total	African-American/ Black (PT)	Hispanic/ Latino (PT)	Asian/ Pacific Islander (PT)	American Indian/ Alaska Native (PT)	Caucasian/ White (PT)	Unknown	Multiethnic (PT)	ADA (PT)	Int'l (PT)
Students	376 (0)	1452 (0)	1828	255 (0)	428 (0)	39 (0)	3 (0)	981 (0)	101 (0)	21 (0)	18 (0)	21 (0)

Financial Information/Assistance

Tuition: Higher tuition cost for this program: Specialist in School Psychology: $710 per credit hour. Tuition is subject to change. Tuition costs vary by program.

Doctoral:
State residents: $970 per credit hour.
Nonstate residents: $970 per credit hour.

Master's:
State residents: $650 per credit hour.
Nonstate residents: $650 per credit hour.

Financial Assistance:

	Teaching Assistantship (% Receiving)	Teaching Assistantship Tuition Remission	Research Assistantship (% Receiving)	Research Assistantship Tuition Remission	Fellowship (% Receiving)	Fellowship Tuition Remission
First-Year Student	NA (NA)	NA	$5,600 (NA)	NA	NA (NA)	NA
Advanced Student	$2,000 (NA)	NA	$5,600 (NA)	NA	NA (NA)	Partial

For additional information on financial assistance, visit http://www.nova.edu/financialaid/.

Employment of Department Graduates

Master's:
Enrolled in a psychology doctoral program: 5
Enrolled in another graduate/professional program: 6
Employed in academic position at a 2-year/4-year college: 3
Employed in other positions at a higher education institution: 10
Employed in a professional position in a school system: 80
Employed in business or industry: 25
Employed in government agency: 7
Employed in a community mental health/counseling center: 65
Employed in a hospital/medical center: 14
Other employment position: 75
Do not know: 80
Total: 370

Doctoral:
Enrolled in a postdoctoral residency/fellowship: 70
Employed in an academic position at a university: 3
Employed in other positions at a higher education institution: 1
Employed in government agency: 2
Employed in a community mental health/counseling center: 1
Employed in a hospital/medical center: 3
Do not know: 8
Total: 88

Additional Information

Housing and Day Care: On-campus housing is available. On-campus day care facilities are available. See the following website for more information: http://www.nova.edu/humandevelopment/earlylearning/index.html.

Information for Students With Physical Disabilities: See the following website: http://www.nova.edu/disabilityservices/.

Special Facilities or Resources: The Center for Psychological Studies is housed in the Maltz Psychology Building, a 65,000 square-foot facility that includes classrooms with state-of-the-art computer technology, a microcomputer lab with 30 multimedia computers connected to major databases and the Internet, study carrels, lounges and meeting rooms, and the Psychology Services Center where there are therapy rooms with audio and video monitoring capability, play-therapy rooms, and workstations for practicum students assigned to faculty specialty clinical programs. As a university-based professional school, CPS provides access to the

NSU 325,000 square-foot Library, Research and Information Technology Center, as well as NSU's Schools of Law, Business and Systemic Studies, the colleges of its Health Professions Division (Medicine, Dentistry, Pharmacy, Allied Health, and Optometry), and its Family and School Center. Also included on NSU's 232-acre+ campus are five residence halls, recreation facilities, and the Miami Dolphins Training Center.

Application Information: Enrollment Processing Services, Attn: Center for Psychological Studies, P.O. Box 299000, Fort Lauderdale, FL 33329-9905. *Fee:* $50. *Online application:* https://webstar.nova.edu/pls/PROD/bwskalog.P_DispLoginNon.

Nova Southeastern University

Department of Psychology and Neuroscience
College of Psychology
3301 College Avenue
Fort Lauderdale, FL 33314-7796
Telephone: (954) 262-7941
Chairperson: Dr. Glenn Scheyd

E-mail: scheydjr@nova.edu
Web: http://psychology.nova.edu/index.html

Orientation, Objectives, and Emphasis of Department

The Master of Science in Experimental Psychology degree program provides students with a strong academic foundation in the theories and concepts of experimental psychology. Through focused coursework and the experience of mentored independent research, students are equipped with comprehensive skills in scientific inquiry and research methodology. The Master's degree program in General Psychology is a 30-credit online program that will prepare students to develop foundational knowledge in psychological theory and research. Local, national, and international students may select this MS degree as an opportunity to obtain prerequisite courses to meet eligibility requirements for application to other psychology programs, including advanced doctoral studies, and through its specialty tracks, allows a variety of professionals within the fields of education, human services, counseling, and allied health to access coursework both as degree-seeking and non-degree seeking students in order to advance their psychological knowledge and use of psychological applications in their respective fields. The Master's degree program in Forensic Psychology is a 36-credit online program that will present information at the intersection of legal issues and psychology. Students will be prepared to understand what forensic psychologists do, as well as to apply this training in a variety of professional settings.

Programs and Degrees Offered

Program	Degree	Application Deadline	Applica-tions Received	Accepted	New Admits Enrolled (PT)	Total Enrolled (PT)	Degrees Awarded in 2014–2015	Median Years to Complete Degree	Dismissed/Withdrew
Experimental Psychology	MA/MS	June 1 (Fall), Rolling	14	9	3 (0)	6 (0)	7	2	1
Forensic Psychology	MA/MS	July 7 (Fall), December 1 (Winter), March 29 (Summer)			35	113			
General Psychology	MA/MS	July 7 (Fall), December 1 (Winter), March 29 (Summer)			35	100			

Admissions

Entries appear in the following order: required test or GPA, minimum score (if required)/median score of students entering in 2015–2016.

Program	Degree	GRE-V	GRE-Q	GRE-Writing	GRE-Subject	Under-graduate GPA	Last 2 Years GPA	Psychol-ogy GPA	Master's GPA
Experimental Psychology	MA/MS	NA/154	NA/149	Not specified	Not specified	Not specified	Not specified	Not specified	Not specified

Admissions *(con't.)*

Program	Degree	GRE-V	GRE-Q	GRE-Writing	GRE-Subject	Under-graduate GPA	Last 2 Years GPA	Psychology GPA	Master's GPA
Forensic Psychology	MA/MS	Not specified	Not specified	Not specified	Not specified	Not specified	Not specified	Not specified	Not specified
General Psychology	MA/MS	Not specified	Not specified	Not specified	Not specified	Not specified	Not specified	Not specified	Not specified

Admissions Requirements:

Degree	GRE	GRE-Subject	Letters of Recommendation	Research Statement	Writing Sample	CV	Interview
Master's/Specialist	Required	Required	3	Required	Optional	Optional	Optional

Please note if these criteria vary for different programs: The criteria listed above apply to the Master's in Experimental Psychology. The programs in Forensic and General Psychology consider GREs optional and only request 2 letters of recommendation.

Admissions Criteria:
GRE scores—high
Research experience—low
Work experience—low
Clinically related public service—low

GPA—high
Letters of recommendation—high
Statement of goals and objectives—high
Undergraduate psychology preparation—low

Department Demographics

	Male (PT)	Female (PT)	Total	African American/ Black (PT)	Hispanic/ Latino (PT)	Asian/ Pacific Islander (PT)	American Indian/ Alaska Native (PT)	Caucasian/ White (PT)	Unknown (PT)	Multiethnic (PT)	ADA (PT)	Int'l (PT)
Students	70 (0)	132 (0)	202	(0)	(0)	0 (0)	0 (0)	0 (0)	202 (0)	0 (0)	0 (0)	(0)

Financial Information/Assistance

Tuition: Tuition is subject to change. Tuition costs vary by program.

Master's:
State residents: $670 per credit hour.
Nonstate residents: $670 per credit hour.

Financial Assistance:

	Teaching Assistantship (% Receiving)	Teaching Assistantship Tuition Remission	Research Assistantship (% Receiving)	Research Assistantship Tuition Remission	Fellowship (% Receiving)	Fellowship Tuition Remission
First-Year Student	NA (NA)	NA	NA (NA)	NA	NA (NA)	NA
Advanced Student	NA (NA)	NA	NA (NA)	NA	NA (NA)	NA

For additional information on financial assistance, visit http://www.nova.edu/financialaid/index.html.

Employment of Department Graduates

No information provided.

Additional Information

Housing and Day Care: On-campus housing is available. See the following website for more information: http://www.nova.edu/housing/graduate/index.html. No on-campus day care facilities are available.

Information for Students With Physical Disabilities: See the following website: http://www.nova.edu/disabilityservices/.

Application Information: Nova Southeastern University, Enrollment Processing Services, Attn: College of Psychology, 3301 College Avenue, P.O. Box 299000, Fort Lauderdale, Florida 33329-9905. *Fee:* $50. *Online application:* http://www.nova.edu/apply/index.html.

South Florida, University of
Department of Educational and Psychological Studies
College of Education
EDU 105
Tampa, FL 33620-7750
Telephone: (813) 974-4614
Chairperson: Kathy Bradley-Klug, PhD

E-mail: batsche@usf.edu
Web: http://www.coedu.usf.edu/schoolpsych/

Orientation, Objectives, and Emphasis of Department

Thorough admissions procedures result in the selection of outstanding students. This makes possible a faculty commitment to do everything possible to guide each student to a high level of professional competence. The curriculum is well organized and explicit such that students are always aware of program expectations and their progress in relation to these expectations. The student body is kept small, resulting in greater student-faculty contact than would otherwise be possible. Skills of practice are developed through non-threatening apprenticeship networks established with local school systems. This model encourages students to assist several professors and practicing school psychologists throughout their training. The notion here is to provide positive environments, containing rich feedback, in which competent psychological skills develop. We emphasize a scientist–practitioner model representing primarily a cognitive-behavioral orientation. Further, we support comprehensive school psychology, including consultation, prevention, intervention, and program evaluation.

Programs and Degrees Offered

Program	Degree	Application Deadline	Applica-tions Received	Accepted	New Admits Enrolled (PT)	Total Enrolled (PT)	Degrees Awarded in 2014–2015	Median Years to Complete Degree	Dismissed/ Withdrew
School Psychology	PhD	January 1 (Fall)	56	11	7 (0)	41 (0)	3	5	0
School Psychology	EdS	January 1 (Fall)	39	7	3 (0)	8 (0)	2		0

APA Accreditation

School PhD: Student Outcome Data website: http://www.coedu.usf.edu/schoolpsych/Program/program_outcomes.htm.

Doctoral Degree (PhD School Psychology): For those doctoral students for whom a professional internship was required in this program prior to graduation:
Total students who applied for an internship: 4
Total students who obtained an internship: 4
Total students who obtained a paid internship: 4
Total students who obtained an unpaid internship: 0
Total students who were placed in APA/CPA-accredited internships: 1
Total students placed in internships not APA/CPA-accredited, but listed with the Association of Psychology Postdoctoral and Internship Centers (APPIC): 0
Total students placed in internships conforming to guidelines of the Council of Directors of School Psychology Programs (CDSPP): 3
Total students placed in internships that were not APA/CPA-accredited, APPIC or CDSSP listed: 0

Internships/Practica

Our practica and internships integrate home, school, and community service programs for students at risk for educational failure and their families, including students with disabilities. We focus especially on the priorities of researching and promoting effective educational and mental health practices for all children, youth and their families. All doctoral students participate in practica during the first three years of the program. Practicum settings include schools (public, charter, alternative), hospital settings, research settings, university-affiliated agencies (e.g., USF Dept. of Pediatrics, Florida Mental Health Institute) and special programs (e.g., Early Intervention Program). Doctoral students participate in approximately 1000 hours of practicum training prior to internship. All doctoral students complete a 2000-hour predoctoral internship in an APA-accredited/APPIC site or one that meets the APA/APPIC criteria.

Admissions

Entries appear in the following order: required test or GPA, minimum score (if required)/median score of students entering in 2015–2016.

Program	Degree	GRE-V	GRE-Q	GRE-Writing	GRE-Subject	Under-graduate GPA	Last 2 Years GPA	Psychol-ogy GPA	Master's GPA
School Psychology	PhD	NA/NA	NA/NA	NA/NA	Not specified	NA/3.7	NA/3.9	Not specified	NA/4
School Psychology	EdS	NA/NA	NA/NA	NA/NA	Not specified	NA/3.7	Not specified	Not specified	Not specified

Admissions Requirements:

Degree	GRE	GRE-Subject	Letters of Recom-mendation	Research Statement	Writing Sample	CV	Interview
Master's/Specialist	Required	Optional	3	Required	Required	Required	Required
Doctoral	Required	Optional	3	Required	Required	Required	Required

Admissions Criteria:

GRE scores—medium
Research experience—high
Work experience—medium
Clinically related public service—medium
GPA—high

Letters of recommendation—high
Interview—high
Statement of goals and objectives—high
Undergraduate psychology preparation—high
Writing sample—high

For additional information on admission requirements, visit http://www.coedu.usf.edu/schoolpsych/Program/program_admissions.htm.

Department Demographics

	Male (PT)	Female (PT)	Total	African-American/ Black (PT)	Hispanic/ Latino (PT)	Asian/ Pacific Islander (PT)	American Indian/ Alaska Native (PT)	Caucasian/ White (PT)	Unknown	Multiethnic (PT)	ADA (PT)	Int'l (PT)
Students	10 (0)	39 (0)	49	6 (0)	2 (0)	5 (0)	0 (0)	36 (0)	0 (0)	0 (0)	0 (0)	5 (0)

Financial Information/Assistance

Tuition: For information on tuition costs, visit http://www.usf.edu/admission/cost-to-attend.aspx. Tuition is subject to change. Additional fees are assessed to students beyond the costs of tuition for the following: athletic fees, service fees, techology fees, and student union fees.

Doctoral:
State residents: $13,016 per academic year.
State residents: $431 per credit hour.
Nonstate residents: $26,389 per academic year.
Nonstate residents: $877 per credit hour.

Master's:
State residents: $13,016 per academic year.
State residents: $431 per credit hour.
Nonstate residents: $26,389 per academic year.
Nonstate residents: $877 per credit hour.

Financial Assistance:

	Teaching Assistantship (% Receiving)	Teaching Assistantship Tuition Remission	Research Assistantship (% Receiving)	Research Assistantship Tuition Remission	Fellowship (% Receiving)	Fellowship Tuition Remission
First-Year Student	NA (NA)	NA	$11,551 (72)	Full	$12,560 (36)	Full
Advanced Student	$11,551 (14)	Full	$11,551 (55)	Full	$12,560 (25)	Full

For additional information on financial assistance, visit http://www.coedu.usf.edu/schoolpsych/Financial_Aid/financial_aid.htm.

Employment of Department Graduates

Master's:
Enrolled in a psychology doctoral program: 2
Total: 2

Doctoral:
Enrolled in a postdoctoral residency/fellowship: 1
Employed in a professional position in a school system: 1
Employed in a hospital/medical center: 1
Total: 3

Additional Information

Housing and Day Care: On-campus housing is available. See the following website for more information: http://www.housing.usf.edu/. On-campus day care facilities are available. See the following website for more information: http://child-care-preschool.brighthorizons.com/FL/Tampa/usf/; http://www.usfpcl.org/.

Information for Students With Physical Disabilities: See the following website: http://www.usf.edu/student-affairs/student-disabilities-services/.

Special Facilities or Resources: The University of South Florida is a comprehensive Research I (FL) and Doctoral/Research Universities-Extensive (Carnegie) university that has over 45,000 students on a 1,700 acre campus 10 miles northeast of downtown Tampa, a city of over 350,000 people. Amongst its faculty, the School Psychology Program has one APA Fellow, two past presidents of the National Association of School Psychologists, the past president of the Council of Directors of School Psychology Programs, the 2009 recipient of the APA Division 16 Lightner Witmer Award, and faculty who have received over $40 million in federal and state grants over the past years. Students collaborate with professors and researchers in the program, the College of Education, the Departments of Psychology, Psychiatry, and Pediatrics, the Florida Mental Health Institute, Shriner's, Tampa General and St. Joseph's hospitals, the Florida Department of Education and other settings. The program is housed in a new College of Education physical plant that has the latest fiber optic-based technology, clinical and research observation areas, and strong technology support. Strong links exist with community schools and agencies.

Application Information: Linda Raffaele Mendez, Coordinator of Admissions, School Psychology Program, EDU 105, University of South Florida, Tampa, FL 33620-7750. *Fee:* $30. *Online application:* https://secure.vzcollegeapp.com/usf/.

South Florida, University of
Department of Psychology
Arts and Sciences
4202 East Fowler Avenue, PCD 4118G
Tampa, FL 33620-7200
Telephone: (813) 974-2492
Chairperson: Toru Shimizu

E-mail: lpierce@usf.edu
Web: http://psychology.usf.edu/

Orientation, Objectives, and Emphasis of Department
The department attempts to educate graduate students to a high level of proficiency in research and in practice. The department expects its doctoral students to be of such quality as to take their place at major institutions of learning if they choose academic careers and to assume roles of responsibility and importance if they choose professional careers. The doctoral program in clinical psychology provides broad-based professional and research training to prepare students for careers in a variety of applied, research, and teaching settings. The doctoral program in cognition, neuroscience, and social psychology prepares students for research

careers in both applied and academic environments. This program also offers an interdisciplinary degree in Speech, Language, and Hearing Science in conjunction with the Department of Communication Sciences and Disorders. The doctoral program in industrial/organizational psychology provides professional and research training to prepare students for careers in industrial, governmental, academic, and related organizational settings.

Programs and Degrees Offered

Program	Degree	Application Deadline	Applica-tions Received	Accepted	New Admits Enrolled (PT)	Total Enrolled (PT)	Degrees Awarded in 2014–2015	Median Years to Complete Degree	Dismissed/ Withdrew
Clinical Psychology	PhD	December 1 (Fall)	259	16	7 (0)	53 (0)	8	6.5	0
Cognition, Neuroscience, and Social Psychology	PhD	December 1 (Fall)	97	7	4 (0)	28 (0)	3	5.75	4
Industrial/ Organizational Psychology	PhD	December 1 (Fall)	151	8	5 (0)	34 (0)	4	6.04	1

APA Accreditation
Clinical PhD: Student Outcome Data website: http://psychology.usf.edu/grad/clinical/.

Doctoral Degree (PhD Clinical Psychology): For those doctoral students for whom a professional internship was required in this program prior to graduation:
Total students who applied for an internship: 7
Total students who obtained an internship: 7
Total students who obtained a paid internship: 7
Total students who obtained an unpaid internship: 0
Total students who were placed in APA/CPA-accredited internships: 7
Total students placed in internships not APA/CPA-accredited, but listed with the Association of Psychology Postdoctoral and Internship Centers (APPIC): 0
Total students placed in internships conforming to guidelines of the Council of Directors of School Psychology Programs (CDSPP): 0
Total students placed in internships that were not APA/CPA-accredited, APPIC or CDSSP listed: 0

Internships/Practica
The Clinical program operates its own Psychology Clinic within the Psychology Department, providing opportunities for practical training in clinical assessment and clinical psychological interventions. Students are active in the Psychology Clinic throughout their training. Clinical core faculty provide most of the supervision of Clinic cases. The Clinical Psychology program is fortunate to have a unique cluster of campus and community training facilities available for student placement. For example, we have student placements at or near such campus facilities as the USF Florida Mental Health Research Institute, the USF Counseling Center for Human Development, the Moffitt Cancer Center and Research Institute and the Tampa Veterans Administration Hospital as well as carefully selected community agencies. Students in the Industrial/Organizational program are required to complete a predoctoral internship. Placements are made in numerous governmental, corporate and consulting firms both locally and nationally. Recent placements have included the cities of Tampa and Clearwater, GTE, Tampa Electric Company, Personnel Decisions Research Institute, Personnel Decisions, Inc., Florida Power and USF&G.

Admissions
Entries appear in the following order: required test or GPA, minimum score (if required)/median score of students entering in 2015–2016.

Program	Degree	GRE-V	GRE-Q	GRE-Writing	GRE-Subject	Under-graduate GPA	Last 2 Years GPA	Psychol-ogy GPA	Master's GPA
Clinical Psychology	PhD	152/160	152/160	NA/4.5	Not specified	Not specified	3.4/3.79	Not specified	Not specified
Cognition, Neuroscience, and Social Psychology	PhD	152/157	152/158	NA/NA	Not specified	Not specified	3.4/3.73	Not specified	Not specified

Admissions *(con't.)*

Program	Degree	GRE-V	GRE-Q	GRE-Writing	GRE-Subject	Under-graduate GPA	Last 2 Years GPA	Psychology GPA	Master's GPA
Industrial/Organizational Psychology	PhD	152/160	152/160	NA/NA	Not specified	Not specified	3.4/3.55	Not specified	Not specified

Admissions Requirements:

Degree	GRE	GRE-Subject	Letters of Recommendation	Research Statement	Writing Sample	CV	Interview
Doctoral	Required	Optional	3	Required	Optional	Recommended	Recommended

Admissions Criteria:

GRE scores—high
Research experience—high
Work experience—low
Clinically related public service—low

GPA—high
Letters of recommendation—high
Interview—medium
Statement of goals and objectives—high

For additional information on admission requirements, visit http://psychology.usf.edu/grad/admission/adminreq/.

Department Demographics

	Male (PT)	Female (PT)	Total	African-American/Black (PT)	Hispanic/Latino (PT)	Asian/Pacific Islander (PT)	American Indian/Alaska Native (PT)	Caucasian/White (PT)	Unknown (PT)	Multiethnic (PT)	ADA (PT)	Int'l (PT)
Students	36 (0)	79 (0)	115	3 (0)	8 (0)	18 (0)	0 (0)	86 (0)	0 (0)	(0)	3 (0)	12 (0)

Financial Information/Assistance

Tuition: For information on tuition costs, visit http://www.usf.edu/business-finance/controller/student-services/tuition-rates.aspx. Tuition is subject to change. Additional fees are assessed to students beyond the costs of tuition for the following: $37 flat fees, $10 bank card fee, $35 one-time orientation fee, technology fee (varies).

Doctoral:
State residents: $7,765 per academic year.
State residents: $431 per credit hour.
Nonstate residents: $15,789 per academic year.
Nonstate residents: $877 per credit hour.

Financial Assistance:

	Teaching Assistantship (% Receiving)	Teaching Assistantship Tuition Remission	Research Assistantship (% Receiving)	Research Assistantship Tuition Remission	Fellowship (% Receiving)	Fellowship Tuition Remission
First-Year Student	$15,700 (56)	Partial	$15,700 (19)	Partial	$20,100 (NA)	Partial
Advanced Student	$15,700 (45)	Partial	$15,700 (20)	Partial	$20,100 (11)	Partial

For additional information on financial assistance, visit http://www.usf.edu/financial-aid/.

Employment of Department Graduates

Doctoral:
Enrolled in a postdoctoral residency/fellowship: 7
Employed in an academic position at a university: 3
Employed in academic position at a 2-year/4-year college: 2
Employed in business or industry: 3
Total: 15

Additional Information

Housing and Day Care: On-campus housing is available. See the following website for more information: http://www.housing.usf.edu/. On-campus day care facilities are available. See the following website for more information: http://child-care-preschool.brighthorizons.com/FL/Tampa/usf/.

Information for Students With Physical Disabilities: See the following website: http://www.usf.edu/student-affairs/student-disabilities-services/.

Special Facilities or Resources: The Psychology Department houses state-of-the-art facilities and equipment. There is research space for faculty, graduate, and advanced undergraduate students, including a large vivarium. An open-use lab has been equipped with computer terminals that access the mainframe computer on campus. The University Computer Center is available. The Psychological Services Center is operated as the department's facility for clinical practicum work. A state-of-the-art video system permits supervisory capabilities for clinical practica.

Application Information: University of South Florida, Office of Admissions, 4202 East Fowler Avenue, SVC 1036, Tampa, FL 33620. *Fee:* $30. *Online application:* http://www.usf.edu/admissions/graduate/index.aspx.

West Florida, University of
Department of Psychology
College of Health
11000 University Parkway
Pensacola, FL 32514-5751
Telephone: (850) 474-2363
Chairperson: Lisa VanWormer

E-mail: psych@uwf.edu
Web: http://uwf.edu/psychology

Orientation, Objectives, and Emphasis of Department
The Department of Psychology is a member of the Council of Applied Master's Programs in Psychology and is committed to the philosophy of training with a foundation in general psychology (individual, social, biological, and learned bases of behavior) as the basis for training in application of psychology. Applied students receive significant supervised field experience. The department mission is preparation of master's level practitioners and preparation of students for doctoral work as well. The programs in Counseling Psychology and Industrial/Organizational Psychology are accredited by the Master's in Psychology and Counseling Accreditation Council (MPCAC). The department also offers a certificate in Health Psychology. The Counseling Psychology program offers a 60-hour option with coursework comparable to requirements for licensure as a Mental Health Counselor in Florida.

Programs and Degrees Offered

Program	Degree	Application Deadline	Applications Received	Accepted	New Admits Enrolled (PT)	Total Enrolled (PT)	Degrees Awarded in 2014–2015	Median Years to Complete Degree	Dismissed/Withdrew
Counseling Psychology	MA/MS	February 1 (Fall)	34	15	9	28 (1)	5	3	4
Applied Experimental	MA/MS	February 1 (Fall)	20	12	8	16 (2)	3	2	1
Industrial/ Organizational Psychology	MA/MS	February 1 (Fall)	66	36	15	25 (2)	13	2	3

Internships/Practica

Master's students complete a minimum of 1000 hours of practicum/internship for the mental health counseling licensure option. Faculty assist in finding suitable placements in field settings under qualified supervision. The student also prepares a portfolio demonstrating mastery of several specific competencies and includes an integrative paper reflecting on professional development. Practica (required for counseling students, optional for other students) are completed earlier in the program and involve more limited applied experience and closer supervision by faculty. Internship placements for counseling students include a variety of local mental health agencies providing inpatient, outpatient and community outreach services. Internship placements for industrial/organizational students include a variety of business and healthcare settings.

Admissions

Entries appear in the following order: required test or GPA, minimum score (if required)/median score of students entering in 2015–2016.

Program	Degree	GRE-V	GRE-Q	GRE-Writing	GRE-Subject	Under-graduate GPA	Last 2 Years GPA	Psychology GPA	Master's GPA
Counseling Psychology	MA/MS	NA/154	NA/152	Not specified	Not specified	Not specified	3/3.53	Not specified	Not specified
Applied Experimental	MA/MS	NA/154	NA/152	Not specified	Not specified	Not specified	3/3.61	Not specified	Not specified
Industrial/ Organizational Psychology	MA/MS	NA/153	NA/152	Not specified	Not specified	Not specified	3/3.52	Not specified	Not specified

Admissions Requirements:

Degree	GRE	GRE-Subject	Letters of Recommendation	Research Statement	Writing Sample	CV	Interview
Master's/Specialist	Required	None	3	Required	Optional	Optional	Required

Please note if these criteria vary for different programs: Counseling applicants are required to complete an interview.

Admissions Criteria:

GRE scores—high
Research experience—medium
Work experience—medium
Clinically related public service—medium
GPA—high

Letters of recommendation—high
Interview—high
Statement of goals and objectives—high
Undergraduate psychology preparation—high

For additional information on admission requirements, visit http://uwf.edu/coh/departments/psychology/psychology-graduate-admissions/how-to-apply/.

Department Demographics

	Male (PT)	Female (PT)	Total	African-American/ Black (PT)	Hispanic/ Latino (PT)	Asian/ Pacific Islander (PT)	American Indian/ Alaska Native (PT)	Caucasian/ White (PT)	Unknown	Multiethnic (PT)	ADA (PT)	Int'l (PT)
Students	21 (4)	48 (1)	74	3 (0)	9 (0)	2 (0)	0 (1)	51 (4)	0 (0)	4 (0)	1 (0)	0 (0)

Financial Information/Assistance

Tuition: For information on tuition costs, visit http://catalog.uwf.edu/graduate/tuitionandfees/. Tuition is subject to change.

Master's:
State residents: $378 per credit hour.
Nonstate residents: $1,037 per credit hour.

Financial Assistance:

	Teaching Assistantship (% Receiving)	Teaching Assistantship Tuition Remission	Research Assistantship (% Receiving)	Research Assistantship Tuition Remission	Fellowship (% Receiving)	Fellowship Tuition Remission
First-Year Student	NA (NA)	NA	$3,760 (NA)	Partial	$2,000 (NA)	NA
Advanced Student	$3,280 (NA)	Partial	$3,760 (NA)	Partial	$750 (NA)	NA

For additional information on financial assistance, visit http://uwf.edu/finaid/.

Employment of Department Graduates

Master's:
Enrolled in a psychology doctoral program: 4
Employed in business or industry: 10
Employed in a community mental health/counseling center: 5
Other employment position: 2
Total: 21

Additional Information

Housing and Day Care: On-campus housing is available. See the following website for more information: http://uwf.edu/housing/. On-campus day care facilities are available. See the following website for more information: http://uwf.edu/childdev.

Information for Students With Physical Disabilities: See the following website: http://uwf.edu/sdrc/.

Special Facilities or Resources: The Department of Psychology is housed in a modern, 22,000 sq. ft. building with excellent research facilities, including a Neurocognition lab with a Neuroscan Grael EEG Amp System with 40 digital channels. The University of West Florida Center for Applied Psychology (CAP) is a consulting group within the department aimed at optimizing human performance across the lifespan in educational, health, and workplace contexts. The University of West Florida Center on Aging is also housed within the department and its mission is to improve the quality of life of aging adults through the application of science to address challenges associated with aging and to promote healthy aging, with an emphasis on prevention. Other University resources include the Institute for Business and Economic Research and the Institute for Human and Machine Cognition. We have links with CMHCs and local health/mental health professionals and organizations. Community resources include three major hospitals and a large Naval training facility. The school hosts student chapters of Psi Chi, Society for Human Resource Management (SHRM), and Student Psychological Association.

Application Information: UWF Graduate Admissions, University of West Florida, 11000 University Parkway, Pensacola, FL 32514-5751. *Fee:* $30. *Online application:* http://uwf.edu/graduate/apply/apply-now/.

Brenau University

Psychology Department/MS in Clinical Counseling Psychology program
Health Sciences
500 Washington Street
Gainesville, GA 30501
Telephone: (770) 534-6225
Chairperson: Dr. Julie Battle

E-mail: gbauman@brenau.edu
Web: http://www.brenau.edu/?page_id=8173

Orientation, Objectives, and Emphasis of Department

We have a scientific-practitioner model that has three emphases: good clinical skills and experience, research experience culminating in a published thesis, and assessment experiences with opportunity to complete assessment batteries with real clients. We are now located on two campuses. We accept 4 new cohorts of students per year, two on the Gainesville campus and two on the Norcross campus. We accept 12 new students into each cohort with hands-on training, clinical experience and support from faculty. Students learn and grow as individuals and professionals in a very hands-on experience during this program.

Programs and Degrees Offered

Program	Degree	Application Deadline	Applications Received	Accepted	New Admits Enrolled (PT)	Total Enrolled (PT)	Degrees Awarded in 2014–2015	Median Years to Complete Degree	Dismissed/ Withdrew
Clinical Counseling Psychology	MA/MS	March 1 (Fall), October 1 (Spring), April 1 (Summer)	66	46	39 (3)	72 (21)	16	2.5	5

Internships/Practica

We have over 85 contracts with various clinical sites ranging from all ages and populations to work with. We have a fieldwork coordinator who meets with all students to help them to decide at what sites they are interested in working and to prepare them for beginning their practicum experience. We also have a clinic on each campus to use for training as well as a secondary placement site. Students will get hours at least two clinical sites.

Admissions

Entries appear in the following order: required test or GPA, minimum score (if required)/median score of students entering in 2015–2016.

Program	Degree	GRE-V	GRE-Q	GRE-Writing	GRE-Subject	Under-graduate GPA	Last 2 Years GPA	Psychol-ogy GPA	Master's GPA
Clinical Counseling Psychology	MA/MS	Not specified	Not specified	Not specified	Not specified	Not specified	Not specified	Not specified	Not specified

Admissions Requirements:

Degree	GRE	GRE-Subject	Letters of Recom-mendation	Research Statement	Writing Sample	CV	Interview
Master's/Specialist	Required	Required	2	Required	Required	Optional	Required

Admissions Criteria:

GRE scores—medium
Research experience—medium
Work experience—medium
Clinically related public service—medium
GPA—medium

Letters of recommendation—medium
Interview—high
Statement of goals and objectives—medium
Undergraduate psychology preparation—medium

Department Demographics

	Male (PT)	Female (PT)	Total	African-American/ Black (PT)	Hispanic/ Latino (PT)	Asian/ Pacific Islander (PT)	American Indian/ Alaska Native (PT)	Caucasian/ White (PT)	Unknown	Multiethnic (PT)	ADA (PT)	Int'l (PT)
Students	5 (3)	69 (16)	93	16 (3)	4 (1)	3 (0)	0 (0)	50 (15)	0 (0)	1 (0)	0 (0)	3 (0)

Financial Information/Assistance

Tuition: For information on tuition costs, visit http://www.brenau.edu/about/offices-and-resources/tuition-fees-and-accounting-office/. Tuition is subject to change.

Master's:
State residents: $17,500 per academic year.
State residents: $594 per credit hour.
Nonstate residents: $17,500 per academic year.
Nonstate residents: $594 per credit hour.

Financial Assistance:

	Teaching Assistantship (% Receiving)	Teaching Assistantship Tuition Remission	Research Assistantship (% Receiving)	Research Assistantship Tuition Remission	Fellowship (% Receiving)	Fellowship Tuition Remission
First-Year Student	$2,000 (5)	NA	$2,000 (5)	NA	NA (NA)	NA
Advanced Student	$1,000 (15)	NA	NA (NA)	NA	NA (NA)	NA

For additional information on financial assistance, visit http://www.brenau.edu/admissions/financialaid/.

Employment of Department Graduates

Master's:
Enrolled in a psychology doctoral program: 2
Employed in an academic position at a university: 2
Employed in government agency: 1
Employed in a community mental health/counseling center: 8
Do not know: 3
Total: 16

Additional Information

Housing and Day Care: On-campus housing is available. On-campus day care facilities are available. See the following website for more information: http://www.brenau.edu/about/child-development-center/.

Special Facilities or Resources: We have a campus stress lab that students use when working with clients. Students also are able to lead groups on campus and use the clinic for training purposes. We are working on expanding this Stress Lab to our second campus.

Application Information: Admissions. *Fee:* $0. *Online application:* http://www.brenau.edu/apply.

Emory University
Department of Psychology
36 Eagle Row
Atlanta, GA 30322
Telephone: (404) 727-7438
Chairperson: Harold Gouzoules, PhD

E-mail: paula.mitchell@emory.edu
Web: http://www.psychology.emory.edu/

Orientation, Objectives, and Emphasis of Department

The primary emphasis of our clinical curriculum is to provide students with the knowledge and skills they need to function as productive clinical researchers in psychology. This requires a basic understanding of the determinants of human behavior, including biological, psychological, and social factors, and a strong background in research design and quantitative methods. The program in cognition and development at Emory is committed to the principle that cognition and its development are best studied together. The research interests of the faculty span a wide range, and are reflected in our graduate courses, which include memory, emotion, language, perception, and concepts and categories. The program in neuroscience and animal behavior approaches topics within the areas of neuroscience, physiological psychology, acquired behavior, and ethology as a unified entity. Thus, the emphasis is on behavior as a biological phenomenon. Research in neuroscience and physiological psychology explores brain-behavior relationships; research on acquired behavior studies the ongoing and evolutionary factors influenced in individual adaptations; and ethological studies are concerned with understanding how animals function in their natural environment.

Programs and Degrees Offered

Program	Degree	Application Deadline	Applica-tions Received	Accepted	New Admits Enrolled (PT)	Total Enrolled (PT)	Degrees Awarded in 2014–2015	Median Years to Complete Degree	Dismissed/ Withdrew
Clinical Psychology	PhD	December 1 (Fall)	304	10	6 (0)	36 (0)	8	6	1
Cognition & Development	PhD	January 3 (Fall)	59	4	3	25 (0)	4	6	1
Neuroscience& Animal Behavior	PhD	December 8 (Fall)	64	5	4 (0)	23 (0)	0		0

APA Accreditation

Clinical PhD: Student Outcome Data website: http://psychology.emory.edu/home/graduate/clinical/index.html.

Doctoral Degree (PhD Clinical Psychology): For those doctoral students for whom a professional internship was required in this program prior to graduation:
Total students who applied for an internship: 7
Total students who obtained an internship: 7
Total students who obtained a paid internship: 7
Total students who obtained an unpaid internship: 0
Total students who were placed in APA/CPA-accredited internships: 4
Total students placed in internships not APA/CPA-accredited, but listed with the Association of Psychology Postdoctoral and Internship Centers (APPIC): 0
Total students placed in internships conforming to guidelines of the Council of Directors of School Psychology Programs (CDSPP): 0
Total students placed in internships that were not APA/CPA-accredited, APPIC or CDSSP listed: 3

Admissions

Entries appear in the following order: required test or GPA, minimum score (if required)/median score of students entering in 2015–2016.

Program	Degree	GRE-V	GRE-Q	GRE-Writing	GRE-Subject	Under-graduate GPA	Last 2 Years GPA	Psychol-ogy GPA	Master's GPA
Clinical Psychology	PhD	NA/165	NA/159	NA/4.83	Not specified	NA/3.5	Not specified	Not specified	NA/NA

Admissions (con't.)

Program	Degree	GRE-V	GRE-Q	GRE-Writing	GRE-Subject	Under-graduate GPA	Last 2 Years GPA	Psychol-ogy GPA	Master's GPA
Cognition & Development	PhD	NA/156	NA/151	NA/4.5	Not specified	3.5/NA	Not specified	Not specified	NA/NA
Neuroscience & Animal Behavior	PhD	NA/160	NA/151	NA/4.5	Not specified	3.5/NA	Not specified	Not specified	NA/NA

Admissions Requirements:

Degree	GRE	GRE-Subject	Letters of Recom-mendation	Research Statement	Writing Sample	CV	Interview
Doctoral	Required	None	3	Required	None	Required	Required

Please note if these criteria vary for different programs: Clinically related public service is less pertinent to the Cognition & Development and the Neuroscience & Animal Behavior programs.

Admissions Criteria:

GRE scores—high
Research experience—high
Work experience—medium
Clinically related public service—medium
GPA—high

Letters of recommendation—high
Interview—high
Statement of goals and objectives—high
Undergraduate psychology preparation—medium
Faculty research match—high

For additional information on admission requirements, visit http://psychology.emory.edu/home/graduate/admission.html.

Department Demographics

	Male (PT)	Female (PT)	Total	African-American/ Black (PT)	Hispanic/ Latino (PT)	Asian/ Pacific Islander (PT)	American Indian/ Alaska Native (PT)	Caucasian/ White (PT)	Unknown	Multiethnic (PT)	ADA (PT)	Int'l (PT)
Students	29 (0)	55 (0)	84	7 (0)	4 (0)	9 (0)	1 (0)	60 (0)	0 (0)	3 (0)	1 (0)	6 (0)

Financial Information/Assistance

Tuition: For information on tuition costs, visit http://www.gs.emory.edu/funding/tuition.html. Tuition is subject to change. Additional fees are assessed to students beyond the costs of tuition for the following: computing fee, mental health fee, athletic fee, activity fee.

Doctoral:
State residents: $53,045 per academic year.
Nonstate residents: $53,045 per academic year.

Financial Assistance:

	Teaching Assistantship (% Receiving)	Teaching Assistantship Tuition Remission	Research Assistantship (% Receiving)	Research Assistantship Tuition Remission	Fellowship (% Receiving)	Fellowship Tuition Remission
First-Year Student	NA (NA)	NA	NA (NA)	NA	$28,000 (NA)	Full
Advanced Student	$25,000 (NA)	Full	NA (NA)	NA	$28,000 (NA)	Full

For additional information on financial assistance, visit http://www.gs.emory.edu/funding/index.html.

Employment of Department Graduates

Doctoral:
Enrolled in a postdoctoral residency/fellowship: 11
Employed in business or industry: 1
Total: 12

Additional Information

Housing and Day Care: No on-campus housing is available. On-campus day care facilities are available. See the following website for more information: http://thecliftonschool.org/.

Information for Students With Physical Disabilities: See the following website: http://equityandinclusion.emory.edu/access/index.html.

Special Facilities or Resources: The department has affiliations with the Emory Medical School, Yerkes National Primate Center, and the Center for Behavioral Neuroscience. In addition, faculty and students from many of the universities in the Atlanta area meet formally and informally to discuss common research interests.

Application Information: *Fee:* $75. *Online application:* https://www.applyweb.com/apply/emorylgs/.

Georgia School of Professional Psychology at Argosy University
Clinical Psychology
College of Clinical Psychology
980 Hammond Drive, Building 2, Suite 100
Atlanta, GA 30328
Telephone: (888) 671-4777
Chairperson: Timothy C. Brown, PhD

E-mail: tcbrown@argosy.edu
Web: http://www.gsppatlanta.com/

Orientation, Objectives, and Emphasis of Department
The PsyD program at the Georgia School of Professional Psychology at Argosy University follows the practitioner–scholar model of clinical training. We are devoted to preparing students to practice as clinical psychologists. Built upon a solid foundation in the discipline of psychology, our practitioner training is firmly grounded in theoretical constructs and empirical findings that guide clinical practice. The faculty at GSPP represent a wide range of clinical interests and theoretical orientations. No particular approach to clinical practice dominates the program, so that students engage in a theoretically rich and diverse training experience. The PsyD program is comprised of a 98-credit hour curriculum that can be completed over a 5-year period, including the internship year. Our program is designed to provide students with well-rounded generalist training in clinical psychology. We believe this generalist approach is critically important given the growing emphasis on accountability, evidence-based practice, working in multidisciplinary settings, and flexibility in adapting to newly emerging roles. The PsyD program also offers elective courses and clinical training in four concentration areas: general adult clinical, child and family psychology, neuropsychology/geropsychology, and health psychology. Our MA program focuses upon preparing students for doctoral study in professional psychology.

Programs and Degrees Offered

Program	Degree	Application Deadline	Applications Received	Accepted	New Admits Enrolled (PT)	Total Enrolled (PT)	Degrees Awarded in 2014–2015	Median Years to Complete Degree	Dismissed/Withdrew
Clinical Psychology	MA/MS	July 15 (Fall), November 30 (Spring), Rolling	13	13	4 (0)	4 (0)	2	2	1
Clinical Psychology	PsyD	July 15 (Fall), November 30 (Spring), Rolling	81	39	21 (0)	79 (0)	19	6	0

APA Accreditation

Clinical PsyD: Student Outcome Data website: http://clinical.argosy.edu/locations/atlanta/clinical-psychology-doctor-of-psychology.

Doctoral Degree (PsyD Clinical Psychology): For those doctoral students for whom a professional internship was required in this program prior to graduation:

Total students who applied for an internship: 11
Total students who obtained an internship: 9
Total students who obtained a paid internship: 9
Total students who obtained an unpaid internship: 0
Total students who were placed in APA/CPA-accredited internships: 9
Total students placed in internships not APA/CPA-accredited, but listed with the Association of Psychology Postdoctoral and Internship Centers (APPIC): 0
Total students placed in internships conforming to guidelines of the Council of Directors of School Psychology Programs (CDSPP): 0
Total students placed in internships that were not APA/CPA-accredited, APPIC or CDSSP listed: 0

Master's Degree (MA/MS Clinical Psychology): An internship experience, such as a final research project or "capstone" experience is required of graduates.

Internships/Practica

Our PsyD students program advance through a sequence of clinical training experiences that are progressively more challenging. The first year of our 2-year practicum training sequence focuses upon developing students' knowledge and skills in assessment, testing, and diagnosis. Students' second year of practicum training focuses upon developing their knowledge base and skills in providing therapeutic interventions that are grounded in clinical theory and evidence-based practice. Most PsyD students participate in a third year of advanced practicum training, allowing them to specialize further in areas consistent with their interests. GSPP maintains longstanding practicum training relationships with local psychologists, agencies, and facilities—including local and regional medical centers, inpatient psychiatric facilities, specialty clinics, the VA Medical Center, college and university counseling centers, correctional facilities, children's hospitals, neuro-rehabilitation centers, and private practitioners. On practicum, students spend 16-20 hours per week providing services to clients in an agency, program, or professional practice that is formally affiliated with the program. Practicum students receive on-site supervision from licensed psychologists and other mental healthcare providers. During each practicum placement, students must also enroll in a weekly practicum seminar led by a faculty member on-campus, who offers didactic training and opportunities for case consultation

Admissions

Entries appear in the following order: required test or GPA, minimum score (if required)/median score of students entering in 2015–2016.

Program	Degree	GRE-V	GRE-Q	GRE-Writing	GRE-Subject	Under-graduate GPA	Last 2 Years GPA	Psychology GPA	Master's GPA
Clinical Psychology	MA/MS	Not specified	Not specified	Not specified	Not specified	3/3.8	Not specified	Not specified	Not specified
Clinical Psychology	PsyD	Not specified	Not specified	NA/NA	Not specified	3/3.5	Not specified	Not specified	Not specified

Admissions Requirements:

Degree	GRE	GRE-Subject	Letters of Recommendation	Research Statement	Writing Sample	CV	Interview
Master's/Specialist	Recommended	Optional	3	Required	None	Required	Required
Doctoral	Recommended	Optional	3	Required	None	Required	Required

Admissions Criteria:

GRE scores—medium
Research experience—medium
Work experience—high
Clinically related public service—high
GPA—high

Letters of recommendation—high
Interview—high
Statement of goals and objectives—high
Undergraduate psychology preparation—medium

For additional information on admission requirements, visit http://clinical.argosy.edu/locations/atlanta/clinical-psychology-doctor-of-psychology/admissions.

Department Demographics

	Male (PT)	Female (PT)	Total	African-American/ Black (PT)	Hispanic/ Latino (PT)	Asian/ Pacific Islander (PT)	American Indian/ Alaska Native (PT)	Caucasian/ White (PT)	Unknown (PT)	Multiethnic (PT)	ADA (PT)	Int'l (PT)
Students	13 (0)	70 (0)	83	32 (0)	3 (0)	3 (0)	1 (0)	41 (0)	0 (0)	3 (0)	3 (0)	2 (0)

Financial Information/Assistance

Tuition: For information on tuition costs, visit https://www.argosy.edu/affordability/tuition-and-fees. Tuition is subject to change. Additional fees are assessed to students beyond the costs of tuition for the following: Technology Fee: $15/credit hour. Student Activity fee: $25 per year.

Doctoral:
State residents: $1,162 per credit hour.
Nonstate residents: $1,162 per credit hour.

Master's:
State residents: $1,162 per credit hour.
Nonstate residents: $1,162 per credit hour.

Financial Assistance:

	Teaching Assistantship (% Receiving)	Teaching Assistantship Tuition Remission	Research Assistantship (% Receiving)	Research Assistantship Tuition Remission	Fellowship (% Receiving)	Fellowship Tuition Remission
First-Year Student	NA (NA)	NA	NA (NA)	NA	$5,775 (40)	Partial
Advanced Student	$1,095 (29)	NA	$950 (12)	NA	$6,340 (19)	Partial

For additional information on financial assistance, visit https://www.argosy.edu/affordability.

Employment of Department Graduates

Master's:
Enrolled in a psychology doctoral program: 2
Total: 2

Doctoral:
Enrolled in a postdoctoral residency/fellowship: 12
Employed in independent practice: 3
Do not know: 4
Total: 19

Additional Information

Housing and Day Care: No on-campus housing is available. No on-campus day care facilities are available.

Special Facilities or Resources: Our students engage in collaborative research with behavioral healthcare agencies in the metro Atlanta area. GSPP also maintains archival data and therapy session recordings from a major psychotherapy research project. This valuable resource provides both psychotherapy training and research opportunities for our students and faculty. Students in our neuropsychology concentration have participated in ongoing neuropsychological test development research with Dr. Nick DeFilippis.

Application Information: Clinical Psychology Admissions, Georgia School of Professional Psychology, Argosy University Atlanta, 980 Hammond Drive, Building 2, Suite 100, Atlanta, GA 30328. *Fee:* $50. *Online application:* https://apply.argosy.edu/apply.

Georgia Southern University
Department of Psychology
College of Liberal Arts and Social Sciences
P.O. Box 8041
Statesboro, GA 30460-8041
Telephone: (912) 478-5539
Chairperson: Dr. Michael Nielsen

E-mail: mnielsen@georgiasouthern.edu
Web: http://class.georgiasouthern.edu/psychology/

Orientation, Objectives, and Emphasis of Department

The MS program focuses on general psychology and prepares students for doctoral study in psychology. The program consists of coursework and supervised research in traditional areas of interest such as social, developmental, learning, cognitive, physiological, and industrial/organizational and has a thesis requirement. The APA-accredited PsyD program in clinical psychology follows the practitioner–scholar model of training. The program is 5 years, including internship. The program emphasizes training in psychotherapy; consultation, and assessment with adults, children, families, and couples in rural and underserved settings.

Programs and Degrees Offered

Program	Degree	Application Deadline	Applications Received	Accepted	New Admits Enrolled (PT)	Total Enrolled (PT)	Degrees Awarded in 2014–2015	Median Years to Complete Degree	Dismissed/Withdrew
Psychology	MA/MS	July 1 (Fall)	25	12	12 (0)	24 (0)	10	2	0
Clinical Psychology	PsyD	January 15 (Fall)	55	8	8 (0)	43 (0)	7	5	1

APA Accreditation

Clinical PsyD: Student Outcome Data website: http://class.georgiasouthern.edu/psychology/psyd/disclosure/.

Doctoral Degree (PsyD Clinical Psychology): For those doctoral students for whom a professional internship was required in this program prior to graduation:
Total students who applied for an internship: 10
Total students who obtained an internship: 10
Total students who obtained a paid internship: 10
Total students who obtained an unpaid internship: 0
Total students who were placed in APA/CPA-accredited internships: 9
Total students placed in internships not APA/CPA-accredited, but listed with the Association of Psychology Postdoctoral and Internship Centers (APPIC): 1
Total students placed in internships conforming to guidelines of the Council of Directors of School Psychology Programs (CDSPP): 0
Total students placed in internships that were not APA/CPA-accredited, APPIC or CDSSP listed: 0

Master's Degree (MA/MS Psychology): An internship experience, such as a final research project or "capstone" experience is required of graduates.

Internships/Practica

PsyD students engage in practica in their second through fourth years. Sites include the department's clinic, which serves a range of community members, the campus counseling center serving students, and a variety of sites in surrounding communities. Internships are required in the fifth year of the PsyD program.

Admissions

Entries appear in the following order: required test or GPA, minimum score (if required)/median score of students entering in 2015–2016.

Program	Degree	GRE V	GRE-Q	GRE-Writing	GRE-Subject	Undergraduate GPA	Last 2 Years GPA	Psychology GPA	Master's GPA
Psychology	MA/MS	NA/158	NA/151	Not specified	Not specified	3/NA	Not specified	Not specified	Not specified
Clinical Psychology	PsyD	NA/156	NA/152	Not specified	Not specified	NA/3.65	Not specified	Not specified	Not specified

Admissions Requirements:

Degree	GRE	GRE-Subject	Letters of Recommendation	Research Statement	Writing Sample	CV	Interview
Master's/Specialist	Required	None	3	Required	Optional	Optional	Recommended
Doctoral	Required	Required	3	Required	Optional	Required	Required

Please note if these criteria vary for different programs: MS: GRE, grades, research experience all important. PsyD: GRE, grades, statement, interview most important. PsyD applicants who do not have a bachelor's or master's degree in Psychology are required to take the GRE-Subject test.

Admissions Criteria:

GRE scores—medium
Research experience—medium
Work experience—medium
Clinically related public service—medium
GPA—medium

Letters of recommendation—medium
Interview—medium
Statement of goals and objectives—medium
Undergraduate psychology preparation—medium

Department Demographics

	Male (PT)	Female (PT)	Total	African-American/ Black (PT)	Hispanic/ Latino (PT)	Asian/ Pacific Islander (PT)	American Indian/ Alaska Native (PT)	Caucasian/ White (PT)	Unknown (PT)	Multiethnic (PT)	ADA (PT)	Int'l (PT)
Students	22 (0)	43 (0)	65	8 (0)	2 (0)	1 (0)	0 (0)	53 (0)	1 (0)	0 (0)	1 (0)	0 (0)

Financial Information/Assistance

Tuition: For information on tuition costs, visit http://businesssrvs.georgiasouthern.edu/bursar/office-of-student-accounts/tuition-and-fees/. Tuition is subject to change. Additional fees are assessed to students beyond the costs of tuition for the following: technology, health insurance, activity, transit, athletics, sustainability.

Doctoral:
State residents: $9,129 per academic year.
State residents: $277 per credit hour.
Nonstate residents: $36,463 per academic year.
Nonstate residents: $1,105 per credit hour.

Master's:
State residents: $5,540 per academic year.
State residents: $277 per credit hour.
Nonstate residents: $22,100 per academic year.
Nonstate residents: $1,105 per credit hour.

Financial Assistance:

	Teaching Assistantship (% Receiving)	Teaching Assistantship Tuition Remission	Research Assistantship (% Receiving)	Research Assistantship Tuition Remission	Fellowship (% Receiving)	Fellowship Tuition Remission
First-Year Student	$8,000 (NA)	Full	$8,000 (NA)	Full	NA (NA)	NA
Advanced Student	$8,000 (NA)	Full	$8,000 (NA)	Full	NA (NA)	NA

For additional information on financial assistance, visit http://cogs.georgiasouthern.edu/new-current-students/graduate-assistantships-information/.

Employment of Department Graduates

Master's:
Enrolled in a psychology doctoral program: 3
Employed in academic position at a 2-year/4-year college: 1
Employed in other positions at a higher education institution: 2
Employed in business or industry: 2
Still seeking employment: 2
Do not know: 2
Total: 12

Doctoral:
Enrolled in a postdoctoral residency/fellowship: 1
Employed in independent practice: 1
Employed in other positions at a higher education institution: 4
Employed in government agency: 1
Employed in a hospital/medical center: 1
Still seeking employment: 1
Do not know: 1
Total: 10

Additional Information

Housing and Day Care: On-campus housing is available. See the following website for more information: http://auxiliary. georgiasouthern.edu/housing/. On-campus day care facilities are available. See the following website for more information: http://chhs.georgiasouthern.edu/she/cdc/.

Information for Students With Physical Disabilities: See the following website: http://students.georgiasouthern.edu/sdrc/.

Special Facilities or Resources: The department is housed in a newly remodeled building, with research laboratories in a variety of subdisciplines in psychology (social, cognitive, etc.). The department also hosts a community psychology clinic, where students in the PsyD program are supervised in seeing adults from the Statesboro community and surrounding rural areas.

Application Information: Office of Graduate Admissions, Georgia Southern University, P.O. Box 8113, Statesboro, GA 30460-8113. *Fee:* $50. *Online application:* https://app.applyyourself.com/?id=gsu-cogs.

Georgia State University
Counseling and Psychological Services
College of Education
P.O. Box 3980
Atlanta, GA 30302-3980
Telephone: (404) 413-8010
Chairperson: Dr. Brian J. Dew

E-mail: bdew@gsu.edu
Web: http://cps.education.gsu.edu/

Orientation, Objectives, and Emphasis of Department
Based on our commitment to diversity, advocacy and the belief that change is possible, the mission of the Department of Counseling and Psychological Services is to prepare competent professionals in counseling and psychological services to contribute to the body of knowledge that undergirds these professions and to provide service to the profession and the community. The CPS department prepares students for employment in settings such as rehabilitation clinics, public and private schools, correctional agencies, colleges and universities, and mental health facilities. A concerted effort is devoted to providing students with the knowledge and skills to work successfully in these particular environments.

Programs and Degrees Offered

Program	Degree	Application Deadline	Applications Received	Accepted	New Admits Enrolled (PT)	Total Enrolled (PT)	Degrees Awarded in 2014–2015	Median Years to Complete Degree	Dismissed/ Withdrew
Counseling Psychology	PhD	December 1 (Fall)	86	5	4 (0)	17	4	4.5	1
School Psychology	PhD	November 15 (Fall)	20	4	4	14	5	4	1
School Psychology	EdS	December 1 (Fall)	20	12	9 (0)	18 (0)	13	2	1

APA Accreditation
Counseling PhD: Student Outcome Data website: http://cps.education.gsu.edu/programs/counseling-psychology/.
School PhD: Student Outcome Data website: http://cps.education.gsu.edu/programs/school-psychology/school-psychology-doctor-of-philosophy-program/.

Doctoral Degree (PhD Counseling Psychology): For those doctoral students for whom a professional internship was required in this program prior to graduation:
Total students who applied for an internship: 4
Total students who obtained an internship: 4
Total students who obtained a paid internship: 4
Total students who obtained an unpaid internship: 0
Total students who were placed in APA/CPA-accredited internships: 4
Total students placed in internships not APA/CPA-accredited, but listed with the Association of Psychology Postdoctoral and Internship Centers (APPIC): 0

Total students placed in internships conforming to guidelines of the Council of Directors of School Psychology Programs (CDSPP): 0
Total students placed in internships that were not APA/CPA-accredited, APPIC or CDSSP listed: 0

Doctoral Degree (PhD School Psychology): For those doctoral students for whom a professional internship was required in this program prior to graduation:
Total students who applied for an internship: 2
Total students who obtained an internship: 1
Total students who obtained a paid internship: 1
Total students who obtained an unpaid internship: 0
Total students who were placed in APA/CPA-accredited internships: 0
Total students placed in internships not APA/CPA-accredited, but listed with the Association of Psychology Postdoctoral and Internship Centers (APPIC): 0
Total students placed in internships conforming to guidelines of the Council of Directors of School Psychology Programs (CDSPP): 1
Total students placed in internships that were not APA/CPA-accredited, APPIC or CDSSP listed: 0

Admissions

Entries appear in the following order: required test or GPA, minimum score (if required)/median score of students entering in 2015–2016.

Program	Degree	GRE-V	GRE-Q	GRE-Writing	GRE-Subject	Under-graduate GPA	Last 2 Years GPA	Psychology GPA	Master's GPA
Counseling Psychology	PhD	NA/166	NA/156	Not specified	Not specified	NA/3.61	NA/NA	NA/NA	3.3/NA
School Psychology	PhD	NA/153	NA/145	NA/NA	NA/NA	3.3/3.38	NA/NA	NA/NA	NA/NA
School Psychology	EdS	NA/154	NA/150	Not specified	Not specified	NA/3.35	NA/NA	Not specified	Not specified

Admissions Requirements:

Degree	GRE	GRE-Subject	Letters of Recom-mendation	Research Statement	Writing Sample	CV	Interview
Master's/Specialist	Required	None	3	Required	Required	Required	Required
Doctoral	Required	None	3	Required	Required	Required	Required

Admissions Criteria:

GRE scores—high
Research experience—high
Work experience—medium
Clinically related public service—medium
GPA—high

Letters of recommendation—high
Interview—high
Statement of goals and objectives—high
Undergraduate psychology preparation—high

For additional information on admission requirements, visit http://education.gsu.edu/admissions/graduate-admissions/.

Department Demographics

	Male (PT)	Female (PT)	Total	African-American/Black (PT)	Hispanic/Latino (PT)	Asian/Pacific Islander (PT)	American Indian/Alaska Native (PT)	Caucasian/White (PT)	Unknown	Multiethnic (PT)	ADA (PT)	Int'l (PT)
Students	8 (0)	44 (0)	52	15 (0)	3 (0)	3 (0)	1 (0)	30 (0)	0 (0)	0 (0)	0 (0)	0 (0)

Financial Information/Assistance

Tuition: For information on tuition costs, visit http://sfs.gsu.edu/tuition-fees/what-it-costs/tuition-and-fees/. Tuition is subject to change.

Doctoral:
State residents: $9,168 per academic year.
State residents: $382 per credit hour.
Nonstate residents: $29,832 per academic year.
Nonstate residents: $1,243 per credit hour.

Master's:
State residents: $9,168 per academic year.
State residents: $382 per credit hour.
Nonstate residents: $29,832 per academic year.
Nonstate residents: $1,243 per credit hour.

Financial Assistance:

	Teaching Assistantship (% Receiving)	Teaching Assistantship Tuition Remission	Research Assistantship (% Receiving)	Research Assistantship Tuition Remission	Fellowship (% Receiving)	Fellowship Tuition Remission
First-Year Student	NA (NA)	NA	NA (NA)	NA	NA (NA)	NA
Advanced Student	NA (NA)	NA	NA (NA)	NA	NA (NA)	NA

For additional information on financial assistance, visit http://sfs.gsu.edu/the-financial-aid-process/.

Employment of Department Graduates

Doctoral:
Employed in an academic position at a university: 6
Employed in academic position at a 2-year/4-year college: 6
Employed in a professional position in a school system: 3
Total: 15

Additional Information

Housing and Day Care: On-campus housing is available. See the following website for more information: http://myhousing.gsu.edu/. On-campus day care facilities are available. See the following website for more information: http://cdp.education.gsu.edu/.

Information for Students With Physical Disabilities: See the following website: http://disability.gsu.edu/.

Application Information: Georgia State University, Office of Academic Assistance, College of Education, 30 Pryor Street, Suite 300, Atlanta, GA 30303. *Fee:* $50. *Online application:* https://app.applyyourself.com/?id=casgsu.

Georgia State University

Department of Psychology
College of Arts and Sciences
P.O. Box 5010
Atlanta, GA 30302-5010
Telephone: (404) 413-6200
Chairperson: Christopher Henrich

E-mail: kdhill@gsu.edu
Web: http://psychology.gsu.edu/

Orientation, Objectives, and Emphasis of Department

The department is eclectic, and many philosophical perspectives and research interests are represented. The policy of the department is to promote the personal and professional development of students. This includes the discovery of individual interests and goals, the growth of independent scholarship and research skills, the mastery of fundamental psychological knowledge and methodology, and the development of various professional skills (e.g., clinical skills, community intervention).

Programs and Degrees Offered

Program	Degree	Application Deadline	Applica- tions Received	Accepted	New Admits Enrolled (PT)	Total Enrolled (PT)	Degrees Awarded in 2014– 2015	Median Years to Complete Degree	Dismissed/ Withdrew
Clinical Psychology	PhD	December 1 (Fall)	385	18	9	66 (0)	7	7	2
Community Psychology	PhD	January 5 (Fall)	45	4	3 (0)	15 (0)	0		0
Developmental Psychology	PhD	January 5 (Fall)	24	6	3 (0)	22 (0)	0		0
Neuropsychology and Behavioral Neurosciences	PhD	December 1 (Fall)	29	2	2 (0)	4 (0)	0		0
Cognitive Sciences	PhD	December 1 (Fall)	34	6	3 (0)	22 (0)	0		0

APA Accreditation

Clinical PhD: Student Outcome Data website: http://psychology.gsu.edu/graduate/areas-of-study/clinical-program/.

Doctoral Degree (PhD Clinical Psychology): For those doctoral students for whom a professional internship was required in this program prior to graduation:
Total students who applied for an internship: 12
Total students who obtained an internship: 11
Total students who obtained a paid internship: 11
Total students who obtained an unpaid internship: 0
Total students who were placed in APA/CPA-accredited internships: 11
Total students placed in internships not APA/CPA-accredited, but listed with the Association of Psychology Postdoctoral and Internship Centers (APPIC): 0
Total students placed in internships conforming to guidelines of the Council of Directors of School Psychology Programs (CDSPP): 0
Total students placed in internships that were not APA/CPA-accredited, APPIC or CDSSP listed: 0

Internships/Practica

Practicum experiences are an important component of the clinical training program. Supervised therapy and assessment practica are available in a variety of settings. For clinical students, one source of training is the Psychology Clinic which is located within the department. It provides services to students and members of the community in a variety of modalities, including assessment, individual therapy, group therapy, and family therapy. Another facility within the department is the Regent's Center for Learning Disorders, which offers comprehensive psychoeducational assessments to students and members of the community. Student clinicians are the primary providers of services in both of these clinics. In addition, there are numerous off-campus settings that offer supervised practicum experiences in a variety of areas including health psychology, neuropsychological assessment, personality assessment, psychiatric emergency room services, day treatment programs, etc. Many of these practica are available at Grady Memorial Hospital, a major metropolitan full-service facility located two blocks from the center of campus. Community students likewise do practica at various community based organizations. Often this research takes the form of needs assessment, program development, and program evaluation.

Admissions

Entries appear in the following order: required test or GPA, minimum score (if required)/median score of students entering in 2015–2016.

Program	Degree	GRE-V	GRE-Q	GRE- Writing	GRE- Subject	Under- graduate GPA	Last 2 Years GPA	Psychol- ogy GPA	Master's GPA
Clinical Psychology	PhD	NA/161	NA/155	Not specified	Not specified	NA/3.85	Not specified	Not specified	Not specified
Community Psychology	PhD	Not specified	Not specified	Not specified	Not specified	Not specified	Not specified	Not specified	Not specified
Developmental Psychology	PhD	Not specified	Not specified	Not specified	Not specified	Not specified	Not specified	Not specified	Not specified

Admissions *(con't.)*

Program	Degree	GRE-V	GRE-Q	GRE-Writing	GRE-Subject	Under-graduate GPA	Last 2 Years GPA	Psychology GPA	Master's GPA
Neuropsychology and Behavioral Neurosciences	PhD	Not specified	Not specified	Not specified	Not specified	Not specified	Not specified	Not specified	Not specified
Cognitive Sciences	PhD	Not specified	Not specified	Not specified	Not specified	Not specified	Not specified	Not specified	Not specified

Admissions Requirements:

Degree	GRE	GRE-Subject	Letters of Recommendation	Research Statement	Writing Sample	CV	Interview
Doctoral	Required	Optional	3	Required	Optional	Required	Required

Admissions Criteria:

GRE scores—high
Research experience—high
Work experience—medium
Clinically related public service—medium
GPA—high

Letters of recommendation—high
Interview—high
Statement of goals and objectives—high
Undergraduate psychology preparation—high

For additional information on admission requirements, visit http://psychology.gsu.edu/apply/.

Department Demographics

	Male (PT)	Female (PT)	Total	African-American/ Black (PT)	Hispanic/ Latino (PT)	Asian/ Pacific Islander (PT)	American Indian/ Alaska Native (PT)	Caucasian/ White (PT)	Unknown	Multiethnic (PT)	ADA (PT)	Int'l (PT)
Students	20 (0)	99 (0)	119	11 (0)	4 (0)	18 (0)	0 (0)	65 (0)	17 (0)	4 (0)	0 (0)	10 (0)

Financial Information/Assistance

Tuition: For information on tuition costs, visit http://sfs.gsu.edu/tuition-fees/what-it-costs/tuition-and-fees/. Tuition is subject to change.

Doctoral:
State residents: $382 per credit hour.
Nonstate residents: $1,243 per credit hour.

Financial Assistance:

	Teaching Assistantship (% Receiving)	Teaching Assistantship Tuition Remission	Research Assistantship (% Receiving)	Research Assistantship Tuition Remission	Fellowship (% Receiving)	Fellowship Tuition Remission
First-Year Student	$15,000 (NA)	Full	$15,000 (NA)	Full	$21,000 (NA)	Full
Advanced Student	$18,000 (NA)	Full	$18,000 (NA)	Full	$21,000 (NA)	Full

Employment of Department Graduates

No information provided.

Additional Information

Housing and Day Care: On-campus housing is available. See the following website for more information: http://myhousing.gsu.edu/. On-campus day care facilities are available. See the following website for more information: http://cdp.education.gsu.edu/.

Information for Students With Physical Disabilities: See the following website: http://disability.gsu.edu/.

Special Facilities or Resources: The facilities of the department permit work in cognition, development, neuroscience, neuropsychology, learning, infant behavior, sensation and perception, motivation, aging, social psychology, assessment, individual, group and family therapy, behavior therapy, and community psychology. Students may work with both human and nonhuman populations. Human populations include all age ranges and a variety of ethnic and socioeconomic backgrounds. Nonhuman populations include a variety of rodent and nonhuman primates.

Application Information: Office of Graduate Studies—College of Arts and Sciences, Georgia State University, P.O. Box 3993, Atlanta, GA 30302-3993. *Fee:* $50. *Online application:* https://app.applyyourself.com/?id=casgsu.

Georgia, University of

Department of Counseling and Human Development Services
College of Education
402 Aderhold Hall
Athens, GA 30602
Telephone: (706) 542-1812
Department Head: Brian Glaser

E-mail: bheckman@uga.edu
Web: http://www.coe.uga.edu/chds/

Orientation, Objectives, and Emphasis of Department
The goal of the program is to educate students in the scientist–practitioner model of training in professional counseling psychology. The program focuses on professional competency development in three areas: teaching, research, and clinical service. The theoretical orientations of faculty members vary widely including representatives of most major schools of thought. The broad emphases of the program include developmental perspectives, cultural diversity perspectives, cognitive-behavioral approaches, and psychodynamic therapies.

Programs and Degrees Offered

Program	Degree	Application Deadline	Applications Received	Accepted	New Admits Enrolled (PT)	Total Enrolled (PT)	Degrees Awarded in 2014–2015	Median Years to Complete Degree	Dismissed/ Withdrew
Counseling Psychology	PhD	December 1 (Fall)	66	13	13 (0)	53 (1)	6	5	0

APA Accreditation
Counseling PhD: Student Outcome Data website: http://coe.uga.edu/academics/degrees/phd/counseling-psychology.

Doctoral Degree (PhD Counseling Psychology): For those doctoral students for whom a professional internship was required in this program prior to graduation:
Total students who applied for an internship: 15
Total students who obtained an internship: 12
Total students who obtained a paid internship: 12
Total students who obtained an unpaid internship: 0
Total students who were placed in APA/CPA-accredited internships: 11
Total students placed in internships not APA/CPA-accredited, but listed with the Association of Psychology Postdoctoral and Internship Centers (APPIC): 1
Total students placed in internships conforming to guidelines of the Council of Directors of School Psychology Programs (CDSPP): 0
Total students placed in internships that were not APA/CPA-accredited, APPIC or CDSSP listed: 0

Internships/Practica
Practicum opportunities are provided at one of three sites: the Juvenile Counseling and Assessment Program (JCAP), the Counseling and Personal Evaluation Center (department clinic) and Counseling Psychological Services (the university counseling center).

Advanced practica are available in the area and in Atlanta at Georgia Tech, Emory University, Morehouse College, Kennesaw State University, and the Atlanta VA.

Admissions

Entries appear in the following order: required test or GPA, minimum score (if required)/median score of students entering in 2015–2016.

Program	Degree	GRE-V	GRE-Q	GRE-Writing	GRE-Subject	Under-graduate GPA	Last 2 Years GPA	Psychol-ogy GPA	Master's GPA
Counseling Psychology	PhD	NA/NA	NA/NA	NA/NA	Not specified	2.78/3.4	Not specified	Not specified	3.64/3.89

Admissions Requirements:

Degree	GRE	GRE-Subject	Letters of Recom-mendation	Research Statement	Writing Sample	CV	Interview
Doctoral	Required	Optional	3	Required	Optional	Required	Required

Admissions Criteria:

GRE scores—medium
Research experience—high
Work experience—high
Clinically related public service—medium
GPA—medium

Letters of recommendation—high
Interview—high
Statement of goals and objectives—high
Undergraduate psychology preparation—low
Social justice commitment—high

For additional information on admission requirements, visit http://coe.uga.edu/apply/program/phd/counseling-psychology.

Department Demographics

	Male (PT)	Female (PT)	Total	African-American/ Black (PT)	Hispanic/ Latino (PT)	Asian/ Pacific Islander (PT)	American Indian/ Alaska Native (PT)	Caucasian/ White (PT)	Unknown (PT)	Multiethnic (PT)	ADA (PT)	Int'l (PT)
Students	7 (1)	41 (0)	49	18 (0)	2 (0)	1 (0)	0 (0)	27 (0)	0 (0)	0 (1)	0 (0)	2 (0)

Financial Information/Assistance

Tuition: For information on tuition costs, visit http://www.bursar.uga.edu/tuition_fees.html. Tuition is subject to change.

Doctoral:
State residents: $13,233 per academic year.
Nonstate residents: $35,655 per academic year.

Financial Assistance:

	Teaching Assistantship (% Receiving)	Teaching Assistantship Tuition Remission	Research Assistantship (% Receiving)	Research Assistantship Tuition Remission	Fellowship (% Receiving)	Fellowship Tuition Remission
First-Year Student	$11,515 (NA)	Full	$11,515 (NA)	Full	NA (NA)	NA
Advanced Student	$11,515 (NA)	Full	$11,515 (NA)	Full	NA (NA)	NA

For additional information on financial assistance, visit http://osfa.uga.edu/index.html.

Employment of Department Graduates

Doctoral:
Enrolled in a postdoctoral residency/fellowship: 4
Employed in an academic position at a university: 3
Employed in other positions at a higher education institution: 1
Employed in government agency: 1
Still seeking employment: 1
Total: 10

Additional Information

Housing and Day Care: On-campus housing is available. See the following website for more information: https://housing.uga.edu/site/housing_family_graduate. On-campus day care facilities are available. See the following website for more information: http://universitychildcarecenter.uga.edu/.

Information for Students With Physical Disabilities: See the following website: http://drc.uga.edu/.

Special Facilities or Resources: The University, the College, and the Department separately and collectively offer a number of services and fully-equipped facilities to assist students in conducting academic inquiry, including special computer labs, research assistance centers, and major libraries.

Application Information: Fee: $75. *Online application:* https://www.applyweb.com/apply/ugagrad/.

Georgia, University of
Department of Psychology
Franklin College of Arts and Sciences
125 Baldwin Street
Athens, GA 30602-3013
Telephone: (706) 542-2174
Chairperson: W. Keith Campbell

E-mail: bhammond@uga.edu
Web: http://psychology.uga.edu/

Orientation, Objectives, and Emphasis of Department
Our emphasis is on research and the basic science aspects of psychology with a focus on doctoral education. A few state and private facilities provide internships. We have a cooperative liaison with several mental health facilities in the region as well as other universities.

Programs and Degrees Offered

Program	Degree	Application Deadline	Applications Received	Accepted	New Admits Enrolled (PT)	Total Enrolled (PT)	Degrees Awarded in 2014–2015	Median Years to Complete Degree	Dismissed/Withdrew
Clinical Psychology	PhD	November 15 (Fall)	244	13	8	27 (8)	6	6	0
Industrial/ Organizational Psychology	PhD	December 1 (Fall)	93	6	4	21 (7)	3	6	
Behavioral and Brain Sciences	PhD	December 1 (Fall)	63	9	5	27 (1)	4	5.5	0
Industrial/ Organizational Psychology	MA/MS	April 25 (Fall)	78	28			9	2	

APA Accreditation
Clinical PhD: Student Outcome Data website: http://psychology.uga.edu/programs/clinical-doctoral-program.

Doctoral Degree (PhD Clinical Psychology): For those doctoral students for whom a professional internship was required in this program prior to graduation:

Total students who applied for an internship: 8
Total students who obtained an internship: 8
Total students who obtained a paid internship: 8
Total students who obtained an unpaid internship: 0
Total students who were placed in APA/CPA-accredited internships: 8
Total students placed in internships not APA/CPA-accredited, but listed with the Association of Psychology Postdoctoral and Internship Centers (APPIC): 0
Total students placed in internships conforming to guidelines of the Council of Directors of School Psychology Programs (CDSPP): 0
Total students placed in internships that were not APA/CPA-accredited, APPIC or CDSSP listed: 0

Admissions

Entries appear in the following order: required test or GPA, minimum score (if required)/median score of students entering in 2015–2016.

Program	Degree	GRE-V	GRE-Q	GRE-Writing	GRE-Subject	Under-graduate GPA	Last 2 Years GPA	Psychology GPA	Master's GPA
Clinical Psychology	PhD	NA/161	NA/158	NA/NA	Not specified	3/3.81	Not specified	Not specified	Not specified
Industrial/ Organizational Psychology	PhD	NA/NA	NA/NA	NA/NA	Not specified	3.25/3.73	Not specified	Not specified	Not specified
Behavioral and Brain Sciences	PhD	NA/NA	NA/NA	NA/NA	Not specified	3/3.69	Not specified	Not specified	Not specified
Industrial/ Organizational Psychology	MA/MS	Not specified	Not specified	Not specified	Not specified	3/NA	Not specified	Not specified	Not specified

Admissions Requirements:

Degree	GRE	GRE-Subject	Letters of Recom-mendation	Research Statement	Writing Sample	CV	Interview
Master's/Specialist	None	None	1	Required	None	Required	Optional
Doctoral	Required	None	3	Required	Optional	Required	Required

Please note if these criteria vary for different programs: Interviews are required by Clinical but occur for all programs.

Admissions Criteria:

GRE scores—medium
Research experience—high
Work experience—high
Clinically related public service—medium

GPA—medium
Letters of recommendation—medium
Interview—medium
Statement of goals and objectives—high

For additional information on admission requirements, visit http://psychology.uga.edu/prospective-students/how-apply-our-graduate-program.

Department Demographics

	Male (PT)	Female (PT)	Total	African-American/ Black (PT)	Hispanic/ Latino (PT)	Asian/ Pacific Islander (PT)	American Indian/ Alaska Native (PT)	Caucasian/ White (PT)	Unknown	Multiethnic (PT)	ADA (PT)	Int'l (PT)
Students	26 (1)	49 (15)	91	2 (2)	0 (1)	7 (0)	0 (0)	62 (14)	0 (0)	4 (0)	0 (0)	10 (0)

Financial Information/Assistance

Tuition: For information on tuition costs, visit http://www.bursar.uga.edu/tuition_fees.html. Higher tuition cost for this program: professional MA in Industrial/Organizational Psychology. Tuition is subject to change. Additional fees are assessed to students beyond the costs of tuition for the following: transportation, activity, athletic, health, facilities, tech, institutional.

Doctoral:
State residents: $8,592 per academic year.
State residents: $354 per credit hour.
Nonstate residents: $24,090 per academic year.
Nonstate residents: $1,004 per credit hour.

Financial Assistance:

	Teaching Assistantship (% Receiving)	Teaching Assistantship Tuition Remission	Research Assistantship (% Receiving)	Research Assistantship Tuition Remission	Fellowship (% Receiving)	Fellowship Tuition Remission
First-Year Student	$17,076 (62)	Full	$17,076 (37)	Full	$27,000 (NA)	Full
Advanced Student	$17,076 (69)	Full	$17,076 (31)	Full	$27,000 (0)	Full

For additional information on financial assistance, visit http://psychology.uga.edu/funding.

Employment of Department Graduates

Doctoral:
Enrolled in a postdoctoral residency/fellowship: 6
Employed in an academic position at a university: 2
Employed in other positions at a higher education institution: 1
Employed in business or industry: 3
Do not know: 1
Total: 13

Additional Information

Housing and Day Care: On-campus housing is available. See the following website for more information: https://housing.uga.edu/site/housing_family_graduate. On-campus day care facilities are available. See the following website for more information: http://www.fcs.uga.edu/hdfs/research-child-development-lab; http://universitychildcarecenter.uga.edu/.

Information for Students With Physical Disabilities: See the following website: http://drc.uga.edu/.

Special Facilities or Resources: Facilities include the Regents Center for Learning Disabilities, the Institute for Behavioral Research, the Psychology Clinic and the Vision Sciences Laboratory. Our 9000 square foot bioimaging center contains equipment for high-density EEG, MEG, MRI and fMRI. We are also associated with the Biomedical and Health Sciences Institute which focuses on the neurosciences and biomedical applications.

Application Information: Department of Psychology c/o Graduate Coordinator, University of Georgia, Athens, GA 30602-3013. *Fee:* $75. *Online application:* https://www.applyweb.com/apply/ugagrad/.

Georgia, University of

School Psychology Program
Education
323 Aderhold Hall
Athens, GA 30602-7143
Telephone: (706) 542-4110
Program Coordinator: Amy L. Reschly

E-mail: reschly@uga.edu
Web: https://coe.uga.edu/academics/degrees/phd/school-psychology

---

Orientation, Objectives, and Emphasis of Department

The PhD program in school psychology trains research-oriented school psychologists for work in educational settings, hospitals, clinics, and universities in which they can provide leadership in applied practice, research and teaching. The school psychology program follows the scientist–practitioner model, and emphasizes human development, developmental psychopathology, and the central core elements of training.

Programs and Degrees Offered

Program	Degree	Application Deadline	Applications Received	Accepted	New Admits Enrolled (PT)	Total Enrolled (PT)	Degrees Awarded in 2014–2015	Median Years to Complete Degree	Dismissed/ Withdrew
School Psychology	PhD	December 15 (Fall)	46	12	6 (0)	27 (0)	0		1

APA Accreditation

School PhD (Doctor of Philosophy).

Doctoral Degree (PhD School Psychology): For those doctoral students for whom a professional internship was required in this program prior to graduation:
Total students who applied for an internship: 4
Total students who obtained an internship: 4
Total students who obtained a paid internship: 4
Total students who obtained an unpaid internship: 0
Total students who were placed in APA/CPA-accredited internships: 4
Total students placed in internships not APA/CPA-accredited, but listed with the Association of Psychology Postdoctoral and Internship Centers (APPIC): 0
Total students placed in internships conforming to guidelines of the Council of Directors of School Psychology Programs (CDSPP): 0
Total students placed in internships that were not APA/CPA-accredited, APPIC or CDSSP listed: 0

Admissions

Entries appear in the following order: required test or GPA, minimum score (if required)/median score of students entering in 2015–2016.

Program	Degree	GRE-V	GRE-Q	GRE-Writing	GRE-Subject	Under-graduate GPA	Last 2 Years GPA	Psychol-ogy GPA	Master's GPA
School Psychology	PhD	NA/NA	NA/NA	Not specified	Not specified	NA/NA	Not specified	Not specified	NA/NA

Admissions Requirements:

Degree	GRE	GRE-Subject	Letters of Recom-mendation	Research Statement	Writing Sample	CV	Interview
Doctoral	Required	Optional	3	Required	Optional	Required	Required

Admissions Criteria:

GRE scores—medium
Research experience—high
Work experience—low
Clinically related public service—medium
GPA—high

Letters of recommendation—high
Interview—medium
Statement of goals and objectives—medium
Undergraduate psychology preparation—low

For additional information on admission requirements, visit https://coe.uga.edu/apply/program/phd/school-psychology.

Department Demographics

	Male (PT)	Female (PT)	Total	African-American/ Black (PT)	Hispanic/ Latino (PT)	Asian/ Pacific Islander (PT)	American Indian/ Alaska Native (PT)	Caucasian/ White (PT)	Unknown (PT)	Multiethnic (PT)	ADA (PT)	Int'l (PT)
Students	6 (0)	21 (0)	27	1 (0)	1 (0)	3 (0)	0 (0)	22 (0)	0 (0)	0 (0)	0 (0)	0 (0)

Financial Information/Assistance

Tuition: For information on tuition costs, visit http://www.reg.uga.edu/tuition. Tuition is subject to change.

Doctoral:
State residents: $354 per credit hour.
Nonstate residents: $1,004 per credit hour.

Financial Assistance:

	Teaching Assistantship (% Receiving)	Teaching Assistantship Tuition Remission	Research Assistantship (% Receiving)	Research Assistantship Tuition Remission	Fellowship (% Receiving)	Fellowship Tuition Remission
First-Year Student	$12,623 (NA)	Full	$12,623 (NA)	Full	$12,623 (NA)	Full
Advanced Student	$13,643 (NA)	Full	$13,643 (NA)	Full	$13,643 (NA)	Full

For additional information on financial assistance, visit http://grad.uga.edu/index.php/current-students/financial-information/.

Employment of Department Graduates

No information provided.

Additional Information

Housing and Day Care: On-campus housing is available. See the following website for more information: https://housing.uga.edu/site/housing_family_graduate. On-campus day care facilities are available. See the following website for more information: http://universitychildcarecenter.uga.edu/ AND http://www.fcs.uga.edu/hdfs/research-child-development-lab.

Information for Students With Physical Disabilities: See the following website: http://drc.uga.edu/.

Special Facilities or Resources: Special facilities and resources include access to a superior computer center, decentralized computational equipment, a major research library, and faculty members who are extraordinarily accessible to students. The department is strongly committed to affirmative action and fair treatment. Despite the suburban setting (a small urban area of 75,000 over an hour from Atlanta), we attract ethnic minority as well as out-of-state and out-of-region students and faculty. NASP and APA requirements and full accreditation from APA and NCATE form the foundation of our programs.

Application Information: Graduate Admissions Office, Graduate Studies Building, The University of Georgia, Athens, GA 30602. *Fee:* $75. *Online application:* https://www.applyweb.com/apply/ugagrad/.

Mercer University Health Sciences Center
Clinical Medical Psychology
College of Health Professions
3001 Mercer Univeristy Drive, AACC 463-468
Atlanta, GA 30341
Telephone: (678) 547-6591
Chair & Program Director, Clinical Medical Psychology: Steven A. Hobbs
Web: http://medicine.mercer.edu/admissions/psychology/

E-mail: hobbs_sa@mercer.edu

Orientation, Objectives, and Emphasis of Department
The interface of psychology with health and disease represents the focus of doctoral training in Clinical Medical Psychology in the Mercer Health Sciences Center. The Clinical Medical Psychology PhD program began in 2012. The PsyD program was implemented in the 2014-2015 academic year and is eligible to apply for APA accreditation in 2016-2017. Both programs have the mission of training graduates to apply clinical and research skills in an integrated, biopsychosocial approach to healthcare. They are designed to produce graduates who are eligible for licensure as practicing clinical psychologists, particularly in integrative health care settings

(PsyD), or for careers in research and in higher education (PhD). Coursework in clinical psychology is augmented by a focus on medical aspects of healthcare and training in concert with healthcare professionals throughout the Mercer Health Sciences Center. Beyond required courses, students may select coursework in areas such as adult health psychology, pediatric psychology, and neuropsychology.

Programs and Degrees Offered

Program	Degree	Application Deadline	Applica-tions Received	Accepted	New Admits Enrolled (PT)	Total Enrolled (PT)	Degrees Awarded in 2014–2015	Median Years to Complete Degree	Dismissed/ Withdrew
Clinical Medical Psychology	PhD	(Fall), Rolling	6	0	0 (0)	2 (0)			0
Clinical Medical Psychology	PsyD	March 15 (Fall), Rolling	59	16	13 (0)	39 (0)	0		2

Internships/Practica

Practicum training opportunities have been developed in varied healthcare settings in Atlanta and surrounding areas. These include clinical departments affiliated with the Mercer Health Sciences Center, the Woodruff/Emory Health Sciences Center, and other healthcare facilities. Several university counseling centers in the Atlanta area serve as practicum sites.

Admissions

Entries appear in the following order: required test or GPA, minimum score (if required)/median score of students entering in 2015–2016.

Program	Degree	GRE-V	GRE-Q	GRE-Writing	GRE-Subject	Under-graduate GPA	Last 2 Years GPA	Psychol-ogy GPA	Master's GPA
Clinical Medical Psychology	PhD	155/157	151/153	3.5/4	Not specified	3.2/3.3	3.5/3.6	3.4/3.7	Not specified
Clinical Medical Psychology	PsyD	151/156	142/150	3/4	Not specified	2.5/3.4	3/3.6	3/3.8	Not specified

Admissions Requirements:

Degree	GRE	GRE-Subject	Letters of Recom-mendation	Research Statement	Writing Sample	CV	Interview
Doctoral	Required	Required	3	Required	None	Recom-mended	Required

Admissions Criteria:

GRE scores—medium
Research experience—high
Work experience—medium
Clinically related public service—medium
GPA—high

Letters of recommendation—high
Interview—high
Statement of goals and objectives—high
Undergraduate psychology preparation—high

For additional information on admission requirements, visit http://medicine.mercer.edu/admissions/psychology/admissions/.

Department Demographics

	Male (PT)	Female (PT)	Total	African-American/ Black (PT)	Hispanic/ Latino (PT)	Asian/ Pacific Islander (PT)	American Indian/ Alaska Native (PT)	Caucasian/ White (PT)	Unknown	Multiethnic (PT)	ADA (PT)	Int'l (PT)
Students	8 (0)	32 (0)	40	3 (0)	2 (0)	0 (0)	0 (0)	36 (0)	0 (0)	(0)	0 (0)	0 (0)

Financial Information/Assistance

Tuition: For information on tuition costs, visit https://bursar.mercer.edu/macon/cost-of-attendance/. Tuition is subject to change. Additional fees are assessed to students beyond the costs of tuition for the following: Technology fee $150.

Doctoral:
State residents: $987 per credit hour.
Nonstate residents: $987 per credit hour.

Financial Assistance:

	Teaching Assistantship (% Receiving)	Teaching Assistantship Tuition Remission	Research Assistantship (% Receiving)	Research Assistantship Tuition Remission	Fellowship (% Receiving)	Fellowship Tuition Remission
First-Year Student	NA (NA)	NA	$4,800 (70)	NA	NA (NA)	NA
Advanced Student	$4,800 (10)	NA	$4,800 (50)	NA	NA (NA)	NA

For additional information on financial assistance, visit http://medicine.mercer.edu/student-services/financial-aid/.

Employment of Department Graduates

No information provided.

Additional Information

Housing and Day Care: On-campus housing is available. See the following website for more information: http://studentaffairs.mercer.edu/housing/. No on-campus day care facilities are available.

Special Facilities or Resources: Training programs in Clinical Medical Psychology utilize resources available in the College of Health Professions and in other schools in the Mercer Health Sciences Center. All courses are offered in Atlanta on Mercer's Cecil B. Day Graduate and Professional Campus.

Application Information: Office of Admissions, Mercer University College of Health Professions, 2930 Flowers Road South, Atlanta GA 30341. *Fee:* $100. *Online application:* https://psycas.liaisoncas.com.

West Georgia, University of
Department of Psychology
College of Social Sciences
1600 Maple Street
Carrollton, GA 30118
Telephone: (678) 839-6510
Professor and Chair: Donadrian L. Rice

E-mail: drice@westga.edu
Web: http://www.westga.edu/psydept/

Orientation, Objectives, and Emphasis of Department
The department is a pioneer of humanistic-transpersonal psychology. It differs from other programs in that it goes beyond conventional subjects and approaches a holistic and integrative understanding of human experience. Alongside demanding academic work, student growth and personal awareness are inherent to this venture since such reflection is considered an important factor in human understanding. Individual programs are designed according to personal needs and interests; the overall atmosphere is communal, encouraging personal and intellectual dialogue and encounter. Most conventional topic areas are taught. Beyond these are areas almost uniquely explorable in a program such as this: the horizons of consciousness through such vantages as Eastern and transpersonal psychologies, hermeneutics, existential and phenomenological psychologies, and critical psychology. Specific areas include women's studies; aesthetic and sacred experience; myths, dreams, and symbols; and creativity. Areas of applied interest are viewed as correlates of the learning process: skill courses related to human services, prevention and community psychology, counseling psychology, Cross-cultural psychology, organizational development, and growth therapies. The department offers training

in qualitative and traditional methodologies of research. Practicum and internship experience along with individual research and reading are highly encouraged for those who can profit from them.

Programs and Degrees Offered

Program	Degree	Application Deadline	Applications Received	Accepted	New Admits Enrolled (PT)	Total Enrolled (PT)	Degrees Awarded in 2014–2015	Median Years to Complete Degree	Dismissed/ Withdrew
Humanistic/ Transpersonal Psychology	MA/MS	February 15 (Fall), September 1 (Spring)	28	19	15 (11)	55 (15)	16	3	0
Consciousness and Society	PhD	January 10 (Fall)	30	8	9 (0)	38 (0)	1	4.5	2

Internships/Practica

Internships are available at local facilities.

Admissions

Entries appear in the following order: required test or GPA, minimum score (if required)/median score of students entering in 2015–2016.

Program	Degree	GRE-V	GRE-Q	GRE-Writing	GRE-Subject	Under-graduate GPA	Last 2 Years GPA	Psychol-ogy GPA	Master's GPA
Humanistic/ Transpersonal Psychology	MA/MS	146/NA	140/NA	Not specified	Not specified	2.5/NA	Not specified	Not specified	Not specified
Consciousness and Society	PhD	140/NA	140/NA	Not specified	Not specified	3.5/NA	Not specified	Not specified	Not specified

Admissions Requirements:

Degree	GRE	GRE-Subject	Letters of Recom-mendation	Research Statement	Writing Sample	CV	Interview
Master's/Specialist	Required	Optional	3	Required	Optional	Optional	Required
Doctoral	Required	Optional	3	Required	Required	Required	Required

Admissions Criteria:

GRE scores—medium
Research experience—high
Work experience—high
Clinically related public service—high
GPA—high

Letters of recommendation—high
Interview—high
Statement of goals and objectives—high
Undergraduate psychology preparation—high

Department Demographics

	Male (PT)	Female (PT)	Total	African-American/ Black (PT)	Hispanic/ Latino (PT)	Asian/ Pacific Islander (PT)	American Indian/ Alaska Native (PT)	Caucasian/ White (PT)	Unknown	Multiethnic (PT)	ADA (PT)	Int'l (PT)
Students	45 (6)	48 (9)	108	10 (0)	2 (0)	3 (0)	0 (0)	78 (0)	0 (0)	0 (0)	(0)	2 (0)

Financial Information/Assistance

Tuition: For information on tuition costs, visit http://www.westga.edu/bursar/index.php. Tuition is subject to change. Tuition costs vary by program.

Doctoral:
State residents: $307 per credit hour.
Nonstate residents: $1,049 per credit hour.

Master's:
State residents: $222 per credit hour.
Nonstate residents: $861 per credit hour.

Financial Assistance:

	Teaching Assistantship (% Receiving)	Teaching Assistantship Tuition Remission	Research Assistantship (% Receiving)	Research Assistantship Tuition Remission	Fellowship (% Receiving)	Fellowship Tuition Remission
First-Year Student	NA (NA)	NA	$3,000 (NA)	Full	NA (NA)	NA
Advanced Student	$10,000 (NA)	Full	$8,000 (NA)	Full	NA (NA)	NA

For additional information on financial assistance, visit http://www.westga.edu/financialAid/index.php.

Employment of Department Graduates

Master's:
Enrolled in a psychology doctoral program: 4
Enrolled in another graduate/professional program: 8
Employed in an academic position at a university: 2
Employed in academic position at a 2-year/4-year college: 2
Employed in other positions at a higher education institution: 1
Employed in a community mental health/counseling center: 5
Total: 22

Additional Information

Housing and Day Care: No on-campus housing is available. No on-campus day care facilities are available.

Information for Students With Physical Disabilities: See the following website: http://www.westga.edu/counseling/4486.php.

Special Facilities or Resources: Special resources include large library holdings in the areas of humanistic, parapsychology, transpersonal, philosophical, and Asian psychology. The library holds papers of Sidney M. Jourard, Edith Weiskoff-Joelsen and the Psychical Research Foundation Library. The department hosts major conferences, and faculty are associated with several journals and newsletters exploring orientation areas.

Application Information: Director of Graduate Studies, College of Social Sciences, University of West Georgia, Carrollton, GA 30118. *Fee:* $40. *Online application:* https://go.westga.edu/Apply/Pages/Welcome.aspx.

HAWAII

Argosy University, Hawaii

Hawaii School of Professional Psychology at Argosy University
College of Clinical Psychology
1001 Bishop Street, Suite 400
Honolulu, HI 96813
Telephone: (808) 536-5555
Program Dean: Sean W. Scanlan, PhD

E-mail: sscanlan@argosy.edu
Web: http://www.argosy.edu/locations/hawaii/

Orientation, Objectives, and Emphasis of Department

The Clinical Program has been accredited by the APA since 1998. It proudly employs the practitioner–scholar and Local Clinical Scientist models of training, both of which emphasize educating and training doctoral students to become clinicians and practitioners. A driving goal of the program is to prepare students to serve diverse populations. As such, it is comprised of diverse faculty members who devote part of their time to the practice of psychology and have various areas of expertise. The program is designed to educate and train students to function effectively as clinical psychologists. Specific goals include the preparation of practitioners of psychology who (1) ethically deliver diagnostic and therapeutic services effectively to diverse populations; (2) understand the scientific foundations of psychology; (3) operate in the expanding roles of psychology; (4) demonstrate their knowledge of and competence in addressing the needs, values, and experiences of people from diverse, marginalized, or underserved subpopulations during relevant courses and practicum; and (5) evaluate and use the existing and evolving body of knowledge and methods in the practice and science of psychology to enhance applications of psychology.

Programs and Degrees Offered

Program	Degree	Application Deadline	Applications Received	Accepted	New Admits Enrolled (PT)	Total Enrolled (PT)	Degrees Awarded in 2014–2015	Median Years to Complete Degree	Dismissed/Withdrew
Clinical Psychology	PsyD	Rolling	102	49	22 (0)	109 (0)	23	6.75	2
Clinical Psychology	MA/MS	Rolling	15	9	6 (0)	13 (0)	3	2	0

APA Accreditation

Clinical PsyD: Student Outcome Data website: http://clinical.argosy.edu/locations/hawaii/clinical-psychology-doctor-of-psychology.

Doctoral Degree (PsyD Clinical Psychology): For those doctoral students for whom a professional internship was required in this program prior to graduation:
Total students who applied for an internship: 33
Total students who obtained an internship: 31
Total students who obtained a paid internship: 31
Total students who obtained an unpaid internship: 0
Total students who were placed in APA/CPA-accredited internships: 17
Total students placed in internships not APA/CPA-accredited, but listed with the Association of Psychology Postdoctoral and Internship Centers (APPIC): 14
Total students placed in internships conforming to guidelines of the Council of Directors of School Psychology Programs (CDSPP): 0
Total students placed in internships that were not APA/CPA-accredited, APPIC or CDSSP listed: 0

Master's Degree (MA/MS Clinical Psychology): An internship experience, such as a final research project or "capstone" experience is required of graduates.

Internships/Practica

Students in the Master of Arts in Clinical Psychology program are required to complete a 1-year intervention practicum which also includes a seminar for three semesters. They need to be at their sites approximately 20 hours a week totaling 720 hours a year and be supervised by licensed professionals. Sites that are available include hospitals, schools, community agencies, private agencies, and counseling centers. They may work with children and adolescents, adults who have psychiatric problems, medical conditions, personal issues, and learning disabilities. Students in the Doctor of Psychology program are required to complete a

Diagnostic Practicum and an Intervention Practicum. Each is for a year and includes a seminar. Students spend approximately 20 hours a week totaling 720 hours a year being supervised by a licensed psychologist. Typical sites include military installations, hospitals, higher education counseling centers, non-profit community agencies, schools, private agencies, psychologists in private practice, and agencies in rural communities. Clients include the elderly, substance abusers, patients with medical conditions, military personnel and families, children/students in schools, and college students. Some students also elect to enroll in Advanced Practicum. Students are also required to complete a 1-year full-time internship.

Admissions

Entries appear in the following order: required test or GPA, minimum score (if required)/median score of students entering in 2015–2016.

Program	Degree	GRE-V	GRE-Q	GRE-Writing	GRE-Subject	Under-graduate GPA	Last 2 Years GPA	Psychol-ogy GPA	Master's GPA
Clinical Psychology	PsyD	Not specified	Not specified	Not specified	Not specified	3/3.4	Not specified	Not specified	3.25/3.55
Clinical Psychology	MA/MS	Not specified	Not specified	Not specified	Not specified	3/3.55	Not specified	Not specified	Not specified

Admissions Requirements:

Degree	GRE	GRE-Subject	Letters of Recom-mendation	Research Statement	Writing Sample	CV	Interview
Master's/Specialist	Optional	Optional	3	Required	Optional	Required	Required
Doctoral	Optional	Optional	3	Required	Optional	Required	Required

Admissions Criteria:

GRE scores—medium
Research experience—medium
Work experience—medium
Clinically related public service—medium
GPA—high

Letters of recommendation—high
Interview—high
Statement of goals and objectives—high
Undergraduate psychology preparation—high
Relevant experience—medium

For additional information on admission requirements, visit http://clinical.argosy.edu/locations/hawaii/clinical-psychology-doctor-of-psychology/admissions.

Department Demographics

	Male (PT)	Female (PT)	Total	African-American/Black (PT)	Hispanic/Latino (PT)	Asian/Pacific Islander (PT)	American Indian/Alaska Native (PT)	Caucasian/White (PT)	Unknown	Multiethnic (PT)	ADA (PT)	Int'l (PT)
Students	30 (0)	82 (0)	112	11 (0)	0 (0)	41 (0)	0 (0)	38 (0)	1 (0)	21 (0)	0 (0)	0 (0)

Financial Information/Assistance

Tuition: For information on tuition costs, visit https://www.argosy.edu/affordability/tuition-and-fees. Tuition is subject to change. Additional fees are assessed to students beyond the costs of tuition for the following: Technology fee = $15/credit.

Doctoral:
State residents: $1,197 per credit hour.
Nonstate residents: $1,197 per credit hour.

Master's:
State residents: $1,197 per credit hour.
Nonstate residents: $1,197 per credit hour.

Financial Assistance:

	Teaching Assistantship (% Receiving)	Teaching Assistantship Tuition Remission	Research Assistantship (% Receiving)	Research Assistantship Tuition Remission	Fellowship (% Receiving)	Fellowship Tuition Remission
First-Year Student	NA (NA)	NA	NA (NA)	NA	NA (NA)	NA
Advanced Student	$600 (NA)	NA	NA (NA)	NA	$1,797 (NA)	NA

For additional information on financial assistance, visit https://www.argosy.edu/affordability.

Employment of Department Graduates

Doctoral:
Enrolled in a postdoctoral residency/fellowship: 10
Employed in independent practice: 1
Employed in other positions at a higher education institution: 1
Employed in a professional position in a school system: 1
Employed in government agency: 6
Employed in a hospital/medical center: 4
Total: 23

Additional Information

Housing and Day Care: No on-campus housing is available. No on-campus day care facilities are available.

Application Information: Admissions, Hawaii School of Professional Psychology, Argosy University Hawaii, 1001 Bishop Street, Suite 400, Honolulu, HI 96813. *Fee:* $50. *Online application:* https://apply.argosy.edu/apply.

Hawaii, University of
Department of Educational Psychology
College of Education
1776 University Avenue
Honolulu, HI 96822-2463
Telephone: (808) 956-4300
Chairperson: Michael Salzman

E-mail: msalzman@hawaii.edu
Web: https://coe.hawaii.edu/academics/educational-psychology-edep

---

Orientation, Objectives, and Emphasis of Department
The primary objective of graduate training is the development of competent educators and scholars in the discipline of Educational Psychology. Therefore, the faculty seeks students with research interests and abilities, independence of thought, and a willingness to actively participate in both formal and informal teaching and learning experiences. The students' efforts may be directed toward the attainment of the MEd or the PhD degree. Members of the faculty share a commitment to a model of graduate education that is humanistic and inquiry-oriented. An extensive core of quantitative coursework—measurement, statistics, and research methodology—underlies most programs of study, especially at the doctoral level. In addition, core courses in human learning and development give the student a contextual framework within which inquiry methodologies are applied. The small size of the department ensures a high level of interaction among students and faculty in and out of class. Working closely with the faculty, each student creates a degree plan uniquely suited to his or her academic goals. Interdisciplinary study is particularly encouraged.

Programs and Degrees Offered

Program	Degree	Application Deadline	Applications Received	Accepted	New Admits Enrolled (PT)	Total Enrolled (PT)	Degrees Awarded in 2014–2015	Median Years to Complete Degree	Dismissed/ Withdrew
Educational Psychology	Med	February 1 (Fall), September 1 (Spring)	16	9	4 (2)	12 (13)	12	2.5	0

Programs and Degrees Offered *(con't.)*

Program	Degree	Application Deadline	Applica-tions Received	Accepted	New Admits Enrolled (PT)	Total Enrolled (PT)	Degrees Awarded in 2014–2015	Median Years to Complete Degree	Dismissed/Withdrew
Educational Psychology	PhD	February 1 (Fall)	13	5	2 (1)	12 (19)	2	5	0

Admissions

Entries appear in the following order: required test or GPA, minimum score (if required)/median score of students entering in 2015–2016.

Program	Degree	GRE-V	GRE-Q	GRE-Writing	GRE-Subject	Under-graduate GPA	Last 2 Years GPA	Psychol-ogy GPA	Master's GPA
Educational Psychology	Med	Not specified	Not specified	Not specified	Not specified	Not specified	Not specified	Not specified	Not specified
Educational Psychology	PhD	NA/NA	NA/NA	NA/NA	Not specified	NA/3.69	Not specified	Not specified	Not specified

Admissions Requirements:

Degree	GRE	GRE-Subject	Letters of Recom-mendation	Research Statement	Writing Sample	CV	Interview
Master's/Specialist	Optional	Optional	3	Required	Optional	Required	None
Doctoral	Required	Optional	3	Required	Required	Required	None

Please note if these criteria vary for different programs: Criteria below pertain to the PhD program. The MEd program does not require research experience.

Admissions Criteria:

GRE scores—medium
Research experience—medium
Work experience—medium

GPA—high
Letters of recommendation—high
Statement of goals and objectives—high

For additional information on admission requirements, visit https://coe.hawaii.edu/academics/educational-psychology.

Department Demographics

	Male (PT)	Female (PT)	Total	African-American/ Black (PT)	Hispanic/ Latino (PT)	Asian/ Pacific Islander (PT)	American Indian/ Alaska Native (PT)	Caucasian/ White (PT)	Unknown	Multiethnic (PT)	ADA (PT)	Int'l (PT)
Students	8 (7)	16 (25)	56	1 (0)	1 (0)	12 (16)	1 (1)	8 (14)	0 (0)	1 (1)	0 (0)	6 (0)

Financial Information/Assistance

Tuition: For information on tuition costs, visit http://www.hawaii.edu/admissions/tuition.html. Tuition is subject to change.

Doctoral:
State residents: $15,072 per academic year.
State residents: $593 per credit hour.
Nonstate residents: $35,160 per academic year.
Nonstate residents: $1,430 per credit hour.

Master's:
State residents: $15,072 per academic year.
State residents: $593 per credit hour.
Nonstate residents: $35,160 per academic year.
Nonstate residents: $1,430 per credit hour.

Financial Assistance:

	Teaching Assistantship (% Receiving)	Teaching Assistantship Tuition Remission	Research Assistantship (% Receiving)	Research Assistantship Tuition Remission	Fellowship (% Receiving)	Fellowship Tuition Remission
First-Year Student	NA (NA)	NA	NA (NA)	NA	$600 (NA)	NA
Advanced Student	NA (NA)	NA	NA (NA)	NA	$9,000 (NA)	NA

For additional information on financial assistance, visit http://manoa.hawaii.edu/graduate/content/financial-support.

Employment of Department Graduates

Master's:
Enrolled in another graduate/professional program: 3
Employed in other positions at a higher education institution: 1
Employed in a professional position in a school system: 5
Employed in government agency: 1
Do not know: 2
Total: 12

Doctoral:
Employed in an academic position at a university: 1
Employed in a professional position in a school system: 1
Total: 2

Additional Information

Housing and Day Care: On-campus housing is available. See the following website for more information: http://manoa.hawaii.edu/housing/. On-campus day care facilities are available. See the following website for more information: http://www.hawaii.edu/childrenscenter/.

Information for Students With Physical Disabilities: See the following website: http://www.hawaii.edu/kokua/.

Special Facilities or Resources: The college's Curriculum Research and Development Group can afford opportunities for involvement in a wide variety of educational research and program evaluation activities, many of which are centered in the K–12 laboratory school on campus.

Application Information: Department of Educational Psychology, College of Education, 1776 University Avenue, Honolulu, HI 96822. *Fee:* $100. *Online application:* http://apply.hawaii.edu/.

Hawaii, University of, Manoa

Department of Psychology
College of Social Sciences
Sakamaki Hall C400, 2530 Dole Street
Honolulu, HI 96822-2294
Telephone: (808) 956-8414
Chairperson: Ashley E. Maynard, PhD

E-mail: gradpsy@hawaii.edu
Web: http://www.psychology.hawaii.edu/

Orientation, Objectives, and Emphasis of Department

The Department of Psychology's orientation is best characterized as a synthesis of biological, behavioral, social, cognitive, developmental, and community and cultural areas, with an overriding emphasis on empiricism (i.e., the study of psychological phenomena based on sound research findings). The graduate concentrations in clinical, developmental, community and cultural, behavioral neuroscience, experimental psychopathology, social, and cognition emphasize the development of research skills and knowledge that are applicable to a wide range of academic and applied settings. The clinical program adheres to the scientist–practitioner model of training, wherein research and clinical skills are equally emphasized. Research opportunities in all graduate concentrations are available. The faculty is particularly interested in admitting students who intend to pursue academically related careers.

Programs and Degrees Offered

Program	Degree	Application Deadline	Applications Received	Accepted	New Admits Enrolled (PT)	Total Enrolled (PT)	Degrees Awarded in 2014–2015	Median Years to Complete Degree	Dismissed/Withdrew
Behavioral Neuroscience	PhD	December 1 (Fall)	5	0	0	0 (0)	0		0
Clinical Psychology	PhD	December 1 (Fall)	112	8	6 (0)	36 (0)	7	6.5	0
Community and Cultural Psychology	PhD	December 1 (Fall)	20	2	1	8 (0)	2		0
Developmental Psychology	PhD	December 1 (Fall)	5	0	0	5 (0)	1		0
Experimental Psychopathology	PhD	December 1 (Fall)	2	0	0	3 (0)	2		0
Social Psychology	PhD	December 1 (Fall)	12	1	1	5 (0)	5		1
Cognition	PhD	December 1 (Fall)	4	1	0	3 (0)	2		1

APA Accreditation

Clinical PhD: Student Outcome Data website: http://www.psychology.hawaii.edu/concentrations/clinical-psychology.html.

Doctoral Degree (PhD Clinical Psychology): For those doctoral students for whom a professional internship was required in this program prior to graduation:
Total students who applied for an internship: 6
Total students who obtained an internship: 6
Total students who obtained a paid internship: 6
Total students who obtained an unpaid internship: 0
Total students who were placed in APA/CPA-accredited internships: 6
Total students placed in internships not APA/CPA-accredited, but listed with the Association of Psychology Postdoctoral and Internship Centers (APPIC): 0
Total students placed in internships conforming to guidelines of the Council of Directors of School Psychology Programs (CDSPP): 0
Total students placed in internships that were not APA/CPA-accredited, APPIC or CDSSP listed: 0

Internships/Practica

A minimum of 2 years of practicum experience (18–20 hours per week) is required for all second through fourth year graduate students in the Clinical Studies program. A variety of practicum sites are available throughout the state and most include stipend support (average $14,000 per academic year). Sites include the department's Cognitive Behavior Therapy Clinic, community mental health outpatient centers, VA (including PTSD specialty clinics), mental health hospitals, child mental health institutions, UH counseling center, and state-supported work with the seriously mentally disabled population.

Admissions

Entries appear in the following order: required test or GPA, minimum score (if required)/median score of students entering in 2015–2016.

Program	Degree	GRE-V	GRE-Q	GRE-Writing	GRE-Subject	Under-graduate GPA	Last 2 Years GPA	Psychol-ogy GPA	Master's GPA
Behavioral Neuroscience	PhD	NA/NA	NA/NA	NA/NA	Not specified	NA/NA	Not specified	Not specified	NA/NA
Clinical Psychology	PhD	NA/161	NA/153	NA/4.8	Not specified	NA/3.67	Not specified	Not specified	NA/NA
Community and Cultural Psychology	PhD	NA/NA	NA/NA	NA/NA	Not specified	NA/NA	Not specified	Not specified	NA/NA

Admissions *(con't.)*

Program	Degree	GRE-V	GRE-Q	GRE-Writing	GRE-Subject	Under-graduate GPA	Last 2 Years GPA	Psychol-ogy GPA	Master's GPA
Developmental Psychology	PhD	NA/NA	NA/NA	NA/NA	Not specified	NA/NA	Not specified	Not specified	NA/NA
Experimental Psychopathology	PhD	NA/NA	NA/NA	NA/NA	Not specified	NA/NA	Not specified	Not specified	NA/NA
Social Psychology	PhD	NA/NA	NA/NA	NA/NA	Not specified	NA/NA	Not specified	Not specified	NA/NA
Cognition	PhD	NA/NA	NA/NA	NA/NA	Not specified	NA/NA	Not specified	Not specified	NA/NA

Admissions Requirements:

Degree	GRE	GRE-Subject	Letters of Recom-mendation	Research Statement	Writing Sample	CV	Interview
Doctoral	Required	Optional	3	Required	Optional	Required	Optional

Admissions Criteria:

GRE scores—high
Research experience—high
Work experience—low
Clinically related public service—low
GPA—high

Letters of recommendation—high
Interview—low
Statement of goals and objectives—high
Undergraduate psychology preparation—medium

For additional information on admission requirements, visit http://www.psychology.hawaii.edu/graduate/application.html.

Department Demographics

	Male (PT)	Female (PT)	Total	African-American/ Black (PT)	Hispanic/ Latino (PT)	Asian/ Pacific Islander (PT)	American Indian/ Alaska Native (PT)	Caucasian/ White (PT)	Unknown	Multiethnic (PT)	ADA (PT)	Int'l (PT)
Students	14 (0)	46 (0)	60	0 (0)	1 (0)	9 (0)	(0)	37 (0)	0 (0)	13 (0)	0 (0)	(0)

Financial Information/Assistance

Tuition: For information on tuition costs, visit http://www.hawaii.edu/finald/tuition.html. Tuition is subject to change.

Doctoral:
State residents: $14,232 per academic year.
State residents: $593 per credit hour.
Nonstate residents: $34,320 per academic year.
Nonstate residents: $1,430 per credit hour.

Master's:
State residents: $14,232 per academic year.
State residents: $593 per credit hour.
Nonstate residents: $34,320 per academic year.
Nonstate residents: $1,430 per credit hour.

Financial Assistance:

	Teaching Assistantship (% Receiving)	Teaching Assistantship Tuition Remission	Research Assistantship (% Receiving)	Research Assistantship Tuition Remission	Fellowship (% Receiving)	Fellowship Tuition Remission
First-Year Student	$17,502 (NA)	Full	$17,502 (NA)	Full	NA (NA)	NA
Advanced Student	$18,930 (NA)	Full	$18,930 (NA)	Full	NA (NA)	NA

For additional information on financial assistance, visit http://manoa.hawaii.edu/graduate/content/financial-support.

Employment of Department Graduates

Doctoral:
Enrolled in a postdoctoral residency/fellowship: 7
Employed in an academic position at a university: 2
Employed in government agency: 2
Employed in a community mental health/counseling center: 2
Employed in a hospital/medical center: 2
Still seeking employment: 1
Other employment position: 1
Do not know: 1
Total: 18

Additional Information

Housing and Day Care: On-campus housing is available. See the following website for more information: http://manoa.hawaii.edu/housing/. On-campus day care facilities are available. See the following website for more information: http://www.hawaii.edu/childrenscenter/.

Information for Students With Physical Disabilities: See the following website: http://www.hawaii.edu/kokua/.

Special Facilities or Resources: The Psychology Department is mainly housed in Sakamaki Hall. Sakamaki Hall is devoted to facilities for office space, research, and teaching in psychology. Faculty members have specialized laboratories for research, including equipment to support cognitive, social, and developmental work. Graduate students are assigned shared office space in Sakamaki Hall and have access to most departmental facilities. The computing facilities in the department and university are of a high standard, and the campus has good wireless internet coverage. Opportunities for study and research also exist elsewhere at the university and in the community. These include the Pacific Biosciences Research Center, the John A. Burns School of Medicine, the Center for Disability Studies, the Hawaii State Hospital at Kaneohe, Leahi Hospital, the State Departments of Health and Education, and the Osher Lifelong Learning Institute. Beyond the physical facilities available to the department is the unusual opportunity for research provided by the unique social and environmental structure of Hawaii. An important dimension is also provided by the East-West Center for Cultural Interchange, which provides fellowships for Asian and U.S. students and for senior scholars from mainland and foreign universities.

Application Information: Graduate Admissions, Department of Psychology, University of Hawaii at Manoa, Sakamaki Hall C400, 2530 Dole Street, Honolulu, HI 96822. *Fee:* $100. *Online application:* http://apply.hawaii.edu/.

Idaho State University

Department of Psychology
Arts and Sciences
921 South 8th Avenue, Stop 8112
Pocatello, ID 83209-8112
Telephone: (208) 282-2462
Chairperson: Shannon Lynch

E-mail: lyncshan@isu.edu
Web: http://www.isu.edu/psych

Orientation, Objectives, and Emphasis of Department

The doctoral program in Experimental Psychology matriculated its fifth class in Fall 2015. Its mission is to provide educational and research training across core areas of psychological science: cognition, developmental, learning, neuroscience, personality, and social. Five program objectives are defined: research knowledge and expertise; breadth of knowledge and integration across core areas in psychology; competence in research methodology and analysis; effective communication skills; and professional identification and ethical research conduct. The mission of the Clinical doctoral program is to train competent clinical psychologists who can apply and adapt general conceptual and technical skills in diverse regional and professional settings. A scientist–practitioner training model has been adopted. Five objectives are defined: research knowledge and skill; professional knowledge and skill; integration of science and practice; professional identification and ethical practice; and appreciation and knowledge of individual and cultural differences.

Programs and Degrees Offered

Program	Degree	Application Deadline	Applica-tions Received	Accepted	New Admits Enrolled (PT)	Total Enrolled (PT)	Degrees Awarded in 2014–2015	Median Years to Complete Degree	Dismissed/ Withdrew
Clinical Psychology	PhD	December 1 (Fall)	89	9	6 (0)	29 (2)	3	5.1	0
Experimental Psychology	PhD	December 1 (Fall)	18	6	1 (1)	11 (2)	0		1

APA Accreditation

Clinical PhD: Student Outcome Data website: http://www.isu.edu/psych/clinicalprogram.shtml.

Doctoral Degree (PhD Clinical Psychology): For those doctoral students for whom a professional internship was required in this program prior to graduation:
Total students who applied for an internship: 6
Total students who obtained an internship: 6
Total students who obtained a paid internship: 6
Total students who obtained an unpaid internship: 0
Total students who were placed in APA/CPA-accredited internships: 6
Total students placed in internships not APA/CPA-accredited, but listed with the Association of Psychology Postdoctoral and Internship Centers (APPIC): 0
Total students placed in internships conforming to guidelines of the Council of Directors of School Psychology Programs (CDSPP): 0
Total students placed in internships that were not APA/CPA-accredited, APPIC or CDSSP listed: 0

Internships/Practica

First- and second-year students complete practica in the ISU Psychology Clinic under the supervision of clinical faculty. Third- and fourth-year students often participate in community practica and/or clinical externships under the supervision of licensed psychologists or allied health professionals employed by local mental health providers/agencies. One semester on the ISU Interdisciplinary Evaluation Team is also required during the fourth year. Currently, seven clinical externship and/or service sites provide stipends and supervised practice in applied settings; six sites provide community practica.

Admissions

Entries appear in the following order: required test or GPA, minimum score (if required)/median score of students entering in 2015–2016.

Program	Degree	GRE-V	GRE-Q	GRE-Writing	GRE-Subject	Under-graduate GPA	Last 2 Years GPA	Psychology GPA	Master's GPA
Clinical Psychology	PhD	NA/NA	NA/NA	NA/NA	Not specified	Not specified	3/3.91	Not specified	Not specified
Experimental Psychology	PhD	NA/153	NA/155	NA/4.5	Not specified	NA/3.92	NA/NA	Not specified	Not specified

Admissions Requirements:

Degree	GRE	GRE-Subject	Letters of Recom-mendation	Research Statement	Writing Sample	CV	Interview
Doctoral	Required	Optional	3	Required	None	Required	Required

Please note if these criteria vary for different programs: For the experimental doctoral program, clinically related public service is not evaluated.

Admissions Criteria:

GRE scores—medium
Research experience—high
Work experience—low
Clinically related public service—medium
GPA—medium

Letters of recommendation—medium
Interview—medium
Statement of goals and objectives—high
Undergraduate psychology preparation—medium

For additional information on admission requirements, visit http://www.isu.edu/psych/apply.shtml.

Department Demographics

	Male (PT)	Female (PT)	Total	African-American/ Black (PT)	Hispanic/ Latino (PT)	Asian/ Pacific Islander (PT)	American Indian/ Alaska Native (PT)	Caucasian/ White (PT)	Unknown	Multiethnic (PT)	ADA (PT)	Int'l (PT)
Students	17 (0)	23 (4)	44	1 (0)	1 (0)	2 (1)	0 (0)	36 (3)	0 (0)	0 (0)	0 (0)	1 (0)

Financial Information/Assistance

Tuition: For information on tuition costs, visit http://www.isu.edu/finserv/costinfo.shtml. Tuition is subject to change.

Doctoral:
State residents: $8,120 per academic year.
State residents: $406 per credit hour.
Nonstate residents: $21,518 per academic year.
Nonstate residents: $623 per credit hour.

Financial Assistance:

	Teaching Assistantship (% Receiving)	Teaching Assistantship Tuition Remission	Research Assistantship (% Receiving)	Research Assistantship Tuition Remission	Fellowship (% Receiving)	Fellowship Tuition Remission
First-Year Student	$15,184 (50)	Full	$15,184 (25)	Full	$1,015 (12)	Partial
Advanced Student	$15,184 (36)	Full	$15,184 (11)	Full	$600 (3)	Partial

For additional information on financial assistance, visit http://www.isu.edu/graduate/finsupp.shtml.

Employment of Department Graduates

Doctoral:
Enrolled in a postdoctoral residency/fellowship: 1
Employed in government agency: 1
Employed in a community mental health/counseling center: 1
Total: 3

Additional Information

Housing and Day Care: On-campus housing is available. See the following website for more information: http://www.isu.edu/housing/. On-campus day care facilities are available. See the following website for more information: http://www.isu.edu/earlylc/.

Information for Students With Physical Disabilities: See the following website: http://www.isu.edu/ada4isu/.

Special Facilities or Resources: The Psychology Department has office and laboratory space for all faculty. The ISU Psychology Clinic, housed in the same building, provides four individual therapy rooms, two child/family rooms, two testing rooms, and a group therapy room, all equipped with observation systems and videotape capabilities. The ISU Psychology Clinic is adopting electronic medical records in 2015. Student computer access is available in the department, the clinic, and a university center located nearby. The university maintains an animal colony, an Office of Sponsored Programs (grant assistance), and an instructional technical resource center (website assistance). A new student study area has recently been completed. The the Integrative Research Center of the College of Arts and Letters, the department has access to a state-of-the-art eye-tracker, a room with multiple computers, and a 3-D printer.

Application Information: Admissions Committee, 921 South 8th Avenue, Stop 8112, Idaho State University, Pocatello, ID 83209-8112. *Fee:* $55. *Online application:* http://apply.isu.edu/.

Idaho, University of
Department of Psychology and Communication Studies
College of Letters, Arts and Social Sciences
University of Idaho, MS 3043
Moscow, ID 83844-3043
Telephone: (208) 885-6324
Chairperson: Dr. Todd Thorsteinson

E-mail: psyc-comm@uidaho.edu
Web: http://www.uidaho.edu/class/psychcomm

Orientation, Objectives, and Emphasis of Department
In the Land Grant tradition of providing a "practical education," the Department of Psychology and Communication Studies at the University of Idaho offers an MS and PhD degree in Experimental Psychology with an emphasis in Human Factors psychology (human technology interaction, ergonomics, human performance). The program emphasizes developing knowledge and skills germane to a professional position, but also provides students with the foundation for further graduate study. Thus, students are helped to develop analytical and problem solving skills that will serve them well in whatever they choose to do after graduation. The department is small, but is able to address the broad needs of its students through working relationships with various other units on campus (e.g., College of Engineering) and Washington State University's Department of Psychology (only 9 miles away). Student placement figures show that our graduates have been very successful in obtaining positions in technical industries. The Department also offers the MS in Psychology degree to off-campus students by making all required courses available through distance education (e.g., online courses, streaming video).

Programs and Degrees Offered

Program	Degree	Application Deadline	Applications Received	Accepted	New Admits Enrolled (PT)	Total Enrolled (PT)	Degrees Awarded in 2014–2015	Median Years to Complete Degree	Dismissed/ Withdrew
Human Factors	MA/MS	February 15 (Fall)	14	9	4 (3)	11 (12)	12	2.75	1
Human Factors	PhD	January 15 (Fall)	9	5	2 (0)	2 (0)	0		0

Internships/Practica

A few internships are available locally through the university (e.g., usability testing, web analytics). Other internships are regularly available throughout the northwest region (e.g., Idaho National Laboratory and Schweitzer Engineering Laboratory).

Admissions

Entries appear in the following order: required test or GPA, minimum score (if required)/median score of students entering in 2015–2016.

Program	Degree	GRE-V	GRE-Q	GRE-Writing	GRE-Subject	Under-graduate GPA	Last 2 Years GPA	Psychol-ogy GPA	Master's GPA
Human Factors	MA/MS	NA/NA	NA/NA	Not specified	Not specified	3/NA	Not specified	Not specified	Not specified
Human Factors	PhD	Not specified	Not specified	Not specified	Not specified	Not specified	Not specified	Not specified	Not specified

Admissions Requirements:

Degree	GRE	GRE-Subject	Letters of Recom-mendation	Research Statement	Writing Sample	CV	Interview
Master's/Specialist	Required	None	3	Required	None	Required	Optional
Doctoral	Required	None	3	Required	None	Required	Optional

Admissions Criteria:

GRE scores—high
Research experience—high
Work experience—medium
GPA—high

Letters of recommendation—high
Statement of goals and objectives—high
Undergraduate psychology preparation—low

For additional information on admission requirements, visit http://www.uidaho.edu/admissions/graduate/graduate-programs/psychology.

Department Demographics

	Male (PT)	Female (PT)	Total	African-American/ Black (PT)	Hispanic/ Latino (PT)	Asian/ Pacific Islander (PT)	American Indian/ Alaska Native (PT)	Caucasian/ White (PT)	Unknown (PT)	Multiethnic (PT)	ADA (PT)	Int'l (PT)
Students	9 (7)	4 (5)	25	0 (0)	0 (0)	2 (0)	0 (0)	11 (12)	0 (0)	0 (0)	0 (0)	1 (0)

Financial Information/Assistance

Tuition: For information on tuition costs, visit http://www.uidaho.edu/admissions/imagine/scholarships-and-costs. Tuition is subject to change.

Doctoral:
State residents: $8,222 per academic year.
State residents: $457 per credit hour.
Nonstate residents: $22,226 per academic year.
Nonstate residents: $1,235 per credit hour.

Master's:
State residents: $8,222 per academic year.
State residents: $457 per credit hour.
Nonstate residents: $22,226 per academic year.
Nonstate residents: $1,235 per credit hour.

Financial Assistance:

	Teaching Assistantship (% Receiving)	Teaching Assistantship Tuition Remission	Research Assistantship (% Receiving)	Research Assistantship Tuition Remission	Fellowship (% Receiving)	Fellowship Tuition Remission
First-Year Student	$10,000 (100)	Partial	NA (NA)	NA	NA (NA)	NA
Advanced Student	$11,000 (90)	Partial	$11,000 (10)	Partial	NA (NA)	NA

For additional information on financial assistance, visit http://www.uidaho.edu/cogs/finances/.

Employment of Department Graduates

Master's:
Employed in other positions at a higher education institution: 1
Employed in business or industry: 10
Do not know: 1
Total: 12

Additional Information

Housing and Day Care: On-campus housing is available. See the following website for more information: http://www.uidaho.edu/student-life/housing. On-campus day care facilities are available. See the following website for more information: http://www.uidaho.edu/studentaffairs/childrens-center.

Information for Students With Physical Disabilities: See the following website: http://www.uidaho.edu/current-students/asap/dss.

Special Facilities or Resources: The department provides over 3,000 square feet of research space. Labs are equipped with cutting-edge technology (e.g., driving and flight simulators, immersive virtual reality displays, multiple graphics workstations, eye and head-tracking technology, six web cameras with a quad multiplexer to allow for simultaneous recording of four camera views simultaneously). Research opportunities are available at distance-sites, such as the Motion Analysis Lab at Shriners Hospital in Spokane, WA and the Idaho National Laboratory in Idaho Falls, ID.

Application Information: Graduate Admissions, University of Idaho, 875 Perimeter Drive MS 3019, Moscow, ID 83844-3019. *Fee:* $60. *Online application:* http://www.uidaho.edu/graduateadmissions/applynow/apply.

Adler University

Department of Psychology
17 North Dearborn Street
Chicago, IL 60602-4310
Telephone: (312) 662-4100
Chair, Department of Psychology: David Katz, PhD, ABPP

E-mail: dkatz@adler.edu
Web: http://www.adler.edu

Orientation, Objectives, and Emphasis of Department

Established in 1952, Adler University follows in the tradition of Alfred Adler, founder of community psychology. Adlerian theory, especially its emphasis on social responsibility and justice, forms the theoretical basis for training across programs, and as a platform for exposure to a broad array of theoretical approaches. A core principle common to the programs at Adler University is the incorporation of socially responsible practice in didactic, seminar and applied training experiences. In addition to Adlerian psychotherapy, students in the doctoral program are able to obtain training in a variety of theoretical approaches, including cognitive-behavioral, humanistic, psychodynamic and group therapies. In addition, concentrations in specialty areas, such as primary care, trauma-related intervention, child and adolescent treatment and clinical neuropsychology are available. Doctoral program graduates often go on to serve their communities as clinicians, advocates, researchers and policy makers. Students learn to think critically, understand and utilize the available evidence in making informed clinical decisions and incorporate what Adler referred to as Social Interest in all their professional endeavors.

Programs and Degrees Offered

Program	Degree	Application Deadline	Applica- tions Received	Accepted	New Admits Enrolled (PT)	Total Enrolled (PT)	Degrees Awarded in 2014– 2015	Median Years to Complete Degree	Dismissed/ Withdrew
Clinical Psychology	PsyD	February 15 (Fall)	380	224	75	422	50	5	

APA Accreditation

Clinical PsyD: Student Outcome Data website: http://www.adler.edu/page/areas-of-study/chicago/doctor-of-psychology-in-clinical-psychology/overview.

Doctoral Degree (PsyD Clinical Psychology): For those doctoral students for whom a professional internship was required in this program prior to graduation:
Total students who applied for an internship: 76
Total students who obtained an internship: 70
Total students who obtained a paid internship: 69
Total students who obtained an unpaid internship: 1
Total students who were placed in APA/CPA-accredited internships: 42
Total students placed in internships not APA/CPA-accredited, but listed with the Association of Psychology Postdoctoral and Internship Centers (APPIC): 27
Total students placed in internships conforming to guidelines of the Council of Directors of School Psychology Programs (CDSPP): 0
Total students placed in internships that were not APA/CPA-accredited, APPIC or CDSSP listed: 1

Internships/Practica

Practicum training is a core component of the educational experience at Adler University. Students are required to undertake a Community Service Practicum, designed to provide practical application of the principles of socially responsible practice central to the training model. Students also engage in assessment, intervention, and advanced practicum experiences prior to their internship training. The training department works diligently to match student interests and skills with available training venues, and our affiliation with large, regional social service organizations, such as Heartland Alliance, provide students with a wide array of opportunities to work with diverse and traditionally underserved populations in settings ranging from correctional facilities to family service agencies. The Adler Community Health Services, comprised of several mental and general healthcare settings, offers training to practicum students as well as an APA-accredited internship site. The Training Department works to prepare students for the internship application process and Adler University students have enjoyed considerable success in matching for APA-accredited and APPIC-affiliated internships. Training is guided by an emphasis on evidence-based practice and the principles of social responsibility and justice.

Admissions

Entries appear in the following order: required test or GPA, minimum score (if required)/median score of students entering in 2015–2016.

Program	Degree	GRE-V	GRE-Q	GRE-Writing	GRE-Subject	Under-graduate GPA	Last 2 Years GPA	Psychology GPA	Master's GPA
Clinical Psychology	PsyD	NA/NA	NA/NA	NA/NA	Not specified	NA/3.4	Not specified	Not specified	NA/3.58

Admissions Requirements:

Degree	GRE	GRE-Subject	Letters of Recom-mendation	Research Statement	Writing Sample	CV	Interview
Doctoral	Required	None	3	Required	Optional	Required	Required

Admissions Criteria:

GRE scores—high
Research experience—medium
Work experience—medium
Clinically related public service—high
GPA—high

Letters of recommendation—high
Interview—high
Statement of goals and objectives—high
Undergraduate psychology preparation—medium
Interest in mission—high

For additional information on admission requirements, visit http://www.adler.edu/page/campuses/chicago/admission/admission-requirements.

Department Demographics

	Male (PT)	Female (PT)	Total	African-American/ Black (PT)	Hispanic/ Latino (PT)	Asian/ Pacific Islander (PT)	American Indian/ Alaska Native (PT)	Caucasian/ White (PT)	Unknown	Multiethnic (PT)	ADA (PT)	Int'l (PT)
Students	96 (0)	326 (0)	422	50 (0)	41 (0)	21 (0)	1 (0)	271 (0)	28 (0)	10 (0)	15 (0)	23 (0)

Financial Information/Assistance

Tuition: For information on tuition costs, visit http://www.adler.edu/page/campuses/chicago/financial-aid/tuition-and-fees. Tuition is subject to change. Additional fees are assessed to students beyond the costs of tuition for the following: student services fee, lab fee, professional liability insurance fee, UPass (for full time students).

Doctoral:
State residents: $39,900 per academic year.
State residents: $1,330 per credit hour.
Nonstate residents: $39,900 per academic year.
Nonstate residents: $1,330 per credit hour.

Financial Assistance:

	Teaching Assistantship (% Receiving)	Teaching Assistantship Tuition Remission	Research Assistantship (% Receiving)	Research Assistantship Tuition Remission	Fellowship (% Receiving)	Fellowship Tuition Remission
First-Year Student	$3,101 (NA)	NA	$3,101 (NA)	NA	$10,000 (NA)	NA
Advanced Student	$3,101 (NA)	NA	$3,101 (NA)	NA	$5,000 (NA)	NA

For additional information on financial assistance, visit http://www.adler.edu/page/campuses/chicago/financial-aid/funding-your-education.

Employment of Department Graduates

No information provided.

Additional Information

Housing and Day Care: No on-campus housing is available. No on-campus day care facilities are available.

Special Facilities or Resources: Our new facility offers state-of-the-art and accessible computer, classroom, lab and common area facilities located in the heart of downtown Chicago. The Adler Institutes for Social Justice (Institute on Social Exclusion, Institute on Public Safety and Social Justice, and LGBTQ Mental Health and Inclusion Center) sponsor national conferences of interest in the areas of social responsibility and public health. In addition, their affiliations with major community organizations provide students at all levels of training with opportunities for practicum and internship training with culturally diverse and traditionally underserved groups. These placements provide a practical application of the principles of social justice and responsibility that form the core of the training experience at Adler University. The library offers a vast array of electronic journal and print holdings, made more extensive by institutional lending agreements and consortium affiliations. In addition, the library boasts a large collection of the works of both Alfred Adler and the school's founder, Rudolf Dreikurs. The Institutional Review Board is federally registered and the university possesses a Federal Wide Assurance certificate, facilitating efforts to secure extramural funding for research and educational programming.

Application Information: Office of Admissions, 17 North Dearborn Street, 15th Floor, Chicago, IL 60602. *Fee:* $50. *Online application:* https://adler-university.force.com/.

Chicago, University of
Department of Psychology
5848 South University Avenue
Chicago, IL 60637
Telephone: (773) 702-8861
Chairperson: Susan Levine

E-mail: mhalpern@uchicago.edu
Web: http://psychology.uchicago.edu/

Orientation, Objectives, and Emphasis of Department
The Department of Psychology at the University of Chicago has been, for a century, a leading center of scholarship, research and teaching in psychology and related fields. The Department is organized into specialized programs that reflect the contemporary state of the discipline as well as the wide-ranging interests of its own faculty. The four areas are: the Cognition Program, the Developmental Psychology Program, the Integrative Neuroscience Program, and the Social Psychology Program. The interdisciplinary character of the University is further reflected in the close connections the Department of Psychology maintains with other departments in the University.

Programs and Degrees Offered

Program	Degree	Application Deadline	Applica-tions Received	Accepted	New Admits Enrolled (PT)	Total Enrolled (PT)	Degrees Awarded in 2014–2015	Median Years to Complete Degree	Dismissed/ Withdrew
Social Psychology	PhD	December 15 (Fall)	80	2	1 (0)	6 (0)	2	5	0
Developmental Psychology	PhD	December 15 (Fall)	51	12	4 (0)	14 (0)	3	5	0
Integrative Neuroscience	PhD	December 15 (Fall)	70	9	6 (0)	21 (0)	1	7.25	1
Cognition Program	PhD	December 15 (Fall)	67	6	4 (0)	18 (0)	2	6	0

Admissions

Entries appear in the following order: required test or GPA, minimum score (if required)/median score of students entering in 2015–2016.

Program	Degree	GRE-V	GRE-Q	GRE-Writing	GRE-Subject	Under-graduate GPA	Last 2 Years GPA	Psychol-ogy GPA	Master's GPA
Social Psychology	PhD	NA/NA	NA/NA	NA/NA	Not specified	NA/NA	NA/NA	Not specified	Not specified
Developmental Psychology	PhD	NA/NA	NA/NA	NA/NA	Not specified	NA/NA	NA/NA	Not specified	Not specified
Integrative Neuroscience	PhD	NA/NA	NA/NA	NA/NA	Not specified	NA/NA	NA/NA	Not specified	Not specified
Cognition Program	PhD	NA/NA	NA/NA	NA/NA	Not specified	NA/NA	NA/NA	Not specified	Not specified

Admissions Requirements:

Degree	GRE	GRE-Subject	Letters of Recom-mendation	Research Statement	Writing Sample	CV	Interview
Doctoral	Required	None	3	Required	Optional	Required	Required

Please note if these criteria vary for different programs: Some science background is helpful for the Integrative Neuroscience program.

Admissions Criteria:

GRE scores—high
Research experience—high
Work experience—low
GPA—high

Letters of recommendation—high
Interview—high
Statement of goals and objectives—high
Undergraduate psychology preparation—high

For additional information on admission requirements, visit http://psychology.uchicago.edu/academics/doctoral/admissions/overview.shtml.

Department Demographics

	Male (PT)	Female (PT)	Total	African-American/ Black (PT)	Hispanic/ Latino (PT)	Asian/ Pacific Islander (PT)	American Indian/ Alaska Native (PT)	Caucasian/ White (PT)	Unknown	Multiethnic (PT)	ADA (PT)	Int'l (PT)
Students	25 (0)	34 (0)	59	0 (0)	5 (0)	15 (0)	2 (0)	37 (0)	0 (0)	0 (0)	1 (0)	13 (0)

Financial Information/Assistance

Tuition: For information on tuition costs, visit http://bursar.uchicago.edu/page/tuition-rates. Tuition is subject to change. Additional fees are assessed to students beyond the costs of tuition for the following: activity fee, health and wellness fee.

Doctoral:
State residents: $51,624 per academic year.
Nonstate residents: $51,624 per academic year.

Financial Assistance:

	Teaching Assistantship (% Receiving)	Teaching Assistantship Tuition Remission	Research Assistantship (% Receiving)	Research Assistantship Tuition Remission	Fellowship (% Receiving)	Fellowship Tuition Remission
First-Year Student	NA (NA)	NA	NA (NA)	NA	$24,000 (NA)	Full
Advanced Student	$3,000 (NA)	Partial	NA (NA)	NA	$24,000 (NA)	Full

For additional information on financial assistance, visit http://grad.uchicago.edu/admissions/funding-your-education/.

Employment of Department Graduates

Doctoral:
Enrolled in a postdoctoral residency/fellowship: 4
Employed in an academic position at a university: 1
Employed in business or industry: 2
Total: 7

Additional Information

Housing and Day Care: On-campus housing is available. See the following website for more information: http://rp.uchicago.edu/graduate_housing/. On-campus day care facilities are available. See the following website for more information: http://childcare.uchicago.edu/.

Information for Students With Physical Disabilities: See the following website: http://disabilities.uchicago.edu/.

Special Facilities or Resources: Facilities include a Laboratory for Conceptual Psychology, an Audio Visual Laboratory, an Early Childhood Initiative, Institute for Mind and Biology, Center for Cognitive and Social Neuroscience, Spatial Intelligence and Learning Center, Language Development Project, and The Arete Initiative.

Application Information: Social Science Division, Office of Admissions, Foster Hall 105, 1130 East 59th Street, University of Chicago, Chicago, IL 60637. *Fee:* $90. *Online application:* https://apply-ssd.uchicago.edu/apply/.

DePaul University
Department of Psychology
College of Science and Health
2219 North Kenmore, Suite 420
Chicago, IL 60614
Telephone: (773) 325-7887
Chairperson: Alice F. Stuhlmacher, PhD

E-mail: gradpsych@depaul.edu
Web: http://csh.depaul.edu/departments/psychology/

Orientation, Objectives, and Emphasis of Department
In addition to several common training experiences, the Clinical program has two areas of emphasis, or tracks: Child and Community. The Child track emphasizes training in developmental psychopathology, in the development of efficacious treatments for low income African-American and Latino families, and the delivery of services for youth living in urban settings, including schools and community mental health centers. The Community track focuses on prevention, consultation, program development, empowerment, and health promotion, rather than traditional treatment. Applicants select an area of emphasis and are admitted to one of the two tracks. The two areas of emphasis are complimentary to one another. Most of the research and training conducted in the Community track is focused on children, adolescents, and families, and the training received in the Child track is informed by Community principles (e.g., prevention, empowerment, health promotion).

Programs and Degrees Offered

Program	Degree	Application Deadline	Applications Received	Accepted	New Admits Enrolled (PT)	Total Enrolled (PT)	Degrees Awarded in 2014–2015	Median Years to Complete Degree	Dismissed/ Withdrew
Clinical Psychology	PhD	December 1 (Fall)	281	10	6 (0)	42 (0)	7	6.25	0
Psychological Science	PhD	December 15 (Fall)	49	5	4 (0)	15 (0)	4	6.5	0
Industrial/ Organizational Psychology	PhD	December 15 (Fall)	75	5	3 (0)	20 (0)	1	7	0
Community Psychology	PhD	December 5 (Fall)	42	3	3 (0)	20 (0)	3	6.25	1
General Psychology	MA/MS	April 20 (Fall)	51	15	6 (0)	19 (0)	4	2	0

APA Accreditation

Clinical PhD: Student Outcome Data website: http://csh.depaul.edu/departments/psychology/graduate/Pages/clinical-outcomes.aspx.

Doctoral Degree (PhD Clinical Psychology): For those doctoral students for whom a professional internship was required in this program prior to graduation:
Total students who applied for an internship: 6
Total students who obtained an internship: 6
Total students who obtained a paid internship: 6
Total students who obtained an unpaid internship: 0
Total students who were placed in APA/CPA-accredited internships: 6
Total students placed in internships not APA/CPA-accredited, but listed with the Association of Psychology Postdoctoral and Internship Centers (APPIC): 0
Total students placed in internships conforming to guidelines of the Council of Directors of School Psychology Programs (CDSPP): 0
Total students placed in internships that were not APA/CPA-accredited, APPIC or CDSSP listed: 0

Master's Degree (MA/MS General Psychology): An internship experience, such as a final research project or "capstone" experience is required of graduates.

Internships/Practica

All of our clinical students are required to take nine quarters of practicum. Though DePaul does not have an internship program, our students fulfill their internship requirement at top facilities in Chicago and across the nation.

Admissions

Entries appear in the following order: required test or GPA, minimum score (if required)/median score of students entering in 2015–2016.

Program	Degree	GRE-V	GRE-Q	GRE-Writing	GRE-Subject	Undergraduate GPA	Last 2 Years GPA	Psychology GPA	Master's GPA
Clinical Psychology	PhD	152/159	152/156	3.5/4.25	Not specified	3.41/3.78	Not specified	Not specified	NA/NA
Psychological Science	PhD	158/160	156/161	3.5/4.25	Not specified	3.25/3.81	Not specified	Not specified	NA/NA
Industrial/ Organizational Psychology	PhD	152/155	154/154	4/5	Not specified	3.66/3.91	Not specified	NA/NA	NA/NA
Community Psychology	PhD	145/155	141/144	2/3.5	Not specified	3.51/3.63	Not specified	Not specified	3.91/ 3.91
General Psychology	MA/MS	148/158	150/156	3/3.75	Not specified	3.15/3.57	Not specified	NA/NA	Not specified

Admissions Requirements:

Degree	GRE	GRE-Subject	Letters of Recommendation	Research Statement	Writing Sample	CV	Interview
Master's/Specialist	Required	None	3	Required	Optional	Required	None
Doctoral	Required	Optional	3	Required	Optional	Required	Required

Please note if these criteria vary for different programs: Clinically related public service is not applicable for the Community, Psychological Science, Industrial/Organizational or General Psychology programs. Only the Clinical Psychology and Community Psychology programs require interviews.

Admissions Criteria:

GRE scores—high
Research experience—high
Work experience—medium
Clinically related public service—medium
GPA—high

Letters of recommendation—high
Interview—high
Statement of goals and objectives—high
Undergraduate psychology preparation—high

For additional information on admission requirements, visit http://www.depaul.edu/admission-and-aid/types-of-admission/graduate-student/Pages/psychology.aspx.

Department Demographics

	Male (PT)	Female (PT)	Total	African-American/ Black (PT)	Hispanic/ Latino (PT)	Asian/ Pacific Islander (PT)	American Indian/ Alaska Native (PT)	Caucasian/ White (PT)	Unknown	Multiethnic (PT)	ADA (PT)	Int'l (PT)
Students	41 (0)	75 (0)	116	17 (0)	12 (0)	6 (0)	1 (0)	65 (0)	15 (0)	0 (0)	0 (0)	4 (0)

Financial Information/Assistance

Tuition: For information on tuition costs, visit http://www.depaul.edu/admission-and-aid/tuition/Pages/default.aspx. Tuition is subject to change. Tuition costs vary by program.

Doctoral:
State residents: $25,020 per academic year.
State residents: $695 per credit hour.
Nonstate residents: $25,020 per academic year.
Nonstate residents: $695 per credit hour.

Master's:
State residents: $16,680 per academic year.
State residents: $695 per credit hour.
Nonstate residents: $16,680 per academic year.
Nonstate residents: $695 per credit hour.

Financial Assistance:

	Teaching Assistantship (% Receiving)	Teaching Assistantship Tuition Remission	Research Assistantship (% Receiving)	Research Assistantship Tuition Remission	Fellowship (% Receiving)	Fellowship Tuition Remission
First-Year Student	$8,650 (NA)	Full	$8,650 (NA)	Full	NA (NA)	NA
Advanced Student	$8,650 (NA)	Full	$8,650 (NA)	Full	NA (NA)	NA

For additional information on financial assistance, visit http://www.depaul.edu/admission-and-aid/financial-aid/.

Employment of Department Graduates

Doctoral:
Enrolled in a postdoctoral residency/fellowship: 2
Employed in a community mental health/counseling center: 1
Employed in a hospital/medical center: 2
Do not know: 12
Total: 17

Additional Information

Housing and Day Care: On-campus housing is available. See the following website for more information: http://housing.depaul.edu/. No on-campus day care facilities are available.

Special Facilities or Resources: DePaul Family and Community Services (FCS) is located in the same building as the Department of Psychology and serves approximately 150,000 people. Our clinical students gain their initial practicum experiences working in the FCS clinic. There are also many educational opportunities available, including colloquia, lectures, and regional and national organizations and conferences.

Application Information: Office of Graduate Admission, College of Science and Health, DePaul University, 2400 North Sheffield Avenue, Chicago, IL 60614-2215. *Fee:* $40. *Online application:* https://www.applyweb.com/depaul/.

Illinois Institute of Technology

Department of Psychology
Lewis College of Human Sciences
3105 South Dearborn, LS-252
Chicago, IL 60616
Telephone: (312) 567-3500
Chairperson: Michael Young

E-mail: youngm@iit.edu
Web: http://humansciences.iit.edu/psychology

Orientation, Objectives, and Emphasis of Department

The primary emphasis in the Department is on a scientist–practitioner model of training. Our APA-approved clinical psychology program offers intensive clinical and research training with an emphasis on a cognitive theoretical framework, community involvement, and exposure to underserved populations. The MS in rehabilitation and mental health counseling prepares students to perform a vital role as counselors who have specialized knowledge and skills for both mental health and rehabilitation service delivery. The PhD program in rehabilitation psychology prepares students for careers in rehabilitation education, research, and the practice of rehabilitation psychology. Our industrial/organizational program provides a solid scientific background as well as knowledge and expertise in personnel selection, evaluation, training and development, motivation, and organizational behavior.

Programs and Degrees Offered

Program	Degree	Application Deadline	Applications Received	Accepted	New Admits Enrolled (PT)	Total Enrolled (PT)	Degrees Awarded in 2014–2015	Median Years to Complete Degree	Dismissed/Withdrew
Clinical Psychology	PhD	January 15 (Fall), January 15 (Summer)	96	28	8 (0)	86 (0)	11	7.2	2
Industrial/ Organizational Psychology	PhD	February 15 (Fall)	45	20	7 (0)	68 (0)	2	7	0
Personnel and Human Resources Development	MA/MS	February 15 (Fall)	63	21	7 (0)	21 (0)	7	2	0

Programs and Degrees Offered *(con't.)*

Program	Degree	Application Deadline	Applications Received	Accepted	New Admits Enrolled (PT)	Total Enrolled (PT)	Degrees Awarded in 2014–2015	Median Years to Complete Degree	Dismissed/Withdrew
Counseling and Rehabilitation Sciences	PhD	March 15 (Fall)	0	0	0 (0)	1 (1)	1	4	0
Rehabilitation and Mental Health Counseling	MA/MS	March 15 (Fall)	50	27	11 (0)	27 (0)	14	2	0

APA Accreditation

Clinical PhD: Student Outcome Data website: http://humansciences.iit.edu/psychology/programs/graduate-programs/clinical-psychology-program-phd.

Doctoral Degree (PhD Clinical Psychology): For those doctoral students for whom a professional internship was required in this program prior to graduation:
Total students who applied for an internship: 14
Total students who obtained an internship: 10
Total students who obtained a paid internship: 10
Total students who obtained an unpaid internship: 0
Total students who were placed in APA/CPA-accredited internships: 10
Total students placed in internships not APA/CPA-accredited, but listed with the Association of Psychology Postdoctoral and Internship Centers (APPIC): 0
Total students placed in internships conforming to guidelines of the Council of Directors of School Psychology Programs (CDSPP): 0
Total students placed in internships that were not APA/CPA-accredited, APPIC or CDSSP listed: 0

Master's Degree (MA/MS Personnel and Human Resources Development): An internship experience, such as a final research project or "capstone" experience is required of graduates. Master's Degree (MA/MS Rehabilitation and Mental Health Counseling): An internship experience, such as a final research project or "capstone" experience is required of graduates.

Internships/Practica

All students are required to complete fieldwork internships and practica. Experiences vary by program. As one of the largest cities in the United States, Chicago provides access to diverse practicum and internship sites.

Admissions

Entries appear in the following order: required test or GPA, minimum score (if required)/median score of students entering in 2015–2016.

Program	Degree	GRE-V	GRE-Q	GRE-Writing	GRE-Subject	Under-graduate GPA	Last 2 Years GPA	Psychology GPA	Master's GPA
Clinical Psychology	PhD	156/166	150/152	3.5/4	Not specified	2.96/3.48	Not specified	Not specified	Not specified
Industrial/Organizational Psychology	PhD	153/NA	150/NA	Not specified	Not specified	3.2/NA	Not specified	Not specified	Not specified
Personnel and Human Resources Development	MA/MS	NA/NA	NA/NA	NA/NA	Not specified	NA/NA	Not specified	Not specified	Not specified
Counseling and Rehabilitation Sciences	PhD	NA/NA	NA/NA	Not specified	Not specified	Not specified	Not specified	Not specified	Not specified

Admissions (con't.)

Program	Degree	GRE-V	GRE-Q	GRE-Writing	GRE-Subject	Under-graduate GPA	Last 2 Years GPA	Psychology GPA	Master's GPA
Rehabilitation and Mental Health Counseling	MA/MS	Not specified	Not specified	Not specified	Not specified	Not specified	Not specified	Not specified	Not specified

Admissions Requirements:

Degree	GRE	GRE-Subject	Letters of Recommendation	Research Statement	Writing Sample	CV	Interview
Master's/Specialist	Required	None	3	Required	None	None	Required
Doctoral	Required	None	3	Required	None	None	Required

Please note if these criteria vary for different programs: GPA and GRE are less important for MS programs; MS in rehabilitation does not require the GRE; MS in Personnel and Human Resources Development does not require an interview.

Admissions Criteria:

GRE scores—high
Research experience—high
Work experience—high
Clinically related public service—medium

GPA—high
Letters of recommendation—high
Interview—high
Statement of goals and objectives—high

For additional information on admission requirements, visit http://humansciences.iit.edu/psychology/programs/graduate-programs/admission.

Department Demographics

	Male (PT)	Female (PT)	Total	African-American/Black (PT)	Hispanic/Latino (PT)	Asian/Pacific Islander (PT)	American Indian/Alaska Native (PT)	Caucasian/White (PT)	Unknown	Multiethnic (PT)	ADA (PT)	Int'l (PT)
Students	55 (0)	167 (0)	222	5 (0)	14 (0)	15 (0)	1 (0)	103 (0)	73 (0)	2 (0)	8 (0)	20 (0)

Financial Information/Assistance

Tuition: For information on tuition costs, visit http://iit.edu/bursar/tuition_and_fees.shtml. Higher tuition cost for this program: Clinical Psychology program charges a higher rate per year. Tuition is subject to change. Tuition costs vary by program.

Doctoral:
State residents: $1,400 per credit hour.
Nonstate residents: $1,400 per credit hour.

Master's:
State residents: $1,400 per credit hour.
Nonstate residents: $1,400 per credit hour.

Financial Assistance:

	Teaching Assistantship (% Receiving)	Teaching Assistantship Tuition Remission	Research Assistantship (% Receiving)	Research Assistantship Tuition Remission	Fellowship (% Receiving)	Fellowship Tuition Remission
First-Year Student	NA (NA)	Partial	NA (NA)	NA	NA (NA)	NA
Advanced Student	$5,000 (NA)	Partial	$2,333 (NA)	Partial	$9,734 (NA)	Partial

For additional information on financial assistance, visit http://www.iit.edu/financial_aid/.

Employment of Department Graduates

No information provided.

Additional Information

Housing and Day Care: On-campus housing is available. See the following website for more information: http://www.iit.edu/housing/. No on-campus day care facilities are available.

Information for Students With Physical Disabilities: See the following website: http://www.iit.edu/cdr/.

Special Facilities or Resources: Facilities include laboratories for human behavior studies, psychophysiological research, infant and maternal attachment, and a testing and interviewing laboratory with attached one-way viewing rooms. Equipment includes programming equipment for learning studies, specialized computer facilities, and videotaping and other audiovisual equipment. There are graduate student offices, a testing library of assessment equipment, and a student lounge. The Disabilities Resource Center is housed within psychology. The department offers professional consulting services through the Center for Research and Service.

Application Information: Department of Psychology, Attention: Admissions, Illinois Institute of Technology, 3105 South Dearborn, Suite 252, Chicago, IL 60616-3793. *Fee:* $60. *Online application:* http://admissions.iit.edu/graduate/apply.

Illinois School of Professional Psychology at Argosy University, Chicago
Clinical Psychology
225 North Michigan, Suite 1300
Chicago, IL 60601
Telephone: (312) 777-7600
Program Dean of the Clinical Psychology Programs: Annemarie Slobig

E-mail: aslobig@argosy.edu
Web: http://www.isppchicago.com

Orientation, Objectives, and Emphasis of Department

The Illinois School of Professional Psychology at Argosy University, Chicago prepares students for contemporary practice through a clinically focused curriculum, taught by practitioner–scholar faculty, with a strong commitment to quality teaching and supervision. The current curricula have been structured to provide students with the fundamental knowledge and skills in psychological assessment and psychotherapy necessary to work with a wide range of traditional clinical populations. In addition, the required curricula include courses and perspectives designed to prepare students for emerging populations from diverse backgrounds and contemporary practice approaches now addressed by clinical psychology. PsyD students may satisfy basic requirements that address the learning of fundamental knowledge and competencies in intervention, assessment, population diversity, and professional practice areas through elective clusters that also provide choices that may conform to their individualized professional goals. As part of the commitment to providing both general and concentrated education and training for doctoral students, the PsyD program offers minors, or optional areas of elective choices, for students wishing to focus their predoctoral studies in particular areas.

Programs and Degrees Offered

Program	Degree	Application Deadline	Applications Received	Accepted	New Admits Enrolled (PT)	Total Enrolled (PT)	Degrees Awarded in 2014–2015	Median Years to Complete Degree	Dismissed/Withdrew
Clinical Psychology	PsyD	January 15 (Fall)	180	65	48 (1)	155 (18)	66	5.9	7

APA Accreditation

Clinical PsyD: Student Outcome Data website: http://clinical.argosy.edu/locations/chicago-downtown/clinical-psychology-doctor-of-psychology.

Doctoral Degree (PsyD Clinical Psychology): For those doctoral students for whom a professional internship was required in this program prior to graduation:
Total students who applied for an internship: 40
Total students who obtained an internship: 35
Total students who obtained a paid internship: 35
Total students who obtained an unpaid internship: 0

Total students who were placed in APA/CPA-accredited internships: 12
Total students placed in internships not APA/CPA-accredited, but listed with the Association of Psychology Postdoctoral and Internship Centers (APPIC): 23
Total students placed in internships conforming to guidelines of the Council of Directors of School Psychology Programs (CDSPP): 0
Total students placed in internships that were not APA/CPA-accredited, APPIC or CDSSP listed: 0

Master's Degree (PsyD Clinical Psychology): An internship experience, such as a final research project or "capstone" experience is required of graduates.

Internships/Practica

The School approves and monitors practicum sites and assists students in locating and applying for internships across the country and in Canada. Both practicum and internship sites offer a wide range of training populations and approaches to students in the programs.

Admissions

Entries appear in the following order: required test or GPA, minimum score (if required)/median score of students entering in 2015–2016.

Program	Degree	GRE-V	GRE-Q	GRE-Writing	GRE-Subject	Under-graduate GPA	Last 2 Years GPA	Psychol-ogy GPA	Master's GPA
Clinical Psychology	PsyD	Not specified	Not specified	Not specified	Not specified	3/3.37	Not specified	Not specified	3.25/3.76

Admissions Requirements:

Degree	GRE	GRE-Subject	Letters of Recom-mendation	Research Statement	Writing Sample	CV	Interview
Doctoral	Optional	Optional	3	Required	Optional	Required	Required

Admissions Criteria:

GRE scores—low
Research experience—medium
Work experience—high
Clinically related public service—high
GPA—high

Letters of recommendation—high
Interview—high
Statement of goals and objectives—high
Undergraduate psychology preparation—high

Department Demographics

	Male (PT)	Female (PT)	Total	African-American/ Black (PT)	Hispanic/ Latino (PT)	Asian/ Pacific Islander (PT)	American Indian/ Alaska Native (PT)	Caucasian/ White (PT)	Unknown	Multiethnic (PT)	ADA (PT)	Int'l (PT)
Students	48 (3)	107 (15)	173	22 (8)	18 (0)	11 (2)	1 (0)	96 (8)	5 (0)	2 (0)	12 (0)	7 (0)

Financial Information/Assistance

Tuition: For information on tuition costs, visit https://www.argosy.edu/affordability/tuition-and-fees. Tuition is subject to change. Additional fees are assessed to students beyond the costs of tuition for the following: testing kit fee, technology fee.

Doctoral:
State residents: $27,888 per academic year.
State residents: $1,162 per credit hour.
Nonstate residents: $27,888 per academic year.
Nonstate residents: $1,162 per credit hour.

Master's:
State residents: $33,117 per academic year.
State residents: $1,162 per credit hour.
Nonstate residents: $33,117 per academic year.
Nonstate residents: $1,162 per credit hour.

Financial Assistance:

	Teaching Assistantship (% Receiving)	Teaching Assistantship Tuition Remission	Research Assistantship (% Receiving)	Research Assistantship Tuition Remission	Fellowship (% Receiving)	Fellowship Tuition Remission
First-Year Student	NA (NA)	NA	NA (NA)	NA	$6,017 (15)	NA
Advanced Student	$1,250 (30)	NA	NA (NA)	NA	$6,156 (13)	NA

For additional information on financial assistance, visit https://www.argosy.edu/affordability/.

Employment of Department Graduates

Doctoral:
Enrolled in a postdoctoral residency/fellowship: 28
Employed in independent practice: 3
Employed in other positions at a higher education institution: 2
Employed in a professional position in a school system: 1
Employed in government agency: 2
Employed in a community mental health/counseling center: 5
Employed in a hospital/medical center: 3
Other employment position: 1
Do not know: 2
Total: 47

Additional Information

Housing and Day Care: No on-campus housing is available. No on-campus day care facilities are available.

Special Facilities or Resources: The Illinois School of Professional Psychology at Argosy University, Chicago offers predoctoral minors which support students' interests in the following areas: Child/Adolescent Psychology, Forensic Psychology, Psychoanalytic Psychology, Client-Centered and Experiential Psychology, Diversity and Multicultural Psychology and Neuropsychology. The Psychological Services Center on campus offers clinical psychology students the opportunity to train in our in-house assessment and therapy clinic. The Center is also the hub of our APPIC-member internship consortium, which provides captive internship training opportunities for ISPP students in a number of clinical settings in the Chicagoland area. The School has a wide variety of practicum sites available for student training in agencies, schools, clinics, hospitals, and practice organizations. The program has a rich tradition of experiential learning through its personal and professional development course, including a first-year, off-campus retreat in Lake Geneva, Wisconsin. Each year students have opportunities to study abroad by taking classes offered in an intensive format for 10–14 days in a foreign country.

Application Information: Illinois School of Professional Psychology at Argosy University, Chicago, 225 North Michigan Avenue, Suite 1300, Chicago, IL 60601. *Fee:* $50. *Online application:* https://apply.argosy.edu/.

Illinois School of Professional Psychology at Argosy University, Schaumburg
Clinical Psychology
College of Clinical Psychology
1000 North Plaza Drive, Suite 300
Schaumburg, IL 60173
Telephone: (847) 969-4900
Program Dean: Cameron Brewer, PhD

E-mail: ccbrewer@argosy.edu
Web: http://clinical.argosy.edu/locations/chicago-schaumburg/

Orientation, Objectives, and Emphasis of Department
The primary purpose of the Clinical Psychology program of the Illinois School of Professional Psychology at Argosy University, Schaumburg is to educate and train students in the major aspects of clinical practice and prepare students for careers as practitioners. To ensure that students are prepared adequately, the curriculum integrates theory, training, research, and practice in preparing students to work with a wide range of populations in need of psychological services. Faculty are both practitioners and scholars

and guide students through coursework and field experiences so that they might learn the work involved in professional psychology and understand how formal knowledge and practice operate to inform and enrich each other. The school has a scholar-practitioner orientation, with faculty skilled in all major theories of assessment and intervention. Working closely with faculty, students are provided with exposure to a variety of diagnostic and therapeutic approaches. Sensitivity to diverse populations, populations with specific needs, and multicultural issues are important components of all programs. The program also has emphasis areas and concentrations in neuropsychology (listed in APA Division 40), forensic psychology, clinical health psychology, and child and family psychology.

Programs and Degrees Offered

Program	Degree	Application Deadline	Applica-tions Received	Accepted	New Admits Enrolled (PT)	Total Enrolled (PT)	Degrees Awarded in 2014–2015	Median Years to Complete Degree	Dismissed/Withdrew
Clinical Psychology	MA/MS	May 15 (Fall), October 15 (Spring)	17	8	4 (0)	17 (6)	6	2	3
Clinical Psychology	PsyD	May 15 (Fall), October 15 (Spring)	56	26	18 (0)	150 (16)	46	5	12

APA Accreditation

Clinical PsyD: Student Outcome Data website: http://clinical.argosy.edu/locations/chicago-schaumburg/clinical-psychology-doctor-of-psychology.

Doctoral Degree (PsyD Clinical Psychology): For those doctoral students for whom a professional internship was required in this program prior to graduation:
Total students who applied for an internship: 28
Total students who obtained an internship: 27
Total students who obtained a paid internship: 27
Total students who obtained an unpaid internship: 0
Total students who were placed in APA/CPA-accredited internships: 7
Total students placed in internships not APA/CPA-accredited, but listed with the Association of Psychology Postdoctoral and Internship Centers (APPIC): 19
Total students placed in internships conforming to guidelines of the Council of Directors of School Psychology Programs (CDSPP): 0
Total students placed in internships that were not APA/CPA-accredited, APPIC or CDSSP listed: 1

Internships/Practica

Clinical field training is a required component of all programs at the Illinois School of Professional Psychology at Argosy University, Schaumburg, and is a direct outgrowth of the practitioner emphasis of professional psychology. The school provides advisement and assistance in placing students in a wide variety of clinical sites, including hospitals, schools, mental health facilities, treatment centers, and non-profit and social service agencies. The MA in clinical psychology requires a minimum of 750 hours of practicum experience. The PsyD program includes 2 years of basic practicum experience, including separate practica for diagnosis and assessment, and psychotherapy, with a minimum of 800 hours per year; there is an additional year of advanced practicum (minimum 600 hours). Clinical field training culminates with a final 1-year, full-time clinical predoctoral internship. In addition to nationwide internship opportunities, our program has developed its own internship consortium, the Northwest Suburban Internship Consortium (NSIC), which is exclusively for our students and is an APPIC member.

Admissions

Entries appear in the following order: required test or GPA, minimum score (if required)/median score of students entering in 2015–2016.

Program	Degree	GRE-V	GRE-Q	GRE-Writing	GRE-Subject	Under-graduate GPA	Last 2 Years GPA	Psychol-ogy GPA	Master's GPA
Clinical Psychology	MA/MS	Not specified	Not specified	Not specified	Not specified	Not specified	Not specified	Not specified	Not specified
Clinical Psychology	PsyD	NA/NA	NA/NA	Not specified	Not specified	Not specified	Not specified	Not specified	Not specified

Admissions Requirements:

Degree	GRE	GRE-Subject	Letters of Recommendation	Research Statement	Writing Sample	CV	Interview
Master's/Specialist	Optional	Optional	3	Required	Optional	Required	Required
Doctoral	Optional	Optional	3	Required	Optional	Required	Required

Admissions Criteria:

GRE scores—low
Research experience—medium
Work experience—medium
Clinically related public service—medium
GPA—high

Letters of recommendation—high
Interview—high
Statement of goals and objectives—high
Undergraduate psychology preparation—high

Department Demographics

	Male (PT)	Female (PT)	Total	African-American/ Black (PT)	Hispanic/ Latino (PT)	Asian/ Pacific Islander (PT)	American Indian/ Alaska Native (PT)	Caucasian/ White (PT)	Unknown (PT)	Multiethnic (PT)	ADA (PT)	Int'l (PT)
Students	27 (3)	140 (19)	189	13 (4)	8 (0)	15 (2)	1 (0)	129 (16)	1 (0)	0 (0)	4 (0)	3 (0)

Financial Information/Assistance

Tuition: For information on tuition costs, visit https://www.argosy.edu/affordability/tuition-and-fees. Tuition is subject to change.

Doctoral:
State residents: $28,469 per academic year.
State residents: $1,162 per credit hour.
Nonstate residents: $28,469 per academic year.
Nonstate residents: $1,162 per credit hour.

Master's:
State residents: $29,050 per academic year.
State residents: $1,162 per credit hour.
Nonstate residents: $29,050 per academic year.
Nonstate residents: $1,162 per credit hour.

Financial Assistance:

	Teaching Assistantship (% Receiving)	Teaching Assistantship Tuition Remission	Research Assistantship (% Receiving)	Research Assistantship Tuition Remission	Fellowship (% Receiving)	Fellowship Tuition Remission
First-Year Student	$2,500 (NA)	NA	NA (NA)	NA	$7,000 (NA)	Partial
Advanced Student	$2,500 (NA)	NA	NA (NA)	NA	$7,000 (NA)	Partial

For additional information on financial assistance, visit https://www.argosy.edu/affordability.

Employment of Department Graduates

Master's:
Enrolled in a psychology doctoral program: 3
Employed in business or industry: 1
Employed in a hospital/medical center: 1
Not seeking employment: 1
Total: 6

Doctoral:
Enrolled in a postdoctoral residency/fellowship: 13
Employed in independent practice: 13
Employed in academic position at a 2-year/4-year college: 1
Employed in a professional position in a school system: 1
Employed in government agency: 2
Employed in a community mental health/counseling center: 10
Employed in a hospital/medical center: 3
Still seeking employment: 1
Other employment position: 1
Do not know: 1
Total: 46

Additional Information

Housing and Day Care: No on-campus housing is available. No on-campus day care facilities are available.

Special Facilities or Resources: The Illinois School of Professional Psychology at Argosy University, Schaumburg has core faculty with extensive experience and training in the following areas: neuropsychology; forensic psychology; clinical health and rehabilitation psychology; substance abuse and addictive disorders; clinical hypnosis; multiculturalism and diversity issues; including sexual orientation and gender issues; severe psychopathology; sleep disorders; eating disorders and self-injury; and multiple models of psychotherapy including child and family therapy, cognitive behavioral therapy, group therapy, client-centered and experiential therapies, emotion-focused therapy and psychodynamic therapies. Faculty members actively encourage student involvement in research projects as a means of fostering mentoring relationships. The program also offers the Dean's Scholarship for selective and exceptional students which pay 25% of the tuition for the entire program. The program also offers full reimbursement of the cost of EPPP licensing preparation by AATBS for all graduating students.

Application Information: Lisa Trumball, Director of Admissions, 1000 North Plaza Drive, Suite 300, Schaumburg, IL 60173. *Fee:* $50. *Online application:* https://apply.argosy.edu/apply.

Illinois State University
Department of Psychology
College of Arts and Sciences
Campus Box 4620
Normal, IL 61790-4620
Telephone: (309) 438-8701
Chairperson: J. Scott Jordan, PhD

E-mail: psygrad@ilstu.edu
Web: http://psychology.illinoisstate.edu/grad/index.shtml

Orientation, Objectives, and Emphasis of Department
The department provides professional training in several fields of psychology that include cognitive and behavioral sciences, clinical-counseling psychology, developmental psychology, industrial/organizational-social psychology, quantitative psychology, and school psychology. Training and research opportunities for graduate students take advantage of the teaching and career experiences of the department faculty in human service settings, schools, and industry so that instruction is both theoretical and practical. Besides required curriculum, graduate study also includes defending a thesis or clinical-counseling capstone project for master's students, or an applied research apprenticeship for specialist students. The doctoral program in school psychology also requires a comprehensive examination and defending a dissertation. The master's degree can be completed with 2 years of full-time graduate study. The specialist degree requires 2 years of full-time coursework and a 9-month full-time professional practice during the third year. The doctoral degree requires 4 years of full-time coursework and a 12-month full-time internship during either the fifth or sixth year of graduate study. Doctoral students are also given an opportunity to teach an undergraduate psychology course.

Programs and Degrees Offered

Program	Degree	Application Deadline	Applications Received	Accepted	New Admits Enrolled (PT)	Total Enrolled (PT)	Degrees Awarded in 2014–2015	Median Years to Complete Degree	Dismissed/Withdrew
Clinical-Counseling Psychology	MA/MS	December 15 (Fall)	51	15	12 (0)	24 (8)	10	2.37	1
Developmental Psychology	MA/MS	January 1 (Fall)	11	4	4 (0)	6 (4)	0		0
Cognitive & Behavioral Sciences	MA/MS	January 1 (Fall)	24	6	5 (0)	10 (5)	4	2.35	1
School Psychology	PhD	November 15 (Fall)	25	9	5 (0)	26 (8)	6	5.85	1
Quantitative Psychology	MA/MS	January 1 (Fall)	12	5	5 (0)	9 (2)	3	3.94	1

Programs and Degrees Offered *(con't.)*

Program	Degree	Application Deadline	Applica-tions Received	Accepted	New Admits Enrolled (PT)	Total Enrolled (PT)	Degrees Awarded in 2014–2015	Median Years to Complete Degree	Dismissed/Withdrew
Industrial/Organizational-Social Psychology	MA/MS	January 1 (Fall)	65	8	5 (0)	9 (10)	3	4.27	3
Specialist in School Psychology	Other	December 1 (Fall)	34	11	5 (0)	17 (0)	7	3.61	0

APA Accreditation

School PhD: Student Outcome Data website: http://psychology.illinoisstate.edu/school/docdata.shtml.

Doctoral Degree (PhD School Psychology): For those doctoral students for whom a professional internship was required in this program prior to graduation:
Total students who applied for an internship: 4
Total students who obtained an internship: 4
Total students who obtained a paid internship: 4
Total students who obtained an unpaid internship: 0
Total students who were placed in APA/CPA-accredited internships: 4
Total students placed in internships not APA/CPA-accredited, but listed with the Association of Psychology Postdoctoral and Internship Centers (APPIC): 0
Total students placed in internships conforming to guidelines of the Council of Directors of School Psychology Programs (CDSPP): 0
Total students placed in internships that were not APA/CPA-accredited, APPIC or CDSSP listed: 0

Master's Degree (MA/MS Clinical-Counseling Psychology): An internship experience, such as a final research project or "capstone" experience is required of graduates. Master's Degree (MA/MS Developmental Psychology): An internship experience, such as a final research project or "capstone" experience is required of graduates. Master's Degree (MA/MS Cognitive & Behavioral Sciences): An internship experience, such as a final research project or "capstone" experience is required of graduates. Master's Degree (MA/MS Quantitative Psychology): An internship experience, such as a final research project or "capstone" experience is required of graduates. Master's Degree (MA/MS Industrial/Organizational-Social Psychology): An internship experience, such as a final research project or "capstone" experience is required of graduates.

Internships/Practica

First-year students in the specialist and doctoral programs in School Psychology are assigned to supervised practica in local public schools, Head Start classrooms, and at The Autism Place. Local school psychologists and advanced doctoral students in School Psychology (under the supervision of a school psychology faculty member) supervise these first-year students. Second-year specialist students, and second- and third-year doctoral students complete practica in local public schools, The Autism Place, and the Psychological Services Center, under the supervision of program faculty and local site supervisors. Advanced doctoral students also complete advanced practica in a variety of settings depending on their interests/career goals, and a 12-month full-time professional internship, usually during their fifth or sixth year in the program. Students in the specialist program must complete a 9-month full-time professional practice experience in a school setting, usually during their third year in the program. During their second year of graduate study, Clinical-Counseling Psychology Program students must complete a 12-month full-time practicum that provides a supervised experience at mental health agencies in the surrounding communities. Students in the Industrial/Organizational-Social Psychology master's sequence have completed part-time internships in the local business community.

Admissions

Entries appear in the following order: required test or GPA, minimum score (if required)/median score of students entering in 2015–2016.

Program	Degree	GRE-V	GRE-Q	GRE-Writing	GRE-Subject	Under-graduate GPA	Last 2 Years GPA	Psychol-ogy GPA	Master's GPA
Clinical-Counseling Psychology	MA/MS	147/151	144/149	3.5/4.5	Not specified	3.3/3.73	3.3/3.79	3.34/3.84	Not specified

Admissions *(con't.)*

Program	Degree	GRE-V	GRE-Q	GRE-Writing	GRE-Subject	Under-graduate GPA	Last 2 Years GPA	Psychology GPA	Master's GPA
Developmental Psychology	MA/MS	146/152	148/151	3/4	Not specified	3.14/3.26	3.15/3.6	3.05/3.55	Not specified
Cognitive & Behavioral Sciences	MA/MS	150/153	149/156	3.5/4	Not specified	3.49/3.7	3.47/3.71	3.42/3.64	Not specified
School Psychology	PhD	155/160	148/152	3.5/4	Not specified	3.36/3.74	3.62/3.85	3.3/3.71	Not specified
Quantitative Psychology	MA/MS	152/155	150/156	3/4.25	Not specified	2.79/3.65	2.48/3.68	2.85/3.51	Not specified
Industrial/Organizational-Social Psychology	MA/MS	146/159	152/156	3.5/4.5	Not specified	3.07/3.9	3.88/3.9	3.5/3.93	Not specified
Specialist in School Psychology	Other	148/155	143/148	3/3.5	Not specified	3.06/3.99	3.27/3.93	3.03/3.48	Not specified

Admissions Requirements:

Degree	GRE	GRE-Subject	Letters of Recommendation	Research Statement	Writing Sample	CV	Interview
Master's/Specialist	Required	None	3	Required	Required	Required	Recommended
Doctoral	Required	Required	3	Required	Required	Required	Required

Please note if these criteria vary for different programs: Doctoral program applicants must take the GRE General Test and Subject Test. Doctoral program applicants must complete 2-day campus interviews with the faculty. Specialist program applicants must complete either campus interviews with the faculty or by Skype, if approved. Clinical-Counseling program applicants must complete campus interviews with the faculty, by telephone, or by Skype. Other master's program applicants are invited to campus for interviews (preferred) or may be contacted for telephone interviews. The Clinical-Counseling Psychology program identifies clinically related public service as a high admission criterion for its applicants. The writing sample is optional for Industrial/Organizational-Social Psychology and Quantitative Psychology applicants.

Admissions Criteria:

GRE scores—high
Research experience—high
Work experience—medium
Clinically related public service—medium
GPA—high

Letters of recommendation—high
Interview—medium
Statement of goals and objectives—medium
Undergraduate psychology preparation—high
CV or resume—medium

For additional information on admission requirements, visit http://psychology.illinoisstate.edu/grad/application/index.shtml.

Department Demographics

	Male (PT)	Female (PT)	Total	African-American/ Black (PT)	Hispanic/ Latino (PT)	Asian/ Pacific Islander (PT)	American Indian/ Alaska Native (PT)	Caucasian/ White (PT)	Unknown	Multiethnic (PT)	ADA (PT)	Int'l (PT)
Students	22 (10)	79 (27)	138	3 (3)	5 (3)	9 (1)	0 (0)	81 (30)	2 (0)	1 (0)	1 (0)	4 (0)

Financial Information/Assistance

Tuition: For information on tuition costs, visit http://studentaccounts.illinoisstate.edu/tuition/graduate.php. Tuition is subject to change. Additional fees are assessed to students beyond the costs of tuition for the following: general fees; student insurance (may be waived with proof of other coverage).

Doctoral:
State residents: $8,976 per academic year.
State residents: $374 per credit hour.
Nonstate residents: $18,648 per academic year.
Nonstate residents: $777 per credit hour.

Master's:
State residents: $8,976 per academic year.
State residents: $374 per credit hour.
Nonstate residents: $18,648 per academic year.
Nonstate residents: $777 per credit hour.

Financial Assistance:

	Teaching Assistantship (% Receiving)	Teaching Assistantship Tuition Remission	Research Assistantship (% Receiving)	Research Assistantship Tuition Remission	Fellowship (% Receiving)	Fellowship Tuition Remission
First-Year Student	$4,050 (37)	Full	$4,050 (39)	Full	$3,600 (1)	Full
Advanced Student	$5,850 (15)	Full	$5,850 (13)	Full	$3,600 (1)	Full

For additional information on financial assistance, visit http://psychology.illinoisstate.edu/grad/financial.shtml.

Employment of Department Graduates

Master's:
Enrolled in a psychology doctoral program: 2
Employed in a professional position in a school system: 7
Employed in business or industry: 8
Employed in a community mental health/counseling center: 8
Employed in a hospital/medical center: 1
Other employment position: 1
Total: 27

Doctoral:
Enrolled in a postdoctoral residency/fellowship: 1
Employed in independent practice: 2
Employed in a professional position in a school system: 3
Total: 6

Additional Information

Housing and Day Care: On-campus housing is available. See the following website for more information: http://www.housing.ilstu.edu/. On-campus day care facilities are available. See the following website for more information: http://childcarecenter.illinoisstate.edu/.

Information for Students With Physical Disabilities: See the following website: http://disabilityconcerns.illinoisstate.edu/.

Special Facilities or Resources: The department has a dedicated computer lab, and human subject and animal laboratories, where students can register and participate in research projects in person and online. The department sponsors the Psychological Services Center (PSC) where graduate clinicians and faculty supervisors provide assessment and clinical services to clients, and work closely with referred children, adolescents, and their families from the community, and college-age students who may exhibit learning disabilities. The PSC services include Child/Adolescent Assessment, Multidisciplinary Psychoeducational Assessment, College Learning Assessment, and Dialectical Behavior Therapy Skills Group. PSC services are provided at the Center, in homes, or at local schools. For the Clinical-Counseling Psychology Program, several local community agencies (hospitals, mental health centers, rehabilitation centers, etc.) provide a 12-month practicum, where students observe, receive work experiences and training by professionals in the field. A School Psychology faculty member manages graduate trainees staff at The Autism Place, an affiliate of The Autism Program of Illinois, which is a network of resources for Autism Spectrum Disorders and an infrastructure of provider networks to help Illinois families.

Application Information: Illinois State University, Admissions, Campus Box 2200, Normal, IL 61790-2200. *Fee:* $50. *Online application:* http://grad.illinoisstate.edu/admission/apply/.

Illinois, University of, Chicago
Department of Educational Psychology
Education (MC 147)
1040 West Harrison Street
Chicago, IL 60607-7133
Telephone: (312) 996-5580
Chairperson: Stacey Horn
Web: http://education.uic.edu/academics-admissions/departments/department-educational-psychology

E-mail: acante2@uic.edu

Orientation, Objectives, and Emphasis of Department
The Department of Educational Psychology is internationally known for its rigorous degree programs, esteemed faculty, and commitment to urban education and test fairness. Our work focuses on understanding how children's ethnicity, culture, class, and gender impact their development and learning, and we are dedicated to developing and applying fair approaches of measurement, statistics, and evaluation to support such efforts. Our research is guided by our commitment to understand what it means to be both a teacher and a learner in an urban context such as Chicago. We research how children's homes, schools, and communities, along with media, contribute to students' learning in various collaborative instructional and play activities. We seek to understand how children construct notions of morality, fairness, and gender, and how they develop resilience in the face of enduring economic difficulties. As part of this endeavor, we seek to contribute to basic scientific understanding of cognition and cognitive development. We strive to advance knowledge in research methodology to address our research questions in a fair manner.

Programs and Degrees Offered

Program	Degree	Application Deadline	Applications Received	Accepted	New Admits Enrolled (PT)	Total Enrolled (PT)	Degrees Awarded in 2014–2015	Median Years to Complete Degree	Dismissed/ Withdrew
Educational Psychology	PhD	December 1 (Fall), December 15 (Summer)	23	6	5 (1)	20 (24)	3	6	0
Measurement, Evaluation, Statistics, & Assm't	Med	March 15 (Fall), October 1 (Spring)	8	6	1	17 (2)	9	2	0
Youth Development	Med	March 15 (Fall)	36	18	15	35	17	2	0

Internships/Practica
Our students in the Youth Development MEd program complete 6 hours of fieldwork that is negotiated with their program advisor and enroll in courses designed to help them maximize the benefits of those experiences.

Admissions
Entries appear in the following order: required test or GPA, minimum score (if required)/median score of students entering in 2015–2016.

Program	Degree	GRE-V	GRE-Q	GRE-Writing	GRE-Subject	Undergraduate GPA	Last 2 Years GPA	Psychology GPA	Master's GPA
Educational Psychology	PhD	150/156	150/160	Not specified	Not specified	3/3.6	Not specified	Not specified	3/3.8
Measurement, Evaluation, Statistics, & Assm't	Med	150/153	150/160	Not specified	Not specified	3/3.5	Not specified	Not specified	Not specified
Youth Development	Med	Not specified	Not specified	Not specified	Not specified	3/3.5	Not specified	Not specified	Not specified

Admissions Requirements:

Degree	GRE	GRE-Subject	Letters of Recommendation	Research Statement	Writing Sample	CV	Interview
Master's/Specialist	Required	None	3	Required	Optional	Optional	None
Doctoral	Required	Optional	3	Required	Optional	Optional	Optional

Please note if these criteria vary for different programs: For students seeking enrollment in the MESA concentration for the PhD Program and the MESA MEd programs, more emphasis is placed on GRE scores and research experience. Students applying to the MESA concentration for the PhD program are expected to have earned a Master's degree in one or more of the relevant areas. For students seeking admission to the MEd in Youth Development, no GRE or other test scores are required. Instead, students must demonstrate more direct involvement in youth development activities.

Admissions Criteria:

GRE scores—medium
Research experience—medium
Work experience—low
Clinically related public service—medium
GPA—medium

Letters of recommendation—high
Statement of goals and objectives—high
Undergraduate psychology preparation—low
Match w/ college mission—high

Department Demographics

	Male (PT)	Female (PT)	Total	African-American/ Black (PT)	Hispanic/ Latino (PT)	Asian/ Pacific Islander (PT)	American Indian/ Alaska Native (PT)	Caucasian/ White (PT)	Unknown	Multiethnic (PT)	ADA (PT)	Int'l (PT)
Students	25 (7)	47 (12)	91	12 (3)	5 (2)	11 (3)	0 (0)	40 (10)	3 (0)	1 (1)	0 (0)	7 (11)

Financial Information/Assistance

Tuition: For information on tuition costs, visit https://admissions.uic.edu/graduate-professional/tuition-fees. Tuition is subject to change. Additional fees are assessed to students beyond the costs of tuition for the following: $4,232 for graduate fees & assessment.

Doctoral:
State residents: $11,480 per academic year.
Nonstate residents: $23,720 per academic year.

Master's:
State residents: $11,480 per academic year.
Nonstate residents: $23,720 per academic year.

Financial Assistance:

	Teaching Assistantship (% Receiving)	Teaching Assistantship Tuition Remission	Research Assistantship (% Receiving)	Research Assistantship Tuition Remission	Fellowship (% Receiving)	Fellowship Tuition Remission
First-Year Student	$17,465 (NA)	Full	$17,465 (NA)	Full	$49,733 (NA)	Full
Advanced Student	$17,465 (NA)	Full	$17,465 (NA)	Full	$49,733 (NA)	Full

For additional information on financial assistance, visit http://education.uic.edu/academics-admissions/tuition-financial-aid.

Employment of Department Graduates

Master's:
Enrolled in a psychology doctoral program: 1
Other employment position: 5
Total: 6

Doctoral:
Enrolled in a postdoctoral residency/fellowship: 1
Employed in other positions at a higher education institution: 2
Employed in a professional position in a school system: 1
Total: 4

Additional Information

Housing and Day Care: On-campus housing is available. See the following website for more information: http://www.housing.uic.edu/halls/graduate.php. On-campus day care facilities are available. See the following website for more information: http://childrenscenter.uic.edu/.

Information for Students With Physical Disabilities: See the following website: http://drc.uic.edu/.

Special Facilities or Resources: UIC is a Research Intensive university and has all the resources that allow for that designation. Our department also has a laboratory that allows faculty and students to obtain measurement, evaluation, statistical, and assessment consulting services as these are used in research.

Application Information: Fee: $60. *Online application:* https://admissions.uic.edu/grad/apply_grad.html.

Illinois, University of, Chicago

Department of Psychology (M/C 285)
Liberal Arts and Sciences
1007 West Harrison Street
Chicago, IL 60607-7137
Telephone: (312) 996-2434
Department Head: Michael Ragozzino

E-mail: pschinfo@uic.edu
Web: http://psch.uic.edu/

Orientation, Objectives, and Emphasis of Department

The goal of the psychology department's doctoral program is to educate scholars and researchers who will contribute to the growth of psychological knowledge, whether they work in academic, applied, or policy settings. Within the framework of satisfying the requirements of a major division and a minor, the department encourages students in consultation with their advisors to construct programs individually tailored to their research interests. The psychology department has more than 30 faculty and nearly 100 graduate students. It has 5 major programs: behavioral neuroscience, clinical, cognitive, community and prevention research, and social and personality. It has a psychology and law minor, a statistics, methods and measurement minor and an interdepartmental specialization in neuroscience. We have close collaborations with the Institute for Juvenile Research, the Institute for Disabilities and Human Development, the School of Public Health, the Center for Urban Educational Research and Development, the Center for the Study of Learning, Instruction and Teacher Development, the Center for Literacy, and the Institute of Government and Public Affairs. These partnerships provide students and faculty with an interest in interdisciplinary research an opportunity to work with scholars from diverse fields.

Programs and Degrees Offered

Program	Degree	Application Deadline	Applications Received	Accepted	New Admits Enrolled (PT)	Total Enrolled (PT)	Degrees Awarded in 2014–2015	Median Years to Complete Degree	Dismissed/ Withdrew
Behavioral Neuroscience	PhD	December 1 (Fall)	13	2	1 (0)	9 (0)	1	6	0
Clinical Psychology	PhD	December 1 (Fall)	249	10	4	34	6	6	0
Cognitive Psychology	PhD	December 1 (Fall)	28	3	3	18	3	6	0
Community and Prevention Research	PhD	December 1 (Fall)	34	4	3	18	5	7.75	0
Social and Personality Psychology	PhD	December 1 (Fall)	50	3	2	14	1	7.75	0

APA Accreditation

Clinical PhD: Student Outcome Data website: http://psch.uic.edu/psychology/programs/clinical/clinical-student-admissions-outcomes-and-other-data.

Doctoral Degree (PhD Clinical Psychology): For those doctoral students for whom a professional internship was required in this program prior to graduation:

Total students who applied for an internship: 6

Total students who obtained an internship: 6

Total students who obtained a paid internship: 6

Total students who obtained an unpaid internship: 0

Total students who were placed in APA/CPA-accredited internships: 6

Total students placed in internships not APA/CPA-accredited, but listed with the Association of Psychology Postdoctoral and Internship Centers (APPIC): 0

Total students placed in internships conforming to guidelines of the Council of Directors of School Psychology Programs (CDSPP): 0

Total students placed in internships that were not APA/CPA-accredited, APPIC or CDSSP listed: 0

Internships/Practica

Access to a wide variety of practicum and research sites is available to advanced students. These include the UIC Counseling Service, Cook County Hospital, Rush-Presbyterian-St. Luke's Medical Center, the Institute for Juvenile Research, the Institute on Disabilities and Human Development, several Veterans Administration hospitals and mental health clinics, schools, and diverse community agencies throughout the Chicago area, in addition to our own Office of Applied Psychology.

Admissions

Entries appear in the following order: required test or GPA, minimum score (if required)/median score of students entering in 2015–2016.

Program	Degree	GRE-V	GRE-Q	GRE-Writing	GRE-Subject	Under-graduate GPA	Last 2 Years GPA	Psychol-ogy GPA	Master's GPA
Behavioral Neuroscience	PhD	NA/154	NA/167	NA/4	Not specified	Not specified	3.2/NA	Not specified	Not specified
Clinical Psychology	PhD	NA/162	NA/162	NA/4.5	Not specified	Not specified	3.2/NA	Not specified	Not specified
Cognitive Psychology	PhD	NA/164	NA/154	NA/4.5	Not specified	Not specified	3.2/NA	Not specified	Not specified
Community and Prevention Research	PhD	NA/148	NA/144	NA/4	Not specified	Not specified	3.2/3.57	Not specified	Not specified
Social and Personality Psychology	PhD	NA/164	NA/159	NA/4.75	Not specified	Not specified	3.2/NA	Not specified	Not specified

Admissions Requirements:

Degree	GRE	GRE-Subject	Letters of Recom-mendation	Research Statement	Writing Sample	CV	Interview
Doctoral	Required	Recom-mended	3	Required	Optional	Required	Required

Admissions Criteria:

GRE scores—medium

Research experience—high

Work experience—medium

Clinically related public service—low

GPA—high

Letters of recommendation—high

Interview—high

Statement of goals and objectives—high

Undergraduate psychology preparation—medium

Fit with faculty research—high

For additional information on admission requirements, visit http://psch.uic.edu/psychology/prospective-graduate-students/application-process.

Department Demographics

	Male (PT)	Female (PT)	Total	African-American/ Black (PT)	Hispanic/ Latino (PT)	Asian/ Pacific Islander (PT)	American Indian/ Alaska Native (PT)	Caucasian/ White (PT)	Unknown	Multiethnic (PT)	ADA (PT)	Int'l (PT)
Students	33 (0)	60 (0)	93	5 (0)	7 (0)	9 (0)	1 (0)	69 (0)	0 (0)	2 (0)	0 (0)	4 (0)

Financial Information/Assistance

Tuition: For information on tuition costs, visit https://registrar.uic.edu/tuition/grad/. Tuition is subject to change.

Doctoral:
State residents: $19,944 per academic year.
Nonstate residents: $32,184 per academic year.

Financial Assistance:

	Teaching Assistantship (% Receiving)	Teaching Assistantship Tuition Remission	Research Assistantship (% Receiving)	Research Assistantship Tuition Remission	Fellowship (% Receiving)	Fellowship Tuition Remission
First-Year Student	$16,065 (NA)	Full	$16,065 (NA)	Full	$22,000 (NA)	Full
Advanced Student	$16,065 (NA)	Full	$16,065 (NA)	Full	$22,000 (NA)	Full

Employment of Department Graduates

Doctoral:
Enrolled in a postdoctoral residency/fellowship: 4
Employed in an academic position at a university: 3
Employed in business or industry: 2
Employed in a hospital/medical center: 1
Do not know: 6
Total: 16

Additional Information

Housing and Day Care: On-campus housing is available. See the following website for more information: http://www.housing.uic.edu/. On-campus day care facilities are available. See the following website for more information: http://childrenscenter.uic.edu/.

Information for Students With Physical Disabilities: See the following website: http://drc.uic.edu/.

Special Facilities or Resources: The department is located in the Behavioral Sciences Building, a fully equipped facility designed to serve the needs of the behavioral and social sciences. Physical facilities include seminar rooms, animal laboratories, human research labs, clinical observation rooms with one-way observational windows and video-recording and biofeedback equipment, a well-equipped electronics and mechanics shop with an on-staff engineer, a department library, the Office of Applied Psychological Services which coordinates clinical and community interventions, the Office of Social Science Research which provides research support, and faculty-student lounge. The Department maintains its own computer lab, in which personal computer workstations connected to a mainframe and standalone PCs (MS-DOS based and Macintosh) are offered for student use. The department also offers wireless internet access.

Application Information: UIC Office of Admission and Records. *Fee:* $60. *Online application:* http://www.uic.edu/depts/oar/grad/apply_grad.html.

Illinois, University of, Urbana Champaign

Department of Educational Psychology
College of Education
210 Education Building, 1310 South Sixth Street
Champaign, IL 61820
Telephone: (217) 333-2245
Chairperson: Daniel Morrow

E-mail: edpsy@illinois.edu
Web: http://education.illinois.edu/edpsy/

Orientation, Objectives, and Emphasis of Department

The Department of Educational Psychology has been a leader in placing students as university/college professors; researchers; professional psychologists; and administrators in educational, private, and government settings. The Department is composed of four divisions, each with a with distinctive program of doctoral study: (1) Counseling Psychology, offering an APA-accredited program, in which students are trained in the scientist–practitioner model from a multicultural perspective; (2) Child Development, focused on the development of children and adolescents, especially as it is relevant to education and educationally relevant outcomes; (3) Studies in Interpretive, Statistical, Measurement, and Evaluative Methodologies for Education (QUERIES), focused on developing and applying new methodologies in educational measurement, statistics, research design, and evaluation; and (4) the Cognitive Science of Teaching and Learning (CSTL), which is concerned with the study of basic processes in learning, cognition, and language understanding, and the principles through which learning is optimized in diverse contexts across the life span, among individuals who vary with respect to abilities, interests, and goals.

Programs and Degrees Offered

Program	Degree	Application Deadline	Applica-tions Received	Accepted	New Admits Enrolled (PT)	Total Enrolled (PT)	Degrees Awarded in 2014–2015	Median Years to Complete Degree	Dismissed/ Withdrew
Counseling Psychology	PhD	December 1 (Fall)	69	3	2 (0)	21 (0)	2	6.17	0
Child Development	PhD	December 1 (Fall)	12	1	1 (0)	8 (0)	2	6.17	0
Measurement and Evaluation (Queries)	PhD	December 1 (Fall)	29	5	2 (0)	16 (0)	3	7.5	0
Cognitive Science Of Teaching and Learning (Cstl)	PhD	December 1 (Fall)	13	2	1 (0)	23 (0)	6	4	1

APA Accreditation

Counseling PhD: Student Outcome Data website: http://education.illinois.edu/edpsy/programs-degrees/counseling-psychology/data.

Doctoral Degree (PhD Counseling Psychology): For those doctoral students for whom a professional internship was required in this program prior to graduation:
Total students who applied for an internship: 3
Total students who obtained an internship: 3
Total students who obtained a paid internship: 3
Total students who obtained an unpaid internship: 0
Total students who were placed in APA/CPA-accredited internships: 3
Total students placed in internships not APA/CPA-accredited, but listed with the Association of Psychology Postdoctoral and Internship Centers (APPIC): 0
Total students placed in internships conforming to guidelines of the Council of Directors of School Psychology Programs (CDSPP): 0
Total students placed in internships that were not APA/CPA-accredited, APPIC or CDSSP listed: 0

Internships/Practica

The Counseling Psychology Division offers a variety of practica in University and community settings. Within the university, students work in agencies such as the Counseling Center, Career Center, McKinley Health Center, and the Disability Resources and Education Services Center at the University of Illinois and the Counseling Center at Illinois State University. Within the community, students work at the Psychological Services Center, the Champaign County Mental Health Center, Carle Clinic (a multi-specialty medical center), Veterans Administration Medical Center, and Cunningham Children's Home. Supervision is provided by on-site supervisors and by faculty members. Each Counseling Psychology doctoral student is required to complete a year-long, full-time predoctoral internship approved by APPIC, or the equivalent. Typical internship sites include university counseling centers, hospitals/VA medical centers, child/adolescent treatment programs, and community mental health agencies.

Admissions

Entries appear in the following order: required test or GPA, minimum score (if required)/median score of students entering in 2015–2016.

Program	Degree	GRE-V	GRE-Q	GRE-Writing	GRE-Subject	Under-graduate GPA	Last 2 Years GPA	Psychol-ogy GPA	Master's GPA
Counseling Psychology	PhD	NA/NA	NA/NA	Not specified	Not specified	Not specified	3.44/3.57	Not specified	3.57/3.76
Child Development	PhD	NA/NA	NA/NA	Not specified	Not specified	Not specified	3.2/3.84	Not specified	4/4
Measurement and Evaluation (Queries)	PhD	NA/NA	NA/NA	Not specified	Not specified	Not specified	3.3/3.58	Not specified	3.6/3.7
Cognitive Science of Teaching and Learning (CSTL)	PhD	NA/NA	NA/NA	Not specified	Not specified	Not specified	3.52/3.6	Not specified	3.96/3.98

Admissions Requirements:

Degree	GRE	GRE-Subject	Letters of Recom-mendation	Research Statement	Writing Sample	CV	Interview
Doctoral	Required	Optional	3	Required	Required	Required	Optional

Admissions Criteria:

GRE scores—medium
Research experience—high
Work experience—medium
Clinically related public service—medium
GPA—medium

Letters of recommendation—high
Interview—low
Statement of goals and objectives—high
Undergraduate psychology preparation—medium
Research interests—high

For additional information on admission requirements, visit http://education.illinois.edu/programs/grad/how-to-apply.

Department Demographics

	Male (PT)	Female (PT)	Total	African-American/ Black (PT)	Hispanic/ Latino (PT)	Asian/ Pacific Islander (PT)	American Indian/ Alaska Native (PT)	Caucasian/ White (PT)	Unknown	Multiethnic (PT)	ADA (PT)	Int'l (PT)
Students	18 (0)	50 (0)	68	6 (0)	6 (0)	26 (0)	1 (0)	26 (0)	1 (0)	2 (0)	0 (0)	23 (0)

Financial Information/Assistance

Tuition: For information on tuition costs, visit https://registrar.illinois.edu/tf-rates-academic-year. Tuition is subject to change.

Doctoral:
State residents: $12,266 per academic year.
Nonstate residents: $26,502 per academic year.

Financial Assistance:

	Teaching Assistantship (% Receiving)	Teaching Assistantship Tuition Remission	Research Assistantship (% Receiving)	Research Assistantship Tuition Remission	Fellowship (% Receiving)	Fellowship Tuition Remission
First-Year Student	$16,042 (NA)	Full	$16,042 (NA)	Full	NA (NA)	Full
Advanced Student	$16,641 (NA)	Full	$16,641 (NA)	Full	NA (NA)	Full

For additional information on financial assistance, visit http://education.illinois.edu/programs/grad/financial-aid.

Employment of Department Graduates

Doctoral:
Enrolled in a postdoctoral residency/fellowship: 1
Employed in an academic position at a university: 6
Employed in other positions at a higher education institution: 1
Employed in a professional position in a school system: 1
Employed in government agency: 1
Other employment position: 1
Total: 11

Additional Information

Housing and Day Care: On-campus housing is available. See the following website for more information: http://www.housing.illinois.edu/. On-campus day care facilities are available. See the following website for more information: http://cdl.illinois.edu/.

Information for Students With Physical Disabilities: See the following website: http://www.disability.illinois.edu/.

Special Facilities or Resources: The Department of Educational Psychology is under the purview of the College of Education, rated one of the nation's top education colleges, with research and support facilities that include the Children's Research Center, Bureau of Educational Research, Office of Educational Technology, Adult Learning Lab (with eye-tracking equipment), Center for the Study of Reading, and classrooms for video demonstration, telecommunications, and computer-based education. Faculty research is funded by the National Science Foundation, National Institutes of Health, Centers for Disease Control, Institute of Educational Sciences, WT Grant Foundation, and the Spencer Foundation. The University of Illinois offers a rich academic environment with top-ranked Departments of Psychology, Computer Science, Engineering, and Speech Communication, as well as the 3rd largest academic library system in the U.S., ranking only behind Harvard and Yale. There are also strong programs in Cognitive Neuroscience (Brain and Cognition Program), Human and Community Development, Gender and Women's Studies, Afro-American Studies and Research Program, and Center for Latin American and Caribbean Studies. Research and support facilities on campus include Beckman Institute for Advanced Science and Technology, Statistical Laboratory for Educational and Psychological Measurement, Language Learning Lab, Survey Research Laboratory, and Illinois Statistical Office (consulting services).

Application Information: Fee: $70. *Online application:* http://www.grad.illinois.edu/admissions/apply.

Illinois, University of, Urbana Champaign
Department of Human Development and Family Studies
Agricultural, Consumer and Environmental Sciences
222 Bevier Hall, MC-180
Urbana, IL 61801
Telephone: (217) 333-2547
Department Head: Susan Silverberg Koerner, PhD

E-mail: roswald@illinois.edu
Web: http://hdfs.illinois.edu/

Orientation, Objectives, and Emphasis of Department
Our Human Development and Family Studies doctoral program focuses on the positive development and resilience of children, youth, and families within everyday life contexts. Emphases include the social and emotional development of children and youth; parent-child and sibling relationships; and racial, ethnic, and sexual orientation diversity. All topics are studied within specific settings.

Faculty have expertise in both qualitative and quantitative research. Students may choose an applied supporting option in program development, evaluation, and outreach.

Programs and Degrees Offered

Program	Degree	Application Deadline	Applications Received	Accepted	New Admits Enrolled (PT)	Total Enrolled (PT)	Degrees Awarded in 2014–2015	Median Years to Complete Degree	Dismissed/ Withdrew
Human Development and Family Studies	PhD	January 15 (Fall)	36	12	9 (0)	32 (0)	4	5.5	1

Internships/Practica

Doctoral students with the applied option complete at least one semester-long internship, usually within a human services setting.

Admissions

Entries appear in the following order: required test or GPA, minimum score (if required)/median score of students entering in 2015–2016.

Program	Degree	GRE-V	GRE-Q	GRE-Writing	GRE-Subject	Under-graduate GPA	Last 2 Years GPA	Psychol-ogy GPA	Master's GPA
Human Development and Family Studies	PhD	145/153	143/150	3.5/4.25	Not specified	Not specified	3/3.8	Not specified	Not specified

Admissions Requirements:

Degree	GRE	GRE-Subject	Letters of Recom-mendation	Research Statement	Writing Sample	CV	Interview
Doctoral	Required	None	3	Required	Optional	Optional	None

Admissions Criteria:

GRE scores—medium
Research experience—high
GPA—medium

Letters of recommendation—high
Statement of goals and objectives—high
Fit with HDFS—high

For additional information on admission requirements, visit http://hdfs.illinois.edu/handbook/admissions-procedures.

Department Demographics

	Male (PT)	Female (PT)	Total	African-American/ Black (PT)	Hispanic/ Latino (PT)	Asian/ Pacific Islander (PT)	American Indian/ Alaska Native (PT)	Caucasian/ White (PT)	Unknown	Multiethnic (PT)	ADA (PT)	Int'l (PT)
Students	5 (0)	27 (0)	32	3 (0)	5 (0)	6 (0)	0 (0)	16 (0)	0 (0)	2 (0)	0 (0)	3 (0)

Financial Information/Assistance

Tuition: For information on tuition costs, visit http://www.registrar.illinois.edu/tuition-fee-rates. Tuition is subject to change.

Doctoral:
State residents: $12,266 per academic year.
Nonstate residents: $29,886 per academic year.

Master's:
State residents: $12,266 per academic year.
Nonstate residents: $29,886 per academic year.

Financial Assistance:

	Teaching Assistantship (% Receiving)	Teaching Assistantship Tuition Remission	Research Assistantship (% Receiving)	Research Assistantship Tuition Remission	Fellowship (% Receiving)	Fellowship Tuition Remission
First-Year Student	$8,100 (15)	Full	$8,100 (75)	Full	$10,000 (100)	Full
Advanced Student	$8,100 (90)	Full	$8,100 (90)	Full	$20,000 (30)	Full

For additional information on financial assistance, visit http://hdfs.illinois.edu/graduate/financial-support.

Employment of Department Graduates

Doctoral:
Enrolled in a postdoctoral residency/fellowship: 1
Employed in an academic position at a university: 1
Employed in other positions at a higher education institution: 1
Employed in government agency: 1
Total: 4

Additional Information

Housing and Day Care: On-campus housing is available. See the following website for more information: http://www.housing.illinois.edu/. On-campus day care facilities are available. See the following website for more information: http://cdl.illinois.edu/.

Information for Students With Physical Disabilities: See the following website: http://www.disability.illinois.edu/.

Special Facilities or Resources: Our department includes two laboratory preschool facilities, a childcare resource and referral service, and the Family Resiliency Center.

Application Information: Graduate Secretary, 222 Bevier Hall, 905 South Goodwin, Urbana, IL, 61801. *Fee:* $70. *Online application:* http://www.grad.illinois.edu/admissions/apply.

Illinois, University of, Urbana Champaign

Department of Psychology
Liberal Arts & Sciences
Psychology Building, 603 East Daniel Street
Champaign, IL 61820
Telephone: (217) 333-2169
Professor and Department Head: Wendy Heller

E-mail: psych-gradstdy@illinois.edu
Web: http://www.psychology.illinois.edu/

Orientation, Objectives, and Emphasis of Department
The department trains students at the doctoral level for basic research in all areas. Students are admitted in one of the nine divisions: behavioral neuroscience, clinical/community, cognitive, cognitive neuroscience, developmental, quantitative, social-personality, industrial/organizational, and visual cognition and human performance. Interactions with faculty in other divisions are quite common; interdisciplinary training is encouraged. Applied research training is offered in measurement and personnel psychology. There is a strong emphasis on individualized training programs in an apprenticeship model. Each student's program is tailored to his or her research interests. Wide opportunities exist for students to participate in ongoing research programs. Students are encouraged to develop their own programs of research.

Programs and Degrees Offered

Program	Degree	Application Deadline	Applications Received	Accepted	New Admits Enrolled (PT)	Total Enrolled (PT)	Degrees Awarded in 2014–2015	Median Years to Complete Degree	Dismissed/ Withdrew
Applied Measurement	MA/MS	December 10 (Fall)	9	0	0 (0)	0 (0)	0		0
Applied Personnel	MA/MS	December 10 (Fall)	15	0	0	0 (0)	0		0
Behavioral Neuroscience	PhD	December 10 (Fall)	13	2	2 (0)	9 (0)	0		1
Clinical/ Community Psychology	PhD	December 10 (Fall)	133	10	3 (0)	31 (0)	3	7.8	1
Cognitive Psychology	PhD	December 10 (Fall)	34	4	3 (0)	18 (0)	2	5.25	0
Developmental Psychology	PhD	December 10 (Fall)	51	13	6 (0)	21 (0)	6	6.33	0
Quantitative Psychology	PhD	December 10 (Fall)	20	4	2 (0)	8 (0)	2	6	0
Cognitive Neuroscience	PhD	December 10 (Fall)	41	3	1 (0)	14 (0)	2	7.25	0
Visual Cognition & Human Performance	PhD	December 10 (Fall)	23	6	5 (0)	15 (0)	3	6.5	0
Social- Personality Psychology	PhD	December 10 (Fall)	85	9	4 (0)	17 (0)	3	6	1
Industrial/ Organizational Psychology	PhD	December 10 (Fall)	75	8	4 (0)	14 (0)	1	6	0

APA Accreditation

Clinical PhD: Student Outcome Data website: http://www.psychology.illinois.edu/people/divisions/clinical/.

Doctoral Degree (PhD Clinical/Community Psychology): For those doctoral students for whom a professional internship was required in this program prior to graduation:

Total students who applied for an internship: 3

Total students who obtained an internship: 3

Total students who obtained a paid internship: 3

Total students who obtained an unpaid internship: 0

Total students who were placed in APA/CPA-accredited internships: 3

Total students placed in internships not APA/CPA-accredited, but listed with the Association of Psychology Postdoctoral and Internship Centers (APPIC): 0

Total students placed in internships conforming to guidelines of the Council of Directors of School Psychology Programs (CDSPP): 0

Total students placed in internships that were not APA/CPA-accredited, APPIC or CDSPP listed: 0

Internships/Practica

Laboratories in Clinical Psychology—Intensive practice in techniques of clinical assessment and behavior modification with emphasis on recent innovations; small sections of the course formed according to the specialized interests of students and staff.

Admissions

Entries appear in the following order: required test or GPA, minimum score (if required)/median score of students entering in 2015–2016.

Program	Degree	GRE-V	GRE-Q	GRE-Writing	GRE-Subject	Under-graduate GPA	Last 2 Years GPA	Psychol-ogy GPA	Master's GPA
Applied Measurement	MA/MS	NA/NA	NA/NA	Not specified	Not specified	3/3.5	Not specified	Not specified	Not specified
Applied Personnel	MA/MS	NA/NA	NA/NA	Not specified	Not specified	3/3.5	Not specified	Not specified	Not specified
Behavioral Neuroscience	PhD	NA/161	NA/158	Not specified	Not specified	3/3.2	Not specified	Not specified	Not specified
Clinical/ Community Psychology	PhD	NA/165	NA/157	Not specified	Not specified	3/3.72	Not specified	Not specified	Not specified
Cognitive Psychology	PhD	NA/165	NA/164	Not specified	Not specified	3/3.81	Not specified	Not specified	Not specified
Developmental Psychology	PhD	NA/160	NA/159	Not specified	Not specified	3/3.69	Not specified	Not specified	Not specified
Quantitative Psychology	PhD	NA/162	NA/162	Not specified	Not specified	3/3.56	Not specified	Not specified	Not specified
Cognitive Neuroscience	PhD	NA/163	NA/158	Not specified	Not specified	3/3.45	Not specified	Not specified	Not specified
Visual Cognition & Human Performance	PhD	NA/163	NA/163	Not specified	Not specified	3/3.9	Not specified	Not specified	Not specified
Social-Personality Psychology	PhD	NA/164	NA/160	Not specified	Not specified	3/3.84	Not specified	Not specified	Not specified
Industrial/ Organizational Psychology	PhD	NA/163	NA/161	Not specified	Not specified	3/3.82	Not specified	Not specified	Not specified

Admissions Requirements:

Degree	GRE	GRE-Subject	Letters of Recom-mendation	Research Statement	Writing Sample	CV	Interview
Master's/Specialist	Required	Recom-mended	3	Required	Optional	Required	Required
Doctoral	Required	Recom-mended	3	Required	Optional	Required	Required

Please note if these criteria vary for different programs: Interviews vary by division.

Admissions Criteria:

GRE scores—high
Research experience—high
Work experience—medium
Clinically related public service—high

GPA—high
Letters of recommendation—high
Interview—high
Statement of goals and objectives—high

For additional information on admission requirements, visit http://www.psychology.illinois.edu/graduate/prospective/application/.

Department Demographics

	Male (PT)	Female (PT)	Total	African-American/ Black (PT)	Hispanic/ Latino (PT)	Asian/ Pacific Islander (PT)	American Indian/ Alaska Native (PT)	Caucasian/ White (PT)	Unknown	Multiethnic (PT)	ADA (PT)	Int'l (PT)
Students	50 (0)	97 (0)	147	5 (0)	7 (0)	51 (0)	0 (0)	78 (0)	2 (0)	4 (0)	1 (0)	41 (0)

Financial Information/Assistance

Tuition: For information on tuition costs, visit http://registrar.illinois.edu/tuition-fee-rates. Tuition is subject to change. Additional fees are assessed to students beyond the costs of tuition for the following: Service, General, Health Insurance, Transportation, Student Initiated, AFMFA, Library/Tech.

Doctoral:
State residents: $12,060 per academic year.
Nonstate residents: $26,058 per academic year.

Master's:
State residents: $12,060 per academic year.
Nonstate residents: $26,058 per academic year.

Financial Assistance:

	Teaching Assistantship (% Receiving)	Teaching Assistantship Tuition Remission	Research Assistantship (% Receiving)	Research Assistantship Tuition Remission	Fellowship (% Receiving)	Fellowship Tuition Remission
First-Year Student	$17,993 (NA)	Full	$17,993 (NA)	Full	$17,993 (NA)	Full
Advanced Student	$17,993 (NA)	Full	$17,993 (NA)	Full	$17,993 (NA)	Full

For additional information on financial assistance, visit http://www.psychology.illinois.edu/graduate/prospective/financial/.

Employment of Department Graduates

Doctoral:
Enrolled in a postdoctoral residency/fellowship: 11
Employed in an academic position at a university: 3
Employed in other positions at a higher education institution: 3
Employed in business or industry: 1
Not seeking employment: 1
Other employment position: 2
Do not know: 1
Total: 22

Additional Information

Housing and Day Care: On-campus housing is available. See the following website for more information: http://www.housing.illinois.edu/. On-campus day care facilities are available. See the following website for more information: http://cdl.illinois.edu/.

Information for Students With Physical Disabilities: See the following website: http://www.disability.illinois.edu/.

Special Facilities or Resources: The department has extensive laboratory facilities in all areas, including behavioral neuroscience/ biological psychology. Excellent departmental and university computer facilities are readily available to graduate students. Most faculty laboratories are computerized. The department maintains computer servers that support data storage and management and communication between laboratories and campus computers. There are very advanced facilities for research in all areas, including psychophysiology, cognitive psychology, neurochemistry, and neuroanatomy. A first-rate animal colony is maintained by the department. There is an excellent machine shop and a fine electronics shop. Programs are coordinated with other campus departments and institutes, including life sciences, communication, labor, education, and child study.

Application Information: Graduate Studies Office, 307 Psychology Building, 603 East Daniel Street, Champaign, IL 61820. *Fee:* $70. *Online application:* https://app.applyyourself.com/?id=uiuc-grad.

Lewis University

Department of Psychology
One University Parkway
Romeoville, IL 60446
Telephone: (815) 836-5594
Director of Graduate Programs in Counseling: Katherine Helm
Web: http://www.lewisu.edu/academics/grad-psychology/index.htm

E-mail: Helmka@lewisu.edu

Orientation, Objectives, and Emphasis of Department

The program in Clinical Mental Health Counseling is oriented toward individuals who have significant interest in becoming a mental health counseling practitioner. Our program trains students to work in a broad range of clinical mental health settings. It is designed primarily as part-time with most courses offered in the evenings, on occasional weekends, and some online course offerings are available. The program has two sub-specialty areas: Adult Clinical Mental Health Counseling and Child and Adolescent Clinical Mental Health Counseling. Clinical Mental Health students also have the option of participating in the Advanced Training Program for Substance Abuse counseling. There is a second program in School Counseling, designed for individuals who want to work in the public or private school systems.

Programs and Degrees Offered

Program	Degree	Application Deadline	Applica- tions Received	Accepted	New Admits Enrolled (PT)	Total Enrolled (PT)	Degrees Awarded in 2014– 2015	Median Years to Complete Degree	Dismissed/ Withdrew
Clinical Mental Health Counseling	MA/MS	Rolling	58	48	5 (20)	12 (108)	36	3	2
School Counseling	MA/MS	Rolling	18	14	2 (12)	10 (58)	23	2.5	3

Internships/Practica

Numerous practicum and internship sites available in the community.

Admissions

Entries appear in the following order: required test or GPA, minimum score (if required)/median score of students entering in 2015–2016.

Program	Degree	GRE-V	GRE-Q	GRE-Writing	GRE-Subject	Under-graduate GPA	Last 2 Years GPA	Psychol-ogy GPA	Master's GPA
Clinical Mental Health Counseling	MA/MS	Not specified	Not specified	Not specified	Not specified	Not specified	Not specified	Not specified	Not specified
School Counseling	MA/MS	Not specified	Not specified	Not specified	Not specified	Not specified	Not specified	Not specified	Not specified

Admissions Requirements:

Degree	GRE	GRE-Subject	Letters of Recom-mendation	Research Statement	Writing Sample	CV	Interview
Master's/Specialist	Optional	None	2	Required	Required	Optional	None

Please note if these criteria vary for different programs: The clinical mental health program requires that applicants have taken 15 hours of undergraduate psychology courses prior to being considered for the program. The school counseling program is a joint program in Psychology and Education. There are no prerequisite psychology courses for this program. Before being admitted to the program student must pass the TAP test (taken through the State of Illinois).

Admissions Criteria:
Research experience—low
Work experience—high
Clinically related public service—high
GPA—high

Letters of recommendation—high
Statement of goals and objectives—high
Undergraduate psychology preparation—medium

For additional information on admission requirements, visit http://www.lewisu.edu/academics/psych/admreq.htm.

Department Demographics

	Male (PT)	Female (PT)	Total	African-American/ Black (PT)	Hispanic/ Latino (PT)	Asian/ Pacific Islander (PT)	American Indian/ Alaska Native (PT)	Caucasian/ White (PT)	Unknown (PT)	Multiethnic (PT)	ADA (PT)	Int'l (PT)
Students	3 (20)	18 (147)	188	2 (18)	4 (13)	0 (4)	0 (0)	10 (140)	0 (0)	1 (2)	0 (2)	0 (0)

Financial Information/Assistance

Tuition: For information on tuition costs, visit http://www.lewisu.edu/welcome/offices/business/bursar/tuitionrates.htm. Tuition is subject to change. Tuition costs vary by program.

Master's:
State residents: $14,976 per academic year.
State residents: $625 per credit hour.
Nonstate residents: $14,976 per academic year.
Nonstate residents: $625 per credit hour.

Financial Assistance:

	Teaching Assistantship (% Receiving)	Teaching Assistantship Tuition Remission	Research Assistantship (% Receiving)	Research Assistantship Tuition Remission	Fellowship (% Receiving)	Fellowship Tuition Remission
First-Year Student	NA (NA)	NA	$11,250 (NA)	Partial	NA (NA)	NA
Advanced Student	NA (NA)	NA	$11,250 (NA)	Partial	NA (NA)	NA

For additional information on financial assistance, visit http://www.lewisu.edu/admissions/finaid/index.htm.

Employment of Department Graduates

No information provided.

Additional Information

Housing and Day Care: No on-campus housing is available. No on-campus day care facilities are available.

Application Information: Graduate Program Director, Department of Psychology, Lewis University, One University Parkway, Romeoville, IL 60446. *Fee:* $40. *Online application:* http://www.lewisu.edu/admissions/application.htm.

Loyola University of Chicago
Counseling Psychology
School of Education
820 North Michigan Avenue
Chicago, IL 60611
Telephone: (312) 915-6311
Program Chair: Steven D. Brown

E-mail: sbrown@luc.edu
Web: http://www.luc.edu/education/

Orientation, Objectives, and Emphasis of Department

The PhD program, accredited by the APA, is based on the scientist–practitioner model of graduate education and emphasizes the interdependence of science and practice. Doctoral students are provided opportunities to collaborate with faculty in terms of research, prevention/intervention, and teaching activities from the first year of enrollment. Faculty research concentrates in three areas: multicultural psychology, preventive psychology, and vocational psychology. Applicant interest in one of these three areas is a major admission criterion since students are expected to apprentice themselves with a faculty member throughout their tenure in the program. Regardless of the field of interest, each student is exposed to the scientist–practitioner model. Graduates are prepared for teaching, research, and professional practice.

Programs and Degrees Offered

Program	Degree	Application Deadline	Applica-tions Received	Accepted	New Admits Enrolled (PT)	Total Enrolled (PT)	Degrees Awarded in 2014–2015	Median Years to Complete Degree	Dismissed/Withdrew
Counseling Psychology	PhD	December 1 (Fall)	38	3	3 (0)	14 (5)	6	5	0
Community Counseling	MA/MS	January 1 (Fall)	28	20	5 (0)	6 (0)	4	2	0
School Counseling	Med	January 1 (Fall)	33	27	12 (0)	14 (3)	9	2.5	0
Clinical Mental Health Counseling	Other	January 1 (Fall)	9	6	6 (0)	12 (3)	4	2	0
Community Counseling	Med	January 1 (Fall)	8	5	3 (1)	7 (2)	11	2	0

APA Accreditation

Counseling PhD: Student Outcome Data website: http://www.luc.edu/education/doctoral/counseling-psychology/.

Doctoral Degree (PhD Counseling Psychology): For those doctoral students for whom a professional internship was required in this program prior to graduation:
Total students who applied for an internship: 2
Total students who obtained an internship: 2
Total students who obtained a paid internship: 2
Total students who obtained an unpaid internship: 0
Total students who were placed in APA/CPA-accredited internships: 2
Total students placed in internships not APA/CPA-accredited, but listed with the Association of Psychology Postdoctoral and Internship Centers (APPIC): 0
Total students placed in internships conforming to guidelines of the Council of Directors of School Psychology Programs (CDSPP): 0
Total students placed in internships that were not APA/CPA-accredited, APPIC or CDSSP listed: 0

Master's Degree (MA/MS Community Counseling): An internship experience, such as a final research project or "capstone" experience is required of graduates.

Internships/Practica

Internships and practica are available at many excellent training facilities in the greater Chicagoland area, including university counseling centers, hospitals, VA centers, and mental health clinics. There are both therapy-oriented and diagnostic/assessment-oriented practica. Most practicum sites serve a diverse clientele.

Admissions

Entries appear in the following order: required test or GPA, minimum score (if required)/median score of students entering in 2015–2016.

Program	Degree	GRE-V	GRE-Q	GRE-Writing	GRE-Subject	Under-graduate GPA	Last 2 Years GPA	Psychol-ogy GPA	Master's GPA
Counseling Psychology	PhD	157/160	146/148	4.5/5	600/600	3.5/NA	3/NA	3/NA	3.5/NA

Admissions (con't.)

Program	Degree	GRE-V	GRE-Q	GRE-Writing	GRE-Subject	Under-graduate GPA	Last 2 Years GPA	Psychol-ogy GPA	Master's GPA
Community Counseling	MA/MS	153/157	144/146	4/4.5	Not specified	3/NA	3/NA	Not specified	Not specified
School Counseling	Med	153/157	144/146	4.5/5	Not specified	3/NA	3/NA	Not specified	Not specified
Clinical Mental Health Counseling	Other	157/160	146/148	4/4.5	Not specified	3/3.5	3/NA	Not specified	Not specified
Community Counseling	Med	153/157	144/146	4/4.5	Not specified	3/3.5	3/3.5	Not specified	Not specified

Admissions Requirements:

Degree	GRE	GRE-Subject	Letters of Recom-mendation	Research Statement	Writing Sample	CV	Interview
Master's/Specialist	Required	None	3	Required	None	Required	None
Doctoral	Required	Required	3	Required	Required	Required	Required

Admissions Criteria:

GRE scores—medium
Research experience—high
Work experience—medium
Clinically related public service—high
GPA—medium

Letters of recommendation—high
Interview—high
Statement of goals and objectives—high
Undergraduate psychology preparation—medium
Match w/ faculty interest—high

For additional information on admission requirements, visit http://www.luc.edu/education/admission/.

Department Demographics

	Male (PT)	Female (PT)	Total	African-American/ Black (PT)	Hispanic/ Latino (PT)	Asian/ Pacific Islander (PT)	American Indian/ Alaska Native (PT)	Caucasian/ White (PT)	Unknown	Multiethnic (PT)	ADA (PT)	Int'l (PT)
Students	6 (3)	47 (10)	66	11 (1)	1 (2)	4 (2)	0 (0)	31 (7)	0 (0)	6 (1)	0 (0)	0 (0)

Financial Information/Assistance

Tuition: For information on tuition costs, visit http://www.luc.edu/bursar/tuition.shtml. Tuition is subject to change. Additional fees are assessed to students beyond the costs of tuition for the following: student development fee, technology fee, course management fee, matriculation fee.

Doctoral:
State residents: $930 per credit hour.
Nonstate residents: $930 per credit hour.

Master's:
State residents: $930 per credit hour.
Nonstate residents: $930 per credit hour.

Financial Assistance:

	Teaching Assistantship (% Receiving)	Teaching Assistantship Tuition Remission	Research Assistantship (% Receiving)	Research Assistantship Tuition Remission	Fellowship (% Receiving)	Fellowship Tuition Remission
First-Year Student	NA (NA)	NA	$14,000 (100)	Full	$16,000 (0)	Full
Advanced Student	$14,000 (0)	Full	$14,000 (50)	Full	$16,000 (50)	Full

For additional information on financial assistance, visit http://www.luc.edu/gradschool/gradstudentfinance/.

Employment of Department Graduates

Master's:
Enrolled in a psychology doctoral program: 3
Employed in a professional position in a school system: 5
Employed in a community mental health/counseling center: 10
Total: 18

Doctoral:
Enrolled in a postdoctoral residency/fellowship: 2
Total: 2

Additional Information

Housing and Day Care: On-campus housing is available. See the following website for more information: http://www.luc.edu/reslife/halls/. No on-campus day care facilities are available.

Information for Students With Physical Disabilities: See the following website: http://www.luc.edu/sswd/index.shtml.

Special Facilities or Resources: The school has excellent library and research facilities and computer resources available to students.

Application Information: Graduate & Professional Enrollment Management, Loyola University Chicago, Lewis Towers, 8th Floor, 820 North Michigan Avenue, Chicago, IL 60611. *Fee:* $50. *Online application:* https://gpem.luc.edu/apply/.

Loyola University of Chicago
Department of Psychology
Arts and Sciences
1032 West Sheridan Road
Chicago, IL 60660
Telephone: (773) 508-3001
Chairperson: James R. Larson, Jr., PhD

E-mail: jlarson4@luc.edu
Web: http://www.luc.edu/psychology/

Orientation, Objectives, and Emphasis of Department
Graduate study is organized into three areas: clinical, developmental, and social. All programs offer the PhD; only the social program offers a terminal MA in applied social psychology. The clinical program emphasizes the scientist–practitioner model, with students receiving extensive training in both areas. Students may specialize in work with children or adults. The developmental program provides training for students wishing to pursue the study of human development, particularly among infants, children, and adolescents. Cognition, social, gender role, and personality development are covered. The social psychology program includes training in both basic and applied social psychology. The emphasis in the applied program is on developing social psychologists who are capable of conducting applied research on the planning, evaluating, and modification of social programs in the areas of law and criminal justice, educational systems, health and/or community services, and organizational behavior.

Programs and Degrees Offered

Program	Degree	Application Deadline	Applica-tions Received	Accepted	New Admits Enrolled (PT)	Total Enrolled (PT)	Degrees Awarded in 2014–2015	Median Years to Complete Degree	Dismissed/ Withdrew
Developmental Psychology	PhD	January 15 (Fall)	30	3	1 (0)	11 (0)	2	6	1
Social Psychology	PhD	January 1 (Fall)	50	5	2 (0)	22 (0)	4	6	0
Applied Social Psychology	MA/MS	January 1 (Fall)	21	4	1	10 (0)	4	2	0
Clinical Psychology	PhD	December 1 (Fall)	260	9	6 (0)	36 (0)	6	6	0

APA Accreditation

Clinical PhD: Student Outcome Data website: http://www.luc.edu/psychology/studentadmissionsoutcomesandotherdata/.

Doctoral Degree (PhD Clinical Psychology): For those doctoral students for whom a professional internship was required in this program prior to graduation:
Total students who applied for an internship: 5
Total students who obtained an internship: 5
Total students who obtained a paid internship: 5
Total students who obtained an unpaid internship: 0
Total students who were placed in APA/CPA-accredited internships: 5
Total students placed in internships not APA/CPA-accredited, but listed with the Association of Psychology Postdoctoral and Internship Centers (APPIC): 0
Total students placed in internships conforming to guidelines of the Council of Directors of School Psychology Programs (CDSPP): 0
Total students placed in internships that were not APA/CPA-accredited, APPIC or CDSSP listed: 0

Master's Degree (MA/MS Applied Social Psychology): An internship experience, such as a final research project or "capstone" experience is required of graduates.

Internships/Practica

Externship experiences are available for clinical psychology students through our in-house Training Clinic at the Wellness Center. In addition, numerous externship training opportunities are available throughout the Chicago metropolitan area and clinical students apply nationally for APA-accredited internships. Students in the doctoral applied social psychology program serve a 1000-hour planning, research and evaluation internship during their third year, while students in the developmental program complete a 250-hour internship. These positions are usually found in health-related, governmental, and research organizations in the Chicago area.

Admissions

Entries appear in the following order: required test or GPA, minimum score (if required)/median score of students entering in 2015–2016.

Program	Degree	GRE-V	GRE-Q	GRE-Writing	GRE-Subject	Under-graduate GPA	Last 2 Years GPA	Psychol-ogy GPA	Master's GPA
Developmental Psychology	PhD	NA/153	NA/157	NA/4.5	NA/NA	NA/3.34	NA/3.8	NA/3.7	Not specified
Social Psychology	PhD	NA/160	NA/162	NA/4	Not specified	Not specified	Not specified	Not specified	Not specified
Applied Social Psychology	MA/MS	NA/154	NA/156	NA/4	Not specified	NA/NA	Not specified	Not specified	Not specified
Clinical Psychology	PhD	NA/161	NA/163	NA/4	NA/NA	NA/3.8	Not specified	Not specified	Not specified

Admissions Requirements:

Degree	GRE	GRE-Subject	Letters of Recommendation	Research Statement	Writing Sample	CV	Interview
Master's/Specialist	Required	Recommended	3	Required	Required	Optional	None
Doctoral	Required	Required	3	Required	Required	Required	Required

Please note if these criteria vary for different programs: Only the Clinical program requires an interview and clinically related public service. Arranging an interview is strongly recommended (but not required) for the Developmental and Social Psychology programs. GRE-Subject test is required for clinical and recommended for developmental and social. Clinical program requires a CV; social and developmental programs require a writing sample in addition to the statement of purpose.

Admissions Criteria:

GRE scores—high
Research experience—high
Work experience—low
Clinically related public service—medium

GPA—high
Letters of recommendation—high
Interview—high
Statement of goals and objectives—high

For additional information on admission requirements, visit http://www.luc.edu/gradschool/applicationinfo.shtml.

Department Demographics

	Male (PT)	Female (PT)	Total	African-American/ Black (PT)	Hispanic/ Latino (PT)	Asian/ Pacific Islander (PT)	American Indian/ Alaska Native (PT)	Caucasian/ White (PT)	Unknown	Multiethnic (PT)	ADA (PT)	Int'l (PT)
Students	18 (0)	61 (0)	79	9 (0)	7 (0)	4 (0)	2 (0)	55 (0)	0 (0)	2 (0)	0 (0)	1 (0)

Financial Information/Assistance

Tuition: For information on tuition costs, visit http://www.luc.edu/bursar/tuition.shtml. Tuition is subject to change. Additional fees are assessed to students beyond the costs of tuition for the following: Activity Fees.

Doctoral:
State residents: $21,603 per academic year.
State residents: $1,003 per credit hour.
Nonstate residents: $21,603 per academic year.
Nonstate residents: $1,003 per credit hour.

Master's:
State residents: $18,054 per academic year.
State residents: $1,003 per credit hour.
Nonstate residents: $18,054 per academic year.
Nonstate residents: $1,003 per credit hour.

Financial Assistance:

	Teaching Assistantship (% Receiving)	Teaching Assistantship Tuition Remission	Research Assistantship (% Receiving)	Research Assistantship Tuition Remission	Fellowship (% Receiving)	Fellowship Tuition Remission
First-Year Student	NA (NA)	NA	$18,000 (NA)	Full	NA (NA)	NA
Advanced Student	$18,000 (NA)	Full	$18,000 (NA)	Full	NA (NA)	NA

For additional information on financial assistance, visit http://www.luc.edu/gradschool/FundingGrad.Education.shtml.

Employment of Department Graduates

Master's:
Enrolled in a psychology doctoral program: 1
Employed in business or industry: 2
Total: 3

Doctoral:
Enrolled in a postdoctoral residency/fellowship: 8
Employed in academic position at a 2-year/4-year college: 4
Employed in a professional position in a school system: 1
Employed in government agency: 1
Employed in a community mental health/counseling center: 1
Total: 15

Additional Information

Housing and Day Care: On-campus housing is available. See the following website for more information: http://www.luc.edu/reslife/. On-campus day care facilities are available. See the following website for more information: http://www.luc.edu/preschool/.

Information for Students With Physical Disabilities: See the following website: http://www.luc.edu/sswd/.

Special Facilities or Resources: Excellent libraries and computer support are available. Departmental facilities include specialized laboratories for audition, vision, and neurophysiology research; a general purpose laboratory for sensory processes; suites of research and observation rooms for clinical research; observation and videotaping rooms and equipment; an extensive psychological test library; a psychophysiology and biofeedback laboratory; and computer facilities.

Application Information: Department of Psychology, Loyola University Chicago, 1032 West Sheridan Road, Chicago, IL 60660. *Fee:* $40. *Online application:* https://gpem.luc.edu/apply/.

Midwestern University
Clinical Psychology Program
College of Health Sciences
555 31st Street
Downers Grove, IL 60515
Telephone: (630) 515-7650
Program Director: Ann Sauer, PhD, ABPP
Web: https://www.midwestern.edu/programs_and_admission/il_clinical_psychology.html

E-mail: asauer@midwestern.edu

Orientation, Objectives, and Emphasis of Department
The program follows a practitioner-scholar model of training entry-level mental health professionals with an eclectic focus who can serve a diverse population. The training model adheres to a competency approach in the development of knowledge, skills, and attitudes related to the practice of clinical psychology. Students are systematically evaluated in the development of competency areas including relationship, assessment, intervention, professionalism, diversity, management and supervision, consultation and education, and research and evaluation. The program emphasizes first-year supervised clinical experiences to produce a foundation for later clinical training. The program provides an individualized mentoring experience for its students.

Programs and Degrees Offered

Program	Degree	Application Deadline	Applica-tions Received	Accepted	New Admits Enrolled (PT)	Total Enrolled (PT)	Degrees Awarded in 2014–2015	Median Years to Complete Degree	Dismissed/ Withdrew
Clinical Psychology	PsyD	Rolling	94	70	28 (0)	105 (0)	6	5	3

APA Accreditation
Clinical PsyD (Doctor of Psychology).

Doctoral Degree (PsyD Clinical Psychology): For those doctoral students for whom a professional internship was required in this program prior to graduation:
Total students who applied for an internship: 16
Total students who obtained an internship: 16
Total students who obtained a paid internship: 16

Total students who obtained an unpaid internship: 0
Total students who were placed in APA/CPA-accredited internships: 9
Total students placed in internships not APA/CPA-accredited, but listed with the Association of Psychology Postdoctoral and Internship Centers (APPIC): 7
Total students placed in internships conforming to guidelines of the Council of Directors of School Psychology Programs (CDSPP): 0
Total students placed in internships that were not APA/CPA-accredited, APPIC or CDSSP listed: 0

Internships/Practica

Students participate in faculty supervised clinical and research clerkships during their first year at various sites. A diagnostic practicum is completed in the second year, followed by a therapy practicum in the third year, and an advanced therapy practicum in the fourth year of study. Midwestern University has numerous affiliation agreements with clinical sites throughout the metropolitan Chicago area, which include a variety of settings and diverse populations. The fifth year consists of a full-time internship obtained through the national APPIC match program and which may be located anywhere in the country. Students are given individualized attention to help secure appropriate clinical training experiences in practica and internship consistent with their interests.

Admissions

Entries appear in the following order: required test or GPA, minimum score (if required)/median score of students entering in 2015–2016.

Program	Degree	GRE-V	GRE-Q	GRE-Writing	GRE-Subject	Under-graduate GPA	Last 2 Years GPA	Psychology GPA	Master's GPA
Clinical Psychology	PsyD	NA/NA	NA/NA	NA/NA	Not specified	3/3.26	Not specified	Not specified	Not specified

Admissions Requirements:

Degree	GRE	GRE-Subject	Letters of Recom-mendation	Research Statement	Writing Sample	CV	Interview
Doctoral	Required	Optional	2	Required	Optional	Required	Required

Admissions Criteria:

GRE scores—medium
Research experience—medium
Work experience—medium
Clinically related public service—high
GPA—high

Letters of recommendation—high
Interview—high
Statement of goals and objectives—medium
Undergraduate psychology preparation—medium
Health care experience—medium

For additional information on admission requirements, visit https://www.midwestern.edu/programs_and_admission/il_clinical_psychology/admission/apply.html.

Department Demographics

	Male (PT)	Female (PT)	Total	African-American/ Black (PT)	Hispanic/ Latino (PT)	Asian/ Pacific Islander (PT)	American Indian/ Alaska Native (PT)	Caucasian/ White (PT)	Unknown (PT)	Multiethnic (PT)	ADA (PT)	Int'l (PT)
Students	20 (0)	85 (0)	105	9 (0)	3 (0)	14 (0)	0 (0)	79 (0)	0 (0)	0 (0)	0 (0)	1 (0)

Financial Information/Assistance

Tuition: For information on tuition costs, visit http://www.midwestern.edu/programs-and-admission/student-financial-services/budgets.html. Tuition is subject to change. Additional fees are assessed to students beyond the costs of tuition for the following: $659 for University fees for insurance, student activities, etc.

Doctoral:
State residents: $27,018 per academic year.
Nonstate residents: $27,018 per academic year.

Financial Assistance:

	Teaching Assistantship (% Receiving)	Teaching Assistantship Tuition Remission	Research Assistantship (% Receiving)	Research Assistantship Tuition Remission	Fellowship (% Receiving)	Fellowship Tuition Remission
First-Year Student	NA (NA)	NA	NA (NA)	NA	NA (NA)	NA
Advanced Student	NA (NA)	NA	NA (NA)	NA	NA (NA)	NA

For additional information on financial assistance, visit https://www.midwestern.edu/programs_and_admission/student_financial_services.html.

Employment of Department Graduates

Doctoral:
Enrolled in a postdoctoral residency/fellowship: 3
Employed in independent practice: 1
Employed in a community mental health/counseling center: 1
Employed in a hospital/medical center: 1
Total: 6

Additional Information

Housing and Day Care: On-campus housing is available. See the following website for more information: https://www.midwestern.edu/downers_grove_campus/housing.html. No on-campus day care facilities are available.

Special Facilities or Resources: The clinical psychology program has the full support of the resources available from Midwestern University, which includes the Chicago College of Osteopathic Medicine, Chicago College of Pharmacy, Chicago Dental Medicine Institute, and the other allied health professional programs in the College of Health Sciences, including research scientists and practicing clinicians. The program is housed on a large wooded campus with numerous buildings and research facilities including a state-of-the-art library. The majority of the physical resources have been constructed or remodeled in the past 5 years. Our location in the Chicago metropolitan area also allows students access to a wide array of clinical training sites and settings, working with a diverse range of patients and conditions.

Application Information: Midwestern University, Office of Admissions, 555 31st Street, Downers Grove, IL 60515. *Fee:* $0. *Online application:* https://online.midwestern.edu/public/initapp.cgi?prog=ADCP.

Northern Illinois University
Department of Psychology
College of Liberal Arts and Sciences
DeKalb, IL 60115-2892
Telephone: (815) 753-0372
Chairperson: Leslie Matuszewich

E-mail: mholliday@niu.edu
Web: http://www.niu.edu/psyc/

Orientation, Objectives, and Emphasis of Department
The PhD program in psychology is designed to prepare graduate students to function in a variety of settings including academic institutions, which emphasize research and/or teaching, non-academic institutions, which emphasize research on mental health, human factors, or skill acquisition, and various consultative modalities, which emphasize practitioner applications and the delivery of human services. Doctorates are awarded in six specialty areas: APA-accredited programs in clinical psychology and school psychology (NASP-approved); cognitive/instructional; developmental; neuroscience and behavior; and social and industrial/organizational psychology. Students are equipped to conduct sophisticated, theoretically based empirical research and to teach at the graduate or undergraduate level. In addition to academic placements, students can also find suitable employment as applied researchers or service practitioners in a variety of mental health (clinical), educational (instructional, developmental, school), physical health (neuroscience), or business (social and industrial/organizational) settings. The overall goal of the graduate program is to produce doctoral graduates who appreciate and are deeply committed to the study of psychological processes and behavior, who

are familiar with fundamental knowledge in the field, and who are well-trained in methodology and modern techniques of data analysis.

Programs and Degrees Offered

Program	Degree	Application Deadline	Applica-tions Received	Accepted	New Admits Enrolled (PT)	Total Enrolled (PT)	Degrees Awarded in 2014–2015	Median Years to Complete Degree	Dismissed/ Withdrew
Clinical Psychology	PhD	December 1 (Fall)	225	21	6 (0)	44 (0)	8	7	0
Neuroscience and Behavior	PhD	January 15 (Fall)	13	3	1	7	2	5.8	0
Social-Industrial/ Organizational Psychology	PhD	January 15 (Fall)	72	12	5 (0)	24 (0)	4	9	0
Cognitive Psychology	PhD	February 1 (Fall)	15	6	4 (0)	11 (2)	2	7.8	0
Developmental Psychology	PhD	February 1 (Fall)	15	2	0 (0)	6 (0)	1	9.66	0
School Psychology	PhD	December 15 (Fall)	24	6	2 (0)	14 (6)	1	12	0

APA Accreditation

Clinical PhD: Student Outcome Data website: http://www.niu.edu/psyc/graduate/clinical/admissions.shtml.
School PhD: Student Outcome Data website: http://www.niu.edu/psyc/graduate/school/outcomes.shtml.

Doctoral Degree (PhD Clinical Psychology): For those doctoral students for whom a professional internship was required in this program prior to graduation:
Total students who applied for an internship: 10
Total students who obtained an internship: 10
Total students who obtained a paid internship: 10
Total students who obtained an unpaid internship: 0
Total students who were placed in APA/CPA-accredited internships: 10
Total students placed in internships not APA/CPA-accredited, but listed with the Association of Psychology Postdoctoral and Internship Centers (APPIC): 0
Total students placed in internships conforming to guidelines of the Council of Directors of School Psychology Programs (CDSPP): 0
Total students placed in internships that were not APA/CPA-accredited, APPIC or CDSSP listed: 0

Doctoral Degree (PhD School Psychology): For those doctoral students for whom a professional internship was required in this program prior to graduation:
Total students who applied for an internship: 5
Total students who obtained an internship: 5
Total students who obtained a paid internship: 5
Total students who obtained an unpaid internship: 0
Total students who were placed in APA/CPA-accredited internships: 5
Total students placed in internships not APA/CPA-accredited, but listed with the Association of Psychology Postdoctoral and Internship Centers (APPIC): 0
Total students placed in internships conforming to guidelines of the Council of Directors of School Psychology Programs (CDSPP): 0
Total students placed in internships that were not APA/CPA-accredited, APPIC or CDSSP listed: 0

Internships/Practica

Clinical and school psychology students will undertake internships. Clinical students also are required to take at least five semesters of clinical practicum in the in-house training clinic during the first three years of training as well as two semesters of an advanced clinical practicum at external placements.

Admissions

Entries appear in the following order: required test or GPA, minimum score (if required)/median score of students entering in 2015–2016.

Program	Degree	GRE-V	GRE-Q	GRE-Writing	GRE-Subject	Under-graduate GPA	Last 2 Years GPA	Psychol-ogy GPA	Master's GPA
Clinical Psychology	PhD	NA/161	NA/155	Not specified	Not specified	3/3.9	Not specified	Not specified	Not specified
Neuroscience and Behavior	PhD	Not specified	Not specified	Not specified	Not specified	Not specified	Not specified	Not specified	Not specified
Social-Industrial/ Organizational Psychology	PhD	NA/157	NA/151	NA/NA	Not specified	NA/3.61	Not specified	Not specified	NA/NA
Cognitive Psychology	PhD	Not specified	Not specified	Not specified	Not specified	Not specified	Not specified	Not specified	Not specified
Developmental Psychology	PhD	Not specified	Not specified	Not specified	Not specified	Not specified	Not specified	Not specified	Not specified
School Psychology	PhD	NA/155	NA/158	NA/4	Not specified	NA/3.97	Not specified	Not specified	Not specified

Admissions Requirements:

Degree	GRE	GRE-Subject	Letters of Recom-mendation	Research Statement	Writing Sample	CV	Interview
Doctoral	Required	Optional	3	Required	Optional	Optional	Required

Please note if these criteria vary for different programs: Clinical and School programs interview students; other programs generally do not.

Admissions Criteria:

GRE scores—high
Research experience—high
Work experience—low
Clinically related public service—low
GPA—high

Letters of recommendation—high
Interview—medium
Statement of goals and objectives—high
Undergraduate psychology preparation—high

For additional information on admission requirements, visit http://www.niu.edu/psyc/graduate/admissions/index.shtml.

Department Demographics

	Male (PT)	Female (PT)	Total	African-American/ Black (PT)	Hispanic/ Latino (PT)	Asian/ Pacific Islander (PT)	American Indian/ Alaska Native (PT)	Caucasian/ White (PT)	Unknown	Multiethnic (PT)	ADA (PT)	Int'l (PT)
Students	29 (3)	77 (5)	114	7 (0)	7 (0)	4 (0)	1 (0)	86 (8)	0 (0)	1 (0)	0 (0)	7 (0)

Financial Information/Assistance

Tuition: For information on tuition costs, visit http://www.niu.edu/Bursar/tuition/graduate.shtml. Tuition is subject to change. Additional fees are assessed to students beyond the costs of tuition for the following: Student health fees.

Doctoral:
State residents: $493 per credit hour.
Nonstate residents: $850 per credit hour.

Master's:
State residents: $493 per credit hour.
Nonstate residents: $850 per credit hour.

Financial Assistance:

	Teaching Assistantship (% Receiving)	Teaching Assistantship Tuition Remission	Research Assistantship (% Receiving)	Research Assistantship Tuition Remission	Fellowship (% Receiving)	Fellowship Tuition Remission
First-Year Student	$12,350 (NA)	Full	$12,350 (NA)	Full	NA (NA)	Full
Advanced Student	$12,350 (NA)	Full	$12,350 (NA)	Full	NA (NA)	Full

For additional information on financial assistance, visit http://www.niu.edu/psyc/graduate/admissions/financial.shtml.

Employment of Department Graduates

Doctoral:
Enrolled in a postdoctoral residency/fellowship: 3
Employed in independent practice: 1
Employed in a professional position in a school system: 1
Employed in a hospital/medical center: 3
Not seeking employment: 1
Total: 9

Additional Information

Housing and Day Care: On-campus housing is available. See the following website for more information: http://www.niu.edu/housing/halls/graduate_housing/index.shtml. On-campus day care facilities are available. See the following website for more information: http://www.niu.edu/ccc/.

Information for Students With Physical Disabilities: See the following website: http://niu.edu/disability/.

Special Facilities or Resources: The department has a modern psychology building with offices for faculty, staff, and graduate students; classrooms; shops; a six-story research wing with research equipment, including computers and direct access to the university computer and Internet applications; and a Psychological Services Center for practicum training in clinical psychology.

Application Information: The Graduate School, Northern Illinois University, 180 Stadium Drive, DeKalb, IL 60115-2828. *Fee:* $40. *Online application:* http://www.grad.niu.edu/grad/admissions/apply/index.shtml.

Northwestern University
Department of Psychology
102 Swift Hall, 2029 Sheridan Road
Evanston, IL 60208-2710
Telephone: (847) 491-7406
Chairperson: Mark Beeman

E-mail: marzena.nowicka@northwestern.edu
Web: http://www.psychology.northwestern.edu/

Orientation, Objectives, and Emphasis of Department
The faculty in each graduate area has designed programs tailored to the needs of students in that area. Whatever a student's field of interest, the department tries to produce doctoral students with a strong research orientation. Administrative barriers between areas are permeable; most faculty members take an active part in the instruction and research programs of more than one interest area. A significant population of postdoctoral fellows enhances the informal professional education of graduate students. In addition, all graduate students are given opportunities for teaching.

Programs and Degrees Offered

Program	Degree	Application Deadline	Applications Received	Accepted	New Admits Enrolled (PT)	Total Enrolled (PT)	Degrees Awarded in 2014–2015	Median Years to Complete Degree	Dismissed/ Withdrew
Clinical Psychology	PhD	December 1 (Fall)	116	7	7 (0)	20 (0)	2	6	0
Cognitive Psychology	PhD	December 1 (Fall)	42	6	3 (0)	23 (0)	4	5	0
Personality and Health Psychology	PhD	December 1 (Fall)	27	2	2 (0)	5 (0)	2	5	0
Brain, Behavior, and Cognition	PhD	December 1 (Fall)	48	6	2 (0)	17 (0)	2	5	0
Social Psychology	PhD	December 1 (Fall)	96	3	1 (0)	14 (0)	1	5	0

APA Accreditation

Clinical PhD: Student Outcome Data website: http://www.psychology.northwestern.edu/graduate/program-areas/clinical/.

Doctoral Degree (PhD Clinical Psychology): For those doctoral students for whom a professional internship was required in this program prior to graduation:
Total students who applied for an internship: 5
Total students who obtained an internship: 3
Total students who obtained a paid internship: 3
Total students who obtained an unpaid internship: 0
Total students who were placed in APA/CPA-accredited internships: 3
Total students placed in internships not APA/CPA-accredited, but listed with the Association of Psychology Postdoctoral and Internship Centers (APPIC): 0
Total students placed in internships conforming to guidelines of the Council of Directors of School Psychology Programs (CDSPP): 0
Total students placed in internships that were not APA/CPA-accredited, APPIC or CDSSP listed: 0

Internships/Practica

A variety of internships in community settings are available.

Admissions

Entries appear in the following order: required test or GPA, minimum score (if required)/median score of students entering in 2015–2016.

Program	Degree	GRE-V	GRE-Q	GRE-Writing	GRE-Subject	Undergraduate GPA	Last 2 Years GPA	Psychology GPA	Master's GPA
Clinical Psychology	PhD	Not specified	Not specified	Not specified	Not specified	Not specified	Not specified	Not specified	Not specified
Cognitive Psychology	PhD	Not specified	Not specified	Not specified	Not specified	Not specified	Not specified	Not specified	Not specified
Personality and Health Psychology	PhD	Not specified	Not specified	Not specified	Not specified	Not specified	Not specified	Not specified	Not specified
Brain, Behavior, and Cognition	PhD	Not specified	Not specified	Not specified	Not specified	Not specified	Not specified	Not specified	Not specified
Social Psychology	PhD	Not specified	Not specified	Not specified	Not specified	Not specified	Not specified	Not specified	Not specified

Admissions Requirements:

Degree	GRE	GRE-Subject	Letters of Recommendation	Research Statement	Writing Sample	CV	Interview
Doctoral	Required	Recommended	3	Required	Optional	Optional	Required

Admissions Criteria:

GRE scores—high
Research experience—high
GPA—high
Letters of recommendation—high

Interview—high
Statement of goals and objectives—medium
Undergraduate psychology preparation—medium

For additional information on admission requirements, visit http://www.psychology.northwestern.edu/graduate/prospective/application-process.html.

Department Demographics

	Male (PT)	Female (PT)	Total	African-American/Black (PT)	Hispanic/Latino (PT)	Asian/Pacific Islander (PT)	American Indian/Alaska Native (PT)	Caucasian/White (PT)	Unknown	Multiethnic (PT)	ADA (PT)	Int'l (PT)
Students	24 (0)	55 (0)	79	6 (0)	5 (0)	9 (0)	2 (0)	54 (0)	0 (0)	3 (0)	0 (0)	5 (0)

Financial Information/Assistance

Tuition: For information on tuition costs, visit http://www.northwestern.edu/sfs/tuition/. Tuition is subject to change.

Doctoral:
State residents: $48,624 per academic year.
Nonstate residents: $48,624 per academic year.

Financial Assistance:

	Teaching Assistantship (% Receiving)	Teaching Assistantship Tuition Remission	Research Assistantship (% Receiving)	Research Assistantship Tuition Remission	Fellowship (% Receiving)	Fellowship Tuition Remission
First-Year Student	NA (NA)	NA	NA (NA)	NA	$29,004 (NA)	Full
Advanced Student	$29,670 (NA)	Full	$29,670 (NA)	Partial	$29,004 (NA)	Full

For additional information on financial assistance, visit http://www.psychology.northwestern.edu/graduate/current/fellowship-and-funding.html.

Employment of Department Graduates

Doctoral:
Enrolled in a postdoctoral residency/fellowship: 9
Employed in independent practice: 2
Employed in an academic position at a university: 4
Employed in a professional position in a school system: 2
Employed in business or industry: 2
Employed in government agency: 1
Employed in a community mental health/counseling center: 1
Employed in a hospital/medical center: 2
Do not know: 5
Total: 28

Additional Information

Housing and Day Care: On-campus housing is available. See the following website for more information: http://www.northwestern.edu/living/. No on-campus day care facilities are available.

Information for Students With Physical Disabilities: See the following website: http://www.northwestern.edu/accessiblenu/.

Application Information: Fee: $100. *Online application:* http://www.tgs.northwestern.edu/admission/index.html.

Northwestern University Feinberg School of Medicine
Department of Psychiatry and Behavioral Sciences, Division of Psychology
Abbott Hall, Suite 1205, 710 North Lake Shore Drive
Chicago, IL 60611
Telephone: (312) 908-8262
Chief: Mark A. Reinecke, PhD

E-mail: clinpsych@northwestern.edu
Web: http://psychiatry.northwestern.edu/education/clinical-psychology-program/index.html

---

Orientation, Objectives, and Emphasis of Department
The goal of our PhD program is to train clinical psychologists who excel with integrating clinical science and practice, ideally for positions in academic healthcare systems. The inter-departmental PhD program takes advantage of its placement within the Feinberg School of Medicine by offering a true balance of research and clinical training. This unique setting provides opportunities for translational research and practice that span molecular to social models of disease, and epidemiologic to clinical and neuroimaging methodologies. Education and training is provided through core and emphasis-specific curricula, intensive research mentoring and training, and at least three years of intensive (15–20 hrs/week) clinical practica. Milestones include a research qualifying paper, a clinical qualifying exam, an empirical dissertation with original research, and an APA-accredited clinical internship. A Master's of Science in Clinical Psychology is available as part of the program. The program is committed to an evidence-based practice process model that provides intensive supervision and training to develop skills in assessment, diagnosis, and treatment. Research labs are organized into four emphases: Behavioral Medicine, Neuropsychology and Behavioral Neuroscience, Policy, and Psychopathology and Treatment. Clinical training is organized into four emphases: Adult Clinical, Behavioral Medicine, Child and Adolescent, and Clinical Neuropsychology.

Programs and Degrees Offered

Program	Degree	Application Deadline	Applications Received	Accepted	New Admits Enrolled (PT)	Total Enrolled (PT)	Degrees Awarded in 2014–2015	Median Years to Complete Degree	Dismissed/Withdrew
Clinical Psychology	PhD	December 1 (Fall)	285	13	7 (0)	44 (0)	2	6.01	0

APA Accreditation
Clinical PhD (Doctor of Philosophy).

Doctoral Degree (PhD Clinical Psychology): For those doctoral students for whom a professional internship was required in this program prior to graduation:
Total students who applied for an internship: 6
Total students who obtained an internship: 5
Total students who obtained a paid internship: 5
Total students who obtained an unpaid internship: 0
Total students who were placed in APA/CPA-accredited internships: 5
Total students placed in internships not APA/CPA-accredited, but listed with the Association of Psychology Postdoctoral and Internship Centers (APPIC): 0
Total students placed in internships conforming to guidelines of the Council of Directors of School Psychology Programs (CDSPP): 0
Total students placed in internships that were not APA/CPA-accredited, APPIC or CDSSP listed: 0

Internships/Practica
We strive to provide guaranteed practicum placements in students' first and second clinical practicum. Practica placements are primarily in academic healthcare systems, such as at Northwestern Medicine (Department of Psychiatry, the Neurobehavior and Memory Health Clinic, Inpatient Neuropsychological Consultation Service, Behavioral Medicine Practicum), Lurie Children's Hospital of Chicago, Rehabilitation Institute of Chicago, Illinois Masonic Hospital, Jessie Brown and Hines VA Medical Centers, Rush University Medical Center, the University of Chicago Medical Center, and the University of Illinois at Chicago Medical Center. We excel at placing our students in some of the best APA-accredited internships in the country.

Admissions

Entries appear in the following order: required test or GPA, minimum score (if required)/median score of students entering in 2015–2016.

Program	Degree	GRE-V	GRE-Q	GRE-Writing	GRE-Subject	Under-graduate GPA	Last 2 Years GPA	Psychol-ogy GPA	Master's GPA
Clinical Psychology	PhD	NA/161	NA/156	NA/4.8	NA/720	NA/3.65	Not specified	Not specified	Not specified

Admissions Requirements:

Degree	GRE	GRE-Subject	Letters of Recom-mendation	Research Statement	Writing Sample	CV	Interview
Doctoral	Required	Recom-mended	3	Required	Recom-mended	Required	Required

Admissions Criteria:

GRE scores—low
Research experience—high
Work experience—medium
Clinically related public service—low
GPA—high

Letters of recommendation—medium
Interview—high
Statement of goals and objectives—high
Undergraduate psychology preparation—medium
Fit with mentors—high

For additional information on admission requirements, visit http://psychiatry.northwestern.edu/education/clinical-psychology-program/admissions/index.html.

Department Demographics

	Male (PT)	Female (PT)	Total	African-American/ Black (PT)	Hispanic/ Latino (PT)	Asian/ Pacific Islander (PT)	American Indian/ Alaska Native (PT)	Caucasian/ White (PT)	Unknown	Multiethnic (PT)	ADA (PT)	Int'l (PT)
Students	4 (0)	40 (0)	44	4 (0)	1 (0)	5 (0)	0 (0)	34 (0)	0 (0)	0 (0)	0 (0)	3 (0)

Financial Information/Assistance

Tuition: For information on tuition costs, visit http://www.northwestern.edu/sfs/tuition/t_grad_s_tuition.html. Tuition is subject to change. Additional fees are assessed to students beyond the costs of tuition for the following: $110 activity fee per quarter (includes city transportation pass).

Doctoral:
State residents: $48,624 per academic year.
Nonstate residents: $48,624 per academic year.

Financial Assistance:

	Teaching Assistantship (% Receiving)	Teaching Assistantship Tuition Remission	Research Assistantship (% Receiving)	Research Assistantship Tuition Remission	Fellowship (% Receiving)	Fellowship Tuition Remission
First-Year Student	NA (NA)	NA	$30,792 (43)	Full	$0 (100)	Partial
Advanced Student	NA (NA)	NA	$30,792 (60)	Full	NA (100)	Partial

For additional information on financial assistance, visit http://psychiatry.northwestern.edu/education/clinical-psychology-program/financial-aid.html.

Employment of Department Graduates

Doctoral:
Enrolled in a postdoctoral residency/fellowship: 2
Total: 2

Additional Information

Housing and Day Care: On-campus housing is available. See the following website for more information: http://www.northwestern.edu/living/. On-campus day care facilities are available. See the following website for more information: http://www.northwestern.edu/hr/work-life/childcare/index.html.

Information for Students With Physical Disabilities: See the following website: http://www.northwestern.edu/accessiblenu/.

Special Facilities or Resources: The PhD program is located within a premier academic medical center and has access to numerous academic and research facilities, such as neuroimaging facilities (e.g., NU's Center for Translational Imaging), genomic services (e.g., NU's Genomics Core), and neuromodulation devices (e.g., Transcranial Magnetic Stimulation). Students in our program have full access to the world-class academic resources associated with Northwestern University, as well resources specific to the Feinberg School of Medicine, such as the Galter Health Sciences Library, the Learning Resources Center, and the Biostatistics Collaboration Center.

Application Information: *Fee:* $95. *Online application:* http://www.tgs.northwestern.edu/admission/.

Roosevelt University
Department of Psychology
Arts and Sciences
430 South Michigan Avenue, Suite GB400
Chicago, IL 60605-1394
Telephone: (312) 341-3760
Chairperson: Dr. Cami K. McBride

E-mail: camcbride@roosevelt.edu
Web: http://www.roosevelt.edu/CAS/Programs/Psychology.aspx

Orientation, Objectives, and Emphasis of Department
Roosevelt University was founded 71 years ago, in 1945, on the principles of social justice and equal educational access for all qualified students. A primary goal of the Department of Psychology is to prepare students to work effectively with diverse cultures in metropolitan settings. Our PhD program in I/O Psychology is based on the scientist–practitioner model of professional training and stresses the importance of apprenticeship, emphasizing working closely with faculty on research and applied projects outside of the classroom. The PsyD program, established in 1996, was the first university-based clinical PsyD program in Illinois. This program is designed to provide generalist training in all facets of clinical practice, in preparation for postdoctoral specialization of the student's choice. At the MA level, we currently have an I/O Psychology, and two Clinical Psychology programs which offer streamlined and personally tailored predoctoral training designed to help qualified students enter PhD or PsyD programs, including our own. The Clinical Psychology (Counseling Practice) program prepares students to apply for the professional counselor license in Illinois and other states. Approximately 85% of our graduates who have applied to doctoral programs have been accepted. We prepare students for professional employment in mental health and I/O psychology services.

Programs and Degrees Offered

Program	Degree	Application Deadline	Applications Received	Accepted	New Admits Enrolled (PT)	Total Enrolled (PT)	Degrees Awarded in 2014–2015	Median Years to Complete Degree	Dismissed/Withdrew
Clinical Psychology	MA/MS	May 1 (Fall), November 1 (Spring)	22	14	1 (2)	12 (2)	9	3	0

Programs and Degrees Offered (con't.)

Program	Degree	Application Deadline	Applications Received	Accepted	New Admits Enrolled (PT)	Total Enrolled (PT)	Degrees Awarded in 2014–2015	Median Years to Complete Degree	Dismissed/ Withdrew
Industrial/ Organizational Psychology	MA/MS	February 1 (Fall), October 15 (Spring), Rolling	88	81	22 (4)	52 (21)	23	2.5	1
Clinical Psychology	PsyD	December 15 (Fall)	225	34	19 (0)	83 (31)	15	6	0
Clinical Psychology (Counseling Practice)	MA/MS	May 1 (Fall), November 1 (Spring)	157	135	48 (8)	115 (76)	40	2.5	5
Industrial/ Organizational Psychology	PhD	February 1 (Fall)	27	8	8 (0)	21 (5)	0		0

APA Accreditation

Clinical PsyD: Student Outcome Data website: http://www.roosevelt.edu/CAS/Programs/Psychology/PsyD.aspx.

Doctoral Degree (PsyD Clinical Psychology): For those doctoral students for whom a professional internship was required in this program prior to graduation:
Total students who applied for an internship: 14
Total students who obtained an internship: 14
Total students who obtained a paid internship: 14
Total students who obtained an unpaid internship: 0
Total students who were placed in APA/CPA-accredited internships: 14
Total students placed in internships not APA/CPA-accredited, but listed with the Association of Psychology Postdoctoral and Internship Centers (APPIC): 0
Total students placed in internships conforming to guidelines of the Council of Directors of School Psychology Programs (CDSPP): 0
Total students placed in internships that were not APA/CPA-accredited, APPIC or CDSSP listed: 0

Master's Degree (MA/MS Clinical Psychology): An internship experience, such as a final research project or "capstone" experience is required of graduates. Master's Degree (MA/MS Industrial/Organizational Psychology): An internship experience, such as a final research project or "capstone" experience is required of graduates. Master's Degree (MA/MS Clinical Psychology [Counseling Practice]): An internship experience, such as a final research project or "capstone" experience is required of graduates.

Internships/Practica

Students in our clinical programs have available over 250 sites in the greater Chicago area for practicum experience. We have a full-time Director of Training to assist students with this process. I/O, Clinical MA, and PsyD students have ample opportunities for training; I/O students nearly always obtain paid practicum experience.

Admissions

Entries appear in the following order: required test or GPA, minimum score (if required)/median score of students entering in 2015–2016.

Program	Degree	GRE-V	GRE-Q	GRE-Writing	GRE-Subject	Under-graduate GPA	Last 2 Years GPA	Psychol-ogy GPA	Master's GPA
Clinical Psychology	MA/MS	Not specified	Not specified	Not specified	Not specified	3/3.4	3/3.5	3/NA	Not specified
Industrial/ Organizational Psychology	MA/MS	NA/150	NA/146	NA/4	Not specified	NA/3.4	Not specified	Not specified	Not specified

Admissions *(con't.)*

Program	Degree	GRE-V	GRE-Q	GRE-Writing	GRE-Subject	Under-graduate GPA	Last 2 Years GPA	Psychology GPA	Master's GPA
Clinical Psychology	PsyD	150/NA	149/NA	4/NA	Not specified	3.25/NA	Not specified	Not specified	Not specified
Clinical Psychology (Counseling Practice)	MA/MS	Not specified	Not specified	Not specified	Not specified	3/3.4	3/3.5	3/NA	Not specified
Industrial/ Organizational Psychology	PhD	NA/156	NA/152	NA/4	Not specified	NA/3.53	Not specified	Not specified	Not specified

Admissions Requirements:

Degree	GRE	GRE-Subject	Letters of Recommendation	Research Statement	Writing Sample	CV	Interview
Master's/Specialist	Required	None	2	Required	None	Recommended	None
Doctoral	Required	Optional	3	Required	None	Required	Required

Please note if these criteria vary for different programs: Criteria section and Doctoral Degree materials are shown for the PsyD program. The Clinical MA program matches the criteria except it has a high criteria rating for the Statement of Goals and Objectives, and the GRE-General is optional. The MA I/O program requires the GRE-General scores as part of its application requirements.

Admissions Criteria:

GRE scores—high
Research experience—medium
Work experience—medium
Clinically related public service—medium
GPA—high

Letters of recommendation—medium
Interview—high
Statement of goals and objectives—medium
Undergraduate psychology preparation—medium

Department Demographics

	Male (PT)	Female (PT)	Total	African-American/ Black (PT)	Hispanic/ Latino (PT)	Asian/ Pacific Islander (PT)	American Indian/ Alaska Native (PT)	Caucasian/ White (PT)	Unknown	Multiethnic (PT)	ADA (PT)	Int'l (PT)
Students	66 (23)	217 (112)	418	26 (14)	35 (15)	19 (7)	1 (0)	190 (94)	3 (2)	9 (3)	3 (2)	12 (0)

Financial Information/Assistance

Tuition: For information on tuition costs, visit http://www.roosevelt.edu/TuitionAndFees.aspx. Higher tuition cost for this program: PsyD: $23,272.00. Tuition is subject to change. Additional fees are assessed to students beyond the costs of tuition for the following: Graduate student fee $150/semester; CTA Ventra U-Pass $138/semester. Tuition costs vary by program.

Doctoral:
State residents: $19,483 per academic year.
Nonstate residents: $19,483 per academic year.

Master's:
State residents: $18,996 per academic year.
State residents: $1,042 per credit hour.
Nonstate residents: $18,996 per academic year.
Nonstate residents: $1,042 per credit hour.

Financial Assistance:

	Teaching Assistantship (% Receiving)	Teaching Assistantship Tuition Remission	Research Assistantship (% Receiving)	Research Assistantship Tuition Remission	Fellowship (% Receiving)	Fellowship Tuition Remission
First-Year Student	NA (NA)	NA	$5,200 (30)	Full	$3,000 (30)	NA
Advanced Student	NA (NA)	NA	$5,200 (15)	Full	$3,000 (30)	NA

For additional information on financial assistance, visit http://www.roosevelt.edu/FinancialAid/InfoPages/Graduate.aspx.

Employment of Department Graduates

Doctoral:
Enrolled in a postdoctoral residency/fellowship: 9
Employed in independent practice: 1
Employed in a community mental health/counseling center: 3
Employed in a hospital/medical center: 1
Do not know: 1
Total: 15

Additional Information

Housing and Day Care: On-campus housing is available. See the following website for more information: http://www.roosevelt.edu/ResidenceLife.aspx. On-campus day care facilities are available. See the following website for more information: http://www.roosevelt.edu/Schaumburg/About/Childcare.aspx.

Information for Students With Physical Disabilities: See the following website: http://www.roosevelt.edu/StudentSuccess/Disability.

Special Facilities or Resources: The Department of Psychology has an exceptional faculty who are actively involved in applied research and clinical practice, supplemented by a large and highly trained adjunct faculty similarly involved in clinical, forensic, and experimental work. In addition to the extensive Roosevelt library and other facilities, there is access to clinical, research, computer, and library facilities of major Chicago universities, hospitals, and clinics. Volunteer research assistantships are available to qualified students interested in doing publishable research. A major resource is the urban location with varied employment, educational, and cultural opportunities. The Organizational Effectiveness Consulting Center aligns I/O students with real-world experiences in the form of applied projects and internships with business, non-profit, government, and educational organizations. The Instructor Development Program prepares PsyD students to teach undergraduate courses during the last 2 years of doctoral training.

Application Information: Roosevelt University, Office of Admission, 1400 North Roosevelt Boulevard, Schaumburg, IL 60173. *Fee:* $25. *Online application:* http://www.roosevelt.edu/apply.

Rosalind Franklin University of Medicine and Science

Department of Psychology
College of Health Professions
3333 Green Bay Road
North Chicago, IL 60064
Telephone: (847) 578-3305
Chairperson: John Calamari, PhD
Web: https://rosalindfranklin.edu/academics/college-of-health-professions/degree-programs/psychology-phd/

E-mail: cathy.mavrolas@rosalindfranklin.edu

Orientation, Objectives, and Emphasis of Department

The Department of Psychology offers an APA-accredited program leading to the PhD degree in clinical psychology. Within the context of the general clinical training program, students select a specialty emphasis in clinical neuropsychology, psychopathology or health/behavioral medicine. The program provides students with intensive training in the methods and theories of clinical practice with emphasis in these specialty areas. Research is a vital part of the program and students work closely with professors throughout their training. Research topics include biopsychosocial issues associated with various medical illnesses (e.g., cancer, diabetes, heart disease), aging, psychopathology (e.g., schizophrenia, OCD, psychopathy; intimate partner violence), and neuropsychological features of various clinical populations (e.g., epilepsy, head injury, multiple sclerosis, AIDS, Alzheimer's disease, dementia, stroke). Subject populations range in age from childhood through adulthood and include those with physical and psychiatric disorders. The Department subscribes to the philosophy that a clinical psychologist is knowledgeable in formulating and solving scientific problems, and skilled in formulating clinical problems and applying empirically supported interventions. To this end, core courses are organized as integrated theory-research-practice units with a problem solving orientation.

Programs and Degrees Offered

Program	Degree	Application Deadline	Applica-tions Received	Accepted	New Admits Enrolled (PT)	Total Enrolled (PT)	Degrees Awarded in 2014–2015	Median Years to Complete Degree	Dismissed/ Withdrew
Clinical Psychology	PhD	December 31 (Fall)	109	16	10	70 (1)	5	6.4	0
Clinical Counseling Psychology	MA/MS	April 15 (Fall)	35	8	7 (0)	17 (1)	13	2	1

APA Accreditation

Clinical PhD: Student Outcome Data website: https://rosalindfranklin.edu/academics/college-of-health-professions/degree-programs/psychology-phd/student-admissions-outcomes/.

Doctoral Degree (PhD Clinical Psychology): For those doctoral students for whom a professional internship was required in this program prior to graduation:
Total students who applied for an internship: 12
Total students who obtained an internship: 10
Total students who obtained a paid internship: 10
Total students who obtained an unpaid internship: 0
Total students who were placed in APA/CPA-accredited internships: 10
Total students placed in internships not APA/CPA-accredited, but listed with the Association of Psychology Postdoctoral and Internship Centers (APPIC): 0
Total students placed in internships conforming to guidelines of the Council of Directors of School Psychology Programs (CDSPP): 0
Total students placed in internships that were not APA/CPA-accredited, APPIC or CDSSP listed: 0

Master's Degree (MA/MS Clinical Counseling Psychology): An internship experience, such as a final research project or "capstone" experience is required of graduates.

Internships/Practica

The Department enjoys formal relationships with many of the major clinical, health and neuropsychology facilities in the catchment area from Chicago to the south and Milwaukee to the north. These include both inpatient and outpatient facilities. Thus, students have the opportunity to obtain experience and clinical training with a diverse range of clinical populations and socio-economic strata. Our students also receive training in our in-house free primary care mental health clinic, Healthy Families, serving the vulnerable and underserved/uninsured in northern Lake County, Illinois.

Admissions

Entries appear in the following order: required test or GPA, minimum score (if required)/median score of students entering in 2015–2016.

Program	Degree	GRE-V	GRE-Q	GRE-Writing	GRE-Subject	Under-graduate GPA	Last 2 Years GPA	Psychol-ogy GPA	Master's GPA
Clinical Psychology	PhD	NA/156	NA/154	NA/4.5	Not specified	Not specified	3.2/NA	Not specified	Not specified
Clinical Counseling Psychology	MA/MS	Not specified	Not specified	Not specified	Not specified	NA/NA	3/NA	Not specified	Not specified

Admissions Requirements:

Degree	GRE	GRE-Subject	Letters of Recommendation	Research Statement	Writing Sample	CV	Interview
Master's/Specialist	Recommended	Recommended	3	Optional	Optional	Optional	Optional
Doctoral	Required	Recommended	3	Required	Optional	Required	Required

Admissions Criteria:

GRE scores—medium
Research experience—high
Work experience—low
Clinically related public service—medium

GPA—high
Letters of recommendation—high
Interview—high
Statement of goals and objectives—high

Department Demographics

	Male (PT)	Female (PT)	Total	African-American/ Black (PT)	Hispanic/ Latino (PT)	Asian/ Pacific Islander (PT)	American Indian/ Alaska Native (PT)	Caucasian/ White (PT)	Unknown	Multiethnic (PT)	ADA (PT)	Int'l (PT)
Students	23 (1)	64 (1)	89	4 (0)	5 (1)	3 (1)	0 (0)	75 (0)	0 (0)	0 (0)	0 (0)	0 (0)

Financial Information/Assistance

Tuition: For information on tuition costs, visit https://rosalindfranklin.edu/admission-aid/financial-services/costs-fees/. Tuition is subject to change.

Doctoral:
State residents: $29,678 per academic year.
Nonstate residents: $29,678 per academic year.

Master's:
State residents: $29,678 per academic year.
Nonstate residents: $29,678 per academic year.

Financial Assistance:

	Teaching Assistantship (% Receiving)	Teaching Assistantship Tuition Remission	Research Assistantship (% Receiving)	Research Assistantship Tuition Remission	Fellowship (% Receiving)	Fellowship Tuition Remission
First-Year Student	NA (NA)	NA	NA (NA)	Partial	NA (NA)	Partial
Advanced Student	$2,000 (NA)	Full	$10,000 (NA)	Full	NA (NA)	Full

For additional information on financial assistance, visit https://rosalindfranklin.edu/admission-aid/financial-services/financial-aid/.

Employment of Department Graduates

Master's:
Enrolled in a psychology doctoral program: 4
Employed in a community mental health/counseling center: 4
Employed in a hospital/medical center: 1
Other employment position: 1
Do not know: 3
Total: 13

Doctoral:
Enrolled in a postdoctoral residency/fellowship: 5
Total: 5

Additional Information

Housing and Day Care: On-campus housing is available. See the following website for more information: https://rosalindfranklin.edu/campus-life/student-housing/. No on-campus day care facilities are available.

Special Facilities or Resources: Research facilities within the Department include an Experimental Neuropsychology Lab, Clinical Health Psychophysiology Lab, Neuroimaging Laboratory, and a Behavioral Therapy Lab. There are ongoing research programs in arthritis, oncology, diabetes, blood pressure regulation, epilepsy, anxiety disorders, schizophrenia, psychopathy, aging and dementia. Collaborative research opportunities are also ongoing with a number of community and academic institutions in the area and include projects using MRI and fMRI to study higher order cognitive processes.

Application Information: Rosalind Franklin University of Medicine and Science, CHP Admissions Office, 3333 Green Bay Road, North Chicago, IL 60064. *Fee:* $50. *Online application:* https://rfucas.liaisoncas.com/.

Southern Illinois University Carbondale

Department of Psychology
College of Liberal Arts
Life Science Building II, Room 281
Carbondale, IL 62901
Telephone: (618) 453-3529
Chairperson: Reza Habib

E-mail: rhabib@siu.edu
Web: http://psychology.siu.edu

Orientation, Objectives, and Emphasis of Department

The department maintains a collaborative learning environment that is responsive to student needs, that promotes professional development, and that sustains high academic standards. In all programs the student selects courses from a rich curriculum that promotes mastery of core material while allowing the pursuit of particular interests. A favorable student-faculty ratio permits close supervision of students, whether in student research, clinical/applied practica, or training assignments that provide graduated experience in research, teaching, and service as a complement to formal coursework. Such training serves to expose students to many of the activities in which they will be engaged after receiving their degrees.

Programs and Degrees Offered

Program	Degree	Application Deadline	Applications Received	Accepted	New Admits Enrolled (PT)	Total Enrolled (PT)	Degrees Awarded in 2014–2015	Median Years to Complete Degree	Dismissed/ Withdrew
Clinical Psychology	PhD	December 1 (Fall)	111	6	6 (0)	36 (0)	7	6	0
Counseling Psychology	PhD	December 1 (Fall)	73	4	4	21 (0)	4	6	0
Applied Psychology	PhD	February 1 (Fall)	20	5	5 (0)	15 (1)	4	6	0
Brain and Cognitive Sciences	PhD	February 1 (Fall)	22	3	3 (0)	14 (0)	3	6	0

APA Accreditation

Clinical PhD: Student Outcome Data website: http://cola.siu.edu/psychology/graduate/doctoral-programs/clinical.php.
Counseling PhD: Student Outcome Data website: http://cola.siu.edu/psychology/graduate/doctoral-programs/counseling/index.php.

Doctoral Degree (PhD Clinical Psychology): For those doctoral students for whom a professional internship was required in this program prior to graduation:
Total students who applied for an internship: 7
Total students who obtained an internship: 6
Total students who obtained a paid internship: 6
Total students who obtained an unpaid internship: 0
Total students who were placed in APA/CPA-accredited internships: 6
Total students placed in internships not APA/CPA-accredited, but listed with the Association of Psychology Postdoctoral and Internship Centers (APPIC): 0
Total students placed in internships conforming to guidelines of the Council of Directors of School Psychology Programs (CDSPP): 0
Total students placed in internships that were not APA/CPA-accredited, APPIC or CDSSP listed: 0

Doctoral Degree (PhD Counseling Psychology): For those doctoral students for whom a professional internship was required in this program prior to graduation:

Total students who applied for an internship: 4
Total students who obtained an internship: 4
Total students who obtained a paid internship: 4
Total students who obtained an unpaid internship: 0
Total students who were placed in APA/CPA-accredited internships: 4
Total students placed in internships not APA/CPA-accredited, but listed with the Association of Psychology Postdoctoral and Internship Centers (APPIC): 0
Total students placed in internships conforming to guidelines of the Council of Directors of School Psychology Programs (CDSPP): 0
Total students placed in internships that were not APA/CPA-accredited, APPIC or CDSSP listed: 0

Internships/Practica

A variety of practicum and field experience sites are available including a Career Development and Resource Clinic; a university clinical center; campus counseling center; campus health service; Applied Research Consultants; and various local mental health centers, hospitals, and human service agencies.

Admissions

Entries appear in the following order: required test or GPA, minimum score (if required)/median score of students entering in 2015–2016.

Program	Degree	GRE-V	GRE-Q	GRE-Writing	GRE-Subject	Under-graduate GPA	Last 2 Years GPA	Psychol-ogy GPA	Master's GPA
Clinical Psychology	PhD	NA/NA	NA/NA	Not specified	Not specified	NA/NA	NA/NA	NA/NA	Not specified
Counseling Psychology	PhD	NA/NA	NA/NA	Not specified	Not specified	NA/NA	NA/NA	NA/NA	Not specified
Applied Psychology	PhD	NA/NA	NA/NA	Not specified	Not specified	NA/NA	NA/NA	NA/NA	Not specified
Brain and Cognitive Sciences	PhD	NA/NA	NA/NA	Not specified	Not specified	NA/NA	NA/NA	NA/NA	Not specified

Admissions Requirements:

Degree	GRE	GRE-Subject	Letters of Recom-mendation	Research Statement	Writing Sample	CV	Interview
Doctoral	Required	Optional	3	Required	Optional	Required	Required

Please note if these criteria vary for different programs: Some variation across programs. Clinical/work experiences relevant to programs are important.

Admissions Criteria:

GRE scores—medium
Research experience—high
Work experience—medium
Clinically related public service—medium
GPA—medium

Letters of recommendation—high
Interview—high
Statement of goals and objectives—high
Undergraduate psychology preparation—medium

For additional information on admission requirements, visit http://cola.siu.edu/psychology/graduate/admissions/dept-application.php.

Department Demographics

	Male (PT)	Female (PT)	Total	African-American/ Black (PT)	Hispanic/ Latino (PT)	Asian/ Pacific Islander (PT)	American Indian/ Alaska Native (PT)	Caucasian/ White (PT)	Unknown	Multiethnic (PT)	ADA (PT)	Int'l (PT)
Students	30 (0)	56 (1)	87	9 (0)	2 (0)	7 (0)	0 (0)	67 (1)	0 (0)	1 (0)	0 (0)	9 (0)

Financial Information/Assistance

Tuition: For information on tuition costs, visit http://tuition.siuc.edu/. Tuition is subject to change. Additional fees are assessed to students beyond the costs of tuition for the following: Health care and activity fees, approximately $2147 per semester.

Doctoral:
State residents: $12,528 per academic year.
State residents: $417 per credit hour.
Nonstate residents: $31,320 per academic year.
Nonstate residents: $1,044 per credit hour.

Financial Assistance:

	Teaching Assistantship (% Receiving)	Teaching Assistantship Tuition Remission	Research Assistantship (% Receiving)	Research Assistantship Tuition Remission	Fellowship (% Receiving)	Fellowship Tuition Remission
First-Year Student	$12,564 (NA)	Full	$12,564 (NA)	Full	$12,564 (NA)	Full
Advanced Student	$14,094 (NA)	Full	$14,094 (NA)	Full	$14,094 (NA)	Full

For additional information on financial assistance, visit http://cola.siu.edu/psychology/graduate/admissions/financial-assistance.php.

Employment of Department Graduates

Doctoral:
Enrolled in a postdoctoral residency/fellowship: 4
Employed in independent practice: 1
Employed in an academic position at a university: 1
Employed in academic position at a 2-year/4-year college: 1
Employed in other positions at a higher education institution: 4
Employed in business or industry: 3
Employed in a hospital/medical center: 1
Still seeking employment: 3
Total: 18

Additional Information

Housing and Day Care: On-campus housing is available. See the following website for more information: http://www.housing.siu.edu/. On-campus day care facilities are available. See the following website for more information: http://rainbowsend.siu.edu/.

Information for Students With Physical Disabilities: See the following website: http://disabilityservices.siu.edu/.

Special Facilities or Resources: The department is located in a building with extensive laboratory facilities for human and animal research available to all students. Additional facilities include a clinic and a counseling center for practicum and research experiences.

Application Information: Psychology Graduate Admissions, Mailcode 6502, Southern Illinois University, Carbondale, IL 62901-6502. *Fee:* $65. *Online application:* http://gradschool.siu.edu/applygrad/.

Southern Illinois University Edwardsville
Department of Psychology
Box 1121
Edwardsville, IL 62026-1121
Telephone: (618) 650-2202
Chairperson: Paul Rose

E-mail: prose@siue.edu
Web: http://www.siue.edu/education/psychology/graduate/

Orientation, Objectives, and Emphasis of Department

The department, faculty and students have won several awards for teaching excellence, educational outcomes, academic excellence, and community contribution. In 2014, the department won the American Psychological Association's Award for Culture of Service in the Psychological Sciences. Students in each specialization are provided with training that is balanced between science and practice.

Programs and Degrees Offered

Program	Degree	Application Deadline	Applica-tions Received	Accepted	New Admits Enrolled (PT)	Total Enrolled (PT)	Degrees Awarded in 2014–2015	Median Years to Complete Degree	Dismissed/ Withdrew
School Psychology	EdS	January 15 (Fall)							
Clinical Psychology	MA/MS	January 15 (Fall)							
Industrial/ Organizational Psychology	MA/MS	January 15 (Fall)							
Clinical Child and School Psychology	MA/MS	January 15 (Fall)							

Internships/Practica

All graduate programs require several credit hours of supervised practicum experience in appropriate professional settings. The specialist degree program also requires an internship.

Admissions

Entries appear in the following order: required test or GPA, minimum score (if required)/median score of students entering in 2015–2016.

Program	Degree	GRE-V	GRE-Q	GRE-Writing	GRE-Subject	Under-graduate GPA	Last 2 Years GPA	Psychol-ogy GPA	Master's GPA
School Psychology	EdS	NA/NA	NA/NA	NA/NA	Not specified	NA/NA	Not specified	Not specified	Not specified
Clinical Psychology	MA/MS	NA/NA	NA/NA	NA/NA	Not specified	NA/NA	Not specified	Not specified	Not specified
Industrial/ Organizational Psychology	MA/MS	NA/NA	NA/NA	NA/NA	Not specified	NA/NA	Not specified	Not specified	Not specified
Clinical Child and School Psychology	MA/MS	NA/NA	NA/NA	NA/NA	Not specified	NA/NA	Not specified	Not specified	Not specified

Admissions Requirements:

Degree	GRE	GRE-Subject	Letters of Recommendation	Research Statement	Writing Sample	CV	Interview
Master's/Specialist	Required	Optional	3	Required	Optional	Required	Required

Admissions Criteria:

GRE scores—medium
Research experience—high
Work experience—medium
Clinically related public service—medium
GPA—high

Letters of recommendation—high
Interview—high
Statement of goals and objectives—high
Undergraduate psychology preparation—medium

For additional information on admission requirements, visit http://www.siue.edu/education/psychology/graduate/apinfo.shtml.

Department Demographics

	Male (PT)	Female (PT)	Total	African-American/ Black (PT)	Hispanic/ Latino (PT)	Asian/ Pacific Islander (PT)	American Indian/ Alaska Native (PT)	Caucasian/ White (PT)	Unknown	Multiethnic (PT)	ADA (PT)	Int'l (PT)
Students	18 (0)	60 (0)	78	5 (0)	3 (0)	2 (0)	0 (0)	68 (0)	0 (0)	0 (0)	2 (0)	2 (0)

Financial Information/Assistance

Tuition: For information on tuition costs, visit http://www.siue.edu/payingforcollege/. Tuition is subject to change. Additional fees are assessed to students beyond the costs of tuition for the following: Some courses have fees.

Master's:
State residents: $8,958 per academic year.
Nonstate residents: $19,514 per academic year.

Financial Assistance:

	Teaching Assistantship (% Receiving)	Teaching Assistantship Tuition Remission	Research Assistantship (% Receiving)	Research Assistantship Tuition Remission	Fellowship (% Receiving)	Fellowship Tuition Remission
First-Year Student	$5,355 (50)	Full	$5,355 (50)	Full	$8,370 (3)	Full
Advanced Student	$5,355 (7)	Full	$5,355 (50)	Full	$8,370 (3)	Full

For additional information on financial assistance, visit http://www.siue.edu/graduatestudents/assistantships.shtml.

Employment of Department Graduates

No information provided.

Additional Information

Housing and Day Care: On-campus housing is available. See the following website for more information: http://www.siue.edu/housing/. On-campus day care facilities are available. See the following website for more information: http://www.siue.edu/earlychildhood/.

Information for Students With Physical Disabilities: See the following website: http://www.siue.edu/dss/.

Special Facilities or Resources: The psychology department houses faculty offices, classrooms, and approximately 9,000 square feet of laboratory space. Resources available include audio and video recording equipment, computers and software for data analysis, books containing thousands of psychological measures, and online survey tools. Funds are also available for student awards and student conference travel.

Application Information: Graduate Admissions, Box 1047, Southern Illinois University Edwardsville, Edwardsville, IL 62026-1047. *Fee:* $40. *Online application:* http://www.siue.edu/education/psychology/graduate/apinfo.shtml.

Western Illinois University

Department of Psychology
Arts and Sciences
Waggoner Hall
Macomb, IL 61455
Telephone: (309) 298-1919
Chairperson: Dr. Karen Sears

E-mail: cj-kreps@wiu.edu
Web: http://www.wiu.edu/cas/psychology/

Orientation, Objectives, and Emphasis of Department

The psychology department offers master's degrees in Clinical/Community Mental Health (C/CMH) and General Experimental Psychology, and a Specialist Degree in School Psychology. The C/CMH and School-Specialist degrees are three year programs with the third year consisting of a paid internship. The emphasis in the C/CMH program is to prepare students to assume professional responsibilities in outpatient mental health settings. Central to the program is the practicum experience offered through the University Psychology Clinic. Graduates of the C/CMH program have found employment in a variety of mental health agencies, with over 90 percent of all graduates currently employed in mental health positions. Students in the general psychology program engage in one to two years of course work in psychology. The opportunity to specialize in industrial/organizational, social, developmental, or experimental psychology is available within the general psychology program. Many students completing the general program have been admitted to PhD programs in psychology. Students in the school psychology program acquire an academic background in psychology and a practical awareness of public school systems. The large majority of students completing the school psychology program receive jobs in a school system directly out of Graduate School.

Programs and Degrees Offered

Program	Degree	Application Deadline	Applica-tions Received	Accepted	New Admits Enrolled (PT)	Total Enrolled (PT)	Degrees Awarded in 2014–2015	Median Years to Complete Degree	Dismissed/ Withdrew
Clinical/ Community Mental Health	MA/MS	February 1 (Fall), Rolling	29	8	6 (0)	16 (0)	6	3	1
General Experimental Psychology	MA/MS	February 1 (Fall)	31	16	9 (0)	18 (0)	5	2	3
Specialist in School Psychology	Other	February 1 (Fall)	18	9	9 (0)	19 (0)	7	3	4

Internships/Practica

The Clinical/Community Mental Health program includes a four semester practicum sequence of intensive, supervised work in the department's Psychology Clinic. An internship for which postgraduate credit is given prepares students for jobs in clinical psychology. Practicum work in community schools and the department's psychoeducational clinic under faculty supervision is required throughout both years of the School Psychology program, and a paid internship for which postgraduate credit is given prepares students for certification in Illinois.

Admissions

Entries appear in the following order: required test or GPA, minimum score (if required)/median score of students entering in 2015–2016.

Program	Degree	GRE-V	GRE-Q	GRE-Writing	GRE-Subject	Under-graduate GPA	Last 2 Years GPA	Psychology GPA	Master's GPA
Clinical/ Community Mental Health	MA/MS	NA/NA	NA/NA	NA/NA	Not specified	Not specified	2.75/3.6	3/3.59	Not specified
General Experimental Psychology	MA/MS	NA/NA	NA/NA	NA/NA	Not specified	2.75/3.42	NA/NA	3.05/3.47	Not specified
Specialist in School Psychology	Other	NA/NA	NA/NA	NA/NA	Not specified	2.93/3.23	NA/NA	NA/NA	Not specified

Admissions Requirements:

Degree	GRE	GRE-Subject	Letters of Recom-mendation	Research Statement	Writing Sample	CV	Interview
Master's/Specialist	Required	None	3	Required	Optional	Optional	None

Admissions Criteria:

GRE scores—high
Research experience—medium
Work experience—medium
Clinically related public service—medium
GPA—high

Letters of recommendation—high
Statement of goals and objectives—high
Undergraduate psychology preparation—high
Biographical Statement—high

For additional information on admission requirements, visit http://wiu.edu/cas/psychology/gradadmission.php.

Department Demographics

	Male (PT)	Female (PT)	Total	African-American/ Black (PT)	Hispanic/ Latino (PT)	Asian/ Pacific Islander (PT)	American Indian/ Alaska Native (PT)	Caucasian/ White (PT)	Unknown	Multiethnic (PT)	ADA (PT)	Int'l (PT)
Students	16 (0)	37 (0)	53	2 (0)	1 (0)	2 (0)	0 (0)	46 (0)	2 (0)	(0)	0 (0)	5 (0)

Financial Information/Assistance

Tuition: For information on tuition costs, visit http://www.wiu.edu/vpas/business_services/tuition/. Tuition is subject to change.

Master's:
State residents: $323 per credit hour.
Nonstate residents: $323 per credit hour.

Financial Assistance:

	Teaching Assistantship (% Receiving)	Teaching Assistantship Tuition Remission	Research Assistantship (% Receiving)	Research Assistantship Tuition Remission	Fellowship (% Receiving)	Fellowship Tuition Remission
First-Year Student	$5,032 (NA)	Partial	$5,032 (NA)	Partial	NA (NA)	NA
Advanced Student	$5,032 (NA)	Partial	$5,032 (NA)	Partial	NA (NA)	NA

For additional information on financial assistance, visit http://www.wiu.edu/student_services/financial_aid/graduate.php.

Employment of Department Graduates

Master's:
Enrolled in another graduate/professional program: 1
Employed in other positions at a higher education institution: 1
Employed in a professional position in a school system: 7
Employed in a community mental health/counseling center: 6
Other employment position: 3
Do not know: 1
Total: 19

Additional Information

Housing and Day Care: On-campus housing is available. See the following website for more information: http://www.wiu.edu/student_services/housing/. On-campus day care facilities are available. See the following website for more information: http://www.wiu.edu/coehs/preschool/.

Information for Students With Physical Disabilities: See the following website: http://www.wiu.edu/student_services/disability_resource_center/.

Special Facilities or Resources: The Department of Psychology is housed in a large modern structure providing facilities for teaching, clinical training, and human and animal research. The department has 55 rooms, including regular classrooms, seminar rooms, observation rooms, small experimental cubicles, and neuroscience labs. Computers are available throughout the department and campus. The department operates a psychology clinic for community referrals, which aids in clinical training, and a psychoeducational clinic for training in school psychology.

Application Information: School of Graduate Studies, Western Illinois University, #1 University Circle, 116 Sherman Hall, Macomb, IL 61455. *Fee:* $30. *Online application:* http://www.wiu.edu/graduate_studies/prospective_students/classification.php.

Wheaton College

Department of Psychology
501 College Avenue
Wheaton, IL 60187-5593
Telephone: (630) 752-5762
Associate Dean: Terri S. Watson, PsyD

E-mail: ted.kahn@wheaton.edu
Web: http://www.wheaton.edu/Graduate-School/Degrees/Psychology

---

Orientation, Objectives, and Emphasis of Department

The doctoral program develops competent scholar-practitioners in clinical psychology who will understand professional practice as service. The primary emphasis of the MA programs is the professional preparation of the master's level therapist for employment in clinical settings; a secondary objective is the preparation of selected students for doctoral studies. The departmental orientation is eclectic, with students exposed to the theory, research, and practical clinical skills of the major clinical models in use today. A pre-eminent concern of all faculty is the interface of psychological theory and practice with Christian faith. Thus, students also take coursework in the theory and practice of integrating psychology and Christian faith, and coursework in theology/biblical studies. Students are encouraged to participate in a growth-oriented group therapy experience or an individual therapy experience. The objectives of the department are to produce mature, capable Master's and doctoral-level clinicians who are well grounded in clinical theory and the essentials of professional practice, and who responsibly and capably relate their Christian faith and professional interests.

Programs and Degrees Offered

Program	Degree	Application Deadline	Applications Received	Accepted	New Admits Enrolled (PT)	Total Enrolled (PT)	Degrees Awarded in 2014–2015	Median Years to Complete Degree	Dismissed/Withdrew
Clinical Psychology	PsyD	December 15 (Fall)	61	29	18 (1)	75 (19)	22	5	3
Marriage and Family Therapy	MA/MS	March 1 (Fall), Rolling	33	30	16 (0)	35 (4)	10	2	1

Programs and Degrees Offered (con't.)

Program	Degree	Application Deadline	Applications Received	Accepted	New Admits Enrolled (PT)	Total Enrolled (PT)	Degrees Awarded in 2014–2015	Median Years to Complete Degree	Dismissed/ Withdrew
Clinical Mental Health Counseling	MA/MS	March 1 (Fall)	36	34	25 (0)	49 (0)	24	2	1

APA Accreditation

Clinical PsyD: Student Outcome Data website: http://www.wheaton.edu/Graduate-School/Degrees/Psychology/Programs/PsyD/Student-Admissions-Outcomes-and-Other-Data.

Doctoral Degree (PsyD Clinical Psychology): For those doctoral students for whom a professional internship was required in this program prior to graduation:
Total students who applied for an internship: 20
Total students who obtained an internship: 20
Total students who obtained a paid internship: 20
Total students who obtained an unpaid internship: 0
Total students who were placed in APA/CPA-accredited internships: 15
Total students placed in internships not APA/CPA-accredited, but listed with the Association of Psychology Postdoctoral and Internship Centers (APPIC): 5
Total students placed in internships conforming to guidelines of the Council of Directors of School Psychology Programs (CDSPP): 0
Total students placed in internships that were not APA/CPA-accredited, APPIC or CDSSP listed: 0

Master's Degree (MA/MS Marriage and Family Therapy): An internship experience, such as a final research project or "capstone" experience is required of graduates. Master's Degree (MA/MS Clinical Mental Health Counseling): An internship experience, such as a final research project or "capstone" experience is required of graduates.

Internships/Practica

The Graduate Psychology Programs have liaisons with over 90 agencies in the Chicago and suburban area with facility types ranging from hospitals, clinics, community agencies, residential, and correctional facilities. The Master's programs (CMHC and MFT) require 600 on-site hours and the PsyD program requires a minimum of 1,200 hours (1,500 strongly recommended). Faculty are involved through professional development groups while students are placed in field assignments.

Admissions

Entries appear in the following order: required test or GPA, minimum score (if required)/median score of students entering in 2015–2016.

Program	Degree	GRE-V	GRE-Q	GRE-Writing	GRE-Subject	Undergraduate GPA	Last 2 Years GPA	Psychology GPA	Master's GPA
Clinical Psychology	PsyD	150/NA	150/NA	NA/NA	Not specified	3/NA	Not specified	Not specified	NA/NA
Marriage and Family Therapy	MA/MS	NA/NA	NA/NA	NA/NA	Not specified	3/NA	Not specified	Not specified	Not specified
Clinical Mental Health Counseling	MA/MS	NA/NA	NA/NA	NA/NA	Not specified	3/NA	Not specified	Not specified	Not specified

Admissions Requirements:

Degree	GRE	GRE-Subject	Letters of Recommendation	Research Statement	Writing Sample	CV	Interview
Master's/Specialist	Required	None	4	Required	None	Required	None
Doctoral	Required	None	3	Required	Required	Required	Required

Admissions Criteria:
GRE scores—high
Research experience—medium
Work experience—medium
Clinically related public service—medium
GPA—medium

Letters of recommendation—high
Interview—high
Statement of goals and objectives—high
Undergraduate psychology preparation—medium

For additional information on admission requirements, visit http://www.wheaton.edu/Graduate-School/Admissions/How-to-Apply/Admission-Requirements.

Department Demographics

	Male (PT)	Female (PT)	Total	African-American/ Black (PT)	Hispanic/ Latino (PT)	Asian/ Pacific Islander (PT)	American Indian/ Alaska Native (PT)	Caucasian/ White (PT)	Unknown	Multiethnic (PT)	ADA (PT)	Int'l (PT)
Students	46 (6)	113 (17)	182	11 (2)	8 (1)	19 (2)	1 (0)	113 (17)	3 (1)	4 (0)	0 (0)	11 (0)

Financial Information/Assistance

Tuition: For information on tuition costs, visit http://www.wheaton.edu/Graduate-School/Financial-Aid/Tuition-and-Fees. Tuition is subject to change. Tuition costs vary by program.

Doctoral:
State residents: $1,005 per credit hour.
Nonstate residents: $1,005 per credit hour.

Master's:
State residents: $795 per credit hour.
Nonstate residents: $795 per credit hour.

Financial Assistance:

	Teaching Assistantship (% Receiving)	Teaching Assistantship Tuition Remission	Research Assistantship (% Receiving)	Research Assistantship Tuition Remission	Fellowship (% Receiving)	Fellowship Tuition Remission
First-Year Student	$3,000 (3)	NA	$3,000 (2)	NA	$8,000 (100)	NA
Advanced Student	$4,000 (7)	NA	$5,000 (4)	NA	$8,000 (100)	NA

For additional information on financial assistance, visit http://www.wheaton.edu/Admissions-and-Aid/Financial-Aid/Graduate-Students.

Employment of Department Graduates

Master's:
Enrolled in a psychology doctoral program: 1
Enrolled in another graduate/professional program: 1
Employed in other positions at a higher education institution: 2
Employed in a professional position in a school system: 2
Employed in government agency: 4
Employed in a community mental health/counseling center: 11
Employed in a hospital/medical center: 1
Still seeking employment: 6
Other employment position: 8
Total: 36

Doctoral:
Employed in independent practice: 9
Employed in other positions at a higher education institution: 1
Employed in a professional position in a school system: 1
Employed in government agency: 1
Employed in a community mental health/counseling center: 5
Employed in a hospital/medical center: 5
Total: 22

Additional Information

Housing and Day Care: On-campus housing is available. See the following website for more information: http://www.wheaton.edu/Graduate-School/Student-Life/Housing. No on-campus day care facilities are available.

Information for Students With Physical Disabilities: See the following website: http://www.wheaton.edu/Student-Life/Student-Care.

Personal Behavior Statement: http://www.wheaton.edu/About-Wheaton/Community-Covenant.

Special Facilities or Resources: The PsyD Program has its own computer lab/reading room for research and study. Many students work with faculty research projects and most faculty have separate lab space within the department.

Application Information: Graduate Admissions Office, Wheaton College, 501 College Avenue, Wheaton, IL, 60187. *Fee:* $50. *Online application:* http://www.wheaton.edu/Graduate-School/Admissions/How-to-Apply.

Ball State University

Department of Counseling Psychology and Guidance Services
Teachers College
Teachers College, Room 605
Muncie, IN 47306-0585
Telephone: (765) 285-8040
Chairperson: Sharon L. Bowman

E-mail: sbowman@bsu.edu
Web: http://www.bsu.edu/counselingpsychology/

Orientation, Objectives, and Emphasis of Department

The objective of the master's counseling programs is to prepare effective counselors by providing students with a common professional core of courses and experiences. The faculty is committed to keeping abreast of trends, skills, and knowledge and to modifying the program to prepare students for their profession. Students will be able to practice in a variety of settings using therapeutic, preventive, or developmental counseling approaches. The counseling programs also prepare students for doctoral study in counseling psychology. The program goals are to develop an atmosphere conducive to inquiry, creativity, and learning and to the discovery of new knowledge through research, counseling, and interactive involvement between students and faculty. The master's program in social psychology provides a conceptual background for those pursuing careers in education, counseling, criminology, personnel work, and so forth, and prepares students for entry into doctoral programs in social psychology. The doctoral program is designed to broaden students' knowledge beyond the master's degree. The rigorous program includes a sound theoretical basis, a substantial experiential component, a research component, and a variety of assistantship assignments. A basic core of courses stresses competence in the social, psychological, biological, cognitive, and affective bases of behavior.

Programs and Degrees Offered

Program	Degree	Application Deadline	Applica-tions Received	Accepted	New Admits Enrolled (PT)	Total Enrolled (PT)	Degrees Awarded in 2014–2015	Median Years to Complete Degree	Dismissed/ Withdrew
Social Psychology	MA/MS	March 1 (Fall), June 15 (Summer)	15	12	10	15 (1)	5	2	0
Counseling	MA/MS	March 1 (Fall)	52	48	35 (2)	85 (15)	45	2	2
Counseling Psychology	PhD	December 1 (Fall)	82	15	10	40 (3)	15	5	1

APA Accreditation

Counseling PhD: Student Outcome Data website: http://www.bsu.edu/counselingpsychology/phdcounpsych/.

Doctoral Degree (PhD Counseling Psychology): For those doctoral students for whom a professional internship was required in this program prior to graduation:
Total students who applied for an internship: 8
Total students who obtained an internship: 8
Total students who obtained a paid internship: 8
Total students who obtained an unpaid internship: 0
Total students who were placed in APA/CPA-accredited internships: 8
Total students placed in internships not APA/CPA-accredited, but listed with the Association of Psychology Postdoctoral and Internship Centers (APPIC): 0
Total students placed in internships conforming to guidelines of the Council of Directors of School Psychology Programs (CDSPP): 0
Total students placed in internships that were not APA/CPA-accredited, APPIC or CDSSP listed: 0

Master's Degree (MA/MS Counseling): An internship experience, such as a final research project or "capstone" experience is required of graduates.

Internships/Practica

The department operates a practicum clinic that serves the surrounding community on a low-cost basis. All counseling master's students and doctoral students are required to complete at least one practicum in this clinic. Other practicum opportunities are available at the university counseling center, a local elementary school, and the nearby medical hospital. Master's students are required to complete an internship prior to graduation. The Master's Internship Director maintains a listing of available sites and assists students in identifying and securing such a site. Most of these sites are unpaid, although a few are paying sites. Doctoral students typically seek APA-approved predoctoral internship sites. There is one such site on campus, in the university's counseling center. Although that site does not guarantee a slot to students from this program, usually one CPSY student a year is matched there.

Admissions

Entries appear in the following order: required test or GPA, minimum score (if required)/median score of students entering in 2015–2016.

Program	Degree	GRE-V	GRE-Q	GRE-Writing	GRE-Subject	Under-graduate GPA	Last 2 Years GPA	Psychol-ogy GPA	Master's GPA
Social Psychology	MA/MS	153/NA	144/NA	Not specified	Not specified	3.5/NA	Not specified	Not specified	Not specified
Counseling	MA/MS	153/NA	144/NA	Not specified	Not specified	3.2/3.6	Not specified	Not specified	Not specified
Counseling Psychology	PhD	144/NA	153/NA	Not specified	Not specified	3.5/NA	Not specified	Not specified	3.54/NA

Admissions Requirements:

Degree	GRE	GRE-Subject	Letters of Recom-mendation	Research Statement	Writing Sample	CV	Interview
Master's/Specialist	Required	None	3	Required	Optional	Required	None
Doctoral	Required	None	3	Required	Optional	Required	Required

Admissions Criteria:

GRE scores—high
Research experience—high
Work experience—high
Clinically related public service—medium
GPA—high

Letters of recommendation—high
Interview—medium
Statement of goals and objectives—high
Undergraduate psychology preparation—low
Diversity interest—high

Department Demographics

	Male (PT)	Female (PT)	Total	African-American/ Black (PT)	Hispanic/ Latino (PT)	Asian/ Pacific Islander (PT)	American Indian/ Alaska Native (PT)	Caucasian/ White (PT)	Unknown	Multiethnic (PT)	ADA (PT)	Int'l (PT)
Students	20 (2)	120 (17)	159	3 (0)	2 (0)	5 (0)	0 (0)	124 (19)	4 (0)	2 (0)	2 (0)	5 (0)

Financial Information/Assistance

Tuition: For information on tuition costs, visit http://cms.bsu.edu/admissions/tuitionandfees/graduate. Tuition is subject to change. Additional fees are assessed to students beyond the costs of tuition for the following: health center, technology, recreation center fees.

Doctoral:
State residents: $7,092 per academic year.
Nonstate residents: $19,404 per academic year.

Master's:
State residents: $7,092 per academic year.
Nonstate residents: $19,404 per academic year.

Financial Assistance:

	Teaching Assistantship (% Receiving)	Teaching Assistantship Tuition Remission	Research Assistantship (% Receiving)	Research Assistantship Tuition Remission	Fellowship (% Receiving)	Fellowship Tuition Remission
First-Year Student	$10,834 (NA)	Full	$10,834 (NA)	Full	NA (NA)	NA
Advanced Student	$10,834 (NA)	Full	$10,834 (NA)	Full	NA (NA)	NA

Employment of Department Graduates

Master's:
Enrolled in a psychology doctoral program: 10
Employed in other positions at a higher education institution: 1
Employed in a professional position in a school system: 9
Employed in government agency: 4
Employed in a community mental health/counseling center: 10
Employed in a hospital/medical center: 2
Other employment position: 4
Do not know: 5
Total: 45

Doctoral:
Enrolled in a postdoctoral residency/fellowship: 4
Employed in independent practice: 1
Employed in an academic position at a university: 2
Employed in other positions at a higher education institution: 3
Employed in government agency: 1
Employed in a community mental health/counseling center: 3
Employed in a hospital/medical center: 1
Do not know: 1
Total: 16

Additional Information

Housing and Day Care: On-campus housing is available. See the following website for more information: http://cms.bsu.edu/CampusLife/Housing.aspx. On-campus day care facilities are available. See the following website for more information: http://cms.bsu.edu/Academics/CentersandInstitutes/ChildStudyCenter.aspx.

Information for Students With Physical Disabilities: See the following website: http://cms.bsu.edu/about/administrativeoffices/disability-services.

Special Facilities or Resources: Departmental, instructional, and research facilities are exceptional. The facilities of the department occupy the sixth floor of the Teachers College building. The department operates an outpatient counseling clinic that serves as the training facility for all counseling graduate students. The clinic includes ten practicum rooms, an observation corridor, several group observation rooms, and digital taping of sessions. The clinic serves clients from Muncie and surrounding communities as well as Ball State faculty/staff. The university operates a separate state-of-the-art counseling center that serves as a training site for a select number of graduate students from the department. The campus is wireless, and offers state-of-the-art emerging media access.

Application Information: Fee: $60. Online application: https://www.applyweb.com/bsug/index.html.

Ball State University
Department of Psychological Science
Sciences and Humanities
104 North Quad
Muncie, IN 47306-0520
Telephone: (765) 285-1690
Chairperson: Guy Mittleman

E-mail: lnlittleford@bsu.edu; slsimondack@bsu.edu
Web: http://cms.bsu.edu/academics/collegesanddepartments/psychology

---

Orientation, Objectives, and Emphasis of Department
We offer two 2-year MA programs in psychology. Our primary mission for both programs is to prepare students for doctoral study by offering quality instruction in the science of psychology and opportunities to conduct psychological research. Students have the opportunity to conduct research with clinical, counseling, experimental, social, developmental, cognitive, and/or industrial/organizational psychologists. Our faculty members have a wide range of research expertise, making it possible for them to mentor students with diverse interests. Students participate in weekly professional development colloquia that offer support, guidance, and mentorship as they complete the program and prepare for their professional goals. Students can tailor their education by completing concentrations in assessment, clinical/counseling, or cultural diversity or certificates in institutional research. We accept 8–10 students each year

for each program, resulting in small class sizes and many opportunities for students to collaborate with faculty on research projects. We are committed to the pursuit of excellence by being inclusive of individuals from all races, religions, colors, sexes, sexual orientations, socioeconomic classes, gender identities/gender expressions, physical or mental disabilities, national origins, ancestries, and ages.

Programs and Degrees Offered

Program	Degree	Application Deadline	Applications Received	Accepted	New Admits Enrolled (PT)	Total Enrolled (PT)	Degrees Awarded in 2014–2015	Median Years to Complete Degree	Dismissed/ Withdrew
Clinical Psychology	MA/MS	February 1 (Fall)	40	17	8 (0)	14 (0)	6	2	0
Cognitive and Social Processes	MA/MS	February 1 (Fall)	16	13	7 (0)	15 (0)	7	2	1

Internships/Practica

Applied and research internships are optional.

Admissions

Entries appear in the following order: required test or GPA, minimum score (if required)/median score of students entering in 2015–2016.

Program	Degree	GRE-V	GRE-Q	GRE-Writing	GRE-Subject	Under-graduate GPA	Last 2 Years GPA	Psychology GPA	Master's GPA
Clinical Psychology	MA/MS	NA/151	NA/149	NA/4	Not specified	NA/3.62	NA/3.81	NA/3.78	Not specified
Cognitive and Social Processes	MA/MS	NA/154	NA/146	NA/3.8	NA/NA	NA/3.31	NA/3.63	NA/3.44	Not specified

Admissions Requirements:

Degree	GRE	GRE-Subject	Letters of Recom-mendation	Research Statement	Writing Sample	CV	Interview
Master's/Specialist	Required	Optional	3	Required	None	Required	Optional

Admissions Criteria:

GRE scores—high
Research experience—high
Work experience—low
Clinically related public service—low
GPA—high

Letters of recommendation—high
Statement of goals and objectives—high
Undergraduate psychology preparation—low
Fit w/ faculty interests—high

For additional information on admission requirements, visit http://cms.bsu.edu/academics/collegesanddepartments/psychology/academicprograms/mastersdeg/howapply.

Department Demographics

	Male (PT)	Female (PT)	Total	African-American/ Black (PT)	Hispanic/ Latino (PT)	Asian/ Pacific Islander (PT)	American Indian/ Alaska Native (PT)	Caucasian/ White (PT)	Unknown	Multiethnic (PT)	ADA (PT)	Int'l (PT)
Students	9 (0)	20 (0)	29	3 (0)	1 (0)	0 (0)	0 (0)	22 (0)	0 (0)	3 (0)	0 (0)	1 (0)

Financial Information/Assistance

Tuition: For information on tuition costs, visit http://cms.bsu.edu/admissions/tuitionandfees/graduate. Tuition is subject to change. Additional fees are assessed to students beyond the costs of tuition for the following: technology, recreation, health center, and transportation.

Master's:
State residents: $7,092 per academic year.
Nonstate residents: $19,404 per academic year.

Financial Assistance:

	Teaching Assistantship (% Receiving)	Teaching Assistantship Tuition Remission	Research Assistantship (% Receiving)	Research Assistantship Tuition Remission	Fellowship (% Receiving)	Fellowship Tuition Remission
First-Year Student	$9,069 (NA)	Partial	$9,069 (NA)	Partial	NA (NA)	Partial
Advanced Student	$9,069 (NA)	Partial	$9,069 (NA)	Partial	NA (NA)	Partial

For additional information on financial assistance, visit http://cms.bsu.edu/academics/collegesanddepartments/psychology/academicprograms/scholarships/payoptions.

Employment of Department Graduates

Master's:
Enrolled in a psychology doctoral program: 8
Enrolled in another graduate/professional program: 1
Employed in other positions at a higher education institution: 2
Other employment position: 3
Total: 14

Additional Information

Housing and Day Care: On-campus housing is available. See the following website for more information: http://cms.bsu.edu/CampusLife/Housing.aspx. On-campus day care facilities are available. See the following website for more information: http://cms.bsu.edu/academics/centersandinstitutes/childstudycenter.

Information for Students With Physical Disabilities: See the following website: http://cms.bsu.edu/about/administrativeoffices/disability-services.

Special Facilities or Resources: Students have access to university and departmental computers and a wireless network. The department maintains space for faculty and student research. Internal grants are available for student research and travel.

Application Information: Fee: $50. *Online application:* https://www.applyweb.com/bsug/index.html.

Ball State University
Educational Psychology
Teachers College
Teachers College Room 505
Muncie, IN 47306
Telephone: (765) 285-8500
Chairperson: Dr. Sharon Paulson

E-mail: spaulson@bsu.edu
Web: http://www.bsu.edu/edpsych

Orientation, Objectives, and Emphasis of Department
The mission of the professional education program at Ball State University is to prepare engaged educational experts who are sensitive and responsive to the contextual bases of teaching, learning, and development. The Department of Educational Psychology

offers an APA-accredited program in School Psychology as well as a PhD program in Educational Psychology and an NASP-approved EdS program in School Psychology.

Programs and Degrees Offered

Program	Degree	Application Deadline	Applications Received	Accepted	New Admits Enrolled (PT)	Total Enrolled (PT)	Degrees Awarded in 2014–2015	Median Years to Complete Degree	Dismissed/ Withdrew
School Psychology	EdS	January 1 (Fall)	29	16	8 (0)	20 (0)	6	3	0
Educational Psychology	PhD	February 15 (Fall)	15	9	5 (0)	20 (0)	1	3	0
School Psychology	PhD	December 1 (Fall)	22	13	6 (0)	36 (0)	2	6.5	1

APA Accreditation

School PhD: Student Outcome Data website: http://cms.bsu.edu/academics/collegesanddepartments/teachers/departments/edpsychology/grad-programs-school-psych/phd-school-psych.

Doctoral Degree (PhD School Psychology): For those doctoral students for whom a professional internship was required in this program prior to graduation:
Total students who applied for an internship: 5
Total students who obtained an internship: 5
Total students who obtained a paid internship: 5
Total students who obtained an unpaid internship: 0
Total students who were placed in APA/CPA-accredited internships: 3
Total students placed in internships not APA/CPA-accredited, but listed with the Association of Psychology Postdoctoral and Internship Centers (APPIC): 2
Total students placed in internships conforming to guidelines of the Council of Directors of School Psychology Programs (CDSPP): 0
Total students placed in internships that were not APA/CPA-accredited, APPIC or CDSSP listed: 0

Internships/Practica

The total minimum number of practicum hours required of all PhD in School Psychology students is 550. Of the 550 hours, at least 200 hours must involve direct service and 100 hours must be met under formally scheduled supervision. Doctoral students complete their practica in two settings: The Muncie Community Schools (Primary) and the Psychoeducational, Diagnostic, and Intervention Clinic (PDIC). The BSU School Psychology Internship Consortium provides internship opportunities for students. The consortium is listed in the Council of Directors of School Psychology Programs Internship Directory and meets the same internship requirements as APPIC members. The program maintains complete control and oversight of the internship ensuring the quality of the internships. Each intern must have at least two licensed psychologists as supervisors, attend weekly group supervision, participate in weekly seminars, and complete at least 2,000 hours of internship over no less than 12 months. In addition, each intern is required to receive no less than 2 hours of individual, face-to-face supervision from a licensed psychologist each week and 2 hours of group supervision each week.

Admissions

Entries appear in the following order: required test or GPA, minimum score (if required)/median score of students entering in 2015–2016.

Program	Degree	GRE-V	GRE-Q	GRE-Writing	GRE-Subject	Undergraduate GPA	Last 2 Years GPA	Psychology GPA	Master's GPA
School Psychology	EdS	NA/154	NA/149	NA/4.19	Not specified	NA/3.62	Not specified	Not specified	Not specified
Educational Psychology	PhD	NA/155	NA/149	NA/4.7	Not specified	NA/2.9	Not specified	Not specified	NA/3.87
School Psychology	PhD	NA/157	NA/152	NA/4.25	Not specified	NA/3.42	Not specified	Not specified	NA/3.61

Admissions Requirements:

Degree	GRE	GRE-Subject	Letters of Recommendation	Research Statement	Writing Sample	CV	Interview
Master's/Specialist	Required	None	3	Required	Optional	Optional	Optional
Doctoral	Required	None	3	Required	Optional	Optional	Required

Please note if these criteria vary for different programs: The Educational Psychology PhD program does not require an interview.

Admissions Criteria:

GRE scores—high
Research experience—medium
Work experience—low
Clinically related public service—low
GPA—high

Letters of recommendation—high
Interview—high
Statement of goals and objectives—high
Undergraduate psychology preparation—low

Department Demographics

	Male (PT)	Female (PT)	Total	African-American/ Black (PT)	Hispanic/ Latino (PT)	Asian/ Pacific Islander (PT)	American Indian/ Alaska Native (PT)	Caucasian/ White (PT)	Unknown	Multiethnic (PT)	ADA (PT)	Int'l (PT)
Students	24 (0)	52 (0)	76	1 (0)	1 (0)	3 (0)	1 (0)	59 (0)	0 (0)	2 (0)	0 (0)	1 (0)

Financial Information/Assistance

Tuition: For information on tuition costs, visit http://cms.bsu.edu/admissions/tuitionandfees/graduate. Tuition is subject to change. Additional fees are assessed to students beyond the costs of tuition for the following: student services, technology, recreation, health, and transportation.

Doctoral:
State residents: $6,948 per academic year.
State residents: $386 per credit hour.
Nonstate residents: $19,062 per academic year.
Nonstate residents: $673 per credit hour.

Master's:
State residents: $6,948 per academic year.
State residents: $386 per credit hour.
Nonstate residents: $19,062 per academic year.
Nonstate residents: $673 per credit hour.

Financial Assistance:

	Teaching Assistantship (% Receiving)	Teaching Assistantship Tuition Remission	Research Assistantship (% Receiving)	Research Assistantship Tuition Remission	Fellowship (% Receiving)	Fellowship Tuition Remission
First-Year Student	NA (NA)	NA	$11,800 (NA)	Full	$14,800 (NA)	Full
Advanced Student	$11,800 (NA)	Full	$11,800 (NA)	Full	$14,800 (NA)	Full

For additional information on financial assistance, visit http://cms.bsu.edu/Academics/CollegesandDepartments/GradSchool/EmploymentandGraduateAssistantships.aspx.

Employment of Department Graduates

Master's:
Employed in a professional position in a school system: 6
Total: 6

Doctoral:
Employed in an academic position at a university: 2
Employed in other positions at a higher education institution: 1
Total: 3

Additional Information

Housing and Day Care: On-campus housing is available. See the following website for more information: http://cms.bsu.edu/campuslife/housing.aspx. On-campus day care facilities are available. See the following website for more information: http://www.bsu.edu/fcs/csc.

Information for Students With Physical Disabilities: See the following website: http://www.bsu.edu/dsd/.

Special Facilities or Resources: For more than 20 years, the Ball State University Psychoeducational Diagnostic Intervention Clinic has conducted psychological and educational assessments of individuals of any age, gender, or race. The Clinic also provides training for MA, EdS, and PhD students in school psychology. The Neuropsychology Laboratory was established in 1984 as a research and teaching facility of the Department of Educational Psychology. The laboratory also serves the larger community by assessment of, and remedial planning for, people with neurologic disorders. The Neuropsychology Laboratory provides support for neuropsychology courses offered through the Department of Educational Psychology's cognate specialization in neuropsychology. The laboratory is also a site for internships in the school psychology doctoral program.

Application Information: Graduate Admissions Specialist. *Fee:* $60. *Online application:* https://www.applyweb.com/bsug/index.html.

Indiana State University
Department of Communication Disorders & Counseling, School, & Educational Psychology
Education
Bayh College of Education
Terre Haute, IN 47809
Telephone: (812) 237-2880
Chairperson: Linda Sperry

E-mail: Benjamin.Pointon@indstate.edu
Web: http://www.indstate.edu/education/cdcsep

Orientation, Objectives, and Emphasis of Department

We currently offer master's degrees in Clinical Mental Health Counseling and School Counseling, both of which are CACREP-accredited. The Clinical Mental Health Counseling program's philosophy is student-centered and developmentally based. It is designed to provide the highest quality training in professional mental health service delivery. Academic and fieldwork experiences are intended to foster a commitment to scientific investigations, to improve problem solving skills and critical thinking, and to develop effective intervention techniques. Our school counselor training program provides a wide variety of experiences designed to graduate 21st Century School Counselors. Graduates are advocates and agents of change, capable of assessing, developing and implementing programs which will effectively close the achievement gap by meeting the educational achievement needs of all students. Students enrolled in this program gain extensive hands-on experience in the K–12 school settings, beginning in the first semester of graduate study. Students establish a two-year relationship with an elementary school, middle school, and high school.

Programs and Degrees Offered

Program	Degree	Application Deadline	Applica-tions Received	Accepted	New Admits Enrolled (PT)	Total Enrolled (PT)	Degrees Awarded in 2014–2015	Median Years to Complete Degree	Dismissed/ Withdrew
Clinical Mental Health Counseling	MA/MS	February 1 (Summer)	48	14	12 (0)	18	9	2	2
School Counseling	Med	February 1 (Summer)	25	13	8 (1)	19	11	2	4

Internships/Practica
Training settings include public and special-need schools, community mental health centers, family service centers, alcohol and substance abuse treatment facilities, college and university counseling centers, psychiatric hospitals, state correctional facilities, and specialized juvenile treatment centers.

Admissions

Entries appear in the following order: required test or GPA, minimum score (if required)/median score of students entering in 2015–2016.

Program	Degree	GRE-V	GRE-Q	GRE-Writing	GRE-Subject	Under-graduate GPA	Last 2 Years GPA	Psychol-ogy GPA	Master's GPA
Clinical Mental Health Counseling	MA/MS	Not specified	Not specified	Not specified	Not specified	Not specified	Not specified	Not specified	Not specified
School Counseling	Med	Not specified	Not specified	Not specified	Not specified	Not specified	Not specified	Not specified	Not specified

Admissions Requirements:

Degree	GRE	GRE-Subject	Letters of Recom-mendation	Research Statement	Writing Sample	CV	Interview
Master's/Specialist	Required	None	3	Required	None	Required	Required

Please note if these criteria vary for different programs: School Counseling program does not require GRE.

Admissions Criteria:

GRE scores—high
Research experience—medium
Work experience—medium
Clinically related public service—medium
GPA—high

Letters of recommendation—high
Interview—high
Statement of goals and objectives—high
Undergraduate psychology preparation—high

Department Demographics

	Male (PT)	Female (PT)	Total	African-American/ Black (PT)	Hispanic/ Latino (PT)	Asian/ Pacific Islander (PT)	American Indian/ Alaska Native (PT)	Caucasian/ White (PT)	Unknown (PT)	Multiethnic (PT)	ADA (PT)	Int'l (PT)
Students	4 (1)	32 (0)	37	6 (0)	0 (0)	0 (0)	0 (0)	28 (1)	0 (0)	2 (0)	0 (0)	1 (0)

Financial Information/Assistance

Tuition: For information on tuition costs, visit http://www2.indstate.edu/tuition/. Tuition is subject to change.

Master's:
State residents: $6,840 per academic year.
State residents: $380 per credit hour.
Nonstate residents: $13,446 per academic year.
Nonstate residents: $747 per credit hour.

Financial Assistance:

	Teaching Assistantship (% Receiving)	Teaching Assistantship Tuition Remission	Research Assistantship (% Receiving)	Research Assistantship Tuition Remission	Fellowship (% Receiving)	Fellowship Tuition Remission
First-Year Student	$6,112 (NA)	Partial	$6,112 (NA)	Partial	NA (NA)	NA
Advanced Student	NA (NA)	NA	NA (NA)	NA	NA (NA)	NA

For additional information on financial assistance, visit http://www.indstate.edu/education/cdcsep/cdcsep-assistantships-and-scholarships.

Employment of Department Graduates

Master's:
Employed in academic position at a 2-year/4-year college: 2
Employed in a professional position in a school system: 8
Employed in government agency: 1
Employed in a community mental health/counseling center: 2
Other employment position: 1
Do not know: 6
Total: 20

Additional Information

Housing and Day Care: On-campus housing is available. See the following website for more information: http://www.indstate.edu/reslife/. On-campus day care facilities are available. See the following website for more information: http://www.indstate.edu/ecec/.

Special Facilities or Resources: The counseling training area is housed in the Bayh College of Education. This area provides faculty and student offices and a departmental clinic (individual and group therapy rooms, videotaping equipment with observation rooms, and a career and testing laboratory). Also available in the building are research stations, microcomputer labs, a statistics laboratory, a psychological evaluation library, testing rooms, and an instructional resource center.

Application Information: Indiana State University, Graduate Admissions, Welcome Center, 318 North 6th Street, Terre Haute, IN 47809-1904. *Fee:* $45. *Online application:* http://www.indstate.edu/graduate/apply.htm.

Indiana State University (2015 data)
Department of Communication Disorders, Counseling, School, and Educational Psychology
College of Education
Terre Haute, IN 47809
Telephone: (812) 237-2880
E-mail: patricia.snyder@indstate.edu
Chairperson: Linda L. Sperry, PhD
Web: http://coe.indstate.edu/cdcsep/counseling/edpsych/index.htm

Orientation, Objectives, and Emphasis of Department
The PhD program in Guidance and Psychological Services, Specialization in School Psychology, follows a scholar-practitioner training model which serves as a foundation upon which program goals and objectives are based. The PhD program and the EdS program in school psychology emphasize experiential learning to develop knowledge and skills in assessment and data-based decision making; prevention and intervention; consultation and collaboration; research and evaluation; and professional practice and standards. Programs emphasize the college mission "to prepare, promote, and advance educational and human service professionals for a diverse and ever-changing world." Values of the college and the programs include student success, collegiality, caring for others, responsibility, openness to change, and social justice and diversity.

Programs and Degrees Offered

Program	Degree	Application Deadline	Applications Received	Accepted	New Admits Enrolled (PT)	Total Enrolled (PT)	Degrees Awarded in 2014–2015	Median Years to Complete Degree	Dismissed/ Withdrew
School Psychology	PhD	December 15 (Fall)	19	4	3 (0)	19 (6)	2	7	1
School Psychology	EdS	December 15 (Fall)	25	5	4 (0)	10 (7)	13	3	0

APA Accreditation
School PhD:

Doctoral Degree (PhD School Psychology): For those doctoral students for whom a professional internship was required in this program prior to graduation:
Total students who applied for an internship: 5
Total students who obtained an internship: 5
Total students who obtained a paid internship: 5

Total students who obtained an unpaid internship: 0
Total students who were placed in APA/CPA-accredited internships: 1
Total students placed in internships not APA/CPA-accredited, but listed with the Association of Psychology Postdoctoral and Internship Centers (APPIC): 0
Total students placed in internships conforming to guidelines of the Council of Directors of School Psychology Programs (CDSPP): 3
Total students placed in internships that were not APA/CPA-accredited, APPIC or CDSSP listed: 1

Internships/Practica

Students in all programs are required to complete field-based practicum hours during each semester they are enrolled in the program. Practicum hours increase with experience and training, from 150 hours in the first year to 450 hours in the second year. PhD students complete an advanced practicum of 600 hours during the third year of full-time enrollment; additional experiences during the fourth year serve to further diversify the range of training experiences and increase autonomy. Practicum experiences include observation, consultation, assessment, counseling and intervention with diverse populations ranging from preschool-aged to school-aged students, as well as with college students, parents, teachers, and other professionals. Practicum sites include public school settings, the Porter School Psychology Center, ISU ADHD Clinic, and the READ Clinic, as well as agencies such as Gibault Children's Services, Inc. and Unlocking the Spectrum. Final experiences include a 1,200+ hour school-based internship for EdS students and a 2,000-hour predoctoral internship in clinical and/or school settings for PhD students. Predoctoral internship sites include public school settings, hospitals and mental health facilities.

Admissions

Entries appear in the following order: required test or GPA, minimum score (if required)/median score of students entering in 2015–2016.

Program	Degree	GRE-V	GRE-Q	GRE-Writing	GRE-Subject	Under-graduate GPA	Last 2 Years GPA	Psychology GPA	Master's GPA
School Psychology	PhD	NA/NA	NA/NA	NA/NA	Not specified	2.7/NA	Not specified	Not specified	Not specified
School Psychology	EdS	NA/NA	NA/NA	NA/NA	Not specified	2.7/NA	Not specified	Not specified	Not specified

Admissions Requirements:

Degree	GRE	GRE-Subject	Letters of Recommendation	Research Statement	Writing Sample	CV	Interview
Master's/Specialist	Required	Required	3	Required	None	Required	Required
Doctoral	Required	Required	3	Required	None	Required	Required

Admissions Criteria:

GRE scores—medium
Research experience—medium
Work experience—medium
Clinically related public service—high
GPA—high

Letters of recommendation—high
Interview—high
Statement of goals and objectives—high
Vita—high

Department Demographics

	Male (PT)	Female (PT)	Total	African-American/ Black (PT)	Hispanic/ Latino (PT)	Asian/ Pacific Islander (PT)	American Indian/ Alaska Native (PT)	Caucasian/ White (PT)	Unknown (PT)	Multiethnic (PT)	ADA (PT)	Int'l (PT)
Students	5 (2)	24 (11)	42	3 (1)	0 (0)	0 (1)	0 (0)	25 (11)	0 (0)	1 (0)	0 (0)	0 (1)

Financial Information/Assistance

Tuition: For information on tuition costs, visit http://www.indstate.edu/tuition/. Tuition is subject to change. Tuition costs vary by program.

Doctoral:
State residents: $8,360 per academic year.
State residents: $380 per credit hour.
Nonstate residents: $17,928 per academic year.
Nonstate residents: $747 per credit hour.

Master's:
State residents: $8,360 per academic year.
State residents: $380 per credit hour.
Nonstate residents: $17,928 per academic year.
Nonstate residents: $747 per credit hour.

Financial Assistance:

	Teaching Assistantship (% Receiving)	Teaching Assistantship Tuition Remission	Research Assistantship (% Receiving)	Research Assistantship Tuition Remission	Fellowship (% Receiving)	Fellowship Tuition Remission
First-Year Student	$6,112 (NA)	Partial	$6,112 (NA)	Partial	$6,112 (NA)	Partial
Advanced Student	$8,475 (NA)	Partial	$8,475 (NA)	Partial	$8,475 (NA)	Partial

For additional information on financial assistance, visit http://www.indstate.edu/finaid/graduate/.

Employment of Department Graduates

Master's:
Enrolled in a psychology doctoral program: 0
Enrolled in another graduate/professional program: 0
Employed in an academic position at a university: 0
Employed in academic position at a 2-year/4-year college: 0
Employed in other positions at a higher education institution: 0
Employed in a professional position in a school system: 12
Employed in business or industry: 0
Employed in government agency: 0
Employed in a community mental health/counseling center: 0
Employed in a hospital/medical center: 0
Still seeking employment: 0
Not seeking employment: 1
Other employment position: 0
Do not know: 0
Total: 13

Doctoral:
Enrolled in a postdoctoral residency/fellowship: 0
Enrolled in another graduate/professional program: 0
Employed in independent practice: 0
Employed in an academic position at a university: 0
Employed in academic position at a 2-year/4-year college: 0
Employed in other positions at a higher education institution: 0
Employed in a professional position in a school system: 2
Employed in business or industry: 0
Employed in government agency: 0
Employed in a community mental health/counseling center: 0
Employed in a hospital/medical center: 0
Still seeking employment: 0
Not seeking employment: 0
Other employment position: 0
Do not know: 0
Total: 2

Additional Information

Housing and Day Care: On-campus housing is available. See the following website for more information: http://www.indstate.edu/reslife/. On-campus day care facilities are available. See the following website for more information: http://web.indstate.edu/ecec/.

Information for Students With Physical Disabilities: See the following website: http://www.indstate.edu/cfss/programs/dss/index.htm.

Special Facilities or Resources: The program participates in an interdisciplinary university-based clinic to provide psychological and educational services to children, youth, and families. The clinic includes programs specifically designed to deliver services in the areas of communication disorders, counseling, and school psychology. Services are provided to individuals and families across the lifespan, with emphasis on serving children, adolescents, and college students within the school psychology area of the clinic. This interdisciplinary clinic provides an opportunity for students to work collaboratively and provide integrated, comprehensive services to clients.

Application Information: Leah Nellis, Director of School Psychology Training Program, Bayh College of Education, Room 302D, Indiana State University, Terre Haute, IN 47809. *Fee:* $35. *Online application:* http://www.indstate.edu/graduate/degree.htm.

Indiana State University

Department of Psychology
Arts and Sciences
424 North 7th Street, Root Hall
Terre Haute, IN 47809
Telephone: (812) 237-2445
Chairperson: Virgil Sheets, PhD

E-mail: Kevin.Bolinskey@indstate.edu
Web: http://www.indstate.edu/psychology

Orientation, Objectives, and Emphasis of Department

The Indiana State University Clinical Psychology Doctoral Program is based on a practitioner–scientist model. The primary goal of the program is to prepare individuals to become competent professional psychologists through balanced training in clinical competencies and research, to contribute to the science of psychology. The program has been APA-accredited for more than 30 years. Our students are required to complete a dissertation, thus we place somewhat more emphasis on research skills than do some PsyD programs. Students interested in a doctoral program that provides rigorous training in clinical skills as well as research opportunities may be particularly suited for our program. The PsyD Program at ISU adheres to the belief that thoughtful training in diversity issues is crucial in developing a professional identity that values and pursues excellence in clinical practice. In addition, we are committed to creating a culture of acceptance and inclusion that values the contribution of diverse perspectives such as those influenced by gender, ethnicity, race, culture, sexual orientation, age, religion, disability and personal experience. The program strives to develop in our students a professional identity grounded in an active sense of social responsibility combined with an appreciation and respect of cultural and individual differences.

Programs and Degrees Offered

Program	Degree	Application Deadline	Applications Received	Accepted	New Admits Enrolled (PT)	Total Enrolled (PT)	Degrees Awarded in 2014–2015	Median Years to Complete Degree	Dismissed/ Withdrew
Clinical Psychology	PsyD	December 5 (Fall)	139	11	5 (0)	40 (0)	6	5	0

APA Accreditation

Clinical PsyD: Student Outcome Data website: http://www.indstate.edu/cas/psychology/psyd-clinical-psychology/psyd-program-clinical-psychology.

Doctoral Degree (PsyD Clinical Psychology): For those doctoral students for whom a professional internship was required in this program prior to graduation:
Total students who applied for an internship: 6
Total students who obtained an internship: 6
Total students who obtained a paid internship: 6
Total students who obtained an unpaid internship: 0
Total students who were placed in APA/CPA-accredited internships: 6
Total students placed in internships not APA/CPA-accredited, but listed with the Association of Psychology Postdoctoral and Internship Centers (APPIC): 0
Total students placed in internships conforming to guidelines of the Council of Directors of School Psychology Programs (CDSPP): 0
Total students placed in internships that were not APA/CPA-accredited, APPIC or CDSSP listed: 0

Internships/Practica

Students in the second and third years in the program are expected to engage in an average of 6–8 hours per week of clinical work in the Psychology Clinic appropriate to their level of training. The number of hours of direct client contact increases throughout the program. Students are assigned to a practicum team during their second and third years in the program based on student preferences, training needs, supervisor availability and staffing. Students in the fourth year engage in clinical work through an external placement. The clinical internship is the culmination of the student's clinical training. Except under unusual circumstances, it is expected that the internship be completed at an APA-accredited internship site.

Admissions

Entries appear in the following order: required test or GPA, minimum score (if required)/median score of students entering in 2015–2016.

Program	Degree	GRE-V	GRE-Q	GRE-Writing	GRE-Subject	Under-graduate GPA	Last 2 Years GPA	Psychology GPA	Master's GPA
Clinical Psychology	PsyD	Not specified	Not specified	Not specified	Not specified	Not specified	Not specified	Not specified	Not specified

Admissions Requirements:

Degree	GRE	GRE-Subject	Letters of Recommendation	Research Statement	Writing Sample	CV	Interview
Doctoral	Required	Optional	3	Required	None	Required	Required

Admissions Criteria:

GRE scores—high
Research experience—high
Work experience—medium
Clinically related public service—medium
GPA—high

Letters of recommendation—high
Interview—high
Statement of goals and objectives—high
Undergraduate psychology preparation—high

For additional information on admission requirements, visit http://www.indstate.edu/cas/psychology/psyd-clinical-psychology/psyd-applying-admission.

Department Demographics

	Male (PT)	Female (PT)	Total	African-American/ Black (PT)	Hispanic/ Latino (PT)	Asian/ Pacific Islander (PT)	American Indian/ Alaska Native (PT)	Caucasian/ White (PT)	Unknown	Multiethnic (PT)	ADA (PT)	Int'l (PT)
Students	12 (0)	28 (0)	40	2 (0)	2 (0)	0 (0)	1 (0)	35 (0)	0 (0)	0 (0)	1 (0)	0 (0)

Financial Information/Assistance

Tuition: For information on tuition costs, visit http://indstate.edu/tuition/. Tuition is subject to change. Additional fees are assessed to students beyond the costs of tuition for the following: $54 per credit hour program fee; $100 per semester recreation center fee

Doctoral:
State residents: $8,148 per academic year.
State residents: $388 per credit hour.
Nonstate residents: $16,002 per academic year.
Nonstate residents: $762 per credit hour.

Financial Assistance:

	Teaching Assistantship (% Receiving)	Teaching Assistantship Tuition Remission	Research Assistantship (% Receiving)	Research Assistantship Tuition Remission	Fellowship (% Receiving)	Fellowship Tuition Remission
First-Year Student	$6,250 (100)	Full	NA (NA)	NA	NA (NA)	NA
Advanced Student	$6,150 (100)	Full	NA (NA)	NA	NA (NA)	NA

For additional information on financial assistance, visit http://www.indstate.edu/cas/psychology/psyd-clinical-psychology/financial-supportscholarship-information.

Employment of Department Graduates

Doctoral:
Enrolled in a postdoctoral residency/fellowship: 3
Employed in independent practice: 2
Employed in government agency: 2
Employed in a community mental health/counseling center: 1
Total: 8

Additional Information

Housing and Day Care: On-campus housing is available. See the following website for more information: http://indstate.edu/reslife/. On-campus day care facilities are available. See the following website for more information: http://indstate.edu/ecec/.

Information for Students With Physical Disabilities: See the following website: http://www.indstate.edu/services/student-success/cfss.

Special Facilities or Resources: The ISU Department of Psychology is located in Root Hall, a modern building that also houses faculty and graduate student offices, research facilities, seminar rooms, and the Psychology Clinic. The Indiana State University Department of Psychology operates its own Psychology Clinic, which provides a wide range of clinical services to the community. The Psychology Clinic has state-of-the-art equipment and provides ample space for clinical and research purposes. Each interview room is equipped with one-way observation mirrors and has video and audio recording capabilities. Computerized testing is available in the Clinic which also has the latest personality, intelligence, achievement, and cognitive ability tests.The department's facilities also include numerous computers for word processing and data analysis, equipment for biofeedback and psycho-physiological measurement, and human research rooms. A full-time shop technician is assigned to the department.

Application Information: Indiana State University, Graduate Admissions, Welcome Center, 318 North Sixth Street, Terre Haute, IN 47809-1904. *Fee:* $45. *Online application:* http://indstate.edu/graduate/apply.htm.

Indiana University
Department of Counseling and Educational Psychology
School of Education
201 North Rose Avenue
Bloomington, IN 47405-1006
Telephone: (812) 856-8300
Chairperson: Ginette Delandshere, PhD

E-mail: gdelands@indiana.edu
Web: http://education.indiana.edu/about/departments/counseling/index.html

---

Orientation, Objectives, and Emphasis of Department
The Department has multiple missions, but at the heart of our enterprise is a community of scholars working to contribute solutions to the problems faced by children, adolescents, and adults in the context of contemporary education. Additionally, the counseling psychology program promotes a broad range of interventions designed to facilitate the maximal adjustment of individuals. Faculty, staff and students share a commitment to open-mindedness and to social justice. We recognize the complex and dynamic nature of the social fabric and welcome qualified students of all ethnic, racial, national, religious, gender, social class, sexual, political, and philosophic orientations. Faculty and students collaboratively investigate numerous facets of child and adolescent development, creativity, learning, metacognition, aging, semiotics, and inquiry methodologies. Our programs require an understanding of both quantitative and qualitative research paradigms. We subscribe to the scientist–practitioner model for preparing professional psychologists. Our graduates work in various research and practice settings; universities, public schools, state departments of education, mental health centers, hospitals, and corporations.

Programs and Degrees Offered

Program	Degree	Application Deadline	Applications Received	Accepted	New Admits Enrolled (PT)	Total Enrolled (PT)	Degrees Awarded in 2014–2015	Median Years to Complete Degree	Dismissed/Withdrew
Counseling Psychology	PhD	December 1 (Fall)	113	10	7	51 (0)	11	5.87	0

Programs and Degrees Offered *(con't.)*

Program	Degree	Application Deadline	Applications Received	Accepted	New Admits Enrolled (PT)	Total Enrolled (PT)	Degrees Awarded in 2014–2015	Median Years to Complete Degree	Dismissed/ Withdrew
Educational Psychology	PhD	December 1 (Fall)	20	9	7	55 (0)	5	8.53	5
School Psychology	PhD	December 1 (Fall)	26	15	6	44 (0)	7	5.81	2
School Psychology	EdS	December 1 (Fall)	42	18	9	23	3	2.85	1
Educational Psychology	MA/MS	December 1 (Fall)	15	14	12	16	1	2	0

APA Accreditation

Counseling PhD: Student Outcome Data website: http://education.indiana.edu/graduate/programs/counseling-psychology/index.html.

School PhD: Student Outcome Data website: http://education.indiana.edu/graduate/programs/school-psychology/index.html.

Doctoral Degree (PhD Counseling Psychology): For those doctoral students for whom a professional internship was required in this program prior to graduation:

Total students who applied for an internship: 5
Total students who obtained an internship: 5
Total students who obtained a paid internship: 5
Total students who obtained an unpaid internship: 0
Total students who were placed in APA/CPA-accredited internships: 5
Total students placed in internships not APA/CPA-accredited, but listed with the Association of Psychology Postdoctoral and Internship Centers (APPIC): 0
Total students placed in internships conforming to guidelines of the Council of Directors of School Psychology Programs (CDSPP): 0
Total students placed in internships that were not APA/CPA-accredited, APPIC or CDSSP listed: 0

Doctoral Degree (PhD School Psychology): For those doctoral students for whom a professional internship was required in this program prior to graduation:

Total students who applied for an internship: 3
Total students who obtained an internship: 3
Total students who obtained a paid internship: 3
Total students who obtained an unpaid internship: 0
Total students who were placed in APA/CPA-accredited internships: 3
Total students placed in internships not APA/CPA-accredited, but listed with the Association of Psychology Postdoctoral and Internship Centers (APPIC): 0
Total students placed in internships conforming to guidelines of the Council of Directors of School Psychology Programs (CDSPP): 0
Total students placed in internships that were not APA/CPA-accredited, APPIC or CDSSP listed: 0

Internships/Practica

All counseling and school psychology students must take both practica and internships.

Admissions

Entries appear in the following order: required test or GPA, minimum score (if required)/median score of students entering in 2015–2016.

Program	Degree	GRE-V	GRE-Q	GRE-Writing	GRE-Subject	Under-graduate GPA	Last 2 Years GPA	Psychology GPA	Master's GPA
Counseling Psychology	PhD	NA/154	NA/152	NA/4.5	Not specified	NA/3.49	Not specified	Not specified	NA/3.89
Educational Psychology	PhD	NA/155	NA/154	NA/4.5	Not specified	NA/3.53	Not specified	Not specified	NA/3.91
School Psychology	PhD	NA/154	NA/160	NA/4	Not specified	NA/3.67	Not specified	Not specified	Not specified

Admissions *(con't.)*

Program	Degree	GRE-V	GRE-Q	GRE-Writing	GRE-Subject	Under-graduate GPA	Last 2 Years GPA	Psychology GPA	Master's GPA
School Psychology	EdS	Not specified	Not specified	Not specified	Not specified	Not specified	Not specified	Not specified	Not specified
Educational Psychology	MA/MS	NA/153	NA/157	NA/4	Not specified	NA/3.53	Not specified	Not specified	Not specified

Admissions Requirements:

Degree	GRE	GRE-Subject	Letters of Recommendation	Research Statement	Writing Sample	CV	Interview
Master's/Specialist	Required	None	3	Required	Optional	Required	None
Doctoral	Required	Optional	3	Required	Required	Required	Required

Please note if these criteria vary for different programs: Personal interviews are required for applicants to the PhD programs. GRE scores are interpreted differently for domestic and international applicants. School Psychology PhD requires a writing sample and CV, EdS requires a CV.

Admissions Criteria:

GRE scores—high
Research experience—medium
Work experience—medium
Clinically related public service—medium

GPA—high
Letters of recommendation—high
Interview—high
Statement of goals and objectives—high

For additional information on admission requirements, visit https://education.indiana.edu/graduate/apply/index.html.

Department Demographics

	Male (PT)	Female (PT)	Total	African-American/ Black (PT)	Hispanic/ Latino (PT)	Asian/ Pacific Islander (PT)	American Indian/ Alaska Native (PT)	Caucasian/ White (PT)	Unknown (PT)	Multiethnic (PT)	ADA (PT)	Int'l (PT)
Students	49 (0)	140 (0)	189	21 (0)	24 (0)	22 (0)	1 (0)	121 (0)	0 (0)	0 (0)	0 (0)	25 (0)

Financial Information/Assistance

Tuition: For information on tuition costs, visit https://bursar.indiana.edu/tuition-fees/fees-semester.html. Tuition is subject to change.

Doctoral:
State residents: $377 per credit hour.
Nonstate residents: $1,222 per credit hour.

Master's:
State residents: $416 per credit hour.
Nonstate residents: $1,222 per credit hour.

Financial Assistance:

	Teaching Assistantship (% Receiving)	Teaching Assistantship Tuition Remission	Research Assistantship (% Receiving)	Research Assistantship Tuition Remission	Fellowship (% Receiving)	Fellowship Tuition Remission
First-Year Student	$15,920 (NA)	Partial	$13,379 (NA)	Partial	$17,000 (NA)	Full
Advanced Student	$15,920 (NA)	Partial	$13,379 (NA)	Partial	$17,000 (NA)	Full

For additional information on financial assistance, visit https://education.indiana.edu/graduate/cost-aid/index.html.

Employment of Department Graduates

Doctoral:
Enrolled in a postdoctoral residency/fellowship: 5
Employed in an academic position at a university: 4
Employed in academic position at a 2-year/4-year college: 1
Employed in other positions at a higher education institution: 5
Employed in a professional position in a school system: 1
Employed in government agency: 1
Employed in a community mental health/counseling center: 2
Other employment position: 1
Do not know: 3
Total: 23

Additional Information

Housing and Day Care: On-campus housing is available. See the following website for more information: http://www.rps.indiana.edu/. On-campus day care facilities are available. See the following website for more information: http://www.childcare.indiana.edu/.

Information for Students With Physical Disabilities: See the following website: https://studentaffairs.indiana.edu/disability-services-students/index.shtml.

Special Facilities or Resources: Special facilities include the Institute for Child Study, Center for Human Growth, Center for Evaluation and Education Policy, Center for Research on Learning & Technology, and the Indiana Institute on Disability and Community.

Application Information: Office of Graduate Studies, Room 2100, W.W. Wright Education Building, 201 North Rose Avenue, Bloomington, IN 47405-1005. *Fee:* $55. *Online application:* http://graduate.indiana.edu/admissions/apply.shtml.

Indiana University
Department of Psychological and Brain Sciences
College of Arts and Sciences
1101 East 10th Street
Bloomington, IN 47405
Telephone: (812) 856-2409
Chairperson: Dr. William Hetrick

E-mail: psychgrd@indiana.edu
Web: http://psych.indiana.edu/

Orientation, Objectives, and Emphasis of Department
The mission of the Department of Psychological and Brain Sciences is to lead scientific advances through state-of-the-art experimentation and theory with the goal of understanding how the entire brain-behavior system works, from molecular neuroscience to cognition to the social behavior of groups. Through the application of cutting-edge discoveries to real world problems, through the training of the next generation of scientists, and through training citizens who will apply their knowledge in many fields from medicine to industry to public service, the department accepts the responsibility to translate scientific knowledge into practical solutions for problems that impact human lives.

Programs and Degrees Offered

Program	Degree	Application Deadline	Applications Received	Accepted	New Admits Enrolled (PT)	Total Enrolled (PT)	Degrees Awarded in 2014–2015	Median Years to Complete Degree	Dismissed/Withdrew
Clinical Science	PhD	December 1 (Fall)	142	7	5	23	4	7.25	0
Cognitive Neuroscience	PhD	December 1 (Fall)	41	6	4 (0)	13 (0)	1	3	0
Cognitive Psychology	PhD	December 1 (Fall)	42	6	2 (0)	27 (0)	3	7.7	0
Mechanisms of Behavior	PhD	December 1 (Fall)	18	2	2 (0)	8 (0)	0		0

Programs and Degrees Offered *(con't.)*

Program	Degree	Application Deadline	Applica-tions Received	Accepted	New Admits Enrolled (PT)	Total Enrolled (PT)	Degrees Awarded in 2014–2015	Median Years to Complete Degree	Dismissed/ Withdrew
Developmental Psychology	PhD	December 1 (Fall)	12	3	1 (0)	9 (0)	1	5	1
Social Psychology	PhD	December 1 (Fall)	73	3	2 (0)	13 (0)	0		
Molecular Systems Neuroscience	PhD	December 1 (Fall)	12	5	4 (0)	13	0		

APA Accreditation

Clinical PhD: Student Outcome Data website: http://psych.indiana.edu/clinical.php.

Doctoral Degree (PhD Clinical Science): For those doctoral students for whom a professional internship was required in this program prior to graduation:

Total students who applied for an internship: 1

Total students who obtained an internship: 1

Total students who obtained a paid internship: 1

Total students who obtained an unpaid internship: 0

Total students who were placed in APA/CPA-accredited internships: 1

Total students placed in internships not APA/CPA-accredited, but listed with the Association of Psychology Postdoctoral and Internship Centers (APPIC): 0

Total students placed in internships conforming to guidelines of the Council of Directors of School Psychology Programs (CDSPP): 0

Total students placed in internships that were not APA/CPA-accredited, APPIC or CDSSP listed: 0

Admissions

Entries appear in the following order: required test or GPA, minimum score (if required)/median score of students entering in 2015–2016.

Program	Degree	GRE-V	GRE-Q	GRE-Writing	GRE-Subject	Under-graduate GPA	Last 2 Years GPA	Psychol-ogy GPA	Master's GPA
Clinical Science	PhD	NA/NA	NA/NA	NA/NA	Not specified	Not specified	Not specified	Not specified	Not specified
Cognitive Neuroscience	PhD	NA/NA	NA/NA	NA/NA	Not specified	Not specified	Not specified	Not specified	Not specified
Cognitive Psychology	PhD	NA/NA	NA/NA	NA/NA	Not specified	Not specified	Not specified	Not specified	Not specified
Mechanisms of Behavior	PhD	NA/NA	NA/NA	NA/NA	Not specified	Not specified	Not specified	Not specified	Not specified
Developmental Psychology	PhD	NA/NA	NA/NA	NA/NA	Not specified	Not specified	Not specified	Not specified	Not specified
Social Psychology	PhD	NA/NA	NA/NA	NA/NA	Not specified	Not specified	Not specified	Not specified	Not specified
Molecular Systems Neuroscience	PhD	NA/NA	NA/NA	NA/NA	Not specified	Not specified	Not specified	Not specified	Not specified

Admissions Requirements:

Degree	GRE	GRE-Subject	Letters of Recommendation	Research Statement	Writing Sample	CV	Interview
Doctoral	Required	Recommended	3	Required	Optional	Optional	Required

Admissions Criteria:

GRE scores—high
Research experience—high
GPA—high
Letters of recommendation—high

Interview—high
Statement of goals and objectives—medium
Undergraduate psychology preparation—high

For additional information on admission requirements, visit http://psych.indiana.edu/grad_admissions.php.

Department Demographics

	Male (PT)	Female (PT)	Total	African-American/ Black (PT)	Hispanic/ Latino (PT)	Asian/ Pacific Islander (PT)	American Indian/ Alaska Native (PT)	Caucasian/ White (PT)	Unknown	Multiethnic (PT)	ADA (PT)	Int'l (PT)
Students	43 (0)	62 (0)	105	4 (0)	4 (0)	6 (0)	2 (0)	72 (0)	18 (0)	0 (0)	1 (0)	23 (0)

Financial Information/Assistance

Tuition: For information on tuition costs, visit https://bursar.indiana.edu/tuition-fees/fees-semester.html. Tuition is subject to change.

Doctoral:
State residents: $8,442 per academic year.
State residents: $351 per credit hour.
Nonstate residents: $26,811 per academic year.
Nonstate residents: $1,117 per credit hour.

Financial Assistance:

	Teaching Assistantship (% Receiving)	Teaching Assistantship Tuition Remission	Research Assistantship (% Receiving)	Research Assistantship Tuition Remission	Fellowship (% Receiving)	Fellowship Tuition Remission
First-Year Student	$24,000 (NA)	Full	$24,000 (NA)	Full	$25,000 (NA)	Full
Advanced Student	$24,000 (NA)	Full	$24,000 (NA)	Full	$25,000 (NA)	Full

For additional information on financial assistance, visit http://graduate.indiana.edu/admissions/financial-support/.

Employment of Department Graduates

Doctoral:
Enrolled in a postdoctoral residency/fellowship: 8
Do not know: 1
Total: 9

Additional Information

Housing and Day Care: On-campus housing is available. See the following website for more information: http://rps.indiana.edu/housing.cfml. On-campus day care facilities are available. See the following website for more information: http://www.childcare.indiana.edu/.

Information for Students With Physical Disabilities: See the following website: http://studentaffairs.indiana.edu/disability-services-students/index.shtml.

Special Facilities or Resources: The Department of Psychological and Brain Sciences is home to the IU Imaging Research Facility. The facility houses a 3T Siemens Magnetom Trio whole body system, used for magnetic resonance imaging (MRI) or functional MRI (fMRI), a noninvasive method for studying patterns of brain activity during mental operations. The facility gives our students the opportunity to be part of research labs doing MRI and fMRI studies and to take classes with the MRI scientists.

Application Information: Indiana University, Graduate Admissions, Psychological and Brain Sciences, 1101 E. 10th Street, Bloomington, IN 47405-7007. *Fee:* $55. *Online application:* http://graduate.indiana.edu/admissions/apply.shtml.

Indiana University-Purdue University Indianapolis
Department of Psychology
School of Science
402 North Blackford Street, LD 124
Indianapolis, IN 46202-3275
Telephone: (317) 274-6945
Chairperson: Peggy Stockdale

E-mail: gradpsy@iupui.edu
Web: http://psych.iupui.edu

Orientation, Objectives, and Emphasis of Department
Graduate education is offered at the PhD level in Clinical Psychology and Addiction Neuroscience. The APA-Accredited Clinical program follows the clinical science model. A rigorous academic and research education is combined with supervised practical training. The clinical program provides specialization in behavioral medicine/health psychology, and severe mental illness/psychiatric rehabilitation. The PhD program in Addiction Neuroscience emphasizes the core content areas of psychology along with specialization in psychobiology and animal models of addiction. Research, scholarship, and close faculty-student mentor relationships are viewed as integral training elements within both programs. Graduate training at the MS level is designed to provide students with theory and practice that will enable them to apply psychological techniques and findings to subsequent jobs. All students are required to take departmental methods courses and then specific area core courses and electives.

Programs and Degrees Offered

Program	Degree	Application Deadline	Applica-tions Received	Accepted	New Admits Enrolled (PT)	Total Enrolled (PT)	Degrees Awarded in 2014–2015	Median Years to Complete Degree	Dismissed/ Withdrew
Industrial/ Organizational Psychology	MA/MS	February 1 (Fall)	88	7	6 (0)	11 (0)	4	2	0
Clinical Psychology	PhD	December 1 (Fall)	123	9	4 (0)	31 (0)	4	6	1
Addiction Neuroscience	PhD	January 1 (Fall)	18	7	2	11 (0)	3	5.5	0

APA Accreditation
Clinical PhD: Student Outcome Data website: http://psych.iupui.edu/graduate/degrees/phd-clinical.

Doctoral Degree (PhD Clinical Psychology): For those doctoral students for whom a professional internship was required in this program prior to graduation:
Total students who applied for an internship: 4
Total students who obtained an internship: 4
Total students who obtained a paid internship: 4
Total students who obtained an unpaid internship: 0
Total students who were placed in APA/CPA-accredited internships: 4
Total students placed in internships not APA/CPA-accredited, but listed with the Association of Psychology Postdoctoral and Internship Centers (APPIC): 0
Total students placed in internships conforming to guidelines of the Council of Directors of School Psychology Programs (CDSPP): 0
Total students placed in internships that were not APA/CPA-accredited, APPIC or CDSSP listed: 0

Master's Degree (MA/MS Industrial/Organizational Psychology): An internship experience, such as a final research project or "capstone" experience, is required of graduates.

Internships/Practica

Clinical practicum sites are located at IUPUI and within the Indianapolis area, and involve supervised clinical training individually tailored for each student. A practicum coordinator, the site supervisor, and the student develop specific contracts that emphasize education and the acquisition of clinical skills and knowledge, rather than experience per se. These contractual activities and goals are monitored and evaluated at the end of each placement. Practicum opportunities are varied and numerous and include many different types of clinical settings with different clinical populations. On-site supervisors are psychologists. Many sites in different settings are available. General practicum sites include a university counseling center and several psychiatric clinics. More advanced settings can be categorized as either Behavioral Medicine/Health Psychology or Severe Mental Illness/Psychiatric Rehabilitation. The I/O master's program offers opportunities to achieve applied experience in business settings. Students have the opportunity to sign up for practicum in the spring of their second year. Students are typically placed in an organization for one 8-hour day each week of the semester. Paid summer internships (15–20 hours per week) in the community are also available.

Admissions

Entries appear in the following order: required test or GPA, minimum score (if required)/median score of students entering in 2015–2016.

Program	Degree	GRE-V	GRE-Q	GRE-Writing	GRE-Subject	Under-graduate GPA	Last 2 Years GPA	Psychology GPA	Master's GPA
Industrial/ Organizational Psychology	MA/MS	151/149	149/151	3.5/4	Not specified	3.36/3.71	Not specified	Not specified	Not specified
Clinical Psychology	PhD	158/159	151/156	3.5/4	530/690	3.2/3.63	Not specified	Not specified	Not specified
Addiction Neuroscience	PhD	155/157	152/153	4/4	Not specified	3/3.21	Not specified	Not specified	Not specified

Admissions Requirements:

Degree	GRE	GRE-Subject	Letters of Recom-mendation	Research Statement	Writing Sample	CV	Interview
Master's/Specialist	Required	None	3	Required	None	Optional	Required
Doctoral	Required	Recom-mended	3	Required	None	Required	Required

Please note if these criteria vary for different programs: The GRE Psychology subject test is recommended for the Clinical PhD application, but not for the Addiction Neuroscience application.

Admissions Criteria:

GRE scores—high
Research experience—high
Work experience—low
GPA—high

Letters of recommendation—high
Interview—high
Statement of goals and objectives—high
Undergraduate psychology preparation—medium

For additional information on admission requirements, visit http://psych.iupui.edu/graduate/admissions.

Department Demographics

	Male (PT)	Female (PT)	Total	African-American/ Black (PT)	Hispanic/ Latino (PT)	Asian/ Pacific Islander (PT)	American Indian/ Alaska Native (PT)	Caucasian/ White (PT)	Unknown	Multiethnic (PT)	ADA (PT)	Int'l (PT)
Students	16 (0)	37 (0)	53	5 (0)	0 (0)	9 (0)	1 (0)	37 (0)	1 (0)	0 (0)	0 (0)	3 (0)

Financial Information/Assistance

Tuition: For information on tuition costs, visit http://bursar.iupui.edu/apps/costestimator.aspx. Tuition is subject to change. Additional fees are assessed to students beyond the costs of tuition for the following: general fee, repair and rehabilitation fee, lab fee for certain classes. Tuition costs vary by program.

Doctoral:
State residents: $339 per credit hour.
Nonstate residents: $957 per credit hour.

Master's:
State residents: $339 per credit hour.
Nonstate residents: $957 per credit hour.

Financial Assistance:

	Teaching Assistantship (% Receiving)	Teaching Assistantship Tuition Remission	Research Assistantship (% Receiving)	Research Assistantship Tuition Remission	Fellowship (% Receiving)	Fellowship Tuition Remission
First-Year Student	$16,500 (NA)	Full	$16,500 (NA)	Full	$22,500 (NA)	Full
Advanced Student	$16,500 (NA)	Full	$16,500 (NA)	Full	$16,500 (NA)	Full

For additional information on financial assistance, visit http://psych.iupui.edu/graduate/financial-support.

Employment of Department Graduates

Master's:
Employed in business or industry: 5
Total: 5

Doctoral:
Enrolled in a postdoctoral residency/fellowship: 6
Total: 6

Additional Information

Housing and Day Care: On-campus housing is available. See the following website for more information: http://housing.iupui.edu/index.shtml. On-campus day care facilities are available. See the following website for more information: http://www.childcare.iupui.edu/.

Information for Students With Physical Disabilities: See the following website: http://aes.iupui.edu/.

Special Facilities or Resources: IUPUI is a unique urban university campus with 27,000 students enrolled in 235 degree programs at the undergraduate and graduate level. The campus includes schools of law, dentistry, and medicine, among others, along with undergraduate programs in the arts, humanities, and science. In addition, there are over 75 research institutes, centers, laboratories and specialized programs. The Department of Psychology at IUPUI occupies teaching and research facilities in a modern science building in the heart of campus. Facilities include a 4,000-square foot space and self-contained area devoted to faculty and graduate student basic animal research in experimental psychology and psychobiology. Many of the research rooms are equipped for online computer recording to one of the faculty offices. Laboratories for human research, research rooms, and teaching laboratories are separately located on the first floor of the building. The Psychology Department maintains ties with the faculty and programs in other schools within IUPUI, including the School of Nursing, and the Departments of Psychiatry, Adolescent Medicine, and Neurology. The clinical program provides an unusually rich array of practicum opportunities in behavioral medicine/health psychology and psychiatric rehabilitation.

Application Information: Heather Sissons, Office Manager and Graduate Coordinator, IUPUI, Department of Psychology, LD124, 402 North Blackford Street, Indianapolis, IN 46202-3275. *Fee:* $60. *Online application:* http://graduate.iupui.edu/admissions/apply.shtml.

Indianapolis, University of

Graduate Psychology Program
School of Psychological Sciences
1400 East Hanna Avenue HEAL 253
Indianapolis, IN 46227
Telephone: (317) 788-3353
Dean: Anita Jones Thomas, PhD

E-mail: psychology@uindy.edu
Web: http://uindy.edu/psychologicalsciences

Orientation, Objectives, and Emphasis of Department

The doctoral program in clinical psychology at the University of Indianapolis is based on a practitioner-scholar model of training. The program trains students in the general, integrative practice of professional psychology through a broad-based exposure to a variety of psychological approaches and modalities. These include in-depth coursework in the theories and psychotherapies associated with psychoanalytical, humanistic-existential, cognitive-behavioral, systems and multi-cultural paradigms. The program is committed to sensitizing students to working with diverse, under-served populations. Scholarship, including scientific inquiry and research is seen as a necessary methodology and discipline for the development of critical thinking, and the foundations of design and statistics are well enough in place to permit professional activity in these areas. In addition, the program offers advanced training in three clinical emphasis areas: health psychology/behavioral medicine, childhood and adolescent psychology and adult psychopathology and psychotherapy. The program offers a master's degree with four tracks: foundational, research, mental health counseling, and mental health counseling and addictions counseling. Each track meets specific academic and career goals. Factors to consider include an interest in future admission to a doctoral program in psychology, or to work as a researcher or a licensed counselor.

Programs and Degrees Offered

Program	Degree	Application Deadline	Applications Received	Accepted	New Admits Enrolled (PT)	Total Enrolled (PT)	Degrees Awarded in 2014–2015	Median Years to Complete Degree	Dismissed/ Withdrew
Clinical Psychology	PsyD	January 10 (Fall)	188	51	29 (0)	117 (4)	22	5	1
Clinical Psychology- Foundational Track	MA/MS	February 25 (Fall)	4	0	0 (0)	0 (0)	3	2.33	0
Clinical Psychology- Mental Health Counseling	MA/MS	February 25 (Fall)	73	27	16 (0)	35 (0)	17	2	0
Clinical Psychology- Research Track	MA/MS	February 25 (Fall)	13	5	0 (0)	5 (0)	0		0
Clinical Psychology- Mental Hlth/ Addictions Counsel	MA/MS	February 25 (Fall)	43	24	6 (0)	9 (0)	0		1

APA Accreditation

Clinical PsyD: Student Outcome Data website: http://uindy.edu/psychologicalsciences/psyd/accreditation.

Doctoral Degree (PsyD Clinical Psychology): For those doctoral students for whom a professional internship was required in this program prior to graduation:
Total students who applied for an internship: 30
Total students who obtained an internship: 28
Total students who obtained a paid internship: 28
Total students who obtained an unpaid internship: 0
Total students who were placed in APA/CPA-accredited internships: 23
Total students placed in internships not APA/CPA-accredited, but listed with the Association of Psychology Postdoctoral and Internship Centers (APPIC): 5
Total students placed in internships conforming to guidelines of the Council of Directors of School Psychology Programs (CDSPP): 0
Total students placed in internships that were not APA/CPA-accredited, APPIC or CDSSP listed: 0

Master's Degree (MA/MS Clinical Psychology-Mental Health Counseling): An internship experience, such as a final research project or "capstone" experience is required of graduates. Master's Degree (MA/MS Clinical Psychology-Research Track): An internship experience, such as a final research project or "capstone" experience is required of graduates. Master's Degree (MA/MS Clinical Psychology-Mental Health/Addictions Counsel): An internship experience, such as a final research project or "capstone" experience is required of graduates.

Internships/Practica

In 2015–2016 there are 57 clinical practicum sites, with 115 openings for doctoral or master's students. The number of practicum openings exceeds the number of applicants ensuring that all students receive placements. Clinical psychology master's students (CP) obtain a minimum of 225 hours of supervised clinical practicum experience, clinical psychology mental health counseling and MHC/Substance abuse students (MHC and MHAC) require 1,000 hours of supervised clinical practicum experience and doctoral students receive a minimum of 1,200 hours of supervised clinical practicum experience. Practica are available at numerous settings, including medical centers, local community hospitals, university counseling centers, forensic settings, private practice placements, schools, social service agencies, and mental health centers. Students gain supervised experience in clinical assessment, testing, psychotherapy, collaboration and consultation with interdisciplinary teams, program development and evaluation, treatment planning and case management, and participation in development and delivery of services to professional staff. Practicum students have opportunities to obtain specific training in forensics, psychodiagnostic assessment, neuropsychology, health psychology, pain, substance abuse/dependence, eating disorders, developmental disabilities, and HIV/AIDS. Doctoral students must also complete a 2,000-hour internship. The Director of Clinical Training develops training sites, assists students in their placement and ensures the quality of practicum and internship training.

Admissions

Entries appear in the following order: required test or GPA, minimum score (if required)/median score of students entering in 2015–2016.

Program	Degree	GRE-V	GRE-Q	GRE-Writing	GRE-Subject	Under-graduate GPA	Last 2 Years GPA	Psychol-ogy GPA	Master's GPA
Clinical Psychology	PsyD	153/156	144/152	4/4.3	Not specified	3/3.75	Not specified	Not specified	Not specified
Clinical Psychology-Foundational Track	MA/MS	153/168	144/147	4/4.1	Not specified	3/3.44	Not specified	Not specified	Not specified
Clinical Psychology-Mental Health Counseling	MA/MS	153/168	144/147	4/4.1	Not specified	3/3.44	Not specified	Not specified	Not specified
Clinical Psychology-Research Track	MA/MS	153/168	144/147	4/4.1	Not specified	3/3.44	Not specified	Not specified	Not specified
Clinical Psychology-Mental Hlth/Addictions Counsel	MA/MS	153/168	144/147	4/4.1	Not specified	3/3.44	Not specified	Not specified	Not specified

Admissions Requirements:

Degree	GRE	GRE-Subject	Letters of Recom-mendation	Research Statement	Writing Sample	CV	Interview
Master's/Specialist	Required	Optional	3	Required	Optional	Required	Required
Doctoral	Required	Recom-mended	3	Required	Optional	Required	Required

Admissions Criteria:

GRE scores—high
Research experience—medium
Work experience—medium
Clinically related public service—medium
GPA—high

Letters of recommendation—high
Interview—high
Statement of goals and objectives—medium
Undergraduate psychology preparation—high

For additional information on admission requirements, visit http://uindy.edu/psychologicalsciences/psyd/admission.

Department Demographics

	Male (PT)	Female (PT)	Total	African-American/ Black (PT)	Hispanic/ Latino (PT)	Asian/ Pacific Islander (PT)	American Indian/ Alaska Native (PT)	Caucasian/ White (PT)	Unknown	Multiethnic (PT)	ADA (PT)	Int'l (PT)
Students	24 (1)	142 (3)	170	5 (1)	9 (1)	15 (0)	2 (0)	134 (2)	0 (0)	1 (0)	1 (0)	5 (0)

Financial Information/Assistance

Tuition: Tuition is subject to change. Additional fees are assessed to students beyond the costs of tuition for the following: health services fee, technology fee, activity fee, lab fees for some classes.

Doctoral:
State residents: $876 per credit hour.
Nonstate residents: $876 per credit hour.

Master's:
State residents: $876 per credit hour.
Nonstate residents: $876 per credit hour.

Financial Assistance:

	Teaching Assistantship (% Receiving)	Teaching Assistantship Tuition Remission	Research Assistantship (% Receiving)	Research Assistantship Tuition Remission	Fellowship (% Receiving)	Fellowship Tuition Remission
First-Year Student	$0 (NA)	Partial	$0 (NA)	Partial	$0 (NA)	Full
Advanced Student	$0 (NA)	Partial	$0 (NA)	Partial	$0 (NA)	Full

For additional information on financial assistance, visit http://uindy.edu/psychologicalsciences/psyd/tuition.

Employment of Department Graduates

Master's:
Enrolled in a psychology doctoral program: 3
Employed in business or industry: 1
Employed in government agency: 1
Employed in a community mental health/counseling center: 5
Employed in a hospital/medical center: 2
Do not know: 8
Total: 20

Doctoral:
Enrolled in a postdoctoral residency/fellowship: 5
Employed in independent practice: 5
Employed in an academic position at a university: 1
Employed in other positions at a higher education institution: 4
Employed in a community mental health/counseling center: 3
Employed in a hospital/medical center: 2
Do not know: 2
Total: 22

Additional Information

Housing and Day Care: On-campus housing is available. See the following website for more information: http://greyhoundvillage.com/. No on-campus day care facilities are available.

Information for Students With Physical Disabilities: See the following website: http://www.uindy.edu/ssd/.

Special Facilities or Resources: Specialized training facilities include several clinical therapy labs designed for supervised assessment, testing, and therapy, and for recording of clinical sessions utilized in feedback and instruction. The Large Groups Lab includes interconnected classrooms used for recording and monitoring of experiential group or class exercises and psychoeducational programs. Individualized Study and Research Labs equipped with computers are available. Computer facilities in the School of Psychological Sciences and throughout the university allow access to the internet, a full range of statistical and office software and library holdings. Wireless internet is available. Psychology classrooms are equipped with large flatscreen monitors readied for notebook display. Direct, online literature searches using a variety of databases (e.g., PsycBOOKS, PsycINFO (with PsycARTICLES), PsycEXTRA, MedLine, PEP) is available. The library subscribes to the major psychology journals and contains the latest publications in the field of clinical psychology. The School also has an on-site Psychological Services Center which offers treatment services to community residents including underserved and marginalized patients on a sliding fee scale. Students receive applied training experience at the Center while conducting intake assessments or providing therapeutic services.

Application Information: University of Indianapolis, School of Psychological Sciences, Director of Communication and Information Systems, 1400 East Hanna Avenue HEAL 227, Indianapolis, IN 46227. *Fee:* $55. *Online application:* https://app.applyyourself.com/?id=uindy.

Notre Dame, University of
Department of Psychology
Arts & Letters
118 Haggar Hall
Notre Dame, IN 46556
Telephone: (574) 631-4501
Chairperson: Daniel K. Lapsley

E-mail: db.watson@nd.edu
Web: http://psychology.nd.edu/

Orientation, Objectives, and Emphasis of Department
The Department of Psychology at the University of Notre Dame is committed to excellence in both basic psychological science and its applications. To realize this commitment, a major focus is on developing knowledge and expertise in the increasingly sophisticated methodology of the discipline. With this methodological core as its major emphasis and integrating link, the department has emphasized four content areas: clinical; cognition, brain, and behavior; developmental; and quantitative psychology. In the context of the mores of the academy, the faculty of each content area organize and coordinate work in the three broad domains of research/scholarship, graduate education and undergraduate education. Using our methodological core as a base, we strive to find intellectual common ground among the content areas within our department and other disciplines throughout the social sciences and the academy. Many of our faculty are members of more than one training area, which helps to foster communication and integration throughout the department.

Programs and Degrees Offered

Program	Degree	Application Deadline	Applications Received	Accepted	New Admits Enrolled (PT)	Total Enrolled (PT)	Degrees Awarded in 2014–2015	Median Years to Complete Degree	Dismissed/Withdrew
Cognition, Brain, and Behavior	PhD	December 1 (Fall)	29	4	2	15	3	6	0
Clinical Psychology	PhD	December 1 (Fall)	137	8	6	23	4	6.5	2
Developmental Psychology	PhD	December 1 (Fall)	22	5	5	17	2	5	0
Quantitative Psychology	PhD	December 1 (Fall)	22	9	3 (0)	16 (0)	2	5.6	0

APA Accreditation
Clinical PhD: Student Outcome Data website: http://psychology.nd.edu/graduate-programs/clinical-program/accreditation-data-outcome/.

Doctoral Degree (PhD Clinical Psychology): For those doctoral students for whom a professional internship was required in this program prior to graduation:
Total students who applied for an internship: 5
Total students who obtained an internship: 5
Total students who obtained a paid internship: 5
Total students who obtained an unpaid internship: 0
Total students who were placed in APA/CPA-accredited internships: 5
Total students placed in internships not APA/CPA-accredited, but listed with the Association of Psychology Postdoctoral and Internship Centers (APPIC): 0
Total students placed in internships conforming to guidelines of the Council of Directors of School Psychology Programs (CDSPP): 0
Total students placed in internships that were not APA/CPA-accredited, APPIC or CDSSP listed: 0

Internships/Practica

All students in the APA-accredited clinical program receive practicum placements at local training sites. Opportunities include the University Counseling Center in Saint Liam Hall, as well as a variety of practicum placements in agencies and institutions in the South Bend community. The University Counseling Center also houses an APA-accredited internship. Advanced students in the clinical program are eligible to apply.

Admissions

Entries appear in the following order: required test or GPA, minimum score (if required)/median score of students entering in 2015–2016.

Program	Degree	GRE-V	GRE-Q	GRE-Writing	GRE-Subject	Under-graduate GPA	Last 2 Years GPA	Psychology GPA	Master's GPA
Cognition, Brain, and Behavior	PhD	154/161	145/154	3/4.5	Not specified	2.78/3.75	Not specified	Not specified	Not specified
Clinical Psychology	PhD	152/161	148/158	4/4.5	Not specified	2.84/3.68	Not specified	Not specified	Not specified
Developmental Psychology	PhD	152/157	144/158	3/4.5	Not specified	2.81/3.73	Not specified	Not specified	Not specified
Quantitative Psychology	PhD	151/156	159/164	3/4.5	Not specified	3/3.63	Not specified	Not specified	Not specified

Admissions Requirements:

Degree	GRE	GRE-Subject	Letters of Recommendation	Research Statement	Writing Sample	CV	Interview
Doctoral	Required	Optional	3	Required	Required	Recommended	Required

Admissions Criteria:

GRE scores—high
Research experience—high
Work experience—low
Clinically related public service—low
GPA—high

Letters of recommendation—high
Interview—medium
Statement of goals and objectives—high
Undergraduate psychology preparation—high

For additional information on admission requirements, visit http://psychology.nd.edu/graduate-programs/admission-and-financial-support/.

Department Demographics

	Male (PT)	Female (PT)	Total	African-American/ Black (PT)	Hispanic/ Latino (PT)	Asian/ Pacific Islander (PT)	American Indian/ Alaska Native (PT)	Caucasian/ White (PT)	Unknown	Multiethnic (PT)	ADA (PT)	Int'l (PT)
Students	24 (0)	47 (0)	71	2 (0)	5 (0)	14 (0)	0 (0)	50 (0)	0 (0)	0 (0)	0 (0)	11 (0)

Financial Information/Assistance

Tuition: For information on tuition costs, visit http://studentaccounts.nd.edu/rates/.

Doctoral:
State residents: $49,450 per academic year.
Nonstate residents: $49,450 per academic year.

Financial Assistance:

	Teaching Assistantship (% Receiving)	Teaching Assistantship Tuition Remission	Research Assistantship (% Receiving)	Research Assistantship Tuition Remission	Fellowship (% Receiving)	Fellowship Tuition Remission
First-Year Student	$21,500 (20)	Full	$21,500 (60)	Full	$26,000 (20)	Full
Advanced Student	$21,500 (50)	Full	$21,500 (30)	Full	$26,000 (20)	Full

For additional information on financial assistance, visit http://graduateschool.nd.edu/admissions/financial-support/.

Employment of Department Graduates

Doctoral:
Enrolled in a postdoctoral residency/fellowship: 1
Employed in an academic position at a university: 4
Employed in academic position at a 2-year/4-year college: 3
Employed in business or industry: 3
Employed in government agency: 1
Employed in a hospital/medical center: 2
Total: 14

Additional Information

Housing and Day Care: On-campus housing is available. See the following website for more information: http://housing.nd.edu/graduate/. On-campus day care facilities are available. See the following website for more information: http://ecdc.nd.edu/.

Information for Students With Physical Disabilities: See the following website: http://disabilityservices.nd.edu/.

Special Facilities or Resources: We are involved in the development of innovative science and practice experiences for undergraduate and graduate students in the local community. Currently, many faculty have excellent relationships with community groups (e.g., the local schools, hospitals, Oaklawn Psychiatric Center, Logan Center, Center for the Homeless, Head Start). Many faculty conduct research with undergraduate and graduate students in these community settings. Over and above these research activities, many students volunteer in these agencies. Finally, clinical psychology graduate students receive supervision to work in such settings as the Memorial Epworth Hospital, Michiana EAP, Oaklawn Psychiatric Center, St. Joseph Medical Center, and the Center for the Homeless.

Application Information: Graduate Admissions, The Graduate School, University of Notre Dame, Notre Dame, IN 46556. *Fee:* $75. *Online application:* https://gradconnect.nd.edu/apply/.

Purdue University
Department of Educational Studies - Counseling Psychology
College of Education
100 North University Street
West Lafayette, IN 47907
Telephone: (765) 494-0837
Training Director: Ayse Ciftci, PhD

E-mail: ayse@purdue.edu
Web: http://www.edst.purdue.edu/counseling_psychology/

Orientation, Objectives, and Emphasis of Department
The counseling psychology program provides training in line with specific training goals. The first goal is to train scientist–practitioners in inquiry skills for use in advancing knowledge of psychology. The second goal is to train scientist–practitioners in inquiry skills for use in psychological conceptualization, diagnosis, intervention, and other counseling professional services to clients and consumers resulting from a sound theoretical and research knowledge base. The third goal is to develop scientist–practitioners who demonstrate ethical and professional behavior consistent with the standards of counseling psychology. Finally, the fourth goal is to prepare scientist–practitioners who can provide competent services that are responsive to individual and cultural differences in a multicultural environment.

Programs and Degrees Offered

Program	Degree	Application Deadline	Applica-tions Received	Accepted	New Admits Enrolled (PT)	Total Enrolled (PT)	Degrees Awarded in 2014–2015	Median Years to Complete Degree	Dismissed/ Withdrew
Counseling Psychology	PhD	December 1 (Fall)	64	8	8 (0)	32	6	6	0

APA Accreditation

Counseling PhD: Student Outcome Data website: http://www.edst.purdue.edu/counseling_psychology/student_admissions_outcomes.html.

Doctoral Degree (PhD Counseling Psychology): For those doctoral students for whom a professional internship was required in this program prior to graduation:

Total students who applied for an internship: 5
Total students who obtained an internship: 5
Total students who obtained a paid internship: 5
Total students who obtained an unpaid internship: 0
Total students who were placed in APA/CPA-accredited internships: 5
Total students placed in internships not APA/CPA-accredited, but listed with the Association of Psychology Postdoctoral and Internship Centers (APPIC): 0
Total students placed in internships conforming to guidelines of the Council of Directors of School Psychology Programs (CDSPP): 0
Total students placed in internships that were not APA/CPA-accredited, APPIC or CDSSP listed. 0

Internships/Practica

Students get practicum and internship placements at community mental health agencies, veterans affairs hospitals, college counseling centers, psychiatric and medical hospitals, prisons and group psychological practices.

Admissions

Entries appear in the following order: required test or GPA, minimum score (if required)/median score of students entering in 2015–2016.

Program	Degree	GRE-V	GRE-Q	GRE-Writing	GRE-Subject	Under-graduate GPA	Last 2 Years GPA	Psychol-ogy GPA	Master's GPA
Counseling Psychology	PhD	NA/NA	NA/NA	NA/NA	Not specified	NA/NA	Not specified	Not specified	NA/NA

Admissions Requirements:

Degree	GRE	GRE-Subject	Letters of Recom-mendation	Research Statement	Writing Sample	CV	Interview
Doctoral	Required	None	3	Required	Optional	Required	Required

Admissions Criteria:

GRE scores—high
Research experience—high
Work experience—medium
Clinically related public service—high
GPA—high

Letters of recommendation—high
Interview—high
Statement of goals and objectives—high
Undergraduate psychology preparation—medium

For additional information on admission requirements, visit http://www.edst.purdue.edu/counseling_psychology/admissions/index.html.

Department Demographics

	Male (PT)	Female (PT)	Total	African-American/ Black (PT)	Hispanic/ Latino (PT)	Asian/ Pacific Islander (PT)	American Indian/ Alaska Native (PT)	Caucasian/ White (PT)	Unknown	Multiethnic (PT)	ADA (PT)	Int'l (PT)
Students	7 (0)	25 (0)	32	2 (0)	2 (0)	10 (0)	0 (0)	13 (0)	5 (0)	0 (0)	0 (0)	9 (0)

Financial Information/Assistance

Tuition: For information on tuition costs, visit http://www.purdue.edu/bursar/tuition/index.html. Tuition is subject to change. Additional fees are assessed to students beyond the costs of tuition for the following: assessment course fees, technology fees, student fitness and wellness fees.

Doctoral:
State residents: $10,002 per academic year.
Nonstate residents: $28,804 per academic year.

Financial Assistance:

	Teaching Assistantship (% Receiving)	Teaching Assistantship Tuition Remission	Research Assistantship (% Receiving)	Research Assistantship Tuition Remission	Fellowship (% Receiving)	Fellowship Tuition Remission
First-Year Student	$14,200 (NA)	Full	$14,200 (NA)	Full	$17,040 (NA)	Full
Advanced Student	$14,200 (NA)	Full	$14,200 (NA)	Full	NA (NA)	NA

For additional information on financial assistance, visit https://www.purdue.edu/gradschool/funding/.

Employment of Department Graduates

Doctoral:
Enrolled in a postdoctoral residency/fellowship: 2
Employed in an academic position at a university: 1
Employed in a community mental health/counseling center: 2
Employed in a hospital/medical center: 1
Total: 6

Additional Information

Housing and Day Care: On-campus housing is available. See the following website for more information: http://www.housing.purdue.edu/. On-campus day care facilities are available. See the following website for more information: http://www.purdue.edu/hr/familyfriendly/purdueChildcare/index.html.

Information for Students With Physical Disabilities: See the following website: https://www.purdue.edu/studentsuccess/specialized/drc/.

Special Facilities or Resources: The Purdue Counseling and Guidance Center (PCGC) is the counseling service and training facility for the College of Education on the Purdue University campus. Students in their second year of training in the counseling psychology program provide counseling under the supervision of a faculty member to clients who are either college students or community members. To facilitate the counselors' training, all sessions are recorded. Recordings are used to help counselors provide competent and effective services. These recordings are used for counselor development and supervision purposes only, are kept confidential, and are then erased. Given these guidelines, individuals who seek counseling at the Counseling and Guidance Center understand and agree to these standards.

Application Information: Purdue University, Office of Graduate Studies, BRNG, Room 6104, 100 North University Street, West Lafayette, IN 47907. *Fee:* $60. *Online application:* https://app.applyyourself.com/?id=purduegrad.

Purdue University

Department of Psychological Sciences
College of Health and Human Sciences
701 Third Street
West Lafayette, IN 47906-2004
Telephone: (765) 494-6067
Professor and Head: Christopher R. Agnew

E-mail: nobrien@psych.purdue.edu
Web: http://www.purdue.edu/hhs/psy/

Orientation, Objectives, and Emphasis of Department

The dominant emphasis of the department is a commitment to research and scholarship as the major core of graduate education. All programs are structured so that students become involved in research activities almost immediately upon beginning their graduate education, and this involvement is expected to continue throughout an individual's entire graduate career.

Programs and Degrees Offered

Program	Degree	Application Deadline	Applications Received	Accepted	New Admits Enrolled (PT)	Total Enrolled (PT)	Degrees Awarded in 2014–2015	Median Years to Complete Degree	Dismissed/ Withdrew
Clinical Psychology	PhD	December 1 (Fall)	128	4	4 (0)	17 (0)	0		0
Cognitive Psychology	PhD	December 1 (Fall)	58	5	2 (0)	10 (0)	2	5	0
Industrial/ Organizational Psychology	PhD	December 1 (Fall)	52	2	2 (0)	12 (0)	1	5	0
Behavioral Neuroscience	PhD	December 1 (Fall)	12	1	1 (0)	9 (0)	2	5	0
Mathematical and Computational Cognitive Science	PhD	December 1 (Fall)	19	3	2 (0)	6 (0)	2	5	0
Social Psychology	PhD	December 1 (Fall)	40	0	0 (0)	11 (0)	4	5	0

APA Accreditation

Clinical PhD: Student Outcome Data website: http://www.purdue.edu/hhs/psy/graduate/research_training_areas/clinical_psychology/index.php.

Doctoral Degree (PhD Clinical Psychology): For those doctoral students for whom a professional internship was required in this program prior to graduation:
Total students who applied for an internship: 1
Total students who obtained an internship: 1
Total students who obtained a paid internship: 1
Total students who obtained an unpaid internship: 0
Total students who were placed in APA/CPA-accredited internships: 1
Total students placed in internships not APA/CPA-accredited, but listed with the Association of Psychology Postdoctoral and Internship Centers (APPIC): 0
Total students placed in internships conforming to guidelines of the Council of Directors of School Psychology Programs (CDSPP): 0
Total students placed in internships that were not APA/CPA-accredited, APPIC or CDSSP listed: 0

Internships/Practica

After the first year requirements, clinical psychology students enroll in clinical practica carried out in the Purdue Psychology Treatment and Research Clinics. Practica include providing services for anxiety disorders, depression, personality disorders, Attention Deficit Hyperactivity Disorder, and oppositional disorders. Practicum training emphasizes use of empirically corroborated interventions for particular problems. A year-long clinical internship is required in order to complete training.

Admissions

Entries appear in the following order: required test or GPA, minimum score (if required)/median score of students entering in 2015–2016.

Program	Degree	GRE-V	GRE-Q	GRE-Writing	GRE-Subject	Under-graduate GPA	Last 2 Years GPA	Psychology GPA	Master's GPA
Clinical Psychology	PhD	NA/160	NA/156	NA/3.5	Not specified	3/3.65	Not specified	Not specified	Not specified
Cognitive Psychology	PhD	NA/NA	NA/NA	NA/NA	Not specified	3/3.42	Not specified	Not specified	Not specified
Industrial/ Organizational Psychology	PhD	NA/NA	NA/NA	NA/NA	Not specified	3/3.54	Not specified	Not specified	Not specified
Behavioral Neuroscience	PhD	NA/NA	NA/NA	NA/NA	Not specified	3/3.4	Not specified	Not specified	Not specified
Mathematical and Computational Cognitive Science	PhD	NA/NA	NA/NA	NA/NA	Not specified	3/3.52	Not specified	Not specified	Not specified
Social Psychology	PhD	NA/NA	NA/NA	NA/NA	Not specified	3/3.51	Not specified	Not specified	Not specified

Admissions Requirements:

Degree	GRE	GRE-Subject	Letters of Recom-mendation	Research Statement	Writing Sample	CV	Interview
Doctoral	Required	Optional	3	Required	Optional	Required	Recom-mended

Please note if these criteria vary for different programs: Not all areas hold formal interviews. Clinically related public service is important if you are applying to the clinical program.

Admissions Criteria:

GRE scores—high
Research experience—medium
Work experience—low
Clinically related public service—medium
GPA—high

Letters of recommendation—high
Interview—high
Statement of goals and objectives—high
Undergraduate psychology preparation—medium

For additional information on admission requirements, visit http://www.purdue.edu/hhs/psy/graduate/prospective_students/applications_admissions.php.

Department Demographics

	Male (PT)	Female (PT)	Total	African-American/ Black (PT)	Hispanic/ Latino (PT)	Asian/ Pacific Islander (PT)	American Indian/ Alaska Native (PT)	Caucasian/ White (PT)	Unknown	Multiethnic (PT)	ADA (PT)	Int'l (PT)
Students	23 (0)	42 (0)	65	4 (0)	2 (0)	5 (0)	1 (0)	53 (0)	0 (0)	0 (0)	0 (0)	13 (0)

Financial Information/Assistance

Tuition: For information on tuition costs, visit http://www.purdue.edu/bursar/tuition/. Tuition is subject to change.

Doctoral:
State residents: $10,002 per academic year.
State residents: $348 per credit hour.
Nonstate residents: $28,804 per academic year.
Nonstate residents: $948 per credit hour.

Financial Assistance:

	Teaching Assistantship (% Receiving)	Teaching Assistantship Tuition Remission	Research Assistantship (% Receiving)	Research Assistantship Tuition Remission	Fellowship (% Receiving)	Fellowship Tuition Remission
First-Year Student	$15,000 (NA)	Full	$15,000 (NA)	Full	$17,000 (NA)	Full
Advanced Student	$16,000 (NA)	Full	$16,000 (NA)	Full	$17,000 (NA)	Full

For additional information on financial assistance, visit http://www.purdue.edu/hhs/psy/graduate/current_students/financial_support.php.

Employment of Department Graduates

Doctoral:
Employed in an academic position at a university: 11
Total: 11

Additional Information

Housing and Day Care: On-campus housing is available. See the following website for more information: http://www.housing.purdue.edu. On-campus day care facilities are available. See the following website for more information: http://www.purdue.edu/hr/familyfriendly/purdueChildcare/index.html.

Information for Students With Physical Disabilities: See the following website: https://www.purdue.edu/studentsuccess/specialized/drc/.

Special Facilities or Resources: Excellent research facilities are available in many areas, including more than 35 computer-controlled laboratories.

Application Information: Nancy O'Brien, Psychological Sciences, Purdue University, 701 Third Street, West Lafayette, IN 47906-2004. *Fee:* $60. *Online application:* https://gradapply.purdue.edu/apply/.

Saint Francis, University of
Psychology and Counseling
School of Liberal Arts and Sciences
2701 Spring Street
Fort Wayne, IN 46808
Telephone: (260) 399-7700 ext 8425
Chairperson: John Brinkman, PhD

E-mail: jbrinkman@sf.edu
Web: http://bhvscience.sf.edu/

Orientation, Objectives, and Emphasis of Department
The MS in Psychology program is designed for people who are either interested in preparation for doctoral work, or furthering their professional careers through a greater understanding of basic psychological principles. The primary goal of the program is to give students a solid, graduate-level grounding in psychology. This program emphasizes a mastery of psychological fundamentals, i.e., theories and research methods, areas of specialization (development, social, abnormal behavior, physiological data, personality development and behavior management techniques). The program of study leading to the MS Degree in Mental Health Counseling is designed to prepare persons to function as Licensed Mental Health Counselors (LMHC) in health care residential, private practice, community agency, governmental, business, and industrial settings.

Programs and Degrees Offered

Program	Degree	Application Deadline	Applica-tions Received	Accepted	New Admits Enrolled (PT)	Total Enrolled (PT)	Degrees Awarded in 2014–2015	Median Years to Complete Degree	Dismissed/ Withdrew
Psychology	MA/MS	Rolling	17	5	2 (0)	2 (3)	8	2	0
Clinical Mental Health Counseling	MA/MS	Rolling	38	17	4 (1)	20 (16)	14	3	0
School Counseling	Med	Rolling	21	14	4 (3)	9 (7)	2	2.5	0

Internships/Practica

General Psychology students can elect to do a practicum experience. This experience would be 150 clock hours (10 hours/week) of supervised practical field experience tailored to the individual needs/interests of the students. Students choosing to have a practicum experience have an on-site supervisor who helps define, mentor, and direct the student's activities. Students also have 15 hours of supervision on campus. This experience is designed to give students an opportunity to integrate formal education with work experience. Mental Health Counseling (MS) has required practicum and internship: Practicum: 1 semester—100 hours/60 face-to-face client contact hours. Internship: 1 or 2 semesters—600 hours/240 face-to-face client contact hours. Advanced Internship: 1 semester—300 hours/120 face-to-face client contact hours. MSEd School Counseling students complete a 105-hour practicum and non-teacher licensed candidates complete a 600-hour, two-semester internship.

Admissions

Entries appear in the following order: required test or GPA, minimum score (if required)/median score of students entering in 2015–2016.

Program	Degree	GRE-V	GRE-Q	GRE-Writing	GRE-Subject	Under-graduate GPA	Last 2 Years GPA	Psychol-ogy GPA	Master's GPA
Psychology	MA/MS	Not specified	Not specified	Not specified	Not specified	3/NA	Not specified	Not specified	Not specified
Clinical Mental Health Counseling	MA/MS	Not specified	Not specified	Not specified	Not specified	3/NA	Not specified	Not specified	Not specified
School Counseling	Med	NA/NA	NA/NA	Not specified	Not specified	3/NA	Not specified	Not specified	Not specified

Admissions Requirements:

Degree	GRE	GRE-Subject	Letters of Recom-mendation	Research Statement	Writing Sample	CV	Interview
Master's/Specialist	Optional	Optional	2	Required	Optional	Optional	Required

Admissions Criteria:

GRE scores—low
Research experience—low
Work experience—high
Clinically related public service—high
GPA—high

Letters of recommendation—high
Interview—high
Statement of goals and objectives—high
Undergraduate psychology preparation—high

Department Demographics

	Male (PT)	Female (PT)	Total	African-American/ Black (PT)	Hispanic/ Latino (PT)	Asian/ Pacific Islander (PT)	American Indian/ Alaska Native (PT)	Caucasian/ White (PT)	Unknown (PT)	Multiethnic (PT)	ADA (PT)	Int'l (PT)
Students	7 (3)	22 (20)	52	2 (3)	1 (2)	0 (0)	1 (0)	21 (18)	3 (0)	1 (0)	1 (0)	0 (0)

Financial Information/Assistance

Tuition: For information on tuition costs, visit http://financialaid.sf.edu/tuition-fees/graduate-tuition/. Tuition is subject to change.

Master's:
State residents: $870 per credit hour.
Nonstate residents: $870 per credit hour.

Financial Assistance:

	Teaching Assistantship (% Receiving)	Teaching Assistantship Tuition Remission	Research Assistantship (% Receiving)	Research Assistantship Tuition Remission	Fellowship (% Receiving)	Fellowship Tuition Remission
First-Year Student	NA (NA)	Partial	NA (NA)	NA	NA (NA)	NA
Advanced Student	NA (NA)	Partial	NA (NA)	NA	NA (NA)	NA

For additional information on financial assistance, visit http://gradschool.sf.edu/financial-aid/paying-graduate-school/.

Employment of Department Graduates

Master's:
Enrolled in a psychology doctoral program: 1
Employed in an academic position at a university: 2
Employed in a professional position in a school system: 5
Employed in business or industry: 1
Employed in government agency: 2
Employed in a community mental health/counseling center: 11
Employed in a hospital/medical center: 1
Still seeking employment: 1
Total: 24

Additional Information

Housing and Day Care: No on-campus housing is available. No on-campus day care facilities are available.

Information for Students With Physical Disabilities: See the following website: http://disabilityservices.sf.edu/.

Application Information: Office of Admissions, Trinity Hall, Room 110A, University of Saint Francis, 2701 Spring Street, Fort Wayne, IN 46808. *Fee:* $20. *Online application:* https://ecampus.sf.edu/ICS/Admissions/.

Valparaiso University
Department of Psychology
1001 Campus Drive South
Valparaiso, IN 46383
Telephone: (219) 464-5440
Director of Graduate Programs in Counseling & Psychology: David B. Simpson, PhD
Web: http://www.valpo.edu/psychology/graduate/index.php

E-mail: David.Simpson@valpo.edu

Orientation, Objectives, and Emphasis of Department

The Clinical Mental Health Counseling program at Valparaiso University serves as an ethical and professional point of entry for individuals from diverse populations interested in acquiring the requisite skills associated with becoming a licensed professional counselor. The CMHC program emphasizes the development of professional identity, awareness of cultural diversity and spirituality, and basic counselor competencies. It is the mission of the Clinical Mental Health Counseling program faculty to prepare counselors who will ethically promote the well-being of individuals, families, mental health organizations and communities located in metropolitan, rural and global settings.

Programs and Degrees Offered

Program	Degree	Application Deadline	Applica-tions Received	Accepted	New Admits Enrolled (PT)	Total Enrolled (PT)	Degrees Awarded in 2014–2015	Median Years to Complete Degree	Dismissed/ Withdrew
Clinical Mental Health Counseling	MA/MS	February 15 (Fall)	37	20	15 (0)	41 (6)	26	2	1

Internships/Practica

Numerous practicum and internship sites are available in the Northwest Indiana region and our proximity to Chicago and southern Michigan provides addition clinical training opportunities for our students. Clinical/experiential training is perhaps the single most important element of a counseling training program. The knowledge, skills, and attitudes acquired through academic coursework may be severely tested by the demands of real world counseling situations. Students are mentored through the process by both faculty and supervisors from each training site.

Admissions

Entries appear in the following order: required test or GPA, minimum score (if required)/median score of students entering in 2015–2016.

Program	Degree	GRE-V	GRE-Q	GRE-Writing	GRE-Subject	Under-graduate GPA	Last 2 Years GPA	Psychol-ogy GPA	Master's GPA
Clinical Mental Health Counseling	MA/MS	Not specified	Not specified	Not specified	Not specified	3/3.33	Not specified	Not specified	Not specified

Admissions Requirements:

Degree	GRE	GRE-Subject	Letters of Recom-mendation	Research Statement	Writing Sample	CV	Interview
Master's/Specialist	Optional	None	3	Required	Required	Required	Recom-mended

Admissions Criteria:

Research experience—low
Work experience—medium
Clinically related public service—medium
GPA—high

Letters of recommendation—high
Interview—high
Statement of goals and objectives—high
Undergraduate psychology preparation—low

For additional information on admission requirements, visit http://www.valpo.edu/psychology/academics/graduate-programs/prospective-students/.

Department Demographics

	Male (PT)	Female (PT)	Total	African-American/ Black (PT)	Hispanic/ Latino (PT)	Asian/ Pacific Islander (PT)	American Indian/ Alaska Native (PT)	Caucasian/ White (PT)	Unknown	Multiethnic (PT)	ADA (PT)	Int'l (PT)
Students	8 (1)	39 (8)	56	3 (1)	2 (1)	0 (0)	0 (0)	26 (4)	8 (1)	2 (0)	0 (0)	0 (0)

Financial Information/Assistance

Tuition: For information on tuition costs, visit http://www.valpo.edu/grad/prospective/tuition.php. Tuition is subject to change. Additional fees are assessed to students beyond the costs of tuition for the following: administrative/graduate student fees.

Master's:
State residents: $615 per credit hour.
Nonstate residents: $615 per credit hour.

Financial Assistance:

	Teaching Assistantship (% Receiving)	Teaching Assistantship Tuition Remission	Research Assistantship (% Receiving)	Research Assistantship Tuition Remission	Fellowship (% Receiving)	Fellowship Tuition Remission
First-Year Student	NA (28)	NA	$2,500 (5)	NA	$3,000 (75)	NA
Advanced Student	NA (NA)	NA	NA (NA)	NA	NA (NA)	NA

For additional information on financial assistance, visit http://www.valpo.edu/grad/prospective/scholarshipintern.php.

Employment of Department Graduates

Master's:
Enrolled in a psychology doctoral program: 1
Employed in other positions at a higher education institution: 1
Employed in a community mental health/counseling center: 18
Employed in a hospital/medical center: 3
Other employment position: 3
Total: 26

Additional Information

Housing and Day Care: On-campus housing is available. See the following website for more information: http://www.valpo.edu/grad/resources/gradhousing.php. No on-campus day care facilities are available.

Information for Students With Physical Disabilities: See the following website: http://www.valpo.edu/disabilityss/.

Application Information: Valparaiso University, Graduate School, 1700 Chapel Drive, Kretzmann Hall, Rm 114, Valparaiso, IN 46383. *Fee:* $30. *Online application:* http://www.valpo.edu/grad/apply.

Iowa State University
Department of Psychology
Liberal Arts & Sciences
Lagomarcino Hall-901 Stange Road
Ames, IA 50011-1041
Telephone: (515) 294-1742
Chairperson: Carolyn Cutrona, PhD

E-mail: psychadm@iastate.edu
Web: http://www.psychology.iastate.edu/

Orientation, Objectives, and Emphasis of Department
Graduate programs emphasize the acquisition of a broad base of knowledge in psychology as well as concentration on the content and methodological skills requisite to performance in teaching, research, and applied activities. A strong research orientation is evident in all areas of the department, with involvement in research being required of all doctoral students throughout their graduate studies. Curriculum requirements for the degrees are based on a core course system, which is designed to enable students to tailor a program best suited to their particular objectives. Subsequent courses, seminars, research, and applied experiences are determined by the student and his or her graduate advisory committee. Additionally, teaching experience is available to all doctoral students, and extensive supervised practicum experience is required of students in the applied programs.

Programs and Degrees Offered

Program	Degree	Application Deadline	Applications Received	Accepted	New Admits Enrolled (PT)	Total Enrolled (PT)	Degrees Awarded in 2014–2015	Median Years to Complete Degree	Dismissed/ Withdrew
Counseling Psychology	PhD	December 1 (Fall)	95	5	4 (0)	30 (0)	2	6	0
Social Psychology	PhD	December 15 (Fall)	61	9	6 (0)	24 (0)	1	5	0
Cognitive Psychology	PhD	December 15 (Fall)	38	1	1 (0)	12 (0)	2	5	0
Quantitative Certificate	Other	Rolling	10	10	7	10	6	1.5	0

APA Accreditation
Counseling PhD: Student Outcome Data website: http://counseling.psych.iastate.edu/.

Doctoral Degree (PhD Counseling Psychology): For those doctoral students for whom a professional internship was required in this program prior to graduation:
Total students who applied for an internship: 2
Total students who obtained an internship: 2
Total students who obtained a paid internship: 2
Total students who obtained an unpaid internship: 0
Total students who were placed in APA/CPA-accredited internships: 2
Total students placed in internships not APA/CPA-accredited, but listed with the Association of Psychology Postdoctoral and Internship Centers (APPIC): 0
Total students placed in internships conforming to guidelines of the Council of Directors of School Psychology Programs (CDSPP): 0
Total students placed in internships that were not APA/CPA-accredited, APPIC or CDSSP listed: 0

Internships/Practica
Sequential, progressive practica provide students in our professional program with individually supervised applied training in their specialty area. All supervision is provided by appropriately certified/licensed faculty and adjuncts in a range of settings, including university counseling centers, major hospitals, outpatient clinics, child and adolescent treatment centers, correctional facilities, and the public school system. Based on such practicum experience and their academic training, ISU students compete successfully for select predoctoral internships across the country.

Admissions

Entries appear in the following order: required test or GPA, minimum score (if required)/median score of students entering in 2015–2016.

Program	Degree	GRE-V	GRE-Q	GRE-Writing	GRE-Subject	Under-graduate GPA	Last 2 Years GPA	Psychology GPA	Master's GPA
Counseling Psychology	PhD	156/168	151/164	4/4.5	NA/655	3.5/3.47	3.66/3.56	3.62/3.6	NA/NA
Social Psychology	PhD	162/171	154/172	4/4.5	Not specified	3.76/3.55	3.95/3.66	3.83/3.68	Not specified
Cognitive Psychology	PhD	156/164	156/155	4/4.5	Not specified	3.62/3.56	3.59/3.64	3.61/3.64	NA/NA
Quantitative Certificate	Other	Not specified	Not specified	Not specified	Not specified	Not specified	Not specified	Not specified	Not specified

Admissions Requirements:

Degree	GRE	GRE-Subject	Letters of Recom-mendation	Research Statement	Writing Sample	CV	Interview
Doctoral	Required	Recom-mended	3	Required	Optional	Optional	Required

Please note if these criteria vary for different programs: Interviews important for Counseling area, less so for Social and Cognitive. Clinically related service or work is more important in Counseling than in the other areas.

Admissions Criteria:

GRE scores—high
Research experience—high
Work experience—low
Clinically related public service—low
GPA—high

Letters of recommendation—high
Interview—high
Statement of goals and objectives—high
Undergraduate psychology preparation—medium
Fit with faculty research—high

For additional information on admission requirements, visit http://www.psychology.iastate.edu/graduate-program/admissions/.

Department Demographics

	Male (PT)	Female (PT)	Total	African-American/ Black (PT)	Hispanic/ Latino (PT)	Asian/ Pacific Islander (PT)	American Indian/ Alaska Native (PT)	Caucasian/ White (PT)	Unknown	Multiethnic (PT)	ADA (PT)	Int'l (PT)
Students	26 (0)	40 (0)	66	2 (0)	6 (0)	3 (0)	1 (0)	39 (0)	8 (0)	0 (0)	0 (0)	8 (0)

Financial Information/Assistance

Tuition: For information on tuition costs, visit http://www.registrar.iastate.edu//fees/. Tuition is subject to change. Additional fees are assessed to students beyond the costs of tuition for the following: activity, student fees assessed, approximately $521/semester.

Doctoral:
State residents: $8,130 per academic year.
Nonstate residents: $21,054 per academic year.

Financial Assistance:

	Teaching Assistantship (% Receiving)	Teaching Assistantship Tuition Remission	Research Assistantship (% Receiving)	Research Assistantship Tuition Remission	Fellowship (% Receiving)	Fellowship Tuition Remission
First-Year Student	$17,100 (NA)	Full	$17,100 (NA)	Full	$17,100 (NA)	Full
Advanced Student	$17,100 (NA)	Full	$17,100 (NA)	Full	NA (NA)	NA

For additional information on financial assistance, visit http://www.psychology.iastate.edu/graduate-program/financial-aid/.

Employment of Department Graduates

Doctoral:
Employed in an academic position at a university: 3
Total: 3

Additional Information

Housing and Day Care: On-campus housing is available. See the following website for more information: http://www.housing.iastate.edu/. On-campus day care facilities are available. See the following website for more information: http://www.hrs.iastate.edu/hrs/node/137.

Information for Students With Physical Disabilities: See the following website: http://www.sdr.dso.iastate.edu/.

Special Facilities or Resources: The department maintains the full array of physical facilities and equipment required for behavioral research. Observational and videotaping facilities are available for research and applied training. The department maintains a microcomputer lab, and the university maintains a superior computation center. We have an eye-tracking lab for faculty and student use. Statistical consulting is also available from faculty jointly appointed with the Statistics Department and the Behavioral and Survey Research Center.

Application Information: Iowa State University, Graduate Admissions, Department of Psychology, W112 Lagomarcino, Ames, IA 50011. *Fee:* $60. *Online application:* https://www.admissions.iastate.edu/apply/online/.

Iowa State University
Human Development & Family Studies
Human Sciences
2330 Palmer
Ames, IA 50011-4380
Telephone: (515) 294-6321
Chairperson: Carl Weems

E-mail: hdfs-grad-adm@iastate.edu
Web: http://www.hdfs.hs.iastate.edu/

Orientation, Objectives, and Emphasis of Department
The mission of the Department of Human Development and Family Studies is to have a positive impact on the quality of life for individuals and families across the lifespan, as well as for schools and communities through research, teaching, extension/outreach, and service. The Department of Human Development and Family Studies offers multidisciplinary educational programs covering a range of human sciences and services related to children and families. Research in the department is focused on three signature areas: early development, care and education; family policy and practice; and lifespan development. Graduates have been successful nationally and internationally in obtaining teaching, research, and service positions in research institutes, human service agencies, and colleges and universities, including the cooperative extension service.

Programs and Degrees Offered

Program	Degree	Application Deadline	Applications Received	Accepted	New Admits Enrolled (PT)	Total Enrolled (PT)	Degrees Awarded in 2014–2015	Median Years to Complete Degree	Dismissed/Withdrew
Human Development and Family Studies	MA/MS	December 1 (Fall)	16	8	6 (1)	7 (1)	11		0
Human Development and Family Studies	PhD	December 1 (Fall)	34	19	17 (0)	29 (0)	4		

Admissions

Entries appear in the following order: required test or GPA, minimum score (if required)/median score of students entering in 2015–2016.

Program	Degree	GRE-V	GRE-Q	GRE-Writing	GRE-Subject	Undergraduate GPA	Last 2 Years GPA	Psychology GPA	Master's GPA
Human Development and Family Studies	MA/MS	NA/NA	NA/NA	NA/NA	Not specified	NA/NA	Not specified	Not specified	Not specified
Human Development and Family Studies	PhD	NA/NA	NA/NA	NA/NA	Not specified	NA/NA	Not specified	Not specified	NA/NA

Admissions Requirements:

Degree	GRE	GRE-Subject	Letters of Recommendation	Research Statement	Writing Sample	CV	Interview
Master's/Specialist	Required	Required	3	Required	None	Required	None
Doctoral	Required	Required	3	Required	None	Required	None

Admissions Criteria:

GRE scores—medium
Research experience—medium
Work experience—medium
Clinically related public service—low

GPA—medium
Letters of recommendation—high
Statement of goals and objectives—medium

For additional information on admission requirements, visit http://www.hdfs.hs.iastate.edu/graduate/apply/.

Department Demographics

	Male (PT)	Female (PT)	Total	African-American/ Black (PT)	Hispanic/ Latino (PT)	Asian/ Pacific Islander (PT)	American Indian/ Alaska Native (PT)	Caucasian/ White (PT)	Unknown (PT)	Multiethnic (PT)	ADA (PT)	Int'l (PT)
Students	5 (1)	31 (0)	37	2 (0)	3 (0)	14 (0)	0 (0)	17 (1)	0 (0)	0 (0)	0 (0)	9 (0)

Financial Information/Assistance

Tuition: For information on tuition costs, visit http://www.registrar.iastate.edu/fees/. Tuition is subject to change. Additional fees are assessed to students beyond the costs of tuition for the following: Activity, Services, Building & Recreation Fee; Health Facility Fee; Health Fee; Technology Fee.

Doctoral:
State residents: $8,130 per academic year.
State residents: $452 per credit hour.
Nonstate residents: $21,054 per academic year.
Nonstate residents: $1,169 per credit hour.

Master's:
State residents: $8,130 per academic year.
State residents: $452 per credit hour.
Nonstate residents: $21,054 per academic year.
Nonstate residents: $1,169 per credit hour.

Financial Assistance:

	Teaching Assistantship (% Receiving)	Teaching Assistantship Tuition Remission	Research Assistantship (% Receiving)	Research Assistantship Tuition Remission	Fellowship (% Receiving)	Fellowship Tuition Remission
First-Year Student	$17,100 (90)	Full	$17,100 (90)	Full	NA (NA)	Full
Advanced Student	$17,100 (90)	Full	$17,100 (90)	Full	NA (NA)	Full

For additional information on financial assistance, visit http://www.hdfs.hs.iastate.edu/graduate/financing/.

Employment of Department Graduates

No information provided.

Additional Information

Housing and Day Care: On-campus housing is available. See the following website for more information: http://www.housing.iastate.edu/. On-campus day care facilities are available. See the following website for more information: http://www.hrs.iastate.edu/hrs/node/137.

Information for Students With Physical Disabilities: See the following website: http://www.sdr.dso.iastate.edu/.

Special Facilities or Resources: Our outreach and engagement programs include: HDFS Family Extension, Iowa State University Child Development Lab, and Financial Counseling Clinic.

Application Information: Fee: $60. *Online application:* http://www.admissions.iastate.edu/apply/graduate.php.

Iowa, University of
Department of Psychological and Brain Sciences
Liberal Arts and Sciences
11 Seashore Hall East
Iowa City, IA 52242-1407
Telephone: (319) 335-2406
Chairperson: Jodie Plumert

E-mail: jodie-plumert@uiowa.edu
Web: http://www.psychology.uiowa.edu

Orientation, Objectives, and Emphasis of Department
The mission of the PhD program is to produce professional scholars who contribute significantly to the advancement of scientific psychological knowledge and who can effectively teach students about the science of psychology. Some of these scholars are also prepared to deliver psychological services. Our goal is to produce PhDs who have developed world-class programs of research, who have published extensively, and who have both broad and deep knowledge. Graduate training is organized into six broad training areas: Behavioral and Cognitive Neuroscience, Clinical Psychology, Cognition and Perception, Developmental Science, Health Psychology, and Social Psychology. The training programs are flexible, and there is considerable overlap and interaction among students and faculty in all areas, leading to an exciting intellectual environment. Students in good standing receive full

support for at least five years. The students–faculty ratio remains quite low, usually less than 2 to 1. The department has been successful in establishing strong ties with other campus units such as Psychiatry, Neurology, the law school, and the business school. Through these associations, one may study such topics as the law and psychology, aging, consumer behavior, and neuroscience.

Programs and Degrees Offered

Program	Degree	Application Deadline	Applica-tions Received	Accepted	New Admits Enrolled (PT)	Total Enrolled (PT)	Degrees Awarded in 2014–2015	Median Years to Complete Degree	Dismissed/Withdrew
Behavioral and Cognitive Neuroscience	PhD	December 1 (Fall)	25	5	2 (0)	15 (0)	2	5.3	0
Clinical Psychology	PhD	December 1 (Fall)	102	8	4 (0)	33 (0)	2	7	0
Cognition and Perception	PhD	December 1 (Fall)	22	5	3 (0)	12 (0)	4	5.8	0
Developmental Science	PhD	December 1 (Fall)	9	4	0 (0)	5 (0)	2	7	2
Social Psychology	PhD	December 1 (Fall)	61	1	1 (0)	8 (0)	2	6	0
Health Psychology	PhD	December 1 (Fall)	9	0	0 (0)	2 (0)	0		0

APA Accreditation

Clinical PhD: Student Outcome Data website: http://www.psychology.uiowa.edu/research/clinical_admissions_outcomes.

Doctoral Degree (PhD Clinical Psychology): For those doctoral students for whom a professional internship was required in this program prior to graduation:
Total students who applied for an internship: 7
Total students who obtained an internship: 7
Total students who obtained a paid internship: 7
Total students who obtained an unpaid internship: 0
Total students who were placed in APA/CPA-accredited internships: 7
Total students placed in internships not APA/CPA-accredited, but listed with the Association of Psychology Postdoctoral and Internship Centers (APPIC): 0
Total students placed in internships conforming to guidelines of the Council of Directors of School Psychology Programs (CDSPP): 0
Total students placed in internships that were not APA/CPA-accredited, APPIC or CDSSP listed: 0

Internships/Practica

Students in our Clinical Psychology program participate in clinical assessment and treatment practica at our department-run clinic (the Carl E. Seashore Psychology Training Clinic) and in clinics run by departments such as Psychiatry and Neurology at the University of Iowa Hospitals and Clinics.

Admissions

Entries appear in the following order: required test or GPA, minimum score (if required)/median score of students entering in 2015–2016.

Program	Degree	GRE-V	GRE-Q	GRE-Writing	GRE-Subject	Under-graduate GPA	Last 2 Years GPA	Psychol-ogy GPA	Master's GPA
Behavioral and Cognitive Neuroscience	PhD	NA/158	NA/155	NA/5	Not specified	NA/NA	Not specified	Not specified	Not specified
Clinical Psychology	PhD	NA/160	NA/158	NA/5	Not specified	NA/3.9	Not specified	Not specified	Not specified
Cognition and Perception	PhD	NA/154	NA/156	NA/4.5	Not specified	NA/NA	Not specified	Not specified	Not specified

Admissions *(con't.)*

Program	Degree	GRE-V	GRE-Q	GRE-Writing	GRE-Subject	Under-graduate GPA	Last 2 Years GPA	Psychology GPA	Master's GPA
Developmental Science	PhD	NA/162	NA/153	NA/4.25	Not specified	NA/NA	Not specified	Not specified	Not specified
Social Psychology	PhD	NA/162	NA/156	NA/5	Not specified	NA/NA	Not specified	Not specified	Not specified
Health Psychology	PhD	NA/164	NA/159	NA/4	Not specified	NA/NA	Not specified	Not specified	Not specified

Admissions Requirements:

Degree	GRE	GRE-Subject	Letters of Recommendation	Research Statement	Writing Sample	CV	Interview
Doctoral	Required	Optional	3	Required	None	Required	Required

Admissions Criteria:

GRE scores—medium
Research experience—high
Work experience—low
Clinically related public service—medium
GPA—medium

Letters of recommendation—high
Interview—high
Statement of goals and objectives—high
Undergraduate psychology preparation—medium

For additional information on admission requirements, visit http://www.psychology.uiowa.edu/graduate-program/application-information.

Department Demographics

	Male (PT)	Female (PT)	Total	African-American/ Black (PT)	Hispanic/ Latino (PT)	Asian/ Pacific Islander (PT)	American Indian/ Alaska Native (PT)	Caucasian/ White (PT)	Unknown (PT)	Multiethnic (PT)	ADA (PT)	Int'l (PT)
Students	21 (0)	54 (0)	75	0 (0)	7 (0)	4 (0)	0 (0)	51 (0)	0 (0)	1 (0)	0 (0)	12 (0)

Financial Information/Assistance

Tuition: For information on tuition costs, visit https://www.maui.uiowa.edu/maui/pub/tuition/rates.page. Tuition is subject to change. Additional fees are assessed to students beyond the costs of tuition for the following: additional student fees of $1,015 per academic year.

Doctoral:
State residents: $8,556 per academic year.
Nonstate residents: $26,060 per academic year.

Financial Assistance:

	Teaching Assistantship (% Receiving)	Teaching Assistantship Tuition Remission	Research Assistantship (% Receiving)	Research Assistantship Tuition Remission	Fellowship (% Receiving)	Fellowship Tuition Remission
First-Year Student	$22,997 (40)	Full	$22,997 (40)	Full	$24,816 (20)	Full
Advanced Student	$22,997 (23)	Full	$22,997 (60)	Full	$24,816 (17)	Full

For additional information on financial assistance, visit http://www.grad.uiowa.edu/funding-your-education.

Employment of Department Graduates

Doctoral:
Enrolled in a postdoctoral residency/fellowship: 6
Employed in an academic position at a university: 3
Employed in academic position at a 2-year/4-year college: 2
Employed in business or industry: 1
Total: 12

Additional Information

Housing and Day Care: On-campus housing is available. See the following website for more information: http://grad.admissions.uiowa.edu/about-iowa/housing. On-campus day care facilities are available. See the following website for more information: http://hr.uiowa.edu/family-services/child-care/.

Information for Students With Physical Disabilities: See the following website: https://sds.studentlife.uiowa.edu/.

Special Facilities or Resources: The Kenneth W. Spence Laboratories of Psychology and adjoining space in Seashore Hall and Stuit Hall include automated data acquisition and analysis systems, extensive computing facilities, observation suites with remote audiovisual control and recording equipment, multiple animal facilities, several surgeries, a histology laboratory, soundproof chambers, closed-circuit TV systems, electrophysiological recording rooms, conditioning laboratories, the Carl E. Seashore Psychology Training Clinic, and well-equipped electronic, mechanical, woodworking, and computer shops. Well over half of the departmental laboratories have been extensively renovated or created anew within the past 5 years. In addition, many resources are available through collaboration with colleagues at the university hospital, the Iowa Veterans Administration Hospital, community service centers, and the Colleges of Medicine, Nursing, Dentistry, Engineering, Business, Education, and Law.

Application Information: Graduate Admissions Office, 11 Seashore Hall East, Iowa City, IA 52242-1407. *Fee:* $60. *Online application:* http://grad.admissions.uiowa.edu/apply.

Iowa, University of
Department of Psychological and Quantitative Foundations
College of Education
361 Lindquist Center
Iowa City, IA 52242
Telephone: (319) 335-5578
Chairperson: Timothy Ansley

E-mail: kunjal-harwani@uiowa.edu
Web: http://www.education.uiowa.edu/pq

Orientation, Objectives, and Emphasis of Department

The counseling psychology program endorses a scientist–practitioner model and expects students to be competent researchers and practitioners at the completion of the program; graduates find positions in various settings such as higher education, counseling centers, clinics, private practice, and hospitals.The school psychology program is committed to training professional psychologists who are knowledgeable about providing services to children in school, medical, and mental health settings; the program's curriculum has been developed to reflect consideration of multicultural issues within psychological theory, research, and professional development. Students who are interested in understanding the psychology of education and learning can choose to do an MA in the learning sciences or a PhD in educational psychology; the online MA has an applied focus, whereas the PhD is research-focused. The educational measurement and statistics graduate programs prepare students for positions in educational measurement, evaluation, research, and statistical methods. Positions are found at universities, state and federal agencies, test publishing organizations, larger school systems, state departments of education, and research centers. The MA in educational measurement and statistics can also be completed online.

Programs and Degrees Offered

Program	Degree	Application Deadline	Applications Received	Accepted	New Admits Enrolled (PT)	Total Enrolled (PT)	Degrees Awarded in 2014–2015	Median Years to Complete Degree	Dismissed/Withdrew
Educational Psychology	PhD	January 15 (Fall)	11	2	2	18	1		0

Programs and Degrees Offered *(con't.)*

Program	Degree	Application Deadline	Applica-tions Received	Accepted	New Admits Enrolled (PT)	Total Enrolled (PT)	Degrees Awarded in 2014–2015	Median Years to Complete Degree	Dismissed/ Withdrew
Educational Measurement and Statistics	MA/MS	December 1 (Fall), October 1 (Spring), March 1 (Summer)	21	10	10	23	13		0
School Psychology	PhD	January 1 (Fall)	24	2	2	35	6	6	0
Counseling Psychology	PhD	December 1 (Fall)	70	6	6	49	4	6	1
Educational Measurement and Statistics	PhD	December 1 (Fall), October 1 (Spring), March 1 (Summer)	34	9	9	39	4		
Educational Psychology-Learning Sciences	MA/MS	January 15 (Fall)	14	4	4	7	6		

APA Accreditation

School PhD: Student Outcome Data website: http://www.education.uiowa.edu/pq/schpsych/student-outcomes.
Counseling PhD: Student Outcome Data website: http://www.education.uiowa.edu/pq/counspsy/student-outcomes.

Doctoral Degree (PhD School Psychology): For those doctoral students for whom a professional internship was required in this program prior to graduation:
Total students who applied for an internship: 5
Total students who obtained an internship: 5
Total students who obtained a paid internship: 5
Total students who obtained an unpaid internship: 0
Total students who were placed in APA/CPA-accredited internships: 2
Total students placed in internships not APA/CPA-accredited, but listed with the Association of Psychology Postdoctoral and Internship Centers (APPIC): 1
Total students placed in internships conforming to guidelines of the Council of Directors of School Psychology Programs (CDSPP): 2
Total students placed in internships that were not APA/CPA-accredited, APPIC or CDSSP listed: 0

Doctoral Degree (PhD Counseling Psychology): For those doctoral students for whom a professional internship was required in this program prior to graduation:
Total students who applied for an internship: 6
Total students who obtained an internship: 6
Total students who obtained a paid internship: 6
Total students who obtained an unpaid internship: 0
Total students who were placed in APA/CPA-accredited internships: 6
Total students placed in internships not APA/CPA-accredited, but listed with the Association of Psychology Postdoctoral and Internship Centers (APPIC): 0
Total students placed in internships conforming to guidelines of the Council of Directors of School Psychology Programs (CDSPP): 0
Total students placed in internships that were not APA/CPA-accredited, APPIC or CDSSP listed: 0

Internships/Practica

Practica are available at university counseling and community mental health centers; at the VA and the University of Iowa Hospitals and Clinics; at the Berlin-Blank International Center for Gifted Education and Talent Development; and in schools.

Admissions

Entries appear in the following order: required test or GPA, minimum score (if required)/median score of students entering in 2015–2016.

Program	Degree	GRE-V	GRE-Q	GRE-Writing	GRE-Subject	Under-graduate GPA	Last 2 Years GPA	Psychol-ogy GPA	Master's GPA
Educational Psychology	PhD	150/NA	152/NA	Not specified	Not specified	NA/NA	Not specified	Not specified	Not specified
Educational Measurement and Statistics	MA/MS	NA/NA	NA/NA	Not specified	Not specified	NA/NA	Not specified	Not specified	Not specified
School Psychology	PhD	NA/NA	NA/NA	Not specified	Not specified	NA/NA	Not specified	Not specified	Not specified
Counseling Psychology	PhD	152/NA	151/NA	Not specified	Not specified	3/NA	Not specified	Not specified	3.5/NA
Educational Measurement and Statistics	PhD	Not specified	Not specified	Not specified	Not specified	Not specified	Not specified	Not specified	Not specified
Educational Psychology-Learning Sciences	MA/MS	Not specified	Not specified	Not specified	Not specified	Not specified	Not specified	Not specified	Not specified

Admissions Requirements:

Degree	GRE	GRE-Subject	Letters of Recom-mendation	Research Statement	Writing Sample	CV	Interview
Master's/Specialist	Required	Optional	3	Required	Optional	Optional	Required
Doctoral	Required	Recom-mended	3	Required	Required	Required	Required

Admissions Criteria:

GRE scores—high
Research experience—high
Work experience—medium
Clinically related public service—high
GPA—high

Letters of recommendation—high
Interview—medium
Statement of goals and objectives—high
Undergraduate psychology preparation—low

For additional information on admission requirements, visit http://grad.admissions.uiowa.edu/colleges/college-education.

Department Demographics

	Male (PT)	Female (PT)	Total	African-American/ Black (PT)	Hispanic/ Latino (PT)	Asian/ Pacific Islander (PT)	American Indian/ Alaska Native (PT)	Caucasian/ White (PT)	Unknown	Multiethnic (PT)	ADA (PT)	Int'l (PT)
Students	38 (19)	89 (31)	177	6 (1)	8 (1)	8 (1)	0 (0)	60 (30)	5 (2)	2 (0)	0 (0)	38 (15)

Financial Information/Assistance

Tuition: For information on tuition costs, visit https://www.maui.uiowa.edu/maui/pub/tuition/rates.page. Additional fees are assessed to students beyond the costs of tuition for the following: technology, activities/events, services/health, buildings/facilities.

Doctoral:
State residents: $10,210 per academic year.
Nonstate residents: $27,682 per academic year.

Master's:
State residents: $10,210 per academic year.
Nonstate residents: $27,682 per academic year.

Financial Assistance:

	Teaching Assistantship (% Receiving)	Teaching Assistantship Tuition Remission	Research Assistantship (% Receiving)	Research Assistantship Tuition Remission	Fellowship (% Receiving)	Fellowship Tuition Remission
First-Year Student	NA (NA)	NA	$18,262 (NA)	Partial	NA (NA)	NA
Advanced Student	$18,262 (NA)	Partial	$18,262 (NA)	Partial	$18,262 (NA)	Partial

For additional information on financial assistance, visit http://grad.admissions.uiowa.edu/finances.

Employment of Department Graduates

Master's:
Enrolled in another graduate/professional program: 10
Employed in other positions at a higher education institution: 1
Employed in a professional position in a school system: 2
Employed in business or industry: 2
Still seeking employment: 1
Other employment position: 1
Total: 17

Doctoral:
Enrolled in a postdoctoral residency/fellowship: 5
Employed in independent practice: 1
Employed in other positions at a higher education institution: 3
Employed in a professional position in a school system: 2
Employed in business or industry: 4
Employed in government agency: 2
Employed in a community mental health/counseling center: 2
Employed in a hospital/medical center: 1
Other employment position: 1
Total: 21

Additional Information

Housing and Day Care: On-campus housing is available. See the following website for more information: http://housing.uiowa.edu/. On-campus day care facilities are available. See the following website for more information: http://hr.uiowa.edu/family-services/child-care.

Information for Students With Physical Disabilities: See the following website: http://diversity.uiowa.edu/disability-resources.

Special Facilities or Resources: There are centers that focus on disability research and education and on assistive technology. Students can use the Statistics Outreach Center or the Writing Resource. Computers are available in the Graduate Commons; in the Educational Technology Center; and in a 24-hour lab. Across the street in the main library (part of University Libraries) is the Learning Commons. The Iowa Testing Programs, which develops the Iowa Assessments, is located in the building: Students have access to test databases for research and may work with faculty or research assistantships that are supported by the Iowa Measurement Research Foundation. The Belin-Blank International Center for Gifted Education and Talent Development also provides opportunities for research, teaching, and counseling experiences as well as assistantship support. The University of Iowa Hospitals and Clinics provide multiple research opportunities. Also located in Iowa City is ACT.

Application Information: Fee: $60. *Online application:* http://grad.admissions.uiowa.edu/apply.

Northern Iowa, University of
Department of Psychology
Social and Behavioral Sciences
1078 Bartlett Hall
Cedar Falls, IA 50614-0505
Telephone: (319) 273-2303
Head: Adam Butler

E-mail: harton@uni.edu
Web: http://www.uni.edu/csbs/psych/psychology-graduate-program

---

Orientation, Objectives, and Emphasis of Department
The MA program provides a strong empirical, research-based approach to the study of human behavior. Students may select one of two emphases: (a) clinical science or (b) social psychology. They may also choose to complete an individualized study program in conjunction with a faculty mentor. The objectives of the program are (a) to develop skills in research methodology, (b) to gain

knowledge of basic areas of scientific psychology, and (c) to obtain competence in research and/or clinical skills. The clinical science emphasis is designed for those who wish to either obtain doctoral degrees in clinical or counseling psychology or become master's-level providers of services operating in clinical settings under appropriate supervision. These students also pursue research-related careers. The social emphasis is designed for students who wish to pursue doctoral degrees in social psychology or master's-level research or teaching positions.

Programs and Degrees Offered

Program	Degree	Application Deadline	Applica-tions Received	Accepted	New Admits Enrolled (PT)	Total Enrolled (PT)	Degrees Awarded in 2014–2015	Median Years to Complete Degree	Dismissed/ Withdrew
Social Psychology	MA/MS	February 1 (Fall), Rolling	23	10	4 (0)	9 (0)	3	2	0
Clinical Science	MA/MS	February 1 (Fall), Rolling	23	8	5 (0)	7 (0)	4	2	0
Individualized Study	MA/MS	February 1 (Fall), Rolling	5	0	0 (0)	1 (1)	1	2	0

Internships/Practica

A variety of practicum sites are available for second year students in the clinical science emphasis. Clinical practicum sites have included the University Counseling Center, the State Psychiatric Hospital, correctional facilities, private hospitals, educational settings, and community-based agencies. Students in the social emphasis conduct independent first-year research projects under faculty supervision and present these research projects at regional and national professional conferences.

Admissions

Entries appear in the following order: required test or GPA, minimum score (if required)/median score of students entering in 2015–2016.

Program	Degree	GRE-V	GRE-Q	GRE-Writing	GRE-Subject	Under-graduate GPA	Last 2 Years GPA	Psychol-ogy GPA	Master's GPA
Social Psychology	MA/MS	NA/150	NA/154	NA/3.5	Not specified	3/3.58	Not specified	Not specified	Not specified
Clinical Science	MA/MS	NA/152	NA/153	NA/4.5	Not specified	3/3.73	Not specified	Not specified	Not specified
Individualized Study	MA/MS	NA/NA	NA/NA	NA/NA	Not specified	NA/NA	Not specified	Not specified	Not specified

Admissions Requirements:

Degree	GRE	GRE-Subject	Letters of Recom-mendation	Research Statement	Writing Sample	CV	Interview
Master's/Specialist	Required	Optional	3	Required	Optional	Optional	Optional

Please note if these criteria vary for different programs: Clinically Related Public Service is important only for the clinical science emphasis.

Admissions Criteria:

GRE scores—high
Research experience—high
Work experience—low
Clinically related public service—medium
GPA—high

Letters of recommendation—high
Interview—medium
Statement of goals and objectives—high
Undergraduate psychology preparation—medium

For additional information on admission requirements, visit http://www.uni.edu/csbs/psych/application-procedure.

Department Demographics

	Male (PT)	Female (PT)	Total	African-American/ Black (PT)	Hispanic/ Latino (PT)	Asian/ Pacific Islander (PT)	American Indian/ Alaska Native (PT)	Caucasian/ White (PT)	Unknown	Multiethnic (PT)	ADA (PT)	Int'l (PT)
Students	5 (1)	11 (0)	17	1 (0)	1 (0)	4 (0)	1 (0)	9 (1)	0 (0)	0 (0)	0 (0)	3 (0)

Financial Information/Assistance

Tuition: For information on tuition costs, visit http://www.uni.edu/tuition/. Tuition is subject to change. Additional fees are assessed to students beyond the costs of tuition for the following: health, technology, recreation, etc.

Master's:
State residents: $8,292 per academic year.
Nonstate residents: $18,766 per academic year.

Financial Assistance:

	Teaching Assistantship (% Receiving)	Teaching Assistantship Tuition Remission	Research Assistantship (% Receiving)	Research Assistantship Tuition Remission	Fellowship (% Receiving)	Fellowship Tuition Remission
First-Year Student	$5,000 (50)	NA	$5,000 (39)	NA	$4,146 (100)	NA
Advanced Student	$5,000 (50)	NA	$5,000 (50)	NA	$4,146 (100)	NA

For additional information on financial assistance, visit http://www.grad.uni.edu/assistantships.

Employment of Department Graduates

Master's:
Enrolled in a psychology doctoral program: 4
Employed in other positions at a higher education institution: 1
Employed in business or industry: 1
Employed in a community mental health/counseling center: 2
Total: 8

Additional Information

Housing and Day Care: On-campus housing is available. See the following website for more information: http://www.uni.edu/dor/. On-campus day care facilities are available. See the following website for more information: http://www.uni.edu/cdc/.

Information for Students With Physical Disabilities: See the following website: http://www.uni.edu/sds/.

Special Facilities or Resources: The department provides laboratory space for research with human participants; access to community facilities and populations for applied research; 24/7 access to computers for graduate students; and office space for graduate students. We are affiliated with a center for social research and students have access to psychiatric, work, and community populations for research projects.

Application Information: Department of the Registrar, University of Northern Iowa, Cedar Falls, IA 50614. *Fee:* $50. *Online application:* http://www.uni.edu/admissions/apply.

Emporia State University

Department of Psychology
The Teachers College
1 Kellogg Circle, Campus Box 4031
Emporia, KS 66801-5087
Telephone: (620) 341-5317
Chairperson: Jim Persinger

E-mail: psych@emporia.edu
Web: http://www.emporia.edu/psych

Orientation, Objectives, and Emphasis of Department

Emporia State offers the Master of Science degree in clinical psychology, school psychology, and industrial/organizational (I/O) psychology. Additionally, students may pursue the EdS degree in school psychology.

Programs and Degrees Offered

Program	Degree	Application Deadline	Applications Received	Accepted	New Admits Enrolled (PT)	Total Enrolled (PT)	Degrees Awarded in 2014–2015	Median Years to Complete Degree	Dismissed/ Withdrew
School Psychology	EdS	Rolling	12	10	10 (0)	18 (5)	6	3	0
Clinical Psychology	MA/MS	Rolling	30	16	8	22 (2)	9	2.5	
Industrial/ Organizational Psychology	MA/MS	Rolling	15	11	8 (0)	28 (5)	8	2	0

Internships/Practica

For Clinical students, internship is 750 clock hours in a mental health setting supervised by a PhD psychologist. For I/O students, the internship is 300 clock hours in a business setting performing I/O-related tasks. School Psychology students do semester internships/practica in the schools. In addition, there is a 1-year, paid, post-EdS internship for School Psychology.

Admissions

Entries appear in the following order: required test or GPA, minimum score (if required)/median score of students entering in 2015–2016.

Program	Degree	GRE-V	GRE-Q	GRE-Writing	GRE-Subject	Undergraduate GPA	Last 2 Years GPA	Psychology GPA	Master's GPA
School Psychology	EdS	NA/NA	NA/NA	Not specified	Not specified	3/NA	Not specified	Not specified	Not specified
Clinical Psychology	MA/MS	NA/NA	NA/NA	Not specified	Not specified	3/NA	3.25/NA	3/NA	Not specified
Industrial/ Organizational Psychology	MA/MS	NA/NA	NA/NA	Not specified	Not specified	3/NA	Not specified	Not specified	Not specified

Admissions Requirements:

Degree	GRE	GRE-Subject	Letters of Recommendation	Research Statement	Writing Sample	CV	Interview
Master's/Specialist	Required	Optional	3	Required	Optional	Recommended	None

Admissions Criteria:

GRE scores—medium
Research experience—medium
Work experience—medium
Clinically related public service—low

GPA—high
Letters of recommendation—high
Statement of goals and objectives—medium
Undergraduate psychology preparation—medium

For additional information on admission requirements, visit http://www.emporia.edu/psych/graduate-programs/.

Department Demographics

	Male (PT)	Female (PT)	Total	African-American/ Black (PT)	Hispanic/ Latino (PT)	Asian/ Pacific Islander (PT)	American Indian/ Alaska Native (PT)	Caucasian/ White (PT)	Unknown	Multiethnic (PT)	ADA (PT)	Int'l (PT)
Students	26 (4)	49 (6)	85	10 (2)	4 (1)	4 (1)	0 (0)	51 (6)	0 (0)	6 (0)	2 (0)	0 (0)

Financial Information/Assistance

Tuition: For information on tuition costs, visit http://www.emporia.edu/busaff/student-information/tuition-and-waivers.html. Tuition is subject to change.

Master's:
State residents: $215 per credit hour.
Nonstate residents: $668 per credit hour.

Financial Assistance:

	Teaching Assistantship (% Receiving)	Teaching Assistantship Tuition Remission	Research Assistantship (% Receiving)	Research Assistantship Tuition Remission	Fellowship (% Receiving)	Fellowship Tuition Remission
First-Year Student	$7,315 (NA)	Full	$7,315 (NA)	Full	$300 (NA)	Partial
Advanced Student	$7,315 (NA)	Full	$7,315 (NA)	Full	$500 (NA)	Partial

For additional information on financial assistance, visit http://www.emporia.edu/grad/financial/.

Employment of Department Graduates

Master's:
Enrolled in a psychology doctoral program: 4
Enrolled in another graduate/professional program: 5
Employed in an academic position at a university: 1
Employed in academic position at a 2-year/4-year college: 2
Employed in other positions at a higher education institution: 1
Employed in a professional position in a school system: 6
Employed in business or industry: 8
Employed in government agency: 2
Employed in a community mental health/counseling center: 7
Employed in a hospital/medical center: 1
Still seeking employment: 1
Do not know: 2
Total: 40

Additional Information

Housing and Day Care: On-campus housing is available. See the following website for more information: http://www.emporia.edu/reslife/. On-campus day care facilities are available. See the following website for more information: http://www.emporia.edu/teach/cece/.

Information for Students With Physical Disabilities: See the following website: http://www.emporia.edu/disabilityservices/.

Special Facilities or Resources: In 2012, all classrooms in the Department of Psychology were upgraded with multimedia technology. Facilities include cognitive, animal behavior, and physiological psychology laboratories; a complete animal vivarium; suites of rooms for administration of psychological tests and observation of testing or clinical and counseling sessions; and microprocessors and mainframe computer facilities. The computers and animal lab have been periodically updated every 3 years.

Application Information: Dean of Graduate Studies and Research, Campus Box 4003, Emporia State University, 1 Kellogg Circle, Emporia, KS 66801. *Fee:* $40. *Online application:* http://www.emporia.edu/grad/admissions/.

Fort Hays State University
Department of Psychology
600 Park Street
Hays, KS 67601-4099
Telephone: (785) 628-4405
Chairperson: Jennifer Bonds-Raacke

E-mail: jmbondsraacke@fhsu.edu
Web: http://www.fhsu.edu/psych/

Orientation, Objectives, and Emphasis of Department
The department emphasizes a research approach to the understanding of behavior. We strive to provide basic empirical and theoretical foundations of psychology to prepare the student for doctoral study, for teaching, or for employment in a service or professional agency. The school program offers broad preparation for students in both psychology and education and includes training as a consultant to work with educators and parents as well as with children. The clinical program emphasizes the preparation of rural mental health workers, although many graduates go on to doctoral programs. The general program is intended to prepare the student for doctoral study.

Programs and Degrees Offered

Program	Degree	Application Deadline	Applications Received	Accepted	New Admits Enrolled (PT)	Total Enrolled (PT)	Degrees Awarded in 2014–2015	Median Years to Complete Degree	Dismissed/ Withdrew
Applied Clinical Psychology	MA/MS	March 15 (Fall), October 15 (Spring)	12	11	8 (0)	16 (0)	3	2	2
General Psychology	MA/MS	Rolling	8	7	0 (6)	4 (6)	0		2
School Psychology	MA/MS	March 15 (Fall), October 15 (Spring), Rolling	36	17	3 (14)	4 (32)	4	2	0
School Psychology	EdS	March 15 (Fall), October 15 (Spring), Rolling	11	7	3 (3)	3 (8)	5	1	0

Internships/Practica
All students in the applied psychology programs (clinical, school) are required to take a practicum in their specialty area. Students in the clinical psychology program receive initial practicum experience in the Kelly Center (an on-campus psychological services center), and then are required to complete an internship at a regional mental health agency or other approved agency. Students in the school psychology program receive initial practicum experience in a school district. School psychology graduates are also required to complete 1 year of paid, supervised post-EdS internship before being recommended for full licensure (certification). Students in the general psychology program have the opportunity to take apprenticeships concentrating on the teaching of psychology.

Admissions

Entries appear in the following order: required test or GPA, minimum score (if required)/median score of students entering in 2015–2016.

Program	Degree	GRE-V	GRE-Q	GRE-Writing	GRE-Subject	Under-graduate GPA	Last 2 Years GPA	Psychol-ogy GPA	Master's GPA
Applied Clinical Psychology	MA/MS	NA/NA	NA/NA	Not specified	Not specified	3/NA	3/NA	3/NA	Not specified
General Psychology	MA/MS	NA/NA	NA/NA	Not specified	Not specified	3/NA	3/NA	3/NA	Not specified
School Psychology	MA/MS	NA/NA	NA/NA	Not specified	Not specified	3/NA	3/NA	3/NA	Not specified
School Psychology	EdS	NA/NA	NA/NA	Not specified	Not specified	3/NA	Not specified	Not specified	Not specified

Admissions Requirements:

Degree	GRE	GRE-Subject	Letters of Recom-mendation	Research Statement	Writing Sample	CV	Interview
Master's/Specialist	Required	None	2	Required	Optional	Optional	None

Admissions Criteria:

GRE scores—medium
Research experience—medium
Work experience—medium
Clinically related public service—medium
GPA—high

Letters of recommendation—high
Interview—medium
Statement of goals and objectives—high
Undergraduate psychology preparation—medium

For additional information on admission requirements, visit http://www.fhsu.edu/psych/graduate-studies/.

Department Demographics

	Male (PT)	Female (PT)	Total	African-American/ Black (PT)	Hispanic/ Latino (PT)	Asian/ Pacific Islander (PT)	American Indian/ Alaska Native (PT)	Caucasian/ White (PT)	Unknown	Multiethnic (PT)	ADA (PT)	Int'l (PT)
Students	6 (11)	21 (35)	73	1 (1)	2 (1)	2 (1)	0 (0)	22 (36)	0 (6)	0 (1)	0 (0)	0 (0)

Financial Information/Assistance

Tuition: For information on tuition costs, visit http://www.fhsu.edu/academic/gradschl/tuition/. Tuition is subject to change.

Master's:
State residents: $214 per credit hour.
Nonstate residents: $543 per credit hour.

Financial Assistance:

	Teaching Assistantship (% Receiving)	Teaching Assistantship Tuition Remission	Research Assistantship (% Receiving)	Research Assistantship Tuition Remission	Fellowship (% Receiving)	Fellowship Tuition Remission
First-Year Student	NA (NA)	Partial	NA (NA)	NA	NA (NA)	NA
Advanced Student	$4,250 (NA)	Full	NA (NA)	NA	$200 (NA)	NA

For additional information on financial assistance, visit http://www.fhsu.edu/academic/gradschl/Graduate-Assistantships/.

Employment of Department Graduates

Master's:
Enrolled in another graduate/professional program: 4
Employed in a professional position in a school system: 4
Employed in business or industry: 1
Employed in a community mental health/counseling center: 3
Total: 12

Additional Information

Housing and Day Care: On-campus housing is available. See the following website for more information: http://www.fhsu.edu/reslife/. On-campus day care facilities are available. See the following website for more information: http://www.fhsu.edu/tigertots/.

Information for Students With Physical Disabilities: See the following website: http://www.fhsu.edu/disability/.

Special Facilities or Resources: The Department of Psychology now occupies a newly remodeled building in the center of campus. Some of the new facilities in this building include: a 25-machine computer facility with separate spaces for individualized research and full Internet connections; testing and observation rooms for children, adults, and small groups; separate research and teaching labs for the major areas of psychology; and several seminar rooms. We are located adjacent to the student psychological services center. There is an active social organization for psychology graduate students. All students at the university have free remote Internet access.

Application Information: Dean of the Graduate School, Fort Hays State University, 600 Park Street, Hays, KS 67601-4099. *Fee:* $40. *Online application:* http://www.fhsu.edu/academic/gradschl/apply/.

Kansas State University

Department of Psychological Sciences
College of Arts and Sciences
492 Bluemont Hall, 1100 Mid-Campus Drive
Manhattan, KS 66506-5302
Telephone: (785) 532-6850
Head: Michael Young

E-mail: psych@ksu.edu
Web: http://www.k-state.edu/psych

Orientation, Objectives, and Emphasis of Department

Both teaching and research are heavily emphasized. Training prepares students for a variety of positions, including teaching and research positions in colleges and universities. Students have also assumed research and evaluative positions in hospitals, clinics, governmental agencies, and industry.

Programs and Degrees Offered

Program	Degree	Application Deadline	Applications Received	Accepted	New Admits Enrolled (PT)	Total Enrolled (PT)	Degrees Awarded in 2014–2015	Median Years to Complete Degree	Dismissed/ Withdrew
Animal Learning/ Behavioral Neuroscience	PhD	December 20 (Fall)	10	2	2 (0)	8 (0)	1	5	1
Cognitive and Human Factors	PhD	December 20 (Fall)	18	3	3 (0)	15 (0)	3	5	0
Social/ Personality Psychology	PhD	December 20 (Fall)	25	3	2	11	4	5	0
Industrial/ Organizational Psychology	PhD	December 20 (Fall)	12	2	1 (0)	12 (0)	1	5	0

Programs and Degrees Offered (cont.)

Program	Degree	Application Deadline	Applications Received	Accepted	New Admits Enrolled (PT)	Total Enrolled (PT)	Degrees Awarded in 2014–2015	Median Years to Complete Degree	Dismissed/Withdrew
Industrial/Organizational (Distance)	MA/MS	April 30 (Fall)	25	10	0 (12)	0 (25)	10	2	0

Internships/Practica

Arrangements for internships in human factors/applied experimental and industrial/organizational psychology vary widely and are made on an individual basis.

Admissions

Entries appear in the following order: required test or GPA, minimum score (if required)/median score of students entering in 2015–2016.

Program	Degree	GRE-V	GRE-Q	GRE-Writing	GRE-Subject	Undergraduate GPA	Last 2 Years GPA	Psychology GPA	Master's GPA
Animal Learning/Behavioral Neuroscience	PhD	Not specified	Not specified	Not specified	Not specified	Not specified	Not specified	Not specified	Not specified
Cognitive and Human Factors	PhD	Not specified	Not specified	Not specified	Not specified	NA/NA	Not specified	Not specified	Not specified
Social/Personality Psychology	PhD	Not specified	Not specified	Not specified	Not specified	Not specified	Not specified	Not specified	Not specified
Industrial/Organizational Psychology	PhD	Not specified	Not specified	Not specified	Not specified	Not specified	Not specified	Not specified	Not specified
Industrial/Organizational (Distance)	MA/MS	Not specified	Not specified	Not specified	Not specified	NA/NA	Not specified	Not specified	Not specified

Admissions Requirements:

Degree	GRE	GRE-Subject	Letters of Recommendation	Research Statement	Writing Sample	CV	Interview
Master's/Specialist	Optional	None	3	Required	Optional	Required	None
Doctoral	Required	Optional	3	Required	Optional	Required	None

Admissions Criteria:

GRE scores—high
Research experience—high
Work experience—low
GPA—high

Letters of recommendation—high
Interview—low
Statement of goals and objectives—high
Undergraduate psychology preparation—medium

For additional information on admission requirements, visit http://www.k-state.edu/psych/graduate/application/procedures.html.

Department Demographics

	Male (PT)	Female (PT)	Total	African-American/Black (PT)	Hispanic/Latino (PT)	Asian/Pacific Islander (PT)	American Indian/Alaska Native (PT)	Caucasian/White (PT)	Unknown	Multiethnic (PT)	ADA (PT)	Int'l (PT)
Students	24 (10)	22 (15)	71	1 (1)	2 (2)	3 (0)	0 (0)	39 (7)	0 (0)	1 (0)	0 (0)	3 (0)

Financial Information/Assistance

Tuition: For information on tuition costs, visit http://www.k-state.edu/sfa/costofattendance/. Tuition is subject to change.

Doctoral:
State residents: $380 per credit hour.
Nonstate residents: $859 per credit hour.

Master's:
State residents: $380 per credit hour.
Nonstate residents: $859 per credit hour.

Financial Assistance:

	Teaching Assistantship (% Receiving)	Teaching Assistantship Tuition Remission	Research Assistantship (% Receiving)	Research Assistantship Tuition Remission	Fellowship (% Receiving)	Fellowship Tuition Remission
First-Year Student	$11,758 (50)	Full	$15,900 (NA)	Partial	NA (NA)	NA
Advanced Student	$12,792 (NA)	Full	$15,900 (NA)	Partial	NA (NA)	NA

For additional information on financial assistance, visit http://www.k-state.edu/psych/graduate/application/financial.html.

Employment of Department Graduates

Doctoral:
Employed in an academic position at a university: 4
Employed in other positions at a higher education institution: 1
Employed in business or industry: 2
Total: 7

Additional Information

Housing and Day Care: On-campus housing is available. See the following website for more information: http://housing.k-state.edu/living-options/apartments/. On-campus day care facilities are available. See the following website for more information: http://www.k-state.edu/ccd/.

Information for Students With Physical Disabilities: See the following website: http://www.k-state.edu/accesscenter/.

Special Facilities or Resources: The department has rooms for individual and group research; several computer laboratories and remote terminal access to mainframe computers; a photographic darkroom; one-way observation facilities; an electrically shielded, light-tight, sound-deadened room for auditory and visual research; laboratories for behavioral research with animals; surgical and histological facilities; and colony rooms.

Application Information: Graduate Admissions, Department of Psychological Sciences, 492 Bluemont Hall, 1100 Mid-campus Drive, Kansas State University, Manhattan, KS 66506-5302. *Fee:* $50. *Online application:* https://www.applyweb.com/kstateg/.

Kansas, University of
Department of Applied Behavioral Science
College of Liberal Arts and Sciences
1000 Sunnyside Avenue
Lawrence, KS 66045-7555
Telephone: (785) 864-4840
Chairperson: Florence DiGennaro Reed

E-mail: absc@ku.edu
Web: http://www.absc.ku.edu/

Orientation, Objectives, and Emphasis of Department
The primary purpose of the program is to train students in basic and applied research in behavior analysis. It features emphases in applied behavior analysis, early childhood, developmental disabilities, organizational behavior management, community health and development, the experimental analysis of human and animal behavior, conceptual issues in behavior analysis, independent living, and rehabilitation. Throughout the PhD training sequence, students work closely as junior colleagues with a faculty adviser

and a research group. Although students typically work with one faculty adviser, they are free to select a different adviser if their interests change during the course of their training. Students participate in research throughout their graduate careers in an individualized, intensive program. As a result, most students complete more research projects than those required for the degree.

Programs and Degrees Offered

Program	Degree	Application Deadline	Applica-tions Received	Accepted	New Admits Enrolled (PT)	Total Enrolled (PT)	Degrees Awarded in 2014–2015	Median Years to Complete Degree	Dismissed/Withdrew
Behavioral Psychology	PhD	December 15 (Fall)	35	2	2	35	9	5	0
Applied Behavioral Science	MA/MS	December 15 (Fall)	26	2	2	7	7	3	0

Internships/Practica

A wide variety of research settings and practicum sites are available to graduate students. They include: Behavioral Pediatrics; Center for Independent Living; Center for the Study of Mental Retardation and Related Problems; Child and Family Research Center; Community Programs for Adults with Mental Retardation; Edna A. Hill Child Development Center; Experimental Analysis of Behavior Laboratories; Performance Management Laboratory; Family Enhancement Project; Gerontology Center; Juniper Gardens Project; Research on Children with Retardation; Schiefelbusch Institute for Life Span Studies; and the Work Group on Health Promotion and Community Development.

Admissions

Entries appear in the following order: required test or GPA, minimum score (if required)/median score of students entering in 2015–2016.

Program	Degree	GRE-V	GRE-Q	GRE-Writing	GRE-Subject	Under-graduate GPA	Last 2 Years GPA	Psychol-ogy GPA	Master's GPA
Behavioral Psychology	PhD	Not specified	Not specified	Not specified	Not specified	Not specified	Not specified	Not specified	Not specified
Applied Behavioral Science	MA/MS	Not specified	Not specified	Not specified	Not specified	Not specified	Not specified	Not specified	Not specified

Admissions Requirements:

Degree	GRE	GRE-Subject	Letters of Recom-mendation	Research Statement	Writing Sample	CV	Interview
Master's/Specialist	Optional	Optional	3	Required	Optional	Required	Recom-mended
Doctoral	Optional	Optional	3	Required	Optional	Required	Recom-mended

Please note if these criteria vary for different programs: Applicants designate individual faculty members whom they want as advisors. Only those faculty members review the applications and make their admission decisions.

Admissions Criteria:

GRE scores—low
Research experience—high
Work experience—high
Clinically related public service—medium
GPA—high

Letters of recommendation—high
Interview—high
Statement of goals and objectives—high
Undergraduate psychology preparation—medium

For additional information on admission requirements, visit http://absc.ku.edu/graduate-admission-tab-3.

Department Demographics

	Male (PT)	Female (PT)	Total	African-American/ Black (PT)	Hispanic/ Latino (PT)	Asian/ Pacific Islander (PT)	American Indian/ Alaska Native (PT)	Caucasian/ White (PT)	Unknown	Multiethnic (PT)	ADA (PT)	Int'l (PT)
Students	14 (0)	28 (0)	42	2 (0)	1 (0)	2 (0)	1 (0)	36 (0)	0 (0)	0 (0)	1 (0)	3 (0)

Financial Information/Assistance

Tuition: For information on tuition costs, visit http://affordability.ku.edu/costs. Tuition is subject to change. Additional fees are assessed to students beyond the costs of tuition for the following: student services. Tuition costs vary by program.

Doctoral:
State residents: $346 per credit hour.
Nonstate residents: $809 per credit hour.

Master's:
State residents: $346 per credit hour.
Nonstate residents: $809 per credit hour.

Financial Assistance:

	Teaching Assistantship (% Receiving)	Teaching Assistantship Tuition Remission	Research Assistantship (% Receiving)	Research Assistantship Tuition Remission	Fellowship (% Receiving)	Fellowship Tuition Remission
First-Year Student	NA (NA)	Full	NA (NA)	Full	NA (NA)	Full
Advanced Student	NA (NA)	Full	NA (NA)	Full	NA (NA)	Full

For additional information on financial assistance, visit http://graduate.ku.edu/funding.

Employment of Department Graduates

Master's:
Enrolled in a psychology doctoral program: 7
Total: 7

Doctoral:
Employed in an academic position at a university: 6
Employed in business or industry: 3
Total: 9

Additional Information

Housing and Day Care: On-campus housing is available. See the following website for more information: http://www.housing.ku.edu/. On-campus day care facilities are available. See the following website for more information: http://www.hilltop.ku.edu/.

Information for Students With Physical Disabilities: See the following website: http://access.ku.edu/.

Special Facilities or Resources: A wide range of research settings are available to graduate students. Populations and settings include both typically developing and disabled infants, toddlers, preschool children, elementary school settings, adolescents, adults, and elders. In addition, the department has an animal laboratory facility.

Application Information: Fee: $65. Online application: https://www.applyweb.com/apply/kugrad/.

Kansas, University of
Department of Psychology
College of Liberal Arts and Sciences
426 Fraser Hall, 1415 Jayhawk Boulevard
Lawrence, KS 66045-7556
Telephone: (785) 864-4195
Chairperson: Ruth Ann Atchley

E-mail: psycgrad@ku.edu
Web: http://psych.ku.edu/

Orientation, Objectives, and Emphasis of Department

With 36 faculty, the department offers a wide range of opportunities for the study and treatment of human psychological and behavioral functioning. Students develop skills in statistics, research methods, and specific content areas with basic and applied emphases, with the flexibility to tailor programs to individual students' needs. Students in all programs (Clinical, Developmental, Quantitative, Cognitive, and Social) may also complete coursework toward a minor in quantitative psychology.

Programs and Degrees Offered

Program	Degree	Application Deadline	Applications Received	Accepted	New Admits Enrolled (PT)	Total Enrolled (PT)	Degrees Awarded in 2014–2015	Median Years to Complete Degree	Dismissed/Withdrew
Clinical Psychology	PhD	December 1 (Fall)	145	6	6 (0)	45 (0)	5	6.5	0
Cognitive Psychology	PhD	December 1 (Fall)	11	2	2	11 (0)	1	6	1
Quantitative Psychology	PhD	December 1 (Fall)	13	1	0	10 (0)	1	6	0
Social Psychology	PhD	December 1 (Fall)	64	10	2	21 (0)	1	6	1
Developmental Psychology	PhD	December 1 (Fall)	0	0	0	1	0		0

APA Accreditation

Clinical PhD: Student Outcome Data website: http://psych.ku.edu/clinical/.

Doctoral Degree (PhD Clinical Psychology): For those doctoral students for whom a professional internship was required in this program prior to graduation:

Total students who applied for an internship: 8
Total students who obtained an internship: 8
Total students who obtained a paid internship: 8
Total students who obtained an unpaid internship: 0
Total students who were placed in APA/CPA-accredited internships: 8
Total students placed in internships not APA/CPA-accredited, but listed with the Association of Psychology Postdoctoral and Internship Centers (APPIC): 0
Total students placed in internships conforming to guidelines of the Council of Directors of School Psychology Programs (CDSPP): 0
Total students placed in internships that were not APA/CPA-accredited, APPIC or CDSSP listed: 0

Admissions

Entries appear in the following order: required test or GPA, minimum score (if required)/median score of students entering in 2015–2016.

Program	Degree	GRE-V	GRE-Q	GRE-Writing	GRE-Subject	Undergraduate GPA	Last 2 Years GPA	Psychology GPA	Master's GPA
Clinical Psychology	PhD	NA/162	NA/159	NA/4.6	Not specified	3/3.63	Not specified	Not specified	Not specified
Cognitive Psychology	PhD	Not specified	Not specified	Not specified	Not specified	Not specified	Not specified	Not specified	Not specified
Quantitative Psychology	PhD	Not specified	Not specified	Not specified	Not specified	Not specified	Not specified	Not specified	Not specified
Social Psychology	PhD	Not specified	Not specified	Not specified	Not specified	Not specified	Not specified	Not specified	Not specified
Developmental Psychology	PhD	Not specified	Not specified	Not specified	Not specified	Not specified	Not specified	Not specified	Not specified

Admissions Requirements:

Degree	GRE	GRE-Subject	Letters of Recommendation	Research Statement	Writing Sample	CV	Interview
Doctoral	Required	Recommended	3	Required	Required	Required	Required

Please note if these criteria vary for different programs: Writing sample for Clinical programs only.

Admissions Criteria:

GRE scores—high
Research experience—high
Work experience—medium
Clinically related public service—medium
GPA—high

Letters of recommendation—high
Interview—high
Statement of goals and objectives—high
Undergraduate psychology preparation—medium

For additional information on admission requirements, visit http://psych.ku.edu/graduate-program.

Department Demographics

	Male (PT)	Female (PT)	Total	African-American/ Black (PT)	Hispanic/ Latino (PT)	Asian/ Pacific Islander (PT)	American Indian/ Alaska Native (PT)	Caucasian/ White (PT)	Unknown	Multiethnic (PT)	ADA (PT)	Int'l (PT)
Students	27 (0)	61 (0)	88	5 (0)	4 (0)	8 (0)	0 (0)	63 (0)	6 (0)	2 (0)	1 (0)	12 (0)

Financial Information/Assistance

Tuition: For information on tuition costs, visit http://affordability.ku.edu/cs/index.shtml. Tuition is subject to change. Additional fees arc assessed to students beyond the costs of tuition for the following: campus fees.

Doctoral:
State residents: $387 per credit hour.
Nonstate residents: $906 per credit hour.

Financial Assistance:

	Teaching Assistantship (% Receiving)	Teaching Assistantship Tuition Remission	Research Assistantship (% Receiving)	Research Assistantship Tuition Remission	Fellowship (% Receiving)	Fellowship Tuition Remission
First-Year Student	$14,250 (NA)	Full	$14,250 (NA)	Full	NA (NA)	NA
Advanced Student	$14,250 (NA)	Full	$14,250 (NA)	Full	NA (NA)	NA

Employment of Department Graduates

Doctoral:
Enrolled in a postdoctoral residency/fellowship: 3
Employed in an academic position at a university: 2
Employed in a hospital/medical center: 1
Still seeking employment: 0
Other employment position: 1
Do not know: 0
Total: 7

Additional Information

Housing and Day Care: On-campus housing is available. See the following website for more information: http://www.housing.ku.edu/. On-campus day care facilities are available. See the following website for more information: http://www.hilltop.ku.edu/.

Information for Students With Physical Disabilities: See the following website: http://access.ku.edu/.

Special Facilities or Resources: The department has well-equipped computer labs and access to university mainframe computers. Clinical and research support facilities include an on-site clinic with a test resource library, individual and group therapy rooms, and play and psychodrama rooms. Specialized research facilities include interview rooms with audio and video capacities, psychophysiological and stress laboratories, ERP facilities, eye-movement monitoring laboratories, and an anechoic chamber. The Kansas University Medical Center houses the Hoglund Brain Imaging Center, a state-of-the-art facility with fMRI and MEG laboratories.

Application Information: The University of Kansas, Graduate School, 1450 Jayhawk Boulevard, Room 313, Lawrence, KS 66045-7535. *Fee:* $65. *Online application:* http://www.graduate.ku.edu/apply.

Kansas, University of

Educational Psychology
School of Education
Joseph R. Pearson Hall, 1122 West Campus Road, Room 621
Lawrence, KS 66045-3101
Telephone: (785) 864-3931
Chairperson: Steven W. Lee, PhD

E-mail: epsy@ku.edu
Web: http://epsy.ku.edu/

Orientation, Objectives, and Emphasis of Department

Educational Psychology offers graduate degrees in three distinct areas. The doctoral programs in Counseling Psychology and School Psychology are APA accredited. The EdS and PhD degrees in School Psychology are NASP accredited. Counseling Psychology trains professionals to possess the generalist skills to function in a wide array of work settings. This program is strongly committed to the training of scientist–practitioners focused on facilitating the personal, social, educational, and vocational development of individuals. School Psychology endorses the training model of the psychoeducational consultant with multifaceted skills drawn from psychology and education to assist children toward greater realization of their potential. The psychoeducational consultant is vitally concerned with enhancing teacher effectiveness, creating a positive classroom environment for children, and influencing educational thought within the school system. The Educational Psychology Program offers instruction in two tracks. The objectives of the program are to prepare students to become faculty members, researchers, and measurement specialists. Students may focus on (a) development and learning, or (b) research, evaluation, measurement, and statistics. Graduate study includes experiences in designing, conducting, and evaluating research and field experiences in a variety of settings.

Programs and Degrees Offered

Program	Degree	Application Deadline	Applications Received	Accepted	New Admits Enrolled (PT)	Total Enrolled (PT)	Degrees Awarded in 2014–2015	Median Years to Complete Degree	Dismissed/ Withdrew
School Psychology	PhD	December 15 (Fall), December 15 (Summer)	19	7	5 (0)	15 (0)	1	5.66	0
Counseling Psychology	MA/MS	January 1 (Fall), January 1 (Summer)	59	24	11 (0)	24 (0)	13	2	0
Educational Psychology and Research	PhD	December 15 (Fall), December 15 (Summer)	16	8	11 (0)	31 (0)	10	6.17	0

Programs and Degrees Offered (con't.)

Program	Degree	Application Deadline	Applications Received	Accepted	New Admits Enrolled (PT)	Total Enrolled (PT)	Degrees Awarded in 2014–2015	Median Years to Complete Degree	Dismissed/ Withdrew
Educational Psychology and Research	MEd	December 15 (Fall), December 15 (Summer)	11	8	2 (0)	6 (0)	4	3.83	0
Counseling Psychology	PhD	December 15 (Fall), December 15 (Summer)	77	10	6 (0)	41 (0)	5	5.33	1
School Psychology	EdS	December 15 (Fall), December 15 (Summer)	28	15	9	16	8	2.17	0

APA Accreditation

School PhD: Student Outcome Data website: http://pre.soe.ku.edu/academics/psy/doctorate.
Counseling PhD: Student Outcome Data website: http://epsy.ku.edu/academics/counseling-psychology/doctorate/overview-benefits.

Doctoral Degree (PhD School Psychology): For those doctoral students for whom a professional internship was required in this program prior to graduation:
Total students who applied for an internship: 2
Total students who obtained an internship: 2
Total students who obtained a paid internship: 2
Total students who obtained an unpaid internship: 0
Total students who were placed in APA/CPA-accredited internships: 0
Total students placed in internships not APA/CPA-accredited, but listed with the Association of Psychology Postdoctoral and Internship Centers (APPIC): 0
Total students placed in internships conforming to guidelines of the Council of Directors of School Psychology Programs (CDSPP): 2
Total students placed in internships that were not APA/CPA-accredited, APPIC or CDSSP listed: 0

Doctoral Degree (PhD Counseling Psychology): For those doctoral students for whom a professional internship was required in this program prior to graduation:
Total students who applied for an internship: 8
Total students who obtained an internship: 8
Total students who obtained a paid internship: 8
Total students who obtained an unpaid internship: 0
Total students who were placed in APA/CPA-accredited internships: 6
Total students placed in internships not APA/CPA-accredited, but listed with the Association of Psychology Postdoctoral and Internship Centers (APPIC): 2
Total students placed in internships conforming to guidelines of the Council of Directors of School Psychology Programs (CDSPP): 0
Total students placed in internships that were not APA/CPA-accredited, APPIC or CDSSP listed: 0

Master's Degree (MA/MS Counseling Psychology): An internship experience, such as a final research project or "capstone" experience is required of graduates.

Internships/Practica

The Counseling Psychology and School Psychology programs require practica and/or internships as part of the degree requirements. Additionally, students enroll in field experience, seminars, and specific EPSY courses to obtain additional training with special populations and/or psychological testing procedures. Counseling Psychology doctoral students must participate in three semesters of practicum and one full year of internship. Both master's and doctoral students in the Counseling Psychology programs complete their practica in a variety of local applied settings. Our doctoral students in Counseling Psychology have been successful in obtaining APA-accredited internships in university counseling centers, veterans' administration medical centers, community mental health centers, and other human service agencies. Students in the School Psychology EdS and PhD programs devote a full year to a school psychology internship. These students obtain internships in a variety of elementary, secondary, and special needs school settings as well as APA-accredited internships throughout the country.

Admissions

Entries appear in the following order: required test or GPA, minimum score (if required)/median score of students entering in 2015–2016.

Program	Degree	GRE-V	GRE-Q	GRE-Writing	GRE-Subject	Under-graduate GPA	Last 2 Years GPA	Psychology GPA	Master's GPA
School Psychology	PhD	NA/159	NA/152	NA/4	Not specified	Not specified	Not specified	Not specified	Not specified
Counseling Psychology	MA/MS	Not specified	Not specified	Not specified	Not specified	Not specified	Not specified	Not specified	Not specified
Educational Psychology and Research	PhD	Not specified	Not specified	Not specified	Not specified	Not specified	Not specified	Not specified	Not specified
Educational Psychology and Research	MEd	Not specified	Not specified	Not specified	Not specified	Not specified	Not specified	Not specified	Not specified
Counseling Psychology	PhD	NA/158	NA/154	NA/4.5	Not specified	NA/3.56	Not specified	Not specified	Not specified
School Psychology	EdS	NA/157	NA/152	NA/4.5	Not specified	Not specified	Not specified	Not specified	Not specified

Admissions Requirements:

Degree	GRE	GRE-Subject	Letters of Recommendation	Research Statement	Writing Sample	CV	Interview
Master's/Specialist	Required	None	3	Required	Optional	Required	None
Doctoral	Required	Recommended	3	Required	Optional	Required	Required

Please note if these criteria vary for different programs: The admission criteria are for applicants to the Counseling Psychology programs. The educational psychology programs place higher emphasis on research experience. School psychology places higher emphasis on GRE scores. No other program requires the GRE-Subject. School Psychology PhD also requires an interview, none of the others do.

Admissions Criteria:

GRE scores—medium
Research experience—medium
Work experience—medium
Clinically related public service—low
GPA—high

Letters of recommendation—high
Interview—high
Statement of goals and objectives—high
Undergraduate psychology preparation—medium
Commit. to Div. & Culture—high

For additional information on admission requirements, visit http://epsy.ku.edu/admission.

Department Demographics

	Male (PT)	Female (PT)	Total	African-American/ Black (PT)	Hispanic/ Latino (PT)	Asian/ Pacific Islander (PT)	American Indian/ Alaska Native (PT)	Caucasian/ White (PT)	Unknown	Multiethnic (PT)	ADA (PT)	Int'l (PT)
Students	31 (0)	102 (0)	133	4 (0)	0 (0)	14 (0)	0 (0)	90 (0)	12 (0)	13 (0)	0 (0)	27 (0)

Financial Information/Assistance

Tuition: For information on tuition costs, visit http://affordability.ku.edu/costs. Higher tuition cost for this program: The School of Education has a differential tuition fee of $26.45/credit hour. Tuition is subject to change. Additional fees are assessed to students beyond the costs of tuition for the following: campus fees- $75.91/credit hour if fewer than 6 hrs or $455.50 if over 6 credit hours.

Doctoral:
State residents: $376 per credit hour.
Nonstate residents: $880 per credit hour.

Master's:
State residents: $376 per credit hour.
Nonstate residents: $880 per credit hour.

Financial Assistance:

	Teaching Assistantship (% Receiving)	Teaching Assistantship Tuition Remission	Research Assistantship (% Receiving)	Research Assistantship Tuition Remission	Fellowship (% Receiving)	Fellowship Tuition Remission
First-Year Student	$14,250 (NA)	Full	$18,000 (NA)	Full	$25,000 (NA)	Full
Advanced Student	$14,250 (NA)	Full	$18,000 (NA)	Full	$25,000 (NA)	Full

For additional information on financial assistance, visit http://soe.ku.edu/admission/scholarships.

Employment of Department Graduates

Master's:
Enrolled in a psychology doctoral program: 3
Employed in a professional position in a school system: 8
Employed in business or industry: 10
Employed in a community mental health/counseling center: 4
Other employment position: 2
Total: 27

Doctoral:
Enrolled in a postdoctoral residency/fellowship: 4
Employed in an academic position at a university: 2
Employed in other positions at a higher education institution: 3
Employed in a professional position in a school system: 2
Employed in a hospital/medical center: 1
Total: 12

Additional Information

Housing and Day Care: On-campus housing is available. See the following website for more information: http://housing.ku.edu/. On-campus day care facilities are available. See the following website for more information: http://hilltop.ku.edu/.

Information for Students With Physical Disabilities: See the following website: http://access.ku.edu/.

Special Facilities or Resources: Students have employment and/or research opportunities with diverse populations in a variety of settings, including university-related facilities and public/private schools. KU's Multicultural Resource Center seeks to reshape notions of education, research, and public service to include a multicultural focus. The America Reads Challenge, Achievement and Assessment Institute (AAI), Center for Educational Testing and Evaluation, Center for Research on Learning, and the Center for Psychoeducational Services are under the umbrella of KU's School of Education. The Center for Psychoeducational Services serves the needs of local schools and community members while offering excellent training opportunities for School Psychology and Counseling Psychology students. Graduate students may work with preschool, school-age children and their families, and college students from the local area. KU's Life Span Institute has numerous programs such as the Juniper Gardens Children's Project, Beach Center on Disability, Research and Training Center on Independent Living, Gerontology Center, and the Work Group for Community Health and Development. The School of Education provides extensive media and internet technology in its state-of-the-art facility, Joseph R. Pearson Hall. Students have access to mediated classrooms and laboratories, instructional and assessment libraries, audio visual resources, and computer labs.

Application Information: KU Educational Psychology, Admissions Committee, 1122 W Campus Road, Room 621 JRP, Lawrence, KS 66045-3101. *Fee:* $65. *Online application:* http://graduate.ku.edu/ku-graduate-application.

Pittsburg State University
Department of Psychology and Counseling
College of Education
207 Whitesitt Hall, 1701 South Broadway
Pittsburg, KS 66762-7551
Telephone: (620) 235-4523
Chairperson: David P. Hurford

E-mail: dphurford@pittstate.edu
Web: http://www.pittstate.edu/college/education/psychology/index.dot

Orientation, Objectives, and Emphasis of Department

The Department of Psychology and Counseling uses an interdisciplinary model to provide broad-based training, understanding and appreciation of the specialties that we represent. The major objective of the department is to prepare graduates with knowledge in scientific foundations and practical applied skills to function as mental health service providers or to pursue study at the doctoral level. Faculty in the department represent a diverse collection of theoretical backgrounds in scientific and applied psychology. All faculty teach coursework in each program area, providing students with the opportunity to learn multidisciplinary approaches and models. The emphasis in the department is on integrated, cross-disciplinary studies within a close faculty-student colleague model that promotes frequent contact and close supervision, aimed at developing practitioner skills. The department is pleased to have the first accredited master's degree program in clinical psychology in the nation (MPAC accreditation received in May 1997). The department also enjoys NCATE accreditation of the MS degree program in school counseling and the EdS degree program in school psychology.

Programs and Degrees Offered

Program	Degree	Application Deadline	Applications Received	Accepted	New Admits Enrolled (PT)	Total Enrolled (PT)	Degrees Awarded in 2014–2015	Median Years to Complete Degree	Dismissed/ Withdrew
Clinical Psychology	MA/MS	March 1 (Fall), October 1 (Spring)	22	18	13	17	1		
General Psychology	MA/MS	March 1 (Fall), October 1 (Spring), March 1 (Summer)	6	4	4	7	4		
School Psychology	EdS	March 1 (Fall), October 1 (Spring), March 1 (Summer)	2	2	2	6 (1)	2		
School Counseling	MA/MS	March 1 (Fall), October 1 (Spring), March 1 (Summer)	8	6	4 (2)	14 (16)	8		

Internships/Practica

All MS and EdS practitioner programs include a 3–8 semester hour (150–400 clock hour) practicum sequence and a 4–32 semester hour (600–1200 clock hour) internship at a site appropriate to the specialty, and under the supervision of faculty and site supervisors. The internship in school psychology is post-degree, and is typically a paid internship. Some internships in other programs are also paid. All internships meet guidelines of the professional association or accrediting body of the specialty (i.e., MPAC, NASP).

Admissions

Entries appear in the following order: required test or GPA, minimum score (if required)/median score of students entering in 2015–2016.

Program	Degree	GRE-V	GRE-Q	GRE-Writing	GRE-Subject	Undergraduate GPA	Last 2 Years GPA	Psychology GPA	Master's GPA
Clinical Psychology	MA/MS	146/NA	141/NA	3.5/NA	Not specified	3/NA	Not specified	Not specified	Not specified
General Psychology	MA/MS	146/NA	141/NA	3.5/NA	Not specified	3/NA	Not specified	Not specified	Not specified
School Psychology	EdS	146/NA	141/NA	3.5/NA	Not specified	3/NA	Not specified	Not specified	Not specified

Admissions *(con't.)*

Program	Degree	GRE-V	GRE-Q	GRE-Writing	GRE-Subject	Under-graduate GPA	Last 2 Years GPA	Psychology GPA	Master's GPA
School Counseling	MA/MS	146/NA	141/NA	3.5/NA	Not specified	3/NA	Not specified	Not specified	Not specified

Admissions Requirements:

Degree	GRE	GRE-Subject	Letters of Recommendation	Research Statement	Writing Sample	CV	Interview
Master's/Specialist	Required	None	3	Required	Optional	Optional	None

Admissions Criteria:

GRE scores—high
Research experience—medium
Work experience—high
Clinically related public service—medium
GPA—high

Letters of recommendation—high
Interview—medium
Statement of goals and objectives—high
Undergraduate psychology preparation—medium

For additional information on admission requirements, visit http://www.pittstate.edu/college/education/psychology/graduate.dot.

Department Demographics

	Male (PT)	Female (PT)	Total	African-American/ Black (PT)	Hispanic/ Latino (PT)	Asian/ Pacific Islander (PT)	American Indian/ Alaska Native (PT)	Caucasian/ White (PT)	Unknown	Multiethnic (PT)	ADA (PT)	Int'l (PT)
Students	12 (2)	32 (15)	61	3 (0)	2 (0)	3 (0)	0 (0)	36 (17)	0 (0)	0 (0)	0 (0)	0 (0)

Financial Information/Assistance

Tuition: For information on tuition costs, visit http://www.pittstate.edu/office/registrar/fees.dot. Tuition is subject to change.

Master's:
State residents: $7,288 per academic year.
State residents: $305 per credit hour.
Nonstate residents: $17,048 per academic year.
Nonstate residents: $711 per credit hour.

Financial Assistance:

	Teaching Assistantship (% Receiving)	Teaching Assistantship Tuition Remission	Research Assistantship (% Receiving)	Research Assistantship Tuition Remission	Fellowship (% Receiving)	Fellowship Tuition Remission
First-Year Student	$5,000 (NA)	Full	NA (NA)	NA	NA (NA)	NA
Advanced Student	$5,000 (NA)	Full	NA (NA)	NA	NA (NA)	NA

For additional information on financial assistance, visit http://www.pittstate.edu/office/financial_aid/index.dot.

Employment of Department Graduates

Master's:
Enrolled in a psychology doctoral program: 2
Enrolled in another graduate/professional program: 3
Employed in an academic position at a university: 1
Employed in academic position at a 2-year/4-year college: 2
Employed in a professional position in a school system: 20
Employed in a community mental health/counseling center: 16
Employed in a hospital/medical center: 2
Still seeking employment: 2
Other employment position: 3
Total: 51

Additional Information

Housing and Day Care: On-campus housing is available. See the following website for more information: http://www.pittstate.edu/office/housing/. No on-campus day care facilities are available.

Information for Students With Physical Disabilities: See the following website: http://www.pittstate.edu/office/eoaa/disability-services/.

Special Facilities or Resources: The department has counseling and psychotherapy training facilities equipped with one-way mirrors and audio and video taping equipment. Microcomputer laboratories with network capacity, word processing, and SAS and SPSS software are available in the department. The university library, in addition to a large book collection, currently maintains over 150 periodical subscriptions in psychology. The department operates the Center for Human Services, an on-campus training, research, and service facility, which includes University Testing Services, a family counseling center, an adult assessment center, The Psycho-Educational Assessment Center, and the Center for Research, Evaluation and Awareness of Dyslexia. The department has a close working relationship with local hospitals and mental health facilities and is a constituent member of the regional community service coalition.

Application Information: Chairperson, Department of Psychology and Counseling, Pittsburg State University, 1701 South Broadway, Pittsburg, KS 66762-7551. *Fee:* $40. *Online application:* http://www.pittstate.edu/office/graduate/.

Washburn University
Department of Psychology
College of Arts and Sciences
1700 SW College Avenue
Topeka, KS 66621
Telephone: (785) 670-1564
Chairperson: Cindy Turk

E-mail: cindy.turk@washburn.edu

Web: http://www.washburn.edu/academics/college-schools/arts-sciences/graduate/psychology/index.html

Orientation, Objectives, and Emphasis of Department
The MA in Psychology with an emphasis in Clinical Skills offers professional training to prepare program graduates for licensure and practice under Kansas statutes. Upon completion of the Master of Arts degree in Psychology with an emphasis in Clinical Skills, graduates should be eligible to sit for the licensure exam in the state of Kansas; be prepared to pass the licensure exam; have appropriate skills and training needed in the Kansas mental health care delivery system; and have a foundation for pursuing doctoral training in clinical (or another area of) psychology in the future. Upon completion of the program students will be able to clearly articulate the application of the peer-reviewed literature to a specific issue or situation relevant to psychology; evaluate, administer, and interpret psychological assessments; understand empirically based therapy techniques and recognize the importance of individual client characteristics and contextual factors in their implementation; and engage in ethical practice, utilize supervision and consultation appropriately, and carry out responsibilities professionally.

Programs and Degrees Offered

Program	Degree	Application Deadline	Applications Received	Accepted	New Admits Enrolled (PT)	Total Enrolled (PT)	Degrees Awarded in 2014–2015	Median Years to Complete Degree	Dismissed/ Withdrew
Clinical Psychology	MA/MS	March 15 (Fall)	30	10	7 (0)	19 (5)	6	3	2

Internships/Practica

Psychological services are offered to the community through a clinic staffed by graduate students enrolled in practica and supervised by licensed, doctoral-level faculty. Services offered focus on remediation of anxiety and depression, and psychological assessment of learning disorders and ADHD. Student therapists practice skills of diagnostic interviewing and integrating interview information with personality and intelligence testing into the formulation of a DSM–5 diagnosis. Under the close supervision of a faculty clinical psychologist, they use this information to conceptualize etiologies and develop and deliver therapeutic treatment options. The therapy processes implemented reflect several theoretical orientations, including Motivational Interviewing, Interpersonal Process, Cognitive/ Behavioral and Brief approaches. Issues of suicide, cross-cultural sensitivity, and individual therapist development are also addressed. An internship consisting of 750 supervised hours over an academic year is required of each student prior to graduation. This requirement is met by working 20 hours per week at an assigned site and meeting 3 hours weekly in a classroom setting. Both onsite and university-based supervisors are available to the student throughout the internship. The types of experiences provided student interns include provision of individual adult and child therapy; co-facilitation of group therapy; psychological testing/assessment; and involvement in multidisciplinary treatment teams.

Admissions

Entries appear in the following order: required test or GPA, minimum score (if required)/median score of students entering in 2015–2016.

Program	Degree	GRE-V	GRE-Q	GRE-Writing	GRE-Subject	Under-graduate GPA	Last 2 Years GPA	Psychology GPA	Master's GPA
Clinical Psychology	MA/MS	NA/NA	NA/NA	Not specified	Not specified	NA/NA	NA/NA	NA/NA	Not specified

Admissions Requirements:

Degree	GRE	GRE-Subject	Letters of Recommendation	Research Statement	Writing Sample	CV	Interview
Master's/Specialist	Required	Optional	3	Required	None	Required	None

Admissions Criteria:

GRE scores—medium
Research experience—medium
Work experience—low
Clinically related public service—medium

GPA—high
Letters of recommendation—high
Statement of goals and objectives—medium
Undergraduate psychology preparation—medium

Department Demographics

	Male (PT)	Female (PT)	Total	African-American/ Black (PT)	Hispanic/ Latino (PT)	Asian/ Pacific Islander (PT)	American Indian/ Alaska Native (PT)	Caucasian/ White (PT)	Unknown	Multiethnic (PT)	ADA (PT)	Int'l (PT)
Students	6 (1)	13 (4)	24	0 (0)	0 (0)	0 (0)	0 (0)	19 (5)	0 (0)	0 (0)	0 (0)	0 (0)

Financial Information/Assistance

Tuition: For information on tuition costs, visit http://www.washburn.edu/current-students/business-office/tuition-fees.html. Tuition is subject to change.

Master's:
State residents: $7,140 per academic year.
State residents: $357 per credit hour.
Nonstate residents: $14,540 per academic year.
Nonstate residents: $727 per credit hour.

Financial Assistance:

	Teaching Assistantship (% Receiving)	Teaching Assistantship Tuition Remission	Research Assistantship (% Receiving)	Research Assistantship Tuition Remission	Fellowship (% Receiving)	Fellowship Tuition Remission
First-Year Student	$3,500 (NA)	NA	$1,500 (NA)	NA	NA (NA)	NA
Advanced Student	$3,500 (NA)	NA	NA (NA)	NA	NA (NA)	NA

For additional information on financial assistance, visit http://www.washburn.edu/admissions/paying-for-college/financial-aid/index.html.

Employment of Department Graduates

Master's:
Enrolled in a psychology doctoral program: 2
Employed in a community mental health/counseling center: 4
Total: 6

Additional Information

Housing and Day Care: On-campus housing is available. See the following website for more information: http://www.washburn.edu/campus-life/housing-dining/index.html. No on-campus day care facilities are available.

Information for Students With Physical Disabilities: See the following website: http://www.washburn.edu/disability-services/index.html.

Special Facilities or Resources: The psychology department, housed with other departments in a modern building, has well-equipped laboratories available for human experimentation. These facilities also include observation areas designed for the direct supervision of psychotherapy and psychological testing. The psychology department provides access to computer hardware and software resources. Thesis research can be conducted by accessing participants from the undergraduate subject pool or in a wide array of community-based agencies.

Application Information: Department of Psychology, Washburn University, Topeka, KS 66621. *Fee:* $40. *Online application:* http://www.washburn.edu/academics/college-schools/arts-sciences/departments/psychology/graduate-degree/application-admission.html.

Wichita State University

Department of Psychology
Fairmount College of Liberal Arts and Sciences
1845 Fairmount
Wichita, KS 67260-0034
Telephone: (316) 978-3170
Chairperson: Rhonda K. Lewis

E-mail: rhonda.lewis@wichita.edu
Web: http://www.wichita.edu/thisis/home/?u=psychology

Orientation, Objectives, and Emphasis of Department

The Psychology Department, open to various theoretical orientations, emphasizes research in its three programs. The Human Factors program is accredited by the Education Committee of the Human Factors and Ergonomics Society. This program provides students with wide exposure to research, training, practice, and literature in the field of Human Factors, as well as to issues in the wider context of basic and applied experimental psychology. Current human factors research involves cognitive functioning, aging, development, human–computer interactions, aerospace issues, perception, attention, vision, and driving related issues, especially with the elderly. The APA-accredited Clinical program seeks to integrate community and clinical psychology. The goal of the program is to educate and license students to be competent clinical psychologists who conceptualize, research, intervene, and treat problems at the individual, group, organizational, and societal levels. Special areas of interest and research include parent–child interaction, treatment and prevention of depression, treatment and prevention of delinquency, adolescent health and development, and assessment of personality and psychopathology. The Community program seeks to educate students in Community Psychology with an emphasis on assessing and solving problems at the group, organizational, and societal levels. Special areas of research and practice include adolescent health and development and self-help groups.

Programs and Degrees Offered

Program	Degree	Application Deadline	Applications Received	Accepted	New Admits Enrolled (PT)	Total Enrolled (PT)	Degrees Awarded in 2014–2015	Median Years to Complete Degree	Dismissed/ Withdrew
Clinical Psychology	PhD	December 1 (Fall)	54	10	4	25 (0)	6	5	0
Human Factors	PhD	January 15 (Fall)	18	7	5	26 (0)	5	5	1
Community Psychology	PhD	January 15 (Fall)	18	12	5	22 (0)	9	3.66	4

APA Accreditation

Clinical PhD: Student Outcome Data website: http://webs.wichita.edu/?u=psychology&p=/graduate/clinical/clinicalphd/.

Doctoral Degree (PhD Clinical Psychology): For those doctoral students for whom a professional internship was required in this program prior to graduation:
Total students who applied for an internship: 3
Total students who obtained an internship: 3
Total students who obtained a paid internship: 3
Total students who obtained an unpaid internship: 0
Total students who were placed in APA/CPA-accredited internships: 3
Total students placed in internships not APA/CPA-accredited, but listed with the Association of Psychology Postdoctoral and Internship Centers (APPIC): 0
Total students placed in internships conforming to guidelines of the Council of Directors of School Psychology Programs (CDSPP): 0
Total students placed in internships that were not APA/CPA-accredited, APPIC or CDSSP listed: 0

Internships/Practica

An important aspect of the Human Factors program is its requirement that all students complete an internship. The internship is designed to provide students with practical experience integrating their education in real-world situations. The internships have included positions with the FAA, Google, Bell Laboratories, IBM, Microsoft, and other similar settings. These placements have often led to post-PhD employment opportunities. In the Clinical and Community programs, practicum opportunities, most of them funded, are available in on-campus training facilities and community agencies. Settings include the Psychology Clinic and the Counseling and Testing Center, both at Wichita State University, the Sedgwick County Department of Mental Health, Head Start, and various community-based projects. Students in the Clinical program are required to complete 1 year of internship experience towards the end of their graduate studies.

Admissions

Entries appear in the following order: required test or GPA, minimum score (if required)/median score of students entering in 2015–2016.

Program	Degree	GRE-V	GRE-Q	GRE-Writing	GRE-Subject	Under-graduate GPA	Last 2 Years GPA	Psychology GPA	Master's GPA
Clinical Psychology	PhD	NA/NA	NA/NA	Not specified	Not specified	Not specified	3/3.81	Not specified	3.25/NA

Admissions *(con't.)*

Program	Degree	GRE-V	GRE-Q	GRE-Writing	GRE-Subject	Under-graduate GPA	Last 2 Years GPA	Psychology GPA	Master's GPA
Human Factors	PhD	NA/NA	NA/NA	Not specified	Not specified	Not specified	3/3.57	Not specified	3.25/NA
Community Psychology	PhD	NA/NA	NA/NA	Not specified	Not specified	Not specified	3/3.86	Not specified	3.25/NA

Admissions Requirements:

Degree	GRE	GRE-Subject	Letters of Recommendation	Research Statement	Writing Sample	CV	Interview
Doctoral	Required	None	3	Required	Optional	Optional	None

Admissions Criteria:

GRE scores—medium
Research experience—high
Work experience—medium
Clinically related public service—medium
GPA—high

Letters of recommendation—medium
Interview—medium
Statement of goals and objectives—high
Undergraduate psychology preparation—low

For additional information on admission requirements, visit http://webs.wichita.edu/?u=psychology&p=/application/gradapplication/.

Department Demographics

	Male (PT)	Female (PT)	Total	African-American/ Black (PT)	Hispanic/ Latino (PT)	Asian/ Pacific Islander (PT)	American Indian/ Alaska Native (PT)	Caucasian/ White (PT)	Unknown (PT)	Multiethnic (PT)	ADA (PT)	Int'l (PT)
Students	25 (0)	48 (0)	73	4 (0)	5 (0)	7 (0)	0 (0)	47 (0)	7 (0)	3 (0)	0 (0)	0 (0)

Financial Information/Assistance

Tuition: For information on tuition costs, visit http://www.wichita.edu/tuitionfees. Tuition is subject to change. Additional fees are assessed to students beyond the costs of tuition for the following: student fees, facility fee, registration fee.

Doctoral:
State residents: $6,603 per academic year.
State residents: $274 per credit hour.
Nonstate residents: $16,167 per academic year.
Nonstate residents: $672 per credit hour.

Financial Assistance:

	Teaching Assistantship (% Receiving)	Teaching Assistantship Tuition Remission	Research Assistantship (% Receiving)	Research Assistantship Tuition Remission	Fellowship (% Receiving)	Fellowship Tuition Remission
First-Year Student	$6,864 (75)	Partial	$10,000 (8)	NA	NA (NA)	NA
Advanced Student	$7,912 (49)	Partial	$10,000 (20)	NA	NA (NA)	NA

For additional information on financial assistance, visit http://webs.wichita.edu/?u=finaid_graduate&p=/index.

Employment of Department Graduates

Doctoral:
Enrolled in a postdoctoral residency/fellowship: 3
Employed in an academic position at a university: 4
Employed in other positions at a higher education institution: 4
Employed in business or industry: 5
Employed in government agency: 3
Employed in a community mental health/counseling center: 1
Do not know: 1
Total: 21

Additional Information

Housing and Day Care: On-campus housing is available. See the following website for more information: http://www.wichita.edu/thisis/home/?u=housing. On-campus day care facilities are available. See the following website for more information: http://www.wichita.edu/childdevelopmentcenter.

Information for Students With Physical Disabilities: See the following website: http://webs.wichita.edu/dss.

Special Facilities or Resources: The department is located in Jabara Hall and maintains fully equipped laboratories. Currently active research groups include the Software Usability Research Lab, Perception & Attention Lab, Visual Psychophysics Lab, Decision Making Research Lab, Child & Family Research Center, Personality Research Lab, and Quantitative Modeling Lab. Our computer facilities are state-of-the-art and are available to students for coursework and research. The department also has access to the National Institute for Aviation Research, the Social Science Research Laboratory, and the University Computing Center. The Psychology Clinic, which is part of the psychology department, provides outpatient services via individual, group, and family modalities. The clinic has facilities for individual and group research. The statewide Civic Engagement Institute, with a computerized database and an 800 number, also operates out of the psychology department. Faculty maintain working relationships with a number of governmental and community agencies which facilitate student involvement in community practice and research. The agencies include the public school system, the Sedgwick County Department of Mental Health, and COMCARE, among others.

Application Information: Graduate Coordinator, Psychology Department. *Fee:* $50. *Online application:* https://apply.wichita.edu/.

Eastern Kentucky University

Department of Psychology
Arts and Sciences
Cammack 127
Richmond, KY 40475
Telephone: (859) 622-1105
Chairperson: Robert G. Brubaker

E-mail: robert.brubaker@eku.edu
Web: http://psychology.eku.edu/

Orientation, Objectives, and Emphasis of Department

The new PsyD program in clinical psychology is designed to train professional psychologists to work in clinics, hospitals, or other agencies, particularly in rural and underserved areas. The PsyS program in school psychology is designed to train professional psychologists to work in schools and school-related agencies. The program involves 71 graduate hours including internship, is NASP and NCATE-accredited, and meets Kentucky certification requirements. The industrial/organizational (I/O) program is designed to meet the education and training guidelines established by the Society for Industrial and Organizational Psychology. The scientist–practitioner I/O program prepares students to work in organizations and/or pursue a doctoral degree. Degree requirements include intensive courses, electives, and practica. The MS in General Psychology program offers a flexible curriculum designed to prepare students for further graduate study in psychology or for a variety of non-applied career options.

Programs and Degrees Offered

Program	Degree	Application Deadline	Applica-tions Received	Accepted	New Admits Enrolled (PT)	Total Enrolled (PT)	Degrees Awarded in 2014–2015	Median Years to Complete Degree	Dismissed/ Withdrew
Clinical Psychology	PsyD	January 15 (Fall)	51	20	19	19	0		1
Industrial/ Organizational Psychology	MA/MS	March 1 (Fall)	43	18	4 (0)	9 (0)	4	2	0
Specialist in School Psychology	Other	March 1 (Fall)	23	14	7 (0)	(0)	5	3	
General Psychology	MA/MS	Rolling	23	6	9 (0)	13 (1)	3	2	2

Internships/Practica

A variety of field placements are available within easy commuting distance from Richmond. Practicum sites have included private psychiatric and VA hospitals, the University counseling center, a residential treatment facility for children, alcohol and drug abuse treatment programs, and several adult and child outpatient mental health centers. Students also gain experience working in the EKU Psychology Clinic, an outpatient mental health facility operated by the Department. School psychology students can choose from a variety of public and private elementary and secondary schools. Students have completed internships in Kentucky as well as many other states. Students in the I/O program work on practicum projects with various for-profit and non-profit organizations in the region.

Admissions

Entries appear in the following order: required test or GPA, minimum score (if required)/median score of students entering in 2015–2016.

Program	Degree	GRE-V	GRE-Q	GRE-Writing	GRE-Subject	Under-graduate GPA	Last 2 Years GPA	Psychol-ogy GPA	Master's GPA
Clinical Psychology	PsyD	NA/154	NA/147	Not specified	Not specified	NA/3.68	NA/NA	NA/NA	Not specified

Admissions *(con't.)*

Program	Degree	GRE-V	GRE-Q	GRE-Writing	GRE-Subject	Under-graduate GPA	Last 2 Years GPA	Psychology GPA	Master's GPA
Industrial/ Organizational Psychology	MA/MS	149/151	144/150	Not specified	Not specified	2.5/3.4	2.75/3.6	NA/3.6	Not specified
Specialist in School Psychology	Other	150/152	143/139	Not specified	Not specified	NA/3.49	NA/3.5	NA/3.7	Not specified
General Psychology	MA/MS	152/157	147/150	Not specified	Not specified	2.78/3.18	NA/3.5	NA/3.6	Not specified

Admissions Requirements:

Degree	GRE	GRE-Subject	Letters of Recom-mendation	Research Statement	Writing Sample	CV	Interview
Master's/Specialist	Required	None	3	Required	Optional	Required	Recom-mended
Doctoral	Required	Recom-mended	3	Required	Optional	Required	Required

Please note if these criteria vary for different programs: The School Psychology program allows applicants to submit GRE scores or Pre-Professional Skills Tests (PPST) scores.

Admissions Criteria:

GRE scores—medium
Research experience—medium
Work experience—medium
Clinically related public service—high

GPA—medium
Letters of recommendation—high
Statement of goals and objectives—high
Undergraduate psychology preparation—medium

For additional information on admission requirements, visit http://psychology.eku.edu/application-admission-graduate-studies.

Department Demographics

	Male (PT)	Female (PT)	Total	African-American/ Black (PT)	Hispanic/ Latino (PT)	Asian/ Pacific Islander (PT)	American Indian/ Alaska Native (PT)	Caucasian/ White (PT)	Unknown	Multiethnic (PT)	ADA (PT)	Int'l (PT)
Students	8 (0)	63 (2)	73	3 (0)	0 (0)	0 (0)	0 (0)	68 (2)	0 (0)	0 (0)	0 (0)	0 (0)

Financial Information/Assistance

Tuition: Tuition is subject to change.

Doctoral:
State residents: $600 per credit hour.
Nonstate residents: $600 per credit hour.

Master's:
State residents: $475 per credit hour.
Nonstate residents: $805 per credit hour.

Financial Assistance:

	Teaching Assistantship (% Receiving)	Teaching Assistantship Tuition Remission	Research Assistantship (% Receiving)	Research Assistantship Tuition Remission	Fellowship (% Receiving)	Fellowship Tuition Remission
First-Year Student	NA (NA)	NA	$5,280 (NA)	Partial	NA (NA)	NA
Advanced Student	$10,480 (NA)	Partial	$5,280 (NA)	Partial	NA (NA)	NA

For additional information on financial assistance, visit http://gradschool.eku.edu/graduate-assistantships.

Employment of Department Graduates

Master's:
Enrolled in a psychology doctoral program: 5
Employed in an academic position at a university: 1
Employed in other positions at a higher education institution: 1
Employed in a professional position in a school system: 10
Employed in business or industry: 2
Employed in government agency: 1
Employed in a community mental health/counseling center: 8
Still seeking employment: 1
Not seeking employment: 2
Other employment position: 1
Total: 32

Additional Information

Housing and Day Care: On-campus housing is available. See the following website for more information: http://housing.eku.edu/. No on-campus day care facilities are available.

Information for Students With Physical Disabilities: See the following website: http://disabilities.eku.edu/.

Special Facilities or Resources: Laboratories include several multipurpose rooms. The clinical training facility includes a group therapy room, individual therapy rooms, a testing room, and a play therapy room. All rooms have one-way mirrors and digital recording facilities. The department operates a psychology training clinic providing outpatient services to the community, with its primary mission the training of students.

Application Information: Graduate School, Eastern Kentucky University, 521 Lancaster Avenue, Richmond, KY 40475. *Fee:* $35. *Online application:* http://gradschool.eku.edu/apply/.

Kentucky, University of
Department of Educational, School, and Counseling Psychology
Education
Dickey Hall, Room 237
Lexington, KY 40506-0017
Telephone: (859) 257-4909
Chairperson: Jeff Reese

E-mail: jeff.reese@uky.edu
Web: https://education.uky.edu/edp/

Orientation, Objectives, and Emphasis of Department
Three programs are housed within the department: counseling psychology, educational psychology, and school psychology. The program faculties in counseling psychology and in school psychology are committed to the scientist–practitioner model for professional training, while educational psychology faculty emphasize the researcher-teacher model. A strong emphasis has been placed upon the psychology core for all professional training. Because we are a graduate department with a professional emphasis, a high premium is placed on professional writing skills throughout—from admissions to course papers to final projects (theses and dissertations) in all programs. Counseling faculty research interests focus upon cultural diversity and social justice, counseling issues for sexual

minorities, family processes, experiential therapies, and rape awareness. The school psychology faculty research interests focus upon evaluation and assessment, positive mental health outcomes, literacy and social development in young children, and direct interventions. The educational psychology faculty research interests include motivation in educational settings, cardiovascular stress in minority children, culture and socialization in relation to cognition, engagement in risky behaviors, and sleep deprivation. Students in each program are encouraged to establish mentoring relationships with their major professor by the beginning of their second semester.

Programs and Degrees Offered

Program	Degree	Application Deadline	Applications Received	Accepted	New Admits Enrolled (PT)	Total Enrolled (PT)	Degrees Awarded in 2014–2015	Median Years to Complete Degree	Dismissed/ Withdrew
Counseling Psychology	MA/MS	February 1 (Fall)	42	26	8 (0)	17 (0)	6	2	0
Educational Psychology	MA/MS	February 1 (Fall)	3	2	2 (0)	5 (0)	2	2	0
Counseling Psychology	PhD	December 1 (Fall)	43	3	1 (0)	26 (0)	9	5.93	1
Educational Psychology	PhD	December 1 (Fall)	10	5	4 (0)	20 (0)	1	5	1
School Psychology	PhD	December 1 (Fall)	12	9	2 (0)	15 (0)	6	6	0
School Psychology	EdS	February 1 (Fall)	35	11	7 (0)	16 (0)	9	3	0
Counseling Psychology	EdS	February 1 (Fall)	2	2	2	5	10	1.5	0

APA Accreditation

Counseling PhD: Student Outcome Data website: https://education.uky.edu/edp/counseling-psychology-overview/.
School PhD: Student Outcome Data website: https://education.uky.edu/edp/school-psychology-overview/.

Doctoral Degree (PhD Counseling Psychology): For those doctoral students for whom a professional internship was required in this program prior to graduation:
Total students who applied for an internship: 4
Total students who obtained an internship: 4
Total students who obtained a paid internship: 4
Total students who obtained an unpaid internship: 0
Total students who were placed in APA/CPA-accredited internships: 3
Total students placed in internships not APA/CPA-accredited, but listed with the Association of Psychology Postdoctoral and Internship Centers (APPIC): 1
Total students placed in internships conforming to guidelines of the Council of Directors of School Psychology Programs (CDSPP): 0
Total students placed in internships that were not APA/CPA-accredited, APPIC or CDSSP listed: 0

Doctoral Degree (PhD School Psychology): For those doctoral students for whom a professional internship was required in this program prior to graduation:
Total students who applied for an internship: 2
Total students who obtained an internship: 2
Total students who obtained a paid internship: 2
Total students who obtained an unpaid internship: 0
Total students who were placed in APA/CPA-accredited internships: 0
Total students placed in internships not APA/CPA-accredited, but listed with the Association of Psychology Postdoctoral and Internship Centers (APPIC): 0
Total students placed in internships conforming to guidelines of the Council of Directors of School Psychology Programs (CDSPP): 2
Total students placed in internships that were not APA/CPA-accredited, APPIC or CDSSP listed: 0

Master's Degree (MA/MS Educational Psychology): An internship experience, such as a final research project or "capstone" experience is required of graduates.

Internships/Practica

The University of Kentucky Counseling Psychology program encourages students to complete their practicum and internship experiences at a variety of sites. A plethora of sites ranging from community mental health agencies, schools, university counseling centers, VA hospitals, inpatient facilities, and correctional facilities are available. The School Psychology program requires students to complete practicum training in the program's training clinic. The clinic offers specialty diagnostic and treatment services for children and families affected by autism. In their third year of training, students complete an advanced practicum experience that may take place in setting approved by the faculty. Recent advanced practicum placements have included a psychiatric hospital, school, alternative school, and autism assessment clinic. Students must complete a full-time predoctoral internship and are encouraged to apply for APA-accredited internship placements.

Admissions

Entries appear in the following order: required test or GPA, minimum score (if required)/median score of students entering in 2015–2016.

Program	Degree	GRE-V	GRE-Q	GRE-Writing	GRE-Subject	Under-graduate GPA	Last 2 Years GPA	Psychology GPA	Master's GPA
Counseling Psychology	MA/MS	148/153	140/147	2.5/4	Not specified	3.15/3.62	Not specified	Not specified	Not specified
Educational Psychology	MA/MS	150/152	143/149	3/3.5	Not specified	3.6/3.61	Not specified	Not specified	Not specified
Counseling Psychology	PhD	147/158	144/148	3/4.5	Not specified	2.8/3.65	Not specified	Not specified	3.36/3.99
Educational Psychology	PhD	145/154	146/148	3.5/4	Not specified	3.47/3.55	Not specified	Not specified	3.18/3.85
School Psychology	PhD	149/152	143/149	3/4	Not specified	2.97/3.46	Not specified	Not specified	3.55/4
School Psychology	EdS	146/154	142/148	3.5/4	Not specified	3/3.73	Not specified	Not specified	Not specified
Counseling Psychology	EdS	154/159	147/150	3.5/4	Not specified	3.15/3.65	Not specified	Not specified	Not specified

Admissions Requirements:

Degree	GRE	GRE-Subject	Letters of Recommendation	Research Statement	Writing Sample	CV	Interview
Master's/Specialist	Required	None	2	Required	None	Required	Required
Doctoral	Required	None	2	Required	Required	Required	Required

Please note if these criteria vary for different programs: Research experience and statement of goals are the highest priority for Educational Psychology programs. Work experiences and clinically related service are more important for School and Counseling programs.

Admissions Criteria:

GRE scores—medium
Research experience—high
Work experience—medium
Clinically related public service—high

GPA—medium
Letters of recommendation—high
Interview—high
Statement of goals and objectives—high

For additional information on admission requirements, visit http://www.gradschool.uky.edu/prospectivestudents/program_reqs/ed_counsel_school_psych.html.

Department Demographics

	Male (PT)	Female (PT)	Total	African-American/ Black (PT)	Hispanic/ Latino (PT)	Asian/ Pacific Islander (PT)	American Indian/ Alaska Native (PT)	Caucasian/ White (PT)	Unknown (PT)	Multiethnic (PT)	ADA (PT)	Int'l (PT)
Students	17 (0)	87 (0)	104	13 (0)	3 (0)	16 (0)	0 (0)	66 (0)	2 (0)	4 (0)	0 (0)	10 (0)

Financial Information/Assistance

Tuition: For information on tuition costs, visit http://www.uky.edu/registrar/tuition-fees. Tuition is subject to change. Additional fees are assessed to students beyond the costs of tuition for the following: University/institution fees or costs $1,249 per year.

Doctoral:
State residents: $11,652 per academic year.
State residents: $617 per credit hour.
Nonstate residents: $24,154 per academic year.
Nonstate residents: $1,423 per credit hour.

Master's:
State residents: $11,652 per academic year.
State residents: $617 per credit hour.
Nonstate residents: $24,154 per academic year.
Nonstate residents: $1,423 per credit hour.

Financial Assistance:

	Teaching Assistantship (% Receiving)	Teaching Assistantship Tuition Remission	Research Assistantship (% Receiving)	Research Assistantship Tuition Remission	Fellowship (% Receiving)	Fellowship Tuition Remission
First-Year Student	$10,907 (31)	Full	$10,367 (42)	Full	$15,000 (0)	Full
Advanced Student	$12,319 (23)	Full	$11,906 (26)	Full	$15,000 (1)	Full

For additional information on financial assistance, visit http://www.research.uky.edu/gs/StudentFunding/fellowships.html.

Employment of Department Graduates

Master's:
Enrolled in a psychology doctoral program: 10
Enrolled in another graduate/professional program: 15
Employed in a professional position in a school system: 4
Employed in a community mental health/counseling center: 6
Do not know: 4
Total: 39

Doctoral:
Employed in an academic position at a university: 3
Employed in other positions at a higher education institution: 1
Employed in a professional position in a school system: 4
Employed in government agency: 1
Total: 9

Additional Information

Housing and Day Care: On-campus housing is available. See the following website for more information: http://www.uky.edu/housing/graduate/about. On-campus day care facilities are available. See the following website for more information: http://www.uky.edu/hr/work-life/resources-for-parents/childcare-options.

Information for Students With Physical Disabilities: See the following website: http://www.uky.edu/StudentAffairs/DisabilityResourceCenter/.

Special Facilities or Resources: The University of Kentucky is located on the western edge of Appalachia, which provides students with the opportunity to interact with a rich and varied American culture. The uniqueness of this potential client and research pool allows our students to examine attributes of the bridge between old, rural America and the future, more technological America. Microcomputer facilities are available within the department and within the college for student use in word processing, model development, simulation and evaluation, and data analysis. The university provides all the facilities and resources expected of a major research institution (e.g., extensive libraries, computer facilities, research environment, and medical center).

Application Information: Fee: $65. *Online application:* https://app.applyyourself.com/?id=ukgrad.

Kentucky, University of
Department of Psychology
Arts and Sciences
Kastle Hall
Lexington, KY 40506-0044
Telephone: (859) 257-9640
Chairperson: Robert Lorch, PhD

E-mail: psychology@uky.edu
Web: http://psychology.as.uky.edu/

Orientation, Objectives, and Emphasis of Department
The goals of the doctoral program depend partly upon the specific program area in which a student enrolls. The program in Clinical Psychology follows the Clinical Science training model. All students are actively engaged in research throughout their graduate training, and the program views the scientific method as the appropriate basis for clinical psychology. Beginning in the second year of study, each student also receives extensive clinical experience via placements in mental or behavioral health settings. Graduates of the program are prepared to pursue an academic career or to be a practitioner. Students in the program receive broad exposure to the major theoretical perspectives influencing clinical psychology. Students in the program in Experimental Psychology, with concentrations in cognitive, developmental, social, animal learning and behavioral neuroscience, are trained as research scientists. They are exposed to the important theoretical perspectives and research paradigms of their respective areas. There is considerable latitude for individuals to define their specific programs of study. Graduates are prepared to pursue an academic career or a research position in an applied setting. All students complete a Master's thesis, written and oral doctoral qualifying examinations, and a dissertation demonstrating accomplishment in independent research.

Programs and Degrees Offered

Program	Degree	Application Deadline	Applications Received	Accepted	New Admits Enrolled (PT)	Total Enrolled (PT)	Degrees Awarded in 2014–2015	Median Years to Complete Degree	Dismissed/ Withdrew
Clinical Psychology	PhD	December 1 (Fall)	171	9	7 (0)	43 (0)	8	6	0
Experimental Psychology	PhD	December 1 (Fall)	80	11	6	47 (0)	6	5	1

APA Accreditation
Clinical PhD: Student Outcome Data website: http://psychology.as.uky.edu/admissions-outcomes-and-other-data.

Doctoral Degree (PhD Clinical Psychology): For those doctoral students for whom a professional internship was required in this program prior to graduation:
Total students who applied for an internship: 7
Total students who obtained an internship: 7
Total students who obtained a paid internship: 7
Total students who obtained an unpaid internship: 0
Total students who were placed in APA/CPA-accredited internships: 7
Total students placed in internships not APA/CPA-accredited, but listed with the Association of Psychology Postdoctoral and Internship Centers (APPIC): 0
Total students placed in internships conforming to guidelines of the Council of Directors of School Psychology Programs (CDSPP): 0
Total students placed in internships that were not APA/CPA-accredited, APPIC or CDSSP listed: 0

Admissions
Entries appear in the following order: required test or GPA, minimum score (if required)/median score of students entering in 2015–2016.

Program	Degree	GRE-V	GRE-Q	GRE-Writing	GRE-Subject	Under-graduate GPA	Last 2 Years GPA	Psychol-ogy GPA	Master's GPA
Clinical Psychology	PhD	NA/162	NA/160	NA/NA	Not specified	NA/3.77	Not specified	NA/NA	NA/NA
Experimental Psychology	PhD	NA/NA	NA/NA	NA/NA	Not specified	NA/3.54	Not specified	NA/NA	NA/NA

Admissions Requirements:

Degree	GRE	GRE-Subject	Letters of Recommendation	Research Statement	Writing Sample	CV	Interview
Doctoral	Required	Optional	3	Required	Recommended	Required	Required

Admissions Criteria:

GRE scores—high
Research experience—high
Work experience—medium
Clinically related public service—medium
GPA—high

Letters of recommendation—high
Interview—high
Statement of goals and objectives—high
Undergraduate psychology preparation—medium
Knowl. of mentor's work—high

For additional information on admission requirements, visit http://psychology.as.uky.edu/psych-application-info.

Department Demographics

	Male (PT)	Female (PT)	Total	African-American/ Black (PT)	Hispanic/ Latino (PT)	Asian/ Pacific Islander (PT)	American Indian/ Alaska Native (PT)	Caucasian/ White (PT)	Unknown	Multiethnic (PT)	ADA (PT)	Int'l (PT)
Students	27 (0)	63 (0)	90	2 (0)	8 (0)	6 (0)	0 (0)	72 (0)	0 (0)	2 (0)	0 (0)	2 (0)

Financial Information/Assistance

Tuition: For information on tuition costs, visit http://www.uky.edu/registrar/tuition-fees. Tuition is subject to change. Additional fees are assessed to students beyond the costs of tuition for the following: Health fee/Recreation fee: total of approximately $500 per semester.

Doctoral:
State residents: $11,652 per academic year.
State residents: $617 per credit hour.
Nonstate residents: $26,154 per academic year.
Nonstate residents: $1,423 per credit hour.

Financial Assistance:

	Teaching Assistantship (% Receiving)	Teaching Assistantship Tuition Remission	Research Assistantship (% Receiving)	Research Assistantship Tuition Remission	Fellowship (% Receiving)	Fellowship Tuition Remission
First-Year Student	$18,000 (NA)	Full	$18,000 (NA)	Full	$15,000 (NA)	Full
Advanced Student	$18,000 (NA)	Full	$18,000 (NA)	Full	$15,000 (NA)	Full

For additional information on financial assistance, visit http://www.research.uky.edu/gs/StudentFunding/funding.html.

Employment of Department Graduates

Doctoral:
Enrolled in a postdoctoral residency/fellowship: 6
Employed in an academic position at a university: 4
Total: 10

Additional Information

Housing and Day Care: On-campus housing is available. See the following website for more information: http://www.uky.edu/housing/graduate/about. On-campus day care facilities are available. See the following website for more information: http://www.uky.edu/hr/work-life/resources-for-parents/childcare-options.

Information for Students With Physical Disabilities: See the following website: http://www.uky.edu/StudentAffairs/DisabilityResourceCenter/.

Special Facilities or Resources: The psychology department occupies its own three-story building located by the computer center and main campus library. Kastle Hall houses faculty and student offices, classrooms, and research space. Research facilities in the building include animal laboratories for behavioral and physiological research; observation rooms with one-way mirrors; extensive video equipment; and microcomputer-equipped rooms for cognitive research. Two additional buildings on campus are available for behavioral research. Current faculty have collaborative arrangements with several facilities on campus, including the neuropsychology laboratories in the Department of Neurology; the OroFacial Pain Clinic in the College of Dentistry; the Central Animal Research Facility; and the Sanders-Brown Center on Aging. The department maintains a large undergraduate subject pool. Clinical training facilities are excellent and include a departmental clinic housed in a separate building and clinical placement arrangements with a variety of mental and behavioral health facilities in Lexington.

Application Information: *Fee:* $65. *Online application:* http://www.research.uky.edu/gs/ProspectiveStudents/Admission.html.

Louisville, University of
Department of Counseling and Human Development
College of Education & Human Development
1905 South 1st Street
Louisville, KY 40292
Telephone: (502) 852-6884
Chairperson: Dr. Mark Leach

E-mail: m.leach@louisville.edu
Web: http://louisville.edu/education/departments/ecpy

Orientation, Objectives, and Emphasis of Department
The Counseling Psychology PhD program adheres to a competencies-based model rooted in a scientist–practitioner framework and we strive to be balanced in each area. We are involved in the community, as our department coordinates two community-based clinics in traditionally underserved areas where students can see clients. Students can also see clients at a wide variety of other applied settings around the city and surrounding area, including community mental health centers, university counseling centers, the VA, hospitals/medical centers, and Ft. Knox. Our faculty emphasize cognitive-behavioral, psychodynamic, and interpersonal models in conjunction with multicultural and feminist approaches. Our research foci include diversity, multi-racial/multi-ethnic identities, prevention of adolescent depression, interpersonal relationships, trauma and resilience, families, forgiveness, religion and spirituality, ethics, and international counseling. Faculty emphasize student collaboration on research projects and most students have a publication prior to graduation.

Programs and Degrees Offered

Program	Degree	Application Deadline	Applica-tions Received	Accepted	New Admits Enrolled (PT)	Total Enrolled (PT)	Degrees Awarded in 2014–2015	Median Years to Complete Degree	Dismissed/Withdrew
Counseling and Personnel Services	PhD	December 1 (Fall)	55	3	3 (0)	33 (2)	5	5	0

APA Accreditation
Counseling PhD: Student Outcome Data website: http://louisville.edu/education/degrees/phd-cps-cp.

Doctoral Degree (PhD Counseling and Personnel Services): For those doctoral students for whom a professional internship was required in this program prior to graduation:
Total students who applied for an internship: 7
Total students who obtained an internship: 7
Total students who obtained a paid internship: 7
Total students who obtained an unpaid internship: 0

Total students who were placed in APA/CPA-accredited internships: 7
Total students placed in internships not APA/CPA-accredited, but listed with the Association of Psychology Postdoctoral and Internship Centers (APPIC): 0
Total students placed in internships conforming to guidelines of the Council of Directors of School Psychology Programs (CDSPP): 0
Total students placed in internships that were not APA/CPA-accredited, APPIC or CDSSP listed: 0

Internships/Practica

Due to the wide variety of practicum placement sites in the city and surrounding area prior to internship, students accept internship positions in counseling centers, hospitals, community mental health centers, and VA settings. Our community sites include the same, which is a strength of our program. With our two community-based clinics, students are learning the complexities of social justice and advocacy work and the intersectionality of multiple identities including class, race, gender and sexual orientation.

Admissions

Entries appear in the following order: required test or GPA, minimum score (if required)/median score of students entering in 2015–2016.

Program	Degree	GRE-V	GRE-Q	GRE-Writing	GRE-Subject	Under-graduate GPA	Last 2 Years GPA	Psychol-ogy GPA	Master's GPA
Counseling and Personnel Services	PhD	153/161	149/152	4.5/4.5	Not specified	3.44/3.5	Not specified	Not specified	Not specified

Admissions Requirements:

Degree	GRE	GRE-Subject	Letters of Recom-mendation	Research Statement	Writing Sample	CV	Interview
Doctoral	Required	None	3	Required	Optional	Required	Required

Admissions Criteria:

GRE scores—high
Research experience—high
Work experience—low
Clinically related public service—low
GPA—high

Letters of recommendation—medium
Interview—high
Statement of goals and objectives—high
Undergraduate psychology preparation—low

For additional information on admission requirements, visit http://louisville.edu/education/degrees/phd-cps-cp.

Department Demographics

	Male (PT)	Female (PT)	Total	African-American/ Black (PT)	Hispanic/ Latino (PT)	Asian/ Pacific Islander (PT)	American Indian/ Alaska Native (PT)	Caucasian/ White (PT)	Unknown	Multiethnic (PT)	ADA (PT)	Int'l (PT)
Students	14 (0)	19 (2)	35	4 (0)	0 (0)	4 (0)	0 (0)	25 (2)	0 (0)	0 (0)	0 (0)	2 (0)

Financial Information/Assistance

Tuition: For information on tuition costs, visit http://louisville.edu/finance/bursar/tuitionfee/tuition. Tuition is subject to change.

Doctoral:
State residents: $15,558 per academic year.
State residents: $649 per credit hour.
Nonstate residents: $32,374 per academic year.
Nonstate residents: $1,350 per credit hour.

Financial Assistance:

	Teaching Assistantship (% Receiving)	Teaching Assistantship Tuition Remission	Research Assistantship (% Receiving)	Research Assistantship Tuition Remission	Fellowship (% Receiving)	Fellowship Tuition Remission
First-Year Student	$18,000 (10)	Full	$18,000 (70)	Full	$18,000 (20)	Full
Advanced Student	$18,000 (10)	Full	$18,000 (70)	Full	$18,000 (20)	Full

For additional information on financial assistance, visit http://louisville.edu/education/financialaid.

Employment of Department Graduates

Doctoral:
Enrolled in a postdoctoral residency/fellowship: 4
Employed in an academic position at a university: 1
Total: 5

Additional Information

Housing and Day Care: On-campus housing is available. See the following website for more information: http://louisville.edu/housing/. On-campus day care facilities are available. See the following website for more information: http://louisville.edu/education/elc.

Information for Students With Physical Disabilities: See the following website: http://louisville.edu/disability.

Special Facilities or Resources: We coordinate two community-based clinics which allow for clinical work and data collection. Students also have opportunities to collect research data at a variety of sites in the city. Depending on the faculty member with whom you work, there may be opportunities in the department. General research space is available in the department. A research lab is housed in the college. Ample computers and training opportunities are available in the college and university.

Application Information: Graduate Admissions Office, University of Louisville, Houchens Room 6, Louisville, KY 40292-0001. *Fee:* $60. *Online application:* https://graduate.louisville.edu/apply.

Louisville, University of
Psychological and Brain Sciences
Arts and Sciences
317 Life Sciences Building
Louisville, KY 40292
Telephone: (502) 852-6775
Chairperson: Suzanne Meeks

E-mail: smeeks@louisville.edu
Web: http://www.louisville.edu/psychology/

Orientation, Objectives, and Emphasis of Department
The Clinical Psychology PhD program adheres to a scientist–practitioner model and is designed to provide training in research, psychological assessment and intervention, ethical and legal issues, and multicultural competence. Faculty research foci are in psychopathology, geropsychology, health psychology, and mental health disparities. Clinical emphases include cognitive-behavioral and acceptance-based interventions. The Experimental Psychology PhD program offers a flexible curriculum tailored to the individual student's interests while providing extensive training in the core processes of psychology, research methodology, and data analysis. Research is an integral component of the Experimental Psychology PhD, thus students begin working in their mentor's laboratory when they arrive on campus. Faculty research interests are varied, but fall into the following areas of strength: Cognitive Science, Developmental Science, Neuroscience, and Vision and Hearing Sciences. Recent graduates are pursuing careers in academic and non-academic fields in numerous settings, including universities and colleges, industry, government, and private consulting organizations.

Programs and Degrees Offered

Program	Degree	Application Deadline	Applications Received	Accepted	New Admits Enrolled (PT)	Total Enrolled (PT)	Degrees Awarded in 2014–2015	Median Years to Complete Degree	Dismissed/Withdrew
Clinical Psychology	PhD	December 1 (Fall)	146	9	7 (0)	40 (0)	6	5	2
Experimental Psychology	PhD	December 1 (Fall)	31	8	5 (0)	26 (0)	3	7	2

APA Accreditation

Clinical PhD: Student Outcome Data website: http://louisville.edu/psychology/graduate/clinical/.

Doctoral Degree (PhD Clinical Psychology): For those doctoral students for whom a professional internship was required in this program prior to graduation:

Total students who applied for an internship: 6

Total students who obtained an internship: 4

Total students who obtained a paid internship: 4

Total students who obtained an unpaid internship: 0

Total students who were placed in APA/CPA-accredited internships: 4

Total students placed in internships not APA/CPA-accredited, but listed with the Association of Psychology Postdoctoral and Internship Centers (APPIC): 0

Total students placed in internships conforming to guidelines of the Council of Directors of School Psychology Programs (CDSPP): 0

Total students placed in internships that were not APA/CPA-accredited, APPIC or CDSSP listed: 0

Internships/Practica

Most practicum experiences take place in our in-house Psychological Services Center. Paid and unpaid practica are available in community and government agencies. These vary from year to year, but include Central State Hospital, Ft. Knox Department of Behavioral Health, private practices, and the Departments of Psychiatry and Behavioral Sciences, Anesthesiology, and Family Medicine.

Admissions

Entries appear in the following order: required test or GPA, minimum score (if required)/median score of students entering in 2015–2016.

Program	Degree	GRE-V	GRE-Q	GRE-Writing	GRE-Subject	Undergraduate GPA	Last 2 Years GPA	Psychology GPA	Master's GPA
Clinical Psychology	PhD	154/160	150/158	Not specified	Not specified	3.5/3.89	Not specified	Not specified	Not specified
Experimental Psychology	PhD	156/157	148/152	Not specified	Not specified	3.67/3.79	3.67/3.92	Not specified	Not specified

Admissions Requirements:

Degree	GRE	GRE-Subject	Letters of Recommendation	Research Statement	Writing Sample	CV	Interview
Doctoral	Required	Optional	3	Required	None	Required	Recommended

Please note if these criteria vary for different programs: Experimental Psychology PhD does not require clinically related public service.

Admissions Criteria:

GRE scores—high

Research experience—high

Work experience—high

Clinically related public service—high

GPA—high

Letters of recommendation—high

Interview—high

Statement of goals and objectives—high

Undergraduate psychology preparation—medium

Department Demographics

	Male (PT)	Female (PT)	Total	African-American/ Black (PT)	Hispanic/ Latino (PT)	Asian/ Pacific Islander (PT)	American Indian/ Alaska Native (PT)	Caucasian/ White (PT)	Unknown	Multiethnic (PT)	ADA (PT)	Int'l (PT)
Students	17 (0)	49 (0)	66	4 (0)	4 (0)	2 (0)	0 (0)	56 (0)	0 (0)	(0)	0 (0)	4 (0)

Financial Information/Assistance

Tuition: For information on tuition costs, visit http://louisville.edu/finance/bursar/tuitionfee/tuition. Tuition is subject to change.

Doctoral:
State residents: $15,558 per academic year.
State residents: $649 per credit hour.
Nonstate residents: $32,374 per academic year.
Nonstate residents: $1,350 per credit hour.

Financial Assistance:

	Teaching Assistantship (% Receiving)	Teaching Assistantship Tuition Remission	Research Assistantship (% Receiving)	Research Assistantship Tuition Remission	Fellowship (% Receiving)	Fellowship Tuition Remission
First-Year Student	$22,000 (NA)	Full	$22,000 (NA)	Full	$22,000 (NA)	Full
Advanced Student	$22,000 (NA)	Full	$22,000 (NA)	Full	$22,000 (NA)	Full

For additional information on financial assistance, visit http://louisville.edu/graduate/current-students/funding-opportunities.

Employment of Department Graduates

Doctoral:
Enrolled in a postdoctoral residency/fellowship: 2
Employed in business or industry: 1
Employed in government agency: 1
Employed in a hospital/medical center: 3
Not seeking employment: 2
Total: 9

Additional Information

Housing and Day Care: On-campus housing is available. See the following website for more information: http://louisville.edu/housing/. On-campus day care facilities are available. See the following website for more information: http://louisville.edu/education/elc/.

Information for Students With Physical Disabilities: See the following website: http://louisville.edu/disability/.

Special Facilities or Resources: Departmental facilities include modern laboratories and a Psychological Services Center. The University Computing resources are available from departmental stations via a campus-wide network. Additional training opportunities are available through such facilities as the Department of Psychiatry and Behavioral Sciences, the Child Evaluation Center, Central State Hospital, and other community agencies.

Application Information: Graduate Admissions Office, University of Louisville, Houchens Room 6, Louisville, KY 40292-0001. *Fee:* $60. *Online application:* https://graduate.louisville.edu/apply.

Morehead State University
Department of Psychology
Science
414 Reed Hall
Morehead, KY 40351
Telephone: (606) 783-2981
Chairperson: Gregory M. Corso

E-mail: g.corso@moreheadstate.edu
Web: http://www.moreheadstate.edu/psych

Orientation, Objectives, and Emphasis of Department
The clinical and counseling programs are designed primarily to train master's-level psychologists to practice in a variety of settings, and lead to certification in many states. However, approximately 30% of our students also enter doctoral level programs upon graduation. The scientist–practitioner model is emphasized in the program, with primary emphasis on acquisition of applied clinical skills and knowledge of the general field of psychology. Consequently, competencies in critical analysis of theories, experimental design, and quantitative data analysis are expected. Clinical and counseling students are encouraged to conduct or participate in ongoing research in the department. Students interested in pursuing doctoral level training are encouraged to complete a thesis.

Programs and Degrees Offered

Program	Degree	Application Deadline	Applications Received	Accepted	New Admits Enrolled (PT)	Total Enrolled (PT)	Degrees Awarded in 2014–2015	Median Years to Complete Degree	Dismissed/ Withdrew
Clinical/ Counseling Psychology	MA/MS	April 1 (Fall)	22	12	8 (0)	19 (0)	7	2.25	2

Internships/Practica
The Department of Psychology maintains clinical affiliation agreements with a number of mental health agencies/facilities in Kentucky and in several other states. Internship and practicum placement sites include community mental health centers, outpatient clinics, hospitals, schools, juvenile justice facilities, and correctional settings.

Admissions
Entries appear in the following order: required test or GPA, minimum score (if required)/median score of students entering in 2015–2016.

Program	Degree	GRE-V	GRE-Q	GRE-Writing	GRE-Subject	Under-graduate GPA	Last 2 Years GPA	Psychology GPA	Master's GPA
Clinical/ Counseling Psychology	MA/MS	143/151	137/144	Not specified	Not specified	2.8/3.42	Not specified	Not specified	Not specified

Admissions Requirements:

Degree	GRE	GRE-Subject	Letters of Recommendation	Research Statement	Writing Sample	CV	Interview
Master's/Specialist	Required	None	3	Required	None	None	Required

Admissions Criteria:
GRE scores—medium
Research experience—medium
Work experience—low
Clinically related public service—low
GPA—medium

Letters of recommendation—medium
Interview—high
Statement of goals and objectives—medium
Undergraduate psychology preparation—low

For additional information on admission requirements, visit http://www.moreheadstate.edu/study/MS-psychology/.

Department Demographics

	Male (PT)	Female (PT)	Total	African-American/ Black (PT)	Hispanic/ Latino (PT)	Asian/ Pacific Islander (PT)	American Indian/ Alaska Native (PT)	Caucasian/ White (PT)	Unknown (PT)	Multiethnic (PT)	ADA (PT)	Int'l (PT)
Students	6 (0)	13 (0)	19	1 (0)	2 (0)	0 (0)	0 (0)	16 (0)	0 (0)	0 (0)	1 (0)	0 (0)

Financial Information/Assistance

Tuition: For information on tuition costs, visit http://www.moreheadstate.edu/tuition/. Tuition is subject to change. Additional fees are assessed to students beyond the costs of tuition for the following: laboratory fees for some courses.

Master's:
State residents: $579 per credit hour.
Nonstate residents: $579 per credit hour.

Financial Assistance:

	Teaching Assistantship (% Receiving)	Teaching Assistantship Tuition Remission	Research Assistantship (% Receiving)	Research Assistantship Tuition Remission	Fellowship (% Receiving)	Fellowship Tuition Remission
First-Year Student	$10,000 (100)	NA	$10,000 (100)	NA	NA (NA)	NA
Advanced Student	$10,000 (100)	NA	$10,000 (100)	NA	NA (NA)	NA

For additional information on financial assistance, visit http://www.moreheadstate.edu/ga/.

Employment of Department Graduates

Master's:
Enrolled in a psychology doctoral program: 2
Employed in government agency: 1
Employed in a community mental health/counseling center: 5
Total: 8

Additional Information

Housing and Day Care: On-campus housing is available. See the following website for more information: http://www.moreheadstate.edu/housing/. No on-campus day care facilities are available.

Information for Students With Physical Disabilities: See the following website: http://www.moreheadstate.edu/disability/.

Special Facilities or Resources: The psychology program provides excellent laboratory facilities for the study of human and animal behavior. Faculty/student research programs are often funded through both intra- and extramural grants.

Application Information: Graduate Office, Morehead State University, 701 Ginger Hall, Morehead, KY 40351. *Fee:* $30. *Online application:* https://admission.moreheadstate.edu/.

Northern Kentucky University
Department of Psychological Science
Arts & Sciences
Nunn Drive
Highland Heights, KY 41099
Telephone: (859) 572-5310
Chairperson: Jeffrey Smith

E-mail: msio@nku.edu
Web: http://msio.nku.edu

Orientation, Objectives, and Emphasis of Department

The Department of Psychological Science at Northern Kentucky University embodies a rigorous, comprehensive, and evidence-based approach to the application of empirical science and research in psychology. The graduate program in Industrial and Organizational Psychology reflects this empirical orientation in developing the critical professional competencies identified by the Society for Industrial and Organizational Psychology as essential for practice and research in I/O psychology. To ensure that the program reflects contemporary trends, an advisory board comprised of I/O psychologists and representatives of major organizations in the greater Cincinnati region provides guidance. Graduate students are encouraged to conduct independent study, practicum, or thesis research with faculty on topics of interest throughout the program. Graduate seminars are presented by four full-time graduate faculty holding doctoral degrees in I/O or social psychology, supplemented by adjunct faculty holding advanced degrees accompanied by specialized knowledge or relevant experience.

Programs and Degrees Offered

Program	Degree	Application Deadline	Applications Received	Accepted	New Admits Enrolled (PT)	Total Enrolled (PT)	Degrees Awarded in 2014–2015	Median Years to Complete Degree	Dismissed/Withdrew
Industrial/Organizational Psychology	MA/MS	August 1 (Fall), December 1 (Spring), May 1 (Summer)	25	21	12 (0)	26 (21)	10	3	2

Internships/Practica

Applied professional experience is gained through internships, which are competitive in nature and become available depending on sponsor funding, and through community engagement projects that allow graduate students to apply their accumulated professional knowledge, statistical skills, and analytic abilities within a consulting framework to challenges confronting regional non-for-profit organizations.

Admissions

Entries appear in the following order: required test or GPA, minimum score (if required)/median score of students entering in 2015–2016.

Program	Degree	GRE-V	GRE-Q	GRE-Writing	GRE-Subject	Undergraduate GPA	Last 2 Years GPA	Psychology GPA	Master's GPA
Industrial/Organizational Psychology	MA/MS	141/154	144/151	3/4	Not specified	3/3.53	NA/NA	Not specified	Not specified

Admissions Requirements:

Degree	GRE	GRE-Subject	Letters of Recommendation	Research Statement	Writing Sample	CV	Interview
Master's/Specialist	Required	None	3	Required	None	Required	None

Admissions Criteria:

GRE scores—high
Research experience—medium
Work experience—medium
GPA—high

Letters of recommendation—medium
Statement of goals and objectives—high
Undergraduate psychology preparation—high
Statistics course—high

For additional information on admission requirements, visit http://artscience.nku.edu/departments/psychology/graduate/applying.html.

Department Demographics

	Male (PT)	Female (PT)	Total	African-American/ Black (PT)	Hispanic/ Latino (PT)	Asian/ Pacific Islander (PT)	American Indian/ Alaska Native (PT)	Caucasian/ White (PT)	Unknown	Multiethnic (PT)	ADA (PT)	Int'l (PT)
Students	4 (7)	19 (11)	41	2 (1)	2 (0)	0 (1)	0 (0)	22 (19)	0 (0)	0 (0)	0 (0)	2 (0)

Financial Information/Assistance

Tuition: For information on tuition costs, visit http://studentaccountservices.nku.edu/tuition.html. Higher tuition cost for this program: Cincinnati Metro Area (IN and OH) Resident Rate $643 per credit hour. Tuition is subject to change.

Master's:
State residents: $534 per credit hour.
Nonstate residents: $822 per credit hour.

Financial Assistance:

	Teaching Assistantship (% Receiving)	Teaching Assistantship Tuition Remission	Research Assistantship (% Receiving)	Research Assistantship Tuition Remission	Fellowship (% Receiving)	Fellowship Tuition Remission
First-Year Student	$5,000 (NA)	Partial	$5,000 (NA)	Partial	NA (NA)	NA
Advanced Student	NA (NA)	Partial	NA (NA)	Partial	NA (NA)	NA

For additional information on financial assistance, visit http://gradschool.nku.edu/admissions/financialaid.html.

Employment of Department Graduates

Master's:
Employed in other positions at a higher education institution: 2
Employed in business or industry: 6
Employed in government agency: 1
Other employment position: 1
Total: 10

Additional Information

Housing and Day Care: On-campus housing is available. See the following website for more information: http://housing.nku.edu/. On-campus day care facilities are available. See the following website for more information: http://earlychildhoodcenter.nku.edu/.

Information for Students With Physical Disabilities: See the following website: http://disability.nku.edu/.

Special Facilities or Resources: The Department of Psychological Science employs two digitally equipped instructional computer labs equipped with 24 and 30 new Dell personal computers and six Apple Macintosh computers for statistics, research methods, and psychometrics seminars. Three additional laboratories are available for graduate student use: a suite of four rooms equipped with 16 Apple Macintosh computers and office; a computer lab equipped with eight Dell desktop computers; and a survey research lab equipped with eight Dell laptop computers. All computer labs are hardwired or linked to the campus wireless network. The Steely Library at NKU subscribes to most major research databases including PsycARTICLES (all APA journals), PsycINFO (APA articles, texts, and books), and Psychology and Behavioral Science Collection (575 journals) through EBSCO Host, and participates in national, regional, and state interlibrary loan systems. The Information Systems group at NKU provides lifetime email accounts to graduate students, and operates a contemporary, professional information management system with full access to the internet from remote (home) log in, including home access to SPSS with full content.

Application Information: Office of Graduate Programs, LAC 302, Northern Kentucky University, 1 Nunn Drive, Highland Heights, KY 41099. *Fee:* $40. *Online application:* http://www.nku.edu/apply/applygrad.html.

Spalding University
School of Professional Psychology
Kosair College of Health and Natural Sciences
845 South Third Street
Louisville, KY 40203
Telephone: (502) 585-7127
Chairperson: Steven Katsikas, PhD

E-mail: esimpson@spalding.edu
Web: http://www.spalding.edu/psychology

Orientation, Objectives, and Emphasis of Department

The School of Professional Psychology (SOPP) offers a comprehensive doctoral program in clinical psychology that is fully accredited by the American Psychological Association and is a member of National Council of Schools and Programs of Professional Psychology (NCSPP). Although strongly grounded in the study of general clinical psychology, our PsyD program strives to meet the demands of a changing, diverse society with the opportunity to obtain additional training in the areas of Adult Psychology, Child/Adolescent/ Family Psychology, Forensic Psychology, and Health Psychology. We are dedicated to providing generalist training in clinical psychology based upon scientific principles, grounded in evidence-based practice, and offered in a collaborative and cooperative setting. Furthermore, to train competent professionals to function in a complex and diverse society, the program emphasizes critical thinking, ethical decision-making, and the promotion of social justice. The faculty share the belief that the most effective approach to training in professional psychology is one of cooperation and mutual support. As such, good relationship skills, compassion, and sensitivity to ethical standards are values in our program.

Programs and Degrees Offered

Program	Degree	Application Deadline	Applica-tions Received	Accepted	New Admits Enrolled (PT)	Total Enrolled (PT)	Degrees Awarded in 2014–2015	Median Years to Complete Degree	Dismissed/ Withdrew
Clinical Psychology	PsyD	January 5 (Fall)	161	79	31 (0)	160 (7)	14	6	4

APA Accreditation

Clinical PsyD: Student Outcome Data website: https://spalding.edu/academics/psychology/student-admissions-outcomes-and-other-data/.

Doctoral Degree (PsyD Clinical Psychology): For those doctoral students for whom a professional internship was required in this program prior to graduation:
Total students who applied for an internship: 29
Total students who obtained an internship: 29
Total students who obtained a paid internship: 29
Total students who obtained an unpaid internship: 0
Total students who were placed in APA/CPA-accredited internships: 25
Total students placed in internships not APA/CPA-accredited, but listed with the Association of Psychology Postdoctoral and Internship Centers (APPIC): 1
Total students placed in internships conforming to guidelines of the Council of Directors of School Psychology Programs (CDSPP): 0
Total students placed in internships that were not APA/CPA-accredited, APPIC or CDSSP listed: 3

Internships/Practica

The Graduate Practicum Program has been designed to give students the opportunity to take their classroom learning into diverse, real-world settings. Over the course of 4 years, students learn to excel in assessment and evidence-based psychotherapy and begin to learn the practice of supervision. With over 60 community sites as practicum partners, students are afforded both a breadth of experience, to develop strong generalist skills, and a depth of experience in a chosen emphasis area. Practicum opportunities are available at sites such as university counseling centers, community agencies, rape crisis centers, inpatient psychiatric and VA hospitals, private practices, schools, and prisons. Further, focused learning opportunities are offered in such areas as behavioral medicine, corrections, pediatrics, neuropsychological assessment, addiction treatment and trauma recovery. Each year, the faculty review the placement preferences and training needs of each student and work diligently to make the best matches possible. Further, faculty are dedicated to ensuring students have the resources and support they need to be effective with their clients. To this end, each student each year is supervised by a site and a university supervisor, both licensed psychologists. The SOPP takes great pride in training professional, competent, ethical psychologists.

Admissions

Entries appear in the following order: required test or GPA, minimum score (if required)/median score of students entering in 2015–2016.

Program	Degree	GRE-V	GRE-Q	GRE-Writing	GRE-Subject	Under-graduate GPA	Last 2 Years GPA	Psychol-ogy GPA	Master's GPA
Clinical Psychology	PsyD	NA/155	NA/149	NA/4	Not specified	NA/3.3	Not specified	Not specified	Not specified

Admissions Requirements:

Degree	GRE	GRE-Subject	Letters of Recommendation	Research Statement	Writing Sample	CV	Interview
Doctoral	Required	None	3	Required	Required	Required	Required

Admissions Criteria:

GRE scores—medium
Research experience—medium
Work experience—medium
Clinically related public service—medium
GPA—medium

Letters of recommendation—medium
Interview—medium
Statement of goals and objectives—medium
Undergraduate psychology preparation—medium

For additional information on admission requirements, visit https://spalding.edu/academics/psychology/about-the-psy-d-program/apply-psyd/.

Department Demographics

	Male (PT)	Female (PT)	Total	African-American/ Black (PT)	Hispanic/ Latino (PT)	Asian/ Pacific Islander (PT)	American Indian/ Alaska Native (PT)	Caucasian/ White (PT)	Unknown	Multiethnic (PT)	ADA (PT)	Int'l (PT)
Students	28 (3)	132 (4)	167	10 (0)	4 (0)	7 (3)	4 (0)	134 (4)	0 (0)	1 (0)	1 (0)	1 (0)

Financial Information/Assistance

Tuition: For information on tuition costs, visit https://spalding.edu/admissions/tuition-and-fees/. Tuition is subject to change.

Doctoral:
State residents: $28,850 per academic year.
State residents: $950 per credit hour.
Nonstate residents: $28,850 per academic year.
Nonstate residents: $950 per credit hour.

Financial Assistance:

	Teaching Assistantship (% Receiving)	Teaching Assistantship Tuition Remission	Research Assistantship (% Receiving)	Research Assistantship Tuition Remission	Fellowship (% Receiving)	Fellowship Tuition Remission
First-Year Student	NA (NA)	NA	NA (NA)	NA	$11,300 (NA)	Partial
Advanced Student	$11,100 (NA)	Partial	NA (NA)	NA	$10,200 (NA)	Partial

For additional information on financial assistance, visit http://spalding.edu/financial-aid/.

Employment of Department Graduates

Doctoral:
Employed in independent practice: 6
Employed in other positions at a higher education institution: 2
Employed in government agency: 1
Employed in a community mental health/counseling center: 1
Employed in a hospital/medical center: 4
Total: 14

Additional Information

Housing and Day Care: On-campus housing is available. See the following website for more information: https://spalding.edu/student-life/housing-and-residence-life/. No on-campus day care facilities are available.

Special Facilities or Resources: The faculty have various areas of expertise and interest and form research and discussion groups around these areas of interest. Current Research and Interest Groups focus on health psychology, forensic psychology, trauma, children and adolescents, substance abuse, stereotype threats, and personal biases. Because we are a professional training program, research is typically conducted in applied settings. About 50% of our current students participate in RIGs, and the majority of participants author papers, articles, or presentations. Students are encouraged to select dissertation and other research projects based on their own desires as well as the interests of the faculty.

Application Information: Administrative Coordinator, School of Professional Psychology, 845 South Third Street, Louisville, KY 40203. *Fee:* $30. *Online application:* https://app.applyyourself.com/?id=spalding.

Western Kentucky University
Department of Psychological Sciences
Ogden College of Science and Engineering
1906 College Heights Boulevard #210130
Bowling Green, KY 42101
Telephone: (270) 745-3918
Chairperson: Kelly L. Madole

E-mail: psychsciences@wku.edu
Web: http://www.wku.edu/psychological-sciences/

Orientation, Objectives, and Emphasis of Department
The Industrial/Organizational (I/O) concentration of the Master of Science program in Psychology is a 2-year graduate program designed for students seeking preparation as MS psychologists in business, industry, service organizations, consulting firms, or government agencies. The objective of the concentration is the development of marketable skills in the areas of test construction and validation, personnel selection and placement, performance appraisal, and training. The development of applied skills is achieved through the integration of practical experience and formal course work. The I/O concentration adheres to a scientist–practitioner model of training. Students learn to evaluate and apply theory and research. The Psychological Science concentration is a 2-year, 36-credit hour research mentorship concentration designed to prepare individuals for continuation in a PhD program and/or for positions where strong research and quantitative skills are needed. The concentration is designed to strengthen students' quantitative skills and provide research experience that will make them more competitive when applying to PhD programs in psychology and/or for positions where these skills are required. The success of our graduates is based on three integrated components of the concentration: active participation in research, small class sizes, and mentoring by faculty members who are professionally active.

Programs and Degrees Offered

Program	Degree	Application Deadline	Applications Received	Accepted	New Admits Enrolled (PT)	Total Enrolled (PT)	Degrees Awarded in 2014–2015	Median Years to Complete Degree	Dismissed/ Withdrew
Psychology	MA/MS	March 1 (Fall)	56	24	14 (0)	33 (0)	18	2	2

Internships/Practica
I/O graduate students participate in an internship in business, industry, service organizations, consulting firms, or governmental agencies the summer following the first year of the program (6 credit hours). Some internship opportunities are provided through our network of WKU I/O program graduates; others placements are secured by the graduate student. The internship experience is

supervised by an I/O faculty member and site host. The faculty member, student, and site host negotiate the specific requirements for the internship. The internship job responsibilities must be substantially related to the field of I/O psychology. Internships develop skills in data management and analysis, technical writing, oral presentation, organizational skills, professionalism, and organizational savvy. Students may collect, analyze, and interpret data as part of their internship experience. Working in the real world introduces students to office politics and the realities of implementing classroom techniques by negotiating with busy managers and workers. Reporting requirements include keeping a daily task journal documenting involvement in organizational projects, submitting a bi-weekly written report (may be done electronically), and writing a comprehensive technical report. A semi-formal presentation of the internship experience is made by each student intern.

Admissions

Entries appear in the following order: required test or GPA, minimum score (if required)/median score of students entering in 2015–2016.

Program	Degree	GRE-V	GRE-Q	GRE-Writing	GRE-Subject	Under-graduate GPA	Last 2 Years GPA	Psychology GPA	Master's GPA
Psychology	MA/MS	Not specified	Not specified	Not specified	Not specified	Not specified	Not specified	Not specified	Not specified

Admissions Requirements:

Degree	GRE	GRE-Subject	Letters of Recom-mendation	Research Statement	Writing Sample	CV	Interview
Master's/Specialist	Required	None	3	Required	None	Optional	None

Please note if these criteria vary for different programs: Industrial/Organization Psychology concentration emphasizes GRE scores and successful completion of quantitative coursework in admissions. Psychological Science concentration emphases GRE scores and undergraduate research experience in admissions.

Admissions Criteria:

GRE scores—medium
Research experience—medium
Work experience—low
GPA—medium

Letters of recommendation—medium
Interview—low
Statement of goals and objectives—medium
Undergraduate psychology preparation—high

For additional information on admission requirements, visit http://www.wku.edu/psychological-sciences/grad/admission.php.

Department Demographics

	Male (PT)	Female (PT)	Total	African-American/ Black (PT)	Hispanic/ Latino (PT)	Asian/ Pacific Islander (PT)	American Indian/ Alaska Native (PT)	Caucasian/ White (PT)	Unknown (PT)	Multiethnic (PT)	ADA (PT)	Int'l (PT)
Students	11 (0)	22 (0)	33	1 (0)	2 (0)	2 (0)	0 (0)	26 (0)	0 (0)	2 (0)	0 (0)	0 (0)

Financial Information/Assistance

Tuition: For information on tuition costs, visit http://www.wku.edu/bursar/home-tuition-fees.php. Tuition is subject to change.

Master's:
State residents: $543 per credit hour.
Nonstate residents: $763 per credit hour.

Financial Assistance:

	Teaching Assistantship (% Receiving)	Teaching Assistantship Tuition Remission	Research Assistantship (% Receiving)	Research Assistantship Tuition Remission	Fellowship (% Receiving)	Fellowship Tuition Remission
First-Year Student	$8,000 (50)	Partial	$8,000 (50)	Partial	NA (NA)	NA
Advanced Student	$8,000 (40)	Partial	$8,000 (50)	Partial	$15,000 (10)	Full

For additional information on financial assistance, visit http://www.wku.edu/graduate/aid/.

Employment of Department Graduates

Master's:
Enrolled in a psychology doctoral program: 3
Employed in other positions at a higher education institution: 3
Employed in business or industry: 9
Employed in government agency: 2
Still seeking employment: 1
Total: 18

Additional Information

Housing and Day Care: No on-campus housing is available. On-campus day care facilities are available. See the following website for more information: http://www.wku.edu/ccc/.

Information for Students With Physical Disabilities: See the following website: https://www.wku.edu/sarc/.

Application Information: Western Kentucky University, The Graduate School, 1906 College Heights Boulevard, #11010, Bowling Green, KY 42101-1010. *Fee:* $60. *Online application:* http://www.wku.edu/apply/.

Louisiana State University

Department of Psychology
College of Humanities and Social Sciences
236 Audubon Hall
Baton Rouge, LA 70803
Telephone: (225) 578-4120
Chairperson: Jason L. Hicks, PhD

E-mail: narnol1@lsu.edu
Web: http://lsu.edu/hss/psychology/

Orientation, Objectives, and Emphasis of Department

The Department of Psychology at Louisiana State University is committed to the view that psychology is both a science and a profession, and it regards all areas of specialization as interdependent. All graduate students, regardless of intended area of specialization, receive broad training to develop the research skills needed to make scholarly contributions to the discipline of psychology throughout their subsequent careers. A student interested in only professional application without regard to research will not be comfortable in the graduate training program in this department. Both faculty and students in psychology recognize, however, that the model of the psychologist as a practitioner is a legitimate one. Those students whose main interest is in research are encouraged to develop familiarity with clinical, industrial, developmental or educational settings as potential research environments. Our program of graduate education reflects an emphasis on research and on professional aspects of psychology.

Programs and Degrees Offered

Program	Degree	Application Deadline	Applications Received	Accepted	New Admits Enrolled (PT)	Total Enrolled (PT)	Degrees Awarded in 2014–2015	Median Years to Complete Degree	Dismissed/ Withdrew
Clinical Psychology	PhD	December 1 (Fall)	168	22	15	60	10	5.5	1
Biological Psychology	PhD	December 1 (Fall)	2	0	0	0	1	5	0
Industrial/ Organizational Psychology	PhD	December 1 (Fall)	1	0	0	1	2	5.25	0
School Psychology	PhD	December 1 (Fall)	36	6	4	25	5	5	1
Cognitive and Brain Sciences	PhD	December 1 (Fall)	24	5	2 (0)	17 (0)	2	5.5	0

APA Accreditation

On Probation PhD: Student Outcome Data website: http://lsu.edu/hss/psychology/grad/prospective-student/areas-of-specialization/clinical.php.
School PhD: Student Outcome Data website: http://lsu.edu/hss/psychology/grad/prospective-student/areas-of-specialization/school.php.

Doctoral Degree (PhD Clinical Psychology): For those doctoral students for whom a professional internship was required in this program prior to graduation:
Total students who applied for an internship: 9
Total students who obtained an internship: 8
Total students who obtained a paid internship: 8
Total students who obtained an unpaid internship: 0
Total students who were placed in APA/CPA-accredited internships: 8
Total students placed in internships not APA/CPA-accredited, but listed with the Association of Psychology Postdoctoral and Internship Centers (APPIC): 0
Total students placed in internships conforming to guidelines of the Council of Directors of School Psychology Programs (CDSPP): 0
Total students placed in internships that were not APA/CPA-accredited, APPIC or CDSSP listed: 0

Doctoral Degree (PhD School Psychology): For those doctoral students for whom a professional internship was required in this program prior to graduation:

Total students who applied for an internship: 1
Total students who obtained an internship: 1
Total students who obtained a paid internship: 1
Total students who obtained an unpaid internship: 0
Total students who were placed in APA/CPA-accredited internships: 1
Total students placed in internships not APA/CPA-accredited, but listed with the Association of Psychology Postdoctoral and Internship Centers (APPIC): 0
Total students placed in internships conforming to guidelines of the Council of Directors of School Psychology Programs (CDSPP): 0
Total students placed in internships that were not APA/CPA-accredited, APPIC or CDSSP listed: 0

Internships/Practica

Internships and practica are primarily used in the clinical and school programs. Examples of practicum sites include: LSU Department of Psychology, Psychological Services Center, Baton Rouge Health Center & Substance Abuse Clinic, Center for Autism & Spectrum Disorders, LSU Medical School Unit, Pennington Biomedical Research Center, Pinecrest Developmental Center and Northshore Supports and Services Center. Recent internship sites include: Boys Town, Omaha, NE; University of Texas HSC, San Antonio, TX; Nationwide Children's Hospital, Columbus, OH; Florida State University, Tallahassee, FL; Medical College of Georgia, VAMC, Augusta, GA; Marcus Autism Center, Atlanta, GA; Central Texas VHCS, Austin, TX; Arise Academy of New Orleans, New Orleans, LA; Tangipahoa Parish School System, Amite, LA; Kennedy Krieger Institute at Johns Hopkins, Baltimore, MD; Wright State University, Dayton, OH; Denver HMO, Denver, CO; Indiana University School of Medicine, Indianapolis, IN; University of Mississippi MC/VA, Jackson, MS; and Munroe-Meyer Institute, Lincoln, NE.

Admissions

Entries appear in the following order: required test or GPA, minimum score (if required)/median score of students entering in 2015–2016.

Program	Degree	GRE-V	GRE-Q	GRE-Writing	GRE-Subject	Under-graduate GPA	Last 2 Years GPA	Psychology GPA	Master's GPA
Clinical Psychology	PhD	150/160	145/156	3/4.5	Not specified	NA/3.68	Not specified	Not specified	NA/3.97
Biological Psychology	PhD	NA/NA	NA/NA	NA/NA	Not specified	NA/NA	Not specified	Not specified	NA/NA
Industrial/ Organizational Psychology	PhD	NA/NA	NA/NA	NA/NA	Not specified	NA/NA	Not specified	Not specified	NA/NA
School Psychology	PhD	150/158	145/155	3/4	Not specified	NA/3.59	Not specified	Not specified	NA/3.9
Cognitive and Brain Sciences	PhD	Not specified	Not specified	Not specified	Not specified	Not specified	Not specified	Not specified	Not specified

Admissions Requirements:

Degree	GRE	GRE-Subject	Letters of Recommendation	Research Statement	Writing Sample	CV	Interview
Doctoral	Required	Optional	3	Required	Optional	Recommended	Required

Admissions Criteria:

GRE scores—high
Research experience—high
Work experience—low
Clinically related public service—low
GPA—high

Letters of recommendation—high
Interview—medium
Statement of goals and objectives—high
Undergraduate psychology preparation—high

For additional information on admission requirements, visit http://lsu.edu/hss/psychology/grad/prospective-student/NatureoftheProgram.php.

Department Demographics

	Male (PT)	Female (PT)	Total	African-American/ Black (PT)	Hispanic/ Latino (PT)	Asian/ Pacific Islander (PT)	American Indian/ Alaska Native (PT)	Caucasian/ White (PT)	Unknown	Multiethnic (PT)	ADA (PT)	Int'l (PT)
Students	28 (0)	75 (0)	103	5 (0)	3 (0)	6 (0)	1 (0)	82 (0)	1 (0)	5 (0)	0 (0)	6 (0)

Financial Information/Assistance

Tuition: For information on tuition costs, visit http://www.lsu.edu/bgtplan/Tuition-Fees/fee-schedules.php. Tuition is subject to change. Additional fees are assessed to students beyond the costs of tuition for the following: Operational fees, technology fee, etc., of roughly $1,500 per year.

Doctoral:
State residents: $10,486 per academic year.
Nonstate residents: $27,710 per academic year.

Financial Assistance:

	Teaching Assistantship (% Receiving)	Teaching Assistantship Tuition Remission	Research Assistantship (% Receiving)	Research Assistantship Tuition Remission	Fellowship (% Receiving)	Fellowship Tuition Remission
First-Year Student	$14,000 (52)	Full	$16,000 (26)	Full	$20,000 (13)	Full
Advanced Student	$14,000 (41)	Full	$16,000 (48)	Full	$20,000 (8)	Full

For additional information on financial assistance, visit http://lsu.edu/hss/psychology/grad/prospective-student/finances.php.

Employment of Department Graduates

Doctoral:
Enrolled in a postdoctoral residency/fellowship: 4
Employed in independent practice: 2
Employed in an academic position at a university: 6
Employed in academic position at a 2-year/4-year college: 3
Employed in a hospital/medical center: 4
Do not know: 1
Total: 20

Additional Information

Housing and Day Care: On-campus housing is available. See the following website for more information: http://www.lsu.edu/housing. On-campus day care facilities are available. See the following website for more information: http://www.lsu.edu/childcare.

Information for Students With Physical Disabilities: See the following website: http://disability.lsu.edu/.

Special Facilities or Resources: The department occupies a centrally located building designed specifically to accommodate our program. Audubon Hall houses faculty offices, instructional space, office space for graduate students, and facilities for a wide array of research. The department also has a Psychological Services Center that provides training for our students and mental health services to the community.

Application Information: Admissions Secretary, LSU Department of Psychology, 236 Audubon Hall, Baton Rouge, LA 70803. *Fee:* $50. *Online application:* http://sites01.lsu.edu/wp/graduateschool/apply-for-admission-to-graduate-study-at-lsu/.

Louisiana State University Shreveport

Department of Psychology
School of Human Sciences
One University Place
Shreveport, LA 71115
Telephone: (318) 797-5044
Chairperson: Yong Dai, PhD

E-mail: yong.dai@LSUS.edu
Web: http://www.lsus.edu/ehd/psyc/

Orientation, Objectives, and Emphasis of Department

The LSUS School Psychology program curriculum is aligned with the training standards recommended by the National Association of School Psychologists (NASP), and the program is fully accredited. The primary focus of training is to develop fluency in data-based problem solving across both academic and behavior domains, and the overarching framework is a tiered model of service delivery based on student response to intervention (RTI). The program features three practicum experiences prior to a culminating 1,200-hour internship in a public school setting. In the MSC program, students are offered a 60 credit hour program that will lead to licensure as a professional counselor. The program follows a practitioner-scientist model of training and is in the process of seeking accreditation by CACREP.

Programs and Degrees Offered

Program	Degree	Application Deadline	Applica-tions Received	Accepted	New Admits Enrolled (PT)	Total Enrolled (PT)	Degrees Awarded in 2014–2015	Median Years to Complete Degree	Dismissed/ Withdrew
School Psychology	EdS	April 30 (Fall)	14	8	5 (0)	11 (7)	3	3	0
Counseling	MA/MS	June 30 (Fall), October 15 (Spring), March 31 (Summer)	20	16	10 (4)	27 (10)	13	2	4

Internships/Practica

Practica for our Specialist degree students are carried out in surrounding parishes which have cooperative agreements with the university for training purposes. There are two distinct practicum experiences for our students. The first involves an observational practicum required during the Introduction to School Psychology course. The second occurs during Psych 754—a formal, 200-plus hour practicum that is done in cooperating parishes with school psychologist field supervisors. All students must complete an appropriate internship to qualify for State certification. Students in the MSC program also are required to serve community-based supervised practicum experiences, in addition to a two-semester internship experience supervised by an LPC or another appropriate mental health professional acceptable to the program. These internships are not CACREP-approved, but currently meet LPC licensure requirements.

Admissions

Entries appear in the following order: required test or GPA, minimum score (if required)/median score of students entering in 2015–2016.

Program	Degree	GRE-V	GRE-Q	GRE-Writing	GRE-Subject	Under-graduate GPA	Last 2 Years GPA	Psychol-ogy GPA	Master's GPA
School Psychology	EdS	142/150	140/146	Not specified	Not specified	2.43/3.29	Not specified	Not specified	Not specified
Counseling	MA/MS	Not specified	Not specified	Not specified	Not specified	Not specified	Not specified	Not specified	Not specified

Admissions Requirements:

Degree	GRE	GRE-Subject	Letters of Recommendation	Research Statement	Writing Sample	CV	Interview
Master's/Specialist	Required	None	2	Required	Optional	Required	Required

Admissions Criteria:

GRE scores—medium
Research experience—low
Work experience—low
Clinically related public service—low
GPA—high

Letters of recommendation—high
Interview—high
Statement of goals and objectives—high
Undergraduate psychology preparation—medium

Department Demographics

	Male (PT)	Female (PT)	Total	African-American/Black (PT)	Hispanic/Latino (PT)	Asian/Pacific Islander (PT)	American Indian/Alaska Native (PT)	Caucasian/White (PT)	Unknown	Multiethnic (PT)	ADA (PT)	Int'l (PT)
Students	2 (0)	13 (4)	19	5 (0)			0 (0)	10 (4)	0 (0)	(0)	0 (0)	1 (0)

Financial Information/Assistance

Tuition: For information on tuition costs, visit http://www.lsus.edu/offices-and-services/accounting-services/tuition-and-fee-schedule. Tuition is subject to change.

Master's:
State residents: $6,952 per academic year.
State residents: $382 per credit hour.
Nonstate residents: $19,450 per academic year.
Nonstate residents: $1,076 per credit hour.

Financial Assistance:

	Teaching Assistantship (% Receiving)	Teaching Assistantship Tuition Remission	Research Assistantship (% Receiving)	Research Assistantship Tuition Remission	Fellowship (% Receiving)	Fellowship Tuition Remission
First-Year Student	NA (NA)	NA	$5,000 (NA)	Full	NA (NA)	NA
Advanced Student	NA (NA)	NA	$5,000 (NA)	Full	NA (NA)	NA

For additional information on financial assistance, visit http://www.lsus.edu/academics/graduate-studies/financial-assistance.

Employment of Department Graduates

Master's:
Enrolled in a psychology doctoral program: 2
Employed in a professional position in a school system: 4
Employed in a community mental health/counseling center: 6
Employed in a hospital/medical center: 2
Other employment position: 2
Total: 16

Additional Information

Housing and Day Care: On-campus housing is available. See the following website for more information: http://www.lsus.edu/student-life/housing. No on-campus day care facilities are available.

Information for Students With Physical Disabilities: See the following website: http://www.lsus.edu/offices-and-services/student-development.

Special Facilities or Resources: The Master's in Counseling and Specialist in School Psychology programs have state-of-the-art audio/video equipment for counseling and intervention techniques and skills, all housed in the psychology clinic and department.

Application Information: Yong Dai, PhD, Chair, Department of Psychology, Louisiana State University Shreveport, 1 University Place, Shreveport, LA 71115. *Fee:* $20. *Online application:* http://www.lsus.edu/admissions-and-financial-aid/graduate-admissions.

Louisiana, University of, Lafayette
Department of Psychology
Liberal Arts
P.O. Box 43644 UL-Lafayette Station
Lafayette, LA 70504-3644
Telephone: (337) 482-6597
Department Head: Cheryl S. Lynch

E-mail: csm5689@louisiana.edu
Web: http://psychology.louisiana.edu/

Orientation, Objectives, and Emphasis of Department
The Department of Psychology at the University of Louisiana at Lafayette strives to promote the study of psychology as a science, as a profession, and as a means of promoting human welfare. A master's program is offered with options enabling tailoring the program to specific areas of specialization in experimental or applied psychology. The program is predoctoral, and all students will complete a thesis as part of their requirements.

Programs and Degrees Offered

Program	Degree	Application Deadline	Applica-tions Received	Accepted	New Admits Enrolled (PT)	Total Enrolled (PT)	Degrees Awarded in 2014–2015	Median Years to Complete Degree	Dismissed/Withdrew
Experimental Psychology	MA/MS	March 1 (Fall)	33	16	13 (0)	29 (11)	10	2.75	0

Internships/Practica
Internships for master's students specializing in applied areas provide training in applied behavior analysis, psychological assessment, and empirically supported individual and group-based therapies. Populations served include, but are not limited to, children with attention, learning, and developmental disabilities, pain or bariatric patients, adults with substance use disorders, offenders, and college students.

Admissions
Entries appear in the following order: required test or GPA, minimum score (if required)/median score of students entering in 2015–2016.

Program	Degree	GRE-V	GRE-Q	GRE-Writing	GRE-Subject	Under-graduate GPA	Last 2 Years GPA	Psychol-ogy GPA	Master's GPA
Experimental Psychology	MA/MS	148/NA	147/NA	Not specified	Not specified	3/NA	3/NA	3/NA	Not specified

Admissions Requirements:

Degree	GRE	GRE-Subject	Letters of Recom-mendation	Research Statement	Writing Sample	CV	Interview
Master's/Specialist	Required	None	3	Required	Recom-mended	Recom-mended	Required

Admissions Criteria:

GRE scores—medium
Research experience—high
Work experience—medium
Clinically related public service—low
GPA—medium

Letters of recommendation—high
Interview—high
Statement of goals and objectives—high
Undergraduate psychology preparation—medium

For additional information on admission requirements, visit http://psychology.louisiana.edu/programs/gr-degrees.shtml.

Department Demographics

	Male (PT)	Female (PT)	Total	African-American/ Black (PT)	Hispanic/ Latino (PT)	Asian/ Pacific Islander (PT)	American Indian/ Alaska Native (PT)	Caucasian/ White (PT)	Unknown (PT)	Multiethnic (PT)	ADA (PT)	Int'l (PT)
Students	12 (3)	17 (8)	40	1 (2)	1 (0)	1 (0)	1 (0)	21 (8)	0 (1)	1 (0)	0 (0)	3 (0)

Financial Information/Assistance

Tuition: For information on tuition costs, visit http://bursar.louisiana.edu/tuition-fees/tuition-fee-schedules. Tuition is subject to change. Tuition costs vary by program.

Master's:
State residents: $9,208 per academic year.
Nonstate residents: $22,936 per academic year.

Financial Assistance:

	Teaching Assistantship (% Receiving)	Teaching Assistantship Tuition Remission	Research Assistantship (% Receiving)	Research Assistantship Tuition Remission	Fellowship (% Receiving)	Fellowship Tuition Remission
First-Year Student	$7,500 (30)	Full	NA (NA)	NA	$9,500 (14)	Full
Advanced Student	$7,500 (30)	Full	NA (NA)	NA	NA (NA)	NA

For additional information on financial assistance, visit http://gradschool.louisiana.edu/prospective-students/tuition-costs.

Employment of Department Graduates

Master's:
Enrolled in another graduate/professional program: 2
Employed in a community mental health/counseling center: 2
Do not know: 6
Total: 10

Additional Information

Housing and Day Care: On-campus housing is available. See the following website for more information: http://housing.louisiana.edu/. On-campus day care facilities are available. See the following website for more information: http://childdev.louisiana.edu/; http://soci-anth.louisiana.edu/programs/NurseryLab.shtml.

Information for Students With Physical Disabilities: See the following website: http://disability.louisiana.edu/.

Special Facilities or Resources: The Psychology Department houses 3 computer laboratories optimized for research. Computer assisted instruction is available for several courses. Major physiological research is conducted at the nearby primate center, The New Iberia Research Center. The University of Louisiana at Lafayette has excellent computer facilities.

Application Information: Graduate School Director, Martin Hall, P.O. Box 44610, University of Louisiana at Lafayette, Lafayette, LA 70504. *Fee:* $25. *Online application:* http://gradschool.louisiana.edu/prospective-students/apply-now.

Louisiana, University of, Monroe
Department of Psychology
College of Business & Social Sciences
700 University Avenue
Monroe, LA 71209
Telephone: (318) 342-1345
Psychology Graduate Admissions & Assistantships Director: Jack A. Palmer

E-mail: palmer@ulm.edu
Web: http://www.ulm.edu/psychology/

Orientation, Objectives, and Emphasis of Department
Three areas of concentration are available in the MS program. The general-experimental option focuses upon the basic science areas of psychology. The psychometric (preclinical) option is structured for those whose primary interest is employment in mental health or related settings. A new concentration in Forensic Psychology has been created which is fully online. All programs require a comprehensive examination and an option of a thesis or research project in conjunction with an internship or grant application.

Programs and Degrees Offered

Program	Degree	Application Deadline	Applications Received	Accepted	New Admits Enrolled (PT)	Total Enrolled (PT)	Degrees Awarded in 2014–2015	Median Years to Complete Degree	Dismissed/ Withdrew
Experimental Psychology	MA/MS	July 1 (Fall), December 1 (Spring)	3	3	3 (2)	12 (4)	1	2	0
Psychometrics	MA/MS	July 1 (Fall), December 1 (Spring)	3		2 (1)	13 (4)	5	2	
Forensic Psychology	MA/MS	July 1 (Fall), December 1 (Spring)	3	3	3 (0)	12 (4)	2	2	

Internships/Practica
Practica and internships are not required but encouraged for the psychometric concentration of the MS program.

Admissions
Entries appear in the following order: required test or GPA, minimum score (if required)/median score of students entering in 2015–2016.

Program	Degree	GRE-V	GRE-Q	GRE-Writing	GRE-Subject	Under-graduate GPA	Last 2 Years GPA	Psychol-ogy GPA	Master's GPA
Experimental Psychology	MA/MS	135/144	138/143	Not specified	Not specified	2.7/3.4	Not specified	Not specified	Not specified
Psychometrics	MA/MS	135/144	138/143	Not specified	Not specified	2.75/3.4	Not specified	Not specified	Not specified
Forensic Psychology	MA/MS	135/144	138/143	Not specified	Not specified	Not specified	Not specified	Not specified	Not specified

Admissions Requirements:

Degree	GRE	GRE-Subject	Letters of Recom-mendation	Research Statement	Writing Sample	CV	Interview
Master's/Specialist	Required	Optional	N/A	Recom-mended	Optional	Optional	Optional

Admissions Criteria:

GRE scores—high
Research experience—medium
Work experience—medium
Clinically related public service—medium
GPA—high

Letters of recommendation—medium
Interview—low
Statement of goals and objectives—low
Undergraduate psychology preparation—medium

For additional information on admission requirements, visit http://ulm.edu/gradschool/ms_psychology.html.

Department Demographics

	Male (PT)	Female (PT)	Total	African-American/ Black (PT)	Hispanic/ Latino (PT)	Asian/ Pacific Islander (PT)	American Indian/ Alaska Native (PT)	Caucasian/ White (PT)	Unknown	Multiethnic (PT)	ADA (PT)	Int'l (PT)
Students	10 (4)	27 (8)	49	10 (5)	2 (0)	3 (0)	0 (0)	22 (7)	0 (0)	0 (0)	0 (0)	7 (0)

Financial Information/Assistance

Tuition: For information on tuition costs, visit http://www.ulm.edu/controller/sas_tuition.html.

Master's:
State residents: $8,004 per academic year.
Nonstate residents: $20,104 per academic year.

Financial Assistance:

	Teaching Assistantship (% Receiving)	Teaching Assistantship Tuition Remission	Research Assistantship (% Receiving)	Research Assistantship Tuition Remission	Fellowship (% Receiving)	Fellowship Tuition Remission
First-Year Student	NA (NA)	NA	$6,000 (33)	Full	NA (NA)	NA
Advanced Student	NA (NA)	NA	$6,000 (33)	Full	NA (NA)	NA

For additional information on financial assistance, visit http://www.ulm.edu/financialaid/.

Employment of Department Graduates

Master's:
Enrolled in a psychology doctoral program: 5
Enrolled in another graduate/professional program: 1
Employed in an academic position at a university: 4
Employed in academic position at a 2-year/4-year college: 1
Employed in other positions at a higher education institution: 1
Employed in business or industry: 1
Employed in government agency: 1
Employed in a community mental health/counseling center: 1
Employed in a hospital/medical center: 3
Total: 18

Additional Information

Housing and Day Care: On-campus housing is available. See the following website for more information: http://www.ulm.edu/reslife/. On-campus day care facilities are available. See the following website for more information: http://www.ulm.edu/cdc/.

Information for Students With Physical Disabilities: See the following website: http://www.ulm.edu/counselingcenter/special.html.

Special Facilities or Resources: A psychological services center includes a test library and special rooms. The department also has a computer room with 16 PCs with a printer for general student use.

Application Information: Graduate School, University of Louisiana-Monroe, 700 University Avenue, Monroe, LA 71209. *Fee:* $20. *Online application:* http://www.ulm.edu/gradschool/applyonline.html.

New Orleans, University of
Department of Psychology
College of Sciences
2001 Geology and Psychology Building
New Orleans, LA 70148
Telephone: (504) 280-6291
Chairperson: Laura Scaramella

E-mail: lscarame@uno.edu
Web: http://www.uno.edu/cos/psychology/

Orientation, Objectives, and Emphasis of Department
The University of New Orleans Department of Psychology offers a PhD program with specializations in applied biopsychology and applied developmental psychology. The program was established in 1980 in response to a growing need for persons who are thoroughly trained in the basic content areas of human development or biopsychology, and who are able to translate that knowledge into practical applications. Both specialties emphasize research and service delivery in applied contexts. The applied developmental program has chosen to focus its training in the area of developmental psychopathology. Graduates are trained to work in a variety of settings where they can advance programmatic research focused on understanding psychopathological conditions from a developmental perspective and where they can make practical applications from this research (e.g., design and implement innovative prevention programs, or develop assessments for at-risk children). Similarly, the applied biopsychology program has chosen to focus its training in the area of the biological bases of psychopathology. Graduates are trained to work in a variety of settings where they can advance programmatic research focused on understanding psychopathological conditions from a biological and neuroscience perspective and where they can make practical applications from this research.

Programs and Degrees Offered

Program	Degree	Application Deadline	Applica-tions Received	Accepted	New Admits Enrolled (PT)	Total Enrolled (PT)	Degrees Awarded in 2014–2015	Median Years to Complete Degree	Dismissed/ Withdrew
Applied Biopsychology	PhD	January 7 (Fall)	11	2	0 (0)	13 (0)	2	6	1
Applied Developmental Psychology	PhD	January 7 (Fall)	33	0	0 (0)	18 (0)	6	5	0

Internships/Practica
Students in both applied specialties are required to complete 12 semester hours of practicum training for the doctoral degree. There are a wide array of practicum experiences available and student's choice of practicum is based on his or her specific career objectives.

Admissions
Entries appear in the following order: required test or GPA, minimum score (if required)/median score of students entering in 2015–2016.

Program	Degree	GRE-V	GRE-Q	GRE-Writing	GRE-Subject	Under-graduate GPA	Last 2 Years GPA	Psychol-ogy GPA	Master's GPA
Applied Biopsychology	PhD	NA/155	NA/152	Not specified	Not specified	NA/3.75	Not specified	Not specified	Not specified
Applied Developmental Psychology	PhD	NA/158	NA/154	Not specified	Not specified	NA/3.64	Not specified	Not specified	Not specified

Admissions Requirements:

Degree	GRE	GRE-Subject	Letters of Recommendation	Research Statement	Writing Sample	CV	Interview
Doctoral	Required	None	3	Required	Optional	Optional	Required

Admissions Criteria:

GRE scores—high
Research experience—high
Work experience—low
Clinically related public service—medium
GPA—high

Letters of recommendation—high
Interview—medium
Statement of goals and objectives—high
Undergraduate psychology preparation—medium

For additional information on admission requirements, visit http://www.uno.edu/cos/psychology/application-info.aspx.

Department Demographics

	Male (PT)	Female (PT)	Total	African-American/Black (PT)	Hispanic/Latino (PT)	Asian/Pacific Islander (PT)	American Indian/Alaska Native (PT)	Caucasian/White (PT)	Unknown	Multiethnic (PT)	ADA (PT)	Int'l (PT)
Students	10 (0)	23 (0)	33	1 (0)	1 (0)	1 (0)	0 (0)	30 (0)	0 (0)	0 (0)	0 (0)	1 (0)

Financial Information/Assistance

Tuition: For information on tuition costs, visit http://www.uno.edu/bursar/TuitionFees/gradfees.aspx. Tuition is subject to change. Additional fees are assessed to students beyond the costs of tuition for the following: graduate enhancement fee, technology fee.

Doctoral:
State residents: $7,234 per academic year.
Nonstate residents: $20,967 per academic year.

Financial Assistance:

	Teaching Assistantship (% Receiving)	Teaching Assistantship Tuition Remission	Research Assistantship (% Receiving)	Research Assistantship Tuition Remission	Fellowship (% Receiving)	Fellowship Tuition Remission
First-Year Student	$11,000 (NA)	Full	$11,000 (NA)	Full	$15,000 (NA)	Full
Advanced Student	$11,000 (NA)	Full	$12,421 (NA)	Full	$15,370 (NA)	Full

For additional information on financial assistance, visit http://www.uno.edu/grad/financing-your-education/index.aspx.

Employment of Department Graduates

Doctoral:
Enrolled in a postdoctoral residency/fellowship: 4
Employed in academic position at a 2-year/4-year college: 1
Employed in other positions at a higher education institution: 1
Employed in a hospital/medical center: 1
Total: 7

Additional Information

Housing and Day Care: On-campus housing is available. See the following website for more information: http://www.uno.edu/housing/lafitte-village.aspx. No on-campus day care facilities are available.

Information for Students With Physical Disabilities: See the following website: http://www.uno.edu/disability-services/.

Application Information: Graduate Coordinator, Department of Psychology, 2001 Geology & Psychology Building, New Orleans, LA 70148. *Fee:* $70. *Online application:* http://www.uno.edu/admissions/apply/.

Southeastern Louisiana University
Department of Psychology
Arts, Humanities, and Social Sciences
SLU 10831
Hammond, LA 70402
Telephone: (985) 549-2154
Department Head: Susan Coats

E-mail: pvarnado@selu.edu
Web: http://www.southeastern.edu/acad_research/depts/psyc/grad_degree/index.html

Orientation, Objectives, and Emphasis of Department
The purposes of offering graduate study in the Department of Psychology are to prepare the student for a PhD program in Psychology through a Master of Arts degree program by providing knowledge and research skills, and to provide students not intending to pursue a PhD degree with a variety of courses that will help prepare them for paraprofessional positions. We also offer an Industrial/Organizational (I/O) concentration for students interested in entering the business professions following graduation with their master's degree. Our program has maintained a strong rate of placement (75%–90%) into doctoral programs over the last 7 years.

Programs and Degrees Offered

Program	Degree	Application Deadline	Applications Received	Accepted	New Admits Enrolled (PT)	Total Enrolled (PT)	Degrees Awarded in 2014–2015	Median Years to Complete Degree	Dismissed/ Withdrew
General Psychology	MA/MS	March 15 (Fall), October 15 (Spring)	35	11	6 (0)	16 (16)	3	3	3
Industrial/ Organizational Psychology	MA/MS	March 15 (Fall), October 15 (Spring)	5	4	3 (0)	5 (3)	2	2.5	0

Internships/Practica
Practica are available in clinical, counseling, and business (for I/O concentration) settings.

Admissions
Entries appear in the following order: required test or GPA, minimum score (if required)/median score of students entering in 2015–2016.

Program	Degree	GRE-V	GRE-Q	GRE-Writing	GRE-Subject	Undergraduate GPA	Last 2 Years GPA	Psychology GPA	Master's GPA
General Psychology	MA/MS	145/155	143/149	Not specified	Not specified	2.89/3.54	Not specified	3.29/3.72	Not specified
Industrial/ Organizational Psychology	MA/MS	143/153	146/150	Not specified	Not specified	2.92/3.14	Not specified	3.16/3.52	Not specified

Admissions Requirements:

Degree	GRE	GRE-Subject	Letters of Recommendation	Research Statement	Writing Sample	CV	Interview
Master's/Specialist	Required	Required	3	Required	Recommended	Required	Optional

Admissions Criteria:

GRE scores—high
Research experience—high
Work experience—low
Clinically related public service—low

GPA—high
Letters of recommendation—high
Statement of goals and objectives—medium
Undergraduate psychology preparation—medium

For additional information on admission requirements, visit http://www.southeastern.edu/acad_research/depts/psyc/grad_degree/app_procedure/index.html.

Department Demographics

	Male (PT)	Female (PT)	Total	African-American/ Black (PT)	Hispanic/ Latino (PT)	Asian/ Pacific Islander (PT)	American Indian/ Alaska Native (PT)	Caucasian/ White (PT)	Unknown (PT)	Multiethnic (PT)	ADA (PT)	Int'l (PT)
Students	5 (4)	16 (15)	40	0 (0)	1 (0)	0 (1)	0 (0)	20 (18)	0 (0)	0 (0)	0 (0)	0 (0)

Financial Information/Assistance

Tuition: For information on tuition costs, visit http://www.southeastern.edu/admin/controller/tuition/index.html. Tuition is subject to change. Additional fees are assessed to students beyond the costs of tuition for the following: rental textbooks; id fee; international fee.

Master's:
State residents: $7,940 per academic year.
Nonstate residents: $20,417 per academic year.

Financial Assistance:

	Teaching Assistantship (% Receiving)	Teaching Assistantship Tuition Remission	Research Assistantship (% Receiving)	Research Assistantship Tuition Remission	Fellowship (% Receiving)	Fellowship Tuition Remission
First-Year Student	NA (NA)	NA	$9,000 (NA)	Full	$12,500 (NA)	Full
Advanced Student	NA (NA)	NA	$9,000 (NA)	Full	$12,500 (NA)	NA

Employment of Department Graduates

Master's:
Employed in business or industry: 3
Still seeking employment: 1
Not seeking employment: 1
Total: 5

Additional Information

Housing and Day Care: On-campus housing is available. See the following website for more information: http://www.southeastern.edu/admin/housing/. No on-campus day care facilities are available.

Information for Students With Physical Disabilities: See the following website: http://www.southeastern.edu/admin/ds/.

Special Facilities or Resources: The department has three 5-room laboratory suites for conducting research with humans. There are about 40 computers and seven printers in the department, about half of which are in a computer laboratory. Statistical packages, such as SPSS, are available on the computers and (via departmental terminal) on the university's mainframe computers.

Application Information: Paula Varnado-Sullivan, PhD, SLU Box 10831, Hammond, LA 70402. *Fee:* $20. *Online application:* http://www.southeastern.edu/apply/graduate/index.html.

Tulane University
Department of Psychology
School of Science and Engineering
2007 Stern Hall
New Orleans, LA 70118
Telephone: (504) 865-5331
Chairperson: Stacy L. Overstreet

E-mail: psych@tulane.edu
Web: http://tulane.edu/sse/psyc/

Orientation, Objectives, and Emphasis of Department
Tulane's Department of Psychology offers the PhD in cognitive/behavioral neuroscience, developmental psychology, school psychology (APA-accredited program) and social psychology. The Department does not offer programs in clinical or counseling psychology. All students are expected to articulate an individualized plan of study by the end of the first year of training, to be developed in consultation with an advisor and a committee of faculty members. Our two broad areas of substantive focus are development (e.g., infant, childhood, adolescence, cognitive aging and neuroscience) and culture and context (e.g., minority youth, stereotyping, ecological systems). Students are required to complete empirical studies for the master's thesis and the dissertation, and are expected to carry out additional research while in training. The APA-accredited program in school psychology, which emphasizes ecological systems and normal developmental processes, will take a minimum of 4 years to complete, with an additional year-long internship.

Programs and Degrees Offered

Program	Degree	Application Deadline	Applications Received	Accepted	New Admits Enrolled (PT)	Total Enrolled (PT)	Degrees Awarded in 2014–2015	Median Years to Complete Degree	Dismissed/ Withdrew
Social Psychology	PhD	December 1 (Fall)	40	2	2	8 (0)	2	4	0
School Psychology	PhD	December 1 (Fall)	40	5	4	22 (0)	5	6	0
Developmental Psychology	PhD	December 1 (Fall)	15	1	1	5 (0)	2		0
Cognitive/ Behavioral Neuroscience	PhD	December 1 (Fall)	30	1	0	2	0		0

APA Accreditation
School PhD: Student Outcome Data website: http://psych.tulane.edu/graduate/School/Aboutourprogram.Outcomes.htm.

Doctoral Degree (PhD School Psychology): For those doctoral students for whom a professional internship was required in this program prior to graduation:
Total students who applied for an internship: 2
Total students who obtained an internship: 2
Total students who obtained a paid internship: 2
Total students who obtained an unpaid internship: 0
Total students who were placed in APA/CPA-accredited internships: 2
Total students placed in internships not APA/CPA-accredited, but listed with the Association of Psychology Postdoctoral and Internship Centers (APPIC): 0
Total students placed in internships conforming to guidelines of the Council of Directors of School Psychology Programs (CDSPP): 0
Total students placed in internships that were not APA/CPA-accredited, APPIC or CDSSP listed: 0

Internships/Practica

Practicum opportunities are available in psychoeducational assessment, school consultation, family-school intervention, and cognitive-behavioral assessment and intervention.

Admissions

Entries appear in the following order: required test or GPA, minimum score (if required)/median score of students entering in 2015–2016.

Program	Degree	GRE-V	GRE-Q	GRE-Writing	GRE-Subject	Under-graduate GPA	Last 2 Years GPA	Psychol-ogy GPA	Master's GPA
Social Psychology	PhD	NA/NA	NA/NA	Not specified	Not specified	Not specified	Not specified	Not specified	Not specified
School Psychology	PhD	NA/NA	NA/NA	Not specified	Not specified	Not specified	Not specified	Not specified	Not specified
Developmental Psychology	PhD	NA/NA	NA/NA	Not specified	Not specified	Not specified	Not specified	Not specified	Not specified
Cognitive/ Behavioral Neuroscience	PhD	NA/NA	NA/NA	Not specified	Not specified	Not specified	Not specified	Not specified	Not specified

Admissions Requirements:

Degree	GRE	GRE-Subject	Letters of Recom-mendation	Research Statement	Writing Sample	CV	Interview
Doctoral	Required	Optional	3	Required	Optional	Optional	Required

Please note if these criteria vary for different programs: Clinical experience and interview important for school psychology. Relevant work experience can be looked upon favorably in other programs (e.g. statistical consulting; market research).

Admissions Criteria:

GRE scores—high
Research experience—high
Work experience—low
Clinically related public service—medium
GPA—high

Letters of recommendation—high
Interview—high
Statement of goals and objectives—medium
Undergraduate psychology preparation—medium

For additional information on admission requirements, visit http://tulane.edu/sse/psyc/academics/graduate/phd-programs/admission.cfm.

Department Demographics

	Male (PT)	Female (PT)	Total	African-American/ Black (PT)	Hispanic/ Latino (PT)	Asian/ Pacific Islander (PT)	American Indian/ Alaska Native (PT)	Caucasian/ White (PT)	Unknown	Multiethnic (PT)	ADA (PT)	Int'l (PT)
Students	9 (0)	28 (0)	37	6 (0)	0 (0)	1 (0)	0 (0)	29 (0)	0 (0)	1 (0)	0 (0)	2 (0)

Financial Information/Assistance

Tuition: For information on tuition costs, visit http://pandora.tcs.tulane.edu/acctrec/tuition.asp.

Doctoral:
State residents: $49,830 per academic year.
Nonstate residents: $49,830 per academic year.

Financial Assistance:

	Teaching Assistantship (% Receiving)	Teaching Assistantship Tuition Remission	Research Assistantship (% Receiving)	Research Assistantship Tuition Remission	Fellowship (% Receiving)	Fellowship Tuition Remission
First-Year Student	$19,000 (NA)	Full	$19,000 (NA)	Full	$26,000 (NA)	Full
Advanced Student	$19,000 (NA)	Full	$19,000 (NA)	Full	$26,000 (NA)	Full

For additional information on financial assistance, visit http://tulane.edu/financialaid/.

Employment of Department Graduates

Doctoral:
Enrolled in a postdoctoral residency/fellowship: 5
Employed in an academic position at a university: 1
Employed in a professional position in a school system: 1
Total: 7

Additional Information

Housing and Day Care: On-campus housing is available. See the following website for more information: http://tulane.edu/studentaffairs/housing/grad/. On-campus day care facilities are available. See the following website for more information: http://tulane.edu/childdevelopmentctrs/.

Information for Students With Physical Disabilities: See the following website: http://tulane.edu/studentaffairs/support/accessibility/index.cfm.

Special Facilities or Resources: The department has research laboratories and computer resources to facilitate research efforts requiring special equipment or space, including physiological, social, sensory, comparative, cognitive, and developmental psychology and human and animal learning. The Newcomb Children's Center, the Hebert facilities at Riverside for natural observation of animals, the laboratories of the Delta Primate Center, and the Audubon Zoological Gardens are available as research sites. There are also opportunities for research in the New Orleans area in organizations and industries, in public and private schools, and in hospitals and other settings serving children.

Application Information: Dean of the School of Science and Engineering, Tulane University, New Orleans, LA 70118. *Fee:* $0. *Online application:* http://tulane.edu/sse/academics/graduate/psycap.cfm.

Maine, University of
Department of Psychology
Liberal Arts and Sciences
5742 Little Hall
Orono, ME 04469-5742
Telephone: (207) 581-2030
Chairperson: Michael A. Robbins

E-mail: michael.robbins@umit.maine.edu
Web: http://www.umaine.edu/psychology/

Orientation, Objectives, and Emphasis of Department
The department believes that the best graduate education involves close working relationships between the faculty and the student. Thus, a high faculty-to-student ratio and small class sizes characterize the department. In addition, incoming students are selected to work with a faculty research mentor. There are also opportunities for individualized study and experience in directed readings, research, and teaching. A faculty committee, selected to represent the student's interests, will assist the student in planning an appropriate graduate program.

Programs and Degrees Offered

Program	Degree	Application Deadline	Applications Received	Accepted	New Admits Enrolled (PT)	Total Enrolled (PT)	Degrees Awarded in 2014–2015	Median Years to Complete Degree	Dismissed/ Withdrew
Clinical Psychology	PhD	December 1 (Fall)	92	7	4 (0)	19 (0)	4	6.5	1
Developmental Psychology	MA/MS	December 31 (Fall)	1	1	1 (0)	0		0
Psychological Sciences	MA/MS	December 31 (Fall)		3	3	4 (0)	0		0
Psychological Sciences	PhD	December 31 (Fall)		1	1	11	0		0

APA Accreditation
Clinical PhD: Student Outcome Data website: http://umaine.edu/clinicalpsychology/admissions/.

Doctoral Degree (PhD Clinical Psychology): For those doctoral students for whom a professional internship was required in this program prior to graduation:
Total students who applied for an internship: 5
Total students who obtained an internship: 5
Total students who obtained a paid internship: 5
Total students who obtained an unpaid internship: 0
Total students who were placed in APA/CPA-accredited internships: 5
Total students placed in internships not APA/CPA-accredited, but listed with the Association of Psychology Postdoctoral and Internship Centers (APPIC): 0
Total students placed in internships conforming to guidelines of the Council of Directors of School Psychology Programs (CDSPP): 0
Total students placed in internships that were not APA/CPA-accredited, APPIC or CDSSP listed: 0

Master's Degree (MA/MS Developmental Psychology): An internship experience, such as a final research project or "capstone" experience is required of graduates.

Internships/Practica
Several settings are used for practicum training: The Psychological Services Center housed within the department, Penobscot Job Corps, Maine General Medical Center, Eastern Maine Medical Center, Health Psychology Maine, Penobscot Community Health Care, School Administrative District #68.

Admissions

Entries appear in the following order: required test or GPA, minimum score (if required)/median score of students entering in 2015–2016.

Program	Degree	GRE-V	GRE-Q	GRE-Writing	GRE-Subject	Under-graduate GPA	Last 2 Years GPA	Psychol-ogy GPA	Master's GPA
Clinical Psychology	PhD	NA/158	NA/156	Not specified	Not specified	NA/3.67	Not specified	Not specified	Not specified
Developmental Psychology	MA/MS	NA/NA	NA/NA	Not specified	Not specified	NA/NA	Not specified	Not specified	Not specified
Psychological Sciences	MA/MS	Not specified	Not specified	Not specified	Not specified	Not specified	Not specified	Not specified	Not specified
Psychological Sciences	PhD	NA/157	NA/162	Not specified	Not specified	NA/3.78	Not specified	Not specified	Not specified

Admissions Requirements:

Degree	GRE	GRE-Subject	Letters of Recom-mendation	Research Statement	Writing Sample	CV	Interview
Master's/Specialist	Required	None	3	Required	Optional	Optional	Optional
Doctoral	Required	None	3	Required	Optional	Optional	Required

Admissions Criteria:

GRE scores—medium
Research experience—high
Work experience –low
Clinically related public service—medium
GPA—high

Letters of recommendation—high
Interview—high
Statement of goals and objectives—high
Undergraduate psychology preparation—high

For additional information on admission requirements, visit http://umaine.edu/psychology/graduate-program/.

Department Demographics

	Male (PT)	Female (PT)	Total	African-American/ Black (PT)	Hispanic/ Latino (PT)	Asian/ Pacific Islander (PT)	American Indian/ Alaska Native (PT)	Caucasian/ White (PT)	Unknown	Multiethnic (PT)	ADA (PT)	Int'l (PT)
Students	14 (0)	21 (0)	35	0 (0)	0 (0)	0 (0)	1 (0)	34 (0)	0 (0)	0 (0)	0 (0)	0 (0)

Financial Information/Assistance

Tuition: For information on tuition costs, visit http://umaine.edu/bursar/tuition-and-fees/. Tuition is subject to change. Additional fees are assessed to students beyond the costs of tuition for the following: $240 for 1–5 credits; $560 for 6–11 credits; unified fee and recreation center fee.

Doctoral:
State residents: $7,524 per academic year.
State residents: $418 per credit hour.
Nonstate residents: $23,580 per academic year.
Nonstate residents: $1,310 per credit hour.

Master's:
State residents: $418 per credit hour.
Nonstate residents: $1,310 per credit hour.

Financial Assistance:

	Teaching Assistantship (% Receiving)	Teaching Assistantship Tuition Remission	Research Assistantship (% Receiving)	Research Assistantship Tuition Remission	Fellowship (% Receiving)	Fellowship Tuition Remission
First-Year Student	$14,600 (NA)	Full	$15,100 (NA)	Full	NA (NA)	NA
Advanced Student	$14,600 (NA)	Full	$15,100 (NA)	Full	NA (NA)	Full

For additional information on financial assistance, visit https://umaine.edu/graduate/funding/.

Employment of Department Graduates

Doctoral:
Enrolled in a postdoctoral residency/fellowship: 4
Total: 4

Additional Information

Housing and Day Care: On-campus housing is available. See the following website for more information: http://umaine.edu/housing/graduate-housing/. On-campus day care facilities are available. See the following website for more information: http://umaine.edu/cntsp/withchildren/childcare/.

Information for Students With Physical Disabilities: See the following website: http://umaine.edu/disability/.

Special Facilities or Resources: Psychophysiological, perception, EEG laboratories; animal research laboratory; on-site practicum training center; department-run preschool.

Application Information: Graduate School, 5782 Winslow Hall, University of Maine, Orono, ME 04469-5782. *Fee:* $65. *Online application:* http://www.umaine.edu/graduate//admissions/admissions.

Baltimore, University of
Division of Applied Behavioral Sciences
Yale Gordon College of Arts and Sciences
1420 North Charles Street
Baltimore, MD 21201-5779
Telephone: (410) 837-5310
Chairperson: Sharon Glazer, PhD
Web: http://www.ubalt.edu/cas/graduate-programs-and-certificates/degree-programs/masters-applied-psychology/

E-mail: eljohnson@ubalt.edu

Orientation, Objectives, and Emphasis of Department
The Division of Applied Behavioral Sciences has a practitioner-oriented faculty of applied psychologists and researchers. The Master of Science program in Applied Psychology prepares students for careers in counseling or industrial/organizational psychology, or for doctoral studies in these fields. The state-of-the-art curriculum provides grounding in psychological theory, research knowledge and skills, ethics, multicultural competencies, and evidence-based practices. Principles drawn from biological, cognitive, and behavioral psychology are learned and applied in seated and hybrid classroom course instruction, independent studies, participation in faculty research, international coursework, theses, and supervised, hands-on experience in practica and internships.

Programs and Degrees Offered

Program	Degree	Application Deadline	Applica-tions Received	Accepted	New Admits Enrolled (PT)	Total Enrolled (PT)	Degrees Awarded in 2014–2015	Median Years to Complete Degree	Dismissed/ Withdrew
Counseling Psychology	MA/MS	July 1 (Fall), December 1 (Spring)	87	67	29 (15)	53 (46)	28	2.25	2
Industrial/ Organizational Psychology	MA/MS	July 1 (Fall), December 1 (Spring)	52	41	19 (2)	30 (13)	12	2	0
Certificate in Professional Counseling Studies	Other	Rolling	22	19	2 (17)	2 (17)	12	1	0

Internships/Practica
The Baltimore/Washington Metropolitan area provides a wide range of settings for paid and unpaid practicum and internships. The academic and site supervisors work closely with the intern to insure a quality experience.

Admissions
Entries appear in the following order: required test or GPA, minimum score (if required)/median score of students entering in 2015–2016.

Program	Degree	GRE-V	GRE-Q	GRE-Writing	GRE-Subject	Under-graduate GPA	Last 2 Years GPA	Psychol-ogy GPA	Master's GPA
Counseling Psychology	MA/MS	NA/152	NA/145	NA/4	Not specified	3/3.28	Not specified	Not specified	Not specified
Industrial/ Organizational Psychology	MA/MS	NA/158	NA/152	Not specified	Not specified	3/3.5	Not specified	Not specified	Not specified
Certificate in Professional Counseling Studies	Other	Not specified	Not specified	Not specified	Not specified	Not specified	Not specified	Not specified	Not specified

Admissions Requirements:

Degree	GRE	GRE-Subject	Letters of Recommendation	Research Statement	Writing Sample	CV	Interview
Master's/Specialist	Required	None	1	Required	Optional	Optional	None

Admissions Criteria:

GRE scores—medium
Research experience—low
Work experience—low
Clinically related public service—low

GPA—high
Letters of recommendation—high
Statement of goals and objectives—medium
Undergraduate psychology preparation—high

For additional information on admission requirements, visit http://www.ubalt.edu/admission/graduate/how-to-apply.cfm.

Department Demographics

	Male (PT)	Female (PT)	Total	African-American/ Black (PT)	Hispanic/ Latino (PT)	Asian/ Pacific Islander (PT)	American Indian/ Alaska Native (PT)	Caucasian/ White (PT)	Unknown	Multiethnic (PT)	ADA (PT)	Int'l (PT)
Students	27 (22)	50 (51)	150	12 (23)	2 (4)	0 (0)	0 (0)	52 (36)	2 (5)	6 (4)	2 (1)	3 (1)

Financial Information/Assistance

Tuition: For information on tuition costs, visit http://www.ubalt.edu/admission/tuition-and-fees/. Tuition is subject to change.

Master's:
State residents: $730 per credit hour.
Nonstate residents: $1,059 per credit hour.

Financial Assistance:

	Teaching Assistantship (% Receiving)	Teaching Assistantship Tuition Remission	Research Assistantship (% Receiving)	Research Assistantship Tuition Remission	Fellowship (% Receiving)	Fellowship Tuition Remission
First-Year Student	NA (NA)	NA	$4,260 (NA)	Full	NA (NA)	NA
Advanced Student	NA (NA)	NA	$4,260 (NA)	Full	NA (NA)	NA

For additional information on financial assistance, visit http://www.ubalt.edu/admission/financial-aid/index.cfm.

Employment of Department Graduates

No information provided.

Additional Information

Housing and Day Care: On-campus housing is available. See the following website for more information: http://www.ubalt.edu/campus-life/housing/. No on-campus day care facilities are available.

Information for Students With Physical Disabilities: See the following website: http://www.ubalt.edu/campus-life/center-for-educational-access/index.cfm.

Special Facilities or Resources: Four different university labs and 100% of our classrooms provide Internet access, MS Office, and SPSS for students and faculty members. The Wagman Psychology Lab provides space for computer based testing and assessment.

Application Information: Office of Graduate Admissions, University of Baltimore, 1420 North Charles Street, Baltimore, MD 21201-5779. *Fee:* $40. *Online application:* http://ubalt.edu/admission/apply-now/.

Frostburg State University
MS in Counseling Psychology Program
College of Liberal Arts and Sciences
Department of Psychology, 101 Braddock Road
Frostburg, MD 21532
Telephone: (301) 687-4446
Graduate Coordinator: Dr. Michael Murtagh

E-mail: mpmurtagh@frostburg.edu
Web: http://www.frostburg.edu/dept/psyc/graduate-information/

Orientation, Objectives, and Emphasis of Department
Providing training in professional psychology at the Master's level, FSU's program is designed for those pursuing further study in science-based counseling psychology. Our theoretical perspective is integrative, including cognitive-behavioral, motivational interviewing, family systems, developmental, multicultural, humanistic, and brief therapies. We emphasize training in empirically supported treatments for adults, children, adolescents, and families. Students develop counseling skills through learning about self, client, counselor-client relationships, and the importance of cultural contexts. Considerable attention is given not only to development of professional skills but also to personal development and multicultural awareness. These emphases reflect our belief that an effective counselor is one who is self-aware and receptive to consultation. For continuing study at the doctoral level, experience and knowledge gained in this program provide a firm foundation. Optional research opportunities prepare students for advanced graduate study in psychology. Two emphasis programs provide specialized training in Addictions Counseling Psychology and Child and Family Counseling Psychology. These can be completed within the 3-year program of study, as well as courses required for licensure. All National Counselor Exam course areas are offered, and FSU offers this exam. The Master's in Psychology Accreditation Council accredits this program.

Programs and Degrees Offered

Program	Degree	Application Deadline	Applications Received	Accepted	New Admits Enrolled (PT)	Total Enrolled (PT)	Degrees Awarded in 2014–2015	Median Years to Complete Degree	Dismissed/ Withdrew
Counseling Psychology	MA/MS	February 15 (Fall)	32	12	11	26 (3)	8	3	2

Internships/Practica
An extensive, two semester internship experience is required which facilitates students' receptivity to supervisory feedback, enhances self-awareness, and provides a setting in which the transition from student to professional is accomplished. In addition to on-site supervision, students participate in individual and group supervision with FSU faculty. Past graduate internship sites for the MS Counseling Psychology program have included outpatient community mental health (the most frequent internship setting); college counseling; inpatient psychiatric; inpatient and outpatient addictions; family services; K–12 psychological assessment and alternative classroom and after school care programs; community health advocacy and counseling; criminal justice system; nursing homes; hospital-based crisis services; hospice; and domestic violence programs. Students construct their internship experiences in order to meet training goals they formulate. Students electing to complete graduate emphasis programs in Addictions Counseling Psychology and Child and Family Counseling Psychology must complete at least 150 hours of direct services in settings consistent with the certificate program's focus. Internship experiences, in addition to at least four academic semesters of study, prepare graduates for positions as mental health counselors, marriage and family counselors, crisis counselors, drug and alcohol counselors, community health specialists, and in supervisory positions in a variety of settings.

Admissions
Entries appear in the following order: required test or GPA, minimum score (if required)/median score of students entering in 2015–2016.

Program	Degree	GRE-V	GRE-Q	GRE-Writing	GRE-Subject	Under-graduate GPA	Last 2 Years GPA	Psychology GPA	Master's GPA
Counseling Psychology	MA/MS	Not specified	Not specified	Not specified	Not specified	3/NA	Not specified	Not specified	Not specified

Admissions Requirements:

Degree	GRE	GRE-Subject	Letters of Recommendation	Research Statement	Writing Sample	CV	Interview
Master's/Specialist	None	None	3	Required	None	Required	Required

Admissions Criteria:

GRE scores—low
Research experience—low
Work experience—high
Clinically related public service—high
GPA—high

Letters of recommendation—medium
Interview—high
Statement of goals and objectives—medium
Undergraduate psychology preparation—medium
People skills—high

For additional information on admission requirements, visit http://www.frostburg.edu/dept/psyc/graduate-information/admissions/.

Department Demographics

	Male (PT)	Female (PT)	Total	African-American/ Black (PT)	Hispanic/ Latino (PT)	Asian/ Pacific Islander (PT)	American Indian/ Alaska Native (PT)	Caucasian/ White (PT)	Unknown (PT)	Multiethnic (PT)	ADA (PT)	Int'l (PT)
Students	5 (1)	21 (2)	29	0 (0)	0 (0)	0 (0)	0 (0)	26 (3)	0 (0)	0 (0)	0 (0)	1 (0)

Financial Information/Assistance

Tuition: For information on tuition costs, visit http://www.frostburg.edu/ungrad/expense/. Tuition is subject to change. Additional fees are assessed to students beyond the costs of tuition for the following: $106 per credit hour.

Master's:
State residents: $382 per credit hour.
Nonstate residents: $491 per credit hour.

Financial Assistance:

	Teaching Assistantship (% Receiving)	Teaching Assistantship Tuition Remission	Research Assistantship (% Receiving)	Research Assistantship Tuition Remission	Fellowship (% Receiving)	Fellowship Tuition Remission
First-Year Student	$6,000 (NA)	Full	$6,000 (NA)	Full	$6,500 (NA)	Full
Advanced Student	$6,000 (NA)	Full	$6,000 (NA)	Full	$6,500 (NA)	Full

For additional information on financial assistance, visit http://www.frostburg.edu/grad/financing-your-education/graduate-assistantships/.

Employment of Department Graduates

No information provided.

Additional Information

Housing and Day Care: On-campus housing is available. See the following website for more information: http://www.frostburg.edu/clife/reslife/. No on-campus day care facilities are available.

Information for Students With Physical Disabilities: See the following website: http://www.frostburg.edu/clife/dss/.

Special Facilities or Resources: Resources include specially designed counseling practice rooms for individual and group counseling. Two-way mirrors with adjacent observation rooms are available for supervision. Audiotaping and videotaping resources are available for faculty and student use. In addition, students' case conceptualization write-ups and all previous internship papers are available for restricted use by students.

Application Information: Office of Graduate Services, 101 Braddock Road, Frostburg State University, Frostburg, MD 21532. *Fee:* $30. *Online application:* http://www.frostburg.edu/grad/apply-to-fsu/.

Johns Hopkins University
Psychological and Brain Sciences
Krieger School of Arts and Sciences
3400 North Charles Street, Ames Hall 232
Baltimore, MD 21218
Telephone: (410) 516-7055
Chairperson: Dr. Susan Courtney

E-mail: pbs@jhu.edu
Web: http://pbs.jhu.edu

Orientation, Objectives, and Emphasis of Department
Since 1883, when the first psychological laboratory in America was founded at JHU, our department has been investigating the most fundamental questions of behavior, mind, and brain. Dedicated to research, not clinical training, the Department of Psychological and Brain Sciences at Johns Hopkins has one of the top-ranked psychology departments in the world. Psychological and brain sciences are concerned with understanding the biological and psychological processes underlying animal and human behavior, and with the effects of environmental influences on behavior at all stages of development. The program for doctoral students in psychological and brain sciences is scientifically oriented and emphasizes research methodology. The broad aims of the graduate program are to train students to become scientists rather than practitioners, and to provide them with the knowledge and skills they need to help solve the problems of contemporary society. The intimate size of the department gives students and faculty significant flexibility to design individual training programs, and promotes an atmosphere of exceptional collegiality. At the same time, the department has at its disposal all the resources of a major research university, as well as the advantages of its connection to one of the world's leading medical institutions.

Programs and Degrees Offered

Program	Degree	Application Deadline	Applications Received	Accepted	New Admits Enrolled (PT)	Total Enrolled (PT)	Degrees Awarded in 2014–2015	Median Years to Complete Degree	Dismissed/Withdrew
Biopsychology	PhD	December 15 (Fall)	17	4	2	8	1	5	0
Cognitive Psychology	PhD	December 15 (Fall)	26	4	2	9	1	5	0
Cognitive Neuroscience	PhD	December 15 (Fall)	32	2	2	12	1	5	0
Developmental Psychology	PhD	December 15 (Fall)	13	2	1	3	1	5	0

Admissions
Entries appear in the following order: required test or GPA, minimum score (if required)/median score of students entering in 2015–2016.

Program	Degree	GRE-V	GRE-Q	GRE-Writing	GRE-Subject	Undergraduate GPA	Last 2 Years GPA	Psychology GPA	Master's GPA
Biopsychology	PhD	Not specified	Not specified	Not specified	Not specified	Not specified	Not specified	Not specified	Not specified
Cognitive Psychology	PhD	Not specified	Not specified	Not specified	Not specified	Not specified	Not specified	Not specified	Not specified
Cognitive Neuroscience	PhD	Not specified	Not specified	Not specified	Not specified	Not specified	Not specified	Not specified	Not specified

Admissions *(con't.)*

Program	Degree	GRE-V	GRE-Q	GRE-Writing	GRE-Subject	Under-graduate GPA	Last 2 Years GPA	Psychology GPA	Master's GPA
Developmental Psychology	PhD	Not specified	Not specified	Not specified	Not specified	Not specified	Not specified	Not specified	Not specified

Admissions Requirements:

Degree	GRE	GRE-Subject	Letters of Recom-mendation	Research Statement	Writing Sample	CV	Interview
Doctoral	Required	None	3	Required	Required	Required	Optional

Admissions Criteria:

GRE scores—high
Research experience—high
Work experience—medium
Clinically related public service—low
GPA—high

Letters of recommendation—high
Interview—high
Statement of goals and objectives—high
Undergraduate psychology preparation—high
Sample of Work—medium

For additional information on admission requirements, visit http://pbs.jhu.edu/graduate/admissions/.

Department Demographics

	Male (PT)	Female (PT)	Total	African-American/ Black (PT)	Hispanic/ Latino (PT)	Asian/ Pacific Islander (PT)	American Indian/ Alaska Native (PT)	Caucasian/ White (PT)	Unknown	Multiethnic (PT)	ADA (PT)	Int'l (PT)
Students	13 (0)	19 (0)	32	1 (0)	2 (0)	13 (0)	1 (0)	13 (0)	0 (0)	2 (0)	0 (0)	15 (0)

Financial Information/Assistance

Tuition: For information on tuition costs, visit http://grad.jhu.edu/cost-of-attendance/tuition-and-fees/. Tuition is subject to change.

Doctoral:
State residents: $50,410 per academic year.
Nonstate residents: $50,410 per academic year.

Financial Assistance:

	Teaching Assistantship (% Receiving)	Teaching Assistantship Tuition Remission	Research Assistantship (% Receiving)	Research Assistantship Tuition Remission	Fellowship (% Receiving)	Fellowship Tuition Remission
First-Year Student	NA (NA)	Full	NA (NA)	Full	NA (NA)	NA
Advanced Student	NA (NA)	Full	NA (NA)	Full	NA (NA)	NA

For additional information on financial assistance, visit http://pbs.jhu.edu/graduate/financial-support.

Employment of Department Graduates

Doctoral:
Enrolled in a postdoctoral residency/fellowship: 2
Employed in an academic position at a university: 1
Employed in government agency: 1
Total: 4

Additional Information

Housing and Day Care: No on-campus housing is available. On-campus day care facilities are available. See the following website for more information: http://homewoodelc.org/.

Information for Students With Physical Disabilities: See the following website: http://web.jhu.edu/disabilities.

Special Facilities or Resources: Each faculty member has a state-of-the-art laboratory for his or her research. The laboratories in developmental and cognitive psychology contain, in addition to extensive computer equipment, special-purpose research equipment, including image-processing and large-format graphics systems, eye-movement monitors, speech-recognition and analysis systems, stereoscopic graphics systems, video equipment, and other stimulus-presentation and response-collection devices (including a TMS rig and an EEG system). The biopsychology labs have outstanding facilities for conducting research in biopsychology, including equipment for behavioral and operant testing, electrophysiology, histology, surgery, neurochemistry, and systems for the analysis and synthesis of audio signals. In addition, there are facilities for psychopharmacology, neuroanatomical imaging, and hormone, neurotransmitter, and immune products analysis. Environmental chambers for the control of light/dark and temperature cycles are used for research in seasonal behavior. Animal colony space and animal care services are excellent. The department is fortunate in that we have an in-house shop dedicated to the design and fabrication of custom research apparatus. Because of its broad scope, the study of psychology and related disciplines extends beyond our department to other departments and organizations within the university.

Application Information: JHU Office of Graduate Admission and Enrollment, 3400 North Charles Street, Shriver Hall 28, Baltimore, MD, 21218. *Fee:* $75. *Online application:* https://app.applyyourself.com/?id=jhu-grad.

Loyola University Maryland
Department of Psychology
4501 North Charles Street
Baltimore, MD 21210
Telephone: (410) 617-2175
Chairperson: Matthew W. Kirkhart, PhD

E-mail: tpmartino@loyola.edu
Web: http://www.loyola.edu/academic/psychology.aspx

Orientation, Objectives, and Emphasis of Department
The master's programs in Clinical and Counseling Psychology at Loyola University Maryland provide training to individuals who wish to promote mental health in individuals, families, organizations, and communities through careers in direct service, leadership, research, and education. We strive to provide a learning environment that facilitates the development of skills in critical thinking, scholarship, assessment and intervention, and that is grounded in an appreciation for both psychological science and human diversity. The goals of the PsyD program in Clinical Psychology are based on the scholar-practitioner model of training, designed to train autonomous practitioners of Health Service Psychology who will deliver mental health services and lead others in service to the general public in diverse settings.

Programs and Degrees Offered

Program	Degree	Application Deadline	Applications Received	Accepted	New Admits Enrolled (PT)	Total Enrolled (PT)	Degrees Awarded in 2014–2015	Median Years to Complete Degree	Dismissed/ Withdrew
Clinical Psychology	MA/MS	March 1 (Fall)	175	138	55 (5)	119 (21)	39	2.5	7
Counseling Psychology	MA/MS	March 1 (Fall)	70	52	11 (1)	41 (6)	25	2.5	2
Clinical Psychology	PsyD	December 1 (Fall)	333	37	17	71	14	4.5	1

APA Accreditation
Clinical PsyD: Student Outcome Data website: http://www.loyola.edu/zbin/external_sites/psychology/psych.html.

Doctoral Degree (PsyD Clinical Psychology): For those doctoral students for whom a professional internship was required in this program prior to graduation:
Total students who applied for an internship: 15

Total students who obtained an internship: 14
Total students who obtained a paid internship: 14
Total students who obtained an unpaid internship: 0
Total students who were placed in APA/CPA-accredited internships: 12
Total students placed in internships not APA/CPA-accredited, but listed with the Association of Psychology Postdoctoral and Internship Centers (APPIC): 0
Total students placed in internships conforming to guidelines of the Council of Directors of School Psychology Programs (CDSPP): 0
Total students placed in internships that were not APA/CPA-accredited, APPIC or CDSSP listed: 2

Master's Degree (MA/MS Clinical Psychology): An internship experience, such as a final research project or "capstone" experience is required of graduates. Master's Degree (MA/MS Counseling Psychology): An internship experience, such as a final research project or "capstone" experience is required of graduates.

Internships/Practica

The MS program, Practitioner Track requires 300 hours of externship experience. The MS program, Thesis Track requires 150 hours of externship experience. Students are able to choose from a wide variety of sites approved by the department. The PsyD program incorporates field placement training throughout the curriculum; a minimum of 1,260 hours of field training is required. The final year of the PsyD program is a full-time internship.

Admissions

Entries appear in the following order: required test or GPA, minimum score (if required)/median score of students entering in 2015–2016.

Program	Degree	GRE-V	GRE-Q	GRE-Writing	GRE-Subject	Under-graduate GPA	Last 2 Years GPA	Psychol-ogy GPA	Master's GPA
Clinical Psychology	MA/MS	NA/155	NA/152	NA/4.5	Not specified	3/NA	Not specified	Not specified	Not specified
Counseling Psychology	MA/MS	NA/155	NA/153	NA/4.5	Not specified	3/3.4	Not specified	Not specified	Not specified
Clinical Psychology	PsyD	NA/157	NA/155	NA/4.4	Not specified	3/3.5	Not specified	Not specified	Not specified

Admissions Requirements:

Degree	GRE	GRE-Subject	Letters of Recom-mendation	Research Statement	Writing Sample	CV	Interview
Master's/Specialist	Required	None	3	Required	None	Required	None
Doctoral	Required	None	3	Required	None	Required	Required

Admissions Criteria:

GRE scores—high
Research experience—high
Work experience—high
Clinically related public service—high
GPA—high

Letters of recommendation—high
Interview—high
Statement of goals and objectives—high
Undergraduate psychology preparation—high

For additional information on admission requirements, visit http://www.loyola.edu/academic/psychology/admission/requirements.

Department Demographics

	Male (PT)	Female (PT)	Total	African-American/ Black (PT)	Hispanic/ Latino (PT)	Asian/ Pacific Islander (PT)	American Indian/ Alaska Native (PT)	Caucasian/ White (PT)	Unknown	Multiethnic (PT)	ADA (PT)	Int'l (PT)
Students	48 (6)	183 (21)	258	30 (2)	18 (1)	18 (0)	0 (0)	152 (24)	11 (0)	2 (0)	0 (0)	5 (0)

Financial Information/Assistance

Tuition: For information on tuition costs, visit http://www.loyola.edu/department/financialservices/studentaccounts/tuition/graduatefees. Tuition is subject to change. Additional fees are assessed to students beyond the costs of tuition for the following: Registration, thesis fees, externship fees, lab fees, graduation. Tuition costs vary by program.

Doctoral:
State residents: $31,060 per academic year.
Nonstate residents: $31,060 per academic year.

Master's:
State residents: $880 per credit hour.
Nonstate residents: $880 per credit hour.

Financial Assistance:

	Teaching Assistantship (% Receiving)	Teaching Assistantship Tuition Remission	Research Assistantship (% Receiving)	Research Assistantship Tuition Remission	Fellowship (% Receiving)	Fellowship Tuition Remission
First-Year Student	NA (NA)	NA	NA (NA)	NA	NA (NA)	NA
Advanced Student	$1,600 (20)	Partial	$1,600 (20)	Partial	NA (NA)	NA

For additional information on financial assistance, visit http://www.loyola.edu/department/financialaid/graduate.

Employment of Department Graduates

Master's:
Enrolled in a psychology doctoral program: 10
Total: 10

Doctoral:
Enrolled in a postdoctoral residency/fellowship: 14
Total: 14

Additional Information

Housing and Day Care: No on-campus housing is available. No on-campus day care facilities are available.

Information for Students With Physical Disabilities: See the following website: http://www.loyola.edu/department/dss.

Special Facilities or Resources: Departmental facilities include the Loyola Clinic, a health psychology/behavioral medicine laboratory, audiovisual recording facilities, assessment and therapy training rooms, and a student lounge. Students have access to a campus-wide computer system, including SPSS and SAS software. All graduate students have e-mail addresses.

Application Information: Loyola University Maryland, Graduate Admission Processing Center, P.O. Box 1447, Beltsville, MD 20704. *Fee:* $60. *Online application:* http://www.loyola.edu/recruiter-grad.

Maryland, University of
Department of Counseling, Higher Education, and Special Education
College of Education
3115 Benjamin Building
College Park, MD 20742-1125
Telephone: (301) 405-2858
Chairperson: Roger Worthington

E-mail: cscott18@umd.edu
Web: http://www.education.umd.edu/CHSE/

Orientation, Objectives, and Emphasis of Department
Both the Counseling Psychology and School Psychology programs espouse the scientist–practitioner model of training. These programs enable students to become psychologists who are trained in general psychology, have expertise in conducting research on a wide range of psychological topics, and are highly competent in providing effective assessment and intervention services from a variety of theoretical perspectives. The Counseling Psychology program is administered collaboratively by the Counseling Psychology, School Psychology and Counselor Education Department, and the Psychology Department.

Programs and Degrees Offered

Program	Degree	Application Deadline	Applica-tions Received	Accepted	New Admits Enrolled (PT)	Total Enrolled (PT)	Degrees Awarded in 2014–2015	Median Years to Complete Degree	Dismissed/ Withdrew
Counseling Psychology	PhD	December 1 (Fall)	242	6	6 (0)	43 (0)	5	6	0
School Psychology	PhD	December 15 (Fall)	43	5	3 (0)	13 (10)	3	7	0

APA Accreditation

Counseling PhD: Student Outcome Data website: http://www.counselingpsychology.umd.edu/counsel2.html.
School PhD: Student Outcome Data website: http://www.education.umd.edu/CHSE/academics/specialization/schoolPsychology.html.

Doctoral Degree (PhD Counseling Psychology): For those doctoral students for whom a professional internship was required in this program prior to graduation:
Total students who applied for an internship: 8
Total students who obtained an internship: 8
Total students who obtained a paid internship: 8
Total students who obtained an unpaid internship: 0
Total students who were placed in APA/CPA-accredited internships: 8
Total students placed in internships not APA/CPA-accredited, but listed with the Association of Psychology Postdoctoral and Internship Centers (APPIC): 0
Total students placed in internships conforming to guidelines of the Council of Directors of School Psychology Programs (CDSPP): 0
Total students placed in internships that were not APA/CPA-accredited, APPIC or CDSSP listed: 0

Doctoral Degree (PhD School Psychology): For those doctoral students for whom a professional internship was required in this program prior to graduation:
Total students who applied for an internship: 3
Total students who obtained an internship: 3
Total students who obtained a paid internship: 3
Total students who obtained an unpaid internship: 0
Total students who were placed in APA/CPA-accredited internships: 0
Total students placed in internships not APA/CPA-accredited, but listed with the Association of Psychology Postdoctoral and Internship Centers (APPIC): 0
Total students placed in internships conforming to guidelines of the Council of Directors of School Psychology Programs (CDSPP): 3
Total students placed in internships that were not APA/CPA-accredited, APPIC or CDSSP listed: 0

Internships/Practica

The Washington, DC area offers an abundance of training settings that supplement our on-campus training facilities. A number of practica are offered at the University of Maryland Counseling Center. In addition, other practica and externships are offered at schools, community agencies, medical centers, and other counseling centers. Counseling Psychology students all complete APA-accredited internships. In order to maximize school-based training, students in the School Psychology program may complete internships that conform to CDSPP guidelines or those that are APA-accredited.

Admissions

Entries appear in the following order: required test or GPA, minimum score (if required)/median score of students entering in 2015–2016.

Program	Degree	GRE-V	GRE-Q	GRE-Writing	GRE-Subject	Under-graduate GPA	Last 2 Years GPA	Psychol-ogy GPA	Master's GPA
Counseling Psychology	PhD	153/170	151/163	4/6	Not specified	3.5/3.85	Not specified	Not specified	3.75/ 3.93
School Psychology	PhD	161/163	150/159	4/5	Not specified	3.54/3.76	Not specified	Not specified	3.76/3.8

Admissions Requirements:

Degree	GRE	GRE-Subject	Letters of Recommendation	Research Statement	Writing Sample	CV	Interview
Doctoral	Required	Optional	3	Required	Optional	Required	Required

Admissions Criteria:

GRE scores—medium
Research experience—high
Work experience—medium
Clinically related public service—low
GPA—high

Letters of recommendation—high
Interview—high
Statement of goals and objectives—high
Undergraduate psychology preparation—medium

For additional information on admission requirements, visit http://www.education.umd.edu/CHSE/admissions/admission_criteria/.

Department Demographics

	Male (PT)	Female (PT)	Total	African-American/ Black (PT)	Hispanic/ Latino (PT)	Asian/ Pacific Islander (PT)	American Indian/ Alaska Native (PT)	Caucasian/ White (PT)	Unknown	Multiethnic (PT)	ADA (PT)	Int'l (PT)
Students	14 (1)	44 (4)	63	4 (1)	1 (0)	15 (0)	0 (0)	37 (4)	0 (0)	1 (0)	0 (0)	1 (0)

Financial Information/Assistance

Tuition: For information on tuition costs, visit http://bursar.umd.edu/Tuitionfees.php. Tuition is subject to change. Additional fees are assessed to students beyond the costs of tuition for the following: various fees total $1520 per year.

Doctoral:
State residents: $14,352 per academic year.
State residents: $632 per credit hour.
Nonstate residents: $28,780 per academic year.
Nonstate residents: $1,363 per credit hour.

Financial Assistance:

	Teaching Assistantship (% Receiving)	Teaching Assistantship Tuition Remission	Research Assistantship (% Receiving)	Research Assistantship Tuition Remission	Fellowship (% Receiving)	Fellowship Tuition Remission
First-Year Student	$20,000 (20)	Full	NA (NA)	NA	$20,000 (80)	Full
Advanced Student	$21,650 (80)	Full	$21,650 (20)	Full	NA (NA)	NA

For additional information on financial assistance, visit http://www.education.umd.edu/CHSE/admissions/finance/.

Employment of Department Graduates

Doctoral:
Enrolled in a postdoctoral residency/fellowship: 4
Employed in other positions at a higher education institution: 1
Employed in a professional position in a school system: 3
Total: 8

Additional Information

Housing and Day Care: On-campus housing is available. On-campus day care facilities are available. See the following website for more information: http://www.education.umd.edu/CYC/.

Information for Students With Physical Disabilities: See the following website: http://www.counseling.umd.edu/DSS/.

Special Facilities or Resources: Observation/training facilities and access to extensive library facilities both on and off campus (e.g., NIH Library of Medicine, Library of Congress).

Application Information: Fee: $75. Online application: https://app.applyyourself.com/?id=umdgrad.

Maryland, University of

Department of Human Development and Quantitative Methodology
College of Education
3304 Benjamin Building
College Park, MD 20742
Telephone: (301) 405-2827
Incoming Chair: Kelly Mix

E-mail: awigfiel@umd.edu
Web: http://www.education.umd.edu/HDQM

Orientation, Objectives, and Emphasis of Department

The Department of Human Development provides an academic environment with characteristics consistent with a culture of scholars model, which is reflected by the mentor-based apprenticeship model of graduate training. The program is designed for the training of graduate students who are preparing for careers as research scientists, college professors, educators, and policy makers informed by research. Included in this area of training are two specializations: (1) Developmental Science, and (2) Educational Psychology. The Developmental Sciences specialization is designed to train students in the areas of social, cognitive, emotional, moral, and biological aspects of human development in normal and clinical populations. Research topics within Developmental Science include peer relationships, parent-child relationships, attachment, neuroscience, emotional development, social–cognitive development, moral development, motivation, social goals, intergroup relationships, prejudice, father involvement, early childhood policy, and cultural influences on development. The specialization in Educational Psychology is designed to mentor students in the areas of cognitive, social, motivational, emotional, and neurobiological aspects of learning and human development. Research topics within Educational Psychology include reading, literacy, parent-child discourse, motivation, civic engagement, social goals, domain of knowledge expertise, learning, and bilingualism. Collaborative research opportunities are available at universities and the NIH in the Washington, DC metropolitan area.

Programs and Degrees Offered

Program	Degree	Application Deadline	Applications Received	Accepted	New Admits Enrolled (PT)	Total Enrolled (PT)	Degrees Awarded in 2014–2015	Median Years to Complete Degree	Dismissed/Withdrew
Developmental Science	PhD	December 15 (Fall)	76	5	4	77	7	5.5	0
Educational Psychology	PhD	December 1 (Fall)	30	4	4 (0)	20 (0)	8	6	0
Educational Measurement and Statistics	PhD	December 15 (Fall)		35	6	38	3	5	

Admissions

Entries appear in the following order: required test or GPA, minimum score (if required)/median score of students entering in 2015–2016.

Program	Degree	GRE-V	GRE-Q	GRE-Writing	GRE-Subject	Undergraduate GPA	Last 2 Years GPA	Psychology GPA	Master's GPA
Developmental Science	PhD	NA/NA	NA/NA	NA/NA	Not specified	3/NA	Not specified	Not specified	Not specified

Admissions (con't.)

Program	Degree	GRE-V	GRE-Q	GRE-Writing	GRE-Subject	Under-graduate GPA	Last 2 Years GPA	Psychology GPA	Master's GPA
Educational Psychology	PhD	NA/NA	NA/NA	NA/NA	Not specified	3/NA	Not specified	Not specified	Not specified
Educational Measurement and Statistics	PhD	Not specified	Not specified	Not specified	Not specified	Not specified	Not specified	Not specified	Not specified

Admissions Requirements:

Degree	GRE	GRE-Subject	Letters of Recom-mendation	Research Statement	Writing Sample	CV	Interview
Doctoral	Required	Optional	3	Required	Optional	Recom-mended	None

Admissions Criteria:

GRE scores—high
Research experience—high
Work experience—medium
Clinically related public service—low
GPA—high

Letters of recommendation—high
Interview—medium
Statement of goals and objectives—high
Undergraduate psychology preparation—medium

For additional information on admission requirements, visit http://www.education.umd.edu/HDQM/admissions/criteria/criteria_HD.html.

Department Demographics

	Male (PT)	Female (PT)	Total	African-American/ Black (PT)	Hispanic/ Latino (PT)	Asian/ Pacific Islander (PT)	American Indian/ Alaska Native (PT)	Caucasian/ White (PT)	Unknown	Multiethnic (PT)	ADA (PT)	Int'l (PT)
Students	6 (4)	42 (18)	70	3 (2)	2 (5)	6 (0)	0 (0)	37 (11)	0 (0)	0 (0)	0 (0)	3 (0)

Financial Information/Assistance

Tuition: For information on tuition costs, visit http://bursar.umd.edu/Tuitionfees.php. Tuition is subject to change. Additional fees are assessed to students beyond the costs of tuition for the following: Campus activities fees.

Doctoral:
State residents: $573 per credit hour.
Nonstate residents: $1,236 per credit hour.

Financial Assistance:

	Teaching Assistantship (% Receiving)	Teaching Assistantship Tuition Remission	Research Assistantship (% Receiving)	Research Assistantship Tuition Remission	Fellowship (% Receiving)	Fellowship Tuition Remission
First Year Student	NA (NA)	NA	$16,000 (NA)	Full	$16,000 (NA)	Full
Advanced Student	$18,000 (10)	Full	$18,000 (35)	Full	$18,000 (45)	Full

For additional information on financial assistance, visit http://www.education.umd.edu/HDQM/admissions/finance/finance_HD.html.

Employment of Department Graduates

Doctoral:
Enrolled in a postdoctoral residency/fellowship: 5
Employed in independent practice: 4
Employed in an academic position at a university: 2
Employed in business or industry: 2
Employed in government agency: 4
Employed in a hospital/medical center: 1
Total: 18

Additional Information

Housing and Day Care: No on-campus housing is available. On-campus day care facilities are available. See the following website for more information: http://www.education.umd.edu/CYC/.

Information for Students With Physical Disabilities: See the following website: http://counseling.umd.edu/DSS/.

Special Facilities or Resources: The Center for Young Children is a university research laboratory school affiliated with the Department of Human Development, which provides on-site research and training opportunities. The Center for Children, Relationships and Culture facilitates national and international collaborative research through hosting visiting scholars as well as coordinating a weekly colloquium series. The Department of Human Development hosts the Institute for Child Study which has a 55-year history of translating research and theory into practice. There are a number of dedicated research laboratories in the department for conducting research with infants, children, and adolescents, both onsite as well as in the regional school systems.

Application Information: The University of Maryland, Enrollment Services Operations, 0130 Mitchell Building, College Park, MD 20742. *Fee:* $75. *Online application:* https://app.applyyourself.com/?id=umdgrad.

Maryland, University of
Department of Psychology
College of Behavioral and Social Sciences
Biology-Psychology Building
College Park, MD 20742-4411
Telephone: (301) 405-1454
Chairperson: Jack Blanchard

E-mail: psycgradstudies@umd.edu
Web: http://psychology.umd.edu/landing/Graduate

Orientation, Objectives, and Emphasis of Department
The department offers a full-time graduate program with an emphasis on intensive individual training made possible by a 3-to-1 student/faculty ratio. All students are expected to participate in a variety of relevant experiences that, in addition to coursework and research training, can include practicum experiences, field training, and teaching. The department offers a variety of programs as well as other emphases that cut across the various specialties. All programs have a strong research emphasis with programs in clinical, counseling, and industrial/organizational advocating the scientist–practitioner model.

Programs and Degrees Offered

Program	Degree	Application Deadline	Applica-tions Received	Accepted	New Admits Enrolled (PT)	Total Enrolled (PT)	Degrees Awarded in 2014–2015	Median Years to Complete Degree	Dismissed/Withdrew
Clinical Psychology	PhD	December 1 (Fall)	306	1	1	28 (0)	4	6.25	0
Developmental Psychology	PhD	December 1 (Fall)	17	0	0	7 (0)	0		0
Counseling Psychology	PhD	December 1 (Fall)	83	0	0	18	2	6.5	0
Cognitive and Neural Systems	PhD	December 1 (Fall)	40	4	3	7	0		0

Programs and Degrees Offered *(con't.)*

Program	Degree	Application Deadline	Applications Received	Accepted	New Admits Enrolled (PT)	Total Enrolled (PT)	Degrees Awarded in 2014–2015	Median Years to Complete Degree	Dismissed/ Withdrew
Social Decision and Organizational Sciences	PhD	December 1 (Fall)	135	3	2	15	3	7	0

APA Accreditation

Clinical PhD: Student Outcome Data website: http://psyc.umd.edu/graduate/clinical.
Counseling PhD: Student Outcome Data website: http://www.counselingpsychology.umd.edu/.

Doctoral Degree (PhD Clinical Psychology): For those doctoral students for whom a professional internship was required in this program prior to graduation:
Total students who applied for an internship: 5
Total students who obtained an internship: 5
Total students who obtained a paid internship: 5
Total students who obtained an unpaid internship: 0
Total students who were placed in APA/CPA-accredited internships: 5
Total students placed in internships not APA/CPA-accredited, but listed with the Association of Psychology Postdoctoral and Internship Centers (APPIC): 0
Total students placed in internships conforming to guidelines of the Council of Directors of School Psychology Programs (CDSPP): 0
Total students placed in internships that were not APA/CPA-accredited, APPIC or CDSSP listed: 0

Doctoral Degree (PhD Counseling Psychology): For those doctoral students for whom a professional internship was required in this program prior to graduation:
Total students who applied for an internship: 2
Total students who obtained an internship: 1
Total students who obtained a paid internship: 1
Total students who obtained an unpaid internship: 0
Total students who were placed in APA/CPA-accredited internships: 1
Total students placed in internships not APA/CPA-accredited, but listed with the Association of Psychology Postdoctoral and Internship Centers (APPIC): 0
Total students placed in internships conforming to guidelines of the Council of Directors of School Psychology Programs (CDSPP): 0
Total students placed in internships that were not APA/CPA-accredited, APPIC or CDSSP listed: 0

Internships/Practica

The specialty areas have established collaborative relationships with several federal and community agencies and hospitals, as well as with businesses and consulting firms, where it is possible for students to arrange for research, practicum, and internship placement. These opportunities are available for Clinical and Counseling students at the National Institutes of Health, Veteran's Administration clinics and hospitals in Washington, DC; Baltimore Perry Point; Coatesville; Martinsburg; and a number of others within a 100-mile radius of the University. Experiences include a wide range of research activities, as well as psychodiagnostic work, psychotherapy, and work within drug and alcohol abuse clinics. Various other hospitals, clinics, and research facilities in the Washington, DC and Baltimore metropolitan area are also available. Industrial/Organizational students also have opportunities for practitioner experiences in organizations such as the U.S. Office of Personnel Management, GEICO, Bell Atlantic, and various consulting firms. The metropolitan area also has many psychologists who can provide students with excellent opportunities for collaboration and/or consultation.

Admissions

Entries appear in the following order: required test or GPA, minimum score (if required)/median score of students entering in 2015–2016.

Program	Degree	GRE-V	GRE-Q	GRE-Writing	GRE-Subject	Under-graduate GPA	Last 2 Years GPA	Psychol-ogy GPA	Master's GPA
Clinical Psychology	PhD	NA/NA	NA/NA	NA/NA	Not specified	NA/NA	Not specified	NA/NA	NA/NA

Admissions *(con't.)*

Program	Degree	GRE-V	GRE-Q	GRE-Writing	GRE-Subject	Under-graduate GPA	Last 2 Years GPA	Psychol-ogy GPA	Master's GPA
Developmental Psychology	PhD	NA/NA	NA/NA	NA/NA	Not specified	NA/NA	Not specified	NA/NA	NA/NA
Counseling Psychology	PhD	NA/NA	NA/NA	NA/NA	Not specified	NA/NA	Not specified	NA/NA	NA/NA
Cognitive and Neural Systems	PhD	NA/NA	NA/NA	NA/NA	Not specified	NA/NA	Not specified	NA/NA	NA/NA
Social Decision and Organizational Sciences	PhD	NA/NA	NA/NA	NA/NA	Not specified	NA/NA	Not specified	NA/NA	NA/NA

Admissions Requirements:

Degree	GRE	GRE-Subject	Letters of Recom-mendation	Research Statement	Writing Sample	CV	Interview
Doctoral	Required	Recom-mended	3	Required	Optional	Required	Required

Admissions Criteria:

GRE scores—high
Research experience—high
Work experience—low
Clinically related public service—low
GPA—high

Letters of recommendation—high
Interview—high
Statement of goals and objectives—high
Undergraduate psychology preparation—medium

For additional information on admission requirements, visit http://psychology.umd.edu/graduate/apply-admission.

Department Demographics

	Male (PT)	Female (PT)	Total	African-American/ Black (PT)	Hispanic/ Latino (PT)	Asian/ Pacific Islander (PT)	American Indian/ Alaska Native (PT)	Caucasian/ White (PT)	Unknown	Multiethnic (PT)	ADA (PT)	Int'l (PT)
Students	13 (0)	62 (0)	75	6 (0)	2 (0)	8 (0)	0 (0)	48 (0)	11 (0)	0 (0)	0 (0)	10 (0)

Financial Information/Assistance

Tuition: For information on tuition costs, visit http://bursar.umd.edu/Tuitionfees.php. Tuition is subject to change. Additional fees are assessed to students beyond the costs of tuition for the following: technology, shuttle bus, athletic, recreation.

Doctoral:
State residents: $632 per credit hour.
Nonstate residents: $1,363 per credit hour.

Financial Assistance:

	Teaching Assistantship (% Receiving)	Teaching Assistantship Tuition Remission	Research Assistantship (% Receiving)	Research Assistantship Tuition Remission	Fellowship (% Receiving)	Fellowship Tuition Remission
First-Year Student	$19,942 (NA)	Full	$19,942 (NA)	Full	$22,000 (NA)	Full
Advanced Student	$22,092 (NA)	Full	$22,092 (NA)	Full	$28,000 (NA)	Full

For additional information on financial assistance, visit http://psychology.umd.edu/graduate/landingtopic/funding-overview.

Employment of Department Graduates

Doctoral:
Enrolled in a postdoctoral residency/fellowship: 6
Employed in other positions at a higher education institution: 1
Employed in government agency: 2
Total: 9

Additional Information

Housing and Day Care: No on-campus housing is available. No on-campus day care facilities are available.

Information for Students With Physical Disabilities: See the following website: http://www.counseling.umd.edu/DSS/.

Special Facilities or Resources: The Department of Psychology has all of the advantages of a large state university, and also has advantages offered by the many resources available in the metropolitan Washington-Baltimore area. The University is approximately 15 miles from the center of Washington, DC and is in close proximity to a number of libraries and state and federal agencies. Students are able to benefit from the excellent additional library resources of the community, such as the Library of Congress, National Library of Medicine, and the National Archives (which is located on the UMCP campus). The building in which the Department is housed was designed by the faculty to incorporate research and educational facilities for all specialty areas. The building contains special centers for research, with acoustical centers, observational units, video equipment, computer facilities, surgical facilities, and radio frequency shielding. Departmental laboratories are well equipped for research in animal behavior, audition, biopsychology, cognition, coordinated motor control, counseling, industrial/organizational psychology, learning, life-span development, psycholinguistics, psychotherapy, social psychology, and vision.

Application Information: *Fee:* $75. *Online application:* http://www.gradschool.umd.edu/welcome/apply_now.html.

Maryland, University of, Baltimore County
Department of Psychology
Arts and Sciences
1000 Hilltop Circle
Baltimore, MD 21250
Telephone: (410) 455-2567
Chairperson: Christopher Murphy, PhD

E-mail: psycdept@umbc.edu
Web: http://psychology.umbc.edu/

Orientation, Objectives, and Emphasis of Department
UMBC Psychology is committed to a scientist–practitioner model and emphasizes science with an applied psychological research focus. The department uses a biopsychosocial interactive framework as the foundation for exploring various problems and issues in psychology. Two doctoral graduate programs are housed in the department: Applied Developmental Psychology (ADP) and Human Services Psychology (HSP). The ADP program has three concentrations: Early Development/Early Intervention, Socioemotional Development of Children, and Educational Contexts of Development; students can affiliate flexibly with one or more concentrations. The ADP program is accredited by the ASPPB/National Register of Health Service Providers in Psychology. The HSP program consists of three subprograms: community/social, behavioral medicine, and an APA-approved clinical subprogram. Many HSP students take cross-area training in clinical/behavioral medicine or clinical/community areas. There is also a master's program in Applied Behavior Analysis, housed at UMBC and in collaboration with the Kennedy Krieger Institute. Faculty represent a broad range of theoretical perspectives and maintain active research programs. The psychology department has many collaborative relationships for research and clinical and practical training opportunities with institutions in the Baltimore-Washington corridor.

Programs and Degrees Offered

Program	Degree	Application Deadline	Applications Received	Accepted	New Admits Enrolled (PT)	Total Enrolled (PT)	Degrees Awarded in 2014–2015	Median Years to Complete Degree	Dismissed/ Withdrew
Applied Behavior Analysis	MA/MS	January 1 (Fall)	65	20	11 (0)	29 (0)	15	2	1

Programs and Degrees Offered (con't.)

Program	Degree	Application Deadline	Applications Received	Accepted	New Admits Enrolled (PT)	Total Enrolled (PT)	Degrees Awarded in 2014–2015	Median Years to Complete Degree	Dismissed/ Withdrew
Applied Developmental Psychology	PhD	January 9 (Fall)	29	5	5 (0)	26 (0)	3	6	1
Human Services Psychology	PhD	December 1 (Fall)	99	16	8 (0)	61 (0)	10	6	1

APA Accreditation

Clinical PhD: Student Outcome Data website: http://psychology.umbc.edu/hsp/clinical/data/.

Doctoral Degree (PhD Human Services Psychology): For those doctoral students for whom a professional internship was required in this program prior to graduation:
Total students who applied for an internship: 10
Total students who obtained an internship: 10
Total students who obtained a paid internship: 10
Total students who obtained an unpaid internship: 0
Total students who were placed in APA/CPA-accredited internships: 10
Total students placed in internships not APA/CPA-accredited, but listed with the Association of Psychology Postdoctoral and Internship Centers (APPIC): 0
Total students placed in internships conforming to guidelines of the Council of Directors of School Psychology Programs (CDSPP): 0
Total students placed in internships that were not APA/CPA-accredited, APPIC or CDSSP listed: 0

Master's Degree (MA/MS Applied Behavior Analysis): An internship experience, such as a final research project or "capstone" experience is required of graduates.

Internships/Practica

Course-linked practica provide students with a focused experience in the application of the skills and knowledge presented in the associated course. The course instructor is responsible for arranging these practica. Beyond the course-linked practica, students in the HSP and ADP programs are required to take a minimum of six additional credits of practicum, usually in their second and third years. These practica, in various clinical, research, and human services settings, are intended to give students a broader and more integrative experience in the application of the skills and knowledge that they have acquired in the various courses they have taken.

Admissions

Entries appear in the following order: required test or GPA, minimum score (if required)/median score of students entering in 2015–2016.

Program	Degree	GRE-V	GRE-Q	GRE-Writing	GRE-Subject	Under-graduate GPA	Last 2 Years GPA	Psychology GPA	Master's GPA
Applied Behavior Analysis	MA/MS	NA/NA	NA/NA	NA/NA	Not specified	NA/NA	Not specified	Not specified	Not specified
Applied Developmental Psychology	PhD	NA/NA	NA/NA	NA/NA	Not specified	3/NA	Not specified	Not specified	Not specified
Human Services Psychology	PhD	NA/NA	NA/NA	NA/NA	NA/NA	3/NA	Not specified	Not specified	NA/NA

Admissions Requirements:

Degree	GRE	GRE-Subject	Letters of Recommendation	Research Statement	Writing Sample	CV	Interview
Master's/Specialist	Required	Optional	3	Required	Optional	Optional	Required
Doctoral	Required	Required	3	Required	Optional	Optional	Required

Please note if these criteria vary for different programs: ADP puts less weight (low) on clinical service than does HSP. ADP does not require the GRE subject test. HSP does.

Admissions Criteria:

GRE scores—high
Research experience—high
Work experience—medium
Clinically related public service—medium
GPA—high

Letters of recommendation—high
Interview—high
Statement of goals and objectives—high
Undergraduate psychology preparation—medium

Department Demographics

	Male (PT)	Female (PT)	Total	African-American/Black (PT)	Hispanic/Latino (PT)	Asian/Pacific Islander (PT)	American Indian/Alaska Native (PT)	Caucasian/White (PT)	Unknown	Multiethnic (PT)	ADA (PT)	Int'l (PT)
Students	20 (0)	96 (0)	116	11 (0)	11 (0)	10 (0)	0 (0)	80 (0)	2 (0)	2 (0)	0 (0)	0 (0)

Financial Information/Assistance

Tuition: For information on tuition costs, visit http://sbs.umbc.edu/tuition-info/. Additional fees are assessed to students beyond the costs of tuition for the following: athletic fee, transportation fee, technology fee, grad program fee.

Doctoral:
State residents: $585 per credit hour.
Nonstate residents: $968 per credit hour.

Master's:
State residents: $585 per credit hour.
Nonstate residents: $968 per credit hour.

Financial Assistance:

	Teaching Assistantship (% Receiving)	Teaching Assistantship Tuition Remission	Research Assistantship (% Receiving)	Research Assistantship Tuition Remission	Fellowship (% Receiving)	Fellowship Tuition Remission
First-Year Student	$16,795 (NA)	Full	$19,890 (NA)	Full	NA (NA)	NA
Advanced Student	$16,795 (NA)	Full	$19,890 (NA)	Full	NA (NA)	NA

For additional information on financial assistance, visit http://gradschool.umbc.edu/funding/assistantships/.

Employment of Department Graduates

Master's:
Enrolled in a psychology doctoral program: 1
Other employment position: 1
Do not know: 13
Total: 15

Doctoral:
Enrolled in a postdoctoral residency/fellowship: 1
Employed in independent practice: 1
Employed in a community mental health/counseling center: 1
Employed in a hospital/medical center: 5
Other employment position: 1
Do not know: 4
Total: 13

Additional Information

Housing and Day Care: On-campus housing is available. See the following website for more information: http://www.umbc.edu/reslife/communities/waa.php. On-campus day care facilities are available. See the following website for more information: http://hr.umbc.edu/preschool/.

Information for Students With Physical Disabilities: See the following website: http://sss.umbc.edu/.

Special Facilities or Resources: The Psychology Department at UMBC has numerous faculty research laboratories on campus in close proximity to faculty offices. Laboratories include equipment for psychological assessment, videotaping and coding, and observation as well as an animal laboratory. The department has access to several large computer laboratories on campus and has a small computer laboratory for graduate students. Through collaborative arrangements with the medical school and other University of Maryland System facilities and Kennedy Krieger Institute, graduate students have access to different patient populations and opportunities for community-based projects.

Application Information: Dean of Graduate School, 1000 Hilltop Circle, Baltimore, MD 21250. *Fee:* $50. *Online application:* https://www.applyweb.com/cgi-bin/app?umbcg2.

Towson University

Department of Psychology
8000 York Road
Towson, MD 21252
Telephone: (410) 704-3080
Chairperson: Geoffrey D. Munro, PhD

E-mail: psychology@towson.edu
Web: http://www.towson.edu/psychology/

Orientation, Objectives, and Emphasis of Department

The experimental psychology program is designed to prepare students for subsequent enrollment in PhD programs or for research jobs in industrial, governmental, private consulting, or hospital settings. The Clinical concentration is ideally suited to meet the needs of individuals who want to provide clinical services that are informed by science, want to work as master's-level psychometricians or behavioral specialists, want to work as research or clinical staff on applied research studies, or are considering pursuing doctoral training in clinical psychology. The Counseling Psychology program trains students to facilitate personal, educational, and vocational adjustment across the lifespan. Graduates from the program may go on to meet the requirements of the Licensed Clinical Professional Counselor, pursue a doctoral degree, and/or find employment in a wide variety of counseling agencies. The School psychology program is fully approved by the National Association of School Psychologists (NASP) and trains graduate students to become school psychologists. The program offers a single 66-credit degree: the Master of Arts in Psychology with a concentration in School Psychology and the Certificate of Advanced Study (CAS) in School Psychology. The HRD Professional Track MS program is ideally suited for people wanting to enter the human resources profession.

Programs and Degrees Offered

Program	Degree	Application Deadline	Applications Received	Accepted	New Admits Enrolled (PT)	Total Enrolled (PT)	Degrees Awarded in 2014–2015	Median Years to Complete Degree	Dismissed/ Withdrew
Clinical Psychology	MA/MS	January 15 (Fall)	94	15	15 (0)	24 (4)	8	2	1
Counseling Psychology	MA/MS	January 15 (Fall)	110	17	16 (1)	34 (5)	10	2	0
Experimental Psychology	MA/MS	January 15 (Fall)	46	17	14 (1)	24 (4)	12	2	0
School Psychology	MA/MS	January 15 (Fall)	58	12	12 (0)	40 (0)	11	3	2
Human Resource Development	MA/MS	May 15 (Fall), September 30 (Spring)	82	51	41 (0)	97 (0)	67	2	0

Internships/Practica

School Psychology students are required to complete two 150-hour practica over two consecutive semesters in a local school system. The program culminates in a 1,200-hour internship that is to be completed full-time over 1 year or part-time over 2 consecutive years. At least 50% of the 1,200 hours must be completed in a public school system; however, most students complete all hours in public schools. Students in clinical psychology complete a required 500-hour, 9-month internship. Students may elect to complete a clinical or research internship depending upon their personal and professional goals. Students on clinical internships provide supervised psychological services to clients in an off-campus mental health setting. Students on research internships will assist an experienced scientist in conducting clinical trials research. Counseling students are required to complete a 240-hour practicum and a 300-hour internship over two semesters. Students are placed in community mental health centers, college counseling centers, drug and alcohol rehabilitation agencies, domestic violence centers, and other mental health service agencies. The HRD program requires graduates to have field work experience in order to graduate. For those not already working in HR, students can complete an internship or practicum for 3 credit hours.

Admissions

Entries appear in the following order: required test or GPA, minimum score (if required)/median score of students entering in 2015–2016.

Program	Degree	GRE-V	GRE-Q	GRE-Writing	GRE-Subject	Under-graduate GPA	Last 2 Years GPA	Psychol-ogy GPA	Master's GPA
Clinical Psychology	MA/MS	144/154	147/153	3.5/4	Not specified	3/3.55	3/NA	Not specified	Not specified
Counseling Psychology	MA/MS	146/155	140/149	3.5/4	Not specified	3/3.5	3/3.6	Not specified	Not specified
Experimental Psychology	MA/MS	Not specified	Not specified	Not specified	Not specified	3/3.68	Not specified	Not specified	Not specified
School Psychology	MA/MS	140/153	NA/NA	3.5/4	Not specified	3.3/3.5	Not specified	Not specified	Not specified
Human Resource Development	MA/MS	Not specified	Not specified	Not specified	Not specified	2.8/3.3	Not specified	Not specified	Not specified

Admissions Requirements:

Degree	GRE	GRE-Subject	Letters of Recom-mendation	Research Statement	Writing Sample	CV	Interview
Master's/Specialist	Required	Optional	2	Required	Optional	Optional	Required

Please note if these criteria vary for different programs: Clinically related public service or experience, letters of recommendation, and interview are all used by the clinical, counseling, and school psychology programs. Research experience is very important for the experimental program and clinical program. Counseling, clinical, experimental, and school psychology also use a letter of intent and consider it very important. The clinical and experimental programs consider GRE scores very important for making initial decisions about whom to interview for admission. The HRD program does not require GRE, but does rely heavily on both GPA and work experience, along with an Application Essay; some applicants may be asked to interview. School and Counseling Psychology require 3 letters of recommendation.

Admissions Criteria:

GRE scores—medium
Research experience—medium
Work experience—medium
Clinically related public service—medium
GPA—high

Letters of recommendation—high
Interview—high
Statement of goals and objectives—medium
Undergraduate psychology preparation—medium

For additional information on admission requirements, visit http://www.towson.edu/cla/departments/psychology/grad/index.html.

Department Demographics

	Male (PT)	Female (PT)	Total	African-American/ Black (PT)	Hispanic/ Latino (PT)	Asian/ Pacific Islander (PT)	American Indian/ Alaska Native (PT)	Caucasian/ White (PT)	Unknown	Multiethnic (PT)	ADA (PT)	Int'l (PT)
Students	42 (4)	182 (9)	237	35 (0)	14 (1)	9 (0)	0 (0)	144 (11)	17 (0)	5 (1)	2 (0)	3 (0)

Financial Information/Assistance

Tuition: For information on tuition costs, visit http://www.towson.edu/bursar/tuition/index.html. Tuition is subject to change. Additional fees are assessed to students beyond the costs of tuition for the following: technology fees: $7 per credit with a $80 cap per term.

Master's:
State residents: $372 per credit hour.
Nonstate residents: $770 per credit hour.

Financial Assistance:

	Teaching Assistantship (% Receiving)	Teaching Assistantship Tuition Remission	Research Assistantship (% Receiving)	Research Assistantship Tuition Remission	Fellowship (% Receiving)	Fellowship Tuition Remission
First-Year Student	$4,000 (NA)	Partial	$5,000 (NA)	Full	NA (NA)	NA
Advanced Student	$4,000 (NA)	Partial	$5,000 (NA)	Full	NA (NA)	NA

For additional information on financial assistance, visit http://www.towson.edu/admissions/financialaid/index.html.

Employment of Department Graduates

No information provided.

Additional Information

Housing and Day Care: No on-campus housing is available. On-campus day care facilities are available. See the following website for more information: https://www.towson.edu/childcare/.

Information for Students With Physical Disabilities: See the following website: http://www.towson.edu/dss/.

Special Facilities or Resources: The new Liberal Arts building houses laboratories for histology and computer analysis as well as specialized space for clinical/counseling training and conducting research in learning/motivation, physiological, comparative, cognitive, social, developmental, and general experimental psychology. Additionally, because of the popularity of the undergraduate psychology major, there are many students willing to participate in research studies.

Application Information: Graduate School, Towson University, Towson, MD 21252. *Fee:* $45. *Online application:* https://www.applyweb.com/towsong/menu.html.

Uniformed Services University of the Health Sciences
Medical and Clinical Psychology
F Edward Hebert School of Medicine
4301 Jones Bridge Road
Bethesda, MD 20814
Telephone: (301) 295-9669
Chairperson: David Riggs, PhD

E-mail: tricia.crum@usuhs.edu
Web: http://www.usuhs.mil/mps/

Orientation, Objectives, and Emphasis of Department

The Department's educational programs provide a background in general psychological principles. Two content areas are emphasized: Health Psychology and Clinical Psychology. Educational and research activities focus on the application of principles and methods of scientific psychology relevant to physical and mental health. The Department is set in a School of Medicine and has an interdisciplinary focus. A Clinical Psychology program for uniformed military personnel and a Medical Psychology clinical track for civilians are APA-accredited and follow the scientist–practitioner model. A research/academic program in Medical Psychology encompasses the fields of Health Psychology and Behavioral Medicine. The Department provides many research opportunities for students in the graduate programs and opportunities for mentorship because of the active and varied research programs conducted by the full-time faculty. Research opportunities available for students all involve the study of behavioral, psychological, and biobehavioral factors in physical and mental health. In addition, several faculty in the Department participate in an NIH-funded predoctoral and postdoctoral training programs in cardiovascular behavioral medicine.

Programs and Degrees Offered

Program	Degree	Application Deadline	Applications Received	Accepted	New Admits Enrolled (PT)	Total Enrolled (PT)	Degrees Awarded in 2014–2015	Median Years to Complete Degree	Dismissed/ Withdrew
Medical Psychology	PhD	December 1 (Fall)	8	0	0 (0)	3 (0)	0	6	0
Clinical Psychology	PhD	December 1 (Fall)	140	6	6 (0)	31 (0)	3	5	0
Medical Psychology (Clinical Track)	PhD	December 1 (Fall)	63	0	0 (0)	8 (0)	0		0

APA Accreditation

Clinical PhD: Student Outcome Data website: https://www.usuhs.edu/mps/clinical-psychology.

Clinical PhD (Doctor of Philosophy).

Doctoral Degree (PhD Clinical Psychology): For those doctoral students for whom a professional internship was required in this program prior to graduation:
Total students who applied for an internship: 6
Total students who obtained an internship: 6
Total students who obtained a paid internship: 6
Total students who obtained an unpaid internship: 0
Total students who were placed in APA/CPA-accredited internships: 6
Total students placed in internships not APA/CPA-accredited, but listed with the Association of Psychology Postdoctoral and Internship Centers (APPIC): 0
Total students placed in internships conforming to guidelines of the Council of Directors of School Psychology Programs (CDSPP): 0
Total students placed in internships that were not APA/CPA-accredited, APPIC or CDSSP listed: 0

Doctoral Degree (PhD Medical Psychology (Clinical Track)): For those doctoral students for whom a professional internship was required in this program prior to graduation:
Total students who applied for an internship: 1
Total students who obtained an internship: 1
Total students who obtained a paid internship: 1
Total students who obtained an unpaid internship: 0
Total students who were placed in APA/CPA-accredited internships: 1
Total students placed in internships not APA/CPA-accredited, but listed with the Association of Psychology Postdoctoral and Internship Centers (APPIC): 0
Total students placed in internships conforming to guidelines of the Council of Directors of School Psychology Programs (CDSPP): 0
Total students placed in internships that were not APA/CPA-accredited, APPIC or CDSSP listed: 0

Internships/Practica

Military Clinical Psychology and Clinical/Medical Psychology students complete the 12-month internship during the fifth and final year of the program within an APA-approved military or civilian clinical psychology training program. Practicum training occurs during the Fall, Winter, and Spring quarters of the second, third, and fourth years. Students work at practicum sites at local facilities for 6 to 10 hours per week.

Admissions

Entries appear in the following order: required test or GPA, minimum score (if required)/median score of students entering in 2015–2016.

Program	Degree	GRE-V	GRE-Q	GRE-Writing	GRE-Subject	Under-graduate GPA	Last 2 Years GPA	Psychol-ogy GPA	Master's GPA
Medical Psychology	PhD	NA/NA	NA/NA	NA/NA	Not specified	3.2/3.5	Not specified	Not specified	Not specified
Clinical Psychology	PhD	NA/NA	NA/NA	NA/NA	Not specified	3.2/3.5	Not specified	Not specified	Not specified
Medical Psychology (Clinical Track)	PhD	NA/NA	NA/NA	NA/NA	Not specified	3.2/3.5	Not specified	Not specified	NA/NA

Admissions Requirements:

Degree	GRE	GRE-Subject	Letters of Recom-mendation	Research Statement	Writing Sample	CV	Interview
Doctoral	Required	Optional	3	Required	Optional	Recom-mended	Required

Admissions Criteria:

GRE scores—high
Research experience—high
Work experience—low
Clinically related public service—medium
GPA—high

Letters of recommendation—high
Interview—high
Statement of goals and objectives—high
Undergraduate psychology preparation—medium

For additional information on admission requirements, visit https://www.usuhs.edu/graded/application.

Department Demographics

	Male (PT)	Female (PT)	Total	African-American/ Black (PT)	Hispanic/ Latino (PT)	Asian/ Pacific Islander (PT)	American Indian/ Alaska Native (PT)	Caucasian/ White (PT)	Unknown (PT)	Multiethnic (PT)	ADA (PT)	Int'l (PT)
Students	10 (0)	33 (0)	43	5 (0)	2 (0)	3 (0)	0 (0)	32 (0)	0 (0)	1 (0)	0 (0)	0 (0)

Financial Information/Assistance

Tuition:

Doctoral:
State residents: $0 per academic year.
Nonstate residents: $0 per academic year.

Financial Assistance:

	Teaching Assistantship (% Receiving)	Teaching Assistantship Tuition Remission	Research Assistantship (% Receiving)	Research Assistantship Tuition Remission	Fellowship (% Receiving)	Fellowship Tuition Remission
First-Year Student	NA (NA)	NA	NA (NA)	NA	$31,000 (NA)	NA
Advanced Student	$26,000 (NA)	NA	$26,000 (NA)	NA	$31,000 (NA)	NA

For additional information on financial assistance, visit https://www.usuhs.edu/graded/prospectivestudents.

Employment of Department Graduates

Doctoral:
Employed in a hospital/medical center: 3
Total: 3

Additional Information

Housing and Day Care: No on-campus housing is available. No on-campus day care facilities are available.

Special Facilities or Resources: The Department has office space, laboratory space for human and animal experimentation, multiple psychophysiology laboratories, and a biochemistry laboratory. There is access to classrooms, conference rooms, an excellent library, a computer center, audiovisual support, teaching hospitals, and a laboratory animal facility that is accredited by the Association for the Assessment and Accreditation of Laboratory Animal Care. The Bethesda campus of the National Institutes of Health (NIH), including the National Library of Medicine, is within walking distance from USUHS. The NIH is a resource for lecture series, specialized courses, funding information, and research collaborations. The major military training hospitals also are nearby, as are all the social and cultural offerings of Washington, DC.

Application Information: Gregory Mueller, PhD, Associate Dean for Graduate Education, USUHS, 4301 Jones Bridge Road, Bethesda, MD 20814. *Fee:* $0. *Online application:* https://registrar.usuhs.edu/.

American International College
Department of Graduate Psychology
1000 State Street
Springfield, MA 01109
Telephone: (800) 242-3142
Chairperson: Lina Racicot, EdD

E-mail: lina.racicot@aic.edu
Web: https://www.aic.edu/school-of-graduate-and-adult-education/

Orientation, Objectives, and Emphasis of Department
All graduate programs are based on a balanced scientist–practitioner model that emphasizes the interrelatedness of theory, research, and practice. Our focus is to develop competent, ethical, and self-aware professionals who can function effectively in a diverse, global, and increasingly interdependent world. Graduates of the MA Program in Clinical Psychology are eligible for master's-level licensure. Graduates of the EdD program in Educational Psychology who are interested in seeking certification or licensure will generally meet academic, experiential, and other requirements depending upon the type of certification/license sought.

Programs and Degrees Offered

Program	Degree	Application Deadline	Applica-tions Received	Accepted	New Admits Enrolled (PT)	Total Enrolled (PT)	Degrees Awarded in 2014–2015	Median Years to Complete Degree	Dismissed/ Withdrew
Clinical Psychology	MA/MS	Rolling	54	28	25 (3)	47 (6)	13	3	
Educational Psychology	MA/MS	Rolling	35	3	3 (0)	6 (0)	3	2	0
Educational Psychology	EdD	Rolling	35	12	10 (2)	32 (2)	6	5	
Forensic Psychology	MA/MS	Rolling	40	15	15 (0)	32 (0)	13	2	0
General Psychology	MA/MS	Rolling	12	12	12	15	1	2	

Doctoral Degree (EdD Educational Psychology): For those doctoral students for whom a professional internship was required in this program prior to graduation:
Total students who applied for an internship: 4
Total students who obtained an internship: 4
Total students who obtained a paid internship: 1
Total students who obtained an unpaid internship: 3
Total students who were placed in APA/CPA-accredited internships: 0
Total students placed in internships not APA/CPA-accredited, but listed with the Association of Psychology Postdoctoral and Internship Centers (APPIC): 0
Total students placed in internships conforming to guidelines of the Council of Directors of School Psychology Programs (CDSPP): 0
Total students placed in internships that were not APA/CPA-accredited, APPIC or CDSSP listed: 4

Master's Degree (MA/MS Clinical Psychology): An internship experience, such as a final research project or "capstone" experience is required of graduates. Master's Degree (MA/MS Forensic Psychology): An internship experience, such as a final research project or "capstone" experience is required of graduates.

Internships/Practica
Internships and practica are secured at various institutions and facilities throughout the area.

Admissions

Entries appear in the following order: required test or GPA, minimum score (if required)/median score of students entering in 2015–2016.

Program	Degree	GRE-V	GRE-Q	GRE-Writing	GRE-Subject	Under-graduate GPA	Last 2 Years GPA	Psychology GPA	Master's GPA
Clinical Psychology	MA/MS	Not specified	Not specified	Not specified	Not specified	2.75/3.25	Not specified	Not specified	Not specified
Educational Psychology	MA/MS	Not specified	Not specified	Not specified	Not specified	3.25/3.5	Not specified	Not specified	Not specified
Educational Psychology	EdD	NA/NA	NA/NA	Not specified	Not specified	3.25/3.59	Not specified	Not specified	3.25/3.5
Forensic Psychology	MA/MS	Not specified	Not specified	Not specified	Not specified	2.75/3	Not specified	Not specified	Not specified
General Psychology	MA/MS	Not specified	Not specified	Not specified	Not specified	Not specified	Not specified	Not specified	Not specified

Admissions Requirements:

Degree	GRE	GRE-Subject	Letters of Recommendation	Research Statement	Writing Sample	CV	Interview
Master's/Specialist	Optional	Optional	2	Required	Optional	Required	Optional
Doctoral	Optional	Optional	3	Required	Optional	Required	Recommended

Admissions Criteria:

GRE scores—medium
Research experience—medium
Work experience—high
Clinically related public service—high
GPA—high

Letters of recommendation—high
Interview—medium
Statement of goals and objectives—high
Undergraduate psychology preparation—medium

Department Demographics

	Male (PT)	Female (PT)	Total	African-American/ Black (PT)	Hispanic/ Latino (PT)	Asian/ Pacific Islander (PT)	American Indian/ Alaska Native (PT)	Caucasian/ White (PT)	Unknown (PT)	Multiethnic (PT)	ADA (PT)	Int'l (PT)
Students	44 (2)	88 (6)	140	36 (2)	26 (2)	2 (0)	0 (0)	68 (2)	0 (0)	0 (0)	1 (0)	5 (0)

Financial Information/Assistance

Tuition: For information on tuition costs, visit https://www.aic.edu/admissions/costs/. Tuition is subject to change.

Doctoral:
State residents: $820 per credit hour.
Nonstate residents: $820 per credit hour.

Master's:
State residents: $820 per credit hour.
Nonstate residents: $820 per credit hour.

Financial Assistance:

	Teaching Assistantship (% Receiving)	Teaching Assistantship Tuition Remission	Research Assistantship (% Receiving)	Research Assistantship Tuition Remission	Fellowship (% Receiving)	Fellowship Tuition Remission
First-Year Student	NA (NA)	NA	NA (NA)	Partial	NA (NA)	Partial
Advanced Student	NA (NA)	Full	NA (NA)	Full	NA (NA)	Full

For additional information on financial assistance, visit https://www.aic.edu/admissions/tuition-and-financial-aid/financial-aid/.

Employment of Department Graduates

No information provided.

Additional Information

Housing and Day Care: No on-campus housing is available. No on-campus day care facilities are available.

Special Facilities or Resources: Curtis Blake Child Development Center.

Application Information: Graduate Admissions Office, American International College, 1000 State Street, Springfield, MA 01109. *Fee:* $50. *Online application:* https://app.applyyourself.com/?id=aic2.

Assumption College
Division of Clinical Counseling Psychology
500 Salisbury Street
Worcester, MA 01609-1296
Telephone: (508) 767-7390
Program Director: Leonard A. Doerfler

E-mail: doerfler@assumption.edu

Web: http://graduate.assumption.edu/counseling-psychology/ma-counseling-psychology-program

---

Orientation, Objectives, and Emphasis of Department
The program is organized to prepare students for entrance into doctoral programs in clinical and counseling psychology and for master's degree entry-level positions in a variety of mental health and related social service settings. Students are given conceptual preparation in a variety of theoretical positions in clinical and counseling psychology. A number of skills courses in counseling, testing, and research are an integral part of the program at both the entry and advanced levels. The goal of the program is to produce master's-level psychologists who show conceptual versatility in theory and practice and depth of preparation in one of several special areas of counseling work. The student takes classes in areas such as personality theory, abnormal psychology, child development, counseling, advanced therapeutic procedure, measurement and research. Outside of class, the student gains applied experience in clinical practice in the one-semester practicum and two-semester internship.

Programs and Degrees Offered

Program	Degree	Application Deadline	Applications Received	Accepted	New Admits Enrolled (PT)	Total Enrolled (PT)	Degrees Awarded in 2014–2015	Median Years to Complete Degree	Dismissed/ Withdrew
Clinical Counseling Psychology	MA/MS	March 6 (Fall), October 3 (Spring), February 6 (Summer)			21 (11)	107 (67)			

Internships/Practica

Practicum and internship placements are available in a wide range of community settings. Students can elect to work in outpatient/community, college counseling, substance abuse, inpatient, residential, and correctional settings. Opportunities to work with children, adolescents, adults, and families are available. The department maintains a close working relationship with the University of Massachusetts Medical Center, McLean Hospital/Harvard Medical School, and other mental health training agencies; students attend clinical case conferences, workshops, and lectures at these agencies. Students often receive training in innovative treatment models like home-based, brief problem-focused, or cognitive-behavioral treatments.

Admissions

Entries appear in the following order: required test or GPA, minimum score (if required)/median score of students entering in 2015–2016.

Program	Degree	GRE-V	GRE-Q	GRE-Writing	GRE-Subject	Under-graduate GPA	Last 2 Years GPA	Psychology GPA	Master's GPA
Clinical Counseling Psychology	MA/MS	Not specified	Not specified	Not specified	Not specified	3/3.4	3/3.4	3/3.5	Not specified

Admissions Requirements:

Degree	GRE	GRE-Subject	Letters of Recom-mendation	Research Statement	Writing Sample	CV	Interview
Master's/Specialist	None	None	3	Required	Optional	Recom-mended	None

Admissions Criteria:

Research experience—low
Work experience—medium
Clinically related public service—medium
GPA—high

Letters of recommendation—high
Statement of goals and objectives—medium
Undergraduate psychology preparation—high

For additional information on admission requirements, visit http://graduate.assumption.edu/counseling-psychology/admission.

Department Demographics

	Male (PT)	Female (PT)	Total	African-American/ Black (PT)	Hispanic/ Latino (PT)	Asian/ Pacific Islander (PT)	American Indian/ Alaska Native (PT)	Caucasian/ White (PT)	Unknown	Multiethnic (PT)	ADA (PT)	Int'l (PT)
Students	11 (7)	96 (60)	174	2 (3)	5 (8)	3 (3)	0 (0)	65 (45)	26 (8)	6 (0)	5 (0)	3 (0)

Financial Information/Assistance

Tuition: For information on tuition costs, visit http://graduate.assumption.edu/financial-aid/tuition-information. Tuition is subject to change. Additional fees are assessed to students beyond the costs of tuition for the following: $20 per semester registration fee and $50 per semester technology fee.

Master's:
State residents: $625 per credit hour.
Nonstate residents: $625 per credit hour.

Financial Assistance:

	Teaching Assistantship (% Receiving)	Teaching Assistantship Tuition Remission	Research Assistantship (% Receiving)	Research Assistantship Tuition Remission	Fellowship (% Receiving)	Fellowship Tuition Remission
First-Year Student	NA (NA)	NA	NA (NA)	NA	NA (NA)	Partial
Advanced Student	NA (NA)	NA	NA (NA)	NA	NA (NA)	Partial

For additional information on financial assistance, visit http://graduate.assumption.edu/financial-aid/tuition-financial-aid.

Employment of Department Graduates

Master's:
Employed in a professional position in a school system: 4
Employed in a community mental health/counseling center: 29
Not seeking employment: 1
Total: 34

Additional Information

Housing and Day Care: No on-campus housing is available. No on-campus day care facilities are available.

Information for Students With Physical Disabilities: See the following website: http://www.assumption.edu/academics/resources/disability-services.

Special Facilities or Resources: Special facilities on campus include a well-equipped media center and an observation laboratory. Students also have access to in-service training at a local medical school, agencies, and hospitals. The college is located within commuting distance of Boston training facilities. College libraries in Worcester operate on a consortium basis.

Application Information: Dean of Graduate Studies, Graduate Office, Assumption College, 500 Salisbury Street, Worcester, MA 01609-1296. *Fee:* $30. *Online application:* https://www.assumption.edu/gradapp/online/.

Boston College
Department of Counseling, Developmental, and Educational Psychology
Lynch School of Education
309 Campion Hall
Chestnut Hill, MA 02467
Telephone: (617) 552-4710
Chairperson: Penny Hauser-Cram, EdD

E-mail: hausercr@bc.edu
Web: http://www.bc.edu/schools/lsoe/academics/departments/cdep.html

---

Orientation, Objectives, and Emphasis of Department
The Programs in Counseling, Developmental and Educational Psychology emphasize a foundation in developmental theory, research skills, and a commitment to preparing professionals to work in public practice, public service, academic or research institutions. The counseling psychology doctoral program espouses a scientist–practitioner model and provides broad-based training with special attention to group and individual counseling processes, theory and skill in research and assessment, and understanding individual development within a social context. Master's counseling students specialize in mental health counseling or school counseling. The program in Applied Developmental and Educational Psychology focuses on application and draws on psychology, educational and community programs, and public policy to enhance the development of individuals and their key institutional contexts- schools, families, and work settings- across the life span. Faculty research interests include psychotherapy; process and outcome; career and moral development; individual differences in cognitive and affective development, including developmental disabilities; influence of gender role strain on the well-being of men; Asian-American and Latino mental health; racial identity; marital and community violence; marital satisfaction; and prevention and intervention for promoting positive development among youth.

Programs and Degrees Offered

Program	Degree	Application Deadline	Applications Received	Accepted	New Admits Enrolled (PT)	Total Enrolled (PT)	Degrees Awarded in 2014–2015	Median Years to Complete Degree	Dismissed/Withdrew
School Counseling	MA/MS	January 31 (Fall)	60	47	14 (2)	33 (4)	13	2	
Counseling Psychology	PhD	December 1 (Fall)	287	6	6 (0)	36 (0)	10	7	
Mental Health Counseling	MA/MS	January 31 (Fall)	288	191	56 (3)	120 (6)	35	2	
Applied Developmental and Educational Psychology	MA/MS	January 31 (Fall)	54	41	10 (0)	15 (4)	10	2	
Applied Developmental and Educational Psychology	PhD	January 31 (Fall)	40	5	4 (0)	19 (0)	4	5	1

APA Accreditation

Counseling PhD: Student Outcome Data website: http://www.bc.edu/schools/lsoe/academics/departments/cdep/counseling-psychology/doctoral-program/AdmissionsOutcomesData.html.

Doctoral Degree (PhD Counseling Psychology): For those doctoral students for whom a professional internship was required in this program prior to graduation:
Total students who applied for an internship: 8
Total students who obtained an internship: 8
Total students who obtained a paid internship: 8
Total students who obtained an unpaid internship: 0
Total students who were placed in APA/CPA-accredited internships: 8
Total students placed in internships not APA/CPA-accredited, but listed with the Association of Psychology Postdoctoral and Internship Centers (APPIC): 0
Total students placed in internships conforming to guidelines of the Council of Directors of School Psychology Programs (CDSPP): 0
Total students placed in internships that were not APA/CPA-accredited, APPIC or CDSSP listed: 0

Master's Degree (MA/MS School Counseling): An internship experience, such as a final research project or "capstone" experience is required of graduates. Master's Degree (MA/MS Mental Health Counseling): An internship experience, such as a final research project or "capstone" experience is required of graduates. Master's Degree (MA/MS Applied Developmental and Educational Psychology): An internship experience, such as a final research project or "capstone" experience is required of graduates.

Internships/Practica

Doctoral students in Counseling Psychology complete two advanced practica in community mental health agencies, schools, clinics, hospitals, and college counseling centers. They also complete a one year predoctoral internship. Master's students in mental health and school counseling work with the Master's Program Coordinator to identify internships that meet requirements for mental health licensure or school counselor certification. Master's students in the Applied Developmental and Educational Psychology program can complete a non-required internship and doctoral students in the Applied Developmental and Educational Psychology program must complete a required internship.

Admissions

Entries appear in the following order: required test or GPA, minimum score (if required)/median score of students entering in 2015–2016.

Program	Degree	GRE-V	GRE-Q	GRE-Writing	GRE-Subject	Undergraduate GPA	Last 2 Years GPA	Psychology GPA	Master's GPA
School Counseling	MA/MS	NA/NA	NA/NA	NA/NA	Not specified	NA/NA	Not specified	Not specified	Not specified
Counseling Psychology	PhD	NA/NA	NA/NA	NA/NA	Not specified	NA/NA	Not specified	Not specified	NA/NA
Mental Health Counseling	MA/MS	NA/NA	NA/NA	NA/NA	Not specified	NA/NA	Not specified	Not specified	Not specified
Applied Developmental and Educational Psychology	MA/MS	NA/NA	NA/NA	NA/NA	Not specified	NA/NA	Not specified	Not specified	Not specified
Applied Developmental and Educational Psychology	PhD	NA/NA	NA/NA	NA/NA	Not specified	NA/NA	Not specified	Not specified	NA/NA

Admissions Requirements:

Degree	GRE	GRE-Subject	Letters of Recommendation	Research Statement	Writing Sample	CV	Interview
Master's/Specialist	Required	None	2	Required	Optional	Required	None
Doctoral	Required	None	3	Required	Required	Required	Required

Admissions Criteria:

GRE scores—medium
Research experience—high
Work experience—medium
Clinically related public service—low
GPA—high

Letters of recommendation—high
Interview—high
Statement of goals and objectives—high
Undergraduate psychology preparation—medium
Social justice commitment—medium

For additional information on admission requirements, visit http://www.bc.edu/schools/lsoe/gradadmission/getting-started.html.

Department Demographics

	Male (PT)	Female (PT)	Total	African-American/ Black (PT)	Hispanic/ Latino (PT)	Asian/ Pacific Islander (PT)	American Indian/ Alaska Native (PT)	Caucasian/ White (PT)	Unknown	Multiethnic (PT)	ADA (PT)	Int'l (PT)
Students	30 (2)	193 (12)	237	14 (2)	20 (1)	16 (1)	0 (0)	113 (7)	53 (3)	7 (0)	5 (0)	27 (1)

Financial Information/Assistance

Tuition: For information on tuition costs, visit http://www.bc.edu/offices/stserv/financial/tuitionandfees.html. Tuition is subject to change.

Doctoral:
State residents: $1,310 per credit hour.
Nonstate residents: $1,310 per credit hour.

Master's:
State residents: $1,310 per credit hour.
Nonstate residents: $1,310 per credit hour.

Financial Assistance:

	Teaching Assistantship (% Receiving)	Teaching Assistantship Tuition Remission	Research Assistantship (% Receiving)	Research Assistantship Tuition Remission	Fellowship (% Receiving)	Fellowship Tuition Remission
First-Year Student	NA (NA)	NA	$17,500 (NA)	Full	NA (NA)	NA
Advanced Student	$17,500 (NA)	Full	$17,500 (NA)	Full	NA (NA)	NA

Employment of Department Graduates

No information provided.

Additional Information

Housing and Day Care: No on-campus housing is available. On-campus day care facilities are available. See the following website for more information: http://www.bc.edu/offices/hr/employees/all-cc-docs.html.

Information for Students With Physical Disabilities: See the following website: http://www.bc.edu/offices/dos/subsidiary_offices/disabilityservices.html.

Special Facilities or Resources: Boston College offers ample student access to computing facilities (Alpha mainframe, Macintosh and PCs) at no charge to students. The Educational Resource Center houses current psychological assessment kits and computerized instructional software. The Thomas P. O'Neill Library is fully automated with all major computerized databases. Through the consortium, students may cross-register in courses in other greater Boston universities (Boston University, Brandeis, and Tufts). The career center provides comprehensive resources and information regarding career planning and placement. The Institute for the Study and Promotion of Race and Culture (ISPRC), under the direction of Dr. Janet E. Helms, promotes the assets and addresses the societal conflicts associated with race or culture in theory and research, mental health practice, education, business, and society at large. The Center for Human Rights and International Justice at Boston College addresses the increasingly interdisciplinary needs of human rights work. Through multidisciplinary training programs, applied research, and the interaction of scholars with practitioners, the Center aims to nurture a new generation of scholars and practitioners in the United States and abroad who draw upon the strengths of many disciplines and the wisdom of rigorous ethical training in the attainment of human rights and international justice.

Application Information: Boston College, LSOE, Data Processing Center, P.O. Box 226, Randolph, MA 02368-9998. *Fee:* $65. *Online application:* https://apply.embark.com/grad/bc/GSOE/16/.

Boston College

Department of Psychology
College of Arts and Sciences
140 Commonwealth Avenue, McGuinn 300
Chestnut Hill, MA 02467
Telephone: (617) 552-4100
Chairperson: Ellen Winner

E-mail: psychoffice@bc.edu
Web: http://www.bc.edu/schools/cas/psych

Orientation, Objectives, and Emphasis of Department

We emphasize rigorous research and a close working relationship between student and professor.

Programs and Degrees Offered

Program	Degree	Application Deadline	Applications Received	Accepted	New Admits Enrolled (PT)	Total Enrolled (PT)	Degrees Awarded in 2014–2015	Median Years to Complete Degree	Dismissed/Withdrew
Cognitive Neuroscience	PhD	December 15 (Fall)	45	1	0	5	0		

Programs and Degrees Offered (con't.)

Program	Degree	Application Deadline	Applications Received	Accepted	New Admits Enrolled (PT)	Total Enrolled (PT)	Degrees Awarded in 2014–2015	Median Years to Complete Degree	Dismissed/ Withdrew
Social Psychology	PhD	December 15 (Fall)	50	0	0	8	1	5	
Developmental Psychology	PhD	December 15 (Fall)	22	0	0	5	1	6	
Behavioral Neuroscience	PhD	December 15 (Fall)	30	2	1	8	1	6	
Quantitative Psychology	PhD	December 15 (Fall)	9	1	1	1	0		

Admissions

Entries appear in the following order: required test or GPA, minimum score (if required)/median score of students entering in 2015–2016.

Program	Degree	GRE-V	GRE-Q	GRE-Writing	GRE-Subject	Under-graduate GPA	Last 2 Years GPA	Psychol-ogy GPA	Master's GPA
Cognitive Neuroscience	PhD	NA/NA	NA/NA	NA/NA	Not specified	NA/NA	Not specified	Not specified	NA/NA
Social Psychology	PhD	NA/NA	NA/NA	NA/NA	Not specified	NA/NA	Not specified	Not specified	NA/NA
Developmental Psychology	PhD	NA/NA	NA/NA	NA/NA	Not specified	NA/NA	Not specified	Not specified	NA/NA
Behavioral Neuroscience	PhD	NA/NA	NA/NA	NA/NA	Not specified	NA/NA	Not specified	Not specified	NA/NA
Quantitative Psychology	PhD	NA/NA	NA/NA	NA/NA	Not specified	NA/NA	Not specified	Not specified	NA/NA

Admissions Requirements:

Degree	GRE	GRE-Subject	Letters of Recom-mendation	Research Statement	Writing Sample	CV	Interview
Doctoral	Required	Optional	3	Required	Required	Required	Required

Admissions Criteria:

GRE scores—high
Research experience—high
Work experience—low
Clinically related public service—low
GPA—high

Letters of recommendation—high
Interview—high
Statement of goals and objectives—high
Undergraduate psychology preparation—medium

For additional information on admission requirements, visit http://www.bc.edu/schools/cas/psych/graduate.html.

Department Demographics

	Male (PT)	Female (PT)	Total	African-American/ Black (PT)	Hispanic/ Latino (PT)	Asian/ Pacific Islander (PT)	American Indian/ Alaska Native (PT)	Caucasian/ White (PT)	Unknown (PT)	Multiethnic (PT)	ADA (PT)	Int'l (PT)
Students	7 (0)	20 (0)	27	0 (0)	1 (0)	4 (0)	0 (0)	22 (0)	0 (0)	0 (0)	0 (0)	5 (0)

Financial Information/Assistance

Tuition: For information on tuition costs, visit http://www.bc.edu/offices/stserv/financial/tuitionandfees.html. Tuition is subject to change.

Doctoral:
State residents: $1,454 per credit hour.
Nonstate residents: $1,454 per credit hour.

Financial Assistance:

	Teaching Assistantship (% Receiving)	Teaching Assistantship Tuition Remission	Research Assistantship (% Receiving)	Research Assistantship Tuition Remission	Fellowship (% Receiving)	Fellowship Tuition Remission
First-Year Student	$22,800 (NA)	Full	NA (NA)	NA	NA (NA)	Full
Advanced Student	$22,800 (NA)	Full	NA (NA)	NA	NA (NA)	Full

For additional information on financial assistance, visit http://www.bc.edu/schools/gsas/admissions/financial-aid.html.

Employment of Department Graduates

Doctoral:
Employed in an academic position at a university: 3
Total: 3

Additional Information

Housing and Day Care: No on-campus housing is available. On-campus day care facilities are available. See the following website for more information: http://www.bc.edu/content/bc/offices/hr/employees/all-cc-docs.html.

Information for Students With Physical Disabilities: See the following website: http://www.bc.edu/disability.

Special Facilities or Resources: Individual faculty maintain separate research laboratories. There is a shared psychophysiology lab. An animal lab facility contains two components: an animal facility and research laboratory space. The animal facility includes small animal housing and behavioral testing rooms, a surgery suite, and special procedure rooms equipped with hoods. The animal research space includes a microscopy suite; dark room; data analysis room; and 3 research labs/wet labs equipped with hoods, sinks, and workspace.

Application Information: Fee: $75. Online application: http://www.bc.edu/schools/gsas/admissions/howtoapply.html.

Boston University
Department of Psychological & Brain Sciences
64 Cummington Mall
Boston, MA 02215
Telephone: (617) 353-2580
Chairperson: David Somers

E-mail: somers@bu.edu
Web: http://www.bu.edu/psych

Orientation, Objectives, and Emphasis of Department
The department offers specialized training leading to the PhD degree in three areas of concentration: clinical; brain, behavior, and cognition; and development science. The PhD degree in psychology is awarded to students of scholarly competence, as reflected by course achievement and by performance on written and oral examinations, and of research competence, as reflected by student's skillful application and communication of knowledge in the area of specialization. Breadth is encouraged within psychology and in related social, behavioral, and biological sciences, but it is also expected that the student will engage in intensive and penetrating study of a specialized area of the field.

Programs and Degrees Offered

Program	Degree	Application Deadline	Applications Received	Accepted	New Admits Enrolled (PT)	Total Enrolled (PT)	Degrees Awarded in 2014–2015	Median Years to Complete Degree	Dismissed/ Withdrew
Brain, Behavior, and Cognition	PhD	December 1 (Fall)	77	1	0 (0)	14 (1)	2	6.25	0
Clinical Psychology	PhD	December 1 (Fall)	652	6	6 (0)	42 (0)	9	6.72	0
General Psychology	MA/MS	May 15 (Fall)	211	99	23 (1)	23 (9)	30	1	1
Developmental Science	PhD	December 1 (Fall)	51	2	2 (0)	13 (0)	2	6	0

APA Accreditation

Clinical PhD: Student Outcome Data website: http://www.bu.edu/psych/graduate/clinical/.

Doctoral Degree (PhD Clinical Psychology): For those doctoral students for whom a professional internship was required in this program prior to graduation:
Total students who applied for an internship: 7
Total students who obtained an internship: 7
Total students who obtained a paid internship: 7
Total students who obtained an unpaid internship: 0
Total students who were placed in APA/CPA-accredited internships: 7
Total students placed in internships not APA/CPA-accredited, but listed with the Association of Psychology Postdoctoral and Internship Centers (APPIC): 0
Total students placed in internships conforming to guidelines of the Council of Directors of School Psychology Programs (CDSPP): 0
Total students placed in internships that were not APA/CPA-accredited, APPIC or CDSSP listed: 0

Master's Degree (MA/MS General Psychology): An internship experience, such as a final research project or "capstone" experience is required of graduates.

Admissions

Entries appear in the following order: required test or GPA, minimum score (if required)/median score of students entering in 2015–2016.

Program	Degree	GRE-V	GRE-Q	GRE-Writing	GRE-Subject	Undergraduate GPA	Last 2 Years GPA	Psychology GPA	Master's GPA
Brain, Behavior, and Cognition	PhD	NA/155	NA/155	NA/3.5	Not specified	NA/3.5	NA/NA	NA/NA	NA/NA
Clinical Psychology	PhD	NA/162	NA/156	NA/4.75	Not specified	NA/3.77	NA/NA	NA/NA	NA/NA
General Psychology	MA/MS	NA/153	NA/154	NA/4.3	Not specified	NA/3.34	NA/NA	NA/NA	Not specified
Developmental Science	PhD	NA/156	NA/160	NA/4.4	Not specified	NA/3.91	NA/NA	NA/NA	NA/NA

Admissions Requirements:

Degree	GRE	GRE-Subject	Letters of Recommendation	Research Statement	Writing Sample	CV	Interview
Master's/Specialist	Required	Optional	3	Required	Optional	Required	None
Doctoral	Required	Optional	3	Required	Optional	Required	Required

Admissions Criteria:

GRE scores—high
Research experience—high
Work experience—low
Clinically related public service—high
GPA—high

Letters of recommendation—high
Interview—high
Statement of goals and objectives—high
Undergraduate psychology preparation—high

For additional information on admission requirements, visit http://www.bu.edu/psych/graduate/prospective/.

Department Demographics

	Male (PT)	Female (PT)	Total	African-American/ Black (PT)	Hispanic/ Latino (PT)	Asian/ Pacific Islander (PT)	American Indian/ Alaska Native (PT)	Caucasian/ White (PT)	Unknown	Multiethnic (PT)	ADA (PT)	Int'l (PT)
Students	19 (3)	73 (7)	102	2 (0)	7 (0)	11 (0)	0 (0)	57 (0)	22 (0)	3 (0)	0 (0)	15 (0)

Financial Information/Assistance

Tuition: For information on tuition costs, visit http://www.bu.edu/reg/registration/tuition-fees/.

Doctoral:
State residents: $48,082 per academic year.
State residents: $1,482 per credit hour.
Nonstate residents: $48,082 per academic year.
Nonstate residents: $1,482 per credit hour.

Master's:
State residents: $48,082 per academic year.
State residents: $1,482 per credit hour.
Nonstate residents: $48,082 per academic year.
Nonstate residents: $1,482 per credit hour.

Financial Assistance:

	Teaching Assistantship (% Receiving)	Teaching Assistantship Tuition Remission	Research Assistantship (% Receiving)	Research Assistantship Tuition Remission	Fellowship (% Receiving)	Fellowship Tuition Remission
First-Year Student	$31,500 (NA)	Full	$31,500 (NA)	Full	$31,500 (NA)	Full
Advanced Student	$31,500 (NA)	Full	$31,500 (NA)	Full	NA (NA)	NA

For additional information on financial assistance, visit http://www.bu.edu/cas/prospective-students/graduate-admissions/graduate-financial-aid/.

Employment of Department Graduates

Doctoral:
Enrolled in a postdoctoral residency/fellowship: 9
Employed in academic position at a 2-year/4-year college: 1
Employed in other positions at a higher education institution: 1
Employed in business or industry: 1
Employed in a hospital/medical center: 1
Total: 13

Additional Information

Housing and Day Care: No on-campus housing is available. No on-campus day care facilities are available.

Information for Students With Physical Disabilities: See the following website: http://www.bu.edu/disability/.

Special Facilities or Resources: Laboratories for research pursuits in animal behavior, behavior disorders, child development, cognition, neurophysiology, molecular biology, addiction, and psychopharmacology add to the department's facilities. The Center for Anxiety and Related Disorders, a nationally recognized clinical research and treatment center, is a recent addition to the department and allows students to engage in a variety of ongoing research projects and receive training in focused clinical interventions. In addition, the Boston area is fortunate to have a number of nationally known hospitals, counseling centers, and community mental health centers directly affiliated with our clinical program, where students have opportunities to gain experience in a variety of clinical settings with different client populations. The New England Regional Primate Center, which is supported by the National Institutes of Health, is also available to Boston University faculty and students.

Application Information: Fee: $95. *Online application:* http://www.bu.edu/cas/prospective-students/graduate-admissions/apply/.

Boston University (2015 data)

Mental Health Counseling and Behavioral Medicine Program
School of Medicine
72 East Concord Street, Robinson Building, Suite B-2903
Boston, MA 02118
Telephone: (617) 414-2320
Chairperson: Stephen Brady

E-mail: nicey@bu.edu
Web: http://www.bumc.bu.edu/mhbm/

Orientation, Objectives, and Emphasis of Department

The mission of the Mental Health Counseling and Behavioral Medicine (MHCBM) Master's Degree Program at Boston University School of Medicine is to provide exceptional academic and clinical fieldwork experience that emphasizes the core competencies of clinical mental health counseling with complementary training in behavioral medicine and neuroscience. Accredited by the Council for Accreditation of Counseling and Related Educational Programs, the MHCBM Program places great value on excellence, diversity, integrity, social justice, advocacy, collegiality, equality of opportunity, and interdisciplinary collaboration. Our program offers theoretical, experiential, clinical, and research-supported activities related to clinical mental health counseling with adults, adolescents, and children on the medical campus as well as in community settings. We accept and educate a broad range of outstanding students who seek careers as clinical mental health counselors. Graduates of the MHCBM Program generally become independently licensed and are trained to work in settings where traditional mental health interventions can be informed by evidence-based practice, an understanding of neuroscience, and strategies to address physical illness and health promotion.

Programs and Degrees Offered

Program	Degree	Application Deadline	Applications Received	Accepted	New Admits Enrolled (PT)	Total Enrolled (PT)	Degrees Awarded in 2014–2015	Median Years to Complete Degree	Dismissed/ Withdrew
Mental Health Counseling and Behavioral Medicine	MA/MS	(Fall), Rolling				56 (0)			

Internships/Practica

One of the most outstanding features of our Masters program is our clinical training model and clinical training field placement opportunities. Individualized attention and advising is given to each student to help create a training track that best meets the clinical and developmental needs of the student. We have a selection of over a 120 sites to choose from. Our clinical field placements represent clinically and ethnically diverse populations. We offer training opportunities to work with clients with emotional, cognitive, behavioral, personality, and health disorders. Students are trained in several modalities of treatment including but not limited to individual, group, and family therapy.

Admissions

Entries appear in the following order: required test or GPA, minimum score (if required)/median score of students entering in 2015–2016.

Program	Degree	GRE-V	GRE-Q	GRE-Writing	GRE-Subject	Under-graduate GPA	Last 2 Years GPA	Psychology GPA	Master's GPA
Mental Health Counseling and Behavioral Medicine	MA/MS	Not specified	Not specified	Not specified	Not specified	Not specified	Not specified	Not specified	Not specified

Admissions Requirements:

Degree	GRE	GRE-Subject	Letters of Recommendation	Research Statement	Writing Sample	CV	Interview
Master's/Specialist	Required	None	3	Required	Optional	Optional	Required

Admissions Criteria:

GRE scores—high
Research experience—low
Work experience—low
Clinically related public service—low
GPA—high

Letters of recommendation—high
Interview—high
Statement of goals and objectives—high
Undergraduate psychology preparation—medium

For additional information on admission requirements, visit http://www.bumc.bu.edu/mhbm/admissions/applying/.

Department Demographics

	Male (PT)	Female (PT)	Total	African-American/ Black (PT)	Hispanic/ Latino (PT)	Asian/ Pacific Islander (PT)	American Indian/ Alaska Native (PT)	Caucasian/ White (PT)	Unknown	Multiethnic (PT)	ADA (PT)	Int'l (PT)
Students	7 (0)	49 (0)	56	6 (0)	1 (0)	3 (0)	4 (0)	42 (0)	0 (0)	0 (0)	0 (0)	3 (0)

Financial Information/Assistance

Tuition: For information on tuition costs, visit http://www.bumc.bu.edu/gms/gateway/prospective/financial-aid/.

Master's:
State residents: $47,422 per academic year
State residents: $1,482 per credit hour.
Nonstate residents: $47,422 per academic year.
Nonstate residents: $1,482 per credit hour.

Financial Assistance:

	Teaching Assistantship (% Receiving)	Teaching Assistantship Tuition Remission	Research Assistantship (% Receiving)	Research Assistantship Tuition Remission	Fellowship (% Receiving)	Fellowship Tuition Remission
First-Year Student	NA (NA)	NA	NA (NA)	NA	NA (NA)	NA
Advanced Student	NA (NA)	NA	NA (NA)	NA	NA (NA)	NA

For additional information on financial assistance, visit http://www.bumc.bu.edu/gms/gateway/prospective/financial-aid/.

Employment of Department Graduates

No information provided.

Additional Information

Housing and Day Care: No on-campus housing is available. No on-campus day care facilities are available.

Information for Students With Physical Disabilities: See the following website: http://www.bu.edu/disability/.

Application Information: Admissions, Division Office of Graduate Medical Sciences, Boston University School of Medicine, 72 East Concord Street, Room L-317, Boston, MA 02118. *Fee:* $75. *Online application:* http://www.bumc.bu.edu/gms/gateway/prospective/.

Brandeis University

Department of Psychology
College of Arts & Sciences
415 South Street, Mail Stop 062
Waltham, MA 02453
Telephone: (781) 736-3300
Chairperson: Prof. Paul DiZio

E-mail: gnat@brandeis.edu
Web: http://www.brandeis.edu/departments/psych

Orientation, Objectives, and Emphasis of Department

The goal of the PhD program is to develop excellent researchers and teachers who will become leaders in psychological science either in academic or applied research settings. Research activity is emphasized from the start of graduate study. The program has an interdisciplinary focus, and it helps students to develop an area of research specialization while providing opportunities to bring various theoretical and methodological perspectives to work in their chosen area of training. Training within the PhD program focuses on Brain, Body, and Behavior Across the Lifespan. Students may elect to specialize in a number of different research areas, including face perception and nonverbal communication; learning and memory; motor control and spatial orientation; neurophysiology of learning and decision making; personality and cognition in adulthood and old age; social, cultural, and affective neuroscience; social relations and health physiology; speech comprehension and memory; taste physiology and psychophysics; and visual perception.

Programs and Degrees Offered

Program	Degree	Application Deadline	Applications Received	Accepted	New Admits Enrolled (PT)	Total Enrolled (PT)	Degrees Awarded in 2014–2015	Median Years to Complete Degree	Dismissed/ Withdrew
General Psychology	MA/MS	May 15 (Fall)	89	15	8 (1)	9 (2)	9	1.5	0
Psychology	PhD	December 1 (Fall)	95	13	5 (0)	27 (0)	3	4.58	0

Admissions

Entries appear in the following order: required test or GPA, minimum score (if required)/median score of students entering in 2015–2016.

Program	Degree	GRE-V	GRE-Q	GRE-Writing	GRE-Subject	Under-graduate GPA	Last 2 Years GPA	Psychol-ogy GPA	Master's GPA
General Psychology	MA/MS	NA/159	NA/160	NA/4	Not specified	NA/3.7	Not specified	Not specified	Not specified
Psychology	PhD	NA/159	NA/158	NA/4	Not specified	NA/3.6	Not specified	Not specified	Not specified

Admissions Requirements:

Degree	GRE	GRE-Subject	Letters of Recom-mendation	Research Statement	Writing Sample	CV	Interview
Master's/Specialist	Required	Recom-mended	3	Required	Optional	Required	Recom-mended
Doctoral	Required	Recom-mended	3	Required	Optional	Required	Required

Admissions Criteria:

GRE scores—high
Research experience—high
Work experience—medium
Clinically related public service—low
GPA—high

Letters of recommendation—high
Interview—high
Statement of goals and objectives—high
Undergraduate psychology preparation—medium

For additional information on admission requirements, visit http://www.brandeis.edu/gsas/programs/psychology.html.

Department Demographics

	Male (PT)	Female (PT)	Total	African-American/ Black (PT)	Hispanic/ Latino (PT)	Asian/ Pacific Islander (PT)	American Indian/ Alaska Native (PT)	Caucasian/ White (PT)	Unknown	Multiethnic (PT)	ADA (PT)	Int'l (PT)
Students	8 (0)	28 (2)	38	1 (0)	2 (0)	3 (0)	0 (0)	22 (1)	4 (1)	4 (0)	0 (0)	9 (0)

Financial Information/Assistance

Tuition: For information on tuition costs, visit http://www.brandeis.edu/gsas/financing/cost.html. Tuition is subject to change.

Doctoral:
State residents: $45,900 per academic year.
State residents: $1,435 per credit hour.
Nonstate residents: $45,900 per academic year.
Nonstate residents: $1,435 per credit hour.

Master's:
State residents: $45,900 per academic year.
State residents: $1,435 per credit hour.
Nonstate residents: $45,900 per academic year.
Nonstate residents: $1,435 per credit hour.

Financial Assistance:

	Teaching Assistantship (% Receiving)	Teaching Assistantship Tuition Remission	Research Assistantship (% Receiving)	Research Assistantship Tuition Remission	Fellowship (% Receiving)	Fellowship Tuition Remission
First-Year Student	NA (NA)	NA	NA (NA)	NA	$22,000 (NA)	Full
Advanced Student	NA (NA)	NA	NA (NA)	NA	$22,000 (NA)	Full

For additional information on financial assistance, visit http://www.brandeis.edu/gsas/financing/.

Employment of Department Graduates

Master's:
Enrolled in a psychology doctoral program: 2
Employed in other positions at a higher education institution: 1
Employed in government agency: 2
Still seeking employment: 1
Do not know: 3
Total: 9

Doctoral:
Enrolled in a postdoctoral residency/fellowship: 1
Employed in other positions at a higher education institution: 1
Employed in a community mental health/counseling center: 1
Total: 3

Additional Information

Housing and Day Care: No on-campus housing is available. On-campus day care facilities are available. See the following website for more information: http://www.brandeis.edu/lemberg/.

Information for Students With Physical Disabilities: See the following website: http://www.brandeis.edu/acserv/disabilities/.

Special Facilities or Resources: Laboratories in the Psychology Department are well-equipped for research on memory, speech recognition, psycholinguistics, visual psychophysics, visual perception, motor control, and spatial orientation, including a NASA-sponsored laboratory for research on human spatial orientation in unusual gravitational environments. Social and developmental psychology laboratories include one-way observation rooms, video-recording and eye-tracking apparatus. There are also opportunities for social neuroscience research through a collaborative grant with the MGH-NMR center. Child development research is facilitated by cooperative relations with the Lemberg Children's Center on the Brandeis campus; applied social research is facilitated by cooperative relations with the Brandeis University Florence Heller Graduate School for Advanced Studies in Social Welfare and the Graduate School of International Economics and Finance. Research on cognitive aging is supported by a training grant from the National Institute on Aging. A special feature of the aging program is an interest in the interaction of cognitive, social and personality factors in healthy aging. The psychology department also participates in an interdisciplinary neuroscience program at the Volen National Center for Complex Systems located on the Brandeis campus.

Application Information: Graduate School of Arts & Sciences, Brandeis University, 415 South Street, MS-031, Waltham, MA 02454-9110. *Fee:* $75. *Online application:* http://www.brandeis.edu/gsas/admissions/apply/.

Bridgewater State University

Department of Psychology
College of Humanities and Social Science
91 Burrill Avenue
Bridgewater, MA 02325
Telephone: (508) 531-1769
Graduate Program Coordinator: John A. Calicchia, PhD
Web: http://www.bridgew.edu/academics/graduate-studies/master-arts-psychology

E-mail: jcalicchia@bridgew.edu

Orientation, Objectives, and Emphasis of Department

The mission of the Master of Arts program in Psychology is to prepare students to become mental health professionals, clinically skilled, and able to contribute to our diverse society. Trained to conduct psychotherapy in a range of contexts, students' education is grounded in a framework of professional ethics and personal responsibility. The faculty seek to provide a high quality and rigorous academic experience that facilitates the development of clinical skills through intensive engagement and experiential learning of both theory and techniques. Moreover, the program seeks to provide students with (1) an empirical theoretical base from scientific psychology; and (2) strong clinical skills that will enable each student to begin a lifetime of clinical work, consultation and/or teaching. Students graduating from the program, once they obtain additional supervised hours, are eligible to become Licensed Mental Health Counselors (LMHC) in the state of Massachusetts and to employ the clinical techniques and knowledge of the profession to improve individual, group, and systemic problems. In line with the mission of the department and the institution, the Psychology MA program emphasizes the value of scientific approaches to psychological understanding, a focus on human development, cultural awareness, and the embodiment of professional ethics.

Programs and Degrees Offered

Program	Degree	Application Deadline	Applications Received	Accepted	New Admits Enrolled (PT)	Total Enrolled (PT)	Degrees Awarded in 2014–2015	Median Years to Complete Degree	Dismissed/ Withdrew
Clinical Psychology	MA/MS	February 15 (Fall)	44	18	7 (3)	35 (11)	9	2.5	1

Internships/Practica

All graduate students are required to engage in both clinical practica and internship for a total of three to five semesters. Students will work closely with their advisors to select an appropriate placement that meets their intended career goals. The practicum and internship fieldwork allows graduate students to continue their training and extend their services to individuals, families, and groups within the community. A variety of both inpatient and outpatient sites are available to graduate students including (but not limited to) community agencies, hospital settings, school settings, and substance-abuse settings.

Admissions

Entries appear in the following order: required test or GPA, minimum score (if required)/median score of students entering in 2015–2016.

Program	Degree	GRE-V	GRE-Q	GRE-Writing	GRE-Subject	Under-graduate GPA	Last 2 Years GPA	Psychology GPA	Master's GPA
Clinical Psychology	MA/MS	145/152	141/147	Not specified	Not specified	2.8/3.4	Not specified	Not specified	Not specified

Admissions Requirements:

Degree	GRE	GRE-Subject	Letters of Recommendation	Research Statement	Writing Sample	CV	Interview
Master's/Specialist	Required	None	3	Required	Required	Required	Required

Admissions Criteria:
GRE scores—medium
Research experience—low
Work experience—high
Clinically related public service—high
GPA—high

Letters of recommendation—high
Interview—high
Statement of goals and objectives—high
Undergraduate psychology preparation—high

Department Demographics

	Male (PT)	Female (PT)	Total	African-American/ Black (PT)	Hispanic/ Latino (PT)	Asian/ Pacific Islander (PT)	American Indian/ Alaska Native (PT)	Caucasian/ White (PT)	Unknown	Multiethnic (PT)	ADA (PT)	Int'l (PT)
Students	5 (2)	30 (9)	46	2 (1)	0 (0)	0 (0)	0 (0)	33 (10)	0 (0)	0 (0)	0 (0)	0 (0)

Financial Information/Assistance

Tuition: For information on tuition costs, visit http://www.bridgew.edu/admissions/cost-attending. Tuition is subject to change.

Master's:
State residents: $6,588 per academic year.
State residents: $397 per credit hour.
Nonstate residents: $6,588 per academic year.
Nonstate residents: $397 per credit hour.

Financial Assistance:

	Teaching Assistantship (% Receiving)	Teaching Assistantship Tuition Remission	Research Assistantship (% Receiving)	Research Assistantship Tuition Remission	Fellowship (% Receiving)	Fellowship Tuition Remission
First-Year Student	$10,500 (NA)	Full	$7,200 (NA)	Partial	$1,000 (NA)	NA
Advanced Student	$12,000 (NA)	Full	$8,000 (NA)	Partial	$1,000 (NA)	NA

Employment of Department Graduates

No information provided.

Additional Information

Housing and Day Care: No on-campus housing is available. No on-campus day care facilities are available.

Information for Students With Physical Disabilities: See the following website: http://www.bridgew.edu/disability-resources.

Special Facilities or Resources: A psychology department research lab is available that provides a standardized, distraction-free testing environment, continuous oversight, and ongoing participation tracking. The psychology department research lab provides a location for graduate students to conduct their research studies and review and analyze their data.

Application Information: Bridgewater State University, College of Graduate Studies, Graduate Admissions, 10 Shaw Road, Bridgewater, MA 02325. *Fee:* $50. *Online application:* http://www.bridgew.edu/admissions/graduate/apply.

Clark University

Frances L. Hiatt School of Psychology
950 Main Street
Worcester, MA 01610
Telephone: (508) 793-7274
Chairperson: Dr. James V. Cordova

E-mail: kboulay@clarku.edu
Web: http://www.clarku.edu/departments/psychology/index.cfm

Orientation, Objectives, and Emphasis of Department

The Department of Psychology at Clark University offers graduate students a unique opportunity to explore a variety of theoretical approaches and to participate in ongoing research programs in the intimate atmosphere of a small research university. We support the intellectual development of our students in ways that make them well qualified for their future careers, whether in academic teaching and research, clinical practice, or elsewhere.

Programs and Degrees Offered

Program	Degree	Application Deadline	Applications Received	Accepted	New Admits Enrolled (PT)	Total Enrolled (PT)	Degrees Awarded in 2014–2015	Median Years to Complete Degree	Dismissed/ Withdrew
Clinical Psychology	PhD	December 15 (Fall)	183	13	7	27	3	6	0
Developmental Psychology	PhD	December 15 (Fall)	15	4	2	9	3	6	1
Social Psychology	PhD	December 15 (Fall)	42	4	1	8	0		0

APA Accreditation

Clinical PhD: Student Outcome Data website: http://www.clarku.edu/departments/psychology/grad/clinical/clinicalstudentdata.cfm.

Doctoral Degree (PhD Clinical Psychology): For those doctoral students for whom a professional internship was required in this program prior to graduation:
Total students who applied for an internship: 4
Total students who obtained an internship: 3
Total students who obtained a paid internship: 3
Total students who obtained an unpaid internship: 0
Total students who were placed in APA/CPA-accredited internships: 3
Total students placed in internships not APA/CPA-accredited, but listed with the Association of Psychology Postdoctoral and Internship Centers (APPIC): 0
Total students placed in internships conforming to guidelines of the Council of Directors of School Psychology Programs (CDSPP): 0
Total students placed in internships that were not APA/CPA-accredited, APPIC or CDSSP listed: 0

Internships/Practica

Students in our APA-accredited clinical PhD program are required to complete psychotherapy, couples, and advanced therapy practica; a part-time externship and a full-time one-year APA-accredited internship. Additional clinical hours are available through several community programs.

Admissions

Entries appear in the following order: required test or GPA, minimum score (if required)/median score of students entering in 2015–2016.

Program	Degree	GRE-V	GRE-Q	GRE-Writing	GRE-Subject	Under-graduate GPA	Last 2 Years GPA	Psychol-ogy GPA	Master's GPA
Clinical Psychology	PhD	Not specified	Not specified	Not specified	Not specified	Not specified	Not specified	Not specified	Not specified
Developmental Psychology	PhD	Not specified	Not specified	Not specified	Not specified	Not specified	Not specified	Not specified	Not specified
Social Psychology	PhD	Not specified	Not specified	Not specified	Not specified	Not specified	Not specified	Not specified	Not specified

Admissions Requirements:

Degree	GRE	GRE-Subject	Letters of Recom-mendation	Research Statement	Writing Sample	CV	Interview
Doctoral	Required	Optional	3	Required	Required	Required	Required

Admissions Criteria:

GRE scores—medium
Research experience—high
Work experience—low
GPA—high

Letters of recommendation—high
Interview—high
Statement of goals and objectives—high
Undergraduate psychology preparation—medium

For additional information on admission requirements, visit http://www.clarku.edu/graduate-admissions/apply/requirements/phd-psychology.cfm.

Department Demographics

	Male (PT)	Female (PT)	Total	African-American/ Black (PT)	Hispanic/ Latino (PT)	Asian/ Pacific Islander (PT)	American Indian/ Alaska Native (PT)	Caucasian/ White (PT)	Unknown (PT)	Multiethnic (PT)	ADA (PT)	Int'l (PT)
Students	9 (0)	35 (0)	44	2 (0)	6 (0)	5 (0)	0 (0)	31 (0)	0 (0)	0 (0)	0 (0)	5 (0)

Financial Information/Assistance

Tuition: For information on tuition costs, visit http://www.clarku.edu/graduate-admissions/admitted/tuition-aid/tuition-intro.cfm. Tuition is subject to change. Additional fees are assessed to students beyond the costs of tuition for the following: Activity fee, enrollment fee, health insurance.

Doctoral:
State residents: $42,800 per academic year.
Nonstate residents: $42,800 per academic year.

Financial Assistance:

	Teaching Assistantship (% Receiving)	Teaching Assistantship Tuition Remission	Research Assistantship (% Receiving)	Research Assistantship Tuition Remission	Fellowship (% Receiving)	Fellowship Tuition Remission
First-Year Student	$17,656 (100)	Full	NA (NA)	NA	NA (NA)	NA
Advanced Student	$17,656 (50)	Full	$17,656 (28)	Full	NA (NA)	NA

For additional information on financial assistance, visit http://www.clarku.edu/departments/psychology/grad/programcosts.cfm.

Employment of Department Graduates

Doctoral:
Enrolled in a postdoctoral residency/fellowship: 3
Employed in an academic position at a university: 3
Employed in academic position at a 2-year/4-year college: 1
Employed in a hospital/medical center: 2
Total: 9

Additional Information

Housing and Day Care: On-campus housing is available. See the following website for more information: http://www.clarku.edu/offices/housing/graduate/index.cfm. No on-campus day care facilities are available.

Information for Students With Physical Disabilities: See the following website: http://www.clarku.edu/offices/aac/ada/.

Application Information: Fee: $75. Online application: http://www.clarku.edu/graduate-admissions/.

Harvard University

Department of Psychology
Faculty of Arts and Sciences
33 Kirkland Street
Cambridge, MA 02138
Telephone: (617) 495-3800
Chairperson: Ken Nakayama

E-mail: psyinfo@wjh.harvard.edu
Web: http://psychology.fas.harvard.edu

Orientation, Objectives, and Emphasis of Department

The psychology department is divided into two main curricula: an APA-accredited clinical science program, and a common curriculum covering all other areas. The aim of the program is to train students for careers in psychological research and teaching. These careers are mainly in academia. The emphasis of the program is heavily on research training; in addition to a small number of required courses, students do a first-year research project, a second-year research project, and the doctoral dissertation. Students take a major examination or intense seminar(s) in their major specialty fields. Since most students prepare for academic careers, there are ample opportunities to serve as teaching fellows.

Programs and Degrees Offered

Program	Degree	Application Deadline	Applications Received	Accepted	New Admits Enrolled (PT)	Total Enrolled (PT)	Degrees Awarded in 2014–2015	Median Years to Complete Degree	Dismissed/ Withdrew
Clinical Psychology	PhD	December 15 (Fall)	291	3	2 (0)	24 (0)	0		0
Common Curriculum	PhD	December 15 (Fall)	312	13	11	54	13	5.92	0

APA Accreditation

Clinical PhD: Student Outcome Data website: http://psychology.fas.harvard.edu/clinical-psychology.

Doctoral Degree (PhD Clinical Psychology): For those doctoral students for whom a professional internship was required in this program prior to graduation:
Total students who applied for an internship: 2
Total students who obtained an internship: 2
Total students who obtained a paid internship: 2
Total students who obtained an unpaid internship: 0
Total students who were placed in APA/CPA-accredited internships: 2
Total students placed in internships not APA/CPA-accredited, but listed with the Association of Psychology Postdoctoral and Internship Centers (APPIC): 0
Total students placed in internships conforming to guidelines of the Council of Directors of School Psychology Programs (CDSPP): 0
Total students placed in internships that were not APA/CPA-accredited, APPIC or CDSSP listed: 0

Internships/Practica

Students in the clinical program will have predoctoral practicum placements in a local Harvard-affiliated hospital. Students are required to have defended their thesis prospectus, and are strongly encouraged to collect most of the data prior to departing for internship, but the thesis project need not be completed before beginning the internship. Clinical internship applicants use the APPIC system.

Admissions

Entries appear in the following order: required test or GPA, minimum score (if required)/median score of students entering in 2015–2016.

Program	Degree	GRE-V	GRE-Q	GRE-Writing	GRE-Subject	Under-graduate GPA	Last 2 Years GPA	Psychol-ogy GPA	Master's GPA
Clinical Psychology	PhD	NA/NA	NA/NA	NA/NA	Not specified	Not specified	Not specified	Not specified	Not specified
Common Curriculum	PhD	NA/NA	NA/NA	NA/NA	Not specified	Not specified	Not specified	Not specified	Not specified

Admissions Requirements:

Degree	GRE	GRE-Subject	Letters of Recommendation	Research Statement	Writing Sample	CV	Interview
Doctoral	Required	None	3	Required	Optional	Required	Required

Admissions Criteria:

GRE scores—high
Research experience—high
Work experience—high
Clinically related public service—medium
GPA—high

Letters of recommendation—high
Interview—high
Statement of goals and objectives—high
Undergraduate psychology preparation—medium

Department Demographics

	Male (PT)	Female (PT)	Total	African-American/Black (PT)	Hispanic/Latino (PT)	Asian/Pacific Islander (PT)	American Indian/Alaska Native (PT)	Caucasian/White (PT)	Unknown	Multiethnic (PT)	ADA (PT)	Int'l (PT)
Students	33 (0)	43 (0)	76	3 (0)	0 (0)	17 (0)	0 (0)	55 (0)	0 (0)	1 (0)	1 (0)	10 (0)

Financial Information/Assistance

Tuition: For information on tuition costs, visit http://www.gsas.harvard.edu/prospective_students/costs_tuition_and_fees.php. Tuition is subject to change.

Doctoral:
State residents: $47,038 per academic year.
Nonstate residents: $47,038 per academic year.

Financial Assistance:

	Teaching Assistantship (% Receiving)	Teaching Assistantship Tuition Remission	Research Assistantship (% Receiving)	Research Assistantship Tuition Remission	Fellowship (% Receiving)	Fellowship Tuition Remission
First-Year Student	NA (NA)	NA	NA (NA)	NA	$33,120 (100)	Full
Advanced Student	$33,120 (NA)	Full	$33,120 (NA)	Full	$33,120 (NA)	Full

For additional information on financial assistance, visit http://www.gsas.harvard.edu/current_students/financial_aid.php.

Employment of Department Graduates

Doctoral:
Enrolled in a postdoctoral residency/fellowship: 5
Employed in business or industry: 6
Total: 11

Additional Information

Housing and Day Care: On-campus housing is available. See the following website for more information: https://www.gsas.harvard.edu/current_students/residential_life.php. On-campus day care facilities are available. See the following website for more information: http://www.childcare.harvard.edu/.

Information for Students With Physical Disabilities: See the following website: http://www.fas.harvard.edu/~aeo/.

Special Facilities or Resources: The department is well equipped with facilities for conducting research. Faculty are the recipients of many grants in various areas of psychology, and graduate students play an essential role in the conduct of most of this research. William James Hall houses a well-staffed computer lab to serve faculty and students. Students are given offices, the use of laboratory space, and a sum of money for research support. The department encourages interdisciplinary study, and students have the benefit of taking courses and working with the faculty at other Harvard graduate schools (Education, Medical School, Public Health, etc.) and at MIT. The Cambridge and Boston areas are well endowed with research facilities and hospitals that offer resources, such as MRI equipment, to students.

Application Information: Harvard University, Office of Admissions, The Graduate School of Arts and Sciences, P.O. Box 9129, Cambridge, MA 02238-9129. *Fee:* $105. *Online application:* http://www.gsas.harvard.edu/apply.

Massachusetts, University of
Department of Psychology
Tobin Hall
Amherst, MA 01003
Telephone: (413) 545-2383
Chairperson: Harold Grotevant

E-mail: mconstantino@psych.umass.edu
Web: http://www.psych.umass.edu/

Orientation, Objectives, and Emphasis of Department
The psychology program is designed to develop research scholars, college teachers, and scientific/professional psychologists in the five areas listed. Individual student programs combine basic courses and seminars in a variety of specialized areas, research experience, and practica in both on- and off-campus settings. In addition, the social area has begun a new specialization in the Psychology of Peace and Prevention of Violence. Students with applied interests, such as clinical and developmental, have ample opportunity for in-depth practical experience.

Programs and Degrees Offered

Program	Degree	Application Deadline	Applica- tions Received	Accepted	New Admits Enrolled (PT)	Total Enrolled (PT)	Degrees Awarded in 2014– 2015	Median Years to Complete Degree	Dismissed/ Withdrew
Clinical Psychology	PhD	December 1 (Fall)	162	8	5	23 (0)	4	6.25	1
Cognitive Psychology	PhD	January 2 (Fall)	47	4	2	12 (0)	0		0
Developmental Science	PhD	January 2 (Fall)	32	4	2 (0)	9 (0)	1		0
Social Psychology	PhD	January 2 (Fall)	61	3	1 (0)	13 (0)	1	5	1
Psychology Of Peace and The Prevention Of Violence	PhD	January 2 (Fall)	32	1	0 (0)	6 (0)	1	5	0

APA Accreditation
Clinical PhD: Student Outcome Data website: http://www.psych.umass.edu/research_and_training/areas_of_training_and_research/clinical_psychology/index.html.

Doctoral Degree (PhD Clinical Psychology): For those doctoral students for whom a professional internship was required in this program prior to graduation:
Total students who applied for an internship: 3
Total students who obtained an internship: 3
Total students who obtained a paid internship: 3
Total students who obtained an unpaid internship: 0
Total students who were placed in APA/CPA-accredited internships: 3

Total students placed in internships not APA/CPA-accredited, but listed with the Association of Psychology Postdoctoral and Internship Centers (APPIC): 0
Total students placed in internships conforming to guidelines of the Council of Directors of School Psychology Programs (CDSPP): 0
Total students placed in internships that were not APA/CPA-accredited, APPIC or CDSSP listed: 0

Internships/Practica
Clinical students must complete an APA-approved clinical internship. None of these required internships are offered by our program.

Admissions
Entries appear in the following order: required test or GPA, minimum score (if required)/median score of students entering in 2015–2016.

Program	Degree	GRE-V	GRE-Q	GRE-Writing	GRE-Subject	Under-graduate GPA	Last 2 Years GPA	Psychology GPA	Master's GPA
Clinical Psychology	PhD	155/164	156/158	4.5/5	Not specified	3.7/3.8	Not specified	Not specified	Not specified
Cognitive Psychology	PhD	NA/NA	NA/NA	NA/NA	Not specified	NA/NA	Not specified	Not specified	Not specified
Developmental Science	PhD	NA/NA	NA/NA	NA/NA	Not specified	NA/NA	Not specified	Not specified	Not specified
Social Psychology	PhD	NA/164	NA/151	NA/NA	Not specified	NA/3.5	Not specified	Not specified	Not specified
Psychology of Peace and the Prevention of Violence	PhD	NA/NA	NA/NA	NA/NA	Not specified	NA/NA	Not specified	Not specified	Not specified

Admissions Requirements:

Degree	GRE	GRE-Subject	Letters of Recom-mendation	Research Statement	Writing Sample	CV	Interview
Doctoral	Required	Optional	3	Required	Optional	Required	Required

Please note if these criteria vary for different programs: Only clinical requires an interview. Clinically related public service also is a criterion (low) in admission to clinical. Undergraduate psychology preparation will be weighed differently depending on division.

Admissions Criteria:
GRE scores—high
Research experience—high
Work experience—low
Clinically related public service—low
GPA—high

Letters of recommendation—high
Interview—medium
Statement of goals and objectives—medium
Undergraduate psychology preparation—medium

For additional information on admission requirements, visit http://www.psych.umass.edu/graduate/program_application/.

Department Demographics

	Male (PT)	Female (PT)	Total	African-American/Black (PT)	Hispanic/Latino (PT)	Asian/Pacific Islander (PT)	American Indian/Alaska Native (PT)	Caucasian/White (PT)	Unknown	Multiethnic (PT)	ADA (PT)	Int'l (PT)
Students	22 (0)	39 (0)	61	1 (0)	2 (0)	6 (0)	0 (0)	38 (0)	13 (0)	1 (0)	1 (0)	10 (0)

Financial Information/Assistance

Tuition: For information on tuition costs, visit http://www.umass.edu/bursar/graduate. Tuition is subject to change.

Doctoral:
State residents: $12,318 per academic year.
Nonstate residents: $23,652 per academic year.

Financial Assistance:

	Teaching Assistantship (% Receiving)	Teaching Assistantship Tuition Remission	Research Assistantship (% Receiving)	Research Assistantship Tuition Remission	Fellowship (% Receiving)	Fellowship Tuition Remission
First-Year Student	$19,174 (NA)	Full	$19,174 (NA)	Full	$19,174 (NA)	Full
Advanced Student	$19,174 (NA)	Full	$19,174 (NA)	Full	$19,174 (NA)	Full

For additional information on financial assistance, visit http://www.psych.umass.edu/graduate/financial_support_and_expenses/.

Employment of Department Graduates

Doctoral:
Enrolled in a postdoctoral residency/fellowship: 3
Employed in an academic position at a university: 1
Employed in government agency: 1
Employed in a hospital/medical center: 2
Still seeking employment: 1
Do not know: 1
Total: 9

Additional Information

Housing and Day Care: On-campus housing is available. See the following website for more information: http://www.umass.edu/living/. On-campus day care facilities are available. See the following website for more information: http://www.umass.edu/ofr/education.php.

Information for Students With Physical Disabilities: See the following website: http://www.umass.edu/disability/.

Special Facilities or Resources: The Department has specialized laboratory facilities, including biochemistry, eyetracking, video data analysis, and other laboratories. It maintains its own clinic for research, clinical training, and service to the community. It provides students with access to microcomputers and to the VAX mainframes at University Computing Services. Departmental facilities and faculty are supplemented by the University's participation in Five College programs (with Amherst, Hampshire, Mount Holyoke, and Smith Colleges) and by cooperation with other University departments including Computer and Information Science, Industrial Engineering, Education, Linguistics, Sociology, and Biology. The University of Massachusetts also offers a separate PhD program in neuroscience and behavior. Many of the students in this program receive the bulk of their training in the Psychology Department and work primarily with Psychology faculty.

Application Information: Graduate Admissions Office, Goodell Building, University of Massachusetts, Amherst, MA 01003. *Fee:* $75. *Online application:* http://www.umass.edu/gradschool/admissions.

Massachusetts, University of, Boston

Department of Psychology
College of Liberal Arts
100 Morrissey Boulevard
Boston, MA 02125
Telephone: (617) 287-6350
Chairperson: Jane Adams

E-mail: jane.adams@umb.edu
Web: http://www.umb.edu/academics/cla/psychology/

Orientation, Objectives, and Emphasis of Department

The Psychology Department offers two PhD programs. APA-accredited, the PhD program in Clinical Psychology adopts the scientist–practitioner model, integrating research and clinical training. This program prepares academics, researchers, and clinicians who have a strong theoretical background in scientific psychology and essential skills in both research and clinical practice. This program prepares students to serve underserved populations by ensuring that they are knowledgeable and skilled in developmentally and culturally competent research and clinical practice. Graduates translate basic psychological knowledge into practical applications to meet the needs of individuals from diverse economic, age, racial, and sociocultural groups. Graduates are qualified to take the Massachusetts Licensing Examination for clinical psychologists and to work in academic, research, and clinical settings. The PhD program in Developmental and Brain Sciences is research-intensive, focused on understanding cognition, perception, and behavior when underlying neural and hormonal mechanisms are developing. Research ranges from cognitive development and psychophysics to neuroendocrinology and behavioral genetics. Students may specialize in Cognitive or Behavioral Neuroscience. All DBS students receive training in methods (dry and wet lab skills, advanced statistics, MATLAB) and multiple levels of investigation including psychophysical and neuropsychological evaluation; functional brain imaging (NIRS, ERP); and neuropharmacological, molecular/cellular, and (epi-)genetic approaches.

Programs and Degrees Offered

Program	Degree	Application Deadline	Applica-tions Received	Accepted	New Admits Enrolled (PT)	Total Enrolled (PT)	Degrees Awarded in 2014–2015	Median Years to Complete Degree	Dismissed/Withdrew
Clinical Psychology	PhD	December 1 (Fall)	260	15	7	58	6	7	1
Developmental Brain Sciences	PhD	December 15 (Fall)	39	5	5 (0)	18 (0)	0		1

APA Accreditation

Clinical PhD: Student Outcome Data website: https://www.umb.edu/academics/cla/psychology/grad/clinical_psychology.

Doctoral Degree (PhD Clinical Psychology): For those doctoral students for whom a professional internship was required in this program prior to graduation:
Total students who applied for an internship: 7
Total students who obtained an internship: 7
Total students who obtained a paid internship: 7
Total students who obtained an unpaid internship: 0
Total students who were placed in APA/CPA-accredited internships: 7
Total students placed in internships not APA/CPA-accredited, but listed with the Association of Psychology Postdoctoral and Internship Centers (APPIC): 0
Total students placed in internships conforming to guidelines of the Council of Directors of School Psychology Programs (CDSPP): 0
Total students placed in internships that were not APA/CPA-accredited, APPIC or CDSSP listed: 0

Internships/Practica

In the Clinical PhD program, students do a 15-hour per week clinical practicum in the University Counseling Center in their second year. They obtain supervised clinical experience doing intake evaluations, short-term dynamic and cognitive behavioral therapy, and some group and couples treatment. Students also do an 18–20-hour per week clinical practicum in a training hospital or community health center in their third year. Examples of external practica include Cambridge Hospital, Children's Hospital, McLean Hospital, the Brookline Center, South Cove Health Center, and Chelsea Memorial Health Center. These agencies all serve a significant number of low income and ethnic minority clients. Students get supervised clinical training in testing and assessment and a range of psychotherapeutic interventions with children, adolescents, and adults at their external practica. Students do a full-time APA-approved clinical internship in their fifth year.

Admissions

Entries appear in the following order: required test or GPA, minimum score (if required)/median score of students entering in 2015–2016.

Program	Degree	GRE-V	GRE-Q	GRE-Writing	GRE-Subject	Under-graduate GPA	Last 2 Years GPA	Psychol-ogy GPA	Master's GPA
Clinical Psychology	PhD	NA/161	NA/158	NA/5	NA/755	NA/3.9	NA/3.9	NA/3.9	NA/3.9

Admissions *(con't.)*

Program	Degree	GRE-V	GRE-Q	GRE-Writing	GRE-Subject	Under-graduate GPA	Last 2 Years GPA	Psychol-ogy GPA	Master's GPA
Developmental Brain Sciences	PhD	149/156	145/154	3/4	Not specified	3/3.94	3.63/3.66	NA/NA	NA/NA

Admissions Requirements:

Degree	GRE	GRE-Subject	Letters of Recom-mendation	Research Statement	Writing Sample	CV	Interview
Doctoral	Required	Required	3	Required	None	Required	Required

Please note if these criteria vary for different programs: The admissions criteria are different for the Developmental Brain Sciences program. Work experience and clinically related public service are rated low for them instead of high.

Admissions Criteria:

GRE scores—medium
Research experience—high
Work experience—high
Clinically related public service—high
GPA—high

Letters of recommendation—high
Interview—high
Statement of goals and objectives—high
Undergraduate psychology preparation—medium

For additional information on admission requirements, visit http://www.umb.edu/academics/cla/psychology/grad.

Department Demographics

	Male (PT)	Female (PT)	Total	African-American/ Black (PT)	Hispanic/ Latino (PT)	Asian/ Pacific Islander (PT)	American Indian/ Alaska Native (PT)	Caucasian/ White (PT)	Unknown	Multiethnic (PT)	ADA (PT)	Int'l (PT)
Students	13 (0)	63 (0)	76	6 (0)	13 (0)	18 (0)	0 (0)	35 (0)	2 (0)	2 (0)	0 (0)	11 (0)

Financial Information/Assistance

Tuition: For information on tuition costs, visit http://www.umb.edu/bursar/tuition_and_fees. Tuition is subject to change. Additional fees are assessed to students beyond the costs of tuition for the following: $413 mandatory fee each semester.

Doctoral:
State residents: $671 per credit hour.
Nonstate residents: $1,297 per credit hour.

Financial Assistance:

	Teaching Assistantship (% Receiving)	Teaching Assistantship Tuition Remission	Research Assistantship (% Receiving)	Research Assistantship Tuition Remission	Fellowship (% Receiving)	Fellowship Tuition Remission
First-Year Student	$17,387 (20)	Full	$17,387 (45)	Full	$17,387 (15)	Full
Advanced Student	$18,858 (59)	Full	$17,387 (14)	Full	$22,000 (27)	Full

Employment of Department Graduates

Doctoral:
Enrolled in a postdoctoral residency/fellowship: 4
Employed in an academic position at a university: 1
Employed in a hospital/medical center: 1
Total: 6

Additional Information

Housing and Day Care: No on-campus housing is available. No on-campus day care facilities are available.

Information for Students With Physical Disabilities: See the following website: http://www.umb.edu/academics/vpass/disability/.

Special Facilities or Resources: For both PhD programs, the Psychology Department's research laboratories support a wide range of research and teaching functions. There are several rooms equipped with one-way mirrors and audio and visual recording that can be used for clinical, social, and developmental research. Human laboratories employ various technologies such as eye-tracking, ERP, and NIRS. Animal laboratories are equipped for research on behavior, genetics, and physiology. The department's laboratory facilities also include woodworking and electronic shops. A technical staff provides programming, electronic, and other related support to the faculty and students. Students in the Clinical program have access to the facilities of other research centers at the university, including the Center for Survey Research, the Center for the Study of Social Acceptance, the William Monroe Trotter Institute for the Study of Black Culture, and the William Joiner Center for the Study of War and Social Consequences. DBS students and faculty may work in collaboration with colleagues and laboratories in Clinical Psychology, Biology, and Computer Science.

Application Information: Graduate Admissions, University of Massachusetts Boston, 100 Morrissey Bouelvard, Boston, MA 02125. *Fee:* $60. *Online application:* http://www.umb.edu/admissions/grad/apply.

Massachusetts, University of, Dartmouth

Psychology Department
College of Arts & Sciences
285 Old Westport Road
North Dartmouth, MA 02747-2300
Telephone: (508) 999-8380
Chairperson: R. Thomas Boone

E-mail: tboone@umassd.edu
Web: http://www.umassd.edu/cas/psychology/

Orientation, Objectives, and Emphasis of Department

The research track of the MA program in psychology is designed to prepare students for doctoral work in psychology and related fields, including cognitive science. The program combines coursework in basic areas of psychology with the opportunity to do collaborative research with faculty members. Students have considerable flexibility to tailor their programs to their individual needs. The outstanding feature of this program is the opportunity for close interaction between faculty and students, both in the classroom and in the laboratory, because of the low student/faculty ratio. The objectives of the Clinical track are (1) to train competent MA-level clinicians; (2) to provide students with applied research and problem-solving skills; (3) to provide students with a broad exposure to a variety of therapy modalities; (4) to provide students with extensive experiential learning opportunities, practica, internships, and intensive supervision; and (5) to prepare students to be Licensed Mental Health Counselors. The Applied Behavior Analysis (ABA) MA track is designed to prepare students to sit for the BCBA (Board Certified Behavior Analyst) exam administered by the Behavior Analyst Certification Board (BACB). The ABA certificate program is designed to prepare individuals with Master's degrees in other areas and appropriate internship experience to sit for the BCBA exam.

Programs and Degrees Offered

Program	Degree	Application Deadline	Applica-tions Received	Accepted	New Admits Enrolled (PT)	Total Enrolled (PT)	Degrees Awarded in 2014–2015	Median Years to Complete Degree	Dismissed/ Withdrew
Clinical Psychology	MA/MS	March 1 (Fall)	55	16	13 (0)	27 (12)	13	3	1
Research Psychology	MA/MS	February 1 (Fall)	15	12	5 (2)	9 (5)	0		0

Programs and Degrees Offered *(con't.)*

Program	Degree	Application Deadline	Applications Received	Accepted	New Admits Enrolled (PT)	Total Enrolled (PT)	Degrees Awarded in 2014–2015	Median Years to Complete Degree	Dismissed/ Withdrew
Applied Behavior Analysis	MA/MS	August 15 (Fall), Rolling	27	26	0 (14)	0 (22)	8	3	0
Applied Behavior Analysis Certificate	Other	August 15 (Fall), Rolling	1	1	0 (0)	0 (0)	0		0

Internships/Practica

We have a wide variety of internship and practicum experiences available for clinical students. Field experiences are tailored to specific student needs. In addition, we can recommend a number of paid internships for students in the ABA track.

Admissions

Entries appear in the following order: required test or GPA, minimum score (if required)/median score of students entering in 2015–2016.

Program	Degree	GRE-V	GRE-Q	GRE-Writing	GRE-Subject	Under-graduate GPA	Last 2 Years GPA	Psychology GPA	Master's GPA
Clinical Psychology	MA/MS	Not specified	Not specified	Not specified	Not specified	2.8/3.54	Not specified	Not specified	Not specified
Research Psychology	MA/MS	NA/154	NA/150	NA/3.5	Not specified	Not specified	Not specified	Not specified	Not specified
Applied Behavior Analysis	MA/MS	NA/NA	NA/NA	NA/NA	Not specified	3/3.27	Not specified	Not specified	Not specified
Applied Behavior Analysis Certificate	Other	Not specified	Not specified	Not specified	Not specified	Not specified	Not specified	Not specified	Not specified

Admissions Requirements:

Degree	GRE	GRE-Subject	Letters of Recommendation	Research Statement	Writing Sample	CV	Interview
Master's/Specialist	Required	Recommended	3	Required	None	Required	Required

Please note if these criteria vary for different programs: These criteria vary across options. The Research track does not require work experience or clinical services. The clinical and ABA tracks do not require research experience. Interview is important for clinical track. Only research track requires GRE scores.

Admissions Criteria:

GRE scores—medium
Research experience—medium
Work experience—high
Clinically related public service—high

GPA—medium
Letters of recommendation—high
Interview—high
Statement of goals and objectives—high

For additional information on admission requirements, visit http://www.umassd.edu/cas/psychology/graduateprograms/.

Department Demographics

	Male (PT)	Female (PT)	Total	African-American/ Black (PT)	Hispanic/ Latino (PT)	Asian/ Pacific Islander (PT)	American Indian/ Alaska Native (PT)	Caucasian/ White (PT)	Unknown	Multiethnic (PT)	ADA (PT)	Int'l (PT)
Students	9 (10)	27 (29)	75	1 (1)	5 (1)	0 (1)	0 (0)	28 (32)	0 (2)	2 (2)	0 (0)	0 (0)

Financial Information/Assistance

Tuition: For information on tuition costs, visit http://www.umassd.edu/graduate/prospectivestudents/tuitionfees/. Tuition is subject to change.

Master's:
State residents: $14,699 per academic year.
State residents: $571 per credit hour.
Nonstate residents: $26,173 per academic year.
Nonstate residents: $1,049 per credit hour.

Financial Assistance:

	Teaching Assistantship (% Receiving)	Teaching Assistantship Tuition Remission	Research Assistantship (% Receiving)	Research Assistantship Tuition Remission	Fellowship (% Receiving)	Fellowship Tuition Remission
First-Year Student	$6,000 (NA)	Full	$12,000 (NA)	Full	NA (NA)	NA
Advanced Student	$6,000 (NA)	Full	$12,000 (NA)	Full	NA (NA)	NA

For additional information on financial assistance, visit http://www.umassd.edu/graduate/fellowshipsfunding/.

Employment of Department Graduates

Master's:
Enrolled in a psychology doctoral program: 1
Enrolled in another graduate/professional program: 1
Employed in business or industry: 2
Employed in a community mental health/counseling center: 1
Do not know: 1
Total: 6

Additional Information

Housing and Day Care: On-campus housing is available. See the following website for more information: http://www.umassd.edu/housing. No on-campus day care facilities are available.

Information for Students With Physical Disabilities: See the following website: http://www.umassd.edu/dss/.

Special Facilities or Resources: The department has two Event-Related Potential (ERP) laboratories as well as behavioral testing laboratories.

Application Information: Office of Graduate Studies. *Fee:* $60. *Online application:* http://www.umassd.edu/graduate/graduateapplication/.

Massachusetts, University of, Lowell

Department of Psychology
Fine Arts, Humanities, & Social Sciences
113 Wilder Street, Suite 300
Lowell, MA 01854-3059
Telephone: (978) 934-3950
Chairperson: Richard Siegel

E-mail: csp@uml.edu; asp@uml.edu; phd-apps@uml.edu
Web: http://www.uml.edu/FAHSS/Psychology/Graduate/default.aspx

Orientation, Objectives, and Emphasis of Department

The Psychology Department offers two master's-level graduate programs: the Community Social Psychology (CSP) program and the Autism Studies program (ASP), as well as a new PhD in Applied Psychology and Prevention Science (APPS). The faculty and students of all programs share a commitment to social justice and the empowerment of all individuals and communities. The CSP program focuses on applying tested psychological knowledge to strengthen community life and to increase individual and community well-being. The ASP provides students with a full appreciation of autism from behavioral, developmental and community perspectives, as well as fully preparing graduates for national Board Certified Behavior Analyst (BCBA)® certification. The APPS program is designed to train students and current practitioners who seek advanced education in the application of psychological theories and methods to address real-world problems, as well as to promote optimal quality of life outcomes. Our goal is to produce graduates with the analytic, creative and practical skills needed to design and implement programs and services that will facilitate positive changes within and across communities—changes that will empower all people to reach their full potential and empower social organizations, public and private, to be more responsive to human needs.

Programs and Degrees Offered

Program	Degree	Application Deadline	Applica-tions Received	Accepted	New Admits Enrolled (PT)	Total Enrolled (PT)	Degrees Awarded in 2014–2015	Median Years to Complete Degree	Dismissed/ Withdrew
Community Social Psychology	MA/MS	March 15 (Fall), Rolling					16	2	
Applied Psychology and Prevention Science	PhD	February 15 (Fall)	0	0	0 (0)	0 (0)	0		0
Autism Studies	MA/MS	March 1 (Fall)	31	14	11 (0)	25 (0)	8	2	2

Internships/Practica

For CSP students, there is a 1-year practicum requirement of 10 to 12 hours a week. Settings vary but much of the fieldwork takes place directly in Lowell, MA, perhaps the most culturally diverse mid-size city in the United States, located just 25 miles from Boston. For ASP students, there is a three-semester practicum requirement of 20 hours per week in a school or agency that applies behavioral intervention methods with individuals on the autism spectrum. Students can also opt to complete an independent fieldwork experience, but all students meet together as a class to share their experiences.

Admissions

Entries appear in the following order: required test or GPA, minimum score (if required)/median score of students entering in 2015–2016.

Program	Degree	GRE-V	GRE-Q	GRE-Writing	GRE-Subject	Under-graduate GPA	Last 2 Years GPA	Psychol-ogy GPA	Master's GPA
Community Social Psychology	MA/MS	NA/NA	NA/NA	NA/NA	Not specified	3/NA	Not specified	Not specified	Not specified

Admissions (con't.)

Program	Degree	GRE-V	GRE-Q	GRE-Writing	GRE-Subject	Under-graduate GPA	Last 2 Years GPA	Psychology GPA	Master's GPA
Applied Psychology and Prevention Science	PhD	Not specified	Not specified	Not specified	Not specified	Not specified	Not specified	Not specified	Not specified
Autism Studies	MA/MS	Not specified	Not specified	Not specified	Not specified	Not specified	Not specified	Not specified	Not specified

Admissions Requirements:

Degree	GRE	GRE-Subject	Letters of Recommendation	Research Statement	Writing Sample	CV	Interview
Master's/Specialist	Required	Optional	3	Required	Optional	Recommended	None
Doctoral	Required	Optional	3	Required	Optional	Required	Required

Admissions Criteria:

GRE scores—medium
Research experience—medium
Work experience—high
Clinically related public service—medium

GPA—high
Letters of recommendation—high
Statement of goals and objectives—high
Undergraduate psychology preparation— medium

Department Demographics

	Male (PT)	Female (PT)	Total	African-American/ Black (PT)	Hispanic/ Latino (PT)	Asian/ Pacific Islander (PT)	American Indian/ Alaska Native (PT)	Caucasian/ White (PT)	Unknown	Multiethnic (PT)	ADA (PT)	Int'l (PT)
Students			0	3 (0)	4 (2)	6 (1)	0 (0)	41 (9)	0 (0)	0 (0)	1 (0)	5 (1)

Financial Information/Assistance

Tuition: For information on tuition costs, visit https://www.uml.edu/thesolutioncenter/bill/tuition-fees/Graduate/default.aspx. Tuition is subject to change.

Master's:
State residents: $13,799 per academic year.
State residents: $766 per credit hour.
Nonstate residents: $24,478 per academic year.
Nonstate residents: $1,359 per credit hour.

Financial Assistance:

	Teaching Assistantship (% Receiving)	Teaching Assistantship Tuition Remission	Research Assistantship (% Receiving)	Research Assistantship Tuition Remission	Fellowship (% Receiving)	Fellowship Tuition Remission
First-Year Student	NA (NA)	NA	NA (NA)	NA	$4,000 (NA)	NA
Advanced Student	NA (NA)	NA	NA (NA)	NA	NA (NA)	NA

For additional information on financial assistance, visit http://www.uml.edu/thesolutioncenter/financial-aid/default.aspx.

Employment of Department Graduates

Master's:
Enrolled in a psychology doctoral program: 1
Employed in an academic position at a university: 2
Employed in a professional position in a school system: 1
Employed in business or industry: 4
Employed in government agency: 2
Still seeking employment: 2
Other employment position: 11
Do not know: 1
Total: 24

Additional Information

Housing and Day Care: On-campus housing is available. See the following website for more information: http://www.uml.edu/student-services/reslife/default.aspx. No on-campus day care facilities are available.

Information for Students With Physical Disabilities: See the following website: http://www.uml.edu/student-services/disability/default.aspx.

Special Facilities or Resources: Special facilities and resources consist of a graduate student lounge/computer lab, grant-related technical services from the Office of Research Administration, numerous research centers such as the Center for Family, Work and Community, the Center for Women and Work, and the Laboratory for Research in Behavior Analysis, and a unique multi-ethnic urban setting in a mid-sized city accessible to Boston.

Application Information: Office of Graduate School Admissions, One University Avenue, Cumnock Hall, Suite 110, Lowell, MA 01854-5130. *Fee:* $50. *Online application:* http://www.uml.edu/Grad/Process/default.aspx.

Northeastern University
Department of Psychology
College of Science
125 Nightingale Hall
Boston, MA 02115
Telephone: (617) 373-3076
Chairperson: Joanne L. Miller

E-mail: j.miller@neu.edu
Web: http://www.northeastern.edu/cos/psychology/

Orientation, Objectives, and Emphasis of Department
The PhD program aims to train students to undertake basic, translational, and interdisciplinary research involving the following areas: behavioral neuroscience; perception; cognition; and social/personality. Students may expect to collaborate with faculty in conducting research in state-of-the-art laboratories. The doctoral program also provides opportunities to gain teaching experience. The program does not provide training in clinical/counseling psychology.

Programs and Degrees Offered

Program	Degree	Application Deadline	Applications Received	Accepted	New Admits Enrolled (PT)	Total Enrolled (PT)	Degrees Awarded in 2014–2015	Median Years to Complete Degree	Dismissed/ Withdrew
Cognition	PhD	January 1 (Fall)	24	0	0 (0)	8 (0)	2	4.5	1
Behavioral Neuroscience	PhD	January 1 (Fall)	36	0	0 (0)	4 (0)	0		1
Social/ Personality Psychology	PhD	January 1 (Fall)	89	4	2 (0)	17 (0)	5	5	1
Perception	PhD	January 1 (Fall)	6	4	1 (0)	4 (0)	1	4	0

Admissions

Entries appear in the following order: required test or GPA, minimum score (if required)/median score of students entering in 2015–2016.

Program	Degree	GRE-V	GRE-Q	GRE-Writing	GRE-Subject	Under-graduate GPA	Last 2 Years GPA	Psychol-ogy GPA	Master's GPA
Cognition	PhD	NA/NA	NA/NA	Not specified	Not specified	Not specified	Not specified	Not specified	Not specified
Behavioral Neuroscience	PhD	NA/NA	NA/NA	Not specified	Not specified	Not specified	Not specified	Not specified	Not specified
Social/ Personality Psychology	PhD	NA/NA	NA/NA	Not specified	Not specified	Not specified	Not specified	Not specified	Not specified
Perception	PhD	NA/NA	NA/NA	Not specified	Not specified	Not specified	Not specified	Not specified	Not specified

Admissions Requirements:

Degree	GRE	GRE-Subject	Letters of Recom-mendation	Research Statement	Writing Sample	CV	Interview
Doctoral	Required	None	3	Required	Required	Required	Required

Admissions Criteria:

GRE scores—high
Research experience—high
Work experience—low
GPA—high

Letters of recommendation—high
Interview—high
Statement of goals and objectives—high
Undergraduate psychology preparation—medium

For additional information on admission requirements, visit http://www.northeastern.edu/cos/future-students/college-of-science-graduate-school/admissions/.

Department Demographics

	Male (PT)	Female (PT)	Total	African-American/ Black (PT)	Hispanic/ Latino (PT)	Asian/ Pacific Islander (PT)	American Indian/ Alaska Native (PT)	Caucasian/ White (PT)	Unknown	Multiethnic (PT)	ADA (PT)	Int'l (PT)
Students	14 (0)	19 (0)	33	1 (0)	1 (0)	8 (0)	0 (0)	23 (0)	0 (0)	0 (0)	0 (0)	6 (0)

Financial Information/Assistance

Tuition: For information on tuition costs, visit http://www.northeastern.edu/financialaid/tuitionandfees/. Tuition is subject to change.

Doctoral:
State residents: $1,325 per credit hour.
Nonstate residents: $1,325 per credit hour.

Financial Assistance:

	Teaching Assistantship (% Receiving)	Teaching Assistantship Tuition Remission	Research Assistantship (% Receiving)	Research Assistantship Tuition Remission	Fellowship (% Receiving)	Fellowship Tuition Remission
First-Year Student	$31,680 (NA)	Full	$31,680 (NA)	Full	NA (NA)	NA
Advanced Student	$31,680 (NA)	Full	$31,680 (NA)	Full	NA (NA)	NA

For additional information on financial assistance, visit http://www.northeastern.edu/cos/future-students/college-of-science-graduate-school/financial-awards/.

Employment of Department Graduates

Doctoral:
Enrolled in a postdoctoral residency/fellowship: 4
Employed in an academic position at a university: 2
Total: 6

Additional Information

Housing and Day Care: No on-campus housing is available. On-campus day care facilities are available. See the following website for more information: http://www.northeastern.edu/hrm/benefits/work-life/index.html.

Information for Students With Physical Disabilities: See the following website: http://www.northeastern.edu/drc/.

Special Facilities or Resources: The department has a wide range of research laboratories containing state-of-the-art facilities in the following main areas: behavioral neuroscience; perception; cognition; and social/personality. These facilities include an array of computer systems used for subject testing, data acquisition and analysis, computational modeling, and graphics, as well as numerous special-purpose systems, such as eye-trackers, histology facilities, multiple electrode EEG, small animal fMRI, and speech processing systems. In addition, laboratory resources outside the department are available to students through the collaborative network the department maintains with other institutions in the Boston/Cambridge area.

Application Information: *Fee:* $75. *Online application:* https://app.applyyourself.com/?id=neu-grad.

Springfield College
Psychology Department
Arts, Sciences and Professional Studies
263 Alden Street
Springfield, MA 01109
Telephone: (413) 748-3664
Program Director, Doctoral Program in Counseling Psychology: Sally M. Hage
Web: http://springfield.edu/academic-programs/psychology/

E-mail: shage@springfieldcollege.edu

Orientation, Objectives, and Emphasis of Department
The doctor of psychology program in counseling psychology is dedicated to the following: educating and developing practitioner-scholars who will lead and serve their communities and the discipline of professional counseling psychology; training students for a variety of work settings and to prepare counseling psychologists to meet state requirements for licensure as psychologists; preparing graduates who can identify and understand individual and cultural differences (ICD) and issues of multiple identities, power, oppression, privilege, and engage in culturally sensitive professional activity; and producing graduates who consistently exhibit ethical knowledge and decision making, professional identity and development as a counseling psychologist, and attitudes and skills that sustain lifelong learning, scholarly inquiry, and professional problem solving. The PsyD program requires approximately 4 years of full-time academic study beyond the master's degree—3 of these years are dedicated to coursework including advanced practica and concentration-specific training. The final year is reserved for the completion of a research project and a year-long, full-time internship.

Programs and Degrees Offered

Program	Degree	Application Deadline	Applica-tions Received	Accepted	New Admits Enrolled (PT)	Total Enrolled (PT)	Degrees Awarded in 2014–2015	Median Years to Complete Degree	Dismissed/ Withdrew
Counseling Psychology	PsyD	January 1 (Fall)	50	14	13	44	0		0

Doctoral Degree (PsyD Counseling Psychology): For those doctoral students for whom a professional internship was required in this program prior to graduation:
Total students who applied for an internship: 7

Total students who obtained an internship: 7
Total students who obtained a paid internship: 7
Total students who obtained an unpaid internship: 0
Total students who were placed in APA/CPA-accredited internships: 3
Total students placed in internships not APA/CPA-accredited, but listed with the Association of Psychology Postdoctoral and Internship Centers (APPIC): 4
Total students placed in internships conforming to guidelines of the Council of Directors of School Psychology Programs (CDSPP): 0
Total students placed in internships that were not APA/CPA-accredited, APPIC or CDSSP listed: 0

Internships/Practica

Clinical training is an integral part of the curriculum in the doctoral program. Practical experience occurs throughout the program and is designed to enhance academic coursework. Utilizing a developmental framework, students receive basic skills training in establishing therapeutic relationships, diagnostic assessment, and intervention with a wide variety of populations in practicum experiences. These are supplemented with advanced training in one of the concentration specialties (mental health, couples and family counseling, or athletic counseling). Internship experiences focus on advanced clinical training in professional counseling with such experiences as treatment planning and evaluation, mentoring, supervision, consultation, and program evaluation. The doctoral practicum and internship training requirements of the Springfield College PsyD program are designed to ensure that students are competent in a variety of counseling modalities, including individual, couples, family, and group counseling; as well as in consultation, supervision, psychological assessment, career counseling, and evaluation of intervention efficacy. These skills include sensitivity to cross cultural counseling and diversity issues. Students are required to complete a minimum of 1500 hours of practicum experience before beginning their predoctoral internship. Students must complete 300 face-to-face contact hours within the student's concentration (i.e., athletic counseling, couples and family counseling, or mental health counseling).

Admissions

Entries appear in the following order: required test or GPA, minimum score (if required)/median score of students entering in 2015–2016.

Program	Degree	GRE-V	GRE-Q	GRE-Writing	GRE-Subject	Under-graduate GPA	Last 2 Years GPA	Psychol-ogy GPA	Master's GPA
Counseling Psychology	PsyD	Not specified	Not specified	Not specified	Not specified	Not specified	Not specified	Not specified	Not specified

Admissions Requirements:

Degree	GRE	GRE-Subject	Letters of Recom-mendation	Research Statement	Writing Sample	CV	Interview
Doctoral	Required	None	3	Required	Optional	Required	Required

Admissions Criteria:

GRE scores—medium
Research experience—medium
Work experience—medium
Clinically related public service—high

GPA—high
Letters of recommendation—high
Interview—high
Statement of goals and objectives—high

Department Demographics

	Male (PT)	Female (PT)	Total	African-American/ Black (PT)	Hispanic/ Latino (PT)	Asian/ Pacific Islander (PT)	American Indian/ Alaska Native (PT)	Caucasian/ White (PT)	Unknown	Multiethnic (PT)	ADA (PT)	Int'l (PT)
Students	33 (0)	156 (0)	189	14 (0)	9 (0)	7 (0)	2 (0)	142 (0)	11 (0)	4 (0)	0 (0)	7 (0)

Financial Information/Assistance

Tuition: Tuition is subject to change.

Doctoral:
State residents: $960 per credit hour.
Nonstate residents: $960 per credit hour.

Financial Assistance:

	Teaching Assistantship (% Receiving)	Teaching Assistantship Tuition Remission	Research Assistantship (% Receiving)	Research Assistantship Tuition Remission	Fellowship (% Receiving)	Fellowship Tuition Remission
First-Year Student	$3,500 (20)	Partial	NA (NA)	NA	$3,500 (80)	Partial
Advanced Student	$3,500 (35)	Partial	NA (NA)	NA	$3,500 (80)	Partial

For additional information on financial assistance, visit http://www.springfieldcollege.edu/admissions/graduate-admissions/graduate-fellowship-and-assistantship-identification-form.

Employment of Department Graduates

No information provided.

Additional Information

Housing and Day Care: On-campus housing is available. See the following website for more information: http://www.springfieldcollege.edu/student-life/residence-life/. On-campus day care facilities are available.

Application Information: Evelyn Cohen, Graduate Admissions. *Fee:* $50. *Online application:* http://www.springfieldcollege.edu/admissions/graduate-admissions/online-application-for-graduate-students.

Suffolk University
Department of Psychology
College of Arts and Sciences
73 Tremont Street
Boston, MA 02108
Telephone: (617) 573-8293
Chairperson: Gary Fireman

E-mail: phd@suffolk.edu
Web: http://www.suffolk.edu/psychology

Orientation, Objectives, and Emphasis of Department
Suffolk University's clinical psychology PhD program is based on the philosophy that practice should be grounded in scientific knowledge and that research should be informed by and relevant to clinical practice (i.e., the Boulder Model). Our faculty approach psychology from a variety of perspectives including developmental, psychodynamic, systemic, behavioral, cognitive-behavioral, humanistic, and integrative/eclectic. Across all aspects of training we strive to train our students to be knowledgeable about and conduct culturally competent clinical practice and research. Our framework recognizes that: (a) knowledge of subdisciplines, such as neuropsychology, developmental psychology, and cultural psychology, is required to be effective; (b) psychologists can complement natural contexts such as families, relationships, schools, and workplaces in fostering development; and (c) psychological pain and conflict can be indicative of ongoing lifespan transformational processes including what is normal as well as psychopathology. Throughout core content and applied areas of training, the program encourages awareness of and respect for diversity of culture, language, national origin, race, gender, age, disability, religious beliefs, sexual orientation, lifestyle, and other individual differences. The program combines a strong theoretical and research background (in both quantitative and qualitative methodologies) with preparation to deliver high-quality psychological services to children, adolescents, and adults.

Programs and Degrees Offered

Program	Degree	Application Deadline	Applications Received	Accepted	New Admits Enrolled (PT)	Total Enrolled (PT)	Degrees Awarded in 2014–2015	Median Years to Complete Degree	Dismissed/ Withdrew
Clinical Psychology	PhD	December 1 (Fall)	234	15	7 (0)	53 (0)	8	6.79	1
Clinical Psychology Respecialization	Respecialization Diploma	February 1 (Fall)	2	1	1 (0)	6 (0)	0		0
Mental Health Counseling	MA/MS	Rolling	86	75	15 (2)	23 (4)	13	2	2

APA Accreditation

Clinical PhD: Student Outcome Data website: http://www.suffolk.edu/college/departments/14059.php.

Doctoral Degree (PhD Clinical Psychology): For those doctoral students for whom a professional internship was required in this program prior to graduation:

Total students who applied for an internship: 11
Total students who obtained an internship: 11
Total students who obtained a paid internship: 11
Total students who obtained an unpaid internship: 0
Total students who were placed in APA/CPA-accredited internships: 11
Total students placed in internships not APA/CPA-accredited, but listed with the Association of Psychology Postdoctoral and Internship Centers (APPIC): 0
Total students placed in internships conforming to guidelines of the Council of Directors of School Psychology Programs (CDSPP): 0
Total students placed in internships that were not APA/CPA-accredited, APPIC or CDSSP listed: 0

Master's Degree (MA/MS Mental Health Counseling): An internship experience, such as a final research project or "capstone" experience is required of graduates.

Internships/Practica

Doctoral students' individualized clinical training programs, which begin their second year, are carefully overseen by the Coordinator and Director of Clinical Training. All students are required to complete at least two years of practicum training, though most elect to do an optional third year. Students are placed with partner sites (e.g., medical centers, psychiatric hospitals, community mental health clinics, university counseling centers, and school psychology centers) in the greater Boston area committed to providing quality supervision and training. Students concurrently take two year-long practicum courses which integrate the external practicum and didactic experience and provide knowledge regarding professional standards and ethics, diversity, treatment and assessment processes and outcomes, consultation and supervision. Students who opt to pursue additional clinical training are supported in their efforts to obtain training experiences consistent with their emerging areas of interest. A limited number of pre-practicum training experiences are also available to students during their first year in the program.

Admissions

Entries appear in the following order: required test or GPA, minimum score (if required)/median score of students entering in 2015–2016.

Program	Degree	GRE-V	GRE-Q	GRE-Writing	GRE-Subject	Undergraduate GPA	Last 2 Years GPA	Psychology GPA	Master's GPA
Clinical Psychology	PhD	NA/159	NA/156	NA/4.25	Not specified	NA/3.62	Not specified	Not specified	Not specified
Clinical Psychology Respecialization	Respecialization Diploma	Not specified	Not specified	Not specified	Not specified	Not specified	Not specified	Not specified	Not specified
Mental Health Counseling	MA/MS	Not specified	Not specified	Not specified	Not specified	Not specified	Not specified	Not specified	Not specified

Admissions Requirements:

Degree	GRE	GRE-Subject	Letters of Recommendation	Research Statement	Writing Sample	CV	Interview
Master's/Specialist	Required	Optional	2	Required	Optional	Required	None
Doctoral	Required	Optional	2	Required	Optional	Required	Required

Please note if these criteria vary for different programs: These criteria only reflect the PhD and Respecialization in Clinical Psychology programs.

Admissions Criteria:

GRE scores—medium
Research experience—high
Work experience—medium
Clinically related public service—medium
GPA—high

Letters of recommendation—high
Interview—high
Statement of goals and objectives—high
Undergraduate psychology preparation—high
Research mentor match—high

Department Demographics

	Male (PT)	Female (PT)	Total	African-American/ Black (PT)	Hispanic/ Latino (PT)	Asian/ Pacific Islander (PT)	American Indian/ Alaska Native (PT)	Caucasian/ White (PT)	Unknown (PT)	Multiethnic (PT)	ADA (PT)	Int'l (PT)
Students	10 (0)	49 (0)	59	4 (0)	7 (0)	7 (0)	0 (0)	38 (0)	3 (0)	0 (0)	0 (0)	1 (0)

Financial Information/Assistance

Tuition: For information on tuition costs, visit http://www.suffolk.edu/explore/16410.php. Tuition is subject to change.

Doctoral:
State residents: $34,810 per academic year.
State residents: $1,450 per credit hour.
Nonstate residents: $34,810 per academic year.
Nonstate residents: $1,450 per credit hour.

Master's:
State residents: $24,802 per academic year.
State residents: $1,029 per credit hour.
Nonstate residents: $24,802 per academic year.
Nonstate residents: $1,029 per credit hour.

Financial Assistance:

	Teaching Assistantship (% Receiving)	Teaching Assistantship Tuition Remission	Research Assistantship (% Receiving)	Research Assistantship Tuition Remission	Fellowship (% Receiving)	Fellowship Tuition Remission
First-Year Student	NA (NA)	NA	$4,800 (NA)	NA	$34,810 (NA)	Full
Advanced Student	NA (NA)	NA	$4,800 (NA)	NA	$34,810 (NA)	Full

For additional information on financial assistance, visit http://www.suffolk.edu/admission/grad/17632.php.

Employment of Department Graduates

Doctoral:
Enrolled in a postdoctoral residency/fellowship: 7
Do not know: 1
Total: 8

Additional Information

Housing and Day Care: No on-campus housing is available. No on-campus day care facilities are available.

Information for Students With Physical Disabilities: See the following website: http://www.suffolk.edu/academics/1316.php.

Special Facilities or Resources: The department has a variety of laboratory spaces available for general use by faculty and doctoral students, with software/hardware accessed by their graduate student teams. Special equipment includes psychophysiological equipment (skin conductance), sleep study equipment, dedicated work stations with brain image analysis software (anatomic and functional images acquired off-site), SPSS software licensed for AMOS (complex statistical modeling software), and video recording equipment. A portion of research occurs off-site with our research collaborators in the clinical, medical and scholastic institutions of the Boston area. Our test library has copies of 518 current psychological tests and measures. Graduate students receive inter-library loan and online document delivery privileges and have access to most of the academic libraries in the Boston area.

Application Information: Office of Graduate Admissions, Suffolk University, 73 Tremont Street, Boston, MA 02108. *Fee:* $50. *Online application:* https://grad.suffolk.edu/apply/?pk=DG.

Tufts University
Department of Education; School Psychology Program
Graduate School of Arts and Sciences
Paige Hall
Medford, MA 02155
Telephone: (617) 627-2390
Co-Director, School Psychology Program: Steven Luz-Alterman
Web: http://ase.tufts.edu/education/programs/SchoolPsychology/index.htm

E-mail: steven.luz-alterman@tufts.edu

Orientation, Objectives, and Emphasis of Department
Our mission is to prepare highly effective, culturally sensitive problem solvers ready to serve all children in general public education and children with disabilities. We are committed to preparing professional school psychologists who will work effectively with children from racially, ethnically, and linguistically diverse backgrounds in a variety of settings. These include urban, urban-rim, suburban, and rural communities. Providing high quality services in urban and urban-rim schools is a program priority. We seek a diverse cohort of students who think critically and are prepared to engage issues of social justice and cultural and linguistic diversity as they are reproduced in our schools.

Programs and Degrees Offered

Program	Degree	Application Deadline	Applica-tions Received	Accepted	New Admits Enrolled (PT)	Total Enrolled (PT)	Degrees Awarded in 2014–2015	Median Years to Complete Degree	Dismissed/ Withdrew
School Psychology	EdS	January 15 (Fall)	60	28	14 (0)	44 (1)	16	3	0

Internships/Practica
Students complete a school-based pre-practicum experience of 150 hours during their first year and a school-based practicum of 600 hours during their second year. Students complete a 1,200-hour internship during their third year. This may be completed through 600 hours in a school setting and 600 hours in a clinical setting, or all 1,200 hours in a school setting. Internship sites must be approved by the program faculty and may be pursued anywhere in the United States, or abroad if the site is approved by the faculty, the student is in good academic standing, and appropriate supervision is provided.

Admissions
Entries appear in the following order: required test or GPA, minimum score (if required)/median score of students entering in 2015–2016.

Program	Degree	GRE-V	GRE-Q	GRE-Writing	GRE-Subject	Under-graduate GPA	Last 2 Years GPA	Psychol-ogy GPA	Master's GPA
School Psychology	EdS	150/NA	150/NA	4.5/NA	Not specified	3/NA	Not specified	Not specified	Not specified

Admissions Requirements:

Degree	GRE	GRE-Subject	Letters of Recommendation	Research Statement	Writing Sample	CV	Interview
Master's/Specialist	Required	None	3	Required	None	Required	Required

Admissions Criteria:

GRE scores—low

Research experience—medium

Work experience—high

Clinically related public service—high

GPA—medium

Letters of recommendation—high

Interview—high

Statement of goals and objectives—high

Undergraduate psychology preparation—medium

Multicultural interest—high

For additional information on admission requirements, visit http://ase.tufts.edu/education/programs/schoolPsychology/apply.htm.

Department Demographics

	Male (PT)	Female (PT)	Total	African-American/Black (PT)	Hispanic/Latino (PT)	Asian/Pacific Islander (PT)	American Indian/Alaska Native (PT)	Caucasian/White (PT)	Unknown (PT)	Multiethnic (PT)	ADA (PT)	Int'l (PT)
Students	8 (1)	36 (0)	45	3 (0)	1 (1)	7 (0)	0 (0)	33 (0)	0 (0)	0 (0)	0 (0)	0 (0)

Financial Information/Assistance

Tuition: For information on tuition costs, visit http://asegrad.tufts.edu/tuition-and-financial-aid. Tuition is not available at this time.

Financial Assistance:

	Teaching Assistantship (% Receiving)	Teaching Assistantship Tuition Remission	Research Assistantship (% Receiving)	Research Assistantship Tuition Remission	Fellowship (% Receiving)	Fellowship Tuition Remission
First-Year Student	$1,500 (NA)	NA	$1,500 (NA)	NA	$17,200 (NA)	Partial
Advanced Student	$1,500 (NA)	NA	$1,500 (NA)	NA	$17,200 (NA)	Partial

Employment of Department Graduates

Master's:

Employed in a professional position in a school system: 16

Total: 16

Additional Information

Housing and Day Care: On-campus housing is available. See the following website for more information: http://ase.tufts.edu/reslife/housing/graduate.asp. On-campus day care facilities are available. See the following website for more information: http://www.brighthorizons.com/teelesquare.

Information for Students With Physical Disabilities: See the following website: http://students.tufts.edu/student-accessibility-services.

Special Facilities or Resources: Tufts offers the resources of a major research university with the campus atmosphere of a small liberal arts college. Several courses of interest are offered through the Eliot-Pearson Department of Child Development. Tufts students may also cross-register for courses at several other Boston area universities at no additional charge through a consortium arrangement. We have a variety of urban, urban-rim, and suburban field sites, including the Step UP Program in Boston. Limited internship stipends are available for practice in urban sites.

Application Information: *Fee:* $75. *Online application:* https://gradase.admissions.tufts.edu/apply/.

Tufts University

Department of Psychology
Psychology Building, 490 Boston Avenue
Medford, MA 02155
Telephone: (617) 627-3523
Chairperson: Lisa Shin

E-mail: cynthia.goddard@tufts.edu
Web: http://ase.tufts.edu/psychology/

Orientation, Objectives, and Emphasis of Department

The Department of Psychology offers a graduate program in experimental psychology, with specializations in cognition, neuroscience, psychopathology, developmental, and social psychology. The program is designed to produce broadly trained graduates who are prepared for careers in teaching, research, or applied psychology. The department does not offer clinical training. Accepted applicants generally possess a substantial college background in psychology, including familiarity with fundamental statistical concepts and research design. The university is a PhD track program, although completion of an MS is required as an integral part of the program. Students who already possess a master's degree may be admitted to the PhD program if a sufficient number of credits are acceptable for transfer and a thesis has been done. Areas of faculty research include infant perception, memory processes, animal cognition and learning, neural and hormonal control of animal sexual behavior, psychopharmacology, event-related brain potentials, neuropsychology of language processes, nutrition and behavior, experimental psychopathology, emotion, human factors, decision making, spatial cognition, psychology and law, and the social psychology of prejudicial attitudes. All graduate students participate in supervised research and/or teaching activities each semester.

Programs and Degrees Offered

Program	Degree	Application Deadline	Applica-tions Received	Accepted	New Admits Enrolled (PT)	Total Enrolled (PT)	Degrees Awarded in 2014–2015	Median Years to Complete Degree	Dismissed/ Withdrew
General Experimental Psychology	PhD	December 15 (Fall)	134	15	10	39	8	5.5	1

Admissions

Entries appear in the following order: required test or GPA, minimum score (if required)/median score of students entering in 2015–2016.

Program	Degree	GRE-V	GRE-Q	GRE-Writing	GRE-Subject	Under-graduate GPA	Last 2 Years GPA	Psychol-ogy GPA	Master's GPA
General Experimental Psychology	PhD	148/161	149/157	Not specified	Not specified	3.16/3.67	NA/NA	Not specified	Not specified

Admissions Requirements:

Degree	GRE	GRE-Subject	Letters of Recom-mendation	Research Statement	Writing Sample	CV	Interview
Doctoral	Required	Recom-mended	3	Required	Recom-mended	Required	Optional

Admissions Criteria:

GRE scores—medium
Research experience—high
Work experience—low
GPA—medium
Letters of recommendation—medium

Interview—medium
Statement of goals and objectives—high
Undergraduate psychology preparation—medium
Research fit—high

For additional information on admission requirements, visit http://ase.tufts.edu/psychology/graduate/prospectives.htm.

Department Demographics

	Male (PT)	Female (PT)	Total	African-American/ Black (PT)	Hispanic/ Latino (PT)	Asian/ Pacific Islander (PT)	American Indian/ Alaska Native (PT)	Caucasian/ White (PT)	Unknown	Multiethnic (PT)	ADA (PT)	Int'l (PT)
Students	14 (0)	25 (0)	39	3 (0)	1 (0)	6 (0)	0 (0)	27 (0)	0 (0)	2 (0)	0 (0)	7 (0)

Financial Information/Assistance

Tuition: For information on tuition costs, visit http://asegrad.tufts.edu/tuition-and-financial-aid. Tuition is subject to change.

Doctoral:
State residents: $27,864 per academic year.
Nonstate residents: $27,864 per academic year.

Financial Assistance:

	Teaching Assistantship (% Receiving)	Teaching Assistantship Tuition Remission	Research Assistantship (% Receiving)	Research Assistantship Tuition Remission	Fellowship (% Receiving)	Fellowship Tuition Remission
First-Year Student	$21,100 (NA)	Full	$21,100 (NA)	Full	NA (NA)	NA
Advanced Student	$21,100 (NA)	Full	$21,100 (NA)	Full	NA (NA)	NA

For additional information on financial assistance, visit http://asegrad.tufts.edu/tuition-and-financial-aid.

Employment of Department Graduates

Doctoral:
Enrolled in a postdoctoral residency/fellowship: 2
Employed in an academic position at a university: 2
Employed in business or industry: 2
Total: 6

Additional Information

Housing and Day Care: No on-campus housing is available. No on-campus day care facilities are available.

Information for Students With Physical Disabilities: See the following website: http://students.tufts.edu/student-accessibility-services.

Special Facilities or Resources: The Department has relatively new research facilities for both human and animal research in areas of cognition, cognitive neuroscience, biopsychology, neuroscience, developmental, and social psychology.

Application Information: Fee: $75. *Online application:* http://asegrad.tufts.edu/admissions.

Tufts University

Eliot-Pearson Department of Child Study and Human Development
105 College Avenue
Medford, MA 02155
Telephone: (617) 627-3355
Chairperson: David Henry Feldman

E-mail: davidhenry.feldman@tufts.edu
Web: http://ase.tufts.edu/epcshd/default.aspx

Orientation, Objectives, and Emphasis of Department

The department prepares students for a variety of careers that have, as their common prerequisite, a comprehensive understanding of children and their development. Students receive a foundation in psychological theory and research concerning the social, emotional, intellectual, linguistic, and physiological growth of children. Course material is complemented with progressively more involved practica encompassing observations and work with children in a wide variety of applied and research settings. The major aim of the program is to train people who can translate their knowledge about development into effective strategies for working with and on behalf of children. We believe that a background in child development is the best possible preparation for teaching and administrative careers in schools, children's advocacy and mental health agencies, hospitals, after-school programs, daycare centers, arts programs, museums, the media, government agencies concerned with the rights and welfare of children, and related fields. There is considerable room for flexibility in the program. Also, students may choose from a rich variety of elective courses that touch upon such diverse topics as child advocacy, the arts and children's development, children and technology, arts and social activism, and children's literature.

Programs and Degrees Offered

Program	Degree	Application Deadline	Applications Received	Accepted	New Admits Enrolled (PT)	Total Enrolled (PT)	Degrees Awarded in 2014–2015	Median Years to Complete Degree	Dismissed/Withdrew
Child Study and Human Development (Thesis)	MA/MS	December 15 (Fall)	0	0	0 (0)	2 (0)	13	2	0
Child Study and Human Development (Applied)	MA/MS	December 15 (Fall)	43	37	20 (3)	31 (5)	35	2	0
Child Study and Human Development	PhD	December 1 (Fall)	48	10	3 (0)	35 (0)	10	5	0
Child Study and Human Development (Mat)	MA/MS	December 15 (Fall)	7	4	2 (0)	7 (0)	8	2	0

Internships/Practica

MA students engage in semester-long internships in applied settings such as hospitals, after-school centers, arts programs, policy centers, museums. PhD students engage in full-time, one-semester or half-time, full-year applied and research internships in varied settings.

Admissions

Entries appear in the following order: required test or GPA, minimum score (if required)/median score of students entering in 2015–2016.

Program	Degree	GRE-V	GRE-Q	GRE-Writing	GRE-Subject	Undergraduate GPA	Last 2 Years GPA	Psychology GPA	Master's GPA
Child Study and Human Development (Thesis)	MA/MS	NA/NA	NA/NA	Not specified	Not specified	NA/NA	NA/NA	Not specified	Not specified

603

Admissions *(con't.)*

Program	Degree	GRE-V	GRE-Q	GRE-Writing	GRE-Subject	Under-graduate GPA	Last 2 Years GPA	Psychol-ogy GPA	Master's GPA
Child Study and Human Development (Applied)	MA/MS	NA/NA	NA/NA	Not specified	Not specified	NA/NA	NA/NA	Not specified	Not specified
Child Study and Human Development	PhD	NA/NA	NA/NA	Not specified	Not specified	NA/NA	NA/NA	Not specified	Not specified
Child Study and Human Development (MAT)	MA/MS	Not specified	Not specified	Not specified	Not specified	Not specified	Not specified	Not specified	Not specified

Admissions Requirements:

Degree	GRE	GRE-Subject	Letters of Recom-mendation	Research Statement	Writing Sample	CV	Interview
Master's/Specialist	Required	Optional	3	Required	Optional	Required	None
Doctoral	Required	Optional	3	Required	Optional	Required	Required

Please note if these criteria vary for different programs: The criteria filled in below is for consideration to our MA programs. The criteria for application to our PhD program is as follows: GRE: high; Research Exp: high; Work Exp: high; Clinically Related Public Serv: low; GPA: high; Letters of Rec: high; Statement of Goals/Obj: high; UG psychology preparation: medium.

Admissions Criteria:

GRE scores—medium
Research experience—low
Work experience—high
Clinically related public service—low

GPA—high
Letters of recommendation—high
Statement of goals and objectives—medium
Undergraduate psychology preparation—medium

Department Demographics

	Male (PT)	Female (PT)	Total	African-American/ Black (PT)	Hispanic/ Latino (PT)	Asian/ Pacific Islander (PT)	American Indian/ Alaska Native (PT)	Caucasian/ White (PT)	Unknown	Multiethnic (PT)	ADA (PT)	Int'l (PT)
Students	7 (1)	68 (4)	80	6 (0)	2 (0)	13 (2)	0 (0)	49 (3)	2 (0)	3 (0)	0 (0)	1 (0)

Financial Information/Assistance

Tuition: For information on tuition costs, visit http://asegrad.tufts.edu/tuition-and-financial-aid. Tuition is subject to change. Tuition costs vary by program.

Doctoral:
State residents: $29,048 per academic year.
Nonstate residents: $29,048 per academic year.

Master's:
State residents: $48,412 per academic year.
Nonstate residents: $48,412 per academic year.

Financial Assistance:

	Teaching Assistantship (% Receiving)	Teaching Assistantship Tuition Remission	Research Assistantship (% Receiving)	Research Assistantship Tuition Remission	Fellowship (% Receiving)	Fellowship Tuition Remission
First-Year Student	$20,000 (NA)	Full	$20,000 (NA)	Full	NA (NA)	Full
Advanced Student	$20,000 (NA)	Full	$20,000 (NA)	Full	NA (NA)	Full

For additional information on financial assistance, visit http://asegrad.tufts.edu/financial-support/scholarships-and-assistantships.

Employment of Department Graduates

No information provided.

Additional Information

Housing and Day Care: On-campus housing is available. See the following website for more information: http://ase.tufts.edu/reslife/. On-campus day care facilities are available.

Special Facilities or Resources: The department is housed in a complex of buildings on the Medford campus. The main building contains faculty and staff offices, class meeting rooms, and a library. Another building houses the Eliot-Pearson Children's School, which serves normal and special-needs children aged 2 to 6. The school has observation booths for student use. Students may work as well as observe. This facility is integrated into faculty research and research training for graduate students.

Application Information: Graduate Admissions, Office of Graduate Admissions, Bendetson Hall, Medford, MA 02155. *Fee:* $75. *Online application:* https://gradase.admissions.tufts.edu/apply/.

William James College
Graduate Education in Psychology
1 Wells Avenue
Newton, MA 02459
Telephone: (617) 327-6777
President: Nicholas A. Covino, PsyD

E-mail: admissions@williamjames.edu
Web: http://www.williamjames.edu/

Orientation, Objectives, and Emphasis of Department
William James College (formerly the Massachusetts School of Professional Psychology) strives to be a preeminent school of psychology that integrates rigorous academic instruction with extensive field education and close attention to professional development. We assume an ongoing social responsibility to create programs to educate specialists of many disciplines to meet the evolving mental health needs of society.

Programs and Degrees Offered

Program	Degree	Application Deadline	Applications Received	Accepted	New Admits Enrolled (PT)	Total Enrolled (PT)	Degrees Awarded in 2014–2015	Median Years to Complete Degree	Dismissed/ Withdrew
Clinical Psychology	PsyD	January 7 (Fall)	354	214	96 (0)	336 (83)	73	4.5	9
Respecialization in Clinical Psychology	Respecialization Diploma	Rolling	2	1	1 (0)	4 (1)			0
School Psychology	MA/MS	January 7 (Fall)	50	37	12	28 (15)	10	3	1

Programs and Degrees Offered *(con't.)*

Program	Degree	Application Deadline	Applications Received	Accepted	New Admits Enrolled (PT)	Total Enrolled (PT)	Degrees Awarded in 2014–2015	Median Years to Complete Degree	Dismissed/ Withdrew
Organizational Psychology	MA/MS	April 1 (Fall)	28	26	23 (0)	19 (10)	30	1	5
School Psychology	PsyD	November 25 (Fall)	7	7	5	32	1	4	2
Leadership Psychology	PsyD	April 1 (Fall)	22	16	14 (0)	27 (0)	0		4
Clinical Mental Health Counseling	MA/MS	Rolling (Fall)	255	130	74	151 (23)	57	2	6
Applied Behavior Analysis Certificate	Other	Rolling (Fall)	0	0	0 (0)	0 (0)	0		0

APA Accreditation

Clinical PsyD: Student Outcome Data website: http://www.williamjames.edu/academics/clinical/psyd/outcomes.cfm.

Doctoral Degree (PsyD Clinical Psychology): For those doctoral students for whom a professional internship was required in this program prior to graduation:
Total students who applied for an internship: 96
Total students who obtained an internship: 96
Total students who obtained a paid internship: 45
Total students who obtained an unpaid internship: 51
Total students who were placed in APA/CPA-accredited internships: 34
Total students placed in internships not APA/CPA-accredited, but listed with the Association of Psychology Postdoctoral and Internship Centers (APPIC): 0
Total students placed in internships conforming to guidelines of the Council of Directors of School Psychology Programs (CDSPP): 0
Total students placed in internships that were not APA/CPA-accredited, APPIC or CDSSP listed: 62

Doctoral Degree (PsyD School Psychology): For those doctoral students for whom a professional internship was required in this program prior to graduation:
Total students who applied for an internship: 6
Total students who obtained an internship: 5
Total students who obtained a paid internship: 1
Total students who obtained an unpaid internship: 4
Total students who were placed in APA/CPA-accredited internships: 0
Total students placed in internships not APA/CPA-accredited, but listed with the Association of Psychology Postdoctoral and Internship Centers (APPIC): 1
Total students placed in internships conforming to guidelines of the Council of Directors of School Psychology Programs (CDSPP): 3
Total students placed in internships that were not APA/CPA-accredited, APPIC or CDSSP listed: 1

Master's Degree (MA/MS School Psychology): An internship experience, such as a final research project or "capstone" experience is required of graduates. Master's Degree (MA/MS Organizational Psychology): An internship experience, such as a final research project or "capstone" experience is required of graduates.

Internships/Practica

Field placements are an integral part of training throughout the duration of the program. The practicum and internship experiences are integrated with the curriculum and individual's educational needs at each level of the program. Over 350 training sites are available in the greater Boston area including hospitals, mental health centers, court clinics, schools, and other agencies offering mental health services. They provide students the opportunity to work with varied populations, life span issues, theoretical orientations, and treatment modalities in the context of supervised training. Our Clinical PsyD students are required to apply for an APA internship.

Admissions

Entries appear in the following order: required test or GPA, minimum score (if required)/median score of students entering in 2015–2016.

Program	Degree	GRE-V	GRE-Q	GRE-Writing	GRE-Subject	Under-graduate GPA	Last 2 Years GPA	Psychol-ogy GPA	Master's GPA
Clinical Psychology	PsyD	NA/NA	NA/NA	NA/NA	Not specified	NA/NA	Not specified	Not specified	Not specified
Respecialization in Clinical Psychology	Respecial-ization Diploma	NA/NA	NA/NA	NA/NA	Not specified	NA/NA	NA/NA	Not specified	Not specified
School Psychology	MA/MS	Not specified	Not specified	Not specified	Not specified	Not specified	Not specified	Not specified	Not specified
Organizational Psychology	MA/MS	Not specified	Not specified	Not specified	Not specified	Not specified	Not specified	Not specified	Not specified
School Psychology	PsyD	NA/NA	NA/NA	NA/NA	Not specified	Not specified	Not specified	Not specified	Not specified
Leadership Psychology	PsyD	Not specified	Not specified	Not specified	Not specified	3/NA	Not specified	Not specified	3/NA
Clinical Mental Health Counseling	MA/MS	Not specified	Not specified	Not specified	Not specified	Not specified	Not specified	Not specified	Not specified
Applied Behavior Analysis Certificate	Other	Not specified	Not specified	Not specified	Not specified	Not specified	Not specified	Not specified	Not specified

Admissions Requirements:

Degree	GRE	GRE-Subject	Letters of Recom-mendation	Research Statement	Writing Sample	CV	Interview
Master's/Specialist	Optional	None	3	Required	Optional	Required	Required
Doctoral	Required	Optional	3	Required	Optional	Required	Required

Admissions Criteria:

GRE scores—medium
Research experience—low
Work experience—medium
Clinically related public service—high
GPA—high

Letters of recommendation—high
Interview—high
Statement of goals and objectives—high
Undergraduate psychology preparation—medium
Community service—high

For additional information on admission requirements, visit http://www.williamjames.edu/admissions/apply/.

Department Demographics

	Male (PT)	Female (PT)	Total	African-American/ Black (PT)	Hispanic/ Latino (PT)	Asian/ Pacific Islander (PT)	American Indian/ Alaska Native (PT)	Caucasian/ White (PT)	Unknown	Multiethnic (PT)	ADA (PT)	Int'l (PT)
Students	141 (35)	456 (97)	729	29 (8)	42 (12)	25 (9)	7 (0)	409 (96)	85 (7)	0 (0)	33 (0)	10 (0)

Financial Information/Assistance

Tuition: For information on tuition costs, visit http://www.williamjames.edu/admissions/tuition-and-aid/tuition-and-fees.cfm. Tuition is subject to change. Additional fees are assessed to students beyond the costs of tuition for the following: Student Services Fee.

Doctoral:
State residents: $37,440 per academic year.
State residents: $1,248 per credit hour.
Nonstate residents: $37,440 per academic year.
Nonstate residents: $1,248 per credit hour.

Master's:
State residents: $37,440 per academic year.
State residents: $1,248 per credit hour.
Nonstate residents: $37,440 per academic year.
Nonstate residents: $1,248 per credit hour.

Financial Assistance:

	Teaching Assistantship (% Receiving)	Teaching Assistantship Tuition Remission	Research Assistantship (% Receiving)	Research Assistantship Tuition Remission	Fellowship (% Receiving)	Fellowship Tuition Remission
First-Year Student	NA (NA)	NA	$4,200 (25)	NA	$5,000 (25)	NA
Advanced Student	$3,500 (10)	NA	$4,200 (25)	NA	$5,000 (25)	NA

For additional information on financial assistance, visit http://www.williamjames.edu/admissions/tuition-and-aid/index.cfm.

Employment of Department Graduates

Master's:
Enrolled in a psychology doctoral program: 9
Enrolled in another graduate/professional program: 1
Employed in a professional position in a school system: 9
Employed in a community mental health/counseling center: 18
Still seeking employment: 4
Other employment position: 12
Do not know: 16
Total: 69

Doctoral:
Enrolled in a postdoctoral residency/fellowship: 32
Employed in other positions at a higher education institution: 5
Employed in business or industry: 1
Employed in a community mental health/counseling center: 7
Employed in a hospital/medical center: 5
Still seeking employment: 3
Not seeking employment: 0
Do not know: 17
Total: 70

Additional Information

Housing and Day Care: No on-campus housing is available. No on-campus day care facilities are available.

Information for Students With Physical Disabilities: See the following website: http://www.williamjames.edu/student-life/services-resources/students-with-d.

Special Facilities or Resources: William James College is located in Newton, Massachusetts. We are a 20 minute drive to downtown Boston. Our facility is state of the art and houses our Centers of Excellence, including the Freedman Center for Child and Family Development, INTERFACE Resource and Referral Service, The Brenner Center for Assessment and Testing, and the Center of Excellence for Children, Families and the Law.

Application Information: Admissions Office, William James College, 1 Wells Avenue, Newton, MA 02459. *Fee:* $60. *Online application:* https://app.applyyourself.com/?id=mspp.

Central Michigan University

Department of Psychology
Humanities and Social and Behavioral Sciences
Sloan Hall
Mt. Pleasant, MI 48859
Telephone: (989) 774-3001
Chairperson: Katrina Rhymer

E-mail: decke1rk@cmich.edu
Web: http://www.chsbs.cmich.edu/psychology

Orientation, Objectives, and Emphasis of Department

Specialization is possible in the areas of clinical, applied experimental, industrial/organizational, and school psychology. There is also a general/experimental MS program with emphasis on foundations, statistics, methodology, and research, which is designed to prepare students for doctoral training or research positions in the public or private sectors. The clinical program follows a practitioner-scientist model, focusing on training for applied settings. The industrial/organizational program is oriented toward training students for careers in research, university, or business settings. The school program prepares school psychologists to provide consultation, intervention, and diagnostic services to schools and school children. The program meets Michigan requirements for certification.

Programs and Degrees Offered

Program	Degree	Application Deadline	Applications Received	Accepted	New Admits Enrolled (PT)	Total Enrolled (PT)	Degrees Awarded in 2014–2015	Median Years to Complete Degree	Dismissed/ Withdrew
Clinical Psychology	PhD	December 1 (Fall)	118	5	5	33 (0)	5	6.85	1
Experimental Psychology	PhD	February 1 (Fall)	28	5	5	22 (0)	2	4.25	
General Psychology	MA/MS	February 1 (Fall)	24	2	2	11 (0)	3	3.5	
School Psychology	PhD	November 15 (Fall)	19	3	3	26	0		
Industrial/ Organizational Psychology	MA/MS	January 1 (Fall)	31	2	2	4	1	2.25	0
Industrial/ Organizational Psychology	PhD	January 1 (Fall)	63	5	5	39	1	6	
Specialist in School Psychology	Other	November 15 (Fall)	12	2	3	12	2	3.5	

APA Accreditation

Clinical PhD: Student Outcome Data website: https://www.cmich.edu/colleges/chsbs/Psychology/Graduate/ClinicalPsychology/Pages/Clinical-Applicant-Data.aspx.
School PhD: Student Outcome Data website: https://www.cmich.edu/colleges/chsbs/Psychology/Graduate/SchoolPsychology/Doctoral/Pages/School-Doctoral-Applicant-Data.aspx.

Doctoral Degree (PhD Clinical Psychology): For those doctoral students for whom a professional internship was required in this program prior to graduation:
Total students who applied for an internship: 5
Total students who obtained an internship: 5
Total students who obtained a paid internship: 5
Total students who obtained an unpaid internship: 0

Total students who were placed in APA/CPA-accredited internships: 5
Total students placed in internships not APA/CPA-accredited, but listed with the Association of Psychology Postdoctoral and Internship Centers (APPIC): 0
Total students placed in internships conforming to guidelines of the Council of Directors of School Psychology Programs (CDSPP): 0
Total students placed in internships that were not APA/CPA-accredited, APPIC or CDSSP listed: 0

Doctoral Degree (PhD School Psychology): For those doctoral students for whom a professional internship was required in this program prior to graduation:
Total students who applied for an internship: 4
Total students who obtained an internship: 4
Total students who obtained a paid internship: 4
Total students who obtained an unpaid internship: 0
Total students who were placed in APA/CPA-accredited internships: 4
Total students placed in internships not APA/CPA-accredited, but listed with the Association of Psychology Postdoctoral and Internship Centers (APPIC): 0
Total students placed in internships conforming to guidelines of the Council of Directors of School Psychology Programs (CDSPP): 0
Total students placed in internships that were not APA/CPA-accredited, APPIC or CDSSP listed: 0

Master's Degree (MA/MS General Psychology): An internship experience, such as a final research project or "capstone" experience is required of graduates. Master's Degree (MA/MS Industrial/Organizational Psychology): An internship experience, such as a final research project or "capstone" experience is required of graduates.

Internships/Practica

Most practica and internships are arranged through agencies and schools outside the University. However, practicum experiences are available through the Department's Psychological Training and Consultation Center. Second-year clinical students routinely have their first practicum at the Center.

Admissions

Entries appear in the following order: required test or GPA, minimum score (if required)/median score of students entering in 2015–2016.

Program	Degree	GRE-V	GRE-Q	GRE-Writing	GRE-Subject	Under-graduate GPA	Last 2 Years GPA	Psychol-ogy GPA	Master's GPA
Clinical Psychology	PhD	NA/158	NA/151	NA/4.3	NA/NA	NA/3.92	Not specified	Not specified	Not specified
Experimental Psychology	PhD	NA/159	NA/152	NA/4.1	Not specified	NA/3.51	Not specified	Not specified	Not specified
General Psychology	MA/MS	NA/158	NA/149	NA/3.5	Not specified	NA/2.91	Not specified	Not specified	Not specified
School Psychology	PhD	NA/154	NA/150	NA/4.5	Not specified	NA/3.68	Not specified	Not specified	Not specified
Industrial/ Organizational Psychology	MA/MS	NA/158	NA/153	NA/4.5	Not specified	NA/3.71	Not specified	Not specified	Not specified
Industrial/ Organizational Psychology	PhD	NA/158	NA/153	NA/4.5	Not specified	NA/3.71	Not specified	Not specified	Not specified
Specialist in School Psychology	Other	NA/150	NA/151	NA/4.17	Not specified	NA/3.7	Not specified	Not specified	Not specified

Admissions Requirements:

Degree	GRE	GRE-Subject	Letters of Recom-mendation	Research Statement	Writing Sample	CV	Interview
Master's/Specialist	Required	None	3	Required	None	Required	Optional
Doctoral	Required	None	3	Required	None	Required	Optional

Please note if these criteria vary for different programs: The Clinical and School programs do interviews with their prospective students. The Experimental and Industrial/Organizational programs do not do interviews.

Admissions Criteria:
GRE scores—medium
Research experience—medium
Work experience—medium
Clinically related public service—medium
GPA—medium

Letters of recommendation—medium
Interview—medium
Statement of goals and objectives—medium
Undergraduate psychology preparation—medium

Department Demographics

	Male (PT)	Female (PT)	Total	African-American/ Black (PT)	Hispanic/ Latino (PT)	Asian/ Pacific Islander (PT)	American Indian/ Alaska Native (PT)	Caucasian/ White (PT)	Unknown	Multiethnic (PT)	ADA (PT)	Int'l (PT)
Students	59 (0)	88 (0)	147	2 (0)	4 (0)	9 (0)	2 (0)	116 (0)	13 (0)	1 (0)	0 (0)	10 (0)

Financial Information/Assistance

Tuition: For information on tuition costs, visit https://www.cmich.edu/ess/registrar/RegistrarRegistration/Pages/Tuition_and_Fee_Schedule.aspx. Tuition is subject to change.

Doctoral:
State residents: $605 per credit hour.
Nonstate residents: $875 per credit hour.

Master's:
State residents: $527 per credit hour.
Nonstate residents: $792 per credit hour.

Financial Assistance:

	Teaching Assistantship (% Receiving)	Teaching Assistantship Tuition Remission	Research Assistantship (% Receiving)	Research Assistantship Tuition Remission	Fellowship (% Receiving)	Fellowship Tuition Remission
First-Year Student	NA (NA)	NA	$10,929 (NA)	Partial	$10,929 (NA)	Partial
Advanced Student	$13,369 (NA)	Partial	$13,369 (NA)	Partial	$13,369 (NA)	Partial

For additional information on financial assistance, visit https://www.cmich.edu/ess/OSFA/Pages/Graduate-Students.aspx.

Employment of Department Graduates

Master's:
Enrolled in a psychology doctoral program: 4
Employed in a professional position in a school system: 2
Total: 6

Doctoral:
Enrolled in a postdoctoral residency/fellowship: 2
Employed in academic position at a 2-year/4-year college: 1
Employed in business or industry: 1
Employed in a hospital/medical center: 3
Do not know: 1
Total: 8

Additional Information

Housing and Day Care: On-campus housing is available. See the following website for more information: https://www.cmich.edu/ess/ResLife/Apartment_Living/About/Pages/Graduate_Housing.aspx. No on-campus day care facilities are available.

Information for Students With Physical Disabilities: See the following website: https://www.cmich.edu/ess/studentaffairs/SDS/.

Special Facilities or Resources: Space is reserved for student research with human subjects. Special equipment permits studies in learning, cognition, human factors, psychophysiology, neuropsychology, and perception. Computer laboratories are available, one specifically designated for clinical and school students. All computer labs have direct email and Internet access, as well as statistical and research software. The Psychology Training and Consultation Center provides training, research, and service functions. In a separate building, space is devoted to animal research and teaching of behavioral neuroscience and experimental behavior analysis. The behavioral neuroscience laboratory contains a fully equipped surgical/histological suite, behavioral testing area and equipment, and a data analysis room including microscopes and an image analysis system. The experimental analysis laboratory is equipped with automated operant chambers for both birds and rodents. A Life-Span Development Research Center has been established in the Department.

Application Information: Psychology Department, Sloan Hall, Central Michigan University, Mt. Pleasant, MI 48859. *Fee:* $45. *Online application:* https://apply.cmich.edu/.

Eastern Michigan University
Department of Psychology
College of Arts and Sciences
341 Science Complex
Ypsilanti, MI 48197
Telephone: (734) 487-1155
Chairperson: Carol Freedman-Doan

E-mail: cfreedman@emich.edu
Web: http://www.emich.edu/psychology

Orientation, Objectives, and Emphasis of Department
The Psychology Department offers three terminal Master's degree programs and courses in several orientations, including behavioral, social, insight, developmental, and physiological. Within the two clinical master's programs, the major emphases are on psychological assessment (General Clinical program) and behavioral treatment (Clinical Behavioral program). Within each program there are a wide variety of theoretical, applied, and research interests. The goal of the Clinical and Clinical Behavioral programs is to give students the background to immediately begin work in clinical treatment settings or to prepare them for entry into doctoral programs, as matches students' educational objectives. The emphasis of the Master's in General Experimental Psychology is to prepare students for entry into higher level study in psychology or as researchers in applied/research settings. Because psychology is considered a natural science at Eastern Michigan University, there is also an emphasis on basing clinical practice on research findings. Theses, although optional in the clinical master's programs, are expected to be research-based. The PhD program in Clinical Psychology is designed to give advanced training in the supervision of mental health professionals in mental health care settings.

Programs and Degrees Offered

Program	Degree	Application Deadline	Applications Received	Accepted	New Admits Enrolled (PT)	Total Enrolled (PT)	Degrees Awarded in 2014–2015	Median Years to Complete Degree	Dismissed/ Withdrew
General Clinical Psychology	MA/MS	February 1 (Fall)	57	15	8 (0)	20 (2)	12	2.25	0
Clinical Behavioral Psychology	MA/MS	February 1 (Fall)	27	14	8 (0)	19 (2)	7	2.53	2
General Experimental Psychology	MA/MS	February 1 (Fall)	15	4	1 (0)	2 (1)	1	2.75	2
Clinical Psychology	PhD	December 1 (Fall)	116	18	10 (0)	40 (0)	6	6.89	2

APA Accreditation
Clinical PhD: Student Outcome Data website: http://www.emich.edu/psychology/programs/phd.php.

Doctoral Degree (PhD Clinical Psychology): For those doctoral students for whom a professional internship was required in this program prior to graduation:
Total students who applied for an internship: 10
Total students who obtained an internship: 8
Total students who obtained a paid internship: 8
Total students who obtained an unpaid internship: 0
Total students who were placed in APA/CPA-accredited internships: 8
Total students placed in internships not APA/CPA-accredited, but listed with the Association of Psychology Postdoctoral and Internship Centers (APPIC): 0

Total students placed in internships conforming to guidelines of the Council of Directors of School Psychology Programs (CDSPP): 0
Total students placed in internships that were not APA/CPA-accredited, APPIC or CDSSP listed: 0

Master's Degree (MA/MS General Clinical Psychology): An internship experience, such as a final research project or "capstone" experience is required of graduates. Master's Degree (MA/MS Clinical Behavioral Psychology): An internship experience, such as a final research project or "capstone" experience is required of graduates. Master's Degree (MA/MS General Experimental Psychology): An internship experience, such as a final research project or "capstone" experience is required of graduates.

Internships/Practica

Practicum settings (unpaid) are available in the surrounding community for clinical and clinical behavioral students. In addition, the university offers mental health services involving practicum experience at both the campus Snow Health Center and the EMU Psychology Clinic. Both terminal MS and PhD programs require sufficient practicum hours to meet the State of Michigan requirements for the Limited License in Psychology (LLP).

Admissions

Entries appear in the following order: required test or GPA, minimum score (if required)/median score of students entering in 2015–2016.

Program	Degree	GRE-V	GRE-Q	GRE-Writing	GRE-Subject	Under-graduate GPA	Last 2 Years GPA	Psychol-ogy GPA	Master's GPA
General Clinical Psychology	MA/MS	152/NA	152/NA	4/NA	Not specified	3/3.5	Not specified	Not specified	Not specified
Clinical Behavioral Psychology	MA/MS	145/NA	145/NA	4/NA	Not specified	3/NA	3/NA	3/NA	Not specified
General Experimental Psychology	MA/MS	150/NA	150/NA	4/NA	Not specified	3/NA	Not specified	Not specified	Not specified
Clinical Psychology	PhD	155/160	155/156	4/4.5	Not specified	3/3.72	3/NA	3/NA	Not specified

Admissions Requirements:

Degree	GRE	GRE-Subject	Letters of Recom-mendation	Research Statement	Writing Sample	CV	Interview
Master's/Specialist	Required	Optional	3	Required	Required	Required	Required
Doctoral	Required	Recom-mended	3	Required	Required	Required	Required

Admissions Criteria:

GRE scores—high
Research experience—medium
Work experience—low
Clinically related public service—medium
GPA—high

Letters of recommendation—medium
Interview—high
Statement of goals and objectives—high
Undergraduate psychology preparation—medium
Fit with faculty research—high

Department Demographics

	Male (PT)	Female (PT)	Total	African-American/ Black (PT)	Hispanic/ Latino (PT)	Asian/ Pacific Islander (PT)	American Indian/ Alaska Native (PT)	Caucasian/ White (PT)	Unknown	Multiethnic (PT)	ADA (PT)	Int'l (PT)
Students	22 (4)	59 (1)	86	3 (0)	4 (0)	6 (1)	1 (0)	72 (4)	0 (0)	0 (0)	0 (0)	3 (1)

Financial Information/Assistance

Tuition: For information on tuition costs, visit http://www.emich.edu/sbs/basics/tuition/index.php. Tuition is subject to change. Additional fees are assessed to students beyond the costs of tuition for the following: general fee, tech fee, student union fee, program fee, assessment lab fees.

Doctoral:
State residents: $695 per credit hour.
Nonstate residents: $1,250 per credit hour.

Master's:
State residents: $597 per credit hour.
Nonstate residents: $873 per credit hour.

Financial Assistance:

	Teaching Assistantship (% Receiving)	Teaching Assistantship Tuition Remission	Research Assistantship (% Receiving)	Research Assistantship Tuition Remission	Fellowship (% Receiving)	Fellowship Tuition Remission
First-Year Student	$9,200 (15)	Partial	NA (NA)	NA	$16,500 (100)	Full
Advanced Student	$9,200 (15)	Partial	NA (NA)	NA	$16,500 (100)	Full

For additional information on financial assistance, visit http://www.emich.edu/graduate/financial_assistance/assistantships.php.

Employment of Department Graduates

Master's:
Enrolled in a psychology doctoral program: 2
Employed in academic position at a 2-year/4-year college: 2
Employed in a community mental health/counseling center: 10
Employed in a hospital/medical center: 6
Still seeking employment: 2
Do not know: 2
Total: 24

Doctoral:
Enrolled in a postdoctoral residency/fellowship: 1
Employed in other positions at a higher education institution: 1
Employed in government agency: 2
Employed in a community mental health/counseling center: 1
Employed in a hospital/medical center: 1
Total: 6

Additional Information

Housing and Day Care: On-campus housing is available. See the following website for more information: http://www.emich.edu/residencelife/. On-campus day care facilities are available. See the following website for more information: http://www.emich.edu/childrensinstitute/.

Information for Students With Physical Disabilities: See the following website: http://www.emich.edu/drc/.

Special Facilities or Resources: The faculty, which consists of approximately 24 full-time members with PhDs and varying number of part-time lecturers, is eclectic in orientation with a wide variety of interests and professional backgrounds. Research interests and publication record of the faculty include psychological test construction and validation, basic behavioral research with humans and non-humans, the history of psychology, applied behavior analysis, physiological psychology, behavioral medicine, PTSD, child and adolescent development, and many more. Student enrollment is intentionally kept low in order to provide the students with ample opportunities to develop close working relationships with the faculty. Students regularly present at regional, national, and international conventions, as well as co-author published papers with faculty. The facilities of the Psychology Department are located in the Mark Jefferson Science Complex and in the Psychology Clinic at 611 West Cross. The department features a state-of-the-art computer laboratory, IEEE 802.11 (AirPort) wireless networking capabilities, human and animal research facilities, seminar rooms, a clinic with one-way observation capabilities, a university library less than one minute away on foot, and other equipment and supplies needed for advanced study.

Application Information: Department of Psychology, Graduate Admissions Committee, 341 Science Complex, Eastern Michigan University, Ypsilanti, MI 48197. *Fee:* $45. *Online application:* http://www.emich.edu/graduate/apply/.

Michigan School of Professional Psychology

26811 Orchard Lake Road
Farmington Hills, MI 48334
Telephone: (248) 476-1122
Program Director, CAO: Fran Brown, PsyD

E-mail: admissions@mispp.edu
Web: http://mispp.edu

Orientation, Objectives, and Emphasis of Department

The Michigan School of Professional Psychology (MiSPP), an independent, not-for-profit graduate school, provides an educational climate which inspires students to live up to their potential, professionally, and personally. The Master of Arts in Clinical Psychology is offered in a 1-year full-time or 2-to 3-year part-time format. The Doctor of Clinical Psychology degree is a full-time, minimum 4-year, post-master's program. The institution has been a leader in clinical, experiential, self-directed education for over 30 years. Its curriculum emphasizes personal growth, authenticity, and creativity as integral parts of the academic process.

Programs and Degrees Offered

Program	Degree	Application Deadline	Applica-tions Received	Accepted	New Admits Enrolled (PT)	Total Enrolled (PT)	Degrees Awarded in 2014–2015	Median Years to Complete Degree	Dismissed/ Withdrew
Clinical Psychology	PsyD	(Fall), Rolling	43	21	14 (0)	70 (2)	19	5.3	1
Clinical Psychology	MA/MS	(Fall), Rolling	116	63	27 (18)	27 (42)	47	1.38	0

Doctoral Degree (PsyD Clinical Psychology): For those doctoral students for whom a professional internship was required in this program prior to graduation:

Total students who applied for an internship: 14
Total students who obtained an internship: 14
Total students who obtained a paid internship: 13
Total students who obtained an unpaid internship: 1
Total students who were placed in APA/CPA-accredited internships: 0
Total students placed in internships not APA/CPA-accredited, but listed with the Association of Psychology Postdoctoral and Internship Centers (APPIC): 0
Total students placed in internships conforming to guidelines of the Council of Directors of School Psychology Programs (CDSPP): 0
Total students placed in internships that were not APA/CPA-accredited, APPIC or CDSSP listed: 14

Master's Degree (MA/MS Clinical Psychology): An internship experience, such as a final research project or "capstone" experience is required of graduates.

Internships/Practica

Master of Arts students complete a 500-hour practicum. Doctoral students complete an 1,800-hour practicum and a 2,000-hour internship.

Admissions

Entries appear in the following order: required test or GPA, minimum score (if required)/median score of students entering in 2015–2016.

Program	Degree	GRE-V	GRE-Q	GRE-Writing	GRE-Subject	Under-graduate GPA	Last 2 Years GPA	Psychol-ogy GPA	Master's GPA
Clinical Psychology	PsyD	NA/NA	NA/NA	NA/NA	Not specified	2.5/3	Not specified	Not specified	3.25/3.5
Clinical Psychology	MA/MS	Not specified	Not specified	Not specified	Not specified	2.5/3	Not specified	Not specified	Not specified

Admissions Requirements:

Degree	GRE	GRE-Subject	Letters of Recom-mendation	Research Statement	Writing Sample	CV	Interview
Master's/Specialist	Optional	Optional	3	Required	Optional	Required	Required
Doctoral	Required	Required	3	Required	Optional	Required	Required

Admissions Criteria:

GRE scores—medium
Research experience—medium
Work experience—high
Clinically related public service—high
GPA—high

Letters of recommendation—high
Interview—high
Statement of goals and objectives—high
Undergraduate psychology preparation—low

For additional information on admission requirements, visit http://mispp.edu/admissions/requirements/.

Department Demographics

	Male (PT)	Female (PT)	Total	African-American/ Black (PT)	Hispanic/ Latino (PT)	Asian/ Pacific Islander (PT)	American Indian/ Alaska Native (PT)	Caucasian/ White (PT)	Unknown	Multiethnic (PT)	ADA (PT)	Int'l (PT)
Students	20 (12)	60 (49)	141	13 (15)	1 (1)	1 (3)	0 (0)	62 (39)	0 (0)	3 (2)	9 (4)	1 (0)

Financial Information/Assistance

Tuition: For information on tuition costs, visit http://mispp.edu/student-services/financial-aid/cost-of-attendance/. Tuition is subject to change. Additional fees are assessed to students beyond the costs of tuition for the following: technology, student engagement, testing, dissertation, supervision, graduation. Tuition costs vary by program.

Doctoral:
State residents: $29,694 per academic year.
State residents: $757 per credit hour.
Nonstate residents: $29,694 per academic year.
Nonstate residents: $757 per credit hour.

Master's:
State residents: $30,279 per academic year.
State residents: $607 per credit hour.
Nonstate residents: $30,279 per academic year.
Nonstate residents: $607 per credit hour.

Financial Assistance:

	Teaching Assistantship (% Receiving)	Teaching Assistantship Tuition Remission	Research Assistantship (% Receiving)	Research Assistantship Tuition Remission	Fellowship (% Receiving)	Fellowship Tuition Remission
First-Year Student	NA (NA)	NA	NA (NA)	NA	NA (NA)	NA
Advanced Student	$13,626 (NA)	NA	NA (NA)	NA	NA (NA)	NA

For additional information on financial assistance, visit http://mispp.edu/student-services/financial-aid/.

Employment of Department Graduates

No information provided.

Additional Information

Housing and Day Care: No on-campus housing is available. No on-campus day care facilities are available.

Application Information: Michigan School of Professional Psychology, Admissions Office, 26811 Orchard Lake Road, Farmington Hills, MI 48334. *Fee:* $75. *Online application:* https://mispp.edu/admissions/apply-now/online-application/.

Michigan State University

Counseling, Educational Psychology, and Special Education/School Psychology Program
College of Education
620 Farm Lane, Room 435 Erickson Hall
East Lansing, MI 49201
Telephone: (517) 432-0843
Chairperson: Richard S. Prawat

E-mail: carlsoj@msu.edu
Web: http://www.educ.msu.edu/cepse/schoolpsychology/

Orientation, Objectives, and Emphasis of Department

The MSU School Psychology program prepares school psychologists to work with educators, children, youth, and families to promote individuals' learning and development particularly in relation to schooling. Our vision for training and practice in school psychology is informed by the standards of the profession including the Specialty Definition of School Psychology by APA Division 16 and the Blueprint for School Psychology published by NASP. The fundamental goal of the MSU School Psychology program is to prepare school psychologists as data-based, system-wide problem-solvers in the educational domain who work with learners of all ages. Our goal for the doctoral program is to prepare psychologists for a wide range of practice that is consistent with contemporary models of school psychological services.

Programs and Degrees Offered

Program	Degree	Application Deadline	Applica-tions Received	Accepted	New Admits Enrolled (PT)	Total Enrolled (PT)	Degrees Awarded in 2014–2015	Median Years to Complete Degree	Dismissed/ Withdrew
School Psychology	PhD	December 1 (Fall)	37	10	2 (0)	35 (0)	7	5.5	0

APA Accreditation

School PhD: Student Outcome Data website: http://www.educ.msu.edu/cepse/SchoolPsychology/student-data.asp.

Doctoral Degree (PhD School Psychology): For those doctoral students for whom a professional internship was required in this program prior to graduation:
Total students who applied for an internship: 6
Total students who obtained an internship: 6
Total students who obtained a paid internship: 5
Total students who obtained an unpaid internship: 1
Total students who were placed in APA/CPA-accredited internships: 1
Total students placed in internships not APA/CPA-accredited, but listed with the Association of Psychology Postdoctoral and Internship Centers (APPIC): 0
Total students placed in internships conforming to guidelines of the Council of Directors of School Psychology Programs (CDSPP): 5
Total students placed in internships that were not APA/CPA-accredited, APPIC or CDSSP listed: 0

Internships/Practica

Practica are completed in school districts and community-based mental health settings, such as hospitals and clinics, where school-aged children receive psychological services. Internships are completed all over the country.

Admissions

Entries appear in the following order: required test or GPA, minimum score (if required)/median score of students entering in 2015–2016.

Program	Degree	GRE-V	GRE-Q	GRE-Writing	GRE-Subject	Under-graduate GPA	Last 2 Years GPA	Psychol-ogy GPA	Master's GPA
School Psychology	PhD	152/155	152/156	3.5/4	Not specified	3.5/3.66	Not specified	Not specified	Not specified

Admissions Requirements:

Degree	GRE	GRE-Subject	Letters of Recommendation	Research Statement	Writing Sample	CV	Interview
Doctoral	Optional	Optional	3	Required	Required	Required	Required

Admissions Criteria:

GRE scores—high
Research experience—high
Work experience—medium
Clinically related public service—medium
GPA—high

Letters of recommendation—high
Interview—high
Statement of goals and objectives—high
Undergraduate psychology preparation—medium
Writing sample—medium

For additional information on admission requirements, visit http://www.educ.msu.edu/cepse/SchoolPsychology/admissions.asp.

Department Demographics

	Male (PT)	Female (PT)	Total	African-American/ Black (PT)	Hispanic/ Latino (PT)	Asian/ Pacific Islander (PT)	American Indian/ Alaska Native (PT)	Caucasian/ White (PT)	Unknown	Multiethnic (PT)	ADA (PT)	Int'l (PT)
Students	6 (0)	29 (0)	35	2 (0)	2 (0)	3 (0)	0 (0)	25 (0)	0 (0)	3 (0)	0 (0)	0 (0)

Financial Information/Assistance

Tuition: For information on tuition costs, visit http://www.ctlr.msu.edu/CoStudentAccounts/Tuition_Fees_MainMenu.aspx. Tuition is subject to change.

Doctoral:
State residents: $16,949 per academic year.
State residents: $672 per credit hour.
Nonstate residents: $32,500 per academic year.
Nonstate residents: $1,320 per credit hour.

Financial Assistance:

	Teaching Assistantship (% Receiving)	Teaching Assistantship Tuition Remission	Research Assistantship (% Receiving)	Research Assistantship Tuition Remission	Fellowship (% Receiving)	Fellowship Tuition Remission
First-Year Student	$14,235 (100)	Partial	$14,235 (100)	Partial	$15,500 (NA)	Partial
Advanced Student	$16,536 (NA)	Partial	$16,536 (NA)	Partial	$20,500 (NA)	Partial

For additional information on financial assistance, visit http://education.msu.edu/cepse/SchoolPsychology/financial.asp.

Employment of Department Graduates

Doctoral:
Enrolled in a postdoctoral residency/fellowship: 4
Employed in academic position at a 2-year/4-year college: 1
Employed in a professional position in a school system: 2
Total: 7

Additional Information

Housing and Day Care: On-campus housing is available. See the following website for more information: http://liveon.msu.edu/. On-campus day care facilities are available. See the following website for more information: http://scdc.msu.edu/; http://hdfs.msu.edu/cdl/.

Information for Students With Physical Disabilities: See the following website: https://www.rcpd.msu.edu/.

Special Facilities or Resources: The College of Education has been ranked as one of the leading universities in the country. The facilities and support for learning are exceptional.

Application Information: Admissions Secretary, Michigan State University, College of Education, CEPSE Department, 620 Farm Lane, Room 447 Erickson Hall, East Lansing, MI 48824. *Fee:* $50. *Online application:* http://grad.msu.edu/apply/.

Michigan State University

Department of Psychology
Social Science
240E Psychology Building
East Lansing, MI 48824-1116
Telephone: (517) 353-5258
Chairperson: Juli Wade

E-mail: psygrad@msu.edu
Web: http://psychology.msu.edu

Orientation, Objectives, and Emphasis of Department

The main objective of our programs is to train researchers who will engage in the generation and application of knowledge in a wide range of areas in psychology.

Programs and Degrees Offered

Program	Degree	Application Deadline	Applications Received	Accepted	New Admits Enrolled (PT)	Total Enrolled (PT)	Degrees Awarded in 2014–2015	Median Years to Complete Degree	Dismissed/Withdrew
Behavioral Neuroscience	PhD	December 1 (Fall)	12	1	1	10 (0)	2	6	1
Clinical Psychology	PhD	December 1 (Fall)	188	6	5	28 (0)	3	6	1
Ecological/ Community Psychology	PhD	December 1 (Fall)	28	7	4	21 (0)	4	6	1
Organizational Psychology	PhD	December 1 (Fall)	81	8	5	21 (0)	4	5	0
Cognition & Cognitive Neuroscience	PhD	December 1 (Fall)	22	7	3	14	2	5	0
Social/ Personality Psychology	PhD	December 1 (Fall)	17	2	0	12 (0)	2	6	0

APA Accreditation

Clinical PhD: Student Outcome Data website: http://psychology.msu.edu/Clinical/ClinicalStudentData.aspx.

Doctoral Degree (PhD Clinical Psychology): For those doctoral students for whom a professional internship was required in this program prior to graduation:
Total students who applied for an internship: 5
Total students who obtained an internship: 5
Total students who obtained a paid internship: 5
Total students who obtained an unpaid internship: 0
Total students who were placed in APA/CPA-accredited internships: 5

Total students placed in internships not APA/CPA-accredited, but listed with the Association of Psychology Postdoctoral and Internship Centers (APPIC): 0

Total students placed in internships conforming to guidelines of the Council of Directors of School Psychology Programs (CDSPP): 0

Total students placed in internships that were not APA/CPA-accredited, APPIC or CDSSP listed: 0

Internships/Practica

Clinical practica provided by the clinical program at the department's Psychological Clinic.

Admissions

Entries appear in the following order: required test or GPA, minimum score (if required)/median score of students entering in 2015–2016.

Program	Degree	GRE-V	GRE-Q	GRE-Writing	GRE-Subject	Under-graduate GPA	Last 2 Years GPA	Psychol-ogy GPA	Master's GPA
Behavioral Neuroscience	PhD	NA/157	NA/150	NA/4	Not specified	Not specified	Not specified	Not specified	Not specified
Clinical Psychology	PhD	NA/165	NA/163	NA/4	NA/NA	NA/3.75	Not specified	Not specified	Not specified
Ecological/ Community Psychology	PhD	NA/170	NA/160	NA/4	Not specified	NA/3.5	NA/NA	NA/NA	NA/NA
Organizational Psychology	PhD	NA/161	NA/163	NA/4	NA/NA	NA/3.65	Not specified	NA/NA	Not specified
Cognition & Cognitive Neuroscience	PhD	NA/158	NA/159	NA/4	NA/NA	Not specified	Not specified	Not specified	Not specified
Social/ Personality Psychology	PhD	NA/165	NA/163	NA/4	NA/NA	NA/3.6	Not specified	NA/NA	Not specified

Admissions Requirements:

Degree	GRE	GRE-Subject	Letters of Recom-mendation	Research Statement	Writing Sample	CV	Interview
Doctoral	Required	Recom-mended	3	Required	Optional	Optional	Optional

Please note if these criteria vary for different programs: Public service and clinical activities are important for applicants to the clinical and ecological/community programs.

Admissions Criteria:

GRE scores—high
Research experience—high
Work experience—medium
Clinically related public service—low
GPA—high

Letters of recommendation—high
Interview—medium
Statement of goals and objectives—high
Undergraduate psychology preparation—medium

For additional information on admission requirements, visit http://psychology.msu.edu/GraduateProgram/ApplicationProcess.aspx.

Department Demographics

	Male (PT)	Female (PT)	Total	African-American/ Black (PT)	Hispanic/ Latino (PT)	Asian/ Pacific Islander (PT)	American Indian/ Alaska Native (PT)	Caucasian/ White (PT)	Unknown	Multiethnic (PT)	ADA (PT)	Int'l (PT)
Students	36 (0)	73 (0)	109	6 (0)	3 (0)	5 (0)	0 (0)	80 (0)	14 (0)	1 (0)	0 (0)	8 (0)

Financial Information/Assistance

Tuition: For information on tuition costs, visit http://www.ctlr.msu.edu/COStudentAccounts/. Tuition is subject to change.

Doctoral:
State residents: $672 per credit hour.
Nonstate residents: $1,320 per credit hour.

Financial Assistance:

	Teaching Assistantship (% Receiving)	Teaching Assistantship Tuition Remission	Research Assistantship (% Receiving)	Research Assistantship Tuition Remission	Fellowship (% Receiving)	Fellowship Tuition Remission
First-Year Student	$22,004 (50)	Full	$22,004 (40)	Full	$27,000 (10)	Full
Advanced Student	$22,004 (30)	Full	$22,004 (60)	Full	$27,000 (10)	Full

For additional information on financial assistance, visit http://www.finaid.msu.edu/grad.asp.

Employment of Department Graduates

No information provided.

Additional Information

Housing and Day Care: On-campus housing is available. See the following website for more information: http://liveon.msu.edu/. On-campus day care facilities are available. See the following website for more information: http://scdc.msu.edu/; http://hdfs.msu.edu/cdl/.

Information for Students With Physical Disabilities: See the following website: https://www.rcpd.msu.edu/.

Special Facilities or Resources: Facilities include the Psychological Clinic for the clinical program, which includes playrooms equipped for audio and video recording, testing equipment, computer-based record keeping system, and neuropsychological assessment lab. The Neuroscience-Biological Psychology Laboratories include research animal facilities, computers, light and electron-microscopy, histology and endocrinology labs. The Vision Research Laboratory, Cognitive Processes Laboratories, Eye-Movement Lab, and Speech Processing Lab provide automated facilities for conducting research in cognitive science. Additional observational labs equipped with video remote control equipment, one-way windows, and automated data recording equipment are available. Computer labs are available within the department and across campus.

Application Information: Fee: $50. *Online application:* http://grad.msu.edu/apply/.

Michigan, University of
Combined Program in Education and Psychology
1406 School of Education, 610 East University Avenue
Ann Arbor, MI 48109-1259
Telephone: (734) 647-0626
Chairperson: Stephanie J. Rowley

E-mail: cpep@umich.edu
Web: http://www.soe.umich.edu/academics/doctoral_programs/ep/

Orientation, Objectives, and Emphasis of Department
The Combined Program in Education and Psychology focuses on research training in instructional psychology, broadly defined. Students are trained to study educational issues and do research in educational settings, on significant educational problems related to learning. There are currently four main research foci: (1) human development in context of schools, families, and communities; (2) cognitive and learning sciences; (3) motivation and self-regulated learning; and (4) resilience and development. Faculty affiliated with the program have ongoing research programs on various important issues. These include projects on children's cognitive development and reading skills, children's achievement motivation, socialization in the schools, how computers are changing the ways in which children learn, and learning and achievement of ethnically diverse students. Students in the program work with faculty

on these projects and learn to design projects in their own areas of interest. They take courses taught by faculty members in the program, and also courses taught by faculty in the Psychology Department and the School of Education. Because the department is an independent interdepartmental unit, students have the unique opportunity to work with faculty in both the Psychology Department and the School of Education, in addition to the faculty directly affiliated with the program.

Programs and Degrees Offered

Program	Degree	Application Deadline	Applications Received	Accepted	New Admits Enrolled (PT)	Total Enrolled (PT)	Degrees Awarded in 2014–2015	Median Years to Complete Degree	Dismissed/ Withdrew
Education and Psychology	PhD	December 1 (Fall)	110	10	5 (0)	38 (0)	6	4.8	1

Admissions

Entries appear in the following order: required test or GPA, minimum score (if required)/median score of students entering in 2015–2016.

Program	Degree	GRE-V	GRE-Q	GRE-Writing	GRE-Subject	Under-graduate GPA	Last 2 Years GPA	Psychology GPA	Master's GPA
Education and Psychology	PhD	NA/159	NA/156	NA/4.5	Not specified	NA/3.59	Not specified	Not specified	Not specified

Admissions Requirements:

Degree	GRE	GRE-Subject	Letters of Recommendation	Research Statement	Writing Sample	CV	Interview
Doctoral	Required	Optional	3	Required	Required	Required	Required

Please note if these criteria vary for different programs: A writing sample is only required from international applicants.

Admissions Criteria:

GRE scores—medium
Research experience—high
Work experience—medium
Clinically related public service—low
GPA—medium

Letters of recommendation—high
Interview—high
Statement of goals and objectives—high
Undergraduate psychology preparation—low
Teaching/education—medium

For additional information on admission requirements, visit http://www.soe.umich.edu/academics/doctoral_programs/ep/ep_applying/.

Department Demographics

	Male (PT)	Female (PT)	Total	African-American/ Black (PT)	Hispanic/ Latino (PT)	Asian/ Pacific Islander (PT)	American Indian/ Alaska Native (PT)	Caucasian/ White (PT)	Unknown	Multiethnic (PT)	ADA (PT)	Int'l (PT)
Students	12 (0)	26 (0)	38	11 (0)	5 (0)	2 (0)	0 (0)	14 (0)	4 (0)	2 (0)	1 (0)	4 (0)

Financial Information/Assistance

Tuition: For information on tuition costs, visit http://ro.umich.edu/tuition/. Tuition is subject to change. Additional fees are assessed to students beyond the costs of tuition for the following: $328.38 (Registration and mandatory fees for combined Fall & Winter terms).

Doctoral:
State residents: $20,966 per academic year.
Nonstate residents: $42,016 per academic year.

Financial Assistance:

	Teaching Assistantship (% Receiving)	Teaching Assistantship Tuition Remission	Research Assistantship (% Receiving)	Research Assistantship Tuition Remission	Fellowship (% Receiving)	Fellowship Tuition Remission
First-Year Student	NA (NA)	NA	$27,526 (30)	Full	$25,200 (70)	Full
Advanced Student	$27,350 (39)	Full	$26,972 (29)	Full	$27,000 (32)	Full

For additional information on financial assistance, visit http://www.soe.umich.edu/academics/doctoral_programs/ep/ep_funding/.

Employment of Department Graduates

Doctoral:
Enrolled in a postdoctoral residency/fellowship: 1
Employed in an academic position at a university: 5
Employed in other positions at a higher education institution: 1
Employed in business or industry: 2
Total: 9

Additional Information

Housing and Day Care: On-campus housing is available. See the following website for more information: http://www.housing.umich.edu. On-campus day care facilities are available. See the following website for more information: http://hr.umich.edu/childcare/.

Information for Students With Physical Disabilities: See the following website: http://ssd.umich.edu/.

Special Facilities or Resources: The University of Michigan provides a rich environment for graduate studies. The faculty in both education and psychology are internationally known for their scholarly productivity, and so students receive excellent training in how to conduct educational research. Faculty in the Psychology Department have ties to school officials in Ann Arbor and the greater Detroit area, which means students receive ample opportunities to work on many different kinds of educational projects. Students can take advantage of the university's excellent library and computer facilities, both of which are among the best in the country. A distinct advantage of the program is that it is interdepartmental in the graduate school with full resources and faculty available from the Psychology Department, the School of Education, the School of Social Work, and the Women's Studies Department. The department has close collaborative relationships with the Center for Human Growth and Development, the Center for Research on Learning and Teaching, the Center for Research on Women and Gender, the Human Performance Center, the Institute of Gerontology, the Institute for Social Research, the Cognitive Science and Machine Intelligence Laboratory, the Evolution and Human Behavior Program, and the Children's Center.

Application Information: Fee: $75. *Online application:* http://www.rackham.umich.edu/admissions/applying.

Michigan, University of
Department of Psychology
Literature, Science & Arts
530 Church Street, 1343 East Hall
Ann Arbor, MI 48109-1043
Telephone: (734) 764-2580
Chairperson: Patricia Reuter-Lorenz

E-mail: psych.saa@umich.edu
Web: https://prod.lsa.umich.edu/psych/

Orientation, Objectives, and Emphasis of Department
The Department of Psychology is committed to a broad mission of excellence in research, teaching, and apprenticeship; to create new scientific knowledge about psychological processes through first-rate scholarship; to teach innovative courses and engage

students in our research and service activities; and to maintain our record of outstanding graduate training that produces tomorrow's leading researchers. We strive to accomplish these goals as a large, diverse and interdisciplinary community of scholars.

Programs and Degrees Offered

Program	Degree	Application Deadline	Applica-tions Received	Accepted	New Admits Enrolled (PT)	Total Enrolled (PT)	Degrees Awarded in 2014–2015	Median Years to Complete Degree	Dismissed/ Withdrew
Biopsychology	PhD	December 1 (Fall)	92	12	4	16	3	5.45	0
Cognition and Cognitive Neuroscience	PhD	December 1 (Fall)	190	9	3	15	7	4.89	0
Developmental Psychology	PhD	December 1 (Fall)	129	10	7	31	4	4.7	0
Social Psychology	PhD	December 1 (Fall)	202	8	5	20	2	5.53	0
Personality and Social Contexts	PhD	December 1 (Fall)	120	2	1 (0)	10 (0)	2	5.07	0
Clinical Science	PhD	December 1 (Fall)	264	9	4	29	2	5.8	0

APA Accreditation

Clinical PhD: Student Outcome Data website: https://prod.lsa.umich.edu/psych/program-areas/clinical-science.html.

Doctoral Degree (PhD Clinical Science): For those doctoral students for whom a professional internship was required in this program prior to graduation:
Total students who applied for an internship: 5
Total students who obtained an internship: 5
Total students who obtained a paid internship: 5
Total students who obtained an unpaid internship: 0
Total students who were placed in APA/CPA-accredited internships: 5
Total students placed in internships not APA/CPA-accredited, but listed with the Association of Psychology Postdoctoral and Internship Centers (APPIC): 0
Total students placed in internships conforming to guidelines of the Council of Directors of School Psychology Programs (CDSPP): 0
Total students placed in internships that were not APA/CPA-accredited, APPIC or CDSSP listed: 0

Internships/Practica

Students in the clinical area begin practica (e.g., psychological testing) during their first year and continue the practicum experience in the second year (usually in local agencies) on a 6–8-hour a week basis. During the same 2-year period, students are engaged in their master's-level research project. Students begin full-time clinical work (internships) usually in their sixth year of training.

Admissions

Entries appear in the following order: required test or GPA, minimum score (if required)/median score of students entering in 2015–2016.

Program	Degree	GRE-V	GRE-Q	GRE-Writing	GRE-Subject	Under-graduate GPA	Last 2 Years GPA	Psychol-ogy GPA	Master's GPA
Biopsychology	PhD	NA/159	NA/156	NA/4	Not specified	NA/3.75	Not specified	Not specified	Not specified
Cognition and Cognitive Neuroscience	PhD	NA/154	NA/160	NA/4	Not specified	NA/3.58	Not specified	Not specified	Not specified
Developmental Psychology	PhD	NA/155	NA/151	NA/5	Not specified	NA/3.71	Not specified	Not specified	Not specified

Admissions *(con't.)*

Program	Degree	GRE-V	GRE-Q	GRE-Writing	GRE-Subject	Under-graduate GPA	Last 2 Years GPA	Psychology GPA	Master's GPA
Social Psychology	PhD	NA/164	NA/162	NA/4.75	Not specified	NA/3.83	Not specified	Not specified	Not specified
Personality and Social Contexts	PhD	NA/164	NA/158	NA/5	Not specified	NA/3.8	Not specified	Not specified	Not specified
Clinical Science	PhD	NA/164	NA/157	Not specified	Not specified	NA/3.71	Not specified	Not specified	Not specified

Admissions Requirements:

Degree	GRE	GRE-Subject	Letters of Recom-mendation	Research Statement	Writing Sample	CV	Interview
Doctoral	Required	Optional	3	Required	Optional	Optional	Recom-mended

Admissions Criteria:

GRE scores—medium
Research experience—high
Work experience—high
Clinically related public service—low
GPA—medium

Letters of recommendation—high
Interview—high
Statement of goals and objectives—high
Undergraduate psychology preparation—medium

For additional information on admission requirements, visit https://prod.lsa.umich.edu/psych/prospective-students/graduate/application-procedures.html.

Department Demographics

	Male (PT)	Female (PT)	Total	African-American/ Black (PT)	Hispanic/ Latino (PT)	Asian/ Pacific Islander (PT)	American Indian/ Alaska Native (PT)	Caucasian/ White (PT)	Unknown	Multiethnic (PT)	ADA (PT)	Int'l (PT)
Students	35 (0)	86 (0)	121	13 (0)	26 (0)	16 (0)	3 (0)	48 (0)	10 (0)	5 (0)	0 (0)	10 (0)

Financial Information/Assistance

Tuition: For information on tuition costs, visit http://ro.umich.edu/tuition/. Tuition is subject to change.

Doctoral:
State residents: $20,638 per academic year.
Nonstate residents: $41,688 per academic year.

Financial Assistance:

	Teaching Assistantship (% Receiving)	Teaching Assistantship Tuition Remission	Research Assistantship (% Receiving)	Research Assistantship Tuition Remission	Fellowship (% Receiving)	Fellowship Tuition Remission
First-Year Student	NA (100)	Partial	NA (NA)	NA	$19,800 (100)	Full
Advanced Student	$26,550 (100)	Full	$29,025 (100)	Full	$19,800 (100)	Full

For additional information on financial assistance, visit https://prod.lsa.umich.edu/psych/prospective-students/graduate/financial-information.html.

Employment of Department Graduates

Doctoral:
Enrolled in a postdoctoral residency/fellowship: 15
Employed in an academic position at a university: 1
Employed in academic position at a 2-year/4-year college: 2
Employed in business or industry: 2
Total: 20

Additional Information

Housing and Day Care: On-campus housing is available. See the following website for more information: http://www.housing. umich.edu. On-campus day care facilities are available. See the following website for more information: http://www.hr.umich.edu/ childcare/.

Information for Students With Physical Disabilities: See the following website: http://ssd.umich.edu/.

Special Facilities or Resources: The University of Michigan is blessed with an extensive scientific-scholarly community of psychologists that is virtually unique in breadth, diversity, and quality. Because of the close collaborative relationships that have evolved over the years, graduate and postgraduate students have the opportunity to learn and work in a wide variety of well-developed specialty centers. These include: the Center for Human Growth and Development, the Center for Research on Learning and Teaching, the Center for Research on Women and Gender, the Human Performance Center, the Institute of Gerontology, the Institute for Social Research (i.e., Survey Research Center, Research Center for Group Dynamics, Center for Political Studies), the NASA Center of Excellence in Man-Systems Research, the Cognitive Science and Machine Intelligence Laboratory, the Human Factors Division of the University of Michigan Transportation Research Institute, the Kresge Hearing Research Institute, the Neuroscience Laboratory, the Evolution and Human Behavior Program, the Children's Center, the Vision Research Laboratory, and the Women's Studies Program. In addition to these resources, the Michigan campus also offers an unusually diverse series of stimulating colloquium and seminar presentations, involving both local and visiting speakers, that contributes significantly to the available opportunities for professional growth and development.

Application Information: Graduate Admissions, Rackham Graduate School, 915 East Washington, Ann Arbor, MI 48109-1070. *Fee:* $75. *Online application:* https://www.applyweb.com/cgi-bin/app?s=umgrad.

Michigan, University of, Dearborn

Masters of Science in Psychology
College of Arts, Sciences, and Letters
4901 Evergreen Road
Dearborn, MI 48128
Telephone: (313) 593-5520
Graduate Program Director: Nancy H. Wrobel

E-mail: nwrobel@umich.edu
Web: http://umdearborn.edu/casl/psychology/

Orientation, Objectives, and Emphasis of Department

The Behavioral Sciences Department at the University of Michigan-Dearborn offers a Master of Science (MS) in Psychology in two specializations. The Master of Science in Clinical Health Psychology program trains mental health care providers to work in primary care settings, as well as more traditional clinical psychology settings. This track provides the coursework necessary to fulfill the state of Michigan requirements for the Limited License in Psychology. The Master of Science in Health Psychology program provides intense research training and is suited for students who wish to continue on to doctoral programs, without first gaining Master's-level licensure as a clinician.

Programs and Degrees Offered

Program	Degree	Application Deadline	Applications Received	Accepted	New Admits Enrolled (PT)	Total Enrolled (PT)	Degrees Awarded in 2014–2015	Median Years to Complete Degree	Dismissed/ Withdrew
Clinical Health Psychology	MA/MS	March 15 (Fall)	45	12	12 (0)	24 (2)			1
Health Psychology	MA/MS	March 15 (Fall)	5	4	4	10 (1)			

Internships/Practica

Students in the Clinical Health Psychology track will undertake practicum training. In practicum, students will attend a weekly class to discuss cases as well as work in a clinical setting approximately 20 hours each week. A variety of placement opportunities are available. Students will meet with the practicum coordinator the semester prior to beginning practicum to discuss practicum sites and locations of interest to the student. Every effort will be made to provide an opportunity for the student to interview at a practicum site within their interest and within a reasonable distance from the students' home. A total of six credit hours will be devoted to practicum over the course of two semesters. 250 hours will be logged each semester, providing the student with 500 hours total clinical experience.

Admissions

Entries appear in the following order: required test or GPA, minimum score (if required)/median score of students entering in 2015–2016.

Program	Degree	GRE-V	GRE-Q	GRE-Writing	GRE-Subject	Under-graduate GPA	Last 2 Years GPA	Psychol-ogy GPA	Master's GPA
Clinical Health Psychology	MA/MS	NA/NA	NA/NA	Not specified	Not specified	3/NA	Not specified	Not specified	Not specified
Health Psychology	MA/MS	NA/NA	NA/NA	Not specified	Not specified	3/NA	Not specified	Not specified	Not specified

Admissions Requirements:

Degree	GRE	GRE-Subject	Letters of Recom-mendation	Research Statement	Writing Sample	CV	Interview
Master's/Specialist	Required	None	3	Required	Optional	Optional	None

Please note if these criteria vary for different programs: Clinical experience would not be of particular consideration for the Health Psychology program.

Admissions Criteria:

GRE scores—high
Research experience—medium
Work experience—low
Clinically related public service—medium

GPA—high
Letters of recommendation—high
Statement of goals and objectives—high
Undergraduate psychology preparation—high

For additional information on admission requirements, visit http://umdearborn.edu/casl/685267/.

Department Demographics

	Male (PT)	Female (PT)	Total	African-American/ Black (PT)	Hispanic/ Latino (PT)	Asian/ Pacific Islander (PT)	American Indian/ Alaska Native (PT)	Caucasian/ White (PT)	Unknown (PT)	Multiethnic (PT)	ADA (PT)	Int'l (PT)
Students	5 (0)	29 (3)	37	0 (0)	1 (0)	2 (0)	0 (0)	28 (3)	0 (0)	3 (0)	0 (0)	2 (0)

Financial Information/Assistance

Tuition: For information on tuition costs, visit http://umdearborn.edu/rr_tuition-fees/. Tuition is subject to change.

Master's:
State residents: $633 per credit hour.
Nonstate residents: $1,133 per credit hour.

Financial Assistance:

	Teaching Assistantship (% Receiving)	Teaching Assistantship Tuition Remission	Research Assistantship (% Receiving)	Research Assistantship Tuition Remission	Fellowship (% Receiving)	Fellowship Tuition Remission
First-Year Student	NA (NA)	NA	NA (NA)	NA	$1,500 (8)	NA
Advanced Student	NA (NA)	NA	NA (NA)	NA	$1,500 (8)	NA

For additional information on financial assistance, visit http://umdearborn.edu/financialaid/.

Employment of Department Graduates

No information provided.

Additional Information

Housing and Day Care: On-campus housing is available. See the following website for more information: http://umdearborn.edu/campus-life/housing. On-campus day care facilities are available. See the following website for more information: http://umdearborn.edu/ecec/.

Information for Students With Physical Disabilities: See the following website: http://umdearborn.edu/cs_disability/.

Application Information: Fee: $60. *Online application:* http://www.casl.umd.umich.edu/695757/.

Northern Michigan University (2015 data)
Psychology Department
Arts and Sciences
1401 Presque Isle Avenue
Marquette, MI 49855
Telephone: (906) 227-2935
Head: Paul Andronis

E-mail: psych@nmu.edu
Web: http://psychology.nmu.edu/

Orientation, Objectives, and Emphasis of Department
The Psychology Department offers a master of science degree that provides students with a thorough grounding in general psychology, preparing the student for doctoral programs and/or positions that require the master's degree. The MS degree in psychology at NMU provides (a) intensive student-initiated training in a variety of areas of psychology, (b) the statistical and methodological knowledge required to examine basic or applied issues and to function as an applied psychologist, and (c) an appreciation of the scientific basis of all fields of psychology. Many graduates of this program will pursue training at the doctoral level while others will be prepared to work in a wide variety of occupations in which an advanced understanding of psychology, research methodology, or human research is of value.

Programs and Degrees Offered

Program	Degree	Application Deadline	Applications Received	Accepted	New Admits Enrolled (PT)	Total Enrolled (PT)	Degrees Awarded in 2014–2015	Median Years to Complete Degree	Dismissed/ Withdrew
Training and Performance Improvement	MA/MS	Rolling							
General Psychology	MA/MS	Rolling							

Admissions

Entries appear in the following order: required test or GPA, minimum score (if required)/median score of students entering in 2015–2016.

Program	Degree	GRE-V	GRE-Q	GRE-Writing	GRE-Subject	Under-graduate GPA	Last 2 Years GPA	Psychol-ogy GPA	Master's GPA
Training and Performance Improvement	MA/MS	Not specified	Not specified	Not specified	Not specified	NA/NA	Not specified	Not specified	Not specified
General Psychology	MA/MS	Not specified	Not specified	Not specified	Not specified	3/NA	Not specified	Not specified	Not specified

Admissions Requirements:

Degree	GRE	GRE-Subject	Letters of Recom-mendation	Research Statement	Writing Sample	CV	Interview
Master's/Specialist	None	None	3	Required	None	Required	None

Admissions Criteria:

Research experience—medium
Work experience—low
GPA—medium

Letters of recommendation—high
Statement of goals and objectives—high

For additional information on admission requirements, visit http://psychology.nmu.edu/grad.php.

Department Demographics

	Male (PT)	Female (PT)	Total	African-American/ Black (PT)	Hispanic/ Latino (PT)	Asian/ Pacific Islander (PT)	American Indian/ Alaska Native (PT)	Caucasian/ White (PT)	Unknown	Multiethnic (PT)	ADA (PT)	Int'l (PT)
Students	30 (10)	32 (20)	92	3 (1)	3 (3)	0 (0)	2 (2)	48 (23)	0 (0)	2 (0)	0 (0)	4 (1)

Financial Information/Assistance

Tuition: For information on tuition costs, visit http://www.nmu.edu/tuition. Tuition is subject to change. Additional fees are assessed to students beyond the costs of tuition for the following: Student Activity Fee and University Fee.

Master's:
State residents: $7,715 per academic year.
State residents: $441 per credit hour.
Nonstate residents: $10,811 per academic year.
Nonstate residents: $634 per credit hour.

Financial Assistance:

	Teaching Assistantship (% Receiving)	Teaching Assistantship Tuition Remission	Research Assistantship (% Receiving)	Research Assistantship Tuition Remission	Fellowship (% Receiving)	Fellowship Tuition Remission
First-Year Student	NA (NA)	Full	NA (NA)	NA	NA (NA)	NA
Advanced Student	NA (NA)	Full	NA (NA)	NA	NA (NA)	NA

For additional information on financial assistance, visit http://www.nmu.edu/graduatestudies/node/53.

Employment of Department Graduates

No information provided.

Additional Information

Housing and Day Care: On-campus housing is available. See the following website for more information: http://www.nmu.edu/housing/. No on-campus day care facilities are available.

Information for Students With Physical Disabilities: See the following website: http://www.nmu.edu/disabilityservices/.

Special Facilities or Resources: The Psychology Department houses active laboratories for human and animal research. These laboratories include an Near-Infrared Optical Imaging, a 64 channel EEG, extensive animal behavioral equipment, confocal laser-scanning microscope, and access to an MRI.

Application Information: Office of Graduate Education and Research, Northern Michigan University, 1401 Presque Isle Avenue, Marquette, MI 49855. *Fee:* $50.

Oakland University

Department of Psychology
College of Arts and Sciences
2200 North Squirrel Road
Rochester, MI 48309
Telephone: (248) 370-2300
Chairperson: Todd Shackelford

E-mail: zeiglerh@oakland.edu
Web: http://www.oakland.edu/psychology

Orientation, Objectives, and Emphasis of Department

Our graduate programs are intended to provide graduate students with the knowledge, skills, and experiences necessary to become successful consumers and producers of psychological science. Psychology is a broad discipline that interfaces with the biological and social sciences and our programs are organized around two concentrations that together encapsulate the breadth of psychological science: (1) Biological and Basic Processes and (2) Social and Behavioral Processes. These concentrations represent two broad areas that focus on phenomena from different orientations in moderately overlapping but distinguishable content areas. Students seeking the MS degree will be broadly exposed to the content and methods in both concentrations. Students seeking the PhD degree will have similar broad exposure to both concentrations which will be extended by an intensive inquiry specialized in one concentration. As a result, students in the PhD degree program will apply for admission in one concentration (either the Biological and Basic Processes concentration or the Social and Behavioral Processes concentration) whereas students in the MS degree program will be required to distribute their course work across these concentrations.

Programs and Degrees Offered

Program	Degree	Application Deadline	Applications Received	Accepted	New Admits Enrolled (PT)	Total Enrolled (PT)	Degrees Awarded in 2014–2015	Median Years to Complete Degree	Dismissed/ Withdrew
Experimental Psychology	MA/MS	January 15 (Fall)	24	11	11	24	9		0
Experimental Psychology	PhD	January 15 (Fall)	58	2	2 (0)	10 (0)	0		0

Admissions

Entries appear in the following order: required test or GPA, minimum score (if required)/median score of students entering in 2015–2016.

Program	Degree	GRE-V	GRE-Q	GRE-Writing	GRE-Subject	Under-graduate GPA	Last 2 Years GPA	Psychology GPA	Master's GPA
Experimental Psychology	MA/MS	Not specified	Not specified	Not specified	Not specified	Not specified	Not specified	Not specified	Not specified

Admissions *(con't.)*

Program	Degree	GRE-V	GRE-Q	GRE-Writing	GRE-Subject	Under-graduate GPA	Last 2 Years GPA	Psychol-ogy GPA	Master's GPA
Experimental Psychology	PhD	Not specified	Not specified	Not specified	Not specified	Not specified	Not specified	Not specified	Not specified

Admissions Requirements:

Degree	GRE	GRE-Subject	Letters of Recom-mendation	Research Statement	Writing Sample	CV	Interview
Master's/Specialist	Required	Optional	3	Required	Optional	Optional	None
Doctoral	Required	Optional	3	Required	Optional	Optional	Required

Admissions Criteria:

GRE scores—high
Research experience—high
GPA—high

Letters of recommendation—high
Interview—high
Statement of goals and objectives—high

Department Demographics

	Male (PT)	Female (PT)	Total	African-American/ Black (PT)	Hispanic/ Latino (PT)	Asian/ Pacific Islander (PT)	American Indian/ Alaska Native (PT)	Caucasian/ White (PT)	Unknown	Multiethnic (PT)	ADA (PT)	Int'l (PT)
Students	17 (0)	13 (0)	30	1 (0)	2 (0)	1 (0)	0 (0)	24 (0)	0 (0)	2 (0)	0 (0)	2 (0)

Financial Information/Assistance

Tuition: For information on tuition costs, visit http://www.oakland.edu/tuition. Tuition is subject to change.

Doctoral:
State residents: $655 per credit hour.
Nonstate residents: $1,027 per credit hour.

Master's:
State residents: $655 per credit hour.
Nonstate residents: $1,027 per credit hour.

Financial Assistance:

	Teaching Assistantship (% Receiving)	Teaching Assistantship Tuition Remission	Research Assistantship (% Receiving)	Research Assistantship Tuition Remission	Fellowship (% Receiving)	Fellowship Tuition Remission
First-Year Student	$14,000 (NA)	Full	NA (NA)	NA	NA (NA)	NA
Advanced Student	$14,000 (NA)	Full	NA (NA)	NA	NA (NA)	NA

For additional information on financial assistance, visit http://www.oakland.edu/financialservices/grad.

Employment of Department Graduates

Master's:
Enrolled in a psychology doctoral program: 3
Enrolled in another graduate/professional program: 2
Employed in other positions at a higher education institution: 1
Employed in business or industry: 4
Still seeking employment: 1
Total: 11

Additional Information

Housing and Day Care: On-campus housing is available. See the following website for more information: http://www.oakland.edu/housing/apply. On-campus day care facilities are available. See the following website for more information: http://www.oakland.edu/lowry/.

Information for Students With Physical Disabilities: See the following website: http://www.oakland.edu/dss.

Application Information: Oakland University, Graduate Admissions, 520 O'Dowd Hall, Rochester, MI 48309-4401. *Fee:* $0. *Online application:* http://www.oakland.edu/grad/apply/.

Wayne State University
Department of Psychology
College of Liberal Arts and Sciences
5057 Woodward Avenue, 7th Floor
Detroit, MI 48202
Telephone: (313) 577-2800
Chairperson: Boris Baltes

E-mail: aallen@wayne.edu
Web: http://clas.wayne.edu/psychology/

Orientation, Objectives, and Emphasis of Department
This department strives to select graduate students with a strong educational background and outstanding potential and to train them to be knowledgeable, ethical practitioners and research scholars in their chosen areas. Initial broad training is followed by specialized training.

Programs and Degrees Offered

Program	Degree	Application Deadline	Applications Received	Accepted	New Admits Enrolled (PT)	Total Enrolled (PT)	Degrees Awarded in 2014–2015	Median Years to Complete Degree	Dismissed/ Withdrew
Clinical Psychology	PhD	December 1 (Fall)	232	12	9	61	7	7	0
Behavioral and Cognitive Neuroscience	PhD	December 1 (Fall)	28	3	2	9	4	6	1
Industrial/ Organizational Psychology	PhD	December 1 (Fall)	54	11	1	19	3	5	2
Cognitive, Developmental & Social Psychology	PhD	December 1 (Fall)	40	7	4	25	2	5	2
Industrial/ Organizational Psychology	MA/MS	May 1 (Fall), September 1 (Winter), January 1 (Summer)	30	15	0 (9)	(24)	8	2	0

APA Accreditation
Clinical PhD: Student Outcome Data website: http://clasweb.clas.wayne.edu/psychology/ClinicalPsychology.

Doctoral Degree (PhD Clinical Psychology): For those doctoral students for whom a professional internship was required in this program prior to graduation:
Total students who applied for an internship: 9
Total students who obtained an internship: 9
Total students who obtained a paid internship: 9

Total students who obtained an unpaid internship: 0
Total students who were placed in APA/CPA-accredited internships: 9
Total students placed in internships not APA/CPA-accredited, but listed with the Association of Psychology Postdoctoral and Internship Centers (APPIC): 0
Total students placed in internships conforming to guidelines of the Council of Directors of School Psychology Programs (CDSPP): 0
Total students placed in internships that were not APA/CPA-accredited, APPIC or CDSSP listed: 0

Internships/Practica

The clinical program has a required 500-hour assessment practicum and a 500-hour therapy practicum at our in-house training clinic. We also have a network of approximately 25 external placements, supervised by psychologists, at a range of clinical settings, which our graduate students attend in their third, fourth, and/or fifth year. All clinical students are expected to complete a full-year predoctoral, APA-accredited internship.

Admissions

Entries appear in the following order: required test or GPA, minimum score (if required)/median score of students entering in 2015–2016.

Program	Degree	GRE-V	GRE-Q	GRE-Writing	GRE-Subject	Under-graduate GPA	Last 2 Years GPA	Psychol-ogy GPA	Master's GPA
Clinical Psychology	PhD	NA/160	NA/158	NA/4.5	Not specified	3/3.79	Not specified	Not specified	Not specified
Behavioral and Cognitive Neuroscience	PhD	NA/NA	NA/NA	NA/NA	Not specified	3/NA	Not specified	Not specified	Not specified
Industrial/ Organizational Psychology	PhD	NA/NA	NA/NA	Not specified	Not specified	3/NA	Not specified	Not specified	Not specified
Cognitive, Developmental & Social Psychology	PhD	NA/NA	NA/NA	NA/NA	Not specified	3/NA	Not specified	Not specified	Not specified
Industrial/ Organizational Psychology	MA/MS	NA/NA	NA/NA	NA/NA	Not specified	3/NA	Not specified	Not specified	Not specified

Admissions Requirements:

Degree	GRE	GRE-Subject	Letters of Recommendation	Research Statement	Writing Sample	CV	Interview
Master's/Specialist	Required	None	2	Required	Optional	Recommended	None
Doctoral	Required	None	3	Required	Optional	Recommended	Optional

Please note if these criteria vary for different programs: Interviews vary by area.

Admissions Criteria:

GRE scores—high
Research experience—high
Work experience—medium
Clinically related public service—medium
GPA—high

Letters of recommendation—high
Interview—high
Statement of goals and objectives—high
Undergraduate psychology preparation—medium

For additional information on admission requirements, visit the following website: http://clasweb.clas.wayne.edu/psychology/DoctoralAdmissionRequirements.

Department Demographics

	Male (PT)	Female (PT)	Total	African-American/ Black (PT)	Hispanic/ Latino (PT)	Asian/ Pacific Islander (PT)	American Indian/ Alaska Native (PT)	Caucasian/ White (PT)	Unknown	Multiethnic (PT)	ADA (PT)	Int'l (PT)
Students	37 (11)	77 (13)	138	6 (1)	4 (1)	12 (2)	3 (0)	88 (20)	0 (0)	0 (0)	0 (0)	9 (0)

Financial Information/Assistance

Tuition: For information on tuition costs, visit http://reg.wayne.edu/students/tuition.php. Tuition is subject to change. Additional fees are assessed to students beyond the costs of tuition for the following: student service credit hour fee: $47.45, registration fee: $274.60.

Doctoral:
State residents: $590 per credit hour.
Nonstate residents: $1,278 per credit hour.

Master's:
State residents: $590 per credit hour.
Nonstate residents: $1,278 per credit hour.

Financial Assistance:

	Teaching Assistantship (% Receiving)	Teaching Assistantship Tuition Remission	Research Assistantship (% Receiving)	Research Assistantship Tuition Remission	Fellowship (% Receiving)	Fellowship Tuition Remission
First-Year Student	$18,000 (NA)	Full	$18,000 (NA)	Full	$18,000 (NA)	Full
Advanced Student	$18,000 (NA)	Full	$18,000 (NA)	Full	$18,000 (NA)	Full

Employment of Department Graduates

No information provided.

Additional Information

Housing and Day Care: On-campus housing is available. See the following website for more information: http://housing.wayne.edu/. On-campus day care facilities are available. See the following website for more information: http://mpsi.wayne.edu/education/childhood.php.

Information for Students With Physical Disabilities: See the following website: http://studentdisability.wayne.edu/.

Special Facilities or Resources: The behavioral and cognitive neuroscience area participates in the university neuroscience program. Excellent laboratory facilities are available in neurobiology, neuropharmacology, psychopharmacology, neuropsychology, and ethology. Several faculty in behavioral and cognitive neuroscience and other areas in the department work in the area of substance abuse. The clinical program emphasizes psychotherapy, community mental health, diagnostics, alcohol abuse issues, neuropsychology, and child and geropsychology. Clinical practice and research experience are obtained in a variety of clinical placements and in our own clinic. The cognitive program emphasizes cognition theory and its application to applied problems. The developmental area emphasizes life-span studies and is affiliated with the Institute of Gerontology. The social psychology program has both basic and applied research emphases. Well-equipped laboratories in the department and at the Merrill-Palmer Institute, which is affiliated with the department, are available for cognitive, social, and developmental research. In addition, social psychology uses its urban setting to carry out field studies. The industrial/organizational area emphasizes organizational psychology, personnel research, and field placements. Excellent computer facilities and libraries support research in all areas.

Application Information: Graduate Office, Psychology Department, WSU, 5057 Woodward Avenue, 7th Floor, Detroit, MI 48202. *Fee:* $0. *Online application:* https://cardinal.wayne.edu/apply/gr.php.

Wayne State University

Division of Theoretical and Behavioral Foundations-Educational Psychology
College of Education
Detroit, MI 48202
Telephone: (313) 557-1614
Chairperson: Stephen B. Hillman

E-mail: s.b.hillman@wayne.edu
Web: http://coe.wayne.edu/tbf/educational-psychology/index.php

Orientation, Objectives, and Emphasis of Department

The department offers a BCBA program leading to either a certificate or an MEd degree, MA programs in School and Community Psychology and Counseling Psychology, and a PhD program in Educational Psychology with a concentration in Learning and Instruction Sciences. The program orientations are eclectic (except for the BCBA program), using the scientist–practitioner model, with emphasis on application of theory at the master's degree level and on theoretical issues at the PhD level.

Programs and Degrees Offered

Program	Degree	Application Deadline	Applica-tions Received	Accepted	New Admits Enrolled (PT)	Total Enrolled (PT)	Degrees Awarded in 2014–2015	Median Years to Complete Degree	Dismissed/ Withdrew
School and Community Psychology	MA/MS	February 15 (Fall)	32	14	14	26 (12)	14	2.25	0
Counseling Psychology	MA/MS	February 15 (Fall)	26	15	15	32	12	2.5	0
Bcba Certificate	Other	Rolling	20	15	(15)	(35)	8	3	4
Learning and Instruction Sciences	PhD	February 15 (Fall)	3	0	0	0	2	6	0

Admissions

Entries appear in the following order: required test or GPA, minimum score (if required)/median score of students entering in 2015–2016.

Program	Degree	GRE-V	GRE-Q	GRE-Writing	GRE-Subject	Under-graduate GPA	Last 2 Years GPA	Psychol-ogy GPA	Master's GPA
School and Community Psychology	MA/MS	NA/NA	NA/NA	NA/NA	Not specified	3/NA	NA/NA	NA/NA	Not specified
Counseling Psychology	MA/MS	NA/NA	NA/NA	NA/NA	Not specified	NA/NA	NA/NA	NA/NA	Not specified
BCBA Certificate	Other	Not specified	Not specified	Not specified	Not specified	Not specified	Not specified	Not specified	Not specified
Learning and Instruction Sciences	PhD	NA/NA	NA/NA	NA/NA	Not specified	NA/NA	NA/NA	NA/NA	NA/NA

Admissions Requirements:

Degree	GRE	GRE-Subject	Letters of Recom-mendation	Research Statement	Writing Sample	CV	Interview
Master's/Specialist	Required	None	3	Required	Optional	Optional	Required
Doctoral	Required	Optional	3	Required	Required	Optional	Required

Admissions Criteria:

GRE scores—medium
Research experience—medium
Work experience—medium
Clinically related public service—medium
GPA—high

Letters of recommendation—high
Interview—high
Statement of goals and objectives—high
Undergraduate psychology preparation—high

Department Demographics

	Male (PT)	Female (PT)	Total	African-American/ Black (PT)	Hispanic/ Latino (PT)	Asian/ Pacific Islander (PT)	American Indian/ Alaska Native (PT)	Caucasian/ White (PT)	Unknown	Multiethnic (PT)	ADA (PT)	Int'l (PT)
Students	2 (3)	24 (9)	38	4 (2)	0 (0)	0 (0)	0 (0)	32 (58)	0 (0)	0 (0)	0 (0)	0 (0)

Financial Information/Assistance

Tuition: For information on tuition costs, visit http://reg.wayne.edu/students/tuition.php. Tuition is subject to change. Additional fees are assessed to students beyond the costs of tuition for the following: testing materials. Tuition costs vary by program.

Doctoral:
State residents: $14,144 per academic year.
State residents: $533 per credit hour.
Nonstate residents: $28,242 per academic year.
Nonstate residents: $1,177 per credit hour.

Master's:
State residents: $14,144 per academic year.
State residents: $533 per credit hour.
Nonstate residents: $28,242 per academic year.
Nonstate residents: $1,177 per credit hour.

Financial Assistance:

	Teaching Assistantship (% Receiving)	Teaching Assistantship Tuition Remission	Research Assistantship (% Receiving)	Research Assistantship Tuition Remission	Fellowship (% Receiving)	Fellowship Tuition Remission
First-Year Student	NA (NA)	NA	NA (NA)	NA	NA (NA)	Full
Advanced Student	NA (NA)	NA	NA (NA)	NA	NA (NA)	Full

For additional information on financial assistance, visit http://coe.wayne.edu/admissions/scholarship.php.

Employment of Department Graduates

Master's:
Enrolled in a psychology doctoral program: 2
Employed in a professional position in a school system: 12
Employed in a community mental health/counseling center: 14
Total: 28

Doctoral:
Employed in independent practice: 3
Employed in a professional position in a school system: 5
Employed in a community mental health/counseling center: 2
Total: 10

Additional Information

Housing and Day Care: On-campus housing is available. See the following website for more information: http://housing.wayne.edu/. On-campus day care facilities are available. See the following website for more information: http://coe.wayne.edu/ted/childhood/ec-center-index.php; http://mpsi.wayne.edu/education/early-childhood.php.

Information for Students With Physical Disabilities: See the following website: http://studentdisability.wayne.edu/.

Application Information: Department Chair. *Fee:* $50. *Online application:* https://cardinal.wayne.edu/apply/gr.php.

Western Michigan University

Counselor Education & Counseling Psychology
College of Education
3521 Sangren Hall, WMU, 1903 West Michigan Avenue
Kalamazoo, MI 49008-5226
Telephone: (269) 387-5100
Chairperson: Patrick H. Munley

E-mail: patrick.munley@wmich.edu
Web: http://www.wmich.edu/cecp/

Orientation, Objectives, and Emphasis of Department

The department prepares competent, ethical and culturally sensitive counseling psychologists at the master's and doctoral levels. The program has a strong emphasis on multicultural training and on maintaining a multicultural/diverse faculty and student body. The faculty remains committed to integrating multiculturalism, with an emphasis on race and racism, into all aspects of the program. The curriculum and practical experiences are designed to ensure professional competency in theory, research, and practice and facilitate their integration. Program graduates are typically employed in a variety of settings including academic departments, university counseling centers, community mental health agencies, hospitals, and independent practices. The curriculum was developed by the Counseling Psychology faculty and is based on guidelines and principles of the American Psychological Association (APA) for accreditation of professional psychology programs. Requirements include course work in the basic scientific core of psychology including research design and statistics, the biological bases of behavior, cognitive-affective bases of behavior, social bases of behavior, individual behavior and human development, and the history and systems of psychology.

Programs and Degrees Offered

Program	Degree	Application Deadline	Applications Received	Accepted	New Admits Enrolled (PT)	Total Enrolled (PT)	Degrees Awarded in 2014–2015	Median Years to Complete Degree	Dismissed/ Withdrew
Counseling Psychology	MA/MS	January 15 (Fall), September 15 (Spring), January 15 (Summer), Rolling	97	79	31 (13)	127 (52)	41		0
Counseling Psychology	PhD	December 10 (Fall)	46	9	9 (0)	44 (10)	8	8	0

APA Accreditation

Counseling PhD: Student Outcome Data website: http://www.wmich.edu/cecp/doctoral-counseling-psychology-outcomes.

Doctoral Degree (PhD Counseling Psychology): For those doctoral students for whom a professional internship was required in this program prior to graduation:
Total students who applied for an internship: 12
Total students who obtained an internship: 12
Total students who obtained a paid internship: 12
Total students who obtained an unpaid internship: 0
Total students who were placed in APA/CPA-accredited internships: 11
Total students placed in internships not APA/CPA-accredited, but listed with the Association of Psychology Postdoctoral and Internship Centers (APPIC): 1
Total students placed in internships conforming to guidelines of the Council of Directors of School Psychology Programs (CDSPP): 0
Total students placed in internships that were not APA/CPA-accredited, APPIC or CDSSP listed: 0

Master's Degree (MA/MS Counseling Psychology): An internship experience, such as a final research project or "capstone" experience is required of graduates.

Internships/Practica

Master's-level practica are available in a wide range of settings. Doctoral practica are also available in hospitals, clinics, university counseling centers, etc. Doctoral students are required to participate in the national match for predoctoral internships and are expected to obtain placement at an APA-accredited site.

Admissions

Entries appear in the following order: required test or GPA, minimum score (if required)/median score of students entering in 2015–2016.

Program	Degree	GRE-V	GRE-Q	GRE-Writing	GRE-Subject	Under-graduate GPA	Last 2 Years GPA	Psychol-ogy GPA	Master's GPA
Counseling Psychology	MA/MS	Not specified	Not specified	Not specified	Not specified	Not specified	Not specified	Not specified	Not specified
Counseling Psychology	PhD	NA/NA	NA/NA	NA/NA	Not specified	NA/NA	Not specified	NA/NA	NA/NA

Admissions Requirements:

Degree	GRE	GRE-Subject	Letters of Recommendation	Research Statement	Writing Sample	CV	Interview
Master's/Specialist	None	None	3	Required	Required	Required	Optional
Doctoral	Required	Recommended	3	Required	Optional	Required	Required

Please note if these criteria vary for different programs: The criteria noted below are primarily for the doctoral program. The master's program is a terminal degree program that places less emphasis on research than does the doctoral program. The General GRE is required for individuals applying to the doctoral program following a master's degree. Applicants to the doctoral program who hold only a bachelor degree must also take the Psychology Subject-GRE. There is no GRE requirement for the master's degree in Counseling Psychology.

Admissions Criteria:

GRE scores—medium
Research experience—high
Work experience—medium
Clinically related public service—low
GPA—high

Letters of recommendation—high
Interview—high
Statement of goals and objectives—high
Undergraduate psychology preparation—medium
Multicultural awareness—high

For additional information on admission requirements, visit http://www.wmich.edu/cecp/admissions.

Department Demographics

	Male (PT)	Female (PT)	Total	African-American/ Black (PT)	Hispanic/ Latino (PT)	Asian/ Pacific Islander (PT)	American Indian/ Alaska Native (PT)	Caucasian/ White (PT)	Unknown	Multiethnic (PT)	ADA (PT)	Int'l (PT)
Students	40 (12)	131 (50)	233	33 (9)	7 (2)	5 (2)	1 (1)	111 (41)	4 (3)	10 (4)	0 (0)	6 (2)

Financial Information/Assistance

Tuition: For information on tuition costs, visit http://www.wmich.edu/registrar/tuition. Tuition is subject to change.

Doctoral:
State residents: $12,727 per academic year.
State residents: $530 per credit hour.
Nonstate residents: $26,958 per academic year.
Nonstate residents: $1,123 per credit hour.

Master's:
State residents: $12,727 per academic year.
State residents: $530 per credit hour.
Nonstate residents: $26,958 per academic year.
Nonstate residents: $1,123 per credit hour.

Financial Assistance:

	Teaching Assistantship (% Receiving)	Teaching Assistantship Tuition Remission	Research Assistantship (% Receiving)	Research Assistantship Tuition Remission	Fellowship (% Receiving)	Fellowship Tuition Remission
First-Year Student	$25,320 (NA)	Full	$25,320 (NA)	Full	NA (NA)	Full
Advanced Student	$25,320 (NA)	Full	$25,320 (NA)	Full	NA (NA)	Full

For additional information on financial assistance, visit http://www.wmich.edu/cecp/scholarships.

Employment of Department Graduates

Doctoral:
Enrolled in a postdoctoral residency/fellowship: 1
Employed in independent practice: 1
Employed in academic position at a 2-year/4-year college: 1
Employed in other positions at a higher education institution: 3
Employed in government agency: 1
Do not know: 1
Total: 8

Additional Information

Housing and Day Care: On-campus housing is available. See the following website for more information: http://www.wmich.edu/housing/. On-campus day care facilities are available. See the following website for more information: http://www.wmich.edu/childcare/index.html.

Information for Students With Physical Disabilities: See the following website: http://www.wmich.edu/disabilityservices/.

Special Facilities or Resources: The department's primary training facility is the Center for Counseling and Psychological Services, which includes interview rooms, two group/family therapy rooms, and a seminar room; it is equipped with audio and video recording systems and provides for observation and telephone supervision. The department also maintains a comparable training clinic at the Graduate Center in Grand Rapids, Michigan. A wide variety of regional resources, including community clinics, schools, hospitals, and private clinics, are available to students.

Application Information: Department of Counselor Education & Counseling Psychology, 1903 West Michigan Avenue, WMU, Kalamazoo, MI 49008-5226. *Fee:* $50. *Online application:* https://app.applyyourself.com/?id=wmichgrad.

Metropolitan State University (2015 data)
Psychology/MA in Psychology Program
College of Health, Community and Professional Studies
1450 Energy Park Drive
St. Paul, MN 55108-5218
Telephone: (651)999-5820
Chairperson: Gary Starr

E-mail: caitlin.mahoney@metrostate.edu
Web: http://www.metrostate.edu/msweb/explore/gradstudies/masters/psych/

Orientation, Objectives, and Emphasis of Department
The Master of Arts in Psychology program emphasizes the application of psychology in the form of community-based interventions that are rooted in the wisdom and work of members of each community. It is an innovative program, rooted in a community psychology model, in which students learn to combine theory, research, and practice to achieve positive social and community change. Prevention (rather than treatment) is a primary focus along with empowerment, health promotion, community organizing and community development. The applied social psychology track provides students with a critical perspective of human behavior in relation to groups, addressing related topics such as conformity, environment and ecology, and social interaction.

Programs and Degrees Offered

Program	Degree	Application Deadline	Applications Received	Accepted	New Admits Enrolled (PT)	Total Enrolled (PT)	Degrees Awarded in 2014–2015	Median Years to Complete Degree	Dismissed/ Withdrew
Psychology	MA/MS	March 1 (Fall), September 1 (Spring)	24	16	2 (5)	8 (16)	2	3.5	1

Internships/Practica
Community-based practica are arranged in consultation with the student and their faculty advisor. Practica are developed and implemented in cooperation with Metropolitan State University's Center for Community Based Learning.

Admissions
Entries appear in the following order: required test or GPA, minimum score (if required)/median score of students entering in 2015–2016.

Program	Degree	GRE-V	GRE-Q	GRE-Writing	GRE-Subject	Under-graduate GPA	Last 2 Years GPA	Psychology GPA	Master's GPA
Psychology	MA/MS	Not specified	Not specified	Not specified	Not specified	3/NA	Not specified	Not specified	Not specified

Admissions Requirements:

Degree	GRE	GRE-Subject	Letters of Recommendation	Research Statement	Writing Sample	CV	Interview
Master's/Specialist	None	None	3	Required	Optional	Required	Recommended

Admissions Criteria:
Research experience—medium
Work experience—medium
GPA—high
Letters of recommendation—high

Interview—high
Statement of goals and objectives—high
Undergraduate psychology preparation—medium
Community-based work—medium

For additional information on admission requirements, visit http://www.metrostate.edu/msweb/explore/gradstudies/masters/psych/applying.html.

Department Demographics

	Male (PT)	Female (PT)	Total	African-American/ Black (PT)	Hispanic/ Latino (PT)	Asian/ Pacific Islander (PT)	American Indian/ Alaska Native (PT)	Caucasian/ White (PT)	Unknown (PT)	Multiethnic (PT)	ADA (PT)	Int'l (PT)
Students	2 (3)	12 (10)	27	4 (2)	0 (0)	1 (0)	0 (1)	9 (10)	0 (0)	0 (0)	0 (0)	0 (0)

Financial Information/Assistance

Tuition: For information on tuition costs, visit http://www.metrostate.edu/msweb/pathway/tuition/costs.html. Tuition is subject to change.

Master's:
State residents: $336 per credit hour.
Nonstate residents: $672 per credit hour.

Financial Assistance:

	Teaching Assistantship (% Receiving)	Teaching Assistantship Tuition Remission	Research Assistantship (% Receiving)	Research Assistantship Tuition Remission	Fellowship (% Receiving)	Fellowship Tuition Remission
First-Year Student	NA (NA)	NA	NA (4)	Full	NA (NA)	NA
Advanced Student	NA (NA)	NA	NA (NA)	NA	NA (NA)	NA

For additional information on financial assistance, visit http://www.metrostate.edu/msweb/pathway/aid/index.html.

Employment of Department Graduates

Master's:
Enrolled in another graduate/professional program: 2
Employed in other positions at a higher education institution: 3
Employed in a professional position in a school system: 1
Employed in business or industry: 2
Not seeking employment: 1
Other employment position: 4
Total: 13

Additional Information

Housing and Day Care: No on-campus housing is available. No on-campus day care facilities are available.

Information for Students With Physical Disabilities: See the following website: http://www.metrostate.edu/msweb/pathway/academic_success/disability/.

Special Facilities or Resources: The graduate division in psychology at Metropolitan State now provides opportunities for students to participate in a variety of community service activities that supplement their graduate academic work experiences (i.e., community gardening programs, volunteer services within the community).

Application Information: MA Psychology Program Coordinator, 1450 Energy Park Drive, St. Paul, MN 55108-5218. *Fee:* $20.

Minnesota School of Professional Psychology at Argosy University

Clinical Psychology
College of Clinical Psychology
1515 Central Parkway
Eagan, MN 55121
Telephone: (651) 286-7953
Program Dean: Donna Johnson, PhD, LP

E-mail: kkile@argosy.edu
Web: http://clinical.argosy.edu/locations/twin-cities/

Orientation, Objectives, and Emphasis of Department

The Clinical Psychology (PsyD) program at the Minnesota School of Professional Psychology at Argosy University emphasizes the development of knowledge, skills, and attitudes essential in the formation of professional psychologists who are committed to the ethical provision of quality services. To prepare students for entry-level practice as clinical psychologists, the doctoral program teaches (1) knowledge in the history and systems of psychology; the theoretical and empirical foundations of clinical psychology, including the developmental, biopsychosocial, cognitive, and affective bases of behavior; and the scientific methodology which serves as the foundation for empirically based clinical practice; (2) skills in the identification, assessment, and diagnosis of clinical concerns; problem remediation and application of empirically supported intervention procedures; and the critical review of empirical literature and objective evaluation of clinical outcomes; (3) attitudes consistent with the ethical principles governing professional clinical practice, including concern for client welfare and respect for client diversity; and (4) skills in interpersonal functioning and the development of therapeutic relationships in a clinical setting.

Programs and Degrees Offered

Program	Degree	Application Deadline	Applica-tions Received	Accepted	New Admits Enrolled (PT)	Total Enrolled (PT)	Degrees Awarded in 2014–2015	Median Years to Complete Degree	Dismissed/Withdrew
Clinical Psychology	PsyD	February 1 (Fall)	72	32	24 (0)	129 (0)	42	6	5

APA Accreditation

Clinical PsyD: Student Outcome Data website: http://clinical.argosy.edu/locations/twin-cities/clinical-psychology-doctor-of-psychology/.

Doctoral Degree (PsyD Clinical Psychology): For those doctoral students for whom a professional internship was required in this program prior to graduation:
Total students who applied for an internship: 25
Total students who obtained an internship: 23
Total students who obtained a paid internship: 23
Total students who obtained an unpaid internship: 0
Total students who were placed in APA/CPA-accredited internships: 10
Total students placed in internships not APA/CPA-accredited, but listed with the Association of Psychology Postdoctoral and Internship Centers (APPIC): 13
Total students placed in internships conforming to guidelines of the Council of Directors of School Psychology Programs (CDSPP): 0
Total students placed in internships that were not APA/CPA-accredited, APPIC or CDSSP listed: 0

Internships/Practica

The Minneapolis/St. Paul Metropolitan Internship Consortium is affiliated with the program and accepts students only from the Minnesota School of Professional Psychology at Argosy University. Currently, two agencies are members of the consortium: Relate Counseling Center and Argosy Counseling Service.

Admissions

Entries appear in the following order: required test or GPA, minimum score (if required)/median score of students entering in 2015–2016.

Program	Degree	GRE-V	GRE-Q	GRE-Writing	GRE-Subject	Under-graduate GPA	Last 2 Years GPA	Psychol-ogy GPA	Master's GPA
Clinical Psychology	PsyD	Not specified	Not specified	Not specified	Not specified	3/NA	Not specified	Not specified	3.5/NA

Admissions Requirements:

Degree	GRE	GRE-Subject	Letters of Recommendation	Research Statement	Writing Sample	CV	Interview
Doctoral	Optional	Optional	3	Required	None	Required	Required

Admissions Criteria:

Research experience—low
Work experience—high
Clinically related public service—medium
GPA—high

Letters of recommendation—high
Interview—high
Statement of goals and objectives—medium
Undergraduate psychology preparation—medium

For additional information on admission requirements, visit http://clinical.argosy.edu/locations/twin-cities/clinical-psychology-doctor-of-psychology/admissions.

Department Demographics

	Male (PT)	Female (PT)	Total	African-American/ Black (PT)	Hispanic/ Latino (PT)	Asian/ Pacific Islander (PT)	American Indian/ Alaska Native (PT)	Caucasian/ White (PT)	Unknown	Multiethnic (PT)	ADA (PT)	Int'l (PT)
Students	37 (0)	92 (0)	129	2 (0)	3 (0)	5 (0)	0 (0)	112 (0)	1 (0)	6 (0)	6 (0)	1 (0)

Financial Information/Assistance

Tuition: For information on tuition costs, visit https://www.argosy.edu/affordability/tuition-and-fees. Tuition is subject to change. Additional fees are assessed to students beyond the costs of tuition for the following: Program Fees: $3,077.

Doctoral:
State residents: $37,184 per academic year.
State residents: $1,162 per credit hour.
Nonstate residents: $37,184 per academic year.
Nonstate residents: $1,162 per credit hour.

Financial Assistance:

	Teaching Assistantship (% Receiving)	Teaching Assistantship Tuition Remission	Research Assistantship (% Receiving)	Research Assistantship Tuition Remission	Fellowship (% Receiving)	Fellowship Tuition Remission
First-Year Student	NA (NA)	NA	NA (NA)	NA	$9,500 (30)	Partial
Advanced Student	$2,880 (10)	NA	NA (NA)	NA	$3,000 (8)	Partial

For additional information on financial assistance, visit https://www.argosy.edu/affordability.

Employment of Department Graduates

No information provided.

Additional Information

Housing and Day Care: No on-campus housing is available. No on-campus day care facilities are available.

Special Facilities or Resources: The program staffs Argosy Counseling Service, providing both practicum and internship opportunities for our students.

Application Information: Clinical Psychology (PsyD) Admissions, Attention: Wendy Assal, Argosy University, Twin Cities, 1515 Central Parkway, Eagan, MN 55121. *Fee:* $50. *Online application:* https://apply.argosy.edu/.

Minnesota State University—Mankato
Department of Psychology
AH 23
Mankato, MN 56001
Telephone: (507) 389-2724
Chairperson: Andrea Lassiter

E-mail: carol.seifert@mnsu.edu
Web: http://sbs.mnsu.edu/psych/

Orientation, Objectives, and Emphasis of Department
The school psychology doctoral program emphasizes data-based decision-making, multiculturalism, mental health, and prevention. Graduates will be prepared to pursue certification and licensure at state and national levels. The clinical program is a research-based, predoctoral program with a strong behavioral emphasis. The goal of the Industrial/Organizational (I/O) program is to provide broad theoretical and technical training for individuals who will function as human resource professionals or who will go on to doctoral programs in I/O psychology.

Programs and Degrees Offered

Program	Degree	Application Deadline	Applications Received	Accepted	New Admits Enrolled (PT)	Total Enrolled (PT)	Degrees Awarded in 2014–2015	Median Years to Complete Degree	Dismissed/ Withdrew
Industrial/ Organizational Psychology	MA/MS	February 15 (Fall)	70	10	10 (0)	19 (0)	10	2	1
School Psychology	PsyD	February 1 (Fall)	10	6	5 (0)	18 (0)	7	5	0
Clinical Psychology	MA/MS	February 15 (Fall)	49	15	7 (0)	17 (0)	9	2	0

Doctoral Degree (PsyD School Psychology): For those doctoral students for whom a professional internship was required in this program prior to graduation:
Total students who applied for an internship: 1
Total students who obtained an internship: 1
Total students who obtained a paid internship: 1
Total students who obtained an unpaid internship: 0
Total students who were placed in APA/CPA-accredited internships: 0
Total students placed in internships not APA/CPA-accredited, but listed with the Association of Psychology Postdoctoral and Internship Centers (APPIC): 0
Total students placed in internships conforming to guidelines of the Council of Directors of School Psychology Programs (CDSPP): 1
Total students placed in internships that were not APA/CPA-accredited, APPIC or CDSSP listed: 0

Master's Degree (MA/MS Industrial/Organizational Psychology): An internship experience, such as a final research project or "capstone" experience is required of graduates. Master's Degree (MA/MS Clinical Psychology): An internship experience, such as a final research project or "capstone" experience is required of graduates.

Internships/Practica
A variety of clinical practica are available to our clinical students. Sites have included The Munroe-Meyer Institute, Minneapolis VA Hospital, Minnesota Veteran's Home, and the MSU, Mankato Counseling Center. I/O internship sites include 360 Solutions (TX), atrain (Germany), Scitrain (OH), Patterson (Mpls), Cargill (Mpls), Center for Rural Policy Development (St. Peter), City of Austin (TX), Federal Management Partners (VA), Hogan Assessments (OK), Kenexa (Mpls), and Walgreens (IL). PsyD students are placed in school districts around the region for practicums and to complete internships. PsyD students are placed in internship sites in school districts across the country including Minnesota, Wisconsin, Iowa, and Colorado.

Admissions

Entries appear in the following order: required test or GPA, minimum score (if required)/median score of students entering in 2015–2016.

Program	Degree	GRE-V	GRE-Q	GRE-Writing	GRE-Subject	Under-graduate GPA	Last 2 Years GPA	Psychology GPA	Master's GPA
Industrial/ Organizational Psychology	MA/MS	148/155	149/157	Not specified	Not specified	3/3.67	Not specified	Not specified	Not specified
School Psychology	PsyD	142/147	135/146	Not specified	Not specified	Not specified	Not specified	Not specified	Not specified
Clinical Psychology	MA/MS	150/NA	150/NA	NA/NA	Not specified	NA/NA	NA/NA	NA/NA	Not specified

Admissions Requirements:

Degree	GRE	GRE-Subject	Letters of Recom-mendation	Research Statement	Writing Sample	CV	Interview
Master's/Specialist	Required	Optional	3	Required	Optional	Required	Optional
Doctoral	Required	Optional	3	Required	Required	Required	Required

Please note if these criteria vary for different programs: Requirements vary slightly depending on graduate program.

Admissions Criteria:

GRE scores—high
Research experience—medium
Work experience—medium
Clinically related public service—medium
GPA—high

Letters of recommendation—high
Interview—low
Statement of goals and objectives—medium
Undergraduate psychology preparation—high

Department Demographics

	Male (PT)	Female (PT)	Total	African-American/ Black (PT)	Hispanic/ Latino (PT)	Asian/ Pacific Islander (PT)	American Indian/ Alaska Native (PT)	Caucasian/ White (PT)	Unknown (PT)	Multiethnic (PT)	ADA (PT)	Int'l (PT)
Students	15 (0)	39 (0)	54	0 (0)	3 (0)	3 (0)	0 (0)	47 (0)	0 (0)	1 (0)	0 (0)	3 (0)

Financial Information/Assistance

Tuition: For information on tuition costs, visit http://www.mnsu.edu/campushub/tuition_fees/. Tuition is subject to change. Tuition costs vary by program.

Doctoral:
State residents: $552 per credit hour.
Nonstate residents: $552 per credit hour.

Master's:
State residents: $380 per credit hour.
Nonstate residents: $380 per credit hour.

Financial Assistance:

	Teaching Assistantship (% Receiving)	Teaching Assistantship Tuition Remission	Research Assistantship (% Receiving)	Research Assistantship Tuition Remission	Fellowship (% Receiving)	Fellowship Tuition Remission
First-Year Student	$4,500 (NA)	Partial	$4,500 (NA)	Partial	NA (NA)	NA
Advanced Student	$4,500 (NA)	Partial	$4,500 (NA)	Partial	NA (NA)	NA

For additional information on financial assistance, visit http://www.mnsu.edu/campushub/programs/.

Employment of Department Graduates

Master's:
Enrolled in a psychology doctoral program: 6
Enrolled in another graduate/professional program: 1
Employed in business or industry: 8
Employed in a community mental health/counseling center: 1
Employed in a hospital/medical center: 2
Other employment position: 1
Total: 19

Doctoral:
Employed in an academic position at a university: 1
Employed in a professional position in a school system: 5
Employed in a community mental health/counseling center: 1
Do not know: 7
Total: 14

Additional Information

Housing and Day Care: On-campus housing is available. See the following website for more information: http://www.mnsu.edu/reslife/. On-campus day care facilities are available. See the following website for more information: http://ed.mnsu.edu/tch/.

Information for Students With Physical Disabilities: See the following website: http://www.mnsu.edu/access/.

Special Facilities or Resources: I/O faculty have research partnerships with major organizations such as U.S. Air Force Office of Special Investigations, JVM South Africa Mining, Catalyst Rx, U.S. Security Associates, and the National Pork Board, to name a few. Clinical faculty maintain professional relationships with long-term care facilities and non-profit organizations. The Clinical Psychology program also runs an assessment clinic. The PsyD program maintains many active partnerships with local and regional school districts.

Application Information: Department of Psychology, AH 23, Minnesota State University-Mankato, Mankato, MN 56001. *Fee:* $40. *Online application:* http://grad.mnsu.edu/applying/.

Minnesota State University—Moorhead

School Psychology Program
College of Science Health and the Environment
1104 7th Avenue South
Moorhead, MN 56563
Telephone: (218) 477-2802
Program Director: Lisa Stewart

E-mail: schpsych@mnstate.edu
Web: http://www.mnstate.edu/schoolpsych/

Orientation, Objectives, and Emphasis of Department

Our goal is to provide the training necessary for our graduates to be skilled problem solvers in dealing with the needs of children, families, and others involved in the learning enterprise. Within a scientist–practitioner model and integrative perspective, the program's primary focus is on educating specialist-level professionals capable of working effectively in educational agencies and in collaboration with other human services providers. Our graduates are highly regarded by the schools and agencies within which they work because of their knowledge of current best practices in the field and because of their skills as team members.

Programs and Degrees Offered

Program	Degree	Application Deadline	Applica-tions Received	Accepted	New Admits Enrolled (PT)	Total Enrolled (PT)	Degrees Awarded in 2014–2015	Median Years to Complete Degree	Dismissed/ Withdrew
School Psychology	EdS	February 15 (Fall)	32	18	12 (0)	29 (0)	8	3	0

Internships/Practica

Field-based practica in both first and second years of study provide hands-on experience to students. Practica are supervised by local educators and school psychologists and are coordinated with on-campus course work so students can apply concepts and techniques learned in class. A 1,200-hour internship during the third year of study serves as a capstone experience for student's training. Internships are usually positions within school districts or special education cooperatives in the tri-state area, however students have completed internships in sites across the country.

Admissions

Entries appear in the following order: required test or GPA, minimum score (if required)/median score of students entering in 2015–2016.

Program	Degree	GRE-V	GRE-Q	GRE-Writing	GRE-Subject	Undergraduate GPA	Last 2 Years GPA	Psychology GPA	Master's GPA
School Psychology	EdS	146/152	142/148	Not specified	Not specified	3/3.4	Not specified	Not specified	Not specified

Admissions Requirements:

Degree	GRE	GRE-Subject	Letters of Recommendation	Research Statement	Writing Sample	CV	Interview
Master's/Specialist	Required	None	3	Required	None	Required	Recommended

Admissions Criteria:

GRE scores—high
Research experience—medium
Work experience—medium
Clinically related public service—low
GPA—high

Letters of recommendation—high
Interview—low
Statement of goals and objectives—high
Undergraduate psychology preparation—low

For additional information on admission requirements, visit http://www.mnstate.edu/schoolpsych/admissions.aspx.

Department Demographics

	Male (PT)	Female (PT)	Total	African-American/ Black (PT)	Hispanic/ Latino (PT)	Asian/ Pacific Islander (PT)	American Indian/ Alaska Native (PT)	Caucasian/ White (PT)	Unknown	Multiethnic (PT)	ADA (PT)	Int'l (PT)
Students	5 (0)	24 (0)	29	0 (0)	0 (0)	0 (0)	2 (0)	27 (0)	0 (0)	0 (0)	0 (0)	0 (0)

Financial Information/Assistance

Tuition: For information on tuition costs, visit http://www.mnstate.edu/business-services/tuition/graduate.aspx. Tuition is subject to change. Additional fees are assessed to students beyond the costs of tuition for the following: university activity, health, etc. fees.

Master's:
State residents: $9,125 per academic year.
State residents: $435 per credit hour.
Nonstate residents: $20,400 per academic year.
Nonstate residents: $850 per credit hour.

Financial Assistance:

	Teaching Assistantship (% Receiving)	Teaching Assistantship Tuition Remission	Research Assistantship (% Receiving)	Research Assistantship Tuition Remission	Fellowship (% Receiving)	Fellowship Tuition Remission
First-Year Student	$1,800 (45)	NA	$1,900 (45)	NA	NA (NA)	NA
Advanced Student	$2,500 (50)	NA	$2,500 (40)	NA	NA (NA)	NA

For additional information on financial assistance, visit http://www.mnstate.edu/graduate/finaid.aspx.

Employment of Department Graduates

Master's:
Employed in a professional position in a school system: 8
Total: 8

Additional Information

Housing and Day Care: On-campus housing is available. See the following website for more information: http://www.mnstate.edu/housing/. On-campus day care facilities are available. See the following website for more information: http://www.mnstate.edu/childcare/.

Information for Students With Physical Disabilities: See the following website: http://www.mnstate.edu/disability/.

Special Facilities or Resources: Our faculty work closely with local schools and reservations to promote opportunities for diverse practicum and research experiences in two states.

Application Information: Graduate Studies Office, Minnesota State University Moorhead, 1104 7th Avenue South, Moorhead, MN 56563. *Fee:* $20. *Online application:* http://www.mnstate.edu/graduate/apply.aspx.

Minnesota, University of

Department of Educational Psychology: Counseling and Student Personnel; School Psychology
Education and Human Development
56 East River Road, 250 EdSciB
Minneapolis, MN 55455
Telephone: (612) 624-4540
Chairperson: Geoffrey Maruyama

E-mail: geoff@umn.edu
Web: http://www.cehd.umn.edu/EdPsych/

Orientation, Objectives, and Emphasis of Department

CSPP: Intended to provide a fundamental body of knowledge/skills to prepare counselors and counseling psychologists for work in a variety of settings—counseling and human development, career development, staff development, student personnel work. While the focus is primarily on facilitating human development in educational settings, it is possible for individuals to prepare for community and agency settings as well. The faculty is committed to addressing current social issues such as diversity concerns and adolescent well-being. The program is designed for a select group of individuals with a demonstrated capacity for leadership and a commitment in the human services. School Psychology: Designed to educate professional psychologists for diverse leadership roles including research, evaluation, administration, practice, consultation, policy analysis, and so forth. The training model is best described as scientist–practitioner because the following components are integral to both didactic coursework and field experiences: (a) the scientific foundation of psychology; and (b) the application of theory and research to address real-life problems of children and youth in applied, academic, and other professional settings. The program's emphasis on empiricism and use of scientific findings in decision making is evident in opportunities provided students to generate knowledge (e.g., research), translate knowledge into practice, and to confirm experientially derived knowledge.

Programs and Degrees Offered

Program	Degree	Application Deadline	Applications Received	Accepted	New Admits Enrolled (PT)	Total Enrolled (PT)	Degrees Awarded in 2014–2015	Median Years to Complete Degree	Dismissed/ Withdrew
Counseling and Student Personnel	MA/MS	January 15 (Fall)	84	64	36 (0)	70 (0)	35	2	1
School Psychology	PhD	November 15 (Fall)	27	13	9 (0)	33 (5)	7	6	1
School Psychology	EdS	November 15 (Fall)	29	15	14 (0)	23 (1)	7	3	1

APA Accreditation

School PhD: Student Outcome Data website: http://www.cehd.umn.edu/EdPsych/Programs/SchoolPsych/outcomes.html.

Doctoral Degree (PhD School Psychology): For those doctoral students for whom a professional internship was required in this program prior to graduation:

Total students who applied for an internship: 8
Total students who obtained an internship: 7
Total students who obtained a paid internship: 7
Total students who obtained an unpaid internship: 0
Total students who were placed in APA/CPA-accredited internships: 2
Total students placed in internships not APA/CPA-accredited, but listed with the Association of Psychology Postdoctoral and Internship Centers (APPIC): 0
Total students placed in internships conforming to guidelines of the Council of Directors of School Psychology Programs (CDSPP): 0
Total students placed in internships that were not APA/CPA-accredited, APPIC or CDSSP listed: 5

Master's Degree (MA/MS Counseling and Student Personnel): An internship experience, such as a final research project or "capstone" experience is required of graduates.

Internships/Practica

Counseling and Student Personnel Psychology MA students complete an academic year practicum in the second year with a focus on community counseling, school counseling, or college student development. The practicum consists of direct work with clients/students, individual on-site supervision, and an academic seminar at the university. Through practicum and internship experiences, school psychology students are exposed to the application of scientific theory and findings to real-life problems in a variety of settings. Program coursework, practica, and internships are designed to facilitate knowledge and skill development in intervention, assessment, consultation, and supervision. All students complete practica during each year of study, with site and university supervision by appropriately credentialed school psychologists or psychologists in the Twin-Cities Metro area schools, clinics, and hospitals. A year-long, full-time internship is required for all school psychology students. PhD students are strongly encouraged to complete internships in APPIC or APA accredited sites.

Admissions

Entries appear in the following order: required test or GPA, minimum score (if required)/median score of students entering in 2015–2016.

Program	Degree	GRE-V	GRE-Q	GRE-Writing	GRE-Subject	Undergraduate GPA	Last 2 Years GPA	Psychology GPA	Master's GPA
Counseling and Student Personnel	MA/MS	NA/155	NA/152	NA/4	Not specified	3/3.69	Not specified	Not specified	Not specified
School Psychology	PhD	NA/162	NA/158	Not specified	Not specified	3/3.78	Not specified	Not specified	Not specified
School Psychology	EdS	NA/159	NA/156	Not specified	Not specified	3/3.74	Not specified	Not specified	Not specified

Admissions Requirements:

Degree	GRE	GRE-Subject	Letters of Recommendation	Research Statement	Writing Sample	CV	Interview
Master's/Specialist	Required	None	3	Required	Required	Required	Required
Doctoral	Required	None	3	Required	Required	Required	Required

Please note if these criteria vary for different programs: School Psychology requires a writing sample; this is optional for Counseling program.

Admissions Criteria:

GRE scores—high
Research experience—medium
Work experience—medium
Clinically related public service—low

GPA—medium
Letters of recommendation—high
Interview—high
Statement of goals and objectives—high

For additional information on admission requirements, visit http://www.cehd.umn.edu/EdPsych/FutureStudents/default.html.

Department Demographics

	Male (PT)	Female (PT)	Total	African-American/ Black (PT)	Hispanic/ Latino (PT)	Asian/ Pacific Islander (PT)	American Indian/ Alaska Native (PT)	Caucasian/ White (PT)	Unknown	Multiethnic (PT)	ADA (PT)	Int'l (PT)
Students	52 (0)	152 (7)	211	5 (1)	5 (2)	7 (0)	1 (0)	155 (4)	3 (0)	9 (0)	0 (0)	19 (0)

Financial Information/Assistance

Tuition: For information on tuition costs, visit http://onestop.umn.edu/finances/costs_and_tuition/index.html. Tuition is subject to change. Additional fees are assessed to students beyond the costs of tuition for the following: General fees, Service & usage fees, College fee.

Doctoral:
State residents: $15,844 per academic year.
State residents: $1,320 per credit hour.
Nonstate residents: $24,508 per academic year.
Nonstate residents: $2,042 per credit hour.

Master's:
State residents: $15,844 per academic year.
State residents: $1,320 per credit hour.
Nonstate residents: $24,508 per academic year.
Nonstate residents: $2,042 per credit hour.

Financial Assistance:

	Teaching Assistantship (% Receiving)	Teaching Assistantship Tuition Remission	Research Assistantship (% Receiving)	Research Assistantship Tuition Remission	Fellowship (% Receiving)	Fellowship Tuition Remission
First-Year Student	$7,071 (NA)	Partial	$7,071 (NA)	Partial	$22,500 (NA)	Full
Advanced Student	$7,071 (NA)	Partial	$7,071 (NA)	Partial	$22,500 (NA)	Full

For additional information on financial assistance, visit http://www.grad.umn.edu/fundingtuition.

Employment of Department Graduates

Master's:
Enrolled in a psychology doctoral program: 4
Employed in other positions at a higher education institution: 4
Employed in a professional position in a school system: 22
Employed in business or industry: 1
Employed in a community mental health/counseling center: 7
Do not know: 4
Total: 42

Doctoral:
Enrolled in a postdoctoral residency/fellowship: 2
Employed in an academic position at a university: 1
Employed in academic position at a 2-year/4-year college: 2
Employed in other positions at a higher education institution: 1
Employed in a professional position in a school system: 6
Employed in a community mental health/counseling center: 5
Total: 17

Additional Information

Housing and Day Care: On-campus housing is available. See the following website for more information: http://www.housing.umn.edu/graduate. On-campus day care facilities are available. See the following website for more information: http://www.sphc.umn.edu/childcare.html.

Information for Students With Physical Disabilities: See the following website: https://diversity.umn.edu/disability/.

Special Facilities or Resources: Our graduate program is located within a major research university where many research projects are ongoing. The program is also located within a state—Minnesota—and major metropolitan area—the Twin Cities—that are known for innovations in human services. The result is that both the research climate and the practice climate are good ones for students. CSPP: Excellent facilities for research opportunities exist throughout the university. There is a time-shared instructional computing laboratory with batch and online computer facilities. Students may borrow video cameras, LCD projectors, and audiorecorders. Students record counseling role-play sessions in a state-of-the-art digital counseling laboratory. School Psychology: The Program maintains a Moodle site for program materials and resources. School Psychology students are provided office space in the Education Science Building. The School Psychology Resource Library is maintained for faculty and students to use both as a resource and a gathering location. This room contains books, test kits, intervention materials, journals, research reports, Master's theses, doctoral dissertations, coursework readings, and computers. The digital counseling lab is also available.

Application Information: Fee: $75. *Online application:* http://www.grad.umn.edu/admissions/.

Minnesota, University of

Department of Psychology
N218 Elliott Hall, 75 East River Road
Minneapolis, MN 55455
Telephone: (612) 626-7762
Chairperson: Monica Luciana

E-mail: psyapply@umn.edu
Web: http://psych.umn.edu/grad/

Orientation, Objectives, and Emphasis of Department

The overall goal of the department is to train the people who will become leaders in their chosen area of specialization. Consequently, the graduate training programs in the department are oriented first to the training of skilled researchers and teachers in psychology, and then to the training of specialists and practitioners. The PhD programs in Clinical Science and Psychopathology Research and Counseling Psychology are APA-accredited. Department faculty also participate in independent degree programs in neuroscience and cognitive science. The Department of Psychology and the Institute of Child Development offer a training program in child clinical psychology focused on the study of psychopathology in the context of development.

Programs and Degrees Offered

Program	Degree	Application Deadline	Applica-tions Received	Accepted	New Admits Enrolled (PT)	Total Enrolled (PT)	Degrees Awarded in 2014–2015	Median Years to Complete Degree	Dismissed/ Withdrew
Biological Psycho-pathology	PhD	December 1 (Fall)	13	1	1 (0)	5 (0)	1	5.8	0
Clinical Science & Psycho-pathology Research	PhD	December 1 (Fall)	168	8	5 (0)	24 (0)	3	6.33	0
Cognitive and Brain Sciences	PhD	December 1 (Fall)	52	5	3 (0)	22 (0)	3	5.75	0
Counseling Psychology	PhD	December 1 (Fall)	110	3	3 (0)	18 (0)	6	5.92	0
Personality, Individual Diff. & Behav. Genetics	PhD	December 1 (Fall)	21	3	1 (0)	10 (0)	1	4.9	0
Industrial/ Organizational Psychology	PhD	December 1 (Fall)	61	6	6 (0)	24 (0)	6	5.38	0
Quantitative/ Psychometric Methods	PhD	December 1 (Fall)	24	5	1 (0)	8 (0)	1	5.8	0
Social Psychology	PhD	December 1 (Fall)	67	6	4 (0)	21 (0)	5	5.7	0

APA Accreditation

Clinical PhD: Student Outcome Data website: http://www.psych.umn.edu/research/areas/clinical/.
Counseling PhD: Student Outcome Data website: http://www.psych.umn.edu/research/areas/counseling/.

Doctoral Degree (PhD Clinical Science & Psychopathology Research): For those doctoral students for whom a professional internship was required in this program prior to graduation:

Total students who applied for an internship: 10
Total students who obtained an internship: 10
Total students who obtained a paid internship: 10
Total students who obtained an unpaid internship: 0
Total students who were placed in APA/CPA-accredited internships: 10
Total students placed in internships not APA/CPA-accredited, but listed with the Association of Psychology Postdoctoral and Internship Centers (APPIC): 0
Total students placed in internships conforming to guidelines of the Council of Directors of School Psychology Programs (CDSPP): 0
Total students placed in internships that were not APA/CPA-accredited, APPIC or CDSSP listed: 0

Doctoral Degree (PhD Counseling Psychology): For those doctoral students for whom a professional internship was required in this program prior to graduation:
Total students who applied for an internship: 1
Total students who obtained an internship: 1
Total students who obtained a paid internship: 1
Total students who obtained an unpaid internship: 0
Total students who were placed in APA/CPA-accredited internships: 1
Total students placed in internships not APA/CPA-accredited, but listed with the Association of Psychology Postdoctoral and Internship Centers (APPIC): 0
Total students placed in internships conforming to guidelines of the Council of Directors of School Psychology Programs (CDSPP): 0
Total students placed in internships that were not APA/CPA-accredited, APPIC or CDSSP listed: 0

Internships/Practica

Internships are available at the university hospitals, the department's Vocational Assessment Clinic, the University Counseling and Consulting Services, the Veterans Administration, and several other governmental and private agencies throughout the area.

Admissions

Entries appear in the following order: required test or GPA, minimum score (if required)/median score of students entering in 2015–2016.

Program	Degree	GRE-V	GRE-Q	GRE-Writing	GRE-Subject	Under-graduate GPA	Last 2 Years GPA	Psychol-ogy GPA	Master's GPA
Biological Psychopathology	PhD	Not specified	Not specified	Not specified	Not specified	Not specified	Not specified	Not specified	Not specified
Clinical Science & Psychopathology Research	PhD	NA/NA	NA/NA	Not specified	Not specified	Not specified	Not specified	Not specified	Not specified
Cognitive and Brain Sciences	PhD	Not specified	Not specified	Not specified	Not specified	Not specified	Not specified	Not specified	Not specified
Counseling Psychology	PhD	NA/NA	NA/NA	Not specified	Not specified	Not specified	Not specified	Not specified	Not specified
Personality, Individual Diff. & Behav. Genetics	PhD	Not specified	Not specified	Not specified	Not specified	Not specified	Not specified	Not specified	Not specified
Industrial/ Organizational Psychology	PhD	Not specified	Not specified	Not specified	Not specified	Not specified	Not specified	Not specified	Not specified
Quantitative/ Psychometric Methods	PhD	Not specified	Not specified	Not specified	Not specified	Not specified	Not specified	Not specified	Not specified
Social Psychology	PhD	Not specified	Not specified	Not specified	Not specified	Not specified	Not specified	Not specified	Not specified

Admissions Requirements:

Degree	GRE	GRE-Subject	Letters of Recommendation	Research Statement	Writing Sample	CV	Interview
Doctoral	Required	Recommended	3	Required	None	Required	Required

Please note if these criteria vary for different programs: Interviews are required for Clinical area only.

Admissions Criteria:

GRE scores—high

Research experience—high

Work experience—medium

Clinically related public service—medium

GPA—high

Letters of recommendation—high

Interview—high

Statement of goals and objectives—high

Undergraduate psychology preparation—medium

For additional information on admission requirements, visit http://www.psych.umn.edu/grad/applying.html.

Department Demographics

	Male (PT)	Female (PT)	Total	African-American/ Black (PT)	Hispanic/ Latino (PT)	Asian/ Pacific Islander (PT)	American Indian/ Alaska Native (PT)	Caucasian/ White (PT)	Unknown	Multiethnic (PT)	ADA (PT)	Int'l (PT)
Students	49 (0)	64 (1)	114	2 (0)	3 (0)	9 (0)	1 (0)	71 (1)	2 (0)	1 (0)	0 (0)	24 (0)

Financial Information/Assistance

Tuition: For information on tuition costs, visit http://onestop.umn.edu/finances/costs_and_tuition/index.html. Tuition is subject to change. Additional fees are assessed to students beyond the costs of tuition for the following: Student services/health insurance fee. Estimated around $700/semester.

Doctoral:

State residents: $15,844 per academic year.

State residents: $1,320 per credit hour.

Nonstate residents: $24,508 per academic year.

Nonstate residents: $2,042 per credit hour.

Financial Assistance:

	Teaching Assistantship (% Receiving)	Teaching Assistantship Tuition Remission	Research Assistantship (% Receiving)	Research Assistantship Tuition Remission	Fellowship (% Receiving)	Fellowship Tuition Remission
First-Year Student	$17,500 (NA)	Full	$17,500 (NA)	Full	$25,000 (NA)	Full
Advanced Student	$17,500 (NA)	Full	$17,500 (NA)	Full	$25,000 (NA)	Full

For additional information on financial assistance, visit http://www.psych.umn.edu/grad/support.html.

Employment of Department Graduates

Doctoral:
Enrolled in a postdoctoral residency/fellowship: 6
Employed in an academic position at a university: 2
Employed in academic position at a 2-year/4-year college: 1
Employed in business or industry: 5
Employed in government agency: 4
Employed in a community mental health/counseling center: 1
Employed in a hospital/medical center: 2
Still seeking employment: 1
Other employment position: 1
Do not know: 1
Total: 24

Additional Information

Housing and Day Care: On-campus housing is available. See the following website for more information: http://www.housing.umn.edu/graduate. On-campus day care facilities are available. See the following website for more information: http://www.cehd.umn.edu/ChildDevelopmentCenter/; http://www.cehd.umn.edu/icd/labschool/.

Information for Students With Physical Disabilities: See the following website: https://diversity.umn.edu/disability/.

Special Facilities or Resources: The department offers extensive laboratory and computer facilities, a wide variety of resources and collaborative relationships both on and off campus, and several federally funded research projects. For example, three research centers are headquartered in the Department: Center for Cognitive Sciences, Center for the Study of Political Psychology, and the Center for the Study of the Individual and Society. Other research centers with which the faculty are involved are located in Neuroscience, Radiology, Epidemiology, and Public Health. We have adjunct faculty at the University of Minnesota Counseling and Consulting Services, Carlson School of Management, Institute of Child Development, and Department of Educational Psychology; and in the VA Medical Center, Hennepin County Medical Center (Minneapolis), Ramsey Medical Center (St. Paul), and Personnel Decisions International (Minneapolis).

Application Information: *Fee:* $75. *Online application:* http://www.grad.umn.edu/admissions/.

Minnesota, University of
Institute of Child Development
College of Education and Human Development
51 East River Parkway
Minneapolis, MN 55455
Telephone: (612) 624-0526
Director: Megan Gunnar

E-mail: icd@umn.edu
Web: http://www.cehd.umn.edu/icd/

Orientation, Objectives, and Emphasis of Department
The Institute program emphasizes training for research and academic careers. The program offers a diversity of substantive and methodological approaches. In the core program, special strengths are in infancy, personality and social development, cognitive processes, language development, biological bases of development, and developmental neuroscience. Formal clinical training is available through the Developmental Psychopathology and Clinical Science (DPCS) joint program. Formal minor programs are offered in Neuroscience, Cognitive Science, Prevention Science, and Interpersonal Relationships Research. Special training is also available through affiliations with the Center for Cognitive Sciences; the Center for Neurobehavioral Development; the Center for Early Education and Development; the Center for Personalized Prevention Research; the Human Capital Research Collaborative; the Institute for Translational Research in Children's Mental Health; and the Consortium on Children, Youth, and Families.

Programs and Degrees Offered

Program	Degree	Application Deadline	Applications Received	Accepted	New Admits Enrolled (PT)	Total Enrolled (PT)	Degrees Awarded in 2014–2015	Median Years to Complete Degree	Dismissed/ Withdrew
Child Psychology	PhD	December 1 (Fall)	39	12	7	25 (0)	3	5	1

Programs and Degrees Offered *(con't.)*

Program	Degree	Application Deadline	Applications Received	Accepted	New Admits Enrolled (PT)	Total Enrolled (PT)	Degrees Awarded in 2014–2015	Median Years to Complete Degree	Dismissed/Withdrew
Child/Clinical Psychology	PhD	December 1 (Fall)	67	3	3	20 (0)	6	6	0

Internships/Practica

Clinical practica and internships are available within the local community to Developmental Psychopathology and Clinical Science students and are offered through the APA-accredited Clinical Science and Psychopathology area of the Psychology Department.

Admissions

Entries appear in the following order: required test or GPA, minimum score (if required)/median score of students entering in 2015–2016.

Program	Degree	GRE-V	GRE-Q	GRE-Writing	GRE-Subject	Undergraduate GPA	Last 2 Years GPA	Psychology GPA	Master's GPA
Child Psychology	PhD	NA/163	NA/159	NA/5	Not specified	NA/3.79	Not specified	Not specified	Not specified
Child/Clinical Psychology	PhD	NA/166	NA/161	NA/5	Not specified	NA/3.8	Not specified	Not specified	Not specified

Admissions Requirements:

Degree	GRE	GRE-Subject	Letters of Recommendation	Research Statement	Writing Sample	CV	Interview
Doctoral	Required	None	3	Required	Optional	Required	Required

Please note if these criteria vary for different programs: Clinically related public service rated low for joint child/clinical program.

Admissions Criteria:

GRE scores—medium
Research experience—high
Work experience—low
Clinically related public service—low
GPA—high

Letters of recommendation—high
Interview—low
Statement of goals and objectives—high
Undergraduate psychology preparation—low

For additional information on admission requirements, visit http://www.cehd.umn.edu/icd/programs/CPSY/Graduate/apply.html.

Department Demographics

	Male (PT)	Female (PT)	Total	African-American/ Black (PT)	Hispanic/ Latino (PT)	Asian/ Pacific Islander (PT)	American Indian/ Alaska Native (PT)	Caucasian/ White (PT)	Unknown	Multiethnic (PT)	ADA (PT)	Int'l (PT)
Students	6 (0)	39 (0)	45	1 (0)	5 (0)	4 (0)	0 (0)	35 (0)	0 (0)	0 (0)	4 (0)	4 (0)

Financial Information/Assistance

Tuition: For information on tuition costs, visit http://onestop.umn.edu/finances/costs_and_tuition/tuition_and_fees/graduate_school_tuition.html. Tuition is subject to change.

Doctoral:
State residents: $15,844 per academic year.

State residents: $1,320 per credit hour.
Nonstate residents: $24,508 per academic year.
Nonstate residents: $2,042 per credit hour.

Financial Assistance:

	Teaching Assistantship (% Receiving)	Teaching Assistantship Tuition Remission	Research Assistantship (% Receiving)	Research Assistantship Tuition Remission	Fellowship (% Receiving)	Fellowship Tuition Remission
First-Year Student	$14,141 (NA)	Full	$14,141 (NA)	Full	$24,000 (NA)	Full
Advanced Student	$14,141 (NA)	Full	$14,141 (NA)	Full	$24,000 (NA)	Full

For additional information on financial assistance, visit http://www.grad.umn.edu/fundingtuition.

Employment of Department Graduates

Doctoral:
Enrolled in a postdoctoral residency/fellowship: 8
Employed in other positions at a higher education institution: 1
Total: 9

Additional Information

Housing and Day Care: On-campus housing is available. See the following website for more information: http://www.housing.umn.edu/graduate/. On-campus day care facilities are available. See the following website for more information: http://www.cehd.umn.edu/ChildDevelopmentCenter/.

Information for Students With Physical Disabilities: See the following website: https://diversity.umn.edu/disability/.

Special Facilities or Resources: Physical and research facilities include an office for every student plus exclusive use of a laptop computer during the program, a reference room with more than 4,500 volumes and 4 computers, 25 experiment rooms, and a laboratory nursery school. In addition, state-of-the-art research facilities and interdisciplinary collaborations facilitate cutting-edge neuroscience research in the areas of cognitive, behavioral, and social/emotional development. Onsite facilities include both high density (128 channels) and low density (32 channels) electrophysiological recording equipment and eyetracking equipment. Facilities at the Center for Neurobehavioral Development include autonomic and electrophysiological laboratories equipped with functional magnetic resonance imaging (fMRI) and event-related potential (ERP) equipment; audiovisual systems for online data collection, videotaping, presentations, and training; research suites, computer workroom, library/conference room; and subject exam rooms and family waiting/play rooms. At the Center for Magnetic Resonance Research, structural and functional MRI equipment is available.

Application Information: *Fee:* $75. *Online application:* https://app.applyyourself.com/?id=UMN-GRAD.

Minnesota, University of, Duluth

Department of Psychology
College of Education and Human Service Professions
320 Bohannon Hall
Duluth, MN 55812
Telephone: (218) 726-7808
Chairperson: Scott Carlson

E-mail: mapsumd@d.umn.edu
Web: http://z.umn.edu/mapsumd

Orientation, Objectives, and Emphasis of Department

Our mission is to prepare graduate students with research-based knowledge and skills that are essential to successful careers in organizational, educational, clinical, and counseling settings. We are one program with three integrated tracks: Clinical-Counseling Psychology, Industrial-Organizational Psychology, and General-Experimental Psychology. For all three tracks, the degree and research-based preparation should also facilitate graduates' admission into PhD and PsyD programs in psychology.

Programs and Degrees Offered

Program	Degree	Application Deadline	Applications Received	Accepted	New Admits Enrolled (PT)	Total Enrolled (PT)	Degrees Awarded in 2014–2015	Median Years to Complete Degree	Dismissed/ Withdrew
Psychological Science	MA/MS	March 1 (Fall)	42	16	13	13	0		0

Internships/Practica

Duluth is home to a variety of organizations which offer opportunities to conduct applied research and provide service for different populations. There are numerous psychological treatment centers in the community which offer opportunities for students to gain real-life clinical experience.

Admissions

Entries appear in the following order: required test or GPA, minimum score (if required)/median score of students entering in 2015–2016.

Program	Degree	GRE-V	GRE-Q	GRE-Writing	GRE-Subject	Under-graduate GPA	Last 2 Years GPA	Psychology GPA	Master's GPA
Psychological Science	MA/MS	NA/NA	NA/NA	Not specified	Not specified	3/NA	Not specified	Not specified	Not specified

Admissions Requirements:

Degree	GRE	GRE-Subject	Letters of Recommendation	Research Statement	Writing Sample	CV	Interview
Master's/Specialist	Required	None	3	Required	Required	Required	None

Please note if these criteria vary for different programs: Interview is required only for clinical-counseling applicants.

Department Demographics

	Male (PT)	Female (PT)	Total	African-American/ Black (PT)	Hispanic/ Latino (PT)	Asian/ Pacific Islander (PT)	American Indian/ Alaska Native (PT)	Caucasian/ White (PT)	Unknown	Multiethnic (PT)	ADA (PT)	Int'l (PT)
Students	11 (0)	14 (0)	25	0 (0)	0 (0)	1 (0)	0 (0)	24 (0)	0 (0)	0 (0)	0 (0)	0 (0)

Financial Information/Assistance

Tuition: For information on tuition costs, visit http://d.umn.edu/onestop/student-finances/tuition-fees/rates/index.html. Tuition is subject to change.

Master's:
State residents: $15,844 per academic year.
State residents: $1,320 per credit hour.
Nonstate residents: $24,508 per academic year.
Nonstate residents: $2,042 per credit hour.

Financial Assistance:

	Teaching Assistantship (% Receiving)	Teaching Assistantship Tuition Remission	Research Assistantship (% Receiving)	Research Assistantship Tuition Remission	Fellowship (% Receiving)	Fellowship Tuition Remission
First-Year Student	NA (NA)	NA	NA (NA)	NA	NA (NA)	NA
Advanced Student	NA (NA)	NA	NA (NA)	NA	NA (NA)	NA

For additional information on financial assistance, visit http://d.umn.edu/onestop/student-finances/financial-aid/index.html.

Employment of Department Graduates

No information provided.

Additional Information

Housing and Day Care: No on-campus housing is available. On-campus day care facilities are available. See the following website for more information: http://cehsp.d.umn.edu/departments-centers/childrens-place.

Information for Students With Physical Disabilities: See the following website: http://www.d.umn.edu/access/.

Special Facilities or Resources: Faculty have lab spaces to facilitate student research. Students in the clinical-counseling track will have access to clinic space with video recording equipment as part of their practicum.

Application Information: Fee: $75. *Online application:* https://app.applyyourself.com/?id=UMN-GRAD.

Saint Mary's University of Minnesota

Counseling and Psychological Services
Graduate School of Health and Human Services
2500 Park Avenue
Minneapolis, MN 55404
Telephone: (612) 238-4548
Program Director: Kenneth Solberg, PhD, LP
Web: http://www.smumn.edu/graduate-home/areas-of-study/graduate-school-of-health-human-services

E-mail: ksolberg@smumn.edu

Orientation, Objectives, and Emphasis of Department

The Master of Arts program in Counseling and Psychological Services prepares graduates for professional work in counseling, psychotherapy, and other psychological services. It is designed to enhance the student's understanding of the complex nature of human behavior and social interaction, and to develop tools for assessing human problems and assisting individuals in developing greater understanding and acceptance of themselves and their relationships with others. The program is designed to meet the educational requirements for Minnesota licensure as a Licensed Professional Counselor. Additional coursework is available for those seeking Minnesota licensure as a Licensed Professional Clinical Counselor. The Counseling and Psychological Services program is offered in Rochester, MN, as well as in Minneapolis. The PsyD program prepares students for licensure as a psychologist in Minnesota and most other states, and has been granted designation status with the National Register. The program has submitted an application for APA accreditation, which is currently in process.

Programs and Degrees Offered

Program	Degree	Application Deadline	Applications Received	Accepted	New Admits Enrolled (PT)	Total Enrolled (PT)	Degrees Awarded in 2014–2015	Median Years to Complete Degree	Dismissed/ Withdrew
Counseling and Psychological Services	MA/MS	Rolling	402	266	90 (22)	301 (149)	103		

Programs and Degrees Offered (con't.)

Program	Degree	Application Deadline	Applica-tions Received	Accepted	New Admits Enrolled (PT)	Total Enrolled (PT)	Degrees Awarded in 2014–2015	Median Years to Complete Degree	Dismissed/Withdrew
Marriage and Family Therapy	MA/MS	February 1 (Fall)	123	36	30 (1)	215 (58)	131		
Addiction Studies Graduate Certificate	Other	Rolling	27	10	2 (1)	5 (15)	5		
Counseling Psychology	PsyD	March 1 (Fall)	49	19	14 (1)	74 (4)	0		

Doctoral Degree (PsyD Counseling Psychology): For those doctoral students for whom a professional internship was required in this program prior to graduation:

Total students who applied for an internship: 12

Total students who obtained an internship: 12

Total students who obtained a paid internship: 12

Total students who obtained an unpaid internship: 0

Total students who were placed in APA/CPA-accredited internships: 1

Total students placed in internships not APA/CPA-accredited, but listed with the Association of Psychology Postdoctoral and Internship Centers (APPIC): 7

Total students placed in internships conforming to guidelines of the Council of Directors of School Psychology Programs (CDSPP): 0

Total students placed in internships that were not APA/CPA-accredited, APPIC or CDSSP listed: 4

Master's Degree (MA/MS Counseling and Psychological Services): An internship experience, such as a final research project or "capstone" experience is required of graduates. Master's Degree (MA/MS Marriage and Family Therapy): An internship experience, such as a final research project or "capstone" experience is required of graduates.

Internships/Practica

A wide variety of practicum sites are available for students. Doctoral students apply for a full-time internship through the APPIC match process.

Admissions

Entries appear in the following order: required test or GPA, minimum score (if required)/median score of students entering in 2015–2016.

Program	Degree	GRE-V	GRE-Q	GRE-Writing	GRE-Subject	Under-graduate GPA	Last 2 Years GPA	Psychol-ogy GPA	Master's GPA
Counseling and Psychological Services	MA/MS	Not specified	Not specified	Not specified	Not specified	2.75/NA	Not specified	Not specified	Not specified
Marriage and Family Therapy	MA/MS	Not specified	Not specified	Not specified	Not specified	2.75/NA	Not specified	Not specified	Not specified
Addiction Studies Graduate Certificate	Other	Not specified	Not specified	Not specified	Not specified	Not specified	Not specified	Not specified	Not specified
Counseling Psychology	PsyD	Not specified	Not specified	Not specified	Not specified	Not specified	Not specified	Not specified	Not specified

Admissions Requirements:

Degree	GRE	GRE-Subject	Letters of Recommendation	Research Statement	Writing Sample	CV	Interview
Master's/Specialist	None	None	3	Required	Required	Required	Required
Doctoral	Optional	Optional	3	Required	Optional	Required	Required

Please note if these criteria vary for different programs: The PsyD program requires completion of a Master's degree in Counseling or a related field prior to admission.

Admissions Criteria:

Research experience—medium
Work experience—high
Clinically related public service—high
GPA—high

Letters of recommendation—high
Interview—high
Statement of goals and objectives—high
Undergraduate psychology preparation—low

Department Demographics

	Male (PT)	Female (PT)	Total	African-American/ Black (PT)	Hispanic/ Latino (PT)	Asian/ Pacific Islander (PT)	American Indian/ Alaska Native (PT)	Caucasian/ White (PT)	Unknown	Multiethnic (PT)	ADA (PT)	Int'l (PT)
Students	114 (35)	481 (191)	821	42 (20)	16 (8)	19 (8)	5 (0)	360 (140)	147 (48)	6 (2)	11 (9)	7 (1)

Financial Information/Assistance

Tuition: For information on tuition costs, visit http://www.smumn.edu/graduate-home/tuition-financial-aid/tuition-fees. Tuition is subject to change. Tuition costs vary by program.

Doctoral:
State residents: $20,888 per academic year.
State residents: $770 per credit hour.
Nonstate residents: $20,888 per academic year.
Nonstate residents: $770 per credit hour.

Master's:
State residents: $450 per credit hour.
Nonstate residents: $450 per credit hour.

Financial Assistance:

	Teaching Assistantship (% Receiving)	Teaching Assistantship Tuition Remission	Research Assistantship (% Receiving)	Research Assistantship Tuition Remission	Fellowship (% Receiving)	Fellowship Tuition Remission
First-Year Student	NA (NA)	NA	NA (NA)	NA	NA (NA)	NA
Advanced Student	NA (NA)	NA	NA (NA)	NA	NA (NA)	NA

For additional information on financial assistance, visit http://www.smumn.edu/graduate-home/tuition-financial-aid.

Employment of Department Graduates

No information provided.

Additional Information

Housing and Day Care: No on-campus housing is available. No on-campus day care facilities are available.

Special Facilities or Resources: The majority of our faculty in the MA programs are adjunct (part-time) instructors with doctorates who are practicing in the field. They bring a wealth of real-world experience to their teaching and possess strong academic credentials.

Since our emphasis is on applied psychological competence, we consider the backgrounds of these practitioner–scholars to be a major strength of the program. The doctoral program employs seven core faculty and a number of adjunct faculty. All have doctorates and appropriate clinical experience.

Application Information: Admissions, Saint Mary's University of Minnesota, 2500 Park Avenue, Minneapolis, MN 55404. *Fee:* $25. *Online application:* http://www.smumn.edu/graduate-home/admission/apply.

St. Cloud State University
Department of Psychology
Social Sciences
720 4th Avenue South
Saint Cloud, MN 56301
Telephone: (320) 308-4157
Chairperson: Dr. Joseph Melcher

E-mail: dsprotolipac@stcloudstate.edu
Web: http://www.stcloudstate.edu/psychology/io/

Orientation, Objectives, and Emphasis of Department
The St. Cloud State University Department of Psychology is dedicated to providing students with a quality graduate education. The Industrial-Organizational Psychology master's degree program is designed to provide graduate students with the knowledge and skills that will prepare them for jobs in consulting, business, and government, or to continue their education. The curriculum reflects a commitment to the scientist–practitioner model of graduate education in psychology by including training in the theoretical and empirical bases of industrial/organizational (I/O) psychology and in the application of these perspectives to work settings. Following the recommendations of the Society for I/O Psychology for master's-level education, students' graduate experience will include (a) training in the core areas of I/O psychology, including personnel selection, training and organizational development, criterion development, and organizational theory; (b) a firm foundation in psychological theory, research methods, statistics, and psychometrics; and (c) the opportunity to obtain both research experience and applied experience while completing their education.

Programs and Degrees Offered

Program	Degree	Application Deadline	Applica-tions Received	Accepted	New Admits Enrolled (PT)	Total Enrolled (PT)	Degrees Awarded in 2014–2015	Median Years to Complete Degree	Dismissed/ Withdrew
Industrial/ Organizational Psychology	MA/MS	February 15 (Fall)	55	15	11 (0)	18 (0)	9	2	1

Internships/Practica
Students pursuing the master's degree in I/O Psychology have the option of completing either a practicum/internship or a thesis. The practicum/internship option is designed for students planning to seek employment upon completion of their degree. The thesis option is designed for students planning to seek a doctoral degree in I/O Psychology.

Admissions
Entries appear in the following order: required test or GPA, minimum score (if required)/median score of students entering in 2015–2016.

Program	Degree	GRE-V	GRE-Q	GRE-Writing	GRE-Subject	Under-graduate GPA	Last 2 Years GPA	Psychol-ogy GPA	Master's GPA
Industrial/ Organizational Psychology	MA/MS	152/NA	144/NA	Not specified	Not specified	2.75/NA	2.75/NA	Not specified	Not specified

Admissions Requirements:

Degree	GRE	GRE-Subject	Letters of Recommendation	Research Statement	Writing Sample	CV	Interview
Master's/Specialist	Required	None	3	Required	Optional	Optional	Optional

Admissions Criteria:

GRE scores—high
Research experience—medium
Work experience—medium

GPA—high
Letters of recommendation—medium
Statement of goals and objectives—medium

For additional information on admission requirements, visit http://www.stcloudstate.edu/psychology/io/application/default.asp.

Department Demographics

	Male (PT)	Female (PT)	Total	African-American/ Black (PT)	Hispanic/ Latino (PT)	Asian/ Pacific Islander (PT)	American Indian/ Alaska Native (PT)	Caucasian/ White (PT)	Unknown	Multiethnic (PT)	ADA (PT)	Int'l (PT)
Students	9 (0)	9 (0)	18	0 (0)	0 (0)	1 (0)	0 (0)	17 (0)	0 (0)	0 (0)	0 (0)	3 (0)

Financial Information/Assistance

Tuition: For information on tuition costs, visit http://www.stcloudstate.edu/srfs/finances/cost-of-attendance.aspx. Tuition is subject to change.

Master's:
State residents: $355 per credit hour.
Nonstate residents: $553 per credit hour.

Financial Assistance:

	Teaching Assistantship (% Receiving)	Teaching Assistantship Tuition Remission	Research Assistantship (% Receiving)	Research Assistantship Tuition Remission	Fellowship (% Receiving)	Fellowship Tuition Remission
First-Year Student	$4,625 (NA)	Partial	$4,625 (NA)	Partial	NA (NA)	NA
Advanced Student	$4,625 (NA)	Partial	$4,625 (NA)	Partial	NA (NA)	NA

For additional information on financial assistance, visit http://www.stcloudstate.edu/gradadmissions/financing-your-education/default.aspx.

Employment of Department Graduates

Master's:
Employed in business or industry: 9
Total: 9

Additional Information

Housing and Day Care: On-campus housing is available. See the following website for more information: http://www.stcloudstate.edu/reslife/. On-campus day care facilities are available. See the following website for more information: http://www.stcloudstate.edu/childcare/.

Information for Students With Physical Disabilities: See the following website: http://www.stcloudstate.edu/sds/.

Special Facilities or Resources: The St. Cloud State University Psychology Department has a dedicated psychology laboratory facility (new space established in 1999). It has 10 rooms for individual and group testing. The lab has networked computers and a laser printer. Activities that take place in this lab include: faculty and student research, meetings of student organizations, research seminars, and classroom demonstrations.

Application Information: School of Graduate Studies, 121 Administrative Services, St. Cloud State University, 720 4th Avenue South, St. Cloud, MN 56301. *Fee:* $40. *Online application:* https://app.applyyourself.com/?id=stcloudg.

St. Thomas, University of
Graduate School of Professional Psychology
College of Education, Leadership and Counseling
1000 LaSalle Avenue, MOH 217
Minneapolis, MN 55403-2005
Telephone: (651) 962-4650
Chairperson: Christopher Vye

E-mail: gradpsych@stthomas.edu
Web: http://www.stthomas.edu/counselingpsychology/

Orientation, Objectives, and Emphasis of Department
The Graduate School of Professional Psychology is dedicated to the development of general practitioners who will make ethical, professional, and creative contributions to their communities and their profession. The programs strive toward leadership in emphasizing a practitioner focus with adult learners. Teaching, scholarship, and service are responsive to diverse perspectives, a blend of practical and reflective inquiry, and social needs. The PsyD program is accredited by the APA.

Programs and Degrees Offered

Program	Degree	Application Deadline	Applications Received	Accepted	New Admits Enrolled (PT)	Total Enrolled (PT)	Degrees Awarded in 2014–2015	Median Years to Complete Degree	Dismissed/ Withdrew
Counseling	MA/MS	February 5 (Fall), October 15 (Spring)	168	104	31 (22)	123 (374)	49	2	5
Counseling Psychology	PsyD	December 15 (Fall)	49	29	9 (9)	23 (186)	13	3.9	0

APA Accreditation
Counseling PsyD: Student Outcome Data website: http://www.stthomas.edu/counselingpsychology/programs/counseling-psychology-doctorate/.

Doctoral Degree (PsyD Counseling Psychology): For those doctoral students for whom a professional internship was required in this program prior to graduation:
Total students who applied for an internship: 14
Total students who obtained an internship: 14
Total students who obtained a paid internship: 14
Total students who obtained an unpaid internship: 0
Total students who were placed in APA/CPA-accredited internships: 8
Total students placed in internships not APA/CPA-accredited, but listed with the Association of Psychology Postdoctoral and Internship Centers (APPIC): 6
Total students placed in internships conforming to guidelines of the Council of Directors of School Psychology Programs (CDSPP): 0
Total students placed in internships that were not APA/CPA-accredited, APPIC or CDSSP listed: 0

Internships/Practica
Master's and doctoral students have available a wide variety of practica and internships in the surrounding community in the Twin Cities area. Application is competitive and supported by the practicum coordinator at UST. Students also participate in predoctoral internships locally and across the country. Recent sites have included community mental health centers, regional hospitals, VA medical centers, residential chemical dependency centers, career and vocational services, college/university counseling and career centers, vocational rehabilitation programs, employee assistance counseling programs, health maintenance organizations, MN state hospitals, and the MN state prison system.

Admissions

Entries appear in the following order: required test or GPA, minimum score (if required)/median score of students entering in 2015–2016.

Program	Degree	GRE-V	GRE-Q	GRE-Writing	GRE-Subject	Under-graduate GPA	Last 2 Years GPA	Psychol-ogy GPA	Master's GPA
Counseling	MA/MS	NA/153	NA/149	NA/4	Not specified	3/NA	Not specified	Not specified	Not specified
Counseling Psychology	PsyD	NA/152	NA/148	NA/4	Not specified	3/NA	Not specified	Not specified	NA/NA

Admissions Requirements:

Degree	GRE	GRE-Subject	Letters of Recom-mendation	Research Statement	Writing Sample	CV	Interview
Master's/Specialist	Required	None	2	Required	None	Required	Required
Doctoral	Required	None	2	Required	Required	Optional	Required

Please note if these criteria vary for different programs: The writing sample is only mandatory for the MA with Direct Admission to PsyD and PsyD admission. Two letters of recommendation are required for the MA and PsyD program, and three letters of recommendation are required for the MA with Direct Admission to PsyD track.

Admissions Criteria:

GRE scores—medium
Research experience—low
Work experience—high
Clinically related public service—high
GPA—high

Letters of recommendation—high
Interview—high
Statement of goals and objectives—high
Undergraduate psychology preparation—low
Writing sample—medium

For additional information on admission requirements, visit http://www.stthomas.edu/counselingpsychology/admissions-and-aid/.

Department Demographics

	Male (PT)	Female (PT)	Total	African-American/ Black (PT)	Hispanic/ Latino (PT)	Asian/ Pacific Islander (PT)	American Indian/ Alaska Native (PT)	Caucasian/ White (PT)	Unknown (PT)	Multiethnic (PT)	ADA (PT)	Int'l (PT)
Students	13 (34)	58 (83)	188	2 (6)	6 (3)	2 (4)	0 (0)	58 (92)	2 (1)	0 (7)	0 (0)	1 (4)

Financial Information/Assistance

Tuition: For information on tuition costs, visit http://www.stthomas.edu/counselingpsychology/tuitionandfees/. Tuition is subject to change. Additional fees are assessed to students beyond the costs of tuition for the following: Technology & Writing Center. Tuition costs vary by program.

Doctoral:
State residents: $23,560 per academic year.
State residents: $995 per credit hour.
Nonstate residents: $23,560 per academic year.
Nonstate residents: $995 per credit hour.

Master's:
State residents: $750 per credit hour.
Nonstate residents: $750 per credit hour.

Financial Assistance:

	Teaching Assistantship (% Receiving)	Teaching Assistantship Tuition Remission	Research Assistantship (% Receiving)	Research Assistantship Tuition Remission	Fellowship (% Receiving)	Fellowship Tuition Remission
First-Year Student	NA (NA)	NA	$3,600 (NA)	Partial	$2,313 (NA)	Partial
Advanced Student	NA (NA)	NA	$3,600 (NA)	Partial	$2,313 (NA)	Partial

For additional information on financial assistance, visit http://www.stthomas.edu/financialaid/graduate/scholarships/.

Employment of Department Graduates

Doctoral:
Enrolled in a postdoctoral residency/fellowship: 8
Employed in independent practice: 1
Employed in other positions at a higher education institution: 1
Employed in government agency: 1
Employed in a community mental health/counseling center: 4
Employed in a hospital/medical center: 2
Total: 17

Additional Information

Housing and Day Care: No on-campus housing is available. On-campus day care facilities are available. See the following website for more information: http://www.stthomas.edu/childdevelopment/.

Information for Students With Physical Disabilities: See the following website: http://www.stthomas.edu/enhancementprog/.

Special Facilities or Resources: UST has developed the Inter-Professional Center (IPC) which is an inter-professional clinic involving counseling psychology, social work and law. This unique center provides free counseling and legal services to underserved populations in the Minneapolis/St. Paul vicinity. This is a practicum and predoctoral internship option for our students.

Application Information: Admissions, Graduate School of Professional Psychology, University of St. Thomas, 1000 LaSalle Avenue, MOH 217, Minneapolis, MN 55403. *Fee:* $0. *Online application:* http://www.stthomas.edu/admissions/graduate/apply/.

Mississippi State University

Department of Counseling, Educational Psychology, and Foundations
College of Education
P.O. Box 9727
Mississippi State, MS 39762-5670
Telephone: (662) 325-3426
Department Head: Dr. David T. Morse

E-mail: ch27@msstate.edu
Web: http://www.cep.msstate.edu

Orientation, Objectives, and Emphasis of Department

Our psychology graduate programs are designed primarily to help develop and train competent and ethical psychologists in the areas of school psychology and educational psychology. The school psychology program is based on a scientist–practitioner model and trains students to implement empirically-based assessment, consultation, and intervention techniques. The flexibility of these offerings gives the student the option of functioning as an educational or school psychologist in a variety of settings, thereby enhancing employment opportunities. The school psychology curriculum has recently been approved by the Behavior Analyst Certification Board (BACB).

Programs and Degrees Offered

Program	Degree	Application Deadline	Applica-tions Received	Accepted	New Admits Enrolled (PT)	Total Enrolled (PT)	Degrees Awarded in 2014–2015	Median Years to Complete Degree	Dismissed/ Withdrew
School Psychology	EdS	January 15 (Fall)	10	5	3 (0)	9 (1)	5	4	1
School Psychology	PhD	January 15 (Fall)	21	12	5 (0)	17 (7)	7	6	3
Educational Psychology	MA/MS	March 15 (Fall)	4	4	0 (0)	2 (2)	0		0
Educational Psychology	PhD	March 15 (Fall)	10	6	1 (0)	5 (3)	0		0

APA Accreditation

School PhD: Student Outcome Data website: http://schoolpsych.msstate.edu/schoolpsych/Student_Admissions,_Outcome,_%26_Other_Data.html.

Doctoral Degree (PhD School Psychology): For those doctoral students for whom a professional internship was required in this program prior to graduation:
Total students who applied for an internship: 3
Total students who obtained an internship: 3
Total students who obtained a paid internship: 3
Total students who obtained an unpaid internship: 0
Total students who were placed in APA/CPA-accredited internships: 3
Total students placed in internships not APA/CPA-accredited, but listed with the Association of Psychology Postdoctoral and Internship Centers (APPIC): 0
Total students placed in internships conforming to guidelines of the Council of Directors of School Psychology Programs (CDSPP): 0
Total students placed in internships that were not APA/CPA-accredited, APPIC or CDSSP listed: 0

Internships/Practica

The School Psychology program offers students numerous practicum and internship opportunities. Most practica are coordinated with local school districts. Students also complete practica in the on-campus School Psychology Services Center. Some externships have also been coordinated with medical centers/hospitals and/or mental health or community counseling centers both within and outside of the state. Doctoral students are strongly encouraged to seek APA-accredited predoctoral internships.

Admissions

Entries appear in the following order: required test or GPA, minimum score (if required)/median score of students entering in 2015–2016.

Program	Degree	GRE-V	GRE-Q	GRE-Writing	GRE-Subject	Under-graduate GPA	Last 2 Years GPA	Psychol-ogy GPA	Master's GPA
School Psychology	EdS	NA/142	NA/140	NA/3.5	Not specified	2.75/3.35	Not specified	Not specified	Not specified
School Psychology	PhD	NA/153	NA/147	NA/4	Not specified	2.75/3.52	Not specified	Not specified	Not specified
Educational Psychology	MA/MS	Not specified	Not specified	Not specified	Not specified	Not specified	Not specified	Not specified	Not specified
Educational Psychology	PhD	NA/152	NA/140	NA/3	Not specified	2.75/3.05	Not specified	Not specified	Not specified

Admissions Requirements:

Degree	GRE	GRE-Subject	Letters of Recom-mendation	Research Statement	Writing Sample	CV	Interview
Master's/Specialist	Required	None	3	Required	Optional	Optional	Required
Doctoral	Required	None	3	Required	Optional	Optional	Required

Admissions Criteria:

GRE scores—high
Research experience—high
Work experience—medium
Clinically related public service—medium
GPA—high

Letters of recommendation—high
Interview—high
Statement of goals and objectives—high
Undergraduate psychology preparation—high

Department Demographics

	Male (PT)	Female (PT)	Total	African-American/ Black (PT)	Hispanic/ Latino (PT)	Asian/ Pacific Islander (PT)	American Indian/ Alaska Native (PT)	Caucasian/ White (PT)	Unknown	Multiethnic (PT)	ADA (PT)	Int'l (PT)
Students	7 (1)	26 (12)	46	3 (2)	1 (0)	1 (2)	0 (0)	20 (9)	6 (0)	2 (0)	1 (0)	5 (0)

Financial Information/Assistance

Tuition: For information on tuition costs, visit http://www.grad.msstate.edu/tuition/fees. Tuition is subject to change. Additional fees are assessed to students beyond the costs of tuition for the following: Assessment laboratory fees for specific courses.

Doctoral:
State residents: $7,392 per academic year.
State residents: $410 per credit hour.
Nonstate residents: $20,032 per academic year.
Nonstate residents: $1,113 per credit hour.

Master's:
State residents: $7,392 per academic year.
State residents: $410 per credit hour.
Nonstate residents: $20,032 per academic year.
Nonstate residents: $1,113 per credit hour.

Financial Assistance:

	Teaching Assistantship (% Receiving)	Teaching Assistantship Tuition Remission	Research Assistantship (% Receiving)	Research Assistantship Tuition Remission	Fellowship (% Receiving)	Fellowship Tuition Remission
First-Year Student	$10,000 (5)	Full	$10,000 (15)	Full	$10,000 (70)	Full
Advanced Student	$12,000 (5)	Full	$12,000 (15)	Full	$12,000 (70)	Full

For additional information on financial assistance, visit http://www.sfa.msstate.edu.

Employment of Department Graduates

Master's:
Enrolled in a psychology doctoral program: 5
Total: 5

Doctoral:
Enrolled in a postdoctoral residency/fellowship: 3
Employed in an academic position at a university: 2
Employed in a professional position in a school system: 2
Employed in a hospital/medical center: 2
Total: 9

Additional Information

Housing and Day Care: On-campus housing is available. See the following website for more information: http://www.housing.msstate.edu. On-campus day care facilities are available. See the following website for more information: http://www.humansci.msstate.edu/cdfsc/; http://www.earlychildhood.msstate.edu/aikenvillage/index.php.

Information for Students With Physical Disabilities: See the following website: http://www.sss.msstate.edu/disabilities/.

Special Facilities or Resources: The Educational and School Psychology faculty maintain close working relationships with faculty in other programs and departments such as Counseling, Psychology, and Special Education. Such relationships afford students the opportunity to work closely with diverse faculty members with various human services backgrounds. Moreover, students are encouraged to work closely with their faculty on various creative projects and research. Additional opportunities exist at the National Research and Training Center on Blindness and Low Vision, the Bureau of Educational Research and Evaluation, and the Research and Curriculum Unit for Vocational-Technical Education, Social Science Research Center, Child Development Center, and T.K. Martin Center for Technology and Disability, all of which are connected with Mississippi State University.

Application Information: Mississippi State University, Office of the Graduate School, P.O. Box G, Mississippi State, MS 39762-5507. *Fee:* $60. *Online application:* http://www.grad.msstate.edu/admissions/.

Mississippi State University
Department of Psychology
Arts and Sciences
P.O. Drawer 6161
Mississippi State, MS 39762
Telephone: (662) 325-3202
Department Head: Mitchell Berman

E-mail: kja3@psychology.msstate.edu
Web: http://psychology.msstate.edu

Orientation, Objectives, and Emphasis of Department
Currently we offer a PhD program in Applied Psychology with concentrations in either Clinical Psychology or Cognitive Science.

Programs and Degrees Offered

Program	Degree	Application Deadline	Applications Received	Accepted	New Admits Enrolled (PT)	Total Enrolled (PT)	Degrees Awarded in 2014–2015	Median Years to Complete Degree	Dismissed/ Withdrew
Clinical Psychology	PhD		41	9	6 (0)	21 (0)	0		0
Cognitive Science	PhD	January 15 (Fall)	5	2	1	12	0		1

Internships/Practica

Students in the PhD program in Applied Psychology, Clinical concentration begin internal practicum in our psychology clinic during the summer following their second year and continue throughout their time in residence. We see clients both from MSU and the broader community and provide both intervention and assessment services for children, adolescents, adults, and older adults. During the summer following the students' second year they begin community practicum placements. These occur in a variety of settings (e.g., state psychiatric hospital, private psychiatric hospital, a neuropsychological practice, a forensic psychology practice, and an inpatient substance-abuse treatment center). Students are exposed to diverse client populations (e.g., in- and outpatient, children and adults with varied diagnoses and ethnic backgrounds). Students are required to complete a 1-year clinical internship prior to graduation.

Admissions

Entries appear in the following order: required test or GPA, minimum score (if required)/median score of students entering in 2015–2016.

Program	Degree	GRE-V	GRE-Q	GRE-Writing	GRE-Subject	Under-graduate GPA	Last 2 Years GPA	Psychology GPA	Master's GPA
Clinical Psychology	PhD	154/157	147/155	3/4	Not specified	3.52/3.8	3.57/3.96	3.87/4	NA/NA
Cognitive Science	PhD	151/156	152/154	4/4	Not specified	3.59/3.94	NA/NA	NA/NA	NA/NA

Admissions Requirements:

Degree	GRE	GRE-Subject	Letters of Recommendation	Research Statement	Writing Sample	CV	Interview
Doctoral	Required	Optional	3	Required	Optional	Optional	Required

Please note if these criteria vary for different programs: The clinically related public service would be relevant for applicants to the Clinical Psychology program. Computer-related experience is relevant to the Cognitive Science program.

Admissions Criteria:

GRE scores—medium
Research experience—high
Work experience—medium
Clinically related public service—medium
GPA—high

Letters of recommendation—high
Interview—high
Statement of goals and objectives—high
Undergraduate psychology preparation—high

For additional information on admission requirements, visit http://psychology.msstate.edu/gradprograms/prospective/howtoapply/index.php.

Department Demographics

	Male (PT)	Female (PT)	Total	African-American/ Black (PT)	Hispanic/ Latino (PT)	Asian/ Pacific Islander (PT)	American Indian/ Alaska Native (PT)	Caucasian/ White (PT)	Unknown	Multiethnic (PT)	ADA (PT)	Int'l (PT)
Students	12 (0)	21 (0)	33	3 (0)	0 (0)	4 (0)	0 (0)	24 (0)	1 (0)	1 (0)	0 (0)	3 (0)

Financial Information/Assistance

Tuition: For information on tuition costs, visit http://www.grad.msstate.edu/tuition/fees/. Tuition is subject to change.

Doctoral:
State residents: $7,392 per academic year.
State residents: $410 per credit hour.
Nonstate residents: $20,032 per academic year.
Nonstate residents: $1,113 per credit hour.

Master's:
State residents: $7,392 per academic year.
State residents: $410 per credit hour.
Nonstate residents: $20,032 per academic year.
Nonstate residents: $1,113 per credit hour.

Financial Assistance:

	Teaching Assistantship (% Receiving)	Teaching Assistantship Tuition Remission	Research Assistantship (% Receiving)	Research Assistantship Tuition Remission	Fellowship (% Receiving)	Fellowship Tuition Remission
First-Year Student	$10,285 (100)	Full	$12,000 (0)	Full	NA (NA)	NA
Advanced Student	$11,000 (46)	Full	$14,000 (54)	Full	NA (NA)	NA

Employment of Department Graduates

Doctoral:
Enrolled in a postdoctoral residency/fellowship: 1
Total: 1

Additional Information

Housing and Day Care: On-campus housing is available. See the following website for more information: http://www.housing.msstate.edu/. On-campus day care facilities are available. See the following website for more information: http://www.earlychildhood.msstate.edu/.

Information for Students With Physical Disabilities: See the following website: http://www.sss.msstate.edu/.

Special Facilities or Resources: All research-active faculty have laboratories that include cutting-edge research tools that are applicable to each faculty member's research program. These include EEG equipment, eye trackers, actigraphy, facial emotional recognition hardware/software, and ePrime software. Additionally, other research facilities on campus house a 3T fMRI magnet, simultaneous EEG/fMRI equipment, and a driving simulator. Finally, clinical students have research/training opportunities in the on-site Psychology Training Clinic and in several off-campus practicum placements.

Application Information: Fee: $60. *Online application:* http://www.grad.msstate.edu/prospective/admissions/domestic.

Mississippi, University of
Department of Psychology
Liberal Arts
205 Peabody Hall
University, MS 38677
Telephone: (662) 915-7383
Chairperson: Michael T. Allen

E-mail: psych@olemiss.edu
Web: http://psychology.olemiss.edu/

Orientation, Objectives, and Emphasis of Department
The Department of Psychology offers programs of study in clinical and experimental psychology leading to the Doctor of Philosophy degree. The clinical program, which is fully accredited by the American Psychological Association, ordinarily requires 5 years beyond the bachelor's level to complete. Four of the 5 years are devoted to coursework and research, and the remaining year entails a clinical internship at an APA-approved training site. Requirements for the master's degree are also fulfilled during this period; however, the MA is considered to be a step in the doctoral training. The clinical program adheres to the scientist–practitioner model and emphasizes an empirical approach to clinical practice. A social learning or behavioral approach characterizes the clinical training offered. The experimental program is designed to prepare psychologists for careers in teaching and research. Specific programs include Behavioral Neuroscience, Cognitive Psychology, and Social Psychology. Students entering the experimental program are assigned a faculty mentor (major professor) whose research interests match their training goals. All students are required to engage in significant research projects.

Programs and Degrees Offered

Program	Degree	Application Deadline	Applications Received	Accepted	New Admits Enrolled (PT)	Total Enrolled (PT)	Degrees Awarded in 2014–2015	Median Years to Complete Degree	Dismissed/ Withdrew
Experimental Psychology	PhD	December 1 (Fall)	21	2	1 (0)	12 (0)	3	6	1
Clinical Psychology	PhD	December 1 (Fall)	125	14	8 (0)	51 (0)	11	6.9	0

APA Accreditation

Clinical PhD: Student Outcome Data website: http://psychology.olemiss.edu/student-admissions-outcomes-and-other-data/.

Doctoral Degree (PhD Clinical Psychology): For those doctoral students for whom a professional internship was required in this program prior to graduation:

Total students who applied for an internship: 11
Total students who obtained an internship: 11
Total students who obtained a paid internship: 11
Total students who obtained an unpaid internship: 0
Total students who were placed in APA/CPA-accredited internships: 10
Total students placed in internships not APA/CPA-accredited, but listed with the Association of Psychology Postdoctoral and Internship Centers (APPIC): 1
Total students placed in internships conforming to guidelines of the Council of Directors of School Psychology Programs (CDSPP): 0
Total students placed in internships that were not APA/CPA-accredited, APPIC or CDSSP listed: 0

Internships/Practica

Practica or field placements are available for clinical students beginning in the second year of the program. Students serve as therapists on practicum teams in our in-house clinic for a minimum of three years under the direct supervision of the members of our clinical faculty, all of whom are licensed psychologists. After students have demonstrated a minimum level of competence in the clinic, they are allowed to apply for practicum positions at field placement agencies in the community, where they are supervised by licensed practitioners who are employed by the field placement agency. In recent years, students have completed field placements at community mental health centers in Oxford and Tupelo, North Mississippi Regional Center in Oxford, St. Jude Children's Research Hospital in Memphis, and others. Students are assisted and advised by faculty in choosing field placements most appropriate to their individual career goals.

Admissions

Entries appear in the following order: required test or GPA, minimum score (if required)/median score of students entering in 2015–2016.

Program	Degree	GRE-V	GRE-Q	GRE-Writing	GRE-Subject	Undergraduate GPA	Last 2 Years GPA	Psychology GPA	Master's GPA
Experimental Psychology	PhD	Not specified	Not specified	Not specified	Not specified	Not specified	Not specified	Not specified	Not specified
Clinical Psychology	PhD	NA/158	NA/156	NA/NA	Not specified	Not specified	Not specified	Not specified	Not specified

Admissions Requirements:

Degree	GRE	GRE-Subject	Letters of Recommendation	Research Statement	Writing Sample	CV	Interview
Doctoral	Required	Optional	3	Required	Optional	Required	Required

Admissions Criteria:

GRE scores—medium
Research experience—high
Work experience—medium
Clinically related public service—medium
GPA—medium

Letters of recommendation—high
Interview—high
Statement of goals and objectives—high
Undergraduate psychology preparation—high

For additional information on admission requirements, visit http://psychology.olemiss.edu/psychology-admissions/.

Department Demographics

	Male (PT)	Female (PT)	Total	African-American/ Black (PT)	Hispanic/ Latino (PT)	Asian/ Pacific Islander (PT)	American Indian/ Alaska Native (PT)	Caucasian/ White (PT)	Unknown	Multiethnic (PT)	ADA (PT)	Int'l (PT)
Students	21 (0)	42 (0)	63	6 (0)	7 (0)	4 (0)	1 (0)	45 (0)	0 (0)	0 (0)	0 (0)	5 (0)

Financial Information/Assistance

Tuition: For information on tuition costs, visit http://www.olemiss.edu/depts/bursar/estimator.html. Tuition is subject to change. Additional fees are assessed to students beyond the costs of tuition for the following: $100.00 Capital improvements fee.

Doctoral:
State residents: $7,344 per academic year.
State residents: $408 per credit hour.
Nonstate residents: $20,574 per academic year.
Nonstate residents: $1,143 per credit hour.

Financial Assistance:

	Teaching Assistantship (% Receiving)	Teaching Assistantship Tuition Remission	Research Assistantship (% Receiving)	Research Assistantship Tuition Remission	Fellowship (% Receiving)	Fellowship Tuition Remission
First-Year Student	$10,000 (NA)	Full	$10,000 (NA)	Full	$3,000 (NA)	NA
Advanced Student	$10,000 (NA)	Full	$10,000 (NA)	Full	$3,000 (NA)	NA

For additional information on financial assistance, visit http://gradschool.olemiss.edu/prospective-students/financial-aid-information/.

Employment of Department Graduates

Doctoral:
Enrolled in a postdoctoral residency/fellowship: 9
Employed in an academic position at a university: 2
Total: 11

Additional Information

Housing and Day Care: On-campus housing is available. See the following website for more information: http://studenthousing. olemiss.edu/. On-campus day care facilities are available. See the following website for more information: http://education.olemiss. edu/willieprice/.

Information for Students With Physical Disabilities: See the following website: http://sds.olemiss.edu/.

Special Facilities or Resources: Most of the department's offices and laboratories are housed in the George Peabody Building. State-of-the-art facilities for animal research are available in a new centralized animal facility on campus. The psychology clinic is in Kinard Hall on campus which provides for a more professional office environment and better client accessibility. The psychology clinic includes multipurpose rooms for evaluation, consultation, and therapy and observation rooms equipped with one-way mirrors and videotape equipment. The department offers computer-based laboratories for psychopharmacology, psychophysiology, operant conditioning, and behavioral toxicology. The department has close ties with the pharmacy and law schools (located on the Oxford campus) and with the medical school in Jackson.

Application Information: Fee: $50. Online application: http://gradschool.olemiss.edu/apply-now/.

Central Missouri, University of

Department of Psychological Science
College of Health, Science, and Technology
Lovinger 1111
Warrensburg, MO 64093
Telephone: (660) 543-4185
Chairperson: David Kreiner

E-mail: kreiner@ucmo.edu
Web: http://www.ucmo.edu/psychology/

Orientation, Objectives, and Emphasis of Department

The department offers two master's programs. In Fall 2017, the first cohort begins a new MS in Behavior Analysis and Therapy. This program meets the educational requirements to sit for the Board Certified Behavior Analyst (BCBA) exam. The MS in Psychology program is focused on predoctoral preparation. It is ideal for students who wish to improve their research skills, co-author articles and presentations with faculty, engage in professional networking, and expand their knowledge of psychology prior to applying or reapplying to PhD programs. The program also prepares students for employment that utilizes acquired psychological knowledge and skills.

Programs and Degrees Offered

Program	Degree	Application Deadline	Applica-tions Received	Accepted	New Admits Enrolled (PT)	Total Enrolled (PT)	Degrees Awarded in 2014–2015	Median Years to Complete Degree	Dismissed/ Withdrew
Psychology	MA/MS	Rolling	27	17	12 (0)	21 (2)	4	2.5	1
Behavior Analysis & Therapy	MA/MS	Rolling	0	0	0 (0)	0 (0)	0		0

Internships/Practica

The MS Behavior Analysis and Therapy requires 6 hours of practica. Practicum sites are available offering a range of experiences with various populations.

Admissions

Entries appear in the following order: required test or GPA, minimum score (if required)/median score of students entering in 2015–2016.

Program	Degree	GRE-V	GRE-Q	GRE-Writing	GRE-Subject	Under-graduate GPA	Last 2 Years GPA	Psychol-ogy GPA	Master's GPA
Psychology	MA/MS	NA/153	NA/145	NA/4	Not specified	Not specified	Not specified	3/NA	Not specified
Behavior Analysis & Therapy	MA/MS	Not specified	Not specified	Not specified	Not specified	Not specified	Not specified	Not specified	Not specified

Admissions Requirements:

Degree	GRE	GRE-Subject	Letters of Recom-mendation	Research Statement	Writing Sample	CV	Interview
Master's/Specialist	Required	None	3	Required	None	Optional	None

Admissions Criteria:

GRE scores—medium
Research experience—medium
Work experience—low
Clinically related public service—low

GPA—high
Letters of recommendation—medium
Statement of goals and objectives—high
Undergraduate psychology preparation—high

For additional information on admission requirements, visit http://www.ucmo.edu/psychology/grad/admit.cfm.

Department Demographics

	Male (PT)	Female (PT)	Total	African-American/ Black (PT)	Hispanic/ Latino (PT)	Asian/ Pacific Islander (PT)	American Indian/ Alaska Native (PT)	Caucasian/ White (PT)	Unknown	Multiethnic (PT)	ADA (PT)	Int'l (PT)
Students	6 (0)	15 (2)	23	0 (0)	2 (0)	1 (0)	0 (0)	18 (2)	0 (0)	0 (0)	1 (0)	2 (0)

Financial Information/Assistance

Tuition: For information on tuition costs, visit http://www.ucmo.edu/costs/. Tuition is subject to change. Additional fees are assessed to students beyond the costs of tuition for the following: athletics, facilities, student activity, student rec center, technology, union.

Master's:
State residents: $278 per credit hour.
Nonstate residents: $557 per credit hour.

Financial Assistance:

	Teaching Assistantship (% Receiving)	Teaching Assistantship Tuition Remission	Research Assistantship (% Receiving)	Research Assistantship Tuition Remission	Fellowship (% Receiving)	Fellowship Tuition Remission
First-Year Student	$7,500 (NA)	Partial	NA (NA)	NA	NA (NA)	NA
Advanced Student	$7,500 (NA)	Partial	NA (NA)	NA	NA (NA)	NA

For additional information on financial assistance, visit http://www.ucmo.edu/graduate/support/.

Employment of Department Graduates

Master's:
Employed in a professional position in a school system: 1
Employed in business or industry: 1
Still seeking employment: 1
Total: 3

Additional Information

Housing and Day Care: On-campus housing is available. See the following website for more information: http://www.ucmo.edu/housing/. On-campus day care facilities are available. See the following website for more information: https://www.ucmo.edu/childcare/.

Information for Students With Physical Disabilities: See the following website: http://www.ucmo.edu/access/.

Special Facilities or Resources: Behavioral Medicine and Biofeedback Laboratory; Neurocognition Laboratory; Eyetracking Laboratory; Experimental Psychology Laboratory; Virtual Reality Laboratory; Social Issues and Assessment of Learning Laboratory.

Application Information: School of Graduate and Extended Studies, Ward Edwards 1800, Warrensburg, MO 64093. *Fee:* $30.
Online application: https://www.ucmo.edu/graduate/admission/apply/secure/.

Missouri State University

Psychology Department
College of Health and Human Services
901 South National Avenue
Springfield, MO 65897
Telephone: (417) 836-4790
Interim Department Head: Robert G. Jones, PhD

E-mail: psychology@missouristate.edu
Web: http://psychology.missouristate.edu

Orientation, Objectives, and Emphasis of Department

We are an eclectic department of 30 full-time faculty serving over 800 undergraduate majors. The faculty have diverse research interests including applied behavior analysis (ABA), clinical, industrial/organizational (I/O), forensic, human learning, language, motivation, human skills, and memory. The department operates the Learning Diagnostic Clinic for diagnosis and remediation of special populations, as well as limited therapy for other psychological disorders.

Programs and Degrees Offered

Program	Degree	Application Deadline	Applica-tions Received	Accepted	New Admits Enrolled (PT)	Total Enrolled (PT)	Degrees Awarded in 2014–2015	Median Years to Complete Degree	Dismissed/ Withdrew
Clinical Psychology	MA/MS	February 15 (Fall)	52	9	9 (0)	19 (1)	7	2.3	0
Experimental Psychology	MA/MS	February 15 (Fall)	18	9	9 (0)	15 (0)	5	2	1
Industrial/ Organizational Psychology	MA/MS	February 15 (Fall)	60	14	14 (0)	26 (0)	14	2	0
Child Forensic Certificate	Other	Rolling	9	9	9 (12)	15 (12)	4	1	1
Applied Behavior Analysis	MA/MS	February 15 (Fall)	10	9	2	7	0		0

Internships/Practica

Clinical—students must complete two 175-contact hour practica. Placements are in a variety of mental health settings. Students who choose a non-thesis option must complete an additional 175-contact hour internship. Experimental—practicum experience is acquired through basic laboratory research work tailored specifically to the graduate student's research area of interest. The goal of the practicum is for the student to develop or acquire competence in various research methods and behavioral/cognitive measurement skills that will prepare the student for later doctoral work.

Admissions

Entries appear in the following order: required test or GPA, minimum score (if required)/median score of students entering in 2015–2016.

Program	Degree	GRE-V	GRE-Q	GRE-Writing	GRE-Subject	Under-graduate GPA	Last 2 Years GPA	Psychol-ogy GPA	Master's GPA
Clinical Psychology	MA/MS	Not specified	Not specified	Not specified	Not specified	Not specified	Not specified	Not specified	Not specified
Experimental Psychology	MA/MS	148/160	146/150	Not specified	Not specified	3.09/3.55	Not specified	NA/NA	Not specified
Industrial/ Organizational Psychology	MA/MS	151/151	142/150	Not specified	Not specified	Not specified	Not specified	Not specified	Not specified
Child Forensic Certificate	Other	Not specified	Not specified	Not specified	Not specified	Not specified	Not specified	Not specified	Not specified

Admissions *(con't.)*

Program	Degree	GRE-V	GRE-Q	GRE-Writing	GRE-Subject	Under-graduate GPA	Last 2 Years GPA	Psychol-ogy GPA	Master's GPA
Applied Behavior Analysis	MA/MS	Not specified	Not specified	Not specified	Not specified	Not specified	Not specified	Not specified	Not specified

Admissions Requirements:

Degree	GRE	GRE-Subject	Letters of Recom-mendation	Research Statement	Writing Sample	CV	Interview
Master's/Specialist	Required	Optional	3	Optional	Optional	Optional	None

Admissions Criteria:

GRE scores—medium
Research experience—high
Work experience—medium
Clinically related public service—high

GPA—high
Letters of recommendation—high
Statement of goals and objectives—high
Undergraduate psychology preparation—high

Department Demographics

	Male (PT)	Female (PT)	Total	African-American/ Black (PT)	Hispanic/ Latino (PT)	Asian/ Pacific Islander (PT)	American Indian/ Alaska Native (PT)	Caucasian/ White (PT)	Unknown	Multiethnic (PT)	ADA (PT)	Int'l (PT)
Students	31 (5)	89 (18)	143	2 (0)	5 (1)	8 (0)	6 (0)	92 (18)	4 (3)	3 (1)	2 (0)	4 (4)

Financial Information/Assistance

Tuition: For information on tuition costs, visit http://www.missouristate.edu/costs/. Tuition is subject to change. Additional fees are assessed to students beyond the costs of tuition for the following: student services fees, supplemental course fees.

Master's:
State residents: $5,500 per academic year.
State residents: $255 per credit hour.
Nonstate residents: $10,108 per academic year.
Nonstate residents: $511 per credit hour.

Financial Assistance:

	Teaching Assistantship (% Receiving)	Teaching Assistantship Tuition Remission	Research Assistantship (% Receiving)	Research Assistantship Tuition Remission	Fellowship (% Receiving)	Fellowship Tuition Remission
First-Year Student	NA (NA)	NA	$8,600 (NA)	Full	NA (NA)	NA
Advanced Student	$8,600 (NA)	Full	$8,600 (NA)	Full	NA (NA)	NA

For additional information on financial assistance, visit http://www.missouristate.edu/FinancialAid/Graduate.htm.

Employment of Department Graduates

No information provided.

Additional Information

Housing and Day Care: On-campus housing is available. See the following website for more information: http://reslife.missouristate. edu/. On-campus day care facilities are available. See the following website for more information: http://education.missouristate. edu/cdc/.

Information for Students With Physical Disabilities: See the following website: http://www.missouristate.edu/disability/.

Special Facilities or Resources: The Psychology Department has 16 research labs serving the Experimental, Industrial/Organizational, and Clinical Master's tracks and the Applied Behavior Analysis program. These labs house well-supported computers and equipment for measuring and recording visual scanning, heart rate, brain evoked potential, behavioral responses, implicit association, mnemonic strategies, psycholinguistic association, and motor skills. Our laboratories support basic research in individual differences, learning and cognition, health and wellness, group performance and decision making, quantitative methods, and applied research in forensic, I/O, social, educational, sport, environmental, and clinical psychology, among others. The department oversees the RStats Institute, which employs graduate students as consultants in quantitative methods. Many other graduate assistantships are also available. Field experiences, which are integral to our applied graduate tracks, are supported both by the Learning Diagnostic Clinic, which is overseen by the department, and by extensive community networks. For example, students in the I/O track engage in field work with local and regional organizations in organizational climate assessment and personnel selection. Students in the Clinical track work with patients in local hospitals and clinics.

Application Information: Psychology Department, Attn: Graduate Application, 901 South National Avenue, Hill Hall 313, Springfield, MO 65897. *Fee:* $35. *Online application:* http://www.missouristate.edu/futurestudents/applynow.aspx.

Missouri Western State University

Psychology
Liberal Arts and Sciences
4525 Downs Drive
St. Joseph, MO 64507
Telephone: (816) 271-4444
Chairperson: Brian Cronk

E-mail: cronk@missouriwestern.edu
Web: http://www.missouriwestern.edu/psychology/

Orientation, Objectives, and Emphasis of Department

Our graduate program combines business and human factors education. We produce students who are able to understand the complex interactions between humans and computing devices. The program highlights the major areas necessary for developing products within a competitive industry environment. The ultimate goal of human factors professionals is to create and transform interactive devices into systems that will make everyone's lives a little easier, safer and more enjoyable.

Programs and Degrees Offered

Program	Degree	Application Deadline	Applications Received	Accepted	New Admits Enrolled (PT)	Total Enrolled (PT)	Degrees Awarded in 2014–2015	Median Years to Complete Degree	Dismissed/ Withdrew
Human Factors and Usability Testing	MA/MS	April 15 (Fall)	8	4	4	8	3	2	0

Admissions

Entries appear in the following order: required test or GPA, minimum score (if required)/median score of students entering in 2015–2016.

Program	Degree	GRE-V	GRF-Q	GRE-Writing	GRE-Subject	Under-graduate GPA	Last 2 Years GPA	Psychology GPA	Master's GPA
Human Factors and Usability Testing	MA/MS	146/NA	141/NA	Not specified	Not specified	2.75/3.5	Not specified	Not specified	Not specified

Admissions Requirements:

Degree	GRE	GRE-Subject	Letters of Recommendation	Research Statement	Writing Sample	CV	Interview
Master's/Specialist	Required	None	1	Required	Required	Required	Recommended

Admissions Criteria:

GRE scores—medium
Research experience—medium
Work experience—medium
Clinically related public service—low

GPA—medium
Letters of recommendation—medium
Interview—low
Statement of goals and objectives—medium

For additional information on admission requirements, visit https://www.missouriwestern.edu/psychology/graduate/admissions-requirements/.

Department Demographics

	Male (PT)	Female (PT)	Total	African-American/ Black (PT)	Hispanic/ Latino (PT)	Asian/ Pacific Islander (PT)	American Indian/ Alaska Native (PT)	Caucasian/ White (PT)	Unknown	Multiethnic (PT)	ADA (PT)	Int'l (PT)
Students	7 (0)	1 (0)	8	0 (0)	0 (0)	0 (0)	0 (0)	8 (0)	0 (0)	0 (0)	0 (0)	0 (0)

Financial Information/Assistance

Tuition: For information on tuition costs, visit https://www.missouriwestern.edu/businessoffice/. Tuition is subject to change.

Master's:
State residents: $6,164 per academic year.
State residents: $315 per credit hour.
Nonstate residents: $10,844 per academic year.
Nonstate residents: $575 per credit hour.

Financial Assistance:

	Teaching Assistantship (% Receiving)	Teaching Assistantship Tuition Remission	Research Assistantship (% Receiving)	Research Assistantship Tuition Remission	Fellowship (% Receiving)	Fellowship Tuition Remission
First-Year Student	NA (NA)	NA	NA (NA)	NA	NA (50)	Partial
Advanced Student	NA (NA)	NA	NA (NA)	NA	NA (NA)	NA

For additional information on financial assistance, visit https://www.missouriwestern.edu/graduate/costs-and-financing/.

Employment of Department Graduates

Master's:
Employed in business or industry: 2
Still seeking employment: 1
Other employment position: 1
Total: 4

Additional Information

Housing and Day Care: No on-campus housing is available. On-campus day care facilities are available. See the following website for more information: http://www.missouriwestern.edu/ykids/.

Information for Students With Physical Disabilities: See the following website: https://www.missouriwestern.edu/arc/.

Application Information: Fee: $15. *Online application:* https://www.missouriwestern.edu/admissions/apply-for-admission/.

Missouri, University of
Department of Psychological Sciences
College of Arts and Science
210 McAlester Hall
Columbia, MO 65211
Telephone: (573) 882-0838
Chairperson: Moshe Naveh-Benjamin

E-mail: gradpsych@missouri.edu
Web: http://psychology.missouri.edu/

Orientation, Objectives, and Emphasis of Department
The Department's mission is defined through research, graduate and undergraduate education, and service. The Department contributes to the theoretical and empirical body of knowledge in the discipline of psychology through research and other scholarly activities, trains graduate students to become contributors to psychology as scientists, disseminates the most current knowledge to students through high quality teaching at both the undergraduate and graduate level, and contributes through community, state, and professional service activities. The clinical program is fully accredited by the American Psychological Association and is a charter member of the Academy of Psychological Clinical Science.

Programs and Degrees Offered

Program	Degree	Application Deadline	Applications Received	Accepted	New Admits Enrolled (PT)	Total Enrolled (PT)	Degrees Awarded in 2014–2015	Median Years to Complete Degree	Dismissed/Withdrew
Clinical Psychology	PhD	December 1 (Fall)	131	13	4 (0)	36 (0)	3	7.75	
Cognition and Neuroscience	PhD	December 1 (Fall)	28	1	1	13 (0)			0
Social/ Personality Psychology	PhD	December 1 (Fall)	47	5	5 (0)	15 (0)			0
Quantitative Psychology	PhD	December 1 (Fall)	21	1	1 (0)	9 (0)			0
Developmental Psychology	PhD	December 1 (Fall)	23	2	2	8			0
Applied Psychometrics	MA/MS	December 1 (Fall)					0		

APA Accreditation
Clinical PhD: Student Outcome Data website: http://psychology.missouri.edu/clinical.

Doctoral Degree (PhD Clinical Psychology): For those doctoral students for whom a professional internship was required in this program prior to graduation:
Total students who applied for an internship: 8
Total students who obtained an internship: 8
Total students who obtained a paid internship: 8
Total students who obtained an unpaid internship: 0
Total students who were placed in APA/CPA-accredited internships: 8
Total students placed in internships not APA/CPA-accredited, but listed with the Association of Psychology Postdoctoral and Internship Centers (APPIC): 0
Total students placed in internships conforming to guidelines of the Council of Directors of School Psychology Programs (CDSPP): 0
Total students placed in internships that were not APA/CPA-accredited, APPIC or CDSSP listed: 0

Admissions

Entries appear in the following order: required test or GPA, minimum score (if required)/median score of students entering in 2015–2016.

Program	Degree	GRE-V	GRE-Q	GRE-Writing	GRE-Subject	Under-graduate GPA	Last 2 Years GPA	Psychol-ogy GPA	Master's GPA
Clinical Psychology	PhD	155/159	150/155	4/4.7	Not specified	3.46/3.68	Not specified	Not specified	Not specified
Cognition and Neuroscience	PhD	148/157	145/148	4/4.2	Not specified	Not specified	Not specified	Not specified	Not specified
Social/ Personality Psychology	PhD	151/158	154/155	4/4.5	Not specified	Not specified	Not specified	Not specified	Not specified
Quantitative Psychology	PhD	151/155	153/157	4/4.5	Not specified	Not specified	Not specified	Not specified	Not specified
Developmental Psychology	PhD	155/155	148/148	4/4	Not specified	Not specified	Not specified	Not specified	Not specified
Applied Psychometrics	MA/MS	Not specified	Not specified	Not specified	Not specified	Not specified	Not specified	Not specified	Not specified

Admissions Requirements:

Degree	GRE	GRE-Subject	Letters of Recommendation	Research Statement	Writing Sample	CV	Interview
Master's/Specialist	Required	None	N/A	None	None	None	None
Doctoral	Required	Recommended	3	Required	Required	Required	Required

Please note if these criteria vary for different programs: The GRE Psychology Subject Test is not required; however, it is strongly recommended for the Clinical program.

Admissions Criteria:

GRE scores—high
Research experience—high
Work experience—low
Clinically related public service—low
GPA—high

Letters of recommendation—high
Interview—high
Statement of goals and objectives—high
Undergraduate psychology preparation—high

For additional information on admission requirements, visit http://psychology.missouri.edu/apply-gen.

Department Demographics

	Male (PT)	Female (PT)	Total	African-American/ Black (PT)	Hispanic/ Latino (PT)	Asian/ Pacific Islander (PT)	American Indian/ Alaska Native (PT)	Caucasian/ White (PT)	Unknown	Multiethnic (PT)	ADA (PT)	Int'l (PT)
Students	27 (0)	54 (0)	81	3 (0)	4 (0)	13 (0)	0 (0)	56 (0)	2 (0)	3 (0)	0 (0)	9 (0)

Financial Information/Assistance

Tuition: For information on tuition costs, visit http://cashiers.missouri.edu/costs/index.html. Tuition is subject to change. Additional fees are assessed to students beyond the costs of tuition for the following: information technology, student activity, recreation facility, health.

Doctoral:
State residents: $350 per credit hour.
Nonstate residents: $937 per credit hour.

Master's:
State residents: $350 per credit hour.
Nonstate residents: $937 per credit hour.

Financial Assistance:

	Teaching Assistantship (% Receiving)	Teaching Assistantship Tuition Remission	Research Assistantship (% Receiving)	Research Assistantship Tuition Remission	Fellowship (% Receiving)	Fellowship Tuition Remission
First-Year Student	$16,095 (NA)	Full	$16,095 (NA)	Full	$16,095 (NA)	Full
Advanced Student	$16,917 (NA)	Full	$16,917 (NA)	Full	$16,917 (NA)	Full

For additional information on financial assistance, visit http://psychology.missouri.edu/grad-financial.

Employment of Department Graduates

Doctoral:
Enrolled in a postdoctoral residency/fellowship: 5
Employed in an academic position at a university: 3
Employed in other positions at a higher education institution: 2
Employed in a community mental health/counseling center: 1
Total: 11

Additional Information

Housing and Day Care: No on-campus housing is available. No on-campus day care facilities are available.

Information for Students With Physical Disabilities: See the following website: http://disabilityservices.missouri.edu.

Special Facilities or Resources: The department has a psychology research facility, a Brain Imaging Center, a psychological clinic, a medical school, a VA hospital, Mid-Missouri Mental Health Center, a counseling center, human experimental laboratories, a university central computer system and departmental computers.

Application Information: *Fee:* $65. *Online application:* https://app.applyyourself.com/?id=umc-grad.

Missouri, University of, Columbia (2015 data)
Department of Educational, School and Counseling Psychology
College of Education
16 Hill Hall
Columbia, MO 65211
Telephone: (573) 882-7731
Associate Division Director: T. Chris Riley-Tillman

E-mail: RileyTillmanT@missouri.edu
Web: http://education.missouri.edu/ESCP/

Orientation, Objectives, and Emphasis of Department
The goals of the department include the preparation of students in the professional specialties of counseling, school and educational psychology, school counseling and student personnel work, and the conduct of research on the applications of psychological knowledge to counseling and educational settings. The department emphasizes general psychological foundations, assessment, career development, counselor training and supervision, group processes, and research on counseling processes and psychological measurement and assessment. The theoretical orientation of the faculty is eclectic.

Programs and Degrees Offered

Program	Degree	Application Deadline	Applica-tions Received	Accepted	New Admits Enrolled (PT)	Total Enrolled (PT)	Degrees Awarded in 2014–2015	Median Years to Complete Degree	Dismissed/ Withdrew
Counseling Psychology	PhD	December 1 (Fall)	142	4	3 (0)	28 (0)	5	6	1

Programs and Degrees Offered *(con't.)*

Program	Degree	Application Deadline	Applica- tions Received	Accepted	New Admits Enrolled (PT)	Total Enrolled (PT)	Degrees Awarded in 2014– 2015	Median Years to Complete Degree	Dismissed/ Withdrew
Counseling Psychology	MEd	December 1 (Fall)	34	20	13 (0)	54 (0)	13	2	0
Educational Psychology	PhD	January 15 (Fall)	10	3	2	10 (0)	3	5	0
Educational Psychology	MEd	January 15 (Fall)	1	0	0	0	1	2	0
Educational Psychology	MA/MS	January 15 (Fall)	5	3	1 (0)	1 (0)	0		0
School Psychology	PhD	December 1 (Fall)	13	7	7 (0)	22 (3)	4	6	0
School Psychology	EdS	December 1 (Fall)	6	4	3 (0)	10 (0)	3	3	0
Educational Research Methods and Analysis	MA/MS	January 15 (Fall)	2	0	1		0		
Educational Research Methods and Analysis	PhD	January 15 (Fall)	5	2	1	10	1	5.5	0
Educational Research Methods and Analysis	MEd	January 15 (Fall)	0	0	0	0	0		0

APA Accreditation

Counseling PhD: Student Outcome Data website: http://education.missouri.edu/ESCP/program_areas/counseling_psychology/index.php.

School PhD: Student Outcome Data website: http://education.missouri.edu/ESCP/program_areas/school_psychology/index.php.

Doctoral Degree (PhD Counseling Psychology): For those doctoral students for whom a professional internship was required in this program prior to graduation:

Total students who applied for an internship: 7

Total students who obtained an internship: 7

Total students who obtained a paid internship: 7

Total students who obtained an unpaid internship: 0

Total students who were placed in APA/CPA-accredited internships: 7

Total students placed in internships not APA/CPA-accredited, but listed with the Association of Psychology Postdoctoral and Internship Centers (APPIC): 0

Total students placed in internships conforming to guidelines of the Council of Directors of School Psychology Programs (CDSPP): 0

Total students placed in internships that were not APA/CPA-accredited, APPIC or CDSSP listed: 0

Doctoral Degree (PhD School Psychology): For those doctoral students for whom a professional internship was required in this program prior to graduation:

Total students who applied for an internship: 3

Total students who obtained an internship: 3

Total students who obtained a paid internship: 3

Total students who obtained an unpaid internship: 0

Total students who were placed in APA/CPA-accredited internships: 1

Total students placed in internships not APA/CPA-accredited, but listed with the Association of Psychology Postdoctoral and Internship Centers (APPIC): 0

Total students placed in internships conforming to guidelines of the Council of Directors of School Psychology Programs (CDSPP): 1

Total students placed in internships that were not APA/CPA-accredited, APPIC or CDSSP listed: 1

Master's Degree (MA/MS Educational Research Methods and Analysis): An internship experience, such as a final research project or "capstone" experience is required of graduates.

Internships/Practica

Internships are available in counseling psychology: VA hospitals, rehabilitation centers, mental health centers, university student counseling services; in school psychology: public schools, schools of medicine; and in school counseling: public schools.

Admissions

Entries appear in the following order: required test or GPA, minimum score (if required)/median score of students entering in 2015–2016.

Program	Degree	GRE-V	GRE-Q	GRE-Writing	GRE-Subject	Under-graduate GPA	Last 2 Years GPA	Psychology GPA	Master's GPA
Counseling Psychology	PhD	150/153	150/151	3/4	Not specified	3/3.5	3/3.6	Not specified	3/3.7
Counseling Psychology	MEd	NA/151	NA/145	NA/3.5	Not specified	NA/3.3	NA/3.4	Not specified	Not specified
Educational Psychology	PhD	150/153	150/152	3/3.5	Not specified	NA/NA	NA/NA	Not specified	NA/NA
Educational Psychology	MEd	150/156	150/163	3/3.5	Not specified	NA/NA	NA/NA	Not specified	Not specified
Educational Psychology	MA/MS	150/152	150/155	3/3.5	Not specified	NA/NA	NA/NA	Not specified	Not specified
School Psychology	PhD	148/156	146/151	3.5/4	Not specified	2.86/3.61	NA/NA	Not specified	4/4
School Psychology	EdS	148/152	143/146	3/3.5	Not specified	3.27/3.55	NA/NA	Not specified	Not specified
Educational Research Methods and Analysis	MA/MS	Not specificd	Not specified	Not specified	Not specified	Not specified	Not specified	Not specified	Not specified
Educational Research Methods and Analysis	PhD	Not specified	Not specified	Not specified	Not specified	Not specified	Not specified	Not specified	Not specified
Educational Research Methods and Analysis	MEd	Not specified	Not specified	Not specified	Not specified	Not specified	Not specified	Not specified	Not specified

Admissions Requirements:

Degree	GRE	GRE-Subject	Letters of Recommendation	Research Statement	Writing Sample	CV	Interview
Master's/Specialist	Required	Optional	3	Required	Optional	Required	Required
Doctoral	Required	Optional	3	Required	Optional	Required	Required

Admissions Criteria:

GRE scores—medium

Research experience—high

Work experience—medium

Clinically related public service—medium

GPA—high

Letters of recommendation—high

Interview—high

Statement of goals and objectives—high

Department Demographics

	Male (PT)	Female (PT)	Total	African-American/ Black (PT)	Hispanic/ Latino (PT)	Asian/ Pacific Islander (PT)	American Indian/ Alaska Native (PT)	Caucasian/ White (PT)	Unknown	Multiethnic (PT)	ADA (PT)	Int'l (PT)
Students	27 (1)	110 (2)	140	16 (0)	8 (0)	3 (0)	2 (0)	63 (3)	4 (0)	1 (0)	1 (0)	35 (0)

Financial Information/Assistance

Tuition: For information on tuition costs, visit http://cashiers.missouri.edu/costs/index.html. Tuition is subject to change. Additional fees are assessed to students beyond the costs of tuition for the following: Health, Recreation, Student Activity Fee, Information Technology Fee.

Doctoral:
State residents: $347 per credit hour.
Nonstate residents: $910 per credit hour.

Master's:
State residents: $347 per credit hour.
Nonstate residents: $910 per credit hour.

Financial Assistance:

	Teaching Assistantship (% Receiving)	Teaching Assistantship Tuition Remission	Research Assistantship (% Receiving)	Research Assistantship Tuition Remission	Fellowship (% Receiving)	Fellowship Tuition Remission
First-Year Student	$5,100 (NA)	Full	$5,100 (NA)	Full	$10,000 (NA)	Full
Advanced Student	$5,610 (NA)	Full	$5,610 (NA)	Full	$10,000 (NA)	Full

Employment of Department Graduates

Master's:
Enrolled in another graduate/professional program: 1
Employed in other positions at a higher education institution: 4
Employed in a professional position in a school system: 8
Employed in a community mental health/counseling center: 1
Total: 14

Doctoral:
Enrolled in a postdoctoral residency/fellowship: 6
Employed in an academic position at a university: 1
Employed in academic position at a 2-year/4-year college: 3
Employed in other positions at a higher education institution: 1
Employed in a professional position in a school system: 1
Employed in business or industry: 1
Total: 13

Additional Information

Housing and Day Care: On-campus housing is available. See the following website for more information: http://reslife.missouri.edu/. No on-campus day care facilities are available.

Information for Students With Physical Disabilities: See the following website: http://disabilitycenter.missouri.edu/.

Special Facilities or Resources: Individual and group counseling and psychological assessment training facilities are available in the department, the College of Education and the department's assessment and consultation clinic, and on campus in the Student Counseling Center. Access to computer services is available across the campus.

Application Information: Graduate Coordinator, 16 Hill Hall, University of Missouri, Educational, School and Counseling Psychology, Columbia, MO 65211. *Fee:* $55. *Online application:* https://app.applyyourself.com/?id=umc-grad.

Missouri, University of, Kansas City
Department of Psychology
5030 Cherry Street, Room 324
Kansas City, MO 64110
Telephone: (816) 235-1318
Chairperson: Jennifer Lundgren, PhD

E-mail: psychology@umkc.edu
Web: http://cas.umkc.edu/Psychology/

Orientation, Objectives, and Emphasis of Department

The psychology program integrates clinical and epidemiological research with the health and life sciences. The department seeks to enhance the public health, broadly defined, through rigorous training of students (education mission); provide an accessible resource for the integration of behavioral sciences and health research and healthcare (service mission); develop knowledge and enhance health outcomes through empirical research (research and evaluation mission); and incorporate integrity and respect for human and intellectual diversity in all our activities (human mission).

Programs and Degrees Offered

Program	Degree	Application Deadline	Applications Received	Accepted	New Admits Enrolled (PT)	Total Enrolled (PT)	Degrees Awarded in 2014–2015	Median Years to Complete Degree	Dismissed/ Withdrew
Clinical Psychology	PhD	December 5 (Fall)	100	3	3 (0)	27 (0)	5	5.9	0
Experimental Health Psychology	PhD	December 5 (Fall)	7	2	2 (0)	8 (0)	0		0

APA Accreditation

Clinical PhD: Student Outcome Data website: http://cas.umkc.edu/psychology/GCPhD.asp.

Doctoral Degree (PhD Clinical Psychology): For those doctoral students for whom a professional internship was required in this program prior to graduation:
Total students who applied for an internship: 4
Total students who obtained an internship: 4
Total students who obtained a paid internship: 4
Total students who obtained an unpaid internship: 0
Total students who were placed in APA/CPA-accredited internships: 4
Total students placed in internships not APA/CPA-accredited, but listed with the Association of Psychology Postdoctoral and Internship Centers (APPIC): 0
Total students placed in internships conforming to guidelines of the Council of Directors of School Psychology Programs (CDSPP): 0
Total students placed in internships that were not APA/CPA-accredited, APPIC or CDSSP listed: 0

Internships/Practica

With a population of over 1.5 million, Kansas City offers numerous practicum and research opportunities. A wide range of formal community practicum opportunities are offered to Clinical Psychology PhD students including placements at community agencies, medical centers, and other applied settings. Clinical psychology students are required to enroll in six semesters of practicum during which they are involved in many different types of clinical experiences, ranging from supervised work in specialized health care programs to more general outpatient settings for psychotherapy and psychological assessment. Basic clinical practica include training in general mental health assessment and treatment areas such as crisis intervention, depression screening, personnel and disability evaluations, and treatment of adjustment problems, depression, and anxiety disorders. Advanced training opportunities are available in the assessment and treatment of obesity and eating disorders, smoking and other substance abuse, and chronic pain. In the fifth year of study, students are required to complete a one-year clinical internship.

Admissions

Entries appear in the following order: required test or GPA, minimum score (if required)/median score of students entering in 2015–2016.

Program	Degree	GRE-V	GRE-Q	GRE-Writing	GRE-Subject	Undergraduate GPA	Last 2 Years GPA	Psychology GPA	Master's GPA
Clinical Psychology	PhD	NA/155	NA/152	NA/4	Not specified	NA/NA	Not specified	Not specified	Not specified
Experimental Health Psychology	PhD	NA/150	NA/151	NA/4	Not specified	Not specified	Not specified	Not specified	Not specified

Admissions Requirements:

Degree	GRE	GRE-Subject	Letters of Recommendation	Research Statement	Writing Sample	CV	Interview
Doctoral	Required	Optional	3	Required	Optional	Required	Required

Admissions Criteria:

GRE scores—high
Research experience—high
Work experience—medium
Clinically related public service—medium
GPA—high

Letters of recommendation—high
Interview—high
Statement of goals and objectives—high
Undergraduate psychology preparation—high

Department Demographics

	Male (PT)	Female (PT)	Total	African-American/ Black (PT)	Hispanic/ Latino (PT)	Asian/ Pacific Islander (PT)	American Indian/ Alaska Native (PT)	Caucasian/ White (PT)	Unknown (PT)	Multiethnic (PT)	ADA (PT)	Int'l (PT)
Students	12 (0)	23 (0)	35	1 (0)	2 (0)	2 (0)	0 (0)	30 (0)	0 (0)	0 (0)	0 (0)	1 (0)

Financial Information/Assistance

Tuition: For information on tuition costs, visit http://www.umkc.edu/finadmin/cashiers/default.asp. Tuition is subject to change. Additional fees are assessed to students beyond the costs of tuition for the following: technology, student health, rec center.

Doctoral:
State residents: $345 per credit hour.
Nonstate residents: $891 per credit hour.

Financial Assistance:

	Teaching Assistantship (% Receiving)	Teaching Assistantship Tuition Remission	Research Assistantship (% Receiving)	Research Assistantship Tuition Remission	Fellowship (% Receiving)	Fellowship Tuition Remission
First-Year Student	$9,513 (NA)	Partial	$9,513 (NA)	Partial	NA (NA)	Partial
Advanced Student	$9,513 (NA)	Partial	$9,513 (NA)	Partial	NA (NA)	Partial

For additional information on financial assistance, visit http://sgs.umkc.edu/scholarships-and-financial-assistance/.

Employment of Department Graduates

Doctoral:
Enrolled in a postdoctoral residency/fellowship: 5
Total: 5

Additional Information

Housing and Day Care: On-campus housing is available. See the following website for more information: http://www.umkc.edu/housing/. On-campus day care facilities are available. See the following website for more information: http://education.umkc.edu/berkley/.

Information for Students With Physical Disabilities: See the following website: http://www.umkc.edu/disability/.

Application Information: UMKC Department of Psychology, 5030 Cherry Street, Room 324, Kansas City, MO 64110. *Fee:* $35.
Online application: http://www.umkc.edu/admissions/ps/apply.cfm.

Missouri, University of, Kansas City
Division of Counseling and Educational Psychology
School of Education
5100 Rockhill Road, ED 215
Kansas City, MO 64110
Telephone: (816) 235-2722
Chairperson: Nancy L. Murdock, PhD
Web: http://education.umkc.edu/our-school/division-of-counseling-and-educational-psychology-cep/

E-mail: umkccep@umkc.edu

Orientation, Objectives, and Emphasis of Department
Consistent with the University of Missouri-Kansas City's (UMKC) urban mission, the UMKC Division of Counseling and Educational Psychology emphasizes cultural and individual diversity within a scientist–practitioner model. Our program model is intended to educate ethical and flexible professionals who can work in a variety of settings. This diverse faculty is committed to educating future counseling psychologists and counselors to improve the welfare of individuals and communities through scholarship and applied interventions.

Programs and Degrees Offered

Program	Degree	Application Deadline	Applications Received	Accepted	New Admits Enrolled (PT)	Total Enrolled (PT)	Degrees Awarded in 2014–2015	Median Years to Complete Degree	Dismissed/ Withdrew
Counseling Psychology	PhD	December 1 (Fall)	63	7	7 (0)	37 (0)	4	6	0
Counseling and Guidance	MA/MS	March 1 (Fall), September 1 (Spring)	32	14	24	33 (21)	20	3	0

APA Accreditation
Counseling PhD: Student Outcome Data website: http://education.umkc.edu/academics/doctoral-degrees/doctorate-of-philosophy-ph-d-in-counseling-psychology/.

Doctoral Degree (PhD Counseling Psychology): For those doctoral students for whom a professional internship was required in this program prior to graduation:
Total students who applied for an internship: 3
Total students who obtained an internship: 3
Total students who obtained a paid internship: 3
Total students who obtained an unpaid internship: 0
Total students who were placed in APA/CPA-accredited internships: 3
Total students placed in internships not APA/CPA-accredited, but listed with the Association of Psychology Postdoctoral and Internship Centers (APPIC): 0
Total students placed in internships conforming to guidelines of the Council of Directors of School Psychology Programs (CDSPP): 0
Total students placed in internships that were not APA/CPA-accredited, APPIC or CDSSP listed: 0

Master's Degree (MA/MS Counseling and Guidance): An internship experience, such as a final research project or "capstone" experience is required of graduates.

Internships/Practica
All programs offer a wide range of practicum and internship placements. The Division of Counseling and Educational Psychology operates the Community Counseling and Assessment Services, an in-house training facility serving individuals, couples, and families in the surrounding community. Advanced practica are also available in a variety of agencies including local community mental health centers, counseling centers, Veterans Affairs hospitals, and other local service provision agencies.

Admissions

Entries appear in the following order: required test or GPA, minimum score (if required)/median score of students entering in 2015–2016.

Program	Degree	GRE-V	GRE-Q	GRE-Writing	GRE-Subject	Under-graduate GPA	Last 2 Years GPA	Psychol-ogy GPA	Master's GPA
Counseling Psychology	PhD	NA/153	NA/154	NA/5	Not specified	3.3/3.45	NA/NA	Not specified	NA/NA
Counseling and Guidance	MA/MS	NA/153	NA/152	NA/4	Not specified	NA/NA	Not specified	Not specified	Not specified

Admissions Requirements:

Degree	GRE	GRE-Subject	Letters of Recom-mendation	Research Statement	Writing Sample	CV	Interview
Master's/Specialist	Required	None	3	Required	None	Optional	None
Doctoral	Required	Optional	3	Required	None	Required	Required

Please note if these criteria vary for different programs: Undergraduate psychology courses are not required for the MA programs but are for the PhD program, unless the student has a graduate degree in counseling or similar field.

Admissions Criteria:

GRE scores—medium
Research experience—medium
Work experience—medium
Clinically related public service—medium
GPA—medium

Letters of recommendation—high
Interview—high
Statement of goals and objectives—high
Undergraduate psychology preparation—medium
Research interests—medium

Department Demographics

	Male (PT)	Female (PT)	Total	African-American/ Black (PT)	Hispanic/ Latino (PT)	Asian/ Pacific Islander (PT)	American Indian/ Alaska Native (PT)	Caucasian/ White (PT)	Unknown	Multiethnic (PT)	ADA (PT)	Int'l (PT)
Students	16 (2)	54 (19)	91	5 (1)	2 (0)	7 (0)	1 (0)	49 (17)	0 (1)	0 (0)	1 (0)	2 (1)

Financial Information/Assistance

Tuition: For information on tuition costs, visit http://www.umkc.edu/adminfinance/finance/cashiers/default.asp. Tuition is subject to change.

Doctoral:
State residents: $7,212 per academic year.
State residents: $444 per credit hour.
Nonstate residents: $17,045 per academic year.
Nonstate residents: $990 per credit hour.

Master's:
State residents: $444 per credit hour.
Nonstate residents: $990 per credit hour.

Financial Assistance:

	Teaching Assistantship (% Receiving)	Teaching Assistantship Tuition Remission	Research Assistantship (% Receiving)	Research Assistantship Tuition Remission	Fellowship (% Receiving)	Fellowship Tuition Remission
First-Year Student	$12,000 (NA)	Partial	$12,000 (NA)	Partial	NA (NA)	NA
Advanced Student	$12,000 (NA)	Partial	$12,000 (NA)	Partial	$10,000 (NA)	Partial

For additional information on financial assistance, visit http://sgs.umkc.edu/scholarships-and-financial-assistance/.

Employment of Department Graduates

Master's:
Employed in a professional position in a school system: 5
Employed in a community mental health/counseling center: 7
Do not know: 33
Total: 45

Doctoral:
Enrolled in a postdoctoral residency/fellowship: 5
Employed in an academic position at a university: 1
Employed in a community mental health/counseling center: 2
Employed in a hospital/medical center: 1
Not seeking employment: 1
Total: 10

Additional Information

Housing and Day Care: On-campus housing is available. See the following website for more information: http://www.umkc.edu/housing/. On-campus day care facilities are available. See the following website for more information: http://education.umkc.edu/berkley/.

Information for Students With Physical Disabilities: See the following website: http://www.umkc.edu/disability/.

Application Information: Division of Counseling & Educational Psychology, Counseling Psychology Program, University of Missouri-Kansas City, 5100 Rockhill Road, ED 215, Kansas City, MO 64110. *Fee:* $35. *Online application:* http://www.umkc.edu/admissions/ps/apply.cfm.

Missouri, University of, St. Louis
Department of Psychological Sciences
Arts & Sciences
1 University Boulevard
St. Louis, MO 63121
Telephone: (314) 516-5393
Chairperson: Michael G. Griffin, PhD

E-mail: griffinm@UMSL.EDU
Web: http://www.umsl.edu/divisions/artscience/psychology/

Orientation, Objectives, and Emphasis of Department
The orientation of the department emphasizes psychology as science yet also recognizes the important social responsibilities of psychology, especially in the clinical and applied areas. Emphasis of behavioral neuroscience is in neuropsychology, cognitive behaviors, psychophysiology and animal models of psychopathology, and behavioral neuropharmacology/endocrinology . The department offers a broad spectrum of high-quality programs at the undergraduate and graduate levels.

Programs and Degrees Offered

Program	Degree	Application Deadline	Applications Received	Accepted	New Admits Enrolled (PT)	Total Enrolled (PT)	Degrees Awarded in 2014–2015	Median Years to Complete Degree	Dismissed/ Withdrew
Clinical Psychology	PhD	December 15 (Fall)	178	9	6 (0)	32 (0)	8	6	2
Industrial/ Organizational Psychology	PhD	January 15 (Fall)	80	3	3 (0)	31 (0)	3	6	1
Behavioral Neuroscience	PhD	January 15 (Fall)	43	6	2 (0)	22 (0)	3	6	0

APA Accreditation
Clinical PhD: Student Outcome Data website: http://www.umsl.edu/divisions/artscience/psychology/psychology/clinical/index.html.

Doctoral Degree (PhD Clinical Psychology): For those doctoral students for whom a professional internship was required in this program prior to graduation:
Total students who applied for an internship: 11
Total students who obtained an internship: 10
Total students who obtained a paid internship: 10

Total students who obtained an unpaid internship: 0
Total students who were placed in APA/CPA-accredited internships: 10
Total students placed in internships not APA/CPA-accredited, but listed with the Association of Psychology Postdoctoral and Internship Centers (APPIC): 0
Total students placed in internships conforming to guidelines of the Council of Directors of School Psychology Programs (CDSPP): 0
Total students placed in internships that were not APA/CPA-accredited, APPIC or CDSSP listed: 0

Internships/Practica

Students (clinical) participate in practica in our Community Psychological Service (the psychology clinic), and a paid clinical clerkship, which may be in a community or university-based program. Advanced students in behavioral neuroscience have internship opportunities with research labs at local medical schools, Washington University and Saint Louis University.

Admissions

Entries appear in the following order: required test or GPA, minimum score (if required)/median score of students entering in 2015–2016.

Program	Degree	GRE-V	GRE-Q	GRE-Writing	GRE-Subject	Under-graduate GPA	Last 2 Years GPA	Psychol-ogy GPA	Master's GPA
Clinical Psychology	PhD	NA/163	NA/157	NA/4.5	Not specified	NA/3.7	Not specified	NA/3.9	Not specified
Industrial/ Organizational Psychology	PhD	NA/158	NA/154	NA/5	Not specified	NA/3.7	Not specified	Not specified	Not specified
Behavioral Neuroscience	PhD	NA/158	NA/153	NA/4	Not specified	NA/3.6	Not specified	NA/3.7	Not specified

Admissions Requirements:

Degree	GRE	GRE-Subject	Letters of Recom-mendation	Research Statement	Writing Sample	CV	Interview
Doctoral	Required	Recom-mended	3	Required	Optional	Required	Required

Please note if these criteria vary for different programs: Importance of criteria varies by program.

Admissions Criteria:

GRE scores—high
Research experience—high
Work experience—medium
Clinically related public service—medium

GPA—high
Letters of recommendation—high
Interview—high
Statement of goals and objectives—high

Department Demographics

	Male (PT)	Female (PT)	Total	African-American/ Black (PT)	Hispanic/ Latino (PT)	Asian/ Pacific Islander (PT)	American Indian/ Alaska Native (PT)	Caucasian/ White (PT)	Unknown	Multiethnic (PT)	ADA (PT)	Int'l (PT)
Students	23 (0)	63 (0)	86	3 (0)	3 (0)	4 (0)	0 (0)	72 (0)	0 (0)	4 (0)	0 (0)	0 (0)

Financial Information/Assistance

Tuition: For information on tuition costs, visit http://www.umsl.edu/cashiers/tuition-fees/index.html. Tuition is subject to change. Additional fees are assessed to students beyond the costs of tuition for the following: computer, parking, activities.

Doctoral:
State residents: $436 per credit hour.
Nonstate residents: $1,049 per credit hour.

Master's:
State residents: $436 per credit hour.
Nonstate residents: $1,049 per credit hour.

Financial Assistance:

	Teaching Assistantship (% Receiving)	Teaching Assistantship Tuition Remission	Research Assistantship (% Receiving)	Research Assistantship Tuition Remission	Fellowship (% Receiving)	Fellowship Tuition Remission
First-Year Student	$11,500 (80)	Full	$12,500 (15)	Full	$4,000 (5)	Full
Advanced Student	$12,500 (50)	Full	$14,000 (30)	Full	$4,000 (10)	Full

For additional information on financial assistance, visit http://www.umsl.edu/services/finaid/.

Employment of Department Graduates

Doctoral:
Enrolled in a postdoctoral residency/fellowship: 10
Employed in business or industry: 1
Total: 11

Additional Information

Housing and Day Care: On-campus housing is available. See the following website for more information: http://www.umsl.edu/services/reslife/. On-campus day care facilities are available. See the following website for more information: http://www.umsl.edu/~kids/.

Information for Students With Physical Disabilities: See the following website: http://www.umsl.edu/services/disability/.

Special Facilities or Resources: The Department of Psychology is housed in Stadler Hall, and research laboratories and computers are conveniently located in the building. The psychological clinic (Community Psychological Service) is also contained within Stadler Hall. The Center for Trauma Recovery and Child Advocacy Center each have community clinics, which are housed on campus. Physical facilities include workshops and animal, social, and human experimental laboratories. A wide range of research equipment is available, including videotaping facilities, computer terminals, and personal computers.

Application Information: Graduate Admissions, University of Missouri-St. Louis, 1 University Boulevard, St. Louis, MO 63121-4499. *Fee:* $35. *Online application:* http://www.umsl.edu/admissions/apply-now.html.

Saint Louis University
Department of Psychology
Arts & Sciences
3511 Laclede Avenue
St. Louis, MO
Telephone: (314) 977-2300
Chairperson: Jeffrey D. Gfeller, PhD

E-mail: gfellerj@slu.edu
Web: http://www.slu.edu/department-of-psychology-home

Orientation, Objectives, and Emphasis of Department
Our mission is to educate students in the discipline of psychology and its applications. We encourage intellectual curiosity, critical thinking, and ethical responsibility in our teaching and research. Our commitment to value-based, holistic education and our enthusiasm for psychology is realized in the products of our research, in our graduates, and in service to others.

Programs and Degrees Offered

Program	Degree	Application Deadline	Applications Received	Accepted	New Admits Enrolled (PT)	Total Enrolled (PT)	Degrees Awarded in 2014–2015	Median Years to Complete Degree	Dismissed/ Withdrew
Clinical Psychology	PhD	December 1 (Fall)	145	14	8	34	8	5.5	0

Programs and Degrees Offered (con't.)

Program	Degree	Application Deadline	Applica- tions Received	Accepted	New Admits Enrolled (PT)	Total Enrolled (PT)	Degrees Awarded in 2014– 2015	Median Years to Complete Degree	Dismissed/ Withdrew
Experimental Psychology	PhD	December 1 (Fall)	48	11	4	27	8	5.5	1
Industrial/ Organizational Psychology	PhD	December 1 (Fall)	45	6	4	26	4	5	0

APA Accreditation

Clinical PhD: Student Outcome Data website: http://www.slu.edu/department-of-psychology-home/graduate-studies/clinical-psychology/student-admission-outcomes-and-other-data.

Doctoral Degree (PhD Clinical Psychology): For those doctoral students for whom a professional internship was required in this program prior to graduation:
Total students who applied for an internship: 9
Total students who obtained an internship: 9
Total students who obtained a paid internship: 9
Total students who obtained an unpaid internship: 0
Total students who were placed in APA/CPA-accredited internships: 9
Total students placed in internships not APA/CPA-accredited, but listed with the Association of Psychology Postdoctoral and Internship Centers (APPIC): 0
Total students placed in internships conforming to guidelines of the Council of Directors of School Psychology Programs (CDSPP): 0
Total students placed in internships that were not APA/CPA-accredited, APPIC or CDSSP listed: 0

Internships/Practica

The Clinical program has established collaborative relationships with various medical centers, agencies, and private practitioners throughout the community to provide advanced practica and training in the science and practice of psychology.

Admissions

Entries appear in the following order: required test or GPA, minimum score (if required)/median score of students entering in 2015–2016.

Program	Degree	GRE-V	GRE-Q	GRE-Writing	GRE-Subject	Under-graduate GPA	Last 2 Years GPA	Psychol-ogy GPA	Master's GPA
Clinical Psychology	PhD	NA/162	NA/165	NA/4.5	Not specified	NA/3.6	Not specified	NA/3.8	Not specified
Experimental Psychology	PhD	NA/155	NA/157	NA/4.5	Not specified	NA/3.9	Not specified	NA/3.9	Not specified
Industrial/ Organizational Psychology	PhD	153/160	153/164	3.5/4.5	Not specified	3.3/3.7	Not specified	Not specified	Not specified

Admissions Requirements:

Degree	GRE	GRE-Subject	Letters of Recom-mendation	Research Statement	Writing Sample	CV	Interview
Doctoral	Required	Optional	3	Required	Optional	Required	Required

Please note if these criteria vary for different programs: These criteria may vary for different program areas.

Admissions Criteria:

GRE scores—medium
Research experience—high
Work experience—medium
Clinically related public service—medium
GPA—high

Letters of recommendation—medium
Interview—high
Statement of goals and objectives—high
Undergraduate psychology preparation—high

Department Demographics

	Male (PT)	Female (PT)	Total	African-American/ Black (PT)	Hispanic/ Latino (PT)	Asian/ Pacific Islander (PT)	American Indian/ Alaska Native (PT)	Caucasian/ White (PT)	Unknown	Multiethnic (PT)	ADA (PT)	Int'l (PT)
Students	25 (0)	62 (0)	87	7 (0)	4 (0)	5 (0)	0 (0)	68 (0)	0 (0)	5 (0)	3 (0)	2 (0)

Financial Information/Assistance

Tuition: For information on tuition costs, visit http://www.slu.edu/student-financial-services/financing-a-slu-education/tuition-room-and-board-rates. Tuition is subject to change. Additional fees are assessed to students beyond the costs of tuition for the following: Student Graduate Association Fee, Student Union Fee.

Doctoral:
State residents: $1,050 per credit hour.
Nonstate residents: $1,050 per credit hour.

Financial Assistance:

	Teaching Assistantship (% Receiving)	Teaching Assistantship Tuition Remission	Research Assistantship (% Receiving)	Research Assistantship Tuition Remission	Fellowship (% Receiving)	Fellowship Tuition Remission
First-Year Student	$18,000 (NA)	Partial	$22,000 (NA)	Full	NA (NA)	NA
Advanced Student	$9,000 (NA)	Partial	$9,000 (NA)	Partial	NA (NA)	NA

For additional information on financial assistance, visit http://www.slu.edu/graduate-admission-home/affording-graduate-education.

Employment of Department Graduates

Doctoral:
Enrolled in a postdoctoral residency/fellowship: 8
Employed in an academic position at a university: 2
Employed in other positions at a higher education institution: 2
Employed in business or industry: 3
Employed in a hospital/medical center: 5
Other employment position: 2
Do not know: 1
Total: 23

Additional Information

Housing and Day Care: On-campus housing is available. See the following website for more information: http://www.slu.edu/reslife. No on-campus day care facilities are available.

Information for Students With Physical Disabilities: See the following website: http://www.slu.edu/retention-and-academic-success/disability-services.

Special Facilities or Resources: The Clinical program operates an on-campus Psychological Services Center, which serves as a primary site for supervised clinical experiences with children, adolescents, adults, couples and families. Resources available to

Experimental students include animal housing and several laboratory suites for social, cognitive, developmental, and neuroscience research. In addition to space for laboratory research, the students in the Industrial/Organizational program are involved with the Center for the Application of Behavioral Sciences. Housed within the department, this Center provides opportunities for training in organizational consulting and program evaluation in a field setting.

Application Information: Office of Admission, DuBourg Hall, Room 119, Saint Louis University, 1 North Grand Boulevard, Saint Louis, MO 63103. *Fee:* $55. *Online application:* https://www.applyweb.com/slugrad/.

Washington University in St. Louis
Department of Psychological & Brain Sciences
Arts & Sciences
One Brookings Drive, Campus Box 1125
St. Louis, MO 63130
Telephone: (314) 935-6520
Chairperson: Deanna Barch

E-mail: mcclelland@wustl.edu
Web: http://psychweb.wustl.edu/

Orientation, Objectives, and Emphasis of Department
The emphasis within the clinical program is on training clinical scientists and promoting an integration of science and practice. Its goal is to train students who will lead the search for knowledge regarding the assessment, understanding, and treatment of psychological disorders. In the experimental programs, the development of generalists with one or more areas of specialization is the department's orientation.

Programs and Degrees Offered

Program	Degree	Application Deadline	Applications Received	Accepted	New Admits Enrolled (PT)	Total Enrolled (PT)	Degrees Awarded in 2014–2015	Median Years to Complete Degree	Dismissed/ Withdrew
Clinical Psychology	PhD	December 1 (Fall)	233	7	5 (0)	28 (0)	3	6	0
Aging and Development	PhD	December 1 (Fall)	15	0	0 (0)	10 (0)	2	6	0
Behavior/ Brain/ Cognition	PhD	December 1 (Fall)	74	16	13 (0)	30 (0)	6	6	0
Social/ Personality Psychology	PhD	December 1 (Fall)	41	5	3 (0)	13 (0)	1	5	0

APA Accreditation
Clinical PhD: Student Outcome Data website: http://psychweb.wustl.edu/graduate/clinical-psychology/student-admissions-outcomes-and-other-data.

Doctoral Degree (PhD Clinical Psychology): For those doctoral students for whom a professional internship was required in this program prior to graduation:
Total students who applied for an internship: 2
Total students who obtained an internship: 2
Total students who obtained a paid internship: 2
Total students who obtained an unpaid internship: 0
Total students who were placed in APA/CPA-accredited internships: 2
Total students placed in internships not APA/CPA-accredited, but listed with the Association of Psychology Postdoctoral and Internship Centers (APPIC): 0
Total students placed in internships conforming to guidelines of the Council of Directors of School Psychology Programs (CDSPP): 0
Total students placed in internships that were not APA/CPA-accredited, APPIC or CDSSP listed: 0

Admissions

Entries appear in the following order: required test or GPA, minimum score (if required)/median score of students entering in 2015–2016.

Program	Degree	GRE-V	GRE-Q	GRE-Writing	GRE-Subject	Under-graduate GPA	Last 2 Years GPA	Psychology GPA	Master's GPA
Clinical Psychology	PhD	161/164	154/159	4/4.5	Not specified	3.3/3.59	Not specified	Not specified	Not specified
Aging and Development	PhD	NA/NA	NA/NA	NA/NA	Not specified	NA/NA	Not specified	Not specified	Not specified
Behavior/Brain/Cognition	PhD	155/159	155/161	3/4.5	Not specified	3.11/3.72	Not specified	Not specified	Not specified
Social/Personality Psychology	PhD	158/163	155/159	4.5/4.5	Not specified	3.07/3.24	Not specified	Not specified	Not specified

Admissions Requirements:

Degree	GRE	GRE-Subject	Letters of Recommendation	Research Statement	Writing Sample	CV	Interview
Doctoral	Required	Recommended	3	Required	Optional	Optional	Required

Please note if these criteria vary for different programs: Interview (by invitation only) is required for applicants prior to acceptance. Phone and/or Skype interviews are possible for applicants who live abroad.

Admissions Criteria:

GRE scores—high
Research experience—high
Work experience—low
Clinically related public service—low
GPA—high

Letters of recommendation—high
Interview—high
Statement of goals and objectives—high
Undergraduate psychology preparation—high

For additional information on admission requirements, visit http://psychweb.wustl.edu/graduate-alternative/admission-financial-aid.

Department Demographics

	Male (PT)	Female (PT)	Total	African-American/ Black (PT)	Hispanic/ Latino (PT)	Asian/ Pacific Islander (PT)	American Indian/ Alaska Native (PT)	Caucasian/ White (PT)	Unknown	Multiethnic (PT)	ADA (PT)	Int'l (PT)
Students	22 (0)	59 (0)	81	6 (0)	2 (0)	11 (0)	0 (0)	46 (0)	13 (0)	3 (0)	0 (0)	10 (0)

Financial Information/Assistance

Tuition: For information on tuition costs, visit http://graduateschool.wustl.edu/prospective_students/financial-information/tuition-and-fees. Tuition is subject to change.

Doctoral:
State residents: $48,950 per academic year.
Nonstate residents: $48,950 per academic year.

Financial Assistance:

	Teaching Assistantship (% Receiving)	Teaching Assistantship Tuition Remission	Research Assistantship (% Receiving)	Research Assistantship Tuition Remission	Fellowship (% Receiving)	Fellowship Tuition Remission
First-Year Student	NA (NA)	NA	$22,220 (0)	Full	$22,220 (100)	Full
Advanced Student	$22,220 (33)	Full	$22,220 (5)	Full	$22,220 (62)	Full

For additional information on financial assistance, visit http://graduateschool.wustl.edu/prospective_students/financial-information.

Employment of Department Graduates

Doctoral:
Enrolled in a postdoctoral residency/fellowship: 6
Employed in an academic position at a university: 3
Employed in business or industry: 1
Employed in government agency: 1
Still seeking employment: 1
Total: 12

Additional Information

Housing and Day Care: No on-campus housing is available. On-campus day care facilities are available. See the following website for more information: http://nurseryschool.wustl.edu/; http://childcare.wustl.edu/.

Information for Students With Physical Disabilities: See the following website: http://cornerstone.wustl.edu/disability-resources/.

Special Facilities or Resources: The department's extensive facilities include animal, human psychophysiological, psychoacoustic, and clinical training laboratories; computer labs; closed circuit TV; and Neuroimaging (fMRI) and Image Analysis Laboratory.

Application Information: Meg McClelland, Graduate Program Coordinator, Washington University, Department of Psychology, Campus Box 1125, St. Louis, MO 63130-4899. *Fee:* $45. *Online application:* https://gsasapply.wustl.edu/apply/.

Montana State University Billings (2015 data)

Department of Psychology
College of Arts and Sciences
1500 North University Drive
Billings, MT 59101
Telephone: (406) 657-2242
Chairperson: Dr. Michael Havens

E-mail: mhavens@msubillings.edu
Web: http://www.msubillings.edu/grad/Program-Psychology.htm

Orientation, Objectives, and Emphasis of Department

Ours is a fairly small department with faculty members representing clinical, social, developmental, and physiological psychology. We have been successful in preparing students for doctoral training, mostly in clinical psychology programs. Some of our students have gone on to successful careers as master's-level clinicians.

Programs and Degrees Offered

Program	Degree	Application Deadline	Applications Received	Accepted	New Admits Enrolled (PT)	Total Enrolled (PT)	Degrees Awarded in 2014–2015	Median Years to Complete Degree	Dismissed/ Withdrew
Psychology	MA/MS	April 15 (Fall)	12	8	7 (0)	12 (0)	8	2	1

Internships/Practica

Our students do internships at several clinics around Billings, including two residential treatment facilities for children and adolescents and a prison prerelease center. Clinical psychologists in private practice also frequently take on our students as testing technicians. Graduate students interested in a teaching career are offered the opportunity to teach undergraduate courses in our department.

Admissions

Entries appear in the following order: required test or GPA, minimum score (if required)/median score of students entering in 2015–2016.

Program	Degree	GRE-V	GRE-Q	GRE-Writing	GRE-Subject	Under-graduate GPA	Last 2 Years GPA	Psychology GPA	Master's GPA
Psychology	MA/MS	NA/NA	NA/NA	NA/NA	Not specified	NA/3.12	Not specified	Not specified	Not specified

Admissions Requirements:

Degree	GRE	GRE-Subject	Letters of Recommendation	Research Statement	Writing Sample	CV	Interview
Master's/Specialist	Required	Optional	3	Required	None	Required	Optional

Admissions Criteria:

GRE scores—medium
Research experience—medium
Work experience—low
Clinically related public service—low

GPA—high
Letters of recommendation—high
Statement of goals and objectives—high

For additional information on admission requirements, visit http://www.msubillings.edu/grad/Admission.htm.

Department Demographics

	Male (PT)	Female (PT)	Total	African-American/ Black (PT)	Hispanic/ Latino (PT)	Asian/ Pacific Islander (PT)	American Indian/ Alaska Native (PT)	Caucasian/ White (PT)	Unknown	Multiethnic (PT)	ADA (PT)	Int'l (PT)
Students	4 (0)	8 (0)	12	0 (0)	1 (0)	0 (0)	0 (0)	11 (0)	0 (0)	0 (0)	0 (0)	1 (0)

Financial Information/Assistance

Tuition: For information on tuition costs, visit http://www.msubillings.edu/future/cost-GradStudies.htm. Tuition is subject to change. Additional fees are assessed to students beyond the costs of tuition for the following: online course fees and lab fees.

Master's:
State residents: $3,312 per academic year.
Nonstate residents: $8,985 per academic year.

Financial Assistance:

	Teaching Assistantship (% Receiving)	Teaching Assistantship Tuition Remission	Research Assistantship (% Receiving)	Research Assistantship Tuition Remission	Fellowship (% Receiving)	Fellowship Tuition Remission
First-Year Student	$4,500 (NA)	Full	$4,500 (NA)	Full	NA (NA)	NA
Advanced Student	$4,500 (NA)	Full	$4,500 (NA)	Full	NA (NA)	NA

For additional information on financial assistance, visit http://www.msubillings.edu/finaid/.

Employment of Department Graduates

Master's:
Enrolled in a psychology doctoral program: 1
Enrolled in another graduate/professional program: 3
Total: 4

Additional Information

Housing and Day Care: On-campus housing is available. See the following website for more information: http://www.msubillings.edu/reslife/. On-campus day care facilities are available. See the following website for more information: http://www.msubillings.edu/childcare/.

Information for Students With Physical Disabilities: See the following website: http://www.msubillings.edu/dss/.

Special Facilities or Resources: One faculty member is conducting research on non-pharmaceutical treatment of ADHD in residents of a prison prerelease center. Another is studying attachment styles and their relation to addiction and other maladaptive behaviors. Students participate in some of this research. We have a newly renovated assessment laboratory for use by graduate students.

Application Information: Office of Graduate Studies. *Fee:* $40. *Online application:* https://www.applyweb.com/apply/msubillg/.

Montana, University of
Department of Psychology
Humanities and Sciences
143 Skaggs Building
Missoula, MT 59812-1584
Telephone: (406) 243-4521
Chairperson: Christine Fiore

E-mail: christine.fiore@umontana.edu
Web: http://hs.umt.edu/psychology/

Orientation, Objectives, and Emphasis of Department

The Clinical Psychology PhD program trains students in basic psychological science and clinical skills including assessment, diagnosis, and therapeutic interventions. The program is based on the scientist–practitioner model and a variety of theoretical orientations are represented and taught. The training is a balanced combination of coursework, practica, and research. Upon completion of the program, graduates are well prepared for health service psychology careers as clinical psychologists in institutional, academic, and private settings. In addition to generalist training, two specialty emphases are also offered: child and family and neuropsychology. The Experimental Psychology PhD program offers research specializations in the fields of animal behavior, cognition, developmental psychology, social psychology, and quantitative psychology. Graduates have found placement in academic, research, and applied settings. The School Psychology program offers both doctoral (PhD) and specialist (EdS) level training based on the scientist–scholar–practitioner model and is aimed at professional preparation of school psychologists who are grounded thoroughly in the principles of human development, behavior, and educational psychology. Doctoral candidates are trained to assume leadership roles in academia, research, and clinical/school practice. Specialist-level candidates are trained to provide psychoeducational services on a systems and individual basis.

Programs and Degrees Offered

Program	Degree	Application Deadline	Applications Received	Accepted	New Admits Enrolled (PT)	Total Enrolled (PT)	Degrees Awarded in 2014–2015	Median Years to Complete Degree	Dismissed/ Withdrew
Clinical Psychology	PhD	December 1 (Fall)	169	5	5 (0)	20 (16)	9	7	0
School Psychology	EdS	December 1 (Fall)	14	7	7 (0)	15 (6)	3	3	0
School Psychology	PhD	December 1 (Fall)	12	2	2 (0)	6 (1)	1	6	1
Experimental Psychology	PhD	January 1 (Fall)	8	1	1	6 (2)	1	4	0

APA Accreditation

Clinical PhD: Student Outcome Data website: http://hs.umt.edu/psychology/clinical-psychology/studentData.php.

Doctoral Degree (PhD Clinical Psychology): For those doctoral students for whom a professional internship was required in this program prior to graduation:
Total students who applied for an internship: 5
Total students who obtained an internship: 4
Total students who obtained a paid internship: 4
Total students who obtained an unpaid internship: 0
Total students who were placed in APA/CPA-accredited internships: 4
Total students placed in internships not APA/CPA-accredited, but listed with the Association of Psychology Postdoctoral and Internship Centers (APPIC): 0
Total students placed in internships conforming to guidelines of the Council of Directors of School Psychology Programs (CDSPP): 0
Total students placed in internships that were not APA/CPA-accredited, APPIC or CDSSP listed: 0

Doctoral Degree (PhD School Psychology): For those doctoral students for whom a professional internship was required in this program prior to graduation:
Total students who applied for an internship: 1
Total students who obtained an internship: 1
Total students who obtained a paid internship: 1
Total students who obtained an unpaid internship: 0
Total students who were placed in APA/CPA-accredited internships: 1
Total students placed in internships not APA/CPA-accredited, but listed with the Association of Psychology Postdoctoral and Internship Centers (APPIC): 0
Total students placed in internships conforming to guidelines of the Council of Directors of School Psychology Programs (CDSPP): 0
Total students placed in internships that were not APA/CPA-accredited, APPIC or CDSSP listed: 0

Admissions

Entries appear in the following order: required test or GPA, minimum score (if required)/median score of students entering in 2015–2016.

Program	Degree	GRE-V	GRE-Q	GRE-Writing	GRE-Subject	Under-graduate GPA	Last 2 Years GPA	Psychol-ogy GPA	Master's GPA
Clinical Psychology	PhD	NA/158	NA/152	NA/NA	Not specified	Not specified	Not specified	Not specified	Not specified
School Psychology	EdS	NA/155	NA/150	NA/NA	Not specified	Not specified	Not specified	Not specified	Not specified
School Psychology	PhD	NA/153	NA/148	NA/NA	Not specified	NA/NA	Not specified	Not specified	Not specified
Experimental Psychology	PhD	NA/154	NA/154	NA/NA	NA/NA	NA/3.67	Not specified	Not specified	Not specified

Admissions Requirements:

Degree	GRE	GRE-Subject	Letters of Recom-mendation	Research Statement	Writing Sample	CV	Interview
Master's/Specialist	Required	None	3	Required	Optional	Required	Required
Doctoral	Required	Required	3	Required	Optional	Required	Required

Please note if these criteria vary for different programs: Clinical service is a criterion for clinical program only. Clinical faculty place higher importance on the statement of goals and objectives and the interview (phone and/or live), and medium importance on GRE scores. Experimental program applicants only are required to take the GRE-Subject test.

Admissions Criteria:

GRE scores—medium
Research experience—high
Work experience—medium
Clinically related public service—medium
GPA—high

Letters of recommendation—high
Interview—high
Statement of goals and objectives—high
Undergraduate psychology preparation—medium

For additional information on admission requirements, visit http://hs.umt.edu/psychology/graduates/how-to-apply/default.php.

Department Demographics

	Male (PT)	Female (PT)	Total	African-American/ Black (PT)	Hispanic/ Latino (PT)	Asian/ Pacific Islander (PT)	American Indian/ Alaska Native (PT)	Caucasian/ White (PT)	Unknown	Multiethnic (PT)	ADA (PT)	Int'l (PT)
Students	10 (5)	37 (20)	72	0 (0)	1 (1)	2 (0)	4 (4)	36 (16)	4 (3)	0 (1)	0 (0)	2 (0)

Financial Information/Assistance

Tuition: For information on tuition costs, visit http://www.umt.edu/business-services/Students/Tuition and Fees/default.php. Tuition is subject to change. Additional fees are assessed to students beyond the costs of tuition for the following: registration, facilities, equip, tech, ASUM, campus rec, transportation, etc.

Doctoral:
State residents: $5,848 per academic year.
State residents: $244 per credit hour.
Nonstate residents: $18,884 per academic year.
Nonstate residents: $787 per credit hour.

Master's:
State residents: $5,176 per academic year.
State residents: $216 per credit hour.
Nonstate residents: $18,614 per academic year.
Nonstate residents: $775 per credit hour.

Financial Assistance:

	Teaching Assistantship (% Receiving)	Teaching Assistantship Tuition Remission	Research Assistantship (% Receiving)	Research Assistantship Tuition Remission	Fellowship (% Receiving)	Fellowship Tuition Remission
First-Year Student	$14,800 (NA)	Full	NA (NA)	NA	NA (NA)	NA
Advanced Student	$14,800 (NA)	Full	$14,800 (NA)	Partial	NA (NA)	NA

For additional information on financial assistance, visit http://hs.umt.edu/psychology/graduates/funding-opportunities/default.php.

Employment of Department Graduates

Master's:
Enrolled in another graduate/professional program: 1
Employed in a professional position in a school system: 2
Total: 3

Doctoral:
Enrolled in a postdoctoral residency/fellowship: 8
Employed in an academic position at a university: 1
Employed in a hospital/medical center: 2
Total: 11

Additional Information

Housing and Day Care: On-campus housing is available. See the following website for more information: http://www.umt.edu/residencelife/. On-campus day care facilities are available. See the following website for more information: http://www.umt.edu/childcare.

Information for Students With Physical Disabilities: See the following website: http://www.umt.edu/dss/.

Special Facilities or Resources: The Department of Psychology is housed on the main campus of the University of Montana. Classrooms, offices, and research laboratories for all areas are found in the Skaggs Building and in the Clinical Psychology Center. The Clinical Psychology Center serves as a meeting place for classes, seminars, and research groups, and provides services for the Missoula community on a sliding fee scale.

Application Information: Graduate Admissions, Department of Psychology, The University of Montana, Skaggs Building 143, Missoula, MT 59812-1584. *Fee:* $60. *Online application:* http://www.applyweb.com/apply/uomont/menu.html.

Nebraska, University of, Lincoln

Department of Educational Psychology
College of Education and Human Sciences
114 Teachers College Hall
Lincoln, NE 68588-0345
Telephone: (402) 472-2223
Chairperson: R.J. De Ayala

E-mail: rdeayala@unlserve.unl.edu
Web: http://cehs.unl.edu/edpsych/

Orientation, Objectives, and Emphasis of Department

Our objective is to develop applied behavioral scientists that are able to function in a variety of settings and roles ranging from educational settings to private practice. The department's broad base offers a diversity of orientations and role models for students.

Programs and Degrees Offered

Program	Degree	Application Deadline	Applications Received	Accepted	New Admits Enrolled (PT)	Total Enrolled (PT)	Degrees Awarded in 2014–2015	Median Years to Complete Degree	Dismissed/ Withdrew
Cognition, Learning, and Development	PhD	January 15 (Fall), October 1 (Spring)	23	14	9	37 (1)	10		
Counseling Psychology	PhD	December 5 (Fall)	73	12	5	40	10	5	
Quantitative, Qualitative, & Psychometric Methods	PhD	January 15 (Fall), October 1 (Spring)	14	9	2	32 (3)	5		
School Psychology	PhD	December 1 (Fall)	36	11	9	36 (0)	5	6	

APA Accreditation

Counseling PhD: Student Outcome Data website: http://cehs.unl.edu/edpsych/counseling-psychology/.
School PhD: Student Outcome Data website: http://cehs.unl.edu/edpsych/school-psychology/.

Doctoral Degree (PhD Counseling Psychology): For those doctoral students for whom a professional internship was required in this program prior to graduation:
Total students who applied for an internship: 4
Total students who obtained an internship: 4
Total students who obtained a paid internship: 4
Total students who obtained an unpaid internship: 0
Total students who were placed in APA/CPA-accredited internships: 4
Total students placed in internships not APA/CPA-accredited, but listed with the Association of Psychology Postdoctoral and Internship Centers (APPIC): 0
Total students placed in internships conforming to guidelines of the Council of Directors of School Psychology Programs (CDSPP): 0
Total students placed in internships that were not APA/CPA-accredited, APPIC or CDSSP listed: 0

Doctoral Degree (PhD School Psychology): For those doctoral students for whom a professional internship was required in this program prior to graduation:
Total students who applied for an internship: 5
Total students who obtained an internship: 5
Total students who obtained a paid internship: 5
Total students who obtained an unpaid internship: 0
Total students who were placed in APA/CPA-accredited internships: 5

Total students placed in internships not APA/CPA-accredited, but listed with the Association of Psychology Postdoctoral and Internship Centers (APPIC): 0

Total students placed in internships conforming to guidelines of the Council of Directors of School Psychology Programs (CDSPP): 0

Total students placed in internships that were not APA/CPA-accredited, APPIC or CDSSP listed: 0

Internships/Practica

The Counseling Psychology and School Psychology programs each have practicum courses wherein students provide direct and consultation services to students, staff, and families in urban school settings. The Nebraska Internship Consortium in Professional Psychology is affiliated with the Counseling and School Psychology programs. Doctoral students in the QQPM program are encouraged to obtain internships.

Admissions

Entries appear in the following order: required test or GPA, minimum score (if required)/median score of students entering in 2015–2016.

Program	Degree	GRE-V	GRE-Q	GRE-Writing	GRE-Subject	Under-graduate GPA	Last 2 Years GPA	Psychol-ogy GPA	Master's GPA
Cognition, Learning, and Development	PhD	NA/152	NA/148	Not specified	Not specified	Not specified	Not specified	Not specified	Not specified
Counseling Psychology	PhD	NA/152	NA/145	Not specified	Not specified	NA/3.51	Not specified	Not specified	Not specified
Quantitative, Qualitative, & Psychometric Methods	PhD	NA/160	NA/155	Not specified	Not specified	Not specified	Not specified	Not specified	Not specified
School Psychology	PhD	NA/154	NA/154	Not specified	Not specified	Not specified	Not specified	Not specified	Not specified

Admissions Requirements:

Degree	GRE	GRE-Subject	Letters of Recom-mendation	Research Statement	Writing Sample	CV	Interview
Doctoral	Required	Optional	3	Required	Recom-mended	Required	Required

Admissions Criteria:

GRE scores—high
Research experience—high
Work experience—high
Clinically related public service—high

GPA—high
Letters of recommendation—high
Interview—high
Statement of goals and objectives—high

For additional information on admission requirements, visit http://cehs.unl.edu/edpsych/how-apply/.

Department Demographics

	Male (PT)	Female (PT)	Total	African-American/ Black (PT)	Hispanic/ Latino (PT)	Asian/ Pacific Islander (PT)	American Indian/ Alaska Native (PT)	Caucasian/ White (PT)	Unknown	Multiethnic (PT)	ADA (PT)	Int'l (PT)
Students	39 (1)	106 (3)	149	10 (1)	16 (0)	21 (0)	0 (0)	94 (3)	2 (0)	2 (0)	0 (0)	23 (0)

Financial Information/Assistance

Tuition: For information on tuition costs, visit http://studentaccounts.unl.edu/tuitionfee. Tuition is subject to change. Additional fees are assessed to students beyond the costs of tuition for the following: program and facilities fees, library and technology fees, dependent on courseload.

Doctoral:
State residents: $290 per credit hour.
Nonstate residents: $829 per credit hour.

Master's:
State residents: $290 per credit hour.
Nonstate residents: $829 per credit hour.

Financial Assistance:

	Teaching Assistantship (% Receiving)	Teaching Assistantship Tuition Remission	Research Assistantship (% Receiving)	Research Assistantship Tuition Remission	Fellowship (% Receiving)	Fellowship Tuition Remission
First-Year Student	$16,000 (NA)	Full	$16,000 (NA)	Full	$10,400 (NA)	Full
Advanced Student	NA (NA)	Full	NA (NA)	Full	NA (NA)	NA

For additional information on financial assistance, visit http://cehs.unl.edu/edpsych/graduate-assistantships/.

Employment of Department Graduates

No information provided.

Additional Information

Housing and Day Care: On-campus housing is available. See the following website for more information: http://housing.unl.edu/. On-campus day care facilities are available. See the following website for more information: http://childcare.unl.edu/.

Information for Students With Physical Disabilities: See the following website: http://www.unl.edu/ssd/.

Special Facilities or Resources: The department-operated Counseling and School Psychology Clinic serves as a practicum site for the School Psychology and Counseling Psychology programs. In addition, the department's excellent contacts with the community promote access to practical experiences and research subject pools. The department contains the Buros Center for Testing and its comprehensive reference library of assessment devices. The department is also home to the Center for Instructional Innovation, which conducts research on teaching and learning, and the Nebraska Prevention Center for Alcohol and Drug Abuse, as well as connections with the Nebraska Research Center on Children, Youth, Families and Schools.

Application Information: Admissions Coordinator, Department of Educational Psychology, 114 Teachers College Hall, University of Nebraska-Lincoln, Lincoln, NE 68588. *Fee:* $50. *Online application:* http://go.unl.edu/gradapp.

Nebraska, University of, Lincoln
Department of Psychology
Arts & Sciences
238 Burnett Hall
Lincoln, NE 68588-0308
Telephone: (402) 472-3721
Chairperson: Rick A. Bevins

E-mail: jamie.longwell@unl.edu
Web: http://psychology.unl.edu/

Orientation, Objectives, and Emphasis of Department
The Department of Psychology at the University of Nebraska-Lincoln offers PhD programs that emphasize the development of research and teaching excellence, collegial partnerships between students and faculty, and the cross-fertilization of ideas between specializations in the context of a rigorous, but flexible, training program. The goal of the clinical program is to produce broadly trained, scientifically oriented psychologists who have skills in both research and professional activities. The social cognitive, neuroscience and behavior, and developmental programs all emphasize research training but also place equal importance upon

training for college or university teaching and policy/applied careers. Students in the PhD/JD program take their first year in the Law College, and then concentrate on psychology plus law to graduate with a double doctorate.

Programs and Degrees Offered

Program	Degree	Application Deadline	Applica-tions Received	Accepted	New Admits Enrolled (PT)	Total Enrolled (PT)	Degrees Awarded in 2014–2015	Median Years to Complete Degree	Dismissed/ Withdrew
Clinical Psychology	PhD	December 1 (Fall)	198	7	7	51	5	6	0
Law and Psychology	PhD	December 15 (Fall)	12	0	0 (0)	16 (0)	1	12.7	0
Neuroscience & Behavior	PhD	December 15 (Fall)	16	3	3 (0)	16 (0)	4	5.25	0
Developmental Psychology	PhD	December 15 (Fall)	3	1	1 (0)	9 (0)	5	5	1
Social Cognitive Psychology	PhD	December 15 (Fall)	53	3	3	22	0		0

APA Accreditation

Clinical PhD: Student Outcome Data website: http://psychology.unl.edu/clinical.

Doctoral Degree (PhD Clinical Psychology): For those doctoral students for whom a professional internship was required in this program prior to graduation:
Total students who applied for an internship: 5
Total students who obtained an internship: 5
Total students who obtained a paid internship: 5
Total students who obtained an unpaid internship: 0
Total students who were placed in APA/CPA-accredited internships: 5
Total students placed in internships not APA/CPA-accredited, but listed with the Association of Psychology Postdoctoral and Internship Centers (APPIC): 0
Total students placed in internships conforming to guidelines of the Council of Directors of School Psychology Programs (CDSPP): 0
Total students placed in internships that were not APA/CPA-accredited, APPIC or CDSSP listed: 0

Internships/Practica

The clinical program offers numerous internship opportunities for students. We have an excellent record of placements for our students at high-quality internship sites throughout North America and participate in the APPIC internship match process.

Admissions

Entries appear in the following order: required test or GPA, minimum score (if required)/median score of students entering in 2015–2016.

Program	Degree	GRE-V	GRE-Q	GRE-Writing	GRE-Subject	Under-graduate GPA	Last 2 Years GPA	Psychol-ogy GPA	Master's GPA
Clinical Psychology	PhD	NA/158	NA/152	NA/NA	Not specified	NA/3.84	Not specified	NA/NA	NA/NA
Law and Psychology	PhD	NA/NA	NA/NA	NA/NA	Not specified	NA/NA	Not specified	NA/NA	NA/NA
Neuroscience & Behavior	PhD	NA/NA	NA/NA	NA/NA	Not specified	NA/NA	Not specified	NA/NA	NA/NA
Developmental Psychology	PhD	NA/149	NA/160	NA/3	Not specified	NA/3.76	Not specified	NA/NA	NA/NA
Social Cognitive Psychology	PhD	Not specified	Not specified	Not specified	Not specified	Not specified	Not specified	Not specified	Not specified

Admissions Requirements:

Degree	GRE	GRE-Subject	Letters of Recommendation	Research Statement	Writing Sample	CV	Interview
Doctoral	Required	Required	3	Required	Optional	Optional	None

Admissions Criteria:

GRE scores—medium
Research experience—medium
Work experience—medium
Clinically related public service—medium
GPA—medium

Letters of recommendation—high
Interview—medium
Statement of goals and objectives—medium
Undergraduate psychology preparation—medium

For additional information on admission requirements, visit http://psychology.unl.edu/graduate-program-procedures-and-materials.

Department Demographics

	Male (PT)	Female (PT)	Total	African-American/ Black (PT)	Hispanic/ Latino (PT)	Asian/ Pacific Islander (PT)	American Indian/ Alaska Native (PT)	Caucasian/ White (PT)	Unknown	Multiethnic (PT)	ADA (PT)	Int'l (PT)
Students	33 (0)	81 (0)	114	2 (0)	8 (0)	6 (0)	(0)	93 (0)	2 (0)	3 (0)	1 (0)	7 (0)

Financial Information/Assistance

Tuition: For information on tuition costs, visit http://studentaccounts.unl.edu/tuitionfee. Tuition is subject to change. Additional fees are assessed to students beyond the costs of tuition for the following: University Program and Facilities fees.

Doctoral:
State residents: $290 per credit hour.
Nonstate residents: $829 per credit hour.

Financial Assistance:

	Teaching Assistantship (% Receiving)	Teaching Assistantship Tuition Remission	Research Assistantship (% Receiving)	Research Assistantship Tuition Remission	Fellowship (% Receiving)	Fellowship Tuition Remission
First-Year Student	$12,350 (25)	Full	$12,350 (75)	Full	NA (NA)	NA
Advanced Student	NA (NA)	Full	NA (NA)	Full	NA (NA)	NA

For additional information on financial assistance, visit http://www.unl.edu/gradstudies/prospective/money.

Employment of Department Graduates

Doctoral:
Enrolled in a postdoctoral residency/fellowship: 10
Employed in independent practice: 1
Employed in an academic position at a university: 1
Employed in academic position at a 2-year/4-year college: 2
Other employment position: 1
Total: 15

Additional Information

Housing and Day Care: On-campus housing is available. See the following website for more information: http://housing.unl.edu/. On-campus day care facilities are available. See the following website for more information: http://childcare.unl.edu/.

Information for Students With Physical Disabilities: See the following website: http://www.unl.edu/ssd/.

Special Facilities or Resources: The department has a number of resources including the Ruth Staples Child Development Laboratory, the Center for Children, Families and the Law, the BUROS Mental Measurement Institute, the NEAR Center, the UNL Public Policy Center, and the Lincoln Regional Mental Health Center.

Application Information: Fee: $45. *Online application:* http://go.unl.edu/gradapp.

Nebraska, University of, Omaha
Department of Psychology
Arts and Sciences
6001 Dodge Street
Omaha, NE 68182-0274
Telephone: (402) 554-2592
Chairperson: Brigette Ryalls

E-mail: josephbrown@unomaha.edu
Web: http://www.unomaha.edu/psych/

Orientation, Objectives, and Emphasis of Department
The department is broadly eclectic, placing emphasis on theory, research, and application. The MA program is primarily for students who anticipate continuing their education at the PhD level. The MA degree may be completed in eight areas of psychology. The MS program is primarily for students who view the master's degree as terminal and who wish to emphasize application in the fields of educational-school or industrial/organizational psychology. These two areas may be emphasized within the MA program as well.

Programs and Degrees Offered

Program	Degree	Application Deadline	Applications Received	Accepted	New Admits Enrolled (PT)	Total Enrolled (PT)	Degrees Awarded in 2014–2015	Median Years to Complete Degree	Dismissed/ Withdrew
Developmental Psychology	PhD	January 5 (Fall)	2	2	1 (0)	8 (0)	1		0
School Psychology	EdS	December 15 (Fall)	6	6	6 (0)	9 (0)	7	4	0
Industrial/ Organizational Psychology	MA/MS	January 5 (Fall)	28	5	5 (0)	10 (0)	3	2	2
School Psychology	MA/MS	December 15 (Fall)	17	9	9	18 (0)	6	2	0
Neuroscience & Behavior	PhD	January 5 (Fall)	8	6	6 (0)	9 (0)	1		0
Developmental Psychology	MA/MS	January 5 (Fall)	7	2	0	3 (0)	0		0
Experimental Psychology	MA/MS	January 5 (Fall)	6	2	2 (0)	4 (0)	0		0
Industrial/ Organizational Psychology	MA/MS	January 5 (Fall)	28	8	8 (0)	18 (0)	3	3	0
Industrial/ Organizational Psychology	PhD	January 5 (Fall)	10	6	6	16	6		3
Neuroscience & Behavior	MA/MS	January 5 (Fall)	21	6	6	7	1		0
Applied Behavior Analysis	MA/MS	January 5 (Fall)	22	9	5	12	5	2	0

Internships/Practica

An internship in school psychology is available and required within the EdS program leading to certification in the field of school psychology. Practica are also available (and for some degrees required) in industrial/organizational psychology and developmental psychology.

Admissions

Entries appear in the following order: required test or GPA, minimum score (if required)/median score of students entering in 2015–2016.

Program	Degree	GRE-V	GRE-Q	GRE-Writing	GRE-Subject	Under-graduate GPA	Last 2 Years GPA	Psychology GPA	Master's GPA
Developmental Psychology	PhD	Not specified	Not specified	Not specified	Not specified	Not specified	Not specified	Not specified	Not specified
School Psychology	EdS	Not specified	Not specified	Not specified	Not specified	Not specified	Not specified	Not specified	Not specified
Industrial/ Organizational Psychology	MA/MS	Not specified	Not specified	Not specified	Not specified	Not specified	Not specified	Not specified	Not specified
School Psychology	MA/MS	Not specified	Not specified	Not specified	Not specified	Not specified	Not specified	Not specified	Not specified
Neuroscience & Behavior	PhD	Not specified	Not specified	Not specified	Not specified	Not specified	Not specified	Not specified	Not specified
Developmental Psychology	MA/MS	Not specified	Not specified	Not specified	Not specified	Not specified	Not specified	Not specified	Not specified
Experimental Psychology	MA/MS	Not specified	Not specified	Not specified	Not specified	Not specified	Not specified	Not specified	Not specified
Industrial/ Organizational Psychology	MA/MS	Not specified	Not specified	Not specified	Not specified	Not specified	Not specified	Not specified	Not specified
Industrial/ Organizational Psychology	PhD	NA/NA	NA/NA	Not specified	Not specified	Not specified	Not specified	Not specified	Not specified
Neuroscience & Behavior	MA/MS	Not specified	Not specified	Not specified	Not specified	Not specified	Not specified	Not specified	Not specified
Applied Behavior Analysis	MA/MS	NA/NA	NA/NA	Not specified	Not specified	Not specified	Not specified	Not specified	Not specified

Admissions Requirements:

Degree	GRE	GRE-Subject	Letters of Recommendation	Research Statement	Writing Sample	CV	Interview
Master's/Specialist	Required	Optional	3	Required	Required	Required	Required
Doctoral	Required	Optional	3	Required	Required	Required	Required

Admissions Criteria:

GRE scores—high
Research experience—high
Work experience—medium
Clinically related public service—low
GPA—high

Letters of recommendation—high
Interview—medium
Statement of goals and objectives—high
Undergraduate psychology preparation—medium

For additional information on admission requirements, visit http://www.unomaha.edu/college-of-arts-and-sciences/psychology/academics/graduate-programs/index.php.

Department Demographics

	Male (PT)	Female (PT)	Total	African-American/ Black (PT)	Hispanic/ Latino (PT)	Asian/ Pacific Islander (PT)	American Indian/ Alaska Native (PT)	Caucasian/ White (PT)	Unknown	Multiethnic (PT)	ADA (PT)	Int'l (PT)
Students	36 (0)	78 (0)	114	2 (0)	2 (0)	3 (0)	0 (0)	107 (0)	0 (0)	0 (0)	0 (0)	2 (0)

Financial Information/Assistance

Tuition: For information on tuition costs, visit http://cashiering.unomaha.edu/tuition.php. Tuition is subject to change. Additional fees are assessed to students beyond the costs of tuition for the following: Library, technology, lab, student access, Mavcard services.

Doctoral:
State residents: $250 per credit hour.
Nonstate residents: $697 per credit hour.

Master's:
State residents: $250 per credit hour.
Nonstate residents: $697 per credit hour.

Financial Assistance:

	Teaching Assistantship (% Receiving)	Teaching Assistantship Tuition Remission	Research Assistantship (% Receiving)	Research Assistantship Tuition Remission	Fellowship (% Receiving)	Fellowship Tuition Remission
First-Year Student	$13,030 (NA)	Full	$13,030 (NA)	Full	$13,030 (NA)	Full
Advanced Student	$13,030 (NA)	Full	$13,030 (NA)	Full	$13,030 (NA)	Full

For additional information on financial assistance, visit http://www.unomaha.edu/admissions/financial-support-and-scholarships/.

Employment of Department Graduates

No information provided.

Additional Information

Housing and Day Care: On-campus housing is available. See the following website for more information: http://housing.unomaha.edu/index.php. On-campus day care facilities are available. See the following website for more information: http://www.unomaha.edu/child-care-center/index.php.

Information for Students With Physical Disabilities: See the following website: http://www.unomaha.edu/disability/.

Special Facilities or Resources: The department maintains extensive laboratory facilities in a variety of experimental areas, both human and animal. The animal colony consists of rats, gerbils, mice, and golden lion tamarins. Up-to-date interactive computer facilities are readily available. The Center for Applied Psychological Services is a departmentally-controlled, faculty-student consulting service that provides an opportunity to gain practical experience in industrial psychology and school psychology. The department maintains working relationships with the Children's Rehabilitation Institute, the Department of Pediatrics, the Department of Physiology, and the University of Nebraska Medical Center. In addition, contact exists with the Boys Town Institute, Boys Town Home, Henry Doorly Zoo, Union Pacific Railroad, and Mutual of Omaha.

Application Information: Graduate Studies Admissions, 6001 Dodge Street, EAB 203, Omaha, NE 68182-0274. *Fee:* $45. *Online application:* https://apply.unomaha.edu/.

Nevada, University of, Las Vegas
Department of Psychology
Liberal Arts
4505 South Maryland Parkway, Box 455030
Las Vegas, NV 89154-5030
Telephone: (702) 895-3305
Chairperson: Christopher A. Kearney

E-mail: chris.kearney@unlv.edu
Web: http://www.unlv.edu/psychology

Orientation, Objectives, and Emphasis of Department
The department has the following goals: generating new psychological knowledge through original scholarly research; disseminating psychological knowledge through scholarly articles, books, and other relevant media, through the development of professional conduct by mentorship and supervision of graduate and undergraduate students, and through effective teaching at the graduate and undergraduate levels; promoting self-exploration and self-awareness among students to develop an appreciation of diversity; creating a just, diverse, and humane working and learning environment; enhancing organizational climate, research, teaching/mentoring, and services related to multiculturalism and diversity; creating an effective and responsive administrative infrastructure to serve all stakeholders, including faculty, graduate and undergraduate students, other administrative units within the College and University, and the larger public; and serving the community by bringing faculty and student expertise to bear on important local and regional issues.

Programs and Degrees Offered

Program	Degree	Application Deadline	Applications Received	Accepted	New Admits Enrolled (PT)	Total Enrolled (PT)	Degrees Awarded in 2014–2015	Median Years to Complete Degree	Dismissed/ Withdrew
Clinical Psychology	PhD	December 1 (Fall)	80	8	8 (0)	38 (0)	8	6.6	1
Experimental Psychology	PhD	December 1 (Fall)	33	11	6 (0)	28 (0)	4	6.75	1

APA Accreditation
Clinical PhD: Student Outcome Data website: https://www.unlv.edu/psychology/graduateprograms/phd-clinical.

Doctoral Degree (PhD Clinical Psychology): For those doctoral students for whom a professional internship was required in this program prior to graduation:
Total students who applied for an internship: 2
Total students who obtained an internship: 2
Total students who obtained a paid internship: 2
Total students who obtained an unpaid internship: 0
Total students who were placed in APA/CPA-accredited internships: 2
Total students placed in internships not APA/CPA-accredited, but listed with the Association of Psychology Postdoctoral and Internship Centers (APPIC): 0
Total students placed in internships conforming to guidelines of the Council of Directors of School Psychology Programs (CDSPP): 0
Total students placed in internships that were not APA/CPA-accredited, APPIC or CDSSP listed: 0

Internships/Practica
Students work in various community practicum settings as part of their training experience.

Admissions

Entries appear in the following order: required test or GPA, minimum score (if required)/median score of students entering in 2015–2016.

Program	Degree	GRE-V	GRE-Q	GRE-Writing	GRE-Subject	Under-graduate GPA	Last 2 Years GPA	Psychol-ogy GPA	Master's GPA
Clinical Psychology	PhD	NA/158	NA/155	Not specified	Not specified	NA/3.8	Not specified	NA/NA	Not specified
Experimental Psychology	PhD	NA/155	NA/154	Not specified	Not specified	NA/3.54	Not specified	NA/NA	Not specified

Admissions Requirements:

Degree	GRE	GRE-Subject	Letters of Recom-mendation	Research Statement	Writing Sample	CV	Interview
Doctoral	Required	Required	3	Required	Optional	Required	Required

Please note if these criteria vary for different programs: Our experimental program ranks clinically related public service as low. Only Clinical program requires GRE-Subject test.

Admissions Criteria:

GRE scores—high
Research experience—high
Work experience—medium
Clinically related public service—medium
GPA—high

Letters of recommendation—high
Interview—high
Statement of goals and objectives—high
Undergraduate psychology preparation—high

Department Demographics

	Male (PT)	Female (PT)	Total	African-American/ Black (PT)	Hispanic/ Latino (PT)	Asian/ Pacific Islander (PT)	American Indian/ Alaska Native (PT)	Caucasian/ White (PT)	Unknown	Multiethnic (PT)	ADA (PT)	Int'l (PT)
Students	17 (0)	49 (0)	66	0 (0)	5 (0)	4 (0)	0 (0)	44 (0)	12 (0)	1 (0)	1 (0)	4 (0)

Financial Information/Assistance

Tuition: For information on tuition costs, visit https://www.unlv.edu/cashiering/tuition-fees. Tuition is subject to change. Additional fees are assessed to students beyond the costs of tuition for the following: lab assessment materials for some courses.

Doctoral:
State residents: $7,128 per academic year.
Nonstate residents: $18,937 per academic year.

Financial Assistance:

	Teaching Assistantship (% Receiving)	Teaching Assistantship Tuition Remission	Research Assistantship (% Receiving)	Research Assistantship Tuition Remission	Fellowship (% Receiving)	Fellowship Tuition Remission
First-Year Student	$15,500 (NA)	Partial	$15,500 (NA)	Partial	NA (NA)	NA
Advanced Student	$15,500 (NA)	Partial	$15,500 (NA)	Partial	$15,000 (NA)	Full

For additional information on financial assistance, visit https://www.unlv.edu/graduatecollege/financing.

Employment of Department Graduates

No information provided.

Additional Information

Housing and Day Care: No on-campus housing is available. On-campus day care facilities are available. See the following website for more information: http://preschool.unlv.edu/.

Information for Students With Physical Disabilities: See the following website: http://drc.unlv.edu/.

Special Facilities or Resources: The strongest resource of the UNLV Psychology Department is the many talents of its diverse faculty. Our graduate program is small enough to provide close personal interaction experiences for training, and yet we encourage students to demonstrate initiative and to undertake the major responsibility for their graduate learning experiences. Student research is encouraged within the department and throughout the university.

Application Information: Fee: $75. Online application: https://unlv-gradcollege.force.com/Portal_Login.

Nevada, University of, Reno

Department of Psychology
Liberal Arts
1664 North Virginia Street, Mail Stop 0296
Reno, NV 89557
Telephone: (775) 784-6828
Chairperson: Michael A. Crognale

E-mail: maustin@unr.edu
Web: http://www.unr.edu/psychology

Orientation, Objectives, and Emphasis of Department

The Cognitive and Brain Science (previously Experimental) program in psychology is research-oriented. The division offers specialized work in human cognition and cognitive neuroscience; learning, perception and psychophysics; and animal communication. The clinical program has a scientist–practitioner emphasis and offers skills in psychotherapy, assessment, evaluation, and community psychology. The behavior analysis program emphasizes applied behavior analysis, especially in institutional settings, and examines both the theoretical and applied ramifications of the behavioral programs.

Programs and Degrees Offered

Program	Degree	Application Deadline	Applica-tions Received	Accepted	New Admits Enrolled (PT)	Total Enrolled (PT)	Degrees Awarded in 2014–2015	Median Years to Complete Degree	Dismissed/ Withdrew
Behavior Analysis	PhD	January 1 (Fall)	52	13	13 (0)	69 (0)	8	4	0
Clinical Psychology	PhD	January 1 (Fall)	73	5	5 (0)	42 (0)	4	6	0
Cognitive and Brain Sciences	PhD	January 1 (Fall)	23	10	6 (0)	29 (0)	5	5	0

APA Accreditation

Clinical PhD: Student Outcome Data website: http://www.unr.edu/psychology/degrees/clinical-phd/apa.

Doctoral Degree (PhD Clinical Psychology): For those doctoral students for whom a professional internship was required in this program prior to graduation:
Total students who applied for an internship: 5
Total students who obtained an internship: 5
Total students who obtained a paid internship: 5
Total students who obtained an unpaid internship: 0
Total students who were placed in APA/CPA-accredited internships: 5
Total students placed in internships not APA/CPA-accredited, but listed with the Association of Psychology Postdoctoral and Internship Centers (APPIC): 0
Total students placed in internships conforming to guidelines of the Council of Directors of School Psychology Programs (CDSPP): 0
Total students placed in internships that were not APA/CPA-accredited, APPIC or CDSSP listed: 0

Internships/Practica

From the last half of the first year through the third year, clinical students see clients at the Psychological Service Center, an in-house clinic. During the fourth year, students are required to complete a 1000-hour practicum (externship) on campus or at agencies in the area. Finally, students are required to complete a 2000-hour, APA-approved internship during their final year.

Admissions

Entries appear in the following order: required test or GPA, minimum score (if required)/median score of students entering in 2015–2016.

Program	Degree	GRE-V	GRE-Q	GRE-Writing	GRE-Subject	Under-graduate GPA	Last 2 Years GPA	Psychol-ogy GPA	Master's GPA
Behavior Analysis	PhD	Not specified	Not specified	Not specified	Not specified	Not specified	Not specified	Not specified	Not specified
Clinical Psychology	PhD	NA/165	NA/161	Not specified	NA/NA	NA/3.6	Not specified	Not specified	Not specified
Cognitive and Brain Sciences	PhD	Not specified	Not specified	Not specified	Not specified	Not specified	Not specified	Not specified	Not specified

Admissions Requirements:

Degree	GRE	GRE-Subject	Letters of Recom-mendation	Research Statement	Writing Sample	CV	Interview
Doctoral	Required	Recom-mended	3	Required	Optional	Required	Required

Please note if these criteria vary for different programs: Interview for admission in Behavior Analysis and Clinical Psychology is required.

Admissions Criteria:

GRE scores—high
Research experience—high
Work experience—medium
Clinically related public service—medium
GPA—high

Letters of recommendation—high
Interview—high
Statement of goals and objectives—medium
Undergraduate psychology preparation—high

For additional information on admission requirements, visit http://www.unr.edu/psychology/degrees.

Department Demographics

	Male (PT)	Female (PT)	Total	African-American/ Black (PT)	Hispanic/ Latino (PT)	Asian/ Pacific Islander (PT)	American Indian/ Alaska Native (PT)	Caucasian/ White (PT)	Unknown	Multiethnic (PT)	ADA (PT)	Int'l (PT)
Students	50 (0)	90 (0)	140	0 (0)	11 (0)	20 (0)	0 (0)	105 (0)	4 (0)	0 (0)	0 (0)	11 (0)

Financial Information/Assistance

Tuition: For information on tuition costs, visit http://www.unr.edu/tuition-and-fees. Tuition is subject to change. Additional fees are assessed to students beyond the costs of tuition for the following: Health Center (if enrolled in 6 credits or more) $135.50.

Doctoral:
State residents: $11,088 per academic year.
State residents: $264 per credit hour.
Nonstate residents: $24,998 per academic year.

Financial Assistance:

	Teaching Assistantship (% Receiving)	Teaching Assistantship Tuition Remission	Research Assistantship (% Receiving)	Research Assistantship Tuition Remission	Fellowship (% Receiving)	Fellowship Tuition Remission
First-Year Student	$17,000 (NA)	Full	$17,000 (NA)	Full	NA (NA)	NA
Advanced Student	$18,000 (NA)	Full	$18,000 (NA)	Full	NA (NA)	NA

For additional information on financial assistance, visit http://www.unr.edu/grad/funding.

Employment of Department Graduates

No information provided.

Additional Information

Housing and Day Care: On-campus housing is available. See the following website for more information: http://www.unr.edu/housing/on-campus-housing/graduate-housing. On-campus day care facilities are available. See the following website for more information: http://www.unr.edu/education/centers/cfrc/programs-and-services.

Information for Students With Physical Disabilities: See the following website: http://www.unr.edu/drc.

Special Facilities or Resources: The cognitive and brain science program has active labs with facilities for research in visual perception, memory, cognition, and animal behavior and communication (including opportunities for research at the primate center at Central Washington University). The behavior analysis program has a lab where students work with autistic children and developmentally-disabled clients. The primary academic/research facility of the clinical program is the Psychological Service Center, an in-house training clinic that serves the community by offering services on a sliding fee basis.

Application Information: Admissions, Psychology Department/296, University of Nevada, Reno, NV 89557. *Fee:* $60. *Online application:* http://www.unr.edu/grad/admissions.

Antioch University New England
Clinical Psychology
40 Avon Street
Keene, NH 03431-3516
Telephone: (603) 283-2183
Chairperson: George Tremblay, PhD

E-mail: cpeterson@antioch.edu
Web: http://www.antiochne.edu/cp/

Orientation, Objectives, and Emphasis of Department
Our practitioner-scholar program prepares clinicians to undertake multiple roles for the expanded world of future clinical psychology practice. Our graduates see clients; supervise other clinicians; consult, train, and teach; perform complex assessments; develop and administer programs; act as advocates to influence public policy; and conduct applied research such as evaluating treatment effectiveness, conducting needs assessments, and performing program evaluations. Our program includes broad training, offering a range of theoretical perspectives, a sound psychological knowledge base, and supervised practice. With a commitment to social responsibility, social justice, and diversity, we emphasize a social vision of clinical psychology, responsive to the needs of the larger society. We view research in clinical psychology as being rooted in solving professional and social problems, where science and practice are integrated and complementary. Preparation as local clinical scientists includes training in an array of methodologies and encourages students to explore their professional interests within the required dissertation and other research, elective course/concentration, and clinical opportunities. Our students learn to engage in reflective practice with self-awareness and an understanding of the importance of all professional relationships. Our pedagogy brings together theory, research, and practice through integrative, reflective learning experiences which help students develop their professional voice.

Programs and Degrees Offered

Program	Degree	Application Deadline	Applications Received	Accepted	New Admits Enrolled (PT)	Total Enrolled (PT)	Degrees Awarded in 2014–2015	Median Years to Complete Degree	Dismissed/ Withdrew
Clinical Psychology	PsyD	January 5 (Fall)	86	45	22 (0)	135 (0)	19	6	2

APA Accreditation

Clinical PsyD (Doctor of Psychology).

Doctoral Degree (PsyD Clinical Psychology): For those doctoral students for whom a professional internship was required in this program prior to graduation:
Total students who applied for an internship: 19
Total students who obtained an internship: 14
Total students who obtained a paid internship: 14
Total students who obtained an unpaid internship: 0
Total students who were placed in APA/CPA-accredited internships: 10
Total students placed in internships not APA/CPA-accredited, but listed with the Association of Psychology Postdoctoral and Internship Centers (APPIC): 3
Total students placed in internships conforming to guidelines of the Council of Directors of School Psychology Programs (CDSPP): 0
Total students placed in internships that were not APA/CPA-accredited, APPIC or CDSSP listed: 1

Internships/Practica
Students complete practica at agencies throughout New England. Approximately 14 students per year are placed at our department-run training clinic, the Antioch Psychological Services Center (PSC). PSC student clinicians provide individual, couple and family therapy; counseling to students from other Antioch departments; psychological assessments for all ages; psychological services in the county jail, local hospital, and regional schools; prevention services for families identified as at risk for abuse; community outreach, consultation, and psychoeducation; and other services. Our external practicum sites offer training to work with a wide range of client populations, problems, and settings. Internship students enter the national APPIC match, and have had great success at obtaining general and focused internships at sites throughout the U.S. and Canada. Practicum and internship students work in: college counseling centers, elementary and secondary schools, mental health centers, community clinics, integrated primary care settings, general and psychiatric hospitals, VA hospitals, the military, rehabilitation centers, neuropsychiatric settings, geriatric centers, jails and prisons, juvenile detention centers, and many other settings.

Admissions

Entries appear in the following order: required test or GPA, minimum score (if required)/median score of students entering in 2015–2016.

Program	Degree	GRE-V	GRE-Q	GRE-Writing	GRE-Subject	Under-graduate GPA	Last 2 Years GPA	Psychol-ogy GPA	Master's GPA
Clinical Psychology	PsyD	142/157	136/151	4/4	440/600	3.2/3.7	Not specified	Not specified	Not specified

Admissions Requirements:

Degree	GRE	GRE-Subject	Letters of Recom-mendation	Research Statement	Writing Sample	CV	Interview
Doctoral	Required	Optional	3	Required	Required	Required	Required

Admissions Criteria:

GRE scores—high
Research experience—medium
Work experience—medium
Clinically related public service—medium
GPA—high

Letters of recommendation—high
Interview—high
Statement of goals and objectives—high
Undergraduate psychology preparation—low

For additional information on admission requirements, visit http://www.antiochne.edu/admissions/approcess_psyd/.

Department Demographics

	Male (PT)	Female (PT)	Total	African-American/ Black (PT)	Hispanic/ Latino (PT)	Asian/ Pacific Islander (PT)	American Indian/ Alaska Native (PT)	Caucasian/ White (PT)	Unknown	Multiethnic (PT)	ADA (PT)	Int'l (PT)
Students	20 (0)	115 (0)	135	4 (0)	2 (0)	2 (0)	2 (0)	102 (0)	18 (1)	2 (0)	4 (0)	2 (0)

Financial Information/Assistance

Tuition: For information on tuition costs, visit http://www.antiochne.edu/financial/clinical-psychology-department-program-tuition-and-fees/. Tuition is subject to change.

Doctoral:
State residents: $37,436 per academic year.
Nonstate residents: $37,436 per academic year.

Financial Assistance:

	Teaching Assistantship (% Receiving)	Teaching Assistantship Tuition Remission	Research Assistantship (% Receiving)	Research Assistantship Tuition Remission	Fellowship (% Receiving)	Fellowship Tuition Remission
First-Year Student	NA (NA)	NA	$2,496 (NA)	NA	$3,117 (NA)	NA
Advanced Student	$1,362 (NA)	NA	$4,352 (NA)	NA	$3,205 (NA)	NA

For additional information on financial assistance, visit http://www.antiochne.edu/financial/how-to-apply/.

Employment of Department Graduates

Doctoral:
Enrolled in a postdoctoral residency/fellowship: 14
Employed in other positions at a higher education institution: 4
Employed in a community mental health/counseling center: 1
Total: 19

Additional Information

Housing and Day Care: No on-campus housing is available. No on-campus day care facilities are available.

Information for Students With Physical Disabilities: See the following website: http://www.antiochne.edu/sds/.

Special Facilities or Resources: In addition to our PSC (above), we run two innovative centers, the Center for Behavioral Health Innovation (BHI) and the Multicultural Center for Research and Practice (MCC). Each is directed by core faculty members and staffed in part by our PsyD students. First launched by Antioch University New England's (AUNE) PsyD Program in 1996, BHI partners with community agencies to design, evaluate and transform clinical service systems. Our team includes 6 faculty and staff and about a dozen students, all supported by external grants and contracts, integrating behavioral health expertise into schools, primary care clinics, and other community settings. Established in 2000, Antioch's MCC promotes multiculturalism within a social justice orientation. Multicultural is applied broadly to include issues of minority or marginalized status (e.g., race, ethnicity, culture, gender, sexual orientation, gender identity, disability, religion, spirituality, country or language of origin, class, and the elderly). The MCC focuses on culturally diverse and immigrant youth, adults, and families in New England.

Application Information: Office of Doctoral (PsyD) Admissions, Antioch University New England, 40 Avon Street, Keene, NH, 03431-3552. *Fee:* $75. *Online application:* https://app.applyyourself.com/?id=antioch-u.

New Hampshire, University of
Department of Psychology
College of Liberal Arts
McConnell Hall
Durham, NH 3824
Telephone: (603) 862-2360
Chairperson: Wm Wren Stine

E-mail: robin.scholefield@unh.edu
Web: http://www.unh.edu/psychology/

Orientation, Objectives, and Emphasis of Department
The program's basic goal is the preparation of doctoral students for academic careers. We focus on the development of psychologists who have broad knowledge of psychology, who can teach and communicate effectively, and who can carry out sound research. Specialties are offered in the following areas: Brain, Behavior and Cognition (behavioral and cognitive neuroscience, cognition, vision); Developmental Psychology; and Social/Personality Psychology. Besides completing academic courses, our program places a distinctive emphasis on preparing graduate students for future roles as faculty members in college or university settings. Students complete a year-long seminar and practicum in the teaching of psychology, which introduces them to the theory and practice of teaching, while they concurrently teach under the supervision of master-teachers. Students also gain experience in other faculty roles such as sponsoring undergraduate students' research and serving on committees. Students are involved in research activities throughout the program. After graduation, most students secure academic positions.

Programs and Degrees Offered

Program	Degree	Application Deadline	Applications Received	Accepted	New Admits Enrolled (PT)	Total Enrolled (PT)	Degrees Awarded in 2014–2015	Median Years to Complete Degree	Dismissed/ Withdrew
Developmental Psychology	PhD	(Fall), Rolling	6	0	0	5	0		0
Social/ Personality Psychology	PhD	(Fall), Rolling	46	3	3	14	2		0
Brain, Behavior and Cognition	PhD	(Fall), Rolling	16	1	3 (0)	10 (0)	1	5	0

Admissions

Entries appear in the following order: required test or GPA, minimum score (if required)/median score of students entering in 2015–2016.

Program	Degree	GRE-V	GRE-Q	GRE-Writing	GRE-Subject	Under-graduate GPA	Last 2 Years GPA	Psychol-ogy GPA	Master's GPA
Developmental Psychology	PhD	NA/NA	NA/NA	NA/NA	Not specified	NA/NA	Not specified	Not specified	Not specified
Social/ Personality Psychology	PhD	NA/NA	NA/NA	NA/NA	Not specified	NA/NA	Not specified	Not specified	Not specified
Brain, Behavior and Cognition	PhD	NA/NA	NA/NA	NA/NA	Not specified	NA/NA	Not specified	Not specified	Not specified

Admissions Requirements:

Degree	GRE	GRE-Subject	Letters of Recom-mendation	Research Statement	Writing Sample	CV	Interview
Doctoral	Required	Optional	3	Required	Optional	Optional	Recom-mended

Admissions Criteria:

GRE scores—high
Research experience—high
Work experience—low
GPA—high
Letters of recommendation—high

Interview—low
Statement of goals and objectives—high
Undergraduate psychology preparation—medium
Interests match program—high

For additional information on admission requirements, visit http://cola.unh.edu/psychology/how-apply.

Department Demographics

	Male (PT)	Female (PT)	Total	African-American/ Black (PT)	Hispanic/ Latino (PT)	Asian/ Pacific Islander (PT)	American Indian/ Alaska Native (PT)	Caucasian/ White (PT)	Unknown (PT)	Multiethnic (PT)	ADA (PT)	Int'l (PT)
Students	8 (0)	21 (0)	29	0 (0)	1 (0)	0 (0)	0 (0)	28 (0)	0 (0)	0 (0)	0 (0)	1 (0)

Financial Information/Assistance

Tuition: For information on tuition costs, visit http://www.unh.edu/business-services/tuitgrad.html. Tuition is subject to change.

Doctoral:
State residents: $13,500 per academic year.
State residents: $750 per credit hour.
Nonstate residents: $26,200 per academic year.
Nonstate residents: $1,089 per credit hour.

Financial Assistance:

	Teaching Assistantship (% Receiving)	Teaching Assistantship Tuition Remission	Research Assistantship (% Receiving)	Research Assistantship Tuition Remission	Fellowship (% Receiving)	Fellowship Tuition Remission
First-Year Student	$15,550 (NA)	Full	NA (NA)	NA	NA (NA)	NA

Financial Assistance (con't.):

	Teaching Assistantship (% Receiving)	Teaching Assistantship Tuition Remission	Research Assistantship (% Receiving)	Research Assistantship Tuition Remission	Fellowship (% Receiving)	Fellowship Tuition Remission
Advanced Student	$17,800 (NA)	Full	NA (NA)	NA	$17,800 (NA)	Full

For additional information on financial assistance, visit http://www.gradschool.unh.edu/grad_aid.php.

Employment of Department Graduates

Doctoral:
Enrolled in a postdoctoral residency/fellowship: 1
Employed in an academic position at a university: 2
Total: 3

Additional Information

Housing and Day Care: On-campus housing is available. See the following website for more information: http://www.unh.edu/housing/graduate-family. On-campus day care facilities are available. See the following website for more information: http://chhs.unh.edu/csdc.

Information for Students With Physical Disabilities: See the following website: http://www.unh.edu/disabilityservices/.

Special Facilities or Resources: The department occupies several buildings and offers research facilities, equipment, and resources in all of its areas of specialization. In addition, the department has up-to-date computing and related resources.

Application Information: Dean of the Graduate School, University of New Hampshire, Thompson Hall, Durham, NH 03824. *Fee:* $65. *Online application:* http://www.gradschool.unh.edu/apply.php.

Rivier University
Department of Education
420 South Main Street
Nashua, NH 3060
Telephone: (603) 897-8589
Dean: John Gleason, EdD

E-mail: gadmissions@rivier.edu
Web: http://www.rivier.edu/academics.aspx?menu=66&id=504

Orientation, Objectives, and Emphasis of Department
Founded in 1933 by the Sisters of the Presentation of Mary, Rivier University is a Catholic institution of higher education dedicated to transforming hearts and minds to serve the world. As a co-educational institution of higher learning, the University is dedicated to the education of undergraduate and graduate students in both the liberal arts and professional courses of study. The Rivier University doctoral program in counseling and school psychology follows the accepted practitioner-scholar model. Students are prepared as critical thinkers and problem solvers who work in applied settings and draw upon the theory and evidence base of psychology and education to deliver a continuum of empirically supported services. Students are trained in a cohort model to be consumers of research to inform practice as highly skilled professionals delivering assessment, intervention, consultation and preventive services to their constituents.

Programs and Degrees Offered

Program	Degree	Application Deadline	Applications Received	Accepted	New Admits Enrolled (PT)	Total Enrolled (PT)	Degrees Awarded in 2014–2015	Median Years to Complete Degree	Dismissed/ Withdrew
Counseling and School Psychology	PsyD	February 1 (Fall)	12	12	6 (0)	22 (0)	0		2

Programs and Degrees Offered *(con't.)*

Program	Degree	Application Deadline	Applica-tions Received	Accepted	New Admits Enrolled (PT)	Total Enrolled (PT)	Degrees Awarded in 2014–2015	Median Years to Complete Degree	Dismissed/ Withdrew
School Psychology	EdS	Rolling				14	7	3	0
Clinical Mental Health Counseling	MA/MS	Rolling				55	21	3	

Doctoral Degree (PsyD Counseling and School Psychology): For those doctoral students for whom a professional internship was required in this program prior to graduation:

Total students who applied for an internship: 2
Total students who obtained an internship: 1
Total students who obtained a paid internship: 1
Total students who obtained an unpaid internship: 0
Total students who were placed in APA/CPA-accredited internships: 0
Total students placed in internships not APA/CPA-accredited, but listed with the Association of Psychology Postdoctoral and Internship Centers (APPIC): 1
Total students placed in internships conforming to guidelines of the Council of Directors of School Psychology Programs (CDSPP): 0
Total students placed in internships that were not APA/CPA-accredited, APPIC or CDSSP listed: 0

Internships/Practica

Students have worked in many internship and practicum sites including school, mental health centers, hospital inpatient units, and area mental health and developmental service agencies.

Admissions

Entries appear in the following order: required test or GPA, minimum score (if required)/median score of students entering in 2015–2016.

Program	Degree	GRE-V	GRE-Q	GRE-Writing	GRE-Subject	Under-graduate GPA	Last 2 Years GPA	Psychol-ogy GPA	Master's GPA
Counseling and School Psychology	PsyD	Not specified	Not specified	Not specified	Not specified	Not specified	Not specified	Not specified	Not specified
School Psychology	EdS	Not specified	Not specified	Not specified	Not specified	Not specified	Not specified	Not specified	Not specified
Clinical Mental Health Counseling	MA/MS	Not specified	Not specified	Not specified	Not specified	Not specified	Not specified	Not specified	Not specified

Admissions Requirements:

Degree	GRE	GRE-Subject	Letters of Recom-mendation	Research Statement	Writing Sample	CV	Interview
Master's/Specialist	None	None	3	Required	None	Required	Required
Doctoral	Required	Required	3	Required	None	Required	Required

Admissions Criteria:

GRE scores—medium
Research experience—low
Work experience—high
Clinically related public service—medium
GPA—medium

Letters of recommendation—high
Interview—high
Statement of goals and objectives—medium
Undergraduate psychology preparation—medium

Department Demographics

	Male (PT)	Female (PT)	Total	African-American/ Black (PT)	Hispanic/ Latino (PT)	Asian/ Pacific Islander (PT)	American Indian/ Alaska Native (PT)	Caucasian/ White (PT)	Unknown (PT)	Multiethnic (PT)	ADA (PT)	Int'l (PT)
Students	0 (0)	0 (0)	0	0 (0)	0 (0)	0 (0)	0 (0)	0 (0)	0 (0)	0 (0)	0 (0)	0 (0)

Financial Information/Assistance

Tuition: For information on tuition costs, visit http://www.rivier.edu/about.aspx?menu=119&id=4115. Tuition is subject to change. Tuition costs vary by program.

Doctoral:
State residents: $820 per credit hour.
Nonstate residents: $820 per credit hour.

Master's:
State residents: $530 per credit hour.
Nonstate residents: $530 per credit hour.

Financial Assistance:

	Teaching Assistantship (% Receiving)	Teaching Assistantship Tuition Remission	Research Assistantship (% Receiving)	Research Assistantship Tuition Remission	Fellowship (% Receiving)	Fellowship Tuition Remission
First-Year Student	NA (NA)	NA	NA (NA)	NA	NA (NA)	NA
Advanced Student	NA (NA)	NA	NA (NA)	NA	NA (NA)	NA

Employment of Department Graduates

No information provided.

Additional Information

Housing and Day Care: On-campus housing is available. See the following website for more information: http://www.rivier.edu/student.aspx?id=90. On-campus day care facilities are available. See the following website for more information: http://www.rivier.edu/about.aspx?menu=136&rand=242&id=1350.

Information for Students With Physical Disabilities: See the following website: http://www.rivier.edu/academics.aspx?id=1960.

Application Information: Rivier University, Office of Graduate Admissions, 420 South Main Street, Nashua, NH 03060. *Fee:* $100. *Online application:* https://www.rivier.edu/admissions/freeapplication/public/account.aspx.

Rivier University
Psychology
420 South Main Street
Nashua, NH 3060
Telephone: (603) 897-8596
Department Coordinator: Elizabeth Harwood, PhD

E-mail: eharwood@rivier.edu
Web: http://www.rivier.edu/academics.aspx?menu=80&id=527

Orientation, Objectives, and Emphasis of Department
The Department of Psychology offers a Master of Science degree program in Experimental and Clinical Psychology. Both are day programs and may be completed on either a full-time or part-time basis. The vision of the programs is one of collegiality and mentorship. Students develop a sense of mutual support and identity under the guidance of a faculty mentor and gain practical research and/or clinical experience in the Behavioral Science Lab or Clinical Psychology internship program. As day programs that provide students with a dedicated space in support of their research and clinical training, Rivier's graduate programs help build a

sense of camaraderie between graduate students and their professors and create an environment in which integrated learning is the shared responsibility of all. The master's programs put into practice the Boulder scientist–practitioner model of graduate psychology education by providing students with solid foundation in both the biopsychosocial bases of behavior and the methodological and quantitative skills acquired through research design, data collection, analysis, and evaluation. These skills will prepare students to progress to PhD or PsyD programs, teach in higher education on a part-time basis, or find employment in academic, business, governmental, or human service settings.

Programs and Degrees Offered

Program	Degree	Application Deadline	Applications Received	Accepted	New Admits Enrolled (PT)	Total Enrolled (PT)	Degrees Awarded in 2014–2015	Median Years to Complete Degree	Dismissed/ Withdrew
Clinical Psychology	MA/MS	Rolling	25	22	7 (1)	14 (1)	11	2	0
Experimental Psychology	MA/MS	Rolling		1	1	3	4	2	0

Internships/Practica

Graduate internships are arranged individually based on the student's prior experience and the learning opportunities provided at the internship setting. We currently have internship sites in a variety of settings and working with a variety of populations. These include working with children in schools, after-school prevention programs and clinical child care facilities. Also available are internships with older adults in nursing homes, senior activity centers and assisted living facilities. Internships in juvenile justice settings as well as group homes for adolescents; in hospital settings for individuals with both chronic developmental disabilities and acquired brain injuries; day treatment programs for adults with developmental disabilities; and transitional living programs are other settings. Our connection with a longitudinal research study at Judge Baker Guidance in Boston, MA has provided a number of our students who are interested in research with opportunities to pursue that interest. Similarly, research opportunities are available through an annual statewide study of homelessness in New Hampshire.

Admissions

Entries appear in the following order: required test or GPA, minimum score (if required)/median score of students entering in 2015–2016.

Program	Degree	GRE-V	GRE-Q	GRE-Writing	GRE-Subject	Under-graduate GPA	Last 2 Years GPA	Psychol-ogy GPA	Master's GPA
Clinical Psychology	MA/MS	Not specified	Not specified	Not specified	Not specified	3/NA	3/NA	3/NA	Not specified
Experimental Psychology	MA/MS	Not specified	Not specified	Not specified	Not specified	3/NA	3/NA	3/NA	Not specified

Admissions Requirements:

Degree	GRE	GRE-Subject	Letters of Recom-mendation	Research Statement	Writing Sample	CV	Interview
Master's/Specialist	Optional	Optional	1	Required	Optional	Optional	Required

Admissions Criteria:

Research experience—low
Work experience—low
Clinically related public service—low
GPA—high
Letters of recommendation—medium

Interview—medium
Statement of goals and objectives—high
Undergraduate psychology preparation—medium
Fit with program—medium

Department Demographics

	Male (PT)	Female (PT)	Total	African-American/ Black (PT)	Hispanic/ Latino (PT)	Asian/ Pacific Islander (PT)	American Indian/ Alaska Native (PT)	Caucasian/ White (PT)	Unknown	Multiethnic (PT)	ADA (PT)	Int'l (PT)
Students	5 (1)	12 (0)	18	1 (0)	3 (0)	2 (0)	0 (0)	11 (1)	0 (0)	0 (0)	0 (0)	1 (0)

Financial Information/Assistance

Tuition: For information on tuition costs, visit http://www.rivier.edu/about.aspx?menu=119&id=4115. Tuition is subject to change.

Master's:
State residents: $545 per credit hour.
Nonstate residents: $545 per credit hour.

Financial Assistance:

	Teaching Assistantship (% Receiving)	Teaching Assistantship Tuition Remission	Research Assistantship (% Receiving)	Research Assistantship Tuition Remission	Fellowship (% Receiving)	Fellowship Tuition Remission
First-Year Student	NA (NA)	NA	NA (NA)	NA	NA (NA)	NA
Advanced Student	NA (NA)	NA	NA (NA)	Partial	NA (NA)	NA

For additional information on financial assistance, visit https://www.rivier.edu/admissions.aspx?menu=98&id=665&act=67.

Employment of Department Graduates

Master's:
Enrolled in a psychology doctoral program: 2
Enrolled in another graduate/professional program: 1
Employed in other positions at a higher education institution: 1
Employed in a community mental health/counseling center: 2
Employed in a hospital/medical center: 1
Other employment position: 1
Total: 8

Additional Information

Housing and Day Care: On-campus housing is available. See the following website for more information: http://www.rivier.edu/student.aspx?id=90. On-campus day care facilities are available. See the following website for more information: http://www.rivier.edu/about.aspx?menu=136&rand=242&id=1350.

Information for Students With Physical Disabilities: See the following website: http://www.rivier.edu/academics.aspx?menu=163&id=1960.

Special Facilities or Resources: The psychology department has two dedicated facilities: the Behavioral Science Laboratory and the Clinical Psychology Laboratory. The Behavioral Science Laboratory (BSL) provides graduate students with access to the tools necessary for studying, characterizing, and analyzing human behavior. The BSL has six computer stations (five experimental and one researcher) equipped with state-of-the-art data acquisition and analysis software. The 400 sq. ft. facility also features reference texts on design and analysis, peer-reviewed psychology journals, and a 10-foot modular conference table that facilitates interaction among graduate students and between students and faculty. The Clinical Psychology Laboratory includes a classroom, an observation room with a one-way mirror, and a research room with three computers for student use. In addition, the facility is equipped with audio/video recording capability; a widescreen television for video presentations; and a general use area where students may interact, study, or just relax. Much like the BSL, this facility is used for both educational and research purposes.

Application Information: Rivier University, Office of Graduate Admissions, 420 South Main Street, Nashua, NH 03060. *Fee:* $25.
Online application: https://www.rivier.edu/admissions/freeapplication/public/login.aspx.

Fairleigh Dickinson University, Metropolitan Campus
School of Psychology
University College: Arts-Sciences-Professional Studies
1000 River Road
Teaneck, NJ 7666
Telephone: (201) 692-2300
Director: Ron Dumont Ed.D., NCSP

E-mail: dumont@fdu.edu
Web: http://view2.fdu.edu/academics/university-college/school-of-psychology/

Orientation, Objectives, and Emphasis of Department
The orientation of the department is essentially based on the scientist–practitioner model. In terms of theoretical orientations, some faculty are dynamicists, some behaviorists, and some humanists, though there is a sense of eclecticism that pervades those who are practitioners. There is a considerable emphasis on empirical research as the preferred basis for developing a theoretical orientation.

Programs and Degrees Offered

Program	Degree	Application Deadline	Applications Received	Accepted	New Admits Enrolled (PT)	Total Enrolled (PT)	Degrees Awarded in 2014–2015	Median Years to Complete Degree	Dismissed/ Withdrew
General/ Theoretical Psychology	MA/MS	Rolling	30	25	8 (1)	16 (3)	4	2	0
Clinical Psychology	PhD	December 15 (Fall)	225	23	12 (0)	74 (0)	14	6.5	1
School Psychology	PsyD	March 1 (Fall)	42	13	13 (0)	60	9	3.5	0
Clinical Psycho-pharmacology	MA/MS	July 15 (Fall), November 15 (Spring)	58	58	0 (49)	0 (105)	27	2	9
School Psychology	MA/MS	March 15 (Fall)	24	12	8	19	9	3	1
Forensic Psychology	MA/MS	March 15 (Fall)	75	25	14 (0)	26 (0)	13	1.5	1

APA Accreditation
Clinical PhD: Student Outcome Data website: http://view2.fdu.edu/academics/university-college/school-of-psychology/ph-d-program-in-clinical-psychology/admissions-outcomes/.

Doctoral Degree (PhD Clinical Psychology): For those doctoral students for whom a professional internship was required in this program prior to graduation:
Total students who applied for an internship: 11
Total students who obtained an internship: 10
Total students who obtained a paid internship: 10
Total students who obtained an unpaid internship: 0
Total students who were placed in APA/CPA-accredited internships: 9
Total students placed in internships not APA/CPA-accredited, but listed with the Association of Psychology Postdoctoral and Internship Centers (APPIC): 1
Total students placed in internships conforming to guidelines of the Council of Directors of School Psychology Programs (CDSPP): 0
Total students placed in internships that were not APA/CPA-accredited, APPIC or CDSSP listed: 0

Doctoral Degree (PsyD School Psychology): For those doctoral students for whom a professional internship was required in this program prior to graduation:

Total students who applied for an internship: 12
Total students who obtained an internship: 12
Total students who obtained a paid internship: 12
Total students who obtained an unpaid internship: 0
Total students who were placed in APA/CPA-accredited internships: 0
Total students placed in internships not APA/CPA-accredited, but listed with the Association of Psychology Postdoctoral and Internship Centers (APPIC): 0
Total students placed in internships conforming to guidelines of the Council of Directors of School Psychology Programs (CDSPP): 1
Total students placed in internships that were not APA/CPA-accredited, APPIC or CDSSP listed: 11

Master's Degree (MA/MS Clinical Psychopharmacology): An internship experience, such as a final research project or "capstone" experience is required of graduates. Master's Degree (MA/MS School Psychology): An internship experience, such as a final research project or "capstone" experience is required of graduates. Master's Degree (MA/MS Forensic Psychology): An internship experience, such as a final research project or "capstone" experience is required of graduates.

Internships/Practica
All PhD students are required to complete research and clinical practica during their first 3 years. Clinical practica may be completed on campus at the University's Center for Psychological Services. Externships are required for the Forensic and School MA programs. PsyD students must complete a 1-year internship.

Admissions
Entries appear in the following order: required test or GPA, minimum score (if required)/median score of students entering in 2015–2016.

Program	Degree	GRE-V	GRE-Q	GRE-Writing	GRE-Subject	Under-graduate GPA	Last 2 Years GPA	Psychology GPA	Master's GPA
General/ Theoretical Psychology	MA/MS	NA/NA	NA/NA	NA/NA	NA/NA	Not specified	Not specified	Not specified	Not specified
Clinical Psychology	PhD	NA/156	NA/153	NA/NA	NA/NA	Not specified	Not specified	Not specified	Not specified
School Psychology	PsyD	Not specified	Not specified	Not specified	Not specified	Not specified	Not specified	Not specified	Not specified
Clinical Psycho-pharmacology	MA/MS	Not specified	Not specified	Not specified	Not specified	Not specified	Not specified	Not specified	Not specified
School Psychology	MA/MS	Not specified	Not specified	Not specified	Not specified	Not specified	Not specified	Not specified	Not specified
Forensic Psychology	MA/MS	NA/NA	NA/NA	Not specified	Not specified	3.5/3.7	Not specified	Not specified	Not specified

Admissions Requirements:

Degree	GRE	GRE-Subject	Letters of Recom-mendation	Research Statement	Writing Sample	CV	Interview
Master's/Specialist	Required	Required	3	Optional	Optional	Optional	Required
Doctoral	Required	Required	3	Required	Optional	Required	Required

Please note if these criteria vary for different programs: These criteria are used for admission to PhD and PsyD programs. For PsyD program, research experience would be low and work experience would be medium-high. School Psychology MA and PsyD require GRE-Subject test; it is required the PhD Clinical program unless the applicant majored in psychology. Forensic Psychology only requires two letters of recommendation. Interviews for School Psychology programs only.

Admissions Criteria:
GRE scores—medium
Research experience—high
Work experience—medium
Clinically related public service—high
GPA—medium

Letters of recommendation—high
Interview—high
Statement of goals and objectives—high
Undergraduate psychology preparation—medium

Department Demographics

	Male (PT)	Female (PT)	Total	African-American/ Black (PT)	Hispanic/ Latino (PT)	Asian/ Pacific Islander (PT)	American Indian/ Alaska Native (PT)	Caucasian/ White (PT)	Unknown	Multiethnic (PT)	ADA (PT)	Int'l (PT)
Students	72 (50)	123 (57)	302	0 (0)	0 (0)	0 (0)	0 (0)	0 (0)	0 (0)	0 (0)	0 (0)	0 (0)

Financial Information/Assistance

Tuition: For information on tuition costs, visit http://view.fdu.edu/default.aspx?id=438. Tuition is subject to change. Tuition costs vary by program.

Doctoral:
State residents: $37,768 per academic year.
Nonstate residents: $37,768 per academic year.

Master's:
State residents: $1,272 per credit hour.
Nonstate residents: $1,272 per credit hour.

Financial Assistance:

	Teaching Assistantship (% Receiving)	Teaching Assistantship Tuition Remission	Research Assistantship (% Receiving)	Research Assistantship Tuition Remission	Fellowship (% Receiving)	Fellowship Tuition Remission
First-Year Student	NA (NA)	NA	$18,884 (NA)	NA	NA (NA)	NA
Advanced Student	NA (NA)	NA	$18,884 (NA)	NA	NA (NA)	NA

For additional information on financial assistance, visit http://view2.fdu.edu/admissions/graduate-admissions/graduate-financial-aid/.

Employment of Department Graduates

No information provided.

Additional Information

Housing and Day Care: No on-campus housing is available. No on-campus day care facilities are available.

Information for Students With Physical Disabilities: See the following website: http://view2.fdu.edu/metropolitan-campus/disability-support-services/.

Special Facilities or Resources: The department operates the Center for Psychological Services, which provides students in the PhD and PsyD programs opportunities in therapy and assessment with adults, children, families, and couples. The department has research laboratories equipped for experiments with humans as well as with small animals. Equipment includes computer facilities (both micro- and mainframe), a four-channel physiograph, electrophysiological stimulating and recording equipment, operant equipment for programming and recording behavior, two- and four-channel tachistoscopes, various other sensory apparatuses, standard and computer-based EEG recorders, and equipment and supplies for psychopharmacological studies.

Application Information: School of Psychology (T-WH1-01), Fairleigh Dickinson University, 1000 River Road, Teaneck, NJ 07666. *Fee:* $40. *Online application:* http://view2.fdu.edu/admissions/graduate-admissions/apply-online/.

Georgian Court University (2015 data)
Department of Psychology and Counseling
School of Arts & Sciences
900 Lakewood Avenue
Lakewood, NJ 8701
Telephone: (732) 987-2636
Chairperson: Susan E. O. Field, PhD

E-mail: field@georgian.edu
Web: http://www.georgian.edu/psychology/index.htm

Orientation, Objectives, and Emphasis of Department

The graduate programs in Clinical Mental Health Counseling, School Psychology, and Applied Behavior Analysis reflect the University's mission and core values of respect, integrity, service, justice, and compassion. We are committed to preparing professionals to address the needs of individuals, their families, and the community emphasizing issues of diversity and social justice. The program philosophy is to promote professional practice by developing competent, socially conscious professionals capable of providing evidence-based services to individuals and organizations in the community.

Programs and Degrees Offered

Program	Degree	Application Deadline	Applications Received	Accepted	New Admits Enrolled (PT)	Total Enrolled (PT)	Degrees Awarded in 2014–2015	Median Years to Complete Degree	Dismissed/ Withdrew
Clinical Mental Health Counseling	MA/MS	(Fall)	51	17	15 (2)		11	3	0
Applied Behavior Analysis	MA/MS	(Summer)		17			7		
School Psychology	MA/MS	(Fall)	25	15	15 (0)		12	4	1

Internships/Practica

The School Psychology program includes a 300 clock-hour practicum and a 1,200-hour, year-long externship in the public schools. The Clinical Mental Health Counseling program includes a 100 clock-hour practicum and a 600-hour, year-long internship with triadic supervision.

Admissions

Entries appear in the following order: required test or GPA, minimum score (if required)/median score of students entering in 2015–2016.

Program	Degree	GRE-V	GRE-Q	GRE-Writing	GRE-Subject	Under-graduate GPA	Last 2 Years GPA	Psychology GPA	Master's GPA
Clinical Mental Health Counseling	MA/MS	Not specified	Not specified	Not specified	Not specified	3/3.27	Not specified	Not specified	Not specified
Applied Behavior Analysis	MA/MS	Not specified	Not specified	Not specified	Not specified	3/3.56	Not specified	Not specified	Not specified
School Psychology	MA/MS	Not specified	Not specified	Not specified	Not specified	3/3.47	Not specified	Not specified	Not specified

Admissions Requirements:

Degree	GRE	GRE-Subject	Letters of Recommendation	Research Statement	Writing Sample	CV	Interview
Master's/Specialist	Required	None	3	Required	None	Required	Required

Please note if these criteria vary for different programs: School Psychology requires the MAT. Clinical Mental Health Counseling requires MAT or GRE. ABA requires either MAT, Praxis, or GRE.

Admissions Criteria:

GRE scores— medium
Research experience—low
Work experience—low
Clinically related public service—low
GPA—high

Letters of recommendation—high
Interview—high
Statement of goals and objectives—medium
Undergraduate psychology preparation—medium
GRE or MAT or Praxis—medium

Department Demographics

	Male (PT)	Female (PT)	Total	African-American/ Black (PT)	Hispanic/ Latino (PT)	Asian/ Pacific Islander (PT)	American Indian/ Alaska Native (PT)	Caucasian/ White (PT)	Unknown	Multiethnic (PT)	ADA (PT)	Int'l (PT)
Students			0				0 (0)	0 (0)	0 (0)		0 (0)	0 (0)

Financial Information/Assistance

Tuition: For information on tuition costs, visit http://www.georgian.edu/student_accounts/grad_costs.htm. Tuition is subject to change. Additional fees are assessed to students beyond the costs of tuition for the following: Some courses include lab fees and/or assessment protocol fees.

Master's:
State residents: $839 per credit hour.
Nonstate residents: $839 per credit hour.

Financial Assistance:

	Teaching Assistantship (% Receiving)	Teaching Assistantship Tuition Remission	Research Assistantship (% Receiving)	Research Assistantship Tuition Remission	Fellowship (% Receiving)	Fellowship Tuition Remission
First-Year Student	NA (NA)	NA	NA (NA)	NA	NA (NA)	NA
Advanced Student	NA (NA)	Partial	NA (NA)	NA	NA (NA)	NA

Employment of Department Graduates

No information provided.

Additional Information

Housing and Day Care: On-campus housing is available. No on-campus day care facilities are available.

Special Facilities or Resources: Our programs have observation rooms for counseling practicum and a lab for experimental and group work. Internships and practica are typically served in community-based programs and schools. The GCU Evaluation center is a New Jersey D.O.E. approved clinic/agency which is staffed by faculty in the department along with faculty from the School of Education.

Application Information: Mr. Patrick Givens, Director of Admissions, Georgian Court University, 900 Lakewood Avenue, Lakewood, NJ 08701. *Fee:* $40. *Online application:* http://www.georgian.edu/admissions/.

Kean University
Department of Psychology; Department of Advanced Studies in Psychology
Nathan Weiss Graduate College
1000 Morris Avenue
Union, NJ 7083
Telephone: (908) 737-5870
Chairperson: Dr. Paula Avioli; Dr. Andrew Wolanin

E-mail: pavioli@kean.edu and awolanin@kean.edu
Web: http://www.kean.edu

Orientation, Objectives, and Emphasis of Department

Our academic emphasis is eclectic including cognitive behavioral, mindfulness and acceptance based approaches, family systems, and psychodynamic approaches. All classes are small, which is conducive to the learning environment and facilitates the opportunity for professional growth. The PsyD program in Combined School and Clinical Psychology places an equal emphasis on research and clinical training. Students acquire the knowledge and skills necessary to practice in a variety of settings. In addition to extensive clinical training, students are able to engage in research throughout the program.

Programs and Degrees Offered

Program	Degree	Application Deadline	Applications Received	Accepted	New Admits Enrolled (PT)	Total Enrolled (PT)	Degrees Awarded in 2014–2015	Median Years to Complete Degree	Dismissed/ Withdrew
School Psychology Diploma	Other	March 2 (Fall)			16 (0)	34 (0)	8	3	1
School and Clinical Psychology	PsyD	February 1 (Fall)	51	18	11 (0)	50 (0)	8	5	0

Doctoral Degree (PsyD School and Clinical Psychology): For those doctoral students for whom a professional internship was required in this program prior to graduation:

Total students who applied for an internship: 8
Total students who obtained an internship: 8
Total students who obtained a paid internship: 7
Total students who obtained an unpaid internship: 1
Total students who were placed in APA/CPA-accredited internships: 3
Total students placed in internships not APA/CPA-accredited, but listed with the Association of Psychology Postdoctoral and Internship Centers (APPIC): 4
Total students placed in internships conforming to guidelines of the Council of Directors of School Psychology Programs (CDSPP): 0
Total students placed in internships that were not APA/CPA-accredited, APPIC or CDSSP listed: 1

Internships/Practica

Internships/practica in a variety of settings are available for students in the professional diploma program in school psychology. Doctoral students obtain externships in both school and clinical settings.

Admissions

Entries appear in the following order: required test or GPA, minimum score (if required)/median score of students entering in 2015–2016.

Program	Degree	GRE-V	GRE-Q	GRE-Writing	GRE-Subject	Under-graduate GPA	Last 2 Years GPA	Psychology GPA	Master's GPA
School Psychology Diploma	Other	153/NA	144/NA	NA/NA	Not specified	3.3/NA	NA/NA	Not specified	Not specified
School and Clinical Psychology	PsyD	NA/158	NA/152	NA/4	NA/703	NA/3.4	NA/NA	Not specified	NA/3.45

Admissions Requirements:

Degree	GRE	GRE-Subject	Letters of Recommendation	Research Statement	Writing Sample	CV	Interview
Master's/Specialist	Required	None	3	Required	Optional	Required	Required
Doctoral	Required	Recommended	3	Required	Required	Required	Required

Admissions Criteria:

GRE scores—medium
Research experience—medium
Work experience—medium
Clinically related public service—high
GPA—medium

Letters of recommendation—high
Interview—high
Statement of goals and objectives—medium
Undergraduate psychology preparation—medium

For additional information on admission requirements, visit http://grad.kean.edu/application-requirements.

Department Demographics

	Male (PT)	Female (PT)	Total	African-American/ Black (PT)	Hispanic/ Latino (PT)	Asian/ Pacific Islander (PT)	American Indian/ Alaska Native (PT)	Caucasian/ White (PT)	Unknown	Multiethnic (PT)	ADA (PT)	Int'l (PT)
Students	9 (0)	75 (0)	84					0 (0)	0 (0)	0 (0)	0 (0)	(0)

Financial Information/Assistance

Tuition: For information on tuition costs, visit http://grad.kean.edu/tuition-and-fees. Tuition is subject to change. Additional fees are assessed to students beyond the costs of tuition for the following: PsyD students pay a clinic fee.

Doctoral:
State residents: $798 per credit hour.
Nonstate residents: $928 per credit hour.

Master's:
State residents: $772 per credit hour.
Nonstate residents: $913 per credit hour.

Financial Assistance:

	Teaching Assistantship (% Receiving)	Teaching Assistantship Tuition Remission	Research Assistantship (% Receiving)	Research Assistantship Tuition Remission	Fellowship (% Receiving)	Fellowship Tuition Remission
First-Year Student	$6,000 (NA)	Full	NA (NA)	NA	NA (NA)	NA
Advanced Student	$6,000 (NA)	Full	NA (NA)	NA	NA (NA)	NA

For additional information on financial assistance, visit http://grad.kean.edu/graduate-financial-aid.

Employment of Department Graduates

No information provided.

Additional Information

Housing and Day Care: No on-campus housing is available. On-campus day care facilities are available. See the following website for more information: http://www.kean.edu/offices/child-care-center.

Information for Students With Physical Disabilities: See the following website: http://www.kean.edu/offices/disability-services.

Special Facilities or Resources: Special resources include computer facilities that are integrated with statistics, measurements, and professional psychology testing courses. The PsyD Program in Combined School and Clinical Psychology has a dedicated training clinic where students provide psychological services.

Application Information: Fee: $75. Online application: http://apply.kean.edu/.

Rider University
School Psychology Program
College of Liberal Arts, Education and Science
2083 Lawrenceville Road
Lawrenceville, NJ 8648
Telephone: (609) 896-5353
Program Director: Stefan C. Dombrowski, PhD
Web: http://www.rider.edu/academics/colleges-schools/claes/school-education/graduate-programs/school-psychology

E-mail: sdombrowski@rider.edu

Orientation, Objectives, and Emphasis of Department
The Rider University School Psychology program is dedicated to educating future school psychologists within a climate of scholarly inquiry and the context of a scientist–practitioner model of service delivery. Rider University's School Psychology program is fully approved by the National Association of School Psychologists (NASP), preparing students to become certified School Psychologists at the state and national level. The 67-credit degree program offers a blend of traditional and contemporary training and innovative practica that result in our graduates being actively recruited by employers. Problem-solving and data-based decision-making permeate all aspects of training with the ultimate goal of fostering the knowledge base, skill set, reflective practice, and professional commitment to improve the educational and mental health of children and adolescents in the schools. The program offers a highly-structured, developmental curriculum that builds upon preceding coursework and experience. Through a variety of theoretical, conceptual, and experiential pedagogical activities, students are prepared to provide a range of evidence-based services including consultation, psychological assessment, behavioral and academic intervention, prevention, counseling, and program planning/evaluation. Students also receive training in sensitively working with clients from diverse cultural and individual backgrounds.

Programs and Degrees Offered

Program	Degree	Application Deadline	Applications Received	Accepted	New Admits Enrolled (PT)	Total Enrolled (PT)	Degrees Awarded in 2014–2015	Median Years to Complete Degree	Dismissed/ Withdrew
School Psychology	EdS	January 1 (Fall)	57	20	12	30	14	3	1

Internships/Practica
Internship is a culminating experience consisting of 1,200 clock hours. The internship occurs on a full-time basis over a period of 1 year or on a part-time basis over 2 consecutive years. Interns are expected to perform all of the roles and functions of a professional school psychologist. As the intern progresses in the experience, greater levels of independence in practice are expected. Internship sites are selected in conjunction with program faculty. NASP guidelines mandate that the 1,200-hour internship must be completed under the following stipulations so as to assure a comprehensive experience: an intern shall work a minimum of 2.5 days per week over 2 consecutive years; a minimum of 600 hours must be completed in a school setting. Up to 600 hours may be served in a non-school setting that is related to the practice of school psychology.

Admissions
Entries appear in the following order: required test or GPA, minimum score (if required)/median score of students entering in 2015–2016.

Program	Degree	GRE-V	GRE-Q	GRE-Writing	GRE-Subject	Under-graduate GPA	Last 2 Years GPA	Psychol-ogy GPA	Master's GPA
School Psychology	EdS	144/155	144/155	3/4	Not specified	2.75/3.6	2.75/3.7	Not specified	Not specified

Admissions Requirements:

Degree	GRE	GRE-Subject	Letters of Recom-mendation	Research Statement	Writing Sample	CV	Interview
Master's/Specialist	Required	Optional	2	Required	Optional	Required	Required

Admissions Criteria:

GRE scores—medium
Research experience—medium
Work experience—medium
GPA—medium

Letters of recommendation—medium
Interview—medium
Statement of goals and objectives—medium

For additional information on admission requirements, visit http://www.rider.edu/admissions/graduate/how-apply/graduate-education-counseling-leadership-students.

Department Demographics

	Male (PT)	Female (PT)	Total	African-American/ Black (PT)	Hispanic/ Latino (PT)	Asian/ Pacific Islander (PT)	American Indian/ Alaska Native (PT)	Caucasian/ White (PT)	Unknown	Multiethnic (PT)	ADA (PT)	Int'l (PT)
Students	3 (0)	27 (0)	30	3 (0)	2 (0)	1 (0)	0 (0)	24 (0)	0 (0)	0 (0)	1 (0)	0 (0)

Financial Information/Assistance

Tuition: For information on tuition costs, visit http://www.rider.edu/offices-services/finaid/tuition-fees/graduate-tuition-fees. Tuition is subject to change. Additional fees are assessed to students beyond the costs of tuition for the following: Technology fee of $35 per course.

Master's:
State residents: $730 per credit hour.
Nonstate residents: $730 per credit hour.

Financial Assistance:

	Teaching Assistantship (% Receiving)	Teaching Assistantship Tuition Remission	Research Assistantship (% Receiving)	Research Assistantship Tuition Remission	Fellowship (% Receiving)	Fellowship Tuition Remission
First-Year Student	NA (NA)	NA	NA (NA)	Partial	$2,000 (NA)	Partial
Advanced Student	NA (NA)	NA	NA (NA)	Partial	$2,000 (NA)	NA

For additional information on financial assistance, visit http://www.rider.edu/offices-services/finaid/scholarships-grants/graduate-scholarships.

Employment of Department Graduates

Master's:
Employed in a professional position in a school system: 12
Total: 12

Additional Information

Housing and Day Care: On-campus housing is available. See the following website for more information: http://www.rider.edu/housing. No on-campus day care facilities are available.

Information for Students With Physical Disabilities: See the following website: http://www.rider.edu/academics/academic-support-services.

Application Information: Rider University, Office of Graduate Admission, 2083 Lawrenceville Road, Lawrenceville, NJ 08648-3099. *Fee:* $50. *Online application:* http://www.applyweb.com/apply/rider/.

Rowan University

Department of Psychology
College of Science and Mathemathics
Robinson Hall
Glassboro, NJ 8028
Telephone: (856) 256-4500 x3171
Department Head: Mary Louise Kerwin, PhD, BCBA-D

E-mail: clinicalpsych@rowan.edu
Web: http://www.rowan.edu/clinicalpsych

Orientation, Objectives, and Emphasis of Department

The Clinical PhD Program at Rowan University is recruiting its first class for the academic year 2016-2017. While the program is focused on health and integrated primary care, all of the faculty members' clinical and research areas are grounded in evidence-based approaches (e.g., cognitive behavioral therapy, person-centered, applied behavioral analysis, integrative, and family systems). The core clinical faculty work in tandem with faculty at Rowan University's Cooper Medical School, School of Osteopathic Medicine, MD Anderson Cancer Center, Psychiatry Department, Center on Aging, and other programs in the region. Numerous faculty members assess the bio-psycho-social aspects of persons with physical and mental health concerns.

Programs and Degrees Offered

Program	Degree	Application Deadline	Applica-tions Received	Accepted	New Admits Enrolled (PT)	Total Enrolled (PT)	Degrees Awarded in 2014–2015	Median Years to Complete Degree	Dismissed/ Withdrew
Clinical Psychology	PhD	January 1 (Fall)	0	0	0 (0)	0 (0)	0		0

Internships/Practica

The clinical training model in health psychology and integrated primary care starts with a second year internal practicum at Rowan University's Wellness Center. Students will spend 6 months on the mental health side and the remaining 6 months on the physical health side. There are additional placements for third and fourth year students.

Admissions

Entries appear in the following order: required test or GPA, minimum score (if required)/median score of students entering in 2015–2016.

Program	Degree	GRE-V	GRE-Q	GRE-Writing	GRE-Subject	Under-graduate GPA	Last 2 Years GPA	Psychol-ogy GPA	Master's GPA
Clinical Psychology	PhD	Not specified	Not specified	Not specified	Not specified	Not specified	Not specified	Not specified	Not specified

Admissions Requirements:

Degree	GRE	GRE-Subject	Letters of Recom-mendation	Research Statement	Writing Sample	CV	Interview
Doctoral	Required	Recom-mended	3	Required	Optional	Required	Required

Please note if these criteria vary for different programs: The GRE Psychology test is required for applicants who were not psychology majors.

Admissions Criteria:

GRE scores—high
Research experience—high
Work experience—low
Clinically related public service—low
GPA—high

Letters of recommendation—high
Interview—high
Statement of goals and objectives—high
Undergraduate psychology preparation—high

For additional information on admission requirements, visit http://www.rowan.edu/colleges/csm/departments/psychology/clinical/prospective/applicationinfo.html.

Department Demographics

	Male (PT)	Female (PT)	Total	African-American/ Black (PT)	Hispanic/ Latino (PT)	Asian/ Pacific Islander (PT)	American Indian/ Alaska Native (PT)	Caucasian/ White (PT)	Unknown (PT)	Multiethnic (PT)	ADA (PT)	Int'l (PT)
Students	0 (0)	0 (0)	0	0 (0)	0 (0)	0 (0)	0 (0)	0 (0)	0 (0)	0 (0)	0 (0)	0 (0)

Financial Information/Assistance

Tuition: For information on tuition costs, visit http://www.rowanu.com/tuition. Tuition is subject to change.

Doctoral:
State residents: $11,500 per academic year.
Nonstate residents: $11,500 per academic year.

Financial Assistance:

	Teaching Assistantship (% Receiving)	Teaching Assistantship Tuition Remission	Research Assistantship (% Receiving)	Research Assistantship Tuition Remission	Fellowship (% Receiving)	Fellowship Tuition Remission
First-Year Student	NA (NA)	NA	NA (NA)	NA	NA (NA)	NA
Advanced Student	$8,396 (NA)	NA	NA (NA)	NA	NA (NA)	NA

For additional information on financial assistance, visit http://www.rowan.edu/home/financial-aid/graduate-aid.

Employment of Department Graduates

No information provided.

Additional Information

Housing and Day Care: On-campus housing is available. On-campus day care facilities are available. See the following website for more information: http://www.rowan.edu/colleges/education/childcare/.

Information for Students With Physical Disabilities: See the following website: http://www.rowan.edu/studentaffairs/asc/disabilityresources/.

Application Information: Rowan Global. *Fee:* $65. *Online application:* http://rowanu.com/apply.

Rowan University
Department of Psychology-Master's in Clinical Mental Health Counseling Program
College of Science and Mathematics
201 Mullica Hill Road
Glassboro, NJ 08028-1701
Telephone: (856) 256-4500 ext 3757
Program Coordinator: Ginean Crawford, MFT, LPC, NCC, ACS
Web: http://www.rowan.edu/colleges/csm/departments/psychology/maCounseling/index.html

E-mail: crawfordg@rowan.edu

Orientation, Objectives, and Emphasis of Department
The program is designed to be consistent with an evidence-based practice model. This 60-credit Master's program prepares students to become mental health counselors and is designed to meet the coursework and practicum requirements for licensure (LAC/LPC). The program offers two tracks to meet students' interests: the Advanced Clinical Track and the Thesis Track.

Programs and Degrees Offered

Program	Degree	Application Deadline	Applications Received	Accepted	New Admits Enrolled (PT)	Total Enrolled (PT)	Degrees Awarded in 2014–2015	Median Years to Complete Degree	Dismissed/ Withdrew
Clinical Mental Health Counseling	MA/MS	February 15 (Fall)	38	15	13 (0)	17 (2)	7	2	2
Mental Health Counseling Certificate (Cags)	Other	Rolling	12	12	0 (12)	0 (12)	4	2	1

Internships/Practica

Practica are available in a wide range of mental health settings.

Admissions

Entries appear in the following order: required test or GPA, minimum score (if required)/median score of students entering in 2015–2016.

Program	Degree	GRE-V	GRE-Q	GRE-Writing	GRE-Subject	Under-graduate GPA	Last 2 Years GPA	Psychology GPA	Master's GPA
Clinical Mental Health Counseling	MA/MS	NA/NA	NA/NA	NA/NA	Not specified	3/NA	Not specified	Not specified	Not specified
Mental Health Counseling Certificate (CAGS)	Other	NA/NA	NA/NA	NA/NA	Not specified	NA/NA	NA/NA	NA/NA	Not specified

Admissions Requirements:

Degree	GRE	GRE-Subject	Letters of Recommendation	Research Statement	Writing Sample	CV	Interview
Master's/Specialist	Recommended	Recommended	2	Required	Optional	Required	Required

Please note if these criteria vary for different programs: GRE's are not required, but are highly recommended.

Admissions Criteria:

GRE scores—medium
Research experience—medium
Work experience—medium
Clinically related public service—high
GPA—high

Letters of recommendation—high
Interview—high
Statement of goals and objectives—high
Undergraduate psychology preparation—medium

For additional information on admission requirements, visit http://rowanu.com/programs/62.

Department Demographics

	Male (PT)	Female (PT)	Total	African-American/ Black (PT)	Hispanic/ Latino (PT)	Asian/ Pacific Islander (PT)	American Indian/ Alaska Native (PT)	Caucasian/ White (PT)	Unknown	Multiethnic (PT)	ADA (PT)	Int'l (PT)
Students	3 (1)	15 (1)	20	2 (0)	0 (1)	1 (0)	0 (0)	14 (1)	1 (0)	0 (0)	0 (0)	0 (0)

Financial Information/Assistance

Tuition: For information on tuition costs, visit https://rowanu.com/tuition. Tuition is subject to change.

Master's:
State residents: $808 per credit hour.
Nonstate residents: $808 per credit hour.

Financial Assistance:

	Teaching Assistantship (% Receiving)	Teaching Assistantship Tuition Remission	Research Assistantship (% Receiving)	Research Assistantship Tuition Remission	Fellowship (% Receiving)	Fellowship Tuition Remission
First-Year Student	NA (NA)	NA	NA (NA)	NA	NA (NA)	NA
Advanced Student	NA (NA)	NA	NA (NA)	NA	NA (NA)	NA

For additional information on financial assistance, visit http://www.rowan.edu/colleges/csm/departments/psychology/maCounseling/financialInfo/.

Employment of Department Graduates

Master's:
Employed in other positions at a higher education institution: 1
Employed in a community mental health/counseling center: 6
Employed in a hospital/medical center: 2
Do not know: 4
Total: 13

Additional Information

Housing and Day Care: On-campus housing is available. See the following website for more information: http://www.rowan.edu/studentaffairs/reslife/. On-campus day care facilities are available. See the following website for more information: http://www.rowan.edu/ecdc/index.html.

Information for Students With Physical Disabilities: See the following website: http://www.rowan.edu/studentaffairs/asc/disabilityresources/.

Application Information: Rowan Global Learning & Partnerships, Admissions Processing, Enterprise Center, Suite 200, 225 Rowan Boulevard, Glassboro, NJ 08028. *Fee:* $65. *Online application:* https://rowanu.com/apply.

Rutgers—The State University of New Jersey
Department of Applied Psychology
Graduate School of Applied and Professional Psychology
152 Frelinghuysen Road, Busch Campus, Psychology Building Addition
Piscataway, NJ 8854
Telephone: (848) 445-3973
Chairperson: Susan G. Forman, PhD

E-mail: sgforman@rci.rutgers.edu
Web: http://gsappweb.rutgers.edu/programs/school/index.php

Orientation, Objectives, and Emphasis of Department
The department of applied psychology is a unit dedicated to (1) enhancement of mental health and learning of children, adolescents, and adults in schools and related educational settings, and (2) development of organizations that allow schooling to occur in effective and efficient ways. Three interrelated dimensions serve to structure the department. An applied research dimension signifies the important weight placed on generating new knowledge; an education and training dimension reflects concern for development of high-level practitioners and leaders of school psychology; and an organizational and community services dimension is targeted at providing schools and related educational settings with consultation and technical assistance in areas of instruction and learning.

A continuum of instruction ranges from observation and assessment through intervention models that include supervised experience as an essential component of didactic instruction. Core faculty are augmented by senior psychologists whose major professional involvement is in the schools or organizational and community settings.

Programs and Degrees Offered

Program	Degree	Application Deadline	Applica-tions Received	Accepted	New Admits Enrolled (PT)	Total Enrolled (PT)	Degrees Awarded in 2014–2015	Median Years to Complete Degree	Dismissed/Withdrew
School Psychology	PsyD	January 9 (Fall)	76	26	18 (0)	84 (0)	23	4.12	2

APA Accreditation

School PsyD (Doctor of Psychology).

Doctoral Degree (PsyD School Psychology): For those doctoral students for whom a professional internship was required in this program prior to graduation:
Total students who applied for an internship: 14
Total students who obtained an internship: 14
Total students who obtained a paid internship: 14
Total students who obtained an unpaid internship: 0
Total students who were placed in APA/CPA-accredited internships: 0
Total students placed in internships not APA/CPA-accredited, but listed with the Association of Psychology Postdoctoral and Internship Centers (APPIC): 2
Total students placed in internships conforming to guidelines of the Council of Directors of School Psychology Programs (CDSPP): 6
Total students placed in internships that were not APA/CPA-accredited, APPIC or CDSSP listed: 6

Internships/Practica

A special component of the student's training is the integration of practicum experiences with didactic courses from the second semester of the first year throughout the remaining semesters of training. These experiences begin by introducing the student to the roles and functions of a school psychologist, the functioning of child study teams, and a variety of schooling issues. For three consecutive semesters, students spend a minimum of 1 day per week in a public school with a doctoral level school psychologist supervisor/mentor. During the fifth and sixth semester, students may elect a different practicum experience from their first based upon their interests. These practica are supervised by on-site doctoral school psychologists and by on-campus faculty. The courses, the practica, and the supervision comprise the planned scaffold for educating students. In addition, there are numerous opportunities for learning and practice through colloquia, symposia, informal discussions, faculty projects, the psychological clinic, and the Center for Applied Psychology.

Admissions

Entries appear in the following order: required test or GPA, minimum score (if required)/median score of students entering in 2015–2016.

Program	Degree	GRE-V	GRE-Q	GRE-Writing	GRE-Subject	Under-graduate GPA	Last 2 Years GPA	Psychol-ogy GPA	Master's GPA
School Psychology	PsyD	NA/153	NA/151	NA/4	Not specified	NA/3.53	Not specified	Not specified	Not specified

Admissions Requirements:

Degree	GRE	GRE-Subject	Letters of Recom-mendation	Research Statement	Writing Sample	CV	Interview
Doctoral	Required	Optional	3	Required	Optional	Required	Required

Admissions Criteria:

GRE scores—high
Research experience—medium
Work experience—high
Clinically related public service—high
GPA—high

Letters of recommendation—high
Interview—high
Statement of goals and objectives—high
Undergraduate psychology preparation—high

For additional information on admission requirements, visit http://gsappweb.rutgers.edu/pstudents/admissions.php.

Department Demographics

	Male (PT)	Female (PT)	Total	African-American/ Black (PT)	Hispanic/ Latino (PT)	Asian/ Pacific Islander (PT)	American Indian/ Alaska Native (PT)	Caucasian/ White (PT)	Unknown	Multiethnic (PT)	ADA (PT)	Int'l (PT)
Students	21 (0)	63 (0)	84	8 (0)	8 (0)	7 (0)	0 (0)	58 (0)	3 (0)	0 (0)	0 (0)	0 (0)

Financial Information/Assistance

Tuition: For information on tuition costs, visit http://www.studentabc.rutgers.edu/tuition-and-fees. Tuition is subject to change. Additional fees are assessed to students beyond the costs of tuition for the following: campus fee, computer fee, and school fee.

Doctoral:
State residents: $20,592 per academic year.
State residents: $858 per credit hour.
Nonstate residents: $34,272 per academic year.
Nonstate residents: $1,428 per credit hour.

Financial Assistance:

	Teaching Assistantship (% Receiving)	Teaching Assistantship Tuition Remission	Research Assistantship (% Receiving)	Research Assistantship Tuition Remission	Fellowship (% Receiving)	Fellowship Tuition Remission
First-Year Student	NA (NA)	NA	NA (NA)	NA	$15,000 (NA)	Partial
Advanced Student	$23,000 (NA)	Full	NA (NA)	NA	$15,000 (NA)	Partial

For additional information on financial assistance, visit http://gradstudy.rutgers.edu/financial/financial-information.

Employment of Department Graduates

No information provided.

Additional Information

Housing and Day Care: On-campus housing is available. See the following website for more information: http://ruoncampus.rutgers.edu/on-campus-life/graduate-students. On-campus day care facilities are available. See the following website for more information: http://uhr.rutgers.edu/child-care-and-development-centers.

Information for Students With Physical Disabilities: See the following website: https://ods.rutgers.edu/.

Special Facilities or Resources: There are two special facilities that are an integrated part of the training program. One is an on-site psychological clinic which serves the university and state communities. Assessment and intervention programs are offered. The other is the Center for Applied Psychology, a division of GSAPP that develops, implements, and evaluates projects involving faculty, students and others from the community. Included in these projects are the Eating Disorders Clinic, Foster Care Counseling, and a home-based intervention program for developmentally disabled individuals.

Application Information: Graduate Admissions, 56 College Avenue, New Brunswick, NJ 08901-8541. *Fee:* $65. *Online application:* http://gradstudy.rutgers.edu/apply/overview.

Rutgers—The State University of New Jersey

Department of Clinical Psychology
Graduate School of Applied and Professional Psychology
152 Frelinghuysen Road
Piscataway, NJ 8854
Telephone: (848) 445-3980
Chairperson: James Walkup

E-mail: walkup@rci.rutgers.edu
Web: http://gsappweb.rutgers.edu/programs/clinical/index.php

Orientation, Objectives, and Emphasis of Department

The PsyD program emphasizes pragmatic training in problem solving and planned change techniques. Didactic training in basic psychological principles is coupled with practical, graduate instruction in a range of assessment and intervention modes. The level of involvement becomes progressively more intense during the student's course of training. Most courses include (1) a seminar component oriented around case discussions and substantive theoretical issues of clinical import, (2) a practicum component during which students see clients in the intervention mode or problem area under study, and (3) a supervision component by which the student receives guidance from an experienced clinical instructor in a wide range of applied clinical settings. All three components are coordinated around a central conceptual issue, such as a mode of intervention or a clinical problem area. Instruction and supervision are offered by full-time faculty and senior psychologists whose primary professional involvement is in applied clinical settings throughout the state. In addition to required general core courses, students may emphasize training within any of three perspectives: psychodynamic, behavioral, or systems approaches. This last perspective focuses on family, organizational, and community services.

Programs and Degrees Offered

Program	Degree	Application Deadline	Applications Received	Accepted	New Admits Enrolled (PT)	Total Enrolled (PT)	Degrees Awarded in 2014–2015	Median Years to Complete Degree	Dismissed/ Withdrew
Clinical Psychology	PsyD	January 9 (Fall)	358	34	19 (0)	79 (17)	20	6	0

APA Accreditation

Clinical PsyD (Doctor of Psychology).

Doctoral Degree (PsyD Clinical Psychology): For those doctoral students for whom a professional internship was required in this program prior to graduation:
Total students who applied for an internship: 22
Total students who obtained an internship: 22
Total students who obtained a paid internship: 22
Total students who obtained an unpaid internship: 0
Total students who were placed in APA/CPA-accredited internships: 22
Total students placed in internships not APA/CPA-accredited, but listed with the Association of Psychology Postdoctoral and Internship Centers (APPIC): 0
Total students placed in internships conforming to guidelines of the Council of Directors of School Psychology Programs (CDSPP): 0
Total students placed in internships that were not APA/CPA-accredited, APPIC or CDSSP listed: 0

Internships/Practica

The PsyD program provides a broadly based practicum program which is structured around the needs and interests of our students. Students can choose placements in hospitals that include a hospice program, neuropsych testing, and long- and short-term inpatient treatment programs for both adolescents and adults. They can choose to be placed in university-based specialty clinics, traditional community mental health centers, college counseling centers, and specialized schools for children (autism, learning disabled, emotionally disturbed). Students can be placed in public school-based mental health clinics, in programs which provide service to at-risk youth, those with serious mental illness, and those with addictive disorders. Our programs are selected for their attention to supervision but also for their balance regarding gender, race, and socioeconomic levels.

Admissions

Entries appear in the following order: required test or GPA, minimum score (if required)/median score of students entering in 2015–2016.

Program	Degree	GRE-V	GRE-Q	GRE-Writing	GRE-Subject	Undergraduate GPA	Last 2 Years GPA	Psychology GPA	Master's GPA
Clinical Psychology	PsyD	NA/157	NA/152	NA/NA	NA/NA	NA/3.57	Not specified	Not specified	Not specified

Admissions Requirements:

Degree	GRE	GRE-Subject	Letters of Recommendation	Research Statement	Writing Sample	CV	Interview
Doctoral	Required	Required	3	Required	Optional	Required	Required

Admissions Criteria:

GRE scores—medium
Research experience—medium
Work experience—high
Clinically related public service—high
GPA—high

Letters of recommendation—high
Interview—high
Statement of goals and objectives—high
Undergraduate psychology preparation—medium

For additional information on admission requirements, visit http://gsappweb.rutgers.edu/pstudents/admissions.php.

Department Demographics

	Male (PT)	Female (PT)	Total	African-American/ Black (PT)	Hispanic/ Latino (PT)	Asian/ Pacific Islander (PT)	American Indian/ Alaska Native (PT)	Caucasian/ White (PT)	Unknown	Multiethnic (PT)	ADA (PT)	Int'l (PT)
Students	29 (6)	50 (11)	96	12 (0)	14 (0)	8 (0)	1 (0)	58 (0)	0 (0)	3 (1)	0 (0)	0 (0)

Financial Information/Assistance

Tuition: For information on tuition costs, visit http://www.studentabc.rutgers.edu/tuition-and-fees. Tuition is subject to change. Additional fees are assessed to students beyond the costs of tuition for the following: college fees and computer fees.

Doctoral:
State residents: $20,592 per academic year.
State residents: $858 per credit hour.
Nonstate residents: $34,272 per academic year.
Nonstate residents: $1,428 per credit hour.

Financial Assistance:

	Teaching Assistantship (% Receiving)	Teaching Assistantship Tuition Remission	Research Assistantship (% Receiving)	Research Assistantship Tuition Remission	Fellowship (% Receiving)	Fellowship Tuition Remission
First-Year Student	NA (NA)	NA	NA (NA)	NA	$15,000 (NA)	Partial
Advanced Student	$25,969 (NA)	Full	$17,000 (NA)	NA	$15,000 (NA)	Partial

Employment of Department Graduates

Doctoral:
Enrolled in a postdoctoral residency/fellowship: 1
Total: 1

Additional Information

Housing and Day Care: On-campus housing is available. See the following website for more information: http://ruoncampus.rutgers.edu/on-campus-life/graduate-students. On-campus day care facilities are available. See the following website for more information: http://uhr.rutgers.edu/child-care-and-development-centers.

Information for Students With Physical Disabilities: See the following website: https://ods.rutgers.edu/.

Special Facilities or Resources: The Center for Applied Psychology at GSAPP is the focal point for the field experiences that are critical in the development of professional psychologists. The projects overseen by the Center are cornerstones of training for our students; the GSAPP Psychological Clinic, the Foster Care Counseling project, the Natural Setting Therapeutic Management program, the Anxiety Disorders Clinic, and our extensive network of practicum placements are all available to our students. Students are placed in community-based organizations where the recipients of the services we provide are often underserved. These placements include community mental health centers, hospitals, special schools, and other programs. All students are placed in a practicum setting for at least one full day per week during their years at GSAPP. All students see clients through our Clinic and receive one hour of individual supervision for each hour of therapy. The Clinic has specialty sub-clinics which will allow students to gain experience and supervision in specific treatment approaches working with faculty experts.

Application Information: Graduate and Professional Admissions, Rutgers, The State University of New Jersey, 56 College Avenue, New Brunswick, NJ 08901-8541. *Fee:* $65. *Online application:* http://gradstudy.rutgers.edu/apply/overview.

Seton Hall University
Experimental Psychology
College of Arts and Sciences
400 South Orange Avenue
South Orange, NJ 7079
Telephone: (973) 761-9498
Director of Graduate Studies: Dr. Kelly M. Goedert

E-mail: psych@shu.edu
Web: http://www.shu.edu/academics/artsci/ms-psychology/

Orientation, Objectives, and Emphasis of Department
The primary goal of our program is to prepare students to be competitive for admittance into a PhD program or for direct entry into research-intensive jobs. Students experience individualized one-on-one research training and mentoring with faculty whose expertise covers diverse areas within experimental psychology: behavioral neuroscience, developmental, cognitive, social, and clinical psychology. Students choose from three thesis concentrations (intended to prepare students for eventual PhD study): Behavioral Neuroscience, Cognitive Neuroscience, Behavioral Sciences; or one of two non-thesis concentrations (intended to prepare students for direct entry into research intensive jobs): Data Visualization and Analysis, General. We also offer an optional specialist certificate in Data Visualization and Analysis. All students complete 36 hours of coursework, or three classes per semester, for 2 years. All students begin working with a faculty member by the end of their first semester. Thesis students develop a proposal in their second semester, and collect data and defend their thesis by the end of Year 2. Non-thesis students work in faculty laboratories as part of their research coursework, developing skills in data collection, data management and analysis. This work culminates either in a literature review or data visualization project by the end of Year 2.

Programs and Degrees Offered

Program	Degree	Application Deadline	Applications Received	Accepted	New Admits Enrolled (PT)	Total Enrolled (PT)	Degrees Awarded in 2014–2015	Median Years to Complete Degree	Dismissed/Withdrew
Experimental Psychology	MA/MS	April 1 (Fall), Rolling	26	17	10 (0)	23 (1)	7	2	1

Admissions

Entries appear in the following order: required test or GPA, minimum score (if required)/median score of students entering in 2015–2016.

Program	Degree	GRE-V	GRE-Q	GRE-Writing	GRE-Subject	Under-graduate GPA	Last 2 Years GPA	Psychol-ogy GPA	Master's GPA
Experimental Psychology	MA/MS	Not specified	Not specified	Not specified	Not specified	Not specified	Not specified	Not specified	Not specified

Admissions Requirements:

Degree	GRE	GRE-Subject	Letters of Recom-mendation	Research Statement	Writing Sample	CV	Interview
Master's/Specialist	Required	Optional	3	Required	None	Required	Optional

Admissions Criteria:

GRE scores—high
Research experience—high
Work experience—low
GPA—high

Letters of recommendation—high
Statement of goals and objectives—medium
Undergraduate psychology preparation—medium

For additional information on admission requirements, visit http://www.shu.edu/academics/artsci/ms-psychology/admissions.cfm.

Department Demographics

	Male (PT)	Female (PT)	Total	African-American/ Black (PT)	Hispanic/ Latino (PT)	Asian/ Pacific Islander (PT)	American Indian/ Alaska Native (PT)	Caucasian/ White (PT)	Unknown	Multiethnic (PT)	ADA (PT)	Int'l (PT)
Students	10 (0)	13 (1)	24	0 (1)	0 (0)	1 (0)	0 (0)	22 (0)	0 (0)	0 (0)	0 (0)	0 (0)

Financial Information/Assistance

Tuition: For information on tuition costs, visit http://www.shu.edu/offices/bursar/tuition-and-fees.cfm. Additional fees are assessed to students beyond the costs of tuition for the following: University and Technology Fees, $318 per semester.

Master's:
State residents: $1,135 per credit hour.
Nonstate residents: $1,135 per credit hour.

Financial Assistance:

	Teaching Assistantship (% Receiving)	Teaching Assistantship Tuition Remission	Research Assistantship (% Receiving)	Research Assistantship Tuition Remission	Fellowship (% Receiving)	Fellowship Tuition Remission
First-Year Student	$4,250 (9)	Partial	$2,600 (35)	Partial	NA (22)	Partial
Advanced Student	NA (NA)	NA	NA (NA)	NA	NA (NA)	NA

For additional information on financial assistance, visit http://www.shu.edu/applying/graduate/grad-finaid.cfm.

Employment of Department Graduates

Master's:
Enrolled in a psychology doctoral program: 3
Employed in other positions at a higher education institution: 1
Employed in business or industry: 1
Other employment position: 1
Total: 6

Additional Information

Housing and Day Care: On-campus housing is available. See the following website for more information: http://www.shu.edu/offices/housing-residence-life/. No on-campus day care facilities are available.

Information for Students With Physical Disabilities: See the following website: https://www.shu.edu/offices/disability-support-services/.

Special Facilities or Resources: The program enjoys state-of-the-art research facilities for both animal and human work. The human laboratory spaces include a 500-square foot research suite with both dedicated and flexibly allocated cubicles for human data collection at standard computer stations. Additional human laboratory spaces include a 350-square foot developmental laboratory and an eye tracking lab. The animal space includes rodent laboratory facilities with two animal colony rooms and approximately 400-square feet of space for surgical preparations, histology, and behavioral testing.

Application Information: *Fee:* $75. *Online application:* http://grad.shuadmissions.org/.

Seton Hall University

Professional Psychology and Family Therapy
Education and Human Services
400 South Orange Avenue
South Orange, NJ 7079
Telephone: (973) 761-9451
Chairperson: Ben Beitin, PhD

E-mail: ben.beitin@shu.edu
Web: http://www.shu.edu/academics/education/professional-psychology/

Orientation, Objectives, and Emphasis of Department

The Marriage and Family program is based on a systemic orientation to family psychology and family therapy. The goals of Counseling Psychology encompass knowledge of the science of psychology and counseling psychology as a specialty, integration of research and practice, and commitment to ongoing professional development. Professional counselors are mental health practitioners trained to help individual clients and groups address common developmental challenges and transitions as well as more severe emotional difficulties. School psychology students learn to specialize in assessment and evaluations in schools. Programs listed as MA/EdS are combined programs in which students are afforded the opportunity to continue their studies without applying for the advanced degree.

Programs and Degrees Offered

Program	Degree	Application Deadline	Applica-tions Received	Accepted	New Admits Enrolled (PT)	Total Enrolled (PT)	Degrees Awarded in 2014–2015	Median Years to Complete Degree	Dismissed/Withdrew
Counseling Psychology	PhD	December 1 (Fall)	134	0	0 (0)	21 (0)	5	5	0
Counseling/ Professional Counseling	EdS	April 1 (Fall), November 1 (Spring)	18	14	14 (0)	33 (0)	11	3.5	0
School and Community Psychology	EdS	April 1 (Fall)	11	8	8 (0)	26 (0)	5	2	1

Programs and Degrees Offered *(con't.)*

Program	Degree	Application Deadline	Applications Received	Accepted	New Admits Enrolled (PT)	Total Enrolled (PT)	Degrees Awarded in 2014–2015	Median Years to Complete Degree	Dismissed/ Withdrew
Counseling/ Professional Counseling (Online)	MA/MS	Rolling	81	41	31	81	51	2.5	5
Psychological Studies	MA/MS	Rolling	14	10	5 (5)	12 (16)	10	2	1
School Counseling (Online)	MA/MS	Rolling	105	68	38	103	29	2.5	0
School Counseling	MA/MS	April 1 (Fall), November 1 (Spring)	13	8	8 (0)	33 (0)	5	2.5	0
Marriage and Family Therapy MA/ EdS	EdS	January 15 (Fall)	44	11	11	43	6	3	0

APA Accreditation

Counseling PhD: Student Outcome Data website: http://www.shu.edu/academics/education/phd-counseling-psychology/index.cfm.

Doctoral Degree (PhD Counseling Psychology): For those doctoral students for whom a professional internship was required in this program prior to graduation:
Total students who applied for an internship: 5
Total students who obtained an internship: 5
Total students who obtained a paid internship: 5
Total students who obtained an unpaid internship: 0
Total students who were placed in APA/CPA-accredited internships: 4
Total students placed in internships not APA/CPA-accredited, but listed with the Association of Psychology Postdoctoral and Internship Centers (APPIC): 1
Total students placed in internships conforming to guidelines of the Council of Directors of School Psychology Programs (CDSPP): 0
Total students placed in internships that were not APA/CPA-accredited, APPIC or CDSSP listed: 0

Master's Degree (MA/MS Counseling/Professional Counseling (Online)): An internship experience, such as a final research project or "capstone" experience is required of graduates. Master's Degree (MA/MS School Counseling (Online)): An internship experience, such as a final research project or "capstone" experience is required of graduates. Master's Degree (MA/MS School Counseling): An internship experience, such as a final research project or "capstone" experience is required of graduates.

Internships/Practica

The Marriage and Family students follow the standards of the Commission on Accreditation for Marriage and Family Therapy Education. The doctoral students adhere to Psychology guidelines. The students in all MA and EdS programs (except psychological studies) complete an internship/practicum sequence consistent with their professional training models.

Admissions

Entries appear in the following order: required test or GPA, minimum score (if required)/median score of students entering in 2015–2016.

Program	Degree	GRE-V	GRE-Q	GRE-Writing	GRE-Subject	Undergraduate GPA	Last 2 Years GPA	Psychology GPA	Master's GPA
Counseling Psychology	PhD	155/155	144/152	Not specified	Not specified	3/3.2	Not specified	Not specified	3.5/3.92

Admissions (con't.)

Program	Degree	GRE-V	GRE-Q	GRE-Writing	GRE-Subject	Under-graduate GPA	Last 2 Years GPA	Psychol-ogy GPA	Master's GPA
Counseling/ Professional Counseling	EdS	132/145	132/141	2.5/3.5	Not specified	2.5/3.3	NA/NA	Not specified	Not specified
School and Community Psychology	EdS	140/NA	140/NA	Not specified	Not specified	3/NA	Not specified	Not specified	Not specified
Counseling/ Professional Counseling (Online)	MA/MS	NA/144	NA/148	NA/3.5	Not specified	3/3.31	NA/NA	Not specified	Not specified
Psychological Studies	MA/MS	NA/NA	NA/NA	NA/NA	Not specified	NA/NA	NA/NA	Not specified	Not specified
School Counseling (Online)	MA/MS	NA/134	NA/138	NA/3.5	Not specified	3/3.33	3.23/ 3.75	Not specified	Not specified
School Counseling	MA/MS	142/145	135/139	3/3.5	Not specified	3/3.5	NA/NA	Not specified	Not specified
Marriage and Family Therapy MA/EdS	EdS	NA/148	NA/144	NA/3.5	Not specified	3/3.42	Not specified	Not specified	Not specified

Admissions Requirements:

Degree	GRE	GRE-Subject	Letters of Recom-mendation	Research Statement	Writing Sample	CV	Interview
Master's/Specialist	Required	Optional	3	Required	Optional	Required	Required
Doctoral	Required	Recom-mended	3	Required	Required	Required	Required

Please note if these criteria vary for different programs: EdS in Marriage and Family Therapy requires a Master's degree in psychology, counseling, or a related field. No interview required for the online programs.

Admissions Criteria:

GRE scores—medium
Research experience—high
Work experience—medium
Clinically related public service—medium
GPA—high

Letters of recommendation—high
Interview—high
Statement of goals and objectives—high
Undergraduate psychology preparation—medium

Department Demographics

	Male (PT)	Female (PT)	Total	African-American/ Black (PT)	Hispanic/ Latino (PT)	Asian/ Pacific Islander (PT)	American Indian/ Alaska Native (PT)	Caucasian/ White (PT)	Unknown	Multiethnic (PT)	ADA (PT)	Int'l (PT)
Students	83 (0)	269 (16)	368	40 (0)	22 (0)	12 (0)	0 (0)	115 (0)	160 (16)	3 (0)	0 (0)	0 (0)

Financial Information/Assistance

Tuition: For information on tuition costs, visit http://www.shu.edu/offices/bursar/tuition-and-fees.cfm. Higher tuition cost for this program: There is a different fee structure for the online master's and EdS degrees. Tuition is subject to change. Additional fees are assessed to students beyond the costs of tuition for the following: University Fee $200; Technology Fee $114. Tuition costs vary by program.

Doctoral:
State residents: $1,100 per credit hour.
Nonstate residents: $1,100 per credit hour.

Master's:
State residents: $1,100 per credit hour.
Nonstate residents: $1,100 per credit hour.

Financial Assistance:

	Teaching Assistantship (% Receiving)	Teaching Assistantship Tuition Remission	Research Assistantship (% Receiving)	Research Assistantship Tuition Remission	Fellowship (% Receiving)	Fellowship Tuition Remission
First-Year Student	NA (NA)	NA	$4,500 (NA)	Full	NA (NA)	NA
Advanced Student	NA (NA)	NA	$4,500 (NA)	Full	$5,000 (NA)	NA

For additional information on financial assistance, visit http://www.shu.edu/offices/financial-aid/index.cfm.

Employment of Department Graduates

No information provided.

Additional Information

Housing and Day Care: No on-campus housing is available. No on-campus day care facilities are available.

Information for Students With Physical Disabilities: See the following website: http://www.shu.edu/offices/disability-support-services.

Special Facilities or Resources: The department has individual counseling/assessment rooms, family and couple laboratories, and group therapy rooms, all of which are wired with audiovisual equipment with centralized viewing in a control room. There are rooms for data analysis as well. Seton Hall University has a beautiful campus located 25 miles west of New York City. Students attending on-campus programs have access to a broad range of clinical training sites, including, but not limited to community-based public and private schools, community mental health centers, large university teaching hospitals, college and university counseling centers, alcohol and drug rehabilitation centers, assisted living programs, therapeutic nurseries, prisons, programs serving military personnel and their families, and programs that provide couples and family therapy—to name a few. Additionally, students in the Counseling Psychology doctoral program benefit from two annual international training experiences, which take place in Trinidad and Tobago.

Application Information: Graduate Admissions, College of Education and Human Services, Seton Hall University, 400 South Orange Avenue, South Orange, NJ 07079. *Fee:* $75. *Online application:* https://grad.shuadmissions.org/.

William Paterson University
Psychology
Humanities & Social Sciences
300 Pompton Road
Wayne, NJ 7470
Telephone: (973) 720-3629
Chairperson: Dr. Michael Gordon

E-mail: Psychgrad@wpunj.edu
Web: http://www.wpunj.edu/cohss/departments/psychology/

Orientation, Objectives, and Emphasis of Department
The Master's program in Clinical and Counseling Psychology prepares students for the professional practice of counseling, assessment, and/or mental health research. The curriculum provides a solid grounding in both theories and interventions that can be

applied to a wide variety of mental health, academic, and research settings. We emphasize professional competency, ethical responsibility, cultural competency, self-awareness, and current body of knowledge in the scientific, methodological, and theoretical foundations of practice. Our program expects students to become compassionate and caring scientist–practitioners with motivation to continue learning and furthering their development throughout their professional careers. The PsyD program is a 96-credit program based on the practitioner–scholar model. The program, which admitted its first class of students in 2015, prepares clinicians, researchers, and teachers in the area of clinical psychology; includes training and coursework in clinical practice and research; and includes faculty with diverse clinical and research interests. The program emphasizes knowledge in clinical theory, empiricism, and the application of clinical and research techniques and procedures to individuals and groups in an ethically, socially, and culturally sensitive context. The program, which requires a dissertation of publishable quality, is designed to meet American Psychological Association accreditation standards.

Programs and Degrees Offered

Program	Degree	Application Deadline	Applications Received	Accepted	New Admits Enrolled (PT)	Total Enrolled (PT)	Degrees Awarded in 2014–2015	Median Years to Complete Degree	Dismissed/ Withdrew
Clinical and Counseling Psychology	MA/MS	May 1 (Fall)	36	18	11 (1)	23 (6)	14	2	1
Clinical Psychology	PsyD	December 15 (Fall)	0	0	7 (0)	7 (0)	0		0

Internships/Practica

Graduates and interns work in a wide variety of inpatient and outpatient settings including hospitals; community mental health clinics; wellness centers; health maintenance facilities; local, regional, national, and international health care organizations; group homes; drug treatment facilities; rehabilitation centers; correctional facilities; and gerontology programs. With appropriate licensing and/or under proper licensed supervision, graduates of our program are able to conduct assessments; provide clinical and health-related services to individuals, groups and families using appropriate diagnostic and intervention techniques; participate in institutional and organizational research; and work on an elective basis with a variety of populations (e.g., chronic and acute diseases and disorders, children, adolescents, the elderly, the severely mentally ill, the neurologically impaired, substance abusers, and others).

Admissions

Entries appear in the following order: required test or GPA, minimum score (if required)/median score of students entering in 2015–2016.

Program	Degree	GRE-V	GRE-Q	GRE-Writing	GRE-Subject	Undergraduate GPA	Last 2 Years GPA	Psychology GPA	Master's GPA
Clinical and Counseling Psychology	MA/MS	151/NA	152/NA	4/NA	Not specified	3/NA	Not specified	Not specified	Not specified
Clinical Psychology	PsyD	Not specified	Not specified	Not specified	Not specified	Not specified	Not specified	Not specified	Not specified

Admissions Requirements:

Degree	GRE	GRE-Subject	Letters of Recommendation	Research Statement	Writing Sample	CV	Interview
Master's/Specialist	Required	None	3	Required	None	Required	Required
Doctoral	Required	Optional	3	Required	Optional	Required	Required

Admissions Criteria:

GRE scores—high

Research experience—medium

Work experience—medium

Clinically related public service—high

GPA—high

Letters of recommendation—high

Interview—medium

Statement of goals and objectives—high

Undergraduate psychology preparation—medium

Department Demographics

	Male (PT)	Female (PT)	Total	African-American/ Black (PT)	Hispanic/ Latino (PT)	Asian/ Pacific Islander (PT)	American Indian/ Alaska Native (PT)	Caucasian/ White (PT)	Unknown (PT)	Multiethnic (PT)	ADA (PT)	Int'l (PT)
Students	7 (2)	23 (4)	36	2 (0)	5 (2)	3 (0)	0 (0)	22 (2)	0 (0)	0 (0)	0 (0)	0 (0)

Financial Information/Assistance

Tuition: For information on tuition costs, visit http://www.wpunj.edu/studentaccounts/tuition-and-fees/graduate.dot. Tuition is subject to change.

Doctoral:

State residents: $8,754 per academic year.

State residents: $633 per credit hour.

Nonstate residents: $12,750 per academic year.

Nonstate residents: $966 per credit hour.

Master's:

State residents: $8,754 per academic year.

State residents: $577 per credit hour.

Nonstate residents: $12,750 per academic year.

Nonstate residents: $951 per credit hour.

Financial Assistance:

	Teaching Assistantship (% Receiving)	Teaching Assistantship Tuition Remission	Research Assistantship (% Receiving)	Research Assistantship Tuition Remission	Fellowship (% Receiving)	Fellowship Tuition Remission
First-Year Student	$6,000 (NA)	Full	$6,000 (NA)	Full	NA (NA)	NA
Advanced Student	$6,000 (NA)	Full	$6,000 (NA)	Full	NA (NA)	NA

For additional information on financial assistance, visit http://www.wpunj.edu/admissions/graduate/prospective-students/financial-support.dot.

Employment of Department Graduates

Master's:

Enrolled in a psychology doctoral program: 2

Employed in an academic position at a university: 1

Employed in a professional position in a school system: 2

Employed in government agency: 2

Employed in a community mental health/counseling center: 5

Employed in a hospital/medical center: 4

Not seeking employment: 1

Total: 17

Additional Information

Housing and Day Care: On-campus housing is available. See the following website for more information: http://www.wpunj.edu/reslife/. On-campus day care facilities are available. See the following website for more information: http://www.wpunj.edu/child-development/.

Information for Students With Physical Disabilities: See the following website: http://www.wpunj.edu/disabilityservices/.

Special Facilities or Resources: The program recently moved into new and renovated space within Science Hall-East. The facility provides students and faculty with a Clinical Teaching Suite that includes training rooms equipped with state-of-the-art video recording and viewing capabilities. The new facilities also include a Testing and Media Instructional Room, research labs, teaching spaces, and a Graduate Study Room where students can study, converse, relax, practice their presentations, and develop a sense of community. The program maintains a wide array of assessment instruments, videos, and equipment that are available to faculty and students. The University has a library with numerous online databases, media, and study areas. The campus is wireless and includes labs equipped with software applications for teaching, research, and meeting student needs. The campus also has an Instructional Research Technology Lab that helps support IT-related activities.

Application Information: Graduate Admissions, William Paterson University, 300 Pompton Road, Wayne, NJ 07470. *Fee:* $50. *Online application:* http://www.wpunj.edu/admissions/graduate/apply-now.dot.

New Mexico Highlands University

Master of Science in Psychology
Box 9000
Las Vegas, NM 87701
Graduate Coordinator: David Pan, PhD
E-mail: dpan@nmhu.edu
Web: http://www.nmhu.edu/current-students/graduate/arts-and-sciences/social-and-behavioral-sciences/masters-of-science-degree-in-psychology/

Orientation, Objectives, and Emphasis of Department

The department offers two tracks that lead to a Master of Science degree in psychology. The General Psychology track is intended to provide a background similar to that given in many PhD programs. This track is especially useful for those students whose goals include either entering a PhD program or working in a non-clinical position (research, etc.) upon completing the master's degree. The Clinical Psychology/Counseling track has a cognitive-behavioral orientation and is unique in that it is one of the few programs in the U.S. providing comprehensive training in psychological training and assessment. In addition to the general core of courses required in the general psychology emphasis area, this track provides the opportunity to gain solid psychological testing and assessment skills in four areas: neuropsychological, behavioral, intelligence, and personality. This clinical psychology/counseling track is designed to prepare students to continue their education at the doctoral level or to work as a master's-level clinician. The student successfully completing this track will qualify for licensure as a counselor in the state of New Mexico as well as a master's-level clinician in approximately 40 other states.

Programs and Degrees Offered

Program	Degree	Application Deadline	Applications Received	Accepted	New Admits Enrolled (PT)	Total Enrolled (PT)	Degrees Awarded in 2014–2015	Median Years to Complete Degree	Dismissed/ Withdrew
Psychology	MA/MS	Rolling			8	14 (10)			1

Internships/Practica

Practicum sites include the New Mexico Behavioral Health Institute, school system, and community-based mental health services.

Admissions

Entries appear in the following order: required test or GPA, minimum score (if required)/median score of students entering in 2015–2016.

Program	Degree	GRE-V	GRE-Q	GRE-Writing	GRE-Subject	Undergraduate GPA	Last 2 Years GPA	Psychology GPA	Master's GPA
Psychology	MA/MS	Not specified	Not specified	Not specified	Not specified	Not specified	Not specified	Not specified	Not specified

Admissions Requirements:

Degree	GRE	GRE-Subject	Letters of Recommendation	Research Statement	Writing Sample	CV	Interview
Master's/Specialist	Optional	Optional	2	Required	Required	Optional	None

Admissions Criteria:

GRE scores—low
Research experience—medium
Work experience—low
Clinically related public service—low

GPA—medium
Letters of recommendation—high
Statement of goals and objectives—high
Undergraduate psychology preparation—medium

Department Demographics

	Male (PT)	Female (PT)	Total	African-American/ Black (PT)	Hispanic/ Latino (PT)	Asian/ Pacific Islander (PT)	American Indian/ Alaska Native (PT)	Caucasian/ White (PT)	Unknown	Multiethnic (PT)	ADA (PT)	Int'l (PT)
Students	5 (4)	9 (6)	24	0 (1)	7 (5)	1 (0)	0 (0)	5 (4)	0 (0)	1 (0)	0 (0)	0 (0)

Financial Information/Assistance

Tuition: For information on tuition costs, visit http://www.nmhu.edu/office-of-the-registrar/tuition-and-fees/. Tuition is subject to change.

Master's:
State residents: $3,194 per academic year.
Nonstate residents: $5,634 per academic year.

Financial Assistance:

	Teaching Assistantship (% Receiving)	Teaching Assistantship Tuition Remission	Research Assistantship (% Receiving)	Research Assistantship Tuition Remission	Fellowship (% Receiving)	Fellowship Tuition Remission
First-Year Student	$5,250 (90)	Partial	NA (NA)	NA	NA (NA)	NA
Advanced Student	$3,500 (75)	Partial	NA (NA)	NA	NA (NA)	NA

For additional information on financial assistance, visit http://www.nmhu.edu/financial-aid/.

Employment of Department Graduates

No information provided.

Additional Information

Housing and Day Care: On-campus housing is available. No on-campus day care facilities are available.

Information for Students With Physical Disabilities: See the following website: http://www.nmhu.edu/accessibility-services/.

Application Information: Office of Graduate Studies, Box 9000, Las Vegas, New Mexico 87701-9000. Fee: $15.

New Mexico State University
Counseling and Educational Psychology
College of Education
Box 30001 MSC 3CEP
Las Cruces, NM 88003-8001
Telephone: (575) 646-2121
Interim Department Head: Gladys DeNecochea, PhD

E-mail: eadams@nmsu.edu
Web: http://cep.education.nmsu.edu/

Orientation, Objectives, and Emphasis of Department
The major thrust of the department is the preparation of professionals for licensure and positions in counseling psychology; mental health and school counseling; school psychology, and related areas. Three graduate degrees are available: (1) Doctor of Philosophy, (2) Masters of Arts, and (3) Specialist in Education. The PhD in Counseling Psychology, which is accredited by the American Psychological Association, is based on the scientist–practitioner model through which both research and service delivery skills are acquired. Graduates of the program are prepared to conduct research, provide service, teach, and supervise. Emphases in the

Counseling Psychology program include cultural diversity, generalist training in a variety of modalities, supervision and behavioral health consultation. The Master of Arts in Counseling and Guidance prepares professional counselors to offer individual, family, and group counseling in schools, agencies, hospitals, and private practice. The curriculum covers human development; appraisal; diagnosis; treatment planning; and individual and professional issues. The School Psychology Program (EdS) prepares professionals for positions in public schools and other organizations which require advanced assessment, counseling, consultation and supervision skills. A major research project (thesis) is a degree requirement.

Programs and Degrees Offered

Program	Degree	Application Deadline	Applica- tions Received	Accepted	New Admits Enrolled (PT)	Total Enrolled (PT)	Degrees Awarded in 2014– 2015	Median Years to Complete Degree	Dismissed/ Withdrew
Counseling and Guidance	MA/MS	February 1 (Summer)	45	12	5 (7)	16 (15)	10	2	0
School Psychology	EdS	March 1 (Summer), Rolling	18	9	7 (2)	19 (5)	3	3	0
Counseling Psychology	PhD	December 15 (Summer)	80	6	6 (0)	29 (1)	6	5	0

APA Accreditation

Counseling PhD: Student Outcome Data website: http://cep.education.nmsu.edu/academic-programs/counseling-psychology-phd/.

Doctoral Degree (PhD Counseling Psychology): For those doctoral students for whom a professional internship was required in this program prior to graduation:
Total students who applied for an internship: 5
Total students who obtained an internship: 5
Total students who obtained a paid internship: 5
Total students who obtained an unpaid internship: 0
Total students who were placed in APA/CPA-accredited internships: 4
Total students placed in internships not APA/CPA-accredited, but listed with the Association of Psychology Postdoctoral and Internship Centers (APPIC): 1
Total students placed in internships conforming to guidelines of the Council of Directors of School Psychology Programs (CDSPP): 0
Total students placed in internships that were not APA/CPA-accredited, APPIC or CDSSP listed: 0

Master's Degree (MA/MS Counseling and Guidance): An internship experience, such as a final research project or "capstone" experience is required of graduates.

Internships/Practica

Practicum placements include university counseling centers, public schools, a primary care setting, community mental health centers, hospitals, adolescent residential centers, the Department of Vocational Rehabilitation, military bases, substance abuse treatment centers, and nursing homes.

Admissions

Entries appear in the following order: required test or GPA, minimum score (if required)/median score of students entering in 2015–2016.

Program	Degree	GRE-V	GRE-Q	GRE-Writing	GRE-Subject	Under-graduate GPA	Last 2 Years GPA	Psychol-ogy GPA	Master's GPA
Counseling and Guidance	MA/MS	NA/NA	NA/NA	Not specified	Not specified	Not specified	Not specified	Not specified	Not specified
School Psychology	EdS	Not specified	Not specified	Not specified	Not specified	Not specified	Not specified	Not specified	Not specified
Counseling Psychology	PhD	NA/155	NA/146	NA/4	Not specified	NA/3.7	Not specified	Not specified	Not specified

Admissions Requirements:

Degree	GRE	GRE-Subject	Letters of Recommendation	Research Statement	Writing Sample	CV	Interview
Master's/Specialist	Required	None	3	Required	Optional	Required	Required
Doctoral	Required	Optional	3	Required	Required	Required	Required

Admissions Criteria:

GRE scores—medium
Research experience—high
Work experience—medium
Clinically related public service—high
GPA—high

Letters of recommendation—high
Interview—high
Statement of goals and objectives—high
Undergraduate psychology preparation—medium
Writing sample—medium

For additional information on admission requirements, visit http://cep.education.nmsu.edu/academic-programs/.

Department Demographics

	Male (PT)	Female (PT)	Total	African-American/ Black (PT)	Hispanic/ Latino (PT)	Asian/ Pacific Islander (PT)	American Indian/ Alaska Native (PT)	Caucasian/ White (PT)	Unknown	Multiethnic (PT)	ADA (PT)	Int'l (PT)
Students	10 (8)	54 (13)	85	2 (1)	20 (6)	4 (1)	0 (1)	33 (12)	0 (0)	5 (0)	0 (0)	0 (1)

Financial Information/Assistance

Tuition: For information on tuition costs, visit http://uar.nmsu.edu/tuition-fees/tuition-rates/. Tuition is subject to change. Additional fees are assessed to students beyond the costs of tuition for the following: Assessment fees.

Doctoral:
State residents: $6,708 per academic year.
State residents: $280 per credit hour.
Nonstate residents: $20,130 per academic year.
Nonstate residents: $839 per credit hour.

Master's:
State residents: $6,708 per academic year.
State residents: $280 per credit hour.
Nonstate residents: $20,130 per academic year.
Nonstate residents: $839 per credit hour.

Financial Assistance:

	Teaching Assistantship (% Receiving)	Teaching Assistantship Tuition Remission	Research Assistantship (% Receiving)	Research Assistantship Tuition Remission	Fellowship (% Receiving)	Fellowship Tuition Remission
First-Year Student	$8,000 (100)	Partial	NA (NA)	NA	$15,000 (80)	Full
Advanced Student	$8,200 (100)	Partial	NA (NA)	NA	$15,000 (80)	Full

For additional information on financial assistance, visit http://gradschool.nmsu.edu/ga/index.htm.

Employment of Department Graduates

Master's:
Enrolled in a psychology doctoral program: 2
Employed in a professional position in a school system: 2
Employed in a community mental health/counseling center: 4
Employed in a hospital/medical center: 1
Not seeking employment: 1
Total: 10

Doctoral:
Enrolled in a postdoctoral residency/fellowship: 2
Employed in independent practice: 1
Employed in a community mental health/counseling center: 2
Employed in a hospital/medical center: 1
Total: 6

Additional Information

Housing and Day Care: On-campus housing is available. See the following website for more information: http://housing.nmsu.edu/graduatehousing/. On-campus day care facilities are available. See the following website for more information: http://ci.nmsu.edu/programs/concentrations/eced/mcvi/.

Information for Students With Physical Disabilities: See the following website: http://sas.nmsu.edu/.

Special Facilities or Resources: The NMSU Mental Health & Wellness Clinic is a training/service facility sponsored by the Department of Counseling and Educational Psychology which provides excellent opportunities for supervised counseling and supervision-of-supervision. Four rooms are available for videotaping, and have one-way mirrors, telephones, and microphone-speakers for live supervision of counseling and live supervision of supervision. The facility has a "state-of-the-art" bug in the ear system which helps facilitate live supervision for immediate feedback to the counselor in training. We also have extensive training with similar supervisory capabilities at the Family Medicine Center, a primary care center staffed by Family Medicine residents and La Clinica de Familia, a Federally-Qualified Health Center.

Application Information: Fee: $40. *Online application:* http://gradadmissions.nmsu.edu/.

New Mexico State University

Department of Psychology
College of Arts and Sciences
Department 3452, P.O. Box 30001
Las Cruces, NM 88003
Telephone: (575) 646-2502
Head: Dominic A. Simon

E-mail: lmadson@nmsu.edu
Web: http://psychology.nmsu.edu

Orientation, Objectives, and Emphasis of Department

The department offers an MA degree in general experimental psychology that allows an emphasis in cognitive, engineering, or social psychology. The PhD is offered in the major areas of cognitive, engineering, and social psychology. Students must earn an MA degree before being admitted to the doctoral program. All programs are experimentally oriented and have the distinctive characteristic of pursuing and extending basic research questions in applied settings.

Programs and Degrees Offered

Program	Degree	Application Deadline	Applica-tions Received	Accepted	New Admits Enrolled (PT)	Total Enrolled (PT)	Degrees Awarded in 2014–2015	Median Years to Complete Degree	Dismissed/Withdrew
Cognitive Psychology	PhD	January 15 (Fall)	1	1	1 (0)	7 (0)	0		0
Engineering Psychology	PhD	January 15 (Fall)	0	0	0 (0)	1 (0)	0		0
Social Psychology	PhD	January 15 (Fall)	4	2	1 (0)	13 (0)	1	5	0
General Experimental Psychology	MA/MS	January 15 (Fall)	15	8	6 (0)	14 (0)	5	2.5	0

Internships/Practica

For the PhD degree, students must either complete an internship of at least three month duration or independently teach an undergraduate course. Many master's students spend a summer or half-year as an intern in industry, but it is not required for the MA degree.

Admissions

Entries appear in the following order: required test or GPA, minimum score (if required)/median score of students entering in 2015–2016.

Program	Degree	GRE-V	GRE-Q	GRE-Writing	GRE-Subject	Under-graduate GPA	Last 2 Years GPA	Psychol-ogy GPA	Master's GPA
Cognitive Psychology	PhD	158/NA	159/NA	4.5/NA	Not specified	3/NA	Not specified	Not specified	3/NA
Engineering Psychology	PhD	158/NA	159/NA	4.5/NA	Not specified	3/NA	Not specified	Not specified	3/NA
Social Psychology	PhD	158/NA	159/NA	4.5/NA	Not specified	3/NA	Not specified	Not specified	3/NA
General Experimental Psychology	MA/MS	155/NA	156/NA	4.5/NA	Not specified	3/NA	Not specified	Not specified	Not specified

Admissions Requirements:

Degree	GRE	GRE-Subject	Letters of Recom-mendation	Research Statement	Writing Sample	CV	Interview
Master's/Specialist	Required	None	3	Required	Required	Required	Recom-mended
Doctoral	Required	None	3	Required	Required	Required	Recom-mended

Admissions Criteria:

GRE scores—high

Research experience—medium

Work experience—low

GPA—high

Letters of recommendation—high

Statement of goals and objectives—high

Undergraduate psychology preparation—medium

Applicant's interests—high

For additional information on admission requirements, visit https://psychology.nmsu.edu/graduate/admissions/.

Department Demographics

	Male (PT)	Female (PT)	Total	African-American/ Black (PT)	Hispanic/ Latino (PT)	Asian/ Pacific Islander (PT)	American Indian/ Alaska Native (PT)	Caucasian/ White (PT)	Unknown (PT)	Multiethnic (PT)	ADA (PT)	Int'l (PT)
Students	20 (0)	15 (0)	35	0 (0)	2 (0)	5 (0)	0 (0)	28 (0)	0 (0)	0 (0)	0 (0)	4 (0)

Financial Information/Assistance

Tuition: For information on tuition costs, visit http://uar.nmsu.edu/tuition-fees/tuition-rates/. Tuition is subject to change. Additional fees are assessed to students beyond the costs of tuition for the following: wellness fee, Associated Students of NMSU fee.

Doctoral:

State residents: $4,941 per academic year.

State residents: $275 per credit hour.

Nonstate residents: $15,108 per academic year.

Nonstate residents: $839 per credit hour.

Master's:

State residents: $4,941 per academic year.

State residents: $275 per credit hour.

Nonstate residents: $15,108 per academic year.

Nonstate residents: $839 per credit hour.

Financial Assistance:

	Teaching Assistantship (% Receiving)	Teaching Assistantship Tuition Remission	Research Assistantship (% Receiving)	Research Assistantship Tuition Remission	Fellowship (% Receiving)	Fellowship Tuition Remission
First-Year Student	$16,964 (90)	Partial	$16,964 (5)	Partial	NA (5)	Partial
Advanced Student	$17,772 (90)	Partial	$17,772 (10)	Partial	NA (NA)	Partial

For additional information on financial assistance, visit http://gradschool.nmsu.edu/gradschool/announcements.html.

Employment of Department Graduates

Master's:
Enrolled in a psychology doctoral program: 1
Employed in business or industry: 3
Not seeking employment: 1
Total: 5

Additional Information

Housing and Day Care: On-campus housing is available. See the following website for more information: http://housing.nmsu.edu/graduatehousing/. On-campus day care facilities are available. See the following website for more information: http://ci.nmsu.edu/programs/concentrations/eced/mcvi/.

Information for Students With Physical Disabilities: See the following website: http://sas.nmsu.edu/.

Special Facilities or Resources: All faculty members have specialized laboratories with a wide variety of computer hardware and software. These include auditory perception and eye tracking labs used to study perceptual and cognitive issues, a biopsychology lab equipped to measure ERPs, an automation lab used to study human interactions with automated systems including unmanned aerial vehicles, and a developmental laboratory equipped with sophisticated equipment for recording, analyzing, and editing mother-infant interactions, etc.

Application Information: Chair of Graduate Committee, Department of Psychology, MSC 3452, New Mexico State University, Las Cruces, NM 88003-8001. *Fee:* $40. *Online application:* http://gradadmissions.nmsu.edu/.

New Mexico, University of
Department of Psychology
Arts and Science
Logan Hall, MSC03 2220
Albuquerque, NM 87131-0001
Telephone: (505) 277-4121
Chairperson: Jane Ellen Smith

E-mail: psych@unm.edu
Web: http://psych.unm.edu

Orientation, Objectives, and Emphasis of Department
Founded in 1960, the doctoral program in psychology is based on the premise that psychology, in all of its areas, is fundamentally a scientific discipline. All students acquire a solid foundation in both scientific methodology and general psychology. Furthermore, the clinical psychology program is now a member of the Academy of Psychological Clinical Science. The department trains individuals who combine competence in the general discipline of psychology with excellence in their chosen specialization.

Programs and Degrees Offered

Program	Degree	Application Deadline	Applications Received	Accepted	New Admits Enrolled (PT)	Total Enrolled (PT)	Degrees Awarded in 2014–2015	Median Years to Complete Degree	Dismissed/Withdrew
Clinical Psychology	PhD	December 15 (Fall)	149	9	8 (0)	45 (0)	5	7	0

Programs and Degrees Offered *(con't.)*

Program	Degree	Application Deadline	Applications Received	Accepted	New Admits Enrolled (PT)	Total Enrolled (PT)	Degrees Awarded in 2014–2015	Median Years to Complete Degree	Dismissed/Withdrew
Developmental Psychology	PhD	December 15 (Fall)	19	0	0 (0)	1 (0)	2	7.5	0
Evolutionary Psychology	PhD	December 15 (Fall)	31	2	1 (0)	5 (0)	2		0
Cognition, Brain and Behavior	PhD	December 15 (Fall)	64	9	3 (0)	20 (0)	1	5	4
Health Psychology	PhD	December 15 (Fall)	40	0	0	3	0		0
Quantitative Methodology	PhD	December 15 (Fall)	2	0	0	3	0		1

APA Accreditation

Clinical PhD: Student Outcome Data website: http://psych.unm.edu/research-areas/clinical-psychology.html.

Doctoral Degree (PhD Clinical Psychology): For those doctoral students for whom a professional internship was required in this program prior to graduation:
Total students who applied for an internship: 7
Total students who obtained an internship: 7
Total students who obtained a paid internship: 7
Total students who obtained an unpaid internship: 0
Total students who were placed in APA/CPA-accredited internships: 7
Total students placed in internships not APA/CPA-accredited, but listed with the Association of Psychology Postdoctoral and Internship Centers (APPIC): 0
Total students placed in internships conforming to guidelines of the Council of Directors of School Psychology Programs (CDSPP): 0
Total students placed in internships that were not APA/CPA-accredited, APPIC or CDSSP listed: 0

Internships/Practica

The department has a number of options for practicum or internship settings including, but not limited to: the department's own outpatient training clinic; specialty clinics in alcoholism, anxiety disorders, behavioral medicine, and multicultural (diversity) issues; the MIND Institute; the Center on Alcoholism, Substance Abuse, and Addictions (CASAA); the UNM Hospital; and the Veterans Administration Hospital.

Admissions

Entries appear in the following order: required test or GPA, minimum score (if required)/median score of students entering in 2015–2016.

Program	Degree	GRE-V	GRE-Q	GRE-Writing	GRE-Subject	Under-graduate GPA	Last 2 Years GPA	Psychology GPA	Master's GPA
Clinical Psychology	PhD	NA/158	NA/154	NA/4	NA/690	Not specified	Not specified	Not specified	Not specified
Developmental Psychology	PhD	NA/154	NA/153	NA/4	NA/740	Not specified	Not specified	Not specified	Not specified
Evolutionary Psychology	PhD	NA/159	NA/154	NA/4	NA/700	Not specified	Not specified	Not specified	Not specified
Cognition, Brain and Behavior	PhD	NA/157	NA/154	NA/4	NA/700	Not specified	Not specified	Not specified	Not specified
Health Psychology	PhD	NA/157	NA/154	NA/4	NA/695	Not specified	Not specified	Not specified	Not specified
Quantitative Methodology	PhD	NA/159	NA/151	NA/4	NA/NA	Not specified	Not specified	Not specified	Not specified

Admissions Requirements:

Degree	GRE	GRE-Subject	Letters of Recommendation	Research Statement	Writing Sample	CV	Interview
Doctoral	Required	Recommended	3	Required	Recommended	Required	Required

Please note if these criteria vary for different programs: Interview is required for the Clinical area, but is only recommended for the other areas of study.

Admissions Criteria:

GRE scores—high   Letters of recommendation—high
Research experience—high   Interview—high
Work experience—medium   Statement of goals and objectives—high
Clinically related public service—medium   Undergraduate psychology preparation—medium
GPA—high

For additional information on admission requirements, visit http://psych.unm.edu/graduate-studies/graduate-admissions.html.

Department Demographics

	Male (PT)	Female (PT)	Total	African-American/ Black (PT)	Hispanic/ Latino (PT)	Asian/ Pacific Islander (PT)	American Indian/ Alaska Native (PT)	Caucasian/ White (PT)	Unknown	Multiethnic (PT)	ADA (PT)	Int'l (PT)
Students	30 (0)	47 (0)	77	2 (0)	11 (0)	2 (0)	3 (0)	52 (0)	6 (0)	1 (0)	0 (0)	2 (0)

Financial Information/Assistance

Tuition: For information on tuition costs, visit http://bursar.unm.edu/tuition-info/tuition-and-fee-rates.html. Tuition is subject to change. Additional fees are assessed to students beyond the costs of tuition for the following: GPSA, course fees.

Doctoral:
State residents: $311 per credit hour.
Nonstate residents: $916 per credit hour.

Financial Assistance:

	Teaching Assistantship (% Receiving)	Teaching Assistantship Tuition Remission	Research Assistantship (% Receiving)	Research Assistantship Tuition Remission	Fellowship (% Receiving)	Fellowship Tuition Remission
First-Year Student	$13,907 (50)	Full	$13,907 (50)	Full	NA (NA)	NA
Advanced Student	$15,198 (77)	Full	$15,198 (17)	Full	$23,000 (6)	Full

For additional information on financial assistance, visit http://psych.unm.edu/graduate-studies/graduate-program-costs.html.

Employment of Department Graduates

Doctoral:
Employed in an academic position at a university: 1
Employed in academic position at a 2-year/4-year college: 1
Employed in business or industry: 1
Do not know: 7
Total: 10

Additional Information

Housing and Day Care: On-campus housing is available. See the following website for more information: http://housing.unm.edu/. On-campus day care facilities are available. See the following website for more information: http://childcare.unm.edu/.

Information for Students With Physical Disabilities: See the following website: http://as2.unm.edu/.

Special Facilities or Resources: The department is housed in a building on the central campus. In addition to faculty and administrative offices and seminar rooms, the building is equipped for sophisticated research. Our recently remodeled 9,000 square-foot Psychology Clinical Neuroscience Center (PCNC) contains state-of-the-art laboratories (Pediatric and Adult EEG, Transcranial Stimulation), imaging and data analysis centers with high-speed IT links, neuropsychological testing rooms, collaborative/computerized work areas, a server room, secure data storage and the state's only system for stereotactic transcranial magnetic stimulation (TMS) with a TMS-compatible EEG. The building also has a large animal research facility which is equipped for surgery and for delicate measurements of brain activities as well as for tests of physical, cognitive, and emotional responses. The Department of Psychology also operates a clinic, opened in 1982, which offers diagnostic and therapeutic services to the Albuquerque community while providing an excellent training facility for clinical students.

Application Information: *Fee:* $50. *Online application:* https://app.applyyourself.com/?id=unmgrad.

Adelphi University

The Derner Institute of Advanced Psychological Studies
158 Cambridge Avenue
Garden City, NY 11530
Telephone: (516) 877-4801
Dean: Jacques P. Barber

E-mail: jcmuran@adelphi.edu; kannenge@adelphi.edu
Web: http://derner.adelphi.edu/

Orientation, Objectives, and Emphasis of Department

The Derner Institute of Advanced Psychological Studies is the first university-based professional school of psychology. The orientation is psychodynamic and the model is scholar–practitioner. The doctoral program in clinical and the respecialization program are oriented toward community service and prepare the students for careers in clinical service; the postgraduate programs prepare graduates for the practice of psychoanalysis and psychotherapy. All doctoral programs offer supervised experience in research and theory. The clinical program consists of 4 years of coursework, which includes at least 1 day a week of supervised practice each year and a fifth-year full-time internship; the respecialization program consists of 2 years of coursework, including at least 1 day a week of supervised practice each year and a third-year full-time internship. There are several postdoctoral programs: the original program in psychoanalysis is still the best-known, and it consists of 4 years of seminars, case conferences, personal therapy, and supervised practice. There are also programs of shorter duration, including Child Psychotherapy, Group Psychotherapy, Marriage and Couples Therapy, and Psychodynamic School Psychology. The General MA program is a 36-credit program, and students often graduate in 1 year.

Programs and Degrees Offered

Program	Degree	Application Deadline	Applications Received	Accepted	New Admits Enrolled (PT)	Total Enrolled (PT)	Degrees Awarded in 2014–2015	Median Years to Complete Degree	Dismissed/Withdrew
Clinical Psychology	PhD	December 1 (Fall)	163	63	20	82 (0)	25	5.5	1
Psychotherapy Postgraduate Certificate	Other	Rolling	19	6	0 (6)	0 (10)	8	4	0
Clinical Psychology Respecialization	Respecialization Diploma	Rolling	0	0	0 (0)	0 (0)	0		0
General Psychology	MA/MS	Rolling	83	79	36	70	31	1	3
School Psychology	MA/MS	March 1 (Fall)	58	33	16 (0)	57 (0)	14	3	0
Mental Health Counseling	MA/MS	March 1 (Fall)	52	45	14	32 (0)	15	2	0

APA Accreditation

Clinical PhD: Student Outcome Data website: http://derner.adelphi.edu/psychology/doctoral-program/.

Doctoral Degree (PhD Clinical Psychology): For those doctoral students for whom a professional internship was required in this program prior to graduation:
Total students who applied for an internship: 16
Total students who obtained an internship: 15
Total students who obtained a paid internship: 15
Total students who obtained an unpaid internship: 0
Total students who were placed in APA/CPA-accredited internships: 12
Total students placed in internships not APA/CPA-accredited, but listed with the Association of Psychology Postdoctoral and Internship Centers (APPIC): 3
Total students placed in internships conforming to guidelines of the Council of Directors of School Psychology Programs (CDSPP): 0
Total students placed in internships that were not APA/CPA-accredited, APPIC or CDSSP listed: 0

Doctoral Degree (Respecialization Diploma Clinical Psychology Respecialization): For those doctoral students for whom a professional internship was required in this program prior to graduation:
Total students who applied for an internship: 1
Total students who obtained an internship: 1
Total students who obtained a paid internship: 1
Total students who obtained an unpaid internship: 0
Total students who were placed in APA/CPA-accredited internships: 0
Total students placed in internships not APA/CPA-accredited, but listed with the Association of Psychology Postdoctoral and Internship Centers (APPIC): 0
Total students placed in internships conforming to guidelines of the Council of Directors of School Psychology Programs (CDSPP): 0
Total students placed in internships that were not APA/CPA-accredited, APPIC or CDSSP listed: 1

Master's Degree (MA/MS General Psychology): An internship experience, such as a final research project or "capstone" experience is required of graduates. Master's Degree (MA/MS School Psychology): An internship experience, such as a final research project or "capstone" experience is required of graduates. Master's Degree (MA/MS Mental Health Counseling): An internship experience, such as a final research project or "capstone" experience is required of graduates.

Internships/Practica

For the doctoral program, students are assigned to the Psychological Services Clinic, the training facility of the PhD Program. Beginning in the first year of the doctoral program, students are trained to perform intake evaluations. In the following years, students are trained to perform psychodiagnostic evaluations and psychotherapy. Students are also assigned to their first externship, usually a 1-day-a-week experience, at a full-service mental health centers during their second year of training. They apply to a second, 2-day-a-week externship during their third year. During their fifth year, students complete a 1-year internship in clinical psychology. For the Postgraduate Programs, students are assigned to the Postdoctoral Psychotherapy Center, the training facility of the Postdoctoral Program.

Admissions

Entries appear in the following order: required test or GPA, minimum score (if required)/median score of students entering in 2015–2016.

Program	Degree	GRE-V	GRE-Q	GRE-Writing	GRE-Subject	Under-graduate GPA	Last 2 Years GPA	Psychology GPA	Master's GPA
Clinical Psychology	PhD	149/157	144/154	Not specified	460/720	3/3.65	Not specified	Not specified	NA/NA
Psychotherapy Postgraduate Certificate	Other	Not specified	Not specified	Not specified	Not specified	Not specified	Not specified	Not specified	Not specified
Clinical Psychology Respecialization	Respecial-ization Diploma	Not specified	Not specified	Not specified	Not specified	Not specified	Not specified	Not specified	Not specified
General Psychology	MA/MS	Not specified	Not specified	Not specified	Not specified	2.33/3.21	Not specified	Not specified	Not specified
School Psychology	MA/MS	Not specified	Not specified	Not specified	Not specified	3.03/3.4	Not specified	Not specified	Not specified
Mental Health Counseling	MA/MS	142/148	135/143	Not specified	Not specified	NA/3.3	Not specified	Not specified	Not specified

Admissions Requirements:

Degree	GRE	GRE-Subject	Letters of Recommendation	Research Statement	Writing Sample	CV	Interview
Master's/Specialist	Required	None	3	Required	None	Optional	Optional
Doctoral	Required	Required	3	Required	Required	Required	Required

Please note if these criteria vary for different programs: The criteria vary for different programs.

Admissions Criteria:

GRE scores—high
Research experience—high
Work experience—high
Clinically related public service—high
GPA—high

Letters of recommendation—high
Interview—high
Statement of goals and objectives—high
Undergraduate psychology preparation—high

For additional information on admission requirements, visit http://derner.adelphi.edu/admissions/graduate/.

Department Demographics

	Male (PT)	Female (PT)	Total	African-American/ Black (PT)	Hispanic/ Latino (PT)	Asian/ Pacific Islander (PT)	American Indian/ Alaska Native (PT)	Caucasian/ White (PT)	Unknown	Multiethnic (PT)	ADA (PT)	Int'l (PT)
Students	47 (1)	194 (9)	251	25 (1)	11 (0)	20 (0)	0 (0)	167 (9)	14 (0)	4 (0)	0 (0)	16 (0)

Financial Information/Assistance

Tuition: For information on tuition costs, visit http://financial-aid.adelphi.edu/tuition/.

Doctoral:
State residents: $43,320 per academic year.
Nonstate residents: $43,320 per academic year.

Master's:
State residents: $1,110 per credit hour.
Nonstate residents: $1,110 per credit hour.

Financial Assistance:

	Teaching Assistantship (% Receiving)	Teaching Assistantship Tuition Remission	Research Assistantship (% Receiving)	Research Assistantship Tuition Remission	Fellowship (% Receiving)	Fellowship Tuition Remission
First-Year Student	$10,000 (NA)	Partial	$10,000 (NA)	Partial	NA (NA)	NA
Advanced Student	$12,500 (NA)	Partial	$12,500 (NA)	Partial	$12,500 (NA)	Partial

For additional information on financial assistance, visit http://financial-aid.adelphi.edu/.

Employment of Department Graduates

Master's:
Enrolled in a psychology doctoral program: 19
Enrolled in another graduate/professional program: 11
Employed in a professional position in a school system: 14
Employed in business or industry: 6
Employed in a community mental health/counseling center: 8
Employed in a hospital/medical center: 6
Do not know: 4
Total: 68

Doctoral:
Enrolled in a postdoctoral residency/fellowship: 7
Employed in an academic position at a university: 1
Employed in other positions at a higher education institution: 4
Employed in a community mental health/counseling center: 3
Employed in a hospital/medical center: 10
Total: 25

Additional Information

Housing and Day Care: No on-campus housing is available. On-campus day care facilities are available. See the following website for more information: http://elc.adelphi.edu/.

Information for Students With Physical Disabilities: See the following website: http://dss.adelphi.edu/.

Special Facilities or Resources: Facilities include videotape recording studios and perception, learning, developmental, cognition, and applied research laboratories. The Institute has close interaction with two health-related professional schools, the Adelphi School of Nursing and the Adelphi School of Social Work, and with affiliated community school and clinical facilities. The Institute maintains two major clinical facilities, the Adelphi University Psychological Services Center and the Postdoctoral Psychotherapy Center. An APA-accredited continuing education program brings a series of distinguished workshops to the campus.

Application Information: *Fee:* $50. *Online application:* https://connect.adelphi.edu/apply/.

Alfred University
Division of Counseling and School Psychology
Graduate School
One Saxon Drive
Alfred, NY 14802-1205
Telephone: (607) 871-2212
Director of School Psychology Program: Cris W. Lauback

E-mail: laubackc@alfred.edu
Web: http://www.alfred.edu/gradschool/school-psychology/

Orientation, Objectives, and Emphasis of Department
The Alfred School Psychology programs emphasize a field-centered, systems-oriented, practitioner-scientist approach. The primary goal of the programs is the preparation of problem-solving psychologists with special concern for the application of psychological knowledge in a variety of child and family related settings. Students acquire knowledge in a wide variety of psychological theories and practices; skills are learned and then demonstrated in a number of different applied settings. They develop the personal characteristics and academic competencies necessary to work effectively with others in the identification, prevention and remediation of psychological and educational problems with children and adults. Training in school psychology at Alfred University offers extensive one-to-one contact between students and faculty members to encourage the personalized learning process. PsyD students are involved in field experience and research orientation from the first semester on. Training in the following areas is provided: knowledge base in psychology and education; assessment, intervention and remediation including counseling, play therapy and family work; consulting/training with teachers, administrators and parents; research methodology; program evaluation; and professional identification and functioning. Training at the doctoral level emphasizes applied research and the development of an area of specialization.

Programs and Degrees Offered

Program	Degree	Application Deadline	Applications Received	Accepted	New Admits Enrolled (PT)	Total Enrolled (PT)	Degrees Awarded in 2014–2015	Median Years to Complete Degree	Dismissed/ Withdrew
School Psychology	PsyD	January 15 (Fall)	23	11	6 (0)	21 (27)	4	5.5	2
School Psychology Specialist	MA/MS	February 1 (Fall)	21	12	8 (0)	22 (2)	7	3	1

APA Accreditation
School PsyD: Student Outcome Data website: http://www.alfred.edu/gradschool/school-psychology/psyd-specialization.cfm.

Doctoral Degree (PsyD School Psychology): For those doctoral students for whom a professional internship was required in this program prior to graduation:
Total students who applied for an internship: 4
Total students who obtained an internship: 4
Total students who obtained a paid internship: 4
Total students who obtained an unpaid internship: 0
Total students who were placed in APA/CPA-accredited internships: 0
Total students placed in internships not APA/CPA-accredited, but listed with the Association of Psychology Postdoctoral and Internship Centers (APPIC): 0
Total students placed in internships conforming to guidelines of the Council of Directors of School Psychology Programs (CDSPP): 4
Total students placed in internships that were not APA/CPA-accredited, APPIC or CDSSP listed: 0

Master's Degree (MA/MS School Psychology Specialist): An internship experience, such as a final research project or "capstone" experience is required of graduates.

Internships/Practica
Students obtaining the specialist degree (MA/CAS) and doctoral degree (PsyD) may pursue internships any place in the United States. Specialist students choose sites at public schools across New York State and northern Pennsylvania, yet other routinely

obtain internships in states such as Colorado, Maryland, Connecticut, Virginia, and even Hawaii. Doctoral students secure internships in these same regions, are required to complete a portion of their internship in a school setting, but many also choose sites and internship experiences in both school and clinical settings. All doctoral interns must have at least one site supervisor that is a licensed psychologist. A portion of doctoral students each year choose to intern at APPIC- and APA-accredited sites.

Admissions

Entries appear in the following order: required test or GPA, minimum score (if required)/median score of students entering in 2015–2016.

Program	Degree	GRE-V	GRE-Q	GRE-Writing	GRE-Subject	Undergraduate GPA	Last 2 Years GPA	Psychology GPA	Master's GPA
School Psychology	PsyD	145/155	141/152	3/4	Not specified	2.5/3.5	Not specified	Not specified	Not specified
School Psychology Specialist	MA/MS	141/148	137/147	3/4	Not specified	2.76/3.2	Not specified	Not specified	Not specified

Admissions Requirements:

Degree	GRE	GRE-Subject	Letters of Recommendation	Research Statement	Writing Sample	CV	Interview
Master's/Specialist	Required	Optional	3	Required	Optional	Required	Required
Doctoral	Required	Optional	3	Required	Optional	Required	Required

Please note if these criteria vary for different programs: The PsyD program places a higher emphasis on research experience as an undergraduate, and requires a statement of research interests.

Admissions Criteria:

GRE scores—medium
Research experience—medium
Work experience—medium
Clinically related public service—low
GPA—high

Letters of recommendation—high
Interview—high
Statement of goals and objectives—high
Undergraduate psychology preparation—medium
Sch. Psych. awareness—medium

For additional information on admission requirements, visit http://www.alfred.edu/gradschool/school-psychology/applying.cfm.

Department Demographics

	Male (PT)	Female (PT)	Total	African-American/ Black (PT)	Hispanic/ Latino (PT)	Asian/ Pacific Islander (PT)	American Indian/ Alaska Native (PT)	Caucasian/ White (PT)	Unknown	Multiethnic (PT)	ADA (PT)	Int'l (PT)
Students	10 (5)	38 (20)	73	4 (3)	1 (3)	1 (0)	0 (0)	41 (19)	0 (0)	1 (0)	1 (1)	0 (0)

Financial Information/Assistance

Tuition: For information on tuition costs, visit https://www.alfred.edu/finaid/graduate/cost.cfm. Tuition is subject to change.

Doctoral:
State residents: $38,020 per academic year.
State residents: $810 per credit hour.
Nonstate residents: $38,020 per academic year.
Nonstate residents: $810 per credit hour.

Master's:
State residents: $38,020 per academic year.
State residents: $810 per credit hour.
Nonstate residents: $38,020 per academic year.
Nonstate residents: $810 per credit hour.

Financial Assistance:

	Teaching Assistantship (% Receiving)	Teaching Assistantship Tuition Remission	Research Assistantship (% Receiving)	Research Assistantship Tuition Remission	Fellowship (% Receiving)	Fellowship Tuition Remission
First-Year Student	NA (NA)	NA	$19,010 (100)	Partial	$9,236 (100)	Partial
Advanced Student	NA (NA)	NA	$19,010 (36)	Partial	$38,020 (63)	Full

For additional information on financial assistance, visit http://www.alfred.edu/gradschool/school-psychology/grants.cfm.

Employment of Department Graduates

Master's:
Employed in a professional position in a school system: 7
Total: 7

Doctoral:
Employed in a professional position in a school system: 3
Employed in a community mental health/counseling center: 1
Total: 4

Additional Information

Housing and Day Care: On-campus housing is available. See the following website for more information: http://www.alfred.edu/students/living_at_au/residence_life-53.cfm. No on-campus day care facilities are available.

Information for Students With Physical Disabilities: See the following website: http://www.alfred.edu/academics/cas.cfm.

Special Facilities or Resources: Departmental resources include an extensive library of psychological and educational assessment tools, a media library of assessment and psychotherapy processes, as well as a library of psychotherapy and intervention materials. All first-year graduate students complete a year-long practicum in a school setting; second-year students complete a year-long practicum in our on-campus mental health clinic (Lea R. Powell Institute's Child and Family Services Center). The Center provides consultation, assessment, and psychotherapy services to children and families in the local community. The Center is a state-of-the-art facility which utilizes group supervision in combination with digital recording of sessions and use of MacBooks to communicate with supervisors. Additionally, a graduate student workroom houses PCs and printers for student use which have necessary assessment scoring software; a student lounge is also available.

Application Information: Ms. Sara Love, Director of Graduate Admissions, Alfred University, One Saxon Drive, Alfred, NY 14802. *Fee:* $60. *Online application:* http://www.alfred.edu/admissions/apply/graduate.cfm.

City University of New York: Brooklyn College
Department of Psychology
School of Natural and Behavioral Sciences
2900 Bedford Avenue
Brooklyn, NY 11210
Telephone: (718) 951-5601
Chairperson: Margaret-Ellen Pipe
Web: http://www.brooklyn.cuny.edu/web/academics/schools/naturalsciences/graduate/psychology.php

E-mail: BChanowitz@brooklyn.cuny.edu

Orientation, Objectives, and Emphasis of Department
The Industrial/Organizational Psychology MA program offers training in two tracks: Human Relations, with focus on the group, and Organizational Behavior, with focus on the organization. Graduates from both tracks are prepared for entry-level, executive positions in Human Resources and Personnel. The MA program in Mental Health Counseling provides experiential learning with counseling practicum experience in mental health settings, along with comprehensive course work that prepares students for practice in mental health counseling. Graduates are eligible to take the NYS licensing exam which permits private/independent practice of counseling. The Experimental Psychology program offers training in classical and current psychological theories and research, methods of data collection and analysis, effective communication and ethical conduct. Graduates of the program pursue a wide range of careers in research, health care, government agencies and the private sector, and for admittance to competitive doctoral programs.

Programs and Degrees Offered

Program	Degree	Application Deadline	Applica-tions Received	Accepted	New Admits Enrolled (PT)	Total Enrolled (PT)	Degrees Awarded in 2014–2015	Median Years to Complete Degree	Dismissed/Withdrew
Experimental Psychology	MA/MS	March 1 (Fall), November 1 (Spring), Rolling	57	22	4 (12)	8 (33)	13	3	0
Industrial/ Organizational Psychology	MA/MS	March 1 (Fall), Rolling	110	49	8 (32)	16 (86)	39	3	0
Mental Health Counseling	MA/MS	March 1 (Fall), Rolling	170	61	36 (0)	79 (0)	36	2	0

Internships/Practica

The MA program in Industrial and Organizational psychology has an internship component that most students avail themselves of. It functions as both training and as an opportunity to experience the hands-on application of principles in a work setting. The MA program in Mental Health Counseling requires two semesters of pre-degree supervised practica and two semesters of internship. An additional 3000 hours of post-degree supervised internship is required for licensure.

Admissions

Entries appear in the following order: required test or GPA, minimum score (if required)/median score of students entering in 2015–2016.

Program	Degree	GRE-V	GRE-Q	GRE-Writing	GRE-Subject	Under-graduate GPA	Last 2 Years GPA	Psychol-ogy GPA	Master's GPA
Experimental Psychology	MA/MS	Not specified	Not specified	Not specified	Not specified	3/NA	Not specified	Not specified	Not specified
Industrial/ Organizational Psychology	MA/MS	Not specified	Not specified	Not specified	Not specified	3/3.45	Not specified	Not specified	Not specified
Mental Health Counseling	MA/MS	Not specified	Not specified	Not specified	Not specified	3/3.3	Not specified	Not specified	Not specified

Admissions Requirements:

Degree	GRE	GRE-Subject	Letters of Recom-mendation	Research Statement	Writing Sample	CV	Interview
Master's/Specialist	Recom-mended	Recom-mended	2	Required	None	Recom-mended	None

Please note if these criteria vary for different programs: The MA programs in Industrial and Organizational have a greater emphasis on applications of psychology. Prior research experience is a plus. Include CV and two academic letters of reference; a third letter may be submitted to the Graduate Admissions office. GRE scores are recommended but not required. The MA in Experimental Psychology focuses on a strong background in research. All these programs require that applicants have 12 undergraduate credits in psychology with (a B or better for) courses in statistics and in research methods. The MA program in Mental Health Counseling requires that applicants have 15 credits, with only a statistics course. The MA program in Mental Health Counseling (MHC) has a greater emphasis on work, internship or volunteer experience in human services; research experience is less important. For the MHC program, an interview is part of the admissions process and a third letter of reference is required.

Admissions Criteria:

Research experience—high
Work experience—medium
Clinically related public service—low
GPA—high

Letters of recommendation—high
Interview—medium
Statement of goals and objectives—high
Undergraduate psychology preparation—high

For additional information on admission requirements, visit http://www.brooklyn.cuny.edu/web/academics/schools/naturalsciences/graduate/psychology/programs.php.

Department Demographics

	Male (PT)	Female (PT)	Total	African-American/ Black (PT)	Hispanic/ Latino (PT)	Asian/ Pacific Islander (PT)	American Indian/ Alaska Native (PT)	Caucasian/ White (PT)	Unknown (PT)	Multiethnic (PT)	ADA (PT)	Int'l (PT)
Students	30 (38)	73 (81)	222	20 (26)	19 (23)	17 (18)	0 (0)	47 (52)	0 (0)	0 (0)	1 (1)	13 (0)

Financial Information/Assistance

Tuition: For information on tuition costs, visit http://www.brooklyn.cuny.edu/web/about/offices/bursar/tuition/graduate.php. Tuition is subject to change. Additional fees are assessed to students beyond the costs of tuition for the following: student technology fee, student activity fee, CUNY consolidation fee.

Master's:
State residents: $10,130 per academic year.
State residents: $425 per credit hour.
Nonstate residents: $780 per credit hour.

Financial Assistance:

	Teaching Assistantship (% Receiving)	Teaching Assistantship Tuition Remission	Research Assistantship (% Receiving)	Research Assistantship Tuition Remission	Fellowship (% Receiving)	Fellowship Tuition Remission
First-Year Student	NA (NA)	NA	NA (NA)	NA	NA (NA)	Partial
Advanced Student	NA (NA)	NA	NA (NA)	NA	NA (NA)	Partial

For additional information on financial assistance, visit http://www.brooklyn.cuny.edu/web/about/administration/enrollment/financial/graduate.php.

Employment of Department Graduates

No information provided.

Additional Information

Housing and Day Care: No on-campus housing is available. On-campus day care facilities are available. See the following website for more information: http://www.brooklyn.cuny.edu/web/academics/schools/education/partnerships/ecc.php.

Information for Students With Physical Disabilities: See the following website: http://www.brooklyn.cuny.edu/web/about/offices/disability.php.

Special Facilities or Resources: There are over two dozen active laboratories in the department focusing on topics such as the physiology of taste and preference formation, children's acquisition of spatial knowledge, transactive knowledge in organizations, teams and culture and diversity, lifespan development and motivation, creativity and cognition in the arts, comparative psychology in cephalopods, amphibians, and crustaceans, hippocampal atrophy in early Alzheimer's disease, implicit impression formation, biomimetic robotics, neurodegeneration in the aged, and parent-child communication. All labs are well equipped and some supported by grants from NSF, NIH, NASA, DARPA, and other organizations. Several faculty have appointments and working collaborations with research labs in city hospitals and medical schools with access to technologies such as fMRI.

Application Information: Office of Graduate Admissions, Brooklyn College, 2900 Bedford Avenue, Brooklyn, NY 11210. *Fee:* $125. *Online application:* http://www.brooklyn.cuny.edu/web/admissions/graduate/apply.php.

City University of New York: Brooklyn College

Department of School Psychology, Counseling and Leadership/School Psychologist Graduate Program
Brooklyn College
2900 Bedford Avenue, Room 1107 James
Brooklyn, NY 11210
Telephone: (718) 951-5876
Program Coordinator: Paul McCabe
Web: http://www.brooklyn.cuny.edu/web/academics/schools/education/graduate/psychology.php

E-mail: paulmc@brooklyn.cuny.edu

Orientation, Objectives, and Emphasis of Department

The aim of the school psychologist training program is to meet the community needs for professionally competent personnel to function in the schools as consultants on psychological aspects of learning and mental health. Students are prepared to make assessments of situations involving children, parents, and school personnel to achieve the more optimal functioning of children in the school setting. Coursework will prepare students in the areas of measurement and evaluation, personality understanding, educational objectives and procedures, curriculum development, and research. Students will also be trained to achieve greater integration between school and community. Elements of the program will provide students with opportunities for self-reflection, collaboration with other professionals and families, and engagement in issues of diversity and social justice.

Programs and Degrees Offered

Program	Degree	Application Deadline	Applica-tions Received	Accepted	New Admits Enrolled (PT)	Total Enrolled (PT)	Degrees Awarded in 2014–2015	Median Years to Complete Degree	Dismissed/ Withdrew
School Psychology	MA/MS	March 1 (Fall)	130	42	20 (10)	39 (47)	35	3	2
School Psychology (Bilingual)	MA/MS	March 1 (Fall)	12	12	5 (7)	5 (7)	6	3	0

Internships/Practica

Internships are available and coordinated through our program with various schools, both public and private, working with both the mainstream population as well as special populations. In addition, internships are available in mental health clinics, agencies, and hospitals. Practica in assessment, intervention, consultation, and counseling are designed to reinforce students' coursework. Students in the bilingual certificate program whose focus language is in an area of need are eligible to apply for the NYC Psychologists in Training (PIT) internship, which is a funded internship program.

Admissions

Entries appear in the following order: required test or GPA, minimum score (if required)/median score of students entering in 2015–2016.

Program	Degree	GRE-V	GRE-Q	GRE-Writing	GRE-Subject	Under-graduate GPA	Last 2 Years GPA	Psychol-ogy GPA	Master's GPA
School Psychology	MA/MS	Not specified	Not specified	Not specified	Not specified	3/NA	Not specified	3/NA	Not specified
School Psychology (Bilingual)	MA/MS	Not specified	Not specified	Not specified	Not specified	3/NA	Not specified	3/NA	Not specified

Admissions Requirements:

Degree	GRE	GRE-Subject	Letters of Recom-mendation	Research Statement	Writing Sample	CV	Interview
Master's/Specialist	Optional	Optional	2	Required	Optional	Required	Required

Admissions Criteria:
Research experience—medium
Work experience—high
Clinically related public service—high
GPA—high
Letters of recommendation—high

Interview—high
Statement of goals and objectives—high
Undergraduate psychology preparation—medium
Writing sample—high

Department Demographics

	Male (PT)	Female (PT)	Total	African-American/ Black (PT)	Hispanic/ Latino (PT)	Asian/ Pacific Islander (PT)	American Indian/ Alaska Native (PT)	Caucasian/ White (PT)	Unknown	Multiethnic (PT)	ADA (PT)	Int'l (PT)
Students	4 (8)	36 (46)	94	6 (11)	7 (10)	9 (4)	0 (0)	16 (19)	2 (10)	0 (0)	0 (0)	0 (0)

Financial Information/Assistance

Tuition: For information on tuition costs, visit http://www.brooklyn.cuny.edu/web/about/offices/bursar/tuition/graduate.php. Additional fees are assessed to students beyond the costs of tuition for the following: student technology fee ($125), student activity fee ($74.25).

Master's:
State residents: $9,170 per academic year.
State residents: $385 per credit hour.
Nonstate residents: $710 per credit hour.

Financial Assistance:

	Teaching Assistantship (% Receiving)	Teaching Assistantship Tuition Remission	Research Assistantship (% Receiving)	Research Assistantship Tuition Remission	Fellowship (% Receiving)	Fellowship Tuition Remission
First-Year Student	NA (NA)	NA	NA (NA)	NA	NA (NA)	NA
Advanced Student	NA (NA)	NA	NA (NA)	NA	NA (NA)	NA

For additional information on financial assistance, visit http://www.brooklyn.cuny.edu/web/about/offices/finiad.php.

Employment of Department Graduates

Master's:
Enrolled in a psychology doctoral program: 2
Employed in a professional position in a school system: 25
Total: 27

Additional Information

Housing and Day Care: On-campus housing is available. See the following website for more information: http://www.1kenilworth. com/. On-campus day care facilities are available. See the following website for more information: http://www.brooklyn.cuny.edu/web/academics/schools/education/partnerships/ecc.php.

Information for Students With Physical Disabilities: See the following website: http://www.brooklyn.cuny.edu/web/about/offices/disability.php.

Special Facilities or Resources: In addition to the use of the Brooklyn College library, students are welcome to use all the libraries at other colleges within the CUNY system. The School Psychology program also has a small library of texts and journals for the students' use. The Program has an extensive library of assessment kits that students are allowed to check out for their assessment classes.

Application Information: Brooklyn College, Admissions Office, 2900 Bedford Avenue, Brooklyn, NY 11210. *Fee:* $125. *Online application:* http://www.brooklyn.cuny.edu/web/graduateapplication.php.

City University of New York: Graduate Center

Behavior Analysis Training Area
Queens College
65-30 Kissena Boulevard
Flushing, NY 11367
Telephone: (718) 997-3630
Coordinator: Bruce L. Brown
Web: http://www.gc.cuny.edu/Page-Elements/Academics-Research-Centers-Initiatives/Doctoral-Programs/Psychology/Training-
   Areas/Behavior-Analysis

E-mail: bruce.brown@qc.cuny.edu

Orientation, Objectives, and Emphasis of Department

The Behavior Analysis Training Area (BA) offers doctoral students in psychology training in the experimental analysis of human and animal behavior and in applied behavior analysis. Students and faculty investigate a wide spectrum of behavioral processes through lectures, experimental laboratory course work, advanced seminars, informal student-faculty discussions, practica, and individual research projects. Faculty and students publish regularly in peer-reviewed journals and are strongly represented at major national and international conferences. Their current research interests include such topics as equivalence class formation, language acquisition, affective behavior, behavioral assessment, human and animal timing, pattern recognition, stimulus control, behavioral community psychology, performance feedback, education and training of children with autism, joint attention, and staff training in organizational settings. The BA program is accredited in behavior analysis by the Association for Behavior Analysis, and is seeking continuation of licensure-qualification in New York State. The Behavior Analysis Certification Board, Inc. has approved a subset of the curriculum as a course sequence that meets the coursework requirements for eligibility to take the Board Certified Behavior Analyst examination. Applicants will have to meet additional requirements to qualify.

Programs and Degrees Offered

Program	Degree	Application Deadline	Applica- tions Received	Accepted	New Admits Enrolled (PT)	Total Enrolled (PT)	Degrees Awarded in 2014– 2015	Median Years to Complete Degree	Dismissed/ Withdrew
Behavior Analysis	PhD	December 1 (Fall)	20	4	4 (0)	28 (0)	3	6.5	1

Admissions

Entries appear in the following order: required test or GPA, minimum score (if required)/median score of students entering in 2015–2016.

Program	Degree	GRE-V	GRE-Q	GRE- Writing	GRE- Subject	Under- graduate GPA	Last 2 Years GPA	Psychol- ogy GPA	Master's GPA
Behavior Analysis	PhD	Not specified	Not specified	Not specified	Not specified	Not specified	Not specified	Not specified	Not specified

Admissions Requirements:

Degree	GRE	GRE- Subject	Letters of Recom- mendation	Research Statement	Writing Sample	CV	Interview
Doctoral	Required	Required	2	Required	Optional	Required	Required

Admissions Criteria:

GRE scores—high
Research experience—high
Work experience—low
Clinically related public service—low
GPA—high

Letters of recommendation—high
Interview—high
Statement of goals and objectives—high
Undergraduate psychology preparation—medium

For additional information on admission requirements, visit http://www.gc.cuny.edu/Prospective-Current-Students/Prospective-Students/Admission-Requirements.

Department Demographics

	Male (PT)	Female (PT)	Total	African-American/ Black (PT)	Hispanic/ Latino (PT)	Asian/ Pacific Islander (PT)	American Indian/ Alaska Native (PT)	Caucasian/ White (PT)	Unknown (PT)	Multiethnic (PT)	ADA (PT)	Int'l (PT)
Students	4 (0)	24 (0)	28	0 (0)	2 (0)	1 (0)	0 (0)	24 (0)	1 (0)	0 (0)	0 (0)	3 (0)

Financial Information/Assistance

Tuition: For information on tuition costs, visit http://www.gc.cuny.edu/Prospective-Current-Students/Current-Students/Tuition-Fees. Tuition is subject to change. Additional fees are assessed to students beyond the costs of tuition for the following: Student Activities Fee, Technology Fee.

Doctoral:
State residents: $9,060 per academic year.
Nonstate residents: $875 per credit hour.

Financial Assistance:

	Teaching Assistantship (% Receiving)	Teaching Assistantship Tuition Remission	Research Assistantship (% Receiving)	Research Assistantship Tuition Remission	Fellowship (% Receiving)	Fellowship Tuition Remission
First-Year Student	NA (NA)	NA	NA (NA)	Full	$25,000 (NA)	Full
Advanced Student	$10,000 (NA)	Full	NA (NA)	NA	$10,000 (NA)	Full

For additional information on financial assistance, visit http://www.gc.cuny.edu/Prospective-Current-Students/Current-Students/Financial-Assistance.

Employment of Department Graduates

Doctoral:
Employed in academic position at a 2-year/4-year college: 1
Employed in a community mental health/counseling center: 2
Total: 3

Additional Information

Housing and Day Care: On-campus housing is available. See the following website for more information: http://queenscollegehousing.com/. On-campus day care facilities are available. See the following website for more information: http://www.qc.cuny.edu/StudentLife/services/ChildDevelopment/.

Information for Students With Physical Disabilities: See the following website: http://www.gc.cuny.edu/Prospective-Current-Students/Student-Life/Resources.

Application Information: Office of Admissions, The Graduate School & University Center of the City University of New York, 365 Fifth Avenue, New York, NY 10016-4309. *Fee:* $125. *Online application:* http://www.gc.cuny.edu/Prospective-Current-Students/New-Online-Application.

City University of New York: Graduate School and University Center

PhD Program in Educational Psychology
365 Fifth Avenue
New York, NY 10016-4309
Telephone: (212) 817-8285
Executive Officer: Bruce D. Homer

E-mail: bhomer@gc.cuny.edu
Web: http://www.gc.cuny.edu/educationalpsychology

Orientation, Objectives, and Emphasis of Department

The PhD program in Educational Psychology is research-oriented, preparing students for teaching, research, and program development in various educational settings such as universities, school systems, research institutions, and community agencies, as well as in educational publishing, television, and other agencies with training programs. Three areas of concentration are offered: quantitative methods in educational and psychological research, educational policy analysis, and learning development and instruction.

Programs and Degrees Offered

Program	Degree	Application Deadline	Applica-tions Received	Accepted	New Admits Enrolled (PT)	Total Enrolled (PT)	Degrees Awarded in 2014–2015	Median Years to Complete Degree	Dismissed/ Withdrew
Educational Psychology	PhD	December 15 (Fall)	36	9	6	69	15	5	1

Doctoral Degree (PhD Educational Psychology): For those doctoral students for whom a professional internship was required in this program prior to graduation:

Total students who applied for an internship: 1

Total students who obtained an internship: 1

Total students who obtained a paid internship: 1

Total students who obtained an unpaid internship: 0

Total students who were placed in APA/CPA-accredited internships: 0

Total students placed in internships not APA/CPA-accredited, but listed with the Association of Psychology Postdoctoral and Internship Centers (APPIC): 0

Total students placed in internships conforming to guidelines of the Council of Directors of School Psychology Programs (CDSPP): 1

Total students placed in internships that were not APA/CPA-accredited, APPIC or CDSSP listed: 0

Admissions

Entries appear in the following order: required test or GPA, minimum score (if required)/median score of students entering in 2015–2016.

Program	Degree	GRE-V	GRE-Q	GRE-Writing	GRE-Subject	Under-graduate GPA	Last 2 Years GPA	Psychol-ogy GPA	Master's GPA
Educational Psychology	PhD	NA/159	NA/156	Not specified	Not specified	Not specified	Not specified	Not specified	Not specified

Admissions Requirements:

Degree	GRE	GRE-Subject	Letters of Recom-mendation	Research Statement	Writing Sample	CV	Interview
Doctoral	Required	Optional	3	Required	Required	Required	Required

Admissions Criteria:

GRE scores—high

Research experience—medium

Work experience—medium

Clinically related public service—low

GPA—medium

Letters of recommendation—high

Interview—high

Statement of goals and objectives—high

Undergraduate psychology preparation—low

For additional information on admission requirements, visit http://www.gc.cuny.edu/Prospective-Current-Students/Prospective-Students/Admissions.

Department Demographics

	Male (PT)	Female (PT)	Total	African-American/ Black (PT)	Hispanic/ Latino (PT)	Asian/ Pacific Islander (PT)	American Indian/ Alaska Native (PT)	Caucasian/ White (PT)	Unknown	Multiethnic (PT)	ADA (PT)	Int'l (PT)
Students	19 (0)	50 (0)	69	8 (0)	4 (0)	6 (0)	0 (0)	47 (0)	4 (0)	0 (0)	0 (0)	1 (0)

Financial Information/Assistance

Tuition: For information on tuition costs, visit http://www.gc.cuny.edu/Prospective-Current-Students/Current-Students/Tuition-Fees. Additional fees are assessed to students beyond the costs of tuition for the following: student activities fee; University Consolidated Services fee; technology fee.

Doctoral:
State residents: $9,060 per academic year.
State residents: $515 per credit hour.
Nonstate residents: $875 per credit hour.

Financial Assistance:

	Teaching Assistantship (% Receiving)	Teaching Assistantship Tuition Remission	Research Assistantship (% Receiving)	Research Assistantship Tuition Remission	Fellowship (% Receiving)	Fellowship Tuition Remission
First-Year Student	NA (NA)	NA	$8,200 (60)	Full	$25,000 (40)	Full
Advanced Student	$5,000 (20)	Full	$8,200 (20)	NA	$25,000 (30)	Full

For additional information on financial assistance, visit http://www.gc.cuny.edu/Prospective-Current-Students/Current-Students/Financial-Assistance.

Employment of Department Graduates

Doctoral:
Enrolled in a postdoctoral residency/fellowship: 2
Employed in other positions at a higher education institution: 4
Employed in a professional position in a school system: 5
Still seeking employment: 1
Other employment position: 2
Do not know: 1
Total: 15

Additional Information

Housing and Day Care: On-campus housing is available. See the following website for more information: http://www.gc.cuny.edu/Prospective-Current-Students/Student-Life/Housing. On-campus day care facilities are available. See the following website for more information: http://www.gc.cuny.edu/Prospective-Current-Students/Student-Life/Resources/Child-Development-and-Learning-Center.

Information for Students With Physical Disabilities: See the following website: http://www.gc.cuny.edu/Prospective-Current-Students/Student-Life/Resources.

Special Facilities or Resources: The Educational Psychology program is affiliated with a university based research institute, CASE (Center for Advanced Study in Education). CASE is heavily involved in the evaluation and implementation of various applied educational programs. Our faculty and students have worked as principal investigators and research assistants on CASE projects.

Application Information: Admissions Office, CUNY Graduate Center, 365 Fifth Avenue, New York, NY 10016-4309. *Fee:* $125. *Online application:* https://app.applyyourself.com/?id=cunygc.

City University of New York: John Jay College of Criminal Justice

Department of Psychology
John Jay College of Criminal Justice, CUNY
524 West 59th Street, 10th Floor
New York, NY 10019
Telephone: (212) 237-8782
Director, MA Program: James S. Wulach, PhD, JD

E-mail: Jwulach@jjay.cuny.edu
Web: http://www.jjay.cuny.edu/department-psychology

Orientation, Objectives, and Emphasis of Department

The 42-credit MA Program in Forensic Psychology program is designed to train students to provide professional MA-level services to, and within, the legal system—especially the criminal justice system; and to provide a background for psychology doctoral study in the future. We offer traditional master's level clinical psychology courses, as well as specialized courses in several areas of study. There is a research track for advanced students to work on MA theses with professors. Many of our full-time faculty members have postdoctoral psychological certifications, are lawyers as well as psychologists, and/or have extensive forensic experience as practitioners and/or researchers. Some of our graduates become MA psychologists within the criminal justice system, working with offenders, delinquents, and victims. Other graduates enhance their present careers in law enforcement, probation, or parole by completing the program. Many of our graduates continue their education in psychology doctoral programs, or in law. We also offer a 60-credit Master's degree in Forensic Mental Health Counseling. This program, developed within the Psychology Department, has been approved by New York State as a "license eligible" academic program. It develops skills in interviewing, counseling, and assessment, based upon established principles and research regarding human development, personality, psychopathology, and counseling.

Programs and Degrees Offered

Program	Degree	Application Deadline	Applications Received	Accepted	New Admits Enrolled (PT)	Total Enrolled (PT)	Degrees Awarded in 2014–2015	Median Years to Complete Degree	Dismissed/ Withdrew
Forensic Psychology	MA/MS	May 15 (Fall), December 1 (Spring)	285	124	50 (5)	101 (90)	89	2	
Forensic Mental Health Counseling	MA/MS	April 15 (Fall), October 15 (Spring)	180	81	20 (9)	81 (76)	49	2.5	0
Postgraduate Certificate in Forensic Psychology	Other	May 15 (Fall), (Spring)	10	6	0	0 (5)	4		1
MA-JD in Forensic Psychology & Law	Other	May 15 (Fall)			5 (0)	5 (0)			

Internships/Practica

Many students in the Forensic Psychology program complete a 300-hour externship in local forensic psychology settings, such as hospitals or prisons. A majority of the hours performed need to involve direct clinical contact with patients or clients. Most students in the Forensic Mental Health Counseling program complete a 600-hour externship in local forensic psychology settings.

Admissions

Entries appear in the following order: required test or GPA, minimum score (if required)/median score of students entering in 2015–2016.

Program	Degree	GRE-V	GRE-Q	GRE-Writing	GRE-Subject	Undergraduate GPA	Last 2 Years GPA	Psychology GPA	Master's GPA
Forensic Psychology	MA/MS	145/NA	145/NA	NA/NA	Not specified	3/3.2	Not specified	Not specified	Not specified
Forensic Mental Health Counseling	MA/MS	NA/150	NA/150	NA/3.5	Not specified	3/3.2	Not specified	Not specified	Not specified
Postgraduate Certificate in Forensic Psychology	Other	NA/NA	NA/NA	Not specified	Not specified	3/3.2	Not specified	Not specified	Not specified
MA-JD in Forensic Psychology & Law	Other	145/150	145/150	3/3.5	Not specified	3/3.2	Not specified	Not specified	Not specified

Admissions Requirements:

Degree	GRE	GRE-Subject	Letters of Recommendation	Research Statement	Writing Sample	CV	Interview
Master's/Specialist	Required	None	3	Required	Optional	Optional	None

Please note if these criteria vary for different programs: MA Program: GPA & GRE Scores weighted most heavily.

Admissions Criteria:

GRE scores—high
Research experience—low
Work experience—low
GPA—high

Letters of recommendation—medium
Statement of goals and objectives—low
Undergraduate psychology preparation—high

For additional information on admission requirements, visit http://www.jjay.cuny.edu/general-admission-requirements.

Department Demographics

	Male (PT)	Female (PT)	Total	African-American/ Black (PT)	Hispanic/ Latino (PT)	Asian/ Pacific Islander (PT)	American Indian/ Alaska Native (PT)	Caucasian/ White (PT)	Unknown (PT)	Multiethnic (PT)	ADA (PT)	Int'l (PT)
Students	73 (39)	114 (132)	358	27 (21)	36 (33)	14 (16)	1 (2)	109 (99)	0 (0)	0 (0)		9 (11)

Financial Information/Assistance

Tuition: For information on tuition costs, visit http://www.jjay.cuny.edu/graduate-tuition-and-fees. Tuition is subject to change. Additional fees are assessed to students beyond the costs of tuition for the following: Students who are enrolled in these programs pay an additional excellence fee of $125 per course.

Master's:
State residents: $10,130 per academic year.
State residents: $425 per credit hour.
Nonstate residents: $18,720 per academic year.
Nonstate residents: $780 per credit hour.

Financial Assistance:

	Teaching Assistantship (% Receiving)	Teaching Assistantship Tuition Remission	Research Assistantship (% Receiving)	Research Assistantship Tuition Remission	Fellowship (% Receiving)	Fellowship Tuition Remission
First-Year Student	NA (NA)	NA	NA (NA)	NA	NA (NA)	NA
Advanced Student	NA (NA)	NA	NA (NA)	NA	NA (NA)	NA

For additional information on financial assistance, visit http://www.jjay.cuny.edu/graduate-financial-aid.

Employment of Department Graduates

No information provided.

Additional Information

Housing and Day Care: No on-campus housing is available. On-campus day care facilities are available. See the following website for more information: http://www.jjay.cuny.edu/childrens-center.

Information for Students With Physical Disabilities: See the following website: http://www.jjay.cuny.edu/office-accessibility-services.

Special Facilities or Resources: The department maintains affiliations with the major forensic psychology institutions in the New York metropolitan area. The program is endowed for student psychology research in the Forensic Psychology Research Institute. In addition, the full academic resources and educational milieu of John Jay College of Criminal Justice, CUNY, are available to our students.

Application Information: Graduate Admissions, John Jay College of Criminal Justice, CUNY, 524 West 59th Street, New York, NY 10019. *Fee:* $125. *Online application:* https://app.applyyourself.com/?id=cunyjjaygr.

City University of New York: The Graduate Center
Clinical Psychology at Queens College
Queens College
65-30 Kissena Boulevard
Queens, NY 11367
Telephone: (718) 997-3630
Director of Clinical Training: Joel R. Sneed, PhD
E-mail: joel.sneed@qc.cuny.edu
Web: http://www.gc.cuny.edu/Page-Elements/Academics-Research-Centers-Initiatives/Doctoral-Programs/Psychology/Training-Areas/Clinical-Queens

---

Orientation, Objectives, and Emphasis of Department
The Clinical Psychology PhD program is an academically oriented PhD program with a core philosophy based on two premises. The first of these is that productive research, effective teaching, and responsible clinical practice are integrally interdependent. That is, effective teaching must include critical analysis of current research data, and clinical assessment and treatment procedures must be empirically validated. The second premise is that the understanding of impaired or disordered brain function in humans requires rigorous training in the neurosciences as well as in traditional clinical topics. The program is designed to train professionals with competence in research and/or teaching of Clinical Psychology as well as in the area of brain-behavior relationships, and in the application of these competencies in clinical settings. The clinical program requires 90 credits including at least 2 years of clinical practicum training. The program provides students the opportunity to acquire and apply the skills appropriate to the practice of clinical psychology and clinical neuropsychology. Students receive training in the evidence-based treatments, in psychotherapeutic and remediation techniques, and in evaluation of psychological and neuropsychological functions in various clinical populations including children, young or older adults, as well as psychiatric, rehabilitation, medical, neurological and/or neurosurgical populations.

Programs and Degrees Offered

Program	Degree	Application Deadline	Applications Received	Accepted	New Admits Enrolled (PT)	Total Enrolled (PT)	Degrees Awarded in 2014–2015	Median Years to Complete Degree	Dismissed/ Withdrew
Clinical Psychology	PhD	December 1 (Fall)	59	5	5	46	6	7	1

APA Accreditation

Clinical PhD (Doctor of Philosophy).

Doctoral Degree (PhD Clinical Psychology): For those doctoral students for whom a professional internship was required in this program prior to graduation:
Total students who applied for an internship: 6
Total students who obtained an internship: 5
Total students who obtained a paid internship: 5
Total students who obtained an unpaid internship: 0
Total students who were placed in APA/CPA-accredited internships: 4
Total students placed in internships not APA/CPA-accredited, but listed with the Association of Psychology Postdoctoral and Internship Centers (APPIC): 0
Total students placed in internships conforming to guidelines of the Council of Directors of School Psychology Programs (CDSPP): 0
Total students placed in internships that were not APA/CPA-accredited, APPIC or CDSSP listed: 1

Internships/Practica

Students experience three different clinical practicum placements in the greater NY area in medical institutions including Departments of Neurology, Psychiatry, Rehabilitation, or Medicine. The predoctoral clinical internships can be completed around the region or anywhere in the United States.

Admissions

Entries appear in the following order: required test or GPA, minimum score (if required)/median score of students entering in 2015–2016.

Program	Degree	GRE-V	GRE-Q	GRE-Writing	GRE-Subject	Undergraduate GPA	Last 2 Years GPA	Psychology GPA	Master's GPA
Clinical Psychology	PhD	156/159	153/160	NA/NA	660/710	3.34/3.8	NA/NA	Not specified	Not specified

Admissions Requirements:

Degree	GRE	GRE-Subject	Letters of Recommendation	Research Statement	Writing Sample	CV	Interview
Doctoral	Required	Recommended	3	Required	Optional	Required	Required

Admissions Criteria:

GRE scores—medium
Research experience—high
Work experience—high
Clinically related public service—medium
GPA—high

Letters of recommendation—high
Interview—high
Statement of goals and objectives—high
Undergraduate psychology preparation—medium

For additional information on admission requirements, visit http://www.gc.cuny.edu/Prospective-Current-Students/Prospective-Students/Admission-Requirements.

Department Demographics

	Male (PT)	Female (PT)	Total	African-American/ Black (PT)	Hispanic/ Latino (PT)	Asian/ Pacific Islander (PT)	American Indian/ Alaska Native (PT)	Caucasian/ White (PT)	Unknown	Multiethnic (PT)	ADA (PT)	Int'l (PT)
Students	8 (0)	38 (0)	46	1 (0)	3 (0)	2 (0)	0 (0)	36 (0)	0 (0)	4 (0)	1 (0)	3 (0)

Financial Information/Assistance

Tuition: For information on tuition costs, visit http://www.gc.cuny.edu/Prospective-Current-Students/Current-Students/Tuition-Fees. Tuition is subject to change. Additional fees are assessed to students beyond the costs of tuition for the following: Student Activity Fee, Student Technology Fee, Student Health Fee.

Doctoral:
State residents: $9,060 per academic year.
Nonstate residents: $875 per credit hour.

Financial Assistance:

	Teaching Assistantship (% Receiving)	Teaching Assistantship Tuition Remission	Research Assistantship (% Receiving)	Research Assistantship Tuition Remission	Fellowship (% Receiving)	Fellowship Tuition Remission
First-Year Student	$8,630 (60)	Full	NA (NA)	NA	$25,000 (40)	Full
Advanced Student	$7,779 (81)	Full	$1,200 (10)	Full	$14,735 (55)	Full

For additional information on financial assistance, visit http://www.gc.cuny.edu/Prospective-Current-Students/Current-Students/Financial-Assistance.

Employment of Department Graduates

Doctoral:
Enrolled in a postdoctoral residency/fellowship: 4
Employed in a hospital/medical center: 1
Total: 5

Additional Information

Housing and Day Care: On-campus housing is available. See the following website for more information: http://queenscollegehousing.com/. On-campus day care facilities are available. See the following website for more information: http://qcpages.qc.cuny.edu/qcchild/.

Information for Students With Physical Disabilities: See the following website: http://www.qc.cuny.edu/StudentLife/services/specialserv.

Special Facilities or Resources: The Program has well equipped research laboratories and clinical facilities for clinical psychology, including individual faculty who focus on human research and faculty who use animal models for their research. The campus runs the Queens College Psychology Clinic, which provides supervised training for students early in their career.

Application Information: Office of Admissions, The Graduate School & University Center of the City University of New York, 365 Fifth Avenue, New York, NY 10016-4309. *Fee:* $125. *Online application:* https://app.applyyourself.com/?id=cunygc.

Columbia University

Department of Counseling and Clinical Psychology
Teachers College
Box 102, 525 West 120th Street
New York, NY 10027-6696
Telephone: (212) 678-8127
Chairperson: Marie L Miville

E-mail: miville@tc.columbia.edu
Web: http://www.tc.edu/ccp

Orientation, Objectives, and Emphasis of Department

This department prepares students to investigate and address the psychological needs of individuals, families, groups, organizations/institutions and communities. Counseling psychology focuses on normal and optimal development across the lifespan, with particular attention to expanding knowledge and skills in occupational choice and transitions, and multicultural and group counseling. Clinical Psychology primarily uses a broad-based psychodynamic perspective to study and treat a variety of psychological and psychoeducational problems. In addition to sharing an interest and appreciation for the critical role of culture in development and adaptation, both programs highly value the teaching of clinical and research skills. Thus, students in this department are trained to become knowledgeable and proficient researchers, to provide psychological and educational leadership, and to be effective practitioners. Specifically, graduates from these programs seek positions in teaching, research, policy, administration, psychotherapy, and counseling.

Programs and Degrees Offered

Program	Degree	Application Deadline	Applications Received	Accepted	New Admits Enrolled (PT)	Total Enrolled (PT)	Degrees Awarded in 2014–2015	Median Years to Complete Degree	Dismissed/ Withdrew
Clinical Psychology	PhD	December 15 (Fall)	370	10	9	36 (16)	9	6.5	0
Applied Psychology	MA/MS	April 15 (Fall)	250	140	98 (20)	144 (38)	82	1.5	2
Counseling Psychology	PhD	December 15 (Fall)	193	5	5	38	4	7	0
Psychological Counseling	MEd	April 15 (Fall)	243	199	(93)	(200)	90	2.2	4

APA Accreditation

Clinical PhD: Student Outcome Data website: http://www.tc.columbia.edu/counseling-and-clinical-psychology/clinical/phd-program/.
Counseling PhD: Student Outcome Data website: http://www.tc.columbia.edu/counseling-and-clinical-psychology/counseling/academics/doctor-of-philosophy/.

Doctoral Degree (PhD Clinical Psychology): For those doctoral students for whom a professional internship was required in this program prior to graduation:
Total students who applied for an internship: 8
Total students who obtained an internship: 7
Total students who obtained a paid internship: 7
Total students who obtained an unpaid internship: 0
Total students who were placed in APA/CPA-accredited internships: 7
Total students placed in internships not APA/CPA-accredited, but listed with the Association of Psychology Postdoctoral and Internship Centers (APPIC): 0
Total students placed in internships conforming to guidelines of the Council of Directors of School Psychology Programs (CDSPP): 0
Total students placed in internships that were not APA/CPA-accredited, APPIC or CDSSP listed: 0

Doctoral Degree (PhD Counseling Psychology): For those doctoral students for whom a professional internship was required in this program prior to graduation:
Total students who applied for an internship: 3
Total students who obtained an internship: 3
Total students who obtained a paid internship: 3
Total students who obtained an unpaid internship: 0
Total students who were placed in APA/CPA-accredited internships: 2

Total students placed in internships not APA/CPA-accredited, but listed with the Association of Psychology Postdoctoral and Internship Centers (APPIC): 1
Total students placed in internships conforming to guidelines of the Council of Directors of School Psychology Programs (CDSPP): 0
Total students placed in internships that were not APA/CPA-accredited, APPIC or CDSSP listed: 0

Master's Degree (MA/MS Applied Psychology): An internship experience, such as a final research project or "capstone" experience is required of graduates.

Internships/Practica
Master's students in the Department of Counseling and Clinical Psychology complete fieldwork appropriate to their track or area of interest in a variety of settings including schools, hospitals, diverse mental health clinics, and rehabilitation centers. Doctoral students do externships in settings similar to the ones indicated above, in preparation for their required APA-approved internships. In addition, all PhD students as well as the MEd students engage in practicum experiences at the Center for Educational and Psychological Services at the College. The Center is a community resource that provides low-cost services for the public utilizing graduate students from several departments within the College. All students receive supervision provided by full-time and adjunct faculty. PhD students in the clinical and counseling programs complete a 1-year (or equivalent) full-time internship.

Admissions
Entries appear in the following order: required test or GPA, minimum score (if required)/median score of students entering in 2015–2016.

Program	Degree	GRE-V	GRE-Q	GRE-Writing	GRE-Subject	Under-graduate GPA	Last 2 Years GPA	Psychol-ogy GPA	Master's GPA
Clinical Psychology	PhD	NA/NA	NA/NA	NA/NA	NA/NA	NA/NA	NA/NA	NA/NA	Not specified
Applied Psychology	MA/MS	NA/NA	NA/NA	NA/NA	Not specified	2.5/3.4	Not specified	Not specified	Not specified
Counseling Psychology	PhD	Not specified	Not specified	Not specified	Not specified	Not specified	Not specified	Not specified	Not specified
Psychological Counseling	MEd	Not specified	Not specified	Not specified	Not specified	Not specified	Not specified	Not specified	Not specified

Admissions Requirements:

Degree	GRE	GRE-Subject	Letters of Recommendation	Research Statement	Writing Sample	CV	Interview
Master's/Specialist	Optional	None	2	Required	Optional	Required	Recommended
Doctoral	Required	Optional	2	Required	Required	Required	Required

Please note if these criteria vary for different programs: Only Counseling PhD requires a writing sample.

Admissions Criteria:
GRE scores—high
Research experience—high
Work experience—high
Clinically related public service—medium
GPA—medium

Letters of recommendation—high
Interview—high
Statement of goals and objectives—medium
Undergraduate psychology preparation—medium

For additional information on admission requirements, visit http://www.tc.columbia.edu/admissions/areas-of-study/psychology/.

Department Demographics

	Male (PT)	Female (PT)	Total	African-American/ Black (PT)	Hispanic/ Latino (PT)	Asian/ Pacific Islander (PT)	American Indian/ Alaska Native (PT)	Caucasian/ White (PT)	Unknown	Multiethnic (PT)	ADA (PT)	Int'l (PT)
Students	89 (50)	200 (102)	441	21 (10)	17 (6)	33 (4)	1 (0)	199 (118)	0 (0)	14 (2)	3 (0)	3 (0)

Financial Information/Assistance

Tuition: For information on tuition costs, visit http://www.tc.columbia.edu/admissions/tuition-and-fees/. Tuition is subject to change.

Doctoral:
State residents: $1,454 per credit hour.
Nonstate residents: $1,454 per credit hour.

Master's:
State residents: $1,454 per credit hour.
Nonstate residents: $1,454 per credit hour.

Financial Assistance:

	Teaching Assistantship (% Receiving)	Teaching Assistantship Tuition Remission	Research Assistantship (% Receiving)	Research Assistantship Tuition Remission	Fellowship (% Receiving)	Fellowship Tuition Remission
First-Year Student	NA (NA)	NA	$20,000 (NA)	Partial	$20,000 (NA)	Partial
Advanced Student	$1,600 (NA)	NA	$20,000 (NA)	Partial	$20,000 (NA)	Partial

For additional information on financial assistance, visit http://www.tc.columbia.edu/financialaid/.

Employment of Department Graduates

Doctoral:
Enrolled in a postdoctoral residency/fellowship: 8
Employed in independent practice: 7
Employed in an academic position at a university: 4
Employed in academic position at a 2-year/4-year college: 4
Employed in other positions at a higher education institution: 2
Employed in a professional position in a school system: 3
Employed in business or industry: 2
Employed in government agency: 1
Employed in a community mental health/counseling center: 2
Employed in a hospital/medical center: 4
Still seeking employment: 1
Total: 38

Additional Information

Housing and Day Care: On-campus housing is available. See the following website for more information: http://www.tc.columbia.edu/housing/. On-campus day care facilities are available. See the following website for more information: http://www.tc.columbia.edu/centers/hollingworth/index.asp; http://www.tc.edu/ritagold/.

Information for Students With Physical Disabilities: See the following website: http://www.tc.columbia.edu/oasid/.

Special Facilities or Resources: The College provides academic/research support in several ways. Students of the College have access to all the libraries of Columbia University. Of particular interest in addition to the Milbank Memorial Library here at Teachers College, are the Psychology Library on the main Columbia campus and the library at the School of Social Work. Technology has transformed most libraries to computer-oriented environments with immediate access to information. The Library not only provides the access but instruction to students so they may avail themselves of the new technology. The ERIC system as well as Inter-Library Loan are also available.

Application Information: Teachers College, Office of Admission, Thorndike Hall, 3rd Floor, 525 West 120th Street, New York, NY 10027-6696. *Fee:* $65. *Online application:* https://apply.tc.edu/apply/.

Columbia University

Health and Behavior Studies/School Psychology
Teachers College
525 West 120th Street, Box 120
New York, NY 10027
Telephone: (212) 678-3942
Chairperson: Stephen Peverly

E-mail: brassard@tc.edu
Web: http://www.tc.columbia.edu/hbs/schoolpsych/

Orientation, Objectives, and Emphasis of Department

The Applied Educational Psychology: School Psychology Program at Teachers College, Columbia University offers doctoral (PhD) and master of education (MEd) degrees with a focus on the application of psychological science to the promotion of learning and mental health in schools and other educational and mental health contexts. We also offer a BCBA certificate that adds 9 credits to the MEd program and extra supervised hours in a ABA school. Our goal is to train beginning-level masters school psychologists to work in schools and doctoral-level school psychologists to work in schools, universities, research centers, hospitals, testing companies, and clinics that serve the educational and mental health needs of children, youth, and their families. Theory and practice are integrated throughout training and all students are engaged in closely supervised practice from the beginning of the program. Under the supervision of faculty, PhD students apprentice in teaching (modules for assessment courses) and supervision of first-year students with practicum clients at the Dean Hope Center. Doctoral students also take on leadership roles in research labs, admissions, faculty searches, and in mentoring younger PhD students.

Programs and Degrees Offered

Program	Degree	Application Deadline	Applica-tions Received	Accepted	New Admits Enrolled (PT)	Total Enrolled (PT)	Degrees Awarded in 2014–2015	Median Years to Complete Degree	Dismissed/ Withdrew
School Psychology	PhD	December 15 (Fall)	68	5	4 (0)	18	3	4.6	0
School Psychology	MEd	December 15 (Fall), Rolling	78	34	20 (0)	59 (0)	18	3	1

APA Accreditation

School PhD: Student Outcome Data website: http://www.tc.columbia.edu/health-and-behavior-studies/school-psychology/resourses/student-admissions-outcomes-and-other-data/.

Doctoral Degree (PhD School Psychology): For those doctoral students for whom a professional internship was required in this program prior to graduation:
Total students who applied for an internship: 4
Total students who obtained an internship: 4
Total students who obtained a paid internship: 4
Total students who obtained an unpaid internship: 0
Total students who were placed in APA/CPA-accredited internships: 4
Total students placed in internships not APA/CPA-accredited, but listed with the Association of Psychology Postdoctoral and Internship Centers (APPIC): 0
Total students placed in internships conforming to guidelines of the Council of Directors of School Psychology Programs (CDSPP): 0
Total students placed in internships that were not APA/CPA-accredited, APPIC or CDSSP listed: 0

Internships/Practica

The first year involves two practica in our Dean Hope Center for Educational and Psychological Services: (1) Practicum in Assessment of Reading and School Subject Difficulties (Fall); (2) Practicum in Psychoeducational Assessment with Culturally Diverse Students (Spring). Second-year students engage in fieldwork (2 days/week over the academic year in one of our cooperating inner-city schools) and a practicum in psychoeducational groups (the groups are run within students' fieldwork sites). In the third year, MEd students do a yearlong internship in the schools while PhD students have externship (2 days/week over an academic year; most students are required to do 2 externships: one in a school and one in a hospital or clinic). PhD students do their internship in the fifth year (full calendar year; students must have an approved dissertation proposal before they begin to do the internship after completing most or all of their dissertation). All students enter the APPIC match to obtain an internship.

Admissions

Entries appear in the following order: required test or GPA, minimum score (if required)/median score of students entering in 2015–2016.

Program	Degree	GRE-V	GRE-Q	GRE-Writing	GRE-Subject	Under-graduate GPA	Last 2 Years GPA	Psychol-ogy GPA	Master's GPA
School Psychology	PhD	155/160	150/155	4/4.5	Not specified	3.32/3.68	Not specified	Not specified	NA/NA
School Psychology	MEd	144/153	143/152	3/4	Not specified	2.7/3.47	Not specified	Not specified	Not specified

Admissions Requirements:

Degree	GRE	GRE-Subject	Letters of Recom-mendation	Research Statement	Writing Sample	CV	Interview
Master's/Specialist	Required	None	2	Required	Required	Required	Optional
Doctoral	Required	None	2	Required	Required	Required	Optional

Please note if these criteria vary for different programs: Research is important for the PhD, not the EdM.

Admissions Criteria:

GRE scores—high
Research experience—high
Work experience—low
Clinically related public service—low
GPA—high

Letters of recommendation—high
Interview—high
Statement of goals and objectives—high
Undergraduate psychology preparation—medium

Department Demographics

	Male (PT)	Female (PT)	Total	African-American/ Black (PT)	Hispanic/ Latino (PT)	Asian/ Pacific Islander (PT)	American Indian/ Alaska Native (PT)	Caucasian/ White (PT)	Unknown	Multiethnic (PT)	ADA (PT)	Int'l (PT)
Students	6 (0)	71 (0)	77	4 (0)	4 (0)	12 (0)	0 (0)	57 (0)	0 (0)	0 (0)	0 (0)	7 (0)

Financial Information/Assistance

Tuition: For information on tuition costs, visit http://www.tc.columbia.edu/admissions/tuition-and-fees/. Additional fees are assessed to students beyond the costs of tuition for the following: college fee, medical fee, research fee.

Doctoral:
State residents: $1,454 per credit hour.
Nonstate residents: $1,454 per credit hour.

Master's:
State residents: $1,454 per credit hour.
Nonstate residents: $1,454 per credit hour.

Financial Assistance:

	Teaching Assistantship (% Receiving)	Teaching Assistantship Tuition Remission	Research Assistantship (% Receiving)	Research Assistantship Tuition Remission	Fellowship (% Receiving)	Fellowship Tuition Remission
First-Year Student	NA (NA)	NA	NA (NA)	NA	$25,000 (100)	Partial
Advanced Student	$14,400 (100)	Partial	NA (NA)	NA	NA (NA)	Partial

For additional information on financial assistance, visit http://www.tc.columbia.edu/financialaid.

Employment of Department Graduates

Master's:
Enrolled in a psychology doctoral program: 2
Employed in a professional position in a school system: 17
Employed in a community mental health/counseling center: 1
Total: 20

Doctoral:
Enrolled in a postdoctoral residency/fellowship: 1
Employed in a professional position in a school system: 3
Total: 4

Additional Information

Housing and Day Care: On-campus housing is available. See the following website for more information: http://www.tc.columbia.edu/housing/. On-campus day care facilities are available. See the following website for more information: htp://www.tc.columbia.edu/centers/ritagold/.

Information for Students With Physical Disabilities: See the following website: http://www.tc.columbia.edu/oasid/.

Special Facilities or Resources: The School Psychology program has a state-of-the-art clinic and test library with a large student room for first-year school psychology students, strong collaborative relationships with seven inner-city schools that serve as fieldwork (practicum) sites for our master's and doctoral students in the second year, and the program participates in the NYC metro-wide externship network for third-year (and sometimes fifth-year) doctoral students.

Application Information: Office of Admissions, Box 302, Teachers College, Columbia University, 525 West 120th Street, New York, NY 10027. *Fee:* $65. *Online application:* https://apply.tc.edu/apply/.

Cornell University
Department of Human Development
The New York State College of Human Ecology
G77 Martha Van Rensselaer Hall
Ithaca, NY 14853-4401
Telephone: (607) 255-7620
Chairperson: Charles Brainerd

E-mail: blb5@cornell.edu
Web: http://www.human.cornell.edu/hd/index.cfm

Orientation, Objectives, and Emphasis of Department
The graduate program trains researchers and prepares students for research and teaching careers in academic life, work in government agencies, and careers as researchers on projects carried out in a variety of public and private sector settings. We offer training in six broad categories: Aging and Health; Cognitive Development; Group Disparities in Development; Human Neuroscience; Law, Psychology, and Human Development; and Social and Personality Development. We do not offer training in counseling psychology, marriage counseling, or family therapy. The doctoral program in Human Development has 37 faculty; 25 are members of the Department of Human Development and 12 have primary appointments in the departments of Psychology, Design and Environmental Analysis, Policy Analysis and Management, the Law school, or in the Weill Cornell Medical College. The faculty includes 25 psychologists and two sociologists. There are approximately 40 graduate students in the program.

Programs and Degrees Offered

Program	Degree	Application Deadline	Applica-tions Received	Accepted	New Admits Enrolled (PT)	Total Enrolled (PT)	Degrees Awarded in 2014–2015	Median Years to Complete Degree	Dismissed/ Withdrew
Developmental Psychology	PhD	December 1 (Fall)	46	7	3 (0)	37 (0)	7	5.5	0
Human Development and Family Studies	PhD	December 1 (Fall)	23	4	1 (0)	2 (0)	1	6	0

Admissions

Entries appear in the following order: required test or GPA, minimum score (if required)/median score of students entering in 2015–2016.

Program	Degree	GRE-V	GRE-Q	GRE-Writing	GRE-Subject	Under-graduate GPA	Last 2 Years GPA	Psychology GPA	Master's GPA
Developmental Psychology	PhD	162/164	157/163	Not specified	Not specified	Not specified	Not specified	Not specified	Not specified
Human Development and Family Studies	PhD	162/164	157/163	Not specified	Not specified	Not specified	Not specified	Not specified	Not specified

Admissions Requirements:

Degree	GRE	GRE-Subject	Letters of Recommendation	Research Statement	Writing Sample	CV	Interview
Doctoral	Required	Optional	3	Required	Required	Optional	Required

Admissions Criteria:

GRE scores—high
Research experience—high
Work experience—low
Clinically related public service—low
GPA—high

Letters of recommendation—high
Interview—medium
Statement of goals and objectives—high
Undergraduate psychology preparation—low

For additional information on admission requirements, visit http://www.human.cornell.edu/hd/graduate/admissions-funding.cfm.

Department Demographics

	Male (PT)	Female (PT)	Total	African-American/ Black (PT)	Hispanic/ Latino (PT)	Asian/ Pacific Islander (PT)	American Indian/ Alaska Native (PT)	Caucasian/ White (PT)	Unknown	Multiethnic (PT)	ADA (PT)	Int'l (PT)
Students	9 (0)	30 (0)	39	2 (0)	2 (0)	1 (0)	(0)	33 (0)	0 (0)	1 (0)	0 (0)	12 (0)

Financial Information/Assistance

Tuition: For information on tuition costs, visit http://gradschool.cornell.edu/tuition. Tuition is subject to change.

Doctoral:
State residents: $20,800 per academic year.
Nonstate residents: $20,800 per academic year.

Financial Assistance:

	Teaching Assistantship (% Receiving)	Teaching Assistantship Tuition Remission	Research Assistantship (% Receiving)	Research Assistantship Tuition Remission	Fellowship (% Receiving)	Fellowship Tuition Remission
First-Year Student	$24,658 (NA)	Full	$24,658 (NA)	Full	$24,658 (NA)	Full
Advanced Student	$24,658 (NA)	Full	$24,658 (NA)	Full	$24,658 (NA)	Full

For additional information on financial assistance, visit http://gradschool.cornell.edu/costs-and-funding/.

Employment of Department Graduates

Doctoral:
Enrolled in a postdoctoral residency/fellowship: 2
Employed in an academic position at a university: 1
Employed in a professional position in a school system: 1
Employed in business or industry: 1
Do not know: 2
Total: 7

Additional Information

Housing and Day Care: On-campus housing is available. See the following website for more information: http://living.sas.cornell.edu/live/wheretolive/gradhousing/. On-campus day care facilities are available. See the following website for more information: https://www.hr.cornell.edu/life/support/child_care_center.html.

Information for Students With Physical Disabilities: See the following website: http://sds.cornell.edu/.

Special Facilities or Resources: The department houses a number of laboratories dedicated to individual projects as well as several non-dedicated laboratories and research rooms, including rooms with audio and visual recording capability. Dedicated space within the department also houses fMRI facilities and a psychophysiology laboratory. There are numerous opportunities for research collaboration with area schools, day care centers, after school programs, youth agencies, and senior housing and other centers. Several faculty in the department also have appointments and affiliations with the Bronfenbrenner Center for Translational Research, the Cornell Edward R. Roybal Center for Translational Research on Aging, Weill Cornell Medical College in New York City, the Cornell Population Program, and the Center for the Study of Inequality. The department also maintains graduate student computer facilities with statistical software and experimental management programs such as E-prime. A comprehensive, continually updated set of statistical analysis programs are available to all graduate students through the Cornell Institute for Social and Economic Research. Free data management and analysis support is provided by the Cornell Statistical Consulting Unit.

Application Information: *Fee:* $85. *Online application:* https://www.applyweb.com/cgi-bin/app?s=cornellg.

Cornell University

Graduate Field of Psychology
Arts & Sciences
211 Uris Hall
Ithaca, NY 14853-7601
Telephone: (607) 255-3834
Director of Graduate Studies: David J. Field

E-mail: pac34@cornell.edu
Web: http://www.psych.cornell.edu/

Orientation, Objectives, and Emphasis of Department

The Psychology Department of the College of Arts and Sciences at Cornell has a faculty of 25 psychologists and is divided into three areas—perception, cognition and development (encompassing cognition, language, perception, and its developmental perspectives), behavioral and evolutionary neuroscience (focusing on hormones and behavior, neural development, and sensory systems), and social and personality psychology (social cognition, judgment, and decision making). We do not have clinical, community, or counseling programs. We have a strong research orientation, training our students to become professional academics or researchers. Our 39 students design their graduate programs under the supervision of their special committees. These committees consist of at least four members of the graduate faculty at Cornell; at least three are from within the department. The chair of the committee is a member of the Graduate Field of Psychology, which consists of the 26 members of our department plus 20 researchers in allied fields (human development, education, industrial and labor relations, and neurobiology and behavior). Two other committee members serve as minor members, one of whom can be outside the Graduate Field of Psychology, and the fourth member oversees breadth requirements.

Programs and Degrees Offered

Program	Degree	Application Deadline	Applications Received	Accepted	New Admits Enrolled (PT)	Total Enrolled (PT)	Degrees Awarded in 2014–2015	Median Years to Complete Degree	Dismissed/Withdrew
Behavioral and Evolutionary Neuroscience	PhD	December 1 (Fall)	29	4	2	13 (0)	3	6	0

Programs and Degrees Offered (con't.)

Program	Degree	Application Deadline	Applications Received	Accepted	New Admits Enrolled (PT)	Total Enrolled (PT)	Degrees Awarded in 2014–2015	Median Years to Complete Degree	Dismissed/ Withdrew
Perception, Cognition and Development	PhD	December 1 (Fall)	47	2	2	17 (0)	3	5	0
Social and Personality Psychology	PhD	December 1 (Fall)	106	2	2	10 (0)	2	5	0

Admissions

Entries appear in the following order: required test or GPA, minimum score (if required)/median score of students entering in 2015–2016.

Program	Degree	GRE-V	GRE-Q	GRE-Writing	GRE-Subject	Under-graduate GPA	Last 2 Years GPA	Psychology GPA	Master's GPA
Behavioral and Evolutionary Neuroscience	PhD	Not specified	Not specified	Not specified	Not specified	Not specified	Not specified	Not specified	Not specified
Perception, Cognition and Development	PhD	Not specified	Not specified	Not specified	Not specified	Not specified	Not specified	Not specified	Not specified
Social and Personality Psychology	PhD	Not specified	Not specified	Not specified	Not specified	Not specified	Not specified	Not specified	Not specified

Admissions Requirements:

Degree	GRE	GRE-Subject	Letters of Recom-mendation	Research Statement	Writing Sample	CV	Interview
Doctoral	Required	Required	3	Required	Optional	Optional	None

Admissions Criteria:

GRE scores—high
Research experience—high
Work experience—low

GPA—high
Letters of recommendation—high
Statement of goals and objectives—high

For additional information on admission requirements, visit http://www.psych.cornell.edu/graduate/.

Department Demographics

	Male (PT)	Female (PT)	Total	African-American/ Black (PT)	Hispanic/ Latino (PT)	Asian/ Pacific Islander (PT)	American Indian/ Alaska Native (PT)	Caucasian/ White (PT)	Unknown (PT)	Multiethnic (PT)	ADA (PT)	Int'l (PT)
Students	18 (0)	22 (0)	40	1 (0)	3 (0)	11 (0)	0 (0)	25 (0)	0 (0)	0 (0)	0 (0)	14 (0)

Financial Information/Assistance

Tuition: For information on tuition costs, visit http://gradschool.cornell.edu/costs-and-funding/tuition-and-costs. Tuition is subject to change.

Doctoral:
State residents: $29,500 per academic year.
Nonstate residents: $29,500 per academic year.

Financial Assistance:

	Teaching Assistantship (% Receiving)	Teaching Assistantship Tuition Remission	Research Assistantship (% Receiving)	Research Assistantship Tuition Remission	Fellowship (% Receiving)	Fellowship Tuition Remission
First-Year Student	$25,152 (NA)	NA	NA (NA)	NA	$25,152 (NA)	NA
Advanced Student	$25,152 (NA)	NA	NA (NA)	NA	$25,152 (NA)	NA

For additional information on financial assistance, visit http://www.gradschool.cornell.edu/costs-and-funding.

Employment of Department Graduates

No information provided.

Additional Information

Housing and Day Care: On-campus housing is available. See the following website for more information: http://living.sas.cornell.edu/live/. On-campus day care facilities are available. See the following website for more information: https://www.hr.cornell.edu/life/support/child_care_center.html.

Information for Students With Physical Disabilities: See the following website: http://sds.cornell.edu/.

Special Facilities or Resources: The three areas of our program each have laboratories associated with them. Each of the members of the perception, cognition and development program has a separate laboratory, fully equipped with state-of-the-art computer equipment. In addition, the program has several computer-based teaching laboratories. The Behavioral Evolutionary Neuroscience (B.E.N.) group each has separate labs and computers, and animal housing facilities where relevant, but they share much of their equipment and lab space. There is also a teaching lab associated with B.E.N.'s group labs. The social and personality psychologists all have their own individual labs, with state-of-the-art computer equipment, and ample space for a full range of behavioral experiments. Also available are a set of cubicles with networked computers, observation rooms with one-way mirrors, video observation cameras and recorders, and fully equipped ERP lab.

Application Information: Fee: $85. *Online application:* https://www.applyweb.com/cgi-bin/app?s=cornellg.

Fordham University (2015 data)

Department of Psychology
Arts and Sciences
441 East Fordham Road
Bronx, NY 10458
Telephone: (718) 817-3775
Chairperson: Barry Rosenfeld

E-mail: rosenfeld@fordham.edu
Web: http://www.fordham.edu/psychology/

Orientation, Objectives, and Emphasis of Department

Clinical psychology prepares students for practice, research, and teaching in the clinical field as both professionals and scientists. Courses can be grouped under four major areas: clinical theory and methodology, research topics and methods, behavioral classification and assessment, and treatment approaches. Specializations include Family and Child, Health/Neuropsychology, and Forensics. Applied Developmental Psychology (ADP) trains professionals who can conduct both basic and applied research in developmental processes across the lifespan and who can share their knowledge in academic and community-based settings. ADP focuses on the interplay between developmental processes and social contexts including design and evaluation of programs; consultation to public policy makers; development and evaluation of programs and materials directed at children and families; and parent/family education. The Psychometrics and Quantitative Psychology program focuses on the quantitative and research-oriented commonalities relevant to most of the behavioral sciences and their applications in industry, education, and the health services. Students become familiar with statistics, psychological testing, computer systems, and other research techniques as well as with the psychology of individual differences. The MS in Applied Psychological Methods provides training in research, psychometrics, data mining, and program evaluation to foster research and evaluation skills in individuals working in corporate and non-profit settings.

Programs and Degrees Offered

Program	Degree	Application Deadline	Applica-tions Received	Accepted	New Admits Enrolled (PT)	Total Enrolled (PT)	Degrees Awarded in 2014–2015	Median Years to Complete Degree	Dismissed/ Withdrew
Clinical Psychology	PhD	December 1 (Fall)	630	9	9 (0)	65 (0)	9	6	0
Psychometrics and Quantitative Psychology	PhD	December 1 (Fall)	27	7	2 (0)	15 (0)	2	4.7	0
Applied Developmental Psychology	PhD	December 1 (Fall)	32	6	2 (0)	25	4	4.7	2
Applied Psychological Methods	MA/MS	Rolling	34	18	1 (3)	1 (7)	2	2	0
Clinical Research Methods	MA/MS	(Fall), (Spring), (Summer), Rolling	0	8	5	5	0		0

APA Accreditation
Clinical PhD (Doctor of Philosophy).

Doctoral Degree (PhD Clinical Psychology): For those doctoral students for whom a professional internship was required in this program prior to graduation:
Total students who applied for an internship: 11
Total students who obtained an internship: 10
Total students who obtained a paid internship: 10
Total students who obtained an unpaid internship: 0
Total students who were placed in APA/CPA-accredited internships: 10
Total students placed in internships not APA/CPA-accredited, but listed with the Association of Psychology Postdoctoral and Internship Centers (APPIC): 0
Total students placed in internships conforming to guidelines of the Council of Directors of School Psychology Programs (CDSPP): 0
Total students placed in internships that were not APA/CPA-accredited, APPIC or CDSSP listed: 0

Master's Degree (MA/MS Applied Psychological Methods): An internship experience, such as a final research project or "capstone" experience is required of graduates. Master's Degree (MA/MS Clinical Research Methods): An internship experience, such as a final research project or "capstone" experience is required of graduates.

Internships/Practica
Internships in a variety of public and private facilities are available for students during and after coursework. Clinical requires an internship after the dissertation has been proposed. All four programs offer multiple one-semester externships in relevant settings.

Admissions
Entries appear in the following order: required test or GPA, minimum score (if required)/median score of students entering in 2015–2016.

Program	Degree	GRE-V	GRE-Q	GRE-Writing	GRE-Subject	Under-graduate GPA	Last 2 Years GPA	Psychol-ogy GPA	Master's GPA
Clinical Psychology	PhD	151/161	148/154	3/5	Not specified	3.1/3.75	Not specified	Not specified	Not specified

Admissions *(con't.)*

Program	Degree	GRE-V	GRE-Q	GRE-Writing	GRE-Subject	Under-graduate GPA	Last 2 Years GPA	Psychol-ogy GPA	Master's GPA
Psychometrics and Quantitative Psychology	PhD	142/158	155/164	3/4	Not specified	3.28/3.28	Not specified	Not specified	Not specified
Applied Developmental Psychology	PhD	147/160	146/156	4/4.5	Not specified	3.6/3.88	Not specified	Not specified	Not specified
Applied Psychological Methods	MA/MS	Not specified	Not specified	Not specified	Not specified	Not specified	Not specified	Not specified	Not specified
Clinical Research Methods	MA/MS	Not specified	Not specified	Not specified	Not specified	Not specified	Not specified	Not specified	Not specified

Admissions Requirements:

Degree	GRE	GRE-Subject	Letters of Recom-mendation	Research Statement	Writing Sample	CV	Interview
Master's/Specialist	Required	Recom-mended	3	Required	Required	Required	Required
Doctoral	Required	Recom-mended	3	Required	Required	Required	Required

Admissions Criteria:

GRE scores—high
Research experience—high
Work experience—high
Clinically related public service—medium
GPA—high

Letters of recommendation—high
Interview—high
Statement of goals and objectives—high
Undergraduate psychology preparation—high

Department Demographics

	Male (PT)	Female (PT)	Total	African-American/ Black (PT)	Hispanic/ Latino (PT)	Asian/ Pacific Islander (PT)	American Indian/ Alaska Native (PT)	Caucasian/ White (PT)	Unknown	Multiethnic (PT)	ADA (PT)	Int'l (PT)
Students	15 (4)	95 (3)	117	5 (0)	10 (0)	12 (4)	0 (0)	83 (3)	0 (0)	0 (0)	0 (0)	3 (2)

Financial Information/Assistance

Tuition: Tuition is subject to change.

Doctoral:
State residents: $1,320 per credit hour.
Nonstate residents: $1,320 per credit hour.

Master's:
State residents: $1,320 per credit hour.
Nonstate residents: $1,320 per credit hour.

Financial Assistance:

	Teaching Assistantship (% Receiving)	Teaching Assistantship Tuition Remission	Research Assistantship (% Receiving)	Research Assistantship Tuition Remission	Fellowship (% Receiving)	Fellowship Tuition Remission
First-Year Student	$21,800 (75)	Full	$21,800 (20)	Full	$24,000 (5)	Full
Advanced Student	$23,200 (70)	Full	$23,200 (20)	Full	$27,100 (10)	Full

Employment of Department Graduates

Doctoral:
Enrolled in a postdoctoral residency/fellowship: 3
Enrolled in another graduate/professional program: 0
Employed in an academic position at a university: 1
Employed in academic position at a 2-year/4-year college: 1
Employed in business or industry: 1
Employed in government agency: 1
Employed in a community mental health/counseling center: 4
Other employment position: 3
Total: 14

Additional Information

Housing and Day Care: No on-campus housing is available. No on-campus day care facilities are available.

Information for Students With Physical Disabilities: See the following website: http://www.fordham.edu/info/20174/disability_services.

Special Facilities or Resources: The Clinical program takes advantage of a wide array of training sites and research sites in the New York City area (Bellevue, Sloan Kettering, Mt. Sinai, AECOM, etc.). The program also has its own clinical research site. Applied Developmental students and faculty conduct research and program evaluation with local schools and hospitals; the program is also a member of a coalition of community service groups in the Northwest Bronx. A Bronx Community Center for Engaged Research has been developed to foster these activities. Psychometric students and faculty work closely with ETS and the College Board and also hospitals (Sloan Kettering, Mt. Sinai, etc.) around measurement issues. The new MS in Applied Psychological Methods draws upon these same resources for the development of one-semester capstone internships.

Application Information: Fordham University, Graduate Admissions Office, Keating 216, 441 East Fordham Rd, Bronx, NY 10458. *Fee:* $70. *Online application:* https://gradadmissions.fordham.edu/apply/.

Fordham University
Division of Psychological and Educational Services
Graduate School of Education
113 West 60th Street, Room 1008
New York, NY 10023
Telephone: (212) 636-6460
Chairperson: Anthony Cancelli

E-mail: cancelli@fordham.edu
Web: http://www.fordham.edu/gse

Orientation, Objectives, and Emphasis of Department
Prepares professionals for positions in PreK–12 schools; mental health settings; and counseling services in higher education, adult education, business, industry, and independent psychological practice. Also provides advanced training for teachers and individuals interested in research or the development and evaluation of educational programs and materials.

Programs and Degrees Offered

Program	Degree	Application Deadline	Applications Received	Accepted	New Admits Enrolled (PT)	Total Enrolled (PT)	Degrees Awarded in 2014–2015	Median Years to Complete Degree	Dismissed/ Withdrew
Counseling Psychology	PhD	December 15 (Fall)	130	21	12 (0)	26 (29)	10	6.25	0
School Psychology	PhD	January 15 (Fall)	80	37	8 (3)	26 (50)	13	7.5	0
School Psychology Diploma	Other	January 15 (Fall)	32	28	6 (3)	20 (18)	14	3	0
Bilingual School Psychology Diploma	Other	January 15 (Fall)	17	16	6 (3)	11 (6)	3	3	0
School Counseling	MEd	February 1 (Fall)	60	45	7 (0)	13 (8)	7	2	0
Mental Health Counseling	MEd	February 1 (Fall)	135	87	15 (3)	48 (11)	31	2	0

APA Accreditation

Counseling PhD: Student Outcome Data website: http://www.fordham.edu/info/21017/counseling_and_counseling_psychology/2911/counseling_psychology_phd.

School PhD: Student Outcome Data website: http://www.fordham.edu/info/21019/school_psychology/2958/school_psychology_phd.

Doctoral Degree (PhD Counseling Psychology): For those doctoral students for whom a professional internship was required in this program prior to graduation:

Total students who applied for an internship: 9
Total students who obtained an internship: 9
Total students who obtained a paid internship: 9
Total students who obtained an unpaid internship: 0
Total students who were placed in APA/CPA-accredited internships: 9
Total students placed in internships not APA/CPA-accredited, but listed with the Association of Psychology Postdoctoral and Internship Centers (APPIC): 0
Total students placed in internships conforming to guidelines of the Council of Directors of School Psychology Programs (CDSPP): 0
Total students placed in internships that were not APA/CPA-accredited, APPIC or CDSSP listed: 0

Doctoral Degree (PhD School Psychology): For those doctoral students for whom a professional internship was required in this program prior to graduation:

Total students who applied for an internship: 11
Total students who obtained an internship: 11
Total students who obtained a paid internship: 3
Total students who obtained an unpaid internship: 8
Total students who were placed in APA/CPA-accredited internships: 0
Total students placed in internships not APA/CPA-accredited, but listed with the Association of Psychology Postdoctoral and Internship Centers (APPIC): 1
Total students placed in internships conforming to guidelines of the Council of Directors of School Psychology Programs (CDSPP): 10
Total students placed in internships that were not APA/CPA-accredited, APPIC or CDSSP listed: 0

Internships/Practica

Students complete practica, field experiences, externships, and internships in a wide variety of sites throughout the metropolitan NYC area. Sites such as P–12 schools, hospitals, mental health agencies and clinics, and college counseling centers all vary by setting, type, and diversity of the population served.

Admissions

Entries appear in the following order: required test or GPA, minimum score (if required)/median score of students entering in 2015–2016.

Program	Degree	GRE-V	GRE-Q	GRE-Writing	GRE-Subject	Under-graduate GPA	Last 2 Years GPA	Psychol-ogy GPA	Master's GPA
Counseling Psychology	PhD	NA/159	NA/160	Not specified	Not specified	NA/3.64	Not specified	Not specified	Not specified
School Psychology	PhD	145/158	141/155	4/5	Not specified	3.2/3.53	Not specified	Not specified	Not specified
School Psychology Diploma	Other	Not specified	Not specified	Not specified	Not specified	Not specified	Not specified	Not specified	Not specified
Bilingual School Psychology Diploma	Other	Not specified	Not specified	Not specified	Not specified	Not specified	Not specified	Not specified	Not specified
School Counseling	MEd	Not specified	Not specified	Not specified	Not specified	Not specified	Not specified	Not specified	Not specified
Mental Health Counseling	MEd	Not specified	Not specified	Not specified	Not specified	Not specified	Not specified	Not specified	Not specified

Admissions Requirements:

Degree	GRE	GRE-Subject	Letters of Recommendation	Research Statement	Writing Sample	CV	Interview
Master's/Specialist	None	None	2	Required	None	Required	Optional
Doctoral	Required	Required	2	Required	Optional	Required	Required

Admissions Criteria:

GRE scores—medium
Research experience—medium
Work experience—medium
Clinically related public service—medium
GPA—high

Letters of recommendation—high
Interview—medium
Statement of goals and objectives—high
Undergraduate psychology preparation—medium

For additional information on admission requirements, visit http://www.fordham.edu/info/21025/application_process/2966/how_to_apply.

Department Demographics

	Male (PT)	Female (PT)	Total	African-American/Black (PT)	Hispanic/Latino (PT)	Asian/Pacific Islander (PT)	American Indian/Alaska Native (PT)	Caucasian/White (PT)	Unknown	Multiethnic (PT)	ADA (PT)	Int'l (PT)
Students	16 (21)	128 (101)	266	16 (14)	14 (13)	23 (15)	2 (1)	89 (79)	0 (0)	0 (0)	0 (0)	17 (8)

Financial Information/Assistance

Tuition: For information on tuition costs, visit http://www.fordham.edu/info/21259/tuition_and_fees/5702/graduate_school_of_education. Tuition is subject to change. Additional fees are assessed to students beyond the costs of tuition for the following: Insurance, Technology Fees.

Doctoral:
State residents: $1,302 per credit hour.
Nonstate residents: $1,302 per credit hour.

Master's:
State residents: $1,302 per credit hour.
Nonstate residents: $1,302 per credit hour.

Financial Assistance:

	Teaching Assistantship (% Receiving)	Teaching Assistantship Tuition Remission	Research Assistantship (% Receiving)	Research Assistantship Tuition Remission	Fellowship (% Receiving)	Fellowship Tuition Remission
First-Year Student	NA (NA)	NA	NA (NA)	Partial	NA (NA)	Partial
Advanced Student	NA (NA)	NA	NA (NA)	Partial	NA (NA)	Partial

For additional information on financial assistance, visit http://www.fordham.edu/info/21026/tuition_and_financial_assistance.

Employment of Department Graduates

Master's:
Employed in a professional position in a school system: 5
Employed in a community mental health/counseling center: 6
Do not know: 44
Total: 55

Doctoral:
Enrolled in a postdoctoral residency/fellowship: 5
Employed in other positions at a higher education institution: 1
Do not know: 17
Total: 23

Additional Information

Housing and Day Care: No on-campus housing is available. No on-campus day care facilities are available.

Information for Students With Physical Disabilities: See the following website: http://www.fordham.edu/info/20174/disability_services.

Special Facilities or Resources: Fordham University's Graduate School of Education offers several higher learning and community-based centers and institutes: The Center for Educational Partnerships, The Rosa A. Hagin School Consultation Center and Early Childhood Center, The Center for Catholic Leadership and Faith-Based Education, The Center for Learning in Unsupervised Environments, Human Resiliency, Advanced Placement Summer Institute and the Psychological Services Institute.

Application Information: *Fee:* $70. *Online application:* https://gradadmissions.fordham.edu/apply/.

Hofstra University
Department of Psychology
Hofstra College of Liberal Arts and Sciences
135 Hofstra University
Hempstead, NY 11549
Telephone: (516) 463-5624
Chairperson: Keith M. Shafritz, PhD

E-mail: keith.shafritz@hofstra.edu
Web: http://www.hofstra.edu/Academics/Colleges/HCLAS/PSY/index.html

---

Orientation, Objectives, and Emphasis of Department
The PhD program in Clinical Psychology is designed to provide doctoral students with assessment and therapeutic skill competence along with a solid scientific foundation for careers working with the variety of psychopathology found among those with mental health disorders. The program employs a scientist–practitioner model of education. Program graduates have readily found employment in a wide variety of mental health clinics, group practices, public and private agencies, as well as hospitals and medical centers. Many have chosen academic paths by becoming college and university faculty members, medical school faculty, research scientists, expert consultants, or editors for psychological publishers. The clinical psychology program is based upon cognitive-behavioral theory and represents the full psychotherapeutic spectrum of this orientation. The APA-accredited PsyD program in School-Community Psychology trains practitioners who are skilled in providing psychological services to children, families, and schools. Schools are viewed as being part of the larger community. Thus, in addition to being trained in a school-based, direct service model, emphasis is placed upon training students whose subject of study is the educational or community system in which children develop. PsyD students are trained as consultants who may be involved in educational and mental health program implementation and evaluation.

Programs and Degrees Offered

Program	Degree	Application Deadline	Applica-tions Received	Accepted	New Admits Enrolled (PT)	Total Enrolled (PT)	Degrees Awarded in 2014–2015	Median Years to Complete Degree	Dismissed/ Withdrew
Clinical Psychology	PhD	December 31 (Fall)	131	17	12	77 (0)	14	6	1
Industrial/ Organizational Psychology	MA/MS	(Fall), Rolling	83	64	22 (6)	50 (6)	24	2	3
School-Community Psychology	PsyD	January 15 (Fall)	80	23	10 (2)	44 (8)	11	5.1	0
Applied Organizational Psychology	PhD	February 1 (Fall)	29	20	9 (0)	34 (0)	5	3.5	0

APA Accreditation

Clinical PhD: Student Outcome Data website: http://www.hofstra.edu/Academics/Colleges/HCLAS/PSY/phdcp/.

School PsyD: Student Outcome Data website: http://www.hofstra.edu/academics/colleges/hclas/psy/psydsc/psydsc_StudentAdmissions_Outcomes_OtherData.html.

Doctoral Degree (PhD Clinical Psychology): For those doctoral students for whom a professional internship was required in this program prior to graduation:

Total students who applied for an internship: 10

Total students who obtained an internship: 10

Total students who obtained a paid internship: 10

Total students who obtained an unpaid internship: 0

Total students who were placed in APA/CPA-accredited internships: 10

Total students placed in internships not APA/CPA-accredited, but listed with the Association of Psychology Postdoctoral and Internship Centers (APPIC): 0

Total students placed in internships conforming to guidelines of the Council of Directors of School Psychology Programs (CDSPP): 0

Total students placed in internships that were not APA/CPA-accredited, APPIC or CDSSP listed: 0

Doctoral Degree (PsyD School-Community Psychology): For those doctoral students for whom a professional internship was required in this program prior to graduation:

Total students who applied for an internship: 16

Total students who obtained an internship: 16

Total students who obtained a paid internship: 7

Total students who obtained an unpaid internship: 9

Total students who were placed in APA/CPA-accredited internships: 0

Total students placed in internships not APA/CPA-accredited, but listed with the Association of Psychology Postdoctoral and Internship Centers (APPIC): 0

Total students placed in internships conforming to guidelines of the Council of Directors of School Psychology Programs (CDSPP): 9

Total students placed in internships that were not APA/CPA-accredited, APPIC or CDSSP listed: 7

Master's Degree (MA/MS Industrial/Organizational Psychology): An internship experience, such as a final research project or "capstone" experience is required of graduates.

Internships/Practica

In the clinical PhD and PsyD programs students complete a series of practica in which assessment, testing, and interviewing skills are developed. PhD students complete various courses and role playing experiences in adult psychotherapy. PhD students are required to apply for internships using the APPIC national match process following the completion of all coursework and the defense of a dissertation proposal. PsyD students complete a diversified and extended internship over a 2-year period. The students are first placed in a school (3 days per week) and then in a community agency (3 days per week). In the PhD program in Applied Organizational Psychology, a major part of the student's training, including a paid internship, research courses, and doctoral dissertation, will involve projects in organizations. The internship provides practical experience working for an organization for approximately 20 hours per week, under the supervision of a manager designated by the organization and approved by the program faculty. All research projects, including the dissertation, must serve the educational needs of the students and advance scientific knowledge in the field of organizational psychology; they cannot only serve the interests of the organization. Dissertation research may be conducted in the laboratory, the organization, or both.

Admissions

Entries appear in the following order: required test or GPA, minimum score (if required)/median score of students entering in 2015–2016.

Program	Degree	GRE-V	GRE-Q	GRE-Writing	GRE-Subject	Under-graduate GPA	Last 2 Years GPA	Psychology GPA	Master's GPA
Clinical Psychology	PhD	NA/160	NA/155	NA/4.5	NA/711	NA/3.7	Not specified	NA/NA	NA/NA
Industrial/ Organizational Psychology	MA/MS	NA/153	NA/153	Not specified	Not specified	3/3.7	Not specified	Not specified	Not specified
School-Community Psychology	PsyD	153/NA	144/NA	NA/NA	NA/600	NA/3.5	Not specified	Not specified	Not specified
Applied Organizational Psychology	PhD	NA/NA	NA/NA	NA/NA	Not specified	Not specified	Not specified	Not specified	3/3.5

Admissions Requirements:

Degree	GRE	GRE-Subject	Letters of Recom-mendation	Research Statement	Writing Sample	CV	Interview
Master's/Specialist	Required	None	N/A	Required	Optional	Optional	Required
Doctoral	Required	Required	3	Required	Optional	Required	Required

Please note if these criteria vary for different programs: For Clinical PhD program: research experience high, especially professional presentations and publications, clinically related public service high, statement of goals and objectives high. GRE-Subject test required. For PsyD program: research experience low, clinically related public service medium, statement of goals and objectives medium. For PhD in Applied Organizational Psychology, a master's degree in one of the social sciences or in business is required. Only 2 letters of recommendation are required.

Admissions Criteria:

GRE scores—high
Research experience—high
Work experience—medium
Clinically related public service—medium
GPA—high

Letters of recommendation—medium
Interview—high
Statement of goals and objectives—medium
Undergraduate psychology preparation—medium

For additional information on admission requirements, visit http://www.hofstra.edu/Academics/Colleges/HCLAS/PSY/psy_proggrad.html.

Department Demographics

	Male (PT)	Female (PT)	Total	African-American/ Black (PT)	Hispanic/ Latino (PT)	Asian/ Pacific Islander (PT)	American Indian/ Alaska Native (PT)	Caucasian/ White (PT)	Unknown (PT)	Multiethnic (PT)	ADA (PT)	Int'l (PT)
Students	75 (4)	135 (10)	224	11 (1)	3 (0)	13 (0)	0 (0)	183 (13)	0 (0)	0 (0)	0 (0)	5 (0)

Financial Information/Assistance

Tuition: For information on tuition costs, visit http://www.hofstra.edu/sfs/bursar/bursar_tuition.html. Tuition is subject to change. Additional fees are assessed to students beyond the costs of tuition for the following: university, technology and activity fees. Tuition costs vary by program.

Doctoral:
State residents: $1,218 per credit hour.
Nonstate residents: $1,218 per credit hour.

Master's:
State residents: $1,218 per credit hour.
Nonstate residents: $1,218 per credit hour.

Financial Assistance:

	Teaching Assistantship (% Receiving)	Teaching Assistantship Tuition Remission	Research Assistantship (% Receiving)	Research Assistantship Tuition Remission	Fellowship (% Receiving)	Fellowship Tuition Remission
First-Year Student	NA (NA)	NA	NA (NA)	Partial	NA (NA)	Full
Advanced Student	NA (NA)	NA	NA (NA)	Partial	NA (NA)	Full

For additional information on financial assistance, visit http://www.hofstra.edu/Academics/grad/grad_fa_scholarships.html.

Employment of Department Graduates

Master's:
Employed in an academic position at a university: 2
Employed in business or industry: 13
Do not know: 9
Total: 24

Doctoral:
Enrolled in a postdoctoral residency/fellowship: 3
Employed in independent practice: 2
Employed in an academic position at a university: 1
Employed in academic position at a 2-year/4-year college: 1
Employed in a professional position in a school system: 6
Employed in business or industry: 6
Employed in government agency: 2
Employed in a community mental health/counseling center: 7
Employed in a hospital/medical center: 2
Total: 30

Additional Information

Housing and Day Care: On-campus housing is available. See the following website for more information: http://www.hofstra.edu/StudentAffairs/StudentServices/ResLife/. On-campus day care facilities are available. See the following website for more information: http://www.hofstra.edu/community/slzctr/slzctr_childcare.html.

Information for Students With Physical Disabilities: See the following website: http://www.hofstra.edu/studentaffairs/stddis/.

Special Facilities or Resources: A community services center, the Psychological Evaluation, Research and Counseling Clinic (PERCC), provides practicum experiences for students in the areas of assessment, intervention, and research. All rooms are wired for video recording; some have observation mirrors and are thus equipped to handle research in areas of interviewing, communication, problem solving, psychotherapy, and team building. An outstanding library and a computer center are also available, as are many department computers and lab facilities. A student workroom has computers for exclusive doctoral student use and all major software programs are available for student use.

Application Information: Fee: $70. Online application: http://www.hofstra.edu/Academics/grad/grad_apply.html.

Iona College

Department of Psychology/Masters of Arts in Psychology
715 North Avenue
New Rochelle, NY 10801
Telephone: (914) 637-7788
Chairperson: Patricia Oswald, PhD

E-mail: agotlieb@iona.edu
Web: http://www.iona.edu/Academics/School-of-Arts-Science/Departments/Psychology.aspx

---

Orientation, Objectives, and Emphasis of Department

The Psychology Department offers separate MA degrees in School Psychology, Mental Health Counseling, Industrial/Organizational (I/O) Psychology, and General-Experimental Psychology. All degree programs have been approved by the Education Department of New York State. The School Psychology program has been approved by NASP. The MA in Mental Health Counseling fulfills the academic requirements to take the licensing exam in New York. All programs have been designed for persons who are considering a career in psychology, who are en route to doctoral study in psychology, or are already employed in the field. The programs provide a balance of theoretical, methodological and practical expertise, as well as extensive training in written and oral expression. They are designed to provide pertinent new experiences, enhance knowledge in substantive areas, and facilitate maximum development of essential professional competencies and attitudes.

Programs and Degrees Offered

Program	Degree	Application Deadline	Applications Received	Accepted	New Admits Enrolled (PT)	Total Enrolled (PT)	Degrees Awarded in 2014–2015	Median Years to Complete Degree	Dismissed/ Withdrew
School Psychology	MA/MS	Rolling	34	29	7 (3)	11 (9)	9	2.75	0
Industrial-Organizational Psychology	MA/MS	Rolling	32	28	12 (1)	22 (1)	11	1.75	0
Mental Health Counseling	MA/MS	Rolling	25	21	8 (1)	16 (16)	4	3.25	1
General-Experimental Psychology	MA/MS	Rolling	5	5	1 (0)	1 (0)	2	1.33	0

Internships/Practica

School Psychology students complete a 1200-hour internship in a school setting under the supervision of a certified school psychologist. Mental Health Counseling students complete 600 hours of internship training in a variety of clinical settings and are supervised by experienced and qualified practitioners. Industrial/Organizational students complete 300 hours of internship in a variety of organizational settings under the supervision of trained I/O professionals. General-Experimental students are not required to complete an internship.

Admissions

Entries appear in the following order: required test or GPA, minimum score (if required)/median score of students entering in 2015–2016.

Program	Degree	GRE-V	GRE-Q	GRE-Writing	GRE-Subject	Under-graduate GPA	Last 2 Years GPA	Psychology GPA	Master's GPA
School Psychology	MA/MS	Not specified	Not specified	Not specified	Not specified	3/3.24	Not specified	3/NA	Not specified
Industrial-Organizational Psychology	MA/MS	Not specified	Not specified	Not specified	Not specified	3/3.38	Not specified	3/NA	Not specified
Mental Health Counseling	MA/MS	Not specified	Not specified	Not specified	Not specified	3/3.14	Not specified	3/NA	Not specified
General-Experimental Psychology	MA/MS	Not specified	Not specified	Not specified	Not specified	3/3.22	NA/NA	3/NA	Not specified

Admissions Requirements:

Degree	GRE	GRE-Subject	Letters of Recommendation	Research Statement	Writing Sample	CV	Interview
Master's/Specialist	None	None	2	Optional	None	Recommended	Optional

Admissions Criteria:
Research experience—medium
Work experience—medium
Clinically related public service—medium
GPA—high

Letters of recommendation—high
Interview—low
Statement of goals and objectives—low
Undergraduate psychology preparation—high

Department Demographics

	Male (PT)	Female (PT)	Total	African-American/ Black (PT)	Hispanic/ Latino (PT)	Asian/ Pacific Islander (PT)	American Indian/ Alaska Native (PT)	Caucasian/ White (PT)	Unknown	Multiethnic (PT)	ADA (PT)	Int'l (PT)
Students	18 (5)	32 (21)	76	8 (5)	7 (7)	1 (1)	0 (0)	31 (8)	3 (4)	0 (1)	0 (0)	1 (0)

Financial Information/Assistance

Tuition: For information on tuition costs, visit http://www.iona.edu/Admissions/Graduate-Admissions/Tuition-Fees.aspx. Additional fees are assessed to students beyond the costs of tuition for the following: program/student service fees—$245 per term.

Master's:
State residents: $1,062 per credit hour.
Nonstate residents: $1,062 per credit hour.

Financial Assistance:

	Teaching Assistantship (% Receiving)	Teaching Assistantship Tuition Remission	Research Assistantship (% Receiving)	Research Assistantship Tuition Remission	Fellowship (% Receiving)	Fellowship Tuition Remission
First-Year Student	NA (NA)	NA	NA (NA)	NA	$20,744 (7)	Partial
Advanced Student	NA (NA)	NA	NA (NA)	NA	$20,744 (7)	Partial

For additional information on financial assistance, visit http://www.iona.edu/Admissions/Graduate-Admissions/Financial-Aid-and-Scholarship.aspx.

Employment of Department Graduates

No information provided.

Additional Information

Housing and Day Care: On-campus housing is available. See the following website for more information: http://www.iona.edu/Student-Life/Housing-Living-Environments/Graduate-Housing.aspx. No on-campus day care facilities are available.

Special Facilities or Resources: The Department contains space dedicated to supporting research projects in specialties of psychology including social, perception, learning, treatment, and cognition. Extensive computer and software capabilities are available. In addition, assessment/testing kits, including the WISC, WAIS, WPPSI, Bailey and ADOS, are available for student use. The department has an assessment lab that includes computerized software such as the MMPI, 16PF and BASC.

Application Information: Office of Graduate Admissions, School of Arts and Sciences, 715 North Avenue, New Rochelle, NY 10801. *Fee:* $50. *Online application:* https://www.applyweb.com/iona/gradas_menu.html.

Long Island University

Department of Psychology
College of Liberal Arts and Sciences
720 Northern Boulevard
Brookville, NY 11548
Telephone: (516) 299-2377
Chairperson: Gerald D. Lachter

E-mail: gerald.lachter@liu.edu
Web: http://liu.edu/CWPost/Academics/Schools/CLAS/Dept/Psychology

Orientation, Objectives, and Emphasis of Department

The Master's degree programs in Experimental Psychology or Behavior Analysis give students a broad background in Experimental Psychology and/or Behavior Analysis. Faculty interests include Behavior Analysis, Cognition and Perception, and Neuroscience. The program is designed to prepare students for admission to doctoral programs, or to give them the skills necessary to obtain employment. The Clinical Psychology Doctoral Program at the C.W. Post Campus of Long Island University offers a Doctor of Psychology (PsyD) degree and has as its basic purpose the training of doctoral level clinical psychologists who will exhibit professional attitudes and apply current knowledge and practice skills for the prevention and alleviation of psychological problems. The program is also committed to training students who will provide services in public sector settings to traditionally underserved groups. While the mission is to broadly train clinical psychologists, the program also seeks to provide each student with special competencies in one of three areas: family violence, applied child, and serious and persistent mental illness. The program also provides its graduates with clinical and theoretical training in two major orientations: cognitive-behavioral and psychoanalytic. The Clinical Psychology doctoral program is fully accredited by the American Psychological Association.

Programs and Degrees Offered

Program	Degree	Application Deadline	Applica-tions Received	Accepted	New Admits Enrolled (PT)	Total Enrolled (PT)	Degrees Awarded in 2014–2015	Median Years to Complete Degree	Dismissed/ Withdrew
Experimental Psychology	MA/MS	August 1 (Fall)	15	8	6	6	3	2	0
Clinical Psychology	PsyD	January 15 (Fall)	275	45	20	100	20	5	0
Applied Behavior Analysis Certificate	Other	August 1 (Fall)	40	32	(26)	(26)	21	1	0
Behavior Analysis	MA/MS	August 1 (Fall), Rolling	19	13	9	9	0		0

APA Accreditation

Clinical PsyD: Student Outcome Data website: http://liu.edu/CWPost/Academics/College-of-Liberal-Arts-and-Sciences/Doctor-of-Psychology/Student-Data.

Doctoral Degree (PsyD Clinical Psychology): For those doctoral students for whom a professional internship was required in this program prior to graduation:
Total students who applied for an internship: 20
Total students who obtained an internship: 18
Total students who obtained a paid internship: 18
Total students who obtained an unpaid internship: 0
Total students who were placed in APA/CPA-accredited internships: 18
Total students placed in internships not APA/CPA-accredited, but listed with the Association of Psychology Postdoctoral and Internship Centers (APPIC): 0
Total students placed in internships conforming to guidelines of the Council of Directors of School Psychology Programs (CDSPP): 0
Total students placed in internships that were not APA/CPA-accredited, APPIC or CDSSP listed: 0

Master's Degree (MA/MS Experimental Psychology): An internship experience, such as a final research project or "capstone" experience is required of graduates. Master's Degree (MA/MS Behavior Analysis): An internship experience, such as a final research project or "capstone" experience is required of graduates.

Internships/Practica
A wide range of internship and practicum placements are available.

Admissions
Entries appear in the following order: required test or GPA, minimum score (if required)/median score of students entering in 2015–2016.

Program	Degree	GRE-V	GRE-Q	GRE-Writing	GRE-Subject	Under-graduate GPA	Last 2 Years GPA	Psychol-ogy GPA	Master's GPA
Experimental Psychology	MA/MS	NA/154	NA/152	NA/NA	Not specified	3.2/3.5	Not specified	3.4/3.6	Not specified
Clinical Psychology	PsyD	NA/158	NA/152	NA/4.4	NA/659	NA/3.65	Not specified	NA/NA	Not specified
Applied Behavior Analysis Certificate	Other	Not specified	Not specified	Not specified	Not specified	3/3.4	NA/NA	Not specified	Not specified
Behavior Analysis	MA/MS	NA/150	NA/146	NA/NA	Not specified	3.2/3.45	NA/NA	NA/NA	Not specified

Admissions Requirements:

Degree	GRE	GRE-Subject	Letters of Recom-mendation	Research Statement	Writing Sample	CV	Interview
Master's/Specialist	Required	None	2	Required	Optional	Required	Optional
Doctoral	Required	Required	2	Required	Recom-mended	Required	Required

Please note if these criteria vary for different programs: Clinical experience not rated highly for MA programs. Research experience rated highly for MA programs.

Admissions Criteria:
GRE scores—medium
Research experience—high
Work experience—high
Clinically related public service—high
GPA—high

Letters of recommendation—high
Interview—high
Statement of goals and objectives—medium
Undergraduate psychology preparation—medium

Department Demographics

	Male (PT)	Female (PT)	Total	African-American/ Black (PT)	Hispanic/ Latino (PT)	Asian/ Pacific Islander (PT)	American Indian/ Alaska Native (PT)	Caucasian/ White (PT)	Unknown (PT)	Multiethnic (PT)	ADA (PT)	Int'l (PT)
Students	20 (2)	80 (18)	120	4 (2)	8 (3)	3 (0)	0 (0)	80 (15)	5 (0)	0 (0)	0 (0)	5 (0)

Financial Information/Assistance

Tuition: For information on tuition costs, visit http://www.liu.edu/SFS/Tuition. Tuition is subject to change. Additional fees are assessed to students beyond the costs of tuition for the following: $100/semester activity fee.

Doctoral:
State residents: $48,962 per academic year.
Nonstate residents: $48,962 per academic year.

Master's:
State residents: $1,178 per credit hour.
Nonstate residents: $1,178 per credit hour.

Financial Assistance:

	Teaching Assistantship (% Receiving)	Teaching Assistantship Tuition Remission	Research Assistantship (% Receiving)	Research Assistantship Tuition Remission	Fellowship (% Receiving)	Fellowship Tuition Remission
First-Year Student	NA (NA)	Partial	NA (NA)	Partial	NA (NA)	Partial
Advanced Student	NA (NA)	Partial	NA (NA)	Partial	NA (NA)	Partial

For additional information on financial assistance, visit http://liu.edu/CWPost/Financial-Assistance.

Employment of Department Graduates

Master's:
Enrolled in a psychology doctoral program: 2
Enrolled in another graduate/professional program: 2
Total: 4

Doctoral:
Employed in a community mental health/counseling center: 12
Employed in a hospital/medical center: 5
Other employment position: 2
Total: 19

Additional Information

Housing and Day Care: On-campus housing is available. See the following website for more information: http://www.liu.edu/CWPost/StudentLife/ResLife.aspx. No on-campus day care facilities are available.

Information for Students With Physical Disabilities: See the following website: http://www.liu.edu/CWPost/StudentLife/Services/LSC/DSS.

Special Facilities or Resources: Laboratories exist for the study of animal and human learning, cognition and perception, and neuroscience. The PsyD program has its own Psychological Services Center that provides mental health services to the community as well as serving as a site for training students.

Application Information: Graduate Admissions, LIU Post, Brookville, NY 11548. *Fee:* $40. *Online application:* https://apply.liu.edu/quickapp/.

Long Island University
Psychology/Clinical Psychology
Richard L. Conolly College
1 University Plaza
Brooklyn, NY 11201
Telephone: (718) 488-1164
Director, PhD Program in Clinical Psychology: Philip S. Wong, PhD
E-mail: Philip.Wong@liu.edu
Web: http://www.liu.edu/Brooklyn/Academics/Liberal-Arts-Sciences/Social-Science-Programs/Psychology/

Orientation, Objectives, and Emphasis of Department
The PhD and MA programs are housed in an urban institution with a multicultural undergraduate student body. This diversity enriches the students' appreciation of the complexity of the clinical and theoretical issues relevant to work in psychology. The theoretical orientation of the clinical training sequence reflects the spectrum of psychodynamic approaches to treatment and familiarizes students with dialectical behavior therapy, cognitive–behavioral and family systems approaches as well. Clinical students are exposed, in a graded series of practicum experiences, to both short-term and longer term approaches to psychotherapy with the New York area's culturally diverse clinical populations. Students are also trained in a range of psychological assessment procedures including cognitive, projective, and neuropsychological testing. The program also seeks to train clinical psychologists who are competent in research and grounded in the science of psychology. To this end, doctoral students receive extensive training in research design and statistics early in their coursework and complete a second-year research project prior to beginning their dissertation. The final goal and emphasis of the department and the PhD program is to enable students to develop a broad base of knowledge in clinical psychology. Doctoral students are provided with opportunities for clinical training with all age ranges.

Programs and Degrees Offered

Program	Degree	Application Deadline	Applications Received	Accepted	New Admits Enrolled (PT)	Total Enrolled (PT)	Degrees Awarded in 2014–2015	Median Years to Complete Degree	Dismissed/Withdrew
Clinical Psychology	PhD	January 5 (Fall)	225	25	16 (0)	98 (0)	6	6	0
General Psychology	MA/MS	Rolling	20	15	5 (10)	18 (42)	12	4	0

APA Accreditation

Clinical PhD (Doctor of Philosophy).

Doctoral Degree (PhD Clinical Psychology): For those doctoral students for whom a professional internship was required in this program prior to graduation:
Total students who applied for an internship: 10
Total students who obtained an internship: 9
Total students who obtained a paid internship: 9
Total students who obtained an unpaid internship: 0
Total students who were placed in APA/CPA-accredited internships: 9
Total students placed in internships not APA/CPA-accredited, but listed with the Association of Psychology Postdoctoral and Internship Centers (APPIC): 0
Total students placed in internships conforming to guidelines of the Council of Directors of School Psychology Programs (CDSPP): 0
Total students placed in internships that were not APA/CPA-accredited, APPIC or CDSSP listed: 0

Internships/Practica

Students in the MA program have a variety of practica available to them. Doctoral externships and internships in the New York City region are among the best in the country and offer training with a wide range of clients and specializations. Among these are child training, family training, neuropsychology, and forensic training. Students in the PhD program regularly train in the most competitive of these externship and internship settings. From 2007 to 2014 the percentage of doctoral students matching in externships and internships was 95%–100%. This is an exceptional record of being accepted at the some of the finest clinical training sites in the country.

Admissions

Entries appear in the following order: required test or GPA, minimum score (if required)/median score of students entering in 2015–2016.

Program	Degree	GRE-V	GRE-Q	GRE-Writing	GRE-Subject	Under-graduate GPA	Last 2 Years GPA	Psychology GPA	Master's GPA
Clinical Psychology	PhD	NA/NA	NA/NA	NA/NA	550/NA	3.2/NA	NA/NA	3.4/NA	Not specified
General Psychology	MA/MS	Not specified	Not specified	Not specified	Not specified	NA/NA	Not specified	Not specified	Not specified

Admissions Requirements:

Degree	GRE	GRE-Subject	Letters of Recommendation	Research Statement	Writing Sample	CV	Interview
Master's/Specialist	Optional	None	2	Required	Optional	Optional	Optional
Doctoral	Required	Required	3	Required	Optional	Required	Required

Please note if these criteria vary for different programs: The requirements are for the PhD Program in Clinical Psychology are different from the MA Program. Requirements for the MA Program include a minimum GPA of 2.75, good letters of recommendation, and a commitment to pursue a scholarly foundation at the graduate level in psychology.

Admissions Criteria:

GRE scores—high	Letters of recommendation—high
Research experience—high	Interview—high
Work experience—high	Statement of goals and objectives—high
Clinically related public service—medium	Undergraduate psychology preparation—medium
GPA—high	Publications and posters—medium

Department Demographics

	Male (PT)	Female (PT)	Total	African-American/Black (PT)	Hispanic/Latino (PT)	Asian/Pacific Islander (PT)	American Indian/Alaska Native (PT)	Caucasian/White (PT)	Unknown	Multiethnic (PT)	ADA (PT)	Int'l (PT)
Students	35 (15)	81 (27)	158	9 (11)	14 (9)	8 (6)	0 (0)	85 (16)	0 (0)	11 (0)	0 (0)	5 (0)

Financial Information/Assistance

Tuition: For information on tuition costs, visit http://www.liu.edu/Brooklyn/Enrollment-Services/Tuition. Tuition is subject to change.

Doctoral:
State residents: $47,972 per academic year.
State residents: $1,535 per credit hour.
Nonstate residents: $47,972 per academic year.
Nonstate residents: $1,535 per credit hour.

Master's:
State residents: $1,155 per credit hour.
Nonstate residents: $1,155 per credit hour.

Financial Assistance:

	Teaching Assistantship (% Receiving)	Teaching Assistantship Tuition Remission	Research Assistantship (% Receiving)	Research Assistantship Tuition Remission	Fellowship (% Receiving)	Fellowship Tuition Remission
First-Year Student	NA (NA)	NA	$1,250 (NA)	Partial	$3,500 (NA)	Full
Advanced Student	$2,400 (NA)	Partial	$1,250 (NA)	Partial	$3,500 (NA)	Full

For additional information on financial assistance, visit http://www.liu.edu/Brooklyn/Enrollment-Services/Financial-Aid.

Employment of Department Graduates

Master's:
Enrolled in a psychology doctoral program: 2
Employed in a professional position in a school system: 4
Employed in government agency: 2
Employed in a community mental health/counseling center: 2
Employed in a hospital/medical center: 2
Total: 12

Doctoral:
Enrolled in a postdoctoral residency/fellowship: 2
Employed in a community mental health/counseling center: 2
Employed in a hospital/medical center: 2
Total: 6

Additional Information

Housing and Day Care: On-campus housing is available. See the following website for more information: http://www.liu.edu/Brooklyn/Campus-Life. No on-campus day care facilities are available.

Special Facilities or Resources: The Department of Psychology has access to: an on-site Psychological Services Center where PhD trainees are carefully supervised by the doctoral faculty; an ongoing psychotherapy research group; research labs for the study of unconscious cognitive processes and personality and mood/anxiety disorders; training in child and adolescent clinical work at several New York area clinical training facilities; specialized electives in neuropsychology; and computer training and facilities. Students in the PhD program have the spectrum of New York City's clinical and educational facilities available, with many collaborative projects underway between the PhD program faculty and NYC hospitals and research institutions.

Application Information: Fee: $50. Online application: https://apply.liu.edu/new/UserLogin.aspx.

Marist College
Department of Psychology
School of Social & Behavioral Sciences
3399 North Road
Poughkeepsie, NY 12601
Telephone: (845) 575-3000
Graduate Program Director: James Regan, PhD

E-mail: james.regan@marist.edu
Web: http://www.marist.edu/sbs/graduate/

Orientation, Objectives, and Emphasis of Department
The Master of Arts program focuses on either mental health counseling or school psychology. The program's goals include providing students with the relevant theory, skills, and practical experience that will enable them to perform competently in assessing individual differences, in counseling, and in planning and implementing effective individual, group, and systems-level interventions. Students interested in working in community settings will find a variety of opportunities for "hands-on" experience. The mental health counseling program fulfills the academic component for students who want to be licensed in New York State as Mental Health Counselors and the school psychology program leads to New York certification as a school psychologist.

Programs and Degrees Offered

Program	Degree	Application Deadline	Applications Received	Accepted	New Admits Enrolled (PT)	Total Enrolled (PT)	Degrees Awarded in 2014–2015	Median Years to Complete Degree	Dismissed/ Withdrew
School Psychology	MA/MS	April 15 (Fall)	23	14	9 (0)	30 (0)	14	3	7
Mental Health Counseling	MA/MS	April 15 (Fall)	22	15	12 (0)	20 (2)	17	2	1
Educational Psychology	MA/MS	April 15 (Fall), December 1 (Spring), April 1 (Summer)	26	12	4 (8)	44 (23)	20	2	0

Internships/Practica
The Mid-Hudson area has many public and private agencies dealing with mental health, developmental disabilities, criminal justice, and social services. In addition, numerous school districts participate with the school psychology program. Students choose their own placement site in consultation with their faculty supervisor.

Admissions
Entries appear in the following order: required test or GPA, minimum score (if required)/median score of students entering in 2015–2016.

Program	Degree	GRE-V	GRE-Q	GRE-Writing	GRE-Subject	Under-graduate GPA	Last 2 Years GPA	Psychol-ogy GPA	Master's GPA
School Psychology	MA/MS	NA/NA	NA/NA	Not specified	Not specified	3/NA	Not specified	Not specified	Not specified
Mental Health Counseling	MA/MS	NA/150	NA/146	NA/3.8	Not specified	3/3.59	3/NA	3/NA	Not specified
Educational Psychology	MA/MS	Not specified	Not specified	Not specified	Not specified	3/NA	Not specified	Not specified	Not specified

Admissions Requirements:

Degree	GRE	GRF-Subject	Letters of Recom-mendation	Research Statement	Writing Sample	CV	Interview
Master's/Specialist	Required	None	3	Required	Optional	Required	Required

Please note if these criteria vary for different programs: Educational Psychology only requires 2 letters of recommendation. GRE scores are only required for Mental Health Counseling program.

Admissions Criteria:

GRE scores—low
Research experience—low
Work experience—medium
Clinically related public service—medium
GPA—low

Letters of recommendation—high
Interview—high
Statement of goals and objectives—low
Undergraduate psychology preparation—low

For additional information on admission requirements, visit http://www.marist.edu/admission/graduate/deadlines.html.

Department Demographics

	Male (PT)	Female (PT)	Total	African-American/ Black (PT)	Hispanic/ Latino (PT)	Asian/ Pacific Islander (PT)	American Indian/ Alaska Native (PT)	Caucasian/ White (PT)	Unknown (PT)	Multiethnic (PT)	ADA (PT)	Int'l (PT)
Students	9 (5)	87 (17)	118	6 (0)	5 (1)	0 (0)	0 (0)	86 (25)	0 (0)	0 (0)	1 (2)	0 (0)

Financial Information/Assistance

Tuition: For information on tuition costs, visit http://www.marist.edu/financialaid/graduate/tuitionandfees.html. Tuition is subject to change. Tuition costs vary by program.

Master's:
State residents: $16,680 per academic year.
State residents: $720 per credit hour.
Nonstate residents: $16,680 per academic year.
Nonstate residents: $720 per credit hour.

Financial Assistance:

	Teaching Assistantship (% Receiving)	Teaching Assistantship Tuition Remission	Research Assistantship (% Receiving)	Research Assistantship Tuition Remission	Fellowship (% Receiving)	Fellowship Tuition Remission
First-Year Student	NA (NA)	NA	$4,500 (NA)	Partial	NA (NA)	NA
Advanced Student	NA (NA)	NA	$4,500 (NA)	Partial	NA (NA)	NA

For additional information on financial assistance, visit http://www.marist.edu/financialaid/graduate/.

Employment of Department Graduates

Master's:
Enrolled in a psychology doctoral program: 13
Enrolled in another graduate/professional program: 7
Employed in academic position at a 2-year/4-year college: 1
Employed in other positions at a higher education institution: 3
Employed in a professional position in a school system: 22
Employed in business or industry: 2
Employed in government agency: 2
Employed in a community mental health/counseling center: 8
Employed in a hospital/medical center: 2
Still seeking employment: 2
Total: 62

Additional Information

Housing and Day Care: No on-campus housing is available. No on-campus day care facilities are available.

Information for Students With Physical Disabilities: See the following website: http://www.marist.edu/specialservices/.

Special Facilities or Resources: Interested students can assist in research at facilities such as the Nathan Kline Research Institute, The Center for Advanced Brain Imaging, The Marist Institute for Community Research, Dutchess County Department of Mental Hygiene and Public Health, and the Montrose and Castle Point Veterans Hospitals.

Application Information: Director of Graduate Admissions, Marist College, Poughkeepsie, NY 12601. *Fee:* $50. *Online application:* http://www.marist.edu/admission/graduate/apply.html.

New York University (2015 data)
Department of Applied Psychology
Steinhardt School of Culture, Education, & Human Development
246 Greene Street - Kimball Hall
New York, NY 10003
Telephone: (212) 998-5555
Chairperson: Dr. LaRue Allen

E-mail: applied.psychology@nyu.edu
Web: http://steinhardt.nyu.edu/appsych

Orientation, Objectives, and Emphasis of Department
The cornerstone of our department is the marriage of theory and practice driven by the University's commitment to being a private university in the public service. To this end, the department's programs reflect both a concern for excellence in teaching and the opportunity to learn from involvement in community-based data collection. Emphases and specific core requirements differ somewhat from program to program, but include a solid foundation in the basic psychological disciplines. Departmental faculty have ongoing research projects in many areas, including: cognition; language; social and emotional development; health and human development; applied measurement and research methods; working people's lives; spirituality; multicultural assessment; group and organizational dynamics; psychopathology and personality; sexual and gender identity; communication and creative expression; trauma and resilience; parenting; immigration.

Programs and Degrees Offered

Program	Degree	Application Deadline	Applications Received	Accepted	New Admits Enrolled (PT)	Total Enrolled (PT)	Degrees Awarded in 2014–2015	Median Years to Complete Degree	Dismissed/ Withdrew
Counseling and Guidance	MA/MS	(Fall)	434	210	65 (5)	113 (35)	89	2	0
Counseling Psychology	PhD	December 1 (Fall)	229	6	2 (0)	28 (0)	7	8	0
Psychological Development	PhD	December 1 (Fall)	45	5	2 (0)	19 (0)	2	6	0
Psychology and Social Intervention	PhD	December 1 (Fall)	56	5	2 (0)	15 (0)	2	5	0
Human Development and Social Intervention	MA/MS	February 1 (Fall)	50	26	7 (2)	26 (3)	16	2	0

APA Accreditation
Counseling PhD:

Doctoral Degree (PhD Counseling Psychology): For those doctoral students for whom a professional internship was required in this program prior to graduation:
Total students who applied for an internship: 6
Total students who obtained an internship: 6
Total students who obtained a paid internship: 5
Total students who obtained an unpaid internship: 1
Total students who were placed in APA/CPA-accredited internships: 5
Total students placed in internships not APA/CPA-accredited, but listed with the Association of Psychology Postdoctoral and Internship Centers (APPIC): 0

Total students placed in internships conforming to guidelines of the Council of Directors of School Psychology Programs (CDSPP): 0
Total students placed in internships that were not APA/CPA-accredited, APPIC or CDSSP listed: 1

Master's Degree (MA/MS Counseling and Guidance): An internship experience, such as a final research project or "capstone" experience is required of graduates. Master's Degree (MA/MS Human Development and Social Intervention): An internship experience, such as a final research project or "capstone" experience is required of graduates.

Internships/Practica

Internships and practica are available in the following areas: school and university counseling; counseling in community agencies, hospitals, and business; psychological development; measurement and evaluation.

Admissions

Entries appear in the following order: required test or GPA, minimum score (if required)/median score of students entering in 2015–2016.

Program	Degree	GRE-V	GRE-Q	GRE-Writing	GRE-Subject	Under-graduate GPA	Last 2 Years GPA	Psychol-ogy GPA	Master's GPA
Counseling and Guidance	MA/MS	Not specified	Not specified	Not specified	Not specified	3/3.5	3/3.5	Not specified	Not specified
Counseling Psychology	PhD	NA/NA	NA/NA	Not specified	Not specified	Not specified	3/3.5	3/3.5	Not specified
Psychological Development	PhD	NA/NA	NA/NA	Not specified	Not specified	3/3	3.5/3.5	Not specified	Not specified
Psychology and Social Intervention	PhD	NA/NA	NA/NA	Not specified	Not specified	3/3	3.5/3.5	Not specified	Not specified
Human Development and Social Intervention	MA/MS	NA/NA	NA/NA	Not specified	Not specified	3/3.5	3/3.5	Not specified	Not specified

Admissions Requirements:

Degree	GRE	GRE-Subject	Letters of Recom-mendation	Research Statement	Writing Sample	CV	Interview
Master's/Specialist	None	None	2	Required	None	Required	None
Doctoral	Required	None	3	Required	Required	Required	Required

Please note if these criteria vary for different programs: The criteria range from "medium" to "high" for admission into the doctoral programs. Master's programs primarily consider GPA, statement of goals and objectives, and letters of recommendation; interviews sometimes required for master's applicants.

Admissions Criteria:

GRE scores—medium
Research experience—high
Work experience—medium
Clinically related public service—medium

GPA—high
Letters of recommendation—high
Interview—high
Statement of goals and objectives—high

Department Demographics

	Male (PT)	Female (PT)	Total	African-American/ Black (PT)	Hispanic/ Latino (PT)	Asian/ Pacific Islander (PT)	American Indian/ Alaska Native (PT)	Caucasian/ White (PT)	Unknown	Multiethnic (PT)	ADA (PT)	Int'l (PT)
Students	35 (5)	154 (32)	226	27 (3)	34 (7)	23 (0)	0 (0)	91 (23)	24 (4)	2 (1)	1 (0)	17 (0)

Financial Information/Assistance

Tuition: For information on tuition costs, visit http://steinhardt.nyu.edu/graduate_admissions/tuition. Tuition is subject to change. Additional fees are assessed to students beyond the costs of tuition for the following: Registration fee for first credit: $461; $65 per additional credit.

Doctoral:
State residents: $34,128 per academic year.
State residents: $1,479 per credit hour.
Nonstate residents: $34,128 per academic year.
Nonstate residents: $1,479 per credit hour.

Master's:
State residents: $34,128 per academic year.
State residents: $1,479 per credit hour.
Nonstate residents: $34,128 per academic year.
Nonstate residents: $1,479 per credit hour.

Financial Assistance:

	Teaching Assistantship (% Receiving)	Teaching Assistantship Tuition Remission	Research Assistantship (% Receiving)	Research Assistantship Tuition Remission	Fellowship (% Receiving)	Fellowship Tuition Remission
First-Year Student	NA (NA)	NA	$25,060 (NA)	Full	$25,060 (NA)	Full
Advanced Student	NA (NA)	NA	$25,060 (NA)	Full	$18,000 (NA)	Full

For additional information on financial assistance, visit http://steinhardt.nyu.edu/financial_aid/.

Employment of Department Graduates

No information provided.

Additional Information

Housing and Day Care: On-campus housing is available. See the following website for more information: http://www.nyu.edu/life/living-at-nyu/on-campus-living.html. No on-campus day care facilities are available.

Information for Students With Physical Disabilities: See the following website: http://www.nyu.edu/csd/.

Special Facilities or Resources: The Measurement Laboratory contains educational and psychological tests and reference books. PCs are available for data analysis and word processing. The Institute for Human Development and Social Change aims to break new intellectual ground through its support for interdisciplinary research and training across, social, behavioral, health, and policy sciences. In the spirit of the common enterprise university, it brings together faculty, graduate students and undergraduate students from professional schools and the Faculty of Arts and Science. The Center for Research on Culture, Development and Education conducts longitudinal research on the pathways to educational success in early childhood and early adolescence among New York City families of five ethnic groups. The Center for Health, Identity, Behavior, and Prevention Studies (CHIBPS) conducts formative and intervention research on social and psychological factors that contribute to HIV transmission and the synergy between drug use, mental health, and HIV transmission. The Child and Family Policy Center conducts research, offers technical assistance, and works to disseminate state-of-the-field knowledge to bring children's healthy development and school success to the forefront of policymaking, program design, and practice.

Application Information: Fee: $75. Online application: http://steinhardt.nyu.edu/application/.

New York University, Graduate School of Arts and Science

Department of Psychology
6 Washington Place, Room 550
New York, NY 10003
Telephone: (212) 998-7900
Chairperson: Peter Gollwitzer

E-mail: marc.skurski@nyu.edu
Web: http://www.psych.nyu.edu

Orientation, Objectives, and Emphasis of Department

Both doctoral programs emphasize research. The cognition–perception faculty's research focuses on memory, emotion, psycholinguistics, categorization, cognitive neuroscience, visual perception and attention. The social program trains researchers in the theory and methods for understanding individuals and groups in social and organizational contexts. Training is provided in subareas ranging from social cognition to motivation, personality, close relationships, and groups and organizations. The concentration in developmental psychology emphasizes research-training that bridges several traditional areas of psychology. Students may minor in quantitative psychology or in any of the above programs. The Master's program in General Psychology offers students the flexibility to explore several areas of psychology in order to discover the area that interests them most. It is also suitable for students who wish to shape their course of study to fit special interests and needs, including preparation for admission to a doctoral program. The Master's program in Industrial/Organizational Psychology prepares graduates who are able to apply research and principles of human behavior to a variety of organizational settings, such as human resources departments and management consulting firms. The program can also be modified for students who are preparing for admission to doctoral programs in Industrial/Organizational and related fields.

Programs and Degrees Offered

Program	Degree	Application Deadline	Applications Received	Accepted	New Admits Enrolled (PT)	Total Enrolled (PT)	Degrees Awarded in 2014–2015	Median Years to Complete Degree	Dismissed/ Withdrew
General Psychology	MA/MS	March 1 (Fall), October 1 (Spring), January 15 (Summer)			80 (13)	161 (62)	79		
Industrial/ Organizational	MA/MS	January 15 (Fall), October 1 (Spring), January 15 (Summer)			18 (3)	23 (20)	19		
Cognition and Perception	PhD	December 1 (Fall)			9	50	8		1
Social	PhD	December 1 (Fall)			7	32	3		0

Internships/Practica

Master's students may opt to take Fieldwork, which would enable them to obtain supervised experience in selected agencies, clinics, and industrial and non-profit organizations relevant to the career or academic objectives of the student.

Admissions

Entries appear in the following order: required test or GPA, minimum score (if required)/median score of students entering in 2015–2016.

Program	Degree	GRE-V	GRE-Q	GRE-Writing	GRE-Subject	Undergraduate GPA	Last 2 Years GPA	Psychology GPA	Master's GPA
General Psychology	MA/MS	Not specified	Not specified	Not specified	Not specified	Not specified	Not specified	Not specified	Not specified

Admissions *(con't.)*

Program	Degree	GRE-V	GRE-Q	GRE-Writing	GRE-Subject	Under-graduate GPA	Last 2 Years GPA	Psychol-ogy GPA	Master's GPA
Industrial/ Organizational	MA/MS	Not specified	Not specified	Not specified	Not specified	Not specified	Not specified	Not specified	Not specified
Cognition and Perception	PhD	Not specified	Not specified	Not specified	Not specified	Not specified	Not specified	Not specified	Not specified
Social	PhD	Not specified	Not specified	Not specified	Not specified	Not specified	Not specified	Not specified	Not specified

Admissions Requirements:

Degree	GRE	GRE-Subject	Letters of Recom-mendation	Research Statement	Writing Sample	CV	Interview
Master's/Specialist	Required	None	3	Required	None	Required	None
Doctoral	Required	None	3	Required	None	Required	Required

Please note if these criteria vary for different programs: Admissions Criteria rankings are for the PhD only. For master's program, letters of recommendation and statement of goals and objectives have high importance; other criteria are low; no interviews are given. GRE/GPA varies by program.

Admissions Criteria:
GRE scores—medium
Research experience—high
Work experience—low
Clinically related public service—low

GPA—medium
Letters of recommendation—high
Statement of goals and objectives—high

For additional information on admission requirements, visit http://gsas.nyu.edu/object/gsas.prd.psye.

Department Demographics

	Male (PT)	Female (PT)	Total	African-American/ Black (PT)	Hispanic/ Latino (PT)	Asian/ Pacific Islander (PT)	American Indian/ Alaska Native (PT)	Caucasian/ White (PT)	Unknown	Multiethnic (PT)	ADA (PT)	Int'l (PT)
Students	90 (20)	176 (62)	348	6 (4)	13 (7)	17 (11)	0 (0)	102 (49)	121 (9)	7 (2)	0 (0)	112 (0)

Financial Information/Assistance

Tuition: For information on tuition costs, visit http://www.nyu.edu/bursar/tuition.fees/. Tuition costs vary by program.

Doctoral:
State residents: $1,608 per credit hour.
Nonstate residents: $1,608 per credit hour.

Master's:
State residents: $1,608 per credit hour.
Nonstate residents: $1,608 per credit hour.

Financial Assistance:

	Teaching Assistantship (% Receiving)	Teaching Assistantship Tuition Remission	Research Assistantship (% Receiving)	Research Assistantship Tuition Remission	Fellowship (% Receiving)	Fellowship Tuition Remission
First-Year Student	NA (NA)	NA	$34,000 (NA)	Full	$34,000 (NA)	Full
Advanced Student	NA (NA)	NA	$26,855 (NA)	Full	$26,855 (NA)	Full

For additional information on financial assistance, visit http://gsas.nyu.edu/page/grad.financialaid.html.

Employment of Department Graduates

No information provided.

Additional Information

Housing and Day Care: On-campus housing is available. See the following website for more information: http://www.nyu.edu/life/living-at-nyu.html. No on-campus day care facilities are available.

Information for Students With Physical Disabilities: See the following website: http://www.nyu.edu/life/safety-health-wellness/students-with-disabilities.

Special Facilities or Resources: The Department of Psychology maintains modern laboratories, classrooms, project rooms, an MEG system, and a magnetic resonance (MR) neuro-imaging facility in an 11-story building near Washington Square Park. The laboratories are continually improved through grants from foundations and federal agencies. The Center for Brain Imaging (CBI) is a shared research center, dedicated for research and instruction in human neuroscience. The Center houses a Siemens Allegra 3T head-only MRI scanner specifically designed for brain research with an extremely flexible development environment. The magnet itself is very compact and actively shielded, resulting in a fringe field comparable to that of a 1.5T whole-body system. Also within the Center are many ancillary equipment options, including visual display, auditory stimulation, button box/MR compatible keyboards, eye movement monitoring, motion capture systems, psychophysiology, and a mock/training scanner laboratory. Additionally, CBI also maintains a 128-channel electroencephalogram (EEG) facility using Geodesic Sensor Net technology developed by Electrical Geodesics Inc., as well as a transcranial magnetic stimulation (TMS) facility, which houses a MagStim Rapid2 stimulator. The MEG Lab houses a 160 channel axial gradiometer system open for use by faculty and students studying neural responses in cognitive and perceptual experiments.

Application Information: Fee: $100. *Online application:* http://gsas.nyu.edu/object/grad.admissions.onlineapp.

Pace University

Department of Psychology
Dyson College of Arts and Sciences
One Pace Plaza
New York, NY 10038
Telephone: (212) 346-1506
Chairperson: Sonia Suchday

E-mail: ssuchday@pace.edu
Web: http://www.pace.edu/dyson/departments/psychology-nyc

Orientation, Objectives, and Emphasis of Department

Pace University's PsyD in School-Clinical Child Psychology program prepares professional psychologists as health service providers with expertise in school and clinical psychology. These professional psychologists will be prepared to develop, provide, supervise, and research a full range of evidence-based psychological services. They will be uniquely prepared to utilize clinical, consultation, and educational expertise within school and clinical settings in order to best serve children and families across a variety of systems of service delivery. The program relies on a practitioner–scholar training model that prepares psychologists to provide direct and indirect services from a variety of theoretical perspectives, appreciate cultural and other forms of diversity, and function within the ethical guidelines provided by the American Psychological Association (APA) and the National Association of School Psychologists (NASP). Among the specific goals related to student learning in the PsyD program are the following: to develop a stable professional identity; a specific approach to knowledge generation and scientific foundations for evaluating practices, interventions, and programs; a firm appreciation of all facets of diversity; and development of ethical awareness.

Programs and Degrees Offered

Program	Degree	Application Deadline	Applications Received	Accepted	New Admits Enrolled (PT)	Total Enrolled (PT)	Degrees Awarded in 2014–2015	Median Years to Complete Degree	Dismissed/Withdrew
Psychology	MA/MS	August 1 (Fall), December 1 (Spring), May 1 (Summer)	56	39	11 (4)	16 (9)	8	2	1

Programs and Degrees Offered (con't.)

Program	Degree	Application Deadline	Applications Received	Accepted	New Admits Enrolled (PT)	Total Enrolled (PT)	Degrees Awarded in 2014–2015	Median Years to Complete Degree	Dismissed/ Withdrew
School-Clinical Child Psychology	PsyD	January 15 (Fall)	199	51	15 (0)	98 (0)	21	5	2
School Psychology	EdS	January 15 (Fall)	30	1	1 (0)	2 (0)	22	3.5	0

APA Accreditation

Combination PsyD: Student Outcome Data website: http://www.pace.edu/dyson/programs/psyd-school-clinical-child-psych-nyc.

Doctoral Degree (PsyD School-Clinical Child Psychology): For those doctoral students for whom a professional internship was required in this program prior to graduation:
Total students who applied for an internship: 25
Total students who obtained an internship: 25
Total students who obtained a paid internship: 20
Total students who obtained an unpaid internship: 5
Total students who were placed in APA/CPA-accredited internships: 14
Total students placed in internships not APA/CPA-accredited, but listed with the Association of Psychology Postdoctoral and Internship Centers (APPIC): 3
Total students placed in internships conforming to guidelines of the Council of Directors of School Psychology Programs (CDSPP): 0
Total students placed in internships that were not APA/CPA-accredited, APPIC or CDSSP listed: 8

Internships/Practica

Most school psychology and bilingual school psychology internships occur in the New York metropolitan region, including Long Island, Westchester County, and school districts throughout northern and central New Jersey. Doctoral internships are typically secured through the APPIC system; the doctoral program also utilizes CDSPP guidelines in approving internships. Doctoral students often secure internships in the New York metropolitan region.

Admissions

Entries appear in the following order: required test or GPA, minimum score (if required)/median score of students entering in 2015–2016.

Program	Degree	GRE-V	GRE-Q	GRE-Writing	GRE-Subject	Undergraduate GPA	Last 2 Years GPA	Psychology GPA	Master's GPA
Psychology	MA/MS	NA/NA	NA/NA	Not specified	Not specified	NA/NA	Not specified	Not specified	Not specified
School-Clinical Child Psychology	PsyD	144/158	142/151	Not specified	Not specified	NA/NA	Not specified	Not specified	Not specified
School Psychology	EdS	NA/NA	NA/NA	Not specified	Not specified	NA/NA	Not specified	Not specified	Not specified

Admissions Requirements:

Degree	GRE	GRE-Subject	Letters of Recommendation	Research Statement	Writing Sample	CV	Interview
Master's/Specialist	Required	Optional	3	Required	None	Required	Required
Doctoral	Required	Optional	3	Required	None	Required	Required

Admissions Criteria:

GRE scores—high
Research experience—medium
Work experience—medium
Clinically related public service—medium
GPA—high

Letters of recommendation—high
Interview—high
Statement of goals and objectives—high
Undergraduate psychology preparation—high

Department Demographics

	Male (PT)	Female (PT)	Total	African-American/ Black (PT)	Hispanic/ Latino (PT)	Asian/ Pacific Islander (PT)	American Indian/ Alaska Native (PT)	Caucasian/ White (PT)	Unknown (PT)	Multiethnic (PT)	ADA (PT)	Int'l (PT)
Students	21 (0)	99 (5)	125	6 (1)	11 (2)	11 (0)		82 (2)	2 (0)	8 (0)	3 (0)	5 (0)

Financial Information/Assistance

Tuition: For information on tuition costs, visit http://www.pace.edu/admission-aid/graduate-admission/graduates/tuition-and-fees. Higher tuition cost for this program: MSEd/PsyD courses each have a $50 per credit additional fee. Tuition is subject to change. Tuition costs vary by program.

Doctoral:
State residents: $1,205 per credit hour.
Nonstate residents: $1,205 per credit hour.

Master's:
State residents: $1,150 per credit hour.
Nonstate residents: $1,150 per credit hour.

Financial Assistance:

	Teaching Assistantship (% Receiving)	Teaching Assistantship Tuition Remission	Research Assistantship (% Receiving)	Research Assistantship Tuition Remission	Fellowship (% Receiving)	Fellowship Tuition Remission
First-Year Student	NA (NA)	NA	$2,500 (19)	Partial	$5,000 (52)	NA
Advanced Student	NA (NA)	NA	NA (NA)	NA	$5,000 (100)	NA

For additional information on financial assistance, visit http://www.pace.edu/admission-aid/graduate-admission/graduates/financial-aid.

Employment of Department Graduates

Doctoral:
Enrolled in a postdoctoral residency/fellowship: 13
Employed in a professional position in a school system: 1
Employed in a community mental health/counseling center: 4
Not seeking employment: 1
Other employment position: 1
Do not know: 1
Total: 21

Additional Information

Housing and Day Care: On-campus housing is available. See the following website for more information: http://www.pace.edu/nyc-housing. No on-campus day care facilities are available.

Information for Students With Physical Disabilities: See the following website: http://www.pace.edu/counseling/office-of-disability-services.

Special Facilities or Resources: The Psychology Department maintains the McShane Center for Psychological Services. This on-site training facility provides practicum training for students in the MSEd and PsyD programs. For example, training opportunities include interviewing, parent-infant observations, psychodiagnostics, and psychotherapy.

Application Information: Office of Graduate Admissions, Pace University, 1 Pace Plaza, New York, NY 10038. *Fee:* $70. *Online application:* http://www.pace.edu/admissions-aid/apply-now.

Roberts Wesleyan College
Department of Psychology/Graduate Psychology Program
School of Liberal Arts & Sciences
2301 Westside Drive
Rochester, NY 14624-1997
Telephone: (585) 594-6680
Director, Graduate Psychology Programs: Cheryl L. Repass, PsyD, NCSP

E-mail: repass_cheryl@roberts.edu
Web: http://www.roberts.edu/gradpsych

Orientation, Objectives, and Emphasis of Department
The mission of the School Psychology and School Counseling programs is to prepare students, in a Christian context, for effective, compassionate, professional practice. The programs aim to prepare students for exemplary service and leadership in private and public agencies/educational institutions, utilizing a scientist–practitioner approach, with special attention given to the Christian community, locally, nationally, and internationally.

Programs and Degrees Offered

Program	Degree	Application Deadline	Applications Received	Accepted	New Admits Enrolled (PT)	Total Enrolled (PT)	Degrees Awarded in 2014–2015	Median Years to Complete Degree	Dismissed/ Withdrew
School Psychology	MA/MS	February 1 (Fall), Rolling	16	12	7 (2)	17 (6)	10	3	0
School Counseling	MA/MS	February 1 (Fall), Rolling	16	11	4 (7)	13 (7)	2	2	2

Internships/Practica
Students in school psychology complete a 1,200-hour internship their third year, which typically includes a stipend paid by the school district. Out-of-state internships are also a possibility. These internships pay anywhere from $28,000 to $40,000 and are also contracted for 1,200 hours. Students in school counseling secure local unpaid internships for 600 hours during their second year.

Admissions
Entries appear in the following order: required test or GPA, minimum score (if required)/median score of students entering in 2015–2016.

Program	Degree	GRE-V	GRE-Q	GRE-Writing	GRE-Subject	Under-graduate GPA	Last 2 Years GPA	Psychology GPA	Master's GPA
School Psychology	MA/MS	NA/NA	NA/NA	NA/NA	Not specified	3/NA	Not specified	Not specified	Not specified
School Counseling	MA/MS	Not specified	Not specified	Not specified	Not specified	3/NA	Not specified	Not specified	Not specified

Admissions Requirements:

Degree	GRE	GRE-Subject	Letters of Recommendation	Research Statement	Writing Sample	CV	Interview
Master's/Specialist	Required	None	3	Required	Optional	Required	None

Please note if these criteria vary for different programs: GRE Scores not required for School Counseling Program.

Admissions Criteria:
GRE scores—medium
Work experience—medium
Clinically related public service—low
GPA—high
Letters of recommendation—high

Interview—high
Statement of goals and objectives—high
Undergraduate psychology preparation—high
Fit w/ College's mission—high

Department Demographics

	Male (PT)	Female (PT)	Total	African-American/ Black (PT)	Hispanic/ Latino (PT)	Asian/ Pacific Islander (PT)	American Indian/ Alaska Native (PT)	Caucasian/ White (PT)	Unknown	Multiethnic (PT)	ADA (PT)	Int'l (PT)
Students	6 (3)	24 (10)	43	5 (3)	1 (0)	2 (0)		0 (0)	22 (10)		0 (0)	1 (0)

Financial Information/Assistance

Tuition: Tuition is subject to change. Additional fees are assessed to students beyond the costs of tuition for the following: One-time student fee—$300; health/counseling—$110/semester; PSY 522—$130; student association—$35.

Master's:
State residents: $631 per credit hour.
Nonstate residents: $631 per credit hour.

Financial Assistance:

	Teaching Assistantship (% Receiving)	Teaching Assistantship Tuition Remission	Research Assistantship (% Receiving)	Research Assistantship Tuition Remission	Fellowship (% Receiving)	Fellowship Tuition Remission
First-Year Student	NA (NA)	NA	NA (NA)	NA	$2,192 (NA)	NA
Advanced Student	$900 (NA)	NA	NA (NA)	NA	NA (NA)	NA

Employment of Department Graduates

Master's:
Employed in a professional position in a school system: 12
Total: 12

Additional Information

Housing and Day Care: On-campus housing is available. See the following website for more information: https://www.roberts.edu/student-experience/residence-life.aspx. No on-campus day care facilities are available.

Information for Students With Physical Disabilities: See the following website: https://www.roberts.edu/student-experience/disability-services.aspx.

Application Information: Department of Psychology, Graduate Admissions Office, Roberts Wesleyan College, 2301 Westside Drive, Rochester, NY 14624-1997. *Fee:* $35. *Online application:* http://www.roberts.edu/graduate-online-application.aspx.

Sage Colleges, The (2015 data)
Department of Psychology
65 First Street
Troy, NY 12180
Telephone: (518) 244-2221
Chairperson: Dr. Patricia O'Connor

E-mail: morseg@sage.edu
Web: http://www.sage.edu/academics/health-sciences/

Orientation, Objectives, and Emphasis of Department
Our two degrees (MA in Community Psychology, and MA in Counseling/Community Psychology) provide students with the academic and skills training to become practitioners at the master's level. The programs range in credits from 42 to 60, depending on degree. The emphasis is on developing and strengthening student skills for application (whether individual or systems level) in the context

of strong theoretical foundations. Graduates of MA in Counseling/Community Psychology are eligible to sit for licensure as mental health counselors (LMHC) in New York State.

Programs and Degrees Offered

Program	Degree	Application Deadline	Applica-tions Received	Accepted	New Admits Enrolled (PT)	Total Enrolled (PT)	Degrees Awarded in 2014–2015	Median Years to Complete Degree	Dismissed/ Withdrew
Community Psychology	MA/MS	Rolling	2	1	0 (0)	7 (1)	4	3.5	0
Counseling and Community Psychology	MA/MS	April 1 (Fall)	45	29	26 (4)	55 (10)	20	3	0
Forensic Mental Health Certificate	Other	April 1 (Fall)	20	15	10 (2)	29 (22)	10	3	0

Internships/Practica

As part of each degree, all students are required to complete an internship (direct services) and/or externship (not direct services) placement, depending upon the selected area of concentration. Internships comprise one-year counseling placements in a setting appropriate to the student's interests; externships are one-semester projects in a setting of the student's choice.

Admissions

Entries appear in the following order: required test or GPA, minimum score (if required)/median score of students entering in 2015–2016.

Program	Degree	GRE-V	GRE-Q	GRF-Writing	GRE-Subject	Under-graduate GPA	Last 2 Years GPA	Psychol-ogy GPA	Master's GPA
Community Psychology	MA/MS	Not specified	Not specified	Not specified	Not specified	3/NA	Not specified	Not specified	Not specified
Counseling and Community Psychology	MA/MS	Not specified	Not specified	Not specified	Not specified	3/NA	Not specified	Not specified	Not specified
Forensic Mental Health Certificate	Other	Not specified	Not specified	Not specified	Not specified	Not specified	Not specified	Not specified	Not specified

Admissions Requirements:

Degree	GRE	GRE-Subject	Letters of Recom-mendation	Research Statement	Writing Sample	CV	Interview
Master's/Specialist	None	None	2	Required	None	Required	Optional

Admissions Criteria:

Research experience—low
Work experience—medium
Clinically related public service—medium
GPA—high

Letters of recommendation—high
Interview—medium
Statement of goals and objectives—high
Undergraduate psychology preparation—medium

For additional information on admission requirements, visit http://www.sage.edu/admission/graduate/procedures/.

Department Demographics

	Male (PT)	Female (PT)	Total	African-American/ Black (PT)	Hispanic/ Latino (PT)	Asian/ Pacific Islander (PT)	American Indian/ Alaska Native (PT)	Caucasian/ White (PT)	Unknown	Multiethnic (PT)	ADA (PT)	Int'l (PT)
Students	15 (3)	73 (12)	103	7 (0)	8 (0)	0 (1)	0 (0)	73 (13)	0 (0)	0 (1)	0 (0)	0 (0)

Financial Information/Assistance

Tuition: For information on tuition costs, visit http://www.sage.edu/costaid/tuition/sgs/. Tuition is subject to change.

Master's:
State residents: $680 per credit hour.
Nonstate residents: $680 per credit hour.

Financial Assistance:

	Teaching Assistantship (% Receiving)	Teaching Assistantship Tuition Remission	Research Assistantship (% Receiving)	Research Assistantship Tuition Remission	Fellowship (% Receiving)	Fellowship Tuition Remission
First-Year Student	NA (NA)	NA	$3,000 (NA)	Partial	NA (NA)	NA
Advanced Student	NA (NA)	NA	$3,000 (NA)	Partial	NA (NA)	NA

For additional information on financial assistance, visit http://www.sage.edu/resources/student_services/financial_aid/.

Employment of Department Graduates

No information provided.

Additional Information

Housing and Day Care: On-campus housing is available. See the following website for more information: http://www.sage.edu/sgs/studentlife/. No on-campus day care facilities are available.

Information for Students With Physical Disabilities: See the following website: http://www.sage.edu/studentlife/disabilities_services/.

Special Facilities or Resources: In addition to the faculty resources one would assume at the master's level, a particular advantage for psychology programs at Sage Graduate School is our prime location in the Capital District area of New York State. The geographic size, population density, and availability of widely varied populations make possible a wide variety of experiences.

Application Information: Graduate Admissions, The Sage Colleges, 65 Ferry Street, Troy, New York 12180. *Fee:* $50. *Online application:* http://www.sage.edu/apply.

St. John's University

Department of Psychology
St. John's College of Liberal Arts & Science, Graduate Division
8000 Utopia Parkway
Queens, NY 11439
Telephone: (718) 990-5541
Chairperson: William Chaplin, PhD
Web: http://www.stjohns.edu/academics/schools-and-colleges/st-johns-college-liberal-arts-and-sciences/psychology

E-mail: chaplinw@stjohns.edu

Orientation, Objectives, and Emphasis of Department

Our department emphasizes rigorous training in methodology, data analysis, and measurement as the foundation for effective research and practice. In addition we recognize the interrelatedness among the various content areas of psychology and emphasize broad exposure to these areas in all our graduate programs. Although our primary focus is on applied areas of psychology we appreciate that most applications can be traced to basic findings concerning human behavior, thought, and feeling. Our department is best described as cooperative as opposed to competitive and we recognize that there is no one orientation, theory, or method that can fully address all issues in psychology. It is through a multiplicity of theories and methods that we can most effectively understand psychology. We also appreciate that diversity in scientific, cultural, and value perspectives are most likely to lead to sustainable and comprehensive explanations.

Programs and Degrees Offered

Program	Degree	Application Deadline	Applica-tions Received	Accepted	New Admits Enrolled (PT)	Total Enrolled (PT)	Degrees Awarded in 2014–2015	Median Years to Complete Degree	Dismissed/ Withdrew
Clinical Psychology	PhD	December 31 (Fall)	295	10	10 (0)	58	13	5	
General-Experimental Psychology	MA/MS	Rolling	29	18	4	17 (1)	10	2	0
School Psychology	MA/MS	Rolling	40	25	12		11	3	1
School Psychology	PsyD	December 31 (Fall)	79	39	21 (0)		20	5	0

APA Accreditation

Clinical PhD: Student Outcome Data website: http://www.stjohns.edu/academics/schools-and-colleges/st-johns-college-liberal-arts-and-sciences/psychology/clinical-psychology-phd.
School PsyD: Student Outcome Data website: http://www.stjohns.edu/academics/schools-and-colleges/st-johns-college-liberal-arts-and-sciences/psychology/school-psychology-psyd.

Doctoral Degree (PhD Clinical Psychology): For those doctoral students for whom a professional internship was required in this program prior to graduation:
Total students who applied for an internship: 10
Total students who obtained an internship: 10
Total students who obtained a paid internship: 10
Total students who obtained an unpaid internship: 0
Total students who were placed in APA/CPA-accredited internships: 9
Total students placed in internships not APA/CPA-accredited, but listed with the Association of Psychology Postdoctoral and Internship Centers (APPIC): 1
Total students placed in internships conforming to guidelines of the Council of Directors of School Psychology Programs (CDSPP): 0
Total students placed in internships that were not APA/CPA-accredited, APPIC or CDSSP listed: 0

Doctoral Degree (PsyD School Psychology): For those doctoral students for whom a professional internship was required in this program prior to graduation:
Total students who applied for an internship: 16
Total students who obtained an internship: 15
Total students who obtained a paid internship: 3
Total students who obtained an unpaid internship: 12
Total students who were placed in APA/CPA-accredited internships: 2
Total students placed in internships not APA/CPA-accredited, but listed with the Association of Psychology Postdoctoral and Internship Centers (APPIC): 0
Total students placed in internships conforming to guidelines of the Council of Directors of School Psychology Programs (CDSPP): 0
Total students placed in internships that were not APA/CPA-accredited, APPIC or CDSSP listed: 13

Master's Degree (MA/MS School Psychology): An internship experience, such as a final research project or "capstone" experience is required of graduates.

Internships/Practica

We require 2 years of supervised externship experiences in our school and clinical programs. Externships are available in clinics, schools, medical centers, and public and private agencies throughout the greater New York area. In addition, students are required to complete a 1-year internship as part of the doctoral degree.

Admissions

Entries appear in the following order: required test or GPA, minimum score (if required)/median score of students entering in 2015–2016.

Program	Degree	GRE-V	GRE-Q	GRE-Writing	GRE-Subject	Under-graduate GPA	Last 2 Years GPA	Psychology GPA	Master's GPA
Clinical Psychology	PhD	Not specified	Not specified	Not specified	Not specified	Not specified	Not specified	Not specified	Not specified
General-Experimental Psychology	MA/MS	Not specified	Not specified	Not specified	Not specified	Not specified	Not specified	Not specified	Not specified
School Psychology	MA/MS	Not specified	Not specified	Not specified	Not specified	Not specified	Not specified	Not specified	Not specified
School Psychology	PsyD	Not specified	Not specified	Not specified	Not specified	Not specified	Not specified	Not specified	Not specified

Admissions Requirements:

Degree	GRE	GRE-Subject	Letters of Recommendation	Research Statement	Writing Sample	CV	Interview
Master's/Specialist	Required	Optional	3	Required	Required	Required	Required
Doctoral	Required	Optional	3	Required	Required	Required	Required

Please note if these criteria vary for different programs: The General Experimental MA program does not require GREs and interview.

Admissions Criteria:

GRE scores—medium
Research experience—high
Work experience—medium
Clinically related public service—high
GPA—medium

Letters of recommendation—high
Interview—high
Statement of goals and objectives—medium
Undergraduate psychology preparation—medium

Department Demographics

	Male (PT)	Female (PT)	Total	African-American/ Black (PT)	Hispanic/ Latino (PT)	Asian/ Pacific Islander (PT)	American Indian/ Alaska Native (PT)	Caucasian/ White (PT)	Unknown (PT)	Multiethnic (PT)	ADA (PT)	Int'l (PT)
Students	49 (0)	193 (0)	242	15 (0)	19 (0)	22 (0)	0 (0)	180 (0)	3 (0)	3 (0)	0 (0)	5 (0)

Financial Information/Assistance

Tuition: For information on tuition costs, visit http://www.stjohns.edu/admission-aid/tuition-and-financial-aid/tuition/graduate-tuition. Higher tuition cost for this program: Clinical PhD is $41,250/year; $1,375/credit. General MA is $27,480/year; $1145/credit.

Doctoral:
State residents: $36,750 per academic year.
State residents: $1,225 per credit hour.
Nonstate residents: $36,750 per academic year.
Nonstate residents: $1,225 per credit hour.

Master's:
State residents: $36,750 per academic year.
State residents: $1,225 per credit hour.
Nonstate residents: $36,750 per academic year.
Nonstate residents: $1,225 per credit hour.

Financial Assistance:

	Teaching Assistantship (% Receiving)	Teaching Assistantship Tuition Remission	Research Assistantship (% Receiving)	Research Assistantship Tuition Remission	Fellowship (% Receiving)	Fellowship Tuition Remission
First-Year Student	NA (NA)	NA	$16,000 (60)	Full	NA (NA)	NA
Advanced Student	NA (NA)	NA	$16,000 (NA)	Full	NA (NA)	NA

For additional information on financial assistance, visit http://www.stjohns.edu/admission-aid/tuition-and-financial-aid/graduate/law-aid.

Employment of Department Graduates

Master's:
Employed in other positions at a higher education institution: 2
Employed in a professional position in a school system: 25
Employed in business or industry: 4
Do not know: 7
Total: 38

Doctoral:
Enrolled in a postdoctoral residency/fellowship: 6
Employed in a professional position in a school system: 14
Employed in a community mental health/counseling center: 6
Employed in a hospital/medical center: 4
Other employment position: 2
Do not know: 2
Total: 34

Additional Information

Housing and Day Care: On-campus housing is available. See the following website for more information: http://www.stjohns.edu/student-life/queens-campus-life/residence-life. No on-campus day care facilities are available.

Special Facilities or Resources: Our department is located in one of the most culturally and linguistically diverse areas in the United States and thus we have unique access to people from many backgrounds for our training and research. We also have a full time Psychological Services Center which serves as a community-based mental health training clinic. Students and faculty also partner with the major medical facilities in New York to conduct research. A number of our faculty have developed specific out reach programs including childhood trauma, parent training, medical consultation, and anger management.

Application Information: Graduate Admission Processing Service Center, St. John's University, P.O. Box 811, Randolph, MA 02368-0811. *Fee:* $70. *Online application:* http://apply.embark.com/grad/stjohns/.

State University of New York at New Paltz
Department of Psychology/Counseling Graduate Program
JFT 314, 600 Hawk Drive
New Paltz, NY 12561-2440
Telephone: (845) 257-3467
Chairperson: Glenn Geher

E-mail: gradpsych@newpaltz.edu; counsgradprogram@newpaltz.edu
Web: http://www.newpaltz.edu/psychology/graduate

Orientation, Objectives, and Emphasis of Department
Founded in 1828, America's 99th oldest university is an exciting blend of tradition and vision, providing students with the skills and knowledge needed to meet the challenges of the 21st century. SUNY New Paltz offers graduate training in psychology and mental health counseling. The 36-credit MA in psychology program offers general graduate training in psychology. The program provides students with the opportunity to select electives in a variety of fields including social, experimental, and organizational psychology as well as counseling. The program may serve as preparation for entry into a doctoral program or as additional training for those who plan to enter or are already involved in applied areas of psychology. The 48-credit MS in mental health counseling program serves both students looking to become licensed as mental health counselors and those seeking to eventually proceed into doctoral training programs. Degree requirements cover a core curriculum and specialization courses. Three fieldwork courses provide hands-on mental health counseling training experiences under supervision of licensed professionals. The program is registered with the State Education Department as meeting the educational requirements necessary for mental health counseling licensure in New York, making this a very marketable degree.

Programs and Degrees Offered

Program	Degree	Application Deadline	Applica-tions Received	Accepted	New Admits Enrolled (PT)	Total Enrolled (PT)	Degrees Awarded in 2014–2015	Median Years to Complete Degree	Dismissed/ Withdrew
Psychology	MA/MS	February 15 (Fall), November 15 (Spring)	19	9		19 (0)	11	2	1
Mental Health Counseling	MA/MS	February 1 (Fall)	37		11 (3)	27 (6)	7		
School Counseling	MA/MS	February 1 (Fall)	35	5	8		6		0
Advanced Certificate in Mental Health Counseling	Other	November 1 (Spring)	2		2	2	2		

Internships/Practica

All students in the mental health counseling program complete a practicum at the college counseling center and the career advising center. Additional internship opportunities are available with regional public and private mental health agencies. In addition to practicum and internship requirements, mental health counseling students complete a curriculum of mental health counseling coursework. All students in the school counseling program must complete a practicum and an internship experience at one of several area school districts. The practicum and internship may be completed within an elementary, middle, or high school setting. Students will have the option of completing the practicum and internship within the same school/school district or to change the school, school district, and/or grade level to gain a wide range of experience.

Admissions

Entries appear in the following order: required test or GPA, minimum score (if required)/median score of students entering in 2015–2016.

Program	Degree	GRE-V	GRE-Q	GRE-Writing	GRE-Subject	Under-graduate GPA	Last 2 Years GPA	Psychol-ogy GPA	Master's GPA
Psychology	MA/MS	NA/NA	NA/NA	NA/NA	Not specified	3/NA	Not specified	3/NA	Not specified
Mental Health Counseling	MA/MS	NA/NA	NA/NA	NA/NA	Not specified	3/NA	Not specified	Not specified	Not specified
School Counseling	MA/MS	NA/NA	NA/NA	NA/NA	Not specified	3/NA	Not specified	Not specified	Not specified
Advanced Certificate in Mental Health Counseling	Other	Not specified	Not specified	Not specified	Not specified	Not specified	Not specified	Not specified	Not specified

Admissions Requirements:

Degree	GRE	GRE-Subject	Letters of Recom-mendation	Research Statement	Writing Sample	CV	Interview
Master's/Specialist	Required	Optional	3	Required	None	None	Required

Please note if these criteria vary for different programs: Admissions criteria are weighted differently for the counseling and psychology programs. Work experience and clinically related public service are low in importance for the MA Psychology program, while research experience is only medium for counseling. The Advanced Certificate in Mental Health Counseling does not require GRE scores, but the other programs all do. The MA program does require an interview.

Admissions Criteria:

GRE scores—medium
Research experience—high
Work experience—medium
Clinically related public service—high
GPA—high

Letters of recommendation—high
Interview—medium
Statement of goals and objectives—high
Undergraduate psychology preparation—medium
Writing ability—high

Department Demographics

	Male (PT)	Female (PT)	Total	African-American/ Black (PT)	Hispanic/ Latino (PT)	Asian/ Pacific Islander (PT)	American Indian/ Alaska Native (PT)	Caucasian/ White (PT)	Unknown	Multiethnic (PT)	ADA (PT)	Int'l (PT)
Students	9 (3)	43 (1)	56					0 (0)	0 (0)			

Financial Information/Assistance

Tuition: For information on tuition costs, visit http://www.newpaltz.edu/financialaid/tuition.php. Tuition is subject to change.

Master's:
State residents: $10,870 per academic year.
State residents: $453 per credit hour.
Nonstate residents: $22,210 per academic year.
Nonstate residents: $925 per credit hour.

Financial Assistance:

	Teaching Assistantship (% Receiving)	Teaching Assistantship Tuition Remission	Research Assistantship (% Receiving)	Research Assistantship Tuition Remission	Fellowship (% Receiving)	Fellowship Tuition Remission
First-Year Student	$5,000 (NA)	Partial	NA (NA)	NA	NA (NA)	Partial
Advanced Student	$5,000 (NA)	Partial	NA (NA)	NA	NA (NA)	Partial

For additional information on financial assistance, visit http://www.newpaltz.edu/financialaid.

Employment of Department Graduates

Master's:
Enrolled in a psychology doctoral program: 5
Employed in a professional position in a school system: 2
Employed in a community mental health/counseling center: 4
Do not know: 2
Total: 13

Additional Information

Housing and Day Care: On-campus housing is available. See the following website for more information: http://www.newpaltz.edu/reslife/. On-campus day care facilities are available. See the following website for more information: http://www.newpaltz.edu/childrenscenter/.

Information for Students With Physical Disabilities: See the following website: http://www.newpaltz.edu/drc.

Special Facilities or Resources: Laboratory facilities and equipment (computers, videotaping equipment) are available to support student and faculty research in a variety of research areas. The department also maintains links to local and community organizations for research opportunities. In addition, the department has a computer lab for research and instruction with Internet access. All graduate students have access to word processing, SPSS, and the world-wide Web through the campus computer network.

Application Information: The Graduate School, SUNY New Paltz, 1 Hawk Drive, New Paltz, NY 12561-2443. *Fee:* $50. *Online application:* http://www.newpaltz.edu/graduate/online.html.

State University of New York, Binghamton University

Psychology
Arts and Sciences
P.O. Box 6000
Binghamton, NY 13902-6000
Telephone: (607) 777-2334
Chairperson: Christopher Bishop

E-mail: rmattson@binghamton.edu
Web: http://www.binghamton.edu/psychology/

Orientation, Objectives, and Emphasis of Department

The psychology department emphasizes basic and applied research in its three areas of specialization: clinical psychology, cognitive psychology, and behavioral neuroscience. The goal of our APA-accredited clinical program is to develop scientists and practitioners. By virtue of ongoing research involvement, students are expected to contribute to knowledge about psychopathology, assessment, and treatment. Our cognitive program has two major research emphases, one focused on learning and memory and the other focused on perception and language (in both the visual and auditory domains). Researchers in this area also work in industrial settings and collaborate with local industry. Our behavioral neuroscience program emphasizes the study of neural and hormonal bases of normal and abnormal behavior and their developmental antecedents in preclinical animal models.

Programs and Degrees Offered

Program	Degree	Application Deadline	Applications Received	Accepted	New Admits Enrolled (PT)	Total Enrolled (PT)	Degrees Awarded in 2014–2015	Median Years to Complete Degree	Dismissed/ Withdrew
Behavioral Neuroscience	PhD	December 15 (Fall)	31	13	5 (0)	23 (0)	3	6	0
Clinical Psychology	PhD	December 15 (Fall)	226	17	7 (0)	40 (0)	7	6	0
Cognitive Psychology	PhD	December 31 (Fall)	30	10	5 (0)	21 (0)	3	6.5	0

APA Accreditation

Clinical PhD: Student Outcome Data website: http://www.binghamton.edu/psychology/graduate/clinical-psychology/index.html.

Doctoral Degree (PhD Clinical Psychology): For those doctoral students for whom a professional internship was required in this program prior to graduation:
Total students who applied for an internship: 10
Total students who obtained an internship: 8
Total students who obtained a paid internship: 8
Total students who obtained an unpaid internship: 0
Total students who were placed in APA/CPA-accredited internships: 8
Total students placed in internships not APA/CPA-accredited, but listed with the Association of Psychology Postdoctoral and Internship Centers (APPIC): 0
Total students placed in internships conforming to guidelines of the Council of Directors of School Psychology Programs (CDSPP): 0
Total students placed in internships that were not APA/CPA-accredited, APPIC or CDSSP listed: 0

Internships/Practica

Students in the clinical area are required to complete two practica—a psychotherapy practicum and a community practicum. The psychotherapy practicum is conducted in the department clinic under the supervision of a faculty member and generally involves the joint treatment of a variety of problems across a broad range of ages and diagnoses. The community practicum consists of supervised clinical activity and/or research at one of a wide range of local agencies, hospitals, and clinics. Students in cognitive psychology are invited—but not required—to complete a research-related practicum in industry. Past internships included training at GE, IBM, Microsoft, Lockheed Martin, and others.

Admissions

Entries appear in the following order: required test or GPA, minimum score (if required)/median score of students entering in 2015–2016.

Program	Degree	GRE-V	GRE-Q	GRE-Writing	GRE-Subject	Under-graduate GPA	Last 2 Years GPA	Psychol-ogy GPA	Master's GPA
Behavioral Neuroscience	PhD	157/166	152/156	4/5	Not specified	3.1/3.3	Not specified	Not specified	Not specified
Clinical Psychology	PhD	152/163	158/169	3.5/4	Not specified	3.35/3.52	Not specified	Not specified	Not specified
Cognitive Psychology	PhD	155/158	157/159	3.5/4.25	Not specified	3.2/3.59	Not specified	Not specified	Not specified

Admissions Requirements:

Degree	GRE	GRE-Subject	Letters of Recom-mendation	Research Statement	Writing Sample	CV	Interview
Doctoral	Required	Required	3	Required	Optional	Required	Required

Please note if these criteria vary for different programs: Clinical Psychology program requires GRE-Subject scores, other programs do not.

Admissions Criteria:

GRE scores—high
Research experience—high
Work experience— medium
Clinically related public service—medium
GPA—high

Letters of recommendation—high
Interview—high
Statement of goals and objectives— high
Undergraduate psychology preparation—medium

For additional information on admission requirements, visit http://www.binghamton.edu/psychology/graduate/admission.html.

Department Demographics

	Male (PT)	Female (PT)	Total	African-American/ Black (PT)	Hispanic/ Latino (PT)	Asian/ Pacific Islander (PT)	American Indian/ Alaska Native (PT)	Caucasian/ White (PT)	Unknown	Multiethnic (PT)	ADA (PT)	Int'l (PT)
Students	30 (0)	54 (0)	84	7 (0)	4 (0)	2 (0)	0 (0)	71 (0)	0 (0)	0 (0)	0 (0)	3 (0)

Financial Information/Assistance

Tuition: For information on tuition costs, visit http://www.binghamton.edu/student-accounts/. Tuition is subject to change.

Doctoral:
State residents: $10,870 per academic year.
State residents: $453 per credit hour.
Nonstate residents: $22,210 per academic year.
Nonstate residents: $1,850 per credit hour.

Financial Assistance:

	Teaching Assistantship (% Receiving)	Teaching Assistantship Tuition Remission	Research Assistantship (% Receiving)	Research Assistantship Tuition Remission	Fellowship (% Receiving)	Fellowship Tuition Remission
First-Year Student	$16,500 (NA)	Full	$16,500 (NA)	Full	$16,500 (NA)	Full
Advanced Student	$16,500 (NA)	Full	$16,500 (NA)	Full	$16,500 (NA)	Full

For additional information on financial assistance, visit http://www.binghamton.edu/grad-school/cost-aid-funding/financial-support/.

Employment of Department Graduates

Doctoral:
Enrolled in a postdoctoral residency/fellowship: 8
Employed in an academic position at a university: 2
Employed in other positions at a higher education institution: 1
Employed in a hospital/medical center: 2
Total: 13

Additional Information

Housing and Day Care: No on-campus housing is available. On-campus day care facilities are available. See the following website for more information: http://www.binghamton.edu/campus-pre-school/.

Information for Students With Physical Disabilities: See the following website: http://www.binghamton.edu/ssd/.

Special Facilities or Resources: All faculty have state-of-the-art, spacious laboratories. The clinical program supports an active in-house mental health clinic. Members of the cognitive area have access to sophisticated systems for the manipulation of auditory and visual stimuli and the online measurement of evoked response potentials, eyetracking, and cognitive processes. Members of the behavioral neurosciences area share multi-user histology, microneuroimaging, and neurochemistry laboratories. A new building for animal research has recently been completed. The faculty and graduate students are members of a number of interdisciplinary centers at housed exclusively at SUNY-Binghamton or shared with other research universities.

Application Information: Fee: $75. *Online application:* http://www.binghamton.edu/grad-school/admissions/apply/.

State University of New York, College at Plattsburgh
Psychology Department
Beaumont Hall, 101 Broad Street
Plattsburgh, NY 12901
Telephone: (518) 564-3076
Chairperson: Drs. Dunham and Morales, Cochairs

E-mail: dunhamkt@plattsburgh.edu
Web: http://www.plattsburgh.edu/academics/psychology

Orientation, Objectives, and Emphasis of Department
The curriculum is a three-year, 70-hour MA program in psychology. The program offers coursework in psychological theories and skill development and applied experiences in area schools and community agencies. The goal of the program is to enable students to work effectively with individuals and groups and to act as psychological resources in schools and the community. A unique feature of the program is that many courses, beginning in the first semester, combine theory and research with practicum experiences in school and clinical work. Students develop competency in personality, research methods, psychological assessment, behavior modification, individual and group psychotherapy, and community mental health. An important aspect of graduate training is the internship served the third year of graduate study at area schools. The Psychology Department and the agencies involved provide extensive supervision of students' work.

Programs and Degrees Offered

Program	Degree	Application Deadline	Applica-tions Received	Accepted	New Admits Enrolled (PT)	Total Enrolled (PT)	Degrees Awarded in 2014–2015	Median Years to Complete Degree	Dismissed/Withdrew
School Psychology	MA/MS	February 1 (Fall)	27	8	8 (0)	21 (0)	7	3	0

Internships/Practica

During the third and final year of graduate study, students are placed within school districts on a full-time basis. School districts sometimes offer a stipend under contractual agreement with the graduate student and the University. Stipends range from $7,000 to $14,000. Relocating to a school district in order to receive a stipend might be necessary.

Admissions

Entries appear in the following order: required test or GPA, minimum score (if required)/median score of students entering in 2015–2016.

Program	Degree	GRE-V	GRE-Q	GRE-Writing	GRE-Subject	Under-graduate GPA	Last 2 Years GPA	Psychol-ogy GPA	Master's GPA
School Psychology	MA/MS	Not specified	Not specified	Not specified	Not specified	3/NA	Not specified	Not specified	Not specified

Admissions Requirements:

Degree	GRE	GRE-Subject	Letters of Recom-mendation	Research Statement	Writing Sample	CV	Interview
Master's/Specialist	None	None	3	Required	Optional	Required	Optional

Admissions Criteria:

GRE scores—low
Research experience—medium
Work experience—high
Clinically related public service—high
GPA—high

Letters of recommendation—medium
Interview—medium
Statement of goals and objectives—high
Undergraduate psychology preparation—high

For additional information on admission requirements, visit http://www.plattsburgh.edu/academics/psychology/graduateprogram/graduateadmissions.php.

Department Demographics

	Male (PT)	Female (PT)	Total	African-American/Black (PT)	Hispanic/Latino (PT)	Asian/Pacific Islander (PT)	American Indian/Alaska Native (PT)	Caucasian/White (PT)	Unknown (PT)	Multiethnic (PT)	ADA (PT)	Int'l (PT)
Students	1 (0)	20 (0)	21	0 (0)	1 (0)	1 (0)	0 (0)	18 (0)	0 (0)	0 (0)	0 (0)	1 (0)

Financial Information/Assistance

Tuition: For information on tuition costs, visit http://www.plattsburgh.edu/studentlife/studentaccounts/summary.php. Tuition is subject to change.

Master's:
State residents: $9,370 per academic year.
Nonstate residents: $16,680 per academic year.

Financial Assistance:

	Teaching Assistantship (% Receiving)	Teaching Assistantship Tuition Remission	Research Assistantship (% Receiving)	Research Assistantship Tuition Remission	Fellowship (% Receiving)	Fellowship Tuition Remission
First-Year Student	NA (NA)	NA	NA (NA)	NA	NA (NA)	NA
Advanced Student	NA (NA)	NA	NA (NA)	NA	NA (NA)	NA

For additional information on financial assistance, visit http://www.plattsburgh.edu/admissions/graduate/assistantships/.

Employment of Department Graduates

Master's:
Employed in a professional position in a school system: 8
Total: 8

Additional Information

Housing and Day Care: On-campus housing is available. See the following website for more information: http://www.plattsburgh.edu/studentlife/housing/. On-campus day care facilities are available. See the following website for more information: http://www.plattsburgh.edu/offices/buildings/childcare.php.

Information for Students With Physical Disabilities: See the following website: http://www.plattsburgh.edu/offices/support/sss/.

Special Facilities or Resources: All students participate in off-site practicum experiences in local schools. The Neuropsychology Clinic and Psychoeducational Services center provides some graduate students with on-site practicum experiences. The Nexus program (an after school program for children diagnosed with Autism Spectrum Disorders) provides some graduate students with on-site practicum experiences.

Application Information: Graduate Admissions, Kehoe Hall, SUNY-Plattsburgh, 101 Broad Street, Plattsburgh, NY 12901. *Fee:* $100.

State University of New York, University of Albany
Educational and Counseling Psychology
School of Education
1400 Washington Avenue
Albany, NY 12222
Telephone: (518) 442-5050
Chairperson: Kevin P. Quinn

E-mail: ecpyinfo@albany.edu
Web: http://www.albany.edu/education/edpsych.php

Orientation, Objectives, and Emphasis of Department
The master's program in mental health counseling (nationally accredited by MPCAC) and the certificate of advanced study program in school psychology are practitioner-focused, leading to certification/licensure in NY State. In the APA-accredited school psychology and counseling psychology doctoral programs, practice and science are viewed as complementary and interdependent, implemented through coursework in psychological foundations, research methods, intervention theory and assessment, and by research and practice opportunities via assistantships, professional development activities, practica, and specialized coursework. Our generalist training emphasizes normal development and theory and methods related to prevention and remediation of intra- and interpersonal human concerns. We have many opportunities to explore issues of individual and multicultural diversity, to learn a variety of theoretical orientations, to pursue a range of research topics and methods, to study with a multicultural array of colleagues, to work with diverse client populations in multiple work settings, and to engage in varied professional roles. The master's program in educational psychology and methodology focuses on research-based knowledge of human development, learning and individual differences, and the development of skills and understanding of research methods and statistics. An important role of this program is to provide introductory graduate work in psychology and education.

Programs and Degrees Offered

Program	Degree	Application Deadline	Applications Received	Accepted	New Admits Enrolled (PT)	Total Enrolled (PT)	Degrees Awarded in 2014–2015	Median Years to Complete Degree	Dismissed/ Withdrew
Counseling Psychology	PhD	December 1 (Fall)	86	12	7 (0)	37 (3)	5	6	0
Educational Psychology	MA/MS	Rolling	25	22	6 (2)	22 (1)	10	1.5	0
School Psychology Certificate	Other	January 31 (Fall)	29	20	5 (0)	20 (0)	8	3	0
Mental Health Counseling	MA/MS	December 15 (Summer)	80	33	33 (0)	62 (2)	29	1.5	1
Educational Psychology	PhD	January 15 (Fall)	29	14	5 (0)	40 (12)	5	5.5	1
School Psychology	PsyD	January 2 (Fall)	36	15	6 (0)	24 (0)	4	5.5	0

APA Accreditation

Counseling PhD: Student Outcome Data website: http://www.albany.edu/counseling_psych/phd_statistics.php.
School PsyD: Student Outcome Data website: http://www.albany.edu/schoolpsych/doctor-of-psychology.php.

Doctoral Degree (PhD Counseling Psychology): For those doctoral students for whom a professional internship was required in this program prior to graduation:
Total students who applied for an internship: 4
Total students who obtained an internship: 4
Total students who obtained a paid internship: 4
Total students who obtained an unpaid internship: 0
Total students who were placed in APA/CPA-accredited internships: 4
Total students placed in internships not APA/CPA-accredited, but listed with the Association of Psychology Postdoctoral and Internship Centers (APPIC): 0
Total students placed in internships conforming to guidelines of the Council of Directors of School Psychology Programs (CDSPP): 0
Total students placed in internships that were not APA/CPA-accredited, APPIC or CDSSP listed: 0

Doctoral Degree (PsyD School Psychology): For those doctoral students for whom a professional internship was required in this program prior to graduation:
Total students who applied for an internship: 5
Total students who obtained an internship: 5
Total students who obtained a paid internship: 5
Total students who obtained an unpaid internship: 0
Total students who were placed in APA/CPA-accredited internships: 0
Total students placed in internships not APA/CPA-accredited, but listed with the Association of Psychology Postdoctoral and Internship Centers (APPIC): 0
Total students placed in internships conforming to guidelines of the Council of Directors of School Psychology Programs (CDSPP): 5
Total students placed in internships that were not APA/CPA-accredited, APPIC or CDSSP listed: 0

Master's Degree (MA/MS Educational Psychology): An internship experience, such as a final research project or "capstone" experience is required of graduates. Master's Degree (MA/MS Mental Health Counseling): An internship experience, such as a final research project or "capstone" experience is required of graduates.

Internships/Practica

In counseling psychology, PhD students take beginning and advanced practica and practica in specialized procedures. The initial, year-long practicum is taken at the University-operated Psychological Services Center, a training facility for graduate students in the counseling and clinical psychology programs. Opportunities for advanced practica are community-based, and include outpatient and inpatient therapy and assessment in hospitals (private and VA), college counseling centers, community mental health centers, and residential treatment settings for youth. Our doctoral students have been highly successful in obtaining their preferred APA-accredited internships. Master's students in mental health counseling take practica in community agencies and hospitals. Both PsyD and Certificate of Advanced Study students in school psychology complete school-based practica. Students obtain supervised experience in assessment, individual and group counseling, classroom interventions, and consultation. Doctoral students in school psychology complete additional field training experiences in local schools and agencies to reinforce basic skills and to develop additional expertise in consultation, prevention, and systems issues. Certificate students in school psychology complete a one-year, full-time internship in a public school system to develop and reinforce basic skill competencies needed for future employment.

Admissions

Entries appear in the following order: required test or GPA, minimum score (if required)/median score of students entering in 2015–2016.

Program	Degree	GRE-V	GRE-Q	GRE-Writing	GRE-Subject	Under-graduate GPA	Last 2 Years GPA	Psychol-ogy GPA	Master's GPA
Counseling Psychology	PhD	NA/156	NA/151	NA/4.5	Not specified	NA/3.59	Not specified	NA/NA	Not specified
Educational Psychology	MA/MS	Not specified	Not specified	Not specified	Not specified	3/NA	Not specified	Not specified	Not specified
School Psychology Certificate	Other	145/153	145/149	3/4	Not specified	3/NA	Not specified	Not specified	Not specified
Mental Health Counseling	MA/MS	NA/156	NA/152	NA/NA	Not specified	NA/3.6	Not specified	NA/3.8	Not specified
Educational Psychology	PhD	NA/NA	NA/NA	Not specified	Not specified	NA/NA	Not specified	Not specified	NA/NA
School Psychology	PsyD	147/155	144/153	3/4	Not specified	3/NA	Not specified	Not specified	Not specified

Admissions Requirements:

Degree	GRE	GRE-Subject	Letters of Recom-mendation	Research Statement	Writing Sample	CV	Interview
Master's/Specialist	Required	None	3	Required	Optional	Optional	Required
Doctoral	Required	Recom-mended	3	Required	Optional	Required	Required

Please note if these criteria vary for different programs: The counseling psychology PhD and school psychology PsyD programs do require interviews, whereas the educational psychology PhD program does not. The GRE Psychology subject test is recommended for the PhD program in counseling psychology (only) but is not required. Undergraduate psychology preparation is not a high priority for the educational psychology PhD. Applicants for the MS in educational psychology do not need to submit GREs. Research experience is not required for the master's in mental health counseling or for the CAS in school psychology.

Admissions Criteria:

GRE scores—high
Research experience—high
Work experience—medium
Clinically related public service—low
GPA—high

Letters of recommendation—medium
Interview—medium
Statement of goals and objectives—high
Undergraduate psychology preparation—medium

For additional information on admission requirements, visit http://www.albany.edu/education/admissions_education.php.

Department Demographics

	Male (PT)	Female (PT)	Total	African-American/ Black (PT)	Hispanic/ Latino (PT)	Asian/ Pacific Islander (PT)	American Indian/ Alaska Native (PT)	Caucasian/ White (PT)	Unknown (PT)	Multiethnic (PT)	ADA (PT)	Int'l (PT)
Students	34 (2)	171 (16)	223	16 (0)	9 (2)	34 (0)	0 (0)	138 (16)	2 (0)	6 (0)	5 (0)	30 (0)

Financial Information/Assistance

Tuition: For information on tuition costs, visit http://www.albany.edu/studentservices/. Tuition is subject to change. Additional fees are assessed to students beyond the costs of tuition for the following: university fee, student activity fee, comprehensive fee, grad student organization fee.

Doctoral:
State residents: $10,870 per academic year.
State residents: $453 per credit hour.
Nonstate residents: $22,210 per academic year.
Nonstate residents: $925 per credit hour.

Master's:
State residents: $10,870 per academic year.
State residents: $453 per credit hour.
Nonstate residents: $22,210 per academic year.
Nonstate residents: $925 per credit hour.

Financial Assistance:

	Teaching Assistantship (% Receiving)	Teaching Assistantship Tuition Remission	Research Assistantship (% Receiving)	Research Assistantship Tuition Remission	Fellowship (% Receiving)	Fellowship Tuition Remission
First-Year Student	NA (NA)	NA	$15,300 (NA)	Full	NA (NA)	NA
Advanced Student	$15,300 (NA)	Full	$15,300 (NA)	Full	$15,300 (NA)	Full

For additional information on financial assistance, visit http://www.albany.edu/graduate/funding-graduate-study.php.

Employment of Department Graduates

Master's:
Enrolled in a psychology doctoral program: 5
Employed in a professional position in a school system: 9
Employed in business or industry: 2
Employed in a community mental health/counseling center: 18
Other employment position: 1
Do not know: 16
Total: 51

Doctoral:
Employed in independent practice: 3
Employed in other positions at a higher education institution: 3
Employed in a professional position in a school system: 3
Employed in a community mental health/counseling center: 1
Employed in a hospital/medical center: 3
Do not know: 4
Total: 17

Additional Information

Housing and Day Care: No on-campus housing is available. On-campus day care facilities are available. See the following website for more information: http://www.albany.edu/ukids/.

Information for Students With Physical Disabilities: See the following website: http://www.albany.edu/disability/.

Special Facilities or Resources: Our fee-for-service community training clinic, the Psychological Services Center, is directed by a licensed psychologist. Second-year doctoral students in counseling psychology are supervised by licensed faculty using live and recorded video monitoring. Advanced doctoral students may have clinical assistantships at the Center, where they gain additional experience in psychodiagnostic assessment and psychotherapy. One unique aspect of the program in Counseling Psychology is the opportunity for PhD students who are reasonably fluent in Spanish to participate in an exchange program with a family therapy graduate training program in northwestern Spain (Galicia). The Division of School Psychology maintains ongoing training partnerships with a number of local school districts and community agencies. Faculty in the Educational Psychology and Methodology Division are associated with two centers that provide students with opportunities to gain experience to supplement their coursework. The Child Research and Study Center undertakes research into the acquisition and remediation of reading skills and consults with schools and parents regarding children's school-related difficulties. The Evaluation Consortium contracts to evaluate a wide variety of programs provided by schools and agencies.

Application Information: Office of Graduate Studies, University at Albany, 1400 Washington Avenue, Albany, NY 12222. *Fee:* $75. *Online application:* http://www.albany.edu/graduate/apply-now.php.

Stony Brook University (2015 data)
Department of Psychology
Stony Brook, NY 11794-2500
Telephone: (631) 632-7855
Chairperson: Arthur Samuel

E-mail: marilynn.wollmuth@stonybrook.edu
Web: http://www.psychology.sunysb.edu

Orientation, Objectives, and Emphasis of Department
In all areas, the primary emphasis is on research training through research advisement and apprenticeship. Students are encouraged to become involved in ongoing research immediately and to engage in independent research when sufficient skills and knowledge permit, with the goal of becoming active and original contributors. As the first behavioral clinical curriculum in the country, Stony Brook has served as a model for a number of other behaviorally oriented clinical programs and continues to be a leader in that field. Research in the experimental area focuses on human perception and cognition and now includes visual cognition, psycholinguistics, memory, attention, and perception. The biopsychology research of core faculty spans the fields of behavioral neuroscience, molecular biology, cognitive neuroscience, and affective neuroscience. Students obtain a broad foundation in neuroscience while developing expertise in a focused research program. Research in social and health psychology includes the study of close relationships in adults and children; prejudice, racism, and stereotyping; and the representation and processing of social experience, motivation, and self-regulation.

Programs and Degrees Offered

Program	Degree	Application Deadline	Applications Received	Accepted	New Admits Enrolled (PT)	Total Enrolled (PT)	Degrees Awarded in 2014–2015	Median Years to Complete Degree	Dismissed/ Withdrew
Integrative Neuroscience	PhD	December 15 (Fall)	30	2	2	14	3	5	0
Clinical Psychology	PhD	December 15 (Fall)	328	8	8	33	6	6	2
Cognitive Science	PhD	December 15 (Fall)	40	3	3	20	3	5	0
Social/Health Psychology	PhD	December 15 (Fall)	70	2	2	16	2	5	0
General Psychology	MA/MS	February 28 (Summer)	101		14	14	12	1	0

APA Accreditation
Clinical PhD:

Doctoral Degree (PhD Clinical Psychology): For those doctoral students for whom a professional internship was required in this program prior to graduation:
Total students who applied for an internship: 6
Total students who obtained an internship: 6
Total students who obtained a paid internship: 6
Total students who obtained an unpaid internship: 0
Total students who were placed in APA/CPA-accredited internships: 6
Total students placed in internships not APA/CPA-accredited, but listed with the Association of Psychology Postdoctoral and Internship Centers (APPIC): 0
Total students placed in internships conforming to guidelines of the Council of Directors of School Psychology Programs (CDSPP): 0
Total students placed in internships that were not APA/CPA-accredited, APPIC or CDSSP listed: 0

Admissions

Entries appear in the following order: required test or GPA, minimum score (if required)/median score of students entering in 2015–2016.

Program	Degree	GRE-V	GRE-Q	GRE-Writing	GRE-Subject	Under-graduate GPA	Last 2 Years GPA	Psychology GPA	Master's GPA
Integrative Neuroscience	PhD	155/156	147/151	3/3.5	Not specified	Not specified	Not specified	Not specified	Not specified
Clinical Psychology	PhD	NA/NA	NA/NA	NA/NA	Not specified	NA/3.83	Not specified	Not specified	Not specified
Cognitive Science	PhD	157/160	151/154	Not specified	Not specified	Not specified	Not specified	Not specified	Not specified
Social/Health Psychology	PhD	NA/NA	NA/NA	NA/NA	Not specified	Not specified	Not specified	Not specified	Not specified
General Psychology	MA/MS	Not specified	Not specified	Not specified	Not specified	Not specified	Not specified	Not specified	Not specified

Admissions Requirements:

Degree	GRE	GRE-Subject	Letters of Recommendation	Research Statement	Writing Sample	CV	Interview
Master's/Specialist	None	None	3	Required	None	Recommended	Optional
Doctoral	Required	Optional	3	Required	Optional	Recommended	Optional

Admissions Criteria:

GRE scores—high
Research experience—high
Work experience—low
Clinically related public service—low

GPA—medium
Letters of recommendation—high
Interview—medium
Statement of goals and objectives—high

Department Demographics

	Male (PT)	Female (PT)	Total	African-American/ Black (PT)	Hispanic/ Latino (PT)	Asian/ Pacific Islander (PT)	American Indian/ Alaska Native (PT)	Caucasian/ White (PT)	Unknown	Multiethnic (PT)	ADA (PT)	Int'l (PT)
Students	23 (0)	74 (0)	97	2 (0)	4 (0)	11 (0)	0 (0)	75 (0)	0 (0)	6 (0)	0 (0)	11 (0)

Financial Information/Assistance

Tuition: For information on tuition costs, visit http://www.stonybrook.edu/bursar/tuition/tuition-and-fee-rates.shtml. Tuition is subject to change. Additional fees are assessed to students beyond the costs of tuition for the following: Student fees and health insurance are additional costs.

Doctoral:
State residents: $10,370 per academic year.
State residents: $10,370 per credit hour.
Nonstate residents: $20,190 per academic year.
Nonstate residents: $841 per credit hour.

Master's:
State residents: $10,370 per academic year.
State residents: $432 per credit hour.
Nonstate residents: $20,190 per academic year.
Nonstate residents: $841 per credit hour.

Financial Assistance:

	Teaching Assistantship (% Receiving)	Teaching Assistantship Tuition Remission	Research Assistantship (% Receiving)	Research Assistantship Tuition Remission	Fellowship (% Receiving)	Fellowship Tuition Remission
First-Year Student	$17,502 (100)	Full	$17,502 (100)	Full	$26,542 (100)	Full
Advanced Student	$17,502 (NA)	Full	$17,502 (NA)	Full	$26,542 (NA)	Full

Employment of Department Graduates

No information provided.

Additional Information

Housing and Day Care: On-campus housing is available. See the following website for more information: http://studentaffairs. stonybrook.edu/res/index.shtml. On-campus day care facilities are available. See the following website for more information: http://www.stonybrook.edu/childcare/.

Information for Students With Physical Disabilities: See the following website: http://studentaffairs.stonybrook.edu/dss/.

Special Facilities or Resources: Besides faculty laboratories for human, animal, and physiological research, and electronics and machine shops, other campus facilities for research and graduate training include: Psychological Center, the training, research, and service unit for clinical psychology; Point of Woods Laboratory School with a special education class for elementary students; University Preschool with children from 18 months to 5 years of age; University Marital Therapy Clinic; and Suffolk Child Development Center, a private school for autistic, retarded, aphasic, and developmentally delayed children. Clinical neuropsychology uses affiliations with the University Health Sciences Center, local schools, an agency for the intellectually disabled, and a Veterans Administration hospital. Departmental CRT terminals and 12 additional terminals and two printers in the division's Social Science Data Laboratory are used with campus computers.

Application Information: Graduate Office, Department of Psychology, Stony Brook University, Stony Brook, NY 11794-2500. *Fee:* $100. *Online application:* https://app.applyyourself.com/?id=sunysb-gs.

Syracuse University
Department of Psychology
Arts & Sciences
430 Huntington Hall, 150 Marshall Street
Syracuse, NY 13244-2340
Telephone: (315) 443-1210
Interim Department Chair: Lawrence J. Lewandowski

E-mail: ljlewand@syr.edu
Web: http://psychology.syr.edu/

Orientation, Objectives, and Emphasis of Department
Our department is home to doctoral programs in Clinical Psychology, Experimental Psychology (the Cognition, Brain and Behavior program), School Psychology, and Social Psychology. Students work closely with a faculty mentor whose research interests are similar to the student's. Our APA-approved programs in clinical and school psychology are based on the scientist–practitioner model. Students enrolled in the clinical and school psychology programs gain clinical experience through our university-based psychological services center and placement in area hospitals and schools. Across all of the doctoral programs, students are active members in faculty-led research labs, develop teaching skills and, as advanced students, have the opportunity to serve as the instructor of record for an undergraduate course.

Programs and Degrees Offered

Program	Degree	Application Deadline	Applications Received	Accepted	New Admits Enrolled (PT)	Total Enrolled (PT)	Degrees Awarded in 2014–2015	Median Years to Complete Degree	Dismissed/ Withdrew
Clinical Psychology	PhD	December 1 (Fall)	183	7	4 (0)	27 (0)	5	6	2
Experimental Psychology	PhD	December 1 (Fall)	19	5	4 (0)	8 (0)	1	6	0
School Psychology	PhD	December 1 (Fall)	50	6	6 (0)	23 (0)	3	5	3
Social Psychology	PhD	December 1 (Fall)	34	3	1 (0)	7 (0)	1	5	1

APA Accreditation

Clinical PhD: Student Outcome Data website: http://psychology.syr.edu/graduate/Clinical.html.
School PhD: Student Outcome Data website: http://psychology.syr.edu/graduate/School_Psychology_Program.html.

Doctoral Degree (PhD Clinical Psychology): For those doctoral students for whom a professional internship was required in this program prior to graduation:
Total students who applied for an internship: 3
Total students who obtained an internship: 2
Total students who obtained a paid internship: 2
Total students who obtained an unpaid internship: 0
Total students who were placed in APA/CPA-accredited internships: 2
Total students placed in internships not APA/CPA-accredited, but listed with the Association of Psychology Postdoctoral and Internship Centers (APPIC): 0
Total students placed in internships conforming to guidelines of the Council of Directors of School Psychology Programs (CDSPP): 0
Total students placed in internships that were not APA/CPA-accredited, APPIC or CDSSP listed: 0

Doctoral Degree (PhD School Psychology): For those doctoral students for whom a professional internship was required in this program prior to graduation:
Total students who applied for an internship: 2
Total students who obtained an internship: 2
Total students who obtained a paid internship: 2
Total students who obtained an unpaid internship: 0
Total students who were placed in APA/CPA-accredited internships: 0
Total students placed in internships not APA/CPA-accredited, but listed with the Association of Psychology Postdoctoral and Internship Centers (APPIC): 0
Total students placed in internships conforming to guidelines of the Council of Directors of School Psychology Programs (CDSPP): 2
Total students placed in internships that were not APA/CPA-accredited, APPIC or CDSSP listed: 0

Internships/Practica

Students in the clinical and school psychology training programs have appropriate internship and practicum experiences available in hospitals, schools, and other community and University settings. Following completion of their coursework, clinical students complete APA-approved internships as part of their required program of study.

Admissions

Entries appear in the following order: required test or GPA, minimum score (if required)/median score of students entering in 2015–2016.

Program	Degree	GRE-V	GRE-Q	GRE-Writing	GRE-Subject	Undergraduate GPA	Last 2 Years GPA	Psychology GPA	Master's GPA
Clinical Psychology	PhD	159/161	151/157	4/5	Not specified	3.28/3.68	Not specified	Not specified	Not specified
Experimental Psychology	PhD	148/155	158/161	2.5/4	Not specified	3/3	Not specified	Not specified	Not specified

Admissions (con't.)

Program	Degree	GRE-V	GRE-Q	GRE-Writing	GRE-Subject	Under-graduate GPA	Last 2 Years GPA	Psychology GPA	Master's GPA
School Psychology	PhD	150/147	155/151	3/4	Not specified	3.34/3.69	Not specified	Not specified	Not specified
Social Psychology	PhD	149/160	147/155	4/4.3	Not specified	3.47/3.64	Not specified	Not specified	Not specified

Admissions Requirements:

Degree	GRE	GRE-Subject	Letters of Recommendation	Research Statement	Writing Sample	CV	Interview
Doctoral	Required	Optional	3	Required	Optional	Required	Required

Please note if these criteria vary for different programs: Interview requirements vary from program to program.

Admissions Criteria:
GRE scores—high
Research experience—high
Work experience—medium
Clinically related public service—medium
GPA—high

Letters of recommendation—high
Interview—high
Statement of goals and objectives—high
Undergraduate psychology preparation—high

Department Demographics

	Male (PT)	Female (PT)	Total	African-American/ Black (PT)	Hispanic/ Latino (PT)	Asian/ Pacific Islander (PT)	American Indian/ Alaska Native (PT)	Caucasian/ White (PT)	Unknown	Multiethnic (PT)	ADA (PT)	Int'l (PT)
Students	16 (0)	49 (0)	65	4 (0)	1 (0)	8 (0)	0 (0)	48 (0)	4 (0)	0 (0)	0 (0)	6 (0)

Financial Information/Assistance

Tuition: For information on tuition costs, visit http://financialaid.syr.edu/costofattendance/graduate/. Tuition is subject to change.

Doctoral:
State residents: $33,312 per academic year.
State residents: $1,388 per credit hour.
Nonstate residents: $33,312 per academic year.
Nonstate residents: $1,388 per credit hour.

Financial Assistance:

	Teaching Assistantship (% Receiving)	Teaching Assistantship Tuition Remission	Research Assistantship (% Receiving)	Research Assistantship Tuition Remission	Fellowship (% Receiving)	Fellowship Tuition Remission
First-Year Student	$14,250 (NA)	Full	$14,250 (NA)	Full	$23,830 (NA)	Full
Advanced Student	$14,250 (NA)	Full	$14,250 (NA)	Full	$23,830 (NA)	Full

For additional information on financial assistance, visit http://financialaid.syr.edu/whoareyou/graduatestudents/.

Employment of Department Graduates

Doctoral:
Enrolled in a postdoctoral residency/fellowship: 6
Employed in an academic position at a university: 4
Employed in government agency: 2
Employed in a hospital/medical center: 1
Total: 13

Additional Information

Housing and Day Care: On-campus housing is available. See the following website for more information: http://housingmealplans.syr.edu. On-campus day care facilities are available. See the following website for more information: http://falk.syr.edu/ChildFamilyStudies/BMW.aspx; http://eeccc.syr.edu/.

Information for Students With Physical Disabilities: See the following website: http://disabilityservices.syr.edu/.

Special Facilities or Resources: The Department of Psychology is housed in Huntington Hall, an historic building that has been remodeled to provide offices and seminar rooms, as well as laboratories for the study of cognition, social psychology, behavioral medicine, family interaction, and group processes. Labs and offices are equipped with microcomputers for data collection and analysis. A separate wing houses the department's Psychological Services Center, which offers facilities for clinical and school psychology practicum training and research. In addition, the Department has two facilities on campus and two facilities off campus that provide additional lab space. Other facilities are available through faculty collaborations with researchers at the Upstate Medical University, which is adjacent to Huntington Hall. The Department and its Center for Health and Behavior support two full-time computer technicians.

Application Information: Enrollment Management Processing Center, Syracuse University, Graduate Admissions Processing, 716 East Washington Street, Suite 200, Syracuse, New York 13210-1572. *Fee:* $75. *Online application:* http://graduateadmissions.syr.edu/howtoapply/.

The College at Brockport - State University of New York

Department of Psychology
350 New Campus Drive
Brockport, NY 14420
Telephone: (585) 395-2488
Chairperson: David Abwender

E-mail: psychdpt@brockport.edu
Web: http://www.brockport.edu/psh/grad/

Orientation, Objectives, and Emphasis of Department

The MA in Psychology program provides promising students with challenging and engaging graduate-level educational experiences. Its three tracks are customized to help students meet their personal academic goals, such as becoming more competitive for admission into doctoral programs or securing master's-level positions in human services and the mental health fields. In the clinically-focused track, students are trained as scientists and practitioners, concerned with the application of psychological principles to the treatment and prevention of behavior disorders. Courses provide theoretical and practical training in contemporary methods of assessment, behavioral and cognitive-behavioral clinical intervention, and program evaluation. In the research-intensive tracks, students deepen their core knowledge of psychology and show their ability to thrive amongst other talented students in graduate study. Moreover, students work closely with their individual faculty mentors to sharpen their research skills and generate scholarly products. In this way, these tracks can be a springboard to doctoral-level study in clinical or non-clinical fields. One of our program's greatest strengths is its emphasis in methods of observation, intervention, and research with behavior disorders and developmental disabilities, but students will be able to explore research opportunities with faculty members with expertise in many different areas of psychology.

Programs and Degrees Offered

Program	Degree	Application Deadline	Applications Received	Accepted	New Admits Enrolled (PT)	Total Enrolled (PT)	Degrees Awarded in 2014–2015	Median Years to Complete Degree	Dismissed/Withdrew
Clinical Psychology — Applied Emphasis	MA/MS	April 1 (Fall)		3	3	4		2	

Programs and Degrees Offered (con't.)

Program	Degree	Application Deadline	Applica-tions Received	Accepted	New Admits Enrolled (PT)	Total Enrolled (PT)	Degrees Awarded in 2014–2015	Median Years to Complete Degree	Dismissed/ Withdrew
Clinical Psychology — Research Emphasis	MA/MS	April 1 (Fall)		3	3	14			
General Psychology	MA/MS	April 1 (Fall)		2		6			

Internships/Practica

Practical experience is available in nearly 50 human service agencies in western New York, including the college counseling center, VA and academic medical centers, and state and local mental health, developmental disability/autism centers, and other community service agencies. Each practicum placement is developed individually, based on the specific student and agency involved. Each practicum is supervised by an agency staff member as well as a faculty member from the Department of Psychology. Students must successfully complete all required coursework before beginning the practicum.

Admissions

Entries appear in the following order: required test or GPA, minimum score (if required)/median score of students entering in 2015–2016.

Program	Degree	GRE-V	GRE-Q	GRE-Writing	GRE-Subject	Under-graduate GPA	Last 2 Years GPA	Psychol-ogy GPA	Master's GPA
Clinical Psychology — Applied Emphasis	MA/MS	NA/NA	NA/NA	NA/NA	Not specified	NA/NA	NA/NA	NA/NA	Not specified
Clinical Psychology — Research Emphasis	MA/MS	NA/NA	NA/NA	NA/NA	Not specified	NA/NA	NA/NA	NA/NA	Not specified
General Psychology	MA/MS	NA/NA	NA/NA	NA/NA	Not specified	NA/NA	NA/NA	NA/NA	Not specified

Admissions Requirements:

Degree	GRE	GRE-Subject	Letters of Recom-mendation	Research Statement	Writing Sample	CV	Interview
Master's/Specialist	Required	None	3	Required	Optional	Required	Required

Admissions Criteria:

GRE scores—medium
Research experience—medium
Work experience—medium
Clinically related public service—medium
GPA—high

Letters of recommendation—high
Interview—high
Statement of goals and objectives—high
Undergraduate psychology preparation—medium

For additional information on admission requirements, visit http://www.brockport.edu/psh/grad/admission.html.

Department Demographics

	Male (PT)	Female (PT)	Total	African-American/ Black (PT)	Hispanic/ Latino (PT)	Asian/ Pacific Islander (PT)	American Indian/ Alaska Native (PT)	Caucasian/ White (PT)	Unknown	Multiethnic (PT)	ADA (PT)	Int'l (PT)
Students	6 (0)	15 (0)	21					0 (0)	0 (0)		0 (0)	0 (0)

Financial Information/Assistance

Tuition: For information on tuition costs, visit http://www.brockport.edu/student_accounts/bill-pay-refund/tuitioncost.html. Tuition is subject to change.

Master's:
State residents: $10,370 per academic year.
Nonstate residents: $20,190 per academic year.

Financial Assistance:

	Teaching Assistantship (% Receiving)	Teaching Assistantship Tuition Remission	Research Assistantship (% Receiving)	Research Assistantship Tuition Remission	Fellowship (% Receiving)	Fellowship Tuition Remission
First-Year Student	$6,000 (NA)	Full	NA (NA)	NA	NA (NA)	NA
Advanced Student	$6,000 (NA)	Full	NA (NA)	NA	NA (NA)	NA

For additional information on financial assistance, visit http://www.brockport.edu/finaid/.

Employment of Department Graduates

No information provided.

Additional Information

Housing and Day Care: No on-campus housing is available. On-campus day care facilities are available. See the following website for more information: http://www.brockport.edu/child_development_center/.

Information for Students With Physical Disabilities: See the following website: http://www.brockport.edu/osd/.

Special Facilities or Resources: The department has facilities for research in the biobehavioral sciences, as well as sensory-perceptual, clinical, developmental, and personality psychology topics; and assessment/intervention training. Laboratory space, computer equipment, and an extensive file of psychological assessment instruments are also available.

Application Information: The Graduate School, The College at Brockport, 350 New Campus Drive, Brockport, NY 14420-2914. *Fee:* $50. *Online application:* http://www.brockport.edu/bounce/webapp.

The New School for Social Research
Department of Psychology
80 Fifth Avenue, 7th Floor
New York, NY 10011
Telephone: (212) 229-5727
Chairperson: Jeremy Safran; Emanuele Castano

E-mail: gfpsych@newschool.edu
Web: http://www.newschool.edu/nssr/psychology/

Orientation, Objectives, and Emphasis of Department

The Psychology Department provides a broad theoretical background emphasizing the scientific study of human behavior. The master's program accommodates both full- and part-time students, with courses in cognitive, developmental, social, and clinical psychology. All MA students design and carry out original individual research projects. At the PhD level, students may specialize either in research psychology or in clinical psychology. The doctoral program reflects an apprenticeship model in which students work closely with individual faculty on collaborative research. Admission to doctoral candidacy is based on students' academic performance in our master's program, interviews with faculty, a personal essay, and passing the psychology comprehensive examination. There is a strong emphasis on cultural psychology as a framework for understanding basic psychological theories, and on approaching psychology in ways that are sensitive to socio-cultural diversity. Students enrolled in the PhD program in Cognitive, Social, and Developmental Psychology (CSD) are prepared for careers in academics as well as in applied settings. Within the clinical psychology doctoral program, there is a strong emphasis on both theory and research. Clinical students have opportunities to gain clinical experience and are prepared as scientist–practitioners equally at home in clinical, research, and teaching settings.

Programs and Degrees Offered

Program	Degree	Application Deadline	Applica-tions Received	Accepted	New Admits Enrolled (PT)	Total Enrolled (PT)	Degrees Awarded in 2014–2015	Median Years to Complete Degree	Dismissed/ Withdrew
Clinical Psychology	PhD	February 1 (Fall)	26	13	11 (0)	69 (0)	19	5.5	1
Cognitive, Social, Developmental Psychology (Csd)	PhD	February 1 (Fall)	7	6	5 (0)	24	6	5	1
General Psychology	MA/MS	January 15 (Fall), October 15 (Spring), Rolling	201	171	48 (2)	112 (2)	52	2	3

APA Accreditation

Clinical PhD: Student Outcome Data website: http://www.newschool.edu/nssr/phd-clinical-psychology/.

Doctoral Degree (PhD Clinical Psychology): For those doctoral students for whom a professional internship was required in this program prior to graduation:
Total students who applied for an internship: 13
Total students who obtained an internship: 13
Total students who obtained a paid internship: 13
Total students who obtained an unpaid internship: 0
Total students who were placed in APA/CPA-accredited internships: 13
Total students placed in internships not APA/CPA-accredited, but listed with the Association of Psychology Postdoctoral and Internship Centers (APPIC): 0
Total students placed in internships conforming to guidelines of the Council of Directors of School Psychology Programs (CDSPP): 0
Total students placed in internships that were not APA/CPA-accredited, APPIC or CDSSP listed: 0

Internships/Practica

Depending on their research areas, students pursuing general psychology can gain internship and work experience in a range of applied settings, including industry research labs and non-profit organizations. Master's level psychology students who are interested in applying to the Clinical PhD program are strongly encouraged to pursue volunteer clinical positions available at local hospitals or institutes. First-year doctoral students in the clinical program participate in an integrated program designed to help them develop as scientist–practitioners. The practicum is based at Beth Israel Medical Center and involves supervised psychotherapy and Structured Clinical Interview for DSM–5 (SCID) training within the Brief Psychotherapy Research Program established at Beth Israel. Students also spend 4 hours per week on an inpatient rotation, co-leading groups and attending relevant unit meetings. Clinical supervision is provided by The New School faculty and by Beth Israel staff psychologists and psychiatrists. This experience provides strong preparation for the 16–20 hour per week externships in their second and third years of PhD level study at approved, affiliated sites. After completing their dissertation proposals, all Clinical PhD students are required to complete an APA-accredited predoctoral internship.

Admissions

Entries appear in the following order: required test or GPA, minimum score (if required)/median score of students entering in 2015–2016.

Program	Degree	GRE-V	GRE-Q	GRE-Writing	GRE-Subject	Under-graduate GPA	Last 2 Years GPA	Psychology GPA	Master's GPA
Clinical Psychology	PhD	Not specified	Not specified	Not specified	Not specified	Not specified	Not specified	Not specified	3.5/NA
Cognitive, Social, Developmental Psychology (CSD)	PhD	Not specified	Not specified	Not specified	Not specified	Not specified	Not specified	Not specified	3.7/NA
General Psychology	MA/MS	NA/NA	NA/NA	Not specified	Not specified	Not specified	Not specified	Not specified	Not specified

Admissions Requirements:

Degree	GRE	GRE-Subject	Letters of Recommendation	Research Statement	Writing Sample	CV	Interview
Master's/Specialist	Recommended	Recommended	3	Required	Required	Recommended	None
Doctoral	Required	Required	2	Required	Optional	Required	Required

Please note if these criteria vary for different programs: Only Master's students at The New School for Social Research are eligible to apply to our PhD programs. Outside applicants with previous graduate credit must apply first to the MA program at The New School for Social Research, then once they complete 12 credits of coursework here, they may transfer credits from a previous degree.

Admissions Criteria:

GRE scores—medium
Research experience—medium
Work experience—medium
Clinically related public service—medium
GPA—high

Letters of recommendation—high
Statement of goals and objectives—high
Undergraduate psychology preparation—high
Writing sample—high

Department Demographics

	Male (PT)	Female (PT)	Total	African-American/ Black (PT)	Hispanic/ Latino (PT)	Asian/ Pacific Islander (PT)	American Indian/ Alaska Native (PT)	Caucasian/ White (PT)	Unknown	Multiethnic (PT)	ADA (PT)	Int'l (PT)
Students	49 (0)	156 (2)	207	10 (1)	5 (1)	4 (0)	0 (0)	182 (0)	4 (0)	0 (0)	1 (0)	19 (0)

Financial Information/Assistance

Tuition: For information on tuition costs, visit http://www.newschool.edu/registrar/tuition-and-fees/. Tuition is subject to change. Additional fees are assessed to students beyond the costs of tuition for the following: university service fee $130.

Doctoral:
State residents: $1,950 per credit hour.
Nonstate residents: $1,950 per credit hour.

Master's:
State residents: $1,950 per credit hour.
Nonstate residents: $1,950 per credit hour.

Financial Assistance:

	Teaching Assistantship (% Receiving)	Teaching Assistantship Tuition Remission	Research Assistantship (% Receiving)	Research Assistantship Tuition Remission	Fellowship (% Receiving)	Fellowship Tuition Remission
First-Year Student	NA (NA)	NA	NA (NA)	NA	$7,800 (NA)	Partial
Advanced Student	$8,712 (40)	NA	$8,078 (25)	NA	$9,660 (NA)	Partial

For additional information on financial assistance, visit http://www.newschool.edu/student-services/student-financial-services/.

Employment of Department Graduates

Doctoral:
Enrolled in a postdoctoral residency/fellowship: 15
Enrolled in another graduate/professional program: 2
Employed in government agency: 1
Employed in a hospital/medical center: 9
Total: 27

Additional Information

Housing and Day Care: On-campus housing is available. See the following website for more information: http://www.newschool.edu/student-housing/. No on-campus day care facilities are available.

Information for Students With Physical Disabilities: See the following website: http://www.newschool.edu/student-disability-services/.

Special Facilities or Resources: All students may participate in collaborative research projects with faculty in labs that feature equipment and software dedicated to the particular research carried out by department members. Students have library access not only at New School social science libraries but also at NYU's Bobst library, the Cooper Union Library, and other libraries within a New York consortium. Various state-of-the-art computing facilities are also available. For clinical PhD students, the New School-Beth Israel Center for Clinical Training and Research provides unusually broad training in outpatient clinics, inpatient units, and clinical research programs. First year clinical PhD students have access to the Psychology library at Beth Israel Medical Center, perform intake evaluations on Beth Israel's psychiatry outpatient clinic and provide group therapy on adult inpatient units. They also attend psychiatry grand rounds and training seminars on child abuse and assault prevention. Second and third-year clinical students may continue work at Beth Israel Medical Center conducting therapy through the Brief Psychotherapy Research Project. Psychotherapy sessions are videotaped with patients' consent, and students review these sessions in supervision with Beth Israel supervising psychologists. Cases are also discussed in externship seminars with New School faculty.

Application Information: *Fee:* $50. *Online application:* http://www.newschool.edu/admission/apply-online/.

University at Albany, State University of New York
Department of Psychology
College of Arts and Sciences
1400 Washington Avenue
Albany, NY 12222
Telephone: (518) 442-4820
Chairperson: Christine K. Wagner

E-mail: psychology@albany.edu
Web: http://www.albany.edu/psychology

Orientation, Objectives, and Emphasis of Department
All facets of the graduate program reflect a commitment to the empirical tradition in psychology. Thus, involvement in research is stressed in all areas of study. Students begin an apprentice relationship with faculty members upon entry into the department and are expected to remain actively involved in research throughout their graduate careers. A major goal of the department is to train individuals who will make research contributions to the field. Admission is offered in five areas: behavioral neuroscience, clinical, cognitive, industrial/organizational, and social-personality. All areas of concentration train students for careers as teachers and

research scientists. In addition, the social, clinical, and industrial/organizational areas prepare students for careers in applied settings. The orientation of the clinical program emphasizes cognitive and behavioral approaches.

Programs and Degrees Offered

Program	Degree	Application Deadline	Applications Received	Accepted	New Admits Enrolled (PT)	Total Enrolled (PT)	Degrees Awarded in 2014–2015	Median Years to Complete Degree	Dismissed/ Withdrew
Behavioral Neuroscience	PhD	January 15 (Fall)	20	2	1 (0)	12 (0)	2	6	0
Clinical Psychology	PhD	December 1 (Fall)	145	11	7 (0)	39 (0)	5	6	1
Cognitive Psychology	PhD	January 15 (Fall)	7	3	1 (0)	10 (0)	1	6	0
Industrial/ Organizational Psychology	PhD	January 15 (Fall)	59	6	2 (0)	18 (0)	0		0
Social/ Personality Psychology	PhD	January 15 (Fall)	26	4	3 (0)	10 (0)	2	5.5	0
Industrial/ Organizational Psychology	MA/MS	March 1 (Fall)	63	18	10 (0)	12 (1)	3	2	1

APA Accreditation

Clinical PhD: Student Outcome Data website: http://www.albany.edu/psychology/clinical_psychology.php.

Doctoral Degree (PhD Clinical Psychology): For those doctoral students for whom a professional internship was required in this program prior to graduation:
Total students who applied for an internship: 7
Total students who obtained an internship: 6
Total students who obtained a paid internship: 6
Total students who obtained an unpaid internship: 0
Total students who were placed in APA/CPA-accredited internships: 6
Total students placed in internships not APA/CPA-accredited, but listed with the Association of Psychology Postdoctoral and Internship Centers (APPIC): 0
Total students placed in internships conforming to guidelines of the Council of Directors of School Psychology Programs (CDSPP): 0
Total students placed in internships that were not APA/CPA-accredited, APPIC or CDSSP listed: 0

Master's Degree (MA/MS Industrial/Organizational Psychology): An internship experience, such as a final research project or "capstone" experience is required of graduates.

Internships/Practica

During the second year of our doctoral program in Clinical Psychology, students are placed at the Psychological Services Center, a University-operated center that serves the general population of the city of Albany. During this placement, students are supervised by members of the Clinical faculty. In their third year, students are required to participate in a community-based practicum. These may include placements in community mental health centers, VA inpatient and outpatient centers, inpatient and outpatient clinics in community hospitals and rehabilitation centers, residential facilities for youth, and the University's counseling center. Students may also elect to participate in an additional community-based practicum experience during their fourth year of training. Students are encouraged to attend APA-accredited internships during their fifth year of study. Our students have attended internships in a variety of settings including children's hospitals, psychiatric hospitals, VA hospitals, university-affiliated medical centers, general hospitals, and rehabilitation centers. Practicum and internship placements for doctoral students in the Industrial/Organizational (I/O) Psychology specialization are possible with a number of local and national corporations and government agencies.

Admissions

Entries appear in the following order: required test or GPA, minimum score (if required)/median score of students entering in 2015–2016.

Program	Degree	GRE-V	GRE-Q	GRE-Writing	GRE-Subject	Under-graduate GPA	Last 2 Years GPA	Psychology GPA	Master's GPA
Behavioral Neuroscience	PhD	Not specified	Not specified	Not specified	Not specified	Not specified	Not specified	Not specified	Not specified
Clinical Psychology	PhD	NA/163	NA/159	NA/5	NA/712	NA/3.8	Not specified	NA/3.83	Not specified
Cognitive Psychology	PhD	NA/157	NA/151	Not specified	Not specified	NA/NA	Not specified	Not specified	Not specified
Industrial/ Organizational Psychology	PhD	NA/163	NA/162	NA/4.5	NA/NA	NA/NA	Not specified	NA/NA	Not specified
Social/ Personality Psychology	PhD	NA/164	NA/151	NA/5	NA/NA	NA/NA	Not specified	NA/NA	Not specified
Industrial/ Organizational Psychology	MA/MS	NA/154	NA/154	NA/4	Not specified	NA/NA	Not specified	NA/NA	Not specified

Admissions Requirements:

Degree	GRE	GRE-Subject	Letters of Recom-mendation	Research Statement	Writing Sample	CV	Interview
Master's/Specialist	Required	None	3	Required	None	Optional	None
Doctoral	Required	Required	3	Required	Optional	Optional	Required

Please note if these criteria vary for different programs: The interview process and clinically related service are relevant for the clinical psychology PhD program only. The GRE Subject exam is only required for the clinical, cognitive, and I/O PhD programs.

Admissions Criteria:

GRE scores—high
Research experience—high
Work experience—low
Clinically related public service—medium
GPA—high

Letters of recommendation—high
Interview—high
Statement of goals and objectives—high
Undergraduate psychology preparation—high

For additional information on admission requirements, visit http://www.albany.edu/psychology/how_to_apply.php.

Department Demographics

	Male (PT)	Female (PT)	Total	African-American/ Black (PT)	Hispanic/ Latino (PT)	Asian/ Pacific Islander (PT)	American Indian/ Alaska Native (PT)	Caucasian/ White (PT)	Unknown	Multiethnic (PT)	ADA (PT)	Int'l (PT)
Students	30 (0)	71 (1)	102	(0)	7 (0)	18 (0)	1 (0)	71 (1)	0 (0)	4 (0)	0 (0)	0 (0)

Financial Information/Assistance

Tuition: For information on tuition costs, visit http://www.albany.edu/studentaccounts/tuition.php. Tuition is subject to change. Additional fees are assessed to students beyond the costs of tuition for the following: university fee, comprehensive service fee, grad student organization fee.

Doctoral:
State residents: $10,870 per academic year.
State residents: $453 per credit hour.
Nonstate residents: $22,210 per academic year.
Nonstate residents: $925 per credit hour.

Master's:
State residents: $10,870 per academic year.
State residents: $453 per credit hour.
Nonstate residents: $22,210 per academic year.
Nonstate residents: $925 per credit hour.

Financial Assistance:

	Teaching Assistantship (% Receiving)	Teaching Assistantship Tuition Remission	Research Assistantship (% Receiving)	Research Assistantship Tuition Remission	Fellowship (% Receiving)	Fellowship Tuition Remission
First-Year Student	$16,320 (100)	Full	NA (NA)	NA	NA (NA)	NA
Advanced Student	$16,320 (75)	Full	NA (NA)	NA	NA (NA)	NA

For additional information on financial assistance, visit http://www.albany.edu/graduate/funding-graduate-study.php.

Employment of Department Graduates

Master's:
Do not know: 3
Total: 3

Doctoral:
Employed in an academic position at a university: 1
Employed in academic position at a 2-year/4-year college: 1
Employed in other positions at a higher education institution: 5
Employed in a hospital/medical center: 3
Total: 10

Additional Information

Housing and Day Care: On-campus housing is available. See the following website for more information: http://www.albany.edu/housing/. On-campus day care facilities are available. See the following website for more information: http://www.albany.edu/uklds/.

Information for Students With Physical Disabilities: See the following website: http://www.albany.edu/disability/.

Special Facilities or Resources: Resources and facilities include university- and grant-funded student stipends, plus stipends from other campus sources; a state-of-the-art animal facility and research laboratories in the Life Sciences Building; several human research laboratories; grant-supported research and treatment clinics; the Psychological Services Center for practicum training; and a variety of research equipment.

Application Information: Office of Graduate Admissions, UAB 121, 1400 Washington Avenue, Albany, NY 12222. *Fee:* $75. *Online application:* http://www.albany.edu/graduate/apply-now.php.

University at Buffalo, State University of New York

Department of Counseling, School, and Educational Psychology
Graduate School of Education
409 Baldy Hall
Buffalo, NY 14260-1000
Telephone: (716) 645-2484
Chairperson: Jeremy D. Finn

E-mail: nmyers@buffalo.edu
Web: http://gse.buffalo.edu/cscp

Orientation, Objectives, and Emphasis of Department

Departmental emphasis is on research based counseling with adults, college students, adolescents, children, and persons with disabilities. Doctoral programs follow the scientist–practitioner model. Some focus on preparing college faculty. Increased integration of counseling, school, and educational psychology programs is developing. Field experience and research experience are continuous through the programs.

845

Programs and Degrees Offered

Program	Degree	Application Deadline	Applica- tions Received	Accepted	New Admits Enrolled (PT)	Total Enrolled (PT)	Degrees Awarded in 2014– 2015	Median Years to Complete Degree	Dismissed/ Withdrew
Counselor Education	PhD	Rolling	11	2	1 (1)	3 (11)	2	6	0
Educational Psychology & Quantitative Methods	PhD	Rolling	14	4	2 (2)	4 (9)	1	6	0
Rehabilitation Counseling	MA/MS	March 31 (Fall)	77	34	10 (22)	18 (67)	35	2	2
School Counseling	MEd	February 1 (Fall)	20	10	9 (1)	11 (1)	10	1	0
Counseling/ School Psychology	PhD	December 1 (Fall)	74	11	11 (0)	46 (0)	11	5	0
Educational Psychology & Quantitative Methods	MA/MS	Rolling	14	9	5 (1)	9 (9)	6	2	0
School Psychology	MA/MS	February 1 (Fall)	36	10	10 (0)	8 (0)	8	3	
Mental Health Counseling	MA/MS	February 15 (Fall)	46	16	16 (0)	32 (3)	14	2.5	0
Certificate in Applied Statistical Analysis	Other	Rolling	15	15	0 (15)	0 (18)	2	2	0
Certificate in School Counseling	Other	Rolling	17	11	11 (0)	14 (2)	7	1	6
Certificate in Mental Health Counseling	Other	February 15 (Fall)	53	35	0 (26)	0 (36)	12	1.5	5
Certificate in Rehabilitation Counseling	Other	March 31 (Fall), November 15 (Spring)	7	4	0 (3)	0 (4)	4	1.5	1

APA Accreditation

Combination PhD: Student Outcome Data website: http://gse.buffalo.edu/programs/cpsp/outcomes.

Doctoral Degree (PhD Counseling/School Psychology): For those doctoral students for whom a professional internship was required in this program prior to graduation:
Total students who applied for an internship: 11
Total students who obtained an internship: 11
Total students who obtained a paid internship: 11
Total students who obtained an unpaid internship: 0
Total students who were placed in APA/CPA-accredited internships: 7
Total students placed in internships not APA/CPA-accredited, but listed with the Association of Psychology Postdoctoral and Internship Centers (APPIC): 2
Total students placed in internships conforming to guidelines of the Council of Directors of School Psychology Programs (CDSPP): 1
Total students placed in internships that were not APA/CPA-accredited, APPIC or CDSSP listed: 1

Master's Degree (MA/MS Rehabilitation Counseling): An internship experience, such as a final research project or "capstone" experience is required of graduates. Master's Degree (MA/MS Educational Psychology & Quantitative Methods): An internship experience, such as a final research project or "capstone" experience is required of graduates. Master's Degree (MA/MS School Psychology): An internship experience, such as a final research project or "capstone" experience is required of graduates. Master's Degree (MA/MS Mental Health Counseling): An internship experience, such as a final research project or "capstone" experience is required of graduates.

Internships/Practica

Practica and internships available at area schools, community agencies, and hospitals. Experience with death and end of life issues, forensics, persons with disabilities, and assessment is available.

Admissions

Entries appear in the following order: required test or GPA, minimum score (if required)/median score of students entering in 2015–2016.

Program	Degree	GRE-V	GRE-Q	GRE-Writing	GRE-Subject	Under-graduate GPA	Last 2 Years GPA	Psychol-ogy GPA	Master's GPA
Counselor Education	PhD	140/147	140/141	4/4.5	Not specified	3/3.2	Not specified	Not specified	3/3.75
Educational Psychology & Quantitative Methods	PhD	NA/150	NA/154	NA/3.5	Not specified	NA/3.69	Not specified	Not specified	3/NA
Rehabilitation Counseling	MA/MS	Not specified	Not specified	Not specified	Not specified	3/3.26	Not specified	Not specified	Not specified
School Counseling	MEd	NA/139	NA/139	NA/3.5	Not specified	3/3.23	Not specified	Not specified	Not specified
Counseling/School Psychology	PhD	NA/150	NA/151	NA/4.5	Not specified	3/3.61	Not specified	Not specified	Not specified
Educational Psychology & Quantitative Methods	MA/MS	NA/147	NA/151	NA/3.5	Not specified	3/3.53	Not specified	Not specified	Not specified
School Psychology	MA/MS	NA/151	NA/151	3/4.5	Not specified	3/3.58	Not specified	Not specified	Not specified
Mental Health Counseling	MA/MS	NA/150	NA/146	NA/4	Not specified	3/3.54	Not specified	Not specified	Not specified
Certificate in Applied Statistical Analysis	Other	Not specified	Not specified	Not specified	Not specified	Not specified	Not specified	Not specified	Not specified
Certificate in School Counseling	Other	Not specified	Not specified	Not specified	Not specified	Not specified	Not specified	Not specified	Not specified
Certificate in Mental Health Counseling	Other	Not specified	Not specified	Not specified	Not specified	Not specified	Not specified	Not specified	Not specified
Certificate in Rehabilitation Counseling	Other	Not specified	Not specified	Not specified	Not specified	Not specified	Not specified	Not specified	Not specified

Admissions Requirements:

Degree	GRE	GRE-Subject	Letters of Recommendation	Research Statement	Writing Sample	CV	Interview
Master's/Specialist	Required	Optional	3	Required	Optional	Optional	Required
Doctoral	Required	None	3	Required	Optional	Optional	Required

Please note if these criteria vary for different programs: Most programs conduct personal interviews, but not all.

Admissions Criteria:

GRE scores—high
Research experience—medium
Work experience—medium
Clinically related public service—medium
GPA—high

Letters of recommendation—high
Interview—high
Statement of goals and objectives—high
Undergraduate psychology preparation—medium

For additional information on admission requirements, visit http://gse.buffalo.edu/apply.

Department Demographics

	Male (PT)	Female (PT)	Total	African-American/ Black (PT)	Hispanic/ Latino (PT)	Asian/ Pacific Islander (PT)	American Indian/ Alaska Native (PT)	Caucasian/ White (PT)	Unknown	Multiethnic (PT)	ADA (PT)	Int'l (PT)
Students	41 (30)	151 (132)	354	21 (17)	5 (7)	19 (4)	1 (1)	129 (106)	16 (19)	1 (6)	0 (1)	21 (8)

Financial Information/Assistance

Tuition: For information on tuition costs, visit http://studentaccounts.buffalo.edu/tuition/index.php. Tuition is subject to change.

Doctoral:
State residents: $13,165 per academic year.
State residents: $611 per credit hour.
Nonstate residents: $22,210 per academic year.
Nonstate residents: $1,083 per credit hour.

Master's:
State residents: $13,165 per academic year.
State residents: $611 per credit hour.
Nonstate residents: $22,210 per academic year.
Nonstate residents: $1,083 per credit hour.

Financial Assistance:

	Teaching Assistantship (% Receiving)	Teaching Assistantship Tuition Remission	Research Assistantship (% Receiving)	Research Assistantship Tuition Remission	Fellowship (% Receiving)	Fellowship Tuition Remission
First-Year Student	NA (NA)	NA	$9,000 (3)	Full	NA (NA)	NA
Advanced Student	NA (NA)	NA	$9,000 (3)	Full	NA (NA)	NA

For additional information on financial assistance, visit http://gse.buffalo.edu/admissions/fin-aid.

Employment of Department Graduates

Master's:
Enrolled in a psychology doctoral program: 1
Enrolled in another graduate/professional program: 5
Employed in a professional position in a school system: 14
Employed in government agency: 25
Employed in a community mental health/counseling center: 7
Employed in a hospital/medical center: 8
Still seeking employment: 3
Other employment position: 4
Do not know: 6
Total: 73

Doctoral:
Enrolled in a postdoctoral residency/fellowship: 5
Employed in an academic position at a university: 1
Employed in other positions at a higher education institution: 3
Employed in government agency: 1
Employed in a community mental health/counseling center: 4
Total: 14

Additional Information

Housing and Day Care: On-campus housing is available. See the following website for more information: http://www.student-affairs.buffalo.edu/housing/apartments.php. On-campus day care facilities are available. See the following website for more information: http://www.ubccc.buffalo.edu/; http://ecrc.buffalo.edu/.

Information for Students With Physical Disabilities: See the following website: http://www.buffalo.edu/accessibility/.

Special Facilities or Resources: Department offers training experiences in a wide variety of schools, agencies, and colleges in both urban and suburban settings.

Application Information: Office of Graduate Admissions, Graduate School of Education, 366 Baldy Hall, University at Buffalo, SUNY, Buffalo, NY 14260-1000. *Fee:* $50. *Online application:* http://gse.buffalo.edu/apply.

University at Buffalo, State University of New York

Department of Psychology
College of Arts and Sciences
206 Park Hall
Buffalo, NY 14260-4110
Telephone: (716) 645-3651
Chairperson: Stephen T. Tiffany

E-mail: ccolder@buffalo.edu
Web: http://psychology.buffalo.edu/

Orientation, Objectives, and Emphasis of Department

The Department of Psychology offers doctoral degrees in Behavioral Neuroscience, Clinical Psychology, Cognitive Psychology, and Social-Personality Psychology and a master's degree in psychology with several specializations. The department has as its defining characteristic and distinguishing mission the conduct and communication of research and scholarship that contributes to the scientific understanding of psychology and the provision of high-quality graduate education and training. The department is dedicated to offering state-of-the-art education and training to its graduate students to prepare them to become leading researchers and to assume important positions in academic institutions or professional practice. We offer students a learning environment that is exciting and challenging, one that will allow them to follow their interests and fully develop their research skills. The research emphasis in Behavioral Neuroscience is on the neural, endocrine, and molecular bases of behavior. Clinical Psychology specializations include adult mood and anxiety disorders, relationship dysfunction, behavioral medicine, attention deficit/hyperactivity disorder, and child and adolescent aggression and substance abuse. Cognitive Psychology focuses on the processes underlying perception, attention, memory, spoken and written language comprehension, language acquisition, categorization, problem solving, and thinking. Social-Personality specializations include close relationships, automatic processes, self-esteem, self-construal, and stress and coping.

Programs and Degrees Offered

Program	Degree	Application Deadline	Applications Received	Accepted	New Admits Enrolled (PT)	Total Enrolled (PT)	Degrees Awarded in 2014–2015	Median Years to Complete Degree	Dismissed/ Withdrew
Behavioral Neuroscience	PhD	December 1 (Fall)	25	8	5 (0)	10 (0)	2	6	0
Clinical Psychology	PhD	December 1 (Fall)	165	13	9 (0)	35 (1)	6	7	0
Cognitive Psychology	PhD	December 1 (Fall)	20	10	6 (0)	17 (0)	0		0
Social-Personality Psychology	PhD	December 1 (Fall)	44	4	1	14 (0)	3	7	0
General Psychology	MA/MS	March 1 (Fall)	95	25	17 (0)	26 (3)	7	2	1

APA Accreditation

Clinical PhD: Student Outcome Data website: http://psychology.buffalo.edu/graduate/ph-d/clinical/admissions-outcomes-statistics/.

Doctoral Degree (PhD Clinical Psychology): For those doctoral students for whom a professional internship was required in this program prior to graduation:

Total students who applied for an internship: 7
Total students who obtained an internship: 6
Total students who obtained a paid internship: 6
Total students who obtained an unpaid internship: 0
Total students who were placed in APA/CPA-accredited internships: 6
Total students placed in internships not APA/CPA-accredited, but listed with the Association of Psychology Postdoctoral and Internship Centers (APPIC): 0
Total students placed in internships conforming to guidelines of the Council of Directors of School Psychology Programs (CDSPP): 0
Total students placed in internships that were not APA/CPA-accredited, APPIC or CDSSP listed: 0

Master's Degree (MA/MS General Psychology): An internship experience, such as a final research project or "capstone" experience is required of graduates.

Internships/Practica

Several clinical practica are offered each year for students in the doctoral program in Clinical Psychology and for other doctoral students with permission of the instructor.

Admissions

Entries appear in the following order: required test or GPA, minimum score (if required)/median score of students entering in 2015–2016.

Program	Degree	GRE-V	GRE-Q	GRE-Writing	GRE-Subject	Under-graduate GPA	Last 2 Years GPA	Psychol-ogy GPA	Master's GPA
Behavioral Neuroscience	PhD	NA/161	NA/156	NA/4.5	Not specified	3/3.43	Not specified	Not specified	Not specified
Clinical Psychology	PhD	NA/160	NA/158	NA/4.5	Not specified	3/3.8	Not specified	Not specified	Not specified
Cognitive Psychology	PhD	NA/157	NA/155	NA/4.5	Not specified	NA/3.77	Not specified	Not specified	Not specified
Social-Personality Psychology	PhD	NA/162	NA/162	NA/5	Not specified	3/3.8	Not specified	Not specified	Not specified
General Psychology	MA/MS	NA/154	NA/152	NA/4	Not specified	3/3.52	Not specified	Not specified	Not specified

Admissions Requirements:

Degree	GRE	GRE-Subject	Letters of Recom-mendation	Research Statement	Writing Sample	CV	Interview
Master's/Specialist	Required	Optional	3	Required	Optional	Optional	Recom-mended
Doctoral	Required	Optional	3	Required	Optional	Optional	Recom-mended

Please note if these criteria vary for different programs: Interview for clinical only.

Admissions Criteria:

GRE scores—medium
Research experience—high
Work experience—low
Clinically related public service—medium
GPA—high

Letters of recommendation—high
Interview—medium
Statement of goals and objectives—high
Undergraduate psychology preparation—medium

For additional information on admission requirements, visit http://psychology.buffalo.edu/graduate/apply/.

Department Demographics

	Male (PT)	Female (PT)	Total	African-American/ Black (PT)	Hispanic/ Latino (PT)	Asian/ Pacific Islander (PT)	American Indian/ Alaska Native (PT)	Caucasian/ White (PT)	Unknown	Multiethnic (PT)	ADA (PT)	Int'l (PT)
Students	31 (1)	71 (3)	106	1 (0)	6 (0)	6 (1)	1 (0)	72 (2)	2 (0)	0 (0)	0 (0)	7 (0)

Financial Information/Assistance

Tuition: For information on tuition costs, visit http://studentaccounts.buffalo.edu/tuition/. Tuition is subject to change. Additional fees are assessed to students beyond the costs of tuition for the following: comprehensive, academic excellence and activity fees.

Doctoral:
State residents: $10,870 per academic year.
State residents: $453 per credit hour.
Nonstate residents: $22,210 per academic year.
Nonstate residents: $925 per credit hour.

Master's:
State residents: $10,870 per academic year.
State residents: $453 per credit hour.
Nonstate residents: $22,210 per academic year.
Nonstate residents: $925 per credit hour.

Financial Assistance:

	Teaching Assistantship (% Receiving)	Teaching Assistantship Tuition Remission	Research Assistantship (% Receiving)	Research Assistantship Tuition Remission	Fellowship (% Receiving)	Fellowship Tuition Remission
First-Year Student	$14,000 (67)	Full	$14,000 (19)	Full	$14,000 (14)	Full
Advanced Student	$14,400 (37)	Full	$14,400 (15)	Full	$13,500 (1)	Full

For additional information on financial assistance, visit http://psychology.buffalo.edu/graduate/financial-support-fees/.

Employment of Department Graduates

Master's:
Employed in other positions at a higher education institution: 2
Employed in business or industry: 1
Employed in a community mental health/counseling center: 1
Employed in a hospital/medical center: 2
Do not know: 1
Total: 7

Doctoral:
Enrolled in a postdoctoral residency/fellowship: 7
Employed in an academic position at a university: 1
Employed in other positions at a higher education institution: 1
Employed in business or industry: 1
Employed in a hospital/medical center: 1
Total: 11

Additional Information

Housing and Day Care: On-campus housing is available. See the following website for more information: http://www.ub-housing. buffalo.edu/. On-campus day care facilities are available. See the following website for more information: http://www.buffalo.edu/ubccc.html.

Information for Students With Physical Disabilities: See the following website: http://www.student-affairs.buffalo.edu/ods/.

Special Facilities or Resources: The Department of Psychology has specialized research facilities for the study of language comprehension, auditory and speech perception, memory, categorization, animal cognition, visual perception, attention, social interaction, small group processes, animal surgery research, behavior therapy, human psychophysiology and biofeedback, and neurochemical and electrophysiological investigations into the physiological bases of behavior. Many of these laboratories are computer-based. The department also has ample facilities for individual and group therapy, marriage counseling, and therapeutic work with children. One-way vision screens and videotape equipment are available for observation and supervision. Internships are available through the department's Psychological Services Center. Excellent facilities are available for working with animals. Students have liberal access to the University's computing services on the North Campus.

Application Information: Director of Graduate Admissions, Department of Psychology, University at Buffalo, The State University of New York, Park Hall Room 213, Buffalo, NY 14260-4110. *Fee:* $75. *Online application:* https://www.gradmit.buffalo.edu.

Yeshiva University

Ferkauf Graduate School of Psychology
Albert Einstein College of Medicine
1300 Morris Park Avenue
Bronx, NY 10461-1602
Telephone: (718) 430-3850
Dean: Lawrence J. Siegel, PhD, ABPP

E-mail: michael.gill@einstein.yu.edu
Web: http://www.yu.edu/ferkauf

Orientation, Objectives, and Emphasis of Department

The objective of the Ferkauf Graduate School of Psychology is to promote a balance between the scientific-research orientation and the practitioner model. Ferkauf offers PhD and PsyD degrees, placing emphasis on research in the former and on application in the latter. The Clinical Psychology (Health Emphasis) program places greater emphasis upon applied and basic research, whereas the Clinical and School-Clinical Child Psychology programs focus on the scientist–practitioner model with integrated clinical research and supervised practicum experiences. A comprehensive theoretical orientation is offered with a psychodynamic focus and an applied behavioral emphasis. In all specialty areas, and at all levels of training, there is a strong commitment to the foundations of psychology, and a core of basic courses is required in all programs. Collaborations with the major NYC health and hospital institutions and schools are well established for all programs.

Programs and Degrees Offered

Program	Degree	Application Deadline	Applica-tions Received	Accepted	New Admits Enrolled (PT)	Total Enrolled (PT)	Degrees Awarded in 2014–2015	Median Years to Complete Degree	Dismissed/Withdrew
Clinical Psychology	PsyD	January 1 (Fall)	350	80	21	111 (12)	20	5	1
School/Clinical Child Psychology	PsyD	February 1 (Fall)	220	43	24	101 (9)	21	5	1
Mental Health Counseling	MA/MS	February 15 (Fall)	300	111	18 (2)	36 (2)	10	2.5	0
Clinical Health Psychology	PhD	January 15 (Fall)	120	55	15 (4)	83 (11)	13	5	1

APA Accreditation

Clinical PsyD: Student Outcome Data website: http://www.yu.edu/ferkauf/clinical-psychology/.
Combination PsyD: Student Outcome Data website: http://www.yu.edu/ferkauf/school-clinical-child-psychology/.

Clinical PhD (Doctor of Philosophy).

Doctoral Degree (PsyD Clinical Psychology): For those doctoral students for whom a professional internship was required in this program prior to graduation:
Total students who applied for an internship: 25
Total students who obtained an internship: 25
Total students who obtained a paid internship: 25
Total students who obtained an unpaid internship: 0
Total students who were placed in APA/CPA-accredited internships: 23
Total students placed in internships not APA/CPA-accredited, but listed with the Association of Psychology Postdoctoral and Internship Centers (APPIC): 2
Total students placed in internships conforming to guidelines of the Council of Directors of School Psychology Programs (CDSPP): 0
Total students placed in internships that were not APA/CPA-accredited, APPIC or CDSSP listed: 0

Doctoral Degree (PsyD School/Clinical Child Psychology): For those doctoral students for whom a professional internship was required in this program prior to graduation:
Total students who applied for an internship: 15
Total students who obtained an internship: 15
Total students who obtained a paid internship: 13
Total students who obtained an unpaid internship: 2

Total students who were placed in APA/CPA-accredited internships: 9
Total students placed in internships not APA/CPA-accredited, but listed with the Association of Psychology Postdoctoral and Internship Centers (APPIC): 0
Total students placed in internships conforming to guidelines of the Council of Directors of School Psychology Programs (CDSPP): 1
Total students placed in internships that were not APA/CPA-accredited, APPIC or CDSSP listed: 5

Doctoral Degree (PhD Clinical Health Psychology): For those doctoral students for whom a professional internship was required in this program prior to graduation:
Total students who applied for an internship: 13
Total students who obtained an internship: 13
Total students who obtained a paid internship: 11
Total students who obtained an unpaid internship: 2
Total students who were placed in APA/CPA-accredited internships: 10
Total students placed in internships not APA/CPA-accredited, but listed with the Association of Psychology Postdoctoral and Internship Centers (APPIC): 2
Total students placed in internships conforming to guidelines of the Council of Directors of School Psychology Programs (CDSPP): 0
Total students placed in internships that were not APA/CPA-accredited, APPIC or CDSSP listed: 1

Master's Degree (MA/MS Mental Health Counseling): An internship experience, such as a final research project or "capstone" experience is required of graduates.

Admissions

Entries appear in the following order: required test or GPA, minimum score (if required)/median score of students entering in 2015–2016.

Program	Degree	GRE-V	GRE-Q	GRE-Writing	GRE-Subject	Under-graduate GPA	Last 2 Years GPA	Psychol-ogy GPA	Master's GPA
Clinical Psychology	PsyD	NA/NA	NA/NA	Not specified	Not specified	NA/NA	Not specified	NA/NA	Not specified
School/Clinical Child Psychology	PsyD	NA/159	NA/155	Not specified	Not specified	NA/3.52	Not specified	NA/NA	Not specified
Mental Health Counseling	MA/MS	NA/NA	NA/NA	Not specified	Not specified	NA/NA	Not specified	NA/NA	Not specified
Clinical Health Psychology	PhD	NA/158	NA/156	Not specified	Not specified	NA/3.6	Not specified	NA/NA	Not specified

Admissions Requirements:

Degree	GRE	GRE-Subject	Letters of Recom-mendation	Research Statement	Writing Sample	CV	Interview
Master's/Specialist	Required	Recom-mended	3	Required	Optional	Required	Required
Doctoral	Required	Recom-mended	3	Required	Optional	Required	Required

Admissions Criteria:

GRE scores—high
Research experience—high
Work experience—high
Clinically related public service—high
GPA—high

Letters of recommendation—high
Interview—high
Statement of goals and objectives—high
Undergraduate psychology preparation—medium

For additional information on admission requirements, visit http://yu.edu/Admissions/Graduate/Ferkauf/.

Department Demographics

	Male (PT)	Female (PT)	Total	African-American/ Black (PT)	Hispanic/ Latino (PT)	Asian/ Pacific Islander (PT)	American Indian/ Alaska Native (PT)	Caucasian/ White (PT)	Unknown	Multiethnic (PT)	ADA (PT)	Int'l (PT)
Students	87 (15)	244 (19)	365	11 (0)	21 (2)	10 (3)	0 (0)	284 (27)	1 (1)	4 (1)	1 (1)	10 (3)

Financial Information/Assistance

Tuition: For information on tuition costs, visit http://yu.edu/osf/tuition-fees/ferkauf/. Tuition is subject to change. Additional fees are assessed to students beyond the costs of tuition for the following: student activities fee; materials fee; registration fee.

Doctoral:
State residents: $35,750 per academic year.
State residents: $1,640 per credit hour.
Nonstate residents: $35,750 per academic year.
Nonstate residents: $1,640 per credit hour.

Master's:
State residents: $35,750 per academic year.
State residents: $1,640 per credit hour.
Nonstate residents: $35,750 per academic year.
Nonstate residents: $1,640 per credit hour.

Financial Assistance:

	Teaching Assistantship (% Receiving)	Teaching Assistantship Tuition Remission	Research Assistantship (% Receiving)	Research Assistantship Tuition Remission	Fellowship (% Receiving)	Fellowship Tuition Remission
First-Year Student	$4,000 (NA)	NA	$2,000 (NA)	NA	$20,000 (NA)	NA
Advanced Student	$4,000 (NA)	NA	$10,000 (NA)	NA	$20,000 (NA)	NA

For additional information on financial assistance, visit http://yu.edu/admissions/graduate/ferkauf/finance/.

Employment of Department Graduates

Master's:
Enrolled in a psychology doctoral program: 25
Enrolled in another graduate/professional program: 5
Do not know: 5
Total: 35

Doctoral:
Enrolled in a postdoctoral residency/fellowship: 3
Employed in independent practice: 7
Employed in an academic position at a university: 2
Employed in academic position at a 2-year/4-year college: 2
Employed in other positions at a higher education institution: 1
Employed in a professional position in a school system: 15
Employed in business or industry: 3
Employed in a community mental health/counseling center: 11
Employed in a hospital/medical center: 20
Still seeking employment: 1
Other employment position: 2
Do not know: 1
Total: 68

Additional Information

Housing and Day Care: No on-campus housing is available. On-campus day care facilities are available.

Information for Students With Physical Disabilities: See the following website: http://yu.edu/student-life/resources-and-services/disability-services.

Special Facilities or Resources: All psychology programs offer practicum experience through Ferkauf's Center for Psychological and Psychoeducational Services. The Center provides a wide range of evaluation, remediation, and therapeutic services for children, adolescents, and adults in the neighboring communities, in addition to consultation services directly to the local schools. Ferkauf is located on Yeshiva University's campus of the Albert Einstein College of Medicine which has led to the development of cooperative programs and activities with various disciplines in medicine as well as added training opportunities for students at the various service delivery agencies affiliated with the medical college.

Application Information: Director of Admissions, Ferkauf Graduate School of Psychology, 1300 Morris Park Avenue, Bronx, NY 10461. *Fee:* $50. *Online application:* http://yu.edu/Admissions/Graduate/Ferkauf/.

Appalachian State University

Department of Psychology
Arts and Science
Smith-Wright Hall
Boone, NC 28608
Telephone: (828) 262-2272
Chairperson: James C. Denniston

E-mail: dennistonjc@appstate.edu
Web: http://psych.appstate.edu

Orientation, Objectives, and Emphasis of Department

The department is student oriented, with a Program Director for each graduate program. The Experimental program is primarily predoctoral for experimental psychology, but one can structure an applied orientation. The Clinical program trains professionals for master's level licensure as LPAs and applied practice in mental health and medical settings or for doctoral study in clinical psychology. The School Psychology program is NCATE/NASP accredited and offers the master's and specialist degree. The Industrial/Organizational–Human Resource Management program integrates with the Department of Management in the College of Business and trains professionals to work in business, industry, and government.

Programs and Degrees Offered

Program	Degree	Application Deadline	Applications Received	Accepted	New Admits Enrolled (PT)	Total Enrolled (PT)	Degrees Awarded in 2014–2015	Median Years to Complete Degree	Dismissed/Withdrew
Experimental Psychology	MA/MS	March 1 (Fall)	35	10	7 (0)	15 (0)	6	2.4	1
Industrial-Organizational Psychology Hr Management	MA/MS	February 15 (Fall)	120	20	13 (0)	24 (0)	9	2	0
Clinical Psychology	MA/MS	February 1 (Fall)	92	8	8	16 (6)	9	2.7	0
Specialist in School Psychology	Other	February 1 (Fall)	41	11	8 (0)	24 (0)	5	3	1

Internships/Practica

Clinical students complete two semester-long practica. These are often at the University Counseling Center, the Psychology Clinic, a school-based mental health clinic, or at other regional mental health centers. Students also complete a 600–1,000-hour internship at a medical or mental health setting. School students complete two semester-long practica in public schools and a 1,200-hour internship, half of which must be in a public school setting. Industrial/Organizational-Human Resources Management students typically complete a 450-hour internship in human resources, organizational development or related areas.

Admissions

Entries appear in the following order: required test or GPA, minimum score (if required)/median score of students entering in 2015–2016.

Program	Degree	GRE-V	GRE-Q	GRE-Writing	GRE-Subject	Under-graduate GPA	Last 2 Years GPA	Psychol-ogy GPA	Master's GPA
Experimental Psychology	MA/MS	147/159	147/157	4/4.5	Not specified	3.4/3.8	Not specified	Not specified	Not specified
Industrial-Organizational Psychology HR Management	MA/MS	NA/155	NA/156	Not specified	Not specified	NA/3.65	Not specified	Not specified	Not specified

Admissions *(con't.)*

Program	Degree	GRE-V	GRE-Q	GRE-Writing	GRE-Subject	Under-graduate GPA	Last 2 Years GPA	Psychol-ogy GPA	Master's GPA
Clinical Psychology	MA/MS	155/155	153/153	3.5/4	Not specified	3.1/3.7	Not specified	Not specified	Not specified
Specialist in School Psychology	Other	144/155	145/153	2.5/4	Not specified	2.9/3.46	Not specified	Not specified	Not specified

Admissions Requirements:

Degree	GRE	GRE-Subject	Letters of Recom-mendation	Research Statement	Writing Sample	CV	Interview
Master's/Specialist	Required	Optional	3	Required	Optional	Required	Required

Please note if these criteria vary for different programs: An interview is not required for IOHRM or Experimental Psychology. Interviews are given high importance for the Clinical and School Psychology programs.

Admissions Criteria:

GRE scores—high
Research experience—medium
Work experience—low
Clinically related public service—low
GPA—high

Letters of recommendation—medium
Interview—high
Statement of goals and objectives—high
Undergraduate psychology preparation– medium

For additional information on admission requirements, visit http://psych.appstate.edu/students/graduate.

Department Demographics

	Male (PT)	Female (PT)	Total	African-American/ Black (PT)	Hispanic/ Latino (PT)	Asian/ Pacific Islander (PT)	American Indian/ Alaska Native (PT)	Caucasian/ White (PT)	Unknown (PT)	Multiethnic (PT)	ADA (PT)	Int'l (PT)
Students	22 (0)	54 (0)	76	5 (0)	0 (0)	4 (0)	0 (0)	72 (0)	0 (0)	0 (0)	1 (0)	1 (0)

Financial Information/Assistance

Tuition: For information on tuition costs, visit http://studentaccounts.appstate.edu/tuition-and-fees. Tuition is subject to change.

Master's:
State residents: $7,409 per academic year.
Nonstate residents: $19,951 per academic year.

Financial Assistance:

	Teaching Assistantship (% Receiving)	Teaching Assistantship Tuition Remission	Research Assistantship (% Receiving)	Research Assistantship Tuition Remission	Fellowship (% Receiving)	Fellowship Tuition Remission
First-Year Student	$5,000 (29)	NA	$7,500 (36)	NA	$12,000 (36)	NA
Advanced Student	$8,000 (26)	NA	$7,500 (NA)	NA	$12,000 (3)	NA

For additional information on financial assistance, visit http://www.graduate.appstate.edu/admissions/financial.html.

Employment of Department Graduates

Master's:
Enrolled in a psychology doctoral program: 6
Employed in other positions at a higher education institution: 1
Employed in a professional position in a school system: 5
Employed in business or industry: 9
Employed in government agency: 1
Employed in a community mental health/counseling center: 4
Do not know: 1
Total: 27

Additional Information

Housing and Day Care: No on-campus housing is available. On-campus day care facilities are available. See the following website for more information: http://lucybrock.appstate.edu/; http://childdevelopment.appstate.edu/.

Information for Students With Physical Disabilities: See the following website: http://ods.appstate.edu/.

Special Facilities or Resources: Biofeedback facilities, student computer laboratory, neuroscience laboratory, an animal operant conditioning laboratory, and a Psychology Clinic are available.

Application Information: The Dean, Cratis D. Williams Graduate School, John E. Thomas Building, Appalachian State University, Boone, NC 28608. *Fee:* $55. *Online application:* http://www.gradadmissions1.appstate.edu/.

Duke University

Department of Psychology and Neuroscience
229 Psychology / Sociology Building, P.O. Box 90085
9 Flowers Drive
Durham, NC 27708
Telephone: (919) 660-5715
Chairperson: Dr. Scott Huettel

E-mail: morrell@duke.edu
Web: http://psychandneuro.duke.edu/

Orientation, Objectives, and Emphasis of Department

The department features a strong mentor-oriented training program with areas of specialization in clinical health, adult and child psychology, as well as programs in developmental and social psychology. Emphasis is placed on informal interaction among faculty and students; seminars and small groups of faculty and graduate students meet regularly.

Programs and Degrees Offered

Program	Degree	Application Deadline	Applica-tions Received	Accepted	New Admits Enrolled (PT)	Total Enrolled (PT)	Degrees Awarded in 2014–2015	Median Years to Complete Degree	Dismissed/Withdrew
Clinical Psychology	PhD	December 1 (Fall)	289	7	4 (0)	30 (0)	8	7.3	0
Developmental Psychology	PhD	December 8 (Fall)	22	1	1 (0)	6 (0)	2		0
Social Psychology	PhD	December 8 (Fall)	35	0	0 (0)	11 (0)	1		0
Systems & Integrative Neuroscience	PhD	December 8 (Fall)	15	0	0 (0)	9 (0)	4	5	0
Cognition & Cognitive Neuroscience	PhD	December 8 (Fall)	117	3	3 (0)	20 (0)	9	5	0
Jd/Ma Social and Health Sciences	MA/MS	February 15 (Fall)	1	1	0 (0)	0 (3)	0		0

APA Accreditation

Clinical PhD: Student Outcome Data website: http://psychandneuro.duke.edu/graduate/clinical.

Doctoral Degree (PhD Clinical Psychology): For those doctoral students for whom a professional internship was required in this program prior to graduation:

Total students who applied for an internship: 5

Total students who obtained an internship: 4

Total students who obtained a paid internship: 4

Total students who obtained an unpaid internship: 0

Total students who were placed in APA/CPA-accredited internships: 4

Total students placed in internships not APA/CPA-accredited, but listed with the Association of Psychology Postdoctoral and Internship Centers (APPIC): 0

Total students placed in internships conforming to guidelines of the Council of Directors of School Psychology Programs (CDSPP): 0

Total students placed in internships that were not APA/CPA-accredited, APPIC or CDSSP listed: 0

Internships/Practica

Doctoral students in our clinical program receive experience in our own departmental clinic as well as a great number of local institutions and medical center facilities.

Admissions

Entries appear in the following order: required test or GPA, minimum score (if required)/median score of students entering in 2015–2016.

Program	Degree	GRE-V	GRE-Q	GRE-Writing	GRE-Subject	Under-graduate GPA	Last 2 Years GPA	Psychol-ogy GPA	Master's GPA
Clinical Psychology	PhD	NA/165	NA/168	NA/5.4	Not specified	NA/3.7	Not specified	Not specified	Not specified
Developmental Psychology	PhD	NA/161	NA/160	NA/4	Not specified	NA/3.9	Not specified	Not specified	Not specified
Social Psychology	PhD	NA/NA	NA/NA	NA/NA	Not specified	NA/NA	Not specified	Not specified	Not specified
Systems & Integrative Neuroscience	PhD	NA/NA	NA/NA	NA/NA	Not specified	NA/NA	Not specified	Not specified	Not specified
Cognition & Cognitive Neuroscience	PhD	NA/167	NA/164	NA/4.5	Not specified	NA/3.7	Not specified	Not specified	Not specified
JD/MA Social and Health Sciences	MA/MS	Not specified	Not specified	Not specified	Not specified	Not specified	Not specified	Not specified	Not specified

Admissions Requirements:

Degree	GRE	GRE-Subject	Letters of Recom-mendation	Research Statement	Writing Sample	CV	Interview
Doctoral	Required	Recom-mended	3	Required	Optional	Optional	Required

Please note if these criteria vary for different programs: Clinically Related Public Service is not required for Developmental, Social, Cognitive, or Neuro. We recommend that applicants to the clinical program who did not major in Psychology take the GRE-Subject test.

Admissions Criteria:

GRE scores—high
Research experience—high
Work experience—high
Clinically related public service—medium
GPA—high

Letters of recommendation—high
Interview—high
Statement of goals and objectives—high
Undergraduate psychology preparation—medium

For additional information on admission requirements, visit http://psychandneuro.duke.edu/graduate/for-applicants.

Department Demographics

	Male (PT)	Female (PT)	Total	African-American/ Black (PT)	Hispanic/ Latino (PT)	Asian/ Pacific Islander (PT)	American Indian/ Alaska Native (PT)	Caucasian/ White (PT)	Unknown (PT)	Multiethnic (PT)	ADA (PT)	Int'l (PT)
Students	22 (1)	54 (2)	79	5 (0)	6 (0)	10 (0)	1 (0)	53 (3)	1 (0)	0 (0)	0 (0)	10 (0)

Financial Information/Assistance

Tuition: For information on tuition costs, visit https://gradschool.duke.edu/financial-support/cost-attend. Tuition is subject to change. Additional fees are assessed to students beyond the costs of tuition for the following: activity, health, and recreation fees.

Doctoral:
State residents: $47,590 per academic year.
Nonstate residents: $47,590 per academic year.

Financial Assistance:

	Teaching Assistantship (% Receiving)	Teaching Assistantship Tuition Remission	Research Assistantship (% Receiving)	Research Assistantship Tuition Remission	Fellowship (% Receiving)	Fellowship Tuition Remission
First-Year Student	$23,795 (NA)	Full	$23,795 (NA)	Full	$23,795 (NA)	Full
Advanced Student	$23,795 (NA)	Full	$23,795 (NA)	Full	$23,795 (NA)	Full

For additional information on financial assistance, visit http://gradschool.duke.edu/financial_support/.

Employment of Department Graduates

Doctoral:
Enrolled in a postdoctoral residency/fellowship: 16
Employed in independent practice: 1
Employed in an academic position at a university: 3
Employed in academic position at a 2-year/4-year college: 2
Employed in business or industry: 1
Still seeking employment: 1
Total: 24

Additional Information

Housing and Day Care: On-campus housing is available. See the following website for more information: https://studentaffairs.duke.edu/hdrl/graduate-professional-students. On-campus day care facilities are available. See the following website for more information: http://www.hr.duke.edu/benefits/family/care/onsite/.

Information for Students With Physical Disabilities: See the following website: http://access.duke.edu/.

Special Facilities or Resources: The department has collaborative ties with the Center for Child and Family Policy, the Center for Cognitive Neuroscience, the Center for the Study of Aging and Human Development, the Fuqua School of Business, Medical Psychology, the Center for Aging and Human Development, the Center for Child and Family Policy, and the Carolina Consortium on Human Development and UNC-Duke Collaborative Graduate Certificate Program in Developmental Psychology. State-of-the-art facilities, including specially equipped laboratories and clinics, are available for student use. These include computational facilities for word processing, data analysis, and experimental programming.

Application Information: Fee: $85. *Online application:* https://app.applyyourself.com/?id=dukegrad.

East Carolina University

Department of Psychology
Arts & Sciences
104 Rawl
Greenville, NC 27858-4353
Telephone: (252) 328-6800
Chairperson: Susan McCammon

E-mail: bakerr@ecu.edu
Web: http://www.ecu.edu/psyc/

Orientation, Objectives, and Emphasis of Department

ECU Psychology prepares students for careers in health care, education and business, and provides leadership within the field through cutting-edge research and prominent national roles. Graduate Programs in the Department include: School Psychology MA/CAS (NASP-approved); MA in Industrial/Organizational psychology; and PhD in Health Psychology with three separate and specific concentrations: Clinical Health Psychology (CHP), Pediatric School Psychology (PSP), and Occupational Health Psychology (OHP). The clinical program espouses a scientist–practitioner model with a health emphasis, training graduates to work within primary care teams, hospitals, health organizations, etc. and academic settings. PSP prepares students to advance school psychology through original research and to professionally apply health psychology principles to school psychology practices across a three-tier model of service delivery. CHP is APA-accredited as a Clinical psychology program and PSP is APA-accredited as a School psychology program. Students from CHP and PSP are eligible for licensure as Licensed Psychologists and Health Services Providers by NC Board of Psychology; PSP graduates are also eligible for school-level licensure. OHP trains occupational health professionals to improve the quality of working life and enhance the safety, health, and well-being of workers across occupations.

Programs and Degrees Offered

Program	Degree	Application Deadline	Applications Received	Accepted	New Admits Enrolled (PT)	Total Enrolled (PT)	Degrees Awarded in 2014–2015	Median Years to Complete Degree	Dismissed/Withdrew
School Psychology	MA/MS	January 15 (Fall)	36	12	7 (0)	20 (0)	6	3	0
Industrial/Organizational Psychology	MA/MS	March 1 (Fall)	100	28	9 (0)	17 (0)	8	2	0
Clinical Health Psychology	PhD	December 1 (Fall)	129	6	6 (0)	24 (0)	7	6	1
Pediatric School Psychology	PhD	December 1 (Fall)	24	5	3 (0)	16 (0)	5	6	0
Occupational Health Psychology	PhD	December 1 (Fall)	17	5	3 (0)	6 (0)	0		1

APA Accreditation

Clinical PhD: Student Outcome Data website: http://www.ecu.edu/cs-cas/psyc/CH-main-new.cfm.
School PhD: Student Outcome Data website: http://www.ecu.edu/cs-cas/psyc/PSP-base-2014.cfm.

Doctoral Degree (PhD Clinical Health Psychology): For those doctoral students for whom a professional internship was required in this program prior to graduation:
Total students who applied for an internship: 3
Total students who obtained an internship: 3
Total students who obtained a paid internship: 3
Total students who obtained an unpaid internship: 0
Total students who were placed in APA/CPA-accredited internships: 2
Total students placed in internships not APA/CPA-accredited, but listed with the Association of Psychology Postdoctoral and Internship Centers (APPIC): 1
Total students placed in internships conforming to guidelines of the Council of Directors of School Psychology Programs (CDSPP): 0
Total students placed in internships that were not APA/CPA-accredited, APPIC or CDSSP listed: 0

Doctoral Degree (PhD Pediatric School Psychology): For those doctoral students for whom a professional internship was required in this program prior to graduation:
Total students who applied for an internship: 1
Total students who obtained an internship: 1
Total students who obtained a paid internship: 1
Total students who obtained an unpaid internship: 0
Total students who were placed in APA/CPA-accredited internships: 0
Total students placed in internships not APA/CPA-accredited, but listed with the Association of Psychology Postdoctoral and Internship Centers (APPIC): 0
Total students placed in internships conforming to guidelines of the Council of Directors of School Psychology Programs (CDSPP): 1
Total students placed in internships that were not APA/CPA-accredited, APPIC or CDSSP listed: 0

Master's Degree (MA/MS School Psychology): An internship experience, such as a final research project or "capstone" experience is required of graduates. Master's Degree (MA/MS Industrial/Organizational Psychology): An internship experience, such as a final research project or "capstone" experience is required of graduates.

Internships/Practica
Doctoral Internships for CHP and PSP are sought primarily via APPIC. Some School Psychology doctoral students choose internships within public school systems. Doctoral practica include placements in the Brody School of Medicine Cardiac Psychology, Family Medicine, and Psychiatry Clinics; Vidant Medical Center Rehabilitation, Behavioral Health, and NICU Follow-up Clinics; Veterans Administration Outpatient Clinic; General Adult Neuropsychology Clinic; Cherry Psychiatric Hospital; school-based mental health services (Greene/Rocky Mt. County Schools); Pitt County Schools Transdisciplinary Play-based Assessment Teams; and ECU Psychological Assessment and Specialty Services (PASS; in-house clinic): Adult Healthy Weight Clinic, Pediatric Healthy Weight Clinic, Women's Health Psychology Clinic, and Pediatric Behavioral Health Clinic. Specialist-level School Psychology students have practica and internships in various public school systems across the state and region. I/O Master's students completing their first year of training are required to complete a 400-hour internship in various organizational/health/business settings.

Admissions
Entries appear in the following order: required test or GPA, minimum score (if required)/median score of students entering in 2015–2016.

Program	Degree	GRE-V	GRE-Q	GRE-Writing	GRE-Subject	Under-graduate GPA	Last 2 Years GPA	Psychology GPA	Master's GPA
School Psychology	MA/MS	NA/154	NA/147	NA/4	Not specified	NA/3.51	Not specified	Not specified	Not specified
Industrial/ Organizational Psychology	MA/MS	NA/154	NA/154	Not specified	Not specified	3/3.54	Not specified	Not specified	Not specified
Clinical Health Psychology	PhD	NA/156	NA/154	NA/4	Not specified	NA/3.7	Not specified	Not specified	Not specified
Pediatric School Psychology	PhD	NA/155	NA/148	NA/4	Not specified	Not specified	Not specified	Not specified	Not specified
Occupational Health Psychology	PhD	NA/155	NA/153	NA/4	Not specified	Not specified	Not specified	Not specified	Not specified

Admissions Requirements:

Degree	GRE	GRE-Subject	Letters of Recommendation	Research Statement	Writing Sample	CV	Interview
Master's/Specialist	Required	None	2	Required	None	Required	None
Doctoral	Required	None	3	Required	None	Required	Required

Please note if these criteria vary for different programs: We require two letters of recommendation for the I/O program, and three for the MA/CAS in School Psychology. All three doctoral concentrations require three letters of recommendation.

Admissions Criteria:
GRE scores—high
Research experience—high
Work experience—medium
Clinically related public service—medium
GPA—high

Letters of recommendation—high
Interview—high
Statement of goals and objectives—high
Undergraduate psychology preparation—high

For additional information on admission requirements, visit http://www.ecu.edu/cs-cas/psyc/Applications.cfm.

Department Demographics

	Male (PT)	Female (PT)	Total	African-American/ Black (PT)	Hispanic/ Latino (PT)	Asian/ Pacific Islander (PT)	American Indian/ Alaska Native (PT)	Caucasian/ White (PT)	Unknown (PT)	Multiethnic (PT)	ADA (PT)	Int'l (PT)
Students	23 (0)	60 (0)	83	5 (0)	3 (0)	1 (0)	0 (0)	73 (0)	0 (0)	1 (0)	0 (0)	1 (0)

Financial Information/Assistance

Tuition: For information on tuition costs, visit http://www.ecu.edu/cashier/tufee.cfm. Tuition is subject to change. Additional fees are assessed to students beyond the costs of tuition for the following: university fees, health service fee, educational/technology fee, safety & security fee.

Doctoral:
State residents: $4,434 per academic year.
Nonstate residents: $17,036 per academic year.

Master's:
State residents: $4,434 per academic year.
Nonstate residents: $17,036 per academic year.

Financial Assistance:

	Teaching Assistantship (% Receiving)	Teaching Assistantship Tuition Remission	Research Assistantship (% Receiving)	Research Assistantship Tuition Remission	Fellowship (% Receiving)	Fellowship Tuition Remission
First-Year Student	$4,500 (42)	Partial	$4,500 (29)	Partial	NA (NA)	NA
Advanced Student	$15,000 (43)	Full	$15,000 (39)	Full	$3,000 (NA)	NA

For additional information on financial assistance, visit http://www.ecu.edu/cs-acad/gradschool/Graduate-School-Financial-Resources.cfm.

Employment of Department Graduates

Master's:
Enrolled in a psychology doctoral program: 2
Employed in a professional position in a school system: 6
Employed in business or industry: 4
Do not know: 2
Total: 14

Doctoral:
Enrolled in a postdoctoral residency/fellowship: 5
Employed in academic position at a 2-year/4-year college: 1
Employed in a professional position in a school system: 2
Employed in government agency: 1
Employed in a hospital/medical center: 2
Still seeking employment: 1
Total: 12

Additional Information

Housing and Day Care: On-campus housing is available. See the following website for more information: http://www.ecu.edu/campusliving/. On-campus day care facilities are available. See the following website for more information: http://www.ecu.edu/cs-hhp/hdfs/ndcdc.cfm.

Information for Students With Physical Disabilities: See the following website: http://www.ecu.edu/cs-admin/accessibility/.

Special Facilities or Resources: The department has a student lounge dedicated to Graduate Students, interview and testing facilities, the PASS Clinic, and an animal laboratory. The school program works closely with community schools and mental health agencies. The doctoral health psychology program works closely with the Brody School of Medicine, family care practices, state health agencies, as well as with the Sleep Disorders Center, the Heart Center, pediatric specialty clinic and psychiatric medicine.

Application Information: East Carolina University Graduate School, 131 Ragsdale Hall, Mail Stop 570, Greenville, NC 27858-4353. *Fee:* $70. *Online application:* https://gradapply.ecu.edu/.

East Carolina University

Medical Family Therapy
College of Health and Human Performance
114 Redditt House
Greenville, NC 27858
Telephone: (252) 328-1349
Program Director: Dr. Jennifer Hodgson

E-mail: hodgsonj@ecu.edu
Web: http://www.ecu.edu/cs-hhp/hdfs/phd-mft.cfm

Orientation, Objectives, and Emphasis of Department

The mission of the doctoral program in Medical Family Therapy (MedFT) is to advance students' learning in the areas of research, theory, clinical practice, leadership, supervision, and teaching in order to prepare and qualify them to pursue employment as researchers, educators, administrators, and/or clinicians in the field of medical family therapy.

Programs and Degrees Offered

Program	Degree	Application Deadline	Applica-tions Received	Accepted	New Admits Enrolled (PT)	Total Enrolled (PT)	Degrees Awarded in 2014–2015	Median Years to Complete Degree	Dismissed/ Withdrew
Medical Family Therapy	PhD	January 1 (Fall)	20	3	4 (0)	11 (0)	2	3	0

Internships/Practica

Each doctoral student is required to complete an internship lasting a minimum of 9 months in duration. The internship must meet the site requirements and those set forth by the program and in agreement with the MFT educational guidelines. The ECU MedFT program further requires that each internship site be situated in a medical context or in a context where students will have access to working with medical populations (research and/or clinical).

Admissions

Entries appear in the following order: required test or GPA, minimum score (if required)/median score of students entering in 2015–2016.

Program	Degree	GRE-V	GRE-Q	GRE-Writing	GRE-Subject	Under-graduate GPA	Last 2 Years GPA	Psychol-ogy GPA	Master's GPA
Medical Family Therapy	PhD	150/NA	150/NA	4/NA	Not specified	2.75/NA	Not specified	Not specified	3/NA

Admissions Requirements:

Degree	GRE	GRE-Subject	Letters of Recom-mendation	Research Statement	Writing Sample	CV	Interview
Doctoral	Required	None	3	Required	Required	Recom-mended	Required

Admissions Criteria:

GRE scores—high
Research experience—high
Work experience—medium
Clinically related public service—medium
GPA—high

Letters of recommendation—high
Interview—high
Statement of goals and objectives—high
Undergraduate psychology preparation—low

For additional information on admission requirements, visit http://www.ecu.edu/cs-hhp/hdfs/phd-mft-admission.cfm.

Department Demographics

	Male (PT)	Female (PT)	Total	African-American/ Black (PT)	Hispanic/ Latino (PT)	Asian/ Pacific Islander (PT)	American Indian/ Alaska Native (PT)	Caucasian/ White (PT)	Unknown	Multiethnic (PT)	ADA (PT)	Int'l (PT)
Students	3 (0)	8 (0)	11	1 (0)	1 (0)	0 (0)	1 (0)	7 (0)	0 (0)	1 (0)	0 (0)	0 (0)

Financial Information/Assistance

Tuition: For information on tuition costs, visit http://www.ecu.edu/cashier/tufee.cfm. Tuition is subject to change. Additional fees are assessed to students beyond the costs of tuition for the following: University fees, education/technology fees, health service fee, safety & security fee.

Doctoral:
State residents: $6,827 per academic year.
State residents: $564 per credit hour.
Nonstate residents: $19,429 per academic year.
Nonstate residents: $2,129 per credit hour.

Financial Assistance:

	Teaching Assistantship (% Receiving)	Teaching Assistantship Tuition Remission	Research Assistantship (% Receiving)	Research Assistantship Tuition Remission	Fellowship (% Receiving)	Fellowship Tuition Remission
First-Year Student	$26,000 (NA)	Full	$26,000 (NA)	Full	NA (NA)	NA
Advanced Student	$26,000 (NA)	Full	$26,000 (NA)	Full	NA (NA)	NA

For additional information on financial assistance, visit http://www.ecu.edu/financial/.

Employment of Department Graduates

Doctoral:
Employed in an academic position at a university: 1
Other employment position: 1
Total: 2

Additional Information

Housing and Day Care: No on-campus housing is available. On-campus day care facilities are available. See the following website for more information: http://www.ecu.edu/cs-hhp/hdfs/ndcdc.cfm.

Information for Students With Physical Disabilities: See the following website: http://www.ecu.edu/accessibility/.

Special Facilities or Resources: In August of 2011, the Redditt House: Medical Family Therapy Research Academy opened and serves as a research and training site for faculty and MedFT students to further strengthen the capacity for unique research training opportunities. The ECU Family Therapy Clinic opened in 1991 and serves as a training facility for our MFT and MedFT students.

The clinic offers a way for faculty to provide co-therapy with Master's and doctoral-level therapists and is also a great location for supervision of students in the program.

Application Information: ECU Graduate School, 131 Ragsdale, Greenville, NC 27858-4353. *Fee:* $70. *Online application:* https://gradapply.ecu.edu.

Fayetteville State University

Psychology
Arts and Sciences
1200 Murchison Road
Fayetteville, NC 28301
Telephone: (910) 672-1413
Chairperson: Timothy O. Moore, PhD

E-mail: tmoore40@uncfsu.edu
Web: http://www.uncfsu.edu/psychology

Orientation, Objectives, and Emphasis of Department

The mission of the 60-semester hour Counseling Track is threefold: to produce highly skilled, license-eligible graduates in counseling and the community human service/mental health movement; to increase the awareness, knowledge, and skills of students, and professionals in the area of multicultural counseling; and to provide practicum experiences that reflect the present and projected community counseling, health, and service needs of an increasingly pluralistic society. In the Counseling track, the program provides curricular experiences and eight core areas including Professional Identity, Social and Cultural Diversity, Human Growth and Development, Career Development, Helping Relationships, Group Work, Assessment, and Research and Program Evaluation. Practica permit the integration of theory, research, and application. Placements have included, but are not limited to: counseling agencies, mental health clinics, correctional facilities, and college-level student services departments. Finally, we encourage the maintenance and development of individual counseling styles and are committed to excellence in counseling through participation in individual and group counseling experiences.

Programs and Degrees Offered

Program	Degree	Application Deadline	Applica-tions Received	Accepted	New Admits Enrolled (PT)	Total Enrolled (PT)	Degrees Awarded in 2014–2015	Median Years to Complete Degree	Dismissed/Withdrew
Counseling Psychology	MA/MS	March 15 (Fall), October 15 (Spring)	30	15	(0)	20 (0)	9	2.5	0
Experimental Psychology	MA/MS	March 15 (Fall)	6	6	6	10	0		0

Internships/Practica

There are numerous internship opportunities in Fayetteville, NC and throughout the surrounding community. Regionally, Cumberland County has many sites for obtaining internship/practicum experience.

Admissions

Entries appear in the following order: required test or GPA, minimum score (if required)/median score of students entering in 2015–2016.

Program	Degree	GRE-V	GRE-Q	GRE-Writing	GRE-Subject	Under-graduate GPA	Last 2 Years GPA	Psychol-ogy GPA	Master's GPA
Counseling Psychology	MA/MS	NA/NA	NA/NA	Not specified	Not specified	2.7/3.4	2.7/3	Not specified	Not specified
Experimental Psychology	MA/MS	NA/NA	NA/NA	Not specified	Not specified	2.7/3.4	2.7/3	Not specified	Not specified

Admissions Requirements:

Degree	GRE	GRE-Subject	Letters of Recommendation	Research Statement	Writing Sample	CV	Interview
Master's/Specialist	Required	None	2	Required	Optional	Required	None

Please note if these criteria vary for different programs: Counseling Program requires a Supplemental Application-Personal Statement. Experimental Program requires an essay describing your interest in psychology.

Admissions Criteria:

GRE scores—high
Research experience—medium
Work experience—medium
Clinically related public service—medium

GPA—high
Letters of recommendation—medium
Statement of goals and objectives—low
Undergraduate psychology preparation—high

For additional information on admission requirements, visit http://www.uncfsu.edu/psychology/graduate-program.

Department Demographics

	Male (PT)	Female (PT)	Total	African-American/ Black (PT)	Hispanic/ Latino (PT)	Asian/ Pacific Islander (PT)	American Indian/ Alaska Native (PT)	Caucasian/ White (PT)	Unknown (PT)	Multiethnic (PT)	ADA (PT)	Int'l (PT)
Students	2 (0)	24 (0)	26	22 (0)	0 (0)	0 (0)	1 (0)	8 (0)	0 (0)	0 (0)	0 (0)	0 (0)

Financial Information/Assistance

Tuition: For information on tuition costs, visit http://www.uncfsu.edu/bursar/fees.

Master's:
State residents: $7,439 per academic year.
Nonstate residents: $18,288 per academic year.

Financial Assistance:

	Teaching Assistantship (% Receiving)	Teaching Assistantship Tuition Remission	Research Assistantship (% Receiving)	Research Assistantship Tuition Remission	Fellowship (% Receiving)	Fellowship Tuition Remission
First-Year Student	NA (NA)	NA	$3,000 (NA)	Partial	NA (NA)	NA
Advanced Student	NA (NA)	NA	$3,000 (NA)	Partial	NA (NA)	NA

For additional information on financial assistance, visit http://finaid.uncfsu.edu/.

Employment of Department Graduates

Master's:
Enrolled in a psychology doctoral program: 1
Employed in a professional position in a school system: 3
Employed in government agency: 3
Employed in a community mental health/counseling center: 5
Total: 12

Additional Information

Housing and Day Care: On-campus housing is available. See the following website for more information: http://www.uncfsu.edu/reslife/. On-campus day care facilities are available. See the following website for more information: http://www.uncfsu.edu/eclc.

Information for Students With Physical Disabilities: See the following website: http://www.uncfsu.edu/studentaffairs/cfpd/disabled-student-services.

Special Facilities or Resources: The department is located on the eastside of campus near the library in the Nursing Education and Research Building (NERC). Along with the Departments of Nursing and Social Work, the Department of Psychology is part of the Collaborative Institute for Interprofessional Education and Practice (CI-PEP). The opportunity to work with CI-PEP can provide additional professional experience to serve the military. Fayetteville is located near a major military installation (Fort Bragg), so programs benefitting veterans, active military, and the families of military personnel are provided by the Department of Psychology.

Application Information: 102 Continuing Education Building, 1200 Murchison Road, Fayetteville NC 28301-4252. *Fee:* $40. *Online application:* http://www.uncfsu.edu/admissions/graduate.

North Carolina State University

Department of Psychology
Humanities and Social Sciences
640 Poe Hall, Box 7650
Raleigh, NC 27695-7650
Telephone: (919) 515-2251
Department Head: Adam Meade

E-mail: psych@ncsu.edu
Web: http://psychology.chass.ncsu.edu/

Orientation, Objectives, and Emphasis of Department

The department trains in the scientist–practitioner model. Students are expected to become knowledgeable about both research and application within their area of study. There are five specialty areas with different emphases. Lifespan Developmental Psychology stresses a balance of conceptual, research-analytical, and application skills and encompasses social and cognitive development from early childhood to old age. Human Factors and Applied Cognition emphasizes the cognitive/perceptual aspects of human factors, including research on visual displays, visual/auditory spatial judgments, ergonomics for older adults and the effective information transfer for complex systems. This track has a cooperative relationship with the Ergonomics/Biomechanics Program in Industrial and Systems Engineering. The Applied Social and Community Psychology program is problem-oriented and deals with research and professional issues in communities and social systems. Heath is a topic of considerable interest. Industrial/Organizational (I/O) students may concentrate in areas such as performance appraisal, selection, training, job analysis, work motivation, organizational theory/development, and the interface of technology with I/O issues. School Psychology develops behavioral scientists who apply psychological knowledge and techniques in school and family settings to help students, parents, and teachers.

Programs and Degrees Offered

Program	Degree	Application Deadline	Applications Received	Accepted	New Admits Enrolled (PT)	Total Enrolled (PT)	Degrees Awarded in 2014–2015	Median Years to Complete Degree	Dismissed/Withdrew
Human Factors & Applied Cognitive Psychology	PhD	January 5 (Fall)	34	11	4 (0)	26 (3)	3	6	0
Lifespan Developmental Psychology	PhD	January 5 (Fall)	28	8	4 (0)	15 (5)	3	5.5	0
Industrial/ Organizational Psychology	PhD	January 5 (Fall)	118	7	4 (0)	27 (2)	7	8.5	0
Applied Social & Community Psychlogy	PhD	January 5 (Fall)	36	6	4 (0)	21 (1)	6	8.5	0
School Psychology	PhD	December 15 (Fall)	54	7	2 (0)	10 (1)	3	5.5	0

APA Accreditation

School PhD: Student Outcome Data website: http://psychology.chass.ncsu.edu/pss/student-data.php.

Doctoral Degree (PhD School Psychology): For those doctoral students for whom a professional internship was required in this program prior to graduation:

Total students who applied for an internship: 2

Total students who obtained an internship: 2

Total students who obtained a paid internship: 2

Total students who obtained an unpaid internship: 0

Total students who were placed in APA/CPA-accredited internships: 0

Total students placed in internships not APA/CPA-accredited, but listed with the Association of Psychology Postdoctoral and Internship Centers (APPIC): 0

Total students placed in internships conforming to guidelines of the Council of Directors of School Psychology Programs (CDSPP): 2

Total students placed in internships that were not APA/CPA-accredited, APPIC or CDSSP listed: 0

Internships/Practica

Practica and internships are required for doctoral students in the School Psychology program. These include supervised experiences in assessment, consultation, intervention, research, and professional school psychology in a wide variety of school-related settings. Students in Human Factors and Applied Cognition are also expected to obtain employment for at least one summer/semester in one of the many suitable companies located in the Research Triangle area. The Applied Social and Community Psychology program recently added an internship requirement.

Admissions

Entries appear in the following order: required test or GPA, minimum score (if required)/median score of students entering in 2015–2016.

Program	Degree	GRE-V	GRE-Q	GRE-Writing	GRE-Subject	Under-graduate GPA	Last 2 Years GPA	Psychol-ogy GPA	Master's GPA
Human Factors & Applied Cognitive Psychology	PhD	150/NA	150/NA	4/NA	Not specified	3/NA	3/NA	3/NA	Not specified
Lifespan Developmental Psychology	PhD	150/NA	150/NA	4/NA	Not specified	3/NA	3/NA	3/NA	Not specified
Industrial/ Organizational Psychology	PhD	150/NA	150/NA	4/NA	Not specified	3/NA	3/NA	3/NA	Not specified
Applied Social & Community Psychology	PhD	150/NA	150/NA	4/NA	Not specified	3/NA	3/NA	3/NA	Not specified
School Psychology	PhD	150/NA	150/NA	4/NA	Not specified	3/NA	3/NA	3/NA	Not specified

Admissions Requirements:

Degree	GRE	GRE-Subject	Letters of Recom-mendation	Research Statement	Writing Sample	CV	Interview
Doctoral	Required	Optional	3	Required	Optional	Optional	Recom-mended

Please note if these criteria vary for different programs: The Applied Social and Community Psychology program gives greater weight to work experience and public service than do other program areas. The Human Factors and Applied Cognitive Psychology Program has a special interest in applicants' backgrounds in mathematics and computer science. The School Psychology Program requires interviews; other areas encourage interviews by invitation during a Visiting Day held each spring semester, generally in February.

Admissions Criteria:

GRE scores—high
Research experience—high
Work experience—medium
Clinically related public service—medium
GPA—high

Letters of recommendation—high
Interview—high
Statement of goals and objectives—high
Undergraduate psychology preparation—high
Research interests—high

For additional information on admission requirements, visit http://psychology.chass.ncsu.edu/graduate/admissions.php.

Department Demographics

	Male (PT)	Female (PT)	Total	African-American/ Black (PT)	Hispanic/ Latino (PT)	Asian/ Pacific Islander (PT)	American Indian/ Alaska Native (PT)	Caucasian/ White (PT)	Unknown	Multiethnic (PT)	ADA (PT)	Int'l (PT)
Students	39 (2)	60 (10)	111	6 (0)	1 (0)	7 (2)	1 (0)	77 (9)	1 (0)	6 (1)	0 (0)	7 (0)

Financial Information/Assistance

Tuition: For information on tuition costs, visit https://treasurer.ofb.ncsu.edu/cashier/tuition/tuition_index.php. Tuition is subject to change. Additional fees are assessed to students beyond the costs of tuition for the following: A required fee of $1,170.94 per semester (regardless of residency) is assessed.

Doctoral:
State residents: $7,852 per academic year.
Nonstate residents: $21,951 per academic year.

Financial Assistance:

	Teaching Assistantship (% Receiving)	Teaching Assistantship Tuition Remission	Research Assistantship (% Receiving)	Research Assistantship Tuition Remission	Fellowship (% Receiving)	Fellowship Tuition Remission
First-Year Student	$14,000 (51)	Full	$14,000 (10)	Full	$22,000 (10)	Full
Advanced Student	$14,000 (46)	Full	$18,000 (14)	Full	$20,000 (1)	Full

For additional information on financial assistance, visit https://grad.ncsu.edu/admissions/financial-support/.

Employment of Department Graduates

Doctoral:
Enrolled in a postdoctoral residency/fellowship: 3
Employed in an academic position at a university: 1
Employed in other positions at a higher education institution: 5
Employed in a professional position in a school system: 1
Employed in business or industry: 12
Employed in government agency: 1
Still seeking employment: 1
Total: 24

Additional Information

Housing and Day Care: On-campus housing is available. See the following website for more information: http://housing.ncsu.edu/. On-campus day care facilities are available. See the following website for more information: http://www.ncsu.edu/human_resources/benefits/Childcare/center.php.

Information for Students With Physical Disabilities: See the following website: http://dso.dasa.ncsu.edu/.

Special Facilities or Resources: The department is housed primarily on two floors of a modern building. Teaching Assistants share office space; Research Assistants have space within faculty research areas. All programs have appropriate equipment, laboratory space and facilities. Human Factors and Applied Cognition, I/O, Applied Social and Community and School students may have opportunities to work in state government, industry, schools, and community agencies to gain practical and research experience. Students are, however, required to maintain continuous registration and carry an adequate course load each semester. Students are permitted to enroll in courses at the University of North Carolina-Chapel Hill and at Duke University, as if the courses were offered on their home campus. Beyond basic research, statistics, and program/departmental course requirements, students have considerable flexibility in developing individually-tailored plans of study.

Application Information: Fee: $75. Online application: http://www2.acs.ncsu.edu/grad/applygrad.htm.

North Carolina, University of, Chapel Hill
Department of Psychology
Arts and Sciences
CB #3270
Chapel Hill, NC 27599-3270
Telephone: (919) 962-4153
Chairperson: Donald T. Lysle

E-mail: lmingo@email.unc.edu
Web: http://psychology.unc.edu/

Orientation, Objectives, and Emphasis of Department
Each graduate training program is designed to acquaint students with the theoretical and research content of their specialty and to train them in the research and teaching skills needed to make contributions to science and society. In addition, certain programs (for example, the clinical program) include an emphasis on the development of competence in appropriate professional skills. Faculty members maintain a balanced commitment to research, teaching and service.

Programs and Degrees Offered

Program	Degree	Application Deadline	Applica-tions Received	Accepted	New Admits Enrolled (PT)	Total Enrolled (PT)	Degrees Awarded in 2014–2015	Median Years to Complete Degree	Dismissed/Withdrew
Clinical Psychology	PhD	December 6 (Fall)	599	11	10 (0)	48 (0)	8	6	0
Cognitive Psychology	PhD	December 6 (Fall)	53	7	4 (0)	17	2	5	1
Developmental Psychology	PhD	December 6 (Fall)	39	4	2 (0)	16 (0)	6	5	0
Behavioral Neuroscience	PhD	December 6 (Fall)	63	5	4 (0)	16 (0)	6	5	
Quantitative Psychology	PhD	December 6 (Fall)	45	4	2	12 (0)	4		0
Social Psychology	PhD	December 6 (Fall)	123	4	2	20 (0)	5	5	1

APA Accreditation
Clinical PhD: Student Outcome Data website: http://clinicalpsych.unc.edu/.

Doctoral Degree (PhD Clinical Psychology): For those doctoral students for whom a professional internship was required in this program prior to graduation:
Total students who applied for an internship: 7
Total students who obtained an internship: 7
Total students who obtained a paid internship: 7
Total students who obtained an unpaid internship: 0
Total students who were placed in APA/CPA-accredited internships: 7
Total students placed in internships not APA/CPA-accredited, but listed with the Association of Psychology Postdoctoral and Internship Centers (APPIC): 0

Total students placed in internships conforming to guidelines of the Council of Directors of School Psychology Programs (CDSPP): 0
Total students placed in internships that were not APA/CPA-accredited, APPIC or CDSSP listed: 0

Internships/Practica

Students within the doctoral program in clinical psychology engage in a wide range of clinical practicum activities beginning in the second year of doctoral study. A variety of practicum sites are available. One of these sites is the University of North Carolina Medical School, which includes opportunities in a number of areas including child, family, adolescent, and adults. There are also specialized opportunities at that site to work with children with developmental disabilities and college students in a university counseling setting. Students also can receive training at Central Regional Hospital, a state psychiatric hospital; opportunities there range from child, adolescent, adult, and geriatric patients. All students are involved in our Psychology Department Psychological Services Clinic, our in-house outpatient treatment facility. Students work with a wide variety of clients within that context, with specialized opportunities in anxiety disorders and marital therapy. Students provide consultation to the local school system, to the Orange-Person-Chatham Mental Health Center, and to a variety of other sites that are arranged on an as-needed basis.

Admissions

Entries appear in the following order: required test or GPA, minimum score (if required)/median score of students entering in 2015–2016.

Program	Degree	GRE-V	GRE-Q	GRE-Writing	GRE-Subject	Under-graduate GPA	Last 2 Years GPA	Psychol-ogy GPA	Master's GPA
Clinical Psychology	PhD	NA/162	NA/158	Not specified	Not specified	3/3.77	Not specified	Not specified	Not specified
Cognitive Psychology	PhD	NA/163	NA/156	Not specified	Not specified	3/3.71	Not specified	Not specified	Not specified
Developmental Psychology	PhD	NA/159	NA/153	Not specified	Not specified	3/3.75	Not specified	Not specified	Not specified
Behavioral Neuroscience	PhD	NA/157	NA/153	Not specified	Not specified	3/3.4	Not specified	Not specified	Not specified
Quantitative Psychology	PhD	NA/163	NA/160	Not specified	Not specified	3/3.8	Not specified	Not specified	Not specified
Social Psychology	PhD	NA/164	NA/160	Not specified	Not specified	3/3.87	Not specified	Not specified	Not specified

Admissions Requirements:

Degree	GRE	GRE-Subject	Letters of Recom-mendation	Research Statement	Writing Sample	CV	Interview
Doctoral	Required	Optional	3	Required	Optional	Required	Required

Admissions Criteria:

GRE scores—high
Research experience—high
Work experience—medium
Clinically related public service—medium
GPA—high

Letters of recommendation—high
Interview—medium
Statement of goals and objectives—high
Undergraduate psychology preparation—medium

For additional information on admission requirements, visit http://psychology.unc.edu/application-process/.

Department Demographics

	Male (PT)	Female (PT)	Total	African-American/ Black (PT)	Hispanic/ Latino (PT)	Asian/ Pacific Islander (PT)	American Indian/ Alaska Native (PT)	Caucasian/ White (PT)	Unknown (PT)	Multiethnic (PT)	ADA (PT)	Int'l (PT)
Students	46 (0)	81 (0)	127	10 (0)	3 (0)	13 (0)	1 (0)	83 (0)	10 (0)	7 (0)	0 (0)	8 (0)

Financial Information/Assistance

Tuition: For information on tuition costs, visit http://finance.unc.edu/saur/student-account-services/tuition-and-fees/. Tuition is subject to change. Additional fees are assessed to students beyond the costs of tuition for the following: student fees are currently $966 per semester, subject to legislative change.

Doctoral:
State residents: $9,143 per academic year.
Nonstate residents: $26,354 per academic year.

Financial Assistance:

	Teaching Assistantship (% Receiving)	Teaching Assistantship Tuition Remission	Research Assistantship (% Receiving)	Research Assistantship Tuition Remission	Fellowship (% Receiving)	Fellowship Tuition Remission
First-Year Student	$18,000 (NA)	Full	$18,000 (NA)	Full	$20,000 (NA)	Full
Advanced Student	$19,000 (NA)	Full	$22,920 (NA)	Full	$20,000 (NA)	Full

Employment of Department Graduates

No information provided.

Additional Information

Housing and Day Care: On-campus housing is available. See the following website for more information: http://housing.unc.edu/. No on-campus day care facilities are available.

Information for Students With Physical Disabilities: See the following website: http://accessibility.unc.edu/.

Special Facilities or Resources: Affiliated clinical and research facilities are: the Psychological Services Clinic, Psychology Department; Central Regional Hospital, Butner, NC; North Carolina Memorial Hospital, Chapel Hill; Murdoch Developmental Center, Butner; Center for Developmental Science, Chapel Hill; VA Hospital, Durham; Frank Porter Graham Child Development Center, Chapel Hill; Carolina Population Center, Chapel Hill; North Carolina Highway Safety Research Center, Chapel Hill; L.L. Thurstone Psychometric Laboratory, Chapel Hill; the Positive Emotions and Psychophysiology Laboratory, Chapel Hill; the Odum Institute for Research in Social Sciences, Chapel Hill; Neurobiology Curriculum, University of North Carolina; Research Laboratories of the U.S. Environmental Protection Agency, Research Triangle Park; and TEACCH Division, North Carolina Memorial Hospital, specializing in the treatment and education of victims of autism and related disorders of communication.

Application Information: Fee: $85. *Online application:* https://app.applyyourself.com/?id=unc-ch.

North Carolina, University of, Charlotte
Department of Psychology
Liberal Arts and Sciences
9201 University City Boulevard
Charlotte, NC 28223-0001
Telephone: (704) 687-1358
E-mail: rtedesch@uncc.edu; vgilriva@uncc.edu
Graduate Coordinator MA/Program Director PhD: Dr. Richard Tedeschi/Dr. Virginia Gil-Rivas
Web: http://psych.uncc.edu/

Orientation, Objectives, and Emphasis of Department
The Department of Psychology works to advance the science of psychology through high quality research, teaching, and service. Faculty and students conduct research on a wide range of topics in psychology and engage in interdisciplinary research in areas such as Health Psychology, Organizational Sciences, and Cognitive Sciences. The high quality teaching of psychology in the department has been recognized through awards to individual faculty and to the department, which was the first winner of the university's Provost's Award for Excellence in Teaching. In addition to the 1,200 majors in our undergraduate program, the department has over 130 graduate students in a master's programs in Industrial/Organizational Psychology and doctoral programs in Health Psychology (providing training in Community, Clinical and General tracks) and Organizational Sciences.

Programs and Degrees Offered

Program	Degree	Application Deadline	Applications Received	Accepted	New Admits Enrolled (PT)	Total Enrolled (PT)	Degrees Awarded in 2014–2015	Median Years to Complete Degree	Dismissed/ Withdrew
Industrial/ Organizational Psychology	MA/MS	March 1 (Fall)	155	13	14 (0)	14 (0)	0		0
Organizational Science	PhD	December 15 (Fall)	80	6	6	25 (0)	5	5	0
Health Psychology	PhD	November 15 (Fall)	156	8	6	42	4	5	0

APA Accreditation

Clinical PhD: Student Outcome Data website: http://healthpsych.uncc.edu/program-description.

Doctoral Degree (PhD Health Psychology): For those doctoral students for whom a professional internship was required in this program prior to graduation:

Total students who applied for an internship: 4
Total students who obtained an internship: 4
Total students who obtained a paid internship: 4
Total students who obtained an unpaid internship: 0
Total students who were placed in APA/CPA-accredited internships: 4
Total students placed in internships not APA/CPA-accredited, but listed with the Association of Psychology Postdoctoral and Internship Centers (APPIC): 0
Total students placed in internships conforming to guidelines of the Council of Directors of School Psychology Programs (CDSPP): 0
Total students placed in internships that were not APA/CPA-accredited, APPIC or CDSSP listed: 0

Master's Degree (MA/MS Industrial/Organizational Psychology): An internship experience, such as a final research project or "capstone" experience is required of graduates.

Admissions

Entries appear in the following order: required test or GPA, minimum score (if required)/median score of students entering in 2015–2016.

Program	Degree	GRE-V	GRE-Q	GRE-Writing	GRE-Subject	Under-graduate GPA	Last 2 Years GPA	Psychology GPA	Master's GPA
Industrial/ Organizational Psychology	MA/MS	NA/154	NA/153	Not specified	Not specified	3/3.45	Not specified	Not specified	Not specified
Organizational Science	PhD	150/159	150/154	4/4	Not specified	3/NA	Not specified	Not specified	Not specified
Health Psychology	PhD	151/159	153/155	4/4	Not specified	3/3.5	Not specified	3/3.87	Not specified

Admissions Requirements:

Degree	GRE	GRE-Subject	Letters of Recom-mendation	Research Statement	Writing Sample	CV	Interview
Master's/Specialist	Required	None	2	Required	Optional	Optional	None
Doctoral	Required	Optional	3	Required	Optional	Required	Required

Please note if these criteria vary for different programs: Health Psychology: Clinical work important for clinical emphasis; community work important for community emphasis. Organizational Science does not interview applicants and highly rates an interest in interdisciplinary education.

Admissions Criteria:
GRE scores—high
Research experience—high
Work experience—medium
Clinically related public service—medium
GPA—high

Letters of recommendation—high
Interview—medium
Statement of goals and objectives—high
Undergraduate psychology preparation—medium

For additional information on admission requirements, visit http://psych.uncc.edu/graduate-programs.

Department Demographics

	Male (PT)	Female (PT)	Total	African-American/ Black (PT)	Hispanic/ Latino (PT)	Asian/ Pacific Islander (PT)	American Indian/ Alaska Native (PT)	Caucasian/ White (PT)	Unknown (PT)	Multiethnic (PT)	ADA (PT)	Int'l (PT)
Students	21 (0)	68 (0)	89	8 (0)	4 (0)	2 (0)	0 (0)	75 (0)	0 (0)	0 (0)	0 (0)	0 (0)

Financial Information/Assistance

Tuition: For information on tuition costs, visit http://finance.uncc.edu/student-accounts/tuition-and-fees. Tuition is subject to change.

Doctoral:
State residents: $7,032 per academic year.
Nonstate residents: $19,703 per academic year.

Master's:
State residents: $7,032 per academic year.
Nonstate residents: $19,703 per academic year.

Financial Assistance:

	Teaching Assistantship (% Receiving)	Teaching Assistantship Tuition Remission	Research Assistantship (% Receiving)	Research Assistantship Tuition Remission	Fellowship (% Receiving)	Fellowship Tuition Remission
First-Year Student	$9,000 (NA)	NA	$8,500 (NA)	NA	$2,150 (NA)	NA
Advanced Student	$13,000 (80)	Full	$13,000 (20)	Full	$15,000 (0)	Full

For additional information on financial assistance, visit http://gradadmissions.uncc.edu/funding.

Employment of Department Graduates

Doctoral:
Enrolled in a postdoctoral residency/fellowship: 2
Employed in independent practice: 2
Employed in an academic position at a university: 2
Employed in academic position at a 2-year/4-year college: 2
Employed in business or industry: 2
Employed in a hospital/medical center: 4
Total: 14

Additional Information

Housing and Day Care: On-campus housing is available. See the following website for more information: http://housing.uncc.edu/. No on-campus day care facilities are available.

Information for Students With Physical Disabilities: See the following website: http://ds.uncc.edu/.

Special Facilities or Resources: The psychology department is housed in a modern classroom office building that provides offices, demonstration rooms, a workshop, and specialty laboratories for research. Facilities include a computerized laboratory with 37 microcomputers; many small testing, training, and interview rooms with one-way mirrors for direct observation; audio intercommunications; and closed circuit television. There is extensive audio and video equipment available as well as a research trailer, tachistoscopes, programming and timing equipment, and microcomputers. The psychometric laboratory contains an extensive inventory of current tests of intelligence, personality, and interest, as well as calculators and microcomputers for testing, test score evaluation and data analysis. A well-equipped physiological laboratory is available for work including human electrophysiology.

Application Information: Graduate Admissions, UNC-Charlotte, 9201 University City Boulevard, Charlotte, NC 28223. *Fee:* $75. *Online application:* https://mygradschool.uncc.edu/.

North Carolina, University of, Greensboro
Psychology
Arts and Science
Department of Psychology, 296 Eberhart Building, P.O. Box 26170
Greensboro, NC 27402
Telephone: (336) 334-5014
Chairperson: Stuart Marcovitch

E-mail: psychology@uncg.edu
Web: https://psy.uncg.edu/

Orientation, Objectives, and Emphasis of Department
The objective is to provide scholarship and methodological and practical skills to enable the student to function in a variety of academic, research, and service settings. The program has an experimental orientation, with four major areas of concentration: (1) clinical, which includes applied training and clinical research training in a variety of service settings; (2) developmental, which includes basic research in behavioral, cognitive, language, and social development in infant, child, adolescent, and adult humans and in animals; (3) cognitive, which includes basic research in human memory, cognition, and language; and (4) social, designed to introduce students to theoretical issues and to applied, biological, and developmental perspectives in social psychology. All General Experimental applicants are expected to earn an MA as their terminal degree. For the PhD applicants, the program is oriented toward the PhD as the terminal degree, although an applicant with a bachelor's degree is admitted into the master's program. Upon successful completion of the requirements for the master's degree, the student's work is reviewed for admission into the PhD program. An applicant entering with a master's degree will be officially reviewed for entry into the PhD program after 1 year.

Programs and Degrees Offered

Program	Degree	Application Deadline	Applica-tions Received	Accepted	New Admits Enrolled (PT)	Total Enrolled (PT)	Degrees Awarded in 2014–2015	Median Years to Complete Degree	Dismissed/ Withdrew
Clinical Psychology	PhD	December 1 (Fall)	226	10	5 (0)	33 (0)	4	6.5	0
Cognitive Psychology	PhD	December 1 (Fall)	21	3	1	6	3	6	0
Developmental Psychology	PhD	December 1 (Fall)	15	2	2	6	3	7	0
Social Psychology	PhD	December 1 (Fall)	16	1	2	3	2	5	0
General Experimental Psychology	MA/MS	April 20 (Fall)	14	1	1	2	2	2	0

APA Accreditation
Clinical PhD: Student Outcome Data website: https://psy.uncg.edu/graduate/clinical-psychology/student-admissions-outcomes-and-other-data/.

Doctoral Degree (PhD Clinical Psychology): For those doctoral students for whom a professional internship was required in this program prior to graduation:
Total students who applied for an internship: 3
Total students who obtained an internship: 3
Total students who obtained a paid internship: 3
Total students who obtained an unpaid internship: 0
Total students who were placed in APA/CPA-accredited internships: 3

Total students placed in internships not APA/CPA-accredited, but listed with the Association of Psychology Postdoctoral and Internship Centers (APPIC): 0

Total students placed in internships conforming to guidelines of the Council of Directors of School Psychology Programs (CDSPP): 0

Total students placed in internships that were not APA/CPA-accredited, APPIC or CDSSP listed: 0

Master's Degree (MA/MS General Experimental Psychology): An internship experience, such as a final research project or "capstone" experience is required of graduates.

Admissions

Entries appear in the following order: required test or GPA, minimum score (if required)/median score of students entering in 2015–2016.

Program	Degree	GRE-V	GRE-Q	GRE-Writing	GRE-Subject	Under-graduate GPA	Last 2 Years GPA	Psychology GPA	Master's GPA
Clinical Psychology	PhD	NA/159	NA/157	NA/4.5	Not specified	NA/3.75	Not specified	Not specified	NA/NA
Cognitive Psychology	PhD	Not specified	Not specified	Not specified	Not specified	Not specified	Not specified	Not specified	Not specified
Developmental Psychology	PhD	Not specified	Not specified	Not specified	Not specified	Not specified	Not specified	Not specified	Not specified
Social Psychology	PhD	Not specified	Not specified	Not specified	Not specified	Not specified	Not specified	Not specified	Not specified
General Experimental Psychology	MA/MS	Not specified	Not specified	Not specified	Not specified	Not specified	Not specified	Not specified	Not specified

Admissions Requirements:

Degree	GRE	GRE-Subject	Letters of Recommendation	Research Statement	Writing Sample	CV	Interview
Master's/Specialist	Required	None	3	Required	None	Required	Required
Doctoral	Required	Recommended	3	Required	None	Required	Required

Admissions Criteria:

GRE scores—high
Research experience—high
Work experience—low
Clinically related public service—low
GPA—high

Letters of recommendation—high
Interview—high
Statement of goals and objectives—high
Undergraduate psychology preparation—medium

For additional information on admission requirements, visit https://psy.uncg.edu/graduate/applying/.

Department Demographics

	Male (PT)	Female (PT)	Total	African-American/ Black (PT)	Hispanic/ Latino (PT)	Asian/ Pacific Islander (PT)	American Indian/ Alaska Native (PT)	Caucasian/ White (PT)	Unknown	Multiethnic (PT)	ADA (PT)	Int'l (PT)
Students	12 (0)	38 (0)	50	1 (0)	5 (0)	1 (0)	0 (0)	39 (0)	2 (0)	2 (0)	0 (0)	2 (0)

Financial Information/Assistance

Tuition: For information on tuition costs, visit http://csh.uncg.edu/. Additional fees are assessed to students beyond the costs of tuition for the following: student fees.

Doctoral:
State residents: $4,541 per academic year.
Nonstate residents: $17,990 per academic year.

Master's:
State residents: $4,541 per academic year.
Nonstate residents: $17,990 per academic year.

Financial Assistance:

	Teaching Assistantship (% Receiving)	Teaching Assistantship Tuition Remission	Research Assistantship (% Receiving)	Research Assistantship Tuition Remission	Fellowship (% Receiving)	Fellowship Tuition Remission
First-Year Student	$13,000 (100)	Full	NA (NA)	NA	NA (NA)	NA
Advanced Student	$14,000 (55)	Partial	$14,000 (40)	Partial	NA (NA)	NA

For additional information on financial assistance, visit http://grs.uncg.edu/financial/.

Employment of Department Graduates

Master's:
Not seeking employment: 1
Total: 1

Doctoral:
Enrolled in a postdoctoral residency/fellowship: 6
Employed in independent practice: 1
Employed in an academic position at a university: 2
Employed in business or industry: 1
Total: 10

Additional Information

Housing and Day Care: On-campus housing is available. See the following website for more information: http://hrl.uncg.edu/. On-campus day care facilities are available. See the following website for more information: http://ccep.uncg.edu/.

Information for Students With Physical Disabilities: See the following website: http://ods.uncg.edu/.

Special Facilities or Resources: The Department of Psychology is located in the Eberhart Life Sciences Building. Space is devoted to classrooms; research laboratories; vivaria; and faculty, student, and secretarial offices. Graduate students are typically assigned office space in the research labs of their primary advisers. Active research laboratories in each of the specialty areas contain an assortment of items: ERP equipment used to study the neurocorrelates of behavior; state-of-the-art computers used to conduct experiments; up-to-date clinical measures; age-appropriate settings for research across the life span; observation rooms with one-way mirrors, and video equipment. All required practicum training is completed at the UNCG Psychology Clinic, which is a community-based clinic that serves a very diverse population of individuals in terms of age, ethnicity, socioeconomic status, and presenting problem. Students complete required practicum training in Years 2, 3, and 4 of the program. The University library has an excellent collection of journals and books, along with an award-winning online access system.

Application Information: Fee: $65. *Online application:* http://grs.uncg.edu/apply-online/.

North Carolina, University of, Wilmington (2015 data)
Psychology
Arts and Sciences
601 South College Road
Wilmington, NC 28403-5612
Telephone: (910) 962-7795
Chairperson: Richard Ogle, PhD

E-mail: hughesc@uncw.edu
Web: http://www.uncw.edu/psy/

Orientation, Objectives, and Emphasis of Department

The department is committed to fostering an understanding of psychological research and practice and emphasizes the importance of faculty as student mentors. Research methodology and application are emphasized for all students regardless of concentration. Students in the General Psychology concentration are prepared to continue to the PhD in a variety of content areas. Students completing the clinical concentration in Substance Abuse Treatment are prepared to work with dual diagnosis clients in mental health clinics and other public service agencies. The clinical Applied Behavior Analysis concentration prepares students for work primarily with autistic and mentally retarded individuals. The SATP and ABA graduates meet all academic requirements to apply for North Carolina state licensure as a Psychological Associate and either North Carolina State certification as a Licensed Clinical Addictions Specialist (SATP concentration) or National Board Certification as a Behavior Analyst (BCBA concentration).

Programs and Degrees Offered

Program	Degree	Application Deadline	Applica-tions Received	Accepted	New Admits Enrolled (PT)	Total Enrolled (PT)	Degrees Awarded in 2014–2015	Median Years to Complete Degree	Dismissed/Withdrew
General Psychology	MA/MS	January 15 (Fall)	63	23	17 (0)	46 (0)	13	2	1
Applied Behavior Analysis	MA/MS	January 15 (Fall)	60	8	7 (0)	20 (0)	7	3	0
Substance Abuse Treatment	MA/MS	January 15 (Fall)	27	6	6 (0)	19	6	3	

Internships/Practica

In the Substance Abuse Treatment Psychology concentration and the Applied Behavior Analysis concentration, students are prepared for work with dual diagnosis clients or with developmentally disabled clients through the completion of a required practicum and internship. The required practicum course and internship consist of at least 1,500 hours total of supervised experience working with substance abuse, autism, mental retardation, and other psychological and behavioral problems. Training sites include community mental health centers; correctional institutions; university counseling centers; inpatient and outpatient substance abuse treatment centers; and residential centers for individuals with autism, intellectual disabilities, and other developmental delays.

Admissions

Entries appear in the following order: required test or GPA, minimum score (if required)/median score of students entering in 2015–2016.

Program	Degree	GRE-V	GRE-Q	GRE-Writing	GRE-Subject	Under-graduate GPA	Last 2 Years GPA	Psychol-ogy GPA	Master's GPA
General Psychology	MA/MS	NA/155	NA/151	NA/4	Not specified	NA/3.67	NA/NA	Not specified	Not specified
Applied Behavior Analysis	MA/MS	NA/152	NA/151	NA/4	Not specified	NA/3.53	NA/NA	Not specified	Not specified
Substance Abuse Treatment	MA/MS	NA/152	NA/152	NA/4.25	Not specified	NA/3.46	Not specified	Not specified	Not specified

Admissions Requirements:

Degree	GRE	GRE-Subject	Letters of Recom-mendation	Research Statement	Writing Sample	CV	Interview
Master's/Specialist	Required	Required	3	Required	Optional	Required	Required

Please note if these criteria vary for different programs: In the Substance Abuse Treatment Psychology concentration, clinically related public service may be given more weight, since this concentration emphasizes the development of clinical as well as research skills. In the Applied Behavior Analysis concentration, previous experience—volunteer or paid— working in the field of applied behavior analysis with people with disabilities is very important. Coursework in learning/behavior analysis and applied behavior analysis/ principles of behavior change are also highly desirable. Applicants who did not major in psychology must also take the GRE-Subject test.

Admissions Criteria:

GRE scores—high
Research experience—high
Work experience—low
Clinically related public service—medium
GPA—high

Letters of recommendation—high
Interview—high
Statement of goals and objectives—high
Undergraduate psychology preparation—high

For additional information on admission requirements, visit http://www.uncw.edu/psy/grad/grad-application.html.

Department Demographics

	Male (PT)	Female (PT)	Total	African-American/ Black (PT)	Hispanic/ Latino (PT)	Asian/ Pacific Islander (PT)	American Indian/ Alaska Native (PT)	Caucasian/ White (PT)	Unknown (PT)	Multiethnic (PT)	ADA (PT)	Int'l (PT)
Students	21 (0)	64 (0)	85	1 (0)	4 (0)	1 (0)	0 (0)	79 (0)	0 (0)	0 (0)	0 (0)	2 (0)

Financial Information/Assistance

Tuition: For information on tuition costs, visit http://www.uncw.edu/studentaccounts/tuition_fees.html. Tuition is subject to change.

Master's:
State residents: $6,528 per academic year.
Nonstate residents: $18,463 per academic year.

Financial Assistance:

	Teaching Assistantship (% Receiving)	Teaching Assistantship Tuition Remission	Research Assistantship (% Receiving)	Research Assistantship Tuition Remission	Fellowship (% Receiving)	Fellowship Tuition Remission
First-Year Student	$11,000 (NA)	Partial	$11,000 (NA)	Partial	$2,000 (NA)	NA
Advanced Student	$11,000 (NA)	NA	$11,000 (NA)	NA	NA (NA)	NA

For additional information on financial assistance, visit http://www.uncw.edu/psy/grad/grad-financial.html.

Employment of Department Graduates

Master's:
Enrolled in a psychology doctoral program: 9
Enrolled in another graduate/professional program: 1
Employed in other positions at a higher education institution: 1
Employed in business or industry: 1
Employed in a community mental health/counseling center: 12
Not seeking employment: 1
Do not know: 1
Total: 26

Additional Information

Housing and Day Care: On-campus housing is available. See the following website for more information: http://www.uncw.edu/stuaff/housing/. No on-campus day care facilities are available.

Information for Students With Physical Disabilities: See the following website: http://www.uncw.edu/disability/.

Special Facilities or Resources: Special facilities or resources include research laboratories (behavioral pharmacology, human, and animal). All students have access to word processing software, SAS, and SPSS on the university computer system. The Psychology Department occupies a new 80,000 square foot building with research laboratories for 32 faculty and their students.

Application Information: Graduate School, University of North Carolina Wilmington, 601 South College Road, Wilmington, NC 28403-5955. *Fee:* $60. *Online application:* http://www.uncw.edu/gradschool/admissions.html.

Wake Forest University
Department of Psychology
Arts & Sciences
P.O. Box 7778
Winston-Salem, NC 27109
Telephone: (336) 758-5424
Chairperson: Dale Dagenbach

E-mail: psygrad@wfu.edu
Web: http://college.wfu.edu/psychology/

Orientation, Objectives, and Emphasis of Department
The department aims to provide rigorous master's-level training with an emphasis on mastery of theory, research methodology, and content in the basic areas of psychology. This is a general, research-oriented MA program for capable students, most of whom will continue to the PhD.

Programs and Degrees Offered

Program	Degree	Application Deadline	Applications Received	Accepted	New Admits Enrolled (PT)	Total Enrolled (PT)	Degrees Awarded in 2014–2015	Median Years to Complete Degree	Dismissed/ Withdrew
General Psychology	MA/MS	January 15 (Fall)	88	13	13 (0)	23 (0)	9	2	0

Admissions
Entries appear in the following order: required test or GPA, minimum score (if required)/median score of students entering in 2015–2016.

Program	Degree	GRE-V	GRE-Q	GRE-Writing	GRE-Subject	Under-graduate GPA	Last 2 Years GPA	Psychol-ogy GPA	Master's GPA
General Psychology	MA/MS	NA/161	NA/154	NA/NA	Not specified	NA/3.76	NA/NA	NA/NA	Not specified

Admissions Requirements:

Degree	GRE	GRE-Subject	Letters of Recom-mendation	Research Statement	Writing Sample	CV	Interview
Master's/Specialist	Required	Recom-mended	3	Required	Optional	Required	None

Admissions Criteria:
GRE scores—medium
Research experience—high
GPA—high

Letters of recommendation—high
Statement of goals and objectives—medium

Department Demographics

	Male (PT)	Female (PT)	Total	African-American/ Black (PT)	Hispanic/ Latino (PT)	Asian/ Pacific Islander (PT)	American Indian/ Alaska Native (PT)	Caucasian/ White (PT)	Unknown	Multiethnic (PT)	ADA (PT)	Int'l (PT)
Students	9 (0)	14 (0)	23	2 (0)	0 (0)	1 (0)	0 (0)	20 (0)	0 (0)	0 (0)	0 (0)	0 (0)

Financial Information/Assistance

Tuition: For information on tuition costs, visit http://graduate.wfu.edu/admissions/costofstudy-RC.html. Tuition is subject to change.

Master's:
State residents: $36,420 per academic year.
State residents: $1,300 per credit hour.
Nonstate residents: $36,420 per academic year.
Nonstate residents: $1,300 per credit hour.

Financial Assistance:

	Teaching Assistantship (% Receiving)	Teaching Assistantship Tuition Remission	Research Assistantship (% Receiving)	Research Assistantship Tuition Remission	Fellowship (% Receiving)	Fellowship Tuition Remission
First-Year Student	$10,125 (NA)	Full	$10,125 (NA)	Full	NA (NA)	Full
Advanced Student	$10,125 (NA)	Full	$10,125 (NA)	Full	NA (NA)	Full

For additional information on financial assistance, visit http://graduate.wfu.edu/admissions/costofstudy-RC.html.

Employment of Department Graduates

Master's:
Enrolled in a psychology doctoral program: 6
Enrolled in another graduate/professional program: 2
Employed in business or industry: 1
Do not know: 1
Total: 10

Additional Information

Housing and Day Care: No on-campus housing is available. No on-campus day care facilities are available.

Information for Students With Physical Disabilities: See the following website: http://lac.wfu.edu/disability-services/.

Special Facilities or Resources: The Department of Psychology occupies a beautiful and spacious building that is equipped with state-of-the-art teaching and laboratory facilities. Learning resources include in-class multimedia instruction equipment, departmental mini- and microcomputers, departmental and university libraries, and information technology centers. Ample research space is available, including social, developmental, cognitive, perception, physiological, and animal behavior laboratories. Office space is available for graduate students. The department has links with the Wake Forest University School of Medicine (e.g., Neuroscience) which can provide opportunities for students. All students work closely with individual faculty on research during both years (2:1 student/faculty ratio). Wake Forest University offers the academic and technological resources, facilities, and Division I athletic programs, music, theater, and art associated with a larger university, with the individual attention that a smaller university can provide.

Application Information: Dean of the Graduate School, Wake Forest University, 1834 Wake Forest Road, Room 124, Reynolda Hall, P.O. Box 7487 Reynolda Station, Winston-Salem, NC 27109-7487. *Fee:* $75. *Online application:* http://graduate.wfu.edu/admissions/onlineapp.html.

North Dakota State University (2015 data)

Department of Psychology
Science and Mathematics
232 Minard Hall
Fargo, ND 58105
Telephone: (701) 231-8622
Chairperson: James Council

E-mail: NDSU.psych@ndsu.edu
Web: http://www.ndsu.edu/psychology/

Orientation, Objectives, and Emphasis of Department

Our strong research tradition has earned us a reputation as one of the best small psychology departments in the nation. PhD training is designed to produce graduates with records in research and teaching, which will make them highly competitive for employment in both traditional academic and nontraditional government and private sector settings. Our programs are based on a mentoring model, in which students work closely with specific faculty members who match their research interests.

Programs and Degrees Offered

Program	Degree	Application Deadline	Applications Received	Accepted	New Admits Enrolled (PT)	Total Enrolled (PT)	Degrees Awarded in 2014–2015	Median Years to Complete Degree	Dismissed/Withdrew
Cognitive and Visual Neuroscience	PhD	February 1 (Fall)	15	3	2 (0)	6 (0)	1	4	0
Health/Social Psychology	PhD	February 1 (Fall)	16	2	2 (0)	5 (0)	1	4	0
Psychological Clinical Science	PhD	February 1 (Fall)	19	2	0 (0)	8 (0)	0		0

Internships/Practica

Research practica are available for doctoral students who wish to develop applied research skills and experiences. Sites include a private foundation for research on addictions and eating disorders, a nationally prominent organization for clinical drug trials, a chronic pain treatment program, a community mental health center, and several sites devoted to survey research.

Admissions

Entries appear in the following order: required test or GPA, minimum score (if required)/median score of students entering in 2015–2016.

Program	Degree	GRE-V	GRE-Q	GRE-Writing	GRE-Subject	Undergraduate GPA	Last 2 Years GPA	Psychology GPA	Master's GPA
Cognitive and Visual Neuroscience	PhD	Not specified	Not specified	Not specified	Not specified	Not specified	Not specified	Not specified	Not specified
Health/Social Psychology	PhD	Not specified	Not specified	Not specified	Not specified	Not specified	Not specified	Not specified	Not specified
Psychological Clinical Science	PhD	NA/NA	NA/NA	Not specified	Not specified	3/NA	Not specified	Not specified	Not specified

Admissions Requirements:

Degree	GRE	GRE-Subject	Letters of Recommendation	Research Statement	Writing Sample	CV	Interview
Doctoral	Required	Optional	3	Required	Optional	Optional	Optional

Admissions Criteria:

GRE scores—high
Research experience—high
GPA—high

Letters of recommendation—high
Statement of goals and objectives—high

For additional information on admission requirements, visit http://www.ndsu.edu/psychology/graduate_programs/application_procedures/.

Department Demographics

	Male (PT)	Female (PT)	Total	African-American/ Black (PT)	Hispanic/ Latino (PT)	Asian/ Pacific Islander (PT)	American Indian/ Alaska Native (PT)	Caucasian/ White (PT)	Unknown	Multiethnic (PT)	ADA (PT)	Int'l (PT)
Students	10 (0)	11 (1)	22	0 (0)	2 (0)	4 (1)	0 (0)	15 (0)	0 (0)	0 (0)	0 (0)	(0)

Financial Information/Assistance

Tuition: For information on tuition costs, visit http://www.ndsu.edu/bisonconnection/accounts/tuition/. Additional fees are assessed to students beyond the costs of tuition for the following: wellness center, technology access, athletic events.

Doctoral:
State residents: $346 per credit hour.
Nonstate residents: $839 per credit hour.

Financial Assistance:

	Teaching Assistantship (% Receiving)	Teaching Assistantship Tuition Remission	Research Assistantship (% Receiving)	Research Assistantship Tuition Remission	Fellowship (% Receiving)	Fellowship Tuition Remission
First-Year Student	$16,000 (NA)	Full	$16,000 (NA)	Full	NA (NA)	NA
Advanced Student	$16,000 (NA)	Full	$16,000 (NA)	Full	$16,000 (NA)	Full

For additional information on financial assistance, visit http://www.ndsu.edu/bisonconnection/finaid/.

Employment of Department Graduates

Doctoral:
Employed in academic position at a 2-year/4-year college: 1
Employed in business or industry: 1
Total: 2

Additional Information

Housing and Day Care: On-campus housing is available. See the following website for more information: http://www.ndsu.edu/reslife/. On-campus day care facilities are available. See the following website for more information: http://www.ndsu.edu/childcenter/.

Information for Students With Physical Disabilities: See the following website: http://www.ndsu.edu/disabilityservices/.

Special Facilities or Resources: The department has state-of-the-art facilities for research in electrophysiology (including EEG), vision, and cognition, as well as ample space for other research projects. A center for research on virtual reality, multi-sensory integration, and driving simulation is very active. As the largest population center in the region, Fargo-Moorhead serves as a center for medical services for a large geographic area. There are three major hospitals (including a VA), a medical school Department of Neuroscience, a psychiatric hospital, a neuroscience research institute, and a private pharmaceutical research institute, which offer opportunities for collaboration. NDSU also has a Research and Technology Park which may offer research experiences involving advanced technology.

Application Information: NDSU Graduate School, NDSU Dept. 2820, P.O. Box 6050, Fargo, ND 58108. *Fee:* $35. *Online application:* http://www.ndsu.edu/gradschool/.

North Dakota State University

Developmental Science
Human Development and Education
NDSU Dept. 2615, P.O. Box 6050
Fargo, ND 58108-6050
Telephone: (701) 231-8268
Chairperson: Joel Hektner

E-mail: joel.hektner@ndsu.edu
Web: http://www.ndsu.edu/hdfs/academic_programs_admission/graduate/ds/

Orientation, Objectives, and Emphasis of Department

The Developmental Science program combines elements of Developmental Psychology and Human Development by integrating the biological, cognitive, and socioemotional underpinnings of lifespan development and incorporating familial, social, institutional and cultural contexts. Developmental Science stands in contrast to more traditional fields by incorporating diverse disciplinary perspectives into a cohesive framework. The doctoral curriculum incorporates a substantial research apprenticeship that requires students to participate in presenting and publishing research above and beyond their theses and dissertations. This requirement serves to build students' scholarly records and employability, and graduates of the program will be well-positioned to become leaders of this emerging field.

Programs and Degrees Offered

Program	Degree	Application Deadline	Applica-tions Received	Accepted	New Admits Enrolled (PT)	Total Enrolled (PT)	Degrees Awarded in 2014–2015	Median Years to Complete Degree	Dismissed/ Withdrew
Developmental Science	PhD	February 1 (Fall)	7	1	1 (0)	7 (0)	1	3	0

Internships/Practica

Internships are available for students who want to explore careers outside of academia.

Admissions

Entries appear in the following order: required test or GPA, minimum score (if required)/median score of students entering in 2015–2016.

Program	Degree	GRE-V	GRE-Q	GRE-Writing	GRE-Subject	Under-graduate GPA	Last 2 Years GPA	Psychol-ogy GPA	Master's GPA
Developmental Science	PhD	155/NA	155/NA	Not specified	Not specified	3/NA	Not specified	Not specified	3.5/NA

Admissions Requirements:

Degree	GRE	GRE-Subject	Letters of Recom-mendation	Research Statement	Writing Sample	CV	Interview
Doctoral	Required	Optional	3	Required	Required	Required	Optional

Admissions Criteria:

GRE scores—high
Research experience—high
Work experience—low
GPA—high
Letters of recommendation—high

Interview—low
Statement of goals and objectives—high
Undergraduate psychology preparation—medium
Research interest match—medium

For additional information on admission requirements, visit http://www.ndsu.edu/hdfs/academic_programs_admission/graduate/ds/ application_process/.

Department Demographics

	Male (PT)	Female (PT)	Total	African-American/ Black (PT)	Hispanic/ Latino (PT)	Asian/ Pacific Islander (PT)	American Indian/ Alaska Native (PT)	Caucasian/ White (PT)	Unknown	Multiethnic (PT)	ADA (PT)	Int'l (PT)
Students	2 (0)	5 (0)	7	1 (0)	0 (0)	1 (0)	0 (0)	5 (0)	0 (0)	0 (0)	0 (0)	3 (0)

Financial Information/Assistance

Tuition: For information on tuition costs, visit https://www.ndsu.edu/bisonconnection/accounts/tuition/graduate_tuition_full_time/. Tuition is subject to change. Additional fees are assessed to students beyond the costs of tuition for the following: Miscellaneous student services.

Doctoral:
State residents: $7,253 per academic year.
State residents: $302 per credit hour.
Nonstate residents: $19,365 per academic year.
Nonstate residents: $807 per credit hour.

Financial Assistance:

	Teaching Assistantship (% Receiving)	Teaching Assistantship Tuition Remission	Research Assistantship (% Receiving)	Research Assistantship Tuition Remission	Fellowship (% Receiving)	Fellowship Tuition Remission
First-Year Student	$12,000 (0)	Full	$12,000 (100)	Full	NA (NA)	NA
Advanced Student	$12,000 (15)	Full	$12,000 (70)	Full	$12,000 (15)	Full

Employment of Department Graduates

Doctoral:
Employed in an academic position at a university: 1
Total: 1

Additional Information

Housing and Day Care: On-campus housing is available. See the following website for more information: http://www.ndsu.edu/reslife/. No on-campus day care facilities are available.

Information for Students With Physical Disabilities: See the following website: http://www.ndsu.edu/disabilityservices/.

Special Facilities or Resources: The department maintains a lab equipped with a one-way mirror and state-of-the-art video equipment for observational research. We utilize Noldus' The Observer software for the collection, analysis, and presentation of observational data. We also have eye-tracking equipment and software. Graduate students are provided office space in research labs.

Application Information: Elizabeth Blodgett Salafia, Developmental Science Coordinator. *Fee:* $35. *Online application:* http://www.ndsu.edu/gradschool/prospective_students/.

North Dakota, University of
Counseling Psychology and Community Services
Education and Human Development
231 Centennial Drive, Stop 8255
Grand Forks, ND 58202-8255
Telephone: (701) 777-2729
Chairperson: Rachel Navarro

E-mail: cindy.juntunen@email.und.edu
Web: http://education.und.edu/counseling-psychology-and-community-services/

Orientation, Objectives, and Emphasis of Department

The Department's graduate programs consist of the PhD in Counseling Psychology and the MA in Counseling. The MA program has 3 areas of emphasis offered on-campus: Mental Health, Addictions, and Rehabilitation Counseling. A school counseling MA is offered online. The PhD program is accredited by the American Psychological Association and provides generalist training as a scientist–practitioner. The overarching goal of the PhD program in Counseling Psychology is to prepare entry level counseling psychologists who are well-trained and competent in both the practice and science of the profession. This is achieved through six training goals that are anchored in the foundational and functional competencies of health-service and counseling psychology. Both programs emphasize multicultural competence and an emphasis on social justice and advocacy. The PhD program participates in the Western Region Graduate Program sponsored by WICHE, which offers tuition support for WICHE residents. The PhD program is also support by a HRSA GPE grant, to provide specialized training in integrated behavioral health care in rural communities.

Programs and Degrees Offered

Program	Degree	Application Deadline	Applications Received	Accepted	New Admits Enrolled (PT)	Total Enrolled (PT)	Degrees Awarded in 2014–2015	Median Years to Complete Degree	Dismissed/ Withdrew
Counseling Psychology	PhD	December 10 (Fall)	58	10	6 (0)	35 (2)	2	4	0
Counseling - School Counseling	MA/MS	November 1 (Spring)	59	15	15 (0)	35 (3)	17	2.25	
Counseling - Addictions Emphasis	MA/MS	May 1 (Fall), May 1 (Summer)	4	2	1 (1)	2 (1)	2	2.5	0
Counseling - Rehabilitation Counseling	MA/MS	May 1 (Fall), May 1 (Summer)	5	4	4 (0)	6 (2)	4	2	0
Counseling - Mental Health Counseling	MA/MS	May 1 (Fall), May 1 (Summer)	28	24	16 (2)	34 (8)	16	2.1	1

APA Accreditation

Counseling PhD: Student Outcome Data website: http://education.und.edu/counseling-psychology-and-community-services/phd/index.cfm.

Doctoral Degree (PhD Counseling Psychology): For those doctoral students for whom a professional internship was required in this program prior to graduation:
Total students who applied for an internship: 13
Total students who obtained an internship: 12
Total students who obtained a paid internship: 12
Total students who obtained an unpaid internship: 0
Total students who were placed in APA/CPA-accredited internships: 12
Total students placed in internships not APA/CPA-accredited, but listed with the Association of Psychology Postdoctoral and Internship Centers (APPIC): 0
Total students placed in internships conforming to guidelines of the Council of Directors of School Psychology Programs (CDSPP): 0
Total students placed in internships that were not APA/CPA-accredited, APPIC or CDSSP listed: 0

Master's Degree (MA/MS Counseling - School Counseling): An internship experience, such as a final research project or "capstone" experience is required of graduates. Master's Degree (MA/MS Counseling - Addictions Emphasis): An internship experience, such as a final research project or "capstone" experience is required of graduates. Master's Degree (MA/MS Counseling - Rehabilitation Counseling): An internship experience, such as a final research project or "capstone" experience is required of graduates. Master's Degree (MA/MS Counseling - Mental Health Counseling): An internship experience, such as a final research project or "capstone" experience is required of graduates.

Internships/Practica

We have practicum training partners at a wide range of sites. Students in both the MA and PhD programs are placed in several university counseling centers and community mental health agencies in Grand Forks and the surrounding region. Students in the school counseling program complete placements in local schools. Several doctoral practicum placements are available in hospital, medical, and integrated care settings. We also have doctoral placements with the Grand Forks Air Force Based and one correctional center. Most practicum placements are located in within an hour's drive of Grand Forks, although a few sites require greater travel commitment. The program has a focused effort on rural behavioral health, providing opportunities for rural practicum placements. Doctoral students are required to establish a written Practicum Training Plan with their advisors during their first year of study, in order to make the best use of practicum toward their ultimate career goals.

Admissions

Entries appear in the following order: required test or GPA, minimum score (if required)/median score of students entering in 2015–2016.

Program	Degree	GRE-V	GRE-Q	GRE-Writing	GRE-Subject	Under-graduate GPA	Last 2 Years GPA	Psychol-ogy GPA	Master's GPA
Counseling Psychology	PhD	NA/152	NA/142	NA/4.5	Not specified	2.75/3.72	2.75/3.75	2.75/3.75	Not specified
Counseling - School Counseling	MA/MS	Not specified	Not specified	Not specified	Not specified	2.75/3.46	2.75/NA	Not specified	Not specified
Counseling - Addictions Emphasis	MA/MS	Not specified	Not specified	Not specified	Not specified	Not specified	Not specified	Not specified	Not specified
Counseling - Rehabilitation Counseling	MA/MS	Not specified	Not specified	Not specified	Not specified	Not specified	Not specified	Not specified	Not specified
Counseling - Mental Health Counseling	MA/MS	Not specified	Not specified	Not specified	Not specified	Not specified	Not specified	Not specified	Not specified

Admissions Requirements:

Degree	GRE	GRE-Subject	Letters of Recom-mendation	Research Statement	Writing Sample	CV	Interview
Master's/Specialist	Recom-mended	Optional	3	Required	None	Recom-mended	Required
Doctoral	Required	Optional	3	Required	Optional	Recom-mended	Required

Please note if these criteria vary for different programs: GRE is required for PhD; MAT or GRE is required for MA degree; the School Counseling program does not require the GRE.

Admissions Criteria:

GRE scores—medium
Research experience—high
Work experience—medium
Clinically related public service—medium
GPA—high

Letters of recommendation—high
Interview—high
Statement of goals and objectives—high
Undergraduate psychology preparation—medium

Department Demographics

	Male (PT)	Female (PT)	Total	African-American/Black (PT)	Hispanic/Latino (PT)	Asian/Pacific Islander (PT)	American Indian/Alaska Native (PT)	Caucasian/White (PT)	Unknown	Multiethnic (PT)	ADA (PT)	Int'l (PT)
Students	16 (3)	96 (13)	128	5 (0)	7 (0)	2 (0)	6 (2)	84 (14)	4 (0)	4 (0)	5 (1)	5 (0)

Financial Information/Assistance

Tuition: For information on tuition costs, visit http://und.edu/admissions/student-account-services/tuition-rates.cfm. Tuition is subject to change. Additional fees are assessed to students beyond the costs of tuition for the following: technology, university services, system services, course fees for practica and assessment. Tuition costs vary by program.

Doctoral:
State residents: $8,225 per academic year.
State residents: $343 per credit hour.
Nonstate residents: $19,703 per academic year.
Nonstate residents: $821 per credit hour.

Master's:
State residents: $7,200 per academic year.
State residents: $332 per credit hour.
Nonstate residents: $18,900 per academic year.
Nonstate residents: $790 per credit hour.

Financial Assistance:

	Teaching Assistantship (% Receiving)	Teaching Assistantship Tuition Remission	Research Assistantship (% Receiving)	Research Assistantship Tuition Remission	Fellowship (% Receiving)	Fellowship Tuition Remission
First-Year Student	$8,060 (60)	Full	$8,060 (40)	Full	$2,575 (NA)	NA
Advanced Student	$8,060 (50)	Partial	$8,060 (50)	Partial	NA (NA)	NA

For additional information on financial assistance, visit http://graduateschool.und.edu/graduate-students/financial-assistance/index.cfm.

Employment of Department Graduates

Master's:
Enrolled in a psychology doctoral program: 2
Employed in an academic position at a university: 1
Employed in other positions at a higher education institution: 1
Employed in a professional position in a school system: 15
Employed in a community mental health/counseling center: 8
Employed in a hospital/medical center: 3
Not seeking employment: 1
Do not know: 4
Total: 35

Doctoral:
Enrolled in a postdoctoral residency/fellowship: 1
Employed in independent practice: 1
Employed in an academic position at a university: 1
Employed in other positions at a higher education institution: 1
Employed in a community mental health/counseling center: 1
Employed in a hospital/medical center: 2
Total: 7

Additional Information

Housing and Day Care: On-campus housing is available. See the following website for more information: http://und.edu/student-life/housing/. On-campus day care facilities are available. See the following website for more information: http://und.edu/centers/childrens/.

Information for Students With Physical Disabilities: See the following website: http://und.edu/disability-services/.

Special Facilities or Resources: The department has office space for doctoral students, observation labs for practicing counseling and assessment skills, and access to significant research space. The college in which the department is housed (Education and Human Development) completed a major renovation and expansion in September, 2011, so new state-of-the-art classrooms and meeting rooms are readily available. The department has established numerous community partnerships to support training opportunities for graduate students. Both MA and PhD students can be trained in telepractice through our on-campus training clinic, the Northern Lights Behavioral Health Center.

Application Information: Fee: $35. *Online application:* http://graduateschool.und.edu/my-gradspace.cfm.

North Dakota, University of
Psychology
Arts & Sciences
319 Harvard Street, Corwin-Larimore Hall, Room 215, Stop 8380
Grand Forks, ND 58202-8380
Telephone: (701) 777-3451
Chairperson: Jeffrey E. Holm

E-mail: und.chairpsych@und.edu
Web: http://arts-sciences.und.edu/psychology/

Orientation, Objectives, and Emphasis of Department

The Psychology Department at the University of North Dakota has a multidimensional mission to provide quality undergraduate and graduate education, student advisement at both the baccalaureate and post-baccalaureate levels, teacher education for graduate students pursuing higher education positions, and a high level of faculty and student scholarship. The department also commits to efforts to enhance mental health care service delivery in underserved populations by underrepresented emerging professionals via our Indians in Psychology Doctoral Education (INPSYDE) clinical training program. The PhD programs are scientifically-oriented and offer intensive training in the scholarly research and applied aspects of their areas. They are designed to produce respected scholars in the field as manifested in the generation of high-quality research which is disseminated in lecturing, writing, and presentations. We also expect students to apply scientific findings in their respective area of specialization and to integrate scientific and applied activities as a method of further enhancing the quality of each.

Programs and Degrees Offered

Program	Degree	Application Deadline	Applica-tions Received	Accepted	New Admits Enrolled (PT)	Total Enrolled (PT)	Degrees Awarded in 2014–2015	Median Years to Complete Degree	Dismissed/ Withdrew
Clinical Psychology	PhD	January 1 (Fall)	70	7	7 (0)	39 (0)	5	6.2	0
Experimental Psychology	PhD	January 1 (Fall)	10	3	3 (0)	12 (0)	3	4.5	0
Forensic Psychology	MA/MS	January 1 (Fall)	12	3	2 (0)	4 (0)	2	2.5	0
Forensic Psychology (Online)	MA/MS	April 1 (Fall), October 1 (Spring)	250	50	0 (50)	0 (106)	32	3	3

APA Accreditation

Clinical PhD: Student Outcome Data website: http://arts-sciences.und.edu/psychology/clinical/.

Doctoral Degree (PhD Clinical Psychology): For those doctoral students for whom a professional internship was required in this program prior to graduation:
Total students who applied for an internship: 11
Total students who obtained an internship: 9
Total students who obtained a paid internship: 9
Total students who obtained an unpaid internship: 0
Total students who were placed in APA/CPA-accredited internships: 9
Total students placed in internships not APA/CPA-accredited, but listed with the Association of Psychology Postdoctoral and Internship Centers (APPIC): 0
Total students placed in internships conforming to guidelines of the Council of Directors of School Psychology Programs (CDSPP): 0
Total students placed in internships that were not APA/CPA-accredited, APPIC or CDSSP listed: 0

Master's Degree (MA/MS Forensic Psychology): An internship experience, such as a final research project or "capstone" experience is required of graduates. Master's Degree (MA/MS Forensic Psychology [Online]): An internship experience, such as a final research project or "capstone" experience is required of graduates.

Internships/Practica

The department maintains agreements with a variety of institutions in the surrounding area to provide more extensive training opportunities for students. Clinical students are required to complete 1 full year (16–20 hours/week) placement prior to internship, with most students completing 2 years. Forensic MS students occasionally complete community practica in forensic/judicial/correctional settings. Experimental doctoral students have the opportunity to complete teaching practica at local 2- and 4-year colleges as well as research practica at the medical school or other university-affiliated institutions.

Admissions

Entries appear in the following order: required test or GPA, minimum score (if required)/median score of students entering in 2015–2016.

Program	Degree	GRE-V	GRE-Q	GRE-Writing	GRE-Subject	Under-graduate GPA	Last 2 Years GPA	Psychol-ogy GPA	Master's GPA
Clinical Psychology	PhD	Not specified	Not specified	Not specified	Not specified	Not specified	Not specified	Not specified	Not specified
Experimental Psychology	PhD	Not specified	Not specified	Not specified	Not specified	Not specified	Not specified	Not specified	Not specified
Forensic Psychology	MA/MS	Not specified	Not specified	Not specified	Not specified	Not specified	Not specified	Not specified	Not specified
Forensic Psychology (Online)	MA/MS	Not specified	Not specified	Not specified	Not specified	Not specified	Not specified	Not specified	Not specified

Admissions Requirements:

Degree	GRE	GRE-Subject	Letters of Recom-mendation	Research Statement	Writing Sample	CV	Interview
Master's/Specialist	Required	None	3	Required	Optional	Required	Required
Doctoral	Required	Required	3	Required	Optional	Required	Required

Please note if these criteria vary for different programs: The Forensic MA (online) program does not require General or Subject GRE scores or interviews.

Admissions Criteria:

GRE scores—high
Research experience—high
Work experience—low
Clinically related public service—low
GPA—high

Letters of recommendation —medium
Interview—medium
Statement of goals and objectives—medium
Undergraduate psychology preparation—low

Department Demographics

	Male (PT)	Female (PT)	Total	African-American/ Black (PT)	Hispanic/ Latino (PT)	Asian/ Pacific Islander (PT)	American Indian/ Alaska Native (PT)	Caucasian/ White (PT)	Unknown	Multiethnic (PT)	ADA (PT)	Int'l (PT)
Students	6 (25)	49 (81)	161	1 (0)	1 (0)	1 (0)	10 (0)	39 (0)	2 (106)	1 (0)	0 (0)	1 (0)

Financial Information/Assistance

Tuition: For information on tuition costs, visit http://und.edu/admissions/student-account-services/tuition-rates.cfm. Tuition is subject to change. Additional fees are assessed to students beyond the costs of tuition for the following: health, technology, student facilities use. Tuition costs vary by program.

Doctoral:
State residents: $7,740 per academic year.
State residents: $333 per credit hour.
Nonstate residents: $18,408 per academic year.
Nonstate residents: $768 per credit hour.

Master's:
State residents: $7,740 per academic year.
State residents: $333 per credit hour.
Nonstate residents: $18,408 per academic year.
Nonstate residents: $768 per credit hour.

Financial Assistance:

	Teaching Assistantship (% Receiving)	Teaching Assistantship Tuition Remission	Research Assistantship (% Receiving)	Research Assistantship Tuition Remission	Fellowship (% Receiving)	Fellowship Tuition Remission
First-Year Student	$15,000 (100)	Full	NA (NA)	NA	NA (NA)	NA
Advanced Student	$18,000 (90)	Full	$18,000 (10)	Full	$1,000 (10)	NA

For additional information on financial assistance, visit http://graduateschool.und.edu/graduate-students/financial-assistance/index.cfm.

Employment of Department Graduates

Master's:
Enrolled in a psychology doctoral program: 1
Employed in a community mental health/counseling center: 1
Do not know: 30
Total: 32

Doctoral:
Enrolled in a postdoctoral residency/fellowship: 1
Employed in an academic position at a university: 2
Employed in academic position at a 2-year/4-year college: 1
Employed in a community mental health/counseling center: 1
Employed in a hospital/medical center: 3
Total: 8

Additional Information

Housing and Day Care: On-campus housing is available. See the following website for more information: http://und.edu/student-life/housing/. On-campus day care facilities are available. See the following website for more information: http://und.edu/centers/childrens/.

Information for Students With Physical Disabilities: See the following website: http://und.edu/disability-services/.

Special Facilities or Resources: The department faculty are part of the interdisciplinary research facility Northern Plains Center for Behavioral Research (NPCBR). NPCBR consists of research laboratories where department faculty and graduate students collaborate on research with faculty and graduate students from many other departments spanning three colleges/schools (e.g., nursing, nutrition, aerospace, educational technology).

Application Information: Fee: $35. *Online application:* http://graduateschool.und.edu/new-students/my-gradspace.cfm.

Akron, University of

Department of Psychology
Buchtel College of Arts and Sciences
College of Arts & Sciences Building, 290 East Buchtel Avenue
Akron, OH 44325-4301
Telephone: (330) 972-7280
Chairperson: Paul E. Levy

E-mail: plevy@uakron.edu
Web: http://www.uakron.edu/psychology

Orientation, Objectives, and Emphasis of Department

The department's goals are to: (1) increase and diffuse psychological knowledge by advancing the discipline both as a science and as a means of promoting human welfare; (2) promote psychology in all its branches in the broadest and most liberal manner; (3) encourage research in psychology; and (4) advance high standards of education, achievement, professional ethics and conduct. The department subscribes to a scientist–practitioner model of training. Graduate students take a common set of courses in foundational areas of psychology in addition to their specialty coursework, with study in the specialty area beginning early in graduate training. The emphasis is on preparation for teaching as well as for research, industrial, or mental health services career paths. Industrial/organizational, gerontological, and counseling psychology are the specialty emphases at the MA and PhD level.

Programs and Degrees Offered

Program	Degree	Application Deadline	Applica-tions Received	Accepted	New Admits Enrolled (PT)	Total Enrolled (PT)	Degrees Awarded in 2014–2015	Median Years to Complete Degree	Dismissed/Withdrew
Counseling Psychology	PhD	December 1 (Fall)	51	6	5 (0)	25 (10)	4	6	1
Industrial/ Organizational Psychology	MA/MS	January 15 (Fall)	49	8	3 (0)	8 (0)	4	2	0
Industrial/ Organizational Psychology	PhD	January 15 (Fall)	56	9	4 (0)	26 (11)	3	6	0
Adult Development and Aging	PhD	January 15 (Fall)	6	2	1 (0)	8 (2)	0		0

APA Accreditation

Counseling PhD: Student Outcome Data website: http://www.uakron.edu/psychology/academics/cpcp/program-outcome-data.dot.

Doctoral Degree (PhD Counseling Psychology): For those doctoral students for whom a professional internship was required in this program prior to graduation:
Total students who applied for an internship: 2
Total students who obtained an internship: 2
Total students who obtained a paid internship: 2
Total students who obtained an unpaid internship: 0
Total students who were placed in APA/CPA-accredited internships: 2
Total students placed in internships not APA/CPA-accredited, but listed with the Association of Psychology Postdoctoral and Internship Centers (APPIC): 0
Total students placed in internships conforming to guidelines of the Council of Directors of School Psychology Programs (CDSPP): 0
Total students placed in internships that were not APA/CPA-accredited, APPIC or CDSSP listed: 0

Master's Degree (MA/MS Industrial/Organizational Psychology): An internship experience, such as a final research project or "capstone" experience is required of graduates.

Internships/Practica

Practica are offered in the department's own Counseling Training Clinic and Center for Organizational Research. Students also have access to a wide variety of community-based practica in industrial and public settings, hospitals, the University's Counseling Testing and Careers Center, and community mental health centers.

Admissions

Entries appear in the following order: required test or GPA, minimum score (if required)/median score of students entering in 2015–2016.

Program	Degree	GRE-V	GRE-Q	GRE-Writing	GRE-Subject	Under-graduate GPA	Last 2 Years GPA	Psychol-ogy GPA	Master's GPA
Counseling Psychology	PhD	148/156	150/153	3/3.5	Not specified	3.27/3.62	Not specified	NA/NA	Not specified
Industrial/ Organizational Psychology	MA/MS	151/158	150/152	4/4.5	Not specified	3.13/3.73	Not specified	NA/NA	Not specified
Industrial/ Organizational Psychology	PhD	157/160	154/158	4.5/4.75	Not specified	3.33/3.69	Not specified	NA/NA	Not specified
Adult Development and Aging	PhD	NA/162	NA/152	NA/5	Not specified	NA/3.62	Not specified	NA/NA	Not specified

Admissions Requirements:

Degree	GRE	GRE-Subject	Letters of Recom-mendation	Research Statement	Writing Sample	CV	Interview
Master's/Specialist	Required	Optional	3	Required	Optional	Required	Optional
Doctoral	Required	Optional	3	Required	Optional	Required	Optional

Please note if these criteria vary for different programs: On campus interviews and telephone interviews are used as a selection criterion only in the Counseling Psychology program. I/O program does telephone screening of those that it intends to accept and on campus interviews.

Admissions Criteria:

GRE scores—high
Research experience—high
Work experience—low
Clinically related public service—low

GPA—high
Letters of recommendation—medium
Interview—medium
Statement of goals and objectives—high

Department Demographics

	Male (PT)	Female (PT)	Total	African-American/ Black (PT)	Hispanic/ Latino (PT)	Asian/ Pacific Islander (PT)	American Indian/ Alaska Native (PT)	Caucasian/ White (PT)	Unknown	Multiethnic (PT)	ADA (PT)	Int'l (PT)
Students	24 (8)	43 (15)	90	7 (2)	4 (0)	9 (1)	0 (0)	46 (20)	1 (0)	0 (0)	0 (0)	4 (0)

Financial Information/Assistance

Tuition: For information on tuition costs, visit http://www.uakron.edu/student-accounts/costs/index.dot. Tuition is subject to change. Additional fees are assessed to students beyond the costs of tuition for the following: General Service Fee, Facilities Fee.

Doctoral:
State residents: $11,448 per academic year.
State residents: $477 per credit hour.
Nonstate residents: $18,792 per academic year.
Nonstate residents: $783 per credit hour.

Master's:
State residents: $11,448 per academic year.
State residents: $477 per credit hour.
Nonstate residents: $18,792 per academic year.
Nonstate residents: $783 per credit hour.

Financial Assistance:

	Teaching Assistantship (% Receiving)	Teaching Assistantship Tuition Remission	Research Assistantship (% Receiving)	Research Assistantship Tuition Remission	Fellowship (% Receiving)	Fellowship Tuition Remission
First-Year Student	$11,500 (NA)	Full	NA (NA)	NA	NA (NA)	NA
Advanced Student	$12,500 (NA)	Full	$12,500 (NA)	Full	NA (NA)	NA

For additional information on financial assistance, visit http://www.uakron.edu/gradsch/financial-assistance/.

Employment of Department Graduates

Master's:
Employed in other positions at a higher education institution: 1
Employed in business or industry: 2
Do not know: 1
Total: 4

Doctoral:
Enrolled in a postdoctoral residency/fellowship: 2
Employed in independent practice: 1
Employed in an academic position at a university: 2
Employed in business or industry: 2
Total: 7

Additional Information

Housing and Day Care: On-campus housing is available. See the following website for more information: http://www.uakron.edu/reslife. On-campus day care facilities are available. See the following website for more information: http://www.uakron.edu/education/community-engagement/ccd.

Information for Students With Physical Disabilities: See the following website: http://www.uakron.edu/access.

Special Facilities or Resources: To enhance research and instruction, we maintain a number of psychological research laboratories designed for individual and group studies, equipped with computers, one-way viewing mirrors, video equipment, and so forth. Over 60 computers are available to faculty and students for word processing, statistical analysis, classroom instruction, e-mail correspondence, and web access. A programmer/technician provides full-time support for the hardware and software for the department and writes custom software for experimental control, stimulus display, and data collection. We maintain an in-house library of teaching resources for graduate teaching assistants, as well as a test library with over 100 tests and manuals for assessment of a broad range of constructs. We are affiliated with the university's Institute for Life-Span Development and Gerontology and the Center for the History of Psychology.

Application Information: Graduate School, The University of Akron, Polsky Building, Room 469, Akron, OH 44325-2101. Fee: $45. *Online application:* http://www.uakron.edu/gradsch/apply-online/.

Akron, University of (2015 data)
School of Counseling/Collaborative Program in Counseling Psychology
The College of Health Professions
27 South Forge Street
Akron, OH 44325-5007
Telephone: (330) 972- 7779
Chairperson: Dr. Karin Jordan

E-mail: queener@uakron.edu
Web: http://www.uakron.edu/soc/index.dot

Orientation, Objectives, and Emphasis of Department
The department subscribes to a scientist–practitioner model of training. Its objective is to provide a core of courses in general psychology and courses in the specialty of counseling psychology. The emphasis is on preparation for teaching, research, and practice career paths.

Programs and Degrees Offered

Program	Degree	Application Deadline	Applica-tions Received	Accepted	New Admits Enrolled (PT)	Total Enrolled (PT)	Degrees Awarded in 2014–2015	Median Years to Complete Degree	Dismissed/ Withdrew
Collaborative Program in Counseling Psychology	PhD	December 1 (Fall)	39	4	4 (0)	11 (14)	4	7.1	1

APA Accreditation

Counseling PhD: Student Outcome Data website: http://www.uakron.edu/psychology/academics/cpcp/program-outcome-data.dot.

Doctoral Degree (PhD Collaborative Program in Counseling Psychology): For those doctoral students for whom a professional internship was required in this program prior to graduation:

Total students who applied for an internship: 8
Total students who obtained an internship: 7
Total students who obtained a paid internship: 7
Total students who obtained an unpaid internship: 0
Total students who were placed in APA/CPA-accredited internships: 7
Total students placed in internships not APA/CPA-accredited, but listed with the Association of Psychology Postdoctoral and Internship Centers (APPIC): 0
Total students placed in internships conforming to guidelines of the Council of Directors of School Psychology Programs (CDSPP): 0
Total students placed in internships that were not APA/CPA-accredited, APPIC or CDSSP listed: 0

Internships/Practica

Practica are offered in the department's clinic, the counseling center on campus, and a broad range of settings in the community.

Admissions

Entries appear in the following order: required test or GPA, minimum score (if required)/median score of students entering in 2015–2016.

Program	Degree	GRE-V	GRE-Q	GRE-Writing	GRE-Subject	Under-graduate GPA	Last 2 Years GPA	Psychol-ogy GPA	Master's GPA
Collaborative Program in Counseling Psychology	PhD	NA/NA	NA/NA	Not specified	NA/NA	2.75/NA	3/NA	Not specified	3.25/NA

Admissions Requirements:

Degree	GRE	GRE-Subject	Letters of Recom-mendation	Research Statement	Writing Sample	CV	Interview
Doctoral	Required	Recom-mended	3	Required	Optional	Required	Required

Admissions Criteria:

GRE scores—high
Research experience—high
Work experience—medium
Clinically related public service—low

GPA—high
Letters of recommendation—high
Interview—high
Statement of goals and objectives—high

For additional information on admission requirements, visit http://www.uakron.edu/psychology/academics/cpcp/admissions/index.dot.

Department Demographics

	Male (PT)	Female (PT)	Total	African-American/ Black (PT)	Hispanic/ Latino (PT)	Asian/ Pacific Islander (PT)	American Indian/ Alaska Native (PT)	Caucasian/ White (PT)	Unknown	Multiethnic (PT)	ADA (PT)	Int'l (PT)
Students	4 (4)	16 (7)	31	4 (0)	1 (0)	1 (0)	0 (0)	14 (0)	0 (0)	0 (0)	0 (1)	0 (0)

Financial Information/Assistance

Tuition: For information on tuition costs, visit http://www.uakron.edu/student-accounts/costs/. Tuition is subject to change.

Doctoral:
State residents: $421 per credit hour.
Nonstate residents: $755 per credit hour.

Financial Assistance:

	Teaching Assistantship (% Receiving)	Teaching Assistantship Tuition Remission	Research Assistantship (% Receiving)	Research Assistantship Tuition Remission	Fellowship (% Receiving)	Fellowship Tuition Remission
First-Year Student	$10,500 (NA)	Full	$10,500 (NA)	Full	NA (NA)	NA
Advanced Student	$10,500 (NA)	Full	$10,500 (NA)	Full	NA (NA)	NA

For additional information on financial assistance, visit http://www.uakron.edu/gradsch/financial-assistance/.

Employment of Department Graduates

Doctoral:
Enrolled in a postdoctoral residency/fellowship: 2
Employed in a community mental health/counseling center: 2
Total: 4

Additional Information

Housing and Day Care: On-campus housing is available. See the following website for more information: http://www.uakron.edu/reslife/. On-campus day care facilities are available. See the following website for more information: http://www.uakron.edu/education/community-engagement/ccd/index.dot.

Information for Students With Physical Disabilities: See the following website: http://www.uakron.edu/access/.

Special Facilities or Resources: The department has its own computer lab and houses the College of Health Professions Clinic for Individual and Family Counseling.

Application Information: The Graduate School, Polsky Building, Room 469, The University of Akron, Akron, OH 44325-2101. *Fee:* $40. *Online application:* http://www.uakron.edu/gradsch/apply-online/docdegr.dot.

Bowling Green State University

Department of Psychology
Bowling Green, OH 43403
Telephone: (419) 372-2306
Chairperson: Michael Zickar

E-mail: pwatson@bgsu.edu
Web: http://www.bgsu.edu/arts-and-sciences/psychology.html

Orientation, Objectives, and Emphasis of Department

The primary goal of the PhD program is the development of scientists capable of advancing psychological knowledge. The program is characterized by both an emphasis on extensive academic training in general psychology and an early and continuing commitment to research. Although each graduate student will seek an area in which to develop his or her own expertise, students will be expected to be knowledgeable about many areas and will be encouraged to pursue interests that cross conventional specialty lines. The program is research-oriented. Each student normally works in close association with a sponsor or chairperson whose special competence matches the student's interest, but students are free to pursue research interests with any faculty member and in any area(s) they choose. Both basic and applied research are well represented within the department. The clinical program has concentrations in clinical child, behavioral medicine, and community, as well as general clinical.

Programs and Degrees Offered

Program	Degree	Application Deadline	Applica-tions Received	Accepted	New Admits Enrolled (PT)	Total Enrolled (PT)	Degrees Awarded in 2014–2015	Median Years to Complete Degree	Dismissed/ Withdrew
Clinical Psychology	PhD	December 15 (Fall)	120	19	11 (0)	55 (0)	5	6	0
Developmental Psychology	PhD	January 1 (Fall)	6	0	0 (0)	6 (0)	1	4.9	0
Neural & Cognitive Sciences	PhD	January 1 (Fall)	24	7	3	19	1	5	0
Industrial/ Organizational Psychology	PhD	December 1 (Fall)	127	10	6	27	5	5.4	0

APA Accreditation

Clinical PhD: Student Outcome Data website: http://www.bgsu.edu/arts-and-sciences/psychology/graduate-program/clinical.html.

Doctoral Degree (PhD Clinical Psychology): For those doctoral students for whom a professional internship was required in this program prior to graduation:
Total students who applied for an internship: 7
Total students who obtained an internship: 7
Total students who obtained a paid internship: 7
Total students who obtained an unpaid internship: 0
Total students who were placed in APA/CPA-accredited internships: 7
Total students placed in internships not APA/CPA-accredited, but listed with the Association of Psychology Postdoctoral and Internship Centers (APPIC): 0
Total students placed in internships conforming to guidelines of the Council of Directors of School Psychology Programs (CDSPP): 0
Total students placed in internships that were not APA/CPA-accredited, APPIC or CDSSP listed: 0

Internships/Practica

In their beginning years, clinical students are placed on Basic Clinical Skills practicum teams through the Department's Psychological Services Center (PSC) that provide experience with a broad range of clients and clinical problems. Students focus on the application of such basic clinical skills as psychological assessment and interventions, the integration of science and practice, case conceptualization, clinical judgment and decision-making and report writing. In their second year, students begin receiving in-house training in psychotherapy through the PSC. As clinical students progress through the program, they are placed on Advanced Clinical Skills teams that involve them in current projects providing "hands-on" experience with the integration of research and practice as it applies to individuals, health/behavioral medicine, the community, or special populations (e.g., children, problem drinkers). More advanced clinical students are provided practicum opportunities consistent with their interest through a number of outside placements, such as community mental health centers, a nearby medical college, the university counseling center and health service, an inpatient child and adolescent facility, hospital-based rehabilitation centers, treatment centers for children and families, and programs for individuals with severe mental disabilities and emotional disorders. Industrial/Organizational students are strongly encouraged to apply for a formal internship after completion of prelims.

Admissions

Entries appear in the following order: required test or GPA, minimum score (if required)/median score of students entering in 2015–2016.

Program	Degree	GRE-V	GRE-Q	GRE-Writing	GRE-Subject	Under-graduate GPA	Last 2 Years GPA	Psychology GPA	Master's GPA
Clinical Psychology	PhD	NA/NA	NA/NA	Not specified	Not specified	NA/3.88	Not specified	Not specified	Not specified
Developmental Psychology	PhD	NA/NA	NA/NA	Not specified	Not specified	NA/NA	Not specified	Not specified	Not specified
Neural & Cognitive Sciences	PhD	NA/NA	NA/NA	Not specified	Not specified	NA/3.7	Not specified	Not specified	Not specified
Industrial/ Organizational Psychology	PhD	NA/NA	NA/NA	Not specified	Not specified	NA/3.73	Not specified	Not specified	Not specified

Admissions Requirements:

Degree	GRE	GRE-Subject	Letters of Recom-mendation	Research Statement	Writing Sample	CV	Interview
Doctoral	Required	Optional	3	Required	Required	Required	Recom-mended

Please note if these criteria vary for different programs: Clinically related public service and interview are high for Clinical program only.

Admissions Criteria:

GRE scores—high
Research experience—high
Work experience—medium
Clinically related public service—high

GPA—high
Letters of recommendation—high
Interview—high
Statement of goals and objectives—high

For additional information on admission requirements, visit http://www.bgsu.edu/arts-and-sciences/psychology/graduate-program/prospective-students.html.

Department Demographics

	Male (PT)	Female (PT)	Total	African-American/ Black (PT)	Hispanic/ Latino (PT)	Asian/ Pacific Islander (PT)	American Indian/ Alaska Native (PT)	Caucasian/ White (PT)	Unknown	Multiethnic (PT)	ADA (PT)	Int'l (PT)
Students	34 (0)	73 (0)	107	1 (0)	1 (0)	10 (0)	2 (0)	83 (0)	10 (0)	0 (0)	0 (0)	10 (0)

Financial Information/Assistance

Tuition: For information on tuition costs, visit http://www.bgsu.edu/bursar.html. Tuition is subject to change. Additional fees are assessed to students beyond the costs of tuition for the following: general fee; registration fee; graduate fee, green fee (optional); legal fee (optional).

Doctoral:
State residents: $11,661 per academic year.
State residents: $486 per credit hour.
Nonstate residents: $18,969 per academic year.
Nonstate residents: $800 per credit hour.

Financial Assistance:

	Teaching Assistantship (% Receiving)	Teaching Assistantship Tuition Remission	Research Assistantship (% Receiving)	Research Assistantship Tuition Remission	Fellowship (% Receiving)	Fellowship Tuition Remission
First-Year Student	$13,000 (NA)	Partial	$13,000 (NA)	Partial	NA (NA)	NA
Advanced Student	$13,000 (NA)	Partial	$13,000 (NA)	Partial	NA (NA)	NA

Employment of Department Graduates

No information provided.

Additional Information

Housing and Day Care: No on-campus housing is available. No on-campus day care facilities are available.

Information for Students With Physical Disabilities: See the following website: http://www.bgsu.edu/disability-services.html.

Special Facilities or Resources: The department is located in the psychology building with excellent facilities for all forms of research. The building houses all faculty and graduate students. The department operates a community-oriented Psychological Services Center and the Institute for Psychological Research and Application.

Application Information: Fee: $45. Online application: http://www.bgsu.edu/graduate/admissions.html.

Cincinnati, University of
Department of Psychology
Arts and Sciences
4130 Edwards I
Cincinnati, OH 45221-0376
Telephone: (513) 556-5577
Interim Head: Kevin Shockley, PhD

E-mail: kevin.shockley@uc.edu
Web: http://www.artsci.uc.edu/departments/psychology.html

Orientation, Objectives, and Emphasis of Department
The University of Cincinnati offers the PhD in Psychology, including an APA-accredited training program in Clinical Psychology. Clinical students must specify a specialty training area (e.g., neuropsychology, health psychology). For students who are seeking an Experimental degree, we offer training primarily in Cognition, Action and Perception; Human Robotic Interaction; Social Psychology; Industrial/Organizational and Experimental Neuropsychology. The doctoral program is limited to full-time students who show outstanding promise. Students are admitted to the doctoral program to work with a faculty research mentor. Faculty mentors are responsible for ensuring that students are actively engaged in doing research from the very start of their graduate school career, and that this work leads successfully to a master's thesis and a dissertation. The department offers a terminal master's program, which has two primary areas of focus: Organizational and Community Psychology. Both areas rely on a solid foundation in psychology, including an understanding of the factors that influence behavior (social psychology) and how individuals think, process information, and make decisions (cognitive psychology). Both areas also emphasize the development of statistical and methodological skills.

Programs and Degrees Offered

Program	Degree	Application Deadline	Applications Received	Accepted	New Admits Enrolled (PT)	Total Enrolled (PT)	Degrees Awarded in 2014–2015	Median Years to Complete Degree	Dismissed/ Withdrew
Clinical Psychology	PhD	December 5 (Fall)	157	6	6 (0)	24 (8)	5	6	0

Programs and Degrees Offered *(con't.)*

Program	Degree	Application Deadline	Applica-tions Received	Accepted	New Admits Enrolled (PT)	Total Enrolled (PT)	Degrees Awarded in 2014–2015	Median Years to Complete Degree	Dismissed/ Withdrew
Experimental Psychology	PhD	December 5 (Fall)	32	6	6 (0)	30 (1)	2	6	0
Applied Psychology	MA/MS	March 15 (Fall)	12	8	8	8	0		0

APA Accreditation
Clinical PhD (Doctor of Philosophy).

Doctoral Degree (PhD Clinical Psychology): For those doctoral students for whom a professional internship was required in this program prior to graduation:
Total students who applied for an internship: 4
Total students who obtained an internship: 3
Total students who obtained a paid internship: 3
Total students who obtained an unpaid internship: 0
Total students who were placed in APA/CPA-accredited internships: 3
Total students placed in internships not APA/CPA-accredited, but listed with the Association of Psychology Postdoctoral and Internship Centers (APPIC): 0
Total students placed in internships conforming to guidelines of the Council of Directors of School Psychology Programs (CDSPP): 0
Total students placed in internships that were not APA/CPA-accredited, APPIC or CDSSP listed: 0

Master's Degree (MA/MS Applied Psychology): An internship experience, such as a final research project or "capstone" experience is required of graduates.

Internships/Practica
All clinical students in Years 3 and 4 typically perform a paid, 20-hour/week clinical (or clinical research) training placement at an external site in the Greater Cincinnati area. Often these placements are at the University of Cincinnati Medical Center, the Cincinnati Children's Hospital Medical Center, or a variety of community agencies. If students need a fifth year of support prior to beginning an APA-accredited clinical internship, we can generally arrange a clinical training opportunity, although priority for placements goes to students in Years 1 through 4. While most of our experimental students do their paid training assignments within the department, there are also paid external training slots available for some of our students in private industry or with the federal government.

Admissions
Entries appear in the following order: required test or GPA, minimum score (if required)/median score of students entering in 2015–2016.

Program	Degree	GRE-V	GRE-Q	GRE-Writing	GRE Subject	Under-graduate GPA	Last 2 Years GPA	Psychol-ogy GPA	Master's GPA
Clinical Psychology	PhD	142/162	139/161	3.5/4.5	Not specified	3.5/3.6	Not specified	Not specified	Not specified
Experimental Psychology	PhD	139/156	138/156	3/4.25	Not specified	2.8/3.7	Not specified	Not specified	Not specified
Applied Psychology	MA/MS	Not specified	Not specified	Not specified	Not specified	Not specified	Not specified	Not specified	Not specified

Admissions Requirements:

Degree	GRE	GRE-Subject	Letters of Recom-mendation	Research Statement	Writing Sample	CV	Interview
Master's/Specialist	Required	Optional	3	Required	Optional	Required	Optional
Doctoral	Required	Optional	3	Required	Optional	Required	Required

Please note if these criteria vary for different programs: Clinically related public service is only considered strongly for students applying for clinical training. Prior research training is required only for doctoral applicants.

Admissions Criteria:

GRE scores—medium
Research experience—high
Work experience—high
Clinically related public service—medium
GPA—medium

Letters of recommendation—high
Interview—high
Statement of goals and objectives—high
Undergraduate psychology preparation—medium

Department Demographics

	Male (PT)	Female (PT)	Total	African-American/ Black (PT)	Hispanic/ Latino (PT)	Asian/ Pacific Islander (PT)	American Indian/ Alaska Native (PT)	Caucasian/ White (PT)	Unknown	Multiethnic (PT)	ADA (PT)	Int'l (PT)
Students	22 (1)	40 (8)	71	9 (1)	7 (0)	1 (1)	0 (0)	41 (6)	0 (0)	4 (1)	3 (0)	2 (1)

Financial Information/Assistance

Tuition: For information on tuition costs, visit http://www.uc.edu/bursar/fees.html. Tuition is subject to change. Additional fees are assessed to students beyond the costs of tuition for the following: computer fees & health insurance.

Doctoral:
State residents: $14,468 per academic year.
State residents: $724 per credit hour.
Nonstate residents: $26,210 per academic year.
Nonstate residents: $1,311 per credit hour.

Master's:
State residents: $14,468 per academic year.
State residents: $724 per credit hour.
Nonstate residents: $26,210 per academic year.
Nonstate residents: $1,311 per credit hour.

Financial Assistance:

	Teaching Assistantship (% Receiving)	Teaching Assistantship Tuition Remission	Research Assistantship (% Receiving)	Research Assistantship Tuition Remission	Fellowship (% Receiving)	Fellowship Tuition Remission
First-Year Student	$16,000 (89)	Full	$16,000 (11)	Full	NA (NA)	Full
Advanced Student	$16,000 (40)	Full	$16,000 (20)	Full	$16,000 (40)	Full

For additional information on financial assistance, visit http://financialaid.uc.edu/gradstudents.html.

Employment of Department Graduates

Doctoral:
Enrolled in a postdoctoral residency/fellowship: 6
Employed in an academic position at a university: 1
Total: 7

Additional Information

Housing and Day Care: No on-campus housing is available. On-campus day care facilities are available. See the following website for more information: http://www.uc.edu/elc.html; http://cech.uc.edu/centers/arlitt.html.

Information for Students With Physical Disabilities: See the following website: http://www.uc.edu/aess/disability.html.

Special Facilities or Resources: The department's clinical program has close ties to the UC College of Medicine, the UC Center for Imaging Research, Cincinnati Children's Hospital Medical Center, and a wide range of community agencies. The experimental program has close collaborations with the UC College of Medicine, the College of Engineering, and agencies including Wright

Patterson Air Force Base and the National Institute for Occupational Safety and Health. The department houses the Center for Cognition, Action, & Perception which includes motion-capture, eye-tracking, and other research facilities.

Application Information: Graduate Coordinator, Department of Psychology, University of Cincinnati, P.O. Box 210376, Cincinnati, OH 45221-0376. *Fee:* $70. *Online application:* http://grad.uc.edu/admissions.html.

Cincinnati, University of
School Psychology
Education, Criminal Justice, and Human Services
P.O. Box 210068
Cincinnati, OH 45221-0068
Telephone: (513) 556-3342
Program Coordinator: Renee Hawkins

E-mail: renee.hawkins@uc.edu
Web: http://cech.uc.edu/programs/school_psychology.html

Orientation, Objectives, and Emphasis of Department
The School Psychology Program at the University of Cincinnati is dedicated to preparing highly competent professional school psychologists, at the specialist (EdS) and doctoral (PhD) levels, according to the scientist–practitioner model. The program builds on foundations in psychology and education, and fosters a special sensitivity to cultural diversity of all people and respect for the uniqueness and human dignity of each person. The program emphasizes the delivery of school psychological services within a tiered services delivery model (prevention to targeted intervention) using a collaborative consultation model from an ecological/behavioral orientation. Students learn to view problems from an ecological/systems perspective focusing on child, family, school and community and to provide comprehensive intervention-based services utilizing data-based decision making to design, implement, and evaluate strategies for preventing and resolving learning and adjustment problem situations across a tiered service delivery model. A child advocacy perspective, built on a scientist–practitioner foundation, provides a framework for guiding decisions and practices to support positive outcomes for all children. Both theoretical and empirical bases of professional practice are emphasized and a diverse range of practical experiences are provided throughout all preparation (preschool to high school, in urban, suburban, and rural settings).

Programs and Degrees Offered

Program	Degree	Application Deadline	Applications Received	Accepted	New Admits Enrolled (PT)	Total Enrolled (PT)	Degrees Awarded in 2014–2015	Median Years to Complete Degree	Dismissed/Withdrew
School Psychology	PhD	January 15 (Fall)	13	6	6 (0)	18 (1)	3	5	1
School Psychology	EdS	January 15 (Fall)	50	25	11 (0)	24 (0)	12	3	0

Doctoral Degree (PhD School Psychology): For those doctoral students for whom a professional internship was required in this program prior to graduation:
Total students who applied for an internship: 3
Total students who obtained an internship: 3
Total students who obtained a paid internship: 3
Total students who obtained an unpaid internship: 0
Total students who were placed in APA/CPA-accredited internships: 1
Total students placed in internships not APA/CPA-accredited, but listed with the Association of Psychology Postdoctoral and Internship Centers (APPIC): 0
Total students placed in internships conforming to guidelines of the Council of Directors of School Psychology Programs (CDSPP): 2
Total students placed in internships that were not APA/CPA-accredited, APPIC or CDSSP listed: 0

Internships/Practica
All students, specialist and doctoral level, complete extensive practica prior to internship in field settings that include local school districts and educational agencies. In the first year, students are placed in schools (urban settings, K–12) to learn about schooling, educational issues, effective instruction, and roles and responsibilities of various personnel. Field experiences also occur to support foundation skills in applied behavior analysis and academic and behavioral intervention. Throughout the second year, students are enrolled in an integrated practicum experience, in which students obtain extensive supervised experience in delivery of services from a consultative, intervention-based tiered services delivery model. Students collaborate to design, implement, and evaluate

prevention and intervention plans in the practicum, incorporating elements of their learning from across course work. In addition, they complete field experiences in behavioral counseling and functional assessment. Specialist-level students then complete a 10-month, 1,500-hour school-based paid internship, arranged through the program. In the internship, students provide a full range of comprehensive school psychological services, with supervision from a licensed school psychologist. Doctoral students complete advanced field work in years 3 and 4, prior to completing internship in Year 5. Doctoral students are actively engaged in research across years in the program.

Admissions

Entries appear in the following order: required test or GPA, minimum score (if required)/median score of students entering in 2015–2016.

Program	Degree	GRE-V	GRE-Q	GRE-Writing	GRE-Subject	Under-graduate GPA	Last 2 Years GPA	Psychology GPA	Master's GPA
School Psychology	PhD	NA/153	NA/150	NA/4.5	Not specified	NA/3.74	NA/3.9	NA/NA	Not specified
School Psychology	EdS	NA/150	NA/148	NA/4	Not specified	NA/3.5	NA/3.74	NA/NA	Not specified

Admissions Requirements:

Degree	GRE	GRE-Subject	Letters of Recommendation	Research Statement	Writing Sample	CV	Interview
Master's/Specialist	Required	None	3	Required	None	Required	Required
Doctoral	Required	Optional	3	Required	None	Required	Required

Please note if these criteria vary for different programs: Specific, focused goals aligned with doctoral study (including research) are expected for doctoral applicants.

Admissions Criteria:

GRE scores—medium
Research experience—medium
Work experience—medium
Clinically related public service—high
GPA—high

Letters of recommendation—high
Interview—high
Statement of goals and objectives—high
Undergraduate psychology preparation—medium

For additional information on admission requirements, visit http://cech.uc.edu/programs/school_psychology/future_students/the-admissions-process.html.

Department Demographics

	Male (PT)	Female (PT)	Total	African-American/ Black (PT)	Hispanic/ Latino (PT)	Asian/ Pacific Islander (PT)	American Indian/ Alaska Native (PT)	Caucasian/ White (PT)	Unknown	Multiethnic (PT)	ADA (PT)	Int'l (PT)
Students	3 (0)	39 (1)	43	3 (0)	2 (0)	1 (0)	0 (0)	36 (1)	0 (0)	0 (0)	0 (0)	0 (0)

Financial Information/Assistance

Tuition: For information on tuition costs, visit http://www.uc.edu/bursar/fees.html. Tuition is subject to change.

Doctoral:
State residents: $14,182 per academic year.
State residents: $710 per credit hour.
Nonstate residents: $25,696 per academic year.
Nonstate residents: $1,285 per credit hour.

Master's:
State residents: $14,182 per academic year.
State residents: $710 per credit hour.
Nonstate residents: $25,696 per academic year.
Nonstate residents: $1,285 per credit hour.

Financial Assistance:

	Teaching Assistantship (% Receiving)	Teaching Assistantship Tuition Remission	Research Assistantship (% Receiving)	Research Assistantship Tuition Remission	Fellowship (% Receiving)	Fellowship Tuition Remission
First-Year Student	NA (NA)	NA	$11,115 (60)	Full	$15,000 (40)	NA
Advanced Student	$11,115 (10)	Full	$11,115 (40)	Full	$15,000 (30)	Full

For additional information on financial assistance, visit http://cech.uc.edu/programs/school_psychology/future_students/financial_assistance_information.html.

Employment of Department Graduates

Master's:
Employed in a professional position in a school system: 12
Total: 12

Doctoral:
Employed in an academic position at a university: 1
Employed in a professional position in a school system: 2
Total: 3

Additional Information

Housing and Day Care: No on-campus housing is available. On-campus day care facilities are available. See the following website for more information: http://www.uc.edu/elc.html.

Information for Students With Physical Disabilities: See the following website: http://www.uc.edu/aess/disability.html.

Special Facilities or Resources: The program has access to excellent field-based training and research partnerships through collaborative relationships with several local school districts, educational agencies, and Head Start programs. Research facilities include statistical consultation for students, a college evaluation services center, and support for student research through college-sponsored mentoring grants.

Application Information: *Fee:* $45. *Online application:* http://grad.uc.edu/admissions.html.

Cleveland State University
Counseling Psychology
Education and Human Services
2121 Euclid Avenue
Cleveland, OH 44115
Telephone: (216) 687-4697
Director, Office of Doctoral Studies: Dr. Graham Stead
Web: http://www.csuohio.edu/cehs/doc/specializations-counseling-psychology

E-mail: d.schultheiss@csuohio.edu

Orientation, Objectives, and Emphasis of Department
The Counseling Psychology program at Cleveland State University is based on a scientist–practitioner model of training and practice. The program emphasizes counseling psychology as a scientific discipline based in the tradition of studying individual differences and the social and cultural context of human behavior. It provides extensive study of multicultural aspects of human behavior with particular emphasis on the impact of urban environments. Its mission is to educate counseling psychologists with strong professional identification with the discipline and with the knowledge, skills, and attitudes to work effectively with diverse populations. As a university committed to serving a diverse urban population, the program's mission is consistent with the mission of Cleveland State University and the College of Education and Human Services which is to prepare professionals who reflect our commitment to educational excellence across the life-span through teaching, research, and service focused on leadership, social justice, and partnerships in addressing contemporary urban needs.

Programs and Degrees Offered

Program	Degree	Application Deadline	Applications Received	Accepted	New Admits Enrolled (PT)	Total Enrolled (PT)	Degrees Awarded in 2014–2015	Median Years to Complete Degree	Dismissed/ Withdrew
Counseling Psychology	PhD	January 15 (Fall)	22	4	2 (0)	27 (0)	5	7	1
Clinical Mental Health Counseling	MEd	July 1 (Fall), November 15 (Spring), April 1 (Summer)	113	64	16 (8)	43 (84)	16	2.7	0
School Counseling	MEd	July 1 (Fall), November 15 (Spring), April 1 (Summer)	80	40	7 (9)	15 (44)	14	2.32	0

APA Accreditation

Counseling PhD: Student Outcome Data website: http://www.csuohio.edu/cehs/doc/student-admissions-outcomes-and-other-data.

Doctoral Degree (PhD Counseling Psychology): For those doctoral students for whom a professional internship was required in this program prior to graduation:
Total students who applied for an internship: 2
Total students who obtained an internship: 2
Total students who obtained a paid internship: 2
Total students who obtained an unpaid internship: 0
Total students who were placed in APA/CPA-accredited internships: 2
Total students placed in internships not APA/CPA-accredited, but listed with the Association of Psychology Postdoctoral and Internship Centers (APPIC): 0
Total students placed in internships conforming to guidelines of the Council of Directors of School Psychology Programs (CDSPP): 0
Total students placed in internships that were not APA/CPA-accredited, APPIC or CDSSP listed: 0

Internships/Practica

Consistent with the program's focus on serving diverse urban populations, all practicum sites are situated in Northeast Ohio, and most are located in the heart of the greater Cleveland area (e.g., Guidestone, University Hospitals, Cleveland State University, Cleveland Clinic). Our sites include mental health agencies, hospitals, and college counseling centers. As such, students have a rich opportunity to gain exposure to clients from a variety of backgrounds. This also ensures that students have ample opportunity to be trained across the spectrum of functioning and a wide continuum of roles, including testing, community outreach, prevention, and intervention, including applications of empirically supported intervention procedures. For example, students placed at University Hospitals and Cleveland State University Counseling Center received training in Cognitive Behavioral Therapy. Oberlin Counseling Center also provided training in Cognitive Behavioral Therapy and Motivational Interviewing. Students participate in the APPIC match for internship.

Admissions

Entries appear in the following order: required test or GPA, minimum score (if required)/median score of students entering in 2015–2016.

Program	Degree	GRE-V	GRE-Q	GRE-Writing	GRE-Subject	Undergraduate GPA	Last 2 Years GPA	Psychology GPA	Master's GPA
Counseling Psychology	PhD	NA/153	NA/148	NA/4	Not specified	NA/3.3	Not specified	Not specified	NA/3.95
Clinical Mental Health Counseling	MEd	136/146	132/143	Not specified	Not specified	NA/NA	Not specified	Not specified	Not specified
School Counseling	MEd	133/145	136/142	Not specified	Not specified	NA/NA	Not specified	Not specified	Not specified

Admissions Requirements:

Degree	GRE	GRE-Subject	Letters of Recommendation	Research Statement	Writing Sample	CV	Interview
Master's/Specialist	Required	None	2	Required	None	None	None
Doctoral	Required	None	3	Required	None	Required	Required

Admissions Criteria:

GRE scores—high
Research experience—high
Work experience—low
Clinically related public service—medium

GPA—high
Letters of recommendation—medium
Interview—medium
Statement of goals and objectives—medium

Department Demographics

	Male (PT)	Female (PT)	Total	African-American/ Black (PT)	Hispanic/ Latino (PT)	Asian/ Pacific Islander (PT)	American Indian/ Alaska Native (PT)	Caucasian/ White (PT)	Unknown	Multiethnic (PT)	ADA (PT)	Int'l (PT)
Students	14 (26)	71 (102)	213	14 (47)	3 (6)	4 (0)	0 (0)	61 (71)	1 (3)	2 (1)	0 (0)	3 (0)

Financial Information/Assistance

Tuition: For information on tuition costs, visit http://www.csuohio.edu/treasury-services/tuition-and-fees. Tuition is subject to change. Additional fees are assessed to students beyond the costs of tuition for the following: Instructional fee, General fee, Technology fee.

Doctoral:
State residents: $13,816 per academic year.
State residents: $531 per credit hour.
Nonstate residents: $18,678 per academic year.
Nonstate residents: $718 per credit hour.

Master's:
State residents: $13,816 per academic year.
State residents: $531 per credit hour.
Nonstate residents: $25,971 per academic year.
Nonstate residents: $998 per credit hour.

Financial Assistance:

	Teaching Assistantship (% Receiving)	Teaching Assistantship Tuition Remission	Research Assistantship (% Receiving)	Research Assistantship Tuition Remission	Fellowship (% Receiving)	Fellowship Tuition Remission
First-Year Student	$5,900 (NA)	Partial	$5,900 (NA)	Partial	NA (NA)	NA
Advanced Student	$5,900 (NA)	Partial	$5,900 (NA)	Partial	NA (NA)	NA

For additional information on financial assistance, visit http://www.csuohio.edu/financial-aid/financial-aid.

Employment of Department Graduates

Doctoral:
Enrolled in a postdoctoral residency/fellowship: 2
Total: 2

Additional Information

Housing and Day Care: On-campus housing is available. See the following website for more information: https://www.csuohio.edu/residence-life/residence-life. No on-campus day care facilities are available.

Information for Students With Physical Disabilities: See the following website: https://www.csuohio.edu/disability/disability.

Special Facilities or Resources: A new college building opened in May, 2010 that houses the counseling psychology program. Offices have up-to-date computer equipment, and have adequate workspace (with laptops) for students. Faculty and students have access to current library, media, and electronic information. The University Library works closely with the college to meet the needs of the faculty and students, now housing over 40,000 volumes. The University Library provides an annual budget for the college for acquisitions. In recent years, the university has moved to significant online access to materials. SCHOLAR, the library's online Bulletin, provides information about the 2,000,000 items available in the University Library. Cleveland State University is a member of OhioLINK, the consortium of 84 public and private institutions in Ohio, sharing a central Bulletin of over 38.1 million items accessible by any member of the OhioLINK community through patron-initiated borrowing. OhioLINK also provides access to about 100 research databases. OhioLINK also provides full-text access to over 4,700 scholarly journals through its Electronic Journal Center. The Library has developed a Subject Portal for every discipline. This gives access to many selected Internet sites in areas such as Tests and Mental Measurements, and Statistics.

Application Information: *Fee:* $40. *Online application:* http://www.csuohio.edu/graduate-admissions/how-apply.

Cleveland State University

Department of Psychology
College of Sciences and Health Professions
2121 Euclid Avenue
Cleveland, OH 44115
Telephone: (216) 687-2544
Chairperson: Kathy McNamara

E-mail: k.mcnamara@csuohio.edu
Web: http://www.csuohio.edu/sciences/psychology/

Orientation, Objectives, and Emphasis of Department

Departmental faculty provide significant breadth across the entire discipline as well as considerable depth in professional and applied areas. The Clinical program emphasizes theory, principles, and application, which prepares students for more advanced training (PhD, PsyD, EdD) or for jobs requiring psychological service in clinical, community, and educational settings. Orientations include cognitive and behavioral viewpoints in assessment and intervention. The School program is NASP-accredited. A post-MA year fulfills requirements for the Psychology Specialist degree. The primary goals of the Experimental Research program are to train students to conduct scientific research in a chosen area of psychology and to prepare students for further graduate work in psychology or employment in research settings and institutions. The Consumer/Industrial Research program prepares students to apply psychological concepts and research techniques in business and institutional settings. It combines advanced quantitative research with hands-on experience involving problems and issues encountered in industrial and service organizations. The department also jointly operates a PhD program in Adult Development and Aging with the University of Akron. Upon completion of the program, students will be able to teach, carry out research, and serve as community consultants on the cognitive, motor, perceptual, and social functioning of adults throughout their lifespan.

Programs and Degrees Offered

Program	Degree	Application Deadline	Applications Received	Accepted	New Admits Enrolled (PT)	Total Enrolled (PT)	Degrees Awarded in 2014–2015	Median Years to Complete Degree	Dismissed/ Withdrew
Clinical Psychology	MA/MS	February 1 (Fall)	103	14	9	15	6	2.5	0
Adult Development and Aging	PhD	January 15 (Fall)	16	1	1				
Specialist in School Psychology	Other	January 10 (Fall)	62	24	12	31	10	3	
Experimental Research	MA/MS	February 10 (Fall)	18	11	3	10	5	3	0
Diversity Management	MA/MS	May 15 (Fall)	13	10	8	16	10	2.5	0
Industrial-Organizational Research	MA/MS	February 10 (Fall)	37	17	6	12	3	2.5	

Internships/Practica

Clinical students and third-year School Psychology students complete a 20-hour/40-hour per week internship (respectively) as part of the degree requirements. Consumer and Industrial Research program students are encouraged to apply for paid internships in business settings to earn hands-on consulting or research experience. Practica during the two-year curriculum are integrated into coursework.

Admissions

Entries appear in the following order: required test or GPA, minimum score (if required)/median score of students entering in 2015–2016.

Program	Degree	GRE-V	GRE-Q	GRE-Writing	GRE-Subject	Under-graduate GPA	Last 2 Years GPA	Psychol-ogy GPA	Master's GPA
Clinical Psychology	MA/MS	153/151	144/146	NA/NA	Not specified	3/3.4	Not specified	Not specified	Not specified
Adult Development and Aging	PhD	156/157	150/152	NA/NA	Not specified	3.25/3.8	Not specified	Not specified	Not specified
Specialist in School Psychology	Other	153/154	144/145	NA/NA	Not specified	2.75/3.3	Not specified	Not specified	Not specified
Experimental Research	MA/MS	153/153	144/145	NA/NA	Not specified	Not specified	Not specified	Not specified	Not specified
Diversity Management	MA/MS	Not specified	Not specified	Not specified	Not specified	Not specified	Not specified	Not specified	Not specified
Industrial-Organizational Research	MA/MS	Not specified	Not specified	Not specified	Not specified	Not specified	Not specified	Not specified	Not specified

Admissions Requirements:

Degree	GRE	GRE-Subject	Letters of Recom-mendation	Research Statement	Writing Sample	CV	Interview
Master's/Specialist	Required	None	2	Required	Required	Recom-mended	Required
Doctoral	Required	Optional	3	Required	Required	Recom-mended	Optional

Admissions Criteria:

GRE scores—high
Research experience—high
Work experience—medium
Clinically related public service—low
GPA—high

Letters of recommendation—high
Interview—high
Statement of goals and objectives—high
Undergraduate psychology preparation—medium

For additional information on admission requirements, visit http://www.csuohio.edu/sciences/psychology/applying-for-graduate-admissions.

Department Demographics

	Male (PT)	Female (PT)	Total	African-American/ Black (PT)	Hispanic/ Latino (PT)	Asian/ Pacific Islander (PT)	American Indian/ Alaska Native (PT)	Caucasian/ White (PT)	Unknown (PT)	Multiethnic (PT)	ADA (PT)	Int'l (PT)
Students	11 (0)	73 (0)	84	2 (0)	0 (0)	2 (0)	0 (0)	80 (0)	0 (0)	0 (0)	0 (0)	(0)

Financial Information/Assistance

Tuition: For information on tuition costs, visit http://www.csuohio.edu/treasury-services/tuition-and-fees. Higher tuition cost for this program: Diversity Management.

Doctoral:
State residents: $547 per credit hour.
Nonstate residents: $741 per credit hour.

Master's:
State residents: $547 per credit hour.
Nonstate residents: $1,031 per credit hour.

Financial Assistance:

	Teaching Assistantship (% Receiving)	Teaching Assistantship Tuition Remission	Research Assistantship (% Receiving)	Research Assistantship Tuition Remission	Fellowship (% Receiving)	Fellowship Tuition Remission
First-Year Student	$2,400 (60)	Partial	$2,400 (40)	Partial	NA (NA)	NA
Advanced Student	$15,500 (25)	Full	$15,500 (75)	Full	NA (NA)	NA

For additional information on financial assistance, visit http://www.csuohio.edu/sciences/psychology/assistantship-information-4.

Employment of Department Graduates

Master's:
Enrolled in a psychology doctoral program: 7
Employed in a professional position in a school system: 12
Employed in business or industry: 4
Employed in a hospital/medical center: 2
Total: 25

Doctoral:
Employed in an academic position at a university: 2
Total: 2

Additional Information

Housing and Day Care: No on-campus housing is available. No on-campus day care facilities are available.

Information for Students With Physical Disabilities: See the following website: http://www.csuohio.edu/disability/.

Application Information: Cleveland State University, Graduate Admissions, 2121 Euclid Avenue, Cleveland, OH 44115. *Fee:* $30.
Online application: http://www.csuohio.edu/graduate-admissions/how-apply.

Dayton, University of
Department of Counselor Education & Human Services/School Psychology
School of Education and Allied Professions
300 College Park
Dayton, OH 45469-0530
Telephone: (937) 229-3644
Chairperson: Alan Demmitt, PhD

E-mail: sdavies1@udayton.edu
Web: https://www.udayton.edu/education/departments_and_programs/edc/index.php

---

Orientation, Objectives, and Emphasis of Department
The Department of Counselor Education and Human Services is dedicated to developing human service practitioners committed to promoting individual and community growth. Our department embraces the university's Catholic and Marianist tradition and the School of Education & Health Sciences's conceptual framework: Building Learning Communities through Critical Reflection. Each program is comprehensive, integrated, and sequential. Courses reflect the most current advances in the field with integration of the most current technology applications. Each program is structured so that course content blends effectively with field experience.

Programs and Degrees Offered

Program	Degree	Application Deadline	Applications Received	Accepted	New Admits Enrolled (PT)	Total Enrolled (PT)	Degrees Awarded in 2014–2015	Median Years to Complete Degree	Dismissed/ Withdrew
School Psychology	EdS	January 10 (Fall)	54	15	9 (1)	27 (6)	11	3	0

Internships/Practica

The practicum experience provides supervised opportunities to hone skills required in professional practice. This experience also includes a complementary course individually based on setting and field experience. The culminating internship provides an opportunity to develop professionally under the guidance of professionals. For School Psychology, the paid internship is completed on a full-time basis for one year in a school district supervised by qualified school psychologists.

Admissions

Entries appear in the following order: required test or GPA, minimum score (if required)/median score of students entering in 2015–2016.

Program	Degree	GRE-V	GRE-Q	GRE-Writing	GRE-Subject	Under-graduate GPA	Last 2 Years GPA	Psychology GPA	Master's GPA
School Psychology	EdS	Not specified	Not specified	Not specified	Not specified	Not specified	Not specified	Not specified	Not specified

Admissions Requirements:

Degree	GRE	GRE-Subject	Letters of Recommendation	Research Statement	Writing Sample	CV	Interview
Master's/Specialist	Required	Optional	3	Required	None	Required	Required

Admissions Criteria:

GRE scores—medium
Research experience—medium
Work experience—medium
Clinically related public service—low
GPA—medium

Letters of recommendation—medium
Interview—high
Statement of goals and objectives—medium
Undergraduate psychology preparation—medium

For additional information on admission requirements, visit https://www.udayton.edu/education/departments_and_programs/edc/programs/school_psychology/apply.php.

Department Demographics

	Male (PT)	Female (PT)	Total	African-American/ Black (PT)	Hispanic/ Latino (PT)	Asian/ Pacific Islander (PT)	American Indian/ Alaska Native (PT)	Caucasian/ White (PT)	Unknown (PT)	Multiethnic (PT)	ADA (PT)	Int'l (PT)
Students	24 (12)	120 (51)	207	0 (0)	0 (0)	0 (0)	0 (0)	0 (0)	0 (0)	0 (0)	0 (0)	0 (0)

Financial Information/Assistance

Tuition: For information on tuition costs, visit https://www.udayton.edu/studentaccounts/tuitionfees/. Higher tuition cost for this program: Educational Specialist degree after completing Master's is $722 per credit hour. Tuition is subject to change. Additional fees are assessed to students beyond the costs of tuition for the following: $25 University Fee.

Master's:
State residents: $603 per credit hour.
Nonstate residents: $600 per credit hour.

Financial Assistance:

	Teaching Assistantship (% Receiving)	Teaching Assistantship Tuition Remission	Research Assistantship (% Receiving)	Research Assistantship Tuition Remission	Fellowship (% Receiving)	Fellowship Tuition Remission
First-Year Student	NA (NA)	NA	$8,900 (NA)	Partial	NA (NA)	NA
Advanced Student	NA (NA)	NA	$9,100 (NA)	Partial	$22,000 (NA)	NA

For additional information on financial assistance, visit http://www.udayton.edu/flyersfirst/financialaid/grad/.

Employment of Department Graduates

No information provided.

Additional Information

Housing and Day Care: On-campus housing is available. See the following website for more information: https://www.udayton.edu/studev/housing/newstudents/graduate-and-law/index.php. On-campus day care facilities are available. See the following website for more information: https://www.udayton.edu/education/offices_and_centers/cel/index.php.

Information for Students With Physical Disabilities: See the following website: http://www.udayton.edu/ltc/learningresources/.

Special Facilities or Resources: We are pleased to have new facilities housing graduate classes. Fitz Hall's newly renovated 6th floor welcomes graduate students in the School of Education and Health Sciences. This beautiful facility has a wide range of interactive classroom space as well as a curriculum materials center for students.

Application Information: University of Dayton, Graduate Admissions, 300 College Park, Dayton, OH 45469-1670. *Fee:* $0. *Online application:* https://apex.udayton.edu/admission/grad/.

Dayton, University of
Department of Psychology
300 College Park Avenue
Dayton, OH 45469-1430
Telephone: (937) 229-2713
Chairperson: Keri Brown Kirschman

E-mail: kkirschman1@udayton.edu
Web: http://www.udayton.edu/artssciences/psychology/index.php

---

Orientation, Objectives, and Emphasis of Department
The Department of Psychology offers graduate programs leading to the MA degree in clinical and general psychology. Emphasis is placed on integrating theory and literature with appropriate applied experience and on competence in the development of relevant research. This is the product of individual supervision and a low student-to-faculty ratio. The aim of the department is to prepare the student for doctoral training or employment at the MA level in an applied/community setting, in research, or in teaching. A recent survey has shown that over 60% of our MA graduates who applied for doctoral programs in the last 6 years were accepted. Also, 98% of our MA graduates seeking employment have found jobs in psychologically related areas.

Programs and Degrees Offered

Program	Degree	Application Deadline	Applications Received	Accepted	New Admits Enrolled (PT)	Total Enrolled (PT)	Degrees Awarded in 2014–2015	Median Years to Complete Degree	Dismissed/ Withdrew
Clinical Psychology	MA/MS	March 1 (Fall)	62	6	6 (0)	13 (0)	7	2	0
General Psychology	MA/MS	March 1 (Fall)	25	4	2 (0)	5 (0)	1	3	0

Internships/Practica

A limited number of paid traineeship placements at local mental health agencies and two childrens medical centers are available for both first and second year clinical students. These traineeships satisfy the program's practicum requirements and include partial tuition remission.

Admissions

Entries appear in the following order: required test or GPA, minimum score (if required)/median score of students entering in 2015–2016.

Program	Degree	GRE-V	GRE-Q	GRE-Writing	GRE-Subject	Under-graduate GPA	Last 2 Years GPA	Psychol-ogy GPA	Master's GPA
Clinical Psychology	MA/MS	NA/NA	NA/NA	NA/NA	Not specified	NA/NA	Not specified	NA/NA	Not specified
General Psychology	MA/MS	NA/NA	NA/NA	NA/NA	Not specified	NA/NA	Not specified	NA/NA	Not specified

Admissions Requirements:

Degree	GRE	GRE-Subject	Letters of Recom-mendation	Research Statement	Writing Sample	CV	Interview
Master's/Specialist	Required	Recom-mended	3	Required	Optional	Recom-mended	Optional

Admissions Criteria:

GRE scores—high
Research experience—high
Work experience—medium
Clinically related public service—low

GPA—high
Letters of recommendation—high
Statement of goals and objectives—high
Undergraduate psychology preparation—medium

Department Demographics

	Male (PT)	Female (PT)	Total	African-American/ Black (PT)	Hispanic/ Latino (PT)	Asian/ Pacific Islander (PT)	American Indian/ Alaska Native (PT)	Caucasian/ White (PT)	Unknown	Multiethnic (PT)	ADA (PT)	Int'l (PT)
Students	4 (0)	14 (0)	18	1 (0)	1 (0)	0 (0)	0 (0)	16 (0)	0 (0)	0 (0)	0 (0)	0 (0)

Financial Information/Assistance

Tuition: For information on tuition costs, visit https://www.udayton.edu/studentaccounts/tuitionfees/index.php. Tuition is subject to change.

Master's:
State residents: $873 per credit hour.
Nonstate residents: $873 per credit hour.

Financial Assistance:

	Teaching Assistantship (% Receiving)	Teaching Assistantship Tuition Remission	Research Assistantship (% Receiving)	Research Assistantship Tuition Remission	Fellowship (% Receiving)	Fellowship Tuition Remission
First-Year Student	$11,120 (NA)	Full	$11,120 (NA)	Full	NA (NA)	NA
Advanced Student	$11,120 (NA)	Full	$11,120 (NA)	Full	NA (NA)	NA

For additional information on financial assistance, visit http://www.udayton.edu/flyersfirst/financialaid/grad/index.php.

Employment of Department Graduates

Master's:
Enrolled in a psychology doctoral program: 4
Employed in a community mental health/counseling center: 1
Employed in a hospital/medical center: 3
Other employment position: 1
Do not know: 1
Total: 10

Additional Information

Housing and Day Care: On-campus housing is available. See the following website for more information: https://www.udayton.edu/studev/housing/residential-facilities/graduate-and-law/index.php. On-campus day care facilities are available. See the following website for more information: https://www.udayton.edu/education/offices_and_centers/cel/index.php.

Information for Students With Physical Disabilities: See the following website: https://www.udayton.edu/ltc/learningresources/disability/index.php.

Special Facilities or Resources: Laboratory and computer facilities are available to support student and faculty research. These include computer-based facilities for research in cognitive science, human factors, social psychology, and clinical psychology. In addition, research opportunities are available through faculty collaborations with the University's Research Institute, the Fitz Center for Leadership in Community, local shelters for homeless individuals, children's hospitals, and community mental health agencies.

Application Information: *Fee:* $0. *Online application:* https://apex.udayton.edu/admission/grad/.

Kent State University

Department of Psychological Sciences
College of Arts and Sciences
P.O. Box 5190
Kent, OH 44242-0001
Telephone: (330) 672-2166
Chairperson: Maria Zaragoza, PhD

E-mail: gradpsyc@kent.edu
Web: http://www.kent.edu/psychology

Orientation, Objectives, and Emphasis of Department

The programs' objectives are to train those who can contribute through research, teaching, service, innovation, and administration. Graduate students in clinical psychology may specialize in adult psychopathology, assessment, child clinical and adolescent, neuropsychology, or health. Graduate students in experimental psychology may specialize in behavioral neuroscience, cognitive, developmental, health, or social psychology. Students in both programs may obtain a minor in quantitative methods. A common program of basic core courses is required of all students. Training facilities and laboratories are freely available to graduate students.

Programs and Degrees Offered

Program	Degree	Application Deadline	Applications Received	Accepted	New Admits Enrolled (PT)	Total Enrolled (PT)	Degrees Awarded in 2014–2015	Median Years to Complete Degree	Dismissed/Withdrew
Clinical Psychology	PhD	December 15 (Fall)	373	8	8 (0)	52 (0)	12	6	0
Psychological Science	PhD	December 15 (Fall)	109	4	4 (0)	33 (0)	6	5.8	1

APA Accreditation

Clinical PhD: Student Outcome Data website: http://www.kent.edu/node/student-admissions-outcomes-and-other-data.

Doctoral Degree (PhD Clinical Psychology): For those doctoral students for whom a professional internship was required in this program prior to graduation:
Total students who applied for an internship: 13
Total students who obtained an internship: 13

Total students who obtained a paid internship: 13
Total students who obtained an unpaid internship: 0
Total students who were placed in APA/CPA-accredited internships: 13
Total students placed in internships not APA/CPA-accredited, but listed with the Association of Psychology Postdoctoral and Internship Centers (APPIC): 0
Total students placed in internships conforming to guidelines of the Council of Directors of School Psychology Programs (CDSPP): 0
Total students placed in internships that were not APA/CPA-accredited, APPIC or CDSSP listed: 0

Internships/Practica

For Clinical Psychology PhD students, two semesters of didactic practica and five semesters of clinical practica in the Department's Psychological Clinic are required. Clinical students also must complete a minimum of 1,000 hours of supervised clinical experience at local placement sites and a 2,000 hour supervised clinical internship in an internship program accredited by the American Psychological Association (these are competitive internships).

Admissions

Entries appear in the following order: required test or GPA, minimum score (if required)/median score of students entering in 2015–2016.

Program	Degree	GRE-V	GRE-Q	GRE-Writing	GRE-Subject	Under-graduate GPA	Last 2 Years GPA	Psychology GPA	Master's GPA
Clinical Psychology	PhD	NA/159	NA/156	Not specified	Not specified	3/3.76	3/NA	Not specified	Not specified
Psychological Science	PhD	NA/155	NA/153	Not specified	Not specified	3/3.6	3/NA	Not specified	Not specified

Admissions Requirements:

Degree	GRE	GRE-Subject	Letters of Recom-mendation	Research Statement	Writing Sample	CV	Interview
Doctoral	Required	Optional	3	Required	Recom-mended	Recom-mended	Required

Admissions Criteria:

GRE scores—high
Research experience—high
Work experience—low
Clinically related public service—low
GPA—high

Letters of recommendation—high
Interview—high
Statement of goals and objectives—high
Undergraduate psychology preparation—medium

For additional information on admission requirements, visit https://www.kent.edu/psychology/how-apply.

Department Demographics

	Male (PT)	Female (PT)	Total	African-American/ Black (PT)	Hispanic/ Latino (PT)	Asian/ Pacific Islander (PT)	American Indian/ Alaska Native (PT)	Caucasian/ White (PT)	Unknown	Multiethnic (PT)	ADA (PT)	Int'l (PT)
Students	26 (0)	68 (0)	94	6 (0)	3 (0)	2 (0)	0 (0)	78 (0)	0 (0)	0 (0)		5 (0)

Financial Information/Assistance

Tuition: For information on tuition costs, visit http://www.kent.edu/tuition. Tuition is subject to change.

Doctoral:
State residents: $495 per credit hour.
Nonstate residents: $837 per credit hour.

Financial Assistance:

	Teaching Assistantship (% Receiving)	Teaching Assistantship Tuition Remission	Research Assistantship (% Receiving)	Research Assistantship Tuition Remission	Fellowship (% Receiving)	Fellowship Tuition Remission
First-Year Student	$15,429 (NA)	Full	$15,429 (NA)	Full	NA (NA)	NA
Advanced Student	$15,429 (NA)	Full	$15,429 (NA)	Full	NA (NA)	NA

For additional information on financial assistance, visit https://www.kent.edu/graduatestudies/aid-assistantships.

Employment of Department Graduates

Doctoral:
Enrolled in a postdoctoral residency/fellowship: 12
Employed in an academic position at a university: 3
Employed in other positions at a higher education institution: 1
Employed in business or industry: 1
Total: 17

Additional Information

Housing and Day Care: On-campus housing is available. See the following website for more information: https://www.kent.edu/housing. On-campus day care facilities are available. See the following website for more information: https://www.kent.edu/ehhs/centers/cdc.

Information for Students With Physical Disabilities: See the following website: http://www.kent.edu/sas/.

Special Facilities or Resources: The Department has well-equipped laboratories available for human and animal research. Research opportunities also are available in various mental health and hospital settings in the area. Clinical training opportunities are available in the Psychological Clinic, which is staffed by clinical faculty and graduate students. The Applied Psychology Center supports research focused on psychological problems of social significance.

Application Information: Division of Graduate Studies, Cartwright Hall, 650 Hilltop Drive, Kent State University, Kent, OH 44242. *Fee:* $45. *Online application:* http://www.kent.edu/admissions/apply/graduate/.

Kent State University
School Psychology Program
College of Education, Health, and Human Services
Lifespan Development and Educational Sciences, 405 White Hall
Kent, OH 44242
Telephone: (330) 672-2294
School Director: Dr. Mary Dellman-Jenkins

E-mail: fsansost@kent.edu
Web: https://www.kent.edu/ehhs/ldes/spsy

Orientation, Objectives, and Emphasis of Department
The KSU school psychology program embraces a preventive mental health model as a context for the study of psychological and educational principles that influence the adjustment of individuals and systems. A commitment to using the science of psychology to promote human welfare is emphasized. In addition, recognizing the pluralistic nature of our society, the program is committed to fostering in its students sensitivity to, appreciation for, and understanding of all individual differences. The program emphasizes the provision of services to individual schools and children, in addition to attaining a functional understanding of systems-consultation and the ability to promote and implement primary and secondary prevention programs to optimize adjustment. The KSU doctoral (PhD) program in school psychology adheres to a scientist–practitioner model of training, which conceptualizes school psychologists as data-oriented problem-solvers and transmitters of psychological knowledge and skill. Since the doctoral program's emphasis is on the application of psychology in applied educational and mental health settings, students are required to demonstrate competence in the substantive content areas of psychological and educational theory and practice.

Programs and Degrees Offered

Program	Degree	Application Deadline	Applications Received	Accepted	New Admits Enrolled (PT)	Total Enrolled (PT)	Degrees Awarded in 2014–2015	Median Years to Complete Degree	Dismissed/Withdrew
School Psychology	PhD	June 1 (Fall), October 1 (Spring), December 15 (Summer)	12	6	4 (0)	8 (7)	1	10	0
School Psychology	EdS	June 1 (Fall), October 1 (Spring), December 15 (Summer)	35	25	15 (0)	47 (0)	18	3	0

APA Accreditation

School PhD: Student Outcome Data website: https://www.kent.edu/ehhs/ldes/spsy/phd-program.

Doctoral Degree (PhD School Psychology): For those doctoral students for whom a professional internship was required in this program prior to graduation:

Total students who applied for an internship: 0
Total students who obtained an internship: 0
Total students who obtained a paid internship: 0
Total students who obtained an unpaid internship: 0
Total students who were placed in APA/CPA-accredited internships: 0
Total students placed in internships not APA/CPA-accredited, but listed with the Association of Psychology Postdoctoral and Internship Centers (APPIC): 0
Total students placed in internships conforming to guidelines of the Council of Directors of School Psychology Programs (CDSPP): 0
Total students placed in internships that were not APA/CPA-accredited, APPIC or CDSSP listed: 0

Internships/Practica

Practica occur in educational and mental health settings that are chosen to provide (a) comprehensive experiences that complement previous and current preparation; (b) appropriate supervision and mentorship; and (c) applied experiences to address individual and program objectives. EdS students take 2 years of practica prior to internship. Doctoral students participate in multiple years of practica. Both the Specialist and Doctoral internships in school psychology follow the completion of all course work and practica. Specialist-level internships are full-time for an academic year, and must occur in school settings. If completed in Ohio, the internship must conform to the Ohio Internship in School Psychology Guidelines. These internships have historically been state-supported, and students receive a generous training stipend. A variety of approved settings may be appropriate for the doctoral internship, including educational settings, hospitals, and mental health centers.

Admissions

Entries appear in the following order: required test or GPA, minimum score (if required)/median score of students entering in 2015–2016.

Program	Degree	GRE-V	GRE-Q	GRE-Writing	GRE-Subject	Under-graduate GPA	Last 2 Years GPA	Psychology GPA	Master's GPA
School Psychology	PhD	NA/NA	NA/NA	NA/NA	Not specified	3/NA	Not specified	Not specified	Not specified
School Psychology	EdS	NA/NA	NA/NA	NA/NA	Not specified	3/NA	Not specified	Not specified	Not specified

Admissions Requirements:

Degree	GRE	GRE-Subject	Letters of Recommendation	Research Statement	Writing Sample	CV	Interview
Master's/Specialist	Required	None	2	Required	Required	Required	Required
Doctoral	Required	None	2	Required	Required	Required	Required

Admissions Criteria:

GRE scores—high
Research experience—high
Work experience—medium
Clinically related public service—medium
GPA—high

Letters of recommendation—high
Interview—high
Statement of goals and objectives—high
Undergraduate psychology preparation—low

For additional information on admission requirements, visit https://www.kent.edu/ehhs/ldes/spsy/application-admissions.

Department Demographics

	Male (PT)	Female (PT)	Total	African-American/ Black (PT)	Hispanic/ Latino (PT)	Asian/ Pacific Islander (PT)	American Indian/ Alaska Native (PT)	Caucasian/ White (PT)	Unknown (PT)	Multiethnic (PT)	ADA (PT)	Int'l (PT)
Students	6 (1)	49 (6)	62	3 (0)	0 (1)	0 (0)	0 (0)	52 (4)	0 (1)	0 (1)	0 (0)	0 (0)

Financial Information/Assistance

Tuition: For information on tuition costs, visit https://www.kent.edu/bursar. Tuition is subject to change. Additional fees are assessed to students beyond the costs of tuition for the following: Some courses (e.g., assessment) require minimal additional materials fees.

Doctoral:
State residents: $10,864 per academic year.
State residents: $495 per credit hour.
Nonstate residents: $18,380 per academic year.
Nonstate residents: $837 per credit hour.

Master's:
State residents: $10,864 per academic year.
State residents: $495 per credit hour.
Nonstate residents: $18,380 per academic year.
Nonstate residents: $837 per credit hour.

Financial Assistance:

	Teaching Assistantship (% Receiving)	Teaching Assistantship Tuition Remission	Research Assistantship (% Receiving)	Research Assistantship Tuition Remission	Fellowship (% Receiving)	Fellowship Tuition Remission
First-Year Student	NA (NA)	NA	$8,500 (35)	Full	$7,500 (15)	NA
Advanced Student	$12,000 (6)	Full	$12,000 (35)	Full	NA (NA)	NA

For additional information on financial assistance, visit http://www.kent.edu/financialaid.

Employment of Department Graduates

Master's:
Enrolled in a psychology doctoral program: 1
Employed in a professional position in a school system: 10
Total: 11

Doctoral:
Employed in a professional position in a school system: 1
Total: 1

Additional Information

Housing and Day Care: On-campus housing is available. See the following website for more information: http://www.kent.edu/housing. On-campus day care facilities are available. See the following website for more information: https://www.kent.edu/ehhs/centers/cdc.

Information for Students With Physical Disabilities: See the following website: http://www.kent.edu/sas.

Special Facilities or Resources: The Center for Disability Studies provides interdisciplinary research support for faculty and graduate students engaged in research on disability issues. The Child Development Center, an early childhood model laboratory school, provides opportunities for faculty and student research and practice. The Family Child Learning Center, which offers early intervention services to infants and toddlers with disabilities and their families, offers a training location for grant-funded school psychology students and for faculty research. The Bureau of Educational Research provides a source of support for students who are engaged in research activities, including data entry and analysis.

Application Information: Kent State University, Graduate Studies, Cartwright Hall, 650 Hilltop Drive, Kent, OH 44242. *Fee:* $30. *Online application:* https://www.kent.edu/admissions/apply/graduate.

Marietta College

Department of Psychology
215 Fifth Street
Marietta, OH 45750
Telephone: (740) 376-4795
Director of the Master of Arts Program in Psychology: Dr. Christopher Klein

E-mail: chris.klein@marietta.edu
Web: https://psychology.marietta.edu

Orientation, Objectives, and Emphasis of Department

The Psychology Department at Marietta College offers a 2-year Master of Arts degree in General Psychology. The program is designed to give students a strong graduate-level foundation in psychology so students may pursue further education in psychology at the PhD level or to aid students in securing employment in a field related to psychology. The orientation of the department faculty is that psychology is a science, and that psychological research and knowledge can be applied to improving people's lives. The 2-year program consists of 24 core content hours in psychology, 6 hours of applied practicum electives in an area of professional psychology (e.g., clinical internship, developmental internship, teaching of psychology), and 6 hours of supervised thesis research. The program offers the opportunity for students to pursue research interests in clinical, social, developmental, cognitive, or biological psychology. Faculty have high expectations for students' academic performance, yet are committed to mentoring students and helping students achieve their educational and professional goals. The program limits courses to 2 or 3 days per week so that students may also work or complete internship work during the rest of the week.

Programs and Degrees Offered

Program	Degree	Application Deadline	Applications Received	Accepted	New Admits Enrolled (PT)	Total Enrolled (PT)	Degrees Awarded in 2014–2015	Median Years to Complete Degree	Dismissed/ Withdrew
General Psychology	MA/MS	Rolling	16	10	6 (0)	13 (0)	3	2.5	2

Internships/Practica

Students select two 3-credit electives in an applied professional practicum experience. The practicum is designed to provide students with an applied experience relating to their career interests in psychology. Students choose electives from the following areas: Teaching of Psychology: designed to train students to be effective instructors of psychology; Supervised Internship: internships in the area of clinical, developmental, or applied psychology (e.g., business/law); and Directed Independent Research: students pursue their own research interests under the direction of a faculty member leading to presentation/publication. The department also has opportunities for grant-funded training and placements in psychometric testing and measurement in under served populations in the region.

Admissions

Entries appear in the following order: required test or GPA, minimum score (if required)/median score of students entering in 2015–2016.

Program	Degree	GRE-V	GRE-Q	GRE-Writing	GRE-Subject	Under-graduate GPA	Last 2 Years GPA	Psychology GPA	Master's GPA
General Psychology	MA/MS	NA/NA	NA/NA	NA/NA	Not specified	3/NA	Not specified	3/NA	Not specified

Admissions Requirements:

Degree	GRE	GRE-Subject	Letters of Recommendation	Research Statement	Writing Sample	CV	Interview
Master's/Specialist	Required	None	2	Required	Optional	Optional	None

Admissions Criteria:

GRE scores—low
Research experience—medium
Work experience—low
Clinically related public service—low

GPA—medium
Letters of recommendation—high
Statement of goals and objectives—medium
Undergraduate psychology preparation—low

For additional information on admission requirements, visit https://psychology.marietta.edu/graduate/prospective-students.

Department Demographics

	Male (PT)	Female (PT)	Total	African-American/ Black (PT)	Hispanic/ Latino (PT)	Asian/ Pacific Islander (PT)	American Indian/ Alaska Native (PT)	Caucasian/ White (PT)	Unknown (PT)	Multiethnic (PT)	ADA (PT)	Int'l (PT)
Students	3 (0)	10 (0)	13	0 (0)	0 (0)	1 (0)	0 (0)	12 (0)	0 (0)	0 (0)	0 (0)	1 (0)

Financial Information/Assistance

Tuition: Tuition is subject to change.

Master's:
State residents: $750 per credit hour.
Nonstate residents: $750 per credit hour.

Financial Assistance:

	Teaching Assistantship (% Receiving)	Teaching Assistantship Tuition Remission	Research Assistantship (% Receiving)	Research Assistantship Tuition Remission	Fellowship (% Receiving)	Fellowship Tuition Remission
First-Year Student	$4,000 (25)	NA	$4,000 (25)	NA	NA (NA)	NA
Advanced Student	$4,000 (25)	NA	$4,000 (25)	NA	NA (NA)	NA

Employment of Department Graduates

Master's:
Enrolled in a psychology doctoral program: 2
Enrolled in another graduate/professional program: 1
Other employment position: 1
Do not know: 1
Total: 5

Additional Information

Housing and Day Care: On-campus housing is available. No on-campus day care facilities are available.

Information for Students With Physical Disabilities: See the following website: http://www.marietta.edu/Academics/resources/ARC/disability.html.

Special Facilities or Resources: The Psychology Department at Marietta College has a newly remodeled human research laboratory equipped with research cubicles, video equipment, one-way observational windows, and specialized cognitive and physiological equipment and software, including BioPac, EPrime, Inquisit, and Qualtrics. Students may apply within the college for graduate research and conference travel funds. Other facilities include a graduate seminar room, graduate student office, and student lounge.

Application Information: Dr. Christopher Klein, Director of the MAP Program, Department of Psychology, Marietta College, 215 Fifth Street, Marietta, OH 45750. *Fee:* $25.

Miami University of Ohio
Department of Psychology
90 North Patterson Avenue
Oxford, OH 45056
Telephone: (513) 529-2400
Chairperson: Cecilia Shore

E-mail: WolfeCR@miamioh.edu
Web: http://www.miamioh.edu/psychology

Orientation, Objectives, and Emphasis of Department
The goal of the department is to provide an environment in which students thrive intellectually. We strive for a balance between enough structure to gauge student progress and provide grounding in the breadth of psychology and enough freedom for students to design programs optimal to their own professional goals. The department provides training and experience in research, teaching, and application of psychology. The department offers basic and applied research orientations in all programs. The clinical program emphasizes a theory-research-practicum combination, so that graduates will be able to function in a variety of academic and service settings. The objective of the department is to produce skilled, informed, and enthusiastic psychologists, capable of contributing to their field in a variety of ways.

Programs and Degrees Offered

Program	Degree	Application Deadline	Applications Received	Accepted	New Admits Enrolled (PT)	Total Enrolled (PT)	Degrees Awarded in 2014–2015	Median Years to Complete Degree	Dismissed/Withdrew
Clinical Psychology	PhD	December 1 (Fall)	146	6	6 (0)	39 (0)	6	6.33	0
Brain/Cognitive/Developmental	PhD	January 1 (Fall)	31	6	5 (0)	14 (0)	3	5	1
Social Psychology	PhD	December 1 (Fall)	28	7	1 (0)	11 (0)	2	5	1

APA Accreditation
Clinical PhD: Student Outcome Data website: http://miamioh.edu/cas/academics/departments/psychology/about/outcomes/.

Doctoral Degree (PhD Clinical Psychology): For those doctoral students for whom a professional internship was required in this program prior to graduation:
Total students who applied for an internship: 9
Total students who obtained an internship: 9
Total students who obtained a paid internship: 9
Total students who obtained an unpaid internship: 0
Total students who were placed in APA/CPA-accredited internships: 9
Total students placed in internships not APA/CPA-accredited, but listed with the Association of Psychology Postdoctoral and Internship Centers (APPIC): 0
Total students placed in internships conforming to guidelines of the Council of Directors of School Psychology Programs (CDSPP): 0
Total students placed in internships that were not APA/CPA-accredited, APPIC or CDSSP listed: 0

Internships/Practica

There are opportunities for students to engage in practica and internships as well as conduct applied research. Traineeships for advanced clinical students are available in a wide range of settings including community mental health centers, hospitals, and school systems.

Admissions

Entries appear in the following order: required test or GPA, minimum score (if required)/median score of students entering in 2015–2016.

Program	Degree	GRE-V	GRE-Q	GRE-Writing	GRE-Subject	Under-graduate GPA	Last 2 Years GPA	Psychology GPA	Master's GPA
Clinical Psychology	PhD	Not specified	Not specified	Not specified	Not specified	Not specified	Not specified	Not specified	Not specified
Brain/Cognitive/Developmental	PhD	140/152	136/153	3/3.83	Not specified	2.85/3.51	Not specified	Not specified	Not specified
Social Psychology	PhD	142/157	135/154	2/4.5	Not specified	2.7/3.6	Not specified	Not specified	Not specified

Admissions Requirements:

Degree	GRE	GRE-Subject	Letters of Recommendation	Research Statement	Writing Sample	CV	Interview
Doctoral	Required	Optional	3	Required	Optional	Required	Required

Please note if these criteria vary for different programs: Clinical and Social programs employ an interview; Brain/Cognitive/Developmental area offers an "Open House/Visit" day for students offered admission.

Admissions Criteria:

GRE scores—medium
Research experience—high
Work experience—low
Clinically related public service—medium
GPA—high

Letters of recommendation—high
Interview—high
Statement of goals and objectives—high
Undergraduate psychology preparation—medium

For additional information on admission requirements, visit http://miamioh.edu/cas/academics/departments/psychology/admission/graduate-admission/.

Department Demographics

	Male (PT)	Female (PT)	Total	African-American/ Black (PT)	Hispanic/ Latino (PT)	Asian/ Pacific Islander (PT)	American Indian/ Alaska Native (PT)	Caucasian/ White (PT)	Unknown	Multiethnic (PT)	ADA (PT)	Int'l (PT)
Students	17 (0)	47 (0)	64	1 (0)	5 (0)	8 (0)	1 (0)	47 (0)	0 (0)	2 (0)	0 (0)	7 (0)

Financial Information/Assistance

Tuition: For information on tuition costs, visit http://miamioh.edu/onestop/your-money/tuition-fees/index.html. Tuition is subject to change.

Doctoral:
State residents: $12,888 per academic year.
State residents: $537 per credit hour.
Nonstate residents: $29,022 per academic year.
Nonstate residents: $1,209 per credit hour.

Financial Assistance:

	Teaching Assistantship (% Receiving)	Teaching Assistantship Tuition Remission	Research Assistantship (% Receiving)	Research Assistantship Tuition Remission	Fellowship (% Receiving)	Fellowship Tuition Remission
First-Year Student	$22,265 (NA)	Full	$16,581 (NA)	Full	$22,265 (NA)	Full
Advanced Student	$22,265 (NA)	Full	$22,265 (NA)	Full	$22,265 (NA)	Full

For additional information on financial assistance, visit http://miamioh.edu/onestop/grad-students/index.html.

Employment of Department Graduates

Doctoral:
Enrolled in a postdoctoral residency/fellowship: 1
Employed in an academic position at a university: 4
Employed in a professional position in a school system: 2
Employed in business or industry: 1
Employed in government agency: 1
Employed in a hospital/medical center: 2
Total: 11

Additional Information

Housing and Day Care: On-campus housing is available. See the following website for more information: http://www.hdg.muohio.edu/Housing/. On-campus day care facilities are available. See the following website for more information: http://www.miniuniversity.net/Miami-University.asp.

Information for Students With Physical Disabilities: See the following website: http://miamioh.edu/student-life/sds/.

Special Facilities or Resources: The department has laboratories dedicated to the study of social cognition, group processes and social interaction, as well as cognitive processes including higher-order cognition, decision-making, perception, spatial cognition, and motor control. One laboratory uses virtual environments to study spatial cognition and posture. Two biological psychology laboratories offer advanced facilities for neurological recording, drug delivery, and pharmacological and histological analyses. The Center for Human Psychophysiology offers access to EEG and other psychophysiological measurement tools. The Center for Psychological Inquiry facilitates undergraduate research. The Psychology Clinic includes group and child therapy rooms, individual assessment and therapy rooms, a test library, conference room, and offices for the clinic director and a full-time secretary. Clinical services are offered in a training or research context to university students and the Oxford community, including a school-based mental health program. Research with children is facilitated by a good relationship with local public school systems and childcare facilities. Access to clinical populations is available through the Psychology Clinic and through cooperative arrangements with nearby mental health centers. Several faculty are engaged in community action projects related to mental health needs in local communities.

Application Information: The Graduate School, 102 Roudebush, Miami University, Oxford, OH 45056. *Fee:* $50. *Online application:* http://miamioh.edu/graduate-school/admission/.

Ohio State University (2015 data)
Department of Educational Services
College of Education and Human Ecology
100A PAES Building, 305 West 17th Avenue
Columbus, OH 43210
Telephone: (614) 292-5909
Director: Eric Anderman

E-mail: joseph.21@osu.edu
Web: http://ehe.osu.edu/educational-studies/school-psychology/

Orientation, Objectives, and Emphasis of Department
The foundation for the School Psychology program at The Ohio State University is based on socio-cultural theories of psychological and educational practices with youth. Socio-cultural theories encompass social cognition and social behavioral principles of under-

standing and working with a diversity of youth in America's schools. Children do not experience life in a vacuum, but do so within socio-cultural contexts such as school, home, and community. The focus of the School Psychology program is service delivery across many different settings with a particular emphasis on children in urban settings. Within this framework, students are trained as scientist–practitioners who function as data-based decision makers and collaborative problem solvers. The program has a commitment to diversity at the research, training, and service level.

Programs and Degrees Offered

Program	Degree	Application Deadline	Applications Received	Accepted	New Admits Enrolled (PT)	Total Enrolled (PT)	Degrees Awarded in 2014–2015	Median Years to Complete Degree	Dismissed/ Withdrew
School Psychology	EdS	December 1 (Fall)	45	21	10	40 (0)	16	3	0
School Psychology	PhD	December 1 (Fall)	15	5	2	15	5	5	0

Doctoral Degree (PhD School Psychology): For those doctoral students for whom a professional internship was required in this program prior to graduation:
Total students who applied for an internship: 3
Total students who obtained an internship: 3
Total students who obtained a paid internship: 3
Total students who obtained an unpaid internship: 0
Total students who were placed in APA/CPA-accredited internships: 0
Total students placed in internships not APA/CPA-accredited, but listed with the Association of Psychology Postdoctoral and Internship Centers (APPIC): 0
Total students placed in internships conforming to guidelines of the Council of Directors of School Psychology Programs (CDSPP): 0
Total students placed in internships that were not APA/CPA-accredited, APPIC or CDSSP listed: 3

Internships/Practica
Specialist students are engaged in practica during their three years of study. All students gain experience in an urban school district as well as either a rural or suburban setting. Students are involved in a 9-month school-based internship in the Central Ohio area. Internships are paid.

Admissions
Entries appear in the following order: required test or GPA, minimum score (if required)/median score of students entering in 2015–2016.

Program	Degree	GRE-V	GRE-Q	GRE-Writing	GRE-Subject	Under-graduate GPA	Last 2 Years GPA	Psychol-ogy GPA	Master's GPA
School Psychology	EdS	151/NA	147/NA	Not specified	Not specified	3/NA	Not specified	Not specified	Not specified
School Psychology	PhD	151/NA	147/NA	Not specified	Not specified	3/NA	Not specified	Not specified	Not specified

Admissions Requirements:

Degree	GRE	GRE-Subject	Letters of Recommendation	Research Statement	Writing Sample	CV	Interview
Master's/Specialist	Required	None	3	Required	Optional	Required	Required
Doctoral	Required	None	3	Required	Optional	Required	Required

Admissions Criteria:
GRE scores—high
Research experience—high
Work experience—medium
Clinically related public service—medium

GPA—high
Letters of recommendation—high
Interview—high
Statement of goals and objectives—high

For additional information on admission requirements, visit http://ehe.osu.edu/educational-studies/prospective-students/application-faqs/.

Department Demographics

	Male (PT)	Female (PT)	Total	African-American/ Black (PT)	Hispanic/ Latino (PT)	Asian/ Pacific Islander (PT)	American Indian/ Alaska Native (PT)	Caucasian/ White (PT)	Unknown (PT)	Multiethnic (PT)	ADA (PT)	Int'l (PT)
Students	2 (0)	36 (0)	38	2 (0)	1 (0)	1 (0)	0 (0)	34 (0)	0 (0)	0 (0)	0 (0)	2 (0)

Financial Information/Assistance

Tuition: For information on tuition costs, visit http://registrar.osu.edu/feetables/mainfeetables.asp. Tuition is subject to change.

Doctoral:
State residents: $444 per credit hour.
Nonstate residents: $996 per credit hour.

Master's:
State residents: $444 per credit hour.
Nonstate residents: $996 per credit hour.

Financial Assistance:

	Teaching Assistantship (% Receiving)	Teaching Assistantship Tuition Remission	Research Assistantship (% Receiving)	Research Assistantship Tuition Remission	Fellowship (% Receiving)	Fellowship Tuition Remission
First-Year Student	NA (NA)	NA	NA (NA)	NA	$10,000 (NA)	Full
Advanced Student	NA (NA)	NA	NA (NA)	NA	$10,000 (NA)	Full

For additional information on financial assistance, visit http://ehe.osu.edu/educational-studies/students/funding-opportunities/.

Employment of Department Graduates

Master's:
Employed in academic position at a 2-year/4-year college: 3
Employed in a professional position in a school system: 21
Total: 24

Additional Information

Housing and Day Care: On-campus housing is available. On-campus day care facilities are available. See the following website for more information: http://hr.osu.edu/childcare/.

Information for Students With Physical Disabilities: See the following website: http://www.ods.ohio-state.edu/.

Application Information: Fee: $40. Online application: http://gpadmissions.osu.edu.

Ohio State University
Department of Psychology
College of Social and Behavioral Sciences
225 Psychology Building, 1835 Neil Avenue
Columbus, OH 43210
Telephone: (614) 292-4112
Chairperson: John Bruno, PhD

E-mail: jones.3308@osu.edu
Web: http://www.psy.ohio-state.edu

Orientation, Objectives, and Emphasis of Department

The department is comprehensive in nature, with PhD programs in nearly all the major fields of study in psychology. The programs all strive to educate psychological scientists, and there is consequently a strong emphasis on research training in the doctoral programs, even in the applied areas. Our objective is to prepare theoretically sophisticated psychologists who leave us with effective skills to build upon in their later careers and with the ability to grow as psychology develops as a science and profession.

Programs and Degrees Offered

Program	Degree	Application Deadline	Applications Received	Accepted	New Admits Enrolled (PT)	Total Enrolled (PT)	Degrees Awarded in 2014–2015	Median Years to Complete Degree	Dismissed/ Withdrew
Clinical Psychology	PhD	December 1 (Fall)	234	9	7 (0)	53 (0)	15	7.85	0
Cognitive Psychology	PhD	December 1 (Fall)	42	9	6 (0)	22 (0)	4	7	3
Developmental Psychology	PhD	December 1 (Fall)	20	6	3 (0)	13 (0)	1	6	1
Intellectual and Developmental Disabilities	PhD	December 1 (Fall)	23	5	4 (0)	13 (0)	3	6.6	0
Behavioral Neuroscience	PhD	December 1 (Fall)	18	1	1 (0)	4 (0)	3	7	0
Quantitative Psychology	PhD	December 1 (Fall)	27	8	4 (0)	16 (0)	4	7.5	1
Social Psychology	PhD	December 1 (Fall)	89	11	4 (0)	25 (0)	9	7.5	

APA Accreditation

Clinical PhD: Student Outcome Data website: http://www.psy.ohio-state.edu/programs/clinical/admissions-outcomes.php.

Doctoral Degree (PhD Clinical Psychology): For those doctoral students for whom a professional internship was required in this program prior to graduation:

Total students who applied for an internship: 7
Total students who obtained an internship: 7
Total students who obtained a paid internship: 7
Total students who obtained an unpaid internship: 0
Total students who were placed in APA/CPA-accredited internships: 7
Total students placed in internships not APA/CPA-accredited, but listed with the Association of Psychology Postdoctoral and Internship Centers (APPIC): 0
Total students placed in internships conforming to guidelines of the Council of Directors of School Psychology Programs (CDSPP): 0
Total students placed in internships that were not APA/CPA-accredited, APPIC or CDSSP listed: 0

Internships/Practica

For students in the clinical training program, initial practica are conducted at the in-house Psychological Services Center (PSC), supervised by core clinical faculty. Following 1 year of in-house training, students progress to advanced clinical experiences at program-approved externship sites throughout the community, where they gain clinical assessment and treatment experience in a variety of settings consistent with the program's three training tracks: Adult Psychopathology, Health Psychology, and Child-Clinical Psychology. Advanced students also have the opportunity to continue treating clients in the in-house PSC while receiving supervision from adjunct faculty in the community. Additionally, all students must complete a 1-year full-time internship in clinical psychology prior to the awarding of the doctoral degree.

Admissions

Entries appear in the following order: required test or GPA, minimum score (if required)/median score of students entering in 2015–2016.

Program	Degree	GRE-V	GRE-Q	GRE-Writing	GRE-Subject	Under-graduate GPA	Last 2 Years GPA	Psychol-ogy GPA	Master's GPA
Clinical Psychology	PhD	NA/NA	NA/NA	NA/NA	Not specified	3/3.81	Not specified	Not specified	Not specified

Admissions (con't.)

Program	Degree	GRE-V	GRE-Q	GRE-Writing	GRE-Subject	Under-graduate GPA	Last 2 Years GPA	Psychology GPA	Master's GPA
Cognitive Psychology	PhD	NA/NA	NA/NA	NA/NA	Not specified	3/3.88	Not specified	Not specified	Not specified
Developmental Psychology	PhD	NA/NA	NA/NA	NA/NA	Not specified	3/3.74	Not specified	Not specified	Not specified
Intellectual and Developmental Disabilities	PhD	NA/NA	NA/NA	NA/NA	Not specified	3/3.93	Not specified	Not specified	Not specified
Behavioral Neuroscience	PhD	NA/NA	NA/NA	NA/NA	Not specified	3/3.98	Not specified	Not specified	Not specified
Quantitative Psychology	PhD	NA/NA	NA/NA	NA/NA	Not specified	3/3.88	Not specified	Not specified	Not specified
Social Psychology	PhD	NA/NA	NA/NA	NA/NA	Not specified	3/3.86	Not specified	Not specified	Not specified

Admissions Requirements:

Degree	GRE	GRE-Subject	Letters of Recom-mendation	Research Statement	Writing Sample	CV	Interview
Doctoral	Required	Optional	3	Required	None	Required	Optional

Please note if these criteria vary for different programs: Clinical area ranks Interview as High.

Admissions Criteria:

GRE scores—high
Research experience—high
Work experience—low
Clinically related public service—low
GPA—high

Letters of recommendation—high
Interview—medium
Statement of goals and objectives—medium
Undergraduate psychology preparation—medium

For additional information on admission requirements, visit http://www.psy.ohio-state.edu/graduate/application.php.

Department Demographics

	Male (PT)	Female (PT)	Total	African-American/ Black (PT)	Hispanic/ Latino (PT)	Asian/ Pacific Islander (PT)	American Indian/ Alaska Native (PT)	Caucasian/ White (PT)	Unknown	Multiethnic (PT)	ADA (PT)	Int'l (PT)
Students	70 (0)	88 (0)	158	7 (0)	9 (0)	11 (0)	3 (0)	94 (0)	7 (0)	27 (0)	0 (0)	30 (0)

Financial Information/Assistance

Tuition: For information on tuition costs, visit http://registrar.osu.edu/FeeTables/MainFeeTables.asp. Tuition is subject to change. Additional fees are assessed to students beyond the costs of tuition for the following: Student Activity Fee, Student Union Fee, COTA fee, General Fee, Rec Fee.

Doctoral:
State residents: $12,424 per academic year.
State residents: $722 per credit hour.
Nonstate residents: $29,924 per academic year.
Nonstate residents: $1,939 per credit hour.

Financial Assistance:

	Teaching Assistantship (% Receiving)	Teaching Assistantship Tuition Remission	Research Assistantship (% Receiving)	Research Assistantship Tuition Remission	Fellowship (% Receiving)	Fellowship Tuition Remission
First-Year Student	$14,400 (NA)	Full	$14,400 (NA)	Full	$21,852 (NA)	Full
Advanced Student	$18,000 (NA)	Full	$18,000 (NA)	Full	$27,312 (NA)	Full

Employment of Department Graduates

Doctoral:
Enrolled in a postdoctoral residency/fellowship: 6
Employed in an academic position at a university: 6
Employed in academic position at a 2-year/4-year college: 3
Employed in other positions at a higher education institution: 2
Employed in business or industry: 5
Employed in a hospital/medical center: 6
Still seeking employment: 6
Do not know: 5
Total: 39

Additional Information

Housing and Day Care: On-campus housing is available. See the following website for more information: http://housing.osu.edu/living-on-campus/graduate-professional-and-non-traditional-housing/. On-campus day care facilities are available. See the following website for more information: https://hr.osu.edu/child-care-program/.

Information for Students With Physical Disabilities: See the following website: http://www.ods.ohio-state.edu/.

Special Facilities or Resources: There are several research labs specializing in the various programs of the OSU psychology department. In addition, since The Ohio State University is a well-known and well-established research institution, there are several non-department labs located throughout the campus that would be of possible interest to psychology graduate students.

Application Information: Graduate Program Coordinator, Department of Psychology, 1835 Neil Avenue, Room 211, Columbus, OH 43210. *Fee:* $60. *Online application:* http://gradadmissions.osu.edu/grad_apply.html.

Ohio University
Department of Psychology
Arts and Sciences
200 Porter Hall
Athens, OH 45701-2979
Telephone: (740) 593-1707
Chairperson: Bruce Carlson, PhD

E-mail: carlsonb@ohio.edu
Web: https://www.ohio.edu/cas/psychology/

Orientation, Objectives, and Emphasis of Department
The clinical doctoral program is a scientist–practitioner program, offering balanced training in research and clinical skills. Practicum training is offered in intellectual and personality assessment. Therapy sequences are offered in health psychology, individual and group psychotherapy, behavior modification, and child psychology. Traineeships are available at the university counseling center and area mental health agencies and clinics. The department has a psychology training clinic. The doctoral program in experimental psychology provides intensive training in scholarly and research activities, preparing the student for positions in academic and research settings. The department offers an applied quantitative psychology track. This track offers advanced training in quantitative methods to graduate students who are concurrently studying in one of the other experimental or clinical psychology programs. Besides the usual coursework in psychology, students who select this track receive extensive training in mathematics, computer science, and statistics.

Programs and Degrees Offered

Program	Degree	Application Deadline	Applications Received	Accepted	New Admits Enrolled (PT)	Total Enrolled (PT)	Degrees Awarded in 2014–2015	Median Years to Complete Degree	Dismissed/Withdrew
Clinical Psychology	PhD	December 1 (Fall)	122	5	5	48	9	7	0
Industrial/ Organizational Psychology	PhD	December 1 (Fall)	20	2	2	9 (0)	2	6	0
Social Psychology	PhD	December 1 (Fall)	26	2	2	12	3	7.3	0
Cognitive Psychology	PhD	December 1 (Fall)	6	1	1	5	0		0
Health Psychology	PhD	December 1 (Fall)	3	0	0	7	0		0
Applied Quantitative Psychology	PhD	December 1 (Fall)	1	0	0	5	0		0

APA Accreditation

Clinical PhD: Student Outcome Data website: https://www.ohio.edu/cas/psychology/grad/clinical-psych/admissions-outcomes-data.cfm.

Doctoral Degree (PhD Clinical Psychology): For those doctoral students for whom a professional internship was required in this program prior to graduation:

Total students who applied for an internship: 6
Total students who obtained an internship: 6
Total students who obtained a paid internship: 6
Total students who obtained an unpaid internship: 0
Total students who were placed in APA/CPA-accredited internships: 6
Total students placed in internships not APA/CPA-accredited, but listed with the Association of Psychology Postdoctoral and Internship Centers (APPIC): 0
Total students placed in internships conforming to guidelines of the Council of Directors of School Psychology Programs (CDSPP): 0
Total students placed in internships that were not APA/CPA-accredited, APPIC or CDSSP listed: 0

Internships/Practica

Clinical doctoral interns are placed in APA-approved, one-year internships throughout the country. Supervised training in clinical skills is provided for all clinical students in area mental health agencies, clinics, and the departmental psychology clinic. Such training is in addition to traineeships and internships. Supervised practicum experience is provided for organizational students in area industries and organizations.

Admissions

Entries appear in the following order: required test or GPA, minimum score (if required)/median score of students entering in 2015–2016.

Program	Degree	GRE-V	GRE-Q	GRE-Writing	GRE-Subject	Under-graduate GPA	Last 2 Years GPA	Psychol-ogy GPA	Master's GPA
Clinical Psychology	PhD	NA/160	NA/156	Not specified	Not specified	NA/3.72	Not specified	Not specified	Not specified
Industrial/ Organizational Psychology	PhD	NA/155	NA/154	Not specified	Not specified	NA/3.62	Not specified	Not specified	Not specified
Social Psychology	PhD	NA/161	NA/156	Not specified	Not specified	NA/3.32	Not specified	Not specified	Not specified

Admissions *(con't.)*

Program	Degree	GRE-V	GRE-Q	GRE-Writing	GRE-Subject	Under-graduate GPA	Last 2 Years GPA	Psychol-ogy GPA	Master's GPA
Cognitive Psychology	PhD	NA/164	NA/162	Not specified	Not specified	NA/3.04	Not specified	Not specified	Not specified
Health Psychology	PhD	NA/NA	NA/NA	Not specified	Not specified	NA/NA	Not specified	Not specified	Not specified
Applied Quantitative Psychology	PhD	NA/NA	NA/NA	Not specified	Not specified	NA/NA	Not specified	Not specified	Not specified

Admissions Requirements:

Degree	GRE	GRE-Subject	Letters of Recom-mendation	Research Statement	Writing Sample	CV	Interview
Doctoral	Required	Optional	3	Required	Optional	Required	Required

Admissions Criteria:

GRE scores—high
Research experience—high
Work experience—low
Clinically related public service—medium
GPA—high

Letters of recommendation—high
Interview—medium
Statement of goals and objectives—medium
Undergraduate psychology preparation—low

Department Demographics

	Male (PT)	Female (PT)	Total	African-American/ Black (PT)	Hispanic/ Latino (PT)	Asian/ Pacific Islander (PT)	American Indian/ Alaska Native (PT)	Caucasian/ White (PT)	Unknown	Multiethnic (PT)	ADA (PT)	Int'l (PT)
Students	31 (0)	55 (0)	86	1 (0)	0 (0)	10 (0)	2 (0)	73 (0)	0 (0)	0 (0)	0 (0)	10 (0)

Financial Information/Assistance

Tuition: For information on tuition costs, visit http://www.ohio.edu/finance/bursar/tuitionfees.cfm. Tuition is subject to change. Additional fees are assessed to students beyond the costs of tuition for the following: general, technology, medical (optional), and legal (optional) fees.

Doctoral:
State residents: $9,444 per academic year.
Nonstate residents: $17,436 per academic year.

Financial Assistance:

	Teaching Assistantship (% Receiving)	Teaching Assistantship Tuition Remission	Research Assistantship (% Receiving)	Research Assistantship Tuition Remission	Fellowship (% Receiving)	Fellowship Tuition Remission
First-Year Student	$15,000 (NA)	Full	$15,000 (NA)	Full	$19,000 (NA)	Full
Advanced Student	$15,000 (NA)	Full	$15,000 (NA)	Full	$19,000 (NA)	Full

For additional information on financial assistance, visit https://www.ohio.edu/graduate/prospect/finaid.cfm.

Employment of Department Graduates

Doctoral:
Enrolled in a postdoctoral residency/fellowship: 3
Employed in an academic position at a university: 1
Employed in other positions at a higher education institution: 1
Employed in business or industry: 2
Employed in a community mental health/counseling center: 3
Employed in a hospital/medical center: 1
Other employment position: 3
Total: 14

Additional Information

Housing and Day Care: On-campus housing is available. See the following website for more information: http://www.ohio.edu/graduate/newadmit/housing.cfm. On-campus day care facilities are available. See the following website for more information: http://www.ohio.edu/childdevcenter/.

Information for Students With Physical Disabilities: See the following website: https://www.ohio.edu/uc/sas/.

Special Facilities or Resources: An addition to Porter Hall, where the Department of Psychology is housed, was completed in the Fall of 2008. This addition contains numerous research labs equipped for a wide variety of human research activities, including psychophysiology, cognitive, social, and health. The department has its own clinic, which is used to train clinical doctoral students. Two computer laboratories in the Psychology Department, one with 30 computers and one with 4 computers, are also available for student research. All computer services, except for printing, are free of charge.

Application Information: Fee: $50. *Online application:* http://www.ohio.edu/graduate/apply/index.cfm.

Toledo, University of
Department of Psychology
Languages, Literature & Social Sciences
MS#948
Toledo, OH 43606
Telephone: (419) 530-2717
Chairperson: A. John McSweeny

E-mail: john.McSweeny@utoledo.edu
Web: http://www.utoledo.edu/psychology/

Orientation, Objectives, and Emphasis of Department
Our department features an APA-accredited Clinical Psychology PhD program as well as an Experimental Psychology PhD program, offering specializations in Social Psychology, Developmental Psychology, Cognitive Psychology, and Behavioral Neuroscience and Learning. Although these programs differ in many respects, the purpose of both programs is to provide superior training in psychological research methods, statistical procedures, clinical practice, and theoretical comprehension. Our doctoral training emphasizes the inculcation of scientific attitudes with regard to (a) the gathering and evaluation of information, (b) the solving of basic and applied research problems, and in the clinical area, (c) clinical assessment and psychotherapy.

Programs and Degrees Offered

Program	Degree	Application Deadline	Applications Received	Accepted	New Admits Enrolled (PT)	Total Enrolled (PT)	Degrees Awarded in 2014–2015	Median Years to Complete Degree	Dismissed/ Withdrew
Experimental Psychology	PhD	January 15 (Fall)	25	1	1 (0)	17 (0)	2	5.5	0
Clinical Psychology	PhD	December 1 (Fall)	87	7	6 (0)	22 (0)	4	5.5	0

APA Accreditation
Clinical PhD: Student Outcome Data website: http://psychology.utoledo.edu/showpage.asp?name=statistics.

Doctoral Degree (PhD Clinical Psychology): For those doctoral students for whom a professional internship was required in this program prior to graduation:

Total students who applied for an internship: 4
Total students who obtained an internship: 4
Total students who obtained a paid internship: 4
Total students who obtained an unpaid internship: 0
Total students who were placed in APA/CPA-accredited internships: 4
Total students placed in internships not APA/CPA-accredited, but listed with the Association of Psychology Postdoctoral and Internship Centers (APPIC): 0
Total students placed in internships conforming to guidelines of the Council of Directors of School Psychology Programs (CDSPP): 0
Total students placed in internships that were not APA/CPA-accredited, APPIC or CDSSP listed: 0

Admissions

Entries appear in the following order: required test or GPA, minimum score (if required)/median score of students entering in 2015–2016.

Program	Degree	GRE-V	GRE-Q	GRE-Writing	GRE-Subject	Under-graduate GPA	Last 2 Years GPA	Psychol-ogy GPA	Master's GPA
Experimental Psychology	PhD	144/160	141/164	3.5/4	Not specified	Not specified	Not specified	Not specified	Not specified
Clinical Psychology	PhD	153/158	150/153	3.5/4	Not specified	3.44/3.82	Not specified	Not specified	Not specified

Admissions Requirements:

Degree	GRE	GRE-Subject	Letters of Recom-mendation	Research Statement	Writing Sample	CV	Interview
Doctoral	Required	Recom-mended	3	Required	None	Optional	Required

Admissions Criteria:

GRE scores—high
Research experience—high
Work experience—medium
Clinically related public service—low
GPA—high

Letters of recommendation—high
Interview—medium
Statement of goals and objectives—high
Undergraduate psychology preparation—high

Department Demographics

	Male (PT)	Female (PT)	Total	African-American/ Black (PT)	Hispanic/ Latino (PT)	Asian/ Pacific Islander (PT)	American Indian/ Alaska Native (PT)	Caucasian/ White (PT)	Unknown (PT)	Multiethnic (PT)	ADA (PT)	Int'l (PT)
Students	17 (0)	32 (0)	49	0 (0)	2 (0)	4 (0)	0 (0)	43 (0)	0 (0)	0 (0)	0 (0)	6 (0)

Financial Information/Assistance

Tuition: For information on tuition costs, visit https://www.utoledo.edu/offices/treasurer/finance_brochures.html. Tuition is subject to change.

Doctoral:
State residents: $13,165 per academic year.
Nonstate residents: $23,502 per academic year.

Financial Assistance:

	Teaching Assistantship (% Receiving)	Teaching Assistantship Tuition Remission	Research Assistantship (% Receiving)	Research Assistantship Tuition Remission	Fellowship (% Receiving)	Fellowship Tuition Remission
First-Year Student	$13,000 (NA)	Full	$13,000 (NA)	Full	NA (NA)	NA
Advanced Student	$15,000 (NA)	Full	$15,000 (NA)	Full	NA (NA)	NA

For additional information on financial assistance, visit http://psychology.utoledo.edu/showpage.asp?name=financial_support_experimental.

Employment of Department Graduates

Doctoral:
Enrolled in a postdoctoral residency/fellowship: 3
Employed in academic position at a 2-year/4-year college: 2
Employed in a community mental health/counseling center: 2
Employed in a hospital/medical center: 2
Total: 9

Additional Information

Housing and Day Care: On-campus housing is available. See the following website for more information: http://www.utoledo.edu/studentaffairs/reslife/. On-campus day care facilities are available. See the following website for more information: http://www.utoledo.edu/centers/earlylearn/.

Information for Students With Physical Disabilities: See the following website: http://www.utoledo.edu/offices/student-disability-services/.

Application Information: Graduate School, University of Toledo, Toledo, OH 43606. *Fee:* $45. *Online application:* http://www.utoledo.edu/graduate/prospectivestudents/admission/guidelines.html.

Wright State University
Department of Psychology
College of Science and Mathematics
335 Fawcett Hall, 3640 Colonel Glenn Highway
Dayton, OH 45435-0001
Telephone: (937) 775-3348
Chairperson: Debra Steele-Johnson

E-mail: debra.steele-johnson@wright.edu
Web: http://science-math.wright.edu/psychology/

Orientation, Objectives, and Emphasis of Department
The Department offers a PhD degree in Human Factors/Industrial-Organizational Psychology (MS degree is earned along the way). Students specialize in one of these areas, but the program is integrated to foster an understanding of both areas and the importance of considering both aspects in the design of industrial, aerospace, health care, or other systems. The program prepares students for careers in research, teaching, design and practice in government, consulting, business, or industry. It includes course work, research training, and experience with system design and applications. Students work closely with faculty beginning early in the program. Human factors, including cognitive engineering, deals with the characteristics of human beings that are applicable to the design of systems and devices of all kinds while industrial/organizational deals with individual or group behaviors in work settings (macrosystem variables). The department has a critical mass of students and faculty in these areas and is unique because its focus on applied psychology does not include students in clinical psychology. Both areas are strengthened by being located in the Dayton, Ohio metropolitan region, which is a rapidly developing high technology sector, a major human factors research and development center, and a region of considerable industrial and corporate strength.

Programs and Degrees Offered

Program	Degree	Application Deadline	Applica-tions Received	Accepted	New Admits Enrolled (PT)	Total Enrolled (PT)	Degrees Awarded in 2014–2015	Median Years to Complete Degree	Dismissed/ Withdrew
Human Factors/ Industrial-Organizational Psychology	PhD	January 1 (Fall)	102	16	10 (0)	45 (18)	6	5.83	0

Internships/Practica

Students participate in internships and practica with local businesses and Wright Patterson Air Force Base. Students working on internships can receive support.

Admissions

Entries appear in the following order: required test or GPA, minimum score (if required)/median score of students entering in 2015–2016.

Program	Degree	GRE-V	GRE-Q	GRE-Writing	GRE-Subject	Under-graduate GPA	Last 2 Years GPA	Psychol-ogy GPA	Master's GPA
Human Factors/ Industrial-Organizational Psychology	PhD	Not specified	Not specified	Not specified	Not specified	Not specified	Not specified	Not specified	Not specified

Admissions Requirements:

Degree	GRE	GRE-Subject	Letters of Recom-mendation	Research Statement	Writing Sample	CV	Interview
Doctoral	Required	None	3	Required	None	Optional	None

Admissions Criteria:

GRE scores—high
Research experience—high
Work experience—medium
GPA—high

Letters of recommendation—high
Interview—medium
Statement of goals and objectives—high
Undergraduate psychology preparation—medium

For additional information on admission requirements, visit http://science-math.wright.edu/psychology/advising/graduate-admission.

Department Demographics

	Male (PT)	Female (PT)	Total	African-American/ Black (PT)	Hispanic/ Latino (PT)	Asian/ Pacific Islander (PT)	American Indian/ Alaska Native (PT)	Caucasian/ White (PT)	Unknown	Multiethnic (PT)	ADA (PT)	Int'l (PT)
Students	25 (11)	20 (7)	63	1 (1)	1 (4)	4 (0)	0 (0)	39 (12)	0 (0)	0 (1)	1 (0)	1 (0)

Financial Information/Assistance

Tuition: For information on tuition costs, visit http://www.wright.edu/raider-connect/student-accounts-and-bills/tuition-and-fees. Tuition is subject to change.

Doctoral:
State residents: $13,082 per academic year.
State residents: $595 per credit hour.
Nonstate residents: $22,224 per academic year.
Nonstate residents: $1,010 per credit hour.

Financial Assistance:

	Teaching Assistantship (% Receiving)	Teaching Assistantship Tuition Remission	Research Assistantship (% Receiving)	Research Assistantship Tuition Remission	Fellowship (% Receiving)	Fellowship Tuition Remission
First-Year Student	$16,000 (80)	Full	$16,000 (20)	Full	$16,000 (NA)	Full
Advanced Student	$16,000 (70)	Full	$16,000 (30)	Full	$16,000 (NA)	Full

For additional information on financial assistance, visit http://www.wright.edu/graduate-school/admissions/graduate-assistantships.

Employment of Department Graduates

Doctoral:
Enrolled in a postdoctoral residency/fellowship: 1
Employed in business or industry: 4
Employed in government agency: 1
Total: 6

Additional Information

Housing and Day Care: No on-campus housing is available. On-campus day care facilities are available. See the following website for more information: http://www.miniuniversity.net/Wright-State-University.asp.

Information for Students With Physical Disabilities: See the following website: http://www.wright.edu/disability-services.

Special Facilities or Resources: The Department of Psychology has state-of-the-art research laboratories, well-equipped teaching laboratories, and office space for graduate assistants. Specialized equipment in dedicated research laboratories supports research on sensory processes, motor control, spatial orientation, human-computer interaction and display design, flight simulation, cultural cognition, naturalistic decision making, memory, aging, expertise, teamwork, assessment, training, and stress in the workplace. In addition, faculty and students share a number of individual and group testing rooms. Computer facilities include over 350 workstations. The Department works cooperatively with research laboratories, research and development organizations, and corporations in the region. These include facilities for virtual environment generation, including 3-D visual displays, 3-D auditory displays, and tactile/haptic displays. The Virtual Environment Research, Interactive Technology, and Simulation (VERITAS) facility, which is owned and operated by Wright State University but housed at Wright Patterson Air Force Base(AFRL), is unique in the world. The facility includes a room-size display that surrounds the user with interactive 3-D auditory and visual images. The Department of Psychology has an agreement with the U.S. AFRL that facilitates utilization of its sophisticated behavioral laboratories such as flight simulators and the Auditory Localization Facility. AFRL supports research in complex cognition. Departmental facilities support the study of complex team performance/training.

Application Information: The Graduate School, Wright State University, E344 Student Union, 3640 Colonel Glenn Highway, Dayton, OH 45435-0001. *Fee:* $40. *Online application:* http://www.wright.edu/graduate-school/admissions/apply-now.

Wright State University

School of Professional Psychology
3640 Colonel Glenn Highway
Dayton, OH 45435-0001
Telephone: (937) 775-3490
Associate Dean and Professor: Jeffery B. Allen, PhD, ABPP-CN

E-mail: jeffery.allen@wright.edu
Web: http://psychology.wright.edu/

Orientation, Objectives, and Emphasis of Department

The School of Professional Psychology is committed to a practitioner model of professional education that educates students at the doctoral level for the eclectic, general practice of psychology. The School's educational and training philosophy explicitly emphasizes generalist training for the Doctor of Psychology (PsyD) degree. In addition to the generalist area, the doctoral program also offers emphasis areas in Child, Health/Rehabilitation/Neuropsychological and Forensic Psychology. As a part of its educational mission, the school emphasizes cultural and other aspects of diversity in the composition of its student body, faculty, staff and curriculum. The curriculum is organized around seven core competency areas that are fundamental to the practice of psychology currently and in the future, including diversity, research/evaluation/basic science, assessment, intervention, relationship, management-supervision, and consultation-education. In Years 1 and 2, the curriculum is designed around foundation coursework and the development of basic competencies. Years 3 and 4 are devoted to the development of advanced competency levels. Year 5 is dedicated to a predoctoral internship.

Programs and Degrees Offered

Program	Degree	Application Deadline	Applications Received	Accepted	New Admits Enrolled (PT)	Total Enrolled (PT)	Degrees Awarded in 2014–2015	Median Years to Complete Degree	Dismissed/ Withdrew
Clinical Psychology	PsyD	December 1 (Fall)	97	49	29 (0)	112 (2)	26	5	0

APA Accreditation

Clinical PsyD: Student Outcome Data website: http://psychology.wright.edu/admissions.

Doctoral Degree (PsyD Clinical Psychology): For those doctoral students for whom a professional internship was required in this program prior to graduation:

Total students who applied for an internship: 18
Total students who obtained an internship: 18
Total students who obtained a paid internship: 18
Total students who obtained an unpaid internship: 0
Total students who were placed in APA/CPA-accredited internships: 15
Total students placed in internships not APA/CPA-accredited, but listed with the Association of Psychology Postdoctoral and Internship Centers (APPIC): 1
Total students placed in internships conforming to guidelines of the Council of Directors of School Psychology Programs (CDSPP): 0
Total students placed in internships that were not APA/CPA-accredited, APPIC or CDSSP listed: 2

Internships/Practica

SOPP runs an APA-accredited internship program which has six slots annually; selections are made competitively from a national pool of students. SOPP students are eligible to apply for this internship program. Most SOPP students are matched with internship programs outside the local area. SOPP students have a strong match rate with APA-accredited internship programs across the country. During Years 2, 3, and 4 of the doctoral program, students are assigned to year-long practicum placements for 2 days (16–20 hours) per week. A number of practicum placements carry a stipend of $5,500 for a 12-month period. Approximately 25% of practicum placements are located in two clinical/teaching facilities: Counseling and Wellness Services on WSU's campus, which provides psychological services for the university's student body, and the Ellis Human Development Institute, located in Dayton, Ohio which provides a broad range of psychological services and special treatment programs developed in response to the needs of the Dayton community. The remaining practicum placements are located in a broad array of service settings located primarily in Dayton and southwestern Ohio. These practicum settings include public agencies, correctional settings, hospitals, health and mental health clinics, and so forth.

Admissions

Entries appear in the following order: required test or GPA, minimum score (if required)/median score of students entering in 2015–2016.

Program	Degree	GRE-V	GRE-Q	GRE-Writing	GRE-Subject	Undergraduate GPA	Last 2 Years GPA	Psychology GPA	Master's GPA
Clinical Psychology	PsyD	NA/153	NA/149	NA/3.93	NA/567	NA/3.55	Not specified	NA/3.63	Not specified

Admissions Requirements:

Degree	GRE	GRE-Subject	Letters of Recommendation	Research Statement	Writing Sample	CV	Interview
Doctoral	Required	Required	3	Required	Optional	Required	Required

Admissions Criteria:

GRE scores—medium
Research experience—low
Work experience—medium
Clinically related public service—medium
GPA—high

Letters of recommendation—high
Interview—high
Statement of goals and objectives—high
Undergraduate psychology preparation—high
Resume—high

For additional information on admission requirements, visit http://psychology.wright.edu/admissions/admission-and-application.

Department Demographics

	Male (PT)	Female (PT)	Total	African-American/ Black (PT)	Hispanic/ Latino (PT)	Asian/ Pacific Islander (PT)	American Indian/ Alaska Native (PT)	Caucasian/ White (PT)	Unknown	Multiethnic (PT)	ADA (PT)	Int'l (PT)
Students	28 (0)	84 (2)	114	15 (0)	7 (0)	11 (1)	0 (0)	75 (1)	0 (0)	4 (0)	0 (0)	7 (0)

Financial Information/Assistance

Tuition: For information on tuition costs, visit http://www.wright.edu/bursar/tuition-fees. Tuition is subject to change. Additional fees are assessed to students beyond the costs of tuition for the following: $350 fee charged to first year students for assessment materials.

Doctoral:
State residents: $23,040 per academic year.
State residents: $711 per credit hour.
Nonstate residents: $36,816 per academic year.
Nonstate residents: $1,138 per credit hour.

Financial Assistance:

	Teaching Assistantship (% Receiving)	Teaching Assistantship Tuition Remission	Research Assistantship (% Receiving)	Research Assistantship Tuition Remission	Fellowship (% Receiving)	Fellowship Tuition Remission
First-Year Student	NA (NA)	NA	NA (NA)	NA	$7,000 (NA)	NA
Advanced Student	NA (NA)	NA	NA (NA)	NA	$6,645 (NA)	Partial

Employment of Department Graduates

Doctoral:
Enrolled in a postdoctoral residency/fellowship: 17
Employed in independent practice: 2
Employed in an academic position at a university: 2
Employed in other positions at a higher education institution: 7
Employed in government agency: 9
Employed in a community mental health/counseling center: 5
Employed in a hospital/medical center: 6
Total: 48

Additional Information

Housing and Day Care: On-campus housing is available. See the following website for more information: http://www.wright.edu/students/housing/. On-campus day care facilities are available. See the following website for more information: http://miniuniversity.net/Wright-State-University.asp.

Information for Students With Physical Disabilities: See the following website: http://www.wright.edu/disability-services.

Special Facilities or Resources: The doctoral program operates the Ellis Human Development Institute, a large clinical service center that is designed to accommodate academic teaching, clinical training, clinical program development and research. This facility is located in an urban, primarily African-American section of Dayton, Ohio and provides assessment and group/individual therapy to children, adolescents and adults from the Dayton community. Several special treatment programs provide unique opportunities for trainees. These include conducting psychological evaluations of teenage mothers aging out of the system, motivating treatment of women with a history of sex work, drug abuse and trauma to pursue treatment upon release from jail; and offering clinical services to refugees via the use of interpreters. The Ellis Human Development Institute houses trainee and faculty offices and computers for student use in research and training activities. The facility is equipped with state-of-the-art equipment for videotaped and live clinical supervision.

Application Information: Fee: $50. *Online application:* http://www.wright.edu/graduate-school/admissions.

Xavier University

School of Psychology
College of Social Sciences, Health and Education
Elet Hall
Cincinnati, OH 45207-6511
Telephone: (513) 745-3533
Chairperson: Karl W. Stukenberg, PhD, ABPP

E-mail: stukenb@xavier.edu
Web: http://www.xavier.edu/psychology-grad

Orientation, Objectives, and Emphasis of Department

Both the master's and doctoral programs provide students with the knowledge and range of skills necessary to provide psychological services in today's changing professional climate. Our objective for the master's students is to prepare them for immediate employment or entry into a doctoral program in their field. Our objective for the doctoral program is to prepare students to serve as clinical psychologists in their communities. The basic philosophy of the PsyD program is to educate skilled practitioners who have a solid appreciation of the role of science in all aspects of professional activity. It is based on a practitioner-scientist model of training.

Programs and Degrees Offered

Program	Degree	Application Deadline	Applications Received	Accepted	New Admits Enrolled (PT)	Total Enrolled (PT)	Degrees Awarded in 2014–2015	Median Years to Complete Degree	Dismissed/ Withdrew
Clinical Psychology	PsyD	December 1 (Fall)	186	35	16 (0)	92 (8)	15	5.67	2
Experimental Psychology	MA/MS	February 1 (Fall)	8	0	0 (0)	0 (0)	0		0
Industrial/ Organizational Psychology	MA/MS	February 1 (Fall)	62	23	9 (0)	20 (5)	10	2.7	0

APA Accreditation

Clinical PsyD: Student Outcome Data website: http://www.xavier.edu/psychology-doctorate/student-admissions-outcomes-and-other-data.cfm.

Doctoral Degree (PsyD Clinical Psychology): For those doctoral students for whom a professional internship was required in this program prior to graduation:
Total students who applied for an internship: 15
Total students who obtained an internship: 14
Total students who obtained a paid internship: 14

Total students who obtained an unpaid internship: 0
Total students who were placed in APA/CPA-accredited internships: 12
Total students placed in internships not APA/CPA-accredited, but listed with the Association of Psychology Postdoctoral and Internship Centers (APPIC): 0
Total students placed in internships conforming to guidelines of the Council of Directors of School Psychology Programs (CDSPP): 0
Total students placed in internships that were not APA/CPA-accredited, APPIC or CDSSP listed: 2

Master's Degree (MA/MS Experimental Psychology): An internship experience, such as a final research project or "capstone" experience is required of graduates. Master's Degree (MA/MS Industrial/Organizational Psychology): An internship experience, such as a final research project or "capstone" experience is required of graduates.

Internships/Practica

In an urban setting, the university has established relationships with a number of private and public agencies, businesses, hospitals, and mental health care centers. PsyD students are given the opportunity to work with underserved populations within the three ares of interest in our PsyD program: child/adolescent, older adults, and severe mental illness. Industrial/Organizational (I/O) MA students work in settings where we have established relationships for internships.

Admissions

Entries appear in the following order: required test or GPA, minimum score (if required)/median score of students entering in 2015–2016.

Program	Degree	GRE-V	GRE-Q	GRE-Writing	GRE-Subject	Under-graduate GPA	Last 2 Years GPA	Psychol-ogy GPA	Master's GPA
Clinical Psychology	PsyD	NA/NA	NA/NA	NA/NA	Not specified	3/NA	Not specified	3/NA	Not specified
Experimental Psychology	MA/MS	NA/NA	NA/NA	NA/NA	Not specified	3/NA	Not specified	3/NA	Not specified
Industrial/ Organizational Psychology	MA/MS	NA/NA	NA/NA	NA/NA	Not specified	3/NA	Not specified	3/NA	Not specified

Admissions Requirements:

Degree	GRE	GRE-Subject	Letters of Recom-mendation	Research Statement	Writing Sample	CV	Interview
Master's/Specialist	Required	Recom-mended	3	Required	Optional	Required	Required
Doctoral	Required	Recom-mended	3	Required	Optional	Required	Required

Please note if these criteria vary for different programs: The graduate programs require a tests and measurements course that, if the student has not completed, he or she can take it online the summer before matriculating. The I/O program requires an undergraduate Industrial/Organizational Psychology course. If the student has not completed, he or she can take it during the summer or take a proficiency exam. GRE-Subject scores are required for applicants who were not psychology majors; they are recommended for everyone else.

Admissions Criteria:

GRE scores—high
Research experience—medium
Work experience—medium
Clinically related public service—medium
GPA—high

Letters of recommendation—high
Interview—medium
Statement of goals and objectives—high
Undergraduate psychology preparation—medium

For additional information on admission requirements, visit http://www.xavier.edu/psychology-doctorate/admission.cfm.

Department Demographics

	Male (PT)	Female (PT)	Total	African-American/ Black (PT)	Hispanic/ Latino (PT)	Asian/ Pacific Islander (PT)	American Indian/ Alaska Native (PT)	Caucasian/ White (PT)	Unknown	Multiethnic (PT)	ADA (PT)	Int'l (PT)
Students	28 (7)	84 (6)	125	5 (1)	4 (0)	5 (0)	0 (0)	97 (12)	0 (0)	1 (0)	0 (0)	0 (0)

Financial Information/Assistance

Tuition: For information on tuition costs, visit http://www.xavier.edu/financial-aid/tuition.cfm?type=grad. Additional fees are assessed to students beyond the costs of tuition for the following: assessment course materials, diversity course fee, APAGS dues, liability insurance fee and software. Tuition costs vary by program.

Doctoral:
State residents: $20,736 per academic year.
State residents: $780 per credit hour.
Nonstate residents: $20,736 per academic year.
Nonstate residents: $780 per credit hour.

Master's:
State residents: $620 per credit hour.
Nonstate residents: $620 per credit hour.

Financial Assistance:

	Teaching Assistantship (% Receiving)	Teaching Assistantship Tuition Remission	Research Assistantship (% Receiving)	Research Assistantship Tuition Remission	Fellowship (% Receiving)	Fellowship Tuition Remission
First-Year Student	$3,200 (25)	Partial	$2,400 (75)	Partial	NA (NA)	NA
Advanced Student	$3,200 (3)	Partial	$2,400 (10)	Partial	NA (NA)	NA

For additional information on financial assistance, visit http://www.xavier.edu/financial-aid/.

Employment of Department Graduates

Master's:
Employed in business or industry: 5
Total: 5

Doctoral:
Enrolled in a postdoctoral residency/fellowship: 6
Employed in a community mental health/counseling center: 2
Employed in a hospital/medical center: 3
Other employment position: 4
Total: 15

Additional Information

Housing and Day Care: No on-campus housing is available. No on-campus day care facilities are available.

Information for Students With Physical Disabilities: See the following website: http://www.xavier.edu/learning-assistance-center/Disability-Services.cfm.

Special Facilities or Resources: The department has affiliation with the Psychological Services Center on campus, which provides psychological services to both the university population and the Greater Cincinnati community. The Center provides the opportunity for training, service, and research. There are opportunities to work in various other areas (e.g., student development) in the university. The department also has established contact with care providers in the community, which provides the opportunity to learn the delivery of service and research that occurs in such organizations.

Application Information: Margaret Maybury, Director, Academic Program, Psychology Department, Xavier University, 3800 Victory Parkway, Cincinnati, OH 45207-6511. *Fee:* $35. *Online application:* https://admit.xavier.edu/apply/.

Central Oklahoma, University of (2015 data)

Department of Psychology
College of Education & Professional Studies
100 North University Drive
Edmond, OK 73034
Telephone: (405) 974-5707
Chairperson: Mark Hamlin

E-mail: mhamlin@uco.edu
Web: http://www.uco.edu/ceps/dept/Professional-Studies-Programs/psy/index.asp

Orientation, Objectives, and Emphasis of Department

Excellent training to pursue doctoral work with the General experimental option or Licensed Professional Counselor (LPC), or Licensed Behavioral Practitioner (LPB) with the Counseling Psychology option. School Psychometry offered with the School Psychology option. Option for Board Certified Behavior Analysis certification.

Programs and Degrees Offered

Program	Degree	Application Deadline	Applications Received	Accepted	New Admits Enrolled (PT)	Total Enrolled (PT)	Degrees Awarded in 2014–2015	Median Years to Complete Degree	Dismissed/Withdrew
Counseling Psychology	MA/MS	January 15 (Fall)	38	21	16 (0)	25 (17)	11	3	3
General Psychology	MA/MS	Rolling	16	9	8 (0)	10 (4)	3	2	1
Experimental Psychology	MA/MS	Rolling	9	5	4 (0)	9 (5)	7	2	2
School Psychology	MA/MS	January 15 (Fall)	10	6	6 (0)	17 (6)	5	3	0
Forensic Psychology	MA/MS	January 15 (Fall)	4	4	3 (0)	7 (4)	1	2	0

Internships/Practica

Practica are available in teaching and research for students in all our programs. In our MA Counseling program, two separate practica are required where students initially work in our departmental clinic and then are placed off-campus in community mental health clinics in our area. For the MA School program, three separate practica are required. Practica are school-based through local placement sites and our UCO Learning & Behavior Clinic. After graduation, a 1 year postgraduate internship is required at a pre-approved clinic or school location.

Admissions

Entries appear in the following order: required test or GPA, minimum score (if required)/median score of students entering in 2015–2016.

Program	Degree	GRE-V	GRE-Q	GRE-Writing	GRE-Subject	Under-graduate GPA	Last 2 Years GPA	Psychology GPA	Master's GPA
Counseling Psychology	MA/MS	145/151	145/146	3.5/4	Not specified	3/3.5	Not specified	Not specified	Not specified
General Psychology	MA/MS	145/149	145/148	3.5/3.75	Not specified	2.75/3.09	Not specified	Not specified	Not specified
Experimental Psychology	MA/MS	145/150	145/150	3.5/3.5	Not specified	2.75/3.21	Not specified	Not specified	Not specified
School Psychology	MA/MS	145/152	145/145	3.5/4	Not specified	3/3.39	Not specified	Not specified	Not specified

Admissions *(con't.)*

Program	Degree	GRE-V	GRE-Q	GRE-Writing	GRE-Subject	Under-graduate GPA	Last 2 Years GPA	Psychology GPA	Master's GPA
Forensic Psychology	MA/MS	145/149	145/149	3.5/4	Not specified	3/3.41	Not specified	Not specified	Not specified

Admissions Requirements:

Degree	GRE	GRE-Subject	Letters of Recom-mendation	Research Statement	Writing Sample	CV	Interview
Master's/Specialist	Required	None	3	Recom-mended	None	Required	None

Please note if these criteria vary for different programs: General and Experimental programs do not require letters of recommendation or a personal statement. School and Counseling programs have an additional supplementary application and require a CV.

Admissions Criteria:

GRE scores—medium
Research experience—high
Work experience—medium
Clinically related public service—high

GPA—high
Letters of recommendation—high
Interview—low
Statement of goals and objectives—medium

For additional information on admission requirements, visit http://www.uco.edu/ceps/dept/Professional-Studies-Programs/psy/psychology-ma.asp.

Department Demographics

	Male (PT)	Female (PT)	Total	African-American/ Black (PT)	Hispanic/ Latino (PT)	Asian/ Pacific Islander (PT)	American Indian/ Alaska Native (PT)	Caucasian/ White (PT)	Unknown	Multiethnic (PT)	ADA (PT)	Int'l (PT)
Students	14 (9)	50 (24)	97	5 (4)	0 (0)	7 (2)	3 (3)	49 (24)	0 (0)	0 (0)	0 (0)	5 (0)

Financial Information/Assistance

Tuition: For information on tuition costs, visit http://www.uco.edu/em/registrar/tuitionandfees.asp. Tuition is subject to change.

Master's:
State residents: $230 per credit hour.
Nonstate residents: $542 per credit hour.

Financial Assistance:

	Teaching Assistantship (% Receiving)	Teaching Assistantship Tuition Remission	Research Assistantship (% Receiving)	Research Assistantship Tuition Remission	Fellowship (% Receiving)	Fellowship Tuition Remission
First-Year Student	$3,640 (NA)	Partial	$1,690 (NA)	Partial	NA (NA)	NA
Advanced Student	$3,640 (NA)	Partial	$1,690 (NA)	Partial	NA (NA)	NA

For additional information on financial assistance, visit http://www.uco.edu/graduate/financial/index.asp.

Employment of Department Graduates

Master's:
Employed in a professional position in a school system: 5
Employed in a hospital/medical center: 1
Total: 6

Additional Information

Housing and Day Care: On-campus housing is available. See the following website for more information: http://www.uco.edu/administration/housing/. No on-campus day care facilities are available.

Information for Students With Physical Disabilities: See the following website: http://www.uco.edu/student-affairs/dss/index.asp.

Special Facilities or Resources: The department has excellent computer facilities. It has counseling clinic facilities in our Psychology Center with audiovisual equipment to train students in community counseling. There is a Cognitive Research Laboratory that includes shared research space with two psychophysiological units capable of collecting EEG, EMG, and cardiovascular data; a unit to collect eye tracking data; and several data collection software packages for the precise presentation of experimental stimuli. We have the UCO Learning & Behavior Clinic off-site for testing and training. In cooperation with a local hospital and the Catholic archdiocese, UCO has a lab/school for children with autism.

Application Information: Dean of the Graduate College, 100 North University Drive, University of Central Oklahoma, Edmond, OK 73034. *Fee:* $50. *Online application:* http://www.uco.edu/graduate/admissions/index.asp.

Oklahoma City University

MEd in Applied Behavioral Studies: Professional Counseling
Petree College of Arts & Sciences (Department of Education)
2501 North Blackwelder
Oklahoma City, OK 73106
Telephone: (405) 208-5387
Professor & Director: Dr. Bryan Farha

E-mail: bfarha@okcu.edu
Web: http://www.okcu.edu/artsci/education/programs/graduate/professional-counseling/

Orientation, Objectives, and Emphasis of Department

The Petree College offers the Master of Education (MEd) degree in Applied Behavioral Studies: Professional Counseling in the Division of Education and Professional Studies (Department of Education). The program is designed to train students to become professional counselors and render services to individuals, groups, and families experiencing normal adjustment difficulties of a personal, social, or career nature in settings such as community counseling centers, mental health clinics, youth and guidance centers, human service agencies, drug and alcohol treatment facilities, university counseling centers, abuse shelters, religious counseling centers, and private practice (once licensed). Students are encouraged to secure internships in settings consistent with their specific areas of professional interest. To attain the professional counseling concentration, students must accrue at least 60 credit hours, including field experience. The sequenced mental health program of study is designed to meet the Oklahoma Board of Behavioral Health's academic requirements to become a Licensed Professional Counselor (LPC).

Programs and Degrees Offered

Program	Degree	Application Deadline	Applications Received	Accepted	New Admits Enrolled (PT)	Total Enrolled (PT)	Degrees Awarded in 2014–2015	Median Years to Complete Degree	Dismissed/Withdrew
Applied Behavioral Studies: Professional Counseling	MEd					31 (7)			

Internships/Practica

We place interns in settings such as community counseling centers, mental health clinics, university counseling centers, and hospitals and other health care facilities.

Admissions

Entries appear in the following order: required test or GPA, minimum score (if required)/median score of students entering in 2015–2016.

Program	Degree	GRE-V	GRE-Q	GRE-Writing	GRE-Subject	Under-graduate GPA	Last 2 Years GPA	Psychology GPA	Master's GPA
Applied Behavioral Studies: Professional Counseling	MEd	Not specified	Not specified	Not specified	Not specified	3/NA	Not specified	Not specified	Not specified

Admissions Requirements:

Degree	GRE	GRE-Subject	Letters of Recommendation	Research Statement	Writing Sample	CV	Interview
Master's/Specialist	None	None	2	Required	Required	None	Optional

Admissions Criteria:

GPA—high
Letters of recommendation—high
Interview—high

Statement of goals and objectives—medium
Undergraduate psychology preparation—low
Effective English ability—medium

For additional information on admission requirements, visit http://www.okcu.edu/petree/education/counseling.aspx.

Department Demographics

	Male (PT)	Female (PT)	Total	African-American/Black (PT)	Hispanic/Latino (PT)	Asian/Pacific Islander (PT)	American Indian/Alaska Native (PT)	Caucasian/White (PT)	Unknown	Multiethnic (PT)	ADA (PT)	Int'l (PT)
Students	5 (2)	26 (5)	38	5 (0)	2 (0)	2 (0)	1 (0)	18 (5)	0 (0)	0 (2)	0 (0)	3 (0)

Financial Information/Assistance

Tuition: Tuition is subject to change.

Master's:
State residents: $530 per credit hour.
Nonstate residents: $530 per credit hour.

Financial Assistance:

	Teaching Assistantship (% Receiving)	Teaching Assistantship Tuition Remission	Research Assistantship (% Receiving)	Research Assistantship Tuition Remission	Fellowship (% Receiving)	Fellowship Tuition Remission
First-Year Student	NA (NA)	NA	NA (NA)	NA	NA (NA)	NA
Advanced Student	NA (NA)	NA	NA (NA)	NA	NA (NA)	NA

For additional information on financial assistance, visit http://www.okcu.edu/financialaid/.

Employment of Department Graduates

Master's:
Enrolled in a psychology doctoral program: 1
Employed in academic position at a 2-year/4-year college: 1
Total: 2

Additional Information

Housing and Day Care: On-campus housing is available. See the following website for more information: http://www.okcu.edu/campus/residencelife/. No on-campus day care facilities are available.

Information for Students With Physical Disabilities: See the following website: http://www.okcu.edu/campus/resources/disability/.

Application Information: Oklahoma City University, Office of Admission, 2501 North Blackwelder, Oklahoma City, OK 73106. *Fee:* $50. *Online application:* https://app.applyyourself.com/?id=okcugrad.

Oklahoma State University
Department of Psychology
Arts & Sciences
116 North Murray Hall
Stillwater, OK 74078-3064
Telephone: (405) 744-6027
Chairperson: Thad Leffingwell

E-mail: Thad.leffingwell@okstate.edu
Web: http://psychology.okstate.edu

Orientation, Objectives, and Emphasis of Department
The doctoral program in clinical psychology is officially accredited as a scientist–practitioner program. We will be formally changing our model to clinical science in January 2017. The program emphasizes the development of knowledge and skills in basic psychology, research methods, clinical theory, and assessment and treatment procedures. Practicum placements, coursework, and internships are selected to enhance the student's interests. Students are expected, through additional coursework, specialized practica, and research, to develop a subspecialty in adult psychopathology, clinical child, pediatric, or health psychology. The central focus of the Experimental Psychology program is on the understanding, prediction, and enhancement of individual behavior from a variety of perspectives. These perspectives may include cognitive neuroscience; the biological and physiological bases of behavior; behavior in social environments; the assessment of individual differences in personality; the developmental changes that impact behavior; and the quantitative modeling of individual performance. To accommodate this broad spectrum, our program includes Cognitive, Comparative-Neurobiology, Developmental and Social-Personality tracks.

Programs and Degrees Offered

Program	Degree	Application Deadline	Applications Received	Accepted	New Admits Enrolled (PT)	Total Enrolled (PT)	Degrees Awarded in 2014–2015	Median Years to Complete Degree	Dismissed/ Withdrew
Clinical Psychology	PhD	December 1 (Fall)	167	7	7 (0)	40 (0)	3	5.71	0
Experimental Psychology	PhD	December 1 (Fall)	25	7	7 (0)	17 (0)	8	5.75	0

APA Accreditation
Clinical PhD: Student Outcome Data website: http://psychology.okstate.edu/graduate-programs/clinical-psychology-program.

Doctoral Degree (PhD Clinical Psychology): For those doctoral students for whom a professional internship was required in this program prior to graduation:
Total students who applied for an internship: 7
Total students who obtained an internship: 7
Total students who obtained a paid internship: 7
Total students who obtained an unpaid internship: 0
Total students who were placed in APA/CPA-accredited internships: 7

Total students placed in internships not APA/CPA-accredited, but listed with the Association of Psychology Postdoctoral and Internship Centers (APPIC): 0
Total students placed in internships conforming to guidelines of the Council of Directors of School Psychology Programs (CDSPP): 0
Total students placed in internships that were not APA/CPA-accredited, APPIC or CDSSP listed: 0

Internships/Practica

For clinical students, the first 2 years of practicum experience are through our on-site clinic. Advanced students are eligible to participate in external supervised practicum experiences at affiliated agencies.

Admissions

Entries appear in the following order: required test or GPA, minimum score (if required)/median score of students entering in 2015–2016.

Program	Degree	GRE-V	GRE-Q	GRE-Writing	GRE-Subject	Under-graduate GPA	Last 2 Years GPA	Psychol-ogy GPA	Master's GPA
Clinical Psychology	PhD	NA/159	NA/153	NA/4.4	Not specified	NA/3.77	NA/3.79	NA/3.8	Not specified
Experimental Psychology	PhD	NA/155	NA/153	NA/4.3	Not specified	NA/3.6	NA/NA	NA/3.72	Not specified

Admissions Requirements:

Degree	GRE	GRE-Subject	Letters of Recom-mendation	Research Statement	Writing Sample	CV	Interview
Doctoral	Required	None	3	Required	Required	Required	Required

Admissions Criteria:

GRE scores—high
Research experience—high
Work experience—low
Clinically related public service—low
GPA—high

Letters of recommendation—high
Interview—high
Statement of goals and objectives—high
Undergraduate psychology preparation—medium

For additional information on admission requirements, visit http://psychology.okstate.edu/graduate-programs/overview.

Department Demographics

	Male (PT)	Female (PT)	Total	African-American/ Black (PT)	Hispanic/ Latino (PT)	Asian/ Pacific Islander (PT)	American Indian/ Alaska Native (PT)	Caucasian/ White (PT)	Unknown (PT)	Multiethnic (PT)	ADA (PT)	Int'l (PT)
Students	17 (0)	40 (0)	57	2 (0)	1 (0)	2 (0)	7 (0)	45 (0)	0 (0)	0 (0)	1 (0)	1 (0)

Financial Information/Assistance

Tuition: For information on tuition costs, visit http://bursar.okstate.edu/tuition-and-fees. Tuition is subject to change. Additional fees are assessed to students beyond the costs of tuition for the following: Health services, activities, technology.

Doctoral:
State residents: $196 per credit hour.
Nonstate residents: $785 per credit hour.

Financial Assistance:

	Teaching Assistantship (% Receiving)	Teaching Assistantship Tuition Remission	Research Assistantship (% Receiving)	Research Assistantship Tuition Remission	Fellowship (% Receiving)	Fellowship Tuition Remission
First-Year Student	$11,106 (100)	Full	$11,106 (100)	Full	NA (NA)	NA
Advanced Student	$13,032 (100)	Full	$13,032 (100)	Full	NA (NA)	NA

Employment of Department Graduates

Doctoral:
Enrolled in a postdoctoral residency/fellowship: 2
Employed in an academic position at a university: 5
Employed in academic position at a 2-year/4-year college: 2
Employed in business or industry: 1
Total: 10

Additional Information

Housing and Day Care: On-campus housing is available. See the following website for more information: http://www.reslife.okstate.edu. No on-campus day care facilities are available.

Information for Students With Physical Disabilities: See the following website: http://sds.okstate.edu/.

Special Facilities or Resources: The Department of Psychology is located in North Murray Hall near the center of the OSU campus. All students are provided office space that they share with two–four others. Offices are equipped with personal computers with access to SPSS, MS Office, internet, and printers. Wireless internet access is available in North Murray Hall. Every student is also provided a free e-mail account. Graduate students also share a common room with a refrigerator, microwave oven, two additional computers with Adobe Professional, and a color printer. In addition, the Department of Psychology maintains a 24-station computer lab for student research, teaching, and other endeavors. The department operates the Psychological Services Center, an on-campus facility for clinical work and research. The center has equipment and facilities to accommodate a number of specialized services and functions, including videotaping, direct observation of clinical work using one-way mirrors, and direct supervision through telephones placed in therapy rooms. The department maintains liaisons with many off-campus organizations and agencies which provide the student with access to special populations for research as well as clinical activities. The department offers a variety of support services through the Psychology Diversified Students Program and the Psychology Graduate Students Association.

Application Information: Department Head, Department of Psychology, OSU, 116 North Murray Hall, Stillwater, OK 74078-3064. *Fee:* $50. *Online application:* https://www.applyweb.com/oksugrad/.

Oklahoma State University

School of Applied Health and Educational Psychology
College of Education
434 Willard Hall
Stillwater, OK 74078
Telephone: (405) 744-6040
Training Director: Julie Koch, PhD

E-mail: julie.koch@okstate.edu
Web: http://education.okstate.edu/sahep

Orientation, Objectives, and Emphasis of Department

The orientation of the Counseling Psychology program is consistent both with the historical development of counseling psychology and with the current roles and functions of counseling psychology. We give major emphasis to prevention/developmental/educational interventions, and to remediation of problems that arise in the normal development of relatively well functioning people. The focus on prevention and developmental change brings us to seek knowledge and skills related to facilitation of growth, such as training in education, consultation, environmental change and self-help. It is the focus upon the assets, skills and strengths, and possibilities for further development of persons that is most reflective of the general philosophical orientation, of counseling psychology and of this program. The School Psychology program is based on the scientist–practitioner model, which emphasizes the application of the scientific knowledge base and methodological rigor in the delivery of school psychology services and in conducting research. Training in the scientist–practitioner model at OSU is for the purpose of developing a Science-Based Learner Success (SBLS) orientation in our students. Our philosophy is that all children and youth have the right to be successful and school psychologists are important agents who assist children, families, and others to be successful.

Programs and Degrees Offered

Program	Degree	Application Deadline	Applications Received	Accepted	New Admits Enrolled (PT)	Total Enrolled (PT)	Degrees Awarded in 2014–2015	Median Years to Complete Degree	Dismissed/ Withdrew
Counseling Psychology	PhD	December 1 (Fall)	72	8	8 (0)	39 (4)	8	5.14	0
School Psychology	PhD	February 1 (Fall)	14	6	6 (0)	32 (1)	6	5.15	0
School Psychology	EdS	March 1 (Fall)	9	7	7 (0)	14 (0)	4	4	
Educational Psychology	PhD	February 1 (Fall)	12	6	3 (3)	6 (15)	2	5	0

APA Accreditation

Counseling PhD: Student Outcome Data website: http://education.okstate.edu/cpsy.
School PhD: Student Outcome Data website: http://education.okstate.edu/spsy.

Doctoral Degree (PhD Counseling Psychology): For those doctoral students for whom a professional internship was required in this program prior to graduation:
Total students who applied for an internship: 12
Total students who obtained an internship: 12
Total students who obtained a paid internship: 12
Total students who obtained an unpaid internship: 0
Total students who were placed in APA/CPA-accredited internships: 12
Total students placed in internships not APA/CPA-accredited, but listed with the Association of Psychology Postdoctoral and Internship Centers (APPIC): 0
Total students placed in internships conforming to guidelines of the Council of Directors of School Psychology Programs (CDSPP): 0
Total students placed in internships that were not APA/CPA-accredited, APPIC or CDSSP listed: 0

Doctoral Degree (PhD School Psychology): For those doctoral students for whom a professional internship was required in this program prior to graduation:
Total students who applied for an internship: 7
Total students who obtained an internship: 7
Total students who obtained a paid internship: 7
Total students who obtained an unpaid internship: 0
Total students who were placed in APA/CPA-accredited internships: 5
Total students placed in internships not APA/CPA-accredited, but listed with the Association of Psychology Postdoctoral and Internship Centers (APPIC): 0
Total students placed in internships conforming to guidelines of the Council of Directors of School Psychology Programs (CDSPP): 2
Total students placed in internships that were not APA/CPA-accredited, APPIC or CDSSP listed: 0

Internships/Practica

Multiple settings for internship experiences are available nationally on a competitive basis, faculty must approve site selection. Students have obtained internships in a wide variety of settings (i.e., health centers, hospital settings). Internships must meet established standards for predoctoral internships in counseling psychology. Practica are available at on-campus agencies, including a university counseling service, a mental health clinic at the student hospital, a career information center, and a marriage and family counseling service. Several off-campus placements are within a 75 mile radius of Stillwater, particularly in and around Tulsa and Oklahoma City, and sites include a stipend and public school settings. School Psychology PhD students are required to compete for internship through APPIC. There has been 100% match for school psychology students. School Psychology EdS students complete the internship in approved public school settings. Practica are completed in public school settings and in the School Psychology Center.

Admissions

Entries appear in the following order: required test or GPA, minimum score (if required)/median score of students entering in 2015–2016.

Program	Degree	GRE-V	GRE-Q	GRE-Writing	GRE-Subject	Under-graduate GPA	Last 2 Years GPA	Psychology GPA	Master's GPA
Counseling Psychology	PhD	Not specified	Not specified	Not specified	Not specified	NA/3.81	Not specified	Not specified	Not specified
School Psychology	PhD	Not specified	Not specified	Not specified	Not specified	Not specified	Not specified	Not specified	Not specified
School Psychology	EdS	Not specified	Not specified	Not specified	Not specified	Not specified	Not specified	Not specified	Not specified
Educational Psychology	PhD	Not specified	Not specified	Not specified	Not specified	Not specified	Not specified	Not specified	Not specified

Admissions Requirements:

Degree	GRE	GRE-Subject	Letters of Recommendation	Research Statement	Writing Sample	CV	Interview
Master's/Specialist	Required	None	3	Required	Required	Required	Required
Doctoral	Required	None	4	Required	Required	Required	Required

Please note if these criteria vary for different programs: School Psychology: work experience and clinically related public service low, letters and interview are high. Statement of Goals-High. Counseling Psychology only requires 3 letters of recommendation. Applicants to the Educational Psychology PhD must have a master's degree.

Admissions Criteria:

GRE scores—high
Research experience—high
Work experience—medium
Clinically related public service—medium

GPA—high
Letters of recommendation—high
Interview—high
Statement of goals and objectives—high

Department Demographics

	Male (PT)	Female (PT)	Total	African-American/ Black (PT)	Hispanic/ Latino (PT)	Asian/ Pacific Islander (PT)	American Indian/ Alaska Native (PT)	Caucasian/ White (PT)	Unknown	Multiethnic (PT)	ADA (PT)	Int'l (PT)
Students	41 (10)	50 (11)	112	5 (2)	6 (3)	4 (0)	1 (1)	73 (11)	0 (0)	2 (4)	1 (0)	0 (0)

Financial Information/Assistance

Tuition: For information on tuition costs, visit http://bursar.okstate.edu/tuition-and-fees. Tuition is subject to change.

Doctoral:
State residents: $2,664 per academic year.
State residents: $168 per credit hour.
Nonstate residents: $9,985 per academic year.
Nonstate residents: $667 per credit hour.

Master's:
State residents: $2,664 per academic year.
State residents: $168 per credit hour.
Nonstate residents: $9,985 per academic year.
Nonstate residents: $667 per credit hour.

Financial Assistance:

	Teaching Assistantship (% Receiving)	Teaching Assistantship Tuition Remission	Research Assistantship (% Receiving)	Research Assistantship Tuition Remission	Fellowship (% Receiving)	Fellowship Tuition Remission
First-Year Student	$4,005 (NA)	Full	$8,010 (NA)	Full	NA (NA)	NA
Advanced Student	$4,635 (NA)	Full	$4,635 (NA)	Full	$250 (NA)	Partial

For additional information on financial assistance, visit http://gradcollege.okstate.edu/assistantship.

Employment of Department Graduates

Doctoral:
Employed in independent practice: 4
Employed in an academic position at a university: 1
Employed in other positions at a higher education institution: 1
Employed in a professional position in a school system: 2
Employed in a community mental health/counseling center: 2
Employed in a hospital/medical center: 1
Total: 11

Additional Information

Housing and Day Care: On-campus housing is available. See the following website for more information: http://www.reslife.okstate.edu/fgsh/. No on-campus day care facilities are available.

Information for Students With Physical Disabilities: See the following website: http://sds.okstate.edu/.

Special Facilities or Resources: Community/School Services, Counseling Psychology Clinic and the School Psychology Clinic.

Application Information: College of Education, Graduate Studies Records, Oklahoma State University, 325 Willard, Stillwater, OK, 74078. *Fee:* $40. *Online application:* https://www.applyweb.com/oksugrad/.

Oklahoma, University of
Department of Educational Psychology
The Jeannine Rainbolt College of Education
820 Van Vleet Oval, Room 321
Norman, OK 73019-2041
Telephone: (405) 325-5974
Chairperson: Dr. Nancy Marchand-Martella

E-mail: edpsych@ou.edu
Web: http://www.ou.edu/education/edpy

Orientation, Objectives, and Emphasis of Department
The department is committed to developing and disseminating new knowledge through research and scholarly activity, delivering quality instruction and professional training, and pursuing research and training opportunities at the junctures of the disciplines within the department.

Programs and Degrees Offered

Program	Degree	Application Deadline	Applica-tions Received	Accepted	New Admits Enrolled (PT)	Total Enrolled (PT)	Degrees Awarded in 2014–2015	Median Years to Complete Degree	Dismissed/Withdrew
Counseling Psychology	PhD	December 7 (Fall)	31	2	2 (0)	23 (0)	6	5.39	0
Professional Counseling	Med	January 31 (Fall)	38	17	17 (0)	37 (1)	13	2	
Instructional Psychology and Technology	Med	March 1 (Fall), October 1 (Spring)	14	7	5 (2)	19 (16)	10	1.83	0
Instructional Psychology and Technology	PhD	February 1 (Fall)	7	4	3 (1)	7 (6)	4	2.5	

APA Accreditation
Counseling PhD: Student Outcome Data website: http://www.ou.edu/content/education/edpy/counseling-psychology-degrees-and-programs/program-outcomes.html.

Doctoral Degree (PhD Counseling Psychology): For those doctoral students for whom a professional internship was required in this program prior to graduation:

Total students who applied for an internship: 8
Total students who obtained an internship: 8
Total students who obtained a paid internship: 8
Total students who obtained an unpaid internship: 0
Total students who were placed in APA/CPA-accredited internships: 8
Total students placed in internships not APA/CPA-accredited, but listed with the Association of Psychology Postdoctoral and Internship Centers (APPIC): 0
Total students placed in internships conforming to guidelines of the Council of Directors of School Psychology Programs (CDSPP): 0
Total students placed in internships that were not APA/CPA-accredited, APPIC or CDSSP listed: 0

Internships/Practica

Master's: Numerous hospitals and clinics in the local area. Doctoral: Students choose from APA-accredited sites (two in the local area and others across the nation).

Admissions

Entries appear in the following order: required test or GPA, minimum score (if required)/median score of students entering in 2015–2016.

Program	Degree	GRE-V	GRE-Q	GRE-Writing	GRE-Subject	Under-graduate GPA	Last 2 Years GPA	Psychol-ogy GPA	Master's GPA
Counseling Psychology	PhD	NA/NA	NA/NA	Not specified	Not specified	Not specified	Not specified	Not specified	NA/3.95
Professional Counseling	MEd	NA/154	NA/148	NA/3.82	Not specified	NA/3.25	Not specified	Not specified	Not specified
Instructional Psychology and Technology	MEd	Not specified	Not specified	Not specified	Not specified	Not specified	NA/NA	Not specified	Not specified
Instructional Psychology and Technology	PhD	NA/NA	NA/NA	NA/NA	Not specified	Not specified	Not specified	Not specified	NA/3.78

Admissions Requirements:

Degree	GRE	GRE-Subject	Letters of Recom-mendation	Research Statement	Writing Sample	CV	Interview
Master's/Specialist	Required	Optional	3	Required	Optional	Required	None
Doctoral	Required	Optional	3	Required	Optional	Required	Required

Please note if these criteria vary for different programs: The Instructional Psychology and Technology programs do not require interviews for all applicants. However, the Admissions Committee may require some students to interview in order to make final decisions regarding admission.

Admissions Criteria:

GRE scores—medium
Research experience—medium
Work experience—medium
Clinically related public service—medium

GPA—high
Letters of recommendation—medium
Interview—high
Statement of goals and objectives—medium

For additional information on admission requirements, visit http://www.ou.edu/content/education/edpy/apply.html.

Department Demographics

	Male (PT)	Female (PT)	Total	African-American/ Black (PT)	Hispanic/ Latino (PT)	Asian/ Pacific Islander (PT)	American Indian/ Alaska Native (PT)	Caucasian/ White (PT)	Unknown	Multiethnic (PT)	ADA (PT)	Int'l (PT)
Students	29 (13)	128 (38)	208	11 (3)	9 (7)	4 (1)	7 (2)	108 (33)	6 (2)	12 (3)		16 (4)

Financial Information/Assistance

Tuition: For information on tuition costs, visit http://www.ou.edu/content/bursar/tuition_fees.html. Tuition is subject to change. Additional fees are assessed to students beyond the costs of tuition for the following: university services, course materials, and technology. Tuition costs vary by program.

Doctoral:
State residents: $190 per credit hour.
Nonstate residents: $739 per credit hour.

Master's:
State residents: $190 per credit hour.
Nonstate residents: $739 per credit hour.

Financial Assistance:

	Teaching Assistantship (% Receiving)	Teaching Assistantship Tuition Remission	Research Assistantship (% Receiving)	Research Assistantship Tuition Remission	Fellowship (% Receiving)	Fellowship Tuition Remission
First-Year Student	$10,197 (NA)	Full	$10,197 (NA)	Full	$15,197 (NA)	Full
Advanced Student	$10,197 (NA)	Full	$10,197 (NA)	Full	$15,197 (NA)	Full

For additional information on financial assistance, visit http://www.ou.edu/content/gradweb/funding_and_aid.html.

Employment of Department Graduates

Master's:
Employed in a professional position in a school system: 4
Employed in business or industry: 1
Employed in government agency: 1
Employed in a community mental health/counseling center: 1
Still seeking employment: 1
Do not know: 12
Total: 20

Doctoral:
Enrolled in a postdoctoral residency/fellowship: 3
Employed in independent practice: 2
Employed in an academic position at a university: 1
Employed in other positions at a higher education institution: 1
Employed in government agency: 1
Not seeking employment: 1
Other employment position: 2
Do not know: 1
Total: 12

Additional Information

Housing and Day Care: On-campus housing is available. See the following website for more information: http://www.housing.ou.edu. On-campus day care facilities are available. See the following website for more information: http://www.ou.edu/education/centers-and-partnerships/institute-of-child-development.

Information for Students With Physical Disabilities: See the following website: http://drc.ou.edu/.

Special Facilities or Resources: The Counseling Psychology Clinic is a community-based training site for our students. The clientele reflects diverse diagnostic classifications with some cultural diversity. Couples, children, and families make up a large proportion of the population served by the clinic.

Application Information: Graduate Programs Officer, Dept. of Educational Psychology, University of Oklahoma, 820 Van Vleet Oval, Room 321, Norman, OK 73019-2041. *Fee:* $50. *Online application:* https://www.applyweb.com/apply/ougrad.

Oklahoma, University of
Department of Psychology
Arts and Sciences
455 West Lindsey
Norman, OK 73019-2007
Telephone: (405) 325-4511
Chairperson: Jorge Mendoza

E-mail: kpaine@ou.edu
Web: http://www.ou.edu/cas/psychology/

Orientation, Objectives, and Emphasis of Department

All programs are highly research oriented within the broad framework of experimental psychology. The department aims to produce creative and productive psychologists to function in academic and research settings, and toward this end emphasizes early and continuing involvement in research. Achievement of orientation and objectives is demonstrated by the excellent placement record of doctoral graduates, and by the department's recent rating as ninth in the nation in percent of publishing faculty. An excellent program in Quantitative Methods in Psychology is an especially attractive feature of the quality graduate training offered.

Programs and Degrees Offered

Program	Degree	Application Deadline	Applica-tions Received	Accepted	New Admits Enrolled (PT)	Total Enrolled (PT)	Degrees Awarded in 2014–2015	Median Years to Complete Degree	Dismissed/ Withdrew
Industrial/ Organizational Psychology	MA/MS	January 1 (Fall)	6	0	0 (0)	0 (0)	0		
Social Psychology	PhD	January 1 (Fall)	32	1	9 (0)	14 (0)	3	5.5	0
Cognitive Psychology	PhD	January 1 (Fall)	16	6	6 (0)	15 (0)	4	5	0
Industrial/ Organizational Psychology	PhD	January 1 (Fall)	64	11	7 (0)	23	6	5	0
Quantitative/ Measurement	PhD	January 1 (Fall)	15	2	1	5 (0)	1	5.5	0

Admissions

Entries appear in the following order: required test or GPA, minimum score (if required)/median score of students entering in 2015–2016.

Program	Degree	GRE-V	GRE-Q	GRE-Writing	GRE-Subject	Under-graduate GPA	Last 2 Years GPA	Psychol-ogy GPA	Master's GPA
Industrial/ Organizational Psychology	MA/MS	NA/155	NA/154	NA/4.8	Not specified	3/3.6	NA/3.8	Not specified	Not specified
Social Psychology	PhD	NA/155	NA/154	NA/5	Not specified	3/3.7	NA/3.8	Not specified	Not specified
Cognitive Psychology	PhD	NA/155	NA/154	NA/5	Not specified	3/3.6	NA/3.8	Not specified	NA/3.8
Industrial/ Organizational Psychology	PhD	NA/156	NA/154	NA/5	Not specified	3/3.8	NA/3.8	Not specified	Not specified
Quantitative/ Measurement	PhD	NA/155	NA/157	NA/4.6	Not specified	3/3.8	NA/3.9	Not specified	Not specified

Admissions Requirements:

Degree	GRE	GRE-Subject	Letters of Recommendation	Research Statement	Writing Sample	CV	Interview
Master's/Specialist	Required	None	3	Required	Optional	Optional	Recommended
Doctoral	Required	None	3	Required	Optional	Optional	Recommended

Please note if these criteria vary for different programs: Work experience is more important to the I/O program.

Admissions Criteria:

GRE scores—high
Research experience—high
Work experience—medium
GPA—high

Letters of recommendation—high
Interview—medium
Statement of goals and objectives—high
Undergraduate psychology preparation—medium

Department Demographics

	Male (PT)	Female (PT)	Total	African-American/ Black (PT)	Hispanic/ Latino (PT)	Asian/ Pacific Islander (PT)	American Indian/ Alaska Native (PT)	Caucasian/ White (PT)	Unknown	Multiethnic (PT)	ADA (PT)	Int'l (PT)
Students	26 (0)	31 (0)	57	1 (0)	2 (0)	8 (0)	3 (0)	41 (0)	0 (0)	2 (0)	1 (0)	3 (0)

Financial Information/Assistance

Tuition: For information on tuition costs, visit https://www.ou.edu/content/bursar/tuition_fees.html. Additional fees are assessed to students beyond the costs of tuition for the following: semester fees and course fees.

Doctoral:
State residents: $191 per credit hour.
Nonstate residents: $740 per credit hour.

Master's:
State residents: $191 per credit hour.
Nonstate residents: $740 per credit hour.

Financial Assistance:

	Teaching Assistantship (% Receiving)	Teaching Assistantship Tuition Remission	Research Assistantship (% Receiving)	Research Assistantship Tuition Remission	Fellowship (% Receiving)	Fellowship Tuition Remission
First-Year Student	$13,482 (NA)	Full	$13,482 (NA)	Full	$16,982 (NA)	Full
Advanced Student	$14,490 (NA)	Full	$14,490 (NA)	Full	NA (NA)	NA

For additional information on financial assistance, visit http://www.ou.edu/content/cas/psychology/graduate-studies/financial-support.html.

Employment of Department Graduates

Doctoral:
Employed in an academic position at a university: 7
Employed in academic position at a 2-year/4-year college: 2
Employed in a professional position in a school system: 2
Employed in business or industry: 1
Employed in government agency: 1
Do not know: 1
Total: 14

Additional Information

Housing and Day Care: On-campus housing is available. See the following website for more information: http://www.ou.edu/housingandfood.html. On-campus day care facilities are available.

Information for Students With Physical Disabilities: See the following website: http://www.ou.edu/content/drc.html.

Special Facilities or Resources: The research facilities of the Department are housed primarily in a social science complex. In this complex, modern research laboratories exist for cognitive processes, personality psychology, and social psychology. The I/O psychology program has a large amount of dedicated research space. This space is designed to support a variety of relevant research activities. Specifically, this space provides graduate students with the resources needed for data collection, data management, data analysis, and general computer use. The University's Computing Center is available for faculty-student research and extensive computing facilities are periodically updated and maintained by the Department. Training is routinely available within the department (including formal courses) on the use of computers for experimentation and for statistical analysis.

Application Information: Kathryn Paine. *Fee:* $40. *Online application:* https://www.applyweb.com/ougrad/.

Tulsa, University of

Department of Psychology
Henry Kendall College of Arts and Sciences
800 South Tucker Drive
Tulsa, OK 74104-3189
Telephone: (918) 631-2894
Chairperson: Dr. John McNulty
E-mail: dani-veit@utulsa.edu
Web: http://artsandsciences.utulsa.edu/academics/departments-schools/psychology/

Orientation, Objectives, and Emphasis of Department

Our graduate programs in applied psychology are central to the departmental mission, which is: to generate new psychological knowledge to help individuals, organizations, and communities make decisions and solve problems; to offer a future-oriented, intellectually challenging, and socially relevant curriculum; and to equip students to make a difference through their work by providing them with an extensive knowledge base as well as the analytical and practical skills needed to apply knowledge wisely. Our programs train students to do what applied psychologists actually do in today's society. The programs in I/O psychology emphasize personnel psychology and organizational development, theory and behavior, with a special focus on individual assessment. The doctoral program in clinical psychology develops scientist–practitioners using the following training components. First, coursework is distributed across clinical core, general psychology, methodology core, and elective offerings. Second, research mentoring is experienced in the precandidacy and dissertation projects. Third, procedural knowledge is developed in clinical practicum and internship training. Fourth, declarative knowledge is developed through comprehensive written and oral examinations covering general psychological knowledge and methods, and clinical psychology.

Programs and Degrees Offered

Program	Degree	Application Deadline	Applications Received	Accepted	New Admits Enrolled (PT)	Total Enrolled (PT)	Degrees Awarded in 2014–2015	Median Years to Complete Degree	Dismissed/Withdrew
Industrial/ Organizational Psychology	PhD	December 15 (Fall)	21	3	3 (0)	11 (0)	1	5.9	0
Clinical Psychology Ma/Jd	MA/MS	December 1 (Fall)	1	0	0 (0)	0 (0)	0		0
Industrial/ Organizational Psychology Ma/Jd	MA/MS	December 15 (Fall)	1	1	1 (0)	1 (0)	0		0
Industrial/ Organizational Psychology	MA/MS	December 15 (Fall)	24	7	2 (0)	12 (0)	10	2.4	

Programs and Degrees Offered *(con't.)*

Program	Degree	Application Deadline	Applica-tions Received	Accepted	New Admits Enrolled (PT)	Total Enrolled (PT)	Degrees Awarded in 2014–2015	Median Years to Complete Degree	Dismissed/ Withdrew
Clinical Psychology	PhD	December 1 (Fall)	84	5	6 (0)	41 (0)	5	6	1
Clinical Psychology	MA/MS	December 1 (Fall)	15	0	0	6	3	4	2

APA Accreditation

Clinical PhD: Student Outcome Data website: https://artsandsciences.utulsa.edu/academics/departments-schools/psychology/clinical-psychology-graduate-programs/.

Doctoral Degree (PhD Clinical Psychology): For those doctoral students for whom a professional internship was required in this program prior to graduation:

Total students who applied for an internship: 7
Total students who obtained an internship: 7
Total students who obtained a paid internship: 7
Total students who obtained an unpaid internship: 0
Total students who were placed in APA/CPA-accredited internships: 6
Total students placed in internships not APA/CPA-accredited, but listed with the Association of Psychology Postdoctoral and Internship Centers (APPIC): 1
Total students placed in internships conforming to guidelines of the Council of Directors of School Psychology Programs (CDSPP): 0
Total students placed in internships that were not APA/CPA-accredited, APPIC or CDSSP listed: 0

Master's Degree (MA/MS Industrial/Organizational Psychology): An internship experience, such as a final research project or "capstone" experience is required of graduates.

Internships/Practica

In the clinical program, supervised applied training begins early in the program. Practicum experiences occur primarily in community settings, utilizing the wide variety of agencies with which the department has relationships and allowing the student to interact with various mental health professionals. Placements include the university health center, community mental health centers, hospitals, community service agencies, and private practice groups. Attempts are made to allow students to choose practicum activities that are most consistent with their professional goals, although it is recognized that a diversity of experiences can provide a strong foundation for professional development. Practicum activities are supervised by an on-site professional, and the practicum experience is organized and monitored by the Coordinator of Practicum Training in conjunction with the Clinical Program Committee.

Admissions

Entries appear in the following order: required test or GPA, minimum score (if required)/median score of students entering in 2015–2016.

Program	Degree	GRE-V	GRE-Q	GRE-Writing	GRE-Subject	Under-graduate GPA	Last 2 Years GPA	Psychol-ogy GPA	Master's GPA
Industrial/ Organizational Psychology	PhD	NA/157	NA/154	NA/3.9	Not specified	3/4	Not specified	Not specified	Not specified
Clinical Psychology MA/JD	MA/MS	NA/NA	NA/NA	NA/NA	Not specified	3/NA	Not specified	Not specified	Not specified
Industrial/ Organizational Psychology MA/JD	MA/MS	NA/NA	NA/NA	NA/NA	Not specified	3/NA	Not specified	Not specified	Not specified
Industrial/ Organizational Psychology	MA/MS	NA/152	NA/148	NA/3.8	Not specified	3/3.4	Not specified	Not specified	Not specified

Admissions *(con't.)*

Program	Degree	GRE-V	GRE-Q	GRE-Writing	GRE-Subject	Undergraduate GPA	Last 2 Years GPA	Psychology GPA	Master's GPA
Clinical Psychology	PhD	NA/159	NA/151	NA/4.7	Not specified	3/3.6	Not specified	Not specified	NA/3.9
Clinical Psychology	MA/MS	Not specified	Not specified	Not specified	Not specified	Not specified	Not specified	Not specified	Not specified

Admissions Requirements:

Degree	GRE	GRE-Subject	Letters of Recommendation	Research Statement	Writing Sample	CV	Interview
Master's/Specialist	Required	None	3	Required	Optional	Required	None
Doctoral	Required	Optional	3	Required	Optional	Required	Required

Please note if these criteria vary for different programs: Resume or CV required for clinical program applicants. Interview for clinical PhD only.

Admissions Criteria:

GRE scores—high
Research experience—high
Work experience—low
Clinically related public service—medium
GPA—high

Letters of recommendation—high
Interview—high
Statement of goals and objectives—high
Undergraduate psychology preparation—medium
Quality of undergrad inst—medium

Department Demographics

	Male (PT)	Female (PT)	Total	African-American/ Black (PT)	Hispanic/ Latino (PT)	Asian/ Pacific Islander (PT)	American Indian/ Alaska Native (PT)	Caucasian/ White (PT)	Unknown	Multiethnic (PT)	ADA (PT)	Int'l (PT)
Students	21 (0)	50 (0)	71	1 (0)	5 (0)	10 (0)	3 (0)	37 (0)	13 (0)	1 (0)	0 (0)	5 (0)

Financial Information/Assistance

Tuition: For information on tuition costs, visit https://graduate.utulsa.edu/admission/tuition-expenses/. Tuition is subject to change. Additional fees are assessed to students beyond the costs of tuition for the following: student association fee - $60; community fee - $100/sem.

Doctoral:
State residents: $1,176 per credit hour.
Nonstate residents: $1,176 per credit hour.

Master's:
State residents: $1,176 per credit hour.
Nonstate residents: $1,176 per credit hour.

Financial Assistance:

	Teaching Assistantship (% Receiving)	Teaching Assistantship Tuition Remission	Research Assistantship (% Receiving)	Research Assistantship Tuition Remission	Fellowship (% Receiving)	Fellowship Tuition Remission
First-Year Student	$13,908 (43)	Full	$13,908 (57)	Full	NA (0)	Full
Advanced Student	$13,908 (23)	Full	$13,908 (58)	Full	NA (19)	Full

For additional information on financial assistance, visit http://admission.utulsa.edu/financial-aid/.

Employment of Department Graduates

Master's:
Enrolled in a psychology doctoral program: 6
Employed in business or industry: 12
Total: 18

Doctoral:
Employed in a community mental health/counseling center: 2
Total: 2

Additional Information

Housing and Day Care: On-campus housing is available. See the following website for more information: http://utulsa.edu/campus-life/housing-dining/. On-campus day care facilities are available. See the following website for more information: http://www.kindercare.com/our-centers/tulsa/ok/000859/.

Special Facilities or Resources: The Department of Psychology is located in Lorton Hall, a building located near the center of the TU campus. The building contains faculty offices, classrooms, offices for graduate students on assistantships, a graduate student lounge, research space, and clinical training space. McFarlin Library, a 2-minute walk from Lorton Hall, contains more than 3 million items and more than 6,000 periodical subscriptions. The library's catalogue is computerized and is accessible from terminals across campus. Computer searches of the major information databases in psychology are available to students at no charge. Major computer application suites and statistical packages (e.g., SPSS) are available for word processing, data analyses, test interpretation, and other tasks. The university has several computer labs with a variety of hardware configurations and software packages for student use. Visiting scholars and professionals often join the graduate faculty in presenting special courses, workshops, and seminars. Each year, colloquium speakers offer opinions, ideas, and research on topics of current interest in psychology.

Application Information: Graduate School, University of Tulsa, 800 S. Tucker Drive, Tulsa, OK 74104. *Fee:* $40. *Online application:* https://applynow.utulsa.edu/.

George Fox University

Graduate Department of Clinical Psychology
School of Behavioral and Health Sciences
414 North Meridian Street #V104
Newberg, OR 97132-2697
Telephone: (503) 554-2370
Chairperson: Mary Peterson

E-mail: psyd@georgefox.edu
Web: http://psyd.georgefox.edu

Orientation, Objectives, and Emphasis of Department

The goal of the Graduate Department of Clinical Psychology (GDCP) is to prepare professional psychologists who are competent to provide psychological services in a wide variety of clinical settings, who are knowledgeable in critical evaluation and application of psychological research, and who are committed to the highest standards of professional ethics. The central distinctive feature of the program is the integration of a Christian worldview and the science of psychology at philosophical, practical and personal levels. Graduates are trained broadly but also as specialists in meeting the unique psychological needs of the Christian community and others who wish a spiritual dimension to be included in their treatment. Other distinctive aspects of the program include close mentoring using clinical and research team models and an option for training emphases in Assessment, Child & Adolescent and Health Psychology. Graduates are prepared for licensure as clinical psychologists. Alumni of the GDCP are licensed in numerous states throughout the U.S. They engage in practice in a variety of settings, including independent and group practice, hospitals, community mental health clinics, government, corrections, public health agencies, and church and para-church organizations. Graduates also provide consultation and teach in a variety of settings.

Programs and Degrees Offered

Program	Degree	Application Deadline	Applica-tions Received	Accepted	New Admits Enrolled (PT)	Total Enrolled (PT)	Degrees Awarded in 2014–2015	Median Years to Complete Degree	Dismissed/ Withdrew
Clinical Psychology	PsyD	January 15 (Fall)	86	37	24 (0)	112 (7)	16	5.33	0

APA Accreditation

Clinical PsyD (Doctor of Psychology).

Doctoral Degree (PsyD Clinical Psychology): For those doctoral students for whom a professional internship was required in this program prior to graduation:
Total students who applied for an internship: 24
Total students who obtained an internship: 24
Total students who obtained a paid internship: 24
Total students who obtained an unpaid internship: 0
Total students who were placed in APA/CPA-accredited internships: 19
Total students placed in internships not APA/CPA-accredited, but listed with the Association of Psychology Postdoctoral and Internship Centers (APPIC): 3
Total students placed in internships conforming to guidelines of the Council of Directors of School Psychology Programs (CDSPP): 0
Total students placed in internships that were not APA/CPA-accredited, APPIC or CDSSP listed: 2

Internships/Practica

Students are required to complete four years of practicum (minimum of 1,500 hours) in a variety of settings in the greater Portland metropolitan area. Practicum settings include hospitals, primary care medical settings, community mental health agencies, drug and alcohol programs, schools, and prisons. In-patient and out-patient experiences are available. All practicum experience is gained under the careful supervision of licensed psychologists at the practicum sites. Additionally, students receive weekly clinical oversight on campus by core faculty. Students apply for internships within the system developed by the Association of Psychology Postdoctoral and Internship Centers (APPIC). Students complete a one-year full-time internship (2,000 hours) at an approved internship site during their fifth year in the program. Usually, 95% of applicants obtain an APA- and/or APPIC-approved internship sites.

Admissions

Entries appear in the following order: required test or GPA, minimum score (if required)/median score of students entering in 2015–2016.

Program	Degree	GRE-V	GRE-Q	GRE-Writing	GRE-Subject	Under-graduate GPA	Last 2 Years GPA	Psychol-ogy GPA	Master's GPA
Clinical Psychology	PsyD	NA/NA	NA/NA	Not specified	Not specified	3/3.4	Not specified	Not specified	Not specified

Admissions Requirements:

Degree	GRE	GRE-Subject	Letters of Recom-mendation	Research Statement	Writing Sample	CV	Interview
Doctoral	Required	Optional	4	Required	Required	Required	Required

Admissions Criteria:

GRE scores—high
Research experience—low
Work experience—medium
Clinically related public service—medium
GPA—high

Letters of recommendation—high
Interview—high
Statement of goals and objectives—high
Undergraduate psychology preparation—medium
Christian worldview—high

For additional information on admission requirements, visit http://www.georgefox.edu/psyd/admission/index.html.

Department Demographics

	Male (PT)	Female (PT)	Total	African-American/ Black (PT)	Hispanic/ Latino (PT)	Asian/ Pacific Islander (PT)	American Indian/ Alaska Native (PT)	Caucasian/ White (PT)	Unknown	Multiethnic (PT)	ADA (PT)	Int'l (PT)
Students	45 (2)	67 (5)	119	4 (0)	9 (0)	7 (0)	3 (0)	85 (7)	0 (0)	4 (0)	0 (0)	1 (0)

Financial Information/Assistance

Tuition: For information on tuition costs, visit http://www.georgefox.edu/offices/student-accounts/grad/tuition/psyd/index.html. Tuition is subject to change. Additional fees are assessed to students beyond the costs of tuition for the following: Student body, health/counseling.

Doctoral:
State residents: $26,218 per academic year.
State residents: $839 per credit hour.
Nonstate residents: $26,218 per academic year.
Nonstate residents: $839 per credit hour.

Financial Assistance:

	Teaching Assistantship (% Receiving)	Teaching Assistantship Tuition Remission	Research Assistantship (% Receiving)	Research Assistantship Tuition Remission	Fellowship (% Receiving)	Fellowship Tuition Remission
First-Year Student	NA (NA)	NA	NA (NA)	NA	$4,000 (NA)	Partial
Advanced Student	$3,000 (42)	NA	$2,100 (3)	NA	$4,000 (18)	Partial

For additional information on financial assistance, visit http://www.georgefox.edu/offices/financial-aid/grad/index.html.

Employment of Department Graduates

Doctoral:
Enrolled in a postdoctoral residency/fellowship: 24
Total: 24

Additional Information

Housing and Day Care: No on-campus housing is available. No on-campus day care facilities are available.

Information for Students With Physical Disabilities: See the following website: http://www.georgefox.edu/offices/dso/.

Personal Behavior Statement: http://www.georgefox.edu/psyd/about/beliefs.html.

Special Facilities or Resources: High-speed microcomputers, laser printers, and complete statistical (SPSS PC+) and graphics software are provided in a computer lab. The Murdock Learning Resource Center provides library support for the psychology program. The library has excellent access to materials important to contemporary clinical and empirical work in most areas of clinical psychology. In addition, the library receives more than 140 periodicals in psychology and related disciplines, most available electronically. Students also have online access to major computerized databases through library services, including PsycInfo, DIALOG, ERIC, and many others. In addition to full-text access to many psychology journals, George Fox University maintains cooperative arrangements with other local educational institutions, providing psychology students with a full range of user services, including interlibrary loans and direct borrowing privileges. The PsyD building includes classrooms, faculty offices, student lounge area, computer lab, cafe, conference rooms, clinical demonstration and videotaping rooms, and student parking.

Application Information: Megan Janes, Graduate Admissions, George Fox University, 12753 SW 68th Avenue #P110, Portland, OR 97223. *Fee:* $40. *Online application:* https://www.georgefox.edu/online-application/.

Oregon, University of (2015 data)
Counseling Psychology
College of Education
5251 University of Oregon
Eugene, OR 97403-5251
Telephone: (541) 346-2456
Department Head: Benedict McWhirter

E-mail: cpsy@uoregon.edu
Web: https://education.uoregon.edu/program/counseling-psychology

---

Orientation, Objectives, and Emphasis of Department

Accredited by the American Psychological Association (APA) since 1955, the UO doctoral program in Counseling Psychology emphasizes an ecological model of training, research, and practice. Student research and training focuses on prevention and treatment relevant to work with children, adolescents, families, and adults. The ecological model holds that human behavior occurs within a context of multiple interacting systems, influenced by unique social, historical, political, and cultural factors. Students in the CPSY program are trained to view assessment, intervention, and research within the contexts of these systems. Development of multicultural competencies is emphasized throughout the curriculum.

Programs and Degrees Offered

Program	Degree	Application Deadline	Applications Received	Accepted	New Admits Enrolled (PT)	Total Enrolled (PT)	Degrees Awarded in 2014–2015	Median Years to Complete Degree	Dismissed/Withdrew
Counseling Psychology	PhD	December 15 (Fall)	206	12	7 (0)	43 (0)	8	6	0

APA Accreditation

Counseling PhD: Student Outcome Data website: https://education.uoregon.edu/program/counseling-psychology.

Doctoral Degree (PhD Counseling Psychology): For those doctoral students for whom a professional internship was required in this program prior to graduation:
Total students who applied for an internship: 6
Total students who obtained an internship: 6
Total students who obtained a paid internship: 6

Total students who obtained an unpaid internship: 0
Total students who were placed in APA/CPA-accredited internships: 6
Total students placed in internships not APA/CPA-accredited, but listed with the Association of Psychology Postdoctoral and Internship Centers (APPIC): 0
Total students placed in internships conforming to guidelines of the Council of Directors of School Psychology Programs (CDSPP): 0
Total students placed in internships that were not APA/CPA-accredited, APPIC or CDSSP listed: 0

Internships/Practica

All students are required to participate in one year each of both adult and child/family practica. Numerous externship opportunities exist throughout the community.

Admissions

Entries appear in the following order: required test or GPA, minimum score (if required)/median score of students entering in 2015–2016.

Program	Degree	GRE-V	GRE-Q	GRE-Writing	GRE-Subject	Under-graduate GPA	Last 2 Years GPA	Psychol-ogy GPA	Master's GPA
Counseling Psychology	PhD	NA/158	NA/155	NA/4.5	Not specified	NA/3.45	Not specified	Not specified	Not specified

Admissions Requirements:

Degree	GRE	GRE-Subject	Letters of Recom-mendation	Research Statement	Writing Sample	CV	Interview
Doctoral	Required	None	3	Required	None	Required	Required

Admissions Criteria:

GRE scores—medium
Research experience—high
Work experience—high
Clinically related public service—medium
GPA—high

Letters of recommendation—high
Interview—high
Statement of goals and objectives—high
Second language skills—low

For additional information on admission requirements, visit https://education.uoregon.edu/counseling-psychology/admissions.

Department Demographics

	Male (PT)	Female (PT)	Total	African-American/ Black (PT)	Hispanic/ Latino (PT)	Asian/ Pacific Islander (PT)	American Indian/ Alaska Native (PT)	Caucasian/ White (PT)	Unknown	Multiethnic (PT)	ADA (PT)	Int'l (PT)
Students	9 (0)	34 (0)	43	1 (0)	8 (0)	7 (0)	0 (0)	20 (0)	0 (0)	7 (0)	1 (0)	0 (0)

Financial Information/Assistance

Tuition: For information on tuition costs, visit http://registrar.uoregon.edu/costs/tuition-fees. Tuition is subject to change. Additional fees are assessed to students beyond the costs of tuition for the following: practicum courses have a $60 fee. Tuition costs vary by program.

Doctoral:
State residents: $18,978 per academic year.
State residents: $395 per credit hour.
Nonstate residents: $25,671 per academic year.
Nonstate residents: $535 per credit hour.

Financial Assistance:

	Teaching Assistantship (% Receiving)	Teaching Assistantship Tuition Remission	Research Assistantship (% Receiving)	Research Assistantship Tuition Remission	Fellowship (% Receiving)	Fellowship Tuition Remission
First-Year Student	$26,151 (100)	Full	NA (NA)	NA	$3,000 (25)	Full
Advanced Student	$31,191 (90)	Full	NA (NA)	NA	$3,000 (90)	Full

For additional information on financial assistance, visit https://education.uoregon.edu/counseling-psychology/student-funding.

Employment of Department Graduates

Doctoral:
Enrolled in a postdoctoral residency/fellowship: 3
Employed in other positions at a higher education institution: 1
Employed in business or industry: 1
Employed in a community mental health/counseling center: 2
Not seeking employment: 1
Total: 8

Additional Information

Housing and Day Care: On-campus housing is available. See the following website for more information: http://housing.uoregon.edu/. On-campus day care facilities are available. See the following website for more information: http://hr.uoregon.edu/content/child-care-campus.

Information for Students With Physical Disabilities: See the following website: http://aec.uoregon.edu/.

Special Facilities or Resources: Students work cooperatively in research areas at the Oregon Social Learning Center, the Oregon Research Institute, and the Prevention Science Institute.

Application Information: Office of Admissions, 1217 University of Oregon, Eugene, OR 97403-1217. *Fee:* $50. *Online application:* https://gradweb.uoregon.edu/online_app/application/guidelines1.asp.

Oregon, University of
Department of Psychology
College of Arts and Sciences
1227 University of Oregon
Eugene, OR 97403-1227
Telephone: (541) 346-5060
Department Head: Ulrich Mayr, PhD

E-mail: lolsen@uoregon.edu
Web: http://psychology.uoregon.edu/

Orientation, Objectives, and Emphasis of Department
The course of study is tailored largely to the student's particular needs. There are minimal formal requirements for the doctorate, which include three course sequences (contemporary issues in psychology, statistics, and a first-year research practicum); a supporting area requirement, consisting of at least two graduate-level, graded courses, and a major project, such as a paper or teaching an original course; a major preliminary examination; and, of course, the doctoral dissertation. Clinical students engage in additional coursework and several practica beginning in the first year. All programs require and are organized to facilitate student research from the first year.

Programs and Degrees Offered

Program	Degree	Application Deadline	Applica-tions Received	Accepted	New Admits Enrolled (PT)	Total Enrolled (PT)	Degrees Awarded in 2014–2015	Median Years to Complete Degree	Dismissed/ Withdrew
Clinical Psychology	PhD	December 1 (Fall)	288	5	5	27 (2)	1	7.3	
Cognitive/ Systems Neuroscience	PhD	December 1 (Fall)	100	4	3	17	3		0
Developmental Psychology	PhD	December 1 (Fall)	36	3	2	13 (1)	1		
Individualized Master's	MA/MS	May 15 (Fall)	48	4	4	7	11		
Social/ Personality Psychology	PhD	December 1 (Fall)	121	5	2	26 (1)	2		

APA Accreditation

Clinical PhD: Student Outcome Data website: http://psychology.uoregon.edu/research/research-areas/clinical/.

Doctoral Degree (PhD Clinical Psychology): For those doctoral students for whom a professional internship was required in this program prior to graduation:
Total students who applied for an internship: 3
Total students who obtained an internship: 3
Total students who obtained a paid internship: 3
Total students who obtained an unpaid internship: 0
Total students who were placed in APA/CPA-accredited internships: 3
Total students placed in internships not APA/CPA-accredited, but listed with the Association of Psychology Postdoctoral and Internship Centers (APPIC): 0
Total students placed in internships conforming to guidelines of the Council of Directors of School Psychology Programs (CDSPP): 0
Total students placed in internships that were not APA/CPA-accredited, APPIC or CDSSP listed: 0

Master's Degree (MA/MS Individualized Master's): An internship experience, such as a final research project or "capstone" experience is required of graduates.

Admissions

Entries appear in the following order: required test or GPA, minimum score (if required)/median score of students entering in 2015–2016.

Program	Degree	GRE-V	GRE-Q	GRE-Writing	GRE-Subject	Under-graduate GPA	Last 2 Years GPA	Psychol-ogy GPA	Master's GPA
Clinical Psychology	PhD	NA/160	NA/156	NA/4.5	Not specified	NA/3.8	NA/NA	NA/NA	Not specified
Cognitive/ Systems Neuroscience	PhD	NA/NA	NA/NA	NA/NA	Not specified	NA/NA	NA/NA	NA/NA	Not specified
Developmental Psychology	PhD	NA/NA	NA/NA	NA/NA	Not specified	NA/NA	NA/NA	NA/NA	Not specified
Individualized Master's	MA/MS	NA/NA	NA/NA	NA/NA	Not specified	NA/NA	NA/NA	NA/NA	Not specified
Social/ Personality Psychology	PhD	NA/NA	NA/NA	NA/NA	Not specified	NA/NA	NA/NA	NA/NA	Not specified

Admissions Requirements:

Degree	GRE	GRE-Subject	Letters of Recommendation	Research Statement	Writing Sample	CV	Interview
Master's/Specialist	Required	None	3	Required	Required	Required	None
Doctoral	Required	None	3	Required	Required	Required	Required

Please note if these criteria vary for different programs: Please check with department regarding interviews.

Admissions Criteria:

GRE scores—high
Research experience—high
Work experience—low
Clinically related public service—medium

GPA—high
Letters of recommendation—high
Interview—high
Statement of goals and objectives—high

For additional information on admission requirements, visit http://psychology.uoregon.edu/graduate/prospective-students/.

Department Demographics

	Male (PT)	Female (PT)	Total	African-American/ Black (PT)	Hispanic/ Latino (PT)	Asian/ Pacific Islander (PT)	American Indian/ Alaska Native (PT)	Caucasian/ White (PT)	Unknown	Multiethnic (PT)	ADA (PT)	Int'l (PT)
Students	33 (2)	57 (2)	94	2 (0)	5 (0)	10 (0)	0 (0)	52 (4)	21 (0)	0 (0)	0 (0)	11 (1)

Financial Information/Assistance

Tuition: For information on tuition costs, visit http://registrar.uoregon.edu/costs/tuition-fees.

Doctoral:
State residents: $17,299 per academic year.
Nonstate residents: $17,299 per academic year.

Master's:
State residents: $10,692 per academic year.
Nonstate residents: $10,692 per academic year.

Financial Assistance:

	Teaching Assistantship (% Receiving)	Teaching Assistantship Tuition Remission	Research Assistantship (% Receiving)	Research Assistantship Tuition Remission	Fellowship (% Receiving)	Fellowship Tuition Remission
First-Year Student	NA (NA)	Full	NA (NA)	Full	NA (NA)	Partial
Advanced Student	NA (NA)	Full	NA (NA)	Full	NA (NA)	Partial

For additional information on financial assistance, visit http://gradschool.uoregon.edu/funding-awards.

Employment of Department Graduates

No information provided.

Additional Information

Housing and Day Care: On-campus housing is available. See the following website for more information: http://housing.uoregon.edu/. On-campus day care facilities are available. See the following website for more information: http://hr.uoregon.edu/worklife/children-elders-family/child-care-campus.

Information for Students With Physical Disabilities: See the following website: http://aec.uoregon.edu/.

Application Information: Graduate Secretary, Department of Psychology, 1227 University of Oregon, Eugene, OR 97403-1227. *Fee:* $50. *Online application:* https://gradweb.uoregon.edu/online_app/application/guidelines1.asp.

Pacific University

School of Professional Psychology
College of Health Professions
Pacific University, 190 SE 8th Avenue, Suite 260
Hillsboro, OR 97123
Telephone: (503) 352-7277
Dean: Christiane Brems

E-mail: waldronk@pacificu.edu
Web: http://www.pacificu.edu/spp/

Orientation, Objectives, and Emphasis of Department

Pacific University's School of Professional Psychology prepares psychological professionals who foster collaborative relationships, have inquiring minds, create meaningful change, and dedicate themselves to models of health and well-being that support diversity and social justice. The curriculum is designed to build and integrate these components of professional practice. The School emphasizes community involvement and flexible, diversity-appropriate, practical applications of scientific psychology. The clinical psychology PsyD program follows a practitioner–scholar model of professional education, with coursework reflecting the latest empirical findings in the field. The Clinical Psychology PhD program follows a scientist–practitioner model of professional education.Students are trained to integrate the science and practice of psychology by completing specific requirements in didactic instruction and experiential practica. We present students with a broad range of theoretical perspectives and expose them to assessment, intervention, research/evaluation, consultation/education, and management/supervision. The Applied Psychological Science program is designed to prepare students for employment at the Master's level or for further training in psychology at the doctoral level. The use of the latest and best scientific findings is a mainstay of our professional training. The faculty encourage students to use the scientific method and an empirical approach in their work.

Programs and Degrees Offered

Program	Degree	Application Deadline	Applica-tions Received	Accepted	New Admits Enrolled (PT)	Total Enrolled (PT)	Degrees Awarded in 2014–2015	Median Years to Complete Degree	Dismissed/Withdrew
Clinical Psychology	PsyD	January 9 (Fall)	204	109	53 (0)	268 (24)	48	5	3
Clinical Psychology	PhD	January 9 (Fall)	45	13	9 (0)	21 (0)	0		0
Applied Psychological Science	MA/MS	April 6 (Fall)	83	72	30 (0)	30 (0)	0		0

APA Accreditation

Clinical PsyD: Student Outcome Data website: http://www.pacificu.edu/spp/program_stats.cfm.

Doctoral Degree (PsyD Clinical Psychology): For those doctoral students for whom a professional internship was required in this program prior to graduation:
Total students who applied for an internship: 46
Total students who obtained an internship: 43
Total students who obtained a paid internship: 43
Total students who obtained an unpaid internship: 0
Total students who were placed in APA/CPA-accredited internships: 30
Total students placed in internships not APA/CPA-accredited, but listed with the Association of Psychology Postdoctoral and Internship Centers (APPIC): 13
Total students placed in internships conforming to guidelines of the Council of Directors of School Psychology Programs (CDSPP): 0
Total students placed in internships that were not APA/CPA-accredited, APPIC or CDSSP listed: 0

Master's Degree (MA/MS Applied Psychological Science): An internship experience, such as a final research project or "capstone" experience is required of graduates.

Internships/Practica

Each student in the doctoral programs is required to complete six terms (2 years) of practicum. Training entails integration of theoretical knowledge through its application in clinical practice. The experience includes supervised practice in the application of professional psychological competencies with a range of client populations, age groups, and clinical problems. Doctoral students complete their 2 years of required practicum while they are taking courses in the program. The practicum experience includes a minimum of 500 training hours per year, of which approximately one third to one half are in direct service, one fourth in supervisory and training activities, and the remainder in administrative/clerical duties related to the above. All students gain some practicum experience at the program's own training clinic, and other community sites in the Portland area are also available, allowing for exposure to varied sites and populations. The Pacific Psychology and Comprehensive Health Clinic operates an APPIC member/APA-approved internship program. There are four intern positions. The MA in Applied Psychological Science students complete 500 hours (12 credits over three terms) of internship in their second year.

Admissions

Entries appear in the following order: required test or GPA, minimum score (if required)/median score of students entering in 2015–2016.

Program	Degree	GRE-V	GRE-Q	GRE-Writing	GRE-Subject	Under-graduate GPA	Last 2 Years GPA	Psychol-ogy GPA	Master's GPA
Clinical Psychology	PsyD	NA/154	NA/150	NA/4	Not specified	NA/3.47	Not specified	Not specified	NA/3.89
Clinical Psychology	PhD	NA/154	NA/149	NA/4	Not specified	3.3/3.39	Not specified	Not specified	NA/3.96
Applied Psychological Science	MA/MS	Not specified	Not specified	Not specified	Not specified	NA/3.3	NA/3.43	Not specified	Not specified

Admissions Requirements:

Degree	GRE	GRE-Subject	Letters of Recom-mendation	Research Statement	Writing Sample	CV	Interview
Master's/Specialist	None	None	3	Required	Optional	Required	Recom-mended
Doctoral	Required	Optional	3	Required	Required	Required	Required

Please note if these criteria vary for different programs: Applicants with an advanced degree (Master's or above) may apply for a waiver of the GRE requirement for the PsyD program.

Admissions Criteria:

GRE scores—medium
Research experience—medium
Work experience—medium
Clinically related public service—low
GPA—medium

Letters of recommendation—high
Interview—high
Statement of goals and objectives—high
Undergraduate psychology preparation—medium
Fit with program—high

Department Demographics

	Male (PT)	Female (PT)	Total	African-American/ Black (PT)	Hispanic/ Latino (PT)	Asian/ Pacific Islander (PT)	American Indian/ Alaska Native (PT)	Caucasian/ White (PT)	Unknown (PT)	Multiethnic (PT)	ADA (PT)	Int'l (PT)
Students	74 (7)	245 (17)	343	6 (0)	24 (0)	28 (1)	2 (1)	197 (20)	27 (2)	35 (0)	22 (4)	2 (1)

Financial Information/Assistance

Tuition: Tuition is subject to change. Additional fees are assessed to students beyond the costs of tuition for the following: Background check: $70; Dissertation Fee (PsyD/PhD): $75; Clinical Competency Exam (PsyD): $75. Tuition costs vary by program.

Doctoral:
State residents: $32,813 per academic year.
State residents: $994 per credit hour.
Nonstate residents: $32,813 per academic year.
Nonstate residents: $994 per credit hour.

Master's:
State residents: $24,362 per academic year.
State residents: $986 per credit hour.
Nonstate residents: $24,362 per academic year.
Nonstate residents: $986 per credit hour.

Financial Assistance:

	Teaching Assistantship (% Receiving)	Teaching Assistantship Tuition Remission	Research Assistantship (% Receiving)	Research Assistantship Tuition Remission	Fellowship (% Receiving)	Fellowship Tuition Remission
First-Year Student	NA (NA)	NA	$5,000 (100)	NA	$3,000 (5)	Partial
Advanced Student	$1,200 (15)	NA	NA (NA)	NA	$3,000 (5)	Partial

For additional information on financial assistance, visit http://www.pacificu.edu/future-graduate-professional/graduate-admissions/graduate-professional-financial-aid.

Employment of Department Graduates

Doctoral:
Enrolled in a postdoctoral residency/fellowship: 25
Employed in other positions at a higher education institution: 4
Employed in government agency: 4
Employed in a community mental health/counseling center: 5
Employed in a hospital/medical center: 2
Other employment position: 4
Do not know: 4
Total: 48

Additional Information

Housing and Day Care: No on-campus housing is available. No on-campus day care facilities are available.

Information for Students With Physical Disabilities: See the following website: http://www.pacificu.edu/about-us/offices/learning-support-services.

Special Facilities or Resources: The School maintains the Pacific Psychology and Comprehensive Health Clinic, a training clinic at two sites. The Hillsboro clinic is located on the Hillsboro Campus, and provides services in both Spanish and English. The Portland clinic is located in downtown Portland. These clinics offer a wide range of psychological services to the community.

Application Information: Pacific University, Graduate and Professional Programs Office of Admissions, 190 SE 8th Avenue, Suite 181, Hillsboro, OR 97123. *Fee:* $40. *Online application:* https://www.applyweb.com/apply/pup/index.html.

Portland State University
Psychology Department
College of Liberal Arts & Sciences
P.O. Box 751
Portland, OR 97207-0751
Telephone: (503) 725-3923
Chairperson: Ellen Skinner, PhD

E-mail: tbodner@pdx.edu
Web: http://www.pdx.edu/psy/

Orientation, Objectives, and Emphasis of Department

Students are given a broad background in applied psychology, which prepares them for careers in academics, research, or various applied settings, such as governmental agencies, manufacturing and service industries, health organizations and labor organizations. Doctoral students major in one specialty area and minor in a second (e.g., research methods, Occupational Health Psychology). Major areas include Applied Developmental Psychology, focusing on how knowledge and research regarding human development can be used to help solve real-world problems. The major focus is Developmental Science and Education, with special attention to the development of motivation, mindfulness, self and identity, and coping in the context of relationships with parents, teachers, and peers. Industrial/Organizational (I/O) Psychology concerns the application of psychological theories, research methods, and intervention strategies to workplace issues, with a goal of helping organizations to be highly productive while ensuring that their workers are able to lead physically and psychologically healthy work lives. The Applied Social and Community area faculty/students share an interest in urban health and community well-being, which includes work promoting mental and physical health, as well as healthy social outcomes and remediating negative influences like discrimination. Graduate students in the area specialize in either the Applied Social or Community Psychology track.

Programs and Degrees Offered

Program	Degree	Application Deadline	Applications Received	Accepted	New Admits Enrolled (PT)	Total Enrolled (PT)	Degrees Awarded in 2014–2015	Median Years to Complete Degree	Dismissed/Withdrew
Applied Developmental	PhD	December 15 (Fall)	28	2	2	17 (0)	1		0
Applied Social & Community	PhD	December 15 (Fall)	67	3	3 (0)	17 (0)	2	6	0
Industrial/ Organizational Psychology	PhD	December 15 (Fall)	124	3	3 (0)	15 (0)	2	5	0

Internships/Practica

The university is located in downtown Portland, the major metropolitan area in the state of Oregon. Consequently, internships are readily available in a variety of applied settings. Since the program emphasizes applied psychology, students receive training in their area of specialty not only through close work with faculty but also through structured participation in community organizations.

Admissions

Entries appear in the following order: required test or GPA, minimum score (if required)/median score of students entering in 2015–2016.

Program	Degree	GRE-V	GRE-Q	GRE-Writing	GRE-Subject	Undergraduate GPA	Last 2 Years GPA	Psychology GPA	Master's GPA
Applied Developmental	PhD	NA/161	NA/158	NA/5.5	Not specified	3.25/3.95	NA/NA	Not specified	Not specified
Applied Social & Community	PhD	NA/161	NA/154	NA/4.3	Not specified	3.25/3.76	NA/NA	Not specified	Not specified
Industrial/ Organizational Psychology	PhD	NA/160	NA/159	NA/4.8	Not specified	3.25/3.85	NA/NA	Not specified	Not specified

Admissions Requirements:

Degree	GRE	GRE-Subject	Letters of Recommendation	Research Statement	Writing Sample	CV	Interview
Doctoral	Required	Optional	3	Required	Optional	Required	None

Admissions Criteria:

GRE scores—high

Research experience—high

Work experience—medium

Clinically related public service—low

GPA—high

Letters of recommendation—high

Statement of goals and objectives—high

Undergraduate psychology preparation—medium

For additional information on admission requirements, visit http://www.pdx.edu/psy/application-instructions.

Department Demographics

	Male (PT)	Female (PT)	Total	African-American/ Black (PT)	Hispanic/ Latino (PT)	Asian/ Pacific Islander (PT)	American Indian/ Alaska Native (PT)	Caucasian/ White (PT)	Unknown (PT)	Multiethnic (PT)	ADA (PT)	Int'l (PT)
Students	12 (0)	37 (0)	49	0 (0)	1 (0)	1 (0)	0 (0)	0 (0)	47 (0)	0 (0)	0 (0)	0 (0)

Financial Information/Assistance

Tuition: For information on tuition costs, visit http://www.pdx.edu/financial-services/tuition-fees. Tuition is subject to change. Additional fees are assessed to students beyond the costs of tuition for the following: health services, building, campus recreation.

Doctoral:

State residents: $10,017 per academic year.

State residents: $371 per credit hour.

Nonstate residents: $15,417 per academic year.

Nonstate residents: $571 per credit hour.

Financial Assistance:

	Teaching Assistantship (% Receiving)	Teaching Assistantship Tuition Remission	Research Assistantship (% Receiving)	Research Assistantship Tuition Remission	Fellowship (% Receiving)	Fellowship Tuition Remission
First-Year Student	$10,800 (NA)	Full	$10,800 (NA)	Full	$10,800 (NA)	Full
Advanced Student	$12,250 (NA)	Full	$11,760 (NA)	Full	$11,760 (NA)	Full

For additional information on financial assistance, visit http://www.pdx.edu/psy/funding-possibilities.

Employment of Department Graduates

Doctoral:

Enrolled in a postdoctoral residency/fellowship: 1

Employed in other positions at a higher education institution: 6

Employed in business or industry: 1

Total: 8

Additional Information

Housing and Day Care: On-campus housing is available. See the following website for more information: http://www.pdx.edu/housing/. On-campus day care facilities are available. See the following website for more information: http://www.pdx.edu/helen-gordon-center/.

Information for Students With Physical Disabilities: See the following website: http://www.pdx.edu/drc/.

Special Facilities or Resources: The Department of Psychology's location in the heart of downtown Portland offers unique academic and research opportunities in the service of the department's applied mission. Strong collaborative relationships with local industry, organizations, and community agencies offer venues for course related projects, faculty research initiatives, practicum placements, and required student research. A number of University-based resources also enhance our students' skills and experiences. For example, the University's writing center allows faculty and students to hone technical writing skills. The Instructional Development Support Center provides training in computer and media-based applications to foster improved teaching and more sophisticated research approaches.

Application Information: Portland State University, P.O. Box 751, Portland, OR 97207-0751. *Fee:* $50. *Online application:* http://www.pdx.edu/ogs/graduate-admissions.

Southern Oregon University

Master's in Clinical Mental Health Counseling
1250 Siskiyou Boulevard
Ashland, OR 97520
Telephone: (541) 552-6947
Chairperson: Paul Murray, PhD

E-mail: MHC@sou.edu
Web: http://www.sou.edu/psychology/mhc/

Orientation, Objectives, and Emphasis of Department

The principle objective of the Master's degree in Clinical Mental Health Counseling is to provide professional training in the application of psychological principles and methodologies in order to increase functioning and service delivery in public and private agencies, organizations, and communities. The Clinical Mental Health Counseling program is based on a common integrated core of courses. The central goal of this core is to train master's-level practitioners who are grounded in professional ethics and values, well-versed in the empirical nature of their professions, and sensitive to and supportive of the increasing multicultural diversity of our communities. The Clinical Mental Health Counseling program is accredited by the Council for Accreditation of Counseling and Related Educational Programs (CACREP). This program is also recognized by the Oregon Board of Licensed Professional Counselors and Therapists (OBLPCT) as meeting the educational requirements for application for licensure at a Licensed Professional Counselor.

Programs and Degrees Offered

Program	Degree	Application Deadline	Applica- tions Received	Accepted	New Admits Enrolled (PT)	Total Enrolled (PT)	Degrees Awarded in 2014– 2015	Median Years to Complete Degree	Dismissed/ Withdrew
Clinical Mental Health Counseling	MA/MS	February 1 (Fall)	59	23	23 (0)	44 (0)	18	2	2

Internships/Practica

The Clinical Mental Health Counseling program requires on-campus practica during the first year of coursework. Internship placement in the community for students in the second year is required to help fulfill state license requirements.

Admissions

Entries appear in the following order: required test or GPA, minimum score (if required)/median score of students entering in 2015–2016.

Program	Degree	GRE-V	GRE-Q	GRE- Writing	GRE- Subject	Under- graduate GPA	Last 2 Years GPA	Psychol- ogy GPA	Master's GPA
Clinical Mental Health Counseling	MA/MS	NA/153	NA/147	NA/3.9	Not specified	2.5/3.6	3.2/3.6	2.98/3.6	Not specified

Admissions Requirements:

Degree	GRE	GRE- Subject	Letters of Recom- mendation	Research Statement	Writing Sample	CV	Interview
Master's/Specialist	Required	None	3	Required	Required	Optional	None

Admissions Criteria:

GRE scores—high
Research experience—medium
Work experience—medium
Clinically related public service—low

GPA—high
Letters of recommendation—high
Statement of goals and objectives—high
Undergraduate psychology preparation—medium

For additional information on admission requirements, visit http://www.sou.edu/psychology/mhc/requirements.html.

Department Demographics

	Male (PT)	Female (PT)	Total	African-American/ Black (PT)	Hispanic/ Latino (PT)	Asian/ Pacific Islander (PT)	American Indian/ Alaska Native (PT)	Caucasian/ White (PT)	Unknown	Multiethnic (PT)	ADA (PT)	Int'l (PT)
Students	10 (0)	34 (0)	44	0 (0)	3 (0)	1 (0)	3 (0)	27 (0)	8 (0)	2 (0)	1 (0)	0 (0)

Financial Information/Assistance

Tuition: For information on tuition costs, visit http://sou.edu/enrollment/tuitionandfees.html. Tuition is subject to change. Additional fees are assessed to students beyond the costs of tuition for the following: Building, Incidental & Green Tag, Health Service, Student Rec Center.

Master's:
State residents: $19,056 per academic year.
State residents: $397 per credit hour.
Nonstate residents: $23,856 per academic year.
Nonstate residents: $497 per credit hour.

Financial Assistance:

	Teaching Assistantship (% Receiving)	Teaching Assistantship Tuition Remission	Research Assistantship (% Receiving)	Research Assistantship Tuition Remission	Fellowship (% Receiving)	Fellowship Tuition Remission
First-Year Student	$4,200 (9)	Partial	NA (NA)	NA	NA (NA)	NA
Advanced Student	$4,200 (9)	Partial	NA (NA)	NA	NA (NA)	NA

For additional information on financial assistance, visit http://sou.edu/enrollment/financial-aid/.

Employment of Department Graduates

Master's:
Employed in a professional position in a school system: 2
Employed in government agency: 5
Employed in a community mental health/counseling center: 10
Employed in a hospital/medical center: 1
Total: 18

Additional Information

Housing and Day Care: On-campus housing is available. See the following website for more information: http://www.sou.edu/housing/. On-campus day care facilities are available. See the following website for more information: http://www.souchildcare.com/.

Information for Students With Physical Disabilities: See the following website: http://www.sou.edu/dr/index.html.

Application Information: Joanna Steinman, Graduate Program Studies, Master in Clinical Mental Health Counseling, Southern Oregon University, 1250 Siskiyou Boulevard, Ashland, OR 97520. *Fee:* $60. *Online application:* http://www.sou.edu/admissions/graduate/gr-apply.html.

Bucknell University

Department of Psychology
203 O'Leary Center
Lewisburg, PA 17837
Telephone: (570) 577-1200
Chairperson: J.T. Ptacek, PhD

E-mail: jwade@bucknell.edu
Web: http://www.bucknell.edu/Psychology

Orientation, Objectives, and Emphasis of Department

The objective of our MS program in general/experimental psychology is to provide additional coursework and closely mentored research experience to students who have completed an undergraduate degree and who wish to go on to pursue doctoral-level training in psychology.

Programs and Degrees Offered

Program	Degree	Application Deadline	Applications Received	Accepted	New Admits Enrolled (PT)	Total Enrolled (PT)	Degrees Awarded in 2014–2015	Median Years to Complete Degree	Dismissed/ Withdrew
General/ Experimental Psychology	MA/MS	February 1 (Fall), Rolling	4	2	2	3	1	2	0

Admissions

Entries appear in the following order: required test or GPA, minimum score (if required)/median score of students entering in 2015–2016.

Program	Degree	GRE-V	GRE-Q	GRE-Writing	GRE-Subject	Under-graduate GPA	Last 2 Years GPA	Psychol-ogy GPA	Master's GPA
General/ Experimental Psychology	MA/MS	NA/NA	NA/NA	NA/NA	NA/NA	3/NA	Not specified	Not specified	Not specified

Admissions Requirements:

Degree	GRE	GRE-Subject	Letters of Recom-mendation	Research Statement	Writing Sample	CV	Interview
Master's/Specialist	Required	Recom-mended	3	Required	Recom-mended	Required	Optional

Admissions Criteria:

GRE scores—medium
Research experience—medium
Work experience—low
Clinically related public service—low

GPA—medium
Letters of recommendation—high
Statement of goals and objectives—high
Undergraduate psychology preparation—medium

For additional information on admission requirements, visit http://www.bucknell.edu/graduate-studies/how-to-apply.html.

Department Demographics

	Male (PT)	Female (PT)	Total	African-American/ Black (PT)	Hispanic/ Latino (PT)	Asian/ Pacific Islander (PT)	American Indian/ Alaska Native (PT)	Caucasian/ White (PT)	Unknown	Multiethnic (PT)	ADA (PT)	Int'l (PT)
Students	2 (0)	1 (0)	3	0 (0)	0 (0)	0 (0)	0 (0)	3 (0)	0 (0)	0 (0)	0 (0)	0 (0)

Financial Information/Assistance

Tuition: For information on tuition costs, visit http://www.bucknell.edu/graduate-studies/expenses-and-financial-aid.html.

Master's:
State residents: $1,324 per credit hour.
Nonstate residents: $1,324 per credit hour.

Financial Assistance:

	Teaching Assistantship (% Receiving)	Teaching Assistantship Tuition Remission	Research Assistantship (% Receiving)	Research Assistantship Tuition Remission	Fellowship (% Receiving)	Fellowship Tuition Remission
First-Year Student	NA (100)	Full	NA (NA)	NA	NA (NA)	NA
Advanced Student	NA (100)	Full	NA (NA)	NA	NA (NA)	NA

Employment of Department Graduates

Master's:
Enrolled in a psychology doctoral program: 1
Total: 1

Additional Information

Housing and Day Care: No on-campus housing is available. On-campus day care facilities are available. See the following website for more information: http://www.sunflowercc.org/.

Information for Students With Physical Disabilities: See the following website: http://www.bucknell.edu/Accessibility.

Special Facilities or Resources: All department faculty have research lab suites, including facilities for human and animal research. Graduate students share office space in the Psychology building, near the faculty offices and labs.

Application Information: Graduate Studies, 228 Marts Hall, Bucknell University, Lewisburg, PA 17837. *Fee:* $50. *Online application:* https://www.bucknell.edu/script/provost/GradAdmissionApp/.

Carnegie Mellon University
Department of Psychology
Humanities and Social Sciences
Baker Hall 332D
Pittsburgh, PA 15213
Telephone: (412) 268-6026
Head: Michael Tarr

E-mail: donahoe@andrew.cmu.edu
Web: http://www.cmu.edu/dietrich/psychology/

Orientation, Objectives, and Emphasis of Department
The department offers doctoral programs in the areas of cognitive psychology, cognitive neuroscience, social-personality psychology, and developmental psychology. Because the graduate program is small, the student's course of study can be tailored to meet individual needs and interests. Further, students have many opportunities to work closely with faculty members on research projects of mutual interest. Carnegie Mellon University has a strong tradition of interdisciplinary research, and it is easy for students to

interact with faculty and students from other graduate programs on campus. Many of our students take courses or engage in research with people from the Departments of Computer Science, Statistics, Social Science, English, Philosophy, and the Graduate School of Industrial Administration.

Programs and Degrees Offered

Program	Degree	Application Deadline	Applications Received	Accepted	New Admits Enrolled (PT)	Total Enrolled (PT)	Degrees Awarded in 2014–2015	Median Years to Complete Degree	Dismissed/ Withdrew
Cognitive/ Cognitive Neuroscience	PhD	December 1 (Fall)	53	6	3 (0)	14 (0)	3	5	0
Developmental Psychology	PhD	December 1 (Fall)	12	0	0 (0)	6 (0)	0		0
Social/Health/ Personality Psychology	PhD	December 1 (Fall)	49	2	2 (0)	8 (0)	2	5	0

Admissions

Entries appear in the following order: required test or GPA, minimum score (if required)/median score of students entering in 2015–2016.

Program	Degree	GRE-V	GRE-Q	GRE-Writing	GRE-Subject	Undergraduate GPA	Last 2 Years GPA	Psychology GPA	Master's GPA
Cognitive/ Cognitive Neuroscience	PhD	160/NA	148/NA	Not specified	Not specified	3.7/NA	Not specified	Not specified	Not specified
Developmental Psychology	PhD	160/NA	148/NA	Not specified	Not specified	3.7/NA	Not specified	Not specified	Not specified
Social/Health/ Personality Psychology	PhD	160/NA	148/NA	Not specified	Not specified	3.7/NA	Not specified	Not specified	Not specified

Admissions Requirements:

Degree	GRE	GRE-Subject	Letters of Recommendation	Research Statement	Writing Sample	CV	Interview
Doctoral	Required	None	3	Required	Optional	Required	None

Admissions Criteria:

GRE scores—high
Research experience—high
Work experience—low
GPA—high

Letters of recommendation—high
Interview—high
Statement of goals and objectives—high
Undergraduate psychology preparation—medium

For additional information on admission requirements, visit http://www.cmu.edu/dietrich/psychology/graduate/admissions/application-requirements/index.html.

Department Demographics

	Male (PT)	Female (PT)	Total	African-American/ Black (PT)	Hispanic/ Latino (PT)	Asian/ Pacific Islander (PT)	American Indian/ Alaska Native (PT)	Caucasian/ White (PT)	Unknown (PT)	Multiethnic (PT)	ADA (PT)	Int'l (PT)
Students	11 (0)	17 (0)	28	2 (0)	0 (0)	3 (0)	0 (0)	17 (0)	6 (0)	0 (0)	0 (0)	3 (0)

Financial Information/Assistance

Tuition: For information on tuition costs, visit http://www.cmu.edu/hub/tuition/graduate/index.html. Tuition is subject to change. Additional fees are assessed to students beyond the costs of tuition for the following: Technology Fee, Activities Fee, Transportation Fee, and Health Insurance.

Doctoral:
State residents: $40,310 per academic year.
Nonstate residents: $40,310 per academic year.

Financial Assistance:

	Teaching Assistantship (% Receiving)	Teaching Assistantship Tuition Remission	Research Assistantship (% Receiving)	Research Assistantship Tuition Remission	Fellowship (% Receiving)	Fellowship Tuition Remission
First-Year Student	NA (NA)	NA	$25,500 (NA)	Full	$25,500 (NA)	Full
Advanced Student	NA (NA)	NA	$25,500 (NA)	Full	$25,500 (NA)	Full

Employment of Department Graduates

Doctoral:
Enrolled in a postdoctoral residency/fellowship: 3
Employed in business or industry: 2
Total: 5

Additional Information

Housing and Day Care: No on-campus housing is available. On-campus day care facilities are available. See the following website for more information: http://www.cmu.edu/cyert-center/.

Information for Students With Physical Disabilities: See the following website: http://www.cmu.edu/hr/eos/disability/index.html.

Application Information: Graduate Program Manager, Department of Psychology, Carnegie Mellon University, Pittsburgh, PA 15213. *Fee:* $70. *Online application:* https://applygrad-dietrich.cs.cmu.edu/apply/.

Carnegie Mellon University
Organizational Behavior and Theory
Tepper School of Business
5000 Forbes Avenue
Pittsburgh, PA 15213
Telephone: (412) 268-1319
OB PhD Coordinator: Brandy Aven
Web: http://tepper.cmu.edu/prospective-students/phd/program/organizational-behavior-and-theory

E-mail: lrapp@andrew.cmu.edu

Orientation, Objectives, and Emphasis of Department
The goal of the doctoral program in Organizational Behavior and Theory at the Tepper School of Business is to produce scientists who will make significant research contributions to our understanding of the structure and functioning of organizations. To achieve this goal the student is placed in a learning environment where a unique set of quantitative and discipline-based skills can be acquired. The opportunities for interdisciplinary work at Tepper provide new avenues for approaching organizational problems. The program attempts to combine structure and flexibility. Structure is achieved by identifying a set of core areas in which the student should become competent. These are quantitative methods, design and measurement, organization theory, and a selected specialty area. Flexibility in the program is achieved by having students and their advisers work out a combination of learning activities consistent with the students' interests and needs. Courses, participation in research projects, summer papers, and special tutorials with individual faculty are some of these learning activities.

Programs and Degrees Offered

Program	Degree	Application Deadline	Applications Received	Accepted	New Admits Enrolled (PT)	Total Enrolled (PT)	Degrees Awarded in 2014–2015	Median Years to Complete Degree	Dismissed/ Withdrew
Organizational Behavior and Theory	PhD	January 15 (Fall)	129	4	2	12	1	6	0

Admissions

Entries appear in the following order: required test or GPA, minimum score (if required)/median score of students entering in 2015–2016.

Program	Degree	GRE-V	GRE-Q	GRE-Writing	GRE-Subject	Under-graduate GPA	Last 2 Years GPA	Psychology GPA	Master's GPA
Organizational Behavior and Theory	PhD	NA/NA	NA/NA	Not specified	Not specified	Not specified	Not specified	Not specified	Not specified

Admissions Requirements:

Degree	GRE	GRE-Subject	Letters of Recommendation	Research Statement	Writing Sample	CV	Interview
Doctoral	Required	None	3	Required	Optional	Required	None

Admissions Criteria:

GRE scores—high
Research experience—medium
GPA—high

Letters of recommendation—high
Statement of goals and objectives—high

Department Demographics

	Male (PT)	Female (PT)	Total	African-American/ Black (PT)	Hispanic/ Latino (PT)	Asian/ Pacific Islander (PT)	American Indian/ Alaska Native (PT)	Caucasian/ White (PT)	Unknown	Multiethnic (PT)	ADA (PT)	Int'l (PT)
Students	4 (0)	8 (0)	12	1 (0)	0 (0)	1 (0)	0 (0)	6 (0)	0 (0)	0 (0)	0 (0)	4 (0)

Financial Information/Assistance

Tuition: For information on tuition costs, visit http://tepper.cmu.edu/prospective-students/phd/tuition-and-financial-aid. Additional fees are assessed to students beyond the costs of tuition for the following: student activity fee, technology fee, transportation fee.

Doctoral:
State residents: $60,000 per academic year.
Nonstate residents: $60,000 per academic year.

Financial Assistance:

	Teaching Assistantship (% Receiving)	Teaching Assistantship Tuition Remission	Research Assistantship (% Receiving)	Research Assistantship Tuition Remission	Fellowship (% Receiving)	Fellowship Tuition Remission
First-Year Student	NA (NA)	NA	NA (NA)	NA	$30,000 (NA)	Full
Advanced Student	NA (NA)	NA	NA (NA)	NA	$30,000 (NA)	Full

For additional information on financial assistance, visit http://tepper.cmu.edu/prospective-students/phd/tuition-and-financial-aid.

Employment of Department Graduates

Doctoral:
Employed in academic position at a 2-year/4-year college: 1
Total: 1

Additional Information

Housing and Day Care: No on-campus housing is available. No on-campus day care facilities are available.

Information for Students With Physical Disabilities: See the following website: http://www.cmu.edu/hr/eos/disability/.

Application Information: Doctoral Program Applications, 247 Posner Hall, Tepper School of Business, Carnegie Mellon University, Pittsburgh, PA 15213-3890. *Fee:* $70. *Online application:* https://app.applyyourself.com/?id=cmu-phd.

Chestnut Hill College
Department of Professional Psychology
9601 Germantown Avenue
Philadelphia, PA 19118-2693
Telephone: (215) 248-7077
Chairperson: Cheryll Rothery, PsyD, ABPP

E-mail: profpsyc@chc.edu
Web: http://www.chc.edu/psyd

Orientation, Objectives, and Emphasis of Department

The theoretical base of the Department of Professional Psychology at Chestnut Hill College is a complementary blend of psychodynamic and systems theories. The insights of psychodynamic theory serve as a method for understanding the individual. Likewise, the perspective of systems theory addresses ways individuals, families and communities influence one another. This synergistic blend of psychodynamic and systems theories promotes a holistic understanding of human behavior within family and social contexts. A structured sequence of mentoring and advising is designed to enable the student to complete the dissertation in a step-by-step manner prior to internship.

Programs and Degrees Offered

Program	Degree	Application Deadline	Applications Received	Accepted	New Admits Enrolled (PT)	Total Enrolled (PT)	Degrees Awarded in 2014–2015	Median Years to Complete Degree	Dismissed/ Withdrew
Clinical Psychology	PsyD	January 15 (Fall)	127	45	17 (0)	109 (9)	20	5.99	3
Clinical and Counseling Psychology	MA/MS	July 1 (Fall), November 1 (Spring), April 1 (Summer), Rolling	74	56	49 (43)	92 (126)	87	3.08	

APA Accreditation

Clinical PsyD: Student Outcome Data website: http://www.chc.edu/psyd/outcome_data.

Doctoral Degree (PsyD Clinical Psychology): For those doctoral students for whom a professional internship was required in this program prior to graduation:
Total students who applied for an internship: 17
Total students who obtained an internship: 17
Total students who obtained a paid internship: 17
Total students who obtained an unpaid internship: 0
Total students who were placed in APA/CPA-accredited internships: 8
Total students placed in internships not APA/CPA-accredited, but listed with the Association of Psychology Postdoctoral and Internship Centers (APPIC): 9
Total students placed in internships conforming to guidelines of the Council of Directors of School Psychology Programs (CDSPP): 0
Total students placed in internships that were not APA/CPA-accredited, APPIC or CDSSP listed: 0

Master's Degree (MA/MS Clinical and Counseling Psychology): An internship experience, such as a final research project or "capstone" experience is required of graduates.

Internships/Practica

Students in the master's program must complete three semesters of practicum training. Students in the doctoral program are required to complete 3 years of practicum (1 year of which may be waived if the student completed a practicum prior to admission as part of their master's program) and a full-time internship. Doctoral students have the option of completing an APA-accredited, APPIC, or other program approved internship. At the present time, there are over 50 mental health facilities that the program has approved as sites for practica and internships. Two faculty members are dedicated to assisting students in securing the most appropriate site for their practicum and internship experiences.

Admissions

Entries appear in the following order: required test or GPA, minimum score (if required)/median score of students entering in 2015–2016.

Program	Degree	GRE-V	GRE-Q	GRE-Writing	GRE-Subject	Under-graduate GPA	Last 2 Years GPA	Psychol-ogy GPA	Master's GPA
Clinical Psychology	PsyD	NA/155	NA/148	NA/4.3	Not specified	NA/3.56	Not specified	Not specified	Not specified
Clinical and Counseling Psychology	MA/MS	Not specified	Not specified	Not specified	Not specified	Not specified	Not specified	Not specified	Not specified

Admissions Requirements:

Degree	GRE	GRE-Subject	Letters of Recom-mendation	Research Statement	Writing Sample	CV	Interview
Master's/Specialist	Required	Required	3	Required	Optional	Optional	Required
Doctoral	Required	Required	3	Required	Optional	Optional	Required

Please note if these criteria vary for different programs: Writing ability is a criterion for the PsyD program. Applicants to the PsyD program must have completed at least four undergraduate courses in psychology including General Psychology, Abnormal Psychology, and Statistics.

Admissions Criteria:

GRE scores—high
Research experience—low
Work experience—low
Clinically related public service—medium
GPA—high

Letters of recommendation—high
Interview—high
Statement of goals and objectives—high
Undergraduate psychology preparation—medium
Writing ability—high

For additional information on admission requirements, visit http://www.chc.edu/psyd/admissions.

Department Demographics

	Male (PT)	Female (PT)	Total	African-American/ Black (PT)	Hispanic/ Latino (PT)	Asian/ Pacific Islander (PT)	American Indian/ Alaska Native (PT)	Caucasian/ White (PT)	Unknown	Multiethnic (PT)	ADA (PT)	Int'l (PT)
Students	47 (24)	174 (143)	388	23 (30)	21 (8)	7 (1)	0 (0)	158 (109)	9 (17)	3 (2)	4 (0)	5 (0)

Financial Information/Assistance

Tuition: For information on tuition costs, visit http://www.chc.edu/financial-services/graduate/graduate-tuition-and-fees. Tuition is subject to change.

Doctoral:
State residents: $985 per credit hour.
Nonstate residents: $985 per credit hour.

Master's:
State residents: $690 per credit hour.
Nonstate residents: $690 per credit hour.

Financial Assistance:

	Teaching Assistantship (% Receiving)	Teaching Assistantship Tuition Remission	Research Assistantship (% Receiving)	Research Assistantship Tuition Remission	Fellowship (% Receiving)	Fellowship Tuition Remission
First-Year Student	$5,910 (14)	Partial	$8,865 (7)	Partial	NA (NA)	NA
Advanced Student	$5,910 (5)	Partial	$8,865 (7)	Partial	NA (NA)	NA

For additional information on financial assistance, visit http://www.chc.edu/psyd/graduate/financial-aid.

Employment of Department Graduates

Doctoral:
Enrolled in a postdoctoral residency/fellowship: 4
Employed in independent practice: 6
Employed in an academic position at a university: 1
Employed in other positions at a higher education institution: 2
Employed in government agency: 1
Employed in a community mental health/counseling center: 4
Employed in a hospital/medical center: 2
Total: 20

Additional Information

Housing and Day Care: No on-campus housing is available. No on-campus day care facilities are available.

Information for Students With Physical Disabilities: See the following website: https://www.chc.edu/node/248.

Special Facilities or Resources: All classrooms are fully equipped for multimedia presentations, and many classrooms have SmartBoard technology. Observation rooms are available for recording and observing clinical sessions. An extensive library of psychological testing equipment is available for student use. The college is part of a library consortium that increases available lending privileges offered to each student. Doctoral students have free interlibrary loan privileges. Students have access to statistical software and test scoring/interpretation software. Advanced doctoral students may teach a master's level course under the direct supervision of a faculty member. The Psychological Services Clinic of Chestnut Hill College provides supervised internship and practica experiences. The CHC Internship Consortium provides 11 paid internships in 7 sites.

Application Information: Director of Graduate Admissions, Chestnut Hill College, 9601 Germantown Avenue, Philadelphia, PA 19118-2693. *Fee:* $60. *Online application:* https://www.chc.edu/apply.

Drexel University
Department of Psychology
College of Arts and Sciences
119 Stratton Hall, 3141 Chestnut Street
Philadelphia, PA 19104
Telephone: (215) 762-7249
Chairperson: Kirk Heilbrun

E-mail: kirk.heilbrun@drexel.edu
Web: http://www.drexel.edu/psychology/

Orientation, Objectives, and Emphasis of Department
The Drexel University Department of Psychology's doctoral program in clinical psychology is based heavily upon a scientist–practitioner model of training, designed to place emphasis on both components, but with somewhat greater emphasis on research. The theoretical orientation is based largely on Social Learning Theory, in which students gain proficiency in the theory and practice of broad-spectrum behavioral approaches to assessment and intervention. The clinical PhD program offers concentrations in health psychology, neuropsychology, and forensic psychology. The program in Applied Cognitive and Brain Sciences is focused primarily on cognitive psychology and cognitive neuroscience, although the research emphasis is of an applied nature. The MS program (non-clinical) is designed to provide students with research skills in preparation for applying for doctoral training or for employment with researchers in academia, industry, or public sector settings.

Programs and Degrees Offered

Program	Degree	Application Deadline	Applications Received	Accepted	New Admits Enrolled (PT)	Total Enrolled (PT)	Degrees Awarded in 2014–2015	Median Years to Complete Degree	Dismissed/ Withdrew
Clinical Psychology	PhD	December 1 (Fall)	640	12	8 (0)	49 (0)	9	5	0
Psychology	MA/MS	February 1 (Fall)	33	21	8	18	9	2	0
Law-Psychology	PhD	December 1 (Fall)	18	2	1	10	2	7	0
Applied Cognitive and Brain Sciences	PhD	December 1 (Fall)	20	3	0 (0)	3 (0)	0		0

APA Accreditation

Clinical PhD: Student Outcome Data website: http://drexel.edu/coas/academics/graduate-programs/psychology-clinical/student-admissions-outcomes-data/.

Clinical PhD (Doctor of Philosophy).

Doctoral Degree (PhD Clinical Psychology): For those doctoral students for whom a professional internship was required in this program prior to graduation:
Total students who applied for an internship: 10
Total students who obtained an internship: 10
Total students who obtained a paid internship: 10
Total students who obtained an unpaid internship: 0
Total students who were placed in APA/CPA-accredited internships: 10
Total students placed in internships not APA/CPA-accredited, but listed with the Association of Psychology Postdoctoral and Internship Centers (APPIC): 0
Total students placed in internships conforming to guidelines of the Council of Directors of School Psychology Programs (CDSPP): 0
Total students placed in internships that were not APA/CPA-accredited, APPIC or CDSSP listed: 0

Doctoral Degree (PhD Law-Psychology): For those doctoral students for whom a professional internship was required in this program prior to graduation:
Total students who applied for an internship: 1
Total students who obtained an internship: 1
Total students who obtained a paid internship: 1
Total students who obtained an unpaid internship: 0
Total students who were placed in APA/CPA-accredited internships: 1
Total students placed in internships not APA/CPA-accredited, but listed with the Association of Psychology Postdoctoral and Internship Centers (APPIC): 0
Total students placed in internships conforming to guidelines of the Council of Directors of School Psychology Programs (CDSPP): 0
Total students placed in internships that were not APA/CPA-accredited, APPIC or CDSSP listed: 0

Master's Degree (MA/MS Psychology): An internship experience, such as a final research project or "capstone" experience is required of graduates.

Internships/Practica

On-campus practicum sites include the Forensic Clinic, the Heart Failure/Cardiac Transplant Center, the Anxiety Treatment and Research Center, and the Laboratory for Innovations in Health-Related Behavior Change. Off-campus practicum sites include a variety of in- and outpatient psychiatric units, University of Pennsylvania Center for the Treatment and Study of Anxiety, University of Pennsylvania Center for Weight and Eating Disorders, Children's Hospital of Philadelphia and approximately sixty other practicum sites.

Admissions

Entries appear in the following order: required test or GPA, minimum score (if required)/median score of students entering in 2015–2016.

Program	Degree	GRE-V	GRE-Q	GRE-Writing	GRE-Subject	Under-graduate GPA	Last 2 Years GPA	Psychology GPA	Master's GPA
Clinical Psychology	PhD	NA/161	NA/158	Not specified	4.5/5	NA/3.7	NA/3.8	NA/3.8	Not specified
Psychology	MA/MS	NA/156	NA/154	Not specified	4/4.5	3.1/3.3	3.2/3.5	3.3/3.6	Not specified
Law-Psychology	PhD	159/159	158/158	Not specified	4.5/4.5	3.5/3.5	3.6/3.6	3.7/3.7	Not specified
Applied Cognitive and Brain Sciences	PhD	NA/NA	NA/NA	Not specified	NA/NA	NA/NA	NA/NA	NA/NA	Not specified

Admissions Requirements:

Degree	GRE	GRE-Subject	Letters of Recommendation	Research Statement	Writing Sample	CV	Interview
Master's/Specialist	Required	Recommended	3	Required	Optional	Required	Required
Doctoral	Required	Required	3	Required	Optional	Required	Required

Please note if these criteria vary for different programs: Clinical experience is not considered for ACBS or MS programs. Research experience is weighted less heavily for applicants for the MS program.

Admissions Criteria:

GRE scores—high
Research experience—high
Work experience—low
Clinically related public service—medium
GPA—high

Letters of recommendation—high
Interview—high
Statement of goals and objectives—high
Undergraduate psychology preparation—medium
Fit with faculty mentor—high

Department Demographics

	Male (PT)	Female (PT)	Total	African-American/ Black (PT)	Hispanic/ Latino (PT)	Asian/ Pacific Islander (PT)	American Indian/ Alaska Native (PT)	Caucasian/ White (PT)	Unknown	Multiethnic (PT)	ADA (PT)	Int'l (PT)
Students	12 (0)	68 (0)	80	3 (0)	3 (0)	2 (0)	0 (0)	72 (0)	0 (0)	0 (0)	4 (0)	1 (0)

Financial Information/Assistance

Tuition: For information on tuition costs, visit http://drexel.edu/grad/financing/tuition/. Tuition is subject to change. Additional fees are assessed to students beyond the costs of tuition for the following: General fee of $280 per quarter.

Doctoral:
State residents: $1,160 per credit hour.
Nonstate residents: $1,160 per credit hour.

Master's:
State residents: $1,160 per credit hour.
Nonstate residents: $1,160 per credit hour.

Financial Assistance:

	Teaching Assistantship (% Receiving)	Teaching Assistantship Tuition Remission	Research Assistantship (% Receiving)	Research Assistantship Tuition Remission	Fellowship (% Receiving)	Fellowship Tuition Remission
First-Year Student	$15,000 (NA)	Full	$15,000 (NA)	Full	$5,000 (NA)	Full
Advanced Student	NA (NA)	NA	$15,000 (NA)	Full	$5,000 (NA)	Full

For additional information on financial assistance, visit http://drexel.edu/drexelcentral/finaid/.

Employment of Department Graduates

Master's:
Enrolled in a psychology doctoral program: 4
Employed in business or industry: 1
Employed in a community mental health/counseling center: 1
Other employment position: 2
Do not know: 1
Total: 9

Doctoral:
Enrolled in a postdoctoral residency/fellowship: 5
Employed in an academic position at a university: 1
Employed in other positions at a higher education institution: 2
Other employment position: 1
Total: 9

Additional Information

Housing and Day Care: On-campus housing is available. See the following website for more information: http://www.drexel.edu/dbs/universityHousing/graduate-housing/. No on-campus day care facilities are available.

Information for Students With Physical Disabilities: See the following website: http://www.drexel.edu/oed/disabilityResources/.

Special Facilities or Resources: Drexel has a major tertiary care medical center that provides exceptional opportunities in health-related areas for psychology. In addition, a Division of Behavioral Neurobiology and the University Neurobiology program, as well as the University Neurosciences program, provide opportunities for learning and collaboration on research at neuropharmacologic and neurophysiologic levels to complement our neuropsychological training. We are surrounded by a wealth of top-notch medical centers including the University of Pennsylvania, Children's Hospital of Philadelphia, Jefferson University Hospitals, and Temple University.

Application Information: Graduate Admission, Drexel University, 3141 Chestnut Street, Suite 212, Philadelphia, PA 19104. *Fee:* $0. *Online application:* http://www.drexel.edu/grad/apply/online-app/.

Duquesne University
Department of Counseling, Psychology and Special Education, School Psychology Program
School of Education
G3 Canevin Hall
Pittsburgh, PA 15282
Telephone: (412) 396-1058
Program Director: Ara J. Schmitt, PhD

E-mail: czwalgaa@duq.edu
Web: http://www.duq.edu/academics/schools/education/

Orientation, Objectives, and Emphasis of Department
The Duquesne University School Psychology program, guided by the belief that all children can learn, is dedicated to providing both breadth and depth of professional training in a theoretically integrated, research-based learning environment. The program prepares ethical practitioners, scientists, and scholars who are life-long learners committed to enhancing the well-being of youth, their families, and the systems that serve them. The program achieves this by engaging in scholarly activities that advance the field of school psychology, maintaining a modern curriculum that employs aspects of multiculturalism and diversity, examining emerging trends in the profession, conducting continuous outcome assessment for program improvement, and providing support to our graduates.

Programs and Degrees Offered

Program	Degree	Application Deadline	Applications Received	Accepted	New Admits Enrolled (PT)	Total Enrolled (PT)	Degrees Awarded in 2014–2015	Median Years to Complete Degree	Dismissed/ Withdrew
Child Psychology	MEd	August 1 (Fall), December 1 (Spring), May 1 (Summer), Rolling	29	13	4 (0)	11 (2)	6	2	0
School Psychology	PhD	January 15 (Fall)	36	16	6 (0)	58 (0)	7	5	0
School Psychology	PsyD	January 15 (Fall)	34	19	12 (0)	102 (4)	10	4	0

APA Accreditation

School PhD (Doctor of Philosophy).

Doctoral Degree (PhD School Psychology): For those doctoral students for whom a professional internship was required in this program prior to graduation:
Total students who applied for an internship: 6
Total students who obtained an internship: 6
Total students who obtained a paid internship: 5
Total students who obtained an unpaid internship: 1
Total students who were placed in APA/CPA-accredited internships: 2
Total students placed in internships not APA/CPA-accredited, but listed with the Association of Psychology Postdoctoral and Internship Centers (APPIC): 1
Total students placed in internships conforming to guidelines of the Council of Directors of School Psychology Programs (CDSPP): 3
Total students placed in internships that were not APA/CPA-accredited, APPIC or CDSSP listed: 0

Doctoral Degree (PsyD School Psychology): For those doctoral students for whom a professional internship was required in this program prior to graduation:
Total students who applied for an internship: 11
Total students who obtained an internship: 11
Total students who obtained a paid internship: 11
Total students who obtained an unpaid internship: 0
Total students who were placed in APA/CPA-accredited internships: 0
Total students placed in internships not APA/CPA-accredited, but listed with the Association of Psychology Postdoctoral and Internship Centers (APPIC): 1
Total students placed in internships conforming to guidelines of the Council of Directors of School Psychology Programs (CDSPP): 10
Total students placed in internships that were not APA/CPA-accredited, APPIC or CDSSP listed: 0

Internships/Practica
Doctoral programs require two practica, one doctoral practicum and an internship.

Admissions
Entries appear in the following order: required test or GPA, minimum score (if required)/median score of students entering in 2015–2016.

Program	Degree	GRE-V	GRE-Q	GRE-Writing	GRE-Subject	Under-graduate GPA	Last 2 Years GPA	Psychol-ogy GPA	Master's GPA
Child Psychology	MEd	Not specified	Not specified	Not specified	Not specified	3/NA	Not specified	Not specified	Not specified
School Psychology	PhD	NA/152	NA/150	NA/4	Not specified	NA/NA	Not specified	Not specified	Not specified

Admissions (con't.)

Program	Degree	GRE-V	GRE-Q	GRE-Writing	GRE-Subject	Undergraduate GPA	Last 2 Years GPA	Psychology GPA	Master's GPA
School Psychology	PsyD	NA/153	NA/148	NA/4	Not specified	NA/NA	Not specified	Not specified	Not specified

Admissions Requirements:

Degree	GRE	GRE-Subject	Letters of Recommendation	Research Statement	Writing Sample	CV	Interview
Master's/Specialist	Optional	Optional	N/A	Optional	Optional	Optional	None
Doctoral	Required	Required	3	Required	Optional	Optional	Required

Admissions Criteria:

GRE scores—high
Research experience—medium
Work experience—medium
Clinically related public service—low
GPA—high

Letters of recommendation—medium
Interview—high
Statement of goals and objectives—high
Undergraduate psychology preparation—high

Department Demographics

	Male (PT)	Female (PT)	Total	African-American/ Black (PT)	Hispanic/ Latino (PT)	Asian/ Pacific Islander (PT)	American Indian/ Alaska Native (PT)	Caucasian/ White (PT)	Unknown	Multiethnic (PT)	ADA (PT)	Int'l (PT)
Students	31 (1)	140 (5)	177	8 (1)	0 (0)	0 (0)	0 (0)	128 (4)	35 (1)	0 (0)	0 (0)	1 (1)

Financial Information/Assistance

Tuition: For information on tuition costs, visit http://www.duq.edu/admissions-and-aid/tuition/graduate-tuition-rates. Tuition is subject to change.

Doctoral:
State residents: $26,396 per academic year.
State residents: $1,189 per credit hour.
Nonstate residents: $26,396 per academic year.
Nonstate residents: $1,189 per credit hour.

Master's:
State residents: $17,835 per academic year.
State residents: $1,189 per credit hour.
Nonstate residents: $17,835 per academic year.
Nonstate residents: $1,189 per credit hour.

Financial Assistance:

	Teaching Assistantship (% Receiving)	Teaching Assistantship Tuition Remission	Research Assistantship (% Receiving)	Research Assistantship Tuition Remission	Fellowship (% Receiving)	Fellowship Tuition Remission
First-Year Student	NA (NA)	NA	NA (NA)	Partial	NA (NA)	NA
Advanced Student	NA (NA)	Partial	NA (NA)	Partial	NA (NA)	NA

For additional information on financial assistance, visit http://www.duq.edu/admissions-and-aid/graduate-admissions/graduate-financing.

Employment of Department Graduates

Doctoral:
Enrolled in a postdoctoral residency/fellowship: 3
Employed in a professional position in a school system: 13
Employed in a hospital/medical center: 1
Total: 17

Additional Information

Housing and Day Care: On-campus housing is available. See the following website for more information: http://www.duq.edu/residence-life/. On-campus day care facilities are available. See the following website for more information: http://www.duq.edu/work-at-du/benefits/other-benefits/campus-services/child-care-services.

Information for Students With Physical Disabilities: See the following website: http://www.duq.edu/special-students/.

Special Facilities or Resources: The program has a curriculum library of current psychological and educational tests for training and research purposes.

Application Information: Dr. Ara J. Schmitt, School Psychology Program, G3B Canevin Hall, Pittsburgh, PA 15282. *Fee:* $50. *Online application:* https://myapplication.duq.edu/Apply/Pages/Welcome.aspx.

Duquesne University
Department of Psychology
McAnulty College and Graduate School of Liberal Arts
600 Forbes Avenue
Pittsburgh, PA 15282
Telephone: (412) 396-6520   E-mail: psychology@duq.edu
Chairperson: Leswin Laubscher, PhD
Web: http://www.duq.edu/academics/schools/liberal-arts/graduate-school/programs/clinical-psychology

---

Orientation, Objectives, and Emphasis of Department
The Department of Psychology at Duquesne University educates students who are sensitive to the assumptions that underlie any effort to understand human beings, as well as the historical, cultural, relational, and embodied character of all human thought and activity. Accordingly, faculty and graduates are sensitive to the multiple meanings of existence, work towards the liberation and well being of persons individually as well as in community, and do so with a deep and abiding consideration of ethics.

Programs and Degrees Offered

Program	Degree	Application Deadline	Applica-tions Received	Accepted	New Admits Enrolled (PT)	Total Enrolled (PT)	Degrees Awarded in 2014–2015	Median Years to Complete Degree	Dismissed/ Withdrew
Clinical Psychology	PhD	December 1 (Fall)	105	7	7 (0)	49 (0)	7	6.5	1

APA Accreditation

Clinical PhD (Doctor of Philosophy).

Doctoral Degree (PhD Clinical Psychology): For those doctoral students for whom a professional internship was required in this program prior to graduation:
Total students who applied for an internship: 6
Total students who obtained an internship: 6
Total students who obtained a paid internship: 6
Total students who obtained an unpaid internship: 0
Total students who were placed in APA/CPA-accredited internships: 5
Total students placed in internships not APA/CPA-accredited, but listed with the Association of Psychology Postdoctoral and Internship Centers (APPIC): 1
Total students placed in internships conforming to guidelines of the Council of Directors of School Psychology Programs (CDSPP): 0
Total students placed in internships that were not APA/CPA-accredited, APPIC or CDSSP listed: 0

Internships/Practica

The Duquesne University Psychology Clinic, which serves more than 70 clients weekly, is the primary training facility for the doctoral students. All services, including assessment and psychotherapy for Duquesne University students, employees, and members of the greater Pittsburgh communities, are provided by the doctoral students. Licensed clinical faculty members and selected licensed adjunct faculty psychologists in the community are involved in the supervision of all doctoral students. The first 4 years of the doctoral program typically involve case work at the Clinic. Additionally, students attend at least 1 academic year of external practicum placement in settings such as hospitals, university counseling centers, and VA centers. External practica are typically completed during the third year of the program. A second year of external practicum training, taken in the fourth year, is strongly recommended.

Admissions

Entries appear in the following order: required test or GPA, minimum score (if required)/median score of students entering in 2015–2016.

Program	Degree	GRE-V	GRE-Q	GRE-Writing	GRE-Subject	Under-graduate GPA	Last 2 Years GPA	Psychol-ogy GPA	Master's GPA
Clinical Psychology	PhD	NA/163	NA/151	NA/4.5	Not specified	Not specified	Not specified	Not specified	Not specified

Admissions Requirements:

Degree	GRE	GRE-Subject	Letters of Recom-mendation	Research Statement	Writing Sample	CV	Interview
Doctoral	Required	Optional	3	Required	Required	Required	Optional

Admissions Criteria:

GRE scores—medium
Research experience—medium
Work experience—medium
Clinically related public service—medium
GPA—medium

Letters of recommendation—high
Interview—high
Statement of goals and objectives—high
Undergraduate psychology preparation—medium

Department Demographics

	Male (PT)	Female (PT)	Total	African-American/ Black (PT)	Hispanic/ Latino (PT)	Asian/ Pacific Islander (PT)	American Indian/ Alaska Native (PT)	Caucasian/ White (PT)	Unknown	Multiethnic (PT)	ADA (PT)	Int'l (PT)
Students	22 (0)	27 (0)	49	2 (0)	2 (0)	6 (0)	0 (0)	38 (0)	0 (0)	1 (0)	3 (0)	7 (0)

Financial Information/Assistance

Tuition: For information on tuition costs, visit http://www.duq.edu/admissions-and-aid/tuition/graduate-tuition-rates. Tuition is subject to change.

Doctoral:
State residents: $33,778 per academic year.
State residents: $1,189 per credit hour.
Nonstate residents: $33,778 per academic year.
Nonstate residents: $1,189 per credit hour.

Financial Assistance:

	Teaching Assistantship (% Receiving)	Teaching Assistantship Tuition Remission	Research Assistantship (% Receiving)	Research Assistantship Tuition Remission	Fellowship (% Receiving)	Fellowship Tuition Remission
First-Year Student	NA (NA)	NA	$17,000 (NA)	Full	NA (NA)	NA
Advanced Student	$17,000 (NA)	Full	$17,000 (NA)	Full	NA (NA)	NA

For additional information on financial assistance, visit http://www.duq.edu/admissions-and-aid/financial-aid.

Employment of Department Graduates

Doctoral:
Employed in independent practice: 1
Employed in a community mental health/counseling center: 1
Employed in a hospital/medical center: 4
Do not know: 1
Total: 7

Additional Information

Housing and Day Care: On-campus housing is available. See the following website for more information: http://www.duq.edu/life-at-duquesne/residence-life. On-campus day care facilities are available. See the following website for more information: http://www.duq.edu/work-at-du/benefits/other-benefits/campus-services/child-care-services.

Information for Students With Physical Disabilities: See the following website: http://www.duq.edu/life-at-duquesne/student-services/special-services.

Special Facilities or Resources: The psychology clinic provides the opportunity for supervised training in personal counseling and for research in the field of counseling and psychotherapy. Field placements are available in clinical psychology. The Silverman Center is a research center containing a comprehensive collection of world literature in phenomenology.

Application Information: Fee: $0. *Online application:* http://www.duq.edu/apply/grad.

Geneva College
Master of Arts in Counseling
3200 College Avenue
Beaver Falls, PA 15010
Telephone: (724) 847-6697
MA in Counseling Program Director: Shannan L. Shiderly, PhD

E-mail: counseling@geneva.edu
Web: http://www.geneva.edu/graduate/counseling/

Orientation, Objectives, and Emphasis of Department
The philosophies of counseling in the CACREP-accredited MA in Counseling program at Geneva College are embedded in a Christian view of human nature and God's created world. A growing body of research literature affirms that Christian faith establishes a basis for healthy personality development, interpersonal relations, and mental health. A multidimensional holistic view of persons examines the interweaving of physical, emotional, social, cognitive, behavioral, and spiritual aspects of life. Integrative psychotherapeutic conceptualizations based on this multidimensionality promote healing and change. Counseling students and faculty engage in Christian spiritual growth, thus modeling adherence to the faith and values they profess and facilitating academic learning, counseling, effectiveness, and ability to consult in the larger church community and beyond. The MA in Counseling program at Geneva College provides academic training in the development of knowledge, skills, and personal awareness pertinent to the counseling profession and encourages students to integrate Christian faith and Biblical knowledge with the training and practice of counseling. The program is designed so that post-baccalaureate students who complete this degree and acquire the required postgraduate supervised experience in the practice of counseling will be eligible to become Licensed Professional Counselors.

Programs and Degrees Offered

Program	Degree	Application Deadline	Applications Received	Accepted	New Admits Enrolled (PT)	Total Enrolled (PT)	Degrees Awarded in 2014–2015	Median Years to Complete Degree	Dismissed/ Withdrew
Marriage and Family Counseling	MA/MS	August 15 (Fall), January 1 (Spring), Rolling	9	6	5 (4)	12 (19)	13	2.7	1
Clinical Mental Health Counseling	MA/MS	August 15 (Fall), January 1 (Spring), Rolling	20	12	8 (8)	22 (24)	14	2.4	3
School Counseling	MA/MS	August 15 (Fall), January 1 (Spring), Rolling	3	1	4 (0)	7 (3)	10	2	0

Internships/Practica

A practicum and internship program is in place. This practicum and internship experience is in line with the CACREP standards for master's-level counseling programs. Practica are 100 hours in length with individual and group supervision and direct client contact. Marriage, Couple and Family internships are 600 hours in length with direct client contact included; Mental Health internships are 600 hours in length with direct client contact hours included; School internships are 600 hours in length with 300 hours on the elementary level and 300 hours on the secondary level. All internships will involve site placements typically in the Beaver County and Pittsburgh area, with supervision via qualified master's and/or doctoral prepared practitioners onsite as well as on campus. Practica and internships are arranged by the faculty coordinators.

Admissions

Entries appear in the following order: required test or GPA, minimum score (if required)/median score of students entering in 2015–2016.

Program	Degree	GRE-V	GRE-Q	GRE-Writing	GRE-Subject	Under-graduate GPA	Last 2 Years GPA	Psychology GPA	Master's GPA
Marriage and Family Counseling	MA/MS	Not specified	Not specified	Not specified	Not specified	NA/NA	Not specified	Not specified	Not specified
Clinical Mental Health Counseling	MA/MS	Not specified	Not specified	Not specified	Not specified	NA/NA	Not specified	Not specified	Not specified
School Counseling	MA/MS	Not specified	Not specified	Not specified	Not specified	NA/NA	Not specified	Not specified	Not specified

Admissions Requirements:

Degree	GRE	GRE-Subject	Letters of Recom-mendation	Research Statement	Writing Sample	CV	Interview
Master's/Specialist	None	None	3	Required	Required	Required	Required

Please note if these criteria vary for different programs: It is recommended that undergrad courses should include 12 credits in psychology, counseling, sociology or classes in a related field. Successful completion of an undergraduate statistics class is highly recommended but not mandatory.

Admissions Criteria:

Research experience—low
Work experience—medium
Clinically related public service—low
GPA—high

Letters of recommendation—medium
Interview—high
Statement of goals and objectives—high
Undergraduate psychology preparation—medium

For additional information on admission requirements, visit http://www.geneva.edu/graduate/counseling/counseling-admissions/.

Department Demographics

	Male (PT)	Female (PT)	Total	African-American/ Black (PT)	Hispanic/ Latino (PT)	Asian/ Pacific Islander (PT)	American Indian/ Alaska Native (PT)	Caucasian/ White (PT)	Unknown (PT)	Multiethnic (PT)	ADA (PT)	Int'l (PT)
Students	9 (14)	32 (32)	87	5 (7)	0 (0)	0 (0)	0 (0)	35 (39)	1 (0)	0 (0)	2 (1)	0 (0)

Financial Information/Assistance

Tuition: For information on tuition costs, visit https://www.geneva.edu/page/tuition_costs. Tuition is subject to change.

Master's:
State residents: $670 per credit hour.
Nonstate residents: $670 per credit hour.

Financial Assistance:

	Teaching Assistantship (% Receiving)	Teaching Assistantship Tuition Remission	Research Assistantship (% Receiving)	Research Assistantship Tuition Remission	Fellowship (% Receiving)	Fellowship Tuition Remission
First-Year Student	NA (NA)	NA	$400 (NA)	NA	NA (NA)	NA
Advanced Student	$800 (NA)	NA	$400 (NA)	NA	NA (NA)	NA

For additional information on financial assistance, visit http://www.geneva.edu/financial-aid/fin_aid_graduate_financial_aid.

Employment of Department Graduates

Master's:
Employed in academic position at a 2-year/4-year college: 1
Employed in a professional position in a school system: 4
Employed in a community mental health/counseling center: 15
Do not know: 14
Total: 34

Additional Information

Housing and Day Care: No on-campus housing is available. No on-campus day care facilities are available.

Information for Students With Physical Disabilities: See the following website: https://www.geneva.edu/student-life/services/ssc/disability-services/.

Special Facilities or Resources: On the Beaver Falls main campus, department facilities include a computer lab and a modern clinical counseling facility. The computer lab is equipped with Windows and various experimental and clinical software resources. Various classes in the MA in Counseling program are also offered at the RLA building in Cranberry Township, PA. The entire facility is technology-based with all classrooms and all other rooms equipped with wireless internet access, LCD projector, laptop, screen, microphones and speakers. Staffing and IT help are always available. For assistance with scholarly writing, a Writing Center is available at both locations.

Application Information: MA in Counseling Program Manager, Geneva College, 3200 College Avenue, Beaver Falls, PA 15010. *Fee:* $50. *Online application:* http://www.geneva.edu/object/counseling_onlineapp.

Immaculata University
Department of Graduate Psychology
College of Graduate Studies
1145 King Road, Loyola Hall 130
Immaculata, PA 19345
Telephone: (610) 647-4400 ext. 3509
Chairperson: Jed Yalof

E-mail: jyalof@immaculata.edu
Web: http://www.immaculata.edu/academics/departments/graduate_psychology

Orientation, Objectives, and Emphasis of Department
At the master's level, the department's orientation is the professional preparation of the mental health counselor through the Clinical Mental Health Counseling (CMHC) programs in relation to CACREP standards and counselor licensure in PA. The department also prepares students for preK–12 counselor certification. The department also offers an EdS in School Psychology. The PsyD program in Clinical Psychology is APA-accredited and offers opportunities to emphasize studies in the areas of psychological testing, integrative psychotherapy, forensic psychology, human and cultural diversity, psychodynamic psychotherapy, and neuropsychology. The department also has a consortium internship that is APA-accredited.

Programs and Degrees Offered

Program	Degree	Application Deadline	Applications Received	Accepted	New Admits Enrolled (PT)	Total Enrolled (PT)	Degrees Awarded in 2014–2015	Median Years to Complete Degree	Dismissed/ Withdrew
Clinical Psychology	PsyD	January 15 (Fall), January 15 (Summer)	96	40	20	95 (52)	29	6	2
Clinical Mental Health Counseling W/ Prek-12 Cert	MA/MS	Rolling	0	0		6 (9)	0		0
Clinical Mental Health Counseling	MA/MS	Rolling	82	55	(41)	47 (73)	0		4
School Psychology	EdS	Rolling	11	7	4	5 (2)	0		0

APA Accreditation
Clinical PsyD: Student Outcome Data website: http://www.immaculata.edu/academics/departments/graduatepsychology/outcomes.

Doctoral Degree (PsyD Clinical Psychology): For those doctoral students for whom a professional internship was required in this program prior to graduation:
Total students who applied for an internship: 16
Total students who obtained an internship: 16
Total students who obtained a paid internship: 16
Total students who obtained an unpaid internship: 0
Total students who were placed in APA/CPA-accredited internships: 15
Total students placed in internships not APA/CPA-accredited, but listed with the Association of Psychology Postdoctoral and Internship Centers (APPIC): 1
Total students placed in internships conforming to guidelines of the Council of Directors of School Psychology Programs (CDSPP): 0
Total students placed in internships that were not APA/CPA-accredited, APPIC or CDSSP listed: 0

Master's Degree (MA/MS Clinical Mental Health Counseling w/ PreK-12 Cert): An internship experience, such as a final research project or "capstone" experience is required of graduates. Master's Degree (MA/MS Clinical Mental Health Counseling): An internship experience, such as a final research project or "capstone" experience is required of graduates.

Internships/Practica

The Graduate Psychology Department places counseling psychology, school psychology, and clinical psychology students at sites throughout the Philadelphia and tri-county area and with supervisors with qualifications specific to student and program requirements. The department has an APPIC-member and APA-accredited internship consortium. Students are required to apply to the department's consortium, in addition to applying to APA-accredited sites and other APPIC internships both locally and nationally. The consortium offers only full time placements. Clinical doctoral students complete diagnostic and therapy placements prior to internship. Students work with either the Master's field site coordinator or doctoral field site and predoctoral internship coordinator to identify prospective field placements for their different programs of study.

Admissions

Entries appear in the following order: required test or GPA, minimum score (if required)/median score of students entering in 2015–2016.

Program	Degree	GRE-V	GRE-Q	GRE-Writing	GRE-Subject	Under-graduate GPA	Last 2 Years GPA	Psychol-ogy GPA	Master's GPA
Clinical Psychology	PsyD	Not specified	Not specified	Not specified	Not specified	Not specified	Not specified	Not specified	Not specified
Clinical Mental Health Counseling w/ PreK-12 Cert	MA/MS	Not specified	Not specified	Not specified	Not specified	Not specified	Not specified	Not specified	Not specified
Clinical Mental Health Counseling	MA/MS	Not specified	Not specified	Not specified	Not specified	Not specified	Not specified	Not specified	Not specified
School Psychology	EdS	Not specified	Not specified	Not specified	Not specified	Not specified	Not specified	Not specified	Not specified

Admissions Requirements:

Degree	GRE	GRE-Subject	Letters of Recom-mendation	Research Statement	Writing Sample	CV	Interview
Master's/Specialist	Required	None	2	Required	Optional	Optional	None
Doctoral	Required	None	3	Required	Optional	Optional	None

Admissions Criteria:

GRE scores—medium
GPA—high
Letters of recommendation—medium

Interview—high
Statement of goals and objectives—medium

For additional information on admission requirements, visit http://www.immaculata.edu/admissions/graduate/requirements.

Department Demographics

	Male (PT)	Female (PT)	Total	African-American/ Black (PT)	Hispanic/ Latino (PT)	Asian/ Pacific Islander (PT)	American Indian/ Alaska Native (PT)	Caucasian/ White (PT)	Unknown	Multiethnic (PT)	ADA (PT)	Int'l (PT)
Students	26 (25)	127 (111)	289	9 (11)	11 (9)	4 (1)	1 (0)	123 (109)	5 (2)	0 (4)	0 (0)	0 (0)

Financial Information/Assistance

Tuition: For information on tuition costs, visit http://www.immaculata.edu/admissions/graduate/tuition_fees. Tuition is subject to change.

Doctoral:
State residents: $955 per credit hour.
Nonstate residents: $955 per credit hour.

Master's:
State residents: $680 per credit hour.
Nonstate residents: $680 per credit hour.

Financial Assistance:

	Teaching Assistantship (% Receiving)	Teaching Assistantship Tuition Remission	Research Assistantship (% Receiving)	Research Assistantship Tuition Remission	Fellowship (% Receiving)	Fellowship Tuition Remission
First-Year Student	NA (NA)	NA	NA (NA)	NA	NA (NA)	NA
Advanced Student	NA (NA)	NA	NA (NA)	NA	$5,730 (NA)	NA

For additional information on financial assistance, visit http://www.immaculata.edu/admissions/graduate/finaid.

Employment of Department Graduates

No information provided.

Additional Information

Housing and Day Care: On-campus housing is available. See the following website for more information: http://www.immaculata.edu/ResidenceLifeandHousing. No on-campus day care facilities are available.

Information for Students With Physical Disabilities: See the following website: http://www.immaculata.edu/academics/academic_success/accommodations.

Special Facilities or Resources: The college has a comprehensive center for academic computing and modern technology available for student computer needs and utilization. There is a Writing Center and other student support services. The Gabrielle Library was opened in 1993 and houses journals and texts and has online search available to students.

Application Information: Assistant Dean, College of Graduate Studies, Immaculata University, 1145 King Road, Loyola Hall 130, Immaculata, PA 19345. *Fee:* $75. *Online application:* http://www.immaculata.edu/gradapply.

Indiana University of Pennsylvania

Department of Psychology - Clinical Psychology Doctoral Program
Natural Sciences and Mathematics
1020 Oakland Avenue, 201 Uhler Hall
Indiana, PA 15705-1064
Telephone: (724) 357-4519
Chairperson: Raymond Pavloski, PhD

E-mail: David.LaPorte@iup.edu
Web: http://www.iup.edu/psychology/psyd

Orientation, Objectives, and Emphasis of Department

The Psychology Department offers a Doctor of Psychology degree in Clinical Psychology (PsyD) that places emphasis upon professional applications of psychology based on the local clinical scientist model and on a solid grounding in the scientific knowledge base of psychology. Training follows a generalist model with opportunities to develop advanced competencies through courses and special practica. The core curriculum consists of seven areas including elective coursework. Heavy emphasis is placed on integrating psychological knowledge with treatment, evaluation, consultation and service delivery program design. The program is designed to meet the academic requirements of licensure and provide the background to assume responsibilities in appropriate professional settings. Current areas of interest that allow students to begin pre-specialization include: forensic, child clinical, behavioral medicine, clinical neuropsychology, and college counseling.

Programs and Degrees Offered

Program	Degree	Application Deadline	Applications Received	Accepted	New Admits Enrolled (PT)	Total Enrolled (PT)	Degrees Awarded in 2014–2015	Median Years to Complete Degree	Dismissed/ Withdrew
Clinical Psychology	PsyD	December 15 (Fall)	224	48	9 (0)	70 (0)	10	5	2

APA Accreditation

Clinical PsyD: Student Outcome Data website: http://www.iup.edu/psychology/grad/clinical-psychology-psyd/admissions/outcome-data/.

Doctoral Degree (PsyD Clinical Psychology): For those doctoral students for whom a professional internship was required in this program prior to graduation:

Total students who applied for an internship: 17
Total students who obtained an internship: 16
Total students who obtained a paid internship: 16
Total students who obtained an unpaid internship: 0
Total students who were placed in APA/CPA-accredited internships: 14
Total students placed in internships not APA/CPA-accredited, but listed with the Association of Psychology Postdoctoral and Internship Centers (APPIC): 2
Total students placed in internships conforming to guidelines of the Council of Directors of School Psychology Programs (CDSPP): 0
Total students placed in internships that were not APA/CPA-accredited, APPIC or CDSSP listed: 0

Internships/Practica

Students begin clinical experiences in the first year through course-based practica. During the second and later years, students enroll in the department-sponsored Center for Applied Psychology (CAP) training clinics, performing both therapy and assessment. Training in the CAP clinics is supplemented with required external practica, currently available in approximately 40 different sites.

Admissions

Entries appear in the following order: required test or GPA, minimum score (if required)/median score of students entering in 2015–2016.

Program	Degree	GRE-V	GRE-Q	GRE-Writing	GRE-Subject	Under-graduate GPA	Last 2 Years GPA	Psychol-ogy GPA	Master's GPA
Clinical Psychology	PsyD	154/160	152/154	Not specified	Not specified	3.1/3.69	NA/NA	NA/NA	NA/NA

Admissions Requirements:

Degree	GRE	GRE-Subject	Letters of Recom-mendation	Research Statement	Writing Sample	CV	Interview
Doctoral	Required	Recom-mended	3	Required	Optional	Recom-mended	Required

Admissions Criteria:

GRE scores—high
Research experience—high
Work experience—medium
Clinically related public service—high
GPA—high

Letters of recommendation—high
Interview—high
Statement of goals and objectives—high
Undergraduate psychology preparation—high

For additional information on admission requirements, visit http://www.iup.edu/psychology/grad/clinical-psychology-psyd/admissions/criteria/.

Department Demographics

	Male (PT)	Female (PT)	Total	African-American/ Black (PT)	Hispanic/ Latino (PT)	Asian/ Pacific Islander (PT)	American Indian/ Alaska Native (PT)	Caucasian/ White (PT)	Unknown (PT)	Multiethnic (PT)	ADA (PT)	Int'l (PT)
Students	19 (0)	51 (0)	70	0 (0)	1 (0)	3 (0)	0 (0)	65 (0)	0 (0)	1 (0)	1 (0)	3 (0)

Financial Information/Assistance

Tuition: For information on tuition costs, visit http://www.iup.edu/bursar/tuitionfees/graduate/. Tuition is subject to change. Additional fees are assessed to students beyond the costs of tuition for the following: technology, activity, instructional, registration, wellness, transportation, student services.

Doctoral:
State residents: $16,624 per academic year.
State residents: $519 per credit hour.
Nonstate residents: $24,993 per academic year.
Nonstate residents: $779 per credit hour.

Financial Assistance:

	Teaching Assistantship (% Receiving)	Teaching Assistantship Tuition Remission	Research Assistantship (% Receiving)	Research Assistantship Tuition Remission	Fellowship (% Receiving)	Fellowship Tuition Remission
First-Year Student	NA (NA)	NA	$3,265 (100)	Partial	NA (NA)	NA
Advanced Student	$22,398 (8)	NA	$3,265 (92)	Partial	NA (NA)	NA

For additional information on financial assistance, visit http://www.iup.edu/financialaid/student-types/graduate/.

Employment of Department Graduates

Doctoral:
Enrolled in a postdoctoral residency/fellowship: 8
Employed in other positions at a higher education institution: 1
Still seeking employment: 1
Total: 10

Additional Information

Housing and Day Care: On-campus housing is available. See the following website for more information: http://www.iup.edu/housing/housing-options/university-towers/. On-campus day care facilities are available. See the following website for more information: http://www.indikids.org/university-childrens-center.html.

Information for Students With Physical Disabilities: See the following website: http://www.iup.edu/disabilitysupport/.

Special Facilities or Resources: The Department of Psychology includes two 16-computer laboratories, a graduate student computer lab, individual research space with recording capabilities, seminar rooms and a graduate student lounge. Each graduate student office is provided with computer access to the department server and the Internet. The facilities for the CAP include 12 treatment rooms as well as one seminar room, all connected with a master recording system. The CAP also houses computer facilities for test administration and scoring.

Application Information: Graduate Admissions Office, Indiana University of Pennsylvania, Sutton Hall Suite 120, 1011 South Drive, Indiana, PA 15705-1048. *Fee:* $50. *Online application:* http://www.iup.edu/admissions/graduate/howto/.

La Salle University

Counseling and Family Therapy Master's Programs
1900 West Olney Avenue
Philadelphia, PA 19141
Telephone: (215) 951-1767
E-mail: tonrey@lasalle.edu
Director, Counseling and Family Therapy Master's Programs: Donna A. Tonrey, PsyD, LMFT, LPC
Web: http://www.lasalle.edu/counseling-family-therapy/

Orientation, Objectives, and Emphasis of Department

Our Marriage and Family Therapy Master's program is COAMFTE-accredited. Our Professional Clinical Counseling program is CACREP-accredited. Three master's degrees are available within the program: Professional Clinical Counseling; Marriage and Family Therapy; and Industrial/Organizational Psychology. The program stresses skills training and clinical preparation for these degrees, including preparation for licensure as a Professional Counselor or a Marriage and Family Therapist. It also prepares students for doctoral studies. The program is based on a holistic view of the person, which stresses the integration of the psychological, systemic, cultural, and spiritual dimensions of experience.

Programs and Degrees Offered

Program	Degree	Application Deadline	Applications Received	Accepted	New Admits Enrolled (PT)	Total Enrolled (PT)	Degrees Awarded in 2014–2015	Median Years to Complete Degree	Dismissed/Withdrew
Marriage and Family Therapy	MA/MS	August 15 (Fall), December 15 (Spring), April 15 (Summer), Rolling	88	59	5 (25)	25 (100)	19	3.5	1
Professional Clinical Counseling	MA/MS	August 15 (Fall), December 15 (Spring), April 15 (Summer), Rolling	123	70	5 (30)	30 (149)	68	3.5	3
Industrial/ Organizational Psychology	MA/MS	August 15 (Fall)	51	37	(20)	(20)	0		0

Internships/Practica

Seventy-five to a hundred students are placed in sites located throughout the Tri-State area. The internship placements are specific to the areas of concentration and supervised by professionals highly qualified in particular realms of expertise. We have contracts with over 100 sites for our students, and each site is well-informed about our program and the preparation our students gain prior to beginning their internship.

Admissions

Entries appear in the following order: required test or GPA, minimum score (if required)/median score of students entering in 2015–2016.

Program	Degree	GRE-V	GRE-Q	GRE-Writing	GRE-Subject	Under-graduate GPA	Last 2 Years GPA	Psychology GPA	Master's GPA
Marriage and Family Therapy	MA/MS	Not specified	Not specified	Not specified	Not specified	Not specified	Not specified	Not specified	Not specified
Professional Clinical Counseling	MA/MS	Not specified	Not specified	Not specified	Not specified	Not specified	Not specified	Not specified	Not specified
Industrial/ Organizational Psychology	MA/MS	Not specified	Not specified	Not specified	Not specified	Not specified	Not specified	Not specified	Not specified

Admissions Requirements:

Degree	GRE	GRE-Subject	Letters of Recommendation	Research Statement	Writing Sample	CV	Interview
Master's/Specialist	Required	None	3	Required	Optional	Required	Optional

Admissions Criteria:
GRE scores—medium
Research experience—medium
Work experience—medium
Clinically related public service—medium
GPA—high

Letters of recommendation—high
Interview—low
Statement of goals and objectives—high
Undergraduate psychology preparation—high

Department Demographics

	Male (PT)	Female (PT)	Total	African-American/ Black (PT)	Hispanic/ Latino (PT)	Asian/ Pacific Islander (PT)	American Indian/ Alaska Native (PT)	Caucasian/ White (PT)	Unknown (PT)	Multiethnic (PT)	ADA (PT)	Int'l (PT)
Students	7 (48)	48 (221)	324	5 (40)	1 (2)	0 (0)	0 (0)	49 (227)	0 (0)	0 (0)	2 (0)	2 (0)

Financial Information/Assistance

Tuition: For information on tuition costs, visit http://www.lasalle.edu/financialaid/content/tuition.php. Tuition is subject to change. Additional fees are assessed to students beyond the costs of tuition for the following: $100 General University Fee, Technology Fee $100 per semester. Tuition costs vary by program.

Master's:
State residents: $760 per credit hour.
Nonstate residents: $760 per credit hour.

Financial Assistance:

	Teaching Assistantship (% Receiving)	Teaching Assistantship Tuition Remission	Research Assistantship (% Receiving)	Research Assistantship Tuition Remission	Fellowship (% Receiving)	Fellowship Tuition Remission
First-Year Student	NA (NA)	NA	NA (NA)	NA	$4,000 (NA)	NA
Advanced Student	NA (NA)	NA	$1,500 (NA)	NA	NA (NA)	NA

For additional information on financial assistance, visit http://www.lasalle.edu/financialaid/.

Employment of Department Graduates

Master's:
Enrolled in a psychology doctoral program: 4
Employed in a community mental health/counseling center: 110
Total: 114

Additional Information

Housing and Day Care: On-campus housing is available. See the following website for more information: http://www.lasalle.edu/students/dean/admin/housing/gradhousing.htm. On-campus day care facilities are available.

Special Facilities or Resources: Our faculty are highly involved in research and our students have the opportunity to join research teams or take a Graduate Research course that connects to the student's interest.

Application Information: Graduate Enrollment, Box 826, LaSalle University, 1900 West Olney Avenue, Philadelphia, PA 19141. *Fee:* $0. *Online application:* http://www.lasalle.edu/grad/application.html.

Lehigh University

Department of Education and Human Services
Education
Mountain Top Campus, 111 Research Drive
Bethlehem, PA 18015
Telephone: (610) 758-3241
Chairperson: Arpana Inman

E-mail: agi2@lehigh.edu
Web: http://coe.lehigh.edu/

Orientation, Objectives, and Emphasis of Department

The College of Education offers degree programs in counseling and school psychology. The program in school psychology offers training at both educational specialist (NASP-approved) and doctoral (PhD) levels (NASP-approved and APA-accredited). Within the PhD program, subspecializations in Health/Pediatric School Psychology and in Students At-Risk for Disabilities are offered. The program at all levels is systems and behaviorally oriented, emphasizing collaborative problem-solving based research, consultation, behavioral assessment and intervention in the implementation of school psychology services. The program in counseling psychology emphasizes a scientist–practitioner model and trains professional psychologists for employment in educational, industrial, and community settings. The counseling psychology program also offers training at the master's level. The training program emphasizes diversity and multicultural perspectives throughout the curriculum.

Programs and Degrees Offered

Program	Degree	Application Deadline	Applications Received	Accepted	New Admits Enrolled (PT)	Total Enrolled (PT)	Degrees Awarded in 2014–2015	Median Years to Complete Degree	Dismissed/ Withdrew
Counseling Psychology	PhD	December 1 (Fall)	76	6	5 (0)	22 (2)	6	6	0
Counseling and Human Services	MEd	February 1 (Fall)	56	26	12 (1)	23 (8)	14	2.5	0
School Psychology	PhD	January 1 (Fall)	48	14	4 (0)	25 (7)	4	9	0
School Psychology	EdS	January 1 (Fall)	29	10	5 (0)	16	3	3	0
International Counseling	MEd	January 15 (Fall)	25	12	0 (11)	0 (25)	15	3	2
School Counseling	MEd	February 1 (Fall)	24	13	6 (1)	11 (6)	4	3	1

APA Accreditation

Counseling PhD: Student Outcome Data website: http://coe.lehigh.edu/academics/degrees/cp-phd.
School PhD: Student Outcome Data website: http://coe.lehigh.edu/academics/degrees/phdschpsych.

Doctoral Degree (PhD Counseling Psychology): For those doctoral students for whom a professional internship was required in this program prior to graduation:
Total students who applied for an internship: 5
Total students who obtained an internship: 5
Total students who obtained a paid internship: 5
Total students who obtained an unpaid internship: 0
Total students who were placed in APA/CPA-accredited internships: 4
Total students placed in internships not APA/CPA-accredited, but listed with the Association of Psychology Postdoctoral and Internship Centers (APPIC): 1
Total students placed in internships conforming to guidelines of the Council of Directors of School Psychology Programs (CDSPP): 0
Total students placed in internships that were not APA/CPA-accredited, APPIC or CDSSP listed: 0

Doctoral Degree (PhD School Psychology): For those doctoral students for whom a professional internship was required in this program prior to graduation:
Total students who applied for an internship: 3

Total students who obtained an internship: 3
Total students who obtained a paid internship: 3
Total students who obtained an unpaid internship: 0
Total students who were placed in APA/CPA-accredited internships: 0
Total students placed in internships not APA/CPA-accredited, but listed with the Association of Psychology Postdoctoral and Internship Centers (APPIC): 1
Total students placed in internships conforming to guidelines of the Council of Directors of School Psychology Programs (CDSPP): 2
Total students placed in internships that were not APA/CPA-accredited, APPIC or CDSSP listed: 0

Internships/Practica

The Counseling Psychology program maintains contracts with a variety of practicum settings. Training in individual, group, couples, and family counseling is readily available. Students receive at least 2 hours of individual and 2 hours group supervision per week. Many sites provide additional training on specific issues in counseling. The Counseling Psychology programs have established a partnership with a local urban school district to provide enhanced in-school psychological services and integrated mental and general health care in collaboration with St. Luke's Hospital physicians. The School Psychology program also has established partnerships with local schools and health agencies for student practica. Third- and fourth-year doctoral students complete practica two days per week which provides hours toward state certification.

Admissions

Entries appear in the following order: required test or GPA, minimum score (if required)/median score of students entering in 2015–2016.

Program	Degree	GRE-V	GRE-Q	GRE-Writing	GRE-Subject	Under-graduate GPA	Last 2 Years GPA	Psychol-ogy GPA	Master's GPA
Counseling Psychology	PhD	NA/154	NA/151	Not specified	Not specified	3/3.49	Not specified	Not specified	Not specified
Counseling and Human Services	MEd	Not specified	Not specified	Not specified	Not specified	3/NA	Not specified	Not specified	Not specified
School Psychology	PhD	151/159	149/152	3.5/5	Not specified	3.56/3.85	Not specified	Not specified	Not specified
School Psychology	EdS	149/157	143/157	3.5/4	Not specified	3.39/3.77	Not specified	Not specified	Not specified
International Counseling	MEd	Not specified	Not specified	Not specified	Not specified	3/NA	Not specified	Not specified	Not specified
School Counseling	MEd	Not specified	Not specified	Not specified	Not specified	3/NA	Not specified	Not specified	Not specified

Admissions Requirements:

Degree	GRE	GRE-Subject	Letters of Recom-mendation	Research Statement	Writing Sample	CV	Interview
Master's/Specialist	Required	None	2	Required	Optional	Required	Required
Doctoral	Required	Optional	2	Required	Optional	Required	Required

Please note if these criteria vary for different programs: Only EdS and PhD programs require GRE scores. Counseling Psychology interviews at the master's level are conducted via Skype or similar medium. School psychology requires three statements focused on professional or research interests, related experiences, and experiences with diverse populations.

Admissions Criteria:

GRE scores—medium
Research experience—high
Work experience—medium
Clinically related public service—medium
GPA—high

Letters of recommendation—high
Interview—medium
Statement of goals and objectives—high
Undergraduate psychology preparation—medium
Additional statements—high

For additional information on admission requirements, visit http://coe.lehigh.edu/admissions/apply/deadlines-requirements.

Department Demographics

	Male (PT)	Female (PT)	Total	African-American/ Black (PT)	Hispanic/ Latino (PT)	Asian/ Pacific Islander (PT)	American Indian/ Alaska Native (PT)	Caucasian/ White (PT)	Unknown	Multiethnic (PT)	ADA (PT)	Int'l (PT)
Students	26 (8)	185 (67)	286	7 (0)	0 (2)	5 (0)	0 (0)	124 (72)	74 (0)	1 (1)	0 (0)	0 (10)

Financial Information/Assistance

Tuition: For information on tuition costs, visit http://financeadmin.lehigh.edu/content/fee-schedule-0. Tuition is subject to change.

Doctoral:
State residents: $565 per credit hour.
Nonstate residents: $565 per credit hour.

Master's:
State residents: $565 per credit hour.
Nonstate residents: $565 per credit hour.

Financial Assistance:

	Teaching Assistantship (% Receiving)	Teaching Assistantship Tuition Remission	Research Assistantship (% Receiving)	Research Assistantship Tuition Remission	Fellowship (% Receiving)	Fellowship Tuition Remission
First-Year Student	NA (NA)	NA	$16,000 (NA)	Full	$26,000 (NA)	Full
Advanced Student	NA (NA)	NA	$16,000 (NA)	Full	$26,000 (NA)	Full

For additional information on financial assistance, visit http://coe.lehigh.edu/admissions/financial-aid.

Employment of Department Graduates

Master's:
Enrolled in a psychology doctoral program: 8
Employed in academic position at a 2-year/4-year college: 2
Employed in other positions at a higher education institution: 3
Employed in a professional position in a school system: 10
Employed in business or industry: 1
Employed in government agency: 1
Employed in a community mental health/counseling center: 4
Total: 29

Doctoral:
Enrolled in a postdoctoral residency/fellowship: 17
Employed in independent practice: 2
Employed in an academic position at a university: 1
Employed in other positions at a higher education institution: 3
Employed in a professional position in a school system: 4
Other employment position: 4
Total: 31

Additional Information

Housing and Day Care: On-campus housing is available. See the following website for more information: https://financeadmin. lehigh.edu/content/graduate-housing-resources. On-campus day care facilities are available. See the following website for more information: http://financeadmin.lehigh.edu/childcare.

Information for Students With Physical Disabilities: See the following website: http://studentaffairs.lehigh.edu/disabilities.

Special Facilities or Resources: The Counseling Psychology program has a large NIMH-funded project on maternal attachment and infant emotional regulation. The school psychology program has a number of research and training projects that are focused on students with behavior and cognitive disabilities. The department has the Center for Promoting Research to Practice, a unit that houses several major research grants involved in bringing known research findings into school and community settings. The department also has university-affiliated training and research programs that provide living arrangements and day treatment programs for adults with developmental disabilities. The department also operates a laboratory school (Centennial School) for children and adolescents with emotional disturbance. All facilities are integrated into the training of students primarily in the school psychology programs. The counseling psychology program has a lab for videotaping and editing. Both programs have established partnerships with urban school districts. School psychology has established practicum placements in local hospitals and with the Children's Hospital of Philadelphia as part of the pediatric school psychology subspecialization track.

Application Information: Ms. Donna Johnson, College of Education, Lehigh University, 111 Research Drive, Bethlehem, PA 18015.
Fee: $65. *Online application:* https://www.applyweb.com/apply/lehighg/.

Lehigh University

Department of Psychology
Arts and Sciences
17 Memorial Drive East
Bethlehem, PA 18015
Telephone: (610) 758-3630
Chairperson: Gordon Moskowitz

E-mail: djp208@lehigh.edu
Web: http://psychology.cas2.lehigh.edu/

Orientation, Objectives, and Emphasis of Department

We are a research-intensive department, where graduate students and faculty work collaboratively in three areas of psychology: cognitive, developmental, and social. The relatively small size of our graduate program means that students and faculty work very closely together. Most students work with one professor as their primary research adviser, but also collaborate with other faculty and students on projects throughout their time in the program. In fact, collaboration across multiple labs and areas of psychology is strongly encouraged. Our program involves some coursework—statistical training is particularly important—but the focus is on designing, conducting and publishing cutting-edge psychological research. Students also have multiple opportunities to gain teaching experience: most will work as teaching assistants at some point, and all PhD students have the opportunity to teach at least one undergraduate course after completing their MSc degree. We aim to train highly talented psychologists who are well qualified to work in academia, business or government after they graduate. Recent graduates from our PhD program have secured tenure-track faculty positions in the U.S. and internationally, postdoctoral research positions, and jobs in university administration.

Programs and Degrees Offered

Program	Degree	Application Deadline	Applica-tions Received	Accepted	New Admits Enrolled (PT)	Total Enrolled (PT)	Degrees Awarded in 2014–2015	Median Years to Complete Degree	Dismissed/ Withdrew
Cognitive, Developmental and Social Psychology	PhD	January 1 (Fall)	70		1 (0)	14 (2)	4	5	1

Admissions

Entries appear in the following order: required test or GPA, minimum score (if required)/median score of students entering in 2015–2016.

Program	Degree	GRE-V	GRE-Q	GRE-Writing	GRE-Subject	Under-graduate GPA	Last 2 Years GPA	Psychol-ogy GPA	Master's GPA
Cognitive, Developmental and Social Psychology	PhD	NA/NA	NA/NA	NA/NA	Not specified	NA/NA	Not specified	Not specified	Not specified

Admissions Requirements:

Degree	GRE	GRE-Subject	Letters of Recom-mendation	Research Statement	Writing Sample	CV	Interview
Doctoral	Required	Optional	2	Required	None	Required	Optional

Admissions Criteria:

GRE scores—medium
Research experience—high
Work experience—low
GPA—medium

Letters of recommendation—high
Interview—high
Statement of goals and objectives—high
Undergraduate psychology preparation—medium

For additional information on admission requirements, visit http://psychology.cas2.lehigh.edu/node/67.

Department Demographics

	Male (PT)	Female (PT)	Total	African-American/ Black (PT)	Hispanic/ Latino (PT)	Asian/ Pacific Islander (PT)	American Indian/ Alaska Native (PT)	Caucasian/ White (PT)	Unknown	Multiethnic (PT)	ADA (PT)	Int'l (PT)
Students	4 (0)	10 (2)	16	0 (0)	0 (0)	4 (0)	0 (0)	9 (2)	0 (1)	1 (0)	0 (0)	5 (0)

Financial Information/Assistance

Tuition: For information on tuition costs, visit http://financeadmin.lehigh.edu/content/fee-schedule-0. Tuition is subject to change.

Doctoral:
State residents: $1,420 per credit hour.
Nonstate residents: $1,420 per credit hour.

Financial Assistance:

	Teaching Assistantship (% Receiving)	Teaching Assistantship Tuition Remission	Research Assistantship (% Receiving)	Research Assistantship Tuition Remission	Fellowship (% Receiving)	Fellowship Tuition Remission
First-Year Student	$20,400 (NA)	Full	$20,400 (NA)	Full	$20,400 (NA)	Full
Advanced Student	$20,400 (NA)	Full	$20,400 (NA)	Full	$20,400 (NA)	Full

For additional information on financial assistance, visit http://cas.cas2.lehigh.edu/content/financial-aid.

Employment of Department Graduates

No information provided.

Additional Information

Housing and Day Care: On-campus housing is available. See the following website for more information: https://financeadmin.lehigh.edu/content/graduate-housing-resources. On-campus day care facilities are available. See the following website for more information: http://financeadmin.lehigh.edu/childcare.

Information for Students With Physical Disabilities: See the following website: http://studentaffairs.lehigh.edu/disabilities.

Special Facilities or Resources: The department's well-equipped laboratories provide an excellent setting for research. The department has extensive facilities available for graduate student research, including a Child Study Center, and cognitive, developmental, and social laboratories.

Application Information: Graduate Programs Office, Lehigh University, 9 West Packer Avenue, Bethlehem, PA 18015-3075. *Fee:* $75. *Online application:* https://www.applyweb.com/lehighg/index.ftl.

Millersville University
Department of Psychology
Byerly Hall
Millersville, PA 17551
Telephone: (717) 871-7302
Chairperson: Frederick Foster-Clark

E-mail: claudia.haferkamp@millersville.edu
Web: http://www.millersville.edu/psychology/

Orientation, Objectives, and Emphasis of Department

All three graduate programs see professional competence as a function of increased self-awareness and personal growth anchored in solid relationship skills and combined with a strong knowledge base of effective interventions. The Clinical Psychology program's mission is to train competent, ethically and multiculturally informed practitioners with knowledge of empirically supported treatments to work as direct service providers in a wide range of mental health settings or pursue advanced doctoral study. The 60-credit Clinical program meets the educational requirements of the Licensed Professional Counselor (LPC) PA regulations. The program in School Psychology is accredited by the National Association of School Psychologists (NASP) and prepares students for entry-level positions as school psychologists. Knowledge of the educational process, psychological and emotional growth, and data-based decision-making are central to the training program. The MEd in School Counseling programs prepare students as school counselors for grades K–12. Using a predominantly solution-focused model, students develop into professionals who are responsive to the needs of the school setting. School Counseling graduates may also seek licensure as professional counselors in PA.

Programs and Degrees Offered

Program	Degree	Application Deadline	Applications Received	Accepted	New Admits Enrolled (PT)	Total Enrolled (PT)	Degrees Awarded in 2014–2015	Median Years to Complete Degree	Dismissed/ Withdrew
Clinical Psychology	MA/MS	January 15 (Fall), October 1 (Spring)	50	20	6 (3)	39 (20)	20	3	0
School Counseling	MEd	January 15 (Fall), October 1 (Spring)	7	5	9 (1)	14 (19)	19	3	0
School Psychology	MA/MS	January 15 (Fall), October 1 (Spring)	14	4	8 (4)	15 (24)	9	3	0
Supervision Of School Guidance Certificate	Other	January 15 (Fall), October 1 (Spring)	1	1	0 (1)	0 (2)	0		
Supervision Of School Psychology Certificate	Other	January 15 (Fall), October 1 (Spring)	4	4	0 (2)	1 (6)	0		

Internships/Practica

The Department has established collaborative training relationships with diverse schools and mental health agencies in the Lancaster, York and Harrisburg region. Field experiences/internships are required of all students in Clinical, School Counseling, and School Psychology programs. Students in the Certification Program in School Psychology are required to complete a full-time internship over 1 academic year for a minimum of 1,200 hours. After satisfactory completion of all coursework, internships and other requirements, School Psychology students may be certified as School Psychologists in PA. Students in the Clinical program must complete a minimum of 600 hours internship in inpatient or outpatient mental health settings. Students in School Counseling complete their practica as counselors working in K–12 schools.

Admissions

Entries appear in the following order: required test or GPA, minimum score (if required)/median score of students entering in 2015–2016.

Program	Degree	GRE-V	GRE-Q	GRE-Writing	GRE-Subject	Under-graduate GPA	Last 2 Years GPA	Psychol-ogy GPA	Master's GPA
Clinical Psychology	MA/MS	147/NA	148/NA	3.5/NA	Not specified	2.75/NA	Not specified	Not specified	Not specified
School Counseling	MEd	147/NA	148/NA	3.5/NA	Not specified	2.75/NA	Not specified	Not specified	Not specified

Admissions *(con't.)*

Program	Degree	GRE-V	GRE-Q	GRE-Writing	GRE-Subject	Under-graduate GPA	Last 2 Years GPA	Psychol-ogy GPA	Master's GPA
School Psychology	MA/MS	147/NA	148/NA	3.5/NA	Not specified	2.75/NA	Not specified	Not specified	Not specified
Supervision of School Guidance Certificate	Other	Not specified	Not specified	Not specified	Not specified	Not specified	Not specified	Not specified	Not specified
Supervision of School Psychology Certificate	Other	Not specified	Not specified	Not specified	Not specified	Not specified	Not specified	Not specified	Not specified

Admissions Requirements:

Degree	GRE	GRE-Subject	Letters of Recom-mendation	Research Statement	Writing Sample	CV	Interview
Master's/Specialist	Required	None	3	Required	Required	Optional	Required

Please note if these criteria vary for different programs: The School Counseling MEd program requires applicants to have 6 credits of Psychology courses and 6 credits of education courses. Persons applying to either the Clinical or School Psychology programs who were not Psychology majors must first complete at least 18 credits of undergraduate Psychology coursework before applying. Suggested courses include Intro, Child Development, Statistics/Research; Abnormal, Personality, Counseling Strategies, or related helping skills courses.

Admissions Criteria:

GRE scores—medium
Research experience—medium
Work experience—high
Clinically related public service—high
GPA—high

Letters of recommendation—high
Interview—high
Statement of goals and objectives—high
Undergraduate psychology preparation—high
Writing sample—medium

For additional information on admission requirements, visit http://www.millersville.edu/psychology/graduate/index.php.

Department Demographics

	Male (PT)	Female (PT)	Total	African-American/ Black (PT)	Hispanic/ Latino (PT)	Asian/ Pacific Islander (PT)	American Indian/ Alaska Native (PT)	Caucasian/ White (PT)	Unknown	Multiethnic (PT)	ADA (PT)	Int'l (PT)
Students	4 (17)	65 (54)	140	4 (0)	3 (7)	2 (0)	0 (1)	58 (61)	1 (0)	1 (2)	0 (0)	0 (0)

Financial Information/Assistance

Tuition: For information on tuition costs, visit http://www.millersville.edu/bursar/tuition-fees/gradcosts.php. Tuition is subject to change. Additional fees are assessed to students beyond the costs of tuition for the following: A general fee of $103/credit and technology fee of $24/credit are also charged.

Master's:
State residents: $581 per credit hour.
Nonstate residents: $820 per credit hour.

Financial Assistance:

	Teaching Assistantship (% Receiving)	Teaching Assistantship Tuition Remission	Research Assistantship (% Receiving)	Research Assistantship Tuition Remission	Fellowship (% Receiving)	Fellowship Tuition Remission
First-Year Student	NA (NA)	NA	$5,000 (NA)	Full	NA (NA)	NA
Advanced Student	NA (NA)	NA	$5,400 (NA)	Full	NA (NA)	NA

For additional information on financial assistance, visit http://www.millersville.edu/finaid/studentinfo/graduate.php.

Employment of Department Graduates

No information provided.

Additional Information

Housing and Day Care: No on-campus housing is available. No on-campus day care facilities are available.

Information for Students With Physical Disabilities: See the following website: http://www.millersville.edu/learningservices/disabilityaccom.php.

Special Facilities or Resources: A microcomputer lab with access to the mainframe is available in the department. Millersville's campus is fully wireless. The Department has a clinic with observation and digital recording facilities. Ganser Library houses approximately half a million books and provides access to nearly 3,500 periodical titles. The research and information needs of faculty, staff, and students are met by subject specialists who provide extensive reference service within the library, at off-site locations, and electronically. Scholarly research is supported by a comprehensive and well-developed library collection that is continuously being augmented by the most current resources available, in print and electronic formats. The Library belongs to several statewide and regional library consortia that allows for resource sharing, reciprocal borrowing, and collaborative purchasing.

Application Information: Graduate Studies Office, Millersville University, P.O. Box 1002, Millersville, PA 17551-0302. *Fee:* $40. *Online application:* https://www.applyweb.com/apply/pamillg/apply.html.

Penn State Harrisburg
Psychology Program
777 West Harrisburg Pike
Middletown, PA 17057-4898
Telephone: (717) 948-6063
Program Coordinator: Marissa A. Harrison
Web: https://harrisburg.psu.edu/behavioral-sciences-and-education/social-sciences-and-psychology

E-mail: mah52@psu.edu

Orientation, Objectives, and Emphasis of Department
The Applied Clinical Psychology program offers the educational background to prepare students to work as mental health professionals in various settings. It is intended to provide a broad training program in empirically validated clinical psychology. When accompanied by an additional 12 credits in advanced graduate studies in psychology and/or counseling, this degree can provide the academic training necessary for graduates to apply for master's-level licensure as a Professional Counselor (LPC) in the Commonwealth of Pennsylvania. This MA program requires 48 credits of coursework. The training model is health-oriented rather than pathology-oriented and emphasizes the development of assessment and intervention. The Applied Psychological Research program follows an apprentice model and focuses on the development of research skills within the context of scientific training in psychology. The program requires 35 credits of course work (29 credits of core courses and 6 credits of electives).This degree program is designed to meet the needs of students who plan careers in research or administration within health, human services, or similar organizations. Students can select electives and research experiences, in consultation with their adviser, to reflect their individual interests.

Programs and Degrees Offered

Program	Degree	Application Deadline	Applications Received	Accepted	New Admits Enrolled (PT)	Total Enrolled (PT)	Degrees Awarded in 2014–2015	Median Years to Complete Degree	Dismissed/ Withdrew
Applied Clinical Psychology	MA/MS	April 30 (Fall)	126	30	10 (0)	24 (12)	10	3	1
Applied Psychological Research	MA/MS	April 30 (Fall)	16	2	2 (0)	9 (2)	4	2.5	0

Internships/Practica

Students in the Applied Clinical Psychology program are required to complete 7 credits of supervised clinical internship, for a total of 700 hours. Students in the Applied Psychological Research program are required to complete 6 credits of research in collaboration with the program faculty.

Admissions

Entries appear in the following order: required test or GPA, minimum score (if required)/median score of students entering in 2015–2016.

Program	Degree	GRE-V	GRE-Q	GRE-Writing	GRE-Subject	Under-graduate GPA	Last 2 Years GPA	Psychol-ogy GPA	Master's GPA
Applied Clinical Psychology	MA/MS	146/157	146/152	3.5/4	Not specified	Not specified	3/3.58	Not specified	Not specified
Applied Psychological Research	MA/MS	146/157	146/156	3.5/4.5	Not specified	Not specified	3/3.58	Not specified	Not specified

Admissions Requirements:

Degree	GRE	GRE-Subject	Letters of Recom-mendation	Research Statement	Writing Sample	CV	Interview
Master's/Specialist	Required	None	3	Required	Optional	Optional	Required

Please note if these criteria vary for different programs: A "B" or above is required for both undergraduate statistics and a Psychology research methods course. At least two letters of recommendation must be academic.

Admissions Criteria:

GRE scores—high
Research experience—medium
Work experience—low
Clinically related public service—low
GPA—high

Letters of recommendation—high
Interview—high
Statement of goals and objectives—high
Undergraduate psychology preparation—medium
Statistics/Methods grades—high

For additional information on admission requirements, visit http://hbg.psu.edu/Programs/Graduate/MastersDegrees.php.

Department Demographics

	Male (PT)	Female (PT)	Total	African-American/ Black (PT)	Hispanic/ Latino (PT)	Asian/ Pacific Islander (PT)	American Indian/ Alaska Native (PT)	Caucasian/ White (PT)	Unknown (PT)	Multiethnic (PT)	ADA (PT)	Int'l (PT)
Students	8 (6)	25 (8)	47	1 (1)	0 (0)	1 (0)	0 (1)	31 (12)	0 (0)	0 (0)	0 (0)	1 (0)

Financial Information/Assistance

Tuition: For information on tuition costs, visit http://tuition.psu.edu/. Tuition is subject to change.

Master's:
State residents: $19,328 per academic year.
State residents: $805 per credit hour.
Nonstate residents: $25,530 per academic year.
Nonstate residents: $1,064 per credit hour.

Financial Assistance:

	Teaching Assistantship (% Receiving)	Teaching Assistantship Tuition Remission	Research Assistantship (% Receiving)	Research Assistantship Tuition Remission	Fellowship (% Receiving)	Fellowship Tuition Remission
First-Year Student	NA (NA)	NA	$16,460 (6)	Full	NA (NA)	NA
Advanced Student	NA (NA)	NA	$16,020 (6)	Full	NA (NA)	NA

For additional information on financial assistance, visit http://harrisburg.psu.edu/financial-aid/financial-aid-for-graduate-students.

Employment of Department Graduates

Master's:
Enrolled in a psychology doctoral program: 2
Employed in other positions at a higher education institution: 2
Employed in a community mental health/counseling center: 4
Employed in a hospital/medical center: 1
Total: 9

Additional Information

Housing and Day Care: On-campus housing is available. See the following website for more information: http://harrisburgcampusliving.psu.edu/. On-campus day care facilities are available. See the following website for more information: http://harrisburg.psu.edu/places/childcare-center.

Information for Students With Physical Disabilities: See the following website: http://harrisburg.psu.edu/disability-services.

Special Facilities or Resources: Most students avail themselves of the resources in community hospitals and residential and outpatient institutions for hands-on clinical and research experience. The department maintains an on-campus research facility which is available for use by graduate students working with faculty on research projects.

Application Information: Fee: $65. *Online application:* http://www.gradschool.psu.edu/apply/.

Pennsylvania State University

Department of Human Development and Family Studies
College of Health and Human Development
119 HHD
University Park, PA 16802
Telephone: (814) 863-8000
Professor in Charge of Graduate Program: Eva Lefkowitz

E-mail: csh5007@psu.edu
Web: http://www.hhdev.psu.edu/hdfs/graduate

Orientation, Objectives, and Emphasis of Department

The basic objectives of the human development and family studies (HDFS) program are the following: to expand knowledge about the development and functioning of individuals, small groups, and families; to improve methods for studying processes of human development and change; and to create and disseminate improved techniques and strategies for enhancing individual and family functioning, helping people learn to cope more effectively with problems of living, and preventing normal life problems from becoming serious difficulties. The program takes a life-span perspective, recognizing that the most important aspects of development and types of life tasks and situations vary from infancy and childhood through maturity and old age, as well as through the life cycle of the family, and that each phase of development is a precursor to the next. There is a firm commitment to an interdisciplinary and multiprofessional approach to these objectives and to the development of competence in applying rigorous methods of empirical inquiry. All students are expected to acquire a broad interdisciplinary base of knowledge and to develop competence in depth in one of four primary program areas: family development, individual development, prevention/intervention, or methodology.

Programs and Degrees Offered

Program	Degree	Application Deadline	Applications Received	Accepted	New Admits Enrolled (PT)	Total Enrolled (PT)	Degrees Awarded in 2014–2015	Median Years to Complete Degree	Dismissed/ Withdrew
Human Development and Family Studies	PhD	December 1 (Fall)	79	23	15 (0)	70 (0)	4	5	1

Admissions

Entries appear in the following order: required test or GPA, minimum score (if required)/median score of students entering in 2015–2016.

Program	Degree	GRE-V	GRE-Q	GRE-Writing	GRE-Subject	Under-graduate GPA	Last 2 Years GPA	Psychol-ogy GPA	Master's GPA
Human Development and Family Studies	PhD	NA/162	NA/157	NA/4	Not specified	NA/NA	NA/NA	Not specified	Not specified

Admissions Requirements:

Degree	GRE	GRE-Subject	Letters of Recom-mendation	Research Statement	Writing Sample	CV	Interview
Doctoral	Required	Optional	3	Required	Required	Required	None

Admissions Criteria:

GRE scores—high
Research experience—high
Work experience—low
GPA—high

Letters of recommendation—high
Interview—low
Statement of goals and objectives—high
Writing sample—high

For additional information on admission requirements, visit http://www.hhdev.psu.edu/hdfs/graduate/apply.

Department Demographics

	Male (PT)	Female (PT)	Total	African-American/ Black (PT)	Hispanic/ Latino (PT)	Asian/ Pacific Islander (PT)	American Indian/ Alaska Native (PT)	Caucasian/ White (PT)	Unknown	Multiethnic (PT)	ADA (PT)	Int'l (PT)
Students	9 (0)	61 (0)	70	3 (0)	3 (0)	22 (0)	0 (0)	42 (0)	0 (0)	0 (0)	0 (0)	18 (0)

Financial Information/Assistance

Tuition: For information on tuition costs, visit http://tuition.psu.edu. Tuition is subject to change.

Doctoral:
State residents: $16,460 per academic year.
State residents: $805 per credit hour.
Nonstate residents: $33,142 per academic year.
Nonstate residents: $1,381 per credit hour.

Financial Assistance:

	Teaching Assistantship (% Receiving)	Teaching Assistantship Tuition Remission	Research Assistantship (% Receiving)	Research Assistantship Tuition Remission	Fellowship (% Receiving)	Fellowship Tuition Remission
First-Year Student	$23,000 (NA)	Full	$23,000 (NA)	Full	$23,000 (NA)	Full
Advanced Student	$18,495 (NA)	Full	$18,495 (NA)	Full	$18,495 (NA)	Full

For additional information on financial assistance, visit http://www.hhdev.psu.edu/hdfs/graduate/aid.

Employment of Department Graduates

Doctoral:
Enrolled in a postdoctoral residency/fellowship: 2
Employed in an academic position at a university: 1
Employed in business or industry: 1
Total: 4

Additional Information

Housing and Day Care: On-campus housing is available. See the following website for more information: http://housing.psu.edu/graduate-family-housing. On-campus day care facilities are available. See the following website for more information: http://childcare.psu.edu/.

Information for Students With Physical Disabilities: See the following website: http://equity.psu.edu/ods.

Special Facilities or Resources: Several additional facilities are associated with the College of Health and Human Development that provide significant resources to our Department in terms of graduate training opportunities and student funding. These include the Child Care Center at Hort Woods and Bennett Family Center, which are high-quality early child care programs providing care to children from early infancy through kindergarten. Each unit has observational rooms for the study of individual and group behavior of children and adults. Our students also avail themselves of the resources provided by several College-based centers, including the Prevention Research Center for the Promotion of Human Development, the Methodology Center, the Methodology Consulting Center, the Center for Childhood Obesity, and the Center for Healthy Aging. All of these centers are directed by HDFS faculty and provide a variety of funding and training opportunities for our graduate students. The Centers are direct outgrowths of our program's four core areas: Individual Development, Prevention/Intervention, Methodology, and Family Development.

Application Information: Graduate Admissions c/o Christa Kreps, Penn State University, Department of Human Development and Family Studies, 119 HHD, University Park, PA 16802. *Fee:* $65. *Online application:* http://www.gradschool.psu.edu/apply/.

Pennsylvania State University
Department of Psychology
140 Moore Building
University Park, PA 16802-3104
Telephone: (814) 863-1721
Professor and Head: Melvin M. Mark

E-mail: sbg4@psu.edu
Web: http://psych.la.psu.edu

Orientation, Objectives, and Emphasis of Department

Graduate study in psychology at Penn State is characterized by highly flexible, individualized programs leading to the PhD in Psychology. Each student is associated with one of the five program areas offered in the department: clinical (including child clinical); cognitive; developmental; industrial/organizational; and social. Students in any program area may combine their program of study with a specialization in behavioral neuroscience by choosing appropriate courses and seminars. Students choosing this specialization may pursue the integration of neuroscience methods and theories by applying these approaches to research topics within their program areas. Within each area, certain courses are usually suggested for all students. The details of a student's program, however, are worked out on an individual basis with a faculty advisor. A major specialization and breadth outside the major are required. The major is selected from among the six specialty areas of the department listed above; breadth requirements are flexible and individualized to career goals. Depending upon the individual student's particular program of study, graduates may be employed in academic departments, research institutes, industry, governmental agencies, or various service delivery settings.

Programs and Degrees Offered

Program	Degree	Application Deadline	Applica-tions Received	Accepted	New Admits Enrolled (PT)	Total Enrolled (PT)	Degrees Awarded in 2014–2015	Median Years to Complete Degree	Dismissed/ Withdrew
Clinical Psychology	PhD	December 1 (Fall)	213	6	6	30 (4)	7	6	0
Clinical Child Psychology	PhD	December 1 (Fall)	141	1	1	25 (3)	4	7	0
Cognitive Psychology	PhD	December 1 (Fall)	58	3	3	19 (0)	6	6	1
Developmental Psychology	PhD	December 1 (Fall)	36	3	3	14 (2)	4	5.5	0
Industrial/ Organizational Psychology	PhD	December 1 (Fall)	152	4	4	16 (3)	5	5	0
Social Psychology	PhD	December 1 (Fall)	62	2	2	13 (2)	1	7	2

APA Accreditation

Clinical PhD (Doctor of Philosophy).

Clinical PhD: Student Outcome Data website: http://psych.la.psu.edu/graduate/program-areas/clinical-adult-and-child.

Doctoral Degree (PhD Clinical Psychology): For those doctoral students for whom a professional internship was required in this program prior to graduation:

Total students who applied for an internship: 5

Total students who obtained an internship: 5

Total students who obtained a paid internship: 5

Total students who obtained an unpaid internship: 0

Total students who were placed in APA/CPA-accredited internships: 5

Total students placed in internships not APA/CPA-accredited, but listed with the Association of Psychology Postdoctoral and Internship Centers (APPIC): 0

Total students placed in internships conforming to guidelines of the Council of Directors of School Psychology Programs (CDSPP): 0

Total students placed in internships that were not APA/CPA-accredited, APPIC or CDSSP listed: 0

Doctoral Degree (PhD Clinical Child Psychology): For those doctoral students for whom a professional internship was required in this program prior to graduation:

Total students who applied for an internship: 5

Total students who obtained an internship: 3

Total students who obtained a paid internship: 3

Total students who obtained an unpaid internship: 0

Total students who were placed in APA/CPA-accredited internships: 3

Total students placed in internships not APA/CPA-accredited, but listed with the Association of Psychology Postdoctoral and Internship Centers (APPIC): 0

Total students placed in internships conforming to guidelines of the Council of Directors of School Psychology Programs (CDSPP): 0
Total students placed in internships that were not APA/CPA-accredited, APPIC or CDSSP listed: 0

Admissions

Entries appear in the following order: required test or GPA, minimum score (if required)/median score of students entering in 2015–2016.

Program	Degree	GRE-V	GRE-Q	GRE-Writing	GRE-Subject	Under-graduate GPA	Last 2 Years GPA	Psychology GPA	Master's GPA
Clinical Psychology	PhD	NA/NA	NA/NA	NA/NA	Not specified	Not specified	NA/NA	Not specified	Not specified
Clinical Child Psychology	PhD	NA/NA	NA/NA	NA/NA	Not specified	Not specified	NA/NA	Not specified	Not specified
Cognitive Psychology	PhD	NA/NA	NA/NA	NA/NA	Not specified	Not specified	NA/NA	Not specified	Not specified
Developmental Psychology	PhD	NA/NA	NA/NA	NA/NA	Not specified	Not specified	NA/NA	Not specified	Not specified
Industrial/ Organizational Psychology	PhD	NA/NA	NA/NA	NA/NA	Not specified	Not specified	NA/NA	Not specified	Not specified
Social Psychology	PhD	NA/NA	NA/NA	NA/NA	Not specified	Not specified	NA/NA	Not specified	Not specified

Admissions Requirements:

Degree	GRE	GRE-Subject	Letters of Recom-mendation	Research Statement	Writing Sample	CV	Interview
Doctoral	Required	Optional	3	Required	Required	Recom-mended	Required

Please note if these criteria vary for different programs: Clinical weighs work, clinical experience, and interviews heavily; other areas do not weight these factors strongly.

Admissions Criteria:

GRE scores—high
Research experience—high
Work experience—medium
Clinically related public service—medium
GPA—high

Letters of recommendation—high
Interview—high
Statement of goals and objectives—high
Undergraduate psychology preparation—medium

For additional information on admission requirements, visit http://psych.la.psu.edu/graduate/prospective-students/how-to-apply-to-graduate-school-in-psychology.

Department Demographics

	Male (PT)	Female (PT)	Total	African-American/ Black (PT)	Hispanic/ Latino (PT)	Asian/ Pacific Islander (PT)	American Indian/ Alaska Native (PT)	Caucasian/ White (PT)	Unknown	Multiethnic (PT)	ADA (PT)	Int'l (PT)
Students	49 (3)	87 (11)	150	3 (3)	12 (0)	14 (0)	0 (0)	86 (10)	2 (0)	4 (0)	0 (0)	18 (1)

Financial Information/Assistance

Tuition: For information on tuition costs, visit http://tuition.psu.edu/. Tuition is subject to change.

Doctoral:
State residents: $30,132 per academic year.
Nonstate residents: $40,500 per academic year.

Financial Assistance:

	Teaching Assistantship (% Receiving)	Teaching Assistantship Tuition Remission	Research Assistantship (% Receiving)	Research Assistantship Tuition Remission	Fellowship (% Receiving)	Fellowship Tuition Remission
First-Year Student	$18,495 (NA)	Full	$18,495 (NA)	Full	$27,500 (NA)	Full
Advanced Student	$18,495 (NA)	Full	$18,495 (NA)	Full	$27,500 (NA)	Full

Employment of Department Graduates

Doctoral:
Enrolled in a postdoctoral residency/fellowship: 19
Employed in an academic position at a university: 3
Employed in business or industry: 1
Employed in government agency: 2
Other employment position: 2
Total: 27

Additional Information

Housing and Day Care: On-campus housing is available. See the following website for more information: http://housing.psu.edu/graduate-family-housing. On-campus day care facilities are available. See the following website for more information: http://childcare.psu.edu/.

Information for Students With Physical Disabilities: See the following website: http://equity.psu.edu/ods.

Special Facilities or Resources: The department has clinical, learning-cognition, perception, physiological, psychophysiology, developmental, and social laboratories; microcomputer laboratories; access to the University's mainframe and electronic communication system (e-mail and Internet) and computer laboratories; clinical practica in local mental health centers and hospitals in addition to the department's Psychological Clinic, which functions as a mental health center for the catchment area of central Pennsylvania; industrial/organizational practica in industrial and government organizations; and developmental practica and research opportunities in day care and preschool settings. A number of centers or institutes are housed within, or affiliated with, the department, including a new Child Study Center.

Application Information: *Fee:* $65. *Online application:* http://www.gradschool.psu.edu/index.cfm/apply/.

Pennsylvania, University of
Applied Psychology-Human Development Division
Graduate School of Education
3700 Walnut Street
Philadelphia, PA 19104-6216
Telephone: (215) 573-6851
Chairperson: Michael J. Nakkula, EdD

E-mail: rhambeau@gse.upenn.edu
Web: http://www.gse.upenn.edu/aphd/

Orientation, Objectives, and Emphasis of Department
Our programs provide a foundation in the core concepts of applied psychology: intervention, prevention, assessment, learning/development, and applied practice and/or research, for careers in counseling, mental health, teaching, and research in various settings. The 1-year Counseling and Psychological Services (CAPS) master's program prepares students in the foundations of providing supportive services. The MPhil program in Professional Counseling and Psychology is a continuation for current CAPS students. The Executive Program in School & Mental Health Counseling (SMHC) enables students with full-time careers to earn their degree in 2 years through 1-weekend-a-month and 1-week-in-summer sessions. The MPhil and SMHC programs prepare students for guidance counseling certification and/or licensure as a professional counselor. The Interdisciplinary Studies in Human Development PhD and MSEd programs combine the study of social, emotional, cognitive, and physical aspects of human development that are focused on urban populations, considered within eco-cultural contexts, and relevant to social policies. Students create a specialized program of study of human development across the lifespan. Career interests: traditional academic appointment; youth

programming /services; urban/ethnic studies; adult development/learning; corporate human resources development; international programming (e.g., work with NGOs); foundation administration/program development; collaborative efforts/health care facilities.

Programs and Degrees Offered

Program	Degree	Application Deadline	Applica-tions Received	Accepted	New Admits Enrolled (PT)	Total Enrolled (PT)	Degrees Awarded in 2014–2015	Median Years to Complete Degree	Dismissed/ Withdrew
Counseling and Psychological Services	MEd	Rolling	220	118	36 (9)	110 (8)	54	1	0
Interdisciplinary Studies in Human Development	MA/MS	Rolling	78	62	17 (2)	17 (13)	8	1	
Interdisciplinary Studies in Human Development	PhD	December 8 (Fall), Rolling	86	65	1 (0)	9 (0)	5	5	
Professional Counseling and Psychology	Other	February 1 (Fall)	40	40	10 (3)	10 (3)	36	2	0
School Counseling Certification	Other		13	12	12 (0)	12 (0)	0		
School & Mental Health Counseling	MEd	Rolling	68	35	55 (0)	55 (0)	21	2	1

Internships/Practica

Master's students in Counseling and Psychological Services engage in supervised practica for 8 hours a week for two semesters. Placements include schools, community colleges, career services, clinics, and community agencies. MPhil students are required to complete a supervised two-semester, 20-hour per week internship. The Executive Program in School and Mental Health Counseling is an executive-style master's-degree program for working educators and professionals interested in working as school counselors or Licensed Professional Counselors. The program requires a practicum and an internship.

Admissions

Entries appear in the following order: required test or GPA, minimum score (if required)/median score of students entering in 2015–2016.

Program	Degree	GRE-V	GRE-Q	GRE-Writing	GRE-Subject	Under-graduate GPA	Last 2 Years GPA	Psychol-ogy GPA	Master's GPA
Counseling and Psychological Services	MEd	NA/NA	NA/NA	NA/NA	Not specified	Not specified	Not specified	Not specified	Not specified
Interdisciplinary Studies in Human Development	MA/MS	NA/NA	NA/NA	NA/NA	Not specified	Not specified	Not specified	Not specified	Not specified
Interdisciplinary Studies in Human Development	PhD	NA/NA	NA/NA	NA/NA	NA/NA	Not specified	Not specified	Not specified	Not specified

Admissions (con't.)

Program	Degree	GRE-V	GRE-Q	GRE-Writing	GRE-Subject	Under-graduate GPA	Last 2 Years GPA	Psychology GPA	Master's GPA
Professional Counseling and Psychology	Other	NA/NA	NA/NA	NA/NA	Not specified	Not specified	Not specified	Not specified	Not specified
School Counseling Certification	Other	NA/NA	NA/NA	NA/NA	Not specified	Not specified	Not specified	Not specified	Not specified
School & Mental Health Counseling	MEd	Not specified	Not specified	Not specified	Not specified	Not specified	Not specified	Not specified	Not specified

Admissions Requirements:

Degree	GRE	GRE-Subject	Letters of Recom-mendation	Research Statement	Writing Sample	CV	Interview
Master's/Specialist	Required	None	3	Required	None	Required	Required
Doctoral	Required	None	3	Required	None	Required	Required

Please note if these criteria vary for different programs: The School and Mental Health Counseling program does not require GRE scores.

Admissions Criteria:
GRE scores—high
Research experience—medium
Work experience—medium
Clinically related public service—medium
GPA—high

Letters of recommendation—high
Interview—high
Statement of goals and objectives—high
Undergraduate psychology preparation—medium

For additional information on admission requirements, visit http://www.gse.upenn.edu/admissions_financial/instructions.

Department Demographics

	Male (PT)	Female (PT)	Total	African-American/ Black (PT)	Hispanic/ Latino (PT)	Asian/ Pacific Islander (PT)	American Indian/ Alaska Native (PT)	Caucasian/ White (PT)	Unknown	Multiethnic (PT)	ADA (PT)	Int'l (PT)
Students	14 (3)	110 (17)	144	19 (1)	7 (0)	16 (7)	0 (0)	72 (12)	4 (0)	6 (0)	4 (0)	10 (3)

Financial Information/Assistance

Tuition: For information on tuition costs, visit http://www.gse.upenn.edu/admissions_financial/tuition. Tuition is subject to change. Tuition costs vary by program.

Doctoral:
State residents: $28,768 per academic year.
Nonstate residents: $28,768 per academic year.

Master's:
State residents: $39,914 per academic year.
Nonstate residents: $39,914 per academic year.

Financial Assistance:

	Teaching Assistantship (% Receiving)	Teaching Assistantship Tuition Remission	Research Assistantship (% Receiving)	Research Assistantship Tuition Remission	Fellowship (% Receiving)	Fellowship Tuition Remission
First-Year Student	NA (NA)	Full	NA (NA)	Full	NA (NA)	Full
Advanced Student	NA (NA)	NA	NA (NA)	NA	NA (NA)	NA

For additional information on financial assistance, visit http://www.gse.upenn.edu/admissions_financial/finaid.

Employment of Department Graduates

Master's:
Enrolled in a psychology doctoral program: 8
Enrolled in another graduate/professional program: 2
Employed in an academic position at a university: 5
Employed in academic position at a 2-year/4-year college: 2
Employed in other positions at a higher education institution: 2
Employed in a professional position in a school system: 6
Employed in business or industry: 8
Employed in government agency: 1
Still seeking employment: 5
Total: 39

Additional Information

Housing and Day Care: On-campus housing is available. See the following website for more information: http://www.business-services.upenn.edu/housing/. On-campus day care facilities are available. See the following website for more information: http://cms.business-services.upenn.edu/childcare/.

Information for Students With Physical Disabilities: See the following website: http://www.vpul.upenn.edu/lrc/sds/.

Special Facilities or Resources: Penn GSE houses state-of-the-art computer labs and classrooms, student lounges, and offers wireless access. Many opportunities exist for students to participate in the Faculty's new and ongoing research that address issues of local, national and international populations.

Application Information: Admissions Office, Graduate School of Education, University of Pennsylvania, 3700 Walnut Street, Philadelphia, PA 19104-6216. *Fee:* $0. *Online application:* https://www.applyweb.com/upenng/index.ftl.

Pennsylvania, University of
Department of Psychology
3720 Walnut Street
Philadelphia, PA 19104
Telephone: (215) 898-7300
Chairperson: Dr. Sharon Thompson-Schill

E-mail: grad_coordinator@psych.upenn.edu
Web: http://psychology.sas.upenn.edu/graduate

Orientation, Objectives, and Emphasis of Department
The Department of Psychology at the University of Pennsylvania offers curricular and research opportunities for the study of sensation, perception, cognition, cognitive neuroscience, decision-making, language, learning, motivation, emotion, motor control, psychopathology, and social processes. Biological, cultural, developmental, comparative, experimental, and mathematical approaches to these areas are used in ongoing teaching and research. The department has an APA-accredited clinical program that is designed to prepare students for research careers in interventions, psychopathology and personality. The interests of the faculty and students in the department cover the entire field of research-oriented psychology. Still, the Department of Psychology at Pennsylvania functions as a single unit whose guiding principle is scientific excellence. Students are admitted to the department. The primary determinant of acceptance is academic promise rather than specific area of interest. Faculty join together from different

sub-disciplines for teaching and research purposes so that students become conversant with issues in a number of different areas. A high level of interaction among department members (students and faculty), within and across disciplines, helps generate both a shared set of interests in the theoretical, historical, and philosophical foundations of psychology and active collaboration in research projects.

Programs and Degrees Offered

Program	Degree	Application Deadline	Applica-tions Received	Accepted	New Admits Enrolled (PT)	Total Enrolled (PT)	Degrees Awarded in 2014–2015	Median Years to Complete Degree	Dismissed/ Withdrew
Psychology	PhD	December 15 (Fall)	265	7	6	40	6	5	2
Clinical Psychology	PhD	December 15 (Fall)	414	5	3 (0)	20 (0)	4	6	0

APA Accreditation

Clinical PhD: Student Outcome Data website: http://psychology.sas.upenn.edu/clinical-training-program/student-admissions-outcomes-and-other-data.

Doctoral Degree (PhD Clinical Psychology): For those doctoral students for whom a professional internship was required in this program prior to graduation:
Total students who applied for an internship: 4
Total students who obtained an internship: 4
Total students who obtained a paid internship: 4
Total students who obtained an unpaid internship: 0
Total students who were placed in APA/CPA-accredited internships: 4
Total students placed in internships not APA/CPA-accredited, but listed with the Association of Psychology Postdoctoral and Internship Centers (APPIC): 0
Total students placed in internships conforming to guidelines of the Council of Directors of School Psychology Programs (CDSPP): 0
Total students placed in internships that were not APA/CPA-accredited, APPIC or CDSSP listed: 0

Internships/Practica

Because of the wealth of opportunities for clinical training in the Philadelphia area, Penn does not run an in-house psychological services clinic. Rather, Penn's clinical students have the opportunity to participate in practica at local hospitals, clinics and research facilities staffed and run by world-renowned clinical scientists. The Associate Director of Clinical Training helps students decide which practicum experiences best suit the student's needs and interests, and arranges for placements at the appropriate sites.

Admissions

Entries appear in the following order: required test or GPA, minimum score (if required)/median score of students entering in 2015–2016.

Program	Degree	GRE-V	GRE-Q	GRE-Writing	GRE-Subject	Under-graduate GPA	Last 2 Years GPA	Psychol-ogy GPA	Master's GPA
Psychology	PhD	NA/159	NA/158	NA/4.6	Not specified	NA/3.7	Not specified	Not specified	Not specified
Clinical Psychology	PhD	NA/159	NA/156	NA/4.8	Not specified	NA/3.6	Not specified	Not specified	Not specified

Admissions Requirements:

Degree	GRE	GRE-Subject	Letters of Recom-mendation	Research Statement	Writing Sample	CV	Interview
Doctoral	Required	Optional	3	Required	Recom-mended	Required	Required

Admissions Criteria:

GRE scores—medium
Research experience—high
Work experience—low
Clinically related public service—low
GPA—medium

Letters of recommendation—high
Interview—medium
Statement of goals and objectives—high
Undergraduate psychology preparation—low

For additional information on admission requirements, visit http://psychology.sas.upenn.edu/graduate/information-applicants.

Department Demographics

	Male (PT)	Female (PT)	Total	African-American/ Black (PT)	Hispanic/ Latino (PT)	Asian/ Pacific Islander (PT)	American Indian/ Alaska Native (PT)	Caucasian/ White (PT)	Unknown	Multiethnic (PT)	ADA (PT)	Int'l (PT)
Students	26 (0)	34 (0)	60	0 (0)	1 (0)	11 (0)	0 (0)	41 (0)	0 (0)	7 (0)	0 (0)	15 (0)

Financial Information/Assistance

Tuition: For information on tuition costs, visit http://www.sfs.upenn.edu/tuition/. Tuition is subject to change.

Doctoral:
State residents: $31,068 per academic year.
Nonstate residents: $31,068 per academic year.

Financial Assistance:

	Teaching Assistantship (% Receiving)	Teaching Assistantship Tuition Remission	Research Assistantship (% Receiving)	Research Assistantship Tuition Remission	Fellowship (% Receiving)	Fellowship Tuition Remission
First-Year Student	NA (NA)	NA	NA (NA)	NA	NA (NA)	Full
Advanced Student	NA (NA)	Full	NA (NA)	Full	NA (NA)	Full

Employment of Department Graduates

Doctoral:
Enrolled in a postdoctoral residency/fellowship: 9
Employed in business or industry: 1
Total: 10

Additional Information

Housing and Day Care: On-campus housing is available. See the following website for more information: http://www.upenn.edu/housing. On-campus day care facilities are available. See the following website for more information: http://www.upenn.edu/childcare/.

Information for Students With Physical Disabilities: See the following website: http://www.vpul.upenn.edu/lrc/sds/index.html.

Special Facilities or Resources: The department has facilities for functional magnetic resonance imaging, transcranial magnetic stimulation, high density electroencephalograhy and magneto encephalography, high speed computing capabilities, and high frequency electrophysiology recording. In addition, the department supports a fully equipped wood, metal, and electronics shop. Also readily available for research in the near environs of the department are 4 major University-affiliated hospitals, urban public and private schools.

Application Information: Graduate Division of Arts and Sciences, 3401 Walnut Street, Suite 322A, Philadelphia, PA 19104. *Fee:* $80. *Online application:* https://www.applyweb.com/upenng/.

Philadelphia College of Osteopathic Medicine
Psychology Department
4190 City Avenue
Philadelphia, PA 19131-1693
Telephone: (215) 871-6442
Chairperson: Robert A. DiTomasso, PhD, ABPP

E-mail: RobertD@pcom.edu
Web: http://www.pcom.edu/academics/academic-departments/psychology/

Orientation, Objectives, and Emphasis of Department
The mission of the Department of Psychology at PCOM is to prepare highly skilled, compassionate psychologists and master's level psychological specialists to provide empirically based, active, focused, and collaborative assessments and treatments with sensitivity to cultural and ethnic diversity and the underserved. Grounded in the cognitive-behavioral tradition, the graduate programs in psychology train practitioner–scholars to offer assessment, intervention, consultation, management, and leadership as local clinical scientists, and to engage in scholarly activities, advocacy, and life-long learning in the field of psychology.

Programs and Degrees Offered

Program	Degree	Application Deadline	Applications Received	Accepted	New Admits Enrolled (PT)	Total Enrolled (PT)	Degrees Awarded in 2014–2015	Median Years to Complete Degree	Dismissed/ Withdrew
Certificate Of Advanced Graduate Studies	Other	(Fall), Rolling	8	8	(8)	(8)	5	1	0
Mental Health Couns/Couns & Clinical Health Psych	MA/MS	(Fall), Rolling	84	37	17 (2)	45 (10)	32	2	0
Clinical Psychology	Respecial- ization Diploma	(Fall), Rolling	4	1	1 (0)	1 (0)	0		0
Clinical Psychology	PsyD	(Fall), Rolling	111	44	23 (0)	142 (0)	20	5.4	2
School Psychology	MA/MS	(Summer), Rolling	36	24	17 (0)	17 (0)	17	1.2	2
School Psychology	EdS	(Fall), Rolling	17	17	14 (0)	38 (0)	19	3	1
Organizational Development and Leadership	MA/MS	Rolling	19	13	7 (3)	17 (6)	15	2.5	0
School Psychology	PsyD	(Summer), Rolling	22	18	16 (0)	67 (0)	11	5.5	0
School Psychology	Respecial- ization Diploma	(Fall), Rolling	0	0	0 (0)	0 (0)	0		0
Clinical Health Psychology Postdoc Certificate	Other	(Fall), Rolling	0	0	0 (0)	0 (0)	0		0
Clinical Neuropsychology Postdoc Certificate	Other	(Fall), Rolling	1	1	0 (1)	0 (1)	0		0

APA Accreditation

Clinical PsyD: Student Outcome Data website: http://www.pcom.edu/academics/programs-and-degrees/clinical-psychology/admissions-outcomes-other-data.html.

Doctoral Degree (PsyD Clinical Psychology): For those doctoral students for whom a professional internship was required in this program prior to graduation:
Total students who applied for an internship: 35
Total students who obtained an internship: 35
Total students who obtained a paid internship: 35
Total students who obtained an unpaid internship: 0
Total students who were placed in APA/CPA-accredited internships: 25
Total students placed in internships not APA/CPA-accredited, but listed with the Association of Psychology Postdoctoral and Internship Centers (APPIC): 6
Total students placed in internships conforming to guidelines of the Council of Directors of School Psychology Programs (CDSPP): 0
Total students placed in internships that were not APA/CPA-accredited, APPIC or CDSSP listed: 4

Doctoral Degree (PsyD School Psychology): For those doctoral students for whom a professional internship was required in this program prior to graduation:
Total students who applied for an internship: 19
Total students who obtained an internship: 18
Total students who obtained a paid internship: 15
Total students who obtained an unpaid internship: 3
Total students who were placed in APA/CPA-accredited internships: 0
Total students placed in internships not APA/CPA-accredited, but listed with the Association of Psychology Postdoctoral and Internship Centers (APPIC): 0
Total students placed in internships conforming to guidelines of the Council of Directors of School Psychology Programs (CDSPP): 18
Total students placed in internships that were not APA/CPA-accredited, APPIC or CDSSP listed: 0

Master's Degree (MA/MS Mental Health Couns/Couns & Clinical Health Psych): An internship experience, such as a final research project or "capstone" experience is required of graduates. Master's Degree (MA/MS Organizational Development and Leadership): An internship experience, such as a final research project or "capstone" experience is required of graduates.

Internships/Practica

Practica are fieldwork experiences completed by master's level and doctoral students at a PCOM approved clinical training site. The minimum weekly hour requirements vary from program to program. Practicum sites are committed to excellence in the training of professionals, and provide extensive supervision and formative clinical experiences. They offer a wide range of training, including the use of empirically supported interventions, brief treatment models, cognitive behavioral therapy, and treatment of psychological/medical problems. Students engage in evaluation, psychological testing (EdS and PsyD only), psychotherapy, and professional clinical work. Practica include seminars taught by faculty that provide a place for students to discuss their experiences and help them integrate coursework with on-site training. Students participate in pratica at the Psychology Department's Center for Brief Therapy, a multi-faceted clinical training center, as well as sites including community agencies, hospitals, university counseling centers, prisons, schools, and specialized treatment centers. The department has a broad network of practicum sites in Pennsylvania, New Jersey, Maryland, and Delaware. PsyD students apply for internships through the APPIC matching program.

Admissions

Entries appear in the following order: required test or GPA, minimum score (if required)/median score of students entering in 2015–2016.

Program	Degree	GRE-V	GRE-Q	GRE-Writing	GRE-Subject	Under-graduate GPA	Last 2 Years GPA	Psychol-ogy GPA	Master's GPA
Certificate of Advanced Graduate Studies	Other	Not specified	Not specified	Not specified	Not specified	3/NA	Not specified	Not specified	Not specified
Mental Health Couns/Couns & Clinical Health Psych	MA/MS	Not specified	Not specified	Not specified	Not specified	3/3.3	Not specified	Not specified	Not specified

Admissions (con't.)

Program	Degree	GRE-V	GRE-Q	GRE-Writing	GRE-Subject	Under-graduate GPA	Last 2 Years GPA	Psychol-ogy GPA	Master's GPA
Clinical Psychology	Respecial-ization Diploma	Not specified	Not specified	Not specified	Not specified	3/3.5	Not specified	Not specified	Not specified
Clinical Psychology	PsyD	Not specified	Not specified	Not specified	Not specified	3/3.43	Not specified	Not specified	3.3/3.76
School Psychology	MA/MS	Not specified	Not specified	Not specified	Not specified	3/3.3	Not specified	Not specified	Not specified
School Psychology	EdS	Not specified	Not specified	Not specified	Not specified	3/3.47	Not specified	Not specified	Not specified
Organizational Development and Leadership	MA/MS	Not specified	Not specified	Not specified	Not specified	3/3.14	Not specified	Not specified	Not specified
School Psychology	PsyD	Not specified	Not specified	Not specified	Not specified	3/3.16	Not specified	Not specified	3/3.79
School Psychology	Respecial-ization Diploma	Not specified	Not specified	Not specified	Not specified	3/NA	Not specified	Not specified	Not specified
Clinical Health Psychology Postdoc Certificate	Other	Not specified	Not specified	Not specified	Not specified	3/NA	Not specified	Not specified	Not specified
Clinical Neuropsychology Postdoc Certificate	Other	Not specified	Not specified	Not specified	Not specified	3/3.5	Not specified	Not specified	Not specified

Admissions Requirements:

Degree	GRE	GRE-Subject	Letters of Recom-mendation	Research Statement	Writing Sample	CV	Interview
Master's/Specialist	Required	None	3	Required	Required	Required	Required
Doctoral	None	None	3	Required	Required	Recom-mended	Required

Please note if these criteria vary for different programs: Work experience is weighted medium as an admission criterion for the MS in School Psychology, MS in Mental Health Counseling/Counseling & Clinical Health Psychology, and CAGS programs. Work experience is weighted high as an admissions criterion for the MS in ODL, EdS and PsyD programs. In addition, a master's degree in psychology or a related field is required for admission to the Clinical PsyD program and the School Psychology EdS program; a master's degree in school psychology or a related field and certification in school psychology are required for admissions to the School PsyD program. Only EdS in School Psychology requires GRE-Subject test. The MS in ODL only requires 1 letter of recommendation. Standardized test score requirements vary across all programs.

Admissions Criteria:
GRE scores—medium
Research experience—low
Work experience—high
Clinically related public service—high
GPA—high

Letters of recommendation—high
Interview—high
Statement of goals and objectives—high
Undergraduate psychology preparation—high
Graded writing sample—high

For additional information on admission requirements, visit http://www.pcom.edu/admissions/.

Department Demographics

	Male (PT)	Female (PT)	Total	African-American/ Black (PT)	Hispanic/ Latino (PT)	Asian/ Pacific Islander (PT)	American Indian/ Alaska Native (PT)	Caucasian/ White (PT)	Unknown	Multiethnic (PT)	ADA (PT)	Int'l (PT)
Students	66 (8)	261 (17)	352	53 (6)	7 (2)	13 (1)	1 (0)	231 (14)	15 (1)	7 (1)	9 (0)	4 (2)

Financial Information/Assistance

Tuition: For information on tuition costs, visit http://www.pcom.edu/about/departments/bursar/tuition-rates/tuition-rates-pa-16-17.html. Higher tuition cost for this program: EdS: $908/credit hour; MS in ODL $805/credit hour; PsyD in School Psych: $1084/credit hour. Tuition is subject to change. Additional fees are assessed to students beyond the costs of tuition for the following: Comprehensive fee (each term): $188. Tuition costs vary by program.

Doctoral:
State residents: $1,158 per credit hour.
Nonstate residents: $1,158 per credit hour.

Master's:
State residents: $840 per credit hour.
Nonstate residents: $840 per credit hour.

Financial Assistance:

	Teaching Assistantship (% Receiving)	Teaching Assistantship Tuition Remission	Research Assistantship (% Receiving)	Research Assistantship Tuition Remission	Fellowship (% Receiving)	Fellowship Tuition Remission
First-Year Student	NA (NA)	NA	$9,000 (1)	NA	$3,153 (27)	Partial
Advanced Student	$1,500 (3)	NA	$9,000 (2)	NA	$3,153 (27)	Partial

For additional information on financial assistance, visit http://www.pcom.edu/about/departments/financial-aid/.

Employment of Department Graduates

Master's:
Enrolled in a psychology doctoral program: 4
Enrolled in another graduate/professional program: 16
Employed in business or industry: 14
Employed in government agency: 2
Employed in a community mental health/counseling center: 25
Employed in a hospital/medical center: 5
Other employment position: 1
Total: 67

Doctoral:
Enrolled in a postdoctoral residency/fellowship: 17
Employed in independent practice: 1
Employed in a professional position in a school system: 11
Employed in a community mental health/counseling center: 2
Total: 31

Additional Information

Housing and Day Care: No on-campus housing is available. No on-campus day care facilities are available.

Special Facilities or Resources: The academic facilities at PCOM include state-of-the-art amphitheaters and classroom facilities, computer laboratories with extensive software including PsycLIT and SPSS, a recently renovated library that includes sophisticated online resources, and the HealthNet teleconferencing system. The Center for Brief Therapy, a mental health clinic housed in the Department of Psychology, provides multi-faceted clinical training and research opportunities for students. PCOM also has four neighborhood health care centers in Philadelphia and one in LaPorte, Pennsylvania.

Application Information: Philadelphia College of Osteopathic Medicine, Department of Admissions, 4170 City Avenue, Philadelphia, PA 19131. *Fee:* $75. *Online application:* http://www.pcom.edu/admissions/.

Pittsburgh, University of
Department of Psychology in Education
School of Education
5930 Posvar Hall
Pittsburgh, PA 15260
Telephone: (412) 624-7881
Chairperson: Suzanne Lane

E-mail: psyed@pitt.edu
Web: http://www.education.pitt.edu/AcademicDepartments/PsychologyinEducation.aspx

Orientation, Objectives, and Emphasis of Department
The doctoral program in Applied Developmental Psychology prepares students for academic positions in colleges and universities and for positions as psychological specialists and research specialists in a variety of organizations concerned with education, health, and other human services. The program is oriented toward research and issues that are or can be readily applied to developmental policy and/or practice.

Programs and Degrees Offered

Program	Degree	Application Deadline	Applica-tions Received	Accepted	New Admits Enrolled (PT)	Total Enrolled (PT)	Degrees Awarded in 2014–2015	Median Years to Complete Degree	Dismissed/ Withdrew
Applied Developmental Psychology	PhD	December 1 (Fall)	20	3	2 (0)	10 (4)	1		

Internships/Practica
The Applied Developmental Program maintains extensive connections with community organizations that provide opportunities for internships in programs that serve children, youth and families in many different capacities.

Admissions
Entries appear in the following order: required test or GPA, minimum score (if required)/median score of students entering in 2015–2016.

Program	Degree	GRE-V	GRE-Q	GRE-Writing	GRE-Subject	Under-graduate GPA	Last 2 Years GPA	Psychol-ogy GPA	Master's GPA
Applied Developmental Psychology	PhD	Not specified	Not specified	Not specified	Not specified	Not specified	Not specified	Not specified	Not specified

Admissions Requirements:

Degree	GRE	GRE-Subject	Letters of Recom-mendation	Research Statement	Writing Sample	CV	Interview
Doctoral	Required	None	3	Required	Required	Required	None

Admissions Criteria:
GRE scores—medium
Research experience—medium
Work experience—medium
Clinically related public service—medium

GPA—medium
Letters of recommendation—medium
Statement of goals and objectives—high
Undergraduate psychology preparation—high

Department Demographics

	Male (PT)	Female (PT)	Total	African-American/ Black (PT)	Hispanic/ Latino (PT)	Asian/ Pacific Islander (PT)	American Indian/ Alaska Native (PT)	Caucasian/ White (PT)	Unknown	Multiethnic (PT)	ADA (PT)	Int'l (PT)
Students	3 (4)	45 (25)	77	4 (5)	3 (1)	9 (3)	0 (0)	31 (18)	0 (0)	1 (2)		8 (0)

Financial Information/Assistance

Tuition: For information on tuition costs, visit http://www.education.pitt.edu/FutureStudents/TuitionFinancialAid.aspx. Tuition is subject to change.

Doctoral:
State residents: $21,260 per academic year.
State residents: $858 per credit hour.
Nonstate residents: $34,944 per academic year.
Nonstate residents: $1,429 per credit hour.

Financial Assistance:

	Teaching Assistantship (% Receiving)	Teaching Assistantship Tuition Remission	Research Assistantship (% Receiving)	Research Assistantship Tuition Remission	Fellowship (% Receiving)	Fellowship Tuition Remission
First-Year Student	$26,340 (NA)	Partial	$21,495 (NA)	Full	NA (NA)	NA
Advanced Student	$26,340 (NA)	Full	$21,495 (NA)	Full	NA (NA)	NA

Employment of Department Graduates

Doctoral:
Enrolled in a postdoctoral residency/fellowship: 1
Total: 1

Additional Information

Housing and Day Care: No on-campus housing is available. On-campus day care facilities are available. See the following website for more information: http://www.childdevelopment.pitt.edu/.

Information for Students With Physical Disabilities: See the following website: http://www.studentaffairs.pitt.edu/drs/.

Special Facilities or Resources: The Applied Developmental Program is closely allied with several leading research, policy and service organizations in the University, including the Learning Policy Center, the Office of Child Development, and the University, Community Leaders, and Individuals with Disabilities Center.

Application Information: University of Pittsburgh School of Education, Student Service Center, 5500 Wesley W. Posvar Hall, Pittsburgh, PA 15260. *Fee:* $50. *Online application:* https://app.applyyourself.com/?id=up-ed.

Pittsburgh, University of
Psychology
Kenneth P. Dietrich School of Arts and Sciences
3129 Sennott Square, 210 South Bouquet Street
Pittsburgh, PA 15260
Telephone: (412) 624-4502
Chairperson: Daniel Shaw

E-mail: psygrad@pitt.edu
Web: http://www.psychology.pitt.edu

Orientation, Objectives, and Emphasis of Department
Basic research training is emphasized, and most projects involve research with important practical implications. The graduate programs include Clinical Psychology, Cognitive Psychology and Cognitive Neuroscience, Developmental Psychology, Biological and Health Psychology, Social Psychology, and joint programs in Clinical–Developmental and Clinical–Health Psychology. Some examples of training opportunities are projects on infant socialization, cognitive, language and social development of children, psychological stress on the cardiovascular and immune systems, nicotine and alcohol use, decision making in groups, stereotyping, reading processes, school and non-school learning, and brain models of attention and reading. Seminars are small (5–12 students), and close working relationships are encouraged with faculty, especially the student's advisor. Excellent relationships with other

departments and schools offer unusually flexible opportunities to carry out interdisciplinary work and gain access to scholars in the Pittsburgh community. All students are expected to teach at least one course, and carry out an original research dissertation.

Programs and Degrees Offered

Program	Degree	Application Deadline	Applica-tions Received	Accepted	New Admits Enrolled (PT)	Total Enrolled (PT)	Degrees Awarded in 2014–2015	Median Years to Complete Degree	Dismissed/Withdrew
Clinical Psychology	PhD	December 1 (Fall)	280	6	3	38 (0)	1	7.5	0
Cognitive Psychology	PhD	December 1 (Fall)	78	2	0	23 (0)	4	7.5	0
Developmental Psychology	PhD	December 1 (Fall)	37	3	1	11 (0)	2	7	0
Biological and Health Psychology	PhD	December 1 (Fall)	26	3	1	6	0		0
Social Psychology	PhD	December 1 (Fall)	40	1	1	5 (0)	0		1

APA Accreditation

Clinical PhD: Student Outcome Data website: http://www.psychology.pitt.edu/clinical-program.

Doctoral Degree (PhD Clinical Psychology): For those doctoral students for whom a professional internship was required in this program prior to graduation:
Total students who applied for an internship: 12
Total students who obtained an internship: 12
Total students who obtained a paid internship: 12
Total students who obtained an unpaid internship: 0
Total students who were placed in APA/CPA-accredited internships: 12
Total students placed in internships not APA/CPA-accredited, but listed with the Association of Psychology Postdoctoral and Internship Centers (APPIC): 0
Total students placed in internships conforming to guidelines of the Council of Directors of School Psychology Programs (CDSPP): 0
Total students placed in internships that were not APA/CPA-accredited, APPIC or CDSSP listed: 0

Admissions

Entries appear in the following order: required test or GPA, minimum score (if required)/median score of students entering in 2015–2016.

Program	Degree	GRE-V	GRE-Q	GRE-Writing	GRE-Subject	Under-graduate GPA	Last 2 Years GPA	Psychol-ogy GPA	Master's GPA
Clinical Psychology	PhD	NA/NA	NA/NA	Not specified	Not specified	3/NA	Not specified	Not specified	Not specified
Cognitive Psychology	PhD	Not specified	Not specified	Not specified	Not specified	Not specified	Not specified	Not specified	Not specified
Developmental Psychology	PhD	Not specified	Not specified	Not specified	Not specified	Not specified	Not specified	Not specified	Not specified
Biological and Health Psychology	PhD	Not specified	Not specified	Not specified	Not specified	Not specified	Not specified	Not specified	Not specified
Social Psychology	PhD	Not specified	Not specified	Not specified	Not specified	Not specified	Not specified	Not specified	Not specified

Admissions Requirements:

Degree	GRE	GRE-Subject	Letters of Recommendation	Research Statement	Writing Sample	CV	Interview
Doctoral	Required	Recommended	3	Required	Optional	Required	Required

Admissions Criteria:

GRE scores—high
Research experience—high
Work experience—medium
Clinically related public service—low

GPA—high
Letters of recommendation—high
Interview—high
Statement of goals and objectives—medium

For additional information on admission requirements, visit http://www.psychology.pitt.edu/graduate/graduate-admission-requirements/how-apply.

Department Demographics

	Male (PT)	Female (PT)	Total	African-American/ Black (PT)	Hispanic/ Latino (PT)	Asian/ Pacific Islander (PT)	American Indian/ Alaska Native (PT)	Caucasian/ White (PT)	Unknown	Multiethnic (PT)	ADA (PT)	Int'l (PT)
Students	17 (0)	66 (0)	83	5 (0)	5 (0)	11 (0)	1 (0)	61 (0)	0 (0)	0 (0)	0 (0)	13 (0)

Financial Information/Assistance

Tuition: For information on tuition costs, visit http://www.ir.pitt.edu/tuition/tuitionrates.php. Tuition is subject to change.

Doctoral:
State residents: $21,260 per academic year.
State residents: $858 per credit hour.
Nonstate residents: $34,944 per academic year.
Nonstate residents: $1,429 per credit hour.

Financial Assistance:

	Teaching Assistantship (% Receiving)	Teaching Assistantship Tuition Remission	Research Assistantship (% Receiving)	Research Assistantship Tuition Remission	Fellowship (% Receiving)	Fellowship Tuition Remission
First-Year Student	$17,560 (NA)	Full	$16,000 (NA)	Full	$21,262 (NA)	Full
Advanced Student	$17,800 (NA)	Full	$16,000 (NA)	Full	$21,900 (NA)	Full

Employment of Department Graduates

Doctoral:
Enrolled in a postdoctoral residency/fellowship: 6
Employed in an academic position at a university: 3
Total: 9

Additional Information

Housing and Day Care: No on-campus housing is available. On-campus day care facilities are available. See the following website for more information: http://www.ucdc.pitt.edu/.

Information for Students With Physical Disabilities: See the following website: http://www.studentaffairs.pitt.edu/drs/.

Special Facilities or Resources: The facilities of the department include experimental laboratories, extensive computer facilities, a small-groups laboratory, the Clinical Psychology Center, and the laboratories of the Learning Research and Development Center. These services offer the advanced graduate student opportunities for supervised practicum and research experiences. The department also maintains cooperative arrangements with many organizations in Pittsburgh engaged in various kinds of psychological work. These include the Brain Imaging Research Center, Children's Hospital, Pittsburgh Cancer Institute, the Western Psychiatric Institute and Clinic, and several local agencies of the Veterans Administration Medical Centers. Collaboration with these organizations consists of part-time instruction by the staffs of these agencies, the sharing of laboratory and clinical facilities, and the appointment in those organizations of graduate students in psychology as clinical or research assistants.

Application Information: *Fee:* $50. *Online application:* https://app.applyyourself.com/?id=up-as.

Saint Joseph's University
Department of Psychology
5600 City Avenue
Philadelphia, PA 19131-1395
Telephone: (610) 660-1800
Director, Graduate Psychology Program: Jodi A. Mindell, PhD

E-mail: jmindell@sju.edu
Web: http://www.psychology.sju.edu/

Orientation, Objectives, and Emphasis of Department
The Saint Joseph's University graduate program in Experimental Psychology is designed to provide students with a solid grounding in the scientific study of psychology. Graduates of the program will have a firm foundation in the scientific method and the skills with which to pursue the scientific study of psychological questions. The program offers a traditional and academically oriented 48-credit curriculum, which requires a qualifying comprehensive examination and an empirical thesis project. The program is designed for successful completion over two academic years. The Saint Joseph's University psychology graduate program has been constructed to complement the strengths and interests of the present psychology faculty and facilities and to reflect the current state of the discipline of psychology. The curriculum is composed of three major components: an 8-credit common core required of all students; 24 credits of content based courses; and a 16-credit research component in which students complete the comprehensive examination and research thesis.

Programs and Degrees Offered

Program	Degree	Application Deadline	Applications Received	Accepted	New Admits Enrolled (PT)	Total Enrolled (PT)	Degrees Awarded in 2014–2015	Median Years to Complete Degree	Dismissed/ Withdrew
Experimental Psychology	MA/MS	March 1 (Fall)	55	20	19	36 (0)	12	2	2

Admissions
Entries appear in the following order: required test or GPA, minimum score (if required)/median score of students entering in 2015–2016.

Program	Degree	GRE-V	GRE-Q	GRE-Writing	GRE-Subject	Under-graduate GPA	Last 2 Years GPA	Psychology GPA	Master's GPA
Experimental Psychology	MA/MS	NA/NA	NA/NA	Not specified	Not specified	NA/NA	Not specified	Not specified	Not specified

Admissions Requirements:

Degree	GRE	GRE-Subject	Letters of Recommendation	Research Statement	Writing Sample	CV	Interview
Master's/Specialist	Required	None	2	Required	None	Required	None

Admissions Criteria:

GRE scores—medium	GPA—high
Research experience—high	Letters of recommendation—high
Work experience—low	Statement of goals and objectives—medium
Clinically related public service—low	Undergraduate psychology preparation—medium

For additional information on admission requirements, visit http://www.sju.edu/int/academics/cas/grad/psychology/admission.

Department Demographics

	Male (PT)	Female (PT)	Total	African-American/ Black (PT)	Hispanic/ Latino (PT)	Asian/ Pacific Islander (PT)	American Indian/ Alaska Native (PT)	Caucasian/ White (PT)	Unknown	Multiethnic (PT)	ADA (PT)	Int'l (PT)
Students	14 (0)	20 (0)	34	1 (0)	0 (0)	0 (0)	0 (0)	33 (0)	0 (0)	0 (0)	0 (0)	0 (0)

Financial Information/Assistance

Tuition: For information on tuition costs, visit http://www.sju.edu/int/academics/cas/grad/tuition.html. Tuition is subject to change.

Master's:
State residents: $934 per credit hour.
Nonstate residents: $934 per credit hour.

Financial Assistance:

	Teaching Assistantship (% Receiving)	Teaching Assistantship Tuition Remission	Research Assistantship (% Receiving)	Research Assistantship Tuition Remission	Fellowship (% Receiving)	Fellowship Tuition Remission
First-Year Student	NA (NA)	NA	NA (NA)	NA	NA (NA)	NA
Advanced Student	$7,200 (NA)	Full	$7,200 (NA)	Full	NA (NA)	NA

For additional information on financial assistance, visit http://www.sju.edu/int/academics/cas/grad/finaid.html.

Employment of Department Graduates

Master's:
Enrolled in a psychology doctoral program: 4
Employed in business or industry: 7
Employed in a hospital/medical center: 8
Total: 19

Additional Information

Housing and Day Care: No on-campus housing is available. On-campus day care facilities are available. See the following website for more information: http://www.childrens-school.org/.

Information for Students With Physical Disabilities: See the following website: http://www.sju.edu/int/studentlife/studentresources/thesuccesscenter/ssd/.

Special Facilities or Resources: All psychology faculty have equipped and active research laboratories in which graduate students pursue independent research projects for completion of their thesis requirement. Support facilities for graduate-level research and education are impressive. A vivarium, certifiable by the United States Public Health Service, for the housing of animal subjects is in operation and is fully staffed. For research involving human subjects, the department coordinates a subject pool consisting of approximately 300 subjects per semester. Additionally, the Psychology Department at Saint Joseph's operates PsyNet, a state-of-the-art Macintosh-AppleShare local area network which is connected to the campus-wide computer network. PsyNet consists of 35 Macintosh computers and peripherals for all faculty and staff plus fileservers and laser printers. Two student computer classrooms/

laboratories which include an additional 20 computers are also available within the department. PsyNet software includes various word processing, statistical, spreadsheet, database, graphics, and simulation packages.

Application Information: Graduate Admissions Office, Saint Joseph's University, 5600 City Avenue, Philadelphia, PA 19131-1395. *Fee:* $35. *Online application:* http://www.sju.edu/information/application-process-0.

Seton Hill University
Graduate & Adult Studies/Marriage & Family Therapy MA
1 Seton Drive
Greensburg, PA 15301
Telephone: (724) 838-4208
Program Director: Dr. Demarquis Clarke
Web: https://www.setonhill.edu/academics/graduate-programs/marriage-and-family-therapy-ma/

E-mail: Gadmit@setonhill.edu

Orientation, Objectives, and Emphasis of Department
The objectives of the Master of Arts in Marriage and Family Therapy program are to ensure that students are: educated in family systems theory in general, and to the wide variety of specific family systems theories and therapies; trained to think and act systematically, which includes recognizing the connections that exist between micro-level and macro-level processes; sensitized to issues of power and the ways in which structured inequalities shape family processes and human relationships; taught effective skills and techniques for clinical assessment and intervention; exposed to the latest advances in MFT research and how to critically digest, evaluate, and utilize research in their clinical practice; educated about the landscape of the current mental health delivery system and how the MFT profession is located within that environment; informed of the ethical and legal standards of the profession; encouraged to develop critical thinking skills; encouraged to develop a heightened sense of self-awareness through reflection; and provided with sufficient supervised practical experience to develop a unique style of family therapy practice.

Programs and Degrees Offered

Program	Degree	Application Deadline	Applications Received	Accepted	New Admits Enrolled (PT)	Total Enrolled (PT)	Degrees Awarded in 2014–2015	Median Years to Complete Degree	Dismissed/ Withdrew
Marriage and Family Therapy	MA/MS	Rolling	66	31	14 (1)	22 (5)	8	2.5	0

Admissions
Entries appear in the following order: required test or GPA, minimum score (if required)/median score of students entering in 2015–2016.

Program	Degree	GRE-V	GRE-Q	GRE-Writing	GRE-Subject	Under-graduate GPA	Last 2 Years GPA	Psychology GPA	Master's GPA
Marriage and Family Therapy	MA/MS	Not specified	Not specified	Not specified	Not specified	3/NA	Not specified	Not specified	Not specified

Admissions Requirements:

Degree	GRE	GRE-Subject	Letters of Recom-mendation	Research Statement	Writing Sample	CV	Interview
Master's/Specialist	None	None	3	Required	None	Required	Required

Admissions Criteria:
Work experience—medium
Clinically related public service—medium
GPA—medium
Letters of recommendation—medium

Interview—high
Statement of goals and objectives—medium
Undergraduate psychology preparation—low

Department Demographics

	Male (PT)	Female (PT)	Total	African-American/ Black (PT)	Hispanic/ Latino (PT)	Asian/ Pacific Islander (PT)	American Indian/ Alaska Native (PT)	Caucasian/ White (PT)	Unknown	Multiethnic (PT)	ADA (PT)	Int'l (PT)
Students	2 (2)	23 (2)	29	5 (1)	0 (0)	0 (0)	0 (0)	18 (2)	0 (0)	2 (1)	0 (0)	0 (0)

Financial Information/Assistance

Tuition: For information on tuition costs, visit https://www.setonhill.edu/admissions/tuition-financial-aid/graduate-programs/tuition-fees/. Tuition is subject to change.

Master's:
State residents: $850 per credit hour.
Nonstate residents: $850 per credit hour.

Financial Assistance:

	Teaching Assistantship (% Receiving)	Teaching Assistantship Tuition Remission	Research Assistantship (% Receiving)	Research Assistantship Tuition Remission	Fellowship (% Receiving)	Fellowship Tuition Remission
First-Year Student	NA (NA)	NA	NA (NA)	NA	NA (NA)	NA
Advanced Student	NA (NA)	NA	NA (NA)	NA	NA (NA)	NA

For additional information on financial assistance, visit https://www.setonhill.edu/admissions/tuition-financial-aid/graduate-programs/financial-aid/.

Employment of Department Graduates

Master's:
Employed in a community mental health/counseling center: 9
Total: 9

Additional Information

Housing and Day Care: On-campus housing is available. See the following website for more information: https://www.setonhill.edu/campus-life/housing-dining/. No on-campus day care facilities are available.

Information for Students With Physical Disabilities: See the following website: https://www.setonhill.edu/campus-life/health-safety/disability-services/.

Special Facilities or Resources: The Seton Hill Center for Family Therapy is a community-based mental health center and training site in downtown Greensburg, PA. Therapy services are provided by the advanced graduate students in Seton Hill's Marriage and Family Therapy program, under the mentorship of experienced clinicians on the faculty at Seton Hill. This new facility uses advanced technology and modern design to provide community members with affordable mental health services. Our Center allows our students to gain practical experience in caring for clients in a supportive learning environment.

Application Information: Office of Graduate and Adult Studies, Seton Hill University, 1 Seton Drive, Greensburg, PA 15601. *Fee:* $0. *Online application:* https://apply.setonhill.edu/.

Shippensburg University (2015 data)
Psychology Department
1871 Old Main Drive
Shippensburg, PA 17257
Telephone: (717) 477-1657
Chairperson: Lea T. Adams, PhD

E-mail: psych@ship.edu
Web: http://www.ship.edu/Psychology/

Orientation, Objectives, and Emphasis of Department

The graduate program in psychological science emphasizes the development of psychological knowledge and research skills. The department offers a Master's degree with three possible tracks—general, applied, and research. The General track is designed to meet the needs of those seeking credentials or advancement in their current place of employment. The Applied track appropriate for graduates who are trying to secure employment in industry, government, or non-profit upon graduate with the master's degree. The Research track is appropriate for those seeking degrees beyond the master's level. This track allows students to specialize in a subarea of psychology via elective selection and completion of a thesis. The thesis requirement will increase students' potentials for acceptance into doctoral level programs.

Programs and Degrees Offered

Program	Degree	Application Deadline	Applica-tions Received	Accepted	New Admits Enrolled (PT)	Total Enrolled (PT)	Degrees Awarded in 2014–2015	Median Years to Complete Degree	Dismissed/ Withdrew
Psychological Science - Research Track	MA/MS	Rolling	32	30	8	17	15	2	2
Psychological Science - Applied Track	MA/MS	Rolling	3	2	2	2	2	2	0
Psychological Science - General Track	MA/MS	Rolling	32	30	8 (0)	15 (0)	3	2	2

Admissions

Entries appear in the following order: required test or GPA, minimum score (if required)/median score of students entering in 2015–2016.

Program	Degree	GRE-V	GRE-Q	GRE-Writing	GRE-Subject	Under-graduate GPA	Last 2 Years GPA	Psychol-ogy GPA	Master's GPA
Psychological Science - Research Track	MA/MS	Not specified	Not specified	Not specified	Not specified	2.75/3.45	Not specified	Not specified	Not specified
Psychological Science - Applied Track	MA/MS	Not specified	Not specified	Not specified	Not specified	2.75/3.45	Not specified	Not specified	Not specified
Psychological Science - General Track	MA/MS	Not specified	Not specified	Not specified	Not specified	2.75/3.45	Not specified	Not specified	Not specified

Admissions Requirements:

Degree	GRE	GRE-Subject	Letters of Recom-mendation	Research Statement	Writing Sample	CV	Interview
Master's/Specialist	None	None	N/A	Required	Required	Recom-mended	None

Admissions Criteria:

Research experience—high
Work experience—low
Clinically related public service—low
GPA—high

Letters of recommendation—medium
Statement of goals and objectives—high
Undergraduate psychology preparation—medium
Statistics grades—high

Department Demographics

	Male (PT)	Female (PT)	Total	African-American/ Black (PT)	Hispanic/ Latino (PT)	Asian/ Pacific Islander (PT)	American Indian/ Alaska Native (PT)	Caucasian/ White (PT)	Unknown	Multiethnic (PT)	ADA (PT)	Int'l (PT)
Students	19 (0)	10 (0)	29	1 (0)	0 (0)	0 (0)	0 (0)	27 (0)	1 (0)	0 (0)	0 (0)	1 (0)

Financial Information/Assistance

Tuition: Tuition is subject to change. Additional fees are assessed to students beyond the costs of tuition for the following: Ed Services, Technology, Comprehensive Health, and Student Union ($127 Resident, $137 Non-resident).

Master's:
State residents: $442 per credit hour.
Nonstate residents: $663 per credit hour.

Financial Assistance:

	Teaching Assistantship (% Receiving)	Teaching Assistantship Tuition Remission	Research Assistantship (% Receiving)	Research Assistantship Tuition Remission	Fellowship (% Receiving)	Fellowship Tuition Remission
First-Year Student	NA (NA)	NA	NA (NA)	NA	NA (NA)	NA
Advanced Student	NA (NA)	NA	NA (NA)	NA	NA (NA)	NA

For additional information on financial assistance, visit http://www.ship.edu/financial_aid/.

Employment of Department Graduates

No information provided.

Additional Information

Housing and Day Care: No on-campus housing is available. No on-campus day care facilities are available.

Information for Students With Physical Disabilities: See the following website: http://www.ship.edu/ODS/.

Special Facilities or Resources: The psychology laboratories are housed in Franklin Science Center. The facilities include a computer room for statistical analysis, observation rooms, individual laboratory testing rooms, and animal colony facilities. Other equipment includes video taping facilities, operant conditioning chambers, and psychophysiological research equipment. The Ezra Lehman Memorial Library has a carefully selected collection of psychology books, journals, and periodicals.

Application Information: Fee: $45. *Online application:* http://www.ship.edu/admissions/apply/.

Temple University
Department of Psychology
College of Liberal Arts
1701 North 13th Street, Room 668
Philadelphia, PA 19122-6085
Telephone: (215) 204-7321
Chairperson: Marsha Weinraub

E-mail: marsha.weinraub@temple.edu
Web: http://www.cla.temple.edu/psychology/

Orientation, Objectives, and Emphasis of Department

The psychology department offers graduate training in: brain and cognitive sciences; clinical; developmental; developmental psycho-pathology; neuroscience; decision neuroscience; and social decision making and emotions. All doctoral programs are designed to prepare students for teaching in universities and colleges, conducting research in field and laboratory settings, and providing consultation in applied settings. The clinical program trains scientist–practitioners and provides students with research and clinical experience.

Programs and Degrees Offered

Program	Degree	Application Deadline	Applica-tions Received	Accepted	New Admits Enrolled (PT)	Total Enrolled (PT)	Degrees Awarded in 2014–2015	Median Years to Complete Degree	Dismissed/ Withdrew
Clinical Psychology	PhD	December 1 (Fall)	500	15	10	61 (0)	7	6	0
Developmental Psychology	PhD	December 1 (Fall)	55	10	5	12 (0)	2	5	1
Brain and Cognitive Sciences	PhD	December 1 (Fall)	52	5	5	23 (0)	5	5	2
Social Psychology	PhD	December 1 (Fall)	47	2	2	5 (0)	3	5	0
Developmental Psycho-pathology	PhD	December 1 (Fall)	25	4	2	4 (0)	0		
Neuroscience	PhD	December 1 (Fall)					2	5	

APA Accreditation

Clinical PhD: Student Outcome Data website: http://www.cla.temple.edu/psychology/graduate/clinical-psychology/.

Doctoral Degree (PhD Clinical Psychology): For those doctoral students for whom a professional internship was required in this program prior to graduation:
Total students who applied for an internship: 10
Total students who obtained an internship: 10
Total students who obtained a paid internship: 10
Total students who obtained an unpaid internship: 0
Total students who were placed in APA/CPA-accredited internships: 10
Total students placed in internships not APA/CPA-accredited, but listed with the Association of Psychology Postdoctoral and Internship Centers (APPIC): 0
Total students placed in internships conforming to guidelines of the Council of Directors of School Psychology Programs (CDSPP): 0
Total students placed in internships that were not APA/CPA-accredited, APPIC or CDSSP listed: 0

Internships/Practica

Clinical students complete a 2,000-hour predoctoral internship at an agency or hospital typically in the Philadelphia metropolitan area.

Admissions

Entries appear in the following order: required test or GPA, minimum score (if required)/median score of students entering in 2015–2016.

Program	Degree	GRE-V	GRE-Q	GRE-Writing	GRE-Subject	Under-graduate GPA	Last 2 Years GPA	Psychol-ogy GPA	Master's GPA
Clinical Psychology	PhD	NA/NA	NA/NA	NA/NA	Not specified	NA/3.68	Not specified	NA/NA	Not specified
Developmental Psychology	PhD	NA/NA	NA/NA	NA/NA	Not specified	NA/NA	Not specified	NA/NA	Not specified

Admissions (con't.)

Program	Degree	GRE-V	GRE-Q	GRE-Writing	GRE-Subject	Under-graduate GPA	Last 2 Years GPA	Psychology GPA	Master's GPA
Brain and Cognitive Sciences	PhD	NA/NA	NA/NA	NA/NA	Not specified	NA/NA	Not specified	NA/NA	Not specified
Social Psychology	PhD	NA/NA	NA/NA	NA/NA	Not specified	NA/NA	Not specified	NA/NA	Not specified
Developmental Psychopathology	PhD	NA/NA	NA/NA	NA/NA	Not specified	NA/NA	Not specified	Not specified	Not specified
Neuroscience	PhD	NA/NA	NA/NA	NA/NA	Not specified	NA/NA	Not specified	NA/NA	Not specified

Admissions Requirements:

Degree	GRE	GRE-Subject	Letters of Recom-mendation	Research Statement	Writing Sample	CV	Interview
Doctoral	Required	Optional	3	Required	Optional	Required	Required

Admissions Criteria:

GRE scores—high
Research experience—high
Work experience—low
Clinically related public service—low
GPA—high

Letters of recommendation—high
Interview—high
Statement of goals and objectives—high
Undergraduate psychology preparation—medium

For additional information on admission requirements, visit http://www.cla.temple.edu/psychology/graduate/requirements-for-admission/.

Department Demographics

	Male (PT)	Female (PT)	Total	African-American/ Black (PT)	Hispanic/ Latino (PT)	Asian/ Pacific Islander (PT)	American Indian/ Alaska Native (PT)	Caucasian/ White (PT)	Unknown	Multiethnic (PT)	ADA (PT)	Int'l (PT)
Students	38 (0)	67 (0)	105	4 (0)	0 (0)	5 (0)	0 (0)	0 (0)	0 (0)	0 (0)	0 (0)	0 (0)

Financial Information/Assistance

Tuition: For information on tuition costs, visit http://www.temple.edu/grad/admissions/tuition_fees.htm. Tuition is subject to change. Additional fees are assessed to students beyond the costs of tuition for the following: University Services Fee.

Doctoral:
State residents: $853 per credit hour.
Nonstate residents: $1,169 per credit hour.

Financial Assistance:

	Teaching Assistantship (% Receiving)	Teaching Assistantship Tuition Remission	Research Assistantship (% Receiving)	Research Assistantship Tuition Remission	Fellowship (% Receiving)	Fellowship Tuition Remission
First-Year Student	$18,690 (70)	Full	$18,690 (5)	Full	$23,000 (25)	Full
Advanced Student	$18,690 (70)	Full	$18,690 (5)	Full	$23,000 (25)	Full

Employment of Department Graduates

Doctoral:
Enrolled in a postdoctoral residency/fellowship: 4
Employed in an academic position at a university: 1
Total: 5

Additional Information

Housing and Day Care: No on-campus housing is available. No on-campus day care facilities are available.

Information for Students With Physical Disabilities: See the following website: http://disabilityresources.temple.edu/.

Special Facilities or Resources: The psychology department occupies eight floors of a high-rise building. The physical resources housed in the building include the Psychological Services Center (an in-house mental health facility where clinical students obtain practicum experience in psychotherapy), extensive laboratory space for human research, a human electrophysiology lab, an infant behavior lab, numerous observation rooms with one-way mirrors, audiovisual equipment (including mobile video equipment), and excellent computer facilities.

Application Information: Graduate Administrator. *Fee:* $65. *Online application:* http://www.temple.edu/apply/common/appcheck.asp.

Villanova University
Department of Psychology
800 Lancaster Avenue
Villanova, PA 19085
Telephone: (610) 519-4720
Chairperson: Thomas Toppino

E-mail: psychologyinformation@villanova.edu
Web: http://psychology.villanova.edu

Orientation, Objectives, and Emphasis of Department
The department offers a program of study leading to the Master of Science in psychology. Individually tailored to meet each student's career interests and needs, the program provides a solid foundation in psychology with special emphasis on preparation for doctoral work. All incoming students are required to take a seminar in the foundations of research and a statistics course. All students also take laboratory courses in Cognition & Learning and Biopsychology. Depending upon the student's interest, he or she selects four elective courses from a reasonably broad range of course offerings such as psychopathology, psychological testing, developmental psychology, social psychology, personality, theories of psychotherapy, behavior modification, special topics, and individual research. During the second year, student efforts are concentrated on the thesis project, which is an intensive, empirically based project done under the supervision of a faculty mentor. The student/faculty ratio approaches 2:1, allowing close interaction, careful advisement, and individual attention. The department has an active, research-oriented faculty.

Programs and Degrees Offered

Program	Degree	Application Deadline	Applications Received	Accepted	New Admits Enrolled (PT)	Total Enrolled (PT)	Degrees Awarded in 2014–2015	Median Years to Complete Degree	Dismissed/Withdrew
General Psychology	MA/MS	March 1 (Fall)	125	43	19	35 (10)	18	2.5	4

Admissions
Entries appear in the following order: required test or GPA, minimum score (if required)/median score of students entering in 2015–2016.

Program	Degree	GRE-V	GRE-Q	GRE-Writing	GRE-Subject	Undergraduate GPA	Last 2 Years GPA	Psychology GPA	Master's GPA
General Psychology	MA/MS	NA/160	NA/155	NA/4.6	Not specified	NA/3.7	Not specified	NA/3.8	Not specified

Admissions Requirements:

Degree	GRE	GRE-Subject	Letters of Recommendation	Research Statement	Writing Sample	CV	Interview
Master's/Specialist	Required	Optional	3	Required	Optional	Optional	None

Admissions Criteria:

GRE scores—high
Research experience—medium
Work experience—low
Clinically related public service—low
GPA—high

Letters of recommendation—high
Interview—medium
Statement of goals and objectives—medium
Undergraduate psychology preparation—high

Department Demographics

	Male (PT)	Female (PT)	Total	African-American/ Black (PT)	Hispanic/ Latino (PT)	Asian/ Pacific Islander (PT)	American Indian/ Alaska Native (PT)	Caucasian/ White (PT)	Unknown	Multiethnic (PT)	ADA (PT)	Int'l (PT)
Students	10 (5)	25 (5)	45	1 (0)	2 (1)	1 (0)	0 (0)	29 (4)	2 (5)	0 (0)	0 (0)	0 (1)

Financial Information/Assistance

Tuition: For information on tuition costs, visit http://www1.villanova.edu/villanova/finance/bursar/tuition/gradrates.html. Tuition is subject to change.

Master's:
State residents: $750 per credit hour.
Nonstate residents: $750 per credit hour.

Financial Assistance:

	Teaching Assistantship (% Receiving)	Teaching Assistantship Tuition Remission	Research Assistantship (% Receiving)	Research Assistantship Tuition Remission	Fellowship (% Receiving)	Fellowship Tuition Remission
First-Year Student	NA (NA)	NA	$15,423 (NA)	Full	NA (NA)	Full
Advanced Student	NA (NA)	NA	$15,423 (NA)	Full	NA (NA)	Full

For additional information on financial assistance, visit http://www1.villanova.edu/villanova/artsci/graduate/financing/cost.html.

Employment of Department Graduates

Master's:
Enrolled in a psychology doctoral program: 7
Enrolled in another graduate/professional program: 1
Employed in business or industry: 2
Employed in a community mental health/counseling center: 1
Still seeking employment: 1
Do not know: 2
Total: 14

Additional Information

Housing and Day Care: No on-campus housing is available. No on-campus day care facilities are available.

Information for Students With Physical Disabilities: See the following website: http://www1.villanova.edu/villanova/studentlife/disabilityservices.html.

Special Facilities or Resources: In addition to office space for faculty and all graduate assistants, the department has approximately 5800 square feet available for research. Equipment of particular interest to the graduate student includes: electronic and computer-controlled tachistoscopes; animal conditioning chambers; cognitive/computer labs; complete facilities for surgery and histology, including stereotaxic equipment for brain implantation; environmental chambers and rooms equipped for observation and automated recording of animal behavior; radial mazes; well-equipped vision labs; one-way vision rooms; audio/video recording and playback facilities; facilities for the design and development of experiments; and computer-based teaching labs. University computing facilities are all networked, with hundreds of remote terminals available.

Application Information: Dean, Graduate School, Villanova University, 800 Lancaster Avenue, Villanova, PA 19085. *Fee:* $50. *Online application:* http://www1.villanova.edu/villanova/artsci/graduate/application.html.

West Chester University of Pennsylvania

Department of Psychology
Arts and Sciences
690 South Church Street Peoples Building
West Chester, PA 19383
Telephone: (610) 436-3136
Chairperson: Loretta Rieser-Danner

E-mail: aclarke@wcupa.edu
Web: http://www.wcupa.edu/_academics/sch_cas.psy/

Orientation, Objectives, and Emphasis of Department

The concentration in clinical psychology is designed for students who wish to work in applied settings such as community mental health facilities, hospitals, counseling centers, and other social and rehabilitation agencies, or who wish to continue their education at the doctoral level. Students with the latter goal in mind are strongly encouraged to engage in research in the course of their master's degree training by participating in faculty members' ongoing research programs or conducting their own research under faculty supervision for research report or thesis credit. The industrial/organizational concentration is appropriate for students interested in employment in business or industry, or for those who wish to continue their education at the doctoral level in a related area. A 3-credit internship and 3- to 6-credit research report or thesis are required. With careful selection of electives, internship placement, and research focus, students are able to develop specialization in personnel selection and evaluation, training, employee engagement, or group and organizational processes. The concentration in general psychology, in addition to exposing students to the major traditional subject matter of psychology, also provides the opportunity to explore particular areas of psychology in depth through the appropriate selection of elective coursework and research.

Programs and Degrees Offered

Program	Degree	Application Deadline	Applications Received	Accepted	New Admits Enrolled (PT)	Total Enrolled (PT)	Degrees Awarded in 2014–2015	Median Years to Complete Degree	Dismissed/Withdrew
Clinical Psychology	MA/MS	March 1 (Fall)	77	52	24 (1)	93 (31)	11	2	0
General Psychology	MA/MS	March 1 (Fall)	25	17	8 (2)	18 (11)	7	2	0
Industrial/Organizational Psychology	MA/MS	March 1 (Fall)	58	37	15 (1)	48 (9)	20	2	

Internships/Practica

Clinical students are required to complete 6 credit hours of practicum and internship in a mental health setting. I/O students are required to complete a 3 credit hour internship in business or industry.

Admissions

Entries appear in the following order: required test or GPA, minimum score (if required)/median score of students entering in 2015–2016.

Program	Degree	GRE-V	GRE-Q	GRE-Writing	GRE-Subject	Undergraduate GPA	Last 2 Years GPA	Psychology GPA	Master's GPA
Clinical Psychology	MA/MS	153/NA	144/NA	Not specified	Not specified	3/3.42	Not specified	3.25/3.5	Not specified

Admissions *(con't.)*

Program	Degree	GRE-V	GRE-Q	GRE-Writing	GRE-Subject	Under-graduate GPA	Last 2 Years GPA	Psychology GPA	Master's GPA
General Psychology	MA/MS	153/NA	144/NA	Not specified	Not specified	3/NA	Not specified	3.25/NA	Not specified
Industrial/ Organizational Psychology	MA/MS	153/NA	144/NA	Not specified	Not specified	3/3.4	Not specified	3.25/3.56	Not specified

Admissions Requirements:

Degree	GRE	GRE-Subject	Letters of Recommendation	Research Statement	Writing Sample	CV	Interview
Master's/Specialist	Required	None	3	Required	Optional	Optional	Recommended

Admissions Criteria:

GRE scores—high
Research experience—medium
Work experience—medium
Clinically related public service—medium

GPA—high
Letters of recommendation—high
Statement of goals and objectives—high
Undergraduate psychology preparation—medium

For additional information on admission requirements, visit http://www.wcupa.edu/_academics/sch_cas.psy/gradadmissions.asp.

Department Demographics

	Male (PT)	Female (PT)	Total	African-American/ Black (PT)	Hispanic/ Latino (PT)	Asian/ Pacific Islander (PT)	American Indian/ Alaska Native (PT)	Caucasian/ White (PT)	Unknown	Multiethnic (PT)	ADA (PT)	Int'l (PT)
Students	50 (17)	109 (34)	210	16 (4)	7 (2)	0 (0)	0 (0)	124 (41)	2 (0)	5 (2)	8 (4)	5 (2)

Financial Information/Assistance

Tuition: For information on tuition costs, visit http://www.wcupa.edu/_information/afa/Fiscal/Bursar/tuition.asp. Tuition is subject to change. Additional fees are assessed to students beyond the costs of tuition for the following: general tee for full-time students: $899.25 (9 credits and up); $101.14 per credit (8 credits and below).

Master's:
State residents: $8,172 per academic year.
State residents: $454 per credit hour.
Nonstate residents: $12,258 per academic year.
Nonstate residents: $681 per credit hour.

Financial Assistance:

	Teaching Assistantship (% Receiving)	Teaching Assistantship Tuition Remission	Research Assistantship (% Receiving)	Research Assistantship Tuition Remission	Fellowship (% Receiving)	Fellowship Tuition Remission
First-Year Student	NA (NA)	NA	$2,500 (NA)	Partial	NA (NA)	NA
Advanced Student	NA (NA)	NA	$2,500 (NA)	Partial	NA (NA)	NA

For additional information on financial assistance, visit http://www.wcupa.edu/_SERVICES/FIN_AID/.

Employment of Department Graduates

No information provided.

Additional Information

Housing and Day Care: No on-campus housing is available. No on-campus day care facilities are available.

Information for Students With Physical Disabilities: See the following website: http://www.wcupa.edu/ussss/ossd/.

Special Facilities or Resources: The department has laboratory space and equipment to support a variety of animal and human research.

Application Information: Graduate Studies, McKelvie Hall, 102 West Rosedale Avenue, West Chester, PA 19383. *Fee:* $50. *Online application:* https://www.applyweb.com/apply/wcgrad/menu.html.

Widener University
Institute for Graduate Clinical Psychology
School of Human Service Professions
One University Place
Chester, PA 19013
Telephone: (610) 499-1206
Associate Dean and Director: Sanjay R. Nath, PhD

E-mail: graduate.psychology@widener.edu
Web: http://www.widener.edu/igcp/

Orientation, Objectives, and Emphasis of Department
The PsyD program retains the basic skills and knowledge traditional to clinical psychology, such as psychodiagnostic testing and psychotherapy, while simultaneously exposing the individual to new ideas and practices in the field.

Programs and Degrees Offered

Program	Degree	Application Deadline	Applications Received	Accepted	New Admits Enrolled (PT)	Total Enrolled (PT)	Degrees Awarded in 2014–2015	Median Years to Complete Degree	Dismissed/ Withdrew
Clinical Psychology	PsyD	December 7 (Fall)	305	58	34 (0)	162 (13)	39	5	0

APA Accreditation
Clinical PsyD: Student Outcome Data website: http://www.widener.edu/academics/schools/shsp/psyd/student admissionsandotherdata.aspx.

Doctoral Degree (PsyD Clinical Psychology): For those doctoral students for whom a professional internship was required in this program prior to graduation:
Total students who applied for an internship: 65
Total students who obtained an internship: 65
Total students who obtained a paid internship: 65
Total students who obtained an unpaid internship: 0
Total students who were placed in APA/CPA-accredited internships: 65
Total students placed in internships not APA/CPA-accredited, but listed with the Association of Psychology Postdoctoral and Internship Centers (APPIC): 0
Total students placed in internships conforming to guidelines of the Council of Directors of School Psychology Programs (CDSPP): 0
Total students placed in internships that were not APA/CPA-accredited, APPIC or CDSSP listed: 0

Internships/Practica
The program has an exclusively affiliated internship that is half time over a 2-year period. The APA-accredited internship is housed at Widener University, but placements are within a 50-mile radius of the campus. One hundred percent of fourth- and fifth-year students are placed.

Admissions

Entries appear in the following order: required test or GPA, minimum score (if required)/median score of students entering in 2015–2016.

Program	Degree	GRE-V	GRE-Q	GRE-Writing	GRE-Subject	Under-graduate GPA	Last 2 Years GPA	Psychol-ogy GPA	Master's GPA
Clinical Psychology	PsyD	156/NA	156/NA	4.5/NA	Not specified	3.2/NA	Not specified	Not specified	Not specified

Admissions Requirements:

Degree	GRE	GRE-Subject	Letters of Recom-mendation	Research Statement	Writing Sample	CV	Interview
Doctoral	Required	Recom-mended	3	Required	Required	Required	Required

Please note if these criteria vary for different programs: An undergraduate major in psychology is not required for admission; however, some basic psychology courses are required before enrollment (statistics, research design/experimental psychology, abnormal psychology/psychopathology). We encourage applications from individuals from various disciplines and with a wide range of experiences.

Admissions Criteria:

GRE scores—high
Work experience—medium
Clinically related public service—medium
GPA—high

Letters of recommendation—high
Interview—high
Statement of goals and objectives—high
Undergraduate psychology preparation—low

For additional information on admission requirements, visit http://www.widener.edu/academics/schools/shsp/psyd/admission/default.aspx.

Department Demographics

	Male (PT)	Female (PT)	Total	African-American/ Black (PT)	Hispanic/ Latino (PT)	Asian/ Pacific Islander (PT)	American Indian/ Alaska Native (PT)	Caucasian/ White (PT)	Unknown	Multiethnic (PT)	ADA (PT)	Int'l (PT)
Students	33 (2)	129 (11)	175	10 (1)	5 (0)	15 (2)	0 (0)	125 (10)	0 (0)	7 (0)	1 (1)	6 (0)

Financial Information/Assistance

Tuition: For information on tuition costs, visit http://www.widener.edu/admissions/graduate/tuition.aspx. Tuition is subject to change.

Doctoral:
State residents: $32,915 per academic year.
Nonstate residents: $32,915 per academic year.

Financial Assistance:

	Teaching Assistantship (% Receiving)	Teaching Assistantship Tuition Remission	Research Assistantship (% Receiving)	Research Assistantship Tuition Remission	Fellowship (% Receiving)	Fellowship Tuition Remission
First-Year Student	NA (NA)	NA	NA (NA)	NA	$23,574 (NA)	Partial
Advanced Student	NA (NA)	NA	NA (NA)	NA	$3,000 (10)	Partial

For additional information on financial assistance, visit http://www.widener.edu/admissions/graduate/financial_aid/default.aspx.

Employment of Department Graduates

Doctoral:
Enrolled in a postdoctoral residency/fellowship: 8
Employed in independent practice: 2
Employed in an academic position at a university: 1
Employed in other positions at a higher education institution: 4
Employed in a professional position in a school system: 5
Employed in business or industry: 4
Employed in government agency: 4
Employed in a community mental health/counseling center: 7
Employed in a hospital/medical center: 4
Total: 39

Additional Information

Housing and Day Care: No on-campus housing is available. On-campus day care facilities are available. See the following website for more information: http://cdc.widener.edu/.

Information for Students With Physical Disabilities: See the following website: http://www.widener.edu/academics/support/disabilities/default.aspx.

Special Facilities or Resources: One of the hallmarks of our program is the variety of internship and practicum opportunities available to students, all of which are within driving distance of the university. A corollary resource is the availability of practicing clinicians to teach in the program, a factor that provides breadth, relevance, and enrichment to the curriculum. Widener University is situated near Philadelphia and in the middle of the Eastern corridor between New York and Washington, DC. As a result, our students enjoy a rich diversity of educational resources, field experiences, and employment opportunities.

Application Information: Widener University, Attn: Clinical Psychology Admissions, One University Place, Chester, PA 19013. *Fee:* $50. *Online application:* http://e.widener.edu/graduate/pages/welcome.aspx.

Brown University

Department of Cognitive, Linguistic, and Psychological Sciences
190 Thayer Street
Providence, RI 2912
Telephone: (401) 863-2727
Chairperson: William Heindel

E-mail: CLPS@brown.edu
Web: http://brown.edu/Departments/CLPS

Orientation, Objectives, and Emphasis of Department

Brown University's Department of Cognitive, Linguistic, and Psychological Sciences is a unique interdisciplinary department that offers PhD programs in three fields: Cognitive Science, Linguistics, and Psychology. Graduate students are admitted to the Department as a whole and select a specific PhD program by the end of their first year. Given the interdisciplinary collaborations among faculty in the department, graduate students are able to carry out coursework and research in many areas and from many methodological perspectives. Students are encouraged to compose advising committees with faculty from the different programs to be exposed to multiple approaches and traditions.

Programs and Degrees Offered

Program	Degree	Application Deadline	Applications Received	Accepted	New Admits Enrolled (PT)	Total Enrolled (PT)	Degrees Awarded in 2014–2015	Median Years to Complete Degree	Dismissed/ Withdrew
Psychology	PhD	December 1 (Fall)	128	6	2 (0)	13 (0)	1	6	0
Cognitive Science	PhD	December 1 (Fall)	110	22	7 (0)	25 (1)	5	6	2
Linguistics	PhD	December 1 (Fall)	30	3	2 (0)	4 (0)	0		0

Admissions

Entries appear in the following order: required test or GPA, minimum score (if required)/median score of students entering in 2015–2016.

Program	Degree	GRE-V	GRE-Q	GRE-Writing	GRE-Subject	Under-graduate GPA	Last 2 Years GPA	Psychology GPA	Master's GPA
Psychology	PhD	NA/NA	NA/NA	NA/NA	Not specified	Not specified	Not specified	Not specified	Not specified
Cognitive Science	PhD	NA/NA	NA/NA	NA/NA	Not specified	Not specified	Not specified	Not specified	Not specified
Linguistics	PhD	NA/NA	NA/NA	NA/NA	Not specified	Not specified	Not specified	Not specified	Not specified

Admissions Requirements:

Degree	GRE	GRE-Subject	Letters of Recom-mendation	Research Statement	Writing Sample	CV	Interview
Doctoral	Required	Optional	3	Required	Required	Optional	Required

Please note if these criteria vary for different programs: For each of the three programs (psychology, cognitive science, linguistics), somewhat different prior course work is expected, and undergraduate psychology preparation is irrelevant for linguistics and of low relevance for cognitive science.

Admissions Criteria:

GRE scores—high
Research experience—high
Work experience—low
GPA—high

Letters of recommendation—high
Interview—high
Statement of goals and objectives—high
Undergraduate psychology preparation—low

For additional information on admission requirements, visit http://brown.edu/Departments/CLPS/graduate.

Department Demographics

	Male (PT)	Female (PT)	Total	African-American/ Black (PT)	Hispanic/ Latino (PT)	Asian/ Pacific Islander (PT)	American Indian/ Alaska Native (PT)	Caucasian/ White (PT)	Unknown	Multiethnic (PT)	ADA (PT)	Int'l (PT)
Students	23 (1)	19 (0)	43	0 (0)	0 (0)	1 (0)	(0)	22 (1)	19 (0)	0 (0)	0 (0)	17 (0)

Financial Information/Assistance

Tuition: For information on tuition costs, visit http://www.brown.edu/academics/gradschool/courses-manual/tuition-fees. Tuition is subject to change.

Doctoral:
State residents: $48,272 per academic year.
Nonstate residents: $48,272 per academic year.

Financial Assistance:

	Teaching Assistantship (% Receiving)	Teaching Assistantship Tuition Remission	Research Assistantship (% Receiving)	Research Assistantship Tuition Remission	Fellowship (% Receiving)	Fellowship Tuition Remission
First-Year Student	NA (NA)	NA	NA (NA)	NA	$30,400 (NA)	Full
Advanced Student	$30,400 (NA)	Full	$30,400 (NA)	Full	$30,400 (NA)	Full

For additional information on financial assistance, visit http://www.brown.edu/academics/gradschool/financing-support/phd-funding.

Employment of Department Graduates

Doctoral:
Enrolled in a postdoctoral residency/fellowship: 4
Employed in business or industry: 3
Still seeking employment: 1
Total: 8

Additional Information

Housing and Day Care: On-campus housing is available. See the following website for more information: http://reslife.brown.edu/graduate_students/oncampus.html. No on-campus day care facilities are available.

Information for Students With Physical Disabilities: See the following website: http://www.brown.edu/campus-life/support/accessibility-services/.

Special Facilities or Resources: Ambulatory virtual reality systems; wide-area motion tracking system; high-performance parallel supercomputer; 3.0T MRI system; 64-channel Event Related Potential (ERP) system, multiple eye-trackers; speech and phonetics labs; gait laboratory; high-performance 3-D graphics work stations; animal behavior and communication laboratories; infant and child testing facilities; computerized testing labs; dyadic and group social interaction AV recording facilities.

Application Information: Fee: $75. *Online application:* https://www.applyweb.com/browng/.

Rhode Island College

Psychology Department
Faculty of Arts & Sciences
600 Mt. Pleasant Avenue HM 311
Providence, RI 2908
Telephone: (401) 456-8015
Director, Graduate Programs in Psychology: Christine A. Marco, PhD

E-mail: psychgradprgm@ric.edu
Web: http://www.ric.edu/psychology/psychMa.php

Orientation, Objectives, and Emphasis of Department

The overall mission of the graduate programs in psychology at Rhode Island College is to provide an education in the science of human behavior. The Certificate of Graduate Studies (CGS) in Health Psychology program requires 16 credits of post-baccalaureate coursework in research methods, statistics, health psychology, stress management, epidemiology and health statistics, and public health science, which can be used in a variety of health-related employment settings. The Master of Arts (MA) in Psychology degree is designed to prepare students for doctoral study. Students in the Master's program complete 30 credits of coursework in research methods, statistics, personality, cognitive, developmental, social psychology, plus electives. All students in the Master's program are required to complete a Master's thesis. The psychology department faculty at Rhode Island College have ongoing research interests in the areas of intergroup relations, family violence, chemical dependency, gambling disorders, health psychology, language development, moral development, and neuroscience.

Programs and Degrees Offered

Program	Degree	Application Deadline	Applications Received	Accepted	New Admits Enrolled (PT)	Total Enrolled (PT)	Degrees Awarded in 2014–2015	Median Years to Complete Degree	Dismissed/ Withdrew
Psychology	MA/MS	March 1 (Fall), November 1 (Spring), Rolling	7	4	3	12	2		
Health Psychology Certificate	Other	March 1 (Fall), November 1 (Spring), Rolling	1	1	1	1			

Admissions

Entries appear in the following order: required test or GPA, minimum score (if required)/median score of students entering in 2015–2016.

Program	Degree	GRE-V	GRE-Q	GRE-Writing	GRE-Subject	Under-graduate GPA	Last 2 Years GPA	Psychol-ogy GPA	Master's GPA
Psychology	MA/MS	NA/NA	NA/NA	Not specified	Not specified	3/NA	3/NA	3/NA	Not specified
Health Psychology Certificate	Other	Not specified	Not specified	Not specified	Not specified	3/NA	3/NA	3/NA	Not specified

Admissions Requirements:

Degree	GRE	GRE-Subject	Letters of Recom-mendation	Research Statement	Writing Sample	CV	Interview
Master's/Specialist	Required	Optional	3	Required	None	Required	Optional

Admissions Criteria:

GRE scores—high
Research experience—medium
Work experience—low
GPA—high
Letters of recommendation—high

Interview—high
Statement of goals and objectives—high
Undergraduate psychology preparation—medium
Resume—medium

Department Demographics

	Male (PT)	Female (PT)	Total	African-American/ Black (PT)	Hispanic/ Latino (PT)	Asian/ Pacific Islander (PT)	American Indian/ Alaska Native (PT)	Caucasian/ White (PT)	Unknown	Multiethnic (PT)	ADA (PT)	Int'l (PT)
Students	3 (1)	5 (1)	10	0 (0)	0 (0)	0 (0)	0 (0)	0 (0)	8 (2)	0 (0)	0 (0)	0 (0)

Financial Information/Assistance

Tuition: For information on tuition costs, visit http://www.ric.edu/graduateStudies/financial.php. Higher tuition cost for this program: MA and CT students living within a 50-mile radius receive a discounted tuition rate. Tuition is subject to change. Additional fees are assessed to students beyond the costs of tuition for the following: Registration, Library, Recreation, Technology, Fine Arts, Transportation.

Master's:
State residents: $372 per credit hour.
Nonstate residents: $724 per credit hour.

Financial Assistance:

	Teaching Assistantship (% Receiving)	Teaching Assistantship Tuition Remission	Research Assistantship (% Receiving)	Research Assistantship Tuition Remission	Fellowship (% Receiving)	Fellowship Tuition Remission
First-Year Student	$3,500 (NA)	Full	NA (NA)	NA	$1,000 (NA)	NA
Advanced Student	$3,500 (NA)	Full	NA (NA)	NA	NA (NA)	NA

For additional information on financial assistance, visit http://www.ric.edu/graduateStudies/opportunities.php.

Employment of Department Graduates

No information provided.

Additional Information

Housing and Day Care: No on-campus housing is available. On-campus day care facilities are available. See the following website for more information: http://www.ric.edu/cooperativepreschool/.

Information for Students With Physical Disabilities: See the following website: http://www.ric.edu/disabilityservices/.

Special Facilities or Resources: Research laboratories include areas of social psychology, child and adolescent development, health psychology, addictions and gambling, neuroscience, social identities, learning, political psychology, environmental psychology, interpersonal perception, social psychology and law, and language development.

Application Information: Dean, Faculty of Arts & Sciences, Graduate Admissions, Kaufmann, L.L., Rhode Island College, 600 Mount Pleasant Avenue, Providence, RI 02908. *Fee:* $50. *Online application:* https://www.applyweb.com/ricg/.

Rhode Island, University of (2015 data)
Department of Psychology
Arts and Sciences
142 Flagg Road
Kingston, RI 2881
Telephone: (401) 874-2193
Interim Chairperson: Su Boatright-Horowitz

E-mail: ugpsych@gmail.com
Web: http://web.uri.edu/psychology/

Orientation, Objectives, and Emphasis of Department
Both the Clinical and School Psychology programs of the URI Psychology Department identify as scientist–practitioner programs and are APA-accredited. The Behavior Science program has an applied quantitative emphasis. The department has a strong commitment to diversity and multicultural competence. There is a lively interaction among the programs and access to training in advanced statistical and methodological approaches. The research and professional interests of the faculty fall into six interest areas: (1) health psychology with an emphasis on health promotion/disease prevention; (2) research methodology; (3) gender, diversity, and multicultural psychology; (4) family, child, and developmental psychology; (5) neuropsychology and (6) school psychology practice. Graduates of our programs have developed diverse careers in academia, government service, schools, private industry, the nonprofit sector, and private consulting and practice.

Programs and Degrees Offered

Program	Degree	Application Deadline	Applications Received	Accepted	New Admits Enrolled (PT)	Total Enrolled (PT)	Degrees Awarded in 2014–2015	Median Years to Complete Degree	Dismissed/ Withdrew
Clinical Psychology	PhD	December 1 (Fall)	247	12	6 (0)	43 (0)	4	5.82	0
Behavioral Science	PhD	January 6 (Fall)	41	7	7	39	3	6.5	0
School Psychology	MA/MS	January 15 (Fall)	33	10	3	10	3	3	1
School Psychology	PhD	January 15 (Fall)	28	10	5	31	5	5.5	1

APA Accreditation
Clinical PhD: Student Outcome Data website: http://web.uri.edu/psychology/clinical-psychology-ph-d-program/.
School PhD: Student Outcome Data website: http://web.uri.edu/psychology/school-psychology-ph-d-program/.

Doctoral Degree (PhD Clinical Psychology): For those doctoral students for whom a professional internship was required in this program prior to graduation:
Total students who applied for an internship: 6
Total students who obtained an internship: 6
Total students who obtained a paid internship: 6
Total students who obtained an unpaid internship: 0
Total students who were placed in APA/CPA-accredited internships: 6
Total students placed in internships not APA/CPA-accredited, but listed with the Association of Psychology Postdoctoral and Internship Centers (APPIC): 0
Total students placed in internships conforming to guidelines of the Council of Directors of School Psychology Programs (CDSPP): 0
Total students placed in internships that were not APA/CPA-accredited, APPIC or CDSSP listed: 0

Doctoral Degree (PhD School Psychology): For those doctoral students for whom a professional internship was required in this program prior to graduation:
Total students who applied for an internship: 5
Total students who obtained an internship: 5
Total students who obtained a paid internship: 5
Total students who obtained an unpaid internship: 0
Total students who were placed in APA/CPA-accredited internships: 0
Total students placed in internships not APA/CPA-accredited, but listed with the Association of Psychology Postdoctoral and Internship Centers (APPIC): 0

Total students placed in internships conforming to guidelines of the Council of Directors of School Psychology Programs (CDSPP): 5
Total students placed in internships that were not APA/CPA-accredited, APPIC or CDSSP listed: 0

Master's Degree (MA/MS School Psychology): An internship experience, such as a final research project or "capstone" experience is required of graduates.

Internships/Practica

The Clinical Psychology program has an excellent record of matching students to internship placements. Our students attend top New England and national internship programs. School Psychology students who choose to apply for APPIC internships have had similar success in internship placements. The Clinical program requires five semesters of practicum placement in our on-campus training clinic in cognitive behavior therapy, family therapy, interpersonal process therapy, and multicultural therapy. Students also receive training in working with ethnically diverse clients. From the third year on, clinical students are placed in off-campus externships that include training in areas such as neuropsychological assessment, structured diagnostic interviewing, psychotherapy, university counseling, and pediatric psychology. School students complete school-based practica in Years 1 and 2 of the program. The masters' students complete an internship in Year 3. The doctoral students take advanced practica in Years 3 and 4 in school settings, as well as in a variety of other child and adolescent service delivery settings (e.g., pediatric hospital). In Year 5, the doctoral students in the School Psychology program complete a year-long internship. The School program adheres to the Internship guidelines of the Council of Directors of School Psychology Programs.

Admissions

Entries appear in the following order: required test or GPA, minimum score (if required)/median score of students entering in 2015–2016.

Program	Degree	GRE-V	GRE-Q	GRE-Writing	GRE-Subject	Under-graduate GPA	Last 2 Years GPA	Psychol-ogy GPA	Master's GPA
Clinical Psychology	PhD	NA/155	NA/154	Not specified	Not specified	NA/3.5	Not specified	Not specified	Not specified
Behavioral Science	PhD	NA/157	Not specified	Not specified	Not specified	Not specified	Not specified	Not specified	Not specified
School Psychology	MA/MS	NA/NA	NA/NA	NA/NA	Not specified	NA/3.25	Not specified	Not specified	Not specified
School Psychology	PhD	NA/NA	NA/NA	NA/NA	Not specified	NA/3.5	Not specified	Not specified	Not specified

Admissions Requirements:

Degree	GRE	GRE-Subject	Letters of Recom-mendation	Research Statement	Writing Sample	CV	Interview
Master's/Specialist	Required	None	3	Required	Optional	Required	Required
Doctoral	Required	None	3	Required	Optional	Required	Required

Please note if these criteria vary for different programs: Importance of criteria varies by program. Behavioral Science: High emphasis on research interest and experience; no required interview; we also consider GPA, GRE, focus and quality of personal statement, teaching experience, multicultural interests, reference letters, and program-applicant fit. Clinical Program: Factors we look at are GRE, GPA, program/applicant match, research experience, letters of recommendation, and overall evaluation. Interview required. School Program: Academic aptitude (GRE + GPA); quality of personal statement; research and applied experience; letters of recommendation; fit between applicant goals and program offerings.

Admissions Criteria:
GRE scores—medium
Research experience—high
Work experience—medium
Clinically related public service—medium
GPA—high

Letters of recommendation—high
Interview—high
Statement of goals and objectives—high
Program match—high

Department Demographics

	Male (PT)	Female (PT)	Total	African-American/ Black (PT)	Hispanic/ Latino (PT)	Asian/ Pacific Islander (PT)	American Indian/ Alaska Native (PT)	Caucasian/ White (PT)	Unknown	Multiethnic (PT)	ADA (PT)	Int'l (PT)
Students	28 (0)	95 (0)	123	16 (0)	4 (0)	7 (0)	1 (0)	95 (0)	0 (0)	0 (0)	0 (0)	6 (0)

Financial Information/Assistance

Tuition: Tuition is subject to change. Additional fees are assessed to students beyond the costs of tuition for the following: health services, student services, technology, registration.

Doctoral:
State residents: $11,532 per academic year.
State residents: $641 per credit hour.
Nonstate residents: $23,606 per academic year.
Nonstate residents: $1,311 per credit hour.

Master's:
State residents: $11,532 per academic year.
State residents: $641 per credit hour.
Nonstate residents: $23,606 per academic year.
Nonstate residents: $1,311 per credit hour.

Financial Assistance:

	Teaching Assistantship (% Receiving)	Teaching Assistantship Tuition Remission	Research Assistantship (% Receiving)	Research Assistantship Tuition Remission	Fellowship (% Receiving)	Fellowship Tuition Remission
First-Year Student	$15,844 (NA)	Full	$15,844 (NA)	Full	$15,844 (NA)	Full
Advanced Student	$16,756 (NA)	Full	$16,756 (NA)	Full	$16,756 (NA)	Full

Employment of Department Graduates

Master's:
Employed in a professional position in a school system: 3
Total: 3

Doctoral:
Enrolled in a postdoctoral residency/fellowship: 5
Employed in independent practice: 1
Employed in an academic position at a university: 2
Employed in other positions at a higher education institution: 2
Employed in a professional position in a school system: 1
Employed in business or industry: 1
Employed in government agency: 1
Employed in a community mental health/counseling center: 1
Total: 14

Additional Information

Housing and Day Care: On-campus housing is available. See the following website for more information: http://housing.uri.edu/info/graduate-housing.php. On-campus day care facilities are available. See the following website for more information: http://web.uri.edu/child-development-centers/.

Information for Students With Physical Disabilities: See the following website: http://web.uri.edu/disability/.

Special Facilities or Resources: The Department operates an on-campus training facility, the Psychological Consultation Center, where students train under direct faculty supervision for professional practice service roles with individual clients, families, and children. The department is closely allied with the Cancer Prevention Research Center, one of the nation's leading centers for behavioral health promotion and disease prevention. Students also participate in research and training activities with the Department's Community Research and Services Team, the URI Family Resource Partnership, the Feinstein Hunger Center, as well as with several training partnerships with medical centers and community mental health service agencies.

Application Information: Fee: $65. *Online application:* https://app.applyyourself.com/?id=uri.

Roger Williams University

Department of Psychology
Arts and Sciences
One Old Ferry Road
Bristol, RI 02809-2921
Telephone: (401) 254-5272
Chairperson: Matt Zaitchik, PhD

E-mail: fdicataldo@rwu.edu
Web: http://rwu.edu/academics/schools-colleges/fcas/degree-offerings/psychology/graduate

Orientation, Objectives, and Emphasis of Department

The Psychology Department strives to provide assessment and treatment skills for students interested in employment in a forensic setting or further training at the doctoral level. Faculty members work closely with students to help them develop an understanding and appreciation of the role of psychologists in legal proceedings and the law. Students are prepared to apply these skills to the problems of the community and the larger society. The department stresses tolerance for the views of others and an appreciation of the value of diversity. Other departmental objectives include preparing students to evaluate published research and think critically about their own ideas and the ideas of others.

Programs and Degrees Offered

Program	Degree	Application Deadline	Applica-tions Received	Accepted	New Admits Enrolled (PT)	Total Enrolled (PT)	Degrees Awarded in 2014–2015	Median Years to Complete Degree	Dismissed/ Withdrew
Forensic Psychology	MA/MS	March 15 (Fall)	70	35	13 (0)	23 (0)	14	2	1
Clinical Psychology	MA/MS	March 15 (Fall)	40		5	8	5	2	0

Internships/Practica

The clinical training program for the Master of Arts in Forensic Psychology at Roger Williams University offers a wide range of practicum placement sites in Massachusetts and Rhode Island with opportunities to clinically work with a diversity of forensic populations. We currently have practicum placements within adult and juvenile correctional settings, adult inpatient forensic hospitals and state hospitals, juvenile court clinics, juvenile treatment programs, state and federal correctional programs for the evaluation and treatment of adult sex offenders, community mental health programs, and outpatient substance abuse programs. There are also a few research practicum placements available. Students receive comprehensive training and clinical supervision on-site from practicing forensic psychologists and forensic mental health practitioners in the assessment and treatment of forensic mental health patients and clients. The focus of the clinical practicum placements is to provide the student with an opportunity to apply clinical skills and techniques learned in clinical course work. Students are encouraged to examine case studies, training issues, ethical dilemmas and conflicts within their continued course work on campus. The practicum placements function as a vital place for students to form professional relationships in the field and to network with allied forensic mental health professionals.

Admissions

Entries appear in the following order: required test or GPA, minimum score (if required)/median score of students entering in 2015–2016.

Program	Degree	GRE-V	GRE-Q	GRE-Writing	GRE-Subject	Under-graduate GPA	Last 2 Years GPA	Psychol-ogy GPA	Master's GPA
Forensic Psychology	MA/MS	NA/NA	NA/NA	Not specified	Not specified	3/3.46	Not specified	Not specified	Not specified
Clinical Psychology	MA/MS	Not specified	Not specified	Not specified	Not specified	Not specified	Not specified	Not specified	Not specified

Admissions Requirements:

Degree	GRE	GRE-Subject	Letters of Recom-mendation	Research Statement	Writing Sample	CV	Interview
Master's/Specialist	Required	None	3	Required	Optional	Optional	None

Admissions Criteria:

GRE scores—high
Research experience—high
Work experience—medium
Clinically related public service—medium

GPA—high
Letters of recommendation—high
Statement of goals and objectives—high
Undergraduate psychology preparation—high

Department Demographics

	Male (PT)	Female (PT)	Total	African-American/ Black (PT)	Hispanic/ Latino (PT)	Asian/ Pacific Islander (PT)	American Indian/ Alaska Native (PT)	Caucasian/ White (PT)	Unknown (PT)	Multiethnic (PT)	ADA (PT)	Int'l (PT)
Students	6 (0)	29 (0)	35	1 (0)	2 (0)	0 (0)	0 (0)	32 (0)	0 (0)	0 (0)	0 (0)	0 (0)

Financial Information/Assistance

Tuition: For information on tuition costs, visit http://www.rwu.edu/about/university-offices/bursar/tuition-fees/graduate. Tuition is subject to change.

Master's:
State residents: $17,955 per academic year.
State residents: $818 per credit hour.
Nonstate residents: $17,955 per academic year.
Nonstate residents: $818 per credit hour.

Financial Assistance:

	Teaching Assistantship (% Receiving)	Teaching Assistantship Tuition Remission	Research Assistantship (% Receiving)	Research Assistantship Tuition Remission	Fellowship (% Receiving)	Fellowship Tuition Remission
First-Year Student	NA (NA)	NA	NA (NA)	NA	$5,000 (NA)	NA
Advanced Student	NA (NA)	NA	NA (NA)	NA	$5,000 (NA)	NA

For additional information on financial assistance, visit http://www.rwu.edu/admission-financial-aid/graduate-admission/tuition-financial-aid/financial-aid.

Employment of Department Graduates

No information provided.

Additional Information

Housing and Day Care: On-campus housing is available. See the following website for more information: http://www.rwu.edu/campus-life/housing-dining/living-rwu/residence-halls/graduate-housing-almeida-apartments. No on-campus day care facilities are available.

Information for Students With Physical Disabilities: See the following website: http://www.rwu.edu/academics/academic-services/sas.

Application Information: Office of Graduate Admission, One Old Ferry Road, Bristol, RI 02809. *Fee:* $50. *Online application:* http://www.rwu.edu/admission-financial-aid/graduate-admission/apply-now.

Citadel, The
Department of Psychology
171 Moultrie Street
Charleston, SC 29409
Telephone: (843) 953-5320
Department Head: Steve A. Nida

E-mail: steve.nida@citadel.edu
Web: http://www.citadel.edu/root/psychology

Orientation, Objectives, and Emphasis of Department

The School Psychology program is based on the scientist–practitioner model and emphasizes the school psychologist as a data-based problem-solver who applies psychological principles, knowledge and skill to processes and problems of education and schooling. Students are trained to provide a range of psychological assessment, consultation, intervention, prevention, program development and evaluation services with the goal of maximizing student learning and development. The School Psychology program has been accredited by the National Association of School Psychologists (NASP) since 1988. Students in the Master of Arts in Psychology: Clinical Counseling program are prepared to become scholarly practitioners of psychosocial counseling in community agencies, including college counseling centers, hospitals, mental health centers, and social services agencies. The program's model blends didactic and experience-based training to facilitate students' ability to utilize an empirical approach to assessment, goal development, intervention, and evaluation of services for a wide range of individuals and families experiencing a variety of psychosocial difficulties. The program is accredited by the Master's in Psychology Accreditation Council and is a member of the Council of Applied Master's Programs in Psychology.

Programs and Degrees Offered

Program	Degree	Application Deadline	Applications Received	Accepted	New Admits Enrolled (PT)	Total Enrolled (PT)	Degrees Awarded in 2014–2015	Median Years to Complete Degree	Dismissed/ Withdrew
School Psychology	EdS	March 15 (Fall)	23	14	13 (1)	34 (5)	10	3	1
Clinical Counseling Psychology	MA/MS	March 15 (Fall)	43	21	12 (4)	56 (13)	16	3	9

Internships/Practica

The EdS program in School Psychology requires two practicum courses where students provide services in the public school systems (40 and 125 hours, respectively) and a 1200-hour internship (some are paid), at least 600 of which involve direct services within the public school system. The MA in Clinical Counseling Psychology requires one practicum (150 hours) and one internship (600 hours) where students provide clinical/counseling services in public mental health/substance abuse treatment facilities. These are unpaid field experiences.

Admissions

Entries appear in the following order: required test or GPA, minimum score (if required)/median score of students entering in 2015–2016.

Program	Degree	GRE-V	GRE-Q	GRE-Writing	GRE-Subject	Under-graduate GPA	Last 2 Years GPA	Psychol-ogy GPA	Master's GPA
School Psychology	EdS	153/151	144/149	Not specified	Not specified	3/3.4	Not specified	Not specified	Not specified
Clinical Counseling Psychology	MA/MS	153/157	144/150	Not specified	Not specified	3/3.46	Not specified	Not specified	Not specified

Admissions Requirements:

Degree	GRE	GRE-Subject	Letters of Recommendation	Research Statement	Writing Sample	CV	Interview
Master's/Specialist	Required	Recommended	2	Required	Required	Optional	Required

Please note if these criteria vary for different programs: GRE subject test not used by School Psychology program.

Admissions Criteria:

GRE scores—high
Research experience—medium
Work experience—medium
Clinically related public service—medium
GPA—high

Letters of recommendation—high
Interview—high
Statement of goals and objectives—high
Undergraduate psychology preparation—medium

Department Demographics

	Male (PT)	Female (PT)	Total	African-American/ Black (PT)	Hispanic/ Latino (PT)	Asian/ Pacific Islander (PT)	American Indian/ Alaska Native (PT)	Caucasian/ White (PT)	Unknown (PT)	Multiethnic (PT)	ADA (PT)	Int'l (PT)
Students	11 (0)	71 (8)	90	4 (1)	1 (0)	1 (0)	0 (0)	66 (7)	0 (0)	0 (0)	8 (2)	2 (0)

Financial Information/Assistance

Tuition: For information on tuition costs, visit http://www.citadel.edu/root/tuition-and-fees. Tuition is subject to change. Additional fees are assessed to students beyond the costs of tuition for the following: lab fees in some courses; registration fee; technology fee.

Master's:
State residents: $538 per credit hour.
Nonstate residents: $896 per credit hour.

Financial Assistance:

	Teaching Assistantship (% Receiving)	Teaching Assistantship Tuition Remission	Research Assistantship (% Receiving)	Research Assistantship Tuition Remission	Fellowship (% Receiving)	Fellowship Tuition Remission
First-Year Student	$7,000 (NA)	NA	$7,000 (NA)	NA	NA (NA)	NA
Advanced Student	$7,000 (NA)	NA	$7,000 (NA)	NA	NA (NA)	NA

For additional information on financial assistance, visit http://www.citadel.edu/root/financial-aid-cgc.

Employment of Department Graduates

Master's:
Enrolled in a psychology doctoral program: 1
Employed in an academic position at a university: 1
Employed in other positions at a higher education institution: 1
Employed in a professional position in a school system: 10
Employed in government agency: 1
Employed in a community mental health/counseling center: 9
Other employment position: 1
Do not know: 2
Total: 26

Additional Information

Housing and Day Care: No on-campus housing is available. No on-campus day care facilities are available.

Information for Students With Physical Disabilities: See the following website: http://www.citadel.edu/root/asc-disability-services.

Special Facilities or Resources: The Citadel's Department of Psychology enjoys a strong working relationship with area school districts and agencies that provide mental health/substance abuse services. In addition, the nearby Medical University of South Carolina provides internship opportunities.

Application Information: The Citadel Graduate College, 171 Moultrie Street, Charleston, SC 29409. *Fee:* $40. *Online application:* http://www.citadel.edu/root/graduatecollege-apply/graduate.

Clemson University

Department of Psychology
418 Brackett Hall
Clemson, SC 29634-1355
Telephone: (864) 656-3210
Chairperson: Patrick Raymark

E-mail: rsincla@clemson.edu
Web: http://www.clemson.edu/psych/

Orientation, Objectives, and Emphasis of Department

The faculty of the Psychology Department are committed to excellence in teaching and research. The primary goals of the Master of Science program are to provide students with an essential core of knowledge in applied psychology and to develop applied research skills. The program is specifically designed to provide students with the requisite theoretical foundations, skills in quantitative techniques and experimental design, and the practical problem-solving skills necessary to address real world problems in industry, business, and government. The emphasis is on the direct application of acquired training upon completion of the program. All of our graduate programs have a heavy out-of-the-classroom research component with a required empirical thesis. The PhD programs prepare the student to generate and use knowledge in accordance with the scientist–practitioner model. In addition to the traditional areas of study in Industrial/Organizational Psychology and Human Factors (Engineering) Psychology, a new emphasis area in Occupational Health Psychology has been added to both the MS and PhD degree programs.

Programs and Degrees Offered

Program	Degree	Application Deadline	Applica-tions Received	Accepted	New Admits Enrolled (PT)	Total Enrolled (PT)	Degrees Awarded in 2014–2015	Median Years to Complete Degree	Dismissed/Withdrew
Human Factors	PhD	January 15 (Fall)	40	4	4 (0)	19 (0)	2	5	0
Industrial/ Organizational Psychology	PhD	January 15 (Fall)	144	4	6 (0)	20 (2)	6	5	0
Applied Psychology	MA/MS	January 15 (Fall)	60	1	1	2 (3)	0		1

Internships/Practica

Students typically complete internships or other applied experiences beginning in their second year of the program. The location, content, and length of these experiences varies but nearly all are paid positions.

Admissions

Entries appear in the following order: required test or GPA, minimum score (if required)/median score of students entering in 2015–2016.

Program	Degree	GRE-V	GRE-Q	GRE-Writing	GRE-Subject	Under-graduate GPA	Last 2 Years GPA	Psychol-ogy GPA	Master's GPA
Human Factors	PhD	NA/NA	NA/NA	NA/NA	Not specified	NA/NA	Not specified	Not specified	Not specified

Admissions (con't.)

Program	Degree	GRE-V	GRE-Q	GRE-Writing	GRE-Subject	Under-graduate GPA	Last 2 Years GPA	Psychology GPA	Master's GPA
Industrial/ Organizational Psychology	PhD	NA/NA	NA/NA	NA/NA	Not specified	NA/NA	Not specified	Not specified	Not specified
Applied Psychology	MA/MS	NA/NA	NA/NA	NA/NA	Not specified	NA/NA	Not specified	Not specified	Not specified

Admissions Requirements:

Degree	GRE	GRE-Subject	Letters of Recom-mendation	Research Statement	Writing Sample	CV	Interview
Master's/Specialist	Required	None	3	Required	None	Recom-mended	Required
Doctoral	Required	None	3	Required	None	Recom-mended	Required

Admissions Criteria:

GRE scores—high
Research experience—high
Work experience—low
GPA—high

Letters of recommendation—medium
Interview—medium
Statement of goals and objectives—high
Undergraduate psychology preparation—high

For additional information on admission requirements, visit http://www.clemson.edu/cbbs/departments/psychology/graduate/apply.html.

Department Demographics

	Male (PT)	Female (PT)	Total	African-American/ Black (PT)	Hispanic/ Latino (PT)	Asian/ Pacific Islander (PT)	American Indian/ Alaska Native (PT)	Caucasian/ White (PT)	Unknown	Multiethnic (PT)	ADA (PT)	Int'l (PT)
Students	14 (3)	24 (7)	48	0 (0)	0 (0)	0 (0)	0 (0)	0 (0)	38 (10)	0 (0)	0 (0)	2 (0)

Financial Information/Assistance

Tuition: For information on tuition costs, visit http://grad.clemson.edu/programs/tuition.php. Tuition is subject to change.

Doctoral:
State residents: $10,172 per academic year.
State residents: $1,263 per credit hour.
Nonstate residents: $20,316 per academic year.
Nonstate residents: $1,263 per credit hour.

Master's:
State residents: $10,172 per academic year.
State residents: $630 per credit hour.
Nonstate residents: $20,316 per academic year.
Nonstate residents: $630 per credit hour.

Financial Assistance:

	Teaching Assistantship (% Receiving)	Teaching Assistantship Tuition Remission	Research Assistantship (% Receiving)	Research Assistantship Tuition Remission	Fellowship (% Receiving)	Fellowship Tuition Remission
First-Year Student	$12,000 (NA)	Full	$12,000 (NA)	Full	$7,000 (NA)	NA
Advanced Student	$14,000 (NA)	Full	$14,000 (NA)	Full	$7,000 (NA)	NA

Employment of Department Graduates

Doctoral:
Employed in business or industry: 7
Total: 7

Additional Information

Housing and Day Care: On-campus housing is available. See the following website for more information: http://housing.clemson.edu/. No on-campus day care facilities are available.

Information for Students With Physical Disabilities: See the following website: http://www.clemson.edu/campus-life/campus-services/sds/.

Special Facilities or Resources: The Psychology Department is housed on four floors of Brackett Hall. Students have access to several laboratories, including a Process Control Simulator Lab, Task Performance Lab, Psychophysiology Research Lab, Sleep Research Lab, Perception and Action Lab, Motion Sciences and Uncoupled Motion Simulation Lab, Visual Performance Lab, Driving Simulator Lab, Usability Testing Lab, Personnel Selection and Performance Appraisal Lab, I/O Research Lab, I/O Quant Lab, Social Psychology Lab, Residential Research Facility, Cognitive Aging and Technology Lab, as well as Virtual Reality and Robotics and Teleoperation facilities. To date, nearly 100% of our graduates have either gained employment in their chosen field or have been accepted into PhD programs (in many cases they have had one or more job offers before the completion of their degree). Our Human Factors program is one of only eight Psychology programs accredited by the Human Factors and Ergonomics Society.

Application Information: Fee: $85. *Online application:* https://www.applyweb.com/clemsong/.

Francis Marion University (2015 data)

Department of Psychology
P.O. Box 100547
Florence, SC 29502
Telephone: (843) 661-1641
Chairperson: William P. Wattles, PhD

E-mail: wwattles@fmarion.edu
Web: http://fmupsychology.com/graduate-studies/

Orientation, Objectives, and Emphasis of Department

The primary purpose of the program is to prepare professionals for employment in human services agencies, schools, or similar settings. The program also provides for the continuing education of those individuals currently employed in the helping professions and prepares students for further graduate study.

Programs and Degrees Offered

Program	Degree	Application Deadline	Applications Received	Accepted	New Admits Enrolled (PT)	Total Enrolled (PT)	Degrees Awarded in 2014–2015	Median Years to Complete Degree	Dismissed/ Withdrew
Clinical/ Counseling Psychology	MA/MS	February 15 (Fall), October 15 (Spring)	23	21	9 (0)	29 (1)	7	2.5	1
Specialist in School Psychology	Other	February 15 (Fall)	24	10	8	24	6	3	

Internships/Practica

Internships occur in a variety of community settings. Typically Clinical/Counseling students complete a full-time 6-month internship in state human service agencies. The School Psychology internship is a full-time experience as a school psychologist during a Fall and Spring semester. All interns develop a broad array of skills under supervision.

Admissions

Entries appear in the following order: required test or GPA, minimum score (if required)/median score of students entering in 2015–2016.

Program	Degree	GRE-V	GRE-Q	GRE-Writing	GRE-Subject	Under-graduate GPA	Last 2 Years GPA	Psychol-ogy GPA	Master's GPA
Clinical/ Counseling Psychology	MA/MS	145/NA	145/NA	4/NA	Not specified	3/NA	Not specified	3/NA	Not specified
Specialist in School Psychology	Other	145/152	145/149	4/4	Not specified	3/NA	Not specified	3/NA	Not specified

Admissions Requirements:

Degree	GRE	GRE-Subject	Letters of Recom-mendation	Research Statement	Writing Sample	CV	Interview
Master's/Specialist	Required	None	2	Required	Optional	Optional	None

Admissions Criteria:

GRE scores—high
Research experience—medium
Work experience—medium
Clinically related public service—medium

GPA—high
Letters of recommendation—high
Statement of goals and objectives—high

For additional information on admission requirements, visit http://fmupsychology.com/graduate-studies/admissions/.

Department Demographics

	Male (PT)	Female (PT)	Total	African-American/ Black (PT)	Hispanic/ Latino (PT)	Asian/ Pacific Islander (PT)	American Indian/ Alaska Native (PT)	Caucasian/ White (PT)	Unknown (PT)	Multiethnic (PT)	ADA (PT)	Int'l (PT)
Students	6 (0)	47 (0)	53	7 (1)	1 (1)	0 (0)	1 (0)	44 (0)	0 (0)	0 (0)	0 (0)	2 (0)

Financial Information/Assistance

Tuition: For information on tuition costs, visit http://www.fmarion.edu/about/fees/. Tuition is subject to change.

Master's:
State residents: $9,472 per academic year.
State residents: $473 per credit hour.
Nonstate residents: $19,460 per academic year.
Nonstate residents: $947 per credit hour.

Financial Assistance:

	Teaching Assistantship (% Receiving)	Teaching Assistantship Tuition Remission	Research Assistantship (% Receiving)	Research Assistantship Tuition Remission	Fellowship (% Receiving)	Fellowship Tuition Remission
First-Year Student	$8,000 (NA)	NA	$7,000 (NA)	NA	$500 (NA)	Partial
Advanced Student	$8,000 (NA)	NA	$7,000 (NA)	NA	$500 (NA)	Partial

For additional information on financial assistance, visit http://fmupsychology.com/graduate-studies/financial-resources/.

Employment of Department Graduates

No information provided.

Additional Information

Housing and Day Care: On-campus housing is available. See the following website for more information: http://www.fmuhousing. com/. On-campus day care facilities are available. See the following website for more information: http://www.centerforthechild.org/.

Information for Students With Physical Disabilities: See the following website: http://www.fmarion.edu/students/disabilityservices.

Special Facilities or Resources: The department has excellent laboratory facilities on campus including a computer laboratory. Regional human services facilities, community agencies, and school districts are accessible off campus. In addition, the Richardson Center for the Child is located on campus and provides opportunities for observation as well as training of graduate students.

Application Information: Sharekka Bridges, Administrative Associate, Department of Psychology, Francis Marion University, P.O. Box 100547, Florence, SC 29502-0547. *Fee:* $35.

South Carolina, University of
Department of Psychology
College of Arts and Sciences
1512 Pendleton Street
Columbia, SC 29208
Telephone: (803) 777-2312
Professor & Department Chair: Douglas H. Wedell

E-mail: escorcia@mailbox.sc.edu
Web: http://www.psych.sc.edu/

Orientation, Objectives, and Emphasis of Department

The USC Department of Psychology has an interdisciplinary research emphasis in quantitative methods, developmental cognitive neuroscience, neurodevelopmental disorders, prevention science, reading and language, and ethnic minority health and mental health. Students in the Experimental Psychology program can pursue research interests in behavioral neuroscience, cognitive neuroscience, cognitive, developmental, and quantitative psychology built on broad scientific training in experimental psychology. The School Psychology program includes emphases in child assessment, individual and group consultation, educational research, and professional roles. In Clinical-Community Psychology, there is a wide latitude of choices: assessment, psychotherapy and behavioral interventions, community psychology, and consultation. Regular clinical-community training includes both adults and children, with an option of special emphasis on children or community settings.

Programs and Degrees Offered

Program	Degree	Application Deadline	Applica-tions Received	Accepted	New Admits Enrolled (PT)	Total Enrolled (PT)	Degrees Awarded in 2014–2015	Median Years to Complete Degree	Dismissed/ Withdrew
Clinical-Community Psychology	PhD	December 1 (Fall)	167	12	7 (0)	42 (1)	12	6.87	0
Experimental Psychology	PhD	December 1 (Fall)	29	4	3 (0)	21 (0)	2	4.5	1
School Psychology	PhD	December 1 (Fall)	34	6	5 (0)	26 (0)	6	5.16	0

APA Accreditation

Clinical PhD: Student Outcome Data website: http://www.psych.sc.edu/clinical-community-program-0.
School PhD: Student Outcome Data website: http://psych.sc.edu/school-program.

Doctoral Degree (PhD Clinical-Community Psychology): For those doctoral students for whom a professional internship was required in this program prior to graduation:
Total students who applied for an internship: 9
Total students who obtained an internship: 8
Total students who obtained a paid internship: 8

Total students who obtained an unpaid internship: 0
Total students who were placed in APA/CPA-accredited internships: 5
Total students placed in internships not APA/CPA-accredited, but listed with the Association of Psychology Postdoctoral and Internship Centers (APPIC): 0
Total students placed in internships conforming to guidelines of the Council of Directors of School Psychology Programs (CDSPP): 0
Total students placed in internships that were not APA/CPA-accredited, APPIC or CDSSP listed: 3

Doctoral Degree (PhD School Psychology): For those doctoral students for whom a professional internship was required in this program prior to graduation:
Total students who applied for an internship: 4
Total students who obtained an internship: 4
Total students who obtained a paid internship: 4
Total students who obtained an unpaid internship: 0
Total students who were placed in APA/CPA-accredited internships: 3
Total students placed in internships not APA/CPA-accredited, but listed with the Association of Psychology Postdoctoral and Internship Centers (APPIC): 0
Total students placed in internships conforming to guidelines of the Council of Directors of School Psychology Programs (CDSPP): 1
Total students placed in internships that were not APA/CPA-accredited, APPIC or CDSSP listed: 0

Internships/Practica

Students in School Psychology and Clinical-Community Psychology complete practicum classes throughout their program of study; they are often conducted at the Psychological Services Center, which provides services to the diverse community of Columbia. In addition, many students seek externships in other local agencies which have longstanding ties to the School and Clinical-Community programs. Every student in the APA-accredited programs completes 1 full year of internship at the end of their program, often at APA-accredited internship locations.

Admissions

Entries appear in the following order: required test or GPA, minimum score (if required)/median score of students entering in 2015–2016.

Program	Degree	GRE-V	GRE-Q	GRE-Writing	GRE-Subject	Undergraduate GPA	Last 2 Years GPA	Psychology GPA	Master's GPA
Clinical-Community Psychology	PhD	NA/162	NA/156	NA/4.5	Not specified	NA/3.62	NA/3.75	NA/3.7	Not specified
Experimental Psychology	PhD	NA/162	NA/160	NA/4.6	Not specified	NA/3.82	NA/3.5	Not specified	Not specified
School Psychology	PhD	NA/157	NA/156	NA/4.1	Not specified	NA/3.69	NA/3.5	NA/3.5	Not specified

Admissions Requirements:

Degree	GRE	GRE-Subject	Letters of Recommendation	Research Statement	Writing Sample	CV	Interview
Doctoral	Required	Recommended	3	Required	Optional	Required	Required

Admissions Criteria:

GRE scores—medium
Research experience—high
Work experience—medium
Clinically related public service—medium
GPA—high

Letters of recommendation—high
Interview—high
Statement of goals and objectives—high
Undergraduate psychology preparation—high

Department Demographics

	Male (PT)	Female (PT)	Total	African-American/ Black (PT)	Hispanic/ Latino (PT)	Asian/ Pacific Islander (PT)	American Indian/ Alaska Native (PT)	Caucasian/ White (PT)	Unknown	Multiethnic (PT)	ADA (PT)	Int'l (PT)
Students	26 (1)	61 (0)	88	5 (0)	2 (0)	7 (0)	1 (0)	69 (1)	0 (0)	3 (0)	0 (0)	7 (0)

Financial Information/Assistance

Tuition: For information on tuition costs, visit http://www.sc.edu/bursar/fees.shtml. Tuition is subject to change. Additional fees are assessed to students beyond the costs of tuition for the following: Technology fee, lab fees, & health insurance.

Doctoral:
State residents: $12,384 per academic year.
State residents: $516 per credit hour.
Nonstate residents: $26,520 per academic year.
Nonstate residents: $1,105 per credit hour.

Master's:
State residents: $12,384 per academic year.
State residents: $516 per credit hour.
Nonstate residents: $26,520 per academic year.
Nonstate residents: $1,105 per credit hour.

Financial Assistance:

	Teaching Assistantship (% Receiving)	Teaching Assistantship Tuition Remission	Research Assistantship (% Receiving)	Research Assistantship Tuition Remission	Fellowship (% Receiving)	Fellowship Tuition Remission
First-Year Student	$16,250 (93)	Full	$16,250 (6)	Full	$8,000 (33)	Full
Advanced Student	$16,250 (34)	Full	$16,250 (10)	Full	$9,214 (22)	Full

For additional information on financial assistance, visit http://gradschool.sc.edu/prospective/paying.asp?page=paying.

Employment of Department Graduates

Doctoral:
Enrolled in a postdoctoral residency/fellowship: 12
Employed in independent practice: 1
Employed in an academic position at a university: 1
Employed in a professional position in a school system: 1
Employed in business or industry: 1
Employed in government agency: 1
Employed in a community mental health/counseling center: 1
Employed in a hospital/medical center: 2
Total: 20

Additional Information

Housing and Day Care: No on-campus housing is available. On-campus day care facilities are available. See the following website for more information: http://www.sc.edu/childrenscenter/usccdc.shtml.

Information for Students With Physical Disabilities: See the following website: http://www.sa.sc.edu/sds/.

Special Facilities or Resources: The special facilities and resources of the department include the university-directed Psychology Services Center, the USC Medical School, the VA hospital, mental health centers and other educational and mental health service settings. Other laboratories include the Experimental and Cognitive Processing Labs, the Infant Attention Lab, Judgment and Decision-Making Lab, and Attention and Perception Lab. We are actively involved in community agencies,and the psychiatric training institution.

Application Information: The Graduate School at USC, 901 Sumter Street, Suite 301, Columbia SC, 29208. *Fee:* $50. *Online application:* http://gradschool.sc.edu/prospective/apply.asp?page=apply.

South Carolina, University of, Aiken

Psychology
471 University Parkway
Aiken, SC 29801
Telephone: (803) 641-3358
Chairperson: Ed Callen

E-mail: jstafford@usca.edu
Web: http://web.usca.edu/psychology/academics/ms-psychology/index.dot

Orientation, Objectives, and Emphasis of Department

Our program provides graduate study and clinical experience in preparation for careers in applied clinical and counseling settings and as a foundation for students interested in pursuing doctoral studies. Students enrolled in this program are expected to pursue a plan of study to ensure increased professional competence and breadth of knowledge in the field of clinical and counseling psychology. The degree objectives are designed to enable the student to understand principles of psychology and how they are applied; understand a diversity of theoretical perspectives; interpret and apply statistical and research techniques; understand professional, legal, and ethical principles as they pertain to professional conduct and responsibility; and understand and develop skills in assessment procedures and intervention strategies. A strong emphasis is placed on the need to train students within the tradition of the scientist–practitioner guidelines espoused by the Council of Applied Master's Programs in Psychology. It is the belief of faculty that the master's-level practitioner is well-served by participation in conducting an empirical thesis project and that the critical-thinking skills so essential to sound clinical decision-making are enhanced through research experience. Our program is fully accredited by the Masters in Psychology and Counseling Accreditation Council.

Programs and Degrees Offered

Program	Degree	Application Deadline	Applications Received	Accepted	New Admits Enrolled (PT)	Total Enrolled (PT)	Degrees Awarded in 2014–2015	Median Years to Complete Degree	Dismissed/Withdrew
Applied Clinical Psychology	MA/MS	April 1 (Fall)	44	21	10 (1)	20 (7)	7	2.5	0

Internships/Practica

Most students have paid assistantships in which they work in an agency in the community or on campus. The assistantships for first-year students are in settings such as the school system and developmental centers while second-year students are in agencies such as psychiatric hospitals and the student counseling center, conducting assessments, and/or providing psychotherapy. In addition, we have a training clinic in our department where advanced graduate students conduct individual and group therapy with children and adults and various types of psychological evaluations. Each student is required to take a minimum of two semesters of practicum in which they receive training in the clinic.

Admissions

Entries appear in the following order: required test or GPA, minimum score (if required)/median score of students entering in 2015–2016.

Program	Degree	GRE-V	GRE-Q	GRE-Writing	GRE-Subject	Undergraduate GPA	Last 2 Years GPA	Psychology GPA	Master's GPA
Applied Clinical Psychology	MA/MS	147/156	142/152	2.5/4	Not specified	2.8/3.5	Not specified	3.2/3.75	Not specified

Admissions Requirements:

Degree	GRE	GRE-Subject	Letters of Recommendation	Research Statement	Writing Sample	CV	Interview
Master's/Specialist	Required	Optional	3	Required	Optional	Optional	Required

Admissions Criteria:

GRE scores—high
Research experience—medium
Work experience—low
Clinically related public service—low
GPA—high

Letters of recommendation—high
Interview—medium
Statement of goals and objectives—medium
Undergraduate psychology preparation—high
Conference presentations—medium

For additional information on admission requirements, visit http://web.usca.edu/psychology/academics/ms-psychology/admission.dot.

Department Demographics

	Male (PT)	Female (PT)	Total	African-American/ Black (PT)	Hispanic/ Latino (PT)	Asian/ Pacific Islander (PT)	American Indian/ Alaska Native (PT)	Caucasian/ White (PT)	Unknown	Multiethnic (PT)	ADA (PT)	Int'l (PT)
Students	6 (2)	14 (5)	27	2 (0)	0 (0)	0 (0)	0 (0)	18 (6)	0 (0)	0 (1)	0 (0)	0 (0)

Financial Information/Assistance

Tuition: For information on tuition costs, visit http://web.usca.edu/finance/cost_attendance.dot. Tuition is subject to change.

Master's:
State residents: $12,386 per academic year.
State residents: $516 per credit hour.
Nonstate residents: $26,632 per academic year.
Nonstate residents: $1,106 per credit hour.

Financial Assistance:

	Teaching Assistantship (% Receiving)	Teaching Assistantship Tuition Remission	Research Assistantship (% Receiving)	Research Assistantship Tuition Remission	Fellowship (% Receiving)	Fellowship Tuition Remission
First-Year Student	$5,000 (50)	Partial	NA (NA)	NA	NA (NA)	NA
Advanced Student	$5,000 (0)	Partial	NA (NA)	NA	NA (NA)	NA

For additional information on financial assistance, visit http://web.usca.edu/psychology/academics/ms-psychology/financial-aid.dot.

Employment of Department Graduates

Master's:
Enrolled in a psychology doctoral program: 1
Employed in a professional position in a school system: 1
Employed in government agency: 1
Employed in a community mental health/counseling center: 4
Total: 7

Additional Information

Housing and Day Care: On-campus housing is available. See the following website for more information: http://web.usca.edu/housing/. On-campus day care facilities are available. See the following website for more information: http://web.usca.edu/childrens-center/.

Information for Students With Physical Disabilities: See the following website: http://web.usca.edu/ds/index.dot.

Special Facilities or Resources: We have an animal vivarium and a psychophysiology laboratory. Graduate students may collect their thesis data utilizing either of these facilities or other research facilities in our department or external to the department such as a nearby army base.

Application Information: Dan Robb, Coordinator Graduate Studies, USCA Graduate Office, 471 University Parkway, Aiken, SC 29801. *Fee:* $45. *Online application:* http://web.usca.edu/applynow/.

Winthrop University
Department of Psychology
Arts and Sciences
135 Kinard
Rock Hill, SC 29733
Telephone: (803) 323-2117
Chairperson: Dr. Joe Prus

E-mail: prusj@winthrop.edu
Web: http://www.winthrop.edu/psychology/

Orientation, Objectives, and Emphasis of Department
The Winthrop School Psychology Program prepares practitioners who are competent to provide a full range of school psychological services, including consultation, academic and behavioral intervention, psychoeducational assessment, research and evaluation, and counseling. The 3-year, full-time program leading to both MS and Specialist in School Psychology degrees qualifies graduates for state and national certification as a school psychologist pending attainment of a passing score on the Praxis II exam in school psychology. The program has an outstanding pass rate on the exam, and record of graduate employment. We emphasize evidence-based psychological and psychoeducational methods. Students are prepared to work with diverse clients from birth to adulthood, and with families, teachers, and others in the schools and community. The program includes an applied, competency-based approach to training that progresses sequentially from foundations and practicum courses to a 450-hour traineeship to a 1,200-hour internship and affords maximum individualized supervision. Faculty represent considerable ethnic and experiential diversity. All have advanced degrees and credentials in school psychology; are active in the profession at local, state, and national levels; and view teaching and supervision as their primary roles. Faculty emphasize collaboration among and support for students.

Programs and Degrees Offered

Program	Degree	Application Deadline	Applications Received	Accepted	New Admits Enrolled (PT)	Total Enrolled (PT)	Degrees Awarded in 2014–2015	Median Years to Complete Degree	Dismissed/Withdrew
School Psychology	EdS	January 15 (Fall)	40	11	11 (0)	27 (0)	8	3	0

Internships/Practica
The program provides paid traineeships during the second year and paid internships during the third year in area school districts. Rural, suburban, and urban field settings include diverse student/client populations. The internship includes a full range of school psychological services. Each intern receives individual supervision from both a faculty member and a field-based, credentialed supervisor.

Admissions
Entries appear in the following order: required test or GPA, minimum score (if required)/median score of students entering in 2015–2016.

Program	Degree	GRE-V	GRE-Q	GRE-Writing	GRE-Subject	Under-graduate GPA	Last 2 Years GPA	Psychol-ogy GPA	Master's GPA
School Psychology	EdS	NA/155	NA/148	NA/4	Not specified	NA/3.6	NA/3.7	NA/3.7	Not specified

Admissions Requirements:

Degree	GRE	GRE-Subject	Letters of Recom-mendation	Research Statement	Writing Sample	CV	Interview
Master's/Specialist	Required	None	3	Required	Required	Required	Required

Admissions Criteria:

GRE scores—medium
Research experience—low
Work experience—medium
Clinically related public service—medium
GPA—high

Letters of recommendation—medium
Interview—high
Statement of goals and objectives—medium
Undergraduate psychology preparation—medium
Experience with children—high

For additional information on admission requirements, visit http://www.winthrop.edu/cas/psychology/default-grad.aspx?id=26690.

Department Demographics

	Male (PT)	Female (PT)	Total	African-American/ Black (PT)	Hispanic/ Latino (PT)	Asian/ Pacific Islander (PT)	American Indian/ Alaska Native (PT)	Caucasian/ White (PT)	Unknown	Multiethnic (PT)	ADA (PT)	Int'l (PT)
Students	0 (0)	27 (0)	27	4 (0)	1 (0)	0 (0)	0 (0)	21 (0)	0 (0)	1 (0)	0 (0)	0 (0)

Financial Information/Assistance

Tuition: For information on tuition costs, visit http://www.winthrop.edu/graduateschool/default.aspx?id=5598. Tuition is subject to change. Additional fees are assessed to students beyond the costs of tuition for the following: small lab fees in assessment courses.

Master's:
State residents: $13,828 per academic year.
State residents: $579 per credit hour.
Nonstate residents: $20,910 per academic year.
Nonstate residents: $872 per credit hour.

Financial Assistance:

	Teaching Assistantship (% Receiving)	Teaching Assistantship Tuition Remission	Research Assistantship (% Receiving)	Research Assistantship Tuition Remission	Fellowship (% Receiving)	Fellowship Tuition Remission
First-Year Student	$3,600 (50)	Partial	$3,600 (30)	Partial	NA (NA)	NA
Advanced Student	$4,500 (100)	Partial	NA (NA)	NA	NA (NA)	NA

For additional information on financial assistance, visit http://www.winthrop.edu/graduateschool/default.aspx?id=4497.

Employment of Department Graduates

Master's:
Employed in a professional position in a school system: 8
Total: 8

Additional Information

Housing and Day Care: On-campus housing is available. See the following website for more information: http://www.winthrop.edu/reslife/default.aspx. On-campus day care facilities are available. See the following website for more information: https://www.winthrop.edu/macfeat/default.aspx.

Information for Students With Physical Disabilities: See the following website: http://www.winthrop.edu/disabilities/.

Special Facilities or Resources: Winthrop University is a state-supported institution of about 6,500 students which provides students with access to a state-of-the-art health center, campus center, university library, and a variety of other resources. Access to such department resources as a graduate student workroom, computer lab, and school psychology mini-library and assessment resource center is also available. Winthrop's 418-acre campus is located in the greater Charlotte, NC area, which includes a great variety of resources which may be of personal or professional interest to graduate students in school psychology.

Application Information: The Graduate School, Winthrop University, Rock Hill, SC 29733. *Fee:* $50. *Online application:* http://www.winthrop.edu/graduateschool/.

South Dakota State University

Department of Psychology
College of Arts and Sciences
Scobey Hall
Brookings, SD 57007
Telephone: (605) 688-4927
Department Head: Dr. Bradley Woldt

E-mail: Bradley.Woldt@sdstate.edu
Web: http://www.sdstate.edu/psych/index.cfm

Orientation, Objectives, and Emphasis of Department

The MS degree in Industrial/Organizational (I/O) Psychology at SDSU is designed to train students in the core competencies of I/O Psychology and prepare them with the knowledge and skills necessary for a successful career in the workplace. The curriculum is based on a scientist–practitioner model, which balances the training of research and applied skills, and is the basis of training in the field. The curriculum is designed to be completed in 2 years and follows a cohort model where students progress through the program together. The curriculum provides disciplinary breadth, as students will take content in the areas of Industrial Psychology, Organizational Psychology, Statistics and Applied Research Methods, as well as complete an internship and a master's thesis.

Programs and Degrees Offered

Program	Degree	Application Deadline	Applications Received	Accepted	New Admits Enrolled (PT)	Total Enrolled (PT)	Degrees Awarded in 2014–2015	Median Years to Complete Degree	Dismissed/ Withdrew
Industrial/ Organizational Psychology	MA/MS	March 1 (Fall)	0	0	0 (0)	0 (0)	0		0

Internships/Practica

An internship is required in the I/O program to be completed during the summer term between the first and second year. Students will work in business or government organizations and apply the psychological theories they have learned and practiced in the classroom to real world situations. The psychology department has secured several internship sites and will facilitate a match between each student's interests and potential placement sites. These internships are typically paid. In addition, traineeships are available during the academic year. Average amount paid per academic year for traineeships is $6,250 for an average of 10 hours worked per week. Traineeships also include tuition remission.

Admissions

Entries appear in the following order: required test or GPA, minimum score (if required)/median score of students entering in 2015–2016.

Program	Degree	GRE-V	GRE-Q	GRE-Writing	GRE-Subject	Under-graduate GPA	Last 2 Years GPA	Psychol-ogy GPA	Master's GPA
Industrial/ Organizational Psychology	MA/MS	Not specified	Not specified	Not specified	Not specified	Not specified	Not specified	Not specified	Not specified

Admissions Requirements:

Degree	GRE	GRE-Subject	Letters of Recom-mendation	Research Statement	Writing Sample	CV	Interview
Master's/Specialist	Required	None	3	Required	Required	Required	Required

Admissions Criteria:

GRE scores—high
Research experience—high
Work experience—medium
Clinically related public service—low
GPA—high

Letters of recommendation—high
Interview—high
Statement of goals and objectives—high
Undergraduate psychology preparation—high

For additional information on admission requirements, visit http://www.sdstate.edu/psych/graduate-programs/apply.cfm.

Department Demographics

	Male (PT)	Female (PT)	Total	African-American/ Black (PT)	Hispanic/ Latino (PT)	Asian/ Pacific Islander (PT)	American Indian/ Alaska Native (PT)	Caucasian/ White (PT)	Unknown	Multiethnic (PT)	ADA (PT)	Int'l (PT)
Students	0 (0)	0 (0)	0	0 (0)	0 (0)	0 (0)	0 (0)	0 (0)	0 (0)	0 (0)	0 (0)	0 (0)

Financial Information/Assistance

Tuition: For information on tuition costs, visit http://www.sdstate.edu/graduate/prospective/tuition.cfm. Tuition is subject to change. Additional fees are assessed to students beyond the costs of tuition for the following: University Support Fee and General Activity Fee.

Master's:
State residents: $4,840 per academic year.
State residents: $220 per credit hour.
Nonstate residents: $10,208 per academic year.
Nonstate residents: $464 per credit hour.

Financial Assistance:

	Teaching Assistantship (% Receiving)	Teaching Assistantship Tuition Remission	Research Assistantship (% Receiving)	Research Assistantship Tuition Remission	Fellowship (% Receiving)	Fellowship Tuition Remission
First-Year Student	$6,250 (25)	Full	NA (NA)	NA	NA (NA)	NA
Advanced Student	NA (NA)	NA	NA (NA)	NA	NA (NA)	NA

Employment of Department Graduates

No information provided.

Additional Information

Housing and Day Care: On-campus housing is available. See the following website for more information: http://www.sdstate.edu/reslife/index.cfm. No on-campus day care facilities are available.

Information for Students With Physical Disabilities: See the following website: http://www.sdstate.edu/campus/disability/index.cfm.

Application Information: South Dakota State University Graduate School. *Fee:* $35. *Online application:* https://app.applyyourself.com/?id=SDSTATE-G.

South Dakota, University of
Department of Psychology
414 East Clark Street
Vermillion, SD 57069
Telephone: (605) 677-5351
Chairperson: Randal Quevillon

E-mail: Randy.Quevillon@usd.edu
Web: http://www.usd.edu/arts-and-sciences/psychology/

Orientation, Objectives, and Emphasis of Department
The Department of Psychology seeks to develop scholars who can contribute to the expansion of psychological knowledge. The major goals of the Clinical program are to increase students' knowledge of, and identification with, psychology as a method of inquiry about human behavior and to provide students with the theory, skills, and experience to function in a professional, research, or academic capacity. Training is provided in traditional areas as well as disaster psychology, rural community psychology, cross-cultural issues (particularly work with American Indian populations), and women's issues. The experience serves to broaden professional competencies and increase the versatility of the program's graduates. The overall mission of Human Factors program is to improve living and working through knowledge of the abilities and limitations of the person part of human-machine or socio-technical systems. The program's goal is to train doctoral-level professionals qualified to do research in industry, government, and universities. All graduate students conduct empirical investigations. In recent years, the Human Factors Laboratory has supported studies of information processing, human-computer interfaces, motor performance, program evaluation and testing, traffic safety, and transportation systems.

Programs and Degrees Offered

Program	Degree	Application Deadline	Applica-tions Received	Accepted	New Admits Enrolled (PT)	Total Enrolled (PT)	Degrees Awarded in 2014–2015	Median Years to Complete Degree	Dismissed/Withdrew
Clinical Psychology	PhD	December 15 (Fall)	84	6	6 (0)	36 (0)	7	7.8	1
Human Factors	PhD	February 15 (Fall)	5	3	2	12 (0)	3	6	0

APA Accreditation
Clinical PhD: Student Outcome Data website: http://www.usd.edu/arts-and-sciences/clinical-psychology/student-admissions.

Doctoral Degree (PhD Clinical Psychology): For those doctoral students for whom a professional internship was required in this program prior to graduation:
Total students who applied for an internship: 8
Total students who obtained an internship: 8
Total students who obtained a paid internship: 8
Total students who obtained an unpaid internship: 0
Total students who were placed in APA/CPA-accredited internships: 8
Total students placed in internships not APA/CPA-accredited, but listed with the Association of Psychology Postdoctoral and Internship Centers (APPIC): 0
Total students placed in internships conforming to guidelines of the Council of Directors of School Psychology Programs (CDSPP): 0
Total students placed in internships that were not APA/CPA-accredited, APPIC or CDSSP listed: 0

Internships/Practica
Several internships are available in Human Factors; placements with IBM, Lockheed, Hewlett-Packard, and Intel have been recent examples. In Clinical, a 12-month internship is required in the final year, and we are proud of the record our students have achieved in obtaining top placements. We also have available a series of paid clinical placements. In addition, many graduate courses include practicum components, and clinical students are placed on practicum teams through the Psychological Services Center each semester.

Admissions

Entries appear in the following order: required test or GPA, minimum score (if required)/median score of students entering in 2015–2016.

Program	Degree	GRE-V	GRE-Q	GRE-Writing	GRE-Subject	Under-graduate GPA	Last 2 Years GPA	Psychol-ogy GPA	Master's GPA
Clinical Psychology	PhD	NA/157	NA/152	NA/NA	Not specified	NA/3.5	Not specified	Not specified	Not specified
Human Factors	PhD	NA/NA	NA/NA	Not specified	Not specified	3/NA	Not specified	Not specified	Not specified

Admissions Requirements:

Degree	GRE	GRE-Subject	Letters of Recom-mendation	Research Statement	Writing Sample	CV	Interview
Doctoral	Required	Recom-mended	3	Required	Optional	Required	Required

Please note if these criteria vary for different programs: Applicant's responses to the Supplemental Application questions are highly weighted in the Clinical program admissions process. The Clinical program requires an interview and the Human Factors program does not.

Admissions Criteria:

GRE scores—medium
Research experience—high
Work experience—medium
Clinically related public service—medium
GPA—medium

Letters of recommendation—high
Interview—high
Statement of goals and objectives—medium
Match with program—high

For additional information on admission requirements, visit http://www.usd.edu/arts-and-sciences/psychology/graduate.

Department Demographics

	Male (PT)	Female (PT)	Total	African-American/ Black (PT)	Hispanic/ Latino (PT)	Asian/ Pacific Islander (PT)	American Indian/ Alaska Native (PT)	Caucasian/ White (PT)	Unknown	Multiethnic (PT)	ADA (PT)	Int'l (PT)
Students	22 (0)	26 (0)	48	1 (0)	2 (0)	4 (0)	1 (0)	40 (0)	0 (0)	0 (0)	0 (0)	0 (0)

Financial Information/Assistance

Tuition: For information on tuition costs, visit http://www.usd.edu/financial-affairs/business-office/tuition-and-fees/graduate. Tuition is subject to change.

Doctoral:
State residents: $219 per credit hour.
Nonstate residents: $464 per credit hour.

Financial Assistance:

	Teaching Assistantship (% Receiving)	Teaching Assistantship Tuition Remission	Research Assistantship (% Receiving)	Research Assistantship Tuition Remission	Fellowship (% Receiving)	Fellowship Tuition Remission
First-Year Student	$7,256 (NA)	Partial	$7,256 (NA)	Partial	$9,000 (NA)	Partial
Advanced Student	$7,256 (NA)	Partial	$8,000 (NA)	Partial	$10,000 (NA)	Partial

For additional information on financial assistance, visit http://www.usd.edu/financial-aid/applying-for-aid/graduate-financial-aid.

Employment of Department Graduates

Doctoral:
Enrolled in a postdoctoral residency/fellowship: 1
Employed in academic position at a 2-year/4-year college: 1
Employed in other positions at a higher education institution: 1
Employed in government agency: 1
Employed in a community mental health/counseling center: 1
Employed in a hospital/medical center: 1
Still seeking employment: 1
Total: 7

Additional Information

Housing and Day Care: On-campus housing is available. See the following website for more information: http://www.usd.edu/student-life/university-housing. On-campus day care facilities are available. See the following website for more information: http://www.usd.edu/student-life/childrens-center.

Information for Students With Physical Disabilities: See the following website: http://www.usd.edu/student-life/disability-services.

Special Facilities or Resources: Available to all psychology graduate students are computer lab facilities including word processing and statistical analysis software. Microcomputers are also easily accessible within the department for personal computing and research purposes. Much general purpose, highly adaptable research equipment is available to both Clinical and Human Factors students. The Human Factors Laboratory is particularly well-equipped for experimentation within the specialty areas of current interest to associated faculty. The Department houses the Disaster Mental Health Institute, a South Dakota Board of Regents Center of Excellence, which provides unique research and service opportunities for graduate students as well as specialized coursework and assistantships. The Psychological Services Center, which supplies clinical services for both University students and the general public, accepts referrals from physicians, schools, and other community and state agencies. The Center has offices equipped for a variety of diagnostic and therapeutic activities, including neuropsychological work. The Department's students take full advantage of training and experience available at local, state, and regional mental health facilities.

Application Information: Dean, Graduate School, University of South Dakota, 414 East Clark Street, Vermilion, SD 57069-2390. *Fee:* $35. *Online application:* http://www.usd.edu/graduate-school/apply-now.

Austin Peay State University
Department of Psychological Science & Counseling
601 College Street
Clarksville, TN 37044
Telephone: (931) 221-7232
Chairperson: Dr. Nicole Knickmeyer

E-mail: knickmeyern@apsu.edu
Web: http://www.apsu.edu/psychology/

Orientation, Objectives, and Emphasis of Department

The programs in the department are based on the concept that both a strong foundation in theoretical principles and the development of skills in the application of these principles and techniques is necessary in the training of psychologists or counselors. The Master of Science in Industrial/Organizational (MSIO) Psychology is an online degree program. The program educates students to design, develop, implement, and evaluate psychologically based human resources interventions in organizations.

Programs and Degrees Offered

Program	Degree	Application Deadline	Applica-tions Received	Accepted	New Admits Enrolled (PT)	Total Enrolled (PT)	Degrees Awarded in 2014–2015	Median Years to Complete Degree	Dismissed/ Withdrew
Industrial/ Organizational Psychology	MA/MS	March 1 (Fall), November 1 (Spring)	53	22	17 (2)	41 (4)	12		0

Admissions

Entries appear in the following order: required test or GPA, minimum score (if required)/median score of students entering in 2015–2016.

Program	Degree	GRE-V	GRE-Q	GRE-Writing	GRE-Subject	Under-graduate GPA	Last 2 Years GPA	Psychol-ogy GPA	Master's GPA
Industrial/ Organizational Psychology	MA/MS	143/NA	138/NA	Not specified	Not specified	3/NA	Not specified	Not specified	Not specified

Admissions Requirements:

Degree	GRE	GRE-Subject	Letters of Recom-mendation	Research Statement	Writing Sample	CV	Interview
Master's/Specialist	Required	Optional	3	Required	None	Optional	None

Admissions Criteria:

GRE scores—high
Research experience—low
GPA—high

Letters of recommendation—medium
Statement of goals and objectives—medium
Undergraduate psychology preparation—medium

For additional information on admission requirements, visit http://www.apsu.edu/ioprogram/admission.

Department Demographics

	Male (PT)	Female (PT)	Total	African-American/ Black (PT)	Hispanic/ Latino (PT)	Asian/ Pacific Islander (PT)	American Indian/ Alaska Native (PT)	Caucasian/ White (PT)	Unknown	Multiethnic (PT)	ADA (PT)	Int'l (PT)
Students	0 (0)	0 (0)	0	0 (0)	0 (0)	0 (0)	0 (0)	0 (0)	0 (0)	0 (0)	0 (0)	0 (0)

Financial Information/Assistance

Tuition: For information on tuition costs, visit http://www.apsu.edu/bursar/tuition. Tuition is subject to change. Additional fees are assessed to students beyond the costs of tuition for the following: technology access fee, general access fee.

Master's:
State residents: $6,600 per academic year.
State residents: $364 per credit hour.
Nonstate residents: $18,180 per academic year.
Nonstate residents: $1,010 per credit hour.

Financial Assistance:

	Teaching Assistantship (% Receiving)	Teaching Assistantship Tuition Remission	Research Assistantship (% Receiving)	Research Assistantship Tuition Remission	Fellowship (% Receiving)	Fellowship Tuition Remission
First-Year Student	NA (NA)	Partial	NA (NA)	NA	NA (NA)	NA
Advanced Student	NA (NA)	Partial	NA (NA)	NA	NA (NA)	NA

For additional information on financial assistance, visit http://www.apsu.edu/financialaid/.

Employment of Department Graduates

Master's:
Enrolled in a psychology doctoral program: 2
Employed in an academic position at a university: 2
Employed in academic position at a 2-year/4-year college: 2
Employed in business or industry: 4
Employed in government agency: 2
Total: 12

Additional Information

Housing and Day Care: On-campus housing is available. See the following website for more information: http://www.apsu.edu/housing/Halls/emerald_hill. On-campus day care facilities are available. See the following website for more information: http://www.apsu.edu/clc/.

Information for Students With Physical Disabilities: See the following website: http://www.apsu.edu/disability/.

Special Facilities or Resources: The Department of Psychological Science and Counseling has a variety of facilities to provide learning and research opportunities. Rooms equipped with one-way observation windows, video and other monitoring equipment are available for counseling, testing and human research. Laboratories for vision, infant development, animal learning, and behavioral physiology are available for faculty and student research. The department has numerous microcomputers connected to the University's high-speed fiber-optic network for data collection, analysis, and the preparation of manuscripts.

Application Information: Office of Graduate Admissions, Austin Peay State University, PO Box 4458, Clarksville, TN 37044. *Fee:* $25. *Online application:* http://www.apsu.edu/grad-studies/apply-admission.

East Tennessee State University

Department of Psychology
College of Arts & Sciences
Box 70649 (Psychology)
Johnson City, TN 37614-0649
Telephone: (423) 439-4424
Chairperson: Wallace E. Dixon, Jr.

E-mail: dixonw@etsu.edu
Web: http://www.etsu.edu/cas/psychology

Orientation, Objectives, and Emphasis of Department

The Department of Psychology, College of Arts and Sciences, offers a Doctor of Philosophy in Psychology with concentrations in Clinical and Experimental Psychology. The clinical psychology concentration provides students with training in clinical psychology with an emphasis in integrated rural primary care psychology. The experimental psychology concentration trains students in the application of basic and applied research with a translational focus, and prepares them for future faculty positions through instruction in teaching, grant writing, and the development of long-term, programmatic research.

Programs and Degrees Offered

Program	Degree	Application Deadline	Applica-tions Received	Accepted	New Admits Enrolled (PT)	Total Enrolled (PT)	Degrees Awarded in 2014–2015	Median Years to Complete Degree	Dismissed/Withdrew
Clinical Psychology	PhD	December 1 (Fall)	89	6	6 (0)	25 (0)	6	5	1
Experimental Psychology	PhD	January 15 (Fall)	24	8	2 (0)	14 (0)	3	4	1

APA Accreditation

Clinical PhD: Student Outcome Data website: http://www.etsu.edu/cas/psychology/academic_programs/grad_programs.php.

Doctoral Degree (PhD Clinical Psychology): For those doctoral students for whom a professional internship was required in this program prior to graduation:
Total students who applied for an internship: 3
Total students who obtained an internship: 3
Total students who obtained a paid internship: 3
Total students who obtained an unpaid internship: 0
Total students who were placed in APA/CPA-accredited internships: 2
Total students placed in internships not APA/CPA-accredited, but listed with the Association of Psychology Postdoctoral and Internship Centers (APPIC): 1
Total students placed in internships conforming to guidelines of the Council of Directors of School Psychology Programs (CDSPP): 0
Total students placed in internships that were not APA/CPA-accredited, APPIC or CDSSP listed: 0

Internships/Practica

Clinical internships and practica in assessment and therapy are available to students enrolled in the clinical psychology program. They are conducted in mental health, behavioral health, and primary care facilities under the joint supervision of departmental faculty and adjunct faculty located in the facilities. Students also participate in intensive clinical training in the department's training clinic. Beginning with the second year, experimental students will participate in supervised teaching experiences. They will complete a course in teaching of psychology and then enroll in teaching practica as a part of both masters level and doctoral level training. Second-year students will be responsible for teaching 1-hour laboratory sections of courses. Advanced students will be teacher of record for 3- or 4-hour undergraduate courses.

Admissions

Entries appear in the following order: required test or GPA, minimum score (if required)/median score of students entering in 2015–2016.

Program	Degree	GRE-V	GRE-Q	GRE-Writing	GRE-Subject	Under-graduate GPA	Last 2 Years GPA	Psychol-ogy GPA	Master's GPA
Clinical Psychology	PhD	NA/159	NA/157	NA/4.5	Not specified	NA/3.7	Not specified	Not specified	Not specified

Admissions (con't.)

Program	Degree	GRE-V	GRE-Q	GRE-Writing	GRE-Subject	Under-graduate GPA	Last 2 Years GPA	Psychol-ogy GPA	Master's GPA
Experimental Psychology	PhD	NA/153	NA/152	Not specified	Not specified	3/3.5	Not specified	Not specified	Not specified

Admissions Requirements:

Degree	GRE	GRE-Subject	Letters of Recom-mendation	Research Statement	Writing Sample	CV	Interview
Doctoral	Required	None	3	Required	None	Recom-mended	Required

Please note if these criteria vary for different programs: The Experimental PhD concentration may or may not have in-person interviews. Interviews are often conducted over the telephone. Clinically Related Public Service is also not considered for the Experimental concentration.

Admissions Criteria:

GRE scores—high
Research experience—high
Work experience—medium
Clinically related public service—low
GPA—high

Letters of recommendation—high
Interview—medium
Statement of goals and objectives—high
Undergraduate psychology preparation—medium

For additional information on admission requirements, visit http://www.etsu.edu/cas/psychology/academic_programs/grad_programs.php.

Department Demographics

	Male (PT)	Female (PT)	Total	African-American/ Black (PT)	Hispanic/ Latino (PT)	Asian/ Pacific Islander (PT)	American Indian/ Alaska Native (PT)	Caucasian/ White (PT)	Unknown	Multiethnic (PT)	ADA (PT)	Int'l (PT)
Students	15 (0)	23 (0)	38	3 (0)	0 (0)	0 (0)	0 (0)	34 (0)	0 (0)	1 (0)	(0)	0 (0)

Financial Information/Assistance

Tuition: For information on tuition costs, visit http://www.etsu.edu/fa/fs/bursar/tuitioninfo/feeschedule.aspx. Tuition is subject to change.

Doctoral:
State residents: $8,950 per academic year.
State residents: $434 per credit hour.
Nonstate residents: $22,469 per academic year.
Nonstate residents: $1,292 per credit hour.

Master's:
State residents: $8,950 per academic year.
State residents: $434 per credit hour.
Nonstate residents: $22,469 per academic year.
Nonstate residents: $1,292 per credit hour.

Financial Assistance:

	Teaching Assistantship (% Receiving)	Teaching Assistantship Tuition Remission	Research Assistantship (% Receiving)	Research Assistantship Tuition Remission	Fellowship (% Receiving)	Fellowship Tuition Remission
First-Year Student	NA (NA)	NA	$12,000 (100)	Full	NA (NA)	NA
Advanced Student	NA (NA)	NA	NA (NA)	NA	NA (NA)	NA

For additional information on financial assistance, visit http://www.etsu.edu/gradstud/GATS_FAQ.aspx.

Employment of Department Graduates

Doctoral:
Enrolled in another graduate/professional program: 1
Employed in a community mental health/counseling center: 1
Total: 2

Additional Information

Housing and Day Care: On-campus housing is available. See the following website for more information: http://www.etsu.edu/students/housing/familygraduate/default.aspx. On-campus day care facilities are available. See the following website for more information: http://child.etsu.edu/.

Information for Students With Physical Disabilities: See the following website: http://www.etsu.edu/students/disable/.

Special Facilities or Resources: The psychology department maintains behavioral neuroscience, social psychology, developmental psychology, and clinical psychology laboratory facilities. All laboratories are used for undergraduate and graduate instructional research and for student and faculty research.

Application Information: School of Graduate Studies, East Tennessee State University, P.O. Box 70720, Johnson City, TN 37614-1710. *Fee:* $35. *Online application:* http://www.etsu.edu/gradstud/ApplyNow.aspx.

Memphis, University of
Department of Counseling, Educational Psychology and Research, Program in Counseling Psychology
Education
100 Ball Building
Memphis, TN 38152
Telephone: (901) 678-2841
Chairperson: Dewaine Rice

E-mail: sbridges@memphis.edu
Web: http://www.memphis.edu/cepr/cpsy/

Orientation, Objectives, and Emphasis of Department
The PhD in Counseling Psychology at the University of Memphis is designed to train generalist psychologists who promote human development in the areas of mental health, career development, emotional and social learning, and decision-making in a rapidly changing global environment. Training is grounded in the scientist–practitioner training model (equal emphasis on science and practice) and emphasizes multicultural competency and responsibility and commitment to human welfare. Didactic and experiential activities are designed to anchor students firmly within the discipline of psychology. The program emphasizes research, development, prevention, and remediation in the context of social justice as vehicles for helping all individuals, families, and groups achieve competence and a sense of well-being. The department has a strong commitment to training professionals to work with diverse populations in urban settings. Within the context of the University mission, students are expected to develop the critical thinking skills necessary for lifelong learning and to contribute to the global community. Students are expected to acquire (1) an identity as a counseling psychologist; (2) a knowledge foundation in psychology, research, counseling, psychological evaluation, and professional standards; and (3) competencies in research, practice, and teaching. The program is individualized to meet the student's goals.

Programs and Degrees Offered

Program	Degree	Application Deadline	Applications Received	Accepted	New Admits Enrolled (PT)	Total Enrolled (PT)	Degrees Awarded in 2014–2015	Median Years to Complete Degree	Dismissed/Withdrew
Counseling Psychology	PhD	December 5 (Fall)	40	17	6 (0)	29 (2)	9	4.5	0

APA Accreditation
Counseling PhD: Student Outcome Data website: http://www.memphis.edu/cepr/cpsy/information.php.

Doctoral Degree (PhD Counseling Psychology): For those doctoral students for whom a professional internship was required in this program prior to graduation:
Total students who applied for an internship: 4
Total students who obtained an internship: 4

Total students who obtained a paid internship: 4
Total students who obtained an unpaid internship: 0
Total students who were placed in APA/CPA-accredited internships: 4
Total students placed in internships not APA/CPA-accredited, but listed with the Association of Psychology Postdoctoral and Internship Centers (APPIC): 0
Total students placed in internships conforming to guidelines of the Council of Directors of School Psychology Programs (CDSPP): 0
Total students placed in internships that were not APA/CPA-accredited, APPIC or CDSSP listed: 0

Internships/Practica

Doctoral students complete a minimum of two practica during their 3 years of coursework; many students complete up to five practica. The department has an extensive network of relationships with community agencies for providing practicum placements for students. These placements include university and college counseling centers, VAs/medical settings, community mental health centers, independent practice, neuroassessment, and correctional services. Students are competitive for placement in national internships with 100% of students matching the last 3 years.

Admissions

Entries appear in the following order: required test or GPA, minimum score (if required)/median score of students entering in 2015–2016.

Program	Degree	GRE-V	GRE-Q	GRE-Writing	GRE-Subject	Under-graduate GPA	Last 2 Years GPA	Psychol-ogy GPA	Master's GPA
Counseling Psychology	PhD	NA/NA	NA/NA	NA/NA	Not specified	Not specified	Not specified	Not specified	3.6/3.9

Admissions Requirements:

Degree	GRE	GRE-Subject	Letters of Recommendation	Research Statement	Writing Sample	CV	Interview
Doctoral	Required	Optional	4	Required	None	Required	Required

Admissions Criteria:

GRE scores—high
Research experience—medium
Work experience—medium
Clinically related public service—low
GPA—high

Letters of recommendation—high
Interview—medium
Statement of goals and objectives—high
Fit w/ program philosophy—high

Department Demographics

	Male (PT)	Female (PT)	Total	African-American/Black (PT)	Hispanic/Latino (PT)	Asian/Pacific Islander (PT)	American Indian/Alaska Native (PT)	Caucasian/White (PT)	Unknown	Multiethnic (PT)	ADA (PT)	Int'l (PT)
Students	12 (1)	17 (1)	31	2 (0)	1 (0)	1 (0)	0 (0)	23 (2)	0 (0)	2 (0)	2 (0)	1 (0)

Financial Information/Assistance

Tuition: For information on tuition costs, visit http://www.memphis.edu/bursar/fees/index.php. Tuition is subject to change. Additional fees are assessed to students beyond the costs of tuition for the following: $85.50/credit program service fee for all graduate students.

Doctoral:
State residents: $16,500 per academic year.
State residents: $461 per credit hour.
Nonstate residents: $18,900 per academic year.
Nonstate residents: $488 per credit hour.

Financial Assistance:

	Teaching Assistantship (% Receiving)	Teaching Assistantship Tuition Remission	Research Assistantship (% Receiving)	Research Assistantship Tuition Remission	Fellowship (% Receiving)	Fellowship Tuition Remission
First-Year Student	$7,800 (25)	Full	$7,800 (75)	Full	NA (NA)	NA
Advanced Student	$7,800 (25)	Full	$7,800 (70)	Full	$10,000 (5)	Partial

For additional information on financial assistance, visit http://www.memphis.edu/gradschool/current_students/ga.php.

Employment of Department Graduates

Doctoral:
Employed in independent practice: 7
Employed in a community mental health/counseling center: 2
Total: 9

Additional Information

Housing and Day Care: On-campus housing is available. See the following website for more information: http://memphis.edu/reslife/residencehalls/gsfh.php. On-campus day care facilities are available. See the following website for more information: http://www.memphis.edu/childcare/.

Information for Students With Physical Disabilities: See the following website: http://www.memphis.edu/drs/.

Special Facilities or Resources: Department faculty have research teams that provide opportunities for faculty and students to collaborate on research and consultation products. Many students are also involved in cross-disciplinary research with Psychology and Women's Studies faculty. Students have graduate assistant training opportunities with approved community agencies.

Application Information: Sara K. Bridges, PhD, Counseling Psychology Admissions, 100 Ball Building, The University of Memphis, Memphis, TN 38152. *Fee:* $35. *Online application:* http://www.memphis.edu/graduateadmissions/future/apply_grad.php.

Memphis, University of
Department of Psychology
College of Arts and Sciences
202 Psychology Building
Memphis, TN 38152-3230
Telephone: (901) 678-4340
Chairperson: Frank Andrasik

E-mail: cywshngt@memphis.edu
Web: http://www.memphis.edu/psychology

Orientation, Objectives, and Emphasis of Department
The Department of Psychology at the University of Memphis has been identified as a Center of Excellence in the state of Tennessee and offers PhD programs in Clinical Psychology, Experimental Psychology, and School Psychology; an MA/EdS (non-thesis) program in School Psychology; and an MS (either thesis or non-thesis) program in General Psychology. The department philosophy emphasizes the training of experimentally sophisticated research scientists and practitioners. All programs have a strong research emphasis. Professional training is based upon a research foundation and students are exposed to a broad range of theoretical perspectives. Diversity of professional training activities and collaborative research activities are encouraged. Our faculty emphasize one-on-one Major Professor-Graduate Student relationships and students are afforded freedom to pursue their own interests and tailor programs to their needs. Five research areas are represented across the PhD and master's programs: Clinical Health Psychology, Behavioral Neuroscience, Child and Family Studies, Cognitive Psychology, and Psychotherapy Research.

Programs and Degrees Offered

Program	Degree	Application Deadline	Applications Received	Accepted	New Admits Enrolled (PT)	Total Enrolled (PT)	Degrees Awarded in 2014–2015	Median Years to Complete Degree	Dismissed/ Withdrew
Clinical Psychology	PhD	December 5 (Fall)	209	6	6 (0)	39 (0)	5	6	0
School Psychology	MA/MS	June 15 (Fall)	14	9	9 (0)	15 (0)	6	3	0
General Psychology	MA/MS	May 1 (Fall)	20	9	9 (0)	24 (0)	12	2	1
School Psychology	PhD	February 1 (Fall)	10	3	3 (0)	10 (0)	1	5.3	0
Experimental Psychology	PhD	January 15 (Fall)	14	1	1 (0)	25	7	6	0

APA Accreditation

Clinical PhD: Student Outcome Data website: http://www.memphis.edu/psychology/graduate/clinadmission.php.
School PhD: Student Outcome Data website: http://www.memphis.edu/psychology/graduate/schabout.php.

Doctoral Degree (PhD Clinical Psychology): For those doctoral students for whom a professional internship was required in this program prior to graduation:
Total students who applied for an internship: 5
Total students who obtained an internship: 5
Total students who obtained a paid internship: 5
Total students who obtained an unpaid internship: 0
Total students who were placed in APA/CPA-accredited internships: 5
Total students placed in internships not APA/CPA-accredited, but listed with the Association of Psychology Postdoctoral and Internship Centers (APPIC): 0
Total students placed in internships conforming to guidelines of the Council of Directors of School Psychology Programs (CDSPP): 0
Total students placed in internships that were not APA/CPA-accredited, APPIC or CDSSP listed: 0

Doctoral Degree (PhD School Psychology): For those doctoral students for whom a professional internship was required in this program prior to graduation:
Total students who applied for an internship: 2
Total students who obtained an internship: 2
Total students who obtained a paid internship: 2
Total students who obtained an unpaid internship: 0
Total students who were placed in APA/CPA-accredited internships: 2
Total students placed in internships not APA/CPA-accredited, but listed with the Association of Psychology Postdoctoral and Internship Centers (APPIC): 0
Total students placed in internships conforming to guidelines of the Council of Directors of School Psychology Programs (CDSPP): 0
Total students placed in internships that were not APA/CPA-accredited, APPIC or CDSSP listed: 0

Master's Degree (MA/MS General Psychology): An internship experience, such as a final research project or "capstone" experience is required of graduates.

Internships/Practica

The department has an extensive network of relationships with local agencies for providing practicum experiences for students. Doctoral clinical students work 20 hours per week at one of these practicum sites for a minimum of one year. Our clinical placement sites include facilities such as a multidisciplinary diagnostic center for children with developmental disabilities (UT Boling Center), UT Health Sciences West Cancer Clinic, a therapeutic school for children with emotional/behavioral difficulties, a federal prison, a private practice specializing in assessment, LeBonheur Children's Research Hospital, and St. Jude Children's Research Hospital. In addition, our students often engage in short-term training on a volunteer basis at the Memphis VA Medical Center and a number of other community agencies. The department maintains an in-house Psychological Services Center. Clinical students complete internships during the fifth or sixth year at sites nationwide.

Admissions

Entries appear in the following order: required test or GPA, minimum score (if required)/median score of students entering in 2015–2016.

Program	Degree	GRE-V	GRE-Q	GRE-Writing	GRE-Subject	Under-graduate GPA	Last 2 Years GPA	Psychology GPA	Master's GPA
Clinical Psychology	PhD	NA/157	NA/153	NA/4.5	Not specified	NA/3.73	Not specified	Not specified	Not specified
School Psychology	MA/MS	Not specified	Not specified	Not specified	Not specified	Not specified	Not specified	Not specified	Not specified
General Psychology	MA/MS	NA/156	NA/152	Not specified	Not specified	Not specified	Not specified	Not specified	Not specified
School Psychology	PhD	NA/153	NA/148	Not specified	Not specified	NA/3.53	Not specified	Not specified	Not specified
Experimental Psychology	PhD	NA/150	NA/149	Not specified	Not specified	NA/3.66	Not specified	Not specified	Not specified

Admissions Requirements:

Degree	GRE	GRE-Subject	Letters of Recom-mendation	Research Statement	Writing Sample	CV	Interview
Master's/Specialist	Required	None	3	Required	Optional	Optional	Optional
Doctoral	Required	Optional	3	Required	Optional	Optional	Required

Please note if these criteria vary for different programs: Interview requirement for doctoral applicants may involve campus visits or interviews via other means.

Admissions Criteria:

GRE scores—high
Research experience—high
Work experience—medium
Clinically related public service—low
GPA—high

Letters of recommendation—high
Interview—medium
Statement of goals and objectives—high
Undergraduate psychology preparation—medium

For additional information on admission requirements, visit http://www.memphis.edu/psychology/graduate/apply.php.

Department Demographics

	Male (PT)	Female (PT)	Total	African-American/ Black (PT)	Hispanic/ Latino (PT)	Asian/ Pacific Islander (PT)	American Indian/ Alaska Native (PT)	Caucasian/ White (PT)	Unknown	Multiethnic (PT)	ADA (PT)	Int'l (PT)
Students	40 (0)	73 (0)	113	24 (0)	2 (0)	12 (0)	0 (0)	73 (0)	2 (0)	0 (0)	0 (0)	4 (0)

Financial Information/Assistance

Tuition: For information on tuition costs, visit http://www.memphis.edu/bursar/fees/. Tuition is subject to change.

Doctoral:
State residents: $10,211 per academic year.
State residents: $567 per credit hour.
Nonstate residents: $18,995 per academic year.
Nonstate residents: $1,055 per credit hour.

Master's:
State residents: $10,211 per academic year.
State residents: $567 per credit hour.
Nonstate residents: $18,995 per academic year.
Nonstate residents: $1,055 per credit hour.

Financial Assistance:

	Teaching Assistantship (% Receiving)	Teaching Assistantship Tuition Remission	Research Assistantship (% Receiving)	Research Assistantship Tuition Remission	Fellowship (% Receiving)	Fellowship Tuition Remission
First-Year Student	$15,000 (NA)	Full	$15,000 (NA)	Full	NA (NA)	NA
Advanced Student	$16,000 (NA)	Full	$16,000 (NA)	Full	NA (NA)	NA

Employment of Department Graduates

Master's:
Enrolled in a Psychology doctoral program: 7
Enrolled in another graduate/professional program: 4
Employed in an academic position at a university: 1
Employed in a professional position in a school system: 3
Employed in business or industry: 2
Employed in a hospital/medical center: 1
Total: 18

Doctoral:
Enrolled in a postdoctoral residency/fellowship: 5
Employed in an academic position at a university: 3
Employed in business or industry: 4
Employed in a community mental health/counseling center: 1
Total: 13

Additional Information

Housing and Day Care: On-campus housing is available. See the following website for more information: http://www.memphis.edu/reslife/. On-campus day care facilities are available. See the following website for more information: http://www.memphis.edu/childcare/.

Information for Students With Physical Disabilities: See the following website: http://www.memphis.edu/drs/.

Special Facilities or Resources: The department has a strong research commitment, ranking high nationally among psychology departments in total research and development expenditures. As a recognized Center of Excellence, the state of Tennessee has supported the department with approximately $1 million per year for the past 20 years. The department is housed in a well-equipped building, providing offices and laboratory space for all students. Facilities include the Institute for Intelligent Systems at the FedEx Institute of Technology, and the Psychological Services Center. The Institute for Intelligent Systems is an interdisciplinary enterprise comprised of researchers and students from the fields of cognitive psychology, computer science, mathematics, physics, neuroscience, education, linguistics, philosophy, anthropology, engineering, and business. The Psychological Services Center is a fee-for-service outpatient mental health clinic located in the psychology building, with clients referred from the greater Memphis area. Doctoral students receive intensive supervision as they learn to provide a wide range of assessment and intervention services. The Psychological Services Center also provides an invaluable resource for research projects. Other community opportunities for research and practical experiences include St. Jude Children's Research Hospital, University of Tennessee Health Sciences in Memphis, Shelby County Schools, Methodist/Le Bonheur Healthcare, VA Hospital, and Shelby County Head Start.

Application Information: Graduate Admissions, 101 Wilder Tower, Memphis, TN 38152-3370, University of Memphis, Memphis, TN 38152. *Fee:* $35. *Online application:* http://www.memphis.edu/graduateadmissions/future/apply_grad.php.

Middle Tennessee State University
Department of Psychology
College of Behavioral and Heath Sciences
Box 87
Murfreesboro, TN 37132
Telephone: (615) 898-2706
Chairperson: Dr. Greg Schmidt

E-mail: gschmidt@mtsu.edu
Web: http://www.mtsu.edu/psychology/

Orientation, Objectives, and Emphasis of Department
We have an applied department with research and service priorities. A strong academic program is available for students seeking to improve their backgrounds in core areas of psychology for admission to doctoral programs. Applied programs lead to certification and/or licensure in school psychology and clinical psychology. Our Industrial/Organizational program is nationally acclaimed and our school psychology program is accredited by the National Association of School Psychologists (NASP).

Programs and Degrees Offered

Program	Degree	Application Deadline	Applica-tions Received	Accepted	New Admits Enrolled (PT)	Total Enrolled (PT)	Degrees Awarded in 2014–2015	Median Years to Complete Degree	Dismissed/ Withdrew
Clinical Psychology	MA/MS	March 1 (Fall), October 1 (Spring)	40	28	14 (0)	24 (7)	7	2.33	2
Experimental Psychology	MA/MS	March 1 (Fall), October 1 (Spring)	13	11	6	12 (2)	4	2.5	0
Industrial/ Organizational Psychology	MA/MS	March 1 (Fall)	80	20	14 (0)	27 (0)	13	2	1
Quantitative Psychology	MA/MS	March 1 (Fall), October 1 (Spring)	5	4	3	4 (8)	9	2	0
School Psychology	EdS	March 1 (Fall), October 1 (Spring)	24	19	11	30 (1)	7	3	2

Internships/Practica

Field placements are available in a variety of mental health facilities, inpatient facilities, the VA hospital, drug abuse facilities, K–12 school settings, and industry and government sites.

Admissions

Entries appear in the following order: required test or GPA, minimum score (if required)/median score of students entering in 2015–2016.

Program	Degree	GRE-V	GRE-Q	GRE-Writing	GRE-Subject	Under-graduate GPA	Last 2 Years GPA	Psychol-ogy GPA	Master's GPA
Clinical Psychology	MA/MS	145/151	138/145	2.5/3.5	Not specified	2.93/3.41	Not specified	Not specified	Not specified
Experimental Psychology	MA/MS	146/154	145/147	Not specified	Not specified	3/3.47	Not specified	Not specified	Not specified
Industrial/ Organizational Psychology	MA/MS	Not specified	Not specified	Not specified	Not specified	Not specified	Not specified	Not specified	Not specified
Quantitative Psychology	MA/MS	146/152	146/153	NA/4	Not specified	3/3.7	Not specified	Not specified	Not specified
School Psychology	EdS	141/150	150/146	NA/4.1	Not specified	NA/NA	Not specified	Not specified	Not specified

Admissions Requirements:

Degree	GRE	GRE-Subject	Letters of Recom-mendation	Research Statement	Writing Sample	CV	Interview
Master's/Specialist	Required	None	3	Required	None	Required	None

Please note if these criteria vary for different programs: Even though interviews are not required, a number of prospective students visit the campus and meet with faculty and students about the programs.

Admissions Criteria:

GRE scores—high
Research experience—medium
Work experience—medium
Clinically related public service—medium
GPA—high

Letters of recommendation—high
Interview—low
Statement of goals and objectives—high
Undergraduate psychology preparation—high

Department Demographics

	Male (PT)	Female (PT)	Total	African-American/ Black (PT)	Hispanic/ Latino (PT)	Asian/ Pacific Islander (PT)	American Indian/ Alaska Native (PT)	Caucasian/ White (PT)	Unknown	Multiethnic (PT)	ADA (PT)	Int'l (PT)
Students	22 (4)	75 (14)	115	3 (1)	1 (1)	2 (1)	0 (0)	91 (15)	0 (0)	0 (0)	0 (0)	0 (0)

Financial Information/Assistance

Tuition: For information on tuition costs, visit http://www.mtsu.edu/tuition/index.php. Tuition is subject to change.

Master's:
State residents: $9,000 per academic year.
State residents: $432 per credit hour.
Nonstate residents: $22,000 per academic year.
Nonstate residents: $1,076 per credit hour.

Financial Assistance:

	Teaching Assistantship (% Receiving)	Teaching Assistantship Tuition Remission	Research Assistantship (% Receiving)	Research Assistantship Tuition Remission	Fellowship (% Receiving)	Fellowship Tuition Remission
First-Year Student	NA (NA)	NA	$3,250 (NA)	Partial	NA (NA)	NA
Advanced Student	NA (NA)	NA	$3,250 (NA)	Partial	NA (NA)	NA

For additional information on financial assistance, visit http://www.mtsu.edu/graduate/student/gtas.php.

Employment of Department Graduates

Master's:
Enrolled in a Psychology doctoral program: 2
Employed in academic position at a 2-year/4-year college: 1
Employed in a professional position in a school system: 6
Employed in business or industry: 16
Do not know: 6
Total: 31

Additional Information

Housing and Day Care: On-campus housing is available. See the following website for more information: http://www.mtsu.edu/housing/. On-campus day care facilities are available. See the following website for more information: http://www.mtsu.edu/pcsw/childcare.php.

Information for Students With Physical Disabilities: See the following website: http://www.mtsu.edu/dac/.

Application Information: Office of Graduate Studies, Cope Administration Building, 114, Middle Tennessee State University, Murfreesboro, TN 37132. *Fee:* $35. *Online application:* http://www.mtsu.edu/graduate/apply.php.

Tennessee, University of, Chattanooga

Department of Psychology
College of Arts and Sciences
350 Holt Hall
Chattanooga, TN 37403
Telephone: (423) 425-4262
Department Head: Brian J. O'Leary

E-mail: boleary@utc.edu
Web: http://www.utc.edu/psychology/

Orientation, Objectives, and Emphasis of Department

The MS in Research program is designed primarily to prepare students to pursue doctoral level training. Students work in an apprenticeship model with faculty to develop strong design and analysis skills. The goal of the MS in I/O program is to provide students with the training necessary to pursue a variety of I/O related fields. These include, but are not limited to, positions in human resources, industrial/organizational consulting, training, and organization development. The I/O program can be used as a preparation for the pursuit of doctoral training in I/O related fields of study. The curriculum is organized around specific core knowledge domains particular to I/O psychology. The industrial domain includes content such as job analysis, selection, and training. The organizational domain includes content such as work motivation, attitudes, leadership, organizational development, and group processes. The third domain, research methodology, includes experimental design and univariate and multivariate statistical analysis.

Programs and Degrees Offered

Program	Degree	Application Deadline	Applica-tions Received	Accepted	New Admits Enrolled (PT)	Total Enrolled (PT)	Degrees Awarded in 2014–2015	Median Years to Complete Degree	Dismissed/ Withdrew
Industrial-Organizational Psychology	MA/MS	March 15 (Fall)	70	30	17	31 (0)	14	2	1
Research Psychology	MA/MS	March 15 (Fall)	14	10	6	17 (2)	2	2	0

Internships/Practica

The I/O program requires six credit hours of practicum, or approximately 300 hours of actual work time, as part of the degree requirements. An additional three credit hours (150 work hours) may be taken as a part of the elective portion of the program. The integration of course work and practice throughout the students' graduate academic program is essential to prepare I/O students for applied professional careers. To achieve this end, I/O students become involved in a variety of real life work organization activities through completion of the practicum program. They are encouraged to start this practicum after their second semester of academic work. The practicum is carried out in private and public work organizations in which the students engage in a wide variety of projects under the guidance of field supervisors, coordinated by the I/O faculty.

Admissions

Entries appear in the following order: required test or GPA, minimum score (if required)/median score of students entering in 2015–2016.

Program	Degree	GRE-V	GRE-Q	GRE-Writing	GRE-Subject	Under-graduate GPA	Last 2 Years GPA	Psychol-ogy GPA	Master's GPA
Industrial-Organizational Psychology	MA/MS	NA/NA	NA/NA	NA/NA	Not specified	NA/NA	Not specified	Not specified	Not specified
Research Psychology	MA/MS	NA/NA	NA/NA	NA/NA	Not specified	NA/NA	NA/NA	NA/NA	Not specified

Admissions Requirements:

Degree	GRE	GRE-Subject	Letters of Recommendation	Research Statement	Writing Sample	CV	Interview
Master's/Specialist	Required	None	3	Required	Recommended	Recommended	None

Please note if these criteria vary for different programs: Admission to the Research program requires sponsorship of a faculty member, highly values research experience and an undergraduate major in psychology, and requires a psychology or social science research methods and statistics course.

Admissions Criteria:

GRE scores—high
Research experience—medium
Work experience—low
Clinically related public service—low
GPA—high

Letters of recommendation—medium
Interview—low
Statement of goals and objectives—medium
Undergraduate psychology preparation—medium

Department Demographics

	Male (PT)	Female (PT)	Total	African-American/ Black (PT)	Hispanic/ Latino (PT)	Asian/ Pacific Islander (PT)	American Indian/ Alaska Native (PT)	Caucasian/ White (PT)	Unknown (PT)	Multiethnic (PT)	ADA (PT)	Int'l (PT)
Students	20 (1)	28 (1)	50	2 (0)	3 (0)	0 (1)	0 (0)	43 (1)	0 (0)	0 (0)	0 (0)	0 (0)

Financial Information/Assistance

Tuition: For information on tuition costs, visit http://www.utc.edu/bursar/fee-schedule.php. Tuition is subject to change.

Master's:
State residents: $7,938 per academic year.
State residents: $441 per credit hour.
Nonstate residents: $24,056 per academic year.
Nonstate residents: $1,336 per credit hour.

Financial Assistance:

	Teaching Assistantship (% Receiving)	Teaching Assistantship Tuition Remission	Research Assistantship (% Receiving)	Research Assistantship Tuition Remission	Fellowship (% Receiving)	Fellowship Tuition Remission
First-Year Student	$1,734 (NA)	NA	$3,500 (NA)	Full	NA (NA)	NA
Advanced Student	$4,400 (NA)	NA	$3,500 (NA)	Full	NA (NA)	NA

For additional information on financial assistance, visit http://www.utc.edu/graduate-school/student-resources/assistantships.php.

Employment of Department Graduates

Master's.
Enrolled in a psychology doctoral program: 3
Employed in business or industry: 12
Other employment position: 1
Total: 16

Additional Information

Housing and Day Care: On-campus housing is available. See the following website for more information: http://www.utc.edu/housing/. On-campus day care facilities are available. See the following website for more information: http://www.utc.edu/childrens-center/.

Information for Students With Physical Disabilities: See the following website: http://www.utc.edu/disability-resource-center/.

Application Information: The Graduate School, The University of Tennessee at Chattanooga, Department 5305, 615 McCallie Avenue, Chattanooga, TN 37403. *Fee:* $35. *Online application:* http://www.utc.edu/graduate-school/.

Tennessee, University of, Knoxville

Department of Psychology
Arts & Sciences
312 Austin Peay Building
Knoxville, TN 37996-0900
Telephone: (865) 974-3328
Department Head: Deborah P. Welsh, PhD

E-mail: cjogle@utk.edu
Web: http://psychology.utk.edu/

Orientation, Objectives, and Emphasis of Department

The graduate faculty maintain active research programs in cognition, developmental, ethology, gender, health, organizational, personality, phenomenology, psychobiology, psychometrics, sensation/perception, and social psychology. The MA program is appropriate for students wanting a master's degree as part of their progress toward a doctorate, or for those who wish to complement a degree in a different field. The Experimental PhD program prepares students for academic/research careers and for careers involving the application of psychological principles as practitioners in industrial, forensic, organizational, and community settings. Areas of concentration include applied psychology, child development, cognition, and consciousness, health psychology, phenomenology, and social/personality. The Clinical PhD program combines psychodynamic and research components, requiring exposure to a wide range of theoretical views and technical practices. Minors are available in child development, health psychology, and social psychology. In order to foster appropriate breadth and interdisciplinary training, some cognate work outside the department of psychology is required of all doctoral students. The Counseling Program is designed to enable students to become behavioral scientists, skilled in psychological research and its application. Students are trained to provide services to a wide variety of clients in numerous settings.

Programs and Degrees Offered

Program	Degree	Application Deadline	Applications Received	Accepted	New Admits Enrolled (PT)	Total Enrolled (PT)	Degrees Awarded in 2014–2015	Median Years to Complete Degree	Dismissed/ Withdrew
Clinical Psychology	PhD	December 1 (Fall)	271	6	6	34 (0)	10	6	0
Experimental Psychology	MA/MS	March 15 (Fall)	26	2	2	3 (0)	3	2.5	0
Counseling Psychology	PhD	December 1 (Fall)	156	5	5	23	6	5.5	0
Experimental Psychology	PhD	December 1 (Fall)	64	7	7	24	2	5	0

APA Accreditation

Clinical PhD: Student Outcome Data website: http://psychology.utk.edu/grad/clinic_data.php.
Counseling PhD: Student Outcome Data website: http://psychology.utk.edu/grad/counseling_data.php.

Doctoral Degree (PhD Clinical Psychology): For those doctoral students for whom a professional internship was required in this program prior to graduation:
Total students who applied for an internship: 6
Total students who obtained an internship: 6
Total students who obtained a paid internship: 6
Total students who obtained an unpaid internship: 0

Total students who were placed in APA/CPA-accredited internships: 6
Total students placed in internships not APA/CPA-accredited, but listed with the Association of Psychology Postdoctoral and Internship Centers (APPIC): 0
Total students placed in internships conforming to guidelines of the Council of Directors of School Psychology Programs (CDSPP): 0
Total students placed in internships that were not APA/CPA-accredited, APPIC or CDSSP listed: 0

Doctoral Degree (PhD Counseling Psychology): For those doctoral students for whom a professional internship was required in this program prior to graduation:
Total students who applied for an internship: 5
Total students who obtained an internship: 5
Total students who obtained a paid internship: 5
Total students who obtained an unpaid internship: 0
Total students who were placed in APA/CPA-accredited internships: 5
Total students placed in internships not APA/CPA-accredited, but listed with the Association of Psychology Postdoctoral and Internship Centers (APPIC): 0
Total students placed in internships conforming to guidelines of the Council of Directors of School Psychology Programs (CDSPP): 0
Total students placed in internships that were not APA/CPA-accredited, APPIC or CDSSP listed: 0

Master's Degree (MA/MS Experimental Psychology): An internship experience, such as a final research project or "capstone" experience is required of graduates.

Internships/Practica

All Clinical students are required to participate in two 12-month practica, one in our Departmental Psychological Clinic and the other in a community mental health facility. Both practica are supervised by doctoral-degreed clinical psychologists, and the clientele are children, adolescents, and adults who seek help for their emotional and behavioral problems. In addition, Clinical and Counseling students are required to serve a one-year internship.

Admissions

Entries appear in the following order: required test or GPA, minimum score (if required)/median score of students entering in 2015–2016.

Program	Degree	GRE-V	GRE-Q	GRE-Writing	GRE-Subject	Under-graduate GPA	Last 2 Years GPA	Psychology GPA	Master's GPA
Clinical Psychology	PhD	147/160	145/153	Not specified	Not specified	2.92/3.83	Not specified	Not specified	Not specified
Experimental Psychology	MA/MS	162/162	152/149	Not specified	Not specified	NA/3.62	Not specified	Not specified	Not specified
Counseling Psychology	PhD	148/156	142/149	Not specified	Not specified	2.96/3.31	Not specified	Not specified	Not specified
Experimental Psychology	PhD	143/154	152/157	Not specified	Not specified	3.47/3.76	Not specified	Not specified	Not specified

Admissions Requirements:

Degree	GRE	GRE-Subject	Letters of Recommendation	Research Statement	Writing Sample	CV	Interview
Master's/Specialist	Required	Optional	3	None	None	Required	Required
Doctoral	Required	Optional	3	None	None	Required	Required

Please note if these criteria vary for different programs: For every program, we require essay responses to several questions. These essay questions are in place of personal statements, which are not required or requested.

Admissions Criteria:

GRE scores—medium
Research experience—high
Work experience—low
Clinically related public service—low
GPA—high

Letters of recommendation—high
Interview—high
Statement of goals and objectives—high
Undergraduate psychology preparation—low
Fit with program—high

For additional information on admission requirements, visit http://psychology.utk.edu/grad/admissions.php.

Department Demographics

	Male (PT)	Female (PT)	Total	African-American/ Black (PT)	Hispanic/ Latino (PT)	Asian/ Pacific Islander (PT)	American Indian/ Alaska Native (PT)	Caucasian/ White (PT)	Unknown	Multiethnic (PT)	ADA (PT)	Int'l (PT)
Students	29 (0)	55 (0)	84	8 (0)	5 (0)	2 (0)	(0)	64 (0)	5 (0)	(0)	0 (0)	6 (0)

Financial Information/Assistance

Tuition: For information on tuition costs, visit http://onestop.utk.edu/your-money/tuition-fees/. Tuition is subject to change.

Doctoral:
State residents: $12,356 per academic year.
State residents: $675 per credit hour.
Nonstate residents: $30,774 per academic year.
Nonstate residents: $1,699 per credit hour.

Master's:
State residents: $12,356 per academic year.
State residents: $675 per credit hour.
Nonstate residents: $30,774 per academic year.
Nonstate residents: $1,699 per credit hour.

Financial Assistance:

	Teaching Assistantship (% Receiving)	Teaching Assistantship Tuition Remission	Research Assistantship (% Receiving)	Research Assistantship Tuition Remission	Fellowship (% Receiving)	Fellowship Tuition Remission
First-Year Student	NA (NA)	NA	$14,250 (NA)	Full	NA (NA)	NA
Advanced Student	NA (NA)	Full	NA (NA)	Full	NA (NA)	NA

For additional information on financial assistance, visit http://psychology.utk.edu/grad/finance.php.

Employment of Department Graduates

Master's:
Enrolled in a psychology doctoral program: 2
Employed in other positions at a higher education institution: 1
Do not know: 1
Total: 4

Doctoral:
Enrolled in a postdoctoral residency/fellowship: 4
Employed in independent practice: 4
Employed in an academic position at a university: 2
Employed in academic position at a 2-year/4-year college: 2
Employed in a community mental health/counseling center: 5
Do not know: 4
Total: 21

Additional Information

Housing and Day Care: On-campus housing is available. See the following website for more information: http://housing.utk.edu/. On-campus day care facilities are available. See the following website for more information: http://elc.utk.edu/.

Information for Students With Physical Disabilities: See the following website: http://ods.utk.edu/.

Special Facilities or Resources: Facilities include computer support in equipment and staff, human and animal laboratories, a psychology clinic for training and research, and a new university library with expanded serials holdings.

Application Information: Fee: $60. *Online application:* http://graduateadmissions.utk.edu/new_applicants.shtml.

Vanderbilt University

Human & Organizational Development
Peabody College of Education & Human Development
Peabody #90, 230 Appleton Place
Nashville, TN 37203-5721
Telephone: (615) 322-8484
Chairperson: Paul Speer

E-mail: sherrie.a.lane@vanderbilt.edu
Web: http://peabody.vanderbilt.edu/departments/hod/index.php

Orientation, Objectives, and Emphasis of Department

Although the vast majority of faculty in the department are psychologists, our orientation is interdisciplinary. There are three graduate programs, all oriented to helping diverse communities and individuals identify and develop their strengths: a long-standing Master's in Human Development Counseling (HDC), a Master's in Community Development and Action (CDA), and a PhD in Community Research and Action (CRA, with a terminal master's degree included). The HDC Program prepares students to meet the psychological needs of the normally developing population, who sometimes require professional help. Through a humanistic training model and a 2-to-3-year curriculum, students develop a strong theoretical grounding in lifespan human development, in either school or clinical mental health counseling. The CDA program is for those who desire training for program administration/evaluation work in public or private, international or domestic, community service, planning, or development organizations. The Doctoral Degree in Community Research and Action is designed to train action-researchers for academia or program/policy-related careers in applied community studies (i.e., community psychology, community development, prevention, community health/mental health, organizational change, and ethics). Coursework in qualitative and quantitative methods and evaluation research is required.

Programs and Degrees Offered

Program	Degree	Application Deadline	Applications Received	Accepted	New Admits Enrolled (PT)	Total Enrolled (PT)	Degrees Awarded in 2014–2015	Median Years to Complete Degree	Dismissed/ Withdrew
Human Development Counseling	MEd	December 31 (Fall)	113	67	41 (0)	92 (0)	35	1.5	1
Community Research & Action	PhD	December 1 (Fall)	95	7	4 (0)	24 (0)	8	2.5	0
Community Development and Action	MEd	December 31 (Fall), April 15 (Summer), Rolling	57	27	18 (0)	36 (3)	21	1	2

Internships/Practica

The CDA and CRA programs require a 15-week internship. Possible sites include Mayor's Office/Metro Council/Planning Commission; local community development organization; regional planning or civic design center; youth development center; healthcare corporation; neighborhood health clinic; alcohol and drug treatment center; welfare or housing agency; state health and human service agencies; and Vanderbilt Institute for Public Policy Studies (Centers for Mental Health Policy, Evaluation Research and Methodology, Child and Family Policy, Crime and Justice Policy, Environmental Management Studies, Health Policy, Psychotherapy Research and Policy, State and Local Policy). The HDC Program requires a 1-year internship that provides opportunities to apply knowledge and skills primarily in the areas of social service agencies; mental health centers; schools (K–12); employee assistance programs; and other human services delivery programs. The CRA PhD program requires a 600-hour internship in the areas of youth development and prevention, community health, community development and urban policy, and international human/community development.

Admissions

Entries appear in the following order: required test or GPA, minimum score (if required)/median score of students entering in 2015–2016.

Program	Degree	GRE-V	GRE-Q	GRE-Writing	GRE-Subject	Under-graduate GPA	Last 2 Years GPA	Psychology GPA	Master's GPA
Human Development Counseling	MEd	150/156	150/153	3.5/4.31	Not specified	3/3.42	Not specified	Not specified	Not specified
Community Research & Action	PhD	157/165	157/156	4.5/4.88	Not specified	3/3.62	Not specified	Not specified	3.6/3.75
Community Development and Action	MEd	150/158	150/152	3.5/4.21	Not specified	3/3.5	Not specified	Not specified	Not specified

Admissions Requirements:

Degree	GRE	GRE-Subject	Letters of Recommendation	Research Statement	Writing Sample	CV	Interview
Master's/Specialist	Required	None	3	Required	None	Optional	Recommended
Doctoral	Required	Optional	3	Required	Required	Required	Required

Please note if these criteria vary for different programs: Research experience less important for Master's programs than for the PhD program. Clinically related public service helpful for all programs. Additional writing samples are requested for the application to the PhD program.

Admissions Criteria:

GRE scores—high
Research experience—medium
Work experience—low
Clinically related public service—low
GPA—high

Letters of recommendation—high
Interview—high
Statement of goals and objectives—high
Undergraduate psychology preparation—low
Writing samples for PhD—high

For additional information on admission requirements, visit http://peabody.vanderbilt.edu/departments/hod/graduate-programs/index.php.

Department Demographics

	Male (PT)	Female (PT)	Total	African-American/ Black (PT)	Hispanic/ Latino (PT)	Asian/ Pacific Islander (PT)	American Indian/ Alaska Native (PT)	Caucasian/ White (PT)	Unknown (PT)	Multiethnic (PT)	ADA (PT)	Int'l (PT)
Students	24 (2)	128 (1)	155	18 (1)	9 (1)	6 (0)	1 (0)	112 (1)	0 (0)	6 (0)	0 (0)	0 (0)

Financial Information/Assistance

Tuition: For information on tuition costs, visit http://peabody.vanderbilt.edu/admin-offices/oas/tuition_and_fees.php. Tuition is subject to change. Additional fees are assessed to students beyond the costs of tuition for the following: student health insurance for MEd, student activities and recreation, library fees, transcript fees. Tuition costs vary by program.

Doctoral:
State residents: $32,724 per academic year.
State residents: $1,818 per credit hour.
Nonstate residents: $32,724 per academic year.
Nonstate residents: $1,818 per credit hour.

Master's:
State residents: $27,108 per academic year.
State residents: $1,506 per credit hour.
Nonstate residents: $27,108 per academic year.
Nonstate residents: $1,506 per credit hour.

Financial Assistance:

	Teaching Assistantship (% Receiving)	Teaching Assistantship Tuition Remission	Research Assistantship (% Receiving)	Research Assistantship Tuition Remission	Fellowship (% Receiving)	Fellowship Tuition Remission
First-Year Student	$18,000 (13)	Partial	$18,000 (13)	Partial	$42,000 (13)	Full
Advanced Student	$18,000 (13)	Partial	$18,000 (13)	Partial	$42,000 (13)	Full

For additional information on financial assistance, visit http://peabody.vanderbilt.edu/degrees-programs/masters-edd-tuition-financial-aid/index.php.

Employment of Department Graduates

Master's:
Enrolled in a psychology doctoral program: 1
Employed in a professional position in a school system: 15
Employed in business or industry: 25
Employed in government agency: 5
Employed in a community mental health/counseling center: 10
Total: 56

Doctoral:
Employed in an academic position at a university: 3
Employed in other positions at a higher education institution: 2
Employed in government agency: 2
Still seeking employment: 1
Total: 8

Additional Information

Housing and Day Care: No on-campus housing is available. On-campus day care facilities are available. See the following website for more information: http://www.vanderbilt.edu/child-family-center/child-care-center/index.php.

Information for Students With Physical Disabilities: See the following website: http://www.vanderbilt.edu/ead/.

Special Facilities or Resources: Peabody College has its own library, several computer centers, and nationally known research centers, including the Learning Sciences Institute and the Kennedy Center for Research on Human Development, mental retardation and other disabilities. Also on the beautiful and historic Peabody campus is the Vanderbilt Institute for Public Policy Studies (Centers for Mental Health Policy, Evaluation Research and Methodology, Child and Family Policy, Crime and Justice Policy, Environmental Management Studies, Health Policy, Psychotherapy Research and Policy, State and Local Policy). Located in Nashville, the Tennessee state capital, offers opportunities for research and internships in state and local health and human service agencies and schools.

Application Information: *Fee:* $0. *Online application:* https://apply.vanderbilt.edu/apply/.

Vanderbilt University

Psychological Sciences
Arts and Science and Peabody College
111 21st Avenue South, Wilson Hall or Peabody College #512, 230 Appleton Place
Nashville, TN 37240
Telephone: (615) 322-0080
Chairperson: René Marois & Amy Needham

E-mail: gale.newton@vanderbilt.edu or ally.armstead@vanderbilt.edu
Web: http://www.vanderbilt.edu/psychological_sciences/

Orientation, Objectives, and Emphasis of Department

The doctoral program in Psychological Sciences is offered jointly by the Department of Psychology in the College of Arts and Science and the Department of Psychology and Human Development in the Peabody College at Vanderbilt University. The program focuses on psychological theory and original empirical research. Students are admitted to work toward the PhD in these areas: Clinical Science, Cognition and Cognitive Neuroscience, Developmental Science, Neuroscience, or Quantitative Methods and Evaluation. A major goal is the placement of students in academic settings. The curriculum is designed to: (a) familiarize students with major areas of psychology; (b) provide specialized training in at least one of the five specific areas; and (c) provide students flexibility to enroll in classes consistent with their research interests. Students take core courses in quantitative methods and their substantive area, enroll in advanced seminars, and attend weekly area group colloquia. In addition to coursework, we expect students to be continually involved in research throughout their tenure in our program. We use a one-on-one mentoring model as a primary though not exclusive means of advising for the acquisition of scientific skills by students.

Programs and Degrees Offered

Program	Degree	Application Deadline	Applica-tions Received	Accepted	New Admits Enrolled (PT)	Total Enrolled (PT)	Degrees Awarded in 2014–2015	Median Years to Complete Degree	Dismissed/Withdrew
Neuroscience	PhD	December 1 (Fall)	170	2	2 (0)	12 (0)	1	5	0
Clinical Science	PhD	December 1 (Fall)	524	6	3 (0)	37 (0)	4	7	1

Programs and Degrees Offered (con't.)

Program	Degree	Application Deadline	Applica-tions Received	Accepted	New Admits Enrolled (PT)	Total Enrolled (PT)	Degrees Awarded in 2014–2015	Median Years to Complete Degree	Dismissed/ Withdrew
Cognition and Cognitive Neuroscience	PhD	December 1 (Fall)	301	2	4	22	4	5	0
Developmental Science	PhD	December 1 (Fall)	182	6	0	8	1	5	0
Quantitative Methods and Evaluation	PhD	December 1 (Fall)	88	2	1	7	2	6	0

APA Accreditation

Clinical PhD: Student Outcome Data website: http://www.vanderbilt.edu/psychological_sciences/graduate/programs/clinical.php.

Doctoral Degree (PhD Clinical Science): For those doctoral students for whom a professional internship was required in this program prior to graduation:
Total students who applied for an internship: 5
Total students who obtained an internship: 5
Total students who obtained a paid internship: 5
Total students who obtained an unpaid internship: 0
Total students who were placed in APA/CPA-accredited internships: 5
Total students placed in internships not APA/CPA-accredited, but listed with the Association of Psychology Postdoctoral and Internship Centers (APPIC): 0
Total students placed in internships conforming to guidelines of the Council of Directors of School Psychology Programs (CDSPP): 0
Total students placed in internships that were not APA/CPA-accredited, APPIC or CDSSP listed: 0

Internships/Practica

We offer up to two dozen different placements for students to do their practica. These include two VA Medical Centers, VU Child and Adolescent Psychiatric Hospital, VU Diabetes Center, VU Psychological and Counseling Center, Mobile Crisis Response Service, public school systems, state prison, and mental health facilities for both children and adults.

Admissions

Entries appear in the following order: required test or GPA, minimum score (if required)/median score of students entering in 2015–2016.

Program	Degree	GRE-V	GRE-Q	GRE-Writing	GRE-Subject	Under-graduate GPA	Last 2 Years GPA	Psychol-ogy GPA	Master's GPA
Neuroscience	PhD	NA/162	NA/167	Not specified	Not specified	NA/3.56	Not specified	NA/3.78	Not specified
Clinical Science	PhD	NA/164	NA/160	Not specified	Not specified	NA/3.74	Not specified	NA/3.85	Not specified
Cognition and Cognitive Neuroscience	PhD	NA/157	NA/160	Not specified	Not specified	NA/3.69	Not specified	NA/3.66	Not specified
Developmental Science	PhD	NA/163	NA/159	Not specified	Not specified	NA/3.95	Not specified	NA/3.96	Not specified
Quantitative Methods and Evaluation	PhD	NA/165	NA/163	Not specified	Not specified	NA/3.77	Not specified	NA/3.8	Not specified

Admissions Requirements:

Degree	GRE	GRE-Subject	Letters of Recommendation	Research Statement	Writing Sample	CV	Interview
Doctoral	Required	Optional	3	Required	Optional	Required	Required

Admissions Criteria:

GRE scores—high
Research experience—high
Work experience—low
Clinically related public service—low
GPA—high

Letters of recommendation—high
Interview—high
Statement of goals and objectives—high
Undergraduate psychology preparation—medium

For additional information on admission requirements, visit http://www.vanderbilt.edu/psychological_sciences/graduate/prospective/index.php.

Department Demographics

	Male (PT)	Female (PT)	Total	African-American/Black (PT)	Hispanic/Latino (PT)	Asian/Pacific Islander (PT)	American Indian/Alaska Native (PT)	Caucasian/White (PT)	Unknown	Multiethnic (PT)	ADA (PT)	Int'l (PT)
Students	26 (0)	57 (0)	83	4 (0)	1 (0)	12 (0)	0 (0)	59 (0)	6 (0)	1 (0)	0 (0)	6 (0)

Financial Information/Assistance

Tuition: For information on tuition costs, visit http://gradschool.vanderbilt.edu/funding/fees.php. Tuition is subject to change. Additional fees are assessed to students beyond the costs of tuition for the following: student activity and recreation fees.

Doctoral:
State residents: $43,632 per academic year.
State residents: $1,818 per credit hour.
Nonstate residents: $43,632 per academic year.
Nonstate residents: $1,818 per credit hour.

Financial Assistance:

	Teaching Assistantship (% Receiving)	Teaching Assistantship Tuition Remission	Research Assistantship (% Receiving)	Research Assistantship Tuition Remission	Fellowship (% Receiving)	Fellowship Tuition Remission
First-Year Student	$23,200 (NA)	Full	$23,200 (NA)	Full	$23,200 (100)	Full
Advanced Student	$23,200 (49)	Full	$23,200 (17)	Full	$23,200 (17)	Full

For additional information on financial assistance, visit http://www.vanderbilt.edu/psychological_sciences/graduate/prospective/aid.php.

Employment of Department Graduates

Doctoral:
Enrolled in a postdoctoral residency/fellowship: 9
Employed in independent practice: 1
Employed in a professional position in a school system: 1
Employed in business or industry: 2
Employed in a community mental health/counseling center: 1
Do not know: 3
Total: 17

Additional Information

Housing and Day Care: No on-campus housing is available. On-campus day care facilities are available. See the following website for more information: http://www.vanderbilt.edu/child-family-center//child-care-center/.

Information for Students With Physical Disabilities: See the following website: http://www.vanderbilt.edu/ead/ds_about.html.

Special Facilities or Resources: Psychological Sciences is housed in Wilson Hall, Jesup Psychological Laboratory, and Hobbs Laboratory of Human Development. We have state-of-the-art laboratories for carrying out basic research with humans and animals that include computer stimulus presentation and response collection capabilities, computers for data analysis and computational modeling, and specialized research equipment (including eyetracking environments, virtual reality, and custom experimental hardware and electronics). Research with humans, including both adults and children, and including those with brain damage and mental illness, is conducted in laboratories at Wilson and Hobbs and at laboratories in the Kennedy Center and the Vanderbilt Medical Center. Wilson Hall contains an AAALAC-accredited animal care facility with dedicated and experienced staff to support husbandry, enrichment, and surgery for species used in basic research. Faculty members have their own dedicated laboratory space for conducting clinical, cognitive and cognitive neuroscience, developmental, neuroscience, and quantitative research. Research in Psychological Sciences is enhanced by a number of Research Centers that support a variety of shared research equipment and services: Advanced Computing Center for Research and Education, Center for Integrative and Cognitive Neuroscience, Institute for Imaging Science, Kennedy Center, Learning Sciences Institute and Vanderbilt Vision Research Center.

Application Information: Center for Data Management, Vanderbilt University, PMB 407833, 2301 Vanderbilt Place, Nashville, TN 37240-7833. *Fee:* $0. *Online application:* https://apply.vanderbilt.edu/apply/.

Angelo State University

Department of Psychology, Sociology, and Social Work
College of Health and Human Services
2601 West Avenue N
San Angelo, TX 76909
Telephone: (325) 942-2068
Chairperson: James Forbes

E-mail: james.forbes@angelo.edu
Web: http://www.angelo.edu/dept/psychology_sociology/

Orientation, Objectives, and Emphasis of Department

The department emphasizes personalized training, small class sizes, and a balance between research skills and practitioner skills. We offer the Applied Psychology program completely online.

Programs and Degrees Offered

Program	Degree	Application Deadline	Applica-tions Received	Accepted	New Admits Enrolled (PT)	Total Enrolled (PT)	Degrees Awarded in 2014–2015	Median Years to Complete Degree	Dismissed/ Withdrew
Counseling Psychology	MA/MS	July 15 (Fall), December 1 (Spring), April 30 (Summer)	71	59	29 (4)	41 (18)	24	2	21
Applied Psychology	MA/MS	March 1 (Fall), October 1 (Spring), March 1 (Summer)	62	29	14 (15)	36 (24)	29	2	24
Industrial/ Organizational Psychology	MA/MS	July 15 (Fall), December 1 (Spring), April 30 (Summer)	21	17	15 (0)	20 (0)	12	2	4

Internships/Practica

Practicum opportunities are available in many local public and private mental health facilities and also in local corporate entities.

Admissions

Entries appear in the following order: required test or GPA, minimum score (if required)/median score of students entering in 2015–2016.

Program	Degree	GRE-V	GRE-Q	GRE-Writing	GRE-Subject	Under-graduate GPA	Last 2 Years GPA	Psychol-ogy GPA	Master's GPA
Counseling Psychology	MA/MS	Not specified	Not specified	Not specified	Not specified	Not specified	Not specified	Not specified	Not specified
Applied Psychology	MA/MS	Not specified	Not specified	Not specified	Not specified	Not specified	Not specified	Not specified	Not specified
Industrial/ Organizational Psychology	MA/MS	NA/NA	NA/NA	NA/NA	Not specified	3/3.3	Not specified	3.25/NA	Not specified

Admissions Requirements:

Degree	GRE	GRE-Subject	Letters of Recommendation	Research Statement	Writing Sample	CV	Interview
Master's/Specialist	Recommended	None	3	Required	Optional	Optional	Required

Please note if these criteria vary for different programs: GRE scores are required for applicants whose GPA is below a certain level; GRE is strongly recommended for all applicants to the I/O program. Interview required for I/O program only.

Admissions Criteria:

GRE scores—high
Research experience—low
Work experience—low
GPA—high

Letters of recommendation—medium
Statement of goals and objectives—medium
Undergraduate psychology preparation—low

For additional information on admission requirements, visit http://www.angelo.edu/dept/psychology_sociology/grad_program/.

Department Demographics

	Male (PT)	Female (PT)	Total	African-American/ Black (PT)	Hispanic/ Latino (PT)	Asian/ Pacific Islander (PT)	American Indian/ Alaska Native (PT)	Caucasian/ White (PT)	Unknown	Multiethnic (PT)	ADA (PT)	Int'l (PT)
Students	28 (11)	69 (31)	139	4 (7)	23 (11)	3 (0)	0 (0)	63 (20)	4 (4)	0 (0)	0 (0)	0 (0)

Financial Information/Assistance

Tuition: For information on tuition costs, visit http://www.angelo.edu/services/controller/sa_tuition&fees.php. Tuition is subject to change.

Master's:
State residents: $5,340 per academic year.
State residents: $608 per credit hour.
Nonstate residents: $10,920 per academic year.
Nonstate residents: $918 per credit hour.

Financial Assistance:

	Teaching Assistantship (% Receiving)	Teaching Assistantship Tuition Remission	Research Assistantship (% Receiving)	Research Assistantship Tuition Remission	Fellowship (% Receiving)	Fellowship Tuition Remission
First-Year Student	NA (NA)	NA	$7,490 (NA)	NA	$2,300 (NA)	NA
Advanced Student	$11,095 (NA)	NA	$7,490 (NA)	NA	$2,300 (NA)	NA

For additional information on financial assistance, visit http://www.angelo.edu/dept/psychology_sociology/grad_program/employment.php.

Employment of Department Graduates

No information provided.

Additional Information

Housing and Day Care: On-campus housing is available. See the following website for more information: http://www.angelo.edu/dept/residential_programs/. No on-campus day care facilities are available.

Information for Students With Physical Disabilities: See the following website: http://www.angelo.edu/services/disability-services/.

Special Facilities or Resources: The department is equipped with state-of-the-art psychology and computer laboratories. Training also occurs in local agencies and hospitals, private companies, and university administration offices.

Application Information: Office of the Graduate Dean, Angelo State University, ASU Station #11025, San Angelo, TX 76909-1025. *Fee:* $40. *Online application:* http://www.angelo.edu/graduate_application/.

Baylor University (2015 data)

Department of Psychology and Neuroscience, PhD Program in Psychology
Arts and Sciences
One Bear Place 97334
Waco, TX 76798-7334
Telephone: (254) 710-2961
Chairperson: Charles A. Weaver III, PhD
E-mail: Jim_Patton@baylor.edu
Web: http://www.baylor.edu/psychologyneuroscience

Orientation, Objectives, and Emphasis of Department

The department offers a broad range of courses in the areas of clinical psychology, behavioral neuroscience, social psychology, and general experimental psychology. The Doctor of Psychology (PsyD) program has the longest history of accreditation by the American Psychological Association. The PsyD program emphasizes a professional–scientist model with a goal of developing competencies based on current research and scholarship in clinical psychology. Extensive practicum experience is integrated with concurrent coursework. A formal dissertation involving applied clinical research is also required. The goal of Baylor's PsyD program is to develop professional–psychologists with the conceptual and clinical competencies necessary to deliver psychological services in a manner that is effective and responsive to individual and societal needs both now and in the future. The doctoral program in Psychology (PhD) has three training tracks: Behavioral Neuroscience, Social Psychology, and General Experimental. Doctoral students are expected to acquire sufficient knowledge and expertise to permit them to work as independent scholars at the frontier of their field upon graduation. Extensive training is provided in laboratory research and experimental design for social psychology and behavioral neuroscience students.

Programs and Degrees Offered

Program	Degree	Application Deadline	Applications Received	Accepted	New Admits Enrolled (PT)	Total Enrolled (PT)	Degrees Awarded in 2014–2015	Median Years to Complete Degree	Dismissed/Withdrew
Clinical Psychology	PsyD	January 2 (Summer)	250	7	7	34 (0)	5	5	2
Psychology	PhD	December 15 (Fall)	87	6	6	22	4	5	0

APA Accreditation

Clinical PsyD: Student Outcome Data website: http://www.baylor.edu/psychologyneuroscience/index.php?id=870047.

Doctoral Degree (PsyD Clinical Psychology): For those doctoral students for whom a professional internship was required in this program prior to graduation:
Total students who applied for an internship: 7
Total students who obtained an internship: 7
Total students who obtained a paid internship: 7
Total students who obtained an unpaid internship: 0
Total students who were placed in APA/CPA-accredited internships: 7
Total students placed in internships not APA/CPA-accredited, but listed with the Association of Psychology Postdoctoral and Internship Centers (APPIC): 0
Total students placed in internships conforming to guidelines of the Council of Directors of School Psychology Programs (CDSPP): 0
Total students placed in internships that were not APA/CPA-accredited, APPIC or CDSSP listed: 0

Internships/Practica

The PsyD program incorporates an extensive practicum program with placements available in 16 community agencies and treatment facilities. Of our graduates over the last 11 years, 105 of 107 have obtained APA-accredited internships.

Admissions

Entries appear in the following order: required test or GPA, minimum score (if required)/median score of students entering in 2015–2016.

Program	Degree	GRE-V	GRE-Q	GRE-Writing	GRE-Subject	Undergraduate GPA	Last 2 Years GPA	Psychology GPA	Master's GPA
Clinical Psychology	PsyD	164/NA	157/NA	Not specified	Not specified	3.8/NA	Not specified	3/NA	Not specified
Psychology	PhD	160/NA	160/NA	Not specified	Not specified	Not specified	Not specified	Not specified	Not specified

Admissions Requirements:

Degree	GRE	GRE-Subject	Letters of Recommendation	Research Statement	Writing Sample	CV	Interview
Doctoral	Required	Optional	3	Required	Optional	Required	Required

Admissions Criteria:

GRE scores—high
Research experience—high
Work experience—medium
Clinically related public service—medium
GPA—high

Letters of recommendation—high
Interview—high
Statement of goals and objectives—medium
Program Fit—high

For additional information on admission requirements, visit http://www.baylor.edu/psychologyneuroscience/index.php?id=68521.

Department Demographics

	Male (PT)	Female (PT)	Total	African-American/ Black (PT)	Hispanic/ Latino (PT)	Asian/ Pacific Islander (PT)	American Indian/ Alaska Native (PT)	Caucasian/ White (PT)	Unknown	Multiethnic (PT)	ADA (PT)	Int'l (PT)
Students	16 (0)	40 (0)	56	1 (0)	3 (0)	7 (0)	0 (0)	45 (0)	0 (0)	0 (0)	0 (0)	0 (0)

Financial Information/Assistance

Tuition: For information on tuition costs, visit http://www.baylor.edu/sfs/index.php?id=871014. Tuition is subject to change. Additional fees are assessed to students beyond the costs of tuition for the following: Student Fee: $131 per semester hour.

Doctoral:
State residents: $1,750 per credit hour.
Nonstate residents: $1,750 per credit hour.

Financial Assistance:

	Teaching Assistantship (% Receiving)	Teaching Assistantship Tuition Remission	Research Assistantship (% Receiving)	Research Assistantship Tuition Remission	Fellowship (% Receiving)	Fellowship Tuition Remission
First-Year Student	$21,000 (100)	Full	$21,000 (100)	Full	$3,000 (75)	Partial
Advanced Student	$21,000 (100)	Full	$21,000 (100)	Full	$3,000 (75)	Partial

For additional information on financial assistance, visit http://www.baylor.edu/graduate/index.php?id=97434.

Employment of Department Graduates

Doctoral:
Employed in independent practice: 6
Employed in an academic position at a university: 2
Employed in academic position at a 2-year/4-year college: 1
Employed in government agency: 4
Employed in a community mental health/counseling center: 2
Employed in a hospital/medical center: 2
Total: 17

Additional Information

Housing and Day Care: On-campus housing is available. See the following website for more information: http://www.baylor.edu/graduate/currentstudents/index.php?id=98874. On-campus day care facilities are available. See the following website for more information: http://www.baylor.edu/piper/.

Information for Students With Physical Disabilities: See the following website: http://www.baylor.edu/oala/.

Special Facilities or Resources: The department has a number of well-equipped research laboratories. PhD program: Computer-controlled programmable laboratory in memory and cognition; complete facilities for research on animal learning and behavior (including animal colony); developmental psychobiology laboratory, with facilities for behavioral and pharmacological research, including teratological studies; inhalation chambers for administration of ethanol (and other substances). Single-subject brain-recording (EEG) and electron microscopy facilities are available. The Department also houses a community clinic that facilitates the clinical training and related research activities for PsyD students.

Application Information: Baylor University; Graduate Admissions; One Bear Place 97264; Waco, TX 76798-7264. *Fee:* $50. *Online application:* http://www.baylor.edu/graduate/index.php?id=863015.

Baylor University
Educational Psychology
Education
One Bear Place #97301
Waco, TX 76798-7301
Telephone: (254) 710-3112
Chairperson: Terrill Saxon

E-mail: edp@baylor.edu
Web: http://www.baylor.edu/soe/edp/

Orientation, Objectives, and Emphasis of Department
The PhD program in Educational Psychology affords graduate students the opportunity to select a specialization in Exceptionalities, Learning and Development, or Quantitative Methods. The EdS program in School Psychology prepares students to apply a scientist–practitioner model in their work with school-age children as well as with parents, teachers, and administrators. Students receive extensive experience within the Baylor Center for Developmental Disabilities. This program is approved by the National Association of School Psychologists (NASP). The applied behavior analysis (ABA) specialization option is designed for students who are interested in behavior management such as working with people with developmental disabilities (e.g., autism spectrum disorders).

Programs and Degrees Offered

Program	Degree	Application Deadline	Applica-tions Received	Accepted	New Admits Enrolled (PT)	Total Enrolled (PT)	Degrees Awarded in 2014–2015	Median Years to Complete Degree	Dismissed/Withdrew
School Psychology	EdS	February 1 (Fall)	31	7	7 (0)	21 (0)	5	3	0
Educational Psychology	PhD	August 1 (Fall), December 1 (Spring), May 1 (Summer)	12	5	2 (0)	12 (11)	3	6.75	0

Internships/Practica

School psychology students engage in practica in local schools and the Baylor Center for Developmental Disabilities during their first and second years. Their third and final year consists of an internship in a public school.

Admissions

Entries appear in the following order: required test or GPA, minimum score (if required)/median score of students entering in 2015–2016.

Program	Degree	GRE-V	GRE-Q	GRE-Writing	GRE-Subject	Under-graduate GPA	Last 2 Years GPA	Psychology GPA	Master's GPA
School Psychology	EdS	NA/156	NA/153	NA/4.5	Not specified	3/3.7	NA/NA	Not specified	Not specified
Educational Psychology	PhD	152/NA	152/NA	4/NA	Not specified	3/3.4	Not specified	Not specified	3.5/3.8

Admissions Requirements:

Degree	GRE	GRE-Subject	Letters of Recom-mendation	Research Statement	Writing Sample	CV	Interview
Master's/Specialist	Required	Optional	3	Required	Optional	Required	Required
Doctoral	Required	Optional	3	Required	Required	Required	Required

Please note if these criteria vary for different programs: EdS program is most interested in GRE, GPA, and clinical experience whereas PhD program is most interested in GRE, GPA, and research experience/promise.

Admissions Criteria:

GRE scores—high
Research experience—medium
Work experience—low
Clinically related public service—medium
GPA—high

Letters of recommendation—high
Interview—low
Statement of goals and objectives—high
Undergraduate psychology preparation—medium

Department Demographics

	Male (PT)	Female (PT)	Total	African-American/ Black (PT)	Hispanic/ Latino (PT)	Asian/ Pacific Islander (PT)	American Indian/ Alaska Native (PT)	Caucasian/ White (PT)	Unknown	Multiethnic (PT)	ADA (PT)	Int'l (PT)
Students	5 (0)	28 (13)	46	1 (0)	1 (0)	5 (0)	0 (0)	33 (0)	0 (0)	0 (0)	0 (0)	2 (0)

Financial Information/Assistance

Tuition: For information on tuition costs, visit http://www.baylor.edu/sfs/index.php?id=871014. Tuition is subject to change. Additional fees are assessed to students beyond the costs of tuition for the following: parking, general student fee.

Doctoral:
State residents: $1,357 per credit hour.
Nonstate residents: $1,357 per credit hour.

Master's:
State residents: $1,357 per credit hour.
Nonstate residents: $1,357 per credit hour.

Financial Assistance:

	Teaching Assistantship (% Receiving)	Teaching Assistantship Tuition Remission	Research Assistantship (% Receiving)	Research Assistantship Tuition Remission	Fellowship (% Receiving)	Fellowship Tuition Remission
First-Year Student	NA (0)	Full	NA (50)	Full	NA (50)	Full
Advanced Student	NA (10)	Full	NA (50)	Full	NA (40)	Full

For additional information on financial assistance, visit http://www.baylor.edu/soe/edp/index.php?id=65337.

Employment of Department Graduates

Master's:
Employed in a professional position in a school system: 5
Total: 5

Doctoral:
Employed in other positions at a higher education institution: 1
Employed in a professional position in a school system: 1
Total: 2

Additional Information

Housing and Day Care: On-campus housing is available. See the following website for more information: http://www.baylor.edu/graduate/currentstudents/index.php?id=98874. On-campus day care facilities are available. See the following website for more information: http://www.baylor.edu/piper/.

Information for Students With Physical Disabilities: See the following website: http://www.baylor.edu/oala/.

Special Facilities or Resources: Baylor Center for Developmental Disabilities: research, teaching, and services to children with developmental disabilities and their families. The Psychometric Laboratory supports the faculty and students at Baylor University and other academic institutions in the development, application, and analysis of measurement in educational/psychological research.

Application Information: Baylor University, Department of Educational Psychology, Attn: Admissions, One Bear Place #97301, Waco, TX 76798-7301. *Fee:* $80. *Online application:* https://www.baylor.edu/graduate/gobaylor/index.php?id=99641.

Houston, University of (2015 data)
Department of Psychological, Health, and Learning Sciences
College of Education
491 Farish Hall
Houston, TX 77204-5029
Telephone: (713) 743-5043
Chairperson: Dr. Ezemenari M. Obasi

E-mail: emobasi@uh.edu
Web: http://www.coe.uh.edu/departments/phls/

Orientation, Objectives, and Emphasis of Department
Graduates of the Department of Psychological, Health, and Learning Sciences (PHLS) have made significant contributions to many university faculties, state and national boards, in private practice, in government agencies, and in leadership roles in public and private schools. Students choose PHLS in order to study with our nationally recognized faculty and to participate in innovative research in one of the most diverse research institutions in the country. The Counseling Psychology PhD program (accredited by the American Psychological Association) prepares highly skilled scientist–practitioners. Counseling psychologists can assume several roles in a variety of settings including personal, educational and career counseling services; college and university teaching; research; and consultation to organizations concerned with psychological and interpersonal development. The PhD program in School Psychology (accredited by the American Psychological Association and approved by the National Association of School Psychologists) also prepares professional psychologists in the scientist–practitioner tradition. Graduates are trained to assume leadership, direct service and consultative roles and careers in public and private PK-12 schools, health and mental health related settings, colleges and universities, research institutions, and in independent practice. The Educational Psychology and Individual Differences PhD program is dedicated to the advancement and application of knowledge relevant to learning quantitative methods.

Programs and Degrees Offered

Program	Degree	Application Deadline	Applications Received	Accepted	New Admits Enrolled (PT)	Total Enrolled (PT)	Degrees Awarded in 2014–2015	Median Years to Complete Degree	Dismissed/Withdrew
Counseling Psychology	PhD	December 1 (Fall)	93	8	7 (0)	32 (9)	8	5	0
Educational Psychology & Individual Differences	PhD	February 1 (Fall)	24	9	6 (1)	21 (17)	6	5	
Counseling	MEd	February 15 (Fall), September 15 (Spring)	109	59	22 (12)	54 (48)	53	2.67	
School Psychology	PhD	December 1 (Fall)	35	5	5	24 (9)	2	6.33	0

APA Accreditation

Counseling PhD: Student Outcome Data website: http://www.coe.uh.edu/degree-programs/counseling-psyc-phd/.
School PhD: Student Outcome Data website: http://www.coe.uh.edu/degree-programs/school-psyc-phd/.

Doctoral Degree (PhD Counseling Psychology): For those doctoral students for whom a professional internship was required in this program prior to graduation:
Total students who applied for an internship: 9
Total students who obtained an internship: 9
Total students who obtained a paid internship: 9
Total students who obtained an unpaid internship: 0
Total students who were placed in APA/CPA-accredited internships: 9
Total students placed in internships not APA/CPA-accredited, but listed with the Association of Psychology Postdoctoral and Internship Centers (APPIC): 0
Total students placed in internships conforming to guidelines of the Council of Directors of School Psychology Programs (CDSPP): 0
Total students placed in internships that were not APA/CPA-accredited, APPIC or CDSSP listed: 0

Doctoral Degree (PhD School Psychology): For those doctoral students for whom a professional internship was required in this program prior to graduation:
Total students who applied for an internship: 5
Total students who obtained an internship: 5
Total students who obtained a paid internship: 5
Total students who obtained an unpaid internship: 0
Total students who were placed in APA/CPA-accredited internships: 5
Total students placed in internships not APA/CPA-accredited, but listed with the Association of Psychology Postdoctoral and Internship Centers (APPIC): 0
Total students placed in internships conforming to guidelines of the Council of Directors of School Psychology Programs (CDSPP): 0
Total students placed in internships that were not APA/CPA-accredited, APPIC or CDSSP listed: 0

Internships/Practica

All counseling psychology doctoral students and counseling master's students participate in supervised practica at numerous sites throughout the Houston area. Examples of the types of sites at which students have completed practica include the Texas Children's Hospital, M.D. Anderson Cancer Hospital, Veterans Affairs Medical Center, Baylor College of Medicine, Harris County Juvenile Probation, Harris County Psychiatric Center, counseling centers and school districts. In addition, doctoral counseling psychology students are required to complete a one year, full-time internship approved by the faculty. These sites range widely in orientation, focus and geographic location. All school psychology doctoral students must complete two years of advanced practicum (half-time) as well as a one year, full-time predoctoral internship. Practica are arranged for students, and are available at various sites around the Houston area, including school districts, Texas Children's Hospital, M.D. Anderson Children's Cancer Hospital, Harris County Juvenile Probation, Harris County Children's Psychiatric Center, and the Mental Retardation and Autism Unit of the Harris County Mental Health and Mental Retardation Department. Internship sites are available in a variety of settings in the Houston area and around the country.

Admissions

Entries appear in the following order: required test or GPA, minimum score (if required)/median score of students entering in 2015–2016.

Program	Degree	GRE-V	GRE-Q	GRE-Writing	GRE-Subject	Under-graduate GPA	Last 2 Years GPA	Psychol-ogy GPA	Master's GPA
Counseling Psychology	PhD	146/156	140/149	3/4.5	Not specified	2.47/3.49	Not specified	Not specified	Not specified
Educational Psychology & Individual Differences	PhD	140/152	131/149	3/4	Not specified	Not specified	Not specified	Not specified	Not specified
Counseling	MEd	139/153	137/149	2.5/4	Not specified	2.33/3.48	Not specified	Not specified	Not specified
School Psychology	PhD	146/155	141/149	3/4.5	Not specified	2.14/3.58	Not specified	Not specified	Not specified

Admissions Requirements:

Degree	GRE	GRE-Subject	Letters of Recom-mendation	Research Statement	Writing Sample	CV	Interview
Master's/Specialist	Required	Optional	3	Required	Required	Required	None
Doctoral	Required	Optional	3	Required	Required	Required	Required

Please note if these criteria vary for different programs: PhD programs emphasize research experience and research interests more than do the master's programs.

Admissions Criteria:

GRE scores—high
Research experience—high
Work experience—medium
Clinically related public service—medium
GPA—high

Letters of recommendation—high
Interview—high
Statement of goals and objectives—high
Undergraduate psychology preparation—medium

For additional information on admission requirements, visit http://www.coe.uh.edu/admissions/graduate/.

Department Demographics

	Male (PT)	Female (PT)	Total	African-American/ Black (PT)	Hispanic/ Latino (PT)	Asian/ Pacific Islander (PT)	American Indian/ Alaska Native (PT)	Caucasian/ White (PT)	Unknown	Multiethnic (PT)	ADA (PT)	Int'l (PT)
Students	10 (9)	121 (74)	214	14 (15)	27 (14)	16 (5)	0 (0)	62 (45)	7 (2)	5 (2)	0 (0)	7 (1)

Financial Information/Assistance

Tuition: For information on tuition costs, visit http://www.uh.edu/financial/graduate/tuition-fees/tuition/. Tuition is subject to change. Additional fees are assessed to students beyond the costs of tuition for the following: Student service fee, university center fee, recreation and wellness center.

Doctoral:
State residents: $6,948 per academic year.
State residents: $386 per credit hour.
Nonstate residents: $15,264 per academic year.
Nonstate residents: $848 per credit hour.

Master's:
State residents: $7,290 per academic year.
State residents: $405 per credit hour.
Nonstate residents: $15,606 per academic year.
Nonstate residents: $867 per credit hour.

Financial Assistance:

	Teaching Assistantship (% Receiving)	Teaching Assistantship Tuition Remission	Research Assistantship (% Receiving)	Research Assistantship Tuition Remission	Fellowship (% Receiving)	Fellowship Tuition Remission
First-Year Student	$12,732 (NA)	Full	$12,732 (NA)	Full	$3,000 (NA)	NA
Advanced Student	$15,132 (NA)	Full	$15,132 (NA)	Full	NA (NA)	NA

For additional information on financial assistance, visit http://coe.uh.edu/student-services/fin_aid_scholarships/.

Employment of Department Graduates

Doctoral:
Enrolled in a postdoctoral residency/fellowship: 4
Employed in independent practice: 3
Employed in an academic position at a university: 1
Employed in other positions at a higher education institution: 1
Employed in a professional position in a school system: 4
Employed in a community mental health/counseling center: 1
Employed in a hospital/medical center: 2
Total: 16

Additional Information

Housing and Day Care: On-campus housing is available. See the following website for more information: http://housing.uh.edu/. On-campus day care facilities are available. See the following website for more information: http://www.uh.edu/clc/.

Information for Students With Physical Disabilities: See the following website: http://www.uh.edu/csd/.

Special Facilities or Resources: Located in the heart of a highly diverse metropolitan area with almost 5 million inhabitants, the Department has access to a wealth of community research facilities and resources (e.g., 56 school districts, a range of community-based mental health and specialty clinics and agencies, a large VA Hospital, 20 hospitals within the Texas Medical Center). Within the College of Education, the Center for Information Technology in Education (CITE) Laboratory provides faculty, staff, and students with computing and multimedia environments, technology resources, and timely service-oriented user support. Several faculty have active funded and unfunded research teams that provide students with a range of research options, often in collaboration with major facilities (i.e., medical facilities, schools, community/state organizations) in the Houston community.

Application Information: Graduate Admissions, Department of Psychological, Health, and Learning Sciences, University of Houston, 491 Farish Hall, Houston, TX 77204-5029. *Fee:* $45. *Online application:* https://www.applyweb.com/uhouston/.

Houston, University of
Department of Psychology
College of Liberal Arts and Social Sciences
126 Heyne Building
Houston, TX 77204-5022
Telephone: (713) 743-8508
Chairperson: Jack M. Fletcher

E-mail: ptolar@uh.edu
Web: http://www.psychology.uh.edu

Orientation, Objectives, and Emphasis of Department
Clinical offers APA-approved training in research, assessment, intervention, and consultation related to complex human problems, including behavioral problems having a neurological basis. Industrial/organizational offers broad training in industrial/organizational psychology with options for specialization in either the personnel or organizational subfields. Social emphasizes research careers in behavioral and preventive medicine; interpersonal interaction processes, with an emphasis on close relationships and motivation; and social cognition. Developmental focuses on experimental research in developmental cognitive neuroscience, including perception, speech, language, reading, attention, decision-making, memory, and emotion, using imaging, electrophysiological, and neurochemical techniques in human and animal models.

Programs and Degrees Offered

Program	Degree	Application Deadline	Applica-tions Received	Accepted	New Admits Enrolled (PT)	Total Enrolled (PT)	Degrees Awarded in 2014–2015	Median Years to Complete Degree	Dismissed/ Withdrew
Clinical Psychology	PhD	December 1 (Fall)	368	15	7 (0)	52 (0)	16	6	1
Industrial/ Organizational Psychology	PhD	January 15 (Fall)	120	8	2 (0)	23 (0)	5	6.2	2
Social Psychology	PhD	January 15 (Fall)	43	4	4 (0)	15 (0)	5	6	0
Developmental Psychology	PhD	December 1 (Fall)	21	1	1	18	4	6.25	2

APA Accreditation

Clinical PhD: Student Outcome Data website: http://www.uh.edu/class/psychology/clinical-psych/admissions/index.php.

Doctoral Degree (PhD Clinical Psychology): For those doctoral students for whom a professional internship was required in this program prior to graduation:
Total students who applied for an internship: 8
Total students who obtained an internship: 8
Total students who obtained a paid internship: 8
Total students who obtained an unpaid internship: 0
Total students who were placed in APA/CPA-accredited internships: 8
Total students placed in internships not APA/CPA-accredited, but listed with the Association of Psychology Postdoctoral and Internship Centers (APPIC): 0
Total students placed in internships conforming to guidelines of the Council of Directors of School Psychology Programs (CDSPP): 0
Total students placed in internships that were not APA/CPA-accredited, APPIC or CDSSP listed: 0

Internships/Practica

Internships are available for advanced students at a number of sites that include private industry, medical centers, state hospitals, and private practices.

Admissions

Entries appear in the following order: required test or GPA, minimum score (if required)/median score of students entering in 2015–2016.

Program	Degree	GRE-V	GRE-Q	GRE-Writing	GRE-Subject	Under-graduate GPA	Last 2 Years GPA	Psychol-ogy GPA	Master's GPA
Clinical Psychology	PhD	NA/NA	NA/NA	NA/NA	Not specified	NA/NA	Not specified	NA/NA	Not specified
Industrial/ Organizational Psychology	PhD	NA/NA	NA/NA	NA/NA	Not specified	NA/NA	Not specified	NA/NA	Not specified
Social Psychology	PhD	NA/NA	NA/NA	NA/NA	Not specified	NA/NA	Not specified	NA/NA	Not specified
Developmental Psychology	PhD	NA/NA	NA/NA	NA/NA	Not specified	NA/NA	Not specified	NA/NA	Not specified

Admissions Requirements:

Degree	GRE	GRE-Subject	Letters of Recom-mendation	Research Statement	Writing Sample	CV	Interview
Doctoral	Required	Optional	3	Required	Optional	Optional	Required

Please note if these criteria vary for different programs: Clinically related public service is more relevant to the clinical program.

Admissions Criteria:

GRE scores—medium
Research experience—high
Work experience—medium
Clinically related public service—medium
GPA—medium

Letters of recommendation—high
Interview—high
Statement of goals and objectives—high
Undergraduate psychology preparation—medium

For additional information on admission requirements, visit http://www.uh.edu/class/psychology/graduate/admissions/.

Department Demographics

	Male (PT)	Female (PT)	Total	African-American/ Black (PT)	Hispanic/ Latino (PT)	Asian/ Pacific Islander (PT)	American Indian/ Alaska Native (PT)	Caucasian/ White (PT)	Unknown	Multiethnic (PT)	ADA (PT)	Int'l (PT)
Students	31 (0)	77 (0)	108	4 (0)	7 (0)	9 (0)	0 (0)	88 (0)	0 (0)	0 (0)	0 (0)	12 (0)

Financial Information/Assistance

Tuition: For information on tuition costs, visit http://www.uh.edu/financial/graduate/tuition-fees/. Tuition is subject to change. Additional fees are assessed to students beyond the costs of tuition for the following: $477/semester for student services.

Doctoral:
State residents: $9,600 per academic year.
State residents: $320 per credit hour.
Nonstate residents: $24,300 per academic year.
Nonstate residents: $810 per credit hour.

Financial Assistance:

	Teaching Assistantship (% Receiving)	Teaching Assistantship Tuition Remission	Research Assistantship (% Receiving)	Research Assistantship Tuition Remission	Fellowship (% Receiving)	Fellowship Tuition Remission
First-Year Student	$19,040 (NA)	Full	$19,040 (NA)	Full	$2,000 (NA)	Full
Advanced Student	$20,672 (NA)	Full	$20,672 (NA)	Full	NA (NA)	Full

For additional information on financial assistance, visit http://www.uh.edu/financial/graduate/index.php.

Employment of Department Graduates

No information provided.

Additional Information

Housing and Day Care: On-campus housing is available. See the following website for more information: http://housing.uh.edu/. On-campus day care facilities are available. See the following website for more information: http://www.uh.edu/clc/.

Information for Students With Physical Disabilities: See the following website: http://www.uh.edu/csd/.

Special Facilities or Resources: The facilities of the department are comparable to those of any major department in a large university. A variety of community settings are available for applied research in all areas of specialization. Specialized laboratories have modern equipment for research in family and couple interaction, biofeedback, personnel interviewing, electrophysiology, and animal studies, as well as access to an fMRI scanner. Several research and clinical practica are available within the community and at several hospitals (the Texas Medical Center is one of the largest in the world).

Application Information: Fee: $65. Online application: https://www.applyweb.com/uhouston/.

Lamar University-Beaumont

Department of Psychology
Arts & Sciences
P.O. Box 10036
Beaumont, TX 77710
Telephone: (409) 880-8285
Chairperson: Edythe Kirk

E-mail: edythe.kirk@lamar.edu
Web: http://artssciences.lamar.edu/psychology/index.html

Orientation, Objectives, and Emphasis of Department

The Department of Psychology offers a program of study leading to the Master of Science degree in Applied Psychology. It is designed to prepare professional personnel for employment in business, industry, or community mental health agencies. The track in Clinical Psychology includes training in assessment and therapy techniques for individuals, groups, and families. The track in Industrial/Organizational Psychology integrates the traditional areas of industrial psychology with the more contemporary areas of organizational development and analysis. Both tracks also prepare graduates for entry to doctoral programs.

Programs and Degrees Offered

Program	Degree	Application Deadline	Applications Received	Accepted	New Admits Enrolled (PT)	Total Enrolled (PT)	Degrees Awarded in 2014–2015	Median Years to Complete Degree	Dismissed/Withdrew
Applied Psychology	MA/MS	June 1 (Fall)	19	8	8 (0)	13 (6)	10	2.8	1

Internships/Practica

A variety of community health settings provide useful practicum experiences for Clinical students in child, adolescent and adult counseling and assessment. There is also a clinic in the Psychology Department where students practice counseling under supervision. Practicum experiences for the Industrial/Organizational students place them in a variety of organizational and industrial work environments.

Admissions

Entries appear in the following order: required test or GPA, minimum score (if required)/median score of students entering in 2015–2016.

Program	Degree	GRE-V	GRE-Q	GRE-Writing	GRE-Subject	Undergraduate GPA	Last 2 Years GPA	Psychology GPA	Master's GPA
Applied Psychology	MA/MS	150/151	150/149	Not specified	Not specified	3/3.39	Not specified	Not specified	Not specified

Admissions Requirements:

Degree	GRE	GRE-Subject	Letters of Recommendation	Research Statement	Writing Sample	CV	Interview
Master's/Specialist	Required	Optional	3	Required	Optional	Recommended	None

Admissions Criteria:

GRE scores—high
Research experience—medium
Work experience—low
Clinically related public service—low

GPA—high
Letters of recommendation—high
Statement of goals and objectives—high
Undergraduate psychology preparation—high

For additional information on admission requirements, visit http://artssciences.lamar.edu/psychology/degrees/graduate/index.html.

Department Demographics

	Male (PT)	Female (PT)	Total	African-American/ Black (PT)	Hispanic/ Latino (PT)	Asian/ Pacific Islander (PT)	American Indian/ Alaska Native (PT)	Caucasian/ White (PT)	Unknown	Multiethnic (PT)	ADA (PT)	Int'l (PT)
Students	6 (1)	7 (5)	19	1 (1)	2 (0)	0 (1)	0 (0)	10 (4)	0 (0)	0 (0)	0 (0)	0 (0)

Financial Information/Assistance

Tuition: For information on tuition costs, visit http://students.lamar.edu/paying-for-school/tuition-and-fees.html. Tuition is subject to change. Additional fees are assessed to students beyond the costs of tuition for the following: health center, technology, library, student services. Tuition costs vary by program.

Master's:
State residents: $496 per credit hour.
Nonstate residents: $886 per credit hour.

Financial Assistance:

	Teaching Assistantship (% Receiving)	Teaching Assistantship Tuition Remission	Research Assistantship (% Receiving)	Research Assistantship Tuition Remission	Fellowship (% Receiving)	Fellowship Tuition Remission
First-Year Student	$3,000 (NA)	Partial	NA (NA)	NA	$1,000 (NA)	Partial
Advanced Student	$3,000 (NA)	Partial	NA (NA)	NA	$1,000 (NA)	Partial

For additional information on financial assistance, visit http://financialaid.lamar.edu/index.html.

Employment of Department Graduates

Master's:
Employed in an academic position at a university: 1
Employed in business or industry: 1
Employed in government agency: 2
Employed in a community mental health/counseling center: 3
Do not know: 2
Total: 9

Additional Information

Housing and Day Care: On-campus housing is available. See the following website for more information: http://beacardinal.lamar.edu/housing/. No on-campus day care facilities are available.

Information for Students With Physical Disabilities: See the following website: http://www.lamar.edu/disability-resource-center/.

Special Facilities or Resources: The Department currently maintains a psychological clinic that is used for training and research. It is available to both the student population as well as those in the surrounding community. The department also has a computer lab and research space.

Application Information: Fee: $30. *Online application:* http://beacardinal.lamar.edu/how-to-apply/graduate.html.

Midwestern State University
Department of Psychology
Prothro-Yeager College of Humanities & Social Sciences
3410 Taft Boulevard
Wichita Falls, TX 76308
Telephone: (940) 397-4340
Psychology Graduate Coordinator: Dave Carlston

E-mail: david.carlston@mwsu.edu
Web: http://mwsu.edu/academics/libarts/psychology/ma/

Orientation, Objectives, and Emphasis of Department

The clinical/counseling psychology graduate program is available in either a 50-hour or 60-hour curriculum option and is designed to lead to certification as a Licensed Professional Counselor (LPC) or Licensed Psychological Associate (LPA). Students may pursue thesis or non-thesis options. Although our emphasis is on training the master's level practitioner, we actively encourage our students to pursue doctoral training, and we see the training we provide as a first step toward that goal.

Programs and Degrees Offered

Program	Degree	Application Deadline	Applica-tions Received	Accepted	New Admits Enrolled (PT)	Total Enrolled (PT)	Degrees Awarded in 2014–2015	Median Years to Complete Degree	Dismissed/ Withdrew
Clinical/ Counseling Psychology	MA/MS	May 1 (Fall), November 1 (Spring)	17	9	6 (0)	16 (0)	7	2	1

Internships/Practica

Students completing the 60 hour clinical/counseling program complete 9 credit hours of practicum for a total of 450 clock-hours of work and study in an applied clinical/counseling setting. Students have completed practica at First Step, Inc. (a battered women's shelter), Taft Counseling Center (non-profit, outpatient service provider), the North Texas State Hospital (adult, child, and forensic units), Rose Street Mental Health (for-profit outpatient service provider), Hospice of Wichita Falls, and with a variety of other licensed psychologists in the community.

Admissions

Entries appear in the following order: required test or GPA, minimum score (if required)/median score of students entering in 2015–2016.

Program	Degree	GRE-V	GRE-Q	GRE-Writing	GRE-Subject	Under-graduate GPA	Last 2 Years GPA	Psychol-ogy GPA	Master's GPA
Clinical/ Counseling Psychology	MA/MS	NA/152	NA/150	NA/3.5	Not specified	NA/3.45	NA/NA	NA/NA	Not specified

Admissions Requirements:

Degree	GRE	GRE-Subject	Letters of Recom-mendation	Research Statement	Writing Sample	CV	Interview
Master's/Specialist	Required	Optional	Not Specified	Optional	Optional	Optional	None

Admissions Criteria:

GRE scores—high
Research experience—medium
Work experience—medium
Clinically related public service—low

GPA—high
Letters of recommendation—low
Statement of goals and objectives—low
Undergraduate psychology preparation—medium

For additional information on admission requirements, visit http://www.mwsu.edu/academics/libarts/psychology/ma/admissions-faqs-copy.

Department Demographics

	Male (PT)	Female (PT)	Total	African-American/ Black (PT)	Hispanic/ Latino (PT)	Asian/ Pacific Islander (PT)	American Indian/ Alaska Native (PT)	Caucasian/ White (PT)	Unknown (PT)	Multiethnic (PT)	ADA (PT)	Int'l (PT)
Students	2 (0)	14 (0)	16	2 (0)	1 (0)	1 (0)	0 (0)	12 (0)	0 (0)	0 (0)	0 (0)	2 (0)

Financial Information/Assistance

Tuition: For information on tuition costs, visit http://www.mwsu.edu/busoffice/tuition-and-fee-rates. Tuition is subject to change.

Master's:
State residents: $8,238 per academic year.
Nonstate residents: $10,189 per academic year.

Financial Assistance:

	Teaching Assistantship (% Receiving)	Teaching Assistantship Tuition Remission	Research Assistantship (% Receiving)	Research Assistantship Tuition Remission	Fellowship (% Receiving)	Fellowship Tuition Remission
First-Year Student	NA (NA)	NA	$4,000 (100)	NA	$1,000 (NA)	Partial
Advanced Student	$4,000 (33)	NA	$4,000 (66)	NA	$1,000 (NA)	Partial

For additional information on financial assistance, visit http://www.mwsu.edu/finaid/.

Employment of Department Graduates

Master's:
Enrolled in a psychology doctoral program: 2
Employed in other positions at a higher education institution: 1
Employed in government agency: 1
Employed in a community mental health/counseling center: 1
Other employment position: 2
Total: 7

Additional Information

Housing and Day Care: On-campus housing is available. See the following website for more information: http://www.mwsu.edu/housing/. No on-campus day care facilities are available.

Information for Students With Physical Disabilities: See the following website: http://mwsu.edu/student-life/disability/.

Special Facilities or Resources: Midwestern State University is located near two state hospitals, a regional community mental health and mental retardation treatment center, and two private psychiatric hospitals. A newly remodeled clinic and computer lab are available for student use, and Graduate Research and Teaching Assistants are provided with office space.

Application Information: Amanda Walton, Midwestern State University, Doris McAda Graduate School, 3410 Taft Blvd, Wichita Falls, TX 76308. *Fee:* $35. *Online application:* http://www.mwsu.edu/academics/graduateschool/how-to-apply.

North Texas, University of
Department of Psychology
Arts & Sciences
1155 Union Circle #311280
Denton, TX 76203-5017
Telephone: (940) 565-2671
Chairperson: Dr. Vicki Campbell

E-mail: PSYC-Grad@unt.edu
Web: http://psychology.unt.edu/

Orientation, Objectives, and Emphasis of Department
Our department adopts the scientist–practitioner model, fostering an appreciation of psychology as a science and as a profession. We embrace a multiplicity of theoretical viewpoints and research interests. Students are involved in graded research and/or clinical practicum experiences by integrating experiential with didactic instruction. Behavioral Science (formerly Experimental Psychology) provides a highly individualized program for the students interested in study and research in one of several specialized areas.

Clinical and Counseling Psychology programs support the development of a well-rounded professional psychologist. These purposes include a thorough grounding in scientific methodology and an orientation to the profession, development of competency in psychological assessment and evaluation, and training in various psychotherapeutic and counseling techniques and skills.

Programs and Degrees Offered

Program	Degree	Application Deadline	Applications Received	Accepted	New Admits Enrolled (PT)	Total Enrolled (PT)	Degrees Awarded in 2014–2015	Median Years to Complete Degree	Dismissed/ Withdrew
Clinical Psychology	PhD	December 1 (Fall)	204	6	6	40	11	6	3
Counseling Psychology	PhD	December 1 (Fall)	180	8	7	49	12	7	1
Behavioral Science	PhD	December 1 (Fall)	19	2	2	14	0		1

APA Accreditation

Clinical PhD: Student Outcome Data website: http://psychology.unt.edu/graduate-programs/clinical-psychology/student-admissions-outcomes-and-other-data.
Counseling PhD: Student Outcome Data website: http://psychology.unt.edu/graduate-programs/counseling-psychology/student-admissions-outcomes-and-other-data.

Doctoral Degree (PhD Clinical Psychology): For those doctoral students for whom a professional internship was required in this program prior to graduation:
Total students who applied for an internship: 7
Total students who obtained an internship: 7
Total students who obtained a paid internship: 7
Total students who obtained an unpaid internship: 0
Total students who were placed in APA/CPA-accredited internships: 7
Total students placed in internships not APA/CPA-accredited, but listed with the Association of Psychology Postdoctoral and Internship Centers (APPIC): 0
Total students placed in internships conforming to guidelines of the Council of Directors of School Psychology Programs (CDSPP): 0
Total students placed in internships that were not APA/CPA-accredited, APPIC or CDSSP listed: 0

Doctoral Degree (PhD Counseling Psychology): For those doctoral students for whom a professional internship was required in this program prior to graduation:
Total students who applied for an internship: 7
Total students who obtained an internship: 7
Total students who obtained a paid internship: 7
Total students who obtained an unpaid internship: 0
Total students who were placed in APA/CPA-accredited internships: 7
Total students placed in internships not APA/CPA-accredited, but listed with the Association of Psychology Postdoctoral and Internship Centers (APPIC): 0
Total students placed in internships conforming to guidelines of the Council of Directors of School Psychology Programs (CDSPP): 0
Total students placed in internships that were not APA/CPA-accredited, APPIC or CDSSP listed: 0

Internships/Practica

The applied training experience in Clinical Psychology and Counseling Psychology begins on campus in the first semester. The bulk of applied training occurs at the Psychology Clinic. The Psychology Clinic practicum team is composed of first, second, and third year students and the supervising psychologist.

Admissions

Entries appear in the following order: required test or GPA, minimum score (if required)/median score of students entering in 2015–2016.

Program	Degree	GRE-V	GRE-Q	GRE-Writing	GRE-Subject	Undergraduate GPA	Last 2 Years GPA	Psychology GPA	Master's GPA
Clinical Psychology	PhD	NA/161	NA/156	Not specified	Not specified	3/3.51	3.5/3.71	3.5/3.83	Not specified

Admissions *(con't.)*

Program	Degree	GRE-V	GRE-Q	GRE-Writing	GRE-Subject	Under-graduate GPA	Last 2 Years GPA	Psychol-ogy GPA	Master's GPA
Counseling Psychology	PhD	NA/156	NA/155	Not specified	Not specified	3/3.9	3.5/3.94	3.5/3.62	Not specified
Behavioral Science	PhD	NA/158	NA/152	Not specified	Not specified	3/3.67	3.5/3.71	3.5/3.72	Not specified

Admissions Requirements:

Degree	GRE	GRE-Subject	Letters of Recom-mendation	Research Statement	Writing Sample	CV	Interview
Doctoral	Required	None	3	Required	None	Required	Required

Admissions Criteria:

GRE scores—medium
Research experience—high
Work experience—medium
GPA—high

Letters of recommendation—high
Interview—high
Statement of goals and objectives—high
Undergraduate psychology preparation—medium

For additional information on admission requirements, visit https://psychology.unt.edu/graduate-applications.

Department Demographics

	Male (PT)	Female (PT)	Total	African-American/ Black (PT)	Hispanic/ Latino (PT)	Asian/ Pacific Islander (PT)	American Indian/ Alaska Native (PT)	Caucasian/ White (PT)	Unknown	Multiethnic (PT)	ADA (PT)	Int'l (PT)
Students	38 (0)	86 (0)	124	5 (0)	10 (0)	8 (0)	0 (0)	80 (0)	20 (0)	1 (0)	0 (0)	5 (0)

Financial Information/Assistance

Tuition: For information on tuition costs, visit http://financialaid.unt.edu/costs. Tuition is subject to change. Additional fees are assessed to students beyond the costs of tuition for the following: instructional fees, miscellaneous fees, books.

Doctoral:
State residents: $7,267 per academic year.
Nonstate residents: $16,627 per academic year.

Financial Assistance:

	Teaching Assistantship (% Receiving)	Teaching Assistantship Tuition Remission	Research Assistantship (% Receiving)	Research Assistantship Tuition Remission	Fellowship (% Receiving)	Fellowship Tuition Remission
First-Year Student	$13,138 (NA)	NA	$13,138 (NA)	NA	$13,138 (NA)	NA
Advanced Student	$15,457 (NA)	NA	$15,457 (NA)	NA	$15,457 (NA)	NA

Employment of Department Graduates

Doctoral:
Enrolled in a postdoctoral residency/fellowship: 15
Employed in independent practice: 1

Employed in other positions at a higher education institution: 1
Employed in government agency: 3
Employed in a community mental health/counseling center: 5
Employed in a hospital/medical center: 1
Do not know: 1
Total: 27

Additional Information

Housing and Day Care: On-campus housing is available. See the following website for more information: http://housing.unt.edu/. No on-campus day care facilities are available.

Information for Students With Physical Disabilities: See the following website: http://disability.unt.edu/.

Special Facilities or Resources: The Psychology Clinic provides professional training, scientific research, and community service. Teams of licensed psychologists and doctoral students in the APA-accredited Clinical and Counseling PhD programs provide therapy and psychological testing to adults, adolescents, children, couples, and families and address problems ranging from everyday stress and relationship issues to more serious problems like depression, anxiety, bipolar disorder, ADHD, and chronic medical conditions. Research and service activities of the Clinic involve members of the entire department. The Center for Sport Psychology and Performance Excellence (CSPPE) provides interdisciplinary training for students in psychology and kinesiology who are interested in specializing in sport psychology. Through the Center, students work with Psychology and KHPR faculty in coursework, research, and applied experiences. The Center for Psychosocial Health Research is an interdisciplinary center that conducts research on wellness in a chronic illness context. Research focuses on exploring stigma and forgiveness as a stressor and coping strategy for people living with HIV/AIDS and for the LGBT community. The Sleep and Health research lab focuses on the epidemiology of sleep and health and explores the role insomnia plays as a risk factor for psychological and medical disorders in various populations.

Application Information: *Fee:* $75. *Online application:* http://tsgs.unt.edu/future-students/graduate-admissions.

Our Lady of the Lake University
Psychology
School of Professional Studies
411 SW 24th Street
San Antonio, TX 78207
Telephone: (210) 431-4009
Chairperson: Kathryn B. Anderson, PhD

E-mail: kbanderson@ollusa.edu
Web: http://www.ollusa.edu

Orientation, Objectives, and Emphasis of Department
Graduate psychology programs at OLLU adhere to the practitioner–scholar model of training and emphasize brief, systemic approaches to psychotherapy. Postmodern and multicultural perspectives are infused throughout the curriculum, including practica. A certificate in psychological services for Spanish-speaking populations is available.

Programs and Degrees Offered

Program	Degree	Application Deadline	Applications Received	Accepted	New Admits Enrolled (PT)	Total Enrolled (PT)	Degrees Awarded in 2014–2015	Median Years to Complete Degree	Dismissed/ Withdrew
Counseling Psychology	PsyD	January 15 (Fall)	30	9	8 (0)	33 (7)	7	7	0
School Psychology	MA/MS	June 1 (Fall)	14	12	10 (0)	35 (1)	6	2.66	0
Family, Couple & Indiv. Psychotherapy-San Antonio	MA/MS	June 1 (Fall)	36	22	17 (0)	34 (2)	13	2	0

Programs and Degrees Offered (con't.)

Program	Degree	Application Deadline	Applications Received	Accepted	New Admits Enrolled (PT)	Total Enrolled (PT)	Degrees Awarded in 2014–2015	Median Years to Complete Degree	Dismissed/ Withdrew
Family, Couple, & Indiv. Psychotherapy-Houston	MA/MS	June 1 (Fall)	28	25	22 (0)	50 (4)	6	3	0

APA Accreditation

Counseling PsyD: Student Outcome Data website: http://www.ollusa.edu/s/1190/hybrid/default-hybrid-ollu.aspx?sid=1190&gid=1&pgid=7957.

Doctoral Degree (PsyD Counseling Psychology): For those doctoral students for whom a professional internship was required in this program prior to graduation:
Total students who applied for an internship: 9
Total students who obtained an internship: 7
Total students who obtained a paid internship: 6
Total students who obtained an unpaid internship: 1
Total students who were placed in APA/CPA-accredited internships: 6
Total students placed in internships not APA/CPA-accredited, but listed with the Association of Psychology Postdoctoral and Internship Centers (APPIC): 0
Total students placed in internships conforming to guidelines of the Council of Directors of School Psychology Programs (CDSPP): 0
Total students placed in internships that were not APA/CPA-accredited, APPIC or CDSSP listed: 1

Master's Degree (MA/MS School Psychology): An internship experience, such as a final research project or "capstone" experience is required of graduates.

Internships/Practica

The psychology department operates a training clinic, the Community Counseling Service (CCS), which serves as the initial practicum site for students in the Family, Couple and Individual Psychotherapy master's program in San Antonio and doctoral students. At the CCS, practicum students work in teams of up to six students under the live supervision of psychology faculty. The CCS is located in and serves a low-income, predominantly Mexican-American community. Supervision of Spanish-language psychotherapy is available. A variety of off-campus sites are available to students in their second and subsequent semesters of practicum. Students are placed at off-campus sites according to their career interests and training needs. Available practicum sites include public and private schools, hospitals, and community agencies.

Admissions

Entries appear in the following order: required test or GPA, minimum score (if required)/median score of students entering in 2015–2016.

Program	Degree	GRE-V	GRE-Q	GRE-Writing	GRE-Subject	Under-graduate GPA	Last 2 Years GPA	Psychology GPA	Master's GPA
Counseling Psychology	PsyD	144/153	141/144	3/4	530/610	2.42/3.47	NA/NA	NA/NA	3.76/ 3.89
School Psychology	MA/MS	137/148	140/143	Not specified	Not specified	2.49/3.35	2.78/3.6	2.71/3.65	Not specified
Family, Couple & Indiv. Psychotherapy-San Antonio	MA/MS	140/148	136/147	Not specified	Not specified	2.36/3.05	1.95/ 3.34	Not specified	Not specified
Family, Couple, & Indiv. Psychotherapy-Houston	MA/MS	Not specified	Not specified	Not specified	Not specified	Not specified	Not specified	Not specified	Not specified

Admissions Requirements:

Degree	GRE	GRE-Subject	Letters of Recommendation	Research Statement	Writing Sample	CV	Interview
Master's/Specialist	Required	Optional	2	Required	None	Optional	Required
Doctoral	Required	Required	3	Required	Optional	Required	Required

Please note if these criteria vary for different programs: The MAT exam or the GRE exam are required for the master's programs.

Admissions Criteria:

GRE scores—medium
Research experience—low
Work experience—high
Clinically related public service—medium
GPA—high

Letters of recommendation—high
Interview—high
Statement of goals and objectives—high
Undergraduate psychology preparation—medium

Department Demographics

	Male (PT)	Female (PT)	Total	African-American/Black (PT)	Hispanic/Latino (PT)	Asian/Pacific Islander (PT)	American Indian/Alaska Native (PT)	Caucasian/White (PT)	Unknown (PT)	Multiethnic (PT)	ADA (PT)	Int'l (PT)
Students	19 (0)	133 (14)	166	16 (2)	89 (6)	1 (0)	0 (0)	43 (5)	3 (1)	0 (0)	0 (0)	5 (0)

Financial Information/Assistance

Tuition: For information on tuition costs, visit http://www.ollusa.edu/s/1190/hybrid/default-hybrid-ollu.aspx?sid=1190&gid=1&pgid=7714. Tuition is subject to change. Additional fees are assessed to students beyond the costs of tuition for the following: general student fee; course lab fees; technology fee.

Doctoral:
State residents: $918 per credit hour.
Nonstate residents: $918 per credit hour.

Master's:
State residents: $855 per credit hour.
Nonstate residents: $855 per credit hour.

Financial Assistance:

	Teaching Assistantship (% Receiving)	Teaching Assistantship Tuition Remission	Research Assistantship (% Receiving)	Research Assistantship Tuition Remission	Fellowship (% Receiving)	Fellowship Tuition Remission
First-Year Student	NA (NA)	NA	NA (NA)	NA	NA (12)	Full
Advanced Student	$5,000 (10)	NA	$5,100 (15)	NA	NA (12)	Full

Employment of Department Graduates

Doctoral:
Enrolled in a postdoctoral residency/fellowship: 4
Employed in independent practice: 2
Employed in a hospital/medical center: 1
Total: 7

Additional Information

Housing and Day Care: On-campus housing is available. See the following website for more information: http://www.ollusa.edu/s/1190/hybrid/default-hybrid-ollu.aspx?sid=1190&gid=1&pgid=7575. No on-campus day care facilities are available.

Special Facilities or Resources: The department's training clinic serves as both a training and research facility. Research facilities are also available in the building which houses the psychology department.

Application Information: Graduate Admissions Office, Our Lady of the Lake University, 411 SW 24th Street, San Antonio, TX 78207. *Fee:* $40. *Online application:* https://apply.ollusa.edu/.

Rice University
Department of Psychology
School of Social Sciences
6100 Main Street - MS 25
Houston, TX 77005
Telephone: (713) 348-4856
Chairperson: David Wetter

E-mail: psyc@rice.edu
Web: http://psychology.rice.edu/

Orientation, Objectives, and Emphasis of Department
Our program emphasizes training in basic and applied research and in the skills necessary to conduct research. The content areas to which this emphasis is applied are cognitive psychology (including cognitive neuroscience), industrial/organizational, and human-computer interaction. We believe that training in research and research skills generalizes very broadly to the kinds of tasks that professional psychologists will be asked to perform both in the university laboratory and in addressing such diverse applied questions as organizational management, system design, and program evaluation. Students in the cognitive neuroscience program are encouraged to participate in courses and research opportunities available from our joint program in neuroscience with Baylor College of Medicine. Students are encouraged to develop research interests that combine content areas across the department. Industrial/organizational and human factors psychologists, for example, might collaborate on research dealing with organizational communication via email. Cognitive and industrial/organizational psychologists might investigate cognitive processes underlying performance appraisal; human factors and cognitive psychologists might collaborate on studies of risk perception and the perceptual and attentional properties of computer displays. Although some of our students prefer to devote their energies to laboratory research in preparation for academic positions, many students take advantage of internship opportunities for "real-world" experience.

Programs and Degrees Offered

Program	Degree	Application Deadline	Applica-tions Received	Accepted	New Admits Enrolled (PT)	Total Enrolled (PT)	Degrees Awarded in 2014–2015	Median Years to Complete Degree	Dismissed/Withdrew
Industrial/ Organizational Psychology	PhD	January 15 (Fall)	115	11	9	19	2	5	0
Cognitive Psychology	PhD	January 15 (Fall)	7	0	0 (0)	1 (0)	0		0
Human-Computer Interaction/ Human Factors	PhD	January 15 (Fall)	18	2	1 (0)	2 (0)	5	5.5	0
Training	PhD	January 15 (Fall)	3	0	0 (0)	0 (0)	0		0
Cognitive Neuroscience	PhD	January 15 (Fall)	20	2	0	9	1	7	0

Internships/Practica
Graduate students beyond their third year have the opportunity to work in internships in the Houston area, and the department arranges internships or practica in a wide variety of settings for interested advanced students. Although not required, many of our students have internships at local organizations including NASA, the Texas Medical Center, Hewlett Packard, and a variety of consulting firms. Other students work in summer internships around the country.

Admissions

Entries appear in the following order: required test or GPA, minimum score (if required)/median score of students entering in 2015–2016.

Program	Degree	GRE-V	GRE-Q	GRE-Writing	GRE-Subject	Under-graduate GPA	Last 2 Years GPA	Psychol-ogy GPA	Master's GPA
Industrial/ Organizational Psychology	PhD	NA/160	NA/158	NA/4.5	Not specified	NA/3.89	Not specified	Not specified	Not specified
Cognitive Psychology	PhD	NA/NA	NA/NA	NA/NA	Not specified	NA/NA	Not specified	Not specified	Not specified
Human-Computer Interaction/ Human Factors	PhD	NA/161	NA/164	NA/4.5	Not specified	NA/3.42	Not specified	Not specified	Not specified
Training	PhD	NA/NA	NA/NA	NA/NA	Not specified	NA/NA	Not specified	Not specified	Not specified
Cognitive Neuroscience	PhD	NA/161	NA/168	NA/3.5	Not specified	NA/3.8	Not specified	Not specified	Not specified

Admissions Requirements:

Degree	GRE	GRE-Subject	Letters of Recom-mendation	Research Statement	Writing Sample	CV	Interview
Doctoral	Required	Optional	4	Recom-mended	Recom-mended	Optional	None

Admissions Criteria:

GRE scores—high
Research experience—high
Work experience—low
GPA—high

Letters of recommendation—high
Statement of goals and objectives—high
Undergraduate psychology preparation—medium
Faculty-applicant fit—high

For additional information on admission requirements, visit http://psychology.rice.edu/Content.aspx?id=70.

Department Demographics

	Male (PT)	Female (PT)	Total	African-American/ Black (PT)	Hispanic/ Latino (PT)	Asian/ Pacific Islander (PT)	American Indian/ Alaska Native (PT)	Caucasian/ White (PT)	Unknown	Multiethnic (PT)	ADA (PT)	Int'l (PT)
Students	5 (0)	26 (0)	31	0 (0)	4 (0)	11 (0)	0 (0)	16 (0)	0 (0)	0 (0)	0 (0)	9 (0)

Financial Information/Assistance

Tuition: For information on tuition costs, visit http://students.rice.edu/Standard.aspx?id=2147484504. Tuition is subject to change. Additional fees are assessed to students beyond the costs of tuition for the following: health insurance, student health services, student organizations.

Doctoral:
State residents: $41,560 per academic year.
Nonstate residents: $41,560 per academic year.

Financial Assistance:

	Teaching Assistantship (% Receiving)	Teaching Assistantship Tuition Remission	Research Assistantship (% Receiving)	Research Assistantship Tuition Remission	Fellowship (% Receiving)	Fellowship Tuition Remission
First-Year Student	NA (NA)	NA	$21,500 (70)	Full	$21,500 (30)	Full
Advanced Student	NA (NA)	NA	$21,500 (39)	Full	$21,500 (58)	Full

For additional information on financial assistance, visit http://psychology.rice.edu/Content.aspx?id=71.

Employment of Department Graduates

Doctoral:
Enrolled in a postdoctoral residency/fellowship: 2
Employed in an academic position at a university: 1
Employed in business or industry: 4
Other employment position: 1
Total: 8

Additional Information

Housing and Day Care: On-campus housing is available. See the following website for more information: http://campushousing.rice.edu/graduate. On-campus day care facilities are available. See the following website for more information: http://www.discovercece.org/.

Information for Students With Physical Disabilities: See the following website: http://dss.rice.edu/.

Special Facilities or Resources: Graduate students in the Rice Psychology programs benefit from their access to a large and vital Houston business community, NASA, and over 40 teaching and research centers in the Texas Medical Center. Within the department, graduate students in all programs have ready access to a variety of powerful Macintosh and Windows-based computers that more than meet the needs of students for data collection, simulation, instruction, word processing, and computation. The department contains facilities for the study of dyadic and small group interaction, social judgment, decision making, and computer-interface design. The cognitive neuroscience area has benefited from the recent construction of the 6000-square-foot T. L. L. Temple Foundation Neuroplasticity Lab, which includes a transcranial magnetic stimulation (TMS) device for investigating brain function, an eye-tracking device, workstations for neuroimaging data analysis and 3D rendering of brains from MRI scans, and 32-channel event-related potential (ERP) recording system that allows the detailed description of neural systems. Collaborations with institutions in the nearby Texas Medical Center provide access to functional neuroimaging facilities, which include the Center for Advanced MR Imaging at Baylor College of Medicine and the Human Neuroimaging Lab at the University of Texas Health Science Center-Houston.

Application Information: Graduate Admissions, Psychology Department - MS-25, Rice University, 6100 Main Street, Houston, TX 77005. *Fee:* $85. *Online application:* https://psycgradapps.rice.edu/.

Sam Houston State University
Department of Psychology
Humanities and Social Sciences
Box 2447
Huntsville, TX 77341-2447
Telephone: (936) 294-1174
Chairperson: Christopher Wilson

E-mail: psychology@shsu.edu
Web: http://www.shsu.edu/academics/psychology-and-philosophy/psychology/

Orientation, Objectives, and Emphasis of Department
The Clinical and School Master's programs are applied training programs that develop effective Master's-level practitioners. Students in these programs receive extensive and eclectic training in both psychotherapy and psychometrics and conclude their training with extensive supervised practicum experience. Graduates can seek licensure as psychological associates through Texas State Board

of Examiners of Psychologists. Graduates of the School program can seek national certification from National Association of School Psychologists and licensure as specialists in school psychology in Texas. Other licensures within the state of Texas such as professional counselor's licensure may be available with additional course work. The General track involves broader exposure to psychology's core disciplines and allows the student more elective flexibility to craft an individual specialty. The focus within the General Program is on developing research skills. Graduates of all three programs often progress to doctoral training here or elsewhere. Our clinical doctoral program is a scientist–practitioner program that provides broad and general training in clinical psychology with an emphasis on forensic psychology and the training of legally informed clinicians. In addition to extensive training in general psychological assessment and treatment, students help to conduct a variety of forensic evaluations for the courts.

Programs and Degrees Offered

Program	Degree	Application Deadline	Applica-tions Received	Accepted	New Admits Enrolled (PT)	Total Enrolled (PT)	Degrees Awarded in 2014–2015	Median Years to Complete Degree	Dismissed/Withdrew
Clinical Psychology	MA/MS	February 15 (Fall)	89	34	15 (0)	35 (0)	12	2	1
General Psychology	MA/MS	February 15 (Fall)	15	6	1 (0)	4 (0)	3	2	0
Specialist in School Psychology	Other	February 15 (Fall)	29	18	9 (0)	22 (0)	6	3	0
Clinical Psychology (Forensic Emphasis)	PhD	December 1 (Fall)	149	7	7 (0)	48 (0)	9	5.5	0

APA Accreditation

Clinical PhD: Student Outcome Data website: http://www.shsu.edu/academics/psychology-and-philosophy/psychology/doctoral-program/.

Doctoral Degree (PhD Clinical Psychology (Forensic Emphasis)): For those doctoral students for whom a professional internship was required in this program prior to graduation:
Total students who applied for an internship: 5
Total students who obtained an internship: 5
Total students who obtained a paid internship: 5
Total students who obtained an unpaid internship: 0
Total students who were placed in APA/CPA-accredited internships: 5
Total students placed in internships not APA/CPA-accredited, but listed with the Association of Psychology Postdoctoral and Internship Centers (APPIC): 0
Total students placed in internships conforming to guidelines of the Council of Directors of School Psychology Programs (CDSPP): 0
Total students placed in internships that were not APA/CPA-accredited, APPIC or CDSSP listed: 0

Master's Degree (MA/MS Clinical Psychology): An internship experience, such as a final research project or "capstone" experience is required of graduates.

Internships/Practica

We offer a variety of internships and practica for each of the applied tracks. Students in the School psychology program complete a one-year internship in schools. There are a variety of practicum placements for students in the Clinical psychology master's program, including the University Counseling Center, area community mental health centers, and the psychological services centers of the Texas Department of Criminal Justice (TDCJ). Students in the clinical doctoral program are assigned to a variety of practica, including Ben Taub General Hospital in Houston, ADAPT Counseling, various private facilities and practices, probation departments, and The Institute for Rehabilitation and Research (neuropsychology). These students also work at our on-campus Psychological Services Center, which provides both general mental health services (e.g., individual psychotherapy, couples counseling, psychological assessment), and forensic services (e.g., treatment programs for offender populations and evaluations for the courts).

Admissions

Entries appear in the following order: required test or GPA, minimum score (if required)/median score of students entering in 2015–2016.

Program	Degree	GRE-V	GRE-Q	GRE-Writing	GRE-Subject	Under-graduate GPA	Last 2 Years GPA	Psychol-ogy GPA	Master's GPA
Clinical Psychology	MA/MS	NA/NA	NA/NA	Not specified	Not specified	3/3.7	Not specified	Not specified	Not specified
General Psychology	MA/MS	NA/NA	NA/NA	Not specified	Not specified	3/3.1	Not specified	Not specified	Not specified
Specialist in School Psychology	Other	NA/NA	NA/NA	Not specified	Not specified	3/3.4	Not specified	Not specified	Not specified
Clinical Psychology (Forensic Emphasis)	PhD	NA/149	NA/152	NA/NA	Not specified	NA/3.74	Not specified	Not specified	Not specified

Admissions Requirements:

Degree	GRE	GRE-Subject	Letters of Recom-mendation	Research Statement	Writing Sample	CV	Interview
Master's/Specialist	Required	Recom-mended	3	Required	Optional	Required	None
Doctoral	Required	Recom-mended	3	Required	Recom-mended	Required	Required

Admissions Criteria:

GRE scores—high
Research experience—high
Work experience—low
Clinically related public service—medium
GPA—high

Letters of recommendation—high
Interview—high
Statement of goals and objectives—high
Undergraduate psychology preparation—medium
Fit with the program—high

Department Demographics

	Male (PT)	Female (PT)	Total	African-American/ Black (PT)	Hispanic/ Latino (PT)	Asian/ Pacific Islander (PT)	American Indian/ Alaska Native (PT)	Caucasian/ White (PT)	Unknown (PT)	Multiethnic (PT)	ADA (PT)	Int'l (PT)
Students	22 (0)	87 (0)	109	5 (0)	13 (0)	6 (0)	1 (0)	84 (0)	0 (0)	0 (0)	1 (0)	7 (0)

Financial Information/Assistance

Tuition: For information on tuition costs, visit http://www.shsu.edu/dept/bursar/financial.html. Tuition is subject to change. Additional fees are assessed to students beyond the costs of tuition for the following: student service, student center, computer use, library, advisement, and records.

Doctoral:
State residents: $7,213 per academic year.
State residents: $245 per credit hour.
Nonstate residents: $14,376 per academic year.
Nonstate residents: $599 per credit hour.

Master's:
State residents: $7,213 per academic year.
State residents: $245 per credit hour.
Nonstate residents: $14,376 per academic year.
Nonstate residents: $599 per credit hour.

Financial Assistance:

	Teaching Assistantship (% Receiving)	Teaching Assistantship Tuition Remission	Research Assistantship (% Receiving)	Research Assistantship Tuition Remission	Fellowship (% Receiving)	Fellowship Tuition Remission
First-Year Student	$19,000 (NA)	NA	$19,000 (NA)	NA	$10,000 (NA)	NA
Advanced Student	$19,000 (NA)	NA	$19,000 (NA)	NA	$19,000 (NA)	NA

Employment of Department Graduates

Doctoral:
Enrolled in a postdoctoral residency/fellowship: 5
Employed in government agency: 5
Total: 10

Additional Information

Housing and Day Care: On-campus housing is available. See the following website for more information: http://www.shsu.edu/dept/residence-life/index.html. No on-campus day care facilities are available.

Information for Students With Physical Disabilities: See the following website: http://www.shsu.edu/dept/disability/.

Special Facilities or Resources: The department enjoys ample testing and observation space. The university's computing facilities offer extensive access to personal computers complete with the latest software. The geographical area provides access to a wide variety of clinical and research populations. These include persons housed in medical and mental health facilities located in the Texas Medical Center, as well as juvenile and adult offender populations.

Application Information: Office of Graduate Studies, Sam Houston State University, P.O. Box 2478, Huntsville, TX 77341-2478. *Fee:* $45. *Online application:* http://www.shsu.edu/admissions/apply-texas.html.

Southern Methodist University
Department of Psychology
Dedman College
6116 North Central Expressway, Suite 1300, P.O. Box 750442
Dallas, TX 75206-0442
Telephone: (214) 768-4924
Chairperson: George Holden, PhD
E-mail: lsimpson@smu.edu
Web: http://www.smu.edu/dedman/academics/departments/psychology

---

Orientation, Objectives, and Emphasis of Department
The mission of the doctoral program in Clinical Psychology at Southern Methodist University is to advance clinical science and evidence-based practice by training graduate students to provide meaningful contributions to the psychological research literature and to become expert providers of evidence-based psychological assessment and interventions. Our program provides general training in clinical psychology as well as specific foci in Child/Family Psychology and Health Psychology.

Programs and Degrees Offered

Program	Degree	Application Deadline	Applications Received	Accepted	New Admits Enrolled (PT)	Total Enrolled (PT)	Degrees Awarded in 2014–2015	Median Years to Complete Degree	Dismissed/Withdrew
Clinical Psychology	PhD	December 1 (Fall)	146	9	4	19	2	6	0

APA Accreditation

Clinical PhD: Student Outcome Data website: http://www.smu.edu/Dedman/Academics/Departments/Psychology/GraduateStudies/Admissions.

Doctoral Degree (PhD Clinical Psychology): For those doctoral students for whom a professional internship was required in this program prior to graduation:
Total students who applied for an internship: 3
Total students who obtained an internship: 3
Total students who obtained a paid internship: 3
Total students who obtained an unpaid internship: 0
Total students who were placed in APA/CPA-accredited internships: 3
Total students placed in internships not APA/CPA-accredited, but listed with the Association of Psychology Postdoctoral and Internship Centers (APPIC): 0
Total students placed in internships conforming to guidelines of the Council of Directors of School Psychology Programs (CDSPP): 0
Total students placed in internships that were not APA/CPA-accredited, APPIC or CDSSP listed: 0

Internships/Practica

The internal practicum takes place in the SMU Psychology Clinic, where faculty members supervise assessment and therapy cases. External practica include a variety of supervised experiences in correctional facilities, hospitals, wellness centers, counseling centers, behavioral medicine facilities, and neuropsychological evaluation centers.

Admissions

Entries appear in the following order: required test or GPA, minimum score (if required)/median score of students entering in 2015–2016.

Program	Degree	GRE-V	GRE-Q	GRE-Writing	GRE-Subject	Under-graduate GPA	Last 2 Years GPA	Psychology GPA	Master's GPA
Clinical Psychology	PhD	NA/161	NA/159	NA/NA	Not specified	3.5/3.72	Not specified	Not specified	NA/NA

Admissions Requirements:

Degree	GRE	GRE-Subject	Letters of Recom-mendation	Research Statement	Writing Sample	CV	Interview
Doctoral	Required	Recom-mended	3	Required	Optional	Optional	Required

Admissions Criteria:

GRE scores—high
Research experience—high
Work experience—low
Clinically related public service—medium
GPA—high

Letters of recommendation—high
Interview—high
Statement of goals and objectives—high
Undergraduate psychology preparation—medium
Research interests—high

For additional information on admission requirements, visit http://www.smu.edu/graduate/Admission/ProgramsOffered/Dedman/Psychology.

Department Demographics

	Male (PT)	Female (PT)	Total	African-American/Black (PT)	Hispanic/Latino (PT)	Asian/Pacific Islander (PT)	American Indian/Alaska Native (PT)	Caucasian/White (PT)	Unknown	Multiethnic (PT)	ADA (PT)	Int'l (PT)
Students	2 (0)	17 (0)	19	1 (0)	2 (0)	3 (0)	0 (0)	11 (0)	0 (0)	2 (0)	0 (0)	1 (0)

Financial Information/Assistance

Tuition: For information on tuition costs, visit http://www.smu.edu/EnrollmentServices/Bursar/CostofAttendance/Graduate. Tuition is subject to change.

Doctoral:
State residents: $34,578 per academic year.
State residents: $1,921 per credit hour.
Nonstate residents: $34,578 per academic year.
Nonstate residents: $1,921 per credit hour.

Financial Assistance:

	Teaching Assistantship (% Receiving)	Teaching Assistantship Tuition Remission	Research Assistantship (% Receiving)	Research Assistantship Tuition Remission	Fellowship (% Receiving)	Fellowship Tuition Remission
First-Year Student	$18,500 (100)	Full	NA (NA)	NA	NA (NA)	NA
Advanced Student	$18,500 (100)	Full	NA (NA)	NA	NA (NA)	NA

For additional information on financial assistance, visit http://www.smu.edu/Dedman/Academics/Departments/Psychology/GraduateStudies/Admissions/FinancialSupport.

Employment of Department Graduates

Doctoral:
Employed in government agency: 1
Employed in a hospital/medical center: 1
Total: 2

Additional Information

Housing and Day Care: On-campus housing is available. See the following website for more information: http://smu.edu/housing/. On-campus day care facilities are available. See the following website for more information: http://smu.edu/childcare/.

Information for Students With Physical Disabilities: See the following website: http://www.smu.edu/Provost/ALEC/DASS.

Special Facilities or Resources: The department houses a Psychology Clinic and a number of well-equipped laboratories for research on various topics in clinical psychology.

Application Information: The Office of Research and Graduate Studies. *Fee:* $75. *Online application:* https://gradadmission.smu.edu/apply/.

Stephen F. Austin State University
Department of Psychology
Liberal and Applied Arts
Box 13046, SFA Station
Nacogdoches, TX 75962
Telephone: (936) 468-4402
Chairperson: Dr. Scott Hutchens

E-mail: graduatepsychology@sfasu.edu
Web: http://www.sfasu.edu/sfapsych/114.asp

Orientation, Objectives, and Emphasis of Department
The primary goal of this two-year, General Psychology MA program is to prepare students for admission to doctoral training programs in psychology by enabling them to earn graduate course credit and gain valuable research and teaching experience. Our degree program would also be of interest to persons who would like to earn an MA in psychology as a means of furthering their professional goals (e.g., by augmenting their research skills), even if those goals have no explicit connection to psychology.

Programs and Degrees Offered

Program	Degree	Application Deadline	Applica- tions Received	Accepted	New Admits Enrolled (PT)	Total Enrolled (PT)	Degrees Awarded in 2014– 2015	Median Years to Complete Degree	Dismissed/ Withdrew
General Psychology	MA/MS	Rolling	13	7	5 (0)	12 (2)	6	2	0

Admissions

Entries appear in the following order: required test or GPA, minimum score (if required)/median score of students entering in 2015–2016.

Program	Degree	GRE-V	GRE-Q	GRE-Writing	GRE-Subject	Under- graduate GPA	Last 2 Years GPA	Psychol- ogy GPA	Master's GPA
General Psychology	MA/MS	NA/NA	NA/NA	Not specified	Not specified	3/NA	Not specified	Not specified	Not specified

Admissions Requirements:

Degree	GRE	GRE- Subject	Letters of Recom- mendation	Research Statement	Writing Sample	CV	Interview
Master's/Specialist	Required	None	3	Required	None	Required	None

Admissions Criteria:

GRE scores—medium
Research experience—low
GPA—medium

Letters of recommendation—medium
Statement of goals and objectives—low
Undergraduate psychology preparation—medium

For additional information on admission requirements, visit http://www.sfasu.edu/sfapsych/113.asp.

Department Demographics

	Male (PT)	Female (PT)	Total	African- American/ Black (PT)	Hispanic/ Latino (PT)	Asian/ Pacific Islander (PT)	American Indian/ Alaska Native (PT)	Caucasian/ White (PT)	Unknown (PT)	Multiethnic (PT)	ADA (PT)	Int'l (PT)
Students	10 (1)	9 (1)	21	0 (0)	2 (0)	0 (0)	0 (0)	17 (2)	0 (0)	0 (0)	2 (1)	1 (0)

Financial Information/Assistance

Tuition: For information on tuition costs, visit http://www.sfasu.edu/controller/businessoffice/students/tuition_calc.asp. Tuition is subject to change. Additional fees are assessed to students beyond the costs of tuition for the following: student service, student center, library, publication.

Master's:
State residents: $4,140 per academic year.
State residents: $265 per credit hour.
Nonstate residents: $8,820 per academic year.
Nonstate residents: $655 per credit hour.

Financial Assistance:

	Teaching Assistantship (% Receiving)	Teaching Assistantship Tuition Remission	Research Assistantship (% Receiving)	Research Assistantship Tuition Remission	Fellowship (% Receiving)	Fellowship Tuition Remission
First-Year Student	$9,225 (NA)	NA	$9,225 (NA)	NA	NA (NA)	NA
Advanced Student	$9,225 (NA)	NA	$9,225 (NA)	NA	NA (NA)	NA

For additional information on financial assistance, visit http://www.sfasu.edu/graduate/104.asp.

Employment of Department Graduates

Master's:
Employed in other positions at a higher education institution: 1
Employed in a professional position in a school system: 1
Employed in business or industry: 1
Employed in government agency: 1
Employed in a hospital/medical center: 1
Total: 5

Additional Information

Housing and Day Care: On-campus housing is available. See the following website for more information: http://www.sfasu.edu/reslife/102.asp. On-campus day care facilities are available. See the following website for more information: http://www.sfasu.edu/echl/.

Information for Students With Physical Disabilities: See the following website: http://www.sfasu.edu/disabilityservices/.

Special Facilities or Resources: The department's facilities occupy more than 20,000 square feet. An extensive research suite and other research spaces permit data collection either with individual participants or groups. These spaces include computers with experimental software and as well as software and equipment for psychophysiological data acquisition and analysis. There are also laboratories for human and animal research in learning, cognition, social, developmental, and personality psychology. Supplemental technical assistance from facilities in other departments on campus is available. All department classrooms are supplied with multimedia equipment. The department has an instructional computing laboratory consisting of networked PC microcomputers and extensive supporting hardware and software for computing across the psychology curriculum.

Application Information: Graduate Program Coordinator, Department of Psychology, Stephen F. Austin State University, Box 13046, SFA Station, Nacogdoches, TX 75962. *Fee:* $25. *Online application:* http://www.sfasu.edu/graduate/101.asp.

Texas A&M International University
Department of Psychology and Communication
College of Arts and Sciences
5201 University Boulevard
Laredo, TX 78041-1900
Telephone: (956) 326-2475
Director of Master's Program in Counseling Psychology: Sara M. Castro-Olivo
Web: http://www.tamiu.edu/coas/psy/mastercounpsy/index.shtml

E-mail: sara.castro@tamiu.edu

Orientation, Objectives, and Emphasis of Department
The Master of Arts in Counseling Psychology provides training for counselors with strong foundations in eclectic, humanistic, multicultural, and community perspectives. Students in our international campus and community are self-reflective active learners. The excellent student–faculty ratio (average class = 11) provides extra attention for its students to identify and achieve their own individual goals. There is an advisory board composed of student and faculty representatives, which strives to expand the counseling program to improve the quality of life in South Texas. Students complete courses in counseling theories, techniques, and attitudes; multicultural counseling; human development; psychopathology; ethical and legal issues; group counseling; career counseling;

assessment; and statistical research design. Electives include coursework in crisis counseling, brief collaborative therapy, community interventions, play therapy, elderly mental health, Latino mental health, alcohol and drug counseling, and bilingualism. Faculty are specialists in brief collaborative therapy, crisis intervention, psycholinguistics, memory, multicultural counseling, psychotherapy research, and counselor professional development. Graduates are eligible to sit for the Licensed Professional Counselor (LPC-Texas) Examination. Students can select a thesis track if they are interested in research and further study at the doctoral level. Our program meets every recommendation of the Multicultural Competency Checklist.

Programs and Degrees Offered

Program	Degree	Application Deadline	Applica-tions Received	Accepted	New Admits Enrolled (PT)	Total Enrolled (PT)	Degrees Awarded in 2014–2015	Median Years to Complete Degree	Dismissed/ Withdrew
Counseling Psychology	MA/MS	April 30 (Fall)	27	9	8	31	9	2.75	0

Internships/Practica

The practicum and internships offer unique training opportunities to prepare competent counselors. Competence exercises include alliance and outcome measurement as well as session process analyses, in addition to more conventional training in documentation and treatment planning. Practicum and internships consist of working at settings such as college counseling centers, drug and alcohol counseling/prevention agencies, domestic violence/battered women shelters, child advocacy centers, and professional counseling clinics. On-site supervisors provide 30-minute supervision sessions. Psychologists on campus provide an additional 2.5 hours of supervision in individual, triadic, and group formats. Peer feedback and group cohesiveness are also vital parts of training. All graduates complete Practicum and Counseling Internship I. Students who choose the non-thesis (clinical) track also complete Internship II. The clinical track provides a total of three semesters of practical experience in counseling (600 hours), a minimum of which is 240 hours of face-to-face counseling activities.

Admissions

Entries appear in the following order: required test or GPA, minimum score (if required)/median score of students entering in 2015–2016.

Program	Degree	GRE-V	GRE-Q	GRE-Writing	GRE-Subject	Under-graduate GPA	Last 2 Years GPA	Psychol-ogy GPA	Master's GPA
Counseling Psychology	MA/MS	NA/NA	NA/NA	Not specified	Not specified	NA/NA	3/NA	3/NA	Not specified

Admissions Requirements:

Degree	GRE	GRE-Subject	Letters of Recom-mendation	Research Statement	Writing Sample	CV	Interview
Master's/Specialist	Required	None	3	Required	Optional	Optional	Required

Please note if these criteria vary for different programs: The Master's in Counseling Psychology requires four undergraduate courses be completed with a B average across them. They are abnormal, personality, research methods, and theories and principles of testing.

Admissions Criteria:

GRE scores—medium
Research experience—medium
Work experience—medium
Clinically related public service—high
GPA—medium

Letters of recommendation—medium
Interview—high
Statement of goals and objectives—high
Undergraduate psychology preparation—high

Department Demographics

	Male (PT)	Female (PT)	Total	African-American/ Black (PT)	Hispanic/ Latino (PT)	Asian/ Pacific Islander (PT)	American Indian/ Alaska Native (PT)	Caucasian/ White (PT)	Unknown	Multiethnic (PT)	ADA (PT)	Int'l (PT)
Students	5 (0)	25 (0)	30	0 (0)	25 (0)	0 (0)	0 (0)	1 (0)	0 (0)	0 (0)	1 (0)	3 (0)

Financial Information/Assistance

Tuition: For information on tuition costs, visit http://www.tamiu.edu/adminis/comptroler/cashiers.shtml. Tuition is subject to change.

Master's:
State residents: $5,436 per academic year.
State residents: $496 per credit hour.
Nonstate residents: $12,092 per academic year.
Nonstate residents: $865 per credit hour.

Financial Assistance:

	Teaching Assistantship (% Receiving)	Teaching Assistantship Tuition Remission	Research Assistantship (% Receiving)	Research Assistantship Tuition Remission	Fellowship (% Receiving)	Fellowship Tuition Remission
First-Year Student	$18,000 (NA)	NA	NA (NA)	NA	$9,000 (NA)	NA
Advanced Student	NA (NA)	NA	$17,000 (NA)	NA	NA (NA)	NA

For additional information on financial assistance, visit http://www.tamiu.edu/gradschool/fellowships.shtml.

Employment of Department Graduates

Master's:
Employed in academic position at a 2-year/4-year college: 3
Employed in a professional position in a school system: 1
Employed in government agency: 1
Employed in a community mental health/counseling center: 2
Still seeking employment: 1
Total: 8

Additional Information

Housing and Day Care: On-campus housing is available. See the following website for more information: http://www.tamiu.edu/housing/housing.shtml. No on-campus day care facilities are available.

Information for Students With Physical Disabilities: See the following website: http://www.tamiu.edu/wellness/disability.shtml.

Special Facilities or Resources: The international flavor of the University and Texas/Mexico border community provides a rich milieu for multicultural and community counseling exploration and education. This is one of the program's greatest resources. Texas A&M International is one of the fastest growing university communities in the United States. Additionally, an off-campus community-counseling center, The Texas A&M International University Community Stress Center, offers free bilingual counseling and psycho-educational services. At this center, student-counselors complete practica and internships in direct and indirect community and client interventions with faculty supervision. The Master of Arts in Counseling Psychology (MACP) Program works closely with Career Services, Student Counseling, and Academic Support and Enrichment to provide training and employment opportunities for student-counselors. A departmental computer lab exists that is currently used for cognitive and language research. It is equipped for detailed analysis of research in memory, cognition, psycholinguistics, bilingualism, as well as other research. A Counseling/Research lab is equipped with digital and video recording, internet video conferencing and standard computer programs. It is available for student use in recording counseling sessions and conducting research. Graduate students may apply for a GREAT grant during their first year if they intend to pursue the thesis option.

Application Information: Texas A&M International University, Office of Graduate Studies & Research, 5201 University Blvd., Laredo, TX 78041-1900. *Fee:* $35. *Online application:* http://www.tamiu.edu/gradschool/.

Texas A&M University
Educational Psychology
College of Education & Human Development
704 Harrington Tower, MS 4225
College Station, TX 77843-4225
Telephone: (979) 845-1831
Department Head: Victor Willson

E-mail: v-willson@tamu.edu
Web: http://epsy.tamu.edu/

Orientation, Objectives, and Emphasis of Department
We are among the top-ranked Educational Psychology departments in the nation. We are committed to making a difference through excellence in our research, education and community outreach activities.

Programs and Degrees Offered

Program	Degree	Application Deadline	Applications Received	Accepted	New Admits Enrolled (PT)	Total Enrolled (PT)	Degrees Awarded in 2014–2015	Median Years to Complete Degree	Dismissed/ Withdrew
School Psychology	PhD	December 1 (Fall)	35	21	13 (0)	37 (11)	10	6.5	1
Counseling Psychology	PhD	December 1 (Fall)	86	12	6	29 (12)	6	5.16	1
Educational Psychology	PhD	December 1 (Fall)	39	34	20 (14)	66 (24)	10	6.8	5

APA Accreditation
School PhD: Student Outcome Data website: http://epsy.tamu.edu/degrees-and-programs/graduate-degree-programs/school-psychology.
Counseling PhD: Student Outcome Data website: http://epsy.tamu.edu/degrees-and-programs/graduate-degree-programs/counseling-psychology.

Doctoral Degree (PhD School Psychology): For those doctoral students for whom a professional internship was required in this program prior to graduation:
Total students who applied for an internship: 7
Total students who obtained an internship: 7
Total students who obtained a paid internship: 7
Total students who obtained an unpaid internship: 0
Total students who were placed in APA/CPA-accredited internships: 7
Total students placed in internships not APA/CPA-accredited, but listed with the Association of Psychology Postdoctoral and Internship Centers (APPIC): 0
Total students placed in internships conforming to guidelines of the Council of Directors of School Psychology Programs (CDSPP): 0
Total students placed in internships that were not APA/CPA-accredited, APPIC or CDSSP listed: 0

Doctoral Degree (PhD Counseling Psychology): For those doctoral students for whom a professional internship was required in this program prior to graduation:
Total students who applied for an internship: 4
Total students who obtained an internship: 4
Total students who obtained a paid internship: 4
Total students who obtained an unpaid internship: 0
Total students who were placed in APA/CPA-accredited internships: 4
Total students placed in internships not APA/CPA-accredited, but listed with the Association of Psychology Postdoctoral and Internship Centers (APPIC): 0
Total students placed in internships conforming to guidelines of the Council of Directors of School Psychology Programs (CDSPP): 0
Total students placed in internships that were not APA/CPA-accredited, APPIC or CDSSP listed: 0

Internships/Practica
Students in School Psychology and Counseling Psychology participate in the APPIC match program.

Admissions
Entries appear in the following order: required test or GPA, minimum score (if required)/median score of students entering in 2015–2016.

Program	Degree	GRE-V	GRE-Q	GRE-Writing	GRE-Subject	Under-graduate GPA	Last 2 Years GPA	Psychology GPA	Master's GPA
School Psychology	PhD	NA/NA	NA/NA	Not specified	NA/NA	NA/NA	Not specified	Not specified	Not specified
Counseling Psychology	PhD	NA/NA	NA/NA	Not specified	Not specified	Not specified	Not specified	Not specified	Not specified
Educational Psychology	PhD	NA/NA	NA/NA	NA/NA	Not specified	Not specified	Not specified	Not specified	Not specified

Admissions Requirements:

Degree	GRE	GRE-Subject	Letters of Recom-mendation	Research Statement	Writing Sample	CV	Interview
Doctoral	Required	Optional	3	Required	Optional	Optional	Required

Admissions Criteria:
GRE scores—medium
Research experience—high
Work experience—medium
Clinically related public service—high
GPA—medium

Letters of recommendation—high
Interview—high
Statement of goals and objectives—high
Undergraduate psychology preparation—low
Fit with program—high

For additional information on admission requirements, visit http://epsy.tamu.edu/admissions/graduate-admissions.

Department Demographics

	Male (PT)	Female (PT)	Total	African-American/ Black (PT)	Hispanic/ Latino (PT)	Asian/ Pacific Islander (PT)	American Indian/ Alaska Native (PT)	Caucasian/ White (PT)	Unknown	Multiethnic (PT)	ADA (PT)	Int'l (PT)
Students	26 (15)	104 (32)	177	9 (7)	34 (23)	29 (3)	0 (0)	58 (14)	0 (0)	0 (0)	2 (0)	39 (1)

Financial Information/Assistance

Tuition: For information on tuition costs, visit http://sbs.tamu.edu/accounts-billing/tuition-fees/cost-attendance/. Tuition is subject to change. Tuition costs vary by program.

Doctoral:
State residents: $9,203 per academic year.
State residents: $233 per credit hour.
Nonstate residents: $24,000 per academic year.
Nonstate residents: $637 per credit hour.

Financial Assistance:

	Teaching Assistantship (% Receiving)	Teaching Assistantship Tuition Remission	Research Assistantship (% Receiving)	Research Assistantship Tuition Remission	Fellowship (% Receiving)	Fellowship Tuition Remission
First-Year Student	NA (NA)	NA	$18,000 (NA)	Partial	$25,000 (NA)	Full
Advanced Student	$15,000 (NA)	Partial	$18,000 (NA)	Partial	$20,000 (NA)	Partial

For additional information on financial assistance, visit http://epsy.tamu.edu/student-services/financial-assistance.

Employment of Department Graduates

Doctoral:
Employed in independent practice: 1
Employed in an academic position at a university: 5
Employed in other positions at a higher education institution: 4
Employed in a professional position in a school system: 5
Employed in government agency: 7
Employed in a community mental health/counseling center: 6
Employed in a hospital/medical center: 4
Total: 32

Additional Information

Housing and Day Care: On-campus housing is available. See the following website for more information: http://reslife.tamu.edu/. On-campus day care facilities are available. See the following website for more information: http://bgcc.tamu.edu/.

Information for Students With Physical Disabilities: See the following website: http://disability.tamu.edu/.

Special Facilities or Resources: Education Research Evaluation Laboratory (EREL) and Counseling and Assessment Clinic (CAC) on campus and in Bryan, TX.

Application Information: Fee: $50. *Online application:* http://admissions.tamu.edu/graduate/apply.

Texas A&M University
Psychology
College of Liberal Arts
Department of Psychology, MS 4235
College Station, TX 77843-4235
Telephone: (979) 458-1710
Department Head and Associate Professor: Heather Lench, PhD

E-mail: cpecos@tamu.edu
Web: http://psychology.tamu.edu

Orientation, Objectives, and Emphasis of Department
The goals of the PhD program in Psychology are (1) to prepare students for careers as researchers and teachers at colleges and universities, and (2) to prepare students for careers as scientist–practitioners in clinical psychology and industrial/organizational psychology. The Department offers a PhD in six areas of specialization: Behavioral and Cellular Neuroscience, Clinical (accredited by the APA), Cognition and Cognitive Neuroscience, Developmental, Social and Personality Psychology, and Industrial/Organizational Psychology. The Department enrolls approximately 80 to 90 graduate students and offers numerous opportunities for student collaboration with faculty. The student–faculty ratio is approximately 2:1, which allows individualized attention to develop research and/or professional skills. Over the last decade, all graduates have obtained full-time employment as researchers, teachers, or practitioners. Faculty members are heavily involved in the placement of graduate students.

Programs and Degrees Offered

Program	Degree	Application Deadline	Applications Received	Accepted	New Admits Enrolled (PT)	Total Enrolled (PT)	Degrees Awarded in 2014–2015	Median Years to Complete Degree	Dismissed/Withdrew
Developmental Psychology	PhD	December 1 (Fall)	3	1	0	3	1	5	1
Industrial/Organizational Psychology	PhD	December 1 (Fall)	58	8	3 (0)	16 (0)	1	5	0
Social and Personality Psychology	PhD	December 1 (Fall)	21	8	5	20 (0)	3	5	0
Behavioral and Cellular Neuroscience	PhD	December 1 (Fall)	14	4	2 (0)	4 (0)	1	5	0
Clinical Psychology	PhD	December 1 (Fall)	207	5	3 (0)	24 (0)	2	5.5	0
Cognition and Cognitive Neuroscience	PhD	December 1 (Fall)	11	5	4 (0)	13 (0)	4	5	0

APA Accreditation

Clinical PhD: Student Outcome Data website: http://psychology.tamu.edu/html/clinical-psychology.html.

Doctoral Degree (PhD Clinical Psychology): For those doctoral students for whom a professional internship was required in this program prior to graduation:
Total students who applied for an internship: 2
Total students who obtained an internship: 2
Total students who obtained a paid internship: 2
Total students who obtained an unpaid internship: 0
Total students who were placed in APA/CPA-accredited internships: 2
Total students placed in internships not APA/CPA-accredited, but listed with the Association of Psychology Postdoctoral and Internship Centers (APPIC): 0
Total students placed in internships conforming to guidelines of the Council of Directors of School Psychology Programs (CDSPP): 0
Total students placed in internships that were not APA/CPA-accredited, APPIC or CDSSP listed: 0

Admissions

Entries appear in the following order: required test or GPA, minimum score (if required)/median score of students entering in 2015–2016.

Program	Degree	GRE-V	GRE-Q	GRE-Writing	GRE-Subject	Under-graduate GPA	Last 2 Years GPA	Psychology GPA	Master's GPA
Developmental Psychology	PhD	NA/NA	NA/NA	NA/NA	Not specified	NA/NA	NA/NA	NA/NA	NA/NA
Industrial/Organizational Psychology	PhD	NA/NA	NA/NA	NA/NA	Not specified	NA/NA	NA/NA	NA/NA	NA/NA
Social and Personality Psychology	PhD	NA/NA	NA/NA	NA/NA	Not specified	NA/NA	NA/NA	NA/NA	NA/NA
Behavioral and Cellular Neuroscience	PhD	NA/NA	NA/NA	NA/NA	Not specified	NA/NA	NA/NA	NA/NA	NA/NA
Clinical Psychology	PhD	NA/NA	NA/NA	NA/NA	Not specified	NA/3.59	NA/NA	Not specified	NA/NA

Admissions (con't.)

Program	Degree	GRE-V	GRE-Q	GRE-Writing	GRE-Subject	Under-graduate GPA	Last 2 Years GPA	Psychol-ogy GPA	Master's GPA
Cognition and Cognitive Neuroscience	PhD	NA/NA	NA/NA	NA/NA	Not specified	NA/NA	NA/NA	NA/NA	NA/NA

Admissions Requirements:

Degree	GRE	GRE-Subject	Letters of Recom-mendation	Research Statement	Writing Sample	CV	Interview
Doctoral	Required	Optional	3	Required	None	Required	Required

Please note if these criteria vary for different programs: Interview required only for Clinical Psychology applicants.

Admissions Criteria:

GRE scores—high
Research experience—high
Work experience—medium
Clinically related public service—high
GPA—high

Letters of recommendation—high
Interview—high
Statement of goals and objectives—high
Undergraduate psychology preparation—high

For additional information on admission requirements, visit http://psychology.tamu.edu/html/application-and-admission.html.

Department Demographics

	Male (PT)	Female (PT)	Total	African-American/ Black (PT)	Hispanic/ Latino (PT)	Asian/ Pacific Islander (PT)	American Indian/ Alaska Native (PT)	Caucasian/ White (PT)	Unknown	Multiethnic (PT)	ADA (PT)	Int'l (PT)
Students	30 (0)	50 (0)	80	3 (0)	9 (0)	6 (0)	0 (0)	60 (0)	2 (0)	0 (0)	(0)	12 (0)

Financial Information/Assistance

Tuition: For information on tuition costs, visit http://sbs.tamu.edu/accounts-billing/tuition-fees/schedule/. Tuition is subject to change.

Doctoral:
State residents: $4,202 per academic year.
State residents: $233 per credit hour.
Nonstate residents: $11,348 per academic year.
Nonstate residents: $630 per credit hour.

Financial Assistance:

	Teaching Assistantship (% Receiving)	Teaching Assistantship Tuition Remission	Research Assistantship (% Receiving)	Research Assistantship Tuition Remission	Fellowship (% Receiving)	Fellowship Tuition Remission
First-Year Student	$15,000 (NA)	Full	$15,000 (NA)	Full	$25,000 (NA)	Full
Advanced Student	$15,000 (NA)	Full	$15,000 (NA)	Full	$25,000 (NA)	Full

Employment of Department Graduates

Doctoral:
Enrolled in a postdoctoral residency/fellowship: 6
Employed in an academic position at a university: 2
Employed in academic position at a 2-year/4-year college: 1
Employed in business or industry: 3
Total: 12

Additional Information

Housing and Day Care: No on-campus housing is available. On-campus day care facilities are available. See the following website for more information: http://bgcc.tamu.edu/.

Information for Students With Physical Disabilities: See the following website: http://disability.tamu.edu/.

Special Facilities or Resources: The Department is housed in an attractive four-story building that contains faculty and graduate student offices, research laboratories, administrative offices, and classrooms. Laboratory facilities are excellent, including labs designated for faculty and student research in behavioral and cellular neuroscience, cognitive, developmental, industrial/organizational, and social psychology. The Department also maintains a Psychology Clinic in which Clinical students are trained to provide a range of psychological services and conduct applied research under supervision from the Clinical faculty.

Application Information: Graduate Studies Supervisor, Department of Psychology, Texas A&M University, 4235 TAMU, College Station, TX 77843-4235. *Fee:* $50. *Online application:* https://www.applytexas.org.

Texas A&M University—Commerce
Department of Psychology, Counseling and Special Education
College of Education and Human Services
Binnion Hall
Commerce, TX 75429
Telephone: (903) 886-5200
Department Head: Dr. Jennifer Schroeder
E-mail: Jennifer.Schroeder@tamuc.edu
Web: http://www.tamuc.edu/academics/colleges/educationHumanServices/departments/psychologyCounselingSpecialEducation/

Orientation, Objectives, and Emphasis of Department
The focus of the educational psychology program is human interventions (direct and indirect), statistics and research design, and cognition and instruction. Students will acquire an in-depth knowledge of human learning and cognition, instructional strategies, and research and evaluation. This emphasis will prepare students to integrate knowledge of human cognition and instructional practice across a variety of occupational, educational and content matter domains, with emphasis on applications of learning technologies. The same is true of our Master's program in General/Experimental Psychology, which a student earns as part of our 90-hour doctoral programs. Or, students can enroll in the Master's program as a terminal degree. This is a 36-hour program that can either emphasize research (with a required empirical thesis) or not. The applied master's program is designed to prepare students to meet the requirements for certification as an associate psychologist in the State of Texas. Associate psychologists are employed in a variety of governmental and private organizations, such as mental health centers, clinics, and hospitals. The school psychology program has been approved by the National Association of School Psychologists (NASP).

Programs and Degrees Offered

Program	Degree	Application Deadline	Applications Received	Accepted	New Admits Enrolled (PT)	Total Enrolled (PT)	Degrees Awarded in 2014–2015	Median Years to Complete Degree	Dismissed/ Withdrew
Educational Psychology	PhD	January 31 (Fall), November 15 (Spring), January 31 (Summer), Rolling	22	16	14 (1)	38 (10)	3	7.5	1

Programs and Degrees Offered *(con't.)*

Program	Degree	Application Deadline	Applica-tions Received	Accepted	New Admits Enrolled (PT)	Total Enrolled (PT)	Degrees Awarded in 2014–2015	Median Years to Complete Degree	Dismissed/ Withdrew
School Psychology	EdS	April 15 (Fall), November 15 (Spring), Rolling	10	2	1 (1)	9 (15)	7	3.5	1
Applied Psychology	MA/MS	Rolling	12	8	3 (5)	21 (31)	6	2.33	3
General Experimental Psychology	MA/MS	Rolling	7	5	5 (0)	12 (0)	2	3	0

Internships/Practica

There are on-site university clinic practica for school and applied programs. The school psychology program requires a 1200-hour internship in the public schools.

Admissions

Entries appear in the following order: required test or GPA, minimum score (if required)/median score of students entering in 2015–2016.

Program	Degree	GRE-V	GRE-Q	GRE-Writing	GRE-Subject	Under-graduate GPA	Last 2 Years GPA	Psychol-ogy GPA	Master's GPA
Educational Psychology	PhD	NA/NA	NA/NA	NA/NA	Not specified	NA/NA	Not specified	Not specified	Not specified
School Psychology	EdS	NA/NA	NA/NA	NA/NA	Not specified	NA/NA	Not specified	Not specified	Not specified
Applied Psychology	MA/MS	NA/NA	NA/NA	NA/NA	Not specified	NA/NA	Not specified	Not specified	Not specified
General Experimental Psychology	MA/MS	NA/NA	NA/NA	NA/NA	Not specified	NA/NA	Not specified	Not specified	Not specified

Admissions Requirements:

Degree	GRE	GRE-Subject	Letters of Recom-mendation	Research Statement	Writing Sample	CV	Interview
Master's/Specialist	Required	Optional	3	Required	Optional	Required	Required
Doctoral	Required	Optional	4	Required	Optional	Optional	None

Please note if these criteria vary for different programs: Greater importance would be assigned to prior research experience, graduate education, and publications/scholarly activity for the doctoral program.

Admissions Criteria:

GRE scores—medium
Research experience—medium
Work experience—medium
GPA—medium

Letters of recommendation—medium
Interview—medium
Statement of goals and objectives—high
Undergraduate psychology preparation—low

Department Demographics

	Male (PT)	Female (PT)	Total	African-American/ Black (PT)	Hispanic/ Latino (PT)	Asian/ Pacific Islander (PT)	American Indian/ Alaska Native (PT)	Caucasian/ White (PT)	Unknown (PT)	Multiethnic (PT)	ADA (PT)	Int'l (PT)
Students	21 (10)	40 (45)	116	9 (7)	3 (2)	1 (0)	0 (0)	48 (46)	0 (0)	0 (0)	1 (0)	6 (0)

Financial Information/Assistance

Tuition: For information on tuition costs, visit http://www.tamuc.edu/admissions/tuitionCosts/default.aspx. Tuition is subject to change.

Doctoral:
State residents: $420 per credit hour.
Nonstate residents: $782 per credit hour.

Master's:
State residents: $420 per credit hour.
Nonstate residents: $782 per credit hour.

Financial Assistance:

	Teaching Assistantship (% Receiving)	Teaching Assistantship Tuition Remission	Research Assistantship (% Receiving)	Research Assistantship Tuition Remission	Fellowship (% Receiving)	Fellowship Tuition Remission
First-Year Student	$8,000 (NA)	Partial	$8,000 (NA)	Partial	$1,000 (NA)	Partial
Advanced Student	$10,000 (NA)	Partial	$10,000 (NA)	Partial	$1,000 (NA)	Partial

For additional information on financial assistance, visit http://www.tamuc.edu/academics/graduateSchool/funding/default.aspx.

Employment of Department Graduates

Master's:
Enrolled in a psychology doctoral program: 1
Enrolled in another graduate/professional program: 1
Employed in a professional position in a school system: 6
Employed in government agency: 1
Employed in a community mental health/counseling center: 2
Employed in a hospital/medical center: 1
Not seeking employment: 1
Total: 13

Doctoral:
Employed in an academic position at a university: 2
Not seeking employment: 2
Do not know: 1
Total: 5

Additional Information

Housing and Day Care: On-campus housing is available. See the following website for more information: http://www.tamuc.edu/CampusLife/housing/default.aspx. On-campus day care facilities are available. See the following website for more information: http://www.tamuc.edu/CampusLife/CampusServices/childrensLearningCenter/default.aspx.

Special Facilities or Resources: Multimedia Instructional Lab, multimedia classrooms, on-site Integrated University Clinic, research partnerships with business industry, Center for excellence-learning technologies, support for online learning, Cognitive Developmental Lab, Cognitive Science Lab, Cognition Lab, Health Psychology Lab, Social Cognition Lab, and School Psychology Resource Center.

Application Information: Graduate School, P.O. Box 3011, Texas A&M—Commerce, Commerce, TX 75429-3011. *Fee:* $50. *Online application:* http://www.tamuc.edu/academics/graduateSchool/applyOnline.aspx.

Texas Christian University
Department of Psychology
College of Science and Engineering
TCU Box 298920
Fort Worth, TX 76129
Telephone: (817) 257-7410
Chairperson: Mauricio Papini

E-mail: c.lord@tcu.edu
Web: http://psychology.tcu.edu/

Orientation, Objectives, and Emphasis of Department

The psychology graduate program at Texas Christian University leads to a PhD in general experimental psychology. We do not accept applicants who seek only a terminal master's degree, nor applicants who prefer to specialize in clinical, counseling, or other applied areas. The program is primarily a basic research degree. Within this degree, the student may study diverse areas of interest with emphasis possible in the following: learning-comparative, developmental-cognition, social psychology, and behavioral neuroscience. The environment is stimulating, informal, and conducive to close student-faculty relations. All 13 research faculty have productive research labs and are excited about mentoring PhD students.

Programs and Degrees Offered

Program	Degree	Application Deadline	Applica-tions Received	Accepted	New Admits Enrolled (PT)	Total Enrolled (PT)	Degrees Awarded in 2014–2015	Median Years to Complete Degree	Dismissed/ Withdrew
Experimental Psychology	PhD	February 1 (Fall)	40	5	5 (0)	26 (0)	6	5	0

Admissions

Entries appear in the following order: required test or GPA, minimum score (if required)/median score of students entering in 2015–2016.

Program	Degree	GRE-V	GRE-Q	GRE-Writing	GRE-Subject	Under-graduate GPA	Last 2 Years GPA	Psychol-ogy GPA	Master's GPA
Experimental Psychology	PhD	155/160	148/153	4.2/4.5	Not specified	3.3/3.7	3.5/3.8	3.6/3.8	Not specified

Admissions Requirements:

Degree	GRE	GRE-Subject	Letters of Recom-mendation	Research Statement	Writing Sample	CV	Interview
Doctoral	Required	None	3	Required	None	Required	None

Admissions Criteria:

GRE scores—medium
Research experience—high
GPA—medium

Letters of recommendation—high
Statement of goals and objectives—medium
Undergraduate psychology preparation—medium

For additional information on admission requirements, visit http://psychology.tcu.edu/prospective-students/experimental-ph-d-program/.

Department Demographics

	Male (PT)	Female (PT)	Total	African-American/ Black (PT)	Hispanic/ Latino (PT)	Asian/ Pacific Islander (PT)	American Indian/ Alaska Native (PT)	Caucasian/ White (PT)	Unknown (PT)	Multiethnic (PT)	ADA (PT)	Int'l (PT)
Students	10 (0)	16 (0)	26	0 (0)	1 (0)	0 (0)	0 (0)	25 (0)	0 (0)	0 (0)	0 (0)	0 (0)

Financial Information/Assistance

Tuition: For information on tuition costs, visit http://graduate.tcu.edu/financial-support/tuition-and-fees/. Tuition is subject to change. Additional fees are assessed to students beyond the costs of tuition for the following: student fees.

Doctoral:
State residents: $1,415 per credit hour.
Nonstate residents: $1,415 per credit hour.

Financial Assistance:

	Teaching Assistantship (% Receiving)	Teaching Assistantship Tuition Remission	Research Assistantship (% Receiving)	Research Assistantship Tuition Remission	Fellowship (% Receiving)	Fellowship Tuition Remission
First-Year Student	$19,750 (NA)	Full	NA (NA)	NA	NA (NA)	NA
Advanced Student	$19,750 (NA)	Full	NA (NA)	NA	NA (NA)	NA

For additional information on financial assistance, visit http://graduate.tcu.edu/degrees-and-programs/financial-aid/.

Employment of Department Graduates

Doctoral:
Employed in an academic position at a university: 2
Employed in academic position at a 2-year/4-year college: 1
Employed in business or industry: 2
Employed in government agency: 1
Total: 6

Additional Information

Housing and Day Care: No on-campus housing is available. No on-campus day care facilities are available.

Information for Students With Physical Disabilities: See the following website: http://www.acs.tcu.edu/disability_services.asp.

Special Facilities or Resources: Assuming that physical proximity is conducive to more interdisciplinary work of substance, TCU has located all its science-related activities in or near the Science Research Center. The Department of Psychology occupies two floors of the center's Winton-Scott Hall (equipment for the behavioral neuroscience program is shared with the Biology Department in the same building, but on a different floor). The university library, containing over one million volumes, is located next to the science facilities. About 140 periodicals of psychological interest are available, plus online access to almost all journals. Full-time personnel skilled in electronics, glass blowing, woodworking, and metalworking aid in construction and maintenance of special equipment or instruments. TCU has 10 open computer labs equipped with Windows-based PCs and Macintosh computers (over 100 Windows-based machines and 39 Mac-based machines). All of the labs provide full Internet access and laser printing. Additionally, some of the labs have scanners, zip drives, CD burners, and web cams. The Psychology Department also has a computer lab with six Windows-based PCs, all of which are connected to the Internet, and a networked laser printer. Additionally, all of the research laboratories in the department have networked computers.

Application Information: Sue Dolce. *Fee:* $60. *Online application:* https://www.applyweb.com/tcug/.

Texas Southwestern Medical Center, The University of
Division of Psychology, Graduate Program in Clinical Psychology
5323 Harry Hines Boulevard
Dallas, TX 75390-9044
Telephone: (214) 648-5277
Chairperson: C. Munro Cullum, PhD

E-mail: psychology@utsouthwestern.edu
Web: http://www.utsouthwestern.edu/clinical-psychology

Orientation, Objectives, and Emphasis of Department
The Graduate Program in Clinical Psychology is a 4-year doctoral program with an affiliated predoctoral internship program in clinical psychology, which is separately accredited by the APA. The program provides a combination of experiences in both clinical and research settings reflecting our basic training philosophy, which is a clinician–researcher model. Our specific objectives include offering the student the opportunity to acquire, experience, or develop the following (1) a closely knit integration between basic psychological knowledge (both theoretical and empirical) and responsible professional services; (2) a wide variety of supervised and broadly conceived clinical and consulting experiences; (3) a sensitivity to professional responsibilities in the context of significant social needs; (4) an understanding of research principles, methodology, and skill in formulating, designing, and implementing psychological research; and (5) a competence and confidence in the role of psychology in multidisciplinary settings.

Programs and Degrees Offered

Program	Degree	Application Deadline	Applica-tions Received	Accepted	New Admits Enrolled (PT)	Total Enrolled (PT)	Degrees Awarded in 2014–2015	Median Years to Complete Degree	Dismissed/ Withdrew
Clinical Psychology	PhD	December 1 (Fall)	205	19	10 (0)	40 (0)	10	4	0

APA Accreditation

Clinical PhD (Doctor of Philosophy).

Doctoral Degree (PhD Clinical Psychology): For those doctoral students for whom a professional internship was required in this program prior to graduation:
Total students who applied for an internship: 10
Total students who obtained an internship: 10
Total students who obtained a paid internship: 10
Total students who obtained an unpaid internship: 0
Total students who were placed in APA/CPA-accredited internships: 10
Total students placed in internships not APA/CPA-accredited, but listed with the Association of Psychology Postdoctoral and Internship Centers (APPIC): 0
Total students placed in internships conforming to guidelines of the Council of Directors of School Psychology Programs (CDSPP): 0
Total students placed in internships that were not APA/CPA-accredited, APPIC or CDSSP listed: 0

Internships/Practica

The program provides more than 1000 hours of clinical practica, followed by an affiliated, APA-accredited internship. These clinical experiences are closely supervised. In order to achieve the goal of broad professional preparation, students will have a number of different clinical placements over the course of their practicum and internship assignments. These assignments are carried out at UT Southwestern facilities, agencies, regional medical centers, area schools, community agencies, university counseling centers, and rehabilitation institutes. These clinical training sites include the following: Parkland Memorial Hospital [PMH]; Neuropsychology Service [UTSWMC]; Children's Health; the Mental Health Service of Southern Methodist University; Student Counseling Center at the University of Texas at Arlington; Dallas County Juvenile Department; Baylor University Medical Center; John Peter Smith; Moncrief Cancer Center; and Metrocare Services.

Admissions

Entries appear in the following order: required test or GPA, minimum score (if required)/median score of students entering in 2015–2016.

Program	Degree	GRE-V	GRE-Q	GRE-Writing	GRE-Subject	Under-graduate GPA	Last 2 Years GPA	Psychol-ogy GPA	Master's GPA
Clinical Psychology	PhD	NA/159	NA/159	Not specified	Not specified	3/3.65	Not specified	Not specified	Not specified

Admissions Requirements:

Degree	GRE	GRE-Subject	Letters of Recom-mendation	Research Statement	Writing Sample	CV	Interview
Doctoral	Required	Optional	3	Required	Required	Required	Required

Admissions Criteria:

GRE scores—high
Research experience—high
Work experience—high
Clinically related public service—medium
GPA—high

Letters of recommendation—high
Interview—high
Statement of goals and objectives—high
Undergraduate psychology preparation—medium

Department Demographics

	Male (PT)	Female (PT)	Total	African-American/ Black (PT)	Hispanic/ Latino (PT)	Asian/ Pacific Islander (PT)	American Indian/ Alaska Native (PT)	Caucasian/ White (PT)	Unknown	Multiethnic (PT)	ADA (PT)	Int'l (PT)
Students	16 (0)	24 (0)	40	2 (0)	2 (0)	4 (0)	0 (0)	32 (0)	0 (0)	0 (0)	1 (0)	0 (0)

Financial Information/Assistance

Tuition: For information on tuition costs, visit http://www.utsouthwestern.edu/about-us/administrative-offices/financial-aid/. Tuition is subject to change. Additional fees are assessed to students beyond the costs of tuition for the following: University/institution fees or costs $1220.00.

Doctoral:
State residents: $8,180 per academic year.
Nonstate residents: $21,050 per academic year.

Financial Assistance:

	Teaching Assistantship (% Receiving)	Teaching Assistantship Tuition Remission	Research Assistantship (% Receiving)	Research Assistantship Tuition Remission	Fellowship (% Receiving)	Fellowship Tuition Remission
First-Year Student	NA (NA)	NA	NA (NA)	NA	NA (NA)	NA
Advanced Student	$14,472 (NA)	NA	NA (NA)	NA	NA (NA)	NA

For additional information on financial assistance, visit http://www.utsouthwestern.edu/education/graduate-school/cost-financial-support/clinical-psychology.html.

Employment of Department Graduates

Doctoral:
Enrolled in a postdoctoral residency/fellowship: 9
Employed in independent practice: 1
Total: 10

Additional Information

Housing and Day Care: On-campus housing is available. See the following website for more information: http://www.utsouthwestern.edu/education/student-services/housing/. On-campus day care facilities are available. See the following website for more information: http://www.utsouthwestern.edu/education/student-services/child-care.html.

Special Facilities or Resources: UT Southwestern has a number of laboratories and clinical settings investigating the brain/behavior relationship, as well as many projects focusing on the psychosocial aspects of various medical and psychiatric disorders. Disorders studied include affective illness, anxiety, schizophrenia, sleep-wake dysfunctions, and medical conditions such as Alzheimer's disease, epilepsy, temporomandibular disorder, cystic fibrosis, and organ transplantation. Notable examples of comprehensive clinical research programs at UT Southwestern include the following: an affective disorders research program; a child psychiatry research program; a sleep disorders research laboratory; an Alzheimer's Disease Center; a neuropsychology laboratory; a pain management program; a schizophrenia research program that includes translational research; and research programs in basic neuroscience.

Application Information: Fee: $0. Online application: http://www.utsouthwestern.edu/gradapp.

Texas State University

Psychology Department/Master of Arts in Psychological Research
College of Liberal Arts
601 University Drive
San Marcos, TX 78666-4616
Telephone: (512) 245-2526
Chairperson: William L. Kelemen, PhD

E-mail: psychology@txstate.edu
Web: http://www.psych.txstate.edu

Orientation, Objectives, and Emphasis of Department

The goal of the Master's program in Psychological Research at Texas State University is to foster competence in the methodological foundations and conduct of psychological research across a wide variety of settings. Students will gain expertise regarding the impact of biological, social, emotional, cognitive, and behavioral factors on psychological phenomena. Focus is placed on learning interpersonal/research skills and statistical competencies relevant to the responsible and ethical conduct of both basic and applied psychological research. This program is appropriate for individuals wishing to work in basic and applied research settings or intending to pursue a doctoral degree in psychology. The program requires completion of 38 credit hours, which includes 6 credit hours for completion of a thesis.

Programs and Degrees Offered

Program	Degree	Application Deadline	Applica-tions Received	Accepted	New Admits Enrolled (PT)	Total Enrolled (PT)	Degrees Awarded in 2014–2015	Median Years to Complete Degree	Dismissed/Withdrew
Psychological Research	MA/MS	April 30 (Fall)	42	21	14 (0)	27 (12)	8	1.75	0

Admissions

Entries appear in the following order: required test or GPA, minimum score (if required)/median score of students entering in 2015–2016.

Program	Degree	GRE-V	GRE-Q	GRE-Writing	GRE-Subject	Under-graduate GPA	Last 2 Years GPA	Psychol-ogy GPA	Master's GPA
Psychological Research	MA/MS	NA/NA	NA/NA	Not specified	Not specified	3/NA	3/NA	Not specified	Not specified

Admissions Requirements:

Degree	GRE	GRE-Subject	Letters of Recom-mendation	Research Statement	Writing Sample	CV	Interview
Master's/Specialist	Required	Required	3	Required	None	Required	None

Admissions Criteria:

GRE scores—low
Research experience—medium
Work experience—low
Clinically related public service—low

GPA—high
Letters of recommendation—high
Statement of goals and objectives—high
Undergraduate psychology preparation—medium

For additional information on admission requirements, visit http://www.psych.txstate.edu/degrees-programs/graduate/mapr/applicationrequirements.html.

Department Demographics

	Male (PT)	Female (PT)	Total	African-American/ Black (PT)	Hispanic/ Latino (PT)	Asian/ Pacific Islander (PT)	American Indian/ Alaska Native (PT)	Caucasian/ White (PT)	Unknown	Multiethnic (PT)	ADA (PT)	Int'l (PT)
Students	10 (6)	17 (6)	39	3 (1)	4 (2)	2 (0)	0 (0)	17 (7)	0 (0)	1 (2)	0 (0)	0 (0)

Financial Information/Assistance

Tuition: For information on tuition costs, visit http://www.sbs.txstate.edu/billing/rates-g.html. Tuition is subject to change.

Master's:
State residents: $7,431 per academic year.
Nonstate residents: $14,841 per academic year.

Financial Assistance:

	Teaching Assistantship (% Receiving)	Teaching Assistantship Tuition Remission	Research Assistantship (% Receiving)	Research Assistantship Tuition Remission	Fellowship (% Receiving)	Fellowship Tuition Remission
First-Year Student	$12,150 (50)	NA	$9,855 (21)	NA	$1,000 (21)	NA
Advanced Student	$12,982 (84)	NA	$10,107 (0)	NA	$1,000 (46)	NA

For additional information on financial assistance, visit http://www.finaid.txstate.edu/graduate.html.

Employment of Department Graduates

Master's:
Enrolled in a psychology doctoral program: 2
Employed in other positions at a higher education institution: 1
Employed in business or industry: 1
Employed in a community mental health/counseling center: 1
Still seeking employment: 1
Other employment position: 2
Total: 8

Additional Information

Housing and Day Care: No on-campus housing is available. On-campus day care facilities are available. See the following website for more information: http://www.fcs.txstate.edu/cdc/.

Information for Students With Physical Disabilities: See the following website: http://www.ods.txstate.edu/.

Special Facilities or Resources: The Psychology Department at Texas State University is housed in a LEED-certified building completed in June 2012. Research facilities include electrophysiology labs; behavioral testing labs; an event-related potentials (ERP) lab; a sleep lab; a salivary analysis lab; an eye-tracking lab; a portable transcranial laser Doppler lab; interpersonal interaction labs; and observation, survey, and computer testing labs.

Application Information: The Graduate College, Texas State University, 601 University Drive, San Marcos, TX 78666-4605. *Fee:* $40. *Online application:* http://www.gradcollege.txstate.edu/steps.html.

Texas Tech University
Department of Psychological Sciences
Arts & Sciences
Box 42051
Lubbock, TX 79409-2051
Telephone: (806) 834-1350
Chairperson: Robert D. Morgan, PhD

E-mail: kay.hill@ttu.edu
Web: http://www.depts.ttu.edu/psy/

Orientation, Objectives, and Emphasis of Department
The clinical program adheres to a basic scientist–practitioner model with equal emphasis given to these components of clinical training. The program strives to develop student competencies in the following areas: psychotherapy and other major patterns of

psychological treatment, clinical research, psychodiagnostic assessment, psychopathology, personality, and general psychology. The doctoral specialization in counseling psychology is also firmly committed to a concept of balanced scientist–practitioner training and is designed to foster the development of competence in basic psychology, counseling and psychotherapy, psychological assessment, psychological research, and professional ethics. Programs in experimental psychology (cognitive/applied cognitive, social, human factors) encompass a variety of research interests, both basic and applied. Students in these programs are exposed to the data, methods and theories and a wide variety of basic areas of psychology while at the same time developing a commitment to an area of special interest through research with a faculty mentor. Collaborative work across departmental programs is encouraged, and the department also collaborates with colleagues in management, industrial engineering, neuroscience, neuropsychiatry, the TTU Neuroimaging Institute (fMRI), and the TTU Health Sciences Center.

Programs and Degrees Offered

Program	Degree	Application Deadline	Applications Received	Accepted	New Admits Enrolled (PT)	Total Enrolled (PT)	Degrees Awarded in 2014–2015	Median Years to Complete Degree	Dismissed/ Withdrew
Clinical Psychology	PhD	December 1 (Fall)	120	8	8 (0)	42 (0)	7	5.5	0
Applied Cognitive Psychology	PhD	January 15 (Fall)	14	5	5 (0)	10 (1)	2	5	0
Counseling Psychology	PhD	December 1 (Fall)	80	8	8 (0)	41 (0)	8	5.5	0
Human Factors	PhD	January 15 (Fall)	28	4	4 (0)	16 (1)	3	5	0
Social Psychology	PhD	January 15 (Fall)	24	5	5 (0)	18 (1)	4	5	0

APA Accreditation

Clinical PhD: Student Outcome Data website: http://www.depts.ttu.edu/psy/clinical/.
Counseling PhD: Student Outcome Data website: http://www.depts.ttu.edu/psy/counseling/.

Doctoral Degree (PhD Clinical Psychology): For those doctoral students for whom a professional internship was required in this program prior to graduation:
Total students who applied for an internship: 4
Total students who obtained an internship: 4
Total students who obtained a paid internship: 4
Total students who obtained an unpaid internship: 0
Total students who were placed in APA/CPA-accredited internships: 4
Total students placed in internships not APA/CPA-accredited, but listed with the Association of Psychology Postdoctoral and Internship Centers (APPIC): 0
Total students placed in internships conforming to guidelines of the Council of Directors of School Psychology Programs (CDSPP): 0
Total students placed in internships that were not APA/CPA-accredited, APPIC or CDSSP listed: 0

Doctoral Degree (PhD Counseling Psychology): For those doctoral students for whom a professional internship was required in this program prior to graduation:
Total students who applied for an internship: 7
Total students who obtained an internship: 7
Total students who obtained a paid internship: 7
Total students who obtained an unpaid internship: 0
Total students who were placed in APA/CPA-accredited internships: 7
Total students placed in internships not APA/CPA-accredited, but listed with the Association of Psychology Postdoctoral and Internship Centers (APPIC): 0
Total students placed in internships conforming to guidelines of the Council of Directors of School Psychology Programs (CDSPP): 0
Total students placed in internships that were not APA/CPA-accredited, APPIC or CDSSP listed: 0

Internships/Practica

Nearly 100% of our PhD students in clinical and counseling obtain a predoctoral internship that is accredited by APA. Practica are available in our Psychology Clinic and the Texas Tech University Counseling Center. Paid practica are available in the community. Such placements include a psychiatric prison, the departments of Family Medicine, Oncology, Pediatric Oncology, Internal Medicine, and Neuropsychiatry in the TTU Health Sciences Center, StarCare (CMHC), a community child psychology practice, a community neuropsychology practice, and conducting assessments at the state school and with local psychologists.

Admissions

Entries appear in the following order: required test or GPA, minimum score (if required)/median score of students entering in 2015–2016.

Program	Degree	GRE-V	GRE-Q	GRE-Writing	GRE-Subject	Under-graduate GPA	Last 2 Years GPA	Psychol-ogy GPA	Master's GPA
Clinical Psychology	PhD	NA/161	NA/159	NA/4.5	Not specified	Not specified	Not specified	Not specified	Not specified
Applied Cognitive Psychology	PhD	NA/160	NA/149	NA/4	Not specified	Not specified	Not specified	Not specified	Not specified
Counseling Psychology	PhD	NA/159	NA/152	NA/4	Not specified	Not specified	Not specified	Not specified	Not specified
Human Factors	PhD	NA/155	NA/150	NA/4	Not specified	NA/3.6	Not specified	Not specified	Not specified
Social Psychology	PhD	NA/162	NA/158	Not specified	Not specified	Not specified	Not specified	Not specified	Not specified

Admissions Requirements:

Degree	GRE	GRE-Subject	Letters of Recom-mendation	Research Statement	Writing Sample	CV	Interview
Doctoral	Required	Recom-mended	3	Required	Optional	Required	Required

Please note if these criteria vary for different programs: Work experience for experimental-low, counseling-medium, clinical-high; interview for clinical-high, counseling-high, experimental-medium. Interviews usually held in late January or early February.

Admissions Criteria:

GRE scores—medium
Research experience—high
Work experience—medium
Clinically related public service—medium
GPA—high

Letters of recommendation—high
Interview—high
Statement of goals and objectives—high
Undergraduate psychology preparation—medium

For additional information on admission requirements, visit http://www.depts.ttu.edu/psy/apply.php.

Department Demographics

	Male (PT)	Female (PT)	Total	African-American/ Black (PT)	Hispanic/ Latino (PT)	Asian/ Pacific Islander (PT)	American Indian/ Alaska Native (PT)	Caucasian/ White (PT)	Unknown	Multiethnic (PT)	ADA (PT)	Int'l (PT)
Students	38 (0)	96 (0)	134	12 (0)	31 (0)	9 (0)	0 (0)	72 (0)	8 (0)	2 (0)	1 (0)	4 (0)

Financial Information/Assistance

Tuition: For information on tuition costs, visit http://www.depts.ttu.edu/studentbusinessservices/feeInfo/tuitiongrids.php. Tuition is subject to change.

Doctoral:
State residents: $6,569 per academic year.
Nonstate residents: $16,985 per academic year.

Financial Assistance:

	Teaching Assistantship (% Receiving)	Teaching Assistantship Tuition Remission	Research Assistantship (% Receiving)	Research Assistantship Tuition Remission	Fellowship (% Receiving)	Fellowship Tuition Remission
First-Year Student	$10,549 (100)	Partial	$10,549 (100)	Partial	$4,000 (15)	Partial
Advanced Student	$12,462 (100)	Partial	$12,462 (NA)	Partial	$1,000 (NA)	Partial

For additional information on financial assistance, visit http://www.financialaid.ttu.edu/.

Employment of Department Graduates

Doctoral:
Employed in independent practice: 4
Employed in an academic position at a university: 5
Employed in academic position at a 2-year/4-year college: 4
Employed in business or industry: 2
Employed in government agency: 4
Employed in a community mental health/counseling center: 4
Employed in a hospital/medical center: 3
Do not know: 1
Total: 27

Additional Information

Housing and Day Care: On-campus housing is available. See the following website for more information: http://housing.ttu.edu/. On-campus day care facilities are available. See the following website for more information: http://www.depts.ttu.edu/hs/cdrc/.

Information for Students With Physical Disabilities: See the following website: http://www.depts.ttu.edu/sds/.

Special Facilities or Resources: The department is housed in its own four-story building (plus a basement, for 5 floors total), which includes a large, well-equipped psychology clinic for practicum training, numerous laboratories equipped for human research activities, and sufficient student workspace and offices. We have access to modern large computer and MRI research facilities, along with a University Health Sciences Center. The university maintains constantly expanding computing support systems that can be accessed from computers in the psychology building. The university enjoys an unusually good relationship with the local metropolitan community of over 250,000 residents. Major medical facilities, a private psychiatric hospital, a psychiatric prison and a state school for the developmentally disabled are located within the city, and APA-accredited internship training is available in the TTU Student Counseling Center.

Application Information: Texas Tech University, Admissions, Psychology Department, Box 42051, Lubbock, TX 79409-2051. *Fee:* $60. *Online application:* http://www.depts.ttu.edu/gradschool/admissions/apply.php.

Texas Woman's University
Department of Psychology and Philosophy
Arts & Sciences
P.O. Box 425470
Denton, TX 76204
Telephone: (940) 898-2303
Chairperson: Shannon Scott, PhD

E-mail: sscott@twu.edu
Web: http://www.twu.edu/psychology-philosophy/

Orientation, Objectives, and Emphasis of Department
Both the APA-accredited Counseling Psychology doctoral program and the Counseling Psychology master's program prepare students in the practitioner-scientist model. The programs are grounded in feminist multicultural philosophy and pedagogy. The programs have a particular focus on developing clinicians with a strong understanding of individuals within their gendered and sociocultural contexts. Graduates of the program are expected to be conversant with and competent in the diversity-sensitive

applications of individual, systemic, and integrative theories. The model provides clear training in both practice and science, but emphasizes practice; practice that is informed by science. Graduate training in school psychology at the master's level provides a program emphasizing direct service to school settings. Specific competencies and areas of specialization stressed in coursework and field-based training include child development, psychopathology, theories and principles of learning, behavioral intervention and prevention strategies, diagnostic assessment, and evaluation techniques. The APA-accredited school psychology doctoral program focuses on applied preparation and training experiences in professional school psychology. It prepares students in skills required in direct-to-client services (for example, diagnostic assessment and evaluation skills, therapeutic and intervention techniques, and competencies in the application of learning principles).

Programs and Degrees Offered

Program	Degree	Application Deadline	Applications Received	Accepted	New Admits Enrolled (PT)	Total Enrolled (PT)	Degrees Awarded in 2014–2015	Median Years to Complete Degree	Dismissed/Withdrew
Counseling Psychology	PhD	December 15 (Fall)	49	8	6 (0)	32 (0)	4	8	0
School Psychology	PhD	January 5 (Fall)	20	8	5 (0)	28 (1)	9	5	1
Counseling	MA/MS	February 1 (Fall)	53	10	10 (0)	20 (0)	7	3.4	1
School Psychology	EdS	February 1 (Fall)	9	8	8 (0)	12 (0)	3	3	3

APA Accreditation
Counseling PhD: Student Outcome Data website: http://www.twu.edu/psychology-philosophy/counseling-psych-phd.asp.
School PhD: Student Outcome Data website: http://www.twu.edu/psychology-philosophy/phd-school-psych.asp.

Doctoral Degree (PhD Counseling Psychology): For those doctoral students for whom a professional internship was required in this program prior to graduation:
Total students who applied for an internship: 8
Total students who obtained an internship: 8
Total students who obtained a paid internship: 8
Total students who obtained an unpaid internship: 0
Total students who were placed in APA/CPA-accredited internships: 8
Total students placed in internships not APA/CPA-accredited, but listed with the Association of Psychology Postdoctoral and Internship Centers (APPIC): 0
Total students placed in internships conforming to guidelines of the Council of Directors of School Psychology Programs (CDSPP): 0
Total students placed in internships that were not APA/CPA-accredited, APPIC or CDSSP listed: 0

Doctoral Degree (PhD School Psychology): For those doctoral students for whom a professional internship was required in this program prior to graduation:
Total students who applied for an internship: 10
Total students who obtained an internship: 10
Total students who obtained a paid internship: 10
Total students who obtained an unpaid internship: 0
Total students who were placed in APA/CPA-accredited internships: 6
Total students placed in internships not APA/CPA-accredited, but listed with the Association of Psychology Postdoctoral and Internship Centers (APPIC): 0
Total students placed in internships conforming to guidelines of the Council of Directors of School Psychology Programs (CDSPP): 4
Total students placed in internships that were not APA/CPA-accredited, APPIC or CDSSP listed: 0

Master's Degree (MA/MS Counseling): An internship experience, such as a final research project or "capstone" experience is required of graduates.

Internships/Practica
There are numerous placements in the Dallas-Fort Worth metropolitan area. Doctoral students are expected to use the APPIC Directory for internship placement.

Admissions

Entries appear in the following order: required test or GPA, minimum score (if required)/median score of students entering in 2015–2016.

Program	Degree	GRE-V	GRE-Q	GRE-Writing	GRE-Subject	Under-graduate GPA	Last 2 Years GPA	Psychol-ogy GPA	Master's GPA
Counseling Psychology	PhD	153/155	144/149	4/4.5	Not specified	Not specified	3/3.63	3.5/3.91	Not specified
School Psychology	PhD	154/154	150/147	Not specified	Not specified	3/3.4	3/3.5	3/3.5	3.5/3.8
Counseling	MA/MS	153/NA	144/NA	4/NA	Not specified	3/NA	3/NA	3.5/NA	Not specified
School Psychology	EdS	143/146	146/146	Not specified	Not specified	Not specified	Not specified	Not specified	Not specified

Admissions Requirements:

Degree	GRE	GRE-Subject	Letters of Recom-mendation	Research Statement	Writing Sample	CV	Interview
Master's/Specialist	Required	None	3	Required	Optional	Required	Required
Doctoral	Required	Optional	3	Required	Optional	Required	Required

Admissions Criteria:

GRE scores—medium
Research experience—medium
Work experience—high
Clinically related public service—medium
GPA—high

Letters of recommendation—high
Interview—high
Statement of goals and objectives—high
Writing skills—high

Department Demographics

	Male (PT)	Female (PT)	Total	African-American/ Black (PT)	Hispanic/ Latino (PT)	Asian/ Pacific Islander (PT)	American Indian/ Alaska Native (PT)	Caucasian/ White (PT)	Unknown	Multiethnic (PT)	ADA (PT)	Int'l (PT)
Students	4 (0)	88 (1)	93	11 (0)	12 (0)	7 (0)	1 (0)	58 (1)	0 (0)	3 (0)	2 (0)	0 (0)

Financial Information/Assistance

Tuition: For information on tuition costs, visit http://www.twu.edu/bursar/. Tuition is subject to change. Additional fees are assessed to students beyond the costs of tuition for the following: $501/yr ($3321/yr out-of-state) University fees such as Library fees, Student Union Fees.

Doctoral:
State residents: $6,777 per academic year.
State residents: $251 per credit hour.
Nonstate residents: $17,700 per academic year.
Nonstate residents: $659 per credit hour.

Master's:
State residents: $6,777 per academic year.
State residents: $251 per credit hour.
Nonstate residents: $17,700 per academic year.
Nonstate residents: $659 per credit hour.

Financial Assistance:

	Teaching Assistantship (% Receiving)	Teaching Assistantship Tuition Remission	Research Assistantship (% Receiving)	Research Assistantship Tuition Remission	Fellowship (% Receiving)	Fellowship Tuition Remission
First-Year Student	$11,926 (50)	NA	NA (NA)	NA	NA (NA)	NA
Advanced Student	$11,926 (50)	NA	NA (NA)	NA	NA (NA)	NA

For additional information on financial assistance, visit http://www.twu.edu/finaid/.

Employment of Department Graduates

Master's:
Employed in academic position at a 2-year/4-year college: 1
Employed in a professional position in a school system: 3
Employed in a community mental health/counseling center: 4
Still seeking employment: 1
Not seeking employment: 1
Total: 10

Doctoral:
Enrolled in a postdoctoral residency/fellowship: 4
Employed in independent practice: 3
Employed in an academic position at a university: 1
Employed in a professional position in a school system: 4
Employed in government agency: 1
Employed in a community mental health/counseling center: 1
Employed in a hospital/medical center: 1
Total: 15

Additional Information

Housing and Day Care: On-campus housing is available. See the following website for more information: http://www.twu.edu/housing/. No on-campus day care facilities are available.

Information for Students With Physical Disabilities: See the following website: http://www.twu.edu/disability-support-services/.

Special Facilities or Resources: The University Counseling Center is an APA-approved internship site.

Application Information: Admissions Coordinator, Department of Psychology and Philosophy, Texas Woman's University, P.O. Box 425470, Denton, TX 76204-5470. *Fee:* $50. *Online application:* http://www.twu.edu/admissions/graduate/.

Texas, University of, Arlington
Department of Psychology
College of Science
Department of Psychology, UTA Box 19528
Arlington, TX 76019-0528
Telephone: (817) 272-2281
Chairperson: Perry Fuchs

E-mail: fuchs@uta.edu
Web: http://www.uta.edu/psychology

Orientation, Objectives, and Emphasis of Department
The objective of graduate work in psychology is to educate the student in the methods and basic content of the discipline and to provide an apprenticeship in the execution of creative research in laboratory and/or field settings. The graduate programs provide comprehensive interdisciplinary training in Experimental Psychology, Health Psychology/Neuroscience, and Industrial/Organizational Psychology. All students in the graduate program are broadly trained in statistical and experimental design. The concentration in Experimental Psychology is designed to form a basis for the doctoral program but is open to those seeking a terminal master's degree. The experimental program trains students to be research scientists in areas of interest that include animal behavior, animal learning, cognitive, developmental, evolutionary, neuroscience, quantitative, and social/personality psychology. The concentration in Health Psychology/Neuroscience is designed to train researchers in health and behavior, working at the cutting edge of interdisciplinary, biomedical, and biobehavioral investigation in areas such as pain, stress, psychoimmunology, cancer, and aging. The Master of Science in Industrial/Organizational Psychology combines rigorous course work in experimental design, quantitative methods, and management with practicum experience enabling students to perform effectively in the workplace.

Programs and Degrees Offered

Program	Degree	Application Deadline	Applications Received	Accepted	New Admits Enrolled (PT)	Total Enrolled (PT)	Degrees Awarded in 2014–2015	Median Years to Complete Degree	Dismissed/ Withdrew
Industrial/ Organizational Psychology	MA/MS	February 1 (Fall)	43	23	10 (0)	20 (0)	9	2	0
Health Psychology	PhD	February 1 (Fall)	21	6	6 (0)	20 (0)			0
Experimental Psychology	PhD	February 1 (Fall)	68	4	4 (0)	20 (0)			1

Internships/Practica

The Arlington-Dallas-Fort Worth area is a major center of business and industrial growth in Texas and offers diverse practical opportunities in consulting firms, corporations, government and private agencies, as well as health and health care agencies, social agencies and the like.

Admissions

Entries appear in the following order: required test or GPA, minimum score (if required)/median score of students entering in 2015–2016.

Program	Degree	GRE-V	GRE-Q	GRE-Writing	GRE-Subject	Under-graduate GPA	Last 2 Years GPA	Psychol-ogy GPA	Master's GPA
Industrial/ Organizational Psychology	MA/MS	153/153	144/150	NA/4	Not specified	3/3.51	Not specified	Not specified	Not specified
Health Psychology	PhD	NA/154	NA/153	NA/4	Not specified	NA/3.36	Not specified	Not specified	Not specified
Experimental Psychology	PhD	NA/154	NA/153	NA/4	Not specified	NA/3.36	Not specified	Not specified	Not specified

Admissions Requirements:

Degree	GRE	GRE-Subject	Letters of Recom-mendation	Research Statement	Writing Sample	CV	Interview
Master's/Specialist	Required	None	3	Required	None	Optional	None
Doctoral	Required	None	3	Required	None	Optional	None

Admissions Criteria:

GRE scores—medium
Research experience—high
Clinically related public service—low
GPA—medium

Letters of recommendation—high
Statement of goals and objectives—high
Undergraduate psychology preparation—medium

Department Demographics

	Male (PT)	Female (PT)	Total	African-American/ Black (PT)	Hispanic/ Latino (PT)	Asian/ Pacific Islander (PT)	American Indian/ Alaska Native (PT)	Caucasian/ White (PT)	Unknown	Multiethnic (PT)	ADA (PT)	Int'l (PT)
Students	22 (0)	39 (0)	61	1 (0)	8 (0)	1 (0)	0 (0)	44 (0)	7 (0)	0 (0)	0 (0)	7 (0)

Financial Information/Assistance

Tuition: For information on tuition costs, visit https://www.uta.edu/business-affairs/sfs/description/index.php. Tuition is subject to change.

Doctoral:
State residents: $9,635 per academic year.
Nonstate residents: $19,211 per academic year.

Master's:
State residents: $9,635 per academic year.
Nonstate residents: $19,211 per academic year.

Financial Assistance:

	Teaching Assistantship (% Receiving)	Teaching Assistantship Tuition Remission	Research Assistantship (% Receiving)	Research Assistantship Tuition Remission	Fellowship (% Receiving)	Fellowship Tuition Remission
First-Year Student	$18,000 (NA)	Partial	$18,000 (NA)	Partial	$1,000 (NA)	NA
Advanced Student	$18,000 (NA)	Partial	$18,000 (NA)	Partial	$1,000 (NA)	NA

For additional information on financial assistance, visit http://www.uta.edu/fao/.

Employment of Department Graduates

Doctoral:
Enrolled in another graduate/professional program: 1
Employed in academic position at a 2-year/4-year college: 1
Employed in business or industry: 7
Do not know: 1
Total: 10

Additional Information

Housing and Day Care: On-campus housing is available. See the following website for more information: http://www.uta.edu/housing/. On-campus day care facilities are available.

Information for Students With Physical Disabilities: See the following website: http://www.uta.edu/disability/.

Special Facilities or Resources: Each faculty member who is active in research in the Psychology Department is fortunate to have ample space. The department has approximately 18,000 total square feet of research space; 7,000 square feet for human subject research and 11,000 square feet for animal research. Graduate students work in faculty labs and use their research facilities. The department is able to utilize modern audiovisual technology in the classroom and is equipped with computer facilities for graduate research. Graduate students have in-office network connections as well as computer access in research laboratories and departmental computer labs. In addition to the departmental computer labs, OIT provides students with access to over 500 computers in 9 computer labs across campus. Each computer lab is equipped with high-end PC and/or Macintosh computers, an abundant array of office and general productivity software, as well as discipline specific software, laser printing, and broadband Internet access.

Application Information: Department of Psychology, Box 19528, The University of Texas at Arlington, Arlington, TX 76019-0528. *Fee:* $40. *Online application:* http://www.uta.edu/admissions/graduate/apply/how-to-apply.php.

Texas, University of, Austin

Department of Educational Psychology
College of Education
1912 Speedway, Stop D5800
Austin, TX 78712-1289
Telephone: (512) 471-4155
Chairperson: Cindy I. Carlson

E-mail: nlandes@austin.utexas.edu
Web: http://www.edb.utexas.edu/education/departments/edp/

Orientation, Objectives, and Emphasis of Department

Training in educational psychology relates human behavior to the educational process as it occurs in the home, in peer groups, in nursery school through graduate school, in business and industry, in the military, in institutions for persons with physical or mental disabilities, and in myriad other settings. In so doing, it includes study in the following areas: the biological bases of behavior; history and systems of psychology and of education; the psychology of learning, motivation, cognition, and instruction; developmental, social, and personality psychology; psychological and educational measurement, statistics, evaluation, and research methodology; the professional areas of school psychology and counseling psychology; and general academic educational psychology.

Programs and Degrees Offered

Program	Degree	Application Deadline	Applications Received	Accepted	New Admits Enrolled (PT)	Total Enrolled (PT)	Degrees Awarded in 2014–2015	Median Years to Complete Degree	Dismissed/ Withdrew
Counseling Psychology	PhD	December 1 (Fall)	169	8	8 (0)	35 (7)	9	5.6	1
Quantitative Methods	PhD	January 10 (Fall)	17	5	5 (0)	16 (3)	8	5.6	0
School Psychology	MA/MS	January 10 (Fall)	58	6	5 (2)	12 (5)	4	2.3	1
MA/MEd - Human Dev., Culture, & Learning Sciences	Other	January 10 (Fall)	43	5	4 (1)	13 (1)	7	2.3	0
MA/MEd - Counselor Education	Other	January 10 (Fall)	56	15	11 (4)	27 (10)	22	1.3	0
Quantitative Methods	MEd	January 10 (Fall)	24	4	3 (1)	6 (3)	4	1.3	1
Human Development, Culture, & Learning Sciences	PhD	December 1 (Fall)	54	7	6 (1)	33 (1)	5	5.6	0
School Psychology	PhD	January 10 (Fall)	67	5	7 (0)	33 (11)	9	5.6	0

APA Accreditation

Counseling PhD: Student Outcome Data website: http://www.edb.utexas.edu/education/departments/edp/doctoral/cp/about/apa_statistics/.

School PhD: Student Outcome Data website: http://www.edb.utexas.edu/education/departments/edp/doctoral/sp/about/apa_stats/.

Doctoral Degree (PhD Counseling Psychology): For those doctoral students for whom a professional internship was required in this program prior to graduation:

Total students who applied for an internship: 7
Total students who obtained an internship: 7
Total students who obtained a paid internship: 7
Total students who obtained an unpaid internship: 0
Total students who were placed in APA/CPA-accredited internships: 7
Total students placed in internships not APA/CPA-accredited, but listed with the Association of Psychology Postdoctoral and Internship Centers (APPIC): 0
Total students placed in internships conforming to guidelines of the Council of Directors of School Psychology Programs (CDSPP): 0
Total students placed in internships that were not APA/CPA-accredited, APPIC or CDSSP listed: 0

Doctoral Degree (PhD School Psychology): For those doctoral students for whom a professional internship was required in this program prior to graduation:

Total students who applied for an internship: 8
Total students who obtained an internship: 8

Total students who obtained a paid internship: 8
Total students who obtained an unpaid internship: 0
Total students who were placed in APA/CPA-accredited internships: 8
Total students placed in internships not APA/CPA-accredited, but listed with the Association of Psychology Postdoctoral and Internship Centers (APPIC): 0
Total students placed in internships conforming to guidelines of the Council of Directors of School Psychology Programs (CDSPP): 0
Total students placed in internships that were not APA/CPA-accredited, APPIC or CDSSP listed: 0

Master's Degree (MA/MS School Psychology): An internship experience, such as a final research project or "capstone" experience is required of graduates. Master's Degree (Other MA/MEd - Human Dev., Culture, & Learning Sciences): An internship experience, such as a final research project or "capstone" experience is required of graduates.

Internships/Practica

In the Counseling Psychology program, internships are generally available in APA-approved counseling and mental health centers, other university counseling centers, and community/hospital settings that provide in-depth supervision. In the School Psychology program, internship sites are often in APA-approved school systems and hospital/community settings that have an educational component. Other programs coordinate a variety of practicum settings to provide both research and applied experiences.

Admissions

Entries appear in the following order: required test or GPA, minimum score (if required)/median score of students entering in 2015–2016.

Program	Degree	GRE-V	GRE-Q	GRE-Writing	GRE-Subject	Under-graduate GPA	Last 2 Years GPA	Psychology GPA	Master's GPA
Counseling Psychology	PhD	NA/161	NA/161	NA/5	Not specified	Not specified	NA/3.8	Not specified	Not specified
Quantitative Methods	PhD	NA/158	NA/163	NA/4	Not specified	Not specified	NA/3.6	Not specified	Not specified
School Psychology	MA/MS	NA/158	NA/155	NA/4.2	Not specified	Not specified	NA/3.72	Not specified	Not specified
MA/MEd - Human Dev., Culture, & Learning Sciences	Other	NA/158	NA/156	NA/4.21	Not specified	Not specified	NA/3.61	Not specified	Not specified
MA/MEd - Counselor Education	Other	NA/155	NA/152	NA/4.2	Not specified	Not specified	NA/3.77	Not specified	Not specified
Quantitative Methods	MEd	NA/159	NA/163	NA/3.8	Not specified	Not specified	NA/3.76	Not specified	Not specified
Human Development, Culture, & Learning Sciences	PhD	NA/161	NA/161	NA/4.22	Not specified	Not specified	NA/3.72	Not specified	Not specified
School Psychology	PhD	Not specified	Not specified	Not specified	Not specified	Not specified	Not specified	Not specified	Not specified

Admissions Requirements:

Degree	GRE	GRE-Subject	Letters of Recom-mendation	Research Statement	Writing Sample	CV	Interview
Master's/Specialist	Required	None	3	Required	None	Required	Optional
Doctoral	Required	None	3	Required	None	Required	Optional

Please note if these criteria vary for different programs: Different areas may consider criteria somewhat differently. Interviews are usually conducted for the following programs: Counseling Psychology, School Psychology, and Counselor Education.

Admissions Criteria:

GRE scores—high
Research experience—medium
Work experience—medium
Clinically related public service—medium
GPA—high

Letters of recommendation—high
Interview—medium
Statement of goals and objectives—high
Undergraduate psychology preparation—low

For additional information on admission requirements, visit http://www.edb.utexas.edu/education/departments/edp/admissions/adm_requirements/.

Department Demographics

	Male (PT)	Female (PT)	Total	African-American/ Black (PT)	Hispanic/ Latino (PT)	Asian/ Pacific Islander (PT)	American Indian/ Alaska Native (PT)	Caucasian/ White (PT)	Unknown	Multiethnic (PT)	ADA (PT)	Int'l (PT)
Students	45 (11)	130 (30)	216	11 (2)	9 (7)	6 (3)	0 (0)	98 (21)	25 (3)	26 (5)	1 (0)	20 (0)

Financial Information/Assistance

Tuition: For information on tuition costs, visit http://www.utexas.edu/business/accounting/sar/t_f_rates.html. Tuition is subject to change.

Doctoral:
State residents: $10,356 per academic year.
State residents: $1,173 per credit hour.
Nonstate residents: $20,330 per academic year.
Nonstate residents: $1,771 per credit hour.

Master's:
State residents: $10,356 per academic year.
State residents: $1,173 per credit hour.
Nonstate residents: $20,330 per academic year.
Nonstate residents: $1,771 per credit hour.

Financial Assistance:

	Teaching Assistantship (% Receiving)	Teaching Assistantship Tuition Remission	Research Assistantship (% Receiving)	Research Assistantship Tuition Remission	Fellowship (% Receiving)	Fellowship Tuition Remission
First-Year Student	$12,849 (NA)	Partial	$14,000 (NA)	Partial	$1,500 (NA)	Partial
Advanced Student	$12,849 (NA)	Partial	$14,000 (NA)	Partial	$1,500 (NA)	Partial

For additional information on financial assistance, visit http://www.edb.utexas.edu/education/departments/edp/admissions/financial/.

Employment of Department Graduates

Master's:
Enrolled in another graduate/professional program: 1
Total: 1

Doctoral:
Enrolled in a postdoctoral residency/fellowship: 9
Employed in independent practice: 4
Employed in an academic position at a university: 3
Employed in other positions at a higher education institution: 1
Employed in a community mental health/counseling center: 1
Total: 18

Additional Information

Housing and Day Care: No on-campus housing is available. On-campus day care facilities are available. See the following website for more information: http://childcenter.utexas.edu/.

Information for Students With Physical Disabilities: See the following website: http://ddce.utexas.edu/disability/.

Special Facilities or Resources: The University of Texas at Austin has the fifth largest academic library in the United States and also provides online access to hundreds of electronic databases. Our department also has access, through our college's Learning Technology Center, to several microcomputer and multimedia laboratories, technical assistance, resource materials, and audiovisual equipment and services. Academic computing facilities are extensive, ranging from mainframes to microcomputers. Additional resources include several university-wide centers with which our faculty are associated, including UT's Counseling and Mental Health Center.

Application Information: Fee: $65. *Online application:* http://www.utexas.edu/ogs/admissions/howtous.html.

Texas, University of, Austin

Department of Human Development and Family Sciences
College of Natural Sciences
108 East Dean Keeton Street, Stop A2702
Austin, TX 78712-0141
Telephone: (512) 475-8065
Chairperson: Deborah Jacobvitz, PhD

E-mail: he-hdf@utlists.utexas.edu
Web: https://he.utexas.edu/hdfs/academics/graduate

Orientation, Objectives, and Emphasis of Department

The program leading to the PhD in Human Development and Family Sciences is designed to prepare individuals for research, teaching, and administrative positions in colleges and universities and for positions in research, government, and other public and private settings. The focus of the program is research concerning the interplay between individual development and family relationships. Development of the individual is considered within the context of the family, peer group, community, and culture. The family is studied as a system of relationships, with attention given to roles, communication, conflict resolution and negotiation, socialization, and family members' perceptions and emotions during interactions with one another. The program emphasizes the investigation of the family and other social processes that contribute to competence and optimal development in individuals from birth to maturity and on how such competencies, once developed, are reflected in interpersonal relationships and family interactions.

Programs and Degrees Offered

Program	Degree	Application Deadline	Applications Received	Accepted	New Admits Enrolled (PT)	Total Enrolled (PT)	Degrees Awarded in 2014–2015	Median Years to Complete Degree	Dismissed/ Withdrew
Human Development & Family Sciences	PhD	December 1 (Fall)	39	13	3 (0)	27 (1)	7	5	0

Admissions

Entries appear in the following order: required test or GPA, minimum score (if required)/median score of students entering in 2015–2016.

Program	Degree	GRE-V	GRE-Q	GRE-Writing	GRE-Subject	Under-graduate GPA	Last 2 Years GPA	Psychology GPA	Master's GPA
Human Development & Family Sciences	PhD	NA/NA	NA/NA	NA/NA	Not specified	NA/NA	NA/NA	Not specified	NA/NA

Admissions Requirements:

Degree	GRE	GRE-Subject	Letters of Recom-mendation	Research Statement	Writing Sample	CV	Interview
Doctoral	Required	Optional	3	Required	Required	Required	Required

Admissions Criteria:

GRE scores—high	Letters of recommendation—high
Research experience—high	Interview—high
Work experience—low	Statement of goals and objectives—high
Clinically related public service—low	Undergraduate psychology preparation—low
GPA—high	

For additional information on admission requirements, visit https://he.utexas.edu/hdfs/academics/graduate/how-to-apply.

Department Demographics

	Male (PT)	Female (PT)	Total	African-American/ Black (PT)	Hispanic/ Latino (PT)	Asian/ Pacific Islander (PT)	American Indian/ Alaska Native (PT)	Caucasian/ White (PT)	Unknown	Multiethnic (PT)	ADA (PT)	Int'l (PT)
Students	3 (0)	24 (1)	28	(0)	1 (0)	1 (0)	0 (0)	18 (0)	0 (1)	7 (0)	0 (0)	7 (0)

Financial Information/Assistance

Tuition: For information on tuition costs, visit http://www.utexas.edu/business/accounting/sar/t_f_rates.html. Tuition is subject to change.

Doctoral:
State residents: $8,350 per academic year.
Nonstate residents: $16,454 per academic year.

Financial Assistance:

	Teaching Assistantship (% Receiving)	Teaching Assistantship Tuition Remission	Research Assistantship (% Receiving)	Research Assistantship Tuition Remission	Fellowship (% Receiving)	Fellowship Tuition Remission
First-Year Student	$16,550 (NA)	Partial	$16,718 (NA)	Full	NA (NA)	NA
Advanced Student	$17,610 (NA)	Partial	$17,788 (NA)	Full	NA (NA)	NA

For additional information on financial assistance, visit https://he.utexas.edu/hdfs/academics/graduate/graduate-student-funding.

Employment of Department Graduates

Doctoral:
Enrolled in a postdoctoral residency/fellowship: 1
Employed in an academic position at a university: 4
Employed in business or industry: 3
Employed in government agency: 2
Not seeking employment: 1
Do not know: 1
Total: 12

Additional Information

Housing and Day Care: On-campus housing is available. See the following website for more information: http://gradschool.utexas.edu/services-and-resources/housing. On-campus day care facilities are available. See the following website for more information: http://childcenter.utexas.edu/.

Information for Students With Physical Disabilities: See the following website: http://ddce.utexas.edu/disability/.

Special Facilities or Resources: The graduate program is housed in the Sarah and Charles Seay building, supporting wireless internet service with access to the university's extensive library collection and statistical software packages, and a computer lab reserved for graduate student research. The Seay building contains a number of facilities for data collection, including five rooms in which children, couples, or families can be observed unobtrusively behind a one-way mirror in an observation booth. Students in the program may become involved in the university child and family laboratory, a laboratory preschool with about 80 three- to five-year-old children enrolled each semester. The school contains research rooms and observation facilities. In addition to the departmental resources, the multicultural population of Austin constitutes a rich resource for both research and practicum experiences. The library, computation center, and support services of the University of Texas at Austin are among the best in the nation. Free services available to students include the Learning Skills Center, Career Choice Information Center, and Counseling Center. The Priscilla Pond Flawn Child and Family Laboratory at The University of Texas at Austin is a part of the Department of Human Development and Family Sciences (HDFS) in the School of Human Ecology.

Application Information: Graduate Coordinator, The University of Texas at Austin, Department of Human Development and Family Sciences, 108 East Dean Keeton Street, Stop A2702, Austin, TX 78712-0141. *Fee:* $65. *Online application:* http://gradschool.utexas.edu/admissions/how-to-apply.

Texas, University of, Austin

Department of Psychology
College of Liberal Arts
108 East Dean Keeton, A8000
Austin, TX 78712
Telephone: (512) 471-6398
Chairperson: Jacqueline Woolley

E-mail: kterry@austin.utexas.edu
Web: http://www.utexas.edu/cola/psychology/

Orientation, Objectives, and Emphasis of Department

The major goal of graduate training in the Department of Psychology is to aid in developing the competence and professional commitment that are essential to scholarly contributions in the field of psychology. All students, upon completing the program, are expected to be well informed about general psychology, well qualified to conduct independent research, and prepared to teach in their area of interest. Within certain specialized areas, they will be prepared for professional practice. The program culminates in the PhD degree, and it is designed for the person committed to psychological research and an academic career. All of the graduate study areas have a strong academic research emphasis. All of the areas also recognize the necessity of developing knowledge and skills for applied research positions and, in the clinical area, for professional competence.

Programs and Degrees Offered

Program	Degree	Application Deadline	Applications Received	Accepted	New Admits Enrolled (PT)	Total Enrolled (PT)	Degrees Awarded in 2014–2015	Median Years to Complete Degree	Dismissed/Withdrew
Behavioral Neuroscience	PhD	December 1 (Fall)	28	4	3	11 (1)	5	6	3
Clinical Psychology	PhD	December 1 (Fall)	417	7	6	30 (3)	4	6	0
Developmental Psychology	PhD	December 1 (Fall)	42	2	1	9 (1)	6	6	0
Individual Differences and Evolutionary Psychology	PhD	December 1 (Fall)	47	2	2	7 (0)	2	5	0
Social and Personality Psychology	PhD	December 1 (Fall)	115	4	1	11 (0)	2	5	1
Cognitive Science	PhD	December 1 (Fall)	30	1	1	7	0		0
Perception, Brain, and Behavior	PhD	December 1 (Fall)	11	3	1	3	1	7	0

Programs and Degrees Offered (con't.)

Program	Degree	Application Deadline	Applica-tions Received	Accepted	New Admits Enrolled (PT)	Total Enrolled (PT)	Degrees Awarded in 2014–2015	Median Years to Complete Degree	Dismissed/Withdrew
Cognitive Neuroscience	PhD	December 1 (Fall)	62	5	4	12	1	5	0

APA Accreditation

Clinical PhD: Student Outcome Data website: http://www.utexas.edu/cola/psychology/areas-of-study/clinical/Program Statistics.php.

Doctoral Degree (PhD Clinical Psychology): For those doctoral students for whom a professional internship was required in this program prior to graduation:
Total students who applied for an internship: 2
Total students who obtained an internship: 2
Total students who obtained a paid internship: 2
Total students who obtained an unpaid internship: 0
Total students who were placed in APA/CPA-accredited internships: 2
Total students placed in internships not APA/CPA-accredited, but listed with the Association of Psychology Postdoctoral and Internship Centers (APPIC): 0
Total students placed in internships conforming to guidelines of the Council of Directors of School Psychology Programs (CDSPP): 0
Total students placed in internships that were not APA/CPA-accredited, APPIC or CDSSP listed: 0

Internships/Practica

Clinical students participate in practica at agencies in the Austin area, including the Austin State Hospital, Austin Child Guidance Center, Brown Schools, and the UT Counseling-Psychological Services Center. Most students select an internship at nationally recognized clinical settings such as the Langley Porter Neuropsychiatric Institute, or the University of California San Diego Psychological Internship Consortium. Local settings are also available.

Admissions

Entries appear in the following order: required test or GPA, minimum score (if required)/median score of students entering in 2015–2016.

Program	Degree	GRE-V	GRE-Q	GRE-Writing	GRE-Subject	Under-graduate GPA	Last 2 Years GPA	Psychol-ogy GPA	Master's GPA
Behavioral Neuroscience	PhD	NA/158	NA/153	NA/4	Not specified	Not specified	3/3.87	Not specified	Not specified
Clinical Psychology	PhD	NA/166	NA/160	NA/4	Not specified	Not specified	3/3.82	Not specified	Not specified
Developmental Psychology	PhD	NA/165	NA/160	NA/4	Not specified	Not specified	3/3.51	Not specified	Not specified
Individual Differences and Evolutionary Psychology	PhD	NA/167	NA/161	NA/4	Not specified	Not specified	3/3.78	Not specified	Not specified
Social and Personality Psychology	PhD	NA/164	NA/160	NA/4	Not specified	Not specified	3/3.89	Not specified	NA/NA
Cognitive Science	PhD	NA/164	NA/161	NA/4.5	Not specified	Not specified	NA/3.92	Not specified	Not specified
Perception, Brain, and Behavior	PhD	NA/167	NA/170	NA/4	Not specified	Not specified	3/3.82	Not specified	Not specified
Cognitive Neuroscience	PhD	NA/162	NA/160	NA/4	Not specified	Not specified	3/3.79	Not specified	Not specified

Admissions Requirements:

Degree	GRE	GRE-Subject	Letters of Recommendation	Research Statement	Writing Sample	CV	Interview
Doctoral	Required	None	3	Required	Optional	Required	Required

Please note if these criteria vary for different programs: Other areas would not consider Clinical experience.

Admissions Criteria:

GRE scores—medium
Research experience—high
Work experience—medium
Clinically related public service—medium
GPA—high

Letters of recommendation—high
Interview—high
Statement of goals and objectives—high
Undergraduate psychology preparation—medium

For additional information on admission requirements, visit http://www.utexas.edu/cola/psychology/graduate/admissions/index.php.

Department Demographics

	Male (PT)	Female (PT)	Total	African-American/ Black (PT)	Hispanic/ Latino (PT)	Asian/ Pacific Islander (PT)	American Indian/ Alaska Native (PT)	Caucasian/ White (PT)	Unknown	Multiethnic (PT)	ADA (PT)	Int'l (PT)
Students	30 (0)	60 (5)	95	3 (0)	10 (1)	8 (0)	0 (0)	55 (3)	13 (1)	1 (0)	0 (0)	10 (0)

Financial Information/Assistance

Tuition: For information on tuition costs, visit http://www.utexas.edu/business/accounting/sar/t_f_rates.html. Tuition is subject to change.

Doctoral:
State residents: $9,604 per academic year.
Nonstate residents: $18,828 per academic year.

Financial Assistance:

	Teaching Assistantship (% Receiving)	Teaching Assistantship Tuition Remission	Research Assistantship (% Receiving)	Research Assistantship Tuition Remission	Fellowship (% Receiving)	Fellowship Tuition Remission
First-Year Student	$15,653 (NA)	Full	$15,653 (NA)	Full	$28,000 (NA)	Full
Advanced Student	$17,243 (NA)	Full	$17,243 (NA)	Full	$28,000 (NA)	Full

For additional information on financial assistance, visit http://www.utexas.edu/cola/psychology/graduate/financial.php.

Employment of Department Graduates

Doctoral:
Enrolled in a postdoctoral residency/fellowship: 6
Enrolled in another graduate/professional program: 1
Employed in an academic position at a university: 4
Employed in other positions at a higher education institution: 1
Employed in business or industry: 4
Do not know: 4
Total: 20

Additional Information

Housing and Day Care: On-campus housing is available. See the following website for more information: http://www.utexas.edu/ student/housing/index.php?site=0&scode=2&id=. On-campus day care facilities are available. See the following website for more information: http://childcenter.utexas.edu/.

Information for Students With Physical Disabilities: See the following website: http://ddce.utexas.edu/disability/.

Special Facilities or Resources: The Department of Psychology moved into the Seay Building in May of 2002. This building houses seminar rooms, offices, and research laboratories. The research space includes small rooms for individual testing and larger rooms for group experiments. Some rooms have adjacent observation rooms. An anechoic testing chamber is available for auditory research. All of the departmental laboratories have computers associated with them. Departmental computers are available for student use. Facilities for research with children include the Children's Research Laboratory with numerous experimental suites. The facilities of the Animal Resource Center support research with animals. The support resources of the department include two well-equipped shops with full-time technicians and staff for computer assistance. The support resources of the university include the Computation Center, one of the finest academic computation facilities in the United States, and the Perry-Castaneda Library, one of the largest academic libraries in the country. Faculty members in the Department of Psychology are affiliated with the Center for Perceptual Systems, the Institute for Cognitive Science, and the Institute for Neuroscience.

Application Information: The University of Texas at Austin, Graduate and International Admissions Center, P.O. Box 7608, Austin, TX 78713-7608. *Fee:* $65. *Online application:* http://www.applytexas.org.

Texas, University of, Dallas

Psychological Sciences
School of Behavioral and Brain Sciences
800 West Campbell Road, GR 41
Richardson, TX 75080-3021
Telephone: (972) 883-2355
Program Heads: Dr. Shayla Holub and Dr. Candice Mills

E-mail: psysciencesphd@utdallas.edu
Web: http://www.utdallas.edu/bbs/

Orientation, Objectives, and Emphasis of Department

The Psychological Sciences PhD program is an experimental psychology program that prepares students for leadership roles in research and teaching. Students benefit from the high quality of faculty research, small classes and seminars, extensive professional development, and a rich array of interdisciplinary opportunities within the School of Behavioral and Brain Sciences. Students can select a concentration in developmental psychology, cognitive psychology, or social/personality psychology. From the start of training, students are actively engaged in research laboratories with a faculty mentor. The research requirements include a qualifying thesis research project and a dissertation research project. Students are expected to complete the program coursework and research requirements in 4 to 5 years. Professional development is facilitated through School colloquia, brown bag series, presentations at professional meetings, workshops, and guidance in the development of teaching skills. The Master of Science program, which began in 2008, provides advanced training to prepare serious student scholars for nationally prominent doctoral programs in clinical and experimental psychology. This research-focused program requires active involvement with a research mentor and at least one laboratory throughout the 2-year training. Students complete advanced coursework and have the opportunity to gain applied experience through the internship program. The program does not provide clinical training.

Programs and Degrees Offered

Program	Degree	Application Deadline	Applications Received	Accepted	New Admits Enrolled (PT)	Total Enrolled (PT)	Degrees Awarded in 2014–2015	Median Years to Complete Degree	Dismissed/ Withdrew
Psychological Sciences	PhD	December 1 (Fall)	44	8	4 (0)	22 (3)	2	5.08	1
Psychological Sciences	MA/MS	February 15 (Fall)	53	19	7 (0)	17 (0)	9	2	0

Internships/Practica

Students in the MS program have the opportunity to gain applied experience through the internship program in the School of Behavioral and Brain Sciences, which facilitates networking with a variety of community agencies and programs.

Admissions

Entries appear in the following order: required test or GPA, minimum score (if required)/median score of students entering in 2015–2016.

Program	Degree	GRE-V	GRE-Q	GRE-Writing	GRE-Subject	Undergraduate GPA	Last 2 Years GPA	Psychology GPA	Master's GPA
Psychological Sciences	PhD	153/NA	152/NA	Not specified	Not specified	3/NA	Not specified	Not specified	Not specified
Psychological Sciences	MA/MS	153/NA	144/NA	Not specified	Not specified	3/NA	Not specified	Not specified	Not specified

Admissions Requirements:

Degree	GRE	GRE-Subject	Letters of Recommendation	Research Statement	Writing Sample	CV	Interview
Master's/Specialist	Required	None	3	Required	None	None	Required
Doctoral	Required	None	3	Required	None	None	Required

Admissions Criteria:

GRE scores—high
Research experience—high
Work experience—medium
GPA—high
Letters of recommendation—high

Interview—medium
Statement of goals and objectives—high
Undergraduate psychology preparation—high
Fit w/ faculty mentor—high

For additional information on admission requirements, visit http://bbs.utdallas.edu/psyciphd/prospective.html.

Department Demographics

	Male (PT)	Female (PT)	Total	African-American/ Black (PT)	Hispanic/ Latino (PT)	Asian/ Pacific Islander (PT)	American Indian/ Alaska Native (PT)	Caucasian/ White (PT)	Unknown	Multiethnic (PT)	ADA (PT)	Int'l (PT)
Students	12 (1)	25 (1)	39	2 (0)	6 (1)	3 (0)	1 (0)	24 (1)	1 (0)	0 (0)	0 (0)	1 (0)

Financial Information/Assistance

Tuition: For information on tuition costs, visit http://www.utdallas.edu/bursar/tuition/tables/. Tuition is subject to change.

Doctoral:
State residents: $11,940 per academic year.
Nonstate residents: $22,786 per academic year.

Master's:
State residents: $11,940 per academic year.
Nonstate residents: $22,786 per academic year.

Financial Assistance:

	Teaching Assistantship (% Receiving)	Teaching Assistantship Tuition Remission	Research Assistantship (% Receiving)	Research Assistantship Tuition Remission	Fellowship (% Receiving)	Fellowship Tuition Remission
First-Year Student	$22,476 (NA)	Full	$22,476 (NA)	Full	NA (NA)	NA
Advanced Student	$22,476 (NA)	Full	$22,476 (NA)	Full	NA (NA)	NA

For additional information on financial assistance, visit http://www.utdallas.edu/finaid/.

Employment of Department Graduates

Master's:
Enrolled in a psychology doctoral program: 2
Enrolled in another graduate/professional program: 1
Employed in an academic position at a university: 1
Employed in government agency: 1
Employed in a community mental health/counseling center: 1
Other employment position: 1
Do not know: 2
Total: 9

Doctoral:
Enrolled in a postdoctoral residency/fellowship: 1
Employed in a professional position in a school system: 1
Total: 2

Additional Information

Housing and Day Care: On-campus housing is available. See the following website for more information: http://www.utdallas.edu/housing/uv/. No on-campus day care facilities are available.

Information for Students With Physical Disabilities: See the following website: http://www.utdallas.edu/studentaccess/.

Special Facilities or Resources: The Psychological Sciences program is a part of the U.T. Dallas School of Behavioral and Brain Sciences, which offers exceptional research facilities, including an on-site laboratory preschool, infant research labs, and video observation laboratories. The Psychological Sciences faculty has strong expertise in development from infancy through the lifespan, social relationships at all stages of life, and cognition and neuroscience, including an emerging emphasis on brain imaging. Many of the Psychological Sciences faculty work collaboratively across our doctoral programs in Cognition and Neuroscience, Communication Sciences and Disorders, and Audiology. The doctoral programs are complemented by four research centers: the Center for Brain Health, the Callier Center, the Center for Children and Families, and the Center for Vital Longevity.

Application Information: The University of Texas at Dallas, Admission and Enrollment Services, 800 West Campbell Road, Richardson, TX 75080-3021. *Fee:* $50. *Online application:* http://www.utdallas.edu/gradapp/.

Texas, University of, Permian Basin
Psychology
College of Arts and Sciences
4901 East University
Odessa, TX 79762
Telephone: (432) 552-2020
Chairperson: Kay Ketzenberger
Web: http://www.utpb.edu/cas/academic-departments/psychology-department/psychology/graduate-program

E-mail: olson_j@utpb.edu

Orientation, Objectives, and Emphasis of Department
The Master of Arts program in Psychology offers concentrations in both Clinical and Experimental Psychology. The program offers students the opportunity to prepare themselves to work in mental health centers, juvenile detention centers, child service agencies, specialized school services, residential treatment facilities, and family counseling agencies, to teach in community colleges, or to study at the doctoral level. The Clinical Psychology concentration is aimed at training students in the assessment and treatment of mental disorders, through individual, family, and group therapies. The program offers instruction in child, adolescent, and adult disorders. Successful completion of the Clinical Psychology concentration is designed to provide students with the opportunity to become eligible to take the state examinations for certification as a Psychological Associate (45 hours) or Licensed Professional Counselor (51 hours). The Licensed Professional Counselor certification requires an additional 2,000 supervised hours after the MA degree. The Applied Research concentration focuses on advanced psychological theory (i.e., developmental, personality, social, etc.), research methods, statistics, and manuscript preparation. The Experimental Psychology concentration offers students the opportunity to prepare themselves to serve in government and community colleges or to pursue additional graduate study at the doctoral level.

Programs and Degrees Offered

Program	Degree	Application Deadline	Applications Received	Accepted	New Admits Enrolled (PT)	Total Enrolled (PT)	Degrees Awarded in 2014–2015	Median Years to Complete Degree	Dismissed/ Withdrew
Clinical Psychology	MA/MS	April 22 (Fall), October 22 (Spring)						3	0
Experimental Psychology	MA/MS	April 22 (Fall), October 22 (Spring)						3	

Internships/Practica

The University Counseling Center has opportunities for supervised clinical practica. Other practica are available in the community. Most students accumulate hours leading to Licensed Professional Counselor (LPC) certification in the State of Texas. Students also qualify for certification as Psychology Associates in the State of Texas.

Admissions

Entries appear in the following order: required test or GPA, minimum score (if required)/median score of students entering in 2015–2016.

Program	Degree	GRE-V	GRE-Q	GRE-Writing	GRE-Subject	Undergraduate GPA	Last 2 Years GPA	Psychology GPA	Master's GPA
Clinical Psychology	MA/MS	NA/NA	NA/NA	NA/NA	Not specified	3/NA	NA/NA	NA/NA	Not specified
Experimental Psychology	MA/MS	Not specified	Not specified	Not specified	Not specified	Not specified	Not specified	Not specified	Not specified

Admissions Requirements:

Degree	GRE	GRE-Subject	Letters of Recommendation	Research Statement	Writing Sample	CV	Interview
Master's/Specialist	Required	None	3	Required	Optional	Optional	None

Admissions Criteria:

GRE scores—high
Research experience—low
Work experience—low
Clinically related public service—low

GPA—high
Letters of recommendation—high
Statement of goals and objectives—high
Undergraduate psychology preparation—medium

Department Demographics

	Male (PT)	Female (PT)	Total	African-American/ Black (PT)	Hispanic/ Latino (PT)	Asian/ Pacific Islander (PT)	American Indian/ Alaska Native (PT)	Caucasian/ White (PT)	Unknown	Multiethnic (PT)	ADA (PT)	Int'l (PT)
Students	5 (5)	20 (5)	35	0 (0)	5 (1)	0 (0)	0 (0)	18 (9)	0 (0)	2 (0)	0 (0)	0 (0)

Financial Information/Assistance

Tuition: For information on tuition costs, visit http://www.utpb.edu/services/business-affairs/accounting/cost-of-college/tuition-information. Tuition is subject to change. Additional fees are assessed to students beyond the costs of tuition for the following: Technology, Energy, Medical, Gym, Athletics, Activity Center, Library.

Master's:
State residents: $3,024 per academic year.
State residents: $168 per credit hour.
Nonstate residents: $7,758 per academic year.
Nonstate residents: $431 per credit hour.

Financial Assistance:

	Teaching Assistantship (% Receiving)	Teaching Assistantship Tuition Remission	Research Assistantship (% Receiving)	Research Assistantship Tuition Remission	Fellowship (% Receiving)	Fellowship Tuition Remission
First-Year Student	NA (NA)	NA	$12,000 (NA)	Partial	$500 (NA)	NA
Advanced Student	NA (NA)	Partial	NA (NA)	NA	$500 (NA)	Partial

For additional information on financial assistance, visit http://www.utpb.edu/academics/graduate-studies-and-research/graduate-scholarships-and-assistantships.

Employment of Department Graduates

Master's:
Employed in other positions at a higher education institution: 1
Employed in a professional position in a school system: 1
Employed in a community mental health/counseling center: 3
Still seeking employment: 3
Do not know: 2
Total: 10

Additional Information

Housing and Day Care: On-campus housing is available. See the following website for more information: http://www.utpb.edu/campus-life/student-housing. On-campus day care facilities are available. See the following website for more information: http://www.utpb.edu/campus-life/childcare-center.

Information for Students With Physical Disabilities: See the following website: http://www.utpb.edu/academics/undergraduate-success/TSAAD/ssd.

Special Facilities or Resources: We have a newly remodeled on-campus center that has a counseling area for clinical practica and research space for applied research and thesis projects. In addition, cooperative arrangements are made with community health centers, schools, governmental agencies, and mental health practitioners for research and practicum opportunities.

Application Information: Graduate Studies, The University of Texas of the Permian Basin, 4901 East University, Odessa, TX 79762. *Fee:* $0. *Online application:* http://www.utpb.edu/admissions/apply-now!/graduate.

Texas, University of, Rio Grande Valley (2015 data)
Department of Psychology
College of Liberal Arts
1201 West University Drive, SBSC 358
Edinburg, TX 78539
Telephone: (956) 665-3329
Chairperson: Joseph Hovey, PhD

E-mail: winkelm@utpa.edu
Web: http://www.utpa.edu/psychology

Orientation, Objectives, and Emphasis of Department
The Master's degree in Clinical Psychology is designed to provide research-based assessment and intervention strategies, skills training, diagnostic assessment skills, clinical experience, and supervision of professional practices in the field of applied psychology.

The program is designed to fulfill academic requirements for taking the Texas State Board Exam as a Licensed Psychological Associate (LPA) and/or a Licensed Professional Counselor (LPC). There are thesis and non-thesis tracks. For the Master's degree in Experimental Psychology all students must complete a thesis as this degree is designed to prepare students for admission to research PhD programs. The certificate in BCBA satisfies all requirements (including practicum hours) for taking the national Board Certification exam as a Behavior Analyst.

Programs and Degrees Offered

Program	Degree	Application Deadline	Applications Received	Accepted	New Admits Enrolled (PT)	Total Enrolled (PT)	Degrees Awarded in 2014–2015	Median Years to Complete Degree	Dismissed/ Withdrew
Clinical Psychology	MA/MS	March 31 (Fall)	36	12	12 (0)	12 (2)	6	2	1
Experimental Psychology	MA/MS	March 31 (Fall)	9	5	4 (0)	4 (0)	3	2.5	1
Certificate in BCBA	Other	March 31 (Fall)	17	9	8 (0)	8 (0)	3	2	0

Internships/Practica

Internships in clinical psychology are for 480 clock hours, at least 100 of which must involve direct patient contact. Internship sites include independent licensed psychologists, public and private mental health clinics and hospitals. Practica for the BCBA certificate allow for completion of hours to become eligible to sit for the national certification exam. BCBA practicum sites include public not-for-profit agencies that serve severely disabled children and some independent home placements.

Admissions

Entries appear in the following order: required test or GPA, minimum score (if required)/median score of students entering in 2015–2016.

Program	Degree	GRE-V	GRE-Q	GRE-Writing	GRE-Subject	Under-graduate GPA	Last 2 Years GPA	Psychol-ogy GPA	Master's GPA
Clinical Psychology	MA/MS	NA/NA	NA/NA	Not specified	Not specified	3/NA	Not specified	Not specified	Not specified
Experimental Psychology	MA/MS	NA/NA	NA/NA	Not specified	Not specified	3/NA	Not specified	Not specified	Not specified
Certificate in BCBA	Other	NA/NA	NA/NA	Not specified	Not specified	3/NA	Not specified	Not specified	Not specified

Admissions Requirements:

Degree	GRE	GRE-Subject	Letters of Recom-mendation	Research Statement	Writing Sample	CV	Interview
Master's/Specialist	Required	None	3	Required	Optional	Required	None

Admissions Criteria:

GRE scores—medium
Research experience—medium
Work experience—medium
Clinically related public service—low

GPA—high
Letters of recommendation—high
Statement of goals and objectives—medium

Department Demographics

	Male (PT)	Female (PT)	Total	African-American/ Black (PT)	Hispanic/ Latino (PT)	Asian/ Pacific Islander (PT)	American Indian/ Alaska Native (PT)	Caucasian/ White (PT)	Unknown	Multiethnic (PT)	ADA (PT)	Int'l (PT)
Students	7 (1)	39 (1)	48	0 (0)	43 (1)	0 (0)	0 (0)	5 (1)	0 (0)	0 (0)	0 (0)	0 (0)

Financial Information/Assistance

Tuition: Tuition is subject to change. Additional fees are assessed to students beyond the costs of tuition for the following: $75 course fee per semester.

Master's:
State residents: $5,489 per academic year.
State residents: $277 per credit hour.
Nonstate residents: $12,509 per academic year.
Nonstate residents: $554 per credit hour.

Financial Assistance:

	Teaching Assistantship (% Receiving)	Teaching Assistantship Tuition Remission	Research Assistantship (% Receiving)	Research Assistantship Tuition Remission	Fellowship (% Receiving)	Fellowship Tuition Remission
First-Year Student	$5,000 (NA)	NA	$10,000 (NA)	NA	NA (NA)	NA
Advanced Student	$5,000 (NA)	NA	$10,000 (NA)	NA	NA (NA)	NA

For additional information on financial assistance, visit http://portal.utpa.edu/utpa_main/dess_home/finaid_home.

Employment of Department Graduates

No information provided.

Additional Information

Housing and Day Care: On-campus housing is available. On-campus day care facilities are available.

Application Information: Office of Graduate Studies, Administration Building Room 116, University of Texas - Pan American, 1201 West University Drive, Edinburg, TX 78541. *Fee:* $50. *Online application:* http://www.utrgv.edu/en-us/admissions/how-to-apply.

Texas, University of, San Antonio

Department of Educational Psychology
College of Education and Human Development
501 West Cesar East Chavez Boulevard
San Antonio, TX 78207
Telephone: (210) 458-2650
Chairperson: Dr. Jeremy Sullivan
E-mail: Teresa.Pena@utsa.edu
Web: http://education.utsa.edu/educational_psychology/welcome/

Orientation, Objectives, and Emphasis of Department

The mission of the Department of Educational Psychology is to promote the development and application of scientific knowledge. To do so, our faculty members are committed to: producing high-quality, innovative research and scholarship; providing effective and culturally inclusive instructional technologies to prepare practitioners and researchers to use the tools, resources, and strategies necessary to improve the educational experience of all learners; preparing culturally competent scientist–practitioners and researchers to effectively contribute to the applied psychological development and well-being of children and adolescents; providing responsive educational and psychological services to the local community, schools, and beyond; and engaging in participatory and leadership roles in local, national, and international institutions and organizations.

Programs and Degrees Offered

Program	Degree	Application Deadline	Applications Received	Accepted	New Admits Enrolled (PT)	Total Enrolled (PT)	Degrees Awarded in 2014–2015	Median Years to Complete Degree	Dismissed/ Withdrew
School Psychology	MA/MS	July 1 (Fall), November 1 (Spring), April 1 (Summer)	40	24	18 (6)	48 (40)	16	3.5	2

Internships/Practica

Practicum and internship are culminating, field-based experiences in which knowledge and skills acquired in coursework are applied in professional settings. San Antonio has the advantage of being in the center of a number of urban, suburban, and rural school districts. Surrounding areas offer additional practicum and internship opportunities. The practicum is taken across two semesters, typically during the second year for students on the full-time track. Practicum sites must be approved by program faculty in order to ensure that the site will provide the appropriate learning experiences (e.g., assessment, consultation, counseling) and supervision. The practicum must consist of at least 150 clock hours per semester (total of 300 hours over the course of two semesters). Practicum students will be supervised by site supervisors and university faculty. The internship is taken across two semesters, typically during the third year for students on the full-time track. The internship must consist of at least 1200 clock hours of experience (600 clock hours per semester over the course of two semesters). The internship is a full-time commitment and internship sites must be approved by program faculty in order to ensure that appropriate experiences and supervision will be provided.

Admissions

Entries appear in the following order: required test or GPA, minimum score (if required)/median score of students entering in 2015–2016.

Program	Degree	GRE-V	GRE-Q	GRE-Writing	GRE-Subject	Undergraduate GPA	Last 2 Years GPA	Psychology GPA	Master's GPA
School Psychology	MA/MS	NA/149	NA/142	3/3.8	Not specified	Not specified	3/3.2	Not specified	Not specified

Admissions Requirements:

Degree	GRE	GRE-Subject	Letters of Recommendation	Research Statement	Writing Sample	CV	Interview
Master's/Specialist	Required	None	2	Required	None	None	None

Admissions Criteria:

GRE scores—medium
Research experience—low
Work experience—low
Clinically related public service—low

GPA—high
Letters of recommendation—medium
Statement of goals and objectives—medium
Undergraduate psychology preparation—medium

For additional information on admission requirements, visit http://education.utsa.edu/DEGREES/article/master_of_arts_in_school_psychology1/.

Department Demographics

	Male (PT)	Female (PT)	Total	African-American/ Black (PT)	Hispanic/ Latino (PT)	Asian/ Pacific Islander (PT)	American Indian/ Alaska Native (PT)	Caucasian/ White (PT)	Unknown	Multiethnic (PT)	ADA (PT)	Int'l (PT)
Students	9 (4)	55 (18)	86	5 (2)	22 (20)	0 (1)	0 (0)	19 (12)	1 (0)	3 (0)	0 (0)	0 (0)

Financial Information/Assistance

Tuition: For information on tuition costs, visit http://graduateschool.utsa.edu/funding/graduate-tuition-and-fees/. Tuition is subject to change. Additional fees are assessed to students beyond the costs of tuition for the following: university-required fees, school psychology support fee.

Master's:
State residents: $6,596 per academic year.
Nonstate residents: $19,944 per academic year.

Financial Assistance:

	Teaching Assistantship (% Receiving)	Teaching Assistantship Tuition Remission	Research Assistantship (% Receiving)	Research Assistantship Tuition Remission	Fellowship (% Receiving)	Fellowship Tuition Remission
First-Year Student	NA (NA)	NA	$7,942 (NA)	NA	NA (NA)	NA
Advanced Student	NA (NA)	NA	$7,942 (NA)	NA	NA (NA)	NA

For additional information on financial assistance, visit http://graduateschool.utsa.edu/funding/.

Employment of Department Graduates

Master's:
Employed in a professional position in a school system: 16
Total: 16

Additional Information

Housing and Day Care: On-campus housing is available. See the following website for more information: http://www.utsa.edu/housing/. On-campus day care facilities are available. See the following website for more information: http://www.utsa.edu/cdc/.

Information for Students With Physical Disabilities: See the following website: http://www.utsa.edu/disability/.

Special Facilities or Resources: The Psychological Assessment and Consultation Center (PACC) is an important learning resource for students. Located in Durango Building, the PACC houses all of the assessment instruments used in the psychological assessment courses, and also contains resources to facilitate students' learning such as computers with scoring and interpretive software programs, training rooms where students can practice test administration, equipment for recording practice administrations, and a library that includes references related to assessment, in addition to multimedia materials related to intervention, consultation, psychopathology, and research/statistics. Faculty in the Department of Educational Psychology also use the PACC for research meetings and supervision of clinical activities. Finally, the PACC provides a space to facilitate the provision of community services such as parent consultation.

Application Information: The University of Texas at San Antonio, Attn: The Graduate School, One UTSA Circle, San Antonio, TX 78249. *Fee:* $50. *Online application:* http://graduateschool.utsa.edu/graduate-admissions/graduate-application/.

Texas, University of, Tyler
Department of Psychology and Counseling
3900 University Boulevard
Tyler, TX 75799
Telephone: (903) 566-7130
Chairperson: Charles Barké

E-mail: cbarke@uttyler.edu
Web: http://www.uttyler.edu/psychology/

Orientation, Objectives, and Emphasis of Department
The purpose of our program is to prepare competent, applied practitioners at the master's level. The curriculum is very practical, stressing clinical assessment and intervention, and hands-on experience in relevant areas. Our students have been very successful

in finding employment in mental health settings and in gaining admission to clinical and counseling psychology doctoral programs. Special opportunities are provided for training in clinical neuropsychological assessment and psychopharmacology, for training in marital and family counseling, school counseling or for training to become a licensed specialist in school psychology.

Programs and Degrees Offered

Program	Degree	Application Deadline	Applica-tions Received	Accepted	New Admits Enrolled (PT)	Total Enrolled (PT)	Degrees Awarded in 2014–2015	Median Years to Complete Degree	Dismissed/ Withdrew
Clinical Mental Health Counseling	MA/MS	February 1 (Fall), October 1 (Spring), Rolling	62	44	9 (6)	36 (30)	17	2	4
School Counseling	MA/MS	February 1 (Fall), October 1 (Spring), Rolling	147	141	0 (26)	1 (62)	38	2	6
Clinical Psychology	MA/MS	February 1 (Fall), October 1 (Spring), Rolling	120	35	26 (0)	56 (0)	23	2	6

Internships/Practica

Available practicum sites include nearby private psychiatric hospitals, MHMR facilities, children's therapy facilities, crisis centers and safe houses for abused women, neuropsychology rehabilitation hospitals, prisons, and schools, as well as our own community counseling center.

Admissions

Entries appear in the following order: required test or GPA, minimum score (if required)/median score of students entering in 2015–2016.

Program	Degree	GRE-V	GRE-Q	GRE-Writing	GRE-Subject	Under-graduate GPA	Last 2 Years GPA	Psychol-ogy GPA	Master's GPA
Clinical Mental Health Counseling	MA/MS	NA/NA	NA/NA	Not specified	Not specified	2.75/NA	Not specified	Not specified	Not specified
School Counseling	MA/MS	NA/NA	NA/NA	Not specified	Not specified	2.75/NA	Not specified	Not specified	Not specified
Clinical Psychology	MA/MS	NA/NA	NA/NA	Not specified	Not specified	2.75/NA	3/NA	Not specified	Not specified

Admissions Requirements:

Degree	GRE	GRE-Subject	Letters of Recom-mendation	Research Statement	Writing Sample	CV	Interview
Master's/Specialist	Required	None	3	Required	Optional	Optional	None

Please note if these criteria vary for different programs: Undergraduate psychology preparation not required for CMHC degree.

Admissions Criteria:

GRE scores—medium
Research experience—low
Work experience—low
Clinically related public service—medium

GPA—high
Letters of recommendation—high
Statement of goals and objectives—medium
Undergraduate psychology preparation—medium

For additional information on admission requirements, visit http://www.uttyler.edu/psychology/graduate/admission-requirements.php.

Department Demographics

	Male (PT)	Female (PT)	Total	African-American/ Black (PT)	Hispanic/ Latino (PT)	Asian/ Pacific Islander (PT)	American Indian/ Alaska Native (PT)	Caucasian/ White (PT)	Unknown	Multiethnic (PT)	ADA (PT)	Int'l (PT)
Students	23 (10)	120 (60)	213	5 (0)	24 (9)	7 (2)	0 (0)	112 (40)	0 (0)	11 (3)	0 (0)	4 (3)

Financial Information/Assistance

Tuition: For information on tuition costs, visit http://www.uttyler.edu/graduate/calculator.php. Tuition is subject to change. Additional fees are assessed to students beyond the costs of tuition for the following: Student Service Fee.

Master's:
State residents: $6,142 per academic year.
Nonstate residents: $12,700 per academic year.

Financial Assistance:

	Teaching Assistantship (% Receiving)	Teaching Assistantship Tuition Remission	Research Assistantship (% Receiving)	Research Assistantship Tuition Remission	Fellowship (% Receiving)	Fellowship Tuition Remission
First-Year Student	NA (NA)	NA	NA (NA)	NA	$1,000 (NA)	Partial
Advanced Student	$3,600 (NA)	NA	$4,000 (NA)	Partial	$1,000 (NA)	Partial

For additional information on financial assistance, visit http://www.uttyler.edu/graduate/fin/.

Employment of Department Graduates

Master's:
Enrolled in a psychology doctoral program: 5
Employed in academic position at a 2-year/4-year college: 1
Employed in other positions at a higher education institution: 1
Employed in a professional position in a school system: 32
Employed in a community mental health/counseling center: 18
Still seeking employment: 5
Do not know: 22
Total: 84

Additional Information

Housing and Day Care: On-campus housing is available. See the following website for more information: http://www.uttyler.edu/housing/. No on-campus day care facilities are available.

Information for Students With Physical Disabilities: See the following website: http://www.uttyler.edu/disabilityservices/.

Special Facilities or Resources: We have on-campus counseling/clinical labs, an on-campus Clinic and a Community Clinic, all used for training graduate students in our program. We also have research labs for use by faculty and their graduate students in the areas of Psychophysiology, Psychotic Disorders, Social and Emotional, Developmental and Alzheimer's/Dementia.

Application Information: Psychology Graduate Coordinator, Department of Psychology, University of Texas at Tyler, 3900 University Boulevard, Tyler, TX 75799. *Fee:* $50. *Online application:* https://app.applyyourself.com/?id=uttylerg.

Brigham Young University
Department of Psychology
Family, Home & Social Sciences
1001 SWKT
Provo, UT 84602-5543
Telephone: (801) 422-4287
Chairperson: Dawson W. Hedges

E-mail: lisa_norton@byu.edu
Web: http://psychology.byu.edu

Orientation, Objectives, and Emphasis of Department
The mission of the Psychology Department is to discover, disseminate, and apply principles of psychology within a scholarly framework that is compatible with the values and purposes of Brigham Young University and its sponsor. Two degrees are offered: (1) Psychology PhD (emphasis areas in Applied Social Psychology, Cognitive and Behavioral Neuroscience, and Developmental Psychology with a sub-specialty of Health Psychology); and (2) Clinical Psychology PhD. For the Psychology PhD, students complete a common core of course work during the first 2 years. By the end of the second year, students in both PhD programs complete the requirements for a second-year project and Clinical students are awarded an MS. The philosophy of the clinical psychology program adheres to the scientist–professional model. Training focuses on academic and research competence as well as on theory and practicum experiences necessary to develop strong clinical skills. The program is eclectic in its theoretical approach, drawing from a wide range of orientations in an attempt to give broad exposure to a diversity of traditional and innovative approaches. If they wish, students may elect to complete an emphasis in (1) Child, Adolescent, and Family Clinical Psychology; (2) Clinical Neuropsychology; (3) Clinical Research; or (4) Clinical Health Psychology.

Programs and Degrees Offered

Program	Degree	Application Deadline	Applications Received	Accepted	New Admits Enrolled (PT)	Total Enrolled (PT)	Degrees Awarded in 2014–2015	Median Years to Complete Degree	Dismissed/ Withdrew
Psychology	PhD	December 1 (Fall)	14	6	5	21	3	4.33	0
Clinical Psychology	PhD	December 1 (Fall)	41	11	8	41	11	5	1

APA Accreditation
Clinical PhD: Student Outcome Data website: https://psychology.byu.edu/Pages/Student-Admissions.aspx.

Doctoral Degree (PhD Clinical Psychology): For those doctoral students for whom a professional internship was required in this program prior to graduation:
Total students who applied for an internship: 6
Total students who obtained an internship: 6
Total students who obtained a paid internship: 6
Total students who obtained an unpaid internship: 0
Total students who were placed in APA/CPA-accredited internships: 6
Total students placed in internships not APA/CPA-accredited, but listed with the Association of Psychology Postdoctoral and Internship Centers (APPIC): 0
Total students placed in internships conforming to guidelines of the Council of Directors of School Psychology Programs (CDSPP): 0
Total students placed in internships that were not APA/CPA-accredited, APPIC or CDSSP listed: 0

Internships/Practica
Students in the Psychology PhD program have the opportunity to complete internships in a wide variety of community settings, ranging from mental health to business. Clinical PhD students complete three types of practica: (1) BYU Comprehensive Clinic Integrative Practicum: Students see clients from the community in their first 3 years under the supervision of full-time clinical faculty. The clinic is a unique interdisciplinary training and research facility housing state-of-the-art audiovisual and computer resources for BYU's Clinical Psychology, Marriage and Family Therapy, Social Work, and Communication Disorders programs. (2) Clerkships: Students are required to complete two unpaid clerkships of 60 hours each. The clerkships allow students to work with different service agencies dealing with different focus groups: examples include prison, state hospital, medical centers, residential treatment

centers, and private practices with a variety of age groups and presenting problems. (3) Externships: The clinical program arranges reimbursed training placements for students in over 25 community agencies where students are supervised by onsite licensed professionals, who may hold affiliate appointments in the Psychology Department. These opportunities provide an excellent foundation for the integration of classroom experiences with practical work applications.

Admissions

Entries appear in the following order: required test or GPA, minimum score (if required)/median score of students entering in 2015–2016.

Program	Degree	GRE-V	GRE-Q	GRE-Writing	GRE-Subject	Under-graduate GPA	Last 2 Years GPA	Psychol-ogy GPA	Master's GPA
Psychology	PhD	NA/164	NA/160	NA/4.5	Not specified	Not specified	NA/NA	Not specified	NA/NA
Clinical Psychology	PhD	NA/157	NA/157	NA/4	Not specified	NA/3.72	NA/NA	Not specified	Not specified

Admissions Requirements:

Degree	GRE	GRE-Subject	Letters of Recom-mendation	Research Statement	Writing Sample	CV	Interview
Doctoral	Required	Optional	3	Required	None	Required	Required

Please note if these criteria vary for different programs: Clinically related public service: Relevant to Clinical PhD applicants only. Undergraduate psychology preparation: Students may have completed courses in other departments which would be considered equivalent to having taken certain psychology courses. Applicants from all majors accepted.

Admissions Criteria:

GRE scores—high
Research experience—high
Work experience—medium
Clinically related public service—medium
GPA—high

Letters of recommendation—high
Interview—high
Statement of goals and objectives—high
Undergraduate psychology preparation—medium

For additional information on admission requirements, visit https://psychology.byu.edu/Pages/GradFAQ.aspx.

Department Demographics

	Male (PT)	Female (PT)	Total	African-American/ Black (PT)	Hispanic/ Latino (PT)	Asian/ Pacific Islander (PT)	American Indian/ Alaska Native (PT)	Caucasian/ White (PT)	Unknown	Multiethnic (PT)	ADA (PT)	Int'l (PT)
Students	22 (0)	40 (0)	62	2 (0)	2 (0)	5 (0)	0 (0)	52 (0)	1 (0)	0 (0)	0 (0)	4 (0)

Financial Information/Assistance

Tuition: For information on tuition costs, visit http://finserve.byu.edu/content/tuition-and-general-fees. Higher tuition cost for this program: In-state tuition is paid by LDS students; others pay $16,700 per academic year. Tuition is subject to change.

Doctoral:
State residents: $8,350 per academic year.
State residents: $393 per credit hour.
Nonstate residents: $16,700 per academic year.

Financial Assistance:

	Teaching Assistantship (% Receiving)	Teaching Assistantship Tuition Remission	Research Assistantship (% Receiving)	Research Assistantship Tuition Remission	Fellowship (% Receiving)	Fellowship Tuition Remission
First-Year Student	NA (NA)	NA	$11,000 (100)	Partial	NA (NA)	NA
Advanced Student	NA (NA)	NA	$11,500 (NA)	Partial	NA (NA)	NA

Employment of Department Graduates

Doctoral:
Enrolled in a postdoctoral residency/fellowship: 5
Employed in independent practice: 1
Employed in an academic position at a university: 2
Employed in academic position at a 2-year/4-year college: 1
Employed in other positions at a higher education institution: 1
Employed in business or industry: 1
Employed in a community mental health/counseling center: 2
Employed in a hospital/medical center: 1
Total: 14

Additional Information

Housing and Day Care: On-campus housing is available. See the following website for more information: http://www.byu.edu/oncampushousing/. No on-campus day care facilities are available.

Information for Students With Physical Disabilities: See the following website: http://uac.byu.edu.

Personal Behavior Statement: While the university is sponsored by the LDS (Mormon) Church, non-LDS students are welcome and considered without bias. The university does expect that all students, regardless of religion, maintain the behavioral standards of the university. These include high standards of honor, integrity, and morality; graciousness in personal behavior; and abstinence from such things as tobacco, alcohol, and the nonmedical use of drugs. The text of this agreement can be viewed at http://honorcode.byu.edu.

Special Facilities or Resources: 3 Tesla MRI Research Facility: This new scanner is capable of doing functional MRI and DT, enabling collaborative projects across disciplines. Comprehensive Clinic: The university maintains a large clinic for training and research purposes, serving 200–250 clients each week. Computer Facilities: Extensive computer facilities are available throughout the department, college, and university. Neuroimaging and Behavior Laboratory: Research and training in the area of neuroimaging and cognitive neuroscience are facilitated by a laboratory consisting of multiple computers, video, data storage, and printer workstations. These are supported by software that allows for the capture, processing, isolation, and imaging output of specific areas of the brain from MRI and CT images and from metabolic imaging studies.

Application Information: Fee: $50. *Online application:* https://www.byu.edu/gradstudies/admissions/applynow.php.

Utah State University
Department of Psychology
Education and Human Services
2810 Old Main Hill
Logan, UT 84322-2810
Telephone: (435) 797-1460
Chairperson: Gretchen Peacock, PhD

E-mail: psychology@usu.edu
Web: http://psychology.usu.edu

Orientation, Objectives, and Emphasis of Department
The Utah State University Department of Psychology offers two graduate PhD specializations. The Experimental and Applied Psychological Sciences program offers training in a number of areas including behavior analysis, quantitative psychology, sociobehavi-

oral epidemiology, and cognition. The Combined program offers integrated training across clinical, counseling, and school psychology (accredited by the American Psychological Association since 1975). Emphasis areas within this program include child clinical psychology, rural/multicultural psychology, and health/neuropsychology. The department also offers an EdS program in School Psychology and an MEd program in School Counseling. The School Counseling program is a part-time, distance-based program. The two graduate PhD programs share a common core of doctoral courses intended to provide an advanced overview of several major areas of psychology. All doctoral programs offer extensive training within their specific areas; however, the common core is designed to ensure that no student will complete the PhD without being exposed to the diverse theoretical and methodological perspectives in the field of psychology. The common core also provides students the opportunity to become aware of the scholarly interests of faculty members in all programs.

Programs and Degrees Offered

Program	Degree	Application Deadline	Applica-tions Received	Accepted	New Admits Enrolled (PT)	Total Enrolled (PT)	Degrees Awarded in 2014–2015	Median Years to Complete Degree	Dismissed/ Withdrew
Combined Clinical/ Counseling/ School Psychology	PhD	December 15 (Fall)	89	16	7 (0)	37 (0)	2	7	0
Experimental and Applied Psychological Science	PhD	December 15 (Fall)	29	6	5 (0)	29 (0)	1	5	2
School Psychology	EdS	February 1 (Fall)	24	5	4 (0)	22 (0)	3	3.5	0
School Counseling	MEd	May 1 (Fall)	91	72	0 (61)	0 (151)	30	3	2

APA Accreditation

Combination PhD: Student Outcome Data website: http://psychology.usu.edu/academics/grad/clinical-counseling-school/outcomes-data.

Doctoral Degree (PhD Combined Clinical/Counseling/School Psychology): For those doctoral students for whom a professional internship was required in this program prior to graduation:
Total students who applied for an internship: 5
Total students who obtained an internship: 5
Total students who obtained a paid internship: 5
Total students who obtained an unpaid internship: 0
Total students who were placed in APA/CPA-accredited internships: 5
Total students placed in internships not APA/CPA-accredited, but listed with the Association of Psychology Postdoctoral and Internship Centers (APPIC): 0
Total students placed in internships conforming to guidelines of the Council of Directors of School Psychology Programs (CDSPP): 0
Total students placed in internships that were not APA/CPA-accredited, APPIC or CDSSP listed: 0

Master's Degree (Med School Counseling): An internship experience, such as a final research project or "capstone" experience is required of graduates.

Internships/Practica

Students in the Combined PhD program are placed in a variety of sites for practicum training, including community mental health centers, the USU Counseling Center, the Center for Persons with Disabilities (a University Center for Excellence in Developmental Disabilities), residential eating disorders treatment facility, and medical facilities in the area. Students from the Combined program accept internships across the country. Students in the School Psychology and School Counseling programs complete practica and internships in school districts. Internship experiences can be in Utah or completed out-of-state.

Admissions

Entries appear in the following order: required test or GPA, minimum score (if required)/median score of students entering in 2015–2016.

Program	Degree	GRE-V	GRE-Q	GRE-Writing	GRE-Subject	Under-graduate GPA	Last 2 Years GPA	Psychology GPA	Master's GPA
Combined Clinical/ Counseling/ School Psychology	PhD	NA/157	NA/155	NA/NA	Not specified	NA/3.77	NA/NA	Not specified	Not specified
Experimental and Applied Psychological Science	PhD	NA/NA	NA/NA	NA/NA	Not specified	NA/NA	NA/NA	Not specified	Not specified
School Psychology	EdS	NA/NA	NA/NA	NA/NA	Not specified	NA/NA	NA/NA	Not specified	Not specified
School Counseling	MEd	Not specified	Not specified	Not specified	Not specified	NA/NA	NA/NA	Not specified	Not specified

Admissions Requirements:

Degree	GRE	GRE-Subject	Letters of Recom-mendation	Research Statement	Writing Sample	CV	Interview
Master's/Specialist	Required	None	3	Required	None	Required	Required
Doctoral	Required	None	3	Required	Optional	Required	Required

Please note if these criteria vary for different programs: The different graduate programs weigh the criteria in different ways. For example, research experience is much more important for the two PhD programs. The MEd program accepts the MAT instead of the GRE and does not require an interview or submission of a CV.

Admissions Criteria:

GRE scores—medium
Research experience—medium
Work experience—low
Clinically related public service—medium
GPA—high

Letters of recommendation—medium
Interview—medium
Statement of goals and objectives—high
Undergraduate psychology preparation—medium

For additional information on admission requirements, visit http://psychology.usu.edu/academics/grad/apply.

Department Demographics

	Male (PT)	Female (PT)	Total	African-American/ Black (PT)	Hispanic/ Latino (PT)	Asian/ Pacific Islander (PT)	American Indian/ Alaska Native (PT)	Caucasian/ White (PT)	Unknown	Multiethnic (PT)	ADA (PT)	Int'l (PT)
Students	32 (29)	56 (122)	239	2 (0)	5 (5)	8 (0)	2 (1)	69 (135)	0 (9)	2 (1)	1 (0)	4 (0)

Financial Information/Assistance

Tuition: For information on tuition costs, visit http://www.usu.edu/registrar/htm/tuition/. Tuition is subject to change. Additional fees are assessed to students beyond the costs of tuition for the following: various student fees amount to approximately $1000 per year (including insurance).

Doctoral:
State residents: $6,132 per academic year.
Nonstate residents: $21,466 per academic year.

Master's:
State residents: $6,132 per academic year.
Nonstate residents: $21,466 per academic year.

Financial Assistance:

	Teaching Assistantship (% Receiving)	Teaching Assistantship Tuition Remission	Research Assistantship (% Receiving)	Research Assistantship Tuition Remission	Fellowship (% Receiving)	Fellowship Tuition Remission
First-Year Student	$10,000 (NA)	Full	$10,000 (NA)	Full	$20,000 (NA)	Full
Advanced Student	$10,000 (NA)	Full	$10,000 (NA)	Full	$20,000 (NA)	Full

For additional information on financial assistance, visit http://rgs.usu.edu/graduateschool/finances.

Employment of Department Graduates

Master's:
Employed in other positions at a higher education institution: 1
Employed in a professional position in a school system: 26
Still seeking employment: 1
Other employment position: 3
Total: 31

Doctoral:
Enrolled in a postdoctoral residency/fellowship: 1
Employed in independent practice: 1
Do not know: 1
Total: 3

Additional Information

Housing and Day Care: On-campus housing is available. See the following website for more information: http://www.usu.edu/housing. On-campus day care facilities are available. See the following website for more information: http://www.usu.edu/fchd/community/dde/index.cfm.

Information for Students With Physical Disabilities: See the following website: http://www.usu.edu/drc/.

Special Facilities or Resources: Students in the School Psychology and Combined programs benefit from the department's Psychology Community Clinic. In addition, the department has cooperative relationships with other campus and off-campus facilities that provide excellent settings for student training, including area school districts, the USU Center for Persons with Disabilities, and the USU Counseling Center. Students in the EAPS program work in labs of their faculty supervisors.

Application Information: Utah State University, School of Graduate Studies, Logan, UT 84322-0900. *Fee:* $55. *Online application:* http://rgs.usu.edu/graduateschool/admissions.

Utah, University of
Department of Educational Psychology
College of Education
1721 Campus Center Drive, Room 3220
Salt Lake City, UT 84112-8914
Telephone: (801) 581-7148
Chairperson: Anne E. Cook

E-mail: jo.yates@utah.edu
Web: http://ed-psych.utah.edu/

Orientation, Objectives, and Emphasis of Department
The Department of Educational Psychology at the University of Utah is characterized by an emphasis on the application of behavioral sciences to educational and psychological processes. The department is organized into four program areas: (1) Counseling and Counseling Psychology (MS, MEd, PhD); (2) School Psychology (MS, MEd, PhD); (3) Reading and Literacy (MEd and PhD); and (4) Learning Sciences with three subprograms: Learning and Cognition (MS and PhD), a master's level (MEd) program in Instructional Design and Educational Technology (IDET), and an interdepartmental program that leads to a Master's in Statistics (MStat). The basic master's level programming includes 1 to 2 years of academic work (and in some cases an additional year of internship). Doctoral programs include Counseling Psychology (APA accredited since 1957), School Psychology (APA accredited since 1986), and Learning Sciences (the Learning and Cognition area). The emphasis of the department is on the application of psychological principles in educational and human service settings. In addition, doctoral programs represent a scientist–practitioner model with considerable emphasis on the development of research as well as professional skills.

Programs and Degrees Offered

Program	Degree	Application Deadline	Applica-tions Received	Accepted	New Admits Enrolled (PT)	Total Enrolled (PT)	Degrees Awarded in 2014–2015	Median Years to Complete Degree	Dismissed/ Withdrew
Counseling Psychology	PhD	December 15 (Fall)	57	4	4 (0)	33 (0)	8	5.7	0
School Psychology	PhD	December 15 (Fall)	20	8	4 (0)	28 (0)	8	6.25	1
Learning Sciences	PhD	Rolling	3	1	1 (0)	16 (0)	3	4.5	3
Instructional Design and Educational Technology	MEd	Rolling	14	14	12 (0)	42 (0)	15	2	0
Clinical Mental Health Counseling	MEd	December 15 (Fall)	22	101	9	30	12	3	0
School Counseling	MEd	December 15 (Fall)	34	21	16 (0)	35 (0)	7	2	0
Statistics	MA/MS	Rolling	3	1	1 (0)	5 (0)	1	1.5	0
School Psychology	MEd	December 15 (Fall)	20	8	7	20	3	4	1

APA Accreditation

Counseling PhD: Student Outcome Data website: http://ed-psych.utah.edu/counseling-psych/.
School PhD: Student Outcome Data website: http://ed-psych.utah.edu/school-psych/.

Doctoral Degree (PhD Counseling Psychology): For those doctoral students for whom a professional internship was required in this program prior to graduation:
Total students who applied for an internship: 5
Total students who obtained an internship: 3
Total students who obtained a paid internship: 3
Total students who obtained an unpaid internship: 0
Total students who were placed in APA/CPA-accredited internships: 3
Total students placed in internships not APA/CPA-accredited, but listed with the Association of Psychology Postdoctoral and Internship Centers (APPIC): 0
Total students placed in internships conforming to guidelines of the Council of Directors of School Psychology Programs (CDSPP): 0
Total students placed in internships that were not APA/CPA-accredited, APPIC or CDSSP listed: 0

Doctoral Degree (PhD School Psychology): For those doctoral students for whom a professional internship was required in this program prior to graduation:
Total students who applied for an internship: 3
Total students who obtained an internship: 3
Total students who obtained a paid internship: 3
Total students who obtained an unpaid internship: 0
Total students who were placed in APA/CPA-accredited internships: 3
Total students placed in internships not APA/CPA-accredited, but listed with the Association of Psychology Postdoctoral and Internship Centers (APPIC): 0
Total students placed in internships conforming to guidelines of the Council of Directors of School Psychology Programs (CDSPP): 0
Total students placed in internships that were not APA/CPA-accredited, APPIC or CDSSP listed: 0

Master's Degree (Med Clinical Mental Health Counseling): An Internship experience, such as a final research project or "capstone" experience is required of graduates. Master's Degree (MA/MS Statistics): An internship experience, such as a final research project or "capstone" experience is required of graduates.

Internships/Practica

Practica for Counseling Psychology doctoral students vary and include such settings as University of Utah Counseling Center and other campus services; community mental health settings; hospital settings; and private practice. Predoctoral internships are typically taken nationally in university counseling centers, community mental health settings, veterans hospitals, and specialty settings. School Psychology practica initially focus on participation in an on-campus clinic and gradually move into field-based settings such as the schools and clinics appropriate to the field of school psychology. Specialized practica for school psychology allow for supervised experiences in early childhood settings, "stand-alone" community based clinics, and specialized treatment programs. Predoctoral Internships are completed in local school districts, hospitals and clinics, and other sites that are APA accredited or meet APPIC criteria. In addition, students from any of the graduate programs who teach undergraduate courses take a Practicum in Teaching, through which they are supervised and provided guidance during their first semester of teaching.

Admissions

Entries appear in the following order: required test or GPA, minimum score (if required)/median score of students entering in 2015–2016.

Program	Degree	GRE-V	GRE-Q	GRE-Writing	GRE-Subject	Under-graduate GPA	Last 2 Years GPA	Psychol-ogy GPA	Master's GPA
Counseling Psychology	PhD	148/154	148/152	3/4	Not specified	3.55/3.65	Not specified	Not specified	Not specified
School Psychology	PhD	152/157	148/151	4/4.75	Not specified	3.57/3.97	Not specified	Not specified	Not specified
Learning Sciences	PhD	152/153	152/149	3/4	Not specified	3.2/3.52	Not specified	Not specified	Not specified
Instructional Design and Educational Technology	MEd	Not specified	Not specified	Not specified	Not specified	2.56/3.51	Not specified	Not specified	Not specified
Clinical Mental Health Counseling	MEd	148/155	142/149	3/4	Not specified	3.16/3.44	Not specified	Not specified	Not specified
School Counseling	MEd	144/154	136/150	3/4	Not specified	3.06/3.44	Not specified	Not specified	Not specified
Statistics	MA/MS	138/163	155/160	2.5/2.5	Not specified	2.91/3.5	Not specified	Not specified	Not specified
School Psychology	MEd	148/152	140/143	2.5/3.5	Not specified	2.94/3.38	Not specified	Not specified	Not specified

Admissions Requirements:

Degree	GRE	GRE-Subject	Letters of Recom-mendation	Research Statement	Writing Sample	CV	Interview
Master's/Specialist	Required	Optional	3	Required	Optional	Required	Optional
Doctoral	Required	Recom-mended	3	Required	Recom-mended	Required	Required

Admissions Criteria:
GRE scores—high
Research experience—high
Work experience—high
Clinically related public service—medium
GPA—high

Letters of recommendation—medium
Interview—medium
Statement of goals and objectives—medium
Undergraduate psychology preparation—medium

For additional information on admission requirements, visit http://ed-psych.utah.edu/admissions/index.php.

Department Demographics

	Male (PT)	Female (PT)	Total	African-American/ Black (PT)	Hispanic/ Latino (PT)	Asian/ Pacific Islander (PT)	American Indian/ Alaska Native (PT)	Caucasian/ White (PT)	Unknown	Multiethnic (PT)	ADA (PT)	Int'l (PT)
Students	55 (0)	172 (0)	227	2 (0)	10 (0)	9 (0)	6 (0)	181 (0)	14 (0)	5 (0)	0 (0)	8 (0)

Financial Information/Assistance

Tuition: For information on tuition costs, visit http://fbs.admin.utah.edu/income/tuition/college-of-education/. Tuition is subject to change. Additional fees are assessed to students beyond the costs of tuition for the following: Special course fees and differential tuition courses.

Doctoral:
State residents: $9,600 per academic year.
Nonstate residents: $27,700 per academic year.

Master's:
State residents: $9,600 per academic year.
Nonstate residents: $27,700 per academic year.

Financial Assistance:

	Teaching Assistantship (% Receiving)	Teaching Assistantship Tuition Remission	Research Assistantship (% Receiving)	Research Assistantship Tuition Remission	Fellowship (% Receiving)	Fellowship Tuition Remission
First-Year Student	$14,000 (14)	Full	$14,000 (0)	Full	$14,000 (3)	Full
Advanced Student	$14,000 (15)	Full	$14,000 (2)	Full	$14,000 (4)	Full

For additional information on financial assistance, visit http://ed-psych.utah.edu/grad-assistance.php.

Employment of Department Graduates

Master's:
Enrolled in a psychology doctoral program: 2
Employed in other positions at a higher education institution: 2
Employed in a professional position in a school system: 4
Employed in business or industry: 9
Employed in a community mental health/counseling center: 4
Other employment position: 2
Do not know: 23
Total: 46

Doctoral:
Enrolled in a postdoctoral residency/fellowship: 3
Employed in independent practice: 1
Employed in an academic position at a university: 1
Employed in academic position at a 2-year/4-year college: 1
Employed in other positions at a higher education institution: 1
Employed in a professional position in a school system: 5
Employed in business or industry: 4
Employed in a community mental health/counseling center: 2
Do not know: 1
Total: 19

Additional Information

Housing and Day Care: On-campus housing is available. See the following website for more information: http://housing.utah.edu/options/graduate.php. On-campus day care facilities are available. See the following website for more information: http://childcare.utah.edu/.

Information for Students With Physical Disabilities: See the following website: http://disability.utah.edu/.

Special Facilities or Resources: A variety of research and training opportunities are available to students through relationships the department has developed with various university and community facilities. Included are the University Counseling Center, University Neuropsychiatric Institute, University Health Sciences Center, Carmen B. Pingree Autism Center for Learning, and the adjacent regional Veterans Administration Medical Center. Community facilities also include local school districts, community mental health clinics, children's hospitals, general hospitals, child guidance clinics, and various state social service agencies. The department maintains its own statistics and research laboratories. Students also have the use of computer stations and access to college and University networks through the College of Education Computer Center.

Application Information: Admissions, University of Utah, Department of Educational Psychology, 1721 East Campus Center Drive, SAEC 3220, Salt Lake City, UT 84112-8914. *Fee:* $55. *Online application:* https://app.applyyourself.com/?id=utahgrad.

Utah, University of
Department of Psychology
Social & Behavioral Science
380 South 1530 East, Room 502
Salt Lake City, UT 84112
Telephone: (801) 581-6124
Chairperson: Lisa G. Aspinwall

E-mail: nancy.seegmiller@psych.utah.edu
Web: http://www.psych.utah.edu

Orientation, Objectives, and Emphasis of Department
We offer comprehensive training in psychology, including Clinical (general, child-family, health, and neuropsychology emphases), Developmental, Cognitive and Neural Science, and Social. Students generally receive support throughout their training. Students are selected for area programs with individual faculty advisers. They do research in their areas, and clinical students also receive applied training. Graduates accept jobs in academic departments, research centers, and applied settings.

Programs and Degrees Offered

Program	Degree	Application Deadline	Applications Received	Accepted	New Admits Enrolled (PT)	Total Enrolled (PT)	Degrees Awarded in 2014–2015	Median Years to Complete Degree	Dismissed/ Withdrew
Clinical Psychology	PhD	December 15 (Fall)	261	12	8 (0)	30 (7)	4	7.5	2
Cognition and Neuroscience	PhD	December 15 (Fall)	37	4	3 (0)	14 (0)	3	5.87	0
Developmental Psychology	PhD	December 15 (Fall)	26	2	0 (0)	5 (0)	0		0
Social Psychology	PhD	December 15 (Fall)	41	3	3 (0)	12 (1)	0		0

APA Accreditation
Clinical PhD: Student Outcome Data website: http://www.psych.utah.edu/graduate/clinical.php.

Doctoral Degree (PhD Clinical Psychology): For those doctoral students for whom a professional internship was required in this program prior to graduation:
Total students who applied for an internship: 6
Total students who obtained an internship: 6
Total students who obtained a paid internship: 6
Total students who obtained an unpaid internship: 0
Total students who were placed in APA/CPA-accredited internships: 6
Total students placed in internships not APA/CPA-accredited, but listed with the Association of Psychology Postdoctoral and Internship Centers (APPIC): 0
Total students placed in internships conforming to guidelines of the Council of Directors of School Psychology Programs (CDSPP): 0
Total students placed in internships that were not APA/CPA-accredited, APPIC or CDSSP listed: 0

Internships/Practica
Extensive clinical training experiences are available through close ties with facilities in the community. A sample of these include the Veteran's Administration Hospital, the University Medical Center, Primary Children's Hospital, the Children's Behavioral Therapy Unit, the Juvenile Detention Center, the University Neuropsychiatric Institute, the University Counseling Center, and local community health centers. There are four APA-approved internships in the local community.

Admissions

Entries appear in the following order: required test or GPA, minimum score (if required)/median score of students entering in 2015–2016.

Program	Degree	GRE-V	GRE-Q	GRE-Writing	GRE-Subject	Under-graduate GPA	Last 2 Years GPA	Psychol-ogy GPA	Master's GPA
Clinical Psychology	PhD	Not specified	Not specified	Not specified	Not specified	Not specified	Not specified	Not specified	Not specified
Cognition and Neuroscience	PhD	Not specified	Not specified	Not specified	Not specified	Not specified	Not specified	Not specified	Not specified
Developmental Psychology	PhD	Not specified	Not specified	Not specified	Not specified	Not specified	Not specified	Not specified	Not specified
Social Psychology	PhD	Not specified	Not specified	Not specified	Not specified	Not specified	Not specified	Not specified	Not specified

Admissions Requirements:

Degree	GRE	GRE-Subject	Letters of Recom-mendation	Research Statement	Writing Sample	CV	Interview
Doctoral	Required	Optional	3	Required	Optional	Required	Required

Please note if these criteria vary for different programs: The Clinical Program requires the Subject GRE.

Admissions Criteria:

GRE scores—medium
Research experience—high
Work experience—medium
Clinically related public service—medium
GPA—medium

Letters of recommendation—high
Interview—high
Statement of goals and objectives—high
Undergraduate psychology preparation—medium

For additional information on admission requirements, visit http://www.psych.utah.edu/graduate/apply.php.

Department Demographics

	Male (PT)	Female (PT)	Total	African-American/ Black (PT)	Hispanic/ Latino (PT)	Asian/ Pacific Islander (PT)	American Indian/ Alaska Native (PT)	Caucasian/ White (PT)	Unknown	Multiethnic (PT)	ADA (PT)	Int'l (PT)
Students	18 (2)	43 (6)	69	1 (0)	1 (0)	4 (0)	0 (0)	48 (8)	2 (0)	5 (0)	0 (0)	2 (0)

Financial Information/Assistance

Tuition: For information on tuition costs, visit http://fbs.admin.utah.edu/income/tuition/. Tuition is subject to change.

Doctoral:
State residents: $8,206 per academic year.
Nonstate residents: $26,340 per academic year.

Financial Assistance:

	Teaching Assistantship (% Receiving)	Teaching Assistantship Tuition Remission	Research Assistantship (% Receiving)	Research Assistantship Tuition Remission	Fellowship (% Receiving)	Fellowship Tuition Remission
First-Year Student	$22,000 (NA)	Full	$22,000 (NA)	Full	$22,000 (NA)	Full
Advanced Student	$22,000 (NA)	Full	$22,000 (NA)	Full	$22,000 (NA)	Full

For additional information on financial assistance, visit http://www.psych.utah.edu/graduate/funding.php.

Employment of Department Graduates

Doctoral:
Employed in an academic position at a university: 2
Employed in business or industry: 1
Employed in government agency: 1
Employed in a hospital/medical center: 1
Do not know: 2
Total: 7

Additional Information

Housing and Day Care: On-campus housing is available. See the following website for more information: http://housing.utah.edu/. On-campus day care facilities are available. See the following website for more information: http://childcare.utah.edu/.

Information for Students With Physical Disabilities: See the following website: http://disability.utah.edu/.

Special Facilities or Resources: Special facilities include the Early Childhood Education Center and 3 on-campus hospitals.

Application Information: *Fee:* $55. *Online application:* https://app.applyyourself.com/?id=utahgrad.

Goddard College

MA Psychology & Clinical Mental Health Counseling Program
123 Pitkin Road
Plainfield, VT 5667
Telephone: (802) 454-8311, (800) 468-4888
Chairperson: Steven E. James, PhD

E-mail: Steven.James@goddard.edu
Web: http://www.goddard.edu/academics/ma/master-arts-psychology/

Orientation, Objectives, and Emphasis of Department

Graduate study in Psychology and Counseling consists of a unique combination of intensive campus residencies and directed, independent study off campus. Students design their own emphasis of study or enter into the defined concentrations in organizational development or sexual orientation studies. The primary goal of the program is to develop skills in individual, family, and/or community psychology, grounded in theory and research, personal experience and self-knowledge, and relevant to current social complexities. While pursuing their own specialized interests, students gain mastery in the broad range of subjects necessary for the effective and ethical practice of counseling. Study begins each semester with a week-long residency at the college, a time of planning for the ensuing semester and attending seminars. Returning home, the student begins implementation of the detailed study plan based upon the student's particular interests and needs. Through appropriate design of their study plan, students may meet the educational requirements for master's level licensure or certification in their state. The program is approved by the Council of Applied Master's Programs in Psychology.

Programs and Degrees Offered

Program	Degree	Application Deadline	Applications Received	Accepted	New Admits Enrolled (PT)	Total Enrolled (PT)	Degrees Awarded in 2014–2015	Median Years to Complete Degree	Dismissed/ Withdrew
Clinical Mental Health Counseling	MA/MS	July 15 (Fall), January 15 (Spring)	41	21	20 (6)	55 (12)	14	2.5	2
Psychology	MA/MS	July 15 (Fall), January 15 (Spring)	2	2	2 (0)	2 (1)	1	2.5	0

Internships/Practica

Students are required to complete a minimum of 600 hours of supervised practicum during the program. This practicum takes place at a location convenient to the student that has been reviewed and evaluated by the program faculty as appropriate to the student's plan of study, providing appropriate licensed supervision and offering direct counseling experience. Students propose sites at which they would like to work to the faculty for review and approval.

Admissions

Entries appear in the following order: required test or GPA, minimum score (if required)/median score of students entering in 2015–2016.

Program	Degree	GRE-V	GRE-Q	GRE-Writing	GRE-Subject	Under-graduate GPA	Last 2 Years GPA	Psychol-ogy GPA	Master's GPA
Clinical Mental Health Counseling	MA/MS	Not specified	Not specified	Not specified	Not specified	Not specified	Not specified	Not specified	Not specified
Psychology	MA/MS	Not specified	Not specified	Not specified	Not specified	Not specified	Not specified	Not specified	Not specified

Admissions Requirements:

Degree	GRE	GRE-Subject	Letters of Recommendation	Research Statement	Writing Sample	CV	Interview
Master's/Specialist	Optional	Optional	3	Required	Required	Optional	Optional

Admissions Criteria:

Research experience—low
Work experience—high
Clinically related public service—high
GPA—medium
Letters of recommendation—high

Interview—low
Statement of goals and objectives—high
Undergraduate psychology preparation—high
Iconoclastic intent—high

For additional information on admission requirements, visit http://www.goddard.edu/academics/psychology-counseling/apply/.

Department Demographics

	Male (PT)	Female (PT)	Total	African-American/ Black (PT)	Hispanic/ Latino (PT)	Asian/ Pacific Islander (PT)	American Indian/ Alaska Native (PT)	Caucasian/ White (PT)	Unknown (PT)	Multiethnic (PT)	ADA (PT)	Int'l (PT)
Students	15 (3)	42 (10)	70	2 (1)	2 (1)	0 (0)	0 (0)	31 (11)	20 (0)	2 (0)	3 (0)	0 (1)

Financial Information/Assistance

Tuition: For information on tuition costs, visit http://www.goddard.edu/admissions/tuition-and-fees. Tuition is subject to change.

Master's:
State residents: $18,506 per academic year.
Nonstate residents: $18,506 per academic year.

Financial Assistance:

	Teaching Assistantship (% Receiving)	Teaching Assistantship Tuition Remission	Research Assistantship (% Receiving)	Research Assistantship Tuition Remission	Fellowship (% Receiving)	Fellowship Tuition Remission
First-Year Student	NA (NA)	NA	NA (NA)	NA	$1,445 (NA)	Partial
Advanced Student	NA (NA)	NA	NA (NA)	NA	$1,445 (NA)	Partial

For additional information on financial assistance, visit http://www.goddard.edu/admissions/financial-aid/.

Employment of Department Graduates

Master's:
Enrolled in a psychology doctoral program: 3
Employed in an academic position at a university: 1
Employed in a professional position in a school system: 1
Employed in business or industry: 2
Employed in government agency: 1
Employed in a community mental health/counseling center: 2
Employed in a hospital/medical center: 1
Not seeking employment: 1
Other employment position: 1
Total: 13

Additional Information

Housing and Day Care: On-campus housing is available. No on-campus day care facilities are available.

Application Information: Admissions Office, Goddard College, 123 Pitkin Road, Plainfield, VT 05667. *Fee:* $40. *Online application:* https://admissions.goddard.edu/application/apply.

Saint Michael's College

Psychology Department/Graduate Program in Clinical Psychology
Saint Michael's College
One Winooski Park
Colchester, VT 5439
Telephone: (802) 654-2206
Director: Ronald B. Miller, PhD

E-mail: rmiller@smcvt.edu
Web: http://www.smcvt.edu/graduate/psych/

Orientation, Objectives, and Emphasis of Department

The focus of the MA program in clinical psychology is on the integration of theory, research, and practice in the preparation of professional psychologists. Our goal is to provide an educational milieu that respects the individual educational goals of the student and fosters intellectual, personal, and professional development. The program is eclectic in orientation and the faculty offer a diversity of interests, orientations, and experiences within the framework of our curriculum. We prepare students for professional practice in community agencies, schools, hospitals, and public and private clinics. The curriculum is also designed with two further objectives in mind: (1) the preparation of students for state licensing examinations, and (2) further doctoral study in professional psychology at another institution. All classes are held in the evening, permitting full- or part-time study. The program seeks to integrate a psychodynamic understanding of the therapeutic relationship with humanistic values and a social systems perspective.

Programs and Degrees Offered

Program	Degree	Application Deadline	Applications Received	Accepted	New Admits Enrolled (PT)	Total Enrolled (PT)	Degrees Awarded in 2014–2015	Median Years to Complete Degree	Dismissed/ Withdrew
Clinical Psychology	MA/MS	Rolling	26	14	6 (8)	25 (25)	17	3	1

Internships/Practica

Practicum and internship sites are available in the following settings: community mental health outpatient, crisis, and residential settings; Youth Services Bureau; public and private schools/education programs; college counseling centers; and programs for the elderly.

Admissions

Entries appear in the following order: required test or GPA, minimum score (if required)/median score of students entering in 2015–2016.

Program	Degree	GRE-V	GRE-Q	GRE-Writing	GRE-Subject	Undergraduate GPA	Last 2 Years GPA	Psychology GPA	Master's GPA
Clinical Psychology	MA/MS	Not specified	Not specified	Not specified	Not specified	3/NA	Not specified	3.25/NA	Not specified

Admissions Requirements:

Degree	GRE	GRE-Subject	Letters of Recommendation	Research Statement	Writing Sample	CV	Interview
Master's/Specialist	None	None	2	Required	None	Required	Required

Admissions Criteria:

Research experience—low
Work experience—high
Clinically related public service—high
GPA—high

Letters of recommendation—high
Interview—high
Statement of goals and objectives—high

Department Demographics

	Male (PT)	Female (PT)	Total	African-American/ Black (PT)	Hispanic/ Latino (PT)	Asian/ Pacific Islander (PT)	American Indian/ Alaska Native (PT)	Caucasian/ White (PT)	Unknown	Multiethnic (PT)	ADA (PT)	Int'l (PT)
Students	3 (6)	21 (20)	50	2 (0)	0 (0)	1 (0)	0 (0)	20 (26)	0 (0)	1 (0)	0 (0)	2 (0)

Financial Information/Assistance

Tuition: For information on tuition costs, visit http://www.smcvt.edu/graduate-programs/prospective-students/tuition.aspx. Tuition is subject to change.

Master's:
State residents: $590 per credit hour.
Nonstate residents: $590 per credit hour.

Financial Assistance:

	Teaching Assistantship (% Receiving)	Teaching Assistantship Tuition Remission	Research Assistantship (% Receiving)	Research Assistantship Tuition Remission	Fellowship (% Receiving)	Fellowship Tuition Remission
First-Year Student	NA (NA)	Partial	NA (NA)	NA	NA (NA)	NA
Advanced Student	NA (NA)	NA	NA (NA)	NA	NA (NA)	NA

For additional information on financial assistance, visit http://www.smcvt.edu/graduate-programs/current-students/campus-resources/financial-aid.aspx.

Employment of Department Graduates

Master's:
Enrolled in a psychology doctoral program: 1
Enrolled in another graduate/professional program: 1
Employed in a professional position in a school system: 1
Employed in a community mental health/counseling center: 13
Employed in a hospital/medical center: 1
Total: 17

Additional Information

Housing and Day Care: No on-campus housing is available. On-campus day care facilities are available. See the following website for more information: http://www.smcvt.edu/On-Campus/Offices-and-Services/Early-Learning-Center.aspx.

Information for Students With Physical Disabilities: See the following website: http://www.smcvt.edu/academics/academic-support/accessibility-services.aspx.

Special Facilities or Resources: Saint Michael's College offers the graduate student a faculty committed to teaching and professional training in a non-bureaucratic learning environment. All clinical courses are taught by highly experienced clinical practitioners who serve as part-time faculty. The full-time faculty teach core courses in general, developmental, and social psychology, as well as research methods. The college has excellent computing facilities for the support of social science research.

Application Information: Saint Michael's College, Master's Program in Clinical Psychology, One Winooski Park, Box 288, Colchester, VT 05439. *Fee:* $50. *Online application:* http://www.smcvt.edu/Graduate-Programs/Prospective-Students/Graduate-Admission.aspx.

Vermont, University of

Department of Psychology
Arts and Sciences
2 Colchester Avenue; John Dewey Hall
Burlington, VT 05405-0134
Telephone: (802) 656-2670
Chairperson: John Green, PhD

E-mail: psychology@uvm.edu
Web: http://www.uvm.edu/psychology

Orientation, Objectives, and Emphasis of Department

The clinical psychology program is based upon a scientist–practitioner model and is designed to develop competent professional psychologists who can function in applied academic or research positions. Training stresses early placement in a variety of nearby clinical facilities and simultaneous research training relevant to clinical problems. Clinical orientations are primarily cognitive-behavioral. The general/experimental program admits students in three broad specialty areas: (1) basic and applied developmental and social psychology that includes research on ways in which people simultaneously influence and are influenced by social situations and cultural contexts; (2) biobehavioral psychology that focuses on behavioral and neurobiological approaches to learning, memory, emotion, and drug abuse; and (3) human behavioral pharmacology and substance abuse treatment. Students must fulfill general/experimental program requirements as well as requirements for the specialty area in which they are accepted. Applicants should be as specific as possible about their program interest areas.

Programs and Degrees Offered

Program	Degree	Application Deadline	Applications Received	Accepted	New Admits Enrolled (PT)	Total Enrolled (PT)	Degrees Awarded in 2014–2015	Median Years to Complete Degree	Dismissed/ Withdrew
General/ Experimental Psychology	PhD	January 2 (Fall)	48	4	4 (0)	23 (0)	4	7	1
Clinical Psychology	PhD	December 1 (Fall)	148	3	3 (0)	32 (0)	2	6	1

APA Accreditation

Clinical PhD: Student Outcome Data website: http://www.uvm.edu/psychology/?Page=clinical/clinical_applicant_data.html&SM=clinical/clinicalsubmenu.html.

Doctoral Degree (PhD Clinical Psychology): For those doctoral students for whom a professional internship was required in this program prior to graduation:
Total students who applied for an internship: 2
Total students who obtained an internship: 2
Total students who obtained a paid internship: 2
Total students who obtained an unpaid internship: 0
Total students who were placed in APA/CPA-accredited internships: 2
Total students placed in internships not APA/CPA-accredited, but listed with the Association of Psychology Postdoctoral and Internship Centers (APPIC): 0
Total students placed in internships conforming to guidelines of the Council of Directors of School Psychology Programs (CDSPP): 0
Total students placed in internships that were not APA/CPA-accredited, APPIC or CDSSP listed: 0

Internships/Practica

Multiple clinical practica are available, including outpatient and inpatient adult assessment and psychotherapy, outpatient child and adolescent assessment and psychotherapy, community mental health centers, and medical centers/hospitals. All practica are funded for 20 hours per week.

Admissions

Entries appear in the following order: required test or GPA, minimum score (if required)/median score of students entering in 2015–2016.

Program	Degree	GRE-V	GRE-Q	GRE-Writing	GRE-Subject	Under-graduate GPA	Last 2 Years GPA	Psychol-ogy GPA	Master's GPA
General/Experimental Psychology	PhD	152/160	148/155	Not specified	Not specified	3.25/3.68	Not specified	Not specified	Not specified
Clinical Psychology	PhD	NA/162	NA/157	Not specified	Not specified	NA/3.64	Not specified	Not specified	Not specified

Admissions Requirements:

Degree	GRE	GRE-Subject	Letters of Recom-mendation	Research Statement	Writing Sample	CV	Interview
Doctoral	Required	Recom-mended	3	Required	Required	Required	Required

Please note if these criteria vary for different programs: Clinically related public service is of importance for clinical program only. Writing Sample required for Clinical Program, recommended for Experimental Program. GRE Subject score not required if applicant majored in psychology.

Admissions Criteria:

GRE scores—high
Research experience—high
Work experience—medium
Clinically related public service—medium
GPA—high

Letters of recommendation—high
Interview—high
Statement of goals and objectives—high
Undergraduate psychology preparation—high

For additional information on admission requirements, visit http://www.uvm.edu/psychology/?Page=application_process.html.

Department Demographics

	Male (PT)	Female (PT)	Total	African-American/ Black (PT)	Hispanic/ Latino (PT)	Asian/ Pacific Islander (PT)	American Indian/ Alaska Native (PT)	Caucasian/ White (PT)	Unknown	Multiethnic (PT)	ADA (PT)	Int'l (PT)
Students	13 (0)	32 (0)	45	2 (0)	1 (0)	1 (0)	2 (0)	39 (0)	0 (0)	0 (0)	0 (0)	0 (0)

Financial Information/Assistance

Tuition: For information on tuition costs, visit http://www.uvm.edu/~stdfinsv/?Page=graduate-tuition.html. Tuition is subject to change.

Doctoral:
State residents: $611 per credit hour.
Nonstate residents: $1,544 per credit hour.

Financial Assistance:

	Teaching Assistantship (% Receiving)	Teaching Assistantship Tuition Remission	Research Assistantship (% Receiving)	Research Assistantship Tuition Remission	Fellowship (% Receiving)	Fellowship Tuition Remission
First-Year Student	$18,750 (NA)	Full	$25,000 (NA)	Full	$25,000 (NA)	Full
Advanced Student	$18,750 (NA)	Full	$25,000 (NA)	Full	$25,000 (NA)	Full

For additional information on financial assistance, visit http://www.uvm.edu/~gradcoll/?Page=Funding.html.

Employment of Department Graduates

Doctoral:
Enrolled in a postdoctoral residency/fellowship: 4
Employed in independent practice: 2
Employed in an academic position at a university: 1
Employed in academic position at a 2-year/4-year college: 1
Employed in other positions at a higher education institution: 2
Total: 10

Additional Information

Housing and Day Care: No on-campus housing is available. On-campus day care facilities are available. See the following website for more information: http://www.uvm.edu/~ccschool/.

Information for Students With Physical Disabilities: See the following website: http://www.uvm.edu/access/.

Special Facilities or Resources: The department has excellent laboratories in behavioral neuroscience, group dynamics, developmental, human psychophysiology, and general human testing. Excellent computer facilities and an in-house psychology clinic with clinical research equipment are available.

Application Information: Graduate College, Admissions Office, 330 Waterman Building, University of Vermont, Burlington, VT 05405-0160. *Fee:* $65. *Online application:* https://www.applyweb.com/apply/uvmg/menu.html.

American School of Professional Psychology at Argosy University/Washington, D.C.

Clinical Psychology
American School of Professional Psychology
1550 Wilson Boulevard, Suite 600
Arlington, VA 22209
Telephone: (703) 526-5800
Dean, Clinical Psychology Programs: Michael D. Lynch, PhD, ABPP

E-mail: mdlynch@argosy.edu
Web: http://clinical.argosy.edu/locations/washington-dc/

Orientation, Objectives, and Emphasis of Department

The doctoral program in clinical psychology (PsyD) is designed to educate and train students to function effectively in diverse professional roles. The program emphasizes the development of attitudes, knowledge, and skills essential in the formation of professional psychologists who are committed to the ethical provision of quality services. The school offers a broad-based curriculum, providing a meaningful integration of diverse theoretical perspectives, scholarship, and practice. The program offers concentrations in forensic psychology, health and neuropsychology, child and family, and diversity. Opportunities are available for students to develop expertise in a number of areas including the provision of services to specific populations such as children and families; theoretical perspectives such as cognitive-behavioral, family systems, and psychodynamic; and areas of application such as forensics and health psychology. The master's degree (MA) in clinical psychology is designed to meet the needs of both those students seeking a terminal degree for work in the mental health field and those who eventually plan to pursue a doctoral degree. The program provides a solid core of basic psychology, as well as a strong clinical orientation with an emphasis in psychological assessment.

Programs and Degrees Offered

Program	Degree	Application Deadline	Applications Received	Accepted	New Admits Enrolled (PT)	Total Enrolled (PT)	Degrees Awarded in 2014–2015	Median Years to Complete Degree	Dismissed/ Withdrew
Clinical Psychology	MA/MS	(Fall), (Spring), Rolling	16	9	9 (0)	14 (1)	3	2	2
Clinical Psychology	PsyD	(Fall), (Spring), Rolling	108	53	44 (0)	212 (11)	52	5	4

APA Accreditation

Clinical PsyD: Student Outcome Data website: http://clinical.argosy.edu/locations/washington-dc/clinical-psychology-doctor-of-psychology.

Doctoral Degree (PsyD Clinical Psychology): For those doctoral students for whom a professional internship was required in this program prior to graduation:
Total students who applied for an internship: 48
Total students who obtained an internship: 47
Total students who obtained a paid internship: 47
Total students who obtained an unpaid internship: 0
Total students who were placed in APA/CPA-accredited internships: 40
Total students placed in internships not APA/CPA-accredited, but listed with the Association of Psychology Postdoctoral and Internship Centers (APPIC): 7
Total students placed in internships conforming to guidelines of the Council of Directors of School Psychology Programs (CDSPP): 0
Total students placed in internships that were not APA/CPA-accredited, APPIC or CDSSP listed: 0

Master's Degree (MA/MS Clinical Psychology): An internship experience, such as a final research project or "capstone" experience is required of graduates.

Internships/Practica

Practicum training is designed to give students the opportunity to work under supervision with a clinical population within a mental health delivery system. Students learn to apply their theoretical knowledge; implement, develop, and assess the efficacy of clinical techniques; and develop the professional attitudes important for the identity of a professional psychologist. Doctoral students complete two training practicum sequences (600 hours each) focusing on assessment or psychotherapy skills, or integrating the two. Master's students are required to complete one practicum (600 hours). All doctoral students are required to complete a one year (12 month) internship as a condition for graduation. This intensive and supervised contact with clients is essential for giving greater breadth and depth to the student's overall academic experience. Typically, students will begin the internship during their fourth or fifth year, depending on the student's progress through the curriculum. The Mid Atlantic Internship Consortium received APA accreditation in October 2015, offering 25 positions.

Admissions

Entries appear in the following order: required test or GPA, minimum score (if required)/median score of students entering in 2015–2016.

Program	Degree	GRE-V	GRE-Q	GRE-Writing	GRE-Subject	Under-graduate GPA	Last 2 Years GPA	Psychol-ogy GPA	Master's GPA
Clinical Psychology	MA/MS	Not specified	Not specified	Not specified	Not specified	3/NA	Not specified	Not specified	Not specified
Clinical Psychology	PsyD	Not specified	Not specified	Not specified	Not specified	3.25/NA	Not specified	Not specified	3.25/NA

Admissions Requirements:

Degree	GRE	GRE-Subject	Letters of Recom-mendation	Research Statement	Writing Sample	CV	Interview
Master's/Specialist	Optional	Optional	3	Required	Required	Required	Required
Doctoral	Optional	Optional	3	Required	Required	Required	Required

Admissions Criteria:

GRE scores—low
Research experience—low
Work experience—low
Clinically related public service—high
GPA—high

Letters of recommendation—high
Interview—high
Statement of goals and objectives—high
Undergraduate psychology preparation—high

Department Demographics

	Male (PT)	Female (PT)	Total	African-American/Black (PT)	Hispanic/Latino (PT)	Asian/Pacific Islander (PT)	American Indian/Alaska Native (PT)	Caucasian/White (PT)	Unknown	Multiethnic (PT)	ADA (PT)	Int'l (PT)
Students	41 (0)	185 (12)	238	45 (7)	9 (0)	15 (1)	2 (0)	132 (3)	8 (0)	15 (1)	5 (0)	3 (0)

Financial Information/Assistance

Tuition: For information on tuition costs, visit https://www.argosy.edu/affordability/tuition-and-fees. Tuition is subject to change.

Doctoral:
State residents: $32,536 per academic year.
State residents: $1,162 per credit hour.
Nonstate residents: $32,536 per academic year.
Nonstate residents: $1,162 per credit hour.

Master's:
State residents: $32,536 per academic year.
State residents: $1,162 per credit hour.
Nonstate residents: $32,536 per academic year.
Nonstate residents: $1,162 per credit hour.

Financial Assistance:

	Teaching Assistantship (% Receiving)	Teaching Assistantship Tuition Remission	Research Assistantship (% Receiving)	Research Assistantship Tuition Remission	Fellowship (% Receiving)	Fellowship Tuition Remission
First-Year Student	NA (NA)	NA	NA (NA)	NA	$10,450 (3)	Full
Advanced Student	$3,645 (NA)	NA	$2,430 (NA)	NA	$7,400 (9)	Full

For additional information on financial assistance, visit http://clinical.argosy.edu/locations/washington-dc/financial-aid.

Employment of Department Graduates

Master's:
Enrolled in a psychology doctoral program: 2
Other employment position: 1
Total: 3

Doctoral:
Enrolled in a postdoctoral residency/fellowship: 49
Do not know: 3
Total: 52

Additional Information

Housing and Day Care: No on-campus housing is available. No on-campus day care facilities are available.

Special Facilities or Resources: Argosy University is conveniently located minutes from downtown Washington, DC. The on-site library has developed a focused psychology collection consisting of reference titles and books, journals, diagnostic assessment instruments, and audiovisual equipment. There are two computer labs and students have full access to both computerized literature searches and electronic text of most journals. In addition, students have access to the rich library resources of the Washington, DC area including the National Library of Medicine and the Library of Congress.

Application Information: J. Katrina Holloway, Director of Clinical Psychology Admissions, American School of Professional Psychology at Argosy University, Washington, DC, 1550 Wilson Boulevard, Suite 600, Arlington, VA 22209. *Fee:* $50. *Online application:* https://apply.argosy.edu/apply.

Divine Mercy University
Psychology
Institute for the Psychological Sciences
2001 Jefferson Davis Highway Suite 511
Arlington, VA 22202
Telephone: (703) 416-1441
Academic Dean: William Nordling, PhD

E-mail: ltucker@ipsciences.edu
Web: http://ipsciences.edu/

Orientation, Objectives, and Emphasis of Department
The Department adopts a practitioner-scholar model of training and education of psychologists. In doing so the degree programs train the students to practice psychology based on science integrated with a Catholic worldview.

Programs and Degrees Offered

Program	Degree	Application Deadline	Applications Received	Accepted	New Admits Enrolled (PT)	Total Enrolled (PT)	Degrees Awarded in 2014–2015	Median Years to Complete Degree	Dismissed/ Withdrew
General Psychology	MA/MS	August 30 (Fall), January 3 (Spring), May 3 (Summer)	74	36	36	93	0		0

Programs and Degrees Offered (con't.)

Program	Degree	Application Deadline	Applications Received	Accepted	New Admits Enrolled (PT)	Total Enrolled (PT)	Degrees Awarded in 2014–2015	Median Years to Complete Degree	Dismissed/ Withdrew
Clinical Psychology	PsyD	October 1 (Fall)	10	8	8	38 (0)	6	5	0

Doctoral Degree (PsyD Clinical Psychology): For those doctoral students for whom a professional internship was required in this program prior to graduation:
Total students who applied for an internship: 6
Total students who obtained an internship: 6
Total students who obtained a paid internship: 6
Total students who obtained an unpaid internship: 0
Total students who were placed in APA/CPA-accredited internships: 1
Total students placed in internships not APA/CPA-accredited, but listed with the Association of Psychology Postdoctoral and Internship Centers (APPIC): 5
Total students placed in internships conforming to guidelines of the Council of Directors of School Psychology Programs (CDSPP): 0
Total students placed in internships that were not APA/CPA-accredited, APPIC or CDSSP listed: 0

Master's Degree (MA/MS General Psychology): An internship experience, such as a final research project or "capstone" experience is required of graduates.

Internships/Practica
Students enrolled in the PsyD program complete practicum in the second, third, and fourth year of the program and full-time predoctoral internship in their fifth year in the program.

Admissions
Entries appear in the following order: required test or GPA, minimum score (if required)/median score of students entering in 2015–2016.

Program	Degree	GRE-V	GRE-Q	GRE-Writing	GRE-Subject	Under-graduate GPA	Last 2 Years GPA	Psychology GPA	Master's GPA
General Psychology	MA/MS	Not specified	Not specified	Not specified	Not specified	2.75/NA	NA/NA	2.75/NA	Not specified
Clinical Psychology	PsyD	NA/NA	NA/NA	Not specified	Not specified	3/NA	NA/NA	3/NA	3.5/NA

Admissions Requirements:

Degree	GRE	GRE-Subject	Letters of Recom-mendation	Research Statement	Writing Sample	CV	Interview
Master's/Specialist	Optional	None	2	Required	Optional	Required	None
Doctoral	Required	None	3	Required	Optional	Required	Required

Admissions Criteria:
GRE scores—medium
Research experience—medium
Work experience—high
Clinically related public service—low

GPA—high
Letters of recommendation—medium
Interview—high
Statement of goals and objectives—high

Department Demographics

	Male (PT)	Female (PT)	Total	African-American/ Black (PT)	Hispanic/ Latino (PT)	Asian/ Pacific Islander (PT)	American Indian/ Alaska Native (PT)	Caucasian/ White (PT)	Unknown	Multiethnic (PT)	ADA (PT)	Int'l (PT)
Students	67 (0)	107 (0)	174	6 (0)	11 (0)	6 (0)	2 (0)	138 (0)	11 (0)	0 (0)	0 (0)	3 (0)

Financial Information/Assistance

Tuition: For information on tuition costs, visit http://ipsciences.edu/cost-of-attendance/. Tuition is subject to change. Additional fees are assessed to students beyond the costs of tuition for the following: library, student activities. Tuition costs vary by program.

Doctoral:
State residents: $31,185 per academic year.
State residents: $945 per credit hour.
Nonstate residents: $31,185 per academic year.
Nonstate residents: $945 per credit hour.

Master's:
State residents: $687 per credit hour.
Nonstate residents: $687 per credit hour.

Financial Assistance:

	Teaching Assistantship (% Receiving)	Teaching Assistantship Tuition Remission	Research Assistantship (% Receiving)	Research Assistantship Tuition Remission	Fellowship (% Receiving)	Fellowship Tuition Remission
First-Year Student	NA (NA)	NA	$5,000 (88)	Full	$1,000 (50)	Full
Advanced Student	$7,500 (33)	Full	$7,500 (33)	Full	$1,000 (50)	Full

For additional information on financial assistance, visit http://ipsciences.edu/financing-your-education/.

Employment of Department Graduates

Master's:
Enrolled in a psychology doctoral program: 4
Employed in a community mental health/counseling center: 3
Not seeking employment: 1
Total: 8

Doctoral:
Enrolled in a postdoctoral residency/fellowship: 1
Employed in independent practice: 5
Total: 6

Additional Information

Housing and Day Care: No on-campus housing is available. No on-campus day care facilities are available.

Special Facilities or Resources: The Washington, DC Metro Area is an environment rich in educational and cultural resources for students. In addition to the IPS Library, students have access to the libraries of other universities and centers of learning within the area. The IPS also has a chapel and a chaplain who provides students with opportunities for spiritual development.

Application Information: The Institute for the Psychological Sciences, Attn: Admissions, 2001 Jefferson Davis Highway, Suite 511, Arlington, VA 22202. *Fee:* $55.

George Mason University
Department of Psychology
Humanities and Social Sciences
4400 University Drive, MSN 3F5
Fairfax, VA 22030-4444
Telephone: (703) 993-1548
Chairperson: Reeshad Dalal

E-mail: dwesley@gmu.edu
Web: http://psychology.gmu.edu/

Orientation, Objectives, and Emphasis of Department

All graduate programs emphasize both basic research and the application of research to solving problems in families, schools, industry, government, and health care settings.

Programs and Degrees Offered

Program	Degree	Application Deadline	Applications Received	Accepted	New Admits Enrolled (PT)	Total Enrolled (PT)	Degrees Awarded in 2014–2015	Median Years to Complete Degree	Dismissed/ Withdrew
Clinical Psychology	PhD	December 1 (Fall)	267	6	6 (0)	38 (0)	4	5	
Industrial/ Organizational Psychology	PhD	December 15 (Fall)	164	5	5 (0)	31 (0)	6	5	1
Human Factors and Applied Cognition	PhD	January 1 (Fall)	45	5	4 (0)	35 (0)	4	6	0
Applied Developmental Psychology	PhD	December 1 (Fall)	26	4	4 (0)	18 (0)	6	4	0
School Psychology	MA/MS	January 15 (Fall)	63	11	10 (0)	18 (0)	5	3	0
Industrial/ Organizational Psychology	MA/MS	February 1 (Fall)	163	24	15 (0)	56 (0)	10	2	0
Human Factors and Applied Cognition	MA/MS	February 1 (Fall)	59	22	16 (0)	34 (0)	6	2	0
Applied Developmental Psychology	MA/MS	January 1 (Fall)	31	5	4 (0)	10 (0)	7	2	1
Cognitive and Behavioral Neuroscience	MA/MS	February 1 (Fall)	37	6	4 (0)	11 (0)	4	3	0
Cognitive and Behavioral Neuroscience	PhD	January 1 (Fall)	27	4	4 (0)	15 (0)	1	7	0

APA Accreditation

Clinical PhD: Student Outcome Data website: http://psychology.gmu.edu/clinical/.

Doctoral Degree (PhD Clinical Psychology): For those doctoral students for whom a professional internship was required in this program prior to graduation:
Total students who applied for an internship: 4
Total students who obtained an internship: 4
Total students who obtained a paid internship: 4
Total students who obtained an unpaid internship: 0
Total students who were placed in APA/CPA-accredited internships: 4
Total students placed in internships not APA/CPA-accredited, but listed with the Association of Psychology Postdoctoral and Internship Centers (APPIC): 0
Total students placed in internships conforming to guidelines of the Council of Directors of School Psychology Programs (CDSPP): 0
Total students placed in internships that were not APA/CPA-accredited, APPIC or CDSSP listed: 0

Master's Degree (MA/MS School Psychology): An internship experience, such as a final research project or "capstone" experience is required of graduates. Master's Degree (MA/MS Cognitive and Behavioral Neuroscience): An internship experience, such as a final research project or "capstone" experience is required of graduates.

Internships/Practica

All programs either require or offer practicum placements in a wide variety of settings, including mental health treatment facilities, medical facilities, schools, government agencies, the military, and businesses and organizations.

Admissions

Entries appear in the following order: required test or GPA, minimum score (if required)/median score of students entering in 2015–2016.

Program	Degree	GRE-V	GRE-Q	GRE-Writing	GRE-Subject	Under-graduate GPA	Last 2 Years GPA	Psychol-ogy GPA	Master's GPA
Clinical Psychology	PhD	NA/160	NA/153	Not specified	Not specified	NA/3.72	3.25/NA	3.25/NA	Not specified
Industrial/ Organizational Psychology	PhD	NA/NA	NA/NA	NA/NA	Not specified	NA/NA	3/NA	3.25/NA	Not specified
Human Factors and Applied Cognition	PhD	NA/NA	NA/NA	NA/NA	Not specified	Not specified	3/NA	3.25/NA	Not specified
Applied Developmental Psychology	PhD	NA/NA	NA/NA	NA/NA	Not specified	Not specified	Not specified	3.25/NA	3.25/NA
School Psychology	MA/MS	NA/NA	NA/NA	Not specified	Not specified	NA/NA	3/NA	3.25/NA	Not specified
Industrial/ Organizational Psychology	MA/MS	NA/NA	NA/NA	Not specified	Not specified	NA/NA	3/NA	3.25/NA	Not specified
Human Factors and Applied Cognition	MA/MS	NA/NA	NA/NA	Not specified	Not specified	Not specified	3/NA	3.25/NA	Not specified
Applied Developmental Psychology	MA/MS	NA/NA	NA/NA	NA/NA	Not specified	Not specified	3/NA	3.25/NA	Not specified
Cognitive and Behavioral Neuroscience	MA/MS	NA/NA	NA/NA	NA/NA	Not specified	Not specified	3/NA	3.25/NA	Not specified
Cognitive and Behavioral Neuroscience	PhD	NA/NA	NA/NA	NA/NA	Not specified	Not specified	3/NA	3.25/NA	Not specified

Admissions Requirements:

Degree	GRE	GRE-Subject	Letters of Recom-mendation	Research Statement	Writing Sample	CV	Interview
Master's/Specialist	Required	None	3	Required	Optional	Optional	Recom-mended
Doctoral	Required	Recom-mended	3	Required	Optional	Optional	Recom-mended

Please note if these criteria vary for different programs: The Clinical and School Psychology programs interview a select group by invitation only. The Cognitive and Behavioral Neuroscience, Developmental, Human Factors/Applied Cognition, and Industrial/ Organizational programs do not require an interview but hold an Open House for selected students to attend. Clinical and Applied Developmental PhD are required to submit the PhD Departmental Form where they select two faculty they wish to work with. This is strongly recommended but not required for other concentrations.

Admissions Criteria:

GRE scores—high
Research experience—medium
Work experience—medium
Clinically related public service—medium
GPA—high

Letters of recommendation—high
Interview—high
Statement of goals and objectives—high
Undergraduate psychology preparation—high

For additional information on admission requirements, visit http://psychology.gmu.edu/prospective/for-prospective.

Department Demographics

	Male (PT)	Female (PT)	Total	African-American/ Black (PT)	Hispanic/ Latino (PT)	Asian/ Pacific Islander (PT)	American Indian/ Alaska Native (PT)	Caucasian/ White (PT)	Unknown	Multiethnic (PT)	ADA (PT)	Int'l (PT)
Students	71 (0)	142 (0)	213	7 (0)	5 (0)	22 (0)	1 (0)	193 (0)	35 (0)	3 (0)	0 (0)	10 (0)

Financial Information/Assistance

Tuition: For information on tuition costs, visit http://studentaccounts.gmu.edu/tuition.html. Tuition is subject to change.

Doctoral:
State residents: $9,934 per academic year.
State residents: $546 per credit hour.
Nonstate residents: $23,466 per academic year.
Nonstate residents: $1,301 per credit hour.

Master's:
State residents: $9,934 per academic year.
State residents: $546 per credit hour.
Nonstate residents: $23,466 per academic year.
Nonstate residents: $1,301 per credit hour.

Financial Assistance:

	Teaching Assistantship (% Receiving)	Teaching Assistantship Tuition Remission	Research Assistantship (% Receiving)	Research Assistantship Tuition Remission	Fellowship (% Receiving)	Fellowship Tuition Remission
First-Year Student	$18,400 (NA)	Full	$18,400 (NA)	Full	NA (NA)	NA
Advanced Student	$18,400 (NA)	Full	$18,400 (NA)	Full	NA (NA)	NA

For additional information on financial assistance, visit http://chss.gmu.edu/graduate/college-information-funding.

Employment of Department Graduates

No information provided.

Additional Information

Housing and Day Care: No on-campus housing is available. On-campus day care facilities are available. See the following website for more information: http://hr.gmu.edu/cdc/.

Information for Students With Physical Disabilities: See the following website: http://ods.gmu.edu/.

Special Facilities or Resources: The Developmental research area includes individual test rooms, a family interaction room, and a number of faculty research areas; some of the test rooms are equipped with video and computers. Cognitive and Behavioral Neuroscience includes a rodent colony, modern facilities for behavior testing (including drug self-administration), a Neurolucida system for neuroanatomical evaluation, and extensive histological capability. Cognitive and Behavioral Neuroscience also has collaborative relationships with the Center for Biomedical Genomics and Informatics for gene microarray work and the Krasnow Institute for Advanced Study for neuroanatomy, neurophysiology, and neural modeling work. The Human Factors/Applied Cognitive labs include numerous workstations for computer display and data collection, several eyetrackers, several simulators (including a cockpit simulator) and human electrophysiology; a Near Infrared Imaging System is planned for the very near future. Industrial/ Organizational research space includes laboratory space for work on groups, teamwork, and leadership. Clinical facilities include a professional clinic and research/interview space in faculty labs. The Center for Cognitive Development, housed in the same building as the clinic, works with local school systems and the School and Clinical programs on issues related to child development. Some students use nearby resources for research, such as the National Institutes of Health.

Application Information: Fee: $65. *Online application:* http://admissions.gmu.edu/grad/applynow/.

George Mason University

Division of Educational Psychology, Research Methods & Education Policy
College of Education and Human Development
4400 University Drive, MS 6D2
Fairfax, VA 22030
Telephone: (703) 993-3679
Division Director: Dr. Erin Peters-Burton

E-mail: edpsych@gmu.edu
Web: http://gse.gmu.edu/educational-psychology/

Orientation, Objectives, and Emphasis of Department

The Educational Psychology program is designed to offer individuals the opportunity to: apply principles of learning, cognition and motivation to vital problems in the area of education; develop a solid understanding of research, assessment, and evaluation methodologies; and develop an analytical and scholarly approach to critically assessing theoretical perspectives, research, and practice within and across content domains. Our doctoral program is individualized, interdisciplinary, and experiential. Students, with the guidance of faculty advisors, plan their own programs to meet self-defined goals. To accomplish these goals, students engage in a variety of intensive courses, independent studies, seminars, and internships of a highly practical nature. Success in the program requires a high degree of personal initiative, self-directed learning, and commitment to inquiry as a style of personal and professional growth.

Programs and Degrees Offered

Program	Degree	Application Deadline	Applica-tions Received	Accepted	New Admits Enrolled (PT)	Total Enrolled (PT)	Degrees Awarded in 2014–2015	Median Years to Complete Degree	Dismissed/ Withdrew
Educational Psychology	MA/MS	April 1 (Fall), November 1 (Spring)		30					0
Data-Driven Decision-Making Certificate	Other	April 1 (Fall), November 1 (Spring)							
Educational Psychology	PhD	February 1 (Fall), September 1 (Spring)							

Admissions

Entries appear in the following order: required test or GPA, minimum score (if required)/median score of students entering in 2015–2016.

Program	Degree	GRE-V	GRE-Q	GRE-Writing	GRE-Subject	Under-graduate GPA	Last 2 Years GPA	Psychol-ogy GPA	Master's GPA
Educational Psychology	MA/MS	NA/NA	NA/NA	NA/NA	Not specified	3/NA	3/NA	Not specified	Not specified
Data-Driven Decision-Making Certificate	Other	Not specified	Not specified	Not specified	Not specified	Not specified	Not specified	Not specified	Not specified

Admissions *(con't.)*

Program	Degree	GRE-V	GRE-Q	GRE-Writing	GRE-Subject	Under-graduate GPA	Last 2 Years GPA	Psychol-ogy GPA	Master's GPA
Educational Psychology	PhD	NA/NA	NA/NA	NA/NA	Not specified	Not specified	Not specified	Not specified	Not specified

Admissions Requirements:

Degree	GRE	GRE-Subject	Letters of Recom-mendation	Research Statement	Writing Sample	CV	Interview
Master's/Specialist	Required	None	3	Required	None	Required	None
Doctoral	Required	None	3	Required	Optional	Required	Required

Admissions Criteria:

GRE scores—medium
Research experience—medium
Work experience—medium
Clinically related public service—low

GPA—medium
Letters of recommendation—medium
Statement of goals and objectives—high

Department Demographics

	Male (PT)	Female (PT)	Total	African-American/ Black (PT)	Hispanic/ Latino (PT)	Asian/ Pacific Islander (PT)	American Indian/ Alaska Native (PT)	Caucasian/ White (PT)	Unknown	Multiethnic (PT)	ADA (PT)	Int'l (PT)
Students			0	0 (0)	0 (0)	0 (0)	0 (0)	0 (0)	0 (0)	0 (0)	0 (0)	0 (0)

Financial Information/Assistance

Tuition: For information on tuition costs, visit http://studentaccounts.gmu.edu/tuition-fees/. Tuition is subject to change. Tuition costs vary by program.

Doctoral:
State residents: $546 per credit hour.
Nonstate residents: $1,301 per credit hour.

Master's:
State residents: $546 per credit hour.
Nonstate residents: $1,301 per credit hour.

Financial Assistance:

	Teaching Assistantship (% Receiving)	Teaching Assistantship Tuition Remission	Research Assistantship (% Receiving)	Research Assistantship Tuition Remission	Fellowship (% Receiving)	Fellowship Tuition Remission
First-Year Student	NA (NA)	NA	$10,600 (NA)	Partial	NA (NA)	NA
Advanced Student	NA (NA)	NA	$14,800 (NA)	Partial	NA (NA)	NA

For additional information on financial assistance, visit https://cehd.gmu.edu/admissions/funding-sources-discounts/.

Employment of Department Graduates

No information provided.

Additional Information

Housing and Day Care: No on-campus housing is available. On-campus day care facilities are available. See the following website for more information: http://hr.gmu.edu/cdc/.

Information for Students With Physical Disabilities: See the following website: http://ods.gmu.edu.

Application Information: George Mason University, Graduate Admissions, Johnson Center, Room 245, 4400 University Drive, MSN 4C8, Fairfax, VA 22030. *Fee:* $75. *Online application:* http://admissions.gmu.edu/ApplyNow/.

James Madison University

Department of Graduate Psychology
College of Health and Behavioral Studies
70 Alumnae Drive; MSC 7401
Harrisonburg, VA 22802
Telephone: (540) 568-6439
Academic Unit Head: Robin D. Anderson

E-mail: ander2rd@jmu.edu
Web: http://www.psyc.jmu.edu/gradpsyc/

Orientation, Objectives, and Emphasis of Department

Our department offers eight graduate programs designed for individuals who want to pursue advanced study in psychology or counseling. These programs share the goals of academic enrichment, development of research and applied skills, and personal and professional growth. Each of these programs is innovative and distinctive in preparing practitioners and scholars for the future. Our strong commitment to diversity is evidenced by devoting specific coursework to socio-cultural issues, providing practical experiences with clients from a variety of cultures and backgrounds, recruiting and supporting a diverse student body, and offering internationalized curricula. Special features of our programs include individualized academic advising and concerned, involved faculty. Many classes are conducted in small, seminar-style environments, and have an experiential emphasis. There are numerous research opportunities, and students are encouraged to become active scholars. Financial assistance is widely available in all programs, and students have opportunities to gain experience working in on-campus centers and inter-professional clinics. We view contemporary psychology and counseling as disciplines that intersect with a number of others, including biological and social sciences and the humanities.

Programs and Degrees Offered

Program	Degree	Application Deadline	Applications Received	Accepted	New Admits Enrolled (PT)	Total Enrolled (PT)	Degrees Awarded in 2014–2015	Median Years to Complete Degree	Dismissed/ Withdrew
Clinical Mental Health Counseling	EdS	January 15 (Fall)	90	11	10	27 (4)	13	3	2
School Counseling	MEd	January 15 (Summer)	24	11	11	16 (3)	7	2	0
School Psychology	EdS	February 1 (Fall)	56	10	7	28 (10)	11	3	0
College Student Personnel Administration	MA/MS	January 15 (Fall)	79	12	12 (2)	24 (3)	12	2	0
Psychological Sciences	MA/MS	January 4 (Fall)	53	15	12 (0)	26 (1)	12	2	0
Clinical and School Psychology	PsyD	February 1 (Fall)	55	6	6 (0)	23 (0)	6	4	1
Assessment and Measurement	PhD	January 15 (Fall)	12	4	4 (0)	10 (3)	7	3	0

Programs and Degrees Offered *(con't.)*

Program	Degree	Application Deadline	Applica-tions Received	Accepted	New Admits Enrolled (PT)	Total Enrolled (PT)	Degrees Awarded in 2014–2015	Median Years to Complete Degree	Dismissed/ Withdrew
Counseling and Supervision	PhD	January 15 (Fall), January 15 (Summer)	16	5	2 (4)	2 (7)	1	3	0

APA Accreditation

Combination PsyD: Student Outcome Data website: http://www.psyc.jmu.edu/cipsyd/.

Doctoral Degree (PsyD Clinical and School Psychology): For those doctoral students for whom a professional internship was required in this program prior to graduation:
Total students who applied for an internship: 6
Total students who obtained an internship: 6
Total students who obtained a paid internship: 6
Total students who obtained an unpaid internship: 0
Total students who were placed in APA/CPA-accredited internships: 6
Total students placed in internships not APA/CPA-accredited, but listed with the Association of Psychology Postdoctoral and Internship Centers (APPIC): 0
Total students placed in internships conforming to guidelines of the Council of Directors of School Psychology Programs (CDSPP): 0
Total students placed in internships that were not APA/CPA-accredited, APPIC or CDSSP listed: 0

Master's Degree (Med School Counseling): An internship experience, such as a final research project or "capstone" experience is required of graduates. Master's Degree (MA/MS College Student Personnel Administration): An internship experience, such as a final research project or "capstone" experience is required of graduates.

Admissions

Entries appear in the following order: required test or GPA, minimum score (if required)/median score of students entering in 2015–2016.

Program	Degree	GRE-V	GRE-Q	GRE-Writing	GRE-Subject	Under-graduate GPA	Last 2 Years GPA	Psychol-ogy GPA	Master's GPA
Clinical Mental Health Counseling	EdS	Not specified	Not specified	Not specified	Not specified	Not specified	Not specified	Not specified	Not specified
School Counseling	MEd	Not specified	Not specified	Not specified	Not specified	Not specified	Not specified	Not specified	Not specified
School Psychology	EdS	Not specified	Not specified	Not specified	Not specified	Not specified	Not specified	Not specified	Not specified
College Student Personnel Administration	MA/MS	Not specified	Not specified	Not specified	Not specified	Not specified	Not specified	Not specified	Not specified
Psychological Sciences	MA/MS	Not specified	Not specified	Not specified	Not specified	Not specified	Not specified	Not specified	Not specified
Clinical and School Psychology	PsyD	Not specified	Not specified	Not specified	Not specified	Not specified	Not specified	Not specified	Not specified
Assessment and Measurement	PhD	Not specified	Not specified	Not specified	Not specified	Not specified	Not specified	Not specified	Not specified
Counseling and Supervision	PhD	Not specified	Not specified	Not specified	Not specified	Not specified	Not specified	Not specified	Not specified

Admissions Requirements:

Degree	GRE	GRE-Subject	Letters of Recommendation	Research Statement	Writing Sample	CV	Interview
Master's/Specialist	Required	Optional	3	Required	Required	Required	Required
Doctoral	Required	Required	3	Required	Required	Required	Required

Please note if these criteria vary for different programs: These criteria vary for different program areas. Only Clinical and School combined program requires the GRE-Subject. All three doctoral programs require the applicant to already have a master's degree.

Admissions Criteria:

For additional information on admission requirements, visit http://www.psyc.jmu.edu/gradpsyc/programs.html.

Department Demographics

	Male (PT)	Female (PT)	Total	African-American/ Black (PT)	Hispanic/ Latino (PT)	Asian/ Pacific Islander (PT)	American Indian/ Alaska Native (PT)	Caucasian/ White (PT)	Unknown (PT)	Multiethnic (PT)	ADA (PT)	Int'l (PT)
Students	49 (8)	107 (23)	187	0 (0)	0 (0)	0 (0)	0 (0)	0 (0)	0 (0)	0 (0)	0 (0)	0 (0)

Financial Information/Assistance

Tuition: For information on tuition costs, visit http://www.jmu.edu/ubo/rates/index.shtml. Tuition is subject to change.

Doctoral:
State residents: $10,416 per academic year.
State residents: $434 per credit hour.
Nonstate residents: $27,240 per academic year.
Nonstate residents: $1,135 per credit hour.

Master's:
State residents: $7,812 per academic year.
State residents: $434 per credit hour.
Nonstate residents: $20,430 per academic year.
Nonstate residents: $1,135 per credit hour.

Financial Assistance:

	Teaching Assistantship (% Receiving)	Teaching Assistantship Tuition Remission	Research Assistantship (% Receiving)	Research Assistantship Tuition Remission	Fellowship (% Receiving)	Fellowship Tuition Remission
First-Year Student	$9,014 (NA)	Full	$7,680 (NA)	Full	NA (NA)	NA
Advanced Student	$9,014 (NA)	Full	$7,680 (NA)	Full	NA (NA)	NA

For additional information on financial assistance, visit http://www.jmu.edu/grad/current-students/assistantships/assist_info.shtml.

Employment of Department Graduates

No information provided.

Additional Information

Housing and Day Care: No on-campus housing is available. No on-campus day care facilities are available.

Information for Students With Physical Disabilities: See the following website: http://www.jmu.edu/ods/.

Special Facilities or Resources: There are well-equipped animal laboratories, including equipment for both behavioral and wet lab procedures, as well as several computer-driven perceptual (e.g., psychoacoustic) and cognitive laboratories.

Application Information: *Fee:* $55. *Online application:* https://www.applyweb.com/apply/jmug/index.html.

Marymount University

Department of Forensic and Legal Psychology
School of Education and Human Services
2807 North Glebe Road
Arlington, VA 22207
Telephone: (703) 284-5705
Chairperson: Dr. Mary Lindahl
E-mail: grad.admissions@marymount.edu
Web: http://www.marymount.edu/Academics/School-of-Education-Human-Services/Graduate-Programs/Forensic-Legal-Psychology-(M-A-)

Orientation, Objectives, and Emphasis of Department

The Department of Forensic and Legal Psychology offers a 39-credit Master of Arts in Forensic and Legal Psychology (Psychology and Law). This degree provides graduates with the skills and knowledge they need to provide effective, high quality services in a variety of psycholegal settings. These settings include probation and parole, victim assistance, intelligence, corrections, law enforcement, and other arenas within the legal system. To accomplish this goal, the program balances the acquisition of traditional psychological knowledge and skills with a specialized understanding of the justice system. Once enrolled in the MA program, students may apply for and, if selected, complete a concentration in Intelligence Studies, which provides the knowledge and skills necessary to be competitive in the Intelligence Community and the private-sector companies that support it. An optional dual degree with Clinical Mental Health Counseling is also offered (which involves a separate application/interview process).

Programs and Degrees Offered

Program	Degree	Application Deadline	Applications Received	Accepted	New Admits Enrolled (PT)	Total Enrolled (PT)	Degrees Awarded in 2014–2015	Median Years to Complete Degree	Dismissed/ Withdrew
Forensic and Legal Psychology	MA/MS	February 16 (Fall)	181	90	75 (6)	145 (30)	69	2	0

Internships/Practica

Forensic and Legal psychology students may choose an internship in a wide variety of settings, including local and state correctional facilities, local community mental health treatment centers, victim witness programs, domestic violence programs and shelters, national and local mental health advocacy organizations, child welfare agencies and advocacy organizations, adult services agencies (serving incapacitated and incompetent adults), juvenile court services, state and local law enforcement, federal law enforcement, intelligence and justice agencies, and any and all areas in which psychological expertise and psychological services would be applied in a legal setting.

Admissions

Entries appear in the following order: required test or GPA, minimum score (if required)/median score of students entering in 2015–2016.

Program	Degree	GRE-V	GRE-Q	GRE-Writing	GRE-Subject	Undergraduate GPA	Last 2 Years GPA	Psychology GPA	Master's GPA
Forensic and Legal Psychology	MA/MS	NA/150	NA/147	NA/4	Not specified	3/3.5	Not specified	Not specified	Not specified

Admissions Requirements:

Degree	GRE	GRE-Subject	Letters of Recommendation	Research Statement	Writing Sample	CV	Interview
Master's/Specialist	Required	None	2	Required	None	Required	None

Admissions Criteria:

GRE scores—medium
Research experience—low
Work experience—medium
Clinically related public service—low

GPA—high
Letters of recommendation—medium
Statement of goals and objectives—high
Undergraduate psychology preparation—medium

For additional information on admission requirements, visit http://www.marymount.edu/admissions/graduate/applying.

Department Demographics

	Male (PT)	Female (PT)	Total	African-American/ Black (PT)	Hispanic/ Latino (PT)	Asian/ Pacific Islander (PT)	American Indian/ Alaska Native (PT)	Caucasian/ White (PT)	Unknown	Multiethnic (PT)	ADA (PT)	Int'l (PT)
Students	17 (3)	128 (27)	175	14 (0)	11 (3)	6 (0)	0 (0)	95 (25)	12 (2)	7 (0)		3 (0)

Financial Information/Assistance

Tuition: For information on tuition costs, visit http://www.marymount.edu/Admissions/Student-Accounts/Tuition-Fees. Tuition is subject to change.

Master's:
State residents: $885 per credit hour.
Nonstate residents: $885 per credit hour.

Financial Assistance:

	Teaching Assistantship (% Receiving)	Teaching Assistantship Tuition Remission	Research Assistantship (% Receiving)	Research Assistantship Tuition Remission	Fellowship (% Receiving)	Fellowship Tuition Remission
First-Year Student	NA (NA)	NA	NA (NA)	Partial	NA (NA)	NA
Advanced Student	NA (NA)	NA	NA (NA)	Partial	NA (NA)	NA

For additional information on financial assistance, visit http://www.marymount.edu/Admissions/Financial-Aid/Types-of-Aid/Graduate.

Employment of Department Graduates

No information provided.

Additional Information

Housing and Day Care: On-campus housing is available. See the following website for more information: http://www.marymount.edu/Student-Life/Graduate-Students/University-Sponsored-Residencies. No on-campus day care facilities are available.

Special Facilities or Resources: The location of Marymount in suburban Washington, DC provides our students with a large number of opportunities for internships and employment in the area, especially with federal agencies. The university is a member of the Washington Consortium of College and Universities, which gives students access to the library facilities and classes of most of the major universities in the area. Also, approximately every other summer, students have the opportunity to learn about and experience forensic and legal psychology in the English justice system via a collaborative relationship with the Forensic Psychology MA Program at London Metropolitan University. Other study abroad options are also available.

Application Information: Office of Graduate Admissions, Marymount University, 2807 North Glebe Road, Arlington, VA 22207. *Fee:* $40. *Online application:* https://app.applyyourself.com/?id=Marymount.

Old Dominion University

Department of Psychology
College of Sciences
Mills Godwin Building—Room 250
Norfolk, VA 23529-0267
Telephone: (757) 683-4439
Chairperson: James P. Bliss

E-mail: jbliss@odu.edu
Web: http://www.odu.edu/psychology

Orientation, Objectives, and Emphasis of Department

The department offers PhD programs in Applied Experimental, Human Factors, and Industrial/Organizational Psychology. Concentrations within Applied Experimental include health, community, substance use and abuse, developmental, cognition, memory, and quantitative. Concentrations within Human Factors include medical modeling and simulation, aviation, decision support systems, human-computer interaction, cognitive and behavioral reactions to alarms and alerts, and cognitive and behavioral responses to mild motion (sopite syndrome). Concentrations within Industrial/Organizational include organizational (e.g., leadership, career development, work-family interface, organizational change and development, positive organizations, international and cross-cultural perspectives, and occupational health) and personnel (e.g, game-based training, self-development, training using social media, technology in research and human resource management). The programs are designed to provide in-depth training in applied experimental, human factors, or industrial/organizational psychology and specialized training in an area of concentration. A program of graduate study leading to the degree of Master of Science with a concentration in general experimental psychology is also offered. The department participates in the Virginia Consortium Program in Clinical Psychology which, in collaboration with Eastern Virginia Medical School and Norfolk State University, offers the PhD in Clinical Psychology.

Programs and Degrees Offered

Program	Degree	Application Deadline	Applications Received	Accepted	New Admits Enrolled (PT)	Total Enrolled (PT)	Degrees Awarded in 2014–2015	Median Years to Complete Degree	Dismissed/Withdrew
Human Factors	PhD	January 5 (Fall)	16	4	4	14 (0)	0		0
Applied Experimental Psychology	PhD	January 5 (Fall)	6	1	1	16	2	4.8	2
General Psychology	MA/MS	May 15 (Fall)	45	1	1	20 (0)	4	3.3	0
Industrial/ Organizational Psychology	PhD	January 5 (Fall)	48	3	3	16 (0)	0		0

Internships/Practica

Internships are highly encouraged for those enrolled in all three PhD programs and are available at local businesses, hospitals, and military and government agencies, as well as out-of-state. Practicum and internship experiences are also available for all graduate students.

Admissions

Entries appear in the following order: required test or GPA, minimum score (if required)/median score of students entering in 2015–2016.

Program	Degree	GRE-V	GRE-Q	GRE-Writing	GRE-Subject	Under-graduate GPA	Last 2 Years GPA	Psychology GPA	Master's GPA
Human Factors	PhD	NA/153	NA/150	NA/3.7	Not specified	NA/3.51	Not specified	Not specified	Not specified
Applied Experimental Psychology	PhD	NA/158	NA/152	NA/4	Not specified	NA/3.52	Not specified	Not specified	Not specified
General Psychology	MA/MS	NA/151	NA/144	NA/3.84	Not specified	NA/3.15	Not specified	Not specified	Not specified
Industrial/ Organizational Psychology	PhD	NA/155	NA/153	NA/4.5	Not specified	NA/3.64	Not specified	Not specified	Not specified

Admissions Requirements:

Degree	GRE	GRE-Subject	Letters of Recom-mendation	Research Statement	Writing Sample	CV	Interview
Master's/Specialist	Required	Required	3	Required	Optional	Optional	Recom-mended
Doctoral	Required	Required	3	Required	Required	Required	Required

Please note if these criteria vary for different programs: MS program and doctoral program concentrations require GRE-Subject test if student did not major in psychology.

Admissions Criteria:

GRE scores—high
Research experience—high
Work experience—medium
Clinically related public service—low
GPA—high

Letters of recommendation—high
Interview—high
Statement of goals and objectives—medium
Undergraduate psychology preparation—medium

Department Demographics

	Male (PT)	Female (PT)	Total	African-American/ Black (PT)	Hispanic/ Latino (PT)	Asian/ Pacific Islander (PT)	American Indian/ Alaska Native (PT)	Caucasian/ White (PT)	Unknown (PT)	Multiethnic (PT)	ADA (PT)	Int'l (PT)
Students	20 (0)	37 (0)	57	3 (0)	2 (0)	2 (0)	0 (0)	48 (0)	2 (0)	0 (0)	0 (0)	5 (0)

Financial Information/Assistance

Tuition: For information on tuition costs, visit http://www.odu.edu/admission/costs-tuition/tuition/tuition-rates. Tuition is subject to change.

Doctoral:
State residents: $437 per credit hour.
Nonstate residents: $1,089 per credit hour.

Master's:
State residents: $437 per credit hour.
Nonstate residents: $1,089 per credit hour.

Financial Assistance:

	Teaching Assistantship (% Receiving)	Teaching Assistantship Tuition Remission	Research Assistantship (% Receiving)	Research Assistantship Tuition Remission	Fellowship (% Receiving)	Fellowship Tuition Remission
First-Year Student	$15,000 (NA)	Full	$15,000 (NA)	Full	$18,000 (NA)	Full
Advanced Student	$15,000 (NA)	Full	$15,000 (NA)	Full	$18,000 (NA)	Full

For additional information on financial assistance, visit http://www.odu.edu/admission/financial-aid/graduate.

Employment of Department Graduates

Master's:
Enrolled in a psychology doctoral program: 3
Do not know: 3
Total: 6

Doctoral:
Employed in an academic position at a university: 1
Employed in business or industry: 2
Total: 3

Additional Information

Housing and Day Care: On-campus housing is available. See the following website for more information: http://www.odu.edu/housing. On-campus day care facilities are available. See the following website for more information: http://www.odu.edu/partnerships/community/programs/child-care.

Information for Students With Physical Disabilities: See the following website: http://www.odu.edu/educationalaccessibility.

Special Facilities or Resources: The department has a Human Computer Interaction and Usability Analysis lab, a driving simulator, eye-track recording equipment, a Bar Lab, a Technology iN Training (TNT) lab, computer labs for data collection, and other research facilities. A close collaboration with the Virginia Modeling, Analysis and Simulation Center provides students with opportunities to engage in command and control simulation, surgical simulation, and virtual reality research. The psychology faculty and graduate students also maintain active collaborations with NASA Langley Research Center, Eastern Virginia Medical School, Children's Hospital of the King's Daughters, Norfolk State University and community and government groups, such as Virginia Department of Motor Vehicles, Department of Public Health, and Newport News Shipbuilding. Field research is facilitated by strong connections to industry and a large alumni network.

Application Information: Old Dominion University, Office of Graduate Admissions, 105 Rollins Hall, Norfolk, VA 23529-0050. *Fee:* $50. *Online application:* http://www.odu.edu/admission/apply/graduate.

Radford University
Department of Psychology
Humanities and Behavioral Sciences
P.O. Box 6946
Radford, VA 24142-6946
Telephone: (540) 831-5361
Chairperson: Jeffery Aspelmeier

E-mail: jaspelme@radford.edu
Web: http://www.radford.edu/content/chbs/home/psychology.html

---

Orientation, Objectives, and Emphasis of Department
The department aims to train psychologists who are well versed in both the theoretical and applied aspects of the discipline. The emphasis of the department is eclectic: school, clinical-counseling, experimental, industrial/organizational and counseling options are available at the graduate level. The School program is an EdS program that also provides preparation for certification and licensing as a school psychologist in Virginia. The PsyD program in Counseling Psychology, with an emphasis on rural mental health, was accredited by APA in 2012.

Programs and Degrees Offered

Program	Degree	Application Deadline	Applications Received	Accepted	New Admits Enrolled (PT)	Total Enrolled (PT)	Degrees Awarded in 2014–2015	Median Years to Complete Degree	Dismissed/ Withdrew
Counseling Psychology	PsyD	December 1 (Fall)	19	5	5	15 (0)	5	4	0
Clinical Counseling Psychology	MA/MS	February 15 (Fall)	33	14	6 (0)	11 (0)	6	2	1
Experimental Psychology	MA/MS	February 15 (Fall)	18	12	4 (0)	6 (0)	6	2	0
Industrial/ Organizational Psychology	MA/MS	February 15 (Fall)	70	20	11 (0)	22 (0)	13	2	0
School Psychology	EdS	February 15 (Fall)	30	28	10 (0)	20 (0)	7	3	0

APA Accreditation

Counseling PsyD: Student Outcome Data website: http://www.radford.edu/content/chbs/home/psychology/programs/counseling/Student-Admissions-Outcomes-and-Other-Data.html.

Doctoral Degree (PsyD Counseling Psychology): For those doctoral students for whom a professional internship was required in this program prior to graduation:
Total students who applied for an internship: 5
Total students who obtained an internship: 5
Total students who obtained a paid internship: 5
Total students who obtained an unpaid internship: 0
Total students who were placed in APA/CPA-accredited internships: 3
Total students placed in internships not APA/CPA-accredited, but listed with the Association of Psychology Postdoctoral and Internship Centers (APPIC): 2
Total students placed in internships conforming to guidelines of the Council of Directors of School Psychology Programs (CDSPP): 0
Total students placed in internships that were not APA/CPA-accredited, APPIC or CDSSP listed: 0

Master's Degree (MA/MS Clinical Counseling Psychology): An internship experience, such as a final research project or "capstone" experience is required of graduates. Master's Degree (MA/MS Experimental Psychology): An internship experience, such as a final research project or "capstone" experience is required of graduates. Master's Degree (MA/MS Industrial/Organizational Psychology): An internship experience, such as a final research project or "capstone" experience is required of graduates.

Internships/Practica

Internships and/or practica are required for all programs.

Admissions

Entries appear in the following order: required test or GPA, minimum score (if required)/median score of students entering in 2015–2016.

Program	Degree	GRE-V	GRE-Q	GRE-Writing	GRE-Subject	Under-graduate GPA	Last 2 Years GPA	Psychol-ogy GPA	Master's GPA
Counseling Psychology	PsyD	150/155	148/150	Not specified	Not specified	3.2/3.38	Not specified	Not specified	3.5/NA
Clinical Counseling Psychology	MA/MS	NA/152	NA/150	Not specified	Not specified	3/3.7	Not specified	Not specified	Not specified
Experimental Psychology	MA/MS	150/157	144/150	Not specified	Not specified	3/3.45	Not specified	Not specified	Not specified

Admissions *(con't.)*

Program	Degree	GRE-V	GRE-Q	GRE-Writing	GRE-Subject	Under-graduate GPA	Last 2 Years GPA	Psychology GPA	Master's GPA
Industrial/Organizational Psychology	MA/MS	NA/153	NA/149	Not specified	Not specified	3/3.71	Not specified	Not specified	Not specified
School Psychology	EdS	NA/150	NA/148	Not specified	Not specified	3/3.45	Not specified	Not specified	Not specified

Admissions Requirements:

Degree	GRE	GRE-Subject	Letters of Recommendation	Research Statement	Writing Sample	CV	Interview
Master's/Specialist	Required	Recommended	3	Required	Optional	Required	Optional
Doctoral	Required	Optional	3	Required	Required	Required	Required

Please note if these criteria vary for different programs: GRE-Subject scores are recommended for applicants to the Clinical Counseling and Experimental programs. CV not required for School Psychology and Experimental applicants.

Admissions Criteria:

GRE scores—medium
Research experience—high
Work experience—medium
Clinically related public service—high
GPA—high

Letters of recommendation—high
Interview—high
Statement of goals and objectives—medium
Undergraduate psychology preparation—medium

For additional information on admission requirements, visit http://www.radford.edu/content/chbs/home/psychology/programs.html.

Department Demographics

	Male (PT)	Female (PT)	Total	African-American/Black (PT)	Hispanic/Latino (PT)	Asian/Pacific Islander (PT)	American Indian/Alaska Native (PT)	Caucasian/White (PT)	Unknown	Multiethnic (PT)	ADA (PT)	Int'l (PT)
Students	15 (0)	59 (0)	74	4 (0)	1 (0)	1 (0)	0 (0)	66 (0)	2 (0)	0 (0)	0 (0)	0 (0)

Financial Information/Assistance

Tuition: For information on tuition costs, visit http://www.radford.edu/content/student-accounts/home/accounts/tuition.html. Tuition is subject to change. Tuition costs vary by program.

Master's:
State residents: $10,161 per academic year.
State residents: $424 per credit hour.
Nonstate residents: $19,814 per academic year.
Nonstate residents: $827 per credit hour.

Financial Assistance:

	Teaching Assistantship (% Receiving)	Teaching Assistantship Tuition Remission	Research Assistantship (% Receiving)	Research Assistantship Tuition Remission	Fellowship (% Receiving)	Fellowship Tuition Remission
First-Year Student	$10,000 (NA)	Partial	$9,000 (NA)	NA	$1,000 (NA)	NA
Advanced Student	$11,000 (NA)	Partial	$9,000 (NA)	NA	$600 (NA)	NA

For additional information on financial assistance, visit http://www.radford.edu/content/grad/home/cost/assistantships.html.

Employment of Department Graduates

Master's:
Enrolled in a psychology doctoral program: 5
Enrolled in another graduate/professional program: 1
Employed in other positions at a higher education institution: 2
Employed in a professional position in a school system: 7
Employed in business or industry: 12
Employed in a community mental health/counseling center: 2
Still seeking employment: 1
Other employment position: 2
Do not know: 2
Total: 34

Doctoral:
Employed in other positions at a higher education institution: 2
Employed in a community mental health/counseling center: 2
Other employment position: 1
Total: 5

Additional Information

Housing and Day Care: On-campus housing is available. See the following website for more information: http://www.radford.edu/content/residence-life/home.html. No on-campus day care facilities are available.

Information for Students With Physical Disabilities: See the following website: http://www.radford.edu/content/dro/home.html.

Special Facilities or Resources: In Summer 2016 we are moving to a new building that will house the entire college. The new building features several spaces dedicated to our department. We will have two new computer laboratories and numerous research space for use by graduate students. We will have a state-of-the-art animal lab facility, expanded space for the Center for Assessment and Psychological Services, a new Testing Library, and a new space for the Center for Gender Studies.

Application Information: College of Graduate and Professional Studies, P.O. Box 6928, Radford University, Radford, VA 24142. *Fee:* $50. *Online application:* https://www.applyweb.com/radg/index.ftl.

Regent University
Doctoral Program in Clinical Psychology
School of Psychology & Counseling
1000 Regent University Drive
Virginia Beach, VA 23464
Telephone: (757) 352-4296
Chairperson: Jennifer S. Ripley, PhD

E-mail: jennrip@regent.edu
Web: http://www.regent.edu/acad/schcou/academics/psyd/

Orientation, Objectives, and Emphasis of Department
The Doctoral Program in Clinical Psychology adopts a practitioner-scholar model of clinical training within an educational context committed to the integration of scientific psychology and a Christian worldview. The clinical training is broad and general, however couple and family therapy, clinical child psychology, forensic psychology, and health psychology are emphases among the faculty and in the curriculum.

Programs and Degrees Offered

Program	Degree	Application Deadline	Applica-tions Received	Accepted	New Admits Enrolled (PT)	Total Enrolled (PT)	Degrees Awarded in 2014–2015	Median Years to Complete Degree	Dismissed/ Withdrew
Clinical Psychology	PsyD	December 15 (Fall)	153	38	25 (0)	97 (0)	15	5.75	4
General Psychology	MA/MS	Rolling	99	30	21 (5)	26	0		4

APA Accreditation

Clinical PsyD: Student Outcome Data website: http://www.regent.edu/acad/schcou/aboutus/prog_eval/psyd/index.html.

Doctoral Degree (PsyD Clinical Psychology): For those doctoral students for whom a professional internship was required in this program prior to graduation:
Total students who applied for an internship: 20
Total students who obtained an internship: 19
Total students who obtained a paid internship: 19
Total students who obtained an unpaid internship: 0
Total students who were placed in APA/CPA-accredited internships: 17
Total students placed in internships not APA/CPA-accredited, but listed with the Association of Psychology Postdoctoral and Internship Centers (APPIC): 2
Total students placed in internships conforming to guidelines of the Council of Directors of School Psychology Programs (CDSPP): 0
Total students placed in internships that were not APA/CPA-accredited, APPIC or CDSSP listed: 0

Master's Degree (MA/MS General Psychology): An internship experience, such as a final research project or "capstone" experience is required of graduates.

Internships/Practica

All PsyD students complete a three-semester placement in the campus training clinic, the Psychological Services Center, during their second year. A three-semester practicum placement is completed during the third year and a two-semester practicum in the fourth year at any of a wide variety of community practicum sites such as military and VA clinics, inpatient brain injury units, psychiatric hospitals, group practices, community mental health agencies, outpatient practices, or correctional settings.

Admissions

Entries appear in the following order: required test or GPA, minimum score (if required)/median score of students entering in 2015–2016.

Program	Degree	GRE-V	GRE-Q	GRE-Writing	GRE-Subject	Under-graduate GPA	Last 2 Years GPA	Psychol-ogy GPA	Master's GPA
Clinical Psychology	PsyD	NA/NA	NA/NA	NA/NA	Not specified	3/NA	Not specified	Not specified	Not specified
General Psychology	MA/MS	Not specified	Not specified	Not specified	Not specified	Not specified	Not specified	Not specified	Not specified

Admissions Requirements:

Degree	GRE	GRE-Subject	Letters of Recom-mendation	Research Statement	Writing Sample	CV	Interview
Master's/Specialist	Optional	Optional	3	Required	Required	Required	None
Doctoral	Required	Optional	3	Required	Required	Required	Required

Please note if these criteria vary for different programs: Whole person review is used with an emphasis on academic and interpersonal skills and personal qualities and experiences to add to the learning environment.

Admissions Criteria:

GRE scores—high
Research experience—medium
Work experience—medium
Clinically related public service—medium
GPA—high

Letters of recommendation—medium
Interview—high
Statement of goals and objectives—medium
Undergraduate psychology preparation—medium
Leadership experiences—medium

For additional information on admission requirements, visit http://www.regent.edu/acad/schcou/admissions/adm_psy.htm.

Department Demographics

	Male (PT)	Female (PT)	Total	African-American/ Black (PT)	Hispanic/ Latino (PT)	Asian/ Pacific Islander (PT)	American Indian/ Alaska Native (PT)	Caucasian/ White (PT)	Unknown	Multiethnic (PT)	ADA (PT)	Int'l (PT)
Students	34 (2)	82 (3)	121	23 (1)	3 (0)	4 (0)	0 (0)	81 (4)	7 (0)	0 (0)	3 (0)	5 (0)

Financial Information/Assistance

Tuition: For information on tuition costs, visit http://www.regent.edu/acad/schcou/admissions/financial/cost_of_attendance.htm. Tuition is subject to change. Additional fees are assessed to students beyond the costs of tuition for the following: $200 Technology; $20 Council of Graduate Students; $10 Academic Services.

Doctoral:
State residents: $26,860 per academic year.
State residents: $790 per credit hour.
Nonstate residents: $26,860 per academic year.
Nonstate residents: $790 per credit hour.

Master's:
State residents: $19,500 per academic year.
State residents: $650 per credit hour.
Nonstate residents: $19,500 per academic year.
Nonstate residents: $650 per credit hour.

Financial Assistance:

	Teaching Assistantship (% Receiving)	Teaching Assistantship Tuition Remission	Research Assistantship (% Receiving)	Research Assistantship Tuition Remission	Fellowship (% Receiving)	Fellowship Tuition Remission
First-Year Student	NA (NA)	NA	NA (NA)	NA	$4,900 (100)	Partial
Advanced Student	$7,500 (8)	Partial	$3,500 (10)	NA	$5,200 (100)	NA

For additional information on financial assistance, visit http://www.regent.edu/acad/schcou/admissions/financial/.

Employment of Department Graduates

Doctoral:
Enrolled in a postdoctoral residency/fellowship: 5
Employed in independent practice: 3
Employed in other positions at a higher education institution: 1
Employed in a hospital/medical center: 6
Do not know: 3
Total: 18

Additional Information

Housing and Day Care: On-campus housing is available. See the following website for more information: http://www.regent.edu/campus/housing/. No on-campus day care facilities are available.

Information for Students With Physical Disabilities: See the following website: http://www.regent.edu/admin/stusrv/disabilities/.

Personal Behavior Statement: http://www.regent.edu/admin/stusrv/student_handbook.cfm.

Special Facilities or Resources: Regent is located in Virginia Beach, Virginia which is part of Tidewater, the largest urban area in Virginia. There are numerous community resources for practica. The campus also houses the Psychological Services Center, our doctoral training clinic that provides services to the campus and surrounding community. The PSC includes state-of-the-art technology for videotaping and observation of clinical activities.

Application Information: Enrollment Support Services, 1000 Regent University Drive, LIB 102; Virginia Beach, VA 23464. *Fee:* $50. *Online application:* http://www.regent.edu/admissions/application.html.

Virginia Commonwealth University

Department of Psychology
Humanities and Sciences
806 West Franklin Street, Box 842018
Richmond, VA 23284-2018
Telephone: (804) 828-1193
Chairperson: Wendy Kliewer

E-mail: wkliewer@vcu.edu
Web: http://www.psychology.vcu.edu/

Orientation, Objectives, and Emphasis of Department

The graduate programs in psychology are designed to provide a core education in the basic science of psychology and to enable students to develop skills specific to their area of interest. Students are educated first as psychologists, and are then guided to develop competence in a more specialized area relevant to their scholarly and professional objectives. In addition to formal research requirements for the thesis and dissertation, students in the graduate programs are encouraged to conduct independent research, participate in research teams, or collaborate with faculty conducting research on an ongoing basis. The clinical and counseling psychology programs strongly emphasize the scientist–practitioner model. Students in the clinical program may elect to develop specialized competency in one of two different concentrations: behavioral medicine or clinical child/adolescent. The counseling psychology program prepares students to function in a variety of research and applied settings and has a strong emphasis on leadership development. The general program emphasizes the acquisition of experimental skills as well as advanced training in one of two specialty areas: developmental psychology and social psychology. The health program provides theoretical background of both basic and applied research skills for their students.

Programs and Degrees Offered

Program	Degree	Application Deadline	Applications Received	Accepted	New Admits Enrolled (PT)	Total Enrolled (PT)	Degrees Awarded in 2014–2015	Median Years to Complete Degree	Dismissed/ Withdrew
Clinical Psychology	PhD	December 1 (Fall)	269	14	8 (0)	51 (0)	5	6	0
Counseling Psychology	PhD	December 1 (Fall)	96	7	5	29	5	5	0
Social Psychology	PhD	December 1 (Fall)	43	6	3 (0)	8 (0)	1	5	0
Developmental Psychology	PhD	December 1 (Fall)	20	6	3 (0)	12 (0)	1	8	0
Health Psychology	PhD	December 1 (Fall)	28	9	7 (0)	23 (0)	2	4.75	0

APA Accreditation

Clinical PhD: Student Outcome Data website: http://www.psychology.vcu.edu/clinical/index.shtml.
Counseling PhD: Student Outcome Data website: http://www.psychology.vcu.edu/counseling/program.shtml.

Doctoral Degree (PhD Clinical Psychology): For those doctoral students for whom a professional internship was required in this program prior to graduation:
Total students who applied for an internship. 8
Total students who obtained an internship: 8
Total students who obtained a paid internship: 8
Total students who obtained an unpaid internship: 0
Total students who were placed in APA/CPA-accredited internships: 8
Total students placed in internships not APA/CPA-accredited, but listed with the Association of Psychology Postdoctoral and Internship Centers (APPIC): 0

Total students placed in internships conforming to guidelines of the Council of Directors of School Psychology Programs (CDSPP): 0
Total students placed in internships that were not APA/CPA-accredited, APPIC or CDSSP listed: 0

Doctoral Degree (PhD Counseling Psychology): For those doctoral students for whom a professional internship was required in this program prior to graduation:
Total students who applied for an internship: 5
Total students who obtained an internship: 5
Total students who obtained a paid internship: 5
Total students who obtained an unpaid internship: 0
Total students who were placed in APA/CPA-accredited internships: 4
Total students placed in internships not APA/CPA-accredited, but listed with the Association of Psychology Postdoctoral and Internship Centers (APPIC): 1
Total students placed in internships conforming to guidelines of the Council of Directors of School Psychology Programs (CDSPP): 0
Total students placed in internships that were not APA/CPA-accredited, APPIC or CDSSP listed: 0

Internships/Practica

Practicum (external) and internship are required for clinical and counseling programs. Sites range from the following: VCU Medical Center facilities, VA hospitals, counseling centers, community mental health agencies, Richmond Children's Hospitals, juvenile facilities, and state/federal prisons. Students in the clinical and counseling programs also spend 1 or 2 years at the department's training clinic, the Center for Psychological Services and Development. Students in all programs also have the opportunity to participate as a TA in service learning classes in community agencies/organizations.

Admissions

Entries appear in the following order: required test or GPA, minimum score (if required)/median score of students entering in 2015–2016.

Program	Degree	GRE-V	GRE-Q	GRE-Writing	GRE-Subject	Under-graduate GPA	Last 2 Years GPA	Psychol-ogy GPA	Master's GPA
Clinical Psychology	PhD	NA/160	NA/156	NA/NA	Not specified	NA/3.71	NA/NA	NA/NA	Not specified
Counseling Psychology	PhD	NA/159	NA/154	NA/NA	Not specified	NA/3.62	NA/NA	NA/NA	Not specified
Social Psychology	PhD	NA/NA	NA/NA	NA/NA	Not specified	NA/NA	NA/NA	NA/NA	Not specified
Developmental Psychology	PhD	NA/NA	NA/NA	NA/NA	Not specified	NA/NA	NA/NA	NA/NA	Not specified
Health Psychology	PhD	NA/NA	NA/NA	NA/NA	Not specified	NA/NA	NA/NA	NA/NA	Not specified

Admissions Requirements:

Degree	GRE	GRE-Subject	Letters of Recom-mendation	Research Statement	Writing Sample	CV	Interview
Doctoral	Required	Optional	3	Required	Recom-mended	Required	Required

Please note if these criteria vary for different programs: All programs emphasize research experience, GPA, letters of recommendation, and GREs. The clinical and counseling programs emphasize match between student interests and faculty interests more than the general/experimental and health programs. Clinical and counseling programs also emphasize importance of clinically related experiences.

Admissions Criteria:

GRE scores—high
Research experience—high
Work experience—high
Clinically related public service—medium
GPA—high

Letters of recommendation—high
Interview—medium
Statement of goals and objectives—medium
Undergraduate psychology preparation—medium

For additional information on admission requirements, visit http://www.psychology.vcu.edu/graduate/prospective/index.shtml.

Department Demographics

	Male (PT)	Female (PT)	Total	African-American/ Black (PT)	Hispanic/ Latino (PT)	Asian/ Pacific Islander (PT)	American Indian/ Alaska Native (PT)	Caucasian/ White (PT)	Unknown	Multiethnic (PT)	ADA (PT)	Int'l (PT)
Students	25 (0)	98 (0)	123	19 (0)	9 (0)	5 (0)	0 (0)	89 (0)	0 (0)	1 (0)	0 (0)	6 (0)

Financial Information/Assistance

Tuition: For information on tuition costs, visit http://accounting.vcu.edu/tuition/. Tuition is subject to change. Additional fees are assessed to students beyond the costs of tuition for the following: activity, library, technology, and health fees.

Doctoral:
State residents: $8,768 per academic year.
State residents: $487 per credit hour.
Nonstate residents: $21,469 per academic year.
Nonstate residents: $1,038 per credit hour.

Financial Assistance:

	Teaching Assistantship (% Receiving)	Teaching Assistantship Tuition Remission	Research Assistantship (% Receiving)	Research Assistantship Tuition Remission	Fellowship (% Receiving)	Fellowship Tuition Remission
First-Year Student	$15,000 (89)	Full	$15,000 (11)	Full	NA (NA)	Full
Advanced Student	$15,000 (53)	Full	$15,000 (47)	Full	NA (NA)	Full

For additional information on financial assistance, visit http://www.graduate.vcu.edu/student/financing.html.

Employment of Department Graduates

Doctoral:
Enrolled in a postdoctoral residency/fellowship: 5
Employed in independent practice: 1
Employed in an academic position at a university: 4
Employed in government agency: 1
Do not know: 4
Total: 15

Additional Information

Housing and Day Care: On-campus housing is available. See the following website for more information: http://www.housing.vcu.edu/. On-campus day care facilities are available. See the following website for more information: http://cdc.soe.vcu.edu/.

Information for Students With Physical Disabilities: See the following website: http://www.students.vcu.edu/dss/.

Special Facilities or Resources: The department maintains laboratories for research across all programs. The department also operates the Center for Psychological Services and Development, which provides mental health services for clients referred from throughout the Richmond metropolitan area. Students in the clinical and counseling programs complete practica in the Center and in a variety of off-campus practicum facilities located in the community. Cooperation with a variety of programs and departments at the University's medical school is extensive for both research and training.

Application Information: Virginia Commonwealth University, Graduate School, Moseley House, 1001 Grove Avenue, P.O. Box 843051, Richmond, VA 23284-3051. *Fee:* $65. *Online application:* http://graduate.admissions.vcu.edu/apply/.

Virginia Consortium Program in Clinical Psychology

Program in Clinical Psychology
EVMS, NSU & ODU
c/o Norfolk State University, 700 Park Ave/MCAR-410
Norfolk, VA 23504
Telephone: (757) 451-7733
Director of Clinical Training: Robin J. Lewis, PhD

E-mail: rlewis@odu.edu
Web: http://www.odu.edu/vcpcp/

Orientation, Objectives, and Emphasis of Department

The Virginia Consortium is a single, unified 4+1 clinical psychology program cosponsored by three institutions: Eastern Virginia Medical School, Norfolk State University, and Old Dominion University. We believe clinical psychologists are best educated as scientist–practitioners. Scientific knowledge and methods form the foundation for effective clinical practice which, in turn, informs future research. Thus, it is essential to develop skills to design and conduct research as well as implement empirically based techniques in practice. Our faculty believes that extensive exposure to theory, research, and practice is key in training clinical psychologists. The curriculum is generalist in content and in theoretical orientation. Students are continually involved in research and practicum training from the outset. Knowledge acquired in the classroom is applied in an orderly sequence of supervised practica. In Year 3, the student pursues individual interests by integrating individualized coursework with advanced practica and clinical dissertation. In Year 4, the student continues advanced practica and competes for a full-time clinical internship to be taken in Year 5. An approved dissertation proposal is required to eligible for internship.

Programs and Degrees Offered

Program	Degree	Application Deadline	Applications Received	Accepted	New Admits Enrolled (PT)	Total Enrolled (PT)	Degrees Awarded in 2014–2015	Median Years to Complete Degree	Dismissed/Withdrew
Virginia Consortium Program in Clinical Psychology	PhD	December 1 (Fall)	101	9	6 (0)	32 (0)	2	5.3	0

APA Accreditation

Clinical PhD: Student Outcome Data website: http://sci.odu.edu/vcpcp/outcomes.html.

Doctoral Degree (PhD Virginia Consortium Program in Clinical Psychology): For those doctoral students for whom a professional internship was required in this program prior to graduation:
Total students who applied for an internship: 6
Total students who obtained an internship: 6
Total students who obtained a paid internship: 6
Total students who obtained an unpaid internship: 0
Total students who were placed in APA/CPA-accredited internships: 6
Total students placed in internships not APA/CPA-accredited, but listed with the Association of Psychology Postdoctoral and Internship Centers (APPIC): 0
Total students placed in internships conforming to guidelines of the Council of Directors of School Psychology Programs (CDSPP): 0
Total students placed in internships that were not APA/CPA-accredited, APPIC or CDSSP listed: 0

Internships/Practica

Practicum training is offered in a variety of diverse settings: mental health centers, medical hospitals, children's residential treatment facilities, public school systems, university counseling centers, social services clinics, private practices, and rehabilitation units. Settings include inpatient, residential, and outpatient. Populations include children, adolescents, adults, and the elderly from most socioeconomic levels and ethnic groups. Services include most forms of assessment; individual, group, and some family intervention modalities; and consultative and other indirect services. Placements are arranged to ensure that each student is exposed to several settings and populations.

Admissions

Entries appear in the following order: required test or GPA, minimum score (if required)/median score of students entering in 2015–2016.

Program	Degree	GRE-V	GRE-Q	GRE-Writing	GRE-Subject	Under-graduate GPA	Last 2 Years GPA	Psychol-ogy GPA	Master's GPA
Virginia Consortium Program in Clinical Psychology	PhD	NA/160	NA/155	NA/4.25	Not specified	3/3.54	3/NA	3/NA	3/NA

Admissions Requirements:

Degree	GRE	GRE-Subject	Letters of Recom-mendation	Research Statement	Writing Sample	CV	Interview
Doctoral	Required	Optional	3	Required	None	Required	Required

Admissions Criteria:

GRE scores—medium
Research experience—high
Work experience—low
Clinically related public service—high
GPA—high

Letters of recommendation—medium
Interview—high
Statement of goals and objectives—high
Undergraduate psychology preparation—high

For additional information on admission requirements, visit http://sci.odu.edu/vcpcp/admission1.html.

Department Demographics

	Male (PT)	Female (PT)	Total	African-American/ Black (PT)	Hispanic/ Latino (PT)	Asian/ Pacific Islander (PT)	American Indian/ Alaska Native (PT)	Caucasian/ White (PT)	Unknown	Multiethnic (PT)	ADA (PT)	Int'l (PT)
Students	7 (0)	25 (0)	32	6 (0)	2 (0)	1 (0)	0 (0)	22 (0)	0 (0)	1 (0)	0 (0)	0 (0)

Financial Information/Assistance

Tuition: For information on tuition costs, visit http://sci.odu.edu/vcpcp/admission1.html. Tuition is subject to change. Additional fees are assessed to students beyond the costs of tuition for the following: $150 graduation fee.

Doctoral:
State residents: $6,000 per academic year.
Nonstate residents: $6,000 per academic year.

Financial Assistance:

	Teaching Assistantship (% Receiving)	Teaching Assistantship Tuition Remission	Research Assistantship (% Receiving)	Research Assistantship Tuition Remission	Fellowship (% Receiving)	Fellowship Tuition Remission
First-Year Student	$14,667 (50)	Partial	$9,333 (50)	Partial	NA (NA)	NA
Advanced Student	$11,333 (35)	Partial	$12,375 (52)	Partial	NA (NA)	NA

For additional information on financial assistance, visit http://sci.odu.edu/vcpcp/admission1.html.

Employment of Department Graduates

Doctoral:
Enrolled in a postdoctoral residency/fellowship: 1
Employed in a hospital/medical center: 1
Total: 2

Additional Information

Housing and Day Care: No on-campus housing is available. No on-campus day care facilities are available.

Information for Students With Physical Disabilities: See the following website: https://www.odu.edu/life/diversity/problem/disabilities.

Special Facilities or Resources: Students are considered full-time in all three sponsoring schools. This permits access to: three libraries with several computerized literature search databases and 400 periodicals in psychology; three computing centers; multiple health services; and a variety of athletic facilities.

Application Information: *Fee:* $65. *Online application:* http://www.odu.edu/admission/apply.

Virginia Polytechnic Institute and State University

Department of Psychology
College of Science
109 Williams Hall
Blacksburg, VA 24061
Telephone: (540) 231-6581
Chairperson: Robert S. Stephens

E-mail: jdunsmor@vt.edu
Web: http://www.psyc.vt.edu/

Orientation, Objectives, and Emphasis of Department

The graduate program in each concentration is designed to ensure that students receive excellent preparation in research methods and psychological theory to be successful in academic or applied settings. Training and experience in the teaching of psychology is available. The Clinical Science concentration is based on the clinical scientist model and emphasizes research methods and theory in understanding, preventing, and treating health and mental health problems in adults and children. Clinical foci include child, adult, and health psychology. The Developmental Science concentration trains future scholars through mentored research training coupled with formal coursework in a variety of relevant content areas. Students receive practical experience in research laboratories and develop expertise in their own areas of specialization through individualized plans of study. The Industrial/Organizational Psychology concentration prepares students for research and teaching positions as well as for solution of individual, group, and organizational problems in applied work settings. Psychometrics, research design, and statistics are emphasized. The Biological Psychology concentration trains research-oriented experimental psychologists through mentorship. Training is offered from perspectives of behavioral neuroscience, psychophysiology, and neuropsychology. The primary mission of the concentration is to develop strong experimental researchers who will pursue careers in academic or non-academic settings.

Programs and Degrees Offered

Program	Degree	Application Deadline	Applications Received	Accepted	New Admits Enrolled (PT)	Total Enrolled (PT)	Degrees Awarded in 2014–2015	Median Years to Complete Degree	Dismissed/ Withdrew
Clinical Science	PhD	December 1 (Fall)	163	14	6 (0)	37 (0)	4	6.5	0
Industrial/ Organizational Psychology	PhD	December 1 (Fall)	79	7	4 (0)	17	2	6	1
Developmental Science	PhD	December 1 (Fall)	30	4	4	12	2	5.5	0
Biological Psychology	PhD	December 1 (Fall)	18	2	1	15	1	6	0

APA Accreditation

Clinical PhD: Student Outcome Data website: http://www.psyc.vt.edu/graduate/clinical/.

Doctoral Degree (PhD Clinical Science): For those doctoral students for whom a professional internship was required in this program prior to graduation:
Total students who applied for an internship: 9
Total students who obtained an internship: 8
Total students who obtained a paid internship: 8
Total students who obtained an unpaid internship: 0
Total students who were placed in APA/CPA-accredited internships: 8
Total students placed in internships not APA/CPA-accredited, but listed with the Association of Psychology Postdoctoral and Internship Centers (APPIC): 0
Total students placed in internships conforming to guidelines of the Council of Directors of School Psychology Programs (CDSPP): 0
Total students placed in internships that were not APA/CPA-accredited, APPIC or CDSSP listed: 0

Internships/Practica

Students in Clinical psychology complete practica in department-run, off-campus clinics serving adults and children from the community. They also complete an externship in one of a variety of local agency and hospital settings. They also are required to complete a predoctoral clinical internship as part of the PhD. Students in Industrial/Organizational psychology are encouraged to pursue summer internships.

Admissions

Entries appear in the following order: required test or GPA, minimum score (if required)/median score of students entering in 2015–2016.

Program	Degree	GRE-V	GRE-Q	GRE-Writing	GRE-Subject	Under-graduate GPA	Last 2 Years GPA	Psychol-ogy GPA	Master's GPA
Clinical Science	PhD	NA/160	NA/157	NA/NA	Not specified	NA/3.74	Not specified	Not specified	Not specified
Industrial/ Organizational Psychology	PhD	NA/159	NA/157	NA/NA	Not specified	NA/3.57	Not specified	Not specified	Not specified
Developmental Science	PhD	NA/159	NA/158	NA/NA	Not specified	NA/3.95	Not specified	Not specified	Not specified
Biological Psychology	PhD	NA/154	NA/154	NA/NA	Not specified	NA/3.66	Not specified	Not specified	Not specified

Admissions Requirements:

Degree	GRE	GRE-Subject	Letters of Recom-mendation	Research Statement	Writing Sample	CV	Interview
Doctoral	Required	None	3	Required	Optional	Required	Required

Admissions Criteria:

GRE scores—medium
Research experience—high
Work experience—low
Clinically related public service—medium
GPA—high

Letters of recommendation—high
Interview—medium
Statement of goals and objectives—high
Undergraduate psychology preparation—medium

For additional information on admission requirements, visit http://www.psyc.vt.edu/graduate/.

Department Demographics

	Male (PT)	Female (PT)	Total	African-American/ Black (PT)	Hispanic/ Latino (PT)	Asian/ Pacific Islander (PT)	American Indian/ Alaska Native (PT)	Caucasian/ White (PT)	Unknown	Multiethnic (PT)	ADA (PT)	Int'l (PT)
Students	31 (0)	50 (0)	81	4 (0)	7 (0)	13 (0)	0 (0)	52 (0)	1 (0)	4 (0)	0 (0)	5 (0)

Financial Information/Assistance

Tuition: For information on tuition costs, visit http://www.bursar.vt.edu/tuition/. Tuition is subject to change. Additional fees are assessed to students beyond the costs of tuition for the following: Comprehensive fees: $876; Technology fee: $33; Library fee: $10.

Doctoral:
State residents: $13,023 per academic year.
State residents: $621 per credit hour.
Nonstate residents: $24,588 per academic year.
Nonstate residents: $1,230 per credit hour.

Financial Assistance:

	Teaching Assistantship (% Receiving)	Teaching Assistantship Tuition Remission	Research Assistantship (% Receiving)	Research Assistantship Tuition Remission	Fellowship (% Receiving)	Fellowship Tuition Remission
First-Year Student	$15,066 (NA)	Full	$15,066 (NA)	Full	NA (NA)	NA
Advanced Student	$15,948 (NA)	Full	$15,948 (NA)	Full	NA (NA)	NA

Employment of Department Graduates

Doctoral:
Enrolled in a postdoctoral residency/fellowship: 4
Employed in independent practice: 1
Employed in an academic position at a university: 1
Employed in academic position at a 2-year/4-year college: 1
Employed in other positions at a higher education institution: 1
Employed in government agency: 1
Total: 9

Additional Information

Housing and Day Care: On-campus housing is available. See the following website for more information: http://www.housing.vt. edu. On-campus day care facilities are available. See the following website for more information: http://www.humandevelopment. vt.edu/CDCLR/cdclr.html.

Information for Students With Physical Disabilities: See the following website: http://www.ssd.vt.edu/.

Special Facilities or Resources: The Psychological Services Center and Child Study Center are located off-campus and provide the foundation for practicum and research training in Clinical Psychology. The Center for Research in Health Behavior is also located off-campus and is primarily involved in prevention research supported by the National Institutes of Health. Virginia Tech Community Partners is another off-campus research facility, located in downtown Roanoke. Faculty, students, and staff benefit from Virginia Tech's state-of-the-art communications system that links every dormitory room, laboratory, office, and classroom to computing capabilities, audio and video data, and the World Wide Web. The entire campus has easy access to supercomputers across the country, worldwide libraries and data systems. Department resources also include two state-of-the-art laboratories that are dedicated to undergraduate and graduate teaching and research. The psychophysiological laboratory includes eight computer workstations, five EEG/Evoked Potential work stations (32 channel Neuroscan; Neurosearch-24), eye tracker equipment, Coulbourn physiological units, and extensive perception equipment. The other computer laboratory includes 25 computer workstations with cognitive and neurophysiological experiments, SAS and SPSS statistical packages, and Bilog and Multilog programs. Graduate students also have access to PC and Macintosh computers for word processing and Internet use.

Application Information: Graduate Admissions Coordinator, 109 Williams Hall, Department of Psychology 0436, Virginia Tech, Blacksburg, VA 24061. *Fee:* $75. *Online application:* http://applyto.graduateschool.vt.edu/.

Virginia, University of
Curry Programs in Clinical and School Psychology
Curry School of Education
P.O. Box 400267
Charlottesville, VA 22904-4267
Telephone: (434) 924-7472
Director: Jason Downer

E-mail: jd2fe@virginia.edu
Web: http://curry.virginia.edu/academics/offerings/clinical-school-psychology

Orientation, Objectives, and Emphasis of Department
The primary goal of the training program in the Curry Programs in Clinical and School Psychology is to produce clinical and school psychologists who will make substantial contributions to the field in a variety of professional and scientific roles. The majority of graduates seek leadership positions in settings such as medical centers, schools, and mental health agencies, while others pursue academic and research careers. All students complete a common core of coursework and practica in both basic science and professional skills. Students have the opportunity for specialized training and research in concentration areas such as school interventions, family therapy, forensic psychology, and neuropsychology, among others. The predominant theoretical and practice orientations of the faculty are cognitive behavioral, psychodynamic, and family systems. All students are expected to develop clinical and research skills, and the integration of clinical, classroom, and research experiences is emphasized. Many students in the PhD program pursue training in both clinical and school psychology through the clinical-school track. The program is fully APA-accredited as a Combined Clinical and School Psychology program, and NASP-accredited as a doctoral School Psychology Program.

Programs and Degrees Offered

Program	Degree	Application Deadline	Applications Received	Accepted	New Admits Enrolled (PT)	Total Enrolled (PT)	Degrees Awarded in 2014–2015	Median Years to Complete Degree	Dismissed/ Withdrew
Curry Program in Clinical and School Psychology	PhD	December 15 (Fall)	131	4	4 (0)	22 (0)	6	5	0

APA Accreditation
Combination PhD: Student Outcome Data website: http://curry.virginia.edu/academics/degrees/doctor-of-philosophy/ph.d.-in-clinical-and-school-psychology.

Doctoral Degree (PhD Curry Program in Clinical and School Psychology): For those doctoral students for whom a professional internship was required in this program prior to graduation:
Total students who applied for an internship: 5
Total students who obtained an internship: 5
Total students who obtained a paid internship: 5
Total students who obtained an unpaid internship: 0
Total students who were placed in APA/CPA-accredited internships: 5
Total students placed in internships not APA/CPA-accredited, but listed with the Association of Psychology Postdoctoral and Internship Centers (APPIC): 0
Total students placed in internships conforming to guidelines of the Council of Directors of School Psychology Programs (CDSPP): 0
Total students placed in internships that were not APA/CPA-accredited, APPIC or CDSSP listed: 0

Internships/Practica
Students undertake external clinical practica and school internships in area public and private schools, state mental hospitals/ residential treatment centers for children or adults, a regional medically affiliated children's rehabilitation center, a family stress clinic, a federal correctional facility, and other mental health settings in the university and community. During the fifth year of training, students complete a full-time 1-year internship in clinical psychology.

Admissions

Entries appear in the following order: required test or GPA, minimum score (if required)/median score of students entering in 2015–2016.

Program	Degree	GRE-V	GRE-Q	GRE-Writing	GRE-Subject	Under-graduate GPA	Last 2 Years GPA	Psychol-ogy GPA	Master's GPA
Curry Program in Clinical and School Psychology	PhD	NA/NA	NA/NA	NA/NA	Not specified	NA/3.6	Not specified	Not specified	Not specified

Admissions Requirements:

Degree	GRE	GRE-Subject	Letters of Recommendation	Research Statement	Writing Sample	CV	Interview
Doctoral	Required	Recommended	2	Required	Optional	Required	Required

Admissions Criteria:

GRE scores—medium
Research experience—medium
Work experience—medium
Clinically related public service—medium
GPA—high

Letters of recommendation—high
Interview—high
Statement of goals and objectives—high
Undergraduate psychology preparation—medium

Department Demographics

	Male (PT)	Female (PT)	Total	African-American/Black (PT)	Hispanic/Latino (PT)	Asian/Pacific Islander (PT)	American Indian/Alaska Native (PT)	Caucasian/White (PT)	Unknown	Multiethnic (PT)	ADA (PT)	Int'l (PT)
Students	2 (0)	20 (0)	22	3 (0)	1 (0)	2 (0)	0 (0)	14 (0)	0 (0)	2 (0)	0 (0)	0 (0)

Financial Information/Assistance

Tuition: For information on tuition costs, visit http://sfs.virginia.edu/finances.

Doctoral:
State residents: $18,124 per academic year.
Nonstate residents: $28,598 per academic year.

Financial Assistance:

	Teaching Assistantship (% Receiving)	Teaching Assistantship Tuition Remission	Research Assistantship (% Receiving)	Research Assistantship Tuition Remission	Fellowship (% Receiving)	Fellowship Tuition Remission
First-Year Student	NA (NA)	NA	$7,000 (100)	NA	$7,000 (100)	Full
Advanced Student	$1,000 (20)	NA	$7,000 (100)	NA	$7,000 (100)	Full

Employment of Department Graduates

Doctoral:
Enrolled in a postdoctoral residency/fellowship: 5
Employed in a professional position in a school system: 1
Total: 6

Additional Information

Housing and Day Care: On-campus housing is available. See the following website for more information: http://www.virginia.edu/housing/grad.php. On-campus day care facilities are available. See the following website for more information: http://www.virginia.edu/childdevelopmentcenter/.

Information for Students With Physical Disabilities: See the following website: http://www.virginia.edu/accessibility/.

Special Facilities or Resources: The Curry Program operates a comprehensive psychological clinic, the Center for Clinical Psychology Services, serving families, couples, and individuals of all ages and diverse backgrounds, within the Sheila Johnson Center for Human Services (SJC). The Sheila Johnson Center is well equipped for live and videotaped supervision and conveniently located in Bavaro Hall, with faculty and student offices nearby. In addition, the Program has close working relationships with numerous community agencies, schools, clinics, and hospitals that permit training and research in many different mental health and educational settings. Our students have research and consultation opportunities with numerous projects, including the Center for Positive Youth Development, Young Women Leaders Program, Virginia Youth Violence Project, and the Center for the Advanced Study of Teaching and Learning. The Curry School of Education is a national leader in instructional technology, with outstanding computing facilities, technology support, and smart classrooms. Students enjoy easy access to the extensive University of Virginia Library system, which includes a collection of nearly 5 million volumes and has state-of-the-art electronic library resources.

Application Information: Curry School of Education Graduate Admissions, P.O. Box 401104, Charlottesville, VA 22904. *Fee:* $75. *Online application:* http://curry.virginia.edu/admissions/doctoral-admissions.

Virginia, University of
Department of Psychology
102 Gilmer Hall, P.O. Box 400400
Charlottesville, VA 22904-4400
Telephone: (434) 982-4750
Chairperson: David L. Hill

E-mail: psychology@virginia.edu
Web: http://www.virginia.edu/psychology/

Orientation, Objectives, and Emphasis of Department
The department emphasizes research on a wide spectrum of psychological issues with clinical, developmental, social, cognitive, sensory and systems neuroscience, quantitative, and community specialties. In addition, new tracks are being developed, such as social ecology and development, law and psychology, family, and minority issues.

Programs and Degrees Offered

Program	Degree	Application Deadline	Applica-tions Received	Accepted	New Admits Enrolled (PT)	Total Enrolled (PT)	Degrees Awarded in 2014–2015	Median Years to Complete Degree	Dismissed/Withdrew
Clinical Psychology	PhD	December 15 (Fall)	242	8	3	23 (0)	4	7	0
Cognitive Psychology	PhD	December 15 (Fall)	30	2	0 (0)	8 (0)	0		0
Community Psychology	PhD	December 15 (Fall)	17	2	1 (0)	7 (0)	1	6	0
Developmental Psychology	PhD	December 15 (Fall)	56	2	2 (0)	9 (0)	2	5	0

Programs and Degrees Offered (con't.)

Program	Degree	Application Deadline	Applica-tions Received	Accepted	New Admits Enrolled (PT)	Total Enrolled (PT)	Degrees Awarded in 2014–2015	Median Years to Complete Degree	Dismissed/ Withdrew
Quantitative Psychology	PhD	December 15 (Fall)	28	2	2 (0)	7 (0)	1	5	0
Social Psychology	PhD	December 15 (Fall)	146	4	0 (0)	15 (0)	5	6	0
Sensory and Systems Neuroscience	PhD	December 15 (Fall)	15	1	1 (0)	5 (0)	0		0

APA Accreditation

Clinical PhD: Student Outcome Data website: http://cacsprd.web.virginia.edu/Psych/ResearchAreas/Clinical.

Doctoral Degree (PhD Clinical Psychology): For those doctoral students for whom a professional internship was required in this program prior to graduation:

Total students who applied for an internship: 4
Total students who obtained an internship: 4
Total students who obtained a paid internship: 4
Total students who obtained an unpaid internship: 0
Total students who were placed in APA/CPA-accredited internships: 4
Total students placed in internships not APA/CPA-accredited, but listed with the Association of Psychology Postdoctoral and Internship Centers (APPIC): 0
Total students placed in internships conforming to guidelines of the Council of Directors of School Psychology Programs (CDSPP): 0
Total students placed in internships that were not APA/CPA-accredited, APPIC or CDSSP listed: 0

Internships/Practica

For the clinical program, multiple practica are available at the University Hospital, State Mental Hospital for children and adults, Kluge Children's Center; Community Mental Health Center; Law and Psychiatry Unit; Department Clinic and other places as connections and student interest suggest.

Admissions

Entries appear in the following order: required test or GPA, minimum score (if required)/median score of students entering in 2015–2016.

Program	Degree	GRE-V	GRE-Q	GRE-Writing	GRE-Subject	Under-graduate GPA	Last 2 Years GPA	Psychol-ogy GPA	Master's GPA
Clinical Psychology	PhD	NA/NA	NA/NA	NA/NA	Not specified	NA/3.85	NA/NA	NA/NA	NA/NA
Cognitive Psychology	PhD	NA/NA	NA/NA	NA/NA	Not specified	NA/NA	NA/NA	NA/NA	NA/NA
Community Psychology	PhD	NA/NA	NA/NA	NA/NA	Not specified	NA/NA	NA/NA	NA/NA	NA/NA
Developmental Psychology	PhD	NA/NA	NA/NA	NA/NA	Not specified	NA/NA	NA/NA	NA/NA	NA/NA
Quantitative Psychology	PhD	NA/NA	NA/NA	NA/NA	Not specified	NA/NA	NA/NA	NA/NA	NA/NA
Social Psychology	PhD	NA/NA	NA/NA	NA/NA	Not specified	NA/NA	NA/NA	NA/NA	NA/NA
Sensory and Systems Neuroscience	PhD	NA/NA	NA/NA	NA/NA	Not specified	NA/NA	NA/NA	NA/NA	NA/NA

Admissions Requirements:

Degree	GRE	GRE-Subject	Letters of Recommendation	Research Statement	Writing Sample	CV	Interview
Doctoral	Required	None	3	Required	Recommended	Optional	Required

Please note if these criteria vary for different programs: Publications and presentations at conferences are valued as actual work experience in an area related to the degree sought.

Admissions Criteria:

GRE scores—medium
Research experience—high
Work experience—medium
Clinically related public service—low

GPA—high
Letters of recommendation—high
Interview—medium
Statement of goals and objectives—high

For additional information on admission requirements, visit http://cacsprd.web.virginia.edu/Psych/Graduates/admissions.

Department Demographics

	Male (PT)	Female (PT)	Total	African-American/ Black (PT)	Hispanic/ Latino (PT)	Asian/ Pacific Islander (PT)	American Indian/ Alaska Native (PT)	Caucasian/ White (PT)	Unknown	Multiethnic (PT)	ADA (PT)	Int'l (PT)
Students	21 (0)	53 (0)	74	2 (0)	3 (0)	9 (0)	0 (0)	59 (0)	0 (0)	1 (0)	0 (0)	5 (0)

Financial Information/Assistance

Tuition: For information on tuition costs, visit https://sfs.virginia.edu/grad/tuition. Tuition is subject to change.

Doctoral:
State residents: $14,518 per academic year.
Nonstate residents: $24,316 per academic year.

Financial Assistance:

	Teaching Assistantship (% Receiving)	Teaching Assistantship Tuition Remission	Research Assistantship (% Receiving)	Research Assistantship Tuition Remission	Fellowship (% Receiving)	Fellowship Tuition Remission
First-Year Student	$9,300 (NA)	Full	$20,000 (NA)	Full	$14,700 (NA)	NA
Advanced Student	$9,300 (NA)	Full	$20,000 (NA)	Full	$14,700 (NA)	NA

For additional information on financial assistance, visit http://cacsprd.web.virginia.edu/Psych/Graduates/finaid.

Employment of Department Graduates

Doctoral:
Enrolled in a postdoctoral residency/fellowship: 7
Employed in independent practice: 1
Employed in an academic position at a university: 2
Employed in business or industry: 1
Employed in government agency: 1
Total: 12

Additional Information

Housing and Day Care: On-campus housing is available. See the following website for more information: http://www.virginia.edu/housing/grad.php. On-campus day care facilities are available. See the following website for more information: http://www.virginia.edu/childdevelopmentcenter/.

Information for Students With Physical Disabilities: See the following website: http://www.virginia.edu/studenthealth/sdac/sdac.html.

Special Facilities or Resources: The department has in excess of 50,000 square feet for offices, laboratories, seminar rooms, and classrooms. Special facilities include rooms for psychophysical investigations, a suite of rooms devoted to developmental, clinical, and social laboratories, and specialized research facilities for the study of animal behavior and psychobiology. Sound-attenuated rooms, electrically shielded rooms, numerous one-way vision rooms, surgery and vivarium rooms, and a darkroom are all available. There are ample computer facilities. All labs are connected to a local area network and a university-wide local area network. This allows the labs to connect to other available University machines such as IBM RS/6000 Unix machines.

Application Information: Dean of the Graduate School, The University of Virginia, P.O. Box 400775, 437 Cabell Hall, Charlottesville, VA 22904-4775. *Fee:* $85. *Online application:* http://gsas.virginia.edu/admission.

William and Mary, College of
Department of Psychology/Predoctoral MA Program
P.O. Box 8795
Williamsburg, VA 23187-8795
Telephone: (757) 221-3870
Chairperson: Joshua Burk, PhD

E-mail: lbbolden@wm.edu
Web: http://www.wm.edu/as/psychology/

Orientation, Objectives, and Emphasis of Department
The general psychology MA program is designed to prepare students for admission to PhD programs. Students are not admitted if they are not planning to further their education. There is a heavy research emphasis throughout both years of the program.

Programs and Degrees Offered

Program	Degree	Application Deadline	Applications Received	Accepted	New Admits Enrolled (PT)	Total Enrolled (PT)	Degrees Awarded in 2014–2015	Median Years to Complete Degree	Dismissed/Withdrew
General Psychology	MA/MS	February 1 (Fall)	89	10	10 (0)	18 (0)	8	2	0

Admissions
Entries appear in the following order: required test or GPA, minimum score (if required)/median score of students entering in 2015–2016.

Program	Degree	GRE-V	GRE-Q	GRE-Writing	GRE-Subject	Under-graduate GPA	Last 2 Years GPA	Psychology GPA	Master's GPA
General Psychology	MA/MS	NA/159	NA/155	NA/NA	Not specified	Not specified	Not specified	Not specified	Not specified

Admissions Requirements:

Degree	GRE	GRE-Subject	Letters of Recommendation	Research Statement	Writing Sample	CV	Interview
Master's/Specialist	Required	Optional	3	Optional	Optional	Optional	None

Admissions Criteria:

GRE scores—medium

Research experience—high

Work experience—low

Clinically related public service—low

GPA—medium

Letters of recommendation—high

Statement of goals and objectives—high

Undergraduate psychology preparation—medium

For additional information on admission requirements, visit http://www.wm.edu/as/psychology/gradprogram/admission/index.php.

Department Demographics

	Male (PT)	Female (PT)	Total	African-American/ Black (PT)	Hispanic/ Latino (PT)	Asian/ Pacific Islander (PT)	American Indian/ Alaska Native (PT)	Caucasian/ White (PT)	Unknown	Multiethnic (PT)	ADA (PT)	Int'l (PT)
Students	6 (0)	12 (0)	18	0 (0)	1 (0)	2 (0)	0 (0)	14 (0)	0 (0)	1 (0)	0 (0)	4 (0)

Financial Information/Assistance

Tuition: For information on tuition costs, visit http://www.wm.edu/offices/financialoperations/sa/tuition/index.php. Tuition is subject to change. Additional fees are assessed to students beyond the costs of tuition for the following: General fee, Technology Fee, Student Faculty Fee, Facility Fee, HEETF Fee.

Master's:

State residents: $7,576 per academic year.

State residents: $316 per credit hour.

Nonstate residents: $22,519 per academic year.

Nonstate residents: $938 per credit hour.

Financial Assistance:

	Teaching Assistantship (% Receiving)	Teaching Assistantship Tuition Remission	Research Assistantship (% Receiving)	Research Assistantship Tuition Remission	Fellowship (% Receiving)	Fellowship Tuition Remission
First-Year Student	$13,500 (NA)	Full	$13,500 (NA)	Full	NA (NA)	NA
Advanced Student	$13,500 (NA)	Full	$13,500 (NA)	Full	NA (NA)	NA

For additional information on financial assistance, visit http://www.wm.edu/as/psychology/gradprogram/financial-support/index.php.

Employment of Department Graduates

Master's:

Enrolled in a psychology doctoral program: 6

Employed in an academic position at a university: 1

Other employment position: 1

Total: 8

Additional Information

Housing and Day Care: On-campus housing is available. See the following website for more information: http://www.wm.edu/offices/residencelife/oncampus/residencehalls/graduate/index.php. On-campus day care facilities are available. See the following website for more information: http://www.wm.edu/offices/auxiliary/wccc/.

Special Facilities or Resources: Our faculty members develop and work with the MA students to design, conduct, and analyze research data. These studies are often published in professional journals. Subjects accessible for research include individuals from the community, college students, and rats.

Application Information: Director of Graduate Studies, Psychology Department, The College of William and Mary, P.O. Box 8795, Williamsburg, VA 23187-8795. *Fee:* $45. *Online application:* http://www.wm.edu/as/graduate/admission/index.php.

Antioch University, Seattle

PsyD in Psychology
School of Applied Psychology, Counseling and Family Therapy
2326 6th Avenue
Seattle, WA 98121-1814
Telephone: (206) 268-4828
Chairperson: Jude Bergkamp, PsyD

E-mail: jbergkamp@antioch.edu
Web: http://www.antiochseattle.edu/academics/psyd-clinical-psychology-2/

Orientation, Objectives, and Emphasis of Department

Antioch University Seattle's PsyD program in clinical psychology prepares students for professional careers in psychology. The mission of Antioch University Seattle is to educate students to engage in lifelong reflective learning within the context of social change agency in this ever-changing world. The program follows the practitioner–scholar model, with equal emphasis on practice and research. Antioch invites and supports students to follow their passion, personally and professionally, to promote health, education, social justice, and human welfare. The program offers flexibility in the curriculum to enable adult learners to progress either full time or part time through their graduate studies after completing the first year of full-time studies. The curriculum includes foundational courses as well as an ability to select concentrations while providing treatment through the on-site AUS mental health clinic and/or in community placements. AUS concentrations provide our students with a spectrum of theoretical perspectives and practical experiences along with stimulating professional seminars. The faculty are experienced teachers, clinicians, researchers, and social advocates; many are well-known in both state-wide and national psychology organizations. Faculty members bring a balance of traditional and contemporary perspectives in the field of clinical psychology, educating students to become informed and effective practitioners and scholars.

Programs and Degrees Offered

Program	Degree	Application Deadline	Applica- tions Received	Accepted	New Admits Enrolled (PT)	Total Enrolled (PT)	Degrees Awarded in 2014– 2015	Median Years to Complete Degree	Dismissed/ Withdrew
Clinical Psychology	PsyD	July 31 (Fall), Rolling	30	27	16 (0)	108	17	8	0

Doctoral Degree (PsyD Clinical Psychology): For those doctoral students for whom a professional internship was required in this program prior to graduation:

Total students who applied for an internship: 18
Total students who obtained an internship: 18
Total students who obtained a paid internship: 14
Total students who obtained an unpaid internship: 4
Total students who were placed in APA/CPA-accredited internships: 2
Total students placed in internships not APA/CPA-accredited, but listed with the Association of Psychology Postdoctoral and Internship Centers (APPIC): 14
Total students placed in internships conforming to guidelines of the Council of Directors of School Psychology Programs (CDSPP): 0
Total students placed in internships that were not APA/CPA-accredited, APPIC or CDSSP listed: 2

Internships/Practica

Throughout their experience, Antioch University Seattle students have the opportunity to develop their clinical, applied research, and assessment skills. There is an emphasis on multicultural competency and social justice is woven into the practical training experiences and placements. Practicum, pre-internship, and internship placements may include working in the Antioch University Seattle Clinic and/or a variety of community engagements. Supervision and mentoring are provided by licensed professionals and licensed psychologists. Currently there are opportunities for placement in forensic, clinical child, clinical adult, therapeutic school, neuropsychology assessment, rehabilitation, college counseling centers, community mental health, and health psychology sites. Collaborative relationships with community sites are nurtured to provide ongoing opportunities for dynamic involvement in psychological services provision, applied research, and psychological assessment opportunities. These practical training experiences culminate in the predoctoral internship, which is a full-time, 1-year or half-time, 2-year placement for advanced training in a particular setting in professional psychology. Local predoctoral internship placements are available. In addition, AUS participates in the

Association of Psychology Postdoctoral and Internship Center's (APPIC) internship match program through which students will have the opportunity to apply for internships nationally.

Admissions

Entries appear in the following order: required test or GPA, minimum score (if required)/median score of students entering in 2015–2016.

Program	Degree	GRE-V	GRE-Q	GRE-Writing	GRE-Subject	Under-graduate GPA	Last 2 Years GPA	Psychol-ogy GPA	Master's GPA
Clinical Psychology	PsyD	Not specified	Not specified	Not specified	Not specified	NA/NA	NA/NA	NA/NA	NA/NA

Admissions Requirements:

Degree	GRE	GRE-Subject	Letters of Recom-mendation	Research Statement	Writing Sample	CV	Interview
Doctoral	Required	Optional	2	Required	Required	Required	None

Admissions Criteria:

GRE scores—medium
Research experience—medium
Work experience—medium
Clinically related public service—medium
GPA—medium

Letters of recommendation—high
Interview—high
Statement of goals and objectives—high
Undergraduate psychology preparation—medium

For additional information on admission requirements, visit http://www.antiochseattle.edu/admissions/requirements-and-deadlines/psy-d-psychology/.

Department Demographics

	Male (PT)	Female (PT)	Total	African-American/ Black (PT)	Hispanic/ Latino (PT)	Asian/ Pacific Islander (PT)	American Indian/ Alaska Native (PT)	Caucasian/ White (PT)	Unknown	Multiethnic (PT)	ADA (PT)	Int'l (PT)
Students	21 (0)	87 (0)	108	7 (0)	5 (0)	5 (0)	1 (0)	85 (0)	3 (0)	2 (0)	8 (0)	2 (0)

Financial Information/Assistance

Tuition: For information on tuition costs, visit http://www.antiochseattle.edu/financial-aid-2/tuition-and-fees/. Tuition is subject to change. Additional fees are assessed to students beyond the costs of tuition for the following: quarterly student service fee, fees for assessment labs and technology fee.

Doctoral:
State residents: $29,740 per academic year.
State residents: $810 per credit hour.
Nonstate residents: $29,740 per academic year.
Nonstate residents: $810 per credit hour.

Financial Assistance:

	Teaching Assistantship (% Receiving)	Teaching Assistantship Tuition Remission	Research Assistantship (% Receiving)	Research Assistantship Tuition Remission	Fellowship (% Receiving)	Fellowship Tuition Remission
First-Year Student	NA (NA)	NA	NA (NA)	NA	$15,200 (NA)	NA
Advanced Student	NA (NA)	NA	NA (NA)	NA	$15,200 (NA)	NA

For additional information on financial assistance, visit http://www.antiochseattle.edu/financial-aid-2/.

Employment of Department Graduates

Doctoral:
Enrolled in a postdoctoral residency/fellowship: 2
Employed in independent practice: 2
Do not know: 18
Total: 22

Additional Information

Housing and Day Care: No on-campus housing is available. No on-campus day care facilities are available.

Information for Students With Physical Disabilities: See the following website: http://www.antiochseattle.edu/disability-support-services/.

Special Facilities or Resources: Antioch University Seattle offers opportunities to pursue clinical practice and assessment, as well as academic and research enterprises, in our on-site sliding-scale community clinic. Students who are closely supervised provide high quality psychological services to various populations. AUS Clinic offers high quality psychological services, including counseling and testing, to the Seattle community in a safe and supportive setting. In addition, AUS has arrangements with local specialty treatment facilities so our students can gain experience with additional populations and treatment modalities. Our students also are encouraged to work closely with faculty on cutting-edge research on issues of social justice and social change. For example, working on a multidisciplinary research team with a nationally renowned expert for the Study of War Stress Injuries dedicated to the study, identification, and elimination of contributing factors responsible for cyclic failure in meeting the military mental health needs of the warrior class. Students are an integral part of departmental and university-wide committees, which helps prepare them for future careers in administration, research, therapy, academia, public policy, and higher education. There are also opportunities for students to join community based research teams of their interests.

Application Information: Admissions Office, 2326 6th Avenue, Seattle, WA 98121-1814. *Fee:* $50. *Online application:* http://www.antiochseattle.edu/admissions/apply-now/.

Central Washington University

Department of Psychology
College of the Sciences
400 East University Way
Ellensburg, WA 98926-7575
Telephone: (509) 963-2381
Chairperson: Stephanie Stein

E-mail: steins@cwu.edu
Web: http://www.cwu.edu/psychology/

Orientation, Objectives, and Emphasis of Department

Central Washington University's graduate program in psychology prepares students for professional employment in a variety of settings, including mental health agencies, public schools, community colleges, and business or industry. We also prepare students for successful completion of doctoral degree programs in psychology. The programs include extensive supervision in practicum and internship settings and research partnerships with faculty mentors. Our School Psychology program is NASP-approved. Our Mental Health Counseling program is CACREP-accredited. The educational requirements of the Animal Behavior Society's Associate Applied Animal Behaviorist Certificate can be met by completing the MS Experimental degree program with an appropriate selection of elective courses. The MS in Applied Behavior Analysis provides coursework that is preapproved by the Behavior Analysis Certification Board and fulfills the coursework requirements to allow individuals to sit for the Board Certified Behavior Analyst certification exam.

Programs and Degrees Offered

Program	Degree	Application Deadline	Applica-tions Received	Accepted	New Admits Enrolled (PT)	Total Enrolled (PT)	Degrees Awarded in 2014–2015	Median Years to Complete Degree	Dismissed/Withdrew
Mental Health Counseling	MA/MS	February 1 (Fall)	40	8	8 (0)	15 (0)	7	2.5	0

Programs and Degrees Offered (con't.)

Program	Degree	Application Deadline	Applications Received	Accepted	New Admits Enrolled (PT)	Total Enrolled (PT)	Degrees Awarded in 2014–2015	Median Years to Complete Degree	Dismissed/Withdrew
Experimental Psychology	MA/MS	February 15 (Fall), October 1 (Winter), January 1 (Spring), April 1 (Summer)	23	11	5 (0)	13 (2)	3	2	0
School Psychology	EdS	February 1 (Fall)	18	9	7 (0)	23	4	3	0
Applied Behavior Analysis	MA/MS	February 1 (Fall)	11	4	4 (0)	9 (2)	1	2	0

Internships/Practica

The Mental Health Counseling Psychology program requires three quarters of practicum and a 600-hour internship. The School Psychology program requires two quarters of practicum and a 1-year internship. Recent school psychology internships have been paid positions. Students enrolled in the Applied Behavior Analysis program are required to complete 480 hours of supervised internship that will fulfill a portion of the 1,500 hours of supervised fieldwork required by the Behavior Analysis Certification Board in order to be eligible to sit for the Board Certified Behavior Analyst certification exam.

Admissions

Entries appear in the following order: required test or GPA, minimum score (if required)/median score of students entering in 2015–2016.

Program	Degree	GRE-V	GRE-Q	GRE-Writing	GRE-Subject	Under-graduate GPA	Last 2 Years GPA	Psychology GPA	Master's GPA
Mental Health Counseling	MA/MS	NA/NA	NA/NA	Not specified	Not specified	Not specified	Not specified	Not specified	Not specified
Experimental Psychology	MA/MS	NA/159	NA/153	Not specified	Not specified	Not specified	Not specified	Not specified	Not specified
School Psychology	EdS	NA/NA	NA/NA	Not specified	Not specified	Not specified	3/NA	Not specified	Not specified
Applied Behavior Analysis	MA/MS	NA/NA	NA/NA	Not specified	Not specified	Not specified	Not specified	Not specified	Not specified

Admissions Requirements:

Degree	GRE	GRE-Subject	Letters of Recommendation	Research Statement	Writing Sample	CV	Interview
Master's/Specialist	Required	None	3	Required	Optional	Optional	None

Admissions Criteria:

GRE scores—medium
Research experience—medium
Work experience—medium
Clinically related public service—medium

GPA—high
Letters of recommendation—high
Statement of goals and objectives—high
Undergraduate psychology preparation—medium

Department Demographics

	Male (PT)	Female (PT)	Total	African-American/ Black (PT)	Hispanic/ Latino (PT)	Asian/ Pacific Islander (PT)	American Indian/ Alaska Native (PT)	Caucasian/ White (PT)	Unknown	Multiethnic (PT)	ADA (PT)	Int'l (PT)
Students	16 (2)	44 (2)	64	0 (1)	4 (0)	1 (0)	2 (1)	52 (2)	0 (0)	1 (0)	0 (0)	0 (0)

Financial Information/Assistance

Tuition: For information on tuition costs, visit http://www.cwu.edu/registrar/tuition-and-mandatory-fees. Tuition is subject to change.

Master's:
State residents: $10,377 per academic year.
State residents: $310 per credit hour.
Nonstate residents: $21,903 per academic year.
Nonstate residents: $713 per credit hour.

Financial Assistance:

	Teaching Assistantship (% Receiving)	Teaching Assistantship Tuition Remission	Research Assistantship (% Receiving)	Research Assistantship Tuition Remission	Fellowship (% Receiving)	Fellowship Tuition Remission
First-Year Student	NA (NA)	Full	NA (NA)	Full	NA (NA)	NA
Advanced Student	NA (NA)	Full	NA (NA)	Full	NA (NA)	NA

For additional information on financial assistance, visit http://www.cwu.edu/masters/graduate-student-funding.

Employment of Department Graduates

Master's:
Enrolled in a psychology doctoral program: 1
Employed in an academic position at a university: 1
Employed in a professional position in a school system: 3
Employed in a community mental health/counseling center: 6
Total: 11

Additional Information

Housing and Day Care: On-campus housing is available. See the following website for more information: http://www.cwu.edu/housing/. On-campus day care facilities are available. See the following website for more information: http://www.cwu.edu/early-learning/.

Information for Students With Physical Disabilities: See the following website: http://www.cwu.edu/disability-support/.

Special Facilities or Resources: Our facilities include an on-site community counseling and psychological assessment center for training in counseling and testing; animal research laboratories, including a laboratory for the study of language learning in chimpanzees; a human behavior laboratory; a computer lab; and a complete mechanical and electrical instrumentation services center.

Application Information: Office of Graduate Studies, Central Washington University, 400 East University Way, Ellensburg, WA 98926-7510. *Fee:* $50. *Online application:* https://app.applyyourself.com/?id=cwugrad.

Eastern Washington University

Department of Psychology
College of Social Sciences
135 Martin Hall
Cheney, WA 99004
Telephone: (509) 359-6227
Chairperson: Nick Jackson

E-mail: sruby@ewu.edu
Web: http://www.ewu.edu/css/programs/psychology

Orientation, Objectives, and Emphasis of Department

The Department seeks to promote the acquisition of the core knowledge and principles of psychology; to enhance the student's professional growth and development; to further the student's ability to think analytically, logically, and creatively; and to develop the student's ability to communicate effectively. The Department promotes psychology as a science and a profession through excellence in teaching, research, and service. Specific goals include: maintaining a student-focused learning environment; demonstrating commitment to undergraduate goals and graduate education; demonstrating commitment to accreditation and excellence in all program areas in order to meet state and national standards for professional training; having faculty who represent excellence in teaching, professional expertise, scholarship, and service of the subjects taught; and having faculty working together in mutually supportive ways that support student learning, research, program development, and service.

Programs and Degrees Offered

Program	Degree	Application Deadline	Applications Received	Accepted	New Admits Enrolled (PT)	Total Enrolled (PT)	Degrees Awarded in 2014–2015	Median Years to Complete Degree	Dismissed/Withdrew
School Psychology	EdS	March 1 (Fall)	32	14	10 (0)	31 (2)	14	3.5	1
Clinical and Experimental Psychology	MA/MS	March 1 (Fall)	63	15	13 (0)	24 (1)	8	2	2
School Psychology Respecialization (Online)	EdS	March 1 (Fall)	32	13	5 (2)	22 (2)	4	2	6

Internships/Practica

Students in our MS Psychology program complete a 9–12 month practicum in various clinics and sites during the second year of the program. Clinical Psychology students complete a minimum of 600 hours at their practicum site, including a minimum of 240 direct contact hours. They receive weekly supervision from a licensed mental health professional. Students in our EdS School Psychology program complete a minimum of 320 hours of practicum, including specific hours in early childhood, individual counseling, group counseling, and general school psychology practice. They are supervised by local school psychologists across 10 local school districts. School psychology students complete a minimum of 1,200 hours of internship, with the choice to complete the internship in any school district across the nation that agrees to meet the requirements for internship established by the National Association of School Psychologists.

Admissions

Entries appear in the following order: required test or GPA, minimum score (if required)/median score of students entering in 2015–2016.

Program	Degree	GRE-V	GRE-Q	GRE-Writing	GRE-Subject	Undergraduate GPA	Last 2 Years GPA	Psychology GPA	Master's GPA
School Psychology	EdS	143/NA	144/NA	3/NA	Not specified	Not specified	3/NA	Not specified	Not specified
Clinical and Experimental Psychology	MA/MS	NA/151	NA/146	NA/4	Not specified	Not specified	3/3.86	Not specified	Not specified

Admissions *(con't.)*

Program	Degree	GRE-V	GRE-Q	GRE-Writing	GRE-Subject	Under-graduate GPA	Last 2 Years GPA	Psychol-ogy GPA	Master's GPA
School Psychology Respecialization (Online)	EdS	Not specified	Not specified	Not specified	Not specified	Not specified	Not specified	Not specified	Not specified

Admissions Requirements:

Degree	GRE	GRE-Subject	Letters of Recom-mendation	Research Statement	Writing Sample	CV	Interview
Master's/Specialist	Required	Optional	3	Required	Optional	Required	Required

Please note if these criteria vary for different programs: EdS School Psychology interviews, while the MS Psychology program does not interview. Research experience applicable to the MS Psychology Program for both clinical and experimental tracks.

Admissions Criteria:

GRE scores—medium
Research experience—medium
Work experience—medium
Clinically related public service—medium
GPA—medium

Letters of recommendation—high
Interview—high
Statement of goals and objectives—medium
Undergraduate psychology preparation—medium

For additional information on admission requirements, visit http://www.ewu.edu/css/programs/psychology/graduate-programs/grad-forms.

Department Demographics

	Male (PT)	Female (PT)	Total	African-American/ Black (PT)	Hispanic/ Latino (PT)	Asian/ Pacific Islander (PT)	American Indian/ Alaska Native (PT)	Caucasian/ White (PT)	Unknown	Multiethnic (PT)	ADA (PT)	Int'l (PT)
Students	15 (0)	51 (5)	71	2 (0)	0 (0)	1 (1)	2 (0)	31 (3)	1 (0)	0 (0)	1 (1)	0 (0)

Financial Information/Assistance

Tuition: For information on tuition costs, visit http://access.ewu.edu/student-financial-services/cost-and-fees/tuition-rates. Tuition is subject to change.

Master's:
State residents: $10,919 per academic year.
State residents: $363 per credit hour.
Nonstate residents: $25,384 per academic year.
Nonstate residents: $846 per credit hour.

Financial Assistance:

	Teaching Assistantship (% Receiving)	Teaching Assistantship Tuition Remission	Research Assistantship (% Receiving)	Research Assistantship Tuition Remission	Fellowship (% Receiving)	Fellowship Tuition Remission
First-Year Student	$8,163 (20)	Full	$8,163 (20)	Full	$8,163 (20)	Full
Advanced Student	$8,163 (10)	Full	$8,163 (10)	Full	$8,163 (10)	Full

For additional information on financial assistance, visit http://www.ewu.edu/grad/assistantships-and-tuition-waivers.

Employment of Department Graduates

Master's:
Enrolled in a psychology doctoral program: 3
Enrolled in another graduate/professional program: 1
Employed in a professional position in a school system: 18
Employed in a community mental health/counseling center: 9
Total: 31

Additional Information

Housing and Day Care: On-campus housing is available. See the following website for more information: http://access.ewu.edu/ housing. On-campus day care facilities are available. See the following website for more information: http://access.ewu.edu/sa-budget-services/children-center.

Information for Students With Physical Disabilities: See the following website: http://access.ewu.edu/disability-support-services.

Special Facilities or Resources: Most of our MS Psychology faculty members have research labs with space. We have a cognitive lab with progressive computer systems. Students also have access to space at the EWU Riverpoint Campus. Computer labs are available to students at both Cheney and Riverpoint Campus. The Cheney campus provides an Academic Success Center, a learning commons in our library with group space for hands-on learning and project development.

Application Information: Psychology Department, 135 Martin Hall, Cheney, WA 99004. *Fee:* $50. *Online application:* http://www.ewu.edu/grad/application-procedures.

Gonzaga University (2015 data)
Department of Counselor Education
School of Education
East 501 Boone Avenue
Spokane, WA 99258-0025
Telephone: (509) 313-3512
Chairperson: Mark Young

E-mail: young@gonzaga.edu

Web: http://www.gonzaga.edu/Academics/Colleges-and-Schools/School-of-Education/Majors-Programs/Counselor-Education/

Orientation, Objectives, and Emphasis of Department
The philosophical theme running throughout the university is humanism. A realistic, balanced attitude is a necessary prerequisite for assisting others professionally. Careful selection of students helps to insure the inclusion of healthy individuals with the highest potential for success, as does faculty modeling, encouragement of trust, and communication of clear expectations. Indicators of counselor success are demonstration of skills and conflict resolution, consistent interpersonal behaviors, recognition of strengths and weaknesses, a clear grasp of goals, and self-knowledge of one's impact on others, as well as strong academic performance. Acquisition of counseling competence comes through both personal and professional growth. Immersion in an intensive course of study with a closely linked group of peers encourages open and honest processing, which in turn contributes to personal growth. The department believes that students must possess insight and awareness, and clarity about the boundaries between their personal issues and those of the client. Students training to become professionals must be treated as professionals. Faculty practice collegiality with students, maintain high standards of performance, and furnish an atmosphere of professionalism. Our three US-based programs are CACREP-accredited.

Programs and Degrees Offered

Program	Degree	Application Deadline	Applications Received	Accepted	New Admits Enrolled (PT)	Total Enrolled (PT)	Degrees Awarded in 2014–2015	Median Years to Complete Degree	Dismissed/Withdrew
School Counseling	MA/MS	March 1 (Fall)	40	10	10 (1)	20 (1)	13	2	1
Clinical Mental Health Counseling	MA/MS	March 1 (Fall)	44	27	17 (3)	35 (3)	18	2	4

Programs and Degrees Offered (con't.)

Program	Degree	Application Deadline	Applica-tions Received	Accepted	New Admits Enrolled (PT)	Total Enrolled (PT)	Degrees Awarded in 2014–2015	Median Years to Complete Degree	Dismissed/Withdrew
Marriage and Family Counseling	MA/MS	March 1 (Fall)	35	13	9 (4)	17 (4)	9	2	0
Master Of Counseling	Other	March 15 (Fall)	50	20	16 (0)	35 (0)	16	2	1

Internships/Practica

Students complete a 100-hour practicum and a 600-hour internship at a site chosen by the student to meet his or her professional interests. School track students currently are placed in schools at elementary, junior high, high school, and alternative settings. Agency track students are placed at sites including but not limited to geriatric, hospital, community mental health, adolescent, marriage and family, child, community college, career, and life-skills settings. A strong reputation within our community has enabled students to select quality placements in diverse settings of the student's choosing.

Admissions

Entries appear in the following order: required test or GPA, minimum score (if required)/median score of students entering in 2015–2016.

Program	Degree	GRE-V	GRE-Q	GRE-Writing	GRE-Subject	Under-graduate GPA	Last 2 Years GPA	Psychol-ogy GPA	Master's GPA
School Counseling	MA/MS	Not specified	Not specified	Not specified	Not specified	3/NA	Not specified	Not specified	Not specified
Clinical Mental Health Counseling	MA/MS	Not specified	Not specified	Not specified	Not specified	3/NA	Not specified	Not specified	Not specified
Marriage and Family Counseling	MA/MS	Not specified	Not specified	Not specified	Not specified	3/NA	Not specified	Not specified	Not specified
Master of Counseling	Other	Not specified	Not specified	Not specified	Not specified	3/NA	Not specified	Not specified	Not specified

Admissions Requirements:

Degree	GRE	GRE-Subject	Letters of Recom-mendation	Research Statement	Writing Sample	CV	Interview
Master's/Specialist	Required	Required	2	Required	None	None	Required

Admissions Criteria:

GRE scores—low
Work experience—medium
Clinically related public service—medium
GPA—medium
Letters of recommendation—high

Interview—high
Statement of goals and objectives—high
Undergraduate psychology preparation—medium
Emotional intelligence—high

Department Demographics

	Male (PT)	Female (PT)	Total	African-American/Black (PT)	Hispanic/Latino (PT)	Asian/Pacific Islander (PT)	American Indian/Alaska Native (PT)	Caucasian/White (PT)	Unknown	Multiethnic (PT)	ADA (PT)	Int'l (PT)
Students	16 (1)	91 (7)	115	2 (0)	3 (2)	0 (0)	0 (0)	63 (2)	36 (4)	3 (0)	0 (0)	0 (1)

Financial Information/Assistance

Tuition: For information on tuition costs, visit http://www.gonzaga.edu/studentaccounts. Tuition is subject to change. Tuition costs vary by program.

Master's:
State residents: $925 per credit hour.
Nonstate residents: $925 per credit hour.

Financial Assistance:

	Teaching Assistantship (% Receiving)	Teaching Assistantship Tuition Remission	Research Assistantship (% Receiving)	Research Assistantship Tuition Remission	Fellowship (% Receiving)	Fellowship Tuition Remission
First-Year Student	$3,200 (NA)	NA	$3,200 (NA)	NA	NA (NA)	NA
Advanced Student	$3,200 (NA)	NA	$3,200 (NA)	NA	NA (NA)	NA

Employment of Department Graduates

Master's:
Enrolled in a psychology doctoral program: 4
Enrolled in another graduate/professional program: 3
Employed in other positions at a higher education institution: 1
Employed in a professional position in a school system: 9
Employed in business or industry: 1
Employed in government agency: 1
Employed in a community mental health/counseling center: 19
Employed in a hospital/medical center: 1
Still seeking employment: 1
Other employment position: 3
Total: 43

Additional Information

Housing and Day Care: On-campus housing is available. See the following website for more information: http://www.gonzaga.edu/Student-Life/Residence-Life-and-Dining-Services/. No on-campus day care facilities are available.

Special Facilities or Resources: The Department of Counselor Education is proud to offer a modern and complete clinic training center, with four practicum rooms, a departmental library, and conference room. The clinic has two-way glass and is equipped with audio-video technological equipment which can be operated in the clinic room by either the student (for taping and reviewing personal work) or by any department faculty member from faculty offices (for viewing and/or taping).

Application Information: Graduate Admissions, School of Education, Gonzaga University, 502 East Boone, Spokane, WA 99258-0025. *Fee:* $50. *Online application:* http://www.gonzaga.edu/Admissions/Graduate/Apply/default.asp.

Puget Sound, University of

School of Education
1500 North Warner #1051
Tacoma, WA 98416
Telephone: (253) 879-3344
Director: Grace L. Kirchner
Web: http://www.pugetsound.edu/academics/departments-and-programs/graduate/school-of-education/med/

E-mail: kirchner@pugetsound.edu

Orientation, Objectives, and Emphasis of Department
We are housed in the School of Education and our primary mission is to train school counselors; however, many of our graduates find employment in social service settings.

Programs and Degrees Offered

Program	Degree	Application Deadline	Applications Received	Accepted	New Admits Enrolled (PT)	Total Enrolled (PT)	Degrees Awarded in 2014–2015	Median Years to Complete Degree	Dismissed/ Withdrew
School Counseling	MEd	March 1 (Fall)	14	12	10 (2)	10 (17)	10	2	0
Mental Health Counseling	MEd	March 1 (Fall)	11	3	3 (2)	3 (6)	2	2	0

Internships/Practica

We require a 400-hour internship in a school or agency setting. Prior to the internship, students participate in an on-campus practicum course held once a week for 12 weeks.

Admissions

Entries appear in the following order: required test or GPA, minimum score (if required)/median score of students entering in 2015–2016.

Program	Degree	GRE-V	GRE-Q	GRE-Writing	GRE-Subject	Under-graduate GPA	Last 2 Years GPA	Psychology GPA	Master's GPA
School Counseling	MEd	NA/NA	NA/NA	NA/NA	Not specified	NA/NA	Not specified	Not specified	Not specified
Mental Health Counseling	MEd	NA/NA	NA/NA	NA/NA	Not specified	NA/NA	Not specified	Not specified	Not specified

Admissions Requirements:

Degree	GRE	GRE-Subject	Letters of Recommendation	Research Statement	Writing Sample	CV	Interview
Master's/Specialist	Required	None	2	Required	None	Required	Required

Admissions Criteria:

GRE scores—medium
Research experience—low
Work experience—medium
Clinically related public service—medium

GPA—medium
Letters of recommendation—medium
Interview—high
Statement of goals and objectives—medium

For additional information on admission requirements, visit http://www.pugetsound.edu/admission/apply/graduate-students/education/.

Department Demographics

	Male (PT)	Female (PT)	Total	African-American/ Black (PT)	Hispanic/ Latino (PT)	Asian/ Pacific Islander (PT)	American Indian/ Alaska Native (PT)	Caucasian/ White (PT)	Unknown	Multiethnic (PT)	ADA (PT)	Int'l (PT)
Students	0 (3)	1 (27)	31	0 (1)	0 (3)	0 (0)	0 (0)	1 (21)	0 (2)	0 (3)	0 (0)	0 (0)

Financial Information/Assistance

Tuition: For information on tuition costs, visit http://www.pugetsound.edu/admission/tuition-aid-scholarships/graduate-students/master-of-education/. Tuition is subject to change.

Master's:
State residents: $917 per credit hour.
Nonstate residents: $917 per credit hour.

Financial Assistance:

	Teaching Assistantship (% Receiving)	Teaching Assistantship Tuition Remission	Research Assistantship (% Receiving)	Research Assistantship Tuition Remission	Fellowship (% Receiving)	Fellowship Tuition Remission
First-Year Student	NA (NA)	NA	NA (NA)	NA	NA (NA)	NA
Advanced Student	NA (NA)	NA	NA (NA)	NA	NA (NA)	NA

For additional information on financial assistance, visit http://www.pugetsound.edu/admission/tuition-aid-scholarships/.

Employment of Department Graduates

Master's:
Employed in other positions at a higher education institution: 1
Employed in a professional position in a school system: 10
Employed in a community mental health/counseling center: 1
Total: 12

Additional Information

Housing and Day Care: No on-campus housing is available. No on-campus day care facilities are available.

Information for Students With Physical Disabilities: See the following website: http://www.pugetsound.edu/academics/academic-resources/disability-services/.

Application Information: Office of Admission, 1500 North Warner Street, CMB 1062, Tacoma, WA 98416-1062. *Fee:* $60. *Online application:* http://www.pugetsound.edu/admission/graduate-students/counseling-application/.

Seattle Pacific University

Clinical Psychology Department
School of Psychology, Family and Community
3307 Third Avenue West
Seattle, WA 98119
Telephone: (206) 281-2839
Chairperson: David G. Stewart, PhD

E-mail: clinicalpsyc@spu.edu
Web: http://spu.edu/depts/spfc/

Orientation, Objectives, and Emphasis of Department

The Clinical Psychology PhD program at SPU is designed to provide training in professional psychology in accordance with the Local Clinical Scientist model of doctoral education. The Local Clinical Scientist extends the scientific and professional ideals in the original Boulder Scientist–Practitioner model of clinical psychology. At the same time, we try to encompass broader concepts of science and more explicitly integrate the art of clinical practice. We also endorse the core competencies outlined by the National Council of Schools and Programs of Professional Psychology (NCSPP) and are committed to helping students achieve mastery of the core competencies of clinical skills. Our doctoral program typically requires 4 years of graduate coursework, during which clinical practicum training as well as dissertation research are completed, followed by a 1-year full-time internship (elsewhere) in the fifth year. We are an APA-accredited program in clinical psychology, and also a designated doctoral program with ASPPB/NR, which verifies our curriculum meets the educational requirements for licensing psychologists in the United States.

Programs and Degrees Offered

Program	Degree	Application Deadline	Applications Received	Accepted	New Admits Enrolled (PT)	Total Enrolled (PT)	Degrees Awarded in 2014–2015	Median Years to Complete Degree	Dismissed/ Withdrew
Clinical Psychology	PhD	December 15 (Fall)	144	26	12 (0)	72 (0)	14	5.5	1

APA Accreditation

Clinical PhD: Student Outcome Data website: http://spu.edu/academics/school-of-psychology-family-community/graduate-programs/clinical-psychology-phd.

Doctoral Degree (PhD Clinical Psychology): For those doctoral students for whom a professional internship was required in this program prior to graduation:
Total students who applied for an internship: 10
Total students who obtained an internship: 10
Total students who obtained a paid internship: 10
Total students who obtained an unpaid internship: 0
Total students who were placed in APA/CPA-accredited internships: 10
Total students placed in internships not APA/CPA-accredited, but listed with the Association of Psychology Postdoctoral and Internship Centers (APPIC): 0
Total students placed in internships conforming to guidelines of the Council of Directors of School Psychology Programs (CDSPP): 0
Total students placed in internships that were not APA/CPA-accredited, APPIC or CDSSP listed: 0

Internships/Practica

Clinical training requirements include two 1-year practicum placements during the third and fourth years of the program (part-time, averaging 16 hours/week, resulting in average total practicum experience of approximately 1,200 hours), as well as a full-time 1-year (2,000 hours) clinical psychology internship during the fifth year of the PhD program. Practicum placements are external to the university in a variety of mental health centers, hospitals, medical/dental clinics, and rehabilitation facilities in the greater Puget Sound area. Students apply for their internship in the APPIC Match and each year most obtain placements at competitive mental health and medical centers around the country. Theoretical models and orientations among the faculty include cognitive behavioral, psychodynamic, interpersonal, family systems, and humanistic approaches. Faculty tend to integrate more than one perspective in theories, teaching and professional practice. We incorporate and contribute to evidence-based research and expect our students to utilize clinical science as well as theory in their clinical work.

Admissions

Entries appear in the following order: required test or GPA, minimum score (if required)/median score of students entering in 2015–2016.

Program	Degree	GRE-V	GRE-Q	GRE-Writing	GRE-Subject	Under-graduate GPA	Last 2 Years GPA	Psychol-ogy GPA	Master's GPA
Clinical Psychology	PhD	NA/159	NA/156	Not specified	Not specified	NA/3.68	Not specified	Not specified	Not specified

Admissions Requirements:

Degree	GRE	GRE-Subject	Letters of Recom-mendation	Research Statement	Writing Sample	CV	Interview
Doctoral	Required	Recom-mended	3	Required	Optional	Optional	Required

Admissions Criteria:

GRE scores—high
Research experience—high
Work experience—medium
Clinically related public service—high
GPA—high

Letters of recommendation—high
Interview—high
Statement of goals and objectives—high
Undergraduate psychology preparation—high
Match with faculty—high

Department Demographics

	Male (PT)	Female (PT)	Total	African-American/Black (PT)	Hispanic/Latino (PT)	Asian/Pacific Islander (PT)	American Indian/Alaska Native (PT)	Caucasian/White (PT)	Unknown	Multiethnic (PT)	ADA (PT)	Int'l (PT)
Students	10 (0)	62 (0)	72	3 (0)	0 (0)	6 (0)	0 (0)	59 (0)	2 (0)	2 (0)	0 (0)	1 (0)

Financial Information/Assistance

Tuition: For information on tuition costs, visit http://spu.edu/student-financial-services/costs/grad-tuition-fees. Tuition is subject to change.

Doctoral:
State residents: $28,275 per academic year.
State residents: $725 per credit hour.
Nonstate residents: $28,275 per academic year.
Nonstate residents: $725 per credit hour.

Financial Assistance:

	Teaching Assistantship (% Receiving)	Teaching Assistantship Tuition Remission	Research Assistantship (% Receiving)	Research Assistantship Tuition Remission	Fellowship (% Receiving)	Fellowship Tuition Remission
First-Year Student	NA (NA)	NA	NA (NA)	NA	$5,000 (100)	NA
Advanced Student	$8,000 (NA)	NA	$4,000 (NA)	NA	$8,000 (NA)	NA

For additional information on financial assistance, visit http://spu.edu/student-financial-services.

Employment of Department Graduates

Doctoral:
Enrolled in a postdoctoral residency/fellowship: 10
Employed in independent practice: 1
Employed in government agency: 1
Employed in a hospital/medical center: 1
Do not know: 1
Total: 14

Additional Information

Housing and Day Care: On-campus housing is available. See the following website for more information: http://spu.edu/depts/reslife/gradstudent/index.asp. On-campus day care facilities are available.

Information for Students With Physical Disabilities: See the following website: http://www.spu.edu/depts/cfl/dss/index.asp.

Special Facilities or Resources: The School maintains a fully equipped suite of psychology research laboratories, including a psychophysiological lab, child-developmental lab, and social psychology lab. The University's newly opened Science Building has wet labs, animal learning facilities, and a psychophysiological demonstration classroom. The Department is housed in Marston Hall, which was completely renovated for us in 2001. The University Library is a four-story structure with conference rooms, private study rooms and group meeting rooms. The library contains approximately 10,000 volumes relevant to the field of psychology, including books, media, a test file, and over 500 journals available either in paper, microfilm, and full-text online. In addition to traditional inter-library loan services, Seattle Pacific University is a member of the Orbis Cascade Alliance, a consortium of 26 public and private academic libraries in Washington and Oregon which provides access to a combined collection of over 22 million volumes of books and other materials. Students have access to several computer labs on campus, which have SPSS installed. Students are given an SPU e-mail account and have 24/7 access to our online Blackboard where program forms, syllabi, schedules, and so forth are posted for students to download.

Application Information: Graduate Center, Seattle Pacific University. *Fee:* $75. *Online application:* https://app.applyyourself.com/?id=spu-grad.

Seattle University
Graduate Psychology Program
Arts and Sciences
901 12th Avenue, P.O. Box 222000
Seattle, WA 98122-1090
Telephone: (206) 296-5400
Director, Graduate Program: Kevin Krycka, PsyD

E-mail: krycka@seattleu.edu
Web: https://www.seattleu.edu/artsci/map/

Orientation, Objectives, and Emphasis of Department

With an emphasis on existential-phenomenological psychology, this master's degree is designed to offer an interdisciplinary program focusing on the qualitative, experiential study of psychological events in the context of the person's life. By laying the foundations for a therapeutic attitude, the program prepares students for entrance into the helping professions or for further study of the psychological world. It is humanistic in that it intends to deepen the appreciation for the human condition by rigorous reflection on immediate psychological experiences and on the wisdom accumulated by the long tradition of the humanities. It is phenomenological in that it develops an attitude of openness and wonder toward psychological reality without holding theoretical prejudgments. It is therapeutic in that it focuses on the psychological conditions that help people deal with the difficulties of life.

Programs and Degrees Offered

Program	Degree	Application Deadline	Applications Received	Accepted	New Admits Enrolled (PT)	Total Enrolled (PT)	Degrees Awarded in 2014–2015	Median Years to Complete Degree	Dismissed/ Withdrew
Existential-Phenomenological Psychology	MA/MS	January 15 (Fall)	68	32	19 (1)	33 (6)	20	2	0

Internships/Practica

A variety of supervised internships (typically about 20 hrs/week during second year) in a wide variety of community agencies, hospitals, shelters and clinics.

Admissions

Entries appear in the following order: required test or GPA, minimum score (if required)/median score of students entering in 2015–2016.

Program	Degree	GRE-V	GRE-Q	GRE-Writing	GRE-Subject	Under-graduate GPA	Last 2 Years GPA	Psychol-ogy GPA	Master's GPA
Existential-Phenomenological Psychology	MA/MS	Not specified	Not specified	Not specified	Not specified	3/NA	Not specified	Not specified	Not specified

Admissions Requirements:

Degree	GRE	GRE-Subject	Letters of Recom-mendation	Research Statement	Writing Sample	CV	Interview
Master's/Specialist	None	None	3	Required	Required	Required	Required

Admissions Criteria:

Research experience—low
Work experience—medium
Clinically related public service—high
GPA—high
Letters of recommendation—high

Interview—high
Statement of goals and objectives—medium
Undergraduate psychology preparation—high
Bio/writing sample—high

For additional information on admission requirements, visit https://www.seattleu.edu/artsci/map/prospective-students/admissions-criteria/.

Department Demographics

	Male (PT)	Female (PT)	Total	African-American/ Black (PT)	Hispanic/ Latino (PT)	Asian/ Pacific Islander (PT)	American Indian/ Alaska Native (PT)	Caucasian/ White (PT)	Unknown	Multiethnic (PT)	ADA (PT)	Int'l (PT)
Students	14 (3)	19 (3)	39	2 (0)	1 (0)	6 (0)	0 (0)	22 (6)	1 (0)	1 (0)	0 (0)	2 (0)

Financial Information/Assistance

Tuition: For information on tuition costs, visit https://www.seattleu.edu/graduate-admissions/finances/tuition-and-fees/. Tuition is subject to change.

Master's:
State residents: $24,732 per academic year.
State residents: $687 per credit hour.
Nonstate residents: $24,732 per academic year.
Nonstate residents: $687 per credit hour.

Financial Assistance:

	Teaching Assistantship (% Receiving)	Teaching Assistantship Tuition Remission	Research Assistantship (% Receiving)	Research Assistantship Tuition Remission	Fellowship (% Receiving)	Fellowship Tuition Remission
First-Year Student	NA (NA)	NA	$14,000 (5)	NA	$2,500 (50)	NA
Advanced Student	NA (NA)	NA	$14,000 (5)	NA	$2,500 (50)	NA

For additional information on financial assistance, visit http://www.seattleu.edu/graduate-admissions/finances/.

Employment of Department Graduates

Master's:
Enrolled in a psychology doctoral program: 3
Employed in business or Industry: 2
Employed in a community mental health/counseling center: 22
Still seeking employment: 13
Other employment position: 2
Total: 42

Additional Information

Housing and Day Care: On-campus housing is available. See the following website for more information: http://www.seattleu.edu/housing/. No on-campus day care facilities are available.

Information for Students With Physical Disabilities: See the following website: https://www.seattleu.edu/disabilities-services/.

Special Facilities or Resources: The program has a tradition of involving selected students in qualitative research projects.

Application Information: Graduate Admissions Office, Seattle University, P.O. Box 222000, Seattle, WA 98122-1090. *Fee:* $55. *Online application:* http://www.seattleu.edu/graduate-admissions/apply/.

Washington State University (2015 data)
Department of Psychology
College of Arts and Sciences
P.O. Box 644820
Pullman, WA 99164
Telephone: (509) 335-2631
Chairperson: Rebecca Craft

E-mail: psych@wsu.edu
Web: https://psychology.wsu.edu/

Orientation, Objectives, and Emphasis of Department
The objectives of the graduate programs are to prepare individuals to make contributions and hold leadership positions in basic and applied research, teaching, clinical psychology, public service, or some combination of these areas. The clinical program is a broad, general one requiring student commitment to both research and clinical work. The emphasis areas within the experimental program are cognitive, biological, social and industrial/organizational, and quantitative/health.

Programs and Degrees Offered

Program	Degree	Application Deadline	Applica-tions Received	Accepted	New Admits Enrolled (PT)	Total Enrolled (PT)	Degrees Awarded in 2014–2015	Median Years to Complete Degree	Dismissed/ Withdrew
Clinical Psychology	PhD	December 1 (Fall)	186	11	7 (0)	37 (0)	3	6	2
Experimental Psychology	PhD	December 1 (Fall)	64	7	7 (0)	32 (2)	6	4.7	1

APA Accreditation

Clinical PhD: Student Outcome Data website: https://psychology.wsu.edu/clinical/graduate-clinical/.

Doctoral Degree (PhD Clinical Psychology): For those doctoral students for whom a professional internship was required in this program prior to graduation:
Total students who applied for an internship: 7
Total students who obtained an internship: 7
Total students who obtained a paid internship: 7
Total students who obtained an unpaid internship: 0
Total students who were placed in APA/CPA-accredited internships: 7
Total students placed in internships not APA/CPA-accredited, but listed with the Association of Psychology Postdoctoral and Internship Centers (APPIC): 0
Total students placed in internships conforming to guidelines of the Council of Directors of School Psychology Programs (CDSPP): 0
Total students placed in internships that were not APA/CPA-accredited, APPIC or CDSSP listed: 0

Internships/Practica

Psychology Clinic Practicum; Counseling Services Practicum; Medical Psychology Practicum at University Hospital, Heath psychology practicum at regional hospital, Spokane VA neuropsychology practicum, child psychology practicum at private practice.

Admissions

Entries appear in the following order: required test or GPA, minimum score (if required)/median score of students entering in 2015–2016.

Program	Degree	GRE-V	GRE-Q	GRE-Writing	GRE-Subject	Under-graduate GPA	Last 2 Years GPA	Psychol-ogy GPA	Master's GPA
Clinical Psychology	PhD	NA/162	NA/160	NA/5	Not specified	NA/3.8	NA/NA	NA/NA	Not specified
Experimental Psychology	PhD	NA/NA	NA/NA	Not specified	Not specified	3.3/3.8	Not specified	Not specified	3.5/3.9

Admissions Requirements:

Degree	GRE	GRE-Subject	Letters of Recom-mendation	Research Statement	Writing Sample	CV	Interview
Doctoral	Required	Optional	3	Required	None	Required	Required

Please note if these criteria vary for different programs: Applicants to the Experimental Psychology program are not expected to demonstrate any clinically related public service.

Admissions Criteria:

GRE scores—high
Research experience—high
Work experience—low
Clinically related public service—low
GPA—high

Letters of recommendation—high
Interview—medium
Statement of goals and objectives—high
Undergraduate psychology preparation—medium
Goodness of fit w/ mentor—high

For additional information on admission requirements, visit http://psychology.wsu.edu/clinical/graduate-application/.

Department Demographics

	Male (PT)	Female (PT)	Total	African-American/ Black (PT)	Hispanic/ Latino (PT)	Asian/ Pacific Islander (PT)	American Indian/ Alaska Native (PT)	Caucasian/ White (PT)	Unknown	Multiethnic (PT)	ADA (PT)	Int'l (PT)
Students	20 (0)	49 (2)	71	1 (0)	2 (0)	5 (0)	1 (0)	60 (2)	0 (0)	0 (0)	0 (0)	1 (0)

Financial Information/Assistance

Tuition: For information on tuition costs, visit http://finaid.wsu.edu/cost-of-attendance/. Tuition is subject to change.

Doctoral:
State residents: $11,768 per academic year.
Nonstate residents: $25,200 per academic year.

Financial Assistance:

	Teaching Assistantship (% Receiving)	Teaching Assistantship Tuition Remission	Research Assistantship (% Receiving)	Research Assistantship Tuition Remission	Fellowship (% Receiving)	Fellowship Tuition Remission
First-Year Student	$13,378 (86)	Full	$13,378 (14)	Full	NA (NA)	NA
Advanced Student	$14,197 (70)	Full	$14,197 (30)	Full	NA (NA)	NA

For additional information on financial assistance, visit http://psychology.wsu.edu/clinical/financial-support/.

Employment of Department Graduates

Doctoral:
Enrolled in a postdoctoral residency/fellowship: 2
Employed in a hospital/medical center: 1
Total: 3

Additional Information

Housing and Day Care: On-campus housing is available. See the following website for more information: http://housing.wsu.edu/famgrad/. On-campus day care facilities are available. See the following website for more information: http://childrenscenter.wsu.edu/.

Information for Students With Physical Disabilities: See the following website: http://drc.wsu.edu/.

Special Facilities or Resources: The Department of Psychology is located in Johnson Tower, near the center of campus. Fully equipped laboratories and shop facilities are available for research in social behavior, cognition, perception, human and animal learning, and biopsychology (behavioral neuroscience). The Psychology Clinic is operated as a training facility within the department.

Application Information: Fee: $75. Online application: http://gradschool.wsu.edu/apply/.

Washington State University
Educational Leadership, Sport Studies, and Educational/Counseling Psychology
Education
P.O. Box 642136
Pullman, WA 99164-2136
Telephone: (509) 335-9195
Chairperson: Dr. Kelly Ward

E-mail: gradstudies@wsu.edu
Web: https://education.wsu.edu/college/elssecp/

Orientation, Objectives, and Emphasis of Department

To produce successful professionals in educational psychology who have strong methodological skills, an understanding of researchable topics, the ability to develop a research program, effectively communicate and work with a wide variety of professionals, and skills to understand nuance and ambiguity in the work environment. Job prospects are many and varied, even in these economically difficult times. Graduates of the educational psychology program have been successful in obtaining interesting and well paying positions at universities, federal laboratories, industry, state agencies, and school districts, all places where people educated and trained in educational psychology are needed.

Programs and Degrees Offered

Program	Degree	Application Deadline	Applications Received	Accepted	New Admits Enrolled (PT)	Total Enrolled (PT)	Degrees Awarded in 2014–2015	Median Years to Complete Degree	Dismissed/ Withdrew
Educational Psychology	PhD	Rolling	16	3	2 (0)	10 (3)	3	5.5	0
Educational Psychology	MA/MS	Rolling	7	2	1 (0)	4 (0)	2	2.5	0

Admissions

Entries appear in the following order: required test or GPA, minimum score (if required)/median score of students entering in 2015–2016.

Program	Degree	GRE-V	GRE-Q	GRE-Writing	GRE-Subject	Under-graduate GPA	Last 2 Years GPA	Psychol-ogy GPA	Master's GPA
Educational Psychology	PhD	NA/151	NA/150	Not specified	Not specified	Not specified	Not specified	Not specified	Not specified
Educational Psychology	MA/MS	NA/154	NA/150	Not specified	Not specified	Not specified	Not specified	Not specified	Not specified

Admissions Requirements:

Degree	GRE	GRE-Subject	Letters of Recom-mendation	Research Statement	Writing Sample	CV	Interview
Master's/Specialist	Required	None	3	Required	Optional	Required	None
Doctoral	Required	None	3	Required	Optional	Required	None

Admissions Criteria:

GRE scores—medium
Research experience—medium
Work experience—medium
Clinically related public service—medium

GPA—high
Letters of recommendation—high
Statement of goals and objectives—high

Department Demographics

	Male (PT)	Female (PT)	Total	African-American/ Black (PT)	Hispanic/ Latino (PT)	Asian/ Pacific Islander (PT)	American Indian/ Alaska Native (PT)	Caucasian/ White (PT)	Unknown	Multiethnic (PT)	ADA (PT)	Int'l (PT)
Students	7 (1)	7 (2)	17	0 (0)	3 (1)	0 (0)	0 (0)	4 (1)	1 (0)	0 (0)	0 (0)	4 (1)

Financial Information/Assistance

Tuition: For information on tuition costs, visit http://finaid.wsu.edu/cost-of-attendance/. Tuition is subject to change.

Doctoral:
State residents: $11,784 per academic year.
State residents: $561 per credit hour.
Nonstate residents: $25,216 per academic year.
Nonstate residents: $1,233 per credit hour.

Master's:
State residents: $11,784 per academic year.
State residents: $561 per credit hour.
Nonstate residents: $25,216 per academic year.
Nonstate residents: $1,233 per credit hour.

Financial Assistance:

	Teaching Assistantship (% Receiving)	Teaching Assistantship Tuition Remission	Research Assistantship (% Receiving)	Research Assistantship Tuition Remission	Fellowship (% Receiving)	Fellowship Tuition Remission
First-Year Student	NA (NA)	Full	NA (NA)	Full	NA (NA)	NA
Advanced Student	NA (NA)	Full	NA (NA)	Full	NA (NA)	NA

For additional information on financial assistance, visit https://gradschool.wsu.edu/student-finance-page/.

Employment of Department Graduates

Master's:
Enrolled in a psychology doctoral program: 2
Total: 2

Doctoral:
Employed in government agency: 1
Still seeking employment: 1
Not seeking employment: 1
Total: 3

Additional Information

Housing and Day Care: On-campus housing is available. See the following website for more information: http://housing.wsu.edu/. On-campus day care facilities are available. See the following website for more information: http://childrenscenter.wsu.edu/.

Information for Students With Physical Disabilities: see the following website: http://drc.wsu.edu/.

Special Facilities or Resources: The Learning and Performance Research Center is a service and research center providing educational and social services agencies in Washington State and beyond with assessment and program evaluation assistance. The Pacific Northwest Center for Mestizo and Indigenous Research and Outreach focuses on the generation, transmission, and application of knowledge to serve the needs of Latino/Mestizo and Native/Indigenous communities in the Pacific Northwest.

Application Information: College of Education, Office of Graduate Education, 70 Cleveland Hall, P.O. Box 642114, Pullman, WA 99164-2114. *Fee:* $75. *Online application:* https://www.applyweb.com/wsugrad/index.ftl.

Washington, University of
Department of Psychology
Arts & Sciences
Box 351525
Seattle, WA 98195-1525
Telephone: (206) 543-8687
Chairperson: Sheri J.Y. Mizumori, PhD

E-mail: mizumori@uw.edu
Web: http://www.psych.uw.edu/

Orientation, Objectives, and Emphasis of Department
The program is committed to research-oriented scientific psychology. No degree programs are available in counseling or humanistic psychology. The clinical program emphasizes both clinical and research competencies and has areas of specialization in child clinical, and subspecialties in behavioral medicine, health psychology, and community psychology. Diversity science and quantitative psychology minors are now available to students in our program.

Programs and Degrees Offered

Program	Degree	Application Deadline	Applications Received	Accepted	New Admits Enrolled (PT)	Total Enrolled (PT)	Degrees Awarded in 2014–2015	Median Years to Complete Degree	Dismissed/ Withdrew
Animal Behavior	PhD	December 1 (Fall)	19	2	2 (0)	10 (1)	0	0	0
Clinical Psychology	PhD	December 1 (Fall)	232	6	4 (0)	26 (7)	4	6.5	0
Child Clinical	PhD	December 1 (Fall)	208	7	6 (0)	24 (1)	3	7	0
Cognition and Perception	PhD	December 1 (Fall)	70	5	4 (0)	16 (2)	1	4.75	0
Developmental Psychology	PhD	December 1 (Fall)	49	5	1 (0)	6 (2)	1	5.25	1
Behavioral Neuroscience	PhD	December 1 (Fall)	26	3	2 (0)	10	3	6	1
Social and Personality Psychology	PhD	December 1 (Fall)	107	5	3 (0)	10 (2)	1	6	0
Quantitative Psychology	PhD	December 1 (Fall)	12	0	0	0	0	0	0

APA Accreditation

Clinical PhD: Student Outcome Data website: http://www.psych.uw.edu/psych.php?p=236.

Clinical PhD (Doctor of Philosophy).

Doctoral Degree (PhD Clinical Psychology): For those doctoral students for whom a professional internship was required in this program prior to graduation:
Total students who applied for an internship: 4
Total students who obtained an internship: 4
Total students who obtained a paid internship: 4
Total students who obtained an unpaid internship: 0
Total students who were placed in APA/CPA-accredited internships: 4
Total students placed in internships not APA/CPA-accredited, but listed with the Association of Psychology Postdoctoral and Internship Centers (APPIC): 0
Total students placed in internships conforming to guidelines of the Council of Directors of School Psychology Programs (CDSPP): 0
Total students placed in internships that were not APA/CPA-accredited, APPIC or CDSSP listed: 0

Doctoral Degree (PhD Child Clinical): For those doctoral students for whom a professional internship was required in this program prior to graduation:
Total students who applied for an internship: 4
Total students who obtained an internship: 4
Total students who obtained a paid internship: 4
Total students who obtained an unpaid internship: 0
Total students who were placed in APA/CPA-accredited internships: 4
Total students placed in internships not APA/CPA-accredited, but listed with the Association of Psychology Postdoctoral and Internship Centers (APPIC): 0
Total students placed in internships conforming to guidelines of the Council of Directors of School Psychology Programs (CDSPP): 0
Total students placed in internships that were not APA/CPA-accredited, APPIC or CDSSP listed: 0

Internships/Practica

A variety of local and national predoctoral internships are available in clinical psychology.

Admissions

Entries appear in the following order: required test or GPA, minimum score (if required)/median score of students entering in 2015–2016.

Program	Degree	GRE-V	GRE-Q	GRE-Writing	GRE-Subject	Under-graduate GPA	Last 2 Years GPA	Psychol-ogy GPA	Master's GPA
Animal Behavior	PhD	NA/NA	NA/NA	Not specified	Not specified	NA/NA	NA/NA	Not specified	Not specified
Clinical Psychology	PhD	NA/NA	NA/NA	Not specified	Not specified	NA/NA	NA/NA	Not specified	Not specified
Child Clinical	PhD	NA/NA	NA/NA	Not specified	Not specified	NA/NA	NA/NA	Not specified	Not specified
Cognition and Perception	PhD	NA/NA	NA/NA	Not specified	Not specified	NA/NA	NA/NA	Not specified	Not specified
Developmental Psychology	PhD	NA/NA	NA/NA	Not specified	Not specified	NA/NA	NA/NA	Not specified	Not specified
Behavioral Neuroscience	PhD	NA/NA	NA/NA	Not specified	Not specified	NA/NA	NA/NA	Not specified	Not specified
Social and Personality Psychology	PhD	NA/NA	NA/NA	Not specified	Not specified	NA/NA	NA/NA	Not specified	Not specified
Quantitative Psychology	PhD	NA/NA	NA/NA	Not specified	Not specified	NA/NA	NA/NA	Not specified	Not specified

Admissions Requirements:

Degree	GRE	GRE-Subject	Letters of Recom-mendation	Research Statement	Writing Sample	CV	Interview
Doctoral	Required	Optional	3	Required	None	Optional	Required

Please note if these criteria vary for different programs: Individual areas evaluate applications differently, but all require a strong background in research and/or statistics.

Admissions Criteria:

GRE scores—high
Research experience—high
Work experience—medium
Clinically related public service—low
GPA—medium

Letters of recommendation—high
Interview—high
Statement of goals and objectives—high
Undergraduate psychology preparation—medium

For additional information on admission requirements, visit http://www.psych.uw.edu/psych.php?p=137.

Department Demographics

	Male (PT)	Female (PT)	Total	African-American/ Black (PT)	Hispanic/ Latino (PT)	Asian/ Pacific Islander (PT)	American Indian/ Alaska Native (PT)	Caucasian/ White (PT)	Unknown	Multiethnic (PT)	ADA (PT)	Int'l (PT)
Students	31 (4)	71 (11)	117	4 (0)	8 (0)	21 (5)	1 (0)	66 (9)	0 (0)	2 (1)	0 (0)	7 (0)

Financial Information/Assistance

Tuition: For information on tuition costs, visit http://opb.washington.edu/content/tuition-fees. Tuition is subject to change.

Doctoral:
State residents: $16,278 per academic year.
Nonstate residents: $28,326 per academic year.

Financial Assistance:

	Teaching Assistantship (% Receiving)	Teaching Assistantship Tuition Remission	Research Assistantship (% Receiving)	Research Assistantship Tuition Remission	Fellowship (% Receiving)	Fellowship Tuition Remission
First-Year Student	$20,997 (NA)	Full	$20,997 (NA)	Full	NA (NA)	NA
Advanced Student	$22,572 (NA)	Full	$22,572 (NA)	Full	NA (NA)	NA

Employment of Department Graduates

Doctoral:
Enrolled in a postdoctoral residency/fellowship: 6
Employed in an academic position at a university: 1
Employed in academic position at a 2-year/4-year college: 1
Employed in a professional position in a school system: 1
Employed in business or industry: 2
Do not know: 3
Total: 14

Additional Information

Housing and Day Care: On-campus housing is available. See the following website for more information: https://www.hfs.washington.edu/. On-campus day care facilities are available. See the following website for more information: http://www.washington.edu/admin/hr/benefits/worklife/childcare/.

Information for Students With Physical Disabilities: See the following website: http://www.washington.edu/admin/dso/.

Special Facilities or Resources: University and urban settings provide many resources, including the University of Washington Medical Center, UW Autism Center, Addictive Behaviors Research Center, Psychological Services and Training Center, Behavioral Research and Therapy Clinics, Center for Child and Family Well-Being, Center for Global Field Study, Institute for Learning and Brain Sciences, UW Center for Anxiety and Traumatic Stress, Washington National Primate Research Center, Children's Hospital and Regional Medical Center, nearby Veterans Administration facilities, and Sound Mental Health.

Application Information: Fee: $85. *Online application:* http://grad.uw.edu/admissions/apply-now/.

Marshall University

Department of Psychology
Liberal Arts
One John Marshall Drive
Huntington, WV 25755-2672
Telephone: (304) 696-6446
Chairperson: Marianna Linz

E-mail: linz@marshall.edu
Web: http://www.marshall.edu/psych/

Orientation, Objectives, and Emphasis of Department

Our PsyD program in Clinical Psychology (offered on our Huntington, West Virginia campus) accepted its first students in Fall 2002 and received APA accreditation in the spring of 2006. The program is also recognized as a designated program by the National Register/ASPPC Designation project. The program's emphasis is on preparing scholar–practitioners for rural/underserved populations in Appalachia and other rural areas. Particular foci of the doctoral program include understanding the needs and challenges of working in rural communities, preparing doctoral-level psychologists to work within these communities, and provision of services to those areas through the training program itself. A wide range of theoretical perspectives is represented on our faculty. The MA program can be individualized to address a variety of academic and professional objectives for students. There is an area of emphasis available in clinical psychology (based in our South Charleston, West Virginia campus), which prepares students for entry-level clinical work at the MA level. Students can also take coursework, do research and take field placements in interest areas such as I/O psychology and a variety of disciplinary areas such as developmental, cognitive, and social.

Programs and Degrees Offered

Program	Degree	Application Deadline	Applications Received	Accepted	New Admits Enrolled (PT)	Total Enrolled (PT)	Degrees Awarded in 2014–2015	Median Years to Complete Degree	Dismissed/Withdrew
Clinical Psychology	PsyD	December 1 (Fall)	80	10	10 (0)	34 (8)	11	5	0
Psychology	MA/MS	March 15 (Fall)	44	28	18 (7)	81 (30)	25	2.5	2

APA Accreditation

Clinical PsyD: Student Outcome Data website: http://www.marshall.edu/psych/programs/psyd-program/.

Doctoral Degree (PsyD Clinical Psychology): For those doctoral students for whom a professional internship was required in this program prior to graduation:
Total students who applied for an internship: 10
Total students who obtained an internship: 10
Total students who obtained a paid internship: 10
Total students who obtained an unpaid internship: 0
Total students who were placed in APA/CPA-accredited internships: 7
Total students placed in internships not APA/CPA-accredited, but listed with the Association of Psychology Postdoctoral and Internship Centers (APPIC): 2
Total students placed in internships conforming to guidelines of the Council of Directors of School Psychology Programs (CDSPP): 0
Total students placed in internships that were not APA/CPA-accredited, APPIC or CDSSP listed: 1

Internships/Practica

Second-year students in the PsyD program work in department's clinic in Huntington; third-year students work at variety of sites in the Huntington community; fourth-year students work at rural placements. Some are in collaboration with primary medical facilities; some may require an overnight stay. Students must complete a full-year, full-time or 2-year, part-time predoctoral internship in order to graduate. Clinical MA students work in the department's clinic in Huntington; master's-level interns work in area mental health agencies. MA students interested in I/O have access to a variety of business and organizational field placements.

Admissions

Entries appear in the following order: required test or GPA, minimum score (if required)/median score of students entering in 2015–2016.

Program	Degree	GRE-V	GRE-Q	GRE-Writing	GRE-Subject	Under-graduate GPA	Last 2 Years GPA	Psychol-ogy GPA	Master's GPA
Clinical Psychology	PsyD	150/154	141/153	Not specified	Not specified	NA/3.6	Not specified	Not specified	Not specified
Psychology	MA/MS	150/NA	141/NA	NA/NA	Not specified	3/NA	Not specified	Not specified	Not specified

Admissions Requirements:

Degree	GRE	GRE-Subject	Letters of Recom-mendation	Research Statement	Writing Sample	CV	Interview
Master's/Specialist	Required	Optional	N/A	Optional	Optional	Optional	Optional
Doctoral	Required	Optional	3	Required	Required	Required	Required

Please note if these criteria vary for different programs: MA program admission is based primarily on GPA and GRE scores; PsyD program considers these, plus statement of professional goals, clinical and research experience, commitment to and understanding of rural psychological service delivery, and letters of recommendation. An interview is required of PsyD applicants and applicants to the clinical emphasis of the MA program. We accept PsyD students via two routes—those with masters degrees in psychology and those who are just begining their graduate education. Criteria are similar, but weightings are a bit different for each; professional experience and demonstrated experience with rural issues are weighted more heavily in our post-MA pool.

Admissions Criteria:

GRE scores—medium
Research experience—medium
Work experience—medium
Clinically related public service—medium
GPA—high

Letters of recommendation—medium
Interview—medium
Statement of goals and objectives—high
Undergraduate psychology preparation—medium

Department Demographics

	Male (PT)	Female (PT)	Total	African-American/ Black (PT)	Hispanic/ Latino (PT)	Asian/ Pacific Islander (PT)	American Indian/ Alaska Native (PT)	Caucasian/ White (PT)	Unknown (PT)	Multiethnic (PT)	ADA (PT)	Int'l (PT)
Students	17 (17)	98 (21)	153	3 (0)	1 (0)	0 (0)	1 (0)	110 (38)	0 (0)	0 (0)	0 (0)	0 (0)

Financial Information/Assistance

Tuition: For information on tuition costs, visit http://www.marshall.edu/bursar/tuition-payment/tuitionhousing-rates/. Tuition is subject to change. Tuition costs vary by program.

Doctoral:
State residents: $9,204 per academic year.
State residents: $512 per credit hour.
Nonstate residents: $19,950 per academic year.
Nonstate residents: $1,108 per credit hour.

Master's:
State residents: $7,068 per academic year.
State residents: $393 per credit hour.
Nonstate residents: $17,058 per academic year.
Nonstate residents: $948 per credit hour.

Financial Assistance:

	Teaching Assistantship (% Receiving)	Teaching Assistantship Tuition Remission	Research Assistantship (% Receiving)	Research Assistantship Tuition Remission	Fellowship (% Receiving)	Fellowship Tuition Remission
First-Year Student	$3,000 (NA)	Partial	$3,000 (NA)	Partial	NA (NA)	NA
Advanced Student	$3,000 (NA)	Partial	$3,000 (NA)	Partial	NA (NA)	NA

For additional information on financial assistance, visit http://www.marshall.edu/graduate/costs-and-aid/how-to-finance-your-graduate-education/.

Employment of Department Graduates

Master's:
Enrolled in a psychology doctoral program: 1
Enrolled in another graduate/professional program: 2
Employed in academic position at a 2-year/4-year college: 1
Employed in business or industry: 1
Employed in government agency: 1
Employed in a community mental health/counseling center: 4
Do not know: 15
Total: 25

Doctoral:
Enrolled in a postdoctoral residency/fellowship: 3
Employed in independent practice: 3
Employed in an academic position at a university: 1
Employed in other positions at a higher education institution: 1
Employed in a community mental health/counseling center: 1
Employed in a hospital/medical center: 3
Not seeking employment: 1
Total: 13

Additional Information

Housing and Day Care: On-campus housing is available. See the following website for more information: http://www.marshall.edu/housing/. On-campus day care facilities are available. See the following website for more information: http://www.marshall.edu/cda/.

Information for Students With Physical Disabilities: See the following website: http://www.marshall.edu/disability/.

Special Facilities or Resources: Departmental and university computer facilities are available to students for clinical work and for research projects in all programs. Online library resources are excellent. Through department clinics, clinical students are afforded the opportunity to work, under supervision, with clients from the community and university. Faculty have a variety of active, ongoing research projects available for student collaboration.

Application Information: Admissions Office, Marshall University Graduate College, 100 Angus Peyton Drive, South Charleston, WV 25303-1600. *Fee:* $40. *Online application:* http://www.marshall.edu/admissions/apply/.

West Virginia University

Department of Counseling, Rehabilitation Counseling and Counseling Psychology
Education and Human Services
502 Allen Hall, P.O. Box 6122
Morgantown, WV 26506-6122
Telephone: (304) 293-2172
Chairperson: Jeffrey A. Daniels
E-mail: David.Allen@mail.wvu.edu
Web: http://counseling.wvu.edu

Orientation, Objectives, and Emphasis of Department

The department's faculty represent a variety of theoretical orientations. The objective of the department is to train professionals primarily to serve clients with intact personalities, but who may be experiencing difficulties related to personal adjustment, interpersonal relationships, developmental problems, crises, academic or career stress, or decisions. The employment settings for our graduates typically include college and university counseling and testing services, community mental health agencies, clinics, hospitals, schools, rehabilitation centers, correctional centers, the United States Armed Services, and private practice.

Programs and Degrees Offered

Program	Degree	Application Deadline	Applications Received	Accepted	New Admits Enrolled (PT)	Total Enrolled (PT)	Degrees Awarded in 2014–2015	Median Years to Complete Degree	Dismissed/ Withdrew
Counseling Psychology	PhD	December 1 (Fall)	24	6	6 (0)	22 (4)	7	6	0

APA Accreditation

Counseling PhD: Student Outcome Data website: http://counseling.wvu.edu/counseling_psychology/future_students.

Doctoral Degree (PhD Counseling Psychology): For those doctoral students for whom a professional internship was required in this program prior to graduation:

Total students who applied for an internship: 5
Total students who obtained an internship: 5
Total students who obtained a paid internship: 5
Total students who obtained an unpaid internship: 0
Total students who were placed in APA/CPA-accredited internships: 5
Total students placed in internships not APA/CPA-accredited, but listed with the Association of Psychology Postdoctoral and Internship Centers (APPIC): 0
Total students placed in internships conforming to guidelines of the Council of Directors of School Psychology Programs (CDSPP): 0
Total students placed in internships that were not APA/CPA-accredited, APPIC or CDSSP listed: 0

Internships/Practica

The doctoral program offers a variety of opportunities for practicum training. Some of the placement sites include: the federal prison system, mental health agencies, employee assistant programs, private practices, VAMCs, local school systems, university counseling center, and others. We have been successful in matching interns with programs in college counseling centers, VAMCs, hospitals/clinics, community mental health centers and consortia, and child and adolescent guidance/treatment centers.

Admissions

Entries appear in the following order: required test or GPA, minimum score (if required)/median score of students entering in 2015–2016.

Program	Degree	GRE-V	GRE-Q	GRE-Writing	GRE-Subject	Under-graduate GPA	Last 2 Years GPA	Psychol-ogy GPA	Master's GPA
Counseling Psychology	PhD	153/NA	144/NA	NA/NA	Not specified	Not specified	Not specified	Not specified	3.5/NA

Admissions Requirements:

Degree	GRE	GRE-Subject	Letters of Recom-mendation	Research Statement	Writing Sample	CV	Interview
Doctoral	Required	Optional	3	Required	Optional	Required	Required

Admissions Criteria:

GRE scores—medium
Research experience—medium
Work experience—high
Clinically related public service—medium
GPA—medium

Letters of recommendation—high
Interview—high
Statement of goals and objectives—high
Undergraduate psychology preparation—low
Fit with program—high

For additional information on admission requirements, visit http://counseling.wvu.edu/counseling_psychology/future_students/admissions.

Department Demographics

	Male (PT)	Female (PT)	Total	African-American/ Black (PT)	Hispanic/ Latino (PT)	Asian/ Pacific Islander (PT)	American Indian/ Alaska Native (PT)	Caucasian/ White (PT)	Unknown	Multiethnic (PT)	ADA (PT)	Int'l (PT)
Students	7 (0)	15 (4)	26	0 (0)	0 (0)	2 (0)	0 (0)	20 (4)	0 (0)	0 (0)	0 (0)	0 (0)

Financial Information/Assistance

Tuition: For information on tuition costs, visit http://tuition.wvu.edu/. Tuition is subject to change. Additional fees are assessed to students beyond the costs of tuition for the following: mandatory fees per semester—$910 for in-state and $1,035 for out-of-state.

Doctoral:
State residents: $9,126 per academic year.
State residents: $507 per credit hour.
Nonstate residents: $22,950 per academic year.
Nonstate residents: $1,275 per credit hour.

Financial Assistance:

	Teaching Assistantship (% Receiving)	Teaching Assistantship Tuition Remission	Research Assistantship (% Receiving)	Research Assistantship Tuition Remission	Fellowship (% Receiving)	Fellowship Tuition Remission
First-Year Student	$12,400 (17)	Full	$12,400 (66)	Full	$17,000 (17)	Full
Advanced Student	$12,400 (27)	Full	$12,400 (64)	Full	$17,000 (9)	Full

For additional information on financial assistance, visit http://counseling.wvu.edu/home/financial_aid.

Employment of Department Graduates

Doctoral:
Enrolled in a postdoctoral residency/fellowship: 3
Employed in a community mental health/counseling center: 2
Employed in a hospital/medical center: 1
Other employment position: 1
Total: 7

Additional Information

Housing and Day Care: On-campus housing is available. See the following website for more information: http://housing.wvu.edu/. On-campus day care facilities are available. See the following website for more information: http://childlearningcenter.wvu.edu/.

Information for Students With Physical Disabilities: See the following website: http://accessibilityservices.wvu.edu/.

Special Facilities or Resources: Facilities include an extensive medical center, including video equipment and computer terminals; training and observation rooms; and practicum and internship sites in a variety of settings.

Application Information: Admissions Coordinator, Department of Counseling, Rehabilitation Counseling and Counseling Psychology, West Virginia University, P.O. Box 6122, Morgantown, WV 25606-6122. *Fee:* $60. *Online application:* https://app.applyyourself.com/?id=wvugrad.

West Virginia University

Department of Psychology
Eberly College of Arts and Sciences
P.O. Box 6040
Morgantown, WV 26506-6040
Telephone: (304) 293-2001
Chairperson: Kevin Larkin

E-mail: PsychGradAdmissions@mail.wvu.edu
Web: http://psychology.wvu.edu

Orientation, Objectives, and Emphasis of Department

The Psychology Department offers the Doctor of Philosophy degree in Behavior Analysis, Behavioral Neuroscience, Lifespan Developmental, Clinical Child, and Clinical Psychology. The Department employs a junior colleague model of training, in which graduate students participate fully in research, teaching, and service activities. The Behavior Analysis doctoral program trains students in basic research, theory, and applications of behavioral psychology. These three areas of study are integrated in the Behavior Analysis curriculum; however, a student may emphasize either basic or applied research. The Lifespan Developmental program emphasizes cognitive and social/personality development across the lifespan. It combines breadth of exposure across a variety of perspectives on the lifespan with depth and rigor in research training and the opportunity to specialize in an age period such as infancy, childhood, adolescence, or adulthood and old age. The Clinical programs have a behavioral/cognitive behavioral orientation. They train scientist–practitioners who function effectively in academic, medical center, or clinical applied settings. Specializations in developmental psychology, behavior analysis, and clinical health psychology are available.

Programs and Degrees Offered

Program	Degree	Application Deadline	Applications Received	Accepted	New Admits Enrolled (PT)	Total Enrolled (PT)	Degrees Awarded in 2014–2015	Median Years to Complete Degree	Dismissed/ Withdrew
Lifespan Developmental Psychology	PhD	December 1 (Fall)	26	5	5 (0)	15 (0)	6	4.5	1
Behavior Analysis	PhD	December 1 (Fall)	31	8	5 (0)	13 (0)	4	4.5	4
Clinical Psychology	PhD	December 1 (Fall)	171	11	6 (0)	31 (0)	5	6.2	1
Behavioral Neuroscience	PhD	December 1 (Fall)	19	3	2 (0)	8 (0)	0		2

APA Accreditation

Clinical PhD: Student Outcome Data website: http://psychology.wvu.edu/graduate-students/doctoral-programs/ph-d-in-clinical-psychology.

Doctoral Degree (PhD Clinical Psychology): For those doctoral students for whom a professional internship was required in this program prior to graduation:
Total students who applied for an internship: 4
Total students who obtained an internship: 4
Total students who obtained a paid internship: 4
Total students who obtained an unpaid internship: 0
Total students who were placed in APA/CPA-accredited internships: 4
Total students placed in internships not APA/CPA-accredited, but listed with the Association of Psychology Postdoctoral and Internship Centers (APPIC): 0
Total students placed in internships conforming to guidelines of the Council of Directors of School Psychology Programs (CDSPP): 0
Total students placed in internships that were not APA/CPA-accredited, APPIC or CDSSP listed: 0

Internships/Practica

Paid clinical placements at out-of-department sites are available for doctoral clinical students who have earned master's degrees. These out-of-department practicum sites include WVU Carruth Counseling Center, Kennedy Federal Correctional Institution, Hopemont Hospital, Sharpe Hospital, the Robert C. Byrd Health Sciences Center, a private practice, various behavioral/community mental health agencies, and children and youth services agencies. These sites are located in Morgantown and across the state and region. Stipends for practica range from $13,000 to $16,000, require 16 hours of work per week, and virtually all last 12 months.

Admissions

Entries appear in the following order: required test or GPA, minimum score (if required)/median score of students entering in 2015–2016.

Program	Degree	GRE-V	GRE-Q	GRE-Writing	GRE-Subject	Under-graduate GPA	Last 2 Years GPA	Psychology GPA	Master's GPA
Lifespan Developmental Psychology	PhD	150/155	150/150	3.5/4	Not specified	3/3.78	Not specified	3.7/3.7	Not specified
Behavior Analysis	PhD	150/156	150/155	3.5/4.3	Not specified	3/3.63	Not specified	3.7/3.7	Not specified
Clinical Psychology	PhD	150/162	150/155	3.5/4.25	NA/NA	3/3.75	Not specified	3.7/3.7	Not specified
Behavioral Neuroscience	PhD	150/159	150/150	3.5/4	Not specified	3/3.65	Not specified	3.7/3.7	Not specified

Admissions Requirements:

Degree	GRE	GRE-Subject	Letters of Recommendation	Research Statement	Writing Sample	CV	Interview
Doctoral	Required	Recommended	3	Required	Optional	Required	Required

Please note if these criteria vary for different programs: Match between faculty and student interests is of high importance. Only clinical programs give high value to clinically related public service.

Admissions Criteria:

GRE scores—high
Research experience—high
Work experience—medium
Clinically related public service—medium
GPA—high

Letters of recommendation—high
Interview—high
Statement of goals and objectives—high
Undergraduate psychology preparation—medium

For additional information on admission requirements, visit http://psychology.wvu.edu/graduate-students/application-information.

Department Demographics

	Male (PT)	Female (PT)	Total	African-American/ Black (PT)	Hispanic/ Latino (PT)	Asian/ Pacific Islander (PT)	American Indian/ Alaska Native (PT)	Caucasian/ White (PT)	Unknown	Multiethnic (PT)	ADA (PT)	Int'l (PT)
Students	20 (0)	47 (0)	67	6 (0)	1 (0)	1 (0)	1 (0)	56 (0)	0 (0)	2 (0)	0 (0)	1 (0)

Financial Information/Assistance

Tuition: For information on tuition costs, visit http://tuition.wvu.edu/graduate. Tuition is subject to change. Additional fees are assessed to students beyond the costs of tuition for the following: University Fees = $630 per semester.

Doctoral:
State residents: $7,308 per academic year.
State residents: $406 per credit hour.
Nonstate residents: $20,880 per academic year.
Nonstate residents: $1,160 per credit hour.

Master's:
State residents: $7,308 per academic year.
State residents: $406 per credit hour.
Nonstate residents: $20,880 per academic year.
Nonstate residents: $1,160 per credit hour.

Financial Assistance:

	Teaching Assistantship (% Receiving)	Teaching Assistantship Tuition Remission	Research Assistantship (% Receiving)	Research Assistantship Tuition Remission	Fellowship (% Receiving)	Fellowship Tuition Remission
First-Year Student	$15,000 (NA)	Full	$18,000 (NA)	Full	$17,500 (NA)	Full
Advanced Student	$15,000 (NA)	Full	$18,000 (NA)	Full	$17,500 (NA)	Full

For additional information on financial assistance, visit http://psychology.wvu.edu/graduate-students/application-information/financial-assistance.

Employment of Department Graduates

No information provided.

Additional Information

Housing and Day Care: On-campus housing is available. See the following website for more information: http://universityapartments.wvu.edu/. On-campus day care facilities are available. See the following website for more information: http://childlearningcenter.wvu.edu/.

Information for Students With Physical Disabilities: See the following website: http://accessibilityservices.wvu.edu/.

Special Facilities or Resources: The Department is housed in the Life Sciences Building, which has modern animal research quarters for work with rats, pigeons, and other species. There are several computer-based laboratories and other laboratories for studies of learning in humans and animals, behavioral pharmacology, and neurosciences. There are additional facilities for human research in learning, cognition, small group processes, developmental psychology, social behavior, and psychophysiology. Clinical practicum opportunities are available through the Department's Quin Curtis Center for Psychological Service, Training, and Research, as well as in numerous mental health agencies throughout the state. Videotaping and direct observation equipment and facilities are available. The West Virginia University Medical Center provides facilities for research and training in such departments and areas as behavioral medicine and psychiatry, pediatrics, neurology, and dentistry. Local preschools and public schools have been cooperative in providing access to children and facilities for child development research, local businesses and other agencies offer sites for practice and research in applied behavior analysis, local senior centers and homes provide access to older adult populations, and the University's Center on Aging-Education Unit and Center for Women's Studies facilitate research related to their purviews.

Application Information: West Virginia University, Office of Admissions, One Waterfront Place, P.O. Box 6009, Morgantown, WV 26506. *Fee:* $60. *Online application:* http://graduate.wvu.edu/future-students/application-process/apply.

Marquette University

Counselor Education and Counseling Psychology
College of Education
561 North 15th Street 150 Schroeder Complex
Milwaukee, WI 53233
Telephone: (414) 288-5790
Chairperson: Alan W. Burkard

E-mail: alan.burkard@marquette.edu
Web: http://www.marquette.edu/education/grad/cecp.shtml

Orientation, Objectives, and Emphasis of Department

Our Master's in Counseling and PhD in Counseling Psychology programs are based on a comprehensive biopsychosocial approach to understanding human behavior. We believe that a sensitivity to biological, psychological, social, multicultural, and developmental influences on behavior increases students' effectiveness both as practitioners and as researchers. We use a generalist approach that includes broad preparation in the diverse areas needed to practice competently as psychological scientists and practitioners in today's health care systems. The master's programs in counseling include specializations in school counseling and clinical mental health counseling, with optional specializations in addictions counseling and child/adolescent counseling. The master's programs are accredited by CACREP. The doctoral program in counseling psychology is accredited by APA.

Programs and Degrees Offered

Program	Degree	Application Deadline	Applications Received	Accepted	New Admits Enrolled (PT)	Total Enrolled (PT)	Degrees Awarded in 2014–2015	Median Years to Complete Degree	Dismissed/ Withdrew
Counseling	MA/MS	February 1 (Fall)	69	31	29 (2)	56 (5)	28	2	1
Counseling Psychology	PhD	December 1 (Fall)	47	4	4 (0)	12 (7)	3	4	0

APA Accreditation

Counseling PhD: Student Outcome Data website: http://www.marquette.edu/education/grad/cecp_doctorate_disclosure.shtml.

Doctoral Degree (PhD Counseling Psychology): For those doctoral students for whom a professional internship was required in this program prior to graduation:
Total students who applied for an internship: 4
Total students who obtained an internship: 4
Total students who obtained a paid internship: 4
Total students who obtained an unpaid internship: 0
Total students who were placed in APA/CPA-accredited internships: 4
Total students placed in internships not APA/CPA-accredited, but listed with the Association of Psychology Postdoctoral and Internship Centers (APPIC): 0
Total students placed in internships conforming to guidelines of the Council of Directors of School Psychology Programs (CDSPP): 0
Total students placed in internships that were not APA/CPA-accredited, APPIC or CDSSP listed: 0

Master's Degree (MA/MS Counseling): An internship experience, such as a final research project or "capstone" experience is required of graduates.

Internships/Practica

We work with a wide range of inpatient and outpatient agencies and educational institutions serving a broad range of clients, from children to seniors and from relatively minor adjustment issues to serious psychopathology. We currently work with approximately 60 agencies and schools and continually try to find additional sites offering superior clinical experience and supervision.

Admissions

Entries appear in the following order: required test or GPA, minimum score (if required)/median score of students entering in 2015–2016.

Program	Degree	GRE-V	GRE-Q	GRE-Writing	GRE-Subject	Under-graduate GPA	Last 2 Years GPA	Psychology GPA	Master's GPA
Counseling	MA/MS	NA/151	NA/148	NA/4	Not specified	NA/3.35	Not specified	Not specified	Not specified
Counseling Psychology	PhD	NA/159	NA/156	NA/4	Not specified	NA/3.53	Not specified	Not specified	NA/3.47

Admissions Requirements:

Degree	GRE	GRE-Subject	Letters of Recom-mendation	Research Statement	Writing Sample	CV	Interview
Master's/Specialist	Required	None	3	Required	Optional	Required	Required
Doctoral	Required	Required	3	Required	Optional	Required	Required

Please note if these criteria vary for different programs: Research experience is much more important for admission into our PhD program than it is for our master's programs.

Admissions Criteria:

GRE scores—high
Research experience—high
Work experience—medium
Clinically related public service—medium
GPA—high

Letters of recommendation—high
Interview—high
Statement of goals and objectives—high
Undergraduate psychology preparation—medium

For additional information on admission requirements, visit http://www.marquette.edu/education/grad/cecp.shtml.

Department Demographics

	Male (PT)	Female (PT)	Total	African-American/ Black (PT)	Hispanic/ Latino (PT)	Asian/ Pacific Islander (PT)	American Indian/ Alaska Native (PT)	Caucasian/ White (PT)	Unknown	Multiethnic (PT)	ADA (PT)	Int'l (PT)
Students	16 (2)	53 (7)	78	4 (0)	4 (2)	2 (1)	0 (0)	49 (4)	8 (0)	4 (0)	3 (1)	2 (0)

Financial Information/Assistance

Tuition: For information on tuition costs, visit http://www.marquette.edu/about/tuition-costs.php.

Doctoral:
State residents: $805 per credit hour.
Nonstate residents: $805 per credit hour.

Master's:
State residents: $805 per credit hour.
Nonstate residents: $805 per credit hour.

Financial Assistance:

	Teaching Assistantship (% Receiving)	Teaching Assistantship Tuition Remission	Research Assistantship (% Receiving)	Research Assistantship Tuition Remission	Fellowship (% Receiving)	Fellowship Tuition Remission
First-Year Student	NA (NA)	NA	$7,825 (100)	Full	$7,825 (100)	Full
Advanced Student	NA (NA)	NA	$7,825 (NA)	Full	$15,650 (NA)	Full

For additional information on financial assistance, visit http://marquette.edu/grad/financial-aid.php.

Employment of Department Graduates

Master's:
Enrolled in a psychology doctoral program: 2
Enrolled in another graduate/professional program: 1
Employed in an academic position at a university: 2
Employed in academic position at a 2-year/4-year college: 1
Employed in other positions at a higher education institution: 2
Employed in a professional position in a school system: 7
Employed in business or industry: 1
Employed in a community mental health/counseling center: 3
Employed in a hospital/medical center: 6
Do not know: 5
Total: 30

Doctoral:
Enrolled in a postdoctoral residency/fellowship: 3
Total: 3

Additional Information

Housing and Day Care: On-campus housing is available. See the following website for more information: http://www.marquette.edu/orl/. On-campus day care facilities are available. See the following website for more information: http://www.marquette.edu/child-care-center/.

Information for Students With Physical Disabilities: See the following website: http://www.marquette.edu/disability-services/.

Special Facilities or Resources: Our faculty, and Marquette University as a whole, are committed to offering high quality education. Our coursework, practica, research activities, and other training opportunities are all designed to provide current and comprehensive preparation. Our student body is small, so students receive substantial individual attention. We are also committed to developing students' competencies to work with diverse, multicultural groups, and we welcome applications from individuals with diverse backgrounds. The full-time faculty are engaged in a variety of research projects with which students may become involved. Our close affiliation with the Behavior Clinic, a community-based facility focusing on children 0-5 years of age and their parents, provides counseling and research opportunities for our students.

Application Information: Graduate School, P.O. Box 1881, Milwaukee, WI 53201. *Fee:* $50. *Online application:* http://www.marquette.edu/grad/apply/.

Marquette University
Department of Psychology
Arts and Sciences
P.O. Box 1881
Milwaukee, WI 53201-1881
Telephone: (414) 288-7218
Chairperson: John Grych

E-mail: john.grych@marquette.edu
Web: http://www.marquette.edu/psyc

Orientation, Objectives, and Emphasis of Department
The Clinical Psychology program offers courses and training leading to the degree of Doctor of Philosophy (PhD) in Clinical Psychology. All doctoral students earn a Master of Science degree as they progress toward the doctoral degree. The doctoral program is accredited by the American Psychological Association Commission on Accreditation. The program follows the scientist–practitioner (Boulder) model. Students receive a solid foundation in the scientific study of psychology and in empirically-based intervention. Training in statistics, measurement, and research methods ensures competence in conducting empirical research and in critically evaluating one's own and others' clinical and empirical work. Students become competent in professional practice skills such as assessment, interventions, and consultation. Supervised clinical experiences are planned throughout the curriculum. Graduates of the doctoral program are prepared for employment as academics, researchers, clinical psychologists, consultants, teachers, and administrators.

Programs and Degrees Offered

Program	Degree	Application Deadline	Applications Received	Accepted	New Admits Enrolled (PT)	Total Enrolled (PT)	Degrees Awarded in 2014–2015	Median Years to Complete Degree	Dismissed/Withdrew
Clinical Psychology	PhD	December 1 (Fall)	162	5	5 (0)	34 (0)	7	6	0

APA Accreditation

Clinical PhD: Student Outcome Data website: http://www.marquette.edu/psyc/graduate_overview.shtml.

Doctoral Degree (PhD Clinical Psychology): For those doctoral students for whom a professional internship was required in this program prior to graduation:

Total students who applied for an internship: 7

Total students who obtained an internship: 7

Total students who obtained a paid internship: 7

Total students who obtained an unpaid internship: 0

Total students who were placed in APA/CPA-accredited internships: 7

Total students placed in internships not APA/CPA-accredited, but listed with the Association of Psychology Postdoctoral and Internship Centers (APPIC): 0

Total students placed in internships conforming to guidelines of the Council of Directors of School Psychology Programs (CDSPP): 0

Total students placed in internships that were not APA/CPA-accredited, APPIC or CDSSP listed: 0

Internships/Practica

Doctoral students obtain supervised clinical experience throughout their training. Practica are offered in the Department's training clinic (the Center for Psychological Services or CPS), a local academic medical center (Froedtert Hospital and Children's Hospital of the Medical College of Wisconsin), the Zablocki VA hospital, and numerous other community agencies. All practica are supervised by licensed psychologists. The Department's training clinic (CPS) provides assessment and intervention services to members of the general community under the supervision of program clinical faculty. Recent practicum placements have included hospitals and agencies that provided training in individual and group therapy, neuropsychological assessment, geropsychology, behavioral medicine, pediatric health, and family therapy. Over their course of study, most students have obtained at least 750 hours at CPS, and students typically acquire a total of 1,500 to 2,500 hours of face-to-face practicum experience with clients (plus face-to-face hours of supervision) before attending internship. Marquette University's urban location provides a wealth of training opportunities in the community. Doctoral students are required to complete a 2,000 hour internship. To date, students have completed APA-approved internships in settings located throughout the United States.

Admissions

Entries appear in the following order: required test or GPA, minimum score (if required)/median score of students entering in 2015–2016.

Program	Degree	GRE-V	GRE-Q	GRE-Writing	GRE-Subject	Under-graduate GPA	Last 2 Years GPA	Psychology GPA	Master's GPA
Clinical Psychology	PhD	NA/160	NA/157	NA/4.7	Not specified	NA/3.76	Not specified	Not specified	Not specified

Admissions Requirements:

Degree	GRE	GRE-Subject	Letters of Recom-mendation	Research Statement	Writing Sample	CV	Interview
Doctoral	Required	None	3	Required	Optional	Optional	Required

Admissions Criteria:

GRE scores—medium
Research experience—high
Work experience—low
Clinically related public service—low
GPA—medium

Letters of recommendation—high
Interview—high
Statement of goals and objectives—high
Undergraduate psychology preparation—medium

For additional information on admission requirements, visit http://www.marquette.edu/psyc/graduate_apply.shtml.

Department Demographics

	Male (PT)	Female (PT)	Total	African-American/ Black (PT)	Hispanic/ Latino (PT)	Asian/ Pacific Islander (PT)	American Indian/ Alaska Native (PT)	Caucasian/ White (PT)	Unknown	Multiethnic (PT)	ADA (PT)	Int'l (PT)
Students	6 (0)	28 (0)	34	0 (0)	3 (0)	1 (0)	0 (0)	30 (0)	0 (0)	0 (0)	0 (0)	0 (0)

Financial Information/Assistance

Tuition: For information on tuition costs, visit http://www.marquette.edu/about/tuition-costs.php. Tuition is subject to change.

Doctoral:
State residents: $1,050 per credit hour.
Nonstate residents: $1,050 per credit hour.

Financial Assistance:

	Teaching Assistantship (% Receiving)	Teaching Assistantship Tuition Remission	Research Assistantship (% Receiving)	Research Assistantship Tuition Remission	Fellowship (% Receiving)	Fellowship Tuition Remission
First-Year Student	$15,650 (100)	Full	$15,650 (100)	Full	NA (NA)	NA
Advanced Student	$15,650 (75)	Full	$15,650 (75)	Full	$17,500 (5)	Full

For additional information on financial assistance, visit http://www.marquette.edu/psyc/graduate_finaid.shtml.

Employment of Department Graduates

Doctoral:
Enrolled in a postdoctoral residency/fellowship: 5
Employed in a community mental health/counseling center: 1
Employed in a hospital/medical center: 1
Total: 7

Additional Information

Housing and Day Care: On-campus housing is available. See the following website for more information: http://www.marquette.edu/orl/. On-campus day care facilities are available. See the following website for more information: http://www.marquette.edu/child-care-center/.

Information for Students With Physical Disabilities: See the following website: http://www.marquette.edu/disability-services/.

Special Facilities or Resources: The department is located in modern quarters that include a psychology clinic, an undergraduate teaching laboratory, and ample space for both faculty and student research. A full range of computer services is available at no charge to students. Located in a large metropolitan area, Marquette University is within easy commuting distance to a variety of hospitals and agencies in which training and research opportunities may be available.

Application Information: Fee: $50. Online application: http://www.marquette.edu/grad/apply/.

Wisconsin School of Professional Psychology
Professional School
9120 West Hampton Avenue
Milwaukee, WI 53225
Telephone: (414) 464-9777
President: Kathleen M. Rusch, PhD

E-mail: rusch.kathleen@wspp.edu
Web: http://www.wspp.edu

Orientation, Objectives, and Emphasis of Department
The Wisconsin School of Professional Psychology has as its goal the provision of a doctoral-level education that emphasizes the acquisition of the traditional skills which defined the professional in the past while staying open to new developments as they emerge. Our APA-accredited program balances theoretical and practical coursework, taking its impetus from the American Psychological Association's Vail Conference. The school's curriculum was developed in accordance with APA norms and is continually evaluated to ensure compliance with the requirements of that body. WSPP trains students toward competence in the following areas: self-awareness, assessment, research and evaluation, ethics and professional standards, management and supervision, relationship, intervention, respect for diversity, consultation, social responsibility and community service. In its training philosophy, the school emphasizes clarity of verbal expression in written and oral communication, the development of clinical acumen, and an appreciation

of the link between scientific data and clinical practice. Our program's small size and large faculty create abundant opportunities for mentorship with practicing psychologists in an apprentice-like setting.

Programs and Degrees Offered

Program	Degree	Application Deadline	Applica-tions Received	Accepted	New Admits Enrolled (PT)	Total Enrolled (PT)	Degrees Awarded in 2014–2015	Median Years to Complete Degree	Dismissed/Withdrew
Clinical Psychology	PsyD	January 1 (Fall)	45	16	15 (1)	37 (58)	32	6	1

APA Accreditation

Clinical PsyD: Student Outcome Data website: http://wspp.edu/whywspp/wacompl.

Doctoral Degree (PsyD Clinical Psychology): For those doctoral students for whom a professional internship was required in this program prior to graduation:

Total students who applied for an internship: 15

Total students who obtained an internship: 14

Total students who obtained a paid internship: 14

Total students who obtained an unpaid internship: 0

Total students who were placed in APA/CPA-accredited internships: 9

Total students placed in internships not APA/CPA-accredited, but listed with the Association of Psychology Postdoctoral and Internship Centers (APPIC): 5

Total students placed in internships conforming to guidelines of the Council of Directors of School Psychology Programs (CDSPP): 0

Total students placed in internships that were not APA/CPA-accredited, APPIC or CDSSP listed: 0

Internships/Practica

WSPP has an on-site training clinic, the Psychology Center, which is designed to serve two purposes: to provide supervised training to students and to provide quality clinical services to an inner-city, multicultural, disadvantaged population. The Center also maintains contracts and affiliations with a number of local service agencies to provide on-site services. Regardless of whether on- or off-site, all practica are supervised by WSPP faculty to ensure quality of supervision and communication with our DCT. Some 40 supervisors, all licensed and most National Register listed, are readily available. For assessment practica, WSPP maintains a library of psychological tests available for student use free of charge. Thus, all students are guaranteed ample practicum opportunities (the program requires 2,000 hours) without having to search for sites or supervisors. This high level of clinical training has led to our very high internship placement rate to date.

Admissions

Entries appear in the following order: required test or GPA, minimum score (if required)/median score of students entering in 2015–2016.

Program	Degree	GRE-V	GRE-Q	GRE-Writing	GRE-Subject	Under-graduate GPA	Last 2 Years GPA	Psychol-ogy GPA	Master's GPA
Clinical Psychology	PsyD	NA/153	NA/147	NA/4.1	Not specified	NA/3.5	NA/NA	NA/NA	NA/NA

Admissions Requirements:

Degree	GRE	GRE-Subject	Letters of Recom-mendation	Research Statement	Writing Sample	CV	Interview
Doctoral	Required	None	3	Required	Required	Required	Required

Admissions Criteria:

GRE scores—medium

Research experience—low

Work experience—high

Clinically related public service—high

GPA—medium

Letters of recommendation—high

Interview—high

Statement of goals and objectives—high

Undergraduate psychology preparation—medium

Essay—high

For additional information on admission requirements, visit http://wspp.edu/admissions.

Department Demographics

	Male (PT)	Female (PT)	Total	African-American/ Black (PT)	Hispanic/ Latino (PT)	Asian/ Pacific Islander (PT)	American Indian/ Alaska Native (PT)	Caucasian/ White (PT)	Unknown	Multiethnic (PT)	ADA (PT)	Int'l (PT)
Students	10 (11)	27 (47)	95	1 (3)	2 (4)	0 (2)	2 (0)	32 (49)	0 (0)	0 (0)	1 (1)	0 (0)

Financial Information/Assistance

Tuition: Tuition is subject to change. Additional fees are assessed to students beyond the costs of tuition for the following: $50 materials fee for all assessment courses; $50 tech fee per semester.

Doctoral:
State residents: $22,990 per academic year.
State residents: $950 per credit hour.
Nonstate residents: $22,990 per academic year.
Nonstate residents: $950 per credit hour.

Financial Assistance:

	Teaching Assistantship (% Receiving)	Teaching Assistantship Tuition Remission	Research Assistantship (% Receiving)	Research Assistantship Tuition Remission	Fellowship (% Receiving)	Fellowship Tuition Remission
First-Year Student	$10,000 (13)	Partial	NA (NA)	NA	$4,250 (19)	Partial
Advanced Student	$5,325 (5)	NA	NA (NA)	NA	$1,900 (14)	Partial

For additional information on financial assistance, visit http://wspp.edu/student-support/financial-aid.

Employment of Department Graduates

Master's:
Enrolled in a psychology doctoral program: 18
Total: 18

Doctoral:
Employed in independent practice: 1
Employed in academic position at a 2-year/4-year college: 1
Employed in government agency: 6
Employed in a community mental health/counseling center: 5
Other employment position: 1
Total: 14

Additional Information

Housing and Day Care: No on-campus housing is available. No on-campus day care facilities are available.

Special Facilities or Resources: The Wisconsin School of Professional Psychology maintains a Training Clinic which includes facilities for research and practicum work associated with clinical courses. The Training Center houses an outpatient mental health clinic which serves a primarily inner-city, culturally diverse population, as well as provides opportunities for supervised experience with a wide range of clinical problems and populations. The center offers services to the community on a sliding fee basis. Supervision is provided by faculty.

Application Information: Wisconsin School of Professional Psychology, 9120 West Hampton Avenue, Milwaukee, WI 53225.
Fee: $75.

Wisconsin, University of, Eau Claire (2015 data)
Department of Psychology
Arts and Sciences
University of Wisconsin-Eau Claire
Eau Claire, WI 54702
Telephone: (715) 836-5733
Chairperson: Doug Matthews

E-mail: tusingm@uwec.edu
Web: http://www.uwec.edu/Psyc/graduate/index.htm

Orientation, Objectives, and Emphasis of Department

The School Psychology Program is offered by the Department of Psychology in cooperation with the College of Education and Human Services. The School Psychology Program is based on the scientist–practitioner model. As scientists, students develop a strong data- and research-based orientation as problem solvers in the practice of school psychology. As practitioners, students develop a high level of competence in skills required of school psychologists: assessment, intervention, and evaluation at the individual, group, and systems levels. Two values guide all aspects of the school psychologist's activities and the training program: (1) sensitivity to and respect for individual differences and diversity; and (2) high standards of ethical and professional conduct. The program has two unique features: the Human Development Center and an ongoing collaborative relationship with the Lac du Flambeau American Indian community.

Programs and Degrees Offered

Program	Degree	Application Deadline	Applica-tions Received	Accepted	New Admits Enrolled (PT)	Total Enrolled (PT)	Degrees Awarded in 2014–2015	Median Years to Complete Degree	Dismissed/Withdrew
School Psychology	EdS	January 15 (Fall)	31	8	8 (0)	25 (2)	10	3	0

Internships/Practica

Internships are required for the Educational Specialist degree and comprise the third year of training. Students must complete a year of full-time practice as school psychologists under the supervision of an appropriately credentialed school psychologist. Students may enroll in the internship upon completion of all requirements except the thesis.

Admissions

Entries appear in the following order: required test or GPA, minimum score (if required)/median score of students entering in 2015–2016.

Program	Degree	GRE-V	GRE-Q	GRE-Writing	GRE-Subject	Under-graduate GPA	Last 2 Years GPA	Psychol-ogy GPA	Master's GPA
School Psychology	EdS	NA/151	Not specified	Not specified	Not specified	3/3.45	Not specified	Not specified	Not specified

Admissions Requirements:

Degree	GRE	GRE-Subject	Letters of Recom-mendation	Research Statement	Writing Sample	CV	Interview
Master's/Specialist	Required	None	3	Required	None	Optional	Required

Admissions Criteria:

GRE scores—high
Research experience—medium
Work experience—medium
Clinically related public service—high
GPA—high

Letters of recommendation—high
Interview—high
Statement of goals and objectives—high
Undergraduate psychology preparation—medium

For additional information on admission requirements, visit http://www.uwec.edu/Psyc/graduate/UWECSchoolPsychAdmissions.htm.

Department Demographics

	Male (PT)	Female (PT)	Total	African-American/ Black (PT)	Hispanic/ Latino (PT)	Asian/ Pacific Islander (PT)	American Indian/ Alaska Native (PT)	Caucasian/ White (PT)	Unknown	Multiethnic (PT)	ADA (PT)	Int'l (PT)
Students	2 (0)	23 (2)	27	0 (0)	1 (0)	1 (0)	0 (0)	25 (2)	0 (0)	0 (0)	0 (0)	0 (0)

Financial Information/Assistance

Tuition: For information on tuition costs, visit http://www.uwec.edu/finaid/costs/index.htm. Tuition is subject to change.

Master's:
State residents: $8,420 per academic year.
State residents: $490 per credit hour.
Nonstate residents: $17,950 per academic year.
Nonstate residents: $997 per credit hour.

Financial Assistance:

	Teaching Assistantship (% Receiving)	Teaching Assistantship Tuition Remission	Research Assistantship (% Receiving)	Research Assistantship Tuition Remission	Fellowship (% Receiving)	Fellowship Tuition Remission
First-Year Student	NA (NA)	NA	$7,100 (50)	Partial	$500 (30)	NA
Advanced Student	NA (NA)	NA	$7,100 (100)	Partial	NA (NA)	NA

For additional information on financial assistance, visit http://www.uwec.edu/finaid/index.htm.

Employment of Department Graduates

Master's:
Employed in a professional position in a school system: 7
Total: 7

Additional Information

Housing and Day Care: No on-campus housing is available. On-campus day care facilities are available. See the following website for more information: http://www.uwec.edu/children/index.htm.

Information for Students With Physical Disabilities: See the following website: http://www.uwec.edu/SSD/.

Special Facilities or Resources: Extensive on-campus and field site training opportunities are available. Two interdisciplinary clinics—The Human Development Center (Psychology-School Psychology; Special Education-Learning Disabilities and Early Childhood; Communication Sciences and Disorders; and Elementary Education-Reading) and the Psychological Services Center (Psychology-School Psychology and Nursing)—provide on-campus training in diagnostics and intervention services. Area schools, residential facilities for developmentally disabled, emotionally disturbed youth and adults, and clinics offer an extensive array of additional supervised training settings. In addition, the program has a continuing collaborative relationship with the Lac du Flambeau American Indian community which offers opportunities for short-term or semester-long practicums.

Application Information: Office of Admissions, University of Wisconsin-Eau Claire, Eau Claire, WI 54702-4004. *Fee:* $56. *Online application:* http://www.uwec.edu/graduate/index.htm.

Wisconsin, University of, La Crosse
Department of Psychology/School Psychology
College of Liberal Studies
1725 State Street, 347 Graff Main Hall
La Crosse, WI 54601
Telephone: (608) 785-8441
Chairperson: Ryan A. McKelley

E-mail: schoolpsych@uwlax.edu
Web: http://www.uwlax.edu/school-psychology/

Orientation, Objectives, and Emphasis of Department
The emphasis of this program is to train school psychologists who are effective teacher, parent and school consultants. The program also emphasizes a pupil services model which addresses the educational and mental health needs of all children. The School

Psychology knowledge base includes areas of Professional School Psychology, Educational Psychology, Psychological Foundations, Educational Foundations, and Mental Health. To provide psychological services in education, graduates of the School Psychology program must also have considerable knowledge of curriculum, special education and pupil services. Graduates of the program are employed in public schools or educational agencies which serve public schools.

Programs and Degrees Offered

Program	Degree	Application Deadline	Applications Received	Accepted	New Admits Enrolled (PT)	Total Enrolled (PT)	Degrees Awarded in 2014–2015	Median Years to Complete Degree	Dismissed/ Withdrew
School Psychology	EdS	January 30 (Fall)	55	18	12	23 (11)	12	3	0

Internships/Practica

The School Psychology program prepares graduate students for certification as School Psychologists through academic coursework, 700 hours of supervised school practica, and a 1-year, 1,200-hour school internship. Graduate students are placed in local schools as early and intensively as possible. During their second, third, and fourth semesters, students spend 2 days per week working in local schools under the direct supervision of experienced school psychologists. During these school practica, students develop professional skills in assessment, consultation, intervention, counseling, and case management. Many of the core courses require projects which are completed in the schools during practica.

Admissions

Entries appear in the following order: required test or GPA, minimum score (if required)/median score of students entering in 2015–2016.

Program	Degree	GRE-V	GRE-Q	GRE-Writing	GRE-Subject	Undergraduate GPA	Last 2 Years GPA	Psychology GPA	Master's GPA
School Psychology	EdS	NA/151	NA/150	NA/3.75	Not specified	NA/3.55	NA/3.65	NA/3.56	Not specified

Admissions Requirements:

Degree	GRE	GRE-Subject	Letters of Recommendation	Research Statement	Writing Sample	CV	Interview
Master's/Specialist	Required	Optional	3	Required	Required	Required	Required

Admissions Criteria:

GRE scores—medium
Research experience—medium
Work experience—medium
Clinically related public service—high
GPA—high

Letters of recommendation—high
Interview—high
Statement of goals and objectives—high
Undergraduate psychology preparation—low

For additional information on admission requirements, visit http://www.uwlax.edu/School-Psychology/How-to-apply/.

Department Demographics

	Male (PT)	Female (PT)	Total	African-American/ Black (PT)	Hispanic/ Latino (PT)	Asian/ Pacific Islander (PT)	American Indian/ Alaska Native (PT)	Caucasian/ White (PT)	Unknown	Multiethnic (PT)	ADA (PT)	Int'l (PT)
Students	3 (2)	20 (9)	34	0 (0)	1 (0)	0 (0)	0 (0)	22 (6)	0 (0)	0 (0)	0 (0)	0 (0)

Financial Information/Assistance

Tuition: For information on tuition costs, visit https://www.uwlax.edu/Cashiers/Tuition-and-fee-information/. Tuition is subject to change. Additional fees are assessed to students beyond the costs of tuition for the following: Special fees may be assessed for certain courses for supplemental materials and/or equipment.

Master's:
State residents: $9,914 per academic year.
State residents: $530 per credit hour.
Nonstate residents: $19,884 per academic year.
Nonstate residents: $1,063 per credit hour.

Financial Assistance:

	Teaching Assistantship (% Receiving)	Teaching Assistantship Tuition Remission	Research Assistantship (% Receiving)	Research Assistantship Tuition Remission	Fellowship (% Receiving)	Fellowship Tuition Remission
First-Year Student	NA (NA)	NA	$4,544 (NA)	NA	NA (NA)	NA
Advanced Student	NA (NA)	NA	$4,544 (NA)	NA	NA (NA)	NA

For additional information on financial assistance, visit http://www.uwlax.edu/School-Psychology/Financial-aid/.

Employment of Department Graduates

Master's:
Employed in a professional position in a school system: 11
Total: 11

Additional Information

Housing and Day Care: On-campus housing is available. See the following website for more information: http://www.uwlax.edu/ResLife/. On-campus day care facilities are available. See the following website for more information: http://www.uwlax.edu/campus-child-center/.

Information for Students With Physical Disabilities: See the following website: http://www.uwlax.edu/access-center/.

Special Facilities or Resources: Extensive fieldwork in local schools is a key to professional training. Faculty work closely with field supervisors and observe student performance in the field.

Application Information: School Psychology Admissions, 347 Graff Main Hall, University of Wisconsin-La Crosse, 1725 State Street, La Crosse, WI 54601. *Fee:* $56. *Online application:* http://www.uwlax.edu/Admissions/Graduate-student/.

Wisconsin, University of, Madison
Department of Counseling Psychology, Counseling Psychology Program
School of Education
335 Education Building - 1000 Bascom Mall
Madison, WI 53706-1326
Telephone: (608) 262-4807
Chairperson: Dr. William T. Hoyt

E-mail: counpsych@education.wisc.edu
Web: http://counselingpsych.education.wisc.edu/

Orientation, Objectives, and Emphasis of Department
The master's and doctoral programs are intended to provide a closely integrated didactic experimental curriculum for the preparation of counseling professionals. The master's degree strongly emphasizes service delivery, and its practica/internship components reflect that emphasis. The doctoral degree emphasizes the integration of counseling and psychological theory and practice with substantive development of research skills in the domains encompassed by counseling psychology. The PhD program in counseling

psychology is APA-accredited and utilizes the scientist–practitioner model. Students are prepared for academic, service-delivery, research and administrative positions in professional psychology. The Department infuses principles of multiculturalism throughout the curriculum.

Programs and Degrees Offered

Program	Degree	Application Deadline	Applica-tions Received	Accepted	New Admits Enrolled (PT)	Total Enrolled (PT)	Degrees Awarded in 2014–2015	Median Years to Complete Degree	Dismissed/Withdrew
Counseling	MA/MS	January 5 (Fall)	202	21	9 (0)	23 (2)	14	2	0
Counseling Psychology	PhD	December 1 (Fall)	131	13	3 (0)	37 (2)	2	7	1

APA Accreditation

Counseling PhD: Student Outcome Data website: http://counselingpsych.education.wisc.edu/cp/phd-program.

Doctoral Degree (PhD Counseling Psychology): For those doctoral students for whom a professional internship was required in this program prior to graduation:
Total students who applied for an internship: 3
Total students who obtained an internship: 3
Total students who obtained a paid internship: 3
Total students who obtained an unpaid internship: 0
Total students who were placed in APA/CPA-accredited internships: 3
Total students placed in internships not APA/CPA-accredited, but listed with the Association of Psychology Postdoctoral and Internship Centers (APPIC): 0
Total students placed in internships conforming to guidelines of the Council of Directors of School Psychology Programs (CDSPP): 0
Total students placed in internships that were not APA/CPA-accredited, APPIC or CDSSP listed: 0

Master's Degree (MA/MS Counseling): An internship experience, such as a final research project or "capstone" experience is required of graduates.

Internships/Practica

Both master's and doctoral students are required to take at least two semesters of practica. For doctoral students and some master's students, local sites include Dane County Community Mental Health Agency, Mendota Mental Health Institute, University of Wisconsin Counseling and Consultation Services, Veteran's Administration Hospital, and Family Therapy, Inc. The majority of practicum placements are in the Madison area but some are placed in nearby metropolitan areas in Wisconsin, such as Milwaukee and Green Bay, as well as in rural communities served by regional mental health clinics.

Admissions

Entries appear in the following order: required test or GPA, minimum score (if required)/median score of students entering in 2015–2016.

Program	Degree	GRE-V	GRE-Q	GRE-Writing	GRE-Subject	Under-graduate GPA	Last 2 Years GPA	Psychol-ogy GPA	Master's GPA
Counseling	MA/MS	NA/NA	NA/NA	NA/NA	Not specified	Not specified	3/NA	Not specified	Not specified
Counseling Psychology	PhD	NA/NA	NA/NA	NA/NA	Not specified	Not specified	3/NA	Not specified	Not specified

Admissions Requirements:

Degree	GRE	GRE-Subject	Letters of Recom-mendation	Research Statement	Writing Sample	CV	Interview
Master's/Specialist	Required	Optional	3	Required	Optional	Required	Optional
Doctoral	Required	Optional	3	Required	Optional	Required	Required

Please note if these criteria vary for different programs: The information above applies to our Counseling Psychology PhD program applicants. For Counseling MS applicants, all criteria remain the same except: research experience is low, an interview may not be required and undergraduate psychology preparation is high.

Admissions Criteria:

GRE scores—medium
Research experience—high
Work experience—medium
Clinically related public service—high
GPA—medium

Letters of recommendation—high
Interview—high
Statement of goals and objectives—high
Undergraduate psychology preparation—medium

Department Demographics

	Male (PT)	Female (PT)	Total	African-American/ Black (PT)	Hispanic/ Latino (PT)	Asian/ Pacific Islander (PT)	American Indian/ Alaska Native (PT)	Caucasian/ White (PT)	Unknown	Multiethnic (PT)	ADA (PT)	Int'l (PT)
Students	23 (2)	37 (2)	64	8 (0)	13 (0)	8 (2)	0 (0)	30 (2)	1 (0)	0 (0)	2 (0)	5 (0)

Financial Information/Assistance

Tuition: For information on tuition costs, visit http://registrar.wisc.edu/tuition_&_fees.htm. Tuition is subject to change. Additional fees are assessed to students beyond the costs of tuition for the following: Some courses carry an additional course fee of $50 or $200.

Doctoral:
State residents: $11,870 per academic year.
State residents: $786 per credit hour.
Nonstate residents: $25,196 per academic year.
Nonstate residents: $1,619 per credit hour.

Master's:
State residents: $11,870 per academic year.
State residents: $786 per credit hour.
Nonstate residents: $25,196 per academic year.
Nonstate residents: $1,619 per credit hour.

Financial Assistance:

	Teaching Assistantship (% Receiving)	Teaching Assistantship Tuition Remission	Research Assistantship (% Receiving)	Research Assistantship Tuition Remission	Fellowship (% Receiving)	Fellowship Tuition Remission
First-Year Student	$14,000 (NA)	Full	$14,000 (NA)	Full	$14,000 (NA)	Full
Advanced Student	$14,000 (NA)	Full	$14,000 (NA)	Full	$14,000 (NA)	Full

For additional information on financial assistance, visit http://counselingpsych.education.wisc.edu/cp/phd-program/funding.

Employment of Department Graduates

Master's:
Enrolled in a psychology doctoral program: 4
Employed in other positions at a higher education institution: 2
Employed in government agency: 3
Employed in a community mental health/counseling center: 5
Total: 14

Doctoral:
Enrolled in a postdoctoral residency/fellowship: 2
Total: 2

Additional Information

Housing and Day Care: On-campus housing is available. See the following website for more information: http://www.housing.wisc.edu/apartments.htm. On-campus day care facilities are available. See the following website for more information: http://occfr.wisc.edu/child_care.htm.

Information for Students With Physical Disabilities: See the following website: http://mcburney.wisc.edu/.

Special Facilities or Resources: The department is housed in the newly renovated Education Building, with excellent facilities including office space for department TAs and a Graduate Student Lounge. The campus has full WiFi coverage, and students have access to multiple computer labs and library facilities with electronic access to journal articles and other research materials. We have longstanding working relationships with practicum sites in the community and on campus, including a departmental training clinic.

Application Information: Department of Counseling Psychology, Graduate Admissions, UW-Madison, 335 Education Building - 1000 Bascom Mall, Madison, WI, 53706-1326. *Fee:* $56. *Online application:* http://grad.wisc.edu/apply.

Wisconsin, University of, Madison

Department of Educational Psychology, School Psychology Program
School of Education
1025 West Johnson Street
Madison, WI 53706-1796
Telephone: (608) 262-3432
Chairperson: B. Bradford Brown

E-mail: edpsych@education.wisc.edu
Web: http://edpsych.education.wisc.edu

Orientation, Objectives, and Emphasis of Department

The School Psychology program, within the Department of Educational Psychology, prepares professional psychologists to use knowledge of the behavioral sciences in ways that enhance the learning and adjustment of both normal and exceptional children, their families, and their teachers. A balanced emphasis is placed on developing competencies necessary for functioning in both applied settings, such as schools and community agencies, and in research positions in institutions of higher education. The program's focus is the study of psychological and educational principles that influence the adjustment of individuals from birth to 21 years. Students are required to demonstrate competence in the substantive content areas of psychological and educational theory and practice.

Programs and Degrees Offered

Program	Degree	Application Deadline	Applications Received	Accepted	New Admits Enrolled (PT)	Total Enrolled (PT)	Degrees Awarded in 2014–2015	Median Years to Complete Degree	Dismissed/ Withdrew
School Psychology	PhD	December 1 (Fall)	60	17	9 (0)	37 (1)	12	5	0
Quantitative Psychology	PhD	December 1 (Fall)	23	1	1 (0)	6 (6)	1	6	0
Learning Science	PhD	December 1 (Fall)	28	4	1 (0)	11 (4)	1	7	0
Human Development	PhD	December 1 (Fall)	39	12	8 (0)	13 (15)	2	6.5	0

APA Accreditation

School PhD: Student Outcome Data website: http://edpsych.education.wisc.edu/academics/school-psychology-area.

Doctoral Degree (PhD School Psychology): For those doctoral students for whom a professional internship was required in this program prior to graduation:
Total students who applied for an internship: 10
Total students who obtained an internship: 10
Total students who obtained a paid internship: 10
Total students who obtained an unpaid internship: 0
Total students who were placed in APA/CPA-accredited internships: 10
Total students placed in internships not APA/CPA-accredited, but listed with the Association of Psychology Postdoctoral and Internship Centers (APPIC): 0
Total students placed in internships conforming to guidelines of the Council of Directors of School Psychology Programs (CDSPP): 0
Total students placed in internships that were not APA/CPA-accredited, APPIC or CDSSP listed: 0

Internships/Practica

The School Psychology program admits students interested in obtaining a PhD. Students working toward this goal complete a two-semester clinical practicum experience during Year 2 (300-hour minimum) and a two-semester field practicum during Year 3, which provides a minimum of 600 clock hours of supervised practice at approved field sites. This practicum experience is provided by the department. After the master's, students are required to complete either an APA-approved internship or establish one of their own in a school (public or private), clinic, or hospital, approved by the program, to complete their PhD requirements. It requires a full-time experience (minimum of 2,000 hours) for the academic (or calendar) year or half-time for 2 consecutive academic years. The primary focus of the predoctoral internship program is to provide advanced training for graduate students from a wide variety of cooperating sites where an internship is provided over several rotations. This internship is implemented according to Ethical Principles of Psychologists; the criteria published by the National Register of Health Service Providers in Psychology and the National Association of School Psychologists are also followed. Criteria endorsed by the Council of Directors of School Psychology Programs are also met.

Admissions

Entries appear in the following order: required test or GPA, minimum score (if required)/median score of students entering in 2015–2016.

Program	Degree	GRE-V	GRE-Q	GRE-Writing	GRE-Subject	Under-graduate GPA	Last 2 Years GPA	Psychol-ogy GPA	Master's GPA
School Psychology	PhD	Not specified	Not specified	Not specified	Not specified	3/3.61	Not specified	Not specified	Not specified
Quantitative Psychology	PhD	NA/163	NA/160	Not specified	Not specified	3/3.61	Not specified	Not specified	Not specified
Learning Science	PhD	NA/155	NA/141	Not specified	Not specified	3/3.4	Not specified	Not specified	Not specified
Human Development	PhD	NA/157	NA/144	Not specified	Not specified	3/3.68	Not specified	Not specified	Not specified

Admissions Requirements:

Degree	GRE	GRE-Subject	Letters of Recom-mendation	Research Statement	Writing Sample	CV	Interview
Doctoral	Required	None	3	Required	Optional	Required	Recom-mended

Admissions Criteria:

GRE scores—medium
Research experience—medium
Work experience—medium
Clinically related public service—medium
GPA—medium

Letters of recommendation—high
Interview—high
Statement of goals and objectives—high
Undergraduate psychology preparation—medium

For additional information on admission requirements, visit http://edpsych.education.wisc.edu/admissions/application-materials.

Department Demographics

	Male (PT)	Female (PT)	Total	African-American/ Black (PT)	Hispanic/ Latino (PT)	Asian/ Pacific Islander (PT)	American Indian/ Alaska Native (PT)	Caucasian/ White (PT)	Unknown	Multiethnic (PT)	ADA (PT)	Int'l (PT)
Students	19 (2)	63 (12)	96	7 (1)	2 (0)	7 (1)	0 (0)	51 (3)	3 (0)	0 (0)	0 (0)	11 (6)

Financial Information/Assistance

Tuition: For information on tuition costs, visit http://www.registrar.wisc.edu/tuition_&_fees.htm. Tuition is subject to change.

Doctoral:
State residents: $11,869 per academic year.
State residents: $786 per credit hour.
Nonstate residents: $25,196 per academic year.
Nonstate residents: $1,619 per credit hour.

Master's:
State residents: $11,869 per academic year.
State residents: $786 per credit hour.
Nonstate residents: $25,196 per academic year.
Nonstate residents: $1,619 per credit hour.

Financial Assistance:

	Teaching Assistantship (% Receiving)	Teaching Assistantship Tuition Remission	Research Assistantship (% Receiving)	Research Assistantship Tuition Remission	Fellowship (% Receiving)	Fellowship Tuition Remission
First-Year Student	$15,648 (NA)	Full	$15,648 (15)	Full	$20,300 (4)	Full
Advanced Student	$18,066 (17)	Full	$19,126 (29)	Full	$20,300 (8)	Full

Employment of Department Graduates

Doctoral:
Enrolled in a postdoctoral residency/fellowship: 5
Employed in an academic position at a university: 3
Employed in other positions at a higher education institution: 1
Employed in a professional position in a school system: 5
Still seeking employment: 1
Do not know: 1
Total: 16

Additional Information

Housing and Day Care: On-campus housing is available. See the following website for more information: http://www.housing.wisc.edu. On-campus day care facilities are available. See the following website for more information: http://occfr.wisc.edu/.

Information for Students With Physical Disabilities: See the following website: http://www.mcburney.wisc.edu.

Special Facilities or Resources: The Laboratory of Experimental Design provides assistance to students and faculty in the design and analysis of research. Members of the laboratory include graduate students and faculty in the quantitative area.

Application Information: Graduate Admissions Coordinator, Educational Psychology, 1025 West Johnson Street, Madison, WI 53706-1796. *Fee:* $56. *Online application:* https://www.gradsch.wisc.edu/eapp/eapp.pl.

Wisconsin, University of, Madison

Department of Psychology
College of Letters and Science
W. J. Brogden Psychology Building, 1202 West Johnson Street
Madison, WI 53706
Telephone: (608) 262-2079
Chairperson: Dr. H. Hill Goldsmith

E-mail: gradinfo@psych.wisc.edu
Web: http://psych.wisc.edu/

Orientation, Objectives, and Emphasis of Department

The psychology PhD program is characterized by the following goals: emphasis both on extensive academic training in general psychology and on intensive research training in the student's particular area of concentration, a wide offering of content courses and seminars permitting the student considerable freedom in working out a program of study in collaboration with the major professor, and early and continuing commitment to research. Students are expected to become competent scholars and creative scientists in their own areas of concentration.

Programs and Degrees Offered

Program	Degree	Application Deadline	Applications Received	Accepted	New Admits Enrolled (PT)	Total Enrolled (PT)	Degrees Awarded in 2014–2015	Median Years to Complete Degree	Dismissed/ Withdrew
Biology of Brain & Behavior	PhD	December 1 (Fall)	35	5	4 (0)	11 (0)	0		1

Programs and Degrees Offered *(con't.)*

Program	Degree	Application Deadline	Applica-tions Received	Accepted	New Admits Enrolled (PT)	Total Enrolled (PT)	Degrees Awarded in 2014–2015	Median Years to Complete Degree	Dismissed/ Withdrew
Clinical Psychology	PhD	December 1 (Fall)	139	1	0 (0)	17 (0)	3	7	
Cognitive and Cognitive Neurosciences	PhD	December 1 (Fall)	52	4	3 (0)	16 (0)	2	6	
Developmental Psychology	PhD	December 1 (Fall)	22	1	0	7	1	5.5	
Social Psychology and Personality	PhD	December 1 (Fall)	77	2	2 (0)	16 (0)	3	6	
Individualized Graduate Major	PhD	December 1 (Fall)	17	3	3 (0)	13 (0)	1	7	
Perception	PhD	December 1 (Fall)	5	0	0 (0)	1 (0)	0		0

APA Accreditation

Clinical PhD: Student Outcome Data website: http://psych.wisc.edu/clinical-accreditation-description.htm.

Doctoral Degree (PhD Clinical Psychology): For those doctoral students for whom a professional internship was required in this program prior to graduation:

Total students who applied for an internship: 1
Total students who obtained an internship: 1
Total students who obtained a paid internship: 1
Total students who obtained an unpaid internship: 0
Total students who were placed in APA/CPA-accredited internships: 1
Total students placed in internships not APA/CPA-accredited, but listed with the Association of Psychology Postdoctoral and Internship Centers (APPIC): 0
Total students placed in internships conforming to guidelines of the Council of Directors of School Psychology Programs (CDSPP): 0
Total students placed in internships that were not APA/CPA-accredited, APPIC or CDSSP listed: 0

Internships/Practica

Clinical psychology graduate students are required to complete a minimum of 400 hours of practicum experience, of which at least 150 hours are in direct service experience and at least 75 hours are in formally scheduled supervision. Each student will complete a 160-hour clerkship at a preapproved site which is designed to expose students to diverse clinical populations and the practice of clinical psychology in an applied setting. Also, a one-year internship is required.

Admissions

Entries appear in the following order: required test or GPA, minimum score (if required)/median score of students entering in 2015–2016.

Program	Degree	GRE-V	GRE-Q	GRE-Writing	GRE-Subject	Under-graduate GPA	Last 2 Years GPA	Psychol-ogy GPA	Master's GPA
Biology of Brain & Behavior	PhD	NA/NA	NA/NA	NA/NA	Not specified	3/NA	NA/NA	Not specified	Not specified
Clinical Psychology	PhD	NA/NA	NA/NA	NA/NA	Not specified	3/NA	NA/NA	Not specified	Not specified
Cognitive and Cognitive Neurosciences	PhD	NA/NA	NA/NA	NA/NA	Not specified	3/NA	NA/NA	Not specified	Not specified

Admissions *(con't.)*

Program	Degree	GRE-V	GRE-Q	GRE-Writing	GRE-Subject	Under-graduate GPA	Last 2 Years GPA	Psychology GPA	Master's GPA
Developmental Psychology	PhD	NA/NA	NA/NA	NA/NA	Not specified	3/NA	NA/NA	Not specified	Not specified
Social Psychology and Personality	PhD	NA/NA	NA/NA	NA/NA	Not specified	3/NA	NA/NA	Not specified	Not specified
Individualized Graduate Major	PhD	NA/NA	NA/NA	NA/NA	Not specified	3/NA	NA/NA	Not specified	Not specified
Perception	PhD	NA/NA	NA/NA	NA/NA	Not specified	3/NA	NA/NA	Not specified	Not specified

Admissions Requirements:

Degree	GRE	GRE-Subject	Letters of Recommendation	Research Statement	Writing Sample	CV	Interview
Doctoral	Required	Optional	3	Required	Optional	Required	Required

Admissions Criteria:

GRE scores—high
Research experience—high
GPA—high
Letters of recommendation—high

Interview—high
Statement of goals and objectives—high
Undergraduate psychology preparation—low

For additional information on admission requirements, visit http://psych.wisc.edu/graduate-admission-and-requirements.htm.

Department Demographics

	Male (PT)	Female (PT)	Total	African-American/ Black (PT)	Hispanic/ Latino (PT)	Asian/ Pacific Islander (PT)	American Indian/ Alaska Native (PT)	Caucasian/ White (PT)	Unknown	Multiethnic (PT)	ADA (PT)	Int'l (PT)
Students	32 (0)	49 (0)	81	2 (0)	2 (0)	10 (0)	1 (0)	65 (0)	1 (0)	0 (0)	0 (0)	5 (0)

Financial Information/Assistance

Tuition: For information on tuition costs, visit http://registrar.wisc.edu/tuition_&_fees.htm. Tuition is subject to change.

Doctoral:
State residents: $11,868 per academic year.
Nonstate residents: $25,196 per academic year.

Financial Assistance:

	Teaching Assistantship (% Receiving)	Teaching Assistantship Tuition Remission	Research Assistantship (% Receiving)	Research Assistantship Tuition Remission	Fellowship (% Receiving)	Fellowship Tuition Remission
First-Year Student	$15,649 (NA)	Full	$18,067 (NA)	Full	$20,304 (NA)	Full
Advanced Student	$18,067 (NA)	Full	$18,067 (NA)	Full	$20,304 (NA)	Full

For additional information on financial assistance, visit http://grad.wisc.edu/studentfunding/prospective/.

Employment of Department Graduates

No information provided.

Additional Information

Housing and Day Care: On-campus housing is available. See the following website for more information: http://www.housing.wisc.edu/apartments.htm. On-campus day care facilities are available. See the following website for more information: http://occfr.wisc.edu/child_care.htm.

Information for Students With Physical Disabilities: See the following website: http://mcburney.wisc.edu/.

Special Facilities or Resources: The department has an extraordinary array of research facilities. Virtually all laboratories are fully computer controlled, and the department's general-purpose facilities are freely available to all graduate students. The Brogden and the Harlow Primate Laboratory have special facilities for housing animals, as well as for behavioral, pharmacological, anatomical, immunological, and physiological studies. We are well-equipped for studies of visual, auditory, and language perception and other areas of cognitive psychology. In addition, the Psychology Department Research and Training Clinic is housed in the Brogden Building. Many of the faculty and graduate students are affiliated with the Institute of Aging, the Waisman Center on Mental Retardation and Human Development, the Wisconsin Regional Primate Research Center, the Health Emotions Center, the Neuroscience Training Program, the Keck Neuroimaging Center, the Hearing Training Program, the Institute for Research on Poverty, the NSF National Consortium on Violence Research, and the Women's Studies Research Center. There are strong ties to the departments of Anatomy, Anthropology, Communicative Disorders, Educational Psychology, Entomology, Immunology, Industrial Engineering, Ophthalmology, Psychiatry, Sociology, Wildlife Ecology, Zoology, the Mass Communication Research Center, the Institute for Research on Poverty, and the Survey Research Laboratory.

Application Information: Graduate Admissions, Department of Psychology, University of Wisconsin, 1202 West Johnson Street, Madison, WI 53706. *Fee:* $56. *Online application:* https://apply.grad.wisc.edu/.

Wisconsin, University of, Madison (2015 data)
Human Development & Family Studies
School of Human Ecology
4198 Nancy Nicholas Hall, 1300 Linden Drive
Madison, WI 53706
Telephone: (608) 263-2381
Chairperson: Janean Dilworth-Bart

E-mail: hdfs@mail.sohe.wisc.edu
Web: http://www.sohe.wisc.edu/hdfs/

Orientation, Objectives, and Emphasis of Department
HDFS offers an interdisciplinary approach to family relationships, child and adolescent development, adult development and aging, child and family intervention and prevention programs, and policy studies. Our work with graduate students is oriented around three fundamental principles: (1) Students benefit from the perspectives of multiple disciplines and an understanding of the social, cultural, and historical contexts in which people develop. Our faculty come from diverse professional and disciplinary backgrounds and possess a wide range of experiences and expertise. We also encourage scholarship that takes into account the larger social and cultural contexts in which people live, such as historical change, community, social class, ethnicity, and public policy. (2) The application of knowledge to real-world issues is central to our program and consistent with the Wisconsin Idea of outreach and service. Faculty and students direct their work toward finding solutions to the current challenges facing individuals, families, and communities. Many work closely with policy and community leaders to gather, disseminate, and apply scientific knowledge. (3) Graduate training is most effective when students work closely with faculty to pursue programs of research and outreach that are tailored to their individual interests and aspirations.

Programs and Degrees Offered

Program	Degree	Application Deadline	Applica-tions Received	Accepted	New Admits Enrolled (PT)	Total Enrolled (PT)	Degrees Awarded in 2014–2015	Median Years to Complete Degree	Dismissed/Withdrew
Human Development & Family Studies	PhD	December 1 (Fall)	19	7	4 (0)	14	4	3.5	0

Programs and Degrees Offered (con't.)

Program	Degree	Application Deadline	Applications Received	Accepted	New Admits Enrolled (PT)	Total Enrolled (PT)	Degrees Awarded in 2014–2015	Median Years to Complete Degree	Dismissed/ Withdrew
Human Development & Family Studies	MA/MS	December 1 (Fall)	20	8	4 (0)	13 (0)	4	2.75	0

Admissions

Entries appear in the following order: required test or GPA, minimum score (if required)/median score of students entering in 2015–2016.

Program	Degree	GRE-V	GRE-Q	GRE-Writing	GRE-Subject	Under-graduate GPA	Last 2 Years GPA	Psychology GPA	Master's GPA
Human Development & Family Studies	PhD	NA/155	NA/156	NA/4	Not specified	3/3.67	Not specified	Not specified	Not specified
Human Development & Family Studies	MA/MS	NA/155	NA/156	NA/4	Not specified	3/3.67	Not specified	Not specified	Not specified

Admissions Requirements:

Degree	GRE	GRE-Subject	Letters of Recommendation	Research Statement	Writing Sample	CV	Interview
Master's/Specialist	Required	None	3	Required	Recommended	None	Optional
Doctoral	Required	None	3	Required	Recommended	None	Optional

Admissions Criteria:

GRE scores—medium
Research experience—medium
Work experience—low
GPA—high

Letters of recommendation—high
Interview—low
Statement of goals and objectives—high
Fit w/ faculty interests—high

Department Demographics

	Male (PT)	Female (PT)	Total	African-American/ Black (PT)	Hispanic/ Latino (PT)	Asian/ Pacific Islander (PT)	American Indian/ Alaska Native (PT)	Caucasian/ White (PT)	Unknown (PT)	Multiethnic (PT)	ADA (PT)	Int'l (PT)
Students	2 (0)	25 (0)	27	0 (0)	2 (0)	4 (0)	0 (0)	21 (0)	0 (0)	0 (0)	3 (0)	1 (0)

Financial Information/Assistance

Tuition: For information on tuition costs, visit http://registrar.wisc.edu/tuition_&_fees.htm. Tuition is subject to change.

Doctoral:
State residents: $11,864 per academic year.
State residents: $786 per credit hour.
Nonstate residents: $25,192 per academic year.
Nonstate residents: $1,619 per credit hour.

Master's:
State residents: $11,864 per academic year.
State residents: $786 per credit hour.
Nonstate residents: $25,192 per academic year.
Nonstate residents: $1,619 per credit hour.

Financial Assistance:

	Teaching Assistantship (% Receiving)	Teaching Assistantship Tuition Remission	Research Assistantship (% Receiving)	Research Assistantship Tuition Remission	Fellowship (% Receiving)	Fellowship Tuition Remission
First-Year Student	$10,126 (65)	Full	$17,712 (30)	Full	$19,125 (5)	Full
Advanced Student	$11,690 (NA)	Full	NA (NA)	Full	NA (NA)	Full

For additional information on financial assistance, visit http://grad.wisc.edu/studentfunding/prospective/.

Employment of Department Graduates

Master's:
Do not know: 3
Total: 3

Doctoral:
Do not know: 3
Total: 3

Additional Information

Housing and Day Care: On-campus housing is available. See the following website for more information: http://www.housing.wisc. edu/. On-campus day care facilities are available. See the following website for more information: http://www.occfr.wisc.edu/child_care.htm.

Information for Students With Physical Disabilities: See the following website: http://www.mcburney.wisc.edu/services/.

Special Facilities or Resources: Departmental resources for training and research include a Family Interaction Lab, a Laboratory Preschool, and numerous outreach programs for children and families. HDFS faculty are closely affiliated with a number of University centers including the Center for Child and Family Well-being, the Waisman Center for Human Development, the Center for Community and Nonprofit Studies, and the Institute for Research on Poverty. In addition, many faculty in the program work closely with the statewide UW Cooperative Extension network of community educators.

Application Information: Graduate Admissions, Department of Human Development & Family Studies, University of Wisconsin—Madison, 4198 Nancy Nicholas Hall, 1300 Linden Drive, Madison, WI 53706. *Fee:* $56. *Online application:* https://www.gradsch.wisc.edu/eapp/eapp.pl.

Wisconsin, University of, Milwaukee
Department of Psychology
College of Letters and Science
P.O. Box 413
Milwaukee, WI 53201-0413
Telephone: (414) 229-4746
Chairperson: W. Hobart Davies

E-mail: suelima@uwm.edu
Web: http://uwm.edu/psychology/graduate/

Orientation, Objectives, and Emphasis of Department
The department has an APA-accredited PhD program in clinical psychology, a PhD program in neuroscience, a PhD program in health psychology, and terminal MS programs in health psychology and in behavior analysis. The Behavior Analysis Certification Board, Inc.® has approved our behavior analysis curriculum as meeting the requirements for eligibility to take the Board Certified Behavior Analyst Examination® to become BCBAs. Our PhD program in clinical psychology is a member of the Academy of Psychological Clinical Science; membership is based on a thorough peer review process. Our membership indicates our commitment to excellence in scientific training and to using clinical science as the foundation for designing, implementing, and evaluating assessment and intervention procedures. All students in our department are directly involved in research under the direction of their major professor.

Programs and Degrees Offered

Program	Degree	Application Deadline	Applica-tions Received	Accepted	New Admits Enrolled (PT)	Total Enrolled (PT)	Degrees Awarded in 2014–2015	Median Years to Complete Degree	Dismissed/ Withdrew
Behavior Analysis	MA/MS	December 31 (Fall)	20	5	6 (0)	12 (0)	4	4	0
Health Psychology	MA/MS	December 31 (Fall)	15	1	1 (0)	3 (0)	1	1.5	0
Clinical Psychology	PhD	December 1 (Fall)	223	6	6 (0)	39 (0)	4	6	0
Neuroscience	PhD	December 1 (Fall)	40	6	6	25	2	6.5	0
Health Psychology	PhD	December 1 (Fall)	15	0	0	8	1	7	0
Behavior Analysis	PhD	December 1 (Fall)	9	1	1	4	2	5	0

APA Accreditation

Clinical PhD: Student Outcome Data website: http://uwm.edu/psychology/graduate/phd-program/clinical-psychology/.

Doctoral Degree (PhD Clinical Psychology): For those doctoral students for whom a professional internship was required in this program prior to graduation:
Total students who applied for an internship: 6
Total students who obtained an internship: 6
Total students who obtained a paid internship: 6
Total students who obtained an unpaid internship: 0
Total students who were placed in APA/CPA-accredited internships: 6
Total students placed in internships not APA/CPA-accredited, but listed with the Association of Psychology Postdoctoral and Internship Centers (APPIC): 0
Total students placed in internships conforming to guidelines of the Council of Directors of School Psychology Programs (CDSPP): 0
Total students placed in internships that were not APA/CPA-accredited, APPIC or CDSSP listed: 0

Master's Degree (MA/MS Behavior Analysis): An internship experience, such as a final research project or "capstone" experience is required of graduates. Master's Degree (MA/MS Health Psychology): An internship experience, such as a final research project or "capstone" experience is required of graduates.

Internships/Practica

The clinical PhD program and the behavior analysis programs require practica. Practicum training occurs in the department and at various sites in the greater Milwaukee area. The clinical PhD program requires a full-time extramural internship at an APA-accredited site.

Admissions

Entries appear in the following order: required test or GPA, minimum score (if required)/median score of students entering in 2015–2016.

Program	Degree	GRE-V	GRE-Q	GRE-Writing	GRE-Subject	Under-graduate GPA	Last 2 Years GPA	Psychol-ogy GPA	Master's GPA
Behavior Analysis	MA/MS	NA/NA	NA/NA	NA/NA	Not specified	3/NA	NA/NA	NA/NA	Not specified
Health Psychology	MA/MS	NA/NA	NA/NA	NA/NA	Not specified	3/NA	NA/NA	NA/NA	Not specified
Clinical Psychology	PhD	NA/164	NA/157	NA/5	Not specified	3/3.7	NA/NA	NA/NA	Not specified
Neuroscience	PhD	Not specified	Not specified	Not specified	Not specified	Not specified	Not specified	Not specified	Not specified

Admissions *(con't.)*

Program	Degree	GRE-V	GRE-Q	GRE-Writing	GRE-Subject	Under-graduate GPA	Last 2 Years GPA	Psychology GPA	Master's GPA
Health Psychology	PhD	Not specified	Not specified	Not specified	Not specified	Not specified	Not specified	Not specified	Not specified
Behavior Analysis	PhD	Not specified	Not specified	Not specified	Not specified	Not specified	Not specified	Not specified	Not specified

Admissions Requirements:

Degree	GRE	GRE-Subject	Letters of Recom-mendation	Research Statement	Writing Sample	CV	Interview
Master's/Specialist	Required	None	3	Required	Required	Required	Required
Doctoral	Required	None	3	Required	Required	Required	Required

Admissions Criteria:

GRE scores—high
Research experience—high
Work experience—low
Clinically related public service—medium
GPA—high

Letters of recommendation—high
Interview—high
Statement of goals and objectives—high
Undergraduate psychology preparation—high

For additional information on admission requirements, visit http://uwm.edu/psychology/graduate/application/.

Department Demographics

	Male (PT)	Female (PT)	Total	African-American/ Black (PT)	Hispanic/ Latino (PT)	Asian/ Pacific Islander (PT)	American Indian/ Alaska Native (PT)	Caucasian/ White (PT)	Unknown	Multiethnic (PT)	ADA (PT)	Int'l (PT)
Students	31 (0)	60 (0)	91	1 (0)	5 (0)	7 (0)	0 (0)	78 (0)	0 (0)	0 (0)	0 (0)	10 (0)

Financial Information/Assistance

Tuition: For information on tuition costs, visit http://www4.uwm.edu/bfs/depts/bursar/tuition-rate-schedules.cfm. Tuition is subject to change. Additional fees are assessed to students beyond the costs of tuition for the following: additional student fees vary from $490 to $812 per year.

Doctoral:
State residents: $10,386 per academic year.
State residents: $649 per credit hour.
Nonstate residents: $23,424 per academic year.
Nonstate residents: $1,463 per credit hour.

Master's:
State residents: $10,386 per academic year.
State residents: $649 per credit hour.
Nonstate residents: $23,424 per academic year.
Nonstate residents: $1,463 per credit hour.

Financial Assistance:

	Teaching Assistantship (% Receiving)	Teaching Assistantship Tuition Remission	Research Assistantship (% Receiving)	Research Assistantship Tuition Remission	Fellowship (% Receiving)	Fellowship Tuition Remission
First-Year Student	$12,850 (55)	Full	$17,000 (5)	Full	$15,000 (5)	Full
Advanced Student	$15,000 (45)	Full	$17,000 (14)	Full	$15,000 (19)	Full

Employment of Department Graduates

Master's:
Enrolled in another graduate/professional program: 1
Employed in business or industry: 1
Employed in a community mental health/counseling center: 3
Total: 5

Doctoral:
Enrolled in a postdoctoral residency/fellowship: 6
Employed in an academic position at a university: 1
Employed in a community mental health/counseling center: 2
Total: 9

Additional Information

Housing and Day Care: On-campus housing is available. See the following website for more information: http://uwm.edu/housing/. On-campus day care facilities are available. See the following website for more information: http://uwm.edu/children/.

Information for Students With Physical Disabilities: See the following website: http://uwm.edu/arc/.

Special Facilities or Resources: The department has a separate research laboratory for each member of the faculty and specifically-designed quarters for teaching laboratory courses. There is also a mechanical and woodworking shop and an electronics shop, supervised by a full-time technician. The department training clinic is housed in a separate wing of the building with its own offices, clerical staff, research space, clinic rooms, and full-time director.

Application Information: Chairperson, Graduate Admissions Committee, Department of Psychology, P.O. Box 413, Milwaukee, WI 53201-0413. *Fee:* $56. *Online application:* http://uwm.edu/graduateschool/admission/.

Wisconsin, University of, Milwaukee
Educational Psychology
Education
2400 East Hartford IP0413
Milwaukee, WI 53211
Telephone: (414) 229-4767
Chairperson: Nadya A. Fouad

E-mail: nadya@uwm.edu
Web: http://uwm.edu/education/academics/educational-psychology-department/

Orientation, Objectives, and Emphasis of Department
The department has one MS program with majors in Community Counseling, School Counseling, School Psychology (also EdS), Research Methodology, as well as Learning and Development. The PhD program in Educational Psychology includes specializations in Educational and Statistical Measurement, Learning and Development, School Psychology, and Counseling Psychology. The PhD programs in School Psychology and Counseling Psychology are APA-accredited. The programs are based on the scientist–practitioner model, in which students are trained as psychological scientists with specializations in school or counseling psychology. Our department has a strong, multicultural perspective within each of the programs, with an emphasis on the contextual factors in student's work, and both provide unique training in the psychological, social, and educational needs of multiethnic populations within an urban psychosocial context. Students gain the knowledge, skills, and attitudes to work in a heterogeneous environment. Students are prepared to work in academic, service delivery, research, and administrative positions.

Programs and Degrees Offered

Program	Degree	Application Deadline	Applications Received	Accepted	New Admits Enrolled (PT)	Total Enrolled (PT)	Degrees Awarded in 2014–2015	Median Years to Complete Degree	Dismissed/ Withdrew
Counseling	MA/MS	February 15 (Fall), November 1 (Spring)	76	60	29 (5)	83 (30)	40	2	
School Psychology	EdS	January 4 (Fall)	69	24	14 (0)	28 (11)	10	3	0
Learning and Development	MA/MS	December 1 (Fall), September 1 (Spring)	7	4	0 (1)	3 (3)	2	3	

Programs and Degrees Offered *(con't.)*

Program	Degree	Application Deadline	Applica-tions Received	Accepted	New Admits Enrolled (PT)	Total Enrolled (PT)	Degrees Awarded in 2014–2015	Median Years to Complete Degree	Dismissed/ Withdrew
Counseling Psychology	PhD	December 1 (Fall)	38	11	11 (0)	34 (2)	4	5	
School Psychology	PhD	December 15 (Fall)	21	6	4 (0)	18 (0)	5	5	0
Learning and Development	PhD	December 1 (Fall), September 1 (Spring)	8	3	0 (2)	3 (5)	1	2	0
Educational Statistics and Measurement	MA/MS	February 15 (Fall), October 1 (Spring)	10	4	1 (1)	1 (3)	3	3	
Educational Statistics and Measurement	PhD	February 15 (Fall), October 1 (Spring)	8	3	0 (1)	7 (2)	4	5	

APA Accreditation

Counseling PhD: Student Outcome Data website: http://uwm.edu/education/academics/counseling-psychology/.
School PhD: Student Outcome Data website: http://uwm.edu/education/academics/school-psychology/.

Doctoral Degree (PhD Counseling Psychology): For those doctoral students for whom a professional internship was required in this program prior to graduation:
Total students who applied for an internship: 4
Total students who obtained an internship: 4
Total students who obtained a paid internship: 4
Total students who obtained an unpaid internship: 0
Total students who were placed in APA/CPA-accredited internships: 2
Total students placed in internships not APA/CPA-accredited, but listed with the Association of Psychology Postdoctoral and Internship Centers (APPIC): 1
Total students placed in internships conforming to guidelines of the Council of Directors of School Psychology Programs (CDSPP): 0
Total students placed in internships that were not APA/CPA-accredited, APPIC or CDSSP listed: 1

Doctoral Degree (PhD School Psychology): For those doctoral students for whom a professional internship was required in this program prior to graduation:
Total students who applied for an internship: 5
Total students who obtained an internship: 5
Total students who obtained a paid internship: 5
Total students who obtained an unpaid internship: 0
Total students who were placed in APA/CPA-accredited internships: 4
Total students placed in internships not APA/CPA-accredited, but listed with the Association of Psychology Postdoctoral and Internship Centers (APPIC): 0
Total students placed in internships conforming to guidelines of the Council of Directors of School Psychology Programs (CDSPP): 0
Total students placed in internships that were not APA/CPA-accredited, APPIC or CDSSP listed: 1

Internships/Practica

Students are placed in a variety of educational, business, and community settings as part of their graduate training. Students in the Educational and Statistical Measurements doctoral program will have the opportunity to gain experience in a research assistants in research design, evaluation, scale development, psychometrics, and statistical consulting in the Consulting Office for Research and Evaluation (CORE).

Admissions

Entries appear in the following order: required test or GPA, minimum score (if required)/median score of students entering in 2015–2016.

Program	Degree	GRE-V	GRE-Q	GRE-Writing	GRE-Subject	Under-graduate GPA	Last 2 Years GPA	Psychology GPA	Master's GPA
Counseling	MA/MS	Not specified	Not specified	Not specified	Not specified	3/NA	3/NA	Not specified	Not specified
School Psychology	EdS	Not specified	Not specified	Not specified	Not specified	3/NA	3/NA	Not specified	Not specified
Learning and Development	MA/MS	Not specified	Not specified	Not specified	Not specified	3/NA	3/NA	NA/NA	Not specified
Counseling Psychology	PhD	145/155	143/148	3/3.9	Not specified	NA/NA	Not specified	Not specified	Not specified
School Psychology	PhD	151/155	145/148	4/4.5	Not specified	3/NA	3/NA	Not specified	3/NA
Learning and Development	PhD	158/158	153/153	4/4	Not specified	3/NA	3/NA	Not specified	3/NA
Educational Statistics and Measurement	MA/MS	NA/NA	NA/NA	NA/NA	Not specified	3.5/NA	3.5/NA	Not specified	Not specified
Educational Statistics and Measurement	PhD	152/152	155/155	3.5/3.5	Not specified	3.5/NA	3.5/NA	Not specified	3.5/NA

Admissions Requirements:

Degree	GRE	GRE-Subject	Letters of Recom-mendation	Research Statement	Writing Sample	CV	Interview
Master's/Specialist	Optional	Optional	3	Required	Optional	Optional	None
Doctoral	Required	Recom-mended	3	Required	Optional	Optional	Required

Please note if these criteria vary for different programs: Clinical experience is not required for the Educational Statistics and Measurement or Learning and Development programs.

Admissions Criteria:

GRE scores—high
Research experience—medium
Work experience—low
GPA—medium

Letters of recommendation—high
Interview—medium
Statement of goals and objectives—high
Research interests—high

For additional information on admission requirements, visit http://uwm.edu/graduateschool/admission/.

Department Demographics

	Male (PT)	Female (PT)	Total	African-American/ Black (PT)	Hispanic/ Latino (PT)	Asian/ Pacific Islander (PT)	American Indian/ Alaska Native (PT)	Caucasian/ White (PT)	Unknown	Multiethnic (PT)	ADA (PT)	Int'l (PT)
Students	42 (18)	135 (38)	233	8 (5)	5 (1)	4 (1)	0 (1)	130 (41)	7 (3)	23 (4)		6 (2)

Financial Information/Assistance

Tuition: For information on tuition costs, visit http://www4.uwm.edu/bfs/depts/bursar/tuition.cfm. Tuition is subject to change. Additional fees are assessed to students beyond the costs of tuition for the following: assessment courses have additional course fees.

Doctoral:
State residents: $11,595 per academic year.
State residents: $1,065 per credit hour.
Nonstate residents: $24,061 per academic year.
Nonstate residents: $1,844 per credit hour.

Master's:
State residents: $11,595 per academic year.
State residents: $1,065 per credit hour.
Nonstate residents: $24,061 per academic year.
Nonstate residents: $1,844 per credit hour.

Financial Assistance:

	Teaching Assistantship (% Receiving)	Teaching Assistantship Tuition Remission	Research Assistantship (% Receiving)	Research Assistantship Tuition Remission	Fellowship (% Receiving)	Fellowship Tuition Remission
First-Year Student	$13,723 (9)	Full	$17,000 (4)	Full	$4,008 (7)	Partial
Advanced Student	$13,723 (6)	Full	$17,000 (6)	Full	$5,414 (13)	Partial

Employment of Department Graduates

Master's:
Employed in a professional position in a school system: 12
Total: 12

Additional Information

Housing and Day Care: On-campus housing is available. See the following website for more information: http://uwm.edu/housing/. On-campus day care facilities are available. See the following website for more information: http://uwm.edu/children/.

Information for Students With Physical Disabilities: See the following website: http://uwm.edu/arc/.

Special Facilities or Resources: The department possesses excellent computer facilities. The department enjoys a strong collaborative relationship with the Department of Psychology, working together in an on-campus psychology clinic. We also have strong linkages to urban community and school partners, which provide students with a diverse set of research and practice opportunities.

Application Information: Application Chair, Department of Educational Psychology, University of Wisconsin-Milwaukee, P.O. Box 413, Milwaukee, WI 53201. *Fee:* $56. *Online application:* https://apply.wisconsin.edu/.

Wisconsin, University of, Oshkosh

Psychology
800 Algoma Boulevard CF 29
Oshkosh, WI 54901
Telephone: (920) 424-2302
Chairperson: Dr. David Lishner

E-mail: hongp@uwosh.edu
Web: http://www.uwosh.edu/psychology

Orientation, Objectives, and Emphasis of Department

The MS in Psychological Research (Cognitive and Affective emphasis) is a program designed to train students to conduct research across ALL disciplines of psychology including but not limited to research in: clinical psychology, social psychology, biopsychology, neuroscience, quantitative psychology, cognitive psychology, comparative psychology, and health psychology. Cognition and affect are theoretical constructs that bridge multiple levels of analysis and a variety of psychological phenomena. The program offers students exposure to all faculty who will teach various approaches to the study of psychological experience. This, coupled with high-quality instruction, offers our students the theoretical and practical background and skills necessary for succeeding in diverse careers in academia and in both the public and private sectors. The strength of the MS in Psychological Research program is the strong emphasis on quantitative and methodological training. Students are required to take two quantitative courses and two research method courses, along with electives that are offered on a rotating basis. The program also parallels quantitative training with in-depth coverage of scientific methodology and the process of conducting psychological research. Students are exposed to topics including research design (e.g., experimental versus quasi-experimental), reliability, validity, and research biases.

Programs and Degrees Offered

Program	Degree	Application Deadline	Applications Received	Accepted	New Admits Enrolled (PT)	Total Enrolled (PT)	Degrees Awarded in 2014–2015	Median Years to Complete Degree	Dismissed/ Withdrew
Experimental Cognitive and Affective Science	MA/MS	August 1 (Fall)	9	8	8	16	10	2	1

Admissions

Entries appear in the following order: required test or GPA, minimum score (if required)/median score of students entering in 2015–2016.

Program	Degree	GRE-V	GRE-Q	GRE-Writing	GRE-Subject	Under-graduate GPA	Last 2 Years GPA	Psychology GPA	Master's GPA
Experimental Cognitive and Affective Science	MA/MS	NA/NA	NA/NA	NA/NA	Not specified	3/NA	NA/NA	Not specified	Not specified

Admissions Requirements:

Degree	GRE	GRE-Subject	Letters of Recommendation	Research Statement	Writing Sample	CV	Interview
Master's/Specialist	Required	None	2	Required	Optional	Optional	None

Admissions Criteria:

GRE scores—medium
Research experience—medium
Work experience—low
GPA—medium

Letters of recommendation—medium
Statement of goals and objectives—medium
Undergraduate psychology preparation—medium

For additional information on admission requirements, visit http://www.uwosh.edu/psychology/graduate-studies/apply.

Department Demographics

	Male (PT)	Female (PT)	Total	African-American/ Black (PT)	Hispanic/ Latino (PT)	Asian/ Pacific Islander (PT)	American Indian/ Alaska Native (PT)	Caucasian/ White (PT)	Unknown	Multiethnic (PT)	ADA (PT)	Int'l (PT)
Students	8 (0)	8 (0)	16	0 (0)	0 (0)	1 (0)	0 (0)	15 (0)	0 (0)	0 (0)	0 (0)	1 (0)

Financial Information/Assistance

Tuition: For information on tuition costs, visit http://www.uwosh.edu/student_financial/student-accounts/tuition-and-fees. Tuition is subject to change.

Master's:
State residents: $8,280 per academic year.
State residents: $460 per credit hour.
Nonstate residents: $17,730 per academic year.
Nonstate residents: $985 per credit hour.

Financial Assistance:

	Teaching Assistantship (% Receiving)	Teaching Assistantship Tuition Remission	Research Assistantship (% Receiving)	Research Assistantship Tuition Remission	Fellowship (% Receiving)	Fellowship Tuition Remission
First-Year Student	NA (NA)	NA	$4,000 (NA)	NA	NA (NA)	NA
Advanced Student	NA (NA)	NA	$4,000 (NA)	NA	NA (NA)	NA

For additional information on financial assistance, visit http://financialaid.uwosh.edu/graduates/.

Employment of Department Graduates

Master's:
Enrolled in a psychology doctoral program: 3
Employed in academic position at a 2-year/4-year college: 1
Employed in other positions at a higher education institution: 1
Employed in business or industry: 4
Employed in a hospital/medical center: 1
Total: 10

Additional Information

Housing and Day Care: On-campus housing is available. See the following website for more information: http://www.housing.uwosh.edu/. On-campus day care facilities are available. See the following website for more information: http://childrenscenter.uwosh.edu/.

Information for Students With Physical Disabilities: See the following website: http://www.uwosh.edu/deanofstudents/disability-services.

Special Facilities or Resources: Animal colony; human physiology & neurology lab (EEG).

Application Information: University of Wisconsin Oshkosh Graduate Studies, Dempsey 337, 800 Algoma Boulevard, Oshkosh, WI 54901. *Fee:* $56. *Online application:* https://apply.wisconsin.edu/.

Wisconsin, University of, Stout

Psychology Department / Master of Science in Applied Psychology (MSAP)
College of Education, Hospitality, Health and Human Sciences
473 Harvey Hall
Menomonie, WI 54751-0790
Telephone: (715) 232-2478
Chairperson: Dr. Kathryn Hamilton

E-mail: smithlib@uwstout.edu
Web: http://www.uwstout.edu/programs/msap/index.cfm

Orientation, Objectives, and Emphasis of Department

The MS in Applied Psychology (MSAP) is a 2-year program designed around a core of psychological theories, principles, and research methods. The program emphasizes experiential learning, as over 85% of the required courses involve applied projects. Students choose from among three concentration areas: industrial/organizational psychology, evaluation research, and health promotion and disease prevention. Dual concentrations are typical. The MSAP program is designed to provide students with the knowledge, experience, skills, and abilities to apply theories and methods to the identification of and solution to a variety of 21st century, real-world problems in business and industry, health care, and nonprofit organizations. A majority of classes incorporate real-world, hands-on learning opportunities that involve extensive group work and communication with external stakeholders. Numerous opportunities exist outside of formal courses for additional applied experience.

Programs and Degrees Offered

Program	Degree	Application Deadline	Applica-tions Received	Accepted	New Admits Enrolled (PT)	Total Enrolled (PT)	Degrees Awarded in 2014–2015	Median Years to Complete Degree	Dismissed/ Withdrew
Applied Psychology	MA/MS	February 1 (Fall)	45	31	20 (0)	41 (0)	14	2.75	0

Internships/Practica

MSAP students are required to do a practicum in external consulting and a 240 hour internship. Students are encouraged to seek out placement sites early in their program work. 85% of MSAP courses involve 'hands-on' applied learning, typically through group projects.

Admissions

Entries appear in the following order: required test or GPA, minimum score (if required)/median score of students entering in 2015–2016.

Program	Degree	GRE-V	GRE-Q	GRE-Writing	GRE-Subject	Under-graduate GPA	Last 2 Years GPA	Psychol-ogy GPA	Master's GPA
Applied Psychology	MA/MS	Not specified	Not specified	Not specified	Not specified	3/3.4	Not specified	Not specified	Not specified

Admissions Requirements:

Degree	GRE	GRE-Subject	Letters of Recom-mendation	Research Statement	Writing Sample	CV	Interview
Master's/Specialist	Optional	Optional	3	Required	Required	Required	Optional

Admissions Criteria:

GRE scores—low
Research experience—high
Work experience—high
GPA—medium

Letters of recommendation—high
Statement of goals and objectives—high
Undergraduate psychology preparation—medium

For additional information on admission requirements, visit http://www.uwstout.edu/programs/msap/applying.cfm.

Department Demographics

	Male (PT)	Female (PT)	Total	African-American/ Black (PT)	Hispanic/ Latino (PT)	Asian/ Pacific Islander (PT)	American Indian/ Alaska Native (PT)	Caucasian/ White (PT)	Unknown	Multiethnic (PT)	ADA (PT)	Int'l (PT)
Students	17 (1)	23 (0)	41	1 (0)	0 (0)	5 (0)	1 (0)	31 (1)	2 (0)	0 (0)	0 (0)	6 (0)

Financial Information/Assistance

Tuition: For information on tuition costs, visit http://www.uwstout.edu/stubus/tuitionrate.cfm. Tuition is subject to change. Additional fees are assessed to students beyond the costs of tuition for the following: SPSS and other computer software required; to be purchased by student.

Master's:
State residents: $8,466 per academic year.
State residents: $423 per credit hour.
Nonstate residents: $16,687 per academic year.
Nonstate residents: $834 per credit hour.

Financial Assistance:

	Teaching Assistantship (% Receiving)	Teaching Assistantship Tuition Remission	Research Assistantship (% Receiving)	Research Assistantship Tuition Remission	Fellowship (% Receiving)	Fellowship Tuition Remission
First-Year Student	$5,120 (35)	NA	$5,120 (30)	NA	$1,000 (3)	NA
Advanced Student	$5,120 (15)	NA	$5,120 (67)	NA	$1,000 (3)	NA

For additional information on financial assistance, visit http://www.uwstout.edu/grad/prospect/finance.cfm.

Employment of Department Graduates

Master's:
Employed in other positions at a higher education institution: 3
Employed in business or industry: 10
Do not know: 1
Total: 14

Additional Information

Housing and Day Care: On-campus housing is available. See the following website for more information: http://www.uwstout.edu/housing/. On-campus day care facilities are available. See the following website for more information: http://www.uwstout.edu/soe/cfsc/index.cfm.

Information for Students With Physical Disabilities: See the following website: http://www.uwstout.edu/services/disability/.

Special Facilities or Resources: The university has numerous consulting relationships with local and regional businesses and industries, health-related organizations, governmental agencies, and nonprofit organizations. MSAP students utilize the latest multimedia hardware and software to perform both quantitative and qualitative analyses. Several facilities and labs within the College of Education, Hospitality, Health and Human Services, and the Psychology Department have received lab modernization funds.

Application Information: Libby Smith, MS, Program Director, MS Applied Psychology, Psychology Department, University of Wisconsin-Stout, Menomonie, WI 54751-0790. *Fee:* $56. *Online application:* https://apply.wisconsin.edu/.

Wyoming, University of
Department of Psychology
Arts and Sciences
Department 3415, 1000 East University Avenue
Laramie, WY 82071
Telephone: (307) 766-6303
Chairperson: Karen Bartsch Estes

E-mail: bartsch@uwyo.edu
Web: http://www.uwyo.edu/psychology

Orientation, Objectives, and Emphasis of Department
The University of Wyoming is the only 4-year university in the state of Wyoming. The psychology department has a broad undergraduate teaching mission and has one of the largest number of majors in the College of Arts and Sciences. The graduate curriculum provides breadth of training in psychology and permits specialization in various content areas. The Clinical Psychology PhD Program is based on the scientist–practitioner model. The goal of the clinical program is to provide students with the knowledge base and broad conceptual skills necessary for professional practice and/or research in a variety of settings. The PhD programs in Social Psychology, Cognition/Cognitive Development, and Psychology and Law provide students with broad training that can be used in a variety of academic and applied settings. All programs contain opportunities for both applied and basic research training. Research collaboration across all programs is encouraged.

Programs and Degrees Offered

Program	Degree	Application Deadline	Applications Received	Accepted	New Admits Enrolled (PT)	Total Enrolled (PT)	Degrees Awarded in 2014–2015	Median Years to Complete Degree	Dismissed/ Withdrew
Clinical Psychology	PhD	January 15 (Fall)	121	4	4	27 (0)	3	6	0
Psychology and Law	PhD	January 15 (Fall)	29	1	1	4	1	4	0
Social Psychology	PhD	January 15 (Fall)	19	0	0	3	0		0
Cognition/ Cognitive Development	PhD	January 15 (Fall)	14	2	2 (0)	5 (0)	1	4	0

APA Accreditation
Clinical PhD: Student Outcome Data website: http://www.uwyo.edu/psychology/graduate/prospective/clinical/data.html.

Doctoral Degree (PhD Clinical Psychology): For those doctoral students for whom a professional internship was required in this program prior to graduation:
Total students who applied for an internship: 6
Total students who obtained an internship: 5
Total students who obtained a paid internship: 5
Total students who obtained an unpaid internship: 0
Total students who were placed in APA/CPA-accredited internships: 5
Total students placed in internships not APA/CPA-accredited, but listed with the Association of Psychology Postdoctoral and Internship Centers (APPIC): 0
Total students placed in internships conforming to guidelines of the Council of Directors of School Psychology Programs (CDSPP): 0
Total students placed in internships that were not APA/CPA-accredited, APPIC or CDSSP listed: 0

Internships/Practica
Given Wyoming's large geographic area (approximately 100,000 square miles) and small population (approximately 500,000), we arrange practica and clerkships for Clinical students in various settings throughout the state. Clerkships are typically conducted in the summer for extended periods of time. Practica and clerkships include a variety of clinical populations such as children, adolescents, adults, and elderly people. They occur in a range of placements including outpatient mental health centers, inpatient hospitals, VA

Medical Centers and residential programs. Specialty experiences include forensic evaluation, substance abuse training, and parent training.

Admissions

Entries appear in the following order: required test or GPA, minimum score (if required)/median score of students entering in 2015–2016.

Program	Degree	GRE-V	GRE-Q	GRE-Writing	GRE-Subject	Under-graduate GPA	Last 2 Years GPA	Psychol-ogy GPA	Master's GPA
Clinical Psychology	PhD	NA/157	NA/150	NA/4.8	Not specified	NA/3.7	NA/NA	NA/3.8	NA/NA
Psychology and Law	PhD	NA/155	NA/148	NA/4	Not specified	NA/3.5	NA/NA	NA/3.5	NA/NA
Social Psychology	PhD	NA/NA	NA/NA	NA/NA	Not specified	NA/NA	NA/NA	NA/NA	Not specified
Cognition/ Cognitive Development	PhD	NA/153	NA/152	NA/4.3	Not specified	NA/3.5	NA/NA	NA/3.6	NA/3.7

Admissions Requirements:

Degree	GRE	GRE-Subject	Letters of Recom-mendation	Research Statement	Writing Sample	CV	Interview
Doctoral	Required	Required	3	Recom-mended	None	Optional	Recom-mended

Please note if these criteria vary for different programs: Work Experience and Clinically Related Public Service relevant to the Clinical Program only.

Admissions Criteria:

GRE scores—high
Research experience—high
Work experience—low
Clinically related public service—medium
GPA—medium

Letters of recommendation—high
Interview—high
Statement of goals and objectives—high
Undergraduate psychology preparation—medium

For additional information on admission requirements, visit http://www.uwyo.edu/psychology/graduate/prospective/apply.html.

Department Demographics

	Male (PT)	Female (PT)	Total	African-American/ Black (PT)	Hispanic/ Latino (PT)	Asian/ Pacific Islander (PT)	American Indian/ Alaska Native (PT)	Caucasian/ White (PT)	Unknown	Multiethnic (PT)	ADA (PT)	Int'l (PT)
Students	12 (0)	27 (0)	39	0 (0)	3 (0)	1 (0)	0 (0)	27 (0)	7 (0)	1 (0)	0 (0)	2 (0)

Financial Information/Assistance

Tuition: For information on tuition costs, visit http://www.uwyo.edu/fsbo/accounts-receivable/. Tuition is subject to change. Additional fees are assessed to students beyond the costs of tuition for the following: Student services, health, athletics, transit, computers.

Doctoral:
State residents: $4,176 per academic year.
State residents: $232 per credit hour.
Nonstate residents: $12,474 per academic year.
Nonstate residents: $693 per credit hour.

Financial Assistance:

	Teaching Assistantship (% Receiving)	Teaching Assistantship Tuition Remission	Research Assistantship (% Receiving)	Research Assistantship Tuition Remission	Fellowship (% Receiving)	Fellowship Tuition Remission
First-Year Student	$16,263 (100)	Full	$16,263 (100)	Full	NA (NA)	NA
Advanced Student	$16,263 (91)	Full	$16,263 (NA)	Full	NA (NA)	NA

For additional information on financial assistance, visit http://www.uwyo.edu/psychology/graduate/prospective/finances.html.

Employment of Department Graduates

Doctoral:
Enrolled in a postdoctoral residency/fellowship: 1
Enrolled in another graduate/professional program: 1
Employed in an academic position at a university: 1
Employed in other positions at a higher education institution: 1
Employed in business or industry: 1
Total: 5

Additional Information

Housing and Day Care: On-campus housing is available. See the following website for more information: http://www.uwyo.edu/reslife-dining/. On-campus day care facilities are available. See the following website for more information: http://www.uwyo.edu/ecec/.

Information for Students With Physical Disabilities: See the following website: http://www.uwyo.edu/udss/.

Special Facilities or Resources: The department has approximately 24,000 square feet of laboratory, office, and clinic space in a science complex with direct access to the university's science library and various computer labs. Faculty laboratories range from wet laboratories designed for the biological aspects of human behavior to labs designed to assess mock jurors and jury decision-making. The Psychology Clinic has ample space for individual or small group assessment and treatment. These facilities also have observation mirrors and digital recording capability.

Application Information: Graduate Admissions Committee, Department of Psychology, University of Wyoming, Department 3415, 1000 East University Avenue, Laramie, WY 82071. *Fee:* $50. *Online application:* http://www.uwyo.edu/admissions/graduate/index.html.

Acadia University

Department of Psychology
18 University Avenue
Wolfville, NS B4P 2R6
Telephone: (902) 585-1301
Head: Dr. Sonya Major

E-mail: susan.potter@acadiau.ca
Web: http://psychology.acadiau.ca

Orientation, Objectives, and Emphasis of Department

The department's principle objective is to train MSc students in clinical psychology. The department's orientation is eclectic although there is an emphasis on cognitive-behavioural approaches to problems in psychology. Our curriculum is highly respected, and graduates going on to doctoral programs elsewhere have had recognition of their master's level coursework from Acadia. We are registered with CAMPP.

Programs and Degrees Offered

Program	Degree	Application Deadline	Applica-tions Received	Accepted	New Admits Enrolled (PT)	Total Enrolled (PT)	Degrees Awarded in 2014–2015	Median Years to Complete Degree	Dismissed/Withdrew
Clinical Psychology	MA/MS	February 1 (Fall)	38	5	5	10	5	2	0

Internships/Practica

Two 250-hour internships are mandatory in intervention and assessment.

Admissions

Entries appear in the following order: required test or GPA, minimum score (if required)/median score of students entering in 2015–2016.

Program	Degree	GRE-V	GRE-Q	GRE-Writing	GRE-Subject	Under-graduate GPA	Last 2 Years GPA	Psychol-ogy GPA	Master's GPA
Clinical Psychology	MA/MS	NA/NA	NA/NA	NA/NA	Not specified	3.5/NA	3.5/NA	3.5/NA	Not specified

Admissions Requirements:

Degree	GRE	GRE-Subject	Letters of Recom-mendation	Research Statement	Writing Sample	CV	Interview
Master's/Specialist	Required	Optional	3	Required	Optional	Required	Required

Admissions Criteria:

GRE scores—high
Research experience—high
Work experience—medium
Clinically related public service—medium
GPA—high

Letters of recommendation—high
Interview—high
Statement of goals and objectives—high
Undergraduate psychology preparation—high
Honours degree (UG)—high

For additional information on admission requirements, visit http://psychology.acadiau.ca/admission-requirements.html.

Department Demographics

	Male (PT)	Female (PT)	Total	African-American/ Black (PT)	Hispanic/ Latino (PT)	Asian/ Pacific Islander (PT)	American Indian/ Alaska Native (PT)	Caucasian/ White (PT)	Unknown	Multiethnic (PT)	ADA (PT)	Int'l (PT)
Students	1 (0)	9 (0)	0	0 (0)	0 (0)	0 (0)	0 (0)	10 (0)	0 (0)	0 (0)	0 (0)	0 (0)

Financial Information/Assistance

Tuition: For information on tuition costs, visit http://gradstudies.acadiau.ca/fees_funding.html. Tuition is subject to change.

Master's:
State residents: $4,090 per academic year.
Nonstate residents: $5,373 per academic year.

Financial Assistance:

	Teaching Assistantship (% Receiving)	Teaching Assistantship Tuition Remission	Research Assistantship (% Receiving)	Research Assistantship Tuition Remission	Fellowship (% Receiving)	Fellowship Tuition Remission
First-Year Student	$8,000 (40)	NA	$12,000 (20)	NA	$10,000 (40)	NA
Advanced Student	NA (NA)	NA	$12,000 (20)	NA	$10,000 (80)	NA

Employment of Department Graduates

Master's:
Enrolled in a psychology doctoral program: 2
Employed in a community mental health/counseling center: 2
Employed in a hospital/medical center: 1
Total: 5

Additional Information

Housing and Day Care: On-campus housing is available. See the following website for more information: http://residencelife. acadiau.ca/. No on-campus day care facilities are available.

Information for Students With Physical Disabilities: See the following website: http://accessiblelearning.acadiau.ca/.

Special Facilities or Resources: Students are able to do a thesis under the supervision of the experimental psychology faculty in our department as well as the clinical faculty. Various special equipment including ERP and eye-tracking equipment is available.

Application Information: Office of Research and Graduate Studies, Acadia University, Wolfville, NS, B4P 2R6. *Fee:* $50. *Online application:* http://www2.acadiau.ca/apply_graduate.html.

Alberta, University of (2015 data)
Department of Psychology
P217 Biological Sciences Building
Edmonton, AB T6G 2E9
Telephone: (708) 492-5216
Chairperson: Jeffrey Bisanz

E-mail: jeff.bisanz@ualberta.ca
Web: http://www.psych.ualberta.ca

Orientation, Objectives, and Emphasis of Department
The goal of the graduate program is to train competent and independent researchers who will make significant contributions to the discipline of psychology. The program entails early and sustained involvement in research and ensures that students attain expertise

in focal and related domains. The program offers training that leads to degrees in a range of research areas, including: Behaviour, Systems and Cognitive Neuroscience; Cognition; Comparative Cognition and Behaviour; Developmental Science; and Social and Cultural Psychology. Recent PhD graduates from the Department have successfully found positions in universities and colleges, branches of government, and industry. A reasonably close match between the research interests of prospective students and faculty members is essential because the program involves apprenticeship-style training. Although many faculty members conduct research on problems that have practical and social significance, we do not have programs in clinical, counseling, or industrial/organizational psychology.

Programs and Degrees Offered

Program	Degree	Application Deadline	Applica-tions Received	Accepted	New Admits Enrolled (PT)	Total Enrolled (PT)	Degrees Awarded in 2014–2015	Median Years to Complete Degree	Dismissed/ Withdrew
Psychology	MA/MS	January 15 (Fall)	51	10	3	20	8		0
Psychology	PhD	January 15 (Fall)	17	3	2	39	4		0

Admissions

Entries appear in the following order: required test or GPA, minimum score (if required)/median score of students entering in 2015–2016.

Program	Degree	GRE-V	GRE-Q	GRE-Writing	GRE-Subject	Under-graduate GPA	Last 2 Years GPA	Psychol-ogy GPA	Master's GPA
Psychology	MA/MS	NA/NA	NA/NA	NA/NA	Not specified	NA/NA	NA/NA	Not specified	Not specified
Psychology	PhD	NA/NA	NA/NA	NA/NA	Not specified	NA/NA	NA/NA	Not specified	NA/NA

Admissions Requirements:

Degree	GRE	GRE-Subject	Letters of Recom-mendation	Research Statement	Writing Sample	CV	Interview
Master's/Specialist	Required	None	2	Required	Optional	Required	None
Doctoral	Required	None	2	Required	Optional	Required	None

Admissions Criteria:

GRE scores—high
Research experience—high
Work experience—low

GPA—high
Letters of recommendation—high
Statement of goals and objectives—high

For additional information on admission requirements, visit http://www.psych.ualberta.ca/graduate/appinfo.php.

Department Demographics

	Male (PT)	Female (PT)	Total	African-American/ Black (PT)	Hispanic/ Latino (PT)	Asian/ Pacific Islander (PT)	American Indian/ Alaska Native (PT)	Caucasian/ White (PT)	Unknown	Multiethnic (PT)	ADA (PT)	Int'l (PT)
Students	20 (0)	38 (0)	0		3 (0)	18 (0)		30 (0)	0 (0)	7 (0)	0 (0)	0 (0)

Financial Information/Assistance

Tuition: For information on tuition costs, visit http://uofa.ualberta.ca/graduate-studies/current-students/tuition-and-fees. Tuition is subject to change.

Doctoral:
State residents: $5,500 per academic year.
Nonstate residents: $8,400 per academic year.

Master's:
State residents: $5,500 per academic year.
Nonstate residents: $8,400 per academic year.

Financial Assistance:

	Teaching Assistantship (% Receiving)	Teaching Assistantship Tuition Remission	Research Assistantship (% Receiving)	Research Assistantship Tuition Remission	Fellowship (% Receiving)	Fellowship Tuition Remission
First-Year Student	$16,080 (NA)	NA	$8,040 (NA)	NA	NA (NA)	NA
Advanced Student	$24,393 (NA)	NA	$24,393 (NA)	NA	NA (NA)	NA

For additional information on financial assistance, visit http://www.psych.ualberta.ca/graduate/finsupport.php.

Employment of Department Graduates

Master's:
Enrolled in a psychology doctoral program: 6
Enrolled in another graduate/professional program: 1
Total: 7

Doctoral:
Enrolled in a postdoctoral residency/fellowship: 3
Employed in an academic position at a university: 3
Employed in business or industry: 1
Total: 7

Additional Information

Housing and Day Care: On-campus housing is available. See the following website for more information: http://www.residence.ualberta.ca/. On-campus day care facilities are available. See the following website for more information: http://www.asinfo.ualberta.ca/AffiliatedChildCare.

Information for Students With Physical Disabilities: See the following website: http://www.ssds.ualberta.ca/.

Special Facilities or Resources: The department maintains a number of specialized support facilities for staff and student use including an electronics shop, labs for teaching and research use, and an instructional technology lab to support teaching. In addition, the department maintains a psychology reading room. Department computing resources include approximately 300 computers used in research and 40 additional computers used for administration and instructional needs. All staff and student computers have network capability on the department and campus networks. Technical assistance for research, teaching, and administrative needs is provided by department technical staff. For research services, the department maintains a fully equipped electronics shop staffed by technicians who design, build, and maintain custom laboratory equipment and data acquisition devices for laboratory applications. The shop contains a variety of professional equipment for electronics and fabrication work and stocks supplies for research and equipment needs. Technical staff also provides a full range of assistance with equipment selection and ordering, equipment repair, and new equipment configuration and setup. Other resources include the University Teaching and Learning Program, which improves the teaching skills of graduate students through workshops and practica, and the Community-University Partnership, which facilitates community- and school-based research.

Application Information: Graduate Program Assistant, Department of Psychology, P-217D Biological Sciences, University of Alberta, Edmonton, AB Canada T6G 2E9. *Fee:* $100. *Online application:* https://applygrad.ualberta.ca/.

British Columbia, University of
Department of Psychology
2136 West Mall, Kenny Building
Vancouver, BC V6T 1Z4
Telephone: (604) 822-5002
Head: D. Geoff Hall

E-mail: gradsec@psych.ubc.ca
Web: http://psych.ubc.ca/

Orientation, Objectives, and Emphasis of Department

The department is organized into seven subject content areas with which faculty and graduate students are affiliated. Graduate training emphasizes a high degree of research competence, and from the beginning of the program, students are involved in increasingly independent research activities.

Programs and Degrees Offered

Program	Degree	Application Deadline	Applications Received	Accepted	New Admits Enrolled (PT)	Total Enrolled (PT)	Degrees Awarded in 2014–2015	Median Years to Complete Degree	Dismissed/Withdrew
Behavioral Neuroscience	PhD	December 1 (Fall)	11	3	3 (0)	9 (0)	0		0
Clinical Psychology	PhD	December 1 (Fall)	119	4	4 (0)	37 (0)	4	9	0
Developmental Psychology	PhD	December 1 (Fall)	17	3	3 (0)	13 (0)	0		0
Cognitive Science	PhD	December 1 (Fall)	32	5	5 (0)	27 (0)	5	7	0
Social/ Personality Psychology	PhD	December 1 (Fall)	63	4	4 (0)	19 (0)	3	7	1
Quantitative Methods	PhD	December 1 (Fall)	11	1	0 (0)	2 (0)	0		0
Health Psychology	PhD	December 1 (Fall)	13	1	1 (0)	6 (0)	1	7.5	0

CPA Accreditation

Clinical PhD (Doctor of Philosophy).

Doctoral Degree (PhD Clinical Psychology): For those doctoral students for whom a professional internship was required in this program prior to graduation:
Total students who applied for an internship: 5
Total students who obtained an internship: 5
Total students who obtained a paid internship: 4
Total students who obtained an unpaid internship: 1
Total students who were placed in APA/CPA-accredited internships: 4
Total students placed in internships not APA/CPA-accredited, but listed with the Association of Psychology Postdoctoral and Internship Centers (APPIC): 0
Total students placed in internships conforming to guidelines of the Council of Directors of School Psychology Programs (CDSPP): 0
Total students placed in internships that were not APA/CPA-accredited, APPIC or CDSSP listed: 1

Internships/Practica

Clinical students are required to do 2 years of practicum training in our in-house psychology clinic as well as community-based practica. A CPA- or APA-accredited psychology internship is required for the PhD in clinical psychology.

Admissions

Entries appear in the following order: required test or GPA, minimum score (if required)/median score of students entering in 2015–2016.

Program	Degree	GRE-V	GRE-Q	GRE-Writing	GRE-Subject	Under-graduate GPA	Last 2 Years GPA	Psychol-ogy GPA	Master's GPA
Behavioral Neuroscience	PhD	NA/NA	NA/NA	NA/NA	Not specified	Not specified	NA/3.83	Not specified	Not specified
Clinical Psychology	PhD	NA/NA	NA/NA	NA/NA	Not specified	Not specified	NA/NA	Not specified	Not specified

Admissions *(con't.)*

Program	Degree	GRE-V	GRE-Q	GRE-Writing	GRE-Subject	Under-graduate GPA	Last 2 Years GPA	Psychol-ogy GPA	Master's GPA
Developmental Psychology	PhD	NA/NA	NA/NA	NA/NA	Not specified	Not specified	NA/NA	Not specified	Not specified
Cognitive Science	PhD	NA/NA	NA/NA	NA/NA	Not specified	Not specified	NA/NA	Not specified	Not specified
Social/ Personality Psychology	PhD	NA/NA	NA/NA	NA/NA	Not specified	Not specified	NA/3.63	Not specified	Not specified
Quantitative Methods	PhD	NA/NA	NA/NA	NA/NA	Not specified	Not specified	NA/NA	Not specified	Not specified
Health Psychology	PhD	NA/NA	NA/NA	NA/NA	Not specified	Not specified	NA/3.9	Not specified	Not specified

Admissions Requirements:

Degree	GRE	GRE-Subject	Letters of Recom-mendation	Research Statement	Writing Sample	CV	Interview
Master's/Specialist	Required	Recom-mended	3	Required	Recom-mended	Required	Required
Doctoral	Required	Optional	3	Required	Recom-mended	Required	Required

Admissions Criteria:

GRE scores—medium
Research experience—high
Clinically related public service—low
GPA—high

Letters of recommendation—high
Interview—medium
Statement of goals and objectives—high
Undergraduate psychology preparation—medium

For additional information on admission requirements, visit http://psych.ubc.ca/graduate/apply/.

Department Demographics

	Male (PT)	Female (PT)	Total	African-American/ Black (PT)	Hispanic/ Latino (PT)	Asian/ Pacific Islander (PT)	American Indian/ Alaska Native (PT)	Caucasian/ White (PT)	Unknown	Multiethnic (PT)	ADA (PT)	Int'l (PT)
Students	42 (0)	72 (0)	0	0 (0)	0 (0)	0 (0)	0 (0)	0 (0)	114 (0)	0 (0)	0 (0)	0 (0)

Financial Information/Assistance

Tuition: For information on tuition costs, visit http://www.grad.ubc.ca/prospective-students/tuition-fees-cost-living/graduate-tuition-fees. Tuition is subject to change. Additional fees are assessed to students beyond the costs of tuition for the following: student fees (including transit pass) and extended health care plan.

Doctoral:
State residents: $4,615 per academic year.
Nonstate residents: $8,108 per academic year.

Master's:
State residents: $4,615 per academic year.
Nonstate residents: $8,108 per academic year.

Financial Assistance:

	Teaching Assistantship (% Receiving)	Teaching Assistantship Tuition Remission	Research Assistantship (% Receiving)	Research Assistantship Tuition Remission	Fellowship (% Receiving)	Fellowship Tuition Remission
First-Year Student	$9,227 (67)	NA	$5,644 (33)	NA	$17,500 (67)	NA
Advanced Student	$10,989 (91)	NA	$6,752 (90)	NA	$23,203 (92)	Full

For additional information on financial assistance, visit http://psych.ubc.ca/graduate/awards-and-funding-2/.

Employment of Department Graduates

Master's:
Enrolled in a psychology doctoral program: 12
Total: 12

Doctoral:
Enrolled in a postdoctoral residency/fellowship: 5
Employed in independent practice: 2
Employed in an academic position at a university: 1
Employed in business or industry: 1
Employed in a community mental health/counseling center: 2
Do not know: 1
Total: 12

Additional Information

Housing and Day Care: On-campus housing is available. See the following website for more information: http://www.grad.ubc.ca/campus-community/residential-graduate-colleges. On-campus day care facilities are available. See the following website for more information: http://www.childcare.ubc.ca/.

Information for Students With Physical Disabilities: See the following website: http://students.ubc.ca/success/student-supports/academic-accommodations.

Special Facilities or Resources: The department is housed in an attractive building of about 90,000 square feet, designed for psychological research. The department has well-equipped research facilities including a psychology clinic, observation galleries, and animal, psychophysiological, perceptual, cognitive, and social/personality laboratories.

Application Information: Fee: $96. *Online application:* http://www.grad.ubc.ca/apply/online/.

Calgary, University of
Department of Psychology
2500 University Drive, Northwest
Calgary, AB T2N 1N4
Telephone: (403) 220-5561
Head: Dr. David Hodgins

E-mail: psycgrad@ucalgary.ca
Web: http://psyc.ucalgary.ca/

Orientation, Objectives, and Emphasis of Department
This is a research-oriented department with a strong focus on applied problems. We offer both a clinical psychology and a psychology program. Specific research programs in psychology include Brain and Cognitive Science, Industrial/Organizational Psychology, and Social and Theoretical Psychology.

Programs and Degrees Offered

Program	Degree	Application Deadline	Applications Received	Accepted	New Admits Enrolled (PT)	Total Enrolled (PT)	Degrees Awarded in 2014–2015	Median Years to Complete Degree	Dismissed/Withdrew
Psychology	PhD	December 5 (Fall), October 1 (Winter)	49	11	11	51 (0)	9	5	0
Clinical Psychology	PhD	December 5 (Fall)	102	6	6	38 (0)	9	4	2

CPA Accreditation

Clinical PhD (Doctor of Philosophy).

Doctoral Degree (PhD Clinical Psychology): For those doctoral students for whom a professional internship was required in this program prior to graduation:
Total students who applied for an internship: 4
Total students who obtained an internship: 4
Total students who obtained a paid internship: 4
Total students who obtained an unpaid internship: 0
Total students who were placed in APA/CPA-accredited internships: 4
Total students placed in internships not APA/CPA-accredited, but listed with the Association of Psychology Postdoctoral and Internship Centers (APPIC): 0
Total students placed in internships conforming to guidelines of the Council of Directors of School Psychology Programs (CDSPP): 0
Total students placed in internships that were not APA/CPA-accredited, APPIC or CDSSP listed: 0

Internships/Practica

Practica are available at several settings, including Alberta Health Services and other community services.

Admissions

Entries appear in the following order: required test or GPA, minimum score (if required)/median score of students entering in 2015–2016.

Program	Degree	GRE-V	GRE-Q	GRE-Writing	GRE-Subject	Under-graduate GPA	Last 2 Years GPA	Psychology GPA	Master's GPA
Psychology	PhD	NA/NA	NA/NA	NA/NA	Not specified	3/NA	3.4/NA	Not specified	3.4/NA
Clinical Psychology	PhD	NA/NA	NA/NA	NA/NA	Not specified	3/NA	3.6/NA	Not specified	3.6/NA

Admissions Requirements:

Degree	GRE	GRE-Subject	Letters of Recommendation	Research Statement	Writing Sample	CV	Interview
Doctoral	Required	Required	2	Required	None	Required	Required

Please note if these criteria vary for different programs: Formal interviews are not typically required for the Psychology Graduate Program.

Admissions Criteria:

GRE scores—medium
Research experience—high
Work experience—medium
Clinically related public service—medium
GPA—high

Letters of recommendation—high
Interview—medium
Statement of goals and objectives—medium
Research proposal—medium

For additional information on admission requirements, visit https://psychology.ucalgary.ca/graduate-program.

Department Demographics

	Male (PT)	Female (PT)	Total	African-American/ Black (PT)	Hispanic/ Latino (PT)	Asian/ Pacific Islander (PT)	American Indian/ Alaska Native (PT)	Caucasian/ White (PT)	Unknown	Multiethnic (PT)	ADA (PT)	Int'l (PT)
Students	22 (0)	67 (0)	0	0 (0)	0 (0)	0 (0)	0 (0)	0 (0)	0 (0)	0 (0)	0 (0)	3 (0)

Financial Information/Assistance

Tuition: For information on tuition costs, visit http://grad.ucalgary.ca/future/tuition-fees. Tuition is subject to change.

Doctoral:
State residents: $5,593 per academic year.
Nonstate residents: $12,695 per academic year.

Master's:
State residents: $5,593 per academic year.
Nonstate residents: $12,695 per academic year.

Financial Assistance:

	Teaching Assistantship (% Receiving)	Teaching Assistantship Tuition Remission	Research Assistantship (% Receiving)	Research Assistantship Tuition Remission	Fellowship (% Receiving)	Fellowship Tuition Remission
First-Year Student	$17,266 (NA)	NA	NA (NA)	NA	$2,500 (NA)	NA
Advanced Student	$17,266 (NA)	NA	NA (NA)	NA	$4,000 (NA)	NA

For additional information on financial assistance, visit http://grad.ucalgary.ca/awards.

Employment of Department Graduates

Master's:
Enrolled in a psychology doctoral program: 11
Employed in business or industry: 2
Total: 13

Doctoral:
Employed in an academic position at a university: 1
Employed in government agency: 1
Employed in a hospital/medical center: 4
Total: 6

Additional Information

Housing and Day Care: On-campus housing is available. See the following website for more information: http://www.ucalgary.ca/residence/. On-campus day care facilities are available. See the following website for more information: http://www.ucalgary.ca/uccc/.

Information for Students With Physical Disabilities: See the following website: http://www.ucalgary.ca/access/.

Application Information: Graduate Programs Administrator, Department of Psychology, 2500 University Drive NW, University of Calgary, Calgary, AB T2N 1N4 Canada. *Fee:* $125. *Online application:* https://iac01.ucalgary.ca/StudentAdmission/default.aspx.

Carleton University
Department of Psychology
Faculty of Arts and Social Sciences
1125 Colonel By Drive
Ottawa, ON K1S 5B6
Telephone: (613) 520-4017
Chairperson: Joanna Pozzulo

E-mail: Gradpsychology@carleton.ca
Web: http://www.carleton.ca/psychology/

Orientation, Objectives, and Emphasis of Department

The program is strongly research-oriented, although practical courses such as quantitative methods, testing and behavior modification are available. This degree however does not offer training in applied areas (e.g., clinical, educational, counseling psychology, etc).

Programs and Degrees Offered

Program	Degree	Application Deadline	Applications Received	Accepted	New Admits Enrolled (PT)	Total Enrolled (PT)	Degrees Awarded in 2014–2015	Median Years to Complete Degree	Dismissed/ Withdrew
Psychology	MA/MS	January 15 (Fall), November 1 (Winter)	156	42	35 (1)	65 (2)	17	2	1
Psychology	PhD	January 15 (Fall), November 1 (Winter)	39	14	13 (0)	64 (6)	11	5	0

Admissions

Entries appear in the following order: required test or GPA, minimum score (if required)/median score of students entering in 2015–2016.

Program	Degree	GRE-V	GRE-Q	GRE-Writing	GRE-Subject	Under-graduate GPA	Last 2 Years GPA	Psychology GPA	Master's GPA
Psychology	MA/MS	Not specified	Not specified	Not specified	Not specified	NA/NA	NA/NA	NA/NA	Not specified
Psychology	PhD	Not specified	Not specified	Not specified	Not specified	Not specified	NA/NA	NA/NA	NA/NA

Admissions Requirements:

Degree	GRE	GRE-Subject	Letters of Recom-mendation	Research Statement	Writing Sample	CV	Interview
Master's/Specialist	Optional	Optional	2	Required	Optional	Required	None
Doctoral	Optional	Optional	2	Required	Required	Required	Optional

Admissions Criteria:

Research experience—high
Work experience—medium
GPA—high
Letters of recommendation—high

Interview—low
Statement of goals and objectives—high
Undergraduate psychology preparation—high

For additional information on admission requirements, visit http://carleton.ca/psychology/graduate-studies/graduate/application-instructions/.

Department Demographics

	Male (PT)	Female (PT)	Total	African-American/ Black (PT)	Hispanic/ Latino (PT)	Asian/ Pacific Islander (PT)	American Indian/ Alaska Native (PT)	Caucasian/ White (PT)	Unknown	Multiethnic (PT)	ADA (PT)	Int'l (PT)
Students	31 (6)	98 (2)	0	0 (0)	0 (0)	9 (0)	1 (0)	119 (8)	0 (0)	0 (0)	0 (0)	9 (0)

Financial Information/Assistance

Tuition: For information on tuition costs, visit http://carleton.ca/studentaccounts/tuition-fees/. Tuition is subject to change.

Doctoral:
State residents: $9,450 per academic year.
Nonstate residents: $21,636 per academic year.

Master's:
State residents: $9,575 per academic year.
Nonstate residents: $21,910 per academic year.

Financial Assistance:

	Teaching Assistantship (% Receiving)	Teaching Assistantship Tuition Remission	Research Assistantship (% Receiving)	Research Assistantship Tuition Remission	Fellowship (% Receiving)	Fellowship Tuition Remission
First-Year Student	$10,288 (NA)	NA	$3,000 (NA)	NA	$5,000 (NA)	NA
Advanced Student	$10,288 (NA)	NA	$3,500 (NA)	NA	$8,000 (NA)	NA

For additional information on financial assistance, visit http://gradstudents.carleton.ca/awards-and-funding/.

Employment of Department Graduates

Master's:
Enrolled in a psychology doctoral program: 10
Employed in government agency: 3
Employed in a hospital/medical center: 1
Still seeking employment: 1
Do not know: 2
Total: 17

Doctoral:
Enrolled in a postdoctoral residency/fellowship: 1
Employed in other positions at a higher education institution: 1
Employed in a professional position in a school system: 3
Employed in business or industry: 1
Employed in government agency: 3
Do not know: 1
Total: 10

Additional Information

Housing and Day Care: On-campus housing is available. See the following website for more information: http://housing.carleton.ca/. On-campus day care facilities are available. See the following website for more information: http://carleton.ca/campus/colonel-by-child-care-centre-cc.

Information for Students With Physical Disabilities: See the following website: http://carleton.ca/pmc/.

Application Information: Fee: $100. *Online application:* http://graduate.carleton.ca/apply-online/.

Concordia University (2015 data)
Department of Psychology
Faculty of Arts and Science
7141 Sherbrooke Street West
Montreal, QC H4B 1R6
Telephone: (514) 848-2424 ext. 2205
Chairperson: Virginia Penhune, PhD

E-mail: psychology.graduate@concordia.ca
Web: http://www.concordia.ca

Orientation, Objectives, and Emphasis of Department
Graduate education in both experimental and clinical psychology is strongly research-oriented and intended for students who are planning to complete the PhD degree. The research program for all students is based on an apprentice-type model. An outstanding feature of graduate education at Concordia is that students pursuing only research studies and students pursuing research and clinical studies may conduct their research in the laboratory of any faculty member. A wide variety of contemporary research areas are represented, ranging from behavioral neurobiology, to cognitive and developmental science, to applied interventions with humans. Research findings from numerous areas are integrated in an effort to solve problems associated with appetitive motivation and drug dependence, memory and aging, human cognition and development, developmental psychobiology, adult and child psychopathology,

and sexual dysfunctions, to name several examples. Clinical training is based on the scientist–practitioner model. That is, clinical students meet the same research requirements as other students, and receive extensive professional training in the delivery of psychological services. Students may choose to specialize their clinical training with children or adults.

Programs and Degrees Offered

Program	Degree	Application Deadline	Applications Received	Accepted	New Admits Enrolled (PT)	Total Enrolled (PT)	Degrees Awarded in 2014–2015	Median Years to Complete Degree	Dismissed/ Withdrew
Research and Clinical Training	PhD	December 15 (Fall)	144	11	11 (0)	73 (0)	10	6.5	0
Research	PhD	December 15 (Fall)	44	13	11 (0)	53 (0)	3	5	0

CPA Accreditation
Clinical PhD (Doctor of Philosophy).

Doctoral Degree (PhD Research and Clinical Training): For those doctoral students for whom a professional internship was required in this program prior to graduation:
Total students who applied for an internship: 14
Total students who obtained an internship: 13
Total students who obtained a paid internship: 13
Total students who obtained an unpaid internship: 0
Total students who were placed in APA/CPA-accredited internships: 11
Total students placed in internships not APA/CPA-accredited, but listed with the Association of Psychology Postdoctoral and Internship Centers (APPIC): 1
Total students placed in internships conforming to guidelines of the Council of Directors of School Psychology Programs (CDSPP): 0
Total students placed in internships that were not APA/CPA-accredited, APPIC or CDSSP listed: 1

Internships/Practica
Clinical students complete a variety of practica and internships while in program residence. All clinical students receive extensive practicum experience in psychotherapy and assessment in our on-campus training clinic, the Applied Psychology Center (APC). APC clients are seen by graduate students under the supervision of clinical faculty. The types of services offered by the APC reflect the interests of clinical supervisors and students, and may include individual, family, or marital psychotherapy, behavior therapy for sexual or phobic difficulties, and treatment of child disorders. During the summer of their second year, students also complete a full-time practicum at a mental health facility in the Montreal area. During their final year in the program, students complete their full-time, predoctoral clinical internships. Recent students have undertaken predoctoral internships at a variety of mental health facilities across Canada and the United States. All students are encouraged to seek internship positions in settings accredited by either the Canadian or American Psychological Associations.

Admissions
Entries appear in the following order: required test or GPA, minimum score (if required)/median score of students entering in 2015–2016.

Program	Degree	GRE-V	GRE-Q	GRE-Writing	GRE-Subject	Undergraduate GPA	Last 2 Years GPA	Psychology GPA	Master's GPA
Research and Clinical Training	PhD	Not specified	Not specified	Not specified	Not specified	Not specified	Not specified	Not specified	Not specified
Research	PhD	Not specified	Not specified	Not specified	Not specified	Not specified	Not specified	Not specified	Not specified

Admissions Requirements:

Degree	GRE	GRE-Subject	Letters of Recommendation	Research Statement	Writing Sample	CV	Interview
Master's/Specialist	Optional	Optional	3	Required	Optional	Required	Recommended
Doctoral	Optional	Optional	3	Required	Optional	Required	Recommended

Please note if these criteria vary for different programs: Research Option does not require clinically related service. Thesis Supervisor is required for admission to graduate program.

Admissions Criteria:

GRE scores—medium
Research experience—high
Work experience—medium
Clinically related public service—medium
GPA—medium

Letters of recommendation—high
Interview—high
Statement of goals and objectives—high
Undergraduate psychology preparation—high

Department Demographics

	Male (PT)	Female (PT)	Total	African-American/ Black (PT)	Hispanic/ Latino (PT)	Asian/ Pacific Islander (PT)	American Indian/ Alaska Native (PT)	Caucasian/ White (PT)	Unknown	Multiethnic (PT)	ADA (PT)	Int'l (PT)
Students	33 (1)	93 (1)	0					0 (0)	0 (0)			9 (0)

Financial Information/Assistance

Tuition: For information on tuition costs, visit http://www.concordia.ca/admissions/tuition-fees.html. Tuition is subject to change. Tuition costs vary by program.

Doctoral:
State residents: $3,999 per academic year.
Nonstate residents: $17,537 per academic year.

Master's:
State residents: $3,999 per academic year.
Nonstate residents: $19,299 per academic year.

Financial Assistance:

	Teaching Assistantship (% Receiving)	Teaching Assistantship Tuition Remission	Research Assistantship (% Receiving)	Research Assistantship Tuition Remission	Fellowship (% Receiving)	Fellowship Tuition Remission
First-Year Student	$6,000 (NA)	NA	$10,000 (NA)	NA	$20,000 (NA)	NA
Advanced Student	$6,000 (NA)	NA	$10,000 (NA)	NA	$20,000 (NA)	NA

For additional information on financial assistance, visit http://www.concordia.ca/students/financial-support/graduate-funding.html.

Employment of Department Graduates

Doctoral:
Enrolled in a postdoctoral residency/fellowship: 2
Employed in independent practice: 1
Employed in an academic position at a university: 1
Employed in a professional position in a school system: 1
Employed in government agency: 2

Employed in a community mental health/counseling center: 1
Still seeking employment: 1
Do not know: 1
Total: 10

Additional Information

Housing and Day Care: On-campus housing is available. See the following website for more information: http://www.concordia.ca/campus-life/residences.html. On-campus day care facilities are available. See the following website for more information: http://www.concordia.ca/campus-life/daycares.html.

Information for Students With Physical Disabilities: See the following website: http://www.concordia.ca/offices/acsd.html.

Special Facilities or Resources: The department has extensive animal and human research facilities that are supported by provincial, federal, and U.S. granting agencies as well as various internal and private sector funds. Research laboratories are well equipped. The department also contains two research centers that are jointly funded by the Government of Quebec and the University: the Center for Studies in Behavioral Neurobiology and the Center for Research in Human Development. Both centers coordinate multidisciplinary research programs, provide state-of-the-art laboratory equipment, and sponsor colloquia by specialists from other universities in North America and abroad. All graduate students benefit from activities supported by the research centers.

Application Information: Concordia University, Graduate Admissions Application Centre, P.O. Box 2002, Station H, Montreal, QC H3G 2V4, Canada. *Fee:* $100. *Online application:* http://www.concordia.ca/admissions/apply-now.html.

Dalhousie University
Department of Psychology and Neuroscience
Life Sciences Centre
Halifax, NS B3H 4R2
Telephone: (902) 494-7804
Chairperson: Tara Perrot

E-mail: Gradprog@dal.ca
Web: http://www.dal.ca/faculty/science/psychology_neuroscience.html

---

Orientation, Objectives, and Emphasis of Department
The Department of Psychology offers graduate training leading to MSc and PhD degrees in psychology and in psychology/neuroscience, and to a PhD in clinical psychology. Our graduate programs emphasize training for research. They are best described as apprenticeship programs in which students work closely with a faculty member who has agreed to supervise the student's research. Compared with many other graduate programs, we place less emphasis on coursework and greater emphasis on research, scholarship, and independent thinking. The graduate program in psychology/neuroscience is coordinated by the Psychology Department and an interdisciplinary Neuroscience Program Committee, with representation from the Departments of Anatomy, Biochemistry, Pharmacology, Physiology and Biophysics, and Psychology. Master's level students in psychology and psychology/neuroscience are expected to advance into the corresponding PhD programs. We do not have a terminal Master's program. The PhD program in clinical psychology is cooperatively administered by the Psychology Department and the Clinical Program Committee with representation from Acadia University, Dalhousie University, Mount Saint Vincent University, Saint Mary's University, and professional psychologists from the teaching hospitals.

Programs and Degrees Offered

Program	Degree	Application Deadline	Applications Received	Accepted	New Admits Enrolled (PT)	Total Enrolled (PT)	Degrees Awarded in 2014–2015	Median Years to Complete Degree	Dismissed/ Withdrew
Clinical Psychology	PhD	December 1 (Fall)	120	6	6 (0)	37 (0)	6	5	0
Experimental— Animal	PhD	December 1 (Fall)	0	0	0 (0)	2 (0)	0		0
Experimental— Human	PhD	December 1 (Fall)	1	1	1 (0)	6 (0)	1	5	0
Neuroscience	MA/MS	December 1 (Fall)	25	3	3 (0)	6 (0)	0		0

Programs and Degrees Offered *(con't.)*

Program	Degree	Application Deadline	Applications Received	Accepted	New Admits Enrolled (PT)	Total Enrolled (PT)	Degrees Awarded in 2014–2015	Median Years to Complete Degree	Dismissed/ Withdrew
Experimental— Animal	MA/MS	December 1 (Fall)	20	0	0 (0)	0 (0)	0		0
Neuroscience	PhD	December 1 (Fall)	10	7	7 (0)	16 (0)	0		0
Experimental— Human	MA/MS	December 1 (Fall)	15	1	1 (0)	2 (0)	1	1	0

CPA Accreditation

Clinical PhD (Doctor of Philosophy).

Doctoral Degree (PhD Clinical Psychology): For those doctoral students for whom a professional internship was required in this program prior to graduation:
Total students who applied for an internship: 4
Total students who obtained an internship: 4
Total students who obtained a paid internship: 4
Total students who obtained an unpaid internship: 0
Total students who were placed in APA/CPA-accredited internships: 4
Total students placed in internships not APA/CPA-accredited, but listed with the Association of Psychology Postdoctoral and Internship Centers (APPIC): 0
Total students placed in internships conforming to guidelines of the Council of Directors of School Psychology Programs (CDSPP): 0
Total students placed in internships that were not APA/CPA-accredited, APPIC or CDSSP listed: 0

Internships/Practica

Practicum training is integrated into the Clinical Psychology PhD curriculum to complement knowledge and skills developed through coursework, to provide opportunities to master specific assessment and intervention techniques, and to ensure that students meet expectations with regard to core competencies. Brief practica are incorporated into a number of the core clinical courses; however, the majority of practicum hours are accumulated through community placements, under the supervision of registered psychologists. Dalhousie is situated in close proximity to a variety of excellent health care facilities, including the IWK Health Centre, the QEII Health Centre, the Nova Scotia Hospital, the Canadian Forces Hospital at CFB Stadacona, and the East Coast Forensic Hospital. Under the guidance of the Field Placement Coordinator, students select and complete a program of practicum placements designed to meet their individual training needs. Students are required to complete a minimum of 600 hours of formal practicum training, but it is recognized that additional practicum hours (for a total of about 1,000–1,200 hours) are often necessary to ensure a competitive internship application.

Admissions

Entries appear in the following order: required test or GPA, minimum score (if required)/median score of students entering in 2015–2016.

Program	Degree	GRE-V	GRE-Q	GRE-Writing	GRE-Subject	Under-graduate GPA	Last 2 Years GPA	Psychol-ogy GPA	Master's GPA
Clinical Psychology	PhD	NA/NA	NA/NA	NA/NA	NA/NA	NA/NA	Not specified	NA/NA	Not specified
Experimental— Animal	PhD	NA/NA	NA/NA	NA/NA	Not specified	NA/NA	Not specified	NA/NA	Not specified
Experimental— Human	PhD	NA/NA	NA/NA	NA/NA	Not specified	NA/NA	Not specified	NA/NA	Not specified
Neuroscience	MA/MS	Not specified	Not specified	Not specified	Not specified	NA/NA	Not specified	NA/NA	Not specified
Experimental— Animal	MA/MS	NA/NA	NA/NA	NA/NA	Not specified	NA/NA	Not specified	NA/NA	Not specified

Admissions *(con't.)*

Program	Degree	GRE-V	GRE-Q	GRE-Writing	GRE-Subject	Under-graduate GPA	Last 2 Years GPA	Psychology GPA	Master's GPA
Neuroscience	PhD	Not specified	Not specified	Not specified	Not specified	NA/NA	Not specified	NA/NA	Not specified
Experimental—Human	MA/MS	NA/NA	NA/NA	NA/NA	Not specified	NA/NA	Not specified	NA/NA	Not specified

Admissions Requirements:

Degree	GRE	GRE-Subject	Letters of Recommendation	Research Statement	Writing Sample	CV	Interview
Master's/Specialist	Required	Recommended	2	Required	Optional	Required	None
Doctoral	Required	Recommended	3	Required	Optional	Required	None

Please note if these criteria vary for different programs: Clinically related public service is high for clinical program. GRE-Subject scores are required for Clinical and Experimental Psychology applicants who do not hold a 4-year Honours degree in Psychology and/or are international students. They are recommended for everyone else.

Admissions Criteria:

GRE scores—medium
Research experience—high
Work experience—low
Clinically related public service—high
GPA—high

Letters of recommendation—high
Interview—medium
Statement of goals and objectives—high
Undergraduate psychology preparation—medium
Willing supervisor—high

For additional information on admission requirements, visit http://www.dal.ca/faculty/science/psychology_neuroscience/programs/graduate-programs.html.

Department Demographics

	Male (PT)	Female (PT)	Total	African-American/ Black (PT)	Hispanic/ Latino (PT)	Asian/ Pacific Islander (PT)	American Indian/ Alaska Native (PT)	Caucasian/ White (PT)	Unknown	Multiethnic (PT)	ADA (PT)	Int'l (PT)
Students	24 (0)	45 (0)	0	0 (0)	0 (0)	0 (0)	0 (0)	0 (0)	69 (0)	0 (0)	0 (0)	6 (0)

Financial Information/Assistance

Tuition: For information on tuition costs, visit http://www.dal.ca/admissions/money_matters/tuition_fees_costs.html. Tuition is subject to change. Tuition costs vary by program.

Doctoral:
State residents: $10,100 per academic year.
Nonstate residents: $15,900 per academic year.

Master's:
State residents: $9,900 per academic year.
Nonstate residents: $15,700 per academic year.

Financial Assistance:

	Teaching Assistantship (% Receiving)	Teaching Assistantship Tuition Remission	Research Assistantship (% Receiving)	Research Assistantship Tuition Remission	Fellowship (% Receiving)	Fellowship Tuition Remission
First-Year Student	$2,990 (50)	NA	NA (NA)	NA	$18,000 (NA)	NA
Advanced Student	$2,990 (100)	NA	NA (NA)	NA	$18,300 (NA)	NA

For additional information on financial assistance, visit http://www.dal.ca/faculty/science/psychology_neuroscience/programs/graduate-programs/financial-information.html.

Employment of Department Graduates

Master's:
Enrolled in a psychology doctoral program: 6
Enrolled in another graduate/professional program: 1
Total: 7

Doctoral:
Enrolled in a postdoctoral residency/fellowship: 1
Employed in an academic position at a university: 2
Employed in a hospital/medical center: 2
Do not know: 2
Total: 7

Additional Information

Housing and Day Care: On-campus housing is available. See the following website for more information: http://www.dal.ca/campus_life/residence_housing/residence.html. On-campus day care facilities are available. See the following website for more information: http://ucc.dal.ca.

Information for Students With Physical Disabilities: See the following website: http://dal.ca/accessibility.

Special Facilities or Resources: The Department of Psychology is located in the Life Sciences Centre, which also contains the departments of biology, earth sciences, and oceanography. The psychology building contains very extensive laboratory areas, some with circulating sea-water aquaria, and is designed for research with a range of animal groups (humans, cats, birds, fish, invertebrates) using a range of research techniques in behavior, electrophysiology, neuroanatomy, immunocytochemistry, neurogenetics, and so forth. The department also houses an electronics and woodworking shop, an animal care facility, a surgical facility, a computer lab for word processing, communications, and access to a mainframe; specific neuroscience facilities are in close proximity to hospitals.

Application Information: Graduate Program Office, Department of Psychology and Neuroscience, Dalhousie University, Life Sciences Centre, 1355 Oxford Street, P.O. Box 15000, Halifax, Nova Scotia, Canada, B3H 4R2. *Fee:* $100. *Online application:* http://www.dal.ca/admissions/graduate/admission_process.html.

Guelph, University of
Department of Psychology
College of Social and Applied Human Sciences
4th Floor MacKinnon Extension
Guelph, ON N1G 2W1
Telephone: (519) 824-4120 ext. 53508
Chairperson: Francesco Leri

E-mail: psygsec@psy.uoguelph.ca
Web: http://www.uoguelph.ca/psychology/

Orientation, Objectives, and Emphasis of Department
The Department of Psychology offers graduate programs leading to a Master of Arts and a Doctor of Philosophy in three fields: Applied Social Psychology, Clinical Psychology: Applied Developmental Emphasis, and Industrial/Organizational Psychology. The three fields follow a scientist–practitioner model and provide training in both research and professional skills. The graduate program in Neuroscience and Applied Cognitive Science leads to MSc and PhD, as well as Collaborative MSc and PhD programs in Neuroscience or Toxicology. All fields provide a firm grounding in theory and research in relevant content areas. The PhD Clinical program is accredited by the Canadian Psychological Association.

Programs and Degrees Offered

Program	Degree	Application Deadline	Applications Received	Accepted	New Admits Enrolled (PT)	Total Enrolled (PT)	Degrees Awarded in 2014–2015	Median Years to Complete Degree	Dismissed/ Withdrew
Neuroscience and Applied Cognitive Science	PhD	January 15 (Fall)	4	4	4 (0)	16 (2)	6	4.3	0
Industrial/ Organizational Psychology	PhD	January 4 (Fall)	2	0	0 (0)	9 (0)	1	9.3	0
Applied Social Psychology	PhD	December 15 (Fall)	8	3	3 (0)	18 (1)	2	4.6	1
Clinical Psychology: Applied Developmental Emphasis	PhD	December 15 (Fall)	10	4	4 (0)	24 (9)	2		0
Neuroscience and Applied Cognitive Science	MA/MS	January 15 (Fall)	18	8	8 (0)	14 (0)	5	2.3	0
Applied Social Psychology	MA/MS	December 15 (Fall)	10	1	1 (0)	1 (0)	5	2	0
Clinical Psychology: Applied Developmental Emphasis	MA/MS	December 15 (Fall)	61	6	6 (0)	13 (0)	5	2	0
Industrial/ Organizational Psychology	MA/MS	January 4 (Fall)	21	5	4 (0)	11 (0)	5	2.3	1

CPA Accreditation
Clinical PhD (Doctor of Philosophy).

Doctoral Degree (PhD Clinical Psychology:Applied Developmental Emphasis): For those doctoral students for whom a professional internship was required in this program prior to graduation:
Total students who applied for an internship: 4
Total students who obtained an internship: 4
Total students who obtained a paid internship: 4
Total students who obtained an unpaid internship: 0
Total students who were placed in APA/CPA-accredited internships: 2
Total students placed in internships not APA/CPA-accredited, but listed with the Association of Psychology Postdoctoral and Internship Centers (APPIC): 2
Total students placed in internships conforming to guidelines of the Council of Directors of School Psychology Programs (CDSPP): 0
Total students placed in internships that were not APA/CPA-accredited, APPIC or CDSSP listed: 0

Internships/Practica
Clinical Psychology: Applied Developmental Emphasis students work 2 days per week one semester with the psychological services staff at local public school boards. During a later semester, they are placed 2 days a week for two semesters in a service facility for atypical children. In addition, they complete practica at the Department's in-house training clinic, The Centre for Psychological Services. All students who apply for internship placements typically gain an accredited internship placement of their first choice. Applied Social Psychology students select practica in settings that include community health facilities, correctional and medical treatment settings, and private consulting firms. Industrial/Organizational and Applied Cognitive Science practica take place in academic, industrial, governmental, and/or military settings.

Admissions

Entries appear in the following order: required test or GPA, minimum score (if required)/median score of students entering in 2015–2016.

Program	Degree	GRE-V	GRE-Q	GRE-Writing	GRE-Subject	Under-graduate GPA	Last 2 Years GPA	Psychol-ogy GPA	Master's GPA
Neuroscience and Applied Cognitive Science	PhD	Not specified	Not specified	Not specified	Not specified	Not specified	Not specified	NA/NA	NA/NA
Industrial/ Organizational Psychology	PhD	NA/NA	NA/NA	NA/NA	NA/NA	NA/NA	NA/NA	NA/NA	NA/NA
Applied Social Psychology	PhD	Not specified	Not specified	Not specified	Not specified	Not specified	NA/NA	NA/NA	NA/NA
Clinical Psychology: Applied Developmental Emphasis	PhD	NA/NA	NA/NA	NA/NA	NA/NA	Not specified	NA/NA	NA/NA	NA/NA
Neuroscience and Applied Cognitive Science	MA/MS	Not specified	Not specified	Not specified	Not specified	Not specified	NA/NA	NA/NA	Not specified
Applied Social Psychology	MA/MS	NA/NA	NA/NA	NA/NA	NA/NA	Not specified	NA/NA	NA/NA	Not specified
Clinical Psychology: Applied Developmental Emphasis	MA/MS	NA/NA	NA/NA	NA/NA	NA/NA	Not specified	NA/NA	NA/NA	Not specified
Industrial/ Organizational Psychology	MA/MS	NA/NA	NA/NA	NA/NA	NA/NA	NA/NA	NA/NA	NA/NA	Not specified

Admissions Requirements:

Degree	GRE	GRE-Subject	Letters of Recommendation	Research Statement	Writing Sample	CV	Interview
Master's/Specialist	Required	Required	2	Required	Optional	Required	Optional
Doctoral	Required	Required	2	Required	Optional	Required	Optional

Please note if these criteria vary for different programs: The field of Neuroscience and Applied Cognitive Science accepts applications from candidates with degrees in allied fields. GRE requirements vary depending on the field of study (AS, CP:ADE, I/O, NACS) and program (MA, MSc, PhD) to which you are applying. AS: General test is required, Subject test in Psychology is not mandatory but suggested for admission consideration to the MA program. GREs are not required for consideration to the PhD program. CP:ADE: General and Subject test in Psychology are both required for admission consideration to the MA and PhD programs. I/O: General test is required, Subject test in Psychology is not mandatory but suggested for admission consideration to the MA and PhD programs. NACS: GRES are NOT required for admission consideration to either MSc or PhD programs.

Admissions Criteria:

GRE scores—high
Research experience—high
Work experience—medium
Clinically related public service—low
GPA—high

Letters of recommendation—high
Interview—high
Statement of goals and objectives—high
Undergraduate psychology preparation—high

For additional information on admission requirements, visit https://www.uoguelph.ca/psychology/graduate/admissions.

Department Demographics

	Male (PT)	Female (PT)	Total	African-American/ Black (PT)	Hispanic/ Latino (PT)	Asian/ Pacific Islander (PT)	American Indian/ Alaska Native (PT)	Caucasian/ White (PT)	Unknown	Multiethnic (PT)	ADA (PT)	Int'l (PT)
Students	27 (1)	79 (11)	0	1 (0)	0 (0)	6 (0)	1 (0)	97 (12)	1 (0)	0 (0)	0 (0)	2 (0)

Financial Information/Assistance

Tuition: For information on tuition costs, visit https://www.uoguelph.ca/graduatestudies/future/cost. Tuition is subject to change.

Doctoral:
State residents: $9,042 per academic year.
Nonstate residents: $20,767 per academic year.

Master's:
State residents: $9,042 per academic year.
Nonstate residents: $20,767 per academic year.

Financial Assistance:

	Teaching Assistantship (% Receiving)	Teaching Assistantship Tuition Remission	Research Assistantship (% Receiving)	Research Assistantship Tuition Remission	Fellowship (% Receiving)	Fellowship Tuition Remission
First-Year Student	$11,333 (NA)	NA	$2,000 (NA)	NA	$2,500 (NA)	NA
Advanced Student	$11,333 (NA)	NA	$2,000 (NA)	NA	$5,000 (NA)	NA

For additional information on financial assistance, visit https://www.uoguelph.ca/psychology/graduate/admissions/financialassistance.

Employment of Department Graduates

Master's:
Enrolled in a psychology doctoral program: 14
Enrolled in another graduate/professional program: 1
Employed in a professional position in a school system: 1
Employed in business or industry: 2
Still seeking employment: 1
Do not know: 2
Total: 21

Doctoral:
Enrolled in a postdoctoral residency/fellowship: 4
Employed in independent practice: 2
Employed in a community mental health/counseling center: 4
Total: 10

Additional Information

Housing and Day Care: On-campus housing is available. See the following website for more information: http://housing.uoguelph.ca/. On-campus day care facilities are available. See the following website for more information: https://www.uoguelph.ca/studentaffairs/childcare/.

Information for Students With Physical Disabilities: See the following website: http://www.uoguelph.ca/csd/.

Special Facilities or Resources: Faculty offices and laboratories are located mainly in the MacKinnon Building, Blackwood Hall and Central Animal Facility. Graduate students have office space in all three settings. The department is well-supported with computer facilities. These include a microcomputer laboratory and extensive microcomputer support for research, teaching, data analysis, and word processing. Facilities for neurobiology research include fully equipped surgery rooms, behavioural testing rooms, and wet labs for molecular biology techniques. For research with human subjects, the department possesses portable video-recording equipment, observation rooms, and experimental testing rooms. All of these facilities are supplemented by excellent technical support. The Centre for Psychological Services is a nonprofit organization associated with the Department of Psychology at the University of Guelph. The Centre provides high-quality psychological services at a reasonable cost, working with families and the community. The Centre is involved in training students in Clinical Psychology: Applied Developmental Emphasis and offers workshops and presentations to professionals in the community. Consulting experience is available via coursework to Industrial/Organizational Psychology, allowing them to apply the knowledge gained in their courses.

Application Information: Fee: $110. *Online application:* http://horizon.ouac.on.ca/guelph/grad/.

Manitoba, University of
Psychology
Faculty of Arts
P514 Duff Roblin Building, 190 Dysart Road
Winnipeg, MB R3T 2N2
Telephone: (204) 474-6377
Head: Daniel S. Bailis

E-mail: Psyc_Grad_Office@umanitoba.ca
Web: http://www.umanitoba.ca/psychology

Orientation, Objectives, and Emphasis of Department
The primary purpose of our program is to provide training in several specialized areas of psychology for individuals desiring to advance their level of knowledge, their research skills, and their applied capabilities. The MA program is designed to provide a broad foundation, as well as specialized skills, in the scientific approach to psychology. The PhD program provides a higher degree of specialization coupled with more intensive training in research and application. Specialized areas of training within the department include applied behavioral analysis, brain and cognitive sciences, clinical, developmental, quantitative, school, and social/personality.

Programs and Degrees Offered

Program	Degree	Application Deadline	Applica-tions Received	Accepted	New Admits Enrolled (PT)	Total Enrolled (PT)	Degrees Awarded in 2014–2015	Median Years to Complete Degree	Dismissed/ Withdrew
Applied Behaviour Analysis	PhD	December 15 (Fall)	9	5	4 (0)	17 (0)	1	7	0
Brain and Cognitive Sciences	PhD	December 15 (Fall)	12	7	4 (0)	12 (0)	3	9	0
Clinical Psychology	PhD	December 15 (Fall)	39	5	3 (0)	41 (0)	7	9	1
Developmental Psychology	PhD	December 15 (Fall)	2	0	0 (0)	2 (0)	1	8.5	0
Quantitative	PhD	December 15 (Fall)	4	1	0 (0)	0 (0)	0		0
Social/ Personality Psychology	PhD	December 15 (Fall)	9	3	0 (0)	7 (0)	1	8	0
School Psychology	MA/MS	December 15 (Fall)	24	11	8 (0)	20 (0)	7	2	0

CPA Accreditation
Clinical PhD (Doctor of Philosophy).

Doctoral Degree (PhD Clinical Psychology): For those doctoral students for whom a professional internship was required in this program prior to graduation:
Total students who applied for an internship: 4
Total students who obtained an internship: 4
Total students who obtained a paid internship: 4
Total students who obtained an unpaid internship: 0
Total students who were placed in APA/CPA-accredited internships: 4
Total students placed in internships not APA/CPA-accredited, but listed with the Association of Psychology Postdoctoral and Internship Centers (APPIC): 0
Total students placed in internships conforming to guidelines of the Council of Directors of School Psychology Programs (CDSPP): 0
Total students placed in internships that were not APA/CPA-accredited, APPIC or CDSSP listed: 0

Master's Degree (MA/MS School Psychology): An internship experience, such as a final research project or "capstone" experience is required of graduates.

Internships/Practica

Clinical students have access to practica at our Psychological Service Center. Practica within the community are available for senior graduate students. ABA students have access to practica with a range of clients in a variety of settings. School Psychology students complete 9 credit hours of in-school practica arranged by the Program in partnership with cooperating School Divisions.

Admissions

Entries appear in the following order: required test or GPA, minimum score (if required)/median score of students entering in 2015–2016.

Program	Degree	GRE-V	GRE-Q	GRE-Writing	GRE-Subject	Under-graduate GPA	Last 2 Years GPA	Psychol-ogy GPA	Master's GPA
Applied Behaviour Analysis	PhD	151/154	144/150	4/4	Not specified	Not specified	3.5/3.6	Not specified	Not specified
Brain and Cognitive Sciences	PhD	155/156	150/154	3.5/4	Not specified	Not specified	3.8/3.95	Not specified	Not specified
Clinical Psychology	PhD	157/159	149/150	5/5.5	Not specified	Not specified	NA/NA	Not specified	Not specified
Developmental Psychology	PhD	NA/NA	NA/NA	NA/NA	Not specified	Not specified	NA/NA	Not specified	Not specified
Quantitative	PhD	NA/NA	NA/NA	NA/NA	Not specified	Not specified	NA/NA	Not specified	Not specified
Social/Personality Psychology	PhD	156/158	156/157	4.5/4.5	Not specified	Not specified	NA/NA	Not specified	Not specified
School Psychology	MA/MS	150/157	145/156	4.5/4.5	Not specified	Not specified	3.8/4	Not specified	Not specified

Admissions Requirements:

Degree	GRE	GRE-Subject	Letters of Recom-mendation	Research Statement	Writing Sample	CV	Interview
Master's/Specialist	Required	Optional	2	Required	Optional	Required	None
Doctoral	Required	Optional	2	Required	Optional	Required	None

Admissions Criteria:

GRE scores—high
Research experience—high
Work experience—medium
Clinically related public service—medium
GPA—high

Letters of recommendation—medium
Interview—low
Statement of goals and objectives—low
Undergraduate psychology preparation—high

For additional information on admission requirements, visit http://www.umanitoba.ca/faculties/arts/departments/psychology/graduate/admissions.php.

Department Demographics

	Male (PT)	Female (PT)	Total	African-American/ Black (PT)	Hispanic/ Latino (PT)	Asian/ Pacific Islander (PT)	American Indian/ Alaska Native (PT)	Caucasian/ White (PT)	Unknown	Multiethnic (PT)	ADA (PT)	Int'l (PT)
Students	20 (0)	79 (0)	0	0 (0)	0 (0)	0 (0)	0 (0)	0 (0)	0 (0)	0 (0)	0 (0)	0 (0)

Financial Information/Assistance

Tuition: For information on tuition costs, visit http://umanitoba.ca/student/records/fees/988.html. Tuition is subject to change. Additional fees are assessed to students beyond the costs of tuition for the following: endowment, student organization, technology services, student services, health insurance.

Doctoral:
State residents: $4,540 per academic year.
Nonstate residents: $9,989 per academic year.

Master's:
State residents: $4,540 per academic year.
Nonstate residents: $9,989 per academic year.

Financial Assistance:

	Teaching Assistantship (% Receiving)	Teaching Assistantship Tuition Remission	Research Assistantship (% Receiving)	Research Assistantship Tuition Remission	Fellowship (% Receiving)	Fellowship Tuition Remission
First-Year Student	NA (NA)	NA	NA (NA)	NA	NA (NA)	NA
Advanced Student	NA (NA)	NA	NA (NA)	NA	NA (NA)	NA

For additional information on financial assistance, visit http://www.umanitoba.ca/faculties/arts/departments/psychology/graduate/financial.html.

Employment of Department Graduates

Master's:
Enrolled in a psychology doctoral program: 7
Employed in a professional position in a school system: 7
Do not know: 1
Total: 15

Doctoral:
Employed in independent practice: 6
Employed in an academic position at a university: 3
Employed in other positions at a higher education institution: 3
Employed in business or industry: 1
Employed in a hospital/medical center: 1
Do not know: 1
Total: 15

Additional Information

Housing and Day Care: On-campus housing is available. See the following website for more information: http://umanitoba.ca/student/housing/. On-campus day care facilities are available. See the following website for more information: http://umanitoba.ca/student/resource/playcare/.

Information for Students With Physical Disabilities: See the following website: http://umanitoba.ca/student/saa/accessibility/.

Special Facilities or Resources: Basic research facilities are housed in over 100 dedicated research rooms. We host a large computer lab maintained by a crew of three excellent computer technicians, integrated animal care facilities under the supervision of three dedicated animal care technicians, and a field station at which avian behavior may be studied. These resources are augmented by collaborative relationships we have with other university departments, local hospitals, St. Amant Centre, and the National Research Council: Institute for Biodiagnostics.

Application Information: Faculty of Graduate Studies, 500 University Centre, University of Manitoba, Winnipeg, MB R3T 2N2. *Fee:* $100. *Online application:* http://umanitoba.ca/faculties/graduate_studies/admissions/index.html.

McGill University (2015 data)
Department of Educational and Counselling Psychology
Faculty of Education, Room 614
3700 McTavish Street
Montreal, QC H3A 1Y2
Telephone: (514) 398-4242
Chairperson: Jeffrey L. Derevensky

E-mail: samantha.ryan@mcgill.ca
Web: http://www.mcgill.ca/edu-ecp

Orientation, Objectives, and Emphasis of Department

There are five broad areas of major graduate-level specialization: Counseling Psychology, Human Development, Learning Sciences, Health Professions Education and School/Applied Child Psychology. A substantial base in research methods and statistics is provided and adjusted to students' entering competence. Graduate students in professional school psychology normally enter the Master's and are considered for transfer to the PhD (if that is their goal) after 2 years for an additional 4 to 5 years of training. Graduate studies directed toward research, academic, and leadership careers follow a similar enrollment pattern except that the program normally requires one year less at the doctoral level. Students are welcome to take selected courses in other departments and at other Quebec universities.

Programs and Degrees Offered

Program	Degree	Application Deadline	Applica-tions Received	Accepted	New Admits Enrolled (PT)	Total Enrolled (PT)	Degrees Awarded in 2014–2015	Median Years to Complete Degree	Dismissed/ Withdrew
Counselling Psychology	PhD	December 15 (Fall)	20	6	3 (0)	41 (0)	5	6.33	0
Educational Psychology	PhD	January 15 (Fall)	21	12	11	45	7	5.3	0
School/Applied Child Psychology	PhD	January 15 (Fall)	23	15	12 (0)	54 (0)	6	5.33	0

CPA Accreditation

Counseling PhD (Doctor of Philosophy).

Doctoral Degree (PhD Counselling Psychology): For those doctoral students for whom a professional internship was required in this program prior to graduation:

Total students who applied for an internship: 4

Total students who obtained an internship: 4

Total students who obtained a paid internship: 3

Total students who obtained an unpaid internship: 1

Total students who were placed in APA/CPA-accredited internships: 1

Total students placed in internships not APA/CPA-accredited, but listed with the Association of Psychology Postdoctoral and Internship Centers (APPIC): 1

Total students placed in internships conforming to guidelines of the Council of Directors of School Psychology Programs (CDSPP): 0

Total students placed in internships that were not APA/CPA-accredited, APPIC or CDSSP listed: 2

Doctoral Degree (PhD School/Applied Child Psychology): For those doctoral students for whom a professional internship was required in this program prior to graduation:

Total students who applied for an internship: 3

Total students who obtained an internship: 3

Total students who obtained a paid internship: 3

Total students who obtained an unpaid internship: 0

Total students who were placed in APA/CPA-accredited internships: 2

Total students placed in internships not APA/CPA-accredited, but listed with the Association of Psychology Postdoctoral and Internship Centers (APPIC): 0

Total students placed in internships conforming to guidelines of the Council of Directors of School Psychology Programs (CDSPP): 1

Total students placed in internships that were not APA/CPA-accredited, APPIC or CDSSP listed: 0

Internships/Practica

All students in the professional psychology programs are required to complete internships. According to the program option these may be in mental health facilities, community social service agencies, schools, psychoeducational clinics, and so forth. In some internships, more than one setting is advised or required. New internship opportunities are regularly added, and students are welcome to seek out those which may especially suit their needs, subject to program approval.

Admissions

Entries appear in the following order: required test or GPA, minimum score (if required)/median score of students entering in 2015–2016.

Program	Degree	GRE-V	GRE-Q	GRE-Writing	GRE-Subject	Under-graduate GPA	Last 2 Years GPA	Psychol-ogy GPA	Master's GPA
Counselling Psychology	PhD	Not specified	Not specified	Not specified	Not specified	Not specified	3.2/NA	Not specified	Not specified
Educational Psychology	PhD	Not specified	Not specified	Not specified	Not specified	3/NA	Not specified	Not specified	Not specified
School/Applied Child Psychology	PhD	NA/NA	NA/NA	NA/NA	NA/NA	3/NA	Not specified	Not specified	Not specified

Admissions Requirements:

Degree	GRE	GRE-Subject	Letters of Recom-mendation	Research Statement	Writing Sample	CV	Interview
Doctoral	Required	Required	3	Required	Required	Required	Required

Please note if these criteria vary for different programs: Relative weight of these criteria varies across program areas. Only the School/Applied Child Psychology program requires the GRE. Educational Psychology PhD does not require a writing sample; the other programs do.

Admissions Criteria:

GRE scores—medium
Research experience—high
Work experience—high
Clinically related public service—medium

GPA—high
Letters of recommendation—high
Interview—medium
Statement of goals and objectives—high

For additional information on admission requirements, visit http://www.mcgill.ca/edu-ecp/prospective.

Department Demographics

	Male (PT)	Female (PT)	Total	African-American/ Black (PT)	Hispanic/ Latino (PT)	Asian/ Pacific Islander (PT)	American Indian/ Alaska Native (PT)	Caucasian/ White (PT)	Unknown	Multiethnic (PT)	ADA (PT)	Int'l (PT)
Students	34 (7)	239 (72)	0	0 (0)	0 (0)	0 (0)	0 (0)	0 (0)	0 (0)	0 (0)	0 (0)	0 (0)

Financial Information/Assistance

Tuition: For information on tuition costs, visit http://www.mcgill.ca/student-accounts/tuition-fees/tuition-and-fees. Tuition is subject to change. Tuition costs vary by program.

Doctoral:
State residents: $3,927 per academic year.
Nonstate residents: $16,041 per academic year.

Financial Assistance:

	Teaching Assistantship (% Receiving)	Teaching Assistantship Tuition Remission	Research Assistantship (% Receiving)	Research Assistantship Tuition Remission	Fellowship (% Receiving)	Fellowship Tuition Remission
First-Year Student	NA (NA)	NA	$3,700 (NA)	NA	$10,800 (NA)	NA
Advanced Student	$2,800 (NA)	NA	$8,200 (NA)	NA	$13,800 (NA)	NA

For additional information on financial assistance, visit http://www.mcgill.ca/edu-ecp/students/finances.

Employment of Department Graduates

No information provided.

Additional Information

Housing and Day Care: On-campus housing is available. See the following website for more information: http://www.mcgill.ca/students/housing/. On-campus day care facilities are available. See the following website for more information: http://www.mcgill.ca/daycare/.

Information for Students With Physical Disabilities: See the following website: http://www.mcgill.ca/osd/.

Special Facilities or Resources: The Department has the following facilities/laboratories: CORE (Coping and Resilience) Research Team; Doc Work; Health Psychology Research Group; Heath Research Team; High Ability and Inquiry Research Group (HAIR); Higher Education Research Group; International Centre for Youth Gambling; Laboratory for the Study of Metacognition and Advanced Learning Technologies (SMART Lab); McGill Psychotherapy Process Research Group (MPPRG); McGill Youth Study Team (MYST); Perceptual Neuroscience Laboratory for Autism & Development (PN Lab); Resilience, Pediatric Psychology, & Neurogenetic Connections Lab (The Connections Lab); Self-Injury Outreach & Support; SPARC (Social Policy, Advocacy, Research, Community); Supporting Active Learning and Technological Innovation in Science Education (SALTISE); Talwar Child Development Research Lab; The Online Learning Research Team; Research Laboratory on Social Behavior.

Application Information: Fee: $102. Online application: http://www.mcgill.ca/gradapplicants/apply.

McGill University
Department of Psychology
1205 Avenue Docteur Penfield
Montreal, QC H3A 1B1
Telephone: (514) 398-6124
Chairperson: John Lydon

E-mail: giovanna.locascio@mcgill.ca
Web: http://www.psych.mcgill.ca

Orientation, Objectives, and Emphasis of Department
McGill University's Department of Psychology offers graduate work leading to the PhD degree. The program in experimental psychology includes the areas of cognitive science (perception, learning, and language), developmental, social, personality, quantitative, and behavioral neuroscience. A program in clinical psychology is also offered. The basic purpose of the graduate program is to provide the student with an environment in which he or she is free to develop skills and expertise that will serve during a professional career in teaching, research, or clinical service as a psychologist. Individually conceived and conducted research in the student's area of interest is the single most important activity of all graduate students in the department.

Programs and Degrees Offered

Program	Degree	Application Deadline	Applications Received	Accepted	New Admits Enrolled (PT)	Total Enrolled (PT)	Degrees Awarded in 2014–2015	Median Years to Complete Degree	Dismissed/ Withdrew
Clinical Psychology	PhD	December 1 (Fall)	142	9	8 (0)	40 (0)	6	6	0
Experimental Psychology	PhD	December 1 (Fall)	82	8	7 (0)	38 (0)	10	5	0

CPA Accreditation
Clinical PhD (Doctor of Philosophy).

Doctoral Degree (PhD Clinical Psychology): For those doctoral students for whom a professional internship was required in this program prior to graduation:
Total students who applied for an internship: 5
Total students who obtained an internship: 5
Total students who obtained a paid internship: 5
Total students who obtained an unpaid internship: 0
Total students who were placed in APA/CPA-accredited internships: 5
Total students placed in internships not APA/CPA-accredited, but listed with the Association of Psychology Postdoctoral and Internship Centers (APPIC): 0
Total students placed in internships conforming to guidelines of the Council of Directors of School Psychology Programs (CDSPP): 0
Total students placed in internships that were not APA/CPA-accredited, APPIC or CDSSP listed: 0

Internships/Practica
The majority of students in our clinical program complete their internships within Montreal, especially at McGill-affiliated hospitals. These include three large and two small general hospitals, a large psychiatric hospital, and a large children's hospital, where a wide range of assessment and treatment skills can be acquired. Specialized, advanced training is provided at other institutions in the areas of neuropsychology, hearing impairments, orthopedic disabilities, and rehabilitation. One advantage of having a local internship is that it facilitates the integration of the student's clinical and research activities. In addition, the department is able to monitor the quality of the training at the placements. All placements have active, ongoing commitments to research. Students have also completed internships at a wide variety of settings in other parts of Canada, the United States, and Europe. Settings outside Montreal must meet with staff approval.

Admissions
Entries appear in the following order: required test or GPA, minimum score (if required)/median score of students entering in 2015–2016.

Program	Degree	GRE-V	GRE-Q	GRE-Writing	GRE-Subject	Undergraduate GPA	Last 2 Years GPA	Psychology GPA	Master's GPA
Clinical Psychology	PhD	NA/NA	NA/NA	NA/NA	NA/NA	NA/NA	NA/NA	NA/NA	NA/NA
Experimental Psychology	PhD	NA/NA	NA/NA	NA/NA	NA/NA	NA/NA	NA/NA	NA/NA	NA/NA

Admissions Requirements:

Degree	GRE	GRE-Subject	Letters of Recommendation	Research Statement	Writing Sample	CV	Interview
Doctoral	Required	Recommended	3	Required	None	Required	Required

Admissions Criteria:
GRE scores—high
Research experience—high
Work experience—high
Clinically related public service—medium
GPA—high

Letters of recommendation—high
Interview—high
Statement of goals and objectives—high
Undergraduate psychology preparation—high

For additional information on admission requirements, visit http://www.mcgill.ca/psychology/graduate/prospective-students/admission-requirements-procedures.

Department Demographics

	Male (PT)	Female (PT)	Total	African-American/ Black (PT)	Hispanic/ Latino (PT)	Asian/ Pacific Islander (PT)	American Indian/ Alaska Native (PT)	Caucasian/ White (PT)	Unknown	Multiethnic (PT)	ADA (PT)	Int'l (PT)
Students	19 (0)	59 (0)	0	(0)	0 (0)	0 (0)	0 (0)	0 (0)	0 (0)	0 (0)	0 (0)	0 (0)

Financial Information/Assistance

Tuition: For information on tuition costs, visit http://www.mcgill.ca/student-accounts/tuition-fees/tuition-and-fees. Tuition is subject to change.

Doctoral:
State residents: $4,100 per academic year.
Nonstate residents: $4,100 per academic year.

Master's:
State residents: $4,100 per academic year.
Nonstate residents: $8,800 per academic year.

Financial Assistance:

	Teaching Assistantship (% Receiving)	Teaching Assistantship Tuition Remission	Research Assistantship (% Receiving)	Research Assistantship Tuition Remission	Fellowship (% Receiving)	Fellowship Tuition Remission
First-Year Student	NA (NA)	NA	NA (NA)	NA	NA (NA)	NA
Advanced Student	NA (NA)	NA	NA (NA)	NA	NA (NA)	NA

For additional information on financial assistance, visit http://www.mcgill.ca/psychology/graduate/prospective-students/financial-support.

Employment of Department Graduates

Doctoral:
Enrolled in a postdoctoral residency/fellowship: 6
Employed in government agency: 1
Other employment position: 5
Do not know: 3
Total: 15

Additional Information

Housing and Day Care: On-campus housing is available. See the following website for more information: http://www.mcgill.ca/students/housing/. On-campus day care facilities are available. See the following website for more information: http://www.mcgill.ca/daycare/.

Information for Students With Physical Disabilities: See the following website: http://www.mcgill.ca/osd/.

Application Information: Fee: $104. *Online application:* http://www.mcgill.ca/gradapplicants/apply.

New Brunswick, University of
Department of Psychology
P.O. Box 4400
Fredericton, NB E3B 5A3
Telephone: (506) 453-4707
Chairperson: E. Sandra Byers

E-mail: sronis@unb.ca
Web: http://www.unb.ca/fredericton/arts/departments/psychology/

Orientation, Objectives, and Emphasis of Department

The Department of Psychology offers an integrated MA/PhD degree designed to provide extensive specialized study in either Clinical or Experimental Psychology. The Clinical Program provides graduates with both sufficient skills in assessment and intervention to initiate careers in service settings under appropriate supervision, and with the knowledge and training needed for an academic career. The Experimental Program emphasizes individual training and the development of skills to prepare graduates for a research-oriented career in an academic or applied setting.

Programs and Degrees Offered

Program	Degree	Application Deadline	Applications Received	Accepted	New Admits Enrolled (PT)	Total Enrolled (PT)	Degrees Awarded in 2014–2015	Median Years to Complete Degree	Dismissed/ Withdrew
Clinical Psychology	PhD	January 15 (Fall)	61	7	5 (0)	30 (2)	9	7	1
Experimental Psychology	PhD	January 15 (Fall)	9	1	1 (0)	14 (1)	1	6	0

CPA Accreditation

Clinical PhD (Doctor of Philosophy).

Doctoral Degree (PhD Clinical Psychology): For those doctoral students for whom a professional internship was required in this program prior to graduation:

Total students who applied for an internship: 2
Total students who obtained an internship: 2
Total students who obtained a paid internship: 2
Total students who obtained an unpaid internship: 0
Total students who were placed in APA/CPA-accredited internships: 1
Total students placed in internships not APA/CPA-accredited, but listed with the Association of Psychology Postdoctoral and Internship Centers (APPIC): 1
Total students placed in internships conforming to guidelines of the Council of Directors of School Psychology Programs (CDSPP): 0
Total students placed in internships that were not APA/CPA-accredited, APPIC or CDSSP listed: 0

Internships/Practica

Students in the Clinical program have completed practica in the following types of agencies: mental health clinic, general hospital, university counselling services, psychiatric hospital, or school system.

Admissions

Entries appear in the following order: required test or GPA, minimum score (if required)/median score of students entering in 2015–2016.

Program	Degree	GRE-V	GRE-Q	GRE-Writing	GRE-Subject	Undergraduate GPA	Last 2 Years GPA	Psychology GPA	Master's GPA
Clinical Psychology	PhD	NA/NA	NA/NA	NA/NA	Not specified	NA/NA	Not specified	Not specified	Not specified
Experimental Psychology	PhD	NA/NA	NA/NA	NA/NA	Not specified	NA/NA	Not specified	Not specified	Not specified

Admissions Requirements:

Degree	GRE	GRE-Subject	Letters of Recommendation	Research Statement	Writing Sample	CV	Interview
Doctoral	Required	Optional	3	Required	None	Required	Required

Admissions Criteria:

GRE scores—medium
Research experience—high
Work experience—medium
Clinically related public service—low
GPA—high

Letters of recommendation—high
Interview—high
Statement of goals and objectives—medium
Undergraduate psychology preparation—medium

For additional information on admission requirements, visit http://www.unb.ca/fredericton/arts/graduate/psychology/admissions.html.

Department Demographics

	Male (PT)	Female (PT)	Total	African-American/ Black (PT)	Hispanic/ Latino (PT)	Asian/ Pacific Islander (PT)	American Indian/ Alaska Native (PT)	Caucasian/ White (PT)	Unknown (PT)	Multiethnic (PT)	ADA (PT)	Int'l (PT)
Students	9 (0)	35 (3)	0	0 (0)	0 (0)	3 (0)	0 (0)	41 (3)	0 (0)	0 (0)	1 (0)	5 (0)

Financial Information/Assistance

Tuition: For information on tuition costs, visit http://www.unb.ca/financialservices/students/Masters_and_PhD_Tuition_and_Fees/index.html. Tuition is subject to change.

Doctoral:
State residents: $7,468 per academic year.
Nonstate residents: $12,901 per academic year.

Financial Assistance:

	Teaching Assistantship (% Receiving)	Teaching Assistantship Tuition Remission	Research Assistantship (% Receiving)	Research Assistantship Tuition Remission	Fellowship (% Receiving)	Fellowship Tuition Remission
First-Year Student	$4,719 (100)	NA	NA (NA)	NA	$10,500 (100)	NA
Advanced Student	$4,927 (68)	NA	NA (NA)	NA	$14,000 (68)	NA

For additional information on financial assistance, visit http://www.unb.ca/gradstudies/aid/index.html.

Employment of Department Graduates

Doctoral:
Enrolled in a postdoctoral residency/fellowship: 1
Employed in independent practice: 1
Employed in government agency: 1
Employed in a hospital/medical center: 4
Do not know: 3
Total: 10

Additional Information

Housing and Day Care: On-campus housing is available. See the following website for more information: http://www.unb.ca/fredericton/residence/. On-campus day care facilities are available. See the following website for more information: http://www2.unb.ca/chdc/.

Information for Students With Physical Disabilities: See the following website: http://www.unb.ca/aboutunb/accessibility/.

Special Facilities or Resources: The department occupies Keirstead Hall, which is well supplied with research equipment. The facilities include laboratories for research in human learning, cognition, perception, development, physiology and neuropsychology; a direct line to the computer center; space for research and teaching in clinical, community, behavior therapy, biofeedback, and other areas of applied or clinical psychology. On campus, there also is a wellness (community) clinic and a counselling (students) centre, whose respective directors and some staff are Licensed Psychologists, and where students can complete supervised practica.

Application Information: Fee: $50. Online application: http://www.unb.ca/gradstudies/admissions/index.html.

Ottawa, University of
School of Psychology
Faculty of Social Sciences
Vanier Hall, 136 Jean-Jacques Lussier
Ottawa, ON K1N 6N5
Telephone: (613) 562-5800 X4197
Director and Associate Dean (Acting): Tim Aubry

E-mail: mcote@uottawa.ca
Web: http://socialsciences.uottawa.ca/psy/

Orientation, Objectives, and Emphasis of Department
The objective of the program in Experimental Psychology is to train researchers in one or more of the following areas: neuroimaging; psychopharmacology; psychoneuroendocrinology; psychophysiology; human and animal cognition; perception; learning; language; sleep and dreams; social, cognitive, and emotional development; personality; intergroup relations; motivation; and the social psychology of health, sports, and work. The objective of the Clinical Psychology program is to provide doctoral training in the area of clinical psychology and prepare students to work with adults, children, and youth. Professional training includes cognitive-behavioral, experiential, interpersonal, and community consultation approaches. Thesis supervisors within the clinical program have special expertise in areas such as mental health problems across the lifespan, anxiety, depression, assessment, psychotherapy, couple therapy, family psychology, community psychology, health psychology, human sexuality, cross-cultural psychology, and program evaluation. Clinical students may also elect to choose a thesis supervisor from the Experimental Psychology program or adjunct professors/clinical professors who are members of the Faculty of Graduate and Postdoctoral Studies.

Programs and Degrees Offered

Program	Degree	Application Deadline	Applications Received	Accepted	New Admits Enrolled (PT)	Total Enrolled (PT)	Degrees Awarded in 2014–2015	Median Years to Complete Degree	Dismissed/ Withdrew
Clinical Psychology	PhD	December 15 (Fall)	200	20	15 (0)	91 (8)	16	6.9	0
Experimental Psychology	PhD	December 15 (Fall)	51	20	14 (0)	89 (7)	6	6.3	2

CPA Accreditation
Clinical PhD (Doctor of Philosophy).

Doctoral Degree (PhD Clinical Psychology): For those doctoral students for whom a professional internship was required in this program prior to graduation:
Total students who applied for an internship: 16
Total students who obtained an internship: 16
Total students who obtained a paid internship: 16
Total students who obtained an unpaid internship: 0
Total students who were placed in APA/CPA-accredited internships: 14
Total students placed in internships not APA/CPA-accredited, but listed with the Association of Psychology Postdoctoral and Internship Centers (APPIC): 0
Total students placed in internships conforming to guidelines of the Council of Directors of School Psychology Programs (CDSPP): 0
Total students placed in internships that were not APA/CPA-accredited, APPIC or CDSSP listed: 2

Internships/Practica
Internships, required of all clinical program students, mainly take place in accredited external settings in Canada and the USA as well as in local, approved training units. There is one internal training unit: the Centre for Psychological Services and Research, which offers practicum training as well as an accredited internship. There are twenty-two external units providing practicum training: Brockville General Hospital, Canadian Forces Health Services, Center for Interpersonal Relationships, Center for the Treatment of Sexual Abuse and Childhood Trauma, Children's Hospital of Eastern Ontario, Conseil des écoles catholiques de langue française, Elizabeth Bruyere Hospital, Emerging Minds, Montfort Hospital, Ottawa-Carleton Detention Centre, Ottawa-Carleton District School Board, Ottawa Institute for Cognitive Behavior Therapy, Ottawa Mindfulness Clinic, Royal Ottawa Health Care Group ' Brockville, Royal Ottawa Health Care Group - Ottawa, Santé Familiale de Clarence-Rockland, St Vincent's Hospital, The Children's Aid Society of Ottawa-Carleton, The Ottawa Hospital, The Rehabilitation Centre, Ottawa Children's Treatment Center, and Western Quebec School Board.

Admissions

Entries appear in the following order: required test or GPA, minimum score (if required)/median score of students entering in 2015–2016.

Program	Degree	GRE-V	GRE-Q	GRE-Writing	GRE-Subject	Under-graduate GPA	Last 2 Years GPA	Psychol-ogy GPA	Master's GPA
Clinical Psychology	PhD	Not specified	Not specified	Not specified	Not specified	Not specified	NA/NA	Not specified	Not specified
Experimental Psychology	PhD	Not specified	Not specified	Not specified	Not specified	Not specified	NA/NA	Not specified	Not specified

Admissions Requirements:

Degree	GRE	GRE-Subject	Letters of Recom-mendation	Research Statement	Writing Sample	CV	Interview
Doctoral	None	None	2	Required	None	Required	None

Admissions Criteria:

Research experience—high
Work experience—low
Clinically related public service—medium
GPA—high

Letters of recommendation—high
Statement of goals and objectives—high
Undergraduate thesis—high

For additional information on admission requirements, visit http://socialsciences.uottawa.ca/psychology/programs/clinical-psychology/admission-procedure.

Department Demographics

	Male (PT)	Female (PT)	Total	African-American/ Black (PT)	Hispanic/ Latino (PT)	Asian/ Pacific Islander (PT)	American Indian/ Alaska Native (PT)	Caucasian/ White (PT)	Unknown (PT)	Multiethnic (PT)	ADA (PT)	Int'l (PT)
Students	35 (1)	145 (14)	0	4 (0)	3 (0)	20 (0)	1 (0)	149 (15)	2 (0)	1 (0)	0 (0)	3 (0)

Financial Information/Assistance

Tuition: For information on tuition costs, visit http://www.registrar.uottawa.ca/Default.aspx?tabid=4168. Tuition is subject to change. Additional fees are assessed to students beyond the costs of tuition for the following: Incidental fees, UPass, Dental and Medication Insurance Plan.

Doctoral:
State residents: $7,074 per academic year.
Nonstate residents: $16,334 per academic year.

Financial Assistance:

	Teaching Assistantship (% Receiving)	Teaching Assistantship Tuition Remission	Research Assistantship (% Receiving)	Research Assistantship Tuition Remission	Fellowship (% Receiving)	Fellowship Tuition Remission
First-Year Student	$10,904 (NA)	NA	$10,904 (NA)	NA	$7,500 (NA)	NA
Advanced Student	$10,904 (NA)	NA	$10,904 (NA)	NA	$9,000 (NA)	NA

For additional information on financial assistance, visit http://www.uottawa.ca/graduate-studies/students/awards.

Employment of Department Graduates

Doctoral:
Enrolled in a postdoctoral residency/fellowship: 5
Employed in independent practice: 2
Employed in a professional position in a school system: 2
Employed in a community mental health/counseling center: 7
Employed in a hospital/medical center: 3
Still seeking employment: 1
Other employment position: 1
Do not know: 1
Total: 22

Additional Information

Housing and Day Care: On-campus housing is available. See the following website for more information: http://www.uottawa.ca/housing/. On-campus day care facilities are available. See the following website for more information: http://gbccc.weebly.com/.

Information for Students With Physical Disabilities: See the following website: http://sass.uottawa.ca/en/access.

Special Facilities or Resources: The School of Psychology clinical training unit, the Centre for Psychological Services and Research, offers assessment and treatment for adults, youth, families and couples. The Centre for Research on Educational and Community Services provides program evaluation and consultation services to local social services agencies.

Application Information: Faculty of Social Sciences, 120 University, Social Sciences Hall, Room 3021, Ottawa, ON, K1N 6N5, Canada. *Fee:* $100. *Online application:* http://www.uottawa.ca/graduate-studies/future-students/apply.

Queen's University
Department of Psychology
Humphrey Hall, 62 Arch Street
Kingston, ON K7L 3N6
Telephone: (613) 533-2872
Chairperson: Dr. Wendy Craig

E-mail: psychead@queensu.ca
Web: http://www.queensu.ca/psychology/

Orientation, Objectives, and Emphasis of Department
All programs stress empirical research. The Brain, Behavior, and Cognitive Science program, the Developmental program, and the Social-Personality program emphasize research skills and scholarship, preparing students for either academic positions or for research positions in government, industry, and the like. The Clinical program is based on a scientist–practitioner model of training that emphasizes the integration of research and clinical skills in the understanding, assessment, treatment, and prevention of psychological problems.

Programs and Degrees Offered

Program	Degree	Application Deadline	Applica-tions Received	Accepted	New Admits Enrolled (PT)	Total Enrolled (PT)	Degrees Awarded in 2014–2015	Median Years to Complete Degree	Dismissed/ Withdrew
Brain, Behavior, and Cognitive Science	PhD	December 1 (Fall)	4	0	0 (0)	8 (0)	2	6.5	0
Clinical Psychology	PhD	December 1 (Fall)	21	1	1 (0)	36 (0)	4	6.5	1
Social-Personality Psychology	PhD	December 1 (Fall)	5	2	2 (0)	10 (0)	5	5.4	1
Developmental Psychology	PhD	December 1 (Fall)	2	0	0 (0)	10 (0)	1	8	1

Programs and Degrees Offered *(con't.)*

Program	Degree	Application Deadline	Applications Received	Accepted	New Admits Enrolled (PT)	Total Enrolled (PT)	Degrees Awarded in 2014–2015	Median Years to Complete Degree	Dismissed/Withdrew
Brain, Behavior, and Cognitive Science	MA/MS	December 1 (Fall)	18	5	5 (0)	10 (0)	3	2	0
Clinical Psychology	MA/MS	December 1 (Fall)	105	8	8 (0)	16 (0)	5	2	0
Developmental Psychology	MA/MS	December 1 (Fall)	9	0	0 (0)	2 (0)	2	2	0
Social-Personality Psychology	MA/MS	December 1 (Fall)	8	1	1 (0)	5 (0)	2	2	0

CPA Accreditation

Clinical PhD (Doctor of Philosophy).

Doctoral Degree (PhD Clinical Psychology): For those doctoral students for whom a professional internship was required in this program prior to graduation:
Total students who applied for an internship: 3
Total students who obtained an internship: 3
Total students who obtained a paid internship: 3
Total students who obtained an unpaid internship: 0
Total students who were placed in APA/CPA-accredited internships: 3
Total students placed in internships not APA/CPA-accredited, but listed with the Association of Psychology Postdoctoral and Internship Centers (APPIC): 0
Total students placed in internships conforming to guidelines of the Council of Directors of School Psychology Programs (CDSPP): 0
Total students placed in internships that were not APA/CPA-accredited, APPIC or CDSSP listed: 0

Internships/Practica

Clinical program students must complete a predoctoral internship in an approved setting under the primary supervision of a registered Psychologist. Students are expected to seek placement in a CPA/APA-approved site.

Admissions

Entries appear in the following order: required test or GPA, minimum score (if required)/median score of students entering in 2015–2016.

Program	Degree	GRE-V	GRE-Q	GRE-Writing	GRE-Subject	Undergraduate GPA	Last 2 Years GPA	Psychology GPA	Master's GPA
Brain, Behavior, and Cognitive Science	PhD	NA/NA	NA/NA	NA/NA	NA/NA	Not specified	NA/NA	NA/NA	NA/NA
Clinical Psychology	PhD	NA/NA	NA/NA	NA/NA	NA/NA	Not specified	NA/NA	NA/NA	NA/NA
Social-Personality Psychology	PhD	NA/NA	NA/NA	NA/NA	NA/NA	NA/NA	NA/NA	NA/NA	NA/NA
Developmental Psychology	PhD	NA/NA	NA/NA	NA/NA	NA/NA	NA/NA	NA/NA	NA/NA	NA/NA
Brain, Behavior, and Cognitive Science	MA/MS	NA/NA	NA/NA	NA/NA	NA/NA	NA/NA	NA/NA	Not specified	Not specified

Admissions *(con't.)*

Program	Degree	GRE-V	GRE-Q	GRE-Writing	GRE-Subject	Under-graduate GPA	Last 2 Years GPA	Psychology GPA	Master's GPA
Clinical Psychology	MA/MS	NA/NA	NA/NA	NA/NA	NA/NA	NA/NA	NA/NA	NA/NA	Not specified
Developmental Psychology	MA/MS	NA/NA	NA/NA	NA/NA	NA/NA	NA/NA	NA/NA	Not specified	Not specified
Social-Personality Psychology	MA/MS	NA/NA	NA/NA	NA/NA	NA/NA	NA/NA	NA/NA	Not specified	Not specified

Admissions Requirements:

Degree	GRE	GRE-Subject	Letters of Recom-mendation	Research Statement	Writing Sample	CV	Interview
Master's/Specialist	Required	Required	2	Required	Optional	Optional	None
Doctoral	Required	Required	2	Required	Optional	Optional	None

Please note if these criteria vary for different programs: GRE Subject test only required for applicants who do not have an honours undergraduate degree in psychology. Applicants to the doctoral program must have a master's degree.

Admissions Criteria:

GRE scores—high
Research experience—medium
Work experience—low
Clinically related public service—low
GPA—high

Letters of recommendation—high
Statement of goals and objectives—high
Undergraduate psychology preparation—high
Supervisor availability—high

For additional information on admission requirements, visit http://www.queensu.ca/psychology/graduate/prospective-students.

Department Demographics

	Male (PT)	Female (PT)	Total	African-American/ Black (PT)	Hispanic/ Latino (PT)	Asian/ Pacific Islander (PT)	American Indian/ Alaska Native (PT)	Caucasian/ White (PT)	Unknown	Multiethnic (PT)	ADA (PT)	Int'l (PT)
Students	24 (0)	73 (0)	0	0 (0)	0 (0)	11 (0)	3 (0)	79 (0)	1 (0)	3 (0)	0 (0)	7 (0)

Financial Information/Assistance

Tuition: For information on tuition costs, visit http://www.queensu.ca/registrar/financials/tuition-fees. Tuition is subject to change.

Doctoral:
State residents: $7,508 per academic year.
Nonstate residents: $14,633 per academic year.

Master's:
State residents: $7,508 per academic year.
Nonstate residents: $14,633 per academic year.

Financial Assistance:

	Teaching Assistantship (% Receiving)	Teaching Assistantship Tuition Remission	Research Assistantship (% Receiving)	Research Assistantship Tuition Remission	Fellowship (% Receiving)	Fellowship Tuition Remission
First-Year Student	$8,016 (NA)	NA	NA (NA)	NA	$20,000 (NA)	NA
Advanced Student	$8,016 (NA)	NA	NA (NA)	NA	$20,000 (NA)	NA

For additional information on financial assistance, visit http://www.queensu.ca/psychology/graduate/funding-financial-support.

Employment of Department Graduates

Master's:
Enrolled in a psychology doctoral program: 11
Enrolled in another graduate/professional program: 1
Total: 12

Additional Information

Housing and Day Care: On-campus housing is available. See the following website for more information: http://residences.housing. queensu.ca/. On-campus day care facilities are available. See the following website for more information: http://www.queensu.ca/ daycare/.

Information for Students With Physical Disabilities: See the following website: http://www.queensu.ca/studentwellness/ accessibility-services.

Special Facilities or Resources: Extensive computer and laboratory facilities are available to graduate students for research and clinical experience.

Application Information: The Registrar, School of Graduate Studies and Research, Gordon Hall, Queen's University, Kingston, ON Canada K7L 3N6. *Fee:* $105. *Online application:* https://eservices.queensu.ca/apps/sgsapp/.

Regina, University of
Department of Psychology
3737 Wascana Parkway
Regina, SK S4S 0A2
Telephone: (306) 585-4157
Department Head: Richard MacLennan

E-mail: richard.maclennan@uregina.ca
Web: http://www.uregina.ca/arts/psychology/

Orientation, Objectives, and Emphasis of Department
Teaching and research are oriented toward clinical, social, and applied approaches. The majority of graduate students are in clinical psychology. Faculty orientation is eclectic. Cognitive behavioral and humanistic approaches are represented. Neuropsychology is also well represented.

Programs and Degrees Offered

Program	Degree	Application Deadline	Applications Received	Accepted	New Admits Enrolled (PT)	Total Enrolled (PT)	Degrees Awarded in 2014–2015	Median Years to Complete Degree	Dismissed/ Withdrew
Clinical Psychology	MA/MS	January 15 (Fall)	32	6	6 (0)	12 (0)	9	2	0

Programs and Degrees Offered *(con't.)*

Program	Degree	Application Deadline	Applica-tions Received	Accepted	New Admits Enrolled (PT)	Total Enrolled (PT)	Degrees Awarded in 2014–2015	Median Years to Complete Degree	Dismissed/Withdrew
Experimental and Applied Psychology	MA/MS	January 15 (Fall)	13	6	6 (0)	7 (0)	5	3	0
Experimental and Applied Psychology	PhD	January 15 (Fall)	4	2	2 (0)	11 (0)	1	4	0
Clinical Psychology	PhD	January 15 (Fall)	9	5	5 (0)	26 (0)	11	4	0

CPA Accreditation
Clinical PhD (Doctor of Philosophy).

Doctoral Degree (PhD Clinical Psychology): For those doctoral students for whom a professional internship was required in this program prior to graduation:
Total students who applied for an internship: 6
Total students who obtained an internship: 6
Total students who obtained a paid internship: 6
Total students who obtained an unpaid internship: 0
Total students who were placed in APA/CPA-accredited internships: 6
Total students placed in internships not APA/CPA-accredited, but listed with the Association of Psychology Postdoctoral and Internship Centers (APPIC): 0
Total students placed in internships conforming to guidelines of the Council of Directors of School Psychology Programs (CDSPP): 0
Total students placed in internships that were not APA/CPA-accredited, APPIC or CDSSP listed: 0

Master's Degree (MA/MS Clinical Psychology): An internship experience, such as a final research project or "capstone" experience is required of graduates. Master's Degree (MA/MS Experimental and Applied Psychology): An internship experience, such as a final research project or "capstone" experience is required of graduates.

Internships/Practica
A wide array of community resources are available and well utilized in providing practicum and internship training. The department cannot guarantee placement in these facilities.

Admissions
Entries appear in the following order: required test or GPA, minimum score (if required)/median score of students entering in 2015–2016.

Program	Degree	GRE-V	GRE-Q	GRE-Writing	GRE-Subject	Under-graduate GPA	Last 2 Years GPA	Psychol-ogy GPA	Master's GPA
Clinical Psychology	MA/MS	150/159	150/153	NA/NA	Not specified	NA/NA	Not specified	Not specified	Not specified
Experimental and Applied Psychology	MA/MS	160/160	156/156	NA/NA	Not specified	NA/NA	Not specified	Not specified	Not specified
Experimental and Applied Psychology	PhD	160/160	149/149	NA/NA	Not specified	NA/NA	Not specified	Not specified	Not specified
Clinical Psychology	PhD	151/158	150/154	NA/NA	Not specified	NA/NA	Not specified	Not specified	Not specified

Admissions Requirements:

Degree	GRE	GRE-Subject	Letters of Recommendation	Research Statement	Writing Sample	CV	Interview
Master's/Specialist	Required	Optional	2	Required	Optional	Optional	Required
Doctoral	Required	Optional	2	Required	Optional	Optional	Required

Admissions Criteria:

GRE scores—high
Research experience—medium
Work experience—low
Clinically related public service—medium
GPA—high

Letters of recommendation—high
Interview—medium
Statement of goals and objectives—high
Undergraduate psychology preparation—high

Department Demographics

	Male (PT)	Female (PT)	Total	African-American/ Black (PT)	Hispanic/ Latino (PT)	Asian/ Pacific Islander (PT)	American Indian/ Alaska Native (PT)	Caucasian/ White (PT)	Unknown	Multiethnic (PT)	ADA (PT)	Int'l (PT)
Students	12 (0)	44 (0)	0	0 (0)	0 (0)	2 (0)	0 (0)	52 (0)	0 (0)	0 (0)	0 (0)	2 (0)

Financial Information/Assistance

Tuition: For information on tuition costs, visit http://www.uregina.ca/gradstudies/current-students/tuition-fees/semester.html. Tuition is subject to change.

Doctoral:
State residents: $5,465 per academic year.
Nonstate residents: $8,465 per academic year.

Master's:
State residents: $5,087 per academic year.
Nonstate residents: $8,087 per academic year.

Financial Assistance:

	Teaching Assistantship (% Receiving)	Teaching Assistantship Tuition Remission	Research Assistantship (% Receiving)	Research Assistantship Tuition Remission	Fellowship (% Receiving)	Fellowship Tuition Remission
First-Year Student	$7,501 (NA)	NA	$5,626 (NA)	NA	$6,000 (NA)	NA
Advanced Student	$7,870 (NA)	NA	$5,902 (NA)	NA	$7,000 (NA)	NA

For additional information on financial assistance, visit http://www.uregina.ca/gradstudies/scholarships/.

Employment of Department Graduates

Master's:
Enrolled in a psychology doctoral program: 8
Employed in a community mental health/counseling center: 1
Other employment position: 1
Do not know: 4
Total: 14

Doctoral:
Employed in an academic position at a university: 4
Employed in a community mental health/counseling center: 1
Employed in a hospital/medical center: 7
Total: 12

Additional Information

Housing and Day Care: On-campus housing is available. See the following website for more information: http://www.uregina.ca/student/residence/. On-campus day care facilities are available. See the following website for more information: http://www.uregina.ca/hr/careers/realize/daycare.html.

Information for Students With Physical Disabilities: See the following website: http://www.uregina.ca/student/accessibility/.

Special Facilities or Resources: The department has clinical/counselling rooms for research purposes, a small testing library, permanent space for faculty research, and observation rooms and computer labs. Our new psychology training clinic which covers 3,269 square feet provides an alternative setting for the provision of psychological services to residents in and around Regina, especially those with moderate to mild psychological concerns who may not be able to easily access other services. It has a large meeting room and several smaller meeting and observation rooms.

Application Information: Dean, Faculty of Graduate Studies and Research, University of Regina, 3737 Wascana Parkway, Regina, SK S4S 0A2. *Fee:* $100. *Online application:* http://www.uregina.ca/gradstudies/future-students/application-process.html.

Ryerson University

Department of Psychology
350 Victoria Street
Toronto, ON M5B 2K3
Telephone: (416) 979-5000, ext. 2178
Graduate Program Director: Dr. Julia Spaniol

E-mail: psychgrad@psych.ryerson.ca
Web: http://www.ryerson.ca/psychology/

Orientation, Objectives, and Emphasis of Department

Launched in the fall of 2007, our program offers students opportunities to study in either Clinical Psychology (accredited by the Canadian Psychological Association in May 2012) or Psychological Science. The Psychological Science stream offers opportunities to specialize in research areas that include brain, perception, and cognition; health and community psychology; lifespan development; psychopathology and intervention; and social and forensic psychology. Ryerson's graduate program in Psychology offers an innovative curriculum that combines training in basic and applied research. Trained and recruited from top universities in Canada, the United States, and around the world, the core faculty bring a rigorous and student-centered approach to scientific and clinical training. Based in a department known for its experiential and career-focused learning, the program takes advantage of its downtown Toronto location that includes proximity to major sites for practicum training and clinical research, and offers students access to world-class training opportunities.

Programs and Degrees Offered

Program	Degree	Application Deadline	Applications Received	Accepted	New Admits Enrolled (PT)	Total Enrolled (PT)	Degrees Awarded in 2014–2015	Median Years to Complete Degree	Dismissed/ Withdrew
Clinical Psychology	MA/MS	December 1 (Fall)	276	8	8 (0)	16 (0)	8	2	0
Psychological Science	MA/MS	December 1 (Fall)	51	8	8 (0)	18 (0)	5	2	0
Clinical Psychology	PhD	December 1 (Fall)	32	11	11 (0)	50 (0)	9	4.5	0
Psychological Science	PhD	December 1 (Fall)	11	4	4 (0)	22 (0)	4	4.2	0

CPA Accreditation

Clinical PhD (Doctor of Philosophy).

Doctoral Degree (PhD Clinical Psychology): For those doctoral students for whom a professional internship was required in this program prior to graduation:
Total students who applied for an internship: 15
Total students who obtained an internship: 15
Total students who obtained a paid internship: 15
Total students who obtained an unpaid internship: 0
Total students who were placed in APA/CPA-accredited internships: 15
Total students placed in internships not APA/CPA-accredited, but listed with the Association of Psychology Postdoctoral and Internship Centers (APPIC): 0
Total students placed in internships conforming to guidelines of the Council of Directors of School Psychology Programs (CDSPP): 0
Total students placed in internships that were not APA/CPA-accredited, APPIC or CDSSP listed: 0

Internships/Practica

Practicum placements are available to our Clinical Psychology students at our Clinical Psychology Training Clinic, housed within a family practice clinic of St. Michael's Hospital. Practicum placements at the Clinic provide Clinical Psychology students with the opportunity to gain experience serving a wide range of clients in a hospital-based, interprofessional setting. Our Clinical Psychology students have also been successful at securing practicum placements and predoctoral internships at top training centres, including Baycrest, Center for Addiction and Mental Health, Hamilton Health Sciences, Humber River Regional Hospital, Montefiore Medical Centre (NY), North York General Hospital, St. Joseph's Healthcare Hamilton, Toronto General Hospital, St. Michael's Hospital, University of Chicago Medical Center, and others. With a focus on breadth and depth of training in research methodology, possible practicum placements for the Psychological Science students include both internal sites such as the research labs of faculty in the Ryerson Department of Psychology as well as external sites such as the CAMH, University of Toronto, Boston College, University of Indiana, University of Texas, Duke University Medical Center, Phonak Canada, Hospital for Sick Children, John Jay College of Criminal Justice (NY), Toronto Rehab Institute, Rotman Research Institute, and Wales at Bangor University (UK).

Admissions

Entries appear in the following order: required test or GPA, minimum score (if required)/median score of students entering in 2015–2016.

Program	Degree	GRE-V	GRE-Q	GRE-Writing	GRE-Subject	Under-graduate GPA	Last 2 Years GPA	Psychol-ogy GPA	Master's GPA
Clinical Psychology	MA/MS	NA/NA	NA/NA	NA/NA	Not specified	Not specified	NA/NA	Not specified	Not specified
Psychological Science	MA/MS	NA/NA	NA/NA	NA/NA	Not specified	Not specified	NA/NA	Not specified	Not specified
Clinical Psychology	PhD	NA/NA	NA/NA	NA/NA	Not specified	Not specified	Not specified	Not specified	Not specified
Psychological Science	PhD	NA/NA	NA/NA	NA/NA	Not specified	Not specified	Not specified	Not specified	Not specified

Admissions Requirements:

Degree	GRE	GRE-Subject	Letters of Recom-mendation	Research Statement	Writing Sample	CV	Interview
Master's/Specialist	Required	Optional	2	Required	None	Required	Required
Doctoral	Required	Recom-mended	2	Required	None	Required	Required

Please note if these criteria vary for different programs: Undergraduate major in psychology is strongly recommended for both fields, and is especially important for the clinical psychology field. Generally, a minimum of 70th percentile for GRE-General exam in Verbal, Quantitative, and Writing skills is desired for both fields. The GRE-Subject exam in Psychology is not required, but recommended for both fields.

Admissions Criteria:

GRE scores—medium
Research experience—high
Work experience—medium
Clinically related public service—low
GPA—high

Letters of recommendation—high
Interview—high
Statement of goals and objectives—high
Undergraduate psychology preparation—high

For additional information on admission requirements, visit http://www.ryerson.ca/psychology/graduate/future/admissions/.

Department Demographics

	Male (PT)	Female (PT)	Total	African-American/ Black (PT)	Hispanic/ Latino (PT)	Asian/ Pacific Islander (PT)	American Indian/ Alaska Native (PT)	Caucasian/ White (PT)	Unknown	Multiethnic (PT)	ADA (PT)	Int'l (PT)
Students	14 (0)	92 (0)	0	0 (0)	2 (0)	16 (0)	0 (0)	85 (0)	2 (0)	1 (0)	0 (0)	0 (0)

Financial Information/Assistance

Tuition: For information on tuition costs, visit http://www.ryerson.ca/registrar/fees/detail/graduate.html. Tuition is subject to change.

Doctoral:
State residents: $9,985 per academic year.
Nonstate residents: $19,677 per academic year.

Master's:
State residents: $10,445 per academic year.
Nonstate residents: $20,502 per academic year.

Financial Assistance:

	Teaching Assistantship (% Receiving)	Teaching Assistantship Tuition Remission	Research Assistantship (% Receiving)	Research Assistantship Tuition Remission	Fellowship (% Receiving)	Fellowship Tuition Remission
First-Year Student	$10,134 (NA)	NA	$10,134 (NA)	NA	$9,000 (NA)	NA
Advanced Student	$10,946 (NA)	NA	$10,946 (NA)	NA	$9,000 (NA)	NA

For additional information on financial assistance, visit http://www.ryerson.ca/psychology/graduate/current/finances/.

Employment of Department Graduates

Master's:
Enrolled in a psychology doctoral program: 10
Enrolled in another graduate/professional program: 2
Do not know: 1
Total: 13

Doctoral:
Enrolled in a postdoctoral residency/fellowship: 5
Employed in independent practice: 3
Employed in an academic position at a university: 1
Employed in academic position at a 2-year/4-year college: 1
Employed in a hospital/medical center: 3
Total: 13

Additional Information

Housing and Day Care: No on-campus housing is available. On-campus day care facilities are available. See the following website for more information: http://www.ryerson.ca/ecs/researchlabs/elc/index.html.

Information for Students With Physical Disabilities: See the following website: http://www.ryerson.ca/studentlearningsupport/.

Special Facilities or Resources: The Department has developed a state-of-the-art Psychology Research and Training Centre (PRTC) lab facility that includes over 15,000 square feet of research space. Our Institute for Research on Stress and Wellbeing (or Stress Institute) provides training in and access to research equipment for psychology graduate students to study stress. The Psychology Training Clinic, housed within a family practice clinic of St. Michael's Hospital, provides a unique opportunity for graduate students to gain experience serving a wide range of clients in a hospital-based, interprofessional setting. The Clinic is a state-of-the-art facility, designed according to the latest medical infrastructure standards with unique modifications and accommodations to meet the needs of patients receiving psychological assessments and interventions. These new spaces have been built from the ground up to serve the research and training needs of our psychology graduate students and faculty.

Application Information: Fee: $110. Online application: http://horizon.ouac.on.ca/ryerson/grad.

Saint Mary's University

Department of Psychology
923 Robie Street
Halifax, NS B3H 3C3
Telephone: (902) 420-5846
Chairperson: Dr. Marc Patry

E-mail: Lori.Francis@smu.ca
Web: http://www.smu.ca/academics/departments/psychology.html

Orientation, Objectives, and Emphasis of Department

Masters' students will acquire a background in theory and research that is consistent with the scientist–practitioner model, preparing themselves for employment and/or continued graduate education. Full-time students normally require 2 years to complete the program. Part-time students may take 2 to 4 years longer. Masters' students are normally provided with financial support for 2 years. PhD students will acquire a background in theory and research that is consistent with the scientist–practitioner model, preparing them for an academic career or a career in consulting and/or industry. Full-time students normally require 3 years to complete the program. PhD students are normally provided with financial support for 3 years.

Programs and Degrees Offered

Program	Degree	Application Deadline	Applications Received	Accepted	New Admits Enrolled (PT)	Total Enrolled (PT)	Degrees Awarded in 2014–2015	Median Years to Complete Degree	Dismissed/ Withdrew
Industrial/ Organizational Psychology	MA/MS	December 15 (Fall)	32	6	6 (0)	12 (1)	5	2	0
Industrial/ Organizational Psychology	PhD	December 15 (Fall)	7	4	3 (0)	13 (7)	2	4	0

Internships/Practica

Masters' students are required to complete a supervised, full-time, paid internship (minimum of 500 hours) in the summer following their first year or part-time during their second year. Placements are available in a variety of government agencies, human resource departments, research agencies, and private consulting firms. Salaries range from $7,000 to $14,000 for the 4 months.

Admissions

Entries appear in the following order: required test or GPA, minimum score (if required)/median score of students entering in 2015–2016.

Program	Degree	GRE-V	GRE-Q	GRE-Writing	GRE-Subject	Under-graduate GPA	Last 2 Years GPA	Psychol-ogy GPA	Master's GPA
Industrial/ Organizational Psychology	MA/MS	NA/NA	NA/NA	NA/NA	Not specified	NA/NA	Not specified	Not specified	Not specified
Industrial/ Organizational Psychology	PhD	NA/NA	NA/NA	NA/NA	Not specified	NA/NA	Not specified	Not specified	3.3/NA

Admissions Requirements:

Degree	GRE	GRE-Subject	Letters of Recommendation	Research Statement	Writing Sample	CV	Interview
Master's/Specialist	Required	None	3	Required	Optional	Optional	None
Doctoral	Required	None	3	Required	Optional	Recommended	Optional

Please note if these criteria vary for different programs: Doctoral applicants must have completed a master's degree.

Admissions Criteria:

GRE scores—high
Research experience—high
Work experience—low
GPA—high

Letters of recommendation—medium
Statement of goals and objectives—high
Undergraduate psychology preparation—high
Honours degree—high

For additional information on admission requirements, visit http://www.smu.ca/future-students/applying-to-graduate-studies.html.

Department Demographics

	Male (PT)	Female (PT)	Total	African-American/ Black (PT)	Hispanic/ Latino (PT)	Asian/ Pacific Islander (PT)	American Indian/ Alaska Native (PT)	Caucasian/ White (PT)	Unknown	Multiethnic (PT)	ADA (PT)	Int'l (PT)
Students	10 (0)	22 (8)	0	1 (0)	0 (0)	1 (0)	0 (0)	22 (8)	0 (0)	1 (0)	0 (0)	2 (0)

Financial Information/Assistance

Tuition: For information on tuition costs, visit http://www.smu.ca/future-students/graduate-studies-course-and-program-fees.html. Higher tuition cost for this program: Tuition is higher for international students - MSc-$12,750; PhD-$13,383. Tuition is subject to change.

Doctoral:
State residents: $6,641 per academic year.
Nonstate residents: $7,924 per academic year.

Master's:
State residents: $5,236 per academic year.
Nonstate residents: $6,519 per academic year.

Financial Assistance:

	Teaching Assistantship (% Receiving)	Teaching Assistantship Tuition Remission	Research Assistantship (% Receiving)	Research Assistantship Tuition Remission	Fellowship (% Receiving)	Fellowship Tuition Remission
First-Year Student	$5,000 (100)	NA	$7,000 (20)	NA	$10,000 (100)	NA
Advanced Student	$5,000 (100)	NA	$7,500 (50)	NA	$15,000 (100)	NA

Employment of Department Graduates

Master's:
Enrolled in a psychology doctoral program: 1
Employed in business or industry: 4
Employed in government agency: 1
Total: 6

Doctoral:
Employed in an academic position at a university: 2
Total: 2

Additional Information

Housing and Day Care: On-campus housing is available. See the following website for more information: http://www.smu.ca/campus-life/family-and-graduate-housing.html. On-campus day care facilities are available. See the following website for more information: http://www.ppccc.ca/.

Information for Students With Physical Disabilities: See the following website: http://www.smu.ca/campus-life/fred-smithers-centre.html.

Special Facilities or Resources: General research laboratories, graduate computer lab, small-group research space, graduate student offices, and a tests and measurements library that includes psychological test batteries are available. Support systems include audiovisual equipment, computer facilities, and a technical workshop. Students may be involved in the CN Centre for Occupational Health & Safety, as well as the Centre for Leadership Excellence.

Application Information: Faculty of Graduate Studies & Research, Saint Mary's University, Halifax, NS, Canada B3H 3C3. *Fee:* $70. *Online application:* http://www.smu.ca/future-students/cs-apply-online.html.

Saskatchewan, University of
Department of Psychology
Arts and Science
9 Campus Drive
Saskatoon, SK S7N 5A5
Telephone: (306) 966-6657
Head: Dr. Gordon Sarty

E-mail: psychology.gradadvising@usask.ca
Web: http://artsandscience.usask.ca/psychology/

Orientation, Objectives, and Emphasis of Department

All graduate programs are small and highly selective. The clinical program focuses on PhD training, based on a scientist–practitioner model with an eclectic theoretical perspective. The goal is to train people who will be able to function in a wide variety of community, agency, academic, and research settings. The applied social program attempts to train people at the MA and PhD level for researcher consultant positions in applied (MA) or academic (PhD) settings. Areas of concentration include program development and evaluation, group processes, and organizational development. The cognition and neuroscience programs are individually structured, admitting a few students to work with active research supervisors, most frequently in behavioral neuroscience, neuropsychology, cognitive psychology or culture and development.

Programs and Degrees Offered

Program	Degree	Application Deadline	Applica-tions Received	Accepted	New Admits Enrolled (PT)	Total Enrolled (PT)	Degrees Awarded in 2014–2015	Median Years to Complete Degree	Dismissed/ Withdrew
Clinical Psychology	PhD	January 15 (Fall)	64	5	5 (0)	42 (0)	5	6.6	0
Applied Social Psychology	PhD	January 15 (Fall)	130	9	9 (0)	23 (0)	5	5	0
Cognition and Neuroscience	PhD	January 15 (Fall)	12	3	0 (0)	16 (0)	5	5	0
Culture, Health and Human Development	PhD	January 15 (Fall)	11	2	2	13	1	4	0

CPA Accreditation
Clinical PhD (Doctor of Philosophy).

Doctoral Degree (PhD Clinical Psychology): For those doctoral students for whom a professional internship was required in this program prior to graduation:
Total students who applied for an internship: 7
Total students who obtained an internship: 6
Total students who obtained a paid internship: 6
Total students who obtained an unpaid internship: 0
Total students who were placed in APA/CPA-accredited internships: 6
Total students placed in internships not APA/CPA-accredited, but listed with the Association of Psychology Postdoctoral and Internship Centers (APPIC): 0
Total students placed in internships conforming to guidelines of the Council of Directors of School Psychology Programs (CDSPP): 0
Total students placed in internships that were not APA/CPA-accredited, APPIC or CDSSP listed: 0

Internships/Practica
Full-time internships and practicum training concurrent with coursework are required in both clinical and applied social programs. In the clinical program, 4-month MA internship placements are available at a number of hospital and outpatient clinics throughout the province. At the PhD level, 12-month internships have been arranged in larger clinical settings with diversified client populations in Canada and the United States. The applied social program requires multiple 4-month applied research internships. Practicum and internship placements are arranged in a wide variety of government, institutional, and business settings.

Admissions

Entries appear in the following order: required test or GPA, minimum score (if required)/median score of students entering in 2015–2016.

Program	Degree	GRE-V	GRE-Q	GRE-Writing	GRE-Subject	Under-graduate GPA	Last 2 Years GPA	Psychol-ogy GPA	Master's GPA
Clinical Psychology	PhD	NA/NA	NA/NA	NA/NA	NA/NA	NA/NA	NA/NA	NA/NA	NA/NA
Applied Social Psychology	PhD	Not specified	Not specified	Not specified	Not specified	Not specified	NA/NA	NA/NA	NA/NA
Cognition and Neuroscience	PhD	Not specified	Not specified	Not specified	Not specified	Not specified	NA/NA	NA/NA	NA/NA
Culture, Health and Human Development	PhD	Not specified	Not specified	Not specified	Not specified	Not specified	NA/NA	NA/NA	Not specified

Admissions Requirements:

Degree	GRE	GRE-Subject	Letters of Recom-mendation	Research Statement	Writing Sample	CV	Interview
Doctoral	Required	Recom-mended	3	Required	None	Recom-mended	Required

Please note if these criteria vary for different programs: GRE scores are ONLY required for the Clinical Program and the Applied Social Psychology (ASP) if you are in international applicant.

Admissions Criteria:

GRE scores—medium
Research experience—high
Work experience—medium
Clinically related public service—low
GPA—high

Letters of recommendation—high
Interview—high
Statement of goals and objectives—high
Undergraduate psychology preparation—high

For additional information on admission requirements, visit http://artsandscience.usask.ca/psychology/graduates/applying.php.

Department Demographics

	Male (PT)	Female (PT)	Total	African-American/ Black (PT)	Hispanic/ Latino (PT)	Asian/ Pacific Islander (PT)	American Indian/ Alaska Native (PT)	Caucasian/ White (PT)	Unknown	Multiethnic (PT)	ADA (PT)	Int'l (PT)
Students	26 (0)	68 (0)	0	0 (0)	0 (0)	0 (0)	0 (0)	0 (0)	0 (0)	0 (0)	0 (0)	3 (0)

Financial Information/Assistance

Tuition: For information on tuition costs, visit https://students.usask.ca/money/tuition-fees/graduate-tuition.php. Tuition is subject to change.

Doctoral:
State residents: $3,804 per academic year.
Nonstate residents: $5,706 per academic year.

Financial Assistance:

	Teaching Assistantship (% Receiving)	Teaching Assistantship Tuition Remission	Research Assistantship (% Receiving)	Research Assistantship Tuition Remission	Fellowship (% Receiving)	Fellowship Tuition Remission
First-Year Student	$16,000 (NA)	NA	NA (NA)	NA	$18,000 (NA)	NA
Advanced Student	$16,000 (NA)	NA	NA (NA)	NA	$20,000 (NA)	NA

For additional information on financial assistance, visit http://www.usask.ca/cgsr/funding/index.php.

Employment of Department Graduates

No information provided.

Additional Information

Housing and Day Care: On-campus housing is available. See the following website for more information: http://livewithus.usask.ca/. On-campus day care facilities are available. See the following website for more information: http://ussu.ca/main-page/centres/childcare-centre/.

Special Facilities or Resources: The Department has a Psychological Services Centre, an animal lab, and a cognitive science lab with access to fMRI facilities. There are also numerous microcomputers, excellent mainframe computer facilities, and a good research library. The Women's Studies Research Unit promotes scholarly research by, for, and about women, providing a source of support for all women studying, teaching, researching, and working on campus.

Application Information: Graduate Program Coordinator, University of Saskatchewan, Department of Psychology, 9 Campus Drive, Saskatoon, SK Canada S7N 5A5. *Fee:* $90. *Online application:* http://grad.usask.ca/admissions/how-to-apply.php.

Toronto, University of
Department of Psychology
100 Saint George Street
Toronto, ON M5S 3G3
Telephone: (416) 978-3404
Graduate Chair: Morris Moscovitch

E-mail: grad@psych.utoronto.ca
Web: http://home.psych.utoronto.ca/

Orientation, Objectives, and Emphasis of Department
The purpose of graduate training at the University of Toronto is to prepare students for careers in teaching and research. Teaching and research apprenticeships, therefore, constitute a large portion of such training. Research training is supplemented by courses and seminars. In some cases the courses are designed to provide up-to-date fundamental background information in psychology. The bulk of instruction, however, takes place in informal seminars; these provide an opportunity for the discussion of theoretical issues, the formulation of research problems, and the review of current developments in specific research areas. In the past, most of our graduates have entered academic careers. More recently, graduates have also taken research and managerial positions in research institutes, hospitals, government agencies, and industrial corporations.

Programs and Degrees Offered

Program	Degree	Application Deadline	Applications Received	Accepted	New Admits Enrolled (PT)	Total Enrolled (PT)	Degrees Awarded in 2014–2015	Median Years to Complete Degree	Dismissed/ Withdrew
Behavioral Neuroscience	MA/MS	December 1 (Fall)	16	8	6	6	3	1	0

Programs and Degrees Offered *(con't.)*

Program	Degree	Application Deadline	Applications Received	Accepted	New Admits Enrolled (PT)	Total Enrolled (PT)	Degrees Awarded in 2014–2015	Median Years to Complete Degree	Dismissed/ Withdrew
Behavioral Neuroscience	PhD	December 1 (Fall)	1	0	0	19	3	5	0
Cognition/ Perception	MA/MS	December 1 (Fall)	49	20	9	9	17	1	0
Cognition/ Perception	PhD	December 1 (Fall)	13	2	1	66	13	6	0
Developmental Psychology	MA/MS	December 1 (Fall)	10	1	1	1	5	1	0
Social/ Personality/ Abnormal	MA/MS	December 1 (Fall)	65	6	6	6	7	1	
Developmental Psychology	PhD	December 1 (Fall)	4	1	1	14	2	5	0
Social/ Personality/ Abnormal	PhD	December 1 (Fall)	23	0	0	33	5	5	0

Admissions

Entries appear in the following order: required test or GPA, minimum score (if required)/median score of students entering in 2015–2016.

Program	Degree	GRE-V	GRE-Q	GRE-Writing	GRE-Subject	Under-graduate GPA	Last 2 Years GPA	Psychology GPA	Master's GPA
Behavioral Neuroscience	MA/MS	NA/160	NA/156	NA/5	Not specified	Not specified	NA/NA	Not specified	Not specified
Behavioral Neuroscience	PhD	NA/164	NA/161	NA/4	Not specified	Not specified	NA/NA	Not specified	NA/NA
Cognition/ Perception	MA/MS	NA/160	NA/155	NA/4	Not specified	Not specified	NA/NA	Not specified	Not specified
Cognition/ Perception	PhD	NA/160	NA/155	NA/4	Not specified	Not specified	NA/NA	Not specified	NA/NA
Developmental Psychology	MA/MS	NA/159	NA/159	NA/4.5	Not specified	Not specified	NA/NA	Not specified	Not specified
Social/ Personality/ Abnormal	MA/MS	NA/159	NA/157	NA/5	Not specified	Not specified	NA/NA	Not specified	Not specified
Developmental Psychology	PhD	NA/159	NA/159	NA/4.5	Not specified	Not specified	NA/NA	Not specified	NA/NA
Social/ Personality/ Abnormal	PhD	NA/158	NA/155	NA/4.5	Not specified	Not specified	NA/NA	Not specified	NA/NA

Admissions Requirements:

Degree	GRE	GRE-Subject	Letters of Recommendation	Research Statement	Writing Sample	CV	Interview
Master's/Specialist	Required	Optional	2	Required	None	Optional	Required
Doctoral	Required	Optional	2	Required	None	Optional	Required

Admissions Criteria:

GRE scores—high
Research experience—high
Work experience—low
GPA—high

Letters of recommendation—high
Interview—high
Statement of goals and objectives—high
Undergraduate psychology preparation—medium

For additional information on admission requirements, visit http://home.psych.utoronto.ca/graduate/grad_admission.htm.

Department Demographics

	Male (PT)	Female (PT)	Total	African-American/ Black (PT)	Hispanic/ Latino (PT)	Asian/ Pacific Islander (PT)	American Indian/ Alaska Native (PT)	Caucasian/ White (PT)	Unknown	Multiethnic (PT)	ADA (PT)	Int'l (PT)
Students	63 (0)	91 (0)	0	0 (0)	0 (0)	0 (0)	0 (0)	0 (0)	154 (1)	0 (0)	0 (0)	19 (0)

Financial Information/Assistance

Tuition: For information on tuition costs, visit http://www.provost.utoronto.ca/link/students.htm. Tuition is subject to change.

Doctoral:
State residents: $8,448 per academic year.
Nonstate residents: $20,938 per academic year.

Master's:
State residents: $8,448 per academic year.
Nonstate residents: $20,938 per academic year.

Financial Assistance:

	Teaching Assistantship (% Receiving)	Teaching Assistantship Tuition Remission	Research Assistantship (% Receiving)	Research Assistantship Tuition Remission	Fellowship (% Receiving)	Fellowship Tuition Remission
First-Year Student	$8,231 (100)	NA	NA (NA)	NA	$16,717 (100)	NA
Advanced Student	$7,871 (100)	NA	NA (NA)	NA	$17,077 (100)	NA

For additional information on financial assistance, visit http://www.sgs.utoronto.ca/currentstudents/Pages/Financing-Your-Graduate-Education.aspx.

Employment of Department Graduates

Master's:
Enrolled in a psychology doctoral program: 25
Do not know: 7
Total: 32

Doctoral:
Enrolled in a postdoctoral residency/fellowship: 10
Employed in government agency: 1
Employed in a community mental health/counseling center: 1
Employed in a hospital/medical center: 1
Do not know: 10
Total: 23

Additional Information

Housing and Day Care: On-campus housing is available. See the following website for more information: http://gradhouse.utoronto.ca/. On-campus day care facilities are available. See the following website for more information: http://www.familycare.utoronto.ca/child_care/childcare.html.

Information for Students With Physical Disabilities: See the following website: http://www.studentlife.utoronto.ca/as.

Special Facilities or Resources: The department has modern laboratories at the St. George, Mississauga, and Scarborough campuses, as well as a fully equipped electronic workshop. Students have access to an extensive computer system including the university's central computer, the department's Sun computer, and many advanced microcomputers. The department has close ties to several medical hospitals, as well as the Rotman Research Institute of Baycrest Centre and the Centre for Addiction and Mental Health.

Application Information: Graduate Studies, Department of Psychology, University of Toronto, 100 Saint George Street, Toronto, ON, Canada M5S 3G3. *Fee:* $120. *Online application:* https://apply.sgs.utoronto.ca/.

Victoria, University of
Department of Psychology
P.O. Box 1700 STN CSC
Victoria, BC V8W 2Y2
Telephone: (250) 721-7525
Chairperson: Ulrich Mueller

E-mail: psychgrd@uvic.ca
Web: http://www.uvic.ca/socialsciences/psychology/

Orientation, Objectives, and Emphasis of Department
The graduate program in psychology emphasizes the training of research competence, and, in the case of neuropsychology and lifespan, the acquisition of clinical skills. The department's orientation is strongly empirical, and students are expected to develop mastery of appropriate methods and design as well as of specific content areas of psychology. The program is directed toward the PhD degree, although students must obtain a master's degree as part of the normal requirements. Formal programs of study, involving a coordinated sequence of courses, are offered for both experimental and clinical neuropsychology (up to but not including a clinical internship), lifespan development, clinical lifespan development, social psychology, and cognition and brain sciences. Individual programs of study may be designed according to the interests of individual students and faculty members in such areas as addictions, consumer and industrial psychology, environmental psychology, experimental and applied behavior analysis, psychopathology, and human psychophysiology.

Programs and Degrees Offered

Program	Degree	Application Deadline	Applica-tions Received	Accepted	New Admits Enrolled (PT)	Total Enrolled (PT)	Degrees Awarded in 2014–2015	Median Years to Complete Degree	Dismissed/ Withdrew
Cognition and Brain Science	PhD	December 1 (Fall)	7	0	0	9 (0)	3	5	0
Experimental Neuropsychology	PhD	December 1 (Fall)	0	0	0	2 (0)	0		0
Social Psychology	PhD	December 1 (Fall)	8	0	0	9 (0)	1	5	0
Lifespan Development	PhD	December 1 (Fall)	8	0	0	6	2	5	0
Clinical Psychology	PhD	December 1 (Fall)	149	6	6	44	9	7	
Individualized	PhD	December 1 (Fall)	8	0	0	7	2	6	

CPA Accreditation
Clinical PhD (Doctor of Philosophy).

Doctoral Degree (PhD Clinical Psychology): For those doctoral students for whom a professional internship was required in this program prior to graduation:
Total students who applied for an internship: 5
Total students who obtained an internship: 5
Total students who obtained a paid internship: 5
Total students who obtained an unpaid internship: 0
Total students who were placed in APA/CPA-accredited internships: 5
Total students placed in internships not APA/CPA-accredited, but listed with the Association of Psychology Postdoctoral and Internship Centers (APPIC): 0
Total students placed in internships conforming to guidelines of the Council of Directors of School Psychology Programs (CDSPP): 0
Total students placed in internships that were not APA/CPA-accredited, APPIC or CDSSP listed: 0

Admissions

Entries appear in the following order: required test or GPA, minimum score (if required)/median score of students entering in 2015–2016.

Program	Degree	GRE-V	GRE-Q	GRE-Writing	GRE-Subject	Under-graduate GPA	Last 2 Years GPA	Psychol-ogy GPA	Master's GPA
Cognition and Brain Science	PhD	NA/NA	NA/NA	NA/NA	Not specified	Not specified	NA/NA	Not specified	Not specified
Experimental Neuropsychology	PhD	NA/NA	NA/NA	NA/NA	Not specified	Not specified	NA/NA	Not specified	Not specified
Social Psychology	PhD	NA/NA	NA/NA	NA/NA	NA/NA	Not specified	NA/NA	Not specified	Not specified
Lifespan Development	PhD	NA/NA	NA/NA	NA/NA	NA/NA	Not specified	NA/NA	Not specified	Not specified
Clinical Psychology	PhD	NA/159	NA/158	NA/5	Not specified	Not specified	NA/NA	Not specified	Not specified
Individualized	PhD	NA/NA	NA/NA	NA/NA	Not specified	Not specified	NA/NA	Not specified	Not specified

Admissions Requirements:

Degree	GRE	GRE-Subject	Letters of Recom-mendation	Research Statement	Writing Sample	CV	Interview
Doctoral	Required	Optional	2	Required	Optional	Optional	Required

Please note if these criteria vary for different programs: Group interview required for Clinical Programs only.

Admissions Criteria:

GRE scores—high
Research experience—high
Work experience—medium
Clinically related public service—medium
GPA—high

Letters of recommendation—high
Interview—high
Statement of goals and objectives—high
Undergraduate psychology preparation—medium

For additional information on admission requirements, visit http://www.uvic.ca/socialsciences/psychology/graduate/admissions/index.php.

Department Demographics

	Male (PT)	Female (PT)	Total	African-American/ Black (PT)	Hispanic/ Latino (PT)	Asian/ Pacific Islander (PT)	American Indian/ Alaska Native (PT)	Caucasian/ White (PT)	Unknown	Multiethnic (PT)	ADA (PT)	Int'l (PT)
Students	23 (0)	59 (0)	0	0 (0)	0 (0)	(0)	0 (0)	0 (0)	0 (0)	(0)	0 (0)	0 (0)

Financial Information/Assistance

Tuition: For information on tuition costs, visit http://www.uvic.ca/vpfo/accounting/services/tuition/index.php. Tuition is subject to change. Additional fees are assessed to students beyond the costs of tuition for the following: Grad student society, athletics & recreation, health & dental plan.

Doctoral:
State residents: $5,465 per academic year.
Nonstate residents: $6,503 per academic year.

Master's:
State residents: $5,465 per academic year.
Nonstate residents: $6,503 per academic year.

Financial Assistance:

	Teaching Assistantship (% Receiving)	Teaching Assistantship Tuition Remission	Research Assistantship (% Receiving)	Research Assistantship Tuition Remission	Fellowship (% Receiving)	Fellowship Tuition Remission
First-Year Student	$2,421 (NA)	NA	$3,500 (NA)	NA	$10,000 (NA)	NA
Advanced Student	$2,421 (NA)	NA	$6,000 (NA)	NA	$15,000 (NA)	NA

For additional information on financial assistance, visit http://www.uvic.ca/graduatestudies/finances/financialaid/index.php.

Employment of Department Graduates

Doctoral:
Enrolled in a postdoctoral residency/fellowship: 5
Employed in independent practice: 2
Employed in an academic position at a university: 1
Employed in government agency: 1
Employed in a hospital/medical center: 2
Do not know: 2
Total: 13

Additional Information

Housing and Day Care: On-campus housing is available. See the following website for more information: http://housing.uvic.ca/. On-campus day care facilities are available. See the following website for more information: http://www.uvic.ca/services/childcare/.

Information for Students With Physical Disabilities: See the following website: http://www.uvic.ca/services/rcsd/.

Special Facilities or Resources: Fully equipped facilities include a psychology clinic operating as an out-patient service and teaching clinic; large observation rooms with audio and video recording equipment for the study of group interaction and other social processes; microcomputer-based cognition laboratories; experimental rooms with one-way mirrors; electrophysiological recording rooms; and specialized labs for the study of visual and auditory perception. We have a Brain and Cognition Laboratory featuring two state-of-the-art event-related potential (ERP) systems. We recently began conducting functional magnetic resonance imaging (fMRI) research at nearby Royal Jubilee Hospital. The Department enjoys good community contact with local hospitals (general, rehabilitation, and extended care), schools, and private and government agencies, which provide sites for both research and practicum experiences.

Application Information: Graduate Admissions and Records, University of Victoria, P.O. Box 3025 STN CSC, Victoria, BC V8W 3P2, Canada. *Fee:* $116. *Online application:* http://www.uvic.ca/application.

Waterloo, University of
Department of Psychology
200 University Avenue West
Waterloo, ON N2L 3G1
Telephone: (519) 888-4567
Chairperson: Colin MacLeod

E-mail: cmacleod@uwaterloo.ca
Web: https://uwaterloo.ca/psychology/

Orientation, Objectives, and Emphasis of Department
There is a strong emphasis on research in all six divisions of the PhD program, and MA/MS students are prepared for careers in applied psychology in a variety of areas. Students are involved either through participation in ongoing faculty research or through development of their own ideas; coursework is intended to provide students with general knowledge and intensive preparation in their area of concentration. For some of the programs, the blending of theory and practice is experienced in internship and practicum arrangements.

Programs and Degrees Offered

Program	Degree	Application Deadline	Applications Received	Accepted	New Admits Enrolled (PT)	Total Enrolled (PT)	Degrees Awarded in 2014–2015	Median Years to Complete Degree	Dismissed/Withdrew
Industrial/ Organizational Psychology	PhD	December 15 (Fall)	24	5	3 (0)	17 (2)	3		
Social Psychology	PhD	December 15 (Fall)	30	10	5	15 (0)	5		
Cognitive Psychology	PhD	December 15 (Fall)	14	2	1	11 (0)	3		
Cognitive Neuroscience	PhD	December 15 (Fall)	20	10	5	21 (0)	1		
Clinical Psychology	PhD	December 15 (Fall)	152	12	8	23 (2)	7		
Developmental Psychology	PhD	December 15 (Fall)	12	4	2	8 (0)	1		
Industrial/ Organizational Psychology	MA/MS	December 15 (Fall)	24	3	3	3 (0)	1		
Developmental Psychology	MA/MS	December 15 (Fall)	14	6	6	6	6		

CPA Accreditation

Clinical PhD (Doctor of Philosophy).

Doctoral Degree (PhD Clinical Psychology): For those doctoral students for whom a professional internship was required in this program prior to graduation:
Total students who applied for an internship: 2
Total students who obtained an internship: 2
Total students who obtained a paid internship: 2
Total students who obtained an unpaid internship: 0
Total students who were placed in APA/CPA-accredited internships: 2
Total students placed in internships not APA/CPA-accredited, but listed with the Association of Psychology Postdoctoral and Internship Centers (APPIC): 0
Total students placed in internships conforming to guidelines of the Council of Directors of School Psychology Programs (CDSPP): 0
Total students placed in internships that were not APA/CPA-accredited, APPIC or CDSSP listed: 0

Master's Degree (MA/MS Industrial/Organizational Psychology): An internship experience, such as a final research project or "capstone" experience is required of graduates. Master's Degree (MA/MS Developmental Psychology): An internship experience, such as a final research project or "capstone" experience is required of graduates.

Internships/Practica

The Applied Master's in Industrial/Organizational Psychology program requires a 4-month supervised internship. The Clinical program requires a 4-month practicum the summer after the first year of study and builds to a 12-month internship at the conclusion of the academic program. Most practicum placements are with local hospitals, schools or industries.

Admissions

Entries appear in the following order: required test or GPA, minimum score (if required)/median score of students entering in 2015–2016.

Program	Degree	GRE-V	GRE-Q	GRE-Writing	GRE-Subject	Undergraduate GPA	Last 2 Years GPA	Psychology GPA	Master's GPA
Industrial/ Organizational Psychology	PhD	NA/NA	NA/NA	NA/NA	Not specified	Not specified	NA/NA	Not specified	NA/NA

Admissions *(con't.)*

Program	Degree	GRE-V	GRE-Q	GRE-Writing	GRE-Subject	Under-graduate GPA	Last 2 Years GPA	Psychol-ogy GPA	Master's GPA
Social Psychology	PhD	NA/NA	NA/NA	NA/NA	Not specified	Not specified	NA/NA	Not specified	NA/NA
Cognitive Psychology	PhD	NA/NA	NA/NA	NA/NA	Not specified	Not specified	NA/NA	Not specified	NA/NA
Cognitive Neuroscience	PhD	NA/NA	NA/NA	NA/NA	Not specified	Not specified	NA/NA	Not specified	NA/NA
Clinical Psychology	PhD	NA/NA	NA/NA	NA/NA	Not specified	Not specified	NA/NA	NA/NA	NA/NA
Developmental Psychology	PhD	NA/NA	NA/NA	NA/NA	Not specified	Not specified	NA/NA	Not specified	NA/NA
Industrial/ Organizational Psychology	MA/MS	NA/NA	NA/NA	NA/NA	Not specified	Not specified	NA/NA	Not specified	Not specified
Developmental Psychology	MA/MS	Not specified	Not specified	Not specified	Not specified	Not specified	NA/NA	Not specified	Not specified

Admissions Requirements:

Degree	GRE	GRE-Subject	Letters of Recom-mendation	Research Statement	Writing Sample	CV	Interview
Master's/Specialist	Required	None	3	Required	None	None	None
Doctoral	Required	None	3	Required	None	None	None

Admissions Criteria:

GRE scores—high
Research experience—medium
Work experience—low
Clinically related public service—medium
GPA—high

Letters of recommendation—high
Interview—medium
Statement of goals and objectives—medium
Undergraduate psychology preparation—high

For additional information on admission requirements, visit https://uwaterloo.ca/psychology/future-graduate-students/applying.

Department Demographics

	Male (PT)	Female (PT)	Total	African-American/ Black (PT)	Hispanic/ Latino (PT)	Asian/ Pacific Islander (PT)	American Indian/ Alaska Native (PT)	Caucasian/ White (PT)	Unknown	Multiethnic (PT)	ADA (PT)	Int'l (PT)
Students	43 (0)	61 (4)	0	0 (0)	0 (0)	0 (0)	0 (0)	0 (0)	0 (0)	0 (0)	0 (0)	0 (0)

Financial Information/Assistance

Tuition: For information on tuition costs, visit https://uwaterloo.ca/finance/student-accounts/tuition-fee-schedules. Tuition is subject to change.

Doctoral:
State residents: $8,648 per academic year.
Nonstate residents: $21,218 per academic year.

Master's:
State residents: $8,648 per academic year.
Nonstate residents: $21,218 per academic year.

Financial Assistance:

	Teaching Assistantship (% Receiving)	Teaching Assistantship Tuition Remission	Research Assistantship (% Receiving)	Research Assistantship Tuition Remission	Fellowship (% Receiving)	Fellowship Tuition Remission
First-Year Student	NA (NA)	NA	NA (NA)	NA	NA (NA)	NA
Advanced Student	NA (NA)	NA	NA (NA)	NA	NA (NA)	NA

For additional information on financial assistance, visit https://uwaterloo.ca/psychology/current-graduate-students/funding-awards.

Employment of Department Graduates

Master's:
Enrolled in a psychology doctoral program: 3
Enrolled in another graduate/professional program: 1
Employed in other positions at a higher education institution: 1
Employed in business or industry: 1
Other employment position: 1
Total: 7

Doctoral:
Enrolled in a postdoctoral residency/fellowship: 4
Employed in independent practice: 1
Employed in academic position at a 2-year/4-year college: 1
Employed in other positions at a higher education institution: 3
Employed in business or industry: 7
Employed in a hospital/medical center: 3
Other employment position: 1
Total: 20

Additional Information

Housing and Day Care: On-campus housing is available. See the following website for more information: https://uwaterloo.ca/housing/single-grad-families. On-campus day care facilities are available. See the following website for more information: https://uwaterloo.ca/human-resources/support-employees/campus-resources.

Information for Students With Physical Disabilities: See the following website: http://uwaterloo.ca/disability-services/.

Special Facilities or Resources: Within a large four-story building, extensive laboratory facilities are available for animal and human research. Additional educational and resource centers operate in conjunction with academic and research programs. Research requiring special populations is often carried out at community institutions under the supervision of faculty members. Considerable investment has been made to technical services including excellent computer facilities and consulting personnel who are available for student research and courses.

Application Information: Graduate Studies Office, University of Waterloo, 200 University Avenue West, Waterloo, ON N2L 3G1. *Fee:* $100. *Online application:* https://uwaterloo.ca/graduate-studies/application-admission/apply-online.

Wilfrid Laurier University
Department of Psychology
75 University Avenue, West
Waterloo, ON N2L 3C5
Telephone: (519) 884-1970, Ext. 3371
Chairperson: Dr. Rudy Eikelboom

E-mail: rsharkey@wlu.ca
Web: http://www.wlu.ca/science/psychology

Orientation, Objectives, and Emphasis of Department
Graduate students can obtain an MA, MS, or PhD in one of five fields: (1) Behavioural Neuroscience, (2) Cognitive Neuroscience, (3) Community Psychology, (4) Social, and (5) Developmental. The objective of the MA, MS, and PhD programs in the fields of Behavioural, Cognitive, Social, and Developmental Psychology is to develop competence in designing, conducting, and evaluating research in these fields. Five half-credit courses and a thesis constitute the degree requirements in these MA/MS programs. The purpose of these programs is to prepare students for doctoral studies, or for employment in an environment requiring research skills. Students in good standing can be considered for admission to the PhD programs in these area, which involves seven half-credit courses, two comprehensive papers, and a dissertation. In the field of Community Psychology, the objective is to train scientist–practitioners with skills in community collaboration. Students receive training in theory, research, and practice that will enable them

to analyze the implications of social change for the delivery of community services. Six half-credit courses and a thesis are required for the Community Psychology MA degree.

Programs and Degrees Offered

Program	Degree	Application Deadline	Applica-tions Received	Accepted	New Admits Enrolled (PT)	Total Enrolled (PT)	Degrees Awarded in 2014–2015	Median Years to Complete Degree	Dismissed/ Withdrew
Behavioural Neuroscience	MA/MS	January 15 (Fall)	6	0	0 (0)	2 (0)	4	1.5	0
Cognitive Neuroscience	MA/MS	January 15 (Fall), Rolling	12	3	3 (0)	9 (0)	3	1.7	0
Community Psychology	MA/MS	January 15 (Fall)	19	9	8 (1)	14 (1)	4	1.9	1
Social Psychology	MA/MS	January 15 (Fall)	36	4	4 (0)	10 (0)	0		0
Developmental Psychology	MA/MS	January 15 (Fall)	27	2	2 (0)	6 (0)	7	1.9	0
Behavioural Neuroscience	PhD	January 15 (Fall)	0	0	0	4	0		0
Cognitive Neuroscience	PhD	January 15 (Fall)	3	2	2 (0)	7 (0)	1	3.5	0
Community Psychology	PhD	January 15 (Fall)	4	0	0 (0)	9 (1)	1	3.5	0
Developmental Psychology	PhD	January 15 (Fall)	4	1	1 (0)	8 (4)	1	5.3	0
Social Psychology	PhD	January 15 (Fall)	3	0	0 (0)	12 (0)	1	3.8	0

Admissions

Entries appear in the following order: required test or GPA, minimum score (if required)/median score of students entering in 2015–2016.

Program	Degree	GRE-V	GRE-Q	GRE-Writing	GRE-Subject	Under-graduate GPA	Last 2 Years GPA	Psychol-ogy GPA	Master's GPA
Behavioural Neuroscience	MA/MS	Not specified	Not specified	Not specified	Not specified	Not specified	Not specified	Not specified	Not specified
Cognitive Neuroscience	MA/MS	Not specified	Not specified	Not specified	Not specified	Not specified	Not specified	Not specified	Not specified
Community Psychology	MA/MS	Not specified	Not specified	Not specified	Not specified	Not specified	Not specified	Not specified	Not specified
Social Psychology	MA/MS	Not specified	Not specified	Not specified	Not specified	Not specified	Not specified	Not specified	Not specified
Developmental Psychology	MA/MS	Not specified	Not specified	Not specified	Not specified	Not specified	Not specified	Not specified	Not specified
Behavioural Neuroscience	PhD	Not specified	Not specified	Not specified	Not specified	Not specified	Not specified	Not specified	Not specified
Cognitive Neuroscience	PhD	Not specified	Not specified	Not specified	Not specified	Not specified	Not specified	Not specified	Not specified
Community Psychology	PhD	Not specified	Not specified	Not specified	Not specified	Not specified	Not specified	Not specified	Not specified

Admissions *(con't.)*

Program	Degree	GRE-V	GRE-Q	GRE-Writing	GRE-Subject	Under-graduate GPA	Last 2 Years GPA	Psychol-ogy GPA	Master's GPA
Developmental Psychology	PhD	Not specified	Not specified	Not specified	Not specified	Not specified	Not specified	Not specified	Not specified
Social Psychology	PhD	Not specified	Not specified	Not specified	Not specified	Not specified	Not specified	Not specified	Not specified

Admissions Requirements:

Degree	GRE	GRE-Subject	Letters of Recom-mendation	Research Statement	Writing Sample	CV	Interview
Master's/Specialist	Required	None	2	Required	Required	Required	Required
Doctoral	Required	Optional	2	Required	Required	Required	Required

Please note if these criteria vary for different programs: GRE test score required for applicants to the behavioural neuroscience, cognitive neuroscience and social psychology fields. Two academic letters of references are required for each field except Community Psychology which also requires one professional reference.

Admissions Criteria:
Research experience—medium
Work experience—low
Clinically related public service—low
GPA—high

Letters of recommendation—high
Interview—medium
Statement of goals and objectives—high

For additional information on admission requirements, visit http://www.wlu.ca/academics/faculties/faculty-of-science/department-of-psychology/index.html.

Department Demographics

	Male (PT)	Female (PT)	Total	African-American/ Black (PT)	Hispanic/ Latino (PT)	Asian/ Pacific Islander (PT)	American Indian/ Alaska Native (PT)	Caucasian/ White (PT)	Unknown	Multiethnic (PT)	ADA (PT)	Int'l (PT)
Students	18 (3)	63 (3)	0	0 (0)	0 (0)	8 (1)	1 (0)	72 (5)	0 (0)	0 (0)	0 (0)	1 (0)

Financial Information/Assistance

Tuition: For information on tuition costs, visit http://www.wlu.ca/graduate-and-postdoctoral-studies/tuition-and-fees.html. Tuition is subject to change.

Doctoral:
State residents: $8,570 per academic year.
Nonstate residents: $18,897 per academic year.

Master's:
State residents: $8,570 per academic year.
Nonstate residents: $18,897 per academic year.

Financial Assistance:

	Teaching Assistantship (% Receiving)	Teaching Assistantship Tuition Remission	Research Assistantship (% Receiving)	Research Assistantship Tuition Remission	Fellowship (% Receiving)	Fellowship Tuition Remission
First-Year Student	NA (NA)	NA	NA (NA)	NA	NA (NA)	NA
Advanced Student	NA (NA)	NA	NA (NA)	NA	NA (NA)	NA

For additional information on financial assistance, visit http://wlu.ca/graduate-and-postdoctoral-studies/funding-at-a-glance/index.html.

Employment of Department Graduates

No information provided.

Additional Information

Housing and Day Care: On-campus housing is available. No on-campus day care facilities are available.

Information for Students With Physical Disabilities: See the following website: http://www.wlu.ca/accessible-learning/index.html.

Special Facilities or Resources: The department has free unlimited access to the university computer, microprocessors, extensive electromechanical equipment, full-time electronics research associate, full-time field supervisor, and access to a wide variety of field settings for research and consultation.

Application Information: Fee: $100. *Online application:* http://www.wlu.ca/admissions-toolkits/graduate-admissions-toolkit/index.html.

Windsor, University of
Psychology
Faculty of Arts, Humanities & Social Sciences
401 Sunset Avenue
Windsor, ON N9B 3P4
Telephone: (519) 253-3000, x 2232
Department Head: Greg Chung Yan

E-mail: gcy@uwindsor.ca
Web: http://www.uwindsor.ca/psychology

Orientation, Objectives, and Emphasis of Department
The mission of the graduate programs in the Department of Psychology is to provide graduate students with a foundation of theory, research, and practice to enable them to conduct research and/or apply psychology in a variety of settings including universities, private practice, schools, health/medical organizations, social service agencies, businesses, and basic/applied research firms. Graduate offerings are divided into two areas: clinical and applied social. Students applying for the clinical program apply directly into specialty tracks of adult clinical, child clinical, or clinical neuropsychology. Each of the areas combines theoretical, substantive, and methodological coursework with a variety of applied training experiences.

Programs and Degrees Offered

Program	Degree	Application Deadline	Applications Received	Accepted	New Admits Enrolled (PT)	Total Enrolled (PT)	Degrees Awarded in 2014–2015	Median Years to Complete Degree	Dismissed/ Withdrew
Applied Social Psychology	PhD	December 1 (Fall)	11	4	2 (0)	26 (0)	4	6.3	0
Clinical Psychology	PhD	December 1 (Fall)	89	12	12 (0)	89 (0)	21	7	0

CPA Accreditation
Clinical PhD (Doctor of Philosophy).

Doctoral Degree (PhD Clinical Psychology): For those doctoral students for whom a professional internship was required in this program prior to graduation:
Total students who applied for an internship: 14
Total students who obtained an internship: 14
Total students who obtained a paid internship: 14
Total students who obtained an unpaid internship: 0
Total students who were placed in APA/CPA-accredited internships: 14
Total students placed in internships not APA/CPA-accredited, but listed with the Association of Psychology Postdoctoral and Internship Centers (APPIC): 0
Total students placed in internships conforming to guidelines of the Council of Directors of School Psychology Programs (CDSPP): 0
Total students placed in internships that were not APA/CPA-accredited, APPIC or CDSSP listed: 0

Internships/Practica

A wide variety of clinical practica are available in the Windsor-Detroit area, and clinical students obtain additional summer practicum positions across the country. Students are placed in predoctoral internships throughout Canada and the U.S. Applied Social students obtain practica and internships in business and industry, community and health-related agencies.

Admissions

Entries appear in the following order: required test or GPA, minimum score (if required)/median score of students entering in 2015–2016.

Program	Degree	GRE-V	GRE-Q	GRE-Writing	GRE-Subject	Under-graduate GPA	Last 2 Years GPA	Psychol-ogy GPA	Master's GPA
Applied Social Psychology	PhD	NA/NA	NA/NA	NA/NA	NA/NA	NA/NA	NA/NA	NA/NA	Not specified
Clinical Psychology	PhD	NA/NA	NA/NA	NA/NA	Not specified	NA/NA	NA/NA	Not specified	NA/NA

Admissions Requirements:

Degree	GRE	GRE-Subject	Letters of Recommendation	Research Statement	Writing Sample	CV	Interview
Doctoral	Required	Optional	3	Required	Optional	Required	Required

Admissions Criteria:

GRE scores—high
Research experience—medium
Work experience—low
Clinically related public service—medium
GPA—high

Letters of recommendation—high
Interview—high
Statement of goals and objectives—medium
Undergraduate psychology preparation—high
Honours thesis—high

For additional information on admission requirements, visit http://www1.uwindsor.ca/psychology/88/applying-for-admission-to-our-graduate-programs.

Department Demographics

	Male (PT)	Female (PT)	Total	African-American/ Black (PT)	Hispanic/ Latino (PT)	Asian/ Pacific Islander (PT)	American Indian/ Alaska Native (PT)	Caucasian/ White (PT)	Unknown (PT)	Multiethnic (PT)	ADA (PT)	Int'l (PT)
Students	20 (0)	93 (0)	0	0 (0)	0 (0)	0 (0)	0 (0)	0 (0)	0 (0)	0 (0)	0 (0)	10 (0)

Financial Information/Assistance

Tuition: For information on tuition costs, visit http://web2.uwindsor.ca/finance/fee-estimator/. Tuition is subject to change. Additional fees are assessed to students beyond the costs of tuition for the following: Compulsory incidental fees each term cover a variety of services. Cost approximately $1,500–$1,900 per year.

Doctoral:
State residents: $7,666 per academic year.
Nonstate residents: $18,015 per academic year.

Financial Assistance:

	Teaching Assistantship (% Receiving)	Teaching Assistantship Tuition Remission	Research Assistantship (% Receiving)	Research Assistantship Tuition Remission	Fellowship (% Receiving)	Fellowship Tuition Remission
First-Year Student	$10,270 (90)	NA	$10,270 (9)	NA	$7,000 (95)	Partial
Advanced Student	$11,275 (70)	NA	$11,275 (10)	NA	$6,000 (100)	Partial

Employment of Department Graduates

Doctoral:
Enrolled in a postdoctoral residency/fellowship: 3
Employed in independent practice: 3
Employed in an academic position at a university: 3
Employed in other positions at a higher education institution: 3
Employed in business or industry: 1
Employed in government agency: 2
Employed in a community mental health/counseling center: 4
Employed in a hospital/medical center: 5
Do not know: 4
Total: 28

Additional Information

Housing and Day Care: On-campus housing is available. See the following website for more information: http://www.uwindsor.ca/residence. No on-campus day care facilities are available.

Information for Students With Physical Disabilities: See the following website: http://www.uwindsor.ca/disability/.

Special Facilities or Resources: The Department of Psychology's PhD program is unique in that all areas of specialization (Applied Social, Clinical Neuropsychology, Adult Clinical and Child Clinical) have an applied focus. Applied training and research resources include the Psychological Services & Research Centre, the Child Study Centre, the Emotion-Cognition Research Laboratory, Health Research Centre for the Study of Violence Against Women, Health & Well-Being Laboratory, Concussion Clinic, Studies in the Psychology of Appearance, the Student Counselling Centre, and the Psycholinguistics and Neurolinguistics Laboratory. There are faculty–student research groups in the areas of body image and eating disorders, trauma and psychotherapy, problem gambling, computer-mediated communication, feminist research, emotional competence, culture and diversity, health psychology, neuropsychoanalysis, aging, applied memory, quantitative and educational psychology, multicultural and counselling research, and autism. The department is affiliated with the Summit Centre for Preschool Children with Autism. The university campus has wireless computer access throughout. Researchers have access to a participant pool and web-based participant recruitment as well as systems that allow for web-based data collection.

Application Information: Office of the Registrar, Graduate Studies Division, University of Windsor, 401 Sunset Avenue, Windsor, ON, Canada N9B 3P4. *Fee:* $105. *Online application:* http://horizon.ouac.on.ca/windsor/grad.

York University
Graduate Program in Psychology
4700 Keele Street, Room 297, Behavioural Science Building
Toronto, ON M3J 1P3
Telephone: (416) 736-5290
Director, Graduate Program in Psychology. Dr. Adrienne Perry

E-mail: gradpsyc@yorku.ca
Web: http://psychology.gradstudies.yorku.ca

Orientation, Objectives, and Emphasis of Department
Strength and depth are emphasized in the areas of brain, behaviour and cognitive science (learning, perception, physiological, psychometrics); clinical; clinical-development; developmental cognitive processes; history and theory; quantitative methods; and social-personality. The department prepares students as researchers and practitioners in a given area.

Programs and Degrees Offered

Program	Degree	Application Deadline	Applications Received	Accepted	New Admits Enrolled (PT)	Total Enrolled (PT)	Degrees Awarded in 2014–2015	Median Years to Complete Degree	Dismissed/ Withdrew
Brain, Behaviour and Cognitive Sciences	PhD	December 9 (Fall)	6	5	5 (0)	18 (0)	2	6	1
Clinical Psychology	PhD	December 9 (Fall)	40	8	8 (0)	51 (17)	14	6	1
Clinical-Developmental Psychology	PhD	December 9 (Fall)	19	7	7 (0)	40 (12)	8	6	1
Developmental Science	PhD	December 9 (Fall)	3	1	1 (0)	14 (0)	1	5	0
History and Theory Of Psychology	PhD	December 9 (Fall)	2	2	2 (0)	8 (2)	0		1
Social and Personality Psychology	PhD	December 9 (Fall)	13	4	4 (0)	13 (2)	3	5	2
Quantitative Methods	PhD	December 9 (Fall)	1	1	1 (0)	1 (0)	0		1

CPA Accreditation

Clinical PhD (Doctor of Philosophy). Clinical PhD (Doctor of Philosophy).

Doctoral Degree (PhD Clinical Psychology): For those doctoral students for whom a professional internship was required in this program prior to graduation:
Total students who applied for an internship: 9
Total students who obtained an internship: 9
Total students who obtained a paid internship: 9
Total students who obtained an unpaid internship: 0
Total students who were placed in APA/CPA-accredited internships: 8
Total students placed in internships not APA/CPA-accredited, but listed with the Association of Psychology Postdoctoral and Internship Centers (APPIC): 0
Total students placed in internships conforming to guidelines of the Council of Directors of School Psychology Programs (CDSPP): 0
Total students placed in internships that were not APA/CPA-accredited, APPIC or CDSSP listed: 1

Doctoral Degree (PhD Clinical-Developmental Psychology): For those doctoral students for whom a professional internship was required in this program prior to graduation:
Total students who applied for an internship: 8
Total students who obtained an internship: 8
Total students who obtained a paid internship: 8
Total students who obtained an unpaid internship: 0
Total students who were placed in APA/CPA-accredited internships: 7
Total students placed in internships not APA/CPA-accredited, but listed with the Association of Psychology Postdoctoral and Internship Centers (APPIC): 0
Total students placed in internships conforming to guidelines of the Council of Directors of School Psychology Programs (CDSPP): 0
Total students placed in internships that were not APA/CPA-accredited, APPIC or CDSSP listed: 1

Internships/Practica

Doctoral internships are available; practicum work is done on a half-time basis during the academic year and, when possible, full-time during the summer. Research practica, and a clinical practicum as part of the Clinical Area's programme, are done on campus. Clinical internships are available in the York University Psychology Clinic (newly opened) and a variety of hospitals, clinics, and counseling centers in the city and elsewhere.

Admissions

Entries appear in the following order: required test or GPA, minimum score (if required)/median score of students entering in 2015–2016.

Program	Degree	GRE-V	GRE-Q	GRE-Writing	GRE-Subject	Under-graduate GPA	Last 2 Years GPA	Psychol-ogy GPA	Master's GPA
Brain, Behaviour and Cognitive Sciences	PhD	Not specified	Not specified	Not specified	Not specified	Not specified	NA/NA	Not specified	NA/NA
Clinical Psychology	PhD	Not specified	Not specified	Not specified	Not specified	Not specified	NA/NA	Not specified	NA/NA
Clinical-Developmental Psychology	PhD	Not specified	Not specified	Not specified	Not specified	Not specified	NA/NA	Not specified	NA/NA
Developmental Science	PhD	Not specified	Not specified	Not specified	Not specified	Not specified	NA/NA	Not specified	NA/NA
History and Theory of Psychology	PhD	Not specified	Not specified	Not specified	Not specified	Not specified	NA/NA	Not specified	NA/NA
Social and Personality Psychology	PhD	Not specified	Not specified	Not specified	Not specified	Not specified	NA/NA	Not specified	NA/NA
Quantitative Methods	PhD	Not specified	Not specified	Not specified	Not specified	Not specified	NA/NA	Not specified	NA/NA

Admissions Requirements:

Degree	GRE	GRE-Subject	Letters of Recom-mendation	Research Statement	Writing Sample	CV	Interview
Master's/Specialist	Required	Required	2	Required	None	Required	Optional
Doctoral	None	None	2	Required	None	Required	Optional

Please note if these criteria vary for different programs: The usual prerequisite for admission to the PhD program is a master's degree in psychology. Normally students may not enter the PhD program until they have completed all the master's requirements including the thesis. Students completing their MA at York are not automatically accepted into the PhD program; they must make a formal, but internal, application for advancement into the PhD program.

Admissions Criteria:

GRE scores—high
Research experience—high
Work experience—medium
Clinically related public service—low
GPA—high

Letters of recommendation—high
Interview—medium
Statement of goals and objectives—medium
Undergraduate psychology preparation—high

For additional information on admission requirements, visit http://psychology.gradstudies.yorku.ca/apply/.

Department Demographics

	Male (PT)	Female (PT)	Total	African-American/ Black (PT)	Hispanic/ Latino (PT)	Asian/ Pacific Islander (PT)	American Indian/ Alaska Native (PT)	Caucasian/ White (PT)	Unknown	Multiethnic (PT)	ADA (PT)	Int'l (PT)
Students	42 (2)	196 (34)	0	0 (0)	0 (0)	0 (0)	0 (0)	0 (0)	204 (36)	0 (0)	0 (0)	0 (0)

Financial Information/Assistance

Tuition: For information on tuition costs, visit http://sfs.yorku.ca/fees/courses. Tuition is subject to change.

Doctoral:
State residents: $5,530 per academic year.
Nonstate residents: $19,645 per academic year.

Master's:
State residents: $5,530 per academic year.
Nonstate residents: $20,511 per academic year.

Financial Assistance:

	Teaching Assistantship (% Receiving)	Teaching Assistantship Tuition Remission	Research Assistantship (% Receiving)	Research Assistantship Tuition Remission	Fellowship (% Receiving)	Fellowship Tuition Remission
First-Year Student	$9,408 (100)	NA	$6,000 (NA)	NA	$6,000 (NA)	NA
Advanced Student	$16,870 (100)	NA	$10,000 (NA)	NA	NA (NA)	NA

For additional information on financial assistance, visit http://psychology.gradstudies.yorku.ca/financial/.

Employment of Department Graduates

Master's:
Enrolled in a psychology doctoral program: 28
Enrolled in another graduate/professional program: 1
Do not know: 3
Total: 32

Doctoral:
Enrolled in a postdoctoral residency/fellowship: 3
Employed in a hospital/medical center: 3
Not seeking employment: 1
Do not know: 12
Total: 19

Additional Information

Housing and Day Care: On-campus housing is available. See the following website for more information: http://studenthousing.info.yorku.ca/yorkapts/. On-campus day care facilities are available. See the following website for more information: http://daycare.info.yorku.ca/; http://www.yorku.ca/children/.

Information for Students With Physical Disabilities: See the following website: http://ds.info.yorku.ca/.

Special Facilities or Resources: The department has a vivarium; substantial computing facilities; audiovisual equipment; and observational laboratories with two-way mirrors.

Application Information: Office of Graduate Admissions, P.O. Box GA2300, York University, 4700 Keele Street, Toronto, ON M3J 1P3, Canada. *Fee:* $100. *Online application:* http://futurestudents.yorku.ca/graduate/apply_now.

A

Applied Behavior Analysis
Arizona State University (MA/MS—terminal)
Auburn University (MA/MS—terminal)
Baylor University (EdS, PhD)
California State University, Fresno (MA/MS—terminal)
California State University, Northridge (MA/MS—terminal)
California State University, Sacramento (MA/MS—terminal)
Central Missouri, University of (MA/MS—terminal)
Central Washington University (MA/MS—terminal)
City University of New York: Graduate Center (PhD)
Florida Institute of Technology (MA/MS—terminal, PhD)
Florida State University (MA/MS—terminal)
Florida, University of (PhD)
Georgian Court University (MA/MS—terminal)
Jacksonville State University (MA/MS—terminal)
Long Island University (MA/MS—terminal, Other)
Manitoba, University of (PhD)
Maryland, University of, Baltimore County (MA/MS—terminal)
Massachusetts, University of, Dartmouth (MA/MS—terminal, Other)
Massachusetts, University of, Lowell (MA/MS—terminal)
Missouri State University (MA/MS—terminal)
Nebraska, University of, Omaha (MA/MS—terminal)
Nevada, University of, Reno (PhD)
North Carolina, University of, Wilmington (MA/MS—terminal)
Nova Southeastern University (MA/MS—terminal)
Pacific, University of the (MA/MS—terminal)
Pepperdine University (MA/MS—terminal)
Philadelphia College of Osteopathic Medicine (Other)
Texas, University of, Rio Grande Valley (Other)
Texas, University of, San Antonio (MA/MS—terminal)
The Chicago School of Professional Psychology (MA/MS, PhD, Respecialization Diploma)
Wayne State University (Other)
William James College (Other)
Wisconsin, University of, Milwaukee (MA/MS—terminal, PhD)

B

Behavioral Psychology
American University (PhD)
Boston College (PhD)
California State University, Northridge (MA/MS—terminal)
California, University of, Berkeley (PhD)
California, University of, Los Angeles (PhD)
City University of New York: Graduate Center (PhD)
Claremont Graduate University (MA/MS—terminal, PhD)
Colorado, University of, Boulder (PhD)
Cornell University (PhD)
Drexel University (MA/MS—terminal)
Eastern Michigan University (MA/MS—terminal)
Florida State University (MA/MS—terminal)
Florida, University of (PhD)
Georgia State University (PhD)
Hofstra University (PhD)
Illinois State University (MA/MS—terminal)
Indiana University (PhD)
Iowa, University of (PhD)
Jacksonville State University (MA/MS—terminal)
Kansas, University of (MA/MS—terminal, PhD)
Long Island University (MA/MS—terminal)
Manitoba, University of (PhD)
Maryland, University of, Baltimore County (MA/MS—terminal)
Massachusetts, University of, Dartmouth (Other)
Miami, University of (PhD)
Michigan State University (PhD)
Middle Tennessee State University (MA/MS—terminal)
Minnesota State University-Mankato (MA/MS—terminal)
Minnesota, University of (PhD)
Nebraska, University of, Omaha (MA/MS)
New Mexico, University of (PhD)
North Carolina, University of, Wilmington (MA/MS—terminal)
Northeastern University (PhD)
Ohio State University (PhD)
Pacific, University of the (MA/MS—terminal)
Pepperdine University (MA/MS—terminal)
Rhode Island, University of (PhD)

Southern California, University of, Keck School of Medicine (PhD)
Stanford University (PhD)
State University of New York, Binghamton University (PhD)
Texas, University of, Austin (PhD)
The Chicago School of Professional Psychology (PhD, Respecialization Diploma)
The College at Brockport—State University of New York (MA/MS—terminal)
Toronto, University of (MA/MS, PhD)
University at Buffalo, State University of New York (PhD)
Utah State University (PhD)
Washington University in St. Louis (PhD)
Washington, University of (PhD)
West Virginia University (PhD)
Wilfrid Laurier University (MA/MS—terminal, PhD)
Wisconsin, University of, Milwaukee (MA/MS—terminal, PhD)

Biological Psychology
Arizona, University of (PhD)
British Columbia, University of (PhD)
California, University of, Berkeley (PhD)
California, University of, Davis (PhD)
Florida, University of (PhD)
George Mason University (MA/MS—terminal, PhD)
Georgia, University of (PhD)
Illinois, University of, Chicago (PhD)
Illinois, University of, Urbana Champaign (PhD)
Johns Hopkins University (PhD)
Louisiana State University (PhD)
Maine, University of (PhD)
Michigan, University of (PhD)
Minnesota, University of (PhD)
Nebraska, University of, Lincoln (PhD)
Nebraska, University of, Omaha (MA/MS—terminal)
New Mexico, University of (PhD)
New Orleans, University of (PhD)
North Carolina, University of, Chapel Hill (PhD)
Oklahoma State University (PhD)
Pittsburgh, University of (PhD)
Stony Brook University (PhD)
Texas, University of, Austin (PhD)
Virginia Polytechnic Institute and State University (PhD)
Virginia, University of (PhD)
Washington State University (PhD)
Washington, University of (PhD)
Wayne State University (PhD)
Wisconsin, University of, Madison (PhD)

C

Child and Adolescent Psychology
Alabama, University of, at Birmingham (PhD)

1349

South Florida, University of (PhD)
Southern California, University of (PhD)
Southern Illinois University Carbondale (PhD)
Southern Illinois University Edwardsville (MA/MS—terminal)
Southern Methodist University (PhD)
Spalding University (PsyD)
St. John's University (PhD)
State University of New York, Binghamton University (PhD)
Stony Brook University (PhD)
Suffolk University (PhD, Respecialization Diploma)
Syracuse University (PhD)
Temple University (PhD)
Tennessee, University of, Knoxville (PhD)
Texas A&M University (PhD)
Texas A&M University—Commerce (MA/MS—terminal)
Texas Southwestern Medical Center, The University of (PhD)
Texas Tech University (PhD)
Texas, University of, Austin (PhD)
Texas, University of, Permian Basin (MA/MS—terminal)
Texas, University of, Rio Grande Valley (MA/MS—terminal)
Texas, University of, Tyler (MA/MS—terminal)
The Catholic University of America (PhD)
The Chicago School of Professional Psychology (PsyD)
The College at Brockport—State University of New York (MA/MS—terminal)
The New School for Social Research (PhD)
Toledo, University of (PhD)
Towson University (MA/MS—terminal)
Tulsa, University of (MA/MS—terminal, PhD)
Uniformed Services University of the Health Sciences (PhD)
University at Albany, State University of New York (PhD)
University at Buffalo, State University of New York (PhD)
Utah State University (PhD)
Utah, University of (PhD)
Vanderbilt University (PhD)
Vermont, University of (PhD)
Victoria, University of (PhD)
Virginia Commonwealth University (PhD)
Virginia Consortium Program in Clinical Psychology (PhD)
Virginia Polytechnic Institute and State University (PhD)
Virginia, University of (PhD)
Washburn University (MA/MS—terminal)
Washington State University (PhD)
Washington University in St. Louis (PhD)
Washington, University of (PhD)
Waterloo, University of (PhD)
Wayne State University (PhD)

West Chester University of Pennsylvania (MA/MS—terminal)
West Virginia University (PhD)
Western Illinois University (MA/MS—terminal)
Wheaton College (PsyD)
Wichita State University (PhD)
Widener University (PsyD)
William James College (PsyD, Respecialization Diploma)
William Paterson University (MA/MS—terminal, PsyD)
Windsor, University of (PhD)
Wisconsin School of Professional Psychology (PsyD)
Wisconsin, University of, Madison (PhD)
Wisconsin, University of, Milwaukee (PhD)
Wright Institute (PsyD)
Wright State University (PsyD)
Wyoming, University of (PhD)
Xavier University (PsyD)
Yale University (PhD)
Yeshiva University (PhD, PsyD)
York University (PhD)

Cognitive Psychology

Alabama, University of (PhD)
Arizona State University (MA/MS—terminal, PhD)
Arizona, University of (PhD)
Auburn University (PhD)
Ball State University (MA/MS—terminal)
Boston College (PhD)
Boston University (PhD)
Bowling Green State University (PhD)
British Columbia, University of (PhD)
Brown University (PhD)
Calgary, University of (PhD)
California, University of, Berkeley (PhD)
California, University of, Davis (PhD)
California, University of, Los Angeles (PhD)
California, University of, Riverside (PhD)
California, University of, Santa Cruz (PhD)
Carnegie Mellon University (PhD)
Chicago, University of (PhD)
Claremont Graduate University (MA/MS—terminal, PhD)
Colorado State University (PhD)
Colorado, University of, Boulder (PhD)
Connecticut, University of (PhD)
Cornell University (PhD)
Dayton, University of (MA/MS—terminal)
Delaware, University of (PhD)
Denver, University of (PhD)
Drexel University (PhD)
Duke University (PhD)
Emory University (PhD)
Florida International University (PhD)
Florida State University (PhD)
George Mason University (MA/MS—terminal, PhD)
George Washington University (PhD)
Georgetown University (PhD)
Georgia State University (PhD)
Guelph, University of (MA/MS, PhD)

Hawaii, University of, Manoa (PhD)
Houston, University of (PhD)
Illinois State University (MA/MS—terminal)
Illinois, University of, Chicago (PhD)
Illinois, University of, Urbana Champaign (PhD)
Indiana University (PhD)
Iowa State University (PhD)
Iowa, University of (PhD)
Johns Hopkins University (PhD)
Kansas State University (PhD)
Kansas, University of (PhD)
Lehigh University (PhD)
Louisiana State University (PhD)
Louisville, University of (PhD)
Manitoba, University of (PhD)
Maryland, University of (PhD)
Massachusetts, University of (PhD)
Massachusetts, University of, Lowell (PhD)
Memphis, University of (PhD)
Michigan State University (PhD)
Michigan, University of (PhD)
Middle Tennessee State University (MA/MS—terminal)
Minnesota, University of (PhD)
Mississippi State University (PhD)
Missouri, University of (PhD)
Missouri, University of, St. Louis (PhD)
Nebraska, University of, Lincoln (PhD)
Nevada, University of, Reno (PhD)
New Hampshire, University of (PhD)
New Mexico State University (PhD)
New Mexico, University of (PhD)
New York University, Graduate School of Arts and Science (PhD)
North Carolina, University of, Chapel Hill (PhD)
North Carolina, University of, Greensboro (PhD)
North Dakota State University (PhD)
North Texas, University of (PhD)
Northeastern University (PhD)
Northern Illinois University (PhD)
Northwestern University (PhD)
Notre Dame, University of (PhD)
Ohio State University (PhD)
Ohio University (PhD)
Oklahoma, University of (PhD)
Oregon, University of (MA/MS—terminal, PhD)
Pennsylvania State University (PhD)
Pittsburgh, University of (PhD)
Purdue University (PhD)
Queen's University (MA/MS, PhD)
Rice University (PhD)
Saskatchewan, University of (PhD)
South Florida, University of (PhD)
Southern California, University of (PhD)
Southern Illinois University Carbondale (PhD)
Stanford University (PhD)
State University of New York, Binghamton University (PhD)
Stony Brook University (PhD)
Syracuse University (PhD)
Temple University (PhD)

Texas A&M University (PhD)
Texas A&M University—Commerce
(MA/MS—terminal)
Texas Tech University (PhD)
Texas, University of, Austin (PhD)
The New School for Social Research
(PhD)
Toledo, University of (PhD)
Toronto, University of (MA/MS, PhD)
University at Albany, State University of
New York (PhD)
University at Buffalo, State University of
New York (PhD)
Utah, University of (PhD)
Vanderbilt University (PhD)
Victoria, University of (PhD)
Virginia, University of (PhD)
Washington State University (PhD)
Washington University in St. Louis (PhD)
Washington, University of (PhD)
Waterloo, University of (PhD)
Wayne State University (PhD)
Wilfrid Laurier University (MA/MS—
terminal, PhD)
Wisconsin, University of, Madison (PhD)
Wisconsin, University of, Oshkosh
(MA/MS—terminal)
Wyoming, University of (PhD)
Yale University (PhD)
York University (PhD)

Community Counseling
Alabama, University of, at Birmingham
(PhD)
Alliant International University: Fresno
(MA/MS—terminal)
Alliant International University: San
Francisco (MA/MS—terminal)
American University (PhD)
Cleveland State University (MEd)
Georgia School of Professional
Psychology at Argosy University
(PsyD)
Georgia State University (PhD)
Georgian Court University (MA/MS—
terminal)
Gonzaga University (Other)
Houston, University of (PhD)
Lehigh University (MEd)
Loyola University of Chicago (MA/MS—
terminal, MEd)
Oklahoma City University (MEd)
Oklahoma, University of (MEd)
Suffolk University (PhD, Respecialization
Diploma)
Texas, University of, Austin (PhD)
Texas, University of, Tyler (MA/MS—
terminal)
University at Buffalo, State University of
New York (MA/MS—terminal, Other)
Windsor, University of (PhD)
Wisconsin, University of, Milwaukee
(MA/MS—terminal)

Community Psychology
Alaska, University of,
Anchorage/Fairbanks (PhD)
California, University of, Berkeley (PhD)

Central Connecticut State University
(MA/MS—terminal)
Cincinnati, University of (MA/MS—
terminal)
Cornell University (PhD)
DePaul University (PhD)
George Mason University (PhD)
George Washington University (PhD)
Georgia State University (PhD)
Hawaii, University of, Manoa (PhD)
Hofstra University (PsyD)
Illinois, University of, Chicago (PhD)
Illinois, University of, Urbana Champaign
(PhD)
Maryland, University of, Baltimore
County (PhD)
Massachusetts, University of, Lowell
(MA/MS—terminal)
Metropolitan State University (MA/MS—
terminal)
Miami University of Ohio (PhD)
Michigan State University (PhD)
New Haven, University of (MA/MS—
terminal)
New York University (MA/MS—terminal)
North Carolina State University (PhD)
Portland State University (PhD)
Sage Colleges, The (MA/MS—terminal)
Seton Hall University (EdS)
South Carolina, University of (PhD)
Texas A&M International University
(MA/MS—terminal)
Vanderbilt University (MEd, PhD)
Virginia, University of (PhD)
Wayne State University (MA/MS—
terminal)
Western Illinois University (MA/MS—
terminal)
Wichita State University (PhD)
Wilfrid Laurier University (MA/MS—
terminal, PhD)

Comparative Psychology
York University (PhD)

Consulting Psychology
Alliant International University: Fresno
(MA/MS—terminal, PsyD)
Alliant International University: Los
Angeles (MA/MS—terminal, PhD)
Alliant International University: San
Diego (MA/MS—terminal, PhD)
New Haven, University of (MA/MS—
terminal)
The Chicago School of Professional
Psychology (PhD)
Wayne State University (MA/MS—
terminal, PhD)

Counseling Psychology
Adelphi University (MA/MS—terminal)
Akron, University of (PhD)
Alaska Pacific University (MA/MS—
terminal, PsyD)
Alliant International University: Fresno
(MA/MS—terminal)
Alliant International University: San
Francisco (MA/MS—terminal)

Angelo State University (MA/MS—
terminal)
Arizona State University (PhD)
Assumption College (MA/MS—terminal)
Auburn University (PhD)
Ball State University (PhD)
Baltimore, University of (MA/MS—
terminal, Other)
Boston College (PhD)
Brenau University (MA/MS—terminal)
Central Arkansas, University of (PhD)
Central Oklahoma, University of
(MA/MS—terminal)
Central Washington University
(MA/MS—terminal)
Chestnut Hill College (MA/MS—terminal)
Citadel, The (MA/MS—terminal)
Cleveland State University (PhD)
Colorado State University (PhD)
Columbia University (MEd, PhD)
Denver, University of (PhD)
Fayetteville State University (MA/MS—
terminal)
Florida International University
(MA/MS—terminal)
Florida State University (PhD)
Florida, University of (PhD)
Fordham University (PhD)
Francis Marion University (MA/MS—
terminal)
Frostburg State University (MA/MS—
terminal)
Georgia State University (PhD)
Georgia, University of (PhD)
Goddard College (MA/MS—terminal)
Golden Gate University (MA/MS—
terminal)
Houston, University of (MEd, PhD)
Humboldt State University (MA/MS—
terminal)
Illinois State University (MA/MS—
terminal)
Illinois, University of, Urbana Champaign
(PhD)
Indiana University (PhD)
Iowa State University (PhD)
Iowa, University of (PhD)
James Madison University (MA/MS—
terminal)
John F. Kennedy University (MA/MS—
terminal)
Kansas, University of (MA/MS—terminal,
PhD)
Kentucky, University of (EdS, MA/MS—
terminal, PhD)
Lehigh University (MEd, PhD)
Louisville, University of (PhD)
Loyola University Maryland (MA/MS—
terminal)
Loyola University of Chicago (PhD)
Marquette University (PhD)
Maryland, University of (PhD)
McGill University (PhD)
Memphis, University of (PhD)
Miami, University of (PhD)
Midwestern State University (MA/MS—
terminal)
Millersville University (MA/MS—terminal)

Minnesota, University of (MA/MS—terminal, PhD)
Missouri, University of, Columbia (MEd, PhD)
Missouri, University of, Kansas City (PhD)
Morehead State University (MA/MS—terminal)
Nebraska, University of, Lincoln (PhD)
New Mexico State University (PhD)
New York University (PhD)
North Dakota, University of (PhD)
North Texas, University of (PhD)
Northern Arizona University (PhD)
Northern Colorado, University of (PhD)
Oklahoma State University (PhD)
Oklahoma, University of (PhD)
Oregon, University of (PhD)
Our Lady of the Lake University (PsyD)
Pennsylvania, University of (Other)
Puget Sound, University of (MEd)
Purdue University (PhD)
Radford University (MA/MS—terminal, PsyD)
Rivier University (PsyD)
Roosevelt University (MA/MS—terminal)
Rosalind Franklin University of Medicine and Science (MA/MS—terminal)
Sage Colleges, The (MA/MS—terminal, Other)
Saint Francis, University of (MA/MS—terminal, MEd)
Saint Mary's University of Minnesota (MA/MS—terminal, Other, PsyD)
Santa Clara University (MA/MS—terminal)
Seton Hall University (PhD)
South Alabama, University of (PhD)
Southern Illinois University Carbondale (PhD)
Southern Oregon University (MA/MS—terminal)
Springfield College (PsyD)
St. Thomas, University of (MA/MS—terminal, PsyD)
State University of New York at New Paltz (Other)
State University of New York, University of Albany (PhD)
Tennessee, University of, Knoxville (PhD)
Texas A&M International University (MA/MS—terminal)
Texas A&M University (PhD)
Texas Tech University (PhD)
Texas Woman's University (MA/MS—terminal, PhD)
Texas, University of, Austin (PhD)
The Chicago School of Professional Psychology (MA/MS—terminal, PhD)
Towson University (MA/MS—terminal)
University at Buffalo, State University of New York (PhD)
Utah State University (PhD)
Utah, University of (MEd, PhD)
Virginia Commonwealth University (PhD)
Wayne State University (MA/MS—terminal)

West Georgia, University of (MA/MS—terminal)
West Virginia University (PhD)
Western Michigan University (MA/MS—terminal, PhD)
William James College (MA/MS—terminal)
William Paterson University (MA/MS—terminal)
Wisconsin, University of, Madison (MA/MS—terminal, PhD)
Wisconsin, University of, Milwaukee (PhD)
Yeshiva University (MA/MS—terminal)

D

Developmental Psychology

Akron, University of (PhD)
Alabama, University of (PhD)
Alabama, University of, at Birmingham (PhD)
American International College (MA/MS—terminal)
Arizona State University (PhD)
Boston College (MA/MS—terminal, PhD)
Boston University (PhD)
Bowling Green State University (PhD)
British Columbia, University of (PhD)
California, University of, Berkeley (PhD)
California, University of, Davis (PhD)
California, University of, Los Angeles (PhD)
California, University of, Merced (PhD)
California, University of, Riverside (PhD)
California, University of, Santa Cruz (PhD)
Carnegie Mellon University (PhD)
Chicago, University of (PhD)
Claremont Graduate University (MA/MS—terminal, PhD)
Clark University (PhD)
Cleveland State University (PhD)
Connecticut, University of (PhD)
Cornell University (PhD)
Denver, University of (PhD)
DePaul University (PhD)
Duke University (PhD)
Florida International University (PhD)
Florida State University (PhD)
Florida, University of (PhD)
Fordham University (MA/MS—terminal, PhD)
George Mason University (MA/MS—terminal, PhD)
Georgetown University (PhD)
Georgia State University (PhD)
Guelph, University of (MA/MS, PhD)
Hawaii, University of, Manoa (PhD)
Humboldt State University (MA/MS—terminal)
Illinois State University (MA/MS—terminal)
Illinois, University of, Urbana Champaign (PhD)
Indiana University (MA/MS—terminal, PhD)

Iowa, University of (PhD)
Johns Hopkins University (PhD)
Kansas, University of (PhD)
Louisville, University of (PhD)
Loyola University of Chicago (PhD)
Maine, University of (MA/MS—terminal)
Manitoba, University of (PhD)
Maryland, University of (PhD)
Maryland, University of, Baltimore County (PhD)
Massachusetts, University of (PhD)
Massachusetts, University of, Boston (PhD)
Massachusetts, University of, Lowell (MA/MS—terminal, PhD)
McGill University (PhD)
Miami University of Ohio (PhD)
Miami, University of (PhD)
Michigan, University of (PhD)
Millersville University (MA/MS—terminal, MEd)
Minnesota, University of (PhD)
Missouri, University of (PhD)
Nebraska, University of, Lincoln (PhD)
Nebraska, University of, Omaha (MA/MS—terminal, PhD)
New Hampshire, University of (PhD)
New Mexico, University of (PhD)
New Orleans, University of (PhD)
New York University (PhD)
North Carolina State University (PhD)
North Carolina, University of, Chapel Hill (PhD)
North Carolina, University of, Greensboro (MA/MS—terminal, PhD)
North Dakota State University (PhD)
Northern Illinois University (PhD)
Northwestern University (PhD)
Notre Dame, University of (PhD)
Ohio State University (PhD)
Oklahoma State University (PhD)
Oregon, University of (PhD)
Pennsylvania State University (PhD)
Pennsylvania, University of (MA/MS—terminal, PhD)
Pittsburgh, University of (PhD)
Portland State University (PhD)
Queen's University (MA/MS, PhD)
Saint Louis University (PhD)
San Diego State University (MA/MS—terminal)
San Francisco State University (MA/MS—terminal)
Saskatchewan, University of (PhD)
Southern California, University of (PhD)
Stanford University (PhD)
Temple University (PhD)
Texas A&M University (PhD)
Texas, University of, Austin (Other, PhD)
Texas, University of, Dallas (MA/MS—terminal, PhD)
The Catholic University of America (PhD)
The New School for Social Research (PhD)
Toronto, University of (MA/MS, PhD)
Tulane University (PhD)
Utah, University of (PhD)

Vanderbilt University (PhD)
Victoria, University of (PhD)
Virginia Commonwealth University (PhD)
Virginia Polytechnic Institute and State
   University (PhD)
Virginia, University of (PhD)
Washington University in St. Louis (PhD)
Washington, University of (PhD)
Waterloo, University of (MA/MS—
   terminal, PhD)
West Virginia University (PhD)
Wilfrid Laurier University (MA/MS—
   terminal, PhD)
Wisconsin, University of, Madison (PhD)
Wisconsin, University of, Milwaukee
   (MA/MS—terminal, PhD)
Wyoming, University of (PhD)
Yale University (PhD)
York University (PhD)

E

Educational Psychology
Alliant International University: Irvine
   (MA/MS terminal, PsyD)
Alliant International University: Los
   Angeles (MA/MS—terminal, PsyD)
Alliant International University: San
   Diego (MA/MS—terminal, PsyD)
Alliant International University: San
   Francisco (MA/MS—terminal, PsyD)
American International College (EdD,
   MA/MS)
Ball State University (PhD)
Baylor University (PhD)
Boston College (MA/MS—terminal, PhD)
City University of New York: Graduate
   School and University Center (PhD)
Claremont Graduate University
   (MA/MS—terminal)
Denver, University of (MA/MS)
George Mason University (MA/MS—
   terminal, Other, PhD)
Hawaii, University of (MEd, PhD)
Houston, University of (PhD)
Illinois, University of, Chicago (MEd,
   PhD)
Indiana University (MA/MS—terminal,
   PhD)
Iowa, University of (MA/MS—terminal,
   PhD)
Kansas, University of (EdS, MEd, PhD)
Kentucky, University of (MA/MS—
   terminal, PhD)
Marist College (MA/MS—terminal)
Maryland, University of (PhD)
McGill University (PhD)
Michigan, University of (PhD)
Mississippi State University (MA/MS—
   terminal, PhD)
Missouri, University of, Columbia
   (MA/MS—terminal, MEd, PhD)
Northern Arizona University (MEd)
Oklahoma State University (PhD)
Oklahoma, University of (MEd, PhD)
State University of New York, University
   of Albany (MA/MS—terminal, PhD)

Texas A&M University (PhD)
Texas A&M University—Commerce
   (PhD)
Texas, University of, Austin (Other)
The Chicago School of Professional
   Psychology (EdD)
University at Buffalo, State University of
   New York (MA/MS—terminal, PhD)
Utah, University of (MA/MS—terminal,
   MEd)
Washington State University (MA/MS—
   terminal, PhD)
Wayne State University (PhD)
Wisconsin, University of, Madison (PhD)
Wisconsin, University of, Milwaukee
   (PhD)

Environmental Psychology
Victoria, University of (PhD)

Experimental Psychology (Applied)
Alabama, University of, at Huntsville
   (MA/MS—terminal)
Alberta, University of (MA/MS, PhD)
Angelo State University (MA/MS—
   terminal)
Appalachian State University (MA/MS—
   terminal)
Auburn University (MA/MS—terminal)
California State University, Fresno
   (MA/MS—terminal)
California State University, Long Beach
   (MA/MS—terminal)
Central Florida, University of (PhD)
Central Michigan University (PhD)
Central Washington University
   (MA/MS—terminal)
Clemson University (PhD)
Cleveland State University (MA/MS—
   terminal)
East Tennessee State University (PhD)
Florida International University (PhD)
Fordham University (PhD)
Fort Hays State University (MA/MS—
   terminal)
Hawaii, University of, Manoa (PhD)
Kent State University (PhD)
Louisiana, University of, Lafayette
   (MA/MS—terminal)
Louisiana, University of, Monroe
   (MA/MS—terminal)
Marietta College (MA/MS—terminal)
Missouri State University (MA/MS—
   terminal)
Nebraska, University of, Omaha
   (MA/MS—terminal)
New Mexico State University (MA/MS—
   terminal, PhD)
North Carolina, University of,
   Greensboro (MA/MS—terminal)
North Carolina, University of, Wilmington
   (MA/MS—terminal)
North Dakota, University of (PhD)
North Texas, University of (PhD)
Old Dominion University (PhD)
Pacific University (MA/MS—terminal)
Penn State Harrisburg (MA/MS—
   terminal)

Pennsylvania, University of (PhD)
Regina, University of (MA/MS—terminal,
   PhD)
Rice University (PhD)
Ryerson University (MA/MS, PhD)
Saint Joseph's University (MA/MS—
   terminal)
Shippensburg University (MA/MS—
   terminal)
South Carolina, University of (PhD)
Southeastern Louisiana University
   (MA/MS—terminal)
Tennessee, University of, Chattanooga
   (MA/MS—terminal)
Texas, University of, Permian Basin
   (MA/MS—terminal)
The Catholic University of America
   (PhD)
University at Albany, State University of
   New York (PhD)
West Florida, University of (MA/MS—
   terminal)
West Virginia University (PhD)
Wichita State University (PhD)

Experimental Psychology (General)
Alabama, University of, at Huntsville
   (MA/MS—terminal)
American International College
   (MA/MS—terminal)
American University (MA/MS—terminal)
Appalachian State University (MA/MS—
   terminal)
Arkansas, University of (PhD)
Brandeis University (MA/MS—terminal,
   PhD)
Brown University (PhD)
Bucknell University (MA/MS—terminal)
California State University, Fresno
   (MA/MS—terminal)
California State University, Fullerton
   (MA/MS—terminal)
California State University, Long Beach
   (MA/MS—terminal)
California State University, Northridge
   (MA/MS—terminal)
California State University, San Marcos
   (MA/MS—terminal)
California, University of, San Diego
   (PhD)
Carnegie Mellon University (PhD)
Central Connecticut State University
   (MA/MS—terminal)
Central Michigan University (MA/MS—
   terminal)
Central Missouri, University of (MA/MS—
   terminal)
Central Oklahoma, University of
   (MA/MS—terminal)
Central Washington University
   (MA/MS—terminal)
Chicago, University of (PhD)
Cincinnati, University of (PhD)
City University of New York: Brooklyn
   College (MA/MS—terminal)
Claremont Graduate University (PhD)
Colorado, University of, Colorado
   Springs (MA/MS—terminal)

Dalhousie University (MA/MS, PhD)
Eastern Kentucky University (MA/MS—terminal)
Eastern Michigan University (MA/MS—terminal)
Eastern Washington University (MA/MS—terminal)
Fayetteville State University (MA/MS—terminal)
Florida Atlantic University (MA/MS—terminal, PhD)
Fort Hays State University (MA/MS—terminal)
Fuller Theological Seminary (PhD)
Georgia Southern University (MA/MS—terminal)
Harvard University (PhD)
Idaho State University (PhD)
Indianapolis, University of (MA/MS—terminal)
Iona College (MA/MS—terminal)
James Madison University (MA/MS—terminal)
Kent State University (PhD)
Kentucky, University of (PhD)
Long Island University (MA/MS—terminal)
Louisiana, University of, Lafayette (MA/MS—terminal)
Louisiana, University of, Monroe (MA/MS—terminal)
Maine, University of (MA/MS—terminal)
Marietta College (MA/MS—terminal)
Massachusetts, University of, Dartmouth (MA/MS—terminal)
McGill University (PhD)
Memphis, University of (MA/MS—terminal, PhD)
Middle Tennessee State University (MA/MS—terminal)
Minnesota, University of, Duluth (MA/MS—terminal)
Mississippi, University of (PhD)
Missouri State University (MA/MS—terminal)
Missouri, University of, Kansas City (PhD)
Montana State University Billings (MA/MS—terminal)
Montana, University of (PhD)
Nevada, University of, Las Vegas (PhD)
New Brunswick, University of (PhD)
New Mexico State University (MA/MS—terminal)
New York University, Graduate School of Arts and Science (PhD)
North Carolina, University of, Wilmington (MA/MS—terminal)
North Dakota, University of (PhD)
North Florida, University of (MA/MS—terminal)
Northern Arizona University (MA/MS—terminal)
Northern Michigan University (MA/MS—terminal)
Nova Southeastern University (MA/MS—terminal)

Oakland University (MA/MS—terminal, PhD)
Oklahoma, University of (MA/MS—terminal, PhD)
Old Dominion University (MA/MS—terminal)
Ottawa, University of (PhD)
Pace University (MA/MS—terminal)
Palo Alto University (MA/MS—terminal)
Pennsylvania, University of (PhD)
Pepperdine University (MA/MS—terminal)
Pittsburg State University (MA/MS—terminal)
Queen's University (MA/MS, PhD)
Radford University (MA/MS—terminal)
Rhode Island College (MA/MS—terminal)
Rhode Island, University of (PhD)
Rivier University (MA/MS—terminal)
Ryerson University (MA/MS, PhD)
Saint Joseph's University (MA/MS—terminal)
Sam Houston State University (MA/MS—terminal)
San Francisco State University (MA/MS—terminal)
Seton Hall University (MA/MS—terminal)
Shippensburg University (MA/MS—terminal)
South Alabama, University of (MA/MS—terminal)
Southeastern Louisiana University (MA/MS—terminal)
Southern Connecticut State University (MA/MS—terminal)
St. John's University (MA/MS—terminal)
State University of New York at New Paltz (MA/MS—terminal)
Stephen F. Austin State University (MA/MS—terminal)
Syracuse University (PhD)
Tennessee, University of, Knoxville (MA/MS—terminal, PhD)
Texas A&M University—Commerce (MA/MS—terminal)
Texas State University (MA/MS—terminal)
Texas, University of, Arlington (PhD)
Texas, University of, Permian Basin (MA/MS—terminal)
Texas, University of, Rio Grande Valley (MA/MS—terminal)
The Catholic University of America (MA/MS—terminal)
The College at Brockport—State University of New York (MA/MS—terminal)
Towson University (MA/MS—terminal)
Tufts University (PhD)
University at Buffalo, State University of New York (MA/MS—terminal)
Utah State University (PhD)
Utah, University of (PhD)
Vermont, University of (PhD)
Victoria, University of (PhD)
Villanova University (MA/MS—terminal)

Wake Forest University (MA/MS—terminal)
Wayne State University (PhD)
West Chester University of Pennsylvania (MA/MS—terminal)
Western Illinois University (MA/MS—terminal)
Western Kentucky University (MA/MS—terminal)
William and Mary, College of (MA/MS—terminal)
Wisconsin, University of, Madison (PhD)
Wisconsin, University of, Oshkosh (MA/MS—terminal)
Xavier University (MA/MS—terminal)

F

Family Psychology

Alliant International University: San Diego (PhD, PsyD, Respecialization Diploma)
Antioch University Santa Barbara (PsyD)
Arizona State University (PhD)
Azusa Pacific University (PsyD)
Fuller Theological Seminary (PsyD)
North Carolina State University (PhD)
Seton Hill University (MA/MS—terminal)
The Chicago School of Professional Psychology (MA/MS—terminal, PsyD)
Wayne State University (MA/MS—terminal)

Forensic Psychology

American International College (MA/MS—terminal)
Carleton University (MA/MS—terminal, PhD)
Central Oklahoma, University of (MA/MS—terminal)
City University of New York: John Jay College of Criminal Justice (MA/MS—terminal, Other)
Denver, University of (MA/MS—terminal)
Drexel University (PhD)
Fairleigh Dickinson University, Metropolitan Campus (MA/MS—terminal)
Fielding Graduate University (PhD)
Florida International University (PhD)
Fordham University (MA/MS—terminal)
George Washington University (MA/MS—terminal)
Louisiana, University of, Monroe (MA/MS—terminal)
Marymount University (MA/MS—terminal)
Missouri State University (MA/MS—terminal, Other)
Nebraska, University of, Lincoln (PhD)
North Dakota, University of (MA/MS—terminal)
Nova Southeastern University (MA/MS—terminal)
Roger Williams University (MA/MS—terminal)
Sage Colleges, The (Other)

Sam Houston State University (PhD)
Saskatchewan, University of (PhD)
The Chicago School of Professional
  Psychology (MA/MS—terminal, PsyD)
Tulsa, University of (MA/MS—terminal)
Valparaiso University (MA/MS—terminal)
Wyoming, University of (PhD)

G

Gender Psychology
Hawaii, University of, Manoa (PhD)
Texas Woman's University (MA/MS—
  terminal, PhD)

General Psychology (Theory, History, and Philosophy)
Adelphi University (MA/MS—terminal)
Angelo State University (MA/MS—
  terminal)
Boston University (MA/MS—terminal)
Brandeis University (MA/MS—terminal)
Central Missouri, University of (MA/MS—
  terminal)
Central Oklahoma, University of
  (MA/MS—terminal)
Dayton, University of (MA/MS—terminal)
DePaul University (MA/MS—terminal)
Divine Mercy University (MA/MS—
  terminal)
Drexel University (MA/MS—terminal)
Duke University (MA/MS—terminal)
Eastern Kentucky University (MA/MS—
  terminal)
Fairleigh Dickinson University,
  Metropolitan Campus (MA/MS—
  terminal)
Goddard College (MA/MS—terminal)
Long Island University (MA/MS—
  terminal)
Marshall University (MA/MS—terminal)
Memphis, University of (MA/MS—
  terminal)
New Mexico Highlands University
  (MA/MS—terminal)
New York University, Graduate School
  of Arts and Science (MA/MS—
  terminal)
North Florida, University of (MA/MS—
  terminal)
Northcentral University (MA/MS, PhD)
Northern Iowa, University of (MA/MS—
  terminal)
Nova Southeastern University (MA/MS—
  terminal)
Pace University (MA/MS—terminal)
Palo Alto University (MA/MS—terminal)
Pittsburg State University (MA/MS—
  terminal)
Regent University (MA/MS—terminal)
Saint Francis, University of (MA/MS—
  terminal)
Sam Houston State University
  (MA/MS—terminal)
Seton Hall University (MA/MS—terminal)
Shippensburg University (MA/MS—
  terminal)

Southern Connecticut State University
  (MA/MS—terminal)
State University of New York at New
  Paltz (MA/MS—terminal)
Stephen F. Austin State University
  (MA/MS—terminal)
Stony Brook University (MA/MS)
The Catholic University of America
  (MA/MS—terminal)
The Chicago School of Professional
  Psychology (MA/MS—terminal)
The New School for Social Research
  (MA/MS—terminal)
University at Buffalo, State University of
  New York (MA/MS—terminal)
West Chester University of Pennsylvania
  (MA/MS—terminal)
West Florida, University of (MA/MS—
  terminal)
York University (PhD)

Geropsychology
Akron, University of (PhD)
Cleveland State University (PhD)
Colorado, University of, Colorado
  Springs (PhD)
Florida, University of (PhD)
North Carolina State University (PhD)
Washington University in St. Louis (PhD)
West Virginia University (PhD)

H

Health Psychology
Alabama, University of, at Birmingham
  (PhD)
Alliant International University: Fresno
  (PhD)
British Columbia, University of (PhD)
California State University, Dominguez
  Hills (MA/MS—terminal)
California, University of, Irvine (PhD)
California, University of, Los Angeles
  (PhD)
California, University of, Merced (PhD)
California, University of, Riverside (PhD)
Carnegie Mellon University (PhD)
Central Connecticut State University
  (MA/MS—terminal)
Claremont Graduate University
  (MA/MS—terminal)
Colorado, University of, Denver (PhD)
Connecticut, University of (PhD)
Duke University (PhD)
East Carolina University (PhD)
George Washington University (PhD)
Guelph, University of (MA/MS, PhD)
Houston, University of (PhD)
Indiana University-Purdue University
  Indianapolis (PhD)
Indianapolis, University of (PsyD)
Iowa, University of (PhD)
Kansas, University of (PhD)
Kentucky, University of (PhD)
Mercer University Health Sciences
  Center (PhD, PsyD)

Michigan, University of, Dearborn
  (MA/MS—terminal)
Missouri, University of, Kansas City
  (PhD)
New Mexico State University (PhD)
New Mexico, University of (PhD)
North Carolina State University (PhD)
North Carolina, University of, Charlotte
  (PhD)
North Dakota State University (PhD)
Northern Arizona University (MA/MS—
  terminal)
Northwestern University (PhD)
Northwestern University Feinberg School
  of Medicine (PhD)
Ohio State University (PhD)
Ohio University (PhD)
Old Dominion University (PhD)
Philadelphia College of Osteopathic
  Medicine (MA/MS—terminal, Other)
Pittsburgh, University of (PhD)
Rhode Island College (Other)
Rhode Island, University of (PhD)
Rosalind Franklin University of Medicine
  and Science (PhD)
Rowan University (PhD)
Southern California, University of, Keck
  School of Medicine (PhD)
Stony Brook University (PhD)
Syracuse University (PhD)
Texas, University of, Arlington (PhD)
Uniformed Services University of the
  Health Sciences (PhD)
Utah, University of (PhD)
Virginia Commonwealth University (PhD)
Wisconsin, University of, Milwaukee
  (MA/MS—terminal, PhD)
Wisconsin, University of, Stout
  (MA/MS—terminal)
Yeshiva University (PhD)

Human Development and Family Studies
Arizona State University (PhD)
Cornell University (PhD)
Illinois, University of, Urbana Champaign
  (PhD)
Iowa State University (MA/MS—terminal,
  PhD)
Pennsylvania State University (PhD)
Texas, University of, Austin (PhD)
Wisconsin, University of, Madison
  (MA/MS, PhD)

Human Factors
Arizona State University (MA/MS—
  terminal)
California State University, Long Beach
  (MA/MS—terminal)
Central Florida, University of (PhD)
Clemson University (MA/MS—terminal,
  PhD)
George Mason University (MA/MS—
  terminal, PhD)
Idaho, University of (MA/MS—terminal,
  PhD)
Illinois, University of, Urbana Champaign
  (PhD)

Kansas State University (PhD)
Missouri Western State University
(MA/MS—terminal)
New Mexico State University (PhD)
North Carolina State University (PhD)
Northern Michigan University (MA/MS—
terminal)
Old Dominion University (PhD)
Rice University (PhD)
Shippensburg University (MA/MS—
terminal)
South Dakota, University of (PhD)
Texas Tech University (PhD)
The Catholic University of America
(MA/MS—terminal)
Wichita State University (PhD)
Wright State University (PhD)

Humanistic Psychology
John F. Kennedy University (MA/MS—
terminal)
Seattle University (MA/MS—terminal)
West Georgia, University of (MA/MS—
terminal, PhD)

I

Industrial/Organizational Psychology
Akron, University of (MA/MS—terminal)
Alabama, University of, at Huntsville
(MA/MS—terminal)
Alliant International University: Fresno
(MA/MS—terminal, PsyD)
Alliant International University: Los
Angeles (MA/MS—terminal, PhD)
Alliant International University: San
Diego (MA/MS—terminal, PhD)
Angelo State University (MA/MS—
terminal)
Appalachian State University (MA/MS—
terminal)
Auburn University (PhD)
Austin Peay State University (MA/MS—
terminal)
Baltimore, University of (MA/MS—
terminal)
Bowling Green State University (PhD)
Calgary, University of (PhD)
California State University, Long Beach
(MA/MS—terminal)
California State University, Sacramento
(MA/MS—terminal)
Carnegie Mellon University (PhD)
Central Florida, University of (MA/MS—
terminal, PhD)
Central Michigan University (MA/MS—
terminal, PhD)
Cincinnati, University of (MA/MS—
terminal)
City University of New York: Brooklyn
College (MA/MS—terminal)
Claremont Graduate University
(MA/MS—terminal, PhD)
Clemson University (MA/MS—terminal,
PhD)
Cleveland State University (MA/MS—
terminal)

Colorado State University (MA/MS—
terminal, PhD)
Connecticut, University of (PhD)
DePaul University (PhD)
East Carolina University (MA/MS—
terminal, PhD)
Eastern Kentucky University (MA/MS—
terminal)
Emporia State University (MA/MS—
terminal)
Florida Institute of Technology
(MA/MS—terminal, PhD)
Florida International University (PhD)
George Mason University (MA/MS—
terminal, PhD)
George Washington University (PhD)
Georgia, University of (MA/MS—
terminal, PhD)
Golden Gate University (MA/MS—
terminal)
Guelph, University of (MA/MS, PhD)
Hartford, University of (MA/MS—
terminal)
Hofstra University (MA/MS—terminal,
PhD)
Houston, University of (PhD)
Illinois Institute of Technology (MA/MS—
terminal, PhD)
Illinois State University (MA/MS—
terminal)
Illinois, University of, Urbana Champaign
(MA/MS—terminal, PhD)
Indiana University-Purdue University
Indianapolis (MA/MS—terminal)
Iona College (MA/MS—terminal)
Kansas State University (MA/MS—
terminal, PhD)
La Salle University (MA/MS—terminal)
Lamar University-Beaumont (MA/MS—
terminal)
Louisiana State University (PhD)
Maryland, University of (PhD)
Michigan State University (PhD)
Middle Tennessee State University
(MA/MS—terminal)
Minnesota State University-Mankato
(MA/MS—terminal)
Minnesota, University of (PhD)
Missouri State University (MA/MS—
terminal)
Missouri, University of, St. Louis (PhD)
Nebraska, University of, Omaha
(MA/MS, MA/MS—terminal, PhD)
New Haven, University of (MA/MS—
terminal)
New York University, Graduate School
of Arts and Science (MA/MS—
terminal)
North Carolina State University (PhD)
North Carolina, University of, Charlotte
(MA/MS—terminal, PhD)
Northern Illinois University (PhD)
Northern Kentucky University (MA/MS—
terminal)
Northern Michigan University (MA/MS—
terminal)
Ohio University (PhD)

Oklahoma, University of (MA/MS—
terminal, PhD)
Old Dominion University (PhD)
Pennsylvania State University (PhD)
Philadelphia College of Osteopathic
Medicine (MA/MS—terminal)
Portland State University (PhD)
Purdue University (PhD)
Radford University (MA/MS—terminal)
Rice University (PhD)
Roosevelt University (MA/MS—terminal,
PhD)
Saint Louis University (PhD)
Saint Mary's University (MA/MS—
terminal, PhD)
San Diego State University (MA/MS—
terminal)
San Francisco State University
(MA/MS—terminal)
South Dakota State University
(MA/MS—terminal)
South Florida, University of (PhD)
Southeastern Louisiana University
(MA/MS—terminal)
Southern Illinois University Carbondale
(PhD)
Southern Illinois University Edwardsville
(MA/MS—terminal)
St. Cloud State University (MA/MS—
terminal)
Tennessee, University of, Chattanooga
(MA/MS—terminal)
Texas A&M University (PhD)
Texas, University of, Arlington (MA/MS—
terminal)
The Chicago School of Professional
Psychology (MA/MS—terminal, Other,
PhD)
Towson University (MA/MS—terminal)
Tulsa, University of (MA/MS—terminal,
PhD)
University at Albany, State University of
New York (MA/MS—terminal, PhD)
Virginia Polytechnic Institute and State
University (PhD)
Waterloo, University of (MA/MS—
terminal, PhD)
Wayne State University (MA/MS—
terminal, PhD)
West Chester University of Pennsylvania
(MA/MS—terminal)
West Florida, University of (MA/MS—
terminal)
Western Kentucky University (MA/MS—
terminal)
William James College (MA/MS—
terminal, PsyD)
Windsor, University of (PhD)
Wisconsin, University of, Stout
(MA/MS—terminal)
Wright State University (PhD)
Xavier University (MA/MS—terminal)

M

Marriage and Family Therapy
Alliant International University: Irvine
(MA/MS—terminal, PsyD)

Alliant International University: Los Angeles (MA/MS—terminal, PsyD)
Alliant International University: Sacramento (MA/MS—terminal, PsyD)
Alliant International University: San Diego (MA/MS—terminal, PsyD)
Alliant International University: San Francisco (MA/MS—terminal)
Azusa Pacific University (MA/MS—terminal)
California Polytechnic State University (MA/MS—terminal)
California State Polytechnic University-Pomona (MA/MS—terminal)
East Carolina University (PhD)
Geneva College (MA/MS—terminal)
Golden Gate University (MA/MS—terminal)
Gonzaga University (MA/MS—terminal)
John F. Kennedy University (MA/MS—terminal)
La Salle University (MA/MS—terminal)
Miami, University of (MA/MS—terminal)
Missouri, University of, Kansas City (MA/MS—terminal)
Our Lady of the Lake University (MA/MS—terminal)
Palo Alto University (MA/MS—terminal)
Pepperdine University (MA/MS—terminal)
Saint Mary's University of Minnesota (MA/MS—terminal)
Seton Hall University (EdS)
Seton Hill University (MA/MS—terminal)
Texas, University of, Tyler (MA/MS—terminal)
The Chicago School of Professional Psychology (MA/MS—terminal, PsyD)
Wheaton College (MA/MS—terminal)

Mental Health Counseling
Adelphi University (MA/MS—terminal)
Arizona State University (Other)
Ball State University (MA/MS—terminal)
Barry University (MA/MS—terminal)
Boston College (MA/MS—terminal)
Boston University (MA/MS—termina)
Bridgewater State University (MA/MS—terminal)
Central Arkansas, University of (MA/MS—terminal)
Central Washington University (MA/MS—terminal)
City University of New York: Brooklyn College (MA/MS—terminal)
City University of New York: John Jay College of Criminal Justice (MA/MS—terminal)
Denver, University of (MA/MS—terminal)
Fordham University (MEd)
Geneva College (MA/MS—terminal)
Georgian Court University (MA/MS—terminal)
Goddard College (MA/MS—terminal)
Gonzaga University (MA/MS—terminal)
Illinois Institute of Technology (MA/MS—terminal)

Immaculata University (MA/MS—terminal)
Indiana State University (MA/MS—terminal)
Indianapolis, University of (MA/MS—terminal)
Iona College (MA/MS—terminal)
James Madison University (EdS, PhD)
La Salle University (MA/MS—terminal)
Lehigh University (MEd)
Lewis University (MA/MS—terminal)
Louisiana State University Shreveport (MA/MS—terminal)
Loyola University of Chicago (Other)
Marist College (MA/MS—terminal)
Marquette University (MA/MS—terminal)
Miami, University of (MA/MS—terminal)
Missouri, University of, Kansas City (MA/MS—terminal)
New Mexico State University (MA/MS—terminal)
New York University (MA/MS—terminal)
North Dakota, University of (MA/MS—terminal)
Northern Arizona University (MA/MS—terminal)
Nova Southeastern University (MA/MS—terminal)
Palo Alto University (MA/MS—terminal)
Penn State Harrisburg (MA/MS—terminal)
Pennsylvania, University of (MEd)
Philadelphia College of Osteopathic Medicine (MA/MS—terminal)
Puget Sound, University of (MEd)
Rivier University (MA/MS)
Rosalind Franklin University of Medicine and Science (MA/MS—terminal)
Rowan University (MA/MS—terminal, Other)
Saint Francis, University of (MA/MS—terminal)
Seton Hall University (EdS, MA/MS—terminal)
Southern Oregon University (MA/MS—terminal)
State University of New York at New Paltz (MA/MS—terminal, Other)
State University of New York, University of Albany (MA/MS—terminal)
Suffolk University (MA/MS—terminal)
Texas, University of, Tyler (MA/MS—terminal)
The Chicago School of Professional Psychology (MA/MS—terminal)
University at Buffalo, State University of New York (MA/MS—terminal, Other)
Utah, University of (MEd)
Valparaiso University (MA/MS—terminal)
Vanderbilt University (MEd)
West Florida, University of (MA/MS—terminal)
Wheaton College (MA/MS—terminal)
William James College (MA/MS—terminal)
Yeshiva University (MA/MS—terminal)

Multicultural Psychology
Alliant International University: Los Angeles (PhD, PsyD)
Alliant International University: San Francisco (PhD, PsyD, Respecialization Diploma)
Cleveland State University (MA/MS—terminal)
Denver, University of (PsyD)
Fordham University (Other)
Hawaii, University of, Manoa (PhD)
John F. Kennedy University (PsyD)
New Mexico State University (EdS)
Pennsylvania, University of (PhD)
The Chicago School of Professional Psychology (MA/MS—terminal, PhD)
Vanderbilt University (PhD)

N

Neuropsychology
Arizona, University of (PhD)
Boston University (PhD)
Cincinnati, University of (PhD)
City University of New York: The Graduate Center (PhD)
Colorado State University (PhD)
Concordia University (PhD)
Connecticut, University of (PhD)
Drexel University (PhD)
Duke University (PhD)
Fielding Graduate University (Other)
Fuller Theological Seminary (PhD)
Georgia State University (PhD)
Houston, University of (PhD)
Michigan State University (PhD)
North Carolina, University of, Chapel Hill (PhD)
Philadelphia College of Osteopathic Medicine (Other)
Purdue University (PhD)
Saint Louis University (PhD)
South Florida, University of (PhD)
Temple University (PhD)
Texas, University of, Tyler (MA/MS—terminal)
Utah, University of (PhD)
Victoria, University of (PhD)
Wayne State University (PhD)
Yale University (PhD)

Neuroscience
Alabama, University of, at Birmingham (PhD)
American University (PhD)
Arizona State University (PhD)
Arizona, University of (PhD)
Auburn University (PhD)
Baylor University (PhD)
Boston College (PhD)
Bowling Green State University (PhD)
Brandeis University (PhD)
Brigham Young University (PhD)
British Columbia, University of (PhD)
California, University of, Berkeley (PhD)
California, University of, Davis (PhD)

California, University of, Los Angeles (PhD)
California, University of, Riverside (PhD)
Chicago, University of (PhD)
Colorado, University of, Boulder (PhD)
Concordia University (PhD)
Connecticut, University of (PhD)
Cornell University (PhD)
Dalhousie University (MA/MS, PhD)
Delaware, University of (PhD)
Denver, University of (PhD)
Drexel University (PhD)
Duke University (PhD)
Emory University (PhD)
Florida International University (PhD)
Florida State University (PhD)
Florida, University of (PhD)
George Mason University (MA/MS—terminal, PhD)
George Washington University (PhD)
Georgetown University (PhD)
Guelph, University of (MA/MS, PhD)
Hawaii, University of, Manoa (PhD)
Houston, University of (PhD)
Illinois, University of, Chicago (PhD)
Illinois, University of, Urbana Champaign (PhD)
Indiana University (PhD)
Indiana University-Purdue University Indianapolis (PhD)
Iowa, University of (PhD)
Johns Hopkins University (PhD)
Kansas State University (PhD)
Kansas, University of (PhD)
Louisiana State University (PhD)
Manitoba, University of (PhD)
Maryland, University of (PhD)
Massachusetts, University of, Boston (PhD)
Miami University of Ohio (PhD)
Miami, University of (PhD)
Michigan State University (PhD)
Michigan, University of (PhD)
Missouri, University of (PhD)
Missouri, University of, St. Louis (PhD)
Nebraska, University of, Omaha (MA/MS—terminal, PhD)
Nevada, University of, Las Vegas (PhD)
Nevada, University of, Reno (PhD)
New Hampshire, University of (PhD)
North Dakota State University (PhD)
Northeastern University (PhD)
Northern Illinois University (PhD)
Northern Michigan University (MA/MS—terminal)
Northwestern University (PhD)
Ohio State University (PhD)
Oregon, University of (PhD)
Pittsburgh, University of (PhD)
Rice University (PhD)
Saint Louis University (PhD)
San Francisco State University (MA/MS—terminal)
Saskatchewan, University of (PhD)
Seton Hall University (MA/MS—terminal)
South Alabama, University of (MA/MS—terminal)
Southern California, University of (PhD)

Southern Illinois University Carbondale (PhD)
Stanford University (PhD)
State University of New York, Binghamton University (PhD)
Stony Brook University (PhD)
Temple University (PhD)
Texas A&M University (PhD)
Texas Christian University (PhD)
Texas, University of, Austin (PhD)
Toronto, University of (MA/MS, PhD)
Tulane University (PhD)
University at Buffalo, State University of New York (PhD)
Vanderbilt University (PhD)
Victoria, University of (PhD)
Virginia Polytechnic Institute and State University (PhD)
Virginia, University of (PhD)
Washington, University of (PhD)
Waterloo, University of (PhD)
Wayne State University (PhD)
West Virginia University (PhD)
Wilfrid Laurier University (MA/MS—terminal, PhD)
Wisconsin, University of, Madison (PhD)
Wisconsin, University of, Milwaukee (PhD)
Yale University (PhD)
York University (PhD)

O

Other
Denver, University of (MA/MS—terminal)
Fielding Graduate University (MA/MS—terminal, Other, PhD)
Fuller Theological Seminary (PhD)
Georgetown University (PhD)
Victoria, University of (PhD)
Wisconsin, University of, Madison (PhD)

P

Personality Psychology
Boston College (PhD)
British Columbia, University of (PhD)
California, University of, Berkeley (PhD)
California, University of, Davis (PhD)
Cornell University (PhD)
Florida State University (PhD)
Illinois, University of, Chicago (PhD)
Illinois, University of, Urbana Champaign (PhD)
Iowa, University of (PhD)
Kansas State University (PhD)
Manitoba, University of (PhD)
Michigan State University (PhD)
Michigan, University of (PhD)
Minnesota, University of (PhD)
Missouri, University of (PhD)
New Hampshire, University of (PhD)
Northeastern University (PhD)
Northwestern University (PhD)
Oregon, University of (PhD)

Queen's University (MA/MS, PhD)
Texas A&M University (PhD)
Texas Tech University (PhD)
Toronto, University of (MA/MS, PhD)
Washington University in St. Louis (PhD)
Washington, University of (PhD)
Wisconsin, University of, Madison (PhD)
Yale University (PhD)
York University (PhD)

Physiological Psychology
Alabama, University of, at Birmingham (PhD)
Boston University (PhD)
Nebraska, University of, Lincoln (PhD)
Nebraska, University of, Omaha (PhD)
New Orleans, University of (PhD)
Northeastern University (PhD)
Northwestern University (PhD)
Ohio University (PhD)
Texas A&M University (PhD)
Tulane University (PhD)
West Virginia University (PhD)

Primary Care Psychology
Alliant International University: San Diego (PsyD)
American School of Professional Psychology at Argosy University/Southern California (PsyD)
Delaware, University of (PhD)
Fordham University (PhD)
George Fox University (PsyD)
Lewis University (MA/MS—terminal)
Miami University of Ohio (PhD)
Minnesota, University of (PhD)
Northern Illinois University (PhD)
Regent University (PsyD)
South Carolina, University of (PhD)
South Florida, University of (PhD)
Southern California, University of (PhD)
Wisconsin, University of, Milwaukee (PhD)
Xavier University (PsyD)

Psychoanalytic Psychology
Adelphi University (Other)
The New School for Social Research (PhD)
Yeshiva University (PsyD)

Psycholinguistics
Brown University (PhD)
Denver, University of (PhD)
Illinois, University of, Urbana Champaign (PhD)
Iowa, University of (PhD)
Northeastern University (PhD)

Psychopharmacology
Alliant International University: San Francisco (MA/MS—terminal)
Fairleigh Dickinson University, Metropolitan Campus (MA/MS—terminal)
Iowa, University of (PhD)

State University of New York,
  Binghamton University (PhD)

Q

Quantitative Psychology
Arizona State University (PhD)
Boston College (PhD)
British Columbia, University of (PhD)
California, University of, Davis (PhD)
California, University of, Los Angeles
  (PhD)
California, University of, Merced (PhD)
Claremont Graduate University
  (MA/MS—terminal, PhD)
Fordham University (MA/MS—terminal,
  PhD)
Hawaii, University of, Manoa (PhD)
Houston, University of (PhD)
Illinois State University (MA/MS—
  terminal)
Illinois, University of, Chicago (MEd)
Illinois, University of, Urbana Champaign
  (MA/MS—terminal, PhD)
Iowa State University (Other)
Iowa, University of (MA/MS—terminal,
  PhD)
James Madison University (MA/MS—
  terminal, PhD)
Kansas, University of (MEd, PhD)
Manitoba, University of (PhD)
Maryland, University of (PhD)
Middle Tennessee State University
  (MA/MS—terminal)
Minnesota, University of (PhD)
Missouri, University of (MA/MS—
  terminal, PhD)
Nebraska, University of, Lincoln (PhD)
New Mexico, University of (PhD)
North Carolina State University (PhD)
North Carolina, University of, Chapel Hill
  (PhD)
Notre Dame, University of (PhD)
Ohio State University (PhD)
Ohio University (PhD)
Oklahoma, University of (PhD)
Purdue University (PhD)
South Carolina, University of (PhD)
Southern California, University of (PhD)
Texas, University of, Austin (MEd, PhD)
University at Buffalo, State University of
  New York (MA/MS—terminal, Other,
  PhD)
Utah, University of (MA/MS—terminal,
  MEd, PhD)
Vanderbilt University (PhD)
Virginia, University of (PhD)
Washington, University of (PhD)
Wisconsin, University of, Madison (PhD)
Wisconsin, University of, Milwaukee
  (MA/MS—terminal, PhD)
York University (PhD)

R

Rehabilitation Psychology
Ball State University (MA/MS—terminal)
Illinois Institute of Technology (MA/MS—
  terminal, PhD)

North Dakota, University of (MA/MS—
  terminal)
University at Buffalo, State University of
  New York (MA/MS—terminal, Other)

S

School Counseling
Alliant International University: Irvine
  (MA/MS—terminal)
Alliant International University: Los
  Angeles (MA/MS—terminal)
Alliant International University: San
  Diego (MA/MS—terminal)
Boston College (MA/MS—terminal)
Cleveland State University (MEd)
Columbia University (MEd)
Denver, University of (MA/MS—terminal)
Fordham University (MEd)
Geneva College (MA/MS—terminal)
Gonzaga University (MA/MS—terminal,
  Other)
Immaculata University (MA/MS—
  terminal)
Indiana State University (MEd)
James Madison University (MA/MS—
  terminal, MEd)
Lehigh University (MEd)
Lewis University (MA/MS—terminal)
Louisiana State University Shreveport
  (MA/MS—terminal)
Loyola University of Chicago (MEd)
Marquette University (MA/MS—terminal)
Millersville University (MEd, Other)
New York University (MA/MS—terminal)
North Dakota, University of (MA/MS—
  terminal)
Northern Arizona University (MEd)
Nova Southeastern University (MA/MS—
  terminal)
Pennsylvania, University of (MEd, Other)
Pittsburg State University (MA/MS—
  terminal)
Puget Sound, University of (MEd)
Rivier University (MA/MS)
Roberts Wesleyan College (MA/MS—
  terminal)
Saint Francis, University of (MEd)
Seton Hall University (MA/MS—terminal)
State University of New York at New
  Paltz (MA/MS—terminal)
Texas, University of, Austin (Other)
Texas, University of, Tyler (MA/MS—
  terminal)
University at Buffalo, State University of
  New York (MEd, Other)
Utah State University (MEd)
Utah, University of (MEd)
Vanderbilt University (MEd)
Wisconsin, University of, Milwaukee
  (MA/MS—terminal)

School Psychology
Adelphi University (MA/MS—terminal)
Alfred University (MA/MS—terminal,
  PsyD)

Alliant International University: Irvine
  (MA/MS—terminal, PsyD)
Alliant International University: Los
  Angeles (MA/MS—terminal, PsyD)
Alliant International University: San
  Diego (MA/MS—terminal, PsyD)
Alliant International University: San
  Francisco (MA/MS—terminal, PsyD)
American International College (EdD)
Appalachian State University (MA/MS—
  terminal, Other)
Ball State University (EdS, PhD)
Baylor University (EdS)
California State University, Fresno (EdS)
California, University of, Berkeley (PhD)
California, University of, Santa Barbara
  (PhD)
Central Arkansas, University of
  (MA/MS—terminal, PhD)
Central Michigan University (Other, PhD)
Central Oklahoma, University of
  (MA/MS—terminal)
Central Washington University (EdS)
Cincinnati, University of (EdS, PhD)
Citadel, The (EdS)
City University of New York: Brooklyn
  College (MA/MS)
Claremont Graduate University (PhD)
Clemson University (PhD)
Cleveland State University (Other)
Columbia University (MEd, PhD)
Connecticut, University of (MA/MS—
  terminal, PhD)
Dayton, University of (EdS)
Denver, University of (EdS, PhD)
Duquesne University (PhD, PsyD)
East Carolina University (MA/MS—
  terminal, PhD)
Eastern Kentucky University (Other)
Eastern Washington University (EdS)
Emporia State University (EdS)
Fairleigh Dickinson University,
  Metropolitan Campus (MA/MS—
  terminal, PsyD)
Florida State University (EdS, PhD)
Fordham University (Other, PhD)
Fort Hays State University (EdS,
  MA/MS—terminal)
Francis Marion University (Other)
Gallaudet University (Other)
George Mason University (MA/MS—
  terminal)
Georgia State University (EdS, PhD)
Georgia, University of (PhD)
Georgian Court University (MA/MS)
Hartford, University of (MA/MS—
  terminal)
Hofstra University (PsyD)
Houston, University of (PhD)
Humboldt State University (MA/MS—
  terminal)
Illinois State University (Other, PhD)
Illinois, University of, Urbana Champaign
  (PhD)
Immaculata University (EdS)
Indiana State University (EdS, PhD)
Indiana University (EdS, PhD)
Iona College (MA/MS—terminal)

Social Psychology

Purdue University (PhD)
Queen's University (MA/MS, PhD)
San Diego State University (MA/MS—
terminal)
San Francisco State University
(MA/MS—terminal)
Saskatchewan, University of (PhD)
Southern California, University of (PhD)
Southern Illinois University Carbondale
(PhD)
Stanford University (PhD)
Stony Brook University (PhD)
Syracuse University (PhD)
Temple University (PhD)
Texas A&M University (PhD)
Texas Christian University (PhD)

Texas Tech University (PhD)
Texas, University of, Austin (PhD)
Texas, University of, Dallas (MA/MS—
terminal, PhD)
The New School for Social Research
(MA/MS—terminal)
Toledo, University of (PhD)
Toronto, University of (MA/MS, PhD)
Tulane University (PhD)
University at Albany, State University of
New York (PhD)
University at Buffalo, State University of
New York (PhD)
Utah, University of (PhD)
Victoria, University of (PhD)
Virginia Commonwealth University (PhD)
Virginia, University of (PhD)

Washington University in St. Louis (PhD)
Washington, University of (PhD)
Waterloo, University of (PhD)
Wichita State University (PhD)
Wilfrid Laurier University (MA/MS—
terminal, PhD)
William James College (PsyD)
Windsor, University of (PhD)
Wisconsin, University of, Madison (PhD)
Wyoming, University of (PhD)
Yale University (PhD)
York University (PhD)

Sport Psychology
Denver, University of (MA/MS—terminal)
John F. Kennedy University (MA/MS—
terminal)

ALPHABETICAL INDEX OF INSTITUTIONS

DISCARD

RECEIVED OCT 1 5 2018

34 95

RECEIVED OCT 1 8 2016

16x

DISCARD